Collect

& Directory of Dealers

11th edition

Collectors' Information Bureau

EDITOR
Karen Feil

CONTRIBUTORS:
Susan Elliott
Danforth Walker

DESIGN AND GRAPHICS
Arrow Design
Chicago, IL

The staff of the Collectors' Information Bureau
would like to express our deep appreciation to
our distinguished panel of limited edition
retailers and secondary market experts, whose
knowledge and dedication to the collectibles
industry have helped make this book possible.
Although we would like to recognize them by
name, they have agreed that to be singled out in
this manner may hinder their ability to maintain
an unbiased view of the marketplace.

Contents

About the CIB

Established in 1982, the Collectors' Information Bureau (CIB) is a not-for-profit trade association whose mission is to serve and educate collectors, members and dealers, and to provide them with credible, comprehensive and authoritative information on collectibles and their current values.
To contact the CIB, write to 77 W. Washington St., Chicago, IL 60602, call (312) 379-2940, or e-mail cibmailbox@aol.com. **Visit CIB's web site at www.collectorsinfo.org.**

On the cover:

Front cover: top row, left: *Alyssa–Nature's Angel*, 1995, from Seraphim Classics; the *2001 Annual Ornament* by Swarovski Consumer Goods; *Diamond Lil* from Alexander Doll Co., 1993; the 10 year Collector Society anniversary piece, *Now and Forever*, 1995, from Lladró.
Middle row: *Time for A Little Something*, Winnie the Pooh and Friends, 1995, from The Bradford Exchange. *Johnny Appleseed* nutcracker from Christian Ulbricht. The *Bald Eagle* stein, 2002, from Anheuser-Busch. *Accordian Boy*, 1947, retired in 1994, from Goebel of North America.
Bottom row, *Twinkle Brite Glitter Factory*, 2002, from Department 56; miniature bears from Deb Canham Artist Designs: *Flore*, 1996, *Columbine*, 1997, and *Moonshine Cosmic*, 1997; *Daisy–Friendship Blossoms with Love*, 1993, Cherished Teddies from Enesco Group; *Versailles* from Just the Right Shoe, Willitts Designs, *Cape Hatteras*, Harbour Lights.
Back cover, *The Music Room* by Lena Liu from Imperial Graphics, *1991; Fisherman's Wharf* by Thos. Kinkade, 1993; *Carousel Horse* from Kurt S. Adler, Polonaise Collector's Guild, 1999.

CIB Member Companies

The Alexander Doll Company, Inc.
615 West 131st St.
New York, NY 10027
212-283-5900 Fax: 212-283-4901
www.madamealexander.com

Anheuser-Busch, Inc.
2700 South Broadway
St. Louis, MO 63118
800-305-2582 Fax: 314-577-9656
www.budweiser.com

Armani / Miller Import Corp.
300 Mac Lane
Keasbey, NJ 08832-1200
800-547-2006 Fax: 732-417-0031
E-mail: society202@aol.com
www.the-society.com

Arts Uniq', Inc.
1710 S. Jefferson Avenue
P.O. Box 3085
Cookeville, TN 38502
800-223-5020 Fax: 931-528-8904
E-mail: sales@artsuniq.com
www.artsuniq.com

The Ashton-Drake Galleries
9200 N. Maryland Avenue
Niles, IL 60714
800-634-5164 Fax: 847-966-3026
www.ashtondrake.com
www.collectiblestoday.com

The Boyds Collection Ltd.
PO Box 385
Gettysburg, PA 17325
717-633-9898 Fax: 717-633-5137
www.boydsstuff.com

The Bradford Exchange
9333 Milwaukee Avenue
Niles, IL 60714
800-323-5577 Fax: 847-966-3121
E-mail: custsrv@bradex.com
www.collectiblestoday.com
www.bradex.com

Cast Art Industries, Inc.
1120 California Avenue
Corona, CA 91719
909-371-3025 Fax: 909-270-2852
E-mail: info@castart.com
www.castart.com

Charming Tails
Fitz and Floyd Collectibles
501 Corporate Dr.
Lewisville, TX 75057
800-527-9550 Fax: 972-353-7718
www.charmingtails.com

Christian Ulbricht USA
P.O. Box 99
Angwin, CA 94508
800-770-2362 Fax: 707-965-4199
E-mail: nutcracker@ulbricht.com
www.ulbricht.com

Collectibles Insurance Agency
P.O. Box 1200
Westminster, MD 21158
888-837-9537 Fax: 410-876-9233
E-mail: info@insurecollectibles.com
www.collectinsure.com

Deb Canham Artist
Designs, Inc.
232 Pedro St.
Venice, FL 34285
941-480-1200 Fax: 941-480-1202
www.debcanhamartistdesigns.com

Department 56®, Inc.
6436 City West Parkway
P.O. Box 44456
Eden Prairie, MN 55344-1456
800-548-8696 Fax: 952-943-4500
E-mail: Mslittown@dept56.com
www.dept56.com

Encore
P.O. Box 500780
San Diego, CA 92150
800-621-3647 Fax: 800-929-9653
www.the-encore-group.com

Enesco Group, Inc.
225 Windsor Drive
Itasca, IL 60143
800-632-7968 Fax: 630-875-5350
www.enesco.com
www.enescoclubs.com

Fitz and Floyd
501 Corporate Dr.
Lewisville, TX 75057
800-527-9550 Fax: 972-353-7718
www.fitzandfloyd.com

Fontanini Heirloom Nativities
c/o Roman, Inc.
555 Lawrence Ave.
Roselle, IL 60172-1599
630-529-3000 Fax: 630-529-1121
www.roman.com

G. DeBrekht Artistic Studios /
Russian Gift and Jewelry Center
18025 Sky Park Circle, Suite G.
Irvine, CA 92614
800-727-7442 Fax: 800-RUSSIA-7
E-mail: info@russiangift.com
www.russiangift.com

Goebel of North America
Rte. 31 North
Goebel Plaza
Pennington, NJ 08534
609-737-8700 Fax: 609-737-1545
www.mihummel.com

The Greenwich Workshop
One Greenwich Place
P.O. Box 875
Shelton, CT 06484-0875
800-243-4246 Fax: 203-925-0262
www.greenwichworkshop.com

The Hamilton Collection
7018 A.C. Skinner Parkway, Suite #300
Jacksonville, FL 32256-6935
www.collectiblestoday.com

Harbour Lights
1000 N. Johnson Ave.
El Cajon, CA 92020
800-365-1219 Fax: 888-579-1911
E-mail:
harbourlights@harbourlights.com
www.harbourlights.com

Imperial Graphics, Ltd.
11516 Lake Potomac Dr.
Potomac, MD 20854
301-299-5711 Fax: 301-299-4837
E-mail: lliu@lenaliu.com
www.lenaliu.com

Kurt S. Adler, Inc.
1107 Broadway
New York, NY 10010
800-243-9627 Fax: 212-807-0575
www.kurtadler.com

Lee Middleton Original Dolls, Inc.

480 Old Worthington Rd. Suite 110
Westerville, OH 43082
614-901-0604 Fax: 614-901-0526
www.leemiddleton.com

Lenox Classics
900 Wheeler Way
Langhorne, PA 19047
888-561-8808 Fax: 888-561-2155
www.lenoxclassics.com

Lightpost Publishing/
Media Arts Group, Inc.
900 Lightpost Way
San Jose, CA 95037
800-366-3733 Fax: 800-243-8533
www.thomaskinkade.com
www.mediaarts.com

Little Gem Teddy Bears
Akira Trading Co., Inc.
2311 205th St.
Torrance, CA 90501
310-618-8165 Fax: 310-618-1623
E-mail: littlegem@usa.net

Lladró USA, Inc.
1 Lladró Drive
Moonachie, NJ 07074
800-634-9088 Fax: 201-807-1293
E-mail: lladrosociety@lladro.com
www.lladro.com

Melody In Motion
6280 S. Valley View Blvd.
Suite 404
Las Vegas, NV 89118
702-253-0450 Fax: 702-348-1871
www.melodyinmotion.com

M.I. Hummel / Goebel of North

America
Rte. 31 North
Goebel Plaza
Pennington NJ 08534
800-666-CLUB, Fax: 609-737-1545
www.mihummel.com

Original Appalachian Artworks, Inc.
PO Box 714
Cleveland, GA 30528
706-865-2171 Fax: 706-865-5862
www.cabbagepatchkids.com

OverCoffee Productions
1073 Rockford Road SW
Cedar Rapids, IA 52404
319-221-1424 Fax: 319-363-8280
www.overcoffee.com

Possible Dreams
6 Perry Drive
Foxboro, MA 02035
508-543-6667 Fax: 508-543-4255
www.possibledreams.com

Precious Moments
c/o Enesco Group, Inc.
225 Windsor Drive
Itasca, IL 60143
800-632-7968 Fax: 630-875-5350
www.enesco.com
www.enescoclubs.com

Prizm, Inc./Pipka Collectibles
8877 Green Valley Dr.
Manhattan, KS 66505
785-776-1613 Fax: 785-776-6550
E-mail: prizminc@pipka.com
www.pipka.com

Reco International

138 Haven Avenue
Port Washington, NY 11050
516-767-2400 Fax: 516-767-2409
www.reco.buylink.com

Roman, Inc.
555 Lawrence Avenue
Roselle, IL 60172-1599
630-529-3000 Fax: 630-529-1121
www.roman.com

Royal Copenhagen/ Bing & Grondahl
140 Bradford Dr.
Berlin, NJ 08091
800-431-1992 Fax: 856-768-9726
www.royalscandinavia.com

Royal Doulton USA
701 Cottontail Lane
Somerset, NJ 08873
800-68-CHINA (682-4462) Fax: 732-764-4974
E-mail: inquiries@royaldoultonusa.com
www.royaldoultonusa.com

The San Francisco Music Box
Company
390 North Wiget Lane, Ste. 200
Walnut Creek, CA 94598
925-939-4800 Fax: 925-927-2999
Mail Order: 800-227-2190
www.sfmusicbox.com

Seraphim Classics
c/o Roman, Inc.
555 Lawrence Ave.
Roselle, IL 60172-1599
630-529-3000 Fax: 630-529-1121
www.roman.com

One Kenney Drive
Cranston, RI 02920
800-426-3088 Fax: 800-870-5660
www.swarovski.com

United Design Corporation
1600 N. Main Street
P.O. Box 1200
Noble, OK 73068
800-727-4883 Fax: 800-832-0866
E-mail: udc@ionet.net
www.united-design.com

United Treasures
3351 East Valley Rd. Suite B
Renton, WA 98055
800-678-2545 Fax: 425-656-0299
www.unitedtreasures.com

The Village Chronicle
56 Freeway Dr.
Cranston, RI 02920
401-467-9343 Fax: 401-467-9359
E-mail: Peter@VillageChronicle.com
Jeanne@VillageChronicle.com
www.villagechronicle.com

Walt Disney Art Classics
500 South Buena Vista Street
Burbank, CA 91521
800-932-5749 Fax: 818-238-1099
www.disneyartclassics.com

Willitts Designs
International, Inc.
1129 Industrial Avenue
Petaluma, CA 94952
707-778-7211 Fax: 707-769-0304
E-mail: info@willitts.com
www.willitts.com

Swarovski Consumer Goods Ltd.

Care Tips for Collectibles

Moses, before...

You want to keep your limited edition pieces looking their best, but you also want your favorite works of art to endure so that they can become heirlooms for the next generation! So how do you make sure they retain their original condition and beauty?

We've asked the manufacturers of a broad range of artworks for their advice. And if you follow their directions, you can help ensure that your favorite treasures will be as beautiful in your great-grand-children's homes as they are in yours today.

Manufacturers Know Best

One repair service estimates that about 35% of items brought in for repair were damaged during ordinary cleaning. Follow the manufacturer's instructions for the care of your collection. Your fragile pieces will probably require specific care and attention. When you buy a new piece, look for hangtags or enclosures that include such information. Also check a company's club newsletter or Internet site for tips.

Sunlight and humidity

Avoid placing your collectibles in direct sunlight. This is especially true if you live in a climate with strong sun, since harsh rays can be harmful to the coloring or detail of a collectible. The humidity of your home may impact special adhesives that are used on composite crystal and coldcast pieces, causing them to separate. Re-attaching pieces is a relatively common repair that many of the repair services listed at the end of this article will handle, should your crystal moose unexpectedly shed his antlers.

Select Well-Constructed Displays

Place your collectibles in sturdy displays

that are away from busy traffic areas in your home. Whether you're choosing a curio cabinet, adjustable shelves, plate hangers or a Christmas tree, make sure it's strong and stable enough to support your pieces. Select glassed-in cabinets over open table displays for especially fragile pieces. And if you live in an area where earthquakes may occur, consider using a product like Quake Hold! removable putty or wax, which fastens collectibles in place.

Figurines, Cottages, Steins, Bells

Because of their delicate detail work and crevices, three-dimensional pieces such as figurines, cottages, steins and bells, often require more cleaning than flat works of art. When deeper cleaning is needed, the manufacturer's advice is crucial. For example, Enesco Corporation recommends that its porcelain bisque figurines from the Precious Moments collection be wiped with a damp cloth—never immersed in water.

Roman, Inc. suggests that its Fontanini figurines be cleaned with a damp cloth dipped in clear water. The newer Fontanini pieces are made of a high-density polymer, which means they are impossible to chip, break or nick. However, if subjected to heat or chemicals, they may be damaged beyond repair. "Just be sure not to store or display the figures near a heat source, such as the top of a hot radiator or register," says Jennifer Guley, Fontanini Brand Manager. "Distortion or damage could result," she warns.

Collectors have reported to the CIB that some crystal figurines separated when immersed in warm water, so we recommend that you do not immerse composite crystal pieces as if they were a wine glass. Crystal figurines should be wiped with a damp cloth. Then, let your crystal air-dry or use a polishing cloth or chamois to bring out its sparkle.

...and after

Plates

Although they are breakable, most collectible plates are remarkably durable. In most cases, they can be wiped clean with a damp cloth or even washed gently by hand in a sink with lukewarm water and mild soap. On the other hand, unglazed plate surfaces or hand-painted, unfired plates should never be immersed in water. In these cases, dusting is your best option. If your plate has been hand-signed by the artist, you should completely avoid using water. Do not wash collector's plates in a dishwasher—bas relief plates created in a composite material may disintegrate from exposure to pressur-

ized hot water and detergent.

Plates on secure hangers, displayed on well-sunk nails, are usually safe from most harm. However, if your plates are to be shown in a high-traffic area, you might choose plate frames for more protection against bumps and bangs.

Collectible Dolls

Because of their fabric clothing, synthetic wigs, delicate features, and fingers, it is best to keep collectible dolls in glass cases or wooden displays with glass fronts. Dolls should be kept away from sunlight to avoid damage to fabrics, hair and painting. If a doll's clothing becomes soiled, the best option is to remove it and have it dry-cleaned, unless the manufacturer says the fabric can be washed without damage or shrinking.

If your doll's coiffeur needs attention, it's not advisable to attempt a complete re-style. This often ends in disaster. Instead, use your fingers to gently smooth down any out-of-place hairs.

Ornaments

At one time, ornaments only saw the light of day at Christmas. However, many of today's collectors choose to show these elegant works of art all year. If you still choose to put your collectible ornaments away each January, the best option is to store them in their original boxes.

They can then be stored in boxes with divided compartments or stackable rubber tray containers lined with bubble wrap. Ornaments should never be stored in an attic or basement where water, humidity or extreme temperatures exist.

Graphics

A museum-mounted, framed print is well protected, but it should still be hung out of direct sunlight to avoid fading. Other important rules in preserving your print are to minimize handling and maintain consistent temperatures in your home to prevent the build-up of moisture between the print and glass. Also, be sure never to spray liquid glass cleaner directly onto the glass: it may drip down between the frame and the mat, causing damage. Instead, spray a dry, lint-free cloth with cleaner and then gently wipe the glass. If a canvas reproduction or oil painting cannot be dusted clean with a lint-free silk cloth or brush, take it to a professional framer for cleaning. Unframed prints should be stored within protective acetate sleeves.

If one of your prized collectibles is broken or damaged, don't despair: often it can be restored to its original beauty, if not its original value. Indeed, many collectors love their artwork so much that they prefer to have it restored rather than accept an insurance settlement. A qualified restorer can assist with a variety of collectibles and recover 50% to 100% of the item's original issue price.

The following list of restorers has been recommended through various sources. Because we have not had the occasion to use the services of the businesses listed, CIB cannot guarantee their workmanship, however we do keep on file the satisfaction surveys sent to us from collectors who have used these services. If you have any reservations about using one of these services, you are welcomed to call us for information on the reports we have received.

The CIB recommends that you discuss the estimated interval required to handle your repair. Depending on the backlog of work in an individual shop, repairs may take anywhere from two to six weeks to complete, sometimes longer.

You can also call a restoration expert in your area by checking your local Yellow Pages under China & Crystal Repair.

Cleaning Your Collectibles

1. Do not allow anyone other than yourself to dust or clean your collectibles.

2. When cleaning collectibles, be very careful. Do not use feather dusters unless the piece is very strong with no small parts. For best results on porcelains, spray them with diluted rubbing alcohol and then hold them upside down until they stop dripping, then allow to air dry. A hair dryer set on cold can also be an effective way to blow dust off of extremely delicate pieces.

3. Never use a vacuum cleaner, especially on delicate pieces.

4. Never wipe dust off fine crystal with a paper towel—it can cause scratches.

5. To dust, wipe the dust off with a small, soft cloth wrapped over one finger. If you use the whole cloth it can snag small parts.

6. Always wash collectibles with cool water and mild soap.

7. Be sure to wash the soap off thoroughly to prevent a dull film from being left behind.

8. Never put fine crystal or a collectible in the dishwasher. Fine crystal figurines should be wiped with a damp cloth.

Repair Services

EAST:

Dean Schulefand & Associates Porcelain & Crystal Restoration
324 Guinevere Ridge
Cheshire, CT 06410
203-271-3659
800-669-1327
Specialty: Pottery, jade, ivory, glass, crystal, ceramic, cold cast, resin, porcelain, marble, plaster, china, bronze, silver, pewter and brass.

Rosine Green
Associates , Inc.
89 School St.
Brookline, MA 02446
617-277-8368
Specialty: Porcelain, paintings, wood, ceramic, pottery, resin, jade, marble, lacquer, granite, alabaster, glass, soapstone, cold cast, brass, pewter and bronze.

Trefler and Sons Antique Restoring
Studio, Inc.
29 Tower Rd.
Newton, MA 02464
617-965-3388
Specialty: Crystal, paintings, furniture, silver, resin, glass, pottery, ceramic, wood, ivory, jade and soapstone.

Collector's Clinic
3009 W. Genesee St.
Syracuse, NY 13219
315-488-7123
Specialty: Porcelain, cold cast, resin, antique dolls, frames, pottery, china, ivory, papier mâché, jade and soapstone.

Restorations by Valerie
4 Country Club Ct.
Livingston, NJ 07039
973-992-9270 Fax: 973-992-8509
Porcelain, crystal, soapstone, marble, ivory. Repairs most major brands of collectibles.

A. Ludwig Klein & Son, Inc.
P.O. Box 145
683 Sumneytown Pike
Harleysville, PA 19438
215-256-9004
Specialty: Glass, ivory, jade, metal art, crystal, pottery, leather, statuary and porcelain.

Harry A. Eberhardt & Sons, Inc.
2010 Walnut St.
Philadelphia, PA 19103
215-568-4144
Specialty: Porcelain, glass, metal, crystal and orientalia.

McHugh's
3461 West Cary St.
Richmond, VA 23221
804-353-9596
Specialty: Crystal, glass, ivory, marble, jade, pottery, soapstone and porcelain.

South:
Crystal Restoration
3411 N. Dixie Highway
Ft. Lauderdale, FL 33334
954-565-8877
Crystal, glass, stoneware, re-attaching crystal pieces on figurines.

Beckus Studios
4511 32nd Avenue North
St. Petersburg, FL 33713
727-522-4288
Specialty: Wood, porcelain, metal, ceramic, pottery, ivory, jade, marble, plaster, resin, china and cold cast.

Central:
Old World Restorations, Inc.
5729 Dragon Way
Cincinnati, OH 45227
513-271-5459
Specialty: Porcelain, paintings, glass, frames, works on paper, photographs, furniture, metals and on-site architectural restoration such as murals, frescos and gold leaf.

Antique & Hummel Restoration by Wiebold
413 Terrace Place
Terrace Park, OH 45174
800-321-2541
Specialty: Porcelain, ceramic, pottery, metal art, glass, oil paintings, frames, crystal, jade, marble, soapstone, alabaster and plaster chalk.

Crystal Cave
1183 Wilmette Avenue
Wilmette, IL 60091
847-251-1160 Fax: 847-251-1172
Allcrystal1141@aol.com
www.crystalcaveofchicago.com
Speciality: Glass and crystal repair.

West:
China & Crystal Clinic
1808 N. Scottsdale Rd.
Tempe, AZ 85281
800-658-9197
Specialty: Porcelain and crystal.

T.S. Restoration
2015 N. Dobson Rd. Suite 4
PMB 598
Chandler, AZ 85224
480-963-3148
Speciality: Porcelain.

Pick Up The Pieces
711 W. 17th St. #C12
Costa Mesa, CA 92627
800-934-9278 Fax: 949-645-8381
Specialty: Porcelain, oil paintings and frames, crystal, glass, wood, jade, ivory, bronze, brass, gold, silver, pewter, resin, papier mâché, iron, white metal, soapstone and china.

Crystal Factory
8010 Beach Bvld.
Buena Park, CA 90620
Need phone.
Specialty:

Brookes Restorations
930 S. Robertson Blvd.
Los Angeles, CA 90035
310-659-8253 Fax: 310-659-8262
Specialty: Porcelain, ceramic, jade, marble, ivory, alabaster, wood, crystal, glass, paintings, soapstone, resin and china.

Horowitz & Brookes Restoration
28914 Roadside Dr. Store #5
Agoura Hills, CA 91301
818-880-5232
Speciality: Porcelain, ceramic, jade, marble, ivory, alabaster, wood, crystal, glass, paintings, soapstone.

Venerable Classics
645 Fourth St., Suite 208
Santa Rosa, CA 95404
707-575-3626
800-531-2891
Specialty: Porcelain, ceramic, resin, pottery, glass, crystal, jade, ivory, marble, wood, frames, brass, bronze and pewter.

Geppetto's Restoration
31121 Via Colinas, Suite 1003
Westlake Village, CA 91362
818-889-0901
Fax: 818-889-8922
Specialty: Porcelain, glass, crystal, ivory, jade, marble, ceramics, resin, pottery and wood.

Herbert F. Klug Conservation and Restoration
Box 28002 #16
Denver, CO 80228
303-985-9261
Specialty: Porcelain, marble and ivory.

Sharon Lewis Restoration & Repairs
8902 Deer Haven Rd.
Austin, TX 78737
512-301-2294
Specialty: Porcelain, ceramic, plaster, stoneware, china and pottery.

Canada:
Kingsmen Antique Restoration Inc.
19 Passmore Avenue, Unit 28
Scarborough, ONT M1V 4T5 Canada
416-291-8939
Specialty: Porcelain, bronze, pewter, ivory, pottery, glass, crystal, jade, marble, soapstone, wood, lacquer, papier mâché, brass, iron, white metal and oil paintings.

Artwork Restoration
30 Hillhouse Rd.
Winnipeg, MB R2V 2V9
Canada
Specialty: Crystal, china, glass, marble, pottery, soapstone, ivory, dolls, paintings, wood frames, and porcelain.

Improved insurance from USPS
by Dan Walker

Collectors and dealers now have improved postal insurance coverage for mailing their collectibles. For collectors, the postal insurance coverage is automatically part of the contract. For example, you are paid up to $200 per loss if mailed by USPS; First Class, Priority Mail, Air Mail, Global Priority Mail, Parcel Post, Bound Printed Matter, Media Mail (book rate), including USPS and non-USPS postal equivalents.

Collectors also receive up to $25,000 coverage for USPS Insured Mail and Certified Mail, including USPS and non-USPS postal equivalents, if the recipient is required to sign for the shipment. Also, up to $60,000 for USPS Registered or Express mail including USPS and non-USPS postal equivalents.

This mail coverage applies to items you mail as well as items mailed to you if the mailer does not provide postal insurance.

Mail coverage includes loss and damage in the mail as well as rifled mailings. Coverage includes breakage and irradiation damage. If you are a collector and selling duplicate and unwanted items on the Internet, the mail coverage discussed above is provided for mailing items sold on the Internet. For a collector, if a loss occurs and the loss is more than $50, you are paid in full. For dealers, mail coverage includes first dollar loss; there is no $50 minimum.

Dan Walker is president of Collectibles Insurance Agency, which exclusively sells insurance for over 100 types of collectibles including limited edition collectibles. Collectibles Insurance Agency has 35 years of experience selling collectible insurance. CIA does not require a professional appraisal and only individual items over $5,000 each need to be inventoried. Contact CIA by calling toll free 1-888-837-9537 or visit www.collectinsure.com.

Trends in the Secondary Market—Dealer Views

"Evolving and fractured" is how collectibles expert Dean Genth (Miller's Hallmark & Gift Gallery) describes the secondary market today. "When any secondary market gets overheated there's also a cooling," says Genth, who specializes in M.I. Hummel, Precious Moments and Swarovski Crystal.

Observers point to a number of factors affecting today's market, including online auctions such as eBay, general uncertainty in the economy and the cooling ardor of Beanie Babies collectors.

Clif White of Swan Galleries says, "This is purely a supply and demand market. The Internet has increased the supply while the demand has relatively remained the same."

As Blaine Garfolo of Crystal Reef explains, "Not all people know about the specialists (secondary market retailers and exchanges), but they know about the eBays, which increases the number of pieces going there."

With prices down for many lines, what do collectors want?

"Collectors are still out for the thrill of the hunt, the search, the pieces that make their collection different from the average and the norm," says Genth.

Secondary market specialists interviewed for this year-end report spotlighted the following collectibles as most in demand in 2001:

- Department 56 (Christmas in the City, North Pole Village and Original Snow Village)
- Ebony Visions
- Lenox plates
- Pocket Dragons
- R. John Wright
- Swarovski Crystal (Annuals, Christmas Ornaments, Inspiration Africa, and Mother and Child)
- Wee Forest Folk

Clif White says, "Collectors are getting real savvy about supply and demand. The amount of production is important to collectors and that's why they're moving to

Retailers ran out of the 2001 Snowflake ornament from Swarovski.

lines such as Wee Forest Folk that are truly limited in their production." He also praises Harbour Lights for managing its limits well and providing high quality.

Another experienced secondary market specialist, Dean Rystad of Rystad's Limited Editions receives requests for a wide variety of items. "I've still got a six-page list of things I'm looking for and I run this list in the NALED Exchange [a dealer network] every month. Things on eBay are the ones that are very easy to get. People come to us with requests for things that they can't find on eBay, the more difficult things."

Do collectors have any hesitation about buying online? "People do have some fear of buying online," says Rystad. "I've bought a few things on eBay myself but never paid more than $35 since I figure that it won't affect my lifestyle if I lose the money. I won't buy things for several hundred dollars from an unknown source. I have had customers who have brought in things that they bought on eBay which have had cracks or crazing, or they didn't get a box or certificate."

"Sometimes people are truly ignorant of

Ebony Visions by Thomas Blackshear were in demand in 2001. Above, from 1999 is "Intimacy", an open edition with an issue price of $165.

what they're selling. They don't know that a collectible is supposed to have a certificate or an extra little flower," says Rystad.

Should collectors be concerned about authenticity of what they buy online? "I have noticed some stuff that looks very suspicious," says Rystad. "For example, Royal Copenhagen Christmas plates were counterfeited by an outfit in Portugal a few years ago. I know these fakes immediately now when I see one, but I was fooled the first time. They were done very well. Also, there are seconds out there, and even thirds. If you're not able to detect them you may end up paying far too much."

Dean Genth adds, "Know who you're dealing with. Make certain you're dealing with a reliable dealer when you're buying on the secondary market. You greatly reduce your risk of a fraudulent transaction."

Most experts agreed with Clif White about selling. "Don't sell now, wait. I think that we do have a supply problem now ver-

sus demand. That will sort of correct itself, particularly in the long run and because manufacturers will cut back on their production."

Jimer deVries of Swan Seekers Network says, "It's definitely a buyer's market, so don't sell unless you have to. It's a great time for buyers."

Angie McIntosh of Crystal Exchange America adds, "If you really truly want to sell, be realistic about selling trends. Buy the piece you like. If it goes up in value, great; if it doesn't, you won't feel bad."

Know when to buy and sell

When selling online, Blaine Garfolo suggests you avoid the following times when more people want to raise extra money. If you're buying, expect to find lower prices.
- Early April (pre-tax filing)
- Early summer (pre-vacation)
- Late November (pre-Christmas)

Auctions versus Store Sales

There is no doubt that the growing popularity of Internet auction sites has changed how secondary market sales are made. A common comment from the CIB's secondary market panelists is that Internet auctions have substantially reduced their sales of retired editions.

Auctions that are collector-to-collector based also lack the benefit of experts with a longer view of the value of a piece, which can result in sellers asking for lower minimum bids than the market would support over time. This results in a gap between values dealers report from their transactions and transactions made collector to collector via auctions.

Collectibles Outlet in San Jose, CA reported that 2001 sales of retired editions were "soft," and Robin Yaw of the Crystal Connection in Peoria, Illinois, a specialist in Swarovski, reported that his secondary market volume was down 50% or more last year.

Cindy Morton of Morton's Crystal says, "For the first time ever, there is an abundance of Swarovski items available, and anyone with a computer can easily view current market values. Some items that should be

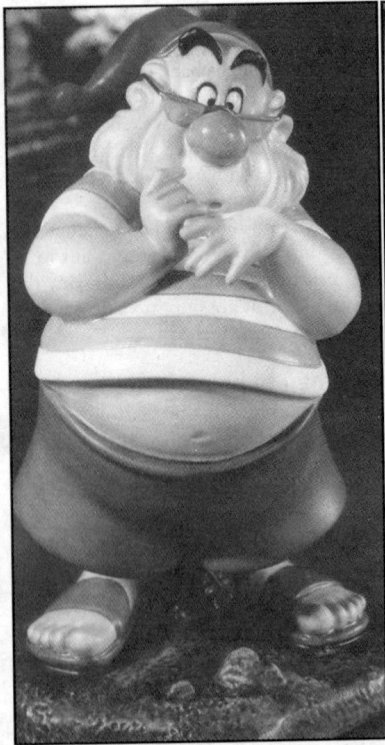

Harder to find: In 2001, Walt Disney Art Classics bought back and destroyed some early pieces from retailers that remained unsold in stores. Items included in the buy-back program included Huey, Duey, and Louis, above, and selected pieces from Disney's animated film classics.

In most cases, special event pieces like Mr. Smee from Peter Pan, left, were not included in the buy-back because they are not widely available from stores at this time.

fairly 'recession-proof' have come down in price, like the Lovebirds and Limited Edition Eagle." Morton is a secondary market specialist in Swarovski.

Morton says that she has seen most of the annual editions drop 10–25 percent in value in 2001. She attributes this change in part to the general economy, and in part to the proliferation of Swarovski on eBay.

"Swarovski is opening up their own stores, and closing many dealers across the U.S.," she explains. Dealers who will no longer be selling the new Swarovski pieces in their stores may list their remaining pieces on Internet auction sites.

Morton says in her view "the pricing probably will not be this good again, because crystal pieces do get broken. Also, lots of first-time collectors are starting collections with the new "Isadora" Annual Edition, which is proving to be very popular. It's a good time for collectors to acquire those retired editions that have been trading at

higher prices prior to the change in the economy," she notes.

Because smaller quantities were made of the earlier editions, Morton speculates that these earlier editions may rebound. She recommends that collectors hold on to the older, rarer items. "Swarovski will continue to be a strong line due to its beauty as an art object and the value of retired pieces," she says.

Matt Lanigan of The Emporium concurs that the collectibles market has been slowing down over the past two years, and Sept. 11 "pushed it to the bottom."

Stein specialist OHI Exchange in New Braunsfels, Texas agreed that sales were much slower last year. Jackson said that auction sites have impacted her secondary sales also.

Secondary specialists like D56 Retirees in Lake Havasu, Arizona have seen "about a 25% increase" in business. Cat's Meow in Glenview, Illinois reported that their sales last year were similar to 2000, and that they

Department 56 village pieces were in demand in 2001. The new "Halloween Village™ Collection was introduced in 2001. It is scaled to work with the Original Snow Village Collection also.

Pocket Dragons from Goebel of N.A. were popular in 2001, according to CIB panel dealers. Right: the Diet Devil from Goebel, with a pitchfork of chocolate candy.

had a lot of the retired pieces in stock that collectors were looking for. In Milton, New Hampshire, Cosmo's Collectibles' secondary market sales were "about 30% better" than 2000.

Mark Rister of Sparkling Rose in Clearwater, Florida saw a great response to many secondary market items in 2001, especially Walt Disney Classics Collection.

"There seems to be more urgency on some of the WDCC items since they had a voluntary buy back program of retired items for dealers to turn in some of the older, slower-moving items," he said. "Disney did the right thing by destroying these retired items, rather than having them surface on eBay or other Internet auction sites at a fraction of the cost," he added.

Lee Zoppa, former director of Walt Disney Art Classics confirmed that Disney pulled off the market and destroyed approximately one million dollars worth of unsold pieces of Walt Disney Classic Collection from dealers. Pieces bought back included items from *101 Dalmatians, Alladin, Alice in Wonderland, Bambi, Hunchback of Notre Dame, American Heroes, Jungle Book, Pinocchio,* and others.

Kemp Weekes of Classic Collectible Exchange in Bucyrus, Ohio says that sales of collectibles in 2002 has started slowly, but it looks like it might be the same or higher than 2001. Cosmo's Collectibles is anticipating that sales of collectibles will grow due to their repeat customers, and their figurine search service for collectors.

Matt Lanigan of The Emporium is predicting moderate to higher sales. He believes that we are coming out of the recession, and that with Americans traveling locally rather than overseas, the sales will stay local, too.

June McGowan of D56 Retirees says January 2002 was up by 31% over January 2001. Like June, Tim Siers of Siers Exchange predicts that business may be a bit higher.

Faye Snodgrass, of The Faye Snodgrass Gallery in Franklin, Tennessee looks forward to higher sales this year because she has a good inventory of secondary market pieces. Her secondary market sales were much higher in 2001 than the prior year.

Mario Pancino at Collector's World in Montrose, California is concerned that their secondary market business may be hurt this year by dealers offering deals on the Internet

If it sounds too good to be true, it just might be! Counterfeit copies of Royal Copenhagen Christmas plates, for issues that had appreciated in value like the "1962 Mermaid" shown above, were being manufactured in Portugal and imported into the U.S. Royal Copenhagen initiated the investigation that shut down the counterfeiters.

Dean Rystad of Rystad's Limited Editions, a specialist in collector's plates, says that on the counterfeit pieces, the trademark on the back of the plate was not raised, like usual; it was printed on.

It pays to work with a retailer you know, who has the experience to recognize a bona fide part of an edition from an imposter.

in an effort to free up cash.

The environment

Clif White of Swan Gallery in Stone Mountain, Georgia predicts that the trend toward staying home, "cocooning" will be positive for collectible sales, as people make their environments pleasing to themselves. Mark Rister of Sparkling Rose thinks that after 9-11, "collectors are buying only what they really want—not because they feel they 'have to have it'."

What dealers are seeking

Charming Tails—the older retired pieces," says Cosmo's Collectibles. D56 Retirees is on the lookout for *St. Paul's Cathedral, Design World*, and *Toot's Model Train* from D56.

Matt Lanigan of The Emporium and Faye Snodgrass of Faye Snodgrass Gallery say they could have used more of Swarovski's *2001 Snowflake* ornament—the CIB also received many calls from collectors looking for this edition in January 2002.

Jim Oliver of J&L Treasures in Midwest City, Oklahoma says he wishes he had bought more Sass-n-Class from Sandy USA. If he'd had a crystal ball, Rich Gernady at Cat's Meow would have bought more Radko, retired Dean Griff figurines, and Woodland Winds. Jean Banks at Cosmo's Collectibles also wishes she had purchased more Charming Tails.

Coca-Cola collectibles are hot at Wad's Antiques. This store could have used more of the early houses from Cavanagh's Coca-Cola Town Square, and more Coca-Cola Santas from Possible Dreams last year.

What collectors are buying

Collectibles Outlet reports that the high-end lines are still selling best: Lladró, Swarovski, and Armani. Collector's World says their store is doing best with price points under $100. The new Cow Parade collection from Westland Gifts is starting to build a collector base. Wee Forest Folk, Mill Creek, Harbour Lights, Lladró, and Swarovski "are holding."

Robin Yaw of Crystal Connection says collectors are looking for bargains in the

Below: Cape Hatteras by Harbour Lights. Harbour Lights has a reputation with dealers for quality and appropriate edition sizes. The Armani line, left, is popular with collectors. Shown is the 1995 piece, Melody, currently valued at $475.
Right: Artist Bev Doolittle has a good track record on the secondary market. Her Prayer for the Wild Things from Greenwich Workshop has an estimated replacement cost of $1650. If you had acquired it as a new issue in 1993, you would have paid $325. In black and white, it is easier to spot the camouflage mountain lion in the lower right.

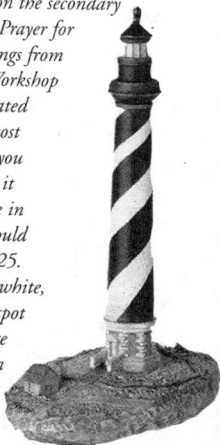

hard-to-find retired Swarovski pieces. Faye Snodgrass is still getting calls for the 2001 Swarovski Silver Christmas ornaments.

June McGowan of D56 Retirees has a very specific list when asked what collectors are looking for: from D56, St. Paul's Cathedral, 12 Drummers Drumming, Nussmacher from Alpine village, and the Starbucks store.

Cat's Meow cites tea sets, dolls and angels as hot categories for their store. Collectors seek out Cat's Meow for Charming Tails, Radko, new Ty pieces, Precious Moments, and D56 Snowbabies.

Using the Dealer Directory

The CIB works with hundreds of collectibles retailers across the U.S. to gather information on replacement costs of the major brands of limited editions. On the following pages, you will find some of the dealers who feature limited edition collectibles. Whether you are looking for a new, or "primary market" piece, or a retired "secondary market" piece, the dealers on the following pages can help you to acquire it.

See the line code chart on the following page to identify the codes for the lines you collect, and look for those codes under the Primary and Secondary detail for each dealer. Dealers are arranged alphabetically by state.

Special thanks to the following secondary market specialists who contributed their expertise for this article: Richard Gernady (Cat's Meow); Robin Yaw (Crystal Connection Ltd.); Angie McIntosh (Crystal Exchange America); Blaine Garfolo (Crystal Reef); Gary McGowan (Department 56 Retirees); Dean Genth (Miller's Hallmark & Gift Gallery); Cindy Morton (Morton's Crystal Inc.); Dean Rystad (Rystad's Limited Editions); Clif White (Swan Galleries); Jimer De Vries (Swan Seekers Network); Jean Banks (Cosmo's Collectibles); Kemp Weeks (Classic Collectible Exchange); Matt Lanigan (The Emporium); Faye Snodgrass (Faye Snodgrass Gallery); Mario Pancino (Collectors' World); Mark Rister (Sparkling Rose); Jean Jackson, (OHI Exchange); Jim Oliver, J&T Treasures.

Line Codes for the Dealer Directory:

Art Affects AAF
Anheuser-Busch AB
All God's Children AGC
Anri AN
Annalee ANNA
Artist Orbis AO
Artists of the World AOW
Applause APP
Armani AR
Artesania Rinconada ART
Ashton-Drake ASH
Arts Uniq' AU
Berlin Design BD
Bradford Exchange BE
Jody Bergsma BERG
Bing & Grondahl BG
Blue Sky BS
Boehm BO
Bovano of Cheshire BOC
Boyds Collection BOY
Brayer horses BR
Brian Baker BB
Bulova miniature clocks BUL
Byer's Choice figures BYER
Tom Clark's Gnomes CA
Cabbage Patch Dolls CAB
Cast Art CAS
Cat's Meow CM
Cavanagh CAV
Charming Tails CHARM
Cherished Teddies CT
Chilmark Pewter CH
Christian Ulbricht CU
Christopher Radko CR
Churchill Gallery CG
Columbus Int'l CI
Cornell, M. COR
Country Artists COUN
Coventry Pewter CP
Crown Parian CROWN
Crystal World CW
Cybis CY
David Grossman DG
David Winter DW
Department 56 D56
Daddy's Long Legs DLL
Dreamscicles DR
Ebony Visions EV
Edna Hibel EH
Emmett Kelly Jr. EK
Emmett Kelly Jr. EKJ
Emmett Kelly Originals EKO
Encore EN
Enchantica ENC

Enesco Group Inc.ENES
Ernst Enterprises EE
Especially For You EFY
Fenton Art Glass FEN
Flambro FL
Fontanini FO
Franklin Mint FM
G. DeBrehkt RUSS
G. Harvey GH
Ganz GA
Gene doll GEN
Goebel of NA GOE
Gorham GO
Greenwich Workshop GW
Halcyon Days HAL
Hadley House HH
Hallmark HA
Hamilton Collection HAM
Harbour Lights HL
Harmony Kingdom HK
Hawthorne Village HAW
Herend HD
Hermann Bears HE
M I Hummel HU
Imperial Graphics IG
Ispanky IS
Jan Hagara JH
June McKenna JM
Just the Right Shoe JTRS
Kurt Adler KA
Knowles China KC
Krystonia KR
Lalique LA
Lance Pewter LAN
Larry Fraga ornaments LF
Lee Middleton LEE
Legends pewter LE
Geo. Zoltan Lefton LEF
Lenox Classics LC
Lilliput Lane LIL
Little People LP
Leo Smith LS
Lladro LL
Longaberger Baskets LB
Lucy & Me LM
Madame Alexander Dolls MA
Margaret Furlong MF
Matchbox Cars MATCH
Mats Jonasson MJ
Marty Bell MB
Melody in Motion MIM
Memories of Yesterday MY
Midwest of Cannon Falls MID
Mill Creek MC

Miss Martha Originals MM
Modern Icons MI
Orrefors OR
Oliver Weber Designs OW
Old World Christmas
OWCOlszewski Studios OS
Papel PA
Pat Buckley Moss PBM
Pen Delfin PEN
Pipka PIP
Pocket Dragons PD
Polonaise ornaments PO
Porsgrund POR
Possible Dreams POSS
Potting Shed PS
Precious Moments PM
R. John Wright RJW
Ray Day RAY
Reco International RE
Reed & Barton RB
Reuge Music Boxes RMB
Rockwell Society RS
Ron Lee Clowns RL
Royal Copenhagen RC
Royal Doulton RD
Roman Inc. ROM
Rosenthal RO
Rostrand ROS
San Francisco Music Box SFMB
Sass 'N Class SNC
Seraphim Angels SA
Schmidt SCH
Shelia's Collectibles SH
Slavic Treasures SLAV
Snow Babies SN
Staffordshire Enamels STAF
Steiff STF
Steinbach Nutcrackers ST
Sven Jensen SJ
Swarovski SW
Thomas Kinkade TK
Towle TOW
Ty Beanie Babies TY
United Treasures UT
Vanmark VA
Wallace WA
Walt Disney Art Classics WD
Waterford Wedgwood WW
Wee Forest Folk WF
Windstone Editions WE
Willitts WIL
Zolan Fine Art ZO

Dealer Directory

The dealers below assist collectors in locating closed or retired editions that are hard to find. Some of the businesses listed below are retail stores, some are not. The lines carried by these dealers, for both new or "Primary Market" pieces, and retired, or "Secondary Market" pieces are shown. See the line code chart at left for the codes corresponding to the lines you collect.

ARIZONA:
CLOCK DOCTOR, THE
10610 N. 71st. Place
SCOTTSDALE, AZ 85254
480-951-8994
Fax: 480-367-1307
clockdr@clockdr.com
www.clockdr.com
Primary:MM, RMB
Secondary: MM, RMB
Buys:Yes, vintage clocks

CRYSTAL WORLD
5750 E. Broadway
TUCSON, AZ 85719
520-745-5991 Fax: same
For lines, call.

DEPARTMENT 56 RETIREES
LAKE HAVASU CITY, AZ 86403
928-505-5655
Fax: 928-505-3709
dept56retirees.com
Secondary: D56
Buys: D56

JULIE & ALAN'S COLLECTIBLES
APACHE JUNCTION, AZ 85220
480-373-5845 Fax: 413-254-4748
gojaco@qwest.net
www.gojaco.com
Secondary: WILL, CHARM, HALL, CT, BOY, TY,PM, JTRS, ENES
Buys: WILL, CHARM, HALL, CT, BOY, TY,PM, JTRS, ENES

SANCHEZ COLLECTIBLES
1555 E. Glendale Ave.
PHOENIX, AZ 85020
602-395-9974 Fax: 602-241-0702
sanchol@primenet.com
primenet.com/nsanchCol
Secondary: LL, SW, WD
Buys: LL,SW

CALIFORNIA:
ALLOVIO GALLERY
1811 Douglas Blvd.
ROSEVILLE, CA 95661
916-782-5330
allovio@surewest.net
WWW.ALLOVIO-GALLERY.COM
Primary: HU, LC
Secondary: DW, EH, WD, HL, WIL
Buys: No

ALWAYS COLLECTORS CORNER
PO Box 1464
Solvang, CA 93464
805-688-0477
Primary: CAV, KA, BA
Secondary: CAV, KA, BA
Buys: Yes

CALEXICO STATIONERS
406 E. Second St.
Calexico, CA 92231
760-357-2751 FAX: 760-357-4388
scw@telecom1.net
Primary: PM, MOY, HU, LL, WD, CT, TV
Secondary: CH, DG, GA, GO

CITY LIGHTS
1212 Knoxville St.
SAN DIEGO, CA 92110
800-262-5335
d56heaven@aol.com
www.citylightscollectibles.com
Primary:D56,BYER,ANNA, FO, SA, MF,
CR,HL, PIP,TK, CHARM, FM, POSS
Buys:Yes, D56, HL

CLASSY COLLECTIBLES
7561 Center Ave #4
HUNTINGTON BEACH, CA 92647
714-897-2229 Fax: 714-899-5966
clacol@aol.com
www.classycollect.com
Primary:AB, MI
Secondary: AB
Buys: No, but assists with sales of AB

COLLECTIBLES OUTLET INC.
1899 W. San Carlos St.
SAN JOSE, CA 95128
408-288-6027   Fax: 408-288-6232
Primary: AR, BOY, WD, HK, HUM, LILI, PM
Secondary: AR, WD, HUM, LILI, LL, PM
Buys: Yes, LL, HUM, WD, PM, SW, WF

COLLECTORS WORLD
2249 Honolulu Ave.
MONTROSE, CA 91020
818-248-9451   Fax: 818-248-0439
collwrld@worldnet.att.net
www.ecollectorsworld.com
Primary:TK, WD, HL, OS, WF
Secondary: TK, WD, HL, OS, WF
Buys: No, consignment only

CRYSTAL REEF
P.O. Box 4455
ANTIOCH, CA 94531
925-778-8146   Fax: 925-778-8186
reefinfo@crystal-reef.com
www.crystal-reef.com
Secondary: PD, WF, SW,WD, ASH, LILI, DW, AR,
CHARM, LL, CR, HK, RJW, STF, CA

CRYSTAL 4U.COM
330 Morro Bay Blvd.
Morro Bay, CA 93442
805-771-8444
Primary: SW, PIP
Secondary: SW, PIP

FAMILY AFFAIR
13330 Paseo del Verano Norte
SAN DIEGO, CA 92128
858-485-5850   Fax: 858-485-7208
Primary: HL, TK
Secondary: HL, TK
Buys: No

FLASH COLLECTIBLES
560 N. Moorpark Rd., PMB #287
THOUSAND OAKS, CA 91360
805 499 9222   Fax: 805 376 5541
flashcoll@aol.com
www.flashcollectibles.com
Secondary: AB
Buys: AB, steins

FRAME GALLERY, THE
305 Third Avenue
CHULA VISTA, CA 91910
619-422-1700 Fax: 619-422-5860
Primary: LC, OS, JTRS, D56, WD, BE, ENES,
WILL
Secondary: HAM, WD, ENES, GOE, BE, WILL
Buys: No

GOLDEN SWAN, THE
881 Lincoln Way
AUBURN, CA 95603
530-823-7739 Fax: 530-823-1945
goldswann@qwest.net
www.goldenswann.com
Primary: LL, SW, AR, DW, HUM, WD, LC
Secondary: LL, SW, AR, DW, HUM, WD, LC
Buys: LL, SW, AR, DW, HUM, WD, LC

HERMANNS CRYSTAL LLC
7561 Center Ave. #45
HUNTINGTON BEACH, CA 92647
714-894-4833 Fax: 714-895-1990
info@hermannsgifts.com
hermannsgifts.com
Primary: ST, LL, D56, HUM, SW, CU
Secondary: ST, LL, D56, HUM, SW, CU

JULIET'S COLLECTIBLES
44060 Margarita Rd.
TEMECULA, CA 92592
909-302-0208 Fax: 909-302-0210
julietming@aol.com
Primary: FEN, PM, HUM, AGC, DW, SAR

LEE'S COLLECTIBLES AND GIFTS
PO Box 3661
CHATSWORTH, CA 91313
818-882-4264
wlee@earthlink.net
http://visitweb/collectibles
Secondary: BE, WD, DW, OS, ZO
Buys: No

NEVADA CITY CRYSTAL & GLASS
110 North Pine St
NEVADA CITY, CA 95959
530-265-3325 Fax: 530-265-3375
nccg@nc-collectibles.com
www.nc-collectibles.com
Primary: SW, DW, HL, WD, MJ, COUN
Secondary: SW, DW, HL, WD,
Buys: No

RYSTAD'S LIMITED EDITIONS
1013 Lincoln Ave.
SAN JOSE, CA 95125
408-279-1960 Fax: 408-279-1960
deanrys@aol.com
Primary: BE, HAM, RC, HK, BG, TK, AGC,
EV, LF
Secondary: BE, HAM, RC, HK, BG, TK, AGC,
EV, LF
Buys: HAM,TK,EV

SWANSEEKERS NETWORK
9740 Campo Rd., Suite 134
SPRING VALLEY, CA 91977
619-462-2333 Fax: 619-462-5517
jimer@swanseekers.com
www.swanseekers.com
Primary: CW
Secondary: SW, CW
Buys: NO, accepts lists

WHISTLESTOP ANTIQUES
350 N. Franklin St.
FT. BRAGG, CA 95437
707-961-0902
Primary: FEN, HL, HK, BOY, LC, LILI
Secondary: FEN, LILI, HK, HL

THE FRAME GALLERY

305 Third Avenue   Chula Vista, California 91910
619.422.1700 fax 619.422.5860

services

Specializes in searching for hard-to-find collectibles. Does not buy outright. Call
for details. All major credit cards accepted.

secondary

All collector plates, prints, figurines, crystal and pewter, including Disney Classics
and Olzewski, Lenox Classics, Hamilton, Enesco, Swarovski, Rockwell, Lilliput
Lane. Autographed celebrity photographs, etc.
A redemption center for Disney Classics, Pocket Dragons, Just The Right Shoe, Cardew, Lilliput Lane,
Krystonia, Myths & Magic, Swarovski, and SnowBabies.

noteworthy

The Frame Gallery began as a framing shop but soon collectors began coming to
the store for advice on the art of framing different collectibles. Before long a
mother daughter team Margaret and Jan, introduced collectibles to their store.

WHOLE BEAN GALLERY, THE
320 E. Main St
SANTA PAULA, CA 93060
805-525-2912 Fax: 805-525-2912
Primary: TK, BE, MB, MP, AA
Secondary: TK, BE, MB, MP, AA

WILSON GALLERIES
6013 N. Palm
Opus 1 Center
FRESNO, CA 93704
559-435-2286 Fax: 559-261-1704
Secondary: AR, WD, TK, CROWN, BE, RE,
          GH, PBM, MB

WINDSOR COTTAGE
8976 S Foothill Blvd.- B10
RANCHO WCAMONGA, CA 91730
909-987-4601 Fax: 909-948-5695
sjmissinlink@ windsorcottage.net
Primary: SW, D56, BYER, ANNA, WF, BOY,
          LC, TK
Secondary: SW, D56, BYER, ANNA, WF, BOY,
          LC, TK
Buys: SW, D56, BYER, ANNA, WF, BOY, LC,
          TK

COLORADO
MICKEY and COMPANY COLLECTIBLES
8475 W. Hampden Avenue, #2-10
LAKEWOOD, CO 80227
303-988-2070
www.mickeyandcompany.com

GIFT HOUSE, THE
98 N. Wadsworth Blvd. Suite 118
Lakewood, CO 80226
303-922-7279
info@the-gifthouse.com
the-gifthouse.com
Primary: PD, CT, PM, BOY, WD, SW, CHARM
Secondary: PD, CT, CHARM

CONNECTICUT
PLATES 'n' STUFF
23 Cemetery Rd.
WILLINGTON, CT 06279
877-684-1553 Fax: 860-684-9384
RBidwell@prodigy.net
ww.auctionworks.com/awstore/platesnst
Primary:BG, RC,BYER,
Buys: No

SUE COFFEE
10 Saunders Hollow Rd.
OLD LYME, CT 06371-1126
860-434-5641 Fax: 860-434-2653
suecoffee@aol.com
www.suecoffee.com
Secondary: ANNA

FLORIDA
CAMERON & SMITH LTD.
P.O. Box 637
VERO BEACH, FL 32961-0637
561-778-7862 Fax: 561-794-0544
Primary: HAL, STAF

CHRISTMAS PLACE, THE
2020 W 64st
HIALEAH, FL 33016
877-667-2474

COLLECTION SHOP, THE
12360 S.W. 132 Ct #211
MIAMI, FL 33186
305-387-1936 Fax: 305-387-1936
info@thecollectionshop.com
www.thecollectionshop.com
Secondary: EV, LE, WD, LL, SW, AR
Buys: Yes, EV, LE, LL, SW, AR, WD

CRYSTAL SEEKERS
5301 Leeward Lane
NEW PORT RICHEY, FL 34652
727-845-5330
ronimo@citicom.com
Secondary: SW

EURASIA COLLECTIBLES
20505 S. Dixie Hwy.#959
MIAMI, FL 33189
305-235-3272 Fax: 305-235-8502
eurasiacolllects@aol.com
www.eurasiacollectibles.com
Primary: SW, LL, EV, AR, HL, D56, HUM, PM
Secondary: SW, LL, WILL, AR, HB, D56,
              HUM, PM
Buys: LL, EV, SW

KATHY'S HALLMARK

11201 Park Boulevard Suite 17
Seminole, Florida 33772
Phone 727.392.2459
Monday-Saturday 10-9
Sunday 12-5

s e r v i c e s

Buy and sell outright.
Visa, MasterCard, American Express, and Discover accepted.

s e c o n d a r y

Swarovski, Collector Plates, Precious Moments, Hallmark Ornaments, and Kiddie
Car Classics, Snowbabies and Hummel.

n o t e w o r t h y

Kathy's Hallmark is a Redemption Center for Swarovski, Precious Moments,
Cherished Teddies, Dreamsicles, and Hallmark. Many past years ornaments and
some 5-piece Christmas promotion sets are available (i.e. Santa and Reindeer,
Snoopy, Bearinger Bears.)
Call or write for specifics.

HEIRLOOM COLLECTIBLES
2516 McMullen Booth Rd
CLEARWATER, FL 33761
727-797-8007 Fax: 727-669-8052

HEIRLOOMS OF TOMORROW
662 NE 125th
NORTH MIAMI, FL 33161
305-899-0920 Fax: 305-899-2877
Primary: AN, LL, GOE, DW, HUM, AR, SW,
       D56, CAB, BE, KR, PM, CH, WD,
       LIL, SCH, ASH, TK, RE,
Secondary: AN, LL, GOE, DW, HUM, AR, SW,
       D56, CAB, BE, KR, PM, CH, WD,
       LIL, SCH, ASH, TK, RE, TY
Buys: Listing service

ILLUM COLLECTIBLES
30 NE FIRST ST
MIAMI, FL 33132
305 373 3918 Fax: 800 984 5586
illumcollectible@aol.com
illumcollectibles.com
Primary: LL, SW, BOE, AR,
Secondary: LL, SW, BOE, AR,
Buys: Yes,call first

KATHY'S HALLMARK
11201 Park Blvd. Suite 17
SEMINOLE, FL 33772
727-392-2459
Secondary: SW, BE, PM, HALL, D56, BA, DR
Buys: Yes

RENA'S COLLECTIBLES
5845 SW 114
MIAMI, FL 33156
305-661-4368
Secondary: GOE, WD, AN, CH

RETIRED COLLECTION, A
550 Harbor Cove Circle
LONGBOAT KEY, FL 34228-3544
941-387-0102 Fax: 941-383-8865
Secondary: LL

SPARKLING ROSE COLLECTIBLES INC.
1261 Gulf Blvd Suite 108
CLEARWATER, FL 33767
727-517-9523 Fax: 727-517-9524
SparklnRos@aol.com
www.sparklingrose.com
Primary: SW, WD, HK, LL, ROM, BOY,
       CHARM
Secondary: SW,WD,HK, CHARM
Buys: HK,WD,SW as needed.

VIKING IMPORT HOUSE, INC.
1516 S. Federal Hwy
FT. LAUDERDALE, FL 33316
954-763-3388 Fax: 954-462-2317
vikimp@aol.com
vikingimporthousee.com
Primary: BG, RC, AB, BD, ROS, POR, SJ, RB
Secondary: BG, RC, BD, ROS, POR, SJ
Buys: Occasionally buys BG, RC

GEORGIA
AREA 51 COLLECTIBLES
NEWNAN, GA
866-272-5592 Fax: 770-253-4147
www.area51collectibles.com
Primary: EKJ, FL
Secondary: EKJ, FL

GALLERY 2A
GA Antique Center #13 6624 NE
ATLANTA, GA 30093
770 458 5858 Fax: 770 458 2001
Primary: EK, GOE, HUM, CT, D56, PM,
       WILL, HL, MA, AGC, ASH, CHARM,
       JTRS
Secondary: EK, PD, HUM, D56
Buys: No

KEEPSAKE EXPRESSIONS
5637 Spring Mall, Suite A
LITHONIA, GA 30038
770-808-1842 Fax: 877-453-3773
info@keepsakeexpressions.com
www.keepsakeexpressions.com
Primary: EV, SAC, JTRS, BOY, AR, DLL,
Secondary: WILL, BOY, AR, DLL, LL, AGC
Buys: Yes

LANIER ARTS & CRAFTS
5977 Main St.
LULA, GA 30554
770-869-3795 Fax: same
jdglac@cs.com
Primary: CAB, BA, LEE, BOY, CT, JH, TY
Secondary: CAB, BA, LEE, BOY, CT, JH, TY
Buys: CAB

SWAN GALLERIES
933 Main St.
STONE MOUNTAIN, GA 30083
770-498-9696 Fax: 770-498-6610
swangal@msn.com
stonemountainvillage.com/swan.htn
Primary: SW, HL, WF, HK, ROM, WILL, MF
Secondary: SW, HL, WF, HK
Buys: SW, WF

THOS. KINKADE
AT THE UPTOWN GALLERY
1013 Broadway
COLUMBUS, GA 31901
706-571-9800 Fax: 706-571-9399
mark@kinkadeartgallery.com
www.kinkadeartgallery.com
Primary: TK
Secondary: TK
Buys: Yes

IDAHO
DONNA'S PLACE
200 Main St., P.O. Box 520
P.O. Box 520
IDAHO CITY, ID 83631
208-392-6000 Fax: 208-392-6006
DPLAC2@Juno.Com
www.donnas-place.com
Primary:AB

MARY LOU'S MUSIC BOXES
1808 19th Avenue
LEWISTON, ID 83501
208-798-8191

ILLINOIS

C.A. JENSEN JEWELERS
709 First St.
LA SALLE, IL 61301
815-223-0377
Primary: CY, IS, BO, WW, LL, LC, BO
Secondary: CY, IS, BO, WW, LL, LC, BO

CAT'S MEOW, THE
1814 Glenview Rd.
GLENVIEW, IL 60025
847-657-6369 Fax: 847-657-9368
Primary: CHARM, PM, TY, LILI HB, CA, CT,
    HK, HL, CM
Secondary: CT, PM, TY, CR
Buys: No

CRYSTAL CONNECTION LTD, THE
8510 N. Knoxville Ave., #218
PEORIA, IL 61615-2034
309-692-2221 Fax: same
crystalconnection@att.net
www.crystal.org
Secondary: SW
Buys: SW

EILEEN'S TREASURES
PO BOX 285
VIRDEN, IL 62690
217-965-3648 Fax: 217-652-2773
eekgak@ctllc.com
Secondary: TY, HALL, PM, MY
Buys: Yes

EUROPEAN IMPORTS & GIFTS
7900 N. Milwaukee Avenue
NILES, IL 60714
847-967-5253 Fax: 847-967-0133
Primary: AB, ANNA, AN, AR, BOY, BB, BYER,
ENES, PM, CT, CHARM, CR, D56, WD, DR,
EV, EKJ, ENC, FEN, FO, GENE, GW, HL,
HK, HAW, HU, JTRS, KR, LILI, LL, MA, PW,
PO, SA, WN, WFF, DW, CU, ST, AGC
Secondary: JTRS, PM, WD, LL, D56, CR, HU
Buys: No

HERITAGE SHOPPE, THE
43 E. Jefferson Ave
NAPERVILLE, IL 60540
630-420-7992 Fax: 630-420-8209
Primary: BYER, BOC
Secondary: BYER, BOC
Buys: BC

INTERNATIONAL HOUSE
15708 LaGrange Rd.
Orland Park, IL 60462
708-349-3366
www.theinternationalhouse.com
Primary: SW, LL, PM, D56, PM, WD, HU, LC,
PIP, HL, CR, CT, BOY, ADG, BE, PD, AR,
JTRS, EV
Secondary: BE, WD
Buys: No

INTERNATIONAL HOUSE
2827 Aurora Ave.
Naperville, IL 60540
630-717-5002
Primary: SW, LL, PM, D56, PM, WD, HU, LC,
PIP, HL, CR, CT, BOY, ADG, BE, PD, AR,
JTRS, EV
Secondary: BE, WD
Buys: No

ROYALE IMPORTS
2775 Maple Avenue
LISLE, IL 60532
630-357-7002
royaleimports@hotmail.com
Primary: SW, WD, HL, HUM, GOE, LIL, CT
Secondary: SW, WD, HL, HUM, GOE, LIL, CT
Buys: SW, HL, LL

STEINLAND GIFTS & COLLECTIBLES
14N679 ROUTE 25 SUITE A
EAST DUNDEE, IL 60118
847-428-3150 Fax: 847-428-3170
steinland@aol.com
www.steinland.com
Primary: AB, MID, COR
Secondary: AB, APP
Buys: AB

INDIANA
CURIO SHOPPE, THE
West Side Square
105 N. Broadway St.
GREENSBURG, IN 47248
812-663-6914 Fax: 812-527-2288
curioshoppe@hotmail.com
curioshoppe.net
Primary: HUM, CT, PM, FO, SA, AN, AB, WF,
MM, AGC, WD, LC, GOE, D56, EKJ,
      LEF, JTRS, DR
Secondary: HUM, CT, PM, FO, SA, AN, AB,
      WF, SCH, MM, AGC, WD, LC,
      GOE, D56, EKJ, LEF, JTRS, DR
Buys: No

GRAHAM'S CRACKERS
5981 E. 86th St
INDIANAPOLIS, IN 46250
317-842-5727 Fax: 317-577-7777
Primary: HU, ST, JTRS, CU, BYER, PD, HK,
BOY, HL, KA, FO, D56

THORPE HOUSE COUNTRY INN, THE
19049 Clayborne St., P.O. Box 36
METAMORA, IN 47030-0036
756-647-5425 Fax: 756-647-6729
thorpe_house@hotmail.com
metamora.com/thorpehouse
Primary: CM
Secondary: CM
Buys: Yes

IOWA
STAMPS N STUFF
8190 Hickmond Rd
DES MOINES, IA 50325
800-999-5964 Fax: 515-331-4957
bkoepp@earthlink.net
stampsnstuff.com
Primary: D56, RD, HUM, AN, CHARM
Secondary: D56, RD, HUM, AN, CHARM
Buys: D56, RD, HUM, AN, CHARM

EILEEN'S TREASURES

P.O. Box 285   Virden, Illinois 62690
217.965.3648 cell 217.494.4561
email eekgak9@ctllc.com Open 9 to 8 daily

s e r v i c e s

Buy & sell. Layaway available. Fair prices. Satisfaction guaranteed.
Large inventory in stock. MasterCard and Visa accepted.
Locator service available.

s e c o n d a r y

Precious Moments (suspended and retired figurines, bells, ornaments, plates),
Memories of Yesterday figurines and ornaments, Hallmark Ornaments, Enesco
Treasury Ornaments and Beanie Babies.

n o t e w o r t h y

Eileen Kruse is an expert on Precious Moments marks, purchasing many early
pieces with original marks. She has expanded her business to include other
Enesco lines and Hallmark ornaments. Eilene attends three to four ornament
and collectible shows in the Illinois area and publishes a price list which is
available upon request.

MASSACHUSETTS

LINDA'S ORIGINALS /
YANKEE CRAFTSMAN
220 Rte. 6A
BREWSTER, MA 02631
508-385-4758 Fax: 508-385-1384
collect8@home.com
YankeeCraftsmen.com
Primary: BYER, SW,HL, D56, TK
Secondary: BYER, SW,HL, D56, TK
Buys: BC

MAINE

EMPORIUM GIFTS & COLLECTIBLES, THE
50 Dock Square
P.O. Box 650-B
KENNEBUNKPORT, ME 04046-1651
207-967-2139
collectme@mainemporium.com
www.mainemporium.com
Primary: LL, SW, HUM, AR, JTRS, CHARM,
          MATCH, VA
Secondary: LL, SW, HUM
Buys: NO

MICHIGAN

COLLECTORS' SOCIETY OF AMERICA
32725 Mc Connell Ct.
WARREN, MI 48092
810-264-8612 Fax: 810-264-8612
ana-collect@hotmail.com
collectors-society.org
Primary: WD, D56, SW, WW, LB, CT, HALL
Secondary: WD, D56, SW, WW, LB, CT, HALL
Buys: No

GENNA'S GIFTS
14600 Lakeside Circle #1347
Lakeside Mall
STERLING HEIGHTS, MI 48313
586-566-5088   Fax: 586-566-6022
gennas@msn.com
Primary: LL, SW, SA, HU, MA, ASH, D56,
WW, PM, BS
Secondary: D56, SW
Buys: No

MOSHER JEWELERS
336 Huron Ave
PORT HURON, MI 48060
810-987-2768 Fax: 810-987-5946
Primary: LL, RD, HAL, RC, B&G, LC, WW.
Secondary: LL, RD, CY, HAL, B&G, LC, WW

MISSOURI

C & N SOUTH FIVE STEINS
324 S. Hwy. 5
Route 1, Box 662 M
CAMDENTON, MO 65020
573-346-6307 Fax: 573-346-4248
Primary: AB
Secondary: AB

TRA-ART LTD
421 West Miller St.
JEFFERSON CITY, MO 65101
573-635-8278 Fax: 573-893-3779
tra-art@socknet.net
Secondary: AB, ANNA, ASH, BERG, BG, BE,
HH, HAM, EH, RE, LIL, MO, OWC, POSS,
PIP, RS, KC, ZOL, ROM, SH

MONTANA

LE BOUTIQUE GIFT CENTER
2545 Central Avenue
BILLINGS, MT 59102
406-656-2815   Fax: 406-656-7307
Primary: AR, BA, BOY, BE, LEF, DW, WD,
DR, EV, GW, JTRS, MA, HL, HK, HUM,
LL, SW, SA

NORTH CAROLINA
CALLAHAN'S OF CALABASH
9973 Beach Rd.
CALABASH, NC 28467
800-344-3816 Fax: 910-579-7209
Secondary: D56

NEBRASKA
COLLECTORS PLATES
7311 Izard St
OMAHA, NE 68114
402-932-9595
collectorsplatesemst@home.com
http://members.home.net/collectorspla
Primary: RC
Secondary: RC, HUM
Buys: RC, BG

AMY'S HALLMARK
415 Norfolk Ave.
NORFOLK, NE 68701
402-379-2130 Fax: 402-644-8115
amyshallmark@conpoint.com
Primary: PIP, D56, ENES, CT, COWS, JTRS,
    DR
Secondary: PIP, D56, ENES, CT, COWS, JTRS,
    DR

NEW HAMPSHIRE
COSMO'S COLLECTIBLES
PO Box 722
MILTON NH 03851
603-652-7101
como@worldpath.net
www.cosnoscollectibles.com
Secondary: CHARM
Buys: Occasionally buys CT

NEW JERSEY
COLLECTIBLE CORNER
41 Clementon Rd. #234
BERLIN, NJ 08009
856-809-9255
jmv1022@aol.com

MORTON'S CRYSTAL INC.
1622 Ash St.
FORT DIX, NJ 08640
201-865-7777 Fax: 201-865-7777
mail@mortonscrystal.com
www.mortonscrystal.com
Primary: SW
Secondary: SW
Buys: SW

PRESTIGE COLLECTIONS
93 Dorsa Ave.
LIVINGSTON, NJ 07039
973-591-0111 Fax: 973-597-9408

NEW YORK
CORNER COLLECTIONS
7979 Main St
HUNTER, NY 12442
518-263-4141 Fax: 518-263-3908
collect@mhonline.net
cornercollections.com
Primary: None
Secondary: SW, WD, AR, HUM, LILI, LC
Buys: SW, WD, AR, HUM, LILI, LC

GLORIOUS TREASURES
1467 E. 70th Street
BROOKLYN, NY 11234
718-241-8185 Fax: 718-241-8184

GOLDRUSH
50 E. 42nd Street
NEW YORK, NY 10017
212-682-5320

JOYCE DOUGLAS
1526 Fox Glen Dr.
HARTSDALE, NY 10530
914-428-3028 Fax: 914-428-3028
Joycry@aol.com
Secondary: SW, HK
Buys: Yes, call first

NATURAL GOODS & FINERY
Main St., P.O. Box 201
ESSEX, NY 12936
518-963-4347

VILLAGE COLLECTORS
12 Hart Place
DIX HILLS, NY 11746
631-242-2457 Fax: 631-243-4607

OHIO
CLASSIC COLECTIBLE EXCHANGE,INC
1397 Winchester W. Rd
BUCYRUS, OH 44820
419-562-9115 Fax: 419-562-9303
clascoll@bright.net
Secondary: WD, AR, PM, CT, SW
Buys: No, will list and try to help sell for customer.

COLONIAL HOUSE of COLLECTIBLES
182 Front St
BEREA, OH 44017
440-826-4169 Fax: 440-826-0839
yworrey@aol.com
Primary: RD, D56, HUM, LL, DW, LILI, WF,
    WD, SW, PM, BG,RC, CT, HK, HL,
    FM, LC, TY
Secondary: RD, D56, HUM, LL, DW, LILI,
    WD, SW, PM, BG,RC, CT, HK, HL,
    LC, TY
Buys: RD, D56, HUM, LL, DW, LILI, WD, SW,
    PM, B&G,RC, CT, HK, HL, LC

CRYSTAL EXCHANGE AMERICA
6505 Browns Run Rd.
MIDDLETOWN, OH 45042
513-423-5272 Fax: 513-423-8318
angie@crystalexchange.com
www.crystalexchange.com
Secondary: SW

CURIO CABINET & CHRISTMAS VILLAGE
679 High St.
WORTHINGTON, OH 43085
614-885-1986 Fax: 614-885-2043
nanaomi@aol.com
www.curiocabinet.com
Primary: WF,CR, D56, WD, RD,
Secondary: WF,CR, D56, WD, RD,
Buys: WF

EMPORIUM DOWNTOWN
154 W. Main Street
LANCASTER, OH 43130
740 653 5717 Fax: 646 390 0921
Emporium@Telocity.com
Primary: AB
Secondary: AB
Buys: Yes, steins

GIFT GARDEN
624 Great Northern Mall
NORTH OLMSTEAD, OH 44070
440-777-0116 Fax: same
Primary: AB

LITTLE RED GIFT HOUSE
State Rte. 113
P.O. Box 36
BIRMINGHAM, OH 44816
440-965-5420
Secondary: HUM, PM, CT, RAY, ENES, SA,
          POSS, BE
Buys: Yes, Rockwell

MILLER'S HALLMARK & GIFT GALLERY
1322 N. Barron St.
EATON, OH 45320
937-456-4151 Fax: 937-456-7851
Primary: HUM

STERLING COLLECTABLES
820 Koogle Rd.
MANSFIELD, OH 44901
419-589-9796 Fax: 419 589 8659
info@sterlingcollectables.com
sterlingcollectables.com
Primary: GO, BG, RC, WW
Secondary: GO, BG, RC, WW
Buys: GO, BG, RC, WW

SHIRLEY MARIE'S DOLLS
7216 Dearborn Ave.
CLEVELAND, OH 44102
216-631-0935
Primary: LEE
Secondary: LEE

WARNERS BLUE RIBBON BOOKS
7163 W Fred-Garland Rd
UNION, OH 45322-9621
937-698-4508
Primary: Reference book for Swarovski

OKLAHOMA
D'S GIFTS & COLLECTIBLES
3420 S. Boulevard
EDMOND, OK 73013
405-348-2367 Fax: 405-348-1870
dsgiftscollect@aol.com
Primary: BOY, CAS, CO, PM
Secondary: BOY, CAS, CT, CR, CO, ENES,
LEF, PA, PM
Buys: No

LITTLE RED GIFT HOUSE
"a unique treasure of a gift shop"
State Route 113 Birmingham, Ohio 44816
440.965.5420
Hours Tuesday-Saturday 10-6 Sunday 12-5 (Sept- December)
Closed Mondays except in December

s e r v i c e s
Specialists in Norman Rockwell figurines and plates. Occasionally buy Rockwell
collections or individual pieces. No consignments. Free appraisals for insurance.
Ship UPS daily. Visa and MasterCard accepted.

s e c o n d a r y
Norman Rockwell figurines and plates.

n o t e w o r t h y
Little Red Gift House has become known nationwide as a major source of
Norman Rockwell collectibles, both new and older pieces. In-stock is a large
inventory of retired, discontinued, and limited edition Rockwell figurines.
Listing of in-stock Rockwell items is available upon request. Little Red Gift House
also carries M.I. Hummel, Precious Moments, Thomas Kinkade, Dept 56,
Collectors Plates, Cherished Teddies, Sports Collectibles, Ray Day, Memories of
Yesterday, Seraphim Angels, Possible Dreams Santas, Bradford, Anheuser-Busch
Steins, Emmet Kelly, Amish Heritage, Jan Hagara, Pretty As a Picture,
Snowbabies and Snowbunnies.

WARNER'S BLUE RIBBON BOOKS

7163 West Fred-Garland Rd. Union, Ohio 45322
Phone 937.698.4508 Fax 937.698.5408 email jane@wbrb.com

Warner's Blue Ribbon Books on Swarovski make collecting and keeping track of
your Swarovski collection more enjoyable.

They currently have five books, each containing photographic illustrations,
designer names, physical dimensions, and other information on Swarovski items.

Their original book, Warner's Blue Ribbon Book on SwarovskiSilver Crystal, is a
comprehensive reference guide that includes information on current and retired,
European and U.S., crystal pieces from 1976 to present. It also includes the SCS
Annual Member pieces.

All books are updated and republished every year to reflect new pieces, new
retirements, and current Estimated Replacement Values (for insurance purposes).
Place your order online using a secure order form.
www.wbrb.com is their online subscription
service with color images.

"The Swarovski Guides Written for Collectors by Collectors"

COLONIAL HOUSE OF COLLECTIBLES

182 Front Street Berea, Ohio 44017
440.826.4169 800.344.9299
Fax 440.826.0839 email yworrey@aol.com
Monday- Friday 9-6 Saturday 10-5

services

Buy/Sell/Trade/Appraise. MasterCard, Visa, Discover and American Express

secondary

Royal Doulton, Department 56, MI Hummel, Lladro, David Winter, Lilliput Lane,
Wee Forest Folk, Disney Classics, Swarovski, Bing & Grondahl, Royal
Copenhagen, Harmony Kingdom, Harbour Lights, Franklin Mint Die Cast Cars,
Looney Tunes Spotlight Collection, Lenox Classics, Beanie Babies.

noteworthy

Colonial House of Collectibles has been in business for over 28 years. For the
past 16 years, they have been located in an 1873 house in the southwest
suburb of Cleveland. A year round Christmas room is always on display. They
are a Redemption Center for Collector club pieces.

J&L TREASURES
6715 E. Reno Ave.
MIDWEST CITY, OK 73110
405 741 2299 Fax: 815 327 2935
JLTreas@SWBell.net
www.Tias.com/stores/JLT
Primary: AB, ART, GOE, ROM, CHARM,
        POSS, UT
Secondary: CT, AB, EK, GOE, CHARM
Buys: No

PICTORAL TREASURES
104 E. 11th St.
PAWHUSKA, OK 74056
918-287-2668 Fax: 507-260-4305
www.artontheweb.com
Primary: GW
Secondary: GW

PINK TURTLE GIFTS
110 W. Main St.
Weatherford, OK 73096
580-772-1666 Fax: same
jmfast@yore.net
www.pinkturtlegifts.com
Primary: D56, CH, HALL, PM, CT, BOY, CA
Secondary: D56, CH, HALL, PM, CT, BOY, CA
Buys: No

SHIRLEY'S COLLECTIBLE EXCHANGE
1500 Ward Rd.
ARDMORE, OK 73401
580-226-6228 Fax: 580-226-6228
shirleys@brightok.net
Secondary: SW, SA, WD, AR, LL, HUM, D56,
        CT, PM, BOY, AGC, BA, HALL,
        MA, LEF, CA
Buys: Yes, HALL

OREGON
CHRISTMAS AT THE ZOO
118 NW 23rd Ave.
PORTLAND, OR 97210
503-223-4048 Fax: 503-225-5892
www.christmaszoo.citysearch.com
Primary: None
Secondary: CR

PENNSYLVANIA
BOB LAMSON BEER STEINS INC.
1728 Allen St
ALLENTOWN, PA 18104
610-435-8611 Fax: 610-435-8188
Firstchoicemal@enter.net
www.lamsonsteins.com
Primary: AB
Secondary: AB
Buys: AB

CRAYON SOUP
King of Prussia Plaza
KING of PRUSSIA, PA 19406
610-265-2446 Fax: 610-265-2979
crayonsoupinc@aol.com
Primary: AGC, AR, WD, EN, LL, LILI, WW,
    SW, DW, ST, PM

EMPORIUM COLLECTIBLES GALLERY
3358 W. 26th Street
ERIE, PA 16506
814-833-2895 Fax: 814-835-5297
Emporiumgallery@aol.com
Primary: LEF, TK, D56, AR,
Secondary: JM, SH, EH, LEF, TK, D56, AR,
Buys: No

GIFTS, GLASS & MUCH MORE
3717 Huckleberry Rd.
Allentown, PA 18104
800-488-5858

SAM'S STEINS & COLLECTIBLES
2207 Lincoln Hwy. EST (Rte. 30)
LANCASTER, PA 17602-1111
717-394-6404
Primary: AB

WORLDWIDE COLLECTIBLES AND GIFTS
PO Box 158, Lakeside Ave
BERWYN, PA 19312-0158
610-644-2442 Fax: 610-899-9549
Secondary: AD

RHODE ISLAND
TONY'S GIFTS & COLLECTIBLES
124 Summit Street
PAWTUCKET, RI 02860
401-724-0440 Fax: 401-722-8566
tony@tonysgifts.com
tonysgifts.com
Primary: LIL, DW, HL, HK
Secondary: LIL, DW
Buys: DW,LILI

TENNESSEE
BARBARA'S GATLINBURG SHOPS
105 Cherokee Orchard Rd.
GATLINBURG, TN 37738
865-436-3454 Fax: 865-436-3219
shop@barbarashops.com
www.Barbarashops.com
Primary: SW, HL, DW, D56, CG, CP, CA
Secondary: SW, HL, DW, D56, CG, CP, CA
Buys: Yes, CHIL

FAYE SNODGRASS GALLERY, THE
320 Main Street
FRANKLIN, TN 37064
615-595-0833 Fax: 615-595-5305
Primary: SW, HUM,
Secondary: WILL, EKO, SW
Buys: No

INCREDIBLE CHRISTMAS PLACE, THE
2470 Parkway Bell Tower Square
PIDGEON FORGE, TN 37863
423-453-0415
Primary: EKJ, FL
Secondary: EMJ, FL

TEXAS:
AFRICAN IMPORTS
3662 W. Camp Wisdon
DALLAS, TX 75237
972-296-9861
Primary: EV, DLL, SNC, AGC, MC

AMANDA'S FINE GIFTS
265 Central Park Mall
San Antonio, TX 78216-5506
800-441-4458   Fax: 210-404-0063
Primary: LL, AR, WD
Secondary: LL, SW, HU, RL, AR, CH, WD

ASHLEY AVERY'S
3811 S. Cooper #1036
ARLINGTON, TX 76015
916-772-1222
Primary: LL, WD, SW, AR, HU, LC, PM, JTRS,
HK, EV, WE, AR, MC, PIP, ST

ASTRAL CASTLE
1028 D Andrews Hwy.
MIDLAND, TX 79702
915-520-6463 Fax: 915-689-5403
thecastle@ccgs.com
www.ccgs.com
Primary: PD, WE
Secondary: PD, WE
Buys: PD, WE

CHERYL M. MC CANTS
13401 Bridgeview Lane
MONTGOMERY, TX 77356
963-449-4088 Fax: 936-597-6267
cmccants@mccantsenamels.com
www.McCantsenamels.com
Primary: HAL
Secondary: HAL
Buys: HAL, call first

GARY'S COLLECTABLES
1217 Trinity Drive
BENBROOK, TX 76126-4209
817 249 2741 Fax: 817-249-6639
gary@garycollectables.com
www.garyscollectables.com
Primary: AR, HL, LL, SW, HUM
Secondary: AR,CT,HL,LL,D56,SW,TY,HUM
Buys: No

MERRY'S CHRISTMAS & CLOWNS
113 N. MacArthur
IRVING, TX 75061
817-329-1431 Fax: 972-259-3528
Primary: LL, TK, CR, PO, POSS, ST, SA, FO,
        RL, D56, BOY
Secondary: D56, LL, SW, TK, BOY, CR, POSS,
        ROM, RL, CT, SW
Buys: RL, ST

MULBERRY BUSH
2304 Highway 281 North
MARBLE FALLS, TX 78654
830-693-8694

OHI EXCHANGE
553 Landa Street
NEW BRAUNFELS, TX 78130
830-629-1191 Fax: 800-606-1118
OHIXCHNG@rx.netcom.com
ohiexchange.com
Primary:Only steins & mugs from Germany.
Buys: No, listing service

SWAN HUNTER 1
C/O Helgas Enterprise
1292-C W. Arkansas Lane
ARLINGTON, TX 76013
817-860-0166
swanhunter@aol.com
Secondary: Price guide to Swarovski.

UTAH
KAREN'S KOLLECTIBLE KLOSET
205 Skyline Drive
BRIGHAM CITY, UT 84302
435-723-5510
karen@brighamnet.com
Secondary: MA, ASH, HAM, LEE, HALL, BA

VIRGINIA
GAZEBO GIFTS of VA INC.
304 Main St
NEWPORT NEWS, VA 23601
757-591-8387 Fax: 757-591-8387
gazebogifts@aol.com
Primary: BOY, D56, GOE, WILL, PIP, MA,
        WD, BE, ASH, HAM, ENES, ENC
Secondary: BOY, D56, GOE, WILL, PIP, MA,
        WD
Buys: D56, HUM, BE

MEMORIES IN MOTION
114 Clark Avenue
ELKTON, VA 22827
540-298-9234
bahorne@rica.net
www.oldornaments.com
Secondary: HALL

WASHINGTON
HEATHER HOUSE
23730 Bothell Everett Hwy. # D
BOTHELL, WA 98021
425-486-8199 Fax: 425-486-3881
Primary: PIP, TK
Secondary: PIP

SIER'S SECONDARY EXCHANGE
6801 98TH Ave. SE
SNOHOMISH, WA 98290
360-568-0107 Fax: 360-568-0107
SecExch@aol.com
Secondary: D56, SW, LE
Buys: Listing service for some items.

WISCONSIN
COUNTRY MOUSE, A
7940 W. Layton Ave.
Milwaukee, WI 53220
414-281-4210
mouse7940@aol.com
Primary: PM, CT, DW, CHARM, JTRS, B&G,
RE, EKJ, BYER, LILI
Secondary: PM, CT, MOY, DW, CHARM, DR,
KR, PD, HU, HK, JTRS, B&G, RE, EKJ, D56,
SN, KR, PD, BYER, CH, LILI, BE, ASH, HK,
SCH, ENES.

CUPOLA HOUSE SHOPS
Box 498
EGG HARBOUR, WI 54209
920-868-3941
cupolahouse@itol.com
cupolahouse.com
Primary: D56, WF, LILI, HL, DLL, AGC
Secondary: D56, WF, LILI, HL, DLL, AGC
Buys: D56, WF, LILI, HL, DLL, AGC

FOLK ART COLLECTION, THE
121 S. Main St.
PO Box 22
FOUNTAIN CITY, WI 54629
608-687-6698
masmith@hbci.com, leosmith.com
Primary: D56, MID
Secondary: D56, MID
Buys: Yes, call first.

Finding Your Way Through CIB's Price Index Is As Easy As 1, 2, 3!

1. Determine the category that your collectible falls into. CIB's Price Index is divided into 10 general categories that are organized alphabetically. They include: Architecture, Bells, Boxes, Dolls/Plush, Figurines, Graphics, Nutcrackers, Ornaments, Plates/Plaques and Steins. Hint: Figurines is by far our most extensive category. If the product you're looking for doesn't fit neatly into one of the other categories, chances are you'll find it in the Figurines section.

2. Locate your manufacturer. Manufacturers are listed alphabetically within each category.

3. Once you turn to the pages that contain information about the manufacturer you're looking for, you'll find that products are listed by line, and by series within each line, if applicable.

TERMS AND ABBREVIATIONS

Annual = Issued once a year.
A/P = Artist Proof.
Closed = An item or series no longer in production
Annual = Issued once a year.
A/P = Artist Proof.
Closed = An item or series no longer in production.
G/P = Gallery Proof.
N/A = Not available at this time.
Numbrd. = Numbered series.
P/P = Publisher's Proof.
Open = Not limited by number or time, available until manufacturer stops production, "retires" or "closes" the item or series.
Retrd. = Retired.
R/E = Renaissance Proof.
S/N = Signed and Numbered.
S/O = Sold Out.
S/P = Studio Proof.
Set = Refers to two or more items issued together for a single price.
Suspd. = Suspended (not currently being produced: may be produced in the future).
Unkn. = Unknown.
Yr. Iss. = Year of issue (limited to a calendar year).
28-day, 10-day, etc. = Limited to this number of production (or firing) days, usually not consecutive.

A Special Note to Beatrix Potter, Boyds Bears, Cherished Teddies, Disney Classics, Goebel Miniatures, M.I. Hummel and Precious Moments Collectors: These collectibles carry special marks which change according to production and/or year. The secondary market value for each piece may vary because of these distinctive markings. Our pricing reflects a range for all marks.

A Special Note to Hallmark Keepsake Ornament Collectors: All quotes in this section are for ornaments in mint condition in their original box.

A Special Note to Department 56 Collectors: Year of Introduction indicates the year in which the piece was designed, sculpted and copyrighted. It is possible these pieces may not be available to collectors until the following calendar year.

Price Index Table of Contents

Price Index Table of Contents

Price Index Table of Contents

Limited Edition
Figurines Architecture Plates/Plaques Dolls/Plush Boxes Ornaments Nutcrackers Graphics Steins Bells

This index includes over 67,000 of the most widely traded limited editions in today's collectibles market. It is based on surveys and interviews with several hundred of the most experienced and informed limited edition dealers in the United States, as well as many independent market advisors. In some cases, dealers outside the U.S. are also consulted.

HOW TO USE THIS INDEX

YEAR ISSUE	EDITION LIMIT	YEAR RETIRED	ISSUE PRICE	QUOTE U.S. $

(1) ARCHITECTURE

(2) Department 56
(3) Alpine Village Series
(4) 1987 Alpine Church 6541-2 Closed 1991 32.00   113-208
                                    (5)   (6)   (7)   (8)

(1) The Price Index is organized by category of collectible. Use the table of contents beginning on page 47A to locate the page number for the category and maker listing that you seek.

(2) Within each category, makers are listed in alphabetical order. The example above shows an item in the Department 56
(3) Alpine Village collection.

(4) The year that the item was introduced, and the title of the item. In some cases, the maker's item number is included as an aid for collectors who may not remember the title of their piece.

(5) This column indicates the production status of the item. In this example, the Alpine Church is out of production.

(6) The year that the item went out of production, when known. In this example, Alpine Church was retired in 1991.

(7) The original issue price for Alpine Church was $32.00 in U.S. dollars

(8) The far right column indicates the estimated replacement cost for this item, from the CIB's survey of limited edition dealers. The estimation is often a range, indicating variances that occur regionally.

ARCHITECTURE

Boyds Collection Ltd.

The Bearly-Built Villages™ - The Boyds Collection

YEAR ISSUE	EDITION LIMIT	YEAR RETD.	ISSUE PRICE	*QUOTE U.S.$
2000 Bailey's Cottage...Friends Make Your Home Glow 19700	Retrd.	2001	56.00	56
2000 Bailey's Cozy Cottage - Boyds Town Village #2 19002	Retrd.	2000	24.00	24
2000 Bearly Well Clinic 19008	Open		30.50	31
2000 Bearly-Able Construction Co. 19011	Open		30.50	31
2000 Boyds Bearly a School - Boyds Town Village #4 19004	Open		23.00	23
2001 The Boyds Town Cathedral 19026	5,200	2001	70.00	70
2001 Boyds Town Depot...Bearsylvania Station 19018	Open		30.50	31
2001 The Boyds Town Police Station 19024	5,200		30.50	31
2002 Boydsenbeary Acres Lil' Country Church 19045	Open		25.00	25
2000 The Chapel in the Woods - Boyds Town Village #3 19003	Open		24.00	24
2000 Cocoa's House of Chocolates 19009	Open		30.50	31
2000 Edmund's Hideaway - Boyds Town Village #5 19005	Retrd.	2001	25.00	25-66
2001 Elves-B-Us Workshop 19034	5,200		30.50	31
2001 Emily's Carrot Cottage 19014	Open		30.50	31
2001 Grenville and Beatrice's Homestead 19019	Open		30.50	31
2001 Hoofer Hall Reindeer Dormitory 19033	5,200		30.50	31
2000 Madge's Beauty Salon & Bait Shop 19010	Open		30.50	31
2001 Martha's Bearly Bloom'n Flower Shop 19016	Open		30.50	31
2001 Mr. Pennypincher's Collectibles Shoppe 19023	5,200		36.00	36
2002 Murphy's Mill & Bakery 19044	Open		25.00	25
2002 Ol' MacDonald's Bank Barn 19047	Open		31.00	31
2002 Ol' MacDonald's Farm House 19046	Open		25.00	25
2001 Pub 'N Grub 19021	5,200		30.50	31
2000 Public Libeary - Boyds Town Village #6 19006	Retrd.	2000	24.00	24
2000 Punky Boobear's Haunted Halloween House 19012	Retrd.	2001	30.50	31
2001 The Roxbeary Theater 19017	Open		30.50	31
2001 Scratch-N-Patch...North Pole Hospital 19032	5,200		30.50	31
2001 The Tea Cozy 19015	Open		30.50	31
2000 Ted E. Bear Shop - Boyds Town Village #1 19001	Open		24.00	24
2001 Trumbles' Mansion 19020	5,200		36.00	36
2000 Volunteer Fire Station 19007	Open		30.50	31
2001 Wee Bear Daycare Center 19025	5,200		30.50	31
2001 Wilson's Books 19022	5,200		30.50	31

The Bearly-Built Villages™ Accessories - The Boyds Collection

YEAR ISSUE	EDITION LIMIT	YEAR RETD.	ISSUE PRICE	*QUOTE U.S.$
2001 Autumn Arboretum Collection 19815	Open		21.00	21
2000 Bailey's Cozy Cottage Accessories 19502-1	Open		8.50	9
2000 Bearly Carolin' Party 19800	Open		16.00	16
2000 Bearly Well Clinic Folks 19508-1	Open		11.00	11
2000 Bearly Well Clinic Spring/Summer Folks 19508-2	Open		11.00	11
2000 Bearly-Able Construction Co. Folks 19511-1	Open		11.00	11
2000 Bearly-Able Construction Co. Spring/Summer Folks 19511-2	Open		11.00	11
2001 Bearly-Built Villages Bushels O' Fun Sparkle Snow 19826	Open		5.00	5
2000 The Boyds Bearly A School Accessories 19504-1	Open		8.50	9
2000 The Boyds Bearly A School Fall/Winter Folks 19504-2	Open		11.00	11
2001 Boyds Town Aboretum Collection 19804	Open		20.50	21
2001 Boyds Town Bearly A Forest Collection 19808	Open		13.00	13
2001 Boyds Town Bearly A Forest Collection 19809	Open		11.00	11
2001 Boyds Town Bearly A Forest Collection 19810	Open		11.00	11
2001 The Boyds Town Cathedral Folks 19526-1	Retrd.	2001	11.00	11
2001 Boyds Town Depot...Bearsylvania Spring/Summer Folks 19518-1	Open		11.00	11
2001 The Boyds Town Fountain 19818	Open		11.00	11
2001 Boyds Town Gas & Electric Co. 19805	Open		11.00	11
2001 The Boyds Town Police Station Folks 19524-1	Open		11.00	11
2001 Boyds Town Spring-is-Sprung Aboretum Collection 19806	Open		16.00	16
2002 Boydsenbeary Acres Lil' Country Church Folks 19545-1	Open		11.00	11
2000 The Chapel in the Woods Accessories 19503-1	Open		8.50	9
2000 The Chapel in the Woods Fall/Winter Folks 19503-2	Open		11.00	11
2001 The Cobblestone Fork in the Road 19814	Open		9.00	9
2001 The Cobblestone Path 19812	Open		9.00	9
2001 The Cobblestone Wall 19811	Open		11.00	11
2000 Cocoa's House of Chocolates Folks 19509-1	Open		11.00	11
2000 Cocoa's House of Chocolates Spring/Summer Folks 19509-2	Open		11.00	11
2000 Edmund's Hideaway Accessories 19505-1	Open		8.50	9
2000 Edmund's Hideaway Fall/Winter Folks 19505-2	Open		11.00	11
2001 Elves-B-Us Workshop Folks 19034-1	Open		11.00	11
2001 Emily's Carrot Cottage Spring/Summer Folks 19514-1	Open		11.00	11
2001 Fall Has Flung Arboretum Collection 19827	Open		18.00	18
2001 Grenville and Beatrice's Homestead Spring/Summer Folks 19519-1	Open		11.00	11
2001 Holly Jolly Christmas Tree 19821	Open		13.00	13
2001 Hoofer Hall Reindeer Dormitory Folks 19033-1	Open		11.00	11
2001 Kringle's Arctic Igloo with Bearly A Snowman 19822	Open		11.00	11
2001 Kringle's Confectionary Fence 19825	Open		11.00	11
2000 Kringle's Retreat...Winter Wishes (waterglobe) 19701	Retrd.	2001	49.00	49
2001 Kringle's Sweet Street 19819	Open		9.00	9
2001 Kringle's Village Gas & Electric Co. Lamp Post 19824	Open		9.00	9
2001 The Lawn & Garden Collection 19807	Open		11.00	11
2001 Little Ben Clock Tower 19803	Open		16.00	16
2000 Madge's Beauty Salon & Bait Shop Folks 19510-1	Open		11.00	11
2001 Martha's Bearly Bloomin' Flower Shop Spring/Summer Folks 19516-1	Open		11.00	11
2001 Matthew's Split Rail Fence, set/4 19802	Open		11.00	11
2001 Mr. Pennypincher's Collectibles Shoppe Folks 19523-1	Open		11.00	11
2002 Murphy's Mill & Bakery Folks 19544-1	Open		11.00	11
2002 Ol' MacDonald's Farm House Folks 19546-1	Open		11.00	11
2002 Ol' MacDonald's FarmBank Barn Folks 19547-1	Open		11.00	11
2001 Pub 'N Grub Folks 19521-1	Open		11.00	11
2000 Public Libeary Accessories 19506-1	Open		8.50	9
2000 Punky Boobear's Haunted Halloween House Folks 19512-1	Open		11.00	11
2001 The Roxbeary Theater Spring/Summer Folks 19517-1	Open		11.00	11
2001 Scratch-N-Patch...North Pole Hospital Folks 19032-1	Open		11.00	11
2001 Sugar Plum Paviiion 19820	Open		11.00	11
2001 Sweet Street Fork in the Road 19828	Open		9.00	9
2001 The Tea Cozy Spring/Summer Folks 19515-1	Open		11.00	11
2000 Ted E. Bear Shop Accessories 19501-1	Open		8.50	9
2000 Ted E. Bear Shop Fall/Winter Folks 19501-2	Open		11.00	11
2001 Trumbles' Mansion Folks 19520-1	Open		11.00	11
2000 Volunteer Fire Station Folks 19507-1	Open		11.00	11
2000 Volunteer Fire Station Spring/Summer Folks 19507-2	Open		11.00	11
2001 Wee Bear Daycare Center Folks 19525-1	Open		11.00	11

YEAR ISSUE	EDITION LIMIT	YEAR RETD.	ISSUE PRICE	*QUOTE U.S.$
2001 Wild Bear Hic-Up Monument 19801	Open		7.00	7
2001 Wilson's Books Folks 19522-1	Open		11.00	11

Route 33 1/3 - The Boyds Collection

2002 Bailey's Frosted Cottage 19900	Open		16.00	16
2002 The Book-O-Love Chapel 19903	Open		16.00	16
2002 Hero's Hook and Ladder Fire House 19901	Open		16.00	16
2002 Miss Macintosh's School of Thought 19904	Open		16.00	16
2002 Ms. Martha's Garden Cottage 19902	Open		16.00	16

Cast Art Industries

Dreamsicles Northern Lights Village - K. Haynes

2000 Ice Castle-60135	Open		59.00	59
2000 The Ice Works-60134	Open		59.00	59
2000 Santa's Place-60131	Open		59.00	59
2000 Ski Lodge-60133	Open		55.00	55
2000 Snowed Inn-60132	Open		49.00	49

Ivy & Innocence-Friends of Ivy Symbol of Membership - S. Reader

1997 Welcome To Ivy 05500	Retrd.	1998	Gift	N/A
1998 Beth's Pastry Cart 05194	Retrd.	1999	Gift	N/A
1998 The Seesaw 05193	Retrd.	2000	15.00	15
1999 All The Latest 05210	Retrd.	2000	Gift	N/A
2000 Rebecca Marie's Visit 05211	Retrd.	2001	Gift	N/A
2001 The Ivy Garden Club 05504	6/02		29.95	30
2001 The Best of Friends 05503	6/02		Gift	N/A

Ivy & Innocence-Accessories - S. Reader

1998 Blooming Beauties (3 pc.) 05191	Retrd.	2000	11.00	11
1999 The Children's Carousel 05196	Retrd.	2000	55.00	55
1997 Cool Water 05185	Retrd.	2000	5.00	5
1997 Emily's Welcome 05182	Retrd.	2000	15.00	15
1998 Flowering Trees (3 pc.) 05192	Retrd.	2000	18.00	18
1998 The Garden Bench 05188	Retrd.	2000	7.00	7
1997 The Garden Gate 05183	Retrd.	2000	7.50	8
1999 The Garden Gazebo 05201	Retrd.	2001	15.00	15
1998 The Garden Path 01590	Retrd.	2000	8.00	8
1998 Glimmering Lamppost 05187	Retrd.	2000	7.00	7
1998 Home Tweet Home 05189	Retrd.	N/A	Gift	N/A
1999 Lighthouse At Ivy Cove 05195	5,000	2000	44.00	44
1999 Miss Virginia Reed 05199	Retrd.	2000	9.50	10
1997 Set A Spell 05186	Retrd.	2000	N/A	N/A
1999 The Sparkling Fountain 05200	Retrd.	2000	12.00	12
1997 Special Delivery 05184	Retrd.	2000	5.00	5
1999 The Tinker's Wagon 05198	Retrd.	2000	20.00	20
1999 Tom The Tinker 05197	Retrd.	2000	9.50	10
1997 The Towering Cottage 05180	10,000	2001	39.00	39

Ivy & Innocence-Chapter One-Parker's Bed & Breakfast - S. Reader

1997 Parker's Bed and Breakfast 05000	Retrd.	1999	29.50	30
1997 Making Wishes Come True (Acc.) 05001	Retrd.	1999	13.00	13
1997 Violet & Ed Peters (Acc.) 05002	Retrd.	1999	15.00	15
1997 Lucinda's Bundle of Joy (Acc.) 05003	Retrd.	1999	9.50	10
1997 Chapter One Display Base 05005	Retrd.	1999	15.00	15

Ivy & Innocence-Chapter Two-Emma's Tea Room - S. Reader

1997 Emma's Tea Room 05030	Retrd.	2000	19.00	19
1997 Tea Party (Acc.) 05031	Retrd.	2001	15.00	15
1997 Tea For Three (Acc.) 05032	Retrd.	2001	9.50	10
1997 Miss Mary Hemmings (Acc.) 05033	Retrd.	2000	7.90	8
1997 Chapter Two Display Base 05035	Retrd.	2001	15.00	15

Ivy & Innocence-Chapter Three-Yates' Antique Shop - S. Reader

1997 Yates' Antique Shop 05060	Retrd.	2000	24.00	24
1997 Winston's Peddler Wagon (Acc.) 05061	Retrd.	2000	17.00	17
1997 Annabelle & Theodore (Acc.) 05062	Retrd.	2000	7.00	7
1997 Jonathan & Giddyup (Acc.) 05063	Retrd.	2000	7.00	7
1997 Timeless Treasures (Acc.) 05064	Retrd.	2000	12.00	12
1997 Chapter Three Display Base 05065	Retrd.	2000	15.00	15

Ivy & Innocence-Chapter Four-The Olde Ivy School - S. Reader

1997 The Olde Ivy School 05090	Retrd.	2000	24.00	24
1997 Long May It Wave (Acc.) 05091	Retrd.	2000	5.00	5
1997 Miss Jenny Morris & Amy (Acc.) 05092	Retrd.	2001	9.50	10
1997 Andrew & Chase (Acc.) 05093	Retrd.	2001	7.00	7
1997 Chapter Four Display Base 05095	Retrd.	2001	15.00	15

Ivy & Innocence-Chapter Five-Greene's Flower Shop - S. Reader

1997 Greene's Flower Shop 05120	Retrd.	2000	24.00	24
1997 Blossom's Flower Cart (Acc.) 05121	Retrd.	2000	15.00	15
1997 Blossom Greene (Acc.) 05122	Retrd.	2000	7.00	7
1997 Katie Jayne Tucker (Acc.) 05123	Retrd.	2000	7.00	7
1997 Chapter Five Display Base 05125	Retrd.	2000	15.00	15

Ivy & Innocence-Chapter Six-A Stitch in Time - S. Reader

1997 A Stitch in Time 05150	Retrd.	2000	24.00	24
1997 The Hearts & Crafts Wagon (Acc.) 05151	Retrd.	2001	17.00	17
1997 The Quilt Tree (Acc.) 05152	Retrd.	2000	23.00	23
1997 Lila & Lucifer (Acc.) 05153	Retrd.	2000	7.90	8
1997 Chapter Six Display Base 05155	Retrd.	2000	15.00	15

Ivy & Innocence-Chapter Seven-The All Faith Chapel - S. Reader

1998 All Faith Chapel 05240	Retrd.	1999	28.00	28
1998 Mary & John Knight, Jr. (Acc.) 05241	Retrd.	1999	11.00	11
1998 Elizabeth Knight (Acc.) 05242	Retrd.	1999	7.00	7
1998 Parson Brown (Acc.) 05243	Retrd.	1999	9.00	9
1998 Joyful News (Acc.) 05244	Retrd.	1999	7.50	8
1998 Chapter Seven Display Base 05245	Retrd.	1999	15.00	15

Ivy & Innocence-Chapter Eight-Ivy Firehouse - S. Reader

1998 Ivy Firehouse 05270	Retrd.	2000	27.00	27
1998 Captain Blaze (Acc.) 05271	Retrd.	2000	9.00	9
1998 Jr. Fire Captain (Acc.) 05272	Retrd.	2000	7.00	7
1998 Sparky's House (Acc.) 05273	Retrd.	2000	8.50	9
1998 Pumper No. 2 (Acc.) 05274	Retrd.	2000	17.00	17
1998 Chapter Eight Display Base 05275	Retrd.	2000	15.00	15

Ivy & Innocence-Chapter Nine-The Toy Shop - S. Reader

1998 The Toy Shop 05300	Retrd.	2000	24.00	24
1998 Ross Harwell & Jimmy (Acc.) 05301	Retrd.	2000	10.00	10
1998 Toys A' Plenty (Acc.) 05302	Retrd.	2000	10.00	10
1998 Mister Snowman (Acc.) 05303	Retrd.	2000	7.00	7
1998 "Greetings" Time (Acc.) 05304	Retrd.	2000	6.00	6
1998 Chapter Nine Display Base 05305	Retrd.	2000	15.00	15

Ivy & Innocence-Chapter Ten-The Old Ivy Church - S. Reader

1999 The Old Ivy Church 05330	Retrd.	2000	30.00	30
1999 Joseph & Priscilla Bracken (Acc.) 05331	Retrd.	2000	11.00	11
1999 Dorothy & Joan Bracken (Acc.) 05332	Retrd.	2000	9.00	9
1999 Away In A Manager (Acc.) 05334	Retrd.	2000	9.00	9
1999 Chapter Ten Display Base 05335	Retrd.	2000	15.00	15

Ivy & Innocence-Chapter Eleven-The Ivy Newspaper Company (Members-Only) - S. Reader

1999 The Ivy Newspaper 05450	Retrd.	2000	29.00	29
1999 Read All About It! 05451	Retrd.	2000	9.00	9
1999 Eddy's Ivy Flier 05452	Retrd.	2000	9.00	9
1999 Newspapers And More 05453	Retrd.	2000	15.00	15

Charming Tails/Fitz and Floyd Collectibles

Charming Tails Squashville Lighted Village - D. Griff

1994 Acorn Street Lamp 87/948	Closed	1997	5.00	10-35
1995 Butternut Squash Dairy 87/562	7,500	1997	45.00	45-155
1996 Candy Apple Candy Store 87/611	9,000	1997	45.00	51-162
1996 Cantaloupe Cathedral 87/597	Closed	1997	45.00	48-125
1995 Carrot Post Office 87/583	Closed	1996	45.00	45-125
1994 Chestnut Chapel 87/521	Closed	1996	45.00	45-125
1995 Great Oak Town Hall 87/584	Closed	1997	45.00	48-139
2002 Holly-Day House 87/128	Open		48.00	48
1994 Leaf Fence 87/947	Closed	1997	6.00	10-25
1995 Mail Box, Bench 87/560	Closed	1995	11.00	16-35
1995 Mushroom Depot 87/563	Closed	1997	45.00	35-139
1994 Old Cob Mill 87/524	7,500	1997	45.00	63-157
1994 Pumpkin Inn 87/522	Closed	1997	45.00	48-119
1995 Street Light/Sign 87/561	Closed	1997	11.00	12-30
1994 Village Sign 87/533	Closed	2000	30.00	30-50

YEAR ISSUE	EDITION LIMIT	YEAR RETD.	ISSUE PRICE	*QUOTE U.S.$
Cherished Teddies/Enesco Group, Inc.				
Our Cherished Neighbearhood - P. Hillman				
1998 Christmas Decorated House 352667	Closed	1999	20.00	20
1998 Winter Church 352659	Closed	1999	20.00	20
1998 Winter Post Office 352675	Closed	1999	20.00	20
1998 Winter Train Depot 352683	Closed	1999	20.00	20
Department 56				
Alpine Village Series - Department 56				
1987 Alpine Church 6541-2	Closed	1991	32.00	160-235
1987 Alpine Church (white) 6541-2	Closed	N/A	32.00	395-485
1992 Alpine Shops 5618-9, set/2	Closed	1997	75.00	80
1992 • Kukuck Uhren 56191	Closed	1998	37.50	38
1992 • Metterniche Wurst 56190	Closed	1997	37.50	40
1986 Alpine Village 6540-4, set/5	Closed	1997	150.00	200
1986 • Apotheke 65407	Closed	1997	39.00	39
1986 • Besson Bierkeller 65405	Closed	1996	30.00	45
1986 • Gasthof Eisl 65406	Closed	1996	30.00	45
1986 • Milch-Kase 65409	Closed	1996	30.00	45
1986 • E. Staubr Backer 65408	Closed	1997	39.00	36-40
2001 Altstadter Bierstube (Alstader Beer House) 56218	Open		65.00	65
1990 Bahnhof 5615-4	Closed	1993	42.00	50-135
1997 Bernhardiner Hundchen 56174	Closed	2000	50.00	50-60
1996 Danube Music Publisher 56173	Closed	2000	55.00	55-64
1998 Federbetten Und Steppdecken 56176	Closed	2001	48.00	48
2002 Getreidemühle Zwettl 56221	Open		85.00	85
1999 Glockenspiel 56210	Open		80.00	80
1988 Grist Mill 5953-6	Closed	1997	42.00	45
1998 Heidi's Grandfather's House 56177	Closed	2001	64.00	64
2000 Hofburg Castle 56216	Open		68.00	68
1987 Josef Engel Farmhouse 5952-8	Closed	1989	33.00	800-925
1995 Kamm Haus 5617-1	Closed	1999	42.00	42-48
2002 Käsehändler Schmitt 56222	Open		55.00	55
1994 Konditorei Schokolade (Bakery & Chocolate Shop) 5614-6	Closed	1998	37.50	30-40
2001 Nussknacker Werkstatt (Nutcracker Workshop) (Anniversary Edition) 59217	5,600	2001	60.00	60-235
2001 Schwarzwalder Kuckucksuhren 56220	Open		65.00	65
1998 The Sound of Music® von Trapp Villa 56178, set/5	Open		130.00	130
1999 The Sound of Music® Wedding Church 56211	Open		60.00	60
1997 Spielzeug Laden 56192	Closed	2000	65.00	65-72
1993 Sport Laden 5612-0	Closed	1998	50.00	40-68
1991 St. Nikolaus Kirche 5617-0	Closed	1999	37.50	37-45
American Pride - Department 56				
2002 American Pride Backdrop 57705	Open		45.00	45
2002 The Jefferson Memorial 57704	Open		65.00	65
2002 The Lincoln Memorial 57702	Open		65.00	65
2002 The White House 57701	Open		75.00	75
Christmas In the City Series - Department 56				
2001 42nd Street Fire Company 58914	Open		80.00	80
1989 5607 Park Avenue Townhouse 5977-3	Closed	1992	48.00	90
1989 5609 Park Avenue Townhouse 5978-1	Closed	1992	48.00	90
1999 5th Avenue Salon 58950	Closed	2001	68.00	68
1991 All Saints Corner Church 5542-5	Closed	1998	96.00	58-110
2002 Architectural Antiques 58926, set/17	Open		75.00	75
1991 Arts Academy 5543-3	Closed	1993	45.00	50-85
2001 Baker Bros. Bagel Bakery 58920	Open		75.00	75
1995 Brighton School 5887-6	Closed	1998	52.00	52-125
1994 Brokerage House 5881-5	Closed	1997	48.00	45-62
1995 Brownstones on the Square 5887-7, set/2	Closed	2000	90.00	90
1995 • Beekman House 5887-8	Closed	2000	45.00	40-52
1995 • Pickford Place 58879	Closed	1998	45.00	51-77
1996 Café Caprice French Restaurant 58882	Closed	2001	45.00	45
1997 The Capitol 58887	Closed	1998	110.00	90-115
1987 The Cathedral 5962-5	Closed	1990	60.00	289-445
2001 Cathedral of St. Paul (Anniversary Piece) 58919	Closed	2001	150.00	150-795
1991 Cathedral Church of St. Mark 5549-2	3,024	1993	120.00	1200-1970
1988 Chocolate Shoppe 5968-4	Closed	1991	40.00	110-150

YEAR ISSUE	EDITION LIMIT	YEAR RETD.	ISSUE PRICE	*QUOTE U.S.$
1987 Christmas In The City 6512-9, set/3	Closed	1990	112.00	535-600
1987 • Bakery 6512-9	Closed	1990	37.50	100-125
1987 • Tower Restaurant 6512-9	Closed	1990	37.50	235-244
1987 • Toy Shop and Pet Store 6512-9	Closed	1990	37.50	185-235
1997 The City Globe 58883	Closed	2000	65.00	65-79
1988 City Hall (small) 5969-2	Closed	1991	65.00	100-159
1988 City Hall (standard) 5969-2	Closed	1991	65.00	110
1999 Clark Street Automat 58954	Closed	2000	68.00	68
1999 The Consulate 58951, set/2	Closed	2000	95.00	95
1991 The Doctor's Office 5544-1	Closed	1994	60.00	70-88
1989 Dorothy's Dress Shop 5974-9	12,500	1991	70.00	235-375
2002 Fenway Park™ Façade 58932	Open		75.00	75
1994 First Metropolitan Bank 5882-3	Closed	1997	60.00	50-95
2001 Foster Pharmacy 58916	Open		85.00	85
2001 Gardengate House 58915	Open		68.00	68
1996 Grand Central Railway Station 58881	Closed	1999	90.00	90-110
1998 The Grand Movie Theater 58870	Closed	1999	50.00	58-75
1988 Hank's Market 5970-6	Closed	1992	40.00	60-85
1994 Heritage Museum of Art 5883-1	Closed	1998	96.00	60-98
1997 Hi-De-Ho Nightclub 58884	Closed	1999	52.00	55-62
1991 Hollydale's Department Store 5534-4	Closed	1997	75.00	60-95
1995 Holy Name Church 5887-5	Closed		96.00	96
1995 Ivy Terrace Apartments 5887-4	Closed	1997	60.00	60-88
2000 Jenny's Corner Book Shop 58912	Open		65.00	65
1997 Johnson's Grocery & Deli 58886	Open		60.00	60
1999 Lafayette's Bakery 58953	Open		62.00	62
1991 Little Italy Ristorante 5538-7	Closed	1995	50.00	75-95
2001 The Majestic Theater (Anniversary Edition) 58913	15,000	2001	100.00	100-195
2001 Midtown News Stand 58974, set/2	Open		32.50	33
1999 Molly O'Brien's Irish Pub 58952	Open		62.00	62
2002 The Monte Carlo Casino 58925	15,000		85.00	85
2001 Mrs. Stover's Bungalow Candies 58917	Open		75.00	75
2002 Nicholas & Co. Toys 58929, set/2	Open		65.00	65
1998 Old Trinity Church 58940	Closed	2000	96.00	96
1987 Palace Theatre 5963-3	Closed	1989	45.00	855-975
2001 Paradise Travel Company 58921	Open		75.00	75
2000 Paramount Hotel 58911	Open		85.00	85
1999 Parkview Hospital 58947	Closed	2000	65.00	65-75
1998 Precinct 25 Police Station 58941	Open		56.00	56
1990 Red Brick Fire Station 5536-0	Closed	1995	55.00	63-85
1989 Ritz Hotel 5973-0	Closed	1994	55.00	58-78
1997 Riverside Row Shops 58888	Open		52.00	52-60
1997 Scottie's Toy Shop Gift Set (Home For the Holidays) 58871, set/10	Yr.Iss.	1998	65.00	85-135
2002 Sterling Jewelers 58926	Open		70.00	70
1987 Sutton Place Brownstones 5961-7	Closed	1989	80.00	599-925
2002 Tavern In The Park Restaurant 58928	Open		75.00	75
1998 The University Club 58945	Closed	2000	60.00	60-78
1992 Uptown Shoppes 5531-0, set/3	Closed	1996	150.00	133-178
1992 • Haberdashery 55311	Closed	1996	30.00	30-58
1992 • City Clockworks 55313	Closed	1996	30.00	45-78
1992 • Music Emporium 55312	Closed	1996	30.00	48-62
1988 Variety Store 5972-2	Closed	1990	45.00	145-180
1996 Washington Street Post Office 58880	Closed	1998	52.00	52-98
1998 The Wedding Gallery 58943	Open		60.00	60
1993 West Village Shops 5880-7, set/2	Closed	1996	90.00	110
1993 • Potters' Tea Seller 58808	Closed	1996	45.00	50-58
1993 • Spring St. Coffee House 58809	Closed	1996	45.00	54-70
1999 Wintergarten Café 58948	Closed	2001	60.00	60-98
1990 Wong's In Chinatown 5537-9	Closed	1994	55.00	85-125
2002 Wrigley Field™ Façade 58933	Open		95.00	95
2001 Yankee Stadium 58923	Open		85.00	85
Dickens' Village Series - Department 56				
2001 Abington Lock Keeper's Residence 58474	Open		58.00	58
2001 Abington Lockside Inn 58473	Open		68.00	68
2001 Abington Locks 58521, set/2	Open		48.00	48
1999 Aldeburgh Music Box Shop 58441	Closed	2000	60.00	60-70
1999 Aldeburgh Music Box Shop (Discover Department 56® Spring Promotion) 58442, gift set/3	35,000	2000	85.00	85-115
1991 Ashbury Inn 5555-7	Closed	1995	50.00	46-85
1997 Ashwick Lane Hose & Ladder 58305	Open		54.00	54
1987 Barley Bree 5900-5, set/2 (Farmhouse, Barn)	Closed	1989	60.00	250-275
1997 Bayham Post Cottage 58324	Closed	2000	48.00	48-86
2002 Bayly's Blacksmith 58495	Open		70.00	70
2002 Bidwell Windmill #2 58489	Open		80.00	80

YEAR ISSUE	EDITION LIMIT	YEAR RETD.	ISSUE PRICE	*QUOTE U.S.$
1990 Bishops Oast House 5567-0	Closed	1992	45.00	50-85
1995 Blenham Street Bank 5833-0	Closed	1998	60.00	44-72
1986 Blythe Pond Mill House 6508-0	Closed	1990	37.00	169-300
1986 By The Pond Mill House 6508-0	Closed	1990	37.00	60-96
1994 Boarding & Lodging School 5810-6	Closed	1998	48.00	48-150
1993 Boarding and Lodging School 5809-2 (Christmas Carol Commemorative Piece)	Yr.Iss.	1993	48.00	55-75
1987 Brick Abbey 6549-8	Closed	1989	33.00	264-385
2001 Burwickglen Golf Clubhouse 58477	Open		96.00	96
1996 Butter Tub Barn 58338	Closed	1999	48.00	48-52
1996 Butter Tub Farmhouse 58337	Closed	1999	40.00	40
1988 C. Fletcher Public House 5904-8	12,500	1999	35.00	390-465
1997 Canadian Trading Co. (Canadian Version) 58306	Closed	1998	65.00	83-160
1986 Chadbury Station and Train 6528-5	Closed	1989	65.00	285-325
1999 Chancery Corner (Discover Department 56® Holiday Program) 58352, set/8	Yr.Iss.	1999	65.00	85-92
1987 Chesterton Manor House 6568-4	7,500	1988	45.00	1100-1390
1999 The China Trader 58447	Closed	2000	72.00	72-88
1986 Christmas Carol Cottages 6500-5, set/3	Closed	1995	75.00	125-185
1986 • The Cottage of Bob Cratchit & Tiny Tim 6500-5	Closed	1995	25.00	60-75
1986 • Fezziwig's Warehouse 6500-5	Closed	1995	25.00	40-48
1986 • Scrooge and Marley Counting House 6500-5	Closed	1995	25.00	42-65
1996 The Christmas Carol Cottages (revisited) 58339	Closed	2000	60.00	60-125
1988 Cobblestone Shops 5924-2, set/3	Closed	1990	95.00	280-325
1988 • Booter and Cobbler 5924-2	Closed	1990	32.00	75-98
1988 • T. Wells Fruit & Spice Shop 5924-2	Closed	1990	32.00	60-85
1988 • The Wool Shop 5924-2	Closed	1990	32.00	100-150
1989 Cobles Police Station 5583-2	Closed	1991	37.50	85-135
1988 Counting House & Silas Thimbleton Barrister 5902-1	Closed	1990	32.00	66-98
2001 Cratchit's Corner 58486	Open		80.00	80
1997 Crooked Fence Cottage 58304	Closed	2000	60.00	60-72
1992 Crown & Cricket Inn (Charles Dickens' Signature Series), 5750-9	Yr.Iss.	1992	100.00	150-185
2001 Crowntree Freckleton Windmill (Anniversary Edition), 58472, set/2	30,000	2001	80.00	80-135
1989 David Copperfield 5550-6, set/3	Closed	1992	125.00	115-190
1989 • Betsy Trotwood's Cottage 5550-6	Closed	1992	42.50	40-70
1989 • Peggotty's Seaside Cottage 5550-6 (green boat)	Closed	1992	42.50	48-75
1989 • Peggotty's Seaside Cottage 5550-6 (tan boat)	Closed	1992	42.50	75-195
1989 • Mr. Wickfield Solicitor 5550-6	Closed	1992	42.50	48-110
1989 David Copperfield 5550-6, set/3 with tan boat	Closed	1992	125.00	170-190
1994 Dedlock Arms 5752-5 (Charles Dickens' Signature Series)	Yr.Iss.	1994	100.00	115-150
1985 Dickens' Cottages 6518-8, set/3	Closed	1988	75.00	850-920
1985 • Stone Cottage 6518-8	Closed	1988	25.00	300-365
1985 • Thatched Cottage 6518-8	Closed	1988	25.00	135-245
1985 • Tudor Cottage 6518-8	Closed	1988	25.00	250-365
2002 Dickens' Gad's Hill Chalet 58488, set/2	Open		65.00	65
1986 Dickens' Lane Shops 6507-2, set/3	Closed	1989	80.00	399-408
1986 • Cottage Toy Shop 6507-2	Closed	1989	27.00	120-175
1986 • Thomas Kersey Coffee House 6507-2	Closed	1989	27.00	105-155
1986 • Tuttle's Pub 6507-2	Closed	1989	27.00	
1985 Dickens' Village Church (lt. cream) 6516-1	Closed	1989	35.00	190-265
1985 Dickens' Village Church (cream-yellow) 6516-1	Closed	1989	35.00	175-200
1985 Dickens' Village Church (dark) 6516-1	Closed	1989	35.00	95-125
1985 Dickens' Village Church (green) 6516-1	Closed	1989	35.00	300-345
1985 Dickens' Village Church (tan) 6516-1	Closed	1989	35.00	98-100
1985 Dickens' Village Mill 6519-6	2,500	1986	35.00	4000-4800
1995 Dudden Cross Church 5834-3	Closed	1997	45.00	40-65
1999 Dudley Docker 58353	Closed	2000	70.00	70-78
1995 Dursley Manor, 5832-9	Closed	1999	50.00	40-68
1997 East Indies Trading Co. 58302	Closed	1999	65.00	55-79
2002 Ebenezer Scrooge's House 58490	Open		85.00	85
1991 Fagin's Hide-A-Way 5552-2	Closed	1995	68.00	40-95
2000 Fezziwig's Ballroom (Discover Department 56® Holiday Program) 58470, set/6	Closed	2000	75.00	75-185
1989 The Flat of Ebenezer Scrooge 5587-5	Closed	2001	37.50	38-65
2002 Fred Holiwell's House 58492	Open		62.00	62
1997 Gad's Hill Place (Charles Dickens' Signature Series), 57535	Yr.Iss.	1997	98.00	58-120
1994 Giggelswick Mutton & Ham, 5822-0	Closed	1997	48.00	32-48
2001 Glendun Cocoa Works 58478	Open		80.00	80
1996 The Grapes Inn, 57534 (Charles Dickens' Signature Series)	Yr.Iss.	1996	120.00	64-135
1993 Great Denton Mill 5812-2	Closed	1997	50.00	35-63
1989 Green Gate Cottage 5586-7	22,500	1990	65.00	175-235
1994 Hather Harness 5823-8	Closed	1997	48.00	32-48
1998 Heathmoor Castle 58313	Closed	1999	90.00	72-102
2001 Hedgerow Garden Cottage 58476	Open		57.00	57
1992 Hembleton Pewterer, 5800-9	Closed	1995	72.00	72-90
1998 The Horse And Hounds Pub 58340	Open		70.00	70
1988 Ivy Glen Church 5927-7	Closed	1991	35.00	50-95
1995 J.D. Nichols Toy Shop 5832-8	Closed	1998	48.00	40-54
1997 J. Lytes Coal Merchant 58323	Closed	1999	50.00	40-64
1987 Kenilworth Castle 5916-1	Closed	1988	70.00	450-595
1998 Kensington Palace (Home For the Holidays) 58309	Yr.Iss.	1998	195.00	110-195
1989 Knottinghill Church 5582-4	Closed	1995	50.00	55-75
1992 King's Road Post Office 5801-7	Closed	1998	45.00	43-65
1993 Kingford's Brewhouse 5811-4	Closed	1996	45.00	43-68
1990 Kings Road 5568-9, set/2	Closed	1996	72.00	83-120
1990 • Tutbury Printer 55690	Closed	1996	36.00	25-50
1990 • C.H. Watt Physician 55691	Closed	1996	36.00	40-50
1997 Leacock Poulterer (Revisited) 58303	Closed	1999	48.00	48-65
1999 Leed's Oyster House 58446	Closed	2001	68.00	68
2001 Lilycott Garden Conservatory (Discover Department 56® Spring Promotion) 58475, gift set/5	Yr.Iss.	2001	65.00	65
1998 Lynton Point Tower 58315	Closed	2001	80.00	80
1995 The Maltings 5833-5	Closed	1998	50.00	36-50
1997 Manchester Square 58301, set/25 (G. Choir's Weights & Scales, Frogmore Chemist, Custom House, Lydby Trunk & Satchel Shop, Manchester Square Accessories, set/7, 12 trees, road, snow)	Closed	2000	250.00	250-310
1997 • G. Choir's Weights & Scales	Closed	2000	N/A	N/A
1997 • Frogmore Chemist	Closed	2000	N/A	N/A
1997 • Custom House	Closed	2000	N/A	N/A
1997 • Lydby Trunk & Satchel Shop	Closed	2000	N/A	N/A
1999 Margrove Orangery 58440	Closed	2001	98.00	98-110
1999 McShane Cottage 58444, set/2	Closed	2001	55.00	55
1996 The Melancholy Tavern (Revisited) 58347	Closed	1999	45.00	40-58
1988 Merchant Shops 5926-9, set/5	Closed	1993	150.00	220-450
1988 • Geo. Weeton Watchmaker 5926-9	Closed	1993	30.00	30-44
1988 • The Mermaid Fish Shoppe 5926-9	Closed	1993	30.00	60-85
1988 • Poulterer 5926-9	Closed	1993	30.00	53-65
1988 • Walpole Tailors 5926-9	Closed	1993	30.00	36-45
1988 • White Horse Bakery 5926-9	Closed	1993	30.00	30-60
2002 Mrs. Brimm's Tea Room 58487, set/4	Open		65.00	65
1996 Mulberrie Court 58345	Closed	1999	90.00	65-88
1991 Nephew Fred's Flat 5557-3	Closed	1994	35.00	60-85
1996 Nettie Quinn Puppets & Marionettes 58344	Closed	2001	50.00	50-62
1988 Nicholas Nickleby 5925-0, set/2	Closed	1991	72.00	135-150
1988 • Nicholas Nickleby Cottage 5925-0	Closed	1991	36.00	48-80
1988 • Wackford Squeers Boarding School 5925-0	Closed	1991	36.00	49-90
1988 Nickolas Nickleby Cottage 5925-0-misspelled	Closed	1991	36.00	70-125
1988 Nickolas Nickleby set/2, 5925-0-misspelled	Closed	1991	36.00	175-200
1986 Norman Church 6502-1	3,500	1987	40.00	3250
1998 North Eastern Sea Fisheries Ltd. 58316	Closed	1999	70.00	70-99
1987 The Old Curiosity Shop 5905-6	Closed	1999	32.00	24-50
1992 Old Michaelchurch, 5562-0	Closed	1996	42.00	50-65
1999 Old Queensbridge Station 58443, set/2	Open		100.00	100
1996 The Olde Camden Town Church (Revisited) 58346	Closed	1999	55.00	44-69
2001 The Olde Curiosity Shop 58482	Open		50.00	50
1991 Oliver Twist 5553-0, set/2	Closed	1993	75.00	70-145
1991 • Brownlow House 5553-0	Closed	1993	38.00	46-85
1991 • Maylie Cottage 5553-0	Closed	1993	38.00	34-70
1984 The Original Shops of Dickens' Village 6515-3, set/7	Closed	1988	175.00	990-1250
1984 • Abel Beesley Butcher 6515-3	Closed	1988	25.00	100-145

YEAR ISSUE	EDITION LIMIT	YEAR RETD.	ISSUE PRICE	*QUOTE U.S.$
1984 • Bean And Son Smithy Shop 6515-3	Closed	1988	25.00	125-175
1984 • Candle Shop 6515-3	Closed	1988	25.00	130-160
1984 • Crowntree Inn 6515-3	Closed	1988	25.00	150-240
1984 • Golden Swan Baker 6515-3	Closed	1988	25.00	122-161
1984 • Green Grocer 6515-3	Closed	1988	25.00	120-215
1984 • Jones & Co. Brush & Basket Shop 6515-3	Closed	1988	25.00	175-240
2002 Piccadilly Gallery 58498	Open		75.00	75
1993 The Pied Bull Inn (Charles Dickens' Signature Series), 5751-7	Closed	1993	100.00	60-150
1994 Portobello Road Thatched Cottages 58246, set/3	Closed	1997	120.00	120-150
1994 • Browning Cottage 58249	Closed	1997	40.00	30-45
1994 • Cobb Cottage 58248	Closed	1997	40.00	30-48
1994 • Mr. & Mrs. Pickle 58247	Closed	1997	40.00	30-47
1993 Pump Lane Shoppes 5808-4, set/3	Closed	1996	112.00	98-145
1993 • Bumpstead Nye Cloaks & Canes 58085	Closed	1996	37.35	25-40
1993 • Lomas Ltd. Molasses 58086	Closed	1996	37.35	30-45
1993 • W.M. Wheat Cakes & Puddings 58087	Closed	1996	37.35	30-51
1996 Quilly's Antiques 58348	Open	1999	46.00	40-65
1996 Ramsford Palace 58336, set/17 (Ramsford Palace, Palace Guards, set/2 Accessory, Palace Gate Accessory, Palace Fountain Accessory, Wall Hedge, set/8 Accessory, Corner Wall Topiaries, set/4 Accessory)	27,500	1996	175.00	275-395
2001 Rockingham School 58479	Open		85.00	85
2001 Royal Staffordshire Porcelains 58481	Open		65.00	65
2001 Royal Stock Exchange 58480	Closed	2001	110.00	110
1989 Ruth Marion Scotch Woolens 5585-9	17,500	1990	65.00	280-360
2001 Scrooge & Marley Counting House 58483	Open		80.00	40-85
1998 Seton Morris, Spice Merchant Gift Set (Home For the Holidays) 58308, set/10	Yr.Iss.	1998	65.00	55-88
2002 Sheffield Manor 58493	Yr.Iss.		130.00	130
1995 Sir John Falstaff Inn 5753-3 (Charles Dickens' Signature Series)	Closed	1995	100.00	63-135
2002 The Slone Hotel 58494, set/2	Open		90.00	90
2001 Somerset Valley Church (Holiday Discover 2001) 58485, set/9 (Christmas Eve Celebration Accessory, 2 walls, trees, snow)	Closed	2001	75.00	75
1999 The Spider Box Locks 58448	Closed	2001	60.00	60
2002 St. Ives Lock House 58495	Open		75.00	75
2000 St. Martin-in-the-Fields Church 58471	Open		96.00	96
1999 Staghorn Lodge 58445	Open		72.00	72
1995 Start A Tradition Set 5832-7, set/13 (The Town Square Carolers Accessory, set/3, 6 Sisal Trees, Bag of Real Plastic Snow, Cobblestone Road)	Closed	1996	85.00	85-90
1995 • Faversham Lamps & Oil	Closed	1996	N/A	63
1995 • Morston Steak and Kidney Pie	Closed	1996	N/A	43
1997 Start A Tradition Set 58322, set/13 (Sudbury Church, Old East Rectory, The Spirit of Giving Accessory, set/3, 6 Sisal Trees, Bag of Real Plastic Snow, Cobblestone Road)	Closed	1998	75.00	100-115
1998 Tattyeave Knoll 58311	Closed	1999	55.00	44-82
1998 Teaman & Crupp China Shop 58314	Open		64.00	64
1989 Theatre Royal 5584-0	Closed	1992	45.00	75-100
1998 Thomas Mudge Timepieces 58307	Closed	2000	60.00	60-80
2002 Thornbury Chapel 58502	Open		60.00	60
1989 Victoria Station 5574-3	Closed	1998	100.00	70-116
1994 Whittlesbourne Church, 5821-1	Closed	1998	85.00	85-90
1999 Wingham Lane Parrot Seller 58449	Closed	2001	68.00	68
1995 Wrenbury Shops 5833-1, set/3	Closed	1997	100.00	100
1995 • The Chop Shop 58333	Closed	1997	35.00	30-48
1995 • Wrenbury Baker 58332	Closed	1997	35.00	35-42
1995 • T. Puddlewick Spectacle Shop 58334	Closed	1998	35.00	36-48

Disney Parks Village Series - Department 56

YEAR ISSUE	EDITION LIMIT	YEAR RETD.	ISSUE PRICE	*QUOTE U.S.$
1994 Fire Station No. 105 5352-0 Disneyland, CA	Closed	1996	45.00	45-50
1994 Fire Station No. 105 744-7 (theme park backstamp) Disneyland, CA	Closed	1996	45.00	63-75
1994 Mickey's Christmas Shop 5350-3, set/2 Disney World, FL	Closed	1996	144.00	144-165

YEAR ISSUE	EDITION LIMIT	YEAR RETD.	ISSUE PRICE	*QUOTE U.S.$
1994 Mickey's Christmas Shop 742-0 (theme park backstamp), set/2 Disney World, FL	Closed	1996	144.00	350-435
1994 Olde World Antiques 5351-1, set/2 Disney World, FL	Closed	1996	90.00	44-96
1994 Olde World Antiques 743-9 (theme park backstamp), set/2 Disney World, FL	Closed	1996	90.00	56-100
1995 Silversmith 5352-1 Disney World, FL	Closed	1996	50.00	215-225
1995 Silversmith 744-8 (theme park backstamp) Disney World, FL	Closed	1996	50.00	225-288
1995 Tinker Bell's Treasures 5352-2 Disney World, FL	Closed	1996	60.00	198-238
1995 Tinker Bell's Treasures 744-9 (theme park backstamp) Disney World, FL	Closed	1996	60.00	235-250

Disney Parks Village Series Accessories - Department 56

YEAR ISSUE	EDITION LIMIT	YEAR RETD.	ISSUE PRICE	*QUOTE U.S.$
1995 The Balloon Seller 5353-9, set/2	Closed	1996	25.00	42-48
1994 Disney Parks Family 5354-6, set/3	Closed	1996	32.50	24-35
1994 Mickey and Minnie 5353-8, set/2	Closed	1996	22.50	25
1994 Olde World Antiques Gate 5355-4	Closed	1996	15.00	18

Event Piece - Heritage Village Collection Accessory - Department 56

YEAR ISSUE	EDITION LIMIT	YEAR RETD.	ISSUE PRICE	*QUOTE U.S.$
1992 Gate House 5530-1	Closed	1992	22.50	40-45
1996 Christmas Bells 98711	Closed	1996	35.00	20-35
1997 The Holly & The Ivy, set/2 56100	Yr.Iss.	1997	17.50	18
1998 Stars And Stripes Forever 55502	Yr.Iss.	1998	50.00	40-58
2001 Lowell Inn (25th Anniversary)	Closed	2001	85.00	225

Heritage Village Collection Accessories Retired - Department 56

YEAR ISSUE	EDITION LIMIT	YEAR RETD.	ISSUE PRICE	*QUOTE U.S.$
1995 The 12 Days of Dickens' Village, A Partridge In A Pear Tree 58351	Closed	1999	35.00	30-38
1995 The 12 Days of Dickens' Village, Two Turtle Doves 58360, set/4	Closed	1999	32.50	32-41
1995 The 12 Days of Dickens' Village, Three French Hens 58378, set/3	Closed	1999	32.50	60-85
1995 The 12 Days of Dickens' Village, Four Calling Birds 58379, set/2	Closed	1999	32.50	55-85
1995 The 12 Days of Dickens' Village, Five Golden Rings 58381, set/2	Closed	1999	27.50	28-50
1995 The 12 Days of Dickens' Village, Six Geese A-Laying 58382, set/2	Closed	1999	30.00	45-50
1996 The 12 Days of Dickens' Village, Seven Swans-A-Swimming 58383, set/4	Closed	2000	27.50	45
1996 The 12 Days of Dickens' Village, Eight Maids A-Milking 58384, set/2	Closed	2000	25.00	25-42
1997 The 12 Days of Dickens' Village, Nine Ladies Dancing 58385, set/3	Closed	2000	30.00	40-95
1997 The 12 Days of Dickens' Village, Ten Pipers Piping 58386, set/3	Closed	2000	30.00	40
1998 The 12 Days of Dickens' Village, Eleven Lords A-Leaping 58413	Closed	2000	27.50	28
1999 The 12 Days of Dickens' Village, Twelve Drummers Drumming 58387	Closed	2000	65.00	65
1999 The 12 Days of Dickens' Village Sign 58467	Closed	2000	20.00	20
1998 1919 Ford® Model-T 58906	Closed	2000	20.00	24-45
2000 1935 Duesenberg® 58964	Closed	2001	20.00	20
1998 Afternoon Sleigh Ride 53322	Closed	2001	27.50	28
1991 All Around the Town 5545-0, set/2	Closed	1993	18.00	20-30
1999 All In Together Girls 58960	Closed	2001	23.50	24
1995 Alpenhorn Player (Alpine Village Sign) 56182	Closed	2001	20.00	16
1987 Alpine Village Sign 6571-4	Closed	1993	6.00	14
1986 Alpine Villagers 6542-0, set/3	Closed	1992	13.00	22-36
1990 Amish Buggy 5949-8	Closed	1992	22.00	45-65
1990 Amish Family 5948-0, set/3	Closed	1992	20.00	28-65
1990 Amish Family, w/Moustache 5948-0, set/3	Closed	1992	20.00	40-75
1997 Animated Ski Mountain With 3 Skiers 52641	Closed	1998	85.00	65-85
1998 An Artist's Touch 56638	Closed	2001	17.00	17
1997 Ashley Pond Skating Party 58405, set/6	Closed	1999	70.00	65-88
1987 Automobiles 5964-1, set/3	Closed	1996	22.00	18-27
1995 Bachman's Squash Cart 753-6	Closed	1996	50.00	75-98
1997 Bachman's Wilcox Truck 880-8	Closed	1997	29.95	44-60
2001 Back From The Orchard 53320	Closed	2001	27.50	28
1991 Baker Elves 5603-0, set/3	Closed	1995	27.50	22-50

ARCHITECTURE

YEAR ISSUE	EDITION LIMIT	YEAR RETD.	ISSUE PRICE	*QUOTE U.S.$
1997 Big Smile For The Camera 58900, set/2	Closed	1999	27.50	20-26
2000 Birch Bench & Table 56927, set/2	Closed	2001	9.00	9
1992 The Bird Seller 5803-3, set/3	Closed	1995	25.00	15-35
1987 Blacksmith 5934-0, set/3	Closed	1990	20.00	55-85
1993 Blue Star Ice Harvesters 5650-2, set/2	Closed	1997	27.50	23-28
1989 Boulevard 5916-6, set/14	Closed	1993	25.00	42-49
1993 Bringing Fleeces To The Mill 58190, set/2	Closed	1998	35.00	24-55
1999 Bringing Home Baby 58909, set/2	Closed	2000	27.50	28
1991 Bringing Home The Yule Log 55581, set/3	Closed	1998	28.00	28-38
1995 Brixton Road Watchman 58390, set/2	Closed	1999	25.00	20-28
1995 A Busy Elf North Pole Sign 56366	Closed	1999	20.00	16-20
1999 Busy Railway Station 58464, set/3	Closed	2001	27.50	28
1990 Busy Sidewalks 5535-2, set/4	Closed	1992	28.00	35-55
1992 Buying Bakers Bread 5619-7, set/2	Closed	1995	20.00	24-30
1993 C. Bradford, Wheelwright & Son 5818-1, set/2	Closed	1996	24.00	22-41
1990 Carolers on the Doorstep 5570-0, set/4	Closed	1993	25.00	20-45
1984 Carolers, w/ Lamppost (bl) 6526-9, set/3	Closed	1990	10.00	35
1984 Carolers, w/ Lamppost (wh) 6526-9, set/3	Closed	1990	10.00	85
1991 Caroling Thru The City 55484, set/3	Closed	1998	27.50	18-28
1994 Chamber Orchestra 58840, set/4	Closed	1998	37.50	38
1995 Charting Santa's Course 56364, set/2	Closed	1997	25.00	26
1999 Check This Out 56711	Closed	2001	13.50	14
1993 Chelsea Lane Shoppers 58165, set/4	Closed	1999	30.00	19-40
1994 Chelsea Market Curiosities Monger & Cart 58270, set/2	Closed	1998	27.50	21-37
1993 Chelsea Market Fish Monger & Cart 5814-9, set/2	Closed	1997	25.00	18-39
1993 Chelsea Market Flower Monger & Cart 58154-7, set/2	Closed	2000	27.50	22-38
1993 Chelsea Market Fruit Monger & Cart 5813-0, set/2	Closed	1997	25.00	16-25
1995 Chelsea Market Hat Monger & Cart 58392, set/2	Closed	2000	27.50	30
1994 Chelsea Market Mistletoe Monger & Cart 58262, set/2	Closed	1998	25.00	25-32
1988 Childe Pond and Skaters 5903-0, set/4	Closed	1991	30.00	32-85
1998 Child's Play 58415, set/2	Closed	2001	25.00	25
1995 Choirboys All-In-A-Row 58892	Closed	1998	20.00	25
1997 Christmas Bazaar...Flapjacks & Hot Cider 56595, set/2	Closed	1999	27.50	26-30
1996 Christmas Bazaar...Handmade Quilts 56594, set/2	Closed	1999	25.00	25
1997 Christmas Bazaar...Sign 56598, set/2	Closed	1999	16.00	14-18
1997 Christmas Bazaar...Toy Vendor & Cart 56597, set/2	Closed	1999	27.50	20-32
1996 Christmas Bazaar...Woolens & Preserves 56595, set/2	Closed	1999	25.00	20-32
1989 Christmas Carol Christmas Spirits 55891, set/4	Closed	2001	27.50	20-28
1986 Christmas Carol Figures 6501-3, set/3	Closed	1990	12.50	50-88
1996 A Christmas Carol Reading by Charles Dickens 58404, set/7 (Charles Dickens' Signature Series)	42,500	1997	75.00	98-115
1996 A Christmas Carol Reading by Charles Dickens 58403, set/4	Closed	2001	45.00	45
1994 Christmas Carol Revisited Holiday Trimming Set 5831-9, set/21	Closed	1997	65.00	45-65
1998 Christmas Fun Run 56434, set/2	Closed	2000	35.00	35
1987 Christmas in the City Sign 5960-9	Closed	1993	6.00	12-16
1997 Christmas Pudding Costermonger 58408, set/3	Closed	2001	32.50	33
1990 Christmas Trash Cans 52094, set/2	Closed	1998	7.00	7-15
1992 Churchyard Fence Extensions 5807-6, set/4	Closed	1997	16.00	18-24
1992 Churchyard Gate & Fence 5806-8, set/3	Closed	1997	15.00	18-30
1992 Churchyard Gate and Fence 5563-8, set/3	Closed	1992	15.00	55-65
1999 The City Ambulance 58910	Closed	2000	15.00	15
1988 City Bus & Milk Truck 5983-8, set/2	Closed	1991	15.00	27-32
1988 City Newsstand 5971-4, set/4	Closed	1991	25.00	70-115
1987 City People 5965-0, set/5	Closed	1990	27.50	45-65
1998 City Police Car 58903	Closed	2001	16.50	17-20
2000 City Professions - Postman & Dairy Delivery Man 58965, set/2	Closed	2001	17.50	18
2000 City Professions - House Painter & Newspaper Boy 58966, set/2	Closed	2001	17.50	18
1991 City Subway Entrance 55417	Closed	1998	15.00	12-18
1996 City Taxi 58894	Closed	2001	12.50	8-13
1987 City Workers 5967-6, set/4	Closed	1988	15.00	35
1993 Climb Every Mountain 56138, set/4	Closed	2001	27.50	28
1995 Cobbler & Clock Peddler 58394, set/2	Closed	1997	25.00	20-38
1994 Coca-Cola® Brand Neon Sign 54828	Closed	1998	16.50	15-17
1991 Come into the Inn, 5560-3	Closed	1994	22.00	20-40
1989 Constables 5579-4, set/3	Closed	1991	17.50	57-72
1992 Courtyard Fence With Steps 52205	Closed	1998	4.00	12
1986 Covered Wooden Bridge 6531-5	Closed	1990	10.00	20-26
1998 Dash Away Delivery 56438	Closed	2001	40.00	40
1989 David Copperfield Characters 5551-4, set/5	Closed	1992	32.50	22-45
1997 Delivering Coal For The Hearth 58326, set/2	Closed	1999	32.50	33-41
1998 Delivering Real Plastic Snow 56435	Closed	2001	17.00	17
1997 Delivering The Christmas Greens 56373, set/2	Closed	2001	27.50	28
1987 Dickens' Village Sign 6569-2	Closed	1993	6.00	13-20
1999 Doctor's House Call 56616, set/2	Closed	2001	27.50	28
1997 Don't Break The Ornaments 56372, set/2	Closed	2001	27.50	28
1992 Don't Drop The Presents! 5532-8, set/2	Closed	1995	25.00	24-38
1987 Dover Coach 6590-0	Closed	1990	18.00	35-65
1987 Dover Coach w/o Mustache 6590-0	Closed	1990	18.00	75-90
1999 Downhill Daredevils 56707, set/2	Closed	2001	16.50	17
1996 Early Rising Elves 56369, set/5	Closed	1999	32.50	26-34
1999 Elf Tree House 56446	Closed	2000	42.00	42
1996 End Of The Line 56370, set/2	Closed	1999	28.00	23-46
1989 Farm Animals 5945-5, set/4	Closed	1991	15.00	22-42
1987 Farm People And Animals 5901-3, set/5	Closed	1989	24.00	70-88
1997 Father Christmas's Journey 58407	Closed	2001	30.00	30
1988 Fezziwig and Friends 5928-5, set/3	Closed	1990	12.50	48-65
1999 Fine Asian Antiques 58642, set/2	Closed	2001	27.50	28
1991 The Fire Brigade 5546-8, set/2	Closed	1995	20.00	20-35
1988 Fire Hydrant & Mailbox 51322, set/2	Closed	1998	6.00	8-19
1991 Fire Truck, "City Fire Dept." 5547-6, set/2	Closed	1995	18.00	21-35
1990 The Flying Scot Train 55735, set/4	Closed	1994	50.00	32-63
1989 For Sale Sign (Bachman's) 51667	Closed	1998	4.50	32-40
1989 For Sale Sign 51667	Closed	1998	4.50	5-10
1995 Fresh Paint (New England Village Sign) 56592	Closed	2001	20.00	20
1999 Fresh Flowers For Sale 58957, set/2	Closed	2001	30.00	30
1998 Fun In The Snow 53323, set/2	Closed	2001	15.00	15
1998 Garden Park Benches 53333, set/4	Closed	2001	12.00	12
2000 Gathering Grapes 53602, set/2	Closed	2001	25.00	25
2001 Ghost of Christmas Present Visits Scrooge 58538	Closed	2001	15.00	15
1996 Gingerbread Vendor 58402, set/2	Closed	2001	22.50	23
1996 Going Home For The Holidays 58896, set/3	Closed	1999	27.50	28
1999 A Good Day's Catch 58420, set/2	Closed	2000	27.50	28
1999 A Happy Harley® Day 56706	Closed	2001	17.00	17
1999 Happy New Year! 56443	Closed	2000	17.50	18
1995 Harvest Pumpkin Wagon 56591	Closed	1999	45.00	45
1992 Harvest Seed Cart 5645-6, set/3	Closed	1995	27.50	35-40
1997 Heidi & Her Goats 56201, set/4	Closed	2000	30.00	22-35
1998 Here We Come A-Wassailing 58410, set/5	Closed	2001	45.00	25-46
1989 Heritage Village Sign 9953-8	Closed	1989	6.00	14-17
1991 Holiday Coach 55611	Closed	1998	70.00	44-70
1996 Holiday Deliveries 56371	Closed	1998	16.50	17
1994 Holiday Field Trip 58858, set/3	Closed	1998	27.50	24-41
1990 Holiday Travelers 5571-9, set/3	Closed	1999	25.00	20-25
1994 Hot Dog Vendor 5886-6, set/3	Closed	1997	27.50	19-35
1995 I'll Need More Toys 56365, set/2	Closed	1998	25.00	25-30
1998 I'm Wishing 53309	Closed	2001	13.00	13
1998 Ivy Vines 53377, set/4	Closed	2001	7.50	8
1997 Johnson's Grocery...Holiday Deliveries 58897	Closed	2001	18.00	18-20
1995 A Key To The City (Christmas In The City Sign) 58893	Closed	2001	20.00	20
1989 King's Road Cab 55816	Closed	1998	30.00	30-42
1999 King's Road Market Cross 58456	Closed	2000	25.00	25
1993 Knife Grinder 5649-9, set/2	Closed	1996	22.50	18-24

6

YEAR ISSUE	EDITION LIMIT	YEAR RETD.	ISSUE PRICE	*QUOTE U.S.$
1994 Last Minute Delivery 56367	Closed	1998	35.00	27-45
1998 Lattice Obelisk 53376, set/2	Closed	2001	8.50	9
1999 Let's Go One More Time 56621, set/3	Closed	2001	30.00	30
1997 Let's Go Shopping In The City 58899, set/3	Closed	1999	35.00	35
1992 Letters for Santa 5604-9, set/3	Closed	1994	30.00	57-75
1986 Lighted Tree With Children & Ladder 6510-2	Closed	1989	35.00	145-250
1992 Lionhead Bridge 5864-5	Closed	1997	22.00	22-38
2000 Little Newlyweds 56805	Closed	2001	16.50	17
1995 Lobster Trappers 56589, set/4	Closed	2000	35.00	35
1999 The Locomotive Shed & Water Tower 58465	Closed	2001	32.50	33
1995 Lumberjacks 56590, set/2	Closed	1998	30.00	32
1991 Mail Box & Fire Hydrant 52140, set/2	Closed	1998	5.00	5-15
1987 Maple Sugaring Shed 6589-7, set/3	Closed	1989	19.00	165-220
1991 Market Day 5641-3, set/3	Closed	1993	35.00	32-50
1999 Master Gardeners 58458, set/2	Closed	2001	30.00	30
1999 Meeting Family At The Railroad Station 58457, set/4	Closed	2001	32.50	33
1999 Members of Parliament 58455, set/2	Closed	2000	19.00	19
1997 A New Batch of Christmas Friends 56175, set/3	Closed	2000	27.50	28
1987 New England Village Sign 6570-6	Closed	1993	6.00	12
1986 New England Winter set 6532-3, set/5	Closed	1990	18.00	30-40
1996 A New Potbellied Stove For Christmas 56593, set/2	Closed	1998	35.00	30-40
1988 Nicholas Nickleby Characters 5929-3, set/4	Closed	1991	20.00	28-30
1996 North Pole Express 56368, set/3	Closed	1999	37.50	30-63
1993 North Pole Gate 56324	Closed	1998	32.50	33
2000 Nuts About Broomball 56926	Closed	2001	20.00	20
1994 The Old Man And The Sea 56553, set/3	Closed	1998	25.00	22-35
1992 The Old Puppeteer 5802-5, set/3	Closed	1995	32.00	40
1991 Oliver Twist Characters 5554-9, set/3	Closed	1993	35.00	40-50
1988 One Horse Open Sleigh 5982-0	Closed	1993	20.00	35-40
1995 One-Man Band And The Dancing Dog 58891, set/2	Closed	1998	17.50	14-30
1995 Open Wide! 56713	Closed	2000	13.00	13
1989 Organ Grinder 5957-9, set/3	Closed	1991	21.00	28-32
1994 Over The River And Through The Woods 56545	Closed	1998	35.00	35
1987 Ox Sled (blue pants) 5951-0	Closed	1989	20.00	78-96
1987 Ox Sled (tan pants) 5951-0	Closed	1989	20.00	255-270
2000 Party in the Hot Tub 56802, set/2	Closed	2001	30.00	30
1998 Peppermint Skating Party 56363, set/2	Closed	2000	64.00	64
1993 Pine Cone Trees 522-13, set/2	Closed	1995	15.00	10-15
1998 Planter Box Topiaries 53334, set/4, 2 asst.	Closed	2001	15.00	15
1993 Playing in the Snow 5556-5, set/3	Closed	1996	25.00	26-35
1997 Poinsettia Delivery Truck 59000	Closed	1999	32.50	25-34
1994 Polka Fest 56073, set/3	Closed	1999	30.00	29-32
1993 Popcorn Vendor 5958-7, set/3	Closed	1992	22.00	24-40
1986 Porcelain Trees 6537-4, set/2	Closed	1992	14.00	27-35
1994 Portobello Road Peddlers 58289, set/3	Closed	1998	27.50	23-41
2000 Postal Pick-up 56641	Closed	2001	14.00	14
1994 Postern 9871-0, (Dickens' Village Ten Year Accessory Anniversary Piece)	Closed	1994	17.50	12-40
1998 Potted Flowers 53331, 12 asst.	Closed	2001	12.50	13
1998 Potted Topiaries 53370, set/4	Closed	2001	15.00	15
1991 Poultry Market 5559-0, set/3	Closed	1995	32.00	36-50
1999 The Queen's Parliamentary Coach 58454	Yr.Iss.	2000	100.00	100
1996 Ready For The Road 58907	Closed	2000	20.00	20
1996 Red Christmas Sulky 58401	Closed	2001	30.00	30
2000 Red Covered Bridge 5987-0	Closed	1994	17.00	24
2000 Reindeer Condo 56886	Closed	2001	70.00	70
1998 Relaxing In A Garden 53307, set/3	Closed	2001	25.00	25
1989 River Street Ice House Cart 5959-5	Closed	1991	20.00	40-58
1989 Royal Coach 5578-6	Closed	1992	55.00	75-85
1988 Salvation Army Band 5985-4, set/6	Closed	1991	24.00	75-98
1990 Santa's Little Helpers 5610-3, set/6	Closed	1993	28.00	50-70
2000 Scissors Wizards 56923, set/2	Closed	2001	25.00	25
1998 Sea Captain & His Mates 56587, set/4	Closed	2000	32.50	33
1987 Shopkeepers 5966-8, set/4	Closed	1988	15.00	32
1987 Silo And Hay Shed 5950-1	Closed	1989	18.00	165
1993 Sing a Song For Santa 5631-6, set/3	Closed	1998	28.00	35
1991 Sisal Wreath 54194, set/6	Closed	1998	4.00	7-10
1991 Skating Party 55239, set/3	Closed	2001	27.50	28
1987 Skating Pond 6545-5	Closed	1990	24.00	38-55
1999 Ski Bums 56710	Closed	2001	22.50	23
1990 Sleepy Hollow Characters 5956-0, set/3	Closed	1992	27.50	45
1986 Sleighride 6511-0	Closed	1990	19.50	45-60
1988 Snow Children 5938-2	Closed	1994	17.00	20-30
1994 Snow Cone Elves 5637-5, set/4	Closed	1997	30.00	30-34
1997 Spirit Of The Season 58898	Closed	1999	20.00	20-26
1997 Steppin' Out On The Town 58885, set/5	Closed	1999	35.00	35-45
1987 Stone Bridge 6546-3	Closed	1990	12.00	15-55
1999 Storybook Village Collection Landscape Set 13179, set/6	Closed	2001	10.00	10
1999 Storybook Village Collection Collection Sign 13169	Closed	2001	10.00	10
1993 Street Musicians 5564-6, set/3	Closed	1997	25.00	20-25
1996 Sunday Morning At The Chapel 53311, set/2	Closed	2001	17.00	17
2000 Tailored For You 56921, set/2	Closed	2001	22.50	23
1995 Tallyho 5839, set/5	Closed	1998	50.00	50-72
1997 Tapping The Maples 56599, set/7	Closed	2001	75.00	75
1999 Tee Time Elves 56442, set/2	Closed	2001	27.50	28
1996 Tending New Calves with Kids 58398, set/3	Closed	1999	30.00	22-38
1998 Tending The Cold Frame 58416, set/3	Closed	1999	32.50	38
1992 Testing The Toys 56057, set/2	Closed	1999	16.50	16-25
1993 Thatchers 5829-7, set/3	Closed	1997	35.00	35-42
1990 Tis the Season 5539-5	Closed	1994	12.95	15-25
1990 Town Crier & Chimney Sweep 55697, set/2	Closed	2001	16.00	16
1999 Town Gate 59794, set/2	Closed	2001	25.00	25
1989 Town Square Gazebo 5513-1	Closed	1997	19.00	21
1995 Town Tinker 5646-4, set/2	Closed	1995	24.00	22-38
1993 Town Tree Trimmers 55662, set/4	Closed	2001	32.50	33
1990 The Toy Peddler 56162, set/3	Closed	1998	22.00	22-28
1991 Toymaker Elves 5602-2, set/3	Closed	1995	27.50	29-40
1999 A Treasure From The Sea 58461, set/2	Closed	2001	22.50	23
1990 Tree-Lined Courtyard Fence 52124	Closed	1998	4.00	4
1990 Trimming the North Pole 5608-1	Closed	1993	10.00	35-45
1994 Two Rivers Bridge 5656-1	Closed	1997	35.00	30-35
1998 Under The Mistletoe 56631	Closed	2001	16.50	17
1997 Untangle The Christmas Lights 56374	Closed	2000	35.00	35
1998 Until We Meet Again 58414, set/2	Closed	2001	27.50	28
1989 U.S. Mail Box and Fire Hydrant 5517-4	Closed	1990	5.00	18-20
1993 Utility Accessories 55123, set/8	Closed	1998	12.50	12-15
1990 Victoria Station Platform 5575-1	Closed	1999	22.00	24-35
1995 Village Arctic Pines 52608, set/3	Closed	1998	12.00	12
1995 Village Autumn Trees 52616, set/3	Closed	1998	13.50	14
1995 Village Cedar Pine Forest 52606, set/3	Closed	1998	15.00	15
1993 Village Chain Link Fence Extensions 52353, set/4	Closed	1998	15.00	9-15
1993 Village Chain Link Fence w/Gate 52345, set/4	Closed	1998	12.00	12
1995 Village Double Pine Trees 52619	Closed	1998	13.50	14
1987 Village Express Train (electric, black),5997-8	Closed	1988	89.95	195-225
1988 Village Express Train 5980-3, set/22	Closed	1996	95.00	138-145
1993 Village Express Van (black), 9951-1	Closed	1993	25.00	35-125
1993 Village Express Van (gold), 9977-5 (promotional)	Closed	1993	N/A	325
1992 Village Express Van (green) 5865-3	Closed	1996	25.00	25-32
1994 Village Express Van-Bachman's 729-3	Closed	1994	22.50	25-60
1994 Village Express Van-Bronner's 737-4	Closed	1994	22.50	25-60
1995 Village Express Van-Canadian 2163-7	Closed	1995	N/A	36-58
1994 Village Express Van-Christmas Dove 730-7	Closed	1994	25.00	20-50
1994 Village Express Van-European Imports 739-0	Closed	1994	22.50	45-50
1994 Village Express Van-Fortunoff's 735-8	Closed	1994	22.50	60-75
1994 Village Express Van-Limited Edition 733-1	Closed	1994	25.00	63-70
1994 Village Express Van-Lock, Stock & Barrel 731-5	Closed	1994	22.50	50-110
1994 Village Express Van-North Pole City 736-6	Closed	1994	25.00	42-54
1995 Village Express Van-Park West 0755-2	Closed	1995	N/A	460
1994 Village Express Van-Robert's Christmas Wonderland 734-0	Closed	1994	22.50	25-40
1995 Village Express Van-St. Nicks 756-0	Closed	1995	25.00	47-55

YEAR ISSUE	EDITION LIMIT	YEAR RETD.	ISSUE PRICE	*QUOTE U.S.$
1994 Village Express Van-Stat's 741-2	Closed	1994	22.50	40-50
1994 Village Express Van-The Incredible Christmas Place (Pigeon Forge) 732-3	Closed	1994	24.98	40-42
1994 Village Express Van-The Lemon Tree 721-8	Closed	1994	30.00	35-40
1994 Village Express Van-William Glen 738-2	Closed	1994	22.50	31-42
1994 Village Express Van-Windsor Shoppe 740-4	Closed	1994	25.00	32-45
1995 Village Frosted Fir Trees 52605, set/4	Closed	1998	15.00	15
1996 Village Frosted Hemlock Tree 52638, set/2	Closed	1998	32.50	33
1991 Village Frosted Norway Pines 51756, set/3	Closed	1998	12.95	13
1988 Village Harvest People 5941-2, set/4	Closed	1991	27.50	44-55
1995 Village Let It Snow Snowman Sign 52594	Closed	1998	12.50	13
1997 Village Lighted Christmas Tree 52690	Closed	1998	48.00	50
1990 Village Mail Box 51985	Closed	1998	3.50	4-10
1996 Village Mini Lights 52626	Closed	1998	10.00	10
1989 Village Parking Meter 51780, set/4	Closed	1998	6.00	6-10
1994 Village Pencil Pines 52469, set/3	Closed	1998	15.00	15-18
1991 Village Pole Pine Forest 55271, set/5	Closed	1998	48.00	38-46
1991 Village Pole Pine Tree, large 55298	Closed	1998	12.50	13-15
1991 Village Pole Pine Tree, small 55280	Closed	1998	10.00	13-15
1995 Village Ponderosa Pines 52607, set/3	Closed	1998	13.00	13
1994 Village Porcelain Pine Trees 5251-5, set/2	Closed	1997	15.00	22-25
1992 Village Porcelain Pine, large 5218-3	Closed	1997	12.50	15-20
1992 Village Porcelain Pine, small 5219-1	Closed	1997	10.00	12-15
1989 Village Sign with Snowman 5572-7	Closed	1994	10.00	12-15
1991 Village Snow Fence 52043	Closed	1998	7.00	7-20
1989 Village Stop Sign 51764, set/2	Closed	1998	5.00	6-10
1992 Village Street Peddlers 5804-1, set/2	Closed	1994	16.00	25-30
1994 Village Streetcar 52400, set/10	Closed	1998	65.00	50-62
1991 Village Town Clock 51101, 2 asst.	Closed	1998	3.00	5
1985 Village Train Brighton 6527-7, set/3	Closed	1986	12.00	295-369
1988 Village Train Trestle 5981-1	Closed	1990	17.00	35-55
1995 Village Wagon Wheel Pine Grove 52617	Closed	1998	22.50	20-23
1987 Village Well And Holy Cross 6547-1, set/2	Closed	1989	13.00	135-145
1996 Village White Picket Fence Extensions 52625, set/6	Closed	1998	10.00	10
1996 Village White Picket Fence With Gate 52624, set/4	Closed	1998	10.00	10
1989 Violet Vendor/Carolers/Chestnut Vendor 5580-8, set/3	Closed	1992	23.00	26-50
1993 Vision of a Christmas Past 5817-3, set/3	Closed	1996	27.50	32-55
1998 Volunteer Firefighters 56635, set/2	Closed	2000	37.50	38
1992 Welcome Home 5533-6, set/3	Closed	1995	27.50	32-40
1994 Winter Sleighride 58254	Closed	2001	18.00	18
1988 Woodcutter And Son 5986-2, set/2	Closed	1990	10.00	29-55
1993 Woodsmen Elves 5630-8, set/3	Closed	1995	27.50	55-64
1991 Wrought Iron Fence 59986, 2 asst.	Closed	1998	2.50	12-17
1991 Wrought Iron Fence Extensions 55158, set/9	Closed	1998	12.50	14-15
1991 Wrought Iron Gate And Fence 55140, set/9	Closed	1998	15.00	14-21
1995 Ye Olde Lamplighter (Dickens' Village Sign) 58393	Closed	2001	20.00	20
1996 Yeomen of the Guard 58397, set/5	Closed	1997	30.00	58-65
1995 Yes, Virginia... 58890, set/2	Closed	2000	12.50	13

Heritage Village Special Edition - Department 56

YEAR ISSUE	EDITION LIMIT	YEAR RETD.	ISSUE PRICE	*QUOTE U.S.$
1999 The Times Tower 55510, set/3	Closed	1999	185.00	210-315
2001 Crystal Ice King and Queen Accessory 58976, set/2	25,000	2001	20.00	20
2001 Crystal Ice Palace 58922, set/9 (Palace Bears Accessory, set/2, 4 sisal trees, an icy path, bag of Snow Crystals)	Closed	2001	165.00	165

The Historical Landmark Series™ - Department 56

YEAR ISSUE	EDITION LIMIT	YEAR RETD.	ISSUE PRICE	*QUOTE U.S.$
1997 The Old Globe Theatre 58501, set/4	Yr.Iss.	1998	175.00	175-245
1997 Tower of London 58500, set/5	Closed	1997	165.00	295
1998 Big Ben 58341, set/2	Closed	2000	95.00	95

YEAR ISSUE	EDITION LIMIT	YEAR RETD.	ISSUE PRICE	*QUOTE U.S.$
1998 Independence Hall 55500	Closed	2000	110.00	110
1999 The Old Royal Observatory 58453, set/2	35,000	2000	95.00	95
2002 Cathedral of St. Paul 58930	Open		150.00	150

Homes For The Holidays - Department 56

YEAR ISSUE	EDITION LIMIT	YEAR RETD.	ISSUE PRICE	*QUOTE U.S.$
1997 Ronald McDonald House ® (Fund Raiser Piece) 8960	Yr.Iss.	1997	N/A	300

Hot Properties Grinch - Department 56

YEAR ISSUE	EDITION LIMIT	YEAR RETD.	ISSUE PRICE	*QUOTE U.S.$
2002 Farfingle's Department Store 59084, set/2	Open		75.00	75
2000 How The Grinch Stole Christmas! "Cindy Lou Who's House", set 59004	Open		75.00	75
2001 How The Grinch Stole Christmas! "Town Hall" 59034	Open		75.00	75

Literary Classics™ Collections - Department 56

YEAR ISSUE	EDITION LIMIT	YEAR RETD.	ISSUE PRICE	*QUOTE U.S.$
1998 Great Expectations - Satis Manor 58310, set/4	Closed	2001	110.00	110
1999 Little Women - The March Residence 56606, set/4	Closed	2000	90.00	92
1999 The Great Gatsby - West Egg Mansion 58939, set/4	Closed	2001	135.00	135
2000 The Adventures of Tom Sawyer - Aunt Polly's House 58600, set/5	Closed	2001	90.00	94
2001 Sherlock Holmes - 221 B Baker Street 58601, set/3	Open		90.00	90

Little Town of Bethlehem Series - Department 56

YEAR ISSUE	EDITION LIMIT	YEAR RETD.	ISSUE PRICE	*QUOTE U.S.$
2001 Carpenter's Shop 59801	Open		72.00	72
2002 Caravansary Corner 59806, set/2	Open		75.00	75
2002 Caravansary's Rooms at the Inn 59807, set/3	Open		110.00	110
1999 Gatekeeper's Dwelling 59797	Closed	2001	55.00	60
2001 Herod's Temple (Anniversary Edition) 59799, set/5	5,600	2001	150.00	150-225
2002 House of The Last Supper 59809, set/2	Open		65.00	65
1999 Innkeeper's Caravansary 59795	Open		70.00	70
1987 Little Town of Bethlehem 5975-7, set/12	Closed	1999	150.00	150-295
1999 Nativity 59796, set/2	Open		55.00	55
2001 Rug Merchant's Colonnade 58902, set/4	Open		110.00	110

New England Village Series - Department 56

YEAR ISSUE	EDITION LIMIT	YEAR RETD.	ISSUE PRICE	*QUOTE U.S.$
1993 A. Bieler Farm 5648-0, set/2	Closed	1996	92.00	90-110
1993 • Pennsylvania Dutch Farmhouse 56481	Closed	1996	46.00	38-88
1993 • Pennsylvania Dutch Barn 56482	Closed	1996	46.00	40-78
1988 Ada's Bed and Boarding House (lemon yellow) 5940-4	Closed	1991	36.00	195-240
1988 Ada's Bed and Boarding House (pale yellow) 5940-4	Closed	1991	36.00	98-112
1996 Apple Valley School 56172	Open		35.00	35
1994 Arlington Falls Church 5651-0	Closed	1997	40.00	26-45
1989 Berkshire House (medium blue) 5942-0	Closed	1991	40.00	122-175
1989 Berkshire House (teal) 5942-0	Closed	1991	40.00	85-115
1993 Blue Star Ice Co. 5647-2	Closed	1997	45.00	45-58
1992 Bluebird Seed and Bulb 5642-1	Closed	1996	48.00	35-48
1996 Bobwhite Cottage 56576	Closed	2001	50.00	50
2002 Breakers Point Lighthouse 56636	Open		85.00	85
1995 Brewster Bay Cottage 5657-0, set/2	Closed	1997	90.00	95
1995 • Jeremiah Brewster House 56568	Closed	1997	45.00	35-48
1995 • Thomas T. Julian House 56569	Closed	1997	45.00	45
1994 Cape Keag Cannery 5652-9	Closed	1998	48.00	48
2002 Captain Kensey's House 56651	Open		55.00	55
1990 Captain's Cottage 5947-1	Closed	1996	40.00	44-56
1988 Cherry Lane Shops 5939-0, set/3	Closed	1990	80.00	320-388
1988 • Anne Shaw Toys 5939-0	Closed	1990	27.00	112-144
1988 • Ben's Barbershop 5939-0	Closed	1990	27.00	75-138
1988 • Otis Hayes Butcher Shop 5939-0	Closed	1990	27.00	80-119
1995 Chowder House 5657-1	Closed	1998	40.00	44
1987 Craggy Cove Lighthouse 5930-7	Closed	1994	35.00	55
2001 The Cranberry House 56627	Open		60.00	60
1998 Deacon's Way Chapel 56604	Closed	2000	68.00	68
1997 East Willet Pottery 56578	Closed	1999	45.00	45
1998 The Emily Louise 56581, set/2	Closed	2000	70.00	70
1998 Franklin Hook & Ladder Co, 56601	Closed	2000	55.00	55
1998 Hale & Hardy House 56610	Closed	2001	60.00	60
1998 Harper's Farm 56605	Open		65.00	65
1999 Harper's Farmhouse 56612	Open		57.00	57

Collectors' Information Bureau

*Quotes have been rounded up to nearest dollar

YEAR ISSUE	EDITION LIMIT	YEAR RETD.	ISSUE PRICE	*QUOTE U.S.$
1996 J. Hudson Stoveworks 56574	Closed	1998	60.00	55-72
1986 Jacob Adams Farmhouse and Barn 6538-2	Closed	1989	65.00	400-500
1989 Jannes Mullet Amish Barn 5944-7	Closed	1992	48.00	70-115
1989 Jannes Mullet Amish Farm House 5943-9	Closed	1992	32.00	86-125
2001 Laurel Hill Church 56629	Open		68.00	68
1991 McGrebe-Cutters & Sleighs 5640-5	Closed	1995	45.00	45-70
1998 Moggin Falls General Store 56602	Open		60.00	60
2001 Mountain View Cabin (Anniversary Edition) 56625	10,000	2001	55.00	55
1996 Navigational Charts & Maps 56575	Closed	1999	48.00	48-62
1986 New England Village 6530-7, set/7	Closed	1989	170.00	1000-1295
1986 • Apothecary Shop 6530-7	Closed	1989	25.00	75-135
1986 • Brick Town Hall 6530-7	Closed	1989	25.00	124-239
1986 • General Store 6530-7	Closed	1989	25.00	250-335
1986 • Livery Stable & Boot Shop 6530-7	Closed	1989	25.00	128-138
1986 • Nathaniel Bingham Fabrics 6530-7	Closed	1989	25.00	138-148
1986 • Red Schoolhouse 6530-7	Closed	1989	25.00	238-290
1986 • Steeple Church (Original) 6530-7	Closed	1989	25.00	139-300
1988 Old North Church 5932-3	Closed	1998	40.00	28-48
2002 Otter Creek Sawmill 56653	Open		70.00	70
1994 Pierce Boat Works 5657-3	Closed	2000	55.00	55
1994 Pigeonhead Lighthouse 5657-7	Closed	1998	50.00	41-55
1999 P.L. Wheeler's Bicycle Shop 56613	Open		57.00	57
1999 Platt's Candles & Wax 56614	Closed	2001	60.00	60
2001 Revere Silver Works 56632, set/2	Open		60.00	60
1990 Semple's Smokehouse 56580	Closed	1999	45.00	45-55
1990 Shingle Creek House 5946-3	Closed	1994	37.50	38-50
1990 Sleepy Hollow 5954-4, set/3	Closed	1993	96.00	160-185
1990 • Ichabod Crane's Cottage 5954-4	Closed	1993	32.00	37-50
1990 • Sleepy Hollow School 5954-4	Closed	1993	32.00	80-100
1990 • Van Tassel Manor 5954-4	Closed	1993	32.00	48
1990 Sleepy Hollow Church 5955-2	Closed	1993	36.00	50
1987 Smythe Woolen Mill 6543-9	7,500	1988	42.00	950-1225
2002 Springfield Studio 56634, set/5	Open		65.00	65
1997 Steen's Maple House (Smoking House) 56579	Closed	2001	60.00	60
1986 Steeple Church (Second Version) 6539-0	Closed	1989	30.00	88-135
1986 Steeple Church (Third Version) 6539-0	Closed	1990	30.00	75
1992 Stoney Brook Town Hall 5644-8	Closed	1995	42.00	42-50
2000 Susquehanna Station 56624, set/2	Open		60.00	60
1997 Timber Knoll Log Cabin 6544-7	Closed	1990	28.00	150-160
1999 Trinity Ledge 56611	Open		85.00	85
1997 Van Guilder's Ornamental Ironworks 56577	Closed	1999	50.00	50-58
2001 Verna Mae's Boutique (Discover Department 56® Spring Promotion) 56626, gift set/3	Yr.Iss.	2001	65.00	65
1987 Weston Train Station 5931-5	Closed	1989	42.00	230-275
2002 Whale Tale Pub & Inn 56652	Open		62.00	62
2002 Whitehill Round Barn 56654	Open		65.00	65
2001 Wm. Walton Fine Clocks & Pocket Pieces 56628	Open		60.00	60
1995 Woodbridge Post Office 5657-2	Closed	1998	40.00	36-45
1992 Yankee Jud Bell Casting 5643-0	Closed	1994	44.00	26-50

North Pole Series - Department 56

YEAR ISSUE	EDITION LIMIT	YEAR RETD.	ISSUE PRICE	*QUOTE U.S.$
2001 ACME Toy Factory (Looney Tunes) 56729, set/5	Open		80.00	80
2002 Barbie™ Boutique 56739	Open		75.00	75
1994 Beard Barber Shop 5634-0	Closed	1997	27.50	25-45
2002 Beard Bros. Sleigh Wash 56740	Open		70.00	70
2001 Caribou Coffee Shop 56736, set/3	Open		62.00	62
1996 Christmas Bread Bakers 56393	Closed	2000	55.00	55
1999 Cold Care Clinic, Elf Land™ 56703	Closed	2000	42.00	42
2000 Crayola® Polar Palette Art Center 56726	Open		65.00	65
1998 Custom Stitchers, Elf Land™ 56400	Closed	2000	37.50	38
2001 The Egg Nog Pub 56737	Open		40.00	40
1999 Elf Mountain Ski Resort 56700	Open		70.00	70
2002 The Elf Spa, Elf Land™ 56402	Open		40.00	40
1992 Elfie's Sleds & Skates 5625-1	Closed	1996	48.00	48-60
1994 Elfin Forge & Assembly Shop 5638-4	Closed	1998	65.00	52-75
1994 Elfin Snow Cone Works 5633-2	Closed	1997	40.00	40
1997 Elsie's Gingerbread (Smoking House) 56398	Yr.Iss.	1998	65.00	85
1995 Elves' Trade School 5638-7	Closed	1998	50.00	40-50
1993 Express Depot 5627-8	Closed	1998	48.00	35-48
2001 Ginny's Cookie Treats 56732	Open		50.00	50
1997 The Glacier Gazette 56394	Closed	1999	48.00	48
1997 Glass Ornament Works 56396	Open		60.00	60
1996 Hall of Records 56392	Closed	1999	50.00	50-63
1999 Jack In The Box Plant No. 2 56705	Yr.Iss.	2000	65.00	65
2001 LEGO Building Creation Station 56735	Open		90.00	90
1999 Marie's Doll Museum 56408	Closed	1999	55.00	55-85
1999 Mini-Donut Shop, Elf Land™ 56702	Closed	2001	42.00	42
1997 Mrs. Claus' Greenhouse 56395	Closed	2001	68.00	68
1991 Neenee's Dolls & Toys 5620-0	Closed	1995	37.50	40-70
1990 North Pole 5601-4, set/2	Closed	1996	70.00	64-86
1990 • Elf Bunkhouse 56016	Closed	1996	35.00	33-60
1990 • Reindeer Barn 56015	Closed	2000	35.00	38-40
2002 North Pole Backdrop 52962	Open		45.00	45
1993 North Pole Chapel 5626-0	Closed	2000	45.00	45-50
1994 North Pole Dolls & Santa's Bear Works 5635-9, set/3 (North Pole Dolls, Santa's Bear Works, Entrance)	Closed	1997	96.00	90-98
1992 North Pole Post Office 5623-5	Closed	1999	45.00	40-50
1991 North Pole Shops 5621-9, set/2	Closed	1995	75.00	120-145
1991 • Orly's Bell & Harness Supply	Closed	1995	37.50	42-55
1991 • Rimpy's Bakery	Closed	1995	37.50	50-85
2001 Northern Lights Fire Station 56730	Open		64.00	64
1999 Northern Lights Stinsel Mill 56704	Open		55.00	55
1992 Obbie's Books & Letrinka's Candy 5624-3	Closed	1996	70.00	68-90
1999 The Peanut Brittle Factory 56701	Open		80.00	80
2002 Polar Palace Theater Elfland™ 56741	Open		45.00	45
1996 Popcorn & Cranberry House 56388	Closed	1997	45.00	85-115
1998 Real Plastic Snow Factory 56403	Closed	2001	80.00	80
1998 Reindeer Flight School 56404	Open		55.00	55
1996 Route 1, North Pole, Home of Mr. & Mrs. Claus 56391	Open		110.00	110
1996 Santa's Bell Repair 56389	Closed	1998	45.00	38-45
1997 Santa's Light Shop 56397	Closed	2000	52.00	52-62
1993 Santa's Lookout Tower 5629-4	Closed	2000	45.00	40-55
1995 Santa's Rooming House 5638-6	Closed	1999	50.00	40-62
2001 Santa's Sleigh Launch (Holiday Discover 2001) 56734, set/5 (All Clear For Take Off, trees, snow)	Closed	2001	75.00	75
1999 Santa's Visiting Center (Discover Department 56® Holiday Program) 56407, set/6	Yr.Iss.	1999	65.00	65-90
1993 Santa's Woodworks 5628-6	Closed	1996	42.00	50-70
1990 Santa's Workshop 5600-6	Closed	1993	72.00	250-400
2002 Starlight Dance Hall 56742	25,000		80.00	80
1996 Start a Tradition Set 56390, set/12 (Candy Cane Elves, set/2 Accessory)	Closed	1996	85.00	64-124
1996 • Candy Cane & Peppermint Shop	Closed	1996	N/A	63-120
1996 • Gift Wrap & Ribbons	Closed	1996	N/A	60
2000 Sweet Rock Candy Co. (Discover Department 56® Holiday Program) 56725, set/9	Yr.Iss.	2000	75.00	75-98
1991 Tassy's Mittens & Hassel's Woolies 5622-7	Closed	1995	50.00	64-90
1998 Tillie's Tiny Cup Café Elf Land™ 56401	Closed	2000	37.50	38
1995 Tin Soldier Shop 5638-3	Closed	1997	42.00	42-48
2001 Toot's Model Train Mfg. (Anniversary Edition) 56728	25,000	2001	110.00	110-235
2002 Twinkle Brite Glitter Factory 56738	Open		65.00	65
1995 Weather & Time Observatory 5638-5	Closed	1999	50.00	40-70
2001 Wedding Bells Chapel 56731	Closed	2001	45.00	45

North Pole Woods - Department 56

YEAR ISSUE	EDITION LIMIT	YEAR RETD.	ISSUE PRICE	*QUOTE U.S.$
2002 Chisel McTimber Art Studio 56887, set/2	Open		65.00	65
2000 Oakwood Post Office Branch 56881, set/2	Open		65.00	65
2000 Reindeer Care & Repair 56882	Open		60.00	60
2001 Reindeer Condo 56886	Open		70.00	70
2001 Rudolph's Condo 56885	Open		50.00	50
2002 Santa's Hot Tub 56888	Open		57.50	58
2001 Santa's Retreat 56883, set/2	Open		70.00	70
2000 Town Meeting Hall 56880	Open		68.00	68
2000 Trim-A-Tree Factory 56884, set/2	Closed	2001	50.00	50

The Original Snow Village Collection - Department 56

YEAR ISSUE	EDITION LIMIT	YEAR RETD.	ISSUE PRICE	*QUOTE U.S.$
1999 2000 Holly Lane (Discover Department 56® Holiday Program) 54977, set/11	Yr.Iss.	1999	65.00	100-115
1986 2101 Maple 5043-1	Closed	1986	32.00	285-360
1992 56 Flavors Ice Cream Parlor 5151-9	Closed	1992	42.00	165-245
2001 Abner's Implement Co. 55052, set/2	Open		85.00	85
1979 Adobe House 5066-6	Closed	1980	18.00	2424-2650

ARCHITECTURE

YEAR ISSUE	EDITION LIMIT	YEAR RETD.	ISSUE PRICE	*QUOTE U.S.$
1992 Airport 5439-9	Closed	1996	60.00	75-95
1992 Al's TV Shop 5423-2	Closed	1995	40.00	40-65
1986 All Saints Church 5070-9	Closed	1997	38.00	45-55
1998 ...Another Man's Treasure Garage 54945, set/22	Closed	2001	60.00	60
1986 Apothecary 5076-8	Closed	1990	34.00	85-95
2002 Armed Forces Recruiting Station 55081	Open		55.00	55
1987 Bachman's Hometown Boarding House 6700-0	Closed	1988	34.00	156
1987 Bachman's Hometown Church 6718-0	Closed	1988	39.00	160
1988 Bachman's Hometown Drugstore 6726-0	Closed	1988	29.00	200
1997 Bachman's Flower Shop 8802-0	Closed	1997	50.00	98-100
1998 Bachman's Greenhouse 2203-0	Closed	1998	60.00	75-92
1999 Bachman's Original Homestead 1885	7,500	1999	75.00	98-115
1981 Bakery 5077-6	Closed	1983	30.00	215-225
1986 Bakery 5077-6	Closed	1991	35.00	75-98
1982 Bank 5024-5	Closed	1983	32.00	490-545
1981 Barn 5074-1	Closed	1984	32.00	295-486
1984 Bayport 5015-6	Closed	1986	30.00	215-250
1986 Beacon Hill House 5065-2	Closed	1988	31.00	121-213
1995 Beacon Hill Victorian 5485-7	Closed	1998	60.00	60-70
1996 Birch Run Ski Chalet 54882	Closed	1999	60.00	60-68
1979 Brownstone 5056-7	Closed	1981	36.00	495-625
1996 Boulder Springs House 54873	Closed	1997	60.00	58-74
1995 Bowling Alley 5485-8	Closed	1998	42.00	42-48
1997 The Brandon Bungalow 54918	Closed	1999	55.00	48-58
2001 Buck's County Farm House 55051	Open		75.00	75
2001 Buck's County Horse Barn 55049	Open		72.00	72
2001 Candlerock Lighthouse Restaurant (Anniversary Edition) 55045	30,000	2001	110.00	110-155
1978 Cape Cod 5013-8	Closed	1980	20.00	400-426
1994 Carmel Cottage 5466-6	Closed	1997	48.00	33-67
1998 The Carnival Carousel (musical) 54933	Open		150.00	150
2000 Carpenter Gothic Bed & Breakfast (American Architecture Series), 55043	Open		75.00	75
1982 Carriage House 5021-0	Closed	1984	28.00	240-348
1986 Carriage House 5071-7	Closed	1988	29.00	94-130
1987 Cathedral Church 5019-9	Closed	1990	50.00	70-100
1980 Cathedral Church 5067-4	Closed	1981	36.00	2740-3500
1999 Cedar Point Cabin 55009	Open		66.00	66
2002 Cedar Ridge School 55070	Open		60.00	60
1982 Centennial House 5020-2	Closed	1984	32.00	260-295
1998 Center For The Arts 54940	Closed	2000	64.00	64
1999 Champsfield Stadium 55001, set/24	Closed	2001	195.00	195
1983 Chateau 5084-9	Closed	1984	35.00	415-507
1997 Christmas Barn Dance 54910	Closed	1999	65.00	55-82
1995 Christmas Cove Lighthouse 5483-6	Closed	2001	60.00	60
2001 Christmas Lake Chalet (Holiday Discover 2001) 55061, set/5	Closed	2001	75.00	75
1996 Christmas Lake High School 54881	Closed	1999	52.00	48-87
1991 The Christmas Shop 5097-0	Closed	1996	37.50	55-68
1985 Church of the Open Door 5048-2	Closed	1988	34.00	85-169
1999 Cinema 56 54978	Closed	2001	85.00	85
1988 Cobblestone Antique Shop 5123-3	Closed	1992	36.00	65-98
1994 Coca-Cola® Brand Bottling Plant 5469-0	Closed	1997	65.00	90-135
1995 Coca-Cola® Brand Corner Drugstore 5484-4	Closed	1998	55.00	80-90
1989 Colonial Church 5119-5	Closed	1992	60.00	58-75
1980 Colonial Farm House 5070-9	Closed	1982	30.00	250-300
1984 Congregational Church 5034-2	Closed	1985	28.00	520-590
1988 Corner Cafe 5124-1	Closed	1991	37.00	85-115
1981 Corner Store 5076-8	Closed	1983	30.00	170-225
1976 Country Church 5004-7	Closed	1979	18.00	375
2002 Country Quilts And Pies 55072, set/2	Open		65.00	65
1979 Countryside Church 5051-8 Meadowland Series	Closed	1980	25.00	360-650
1979 Countryside Church 5058-3	Closed	1984	27.50	200-250
1989 Courthouse 5144-6	Closed	1993	65.00	175-235
1992 Craftsman Cottage (American Architecture Series), 5437-2	Closed	1995	55.00	53-80
2001 Creepy Creek Carriage House 55055	Open		75.00	75
2001 Crosby House 55056	Open		50.00	50
1987 Cumberland House 5024-5	Closed	1995	42.00	60-75
1993 Dairy Barn 5446-1	Closed	1997	55.00	45-75
1984 Delta House 5012-1	Closed	1986	32.00	250-270
1985 Depot and Train w/2 Train Cars 5051-2	Closed	1988	65.00	135-175
1993 Dinah's Drive-In 5447-0	Closed	1996	45.00	138-165
1989 Doctor's House 5143-8	Closed	1992	56.00	100-178
1991 Double Bungalow 5407-0	Closed	1994	45.00	49-70
1985 Duplex 5050-4	Closed	1987	35.00	106-158
1995 Dutch Colonial (American Architecture Series) 5485-6	Closed	1996	45.00	36-70
2000 Elvis Presley's Graceland® (Discover Department 56® Holiday Program) 55041, set/6	Closed	2000	165.00	165
1981 English Church 5078-4	Closed	1982	30.00	400-474
1981 English Cottage 5073-3	Closed	1982	25.00	280-325
1983 English Tudor 5033-4	Closed	1985	30.00	184-262
1987 Farm House 5089-0	Closed	1992	40.00	46-75
1997 Farm House 54912	Closed	2000	50.00	50
1998 The Farmer's Co-op Granary 54946	Closed	2000	64.00	64
1994 Federal House (American Architecture Series) 5465-8	Closed	1997	50.00	50-78
1991 Finkle's Finery: Costume Shop 5405-4	Closed	1993	45.00	65-78
1983 Fire Station 5032-6	Closed	1984	32.00	480-550
1987 Fire Station No. 2 5091-1	Closed	1989	40.00	175-195
1998 Fire Station No. 3 54942	Open		70.00	70
1994 Fisherman's Nook Cabins 5461-5, set/2, (Fisherman's Nook Bass Cabin, Fisherman's Nook Trout Cabin)	Closed	1999	50.00	40-85
1994 Fisherman's Nook Resort 5460-7	Closed	1999	75.00	75-95
1982 Flower Shop 5082-2	Closed	1983	25.00	410-462
2001 Frost And Sons 5 & Dime 55047	Open		68.00	68
1976 Gabled Cottage 5002-1	Closed	1979	20.00	320-390
1982 Gabled House 5081-4	Closed	1983	30.00	360-370
1984 Galena House 5009-1	Closed	1985	32.00	350-402
1978 General Store (gold) 5012-0	Closed	1980	25.00	550
1978 General Store (tan) 5012-0	Closed	1980	25.00	625
1978 General Store (white) 5012-0	Closed	1980	25.00	400-522
1979 Giant Trees 5065-8	Closed	1982	20.00	315-335
1983 Gingerbread House Bank (Non-lighted) 5025-3	Closed	1984	24.00	460-650
1983 Gingerbread House Bank (lighted) 5025-3	Closed	1984	24.00	425
1994 Glenhaven House 5468-2	Closed	1997	45.00	45-58
1992 Good Shepherd Chapel & Church School 5424-0, set/2	Closed	1996	72.00	55-95
1983 Gothic Church 5028-8	Closed	1986	36.00	211
1991 Gothic Farmhouse (American Architecture Series), 5404-6	Closed	1997	48.00	55-95
1983 Governor's Mansion 5003-2	Closed	1985	32.00	350
1997 Gracie's Dry Goods & General Store 54915, set/2	Closed	2000	70.00	70-86
1992 Grandma's Cottage 5420-8	Closed	1996	42.00	59-88
1999 Grimsley Manor 55004	Open		120.00	120
1983 Grocery 5001-6	Closed	1985	35.00	290-348
2002 Gus's Drive-In 55067, set/7	Open		95.00	95
2002 Happy Easter House 55090, set/3	Open		50.00	50
1998 Harley-Davidson® Manufacturing 54948, set/3	Closed	2000	80.00	80-115
1996 Harley-Davidson® Motorcycle Shop 54886	Open		65.00	65
1992 Hartford House 5426-7	Closed	1995	55.00	55-78
2001 Haunted Barn (Halloween Discover 2001) 55060, set/4	Closed	2001	75.00	75-155
1998 Haunted Mansion (black roof) 54935	Closed	2000	110.00	495-745
1998 Haunted Mansion (green roof) 54935	Closed	2000	110.00	195-295
2001 Hauntsburg House 55058	Open		95.00	95
1984 Haversham House 5008-3	Closed	1987	37.00	182-247
1997 Hershey's® Chocolate Shop 54913	Closed	2000	55.00	55
1998 Hidden Ponds House 54944	Closed	2001	50.00	50
1986 Highland Park House 5063-6	Closed	1988	35.00	105-165
2001 The Holiday House 55048	Open		90.00	90
1995 Holly Brothers Garage 5485-4	Closed	1998	48.00	50-96
1999 Holy Spirit Church 55003, set/2	Open		70.00	70
1999 A Home In The Making 54979, set/5	Closed	2001	95.00	95
1988 Home Sweet Home/House & Windmill 5126-8	Closed	1991	60.00	100-125
1978 Homestead 5011-2	Closed	1984	30.00	195-294
1991 Honeymooner Motel 5401-1	Closed	1993	42.00	72-135
1998 The House That Love Built™ 1998 (Home For the Holidays) 2210	Yr.Iss.	1998	N/A	130
2000 How The Grinch Stole Christmas! - Movie Premiere, set/2 55103	Open		17.50	18
1993 Hunting Lodge 5445-3	Closed	1996	50.00	100-216
1976 The Inn 5003-9	Closed	1979	20.00	365
1997 Italianate Villa (American Architecture Series), 54911	Closed	2001	55.00	55-76

*Quotes have been rounded up to nearest dollar

YEAR ISSUE	EDITION LIMIT	YEAR RETD.	ISSUE PRICE	*QUOTE U.S.$
1989 J. Young's Granary 5149-7	Closed	1992	45.00	75-125
1991 Jack's Corner Barber Shop 5406-2	Closed	1994	42.00	75-98
1987 Jefferson School 5082-2	Closed	1991	36.00	129-188
1989 Jingle Belle Houseboat 5114-4	Closed	1991	42.00	150-265
2002 Juliette's School of French Cuisine 55063, set/4	Open		65.00	65
1988 Kenwood House 5054-7	Closed	1990	50.00	100-150
1979 Knob Hill (gold) 5055-9	Closed	1981	30.00	320-370
1979 Knob Hill 5055-9	Closed	1981	30.00	295-358
2002 Krispy Kreme Doughnut Shop 55071, set/2	Open		85.00	85
1981 Large Single Tree 5080-6	Closed	1989	17.00	20-45
1999 Last Stop Gas Station 55012, set/2	Closed	2001	72.00	72-86
1987 Lighthouse 5030-0	Closed	1988	36.00	320-660
1986 Lincoln Park Duplex 5060-1	Closed	1988	33.00	125-140
1997 Linden Hills Country Club 54917, set/2	Closed	2001	60.00	60
1998 Lionel® Electric Train Shop 54947	Closed	2000	55.00	55
1979 Log Cabin 5057-5	Closed	1981	22.00	525-600
1999 Lucky Dragon Restaurant 55011	Closed	2000	75.00	75-95
1997 Main Street Gift Shop 5488-7	Closed	1998	50.00	50-79
1984 Main Street House 5005-9	Closed	1986	27.00	190-250
1990 Mainstreet Hardware Store 5153-5	Closed	1993	42.00	64-119
1977 Mansion (blue-green) 5008-8	Closed	1979	30.00	500-540
1977 Mansion (dark green) 5008-8	Closed	1979	30.00	800-850
1988 Maple Ridge Inn 5121-7	Closed	1990	55.00	70
1994 Marvel's Beauty Salon 5470-4	Closed	1997	37.50	38-50
1997 McDonald's® 54914	Closed	1999	65.00	50-65
2002 McGuire's Irish Pub 55066	Open		50.00	50
1986 Mickey's Diner 5078-4	Closed	1987	22.00	550-690
1979 Mission Church 5062-5	Closed	1980	30.00	1174-1300
1979 Mobile Home 5063-3	Closed	1980	18.00	2200-2800
1990 Morningside House 5152-7	Closed	1992	45.00	48-82
1993 Mount Olivet Church 5442-9	Closed	1996	65.00	56-95
1979 Mountain Lodge 5001-3	Closed	1979	20.00	377-395
1978 Nantucket 5014-6	Closed	1986	25.00	235
1993 Nantucket Renovation 5441-0	Closed	1993	55.00	70-88
1997 New Hope Church 54904	Closed	1998	60.00	58-80
1984 New School House 5037-7	Closed	1986	35.00	199-225
1982 New Stone Church 5083-0	Closed	1984	32.00	350-432
1996 Nick's Tree Farm 54871, set/10 (Nick's Tree Farm, Nick The Tree Farmer Accessory)	Closed	1999	40.00	40-85
1989 North Creek Cottage 5120-9	Closed	1992	45.00	37-79
1991 Oak Grove Tudor 5400-3	Closed	1994	42.00	49-70
1997 Old Chelsea Mansion 54903	Closed	1998	85.00	85-98
1994 The Original Snow Village Starter Set 5462-3 (Sunday School Serenade Accessory, 3 asst. Sisal Trees, 1.5 oz. bag of real plastic snow)	Closed	1996	50.00	40-45
1994 • Shady Oak Church	Closed	1996	N/A	N/A
1986 Pacific Heights House 5066-0	Closed	1988	33.00	75-125
2001 Palm Lounge Supper Club 55046, set/2	Closed	2001	95.00	95
1988 Palos Verdes 5141-1	Closed	1990	37.50	70-82
1989 Paramount Theater 5142-0	Closed	1993	42.00	130-195
1984 Parish Church 5039-3	Closed	1986	32.00	290-354
1983 Parsonage 5029-6	Closed	1985	35.00	365-396
1995 Peppermint Porch Day Care 5485-2	Closed	1997	45.00	68-115
1989 Pinewood Log Cabin 5150-0	Closed	1995	37.50	60-96
1982 Pioneer Church 5022-9	Closed	1984	30.00	372-385
1995 Pisa Pizza 5485-1	Closed	1998	35.00	35-68
1985 Plantation House 5047-4	Closed	1987	37.00	88-138
2002 Polaris Snowmobile Dealership 55078	Open		85.00	85
1992 Post Office 5422-4	Closed	1995	35.00	62-82
1990 Prairie House (American Architecture Series), 5156-0	Closed	1993	42.00	60-96
1992 Print Shop & Village News 5425-9	Closed	1994	37.50	60-115
1990 Queen Anne Victorian (American Architecture Series), 5157-8	Closed	1996	48.00	65-72
1986 Ramsey Hill House 5067-9	Closed	1989	36.00	75-135
1987 Red Barn 5081-4	Closed	1992	38.00	85-135
1988 Redeemer Church 5127-6	Closed	1992	42.00	60-72
1996 Reindeer Bus Depot 54874	Closed	1997	42.00	42-64
1985 Ridgewood 5052-0	Closed	1987	35.00	115-160
1984 River Road House 5010-5	Closed	1987	36.00	125-198
1984 River Road House (open transom) 5010-5	Closed	1987	36.00	330-350
1996 Rockabilly Records 54880	Closed	1998	45.00	45-56
1998 Rock Creek Mill 54932	Closed	1998	64.00	95
1997 Rollerama Roller Rink 54916	Closed	1999	56.00	68
1996 Rosita's Cantina 54883	Closed	1999	50.00	50-88
1995 Ryman Auditorium 5485-5	Closed	1997	75.00	68-107
1986 Saint James Church 5068-7	Closed	1988	37.00	100-194
1979 School House 5060-9	Closed	1982	30.00	370-396
1996 The Secret Garden Florist 54885	Closed	2001	50.00	50
1998 The Secret Garden Greenhouse 54949	Closed	2001	60.00	60
1988 Service Station 5128-4	Closed	1991	37.50	215-225
1999 Shelly's Diner 55008, set/12	Open		110.00	110
1996 Shingle Victorian (American Architecture Series), 54884	Closed	1999	55.00	55
2002 Shipwreck Lighthouse 55088	Open		110.00	110
2000 Silver Bells Christmas Shop (Discover Department 56® Holiday Program) 55040, set/4	Closed	2000	75.00	88-98
1988 Single Car Garage 5125-0	Closed	1990	22.00	35-55
2000 Sitting in the Park, set/4 55100	Open		28.00	28
1994 Skate & Ski Shop 5467-4	Closed	1998	50.00	50-58
1982 Skating Pond 5017-2	Closed	1984	25.00	320-396
1978 Skating Rink, Duck Pond (set) 5015-3	Closed	1979	16.00	898-975
1976 Small Chalet 5006-2	Closed	1979	15.00	456-550
1996 Smokey Mountain Retreat 54872	Closed	2000	65.00	65
1995 Snow Carnival Ice Palace 5485-0	Closed	1998	95.00	70-135
1987 Snow Village Factory 5013-0	Closed	1989	45.00	96-144
1987 Snow Village Resort Lodge 5092-0	Closed	1989	55.00	125-162
1993 Snowy Hills Hospital 5448-8	Closed	1996	48.00	94-125
1998 Snowy Pines Inn Gift Set (Home For the Holidays) 54934, set/9	Yr.Iss.	1998	65.00	75-145
1986 Sonoma House 5062-8	Closed	1988	33.00	115-150
1991 Southern Colonial (American Architecture Series), 5403-8	Closed	1994	48.00	90
1990 Spanish Mission Church 5155-1	Closed	1992	42.00	68-98
2002 The Spooky Schooner 55087	Yr.Iss.		80.00	80
1987 Springfield House 5027-0	Closed	1990	40.00	62
1985 Spruce Place 5049-0	Closed	1987	33.00	235
1987 St. Anthony Hotel & Post Office 5006-7	Closed	1989	40.00	85-135
1992 St. Luke's Church 5421-6	Closed	1994	45.00	55-75
1995 Starbucks Coffee 5485-9	Closed	2000	48.00	48
2001 Stardust Drive-In Theater 55064	Open		68.00	68
2001 Stardust Refreshment Center 55065, set/7	Open		68.00	68
1997 Start A Tradition Set 54902, set/8 (Kringle's Toy Shop, Hot Chocolate Stand, Saturday Morning Downtown accessory, set/4, Bag of Real Plastic Snow, Cobblestone Road)	Closed	1998	75.00	45-100
1976 Steepled Church 5005-4	Closed	1979	25.00	480-600
1998 Stick Style House (American Architecture Series) 54943	Closed	2000	60.00	60-72
1977 Stone Church (10") 5009-6	Closed	1979	35.00	690-800
1979 Stone Church (8") 5059-1	Closed	1980	32.00	780-900
1980 Stone Mill House 5068-2	Closed	1982	30.00	400-546
1988 Stonehurst House 5140-3	Closed	1994	37.50	55-65
1984 Stratford House 5007-5	Closed	1986	28.00	135-155
1982 Street Car 5019-9	Closed	1984	16.00	330-403
1985 Stucco Bungalow 5045-8	Closed	1986	30.00	325-378
1984 Summit House 5036-9	Closed	1985	28.00	300-390
1999 Super Suds Laundromat 55006	Closed	2001	60.00	60
1982 Swiss Chalet 5023-7	Closed	1984	28.00	330-438
1979 Thatched Cottage 5050-0 Meadowland Series	Closed	1980	30.00	680-700
2001 Timberlake Outfitters 55054	Open		75.00	75
2001 Totem Town Souvenir Shop 55053	Open		68.00	68
1980 Town Church 5071-7	Closed	1982	33.00	276-300
1983 Town Hall 5000-8	Closed	1984	32.00	300-360
1986 Toy Shop 5073-3	Closed	1990	36.00	85-125
1980 Train Station (8 window panes) w/ 3 Train Cars 5085-6	Closed	1985	100.00	325-345
1980 Train Station (6 window panes) w/ 3 Train Cars 5085-6	Closed	1985	100.00	395-425
1996 Treetop Tree House 54890	Open		35.00	37
1984 Trinity Church 5035-0	Closed	1986	32.00	200-360
1979 Tudor House 5061-7	Closed	1981	25.00	250-348
2001 Tudor House 55062	Open		60.00	60
1983 Turn of the Century 5004-0	Closed	1986	36.00	195-288
1986 Twin Peaks 5042-3	Closed	1986	32.00	325-462
1998 Uncle Sam's Fireworks Stand 54974, set/2	Closed	2000	45.00	45
1998 Uptown Motors Ford® 54941, set/3	Open		95.00	95
1979 Victorian 5054-2	Closed	1982	30.00	235-360
1983 Victorian Cottage 5002-4	Closed	1984	35.00	300-375
1979 Victorian House 5007-0	Closed	1979	30.00	460-492
1999 Village Bank & Trust 55002	Closed	2001	75.00	75

ARCHITECTURE

YEAR ISSUE	EDITION LIMIT	YEAR RETD.	ISSUE PRICE	*QUOTE U.S.$
1983 Village Church 5026-1	Closed	1984	30.00	400-450
1991 Village Greenhouse 5402-0	Closed	1995	35.00	55-75
2002 Village Legion Hall 55080, set/2	Open		55.00	55
1988 Village Market 5044-0	Closed	1991	39.00	80-125
1995 Village Police Station 5485-3	Closed	1998	48.00	44-67
1993 Village Public Library 5443-7	Closed	1997	55.00	53-82
1990 Village Realty 5154-3	Closed	1997	42.00	58-65
1992 Village Station 5438-0	Closed	1997	65.00	70-98
1988 Village Station and Train 5122-5	Closed	1992	65.00	110-120
2001 Village Town Hall 55044	Open		96.00	96
1992 Village Vet and Pet Shop 5427-5	Closed	1995	32.00	70-100
1989 Village Warming House 5145-4	Closed	1992	42.00	65-89
1986 Waverly Place 5041-5	Closed	1986	35.00	248-305
1994 Wedding Chapel 5464-0	Closed	2001	55.00	55
1985 Williamsburg House 5046-6	Closed	1988	37.00	95-130
1993 Woodbury House 5444-5	Closed	1996	45.00	60-82
1983 Wooden Church 5031-8	Closed	1985	30.00	275-384
1981 Wooden Clapboard 5072-5	Closed	1984	32.00	180-300
2002 Woodlake Chapel 55068, set/2	Open		65.00	65
1999 WSNO Radio 55010	Open		75.00	75

The Original Snow Village Collection Accessories Retired - Department 56

YEAR ISSUE	EDITION LIMIT	YEAR RETD.	ISSUE PRICE	*QUOTE U.S.$
1998 1955 Ford® Automobiles 54950	Closed	2001	10.00	10
1998 1964 1/2 Ford® Mustang 54951	Closed	2001	10.00	10
2000 2001 Space Oddity 55118, set/11	Closed	2001	125.00	125
1987 3 Nuns With Songbooks 5102-0	Closed	1988	6.00	120-154
1998 Another Man's Treasure 54976, set/3	Closed	2001	27.50	28
1988 Apple Girl/Newspaper Boy 5129-2, set/2	Closed	1990	11.00	20-30
1979 Aspen Trees 5052-6, Meadowland Series	Closed	1980	16.00	450-515
1997 At The Barn Dance, It's Allemande Left 54927, set/2	Closed	1999	30.00	30
1985 Auto With Tree 50555	Closed	2001	6.50	7
1999 Before The Big Game 55019, set/4	Closed	2001	37.50	38
1989 Bringing Home The Tree 5169-1	Closed	1992	15.00	16-32
1989 Calling All Cars 5174-8, set/2	Closed	1991	15.00	58-75
1998 The Carnival Carousel 54933	Closed	2001	150.00	150
1998 Carnival Tickets & Cotton Candy 54938, set/3	Closed	2000	30.00	30
1979 Carolers 5064-1	Closed	1986	12.00	95-126
1994 Caroling At The Farm 54631	Closed	1986	35.50	36
1987 Caroling Family 5105-5, set/3	Closed	1990	20.00	30-48
1996 Caroling Through The Snow 54896	Closed	1999	15.00	15
1998 The Catch Of The Day 54956	Closed	2001	30.00	30
1980 Ceramic Car 5069-0	Closed	1986	5.00	45-54
1981 Ceramic Sleigh 5079-2	Closed	1986	5.00	45-54
1993 Check It Out Bookmobile 5451-8, set/3	Closed	1995	25.00	17-38
1998 Couldn't Wait Until Christmas 54972	Closed	2000	17.00	17
1987 Children In Band 5104-7	Closed	1989	15.00	17-40
1989 Choir Kids 5147-0	Closed	1992	15.00	15-26
1993 Christmas at the Farm 5450-0, set/2	Closed	1996	16.00	16-28
1991 Christmas Cadillac 5413-5	Closed	1994	9.00	14-20
1987 Christmas Children 5107-1, set/4	Closed	1990	20.00	19-30
1997 Christmas Kids 54922, set/5	Closed	1999	27.50	28
1992 Christmas Puppies 5432-1, set/2	Closed	1996	27.50	20-35
1998 Christmas Visit To The Florist 54957, set/3	Closed	2001	30.00	30
1993 Classic Cars 54577, set/3	Closed	1998	22.50	15-28
1994 Coca-Cola® Brand Billboard 5481-0	Closed	1997	18.00	15-26
1994 Coca-Cola® Brand Delivery Men 54801, set/2	Closed	1998	25.00	19-26
1994 Coca-Cola® Brand Delivery Truck 54798	Closed	1998	15.00	15-38
1991 Cold Weather Sports 5410-0, set/4	Closed	1994	27.50	23-50
1991 Come Join The Parade 5411-9	Closed	1992	13.00	16-20
1991 Country Harvest 5415-1	Closed	1993	13.00	14-30
1989 Crack the Whip 5171-3, set/3	Closed	1996	25.00	27-36
1988 Doghouse/Cat In Garbage Can 5131-4, set/2	Closed	1992	15.00	25-48
1990 Down the Chimney He Goes 5158-6	Closed	1993	6.50	10-20
1999 The Dragon Parade 55032	Closed	2001	35.00	35
1992 Early Morning Delivery 5431-3, set/3	Closed	1995	27.50	32-40
2000 Elvis Presley's® Autograph 55106, set/3	Closed	2001	27.50	25-48
1997 Everybody Goes Skating At Rollerama 54928, set/2	Closed	1999	25.00	15-25
1985 Family Mom/Kids, Going/Girl 5057-1	Closed	1988	11.00	21-60
1998 Farmer's Flatbed 54955	Closed	2000	17.50	18
1994 Feeding The Birds 5473-9, set/3	Closed	1997	25.00	25-38
1999 Finding The Bird's Song 55020, set/2	Closed	2001	25.00	2
1998 Fireman To The Rescue 54953, set/3	Closed	2001	30.00	3
1995 Firewood Delivery Truck 54864	Closed	1999	15.00	12-1
1999 First Deposit 55023	Closed	2001	14.00	1
1998 First Round Of The Year 54936, set/3	Closed	2001	30.00	3
1989 Flag Pole 51772	Closed	1999	8.50	6-1
1987 For Sale Sign 5108-0	Closed	1989	3.50	4-2
1990 Fresh Frozen Fish 5163-2, set/2	Closed	1993	20.00	34-5
1995 Frosty Playtime 54860, set/3	Closed	1997	30.00	28-4
1986 Girl/Snowman, Boy 5095-4	Closed	1987	11.00	60-7
1999 Gifts On The Go 55035, set/2	Closed	2001	30.00	3
1994 Going To The Chapel 54763, set/2	Closed	2001	20.00	2
1995 Grand Ole Opry Carolers 54867	Closed	1997	25.00	15-3
1996 A Harley-Davidson® Fat Boy® & Softail® 54900	Closed	2001	17.50	1
1996 A Harley-Davidson® Holiday 54898, set/2	Closed	1999	25.00	18-2
1988 Hayride 5117-9	Closed	1990	30.00	34-6
1997 He Led Them Down The Streets Of Town 54927, set/3	Closed	1999	30.00	3
1992 A Heavy Snowfall 54348, set/2	Closed	2001	16.00	1
1993 A Herd Of Holiday Heifers 5455-0, set/3	Closed	1997	18.00	18-2
1990 Here We Come A Caroling 5161-6, set/3	Closed	1992	18.00	14-3
1997 Hitch-up The Buckboard 54930	Closed	1999	40.00	17-3
1996 Holiday Hoops 54893, set/3	Closed	1999	20.00	2
1997 A Holiday Sleigh Ride Together 54921	Closed	2001	32.50	26-3
1990 Home Delivery 5162-4, set/2	Closed	1992	16.00	22-4
1990 A Home For The Holidays 5165-9	Closed	1996	7.00	6-
2000 How The Grinch Stole Christmas - Movie Premiere 55103, set/2	Closed	2001	17.50	1
1999 It's Time For An Icy Treat 55013, set/2	Closed	2001	30.00	3
1986 Kids Around The Tree (large) 5094-6	Closed	1990	15.00	50-6
1986 Kids Around The Tree (small) 5094-6	Closed	1990	15.00	19-4
1997 Kids, Candy Canes....& Ronald Mc Donald® 54926, set/3	Closed	1999	30.00	24-3
1990 Kids Decorating the Village Sign 5134-9	Closed	1993	13.00	25-3
1997 Kids Love Hershey's™! 54924, set/2	Closed	2000	30.00	3
1989 Kids Tree House 5168-3	Closed	1991	25.00	33-5
1999 Laundry Day 55017	Closed	2001	13.00	1
1997 Let It Snow, Let It Snow 54923	Closed	2000	20.00	2
1999 The Looney Toons® Animation Film Festival 54983, set/4	Closed	2001	40.00	
1988 Man On Ladder Hanging Garland 5116-0	Closed	1992	7.50	15-2
1997 McDonald's®...Lights Up The Night 54925	Closed	1999	30.00	28-3
1996 Men At Work 54894, set/5	Closed	1998	27.50	25-3
1982 Monks-A-Caroling 6460-2	Closed	1983	6.00	135-18
1984 Monks-A-Caroling (brown) 5040-7	Closed	1988	6.00	26-3
1983 Monks-A-Caroling (butterscotch) 6459-9	Closed	1984	6.00	45-6
1996 Moving Day 54892, set/3	Closed	1998	32.50	3
1991 Mush! 5474-7, set/2	Closed	1997	20.00	20-2
1992 Nanny and the Preschoolers 5430-5, set/2	Closed	1994	27.50	20-3
1988 Nativity 51357	Closed	2000	7.50	
2000 Now Showing - Elvis Presley® Sign 55105	Closed	2001	30.00	3
1999 On The Way To Ballet Class 55031, set/3	Closed	2001	27.50	
1987 Park Bench (green) 5109-8	Closed	1993	3.00	5-1
1998 Patrolling The Road 54971	Closed	2001	20.00	2
1994 Pets on Parade 54720, set/2	Closed	1998	16.50	18-2
1993 Pick-Up & Delivery 5454-2	Closed	2001	10.00	3
1996 Pick-Up & Delivery (St. Nick's) 5454-2	Closed	1996	10.00	3
1993 Pint-Size Pony Rides 5453-4, set/3	Closed	1996	37.50	37-5
1995 Pizza Delivery 54866, set/2	Closed	1998	20.00	30-3
1995 Poinsettias For Sale 54861, set/3	Closed	1998	30.00	30-3
1987 Praying Monks 5103-9	Closed	1988	6.00	35-4
1998 Quality Service At Ford® 54970, set/2	Closed	2001	27.50	
1996 A Ride On The Reindeer Lines 54875, set/3	Closed	1997	35.00	25-4
1997 Road Construction Sign 52680, set/2	Closed	2001	12.00	1
1992 Round & Round We Go! 5433-0, set/2	Closed	1995	18.00	25-4
1993 Safety Patrol 5449-6, set/4	Closed	1997	27.50	2
1988 Santa/Mailbox 5059-8	Closed	1990	11.00	30-4
1994 Santa Comes To Town, 1995 5477-1	Closed	1995	30.00	30-4
1995 Santa Comes To Town, 1996 54862	Closed	1996	32.50	22-4

YEAR ISSUE	EDITION LIMIT	YEAR RETD.	ISSUE PRICE	*QUOTE U.S.$
1996 Santa Comes To Town, 1997 54899	Closed	1997	35.00	22-50
1997 Santa Comes To Town, 1998 54920	Closed	1998	30.00	30-44
1998 Santa Comes To Town, 1999 54958	Closed	1999	30.00	30
1999 Santa Comes To Town, 2000 55015	Closed	2000	37.50	38
2000 Santa Comes To Town, 2001 55120	Closed	2001	40.00	40
1999 Santa's Little Helpers 55025	Closed	2001	27.50	28
1988 School Bus, Snow Plow 5137-3, set/2	Closed	1991	16.00	50-68
1988 School Children 5118-7, set/3	Closed	1990	15.00	25
1984 Scottie With Tree 5038-5	Closed	1985	3.00	176-220
1999 Send In The Clown! 55021	Closed	2001	13.50	14
1995 Service With a Smile 54865, set/2	Closed	1998	25.00	22-32
1979 Sheep, 9 White, 3 Black 5053-4 Meadowland Series	Closed	1980	12.00	400
1986 Shopping Girls w/Packages (large) 5096-2	Closed	1988	11.00	45-60
1986 Shopping Girls w/Packages (small) 5096-2	Closed	1988	11.00	24-35
1988 Sisal Tree Lot 8183-3	Closed	1991	45.00	50-104
1985 Singing Nuns 5053-9	Closed	1987	6.00	120-136
1991 Skate Faster Mom 5170-5	Closed	1991	13.00	11-35
1984 Skaters & Skiers 54755, set/3	Closed	2001	27.50	28
1990 Sleighride 5160-8	Closed	1992	30.00	43-65
1978 Small Double Trees w/ blue birds 5016-1	Closed	1989	13.50	157-175
1978 Small Double Trees w/ red birds 5016-1	Closed	1989	13.50	45
1990 Sno-Jet Snowmobile 5159-4	Closed	1993	15.00	28-38
1995 Snow Carnival Ice Sculpture 54868, set/2	Closed	1998	27.50	28
1995 Snow Carnival King & Queen 54869	Closed	1998	35.00	35-58
1987 Snow Kids 5113-6, set/4	Closed	1990	20.00	35-60
1985 Snow Kids Sled, Skis 5056-3	Closed	1987	11.00	39-50
1991 Snowball Fort 5414-3, set/3	Closed	1993	27.50	35-40
1982 Snowman With Broom 5018-0	Closed	1990	3.00	10-22
1992 Spirit of Snow Village Airplane 5440-2	Closed	1996	32.50	25-42
1993 Spirit of Snow Village Airplane 5458-5, 2 asst.	Closed	1996	12.50	42-58
1995 Starbucks® Coffee Car 54870, set/2	Closed	2000	27.50	28
1989 Statue of Mark Twain 5173-0	Closed	1991	15.00	30-38
1994 Stuck In The Snow 54712, set/3	Closed	1998	30.00	21-44
1989 Street Sign 5167-5, set/6	Closed	1992	7.50	19-50
1990 SV Special Delivery 5197-7, set/2	Closed	1992	16.00	38-43
1987 Taxi Cab 51063	Closed	2000	6.50	7
1997 Television Antenna 52658, set/4	Closed	1999	5.00	5
1996 Terry's Towing 54895, set/2	Closed	1999	20.00	16-24
1993 Tour The Village 5452-6	Closed	1997	12.50	8-16
1989 Through the Woods 5172-1, set/2	Closed	1991	18.00	12-30
1990 A Tree For Me 5164-0, set/2	Closed	1995	8.00	7-20
1988 Tree Lot 51381	Closed	1999	37.50	30-48
1998 Uncle Sam's Fireworks Stand 54974, set/2	Closed	2000	45.00	45
1998 Uptown Motors Ford® Billboard 52780	Closed	2001	20.00	20
1989 US Mailbox 5179-9	Closed	1990	3.50	8-12
1989 US Special Delivery 51489, (red, white, blue) set/2	Closed	1990	16.00	32-56
1990 US Special Delivery 51977, (red, green) set/2	Closed	1992	16.00	17-34
1990 Village Birds 5180-2, set/6	Closed	1994	3.50	7-16
1989 Village Gazebo 5146-2	Closed	1995	30.00	25-45
1991 Village Greetings 5418-6, set/3	Closed	1994	5.00	6-10
1998 Village Halloween Set 52704, set/22	Closed	2001	50.00	50
1993 Village News Delivery 5459-3, set/2	Closed	1996	15.00	20-36
1991 Village Marching Band 5412-7, set/3	Closed	1992	30.00	40-75
1998 Village Service Vehicles 54959, set/3	Closed	2001	45.00	45
1992 Village Used Car Lot 5428-3, set/5	Closed	1997	45.00	45-52
1988 Water Tower 5133-0	Closed	1991	20.00	69-95
1989 Water Tower-John Deer 568-0	Closed	1991	20.00	650-985
1992 We're Going to a Christmas Pageant 5435-6	Closed	1994	15.00	27
1999 Welcome To The Congregation 55014, set/4	Closed	2001	15.00	15
1997 The Whole Family Goes Shopping 54905, set/3	Closed	1999	25.00	25
1991 Winter Fountain 5409-7	Closed	1993	25.00	37-85
1992 Winter Playground 5436-4	Closed	1995	20.00	30-55
1988 Woodsman and Boy 5130-6, set/2	Closed	1991	13.00	15-26
1988 Woody Station Wagon 5136-5	Closed	1990	6.50	24-28
1991 Wreaths For Sale 5408-9,set/4	Closed	1994	27.50	35-50

Profile Series - Department 56

YEAR ISSUE	EDITION LIMIT	YEAR RETD.	ISSUE PRICE	*QUOTE U.S.$
1996 Heinz House	Closed	1996	28.00	49-95

YEAR ISSUE	EDITION LIMIT	YEAR RETD.	ISSUE PRICE	*QUOTE U.S.$
1997 State Farm Insurance 75th Anniversary 56000	Closed	1997	35.50	68-94

Seasons Bay Series - Department 56

YEAR ISSUE	EDITION LIMIT	YEAR RETD.	ISSUE PRICE	*QUOTE U.S.$
1998 Bay Street Shops 53401, set/2	Open		135.00	135
1998 Bay Street Shops (1st Ed.) 53301, set/2	Closed	1999	135.00	135
2002 Bayport Souvenir And Kite Shop 53450	Open		60.00	60
2001 Breezy Hill Stables 53477	Open		68.00	68
1998 Chapel On The Hill 53402	Closed	2001	72.00	72
1998 Chapel On The Hill (1st Ed.) 53302	Closed	1999	72.00	72
2001 East Cape Cottages 53448, set/2	Open		95.00	95
2001 Garden Valley Vineyards (Anniversary Edition) 53446	5,600	2001	125.00	125
1998 The Grand Creamery 53405	Closed	2001	60.00	60
1998 The Grand Creamery (1st Ed.) 53305	Closed	1999	60.00	60
1998 Grandview Shores Hotel 53400	Closed	2000	150.00	150
1998 Grandview Shores Hotel (1st Ed.) 53300	Closed	1999	150.00	150
1998 Inglenook Cottage #5 53404	Closed	2000	60.00	60
1998 Inglenook Cottage #5 (1st Ed.) 53304	Closed	1999	60.00	60
2000 Mystic Ledge Lighthouse 53445	5,600	2000	96.00	185-235
1999 Parkside Pavilion (Discover Department 56® Spring Promotion) 53412, gift set/9	Closed	2000	75.00	75
1999 Parkside Pavilion 53411, set/2	Open		65.00	65
2001 Seaside Inn 53449	Open		68.00	68
1998 Side Porch Café 53403	Open		50.00	50
1998 Side Porch Café (1st Ed.) 53303	Closed	1999	50.00	50
1999 Springlake Station 53413	Open		90.00	90
1999 Stillwaters Boathouse 53414	Open		70.00	70

Storybook Village - Department 56

YEAR ISSUE	EDITION LIMIT	YEAR RETD.	ISSUE PRICE	*QUOTE U.S.$
1999 The Butcher, Baker and Candlestick Maker 13186, set/2	Closed	2000	75.00	75-155
2002 Christmas House 13249	Open		98.00	98
2001 Cinderella's Dress Shop 13203, set/2	Open		50.00	50
2001 The Emerald City 13201, set/2	Open		95.00	95
2001 Frosty Frolic Castle 13205	Open		95.00	95
2002 Frosty The Snowman Country Nurseries Waterglobe 13216, set/3	Open		55.00	55
1996 Goldilocks Bed And Breakfast 13193, set/4	Closed	1999	75.00	75-165
1998 H.D. Diddle Fiddles 13183, set/4	Open		75.00	75
2001 Hansel and Gretel's Sweets Shop 13210, set/4	Open		50.00	50
1996 Hickory Dickory Dock 13195, set/3	Closed	1998	95.00	95-165
1997 Humpty Dumpty Café 13181, set/4	Closed	2001	75.00	75
1996 Lambsville School 13194, set/5	Closed	1999	75.00	75-175
1999 Lil' Boy Blue Petting Farm 13172, set/4	Closed	2001	75.00	75
2000 Little Bo-Peep's Woolery 13174, set/3	Open		75.00	75
1997 Mary, Quite Contrary Flower Shop 13180, set/5	Closed	2000	75.00	75-165
1999 Mother Goose Book Cellar 13171, set/5	Open		75.00	75
2002 Noah's Ark 13220, set/3	Open		65.00	65
2002 Noah's Ark Waterglobe 13223	Open		42.00	42
1998 Old House In Paris That Was Covered With Vines 13185, set/9	Open		75.00	75
1996 Old Woman Cobbler 13191, set/5	Closed	1999	75.00	75-135
1996 Peter Piper Pickle And Peppers 13192, set/4	Closed	1998	95.00	95-165
1998 Peter Piper's 13184, set/3	Closed	2001	75.00	75
1999 Queen's House of Cards 13173, set/8	Open		85.00	85
2002 Raggedy Ann & Andy's Patchwork House 13207, set/3	Open		50.00	50
2001 Rapunzel's Hair Salon 13204	Open		50.00	50
2001 Rudolph's Bunk House 13206, set/2	Open		75.00	75
2001 Rudolph's Red-Nosed Lighthouse 13202, set/4	Open		95.00	95
1999 Storybook Village Collection Landscape Set 13179, set/6	Open		10.00	10
1999 Storybook Village Collection Sign 13169	Open		10.00	10
1998 T.L. Pigs Brick Factory 13182, set/2	Closed	2000	75.00	75-165

Village CCP Miniatures - Department 56

YEAR ISSUE	EDITION LIMIT	YEAR RETD.	ISSUE PRICE	*QUOTE U.S.$
1987 Christmas Carol Cottages 6561-7, set/3	Closed	1989	30.00	83-93
1987 • The Cottage of Bob Cratchit & Tiny Tim 6561-7	Closed	1989	10.00	38-50
1987 • Fezziwig's Warehouse 6561-7	Closed	1989	10.00	26-30

YEAR ISSUE	EDITION LIMIT	YEAR RETD.	ISSUE PRICE	*QUOTE U.S.$
1987 · Scrooge/ Marley Countinghouse 6561-7	Closed	1989	10.00	40-42
1987 Dickens' Chadbury Station & Train 6592-7	Closed	1989	27.50	50-55
1987 Dickens' Cottages 6559-5, set/3	Closed	1989	30.00	345
1987 · Stone Cottage 6559-5	Closed	1989	10.00	98-130
1987 · Thatched Cottage 6559-5	Closed	1989	10.00	105-125
1987 · Tudor Cottage 6559-5	Closed	1989	10.00	121-140
1988 Dickens' Kenilworth Castle 6565-0	Closed	1989	30.00	120-125
1987 Dickens' Lane Shops 6591-9, set/3	Closed	1989	30.00	140-150
1987 · Cottage Toy Shop 6591-9	Closed	1989	10.00	25-30
1987 · Thomas Kersey Coffee House 6591-9	Closed	1989	10.00	40-56
1987 · Tuttle's Pub 6591-9	Closed	1989	10.00	28-50
1987 Dickens' Village Assorted 6560-9, set/3	Closed	1989	48.00	140
1987 · Blythe Pond Mill House 6560-9	Closed	1989	16.00	40-42
1987 · Dickens Village Church 6560-9	Closed	1989	16.00	38-40
1987 · Norman Church 6560-9	Closed	1989	16.00	130-138
1987 Dickens' Village Assorted 6562-5, set/4	Closed	1989	60.00	300
1987 · Barley Bree Farmhouse 6562-5	Closed	1989	15.00	22-55
1987 · Brick Abbey 6562-5	Closed	1989	15.00	88-105
1987 · Chesterton Manor House 6562-5	Closed	1989	15.00	120-130
1987 · The Old Curiosity Shop 6562-5	Closed	1989	15.00	72-75
1987 Dickens' Village Original 6558-7, set/7	Closed	1989	72.00	219
1987 · Abel Beesley Butcher 6558-7	Closed	1989	12.00	24-30
1987 · Bean and Son Smithy Shop 6558-7	Closed	1989	12.00	32-40
1987 · Candle Shop 6558-7	Closed	1989	12.00	35-40
1987 · Crowntree Inn 6558-7	Closed	1989	12.00	35-38
1987 · Golden Swan Baker 6558-7	Closed	1989	12.00	17-25
1987 · Green Grocer 6558-7	Closed	1989	12.00	17-45
1987 · Jones & Co Brush & Basket Shop 6558-7	Closed	1989	12.00	28-68
1987 Little Town of Bethlehem 5976-5, set/12	Closed	1989	85.00	215-285
1988 New England Village Assorted 5937-4, set/6	Closed	1989	85.00	400-500
1988 · Craggy Cove Lighthouse 5937-4	Closed	1989	14.50	89-105
1988 · Jacob Adams Barn 5937-4	Closed	1989	14.50	49-55
1988 · Jacob Adams Farmhouse 5937-4	Closed	1989	14.50	47-50
1988 · Maple Sugaring Shed 5937-4	Closed	1989	14.50	46-60
1988 · Smythe Wollen Mill 5937-4	Closed	1989	14.50	75-80
1988 · Timber Knoll Log Cabin 5937-4	Closed	1989	14.50	48-50
1988 New England Village Original 5935-8, set/7	Closed	1989	72.00	680
1988 · Apothecary Shop 5935-8	Closed	1989	10.50	38-45
1988 · Brick Town Hall 5935-8	Closed	1989	10.50	55-60
1988 · General Store 5935-8	Closed	1989	10.50	62-70
1988 · Livery Stable & Boot Shop 5935-8	Closed	1989	10.50	55-60
1988 · Nathaniel Bingham Fabrics 5935-8	Closed	1989	10.50	63-65
1988 · Red Schoolhouse 5935-8	Closed	1989	10.50	80-90
1988 · Village Steeple Church 5935-8	Closed	1989	10.50	155-200
1986 Victorian Miniatures 6564-1, set/2	Closed	1987	45.00	219-248
1986 · Church 6564-1	Closed	1987	22.50	40-93
1986 · Estate 6564-1	Closed	1987	22.50	40-88
1986 Victorian Miniatures 6563-3, set/5	Closed	1987	65.00	275
1986 Williamsburg Snowhouse Series, set/6	Closed	1987	60.00	625
1986 · Williamsburg Church, White 6566-8	Closed	1987	10.00	30-62
1986 · Williamsburg House Brown Brick 6566-8	Closed	1987	10.00	61
1986 · Williamsburg House, Blue 6566-8	Closed	1987	10.00	20-50
1986 · Williamsburg House, Brown Clapboard	Closed	1987	10.00	50-75
1986 · Williamsburg House, Red 6566-8	Closed	1987	10.00	20-50
1986 · Williamsburg House, White 6566-8	Closed	1987	10.00	30-62

Encore

Snow Buddies Snowville™ - Encore

2002 Barn	Open		25.00	25
2000 Boot Repair Shop	Closed	2001	25.00	25
2000 Bridge	Open		5.00	5
2000 Church	Open		25.00	25
2001 Circus Tent (4 pc. set)	Closed	2001	25.00	25
2000 Flurry's Home Sweet Home	Open		25.00	25
2001 Gazebo	Open		20.00	20
2000 Hat Shop	Closed	2001	19.00	19
2000 Ice Pond	Open		15.00	15
2000 Knitting School	Closed	2001	25.00	25
2000 Lamp Post	Open		3.00	3

YEAR ISSUE	EDITION LIMIT	YEAR RETD.	ISSUE PRICE	*QUOTE U.S.$
2002 Lighthouse	Open		25.00	25
2000 Sno Cone Shop	Open		15.00	15
2001 Snowville Fire Dept.	Open		25.00	25
2001 Snowville Hotel	Open		29.00	29
2000 Sports Shop	Open		30.00	30
2000 Sports Shop, 20"	Yr.Iss.	2000	350.00	350
2000 Tree, lg.	Open		8.00	8
2000 Tree, med.	Open		4.00	4
2000 Tree, sm.	Open		2.50	3
2000 Welcome To Snowville Sign	Open		4.00	4

Fontanini/Roman, Inc.

Fontanini Club Members Only Exclusives - E. Simonetti

2000 The Harbor	Yr.Iss.	2000	75.00	75
2001 Courtyard	Yr.Iss.	2001	50.00	50
2002 Sewing Corner	Yr.Iss.		35.00	35

Fontanini Life of Christ 5" - E. Simonetti

1999 Crucifixion Scene	Open		100.00	100
2000 Resurrection Scene	Open		85.00	85
2001 Wedding at Cana Canopy Set	Open		45.00	45

Fontanini Nativity Village 2.5" - E. Simonetti

2000 Basket Shop	Retrd.	2000	32.50	33
1998 Carpenter's Shop	Retrd.	2000	32.50	33
1998 Corral	Retrd.	2001	32.50	33
1996 Inn	Retrd.	2000	29.50	30
1996 King's Tent, Blue	Retrd.	2000	17.50	18
1997 King's Tent, Gold	Retrd.	2001	22.50	23
1997 King's Tent, Purple	Retrd.	2000	22.50	23
1997 Marketplace	Retrd.	2000	32.50	33
1997 Pottery Shop	Retrd.	2000	32.50	33
1998 Poultry Shop	Retrd.	2000	32.50	33
1996 Set/6, 1996 w/ lighted base	Retrd.	1998	270.00	270
1996 Shepherd's Camp	Retrd.	1999	29.50	30
1996 Town Building	Retrd.	2000	25.00	25
1997 Town Gate	Retrd.	2001	32.50	33
1996 Town Store	Retrd.	1998	25.00	25
2000 Weaver's Shop	Retrd.	2000	32.50	33

Fontanini Nativity Village 5" - E. Simonetti

1996 Bakery	Retrd.	1999	80.00	80
2001 Baking Oven	Open		22.50	23
2000 Basket Shop	Open		80.00	80
2001 Carpenter's Shed	Open		70.00	70
1998 Carpenter's Shop	Retrd.	2000	90.00	90
1999 Census Building	Retrd.	2001	85.00	85
1998 Corral	Retrd.	2001	90.00	90
2001 Farm Scene with Shelter - 4 pc. Set	Open		50.00	50
2001 Fishing Boat with Wave Base	Open		22.50	23
2000 Home	Open		125.00	125
1996 Inn	Retrd.	2001	85.00	85
2002 Inn Starter Set	Open		100.00	100
2001 King's Pavilion	Open		65.00	65
1996 King's Tent, Blue	Retrd.	2000	50.00	50
1997 King's Tent, Gold	Retrd.	2000	65.00	65
1997 King's Tent, Purple	Retrd.	2000	60.00	65
1997 Marketplace	Retrd.	1999	90.00	90
2002 Pottery Corner	Open		25.00	25
1997 Pottery Shop	Retrd.	2001	90.00	90
1998 Poultry Shop	Retrd.	2000	90.00	90
2002 Produce Market	Open		25.00	25
2002 Rug Tent	Open		25.00	25
1996 Shepherd's Camp	Retrd.	1998	80.00	80
2002 Spice Shop	Open		25.00	25
2002 Synagogue School	Open		25.00	25
1999 Temple	Open		125.00	125
1997 Town Gate	Open		90.00	90
2001 Town Well	Open		35.00	35
2000 Vineyard	Open		80.00	80
1999 Weaver's Shop	Retrd.	2001	75.00	75

Fontanini Nativity Village 7.5" - E. Simonetti

1998 Fish Market	Retrd.	2000	120.00	120
1997 Inn	Retrd.		55.00	55
1997 King's Tent, Blue	Retrd.	2001	99.50	100
1998 King's Tent, Gold	Retrd.	2000	110.00	110
1998 King's Tent, Purple	Retrd.	2000	95.00	95
1999 Marketplace	Retrd.	2001	120.00	120
1997 Marketplace	Retrd.	1998	65.00	65
1997 Town Building	Retrd.	1998	70.00	70

YEAR ISSUE	EDITION LIMIT	YEAR RETD.	ISSUE PRICE	*QUOTE U.S.$
1997 Town Gate	Retrd.	1998	35.00	35
2000 Weaver's Shop	Retrd.	2001	110.00	110
1999 William Blarney 11578	Suspd.		15.00	15
1995 Wood Fence, 36"	Suspd.		5.00	8

G. DeBrekht Artistic Studios/Derévo Collection

Derévo Fairy-Tale Village - G. DeBrekht Artistic Studios

YEAR ISSUE	EDITION LIMIT	YEAR RETD.	ISSUE PRICE	*QUOTE U.S.$
2001 Baba Yaga House 59013	1,200		110.00	110
2001 Bridge 59014	2-Yr.		45.00	45
2001 Church, small (lighted) 59009	1,200		110.00	110
2001 Dog 59069	Open		10.00	10
2001 Round Church (lighted) 59010-2	1,200		129.00	129
2000 Village Church (lighted) 59010	2-Yr.		129.00	129
2000 Village House (lighted) 59011	2-Yr.		119.00	119
2001 Winter Trees, set/3 59050	Open		49.00	49
2001 Wood cut with Mushroom 59056	Open		13.00	13

Geo. Zoltan Lefton Company

Accessories - Lefton

YEAR ISSUE	EDITION LIMIT	YEAR RETD.	ISSUE PRICE	*QUOTE U.S.$
1990 Abe Smith 07483	Suspd.		5.00	10-24
1988 Allison Davis 06547	Suspd.		5.00	22-30
1991 Annette & Rebecca 07827	Suspd.		10.00	10-35
1999 Autumn Colors 11582	Suspd.		13.00	13
1988 Billy O'Malley 06740	Suspd.		7.00	12-32
1990 Bonnie Charles & Spot 07824	Suspd.		10.00	12-35
1999 Brown Tree (11") 12454	Suspd.		6.00	6
1999 Brown Tree (9") 12455	Open		4.00	4
1987 Cab 06459	Suspd.		13.00	25-57
1991 Cart 07830	Suspd.		11.00	15-28
1994 The Convenience 732500	Suspd.		6.00	8-28
1988 CV Express 05826	Suspd.		27.00	99-124
1991 Da Vinci Bros. 00269	Suspd.		12.00	14-32
1990 Dashing Through Snow 07322	Suspd.		16.00	10-16
1988 Dick's Delivery 06548	Suspd.		8.00	27-45
1999 Direction Sign 12130	Suspd.		16.00	16
1987 Doc Olsens' Wagon 06457	Suspd.		14.00	28-60
1988 Double Tree 06467	Suspd.		5.00	10-40
1987 Eberhardt's (4pc./set) 05910	Suspd.		20.00	17-79
1994 The Eberhardts (6 pc./set) 582700	Suspd.		50.00	17-20
1987 Fire Engine Co. NO. 5 06458	Suspd.		14.00	19-50
1991 Frank Pendergast 07776	Suspd.		5.50	10-25
1999 George Blarney 11580	Suspd.		22.00	22
1991 The Griffiths 00661	Suspd.		13.00	10-35
1999 Harvest Pickens 11579	Suspd.		12.00	12
1987 Ivan the Lamplighter 06741	Suspd.		7.00	7-35
2001 Jackson Family, set/2 13674	Yr.Iss.	2001	30.00	30
1991 Jeffrey Sawyer 00659	Suspd.		8.00	10-28
1988 Kalenko Family Choir 06887	Suspd.		13.00	47-67
1988 Large Tree 06465	Suspd.		6.50	10-40
1999 Lillian Blarney 11577	Suspd.		15.00	15
1988 Lisa & Selena 06549	Suspd.		7.00	12-30
1991 Major & Mrs. 00214	Suspd.		12.00	13-30
1999 Maple Tree (10") 12453	Open		13.00	13
1999 Maple Tree (12") 11988	Open		17.00	17
1999 Maple Tree (12") 12452	Open		17.00	17
1990 Mary & Jack Cobb 07825	Suspd.		10.00	12-35
1988 Matt's Milk Wagon 06461	Suspd.		13.00	30-63
1988 Merrymaker Ed 06739	Suspd.		7.00	10-33
1988 Mr. Watts 06742	Suspd.		7.00	9-35
1999 Needle in a Haystack 11581	Suspd.		15.00	15
1988 Nina & Fillipe 06737	Suspd.		9.00	10-35
1994 Nurse Sarah Miller 21700	Suspd.		5.00	6-10
1994 Officer Casey 733000	Suspd.		5.00	6-10
1987 One Horse Open Sleigh 06460	Suspd.		13.00	24-42
1991 The Parkers 00218	Suspd.		13.00	6-13
1999 Peek-A-Boo 11575	Suspd.		13.00	13
1999 Santa's Helpers 698700	Suspd.		5.00	9
1999 Season's Greetings 11585	Suspd.		17.00	17
1999 Sharon Blarney 11576	Suspd.		15.00	15
1988 Small Tree 06466	Suspd.		4.00	10-30
1988 Steven & Stacey 06744	Suspd.		9.00	15-35
1988 Stone Church Carolers 06554	Suspd.		12.00	39-63
1990 Sylvester The Sweep 07778	Suspd.		5.00	12-25
2001 Through The Years, set/6 13672	Yr.Iss.	2001	50.00	50
1992 Tim & Lucy Morgan 00662	Suspd.		9.00	5-9
1999 Trick or Treat 11574	Suspd.		13.00	13
2001 Tyler Family, set/5 13673	Yr.Iss.	2001	40.00	40
1994 The Vanderspeck Kids 782800	Suspd.		6.50	10-15
1994 Water Pump 792300	Suspd.		4.00	15
1994 Well, 5" 792600	Suspd.		8.50	17-25

Colonial Village - Lefton

YEAR ISSUE	EDITION LIMIT	YEAR RETD.	ISSUE PRICE	*QUOTE U.S.$
1993 Antiques & Curiosities 00723	Closed	1998	50.00	50
1995 Applegate-CVRA Exclusive 01327	Closed	1995	50.00	88-110
1990 The Ardmore House 07338	Closed	1995	45.00	35-50
1997 Ashton House-CVRA Exclusive 10829	Closed	2000	50.00	50
2000 Auntie June's House 13517	Closed	2001	50.00	50
1993 Baldwin's Fine Jewelry 00722	Closed	1997	50.00	39-59
2001 Barber Shop 13666	2,000		50.00	50
2000 Bed & Breakfast 13501	Closed	2000	50.00	50
1991 Belle-Union Saloon 07482	Closed	1994	45.00	65-104
1998 Berkely House-CVRA Exclusive 11262	Closed	2000	50.00	50
1989 Bijou Theatre 06897	Closed	1990	40.00	625-691
1994 Black Sheep Tavern 01003	Closed	1999	50.00	35-50
1993 Blacksmith 00720	Closed	2001	47.00	40-63
1999 Blarney Barn/Blarney Silo (Collector's Set) 12330	Closed	1999	150.00	150
1999 Blarney Farmhouse 11587	Closed	2000	50.00	50
1998 Blue Bell Flour 11263	Closed	2000	50.00	50
1999 Bradley House 11999	Closed	2000	65.00	65
1992 Brenner's Apothecary 07961	Closed	2000	45.00	40-50
1996 The Brookfield 11996	5,500	1996	75.00	75 116
1994 Brown's Book Shop 01001	Closed	1999	50.00	50
1993 Burnside 00717	Closed	2000	50.00	50
1989 Capper's Millinery 06904	Closed	2000	40.00	50-94
2001 The Carriage House 13671	Yr.Iss.	2001	50.00	50
1988 City Hall 06340	Closed	2000	40.00	95-194
1989 Cobb's Bootery 06903	Closed	2000	40.00	82-188
1990 Coffee & Tea Shoppe 07342	Closed	2000	45.00	75-188
2001 Colby House 14123	Open		50.00	50
1996 Collectors Set 10740	Closed	1998	100.00	100
1989 Cole's Barn 06750	Closed	1994	40.00	69-94
1998 Colonial Queen Showboat (Collectors' Set - musical)11266	Closed	1998	100.00	100
1995 Colonial Savings and Loan 01321	Closed	1998		40-50
1995 Colonial Village News 01002	Closed	1999	50.00	50
1998 Cooper's Shop 11259	Closed	2000	50.00	50
1999 Cotswold Cottage, set/3 12218	Closed	2000	49.00	49
1990 Country Post Office 07341	Closed	1994	45.00	50-94
1992 County Courthouse 00233	Closed	2000	45.00	45-50
1991 Daisy's Flower Shop 07478	Closed	1996	45.00	55-94
1993 Dentist's Office 00724	Closed	2000	50.00	50
2001 Doan's Blacksmith Shop 14120	Open		50.00	50
1993 Doctor's Office 00721	Closed	2000	50.00	50
2001 Dress & Tailor Shop 13668	Yr.Iss.	2001	50.00	50
1992 Elegant Lady Dress Shop 00232	Closed	2001	45.00	45-94
1988 Engine Co. No. 5 Firehouse 06342	Closed	2000	40.00	50
1996 Fairbanks House 10397	Closed	2000	50.00	50
1988 Faith Church 06333	Closed	1991	40.00	130-360
1990 Fellowship Church 07334	Closed	2000	45.00	78-188
2000 Fellowship Place 02000	3,000		60.00	60
1990 The First Church 07333	Closed	2000	45.00	45-50
1988 First Post Office 06343	Closed	2000	40.00	50
2000 The Fountain 12897	Closed	2000	11.00	11
1988 Franklin College 10393	Closed	1999	50.00	50
1988 Friendship Chapel 06334	Closed	1994	40.00	55-188
2000 Grandma's House 12000	Closed	2001	60.00	60
2000 Gazebo 12898	Closed	2000	24.00	24
1993 Green's Grocery 00725	Closed	2000	50.00	50-63
1988 Greystone House 06339	Closed	1995	40.00	55-100
1989 Gull's Nest Lighthouse 06747	Closed	2000	40.00	45-50
1990 Hampshire House 07336	Closed	1996	45.00	45-157
1996 The Hermitage 10394	Closed	1998	55.00	98-100
1991 Hillside Church 11991	Closed	1991	60.00	469-576
1995 Historical Society Museum 01328	Closed	1999	50.00	98
1998 Holmer's Bait Shop, set/3 11534	Closed	2000	60.00	60
2001 Hope Church 14122	Open		50.00	50
1988 House of Blue Gables 06337	Closed	1995	40.00	50-75
1988 Johnson's Antiques 06346	Closed	1993	40.00	55-125
1993 Joseph House 00718	Closed	2000	50.00	45-50
1999 Kidgloo 12132	Closed	2000	24.00	24
1993 Kirby House-CVRA Exclusive 00716	Closed	1994	50.00	75-157
1999 Kringle's Snow Castle 12129	Closed	1999	150.00	150
1992 Lakehurst House 11992	Closed	1992	55.00	313-388
1996 Lattimore House-CVRA Exclusive 10391	Closed	1997	50.00	63-125
1997 Law Office 10825	Closed	1999	50.00	40-50
2001 The Logan Residence 13670	Yr.Iss.	2001	50.00	50

ARCHITECTURE

YEAR ISSUE	EDITION LIMIT	YEAR RETD.	ISSUE PRICE	*QUOTE U.S.$
1992 Main St. Church 00230	Closed	2000	45.00	50
1989 The Major's Manor 06902	Closed	1998	40.00	63-94
1989 Maple St. Church 06748	Closed	1993	40.00	63-107
1993 Mark Hall 00719	Closed	2000	50.00	50
1989 Miller Bros. Silversmiths 06905	Closed	2001	40.00	100-194
1998 M.S. Miller-Painter 11261	Closed	2000	50.00	50
1997 Montrose Manor 10828	Closed	2000	50.00	50
1999 Mooncrest Mansion 11588	Closed	1999	50.00	50
1999 Mortimer & Friends 11589	Closed	2000	35.00	35
1994 Mt. Zion Church 11994	5,500	1994	70.00	75-113
1994 Mt. Zion Church (Hillside Church-error) 11994	Closed	1994	70.00	255-553
1990 Mulberry Station 07344	Closed	2000	50.00	65
1995 Mundt Manor 01008	Closed	1999	50.00	50
2000 Nativity, set/3 12220	Closed	2000	32.00	32
2000 Nativity, set/4 12221	Closed	2000	44.00	44
1988 New Hope Church (musical) 06470	Closed	2000	40.00	500-750
1990 The Nob Hill 07337	Closed	1995	45.00	52-67
1992 Northpoint School 07960	Closed	2000	45.00	50
1994 Notfel Cabin 01320	Closed	2001	50.00	50
1999 O' Christmas Tree 12113	Closed	1999	33.00	33
1995 O'Doul's Ice House 01324	Closed	2000	50.00	50
1988 Old Stone Church (musical) 06471	Closed	2000	25.00	300-580
1988 Old Time Station 06335	Closed	1997	40.00	69-94
1998 Opera House 11260	Closed	2000	50.00	50
1987 Original Set of 6 05818	Closed	N/A	210.00	N/A
1987 · Charity Chapel 05818 (05895)	Closed	1989	35.00	886-938
1987 · King's Cottage 05818 (05890)	Closed	1997	35.00	39-49
1987 · McCauley House 05818 (05892)	Closed	1988	35.00	519-938
1987 · Nelson House 05818 (05891)	Closed	1989	35.00	688-813
1987 · Old Stone Church 05818 (05825)	Closed	2000	35.00	50
1987 · The Welcome Home 05818 (05824)	Closed	1997	35.00	50
1987 Original Set of 6 05819	Closed	N/A	210.00	N/A
1987 · Church of the Golden Rule 05819 (05820)	Closed	1999	35.00	50
1987 · General Store 05819 (05823)	Closed	1988	35.00	750-920
1987 · Lil Red School House 05819 (05821)	Closed	2001	35.00	50
1987 · Penny House 05819 (05893)	Closed	1988	35.00	750-1000
1987 · Ritter House 05819 (05894)	Closed	1989	35.00	700-850
1987 · Train Station 05819 (05822)	Closed	1989	35.00	1065-1244
1997 Park Vista-Convention Piece 11141	Closed	1997	50.00	250-720
1995 Patriot Bridge 01325	Closed	2000	50.00	50
1997 Photography Studio 10872	Closed	2000	50.00	50
1997 Pierpont-Smithe's Curios 07343	Closed	1993	45.00	63-113
1997 Potter House 10826	Closed	2000	50.00	50
1995 Queensgate 01329	Closed	2000	50.00	50
1989 Quincy's Clock Shop 06899	Closed	2000	40.00	75-188
1995 Rainy Days Barn 01323	Closed	2000	50.00	50
2000 Rathbone Retreat 13518	Closed	2000	50.00	50
1994 Real Estate Office -CVRA Exclusive 01006	Closed	2000	50.00	50
2000 Rhodes Bed & Breakfast 13501	Closed	2000	50.00	50
1988 The Ritz Hotel 06341	Closed	1997	40.00	188-375
1999 River Queen 12216	Closed	2000	50.00	50
1994 Rosamond 00988	Closed	1999	50.00	50
1990 Ryman Auditorium-Special Edition 00810	Closed	2000	50.00	50-113
1992 San Sebastian Mission 00231	Closed	1995	45.00	60-94
1991 Sanderson's Mill 07927	Closed	2000	45.00	50
1997 Sawyer's Creek 11030	Closed	2000	55.00	55
1990 Ship's Chandler's Shop 07339	Closed	2000	45.00	75-157
1997 Sir George's Manor 11997	5,500	1997	75.00	75-113
1994 Smith and Jones Drug Store 01007	Closed	2000	50.00	50
1991 Smith's Smithy 07476	Closed	1991	45.00	732-1063
1994 Springfield 00989	Closed	2001	50.00	50
1993 St. James Cathedral 11993	Closed	1993	75.00	125-213
1996 St. Paul's Church 10735	Closed	1999	50.00	50
1993 St. Peter's Church w/Speaker 00715	Closed	2001	60.00	75-100
1996 Stable 10395	Closed	2000	33.00	33
1988 The State Bank 06345	Closed	1997	40.00	63-94
1992 Stearn's Stable 00228	Closed	1999	50.00	60
1988 The Stone House 06338	Closed	1998	40.00	63-100
1991 Sweet Shop 07481	Closed	2000	45.00	50
1989 Sweetheart's Bridge 06751	Closed	2000	40.00	50-94
2000 Town Meeting Hall 13500	Closed	2001	50.00	50
1991 The Toy Maker's Shop 07477	Closed	2000	45.00	50
1988 Trader Tom's Gen'l Store 06336	Closed	1999	40.00	69-94
1996 Trading Post 10732	Closed	2000	50.00	50
1996 Treviso House 10392	Closed	1999	50.00	50

YEAR ISSUE	EDITION LIMIT	YEAR RETD.	ISSUE PRICE	*QUOTE U.S.$
1998 Trinity Church 11998	5,500	1998	75.00	75-219
2001 Tyler Hometead 13669	Yr.Iss.	2001	50.00	50
1992 Vanderspeck's Mill 00229	Closed	1996	45.00	57-125
1997 Variety Store 10827	Closed	2000	50.00	50
1990 The Victoria House 07335	Closed	1993	45.00	63-94
1989 Victorian Apothecary 06900	Closed	1991	40.00	282-375
1991 Victorian Gazebo 07925	Closed	2000	45.00	25-63
1989 The Village Bakery 06898	Closed	2000	40.00	50
1989 Village Barber Shop 06901	Closed	2000	40.00	50-63
2000 The Village Church 13502	Closed	2000	50.00	50
1986 Village Express 05826	Closed	1990	27.00	94-219
1992 Village Green Gazebo 00227	Closed	2000	22.00	22-32
1990 Village Hardware 07340	Closed	1996	45.00	69-125
1994 Village Hospital 01004	Closed	2000	50.00	50
1992 The Village Inn 07962	Closed	1998	45.00	117
1989 Village Library 06752	Closed	2000	40.00	63-94
2000 Village Meeting Hall 13500	Closed	2000	50.00	50
2000 The Village Lighthouse 13537	Closed	2000	50.00	50
1988 Village Police Station 06344	Closed	2000	40.00	50-82
2001 Village Restaurant 13667	Yr.Iss.	2001	50.00	50
1989 Village School 06749	Closed	1991	40.00	200-432
1991 Watt's Candle Shop 07479	Closed	1994	45.00	63-94
1987 Welcome Home 05824	Closed	1997	50.00	63-105
1994 White's Butcher Shop 01005	Closed	2000	50.00	50
1999 Winter Carnival (set/7) 11584	Closed	2000	120.00	120
1999 Winter Carnival (set/3) 12194	Closed	2000	40.00	40
1999 Winter Carnival (set/2) 12195	Closed	2000	34.00	34
1999 Winter Carnival (set/2) 12196	Closed	2000	34.00	34
1998 Wright's Emporium 11264	Closed	2000	50.00	50
1990 Wig Shop 07480	Closed	2001	45.00	50-100
1995 Wycoff Manor 11995	5,500	1995	75.00	107-150
1995 Zachary Peters Cabinet Maker 01322	Closed	1999	50.00	50

Colonial Village Special Event - Lefton

YEAR ISSUE	EDITION LIMIT	YEAR RETD.	ISSUE PRICE	*QUOTE U.S.$
1995 Bayside Inn 01326	Yr.Iss.	1999	50.00	100-194
1996 Town Hall 10390	Yr.Iss.	1996	50.00	78-132
1997 Meeting House 10830	Yr.Iss.	1997	65.00	65-125
1998 Good Neighbor's Haven 11505	Yr.Iss.	1998	55.00	55-75
1999 Christmas Wishes 12114	Yr.Iss.	1999	25.00	25

Historic American Lighthouse Collection - Lefton

YEAR ISSUE	EDITION LIMIT	YEAR RETD.	ISSUE PRICE	*QUOTE U.S.$
1995 1716 Boston Lighthouse 08607	7,500	1995	50.00	260-300
2000 Abselon, NJ 13522	Open		43.00	43
1994 Admirality Head, WA 01126	Open		40.00	43
1997 Alcatraz Island-1854 08649	9,000	1997	55.00	138-175
1998 Alcatraz, CA 11501	Open		65.00	65
2000 Amelia Isl., FL 13523	Open		43.00	43
1992 Assateaque, VA 00137	Open		40.00	43
1995 Barneget, NJ 01333	Open		40.00	43
1993 Big Sable Point, MI 00885	Open		40.00	43
1998 Biloxi Lighthouse, MS 11522	Open		40.00	43
1996 Block Island, RI 10105	Open		50.00	50
1994 Bodie Island, NC 01118	Open		40.00	43
2000 Boon Isl., ME 12717	Open		45.00	45
1993 Boston Harbor, MA 00881	Open		40.00	43
2001 Branot Point, MA 13897	Open		43.00	43
1996 Buffalo, NY 10076	Closed	2001	40.00	43
1994 Cana Island, WI 01117	Closed	2001	40.00	43
1999 Cape Canaveral, FL 11569	Open		43.00	43
1993 Cape Cod, MA 00882	Open		40.00	43
1994 Cape Florida, FL 01125	Closed	1998	40.00	43
1998 Cape Florida, FL 11537	Open		43.00	43
1992 Cape Hatteras, NC 00133	Closed	1998	40.00	40-125
1998 Cape Hatteras, NC 11533	Open		45.00	45
1997 Cape Henlopen, DE	9,000	1997	55.00	65-125
1992 Cape Henry, VA 00135	Open		40.00	43
1992 Cape Lookout, NC 00134	Open		40.00	43
1994 Cape May, NJ 01013	Closed	1995	40.00	185-272
1995 Cape May, NJ 01013R	Open		40.00	43
1996 Cape Neddick, ME 10106	Open		47.00	47
2000 Cape St. George, FL 13524	Open		43.00	43
1994 Chicago Harbor, IL 01010	Open		40.00	43
1999 Concord Point, MD 11567	Open		47.00	47
2001 Coquille, OR 13906	Open		43.00	43
1997 Currituck Beach, NC 10834	Open		43.00	43
1996 Destruction Island, WA 10108	Open		40.00	43
2000 Diamond Head, HI 12858	Open		43.00	43
1995 Fire Island, NY 01334	Open		40.00	43
2001 Five Finger, AK 13907	7,500		50.00	50
1997 Fort Niagara, NY 10965	Open		40.00	43
1994 Ft. Gratiot, MI 01123	Open		40.00	43

Collectors' Information Bureau

*Quotes have been rounded up to nearest dollar

YEAR ISSUE	EDITION LIMIT	YEAR RETD.	ISSUE PRICE	*QUOTE U.S.$
000 Grand Haven, MI 13525	Open		50.00	50
993 Gray's Harbor, WA 00880	Closed	2001	40.00	43
998 Harbour Town, SC 11527	Open		45.00	45
994 Heceta Head, OR 01122	Open		40.00	43
000 Hereford Inlet, NJ 13526	Open		50.00	50
000 Hillsboro Inlet, FL 13527	Open		50.00	50
996 Holland Harbor, MI 10104	Open		45.00	45
001 Hunting Island, SC 14922	Open		47.00	47
995 Jupiter Inlet, FL 01336	Open		40.00	43
996 Key West, FL 10075	Open		40.00	43
996 Los Angeles Harbor, CA 10109	Open		45.00	45
993 Marblehead, OH 00879	Open		40.00	43
001 Middle Bay, AL 13896	Open		45.00	45
999 Minots Ledge, MA 11568	Open		43.00	43
993 Montauk, NY 00884	Open		40.00	43
998 Morris Island, SC 08657	9,000	1998	50.00	60-155
001 Morris Island, SC 14924	Open		47.00	47
000 Mukilteo Light Possession Sound, WA 12257	Open		56.00	56
001 New Canal, LA 14920	Open		47.00	47
998 New London Harbor, CT 11524	Open		40.00	43
994 New London Ledge, CT 01119	Closed	2001	40.00	43
998 New Presque Isle, MI 11523	Open		40.00	43
000 Oak Island, NC 08683	9,000		45.00	45
001 Oak Island, NC 13895	Open		43.00	43
994 Ocracoke, NC 01124	Open		40.00	43
000 Old Baldy Smith Isl., NC 12256	Open		45.00	45
996 Old Cape Henry, VA 08619	7,500	1996	47.00	202-285
001 Old Cape Henry, VA 14923	Open		47.00	47
999 Old Mackinac Pt., MI 08676	9,000	2000	79.00	79
000 Old Point Comfort, VA 12715	Open		43.00	43
994 Old Point Loma, CA 01011	Open		40.00	43
998 Pemaquid Point, ME 11525	Open		42.00	42
999 Pensacola, FL 11566	Closed	2001	43.00	43
995 Pigeon Point, CA 01289	Open		40.00	43
997 Point Arena, CA 10968	Open		40.00	43
995 Point Betsie, MI 01335	Closed	2001	47.00	47
997 Point Bolivar, TX 10967	Open		40.00	43
995 Point Cabrillo, CA 01330	Open		47.00	47
999 Point Pinos, CA 11571	Open		56.00	56
993 Point Wilson, WA 00883	Closed	2001	40.00	43
995 Ponce De Leon, FL 01332	Open		40.00	43
994 Portland Head, ME 01121	Open		40.00	43
996 Pt. Isabel, TX 10074	Open		40.00	43
000 Racine Reef, WI 68684	9,500	2001	65.00	65
000 Rockland Breakwater, ME 13529	Open		47.00	47
997 Round Island, MI 10969	Open		47.00	47
992 Sandy Hook, NJ 00132	Open		40.00	43
994 Split Rock, MN 01009	Open		40.00	43
994 St. Augustine, FL 01015	Open		40.00	43
001 St. Augustine, FL 14921	Open		47.00	47
000 St. Marks Light, FL 13530	Open		50.00	50
001 St. Simmons, GA 13816	Open		43.00	43
994 St. Simons, GA 01012	Open		40.00	43
001 Sturgeon Point, MI 13817	Open		43.00	43
001 Sullivan, SC 14925	Open		47.00	47
000 Tawas, MI 12716	Open		43.00	43
996 Thomas Point, MO 10107	Open		45.00	45
995 Toledo Harbor, OH 01331	Open		47.00	47
000 Two Harbors, MI 13531	Open		50.00	50
994 Tybee Island, GA 01014	Closed	1999	40.00	40-43
999 Tybee Island, GA 12217	Open		43.00	43
992 West Quoddy Head, ME 00136	Closed	2001	40.00	43
001 White Fish Point, MI 13818	Open		52.00	52
993 White Shoal, MI 00878	Open		40.00	43
997 Wind Point, WI 10966	Open		40.00	43
994 Yerba Buena, CA 01120	Open		40.00	43

Historic American Lighthouse Collection Special Event - Lefton

999 Diamond Head, HI 11570	Yr.Iss.	1999	50.00	50
000 Gays Head, MA 13528	Yr.Iss.	2000	45.00	45

Historic Williamsburg Collection - Lefton

997 Bruton Parish Church 11051	Closed	2000	55.00	55
997 The Capitol 11054	Closed	2000	75.00	75
997 Christiana Campbell's Tavern 11705	Closed	2000	55.00	55
998 Courthouse 11704	Closed	2000	70.00	70
997 George Wythe House 11053	Closed	2000	50.00	50
997 The Govenor's Palace 11052	Closed	2000	75.00	75
997 King Arms Taverns 11050	Closed	2000	50.00	50

YEAR ISSUE	EDITION LIMIT	YEAR RETD.	ISSUE PRICE	*QUOTE U.S.$
1998 Prentis Store 11703	Closed	2000	50.00	50

Lost Lights Collection - Lefton

2000 1854 Cape Hatteras, NC 13557	Closed	2001	50.00	50
2001 Admiralty Head, WA 13652	Closed	2001	50.00	50
2000 Bishop & Clerks, MA 13549	Closed	2001	50.00	50
2001 Bridgeport Harbor, CT 13665	Closed	2001	50.00	50
2000 Bullocks, RI 13550	Closed	2001	50.00	50
2000 Cape Henlopen, DE 13551	Closed	2001	50.00	50
2000 Cleveland, OH 13553	Closed	2001	50.00	50
2000 Fort Sumter, SC 13552	Closed	2001	50.00	50
2001 Franks Island, LA 13664	Closed	2001	50.00	50
2001 Portland Breakwater, ME 13654	Closed	2001	50.00	50
2000 Santa Barbara, CA 13546	Closed	2001	50.00	50
2000 Scotch Cap, AK 13555	Closed	2001	50.00	50
2000 Shinnecoock Bay, NY 13547	Closed	2001	50.00	50
2001 St. Augustine, FL 13653	Closed	2001	50.00	50
2000 St. Croix, ME 13548	Closed	2001	50.00	50
2000 Tuckers Beach, NJ 13554	Closed	2001	50.00	50
2001 Waukegan Light, IL 13651	Closed	2001	50.00	50
2000 Wauega Light, GA 13556	Closed	2001	50.00	50

Goebel/M.I. Hummel

M.I. Hummel Bavarian Village Collection - M.I. Hummel

1996 All Aboard	Open		60.00	60
1995 Angel's Duet	Open		50.00	60
2000 Apple Tree Cottage	Open		65.00	65
1995 The Bench and Tree Set (accessory)	Open		25.00	30
1995 Christmas Mail	Open		50.00	60
2000 Clock Shop	Open		65.00	65
1995 Company's Coming	Open		50.00	60
1997 Evergreen Tree Set (accessory)	Open		30.00	30
1998 Heavenly Harmony Church	Open		60.00	60
1996 Holiday Fountain (accessory)	Open		35.00	35
1997 Holiday Lights (accessory)	Open		30.00	20
1996 Horse With Sled (accessory)	Open		35.00	35
1997 The Mailbox (accessory)	Open		30.00	20
1996 Off for the Holidays	Open		60.00	60
1998 Practice Makes Perfect	Open		65.00	65
1998 Scholarly Thoughts	Open		65.00	65
1996 Shoe Maker Shop	Open		60.00	60
1995 The Sled and Pine Tree Set (accessory)	Open		25.00	30
2000 Tending the Geese	Open		65.00	65
1995 The Village Bakery	Open		50.00	60
1995 The Village Bridge (accessory)	Open		25.00	30
2000 Village Pharmacy	Open		65.00	65
1998 Warm Winter Wishes	Open		65.00	65
1995 Winter's Comfort	Open		50.00	60
1995 The Wishing Well (accessory)	Open		25.00	30

Hamilton Collection

Cherished Teddies Christmas Village - P. Hillman

2000 Boat House	Open		49.95	50
2000 Christmas Cottage	Open		49.95	50
2000 Santa Bear's Sweet Shoppe	Open		49.95	50
2000 Teddies Toy Shop	Open		49.95	50

Dreamsicles Heavenly Village - K. Haynes

1997 Cherub Concerto	Open		49.95	50
1996 Flight School	Open		49.95	50
1996 Star Factory	Open		49.95	50
1997 Wreath Makers	Open		49.95	50

Harbour Lights

Harbour Lights Collector's Society - Harbour Lights

1995 Point Fermin CA 501 (Charter Member Piece)	Retrd.	1996	80.00	250-350
1995 Framed Point Fermin CA Print (numbrd.)	Retrd.	1996	Gift	20-45
1996 Stonington Harbor CT 502	Retrd.	1997	70.00	110-350
1996 Spyglass Collection 503	Retrd.	1997	Gift	75-90
1996 Point Fermin CA (Ornament)	Retrd.	1997	15.00	15-50
1997 Port Sanilac MI 506	Retrd.	1998	80.00	80-200
1997 Amelia Island FL	Retrd.	1998	Gift	55-144
1997 Stonington Harbor CT (Ornament)	Retrd.	1998	15.00	15-63
1998 Sea Girt NJ	Retrd.	1999	80.00	80-150
1998 Cockspur GA	Retrd.	1999	Gift	65-75

ARCHITECTURE

YEAR ISSUE	EDITION LIMIT	YEAR RETD.	ISSUE PRICE	*QUOTE U.S.$
1998 Port Sanilac MI (Ornament)	Retrd.	1999	15.00	15-50
1999 Seven Foot Knoll MD 521	Retrd.	2000	99.00	99
1999 Baltimore MD 524	Retrd.	2000	Gift	N/A
1999 Sea Girt NJ 527 (Ornament)	Retrd.	2000	15.00	15
1999 Pt. Fermin CA (Charter Member 5 Year)	Retrd.	2000	29.00	29
1999 Pt. Fermin CA (Member 5 Year)	Retrd.	2000	29.00	29
2000 Boca Grande FL 531	Retrd.	2001	90.00	90
2000 S.W. Reef LA 530	Retrd.	2001	Gift	N/A
2000 Seven Foot Knoll MD (Ornament) 532	Retrd.	2001	15.00	15
2001 Coney Island NY 534	4/02		90.00	90
2001 Cold Spring Harbor NY 533	4/02		Gift	N/A
2001 Boca Grande FL (Ornament) 535	4/02		15.00	15

Event Piece - Harbour Lights

YEAR ISSUE	EDITION LIMIT	YEAR RETD.	ISSUE PRICE	*QUOTE U.S.$
1996 Sunken Rock NY 602	8,132	1996	25.00	50-70
1997 New Point Loma 604 (1997 Collector's Reunion)	950	1997	70.00	625-1035
1997 New Point Loma-mini 605 (1997 Collector's Reunion)	480	1997	Gift	188-380
1997 Edgartown MA 603	8,008	1997	35.00	55-75
1997 Thumbnail-Assateague	Closed	1997	Gift	15-25
1997 Thumbnail-Cape Hatteras	Closed	1997	Gift	15-25
1997 Thumbnail-Sandy Hook	Closed	1997	Gift	15-25
1997 Thumbnail-St. Simons	Closed	1997	Gift	15-25
1998 Roosevelt Island NY 612	7,884	1998	25.00	50
1998 Rose Island RI 614	700	1998	70.00	100-150
1998 Rose Island RI (mini) 615	700	1998	Gift	50
1998 Rose Island RI (Society Members Only) 616	6,100	1998	70.00	215-300
1998 Thumbnail-Beavertail	Closed	1998	Gift	15
1998 Thumbnail-Point Judith	Closed	1998	Gift	15
1998 Thumbnail-Rose Island	Closed	1998	Gift	15
1998 Thumbnail-SE Block Island	Closed	1998	Gift	15
1999 Kilauea HI 620	Closed	1999	65.00	110-150
2000 Hatteras-on-the-Move 632	Closed	2000	65.00	65
2000 Lady Liberty 627	Closed	2000	125.00	125
2000 Beckoning Beacon 630	Closed	2000	35.00	35
2001 Cape St. George FL 633	Closed	2001	59.00	59
2001 Yerba Buena CA 639	Closed	2001	79.00	79
2002 Mark Twain 654	Yr.Iss.		68.00	68
2002 Fort Tompkins-Spring Regional Piece 652	Yr.Iss.		59.00	59
2002 Fort Tompkins-Summer Regional Piece 653	Yr.Iss.		59.00	59
2002 Fort Tompkins-Fall Regional Piece 655	Yr.Iss.		59.00	59
2002 Fort Tompkins-Winter Regional Piece 656	Yr.Iss.		59.00	59

Chesapeake Series - Harbour Lights

YEAR ISSUE	EDITION LIMIT	YEAR RETD.	ISSUE PRICE	*QUOTE U.S.$
1996 Concord MD 186	8,450	1999	66.00	66-73
1997 Drum Point MD 180	9,500	1997	99.00	99-150
1996 Sandy Point MD 167	9,500	1999	70.00	70-90
1996 Sharps Island MD 185	9,500	1997	70.00	70-120
1996 Thomas Point MD 181	9,500	1996	99.00	175-300

Christmas - Harbour Lights

YEAR ISSUE	EDITION LIMIT	YEAR RETD.	ISSUE PRICE	*QUOTE U.S.$
1995 Christmas 1995 - Big Bay Point MI 700	5,000	1995	75.00	335-500
1996 Christmas 1996 - Colchester VT 701	8,200	1996	75.00	150
1997 Christmas 1997 - White Shoal MI 704	8,000	1997	80.00	120-150
1998 Christmas 1998 - Old Field Point NY 707	10,000	1998	80.00	80-150
1999 Christmas 1999 -East Quoddy Canada 708	10,000	1999	80.00	80-150
2000 Christmas 2000 -Hereford Inlet NJ 710	10,000	2000	75.00	75-100
2001 Christmas 2001 -Michigan City IN 712	10,000	2001	75.00	75

From Glow to Limited - Harbour Lights

YEAR ISSUE	EDITION LIMIT	YEAR RETD.	ISSUE PRICE	*QUOTE U.S.$
1996 Alcatraz CA 407 to 177	Closed	1996	77.00	82-145
1996 Cape Lookout 405 to 175	Closed	1996	64.00	64-88
1996 Fire Island NY 406 to 176	Closed	1996	70.00	70-100
1996 Mukilteo WA 417 to 178	Closed	1996	55.00	55
1996 Spectacle Reef MI 410 to 182	Closed	1996	60.00	60-88
1996 St. Joseph MI 411 to 183	Closed	1996	60.00	60-110
1996 Thirty Mile Point NY 414 to 184	Closed	1996	62.00	60-90

Gone But Not Forgotten - Harbour Lights

YEAR ISSUE	EDITION LIMIT	YEAR RETD.	ISSUE PRICE	*QUOTE U.S.$
2000 Cape Henlopen DE 243	Closed	2001	80.00	80

Great Lakes Region - Harbour Lights

YEAR ISSUE	EDITION LIMIT	YEAR RETD.	ISSUE PRICE	*QUOTE U.S.$
1999 Big Sable MI 228	10,000		70.00	70
1992 Buffalo NY 122	5,500	1996	60.00	95-125
1992 Cana Island WI 119	5,500	1995	60.00	120-150

YEAR ISSUE	EDITION LIMIT	YEAR RETD.	ISSUE PRICE	*QUOTE U.S.$
1996 Charlotte-Genesee NY 165	7,100	1999	77.00	77-
1998 Chicago Harbor IL 208	10,000	2001	73.00	
2001 Cleveland OH 266	5,000		65.00	
2000 Eagle Bluff WI 249	6,500		65.00	
2000 Fairport Harbor OH	6,500		68.00	
2000 Fort Gratiot MI	7,000		65.00	
1991 Fort Niagara NY 113	5,500	1995	60.00	120-2
1998 Grand Haven MI 212	10,000	2001	90.00	
1997 Grand Traverse MI 191	9,500	1999	80.00	80-
1992 Grosse Point IL 120	5,500	1996	60.00	60-1
1994 Holland (Big Red) MI 142	5,500	1995	60.00	2
1992 Lorain OH 207	10,000	2001	75.00	
1992 Marblehead OH 121	5,500	1995	50.00	125-1
1992 Michigan City IN 123	5,500	1996	60.00	94-1
1992 Old Mackinac Point MI 118	5,500	1995	65.00	145-3
1999 Old Mission Point MI 236	10,000		70.00	
1998 Point Betsie MI 218	10,000	2001	70.00	
2002 Point Iroquois MI 270	6,500		68.00	
2002 Presque Isle PA 201	9,500	2000	75.00	
2002 Rock of Ages MI 271	5,500		60.00	
1995 Round Island MI 153	9,500	1999	85.00	65-1
1991 Sand Island WI 112	5,500	1996	60.00	75-1
1995 Selkirk NY 157	6,500	1999	75.00	74-
2001 Sherwood Point WI 265	Yr.Iss.	2001	68.00	
2000 Sister Island NY (Collector's Choice) 252	Closed	2001	68.00	
1999 South Bass Island OH 237	10,000		80.00	
1992 Split Rock MI 124 (incorrect state)	Closed	1992	60.00	1800-250
1992 Split Rock MN 124	5,500	1995	60.00	60-10
1998 Sturgeon Bay WI 217	10,000	2001	90.00	
1995 Tawas Pt. MI 152	5,500	1996	75.00	75-1
1996 Toledo OH 179	6,437	1999	85.00	68-
1999 White River MI 226	10,000		73.00	
2000 Whitefish Point MI 254	6,500		99.00	
1995 Wind Point WI 154	7,783	1999	78.00	62-9

Great Lighthouses of the World - Harbour Lights

YEAR ISSUE	EDITION LIMIT	YEAR RETD.	ISSUE PRICE	*QUOTE U.S.$
1998 Alcatraz CA 417	Open		70.00	
1999 Assateague VA 425	Open		60.00	
1997 Barnegat NJ 414	Closed	1997	45.00	45-5
1998 Barnegat NJ 414R	Open		50.00	5
1998 Bolivar TX 422	Open		65.00	6
1996 Boston Harbor MA 402	Closed	1998	50.00	23
1999 Boston Harbor MA 402R	Open		55.00	5
1998 Cape Canaveral FL 420	Open		50.00	5
2001 Cape Florida FL 432	Open		50.00	5
1994 Cape Hatteras NC 401	Open		50.00	5
2000 Cape Hatteras NC 401R	Open		50.00	5
2000 Cape May NJ 428	Open		55.00	5
1997 Cape Neddick ME 410	Open		50.00	5
2001 Currituck NC 436	Open		50.00	5
1999 Grosse Point IL 426	Open		60.00	6
2002 Highland MA 439	Open		50.00	5
1998 Holland MI 407	Open		50.00	5
2001 Jupiter FL 433	Open		50.00	5
1999 Key West FL 424	Open		65.00	6
2002 Kilauea HI 437	Open		45.00	4
1997 Montauk NY 405	Open		55.00	5
1997 New London Ledge CT 406	Open		55.00	5
1998 Old Mackinac MI 419	Open		65.00	6
2001 Pemaquid ME 435	Open		55.00	5
2000 Pensacola FL 43	Open		60.00	6
1997 Point Loma CA 403	Open		50.00	5
1997 Ponce De Leon FL 408	Open		55.00	5
1995 Portland Head MF 404	Closed	1998	50.00	50-8
1999 Portland Head ME 404R	Open		55.00	5
1996 Sandy Hook NJ 418	Open		50.00	5
2000 Sanibel FL 429	Open		90.00	9
1997 Sea Pines (Hilton Head) SC 415	Open		50.00	5
1995 Southeast Block Island RI 403	Closed	1998	50.00	50
1999 Southeast Block Island RI 403R	Open		55.00	5
1997 St. Augustine FL 411	Open		45.00	4
2001 St. Joseph Pier MI 434	Open		65.00	6
1997 St. Simons GA 416	Open		50.00	5
2002 Statue of Liberty NY 438	Open		45.00	4
1998 Thomas Point MD 421	Open		90.00	9
2001 West Quoddy ME 431	Open		45.00	4

Gulf Coast Region - Harbour Lights

YEAR ISSUE	EDITION LIMIT	YEAR RETD.	ISSUE PRICE	*QUOTE U.S.$
1995 Biloxi MS 149	5,500	1997	60.00	6
1995 Bolivar TX 146	5,500	1997	70.00	90-14

Collectors' Information Bureau   *Quotes have been rounded up to nearest dollar

YEAR ISSUE	EDITION LIMIT	YEAR RETD.	ISSUE PRICE	*QUOTE U.S.$
997 Middle Bay AL 187	9,500	1997	99.00	99-182
995 New Canal LA 148	5,500	1996	65.00	90-105
995 Pensacola FL 150	9,000	1997	80.00	79-175
995 Port Isabel TX 147	5,500	1997	65.00	100-120
000 Round Island MS "Then & Now" 242	Retrd.	2000	65.00	65-75

Hudson River Series - Harbour Lights

YEAR ISSUE	EDITION LIMIT	YEAR RETD.	ISSUE PRICE	*QUOTE U.S.$
999 Esopus Meadows NY 231	10,000		70.00	70
999 Hudson-Athens NY 230	10,000		78.00	78
999 Tarrytown NY 232	10,000		75.00	75

International Series - Harbour Lights

YEAR ISSUE	EDITION LIMIT	YEAR RETD.	ISSUE PRICE	*QUOTE U.S.$
001 Bremerhaven Germany 264	5,000		60.00	60
999 Cape Agulhas South Africa 227	10,000		73.00	73
999 Cove Canada Ontario 233	8,000		68.00	68
001 Eddystone Light UK (10 Year Anniversary) 636	Yr.Iss	2001	99.00	99
999 Fisgard British Columbia 234	8,000		69.00	69
997 Hook Head Ireland 198	9,500	2000	71.00	71
999 La Coruna Spain 235	6,500		65.00	65
000 La Marte Quebec 255	6,500		75.00	75
997 La Jument France 192	9,500	1998	68.00	67-150
997 Longship UK 193	9,500	2000	68.00	68
997 Macquarie Australia 197	9,500	2000	68.00	68
999 Panama (Miraflores & Gutan Locks) Matched Numbered Set 241	4,000	1999	65.00	65
996 Peggy's Cove Canada 169	Closed	1999	68.00	63-100

Lady Lightkeepers - Harbour Lights

YEAR ISSUE	EDITION LIMIT	YEAR RETD.	ISSUE PRICE	*QUOTE U.S.$
996 Chatham MA 172	8,032	1998	70.00	100-150
996 Ida Lewis RI 174	5,886	1999	70.00	70
996 Matinicus ME 173	6,800	1999	77.00	76-100
996 Point Piños CA 170	6,700	1999	70.00	70-100
996 Saugerties NY 171	8,100	1999	75.00	60-75

Northeast Region - Harbour Lights

YEAR ISSUE	EDITION LIMIT	YEAR RETD.	ISSUE PRICE	*QUOTE U.S.$
994 Barnegat NJ (blue water)139	5,500	1995	60.00	315-354
994 Barnegat NJ (green water) 139	5,500	1995	60.00	275-360
998 Bass Harbor ME 214	10,000	2001	75.00	75
997 Beavertail RI (gray) 188	6,500	1999	80.00	80
997 Beavertail RI (tan) 188	3,000	1999	80.00	64
991 Boston Harbor MA 117	5,500	1995	60.00	150-300
995 Brant Point MA 162	Closed	1999	66.00	60-80
998 Cape Elizabeth ME 215	10,000	2001	75.00	75
996 Cape Henry VA 196	9,500	1997	82.00	82-94
996 Cape May NJ 168	9,500	1997	75.00	75-190
995 Cape Neddick (Nubble) ME 141	5,500	1995	66.00	400
991 Castle Hill RI 116	5,500	1996	60.00	120
998 Dunkirk NY 221	10,000	2001	70.00	70
2001 East Point NJ 260	6,500		60.00	60
998 Execution Rock NY 210	10,000	2001	78.00	78
998 Faulkner's Island CT 216	10,000	2001	70.00	70
998 Fenwick DE 213	10,000	2001	82.00	82
996 Fire Island NY 176	9,500	1998	70.00	70-150
998 Gay Head MA 219	10,000	2001	75.00	75
998 Goat Island ME 222	10,000	2001	75.00	75
991 Gt. Captain Island CT 114	5,500	1996	60.00	100
2002 Hendricks Head ME 274	5,500		75.00	75
995 Highland MA (w/o "s") 161	3,500	1998	75.00	150
995 Highlands MA (w/ "s") 161	6,000	1998	75.00	175
998 Horton Point NY 205	10,000	2001	75.00	75
997 Jeffrey's Hook NY 195	9,500	1999	66.00	66-125
2001 Long Beach Bar NY 262	6,500		95.00	95
2001 Marshall Point ME 258	6,500		79.00	79
1992 Minot's Ledge MA (blue water) 131	5,500	1996	60.00	150-275
1992 Minot's Ledge MA (green water) 131	5,500	1996	60.00	200-275
2002 Monomoy MA 269	5,500		75.00	75
1994 Montauk NY 143	5,500	1995	85.00	220
1991 Nauset MA 126	5,500	1995	66.00	200-375
1992 New London Ledge CT (blue water) 129	5,500	1995	66.00	145-175
1992 New London Ledge CT (green water) 129	5,500	1995	66.00	250
1997 Nobska MA 203	9,500	1998	75.00	74-80
1998 Old Saybrook CT 206	10,000	2001	69.00	69
1996 Pemaquid ME 164	9,500	1998	90.00	120-150
1998 Point Judith RI 223	10,000	2001	82.00	82
1992 Portland Breakwater ME 130	5,500	1996	60.00	82-115
1992 Portland Head ME 125	5,500	1994	66.00	600-875
2001 Portsmouth Harbor NH 259	6,500		79.00	79
1996 Pt. Pinos CA 170	6,700	1999	70.00	70
2002 Race Rock NY 272	5,000		69.00	69

YEAR ISSUE	EDITION LIMIT	YEAR RETD.	ISSUE PRICE	*QUOTE U.S.$
1991 Sandy Hook NJ 104	5,500	1994	60.00	275-550
2001 Sankaty MA 250	6,500		68.00	68
1996 Scituate MA 166	9,500	1998	77.00	100-150
2001 Seguin ME 256	6,500		67.00	67
2000 Ship John Shoal DE 245	6,500		68.00	68
1992 Southeast Block Island RI 128	5,500	1994	71.00	369-500
1991 West Quoddy Head ME 103	5,500	1995	60.00	133-313
1992 Whaleback NH 127	5,500	1996	60.00	60-95

Northwest Region - Harbour Lights

YEAR ISSUE	EDITION LIMIT	YEAR RETD.	ISSUE PRICE	*QUOTE U.S.$
2000 Eldred Rock AK 257	4,000	2000	65.00	65

Restoration Series - Harbour Lights

YEAR ISSUE	EDITION LIMIT	YEAR RETD.	ISSUE PRICE	*QUOTE U.S.$
2000 Rockland Breakwater ME 248	6,500		70.00	70
1999 Sapelo Island GA 239	8,000		60.00	60

Signature Series - Harbour Lights

YEAR ISSUE	EDITION LIMIT	YEAR RETD.	ISSUE PRICE	*QUOTE U.S.$
1999 Coquille OR 427, S/N	Open		55.00	55
1998 Thomas Point MD 421, S/N	Open		90.00	90
1998 Tybee GA 423, S/N	Open		65.00	65

Southeast Region - Harbour Lights

YEAR ISSUE	EDITION LIMIT	YEAR RETD.	ISSUE PRICE	*QUOTE U.S.$
2000 American Shoal FL 229	6,500	2000	99.00	99
1994 Assateague VA 145-mold one	988	1994	69.00	150-275
1994 Assateague VA 145-mold two	4,512	1995	69.00	150-188
1996 Bald Head NC 155	9,500	1998	75.00	75-155
1996 Cape Canaveral FL 163	9,500	1996	80.00	175-250
1998 Cape Florida FL 209	10,000	1998	78.00	78-150
1991 Cape Hatteras NC 102 (with house)	Retrd.	1991		3400-3481
1992 Cape Hatteras NC 102R	5,500	1993	60.00	615-1250
2001 Cedar Keys FL 268	8,000		65.00	65
2001 Charleston SC 267	6,500		68.00	68
2000 Fort Jefferson FL 247	8,000		75.00	75
2000 Haig Point SC 246	8,000		75.00	75
1999 Hillsboro FL 225	6,500	1999	125.00	125-238
1993 Hilton Head SC 136	5,500	1994	60.00	420-500
1998 Hunting Island SC 211	10,000	2001	75.00	75
1995 Jupiter FL 151	9,500	1996	77.00	125-195
1993 Key West FL 134	5,500	1995	60.00	275-379
2000 Oak Island NC 240	6,500	2000	78.00	78
1993 Ocracoke NC 135	5,500	1995	60.00	300-450
2000 Old Point Comfort VA 244	8,000		82.00	82
1993 Ponce de Leon FL 132	5,500	1994	60.00	350-469
1997 Sanibel FL 194	9,500	1997	120.00	120-250
1993 St. Augustine FL 138	5,500	1994	71.00	447-500
1999 St. Marks FL 220	10,000	2001	75.00	75
1993 St. Simons GA 137	5,500	1995	66.00	300-375
1993 Tybee GA 133	5,500	1995	60.00	250-295

Special Editions - Harbour Lights

YEAR ISSUE	EDITION LIMIT	YEAR RETD.	ISSUE PRICE	*QUOTE U.S.$
2000 5th Order Fresnel Lens 631	4,000	2000	80.00	80
2000 Beckoning Beacon 628	Open		35.00	35
1999 Bob Younger Memorial 623	Open		10.00	10
1997 Keepers & Friends 606	Open		55.00	55
1995 Legacy Light (blue) 601	Retrd.	1996	65.00	65-150
1995 Legacy Light (red) 600	Retrd.	1996	65.00	65-188
2000 Liberty Enlightening The World 627	Yr.Iss.	2000	125.00	125
1997 Navesink NJ 200	9,500	2000	245.00	245
2001 Point Allerton Lifesaving Station 635	5,000		79.00	79
2001 Point Allerton Men of the Lifesaving Station, set/3 638	Open		60.00	60
1997 Spyglass Collection-New England 607	Open		83.00	83
1998 Spyglass Collection-Southern Belles, set/7 613	Open		83.00	83
2001 St. Helena MI (Lighthouse Appreciation) 634	Closed	2001	79.00	79

Stamp Series - Harbour Lights

YEAR ISSUE	EDITION LIMIT	YEAR RETD.	ISSUE PRICE	*QUOTE U.S.$
1995 Marblehead OH 413	Open		50.00	50
1995 Spectacle Reef MI 182	9,500	1996	60.00	60
1995 Split Rock MN 412	Open		60.00	60
1995 St. Joseph MI 183	9,500	1996	60.00	60-95
1995 Thirty Mile Point NY 184	9,500	1996	62.00	62
1995 Five Piece Matched Numbd. Set 400	5,300	1995	275.00	275-350

Tall Towers - Harbour Lights

YEAR ISSUE	EDITION LIMIT	YEAR RETD.	ISSUE PRICE	*QUOTE U.S.$
1996 Bodie NC 159	9,500	1998	77.00	144-188
1996 Cape Lookout NC 175	9,500	1997	64.00	64-150
1996 Currituck NC 158	9,500	1997	80.00	80-150
1997 Morris Island - Now, SC 190	9,500	1997	65.00	65-163
1997 Morris Island - Then, SC 189	9,500	1997	85.00	85-195
1997 Morris Island - Now & Then, set SC 189	9,500	1997	170.00	175-300

This Little Light of Mine - Harbour Lights

YEAR ISSUE	EDITION LIMIT	YEAR RETD.	ISSUE PRICE	*QUOTE U.S.$
2001 Amelia Island FL 174	Open		12.95	13
2001 Bald Head NC 164	Open		12.95	13
2001 Bass Harbor ME 158	Open		14.95	15
2001 Biloxi MS 165	Open		12.95	13
2001 Bodie Island NC 163	Open		12.95	13
2001 Brant Point MA 166	Open		14.95	15
2001 Cape Henlopen DE 173	Open		12.95	13
2001 Castle Hill RI 162	Open		14.95	15
2001 Cockspur GA 156	Open		12.95	13
2001 Diamond Head HI 145	Open		14.95	15
2001 Eagle Bluff WI 172	Open		14.95	15
2001 Fenwick DE 167	Open		14.95	15
2001 Fire Island NY 176	Open		14.95	15
2001 Gay Head MA 159	Open		12.95	13
2001 Grand Traverse MI 160	Open		14.95	15
2001 Hunting Island SC 175	Open		12.95	13
2001 Jeffrey's Hook NY 168	Open		12.95	13
2001 Kilauea HI 169	Open		12.95	13
2001 Michigan City IN 142	Open		14.95	15
2001 Point Betsie MI 170	Open		14.95	15
2001 Round Island MI 147	Open		14.95	15
2001 Sharps Island MD 154	Open		12.95	13
2001 St. Marks FL 171	Open		14.95	15
2001 Wind Point WI 148	Open		14.95	15

Western Region - Harbour Lights

YEAR ISSUE	EDITION LIMIT	YEAR RETD.	ISSUE PRICE	*QUOTE U.S.$
1991 Admiralty Head WA 101(misspelled)	Closed	1994	60.00	125-188
1991 Admiralty Head WA 101	Retrd.	1994	60.00	87-250
1996 Alcatraz CA 177	9,500	1996	77.00	122-195
1991 Burrows Island OR 108 (incorrect state)	Closed	1991	60.00	1063-1250
1991 Burrows Island WA 108	2,563	1994	60.00	300-425
1991 Cape Blanco OR 109	5,500	1997	60.00	60-94
1999 Cape Disappointment WA 238	8,000		65.00	65
1996 Cape Meares OR 160	5,656	1999	68.00	68-100
1991 Coquille River OR 111	1,138	1993	60.00	2270-2700
1994 Diamond Head HI 140	5,500	1995	60.00	150-325
1997 Gray's Harbor WA 202	9,500	2000	75.00	75
1994 Heceta Head OR 144	5,500	1996	65.00	72-138
2001 Los Angeles Harbor CA 263	6,000		60.00	60
1996 Mukilteo WA 178	9,500	1999	55.00	55
2001 New Dungeness WA 261	5,000		62.00	62
1991 North Head WA 106	5,500	1996	60.00	72-93
1991 Old Point Loma CA 105	5,500	1995	60.00	122-235
1997 Pigeon Point CA 199	9,500	2000	68.00	68
1995 Pt. Arena CA 156	5,428	1996	80.00	128-295
1991 St. George's Reef CA 115	5,500	1996	60.00	63-90
1998 Tillamook OR 224	10,000	2001	75.00	75
1991 Umpqua River OR 107	5,500	1996	60.00	68-125
1997 Yaquina Bay OR 204	9,500	2000	77.00	77-90
1991 Yaquina Head WA 110	5,500	1996	60.00	75-104

Kiddie Car Classics/Hallmark Keepsake Collections

Kiddie Car Corner Collection - L. Sickman

YEAR ISSUE	EDITION LIMIT	YEAR RETD.	ISSUE PRICE	*QUOTE U.S.$
1999 "Cinder says..." QHG3621	Retrd.	2000	30.00	30
1999 "Cinder" & "Ella" Dalmatians QHG3619	Retrd.	2000	15.00	15
1999 Call Box & Fire Hydrant QHG3618	Retrd.	2000	25.00	25
1998 Corner Drive-In QHG3610	39,500	2000	70.00	70
1999 Corner Drive-In Sidewalk Signs QHG3616	Retrd.	2000	15.00	15
2000 Don's Sign QHG3623	Retrd.	2000	16.00	16
1998 Famous Food Sign QHG3614	Retrd.	2000	30.00	30
1999 Fire Station No.1 QHG3617	39,500	2000	70.00	70
1999 Flagpole QHG3620	Retrd.	2000	20.00	20
1997 KC's Garage QHG3601	Retrd.	1998	70.00	70-100
1998 KC's Motor Oil QHG3609	Retrd.	2000	15.00	15
1998 Mechanic's Lift & Tool Box QHG3608	Retrd.	2000	25.00	25
1998 Menu Station with Food Trays QHG3611	Retrd.	2000	30.00	30
1998 Newspaper Box and Trash Can Set QHG3613	Retrd.	2000	20.00	20
2000 Parking Sign QHG3630	Retrd.	2000	8.00	8
1997 Pedal Petroleum QHG3602	Retrd.	1999	25.00	25
1999 Pedal Power Premium Gas Pump QHG3603	Retrd.	1999	30.00	30-50
1997 Sidewalk Sale Signs QHG3605	Retrd.	1999	15.00	15
1997 Sidewalk Service Signs QHG3604	Retrd.	1999	15.00	15-25
1999 Stop Sign QHG3622	Retrd.	2000	10.00	10
2000 Street Signs QHG3629	Retrd.	2000	10.00	10

YEAR ISSUE	EDITION LIMIT	YEAR RETD.	ISSUE PRICE	*QUOTE U.S.$
2000 Streetlamp QHG3624	Retrd.	2000	15.00	
1999 Table & Benches QHG3615	Retrd.	2000	20.00	
1997 Welcome Sign QHG3606	Retrd.	1999	15.00	

Possible Dreams

Crinkle Village - Staff

YEAR ISSUE	EDITION LIMIT	YEAR RETD.	ISSUE PRICE	*QUOTE U.S.$
1997 Crinkle Barn 659654	Open		43.30	
1998 Crinkle Candy Store (lighted) 659661	Open		62.00	
1996 Crinkle Castle (lighted) 659652	Retrd.	1998	70.00	
1996 Crinkle Church (lighted) 659651	Retrd.	1998	70.00	
1997 Crinkle Claus Village Display 965006	Open		10.00	
1996 Crinkle Cottage (lighted) 659653	Retrd.	1998	70.00	
1997 Crinkle Farmhouse 659657	Open		43.30	
1998 Crinkle Fire Station (lighted) 659660	Open		62.00	
1997 Crinkle Grist Mill 659656	Open		43.30	
1997 Crinkle Inn 659655	Open		43.30	
1998 Crinkle Police Station (lighted) 659662	Open		62.00	
1998 Crinkle Post Office (lighted) 659659	Open		62.00	
1998 Crinkle Toy Shop (lighted) 659658	Open		62.00	
1996 Crinkle Workshop (lighted) 659650	Retrd.	1998	70.00	
1996 Santa Castle 659019	Open		15.00	
1996 Santa Christmas House 659017	Open		15.00	
1996 Santa Church 659020	Open		15.00	
1996 Santa Farm House 659018	Open		15.00	
1996 Santa Palace 659016	Open		15.00	
1996 Santa Windmill 659021	Open		15.00	

Prizm, Inc./Pipka

Pipka's Miniature Collection - Pipka

YEAR ISSUE	EDITION LIMIT	YEAR RETD.	ISSUE PRICE	*QUOTE U.S.$
2002 Christmas Cottage 13767	Open		35.00	
2002 Midnight Visitor House 13766	Open		35.00	
2002 Porcelain Trees, set/3 (accessory) 13771	Open		20.00	
2002 Teddy Bear Santa House 13768	Open		35.00	

Pipka's Treasure Boxes - Pipka

YEAR ISSUE	EDITION LIMIT	YEAR RETD.	ISSUE PRICE	*QUOTE U.S.$
2001 Midnight Visitor 11601	Open		40.00	
2001 Star Catcher Santa 11603	Open		40.00	
2001 Starcoat Santa 11602	Open		40.00	

Reco International

Mini Views - Various

YEAR ISSUE	EDITION LIMIT	YEAR RETD.	ISSUE PRICE	*QUOTE U.S.$
1999 Afternoon in Venice - B. Pejman	Open		20.00	
1999 Almost There - R. Lee	Retrd.	2000	20.00	
2000 Angel Lighting the World - D. Gelsinger	Open		20.00	
2000 Anna - H. Fisher	Open		20.00	
2001 The Awakening - J. Bowser	Open		20.00	
2000 Ballerina - N. Mirkovich	Open		20.00	
2000 Beach Duet - P. Brent	Open		20.00	
1999 Birth of Hiawatha - G. Perillo	Retrd.	2000	20.00	
2000 Cape Hatteras - P. Brent	Open		20.00	
2000 Cape Lookout - P. Brent	Open		20.00	
1999 Capri Terrace - B. Pejman	Open		20.00	
2000 Celestial Spirit - J. Bowser	Open		20.00	
1999 Champaign Wishes - S. Hatchett	Open		20.00	
2000 Cherub with Wren - C. Shoresright	Open		20.00	
2000 Chickadees in the Snow - D. Balke	Open		20.00	
2000 Christmas Joy - B. Harris Tustian	Open		20.00	
2000 Christmas Memories - B. Harris Tustian	Open		20.00	
1999 Duck Crossing - R. Lee	Retrd.	2000	20.00	
2000 Dune Hideaway - P. Brent	Open		20.00	
2000 Follow Me - D. DeVary	Open		20.00	
1999 From Santorini With Love - S. Hatchett	Open		20.00	
2000 The Gallery - J. Haney-Neal	Open		20.00	
2001 Goddess of Tides - J. Bowser	Open		20.00	
2000 The Grand Finale - M. Grimball	Open		20.00	
2000 Grandma's Backyard - N. Mirkovich	Open		20.00	
1999 Green Ledge Lighthouse - H. Schaare	Open		20.00	
2000 Hope - P. Church	Open		20.00	
1999 The Hunt - G. Perillo	Retrd.	2000	20.00	
2000 In Disgrace - M. Grimball	Open		20.00	
2000 Jazz - T. Wilson	Open		20.00	
2000 Lilies of the Mohawk - G. Perillo	Open		20.00	
1999 Lily Pond - G. Perillo	Retrd.	2000	20.00	
1999 Love Song - G. Ratinavera	Retrd.	2000	20.00	

YEAR ISSUE	EDITION LIMIT	YEAR RETD.	ISSUE PRICE	*QUOTE U.S.$
2000 Loving Care - C. Shoresright	Open		20.00	20
1999 Memories in Blue - A. Berman	Open		20.00	20
2000 Mystical Santa - D. Gelsinger	Open		20.00	20
2000 The Old Barn - N. Mirkovich	Open		20.00	20
2000 On Guard - M. Grimball	Open		20.00	20
1999 Once Upon a Time - S. Hatchett	Open		20.00	20
2000 The Optimist - J. Haney-Neal	Open		20.00	20
2000 Pansies & Lace - S. Wall	Open		20.00	20
2000 Peace - P. Church	Open		20.00	20
2000 The Rebel - J. Haney-Neal	Open		20.00	20
1999 Rhapsody in Blue - G. Ratinavera	Retrd.	2000	20.00	20
2000 Rhythm - T. Wilson	Open		20.00	20
2000 Ride the Pony - D. DeVary	Open		20.00	20
1999 Room Service - G. Buffet	Open		20.00	20
2000 The Run Away - D. DeVary	Open		20.00	20
1999 The Rustler - G. Perillo	Open		20.00	20
2000 Snowman Family - D. Gelsinger	Open		20.00	20
2000 Still Life - A. Kaercher	Open		20.00	20
2000 Three for Tea - S. Wall	Open		20.00	20
2000 Three Little... - S. Wall	Open		20.00	20
2000 Three Sisters - C. Shoresright	Open		20.00	20
1999 The Vanishing West - D. Cook	Open		20.00	20
2000 Vase of Roses - J. L. Jensen	Open		20.00	20
2001 The Virgin of Humility - G. Starnina	Open		20.00	20
2000 Who's Afraid - M. Grimball	Open		20.00	20

Native American Views - G. Perillo

YEAR ISSUE	EDITION LIMIT	YEAR RETD.	ISSUE PRICE	*QUOTE U.S.$
1999 Anasazis Sanctuary	Open		45.00	45
1999 Cheyenne's Pride	Open		45.00	45
1999 Iroquois Dignity	Open		45.00	45
1999 Navaho's Refuge	Open		45.00	45
1999 Pueblo Abode	Open		45.00	45

Nautical Views - R. Reichardt

YEAR ISSUE	EDITION LIMIT	YEAR RETD.	ISSUE PRICE	*QUOTE U.S.$
1999 Cape Hatteras	2,400		45.00	50

Purr-fect Views - J. Everett

YEAR ISSUE	EDITION LIMIT	YEAR RETD.	ISSUE PRICE	*QUOTE U.S.$
1999 Country Store	Open		40.00	40
1999 The Potting Shed	Open		40.00	40
1999 Townhouse Cats	Open		40.00	40

Rooms With A View - Various

YEAR ISSUE	EDITION LIMIT	YEAR RETD.	ISSUE PRICE	*QUOTE U.S.$
2000 Afternoon Remembered - J. O'Brien	Open		40.00	40
1998 Archway - J. O'Brien	Retrd.	2000	40.00	40
2000 The Arrangement - J. O'Brien	Open		40.00	40
2000 Castle View - J. O'Brien	Open		40.00	40
2000 Country Elegance - E. Dertner	Open		40.00	40
1998 Gourmet Delight - B. Ternay	Open		40.00	40
2000 Grand Ma's Kitchen - E. Dertner	Open		40.00	40
1998 In The Garden - J. O'Brien	Retrd.	2000	40.00	40
1999 Lighthouse - R. Reichardt	Open		40.00	40
1998 Nantucket - F. Ledan	Open		40.00	40
1998 New York Nights - F. Ledan	Open		40.00	40
1998 Remembering - J. O'Brien	Retrd.	2000	40.00	40
1999 Romantic Belliago - S. Hatchett	Open		40.00	40
1998 Rustic Repose - E. Dertner	Open		40.00	40
1998 Salinger Mansion - F. Ledan	Open		40.00	40
1998 Salon Sur La Cite - F. Ledan	Open		40.00	40
2000 Summer's Light - J. O'Brien	Open		40.00	40
1998 Terrasse-Sur-Riviera - F. Ledan	Open		40.00	40
1998 Top of the Morning - E. Dertner	Open		40.00	40
1999 Tropical Hideaway - S. Hatchett	Open		40.00	40
1998 Yellow Roses, Red Poppies - F. Ledan	Open		40.00	40

Rooms With A View-Graceland - Based on Graceland Rooms

YEAR ISSUE	EDITION LIMIT	YEAR RETD.	ISSUE PRICE	*QUOTE U.S.$
1999 The Graceland Mansion	Open		45.00	50
1999 The Jungle Room	Open		45.00	50
1999 The Living Room & Music Room	Open		45.00	50
1999 The Mansion Foyer	Open		45.00	50

Shops With A View - Various

YEAR ISSUE	EDITION LIMIT	YEAR RETD.	ISSUE PRICE	*QUOTE U.S.$
1999 Bottle Brigade - G. Buffet	Open		45.00	45
1999 Clip Art - R. Souders	Open		40.00	40
1999 Diner - W. Ternay	Open		40.00	40
2000 The Flower Shop - J. O'Brien	Open		45.00	45
1999 La Cacioteca - G. Buffet	Open		45.00	45
2000 Menu of the Day - G. Buffet	Open		45.00	45
2000 The Old Antique Shop - J. O'Brien	Open		40.00	40
2000 Palace of Treasures - J. O'Brien	Open		45.00	45
1999 Panetteria - G. Buffet	Open		45.00	45

YEAR ISSUE	EDITION LIMIT	YEAR RETD.	ISSUE PRICE	*QUOTE U.S.$
1999 Pop's - R. Souders	Open		40.00	40

Views of Faith - Various

YEAR ISSUE	EDITION LIMIT	YEAR RETD.	ISSUE PRICE	*QUOTE U.S.$
1999 The Conception - S. Tiepolo	Open		40.00	40
1999 Gett'n Ready - J. Claybrooks	2,400	2001	45.00	45
1999 Madonna in Prayer - S. Tiepolo	Open		40.00	40
1999 Sharing Harmony - S. Kuck	2,400		45.00	45

Shelia's Collectibles

Shelia's Collectors' Society - S. Thompson

YEAR ISSUE	EDITION LIMIT	YEAR RETD.	ISSUE PRICE	*QUOTE U.S.$
1993 Anne Peacock House SOC01	Retrd.	1994	16.00	132-250
1993 Susan B. Anthony CGA93	Retrd.	1994	Gift	94-125
1993 Anne Peacock House SOC01 & Susan B. Anthony CGA93, set/2	Retrd.	1994	16.00	132-300
1993 Anne Peacock House Print	Retrd.	1994	Gift	47-75
1994 Seaview Cottage SOC02	Retrd.	1995	17.00	75-125
1994 Helen Keller's Birthplace-Ivy Green CGA94	Retrd.	1995	Gift	75
1994 Seaview Cottage SOC02 & Helen Keller's Birthplace-Ivy Green CGA94, set/2	Retrd.	1995	17.00	97-113
1994 Collector's Society T-Shirt	Retrd.	1995	Gift	N/A
1995 Pink Lady SOC03	Retrd.	1996	20.00	40-57
1995 Red Cross CGA95	Retrd.	1996	Gift	47-88
1995 Pink Lady SOC03 & Red Cross CGA95, set/2	Retrd.	1996	20.00	50-200
1995 Collector's Society T-Shirt & Collector's Society Pin	Retrd.	1996	Gift	45-115
1996 Tinker Toy House SOC04	Retrd.	1997	20.00	39-47
1996 Tatman House CGA96	Retrd.	1997	Gift	30-50
1996 Tinker Toy House SOC04 & Tatman House CGA96, set/2	Retrd.	1997	20.00	200
1996 Tinker Toy House Ornament	Retrd.	1997	Gift	45
1997 25 Meeting St. SOC97	Retrd.	1998	26.00	45-47
1997 23 Meeting Street CGA97	Retrd.	1998	Gift	45
1997 23 Meeting St. SOC97 & 23 Meeting Street CGA97, set/2	Retrd.	1998	26.00	150
1997 25 Meeting Street Ornament OCS02	Retrd.	1998	Gift	40-63
1998 Old North Church II CGA98	Retrd.	1998	Gift	20-25
1998 Paul Revere's Ride CGA98	Retrd.	1998	Gift	15-20
1998 Munroe Tavern SOC98	Retrd.	1999	26.00	28
1999 Eugenia's Flower Garden SOC99	Retrd.	1999	Gift	N/A
1999 Eugenia's Cottage CGA99	Retrd.	1999	Gift	25
2000 Betsy Ross CSA00	Retrd.	2000	Gift	N/A
2000 Betsy Ross House CGA00	Retrd.	2000	Gift	N/A

Signing & Event Pieces - S. Thompson

YEAR ISSUE	EDITION LIMIT	YEAR RETD.	ISSUE PRICE	*QUOTE U.S.$
1994 Star Barn SOP01	Retrd.	1994	24.00	60-75
1995 Shelia's Real Estate Office SOP02	Retrd.	1995	20.00	20-44
1996 Thompson's Mercantile SOP03	Retrd.	1996	24.00	25-55
1997 27 Meeting St. SOP97	Retrd.	1997	26.00	44-50
1998 The Old Manse SOP98	Retrd.	1998	26.00	26
1999 Gilson Residence EVT99	Retrd.	1999	23.00	23-30
2000 Buckeye Tree SOP04	Retrd.	2000	15.00	15
2000 Golden Gate Bridge SOP05	Retrd.	2000	17.00	17
2000 A Day at the Beach SOP06	Retrd.	2000	N/A	N/A
2000 Thanksgiving Blessings SOP07	Retrd.	2000	N/A	N/A

Accessories - S. Thompson

YEAR ISSUE	EDITION LIMIT	YEAR RETD.	ISSUE PRICE	*QUOTE U.S.$
1994 Amish Quilt Line COL12	Retrd.	1994	18.00	35-48
1993 Apple Tree COL09	Retrd.	1996	12.00	20-35
1996 Autumn Tree ACC09	Open		14.00	15
1996 Barber Gazebo ACC05	Retrd.	2000	13.00	14
1999 Biltmore Conservatory ACC15	Retrd.	2000	24.00	24
1997 Crepe Myrtle ACC13	Open		15.00	15
1993 Dogwood Tree COL08	Retrd.	1996	12.00	24-55
1999 Evergreen Trees ACC16	Open		13.00	13
1992 Fence 5" COL04	Retrd.	1994	9.00	25-30
1992 Fence 7" COL05	Retrd.	1995	10.00	27-35
1995 Flower Garden ACC02	Retrd.	1998	13.00	13-18
1994 Formal Garden COL13	Retrd.	1994	18.00	30-35
1992 Gazebo With Victorian Lady COL02	Retrd.	1995	11.00	25-35
1996 Grazing Cows ACC04	Retrd.	2000	12.00	12
1992 Lake With Swan COL06	Retrd.	1993	11.00	23-35
1997 Magnolia Tree ACC11	Open		15.00	15
1992 Oak Bower COL03	Retrd.	1993	11.00	35-45
1996 Palm Tree ACC07	Open		14.00	15
1995 Real Estate Sign ACC03	Retrd.	1998	12.00	15-18
1997 Sabal Palm ACC12	Open		14.00	14
1996 Sailboat ACC06	Open		12.00	13
1996 Spring Tree ACC10	Open		14.00	15

ARCHITECTURE

YEAR ISSUE	EDITION LIMIT	YEAR RETD.	ISSUE PRICE	*QUOTE U.S.$
1996 Summertime Picket Fence ACC08	Open		12.00	13
1994 Sunrise At 80 Meeting COL10	Retrd.	1994	18.00	30-65
1998 Town Square Evergreen TSN06	Retrd.	1998	10.00	18
1992 Tree With Bush COL07	Retrd.	1996	10.00	24-35
1994 Victorian Arbor COL11	Retrd.	1994	18.00	30-45
1997 White Dogwood ACC14	Open		15.00	15
1995 Wisteria Arbor ACC01	Retrd.	1998	12.00	12-14
1992 Wrought Iron Gate With Magnolias COL01	Retrd.	1993	11.00	30-50

American Barns - S. Thompson

1995 Casey Barn AP BAR04	Retrd.	1997	18.00	20-35
1995 Casey Barn BAR04	Retrd.	1997	18.00	24-27
1999 Dr. Pierce's Barn BAR07	Retrd.	2000	24.00	24
1999 King Midas Barn BAR06	Retrd.	2000	22.00	22
1995 Mail Pouch Barn AP BAR03	Retrd.	1996	18.00	18
1995 Mail Pouch Barn BAR03	Retrd.	1999	18.00	22-25
1996 Mr. Peanut Barn BAR05	Retrd.	2000	19.00	21
1996 Mr. Peanut Barn, AP BAR05	97	1996	24.00	35-60
1995 Pennsylvania Dutch Barn AP BAR02	Retrd.	1995	20.00	90
1995 Pennsylvania Dutch Barn BAR02	Retrd.	1996	18.00	25-35
1994 Rock City Barn AP BAR01	Retrd.	1994	20.00	22-25
1994 Rock City Barn BAR01	Retrd.	1999	18.00	22

Amish Village - S. Thompson

1993 Amish Barn AMS04	Retrd.	1997	17.00	30
1993 Amish Barn, AP AMS04	Retrd.	1993	20.00	30-35
1994 Amish Barn (renovated) AMS04II	Retrd.	1997	17.00	60
1997 Amish Barnraising AMS09	Retrd.	1999	22.00	23
1993 Amish Buggy AMS05	Retrd.	1997	12.00	26-35
1993 Amish Buggy, AP AMS05	Retrd.	1994	16.00	20-35
1994 Amish Buggy (renovated) AMS05II	Retrd.	1997	12.00	20-30
1997 Amish Corn Cribs AMS07	Retrd.	1999	18.00	19-21
1997 Amish Farmhouse AMS08	Retrd.	1999	22.00	23-27
1993 Amish Home AMS01	Retrd.	1994	17.00	31-35
1993 Amish Home, AP AMS01	Retrd.	1993	20.00	35-42
1994 Amish Home (renovated) AMS01II	Retrd.	1997	17.00	28-35
1993 Amish School AMS02	Retrd.	1994	15.00	22-34
1993 Amish School, AP AMS02	Retrd.	1993	20.00	35-60
1994 Amish School (renovated) AMS02II	Retrd.	1997	15.00	20-27
1997 Amish Schoolhouse AMS10	Retrd.	1999	18.00	19
1993 Covered Bridge AMS03	Retrd.	1994	16.00	18-40
1993 Covered Bridge, AP AMS03	Retrd.	1993	20.00	20-60
1994 Covered Bridge (renovated) AMS03II	Retrd.	1997	16.00	28-30
1995 Roadside Stand AMS06	Retrd.	1999	17.00	19-23
1995 Roadside Stand, AP AMS06	Retrd.	1995	24.00	30-35

Arkansas Ladies - S. Thompson

1996 Handford Terry House ARK02	Retrd.	1999	19.00	23-25
1996 Handford Terry House, AP ARK02	50	1996	24.00	47
1996 Pillow-Thompson House ARK04	Retrd.	1999	19.00	23
1996 Pillow-Thompson House, AP ARK04	101	1996	24.00	47-65
1996 Rosalie House ARK01	Retrd.	1999	19.00	23
1996 Rosalie House, AP ARK01	102	1996	24.00	48
1996 Wings ARK03	Retrd.	1999	19.00	23-25
1996 Wings, AP ARK03	103	1996	24.00	47

Artist Choice-American Gothic - S. Thompson

1993 Gothic Revival Cottage ACL01	Retrd.	1993	20.00	37-45
1993 Mele House ACL04	Retrd.	1993	20.00	38-57
1993 Perkins House ACL02	Retrd.	1993	20.00	35-57
1993 Rose Arbor ACL05	Retrd.	1993	14.00	27-65
1993 Roseland Cottage ACL03	Retrd.	1993	20.00	35-43
1993 Set of 5	Retrd.	1993	94.00	219-275

Artist Choice-Barber Houses - S. Thompson

1995 Banta House ACL12	4,000	1995	24.00	45-60
1995 Greenman House ACL11	4,000	1995	24.00	40-45
1995 Riley-Cutler House ACL10	4,000	1995	24.00	32-35
1995 Weller House ACL13	4,000	1995	24.00	40
1995 Set of 4	4,000	1995	96.00	144

Artist Choice-Mail-Order Victorians (Barber Houses) - S. Thompson

1994 Brehaut House ACL09	3,300	1994	24.00	40
1994 Goeller House ACL08	3,300	1994	24.00	40
1994 Henderson House ACL07	3,300	1994	24.00	55
1994 Titman House ACL06	3,300	1994	24.00	75-80
1994 Set of 4	3,300	1994	96.00	145-210

Artist Choice-My Favorite Places - S. Thompson

1997 Garden Bench ACL18	5,000	1997	24.00	25-30
1997 Reflecting Pond ACL19	5,000	1997	24.00	25-30

YEAR ISSUE	EDITION LIMIT	YEAR RETD.	ISSUE PRICE	*QUOTE U.S.$
1997 Sunflower Field ACL21	5,000	1997	21.00	23-25
1997 Tranquil Arbor ACL20	5,000	1997	22.00	25

Artist Choice-Noah's Ark - S. Thompson

1999 Noah's Ark ACL24	5,000		45.00	45
1999 Rainbow ACL25	5,000		set	set

Artist Choice-The Night Before Christmas - S. Thompson

1998 The Night Before Christmas ACL22	7,500		55.00	55
1998 Frozen Lawn ACL23	7,500		set	set

Artist Choice-Winter White Collection - S. Thompson

1996 Drain House ACL16	4,500	1996	25.00	27-40
1996 Moses Bulkeley House ACL14	4,500	1996	25.00	32-43
1996 Paul House ACL17	4,500	1996	25.00	27-43
1996 Penn House ACL15	4,500	1996	25.00	35-40

Atlanta - S. Thompson

1995 Fox Theatre ATL06	Retrd.	1998	19.00	22-35
1995 Fox Theatre, A/P ATL06	Retrd.	1995	24.00	24
1995 Hammond's House ATL05	Retrd.	1997	18.00	19-26
1995 Hammond's House, A/P ATL05	Retrd.	1995	24.00	24
1996 Margaret Mitchell House ATL07	Retrd.	1996	19.00	21-25
1996 Margaret Mitchell House, AP ATL07	89	1996	24.00	35
1995 Swan House ATL03	Retrd.	1998	18.00	22-37
1995 Swan House, A/P ATL03	Retrd.	1995	24.00	25
1995 Tullie Smith House ATL01	Retrd.	1997	17.00	18-35
1995 Tullie Smith House, A/P ATL01	Retrd.	1995	24.00	24
1995 Victorian Playhouse ATL02	Retrd.	1997	17.00	18-35
1995 Victorian Playhouse, A/P ATL02	Retrd.	1995	24.00	24
1995 Wren's Nest ATL04	Retrd.	1998	19.00	22-35
1995 Wren's Nest, A/P ATL04	Retrd.	1995	24.00	24

Charleston - S. Thompson

1991 #2 Meeting Street CHS06	Retrd.	1994	15.00	18-25
1994 #2 Meeting Street (renovated) CHS06II	Retrd.	1997	16.00	31-50
1999 #7 Meeting Street CHS70	Open		24.00	24
1990 90 Church St. CHS17	Retrd.	1993	12.00	45-85
1993 Ashe House CHS51	Retrd.	1994	16.00	26-50
1994 Ashe House (renovated) CHS51II	Retrd.	1997	16.00	45
1991 Beth Elohim Temple CHS20	Retrd.	1993	15.00	30-35
1993 The Citadel CHS22	Retrd.	1994	16.00	31-45
1994 The Citadel (renovated) CHS22II	Retrd.	1997	16.00	40-45
1993 City Hall CHS21	Retrd.	1993	15.00	94
1993 City Hall (No banner) CHS21	Retrd.	1993	15.00	200-450
1993 City Hall (without Spoleto colors) CHS21	Retrd.	1993	15.00	275
1991 City Market (closed gates) CHS07	Retrd.	1991	15.00	100
1991 City Market (open gates) CHS07	Retrd.	1994	15.00	35-50
1994 City Market (renovated) CHS07II	Retrd.	1998	15.00	20-25
1993 College of Charleston CHS40	Retrd.	1994	16.00	30-47
1993 College of Charleston, AP CHS40	Retrd.	1993	20.00	30-69
1994 College of Charleston (renovated) CHS40II	Retrd.	1996	16.00	85
1992 Dock Street Theater (chimney) CHS08	Retrd.	1993	15.00	30-50
1991 Dock Street Theater (no chimney) CHS08	Retrd.	1992	15.00	58-60
1991 Edmonston-Alston CHS04	Retrd.	1994	15.00	31-50
1994 Edmonston-Alston (renovated) CHS04II	Retrd.	1995	16.00	31-50
1990 Exchange Building CHS15	Retrd.	1994	15.00	40
1993 Heyward-Washington House CHS02	Retrd.	1993	15.00	35-40
1993 John Rutledge House Inn CHS50	Retrd.	1994	16.00	30-35
1994 John Rutledge House Inn (renovated) CHS50II	Retrd.	1997	16.00	45
1991 Magnolia Plantation House (beige curtains) CHS03	Retrd.	1994	16.00	45-50
1991 Magnolia Plantation House (white curtains) CHS03	Retrd.	1994	16.00	26-35
1994 Magnolia Plantation House (renovated) CHS03II	Retrd.	1996	16.00	26-50
1990 Manigault House CHS01	Retrd.	1993	15.00	40-57
1990 Middleton Plantation CHS19	Retrd.	1991	9.00	225-260
1999 Open Air City Market CHS69	Open		24.00	24
1990 Pink House CHS18	Retrd.	1993	12.00	35-40
1990 Powder Magazine CHS16	Retrd.	1991	9.00	300-344
1993 Single Side Porch CHS30	Retrd.	1994	16.00	27-35
1993 Single Side Porch, AP CHS30	Retrd.	1993	20.00	20-45
1994 Single Side Porch (renovated) CHS30II	Retrd.	1997	16.00	30-35

Collectors' Information Bureau   *Quotes have been rounded up to nearest dollar

YEAR ISSUE	EDITION LIMIT	YEAR RETD.	ISSUE PRICE	*QUOTE U.S.$
1990 St. Michael's Church CHS14	Retrd.	1994	15.00	33-40
1991 St. Philip's Church CHS05	Retrd.	1994	15.00	32-37
1994 St. Philip's Church (renovated) CHS05II	Retrd.	1996	15.00	55-60
1991 St. Phillip's Church (misspelling Phillips) CHS05	Retrd.	1991	15.00	90

Charleston Battery - S. Thompson

1996 22 South Battery CHB01	Open		19.00	21
1996 22 South Battery, AP CHB01	109	1996	24.00	35
1996 24 South Battery CHB02	Open		19.00	21
1996 24 South Battery, AP CHB02	99	1996	24.00	35
1996 26 South Battery CHB03	Open		19.00	21
1996 26 South Battery, AP CHB03	74	1996	24.00	35
1996 28 South Battery CHB04	Open		19.00	21
1996 28 South Battery, AP CHB04	74	1996	24.00	35
1998 30 South Battery CHB05	Open		21.00	21
1998 30 South Battery, AP CHB05	275		25.00	25

Charleston Gold Seal - S. Thompson

1988 90 Church St. CHS17	Retrd.	1990	9.00	40
1988 CHS31 Rainbow Row-rust	Retrd.	1990	9.00	30-35
1988 CHS32 Rainbow Row-tan	Retrd.	1990	9.00	30-35
1988 CHS33 Rainbow Row-cream	Retrd.	1990	9.00	30-35
1988 CHS34 Rainbow Row-green	Retrd.	1990	9.00	30-35
1988 CHS35 Rainbow Row-lavender	Retrd.	1990	9.00	30-35
1988 CHS36 Rainbow Row-pink	Retrd.	1990	9.00	30-35
1988 CHS37 Rainbow Row-blue	Retrd.	1990	9.00	30-35
1988 CHS38 Rainbow Row-lt. yellow	Retrd.	1990	9.00	30-35
1988 CHS39 Rainbow Row-lt. pink	Retrd.	1990	9.00	30-35
1988 Exchange Building CHS15	Retrd.	1990	9.00	35
1988 Middleton Plantation CHS19	Retrd.	1990	9.00	222
1988 Pink House CHS18	Retrd.	1990	9.00	29-35
1988 Powder Magazine CHS16	Retrd.	1990	9.00	188
1988 St. Michael's Church CHS14	Retrd.	1990	9.00	60

Charleston II - S. Thompson

1995 Boone Hall Plantation CHS56	Retrd.	1999	18.00	22-25
1995 Boone Hall Plantation, AP CHS56	Retrd.	1995	24.00	35-46
1998 Dr. Vincent LeSigneur House CHS68	Open		22.00	22
1998 Dr. Vincent LeSigneur House, AP CHS68	130	1998	43.00	45
1994 Drayton House CHS52	Retrd.	1999	18.00	22-30
1994 Drayton House, AP CHS52	Retrd.	1999	24.00	44-58
1996 Huguenot Church CHS58	Retrd.	1999	19.00	21-25
1996 Huguenot Church, AP CHS58	95	1996	24.00	20-44
1996 Magnolia Garden CHS57	Open		19.00	21
1996 Magnolia Garden, A/P CHS57	Retrd.	1996	24.00	24-35
1998 Middleton Plantation II CHS67	Open		24.00	24-27
1995 O'Donnell's Folly CHS55	Retrd.	1999	18.00	22-24
1995 O'Donnell's Folly, AP CHS55	Retrd.	1995	24.00	46-50
1996 Sotille CHS59	Retrd.	1999	19.00	22
1996 Sotille, AP CHS59	98	1996	24.00	20-45

Charleston III - S. Thompson

1997 South of Broad, Cream CHS65	Retrd.	1999	18.00	19-21
1997 South of Broad, Cream, AP CHS65	197	1998	24.00	35-46
1997 South of Broad, Dark Pink CHS64	Retrd.	1999	18.00	19-21
1997 South of Broad, Dark Pink, AP CHS64	214	1998	24.00	35-46
1997 South of Broad, Lavender CHS63	Retrd.	1999	18.00	19-21
1997 South of Broad, Lavender, AP CHS63	205	1998	24.00	35-46
1997 South of Broad, Light Pink CHS66	Retrd.	1999	18.00	19-21
1997 South of Broad, Light Pink, AP CHS66	207	1998	24.00	35-46
1997 South of Broad, Tan CHS62	Retrd.	1999	18.00	19-21
1997 South of Broad, Tan, AP CHS62	198	1998	24.00	35-46

Charleston Rainbow Row - S. Thompson

1990 CHS31 Rainbow Row-rust	Retrd.	1993	9.00	35-60
1990 CHS32 Rainbow Row-cream	Retrd.	1993	9.00	35-69
1990 CHS33 Rainbow Row-tan	Retrd.	1993	9.00	38-40
1990 CHS34 Rainbow Row-green	Retrd.	1993	9.00	35-40
1990 CHS35 Rainbow Row-lavender	Retrd.	1993	9.00	35-43
1990 CHS36 Rainbow Row-pink	Retrd.	1993	9.00	40-52
1990 CHS37 Rainbow Row-blue	Retrd.	1993	9.00	38-40
1990 CHS38 Rainbow Row-lt. yellow	Retrd.	1993	9.00	40
1990 CHS39 Rainbow Row-lt. pink	Retrd.	1993	9.00	33-42
1993 CHS41 Rainbow Row-aurora	Retrd.	1994	13.00	18-30
1994 CHS41II Rainbow Row-aurora (renovated)	Retrd.	1997	13.00	30
1993 CHS42 Rainbow Row-off-white	Retrd.	1994	13.00	18-30
1994 CHS42II Rainbow Row-off-white (renovated)	Retrd.	1997	13.00	30

YEAR ISSUE	EDITION LIMIT	YEAR RETD.	ISSUE PRICE	*QUOTE U.S.$
1993 CHS43 Rainbow Row-cream	Retrd.	1994	13.00	18-30
1994 CHS43II Rainbow Row-cream (renovated)	Retrd.	1997	13.00	30
1993 CHS44 Rainbow Row-green	Retrd.	1994	13.00	18-26
1994 CHS44II Rainbow Row-green (renovated)	Retrd.	1997	13.00	30
1993 CHS45 Rainbow Row-lavender	Retrd.	1994	13.00	18-30
1994 CHS45II Rainbow Row-lavender (renovated)	Retrd.	1997	13.00	30
1993 CHS46 Rainbow Row-pink	Retrd.	1994	13.00	18-30
1994 CHS46II Rainbow Row-pink (renovated)	Retrd.	1997	13.00	30
1993 CHS47 Rainbow Row-blue	Retrd.	1994	13.00	18-30
1994 CHS47II Rainbow Row-blue (renovated)	Retrd.	1997	13.00	30
1993 CHS48 Rainbow Row-yellow	Retrd.	1994	13.00	18-30
1994 CHS48 Rainbow Row-yellow (renovated)	Retrd.	1997	13.00	30
1993 CHS49 Rainbow Row-gray	Retrd.	1994	13.00	18-21
1994 CHS49II Rainbow Row-gray (renovated)	Retrd.	1997	13.00	30
1993 Rainbow Row Sign	Retrd.	N/A	12.50	25-40

Charleston Rainbow Row '97 - S. Thompson

1997 89 East Bay CRR05	Open		18.00	18
1997 91 East Bay CRR06	Open		18.00	18
1997 93 East Bay CRR07	Open		18.00	18
1997 95 East Bay CRR08	Open		18.00	18
1997 97 East Bay CRR09	Open		18.00	18
1997 99-101 East Bay CRR10	Open		18.00	18
1997 103 East Bay CRR11	Open		18.00	18
1997 105 East Bay CRR12	Open		18.00	18
1997 107 East Bay CRR13	Open		18.00	18

Churches of America - S. Thompson

1999 Old Church on the Hill COA06	Retrd.	2000	23.00	23

Colored Metal Accessories - S. Thompson

1997 Burma Shave Sign: Past...Schoolhouse, set/6 CMA01	Retrd.	1997	17.00	19
1997 Burma Shave Sign: Don't Lose Your Head, set/6 CMA02	Retrd.	1997	17.00	19
1997 Daimler 1910 Car CMA03	Retrd.	1997	18.00	20

Dicken's Village - S. Thompson

1991 Butcher Shop XMS03	Retrd.	1993	15.00	35-40
1991 Evergreen Tree XMS08	Retrd.	1993	11.00	40-50
1991 Gazebo & Carolers XMS06	Retrd.	1993	12.00	35-50
1991 Scrooge & Marley's Shop XMS01	Retrd.	1993	15.00	35-50
1991 Scrooge's Home XMS05	Retrd.	1993	15.00	35-40
1991 Toy Shoppe XMS04	Retrd.	1993	15.00	35-40
1991 Victorian Apartment Building XMS02	Retrd.	1993	15.00	40
1992 Victorian Church XMS09	Retrd.	1993	15.00	100-175
1991 Victorian Skaters XMS07	Retrd.	1993	12.00	30-45
1992 Set of 9	Retrd.	1993	125.00	190-282

Exclusive Designs - S. Thompson

1998 Drayton Hall Privy (Drayton Hall) EXC15	400	1998	17.00	34
1998 Drayton River Front (Drayton Hall) EXC14	300	1998	29.00	44-58
1999 Alladin's Castle (Disney) EXC26	Open		42.00	42
1999 Beauty and the Beast's Castle (Disney) EXC23	Open		42.00	42
1999 Cinderella's Castle (Disney) EXC22	Open		42.00	42
1999 The Little Mermaid's Castle (Disney) EXC25	Open		42.00	42
1999 Sleeping Beauty's Castle (Disney) EXC27	Open		42.00	42
1999 Snow White's Castle (Disney) EXC24	Open		42.00	42
1999 Castles w/certificate, set/6 (Disney)	750		255.00	255
1997 Donald's House (Disney) EXC03	Retrd.	1997	30.00	50
1997 Goofy's House (Disney) EXC02	Retrd.	1997	30.00	50
1997 Mickey's House (Disney) EXC04	Closed	1997	30.00	36-52
1997 Minnie's House (Disney) EXC05	Closed	1997	30.00	30-36
1997 Set of Four Houses w/certificate (Disney)	500	1997	120.00	N/A

Famous Homes of America - S. Thompson

1998 Biltmore FHA03	Open		27.00	27
1998 Biltmore, AP FHA03	130	1998	41.00	50
1998 Monticello FHA01	Open		24.00	24
1998 Monticello, AP FHA01	130	1998	45.00	45
1998 Orchard House FHA02	Retrd.	1999	20.00	21

YEAR ISSUE	EDITION LIMIT	YEAR RETD.	ISSUE PRICE	*QUOTE U.S.$
1998 Orchard House, AP FHA02	130	1998	48.00	48
Food For Thought - S. Thompson				
1999 Doumar's FTO01	Retrd.	2000	23.00	23
1999 Springer's Homemade Ice Cream, NJ (no custom logo) C0053	Retrd.	1999	23.00	23
Galveston - S. Thompson				
1995 Beissner House GLV04	Retrd.	1998	18.00	20-35
1995 Beissner House, A/P GLV04	Retrd.	1995	24.00	24-35
1995 Dancing Pavillion GLV03	Retrd.	1998	18.00	20-35
1995 Dancing Pavillion, A/P GLV03	Retrd.	1995	24.00	24
1995 Frenkel House GLV01	Retrd.	1998	18.00	20-35
1995 Frenkel House, A/P GLV01	Retrd.	1995	24.00	24
1995 Reymershoffer House GLV02	Retrd.	1998	18.00	20-35
1995 Reymershoffer House, A/P GLV02	Retrd.	1995	24.00	35
George Barber - S. Thompson				
1996 Newton House GFB03	Retrd.	1999	19.00	20-25
1996 Newton House, AP GFB03	71	1996	24.00	32
1997 Nunan House GFB05	Retrd.	1999	22.00	25
1996 Phillipi House GFB02	Retrd.	1999	19.00	20-25
1996 Phillipi House, A/P GFB02	46	1996	24.00	32
1996 Pine Crest GFB04	Retrd.	1999	19.00	25
1996 Pine Crest, AP GFB04	95	1996	24.00	32
1996 Renaissance GFB01	Retrd.	1999	19.00	23-25
1996 Renaissance, AP GFB01	67	1996	24.00	33
Ghost House Series - S. Thompson				
1996 31 Legare St. GHO06	Retrd.	1999	19.00	23-25
1997 Catfish Plantation GHO07	Retrd.	1999	22.00	23-25
1997 Catfish Plantation, A/P GHO07	Retrd.	1997	28.00	28
1995 Gaffos House GHO04	Retrd.	1998	19.00	21-45
1995 Gaffos House, A/P GHO04	Retrd.	1995	24.00	24
1997 Hampton Lillbridge Home GHO08	Retrd.	1999	22.00	23
1997 Hampton Lillbridge Home, A/P GHO08	Retrd.	1997	24.00	24
1994 Inside-Outside House GHO01	Retrd.	1996	18.00	19-40
1994 Inside-Outside House, AP GHO01	Retrd.	1994	20.00	30-40
1996 Kings Tavern GHO05	Retrd.	1999	19.00	23
1996 Kings Tavern, AP GHO05	102	1996	24.00	28-46
1994 Pirates' House GHO02	Retrd.	1996	18.00	52-57
1994 Pirates' House, AP GHO02	Retrd.	1994	20.00	75-125
1995 Red Castle GHO03	Retrd.	1998	19.00	21-45
1995 Red Castle, AP GHO03	Retrd.	1995	24.00	24
Gone with the Wind - S. Thompson				
1995 Aunt Pittypat's GWW03	Retrd.	1996	24.00	43-63
1995 Aunt Pittypat's, AP GWW03	Retrd.	1995	30.00	58-75
1998 Butler's Atlanta Mansion GWW09	Retrd.	1998	27.00	28
1998 Butler's Atlanta Mansion, AP GWW09	130	1998	48.00	48
1995 General Store GWW04	Retrd.	1996	24.00	25-63
1995 General Store, AP GWW04	Retrd.	1995	30.00	50-58
1998 Home of Ashley Wilkes GWW08	Retrd.	1998	29.00	35
1998 Home of Ashley Wilkes, AP GWW08	130	1998	50.00	50
1998 Honeymoon Embrace Poster GWW10	Retrd.	1998	20.00	23
1998 Honeymoon Embrace Poster, AP GWW10	130	1998	41.00	41
1995 Loew's Grand GWW05	Retrd.	1995	24.00	75-125
1995 Loew's Grand, AP GWW05	Retrd.	1995	30.00	75-150
1999 Scarlett GWW13	Retrd.	1999	14.00	15
1998 Scarlett's Passion, Tara GWW07	Retrd.	1998	29.00	30-35
1998 Scarlett's Passion, Tara, AP GWW07	130	1998	50.00	50
1996 Silhouette GWW06	Retrd.	1996	16.00	35
1995 Tara GWW01	Retrd.	1996	24.00	35-50
1995 Tara, AP GWW01	Retrd.	1995	30.00	50-60
1999 Tara Revisited GWW11	Retrd.	1999	29.00	30
1999 Twelve Oaks Revisited GWW12	Retrd.	1999	29.00	30
1995 Twelve Oaks GWW02	Retrd.	1996	24.00	35-45
1995 Twelve Oaks, AP GWW02	Retrd.	1995	30.00	40-55
1995 Set of 5, AP	Retrd.	1995	150.00	288
1995 Set of 6 GWW01-GWW06	Retrd.	1995	160.00	230
Heartsville Christmas - S. Thompson				
1999 Heartsville Skaters TSN10	Retrd.	2000	14.00	14
1999 Heartsville Victorian TSN07	Retrd.	2000	23.00	23
Hook Houses - S. Thompson				
1993 #2 Meeting St. HHH14	Retrd.	N/A	25.00	18-32
XX 90 Church St. CHS26	Retrd.	N/A	21.00	85
1993 Amish House HHH19	Retrd.	N/A	25.00	43-63
1993 Anne Peacock House HHH15	Retrd.	N/A	25.00	43-63
1993 Ashe House HHH17	Retrd.	N/A	25.00	18-32
1993 Atlanta Queen Anne HHH16	Retrd.	N/A	25.00	43-63

YEAR ISSUE	EDITION LIMIT	YEAR RETD.	ISSUE PRICE	*QUOTE U.S.$
1993 Cape May Linda Lee HHH18	Retrd.	N/A	25.00	17-33
1993 Cape May Pink House HHH11	Retrd.	N/A	25.00	17-34
1993 Edmonston-Alston HHH13	Retrd.	N/A	25.00	33
1994 Ford Motor Company HHH20	Retrd.	N/A	25.00	17-33
1994 Gingerbread House HHH22	Retrd.	N/A	25.00	43-63
1994 Thomas Point Light HHH21	Retrd.	N/A	25.00	17-38
1993 Victorian Blue Rose HHH12	Retrd.	1993	24.00	17-25
Hook Houses-History For Keeps - S. Thompson				
1996 Chestnut House HFK04	Retrd.	1997	28.00	46
1996 Drayton House HFK01	Retrd.	1997	28.00	46
1996 E.B. Hall House HFK03	Retrd.	1997	28.00	42
1996 Eclectic Blue HFK06	Retrd.	1997	28.00	42
1996 Southernmost House HFK05	Retrd.	1997	28.00	46
1996 Victoria HFK02	Retrd.	1997	28.00	46
Inventor Series - S. Thompson				
1993 Ford Motor Company (green) INV04	Retrd.	1993	17.00	18-50
1993 Ford Motor Company (grey) INV01	Retrd.	1994	17.00	35-50
1993 Ford Motor Company, AP INV01	Retrd.	1993	20.00	20-45
1993 Menlo Park Laboratory (cream) INV02	Retrd.	1993	16.00	17-50
1993 Menlo Park Laboratory (grey) INV02	Retrd.	1994	16.00	40
1993 Menlo Park Laboratory, AP INV02	Retrd.	1993	20.00	35-70
1993 Noah Webster House INV03	Retrd.	1994	15.00	16-50
1993 Noah Webster House, AP INV03	Retrd.	1993	20.00	40-70
1993 Wright Cycle Shop INV04	Retrd.	1994	17.00	18-35
1993 Wright Cycle Shop, AP INV04	Retrd.	1993	20.00	14-27
Jazzy New Orleans Series - S. Thompson				
1994 Beauregard-Keys House (green) JNO04	Retrd.	1996	18.00	26-63
1994 Beauregard-Keys House, AP JNO04	Retrd.	1994	20.00	45-65
1994 Gallier House JNO02	Retrd.	1998	18.00	30-36
1994 Gallier House, AP JNO02	Retrd.	1994	20.00	17-22
1994 La Branche Building JNO01	Retrd.	1998	18.00	30-36
1994 La Branche Building, AP JNO01	Retrd.	1994	20.00	17-22
1994 LePretre House JNO03	Retrd.	1998	18.00	22-36
1994 LePretre House, AP JNO03	Retrd.	1994	20.00	50
Key West - S. Thompson				
1995 Artist House KEY06	Retrd.	1999	19.00	23
1995 Artist House, AP KEY06	Retrd.	1995	24.00	46
1995 Eyebrow House KEY01	Retrd.	1998	18.00	20-23
1995 Eyebrow House, AP KEY01	Retrd.	1995	24.00	36
1995 Hemingway House KEY07	Retrd.	1999	19.00	23
1995 Hemingway House, AP KEY07	Retrd.	1995	24.00	35-46
1995 Illingsworth Gingerbread House KEY05	Retrd.	1999	19.00	23
1995 Illingsworth Gingerbread House, AP KEY05	Retrd.	1995	24.00	46
1995 Shotgun House KEY03	Retrd.	1997	17.00	30-46
1995 Shotgun House, AP KEY03	Retrd.	1995	24.00	24-75
1995 Shotgun Sister KEY04	Retrd.	1997	17.00	30-45
1995 Shotgun Sister, AP KEY04	Retrd.	1995	24.00	24-75
1995 Southernmost House KEY02	Retrd.	1999	19.00	22-28
1995 Southernmost House, AP KEY02	Retrd.	1995	24.00	46
1996 Southernmost Point KEY08	Retrd.	1999	12.00	14-17
Ladies By The Sea - S. Thompson				
1996 Abbey II LBS01	Open		19.00	22
1996 Abbey II, AP LBS01	93	1996	24.00	35
1998 Cape S Cape LBS06	Retrd.	1999	22.00	24
1998 Cape S Cape, AP LBS06	250	1998	26.00	26
1996 Centennial Cottage LBS02	Retrd.	1999	19.00	24
1996 Centennial Cottage, AP LBS02	94	1996	24.00	35
1996 Hall Cottage LBS04	Retrd.	1999	19.00	24
1996 Hall Cottage, AP LBS04	108	1996	24.00	35
1996 Heart Blossom LBS03	Retrd.	1999	19.00	24
1996 Heart Blossom, AP LBS03	107	1996	24.00	24
1998 Ocean Pathway Princess LBS05	Retrd.	1999	22.00	22
1998 Ocean Pathway Princess, AP LBS05	275	1998	26.00	35
Lighthouse Series - S. Thompson				
1991 Anastasia Lighthouse (burgundy) FL103	Retrd.	1991	15.00	22-32
1991 Anastasia Lighthouse (red) FL103	Retrd.	1994	15.00	75-100
1993 Assateague Island Light LTS07	Retrd.	1997	17.00	30-37
1994 Assateague Island Light, AP LTS07	Retrd.	1994	20.00	44
1995 Cape Hatteras Light LTS09	Retrd.	1997	17.00	26-35
1995 Cape Hatteras Light, AP LTS09	Retrd.	1995	24.00	60
1991 Cape Hatteras Lighthouse NC103	Retrd.	1994	15.00	20-50
1993 Charleston Light LTS01	Retrd.	1995	15.00	32
1994 Charleston Light (renovated) LTS01	Retrd.	1995	15.00	60
1993 New London Ledge Light LTS08	Retrd.	1996	17.00	20-35

YEAR ISSUE	EDITION LIMIT	YEAR RETD.	ISSUE PRICE	*QUOTE U.S.$
1994 New London Ledge Light, AP LTS08	Retrd.	1994	20.00	55
1993 Round Island Light LTS06	Retrd.	1997	17.00	18-32
1994 Round Island Light, AP LTS06	Retrd.	1994	20.00	65
1990 Stage Harbor Lighthouse NEW06	Retrd.	1993	15.00	250
1993 Thomas Point Light LTS05	Retrd.	1997	17.00	20-29
1994 Thomas Point Light, AP LTS05	Retrd.	1994	20.00	55-65
1990 Tybee Lighthouse SAV07	Retrd.	1994	15.00	110-150

Limited Pieces - S. Thompson

YEAR ISSUE	EDITION LIMIT	YEAR RETD.	ISSUE PRICE	*QUOTE U.S.$
1991 Bridgetown Library NJ102	Retrd.	N/A	16.00	75-85
1993 Comly-Rich House XXX01	Retrd.	N/A	12.00	77-125
1993 Comley-Rich House (misspelling) XXX01	Retrd.	N/A	12.00	25-77
1991 Delphos City Hall OH101	Retrd.	N/A	15.00	250-265
1991 Historic Burlington County Clubhouse NJ101	Retrd.	N/A	16.00	75-125
1991 Mark Twain Boyhood Home MO101	Retrd.	N/A	15.00	395
1990 Newton County Court House GA101	Retrd.	N/A	16.00	65-100

Lone Star State - S. Thompson

YEAR ISSUE	EDITION LIMIT	YEAR RETD.	ISSUE PRICE	*QUOTE U.S.$
1998 Ashton Villa LSS02	Retrd.	1999	22.00	23
1998 Ashton Villa, AP LSS02	250	1998	26.00	35
1998 Blue Bonnets LSS03	Open		13.00	13
1998 Redington House LSS01	Retrd.	1999	22.00	25
1998 Redington House, AP LSS01	250	1998	26.00	35

Louisiana - S. Thompson

YEAR ISSUE	EDITION LIMIT	YEAR RETD.	ISSUE PRICE	*QUOTE U.S.$
1998 Commander's Palace LOU02	Open		22.00	22
1998 Commander's Palace, AP LOU02	275	1998	26.00	35
1998 Jackson Square LOU01	Open		22.00	22
1998 Jackson Square, AP LOU01	275	1998	26.00	35

Mackinac - S. Thompson

YEAR ISSUE	EDITION LIMIT	YEAR RETD.	ISSUE PRICE	*QUOTE U.S.$
1996 Amberg Cottage MAK01	Open		19.00	22
1996 Amberg Cottage, AP MAK01	102	1996	24.00	26-30
1996 Anne Cottage MAK02	Retrd.	1999	19.00	25-32
1996 Anne Cottage, AP MAK02	95	1996	24.00	28-46
1996 Grand Hotel (3 pc. set) MAK05	Retrd.	1998	57.00	70-80
1996 Grand Hotel (3 pc. set), AP MAK05	95	1996	72.00	72
1996 Rearick Cottage MAK03	Open		19.00	22
1996 Rearick Cottage, AP MAK03	103	1996	24.00	28-46
1996 Windermere Hotel MAK04	Open		19.00	22
1996 Windermere Hotel, AP MAK04	105	1996	24.00	28-46

Martha's Vineyard - S. Thompson

YEAR ISSUE	EDITION LIMIT	YEAR RETD.	ISSUE PRICE	*QUOTE U.S.$
1993 Alice's Wonderland MAR08	Retrd.	1994	16.00	19-25
1993 Alice's Wonderland, AP MAR08	Retrd.	1993	20.00	20-35
1994 Alice's Wonderland (renovated) MAR08II	Retrd.	1998	16.00	20-24
1995 Blue Cottage MAR13	Retrd.	1999	17.00	22
1995 Blue Cottage, AP MAR13	Retrd.	1995	24.00	24-45
1997 Butterfly Cottage MAR14	Open		20.00	20
1993 Campground Cottage MAR07	Retrd.	1995	16.00	35-45
1993 Campground Cottage, AP MAR07	Retrd.	1993	20.00	35-45
1994 Campground Cottage (renovated) MAR07II	Retrd.	1995	16.00	18-35
1993 Gingerbread Cottage-grey MAR09	Retrd.	1996	16.00	35-40
1993 Gingerbread Cottage-grey AP MAR09	Retrd.	1993	20.00	20-40
1994 Gingerbread Cottage-grey (renovated) MAR09II	Retrd.	1996	16.00	25-35
1998 Summer Love MAR16	Open		21.00	21
1998 Summer Love, AP MAR16	275	1998	25.00	25
1995 Trails End MAR11	Retrd.	1998	17.00	21-35
1995 Trails End, AP MAR11	Retrd.	1995	24.00	24-46
1998 Tranquility MAR15	Open		21.00	21
1998 Tranquility, AP MAR15	275	1998	25.00	25
1995 White Cottage MAR12	Open		17.00	20
1995 White Cottage, AP MAR12	Retrd.	1995	24.00	35
1993 Wood Valentine MAR10	Retrd.	1994	16.00	19-25
1993 Wood Valentine, AP MAR10	Retrd.	1993	20.00	20-46
1994 Wood Valentine (renovated) MAR10II	Retrd.	1998	16.00	20-25

Nantucket - S. Thompson

YEAR ISSUE	EDITION LIMIT	YEAR RETD.	ISSUE PRICE	*QUOTE U.S.$
1998 Brant Point Lighthouse NTK01	Open		22.00	22
1998 Brant Point Lighthouse, AP NTK01	265	1998	26.00	35
1998 Pedal Shop NTK03	Open		13.00	13
1998 Swain Cottage NTK02	Open		22.00	22
1998 Swain Cottage, AP NTK02	265	1998	26.00	35

National Park Treasures - S. Thompson

YEAR ISSUE	EDITION LIMIT	YEAR RETD.	ISSUE PRICE	*QUOTE U.S.$
1998 Independence Hall NPT04	Open		21.00	21
1998 Independence Hall, AP NPT04	130	1998	42.00	45
1998 Liberty Bell NPT05	Open		15.00	15
1998 Liberty Bell, AP NPT05	130	1998	36.00	40
1998 Mount Rushmore National Memorial NPT03	Open		20.00	20
1998 Mount Rushmore National Memorial, AP NPT03	130	1998	41.00	45
1998 Statue of Liberty NPT02	Open		20.00	20
1998 Statue of Liberty, AP NPT02	130	1998	41.00	45
1999 Vietnam Veteran's Memorial NPT06	Open		23.00	23
1998 White House NPT01	Open		26.00	26
1998 White House, AP NPT01	130	1998	47.00	50

National Trust Houses - S. Thompson

YEAR ISSUE	EDITION LIMIT	YEAR RETD.	ISSUE PRICE	*QUOTE U.S.$
1997 Cliveden NHP03	Retrd.	1999	24.00	26
1997 Cliveden, AP NHP03	240	1997	30.00	35
1998 Decatur House NHP04	Retrd.	1999	24.00	26
1998 Decatur House, AP NHP04	130	1998	44.00	44
1997 Drayton Hall NHP01	Open		24.00	24
1997 Drayton Hall, AP NHP01	266	1997	30.00	35
1997 Montpelier NHP02	Retrd.	1999	24.00	26
1997 Montpelier, AP NHP02	200	1997	30.00	35-42
1998 Oatlands NHP07	Retrd.	1999	24.00	26
1998 Oatlands, AP NHP07	130	1998	44.00	45
1998 Woodlawn Plantation NHP05	Retrd.	1999	24.00	26
1998 Woodlawn Plantation, AP NHP05	130	1998	44.00	35-44
1998 Woodrow Wilson House NHP06	Retrd.	1999	24.00	26
1998 Woodrow Wilson House, AP NHP06	130	1998	44.00	44

New England - S. Thompson

YEAR ISSUE	EDITION LIMIT	YEAR RETD.	ISSUE PRICE	*QUOTE U.S.$
1991 Faneuil Hall NEW09	Retrd.	1993	15.00	38-50
1990 Longfellow's House NEW01	Retrd.	1993	15.00	28-45
1990 Malden Mass. Victorian Inn NEW05	Retrd.	1992	10.00	63-94
1990 Martha's Vineyard Cottage-blue/mauve MAR06	Retrd.	1993	15.00	60
1990 Martha's Vineyard Cottage-blue/orange MAR05	Retrd.	1993	15.00	30-45
1990 Motif #1 Boathouse NEW02	Retrd.	1993	15.00	50
1990 Old North Church NEW04	Retrd.	1993	15.00	42-45
1990 Paul Revere's Home NEW03	Retrd.	1993	15.00	40-45
1991 President Bush's Home NEW07	Retrd.	1993	15.00	63-75
1991 Wedding Cake House NEW08	Retrd.	1993	15.00	43-63
1991 Set of 10	Retrd.	1993	145.00	385

North Carolina - S. Thompson

YEAR ISSUE	EDITION LIMIT	YEAR RETD.	ISSUE PRICE	*QUOTE U.S.$
1990 Josephus Hall House NC101	Retrd.	1993	15.00	40-45
1990 Presbyterian Bell Tower NC102	Retrd.	1993	15.00	29-32
1991 The Tryon Palace NC104	Retrd.	1993	15.00	36-40

Old-Fashioned Christmas - S. Thompson

YEAR ISSUE	EDITION LIMIT	YEAR RETD.	ISSUE PRICE	*QUOTE U.S.$
1994 Conway Scenic Railroad Station OFC04	Retrd.	1997	18.00	20-30
1994 Conway Scenic Railroad Station, AP OFC04	Retrd.	1994	20.00	28-50
1994 Dwight House OFC02	Retrd.	1996	18.00	22-35
1994 Dwight House, AP OFC02	Retrd.	1994	20.00	50
1994 General Merchandise OFC03	Retrd.	1997	18.00	19-38
1994 General Merchandise, AP OFC03	Retrd.	1994	20.00	28-60
1994 Old First Church OFC01	Retrd.	1997	18.00	23-30
1994 Old First Church, AP OFC01	Retrd.	1994	20.00	29-60
1994 Set of 4 1994 AP	Retrd.	1994	80.00	240
1995 Christmas Inn OFC05	Retrd.	1997	18.00	30-32
1995 Town Square Tree OFC06	Retrd.	1997	18.00	17-21

Painted Ladies I - S. Thompson

YEAR ISSUE	EDITION LIMIT	YEAR RETD.	ISSUE PRICE	*QUOTE U.S.$
1990 The Abbey LAD08	Retrd.	1992	10.00	94-150
1990 Atlanta Queen Anne LAD07	Retrd.	1992	10.00	50-94
1990 Cincinnati Gothic LAD05	Retrd.	1992	10.00	48-113
1990 Colorado Queen Anne LAD04	Retrd.	1992	10.00	50-63
1990 Illinois Queen Anne LAD06	Retrd.	1991	10.00	550-620
1990 San Francisco Italianate-yellow LAD03	Retrd.	1992	10.00	50-94
1990 San Francisco Stick House-blue LAD02	Retrd.	1991	10.00	60-75
1990 San Francisco Stick House-yellow LAD01	Retrd.	1991	10.00	57-70
1990 Painted Ladies I Sign	Retrd.	N/A	12.50	30

Painted Ladies II - S. Thompson

YEAR ISSUE	EDITION LIMIT	YEAR RETD.	ISSUE PRICE	*QUOTE U.S.$
1992 Cape May Gothic LAD13	Retrd.	1994	15.00	30-45
1994 Cape May Gothic (renovated) LAD13II	Retrd.	1995	16.00	31-35
1992 Cape May Victorian Pink House LAD16	Retrd.	1994	15.00	28-63
1994 Cape May Victorian Pink House (renovated) LAD16II	Retrd.	1996	16.00	28-30
1992 The Gingerbread Mansion LAD09	Retrd.	1994	15.00	35-45

ARCHITECTURE

YEAR ISSUE	EDITION LIMIT	YEAR RETD.	ISSUE PRICE	*QUOTE U.S.$
1994 The Gingerbread Mansion (renovated) LAD09II	Retrd.	1994	16.00	30-63
1992 Morningstar Inn LAD15	Retrd.	1994	15.00	25-63
1994 Morningstar Inn (renovated) LAD15II	Retrd.	1994	16.00	18-25
1992 Pitkin House LAD10	Retrd.	1994	15.00	25-57
1994 Pitkin House (renovated) LAD10II	Retrd.	1996	16.00	25-30
1992 Queen Anne Townhouse LAD12	Retrd.	1994	15.00	30-63
1994 Queen Anne Townhouse (renovated) LAD12II	Retrd.	1994	16.00	30-35
1992 The Victorian Blue Rose LAD14	Retrd.	1994	15.00	30-45
1994 The Victorian Blue Rose (renovated) LAD14II	Retrd.	1996	16.00	28-63
1992 The Young-Larson House LAD11	Retrd.	1994	15.00	25-45
1994 The Young-Larson House (renovated) LAD11II	Retrd.	1996	16.00	28-63

Painted Ladies III - S. Thompson

YEAR ISSUE	EDITION LIMIT	YEAR RETD.	ISSUE PRICE	*QUOTE U.S.$
1993 Cape May Green Stockton Row LAD20	Retrd.	1994	16.00	28-35
1994 Cape May Green Stockton Row (renovated) LAD20II	Retrd.	1995	16.00	25-35
1993 Cape May Linda Lee LAD17	Retrd.	1994	16.00	30-40
1994 Cape May Linda Lee (renovated) LAD17II	Retrd.	1996	16.00	20-30
1993 Cape May Pink Stockton Row LAD19	Retrd.	1994	16.00	27-39
1994 Cape May Pink Stockton Row (renovated) LAD19II	Retrd.	1998	16.00	18-23
1993 Cape May Tan Stockton Row LAD18	Retrd.	1994	16.00	25-39
1994 Cape May Tan Stockton Row (renovated) LAD18II	Retrd.	1998	16.00	20-23
1996 Cream Stockton LAD22	Retrd.	1998	19.00	25-40
1996 Cream Stockton, AP LAD22	101	1996	24.00	29-50
1995 Steiner Cottage LAD21	Retrd.	1998	17.00	20-25
1995 Steiner Cottage, AP LAD21	Retrd.	1995	24.00	28-40

Panoramic Lights - S. Thompson

YEAR ISSUE	EDITION LIMIT	YEAR RETD.	ISSUE PRICE	*QUOTE U.S.$
1996 Jeffrys Hook Light PLH02	Retrd.	1999	19.00	23
1996 Jeffrys Hook Light, AP PLH02	97	1996	24.00	35
1996 New Canal Light PLH03	Open		19.00	21
1996 New Canal Light, AP PLH03	104	1996	24.00	24-35
1997 Portland Head Light PLH05	Open		21.00	21
1996 Quoddy Head Light PLH04	Retrd.	1999	19.00	23
1996 Quoddy Head Light, AP PLH04	102	1996	24.00	24-35
1996 Split Rock Light PLH01	Retrd.	1999	19.00	23
1996 Split Rock Light, AP PLH01	105	1996	24.00	35

Philadelphia - S. Thompson

YEAR ISSUE	EDITION LIMIT	YEAR RETD.	ISSUE PRICE	*QUOTE U.S.$
1990 "Besty" Ross House (misspelling) PHI03	Retrd.	1990	15.00	69-94
1990 Betsy Ross House PHI03	Retrd.	1993	15.00	65-80
1990 Carpenter's Hall PHI01	Retrd.	1993	15.00	35-40
1990 Elphreth's Alley PHI05	Retrd.	1993	15.00	42-45
1990 Graff House PHI07	Retrd.	1993	15.00	45-69
1990 Independence Hall PHI04	Retrd.	1993	15.00	90-94
1990 Market St. Post Office PHI02	Retrd.	1993	15.00	38-45
1990 Old City Hall PHI08	Retrd.	1993	15.00	48-57
1990 Old Tavern PHI06	Retrd.	1993	15.00	38-50
1990 Set of 8	Retrd.	1993	120.00	275

Plantations - S. Thompson

YEAR ISSUE	EDITION LIMIT	YEAR RETD.	ISSUE PRICE	*QUOTE U.S.$
1996 Dickey House PLA05	Retrd.	1998	19.00	23-43
1995 Farley PLA04	Retrd.	1996	18.00	22-30
1995 Farley, AP PLA04	Retrd.	1995	24.00	16-28
1995 Longwood PLA02	Retrd.	1998	19.00	22-29
1995 Longwood, AP PLA02	Retrd.	1995	24.00	38-43
1995 Merry Sherwood PLA03	Retrd.	1998	18.00	22-30
1995 Merry Sherwood, AP PLA03	Retrd.	1995	24.00	33-50
1995 San Francisco PLA01	Retrd.	1999	19.00	23-30
1995 San Francisco, AP PLA01	Retrd.	1995	24.00	24-32

San Francisco - S. Thompson

YEAR ISSUE	EDITION LIMIT	YEAR RETD.	ISSUE PRICE	*QUOTE U.S.$
1995 Brandywine SF101	Retrd.	1998	18.00	21-37
1995 Brandywine, AP SF101	Retrd.	1995	24.00	50
1995 Eclectic Blue SF103	Retrd.	1998	19.00	21-38
1995 Eclectic Blue, AP SF103	Retrd.	1995	24.00	50
1995 Edwardian Green SF104	Retrd.	1998	18.00	21-37
1995 Edwardian Green, AP SF104	Retrd.	1995	24.00	50
1995 Queen Rose SF102	Retrd.	1998	19.00	21-38
1995 Queen Rose, AP SF102	Retrd.	1995	24.00	52

San Francisco II/ Postcard Row - S. Thompson

YEAR ISSUE	EDITION LIMIT	YEAR RETD.	ISSUE PRICE	*QUOTE U.S.$
1998 716 Steiner Street SF108	Retrd.	1999	21.00	23
1998 716 Steiner Street, AP SF108	275	1998	25.00	25

YEAR ISSUE	EDITION LIMIT	YEAR RETD.	ISSUE PRICE	*QUOTE U.S.$
1998 718 Steiner Street SF107	Retrd.	1999	21.00	22
1998 718 Steiner Street, AP SF107	275	1998	25.00	25
1998 720 Steiner Street SF106	Retrd.	1999	21.00	22
1998 720 Steiner Street, AP SF106	275	1998	25.00	25
1998 722 Steiner Street SF105	Retrd.	1999	21.00	21
1998 722 Steiner Street, AP SF105	275	1998	25.00	25

Savannah - S. Thompson

YEAR ISSUE	EDITION LIMIT	YEAR RETD.	ISSUE PRICE	*QUOTE U.S.$
1990 Andrew Low Mansion SAV02	Retrd.	1994	15.00	40-57
1996 Asendorf House SAV13	Open		19.00	22
1996 Asendorf House, AP SAV13	100	1996	24.00	32-60
1992 Cathedral of St. John SAV09	Retrd.	1994	16.00	128-138
1994 Cathedral of St. John (renovated) SAV09II	Retrd.	1995	16.00	110-150
1994 Chestnutt House SAV11	Open		18.00	22
1994 Chestnutt House, AP SAV11	Retrd.	1994	24.00	55
1990 Davenport House SAV03	Retrd.	1994	15.00	37-86
1990 Herb House SAV05	Retrd.	1993	15.00	50-75
1990 Juliette Low House (w/logo) SAV04	Retrd.	1994	15.00	22-35
1990 Juliette Low House (w/o logo) SAV04	Retrd.	1990	15.00	100-130
1994 Juliette Low House (renovated) SAV04II	Retrd.	1998	15.00	23-30
1998 King Tisdale SAV14	Open		22.00	22
1995 Mercer House SAV12	Retrd.	1998	18.00	22-45
1995 Mercer House, AP SAV12	Retrd.	1995	24.00	50-225
1990 Mikve Israel Temple SAV06	Retrd.	1994	15.00	50-86
1990 Olde Pink House SAV01	Retrd.	1994	15.00	35-50
1994 Olde Pink House (renovated) SAV01II	Retrd.	1996	15.00	40-195
1993 Owens Thomas House SAV10	Retrd.	1994	16.00	29-40
1993 Owens Thomas House, AP SAV10	Retrd.	1993	20.00	27-140
1994 Owens Thomas House (renovated) SAV10II	Retrd.	1996	16.00	55-80
1990 Savannah Gingerbread House I SAV08	Retrd.	1990	15.00	210-238
1990 Savannah Gingerbread House II SAV08	Retrd.	1992	15.00	325
1998 Tybee Island Light Station II SAV15	Open		23.00	23

Show Pieces - S. Thompson

YEAR ISSUE	EDITION LIMIT	YEAR RETD.	ISSUE PRICE	*QUOTE U.S.$
1995 Baldwin House SHW01	Retrd.	1995	20.00	30-63
1996 The Winnie Watson House SHW02	Retrd.	1996	20.00	30-63

Sights to See - S. Thompson

YEAR ISSUE	EDITION LIMIT	YEAR RETD.	ISSUE PRICE	*QUOTE U.S.$
1998 Space Needle SEE06	Retrd.	2000	24.00	24

South Carolina - S. Thompson

YEAR ISSUE	EDITION LIMIT	YEAR RETD.	ISSUE PRICE	*QUOTE U.S.$
1991 All Saints' Church SC105	Retrd.	1993	15.00	28-45
1990 The Governor's Mansion SC102	Retrd.	1995	15.00	30-45
1990 The Governor's Mansion (misspelling) SC102	Retrd.	1990	15.00	37-100
1994 The Governor's Mansion (renovated) SC102II	Retrd.	1995	15.00	30
1990 The Hermitage SC101	Retrd.	1994	15.00	29-50
1994 The Hermitage (renovated) SC101II	Retrd.	1995	15.00	45-50
1990 The Lace House SC103	Retrd.	1994	15.00	29-32
1994 The Lace House (renovated) SC103II	Retrd.	1995	15.00	15-75
1991 The State Capitol SC104	Retrd.	1994	15.00	29-63
1994 The State Capitol (renovated) SC104II	Retrd.	1994	15.00	22-115

South Carolina Ladies - S. Thompson

YEAR ISSUE	EDITION LIMIT	YEAR RETD.	ISSUE PRICE	*QUOTE U.S.$
1996 Cinnamon Hill SCL04	Retrd.	1999	19.00	23
1996 Cinnamon Hill, AP SCL04	93	1996	24.00	24-35
1996 Davis-Johnsey House SCL02	Retrd.	1999	19.00	23
1996 Davis-Johnsey House, AP SCL02	104	1996	24.00	32-35
1996 Inman House SCL01	Retrd.	1999	19.00	23
1996 Inman House, AP SCL01	107	1996	24.00	28-35
1996 Montgomery House SCL03	Retrd.	1999	19.00	23
1996 Montgomery House, AP SCL03	105	1996	24.00	24-35
1996 Set of 4 APs	Retrd.	1996	96.00	80-96

St. Augustine - S. Thompson

YEAR ISSUE	EDITION LIMIT	YEAR RETD.	ISSUE PRICE	*QUOTE U.S.$
1991 Anastasia Lighthousekeeper's House FL104	Retrd.	1993	15.00	52-88
1991 Mission Nombre deDios FL105	Retrd.	1993	15.00	51-75
1991 Old City Gates FL102	Retrd.	1993	15.00	33-35
1991 The "Oldest House" FL101	Retrd.	1993	15.00	37-42
1991 Set	Retrd.	1993	60.00	130

Texas - S. Thompson

YEAR ISSUE	EDITION LIMIT	YEAR RETD.	ISSUE PRICE	*QUOTE U.S.$
1990 The Alamo TEX01	Retrd.	1993	15.00	157-350
1990 Mission Concepcion TEX04	Retrd.	1993	15.00	45-75
1990 Mission San Francisco TEX03	Retrd.	1993	15.00	45-75
1990 Mission San Jose' TEX02	Retrd.	1993	15.00	47-94

*Quotes have been rounded up to nearest dollar

YEAR ISSUE	EDITION LIMIT	YEAR RETD.	ISSUE PRICE	*QUOTE U.S.$
1990 Texas Sign	Retrd.	N/A	12.50	23

Town Square Nativity Series - S. Thompson

YEAR ISSUE	EDITION LIMIT	YEAR RETD.	ISSUE PRICE	*QUOTE U.S.$
1998 Borrowed Eli TSN04	Retrd.	1998	15.00	16-22
1998 Heartsville Gazebo TSN01	Retrd.	1998	26.00	27
1998 Heartsville's Lil Angels TSN03	Retrd.	1998	19.00	20-30
1998 Michael Keeping Watch TSN02	Retrd.	1998	19.00	20-26
1998 Town Square Church TSN05	Retrd.	1998	22.00	23
1998 Town Square Church, AP TSN05	130	1998	43.00	43-45
1998 Town Square Nativity OFC07L	11,997	1998	27.00	35-40

Victorian Springtime - S. Thompson

YEAR ISSUE	EDITION LIMIT	YEAR RETD.	ISSUE PRICE	*QUOTE U.S.$
1993 Heffron House VST03	Retrd.	1998	17.00	20-50
1993 Heffron House, AP VST03	Retrd.	1993	20.00	45-50
1993 Jacobsen House VST04	Retrd.	1996	17.00	20-45
1993 Jacobsen House, AP VST04	Retrd.	1993	20.00	60
1993 Ralston House VST01	Retrd.	1996	17.00	20-40
1993 Ralston House, AP VST01	Retrd.	1993	20.00	100
1993 Sessions House VST02	Retrd.	1996	17.00	20-44
1993 Sessions House, AP VST02	Retrd.	1993	20.00	70
1993 Set of 4, AP	Retrd.	1993	100.00	169

Victorian Springtime II - S. Thompson

YEAR ISSUE	EDITION LIMIT	YEAR RETD.	ISSUE PRICE	*QUOTE U.S.$
1995 Dragon House VST07	Retrd.	1997	18.00	30-45
1995 Dragon House, AP VST07	Retrd.	1995	24.00	24-60
1995 E.B. Hall House VST08	Retrd.	1997	19.00	30-35
1995 E.B. Hall House, AP VST08	Retrd.	1995	24.00	50-60
1995 Gibney Home VST09	Retrd.	1997	18.00	19-30
1995 Gibney Home, AP VST09	Retrd.	1995	24.00	24-60
1995 Ray Home VST05	Retrd.	1997	18.00	20-30
1995 Ray Home, AP VST05	Retrd.	1995	24.00	24-60
1995 Victoria VST06	Retrd.	1997	18.00	40-46
1995 Victoria, AP VST06	Retrd.	1995	24.00	25-60

Victorian Springtime III - S. Thompson

YEAR ISSUE	EDITION LIMIT	YEAR RETD.	ISSUE PRICE	*QUOTE U.S.$
1996 Clark House VST14	Retrd.	1998	19.00	23-26
1996 Clark House, AP VST14	96	1996	24.00	28-50
1996 Goodwill House VST13	Retrd.	1998	19.00	24
1996 Goodwill House, AP VST13	88	1996	24.00	25-50
1996 Queen-Anne Mansion VST12	Retrd.	1998	19.00	24
1996 Queen-Anne Mansion, AP VST12	103	1996	24.00	28-50
1996 Sheppard House VST11	Retrd.	1998	19.00	24-30
1996 Sheppard House, AP VST11	98	1996	24.00	28-50
1996 Urfer House VST10	Retrd.	1998	19.00	24
1996 Urfer House, AP VST10	71	1996	24.00	25-50

Victorian Springtime IV - S. Thompson

YEAR ISSUE	EDITION LIMIT	YEAR RETD.	ISSUE PRICE	*QUOTE U.S.$
1997 Allyn Mansion VST19	Retrd.	1999	22.00	25
1997 Allyn Mansion, AP VST19	200	1997	28.00	28
1997 Halstead House VST16	Retrd.	1999	22.00	22
1997 Halstead House, AP VST16	217	1997	28.00	28
1997 Harvard House VST15	Retrd.	1999	22.00	25
1997 Harvard House, AP VST15	234	1997	28.00	28
1997 Rosewood VST18	Retrd.	1999	22.00	25
1997 Rosewood, AP VST18	244	1997	28.00	22-28
1997 Zabriskie House VST17	Retrd.	1999	22.00	25
1997 Zabriskie House, AP VST17	230	1997	28.00	28

Washington D.C. - S. Thompson

YEAR ISSUE	EDITION LIMIT	YEAR RETD.	ISSUE PRICE	*QUOTE U.S.$
1992 Cherry Trees DC005	Retrd.	1993	12.00	35-40
1992 Library of Congress DC002	Retrd.	1993	16.00	69-80
1991 National Archives DC001	Retrd.	1993	16.00	47-69
1991 Washington Monument DC004	Retrd.	1993	16.00	40-63
1992 White House DC003	Retrd.	1993	16.00	175-280
1992 Set of 5	Retrd.	1993	76.00	288-500

West Coast Lighthouse Series - S. Thompson

YEAR ISSUE	EDITION LIMIT	YEAR RETD.	ISSUE PRICE	*QUOTE U.S.$
1995 East Brother Light WCL01	Retrd.	1998	19.00	20-25
1995 East Brother Light, AP WCL01	Retrd.	1995	24.00	48
1995 Mukilteo Light WCL02	Retrd.	1998	18.00	20-25
1995 Mukilteo Light, AP WCL02	Retrd.	1995	24.00	48
1995 Point Fermin Light WCL04	Retrd.	1998	18.00	20-23
1995 Point Fermin Light, AP WCL04	Retrd.	1995	24.00	25-48
1995 Yaquina Bay Light WCL03	Retrd.	1998	18.00	20-23
1995 Yaquina Bay Light, AP WCL03	Retrd.	1995	24.00	48

Williamsburg - S. Thompson

YEAR ISSUE	EDITION LIMIT	YEAR RETD.	ISSUE PRICE	*QUOTE U.S.$
1990 Apothecary WIL09	Retrd.	1994	12.00	35-48
1992 Bruton Parish Church WIL13	Retrd.	1994	15.00	17-35
1994 Bruton Parish Church (renovated) WIL13II	Retrd.	1997	15.00	28-30
1995 Capitol WIL15	Retrd.	1999	18.00	19-23
1995 Capitol, AP WIL15	Retrd.	1995	24.00	24-50
1990 Courthouse WIL11	Retrd.	1994	15.00	23-35
1994 Courthouse (renovated) WIL11II	Retrd.	1995	15.00	29-63
1990 The Golden Ball Jeweler WIL07	Retrd.	1994	12.00	34-45
1997 Govenor's Palace Formal Entrance WIL17	Retrd.	1999	22.00	24-30
1997 Govenor's Palace Formal Entrance, AP WIL17	265	1997	28.00	28
1990 Governor's Palace WIL04	Retrd.	1994	15.00	17-48
1994 Governor's Palace (renovated) WIL04II	Retrd.	1997	15.00	22-30
1990 Homesite WIL12	Retrd.	1996	15.00	29-48
1994 Homesite (renovated) WIL12II	Retrd.	1996	15.00	17-35
1990 King's Arm Tavern WIL10	Retrd.	1994	15.00	33-57
1994 King's Arm Tavern (renovated) WIL10II	Retrd.	1995	15.00	32-50
1990 Milliner WIL06	Retrd.	1994	12.00	33-45
1990 Nicolson Shop WIL08	Retrd.	1994	12.00	35-48
1990 The Printing Offices WIL05	Retrd.	1993	12.00	32-35
1995 Raleigh Tavern WIL14	Retrd.	1999	18.00	19-25
1995 Raleigh Tavern, AP WIL14	Retrd.	1995	24.00	24-45
1997 Tayloe House WIL16	Retrd.	1999	21.00	21-23
1997 Tayloe House, AP WIL16	235	1997	27.00	27

ART GLASS & TABLE DÉCOR

Fenton Art Glass Company

Fenton Art Glass Collectors - Fenton

YEAR ISSUE	EDITION LIMIT	YEAR RETD.	ISSUE PRICE	*QUOTE U.S.$
1978 Cranberry Opalescent Baskets w/variety of spot moulds	Yr.Iss.	1978	20.00	175-225
1979 Vasa Murrhina Vases (Variety of colors)	Yr.Iss.	1979	25.00	150-175
1980 Velva Rose Bubble Optic "Melon" Vases	Yr.Iss.	1980	30.00	115-125
1981 Amethyst w/White Hanging Hearts Vases	Yr.Iss.	1981	37.50	195-250
1982 Overlay Baskets in pastel shades (Swirl Optic)	Yr.Iss.	1982	40.00	115-125
1983 Cranberry Opalescent 1 pc. Fairy Lights	Yr.Iss.	1983	40.00	295-350
1984 Blue Burmese w/peloton Treatment Vases	Yr.Iss.	1984	25.00	150-175
1985 Overlay Vases in Dusty Rose w/Mica Flecks	Yr.Iss.	1985	25.00	100-125
1986 Ruby Iridized Art Glass Vase	Yr.Iss.	1986	30.00	295-300
1987 Dusty Rose Overlay/Peach Blow Interior w/dark blue Crest Vase	Yr.Iss.	1987	38.00	110-150
1988 Teal Green and Milk marble Basket	Yr.Iss.	1988	30.00	110-125
1989 Mulberry Opalescent Basket w/Coin Dot Optic	Yr.Iss.	1989	37.50	250-295
1990 Sea Mist Green Opalescent Fern Optic Basket	Yr.Iss.	1990	40.00	75-95
1991 Rosalene Leaf Basket and Peacock & Dahlia Basket	Yr.Iss.	1991	65.00	95
1992 Blue Bubble Optic Vases	Yr.Iss.	1992	35.00	75-95
1993 Cranberry Opalescent "Jonquil" Basket	Yr.Iss.	1993	35.00	110-125
1994 Cranberry Opalescent Jacqueline Pitcher	Yr.Iss.	1994	55.00	125-150
1994 Rosalene Tulip Vase-1994 Convention Pc.	Yr.Iss.	1994	45.00	150-195
1995 Fairy Light-Blue Burmese-1995 Convention Pc.	Yr.Iss.	1995	45.00	295-325
1996 Temple Jar, Burmese-1996 Convention Pc.	Yr.Iss.	1996	65.00	195-225
1997 Mouthblown Egg, Topaz Opal Irid. Hndpt.	Yr.Iss.	1997	65.00	175-195

Collector's Club-Glass Messenger Subscribers Only - Various

YEAR ISSUE	EDITION LIMIT	YEAR RETD.	ISSUE PRICE	*QUOTE U.S.$
1996 Basket, Roselle on Cranberry - M. Reynolds	Yr.Iss.	1996	89.00	130
1997 Vase, French Rose on Rosalene - M. Reynolds	Yr.Iss.	1997	95.00	195-225
1998 Vase, Morning Glory on Burmese - F. Burton	Yr.Iss.	1998	95.00	95
1999 Vase, Blue Harmony - M. Reynolds & F. Burton	Yr.Iss.	1999	95.00	95
2000 Basket, Dancing Windflowers on Lotus Mist - M. Reynolds	Yr.Iss.	2000	95.00	95
2001 Pitcher, Visions on Royal Purple - M. Reynolds	Yr.Iss.	2001	95.00	95

YEAR ISSUE	EDITION LIMIT	YEAR RETD.	ISSUE PRICE	*QUOTE U.S.$
2002 Sunset Overlay Camellia Ginger Jar w/cover - M. Fenton	Yr.Iss.		95.00	95
2002 Iridized Sunset Asian Goldfish - S. Fenton	Yr.Iss.		27.50	28

1983 Connoisseur Collection - Fenton

1983 Basket, 9" Vasa Murrhina	1,000	1983	75.00	125-150
1983 Craftsman Stein, White Satin Carnival	1,500	1983	35.00	50-95
1983 Cruet/Stopper Vasa Murrhina	1,000	1983	75.00	250-295
1983 Epergne Set, 5 pc. Burmese	500	1983	200.00	995-1295
1983 Vase, 4 1/2" Sculptured Rose Quartz	2,000	1983	32.50	125-155
1983 Vase, 7" Sculptured Rose Quartz	1,500	1983	50.00	120-190
1983 Vase, 9" Sculptured Rose Quartz	850	1983	75.00	220-250

1984 Connoisseur Collection - Fenton, unless otherwise noted

1984 Basket, 10" Plated Amberina Velvet	1,250	1984	85.00	250-295
1984 Candy Box w/cover, 3 pc. Blue Burmese	1,250	1984	75.00	250-295
1984 Cane, 18" Plated Amberina Velvet	Yr.Iss.	1984	35.00	195-225
1984 Top Hat, 8" Plated Amberina Velvet	1,500	1984	65.00	250-295
1984 Vase, 9" Rose Velvet Hndpt. Floral - L. Everson	750	1984	75.00	225-295
1984 Vase, 9" Rose Velvet-Mother/Child	750	1984	125.00	250-295
1984 Vase, Swan, 8" Gold Azure	1,500	1984	65.00	295-325

1985 Connoisseur Collection - Fenton, unless otherwise noted

1985 Basket, 8 1/2" Burmese, Hndpt. - L. Everson	1,250	1985	95.00	250-295
1985 Epergne Set, 4 pc. Diamond Lace Green Opal.	1,000	1985	95.00	295-325
1985 Lamp, 22" Burmese-Butterfly, Hndpt. - L. Everson	350	1985	300.00	795-995
1985 Punch Set, 14 pc. Green Opalescent	500	1985	250.00	350-395
1985 Vase, 12" Gabrielle Scul. French Opal.	800	1985	150.00	250-295
1985 Vase, 7 1/2" Burmese-Shell - D. Barbour	950	1985	135.00	300-350
1985 Vase, 7 1/2" Chrysanthemums/ Circlet, Hndpt. - L. Everson	1,000	1985	125.00	175-250

1986 Connoisseur Collection - Fenton, unless otherwise noted

1986 Basket, Top hat Wild Rose/Teal Overlay	1,500	1986	49.00	110-125
1986 Boudoir Lamp, Cranberry Pearl	750	1986	145.00	295-350
1986 Cruet/Stopper, Cranberry Pearl	1,000	1986	75.00	295-350
1986 Handled Urn, 13" Cranberry Satin	1,000	1986	185.00	550-595
1986 Handled Vase, 7" French Royale	1,000	1986	100.00	175-195
1986 Lamp, 20" Burmese Shells Hndpt. - D. Barbour	500	1986	350.00	995
1986 Vanity Set, 4 pc. Blue Ridge	1,000	1986	125.00	225-395
1986 Vase 10 1/2" Danielle Sandcarved - R. Delaney	1,000	1986	95.00	195-225
1986 Vase, 10 1/2" Misty Morn, Hndpt. - L. Everson	1,000	1986	95.00	195-225

1987 Connoisseur Collection - Various

1987 Pitcher, 8" Enameled Azure Hndpt. - L. Everson	950	1987	85.00	125-150
1987 Vase, 7 1/4" Blossom/Bows on Cranberry Hndpt.- D. Barbour	950	1987	95.00	195-225

1988 Connoisseur Collection - Fenton, unless otherwise noted

1988 Basket, Irid. Teal Cased Vasa Murrhina	2,500	1988	65.00	125-150
1988 Candy, Wave Crest, Cranberry Hndpt. - L. Everson	2,000	1988	95.00	225-250
1988 Pitcher, Cased Cranberry/ Opal Teal Ring	3,500	1988	60.00	175-195
1988 Vase, 6" Cased Cranberry/Opal Teal/Irid.	3,500	1988	50.00	125-150

1989 Connoisseur Collection - Fenton, unless otherwise noted

1989 Basket, 7" Cranberry w/Crystal Ring Hndpt.- L. Everson	2,500	1989	85.00	175-195
1989 Candy Box, w/cover, Cranberry, Hndpt. - L. Everson	2,500	1989	85.00	125-195
1989 Epergne Set 5 pc., Rosalene	2,000	1989	250.00	595-795
1989 Lamp, 21" Rosalene Satin Hndpt. - L. Everson	1,000	1989	250.00	550-695
1989 Pitcher, Diamond Optic, Rosalene	2,500	1989	55.00	110-150
1989 Vase, Basketweave, Rosalene	2,500	1989	45.00	85-95

YEAR ISSUE	EDITION LIMIT	YEAR RETD.	ISSUE PRICE	*QUOTE U.S.$
1989 Vase, Pinch, 8" Vasa Murrhina	2,000	1989	65.00	110-125

1990-85th Anniversary Collection - Various

1990 Basket, 5 1/2" Trees on Burmese, Hndpt.- Piper/F. Burton	Closed	1990	57.50	125
1990 Basket, 7" Raspberry on Burmese, Hndpt. - L. Everson	Closed	1990	75.00	150-195
1990 Cruet/Stopper Petite Floral on Burmese, Hndpt. - L. Everson	Closed	1990	85.00	195-250
1990 Epergne Set, 2 pc. Pt. Floral on Burmese, Hndpt. - L. Everson	Closed	1990	125.00	295-350
1990 Lamp, 20" Rose Burmese, Hndpt. - Piper/D. Barbour	Closed	1990	250.00	550-695
1990 Lamp, 21" Raspberry on Burmese, Hndpt. - Piper/D. Barbour	Closed	1990	295.00	695-995
1990 Vase, 6 1/2" Rose Burmese, Hndpt. - Piper/D. Barbour	Closed	1990	45.00	100-110
1990 Vase, 9" Trees on Burmese, Hndpt. - Piper/F. Burton	Closed	1990	75.00	220-250
1990 Vase, Fan 6" Rose Burmese, Hndpt. - Piper/D. Barbour	Closed	1990	49.50	110-125
1990 Water Set, 7 pc. Raspberry on Burmese, Hndpt. - L. Everson	Closed	1990	275.00	895-995

1991 Connoisseur Collection - Various

1991 Basket, Floral on Rosalene, Hndpt. - M. Reynolds	1,500	1991	64.00	130-150
1991 Candy Box, 3 pc. Favrene - Fenton	1,000	1991	90.00	250-295
1991 Fish, Paperweight, Rosalene - Fenton	2,000	1991	30.00	60-75
1991 Lamp, 20" Roses on Burmese, Hndpt. - Piper/F. Burton	500	1991	275.00	595-695
1991 Vase, 7 1/2" Raspberry on Burmese, Hndpt. - L. Everson	1,500	1991	65.00	110-150
1991 Vase, Floral on Favrene, Hndpt. - M. Reynolds	850	1991	125.00	350-395
1991 Vase, Fruit on Favrene, Hndpt. - F. Burton	850	1991	125.00	395-450

1992 Connoisseur Collection - Various

1992 Covered Box, Poppy/Daisy, Hndpt. - F. Burton	1,250	1992	95.00	200-225
1992 Pitcher, 4 1/2" Berries on Burmese, Hndpt. - M. Reynolds	1,500	1992	65.00	150-195
1992 Pitcher, 9" Empire on Cranberry, Hndpt. - M. Reynolds	950	1992	110.00	225-250
1992 Vase, 6 1/2" Raspberry on Burmese - L. Everson	1,500	1992	45.00	150-195
1992 Vase, 8" Seascape, Hndpt. - F. Burton	750	1992	150.00	225-295
1992 Vase, Twining Floral Rosalene Satin, Hndpt. - M. Reynolds	950	1992	110.00	175-195

1993 Connoisseur Collection - Various

1993 Amphora w/Stand, Favrene, Hndpt. - M. Reynolds	850	1993	285.00	350-395
1993 Bowl, Ruby Stretch w/Gold Scrolls, Hndpt. - M. Reynolds	1,250	1993	95.00	150-195
1993 Lamp, Spring Woods Reverse Hndpt. - F. Burton	500	1993	595.00	595-795
1993 Owl Figurine, 6" Favrene - Fenton	1,500	1993	95.00	125-150
1993 Perfume/Stopper, Rose Trellis Rosalene, Hndpt. - F. Burton	1,250	1993	95.00	125
1993 Vase, 9" Gold Leaves Sandcarved on Plum Irid., - M. Reynolds	950	1993	175.00	250-295
1993 Vase, Victorian Roses Persian Blue Opal., Hndpt. - M. Reynolds	950	1993	125.00	150-195

1993 Family Signature Collection - Various

1993 Basket, 8 1/2" Lilacs - Bill Fenton	3,240	1993	65.00	95-125
1993 Vase, 9" Alpine Thistle/Ruby Carnival - Frank M. Fenton	1,205	1993	105.00	195-250
1993 Vase, 9" Cottage Scene - Shelley Fenton	855	1993	90.00	150-195
1993 Vase, 10" Vintage on Plum - Don Fenton	1,614	1993	80.00	150-225
1993 Vase, 11" Cranberry Dec. - George Fenton	1,217	1993	110.00	140-225

1994 Connoisseur Collection - Various

1994 Bowl, 14" Cranberry Cameo Sandcarved - Reynolds/Delaney	500	1994	390.00	390-450
1994 Clock, 4 1/2" Favrene, Hndpt. - F. Burton	850	1994	150.00	175-225
1994 Lamp, Hummingbird Reverse, Hndpt. - F. Burton	300	1994	590.00	600-750

YEAR ISSUE	EDITION LIMIT	YEAR RETD.	ISSUE PRICE	*QUOTE U.S.$
1994 Pitcher, 10" Lattice on Burmese, Hndpt. - F. Burton	750	1994	165.00	225-295
1994 Vase, 7" Favrene, Hndpt. - M. Reynolds	850	1994	185.00	225-250
1994 Vase, 8" Plum Opalescent, Hndpt. - M. Reynolds	750	1994	165.00	175-225
1994 Vase, 11" Gold Amberina, Hndpt. - M. Reynolds	750	1994	175.00	350-395

1994 Family Signature Collection - Various

1994 Basket, 7 1/2" Lilacs - Shelley Fenton	1,459	1994	65.00	95-125
1994 Basket, 8" Stiegel Green - Bill Fenton	Closed	1994	60.00	95-110
1994 Basket, 8 1/2" Ruby Carnival - Tom Fenton	1,499	1994	60.00	110-120
1994 Basket, 11" Autumn Gold Opal - Frank Fenton	1,001	1994	70.00	95-150
1994 Candy w/cover, 9 1/2" Autumn Leaves - Don Fenton	1,301	1994	60.00	75-95
1994 Pitcher, 6 1/2" Cranberry - Frank M. Fenton	Closed	1994	85.00	125-150
1994 Vase, 9 1/2" Pansies on Cranberry - Bill Fenton	1,698	1994	95.00	125
1994 Vase, 10" Fuchsia - George Fenton	1,497	1994	95.00	125-150

1995 Burmese Historic Collection - Various

1995 Basket, 8" "Butterflies" - M Reynolds	790	1995	135.00	195-200
1995 Bowl, 10 1/4" Rolled Rim "Vintage" - M. Reynolds	790	1995	150.00	200-225
1995 Lamp, 33" "Daybreak" - F. Burton	300	1995	495.00	650-795
1995 Pitcher, 10" "Cherry Blossoms & Butterfly" - M. Reynolds	790	1995	175.00	250-295
1995 Vase, 9" "Hummingbird", 11 Family Signatures - M. Reynolds	790	1995	150.00	200-250

1995 Connoisseur Collection - M. Reynolds, unless otherwise noted

1995 Amphora w/stand, 10 1/4" Royal Purple, Hndpt.	890	1995	195.00	300-350
1995 Ginger Jar, 3 Pc. 8 1/2" Favrene, Hndpt.	790	1995	275.00	400-425
1995 Lamp, 21" Butterfly/Floral Reverse, Hndpt. - F. Burton	300	1995	595.00	700-850
1995 Pitcher, 9 1/2" Victorian Art Glass, Hndpt.	490	1995	250.00	295-350
1995 Vase, 7" Aurora Wild Rose, Hndpt.	890	1995	125.00	175-195

1995 Family Signature Collection - Various

1995 Basket, 8 1/2" Trellis - Lynn Fenton	Closed	1995	85.00	85-95
1995 Basket, 9 1/2" Coralene Floral - Frank M./Bill Fenton	Closed	1995	75.00	95-120
1995 Candy w/cover, 9" Red Carnival - Mike Fenton	Closed	1995	65.00	85-120
1995 Pitcher, 9 1/2" Thistle - Don Fenton	Closed	1995	125.00	125-150
1995 Vase, 7" Gold Pansies on Cranberry - George Fenton	Closed	1995	75.00	95-120
1995 Vase, 9" Summer Garden on Spruce - Don Fenton	Closed	1995	85.00	85-95
1995 Vase, 9 1/2" Golden Flax on Cobalt - Shelley Fenton	Closed	1995	95.00	95-110

1996 Connoisseur Collection - Various

1996 Covered Box, 7" Mandarin Red, Hndpt. - K. Plauché	1,250	1996	150.00	150-225
1996 Lamp, 33" Reverse Painted Poppies, Hndpt. - F. Burton	400	1996	750.00	750-895
1996 Pitcher, 8" Dragonfly on Burmese, Hndpt. - F. Burton	1,450	1996	165.00	165-195
1996 Vase, 11" Berries on Wildrose, Hndpt. - M. Reynolds	1,250	1996	195.00	195-295
1996 Vase, 11" Queen's Bird on Burmese, Hndpt. - M. Reynolds	1,350	1996	250.00	250-395
1996 Vase, 7 1/2" Favrene Cut-Back Sandcarved - M. Reynolds	1,250	1996	195.00	250-295
1996 Vase, 8" Trout on Burmese, Hndpt. - R. Spindler	1,450	1996	135.00	135-195

1996 Family Signature Collection - Various

1996 Basket, 7 1/2" Starflower on Cran. Pearl - M. Fenton	2,430	1996	75.00	75-95
1996 Basket, 8" Mountain Berry - Don Fenton	2,033	1996	85.00	85-95
1996 Candy Box w/cover Pansies - Shelley Fenton	2,074	1996	65.00	75-95
1996 Pitcher, 6 1/2" Asters - Lynn Fenton	2,769	1996	70.00	70-95
1996 Vase, 10" Magnolia & Berry on Spruce - Tom Fenton	2,820	1996	85.00	85-95

YEAR ISSUE	EDITION LIMIT	YEAR RETD.	ISSUE PRICE	*QUOTE U.S.$
1996 Vase, 11" Meadow Beauty - Nancy Fenton	3,217	1996	95.00	95-125
1996 Vase, 8 1/2" Blush Rose on Opaline - George Fenton	2,358	1996	75.00	75-95

1996 Mulberry Historic Collection - Various

1996 Basket, 8" "Hummingbird & Wildrose" - M. Reynolds	1,250	1996	95.00	150-195
1996 Lamp, 21" "Evening Blossom w/ Ladybug" - R. Spindler	500	1996	495.00	495-695
1996 Pitcher, 7 1/2" "Evening Blossom w/ Ladybug" - R. Spindler	1,250	1996	95.00	195-225
1996 Vase, 8" Melon Herringbone "Hummingbird" - M. Reynolds	1,250	1996	85.00	150-175
1996 Vase, 9 1/2" "Hummingbird & Wildrose" - M. Reynolds	1,250	1996	95.00	150-195

1997 Connoisseur Collection - Various

1997 Basket, 11 1/2" Burmes Fenced Garden - R. Spindler	1,750	1997	160.00	160-195
1997 Lamp, 24 1/2" Reverse painted Scenic Floral - F. Burton	550	1997	750.00	795
1997 Pitcher, 6 1/2" Wildrose - K. Plauché	1,350	1997	175.00	195
1997 Vase, 8" French Opal, "Tranquility" - R. Spindler	1,500	1997	135.00	135-180
1997 Vase, 9" Faverne Daisy w/Lid - M. Reynolds	1,350	1997	295.00	295-450
1997 Vase, 9" Opaline Floral - M. Reynolds	1,500	1997	95.00	95
1997 Vase, 9 1/2" Trillium - R. Spindler	1,750	1997	195.00	195-295

1997 Family Signature Collection - Various

1997 Basket, 9" Sweetbriar on Plum Overlay - L. Spindler	2,137	1997	85.00	85-120
1997 Fairy Light, 7 1/2" Hydrangeas on Topaz - F. Fenton	2,364	1997	125.00	125-250
1997 Pitcher, 7 1/2" Irises on Misty Blue - D. Fenton	3,043	1997	85.00	85
1997 Pitcher, 8 1/2", Showcase Only - B. Fenton	945	1997	95.00	95
1997 Urn, 13" Magnolia & Berry - G. Fenton	2,108	1997	84.00	84-125
1997 Vase, 6" Field Flowers on Champ. Satin - S. Fenton	4,181	1997	55.00	55-65
1997 Vase, 8" Hydrangeas on Topaz - T. Fenton	1,607	1997	70.00	70-95
1997 Vase, 8" Medallion Collect. Floral on Black - M. Fenton	1,395	1997	75.00	75

1997 Rubina Verde Historic Collection - M. Reynolds

1997 Basket, 7 1/2" Melon	1,750	1997	99.00	125-150
1997 Box, 5 1/4" Melon	1,750	1997	135.00	150-175
1997 Lamp, 24"	650	1997	495.00	495-650
1997 Pitcher, 6"	1,750	1997	95.00	95-150
1997 Vase, 11" Melon	1,750	1997	135.00	135-190
1997 Vase, 8" Reverse Melon	1,750	1997	95.00	110-125

1998 Connoisseur Collection - Various

1998 Basket, 7 1/2" Bouquet - K. Plauché	2,250	1998	135.00	135-275
1998 Lamp, 20" Trysting Place - F. Burton	750	1998	650.00	650
1998 Lamp, 23 1/2" Jacobean Floral - M. Reynolds	750	1998	495.00	495-595
1998 Pitcher, 7" Bountiful Harvest - R. Spindler	2,250	1998	155.00	155-195
1998 Vase, 10" Papillon - K. Plauché	2,250	1998	165.00	165-195
1998 Vase, 6" Alhambra - M. Reynolds	4,604	1998	145.00	145
1998 Vase, 9 1/2" Fields of Gold, Showcase Only - M. Reynolds	1,350	1998	150.00	150-195
1998 Vase, 9" Leaves & Vines - D. Fetty	950	1998	245.00	245-350
1998 Vase, 9" Seasons - M. Reynolds	1,350	1998	250.00	250

1998 Family Signature Collection - Various

1998 Basket, 10 1/2" Topaz - S. Fenton	2,035	1998	135.00	125-135
1998 Basket, Hat 9" - T. Fenton	1,850	1998	95.00	95
1998 Bell, 6 1/2" Royal Purple - D. Fenton	3,068	1998	99.00	99
1998 Clock, 4 1/2" Misty Blue - L. Fenton	1,411	1998	95.00	95
1998 Sleigh, 7 1/2" Twining Berries - M. Fenton	Closed	1998	67.50	45-68
1998 Tulip Vase, Sea Green Satin - N. & G. Fenton	4,851	1998	99.00	99-125
1998 Vase, 8" After The Rain - R. Spindler	2,250	1998	185.00	185

1998 Royal Purple Historic Collection - F. Burton, unless otherwise noted

1998 Basket, 8" "Colonial Scroll"	2,250	1998	115.00	115
1998 Blown Bell, 6 1/2" "Colonial Scroll" - D. Fenton	3,068	1998	99.00	99

ART GLASS & TABLE DÉCOR

YEAR ISSUE	EDITION LIMIT	YEAR RETD.	ISSUE PRICE	*QUOTE U.S.$
1998 Fairy Light, 7 1/2" "Colonial Scroll"	2,250	1998	175.00	175-250
1998 Lamp, 20" "Colonial Scroll"	750	1998	350.00	350
1998 Perfume 6 1/2" "Colonial Scroll"	2,250	1998	125.00	125
1998 Pitcher, 6 1/2" "Colonial Scroll"	2,250	1998	129.00	129
1998 Tumble Up, 6" "Colonial Scroll", Showcase Only	1,049	1998	179.00	179-250
1998 Vase, 6 1/2" "Colonial Scroll"	2,950	1998	145.00	145
1998 Vase, 9 1/2" "Colonial Scroll"	2,250	1998	125.00	125

1999 Connoisseur Collection - Various

1999 Amphora, 14", Mulberry "Mystic Bird" - M. Reynolds	1,250	1999	350.00	350
1999 Basket, 7 1/2", Peach Crest "Roses" 1,750 - K. Plauché	1,750	1999	170.00	170
1999 Basket, 9 1/2", Burmese "Bluebird" - R. Spindler	2,950	1999	150.00	150
1999 Ewer, 7", Burmese "Gourds" - M. Reynolds	2,500	1999	175.00	175
1999 Ginger Jar, 6", Favrene "Orchid" - K. Plauché	1,750	1999	160.00	160
1999 Lamp, 17", Burmese "Memories" - R. Spindler	950	1999	695.00	695
1999 Lamp, 26", Reverse Painted "Tulips" - F. Burton	750	1999	695.00	695
1999 Vase, 13", Burmese "Poppies" - M. Reynolds	2,500	1999	185.00	185

1999 Family Signature Collection - Various

1999 Bellflowers on Tranquility, 9 1/2" - D. Fenton	2,692	1999	109.00	109
1999 Martha's Rose Vase, 8 1/2" - S. Fenton Ash	1,365	1999	89.00	89
1999 Morning Mist Pitcher, 6" - S. Fenton	1,890	1999	70.00	70
1999 Rosalene Basket, 8" - L. Fenton Erb	3,715	1999	99.00	99
1999 Violet Satin Covered Box, 5" - G. Fenton	1,706	1999	70.00	70
1999 Violet Satin Doll, 6 3/4", Showcase Only - N. Fenton	1,629	1999	49.00	49

1999 Gold Amberina Historic Offering - R. Spindler

1999 Basket, Hex, 11"	2,500	1999	149.00	149
1999 Cruet, 7"	2,500	1999	129.00	129
1999 Lamp, 24"	950	1999	449.00	449
1999 Pitcher, 9 1/2"	2,500	1999	145.00	145
1999 Vase, 11"	2,500	1999	135.00	135
1999 Vase, 6 1/2"	2,500	1999	95.00	95

2000 Connoisseur Collection - Various

2000 Lamp, 21", Reverse Painted "Emerald Meadow" - M. Reynolds	950	2000	595.00	595
2000 Basket, 9 1/2", Mulberry "Plum Blossoms" - M. Reynolds	1,950	2000	170.00	170
2000 Bowl w/stand, 10", Plum Opal "Botanical Cadence" - R. Spindler	1,950	2000	135.00	135
2000 Ewer Burmese, 8 1/2" "Rose Bed" - F. Burton	2,750	2000	160.00	160
2000 Ginger Jar Burmese, 8" "Daisy" - R. Spindler	2,500	2000	250.00	250
2000 Lotus Mist Burmese, 11", "Coastal Waters" - M. Reynolds	1,950	2000	295.00	295
2000 Pitcher, 7 3/4", Peach Crest "Asian Garden" - R. Spindler	1,850	2000	185.00	185
2000 Vase, 11", Mulberry, (Showcase Only), D. Fenton - R. Spindler	2,950	2000	120.00	120
2000 Vase, 7 1/2" Willow Green Opal "Hanging Hearts" -N/A	1,250	2000	250.00	250

2000 Family Signature Collection - Various

2000 Angel's Blush Perfume, 6" Willow Green - Lynn Fenton Erb	Closed	2000	89.00	89
2000 Butterfly Garden Pitcher, 5 1/2" Cobalt - D. Fenton	Closed	2000	75.00	75
2000 Butterfly Garden Vase, 8 1/2" Gold - N. Fenton	Closed	2000	95.00	95
2000 Lady Basket, 11" Lavender - T. & S. Fenton	Closed	2000	109.00	109
2000 Provincial Floral Basket, 7" Cranberry - B. Fenton	Closed	2000	85.00	85
2000 Sweet Harvest Ribbed Basket, 9" - M. Fenton	Closed	2000	65.00	65

2000 Lotus Mist Burmese Historic Collection - M. Reynolds

2000 Basket, 8 1/2"	2,950	2000	95.00	95
2000 Cruet, 8" (Showcase Only), - G. Fenton	2,950	2000	120.00	120

2000 Epergne, 9 1/2"	2,950	2000	150.00	150
2000 Lamp, 23"	1,250	2000	450.00	450
2000 Pitcher, 7"	2,950	2000	99.00	99
2000 Vase, 5"	2,950	2000	65.00	65
2000 Vase, 9 1/2"	2,950	2000	95.00	95

2001 Connoisseur Collection - Various

2001 Lamp, 23", Hummingbird Arbor - F. Burton	950	2001	650.00	650
2001 Pitcher, 10 1/2", Garden Glory on Mulberry - K. Plauché	1,850	2001	250.00	250
2001 Vase, 6 1/2", Cut Flowers - D. Fetty	1,450	2001	295.00	295
2001 Vase, 9 1/2", Meadows Poppies on Topaz Amberina - F. Burton	1,750	2001	225.00	225
2001 Vase, 9", Cranberry Splendor - S. Williams	1,750	2001	295.00	295
2001 Vase, 9", Felicity on Favrene - K. Plauché	1,850	2001	250.00	250
2001 Vase, 9", Veil Tail Habitat on Burmese - S. Williams	2,500	2001	150.00	150

2001 Family Signature Collection - Various

2001 Basket, Cranberry Opal. w/Criss-Cross - G. Fenton	Closed	2001	85.00	85
2001 Fairy Light, Atlantis, Red Carnival - T. Fenton	Closed	2001	50.00	50
2001 Melon Candy Box, Pink Chiffon - Shelley Fenton	Closed	2001	99.00	99
2001 Melon Pitcher, 10 1/2" Topaz Opal. - B. Fenton & D. Fenton	Closed	2001	129.50	130
2001 Vase, 7" Willow Green Opal. - Scott Fenton	Closed	2001	79.50	80

2001 Honor Collection - Various

2001 Basket, 8" Purple Passion Flower on Blue Burmese - R. Spindler	2,500	2001	99.50	100
2001 Cat, Symphony on Favrene - S. Williams	3,500	2001	89.50	90
2001 Covered Box, Symphony on Favrene - S. Williams	1,950	2001	175.00	175
2001 Pitcher, 7" Purple Passion Flower on Blue Burmese - R. Spindler	2,500	2001	99.50	100
2001 Vase, 13" Purple Passion Flower on Blue Burmese - R. Spindler	2,500	2001	125.00	125

2001 Legendary Fashions Collection - Fenton

2001 Evening Gown	4,750	2001	72.50	73
2001 Flapper	4,750	2001	72.50	73
2001 Gibson Girl	4,750	2001	72.50	73
2001 Poodle Skirt	4,750	2001	72.50	73
2001 Victorian Lady	4,750	2001	72.50	73

2001 Lotus Mist Burmese - K. Plauché

2001 Basket, Daisy Butterfly hndpt.	2,750	2001	115.00	115
2001 Cat, Daisy Butterfly hndpt.	4,750	2001	47.50	48
2001 Vase, 10" Daisy Butterfly hndpt.	2,750	2001	105.00	105

2001 Topaz Opalescent Historic Collection - S. Williams

2001 Basket	Closed	2001	45.00	45
2001 Basket w/Lily Trail hndpt.	Closed	2001	99.50	100
2001 Cat w/Lily Trail hndpt.	Closed	2001	39.50	40
2001 Covered Candy	Closed	2001	45.00	45
2001 Cruet w/Lily Trail hndpt	Closed	2001	109.00	109-115
2001 Diamond Lace 4 pc. Epergne	Closed	2001	225.00	225
2001 Drape Pitcher, 7 1/2" w/black base	Closed	2001	99.50	100
2001 Elephant	Closed	2001	29.50	30
2001 Elite vase, 8"	Closed	2001	37.50	38
2001 Embossed Leaf 7" Vase	Closed	2001	85.00	85
2001 Fairy light w/Lily Trail hndpt.	Closed	2001	49.50	50
2001 Flip vase, 6" w/Lily Trail hndpt.	Closed	2001	99.50	100
2001 GWTW lamp w/Lily Trail hndpt.	Closed	2001	350.00	350
2001 Hex. vase w/Lily Trail hndpt.	Closed	2001	89.50	90
2001 Melon Slipper	Closed	2001	16.50	17
2001 Mouse w/Lily Trail hndpt.	Closed	2001	29.50	30
2001 Templebells bell	Closed	2001	27.50	28

2002 Honor Collection - D. Gessell

2002 Rosalene Cat Figurine	2,750		49.50	50
2002 Rosalene Fairy Light	1,750		149.00	149
2002 Rosalene Feather Vase	1,750		109.00	109
2002 Rosalene Rose Bowl	2,500		49.50	50
2002 Rosalene Vase	2,500		65.00	65

*Quotes have been rounded up to nearest dollar

YEAR ISSUE	EDITION LIMIT	YEAR RETD.	ISSUE PRICE	*QUOTE U.S.$
2002 Legendary Fashions Collection - Fenton				
2002 Gibson Girl	4,750		72.50	73
2002 Victorian Lady	4,750		72.50	73
American Classic Series - M. Dickinson				
1986 Jupiter Train on Opal Satin, Lamp, 23"	1,000	1986	295.00	400-450
1986 Studebaker-Garford Car on Opal Satin, Lamp, 16"	1,000	1986	235.00	375-450
The Centennial Collection - F. Burton				
2000 Epergne Set, 16 1/2", Willow Green Opal	Closed	2000	350.00	350
2000 Vase, 9", Burmese Hndpt. w/Poppies	Closed	2000	175.00	175
Christmas - Various				
1978 Christmas Morn, Lamp, 16" - M. Dickinson	Yr.Iss.	1978	125.00	250-295
1978 Christmas Morn, Fairy Light - M. Dickinson	Yr.Iss.	1978	25.00	50-95
1979 Nature's Christmas, Lamp, 16" - K. Cunningham	Yr.Iss.	1979	150.00	250-295
1979 Nature's Christmas, Fairy Light - K. Cunningham	Yr.Iss.	1979	30.00	50-95
1980 Going Home, Lamp, 16" - D. Johnson	Yr.Iss.	1980	165.00	250-295
1980 Going Home, Fairy Light - D. Johnson	Yr.Iss.	1980	32.50	50-95
1981 All Is Calm, Lamp, 16" - D. Johnson	Yr.Iss.	1981	175.00	200-295
1981 All Is Calm, Lamp, 20" - D. Johnson	Yr.Iss.	1981	225.00	295-350
1981 All Is Calm, Fairy Light - D. Johnson	Yr.Iss.	1981	35.00	50-95
1982 Country Christmas, Lamp, 16" - R. Spindler	Yr.Iss.	1982	175.00	250-295
1982 Country Christmas, Lamp, 21" - R. Spindler	Yr.Iss.	1982	225.00	250-350
1982 Country Christmas, Fairy Light - R. Spindler	Yr.Iss.	1982	35.00	50-95
1983 Anticipation, Fairy Light - D. Johnson	7,500	1983	35.00	50-95
1984 Expectation, Lamp, 10 1/2" - D. Johnson	7,500	1984	75.00	275-295
1984 Expectation, Fairy Light - D. Johnson	7,500	1984	37.50	50-95
1985 Heart's Desire, Fairy Light - D. Johnson	7,500	1986	37.50	50-95
1987 Sharing The Spirit, Fairy Light - L. Everson	Yr.Iss.	1987	37.50	50-95
1987 Cardinal in the Churchyard, Lamp, 18 1/2" - D. Johnson	500	1987	250.00	295
1987 Cardinal in the Churchyard, Fairy Light - D. Johnson	4,500	1987	29.50	75-95
1988 A Chickadee Ballet, Lamp, 21" - D. Johnson	500	1988	274.00	295
1988 A Chickadee Ballet, Fairy Light - D. Johnson	4,500	1988	29.50	75-95
1989 Downy Pecker, Lamp, 16" - Chisled Song - D. Johnson	500	1989	250.00	295
1989 Downy Pecker, Fairy Light - Chisled Song - D. Johnson	4,500	1989	29.50	75-95
1990 A Blue Bird in Snowfall, Lamp, 21" - D. Johnson	500	1990	250.00	295
1990 A Blue Bird in Snowfall, Fairy Light - D. Johnson	4,500	1990	29.50	75-95
1990 Sleigh Ride, Lamp, 16" - F. Burton	1,000	1990	250.00	295-350
1990 Sleigh Ride, Fairy Light - F. Burton	3,500	1990	39.00	75-95
1991 Christmas Eve, Lamp, 16" - F. Burton	1,000	1991	250.00	295
1991 Christmas Eve, Fairy Light - F. Burton	3,500	1991	39.00	95
1992 Family Tradition, Lamp, 20" - F. Burton	1,000	1992	250.00	295-350
1992 Family Tradition, Fairy Light - F. Burton	3,500	1992	39.00	75-95
1993 Family Holiday, Lamp, 16" - F. Burton	1,000	1993	265.00	295
1993 Family Holiday, Fairy Light - F. Burton	3,500	1993	39.00	75-95
1994 Silent Night, Lamp, 16" - F. Burton	500	1994	275.00	325-350
1994 Silent Night, Fairy Light - F. Burton	1,500	1994	45.00	95-120
1994 Silent Night, Egg on Stand - F. Burton	1,500	1994	45.00	65-95
1995 Our Home Is Blessed, Lamp, 21" - F. Burton	500	1995	275.00	295-350
1995 Our Home Is Blessed, Egg - F. Burton	1,500	1995	45.00	85-95
1995 Our Home Is Blessed, Fairy Light - F. Burton	1,500	1995	45.00	95-120
1996 Star of Wonder, Lamp, 16" - F. Burton	750	1996	175.00	175-250
1996 Star of Wonder, Egg - F. Burton	1,750	1996	45.00	45-65
1996 Star of Wonder, Fairy Light - F. Burton	1,750	1996	48.00	65-95
1997 The Way Home, Lamp, 20" - F. Burton	750	1997	299.00	299-325
1997 The Way Home, Egg - F. Burton	1,750	1997	59.00	59
1997 The Way Home, Fairy Light - F. Burton	1,750	1997	65.00	65
1997 Holy Family Nativity, set/3 (1st ed.) - J. Saffell	Closed	1997	125.00	125
1997 Olde World Santa - M. Reynolds	3,750	1997	75.00	75
1998 Wise Men, set/3 (Melchoir, Caspar, Belthazar) (1st ed.) - J. Saffell	Closed	1998	155.00	155
1998 Santa, 8 1/2" Patriotic - M. Reynolds	4,750	1998	79.00	79
1998 Santa, 8" Northern Lights - R. Spindler	Closed	1998	75.00	75
1998 Angel Girl, 5 3/4" - K. Plauché	Closed	1998	47.50	50
1998 Radiant Angel, 7 1/2" - K. Plauché	Closed	1998	67.50	68
1998 The Arrival, Egg - F. Burton	2,500	1998	49.00	49
1998 The Arrival, Fairy Light - F. Burton	2,500	1998	55.00	36-55
1998 The Arrival, Lamp - F. Burton	850	1998	285.00	285
1999 Golden Age Santa, 8 1/2" - R. Spindler	Closed	1999	75.00	75
1999 Bejeweled Santa, 8" - K. Plauché	Closed	1999	75.00	75
1999 Enjantment Santa, 7" - M. Reynolds	4,750	1999	85.00	85
1999 Angel Bell, Girl, 5 3/4" - M. Reynolds	Closed	1999	47.50	48
1999 Radiant Angel 7 1/2" - M. Reynolds	Closed	1999	89.50	90
1999 The Announcement, Egg - F. Burton	2,500	1999	49.00	49
1999 The Announcement, Fairy Light - F. Burton	2,500	1999	59.00	59
1999 The Announcement, Hurricane Candle - F. Burton	1,750	1999	149.00	149
1999 Gloria Angel, Camel, Donkey - R. Spindler	Closed	1999	145.00	145
2000 Quilted Santa, 8" - M. Reynolds	Closed	2000	85.00	85
2000 Tyrolean Santa, 8 1/2" - K. Plauché	Closed	2000	85.00	85
2000 Americana Santa, 7" - R. Spindler	Closed	2000	85.00	85
2000 Radiant Angel, 7 1/2", Northern Lights - R. Spindler	Closed	2000	75.00	75
2000 Angel Bell, Girl 5 3/4", Northern Lights - R. Spindler	Closed	2000	49.50	50
2000 The Journey, Egg - F. Burton	2,500	2000	49.00	49
2000 The Journey, Fairy Light - F. Burton	2,500	2000	65.00	65
2000 The Journey, Hurricane Candle - F. Burton	1,750	2000	149.00	149
2000 Shepherds, set/3 - R. Spindler	Closed	2000	135.00	135
2001 Christmas Star Holy Family (Joseph, Mary and Baby Jesus) - J. Saffell/K. Plauché	Closed	2001	125.00	125
2001 Northwoods Santa - K. Plauché	Closed	2001	89.50	90
2001 Morning Star Santa - S. Williams	Closed	2001	89.50	90
2001 The Celebration, Egg - F. Burton	2,500	2001	49.50	50
2001 The Celebration, Fairy Light - F. Burton	2,500	2001	67.50	68
2001 The Celebration, Hurricane Lamp - F. Burton	1,750	2001	159.00	159
Designer Series - Various				
1983 Lighthouse Point, Lamp, 23 1/2" - M. Dickinson	150	1983	350.00	450-550
1983 Lighthouse Point, Lamp, 25 1/2" - M. Dickinson	150	1983	350.00	575-695
1983 Down Home, Lamp, 21" - G. Finn	300	1983	300.00	450-495
1984 Smoke 'N Cinders, Lamp, 16" - M. Dickinson	250	1984	195.00	375-495
1984 Smoke 'N Cinders, Lamp, 23" - M. Dickinson	250	1984	350.00	450-595
1984 Majestic Flight, Lamp, 16" - B. Cumberledge	250	1984	195.00	395-495
1984 Majestic Flight, Lamp, 23 1/2" - B. Cumberledge	250	1984	350.00	495-595
1985 In Season, Lamp, 16" - M. Dickinson	250	1985	225.00	450-495
1985 In Season, Lamp, 23" - M. Dickinson	250	1985	295.00	495-550
1985 Nature's Grace, Lamp, 16" - B. Cumberledge	250	1985	225.00	325-450
1985 Nature's Grace, Lamp, 23" - B. Cumberledge	295	1985	295.00	400-495
Easter Series - M. Reynolds				
1995 Fairy Light	Closed	1995	49.00	55-95
Mary Gregory - M. Reynolds				
1994 Basket, 7 1/2" Oval	Closed	1994	59.00	125-150
1995 Basket, 7 1/2" Oval	Closed	1995	65.00	125-150
1995 Egg on stand, 4" - Butterfly Delight	Closed	1995	37.50	45-95
1996 Hat Basket on Cranberry, 6 1/2"	2,000	1996	95.00	95-150
1996 Vase on Cranberry, 9"	1,500	1996	135.00	135-179
1997 Guest Set, 7" Cranberry	1,500	1997	189.00	250-295
1997 Fairy Light, 5" Cranberry	1,500	1997	79.00	150-250
1997 Basket, 8" Cranberry	1,500	1997	115.00	225-250
1998 Basket, Hex 11 1/2" Cranberry	1,950	1998	150.00	155-195
1998 Pitcher, 6 1/2" Cranberry	1,950	1998	135.00	125-175
1998 Perfume, 5 1/2" Cranberry	1,950	1998	115.00	115-195
1999 Basket, 8"	2,250	1999	129.00	129
1999 Pitcher, 7 1/2"	2,250	1999	135.00	135
1999 Lamp, 13"	1,250	1999	259.00	259

ART GLASS & TABLE DÉCOR

YEAR ISSUE	EDITION LIMIT	YEAR RETD.	ISSUE PRICE	*QUOTE U.S.$
1999 Vase, 5"	2,500	1999	69.00	69
2000 First Rain Basket, 9 1/2"	2,350	2000	139.00	139
2000 Lamp, 18"	1,250	2000	359.00	359
2000 Pillar Vase, 9"	2,350	2000	139.00	139
2001 Basket, Bird Watching	2,350		139.00	139
2001 Tumble up, Swinging	2,350		149.00	149
2001 Vase, 7" Along for the Rise	2,350		99.00	99
2001 Vase, 10" Tea Party	2,350		159.00	159

Millennium Collection - R. Spindler

1999 Circular Vase, 6 1/2"	Closed	1999	149.00	149
1999 Happiness Bird, 6"	Closed	1999	39.00	39
1999 Rolled Rim Bowl, 10"	Closed	1999	95.00	95

Miniatures - Fenton

1999 English Daisy Table Set, 5 pc.	1,500	1999	159.00	159
1998 Epergne, 4 1/2" Champagne	Closed	1998	65.00	65
1996 Epergne, 4 1/2" Opaline	Closed	1996	35.00	35-115
1996 Punch Bowl Set, 3 3/4" Dusty Rose	Closed	1996	59.00	59
1997 Punch Bowl Set, 3 3/4" Seamist Green	Closed	1997	59.00	59
1998 Punch Set, 3 3/4" Champagne	Closed	1998	75.00	75
2000 Water Set, 2 3/4" Irid.	Closed	2000	69.00	69
1998 Water Set, 4 1/2" Champagne	Closed	1998	85.00	85

Mother's Day - J. Saffell

1999 Mother and Child Pendent	Closed	1999	39.00	39

Valentine's Day Series - Fenton, unless otherwise noted

1992 Basket, 6" Cranberry Opal/Heart Optic	Closed	1992	50.00	50-150
1992 Vase, 4" Cranberry Opal/Heart Optic	Closed	1992	35.00	95-125
1992 Perfume, w/oval stopper Cranberry Opal/Heart Optic	Closed	1992	60.00	145-150
1993 Basket, 7" Caprice Cranberry Opal/Heart Optic	Closed	1993	59.00	59-170
1993 Trinket Box, 5" Cranberry Opal/Heart Optic	Closed	1993	79.00	79-170
1993 Vase, 5 1/2" Melon Cranberry Opal/Heart Optic	Closed	1993	45.00	95-110
1993 Southern Girl, 8", Hndpt. Opal Satin - M. Reynolds	Closed	1993	49.00	75-95
1993 Southern Girl, 8", Rose Pearl Irid.	Closed	1993	45.00	75-95
1994 Basket, 7" Cranberry Opal/Heart Optic	Closed	1994	65.00	120-175
1994 Vase, 5 1/2" Ribbed Cranberry Opal/Heart Optic	Closed	1994	47.50	75-95
1994 Perfume, w/ stopper, 5" Cranberry Opal/Heart Optic	Closed	1994	75.00	75-150
1995 Basket, 8" Melon Cranberry Opal/Heart Optic	Closed	1995	69.00	69-110
1995 Pitcher, 5 1/2" Melon Cranberry Opal/Heart Optic	Closed	1995	69.00	69-110
1995 Perfume, w/ heart stopper, Kristen's Floral Hndpt. - M. Reynolds	2,500	1995	49.00	49-60
1995 Doll, 7", Kristen's Floral Hndpt. Ivory Satin - M. Reynolds	2,500	1995	49.00	49-60
1996 Basket, 8" Melon Cranberry Opalescent	Closed	1996	75.00	75-110
1996 Perfume, 5" Melon Cranberry Opalescent	Closed	1996	95.00	125-150
1996 Fairy Light, 3 pc. Cranberry Opalescent	Closed	1996	135.00	195-250
1996 Vanity Set, 4 pc. Tea Rose	1,500	1996	250.00	250-295
1996 Doll, w/Musical Base Tea Rose - M. Reynolds	2,500	1996	55.00	55-95
1997 Pitcher, 6 1/2" Cranberry Opal/Heart Optic	Closed	1997	89.00	110-125
1997 Puff Box, 4" Cranberry Opal/Heart Optic	Closed	1997	79.00	120-125
1997 Hat Basket, 7" Cranberry Opal/Heart Optic	Closed	1997	79.00	110-125
1997 Vanity Set, 7" Burmese Floral & Butterfly Hndpt. - K. Reynolds	2,000	1997	225.00	295-350
1997 Girl Figurine, 8" Burmese Floral Hndpt. - R. Spindler	2,000	1997	75.00	125-150
1997 Pendant & Trinket Box, Champagne Satin	2,500	1997	65.00	65-95
1998 Fairy Light, 5", Cranberry Opal/Heart Optic	Closed	1998	65.00	65-125
1998 Vase, 5", Cranberry Opal/Heart Optic	Closed	1998	39.50	40
1998 Covered Box, 4 1/2", Cranberry Opal/Heart Optic	Closed	1998	125.00	125
1998 "Natalie" Ballerina, 6 1/2", Rosalene - R. Spindler	Closed	1998	85.00	85

YEAR ISSUE	EDITION LIMIT	YEAR RETD.	ISSUE PRICE	*QUOTE U.S.$
1998 Vase, 6", Rosebuds on Rosalene - R. Spindler	Closed	1998	69.50	70
1998 Perfume, 6 1/2", Rosebuds on Rosalene - R. Spindler	Closed	1998	85.00	85
1998 Puffbox, 4 1/2", Rosebuds on Rosalene - R. Spindler	Closed	1998	99.50	80-100
1998 Pendant & Earrings Box, Amethyst	Closed	1998	95.00	95
1999 Violets on Rosalene, Perfume, 5" - K. Plauché	Closed	1999	79.00	75-79
1999 Violets on Rosalene, Music Box, 5" - K. Plauché	Closed	1999	85.00	85
1999 Violets on Rosalene, Praying Children, 4" - K. Plauché	Closed	1999	75.00	75
1999 Violets on Rosalene, Doll, 7" - K. Plauché	Closed	1999	49.50	50
1999 Violets on Rosalene, Butterfly, 4 1/2" - K. Plauché	Closed	1999	49.50	50

Hamilton Collection

Spirit Vessels of the Wolf - K. Daniel

2001 Cry of Courage	Open		29.95	30
2001 Loyal Companions	Open		29.95	30
2001 Power of the Pack	Open		29.95	30

Lenox Classics

Home Décor Collection - Lenox

2002 Jeweled Butterfly Vase	Open		76.00	76
2002 Sunshine Meadows Vase	Open		58.50	59

Reco International

Blessings From Heaven - D. Martelli

2001 Grace Fountain	Open		50.00	50
2001 Mercy Fountain	Open		50.00	50

Royal Doulton

Burslem Artwares - C. Noke

1999 Aquatic Bowl	150	1999	1565.00	1565
1999 Bird of Paradise Vase	150	1999	1075.00	1075
1999 Canton Ginger Jar	250	1999	585.00	585
2001 Chaozhou Bowl	300		450.00	450
1999 Chengdu Bowl	250	1999	780.00	780
2001 Covered Sichuan Vase	300	2001	780.00	780
1999 Fanling Vase	250	1999	685.00	685
2000 Fanling Vase, Sung	350	2001	525.00	525
1999 Foshon Jade Vase	250	1999	585.00	585
2000 Fuyang Dragon Vase	200	2001	1325.00	1325
2001 Jianyang Vase	300		660.00	660
2000 Kowloon Dragon Vase	150	1999	1175.00	1175
2000 Kunshan Bowl, Jade	250	2001	785.00	785
2000 Lantao Vase, Sung	350	2001	525.00	525
1999 Lontao Vase, Flambe	250	1999	685.00	685
2001 Nanhai Vase	Open		225.00	225
2001 Ninghai Vase	350		450.00	450
1999 Osprey Vase	75	1999	3900.00	3900
2001 Panyu & Puning Snake Candlesticks (pr.)	250	2001	780.00	780
2000 Sanming Dragon Vase	125	2001	4485.00	4485
2001 Sanming Vase in Chang	125	2001	2950.00	2950
2001 Shantou Vase	Open		225.00	225
2001 Shenlong Dragon	250		1785.00	1785
2001 Tang Horse	250		1950.00	1950
2000 Wenzhou Bowl, Chang	250	2001	1125.00	1125
1999 Wuhan Jade Vase	250	1999	685.00	685
2001 Yantai Vase	Open		270.00	270

Royal Crown Derby Guild - Various

2000 Firecrest - R. Jefferson/S. Rowe	Yr.Iss.	2000	50.00	50
2001 Llama	Yr.Iss.	2001	185.00	185
2000 Orchard Hedgehog - J. Ablitt	Yr.Iss.	2000	125.00	125
2001 Puppy	Yr.Iss.	2001	50.00	50

Royal Crown Derby Paperweights - Various

1990 Angel Fish - R. Jefferson/J. Ledger	Retrd.	1995	140.00	140
1996 Armadillo - J. Ablitt	Retrd.	1999	140.00	145-190
1995 Ashbourne Hedgehog - R. Jefferson/J. Ablitt	500	1995	118.00	118
1990 Baby Rabbit - R. Tabbenor /B. Branscombe	Open		70.00	70

*Quotes have been rounded up to nearest dollar

YEAR ISSUE	EDITION LIMIT	YEAR RETD.	ISSUE PRICE	*QUOTE U.S.$
1986 Badger - R. Jefferson/B. Branscombe	Retrd.	1994	110.00	110
1995 Bakewell Duck - R. Jefferson/J. Ablitt	500	1995	110.00	110
1992 Bald Eagle - R. Jefferson/J. Ledger	Open		500.00	500
1995 Barn Owl - J. Ablitt	Open		150.00	150
1994 Beaver - R. Jefferson/J. Ledger	Retrd.	1997	125.00	125-172
1994 Bengal Tiger - J. Ablitt	Retrd.	1999	435.00	435
1995 Bengal Tiger Cub - J. Ablitt	Retrd.	1999	200.00	200
1995 Blue Jay - J. Ablitt	Retrd.	1999	155.00	155
1994 Blue Tit - R. Jefferson/A. Garton	Open		105.00	105
1998 Brown Pelican - J. Ablitt	Open		155.00	155
1992 Bull - R. Jefferson/J. Ledger	Open		625.00	625
1991 Bulldog - R. Jefferson/J. Ledger	Retrd.	1997	175.00	220-293
1996 Buxton Badger - R. Jefferson/J. Ablitt	500	1996	130.00	130
1996 Camel - J. Ablitt	Open		575.00	575
1985 Cat - R. Jefferson/B. Branscombe	Open		190.00	190
1997 Catnip Kitten - R. Jefferson/L. Adams	Retrd.	1997	50.00	172-196
1989 Chaffinch - R. Jefferson/J. Ledger	Open		120.00	120
1996 Cheshire Cat - R. Jefferson/J. Ablitt	500	1996	170.00	170
1991 Chevroned Butterfly Fish - R. Jefferson/J. Ledger	Retrd.	1995	140.00	140
1986 Chipmunk - R. Jefferson /B. Branscombe	Retrd.	1997	85.00	135
1992 Cockerel - R. Jefferson/J. Ledger	Retrd.	1999	95.00	150-248
1995 Contented Cat - J. Ablitt	Retrd.	1998	155.00	138-150
1996 Contented Kitten - J. Ablitt	Retrd.	1998	75.00	75-80
1995 Coot - J. Ablitt	Retrd.	1997	110.00	120-241
2000 Country Mouse - J. Ablitt	Open		95.00	95
2000 Country Mouse - J. Ablitt	Open		90.00	95
1988 Crab - R. Jefferson/B. Branscombe	Retrd.	1991	120.00	210-241
1990 Crown - R. Jefferson/J. Ledger	Retrd.	1998	160.00	160
2000 Dappled Quail - R. Jefferson/C. Adams	Open		145.00	155
1998 Debonair Bear - J. Ablitt	Retrd.	1998	130.00	130-228
1994 Deer - J. Ablitt	Retrd.	1994	250.00	250
1997 Derby Wren - R. Jefferson/S. Rowe	Retrd.	1998	50.00	50
1987 Dolphin - R. Jefferson /B. & J. Branscombe	Retrd.	1993	120.00	136
1991 Dormouse - R. Jefferson/J. Ledger	Retrd.	1995	80.00	101
1995 Dove - Gold Backstamp - J. Branscombe	50	1995	860.00	860
1995 Dove - J. Branscombe	100	1995	760.00	760
1988 Dragon - R. Jefferson/B. Branscombe	Retrd.	1992	120.00	210
1999 Drummer Bear - J. Ablitt	Open		165.00	180
1981 Duck - R. Jefferson/B. Branscombe	Retrd.	1997	95.00	135-241
1999 Duck Billed Platypus - J. Ablitt	Open		135.00	135
1999 Duck-Billed Platypus	Open		135.00	135
1990 Elephant, lg. - R. Jefferson/J. Ledger	Open		900.00	900
1990 Elephant, sm. - R. Tabbenor/J. Ledger	Open		295.00	295
1996 Fawn - J. Ablitt	Retrd.	1996	200.00	250
1983 Fox - R. Jefferson/B. Branscombe	Retrd.	1987	75.00	75
1983 Fox (Arctic) - R. Jefferson /B. Branscombe	Retrd.	1987	75.00	75
1983 Frog - R. Jefferson/B. Branscombe	Retrd.	1997	95.00	118
1999 Garden Snail - Tien Manh-Dinh /R. Ledger	Yr.Iss.	1999	180.00	180
1990 Ginger Cat - R. Jefferson	Retrd.	1994	125.00	125
1991 Goldcrest - R. Tabbenor/J. Ledger	Open		70.00	70
1986 Golden Carp - R. Jefferson /B. Branscombe	Retrd.	1991	125.00	125
1990 Gourami - R. Jefferson/J. Ledger	Retrd.	1995	140.00	140
1990 Grey Kitten - R. Jefferson /B. Branscombe	Retrd.	1995	95.00	95
1990 Gumps Large Elephant - R. Tabbenor/J. Ledger	100	1990	1000.00	1000
1990 Guppy - R. Jefferson/J. Ledger	Retrd.	1995	140.00	140
1989 Hamster - R. Jefferson/J. Ledger	Retrd.	1992	100.00	162-224
1985 Harvest Mouse - R. Jefferson /B. Branscombe	Retrd.	1994	75.00	80
1983 Hedgehog - R. Jefferson /B. Branscombe	Retrd.	1987	75.00	75
1994 Honey Bear - R. Jefferson/J. Ledger	Retrd.	1997	175.00	250-276
1990 Horse - R. Jefferson/J. Ledger	Retrd.	1993	140.00	140-414
1991 Imari Dormouse - R. Jefferson /J. Ledger	Retrd.	1994	80.00	80
1999 Kangaroo - J. Ablitt	Open		265.00	265
1993 King Charles Spaniel - R. Jefferson/J. Ledger	Retrd.	1995	125.00	125
1993 Kingfisher - R. Jefferson/D. Martin	Retrd.	2001	165.00	165
1993 Kitten - R. Tabbenor/J. Ledger	Open		120.00	120
1988 Koala - R. Jefferson/B. Branscombe	Retrd.	1993	120.00	120
1999 Koala & Baby - J. Ablitt	Open		190.00	190
1991 Koran - R. Jefferson/J. Ledger	Retrd.	1995	140.00	140
1997 Ladybug - Two Spot - J. Ablitt	Retrd.	1998	70.00	70
1992 Lamb - J. Branscombe	Retrd.	1996	75.00	158
1998 Little Owl - J. Ablitt	Open		135.00	135
1997 Majestic Cat - R. Jefferson/C. Roome	3,500	1997	180.00	180
1997 Mallard Duck - J. Ablitt	Open		165.00	165
2000 Millennium Bug - Scarab - J. Ablitt	Yr.Iss.	2000	95.00	95
1995 Mole - R. Jefferson/S. Rowe	Retrd.	1995	90.00	90
1992 Monkey & Baby - R. Jefferson /J. Ledger	Retrd.	1994	230.00	230
1997 Mulberry Hall Elephant - R. Tabbenor/L. Adams	500	1997	1190.00	1190
1996 Mulberry Hall Frog - R. Jefferson /S. Rowe	Retrd.	500	180.00	180
1997 Nesting Bullfinch - J. Ablitt	Retrd.	1999	135.00	135
1997 Nesting Chaffinch - J. Ablitt	Retrd.	1997	135.00	135-241
1997 Nesting Goldfinch - J. Ablitt	Retrd.	1999	135.00	135
1999 Nuthatch - J. Ablitt	Open		115.00	115
1998 Old Imari Frog - R. Jefferson/S. Rowe	4,500	1998	160.00	160-345
1997 Old Imari Honey Bear - R. Jefferson/S. Rowe	Open		220.00	220
1999 Old Imari Rocky Mountain Bear - R. Jefferson/S. Rowe	Open		195.00	195
1981 Owl - R. Jefferson/B. Branscombe	Retrd.	1992	95.00	135
1994 Panda - R. Jefferson/R. Harris	Retrd.	2001	165.00	165
1999 Pelican - J. Ablitt	Open		155.00	155
1981 Penguin - R. Jefferson/B. Branscombe	Retrd.	1992	95.00	95-379
1998 Penguin and Chick - J. Ablitt	Open		150.00	150
1983 Pheasant - R. Jefferson /B. Branscombe	Retrd.	1998	75.00	128
1985 Pig - R. Jefferson/B. Branscombe	Retrd.	1991	95.00	95
1996 Piglet - R. Jefferson/S. Rowe	Retrd.	1999	65.00	98-112
1988 Platypus - R. Jefferson/B.Branscombe	Retrd.	1992	120.00	120
1993 Playful Kitten - R. Tabbenor/J. Ledger	Retrd.	1996	110.00	110-259
1996 Poppy Mouse - R. Jefferson/S. Rowe	Retrd.	1996	50.00	50
1996 Puffin - J. Ablitt	Open		150.00	150
1981 Quail - R. Jefferson/B. Branscombe	Retrd.	1991	95.00	250-379
1981 Rabbit - R. Tabbenor/B. Branscombe	Open		105.00	105
1989 Ram - B. Branscombe/J. Branscombe	Retrd.	1993	250.00	250
1990 Red Fox - R. Jefferson/B. Branscombe	Retrd.	1993	85.00	85
1999 Red Squirrel - J. Ablitt	Open		135.00	135
1997 Regal Goldie Bear - J. Ablitt	1,000	1997	120.00	120
1989 Robin - R. Tabbenor/J. Ledger	Open		95.00	95
1999 Rocky Mountain Bear - R. Jefferson/S. Rowe	Open		195.00	195
1997 Rowsley Rabbit - R. Jefferson /S. Rowe	Retrd.	1997	118.00	118
1991 Russian Bear - R. Jefferson /J. Ledger	Retrd.	1998	85.00	123-224
1999 Santa and Sleigh - J. Ablitt	Open		160.00	165
1998 Santa Claus - J. Ablitt	Open		135.00	135
1991 Seahorse - J. Branscombe	Retrd.	1994	170.00	170
1983 Seal - R. Jefferson/B. Branscombe	Retrd.	1987	95.00	95
1997 Seven Spot Ladybug - J. Ablitt	Open		80.00	80
1991 Sheep - J. Branscombe	Retrd.	1995	140.00	140
1996 Siamese Cat - J. Ablitt/S. Rowe	Retrd.	2001	135.00	135
1996 Siamese Kitten - J. Ablitt/S. Rowe	Retrd.	2001	110.00	110
1999 Sitting Duckling - J. Ablitt	Open		105.00	105
1999 Sitting Piglet - J. Ablitt	Open		105.00	105
1991 Sleeping Kitten - R. Tabbenor /J. Ledger	Open		120.00	120
1999 Sleeping Piglet - J. Ablitt	Open		100.00	100
1985 Snail - R. Jefferson/B. Branscombe	Retrd.	1991	95.00	95
1989 Snake - R. Jefferson/B. Branscombe	Retrd.	1991	175.00	210-241
1991 Squirrel - R. Jefferson/J. Ledger	Retrd.	1996	100.00	100-207
2000 Striped Dolphin - R. Jefferson/S. Rowe	Open		175.00	185
1996 Swan - M. Delf	Retrd.	1999	150.00	170-183
1990 Swee - R. Jefferson/J. Ledger	Retrd.	1995	140.00	140
1990 Sweetlips - R. Jefferson/J. Ledger	Retrd.	1995	140.00	145
1999 Swimming Duckling - J. Ablitt	Open		105.00	105
1997 Teddy Bear - J. Ablitt	Open		140.00	140
1997 Teddy Bear - Red Bow Tie - J. Ablitt	950	1997	120.00	140
1993 Tiger Cub - R. Jefferson/J. Ledger	Retrd.	1995	105.00	105
1983 Turtle - R. Jefferson/B. Branscombe	Retrd.	1998	75.00	172-180
1993 Twin Lambs - J. Branscombe	Retrd.	1997	130.00	130
1987 Walrus - R. Jefferson/B. Branscombe	Retrd.	1991	70.00	210
1995 Waxwing - R. Jefferson/J. Ledger	Retrd.	1998	110.00	150-207
1991 Wren - R. Jefferson/B. Branscombe	Retrd.	2001	105.00	105-113
1995 Zebra - J. Ablitt	Retrd.	1998	375.00	328-862

YEAR ISSUE	EDITION LIMIT	YEAR RETD.	ISSUE PRICE	*QUOTE U.S.$
United Design Corp.				
Cameo Girls™ Lady Vases - Various				
2002 Abigail 1903 Party Line LV-053 - Oldham/Kaspari	2,500		45.00	45
2002 Abigail 1953 "Head's Up" LV-054 - Couch/Oldham/Kaspari	500		50.00	50
2000 Angeline 1847 Blue Bonnet Beauty LV-014 - P. Di Pasquale	Open		38.00	38
2000 Angeline 1924 Prim & Proper LV-015 - P. Di Pasquale	Open		38.00	38
2002 Angeline 1934 Foxy Lady LV-046 - Di Pasquale/Kaspari	Open		38.00	38
2000 Angeline 1952 Garden Club President LV-016 - P. Di Pasquale	Open		38.00	38
2000 Angeline 1964 Très Chic LV-017 - P. Di Pasquale	Open		38.00	38
2000 Angeline 1973 California Natural LV-018 - P. Di Pasquale	Open		38.00	38
2002 Blythe 1875 Winter Beauty LV-050 - B. Tortolani	Open		45.00	45
2001 Blythe 1912 Park Avenue Promenade LV-036 - B. Tortolani	Open		38.00	38
2001 Blythe 1930 Black Magic LV-037 - Tortolani/Kaspari	Open		38.00	38
2001 Blythe 1953 Blonde Enchantress LV-038 - Tortolani/Kaspari	Open		38.00	38
2001 Blythe 1960 Royal Wedding LV-039 - Tortolani/Kaspari	Open		38.00	38
2001 Celeste 1924 Harlem Renaissance LV-040 - Oldham/Kaspari	Open		38.00	38
2002 Celeste 1953 Sunday Best LV-051 - V. Oldham	2,500		45.00	45
2001 Celeste 1965 Moonlight and Pearls LV-041 - Oldham/Kaspari	Open		38.00	38
2001 Celeste 1987 Broadway Star LV-042 - Oldham/Kaspari	Open		38.00	38
2001 Celeste 1999 Toasting the Millennium LV-043 - Oldham/Kaspari	Open		38.00	38
2002 Clarissa 1908 Buffalo Gal LV-047 - Horine/Kaspari	Open		38.00	38
2001 Clarissa 1922 Silent Screen Siren LV-031 - C. Horine	Open		38.00	38
2000 Clarissa 1955 Beatnik Beauty LV-019 - C. Horine	Open		38.00	38
2000 Clarissa 1967 Party Girl LV-020 - C. Horine	Open		38.00	38
2001 Clarissa 1975 Toast of the Town LV-032 - Horine/Kaspari	Open		38.00	38
2002 Clarissa 1996 Blushing Bride LV-048 - Couch/Kaspari	2,500		45.00	45
2001 Eloise 1845 Southern Deb LV-033 - C. Horine	Open		38.00	38
2000 Eloise 1935 Seaside Sweetie LV-021 - C. Horine	Open		38.00	38
2000 Eloise 1944 Girl Next Door LV-022 - C. Horine	Open		38.00	38
2000 Eloise 1972 High School Sweetheart LV-023 - C. Horine	Open		38.00	38
2000 Eve 1926 Flapper Fatale LV-001 - P. Couch	Open		38.00	38
2000 Eve 1935 Uptown Style LV-002 - P. Couch	Open		38.00	38
2000 Eve 1948 Tea Party LV-003 - P. Couch	Open		38.00	38
2000 Eve 1954 Easter Outing LV-004 - P. Couch	Open		38.00	38
2000 Eve 1968 High Society LV-005 - P. Couch	Open		38.00	38
2000 Eve 1973 Folkfest Finery LV-006 - P. Couch	Open		38.00	38
2001 Eve 1987 Grand Entrance LV-027 - Couch/Kaspari	Open		38.00	38
2000 Eve 1998 Dressed for Success LV-007 - P. Couch	Open		38.00	38
2000 Judith 1809 Lovely in Lavender LV-008 - V. Oldham	Open		38.00	38
2002 Judith 1875 Victorian Valentine LV-045 - Oldham/Kaspari	Open		38.00	38
2000 Judith 1910 Transatlantic Lady LV-009 - V. Oldham	Open		38.00	38
2001 Judith 1932 Satin Doll LV-028 - Horine/Oldham	Open		38.00	38

YEAR ISSUE	EDITION LIMIT	YEAR RETD.	ISSUE PRICE	*QUOTE U.S.$
2000 Judith 1948 Big Band Beauty LV-010 - V. Oldham	Open		38.00	38
2000 Judith 1954 Ladies' Auxiliary LV-011 - V. Oldham	Open		38.00	38
2000 Judith 1968 Sorority Sister LV-012 - V. Oldham	Open		38.00	38
2001 Judith 1977 Lady Luck LV-029 - Oldham/Kaspari	Open		38.00	38
2000 Judith 1985 Athletic Allure LV-013 - V. Oldham	Open		38.00	38
2002 Sasha 1776 Stars and Stripes LV-049 - Couch/Zell	2,500		45.00	45
2000 Sasha 1848 Southern Belle LV-024 - L. Zell	Open		38.00	38
2001 Sasha 1910 Joie de Vivre LV-035 - Couch/Kaspari	Open		38.00	38
2001 Sasha 1955 Diamond Dazzler LV-034 - P. Couch	Open		38.00	38
2000 Sasha 1971 Feelin' Groovy LV-025 - L. Zell	Open		38.00	38
2000 Sasha 1983 Disco Fever LV-026 - L. Zell	Open		38.00	38

BELLS

Artists of the World

DeGrazia Bells - T. DeGrazia

YEAR ISSUE	EDITION LIMIT	YEAR RETD.	ISSUE PRICE	*QUOTE U.S.$
1980 Festival of Lights	5,000	N/A	40.00	39-75
1980 Los Ninos	7,500	N/A	40.00	46-80
1980 Los Ninos (signed)	500	N/A	80.00	250

Cherished Teddies/Enesco Group, Inc.

Cherished Teddies Bell - P. Hillman

YEAR ISSUE	EDITION LIMIT	YEAR RETD.	ISSUE PRICE	*QUOTE U.S.$
1992 Angel Bell 906530	Suspd.		20.00	44-117

Fenton Art Glass Company

1996 Designer Bell - Various

YEAR ISSUE	EDITION LIMIT	YEAR RETD.	ISSUE PRICE	*QUOTE U.S.$
1996 Floral Medallion, 6" - M. Reynolds	2,500	1996	50.00	60
1996 Gardenia, 7" - R. Spindler	2,500	1996	55.00	60
1996 Gilded Berry, 6 1/2" - F. Burton	2,500	1996	60.00	75
1996 Wild Rose, 5 1/2" - K. Plauché	2,500	1996	60.00	75

1997 Designer Bell - Various

1997 Butterflies, 6" - M. Reynolds	2,500	1997	59.00	59
1997 Feathers, 6 3/4" - R. Spindler	2,500	1997	59.00	59
1997 Forest Cottage, 7" - F. Burton	2,500	1997	59.00	59
1997 Roses on Ribbons, 6 1/2" - K. Plauché	2,500	1997	59.00	59

1998 Designer Bell - Various

1998 Bleeding Hearts, 7" - R. Spindler	2,500	1998	59.00	59
1998 Fairy Roses, 6" - K. Plauché	2,500	1998	59.00	59
1998 Hibiscus, 6 1/2" - F. Burton	2,500	1998	59.00	59
1998 Topaz Swirl, 7" - M. Reynolds	2,500	1998	59.00	75

1999 Designer Bell - Various

1999 Butterfly on Blue Burmese, 7" - F. Burton	2,500	1999	75.00	95
1999 Deco Fushia, 7" - K. Plauché	2,500	1999	65.00	65
1999 Gilded Daisy, 6" - R. Spindler	2,500	1999	65.00	65
1999 Iridescence, 7" - M. Reynolds	2,500	1999	65.00	65

2000 Designer Bell - Various

2000 Dolphin Frolic, 5 1/2" - K. Plauché	2,500	2000	65.00	65
2000 Lush Garden, 6" - F. Burton	2,500	2000	75.00	75
2000 Victorian Stripes, 6" - M. Reynolds	2,500	2000	65.00	65
2000 Water Lilies, 6 1/2" - R. Spindler	2,500	2000	65.00	65

2001 Designer Bell - Various

2001 Cotton Berry, 7" - K. Plauché	1,500	2001	65.00	65
2001 Midnight Safari, 7" - M. Reynolds	1,500	2001	65.00	65
2001 Morning Peace, 6" R. Spindler	1,500	2001	75.00	75
2001 Rose Court, 6 1/2" - F. Burton	1,500	2001	65.00	65

2002 Designer Bell - Various

2002 Butterfly Breeze - F. Burton	1,500		67.50	68
2002 Desert Moon - S. Williams	1,500		67.50	68
2002 Enchantment - K. Plauché	1,500		67.50	68

BELLS

Fenton Art Glass Company
to Precious Moments/Enesco Group, Inc.

YEAR ISSUE	EDITION LIMIT	YEAR RETD.	ISSUE PRICE	*QUOTE U.S.$
2002 Magical Meadow - R. Spindler	1,500		77.50	78

Christmas - Various

YEAR ISSUE	EDITION LIMIT	YEAR RETD.	ISSUE PRICE	*QUOTE U.S.$
1978 Christmas Morn - M. Dickinson	Yr.Iss.	1978	25.00	50
1979 Nature's Christmas - K. Cunningham	Yr.Iss.	1979	30.00	50
1980 Going Home - D. Johnson	Yr.Iss.	1980	32.50	60
1981 All Is Calm - D. Johnson	Yr.Iss.	1981	35.00	50
1982 Country Christmas - R. Spindler	Yr.Iss.	1982	35.00	50
1983 Anticipation - D. Johnson	7,500	1983	35.00	50
1984 Expectation - D. Johnson	7,500	1984	37.50	50
1985 Heart's Desire - D. Johnson	7,500	1986	37.50	50
1987 Sharing The Spirit - L. Everson	Yr.Iss.	1987	37.50	50
1987 Cardinal in the Churchyard - D. Johnson	4,500	1987	29.50	60
1988 A Chickadee Ballet - D. Johnson	4,500	1988	29.50	50
1989 Downy Pecker - Chisled Song - D. Johnson	4,500	1989	29.50	60
1990 A Blue Bird in Snowfall - D. Johnson	4,500	1990	29.50	55
1990 Sleigh Ride - F. Burton	3,500	1990	39.00	55
1991 Christmas Eve - F. Burton	3,500	1991	35.00	55
1992 Family Tradition - F. Burton	3,500	1992	39.00	55
1993 Family Holiday - F. Burton	3,500	1993	39.50	55
1994 Silent Night - F. Burton	2,500	1994	45.00	65
1995 Our Home Is Blessed - F. Burton	2,500	1995	45.00	65
1996 Star of Wonder - F. Burton	2,500	1996	48.00	65
1997 The Way Home - F. Burton	2,500	1997	65.00	65
1998 The Arrival - F. Burton	2,500	1998	55.00	55
1999 The Announcement - F. Burton	2,500	1999	59.00	59
2000 The Journey - F. Burton	2,500	2000	59.00	59
2001 The Celebration - F. Burton	2,500	2001	65.00	65

Connoisseur Bell - Various

YEAR ISSUE	EDITION LIMIT	YEAR RETD.	ISSUE PRICE	*QUOTE U.S.$
1983 Bell, Burmese Handpainted - L. Everson	2,000	1983	50.00	125
1983 Craftsman Bell, White Satin Carnival - Fenton	3,500	1983	25.00	50
1984 Bell, Famous Women's Ruby Satin Irid. - Fenton	3,500	1984	25.00	65
1985 Bell, 6 1/2" Burmese, Hndpt. - L. Everson	2,500	1985	55.00	125
1986 Bell, Burmese-Shells, Hndpt. - D. Barbour	2,500	1986	60.00	150
1988 Bell, 7" Wisteria, Hndpt. - L. Everson	4,000	1988	45.00	150
1989 Bell, 7" Handpainted Rosalene Satin - L. Everson	3,500	1989	50.00	85
1991 Bell, 7" Roses on Rosalene, Hndpt. - M. Reynolds	2,000	1991	50.00	85

Mary Gregory - M. Reynolds

YEAR ISSUE	EDITION LIMIT	YEAR RETD.	ISSUE PRICE	*QUOTE U.S.$
1993 Bell, 6" Ruby	Closed	1993	49.00	95
1994 Bell, 6" Ruby - Loves Me, Loves Me Not	Closed	1994	49.00	95
1995 Bell, 6 1/2"	Closed	1995	49.00	95
2000 Swan Lake Bell, 6 1/2"	2,350	2000	109.50	110

Goebel/M.I. Hummel

M.I. Hummel Collectibles Annual Bells - M. I. Hummel

YEAR ISSUE	EDITION LIMIT	YEAR RETD.	ISSUE PRICE	*QUOTE U.S.$
1978 Let's Sing 700	Closed	N/A	50.00	20-195
1979 Farewell 701	Closed	N/A	70.00	20-170
1980 Thoughtful 702	Closed	N/A	85.00	20-95
1981 In Tune 703	Closed	N/A	85.00	39-115
1982 She Loves Me, She Loves Me Not 704	Closed	N/A	90.00	20-140
1983 Knit One 705	Closed	N/A	90.00	30-125
1984 Mountaineer 706	Closed	N/A	90.00	20-145
1985 Sweet Song 707	Closed	N/A	90.00	20-145
1986 Sing Along 708	Closed	N/A	100.00	50-150
1987 With Loving Greetings 709	Closed	N/A	110.00	65-150
1988 Busy Student 710	Closed	N/A	120.00	35-225
1989 Latest News 711	Closed	N/A	135.00	40-240
1990 What's New? 712	Closed	N/A	140.00	50-265
1991 Favorite Pet 713	Closed	N/A	150.00	50-245
1992 Whistler's Duet 714	Closed	N/A	160.00	70-165

Greenwich Workshop

The Greenwich Workshop Collection - J. Christensen

YEAR ISSUE	EDITION LIMIT	YEAR RETD.	ISSUE PRICE	*QUOTE U.S.$
1997 The Sound of Christmas	4,896		59.00	59
1997 Christmas Bell	5,000		59.00	59
1998 '98 Mrs. Claus Bell	Open		59.00	59

Lenox China

Songs of Christmas - Unknown

YEAR ISSUE	EDITION LIMIT	YEAR RETD.	ISSUE PRICE	*QUOTE U.S.$
1991 We Wish You a Merry Christmas	Yr.Iss.	1992	49.00	49
1992 Deck the Halls	Yr.Iss.	1993	53.00	53
1993 Jingle Bells	Yr.Iss.	1994	57.00	57
1994 Silver Bells	Yr.Iss.	1995	62.00	62
1995 Hark The Herald Angels Sing	Yr.Iss.	1996	62.50	63

Lenox Crystal

Annual Bell Series - Lenox

YEAR ISSUE	EDITION LIMIT	YEAR RETD.	ISSUE PRICE	*QUOTE U.S.$
1987 Partridge Bell	Yr.Iss.	1990	45.00	45
1988 Angel Bell	Closed	1991	45.00	45
1989 St. Nicholas Bell	Closed	1991	45.00	45
1990 Christmas Tree Bell	Closed	1993	49.00	49
1991 Teddy Bear Bell	Yr.Iss.	1992	49.00	49
1992 Snowman Bell	Yr.Iss.	1993	49.00	49
1993 Nutcracker Bell	Yr.Iss.	1994	49.00	49
1994 Candle Bell	Yr.Iss.	1995	49.00	49
1995 Bell	Yr.Iss.	1996	49.50	50
1996 Bell	Yr.Iss.	1996	49.50	50

Lladró

Four Seasons Bell - Lladró

YEAR ISSUE	EDITION LIMIT	YEAR RETD.	ISSUE PRICE	*QUOTE U.S.$
1991 Spring 17613	Annual	1991	35.00	36-75
1992 Summer 17614	Annual	1992	35.00	35-75
1993 Autumn 17615	Annual	1993	35.00	34-75
1994 Winter 17616	Annual	1994	35.00	36-100

Lladró Bell - Lladró

YEAR ISSUE	EDITION LIMIT	YEAR RETD.	ISSUE PRICE	*QUOTE U.S.$
XX Crystal Wedding Bell L4500	Closed	1985	35.00	195

Lladró Christmas Bell - Lladró

YEAR ISSUE	EDITION LIMIT	YEAR RETD.	ISSUE PRICE	*QUOTE U.S.$
1987 Christmas Bell - L5458M	Annual	1987	29.50	90-150
1988 Christmas Bell - L5525M	Annual	1988	32.50	39-45
1989 Christmas Bell - L5616M	Annual	1989	32.50	100-125
1990 Christmas Bell - L5641M	Annual	1990	35.00	67-75
1991 Christmas Bell - L5803M	Annual	1991	37.50	45-67
1992 Christmas Bell - L5913M	Annual	1992	37.50	45-67
1993 Christmas Bell - L6010M	Annual	1993	39.50	45
1994 Christmas Bell - L6139M	Annual	1994	39.50	45-75
1995 Christmas Bell - L6206M	Annual	1995	39.50	45-60
1996 Christmas Bell - L6297M	Annual	1996	39.50	40-85
1997 Christmas Bell - L6441M	Annual	1997	40.00	45-55
1998 Christmas Bell - 16560	Annual	1998	40.00	45-55
1999 Christmas Bell - 16636	Annual	1999	40.00	45-70
2000 Christmas Bell - 16700	Annual	2000	45.00	45
2001 Christmas Bell - 16718	Annual	2001	40.00	40

Lladró Limited Edition Bell - Lladró

YEAR ISSUE	EDITION LIMIT	YEAR RETD.	ISSUE PRICE	*QUOTE U.S.$
1994 Eternal Love 7542M	Annual	1994	95.00	95-115

Memories of Yesterday/Enesco Group, Inc.

Annual Bells - M. Attwell

YEAR ISSUE	EDITION LIMIT	YEAR RETD.	ISSUE PRICE	*QUOTE U.S.$
1990 Here Comes the Bride-God Bless Her 523100	Retrd.	1999	25.00	25
1994 Time For Bed 525243	Retrd.	1999	25.00	25

Precious Moments/Enesco Group, Inc.

Annual Bells - S. Butcher

YEAR ISSUE	EDITION LIMIT	YEAR RETD.	ISSUE PRICE	*QUOTE U.S.$
1981 Let the Heavens Rejoice E-5622	Yr.Iss.	1981	17.00	82-220
1982 I'll Play My Drum for Him E-2358	Yr.Iss.	1982	17.00	51-60
1983 Surrounded With Joy E-0522	Yr.Iss.	1983	18.00	20-65
1984 Wishing You a Merry Christmas E-5393	Yr.Iss.	1984	19.00	22-47
1985 God Sent His Love 15873	Yr.Iss.	1985	19.00	17-40
1986 Wishing You a Cozy Christmas 102318	Yr.Iss.	1986	20.00	20-42
1987 Love is the Best Gift of All 109835	Yr.Iss.	1987	22.50	20-32
1988 Time To Wish You a Merry Christmas 115304	Yr.Iss.	1988	25.00	25-40
1989 Oh Holy Night 522821	Yr.Iss.	1989	25.00	25-36
1990 Once Upon A Holy Night 523828	Yr.Iss.	1990	25.00	22-38
1991 May Your Christmas Be Merry 524182	Yr.Iss.	1991	25.00	25-38
1992 But The Greatest Of These Is Love 527726	Yr.Iss.	1992	25.00	22-30

YEAR ISSUE	EDITION LIMIT	YEAR RETD.	ISSUE PRICE	*QUOTE U.S.$
1993 Wishing You The Sweetest Christmas 530174	Yr.Iss.	1993	25.00	23-40
1994 You're As Pretty as a Christmas Tree 604216	Yr.Iss.	1994	27.50	28-32

Various Bells - S. Butcher

1981 Jesus Loves Me (B) E-5208	Suspd.		15.00	27-46
1981 Jesus Loves Me (G) E-5209	Suspd.		15.00	38-52
1981 Prayer Changes Things E-5210	Suspd.		15.00	29-48
1981 God Understands E-5211	Retrd.	1984	15.00	27-45
1981 We Have Seen His Star E-5620	Suspd.		15.00	25-32
1981 Jesus Is Born E-5623	Suspd.		15.00	20-50
1982 The Lord Bless You and Keep You E-7175	Suspd.		17.00	19-35
1982 The Lord Bless You and Keep You E-7176	Suspd.		17.00	44
1982 The Lord Bless You and Keep You E-7179	Suspd.		22.50	30-40
1982 Mother Sew Dear E-7181	Suspd.		17.00	25-50
1982 The Purr-fect Grandma E-7183	Suspd.		17.00	25-38

River Shore

Norman Rockwell Single Issues - N. Rockwell

1981 Grandpa's Guardian	7,000	N/A	45.00	45-75
1981 Looking Out to Sea	7,000	N/A	45.00	95-125
1981 Spring Flowers	347	N/A	175.00	150-175

Rockwell Children Series I - N. Rockwell

1977 First Day of School	7,500	N/A	30.00	50-75
1977 Flowers for Mother	7,500	N/A	30.00	50-60
1977 Football Hero	7,500	N/A	30.00	50-75
1977 School Play	7,500	N/A	30.00	50-75

Rockwell Children Series II - N. Rockwell

1978 Dressing Up	15,000	N/A	35.00	50
1978 Five Cents A Glass	15,000	N/A	35.00	40-50
1978 Future All American	15,000	N/A	35.00	50
1978 Garden Girl	15,000	N/A	35.00	40-50

Roman, Inc.

F. Hook Bells - F. Hook

1985 Beach Buddies	15,000	N/A	25.00	28
1986 Sounds of the Sea	15,000	N/A	25.00	28
1987 Bear Hug	15,000	N/A	25.00	28

The Masterpiece Collection - Various

1979 Adoration - F. Lippe	Closed	N/A	20.00	20
1980 Madonna with Grapes - P. Mignard	Closed	N/A	25.00	25
1981 The Holy Family - G. Notti	Closed	N/A	25.00	25
1982 Madonna of the Streets - R. Ferruzzi	Closed	N/A	25.00	25

BOXES & MUSICALS

Artesania Rinconada Collection/John J. Madison Co. Inc.

De Rosa Box Collection - J. & J. Carbajales

2002 601 Elephant	Open		55.00	55
2001 601L Elephant	1,000		55.00	55
2002 602 Turtle	Open		55.00	55
2001 602L Turtle	1,000		55.00	55
2002 604 Owl	Open		55.00	55
2001 604L Owl	1,000		55.00	55
2002 605 Hedgehog	Open		55.00	55
2001 605L Hedgehog	1,000		55.00	55
2002 606 Cat on Pillow	Open		55.00	55
2001 606L Cat on Pillow	1,000		55.00	55
2002 607 Camel	Open		55.00	55
2001 607L Camel	1,000		55.00	55
2002 608 Frog	Open		55.00	55
2001 608L Frog	1,000		55.00	55

Boyds Collection Ltd.

Uncle Ben's Treasure Boxes™ - The Boyds Collection

2000 Candice's Apple Crate w/"Doc" McNibble 392105	6,000		14.00	14
2001 Chanel's Hat Box with Narcissus McNibble 392108	6,000		14.00	14

YEAR ISSUE	EDITION LIMIT	YEAR RETD.	ISSUE PRICE	*QUOTE U.S.$
2001 Chester's Birdhouse with Audubon McNibble 392107	6,000	2001	14.00	14-34
2000 Devon's Pile O'Leaves w/Rake McNibble 392106	6,000	2000	14.00	14-40
2002 Flopsie's Easter Basket with Cocoa McNibble 392118	6,000		14.00	14
2002 Flora's Bloomin' Bunch with Daisy McNibble (Mother's Day) 82510	6,000		14.00	14
2002 Forever Love Wedding Cake with Bride & Groom 392119	6,000		14.00	14
2000 Fuzzface's Yarn Basket w/"Purl Too" McNibble 392104	6,000	2000	14.00	14-40
2000 Indy's Treasure Chest w/Pirate McNibble 392103	6,000	2000	14.00	14-40
2001 Jack's Prize Punkin with Nutmeg McNibble 392115	Retrd.	2001	14.00	14
2001 Kendra's Watering Can with Sprinkle McNibble 392109	6,000	2001	14.00	14-40
2000 Laurel Bearibean w/Picasso Mouski...Hidden Surprises 392100	6,000	2000	14.00	13-40
2001 Lizzie's Berry Basket with Currant McNibble 392110	6,000		14.00	14
2001 Noah's Ark with Drip McNibble 392111	Retrd.	2001	14.00	14
2000 Potter Bloombeary w/Nibbles 392101	6,000	2000	13.00	13
2001 Sugar Chalet with Pudge McNibble 392116	Retrd.	2001	14.00	14
2001 Uncle Bean and McNibble Gang...Treasured Memories 3999	6,000		14.00	14
2002 Wilson's Typewriter with Underwood McNibble 392120	6,000		14.00	14
2000 Zazu's Attic Trunk w/Snoozy McNibble 392102	6,000		14.00	14

Calico Kittens/Enesco Group, Inc.

Christmas - P. Hillman

1993 Girl Kitten w/Hat & Scarf (musical) 629162	Retrd.	1998	60.00	60
1994 Hark, The Herald Angels Sing (musical) 651397	Retrd.	1996	60.00	60
1994 Hark, The Herald Angels Sing (musical) 651397	Retrd.	1996	60.00	60
1995 Hark-A-Herald Angel 144193	Retrd.	1998	17.50	18
1994 Hold On To Friendship 651079	Retrd.	1998	20.00	20
1993 Tan Angel Kitten (musical) 628212	Retrd.	1998	40.00	40
1993 Tan kitten Holding a Snowman (musical waterball) 623806	Retrd.	1998	50.00	50
1994 Tis' The Season For Sharing (musical) 628166	Retrd.	1998	25.00	25
1993 We Wish You a Merry Christmas (musical) 627526	Retrd.	1997	50.00	50
1996 We Wish You A Merry Christmas 932418	Retrd.	1998	17.50	18

Cast Art Industries

Dreamsicles - K. Haynes

1999 Sunflower Birdhouse-10772	Suspd.		19.00	19
1997 Tiny Dancer-10036	Suspd.		19.50	20

Charming Tails/Fitz and Floyd Collectibles

Charming Tails Holiday Gifts - D. Griff

2001 Everybody Sing Waterglobe 93/500	Open		36.00	36
2001 Lidded Box 93/501	Open		14.00	14

Charming Tails Love Is In The Air Gifts - D. Griff

1999 Love Bunny Music Box 93/200	Open		35.00	35
2001 Mini Lidded Ring Box 93/211	Open		15.00	15
1999 Tunnel Of Love Music Box 93/201	Open		49.50	50

Charming Tails Musicals and Waterglobes - D. Griff

2002 Here Comes Santa Claus 87/121	Open		32.00	32
1994 Jawbreakers Musical 87/542	Closed	1995	40.00	77-125
1994 Letter to Santa Waterglobe 87/518	Closed	1994	45.00	65-125
1994 Me Next! Musical 89/555	Closed	1995	45.00	198-240
1994 Mini Surprise Waterglobe 87/956	Closed	1994	22.00	54-125
1994 Mouse on Cheese, Waterglobe 92/224	Closed	1995	44.00	44
1994 Mouse on Rubber Duck, Waterglobe 92/225	Closed	1995	44.00	117-200
1994 My Hero! Waterglobe 89/557	Closed	1995	45.00	81-98
2001 Pumpkin Harvest Music Box 93/107	Open		36.00	36

YEAR ISSUE	EDITION LIMIT	YEAR RETD.	ISSUE PRICE	*QUOTE U.S.$
2001 Pumpkin Harvest Waterglobe Musical 93/112	Open		36.00	36
1995 Pumpkin Playtime Musical 85/778	Closed	1995	35.00	72-104
1993 Rocking Mice Musical 86/790	Closed	1994	65.00	150-202
1994 Sailing Away Waterglobe 87/200	Closed	1994	50.00	90-120
1994 Sharing the Warmth Waterglobe 87/517	Closed	1994	40.00	77-108
1993 Skating Mice Musical 87/511	Closed	1994	25.00	100-360
1994 Sweet Dreams Waterglobe 87/534	Closed	1994	40.00	40-48
1994 Together at Christmas, Mini Waterglobe 87/530	Closed	1995	30.00	54-80
1994 Trimmings for the Tree Waterglobe 87/516	Closed	1994	45.00	104-163
1994 Underwater Explorer Waterglobe 89/556	Closed	1995	45.00	99-250
1994 Up, Up and Away Musical 89/602	Closed	1995	70.00	190-360

Charming Tails Pumpkin Harvest Gifts - D. Griff

2001 Pumpkin Box 93/110	Open		20.00	20

Moon & Star Nursery Gifts - D. Griff

2000 Mini Lidded Box (blue) 93/608	Closed	2001	12.00	12
2000 Mini Lidded Box (pink) 93/605	Closed	2001	12.00	12

Cherished Teddies/Enesco Group, Inc.

Cherished Teddies Covered Box - P. Hillman

2001 Mermaid (2001 Summer Adoption Center Exclusive) 865087	Open		15.00	15

Department 56

Alpine Village Boxes - Department 56

1995 Silent Night Music Box 56180	Closed	1999	32.50	33

Dickens' Hinged Boxes - Department 56

1997 Bah, Humbug! 58430	Closed	2000	15.00	15
1998 Chimney Sweep 58429	Closed	2000	15.00	15
1997 God Bless Us, Every One! 58432	Closed	2000	15.00	15
1998 Royal Coach 57501	Closed	2000	25.00	25
1998 Sleighride 57502	Closed	2000	20.00	20
1997 The Spirit of Christmas 58431	Closed	2000	15.00	15
1998 Town Crier 58433	Closed	2000	15.00	15

Harry Potter Boxes - Department 56

2000 Golden Snitch 59007	Closed	2000	12.50	13
2001 Golden Snitch™ In Flight 59020	Open		13.50	14
2001 Harry And Hagrid At Gringotts 59012	Closed	2001	27.50	28
2000 Harry And The Sorting Hat 59010	Closed	2000	19.50	20
2000 Harry Potter 59008	Closed	2000	19.50	20
2001 Harry's Inheritance 59019	Open		24.00	24
2000 Hedwig The Owl 59009	Closed	2000	19.50	20
2001 Hermione Granger™ 59017	Open		24.00	24
2000 Hermione The Bookworm 59011	Closed	2000	19.50	20
2001 The Mirror of ERISED™ 59018	Open		24.00	24
2001 Professor of Potions 59016	Open		27.50	28
2001 Under The Invisibility Clock 59015	Open		24.00	24

Heritage Village Boxes - Department 56

1998 Stars and Stripes Forever Gazebo Music Box 55502	Closed	1999	50.00	50

Madeline™ Musicals - Department 56

1999 Skater's Waltz Music Box 13100	Closed	2000	40.00	40
1999 We Wish You A Merry Christmas Music Box 13101	Closed	2000	40.00	40

North Pole Hinged Boxes - Department 56

1998 Caroling Elf 57506	Closed	2000	15.00	15
1998 Elf on Sled 57505	Closed	2000	15.00	15

The Original Snow Village Collection Accessories Retired - Department 56

1999 Holy Spirit Baptistery Music Box 55022	Closed	2001	37.50	38

Silhouette Treasures (Winter Silhouette)-Music Boxes - Department 56

1992 Bedtime Stories (waterglobe/music box) 7838-7	Closed	1995	30.00	55-69
1998 Clara & The Nutcracker (waterglobe/music box) 78607	Closed	2001	32.50	33
1992 Decorating The Mantel (waterglobe, music box) 78395	Closed	1999	30.00	30

YEAR ISSUE	EDITION LIMIT	YEAR RETD.	ISSUE PRICE	*QUOTE U.S.$
1996 Father Time: As Time Goes By Music Box 78589	Closed	1999	65.00	65
1996 Father Time: Counting The Minutes Music Box 78588	Closed	1999	75.00	75
1992 Hanging The Ornaments (waterglobe, music box) 78409	Closed	1999	30.00	30
1991 Hanging The Ornaments 7793-3, set/3	Closed	1997	30.00	38-58
2002 Here Comes The Bride (waterglobe, music box) 78727	Open		32.50	33
2002 Journey to Bethlehem (waterglobe, music box) 78691	Open		32.50	33
2002 Lattice And Lace Covered Box 78715	Open		15.00	15
2001 Make A Wish Music Box 78655	Closed	2001	40.00	40
1997 Nativity (waterglobe, music box) 78599	Closed	2001	32.50	33
1995 Naughty Or Nice? Santa (waterglobe/music box) 7859-0	Closed	1997	30.00	31
2002 O' Holy Night (waterglobe, music box) 78690	Open		50.00	50
1993 Sharing A Christmas Moment Music Box 78425	Closed	1999	36.00	36
1995 Sliding In The Snow (waterglobe, music box) 78581	Closed	1999	30.00	30
2002 What Child Is This? (waterglobe, music box) 78726	Open		32.50	33

Snowbabies - Department 56

1999 Fly With Me 68949	Closed	2000	15.00	15
2002 Get Well Soon Sentiment Box 69280	Open		17.50	18
1999 Hard Landing 68948	Closed	2000	15.00	15
1998 Hold On Tight 68884	Closed	1999	15.00	15
2000 Home Sweet Home 69060	Closed	2001	15.00	15
1998 I Love You, (Mother's Day Event Piece) 68867	Closed	1998	15.00	15-25
1998 I'll Ring For You 68928	Closed	2000	15.00	15
1998 Just Imagine (hinged photo frame box) 68929	Closed	2001	15.00	15
2001 Merrily We Roll Along 69096	Open		90.00	90
2002 My Best Teacher Sentiment Box 69281	Open		17.50	18
1998 Once Upon A Time... 68883	Closed	2000	15.00	15
1997 Polar Express 68869	Open		15.00	15
1999 Reach Out 69030	Open		17.50	18
2001 Royal Treasure January 69110	Open		15.00	15
2001 Royal Treasure February 69111	Open		15.00	15
2001 Royal Treasure March 69112	Open		15.00	15
2001 Royal Treasure April 69113	Open		15.00	15
2001 Royal Treasure May 69114	Open		15.00	15
2001 Royal Treasure June 69115	Open		15.00	15
2001 Royal Treasure July 69116	Open		15.00	15
2001 Royal Treasure August 69117	Open		15.00	15
2001 Royal Treasure September 69118	Open		15.00	15
2001 Royal Treasure October 69119	Open		15.00	15
2001 Royal Treasure November 69120	Open		15.00	15
2001 Royal Treasure December 69121	Open		15.00	15
1999 Sending Hugs To You (Discover Department 56® Spring Promotion) 69027	Closed	2000	15.00	15
1999 Super Star 69029	Closed	2001	15.00	15
1997 Sweet Dreams 68868	Open		15.00	15
1998 Sweet Heart (1999 Mother's Day Event) 68930	Closed	1999	15.00	15
1999 Take The First Step 69028	Closed	2001	15.00	15
1999 Time Out 68947	Closed	2000	15.00	15
2002 Unconditional Love Sentiment Box 69282	Open		17.50	18

Snowbabies-Bisque Porcelain Boxes - Department 56

1997 Celebrate 68847	Closed	1999	15.00	15
1997 Polar Express 79782	Closed	2001	15.00	15
1997 Surprise 68846	Closed	2000	15.00	15
1997 Sweet Dreams 68868	Closed	1999	15.00	15
2001 Thread of Hope 69090	Closed	2001	15.00	15
2001 Two For Tea 69089	Closed	2001	15.00	15

Snowbabies-Music Boxes - Department 56

1993 Can I Open it Now?, mini 7648-1	Closed	1994	20.00	28-50
1997 Catch a Falling Star 6871-3	Closed	1997	37.50	32-43
1986 Catch a Falling Star 7950-2	Closed	1987	27.50	553-577
1987 Don't Fall Off 7972-3	Closed	1993	30.00	45-60
1997 Did He See You? 68870	Closed	2001	37.50	38
2002 First Love (Snowbabies Guest Collection™) 69925	Open		32.50	33

BOXES & MUSICALS

YEAR ISSUE	EDITION LIMIT	YEAR RETD.	ISSUE PRICE	*QUOTE U.S.$
1991 Frosty Frolic 7634-1	Closed	1993	110.00	121-138
1993 Frosty Fun, mini 7650-3	Closed	1994	20.00	36-39
1993 I'm So Sleepy 6851-9	Closed	2000	37.50	38
1998 I Love You From The Bottom Of My Heart (1999 Mother's Day Event) 68921	Closed	1999	30.00	30
1998 Just Follow The Star 68916	Closed	2001	48.00	48
1993 Let It Snow 6857-8	Closed	1995	100.00	100-110
2001 O Christmas Tree (The Gift of Christmas) 69130	Open		37.50	38
1996 Once Upon a Time 68832	Closed	1999	30.00	30
1991 Penguin Parade 7633-3	Closed	1994	72.00	52-77
1993 Penguin Parade, mini 7646-5	Closed	1994	20.00	36-50
1995 Play Me a Tune 68809	Closed	1998	37.50	42-45
1993 Play Me a Tune, mini 7651-1	Closed	1994	20.00	36-46
1991 Playing Games Is Fun 7632-5	Closed	1993	72.00	97-105
1993 Reading a Story, mini 7649-0	Closed	1994	20.00	32-46
2002 The Skater's Waltz (Snowbabies Babies on the Farm) 67521	Open		32.50	33
1996 Sliding Through The Milky Way 6883-3	Closed	1999	37.50	38
1999 Swing Your Partner 68953	Closed	2000	37.50	38
2000 Take Me With You 69068	Closed	2001	40.00	40
1991 We Wish You a Merry Christmas (Advent Tree) 7635-0	Closed	1994	135.00	225-245
1992 What Will I Catch? 6826-8	Closed	1998	48.00	48-65
1993 Wishing on a Star 7647-3	Closed	1994	20.00	32-50

Snowbunnies - Department 56

YEAR ISSUE	EDITION LIMIT	YEAR RETD.	ISSUE PRICE	*QUOTE U.S.$
1997 Abracadabra 26298	Closed	1999	15.00	15
1998 Alleluia 26313	Closed	2000	20.00	20
1997 And 'B' Is For Bunny (music box) 26290	Closed	1999	30.00	30
1997 Be My Baby Bunny Bee (music box) 26294	Closed	1999	32.50	35
1999 Bunny in Bloom 26332	Closed	2001	15.00	15
1999 Eye to Eye 26331	Closed	2002	15.00	15
2000 Go Bunny, Go! 26362	Closed	2002	15.00	15
1998 Happy Easter 26310	Closed	2001	15.00	15
1998 I Love You 26305	Closed	2001	15.00	15
1997 Is There Room For Me? (waterglobe, music box) 26295	Closed	2000	25.00	25
1995 Let's Play In The Meadow (waterglobe, music box) 26271	Closed	1998	25.00	25
1999 Look For The Rainbow (music box) 26337	Closed	2001	32.50	33
1995 Look What I've Got! (waterglobe, music box) 26263	Closed	1997	25.00	30-35
1997 Piggyback? 26299	Closed	2000	15.00	15
2000 Rock-A-Bye Birdie 26363	Closed	2002	15.00	15
1996 Rock-A-Bye Bunny (waterglobe, music box) 26285	Closed	1999	25.00	25
1999 Sunny Side Up 26334	Closed	2001	15.00	15
1998 Sweet Dreams 26311	Closed	2001	15.00	15
1999 Sweet Violet 26333	Closed	2001	15.00	15
1999 Talk To The Animals (waterglobe, music box) 26338	Closed	2001	25.00	25
1998 True-Blue Friends 26314	Closed	2001	20.00	20
1997 Tweet, Tweet, Tweet 26297	Closed	2000	15.00	15
1998 Two Of A Kind 26312	Closed	2001	20.00	20
1996 You Make Be Laugh (music box) 26284	Closed	1999	32.50	33-35

Encore

Santa and Snow Buddies™ Musicals - Encore

YEAR ISSUE	EDITION LIMIT	YEAR RETD.	ISSUE PRICE	*QUOTE U.S.$
2000 Buddies Dancing Together	Yr.Iss.	2000	25.00	25
1999 Buddies Musical with Harp	Retrd.	1999	19.00	19
1999 Buddies with Book	Yr.Iss.	2000	19.00	19
2000 Buddy on Horse	Yr.Iss.	2000	25.00	25
2000 Figure 8	Yr.Iss.	2000	24.00	24
2000 Santa at Workbench	Yr.Iss.	2000	19.00	19
2000 Skate with Me	Yr.Iss.	2000	25.00	25

Snow Buddies™ Musicals - Encore

YEAR ISSUE	EDITION LIMIT	YEAR RETD.	ISSUE PRICE	*QUOTE U.S.$
2001 Everybuddies Favorite Things	Closed	2001	20.00	20
2001 Shakin' Things Up!	Closed	2001	20.00	20
2001 Tight Squeeze (musical)	Open		20.00	20
2001 When Duty Calls	Closed	2001	20.00	20

G. DeBrekht Artistic Studios/Russian Gift & Jewelry

Heritage Fairy Tales and Fantasy - G. DeBrekht Artistic Studios

YEAR ISSUE	EDITION LIMIT	YEAR RETD.	ISSUE PRICE	*QUOTE U.S.$
1998 Alenushka	Open		39.00	39
1998 As if by Magic	Open		39.00	39
1998 Bear on Troika	Retrd.	2000	39.00	39
1998 Chase	Retrd.	1999	39.00	39
1998 Dance	Retrd.	2000	39.00	39
1998 Fall	Retrd.	1999	39.00	39
2001 Father Frost	350		150.00	150
1998 Fire Bird KHB/MD#326	Retrd.	1999	39.00	39
1998 Fire Bird KHB/MD#342	Open		39.00	39
1998 Flowers	Open		39.00	39
1998 Gold Cockerel	Open		39.00	39
1998 Ivan Tsarevich	Open		39.00	39
2001 Landscape	350		150.00	150
1998 Lell	Open		39.00	39
2001 The Love Musical Box	350		150.00	150
1998 The Maiden with Looking-Glass	Retrd.	2000	39.00	39
1998 Morozko	Open		39.00	39
1998 Pokrov	Retrd.	1999	39.00	39
1998 Russian North	Retrd.	1999	39.00	39
1998 Russian Winter	Retrd.	1999	39.00	39
1998 Scarlet Flower	Retrd.	1999	39.00	39
2001 Snowmaiden	350		150.00	150
1998 Snow-Maiden	Retrd.	2000	39.00	39
1998 Storm	Retrd.	2000	39.00	39
1998 Suzdal	Retrd.	1999	39.00	39
1998 Troika	Open		39.00	39
2001 Troika	350		150.00	150

Heritage Floral Fantasy - G. DeBrekht Artistic Studios

YEAR ISSUE	EDITION LIMIT	YEAR RETD.	ISSUE PRICE	*QUOTE U.S.$
2000 Bouquet Bounty	Open		47.00	47
2000 Floral Bounty	Open		25.00	25

Goebel/M.I. Hummel

M.I. Hummel Collectibles Boxes - M.I. Hummel

YEAR ISSUE	EDITION LIMIT	YEAR RETD.	ISSUE PRICE	*QUOTE U.S.$
2001 Sweet Greetings 686	Open		50.00	50

Halcyon Days Enamels

Bonbonnieres - Halcyon Days Enamels

YEAR ISSUE	EDITION LIMIT	YEAR RETD.	ISSUE PRICE	*QUOTE U.S.$
1998 Owl & Pussycat	Retrd.	1998	250.00	350-375
1999 Humpty Dumpty	Retrd.	1999	285.00	285
2000 Old Woman in A Shoe	Open		285.00	285

Christmas Boxes - Halcyon Days Enamels

YEAR ISSUE	EDITION LIMIT	YEAR RETD.	ISSUE PRICE	*QUOTE U.S.$
1973 Christmas Box (UK)	Retrd.	1973	25.00	1250-1400
1973 Christmas Box (US)	Retrd.	1973	35.00	900
1974 Christmas Box (UK)	Retrd.	1974	25.00	625-1400
1974 Christmas Box (US)	Retrd.	1974	35.00	675-725
1975 Christmas Box	Retrd.	1975	30.00	575-625
1976 Christmas Box	Retrd.	1976	30.00	450-495
1977 Christmas Box	Retrd.	1977	30.00	195-400
1978 Christmas Box	Retrd.	1978	30.00	350-495
1979 Christmas Box	Retrd.	1979	35.00	350-425
1980 Christmas Box	Retrd.	1980	50.00	380-395
1981 Christmas Box	Retrd.	1981	75.00	335
1982 Christmas Box	Retrd.	1982	75.00	340
1983 Christmas Box	Retrd.	1983	85.00	265
1984 Christmas Box	Retrd.	1984	85.00	295
1985 Christmas Box	Retrd.	1985	95.00	260
1986 Christmas Box	Retrd.	1986	100.00	235
1987 Christmas Box	Retrd.	1987	100.00	235
1988 Christmas Box	Retrd.	1988	110.00	185-210
1989 Christmas Box	Retrd.	1989	110.00	210
1990 Christmas Box	Retrd.	1990	125.00	210
1991 Christmas Box	Retrd.	1991	125.00	195
1992 Christmas Box	Retrd.	1992	135.00	210
1993 Christmas Box	Retrd.	1993	145.00	210
1994 Christmas Box	Retrd.	1994	155.00	210
1995 Christmas Box	Retrd.	1995	155.00	195
1996 Christmas Box	Retrd.	1996	155.00	185
1997 Christmas Box	Retrd.	1997	165.00	185
1998 Christmas Box	Retrd.	1998	175.00	185
1999 Christmas Box	Retrd.	1999	185.00	185
2000 Christmas Box	Retrd.	2000	185.00	185

Collectors' Information Bureau   *Quotes have been rounded up to nearest dollar

YEAR ISSUE	EDITION LIMIT	YEAR RETD.	ISSUE PRICE	*QUOTE U.S.$
Christmas Oval Boxes - Halcyon Days Enamels				
1971 Christmas Box	365	1971	25.00	925-1100
1972 Christmas Box	366	1972	25.00	835-950
1973 Christmas Box	365	1973	35.00	495-550
1974 Christmas Box	365	1974	38.00	495-625
1975 Christmas Box	365	1975	38.00	495
1976 Christmas Box	366	1976	40.00	440-465
1977 Christmas Box	365	1977	40.00	440-465
1978 Christmas Box	365	1978	40.00	400-440
1979 Christmas Box	365	1979	54.00	400-440
1980 Christmas Box	366	1980	73.00	400-440
1981 Christmas Box	365	1981	62.00	435-575
1982 Christmas Box	365	1982	63.00	400-435
Classic Pooh Series - Halcyon Days Enamels				
1995 An Astute & Helpful Bear	1,000	1998	195.00	215
1998 At Mr. Saunders House	2,500	1999	325.00	325
1999 A Bear and His Honey	750	1999	195.00	195
1995 Do Nothing Bear	1,500	1997	95.00	135
1998 Heffalumps	Open		185.00	185
1999 If You're Stuck	500	1999	345.00	345
1997 Just A Smackeral Higher	2,500	1999	195.00	195
1998 Picnic Basket Egg	1,000	1999	235.00	235
1995 Pooh and Honey Pot	Retrd.	1997	80.00	105
1997 Pooh Ornament (Event Piece)	Retrd.	1998	185.00	195
1995 Silly Old Bear Pink	Retrd.	1997	80.00	100
1995 Silly Old Blue Blue	Retrd.	1997	80.00	100
1997 Three Cheers For Pooh	Retrd.	1997	165.00	210-225
1997 Tiggers Don't Like Honey	2,500	1999	250.00	250
1998 Winnie & Fircones	1,500	1999	245.00	245
Disney Boxes - Halcyon Days Enamels				
1995 Winnie the Pooh Christmas Box	Retrd.	1995	165.00	225
1998 Let The Good Times Roll	1,250	1998	165.00	185-195
1998 Goofy Diet	1,250	1998	145.00	150-160
Easter Egg - Halcyon Days Enamels				
1973 Easter Egg	Retrd.	1973	32.00	950
1974 Easter Egg	Retrd.	1974	32.00	595
1975 Easter Egg	Retrd.	1975	32.00	575-595
1976 Easter Egg	Retrd.	1976	32.00	475
1977 Easter Egg	Retrd.	1977	32.00	460
1978 Easter Egg	Retrd.	1978	32.00	325
1979 Easter Egg	Retrd.	1979	35.00	325
1980 Easter Egg	Retrd.	1980	50.00	375
1981 Easter Egg	Retrd.	1981	60.00	295-375
1982 Easter Egg	Retrd.	1982	75.00	275-375
1983 Easter Egg	Retrd.	1983	75.00	295-375
1984 Easter Egg	Retrd.	1984	85.00	265-375
1985 Easter Egg	Retrd.	1985	95.00	265-375
1986 Easter Egg	Retrd.	1986	100.00	265-375
1987 Easter Egg	Retrd.	1987	110.00	265-300
1988 Easter Egg	Retrd.	1988	110.00	265
1989 Easter Egg	Retrd.	1989	110.00	265-300
1990 Easter Egg	Retrd.	1990	145.00	250
1991 Easter Egg	Retrd.	1991	145.00	250
1992 Easter Egg	Retrd.	1992	150.00	235
1993 Easter Egg	Retrd.	1993	165.00	235
1994 Easter Egg	Retrd.	1994	180.00	210
1995 Easter Egg	Retrd.	1995	180.00	200
1996 Easter Egg	Retrd.	1996	185.00	200
1997 Easter Egg	Retrd.	1997	195.00	235
1998 Easter Egg	Retrd.	1998	210.00	210
1999 Easter Egg	Retrd.	1999	225.00	225
2000 Easter Egg	Open		235.00	235
Mickey Christmas Boxes - Halcyon Days Enamels				
1997 Mickey	750	1997	135.00	160
1998 Mickey	750	1998	135.00	145
Millennium - Halcyon Days Enamels				
1998 Architecture	1,000	1999	325.00	350
1998 The Arts	1,000	1999	325.00	350
1999 Champagne 2000	Open		90.00	90
1999 Children of the World	Open		185.00	185
1999 International Box	Open		275.00	275
1999 International Music Box	1,000	1999	495.00	550-575
1999 Millennium Bug	Open		125.00	125
1999 Millennium Globe	Open		295.00	295
2000 Millennium Teddy	Open		125.00	125
1999 Millennium Time Capsule	500	1999	295.00	350-375
1999 Nearly the Millennium	Retrd.	1999	115.00	115-125

YEAR ISSUE	EDITION LIMIT	YEAR RETD.	ISSUE PRICE	*QUOTE U.S.$
1998 The Sciences	1,000	1999	325.00	350
1999 Time Capsule II	Open		295.00	295
2000 Travel Through the Ages	1,000		325.00	325
1999 World 2000	Open		125.00	125
Mother's Day Boxes - Halcyon Days Enamels				
1975 Mother's Day Box	Retrd.	1975	30.00	295-325
1976 Mother's Day Box	Retrd.	1976	30.00	310-319
1977 Mother's Day Box	Retrd.	1977	30.00	300
1978 Mother's Day Box	Retrd.	1978	30.00	265
1979 Mother's Day Box	Retrd.	1979	35.00	265
1980 Mother's Day Box	Retrd.	1980	50.00	250
Non Dated Enamel Boxes - Halcyon Days Enamels				
1999 Arab Tent (based on painting by E. Landseer)	250		725.00	725
1998 Aubrey Beardsley	250	1999	235.00	265
1998 Becket's Casket	250	1999	350.00	395
1996 Birds on a Wire	Retrd.	1999	165.00	200
1999 Book of Common Prayer	450		275.00	275
1998 British Humane Society	500	1999	225.00	250
1998 California Gold Rush	500	1999	295.00	295
1997 Canaletto Tercentenary	300	1997	255.00	425
1985 Cezanne's Blue Vase	250	1986	275.00	525
1992 Christopher Columbus	500	1992	275.00	395
1970 Composer, set/5	1,000	1972	500.00	2750
1999 Fantin-Latour Flowers	500		695.00	695
1996 Front Garden Buckingham Palace	500	1997	350.00	495
1999 George Washington	200	1999	245.00	245
1995 Hancock's Tea Party 25th Anniversary	Retrd.	1995	220.00	285
1999 Hassam Impressionist Garden	500		385.00	385
1997 Hong Kong Box	2,187	1997	295.00	385
1997 It Started with a Mouse (Mickey)	2,500	N/A	225.00	265
1975 Jane Austen Bicentenary	500	1975	80.00	675
1996 Jerusalem 3000th Anniversary	3,000	1996	295.00	375
1999 La Musique Music Box	200	1999	590.00	590
1998 Lady Diane Memento Box	2,965	1998	135.00	160-185
1998 Lady Diane Memorial Box	3,354	1998	225.00	225-265
1976 Liberty Bell	250	1976	45.00	255-275
1996 Monet's House At Argentuil	Retrd.	1998	375.00	395-410
1999 Monet's Lady In A Garden	500		395.00	395
1999 Monet's Sunflowers	250	1999	425.00	425
1991 Moulin Rouge	250	1992	175.00	475
1999 Napoleon Bonbonniere	250		250.00	250
1999 Nelson Bonbonniere	250		250.00	250
1994 Pennsylvania Box	350	1994	250.00	325-345
1999 Pissaro's Boulevard Montmarte	500		475.00	475
1990 Pre Raphaelite	500	1991	200.00	495
1981 Prince Charles & Lady Diana Wedding (oval)	Retrd.	1981	65.00	265-285
1998 The Quakers	200	1999	195.00	195
1990 Queen Mother's 90th Birthday	Retrd.	1990	140.00	195
1998 Renoir's Two Sisters	750	1999	375.00	375
1999 Royal Wedding	500	1999	275.00	275
1994 Rupert Bear	Retrd.	1994	175.00	225
1994 San Marco Venice	Retrd.	1995	250.00	450
1999 Shakespeare 400th Anniversary	200	1999	175.00	240-265
1991 Sherlock Homes Centenary	250	1992	280.00	550
1977 Silver Jubilee	1,000	1977	125.00	925
1972 Silver Wedding Queen Elizabeth	100	1972	95.00	945
1998 Still Life w/Flowers	100	1998	325.00	395
1993 Table of the Grand Commanders	Retrd.	1998	230.00	385
1998 Tissot's Ball on Shipboard	350	1999	425.00	425
1998 Van de Meer's Lady with Guitar Music Box	250	1999	425.00	425
1997 Watership Down	500	1999	325.00	365
1999 Wellington Bonbonniere	250		250.00	250
1998 Whistlejacket (based on painting by Stubbs)	250	1999	575.00	625
1974 Winston Churchill	500	1975	125.00	585
1976 World Wildlife, set/6	750	1976	600.00	2400
State Boxes - Halcyon Days Enamels				
2000 Florida	1,000		295.00	295
2000 Michigan	1,000		295.00	295
Valentines Day Boxes - Halcyon Days Enamels				
1974 Valentine Box	Retrd.	1974	21.00	600-650
1975 Valentine Box	Retrd.	1975	30.00	425
1976 Valentine Box	Retrd.	1976	30.00	385
1977 Valentine Box	Retrd.	1977	30.00	385
1978 Valentine Box	Retrd.	1978	30.00	310

*Quotes have been rounded up to nearest dollar

YEAR ISSUE	EDITION LIMIT	YEAR RETD.	ISSUE PRICE	*QUOTE U.S.$
1979 Valentine Box	Retrd.	1979	35.00	300
1980 Valentine Box	Retrd.	1980	50.00	265-285
1981 Valentine Box	Retrd.	1981	50.00	250
1982 Valentine Box	Retrd.	1982	50.00	240
1983 Valentine Box	Retrd.	1983	60.00	240
1984 Valentine Box	Retrd.	1984	65.00	235
1985 Valentine Box	Retrd.	1985	75.00	235
1986 Valentine Box	Retrd.	1986	80.00	235
1987 Valentine Box	Retrd.	1987	85.00	235
1988 Valentine Box	Retrd.	1988	85.00	200-235
1989 Valentine Box	Retrd.	1989	95.00	235
1990 Valentine Box	Retrd.	1990	95.00	225
1991 Valentine Box	Retrd.	1991	125.00	225

Yearly Boxes - Halcyon Days Enamels

YEAR ISSUE	EDITION LIMIT	YEAR RETD.	ISSUE PRICE	*QUOTE U.S.$
1977 Year Box	Retrd.	1977	25.00	600
1978 Year Box	Retrd.	1978	30.00	365
1979 Year Box	Retrd.	1979	30.00	300
1980 Year Box	Retrd.	1980	35.00	325
1981 Year Box	Retrd.	1981	50.00	225-275
1982 Year Box	Retrd.	1982	65.00	275
1983 Year Box	Retrd.	1983	65.00	250
1984 Year Box	Retrd.	1984	75.00	235
1985 Year Box	Retrd.	1985	85.00	235
1986 Year Box	Retrd.	1986	85.00	225-250
1987 Year Box	Retrd.	1987	95.00	235
1988 Year Box	Retrd.	1988	100.00	225
1989 Year Box	Retrd.	1989	110.00	225
1990 Year Box	Retrd.	1990	125.00	240
1994 Year Box	Retrd.	1994	N/A	232
1999 Year Box	Retrd.	1999	185.00	185
2000 Year Box	Retrd.	2000	185.00	185

Hamilton Collection

Dreamsicles Special Friends Music Box - K. Haynes

YEAR ISSUE	EDITION LIMIT	YEAR RETD.	ISSUE PRICE	*QUOTE U.S.$
1997 The Best Gift of All	Open		29.95	30
1997 Bless Us All	Open		29.95	30
1997 A Heavenly Hoorah!	Open		29.95	30
1997 Heaven's Little Helper	Open		29.95	30
1997 A Hug From The Heart	Open		29.95	30
1997 A Love Like No Other	Open		29.95	30

Sacred Encounters Totem Box - S. Kerhli

YEAR ISSUE	EDITION LIMIT	YEAR RETD.	ISSUE PRICE	*QUOTE U.S.$
1999 Keeper of Courage	Open		39.95	40
1999 Keeper of Dreams	Open		39.95	40
1999 Keeper of Strength	Open		39.95	40
1999 Keeper of Wisdom	Open		39.95	40

Sacred Keepsakes Box Collection - S. Kerhli

YEAR ISSUE	EDITION LIMIT	YEAR RETD.	ISSUE PRICE	*QUOTE U.S.$
1998 Future Pack	Open		29.95	30
1998 Guardian of Tomorrow	Open		29.95	30
1998 Legend of the Wolf	Open		29.95	30
1998 Night Watch	Open		29.95	30
1998 Priceless Treasure	Open		29.95	30
1998 Pride of the Pack	Open		29.95	30
1998 Spirit of the Hunt	Open		29.95	30
1998 Wolf Guide	Open		29.95	30

Harmony Kingdom

Royal Watch™ Collector's Club - Various

YEAR ISSUE	EDITION LIMIT	YEAR RETD.	ISSUE PRICE	*QUOTE U.S.$
1996 Big Blue - P. Calvesbert	Retrd.	1997	75.00	195-337
1996 The Big Day - P. Calvesbert	Retrd.	1996	Gift	150-195
1996 Purrfect Fit - D. Lawrence	Retrd.	1996	Gift	390-450
1996 Complete Charter Member Kit	Retrd.	1996	35.00	390-600
1997 Paper Anniversary - P. Calvesbert	Retrd.	1997	20.00	75-135
1997 Toad Pin - P. Calvesbert	Retrd.	1997	Gift	25-95
1997 Sweet as a Summer's Kiss - D. Lawrence	Retrd.	1997	Gift	72-94
1997 Big Blue 1997 - P. Calvesbert	Retrd.	1997	75.00	150-250
1997 The Sunflower - M. Perry	Retrd.	1997	70.00	125-175
1998 Cat Pin - P. Calvesbert	Retrd.	1998	Gift	30-70
1998 Mutton Chops - P. Calvesbert	Retrd.	1998	Gift	45-125
1998 Behold The King - D. Lawrence	Retrd.	1998	100.00	135-195
1998 The Mushroom - M. Perry	Retrd.	1998	120.00	120-188
1998 April's Fool Pen - D. Lawrence	Retrd.	1998	45.00	45-120
1998 Friends of the Royal Watch - D. Lawrence	526	1998	Gift	375
1999 Beneath the Ever Changing Seas - D. Lawrence	Yr.Iss.	1999	Gift	45-55

YEAR ISSUE	EDITION LIMIT	YEAR RETD.	ISSUE PRICE	*QUOTE U.S.$
1999 Murphy Lapel Pin - M. Perry	Yr.Iss.	1999	Gift	N/A
1999 Pell Mell - D. Lawrence	Yr.Iss.	1999	120.00	120-200
1999 Byron's Lonely Heart Club - M. Perry	Yr.Iss.	1999	65.00	65
1999 The Mouse That Roared - P. Calvesbert	Yr.Iss.	1999	45.00	45-85
1999 Sole Mate - D. Lawrence	Yr.Iss.	1999	35.00	35
2000 Merry-go-round - M. Perry	Yr.Iss.	2000	Gift	N/A
2000 Lover's Leap - M. Perry	Yr.Iss.	2000	Gift	18
2000 Field Day - M. Perry	Yr.Iss.	2000	Gift	N/A
2000 Byron & Bumbles - M. Perry	Yr.Iss.	2000	75.00	75
2000 Cow Town - D. Lawrence	Yr.Iss.	2000	75.00	75
2000 Silk Anniversary - P. Calvesbert	Retrd.	2000	20.00	20
2001 Minx on the Moon - A. Binder	Yr.Iss.	2001	Gift	N/A
2001 Wolfie in Space - P. Calvesbert	Yr.Iss.	2001	Gift	N/A
2001 Holding Court II - P. Calvesbert	Yr.Iss.	2001	65.00	65
2001 Night Watch - M. Baldwin	Yr.Iss.	2001	65.00	65
2001 Wood Anniversary - P. Calvesbert	Open		40.00	40
2001 Moon Rovers - S. Drackett	Yr.Iss.	2001	55.00	55
2002 Rule Britannia - P. Calvesbert			Gift	N/A
2002 Bulldog Pin - M. Baldwin	Yr.Iss.		Gift	N/A
2002 Softly Softly - A. Binder	6/03		72.00	72
2002 Haji's Hero - M. Baldwin	6/03		65.00	65

Event Pieces - Various

YEAR ISSUE	EDITION LIMIT	YEAR RETD.	ISSUE PRICE	*QUOTE U.S.$
1997 Oktobearfest - P. Calvesbert	Retrd.	1997	38.50	63-88
1997 Octobearfest (misprint on label) - P. Calvesbert	Retrd.	1997	38.50	70-95
1998 Pumpkinfest - D. Lawrence	Retrd.	1998	45.00	45-109
1999 Chucky Pig - P. Calvesbert	300	1999	Gift	375-711
1999 Gobblefest - P. Calvesbert	12,000	1999	49.00	49-65
1999 Queen of the Jungle - D. Lawrence	6,000	1999	95.00	94-118
1999 QVC Pin - M. Baldwin	7,000	1999	Gift	12-25
1999 Noah's Hideaway-Carlsbad - Martin Perry Studios	500	1999	75.00	100-150
1999 Noah's Hideaway-Portland - Martin Perry Studios	500	1999	75.00	100-150
1999 Noah's Hideaway-Tampa - Martin Perry Studios	500	1999	75.00	100-150
1999 Noah's Hideaway-Chicago - Martin Perry Studios	500	1999	75.00	100-150
1999 Noah's Hideaway-Rockville - Martin Perry Studios	500	1999	75.00	100-150
1999 Cat's Meow - P. Calvesbert	Retrd.	2000	20.00	20-75
1999 Noah's Hideaway-Merrick, NY - Martin Perry Studios	500	1999	75.00	100-150
2000 Fat Cat's Meow - M. Baldwin	Yr.Iss.	2000	35.00	35
2000 Alley Cat's Meow - M. Baldwin	3,600	2000	45.00	45-66
2000 Cat Nap's Meow - S. Rickett	3,600	2000	35.00	35-66
2000 Clair de Meow - J. Bharucha	3,600	2000	45.00	45-55
2000 Last Cat's Meow - M. Baldwin	2,000	2000	45.00	45-55
2000 Nick & Rudy Winterfest - A. Binder	10,626	2000	56.00	56-88
2001 Lord Foxglove - M. Baldwin	3,000	2001	45.00	45
2001 Bela Hallowfest - A. Binder	5,751	2001	28.00	28
2001 Fang - A. Binder	5,751	2001	28.00	28
2001 Planet Paradise - Baldwin, Calvesbert, Binder	250	2001	N/A	N/A
2001 Memories Dinner Flower Pot	1,000	2001	N/A	N/A
2001 House Party - A. Binder	624	2001	90.00	90
2001 House Party - P. Calvesbert	359	2001	90.00	90

Show Pieces - P. Calvesbert, unless otherwise noted

YEAR ISSUE	EDITION LIMIT	YEAR RETD.	ISSUE PRICE	*QUOTE U.S.$
1996 Secaucus Frog Pendant	210	1996	Gift	300-500
1996 Rosemont Frog Pendant	403	1996	Gift	200-350
1997 Long Beach Rose Pendant	552	1997	Gift	109-205
1997 Rosemont Rose Pendant	847	1997	Gift	132-188
1997 Puffin Pin	177	1997	Gift	300-500
1998 Edison Pendant	Retrd.	1998	Gift	75-237
1998 Newark Pendant	295	1998	Gift	175-265
1998 Rosemont Pendant	1,912	1998	Gift	95-162
1998 Stoneleigh Pendant	270	1998	Gift	150
1998 Tin Cat's Cruise	575	1998	Gift	375-450
1999 Camelot	1,455	1999	Gift	262-650
1999 Crooze Cat	739	1999	45.00	45
1999 Dragon's Breath - Martin Perry Studios	360	1999	Gift	N/A
1999 Long Beach Pendant - M. Baldwin	2,000	1999	Gift	50-111
1999 Primordial Sloop	855	1999	Gift	219-325
1999 Rosemont Pendant - M. Baldwin	1,956	1999	Gift	50-75
1999 Tubs Pin	566	1999	Gift	N/A
2000 Bumbles Pendent - M. Baldwin	2,000	2000	Gift	N/A
2001 Anaheim Minx Pendent - A. Binder	1,435	2001	Gift	N/A
2001 Rosemont Minx Pendant - A. Binder	1,595	2001	Gift	N/A

I.C.E. Piece - P. Calvesbert

YEAR ISSUE	EDITION LIMIT	YEAR RETD.	ISSUE PRICE	*QUOTE U.S.$
1998 Sneak Preview	5,000	1998	65.00	94-149
1999 Swap N Sell	5,000	1999	75.00	75-125
1999 Swap N Sell Groucho	200	1999	75.00	650-750
2000 Signing Line	5,000	2000	75.00	75
2001 Fred & Homer - A. Binder	3,500	2001	56.00	56

GCC Exclusive - P. Calvesbert, unless otherwise noted

YEAR ISSUE	EDITION LIMIT	YEAR RETD.	ISSUE PRICE	*QUOTE U.S.$
1998 Queen's Council	Retrd.	1998	45.00	45-73
1998 Boarding School	Retrd.	1998	45.00	45-75
1999 Thin Ice - Martin Perry Studios	6,000	1999	45.00	55-75
1999 Jump Shot - Martin Perry Studios	3,600	1999	45.00	55-138

Angelique - D. Lawrence

YEAR ISSUE	EDITION LIMIT	YEAR RETD.	ISSUE PRICE	*QUOTE U.S.$
1996 Bon Chance	Retrd.	2001	35.00	35
1996 Fleur-de-lis	7,888	1998	35.00	38-77
1996 Fleur-de-lis (wide-wing)	Retrd.	N/A	35.00	250
1996 Gentil Homme	6,786	1998	35.00	38-99
1996 Ingenue	8,062	1998	35.00	38-83
1996 Joie De Vivre	8,170	1998	35.00	45-90

Disneyana Conventions - Various

YEAR ISSUE	EDITION LIMIT	YEAR RETD.	ISSUE PRICE	*QUOTE U.S.$
2000 Bibbidi Bobbidi Boo - R. King	400	2000	440.00	440

Garden Party - Various

YEAR ISSUE	EDITION LIMIT	YEAR RETD.	ISSUE PRICE	*QUOTE U.S.$
1996 Baroness Trotter - P. Calvesbert	Retrd.	2001	17.50	18
1997 Count Belfry - D. Lawrence	6,978	1999	17.50	18-20
1996 Courtiers At Rest - P. Calvesbert	Retrd.	2001	17.50	18
1997 Duc de Lyon - D. Lawrence	7,220	1999	17.50	18-20
1997 Earl of Oswald - D. Lawrence	9,253	1999	17.50	18-20
1996 Garden Prince - P. Calvesbert	Retrd.	2001	17.50	18
1996 Ladies In Waiting - P. Calvesbert	Retrd.	2001	17.50	18
1997 Lord Busby - D. Lawrence	6,964	1999	17.50	18-39
1997 Major Parker - D. Lawrence	6,262	1999	17.50	18-20
1997 Marquis de Blanc - D. Lawrence	9,222	1999	17.50	18-20
1997 Royal Flotilla - P. Calvesbert	11,488	1998	17.50	18-31
1996 Yeoman Of The Guard - P. Calvesbert	Retrd.	2001	17.50	18

Harmony Circus - D. Lawrence

YEAR ISSUE	EDITION LIMIT	YEAR RETD.	ISSUE PRICE	*QUOTE U.S.$
1996 The Audience	1,359	1998	150.00	150-175
1996 Ball Brothers	2,608	1998	35.00	39-50
1996 Beppo And Barney The Clowns	2,881	1998	35.00	35-50
1996 Circus Ring	640	1998	100.00	80-175
1996 Clever Constantine	1,902	1998	35.00	39-50
1996 Great Escapo	1,733	1998	80.00	80-90
1996 Harmony Circus Arch	734	1998	35.00	35-50
1996 Henry The Human Cannonball	1,886	1998	35.00	35-50
1996 Il Bendi	1,468	1998	35.00	39-50
1996 Lionel Loveless	1,983	1998	35.00	35-50
1996 Mr. Sediments	1,916	1998	35.00	35-50
1996 Olde Time Carousel	3,322	1998	35.00	35-50
1996 Pavareata The Little Big Girl	3,613	1998	35.00	35-50
1996 The Ringmaster	1,649	1998	35.00	39-50
1996 Road Dogs	3,340	1998	35.00	35-50
1996 Suave St. John	1,744	1998	35.00	39-95
1996 Top Hat	3,154	1998	35.00	35-50
1996 Vlad The Impaler	2,538	1998	35.00	35-50
1996 Winston The Lion Tamer	2,716	1998	35.00	35-38
1996 Matched Number Harmony Circus Set	1,000	1998	890.00	890-950
1998 Bozini the Clown	10,000	1998	29.50	30-57
1998 Madeline of the High Wire	10,000	1998	29.50	30-57

Hi-Jinx - P. Calvesbert

YEAR ISSUE	EDITION LIMIT	YEAR RETD.	ISSUE PRICE	*QUOTE U.S.$
1994 Antarctic Antics	3,291	1998	100.00	100-125
1994 Hold That Line	4,740	1998	100.00	100-150
1994 Mad Dogs and Englishmen	4,625	1998	100.00	100-125
1995 Open Mike	3,032	1998	100.00	100-125

Holiday Edition - D. Lawrence, unless otherwise noted

YEAR ISSUE	EDITION LIMIT	YEAR RETD.	ISSUE PRICE	*QUOTE U.S.$
1995 Chatelaine	7,988	1995	35.00	375-420
1996 Bon Enfant	Retrd.	1996	35.00	250-325
1996 Bon Enfant (1st ed.)	Retrd.	1996	35.00	600-700
1996 Nick Of Time - P. Calvesbert	7,804	1996	35.00	175-245
1997 Celeste	Retrd.	1997	45.00	45-70
1997 Something's Gotta Give - P. Calvesbert	16,368	1997	35.00	45-65
1998 La Guardienne	16,130	1998	45.00	45-61
1998 Jingle Bell Rock - P. Calvesbert	19,019	1998	45.00	55-72
1999 Holy Roller - P. Calvesbert	9,948	1999	45.00	48-121
1999 Joyeaux	Retrd.	1999	45.00	45-48
1999 Noel	Retrd.	1999	45.00	45-48

YEAR ISSUE	EDITION LIMIT	YEAR RETD.	ISSUE PRICE	*QUOTE U.S.$
1998 Ruffians' Feast Tile - A. Richmond	Retrd.	2000	55.00	45
1999 Snowdonia Fields - Martin Perry Studios	Retrd.	2000	55.00	55
1999 Purrfect Tidings Tile - A. Richmond	Retrd.	2000	55.00	55
2000 Bon Bon	Yr.Iss.	2000	45.00	45
2000 Pastille	Yr.Iss.	2000	45.00	45
2000 Easy Slider - S. Drackett	Yr.Iss.	2000	45.00	45
2000 King of the Road - P. Calvesbert	Yr.Iss.	2000	55.00	55
2001 Beau Geste - A. Binder	Yr.Iss.	2001	45.00	45
2001 Blue Moon - S. Drackett	Yr.Iss.	2001	35.00	35
2001 Knackered Nick - P. Calvesbert	Yr.Iss.	2001	55.00	55

Large Treasure Jest® - P. Calvesbert, unless otherwise noted

YEAR ISSUE	EDITION LIMIT	YEAR RETD.	ISSUE PRICE	*QUOTE U.S.$
1991 Awaiting A Kiss	Open		55.00	55
1990 Drake's Fancy	4,512	1999	55.00	45-75
1995 Holding Court	Retrd.	2001	55.00	55
1991 Horn A' Plenty	6,910	1997	55.00	75-95
1991 Journey Home	7,011	1999	55.00	55-65
1990 Keeping Current	4,448	1998	55.00	55-75
1992 On A Roll	Retrd.	2000	55.00	55-65
1994 One Step Ahead	Retrd.	1999	55.00	55-70
1991 Pen Pals	Retrd.	2000	55.00	55-88
1990 Pondering	3,918	1997	55.00	110-328
1993 Pride And Joy	10,750	1998	55.00	55-75
1990 Quiet Waters	3,518	1999	55.00	55-65
1993 Standing Guard	3,646	1997	55.00	76-175
1993 Step Aside	Retrd.	2001	55.00	55
1991 Straight From The Hip	Retrd.	2000	55.00	55-85
1991 Sunnyside Up	Retrd.	2001	55.00	55
1999 Tally Ho! - D. Lawrence	Open		65.00	65
1991 Tea For Two	5,384	1999	55.00	55-65
1997 Terra Incognita - D. Lawrence	Open		75.00	75

Limited Editions - Various

YEAR ISSUE	EDITION LIMIT	YEAR RETD.	ISSUE PRICE	*QUOTE U.S.$
2001 Beer Nuts (Canadian Exclusive) - M. Baldwin	2,001	2001	N/A	N/A
1998 Family Reunion - D. Lawrence	7,200	1998	120.00	120-150
2000 Gentle Giant - S. Drackett	5,000	2000	55.00	55
2001 Golden Oldie (Parkwest Exclusive) - M. Baldwin	1,000	2001	45.00	45
1998 Have a Heart - P. Calvesbert	3,600	1998	55.00	200-295
1998 Ivory Tower - D. Lawrence	7,200	1998	120.00	120-250
1997 Killing Time (black sand) - D. Lawrence	3,600	1997	100.00	175-250
1997 Killing Time (gold sand) - D. Lawrence	3,600	1997	100.00	225-275
1995 Noah's Lark (Biblical) - P. Calvesbert	5,000	1998	400.00	400-510
2000 Noah's Quark - M. Ricketts	Yr.Iss.	2000	175.00	175
2000 Nose Bleed - P. Calvesbert	5,000	2000	55.00	55-179
1997 Original Kin (Biblical) - P. Calvesbert	2,500	1998	250.00	400-540
2001 Peony Basket (Longaberger Exclusive) - S. Drackett	3,600	2001	55.00	55
1998 Pieces of Eight (orange) - D. Lawrence	5,000	1998	120.00	650-1200
1998 Pieces of Eight (pink) - D. Lawrence	5,000	1998	120.00	250-450
1998 Pieces of Eight (red) - D. Lawrence	5,000	1998	120.00	120-213
1998 Planet Dustbin - P. Calvesbert	2,230	1998	45.00	45
1998 Play Ball - D. Lawrence	7,200	1998	120.00	120-150
2000 Retired Racers - D. Lawrence	5,000	2000	65.00	65
1999 Road Kill - P. Calvesbert	3,600	1999	55.00	122-225
2001 Road Kill's Revenge - P. Calvesbert	5,000	2001	75.00	75-125
1998 SinCity (Biblical) - P. Calvesbert	5,000	1998	600.00	600-720
2001 Take A Bow (Parkwest Exclusive) - M. Baldwin	2,000	2001	45.00	45
2001 Tamira's Treasure - P. Calvesbert	3,600	2001	150.00	150
1995 Unbearables - P. Calvesbert	2,500	1998	400.00	400-510
1999 Y2HK - Martin Perry Studios	Yr.Iss.	1999	175.00	175-219

Lord Byron's Harmony Garden™ - M. Perry, unless otherwise noted

YEAR ISSUE	EDITION LIMIT	YEAR RETD.	ISSUE PRICE	*QUOTE U.S.$
2000 Albatross - M. Baldwin	Open		45.00	45
1999 Alpine Flower	Open		45.00	45
2001 American Beauty	3,600	2001	175.00	175
1997 Basket of Roses	3,600	1997	65.00	180-250
1998 Begonia	Retrd.	2000	45.00	45-57
1998 Cactus	Open		45.00	45
2001 Carnation - S. Drackett	Open		30.00	30
2000 Cherry Blossom - M. Baldwin	Open		45.00	45
1999 Christmas Bouquet - Martin Perry Studios	5,000	1999	75.00	75-95
1997 Chrysanthemum	Retrd.	2000	38.50	39-88
1997 Cranberry	12,667	1999	38.50	39-83
1997 Daisy	Retrd.	1999	38.50	39-83
2001 Daisy II - S. Drackett	Open		30.00	30

BOXES & MUSICALS

YEAR ISSUE	EDITION LIMIT	YEAR RETD.	ISSUE PRICE	*QUOTE U.S.$
1998 Double Rose (red)	5,000	1998	55.00	95-145
1998 Double Rose (pink)	5,000	1998	55.00	75-94
1998 Double Rose (violet)	5,000	1998	55.00	85-169
1998 Double Rose (yellow)	5,000	1998	55.00	69-94
1999 Double Silver Rose - R. Glover	1,500	1999	500.00	500-516
1999 Easter Bouquet	5,000	1999	75.00	75-132
2000 Egyptian Rose - M. Baldwin	Retrd.	2001	45.00	45
1997 English Chrysanthemum	Retrd.	1997	38.50	82-120
1997 English Cranberry	Retrd.	1997	38.50	82-120
1997 English Daisy	Retrd.	1997	38.50	82-120
1997 English Hyacinth	Retrd.	1997	38.50	69-120
1997 English Hydrangea	Retrd.	1997	38.50	63-120
1997 English Marsh Marigold	Retrd.	1997	38.50	69-120
1997 English Morning Glory	Retrd.	1997	38.50	69-125
1997 English Peace Lily	Retrd.	1997	38.50	75-120
1997 English Rhododendron	Retrd.	1997	38.50	69-120
1997 English Snow Drop	Retrd.	1997	38.50	69-120
1997 English Roses, set/10	Retrd.	1997	385.00	600-875
2000 Fall Bouquet - S. Drackett	5,000	2000	75.00	75
1998 Forget Me Not	Retrd.	2000	45.00	45-48
1998 Gardenia	11,538	1999	45.00	45-63
1999 Gill	Retrd.	1999	45.00	45-63
2000 Grapes - M. Baldwin	Open		45.00	45
1999 Halloween Bouquet - Martin Perry Studios	5,000	1999	75.00	75-95
2001 Hibiscus - S. Drackett	Open		30.00	30
2000 Home Sweet Home	3,600	2000	250.00	250
1999 Hops	Open		45.00	45
1999 Hot Pepper	Retrd.	2001	45.00	45-48
1997 Hyacinth	Retrd.	1999	38.50	39-83
1997 Hydrangea	Retrd.	1999	38.50	39-83
1998 Iris	Open		45.00	45
2001 Iris II	Open		30.00	30
2000 Lemon - M. Baldwin	Open		45.00	45
2001 Lily	Open		30.00	30
2000 Lotus - M. Baldwin	Open		45.00	45
1999 Marigold	Open		45.00	45
1997 Marsh Marigold	Retrd.	1999	38.50	39-83
1999 Morning Glory	Retrd.	2000	38.50	39-69
1999 Mother's Day Bouquet	5,000	1999	75.00	83-132
1999 Orange	Open		45.00	45
1997 Orange Rose	3,600	1998	38.50	75-150
1997 Peace Lily	Open		38.50	39
1997 Peach Rose	3,600	1997	38.50	119-125
1998 Peony	Open		45.00	45
1997 Pink Rose	3,600	1997	38.50	75-144
1999 Pomegranate	Open		45.00	45
2000 Poppy - M. Baldwin	Retrd.	2001	45.00	45
1997 Red Rose	3,600	1997	38.50	188-300
1997 Rhododendron	Retrd.	1999	38.50	39-83
2001 Rose - S. Drackett	Open		30.00	30
1997 Rose Basket	3,600	1997	65.00	155-188
1998 Rose Bud	Open		45.00	45
1998 Rose Party	5,000	1998	100.00	105-175
1998 Snapdragon	Retrd.	2000	45.00	45-57
1997 Snow Drop	11,893	1999	38.50	39-83
2000 Spring Bouquet	5,000	2000	75.00	75
1998 Sterling Rose	1,000	1998	400.00	480-600
2000 Summer Bouquet	5,000	2000	75.00	75
1998 Sunflower	Open		45.00	45
1999 Sunflower II	Retrd.	2002	45.00	45-57
2001 Sunflower III - S. Drackett	Open		30.00	30
1999 Tulip	Retrd.	2002	45.00	45-57
1997 Violet Rose	3,600	1997	38.50	75-188
1997 White Rose	3,600	1997	38.50	75-138
2000 Winter Bouquet - S. Drackett	5,000	2000	75.00	75
1997 Yellow Rose	3,600	1997	38.50	75-150

NALED Special Editions - D. Lawrence, unless otherwise noted

YEAR ISSUE	EDITION LIMIT	YEAR RETD.	ISSUE PRICE	*QUOTE U.S.$
1997 Cat's Cradle	1,000	1997	38.50	260-350
1997 Cat's Cradle Too	1,000	1997	38.50	225-337
1998 Kitty's Kippers	5,600	1998	45.00	45-75
1998 Peace Offering	4,200	1998	45.00	69-144
1999 Beware the Hare	4,200	1999	45.00	48-75
1999 Harmony Bull - P. Calvesbert	5,600		45.00	45

Rather Large Series - P. Calvesbert

YEAR ISSUE	EDITION LIMIT	YEAR RETD.	ISSUE PRICE	*QUOTE U.S.$
1996 Rather Large Friends	9,350	1998	65.00	65-88
1996 Rather Large Hop	4,330	1998	65.00	65-88
1996 Rather Large Huddle	5,423	1998	65.00	65-88

YEAR ISSUE	EDITION LIMIT	YEAR RETD.	ISSUE PRICE	*QUOTE U.S.$
1996 Rather Large Safari	6,692	1998	65.00	65-150

Romance Annual - D. Lawrence, unless otherwise noted

YEAR ISSUE	EDITION LIMIT	YEAR RETD.	ISSUE PRICE	*QUOTE U.S.$
1997 Pillow Talk	Retrd.	1998	120.00	92-160
1998 Love Nest	Retrd.	1998	90.00	90-137
1999 Tender is the Night - Martin Perry Studios	Retrd.	2000	75.00	75
2000 Love and Peace - S. Drackett	Retrd.	2000	75.00	75
2001 Sea of Love - M. Baldwin	Retrd.	2001	55.00	55

Small Treasure Jest® - P. Calvesbert

YEAR ISSUE	EDITION LIMIT	YEAR RETD.	ISSUE PRICE	*QUOTE U.S.$
1998 Algenon (1st Ed.)	3,000	1998	45.00	45-95
1998 Algenon (2nd Ed.)	Open		45.00	45
1994 All Angles Covered	Retrd.	2000	35.00	35-45
1993 All Ears	6,668	1996	35.00	240-250
1993 All Tied Up	4,566	1996	35.00	165-265
1998 Antipasto	Retrd.	1999	45.00	45-75
1998 Aria Amorosa	9,555	1998	45.00	45-77
1993 At Arm's Length	2,029	1996	35.00	360-600
1995 At The Hop	Open		35.00	35
1998 Baby Boomer (1st Ed.)	3,000	1998	45.00	55-95
1998 Baby Boomer (2nd Ed.)	Retrd.	1999	45.00	45
1993 Baby on Board	13,217	1997	35.00	48-77
1993 Back Scratch	554	1995	35.00	3000-5000
2001 Bad to the Bone	Open		45.00	45
1997 Bamboozled	Open		45.00	45
1995 Beak To Beak	12,422	1997	35.00	35-95
2000 Beau Brummel	Open		35.00	35
1996 Brean Sands	Open		35.00	35
1998 Catch A Lot	Retrd.	1999	45.00	45-63
1999 Caw of the Wild	Open		45.00	45
1996 Changing of the Guard	Open		35.00	35
1996 Close Shave	10,913	1998	35.00	38-60
2000 Cookie's Jar	Open		45.00	45
1998 Croc Pot (1st Ed.-w/McD)	3,000	1998	45.00	82-99
1998 Croc Pot (2nd Ed.)	Retrd.	2000	45.00	45
1995 Damnable Plot	16,257	1999	35.00	38-63
1993 Day Dreamer	4,247	1996	35.00	480-675
1999 Dead Ringer	Open		45.00	45
1995 Den Mothers	6,264	1996	35.00	175-200
1994 Dog Days	Retrd.	2001	35.00	35-38
1997 Down Under	Retrd.	1999	35.00	45-63
1997 Driver's Seat	Open		45.00	45
1995 Ed's Safari	Open		35.00	35
1999 Ed's Safari II	Open		35.00	35
2000 Ed's Safari III	Open		45.00	45
1994 Family Tree	Retrd.	2000	35.00	35-38
1997 Faux Paw	Retrd.	1999	35.00	45-60
1992 Forty Winks	5,385	1996	35.00	265-300
1999 Foul Play	Open		45.00	45
1997 Friends in High Places	Open		45.00	45
1995 Fur Ball	Open		35.00	35
2000 Fusspot	Open		45.00	45
1999 The Great Escape	Open		45.00	45
2000 The Great Escape II	Open		45.00	45
1994 Group Therapy	3,170	1996	35.00	151-318
1993 Hammin' It Up	13,217	1996	35.00	125-165
1996 Hog Heaven	Retrd.	2000	35.00	35
1995 Horse Play	1,907	1996	35.00	270-375
1997 In Fine Feather	Retrd.	2000	35.00	45-60
1994 Inside Joke	Retrd.	2000	35.00	35-45
1993 It's A Fine Day	4,916	1996	35.00	400-475
1995 Jersey Belles	Open		35.00	35
1993 Jonah's Hideaway	7,342	1996	35.00	270-365
2001 Kit and Caboodle	Open		45.00	45
1999 The Last Laugh	Open		45.00	45
2000 Leatherneck's Lounge	Open		45.00	45
1994 Let's Do Lunch	1,269	1995	35.00	480-780
1996 Liberty and Justice	Retrd.	2000	45.00	45-55
1995 Life's a Picnic	17,842	1998	35.00	35-55
1994 Love Seat	11,510	1997	35.00	38-77
1995 Major's Mousers	9,372	1997	45.00	99-140
1998 Menage A Trois	Open		45.00	45
1995 Mud Bath	3,958	1997	35.00	90-195
1997 Murphy's Last Stand	10,168	1997	35.00	45-55
1994 Neighborhood Watch	8,837	1997	35.00	95-150
1996 Nic Nac Paddy Whack	Retrd.	2001	35.00	35
1993 Of The Same Stripe	Retrd.	2001	35.00	38-50
1999 Package Tour	Open		45.00	45
1991 Panda	100	1995	35.00	2000-2500
1999 Peace Summit	Open		45.00	45

*Quotes have been rounded up to nearest dollar

YEAR ISSUE	EDITION LIMIT	YEAR RETD.	ISSUE PRICE	*QUOTE U.S.$
1999 Pecking Order	Open		45.00	45
1999 Petty Teddies	Open		45.00	45
1997 Photo Finish	Retrd.	2000	45.00	45
1996 Pink Paradise	Retrd.	2000	35.00	35
1996 Pink Paradise (black beaks)	Retrd.	1996	35.00	35-57
1994 Play School	19,780	1998	35.00	38-55
2001 Pongo's Palm	Open		45.00	45
2001 Powder Room	Open		45.00	45
1992 Princely Thoughts	9,682	1996	35.00	100-328
1995 Puddle Huddle	Open		35.00	35
1994 Purrfect Friends	Retrd.	2000	35.00	35
1991 Ram	100	1995	35.00	1000-1250
1993 Reminiscence	15,957	1996	35.00	125-328
1998 Rocky's Raiders	Retrd.	2000	45.00	45
1997 Rooster	300	1997	35.00	480-650
1996 Rumble Seat	Open		45.00	45
2001 Saint or Sinner	Open		45.00	45
1993 School's Out	33,230	1999	35.00	38-45
2001 Scotland Yard	Open		45.00	45
1997 Shaggy Dog (Sheep Dog)	300	1997	35.00	500-725
1991 Shark	100	1995	35.00	1025-2000
1993 Shell Game	Retrd.	2001	35.00	35-38
1997 Shoe Bill	300	1997	35.00	650-750
1993 Side Steppin'	6,813	1996	35.00	100-185
1997 Sleepy Hollow	Retrd.	2001	35.00	35-45
2001 Slow Dance	Open		45.00	45
2000 Special Delivery	Retrd.	2001	45.00	45
1997 Splashdown	Retrd.	2000	45.00	45-55
1994 Sunday Swim	Open		35.00	35
1993 Swamp Song	16,540	1997	35.00	48-150
1995 Sweet Serenade	Open		35.00	35
1994 Teacher's Pet	7,182	1997	35.00	88-200
1995 Teapot Angel I (UK)	43	1996	20.00	2000-4000
1995 Teapot Angel II (UK)	43	1996	20.00	2000-4000
1996 Tin Cat	14,418	1998	35.00	38-50
1996 Tin Cat (brown boat)	990	1996	35.00	200-207
1994 Tongue And Cheek	Open		35.00	35
1997 Tony's Tabbies	Open		45.00	45
2000 Tony's Tabbies II	Open		45.00	45
1994 Too Much of A Good Thing	15,631	1999	35.00	35-45
1993 Top Banana	1,499	1996	35.00	225-275
1996 Trumpeter's Ball	Open		45.00	45
1996 Trumpeter's Ball w/extra trunk	Retrd.	1996	45.00	250-290
1993 Trunk Show	6,467	1996	35.00	250-350
1999 Turdus Felidae	Open		45.00	45
1995 Unbridled & Groomed	20,382	1998	35.00	45-120
1994 Unexpected Arrival	Retrd.	2000	35.00	38-45
1994 Untouchable	1,889	1995	35.00	360-400
2001 Up to Scratch	Open		45.00	45
1997 Whale of a Time	15,154	1998	35.00	38-76
1999 When Nature Calls	Retrd.	2002	45.00	48-55
1993 Who'd A Thought	935	1995	35.00	1500-2750
1995 Wise Guys	Retrd.	2000	35.00	35
1998 Wishful Thinking (1st Ed.)	3,000	1998	45.00	77-95
1998 Wishful Thinking (1st Ed.-Full Screw)	Retrd.	1998	45.00	75-150
1998 Wishful Thinking (2nd Ed.)	Retrd.	1999	45.00	45-60

Special Edition - P. Calvesbert

YEAR ISSUE	EDITION LIMIT	YEAR RETD.	ISSUE PRICE	*QUOTE U.S.$
1996 Angel Baroque	62	1997	45.00	2000
1995 Primordial Soup	Retrd.	1999	150.00	160-328

Lenox Classics

Lenox Classics-China Lenox Treasures - Lenox

YEAR ISSUE	EDITION LIMIT	YEAR RETD.	ISSUE PRICE	*QUOTE U.S.$
2001 All Aboard	Open		30.00	30
2000 Anchors Away Treasure Box	Open		30.00	30
2002 Bashful	Open		30.00	30
2000 The Cat's Surprise Box	Open		30.00	30
2002 Celebration of Love	Open		30.00	30
2002 Darling Dreamer	Open		30.00	30
2002 Doc	Open		30.00	30
2000 The Dolphin Seascape Box	Open		30.00	30
2000 The Dolphin Splash Box	Open		30.00	30
2002 Dopey	Open		30.00	30
2002 Grumpy	Open		30.00	30
2000 Guardian of Song	Open		30.00	30
2002 Happy	Open		30.00	30
2000 The Light in the Harbor Treasure Box	Open		30.00	30
2001 A Pooh Sort of Christmas	Open		40.00	40
2000 Pooh's Friendship Garden	Open		40.00	40
2001 Rocking Horse	Open		30.00	30

YEAR ISSUE	EDITION LIMIT	YEAR RETD.	ISSUE PRICE	*QUOTE U.S.$
2001 Sailor Girl	Open		30.00	30
2000 Santa's Special Delivery	Open		30.00	30
2000 Skating Adventure Box	Open		30.00	30
2001 Skiing in Style	Open		30.00	30
2002 Sleepy	Open		30.00	30
2002 Sneezy	Open		30.00	30
2002 Snow White	Open		30.00	30
2000 The Snowman's Surprise Box	Open		30.00	30
2000 Sunshine & Sprinkles Box	Open		30.00	30
2001 A Sweet Surprise Gingerbread Box	Open		30.00	30
2000 Time for Tea Treasure Box	Open		30.00	30

Little Angel Publishing

Heaven's Little Angel - D. Gelsinger

YEAR ISSUE	EDITION LIMIT	YEAR RETD.	ISSUE PRICE	*QUOTE U.S.$
1999 Ornament Box	Open		34.99	35
1999 Photo Box	Open		14.99	15

Heaven's Little Angel Heirloom Porcelain Music Box Collection- D. Gelsinger

YEAR ISSUE	EDITION LIMIT	YEAR RETD.	ISSUE PRICE	*QUOTE U.S.$
2000 Precious Blessings	95-day		29.97	30

Heaven's Little Guardian - D. Gelsinger

YEAR ISSUE	EDITION LIMIT	YEAR RETD.	ISSUE PRICE	*QUOTE U.S.$
1999 Angel's Devotion Music Box	95-day		29.95	30
1999 Angel's Love Music Box	95-day		29.95	30
1999 Angel's Prayer Music Box	95-day		29.95	30
1999 Angel's Tenderness Music Box	95-day		29.95	30

Memories of Yesterday/Enesco Group, Inc.

Covered Boxes - M. Attwell

YEAR ISSUE	EDITION LIMIT	YEAR RETD.	ISSUE PRICE	*QUOTE U.S.$
1998 Can I Keep Her, Mommy? 314862	Retrd.	1999	25.00	25
1998 Here Comes The Bride-God Bless Her 314870	Retrd.	1999	25.00	25
1998 Hoping To See You Soon 279706	Retrd.	1999	25.00	25
1998 How 'bout A Little Kiss 279730	Retrd.	1999	25.00	25
1998 I Pray Thee Lord My Soul To Keep 279714	Retrd.	1999	25.00	25
1998 Let Me Be Your Guardian Angel 279722	Retrd.	1999	25.00	25
1998 May Your Birthday Be Happy And Bright 314889	Retrd.	1999	25.00	25
1998 Mommy, I Teared 314897	Retrd.	1999	25.00	25
1998 Now I Lay Me Down To Sleep 279749	Retrd.	1999	25.00	25
1998 Time For Bed 279765	Retrd.	1999	25.00	25

Precious Moments/Enesco Group, Inc.

Precious Moments - S. Butcher

YEAR ISSUE	EDITION LIMIT	YEAR RETD.	ISSUE PRICE	*QUOTE U.S.$
2000 I'll Give You The World (Parkwest Exclusive) 798290	Open		6.25	7
2002 You're Just Too Thweet (Tooth Fairy Pillow Box) 797693	Open		22.50	23

Prizm, Inc./Pipka

Midnight Visitor Collection - Pipka

YEAR ISSUE	EDITION LIMIT	YEAR RETD.	ISSUE PRICE	*QUOTE U.S.$
2002 Midnight Visitor Waterglobe (musical) 11618	Open		30.00	30

Pipka's Boot Boxes - Pipka

YEAR ISSUE	EDITION LIMIT	YEAR RETD.	ISSUE PRICE	*QUOTE U.S.$
2002 Alaskan Santa Boot Box 40042	Open		17.00	17
2002 Czechoslovakian Santa Boot Box 40033	Open		17.00	17
2002 Patriotic Santa Boot Box 40041	Open		17.00	17
2002 Polish Father Christmas Boot Box 40034	Open		17.00	17
2002 Santa's Boot Box 40029	Open		17.00	17
2002 Starcoat Santa Boot Box 40031	Open		17.00	17
2002 Teddy Bear Santa Boot Box 40032	Open		17.00	17
2002 Where's Rudolph? Boot Box 40030	Open		17.00	17

Pipka's Music Boxes - Pipka

YEAR ISSUE	EDITION LIMIT	YEAR RETD.	ISSUE PRICE	*QUOTE U.S.$
2000 Christmas Ark 11604	300	2001	170.00	170
2000 Christmas Tree 11606	200		120.00	120
2000 Teddy Bear Santa 11605	200		120.00	120

Reco International

Hearts & Flowers Music Boxes - S. Kuck

YEAR ISSUE	EDITION LIMIT	YEAR RETD.	ISSUE PRICE	*QUOTE U.S.$
2000 Tea Party	95-day		30.00	30

Precious Child Music Boxes - S. Kuck

YEAR ISSUE	EDITION LIMIT	YEAR RETD.	ISSUE PRICE	*QUOTE U.S.$
2000 Monday's Child	95-day		30.00	30

YEAR ISSUE	EDITION LIMIT	YEAR RETD.	ISSUE PRICE	*QUOTE U.S.$
2000 Tuesday's Child	95-day		30.00	30
2000 Wednesday's Child	95-day		30.00	30
2000 Thursday's Child	95-day		30.00	30
2000 Friday's Child	95-day		30.00	30
2000 Saturday's Child	95-day		30.00	30
2000 Sunday's Child	95-day		30.00	30

San Francisco Music Box Company

Collector's Club - G. Ho
1998 Hanna w/Baby Waterglobe	Open		30.00	30

American Heroes - San Francisco Music Box Company
2000 Air Force Dress Rehearsal	Open		50.00	50
2000 Army Honor Gurard	Open		50.00	50
2001 Army Morning Stroll	Open		50.00	50
2001 Iwo Jima Memorial	Open		60.00	60
2000 Marines The Few	Open		50.00	50
2000 Navy Outward Bound	Open		50.00	50
2001 Seaport Sweetheart	Open		75.00	75

American Treasures Historical Reproduction Musical Carousel Collection - San Francisco Music Box Company
1997 Dentzel Tiger	4,500	1998	59.95	60
1997 Dentzel/Cernigliaro Giraffe	4,500	1998	59.95	60
1997 Dentzel/Cernigliaro Lion	4,500	1998	59.95	60
1997 Herschell-Spillman Hop Toad	4,500	1998	84.95	60
1997 Looff Jumper Horse	4,500	1998	84.95	85
1997 M.C. Illions American Beauty Horse	4,500	1998	84.95	85
1997 Muller Eagle Horse	4,500	1998	84.95	85
1997 PTC Armored Horse	4,500	1998	84.95	85

Angus & Friends™ Cat Collection - San Francisco Music Box Company
2001 All I Need Is Love	9,000		35.00	35
2001 Cats Need 9 Lives	9,000		40.00	40
2001 Mood Swings	9,000		35.00	35
2001 Purrfect Life	9,000		35.00	35
2001 Sewing Room	9,000		45.00	45
2001 She Who Must Be Obeyed	9,000		35.00	35
2001 Snack Time Waterglobe	9,000		30.00	30
2001 Will Move For Food	9,000		40.00	40
2001 You're Late Waterglobe	9,000		30.00	30

Bearhugs™ - B. Giordano
2001 Bearlerina	Open		30.00	30
2001 Birthday Waterglobe	Open		30.00	30
2001 Forever Friends	Open		30.00	30
2001 Love Waterglobe	Open		30.00	30
2001 Mother	Open		30.00	30
2001 Sewing	Open		30.00	30
2001 Sisters	Open		30.00	30
2001 Storytime	Open		30.00	30
2001 Sweetheart	Open		30.00	30
2001 Teacher Waterglobe	Open		30.00	30
2001 Wedding	Open		30.00	30

Bearhugs™ - San Francisco Music Box Company
2002 Friendship Lifts the Spirit Figurine	Open		35.00	35
2002 Heart of Gold	Open		35.00	35
2002 Jewelry Box	Open		35.00	35
2002 Merry-Go-Round	Open		85.00	85
2002 Rotating Figurine	Open		35.00	35
2002 Snowblower Waterglobe	Open		35.00	35
2002 Tea Light Figurine	Open		25.00	25
2002 Umbrella Waterglobe	Open		30.00	30

Boyds Bears Musical Bearstone Figurines - G.M. Lowenthal
1998 20th Anniversary Grace & Jonathon Born to Shop (1st ed.)	3,600	1998	45.00	45
1998 20th Anniversary Grace & Jonathon Born to Shop (2nd ed.)	3,600	1998	45.00	45
1998 20th Anniversary Grace & Jonathon Born to Shop (3rd ed.)	3,600	1998	45.00	45
1998 20th Anniversary Grace & Jonathon Born to Shop (4th ed.)	3,600	1998	45.00	45
1997 Amelia's Enterprise (1st ed.)	3,600	1998	44.95	58-69
1997 Amelia's Enterprise (2nd ed.)	3,600	1998	44.95	45
1995 Arthur on Trunk (1st ed.)	3,600	1997	39.95	67-75
1995 Arthur on Trunk (2nd ed.)	3,600	1997	39.95	47-94
1996 Bailey & Emily (1st ed.)	3,600	1997	44.95	52-65
1996 Bailey & Emily (2nd ed.)	3,600	1997	44.95	45

YEAR ISSUE	EDITION LIMIT	YEAR RETD.	ISSUE PRICE	*QUOTE U.S.$
1998 Bailey Honey Bear (1st ed.)	3,600	1998	44.95	45-86
1998 Bailey Honey Bear (2nd ed.)	3,600	1998	44.95	45
1996 Bailey with Suitcase (1st ed.)	3,600	1997	39.95	58-83
1996 Bailey with Suitcase (2nd ed.)	3,600	1997	39.95	40
1997 Bailey's Birthday (1st ed.)	3,600	1998	44.95	45-63
1997 Bailey's Birthday (2nd ed.)	3,600	1998	44.95	45
1998 Bailey's Heart Desire (1st ed.)	3,600	1998	45.00	45-72
1998 Bailey's Heart Desire (2nd ed.)	3,600	1998	45.00	45
2000 Bud Buzzby Honey Bear	6,000	2000	45.00	45-88
1999 Checkers Waterglobe (1st ed.)	3,600	1999	55.00	55
1999 Checkers Waterglobe (2nd ed.)	3,600	1999	55.00	55
2000 Christmas Helper Waterglobe	6,000	2000	45.00	45
1999 Clara Nurse (1st ed.)	3,600	1999	45.00	45-85
1999 Clara Nurse (2nd ed.)	3,600	1999	45.00	45
1996 Clarence Angel (1st ed.)	3,600	1998	39.95	40-63
1996 Clarence Angel (2nd ed.)	3,600	1998	39.95	40-42
1997 The Collector (1st ed.)	3,600	1998	49.95	50-85
1997 The Collector (2nd ed.)	3,600	1998	49.95	50
1997 Daphne & Eloise (1st ed.)	3,600	1998	44.95	45-63
1997 Daphne & Eloise (2nd ed.)	3,600	1998	44.95	45-69
1999 Elliot... Hero Waterglobe (1st ed.)	3,600	1999	45.00	45
1999 Elliot... Hero Waterglobe (2nd ed.)	3,600	1999	50.00	50
1996 Emma & Bailey Tea Party Waterglobe (1st ed.)	3,600	1997	44.95	58-86
1996 Emma & Bailey Tea Party Waterglobe (2nd ed.)	3,600	1997	44.95	45
1998 Grenville & Beatrice True Love Waterglobe (1st ed.)	3,600	1998	44.95	45
1998 Grenville & Beatrice True Love Waterglobe (2nd ed.)	3,600	1998	44.95	45
1997 Homer on Plate Waterglobe (1st ed.)	3,600	1998	44.95	45-52
1997 Homer on Plate Waterglobe (2nd ed.)	3,600	1998	44.95	45
1998 Justina Message Bearer (1st ed.)	3,600	1998	44.95	47
1998 Justina Message Bearer (2nd ed.)	3,600	1998	44.95	45
1998 Kringle & Co. Waterglobe (1st ed.)	3,600	1999	45.00	45
1998 Kringle & Co. Waterglobe (2nd ed.)	3,600	1999	50.00	50
1999 Love Is The Master Key Waterglobe (1st ed.)	3,600	1999	45.00	45
1999 Love Is The Master Key Waterglobe (2nd ed.)	3,600	1999	45.00	45
2000 McNew Bear Waterglobe	6,000	2000	45.00	45
1996 Miss Bruin & Bailey (1st ed.)	3,600	1998	44.95	45-75
1996 Miss Bruin & Bailey (2nd ed.)	3,600	1998	44.95	45-81
1996 Nelville Bedtime (1st ed.)	3,600	1998	39.95	58-69
1996 Nelville Bedtime (2nd ed.)	3,600	1998	39.95	40
1998 Neville Compubear (1st ed.)	3,600	1998	44.95	47-81
1998 Neville Compubear (2nd ed.)	3,600	1998	44.95	45-79
1999 Quiet Time (1st ed.)	3,600	1999	40.00	40
1999 Quiet Time (2nd ed.)	3,600	1999	40.00	40
2000 Rosemary Bearhugs	6,000	2000	45.00	45
1997 The Secret (1st ed.)	3,600	1998	49.95	50
1997 The Secret (2nd ed.)	3,600	1998	49.95	50
2000 Shipmates	6,000	2000	45.00	45
1995 Ted & Teddy Waterglobe (1st ed.)	3,600	1997	39.95	45-86
1995 Ted & Teddy Waterglobe (2nd ed.)	3,600	1997	39.95	40
1999 Telephone Tied (1st ed.)	3,600	1999	45.00	45-94
1999 Telephone Tied (2nd ed.)	3,600	1999	45.00	45
1995 Wilson with Love Sonnets (1st ed.)	3,600	1995	39.95	45-92
1995 Wilson with Love Sonnets (2nd ed.)	3,600	1997	39.95	40-52

Boyds Bears Musical Dollstone Figurines - G.M. Lowenthal
2000 Ballerina Waterglobe	6,000		45.00	45
2000 By The Sea Waterglobe	6,000	2000	45.00	45
1999 Garden Friends Waterglobe (1st ed.)	4,800	1999	45.00	45
1999 Goin' to Grandma's (1st ed.)	4,800	1999	45.00	45
1999 Momma's Clothes (1st ed.)	4,800	1999	45.00	45
1999 School Days (1st ed.)	4,800	1999	40.00	40-59
2000 Stitched With Love	6,000	2000	45.00	45
1998 Wendy Wash Day (1st ed.)	4,800	1998	45.00	45-72
1998 Wendy Wash Day (2nd ed.)	4,800	1998	45.00	45

Charming Tails Musicals - D. Griff
1996 After Lunch Snooze	Closed	1996	40.00	56
1996 Getting To Know You	Closed	1996	40.00	55
1996 Spring Flowers	Closed	1996	40.00	57
1996 That's What Friends Are For	Closed	1996	40.00	55

Cherish The Thought - San Francisco Music Box Company
1994 Friendship Waterglobe	Closed	2000	45.95	46

Collectors' Information Bureau   *Quotes have been rounded up to nearest dollar

San Francisco Music Box Company
to San Francisco Music Box Company

YEAR ISSUE	EDITION LIMIT	YEAR RETD.	ISSUE PRICE	*QUOTE U.S.$
Christmas - C. Radko				
1999 Carlton Snowman Waterglobe	7,500		115.00	115
1999 Elves Waterglobe	7,500		115.00	115
1999 Gold Balmoral Santa Waterglobe	5,000		95.00	95
1999 Rooftop of London Waterglobe	7,500		115.00	115
1999 Sneak-a-Peak Waterglobe	5,000		95.00	95
1999 Vintage Santa Waterglobe	7,500		95.00	95
1999 Woodland Santa Waterglobe	7,500		115.00	115
Cicely Mary Barker-Flower Fairies™ - San Francisco Music Box Company				
2001 Flower Fairies™ Apple Blossom Figurine	Open		45.00	45
2001 Flower Fairies™ Candytuft Figurine	Open		40.00	40
2001 Flower Fairies™ Chicory Figurine	Open		35.00	35
2001 Flower Fairies™ Sweet Pea Figurine	Open		45.00	45
Crystal Vision - M. Sarnat				
2001 Dragon and Egg	Open		50.00	50
2001 Dragon Lighthouse	Open		70.00	70
2000 Dragon Tarot	Open		70.00	70
2001 Dragon's Gazing Sphere	Open		45.00	45
1999 Hourglass Waterglobe	Closed	2001	100.00	100
1994 Hourglass Waterglobe	Closed	1997	150.00	150
2001 Merlin and Dragon Fountain	Open		45.00	45
2001 Merlin and the Dragon	Open		50.00	50
2000 Merlin/Dragon Chess	Open		70.00	70
2001 Merlin's Castle Waterglobe	Open		70.00	70
1994 Merlin's Library	Closed	1996	150.00	150
2000 Merlin's Study	Open		55.00	55
1999 Millenium Zodiac Hourglass Waterglobe	9,500	2001	100.00	100
Dreamsicles - C. Hayes				
1997 Butterfly Waterglobe	10,000	1998	70.00	70
1998 Dolphins Searching for Hope Waterglobe	10,000	2001	40.00	40
1998 Flying Lesson Waterglobe	10,000	1999	70.00	70
1998 Handmade with Love Waterglobe	10,000	1999	70.00	70
1998 Heart to Heart Waterglobe	10,000	1999	70.00	70
1999 Love Waterglobe	10,000	2001	70.00	70
1998 Time to Dash Waterglobe	10,000	1998	70.00	70
Gone With The Wind™ - San Francisco Music Box Company				
2001 Gone With the Wind™ Poster Laquer Box	Open		45.00	45
2000 Gone With the Wind™ Rhett & Scarlett 120mm Waterglobe	Open		50.00	50
2000 Gone With the Wind™ Rhett & Scarlett Carriage	Open		80.00	80
2001 Gone With the Wind™ Rhett w/Column	Open		50.00	50
2001 Gone With the Wind™ Rhett/Scarlett Seated	Open		75.00	75
2001 Gone With the Wind™ Scarlett & Rhett at Home	Open		75.00	75
2000 Gone With the Wind™ Scarlett & Rhett Lacquer Box	Open		45.00	45
2000 Gone With the Wind™ Scarlett & Rhett Stairs	Open		75.00	75
2000 Gone With the Wind™ Scarlett & Tara 120mm Waterglobe	Closed	2001	50.00	50
2000 Gone With the Wind™ Scarlett Ceramic Box	Open		35.00	35
2000 Gone With the Wind™ Scarlett Figurine	Open		50.00	50
2001 Gone With the Wind™ Scarlett Green Dress	Open		50.00	50
2000 Gone With the Wind™ Scarlett on Bench	Open		70.00	70
Heart Tugs Musical Collection - M. Danko				
1998 20th Anniversary - "Old Friendships are the Best"	2,500	1998	35.00	35
1998 Pie Safe - "Friendship is Homemade"	6,000	1998	49.95	50
1997 Tea Time - "Forever Friends"	6,000	1997	49.95	50
Musical Goose Eggs - V. Damann, unless otherwise noted				
1998 20th Anniversary	300	1999	200.00	200
1998 Blue Pansies	300	1999	165.00	165
2001 Carnival Purple Egg with Egg Pendant	500	2002	350.00	350
1999 Celestial Pendant	500	2000	310.00	310

YEAR ISSUE	EDITION LIMIT	YEAR RETD.	ISSUE PRICE	*QUOTE U.S.$
1999 Cinderella Crystal Slipper Coach	750	2000	495.00	495
1997 Coach	300	1998	450.00	450
1998 Coach with Crown - R. Egg	700	2000	495.00	495
1999 Crystal Flower Coach Egg	500	2000	550.00	550
1999 Crystal Millenium Angel Egg	750	2000	575.00	575
2001 Dangling Jewels Cameo Egg	500		230.00	230
1999 Emeralds Jewel Egg	750	2000	295.00	295
1997 Mauve Cherub	300	1998	195.00	195
1997 Purple Pansies	300	1998	160.00	160
2001 Rhea Egg with Swans	500		495.00	495
1997 Roses	300	1998	160.00	160
1998 Silvery Blue	500	2000	200.00	200
1997 Velvet Romance Carousel - K. Johnson	1,000	1998	240.00	240
Musical Merry-Go-Round Collection - Various				
1998 The American Treasures™ 12-Animal Merry-Go-Round - Team	5,000	1999	500.00	500
1998 The American Treasures™ 6-Animal Merry-Go-Round - Team	5,000	1999	299.00	299
1999 Angel Flight 8" Horse	4,500		90.00	90
1999 Angel Flight Double Horse	4,500		110.00	110
1999 Arabesque Horse, 8" - E. Kamysz	4,500	1999	85.00	85
1998 Baroque Horse - P. Fulton	4,500	1999	85.00	85
1998 Baroque Horse with Canopy - P. Fulton	5,000	1999	65.00	65
1999 Chinese Double Horse with Canopy	4,000		110.00	110
1999 Cloisonne Merry-Go-Round - Scheherazade	500	2000	1500.00	1500
2000 Elizabeth 6-Horse Merry-Go-Round	5,000		325.00	325
1999 Florentine Horse, 8"	4,500	1999	85.00	85
1999 Florentine Single Horse with Canopy	5,000	1999	85.00	85
1998 Four Season Merry-Go-Round - E. Kamysz	5,000		225.00	225
1997 Gardenia 10" Horse - M. Drdak	3,000	1998	87.50	88
1997 Gardenia 8" Horse - M. Drdak	4,500	1998	85.00	85
1997 Gardenia Horse with Canopy	4,000	1998	99.95	100
2001 Jewels of the Empire Jade Porcelain 4-animal Merry-Go-Round	5,000		225.00	225
1998 Jewels of the Empire Jade Porcelain 4-animal Merry-Go-Round	5,000	1999	199.00	199
1997 Les Fleurs D'Amour 6-horse Merry-Go-Round - Team	5,000	1999	299.00	299
1999 Lily Double Horse with Canopy	4,000	1999	100.00	100
1999 Lily Horse, 8"	4,500	1999	85.00	85
1999 Lily Single Horse with Canopy	5,000	1999	85.00	85
1999 Millenium 12-Horse Merry-Go-Round	5,000	2000	499.00	499
1999 Neptune 8" Horse - M. Drdak	4,500		90.00	90
1999 Neptune Double Horse with Canopy - M. Drdak	4,500		110.00	110
1999 Neptune Merry-Go-Round	5,000		225.00	225
1998 Renaissance Horse with Canopy	5,000	1999	85.00	85
1999 Royal Crest Double 6-Horse Merry-Go-Round - Team	5,000	1999	299.00	299
1999 Royal Crest Double Horse with Canopy - Team	4,000	1999	100.00	100
1999 Royal Crest Horse, 10" - Team	3,000	1999	100.00	100
1997 Savannah Horse with Canopy - N. Bailey	5,000	1998	84.95	85
1998 Sultan's Dream 6-Horse Merry-Go-Round	5,000	1999	299.00	299
1998 Sultan's Dream Double Horse with Canopy	4,000	1999	100.00	100
1998 Sultan's Dream Horse, 12"	2,500	1999	125.00	125
1998 Sultan's Dream Horse, 8"	4,500	1999	85.00	85
2000 Venetian Rose 12-Horse Merry-Go-Round	2,500		525.00	525
1997 Venetian Rose Horse	4,500	1998	84.95	85
1997 Venetian Rose Horse with Canopy	5,000	1998	84.95	85
2000 Victoria Rose 12-Horse Merry-Go-Round	2,500		525.00	525
National Geographic Musical Figurines - M. Adams				
2001 African Elephant	7,500		85.00	85
1998 African Lion Family	7,500		125.00	125
1999 Appaloosa	7,500		85.00	85
2001 Assateague Island Ponies	7,500		75.00	75
1998 Baby Chickadee	7,500	2001	55.00	55
1998 Bald Eagle	7,500	2001	125.00	125
2001 Bengal Tiger	7,500		85.00	85
2001 Bottlenose Dolphin	2,500		150.00	150

YEAR ISSUE	EDITION LIMIT	YEAR RETD.	ISSUE PRICE	*QUOTE U.S.$
2001 Dolphin	7,500		60.00	60
1999 Dolphin	7,500		75.00	75
1999 Double Eagle	7,500		125.00	125
2001 Emperor Penguin Creche	7,500		60.00	60
2001 Gray Wolf	7,500		60.00	60
1998 Gray Wolf Pup	Closed	2001	55.00	55
1998 Gray Wolves	7,500		85.00	85
1999 Hummingbirds	7,500		70.00	70
1998 Lion Cub	Closed	2001	55.00	55
1999 Mallards	7,500	2002	85.00	85
2000 Mallards	7,500	2002	85.00	85
1998 Mayan Jaguar	7,500	2001	90.00	90
1998 Mom & Baby Giraffe	Closed	2001	55.00	55
2000 Mom & Baby Giraffe	7,500		60.00	60
2000 Mom & Baby Panda	7,500		60.00	60
1998 Mom & Baby Panda	Closed	2001	55.00	55
1998 Mom & Baby Seal	Closed	2001	55.00	55
2001 Morpho Butterflies	7,500		75.00	75
1998 Mother & Baby Elephant	7,500	2001	100.00	100
1998 Mother Zebra & Baby	7,500	2001	100.00	100
1999 Mustang	7,500		125.00	125
1999 Mustang Rearing	7,500	2001	85.00	85
2001 North American Wildlife Fountain	Open		125.00	125
2000 Polar Bear	7,500		60.00	60
1998 Polar Cub	Closed	2001	55.00	55
1998 Red Eyed Tree Frog	7,500	2001	85.00	85
1998 Scarlet Macaw	7,500	2001	100.00	100
2001 Snowy Owl	7,500		60.00	60

Norman Rockwell The Saturday Evening Post™ Collection - San Francisco Music Box Company

YEAR ISSUE	EDITION LIMIT	YEAR RETD.	ISSUE PRICE	*QUOTE U.S.$
2001 After The Prom 1957	7,500		75.00	75
2000 Catching the Big One Waterglobe 1929	7,500		50.00	50
2000 Doctor and the Doll 1929	7,500		60.00	60
2001 Football Hero 1938	7,500		60.00	60
2000 Girl at Mirror 1954	7,500		60.00	60
2000 Going Out 1933	7,500		60.00	60
2001 Puppy Love 1926	7,500	2002	50.00	50
2000 Santa at the Globe 1926	7,500		60.00	60
2000 Santa Reading Letters Waterglobe	7,500	2002	50.00	50

Phantom of the Opera Collection - San Francisco Music Box Company

YEAR ISSUE	EDITION LIMIT	YEAR RETD.	ISSUE PRICE	*QUOTE U.S.$
1999 Boat Scene Waterglobe	Open		45.00	45
2000 Christine and Raoul Waterglobe	Open		45.00	45
2000 Mirror Scene	5,000		65.00	65
2000 Monkey Musician	Open		55.00	55
1999 Music Box	Open		40.00	40
2000 Phantom Chair	Open		50.00	50
1999 Phantom Waterglobe	Open		40.00	40
2000 Red Death Mask	Open		50.00	50

Rainbow Visions - San Francisco Music Box Company

YEAR ISSUE	EDITION LIMIT	YEAR RETD.	ISSUE PRICE	*QUOTE U.S.$
1993 Castle Hourglass Waterglobe	Closed	1997	150.00	150
2001 Hourglass Waterglobe	9,500		100.00	100

Santa - Harley Davidson

YEAR ISSUE	EDITION LIMIT	YEAR RETD.	ISSUE PRICE	*QUOTE U.S.$
1998 Born to Ride Santa Waterglobe	10,000		55.00	55
1999 Mr. & Mrs. Claus	15,000		65.00	65
1998 Santa in the Sky	10,000		65.00	65
1999 Santa Waterglobe	10,000		50.00	50

Santa - L. Haney

YEAR ISSUE	EDITION LIMIT	YEAR RETD.	ISSUE PRICE	*QUOTE U.S.$
1999 "Bear Hugs"	250	1999	350.00	350
1998 Jolly Santa	300	1998	300.00	300
1999 Santa for a New Century	250	1999	300.00	300
1997 "Splendor of Christmas"	350	1997	300.00	300
1998 Winterfrost Santa	300	1998	300.00	300

Sentimental Rose - San Francisco Music Box Company

YEAR ISSUE	EDITION LIMIT	YEAR RETD.	ISSUE PRICE	*QUOTE U.S.$
2001 26" Rocking Horse	Open		300.00	300
2001 Angel Peace Figurine	Open		45.00	45
2001 Couple in Sleigh	Open		85.00	85
2001 Dove Centerpiece	Open		50.00	50
2000 Father Christmas Figurine	Open		60.00	60

Seraphim Angel Musical Figurines - Seraphim Studios

YEAR ISSUE	EDITION LIMIT	YEAR RETD.	ISSUE PRICE	*QUOTE U.S.$
1999 Ana Lisa	2,000	2000	210.00	210
2001 Angel with Jesus	Open		135.00	135
1997 Ariel	1,202	1997	179.95	180-225
2001 At Heaven's Gate	Open		135.00	135
1998 Avalon	1,410	1998	195.00	195

YEAR ISSUE	EDITION LIMIT	YEAR RETD.	ISSUE PRICE	*QUOTE U.S.$
2001 Bride & Groom	Open		110.00	110
1998 Hope	1,773	1999	179.95	180
2001 Jenna	Open		70.00	70
1998 Monica - 20th Anniversary Special Ed.	Closed	1999	60.00	60-95
1999 Nina	Closed	1999	195.00	195-225

Snow Magic Collection - San Francisco Music Box Company

YEAR ISSUE	EDITION LIMIT	YEAR RETD.	ISSUE PRICE	*QUOTE U.S.$
2000 Believe in Magic Waterglobe	Open		40.00	40
2000 Celebrate The Magic	Open		50.00	50
2000 Celebrate Winterstar Angel	Open		55.00	55
2000 Cold Nose, Warm Heart	Open		35.00	35
2000 Faith Gives Wishes Their Wings Waterglobe	Open		50.00	50
2000 Forever Friends Waterglobe	Open		45.00	45
2000 A Happy Wish or Two	Open		35.00	35
2000 Hope Upon A Star	9,500		60.00	60
2000 Jack Frost in Sleigh	Open		60.00	60
2000 Jack Frost Plate	Open		45.00	45
2000 Jack Frost Waterglobe	Open		85.00	85
2000 Jingle Bell Rock Waterglobe	Open		35.00	35
2000 Love Lights the Season	9,500		35.00	35
2000 May the Miracle of Christmas Waterglobe	Open		40.00	40
2000 May Your Heart Be Light	9,500		50.00	50
2000 Peace and Joy	Open		30.00	30
2000 Winterstar Angel "Rejoice"	9,500		50.00	50
2000 Winterstar Angel with Harp	Open		45.00	45

Teddy Hugs Musical Collection - M. Danko

YEAR ISSUE	EDITION LIMIT	YEAR RETD.	ISSUE PRICE	*QUOTE U.S.$
1998 Praying Bears - "Now I Lay me Down to Sleep" (1st ed.)	3,600	1999	35.00	35
1998 Toy Hutch - "Hugs are for Sharing"	6,000	1999	45.00	45

Wizard of Oz™ - San Francisco Music Box Company

YEAR ISSUE	EDITION LIMIT	YEAR RETD.	ISSUE PRICE	*QUOTE U.S.$
2001 Cowardly Lion Wateglobe	Closed	2002	55.00	55
1999 Dorothy	Closed	2001	45.00	45
2001 Dorothy Waterglobe	Closed	2002	55.00	55
1999 Emerald City Waterglobe	Open		60.00	60
2001 Four Characters Waterglobe	Open		60.00	60
1999 Glinda and Dorothy	Open		55.00	55
1999 Lion	Open		45.00	45
2001 Munchkinland Figurine	Open		85.00	85
2001 Munchkinland Waterglobe	Open		80.00	80
1999 No Place Like Home Waterglobe	Open		60.00	60
1999 Oz Hourglass Waterglobe	Open		125.00	125
1999 Oz Lacquer Box	Open		45.00	45
1999 Ruby Shoes Waterglobe	Open		45.00	45
1999 Scarecrow	Closed	2002	45.00	45
2001 Scarecrow Waterglobe	Closed	2002	55.00	55
1999 Tinman	Closed	2002	45.00	45
2001 Tinman Waterglobe	Closed	2002	55.00	55
2001 Wicked Witch Waterglobe	Open		45.00	45
1999 Witch Ball Waterglobe	Open		75.00	75

Xenis Collection Jester Series - San Francisco Music Box Company

YEAR ISSUE	EDITION LIMIT	YEAR RETD.	ISSUE PRICE	*QUOTE U.S.$
2000 Corbett	1,100	2001	225.00	225
2001 Sweetheart Doll	250		250.00	250

Willitts Designs

The Blackshear Style - T. Blackshear

YEAR ISSUE	EDITION LIMIT	YEAR RETD.	ISSUE PRICE	*QUOTE U.S.$
2000 Father's Keepsake Box	Closed	2001	125.00	125
2000 Heart Treasures Keepsake Box	Closed	2001	50.00	50
2000 Lover's Keepsake Box	Closed	2001	50.00	50
2000 Mother's Keepsake Box	Closed	2001	42.50	43

Carousel Classics/Carousel Memories - A. Dezendorf

YEAR ISSUE	EDITION LIMIT	YEAR RETD.	ISSUE PRICE	*QUOTE U.S.$
1998 American Musical Carousel	9,500	1999	100.00	100
1997 Armoured Lead Horse	9,500	1999	75.00	75
1997 Eagle-Back Stander	9,500	1999	65.00	65
1998 English Musical Carousel	9,500	1999	100.00	100
1998 French Musical Carousel	9,500	1999	100.00	100
1998 German Musical Karussell	9,500	1999	100.00	100
1997 Indian Pony Stander	9,500	1999	75.00	75
1998 Lion with Cherub	9,500	1999	75.00	75
1998 Middle Row Jumper w/Dog	9,500	1999	70.00	70
1997 Outside Row Jumper w/Parrot	9,500	1999	70.00	70
1998 Outside Row Stander w/ Scalloped Saddle	9,500	1999	70.00	70
1997 Outside Row Stander w/Cherub	9,500	1999	70.00	70

*Quotes have been rounded up to nearest dollar

YEAR ISSUE	EDITION LIMIT	YEAR RETD.	ISSUE PRICE	*QUOTE U.S.$
1997 Outside Row Stander w/Gold Mane	9,500	1999	75.00	75
1998 Outside Row Zebra Stander	9,500	1999	75.00	75
1997 Patriotic Outside Row Jumper	9,500	1999	70.00	70
1997 Stander "King" Horse	9,500	1999	70.00	70
1998 Stander w/Roached Mane	9,500	1999	70.00	70

CRYSTAL

Crystal World

All God's Creatures - Various

YEAR ISSUE	EDITION LIMIT	YEAR RETD.	ISSUE PRICE	*QUOTE U.S.$
2001 African Elephant - R. Takii	Open		300.00	300
1997 Allie Gator - R. Nakai	Closed	2000	100.00	100
2000 American Eagle - T. Suzuki	Open		195.00	195
2000 Baby Deer - R. Takii	Open		110.00	110
1990 Baby Dinosaur - T. Suzuki	Closed	1992	50.00	50
1990 Betsy Bunny - T. Suzuki	Closed	1992	32.00	32
2001 Birds of a Feather -T. Suzuki	Open		100.00	100
1997 Buffalo - Team	Closed	2000	350.00	350
2000 Charleston Charlie - T. Suzuki	Open		60.00	60
1990 Clara Cow - T. Suzuki	Closed	1991	32.00	32
2001 Doodle Doo -T. Suzuki	Open		50.00	50
1996 Freddy Frog - R. Nakai	Open		27.00	28
1996 Frieda Frog - R. Nakai	Open		35.00	36
1990 Georgie Giraffe - T. Suzuki	Closed	1992	32.00	32
1997 Giant Sea Turtle - Team	Closed	2000	250.00	250
1990 Henry Hippo - T. Suzuki	Closed	1992	32.00	32
1994 Hoot Owls - N. Mulargia	Closed	1998	45.00	45
1990 Jumbo Elephant - T. Suzuki	Open		32.00	32
1997 Junior (Elephant) - R. Nakai	Closed	2000	110.00	110
1995 Ling Ling - T. Suzuki	Closed	1997	53.00	53
1998 Little Owl - T. Suzuki	Open		100.00	100
1997 Mama Elephant - R. Nakai	Closed	2000	250.00	250
1990 Mikey Monkey - T. Suzuki	Closed	1991	32.00	32
2000 Mother and Cub - R. Takii	Open		175.00	175
1995 Percy Piglet - T. Suzuki	Closed	1996	19.00	19
1993 Pig - N. Mulargia	Closed	1995	50.00	50
1993 Playful Seal - T. Suzuki	Closed	1998	42.00	42
2000 Ponder - T. Suzuki	Open		55.00	55
1997 Proud Peacock - R. Nakai	Open		150.00	150
1994 Seal - R. Nakai	Closed	1996	46.00	46
1999 Thrills 'N Chills - R. Takii	Open		195.00	195
1992 Trumpeting Elephant - T. Suzuki	Closed	1996	50.00	50
1993 Turtle - R. Nakai	Closed	1996	65.00	65
1995 Wilbur in Love - N. Mulargia	Closed	1996	90.00	90
1994 Wilbur the Pig - T. Suzuki	Closed	2001	45.00	45
2001 Young Elephant - R. Takii	Open		125.00	125

Bon Voyage Collection - Various

YEAR ISSUE	EDITION LIMIT	YEAR RETD.	ISSUE PRICE	*QUOTE U.S.$
1990 Airplane, sm. - T. Suzuki	Closed	1993	200.00	200
1995 Amish Buggy - R. Nakai	Closed	1997	160.00	160
1995 Amish Buggy w/Wood Base - R. Nakai	Closed	1997	190.00	190
1994 Bermuda Rig Sailboat - R. Nakai	Open		50.00	60
1998 Bi-Plane - T. Suzuki	Open		40.00	75
1992 Bi-Plane, mini - T. Suzuki	Closed	1998	65.00	65
1991 Cruise Ship - T. Suzuki	1,000	2000	2000.00	2000
1997 Cruise Ship, med. - R. Nakai	Open		550.00	550
1995 Cruise Ship, mini - N. Mulargia	Open		100.00	100
1994 Cruise Ship, sm. - T. Suzuki	Open		250.00	250
1993 Express Train - N. Mulargia	Closed	1993	95.00	100
1998 Float Plane - T. Suzuki	Open		40.00	75
1994 Mainsail Sailboat - R. Nakai	Open		110.00	110
1990 Orbiting Space Shuttle - T. Suzuki	Closed	1997	300.00	300
1991 Orbiting Space Shuttle, sm. - T. Suzuki	Closed	1999	150.00	150
1991 The Rainbow Express - N. Mulargia	Closed	1993	125.00	130
1993 Sailboat - R. Nakai	Closed	2000	90.00	90
1992 Sailing Ship - N. Mulargia	Closed	1998	38.00	38
1991 Schooner - N. Mulargia	Closed	1995	95.00	95
1997 Schooner - R. Nakai	Closed	1998	60.00	60
1990 Space Shuttle Launch, sm. - T. Suzuki	Closed	1996	265.00	270
1994 Spinnaker Sailboat - R. Nakai	Open		130.00	130
1990 Square Rigger - R. Nakai	Open		250.00	270
1995 Tall Ship - R. Nakai	Closed	2000	395.00	395
1998 Titanic -T. Suzuki	1,912		175.00	175
1990 Train Set, lg. - T. Suzuki	Closed	1992	480.00	480
1990 Train Set, sm. - T. Suzuki	Closed	2000	100.00	170
1997 Truckin' - R. Nakai	Open		260.00	260

Castles and Legends - R. Nakai, unless otherwise noted

YEAR ISSUE	EDITION LIMIT	YEAR RETD.	ISSUE PRICE	*QUOTE U.S.$
1991 Castle In The Sky	Closed	1994	150.00	165
1994 Castle Rainbow Rainbow Mtn. Bs.	Closed	2000	1575.00	1600
1994 Castle Royale/Clear Mtn. Bs.	Closed	2000	1300.00	1350
2000 Delilah Shares a Secret - R. Takii	Open		70.00	70
2000 Delilah Welcomes Summer - R. Takii	Open		70.00	70
1989 Dream Castle	Closed	1999	9000.00	10000
1996 Emerald Castle	Closed	1998	105.00	105
1993 Enchanted Castle	750		800.00	850
1993 Fantasy Castle, lg.	Open		230.00	235
1993 Fantasy Castle, med.	Open		130.00	135
1992 Fantasy Castle, mini - N. Mulargia	Closed	2000	40.00	40
1992 Fantasy Castle, sm.	Open		85.00	90
1995 Fantasy Coach, lg. - N. Mulargia	Open		350.00	350
1995 Fantasy Coach, med. - N. Mulargia	Open		150.00	150
1995 Fantasy Coach, sm. - N. Mulargia	Open		95.00	95
1988 Imperial Castle	Closed	1998	320.00	320
1999 Legendary Unicorn - T. Suzuki	Open		125.00	125
1991 Majestic Castle - A. Kato	Closed	1998	390.00	390
1995 Mouse Coach, mini - N. Mulargia	Open		50.00	50
1995 Mouse Coach, sm. - N. Mulargia	Open		90.00	90
1988 Mystic Castle	Open		100.00	100
1987 Rainbow Castle	Open		150.00	190
1989 Rainbow Castle, mini	Open		60.00	60
1990 Rainbow Unicorn - N. Mulargia	Open		50.00	60

Celebration of Life - Various

YEAR ISSUE	EDITION LIMIT	YEAR RETD.	ISSUE PRICE	*QUOTE U.S.$
1998 Baby Booties - R. Nakai	Open		35.00	35
1997 Baby Boy Carriage - T. Suzuki	Closed	1998	50.00	50
1997 Baby Girl Carriage - T. Suzuki	Closed	1998	50.00	50
2001 Bride and Groom - T. Suzuki	Open		100.00	100
2000 First Dance - T. Suzuki	Open		90.00	90
1995 Happy Birthday Cake - R. Nakai	Open		60.00	60
XX Pacifier - Team	Open		30.00	30
1998 Wedding Bells - R. Nakai	Open		125.00	125
1989 Wedding Couple - N. Mulargia	Closed	2000	100.00	100
1995 Wedding Couple, med. - N. Mulargia	Closed	1998	63.00	63
1992 Wedding Couple, mini - N. Mulargia	Closed	1997	30.00	30

Crystal Concerto - Various

YEAR ISSUE	EDITION LIMIT	YEAR RETD.	ISSUE PRICE	*QUOTE U.S.$
2001 Accoustic Guitar - T. Suzuki	Open		65.00	65
1997 Clarinet - J. Makoto	Closed	1999	235.00	235
1998 Grand Piano with Bench - R. Nakai	Open		125.00	125
1999 Violin and Bow - T. Suzuki	Open		80.00	80

Disney Showcase Collection - Various

YEAR ISSUE	EDITION LIMIT	YEAR RETD.	ISSUE PRICE	*QUOTE U.S.$
2001 Bewitched Blossom - R. Nakai	6,750		99.00	99
1998 Cinderella's Castle - T. Suzuki	1,250		1495.00	1495
1999 Cinderella's Coach - R. Nakai	1,450		893.00	893
1998 Cinderella's Slipper - R. Nakai	9,750		49.50	50
1998 Dumbo & Timothy - T. Suzuki	2,750	2001	279.00	279
2001 Eeyore - T. Suzuki	2,750		199.00	199
1998 Gee, You're the Sweetest (Minnie) - R. Nakai	4,750		249.00	249
2001 Jiminy Cricket - T. Suzuki	2,750		159.00	159
1998 Just For You (Mickey) - R. Nakai	4,750		249.00	249
2001 Piglet - T. Suzuki	2,750		109.00	109
1998 Pinocchio & Jiminy Cricket - T. Suzuki	2,750		299.00	299
2000 Sorcerer Mickey Makes Magic - T. Suzuki	2,000		299.00	299
1999 Steamboat Willie - T. Suzuki	2,000		299.00	299
2001 Tigger - T. Suzuki	2,750		179.00	179
1999 Tinker Bell - R. Nakai	3,750		193.00	193
2001 Winnie the Pooh - T. Suzuki	4,750		199.00	199

The Gambler Collection - R. Nakai, unless otherwise noted

YEAR ISSUE	EDITION LIMIT	YEAR RETD.	ISSUE PRICE	*QUOTE U.S.$
1993 Black Jack Teddies - N. Mulargia	Open		97.00	97
1991 Dice, sm.	Closed	1997	27.00	27
1997 Jackpot Teddy - T. Suzuki	Open		62.50	63
1991 Lucky 7	Closed	1992	50.00	50
1997 Lucky Die	Closed	1998	70.00	70
1994 Lucky Roll	Open		95.00	95
1996 One Arm Bandit	Open		70.00	70
1991 Rolling Dice - T. Suzuki	Closed	N/A	110.00	110
1993 Rolling Dice, lg.	Closed	1997	60.00	60
1993 Rolling Dice, med.	Open		45.00	45
1992 Rolling Dice, mini	Open		32.00	32
1993 Rolling Dice, sm.	Closed	1996	40.00	40
1993 Slot Machine, lg. - T. Suzuki	Open		80.00	80
1991 Slot Machine, mini	Open		30.00	35
1991 Slot Machine, sm. - T. Suzuki	Open		60.00	60
1994 Super Slot Machine	Open		295.00	295

CRYSTAL

YEAR ISSUE	EDITION LIMIT	YEAR RETD.	ISSUE PRICE	*QUOTE U.S.$
1999 Teddies on a Roll - R. Takii	Open		100.00	100

Holiday Treasures - R. Nakai, unless otherwise noted

YEAR ISSUE	EDITION LIMIT	YEAR RETD.	ISSUE PRICE	*QUOTE U.S.$
1999 Angel of Joy - T. Suzuki	Open		60.00	60
1999 Angel of Love - T. Suzuki	Open		60.00	60
1999 Angel of Peace - T. Suzuki	Open		60.00	60
1997 Angel with Heart - T. Suzuki	Closed	1998	30.00	30
1995 Angel, lg.	Closed	1998	50.00	50
1994 Angel, mini	Closed	1996	25.00	25
1995 Baby Bear's Christmas - T. Suzuki	Closed	1997	48.00	48
1994 Cathedral w/Rainbow Base	Closed	1996	99.00	99
1994 Christmas Tree, Extra lg.	Open		300.00	300
1985 Christmas Tree, lg.	Open		126.00	130
1985 Christmas Tree, mini	Open		45.00	45
1985 Christmas Tree, sm.	Open		50.00	70
1991 Christmas Wreath Teddy - T. Suzuki	Closed	1992	70.00	75
1994 Country Church	Closed	1997	53.00	53
1994 Country Church w/Rainbow Base	Open		60.00	60
2000 Drumming Toy Soldier - T. Suzuki	Open		60.00	60
1996 Frosty	Closed	2000	41.00	45
1991 Holy Angel Blowing A Trumpet - T. Nakai	Closed	1997	38.00	38
1991 Holy Angel Holding A Candle - T. Nakai	Closed	1998	38.00	38
1991 Holy Angel Playing A Harp - T. Suzuki	Closed	1996	38.00	38
2000 Marching Toy Soldier - T. Suzuki	Open		60.00	60
1991 Merry Christmas Teddy - T. Suzuki	Open		55.00	55
1986 Nativity - N. Mulargia	Open		150.00	170
1991 Nativity, sm. - T. Suzuki	Closed	1998	85.00	85
1991 Santa Bear Christmas - T. Suzuki	Closed	1997	70.00	70
2000 Santa Bear is Coming to Town - T. Suzuki	Open		55.00	55
1991 Santa Bear Sleighride - T. Suzuki	Closed	1997	70.00	70
2000 Santa's Buddy - T. Suzuki	Open		50.00	50
2001 Snowman - T. Suzuki	Open		50.00	50
1987 Teddy Bear Christmas	Open		100.00	100
1991 Trim A Tree Teddy	Closed	1996	50.00	50
1990 Trumpeting Angel	Closed	1991	60.00	60
2000 Trumpeting Toy Soldier - T. Suzuki	Open		60.00	60

Imagination - Various

YEAR ISSUE	EDITION LIMIT	YEAR RETD.	ISSUE PRICE	*QUOTE U.S.$
1996 Bo-Bo The Clown - N. Mulargia	Closed	2000	50.00	50
1998 Carousel Horse - R. Nakai	Open		125.00	125
1992 Fire Engine - T. Suzuki	Closed	1998	80.00	80
1996 Friends Forever - R. Nakai	Closed	1998	75.00	75
1997 Frog Prince - R. Nakai	Open		55.00	55
1998 Glass Slipper - T. Suzuki	Open		30.00	30
1990 I Love You Unicorn - N. Mulargia	Closed	1992	58.00	58
1996 Merry-Go-Round - N. Mulargia	750	2000	265.00	265
1996 Merry-Go-Round, sm. - N. Mulargia	Open		150.00	150
1996 Noah and Friends - N. Mulargia	Open		150.00	150
1990 Pegasus - N. Mulargia	Closed	1991	50.00	50
1996 Pinocchio - T. Suzuki	Open		150.00	150
1999 Rocking Horse - T. Suzuki	Open		150.00	150
1990 Unicorn - N. Mulargia	Closed	1992	38.00	40
1998 Wishin' and a Hoppin' - T. Suzuki	Closed	2000	95.00	95

The Jitterbugs - T. Suzuki, unless otherwise noted

YEAR ISSUE	EDITION LIMIT	YEAR RETD.	ISSUE PRICE	*QUOTE U.S.$
1999 Buzz	Open		70.00	70
1999 Lady	Open		65.00	65
1999 Madame D - R. Takii	Open		65.00	65
1999 Mister G	Open		65.00	65

Limited Edition Collection Series - Various

YEAR ISSUE	EDITION LIMIT	YEAR RETD.	ISSUE PRICE	*QUOTE U.S.$
1993 Country Gristmill - T. Suzuki	1,250	1998	320.00	340
1991 Ellis Island - R. Nakai	Closed	1992	450.00	500
1992 Santa Maria - N. Mulargia	Closed	1993	1000.00	1050
1990 Tower Bridge - T. Suzuki	Closed	1992	600.00	650
1993 Victorian House - N. Mulargia	Closed	1992	190.00	190

New York Collection - R. Nakai, unless otherwise noted

YEAR ISSUE	EDITION LIMIT	YEAR RETD.	ISSUE PRICE	*QUOTE U.S.$
1993 Apple with Red Heart, med.	Closed	1997	37.00	37
1985 Apple, lg.	Open		44.00	65
1985 Apple, med.	Open		30.00	40
1987 Apple, mini	Open		12.50	13
1985 Apple, sm.	Open		15.00	20
1995 Chrysler Building	Closed	1996	275.00	275
1992 Contemp. Empire State Bldg., lg. - A. Kato	Closed	1996	475.00	475
1992 Contemp. Empire State Bldg., med.	Closed	1997	170.00	170
1992 Contemp. Empire State Bldg., sm.	Closed	1996	95.00	95
1992 Contemp. Empire State Bldg., sm. MV	Open		95.00	95

YEAR ISSUE	EDITION LIMIT	YEAR RETD.	ISSUE PRICE	*QUOTE U.S.$
1996 The Empire State Bldg.	475		1315.00	1315
1992 Empire State Bldg. w/Windows, mini	Open		65.00	65
1987 Empire State Bldg., lg.	2,000		650.00	700
1987 Empire State Bldg., med.	Open		250.00	260
1991 Empire State Bldg., mini	Open		60.00	65
1987 Empire State Bldg., sm.	Open		120.00	120
1993 Holiday Empire State building - N. Mulargia	Open		170.00	170
2000 Lady Liberty - R. Takii	Open		89.00	89
2000 Lady Liberty w/colored base - R. Takii	Open		95.00	95
1989 Liberty Sign - N. Mulargia	Open		75.00	80
1990 Manhattan Island	Open		240.00	240
1993 Manhattan Island, sm. - N. Mulargia	Open		80.00	80
1985 The Statue of Liberty	Open		250.00	350
1987 Statue of Liberty, med.	Closed	2000	120.00	155
2000 Statue of Liberty, med. - R. Takii	Open		165.00	165
1992 Statue Of Liberty, mini	Open		40.00	40
1987 Statue of Liberty, sm. - N. Mulargia	Open		50.00	65
1998 Twin Towers, lg.	Open		150.00	150
1992 Twin Towers, sm.	Open		90.00	90
2000 A View of New York - T. Suzuki	Open		450.00	450

North American Wildlife - R. Takii, unless otherwise noted

YEAR ISSUE	EDITION LIMIT	YEAR RETD.	ISSUE PRICE	*QUOTE U.S.$
1997 Majestic Bald Eagle - N. Mulargia	1,250		1100.00	1100
1999 Mountain Lion	Open		195.00	195
2000 Mustang	Open		185.00	185
1998 Timber Wolf - R. Nakai	1,250		175.00	175
1999 White-Tailed Deer	Open		195.00	195

Nostalgia Collection - Various

YEAR ISSUE	EDITION LIMIT	YEAR RETD.	ISSUE PRICE	*QUOTE U.S.$
2000 Antique Gramophone - T. Suzuki	Open		65.00	65
2000 Antique Telephone - T. Suzuki	Open		65.00	65
1991 Cable Car, lg. - T. Suzuki	Open		100.00	100
1992 Cable Car, mini - T. Suzuki	Closed	1996	40.00	40
1991 Cable Car, sm. - T. Suzuki	Closed	1997	70.00	70
2001 Carousel - R. Takii	Open		320.00	320
2001 Carousel, sm. - R. Takii	Open		170.00	170
1996 Classic Motorcycle - T. Suzuki	Closed	1999	400.00	400
1996 Classic Motorcycle, sm. - T. Suzuki	Open		200.00	200
1999 Engine No. 9 - T. Suzuki	Closed	2000	85.00	85
1996 Fabulous Fifties Jukebox - N. Mulargia	Closed	2000	80.00	80
1992 Fire Engine - T. Suzuki	Closed	1998	75.00	80
2001 Formal Arm Chair - T. Suzuki	Open		65.00	65
1997 Grand Cable Car - T. Suzuki	Closed	1998	150.00	150
1993 Riverboat - N. Mulargia	350	1999	570.00	600
1994 Riverboat, sm. - N. Mulargia	Open		100.00	100
1993 San Francisco Cable Car, lg. - R. Nakai	Open		60.00	60
1993 San Francisco Cable Car, sm. - R. Nakai	Open		40.00	40
2000 Tea For Two - T. Suzuki	Open		65.00	65
2001 Victorian Slipper - R. Takii	Open		35.00	35
2001 Victorian Tea Hat - R. Takii	Open		55.00	55

Puppies, Kitties & Friends - T. Suzuki

YEAR ISSUE	EDITION LIMIT	YEAR RETD.	ISSUE PRICE	*QUOTE U.S.$
2001 Trick or Treat	Open		60.00	60

Raining Cats and Dogs (and occasional Mice) - T. Suzuki, unless otherwise noted

YEAR ISSUE	EDITION LIMIT	YEAR RETD.	ISSUE PRICE	*QUOTE U.S.$
1990 Barney Dog	Closed	1992	32.00	32
1991 Calamity Cat	Closed	1998	60.00	60
1990 Cat N Mouse	Closed	1996	45.00	45
1994 Cheese Mouse - R. Nakai	Closed	2000	50.00	50
1998 Coffee Break	Open		50.00	50
1992 Country Cat	Closed	1998	60.00	60
1990 The Curious Cat	Open		60.00	60
1991 Curious Cat, lg.	Closed	1998	90.00	90
1997 CyberMouse - N. Mulargia	Closed	1997	35.00	35
1995 Fido the Dog	Closed	1997	27.00	27
1995 Frisky Fido	Closed	1996	27.00	27
1998 Glamour Puss	Open		70.00	70
1991 Hello Birdie	Open		70.00	70
2000 Karma the Bulldog - R. Takii	Open		60.00	60
1992 Kitten in Basket - C. Kido	Closed	1997	35.00	40
1993 Kitty Kare	Closed	1994	70.00	70
1991 Kitty with Butterfly	Closed	1994	60.00	60
1991 Kitty with Heart	Open		30.00	30
1990 Moonlight Cats - R. Nakai	Closed	1992	100.00	110
1995 Moonlight Kitties	Closed	1997	83.00	83
1994 Mozart	Closed	2000	50.00	50
1991 Peek-A-Boo Kitties	Open		60.00	60
1993 Pinky	Closed	1996	50.00	50
1992 Playful Kitty	Open		32.00	32

Collectors' Information Bureau   *Quotes have been rounded up to nearest dollar

YEAR ISSUE	EDITION LIMIT	YEAR RETD.	ISSUE PRICE	*QUOTE U.S.$
1993 Playful Kitty, lg.	Closed	1996	50.00	50
1990 Playful Pup	Closed	N/A	85.00	85
1994 Playful Pup - T. Suzuki	Closed	1998	53.00	53
1990 Puppy Love	Closed	1992	45.00	45
1993 Puppy-Gram	Open		60.00	60
1991 Rock-A-Bye Kitty - R. Nakai	Closed	2000	80.00	80
2001 Sebastian	Open		40.00	40
1992 See Saw Pals - A. Kato	Closed	1999	40.00	40
1997 Sparkie	Closed	2000	60.00	60
1991 Sparkie - R. Nakai	Closed	1992	50.00	50
1991 Spike - R. Nakai	Closed	1992	50.00	50
1991 Spot	Closed	1992	50.00	50
1991 Strolling Kitties	Closed	1992	65.00	65
1994 Sweetie	Closed	2000	28.00	28
1995 Tea Time - R. Nakai	Closed	1998	50.00	50
1996 Wanna Play?	Closed	1999	65.00	65

Seaside Memories - R. Nakai, unless otherwise noted

YEAR ISSUE	EDITION LIMIT	YEAR RETD.	ISSUE PRICE	*QUOTE U.S.$
1992 Baby Seal - T. Suzuki	Open	1998	21.00	21
1998 Barnegat Lighthouse-NJ	Open		80.00	80
1991 Beaver	Closed	1996	47.00	47
2001 Cape Hatteras Lighthouse	Open		105.00	105
2000 Cape May Lighthouse	Open		110.00	110
1997 Coastal Lighthouse	Open		80.00	80
1996 Crabbie le Crab	Closed	1997	38.00	38
1992 Cute Crab - T. Suzuki	Closed	1997	27.00	27
1998 Dolphin Dreams	1,250	2000	220.00	220
1990 Duck Family	Closed	1992	70.00	70
1993 Extra Large Oyster with Pearl	Closed	1996	75.00	78
1993 Harbor Lighthouse - N. Mulargia	Open		70.00	70
1998 Hatching Sea Turtle - T. Suzuki	Closed	1998	45.00	45
2001 Humpback Whale - R. Rakii	Open		250.00	250
1998 Lobster - T. Suzuki	Closed	2000	125.00	135
1993 Manatee Paperweight - Team	Open		125.00	125
1999 Nubble Lighthouse-Maine	Open		125.00	125
2001 Oliver - T. Suzuki	Open		70.00	70
1994 Oscar Otter - T. Suzuki	Closed	1996	105.00	105
1990 Pearl Oyster, lg.	Open		60.00	60
1990 Pearl Oyster, sm.	Open		25.00	25
1996 Pelican	Closed	1998	65.00	65
1991 Penguin On Cube	Closed	1995	40.00	40
1996 Penguin On Cube	Closed	1998	48.00	48
1996 Playful Dolphin	Closed	1999	125.00	125
1996 Playful Dolphin	Closed	1999	75.00	75
1992 Playful Dolphins - T. Suzuki	Closed	1996	60.00	60
1993 Playful Seal - T. Suzuki	Closed	1996	45.00	45
1998 Sea Turtle at Play - T. Suzuki	Open		85.00	85
1994 Seal	Closed	1996	47.00	50
1992 Seaside Pelican - T. Suzuki	Closed	1995	55.00	55
1998 Splash	Open		80.00	80
1995 Treasure Chest - R. Nakai	Open		60.00	60
1992 Tropical Fish	Closed	1995	95.00	95
1992 Tuxedo Penguin	Closed	1995	75.00	75
2000 Two To Tango - R. Takii	Open		100.00	100
1992 The Whales - T. Suzuki	Closed	1994	60.00	65

Spring Parade Collection - Various

YEAR ISSUE	EDITION LIMIT	YEAR RETD.	ISSUE PRICE	*QUOTE U.S.$
1990 African Violet - I. Nakamura	Open		32.00	32
1996 American Beauty Rose - N. Mulargia	Closed	1997	53.00	53
1992 Barrel Cactus - I. Nakamura	Closed	1995	45.00	45
1998 Blossom Bunny - T. Suzuki	Closed	1998	42.00	42
1991 Bunnies On Ice - T. Suzuki	Closed	1996	58.00	58
1991 Bunny Buddy with Carrot - T. Suzuki	Closed	2000	30.00	30
1992 Candleholder - N. Mulargia	Closed	1995	125.00	125
1993 Cheep Cheep - T. Suzuki	Closed	1998	35.00	35
1998 Cottontail - T. Suzuki	Open		70.00	70
1990 Crocus - N. Nakai	Closed	1991	45.00	45
1992 Cute Bunny - T. Suzuki	Closed	1995	38.00	38
2001 Daffodils - A. Harigae	Open		50.00	50
1995 Desert Cactus - N. Mulargia	Closed	1996	48.00	48
2001 Dogwood Flower - A. Harigae	Open		50.00	50
1994 The Enchanted Rose - R. Nakai	Open		60.00	60
1992 Flowering Cactus - I. Nakamura	Closed	1996	58.00	58
2001 Friendship Bouquet - A. Harigae	Open		45.00	45
2000 Golden Pineapple - R. Nakai	Open		40.00	40
1992 Half Dozen Flower Arrangement - N. Mulargia	Closed	1996	20.00	20
1992 Happy Heart - N. Mulargia	Closed	1996	25.00	25
1992 Hummingbird - T. Suzuki	Open		58.00	58
1992 Hummingbird, mini - T. Suzuki	Open		27.00	27
1990 Hyacinth - I. Nakamura	Closed	1996	50.00	50

YEAR ISSUE	EDITION LIMIT	YEAR RETD.	ISSUE PRICE	*QUOTE U.S.$
2001 Hyacinth- R. Nakai	Open		45.00	45
1995 Long Stem Pink Rose in Vase - R. Nakai	Closed	1998	41.00	41
1992 Long Stem Rose - N. Mulargia	Open		35.00	40
1994 Long Stem Rose in Vase - R. Nakai	Open		40.00	40
1986 Love Swan - N. Mulargia	Closed	N/A	70.00	70
1995 Love Swans - N. Mulargia	Open		80.00	80
1996 Love Swans, lg. - N. Mulargia	Closed	2000	252.00	252
1992 Loving Hearts - N. Mulargia	Open		35.00	35
2001 Pansies - A. Harigae	Open		65.00	65
1996 Pineapple - R. Nakai	Closed	1998	50.00	50
1995 Pink Rose - R. Nakai	Closed	1997	53.00	53
1991 Rainbow Butterfly, mini - R. Nakai	Closed	1996	27.00	27
1994 Rainbow Rose - N. Mulargia	Closed	1996	82.00	82
1987 Red Rose - R. Nakai	Open		50.00	50
1990 Rose Basket - I. Nakamura	Closed	1992	52.00	52
1996 Rose Bouquet, sm. - R. Nakai	Closed	1998	45.00	45
1993 Songbirds - I. Nakamura	Open		90.00	100
1992 Spring Blossoms - T. Suzuki	Closed	1997	40.00	40
1995 Spring Butterfly - R. Nakai	Open		40.00	40
1989 Spring Chick - R. Nakai	Open		50.00	50
2001 Summer Sunflower - R. Takii	Open		60.00	60
2000 Swallowtail Butterfly - R. Takii	Open		85.00	85
1990 Swan Family - T. Suzuki	Closed	N/A	70.00	70
1987 Swan, lg. - R. Nakai	Closed	1996	100.00	100
1987 Swan, med. - R. Nakai	Closed	2000	60.00	60
1987 Swan, mini - R. Nakai	Closed	2000	28.00	28
1987 Swan, sm. - R. Nakai	Open		32.00	45
1996 Water Lily, Medium, AB - R. Nakai	Open		200.00	200
1997 Water Lily, sm. AB - R. Nakai	Open		100.00	100
1992 Waterfront Village - N. Mulargia	Closed	1996	190.00	190
1992 Wedding Couple - N. Mulargia	Closed	2000	100.00	100
2001 Wind Dancer - A. Harigae	Open		110.00	110
1991 Windmill, mini - R. Nakai	Closed	1992	63.00	63

Teddies - T. Suzuki

YEAR ISSUE	EDITION LIMIT	YEAR RETD.	ISSUE PRICE	*QUOTE U.S.$
2001 Bingo!	Open		55.00	55
2001 Halloween Night	Open		70.00	70
2001 Nigel	Open		50.00	50

Teddyland Collection - Various

YEAR ISSUE	EDITION LIMIT	YEAR RETD.	ISSUE PRICE	*QUOTE U.S.$
1990 Baron Von Teddy - T. Suzuki	Closed	1993	60.00	60
1987 Beach Teddies - N. Mulargia	Open		100.00	100
1992 Beach Teddies, sm. - N. Mulargia	Closed	2000	70.00	70
1992 Billard Buddies - T. Suzuki	Closed	1998	70.00	70
1988 Bouquet Teddy, sm. - N. Mulargia	Open		35.00	40
1998 Broadway Ted - R. Nakai	Open		45.00	45
1990 Choo Choo Teddy - T. Suzuki	Closed	1993	100.00	100
1995 CompuBear - N. Mulargia	Open		60.00	60
1996 Cuddly Bear - R. Nakai	Closed	1998	50.00	50
1993 Flower Teddy - T. Suzuki	Closed	1997	50.00	50
1995 Fly A Kite Teddy - T. Suzuki	Closed	1996	41.00	41
1995 Get Well Teddy - R. Nakai	Closed	1996	48.00	48
1989 Golfing Teddies - R. Nakai	Open		100.00	120
1991 Gumball Teddy - T. Suzuki	Closed	1996	63.00	63
1989 Happy Birthday Teddy - R. Nakai	Open		50.00	50
1991 Heart Bear - T. Suzuki	Open		28.00	28
1991 High Chair Teddy - T. Suzuki	Closed	1992	75.00	78
1988 I Love You Teddy - N. Mulargia	Open		40.00	40
1994 I Love You Teddy Couple - N. Mulargia	Open		45.00	45
1992 Ice Cream Teddies - N. Mulargia	Closed	1998	55.00	55
1987 Loving Teddies - N. Mulargia	Closed	1998	75.00	75
1990 Loving Teddies, sm. - N. Mulargia	Open		60.00	65
1991 Luck Of The Irish - R. Nakai	Closed	1992	60.00	60
1990 Mountaineer Teddy - N. Mulargia	Closed	1992	80.00	80
1991 My Favorite Picture - T. Suzuki	Open		45.00	45
1998 Mystic Teddy - R. Nakai	Open		70.00	70
1992 Patriotic Teddy - N. Mulargia	Open		30.00	30
1991 Play It Again Ted - T. Suzuki	Closed	1997	65.00	65
1991 Playground Teddy - R. Kido	Closed	1992	90.00	90
1990 Rainbow Teddies - N. Mulargia	Closed	1993	95.00	95
1990 Rocking Horse Teddy - N. Mulargia	Closed	1992	80.00	80
1991 School Bears - H. Serino	Open		75.00	75
1991 Scuba Bear - T. Suzuki	Closed	1992	65.00	65
1993 Singing Baby Bear - T. Suzuki	Closed	1993	55.00	55
1999 Sophie - T. Suzuki	Open		60.00	60
1989 Speedboat Teddies - R. Nakai	Closed	1998	90.00	90
1990 Storytime Teddies - T. Suzuki	Closed	2000	70.00	80
1991 Swinging Teddies - N. Mulargia	Closed	2000	100.00	120
1988 Teddies At Eight - N. Mulargia	Open		100.00	100

YEAR ISSUE	EDITION LIMIT	YEAR RETD.	ISSUE PRICE	*QUOTE U.S.$
1988 Teddies with Heart - R. Nakai	Open		45.00	50
1994 Teddy Bear with Rainbow Base - R. Nakai	Closed	1996	75.00	75
1991 Teddy with Red Heart, mini - R. Nakai	Open		25.00	25
1995 Teddy's Self Portrait - T. Suzuki	Closed	1996	53.00	53
1999 Theodore - T. Suzuki	Open		55.00	60
1988 Touring Teddies - N. Mulargia	Open		90.00	100
1990 Tricycle Teddy - T. Suzuki	Closed	1993	40.00	40
1997 Up and Away - N. Mulargia	Open		80.00	80

Wildlife - T. Suzuki

2001 Panda Love	Open		115.00	115

Wonders of the World Collection - R. Nakai, unless otherwise noted

1993 Capitol Building, sm. - N. Mulargia	Closed	1996	100.00	100
1997 Capitol Hill	350		1300.00	1300
1991 Chicago Water Tower w/base - T. Suzuki	Closed	1997	300.00	300
1986 The Eiffel Tower - T. Suzuki	2000		1000.00	1350
1988 Eiffel Tower, sm. - T. Suzuki	2000		500.00	625
1995 Independence Hall	750	1999	370.00	370
1990 Le Petit Eiffel - T. Suzuki	Open		240.00	250
1995 The Liberty Bell	Closed	2000	150.00	150
1999 Liberty Bell, sm.	Open		80.00	80
1993 Sears Tower	Closed	1997	150.00	150
1987 Taj Mahal - T. Suzuki	2,000		2000.00	2250
1995 Taj Mahal, med.	Open		790.00	790
1995 Taj Mahal, sm.	Open		210.00	210
1999 Totem Pole	Open		79.00	79
2000 Totem Pole, lg.	Open		145.00	145
2000 Totem Pole, sm.	Open		59.00	59
1987 U.S. Capitol Building	Open		250.00	300
1998 Washington Monument	Open		75.00	75
1992 The White House	Closed	1993	3000.00	3000
1994 White House w/Oct. Mirror, sm. - N. Mulargia	Open		175.00	175

Lenox Classics

Lenox Classics-China Disney Showcase - Lenox

2002 Cinderella's Surprise	3,500		250.00	250
2002 For You, From Pooh	Open		79.00	79
2002 Mrs. Potts and Chip	Open		95.00	95
2002 Pooh and Piglet's Party	Open		50.00	50
2002 Searching for the Sorcerer's Spell	3,500		250.00	250
2002 Tinker Bell	Open		95.00	95

Lenox Classics-Crystal Birds - Lenox

2000 Love and Devotion	2,500		95.00	95

Lenox Classics-Crystal Cats - Lenox

1997 Crystal Jaguar (Cat in Grass)	Retrd.	2000	160.00	175
1996 Fascination (Cat w/Butterfly)	Open		50.00	55
1998 Grace and Glamour (Crystal Cat Pair)	Retrd.	2002	79.00	79
1998 Hugs and Kisses (Crystal Cat Pair)	Retrd.	2000	79.00	79
2000 Majestic Tiger	Open		195.00	195
1997 Morning Stretch (Cat Stretching)	Open		136.00	145
1996 Playtime (Cat w/Ball)	Retrd.	2000	50.00	55
1996 Preen & Serene (Cat Pair)	Open		76.00	79
1998 Prim & Proper	Open		76.00	76
1997 Warm & Cozy (Cat & Kitten)	2,500		110.00	110

Lenox Classics-Crystal Collection - Lenox

2001 The Crystal Buck	Open		154.00	154
2002 Crystal Dolphin Candlesticks	Open		156.00	156
2001 The Crystal Dolphin Vase	Open		119.00	119
2001 Crystal Peacock	Open		136.00	136
2001 Free Spirit	Open		136.00	136
2002 The Lenox Crystal Butterfly Candlesticks	Open		98.00	98
2001 The Lenox Crystal Butterfly Vase	Open		95.00	95
2002 The Lenox Crystal Dolphin Salt and Pepper	Open		25.00	25
2002 The Lenox Crystal Lighthouse Salt and Pepper	Open		25.00	25
2002 The Lenox Jeweled Crystal Cross	Open		40.00	40
2001 The Light at Crystal Point	Open		95.00	95
2000 Racing The Wind	2,500		136.00	136
2000 Sunset Sail	Open		136.00	136
2002 Undersea Paradise Vase	Open		95.00	95

Lenox Classics-Crystal Disney Showcase - Lenox

2000 Flowers From Mickey	Open		80.00	80
2000 Hello Minnie!	Open		80.00	80
2002 Light of Friendship Votive	Open		119.00	119
2002 Piglet	Open		98.00	98
2001 Tigger	Open		98.00	98
2000 Winnie the Pooh	Open		98.00	98

Lenox Classics-Crystal Eagles - Lenox

1997 Protector of the Stars (Patriotic Eagle)	Retrd.	2001	115.00	125
1996 Soaring Majesty (Flying Eagle)	Retrd.	2000	195.00	195
1998 Wings of Brilliance (Eagle Taking Off)	Retrd.	2000	195.00	195
1996 Wings of the Sun (Eagle on Rock)	Retrd.	2001	195.00	195

Lenox Classics-Crystal Elephants - Lenox

1999 Bashful & Bold	Open		79.00	79
1998 Cotton and Candy (Elephant Pair)	Retrd.	2001	79.00	79
1998 Crystal Dancer	Retrd.	2001	136.00	136
1997 Crystal Playmate (Elephant in Grass)	Retrd.	2000	136.00	136
1998 Crystal Repose	Retrd.	2000	136.00	136
1996 Peanuts & Popcorn (Elephant Pair)	Open		76.00	79
2000 Standing Elephant	Open		136.00	136
1999 Tender Embrace	2,500		195.00	195
1997 Touch of Love (Elephant Mother & Calf)	2,500	2000	195.00	195

Lenox Classics-Crystal Inspirational - Lenox

1999 The Ascension	2,500	2001	195.00	195
1999 Footprints	2,500	2001	195.00	195

Lenox Classics-Crystal Safari Animals - Lenox

2000 Giraffe	2,500		154.00	154
2000 Zebra	2,500		136.00	136

Lenox Classics-Crystal Sea Animals - Lenox

1998 Dolphin Duet (Crystal Dolphin pair)	Open		100.00	100
1996 Dolphin's Journey (Mother w/Child)	Retrd.	2000	76.00	100
1999 Dolphin's Love (Mother & Child Dolphin)	2,500		136.00	136
1996 Glorious Dolphin (Dolphin Jumping Up)	Retrd.	2000	76.00	100
1998 Majestic Dolphin	Open		100.00	100
1996 Radiant Dolphin (Dolphin Diving Down)	Retrd.	2000	76.00	100
1999 Sea Surrender (Diving Dolphin)	2,500	2000	125.00	125
1998 Swan King (Crystal Swan on Lake)	Retrd.	2000	65.00	65
1998 Trio of Light	Open		154.00	154
2000 Water Dance	2,500		136.00	136

Lenox Classics-Crystal Seasonal - Lenox

1999 Jolly Santa Claus	2,500	2001	136.00	136
1999 Winter Magic	2,500	2001	60.00	60

Lenox Classics-Crystal Teddies - Lenox

2000 Charming Teddy	2,500		65.00	65
1999 Cute 'N Cuddly (Teddy Bear Pair)	Open		100.00	100

Lenox Classics-Crystal Unicorns - Lenox

1998 Unicorn	Retrd.	2000	136.00	136

Lenox Classics-Crystal Woodland Animals - Lenox

1996 Lord & Lady (Wolf Pair)	Retrd.	2000	76.00	79
1997 Protector of the Wild (Wolf)	Retrd.	2000	100.00	100
1999 Regal Lion (Standing Lion)	2,500	2000	195.00	195
1996 Satin & Silk (Bunny Pair)	Retrd.	2000	76.00	79
1999 Woodland Spirit (Wolf #2 Running)	2,500	2000	100.00	100

Swarovski Consumer Goods Ltd.

Swarovski Crystal Decor - Various

2000 Aladdin Candleholder - J. Desgrippes	Open		390.00	390
2000 Allegra Table Clock - S. Weinberg	Open		590.00	590
1996 Apollo Bowl - B. Sipek	Open		650.00	650
2000 Arcadia Picture Frame - S. Weinberg	Open		280.00	280
1997 Astro Box - A. Putman	Open		355.00	355
1995 Colorado Bowl - J. Desgrippes	Open		355.00	355
1992 Euclid Caviar Bowl - L. Redl	Open		650.00	650
2000 Galeo Card Holder - J. Desgrippes	Open		180.00	180
1992 Helios Tableclock - B. Sipek	Open		355.00	355
2000 Medea Vase - J. Desgrippes	Open		315.00	315
2001 Op Art Box, black - A. Jill	Open		335.00	335
2001 Op Art Box, blue - A. Jill	Open		335.00	335

YEAR ISSUE	EDITION LIMIT	YEAR RETD.	ISSUE PRICE	*QUOTE U.S.$
2001 Op Art Box, green - A. Jill	Open		335.00	335
2001 Op Art Box, white - A. Jill	Open		335.00	335
2001 Op Art Compass - A. Jill	Open		215.00	215
2001 Op Art Tableclock - A. Jill	Open		315.00	315
1992 Petit Vase - J. Desgrippes	Open		650.00	650
1998 Providence Tableclock - S. Weinberg	Open		850.00	850
2001 Rainbow Bottle Stopper (Available in Sapphire, Topaz, or Siam) - J. Desgrippes	Open		105.00	105
2001 Rainbow Candleholder (Available in Topaz/Ovaline, Blue Zircon /Sapphire, Siam/Fuschia) - S. Umdasch	Open		315.00	315
2001 Rainbow Knife Rest (Set/2) (Available in Topaz and Sapphire) - J. Desgrippes	Open		280.00	280
2001 Rainbow Napkin Rings (Set/2) (Available in Blue Zircon, Fuschia, Ovaline, Sapphire, Siam and Topaz) - S. Umdasch	Open		280.00	280
1998 Ren Candleholder - K. Nagai	Open		525.00	525
1992 Soliflor Vase - J. Desgrippes	Open		440.00	440
1994 Stalactite Candleholder - A. Putman	Open		620.00	620
2000 Tim Cardholder - J. Desgrippes	Open		225.00	225
2000 Toasting Flutes - S. Weinberg	Open		280.00	280
1999 Toh Vase - K. Nagai	Open		650.00	650
2000 Trio Candleholders (Set/3) - A. Putman	Open		180.00	180
1997 Wa Bowl - K. Nagai	Open		850.00	850
1999 Yin Yang Candleholder - Tao Ho	Open		620.00	620

Swarovski Crystal Decor-Retired

YEAR ISSUE	EDITION LIMIT	YEAR RETD.	ISSUE PRICE	*QUOTE U.S.$
1992 Boite meli-melo (bowl) 0168008	Retrd.	1995	210.00	210-273
1994 Buchstützen (bookends) 0168342	Retrd.	1996	385.00	360-462
1996 Calix Vase 0210527 - B. Sipek	Retrd.	2000	650.00	650
1992 Cendrier (ashtray) 0168007	Retrd.	1995	190.00	175-190
1995 Cleo Picture Frame 0200085 - M. Zendron	Retrd.	2000	440.00	440
1994 Coupe-papier (letter opener) 0172756	Retrd.	1997	190.00	185-225
1995 Curaçao Tableclock 0200086 - E. Mair	Retrd.	2000	440.00	440
1992 Enigma Tableclock 0168002 - L. Redl	Retrd.	1998	355.00	275-355
1992 Federhalter (pen holder) 0168006	Retrd.	1995	385.00	360-385
1996 Gemini Vase 0206210 - B. Sipek	Retrd.	2000	440.00	440
1992 Grand Contenitore (bowl) 0167997	Retrd.	1995	620.00	600-720
1997 Hong Kong 0222859 - Mae Tsang	1,997	1997	1100.00	1200-2900
1993 Porte-cartes imago (card holder) 0170199	Retrd.	1995	190.00	150-190
1996 Saturn Candleholder 0206211 - B. Sipek	Retrd.	2001	440.00	440
1992 Scatola Piccola con tappo (bowl) 0167998	Retrd.	1995	515.00	480-515
1992 Schmuckdose (jewel box) 0168005	Retrd.	1995	515.00	420-515
1993 Shiva Bowl 0170301 - L. Redl	Retrd.	2001	440.00	440
1994 Stalagmite Ringholder 0182484 - A. Putman	Retrd.	1998	355.00	355-495
1992 Uranus Candleholder 0168004 - B. Sipek	Retrd.	1998	385.00	360-385

Swarovski Crystal Moments-Celebrations

YEAR ISSUE	EDITION LIMIT	YEAR RETD.	ISSUE PRICE	*QUOTE U.S.$
1995 Balloons	Open		32.50	33
1996 Bells	Open		32.50	33
1995 Birthday Cake	Open		32.50	33
1996 Bouquet	Open		40.00	40
1995 Present	Open		32.50	33
1996 Sparkling Wine	Open		32.50	33
1995 Sparkling Wine Cooler w/2 flutes	Open		50.00	50
1999 Wedding Bouquet	Open		50.00	50
1999 Wedding Cake	Open		65.00	65

Swarovski Crystal Moments-Childhood Dreams

YEAR ISSUE	EDITION LIMIT	YEAR RETD.	ISSUE PRICE	*QUOTE U.S.$
1993 Baby Carriage	Open		40.00	40
1997 Baby Shoes	Open		25.00	25
1998 Baby's Rattle	Open		17.50	18
2000 Ballet Slippers	Open		37.50	38
2000 Cradle	Open		55.00	55
1998 Doll	Open		50.00	50
1998 Freight Car	Open		32.50	33
1993 Merry-Go-Round	Open		32.50	33
2002 My Keys	Open		40.00	40
1993 Pacifier	Open		17.50	18
1998 Passenger Car	Open		32.50	33

YEAR ISSUE	EDITION LIMIT	YEAR RETD.	ISSUE PRICE	*QUOTE U.S.$
1996 Rocking Horse	Open		40.00	40
2000 Teddy Bear on Wheels	Open		65.00	65
2000 Toy Elephant	Open		90.00	90
1997 Toy Train	Open		50.00	50
2002 Toy Wagon	Open		65.00	65
1998 Tricycle	Open		40.00	40

Swarovski Crystal Moments-Crystal Garden

YEAR ISSUE	EDITION LIMIT	YEAR RETD.	ISSUE PRICE	*QUOTE U.S.$
2001 Gardening Set	Open		55.00	55

Swarovski Crystal Moments-Dedicated to Music

YEAR ISSUE	EDITION LIMIT	YEAR RETD.	ISSUE PRICE	*QUOTE U.S.$
1993 Piano	Open		40.00	40
1995 Saxophone	Open		40.00	40
1993 Violin	Open		25.00	25

Swarovski Crystal Moments-Home and Desk

YEAR ISSUE	EDITION LIMIT	YEAR RETD.	ISSUE PRICE	*QUOTE U.S.$
2002 Dew Drop Paperweight	Open		55.00	55
2002 Picture Frame/Poetry	Open		75.00	75

Swarovski Crystal Moments-In a Class of Their Own

YEAR ISSUE	EDITION LIMIT	YEAR RETD.	ISSUE PRICE	*QUOTE U.S.$
2000 Bicycle	Open		65.00	65
2000 Binoculars	Open		55.00	55
2002 Blue Dice (set/2)	Open		55.00	55
1997 Camera	Open		32.50	33
1993 Golf Bag	Open		40.00	40
2000 In-Line Skate	Open		40.00	40
2000 Mobile Phone	Open		37.50	38
2002 Red Dice (set/2)	Open		55.00	55
1994 Sailboat	Open		40.00	40

Swarovski Crystal Moments-In Familiar Surroundings

YEAR ISSUE	EDITION LIMIT	YEAR RETD.	ISSUE PRICE	*QUOTE U.S.$
2000 Espresso Machine	Open		55.00	55
2000 Espresso Machine-Small	Open		32.50	33
1993 Tea Set	Open		50.00	50
1999 Wine Set (5 pc.)	Open		65.00	65

Swarovski Crystal Moments-Journeys

YEAR ISSUE	EDITION LIMIT	YEAR RETD.	ISSUE PRICE	*QUOTE U.S.$
1999 Airplane	Open		95.00	95
1999 Carriage	Open		125.00	125
2000 Castle	Open		107.00	110
2000 Cathedral	Open		107.00	110
2001 Chinese Junk	Open		110.00	110
2000 Greek Temple	Open		95.00	95
1999 Hot Air Balloon	Open		85.00	85
2000 Japanese Temple	Open		107.00	110
2000 Lighthouse	Open		65.00	65
1999 Limousine	Open		95.00	95
1999 Locomotive	Open		125.00	125
2000 Mosque	Open		107.00	110
2001 Power Boat	Open		95.00	95
2001 Viking Ship	Open		110.00	110
2001 Wind Mill	Open		85.00	85

Swarovski Crystal Moments-Times Past

YEAR ISSUE	EDITION LIMIT	YEAR RETD.	ISSUE PRICE	*QUOTE U.S.$
1998 Alarm Clock	Open		40.00	40
2001 Balance Scale	Open		65.00	65
1998 Film Camera	Open		50.00	50
1996 Globe	Open		32.50	33
1995 Gramophone	Open		40.00	40
1993 Hourglass	Open		25.00	25
2000 Juke Box	Open		50.00	50
1996 Mantel Clock	Open		32.50	33
2001 Microscope	Open		55.00	55
1998 Radio	Open		32.50	33
2000 Rocking Chair	Open		40.00	40
1994 Telephone	Open		32.50	33
1997 Typewriter	Open		40.00	40
2001 Water Pipe	Open		37.50	38

Swarovski Crystal Moments-Your Special Treasures

YEAR ISSUE	EDITION LIMIT	YEAR RETD.	ISSUE PRICE	*QUOTE U.S.$
1993 Atomizer	Open		17.50	18
1993 Flower Basket	Open		40.00	40
1997 Flower Pot	Open		32.50	33
1993 High-Heeled Shoe	Open		32.50	33
1994 Inkwell with Quill	Open		17.50	18
2001 Paper Clip	Open		55.00	55
1999 Sewing Machine	Open		50.00	50
2002 Weather Frog	Open		35.00	35

Swarovski Crystal Moments-Secrets

YEAR ISSUE	EDITION LIMIT	YEAR RETD.	ISSUE PRICE	*QUOTE U.S.$
1999 Book/Clock	Open		95.00	95
1999 Cactus/Flacon	Open		85.00	85
2001 Dolphin/Flacon	Open		75.00	75

YEAR ISSUE	EDITION LIMIT	YEAR RETD.	ISSUE PRICE	*QUOTE U.S.$
2000 Egg with Garland/Jewelry Box	Open		90.00	90
1999 Flower Basket/Jewelry Box	Open		95.00	95
1997 Gift/Clock	Open		95.00	95
1997 Globe/Clock	Open		95.00	95
2001 Love/Jewelry Box	Open		90.00	90
1997 Rose Vase/Flacon	Open		65.00	65
1997 Suitcase/Picture Frame	Open		75.00	75
1997 Tulip Vase/Flacon	Open		75.00	75
2000 Turtle/Jewelry Box	Open		85.00	85

Swarovski Crystal Moments-Retired

YEAR ISSUE	EDITION LIMIT	YEAR RETD.	ISSUE PRICE	*QUOTE U.S.$
1993 Anchor 9460NR000030	Retrd.	1996	32.50	33-68
1993 Baby's Bottle 9460NR000009	Retrd.	1998	17.50	50
1997 Beauty Case/Jewelry Box 9448000001	Retrd.	2000	85.00	85
1993 Beer Mug 9460NR000022	Retrd.	1997	25.00	25-59
1999 Cactus, Blue Zircon 9460NR000088	Retrd.	2001	50.00	50
1999 Cactus, Light Topaz 9460NR000089	Retrd.	2001	50.00	50
1999 Cactus, Rosaline 9460NR000087	Retrd.	2001	40.00	40
1993 Coffee Mill 9460NR000001	Retrd.	1998	32.50	33-50
1994 Diary 9460NR000055	Retrd.	1999	40.00	35-40
1994 Dinner Bell 9460NR000047	Retrd.	1998	17.50	18-55
1995 Flute 9460000058	Retrd.	2000	40.00	40
1996 Fruit Bowl 9460NR000069	Retrd.	1999	40.00	30-40
1997 Gift/Jewelry Box 9448NR000009	Retrd.	2001	85.00	85
1993 Greek Vase 9460NR000006	Retrd.	1996	32.50	35-70
1993 Guitar 9460000020	Retrd.	2000	32.50	33
1993 Handbag 9460NR000013	Retrd.	1998	32.50	45
1997 Handbag/Clock 9448000002	Retrd.	2000	95.00	95
1994 Ice Cream Sundae 9460NR000046	Retrd.	1998	25.00	25
1994 Ice Skate 9460NR000051	Retrd.	1999	32.50	33-45
1993 Iron 9460NR000002	Retrd.	1996	25.00	30-61
1994 Kettledrum 9460NR000054	Retrd.	1997	32.50	33-69
1994 Knapsack 9460NR000049	Retrd.	1997	32.50	33-69
1993 Knitting Needles and Wool 9460NR000016	Retrd.	1996	32.50	30-67
1993 Lamp 9460NR000039	Retrd.	1997	25.00	30-59
1993 Lantern 9460NR000023	Retrd.	1997	40.00	40-79
1994 Penny Farthing Bicycle 9460NR000043	Retrd.	1998	32.50	33-60
1993 Piece of Cake 9460NR000026	Retrd.	2000	25.00	25
1994 Row Boat 9460NR000034	Retrd.	1999	40.00	35-40
1993 Salt & Pepper 9460NR000045	Retrd.	1996	25.00	30-45
1993 Ski 9460NR000037	Retrd.	1999	25.00	20-25
1994 Spinning Wheel 9460NR000035	Retrd.	1997	40.00	40-76
1997 Spring Flower Vase/Flacon 9448000007	Retrd.	2000	65.00	65
1994 Tennis Racket 9460NR000048	Retrd.	1998	32.50	33-65
1993 Treasure Chest 9460NR000004	Retrd.	1996	40.00	35-76
1993 Treasure Island 9460NR000025	Retrd.	1996	32.50	35-69
1994 Trophy 9460NR000052	Retrd.	1998	40.00	40-50
1993 Umbrella 9460NR000008	Retrd.	1996	32.50	40-69
1993 Watering Can 9460NR000007	Retrd.	1998	32.50	33-70
1993 Wine Set 9460NR000038	Retrd.	1999	49.50	50

Swarovski Collectors Society - Various

YEAR ISSUE	EDITION LIMIT	YEAR RETD.	ISSUE PRICE	*QUOTE U.S.$
1987 Togetherness-The Lovebirds - M. Schreck	Yr.lss.	1987	150.00	3500-4600
1988 Sharing-The Woodpeckers - A. Stocker	Yr.lss.	1988	165.00	1546-1750
1988 Mini Cactus	Yr.lss.	1988	Gift	188-225
1989 Amour-The Turtledoves - A. Stocker	Yr.lss.	1989	195.00	959-1020
1989 The Lovebirds, The Woodpeckers, The Turtledoves	Closed	1989	510.00	4800-7440
1989 SCS Key Chain	Yr.lss.	1989	Gift	147-900
1990 Lead Me-The Dolphins - M. Stamey	Yr.lss.	1990	225.00	885-1295
1990 Mini Chaton	Yr.lss.	1990	Gift	85-110
1991 Save Me-The Seals - M. Stamey	Yr.lss.	1991	225.00	450-595
1991 Dolphin Brooch	Yr.lss.	1991	75.00	100-120
1991 SCS Pin	Yr.lss.	1991	Gift	20-49
1992 Care For Me - The Whales - M. Stamey	Yr.lss.	1992	265.00	375-710
1992 The Dolphins, The Seals, The Whales - M. Stamey	Closed	1992	715.00	1500-2760
1992 SCS Pen	Yr.lss.	1992	Gift	20-48
1992 The Birthday Cake (SCS 5th Anniversary Edition) - G. Stamey	Yr.lss.	1992	85.00	188-295
1993 Inspiration Africa-The Elephant - M. Zendron	Yr.lss.	1993	325.00	1150-1825
1993 Elephant Brooch	Yr.lss.	1993	85.00	85-195
1993 Leather Luggage Tag	Yr.lss.	1993	Gift	35-55

YEAR ISSUE	EDITION LIMIT	YEAR RETD.	ISSUE PRICE	*QUOTE U.S.$
1994 Inspiration Africa-The Kudu - M. Stamey	Yr.lss.	1994	295.00	392-595
1994 Leather Double Picture Frame	Yr.lss.	1994	Gift	18
1995 Inspiration Africa-The Lion - A. Stocker	Yr.lss.	1995	325.00	350-750
1995 Centenary Swan Brooch	Yr.lss.	1995	125.00	110-150
1995 The Elephant, The Kudu, The Lion	Closed	1995	945.00	1440-2375
1995 Miniature Crystal Swan	Yr.lss.	1995	Gift	32-75
1996 Fabulous Creatures-The Unicorn - M. Zendron	Yr.lss.	1996	325.00	360-600
1996 Clear Crystal Heart	Yr.lss.	1996	Gift	85-100
1996 Bag of Hearts (3 Yr. Renewal) SCMR10	Retrd.	1998	Gift	35-75
1997 Fabulous Creatures-The Dragon - G. Stamey	Yr.lss.	1997	325.00	350-595
1997 SCS 10th Anniversary Edition - The Squirrel - A. Hirzinger	Yr.lss.	1997	140.00	75-240
1997 Blue Crystal Heart	Yr.lss.	1997	Gift	59-85
1998 Fabulous Creatures-The Pegasus - A. Stocker	Yr.lss.	1998	350.00	254-500
1998 Red Crystal Heart	Yr.lss.	1998	Gift	35-100
1999 Masquerade-Pierrot	Yr.lss.	1999	350.00	325-475
2000 Masquerade-Columbine - G. Stamey	Yr.lss.	2000	350.00	300-400
2001 Masquerade-Harlequin - A. Hirzinger	Yr.lss.	2001	350.00	350
2002 Magic of Dance-Isadora - A. Stocker	Yr.lss.		370.00	370
2002 The Vase of Roses - G. Stamey (SCS 15th Anniversary Edition)	Yr.lss.		140.00	140

Swarovski Silver Crystal-Worldwide Limited Editions - A. Stocker

YEAR ISSUE	EDITION LIMIT	YEAR RETD.	ISSUE PRICE	*QUOTE U.S.$
1995 Eagle	10,000	1995	1750.00	4800-7200
1998 Peacock	10,000	1998	1800.00	3000-5160
2001 Wild Horses	10,000	2001	4000.00	3100-6000

Swarovski Silver Crystal-Special Editions - A. Hirzinger

YEAR ISSUE	EDITION LIMIT	YEAR RETD.	ISSUE PRICE	*QUOTE U.S.$
1995 Centenary Swan	Yr.lss.	1995	150.00	100-225
2000 Crystal Planet	Yr.lss.	2000	275.00	210-265

Swarovski Silver Crystal-Commemorative Single Issues - Team

YEAR ISSUE	EDITION LIMIT	YEAR RETD.	ISSUE PRICE	*QUOTE U.S.$
1990 Elephant, 7640NR100 (Introduced by Swarovski America as a commemorative item for Design Celebration/January '90 in Walt Disney World)	Closed	1990	125.00	900-1085
1993 Elephant, 7640NR100001 (Introduced by Swarovski America as a commemorative item for Design Celebration/January '93 in Walt Disney World)	Closed	1993	150.00	480-506

Swarovski Silver Crystal-Special Walt Disney Theme Park Specials - Team

YEAR ISSUE	EDITION LIMIT	YEAR RETD.	ISSUE PRICE	*QUOTE U.S.$
1987 Elephant (small tusks, small ears) - A. Stocker	Closed	1987	95.00	2799-4800
1987 Elephant (large tusks, small ears) - A. Stocker	Closed	1987	95.00	2799
1987 Elephant (no tusks, small ears) - A. Stocker	Closed	1987	95.00	2615
1988 Elephant (no tusks, large ears) - A. Stocker	Closed	1988	95.00	3105-4750
1988 Elephant (large tusks, large ears) - A. Stocker	Closed	1988	95.00	3429

Swarovski Silver Crystal-African Wildlife - Various

YEAR ISSUE	EDITION LIMIT	YEAR RETD.	ISSUE PRICE	*QUOTE U.S.$
1995 Baby Elephant - M. Zendron	Open		155.00	155
1999 Baby Giraffe - M. Stamey	Open		260.00	260
2000 Camel - H. Tabertshofer	Open		375.00	375
1994 Cheetah - M. Stamey	Open		275.00	275
1998 Chimpanzee - E. Mair	Open		125.00	125
2000 Cobra - H. Tabertshofer	Open		140.00	140
1989 Elephant-Small - A. Stocker	Open		50.00	65
1997 Leopard - M. Stamey	Open		260.00	260
2001 Lion - M. Zendron	Open		325.00	325
1997 Lion Cub - A. Stocker	Open		125.00	125
2001 Young Gorilla - A. Stocker	Open		140.00	140

Swarovski Silver Crystal-Among Flowers And Foliage - Various

YEAR ISSUE	EDITION LIMIT	YEAR RETD.	ISSUE PRICE	*QUOTE U.S.$
2001 Baby Snails on Leaf - E. Mair	Open		49.50	50
1994 Butterfly on Leaf - C. Schneiderbauer	Open		75.00	85
1995 Dragonfly - C. Schneiderbauer	Open		85.00	85
1992 Hummingbird - C. Schneiderbauer	Open		195.00	210
1996 Snail on Vine-Leaf - E. Mair	Open		65.00	65

CRYSTAL

YEAR ISSUE	EDITION LIMIT	YEAR RETD.	ISSUE PRICE	*QUOTE U.S.$
Swarovski Silver Crystal-Barnyard Friends - Various				
2000 Cockerel - M. Stamey	Open		75.00	75
1984 Medium Pig - M. Schreck	Open		35.00	55
1988 Miniature-Chickens (Set/3) - G. Stamey	Open		35.00	45
1982 Miniature-Pig - M. Schreck	Open		16.00	30
Swarovski Silver Crystal-Beauties of the Lake - Various				
1994 Frog - G. Stamey	Open		49.50	50
1989 Mallard-Giant - M. Stamey	Open		2000.00	4500
1984 Standing Drake-Mini - M. Schreck	Open		20.00	45
1987 Standing Duck-Mini - A. Stocker	Open		22.00	38
2000 Swan Family - A. Stocker	Open		185.00	185
1981 Swan-Large - M. Schreck	Open		55.00	95
1995 Swan-Maxi - A. Hirzinger	Open		4500.00	4500
1981 Swan-Medium - M. Schreck	Open		44.00	85
1982 Swan-Small - M. Schreck	Open		35.00	55
Swarovski Silver Crystal-Chinese Zodiacs - A. Hirzinger				
2001 Zodiac Goat	Open		55.00	55
2001 Zodiac Ox	Open		65.00	65
2001 Zodiac Rat	Open		55.00	55
Swarovski Silver Crystal-Crystal Melodies - Various				
1993 Grand Piano - M. Zendron	Open		250.00	275
1997 Saxophone - M. Zendron	Open		125.00	125
1996 Violin - G. Stamey	Open		140.00	140
Swarovski Silver Crystal-Endangered Species - Various				
1998 Miniature-Alligator - M. Stamey	Open		75.00	75
2001 Anteater - A. Stocker	Open		55.00	55
1993 Baby Panda - A. Stocker	Open		24.50	25
2000 Bald Eagle - A. Stocker	Open		275.00	275
2001 Ibex - H. Tabertshofer	Open		210.00	210
1993 Mother Kangaroo with Baby - G. Stamey	Open		95.00	95
1987 Koala-Large - A. Stocker	Open		50.00	65
1998 Baby Sea Lion - M. Stamey	Open		49.50	50
1998 Baby Tortoises (Set/2) - E. Mair	Open		45.00	45
1993 Mother Panda - A. Stocker	Open		120.00	125
1997 Tortoise - E. Mair	Open		55.00	55
1998 Tiger - M. Stamey	Open		275.00	275
1983 Turtle-Giant - M. Schreck	Open		2500.00	4500
Swarovski Silver Crystal-Exquisite Accents - Various				
1995 Angel - A. Stocker	Open		210.00	210
1981 Birdbath - M. Schreck	Open		150.00	210
1999 Chaton - Team	Open		185.00	185
1990 Chaton-Giant - M. Schreck	Open		4500.00	4500
2001 Christmas Tree - A. Hirzinger	Open		125.00	125
1999 Comet Candleholder - M. Zendron	Open		185.00	185
2000 Flacon Napoleon - A. Hirzinger	Open		185.00	185
1997 Kris Bear Table Clock - M. Zendron	Open		210.00	210
2000 Maxi Flower Arrangement - M. Stamey	Open		525.00	525
1999 Nutcracker - A. Hirzinger	Open		155.00	155
1996 The Orchid-pink - M. Stamey	Open		140.00	140
1997 Oriental Flacon - M. Zendron	Open		185.00	185
1997 Picture Frame w/Butterfly - C. Schneiderbauer	Open		85.00	85
1997 Reindeer - A. Hirzinger	Open		185.00	185
1993 The Rose - M. Stamey	Open		150.00	155
1999 Rose Flacon - M. Zendron	Open		185.00	185
1998 Santa Claus - M. Zendron	Open		155.00	155
1996 Sleigh - M. Zendron	Open		295.00	295
1999 Solaris Table Bell - A. Hirzinger	Open		185.00	185
1998 Solaris Table Clock - A. Stocker	Open		375.00	375
1997 Sweet Heart - E. Mair	Open		110.00	125
Swarovski Silver Crystal-Fairy Tales - Various				
2001 Cinderella - M. Zendron	Open		325.00	325
1999 Dragon - G. Stamey	Open		325.00	325
1996 Red Riding Hood - E. Mair	Open		185.00	185
1996 Wolf - E. Mair	Open		155.00	155
Swarovski Silver Crystal-Feathered Friends - Various				
1996 Baby Lovebirds - A. Stocker	Open		155.00	155
2001 Cockatoo - H. Tabertshofer	Open		140.00	140
1995 Dove - E. Mair	Open		55.00	55
1993 Pelican - A. Hirzinger	Open		37.50	38
2001 Puffins - M. Zendron	Open		155.00	155
1998 Silver Heron - A. Stocker	Open		275.00	275
1999 Toucan - M. Stamey	Open		155.00	155
Swarovski Silver Crystal-Game of Kings - M. Schreck				
1985 Chess Set	Open		950.00	1375
Swarovski Silver Crystal-Horses on Parade - M. Zendron				
1998 Arabian Stallion	Open		260.00	260
1993 White Stallion	Open		250.00	260
Swarovski Silver Crystal-In A Summer Meadow - Various				
1997 Bunny Rabbit - E. Mair	Open		55.00	55
1983 Butterfly-Large - Team	Open		44.00	85
1994 Field Mice (Set/3) - A. Stocker	Open		42.50	45
1991 Field Mouse - A. Stocker	Open		47.50	55
1997 Four-Leaf Clover - A. Hirzinger	Open		49.50	50
1988 Hedgehog-Medium - M. Schreck	Open		70.00	85
1988 Hedgehog-Small - M. Schreck	Open		50.00	55
1995 Ladybug - E. Mair	Open		29.50	30
1986 Miniature-Butterfly - Team	Open		16.00	45
1988 Miniature-Rabbit, sitting - A. Stocker	Open		35.00	45
1988 Mother Rabbit - A. Stocker	Open		60.00	75
Swarovski Silver Crystal-Kingdom Of Ice And Snow - Various				
1997 Baby Penguins (Set/3) - A. Stocker	Open		75.00	75
1985 Miniature-Seal - A. Stocker	Open		30.00	45
Swarovski Silver Crystal-Our Candleholders - Various				
1989 Star-Medium 7600NR143001 - Team	Open		200.00	260
1985 Water Lily-Large 7600NR125 - M. Schreck	Open		200.00	375
1984 Water Lily-Medium 7600NR123 - M. Schreck	Open		150.00	260
1985 Water Lily-Small 7600NR124 - M. Schreck	Open		100.00	175
Swarovski Silver Crystal-Pets' Corner - Various				
1990 Beagle - A. Stocker	Open		40.00	50
1993 Beagle Playing - A. Stocker	Open		49.50	50
1999 German Shepherd - H. Tabertshofer	Open		140.00	140
2000 Mini Cat - M. Schreck	Open		29.50	30
1991 Sitting Cat - M. Stamey	Open		75.00	85
1993 Sitting Poodle - A. Stocker	Open		85.00	85
1996 St. Bernard - E. Mair	Open		95.00	125
1996 Tomcat - A. Hirzinger	Open		45.00	45
Swarovski Silver Crystal-South Sea - Various				
1987 Miniature-Blowfish - Team	Open		22.00	30
1987 Blowfish-Small - Team	Open		35.00	55
1996 Miniature-Crab - M. Stamey	Open		65.00	65
1995 Dolphin - M. Stamey	Open		210.00	210
1998 Maxi Dolphin - M. Stamey	Open		880.00	880
1993 Sea Horse - M. Stamey	Open		85.00	85
1999 Siamese Fighting Fish (blue) - H. Tabertshofer	Open		125.00	125
2000 Siamese Fighting Fish (green) - H. Tabertshofer	Open		125.00	125
2001 Baby Shark - A. Hirzinger	Open		155.00	155
1987 Shell w/Pearl - M. Stamey	Open		120.00	175
1995 Shell - M. Stamey	Open		45.00	45
1995 Starfish - M. Stamey	Open		29.50	30
1995 Conch - M. Stamey	Open		29.50	30
1995 Maritime Trio (Shell, Starfish, Conch) - M. Stamey	Open		104.00	104
Swarovski Silver Crystal-Sparkling Fruit - Various				
1995 Bunch of Grapes - Team	Open		375.00	375
1983 Pineapple-Giant /Gold - M. Schreck	Open		1750.00	3250
1982 Pineapple-Large /Gold - M. Schreck	Open		150.00	260
1987 Pineapple-Small /Gold - M. Schreck	Open		55.00	85
Swarovski Silver Crystal-Symbols - Various				
2001 The Cat - A. Stocker	Open		260.00	260
2001 The Dog - A. Hirzinger	Open		300.00	300
Swarovski Silver Crystal-When We Were Young - Various				
1999 Ballerina - M. Zendron	Open		325.00	325
1999 Celebration Kris Bear - M. Zendron	Open		85.00	85
1995 Kris Bear on Skates - M. Zendron	Open		75.00	75
1997 Kris Bear with Honey Pot - M. Zendron	Open		75.00	75
1999 Kris Bear with Skis - M. Zendron	Open		85.00	85
1988 Locomotive - G. Stamey	Open		150.00	155
1995 Miniature-Train - G. Stamey	Open		125.00	125
1990 Petrol Wagon - G. Stamey	Open		75.00	95

YEAR ISSUE	EDITION LIMIT	YEAR RETD.	ISSUE PRICE	*QUOTE U.S.$
1997 Puppet - G. Stamey	Open		125.00	125
1994 Replica Cat - Team	Open		37.50	38
1994 Replica Hedgehog - Team	Open		37.50	38
1994 Replica Mouse - Team	Open		37.50	38
1994 Rocking Horse - G. Stamey	Open		125.00	125
1994 Sailboat - G. Stamey	Open		195.00	210
1991 Santa Maria - G. Stamey	Open		375.00	375
2000 Snowman - E. Mair	Open		95.00	95
1994 Starter Set - Team	Open		112.50	113
1998 Tank Wagon - G. Stamey	Open		95.00	95
1988 Tender - G. Stamey	Open		55.00	55
1993 Tipping Wagon - G. Stamey	Open		95.00	95
1988 Wagon - G. Stamey	Open		85.00	125
2000 Young Ballerina - E. Mair	Open		155.00	155

Swarovski Silver Crystal-Woodland Friends - Various

YEAR ISSUE	EDITION LIMIT	YEAR RETD.	ISSUE PRICE	*QUOTE U.S.$
1981 Bear-Large - M. Schreck	Open		75.00	95
2000 Doe - M. Zendron	Open		260.00	260
1999 Fawn - M. Zendron	Open		125.00	125
1983 Giant Owl- M. Schreck	Open		1200.00	2000
2000 Grizzly - H. Tabertshofer	Open		325.00	325
2001 Grizzly Cub - H. Tabertshofer	Open		95.00	95
1988 Mini Sitting Fox - A. Stocker	Open		35.00	45
1985 Miniature-Bear - M. Schreck	Open		16.00	55
1981 Miniature-Owl - M. Schreck	Open		16.00	30
1981 Owl-Large - M. Schreck	Open		90.00	125
1985 Squirrel - M. Schreck	Open		35.00	55

Swarovski Silver Crystal-Retired Candleholders - Team, unless otherwise noted

YEAR ISSUE	EDITION LIMIT	YEAR RETD.	ISSUE PRICE	*QUOTE U.S.$
1996 Blue Flower 7600NR146000 - G. Stamey	Retrd.	2001	260.00	260
1981 Candleholder 7600NR101	Retrd.	1981	28.00	95-260
1981 Candleholder 7600NR102 (hole) - H. Koch	Retrd.	1986	40.00	147-500
1981 Candleholder 7600NR102 (pin) - H. Koch	Retrd.	1986	40.00	130-140
1976 Candleholder 7600NR102T (smoked) (pin) - H. Koch	Retrd.	N/A	44.00	468-520
1986 Candleholder 7600NR103 (hole)	Retrd.	1988	40.00	112-172
1986 Candleholder 7600NR103 (pin)	Retrd.	1988	40.00	462
1976 Candleholder 7600NR103 (pin) (European)	Retrd.	1983	N/A	416-719
1986 Candleholder 7600NR104 (hole)	Retrd.	1988	95.00	217-269
1976 Candleholder 7600NR104 (pin) (European)	Retrd.	1989	N/A	438-650
1981 Candleholder 7600NR106 (hole)	Retrd.	1986	100.00	459-784
1981 Candleholder 7600NR106 (pin)	Retrd.	1986	100.00	364-590
1981 Candleholder 7600NR107 (hole)	Retrd.	1985	120.00	480-700
1981 Candleholder 7600NR107 (pin)	Retrd.	1985	120.00	375-390
1976 Candleholder 7600NR108 (pin) (European)	Retrd.	1987	N/A	625-756
1981 Candleholder 7600NR109 (hole)	Retrd.	1985	40.00	155-194
1981 Candleholder 7600NR109 (pin)	Retrd.	1985	40.00	155-320
1981 Candleholder 7600NR110 (hole)	Retrd.	1986	45.00	195
1981 Candleholder 7600NR110 (pin)	Retrd.	1986	45.00	165
1981 Candleholder 7600NR111 (hole)	Retrd.	1985	100.00	457-888
1981 Candleholder 7600NR111 (pin)	Retrd.	1985	100.00	700-813
1981 Candleholder 7600NR112 (hole)	Retrd.	1985	80.00	370-750
1981 Candleholder 7600NR112 (pin)	Retrd.	1985	80.00	315-350
1976 Candleholder 7600NR112T (pin)	Retrd.	N/A	N/A	1940-3450
1976 Candleholder 7600NR113 (Euopean) (pin)	Retrd.	1981	N/A	642-1313
1981 Candleholder 7600NR114 (hole)	Retrd.	1985	40.00	415-545
1981 Candleholder 7600NR114 (pin)	Retrd.	1985	40.00	173-272
1981 Candleholder 7600NR115 (hole)	Retrd.	1986	200.00	800-938
1981 Candleholder 7600NR115 (pin)	Retrd.	1986	200.00	580-700
1981 Candleholder 7600NR116 (hole)	Retrd.	1985	350.00	3100-4680
1981 Candleholder 7600NR116 (pin)	Retrd.	1985	350.00	1610-2350
XX Candleholder 7600NR118 (European) (pin)	Retrd.	N/A	N/A	2170-3500
1977 Candleholder 7600NR119 (European)	Retrd.	1989	N/A	232-532
1986 Candleholder 7600NR122	Retrd.	1986	85.00	625-1250
1985 Candleholder 7600NR125 (with floweret)	Retrd.	N/A	250.00	360-590
1985 Candleholder 7600NR127	Retrd.	1987	65.00	375-775
1985 Candleholder 7600NR128	Retrd.	1987	100.00	422-585
1985 Candleholder 7600NR129	Retrd.	1987	120.00	450-750
1981 Candleholder 7600NR130	Retrd.	1985	300.00	1875-1890
1978 Candleholder 7600NR131, set/6 (European)	Retrd.	1989	N/A	325-468
1986 Candleholder 7600NR138	Retrd.	1986	160.00	750-964

YEAR ISSUE	EDITION LIMIT	YEAR RETD.	ISSUE PRICE	*QUOTE U.S.$
1986 Candleholder 7600NR139	Retrd.	1986	140.00	1063-1200
1986 Candleholder 7600NR140	Retrd.	1986	120.00	1000-1145
1986 Candleholder 7600NR141 (European) - M. Schreck	Retrd.	1991	N/A	750-1400
1986 Candleholder 7600NR142 (European) - M. Schreck	Retrd.	1990	N/A	282-624
1994 Candleholder 7600NR145	Retrd.	N/A	N/A	3000-5880
1982 Candleholder-Baroque 7600NR121	Retrd.	1986	150.00	625-1313
1981 Candleholder-Global-Kg. Sz. 7600NR135	Retrd.	1988	50.00	175-338
1981 Candleholder-Global-Lg. 7600NR134	Retrd.	1990	40.00	150-163
1981 Candleholder-Global-Med. (2) 7600NR133	Retrd.	1990	40.00	163-195
1981 Candleholder-Global-Sm. (4) 7600NR132	Retrd.	1989	60.00	60-195
1988 Candleholder-Neo-Classic-Lg. 7600NR144090 - A. Stocker	Retrd.	1992	220.00	225-275
1990 Candleholder-Neo-Classic-Med. 7600NR144080 - A. Stocker	Retrd.	1992	190.00	195-220
1990 Candleholder-Neo-Classic-Sm. 7600NR144070 - A. Stocker	Retrd.	1992	170.00	105-244
1985 Candleholder-Pineapple-Gold 7600NR136 - M. Schreck	Retrd.	1986	150.00	394-690
1984 Candleholder-Pineapple-Rhodium 7600NR136 - M. Schreck	Retrd.	1986	150.00	500-750
1987 Candleholder-Star-Lg. 7600NR143000	Retrd.	1996	250.00	302-395
1984 Candleholder-w/Flowers-Lg. 7600NR137	Retrd.	1990	150.00	312-407
1986 Candleholder-w/Flowers-Sm. 7600NR120	Retrd.	1987	60.00	450-500
1986 Candleholder-w/Leaves-Sm. 7600NR126	Retrd.	1987	100.00	750-844
1999 Solaris Candleholder 7600NR147000 - A. Stocker	Retrd.	2001	350.00	350

Swarovski Silver Crystal-Retired Paperweights - Team, unless otherwise noted

YEAR ISSUE	EDITION LIMIT	YEAR RETD.	ISSUE PRICE	*QUOTE U.S.$
1981 Pprwgt-Atomic-Crystal Cal 7454NR60095 - M. Schreck	Retrd.	1985	80.00	1134-1500
1981 Pprwgt-Atomic-Vitrl Med. 7454NR60087 - M. Schreck	Retrd.	1985	80.00	1239-1800
1981 Pprwgt-Barrel-Crystal Cal 7453NR60095 - M. Schreck	Retrd.	1988	80.00	302-938
1981 Pprwgt-Barrel-Vitrl Med. 7453NR60087 - M. Schreck	Retrd.	1988	80.00	375-532
1981 Pprwgt-Carousel-Crystal Cal 7451NR60095 - M. Schreck	Retrd.	1985	80.00	438-900
1981 Pprwgt-Carousel-Vitrl Med. 7451NR60087 - M. Schreck	Retrd.	1985	80.00	1250-2000
1976 Pprwgt-Cone Bermuda Blue 7452NR60088 - M. Schreck	Retrd.	1992	N/A	525-754
1982 Pprwgt-Cone Crystal Cal 7452NR60095 - M. Schreck	Retrd.	1982	80.00	280-398
1982 Pprwgt-Cone Vitrl Med. 7452NR60087 - M. Schreck	Retrd.	1982	80.00	315-375
1981 Pprwgt-Egg 7458NR63069 - M. Schreck	Retrd.	1982	60.00	165-313
1987 Pprwgt-Geometric 7432NR57002	Retrd.	1990	75.00	219-313
1987 Pprwgt-Octron-Bermuda Blue 7456NR41088	Retrd.	1991	N/A	315-392
1987 Pprwgt-Octron-Crystal Cal 7456NR41	Retrd.	1991	75.00	115-232
1987 Pprwgt-Octron-Crystal Cal 7456NR41095	Retrd.	1991	95.00	139-157
1988 Pprwgt-Octron-Vitrl Med. 7456NR41087	Retrd.	1991	90.00	128-149
1987 Pprwgt-One Ton 7495NR65	Retrd.	1990	75.00	127-438
1981 Pprwgt-Rd.-Berm Blue 7404NR30	Retrd.	1982	15.00	250
1981 Pprwgt-Rd.-Berm Blue 7404NR40	Retrd.	1981	20.00	82-150
1981 Pprwgt-Rd.-Berm Blue 7404NR50	Retrd.	1982	40.00	94-302
1981 Pprwgt-Rd.-Crystal Cal 7404NR30095/30	Retrd.	1989	15.00	63-125
1981 Pprwgt-Rd.-Crystal Cal 7404NR40095/40	Retrd.	1989	20.00	100-150
1981 Pprwgt-Rd.-Crystal Cal 7404NR50095/50	Retrd.	1989	40.00	195-225
1981 Pprwgt-Rd.-Crystal Cal 7404NR60095/60	Retrd.	1989	50.00	195-200
1981 Pprwgt-Rd.-Green 7404NR30	Retrd.	1982	15.00	100-250
1981 Pprwgt-Rd.-Green 7404NR40	Retrd.	1981	20.00	150-240
1981 Pprwgt-Rd.-Green 7404NR50	Retrd.	1982	40.00	255
1981 Pprwgt-Rd.-Sahara 7404NR30	Retrd.	1982	15.00	195-200
1981 Pprwgt-Rd.-Sahara 7404NR40	Retrd.	1981	20.00	115-195

YEAR ISSUE	EDITION LIMIT	YEAR RETD.	ISSUE PRICE	*QUOTE U.S.$
1981 Pprwgt-Rd.-Sahara 7404NR50	Retrd.	1982	40.00	208-313
1981 Pprwgt-Rd.-Vitrl Med. 7404NR30087	Retrd.	1989	15.00	63-113
1981 Pprwgt-Rd.-Vitrl Med. 7404NR40087	Retrd.	1989	20.00	75-94
1981 Pprwgt-Rd.-Vitrl Med. 7404NR50087	Retrd.	1989	40.00	125-244
1981 Pprwgt-Rd.-Vitrl Med. 7404NR60087	Retrd.	1989	50.00	100-200

Swarovski Silver Crystal-Retired - Various

YEAR ISSUE	EDITION LIMIT	YEAR RETD.	ISSUE PRICE	*QUOTE U.S.$
1990 Airplane 7473NR000002 - A. Stocker	Retrd.	1999	135.00	125-155
1991 Apple 7476NR000001- M. Stamey	Retrd.	1996	175.00	172-325
1984 Apple Photo Stand-Kg. Sz. (Gold) 7504NR060G - M. Schreck	Retrd.	1988	120.00	545-842
1981 Apple Photo Stand-Kg. Sz. (Rhodium) 7504NR060R - M. Schreck	Retrd.	1988	120.00	600-780
1983 Apple Photo Stand-Lg. (Gold) 7504NR050G - M. Schreck	Retrd.	1990	80.00	245-345
1981 Apple Photo Stand-Lg. (Rhodium) 7504NR050R - M. Schreck	Retrd.	1986	80.00	358-465
1983 Apple Photo Stand-Sm. (Gold) 7504NR030G - M. Schreck	Retrd.	1990	40.00	150-250
1981 Apple Photo Stand-Sm. (Rhodium) 7504NR030R - M. Schreck	Retrd.	1986	40.00	249-324
1982 Ashtray 7461NR100 - M. Schreck	Retrd.	1990	150.00	325-332
1981 Ashtray 7501NR061 - Team	Retrd.	1981	45.00	295-380
1997 Baby Carp 7644NR000003 - M. Stamey	Retrd.	2001	49.50	50
1996 Baby Carriage 7473NR000005 - G. Stamey	Retrd.	1999	140.00	103-150
1983 Bear-Giant Size 7637NR112 - M. Schreck	Retrd.	1988	125.00	1765-2700
1983 Bear-King Size (no tail) 7637NR92 - M. Schreck	Retrd.	1987	95.00	1600-2340
1985 Bear-Mini 7670NR32 - M. Schreck	Retrd.	1989	16.00	175-450
1982 Bear-Sm 7637NR054000 - M. Schreck	Retrd.	1995	44.00	65-122
1992 Beaver-Baby Lying 7616NR000003 - A. Stocker	Retrd.	1995	47.50	67-107
1992 Beaver-Baby Sitting 7616NR000002 - A. Stocker	Retrd.	1999	47.50	50-100
1985 Bee (Gold) 7553NR100 - Team	Retrd.	1988	200.00	1488-2964
1985 Bee (Rhodium) 7553NR200 - Team	Retrd.	1986	200.00	1990-4380
1983 Beetle Bottle Opener (Gold) 7505NR76 - Team	Retrd.	1983	80.00	750-1875
1981 Beetle Bottle Opener (Rhodium) 7505NR76 - Team	Retrd.	1983	80.00	886-1421
1987 Birds' Nest 7470NR050000 - Team	Retrd.	1996	90.00	139-260
1985 Blowfish-Lg. 7644NR41 - Team	Retrd.	1991	40.00	150-252
1996 Blue Flower Jewel Box 7464000001 - G. Stamey	Retrd.	2000	210.00	210
1996 Blue Flower Picture Frame 7506000001 - G. Stamey	Retrd.	2000	260.00	260
1992 Bumblebee 7615NR000002 - C. Schneiderbauer	Retrd.	1997	85.00	110-155
1982 Butterfly (gold antenna) 7551NR55000 - Team	Retrd.	N/A	85.00	85-330
1985 Butterfly (Gold) 7551NR100 - Team	Retrd.	1988	200.00	900-1250
1985 Butterfly (Rhodium) 7551NR200	Retrd.	1986	200.00	2400
1991 Butterfly Fish 7644NR077000 - M. Stamey	Retrd.	1998	150.00	145-219
1985 Butterfly-Mini (black tips/rhodium antenna) 7671NR30 - Team	Retrd.	1988	16.00	330
1985 Butterfly-Mini (crystal tips/gold antenna) 7671NR30 - Team	Retrd.	1988	16.00	136
1981 Cardholders-Lg., Set/4 -7403NR30095 - K. Mignon	Retrd.	1989	43.00	295-451
1981 Cardholders-Sm., Set/4-7403NR20095 - K. Mignon	Retrd.	1989	25.00	180-250
1981 Cardholders-Sm., Set/6-7403NR20095 - K. Mignon (European)	Retrd.	1989	25.00	116-375
1984 Cat-Lg 7634NR70 - M. Schreck	Retrd.	1991	44.00	80-145
1983 Cat-Medium 7634NR52 - M. Schreck	Retrd.	1987	38.00	310-530
1983 Cat-Mini (Retired in U.S. only) 7659NR31 - M. Schreck	Retrd.	1991	16.00	50-80
1987 Chaton-Large 7433NR080000 - M. Schreck	Retrd.	1998	190.00	215-265
1987 Chaton-Small 7433NR050000 - M. Schreck	Retrd.	1998	50.00	65-115
1985 Chess Board (mirror) 7700345006 - M. Schreck	Retrd.	1986	N/A	221
1985 Chess Carrying Case - Team	Retrd.	1986	N/A	99
1985 Chess Men 7469100000 - M. Schreck	Retrd.	1986	N/A	337
1985 Chess Set/Wooden Board 7550NR432032 - M. Schreck	Retrd.	1986	950.00	1188-3000
1981 Chicken-Mini 7651NR20 - M. Schreck	Retrd.	1988	16.00	65-80
1978 Cigarette Box 7503NR050 (European)	Retrd.	1983	N/A	1875-2100
1982 Cigarette Holder 7463NR062 - M. Schreck	Retrd.	1990	85.00	115-195
1977 Cigarette Holder Rhodium 7503NR50	Retrd.	1982	160.00	512-1680
1977 Cigarette Lighter Rhodium 7500NR50	Retrd.	1982	130.00	1130-1470
1987 Clock, Athena 9280NR102	Retrd.	1992	330.00	315-350
1987 Clock, Belle Epoque 9280NR104	Retrd.	1992	N/A	545-785
1987 Clock, Colosseum 9280NR105	Retrd.	1992	N/A	410-536
1987 Clock, El Dorado 9280NR106	Retrd.	1992	N/A	509-536
1987 Clock, Napoleon 9280NR101	Retrd.	1992	N/A	300-475
1987 Clock, Polar Star 9280NR103	Retrd.	1992	N/A	419-500
1990 Coin Box no hinge 7400090001	Retrd.	1991	N/A	1008
1991 Coin Box w/hinge 7400090001	Retrd.	1995	N/A	313-420
1985 Dachshund-Lg. 7641NR75 - M. Schreck	Retrd.	1991	48.00	92-157
1985 Dachshund-Mini (wire tail) 7672NR42 - M. Schreck	Retrd.	1988	20.00	130-225
1987 Dachshund-Mini (frosted tail) 7672NR042000 - A. Stocker	Retrd.	1995	20.00	85-110
1993 Dick Gosling 7613NR000004 - A. Stocker	Retrd.	1999	37.50	38-60
1982 Dinner Bell-Lg. 7467NR71 - M. Schreck	Retrd.	1991	80.00	125-180
1987 Dinner Bell-Medium 7467NR54 - M. Schreck	Retrd.	1997	80.00	90-235
1981 Dog (Pluto) 7635NR70 - M. Schreck	Retrd.	1990	44.00	70-195
1983 Duck-Lg. 7653NR75 - M. Schreck	Retrd.	1987	44.00	160-708
1983 Duck-Med. 7653NR55 - M. Schreck	Retrd.	1988	38.00	128-228
1981 Duck-Mini 7653NR45 - M. Schreck	Retrd.	1988	16.00	50-95
1983 Elephant-Lg. 7640NR55 - M. Schreck	Retrd.	1989	90.00	180-290
1988 Elephant-Sm. 7640NR60 - A. Stocker	Retrd.	1995	70.00	65-125
1985 Falcon Head-Lg. 7645NR100 - M. Schreck	Retrd.	1991	600.00	1940-4000
1987 Falcon Head-Sm. 7645NR45 - M. Schreck	Retrd.	1991	60.00	240-250
1987 Fox-Lg. (black nose) 7629NR70 - A. Stocker	Retrd.	1999	50.00	75-157
1987 Fox-Lg. (frosted nose) 7629NR70 - A. Stocker	Retrd.	1988	50.00	170-185
1988 Fox-Mini Running 7677NR055 - A. Stocker	Retrd.	1996	35.00	35-65
1985 Frog (black eyes) 7642NR48 - M. Schreck	Retrd.	1991	30.00	106-151
1984 Frog (clear eyes) 7642NR48 - M. Schreck	Retrd.	1985	30.00	248-285
1996 Goldfish-Mini 7644000002 - M. Stamey	Retrd.	2000	45.00	45
1985 Grapes (European) 7550NR150070 - Team	Retrd.	1989	N/A	1008-1600
1983 Grapes-Lg. 7550NR30015 - Team	Retrd.	1988	250.00	1785-2290
1985 Grapes-Med. (gold & rhodium) 7550NR20029 - Team	Retrd.	1985	N/A	634
1983 Grapes-Med. (gold) 7550NR20029 - Team	Retrd.	1995	300.00	398-495
1983 Grapes-Med. (rhodium) 7550NR20029 - Team	Retrd.	1985	N/A	624-1629
1983 Grapes-Sm. (gold & rhodium) 7550NR20015 - Team	Retrd.	1985	N/A	1278-1420
1983 Grapes-Sm. (gold) 7550NR20015 - Team	Retrd.	1995	200.00	296-390
1983 Grapes-Sm. (rhodium) 7550NR20015 - Team	Retrd.	1985	N/A	1449-1610
1992 Harp 7477NR000003 - M. Zendron	Retrd.	1998	175.00	145-295
1993 Harry Gosling 7613NR000003 - A. Stocker	Retrd.	1999	37.50	40
1982 Hedgehog-Kg. Sz. 7630NR60 - Team	Retrd.	1987	98.00	1170
1981 Hedgehog-Lg. 7630NR50 - M. Schreck	Retrd.	1987	65.00	120-245
1988 Hedgehog-Lg. 7630NR70 - M. Schreck	Retrd.	1996	120.00	165-345
1981 Hedgehog-Med. 7630NR40 - M. Schreck	Retrd.	1987	44.00	68-244
1982 Hedgehog-Sm. 7630NR30 - Team	Retrd.	1987	38.00	413-450
1987 Hen, Mini 7675NR30 - G. Stamey	Retrd.	2001	35.00	45
1988 Hippopotamus 7626NR65 - A. Stocker	Retrd.	1992	70.00	92-188
1989 Hippopotamus-Sm. 7626NR055000 - A. Stocker	Retrd.	1995	70.00	72-122
1985 Hummingbird (Gold) 7552NR100 - Team	Retrd.	1988	200.00	1150-1315

YEAR ISSUE	EDITION LIMIT	YEAR RETD.	ISSUE PRICE	*QUOTE U.S.$
1985 Hummingbird (Rhodium) 7552NR200 - Team	Retrd.	1986	200.00	5200-6266
1990 Kingfisher 7621NR000001 - M. Stamey	Retrd.	1992	75.00	88-204
1991 Kitten 7634NR028000 - M. Stamey	Retrd.	1995	47.50	68-115
1991 Kiwi 7617NR043000 - M. Stamey	Retrd.	1996	37.50	65-175
1987 Koala (right) 7673NR40 - A. Stocker	Retrd.	1993	65.00	95-163
1989 Koala-Mini (left) 7673NR30 - A. Stocker	Retrd.	1993	45.00	45-75
1989 Koala-Mini 7676030000 - A. Stocker	Retrd.	2000	35.00	45
1993 Kris Bear 7637NR000001 - M. Zendron	Retrd.	2001	75.00	75
1997 Kris Bear Picture Frame 7506NR000002 - M. Zendron	Retrd.	2001	95.00	95
1977 Lighter (European) 7500NR050	Retrd.	1983	N/A	1400-3000
1982 Lighter 7462NR062 - M. Schreck	Retrd.	1990	160.00	275-471
1992 Lute 7477NR000004 - M. Zendron	Retrd.	1997	125.00	105-195
1996 Madame Penguin 7661NR000002 - A. Stocker	Retrd.	1999	85.00	60-135
1986 Mallard 7647NR80 - M. Schreck	Retrd.	1994	80.00	175
1992 Mother Beaver 7616NR000001 - A. Stocker	Retrd.	1996	110.00	124-200
1993 Mother Goose 7613NR000001 - A. Stocker	Retrd.	1999	75.00	66-75
1982 Mouse-Kg. Sz. 7631NR60 - M. Schreck	Retrd.	1987	95.00	2250-2700
1982 Mouse-Lg. 7631NR50 - M. Schreck	Retrd.	1987	69.00	580-1188
1976 Mouse-Med. (coil tail) 7631NR040 - M. Schreck	Retrd.	1995	85.00	113-195
1976 Mouse-Med. (floppy tail) 7631NR040 - M. Schreck	Retrd.	1995	60.00	244
1976 Mouse-Med. (leather tail) 7631NR040 - M. Schreck	Retrd.	1995	60.00	1397-1552
1976 Mouse-Med. (stone cut ears) 7631NR040 - M. Schreck	Retrd.	1995	60.00	455-505
1981 Mouse-Mini 7655NR23 - M. Schreck	Retrd.	1988	16.00	65-98
1976 Mouse-Sm. (coil tail) 7631NR30 - M. Schreck	Retrd.	1991	42.50	160-195
1976 Mouse-Sm. (flexible tail) 7631NR30 - M. Schreck	Retrd.	1978	40.00	145-161
1976 Mouse-Sm. (leather tail) 7631NR30 - M. Schreck	Retrd.	1991	40.00	279-310
1989 Mushrooms 7472NR030000 - A. Stocker	Retrd.	1998	35.00	35-82
1992 Nativity Angel 7475NR000009 - Team	Retrd.	1993	65.00	150-225
1991 Nativity Arch 7475NR0010 - Team	Retrd.	1993	N/A	170-207
1991 Nativity Holy Family 7475NR001 - Team	Retrd.	1993	N/A	130-259
1991 Nativity Holy Family w/Arch 7475NR001 - Team	Retrd.	1993	N/A	219-325
1992 Nativity Set (European) 6475NR0000099 - Team	Retrd.	1993	N/A	650
1992 Nativity Shepherd 7475NR000007 - Team	Retrd.	1993	65.00	79-98
1992 Nativity Wise Men (Set/3) 7475NR200000 - Team	Retrd.	1993	175.00	200-278
1996 Night Owl 7636NR000002 - A. Hirzinger	Retrd.	2001	85.00	85
1989 Old Timer Automobile 7473NR000001 - G. Stamey	Retrd.	1995	130.00	200-250
1996 The Orchid-yellow 7478000002 - M. Stamey	Retrd.	2000	140.00	140-200
1989 Owl 7621NR000003 - M. Stamey	Retrd.	1992	70.00	123-269
1989 Owl, Parrot, Kingfisher, Toucan - M. Stamey	Retrd.	N/A	285.00	600-1063
1995 Owlet 7636000001 - A. Hirzinger	Retrd.	2000	45.00	45
1981 Owl-Sm. 7636NR046000 - M. Schreck	Retrd.	1995	59.00	77-155
1989 Parrot 7621NR000004 - M. Stamey	Retrd.	1992	70.00	116-220
1988 Partridge 7625NR50 - A. Stocker	Retrd.	1990	85.00	109-204
1991 Pear 7476NR000002 - M. Stamey	Retrd.	1997	175.00	152-225
1985 Penguin, Mini 7661NR33 - M. Schreck	Retrd.	2001	16.00	38
1984 Penguin-Lg. 7643NR085000 - M. Schreck	Retrd.	1995	44.00	85-179
1997 Picture Frame w/Ladybug 7506000003 - E. Mair	Retrd.	2000	55.00	55
1986 Picture Frame/Oval 7505NR75G - Team	Retrd.	1989	90.00	293-445
1984 Picture Frame/Square 7506NR60G - M. Schreck	Retrd.	1989	100.00	214-425
1983 Picture Frame/Square 7506NR60R - M. Schreck	Retrd.	1987	N/A	211-234
1982 Pig-Lg. 7638NR65 - M. Schreck	Retrd.	1987	50.00	293-663
1984 Pig-Med. (crystal tail) 7638NR50 - M. Schreck	Retrd.	N/A	42.50	268-476
1982 Pig-Mini (crystal tail) 7657NR27 - M. Schreck	Retrd.	1994	29.50	55-139
XX Pillbox 7506NR030	Retrd.	1983	N/A	194
XX Pillbox 7506NR050	Retrd.	1983	N/A	257-543
1983 Pineapple/Rhodium-Giant 7507NR26002 - M. Schreck	Retrd.	1986	1750.00	2115-3750
1982 Pineapple/Rhodium-Lg. 7507NR105002 - M. Schreck	Retrd.	1986	150.00	350-657
1986 Pineapple/Rhodium-Sm. 7507NR060002 - M. Schreck	Retrd.	1986	55.00	116-170
1987 Polar Bear-Large 7649NR85 - A. Stocker	Retrd.	1997	140.00	210-374
1992 Poodle 7619NR000003 - A. Stocker	Retrd.	1997	125.00	115-225
1981 Pyramid-Lg.-Crystal Cal 7450NR50095 - M. Schreck	Retrd.	1993	90.00	100-293
1976 Pyramid-Lg.-Helio 7450NR50 - M. Schreck	Retrd.	1990	N/A	520-680
1981 Pyramid-Lg.-Vitrl Med. 7450NR50087 - M. Schreck	Retrd.	1993	90.00	175-328
1986 Pyramid-Small-Bermuda Blue 7450NR40088 - M. Schreck	Retrd.	1992	N/A	225-241
1987 Pyramid-Small-Crystal Cal. 7450NR40095 - M. Schreck	Retrd.	1997	100.00	145-293
1986 Pyramid-Small-Vitrail Light 7450NR400 - M. Schreck	Retrd.	1990	N/A	555-600
1987 Pyramid-Small-Vitrail Med. 7450NR40087 - M. Schreck	Retrd.	1997	100.00	125-160
1983 Rabbit-Lg. 7652NR45 - M. Schreck	Retrd.	1988	38.00	396-531
1981 Rabbit-Mini 7652NR20 - M. Schreck	Retrd.	1988	16.00	70-100
1988 Rabbit-Mini Lying 7678NR030000 - A. Stocker	Retrd.	1995	35.00	75-107
1988 Rhinoceros-Lg. 7622NR70 - A. Stocker	Retrd.	1992	70.00	105-187
1990 Rhinoceros-Sm. 7622NR060000 - A. Stocker	Retrd.	1995	70.00	92-130
1994 Roe Deer Fawn 7608NR000001 - E. Mair	Retrd.	1998	75.00	75-160
1987 Rooster-Mini 7674045000 - G. Stamey	Retrd.	2000	35.00	55
1982 Salt & Pepper 7508NR068034 - M. Schreck	Retrd.	1988	100.00	367-530
XX Salt & Pepper Rhodium Cruet Set 7502NR030-031-032	Retrd.	1983	N/A	2240-2395
1984 Salt and Pepper Shakers 7508NR068034 - Team	Retrd.	1988	80.00	271-400
1982 Schnapps Glasses, Set/3 7468NR039000 - Team (European)	Retrd.	1990	N/A	225-250
1982 Schnapps Glasses, Set/6 7468NR039000 - Team	Retrd.	1990	150.00	350-480
1990 Scotch Terrier 7619NR000002 - A. Stocker	Retrd.	1996	60.00	73-122
1985 Seal-Large (black nose) 7646NR085000 - M. Schreck	Retrd.	1995	85.00	100-280
1985 Seal-Large (black whiskers-left) 7646NR085000 - M. Schreck	Retrd.	1995	85.00	119-157
1985 Seal-Large (black whiskers-right) 7646NR085000 - M. Schreck	Retrd.	1995	85.00	531
1985 Seal-Large (black whiskers-straight) 7646NR085000 - M. Schreck	Retrd.	1995	85.00	150-300
1985 Seal-Large (silver whiskers) 7646NR085000 - M. Schreck	Retrd.	1995	85.00	95-195
1986 Seal-Mini (black nose) 7663NR46 - A. Stocker	Retrd.	N/A	45.00	205-275
1986 Seal-Mini (silver whiskers) 7663NR46 - A. Stocker	Retrd.	N/A	45.00	60-350
XX Silver Crystal City Espositore, set/8 9097422 - G. Stamey/M. Parma	4,999	1993	N/A	1055-2040
1990 Silver Crystal City-Cathedral 7474NR000021 - G. Stamey	Retrd.	1994	95.00	118-215
1991 Silver Crystal City-City Gates 7474NR000023 - G. Stamey	Retrd.	1994	95.00	91-215
1991 Silver Crystal City-City Tower 7474NR000027 - G. Stamey	Retrd.	1994	37.50	73-120
1990 Silver Crystal City-Houses I & II (Set/2) 7474NR100000 - G. Stamey	Retrd.	1994	75.00	85-150
1990 Silver Crystal City-Houses III & IV (Set/2) 7474NR200000 - G. Stamey	Retrd.	1994	75.00	85-150
1990 Silver Crystal City-Poplars (Set/3) 7474NR020003 - G. Stamey	Retrd.	1994	40.00	110-175
1993 Silver Crystal City-Town Hall 7474NR000027 - G. Stamey	Retrd.	1994	135.00	203-225
1995 Sir Penguin 7661000001 - A. Stocker	Retrd.	2000	85.00	85

Collectors' Information Bureau   *Quotes have been rounded up to nearest dollar

YEAR ISSUE	EDITION LIMIT	YEAR RETD.	ISSUE PRICE	*QUOTE U.S.$
1986 Snail 7648NR030000 - M. Stamey	Retrd.	1995	35.00	85-122
1991 South Sea Shell 7624NR72000 - M. Stamey	Retrd.	1994	110.00	115-170
1992 Sparrow 7650NR000001 - C. Schneiderbauer	Retrd.	1997	29.50	50-85
1983 Sparrow-Lg. 7650NR32 - M. Schreck	Retrd.	1988	38.00	135-180
1981 Sparrow-Mini 7650NR20 - M. Schreck	Retrd.	1991	16.00	50-85
1985 Squirrel (black nut) 7662NR42 - M. Schreck	Retrd.	N/A	55.00	397-441
1985 Squirrel (small ears) 7662NR42 - M. Schreck	Retrd.	1994	55.00	105-204
1977 Swan-Lg. (chandlier) 7633NR63 - M. Schreck	Retrd.	N/A	75.00	75-140
1983 Swan-Mini 7658NR27 - M. Schreck	Retrd.	1988	16.00	125-200
1982 Swan-Small 7633NR38V1 - M. Schreck	Retrd.	1988	35.00	75
1989 Swan-Small 7633NR38V2 - M. Schreck	Retrd.	1995	35.00	50
1997 Sweet Heart Jewel Box 7480NR000002 - E. Mair	Retrd.	2001	140.00	140
1986 Swimming Duck-Mini 7665NR37 - A. Stocker	Retrd.	2001	16.00	38
1987 Table Bell-Small 7467NR039000 - M. Schreck	Retrd.	1999	60.00	65
XX Table Magnifier (gold chain) 7800NR026	Retrd.	1984	N/A	1015-1200
1981 Table Magnifier (no chain) 7510NR01G	Retrd.	1984	70.00	791-1125
1981 Table Magnifier (no chain) 7510NR01R	Retrd.	1984	80.00	915-1125
XX Table Magnifier (rhodium chain) 7800NR026	Retrd.	1984	N/A	787-875
1981 Table Magnifier (with chain) 7510NR01R	Retrd.	1984	80.00	914-1200
1993 Three South Sea Fish 7644NR057000 - M. Stamey	Retrd.	1998	135.00	130-245
1993 Tom Gosling 7613NR000002 - A. Stocker	Retrd.	1999	37.50	32-48
1989 Toucan 7621NR000002 - M. Stamey	Retrd.	1992	70.00	155-195
1982 Treasure Box (Heart/Butterfly) 7465NR52/100 - M. Schreck	Retrd.	1990	80.00	223-331
1982 Treasure Box (Heart/Flower) 7465NR52 - M. Schreck	Retrd.	1988	80.00	220-270
1982 Treasure Box (Oval/Butterfly) 7466NR063100 - M. Schreck	Retrd.	1988	80.00	230-360
1982 Treasure Box (Oval/Flower) 7466NR063000 - M. Schreck	Retrd.	1990	80.00	282-360
1982 Treasure Box (Round/Butterfly) 7464NR50/100 - M. Schreck	Retrd.	1988	80.00	200-295
1982 Treasure Box (Round/Flower) 7464NR50 - M. Schreck	Retrd.	1990	80.00	220-295
1983 Turtle-King Sz. 7632NR75 - M. Schreck	Retrd.	1988	58.00	336-1170
1981 Turtle-Large 7632NR045000 - M. Schreck	Retrd.	1998	48.00	70-115
1981 Turtle-Small 7632NR030000 - M. Schreck	Retrd.	1996	35.00	55-99
1986 Vase 7511NR70 - Team	Retrd.	1990	50.00	169-250
1989 Walrus 7620NR100000 - M. Stamey	Retrd.	1993	120.00	124-277
1987 Whale 7628NR80 - M. Stamey	Retrd.	1991	70.00	245-250
1981 Zoo-Mini (Set/6) 7656NR006 - Team	Retrd.	1982	90.00	800-875

DOLLS & PLUSH

Alexander Doll Company

Madame Alexander Doll Club (M.A.D.C.)-Convention Dolls - Madame Alexander Design Team

1984 Ballerina 8" - Schumburg, IL	360	1984	N/A	N/A
1985 Happy Birthday 8" - Miami, FL	450	1985	N/A	N/A
1986 Scarlett 8" - Atlanta, GA	625	1986	N/A	N/A
1987 Cowboy 8" - San Antonio, TX	720	1987	N/A	275-325
1988 Flapper 10" - Chicago, IL	720	1988	N/A	175
1989 Briar Rose 8" - Los Angelos, CA	804	1989	N/A	225
1990 Riverboat Queen (Lena) 8" - New Orleans, LA	925	1990	N/A	N/A
1991 Queen Charlotte 10" - Charlotte, NC	900	1991	N/A	N/A
1992 Prom Queen (Memories) 8" - Chicago, IL	1,100	1992	N/A	N/A

YEAR ISSUE	EDITION LIMIT	YEAR RETD.	ISSUE PRICE	*QUOTE U.S.$
1993 Diamond Lil (Days Gone By) 10" - Kansas City, MO	876	1993	N/A	N/A
1994 Navajo Women 8" - Phoenix, AZ	835	1994	N/A	N/A
1995 Frances Folsom 10" - Washington DC	Retrd.	1995	N/A	200
1996 Showgirl 10" - Las Vegas, NV	Retrd.	1996	N/A	N/A
1997 A Little Bit of Country 8" - Nashville, TN	Retrd.	1997	N/A	N/A
1998 Rose Queen	Retrd.	1998	N/A	N/A
1999 Orange Blossom	Retrd.	1999	N/A	N/A
1999 Electro	Retrd.	1999	N/A	N/A
2000 Going to MADC 26415	810	2000	N/A	N/A
2000 MADC Angel 26170	Retrd.	2000	N/A	N/A
2001 MADC Ballerina 31490	Retrd.	2001	N/A	N/A
2001 Abagail Adams 31510	Retrd.	2001	N/A	N/A
2001 Suffragette 31495	1	2001	N/A	N/A
2001 MADC Revolutionary Pin 31500	150	2001	N/A	N/A
2001 Fashion Doll Centerpiece 31505	16	2001	N/A	N/A
2001 Charles River Regatta Alex 31506	400	2001	N/A	N/A
2001 Louisa May Alcott 31511	300	2001	N/A	N/A
2001 MADC Aviatrix 31512	500	2001	N/A	N/A
2001 Aviator Travel Doll Centerpiece 31513	30	2001	N/A	N/A
2001 Cissy Diva 31730	26	2001	N/A	N/A
2001 Evening at the Pops Cissy 31735	260	2001	N/A	N/A
2002 Spring Garden Party 34495	Yr.Iss.		N/A	N/A
2002 Cissette Garden Party 34500	Yr.Iss.		N/A	N/A
2002 March Winds Outfit 34505	Yr.Iss.		N/A	N/A
2002 April Fashion Accessory 34510	Yr.Iss.		N/A	N/A

Madame Alexander Annual Member's Only - Madame Alexander Design Team

1989 Wendy 8"	4,878	1989	49.95	100
1990 Polly Pigtails 8"	4,896	1990	49.95	50-100
1991 Miss Liberty 10"	Retrd.	1992	69.95	N/A
1992 Little Miss Godey 8"	Retrd.	1993	79.95	N/A
1994 Wendy's Best Friend Maggie 8"	Retrd.	1994	74.95	N/A
1995 Wendy Joins M.A.D.C. 8"	Retrd.	1995	49.95	125
1996 Wendy Honors Margaret Winson 8"	Retrd.	1996	69.95	N/A
1997 From The Madame's Sketchbook 8"	Retrd.	1997	69.95	N/A

ALEX - Madame Alexander Design Team

2000 Editor in Chief 25570	3,800	2000	89.95	90
2000 Cape Cod outfit by Timothy J. Alberts 25575	Open		39.95	40
2000 Millennium Ball by Timothy J. Alberts 25580	4,000	2000	124.95	125
2000 Alexandra Fairchild Ford by Timothy J. Alberts 26930	3,150	2000	79.95	80
2000 Misty Magic Accessory Pack by Timothy J. Alberts 27015	Open		29.95	30
2000 Pashmina Accessory Pack by Timothy J. Alberts 27075	Open		29.95	30
2000 Dinner and a Movie 27270	Open		39.95	40
2000 Runway Review 27275	2,850	2000	84.95	85
2000 Museum Gala 27280	400	2000	109.95	110
2000 Magazine Launch 27285	2,850	2000	79.95	80
2000 Lunch at 2 by Timothy J. Alberts 27290	3,800	2000	69.95	70
2000 Sensual Essentials Accessory Pack	Open		39.95	40
2000 Crimson Christmas 27660	2,500	2000	159.95	160
2001 New Year's Eve 28445	2,200	2001	149.95	150
2001 Finishing Touches 30350	Open		59.95	60
2001 Tides (blonde hr, green eyes) by Timothy J. Alberts 30620	2,500	2001	79.95	80
2001 Tides (brown hair, brown eyes) by Timothy J. Alberts 30625	2,500	2001	79.95	80
2001 Tides (red hr, bl eyes) by Timothy J. Alberts 30630	2,500	2001	79.95	80
2001 Santa Baby Giftset by Timothy J. Alberts 30635	1,000	2001	229.95	230
2001 Woman of the Year by Timothy J. Alberts 30640	2,500	2001	119.95	120
2001 Atlantico Outfit by Timothy J. Alberts 30800	Open		69.95	70
2001 Laguna outfit by Timothy J. Alberts 30805	Open		54.95	55
2001 Mardi Gras 31155	2,000	2001	229.95	230
2001 Sugar Mountain 31160	Open		49.95	50
2001 Sunset Grille 31165	2,500	2001	109.95	110
2001 Grande Entrance 31170	2,000	2001	189.95	190
2001 La Concorde (Paris) 31175	1,800	2001	89.95	90
2001 Soleil Outfit by Timothy J. Alberts 31195	Open		59.95	60

DOLLS & PLUSH

YEAR ISSUE	EDITION LIMIT	YEAR RETD.	ISSUE PRICE	*QUOTE U.S.$
2001 Tropicana Outfit by Timothy J. Alberts 31205	Open		69.95	70
2001 Cyber Launch 31215	2,500	2001	79.95	80
2001 Music Video Awards 31220	2,500	2001	89.95	90
2001 Milano by Timothy J. Alberts 31221	2,000	2001	99.95	100
2001 Book Tour 31265	1,500	2001	164.95	165
2001 Ocean Drive Outfit by Timothy J. Alberts 31380	Open		44.95	45
2001 Newport Drive 31385	Open		49.95	50
2001 Book Tour Travel Kit 31405	Open		39.95	40
2001 Portrait Sitting Alex 32060	1,000	2001	199.95	200
2001 Gone Gold (Paris) 32065	1,000	2001	149.95	150
2001 Alex Hair Kit 37665	Open		49.95	50
2001 Bon Anniversaire Alex for FAO Schwarz's 140th Anniversary 31645	500	2001	N/A	N/A

Alice in Wonderland - Madame Alexander Design Team

YEAR ISSUE	EDITION LIMIT	YEAR RETD.	ISSUE PRICE	*QUOTE U.S.$
1995 Alice 14508	Retrd.	1996	49.95	50
1995 Queen of Hearts 14511	Retrd.	1996	69.95	70
1995 Caterpillar 14594	Retrd.	1996	79.95	80
1996 Alice w/calendar 13000	Retrd.	1997	69.95	70
1996 Knave 13040	Retrd.	1998	69.95	70-75
1996 King of Hearts 14611	Retrd.	1996	59.95	60
1996 The Duchess 14613	Retrd.	1996	69.95	70
1996 White Rabbit 14616	Retrd.	1996	59.95	60
1997 Red Queen 13010	Retrd.	2000	109.95	110-115
1997 White King 13020	Retrd.	1998	89.95	90-95
1997 Red Queen and White King, set 13030	Retrd.	1997	199.95	200
1997 White Rabbit 13050	Retrd.	1997	59.95	60
1997 Humpty Dumpty 13060	Retrd.	1999	64.95	65-70
1997 Cheshire Cat 13070	Retrd.	1999	54.95	55-60
1998 Alice in Wonderland 13001	Retrd.	2000	69.95	70
1998 Dormouse 13090	Retrd.	2000	89.95	90
1998 Chessboard Quilt 13100	Retrd.	1998	74.95	75
1998 Tweedledum 13110	Retrd.	1998	79.95	80
1998 Tweedledee 13120	Retrd.	1998	79.95	80
1999 Tweedledum and Tweedledee 13080, set	Retrd.	2000	159.95	160-165
1999 Jabberwocky 13580	Retrd.	2000	74.95	75
2000 Knight 25915	Open		74.95	75
2000 Alice in Wonderland, 14" 25905	Open		49.95	50
2001 Alice in Wonderland w/Rabbit 30665	Open		94.95	95

Artist Circle - Madame Alexander Design Team

YEAR ISSUE	EDITION LIMIT	YEAR RETD.	ISSUE PRICE	*QUOTE U.S.$
2001 Prima Donna Cissy by Laura Meisner 31970	100	2001	1200.00	1200
2001 Manhattan Gothic Cissy by Doug James 31965	100	2001	1200.00	1200
2001 Madame de Pompadour Cissy by Timothy J. Alberts 31520	100	2001	1700.00	1700
2002 Equestrian Cissy by Laura Meisner 33965	200		499.95	500
2002 Baby Doe Cissy by Doug James 33960	200		649.95	650
2002 Pompadour Cissy by Tim Alberts 34400	200		799.95	800

Cinderella - Madame Alexander Design Team

YEAR ISSUE	EDITION LIMIT	YEAR RETD.	ISSUE PRICE	*QUOTE U.S.$
1997 Cinderella, 8" 13400	Retrd.	2000	64.95	70
1997 Poor Cinderella, 8" 13410	Retrd.	1999	69.95	75
1997 Cinderella's Prince, 8" 13420	Retrd.	1997	64.95	65
1997 Fairy Godmother, 8" 13430	Retrd.	2000	69.95	75
1997 Ugly Stepsister, 10" 13440	Retrd.	1998	79.95	85
1999 Cinderella's Carriage 13460	Retrd.	2000	174.95	175
1997 Really Ugly Stepsister, 8" 13450	Retrd.	1998	79.95	85
1999 Footmouse 13470	Retrd.	2000	99.95	100
1999 Cinderella's Wedding 13490	Open		89.95	90
1996 Cinderella 14540	Retrd.	1996	N/A	N/A
2000 Fairy Godmother 25920	Open		89.95	90
2000 14" Cinderella 25940	Open		139.95	140
2001 Cinderella at the Ball 30670	Open		79.95	80

Cissette - Madame Alexander Design Team

YEAR ISSUE	EDITION LIMIT	YEAR RETD.	ISSUE PRICE	*QUOTE U.S.$
1997 Cissette Houndstooth (African American) 22193	Retrd.	1999	119.95	120
1997 Cissette Houndstooth 22190	Retrd.	1999	119.95	120
1997 Cissette Onyx 22170	Retrd.	1999	119.95	120
1997 Cissette Café Rose (African American) 22203	Retrd.	1999	119.95	120
1997 Cissette Café Rose 22200	Retrd.	1999	119.95	120

YEAR ISSUE	EDITION LIMIT	YEAR RETD.	ISSUE PRICE	*QUOTE U.S.$
1997 Cissette Leopard w/ Shopping Bag (African American) 22183	Retrd.	1999	119.95	120
1997 Cissette Leopard w/ Shopping Bag 22180	Retrd.	1999	119.95	120
1997 Cissette Onyx (African American) 22173	Retrd.	1999	119.95	120

Cissy - Madame Alexander Design Team

YEAR ISSUE	EDITION LIMIT	YEAR RETD.	ISSUE PRICE	*QUOTE U.S.$
1998 Cissy's Secret Armoire 22250	Retrd.	1999	699.95	700
1998 Paris 22300	1,500	2000	589.95	590
1998 Venice 22310	1,500	2000	589.95	590
1998 Milan 22320	1,500	2000	589.95	590
1998 Barcelona (African American) 22330	1,500	2000	589.95	590
1998 Barcelona 22333	1,500	2000	589.95	590
1998 Budapest 22340	1,500	2000	589.95	590
1999 Madame Alexander 22560	Retrd.	1999	449.95	450
1999 Linda Allard for Ellen Tracy 22570	Retrd.	1999	449.95	450
1999 Scassi 22580	Retrd.	1999	449.95	450
1999 Anna Sui 22590	Retrd.	1999	449.95	450
1999 Fernando Sanchez 22720	Retrd.	1999	449.95	450
1999 Josie Natori 22730	Retrd.	1999	449.95	450
1999 Badgley-Mischka 22740	Retrd.	1999	449.95	450
1999 James Purcell 22760	Retrd.	1999	449.95	450
1999 Dana Buchman 22770	Retrd.	1999	449.95	450
1999 Jessica McClintock 22780	Retrd.	1999	449.95	450
2000 Rome 25555	Retrd.	2000	399.95	400
2000 Cairo 25560	Retrd.	2000	399.95	400
2000 Shanghai 25565	Retrd.	2000	299.95	300
2000 Vienna 25585	Retrd.	2000	399.95	400
2000 Hollywood 26865	Retrd.	2000	449.95	450
2000 Hollywood (African American) 26866	Retrd.	2000	449.95	450
2000 New York 26920	Retrd.	2000	349.95	350
2000 Romantic Dreams 27005	Retrd.	2000	349.95	350
2001 Society Stroll 28415	500	2000	499.95	500
2001 Society Stroll (African American) 28416	500	2000	549.95	550
2001 Day in the Life Trunk Set 28420	500	2000	69.95	70
2001 Hatbox 28425	Retrd.	2000	69.95	70
2001 Black and White Ball 28430	500	2000	549.95	550
2001 Haute Couture 28435	500	2000	499.95	500
2001 On the Avenue-Yardley 28440	500	2000	799.95	800
2001 Royal Reception 28441	500	2000	449.95	450
2001 Shoe Package 28830	500	2000	499.95	500
2001 Promise of Spring 31235	500		N/A	800
2001 Alluring Amethyst 32070	350		N/A	500
2001 140th Anniversary Cissy for FAO Schwarz's 140th Anniversary 31655	40	2001	N/A	N/A
2002 Mamie Cissy 33175	350		499.95	500
2002 Cissy Bluebird - Caucasian 33165	350		499.95	500
2002 Cissy Bluebird - African American 33166	150		499.95	500
2002 Renaissance Garden Cissy 33200	350		499.95	500
2002 Taffeta Romance Cissy 33170	350		549.95	550
2002 Dance the Night Away Cissy 33160	350		449.95	450
2002 Cissy's European Holiday Trunk Set 33190	350		449.95	450

Classics - Madame Alexander Design Team

YEAR ISSUE	EDITION LIMIT	YEAR RETD.	ISSUE PRICE	*QUOTE U.S.$
2000 140th Anniversary Wendy for FAO Schwarz's 140th Anniversary 31660	1,000	2000	N/A	N/A

Coca-Cola™ - Madame Alexander Design Team

YEAR ISSUE	EDITION LIMIT	YEAR RETD.	ISSUE PRICE	*QUOTE U.S.$
1998 10" Coca-Cola™ Celebrates Aviation '98 17380	Retrd.	2000	164.95	165
1998 10" Coca-Cola™ Carhop 17400	Retrd.	2000	114.95	115
1998 10" Coca-Cola™ Fantasy 13210	Retrd.	1999	149.95	150-155
1998 10" Coca-Cola™ Fantasy (African American) 31213	Retrd.	1999	149.95	150-155
1999 10" Coca-Cola™ Victorian Calender Doll 17360	Retrd.	1999	164.95	165
1999 8" Coca-Cola™ Winter Fun Wendy 17370	Retrd.	1999	99.95	100
1999 10" Nostalgia Coca-Cola™ 17490	Retrd.	1999	219.95	220
2000 10" Coca-Cola™ Carhop (Brunette) 17401	Retrd.	2000	114.95	115
2000 8" Off to the North Pole Coca-Cola™ 25245	Open		99.95	100
2000 10" Time Out for Sockhop Coca-Cola™ 26225	Open		114.95	115
2001 8" School Days Coca-Cola™ 28275	Open		119.95	120
2001 1920's Coca-Cola™ 28280	Open		149.95	150
2002 8" Refreshing Coca-Cola™ 33000	Open		89.95	90

YEAR ISSUE	EDITION LIMIT	YEAR RETD.	ISSUE PRICE	*QUOTE U.S.$
The Dionne Quintuplets - Madame Alexander Design Team				
1998 Dionne Quintuplets/Carousel 12230	Retrd.	1999	499.95	500
1998 Yvonne (pink) 12240	Retrd.	1999	84.95	85
1998 Annette (yellow) 12250	Retrd.	1999	84.95	85
1998 Marie (blue) 12260	Retrd.	1999	84.95	85
1998 Cécile (green) 12270	Retrd.	1999	84.95	85
1998 Emilie (lilac) 12280	Retrd.	1999	84.95	85
Disneyana Convention - Madame Alexander Design Team				
1993 Annette	1,000	1993	395.00	510-780
Gone With The Wind™ - Madame Alexander Design Team				
1997 10" Scarlett™ Hoop-Petti 15000	Retrd.	1998	99.95	100
1997 10" Mammy 15010	Retrd.	1999	89.95	95
1997 10" Scarlett™ Hoop-Petti, Mammy™ & Flower Dress 15020	Retrd.	1998	219.95	230
1997 8" Shadow Scarlett™ Rose Picnic 15030	Retrd.	1999	74.95	80
1997 10" Scarlett 15040	Retrd.	1997	109.95	110
1997 10" Rhett 15050	Retrd.	1997	89.95	90
1997 Stand 15060	Retrd.	1998	19.95	20
1997 21" Scarlett™ Rose Picnic Dress 15070	Retrd.	1997	349.95	350
1998 8" Poor Scarlett 14970	Retrd.	1999	94.95	95
1998 Tara™ 14990	Retrd.	1999	189.95	190
1999 10" Portrait Scarlett™ 14980	Retrd.	2000	129.95	130-135
1999 21" Black Mourning Scarlett™ 15170	1,000	2000	499.95	500
1999 8" Sweet 16 Scarlett™ 15180	Retrd.	2000	89.95	90
1999 8" Careen O'Hara™ 15190	Retrd.	1999	79.95	80
1999 8" Suellen O'Hara™ 15200	Retrd.	1999	79.95	80
2000 21" Atlanta Stroll Scarlett™ 25765	Retrd.	2000	449.95	450
2000 10" Sewing Circle Scarlett™ 25770	Retrd.	2000	119.95	120
2000 8" Melanie™ 25775	Retrd.	2000	89.95	90-100
2000 8" Scarlett™ Picnic 26860	Retrd.	2000	89.95	90-100
2001 8" Scarlett O'Hara™ 27825	Retrd.	2001	84.95	85
2001 8" Honeymoon Scarlett™ 28750	Retrd.	2001	94.95	95
2001 10" Atlanta Stroll Scarlett™ 28755	1,500	2001	149.95	150
2001 21" Peachtree Promenade Scarlett™ 28760	500	2001	549.95	550
2001 8" Honeymoon Rhett™ 28765	Retrd.	2001	89.95	90
2001 10" Belle Watling™ 30820	Retrd.	2001	149.95	150
2002 8" Aunt Pitty Pat 33465	Open		89.95	90
2002 10" Scarlett™ in Dressing Gown 33470	750		349.95	350
2002 21" Matron of the Mansion Scarlett™ 33475	250		549.95	550
Hall of Fame 2000 - Madame Alexander Design Team				
2000 Karen Ballerina 10" 25551	Retrd.	2000	119.95	120
2000 1953 Glamour Girl 25600	Retrd.	2000	109.95	110
2000 Madame Alexander Celebrates American Design 25590	Retrd.	2000	159.95	160
2000 1954 Victorian Girl 10" 25605	Open		109.95	110
2000 1954 Mystery Dance 14" 26035	Open		N/A	N/A
2000 Deborah Bride 16" 25595	Open		199.95	200
2000 Little Shaver 10" Grey and Crème 26820	Open		54.95	55
2000 Little Shaver 10" Pink and Green 26825	Open		54.95	55
2000 Little Shaver 6" Grey and Crème 26830	Open		54.95	55
Harley Davidson® - Madame Alexander Design Team				
1998 Cissette, 10" 17390	Retrd.	1998	149.95	150
1997 Billy, 8" 17410	Retrd.	1997	99.95	100
1997 Wendy, 8" 17420	Retrd.	1997	99.95	100
1997 David, 10" 17430	Retrd.	1997	120.00	120
1997 Cissette, 10" 17440	Retrd.	1997	120.00	120
International - Madame Alexander Design Team				
1994 Poland 110523	Retrd.	1994	N/A	N/A
1994 Italy 110524	Retrd.	1994	N/A	N/A
1994 Portugal 110535	Retrd.	1994	N/A	N/A
1994 USA 110536	Retrd.	1994	N/A	N/A
1994 France 110538	Retrd.	1994	N/A	N/A
1994 Austria 110539	Retrd.	1994	N/A	N/A
1994 Russia 110540	Retrd.	1994	N/A	N/A
1994 Ireland 110541	Retrd.	1994	N/A	N/A
1994 Germany 110542	Retrd.	1994	N/A	N/A
1994 Croatia 110543	Retrd.	1994	N/A	N/A
1994 Lithuania 110544	Retrd.	1994	N/A	N/A
1994 Spain 110545	Retrd.	1995	N/A	N/A
1994 Scotland 110546	Retrd.	1994	N/A	N/A

YEAR ISSUE	EDITION LIMIT	YEAR RETD.	ISSUE PRICE	*QUOTE U.S.$
1995 Uncle Sam 10353	Retrd.	1995	N/A	N/A
1995 Cuba 11548	Retrd.	1995	N/A	N/A
1995 Italy 11549	Retrd.	1995	N/A	N/A
1995 China 11550	Retrd.	1995	N/A	N/A
1995 Mexico 11551	Retrd.	1995	N/A	N/A
1995 Irish Lass 11555	Retrd.	1995	N/A	N/A
1996 France 11557	Retrd.	1996	N/A	N/A
1996 Morocco 11559	Retrd.	1996	N/A	N/A
1996 China 11561	Retrd.	1996	N/A	N/A
1996 USA 11562	Retrd.	1996	N/A	N/A
1996 India 11563	Retrd.	1996	N/A	N/A
1996 Brazil 11564	Retrd.	1996	N/A	N/A
1996 Mali 11565	Retrd.	1996	N/A	N/A
1996 Norway 11566	Retrd.	1996	N/A	N/A
1996 Ireland 17028	Retrd.	1996	N/A	N/A
1997 Ireland 21000	Retrd.	1998	N/A	60
1997 USA 24000	Retrd.	1998	N/A	75
1997 Morocco 24010	Retrd.	1997	N/A	N/A
1997 France 24020	Retrd.	1998	N/A	75
1997 India 24030	Retrd.	1997	N/A	N/A
1997 England 24040	Retrd.	1999	79.95	80
1997 Norway 24060	Retrd.	1997	N/A	N/A
1997 China 24080	Retrd.	1997	N/A	N/A
1997 Brazil 24090	Retrd.	1997	N/A	N/A
1997 Mexico 24100	Retrd.	1997	N/A	N/A
1997 Mali 24770	Retrd.	1997	N/A	N/A
1997 Italy 24050	Retrd.	1998	N/A	70
1998 Mexico 24100	Retrd.	1998	N/A	75
1998 Egypt w/ Sarcophagus 24110	Retrd.	2000	99.95	100
1998 Puerto Rico 24120	Retrd.	1999	74.95	75-80
1999 Team Canada 24130	Retrd.	1999	89.95	90
1999 Ireland/ St Patrick's Day 24140	Retrd.	1999	84.95	85
1999 Russia w/Stacking dolls 24150	Open		149.95	150
1999 Spain 24160	Retrd.	2000	89.95	90
1999 USA 24170	Retrd.	2000	84.95	85-90
1999 Guatamala 24180	Retrd.	1999	79.95	80
1999 Father of Vatican City 24190	Retrd.	1999	79.95	80
2000 Germany 25800	Open		149.95	150
2000 China 26280	Open		64.95	65
2000 Switzerland 25795	Open		89.95	90
2001 Japan Geisha 28545	Open		109.95	110
2001 Scotland 28550	Open		84.95	85
2001 England 28560	Open		109.95	110
2001 Las Vegas 28565	Open		84.95	85
2001 Gypsy of the World 28570	Open		74.95	75
2001 USA, Sacajawea 28575	Open		79.95	80
2002 African Safari - Caucasian 33501	Open		79.95	80
2002 African Safari - African American 33500	Open		79.95	80
2002 Ukraine 34325	Open		74.95	75
2002 Shanghai 33520	Open		84.95	85
2002 Morocco 33510	Open		79.95	80
2002 Holland 33490	Open		109.95	110
Leading Ladies/Silver Screen Legends - Madame Alexander Design Team				
2002 Grand Hotel - Greta Garbo 33480	1,500		159.95	160
2002 Meet Me in St. Louis - Judy Garland 32175	1,500		159.95	160
2002 Shanghai Express - Marlene Dietrich 33485	1,500		159.95	160
Little Women - Madame Alexander Design Team				
1995 Jo Goes to NY Trunk 14522	Retrd.	1995	N/A	N/A
1995 8" Jo 14523	Retrd.	1995	N/A	N/A
1995 8" Meg 14524	Retrd.	1995	N/A	N/A
1995 8" Beth 14525	Retrd.	1995	N/A	N/A
1995 8" Amy 14526	Retrd.	1995	N/A	N/A
1995 8" Marmee 14528	Retrd.	1995	N/A	N/A
1996 8" Laurie 14620	Retrd.	1996	N/A	N/A
1996 8" Aunt March 14621	Retrd.	1996	N/A	N/A
1996 10" Amy the Bride 14622	Retrd.	1996	N/A	N/A
1996 10" Amy 14630	Retrd.	1996	N/A	N/A
1996 10" Beth 14631	Retrd.	1996	N/A	N/A
1996 10" Jo 14632	Retrd.	1996	N/A	N/A
1996 10" Meg 14633	Retrd.	1996	N/A	N/A
1996 8" Amy Goes to Paris Trunk 14635	Retrd.	1996	N/A	N/A
1997 16" Amy 18500	Retrd.	1999	99.95	100
1997 16" Beth 18510	Retrd.	1999	99.95	100
1997 16" Jo 18520	Retrd.	1999	99.95	100
1997 16" Meg 18530	Retrd.	1999	99.95	100
1999 16" Marmee 28040	Retrd.	1999	119.95	120

DOLLS & PLUSH

YEAR ISSUE	EDITION LIMIT	YEAR RETD.	ISSUE PRICE	*QUOTE U.S.$
1999 8" Marmee 28120	Retrd.	2000	79.95	80-90
1999 8" Jo 28140	Retrd.	2000	79.95	80-90
1999 8" Meg 28150	Retrd.	2000	79.95	80
1999 8" Beth 28160	Retrd.	2000	79.95	80-90
1999 8" Amy 28170	Retrd.	2000	79.95	80-90
2000 8" Laurie 27765	Retrd.	2000	N/A	N/A
2001 5" Very Little Women Meg 28700	Open		84.95	85
2001 5" Very Little Women Beth 28705	Open		84.95	85
2001 5" Very Little Women Jo 28710	Open		84.95	85
2001 5" Very Little Women Amy 28715	Open		84.95	85
2002 8" Amy 33375	Open		89.95	90
2002 8" Meg 33380	Open		89.95	90
2002 8" Jo 33385	Open		89.95	90
2002 8" Beth 33386	Open		89.95	90

Peter Pan - Madame Alexander Design Team

1994 Peter Pan 140465	Retrd.	1994	N/A	N/A
1994 Wendy 140466	Retrd.	1994	N/A	85
1994 Tinker Bell 140467	Retrd.	1996	N/A	N/A
1996 14" Tinker Bell 87009	Retrd.	1996	N/A	N/A
1997 Tinker Bell 13960	Retrd.	2000	74.95	75
1999 Peter Pan 13660	Open		69.95	70
1999 Wendy 13670	Open		59.95	60
2000 Captain Hook 27060	Open		84.95	85
2001 Tinker Bell 30675	Open		79.95	80
2002 Tinker Bell 34100	Open		79.95	80
2002 Tinker Bell Mini Porcelain Doll 30455	Open		79.95	80

Queen Elizabeth's Coronation - Madame Alexander Design Team

2002 10" Queen Elizabeth Processional 33530	500		349.95	350
2002 21" Queen Elizabeth Recessional 33525	250		949.95	950
2002 8" Palace Guard 33395	1,000		79.95	80
2002 8" Princess Anne & Prince Charles Set 34150	1,000		159.95	160
2002 8" Princess Philip 33495	500		119.95	120
2002 8" Queen Elizabeth Crowning Glory 33660	500		189.95	190

Sleeping Beauty - Madame Alexander Design Team

1997 Sleeping Beauty, 8" 13600	Retrd.	2000	69.95	70
1997 Evil Sorceress, 8" 13610	Retrd.	1997	69.95	75
1997 Fairy of Beauty (pink), 8" 13620	Open		69.95	75
1997 Fairy of Song (green), 8" 13630	Open		69.95	75
1997 Fairy of Virtue (blue), 8" 13640	Open		69.95	75
1999 Sleeping Beauty's Prince w/Castle 13650	Retrd.	1999	79.95	80
2000 Sleeping Beauty's Prince w/bent knee 13651	Retrd.	2000	79.95	80
2000 Sleeping Beauty, 16" 25325	Retrd.	2000	189.95	190
2000 Princess and the Pea, 8" 27745	Open		109.95	110
2001 Sleeping Beauty, 8" 30680	Open		74.95	75

The Sound of Music™ - Madame Alexander Design Team

1998 Mother Superior, 10" 13870	Retrd.	2000	114.95	115
1998 Maria Travel Ensemble, 10" 13880	Retrd.	2000	124.95	125
1998 Maria at the Abbey, 10" 13890	Retrd.	2000	124.95	125
1999 Friedrich Von Trapp™, 10" 14020	Open		99.95	100
1998 Captain Von Trapp™, 10" 14030	Retrd.	2000	124.95	125
1998 Brigitta Von Trapp™, 9" 14040	Open		99.95	100
1998 Marta Von Trapp™, 8" 14050	Open		99.95	100
1998 Gretl Von Trapp™, 8" 14060	Open		99.95	100
1999 Kurt Von Trapp™, 8" 14090	Open		99.95	100
1999 Louisa Von Trapp™, 10" 14160	Open		99.95	100
1999 Liesl Von Trapp™, 10" 14170	Open		99.95	100

Specials - Madame Alexander Design Team

2001 8" Little Miss USA	1,800		65.00	65

The Wizard of Oz™ - Madame Alexander Design Team

1995 The Scarecrow 140430	Retrd.	1996	54.95	55
1995 Cowardly Lion 140431	Retrd.	1996	54.95	55
1995 Tin Woodsman 140432	Retrd.	1996	59.95	60
1995 Dorothy™ 140464	Retrd.	1996	49.95	50
1997 Dorothy™ with Toto 13200	Open		46.95	60
1993 8" The Tin Man 13210	Open		119.95	120
1993 8" The Cowardly Lion™ 13220	Open		54.95	55
1993 8" The Scarecrow 13230	Open		64.95	65
1997 10" Miss Gulch™ with Bicycle and Toto™ 13240	Retrd.	2001	119.95	120-130
1997 10" Glinda the Good Witch™ 13250	Open		64.95	65

YEAR ISSUE	EDITION LIMIT	YEAR RETD.	ISSUE PRICE	*QUOTE U.S.$
1997 There's No Place Like Home 13260	Retrd.	1999	139.95	140-150
1997 10" The Wicked Witch of the West™ 13270	Open		99.95	100
1998 The Wizard™ with State Fair Balloon 13280	Retrd.	2000	139.95	140
1998 The Wizard of Oz™ 23281	Retrd.	2000	94.95	95
1999 Apple Tree™ 13290	Open		79.95	80
1999 Lullaby Munchkin™ 13300	Open		69.95	70
2000 Dorothy™ w/Toto™ and Glitter Shoes 13201	Retrd.	2000	59.95	60-80
2000 15" Dorothy™ 25545	Retrd.	2000	49.95	50
2000 8" Winged Monkey™ 25950	Open		69.95	70
2000 10" Dorothy Yellow Brick Road 26365	Open		24.95	25
2000 Oz Flower Munchkin™ 27035	Open		49.95	50
2000 5" Dorothy™ 27065	Open		69.95	70
2000 5" Lullaby Munchkin™ 27070	Open		84.95	85
2001 15" Glinda the Good Witch™ Soft Sculpture 27570	Open		64.95	65
2001 15" Dorothy™ Soft Sculpture 25546	Open		59.95	60
2001 5" Porcelain Tin Man™ 28685	Open		84.95	85
2001 5" Porcelain Scarecrow™ 28690	Open		84.95	85
2001 5" Porcelain Cowardly Lion™ 28695	Open		84.95	85
2001 5" Daisy Munchkin™ 28770	Open		64.95	65
2001 8" Flower Bonnet Munchkin™ 28775	Open		69.95	70
2001 8" Emerald City Guard 31395	Open		84.95	85
2002 8" O.E.O. Guard 33595	Open		84.95	85
2002 15" Emerald City and Wizard Chambers 25945	Open		349.95	350
2002 8" Hairdresser 33585	Open		64.95	65
2002 8" Dorothy™ with Toto™ 13202	Open		59.95	60
2002 5" Porcelain Glinda the Good Witch™ 33765	Open		84.95	85
2002 5" To Oz™ Bear Set 33634	1,000		109.95	110
2002 5" To Oz Scarecrow™ 33633	1,500		94.95	95
2002 5" To Oz Tin Man™ 33631	1,500		94.95	95
2002 5" To Oz Cowardly Lion™ 33632	1,500		94.95	95
2002 5" Dorothy™ 33630	2,500		84.95	85

Ashton-Drake Galleries

Age of Bear-ius/Plush - D. Henretty

1999 Guthrie	Open		69.99	70
2000 Moonflower	Open		69.99	70
2000 Nash	Open		69.99	70
2000 Meadow	Open		69.99	70

All I Wish For You - J. Good-Krüger

1994 I Wish You Love	Closed	1995	49.95	50
1995 I Wish You Faith	Closed	1998	49.95	50
1995 I Wish You Happiness	Closed	1998	49.95	50
1995 I Wish You Wisdom	Closed	1998	49.95	50
1996 I Wish You Charity	Closed	1999	49.95	50
1996 I Wish You Luck	Closed	1999	49.95	50

All Precious in His Sight - J. Ibarolle

1998 Naomi	Closed	1999	72.99	73
1998 Kristina	Closed	1999	72.99	73
1998 Rosa	Closed	1999	72.99	73
1998 Su-Lee	Closed	1999	72.99	73

Amish Blessings - J. Good-Krüger

1990 Rebeccah	Closed	1993	68.00	95-100
1991 Rachel	Closed	1993	69.00	125
1991 Adam	Closed	1993	75.00	125-150
1992 Ruth	Closed	1993	75.00	90-110
1992 Eli	Closed	1993	79.95	95-125
1993 Sarah	Closed	1993	79.95	125

Anne of Green Gables - J. Kovacik

1995 Anne	Closed	1998	69.95	70
1996 Diana Barry	Closed	1998	69.95	70
1996 Gilbert Blythe	Closed	1998	69.95	70
1996 Josie Pye	Closed	1998	69.95	70

As Cute As Can Be - D. Effner

1993 Sugar Plum	Closed	1994	49.95	95
1994 Puppy Love	Closed	1995	49.95	75-95
1994 Angel Face	Closed	1995	49.95	50-75
1995 Patty Cake	Closed	1998	49.95	50

Babies World of Wonder - K. Barry-Hippensteel

1996 Andrew	Closed	1999	59.95	60
1996 Sarah	Closed	1999	59.95	60

Collectors' Information Bureau   *Quotes have been rounded up to nearest dollar

YEAR ISSUE	EDITION LIMIT	YEAR RETD.	ISSUE PRICE	*QUOTE U.S.$
1997 Jason	Closed	1999	59.95	60
1997 Kristen	Closed	1999	69.95	70
1998 Alex	Closed	1999	69.95	70

Baby Book Treasures - K. Barry-Hippensteel

1990 Elizabeth's Homecoming	Closed	1993	58.00	58
1991 Catherine's Christening	Closed	1994	58.00	58
1991 Christopher's First Smile	Closed	1992	63.00	58-63

Baby Talk - J. Good-Krüger

1994 All Gone	Closed	1995	49.95	75
1994 Bye-Bye	Closed	1995	49.95	50-75
1994 Night, Night	Closed	1995	49.95	50-75

Baby's Own Book - E. Helland

1999 Hannah's Homecoming	Open		59.99	60

Backyard Pool Party - T. Tomescu

1999 Summer Lovin' Tweety	Open		79.99	80

Ballet Recital - P. Bomar

1996 Chloe	Closed	2000	69.95	70
1996 Kylie	Closed	1999	69.95	70
1996 Heidi	Closed	1998	69.95	70

Barely Yours - T. Tomescu

1994 Cute as a Button	Closed	1994	69.95	95-125
1994 Snug as a Bug in a Rug	Closed	1995	75.00	75-125
1995 Clean as a Whistle	Closed	1996	75.00	75-125
1995 Pretty as a Picture	Closed	1996	75.00	75-125
1995 Good as Gold	Closed	1996	75.00	75-125
1996 Cool As A Cucumber	Closed	1999	75.00	75

Beach Babies - C. Jackson

1996 Carly	Closed	1998	79.95	80
1996 Kyle	Closed	1997	79.95	80
1997 Kellie	Closed	1999	79.95	80

Beach Babies - C. Marschner

1995 Sally	Closed	N/A	95.00	95
1996 Lacey	Closed	N/A	95.00	95-120
1997 Cassie	Closed	N/A	95.00	95

Bears of Memories/Plush - B. Ferrier

1997 Cinnamon Bear	Closed	N/A	79.99	80

Beautiful Dreamers - G. Rademann

1992 Katrina	Closed	1993	89.00	125-150
1992 Nicolette	Closed	1994	89.95	95-100
1993 Brigitte	Closed	1994	94.00	94
1993 Isabella	Closed	1994	94.00	94
1993 Gabrielle	Closed	1994	94.00	94-105

Beauty And Grace - B. Hanson

1997 Isabella	Closed	1999	99.95	100
1997 Patrice	Closed	1999	99.95	100
1998 Collette	Closed	2000	99.95	100
1998 Lara	Closed	1999	99.95	100

Bedtime for Bears/Plush - J. Davis

1998 Eliza	Closed	N/A	42.99	43
1998 Genie	Closed	N/A	42.99	43
1998 Jilly	Closed	N/A	42.99	43
1997 Sarah	Closed	N/A	42.99	43

The Bible Tells Me So - R. Miller

1998 Matthew	Open		72.99	73
1998 Mark	Closed	1999	72.99	73
1999 Luke	Open		72.99	73
1999 John	Open		72.99	73

Birthstone Bears/Plush - P. Blair

1997 January Garnet	Open		39.95	40
1997 February Amethyst	Open		39.95	40
1997 March Aquamarine	Open		39.95	40
1997 April Diamond	Open		39.95	40
1997 May Emerald	Open		39.95	40
1997 June Pearl	Open		39.95	40
1997 July Ruby	Open		39.95	40
1997 August Peridot	Open		39.95	40
1997 September Sapphire	Open		39.95	40
1997 October Opal	Open		39.95	40
1997 November Topaz	Open		39.95	40
1997 December Turquoise	Open		39.95	40

YEAR ISSUE	EDITION LIMIT	YEAR RETD.	ISSUE PRICE	*QUOTE U.S.$

Blessed Are The Children - B. Deval

1996 Blessed Are The Peacemakers	Closed	1999	69.95	70
1996 Blessed Are The Pure of Heart	Closed	1998	69.95	70
1997 Blessed Are The Meek	Closed	1998	79.95	80
1997 Blessed Are The Merciful	Closed	1998	79.95	80

Blessings of the Great Spirit - J. Belle

1999 Miracle of the Spirit Wind	Open		99.99	100

Blessings of the Seasons - T. Tomescu

1999 Winter Wonder	Open		99.99	100
2000 The Glory of Summer	Open		99.99	100
2000 The Delight of Spring	Open		99.99	100
2000 The Bounty of Autumn	Open		99.99	100

Blossoming Belles - S. Freeman

1997 Yellow Rose	Closed	2000	82.99	83
1998 Peach Blossom	Closed	1999	82.99	83
1998 Honeysuckle Rose	Closed	1999	82.99	83
1998 Magnolia Blossom	Closed	1999	82.99	83

Born To Be Famous - K. Barry-Hippensteel

1989 Little Sherlock	Closed	1991	87.00	87-90
1990 Little Florence Nightingale	Closed	1991	87.00	87-95
1991 Little Davey Crockett	Closed	1994	92.00	92
1992 Little Christopher Columbus	Closed	1993	95.00	95

Boys & Bears - A. Brown

1996 Cody and Cuddle Bear	Closed	1999	62.99	63
1997 Bobby and Buddy Bear	Closed	2000	62.99	63
1997 Nicky and Naptime Bear	Closed	2001	62.99	63
1998 Sammy and Sharing Bear	Closed	1999	62.99	63

Boys Will Be Bears/Plush - P. Joho & E. Foran

1997 Charlie	Closed	1999	49.95	50
1998 Davey	Closed	1999	49.95	50
1998 Frankie	Open		49.95	50
1998 Jimmy	Closed	2000	49.95	50

Brides of the South - L. Dunsmore

1998 Charlotte	Open		132.99	133
1998 Savannah	Open		132.99	133
1999 Laurel	Open		132.99	133
1999 Florence	Open		132.99	133

Calendar Babies - Ashton-Drake

1995 New Year	Open		24.95	25
1995 Cupid	Open		24.95	25
1995 Leprechaun	Open		24.95	25
1995 April Showers	Open		24.95	25
1995 May Flowers	Open		24.95	25
1995 June Bride	Open		24.95	25
1995 Uncle Sam	Open		24.95	25
1995 Sun & Fun	Open		24.95	25
1995 Back to School	Open		24.95	25
1995 Happy Haunting	Open		24.95	25
1995 Thanksgiving Turkey	Open		24.95	25
1995 Jolly Santa	Open		24.95	25

Catch of the Day/Plush - A. Inman-Looms

1999 Any Minute Now	Open		49.99	50
1999 Early Bear Catches the Worm	Open		49.99	50
2000 The One That Got Away	Open		49.99	50
2000 A Good Day Fishing	Open		49.99	50

Caught In The Act - M. Tretter

1992 Stevie, Catch Me If You Can	Closed	1994	49.95	125-145
1993 Kelly, Don't I Look Pretty?	Closed	1994	49.95	60-135
1994 Mikey (Look It Floats)	Closed	1994	55.00	55
1994 Nickie (Cookie Jar)	Closed	1995	59.95	60
1994 Becky (Kleenex Box)	Closed	1995	59.95	60

Caught In The Act/Plush - M. Tretter

1994 Sandy	Closed	1995	59.95	60

Caught In The Act/Plush - S. Schutt

1995 Bailey	Closed	1999	39.95	40
1995 Bonnie	Closed	1998	39.95	40
1995 Katie	Closed	1999	39.95	40
1995 Nathaniel	Closed	1998	39.95	40

Century of Beautiful Brides - S. Bilotto

1997 Katherine	Closed	1997	62.99	63
1997 Grace	Closed	1998	62.99	63

DOLLS & PLUSH

YEAR ISSUE	EDITION LIMIT	YEAR RETD.	ISSUE PRICE	*QUOTE U.S.$
1998 Donna	Closed	1999	62.99	63
1998 Heather	Closed	1999	62.99	63
1999 Joanna	Closed	1999	62.99	63

Charming Discoveries - S. Freeman

1996 Celeste	Closed	2000	89.95	90-100
1996 Marie	Closed	2000	89.95	90-100
1997 Cynthia	Closed	1998	89.95	90

Children of Christmas - M. Sirko

1994 The Little Drummer Boy	Closed	1995	79.95	125-150
1994 The Littlest Angel	Closed	1995	79.95	80
1995 O Christmas Tree	Closed	1998	79.95	80
1995 Sugar Plum Fairy	Closed	1998	79.95	80

Children of Mother Goose - Y. Bello

1987 Little Bo Peep	Closed	1988	58.00	95-110
1987 Mary Had a Little Lamb	Closed	1989	58.00	85-175
1988 Little Jack Horner	Closed	1989	63.00	63
1989 Miss Muffet	Closed	1991	63.00	63-150

Children of the Great Spirit - S. Simon

1994 Meadowlark	Open		95.00	95
1995 Tashee	Open		95.00	95
1996 Star Dreamer	Open		95.00	95
1996 Sewanka	Open		95.00	95

A Children's Circus - J. McClelland

1990 Tommy The Clown	Closed	1993	78.00	70-125
1991 Katie The Tightrope Walker	Closed	1993	78.00	70-125
1991 Johnnie The Strongman	Closed	1994	83.00	83-125
1992 Maggie The Animal Trainer	Closed	1994	83.00	83-150

A Child's Bedtime Prayer - M. Snyder

1997 Now I Lay Me Down To Sleep	Open		59.95	60
1998 I Pray The Lord My Soul To Keep	Open		59.95	60
1998 Keep Me Safe All Through The Night	Open		59.95	60
1998 Wake Me Up At Morning Light	Open		59.95	60

Christmas Cinderella 1998 - B. Deval

1998 1998 Christmas Cinderella	Closed	1998	114.99	115

Classic Brides of The Century - E. Williams

1990 Flora, The 1900s Bride	Closed	1993	145.00	195-300
1991 Jennifer, The 1980s Bride	Closed	1992	149.00	225-300
1993 Kathleen, The 1930s Bride	Closed	1993	149.95	150

Classic Collection - D. Effner

1996 Hillary	Closed	2000	79.95	80
1996 Willow	Closed	2000	79.95	80
1996 Emily	Closed	1998	79.95	80
1997 Jenny	Closed	2001	79.95	80
1997 Schoolgirl Jenny	Closed	2000	79.95	80

Classic Pooh Storytime - C. McClure

1999 Storytime with Pooh	Open		172.99	173

Country Kids - C. Johnston

1994 Savannah	Closed	1998	79.00	95
1994 Skyler	Closed	1998	95.00	95
1995 Cheyene	Closed	1998	95.00	95
1995 Austin	Closed	1998	95.00	95

Country Sweethearts - M. Tretter

1996 Millie	Closed	1998	62.99	63

Cuddle Chums - K. Barry-Hippensteel

1995 Heather	Closed	1998	59.95	60
1995 Jeffrey	Closed	1998	59.95	60

Decorating The Tree - M. Tretter

1996 Trisha	Closed	2000	59.95	60
1996 Patrick	Closed	2000	59.95	60
1996 Ryan	Closed	2000	59.95	60
1996 Melissa	Closed	2000	59.95	60

Deval's Fairytale Princesses - B. Deval

1996 Cinderella	Closed	2000	92.99	93
1996 Rapunzel	Closed	1999	92.99	93
1997 The Snow Queen	Closed	2001	94.99	95-100
1997 Sleeping Beauty	Closed	1998	94.99	95-100
1997 Princess and the Frog	Closed	1999	94.99	95-100

Dianna Effner's Mother Goose - D. Effner

1990 Mary, Mary, Quite Contrary	Closed	1992	78.00	175-200

YEAR ISSUE	EDITION LIMIT	YEAR RETD.	ISSUE PRICE	*QUOTE U.S.$
1991 The Little Girl With The Curl (Horrid)	Closed	1992	79.00	150-250
1991 The Little Girl With The Curl (Good)	Closed	1993	79.00	125-200
1992 Little Boy Blue	Closed	1993	85.00	75-85
1993 Snips & Snails	Closed	1994	85.00	125-150
1993 Sugar & Spice	Closed	1994	89.95	125-135
1993 Curly Locks	Closed	1995	89.95	90-100

Disney Babies in Dreamland - Y. Bello

1998 Baby Mickey	Open		62.99	63
1998 Baby Minnie	Open		62.99	63
1999 Baby Donald	Open		62.99	63
1999 Baby Pluto	Open		62.99	63
1999 Baby Daisy	Open		62.99	63
1999 Baby Goofy	Open		62.99	63

Down on the Beanbag Farm - R. Clark

1997 Janie	Closed	2000	62.99	63
1998 Emma	Closed	1999	62.99	63
1998 Drew	Closed	1999	62.99	63

Emily Anne's Busy Day - A. Tsalikhan

1996 Emily Anne	Closed	1998	69.95	70
1997 Emily Anne Playing Mommy	Closed	1998	69.95	70
1997 Emily Anne Calling Grandma	Closed	1999	69.95	70
1997 Snacktime	Closed	1999	82.99	83

England's Rose/Plush - L. DeMent

1999 England's Rose	Open		62.99	63

Eternal Love - T. Tomescu

1997 Eternal Love	Closed	1997	92.99	93

European Fairytales - G. Rademann

1994 Little Red Riding Hood	Closed	1995	79.95	80-85
1995 Snow White	Closed	1996	79.95	80

Family Ties - M. Tretter

1994 Welcome Home Baby Brother	Closed	1995	79.95	80
1995 Kiss and Make it Better	Closed	1996	89.95	80-90
1995 Happily Ever Better	Closed	1996	89.95	80-90

First Day at Walt Disney World - T. Tomescu

1998 Disney Girl	Open		99.99	100
1998 Disney Boy	Open		99.99	100
1998 End of a Long Day	Open		99.99	100
1998 Just Being Goofy	Open		99.99	100

Flurry of Activity - T. Tomescu

1996 Making Snowflakes	Closed	1998	72.99	73
1997 Making Icicles	Closed	1997	72.99	73
1997 Making Sunshine	Closed	2000	72.99	73

Forever Starts Today - C. McClure

1996 Melody	Closed	2000	199.95	200
1997 Angelica	Closed	2000	199.95	200
1997 Caroline	Closed	2000	199.95	200
1998 Monique	Open		199.95	200

Four Seasons Carousel - G. Rademann

1998 Winter Splendor (with horse)	Open		124.99	125
1998 Spring Enchantment	Open		62.99	63
1999 Summer Glory	Open		62.99	63
1999 Autumn Radiance	Open		62.99	63

The Friendship Bouquet - P. Parkins

1999 Everything's Coming Up Roses	Open		74.99	75
2000 Love Stems From Friendship	Open		74.99	75
2000 Bloom Where You Are Planted	Open		74.99	75
2000 Pick Your Friends & Love Them Bunches	Open		74.99	75

From This Day Forward - P. Tumminio

1994 Elizabeth	Closed	1995	89.95	150-200
1995 Betty	Closed	1996	89.95	90-150
1995 Beth	Closed	1996	89.95	90-175
1995 Lisa	Closed	1996	89.95	90

Garden of Innocence - D. Richardson

1996 Hope	Closed	1999	92.99	93
1996 Serenity	Closed	2000	92.99	93
1997 Charity	Closed	2001	92.99	93
1997 Grace	Closed	1998	92.99	93
1997 Kindness	Closed	2001	92.99	93

*Quotes have been rounded up to nearest dollar

YEAR ISSUE	EDITION LIMIT	YEAR RETD.	ISSUE PRICE	*QUOTE U.S.$
Garden of Inspirations - B. Hanson				
1994 Gathering Violets	Closed	1995	69.95	75
1994 Daisy Chain	Closed	1995	69.95	70
1995 Heart's Bouquet	Closed	1996	74.95	75
1995 Garden Prayer	Closed	1996	74.95	75
Gentle Joys - J. Good-Krüger				
1997 A Day Filled With Hugs & Kisses	Closed	1998	49.99	50
Gibson Girl in Fashion - S. Bilotto				
1998 Garden Walk	Closed	2001	132.99	133
1998 Evening at the Opera	Closed	2001	132.99	133
1998 Derby Day	Closed	2001	132.99	133
1998 The Masquerade Ball	Closed	2001	132.99	133
Gifts For Mommy - M. Girard-Kassis				
1997 Mother's Day	Closed	2001	62.99	63
1997 Christmas	Closed	2001	62.99	63
1998 Be My Valentine	Closed	2001	62.99	63
1998 Happy Birthday	Closed	2001	62.99	63
Gingham & Bows - S. Freeman				
1995 Gwendolyn	Closed	1998	69.95	70
1996 Mallory	Closed	1999	69.95	70
1996 Ashleigh	Closed	1998	69.95	70
1996 Bridget	Closed	2000	69.95	70
God Hears the Children - B. Conner				
1995 Now I Lay Me Down	Closed	1998	79.95	80
1996 God Is Great, God Is Good	Closed	1999	79.95	80
1996 We Give Thanks For Things We Have	Closed	1999	79.95	80
1996 All Creatures Great & Small	Closed	1998	79.95	80
God Sends an Angel - L. Tierney				
1999 Sleeping Like an Angel	Open		69.99	70
Growing Up Like Wildflowers - B. Madeja				
1996 Annie	Closed	1999	49.95	50
Happily Ever After - G. Rademann				
1998 Cinderella Bride	Closed	2001	82.99	83
1998 Snow White Bride	Closed	2001	82.99	83
1998 Rapunzel Bride	Open		82.99	83
1998 Beauty Bride	Open		82.99	83
Happiness Is Homemade - J. Good-Krüger				
1997 Hugs Made By Hand	Closed	1999	72.99	73
Happiness Is... - K. Barry-Hippensteel				
1991 Patricia (My First Tooth)	Closed	1993	69.00	125
1992 Crystal (Feeding Myself)	Closed	1994	69.95	75-100
1993 Brittany (Blowing Kisses)	Closed	1993	69.95	100
1993 Joy (My First Christmas)	Closed	1993	69.95	75-100
1994 Candy Cane (Holly)	Closed	1994	69.95	70
1994 Patrick (My First Playmate)	Closed	1994	69.95	75
Happy Meals World of Play - Y. Bello				
1997 McDonald's Express	Closed	1999	59.95	60
1997 McDonald's Old West	Closed	1998	64.99	65
Hats Off To The Seasons - L. Dunsmore				
1997 Christmas Carol	Closed	2000	72.99	73
1997 Springtime Robin	Closed	1998	82.99	83
1998 Mary Sunshine	Closed	1999	82.99	83
1998 Autumn Joy	Closed	1999	82.99	83
Heavenly Blessings - C. Walser-Derek				
1998 Love's Gentle Kiss	Open		82.99	83
1999 Friendship's Warm Hug	Open		82.99	83
Heavenly Goodness/Plush - A. Inman-Looms				
1999 Purity	Open		49.99	50
Heavenly Inspirations - C. McClure				
1992 Every Cloud Has a Silver Lining	Closed	1994	59.95	48-75
1993 Wish Upon A Star	Closed	1994	59.95	60-65
1994 Sweet Dreams	Closed	1994	65.00	65
1994 Luck at the End of Rainbow	Closed	1994	65.00	65
1994 Sunshine	Closed	1994	69.95	65-70
1994 Pennies From Heaven	Closed	1995	69.95	65-70
Here Comes Trouble - K. Barry-Hippensteel				
1999 Taz Made Me Do It	Open		79.99	80
2000 Loud but Lovable	Open		79.99	80
2000 Little Tornado	Open		79.99	80
2000 Too Tired for Trouble	Open		79.99	80
Heritage of American Quilting - J. Lundy				
1994 Eleanor	Closed	1995	79.95	80
1995 Abigail	Closed	1996	79.95	80
1995 Louisa	Closed	1996	84.95	85
1995 Ruth Anne	Closed	1996	84.95	85
Heroines from the Fairy Tale Forests - D. Effner				
1988 Little Red Riding Hood	Closed	1990	68.00	195-250
1989 Goldilocks	Closed	1991	68.00	68-95
1990 Snow White	Closed	1992	73.00	175
1991 Rapunzel	Closed	1993	79.00	175-250
1992 Cinderella	Closed	1993	79.00	175-295
1993 Cinderella (Ballgown)	Closed	1994	79.95	175-250
Honkytonk Gals Doll Collection - C. Johnston				
1996 Kendall	Open		95.00	95
I Love Tweety - L. Tierney				
1998 Tweety & Me	Open		74.99	75
1999 Sylvester's Surprise	Open		74.99	75
1999 A Snuggle With Tweety	Open		74.99	75
1999 Let's Have a Birdbath	Open		74.99	75
I Want Mommy - K. Barry-Hippensteel				
1993 Timmy (Mommy I'm Sleepy)	Closed	1994	59.95	145-150
1993 Tommy (Mommy I'm Sorry)	Closed	1994	59.95	125
1994 Up Mommy (Tammy)	Closed	1994	65.00	65
I'd Rather Be Fishin' - M. Tretter				
1996 What A Catch	Closed	2000	72.99	73
1997 Fishin' Buddies	Closed	2001	72.99	73
1997 Hooked on Fishin'	Closed	2001	72.99	73
1997 Fish Story	Closed	2001	72.99	73
I'm a Little Handyman - A. Tsalikhan				
1998 Tools Make the Man	Open		72.99	73
1999 Duct Tape Does it All	Open		72.99	73
1999 Brushing Up on the Job	Open		72.99	73
I'm Just Little - K. Barry-Hippensteel				
1995 I'm a Little Angel	Closed	1996	49.95	50
1995 I'm a Little Devil	Closed	1996	49.95	50
1996 I'm a Little Cutie	Closed	1999	49.95	50
I'm Tarzan Too - T. Tomescu				
1999 Jungle Buddies	Open		79.99	80
Imagine Where He'll Go - R. Miller				
1997 Adam	Closed	1998	62.99	63
In God's Garden - K. Barry-Hippensteel				
1998 Jessica Rose	Open		72.99	73
1998 Lil' Butterfly	Open		72.99	73
1999 Sweet Magnolia	Open		72.99	73
1999 Meadow Shade	Open		72.99	73
Innocence of Spring - C.W. Derek				
1997 Chelsea	Closed	2000	79.00	79
1999 Dori	Closed	1999	79.00	79
1999 Sidney	Open		79.00	79
1999 Leslie	Open		79.00	79
International Festival of Toys and Tots - K. Barry-Hippensteel				
1989 Chen, a Little Boy of China	Closed	1990	78.00	78-150
1989 Natasha	Closed	1992	78.00	78-150
1990 Molly	Closed	1993	83.00	75-99
1991 Hans	Closed	1993	88.00	88
1992 Miki, Eskimo	Closed	1994	88.00	88
It's So Much Friendlier With Pooh - C. McClure				
1998 You Need a Hug Pooh	Closed	2001	72.99	75
1998 You Look Sleepy Pooh	Closed	2001	72.99	73
1998 What's For Lunch Pooh?	Open		72.99	75
1998 Let's Play Pattycake Pooh	Open		72.99	75
1999 It's Our Bedtime Story, Pooh	Open		74.99	75
Joy Forever - C. McClure				
1996 Victorian Serenity	Closed	1998	129.95	130
1997 Victorian Bliss	Closed	1999	129.95	130
1997 Victorian Harmony	Closed	1998	129.95	130

DOLLS & PLUSH

YEAR ISSUE	EDITION LIMIT	YEAR RETD.	ISSUE PRICE	*QUOTE U.S.$
1997 Victorian Peace	Closed	1998	129.95	130
Joys of Summer - K. Barry-Hippensteel				
1993 Tickles	Closed	1994	49.95	110-120
1993 Little Squirt	Closed	1994	49.95	65
1994 Yummy	Closed	1994	55.00	65
1994 Havin' A Ball	Closed	1994	55.00	65
1994 Lil' Scoop	Closed	1994	55.00	65
Just Caught Napping - A. Brown				
1996 Asleep in the Saddle	Closed	1999	69.95	70
1996 Oatmeal Dreams	Closed	1998	69.95	70
1997 Dog Tired	Closed	1998	69.95	70
The King & I - P. Ryan Brooks				
1991 Shall We Dance	Closed	1992	175.00	395
La Quincenera - B. Hanson				
1998 La Quincenera	Open		92.99	93
The Language of Wedding Flowers - B. Hanson				
1998 White Roses	Open		99.99	100
2000 Calla Lilies	Open		99.99	100
2000 Gardenias	Open		99.99	100
2000 Camellias	Open		99.99	100
Lawton's Nursery Rhymes - W. Lawton				
1994 Little Bo Peep	Closed	1995	79.95	80-95
1994 Little Miss Muffet	Closed	1995	79.95	100
1994 Mary, Mary	Closed	1995	85.00	75-95
1994 Mary/Lamb	Closed	1995	85.00	75-95
The Legends of Baseball - Various				
1994 Babe Ruth - T. Tomescu	Closed	1995	79.95	140-175
1994 Lou Gehrig - T. Tomescu	Closed	1995	79.95	80-199
1995 Ty Cobb - E. Shelton	Closed	1996	79.95	80
Let's Play Mother Goose - K. Barry-Hippensteel				
1994 Cow Jumped Over the Moon	Closed	1995	69.95	70
1994 Hickory, Dickory, Dock	Closed	1995	69.95	95
Life's Little Blessings - R. Mattingly				
1997 Charity Is A Blessing	Closed	2001	82.99	83
1997 Kindness Is A Blessing	Closed	1998	72.99	73
1998 Patience Is A Blessing	Closed	2001	72.99	73
Little Ballerina Bears/Plush - A. Cranshaw				
1999 Gracie	Open		52.99	53
Little Girls of Classic Literature - W. Lawton				
1995 Pollyanna	Closed	1998	79.95	80
1996 Laura Ingalls	Closed	1999	79.95	80
1996 Rebecca of Sunnybrook Farm	Closed	1999	79.95	80
Little Gymnast - K. Barry-Hippensteel				
1996 Little Gymnast	Closed	1999	59.95	60
Little House On The Prairie - J. Ibarolle				
1992 Laura	Closed	1993	79.95	95
1993 Mary Ingalls	Closed	1993	79.95	300-395
1993 Nellie Olson	Closed	1994	85.00	145-150
1993 Almanzo	Closed	1994	85.00	95
1994 Carrie	Closed	1994	85.00	95-100
1994 Ma Ingalls	Closed	1995	85.00	85
1994 Pa Ingalls	Closed	1995	85.00	85
1995 Baby Grace	Closed	1996	69.95	75
Little Lacy Sleepyheads - J. Wolf				
1996 Jacqueline	Closed	N/A	99.99	100
The Little Performers - C. McClure				
1997 Joelle	Closed	1998	94.99	95
1997 Lauren	Closed	2001	94.99	95
1998 Nicole	12/02		94.99	95
1998 Alyssa	Closed	1999	94.99	95
Little Rascals™ - S./J. Hoffman				
1992 Spanky	Closed	1999	75.00	90-200
1993 Alfalfa	Closed	1999	75.00	90-175
1994 Darla	Closed	1999	75.00	90-175
1994 Buckwheat	Closed	1999	75.00	90-150
1995 Stymie	Closed	1999	75.00	90-175
Little Women - W. Lawton				
1994 Jo	Closed	1995	59.95	75-150

YEAR ISSUE	EDITION LIMIT	YEAR RETD.	ISSUE PRICE	*QUOTE U.S.$
1994 Meg	Closed	1995	59.95	60-125
1994 Beth	Closed	1996	59.95	125-175
1994 Amy	Closed	1996	59.95	175-250
1995 Marmie	Closed	1996	59.95	75-125
Looney Tunes Cuties - A. Tsalikhan				
1999 Pepe Le Pew	Open		74.99	75
1999 Marvin the Martian	Open		74.99	75
Lots Of Love - T. Menzenbach				
1993 Hannah Needs A Hug	Closed	1994	49.95	100
1993 Kaitlyn	Closed	1994	49.95	95
1994 Nicole	Closed	1995	55.00	55
1995 Felicia	Closed	1998	55.00	55
Love, Marriage, Baby Carriage/Plush - Various				
1996 Sam - B. Dewey	Open		49.95	50
1996 Katherine - M. Sibol	Closed	1999	49.95	50
1997 Carrie - D. Ortega	Closed	1999	49.95	50
The Loving Heart of the Irish Bride - J. Belle				
1999 Erin	Open		99.99	100
Lucky Charmers - C. McClure				
1995 Lucky Star	Closed	1998	69.95	70
1996 Bit O' Luck	Closed	N/A	69.95	70
Madonna & Child - B. Deval				
1996 Madonna & Child	Closed	1999	99.95	100
Magic Moments - K. Barry-Hippensteel				
1996 Birthday Boy	Closed	1999	69.95	70
Magical Moments of Summer - Y. Bello				
1995 Whitney	Closed	1998	59.95	48-60
1996 Zoe	Closed	1999	59.95	60
McDonald's And Me - D. Effner				
1996 You Deserve a Break Today	Closed	N/A	59.95	60-70
1997 Sharing a Good Time	Closed	N/A	59.95	60
McDonald's Future All Stars - B. Madeja				
1997 Joey	Closed	2001	62.99	63
McDonald's Happy Times - K. Barry-Hippensteel				
1997 Ritchie	Closed	2001	62.99	63
McDonald's Learning is Fun - T. Tomescu				
1996 Katie	Closed	1999	79.95	80
McDonald's Pillow Talk - B. Madeja				
1997 Sweet Dreams Ronald	Closed	2000	62.99	63
McDonald's Treats For Tots - Y. Bello				
1996 Erik's First French Fry	Closed	2000	59.95	60
1997 Nathan Picks a Pickle	Closed	2001	59.95	60-80
1998 Krissy's Ice Cream Cone	Closed	2001	59.95	60
Memories of Victorian Childhood - M. Girard-Kassis				
1998 Lydia	Closed	1998	82.99	83-93
1998 Paige	Closed	1999	82.99	83
1998 Olivia	Closed	1999	82.99	83-93
1998 Estelle	Closed	1999	82.99	83
Messages of Hope - T. Tomescu				
1994 Let the Little Children Come to Me	Closed	1995	129.95	175
1995 Good Shepherd	Closed	1996	129.95	130
1995 I Stand at the Door	Closed	1996	129.95	130
1996 Our Father	Closed	1999	129.95	130
Metropolitan Moments - V. Turner				
1998 Deirdre	Open		92.99	93
1998 Cecilia	Open		92.99	93
1999 Rosalind	Open		92.99	93
1999 Alexandra	Open		92.99	93
Miracle of Life - Y. Bello				
1996 Beautiful Newborn	Closed	1999	49.95	50-75
1996 Her Very First Smile	Closed	1999	49.95	50
1996 She's Sitting Pretty	Closed	1998	49.95	50
1996 Watch Her Crawl	Closed	1999	49.95	50
Miracles of Christ - T. Tomescu				
1996 Water Into Wine	Closed	2000	99.95	100
1996 Multiplying the Loaves	Closed	1999	99.95	100

Collectors' Information Bureau *Quotes have been rounded up to nearest dollar

YEAR ISSUE	EDITION LIMIT	YEAR RETD.	ISSUE PRICE	*QUOTE U.S.$
1997 Walking on Water	Closed	1999	99.95	100
1998 Ascension Into Heaven	Closed	1999	99.95	100
Moments To Remember - Y. Bello				
1991 Justin	Closed	1994	75.00	75
1992 Jill	Closed	1993	75.00	75-85
1993 Brandon (Ring Bearer)	Closed	1994	79.95	80-90
1993 Suzanne (Flower Girl)	Closed	1994	79.95	80
Mommy Can I Keep It?/Plush - P. Joho & E. Foran				
1995 Bartholomew & His Goldfish	Closed	1999	49.95	50
1995 Becky & Her Bunny	Closed	1999	49.95	50
1995 Belinda & Her Kitty	Closed	2000	49.95	50
1995 Benjamin & His Puppy	Retrd.	1997	49.95	50
Mommy Can You Fix It?/Plush - A. Cranshaw				
1997 Edgar	Open		49.95	50
1998 Edith	Open		49.95	50
1997 Emma	Open		49.95	50
1996 Emmett	Open		49.95	50
Morning Glories - B. Bambina				
1996 Rosebud	Closed	N/A	49.95	50
1996 Dew Drop	Closed	N/A	49.95	50
A Mother's Work Is Never Done - T. Menzenbach				
1995 Don't Forget To Wash Behind Your Ears	Closed	1998	59.95	60
1996 A Kiss Will Make It Better	Closed	1999	59.95	60
1996 Who Made This Mess	Closed	1999	59.95	60
My Closest Friend - J. Goodyear				
1991 Boo Bear 'N Me	Closed	1992	78.00	125-225
1991 Me and My Blankie	Closed	1993	79.00	95
1992 My Secret Pal (Robbie)	Closed	1993	85.00	85
1992 My Beary Softest Blanket	Closed	1993	79.95	85
My Fair Lady - P. Ryan Brooks				
1991 Eliza at Ascot	Closed	1992	125.00	395-450
My Little Ballerina - K. Barry-Hippensteel				
1994 My Little Ballerina	Closed	1995	59.95	60-75
Naturally Playful - S. Housely				
1997 Peek-A-Boo Bunny	Closed	1999	72.99	73
Noble Native Women - D. Wright				
1994 Sacajawea	Open		135.00	135
1994 Minnehaha	Open		135.00	135
1995 Pine Leaf	Open		135.00	135
1995 Lozen	Open		135.00	135
1997 White Rose	Open		135.00	135
1997 Falling Star	Closed	N/A	135.00	175-178
Nostalgic Toys - C. McClure				
1996 Amelia	Closed	1998	79.95	80
1996 Charlotte	Closed	1998	79.95	80-90
1997 Tess	Closed	1998	79.95	80-90
Nursery Newborns - J. Wolf				
1994 It's A Boy	Closed	1995	79.95	80
1994 It's A Girl	Closed	1995	79.95	80
Nursery Rhyme Favorites/Plush - J. Davis				
1995 Little Bo Peep	Closed	1997	39.95	40
1995 Little Miss Muffet	Open		39.95	40
1995 Mary, Mary	Open		39.95	40
1995 Little Lucy Locket	Open		39.95	40
Oh Holy Night - J. Good-Krüger				
1994 The Holy Family (Jesus, Mary, Joseph)	Closed	1995	129.95	130-140
1995 The Kneeling King	Closed	1995	59.95	60
1995 The Purple King	Closed	1995	59.95	60
1995 The Blue King	Closed	1995	59.95	60
1995 Shepherd with Pipes	Closed	1995	59.95	60
1995 Shepherd with Lamb	Closed	1995	59.95	60
1995 Angel	Closed	1995	59.95	60
Only At Grandma and Grandpa's - Y. Bello				
1996 I'll Finish The Story	Closed	1999	89.95	90
Our Own Ballet Recital - P. Bomar				
1996 Chloe	Closed	1999	69.95	70

YEAR ISSUE	EDITION LIMIT	YEAR RETD.	ISSUE PRICE	*QUOTE U.S.$
Passports to Friendship - J. Ibarolle				
1995 Serena	Closed	1998	79.95	80-90
1996 Kali	Closed	1999	79.95	80
1996 Asha	Closed	1999	79.95	80
1996 Liliana	Closed	2000	79.95	80
Patchwork of Love - J. Good-Krüger				
1995 Warmth of the Heart	Closed	1998	59.95	60
1996 Love One Another	Closed	1999	59.95	60
1996 Family Price	Closed	1999	59.95	60
1996 Simplicity Is Best	Closed	1999	59.95	60
1996 Fondest Memory	Closed	1999	59.95	60
1996 Hard Work Pays	Closed	1999	59.95	60
Peanuts Best Friends - L. Dunsmore				
1999 A Snuggle for Snoopy	Open		79.99	80
Perfect Companions/Plush - Various				
1998 Big Ears - B. Dewey	Open		59.99	60
1998 Big Hugs - A. Cranshaw	Open		59.99	60
Perfect Pairs - B. Bambina				
1995 Amber	Closed	1996	59.95	60
1995 Tiffany	Closed	1996	59.95	60
1995 Carmen	Closed	1996	59.95	60
1996 Susie	Closed	1999	59.95	60
Petting Zoo - Y. Bello				
1995 Andy	Closed	1996	59.95	60
1995 Kendra	Closed	1996	59.95	60
1995 Cory	Closed	1996	59.95	60
1995 Maddie	Closed	1996	59.95	60
Please Come To Tea - R. Miller				
1998 Abby	Closed	1999	62.99	63
1998 Clarissa	Closed	2000	62.99	63
1999 Morgan	Open		62.99	63
1999 Robyn	Closed	2000	62.99	63
Portraits From the Past - C. Haase				
1999 Adele	Open		99.99	100
2000 Penelope	Open		99.99	100
2000 Celeste	Open		99.99	100
2000 Sophia	Open		99.99	100
Portraits of Diana - T. Tomescu				
1998 Diana, The Princess of Wales	Open		132.99	133
1998 Diana, The World's Beloved Rose	Open		132.99	133
1999 Diana, Visionary of Style	Closed	2000	132.99	133
1999 Diana, Emissary of Compassion	Open		132.99	133
Precious Memories of Motherhood - S. Kuck				
1989 Loving Steps	Closed	1991	125.00	125-225
1990 Lullaby	Closed	1993	125.00	130-200
1991 Expectant Moments	Closed	1993	149.00	130-250
1992 Bedtime	Closed	1993	150.00	150-200
Precious Moments - Baby Blessings - P. Archer				
1999 Jesus Loves Me	Open		74.99	75
1999 Heaven Bless You	Open		74.99	75
2000 Someone to Watch Over Me	Open		74.99	75
2000 The Lord is My Shepherd	Open		74.99	75
Precious Moments - Baby's First - S. Butcher				
1999 Baby's First Birthday	Open		74.99	75
1999 Baby's First Pet	Open		74.99	75
2000 Baby's First Christmas	Open		74.99	75
Precious Moments - S. Butcher				
1994 Tell Me the Story of Jesus	Open		79.00	79
1995 God Loveth a Cheerful Giver	Open		79.00	79
1995 Mother Sew Dear	Open		79.00	79
1996 You Are the Type I Love	Open		79.00	79
Precious Moments - Songs of the Spirit - S. Butcher				
1999 Hope is a Gentle Melody	Open		79.99	80
1999 Faith is Heaven's Sweet Song	Open		79.99	80
2000 Love is a Heavenly Song	Open		79.99	80
2000 Happiness is a Song From Heaven	Open		79.99	80
Precious Moments - Tender Twosomes - S. Butcher				
1999 I Love Ewe	Open		82.99	83
1999 You're My Hunny Bunny	Open		82.99	83

DOLLS & PLUSH

YEAR ISSUE	EDITION LIMIT	YEAR RETD.	ISSUE PRICE	*QUOTE U.S.$
Precious Papooses - S. Housely				
1995 Sleeping Bear	Closed	1998	79.95	80
1996 Bright Feather	Closed	1999	79.95	80
1996 Cloud Chaser	Closed	1998	79.95	80
1996 Swift Fox	Closed	1998	79.95	80
Puppies Are People Too - M. Girard-Kassis				
1999 Dottie and Spots	Open		69.99	70
1999 Husty and Red	Open		69.99	70
2000 Curly and Frenchy	Open		69.99	70
2000 Buster and Boxer	Open		69.99	70
Quiet Moments - S. Freeman				
1998 Her Mother's Voice	Open		74.99	75
Rainbow of Love - Y. Bello				
1994 Blue Sky	Closed	1995	59.95	60-80
1994 Yellow Sunshine	Closed	1995	59.95	60
1994 Green Earth	Closed	1995	59.95	60
1994 Pink Flower	Closed	1996	59.95	60
1994 Purple Mountain	Closed	1996	59.95	60
1994 Orange Sunset	Closed	1996	59.95	60
Recipe For Happiness - M. Girard-Kassis				
1999 A Cup of Love	Open		79.99	80
1999 Measure of Faith	Open		79.99	80
2000 Portion of Kindness	Open		79.99	80
2000 Dash of Laughter	Open		79.99	80
Ruffle & Ribbons, Buttons & Bows - B. Madeja				
1998 Ruffles For Rebecca	Closed	2001	62.99	63
1998 Rachel in Ribbons	Closed	2000	62.99	63
1998 Betsy in Buttons	Open		62.99	63
1998 Bows for Belinda	Open		62.99	63
Seasons of Joy - J. Ibarolle				
1997 Nicholas	Closed	1998	74.99	75
1997 Kimberly	Closed	2001	74.99	75
1998 Molly	Closed	2001	74.99	75
1998 Brandon	Closed	1999	74.99	75
Secret Garden - J. Kovacik				
1994 Mary	Closed	1995	69.95	70
1995 Colin	Closed	1996	69.95	70-80
1995 Martha	Closed	1996	69.95	70
1995 Dickon	Closed	1996	69.95	70-85
A Sense of Discovery - K. Barry-Hippensteel				
1993 Sweetie (Sense of Discovery)	Closed	1994	59.95	60
Sense of Security - G. Rademann				
1996 Amy	Closed	1998	62.99	63
She Walks in Beauty - S. Bilotto				
1996 Winter Romance	Closed	2000	92.99	93
1997 Spring Promise	Closed	2001	92.99	93
1997 Summer Dream	Closed	2001	92.99	93
1998 Autumn Reflection	Closed	2001	92.99	93
Siblings Through Time - C. McClure				
1995 Alexandra	Closed	1996	69.95	70
1995 Gracie	Closed	1996	59.95	60
Simple Gifts - J. Good-Krüger				
1996 Roly Poly Harvest	Closed	1998	49.95	50
1997 Sweet Sensation	Closed	1998	49.95	50
1997 Papa's Helper	Closed	1998	49.95	50
1997 Naptime at Noon	Closed	1998	49.95	50
1997 Cuddly Companions	Closed	1999	49.95	50
Simple Pleasures, Special Days - J. Lundy				
1996 Gretchen	Closed	1999	79.95	80
1996 Molly	Closed	1999	79.95	80
1996 Adeline	Closed	N/A	79.95	80
1996 Eliza	Closed	N/A	79.95	80
Sing a Song of Childhood - J. Good-Krüger				
1999 I'm a Little Teapot	Open		79.99	80
Sleepytown Lullabies - P. Parkins				
1995 Nite, Nite Pony	Open		95.00	95
1996 Twice As Nice	Open		95.00	95
1996 Sleep Tight, Sweetheart	Open		95.00	95
1996 Cradled in Love	Open		95.00	95
Snow Babies - T. Tomescu				
1995 Beneath the Mistletoe	Closed	1995	69.95	70
1995 Follow the Leader	Closed	1996	75.00	75
1995 Snow Baby Express	Closed	1996	75.00	75
1996 Slip Slidn'	Closed	1998	75.00	75
1996 Learning To Fly	Closed	1998	75.00	75
1996 Catch of the Day	Closed	1999	75.00	75
Someone to Watch Over Me - K. Barry-Hippensteel				
1994 Sweet Dreams	Closed	1995	69.95	70
1995 Night-Night Angel	Closed	1995	24.95	25
1995 Lullaby Angel	Closed	1995	24.95	25
1995 Sleepyhead Angel	Closed	1996	24.95	25
1995 Stardust Angel	Closed	1996	24.95	25
1995 Tuck-Me-In Angel	Closed	1996	24.95	25
Special Edition Tour 1993 - Y. Bello				
1993 Miguel	Closed	1993	69.95	70-150
1993 Rosa	Closed	1993	69.95	70-150
Spending Time With Grandparents/Plush - B. Conley & T. Roe				
1996 Grandma and Sam	Closed	1998	49.95	50
Spice of Life - Y. Bello				
1997 Ginny	Closed	1998	49.95	46
1997 Megan	Closed	1998	49.95	46
1997 Rosa	Closed	1999	49.95	46
Sunday's Best - C. Jackson				
1996 Brianne	Closed	1996	72.99	73
1997 Jacob	Closed	1999	72.99	73
1997 Tamara	Closed	2000	72.99	73
1997 Jacob	Closed	1999	72.99	73
Sweet Inspirations - V. Turner				
1998 Kathryn Rose	Open		82.99	83
1999 Lily Anne	Open		82.99	83
1999 Dahlia	Open		82.99	83
1999 Iris Diane	Open		82.99	83
Tales From the Nursery - T. Tomescu				
1997 Baby Bo Peep	Closed	2000	82.99	83
1998 Baby Red Riding Hood	Closed	2001	82.99	83
1998 Baby Goldilocks	Closed	1999	82.99	83
1998 Baby Miss Muffet	Closed	1999	82.99	83
To Have and To Hold - A. Brown				
1998 Paulette	Open		99.99	100
Together Forever - S. Krey				
1994 Kirsten	Closed	1995	59.95	60
1994 Courtney	Closed	1995	59.95	60
1994 Kim	Closed	1995	59.95	60
Too Cute to Resist - M. Girard-Kassis				
1997 Ally	Closed	2000	49.99	50
1997 Kayla	Closed	2000	49.99	50
1998 Jennifer	Closed	2001	49.99	50
Toy Chest Treasures/Plush - P. Joho & E. Foran				
1996 Tad	Closed	1998	49.95	50
1997 Theo	Closed	1998	49.95	50
Treasured Togetherness - M. Tretter				
1994 Tender Touch	Closed	1995	99.95	100
1994 Touch of Love	Closed	1995	99.95	100
Tumbling Tots - K. Barry-Hippensteel				
1993 Roly Poly Polly	Closed	1994	69.95	70-95
1994 Handstand Harry	Closed	1995	69.95	70
Twinkle Toes Recital - T. Tomescu				
1997 Little Carnation	Closed	2000	72.99	73
1998 Little Daffodil	Closed	1998	72.99	73
1998 Little Violet	Closed	1998	72.99	73
Two Much To Handle - K. Barry-Hippensteel				
1993 Julie (Flowers For Mommy)	Closed	1994	59.95	60
1993 Kevin (Clean Hands)	Closed	1995	59.95	145
Under Her Wings - P. Bomar				
1995 Guardian Angel	Closed	1998	79.95	80

Collectors' Information Bureau   *Quotes have been rounded up to nearest dollar

YEAR ISSUE	EDITION LIMIT	YEAR RETD.	ISSUE PRICE	*QUOTE U.S.$
Victorian Dreamers - K. Barry-Hippensteel				
1995 Rock-A-Bye/Good Night	Closed	1996	49.95	55
1995 Victorian Storytime	Closed	1996	49.95	50
Victorian Lace - C. Layton				
1993 Alicia	Closed	1994	79.95	125
1994 Colleen	Closed	1995	79.95	85
1994 Olivia	Closed	1995	79.95	80
Victorian Nursery Heirloom - C. McClure				
1994 Victorian Lullaby	Closed	1995	129.95	130-150
1995 Victorian Highchair	Closed	1996	129.95	130-150
1995 Victorian Playtime	Closed	1996	139.95	140
1995 Victorian Bunny Buggy	Closed	1996	139.95	140
Victorian Vanity - S. Freeman				
1998 Melissa	Open		92.99	93
1998 Dorothea	Open		92.99	93
1998 Marianne	Open		92.99	93
Visions Of Our Lady - B. Deval				
1996 Our Lady of Grace	Closed	1999	99.95	100
1996 Our Lady of Lourdes	Closed	2000	99.95	100
1997 Our Lady of Fatima	Closed	2001	99.95	100
1997 Our Lady of Medjugorje	Closed	2001	99.95	100
Wain, Wain Go Away - M. Girard-Kassis				
1999 Melinda	Open		69.99	70
1999 Lexi	Open		69.99	70
1999 Holly	Open		69.99	70
Warner Brothers Baby - A. Tsalikhan				
1998 Tweet Dreams	Closed	2001	74.99	75
1998 Some Bunny Loves You	Open		74.99	75
1999 Mommy's Little Angel	Open		74.99	75
1999 Rock-a-Bye Puddy	Open		74.99	75
We Love The Homerun King - R. Miller				
1999 I Got His Autograph!	Open		79.99	80
1999 Hit It Here, Mark	Open		79.99	80
The Wee Wild West - J. Good-Krüger				
1999 Little Buckaroo	Open		72.99	73
1999 Little Card Shark	Open		72.99	73
1999 Little Lawman	Open		72.99	73
1999 Little Bandit	Open		72.99	73
What Little Girls Are Made Of - D. Effner				
1994 Peaches and Cream	Closed	1995	69.95	80-150
1995 Lavender & Lace	Closed	1998	69.95	70
1995 Sunshine & Lollipops	Closed	1998	69.95	115-135
Where Do Babies Come From - T. Tomescu				
1996 Special Delivery	Closed	1999	79.95	80
1996 Fresh From The Patch	Closed	2000	79.95	80
1996 Just Hatched	Closed	1996	79.95	80
1997 Handle With Care	Closed	2001	79.95	80
Winning Style - B. Hanson				
1998 Winning Style	Closed	1998	99.95	100
Winter Magic - M. Tretter				
1998 Lindsey	Open		64.99	65
1998 Bradley with Snowman	Open		64.99	65
1998 Tyler	Open		64.99	65
1998 Pamela	Open		64.99	65
The Wonderful Wizard of Oz - M. Tretter				
1994 Dorothy	Closed	1995	79.95	125
1994 Scarecrow	Closed	1995	79.95	80-125
1994 Tin Man	Closed	1995	79.95	80
1994 The Cowardly Lion	Closed	1996	79.95	80
A World of Romantic Weddings - T. Tomescu				
1999 Paris Bride	Open		129.99	130
Wreathed in Beauty - G. Rademann				
1996 Winter Elegance	Closed	1999	89.95	90
1997 Spring Promise	Closed	1999	99.99	100
1997 Summer Sweetness	Closed	1999	99.99	100
1997 Autumn Harmony	Closed	1999	99.99	100
A Year With Addie/Plush - B. Conley & T. Roe				
1995 January Ice Skating	Open		39.95	40

YEAR ISSUE	EDITION LIMIT	YEAR RETD.	ISSUE PRICE	*QUOTE U.S.$
1995 February Valentine	Open		39.95	40
1995 March Kite Flying	Open		39.95	40
1995 April Easter Fun	Open		39.95	40
1995 May Gardening Time	Open		39.95	40
1995 June Dress Up	Open		39.95	40
1995 July Summer Fun	Open		39.95	40
1995 August Autumn Adventure	Open		39.95	40
1995 September Back to School	Open		39.95	40
1995 October Masquerade	Open		39.95	40
1995 November Give Thanks	Open		39.95	40
1995 December Trim a Tree	Open		39.95	40
Yesteryear's Bears/Plush - L. DeMent				
1998 Theodora	Open		62.99	63
1999 Jacob	Open		62.99	63
1999 Constance	Open		62.99	63
2000 Alexander	Open		62.99	63
Yolanda's Heaven Scent Babies - Y. Bello				
1993 Meagan Rose	Closed	1994	49.95	75-125
1993 Daisy Anne	Closed	1994	49.95	50
1993 Morning Glory	Closed	1995	49.95	50-65
1993 Sweet Carnation	Closed	1995	54.95	55-70
1993 Lily	Closed	1995	54.95	55
1993 Cherry Blossom	Closed	1995	54.95	55-70
Yolanda's Lullaby Babies - Y. Bello				
1991 Christy (Rock-a-Bye)	Closed	1993	69.00	75-105
1992 Joey (Twinkle, Twinkle)	Closed	1994	69.00	75
1993 Amy (Brahms Lullaby)	Closed	1994	75.00	75
1993 Eddie (Teddy Bear Lullaby)	Closed	1994	75.00	75
1993 Jacob (Silent Night)	Closed	1994	75.00	75
1994 Bonnie (You Are My Sunshine)	Closed	1994	80.00	80
Yolanda's Picture - Perfect Babies - Y. Bello				
1985 Jason	Closed	1988	48.00	650-695
1986 Heather	Closed	1988	48.00	225-250
1987 Jennifer	Closed	1988	58.00	200-225
1987 Matthew	Closed	1990	58.00	195-200
1987 Sarah	Closed	1990	58.00	95-175
1988 Amanda	Closed	1990	63.00	125-150
1989 Jessica	Closed	1993	63.00	85
1990 Michael	Closed	1992	63.00	120-150
1990 Lisa	Closed	1992	63.00	100-150
1991 Emily	Closed	1992	63.00	110-150
1991 Danielle	Closed	1993	69.00	125-250
Yolanda's Playtime Babies - Y. Bello				
1993 Todd	Closed	1994	59.95	60
1993 Lindsey	Closed	1994	59.95	65
1993 Shawna	Closed	1994	59.95	60-75
Yolanda's Precious Playmates - Y. Bello				
1992 David	Closed	1994	69.95	125-250
1993 Paul	Closed	1994	69.95	125
1994 Johnny	Closed	1994	69.95	70-95

Boyds Collection Ltd.

Animal Menagerie™ - The Boyds Collection

YEAR ISSUE	EDITION LIMIT	YEAR RETD.	ISSUE PRICE	*QUOTE U.S.$
2001 Adelaide & Joey Downunder 55222	Open		25.00	25
2002 Archie Strutencrow 55316-05	Open		16.00	16
2000 Bandit Bushytail 55211	Open		12.00	12
1999 bessie moostein 5532	Retrd.	2001	14.00	14
2001 Butch Hoofenutter 55330-07	Open		19.50	20
2001 Corabelle Hoofenutter 55320-11	Open		15.00	15
1998 Dalton Monkbury 55242-08	Retrd.	2001	12.00	12
1998 Darwin Monkbury 55242-05	Retrd.	2001	12.00	12
2002 Dolly Llama 57860	Open		20.00	20
2000 Elford Bullsworth 55330-05	Open		19.00	19
1999 ernestine vanderhoof 55312-05	Retrd.	2001	11.00	11
2002 Ewebey Woolsley 55202-10	Open		16.00	16
2001 Farley O'Pigg 55392-07	Retrd.	2001	13.00	13
2001 Fernando Uttermost 55314-05	Open		12.50	13
2001 Florabelle Uttermost 55314-07	Open		12.50	13
2001 Hamlet 55360	Retrd.	2001	13.00	13
2001 Hannibal Trunkster 55223	Open		40.00	40
2001 I.M. Uproarius 55220	Open		16.00	16
2000 Jim I. Swingster 55241-08	Open		16.00	16
2002 Lambert Fuzzyfleece 55201-06	Open		14.00	14
2001 Liza Fuzzyfleece 55203-01	Open		22.00	22
2001 Lucibelle Fuzzyfleece 55203-06	Retrd.	2001	22.00	22

DOLLS & PLUSH

YEAR ISSUE	EDITION LIMIT	YEAR RETD.	ISSUE PRICE	*QUOTE U.S.$
2000 Matilda Baahead 55200-01	Retrd.	2001	14.00	14
1996 Mendel V.H.M. 5547	Retrd.	2001	8.00	8
2001 Merle B. Squirrel 55214	Retrd.	2001	13.00	13
1998 mike magilla 55251	Open		12.00	12
2001 Oda Parfume 55212	Retrd.	2001	16.00	16
2000 P. Gallery Trunkster 55250	Open		17.00	17
1999 Reggie Foxworthy 55210	Retrd.	2001	12.00	12
1992 Rosie O'Pigg 5536	Retrd.	1998	14.00	14
2001 Sillie Waddlewalk 555002	Open		11.00	11
1999 silo q. vanderhoof 55312-07	Retrd.	2001	11.00	11
1999 tallulah baahead 5520-01	Open		16.00	16
1999 Tuxie Waddlewalk 55500	Retrd.	2001	13.00	13
2002 Willie B. Bacon 55393-09	Open		31.00	31
2000 Willie Waddlewalk 555001	Retrd.	2001	11.00	11
2001 Wilt Stiltwalker 55221	Open		19.00	19

The Archive Series™ - The Boyds Collection

YEAR ISSUE	EDITION LIMIT	YEAR RETD.	ISSUE PRICE	*QUOTE U.S.$
2001 Alfred Q. Rothsbury 57004-11	Open		19.00	19
2001 Auden S. Penworthy 57410-11	Retrd.	2001	13.00	13
1998 Bedford Boneah II 582910-05	Retrd.	2001	23.00	23
2000 Big Ben Bearhugs 500050-05	Retrd.	2001	200.00	200
2000 Blake B. Wordsworth 5745-06	Open		7.50	8
2002 Bradford 57052-08	Open		13.00	13
2002 Bramble B. Thumperton 58340-03	Open		19.00	19
1993 Brie 5756	Retrd.	2001	14.00	14
1997 Brigham Boneah II 582910	Retrd.	2001	23.00	23
2000 Bristol B. Windsor 57052-03	Open		13.00	13
1997 Caledonia 5840-01	Retrd.	2001	9.00	9
2000 Cambridge Q. Bearrister 57003-08	Open		20.00	20
2000 Carlyle Wordsworth 57440-01	Open		7.50	8
2002 Cassie B. Nibbles 58290-01	Open		22.50	23
1993 Chedda 5756-06	Retrd.	2001	6.50	7
2001 Chester B. Bearsworth 57253-05	Open		7.00	7
2000 Cranbeary N. Bear 500100-02	Retrd.	2001	91.00	91
2001 Dawson B. Bearsworth 57150-08	Open		29.00	29
1999 Derry O. Berry 57252-05	Open		7.50	8
2000 Dickens Q. Wordsworth 5745-03	Open		7.50	8
2001 Domino 57004-07	Open		19.00	19
2000 Dover D. Windsor 57051-03	Open		13.00	13
2001 Dreyfus Q. Wordsworth 5745-07	Open		7.50	8
1999 Dunston J. Bearsford 57251-07	Retrd.	2001	7.50	8
1990 Eden 5708	Retrd.	N/A	7.00	35
2000 Emerson T. Penworthy 57410-03	Retrd.	2001	12.00	12
2000 Fairbanks 58070-10	Open		7.50	8
2001 Griffin W. Beasrley 572210-08	Retrd.	2001	53.00	53
2000 Hastings P. Bearsford 57250-11	Open		7.00	7
2000 Hayden T. Bearsford 57250-10	Open		7.00	7
2000 Hazlenut B. Bean 500100-05	Open		7.00	7
1998 Henson 58011-05	Retrd.	2001	20.00	20
2001 Higgins D. Nibbleby 58330	Retrd.	2001	13.00	13
2001 Hucklebeary B. 500100-06	Open		91.00	91
1996 Humboldt 5840-05	Retrd.	2001	9.00	9
2000 Huxley W. Penworthy 57411-08	Open		13.00	13
2001 J.J. Rugsley 500100	Open		91.00	91
1999 J.P. Locksley 57002-08	Open		20.00	20
1999 Jameson J. Bearsford 57251-10	Retrd.	2001	7.50	8
2000 Java B. Bean 500102-07	Open		91.00	91
2001 John Henry 572210-07	Open		53.00	53
1992 Keats 5743	Retrd.	2001	6.50	7
2000 Kelly O. Berry 57252-08	Retrd.	2001	7.50	8
2000 Latte O. Bear 500100-01	Retrd.	2001	9.00	9
2002 Layona Rugsley 500100-08	Open		91.00	91
2001 Lead B. Bottoms 51020	Open		20.00	20
2001 Lula Mae Loppenhop 573304-08	Open		7.00	7
2000 Maximillian 572210-05	Retrd.	2001	53.00	53
2001 Mazie Q. Lightfoot 58300-05	Retrd.	2001	15.00	15
1997 McKenzie 5840-03	Retrd.	2001	9.00	9
2001 Midge Meowsworth 5745-11	Open		7.50	8
2000 Milton R. Penworthy 57410-07	Open		12.00	12
2001 Missie Meowsworth 57411-06	Open		13.00	13
2000 Munster Q. Fondue 5755-06	Open		7.50	8
2000 Natalie Nibblenose 573300-01	Retrd.	2001	7.00	7
2000 Nickie Nibblenose 573303-03	Retrd.	2001	7.00	7
1999 oxford t. bearrister 57001-05	Open		20.00	20
2002 Pandora 500052	Open		91.00	91
1998 Peary 5807-10	Retrd.	2001	28.00	28
2000 Percy 5725-11	Open		6.00	6
2001 Putnam P. Beasrley 572210-08	Retrd.	2001	7.00	7
2000 Quaker O. Brimley 57150-10	Retrd.	2001	31.00	31
1999 Remington Braveheart 57210-03	Open		41.00	41
2000 Rockwell B. Bruin 57211-05	Retrd.	2001	40.00	40

YEAR ISSUE	EDITION LIMIT	YEAR RETD.	ISSUE PRICE	*QUOTE U.S.$
2000 Romano B. Grated 5755	Open		7.50	8
2001 Ruskin K. Woodruff 57052-07	Open		13.00	13
2002 Shane B. Bearsworth 57153-03	Open		31.00	31
2000 Sinclair Bearsford 57150-03	Open		31.00	31
2001 Sir Humpsley 57850	Open		18.00	18
1992 Spencer 5725	Retrd.	2001	6.00	6
2000 Stellina Hopswell 573700-01	Retrd.	2001	14.00	14
2000 Sterling Hopswell 573701-06	Retrd.	2001	14.00	14
2000 Sutton 57051	Open		13.00	13
1999 townsend q. bearrister 57001-03	Retrd.	2001	20.00	20
2001 True Luv B. Mine 57004-01	Open		19.00	19
2002 Tyler T. Bear 57253-03	Open		7.00	7
2002 Vera W. Bearsworth 572211-08	Open		53.00	53
2001 Warner Von Bruin 57151-05	Open		31.00	31
2001 Webster T. Bearsworth 57253-11	Open		7.00	7
2001 Whittington P. Bearsford 57152-08	Open		31.00	31
1999 Woodruff K. Bearsford 57251-05	Retrd.	2001	7.50	8
1998 Yolanda Panda 57701	Retrd.	2001	9.00	9

Baby Boyds™ - The Boyds Collection

YEAR ISSUE	EDITION LIMIT	YEAR RETD.	ISSUE PRICE	*QUOTE U.S.$
1998 Allie Fuzzbucket 51720	Retrd.	2001	7.50	8
1999 Barkley McFarkle 51750	Retrd.	2001	7.50	8
2000 Binky McFarkle 517050-03	Retrd.	2001	5.00	5
2000 Bundles B. Joy & Blankie 56391-04	Open		22.00	22
2000 Bunkie Hoppleby 51740-06	Retrd.	2001	7.50	8
2000 Bunky McFarkle 51750-07	Retrd.	2001	5.00	5
2000 Callie Fuzzbucket 517020-06	Retrd.	2001	5.00	5
2000 Dipsey Baadoodle 51800-01	Retrd.	2001	7.50	8
1999 Foodle McDoodle 51710-05	Retrd.	2001	7.50	8
1999 Goober Padoodle 517010-05	Retrd.	2001	5.00	5
2000 Kookie Snicklefritz 51770-12	Retrd.	2001	14.00	14
1999 Maddie LaMoose 517030-05	Retrd.	2001	5.00	5
1999 Marley Dredlion 51735	Retrd.	2001	7.50	8
2000 Mudpuddle P. Piglet 51790-09	Retrd.	2001	7.50	8
1998 Paddy McDoodle 51710	Retrd.	2001	7.50	8
2000 Poof Pufflebeary & Blankie 51780-03	Open		23.00	23
2000 Pookie C. Hoppleby 517040-01	Retrd.	2001	5.00	5
2000 Snookie Snicklefritz 51770-09	Retrd.	2001	14.00	14
1999 Toodle Padoodle 517010-03	Retrd.	2001	5.00	5
2000 Wookie Snicklefritz 51770-06	Retrd.	2001	14.00	14

Bailey and Friends™ - The Boyds Collection

YEAR ISSUE	EDITION LIMIT	YEAR RETD.	ISSUE PRICE	*QUOTE U.S.$
2000 Bailey & Matthew 9229	Retrd.	2000	64.00	64
1998 Bailey 9199-09	Retrd.	1998	26.00	26
1998 Bailey 9199-10	Retrd.	1998	26.00	26-31
1999 Bailey 9199-11	Retrd.	1999	26.00	26-32
2000 Bailey 9199-14	Retrd.	2000	26.00	26-40
2000 Bailey 9199-15	Retrd.	2000	29.00	29
2001 Bailey 9199-16	Retrd.	2001	29.00	29
2001 Bailey 9199-17	Retrd.	2001	23.00	23
2002 Bailey 9199-18	Open		23.00	23
1999 Bailey with Dottie 9199-12	Retrd.	2000	29.00	29
1998 Edmund 9175-09	Retrd.	1998	25.00	25
1998 Edmund 9175-10	Retrd.	1998	26.00	26
1999 Edmund 9175-11	Retrd.	1999	25.00	25
2000 Edmund 9175-14	Retrd.	2000	25.00	25
2000 Edmund 9175-15	Retrd.	2000	25.00	25
2001 Edmund 9175-16	Retrd.	2001	24.00	24
2001 Edmund 9175-17	Retrd.	2001	20.00	20
2002 Edmund 9175-18	Open		20.00	20
1998 Emily 9150-10	Retrd.	1998	26.00	26-30
2000 Emily 9150-15	Retrd.	2000	26.00	26-30
1998 Emily Babbit 9150-09	Retrd.	1998	26.00	26-30
1999 Emily Babbit 9150-11	Retrd.	1999	26.00	26-30
2000 Emily Babbit 9150-14	Retrd.	2000	26.00	26
2001 Emily Babbit 9150-16	Retrd.	2001	26.00	26
2001 Emily Babbit 9150-17	Retrd.	2001	22.00	22
2002 Emily Babbit 9150-18	Open		22.00	22
1998 Indy 91757-11	Retrd.	1998	11.50	12
1999 Indy 91757-12	Retrd.	2000	11.50	12
2000 Indy 91757-14	Retrd.	2000	12.00	12
2001 Indy 91757-15	Retrd.	2001	11.50	12
1999 Matthew & Bailey Millennium Gala Set 9228	Retrd.	2000	67.00	67
1998 Matthew 91756-10	Retrd.	1998	26.00	26
1999 Matthew 91756-12	Retrd.	2000	25.00	25
2000 Matthew 91756-15	Retrd.	2000	25.00	25
2001 Matthew 91756-17	Retrd.	2001	20.00	20

Bearfoot Friends - The Boyds Collection

YEAR ISSUE	EDITION LIMIT	YEAR RETD.	ISSUE PRICE	*QUOTE U.S.$
2001 Emmie...Button Up 641001	Open		14.00	14
2001 Miles...First Steps 641000	Open		14.00	14

Collectors' Information Bureau   *Quotes have been rounded up to nearest dollar

YEAR ISSUE	EDITION LIMIT	YEAR RETD.	ISSUE PRICE	*QUOTE U.S.$
2002 Mimsie...Weesteps 641004	Open		14.00	14
2001 Nellie...Baby Bundles 641002	Open		14.00	14
2002 Patty...Sunday's Best 641003	Open		14.00	14
2002 Skippy...All Tied Up 641005	Open		14.00	14

Bears In the Attic - The Boyds Collection

YEAR ISSUE	EDITION LIMIT	YEAR RETD.	ISSUE PRICE	*QUOTE U.S.$
2000 Bixby Trufflebeary 56390-10	Retrd.	2001	16.00	16
1998 Bixie 56501-10	Retrd.	2001	16.00	16
1998 Bluebeary 56421-06	Retrd.	2001	11.00	11
2000 Bundles B. Joy & Blankie 56391-04	Open		22.00	22
2001 Buttercup Pufflefluff 56398-12	Open		25.00	25
1998 Ezra R. Ribbit 566470	Open		5.00	5
2001 Fluff Pufflepoof 56380-01	Open		25.00	25
2000 Fuzzball Snicklefritz 51770-12	Retrd.	2001	14.00	14
1998 Muffin 56421-03	Retrd.	2001	11.00	11
2000 Philo Puddlemaker 56551-07	Retrd.	2001	16.00	16
1998 Pixie 56510-05	Retrd.	2001	16.00	16
2000 Poof Pufflebeary & Blankie 51780-03	Retrd.	2000	23.00	23
2000 Snookie Snicklefritz 51770-09	Retrd.	2001	14.00	14
2002 Snoozie 56392-10	Open		22.00	22
2000 Truffles O'Pigg 916010-01	Open		16.00	16
2000 Trundle B. Bear & Blankie 56391-10	Retrd.	2000	22.00	22
2000 Wookie Snicklefritz 51770-06	Retrd.	2001	14.00	14
1996 Zazu 5641-05	Retrd.	2001	25.00	25

Crazee Doos - The Boyds Collection

YEAR ISSUE	EDITION LIMIT	YEAR RETD.	ISSUE PRICE	*QUOTE U.S.$
2002 Celery...The Organic Gardener 4501	Open		7.50	8
2002 Elsie...The Dairy Farmer 4503	Open		7.50	8
2002 Fuchsia...The Fashion Designer 4504	Open		7.50	8
2002 Moonbeam...The Rock Star 4500	Open		7.50	8
2002 Olympic...The Synchronized Swimmer 4505	Open		7.50	8
2002 Sparkle...Future Fairy Godmother 4502	Open		7.50	8

Dressed Artisan Series™ - The Boyds Collection, unless otherwise noted

YEAR ISSUE	EDITION LIMIT	YEAR RETD.	ISSUE PRICE	*QUOTE U.S.$
2002 Andy B. Pattington 92001-06	Open		40.00	40
1999 Bess W. Pattington 92001-02	Retrd.	2001	39.00	39-59
1999 Betsie B. Jodibear 92000-07	Retrd.	2001	20.50	21
1999 Bumbershoot B. Jodibear 92000-03	Open		20.00	20
1999 Denton P. Jodibear 92000-06	Retrd.	2001	20.00	20
2000 Ebenezer S. Jodibear 92000-09	Open		22.50	23
1999 General P.D.Q. Pattington 92001-05	Retrd.	2001	40.00	40
2001 Glenda Jodibear 92000-17 - J. Battaglia	Open		14.00	14
1999 Harry S. Pattington 92001-01	Retrd.	2001	43.00	43-60
1999 Herbert Henry Jodibear 92000-05	Retrd.	2001	20.00	20-27
2000 Jack R. Woodsley 92002-04	Open		19.00	19
2001 Jeanine Jodibear 92000-16 - J. Battaglia	Open		20.00	20
2001 Jeremiah Woodsley 92002-3	Open		21.00	21
2002 Luci T. Jodibear 92000-18	Open		22.50	23
2002 Luke P. Jodibear 92000-19	Open		22.50	23
1999 Margaret T. Pattington 92001-03	Retrd.	2001	20.00	20-51
1999 Maris G. Pattington 92001-04	Retrd.	2001	47.00	47
2000 Mrs. Fezziwig Jodibear 92000-10	Open		22.50	23
1999 Nicklas T. Jodibear 92000-12	Retrd.	2001	23.00	23
2000 Ross G. Jodibear 92000-08	Retrd.	2001	20.50	20-25
1999 Sarah Beth Jodibear 92000-04	Retrd.	2001	18.00	18
2001 Simianne Z. Jodibear 92000-15	Retrd.	2001	18.00	18
2001 Slim B. Woodsley 92002-02	Open		16.00	16
2001 Sniffles T. Woodsley 92002-01	Open		16.00	16
2001 Timothy & Tiny Jodibear 92000-14	Retrd.	2001	17.00	17
2000 Tiny T. Jodibear 92000-11	Open		12.50	13

J.B. Bean & Associates™ - The Boyds Collection

YEAR ISSUE	EDITION LIMIT	YEAR RETD.	ISSUE PRICE	*QUOTE U.S.$
1999 Abercrombie B. Beanster 510400-05	Retrd.	2001	25.00	25
2000 Alabaster B. Bigfoot 51110-01	Open		39.00	39
1998 Amelia R. Hare 5203	Retrd.	2000	13.00	13
2000 Arlington B. Beanster 510400-03	Retrd.	2001	25.00	25
1996 Bedford B. Bean 5121-08	Retrd.	N/A	14.00	88-94
2000 Bennington W. Bruin 510400-08	Retrd.	2001	25.00	25
2000 Bobbi McBobble 510306-01	Open		14.00	14
1999 Boots Alleyruckus 5308-07	Retrd.	2001	22.00	22
2000 Bowser Barksalot 54000	Open		19.00	19
1998 Braxton B. Bear 51081-08	Retrd.	2001	20.00	20
2000 Buffie Bunnyhop 522700-03	Open		10.00	10
1997 Burke P. Bear 5109-05	Retrd.	2001	20.00	20-27
1999 Burlington P. Beanster 510400-07	Retrd.	2001	25.00	25
2000 Carson B. Barker 540300-05	Retrd.	2001	29.00	29
1997 Catherine Q. Fuzzberg 5303-08	Retrd.	2001	10.00	10

YEAR ISSUE	EDITION LIMIT	YEAR RETD.	ISSUE PRICE	*QUOTE U.S.$
2002 Catterina Cuddlepuss 53110-03	Open		29.00	29
2000 Checkers P. Hydrant 54051-07	Retrd.	2001	14.50	15
2001 Chopsticks 51200-07	Open		20.00	20
2001 Clem Cladiddlebear 500070-08	Retrd.	2001	57.00	57
2000 Coalcracker Ninelives 53040-07	Open		17.00	17
1991 Cookie Grimilkin 5306	Retrd.	2001	17.00	17
2002 Cotton Bunnytoes 522801-08	Retrd.	2002	11.00	11
2000 Cranbeary N. Bear 500100-02	Open		9.00	9
1998 Craxton B. Bean 510300-11	Retrd.	2001	14.00	14
1999 D.L. Merrill 51100-05	Retrd.	2000	28.00	28
2001 Dabney P. Powderfoot 58290-10	Open		22.50	23
XX Daryl Bear 5114	Retrd.	N/A	27.00	313
1999 Delanie B. Beansford 51101-10	Retrd.	2000	28.00	28
2001 Dickens 500051	Open		200.00	200
1999 Doolittle Buckshot 51200-08	Retrd.	2001	20.00	20-27
2000 Doomoore Buckshot 51200-03	Open		20.00	20
2001 Duffy P. Hydrant 540301-07	Open		29.00	29
2001 Duncan Doodledog 54040-11	Open		19.00	19
2001 Dutch P. Beansford 510301-08	Open		14.00	14
2002 Dylan T. Beansford 510402-11	Open		25.00	25
1989 Ernest Q. Grimilkin 5304	Retrd.	2001	14.00	14
2001 F.E.B.B. (First Ever Bean Bear) - Limited Edition 510301-03	Retrd.	2001	14.00	14
2000 Felicity N. Hugs 510301-01	Retrd.	2000	11.00	11
2001 Finicky snottykat 53030-10	Open		10.50	11
2000 Fluffie Bunnyhop 522700-01	Open		10.00	10
2000 Gabby Bunnyhop 522700-09	Retrd.	2001	8.00	8
2001 Golda Meow 53030-08	Open		10.50	11
2002 Grumples Q. Beansley 510401-10	Open		25.00	25
2001 Hattie Hopsalot 52401-01	Open		30.00	30
2000 Hooper Q. Hugster 500070-05	Retrd.	2001	57.00	57
1999 Hsing-Hsing Wongbruin 51540-07	Retrd.	2001	20.00	20
2001 Hucklebeary B. Bear 500100-06	Open		9.00	9
2001 Humphrey T. Bigfoot 51110-05	Open		39.00	39
2001 Jasper McBobble 510305-05	Retrd.	2001	14.50	15
2000 Java B. Bean 500102-07	Open		7.00	7
2000 Jaxton B. Bear 510300-10	Retrd.	2001	14.00	14
2001 JoyAnn Hugsbeary 82505	Open		20.00	20
2001 Keefer P. Lightfoot 52200-06	Open		20.00	20
2000 Kemper Forbes 51102-03	Retrd.	2001	28.00	28
1999 Kerry Q. Hopgood 52401-03	Retrd.	2001	28.00	28
2001 Key Lime Thumpster 52010-08	Open		16.00	16
2000 Latte O. Bear 500100-01	Open		9.00	9
2000 Marmalade Sneakypuss 530800-08	Open		22.00	22
2001 Michael David Bearsley 510401-11	Open		25.00	25
2002 Minkles D. Bearsdale 510810-03	Open		20.00	20
2001 Nana Bearhugs 500050-08	Retrd.	2001	200.00	200
2000 Nibbie Bunnyhop 522700-06	Retrd.	2001	8.00	8
2001 Ozzie N. Harrycat 53040-11	Open		17.00	17
2000 Parker B. Pooch 54050-08	Open		14.50	15
1998 Paxton P. Bean 510300-05	Retrd.	2001	14.00	14-27
2002 Peaches Thumpster 52010-06	Open		16.00	16
2001 Penny P. Copperpuss 53080-06	Open		22.00	22
2001 Peppermint P. Bear 510305-01	Retrd.	2001	14.00	14
2001 Peter Potter 515211-10	Open		20.50	21
2001 Petey Thumpster 52010-09	Open		16.00	16
2002 Peyton C. Hopplebuns 500071-01	Open		57.00	57
2002 Polly Bunnytoes 522801-03	Retrd.	2002	11.00	11
XX Pop Bruin 5124	Retrd.	N/A	27.00	27-58
2001 Purrzilla P. Pussytoes 53040-01	Open		17.00	17
2001 Purrsnicitty Snottykat 53050-10	Open		17.00	17
2002 Riley B. Bean 515212-10	Open		20.50	21
2002 Rustley Leadbottoms 51020-11	Open		20.00	20
2001 Sable B. Bearsdale 510810-05	Open		20.00	20
2001 Scratches T. Whiskerpuss 53000	Open		19.00	19
2001 Scruffy S. Beariluved 51000-05	Open		18.00	18
2001 Simon T. Poochley 54052-08	Open		14.50	15
2001 Sly Alleyruckus 53041-07	Retrd.	2002	17.00	17
2001 Smokey Ninelives 53030-06	Open		11.00	11
2001 Snuffy B. Barker 5405	Retrd.	2001	14.50	15
1993 Stanley R. Hare 5201	Retrd.	2000	13.00	13
2000 Stumper A. Potter 515211-11	Open		20.50	21
2001 T. Hopplewhite 52200-01	Open		19.00	19
2001 Tangerine Thumpster 52031-01	Retrd.	2001	16.00	16
2000 Tatters T. Hareloom 52000	Retrd.	2001	18.00	18
2000 Tessa Fluffypaws 5309-01	Open		20.00	20
2001 Theodore-Limited Edition 900300	Open		30.00	30
2001 Timothy T. Beansley 510301-05	Open		14.00	14
1996 Truly D. Bestmom 82506	Retrd.	2001	10.00	10
2001 Twigley Hopsalot 522701-08	Open		11.00	11

DOLLS & PLUSH

YEAR ISSUE	EDITION LIMIT	YEAR RETD.	ISSUE PRICE	*QUOTE U.S.$
2001 Uncle Sam 51100-01	Retrd.	2001	28.00	28
2000 Valerie B. Bearhugs 510301	Retrd.	2001	11.00	11
2001 Venessa V. Fluffypaws 53110-01	Open		29.00	29
1997 Walter Q. Fuzzberg 5303-07	Retrd.	2001	10.00	10
2000 Webber Vanguard 51100-07	Retrd.	2001	28.00	28
1999 Wilcox J. Beansford 51081-05	Retrd.	2001	20.00	20-41
1998 Winstead P. Bear 515210-03	Retrd.	2000	23.00	23-31
2001 Yowley Alleyruckus 53110-06	Open		29.00	29
1999 Zachariah Alleyruckus 5308-06	Retrd.	2001	22.00	22
2002 Zsa-Zsa Yippsalot 54052-01	Open		14.50	15

Little Girls and Boyds - J. Good-Krüger/The Boyds Collection

YEAR ISSUE	EDITION LIMIT	YEAR RETD.	ISSUE PRICE	*QUOTE U.S.$
2002 Abby & Gil...Deep Sea Fishing 4706	Open		61.00	61
2002 B.J. & Kenny...Songs of the Sea 4705	Open		61.00	61
2002 Carlie Mae with Ben...Bunny Watching 4704	Open		61.00	61
2001 Jill with Tumbles...Went Up The Hill 4701	Open		61.00	61
2001 Tina with Tutu...Just Barely Ballet! 4703	Open		61.00	61

The Mohair Bears™ & Friends - The Boyds Collection

YEAR ISSUE	EDITION LIMIT	YEAR RETD.	ISSUE PRICE	*QUOTE U.S.$
2001 Amy Z. Sassycat 590250-10	Retrd.	2001	40.00	40
1999 Armstrong Cattington 590087-07	Retrd.	2000	10.00	10
1999 Arthur C. Bearington 590060-03	Retrd.	2000	28.00	28
2000 Aunt Mamie Bearington 590104	Retrd.	2000	10.50	11
2000 Bamboo Bearington 590030	Retrd.	2000	50.00	50
2000 Bethany Bearington 590053-01	Retrd.	2000	26.00	26
2000 C. Carryout Bearington 590106	Retrd.	2001	10.00	10
2002 Cecelia T. Bearington 590056	Open		31.00	31
2000 Cleveland G. Bearington 590042-03	Retrd.	2001	46.00	46
2000 Dwight D. Bearington 590081-03	Retrd.	2000	14.00	14
1999 Earhart Harington 590086-01	Retrd.	2000	10.00	10
1999 Eastwick Bearington 590101	Retrd.	2000	10.50	11
1999 Edith Q. Harington II 5901600-03	Retrd.	2000	30.00	30
1999 Elfwood Bearington 590100	Retrd.	2000	10.50	11
2000 Hampton T. Bearington 590052-08	Retrd.	2000	35.00	35
2001 Juno Whatt Bearington 590054	Open		33.00	33
2001 Keifer B. Elfington 590055	Open		38.00	38
1999 Lindbergh Cattington 590087-03	Retrd.	2000	10.00	10
2000 Martin V. Moosington 590301-05	Retrd.	2001	31.00	31
2001 McKinley Bearington 590043-01	Retrd.	2001	50.00	50
1999 Milhous N. Moosington 590300	Retrd.	2001	81.00	81
1999 Mondale Cattington 590250-05	Retrd.	2000	28.00	28
1999 Monroe Bearington 590023-11	Retrd.	2000	96.00	96
2000 Nantucket P. Bearington 590102	Retrd.	2001	10.50	11
2001 Nicolas Bearington 590107	Retrd.	2001	10.50	11
1999 Quayle D. Cattington 590270-07	Retrd.	2000	16.00	16
1999 Rosalynn P. Harington II 5901400-01	Retrd.	2000	54.00	54
2001 Scarlett Bearington 590043-02	Open		46.00	46
2000 Uncle Ben Bearington 590103	Retrd.	2000	10.50	11
1999 Yeager Bearington 590085-05	Retrd.	2000	10.00	10

My Best Friend...Doll Collection - J. Good-Krüger/The Boyds Collection

YEAR ISSUE	EDITION LIMIT	YEAR RETD.	ISSUE PRICE	*QUOTE U.S.$
2001 Andrea & LP...Friends Sing the Same Songs 4822	Open		41.00	41
2002 Angie with Robin...Friends Will Fill Our Empty Nest 4837	Open		39.00	39
2001 Candy with Patience...Friends Ease The Pain 4831	Open		39.00	39
2001 Carrie with Atlas...Friends Lighten Our Load 4829	Open		39.00	39
2001 Cinnamon with Spice...Recipe for Friendship (Paw Dealer Exclusive) 4832	Retrd.	2001	39.00	39
2001 Danielle with Chilly...Friends Keep Us Warm 4828	Open		39.00	39
2001 Heather and Gusty...Friends Make Smooth Sailing 4824	Open		39.00	39
2001 Holly with Holiday...Friends Make Good Time Better 4830	Open		39.00	39
2001 Katy & Friends...Friends Stick Together 4826	Open		41.00	41
2001 Lynne & Jigsaw...Friends Help Put Back Our Pieces 4825	Open		40.00	40
2001 Megan & Faithful...Old and Dear Friends 4823	Open		39.00	39
2001 Miss Molly with Penpal...Friends are Everywhere 4827	Open		39.00	39
2002 Morgan With Flora...A Friend Is Always There 4833	Open		39.00	39

YEAR ISSUE	EDITION LIMIT	YEAR RETD.	ISSUE PRICE	*QUOTE U.S.$
2002 Paula With Peek And Boo...Make New Friends 4835	Open		39.00	39
2001 Rachael & Raspbeary...Berry Good Friends 4823	Open		41.00	41

Noah's Ark - The Boyds Collection

YEAR ISSUE	EDITION LIMIT	YEAR RETD.	ISSUE PRICE	*QUOTE U.S.$
2002 Noah 568001	Open		16.00	16
2002 Hsing Hsing and Ling Ling Wongbruin 568002	Open		12.50	13
2002 Stretch and Skye Longnecker 568003	Open		12.50	13
2002 Lawrence and Sheherazade O'Sand 568004	Open		12.50	13
2002 Packy and Dermah Trunkspace 568005	Open		12.50	13
2002 Zeiggy and Roary Tigertooth 568006	Open		12.50	13
2002 Joey and Alice Outback 568007	Open		12.50	13
2002 Noah's Ark 658222	Open		35.00	35

The Raggedymuffs - The Boyds Collection

YEAR ISSUE	EDITION LIMIT	YEAR RETD.	ISSUE PRICE	*QUOTE U.S.$
2002 Cora Belle 744108	Open		19.00	19
2002 Delray 744101	Open		19.00	19
2002 Kissimmee 744103	Retrd.	2002	19.00	19
2002 Mary Jane 744107	Open		19.00	19
2002 Peter Frost 744106	Open		19.00	19
2002 Sanibel 744102	Open		19.00	19

Snuggle-B's - The Boyds Collection

YEAR ISSUE	EDITION LIMIT	YEAR RETD.	ISSUE PRICE	*QUOTE U.S.$
2002 Flossie...Shortcake Dreams 4651	Open		16.00	16
2002 Gertrude...Pulling Weeds 4650	Open		16.00	16
2002 Mabel...Sunday Best 4653	Open		16.00	16
2002 Rose...Smelling the Flowers 4652	Open		16.00	16

T.J.'s Best Dressed™ - The Boyds Collection

YEAR ISSUE	EDITION LIMIT	YEAR RETD.	ISSUE PRICE	*QUOTE U.S.$
2000 Abigail Bramblebeary 913963	Retrd.	2001	12.50	13
2002 Abigail Rose Primsley 912645	Open		43.00	43
2000 Adaline Bearett 918437	Open		10.50	11
2001 Adeline LaBearsley 912657	Open		26.00	26
2000 Agatha Snoopstein 91870	Retrd.	2001	17.00	17
2000 Aissa Witebred 912070	Retrd.	2001	26.00	26
2001 Albert Merrybeary 915212	Open		16.00	16
1998 Alexis Berriman 912022	Retrd.	2001	59.00	59-69
2000 Alice B. Patchbeary 913978	Open		10.50	11
2001 Alouysius Quakenwaddle 91860	Retrd.	2001	21.00	21
1999 Amanda K. Huntington 912025	Retrd.	2001	57.00	57
1998 Anastasia 912081	Open		15.00	25-27
1998 Andrei Berriman 917300-06	Retrd.	2001	13.00	13
1999 Andrew Huntington 918053	Retrd.	2001	12.00	12-20
2001 Angeline Angelfrost 744115-06	Open		21.00	21
1999 Anissa Whittlebear 912650	Retrd.	2001	25.00	25
2001 Antoinette DeBearvoire 918440	Retrd.	2001	12.50	13
1999 Anya Frostfire 912023	Retrd.	2001	57.00	57-83
2002 April Mae 917445	Open		20.00	20
1998 Archibald McBearlie 91393	Retrd.	2001	13.00	13-20
1999 Ashley Huntington 918054	Retrd.	2001	12.00	12
2001 Ashlyn Bloomengrows 912653	Retrd.	2001	26.00	26
2001 Ashlyn LaBearsley 918352	Open		20.00	20
2000 Aubrey Tippeetoes 912054	Open		27.00	27
1998 Aunt Becky Bearchild 912052	Retrd.	2001	58.00	58
1998 Aunt Bessie Skidoo 91931	Open		29.00	29
1999 Aunt Fanny Fremont 918350	Retrd.	2001	22.00	22-27
2002 Aunt Mable with Snowy 90506	Open		33.00	33
1998 Aunt Yvonne Dubeary 918450	Open		24.00	24
1999 Auntie Aleena de Bearvoire 918451	Retrd.	2001	22.00	22
2000 Auntie Lavonne Higgenthorpe 918452	Retrd.	2001	24.00	24
2000 Autumn Fallsbeary 91745	Open		20.00	20
2000 B.A. Blackbelt 917361	Open		21.00	21
2001 B.A. Scholar 917369	Open		25.00	25
2001 B.Y. Lotsaluck 917370	Open		15.00	15
2002 Baakins 91863	Open		21.00	21
2001 Baby Mae Wishkabibble 90503	Open		21.00	21
2001 Baby Noel 912057	Open		21.00	21
2001 The Bearsleys 919810	Open		59.00	59
2002 Benson T. Hopabout 916503	Open		26.00	26
2001 Bernadette DeBearvoire 918443	Retrd.	2001	12.50	13
1999 Bethany Thistlebeary 913955	Retrd.	2001	12.50	13
2002 Betty Jane Maybeary 918454	Open		10.50	11
2000 Biff Grizzwood 912617	Open		29.00	29
2000 Billy Bob Bruin w/Froggie 912622	Retrd.	2001	30.00	30
1998 Boris Berriman 918021	Open		12.00	12
2000 Brady Bearimore 918321	Retrd.	2001	27.00	27
1999 Breezy T. Frostman 91522	Retrd.	2001	13.00	13-37
2000 Brewster T. Bear 912627	Open		24.00	24

*Quotes have been rounded up to nearest dollar

DOLLS & PLUSH

YEAR ISSUE	EDITION LIMIT	YEAR RETD.	ISSUE PRICE	*QUOTE U.S.$
2000 Brianna Tippeetoes 913959	Retrd.	2001	12.50	13
2002 Brittney Q. Hopplebuns 916633	Open		19.00	19
2000 Brooke B. Bearsley 917400	Retrd.	2001	20.00	20
2000 Bumble B. Buzzoff 91773	Retrd.	2001	17.00	17
2001 Buster McRind 915503	Open		15.00	15
2000 C.Z. Comet 917308	Retrd.	2000	16.00	16
2001 Cal Doubleplay 917710	Open		23.00	23
2001 Candy B. Corn 919633	Retrd.	2001	14.00	14
2001 Cara Z. Bunnyhugs 91649	Retrd.	2001	14.00	14
1999 Carmella de Bearvoire 918401	Retrd.	2001	9.00	9
2002 Carol Anne Primsley 913979	Open		10.50	11
2002 Caroline Mayflower 913958	Retrd.	2001	13.50	14
2002 Carrie N. Lotsalove 82518	Open		10.00	10
2000 Cathy J. Hiphop 917030	Retrd.	2001	12.00	12
2000 Catia Clawford 91712	Retrd.	2001	18.00	18
2000 Celeste Angeltrust w/Hope 900101	Open		65.00	65
XX Chamomile Q. Quignapple 91004	Retrd.	2001	23.00	23
2002 Chantelle Chapeau 918448	Open		10.50	11
2000 Chase Bearimore 913930	Open		14.50	15
2002 Cheryl S. Grammykins 912664	Open		29.00	29
1992 Christian 9190	Retrd.	2001	17.00	22-27
2001 Christiana LaBearsley 918446	Open		10.50	11
2001 Christine P. Plumbeary 918355	Open		22.00	22
2001 Chuck Woodbeary 917366	Open		26.00	26
2000 Chutney Cheeseworthy 916710	Retrd.	2001	18.00	18
2001 Cindyrella 91777	Open		28.00	28
2001 Clark S. Bearhugs 918055	Retrd.	2001	9.50	10-27
2001 Claudette Prissypuss 912091-08	Retrd.	2001	26.00	26
1999 Claudine De La Plumete 91710	Open		11.00	11
2001 Claus Kringlebeary 917311-01	Open		39.00	39
1998 Clementine 913953	Retrd.	2001	12.00	12-25
1999 Clover L. Buzzoff 91772	Retrd.	2001	18.00	18-32
2001 Colette Dubeary 918439	Retrd.	2001	10.50	11
2001 Conner D. Devilbear 919632	Open		21.00	21
2001 Cooper T. Wishkabibble 90502	Retrd.	2001	17.00	17
2001 Cora B. Applesmith 912634	Open		33.00	33
2000 Corey Allen Bearsmoore 912616	Open		30.00	30
2001 Cori Bearburg 915211	Retrd.	2001	14.00	14
1999 Cottage McNibble 91673	Retrd.	2001	12.00	12
2002 Cousin Marty with Rover 90508	Open		20.00	20
2002 Cousin Matilda with Ted 90507	Open		20.00	20
2002 Cybill Quackenwaddle 913939	Open		14.00	14
2002 Daisy Bloomengrows 913964	Retrd.	2001	14.00	14
2000 Darby Bearibug 913960	Retrd.	2001	12.00	12
2002 Dazey Ewe 913122	Retrd.	2001	23.00	23
2001 Delanie D. Hopplebuns 912078	Retrd.	2001	39.00	39
1996 Delbert Quignapple 91003	Retrd.	2001	23.00	23
1999 Devin Fallsbeary 912621	Retrd.	2001	39.00	39
2001 Dixie Hackett 918334	Open		24.00	24
2001 Dorchester Catsworth w/Artie 919760	Retrd.	2001	29.00	29
2002 Dorothea Laceley 918345	Open		22.00	22
2002 Dottie B. Bug 913936	Open		14.00	14
2002 Dunkin' 917381	Open		24.00	24
2000 Einstein Q. ScaredyBear 917368	Open		27.00	27
2000 Eleanore Bearsevelt 912010	Retrd.	2001	56.00	56
2001 Elijah Bearringer 912073	Retrd.	2001	30.00	30
2000 Elmer O. Bearroad 911931	Retrd.	2001	26.00	26
1999 Eloise Willoughby 918402	Retrd.	2001	14.00	14-22
2000 Embraceable Ewe 913121	Retrd.	2001	11.00	11
2000 Emmie Bramblebeary 912628	Open		34.00	34
2001 Erin Plumbeary 913970	Open		14.50	15
2001 Ernie Elfbeary 918358	Open		15.00	15
2001 Ernie Z. Foxworthy 913968	Open		11.00	11
2001 Father Kissmoose 917280	Open		24.00	24
2000 Father Kristmas 917310-01	Retrd.	2000	29.00	29
2001 Fawn Woodsbeary 913967	Open		14.00	14
2001 Fearless Fido 918056	Open		11.50	12
2001 Felicia Fuzzbuns 912090	Open		29.00	29
1999 Felina B. Catterwall 919701-01	Retrd.	2001	14.00	14
1998 Fern Blumenshine 91692	Retrd.	2001	12.00	12
1997 Fifi Farklefrost 91361	Open		20.00	20
2000 Fitz Farklefrost 91360	Open		12.50	13
2001 Flakey Bearlfrost 917380	Open		24.00	24
2001 Flora B. Flutterby 917720	Open		18.00	18
2001 Flurry B. Bundleup 913951	Open		15.00	15
1999 Forrest B. Bearsley 91744	Retrd.	2001	20.00	20
2000 Francesca LaFlame 912026	Open		57.00	57
2001 Frazier 913972	Open		14.00	14
2000 Freezy T. Frostman 913962	Retrd.	2001	12.50	13
1999 G. Kelly Ribbit 91320	Retrd.	2001	24.00	24
2001 G.P. Hugabunch 903000	Retrd.	2001	14.00	14
2001 Gala Applesmith 917441	Open		25.00	25
1999 Gary M. Bearenthal 912500	Retrd.	2001	51.00	51
2000 Ginger Snap 91523	Open		18.00	18
2000 Ginnie Higgenthorpe 918442	Retrd.	2001	9.50	10
2001 Ginnie Witebred 912074	Open		33.00	33
2001 Gloria Bearsevelt 912631	Retrd.	2001	37.00	37
1998 Gouda 91671	Retrd.	2001	12.00	12
1999 Grace Bedlington 912072	Retrd.	2001	39.00	40
2001 Graham Quackers 81509	Retrd.	2001	18.00	18
2002 Grammy Beariluv 82516	Open		11.00	11
2001 Grannie Annie Wishkabibble 90504	Open		33.00	33
1999 Gus Ghoulie 919640	Retrd.	2001	20.00	20-22
2000 Gwen Marie Bear 912055	Open		26.00	26
2001 H.B. Bearwish 903003	Open		14.00	14
2001 Haley Angelfrost 917379	Open		19.00	19
2001 Heidi Woodsbeary 918335	Open		26.00	26
1999 Hemingway K. Grizzman 91263	Retrd.	2001	39.00	39-42
1999 Henley Fitzhampton 912034	Retrd.	2001	12.50	13-21
2002 Henrietta MacDonald 917444	Open		20.00	20
2002 Hilby Jamm 917750	Open		20.00	20
2000 Holly Beary 744115-02	Retrd.	2001	20.00	20
1996 Huck 918051	Retrd.	2001	12.00	12-25
2002 Huck, Zach and Mandy (Show Exclusive) 919811	Open		51.00	51
2000 Huney B. Keeper 91774	Retrd.	2000	23.00	23
2000 Hunter Bearsdale w/Greenspan 912625	Retrd.	2000	31.00	31
2001 I.B. Bearyproud 913975	Open		11.00	11
2001 Ido Loveya 903004	Open		14.00	14
2002 Ima Scholar 917369-01	Open		25.00	25
1998 Inky Catterwall 91972	Retrd.	2001	18.00	18
2001 Isadora T. Lightfoot 913201	Retrd.	2001	21.00	21
2001 Ivy Bloomengrows 91602	Open		18.00	18
2001 J.W. VanWinkle & Snuggies 912633	Open		33.00	33
2001 Jack O. Lantern 919631	Open		21.00	21
2001 Jacob Wishkabibble 90505	Open		36.00	36
2001 Jeannie S. Berriman 919809	Retrd.	2001	49.00	49
2002 Jeb MacDonald 912662	Open		26.00	26
2001 Jeffrey T. Treetoes 917376	Open		15.00	15
2001 Jenna D. LaPinne 916630	Retrd.	2001	16.00	16
2001 Jocelyn Bloomengrows 912012	Retrd.	2001	56.00	56
2001 Jonathan Applesmith 913969	Open		10.00	10
2001 Julia Angelbrite 91776	Open		19.00	19
1999 Juliana Hopkins II 911220	Open		15.00	15
2001 Juliet S. Bearlove 912651	Retrd.	2001	23.00	23
2001 Juniper Bunnyhugs 916501	Open		16.00	16
1998 Kaitlin McSwine III 91601-02	Open		16.00	16
2001 Karen A. Mulberry 917364	Open		23.00	23
1999 Karla Mulbeary 915500	Retrd.	2001	20.00	20-25
2002 Katie B. Bearyproud 918341	Open		26.00	26
1999 Katie Berrijam 910062	Retrd.	2001	22.00	22-28
1999 Kayla Mulbeary 913941	Retrd.	2001	14.00	14-21
2001 Kendall B. Learnin 912661	Open		39.00	39
2000 Kevin G. Bearsley 917362	Retrd.	2001	22.00	22
2002 Kimmy 917382	Open		15.00	15
1999 Kitt Purrsley 91711	Open		18.00	18
1998 Klaus Von Fuzzner 91262	Retrd.	2001	39.00	39
2001 Krista Fuzzyfrost 913974	Open		10.00	10
2002 Kristen T. Beansley 919812	Retrd.	2001	27.00	27
2000 Kyle L. Berriman 917401	Retrd.	2001	20.00	20
2001 Lady B. Bug 91775	Open		20.00	20
1999 Laurel S. Berrijam 913954	Retrd.	2001	12.50	13-21
2001 Leisell Bloomengrows 915502	Open		17.00	17
1998 Leo Bruinski 918320	Retrd.	2001	30.00	30
2001 Libby B. Bunster 916502	Retrd.	2001	16.00	16
2002 Lil' Missy Muffet 91778	Open		28.00	28
2000 Lila Hopkins 91124	Open		18.00	18
1998 Lillian K. Bearsley 91743	Open		20.00	20-29
2002 Lily Flutterby 913934	Open		14.50	15
2001 Lindsey P. Prissypuss 912091	Retrd.	2001	30.00	30
2001 Lindsey P. Pussytoes 912091	Retrd.	2001	30.00	30
1998 Lisa T. Bearringer 911950	Retrd.	2001	56.00	56
2001 Little Bearpeep and Friends 912056	Open		44.00	44
1999 Liza J. Berrijam 910061	Retrd.	2001	17.00	17-25
2001 Lizzie (Fall Event) 50003	Retrd.	2000	5.50	6
2000 Lizzie Wishkabibble (Fall Event) 50002	Retrd.	2000	19.50	20-50
1999 Logan Fremont 919611	Retrd.	2001	13.00	13-32
2000 Lois B. Bearlove 913956	Retrd.	2001	12.50	13
1999 Lola Ninelives 919751	Open		23.00	23
2001 Lottie de Lopear 91648	Retrd.	2000	15.00	15
1998 Lou Bearig 91771-06	Retrd.	2001	14.00	14-32

DOLLS & PLUSH

YEAR ISSUE	EDITION LIMIT	YEAR RETD.	ISSUE PRICE	*QUOTE U.S.$
1999 Lucinda de la Fleur 91705	Retrd.	2001	9.00	9
2000 Lynette Bearlove 918433	Retrd.	2001	9.50	10
2001 Macy Sunbeary 911952	Retrd.	2001	40.00	40
1999 Madeline Willoughby 918333	Retrd.	2001	29.00	29
1998 Margarita 911062	Retrd.	2001	20.00	20-22
2002 Margo DeBearvoire 918340	Open		22.00	22
2000 Marie B. Bearlove 912626	Retrd.	2001	30.00	30
2002 Marina Yachtley 918343	Open		23.00	23
2002 Marion T. Bestlove 82514	Open		12.00	12
2002 Maris Q. Yachtley 912018	Open		57.00	57
1999 Marissa P. Pussyfoot 912093	Retrd.	2001	35.00	35
2000 Marla Sprucebeary 915501	Open		20.00	20
2001 Martha S. McBruin 910063	Open		28.00	28
2001 Marwood 917298	Open		43.00	43
2002 Mary Ellen Patchbeary 912643	Open		33.00	33
1995 Maya Berriman 91394	Retrd.	2001	14.00	14-22
2001 The McCoy Family 919808	Retrd.	2001	49.00	49
2000 Megan Berriman 912623	Open		31.00	31
2001 Melanie McRind 912658	Retrd.	2001	27.00	27
2000 Melinda S. Willoughby 913961	Retrd.	2001	12.00	12
1998 Mercedes Fitzbruin 91204	Retrd.	2001	19.00	19
2001 Merci Bearcoo 903001	Open		14.00	14
2001 Meridian Wishkabibble 90500	Retrd.	2001	30.00	30
2001 Merry Beth Angelwish 744110-04	Open		15.00	15
2002 Michele S. Hopplebuns 916629	Open		18.00	18
2000 Mikayla Springsbeary 912624	Retrd.	2001	31.00	31
2002 Mimi Chapeau 918449	Open		10.50	11
2000 Mipsie Blumenshine 917040	Retrd.	2001	12.00	12
2001 Miracle Gardenglow 916632	Retrd.	2001	19.00	19
2000 Miss Hedda Bearimore 918453	Open		22.00	22
2001 Miss Macintosh 912652	Open		33.00	33
2000 Miss Prissy Fussybuns 912094	Open		29.00	29
1999 Mitchell Bearsdale 912615	Retrd.	2001	39.00	39
2001 Momma Bearhugs and Tory 82507	Retrd.	2001	30.00	30
2000 Momma McFuzz and Missy 910080	Retrd.	2001	29.00	29
2001 Momma McNew and Hugsley 910021	Open		26.00	26
2001 Monique LaBearsley 918447	Open		10.50	11
1999 Montana Mooski 917295	Retrd.	2001	29.00	29
1999 Monterey Mouski 91675	Retrd.	2001	12.00	12
2002 Mookins 91862	Open		21.00	21
2002 Mooshell Patchbeary 912096	Open		33.00	33
2002 Morgan T. Yachtley with Bill 912644	Open		33.00	33
2000 Mr. Bojingles 91264	Retrd.	2001	20.00	20-39
2001 Mr. Everlove 912655	Open		32.00	32
2000 Mr. McFarkle 912640	Retrd.	2001	25.00	25
2001 Mr. McSnickers 912641	Retrd.	2001	29.00	29
2000 Mr. Noah and Friends 900100	Retrd.	2001	60.50	61
1998 Mr. Trumbull 918330	Retrd.	2001	27.00	27-37
2000 Mrs. Baybeary 917312	Open		29.00	29
2000 Mrs. Baybeary 917314	Open		26.00	26
2001 Mrs. Everlove 912654	Open		38.00	38
2001 Mrs. Figgy Pudding 917442	Open		29.00	29
1999 Mrs. Mertz 918331	Retrd.	2001	29.00	29
1999 Mrs. Northstar 917303-03	Retrd.	2001	30.00	30-82
1998 Mrs. Partridge 919750	Retrd.	2001	29.00	29
1999 Mrs. Petrie 919752	Retrd.	2001	29.00	29
1998 Mrs. Trumbull 91833	Open		29.00	29
1999 Murphy Mooselfluff 917291	Retrd.	2001	23.00	23
2001 Murtaugh Moosetrax 917297	Open		21.00	21
1999 Nadia Berriman 917420	Retrd.	2001	29.00	29-52
2000 Nanette DuBeary 918432	Retrd.	2001	9.50	10
2000 Naomi Bearlove 913957	Retrd.	2000	13.50	14
1998 Natasha Berriman 918050	Retrd.	2001	12.00	12
2002 Nellie T. Bearypatch 919814	Retrd.	2001	23.00	23
2002 Nibblekins 91861	Open		21.00	21
1996 Niki II 91730-1	Retrd.	2001	12.50	13-25
2000 Noah w/Puddles 918434	Open		37.00	37
2001 Olive T. Leafowitz 912014	Open		57.00	57
1998 Oliver 91110	Retrd.	2001	12.00	12
1999 Omega T. Legacy & Alpha 900099	Retrd.	2001	67.00	67
2000 Paige Willoughby 918351	Retrd.	2001	19.00	19
2002 Pamela P. Patchbeary 912017	Open		57.00	57
2001 Patrick Bearsevelt 913966	Retrd.	2001	13.00	13
2000 Paula Hoppleby 91125	Retrd.	2001	18.00	18
2002 Peepers P. MacDonald 913937	Open		14.00	14
2001 Pepper B. Scaredycat 919700-02	Open		14.00	14
2000 Phoebe Purrsmore 917101	Open		12.00	12
2002 Piper Lapine 918430	Open		10.50	11
2001 Pipley McRind 913965	Open		13.00	13
1999 Polly Quignapple 910020	Retrd.	2001	26.00	26
1998 Primrose III 9160-02	Retrd.	2001	22.00	22
2000 Primrose IV 9160-04	Retrd.	2001	22.00	22
2002 Prissie Hopplebuns 912082	Open		21.00	21
1999 Prudence Bearimore 912053	Retrd.	2001	30.00	30-40
1999 Punkie BooBear 919630	Retrd.	2001	23.00	23
2000 Radcliffe Fitzbruin 912020	Retrd.	2000	43.00	43
2000 Rebecca Bearimore 912028	Retrd.	2001	57.00	57
2001 Redford T. Woodsbeary 912501	Open		57.00	57
2000 Regena Haresford 916490	Retrd.	2001	29.00	29
2002 Roberta 912665	Open		26.00	26
2000 Robyn Purrsmore 915600	Retrd.	2001	11.50	12
2001 Rosalie Bloomengrows 916500	Open		14.00	14
1999 Roscoe P. Bumpercrop 912079	Retrd.	2001	39.00	39
2000 Roslyn Hiphop 912080	Retrd.	2001	30.00	30
2002 Rowen Yachtley 918342	Open		26.00	26
2001 Rowena Prissypuss 915601	Retrd.	2001	15.00	15
2001 Rudy McRind 912630	Retrd.	2001	28.00	28
2000 Rudy Pitoody 91880	Retrd.	2001	21.00	21
2001 Rusty & Scardycrow 912642	Open		24.00	24
1999 Sabrina P. Catterwall 919700-01	Retrd.	2001	14.00	14
2001 Sage Leafowitz 918353	Open		16.00	16
2000 Sally Quignapple and Annie 91009	Retrd.	2001	24.00	24
1999 Samantha Sneakypuss 91979	Retrd.	2001	20.00	20
1998 Samuel 918052	Retrd.	2001	12.00	12-22
2000 Samuel Adams 915210	Open		14.00	14
2002 Sandy Sanditoes 917443	Open		24.00	24
2000 Savannah Buttercup 91650	Retrd.	2001	26.00	26
2001 Serendipity Wishkabibble 90501	Open		20.50	20
2000 Sergei Bearskov 912619	Retrd.	2000	39.00	39
1999 Sharp McNibble 91674	Retrd.	2001	12.00	12
2002 Shelby T. Sanditoes 913981	Open		13.00	13
1998 Sheldon Bearchild 918061	Retrd.	2001	8.00	8
2001 Shivers Snowbeary 918360	Open		14.00	14
2001 Sierra Woodsbeary 912632	Open		34.00	34
2000 Simon Beanster and Andy 910090	Retrd.	2001	24.00	24
2002 Skip B. Yachtley 913976	Open		14.50	15
1999 Skylar Thistlebeary 911951	Retrd.	2001	43.00	43-50
2001 Smith Applewish 918357	Open		14.00	14
2001 Snickersnoodle 91770	Open		18.00	18
2001 Sonja Frostbeary 912058	Open		29.00	29
1998 St. Niklas 917311	Retrd.	2001	21.00	21
2002 Starr B. Bearyproud with Sparkle 912016	Open		57.00	57
2001 Stella 913973	Open		15.00	15
2002 Stephanie W. Bearyproud 919819	Retrd.	2001	29.00	29
1999 Stevenson Q. Bearitage 91736	Retrd.	2001	23.00	23
2000 Stewart MacGregor 91400	Open		18.00	18
2001 Sturbridge Q. Patriot 91524	Retrd.	2001	15.00	15
2001 Sue B. Bearkins 917440	Open		20.00	20
2001 Sugar McRind 91746	Open		23.00	23
2002 Summer Sanditoes 913933	Open		20.00	20
2001 Swiss C. Mouski 91670	Retrd.	2001	12.00	12
2000 Sylvia G. Bearimore 918438	Retrd.	2001	10.50	11
2002 T. Lynne Bearyproud 913932	Open		17.00	17
2000 Tami P. Rally 917367	Open		29.00	29
2000 Taylor Purrski 912095	Retrd.	2001	35.00	35
2002 Teresa D. Bestlove 82512	Open		25.00	25
2001 Tessie T. Nibblenose 917050	Retrd.	2001	12.00	12
1997 Thayer 91570	Retrd.	2001	18.00	18-20
1999 Tomba Bearski 912620	Retrd.	2001	41.00	41
2001 Tommy Leafowitz 918361	Open		17.00	17
2000 Truffles O' Pigg 916010-01	Open		16.00	16
1999 Tundra Northpole 912810	Retrd.	2001	23.00	23-40
1997 Twila Higgenthorpe 91843	Retrd.	2001	9.50	10-17
2001 Twink L. Starbeary 918356	Open		15.00	15
2001 Vanna Hopkins 91113	Retrd.	2001	12.00	12
2001 Victoria L. Plumbeary 912015	Open		57.00	57
2002 Victoria Lynn Primsley 918344	Open		25.00	25
2002 Wade N. Sanditoes with Buster the Crab 913938	Open		14.00	14
1999 Waldo Bearsworth 912045	Retrd.	2001	26.00	26
1999 Wayfer North 917360	Retrd.	2001	25.00	25
1999 Weaver Berrybrook 911930	Retrd.	2001	20.00	20-45
2002 Webb Q. Yachtley 91603	Open		18.00	18
2001 Webster Jopplebuns 916631	Open		19.00	19
2000 Wesley Bearimore 912027	Open		49.00	49
2001 Whilley Frostifeet 918359	Open		11.00	11
1998 Winifred Witebred 912071	Retrd.	2001	33.00	33-42
1998 Winnie II 912071-01	Retrd.	2001	33.00	33
2000 Winnie Stillwithuis 912071-03	Retrd.	2001	33.00	33
2001 Wixie Lee Hackett 918444	Open		10.50	11
1999 Yardley Fitzhampton 912030	Retrd.	2000	26.00	26

*Quotes have been rounded up to nearest dollar

YEAR ISSUE	EDITION LIMIT	YEAR RETD.	ISSUE PRICE	*QUOTE U.S.$
1997 Yogi 91771-02	Retrd.	2001	14.00	14-34
1999 Yvette Dubeary 918431	Retrd.	2001	10.50	11-23
2001 Zelda Z. Witchypuss 919790	Open		24.00	24

Wishkadingles - The Boyds Collection

2002 Ernie 620001	Open		19.00	19
2002 Fred 620003	Open		19.00	19
2002 Jack 620002	Open		19.00	19
2002 Sam 620000	Open		19.00	19

Yesterdays' Child™...The Doll Collection - The Boyds Collection, unless otherwise noted

2002 Alexa with Bon Bon...Mothers Make the Best Friends 4834	Open		39.00	39
1999 Allison with Andy...Bird Watchin' 4802	Retrd.	2001	35.00	35
1999 Alyssa with Caroline & Carla...A Stitch in Time 4928	Retrd.	2000	72.00	72
2001 Amanda & Millie...The Hat Shoppe 4944 - Julie Good-Krüger	12,000		82.00	82
1999 Amy with Edwin...Momma's Clothes 4921	Retrd.	1999	100.00	100
1999 Anne with Rockwell...The Masterpiece 4922	Retrd.	1999	72.00	72
2001 Ariel & Yenta...Finding My Prince 4941 - Julie Good-Krüger	12,000		79.00	79
2000 Autumn with Acorn...Pumpkin Patch 4817	Retrd.	2001	35.00	35
1999 Betsie with Troy...A Day at the Lake 4805	Retrd.	2001	35.00	35
1999 Brittany with Ben...Goin' to Grandma's 4803	Retrd.	2001	35.00	35
1998 Brittany...Life's Journey 4906	Retrd.	1998	71.00	71
2001 Callie & Ladybug...Backyard Safari 4942 - Julie Good-Krüger	12,000		82.00	82
2002 Cameron With ZigZag...Sew Perfect! 4950	Open		77.00	77
1999 Candice with Macintosh...Gathering Apples 4923	Retrd.	1999	72.00	72
2000 Cassidy with Buttons...Dollmaker 4936	Retrd.	2000	86.00	86
1999 Catherine with Doolittle...The Nurse Is In 4806	Retrd.	2001	34.00	34
1999 Cheryl with Ashlie...Nighty Night 4917	Retrd.	1999	69.00	69
2000 Christa with Harvey...Back to School 4937	Retrd.	2000	72.00	72
2001 Elizabeth & Lockslea with Curry...New Best Friends 4946 - Julie Good-Krüger	Open		77.00	77
2000 Emilee with Otis...Forever 4808	Open		35.00	35
2000 Erica with Ferris...Carnival Fun 4809	Retrd.	2001	35.00	35
2000 Erin Lynn with Squirt...Peppermint Lemonade 4810	Retrd.	2001	35.00	35
1998 Jamie...the Last One 4908	Retrd.	1998	66.00	66
1999 Jean with Nutmeg...The Bakers 4919	Retrd.	1999	69.00	69
2001 Jessica with Cuddles 4949	Open		73.00	73
2001 Jocelyn with Glitzy...The Bear Essentials 4945 - Julie Good-Krüger	Open		77.00	77
2000 Joni with Patch...Strawberry Fields 4812	Retrd.	2001	35.00	35
2000 Joy with Smooch...Mistletoe Kisses 4947 - Julie Good-Krüger	Open		77.00	77
2000 Judy Dee with John...Sweater Weather Antiquing 4816	Retrd.	2001	35.00	35
1999 Kayla with Kirby...Harvest Time 4918	Retrd.	1999	72.00	72
2002 Kaylee With Snapshot...Small Miracles 4953	Open		79.00	79
1999 Kellie with Evan...The Fun of Collecting 4804	Open		35.00	35
1998 Lara...Moscow at Midnight 4907	Retrd.	1998	68.00	68
1999 Laura with Lucy...School Days 4801	Retrd.	2001	35.00	35
2001 Laurel & Hyacinth...Garden Party 4943 - Julie Good-Krüger	12,000		82.00	82
2000 Leah with Windy...Summer Breeze 4811	Retrd.	2000	35.00	35
2000 Leslie with Nibbles...Milk & Cookies 4818	Open		35.00	35
2000 Lindsey with Leonard...The Recital 4931	Retrd.	2000	79.00	79
2000 Lucinda with Gilligan...By the Sea 4929	Retrd.	2000	69.00	69
2000 Madison with Colby 4935	Retrd.	2000	72.00	72
2000 Meredith with Jacqueline...Daisy Chain 4933	Retrd.	2000	79.00	79
2000 Molly with Cricket...Winged Friends 4924	Retrd.	2000	72.00	72

YEAR ISSUE	EDITION LIMIT	YEAR RETD.	ISSUE PRICE	*QUOTE U.S.$
1998 Ms. Ashley...the Teacher 4905	Retrd.	1998	66.00	66
2000 Nicole with Buzz...Sweeter Than Honey 4925	Retrd.	2000	72.00	72
2000 Noel...Cranberries and Popcorn 4820	Retrd.	2001	35.00	35
2000 Olivia with Pearl...Coloring Time 4934	Retrd.	2000	72.00	72
1999 Paige with Spinner...Around the World 4807	Retrd.	2001	35.00	35
2000 Priscilla with William...Victorian Lace 4815	Retrd.	2000	72.00	72
2000 Rebecca with Elliot...Birthday 4927	Retrd.	2000	72.00	72
2001 Samantha with Snipper...The Bearmaker 4948 - Julie Good-Krüger	Open		79.00	79
2002 Sidney With Monet...Self Portraits 4952	Open		79.00	79
2000 Sonja with Frosty...A Winter Stroll 4814	Retrd.	2001	35.00	35
2000 Taylor with Jumper...Play Time 4926	Retrd.	2000	69.00	69
2000 Whitney with Wilson...Tea Party 4932	Retrd.	2000	76.00	76

Cast Art Industries

Dreamsicles Angel Hugs™ - K. Haynes

1999 Bluebeary (bear) (1st Generation)-08002	Retrd.	1999	8.00	8
1999 Bubbles (whale)-08013	Retrd.	1999	8.00	8
1999 Creampuff (cherub) (1st Generation)-08001	Retrd.	1999	8.00	8
1999 Cupcake (cherub) (1st Generation)-08003	Retrd.	1999	8.00	8
1999 Daisy (cow) (1st Generation)-08004	Retrd.	1999	8.00	8
1999 Dawn-Millennium Edition-08029	Suspd.		8.00	8
1999 Faith (cherub)-08012	Retrd.	1999	8.00	8
1999 Honey Bunny-08041	Open		8.00	8
1999 Joy (cherub)-08014	Retrd.	1999	8.00	8
1999 Peaches (cherub) (1st Generation)-08005	Retrd.	1999	8.00	8
1999 Peanut (elephant) (1st Generation)-08006	Retrd.	1999	8.00	8
1999 Peg (horse)-08017	Retrd.	1999	8.00	8
1999 Rosebud (cherub)-08016	Retrd.	1999	8.00	8
1999 Rosie - Rosemont ICE Commemorative-08030	750	1999	Gift	N/A
1999 Smooches (cherub)-08039	Open		8.00	8
1999 Splash (frog)-08015	Retrd.	1999	8.00	8
1999 Sugar (cherub)-08038	Open		8.00	8
1999 Sunshine-08040	Open		8.00	8
1999 Sweetie (cherub)-08037	Open		8.00	8
1999 Tooth Fairy-08042	Open		8.00	8

Dreamsicles Angel Hugs™ Event - K. Haynes

2000 I Love Dreamsicles-08057	Retrd.	2000	7.95	8
2001 Dreamsicles Rule-08150	Yr.Iss.	2001	8.00	8

Dreamsicles Angel Hugs™ Holiday - K. Haynes

1999 Candy (cherub)-08021	Retrd.	1999	8.00	8
1999 Crystal (cherub)-08025	Retrd.	1999	8.00	8
1999 Evergreen (bear)-08026	Retrd.	1999	8.00	8
1999 Holly (cherub)-08023	Retrd.	1999	8.00	8
1999 Mittens (snowman)-08022	Retrd.	1999	8.00	8
1999 Moose L. Toe (moose)-08024	Retrd.	1999	8.00	8

Dreamsicles Northern Lights Angel Hugs™ - K. Haynes

1999 Loverboy (Moose)-08051	Suspd.		8.00	8
1999 Shivers (Snowman)-08050	Open		8.00	8
1999 Sparkle (Snow Angel)-08047	Suspd.		8.00	8
1999 Squeak (Penguin)-08049	Open		8.00	8
1999 Sweetheart (Snow Angel)-08046	Open		8.00	8
1999 Twinkle (Snow Angel)-08048	Open		8.00	8

Cherished Teddies/Enesco Group, Inc.

Collectible Plush - P. Hillman

1999 Antique Toy Bear 662240	Open		17.50	18
1999 Antique Toy Bear/Bual 737380	Open	2001	17.50	18
1999 Antique Toy Bear/Bunny 737399	Open		17.50	18
1999 Antique Toy Cow/Teddie 662259	Open	2001	17.50	18
1999 Antique Toy Elephant/Teddie 662275	7,500		17.50	18
1999 Antique Toy Horse/Teddie 662267	Open		17.50	18
1999 Antique Toy Lamb/Teddie 742740	Open	2001	17.50	18
1999 Bear w/Sweater, 2 asst. 649155	Yr.Iss.	1999	25.00	25

DOLLS & PLUSH

YEAR ISSUE	EDITION LIMIT	YEAR RETD.	ISSUE PRICE	*QUOTE U.S.$
2000 Beatrice 798827	Open		25.00	25
2000 Doris 790605	Open		25.00	25
1999 Girls w/velvet Christmas Scarfs 644323	Open		15.00	15-21
1999 Spanky "Friendship Can Sometimes Be Bumpy But It's Worth It" 661597	Open		30.00	30
2000 Toothfairy Wanda 789925	Open		25.00	25
1999 Val 662291	Open		27.50	28
1999 Val 662291L	12,000		27.50	28

Four Seasons Plush, 12" - P. Hillman

2001 Winter Outfit 866067	Open		35.00	35
2001 Spring Sailor 866032	Open		35.00	35
2001 Summer Sundress 866040	Open		35.00	35
2001 Autumn Outfit 866059	Open		35.00	35

Holiday Occasions Plush - P. Hillman

1999 4th of July 637998	Closed	2000	7.00	7
1999 Christmas 638021	Closed	2000	7.00	7
1999 Easter 637955	Closed	2000	7.00	7
1999 Halloween 638005	Closed	2000	7.00	7
1999 Mother's Day 637963	Closed	2000	7.00	7
1999 New Year's 637696	Closed	2000	7.00	7
1999 St. Patrick's Day 637947	Closed	2000	7.00	7
1999 Teacher 637971	Closed	2000	7.00	7
1999 Thanksgiving 638013	Closed	2000	7.00	7
1999 Valentine 637939	Closed	2000	7.00	7

Holiday Plush - P. Hillman

2001 Christmas Tree Bear 867284	Open		15.00	15
2001 Jingle Bell Bear 867268	Open		15.00	15
2001 Star Bear 867276	Open		15.00	15

Monthly Plush - P. Hillman

1999 January 556165	Open		7.00	7
1999 February 556181	Open		7.00	7
1999 March 556203	Open		7.00	7
1999 April 556246	Open		7.00	7
1999 May 556270	Open		7.00	7
1999 June 556289	Open		7.00	7
1999 July 556327	Open		7.00	7
1999 August 556483	Open		7.00	7
1999 September 556688	Open		7.00	7
1999 October 556750	Open		7.00	7
1999 November 556785	Open		7.00	7
1999 December 556793	Open		7.00	7

Columbus International

HERMANN-Spielwaren Annual Bears - U. Hermann

1992 Annual Bear Teddy Black & White	Yr.Iss.	1992	140.00	170-200
1993 Annual Bear Greeny	Yr.Iss.	1993	140.00	180
1994 Annual Bear Rosanna	Yr.Iss.	1994	140.00	175
1995 Annual Bear Symphonie	Yr.Iss.	1995	140.00	160
1996 Annual Bear Kir Royal	Yr.Iss.	1996	140.00	160
1997 Annual Bear Golden Blue	Yr.Iss.	1997	140.00	155-199
1998 Annual Bear Smoky	Yr.Iss.	1998	140.00	140-162
1999 Annual Bear True Love	Yr.Iss.	1999	145.00	145
2000 Annual Bear Green Leaves	Yr.Iss.	2000	150.00	150
2001 Annual Bear Panda Rouge Lg.	Yr.Iss.	2001	150.00	150
2001 Annual Bear Panda Rouge Sm.	Yr.Iss.	2001	138.00	150

HERMANN-Spielwaren Annual Christmas Bears - U. Hermann

1994 Annual Christmas Bear 1994	Yr.Iss.	1994	176.00	240
1995 Annual Christmas Bear 1995	Yr.Iss.	1995	176.00	230
1996 Annual Christmas Bear 1996	Yr.Iss.	1996	176.00	210
1997 Annual Christmas Bear 1997	Yr.Iss.	1997	176.00	200-235
1998 Annual Christmas Bear 1998	Yr.Iss.	1998	176.00	190
1999 Annual Christmas Bear 1999	Yr.Iss.	1999	197.00	197
2000 Annual Christmas Bear 2000	Yr.Iss.	2000	199.00	199
2001 Annual Christmas Bear 2001	Yr.Iss.	2001	180.00	180

HERMANN-Spielwaren Artline Bears - U. Hermann

1996 Artline Bear Bleu	Closed	1996	260.00	415
1996 Artline Bear Rouge	Closed	1996	260.00	415
1996 Artline Bear Vert	Closed	1996	260.00	415
2001 Artline Red Panda	Closed	1996	160.00	250

HERMANN-Spielwaren Collectible Bears - N/A, unless otherwise noted

1960 Baby Bear, Dralon fabric, 26 cm	Closed	N/A	N/A	550

YEAR ISSUE	EDITION LIMIT	YEAR RETD.	ISSUE PRICE	*QUOTE U.S.$
1998 Baby Panda - M. Hermann	500	1999	125.00	125
1998 Chester Bear Michael - M. Hermann	500	1999	159.00	159
1996 Chimney Sweep	500	1999	140.00	140
1998 Edelweiss - M. Hermann	1,000	1999	159.00	159
1954 Flexible Bear, tipped Mohair, 35 cm	Closed	N/A	N/A	3000
1999 Grand Panda	500	1999	160.00	160
2000 Hermann 80th Anniversary Bear - U. Hermann	1,000		150.00	150
1999 Hermann Euro Bear - M. Hermann	500	1999	159.00	300
2000 Hermann Golfer Bear - U. Hermann	2,000		250.00	250
1999 Hilde Hermann-Classic Birthday Bear - M. Hermann	500	1999	199.00	199
1998 Leopold, the little old music bear - M. Hermann	250	1999	150.00	150
1996 Little Old Max	500	1999	160.00	160
1999 Max III - U. Hermann	750	2000	220.00	220
1998 Millennium Bear - M. Hermann	2,000	1999	215.00	215-224
2000 Millennium Set, set/2 - U. Hermann	4-day	2000	500.00	500
1999 New York Toy Fair, 1999 - M. Hermann	333	1999	99.00	99
1998 Papa Panda - M. Hermann	500	1999	140.00	140
2001 Patriot Bear - U. Hermann	1,000	2001	100.00	200
1998 Phantom of the Opera - M. Hermann	500	1999	209.00	209
1999 Polar "Ice" Bear	1,000	1999	160.00	160
1998 Professor Higgins - M. Hermann	500	1999	198.00	198
2000 Red Baron - U. Hermann	500	2000	260.00	260
1996 Robinhood	500	1999	210.00	210
1998 Small Jacob - M. Hermann	500	1999	106.00	106
1965 Speaking Bear, with speak mechanism, 45 cm	Closed	N/A	N/A	550
1940 Teddy, Cotton fabric, 50 cm	Closed	N/A	N/A	600
1950 Teddy, Mohair, 50 cm - M. Hermann	Closed	N/A	N/A	550
1950 Teddy, Mohair, 80 cm - M. Hermann	Closed	N/A	N/A	4250
1920 Teddy, Mohair, 50 cm - M. Hermann	Closed	N/A	N/A	2650
1954 Teddy, Mohair, 55 cm	Closed	N/A	N/A	900
1960 Teddy, short Mohair, 40 cm	Closed	N/A	N/A	900
1955 Teddy, synthetic	Closed	N/A	N/A	800
1955 Teddy, tipped Mohair, 50 cm	Closed	N/A	N/A	1000
1955 Teddy, tipped Mohair, 60 cm	Closed	N/A	N/A	1250
1955 Teddy, tipped Mohair, long nose, 70 cm	Closed	N/A	N/A	1500
1971 Teddybear, synthetic fabric with airbrush	Closed	N/A	N/A	400
1933 Trachtenbären, Artificial Silk, 18 cm - M. Hermann	Closed	N/A	N/A	1750
1998 Wolfgang Amadeus Mozart - M. Hermann	500	1999	225.00	225
2000 XXI - Twenty First Century Bear - U. Hermann	1,000	2001	150.00	150

HERMANN-Spielwaren Columbus International "Columbus Collection™" - U. Hermann

1998 Oktoberfest	250	1998	198.00	250-500
1998 Rosemont Special Edition, 1998	100	1998	199.00	199-250
1999 Oktoberfest	500	1999	220.00	220
1999 Rosemont Special Edition, 1999	191	1999	199.00	199
1999 Snowflake	250	1999	179.00	179
2000 Rosemont Special Edition, 2000	200	2000	198.00	198
2000 Christopher Columbus	780		279.00	279
2001 Rosemont Special Edition, 2001	1,000	2001	199.00	199

HERMANN-Spielwaren Hennef Bears - U. Hermann

1996 Hennef Bär 1996 Shooting Gallerie	85	1996	140.00	250
1997 Hennef Bär 1997 Bear Pocket	85	1997	160.00	200
1998 Hennef Bär 1998 Vario Bear	65	1998	140.00	400

HERMANN-Spielwaren Internet Bears - U. Hermann

1996 HERMANN 1st Internet Bear	250	1997	225.00	800
1999 HERMANN 2nd Internet Bear -Y2K Bug Bear	1,000	2001	198.00	198
1997 Internet Bear Miniature Edtion	500	1998	180.00	450

HERMANN-Spielwaren Neustadter Festival Bears - U. Hermann

1992 Neustadter Festival Bear 1992	100	1992	130.00	1500
1993 Neustadter Festival Bear 1993	100	1993	160.00	1200
1994 Neustadter Festival Bear 1994	100	1994	180.00	1000
1995 Neustadter Festival Bear 1995	100	1995	190.00	800
1996 Neustadter Festival Bear 1996	100	1996	190.00	600
1997 Neustadter Festival Bear 1997	100	1997	190.00	700
1998 Neustadter Festival Bear 1998	100	1998	190.00	400

Collectors' Information Bureau   *Quotes have been rounded up to nearest dollar

HERMANN-Spielwaren Sonneberger Kirmes Bears - U. Hermann

YEAR ISSUE	EDITION LIMIT	YEAR RETD.	ISSUE PRICE	*QUOTE U.S.$
1995 HERMANN Nachkriegsbär	50	1995	103.00	170
1995 Sonneberger Kirmesbär Adelbert	16	1995	103.00	300
1995 Sonneberger Kirmesbär Berta	8	1995	103.00	300
1995 Sonneberger Kirmesbär Casimier	100	1995	84.00	150
1995 Sonneberger Kirmesbär Dieter	100	1995	61.00	100
1995 Sonneberger Kirmesbär Erna	50	1995	57.00	90
1995 Sonneberger Kirmesbär Friedrich	150	1995	61.00	80
1995 Sonneberger Kirmesbär Gerda	25	1995	57.00	80
1995 Sonneberger Kirmesbär Heidi	25	1995	73.00	90
1995 Sonneberger Kirmesbär Inge	60	1995	73.00	90
1995 Sonneberger Kirmesbär Jan	25	1995	57.00	80
1995 Sonneberger Kirmesbär Kurt	25	1995	92.00	140
1995 Sonneberger Kirmesbär Ludwig	20	1995	73.00	100-160
1995 Sonneberger Kirmesbär Moritz	10	1995	73.00	300
1995 Sonneberger Kirmesbär Norbert	85	1995	61.00	100
1995 Sonneberger Kirmesbär Oskar	30	1995	92.00	130-150
1995 Sonneberger Kirmesbär Peter	40	1995	57.00	80
1995 Sonneberger Kirmesbär Quax	150	1996	57.00	80
1995 Sonneberger Kirmesbär Rudolf	250	1996	57.00	70
1995 Sonneberger Kirmesbär Sabine	250	1996	65.00	70
1995 Sonneberger Kirmesbär Tina	50	1995	65.00	100

HERMANN-Spielwaren Special Event Bears - U. Hermann, unless otherwise noted

YEAR ISSUE	EDITION LIMIT	YEAR RETD.	ISSUE PRICE	*QUOTE U.S.$
1994 Soccer Bear "WM 94 USA"	250	1995	400.00	500
1995 HERMANN Raritätenbär, 40 cm	50	1995	400.00	3000
1995 Der Verhüllte Bär (Covered Bear)	100	1995	300.00	650
1996 RGH Bear - Rolf G. Hermann	2,000	1996	235.00	800
2002 Olympic Baer	35	2002	170.00	300
1998 Pustefix Bear	1,000	1998	140.00	180

HERMANN-Spielwaren Yes-No Bear - M. Hermann

YEAR ISSUE	EDITION LIMIT	YEAR RETD.	ISSUE PRICE	*QUOTE U.S.$
1938 Nicky, Yes-No Bear, Mohair, 28 cm	Closed	1950	15.00	2750

Deb Canham Artist Designs Inc.

DCAD Collector's Club - D. Canham

YEAR ISSUE	EDITION LIMIT	YEAR RETD.	ISSUE PRICE	*QUOTE U.S.$
1999 Binker	550	2000	80.00	80
1999 Santa on Holiday	980	2000	80.00	80
1999 Gift	1,500	2000	Gift	N/A
2000 Harvey	950	2000	80.00	80
2000 Molly & Jake	Retrd.	2001	80.00	80
2000 Together Forever	Retrd.	2001	150.00	150
2000 Pin	Retrd.	2001	Gift	N/A
2001 Bumble	5/02		80.00	80
2001 Flutterby	5/02		80.00	80
2001 Ladybug	5/02		80.00	80
2001 Pin	5/02		Gift	N/A

Signing Events - D. Canham

YEAR ISSUE	EDITION LIMIT	YEAR RETD.	ISSUE PRICE	*QUOTE U.S.$
1999 Fluffy	200	2000	60.00	125-450
2000 Kasalopy	100	2000	100.00	150-450
2000 Silkie	100	2000	95.00	150-450
2000 Acorn	100	2000	95.00	95-100
2000 Blitz	100	2000	95.00	95
2000 Rudy	200	2000	105.00	105
2001 Jolly	100	2001	100.00	100-350
2001 Onyx	50	2001	120.00	120-350
2001 Phoebe	100	2001	100.00	100
2001 Summer	100	2001	110.00	110
2001 K. Preston	100	2001	95.00	95
2001 JP	100	2001	95.00	95
2001 Ella Mae	100	2001	95.00	95
2001 Tottie	100	2001	95.00	95
2001 Little Boy Blue	100	2001	95.00	95
2001 Jamie (BIGger bear)	100	2001	95.00	95
2001 Jim Jingle	100	2001	95.00	95
2001 Goldie	100	2002	95.00	95
2002 Cheddar	100	2002	60.00	60
2002 Serendipity	100	2002	60.00	60
2002 Lexie Bunny	100	2002	60.00	60
2002 Karl	100	2002	60.00	60

Alice Collection - D. Canham

YEAR ISSUE	EDITION LIMIT	YEAR RETD.	ISSUE PRICE	*QUOTE U.S.$
2000 Alice	2,500	2002	68.00	68
2000 Carpenter	2,500		56.00	58
2000 Cheshire Cat	2,500		56.00	58
2000 Dormouse	2,500		54.00	54
2000 Herald	2,500	2002	56.00	58
2000 Madhatter	2,500	2002	56.00	58
2000 March Hare	2,500		56.00	58
2000 Queen of Hearts	2,500	2002	56.00	58
2000 Tweedle Dee	2,500		56.00	58
2000 Tweedle Dum	2,500		56.00	58
2000 Walrus	2,500	2001	56.00	58
2000 White Rabbit	2,500		56.00	58

Baby Dappled Dragons - D. Canham

YEAR ISSUE	EDITION LIMIT	YEAR RETD.	ISSUE PRICE	*QUOTE U.S.$
2001 Bubba	1,500	2001	58.00	58
2001 Jingo	1,500	2001	58.00	58
2001 Pebbles	1,500	2001	58.00	58

BIGger Bears (7-12") - D. Canham

YEAR ISSUE	EDITION LIMIT	YEAR RETD.	ISSUE PRICE	*QUOTE U.S.$
2000 Beau	500	2001	110.00	110
2002 Bessie Bunny	200		110.00	110
2000 Big Carrot Top	150		199.00	199
2000 Big Columbine	500		110.00	110
2000 Big Cosmic Moonshine	100	2000	280.00	280
2000 Big Gussie Galactica	100	2000	280.00	280
2000 Big Jingle	150		199.00	199
2000 Big Pananini	150		199.00	199
2000 Big Plum	150		199.00	199
2000 Big Snowflake	500		90.00	90
2000 Blue Elephant	100	2000	100.00	90-100
2002 Cheeky	200		90.00	90
2000 Cissie	500		102.00	102
2001 Fancy Nancy	150		85.00	85
2000 Fleur	500		110.00	110
2001 Harriet	300		66.00	66
2001 Henry	300		66.00	66
2001 Homer	300		66.00	66
2000 Hoppy Rabbit	500	2002	130.00	130
2000 J. Hunter	100	2000	150.00	150-225
1999 Judy	1,000	2001	60.00	60
2000 Kenny	500	2002	80.00	80
2000 Little Blue	500	2002	80.00	80
2001 Lucy Lilac	150		80.00	80
2002 Mischief	200		90.00	90
2001 Nite Nite	200	2002	70.00	70
2002 Ooh La La	200		90.00	90
2001 Perry Panda	150	2002	70.00	70
2001 Petunia	200	2002	70.00	70
2002 Phat Cat	200		90.00	90
2000 Pink Elephant	100	2000	100.00	90-100
2001 Powder Puff	150	2002	98.00	98
2002 Prickles	200		96.00	96
2000 Prissie	150		199.00	199
1999 Punch	1,000		60.00	60
2002 Salute	200		78.00	78
2001 Sammy	100	2002	80.00	80
2002 Sassy	200		150.00	150
2000 Scruffy	500		90.00	90
2002 Sherbet	200		90.00	90
2002 So What	200		98.00	98
2001 Splodge	150	2002	85.00	85
2001 Sweetheart	200		180.00	180
2000 Sweetpea	500	2002	130.00	130
2000 Tiny	100		270.00	270
2000 Toots	100		250.00	250
2000 Violet	500		105.00	105
2002 Whatever	200		98.00	98
2000 Wishi Washi	500	2002	110.00	110

Brenda Power Animals - B. Power

YEAR ISSUE	EDITION LIMIT	YEAR RETD.	ISSUE PRICE	*QUOTE U.S.$
1999 Goosey	400	2000	54.00	54-75
1999 Ping	400	2000	54.00	54-75
1999 Pong	400	2000	54.00	54-75
1999 Quackers	400	2000	54.00	54-75

Brenda Power Collection - B. Power

YEAR ISSUE	EDITION LIMIT	YEAR RETD.	ISSUE PRICE	*QUOTE U.S.$
1998 Penguin	2,000		54.00	55
1998 Rabbit on Wheels	2,000	2000	54.00	54-75
1998 Racoon	2,000		54.00	55
1998 Standing Rabbit	2,000	2000	54.00	54-75

Bunnies - D. Canham

YEAR ISSUE	EDITION LIMIT	YEAR RETD.	ISSUE PRICE	*QUOTE U.S.$
2002 Carrots	1,500		58.00	58
2002 Flo	1,500		58.00	58
2001 Parsley	1,500		58.00	58
2001 Sage	1,500		58.00	58

DOLLS & PLUSH

YEAR ISSUE	EDITION LIMIT	YEAR RETD.	ISSUE PRICE	*QUOTE U.S.$
Camelot Collection - D. Canham, unless otherwise noted				
1998 Guinivere	2,500	2000	54.00	55-57
1998 Jester	2,500		54.00	55
1998 King Arthur	2,500	2000	54.00	55-75
1998 Merlin - L. Sasaki	2,500	1999	54.00	55-75
1998 Sir Dennis	2,500	2000	54.00	54-80
1998 Sir Lancelot	2,500	2000	54.00	54-60
1998 Slap-a-Roo	2,500	2000	54.00	65-80
Cloth Dolls (5") - J. Davis				
2001 Alice	150		120.00	120
2001 Andy Organdy	150		110.00	110
2000 Calico Clown	300		100.00	100
2000 Charlie Calico	300		110.00	110
2001 Daisy Duck	150		120.00	120
2001 Davy Duck	150		120.00	120
2002 Janice	150		120.00	120
2002 Jim	150		120.00	120
2002 Jo Ellen	150		120.00	120
2002 Joey	150		120.00	120
2002 Julia I	150		130.00	130
2002 Julia II	150		130.00	130
2001 Mandy Organdy	150		110.00	110
2000 Tilly Twill	300		130.00	130
Country Collection - D. Canham				
1996 Annalee and Miss Goosey	3,000	1999	40.00	50-93
1996 Missi and Miss Moo	3,000	1999	40.00	50-78
1996 Tom and Mr. H	3,000	1999	40.00	50-67
1996 Zack and Mr. H	3,000	1999	40.00	50-85
Dappled Dragons - D. Canham				
2001 Bella the Ballerina	1,500	2001	58.00	58
2001 Clarissa Style	1,500	2001	58.00	58
2000 Custard	1,500	2000	55.00	55-70
2002 Delphinium	1,000		60.00	60
1999 Dringle	1,500	2000	58.00	58
2001 Drungo the Magnificent	1,500	2001	58.00	58
2001 Gingerbread	1,000		60.00	60
2002 The Graduate	1,000		60.00	60
2002 Hotlips	1,000		60.00	60
1999 Stan	1,500	1999	58.00	58-65
Denizens of Honey Hills - D. Canham				
1996 Bratty Butchy	3,000	1999	60.00	75-90
1996 Gertie Lady of the Bag	3,000	1999	60.00	75-90
1996 Poppo the Wise	3,000	1999	60.00	75-90
1996 Simon the Curious	3,000	1999	60.00	75-90
1996 Willyum the Brave	3,000	1999	60.00	75-110
Gollies - D. Canham, unless otherwise noted				
1999 Nosey	1,500	2001	56.00	58
2002 Polly - K. Apps	1,000		60.00	60
2001 Shine	100	2002	100.00	100
1997 Spangles	2,000	2000	52.00	60-70
1997 Spats	2,000	2000	52.00	60-70
1999 Sunshine	1,500	2001	56.00	58
2002 Wally - K. Apps	1,000		60.00	60
Good Old Days - D. Canham				
1999 Doodle	2,500	2000	58.00	58-65
1999 Ginger	2,500	2001	58.00	58
1999 Old Soldier	2,500	2001	58.00	58
1999 Peaches	2,500	2000	58.00	58
1999 Prue	2,500	2001	58.00	58
Have a Heart Collection - D. Canham, unless otherwise noted				
1998 Angel	2,500	1999	52.00	60
1999 Blush	2,000	2001	56.00	58
2001 Charlie Charm	1,500		58.00	58
2000 Chi Chi	1,200	2001	58.00	58
1998 Crispin	2,500	1999	52.00	54-65
2002 Elliot	1,000		60.00	60
1998 Gus	2,500	1999	52.00	54-65
2002 Jessie - M. Baker	1,000		60.00	60
2000 Kevin	1,200	2001	60.00	60
1998 Lilac Lil	2,500	1999	52.00	65
1998 Mummy's Little Monster	2,500	1999	52.00	56-70
2001 Nellie	1,500	2002	58.00	58
2002 Oliver	1,000		60.00	60
2002 Pansy - M. Baker	1,000		60.00	60

YEAR ISSUE	EDITION LIMIT	YEAR RETD.	ISSUE PRICE	*QUOTE U.S.$
1998 Peppermint	2,500	1999	52.00	65
2000 Rose	1,200	2001	60.00	60
2000 Ruby Red	800	2000	60.00	60
1998 Susie	2,500	1999	52.00	52-60
2002 Tai Chi - M. Baker	1,000		60.00	60
Hermann (Red Tag) Exclusives - D. Canham				
1998 Belinda	Retrd.	2000	60.00	60-150
1998 Benji	Retrd.	2000	60.00	60-150
Mini Mice - D. Canham				
2001 Albert	1,200	2002	58.00	58
2000 Angelina	1,200	2001	58.00	58
2001 Cederik	1,200	2001	58.00	58
2002 Chico	1,000	2002	60.00	60
2000 Cuthbert	1,200	2000	58.00	58
2001 Jack	1,200	2001	58.00	58
2001 Lilly	1,200	2001	58.00	58
2000 Merry	1,200	2000	58.00	58
2002 Missy	1,000		60.00	60
2002 Sink	1,500		64.00	64
2002 Swim	1,500		64.00	64
2001 Victoria	1,200	2002	58.00	58
Mini Mice Special - D. Canham				
2001 Sugar	400	2001	60.00	60
Mohair Collection - D. Canham				
1996 A.J.	5,000	1998	40.00	70-119
1996 B.J.	5,000	1998	40.00	70-87
1996 Benjamin	3,000	1997	40.00	85-125
1996 Flore	3,000	1997	40.00	200-350
1996 Golly Gosh	3,000	1997	40.00	150-225
1996 Panda	5,000	1999	40.00	75-100
1996 Peter	3,000	1997	40.00	95-200
1996 Sorry	5,000	1997	40.00	90-125
1997 Uncle Ernie	700	1997	48.00	75-130
Nutcracker Suite - D. Canham, unless otherwise noted				
1997 Columbine	2,000	1998	52.00	100-175
1997 Harlequin	2,000	1998	52.00	53-75
1997 Magician	2,000	1999	52.00	53-60
1997 Nutcracker Prince - L. Sasaki	2,000	1999	52.00	53-60
1997 Rat King - B. Windell	2,000	1999	52.00	53-60
1997 Snowflake	2,000	1998	52.00	85-150
1997 Sugar Plum	2,000	1999	52.00	55-65
Out of Towners - D. Canham				
2000 Galaxy	1,500	2001	60.00	60
1997 Gussie Galactica	1,000	1998	54.00	238-500
1997 Moonshine Cosmic	1,000	1998	54.00	238-500
2000 Star Bright	1,500		60.00	60
2000 Twinkle	1,500		60.00	60
Oz Collection - D. Canham, unless otherwise noted				
2001 Bad Witch	2,500		58.00	58
2001 Crow	2,500		58.00	58
2001 Dorothy	2,500		70.00	70
2001 Flying Monkey	2,500		58.00	58
2001 Good Witch	2,500		58.00	58
2001 Lion	2,500		58.00	58
2001 Munkin Boy - L. Sasaki	2,500		58.00	58
2001 Munkin Girl - L. Sasaki	2,500		58.00	58
2001 Professor	2,500		58.00	58
2001 Queen of the Field Mouse	2,500		58.00	58
2001 Scarecrow	2,500		64.00	64
2001 Tinman	2,500		58.00	58
Pan Collection - D. Canham				
2002 Hook	1,500		60.00	60
2002 John	1,500		60.00	60
2002 Michael	1,500		60.00	60
2002 Peter	1,500		60.00	60
2002 Tinkerbell	1,500		60.00	60
2002 Wendy	1,500		60.00	60
Rainy Days Collection - D. Canham				
1997 Chuckles	2,000	1999	48.00	55-100
1997 Hattie	2,000	1998	48.00	70-100
1997 Herschel	2,000	1997	48.00	70-125
1997 Lady Ascot	2,000	1999	48.00	50-60
1997 Pilgrim	2,000	1998	48.00	75-90
1997 Sticky Bun	2,000	1999	48.00	50

Collectors' Information Bureau   *Quotes have been rounded up to nearest dollar

YEAR ISSUE	EDITION LIMIT	YEAR RETD.	ISSUE PRICE	*QUOTE U.S.$
Specials - D. Canham, unless otherwise noted				
2001 911 USA Bear Pin	1,500		25.00	25
1999 Billie	39	1999	60.00	300
1998 Button Jester	200	1998	60.00	175-450
2001 Celebration	1,500		60.00	60
2000 Christmas	1,200	2000	60.00	60-250
1999 Clementine	400	2000	60.00	60-100
2000 Coco	400	2000	60.00	60
2002 Edward Rabbit - K. Apps	400	2002	60.00	60
2001 Ernestine The Rabbit - K. Apps	400	2001	60.00	60
2000 Happy Chap	800	2001	60.00	60
2001 Hundentjahrig	1,500	2001	60.00	60
2002 Inky - K. Apps	400	2002	60.00	60
2001 Issac The Elephant - K. Apps	400	2001	60.00	60
1999 Lulu	99	1999	60.00	200-650
2000 Myrtle (Camp Canham Bear)	200	2000	80.00	80
2001 Night Before Xmas	150	2001	140.00	140
2001 Niku	400	2001	90.00	90
1999 Old Punch	20	1999	80.00	300
2000 Popsicle	400	2000	60.00	60
2000 Rusty	500	2000	60.00	60
2000 Snowy	1,000	2000	60.00	60-200
2001 St. Nick	1,000		60.00	60
1998 Swat	27	1999	80.00	350-1200
2000 Titania & Puck (Disney)	150	2000	150.00	150-650
1999 Topper	Retrd.	1999	60.00	100-450
1998 Tulip	400	1998	54.00	175-450
1999 Winnie the Pooh	500	1999	95.00	90-350
The Woebe's - D. Canham				
2001 Okey Dokey	1,500	2002	58.00	58
2001 Righty-O	1,500	2002	58.00	58

Department 56

Heritage Village Doll Collection - Department 56				
1987 Christmas Carol Dolls 1000-6, set/4 (Tiny Tim, Bob Crachet, Mrs. Crachet, Scrooge)	250	1988	1500.00	900-1100
1987 Christmas Carol Dolls 5907-2, set/4 (Tiny Tim, Bob Crachet, Mrs. Crachet, Scrooge)	Closed	1993	250.00	150-315
1988 Mr. & Mrs. Fezziwig 5594-8, set/2	Closed	1995	172.00	125-200
Snowbabies Dolls - Department 56				
1988 Allison & Duncan 7730-5, set/2	Closed	1989	200.00	486-1025
Snowbabies Plush - Department 56				
2000 Frosty Frolic Friends-Penguin 69002	Closed	2001	15.00	15
2000 Frosty Frolic Friends-Polar Bear, large 69000	Closed	2001	20.00	20
2000 Frosty Frolic Friends-Polar Bear, small 69001	Closed	2001	15.00	15
2000 Frosty Frolic Friends-Sled Dog 69003	Closed	2001	15.00	15

Elke's Originals, Ltd.

Elke Hutchens - E. Hutchens				
1991 Alicia	250	N/A	595.00	700-995
1989 Annabelle	250	N/A	575.00	1400-1500
1990 Aubra	250	N/A	575.00	900-1050
1990 Aurora	250	N/A	595.00	900-1050
1991 Bellinda	400	N/A	595.00	1010
1992 Bethany	400	N/A	595.00	1050-1100
1991 Braelyn	400	N/A	595.00	1525
1991 Brianna	400	N/A	595.00	1500
1992 Cecilia	435	N/A	635.00	1050
1992 Charles	435	N/A	635.00	975
1992 Cherie	435	N/A	635.00	1050
1992 Clarissa	435	N/A	635.00	1050
1993 Daphne	435	N/A	675.00	700-850
1993 Deidre	435	N/A	675.00	795
1993 Desirée	435	N/A	675.00	700-900
1990 Kricket	500	N/A	575.00	400
1992 Laurakaye	435	N/A	550.00	875
1990 Little Liebchen	250	N/A	475.00	1000
1990 Victoria	500	N/A	645.00	870

YEAR ISSUE	EDITION LIMIT	YEAR RETD.	ISSUE PRICE	*QUOTE U.S.$
G. DeBrekht Artistic Studios/Russian Gift & Jewelry				
Holiday Surprises-Doll with Ornaments - G. DeBrekht Artistic Studios				
2000 Alenushka	3-Yr.		59.00	59
2001 Children Snowman	3-Yr.		59.00	59
2000 The Couple	3-Yr.		59.00	59
1998 Doll with Ornaments	Retrd.	1999	59.00	59
1998 Egg-Santa	Retrd.	2000	45.00	45
2001 Fairy-tale	3-Yr.		69.00	69
2000 Father Frost	3-Yr.		59.00	59
1998 Girl	Retrd.	2000	45.00	45
2001 Golden Egg	3-Yr.		59.00	59
2001 Holiday Tree	3-Yr.		25.00	25
2001 Ivan/tzarevich	3-Yr.		69.00	69
2001 Marry Wedding	3-Yr.		69.00	69
2000 Morozko	3-Yr.		59.00	59
2001 Nativity	3-Yr.		90.00	90
2001 North Pole Santa	3-Yr.		25.00	25
2001 Nutcracker Doll with Ornaments	3-Yr.		69.00	69
2001 Ovan tzarevich	3-Yr.		69.00	69
1998 Samovar	Retrd.	2000	35.00	35
1998 Santa with Ornament	Open		59.00	59
1998 Santa with Samovar	Retrd.	2000	33.00	33
2001 Tea-time	3-Yr.		69.00	69
2001 Toyful Santa	3-Yr.		49.00	49
2000 Village Toyland	3-Yr.		49.00	49
2001 Whimsical Snowman	3-Yr.		59.00	59
Matryoshka Memories Celebrations - G. DeBrekht Artistic Studios				
1998 Easter	Retrd.	N/A	99.00	99
1998 Romantic	Retrd.	N/A	130.00	130
Matryoshka Memories Childhood Memories - G. DeBrekht Artistic Studios				
1998 Angel	250	2000	330.00	330
1998 Angel of Love 16075	300	2000	250.00	250
1998 Childhood Play	250		300.00	300
1998 Children Always Playing	250	1999	250.00	250
1998 Frog Princess	100	2000	1100.00	1100
1998 Guardian Angel 16025	100	2000	830.00	830
1998 Nutcracker 18017 (Roly-Poly)	100	1999	270.00	270
1998 Nutcracker 18018 (Roly-Poly)	100	1999	270.00	270
2001 Nutcracker 5"	3-Yr.		59.00	59
1998 Nutcracker DA-10/10N	50	1999	1590.00	1590
1998 Russian Fairy-Tales	300	1999	390.00	390
1998 Winter Pleasure (Roly-Poly)	100	1999	270.00	270
Matryoshka Memories Fairytale Dolls - G. DeBrekht Artistic Studios				
2001 Cinderella 7"	2-Yr.		75.00	75
2000 Fairytale 5"	2-Yr.		39.00	39
2001 Fairytale 5"	3-Yr.		49.00	49
2001 Gingerbread 5"	2-Yr.		39.00	39
2001 Ivan tzarevich 10"	2-Yr.		180.00	180
2001 Scarlet Flower 7"	2-Yr.		75.00	75
2001 Snowmaiden 10"	2-Yr.		180.00	180
2001 Turnip Family 5"	3-Yr.		39.00	39
Matryoshka Memories Family Dolls - G. DeBrekht Artistic Studios				
1998 Captain	Retrd.	N/A	49.00	49
1998 Family Man C/PE-3N	Retrd.	N/A	35.00	35
1998 Family Man C/PE-5N	Retrd.	N/A	49.00	49
1998 Family Women	Open		30.00	30
1998 Girl	Retrd.	N/A	49.00	49
1998 Grandma	Open		49.00	49
1998 Merchant	Open		49.00	49
1998 Musician Man	Open		49.00	49
1998 Snow Maiden	Retrd.	N/A	49.00	49
Matryoshka Memories Four Season - G. DeBrekht Artistic Studios				
1998 Spring	500	2000	130.00	150
1998 Summer	500	2000	99.00	125
1998 Winter	500	2000	130.00	150
Matryoshka Memories Musical Roly-Poly Dolls - G. DeBrekht Artistic Studios				
1998 Angel	Retrd.	2001	35.00	35
1998 Animals	Retrd.	2001	35.00	35

DOLLS & PLUSH

YEAR ISSUE	EDITION LIMIT	YEAR RETD.	ISSUE PRICE	*QUOTE U.S.$
1998 Animals	Retrd.	1999	35.00	35
1999 Animated Roly-Poly	Open		35.00	35
2001 Fisherman Cat	Open		35.00	35
1998 Girl	Retrd.	2001	35.00	35
1998 Indian	Retrd.	1999	35.00	35
1998 Nutcracker #1	100	2001	270.00	270
1998 Nutcracker #2	100	2001	270.00	270
1998 Royal Couple, set/2	500	2001	90.00	150
1998 Santa	Retrd.	2001	35.00	35
1998 Snowman's Time	100	2001	270.00	270

Matryoshka Memories Nested Wood Dolls - G. DeBrekht Artistic Studios

YEAR ISSUE	EDITION LIMIT	YEAR RETD.	ISSUE PRICE	*QUOTE U.S.$
1998 Frog Princess Fairy Tale, set/10	250	2001	1100.00	1100
1998 Guardian Angel, set/10	250	2001	830.00	830
1998 Guardian Angel, set/5	750	2001	250.00	250
1998 Nutcracker, set/10	50	2000	1590.00	1590
1998 Village Holidays, set/6	250	2001	300.00	300

Matryoshka Memories Old World Dolls - G. DeBrekht Artistic Studios

YEAR ISSUE	EDITION LIMIT	YEAR RETD.	ISSUE PRICE	*QUOTE U.S.$
2001 Baby Doll Teapot	2-Yr.		49.00	49
2000 Egg-doll Gone Fishing	3-Yr.		45.00	45
1999 Egg-doll Sleighing Kids	3-Yr.		45.00	45
1999 Egg-doll Snow Maiden	3-Yr.		45.00	45
2001 Father Frost Baby Doll	2-Yr.		49.00	49
2001 Morozko Baby Doll	2-Yr.		49.00	49

Matryoshka Memories Russian Elegance - G. DeBrekht Artistic Studios

YEAR ISSUE	EDITION LIMIT	YEAR RETD.	ISSUE PRICE	*QUOTE U.S.$
1998 Holiday	Open		300.00	300
1998 Snowmaiden	Open		300.00	300

Matryoshka Memories Russian Traditions - G. DeBrekht Artistic Studios

YEAR ISSUE	EDITION LIMIT	YEAR RETD.	ISSUE PRICE	*QUOTE U.S.$
1998 Babushka with Bird (5N)	Retrd.	2001	150.00	150
1998 Babushka with Cat (5N)	Retrd.	2001	150.00	150
1998 Babushka with Children (5N)	Retrd.	2001	150.00	150
1998 Babushka with Troika (10N)	500	2001	590.00	590
1998 Ballet (5N)	Retrd.	2000	90.00	90
1998 Fairy-Tale (5N)	Retrd.	2000	40.00	40
1998 Kitty Cats (5N)	Retrd.	2000	150.00	150
1998 Musical Girls (5N)	Retrd.	2000	130.00	130
1998 Royalty	750	2001	90.00	90
1998 Snowmaiden (5N)	Retrd.	2001	130.00	130

Matryoshka Memories Santa Dolls - G. DeBrekht Artistic Studios

YEAR ISSUE	EDITION LIMIT	YEAR RETD.	ISSUE PRICE	*QUOTE U.S.$
1998 All Santas CS/5N#2	Open		49.00	49
1998 Family Santa	Open		49.00	49
2001 Father Frost 3"	2-Yr.		31.00	31
2001 Happy Snowman	3-Yr.		49.00	49
2000 Musical Snowman 5"	2-Yr.		49.00	49
2001 Nutcracker Santa 5"	3-Yr.		49.00	49
2001 Santa 3"	2-Yr.		31.00	31
1998 Santa 6SC/5N-CT/SM	Retrd.	2000	11.00	11
1998 Santa 6SE/LG	Retrd.	2000	15.00	15
1998 Santa Cone/Shape	Open		29.00	29
1998 Santa CS/3N#1	Open		35.00	35
1998 Santa CS/3N#3-SM	Open		23.00	23
1998 Santa CS/3N#4-LG	Open		37.00	37
1998 Santa with Teddy Bear	Retrd.	1999	31.00	31
2001 Santa's Family 5"	3-Yr.		49.00	49

Matryoshka Memories Special Friends Dolls - G. DeBrekht Artistic Studios

YEAR ISSUE	EDITION LIMIT	YEAR RETD.	ISSUE PRICE	*QUOTE U.S.$
1998 Cat 1CAT/5N-MD	Open		35.00	35
1998 Cat E/CAT-5N	Open		35.00	35
1998 Doll with Rabbit, Cat, Pig	Retrd.	2000	27.00	27
1998 Fairy-Tale	Open		35.00	35
1998 Holiday	Open		35.00	35

Matryoshka Memories Timeless Faith Dolls - G. DeBrekht Artistic Studios

YEAR ISSUE	EDITION LIMIT	YEAR RETD.	ISSUE PRICE	*QUOTE U.S.$
1998 Icon Doll D-21/5N	Retrd.	2000	150.00	150
1998 Icon Doll D-21/5N#2	Retrd.	2000	150.00	150

Matryoshka Memories Toy Dolls - G. DeBrekht Artistic Studios

YEAR ISSUE	EDITION LIMIT	YEAR RETD.	ISSUE PRICE	*QUOTE U.S.$
1998 Floral	Open		35.00	35
1998 Girl with Cats	2-Yr.	2000	130.00	130
1998 Squirrel	2-Yr.	2000	130.00	130
1998 Unusual	Open		55.00	55

Matryoshka Memories Toy Land - G. DeBrekht Artistic Studios

YEAR ISSUE	EDITION LIMIT	YEAR RETD.	ISSUE PRICE	*QUOTE U.S.$
1998 Abramtsevo	Open		99.00	99
1998 Girls & Boys	Open		130.00	130
1998 Santa with Children	Retrd.	2001	130.00	130
1998 Teddy Bear	Retrd.	2001	130.00	130

Gene/Ashton-Drake Galleries

Gene Accessories - J. Greene, unless otherwise noted

YEAR ISSUE	EDITION LIMIT	YEAR RETD.	ISSUE PRICE	*QUOTE U.S.$
1999 Birthday Accessory Set 76079 - N/A	Retrd.	2001	29.95	30
2000 Chaise Lounge 94661 - N/A	Open		74.95	75
1999 Director's Chair 76080 - N/A	Open		29.95	30
1996 Dress Form 94390	Open		19.95	20
1999 Dresser 76073 - N/A	Open		79.95	80
1999 Gene Patio Set 94679 - N/A	Open		49.95	50
2000 Gene's Croquet Set 76406 - D. Gibbons	Open		29.95	30
2000 Gene's Dressing Screen 92937 - N/A	Open		44.95	45
2000 Gene's Gazebo 92259 - N/A	Open		44.95	45
1999 Gene's Jewelry Set 92938 - N/A	Open		34.95	35
1999 Gene's Paper Doll Set #1 92931 - N/A	Open		12.95	13
1999 Gene's Paper Doll Set #2 92932 - N/A	Open		12.95	13
1999 Gene's Paper Doll Set #3 92933 - N/A	Open		12.95	13
2002 Gene's Show Set #3 93696 - E. Foran	Open		29.95	30
1996 Gene's Trunk 93504	Open		69.95	70
2000 Gene's Wardrobe Rack 92256 - N/A	Open		44.95	45
2000 Hanger Set 76156 - N/A	Open		14.95	15
2000 Hat Stand 92255 - N/A	Open		14.95	15
2000 Hat/Purse Set #1 92940 - M. Tibbitts	Open		44.95	45
2000 Hat/Purse Set #2 92255 - M. Tibbitts	Open		44.95	45
2000 Hat/Purse Set #3 96314 - M. Tibbitts	Open		44.95	45
2000 Hat/Purse Set #4 96319 - M. Tibbitts	Open		44.95	45
2000 Hearts and Flowers 92939 - E. Foran	Open		34.95	35
1997 Hot Day in Hollywood 93548	Open		34.95	35
1999 Mirror 94678 - N/A	Open		19.95	20
1997 Out For a Stroll 93547 - E. Foran	Retrd.	2001	29.95	30
2000 Panther Lamp 94671 - N/A	Open		34.95	35
1999 Picnic Basket 76072 - N/A	Retrd.	2001	34.95	35
2000 Shoe Set #1 96317 - E. Foran	Open		19.95	20
2000 Shoe Set #2 96318 - E. Foran	Open		19.95	20
2002 Shoe Set #3 93696 - E. Foran	Open		29.95	30
1999 Swan Bed 76087 - N/A	Open		89.95	90
2000 Swan Lamp 93322 - D. Gibbons	Open		49.95	50
2000 Undercover Story (Lingerie) 96316 - N/A	Open		29.95	30
1999 USO Accessory Pack 94677 - N/A	Retrd.	2002	34.95	35
1997 White Christmas 94398	Open		44.95	45

Gene Costumed Dolls by Mel Odom - Various

YEAR ISSUE	EDITION LIMIT	YEAR RETD.	ISSUE PRICE	*QUOTE U.S.$
1999 An American Countess (Parkwest /NALED Exclusive) 76082 - C. Curtis	Retrd.	1999	99.95	100-120
2001 April Showers (Coca-Cola®) 38268 - N/A	Open		125.00	125
2002 Best Bet 76479 - S. Gallen	Yr.Iss.		110.00	110
1997 Bird of Paradise 94397 - W. Long	Retrd.	1999	79.95	80-90
2001 Blue Fox 38259 - T.Kennedy	Open		89.95	90
1996 Blue Goddess 93503 - T. Kennedy	Retrd.	1999	69.95	70-90
2000 Bon Voyage (Star Dealer Exclusive) 92266 - J. Ferrand	3,500		99.95	100
1999 Breathless (Retailer Exclusive) (YDA Winner) 76074 - S. Bruner	9,999	1999	99.95	100-110
1998 Broadway Medley (Convention Exclusive) 94665 - T. Kennedy	800	1998	N/A	250-695
2002 Calendar Girl: That Extra Something (Coca-Cola®) 93650 - Gene Development Team	3,000		125.00	125
1998 Champagne Supper 94662 - T. Kennedy	Retrd.	2000	79.95	80-100
2002 Coca-Cola® Girl: Holiday Shopper (Coca-Cola®) 93655 - Gene Development Team	3,000		125.00	125
1998 Covent Garden (Parkwest/NALED Exclusive) 94664 - T. Kennedy	Closed	1998	99.95	100-199
1998 Crème de Cassis 94685 - T. Alberts	Retrd.	1999	79.95	80-92
2000 Dance With Me 76154 - L. Day	5,000		84.95	85
1998 Daughter of the Nile 94667 - T. Alberts	Retrd.	2000	79.95	80-100
1998 Destiny (YDA Winner) 94656 - M. Esposito	Yr.Iss.	1998	89.95	100-110
2000 Encore (Retailer Exclusive) 76529 - L. Day	5,000		99.95	100

Collectors' Information Bureau   *Quotes have been rounded up to nearest dollar

YEAR ISSUE	EDITION LIMIT	YEAR RETD.	ISSUE PRICE	*QUOTE U.S.$
2001 Everything's Coming up Roses 96375 - J. Ferrand	Yr.Iss.		99.95	100
2001 Garden Party 38240 - D. Silva	5,000		120.00	120
2001 Gene in the Fabulous Costumes of 20th Century Fox 38270 - N/A	5,000		125.00	125
2000 Heart of Hollywood (Parkwest/NALED Exclusive) 96376 - V. Nowell	3,500		99.95	100
1998 Hello Hollywood, Hello 94657 - D. James	Open		79.95	80
2000 I Do 96371 - T. Kennedy	5,000		84.95	85
1997 Iced Coffee 94396 - L. Meisner	Retrd.	1999	79.95	80-92
1998 Incognito 94659 - T. Alberts	Open		79.95	80
1997 The King's Daughter (Retailer Exclusive) (YDA Winner) 93525 - M. Gutierrez	5,000	1997	99.95	200-495
2001 A Lady Knows 38277 - B. Lange	Open		99.95	100
2000 Love At First Sight 76528 - D. Cipolla	5,000		84.95	85
2001 Love in Bloom 38243 - R. Ganem	5,000		120.00	120
1999 Love, Paris 76063 - J. Ferrand	Retrd.	2000	79.95	80-90
2000 Lovely in Lace 76523 - T. Kennedy	Retrd.	2001	84.95	85
1999 Lucky Stripe 93529 - T. Kennedy	Open		79.95	80
2000 Meet Me In Paris (Paris Convention Doll) 93329 - V. Nowell	Closed	2000	N/A	N/A
1998 Midnight Gamble (Retailer Exclusive) 94666 - D. James	9,500	1998	99.95	100-125
1997 Midnight Romance (Parkwest/NALED Exclusive) 93550 - T. Alberts	Closed	1997	89.95	150-295
1995 Monaco 96403 - T. Alberts	Retrd.	1997	69.95	125-150
1999 Mood Music (Convention Exclusive) 76083 - L. Day	Closed	1999	N/A	N/A
1997 My Favorite Witch (Convention Exclusive) 93549 - T. Kennedy	350	1997	N/A	1100-1750
2001 My Heart's Song 38230 - B. Lange	Open		89.95	90
1997 A Night At Versailles (FAO Schwarz Exclusive) 93551 - T. Alberts	5,000	1997	90.00	210-295
1998 On The Avenue (FAO Schwarz Spring Exclusive) 94668 - T. Kennedy	5,000	1998	90.00	95-299
2001 Pierrette (Masquerade) 38255 - L. Day	5,000		99.95	100
1996 Pin-Up 93507 - T. Kennedy	Retrd.	1999	69.95	70-90
1995 Premiere 96401 - T. Kennedy	Retrd.	1996	69.95	700-800
1999 Priceless (FAO Schwarz Exclusive) 76081 - J. Ferrand	Retrd.	1999	110.00	110
1995 Red Venus 96402 - T. Kennedy	Retrd.	2001	69.95	70
1999 Savannah (YDA Winner) 76064 - K. McHale	Retrd.	2001	79.95	80
1999 She'd Rather Dance 76062 - T. Kennedy	Retrd.	2001	79.95	80
2000 Shooting Star 76402 - D. James	5,000		84.95	85
1999 Simply Gene (blond) 93527	Open		49.95	50
1999 Simply Gene (brunette) 93528	Open		49.95	50
2000 Simply Gene (platinum) 76157 - J. Greene	Open		54.95	55
1999 Simply Gene (red) 93526	Open		49.95	50
2001 Simply Gene 2001 38239 - N/A	Open		69.95	70
2002 Simply Gene 2002 76477 - Gene Development Team	Open		59.95	60
1999 Song of Spain 76065 - T. Kennedy	Yr.Iss.	1999	99.95	100
1997 Sparkling Seduction (YDA Winner) 94394 - S. Rinker	Retrd.	2001	79.95	80
2000 Spotted In The Park (FAO Exclusive) (YDA Winner) 93326 - V. Alvarado	3,500		99.95	100
2000 Symphony In G (Ashton-Drake Galleries Exclusive) (YDA Winner) 96379 - T. Butts	Open		99.95	100
1999 Tea Time (FAO Schwarz Exclusive) 76066 - L. Day	Closed	1999	100.00	100
2002 To Have and To Hold 93648 - J. Ferrand	3,750		125.00	125
2000 Twilight Rumba 93325 - D. James	Yr.Iss.	2000	99.95	100
1999 Unforgettable (Ashton-Drake Galleries Exclusive) 76075 - D. Cipolla	Open		99.95	100
1999 USO 76061 - D. James	Retrd.	2002	79.95	80
1998 Warmest Wishes (FAO Schwarz Fall Exclusive) 94663 - T. Kennedy	Closed	1998	110.00	110-155
1997 White Hyacinth 94395 - D. James	Retrd.	1998	79.95	80-155
2002 Winter's Romance 93644 - B. Lange	2,500		110.00	110

Gene Costumes - Various

YEAR ISSUE	EDITION LIMIT	YEAR RETD.	ISSUE PRICE	*QUOTE U.S.$
1996 Afternoon Off 93508 - D. James	Retrd.	1998	29.95	50-88
1999 At Home For The Holidays (Retailer Exclusive) 76084 - T. Kennedy	9,999	1999	49.95	50
1996 Atlantic City Beauty (Convention Exclusive) 94393 - D. James	250	1996	N/A	1200
1999 Avant Garde 76085 - J. Ferrand	Retrd.	2001	39.95	40
2000 Baking Cookies 76239 - T. Kennedy	5,000		34.95	35
2001 Batter Up! (YDA Winner) 38278 - S. Iller-Drachman	Open		44.95	45
1999 Black Ribbon 76088 - T. Kennedy	Retrd.	2001	39.95	40
1995 Blonde Lace 96404 - T. Kennedy	Retrd.	1998	29.95	30-60
1997 Blossoms in the Snow (Retailer Exclusive) 93544 - T. Kennedy	5,000	1997	44.95	150-200
1995 Blue Evening 96409 - T. Alberts	Retrd.	1999	29.95	30-45
2001 Blue Heaven 38245 - L. Day	Open		44.95	45
2000 Bolera (YDA Winner) 76407 - D. Trejo	5,000		39.95	40
2001 Bonnie and Blithe 38275 - C. Curtis	Open		49.95	50
1999 Bridge Club 76069 - V. Nowell	Retrd.	2001	34.95	35
2001 Brunch With Katie 38247 - L. Day	Open		44.95	45
1998 Cameo (YDA Winner) 94655 - K. Johnson	Retrd.	2001	29.95	30
1999 Cognac Evening 76086 - J. Ferrand	Retrd.	2002	44.95	45
2001 Crazy for Calypso 96373 - T. Kennedy	Open		44.95	45
1996 Crescendo 93505 - D. James	Retrd.	2001	39.95	40
1995 Crimson Sun 93502 - D. James	Retrd.	1999	29.95	30-45
2000 Croquet Anyone? 76526 - L. Day	5,000		34.95	35
2000 Don't Fence Me In 76403 - V. Nowell	5,000		34.95	35
1996 El Morocco 93506 - T. Alberts	Retrd.	2000	29.95	30-35
1998 Embassy Luncheon 94652 - L. Meisner	Retrd.	2001	39.95	40
2002 Emerald Eve (Retailer Exclusive) 76660 - L. Day	2,500		69.95	70
1999 Farewell, Golden Moon 76067 - T. Kennedy	Retrd.	2001	44.95	45
2000 First Close Up 76524 - T. Kennedy	5,000		39.95	40
2000 First Stop Chicago 76522 - L. Day	5,000		44.95	45
1998 Forget Me Not 94653 - T. Alberts	Open		39.95	40
2000 Friendly Connection (Ashton-Drake Galleries Exclusive) 76155 - G. Sarofeen	2,500		39.95	40
1995 Goodbye New York 93501 - D. James	Open		34.95	35
2000 Hacienda 76408 - L. Day	5,000		44.95	45
2000 Hearts Afire 76401 - L. Day	5,000		44.95	45
1998 Hi Fi 94669 - D. James	Retrd.	2000	34.95	35
1996 Holiday Magic (Retailer Exclusive) 94392 - T. Kennedy	2,000	1996	44.95	225-395
1999 Honeymoon 93524 - J. Ferrand	Open		44.95	45
2002 It Happened in Monterey 76730 - W. Nilson	2,002		49.95	50
2000 It's A Wrap 76274 - T. Kennedy	5,000		32.95	33
2000 Jazz Note 76273 - D. Cipolla	5,000		44.95	45
1995 The Kiss 96410 - T. Kennedy	Open		29.95	30
2000 Kiss Me, Gene 76271 - L. Day	5,000		44.95	45
2000 The Little Black Dress 93328 - T. Kennedy	5,000		49.95	50
2001 Little Blessings 38274 - V. Nowell	Open		49.95	50
1998 Love After Hours 94658 - T. Kennedy	Open		34.95	35
2000 Love Letters 93327 - J. Ferrand	5,000		39.95	40
1995 Love's Ghost 96406 - D. James	Open		29.95	30
1997 Mandarin Mood 93543 - T. Kennedy	Retrd.	1999	34.95	35-75
1998 Midnight Angel (YDA Winner) 94674 - N. Burke	Retrd.	2001	39.95	40
1998 My Favorite Bow 94686 - T. Kennedy	Retrd.	2000	39.95	40
1999 On the Town (NALED Exclusive) 76071 - L. Day	Closed	1999	49.95	50
2000 The Perfect Gift (YDA Winner) 92269 - R. Ganem	5,000		44.95	45
1997 Personal Secretary 93542 - T. Kennedy	Retrd.	2001	34.95	35
1999 Picnic In The Country 76077 - L. Day	Open		39.95	40-50
1995 Pink Lightening 96405 - T. Kennedy	Retrd.	1998	29.95	40-60
1999 Poolside 76078 - V. Nowell	Retrd.	2001	34.95	35
1999 Press Conference 76068 - D. Cipolla	Retrd.	2001	44.95	45
1997 Promenade 93541 - T. Kennedy	Retrd.	1998	29.95	30-75
1998 Rain Song 94675 - D. James	Open		29.95	30
1998 Ransom in Red (Retailer Exclusive) 94676 - T. Kennedy	7,500	1998	44.95	45-75
1998 Right In Step 38235 - L. Day	Open		54.95	55
1998 Safari 94673 - T. Alberts	Retrd.	2000	39.95	40
1997 Sea Spree 93546 - T. Kennedy	Retrd.	1999	34.95	35-55
1999 Secret Sleuth 93523 - T. Kennedy	Open		39.95	40
2001 Shimmering Star 38269 - G. Sarofeen	5,000		65.00	65

DOLLS & PLUSH

YEAR ISSUE	EDITION LIMIT	YEAR RETD.	ISSUE PRICE	*QUOTE U.S.$
2000 Shorts Story 76234 - V. Nowell	5,000		32.95	33
1998 Smart Set 94687 - D. James	Open		39.95	40
1999 Somewhere Summer 93522 - T. Kennedy	Open		44.95	45
2000 Spellbound (Retailer Exclusive) 76235 - T. Kennedy	5,000		44.95	45
2000 The Spirit of Truth (YDA Winner) 96313 - E. Machnica	5,000		44.95	45
2000 St. Moritz 92257 - L. Day	5,000		49.95	50
1999 Stand Up and Cheer 76070 - D. Cipolla	Open		44.95	45
1995 Striking Gold 96407 - T. Alberts	Retrd.	1998	29.95	44-50
1999 Sunday Afternoon (YDA Winner) 93521 - A. Haskell	Retrd.	2001	39.95	40
1999 Sunset Celebration 76076 - V. Nowell	Retrd.	2001	39.95	40
2000 Table For Two 93145 - J. Ferrand	5,000		34.95	35
1997 Tango 93545 - T. Kennedy	Retrd.	2000	39.95	40
1995 Usherette 96408 - T. Kennedy	Open		29.95	30
2002 Victory Garden 76047 - Gene Development Team	2,002		44.95	45
2000 Will You Marry Me? 96372 - G. Sarofeen	5,000		44.95	45

Madra Lord Accessories - D. Gibbons, unless otherwise noted

2001 Madra's Director's Chair 38249	Open		29.95	30
2000 Madra's Dogs 92258 - D. Gibbons	Open		44.95	45

Madra Lord Costumed Dolls by Mel Odom - Various

2001 Black Ice 38276 - T. Kennedy	Open		99.95	100
2000 Black Widow 96312 - L. Day/J. Greene	2,500		125.00	125
2001 Cold Shoulder 38238 - J. Ferrand	Open		110.00	110
2002 Dark Desire 76659 - G. Sarofeen	3,000		99.95	100
2000 First Encounter 96311 - C. Curtis	Retrd.	2001	110.00	110
2001 Madra in the Fabulous Costumes of 20th Century Fox 38272 - N/A	5,000		125.00	125
2002 Moulin Noire 76770 - R. Benea	2,002		110.00	110
2001 Scarlett Temptress (Retailer Exclusive) 76372 - T. Kennedy	Open		120.00	120
2001 Scorned Woman (Masquerade) 38267 - D. James	5,000		125.00	125
2001 Stolen Moments 38260 - T. Kennedy	Open		99.95	100
2002 Top This 76800 - J. Ferrand	3,500		99.95	100
2001 Turbulence 38234 - L. Day	Open		99.95	100
2002 Ultimately Madra 2002 76159 - Gene Development Team	Open		69.95	70
2001 Ultimately Madra 38244 - N/A	Open		69.95	70
2001 Unsung Melody 38258 - B. Lange	Open		110.00	110

Madra Lord Costumes - Various

2001 Anything But Nice 38289 - G. Sarofeen	Open		49.95	50
2000 Cat Walk 92285 - J. Ferrand	Open		39.95	40
2001 Chocolate Truffle 38288 - J. Howard	Open		59.95	60
2001 Coffee Klatch 38242 - D. Cipolla	Open		49.95	50
2000 Devil May Care 92287 - L. Day	Open		49.95	50
2000 Dressed To Kill 92268 - T. Kennedy	Open		44.95	45
2000 Heartless 92288 - T. Kennedy	Retrd.	2001	44.95	45
2001 Highland Fling 92267 - T. Kennedy	3,500		59.95	60
2001 Mad About Mitzi 38236 - V. Nowell	Open		69.95	70
2002 Midnight Blossoms 76170 - V. Nowell	2,002		49.95	50
2000 Pink With Envy 92286 - B. Lange	Retrd.	2001	44.95	45
2001 Rio Rumba 38248 - T. Kennedy	Open		44.95	45
2000 So Evil My Love 92289 - T. Kennedy	Open		49.95	50
2001 Stormy Weather 38237 - T. Kennedy	Open		59.95	60
2001 Winter/Summer Set 38263 - J. Howard	Open		79.95	80

The Starlight Canteen - Various

2002 Gene 92345 - J. Howard	2,500		110.00	110
2002 Trent 93643 - Gene Development Team	2,500		110.00	110

Trent Osborn Accessories - D. Gibbons

2001 Trent's Director's Chair 38254	Open		29.95	30

Trent Osborn Costumed Dolls by Mel Odom - Various

2001 After Hours 38264 - T. Kennedy	Retrd.	2002	110.00	110
2001 Formal Introduction 38250 - L. Day	Open		110.00	110
2001 Lover in Disguise (Masquerade) 38257 - L. Day	5,000		125.00	125
2002 Neat as a Pin 76680 - L. Day	3,000		110.00	110
2002 Top of the Morning 93649 - Gene Development Team	3,750		125.00	125

YEAR ISSUE	EDITION LIMIT	YEAR RETD.	ISSUE PRICE	*QUOTE U.S.$
2002 Totally Trent 96374 - Gene Development Team	Open		69.95	70
2001 Trent in the Fabulous Costumes of 20th Century Fox 38273 - N/A	5,000		125.00	125

Trent Osborn Costumes - Various

2001 Betting on the Ponies 38253 - D. Cipolla	Open		49.95	50
2001 Kid Valentine 38265 - The Gene Team	Open		59.95	60
2002 Playing the Field 76790 - D. Cipolla	2,002		59.95	60
2001 Royal Military 38266 - G. Sarofeen	Open		59.95	60
2001 Tennis Anyone? 38252 - V. Nowell	Open		69.95	70

Violet Waters Accessories - Various

2002 Violet's Microphone Set 93694 - D. Gibbons/Gene Development Team	Open		39.95	40

Violet Waters Costumed Dolls by Mel Odom - Various

2002 Autumn Lace 76237 - T. Kennedy	3,000		110.00	110
2002 Fascination (Retailer Exclusive) 76720 - L. Day	2,002		99.95	100
2002 Mood Indigo 76710 - J. Ferrand	3,000		99.95	100
2002 Out of the Blue 92165 - Ashton	3,750		110.00	110
2002 Swingtime Serenade 93147 - T. Kennedy	Retrd.	2002	99.95	100
2002 Torch Song 76700 - J. d' Saenz	3,000		125.00	125

Violet Waters Costumes - Various

2002 Evening Sunrise 76750 - T. Kennedy	2,002		59.95	60
2002 My Sunday Chapeau 76740 - D. Cipolla	2,002		59.95	60

Georgetown Collection, Inc./Ashton-Drake Galleries

Age of Romance - J. Reavey

1994 Catherine	Closed	1998	150.00	150

American Diary Dolls - L. Mason

1991 Bridget Quinn	Closed	1996	129.25	130
1991 Christina Merovina	Closed	1996	129.25	130
1990 Jennie Cooper	Closed	1996	129.25	130-155
1994 Lian Ying	Closed	1996	130.00	130
1991 Many Stars	Open		129.25	130
1992 Rachel Williams	Closed	1996	129.25	130
1993 Sarah Turner	Closed	1996	130.00	130
1992 Tulu	100-day		129.25	130

Baby Kisses - T. DeHetre

1992 Michelle	Closed	1996	118.60	119

Blessed Are The Children - J. Reavey

1994 Faith	Closed	2000	83.00	83

Boys Will Be Boys - J. Reavey

1996 Just Like Dad	Closed	2000	96.00	96
1994 Mr. Mischief	100-day		96.00	96
1997 Tyler	100-day		96.80	97

Caught in the Act - J. Reavey

1997 Nicholas	Closed	1998	115.00	121

Children of Main St. - G. Braun

1996 Alice	Closed	2000	130.00	130
1997 Sara	Closed	2000	131.00	131

Children of the Great Spirit - C. Theroux

1993 Buffalo Child	100-day		140.00	140
1994 Golden Flower	Closed	2000	130.00	130
1994 Little Fawn	Closed	1997	114.00	114
1993 Winter Baby	Closed	1997	160.00	160

The Christening Day - J. Reavey

1998 Jasmine	100-day		131.00	131

Class Portraits - J. Kissling

1995 Anna	Closed	1997	140.00	140

The Cottage Garden - P. Phillips

1996 Emily	Closed	2000	131.00	131

Counting Our Blessings - N/A

1998 Tama	100-day		121.00	121

YEAR ISSUE	EDITION LIMIT	YEAR RETD.	ISSUE PRICE	*QUOTE U.S.$
Country Quilt Babies - B. Prusseit				
1996 Hannah	Closed	1998	104.00	104
Cultures of the World - M. Aldred				
1998 Maya	100-day		131.00	131
Dreams Come True - M. Sirko				
1995 Amanda	Closed	1996	120.00	120
Enchanted Garden - S. Blythe				
1998 Floral Whimsies	100-day		94.50	95
Enchanted Nursery - S. Lekven				
1998 Aria	100-day		131.00	131
Faerie Princess - B. Deval				
1989 Faerie Princess	Closed	1996	248.00	248
Fanciful Dreamers - A. Timmerman				
1995 Sweetdreams & Moonbeams	Closed	1997	130.00	130
Faraway Friends - S. Skille				
1994 Dara	Closed	2000	140.00	140
1993 Kristin	Closed	1996	140.00	140
1994 Mariama	100-day		140.00	140
Favorite Friends - K. Murawska				
1997 Brittany	100-day		131.00	131
1995 Christina	100-day		130.00	130
1996 Samantha	100-day		130.00	130
Friendships of the Heart - P. Erff				
1998 Kari & Danielle	100-day		156.00	156
Fuzzy Friends - A. DiMartino				
1996 Sandy & Sam	Closed	2000	130.00	130
Georgetown Collection - Various				
1995 Buffalo Boy - C. Theroux	Open		130.00	130
1993 Quick Fox - L. Mason	Closed	1996	138.95	139
1994 Silver Moon - L. Mason	100-day		140.00	140
Gifts From Heaven - B. Prusseit				
1994 Good as Gold	Closed	1998	88.00	88
1995 Sweet Pea	Closed	2000	88.00	88
Gifts of Endearment - J. Reavey				
1997 Katie	100-day		115.00	115
Hearts in Song - J. Galperin				
1994 Angelique	100-day		150.00	150
1992 Grace	100-day		149.60	150
1993 Michael	Closed	2000	150.00	150
Heavenly Messages - M. Sirko				
1996 David	100-day		104.00	104
1995 Gabrielle	Closed	1997	104.00	104
Hidden Realms - S. Lekven				
1998 Brianna	100-day		153.50	154
A House Just For Me - G. Braun				
1998 Anne	100-day		156.00	156
I Love It - K. Murawska				
1998 Jamila	100-day		131.00	131
Irish Traditions - L. Mason				
1998 Kathleen	100-day		151.00	151
Kindergarten Kids - V. Walker				
1992 Nikki	Closed	1996	129.60	130
Let There Be Light - K. Murawska				
1997 Charlotte	100-day		130.00	130
Let's Play - T. DeHetre				
1992 Eentsy Weentsy Willie	Closed	1996	118.60	119
1992 Peek-A-Boo Beckie	Closed	1996	118.60	119
Linda's Little Ladies - L. Mason				
1993 Shannon's Holiday	Closed	1997	169.95	170
Little Artists of Africa - C. Massey				
1997 Little Ashanti Weaver	100-day		125.00	125
1996 Oluwa Fumike	Closed	2000	131.00	131
Little Bit of Heaven - A. Timmerman				
1996 Adriana	Closed	2000	135.00	135
1994 Arielle	100-day		130.00	130
1995 Cupid	Closed	2000	135.00	135
1995 Noelle	100-day		130.00	130
Little Bloomers - J. Reavey				
1995 Darling Daisy	Closed	1997	99.00	99
Little Dreamers - A. DiMartino				
1994 Beautiful Buttercup	Closed	2000	130.00	130
1995 Julie	Closed	1997	130.00	130
1996 Nicole	Closed	2000	130.00	130
Little Loves - B. Deval				
1988 Emma	Closed	1996	139.20	140
1989 Katie	Closed	1996	139.20	140
1990 Laura	Closed	1996	139.20	140
1989 Megan	Closed	1996	138.00	160
Little Performers - M. Sirko				
1996 Tickled Pink	Closed	1997	100.00	100
Little Sweethearts - J. Reavey				
1997 Melanie & Michael	Closed	2000	152.50	153
Loving Moments - J. Reavey				
1998 A Hug Just Because	Closed	2000	181.00	181
Maud Humphrey's Little Victorians - M. Humphrey				
1996 Papa's Little Sailor	Closed	2000	130.00	130
Messengers of the Great Spirit - Various				
1994 Noatak - L. Mason	Closed	2000	150.00	150
1994 Prayer for the Buffalo - C. Theroux	Closed	2000	120.00	120
Miss Ashley - P. Thompson				
1989 Miss Ashley	Closed	1996	228.00	228
Mommy's World - A. Hollis				
1996 Julia	100-day		136.00	136
Moody Cuties - L. Randolph				
1997 Cece	100-day		130.00	130
1998 Tasha	100-day		136.00	136
My Hero - C. Joniak				
1998 Matthew	Closed	2000	105.00	105
Naturally Curious Kids - A. Hollis				
1996 Jennifer	Closed	1997	100.00	100
Nursery Babies - T. DeHetre				
1990 Baby Bunting	Closed	1996	118.20	150
1991 Diddle, Diddle	Closed	1996	118.20	119
1991 Little Girl	Closed	1996	118.20	119
1990 Patty Cake	Closed	1996	118.20	119
1991 Rock-A-Bye Baby	Closed	1996	118.20	119
1991 This Little Piggy	Closed	1996	118.20	119
Nutcracker Sweethearts - S. Skille				
1995 Sugar Plum	Closed	2000	130.00	130
The Old Country - L. Mason				
1998 Elsa	100-day		136.00	136
Pictures of Innocence - J. Reavey				
1994 Clarissa	Closed	1997	135.00	135
Portraits From the Bible - T. Francirek				
1998 Madonna & Child	100-day		156.00	156
Portraits of a Perfect World - A. Timmerman				
1997 Cherry Pie	100-day		136.00	136
1998 Lemon Drop	100-day		136.00	136
1997 Orange Blossom	100-day		136.00	136
Portraits of Enchantment - A. Timmerman				
1996 Sleeping Beauty	Closed	2000	150.00	150
Portraits of Perfection - A. Timmerman				
1993 Apple Dumpling	100-day		149.60	150
1994 Blackberry Blossom	Closed	2000	149.60	150
1993 Peaches & Cream	100-day		149.60	150
1993 Sweet Strawberry	Closed	2000	149.60	150

DOLLS & PLUSH

YEAR ISSUE	EDITION LIMIT	YEAR RETD.	ISSUE PRICE	*QUOTE U.S.$
Prayers From The Heart - S. Skille				
1995 Hope	Closed	1997	115.00	115
Proud Moments - P. Erff				
1996 Chelsea	100-day		126.00	126
Reflections of Childhood - L. Mason				
1996 Courtney	Closed	1997	152.50	153
Russian Fairy Tales Dolls - B. Deval				
1993 Vasilisa	Closed	N/A	190.00	190
Small Wonders - B. Deval				
1991 Abbey	Closed	1996	97.60	98
1990 Corey	Closed	1996	97.60	98
1992 Sarah	Closed	1996	97.60	98
A Song in My Heart - J. Reavey				
1998 Caitlyn	100-day		121.00	121
Songs of Innocence - J. Reavey				
1997 Andy	Closed	2000	99.00	99
1996 Eric	Closed	2000	105.00	105
1995 Kelsey	Closed	2000	104.00	104
1996 Meagan	Closed	2000	104.00	104
Sugar & Spice - L. Mason				
1992 Little Sunshine	Closed	1996	141.10	142
1991 Little Sweetheart	Closed	1996	118.25	119
1991 Red Hot Pepper	Closed	1996	118.25	119
Sweethearts of Summer - P. Phillips				
1997 Ashley	Closed	2000	135.00	135
1994 Caroline	Closed	2000	140.00	140
1995 Jessica	Closed	2000	140.00	140
1995 Madeleine & Harry	Closed	2000	140.00	140
Sweets For the Sweet - V. Ohms				
1996 Elise	Closed	2000	130.00	130
Tansie - P. Coffer				
1988 Tansie	Closed	1996	81.00	81
Victorian Fantasies - L. Mason				
1995 Amber Afternoon	Closed	2000	150.00	150
1997 Emerald Memories	100-day		145.00	145
1995 Lavender Dreams	Closed	2000	150.00	150
1996 Reflections of Rose	Closed	2000	150.00	150
Victorian Innocence - L. Mason				
1994 Annabelle	100-day		130.00	130
Victorian Splendor - J. Reavey				
1994 Emily	100-day		130.00	130
Warm Hearts in Winter - L. Mason				
1997 Claire	100-day		145.00	145
Warm World - A. Hollis				
1997 Alison & Angus	100-day		140.00	140
The Wedding Day - S. Sauer				
1997 Elizabeth	100-day		121.00	121
What a Beautiful World - R. Hockh				
1996 Marisa	100-day		130.00	130
1996 Mora	100-day		126.00	126
1996 Therese & Tino	100-day		155.00	155
Wings of Love - L. Randolph				
1998 Angel Dreams	100-day		105.00	105
1998 Angel Hugs	100-day		105.00	105
1997 Angel Kisses	100-day		125.00	125
Yesterday's Dreams - P. Phillips				
1994 Mary Elizabeth	100-day		130.00	130
1996 Sophie	100-day		130.00	130
Goebel of North America				
Bob Timberlake Dolls - B. Ball				
1996 Abby Liz 911350	2,000	1997	195.00	195
1996 Ann 911352	2,000	1997	195.00	195
1996 Carter 911351	2,000	1997	195.00	195

YEAR ISSUE	EDITION LIMIT	YEAR RETD.	ISSUE PRICE	*QUOTE U.S.$
1996 Kate 911353	2,000	1997	195.00	195
Cindy Guyer Romance Dolls - B. Ball				
1996 Cordelia 911824	1,000	1997	225.00	225
1996 Cynthia 911830	1,000	1997	225.00	225
1996 Mackenzie 911825	1,000	1997	225.00	225
Collection of the Masters-Beloved Babies - M. Massey				
2001 Rose's Layette 823085	Open		100.00	100
Collection of the Masters-Holiday Treasures - R. Volpi				
2001 Christmas Love 823068	Open		195.00	195
2001 La Befana 823067	Open		175.00	175
2000 Millennium Santa 823018	Open		250.00	250
Collection of the Masters-Journeys of the Heart - S. Blythe				
2001 The Kiss 823079	Open		195.00	195
2001 Secrets 823078	Open		175.00	175
Collection of the Masters-Memories of Childhood - C. Malbon				
2000 Chloe 823014	Open		140.00	140
2001 Emma 823071	Open		150.00	150
2001 Jessica 823058	Open		150.00	150
2000 Mary 823016	Open		150.00	150
2000 Patricia 823015	Open		150.00	150
2001 Summer 823072	Open		150.00	150
Collection of the Masters-Nana's Family - A. Wahl				
2001 Apple Annie 823059	Open		100.00	100
2000 Belle of the Ball 823007	Open		100.00	100
2001 Elmer the Tooth Fairy 823054	Open		100.00	100
2000 The Fireman 823003	Open		100.00	100
2000 The Golfer 823004	Open		100.00	100
2001 Nana's 90th Birthday 823056	Open		100.00	100
2000 The Prayer 823005	Open		100.00	100
2001 Sid and Vera's Night on the Town 823055	Open		180.00	180
2001 Sister Cecilia of the Flowers 823053	Open		100.00	100
2000 Sisters 823006	Open		180.00	180
2001 Uncle Warren 823060	Open		100.00	100
Collection of the Masters-Reminder Angels - A. Wahl				
2000 Be Kind To Animals 823008	Open		37.50	38
2001 Call a Friend 823049	Open		37.50	38
2000 Hang in There 823009	Open		37.50	38
2001 Hug Your Cat 823047	Open		39.50	40
2001 Hug Your Dog 823048	Open		39.50	40
2001 Keep a Song in Your Heart 823052	Open		37.50	38
2000 Keep Smiling 823013	Open		37.50	38
2001 Lend an Ear 823051	Open		37.50	38
2000 One Pound at a Time 823012	Open		37.50	38
2000 Smell the Flowers 823011	Open		37.50	38
2001 Treat Yourself 823050	Open		37.50	38
2000 You're # 1 823010	Open		37.50	38
Collection of the Masters-Story Time Treasures - R. Volpi				
2001 Fairy Godmother 823070	Open		125.00	125
2001 The Sandman 823069	Open		125.00	125
Collection of the Masters-The Precious Years - J. Fischer				
2001 Angel of My Heart 823074	Open		150.00	150
2001 Red Riding Hood 823073	Open		175.00	175
Collection of the Masters-Twelve Elves of Christmas - J. & R. Craeger				
2001 Flicker 823086	Open		100.00	100
2001 Snuggles 82308	Open		100.00	100
Dolly Dingle - B. Ball				
1995 Melvis Bumps 911617	1,000	1997	99.00	99
Goebel Dolls - B. Ball				
1995 Brother Murphy 911100	2,000	1997	125.00	125
Hummel Dolls - B. Ball				
1998 Apple Tree Boy 911213	N/A		250.00	250
1998 Apple Tree Girl 911214	N/A		250.00	250
1998 Kiss Me 911216	N/A		200.00	200
1996 Little Scholar, 14" 911211	N/A		200.00	200
1997 School Girl, 14" 911212	N/A		200.00	200
Hummel Dolls - Goebel				
1998 Ride Into Christmas 911215	Open		195.00	195

Collectors' Information Bureau   *Quotes have been rounded up to nearest dollar

YEAR ISSUE	EDITION LIMIT	YEAR RETD.	ISSUE PRICE	*QUOTE U.S.$

United States Historical Society - B. Ball

YEAR ISSUE	EDITION LIMIT	YEAR RETD.	ISSUE PRICE	*QUOTE U.S.$
1995 Mary-911155	1,500	1997	195.00	195

Victoria Ashlea® Birthstone Dolls - K. Kennedy

YEAR ISSUE	EDITION LIMIT	YEAR RETD.	ISSUE PRICE	*QUOTE U.S.$
1995 January-Garnet-912471	2,500	1996	29.50	30
1995 February-Amethyst-912472	2,500	1996	29.50	30
1995 March-Aquamarine-912473	2,500	1996	29.50	30
1995 April-Diamond-912474	2,500	1996	29.50	30
1995 May-Emerald-912475	2,500	1996	29.50	30
1995 June -Lt. Amethyst-912476	2,500	1996	29.50	30
1995 July-Ruby-912477	2,500	1996	29.50	30
1995 August-Peridot-912478	2,500	1996	29.50	30
1995 September-Sapphire-912479	2,500	1996	29.50	30
1995 October-Rosestone-912480	2,500	1996	29.50	30
1995 November-Topaz-912481	2,500	1996	29.50	30
1995 December-Zircon-912482	2,500	1996	29.50	30

Victoria Ashlea® Originals - B. Ball, unless otherwise noted

YEAR ISSUE	EDITION LIMIT	YEAR RETD.	ISSUE PRICE	*QUOTE U.S.$
1985 Adele-901172	Closed	1989	145.00	275
1989 Alexa-912214	Closed	1991	195.00	195
1989 Alexandria-912273	Closed	1991	275.00	275
1990 Alice-901212	Closed	1991	95.00	135
1990 Alice-912296 - K. Kennedy	Closed	1992	65.00	65
1992 Alicia-912388	500	1994	135.00	135
1992 Allison-912358	Closed	1993	160.00	165
1987 Amanda Pouty-901209	Closed	1991	150.00	215
1988 Amanda-912246	Closed	1991	180.00	180
1993 Amanda-912409	2,000	1995	40.00	40
1984 Amelia-933006	Closed	1988	100.00	100
1990 Amie-912313 - K. Kennedy	Closed	1991	150.00	150
1990 Amy-901262	Closed	1993	110.00	110
1990 Angela-912324 - K. Kennedy	Closed	1994	130.00	135
1988 Angelica-912204	Closed	1991	150.00	150
1992 Angelica-912339	1,000	1995	145.00	145
1990 Annabelle-912278	Closed	1992	200.00	200
1988 Anne-912213	Closed	1991	130.00	150
1990 Annette-912333 - K. Kennedy	Closed	1993	85.00	85
1990 April-901239	Closed	1992	225.00	225
1989 Ashlea-901250	Closed	1992	550.00	550
1988 Ashley-901235	Closed	1991	110.00	110
1992 Ashley-911004	Closed	1994	99.00	105
1986 Ashley-912147	Closed	1989	125.00	125
1986 Baby Brook Beige Dress-912103	Closed	1989	60.00	60
1986 Baby Courtney-912124	Closed	1990	120.00	120
1988 Baby Daryl-912200	Closed	1991	85.00	85
1987 Baby Doll-912184	Closed	1990	75.00	75
1988 Baby Jennifer-912210	Closed	1992	75.00	75
1988 Baby Katie-912222	Closed	1993	70.00	70
1986 Baby Lauren Pink-912086	Closed	1991	120.00	120
1987 Baby Lindsay-912190	Closed	1990	80.00	80
1984 Barbara-901108	Closed	1987	57.00	110
1990 Baryshnicat-912298 - K. Kennedy	Closed	1991	25.00	25
1988 Bernice-901245	Closed	1991	90.00	90
1993 Beth-912430 - K. Kennedy	2,000	1996	45.00	45
1992 Betsy-912390	500	1994	150.00	150
1990 Bettina-912310	Closed	1993	100.00	105
1988 Betty Doll-912220	Closed	1993	90.00	90
1987 Bonnie Pouty-901207	Closed	1992	100.00	100
1990 Brandon-901234	Closed	1992	90.00	90
1990 Brandy-912304 - K. Kennedy	Closed	1992	150.00	150
1987 Bride Allison-901218	Closed	1993	180.00	180
1988 Brittany-912207	Closed	1990	130.00	145
1992 Brittany-912365 - K. Kennedy	Closed	1993	140.00	145
1987 Caitlin-901228	Closed	1991	260.00	260
1988 Campbell Kid-Boy-758701	Closed	1988	13.80	14
1988 Campbell Kid-Girl-758700	Closed	1988	13.80	14
1989 Candace-912288 - K. Kennedy	Closed	1992	70.00	70
1992 Carol-912387 - K. Kennedy	1,000	1996	140.00	140
1987 Caroline-912191	Closed	1990	80.00	80
1990 Carolyn-901261 - K. Kennedy	Closed	1993	200.00	200
1992 Cassandra-912355 - K. Kennedy	1,000	1996	165.00	165
1988 Cat Maude-901247	Closed	1993	85.00	85
1986 Cat/Kitty Cheerful Gr Dr-901179	Closed	1990	60.00	60
1987 Catanova-901227	Closed	1991	75.00	75
1987 Catherine-901242	Closed	1992	240.00	240
XX Charity-912244	Closed	1990	70.00	70
1982 Charleen-912094	Closed	1986	65.00	65
1985 Chauncey-912085	Closed	1988	75.00	110
1988 Christina-901229	Closed	1991	350.00	400
1987 Christine-912168	Closed	1989	75.00	75
1992 Cindy-912384	1,000	1994	185.00	190

YEAR ISSUE	EDITION LIMIT	YEAR RETD.	ISSUE PRICE	*QUOTE U.S.$
1985 Claire-901158	Closed	1988	115.00	160
1984 Claude-901032	Closed	1987	110.00	225
1984 Claudette-901033	Closed	1987	110.00	225
1989 Claudia-901257 - K. Kennedy	Closed	1993	225.00	225
1987 Clementine-901226	Closed	1991	75.00	75
1986 Clown Calypso-912104	Closed	1990	70.00	70
1985 Clown Casey-912078	Closed	1988	40.00	40
1986 Clown Cat Cadwalader-912132	Closed	1988	55.00	55
1987 Clown Champagne-912180	Closed	1989	95.00	95
1986 Clown Christabel-912095	Closed	1988	100.00	150
1985 Clown Christie-912084	Closed	1988	60.00	90
1986 Clown Clarabella-912096	Closed	1989	80.00	80
1986 Clown Clarissa-912123	Closed	1990	75.00	110
1988 Clown Cotton Candy-912199	Closed	1990	67.00	67
1986 Clown Cyd-912093	Closed	1988	70.00	70
1985 Clown Jody-912079	Closed	1988	100.00	150
1982 Clown Jolly-912181	Closed	1991	70.00	70
1986 Clown Kitten-Cleo-912133	Closed	1989	50.00	50
1986 Clown Lollipop-912127	Closed	1989	125.00	225
1984 Clown-901136	Closed	1988	90.00	120
1988 Crystal-912285	Closed	1992	75.00	75
1983 Deborah-901107	Closed	1987	220.00	400
1990 Debra-912319 - K. Kennedy	Closed	1992	120.00	120
1992 Denise-912362 - K. Kennedy	1,000	1994	145.00	175-225
1989 Diana Bride-912277	Closed	1992	180.00	180
1984 Diana-901119	Closed	1987	55.00	135
1988 Diana-912218	Closed	1992	270.00	270
1987 Dominique-901219	Closed	1991	170.00	225
1987 Doreen-912198	Closed	1990	75.00	75
1985 Dorothy-901157	Closed	1988	130.00	275
1992 Dottie-912393 - K. Kennedy	1,000	1996	160.00	160
1988 Elizabeth-901214	Closed	1990	90.00	90
1990 Ellen-901246	Closed	1991	100.00	100
1990 Emily-912303	Closed	1992	150.00	150
1988 Erin-901241	Closed	1991	170.00	170
1990 Fluffer-912293	Closed	1994	135.00	150-225
1985 Garnet-901183	Closed	1988	160.00	295
1990 Gigi-912306 - K. Kennedy	Closed	1994	150.00	150
1986 Gina-901176	Closed	1989	300.00	300
1989 Ginny-912287 - K. Kennedy	Closed	1993	140.00	140
1986 Girl Frog Freda-912105	Closed	1989	20.00	20
1988 Goldilocks-912234 - K. Kennedy	Closed	1992	65.00	65
1986 Googley German Astrid-912109	Closed	1989	60.00	60
1988 Heather-912247	Closed	1990	135.00	150
1990 Heather-912322	Closed	1992	150.00	150
1990 Heidi-901266	2,000	1995	150.00	150
1990 Helene-901249 - K. Kennedy	Closed	1991	160.00	160
1990 Helga-912337	Closed	1994	325.00	325
1984 Henri-901035	Closed	1986	100.00	200
1984 Henrietta-901036	Closed	1986	100.00	200
1992 Hilary-912353	Closed	1993	130.00	135
1992 Holly Belle-912380	500	1994	125.00	125
1982 Holly-901233	Closed	1985	160.00	200
1989 Holly-901254	Closed	1992	180.00	180
1989 Hope Baby w/ Pillow-912292	Closed	1992	110.00	110
1992 Iris-912385 - K. Kennedy	500	1995	165.00	165
1987 Jacqueline-912192	Closed	1990	80.00	80
1990 Jacqueline-912329 - K. Kennedy	Closed	1993	136.00	150-225
1984 Jamie-912061	Closed	1987	65.00	100
1984 Jeannie-901062	Closed	1987	200.00	550
1988 Jennifer-901248	Closed	1991	150.00	150
1987 Jennifer-912221	Closed	1990	80.00	80
1992 Jenny-912374 - K. Kennedy	Closed	1993	150.00	150
1988 Jesse-912231	Closed	1994	110.00	115
1987 Jessica-912195	Closed	1990	120.00	135
1993 Jessica-912410	2,000	1994	40.00	40
1990 Jillian-912323	Closed	1993	150.00	150
1989 Jimmy Baby w/ Pillow-912291 - K. Kennedy	Closed	1992	165.00	165
1989 Jingles-912271	Closed	1991	60.00	60
1990 Joanne-912307 - K. Kennedy	Closed	1991	165.00	165
1987 Joy-912155	Closed	1989	50.00	50
1989 Joy-912289 - K. Kennedy	Closed	1992	110.00	110
1987 Julia-912174	Closed	1989	80.00	80
1990 Julia-912334 - K. Kennedy	Closed	1993	85.00	85
1993 Julie-912435 - K. Kennedy	2,000	1995	45.00	45
1990 Justine-901256	Closed	1992	200.00	200
1988 Karen-912205	Closed	1991	200.00	250
1993 Katie-912412	2,000	1994	40.00	40
1993 Kaylee-912433 - K. Kennedy	2,000	1994	45.00	45
1992 Kelli-912361	1,000	1995	160.00	165

DOLLS & PLUSH

YEAR ISSUE	EDITION LIMIT	YEAR RETD.	ISSUE PRICE	*QUOTE U.S.$
1990 Kelly-912331	Closed	1991	95.00	95
1990 Kimberly-912341	1,000	1996	140.00	145
1987 Kittie Cat-912167	Closed	1989	55.00	55
1987 Kitty Cuddles-901201	Closed	1990	65.00	65
1992 Kris-912345 - K. Kennedy	Closed	1992	160.00	160
1989 Kristin-912285 - K. Kennedy	Closed	1994	90.00	95
1984 Laura-901106	Closed	1987	300.00	575
1988 Laura-912225	Closed	1991	135.00	135
1988 Lauren-912212	Closed	1991	110.00	110
1992 Lauren-912363 - K. Kennedy	1,000	1996	190.00	195
1993 Lauren-912413	2,000	1996	40.00	40
1993 Leslie-912432 - K. Kennedy	2,000	1994	45.00	45
1989 Licorice-912290	Closed	1991	75.00	75
1987 Lillian-901199	Closed	1990	85.00	100
1989 Lindsey-901263	Closed	1991	100.00	100
1989 Lisa-912275	Closed	1991	160.00	160
1989 Loni-912276	Closed	1993	125.00	150-185
1985 Lynn-912144	Closed	1988	90.00	135
1992 Margaret-912354 - K. Kennedy	1,000	1994	150.00	150
1989 Margot-912269	Closed	1991	110.00	110
1989 Maria-912265	Closed	1990	90.00	90
1982 Marie-901231	Closed	1985	95.00	95
1989 Marissa-901252 - K. Kennedy	Closed	1993	225.00	225
1988 Maritta Spanish-912224	Closed	1990	140.00	140
1992 Marjorie-912357	Closed	1993	135.00	135
1990 Marshmallow-912294 - K. Kennedy	Closed	1992	75.00	75
1985 Mary-912126	Closed	1988	60.00	90
1987 Matthew-901251	Closed	1993	100.00	100
1989 Megan-901260	Closed	1993	120.00	120
1989 Megan-912148	Closed	1989	70.00	70
1989 Melanie-912284 - K. Kennedy	Closed	1992	135.00	135
1990 Melinda-912309 - K. Kennedy	Closed	1991	70.00	70
1988 Melissa-901230	Closed	1991	110.00	110
1988 Melissa-912208	Closed	1990	125.00	125
1989 Merry-912249	Closed	1990	200.00	200
1987 Michelle-901222	Closed	1991	90.00	90
1985 Michelle-912066	Closed	1989	100.00	225
1992 Michelle-912381 - K. Kennedy	Closed	1992	175.00	175
1985 Millie-912135	Closed	1988	70.00	125
1989 Missy-912283	Closed	1993	110.00	115
1988 Molly-912211 - K. Kennedy	Closed	1992	75.00	75
1990 Monica-912336 - K. Kennedy	Closed	1993	100.00	105
1990 Monique-912335 - K. Kennedy	Closed	1993	85.00	85
1988 Morgan-912239 - K. Kennedy	Closed	1992	75.00	75
1990 Mrs. Katz-912301	Closed	1993	140.00	145
1993 Nadine-912431 - K. Kennedy	2,000	1995	45.00	45
1989 Nancy-912266	Closed	1990	110.00	110
1987 Nicole-901225	Closed	1991	575.00	575
1993 Nicole-912411	2,000	1996	40.00	40
1987 Noel-912170	Closed	1989	125.00	125
1992 Noelle-912360 - K. Kennedy	1,000	1994	165.00	170
1990 Pamela-912302	Closed	1991	95.00	95
1990 Paula-912316	Closed	1992	100.00	100
1988 Paulette-901244	Closed	1991	90.00	90
1990 Penny-912325 - K. Kennedy	Closed	1993	130.00	150-225
1986 Pepper Rust Dr/Appr-901184	Closed	1990	125.00	200
1985 Phyllis-912067	Closed	1989	60.00	60
1989 Pinky Clown-912268 - K. Kennedy	Closed	1993	70.00	75
1988 Polly-912206	Closed	1990	100.00	125
1990 Priscilla-912300	Closed	1993	185.00	190
1990 Rebecca-901258	Closed	1992	250.00	250
1988 Renae-912245	Closed	1990	120.00	120
1990 Robin-912321	Closed	1993	160.00	165
1985 Rosalind-912087	Closed	1988	145.00	225
1985 Roxanne-901174	Closed	1988	155.00	275
1984 Sabina-901155	Closed	1988	75.00	N/A
1990 Samantha-912314	Closed	1993	185.00	190
1988 Sandy-901240 - K. Kennedy	Closed	1993	115.00	115
1989 Sara-912279	Closed	1991	175.00	175
1988 Sarah w/Pillow-912219	Closed	1991	105.00	105
1987 Sarah-901220	Closed	1992	350.00	350
1993 Sarah-912408	2,000	1996	40.00	40
1993 Shannon-912434 - K. Kennedy	2,000	1996	45.00	45
1990 Sheena-912338	Closed	1992	115.00	115
1984 Sheila-912060	Closed	1988	75.00	135
1990 Sheri-912305 - K. Kennedy	Closed	1992	115.00	115
1992 Sherise-912383 - K. Kennedy	Closed	1992	145.00	145
1989 Sigrid-912282	Closed	1992	145.00	145
1988 Snow White-912235 - K. Kennedy	Closed	1992	65.00	65
1987 Sophia-912173	Closed	1989	40.00	40
1988 Stephanie-912238	Closed	1992	200.00	200
1990 Stephanie-912312	Closed	1993	150.00	150
1984 Stephanie-933012	Closed	1988	115.00	115
1988 Susan-901243	Closed	1991	100.00	100
1990 Susie-912328	Closed	1993	115.00	120
1987 Suzanne-901200	Closed	1990	85.00	100
1989 Suzanne-912286	Closed	1992	120.00	120
1989 Suzy-912295	Closed	1991	110.00	110
1992 Tamika-912382	500	1994	185.00	185
1989 Tammy-912264	Closed	1990	110.00	110
1987 Tasha-901221	Closed	1990	115.00	130
1990 Tasha-912299 - K. Kennedy	Closed	1992	25.00	25
1989 Terry-912281	Closed	1994	125.00	130
1987 Tiffany Pouty-901211	Closed	1991	120.00	160
1990 Tiffany-912326 - K. Kennedy	Closed	1992	180.00	180
1984 Tobie-912023	Closed	1987	30.00	30
1992 Toni-912367 - K. Kennedy	Closed	1993	120.00	120
1990 Tracie-912315	Closed	1993	125.00	125
1992 Trudie-912391	500	1994	135.00	135
1982 Trudy-901232	Closed	1985	100.00	100
1992 Tulip-912385 - K. Kennedy	500	1994	145.00	145
1989 Valerie-901255	Closed	1994	175.00	175
1989 Vanessa-912272	Closed	1991	110.00	110
1984 Victoria-901068	Closed	1987	200.00	1500
1992 Wendy-912330 - K. Kennedy	1,000	1995	125.00	130
1988 Whitney Blk-912232	Closed	1994	62.50	65

Victoria Ashlea® Originals-Birthday Babies - K. Kennedy

YEAR ISSUE	EDITION LIMIT	YEAR RETD.	ISSUE PRICE	*QUOTE U.S.$
1996 January-913017	2,500		30.00	30
1996 February-913018	2,500		30.00	30
1996 March-913019	2,500		30.00	30
1996 April-913020	2,500		30.00	30
1996 May-913021	2,500		30.00	30
1996 June-913022	2,500		30.00	30
1996 July-913023	2,500		30.00	30
1996 August-913024	2,500		30.00	30
1996 September-913025	2,500		30.00	30
1996 October-913026	2,500		30.00	30
1996 November-913027	2,500		30.00	30
1996 December-913028	2,500		30.00	30

Victoria Ashlea® Originals-Collectible Cats - K. Kennedy

YEAR ISSUE	EDITION LIMIT	YEAR RETD.	ISSUE PRICE	*QUOTE U.S.$
1996 Charmer-913005	2,000		39.50	40
1996 Copper-913006	2,000		39.50	40
1996 Cuddles-913007	2,000		39.50	40
1996 Fluffy-913008	2,000		39.50	40
1996 Lollipop-913009	2,000		39.50	40
1996 Mittens-913010	2,000		39.50	40
1996 Patches-913011	2,000		39.50	40
1996 Pebbles-913012	2,000		39.50	40
1996 Pepper-913013	2,000		39.50	40
1996 Ruffles-913014	2,000		39.50	40
1996 Tumbles-913015	2,000		39.50	40
1996 Whiskers-913016	2,000		39.50	40

Victoria Ashlea® Originals-Holiday Babies - K. Kennedy

YEAR ISSUE	EDITION LIMIT	YEAR RETD.	ISSUE PRICE	*QUOTE U.S.$
1996 Boo!-913001	1,000		30.00	30
1996 Happy Easter-913002	1,000		30.00	30
1996 Happy Holidays-913003	1,000		30.00	30
1996 I Love You-913004	1,000		30.00	30

Victoria Ashlea® Originals-Tiny Tot Clowns - K. Kennedy

YEAR ISSUE	EDITION LIMIT	YEAR RETD.	ISSUE PRICE	*QUOTE U.S.$
1994 Danielle-912461	2,000	1996	45.00	45
1994 Lindsey-912463	2,000	1996	45.00	45
1994 Lisa-912458	2,000	1996	45.00	45
1994 Marie-912462	2,000	1996	45.00	45
1994 Megan-912460	2,000	1996	45.00	45
1994 Stacy-912459	2,000	1996	45.00	45

Victoria Ashlea® Originals-Tiny Tot School Girls - K. Kennedy

YEAR ISSUE	EDITION LIMIT	YEAR RETD.	ISSUE PRICE	*QUOTE U.S.$
1994 Andrea- 912456	2,000	1996	47.50	48
1994 Christine- 912450	2,000	1996	47.50	48
1994 Monique- 912455	2,000	1996	47.50	48
1994 Patricia- 912453	2,000	1996	47.50	48
1994 Shawna- 912449	2,000	1996	47.50	48
1994 Susan- 912457	2,000	1996	47.50	48

Goebel/M.I. Hummel

M. I. Hummel Collectible Dolls - M. I. Hummel

YEAR ISSUE	EDITION LIMIT	YEAR RETD.	ISSUE PRICE	*QUOTE U.S.$
1964 Chimney Sweep 1908	Closed	N/A	55.00	200

YEAR ISSUE	EDITION LIMIT	YEAR RETD.	ISSUE PRICE	*QUOTE U.S.$
1964 For Father 1917	Closed	N/A	55.00	100-150
1964 Goose Girl 1914	Closed	N/A	55.00	390
1964 Gretel 1901	Closed	N/A	55.00	200
1964 Hansel 1902	Closed	N/A	55.00	200
1964 Little Knitter 1905	Closed	N/A	55.00	200
1964 Lost Stocking 1926	Closed	N/A	55.00	200
1964 Merry Wanderer 1906	Closed	N/A	55.00	200-390
1964 Merry Wanderer 1925	Closed	N/A	55.00	200-390
1964 On Secret Path 1928	Closed	N/A	55.00	200
1964 Rosa-Blue Baby 1904/B	Closed	N/A	45.00	150
1964 Rosa-Pink Baby 1904/P	Closed	N/A	45.00	150
1964 School Boy 1910	Closed	N/A	55.00	200
1964 School Girl 1909	Closed	N/A	55.00	200
1964 Visiting and Invalid 1927	Closed	N/A	55.00	200

M. I. Hummel Porcelain Dolls - M. I. Hummel

YEAR ISSUE	EDITION LIMIT	YEAR RETD.	ISSUE PRICE	*QUOTE U.S.$
1984 Birthday Serenade/Boy	Closed	N/A	225.00	300-325
1984 Birthday Serenade/Girl	Closed	N/A	225.00	300-325
1985 Carnival	Closed	N/A	225.00	300
1985 Easter Greetings	Closed	N/A	225.00	299-325
1998 Kiss Me 805	Open		200.00	200
1996 Little Scholar 522	Open		200.00	200
1985 Lost Sheep	Closed	N/A	225.00	300
1984 On Holiday	Closed	N/A	225.00	300
1984 Postman	Closed	N/A	225.00	390-520
1996 School Girl 521	Suspd.		200.00	200
1985 Signs of Spring	Closed	N/A	225.00	300

Hamilton Collection/Ashton-Drake Galleries

Abbie Williams Doll Collection - A. Williams

YEAR ISSUE	EDITION LIMIT	YEAR RETD.	ISSUE PRICE	*QUOTE U.S.$
1992 Molly	Closed	N/A	155.00	200

American Country Doll Collection - T. Tucker

1995 Carson	Closed	1997	95.00	95-150
1995 Bonnie	Closed	1997	195.00	195-295
1996 Patsy	Closed	1997	95.00	95-150
1996 Delaney	Closed	1997	95.00	95-150
1996 Arizona	Closed	1997	95.00	95-150
1996 Kendra	Closed	1997	195.00	195-295

Annual Connossieur Doll - N/A

1992 Lara	Closed	1997	295.00	295

The Antique Doll Collection - Unknown

1989 Nicole	Closed	N/A	195.00	195-300
1990 Colette	Closed	1996	195.00	195
1991 Lisette	Closed	1996	195.00	225
1991 Katrina	Closed	1996	195.00	195

Baby Portrait Dolls - B. Parker

1991 Melissa	Closed	1993	135.00	175-200
1992 Jenna	Closed	N/A	135.00	135-200
1992 Bethany	Closed	1996	135.00	150
1993 Mindy	Closed	1996	135.00	150-160

Belles of the Countryside - C. Heath Orange

1992 Erin	Closed	1997	135.00	150
1992 Rose	Closed	1997	135.00	135
1993 Lorna	Closed	1997	135.00	150
1994 Gwyn	Closed	1997	135.00	135

The Bessie Pease Gutmann Doll Collection - B.P. Gutmann

1989 Love is Blind	Closed	N/A	135.00	220
1989 He Won't Bite	Closed	N/A	135.00	135
1991 Virginia	Closed	1996	135.00	135
1991 First Dancing Lesson	Closed	1996	135.00	135
1991 Good Morning	Closed	1996	135.00	135
1991 Love At First Sight	Closed	1996	135.00	135

Best Buddies - C.M. Rolfe

1994 Jodie	Closed	1997	69.00	69-90
1994 Brandy	Closed	1997	69.00	69
1995 Joey	Closed	1997	69.00	69-100
1996 Stacey	Closed	1997	69.00	69

Boehm Christening - Boehm Studio

1994 Elena's First Portrait	Closed	1996	155.00	180-250
1994 Elena	Closed	1996	155.00	180-250

Bridal Elegance - Boehm

1994 Camille	Closed	1996	195.00	225

Bride Dolls - Unknown

YEAR ISSUE	EDITION LIMIT	YEAR RETD.	ISSUE PRICE	*QUOTE U.S.$
1991 Portrait of Innocence	Closed	1996	195.00	210
1992 Portrait of Loveliness	Closed	1996	195.00	250

Brooker Tickler - Harris/Brooker

1995 Nellie	Closed	1997	95.00	95
1996 Callie	Closed	1997	95.00	95

Brooks Wooden Dolls - P. Ryan Brooks

1993 Waiting For Santa	15,000	1994	135.00	200-250
1993 Are You the Easter Bunny?	Closed	1997	135.00	135
1994 Be My Valentine	Closed	1997	135.00	135
1995 Shh! I Only Wanna Peek	Closed	1997	135.00	135

Byi Praying Dolls - C. Byi

1996 Mark & Mary	Closed	1997	89.95	175

Catherine Mather Dolls - C. Mather

1993 Justine	Closed	1997	155.00	155-200

Central Park Skaters - Unknown

1991 Central Park Skaters	Closed	1996	245.00	245

Children To Cherish - Cybis

1991 A Gift of Innocence	Yr.Iss.	1991	135.00	135
1991 A Gift of Beauty	Closed	1996	135.00	135

A Child's Menagerie - B. Van Boxel

1993 Becky	Closed	1996	69.00	69-100
1993 Carrie	Closed	1996	69.00	69
1994 Mandy	Closed	1996	69.00	69
1994 Terry	Closed	1996	69.00	69

Ciambra - M. Ciambra

1995 Chloe	Closed	1997	155.00	135-180
1996 Lydia	Closed	1997	155.00	155

Cindy Marschner Rolfe Dolls - C.M. Rolfe

1993 Shannon	Closed	1996	95.00	95
1993 Julie	Closed	1997	95.00	95
1993 Kayla	Closed	1997	95.00	95
1994 Janey	Closed	1997	95.00	95

Cindy Marschner Rolfe Twins - C.M. Rolfe

1995 Shelby & Sydney	Closed	1996	190.00	190-210

Connie Walser Derek Baby Dolls - C.W. Derek

1990 Jessica	Closed	1993	155.00	350-500
1991 Sara	Closed	1995	155.00	200-250
1991 Andrew	Closed	1996	155.00	155-225
1991 Amanda	Closed	1996	155.00	155-180
1992 Samantha	Closed	1996	155.00	155-225

Connie Walser Derek Baby Dolls II - C.W. Derek

1992 Stephanie	Closed	1996	95.00	200
1992 Beth	Closed	1996	95.00	160

Connie Walser Derek Baby Dolls III - C.W. Derek

1994 Chelsea	Closed	1997	79.00	79
1995 Tina	Closed	1997	79.00	79
1995 Tabitha	Closed	1997	79.00	79
1995 Ginger	Closed	1997	79.00	79

Connie Walser Derek Dolls - C.W. Derek

1992 Baby Jessica	Closed	1996	75.00	75
1993 Baby Sara	Closed	1996	75.00	75

Connie Walser Derek Toddlers - C.W. Derek

1994 Jessie	Closed	1996	79.00	120
1994 Casey	Closed	1996	79.00	120
1995 Angie	Closed	1996	79.00	120
1995 Tori	Closed	1997	79.00	79

Daddy's Little Girls - M. Snyder

1992 Lindsay	Closed	1996	95.00	95
1993 Cassie	Closed	1996	95.00	95
1993 Dana	Closed	1996	95.00	120
1994 Tara	Closed	1996	95.00	95

Dey Recital Dolls - P. Dey

1996 Mallory	Closed	1997	195.00	250

Dolls by Autumn Berwick - A. Berwick

1993 Laura	Closed	1995	135.00	150

DOLLS & PLUSH

YEAR ISSUE	EDITION LIMIT	YEAR RETD.	ISSUE PRICE	*QUOTE U.S.$
Dolls By Kay McKee - K. McKee				
1992 Shy Violet	Closed	1993	135.00	300-320
1992 Robin	Closed	1995	135.00	135
1993 Katie Did It!	Closed	1995	135.00	135-150
1993 Ryan	Closed	1997	135.00	135-180
Dolls of America's Colonial Heritage - A. Elekfy				
1986 Katrina	Closed	1994	55.00	55
1986 Nicole	Closed	1994	55.00	55
1987 Maria	Closed	1994	55.00	55
1987 Priscilla	Closed	1994	55.00	55
1987 Colleen	Closed	1994	55.00	55
1988 Gretchen	Closed	1994	55.00	55
Dreamsicle Dolls - K. Haynes				
1997 Sweet Dreams Teddy	Closed	1997	49.95	50
1998 Story Time With Bunny	Closed	1997	49.95	50
Elaine Campbell Dolls - E. Campbell				
1994 Emma	Closed	1994	95.00	95-120
1995 Abby	Closed	1997	95.00	95
1995 Jana	Closed	1997	95.00	95
1995 Molly	Closed	1997	95.00	95
Eternal Friends Doll Collection - Precious Moments				
1996 Love One Another	Closed	1997	135.00	135
1997 Friendship Hits The Spot	Closed	1997	135.00	135
First Recital - N/A				
1993 Hillary	Closed	1998	135.00	135-195
1994 Olivia	Closed	1998	135.00	135
Grobben Ethnic Babies - J. Grobben				
1994 Jasmine	Closed	1996	135.00	180
1995 Taiya	Closed	1996	135.00	160-175
Grothedde Dolls - N. Grothedde				
1994 Cindy	Closed	1996	69.00	100
1995 Holly	Closed	1997	69.00	69
Hargrave Dolls - M. Hargrave				
1994 Angela	Closed	1997	79.00	79-110
1995 April	Closed	1997	79.00	79-100
Heath Babies - C. Heath Orange				
1995 Hayley	Closed	1997	95.00	95
1996 Ellie	Closed	1997	95.00	95
Heavenly Clowns Doll Collection - K. McKee				
1996 Blue Moon	Closed	1997	95.00	95
Helen Carr Dolls - H. Carr				
1994 Claudia	Closed	1997	135.00	135-185
1995 Jillian	Closed	1997	135.00	135-185
1996 Abigail	Closed	1997	135.00	135-185
1996 Rosalee	Closed	1997	135.00	135-195
Helen Kish II Dolls - H. Kish				
1992 Vanessa	Closed	1997	135.00	135-155
1994 Jordan	Closed	1997	95.00	95
Holiday Carollers - U. Lepp				
1992 Joy	Closed	1996	155.00	155
1993 Noel	Closed	1996	155.00	155
Huckleberry Hill Kids - B. Parker				
1994 Gabrielle	Closed	1997	95.00	95-125
1994 Alexandra	Closed	1997	95.00	95-135
1995 Jeremiah	Closed	1997	95.00	95-135
1996 Sarah	Closed	1997	95.00	95-135
I Love Lucy (Porcelain) - Unknown				
1990 Lucy	Closed	N/A	95.00	240-300
1991 Ricky	Closed	N/A	95.00	294-350
1992 Queen of the Gypsies	Closed	N/A	95.00	245-400
1992 Vitameatavegamin	Closed	N/A	95.00	300-400
I Love Lucy (Vinyl) - Unknown				
1988 Ethel	Closed	N/A	40.00	100
1988 Fred	Closed	N/A	40.00	100
1990 Lucy	Closed	N/A	40.00	100
1991 Ricky	Closed	N/A	40.00	150
1992 Queen of the Gypsies	Closed	1997	40.00	40
1992 Vitameatavegamin	Closed	1997	40.00	40
I'm So Proud Doll Collection - L. Cobabe				
1992 Christina	Closed	1996	95.00	95-125
1993 Jill	Closed	1996	95.00	120
1994 Tammy	Closed	1996	95.00	95-110
1994 Shelly	Closed	1996	95.00	115
Inga Manders - I. Manders				
1995 Miss Priss	Closed	1997	79.00	79
1995 Miss Hollywood	Closed	1997	79.00	79
1995 Miss Glamour	Closed	1997	79.00	79
1996 Miss Sweetheart	Closed	1997	79.00	79
International Children - C. Woodie				
1991 Miko	Closed	N/A	49.50	80
1991 Anastasia	Closed	1996	49.50	50
1991 Angelina	Closed	1996	49.50	50
1992 Lian	Closed	1996	49.50	50
1992 Monique	Closed	1996	49.50	50
1992 Lisa	Closed	1996	49.50	50
Jane Zidjunas Party Dolls - J. Zidjunas				
1991 Kelly	Closed	1994	135.00	135-150
1992 Katie	Closed	1994	135.00	135
1993 Meredith	Closed	1994	135.00	135-140
Jane Zidjunas Sleeping Dolls - J. Zidjunas				
1995 Annie	Closed	1997	79.00	79-110
1995 Jamie	Closed	1997	79.00	79-120
Jane Zidjunas Toddler Dolls - J. Zidjunas				
1991 Jennifer	Closed	1995	135.00	135
1991 Megan	Closed	1995	135.00	160
1992 Kimberly	Closed	1995	135.00	135
1992 Amy	Closed	1995	135.00	175-225
Jane Zidjunas Victorian - J. Zidjunas				
1996 Constance	Closed	1997	195.00	195-210
Jeanne Wilson Dolls - J. Wilson				
1994 Priscilla	Closed	1997	155.00	155
Join The Parade - N/A				
1992 Betsy	Closed	1996	49.50	50
1994 Peggy	Closed	1996	49.50	50
1994 Sandy	Closed	1996	49.50	50
1995 Brian	Closed	1996	49.50	50
Joke Grobben Dolls - J. Grobben				
1992 Heather	Closed	1995	69.00	69-100
1993 Kathleen	Closed	1995	69.00	69-110
1993 Brianna	Closed	1995	69.00	69-125
1994 Bridget	Closed	1995	69.00	69-125
Joke Grobben Tall Dolls - J. Grobben				
1995 Jade	Closed	1997	135.00	135-150
1996 Raven	Closed	1997	135.00	135-150
Just Like Mom - H. Kish				
1991 Ashley	Closed	1993	135.00	250-300
1992 Elizabeth	Closed	1994	135.00	160
1992 Hannah	Closed	1994	135.00	135
1993 Margaret	Closed	1994	135.00	135-145
Kay McKee Downsized Dolls - K. McKee				
1995 Kyle	Closed	1997	79.00	79
1996 Cody	Closed	1997	79.00	79
Kay McKee Klowns - K. McKee				
1993 The Dreamer	15,000	1995	155.00	155-295
1994 The Entertainer	15,000	1996	155.00	180
Kuck Fairy - S. Kuck				
1994 Tooth Fairy	Closed	1996	135.00	135
Laura Cobabe Dolls - L. Cobabe				
1992 Amber	Closed	1994	195.00	225-250
1992 Brooke	Closed	1994	195.00	195
Laura Cobabe Dolls II - L. Cobabe				
1993 Kristen	Closed	1994	75.00	75
Laura Cobabe Ethnic - L. Cobabe				
1995 Nica	Closed	1997	95.00	95-135
1996 Kenu	Closed	1997	95.00	95-135

Collectors' Information Bureau   *Quotes have been rounded up to nearest dollar

Laura Cobabe Indians - L. Cobabe

YEAR ISSUE	EDITION LIMIT	YEAR RETD.	ISSUE PRICE	*QUOTE U.S.$
1994 Snowbird	Closed	1997	135.00	155-200
1995 Little Eagle	Closed	1997	135.00	135-175
1995 Desert Bloom	Closed	1997	135.00	135-185
1996 Call of the Coyote	Closed	1997	135.00	135-175

Laura Cobabe Tall Dolls - L. Cobabe

YEAR ISSUE	EDITION LIMIT	YEAR RETD.	ISSUE PRICE	*QUOTE U.S.$
1994 Cassandra	Closed	1997	195.00	250
1994 Taylor	Closed	1997	195.00	250

Laura Cobabe's Costume Kids - L. Cobabe

YEAR ISSUE	EDITION LIMIT	YEAR RETD.	ISSUE PRICE	*QUOTE U.S.$
1994 Lil' Punkin	Closed	1996	79.00	110-125
1994 Little Ladybug	Closed	1997	79.00	79-150
1995 Miss Dinomite	Closed	1997	79.00	79-150
1995 Miss Flutterby	Closed	1997	79.00	79

Little Gardners - J. Galperin

YEAR ISSUE	EDITION LIMIT	YEAR RETD.	ISSUE PRICE	*QUOTE U.S.$
1996 Daisy	Closed	1997	95.00	95

Littlest Members of the Wedding - J. Esteban

YEAR ISSUE	EDITION LIMIT	YEAR RETD.	ISSUE PRICE	*QUOTE U.S.$
1993 Matthew & Melanie	Closed	1995	195.00	195

Lucy Dolls - Unknown

YEAR ISSUE	EDITION LIMIT	YEAR RETD.	ISSUE PRICE	*QUOTE U.S.$
1996 Lucy	Closed	1997	95.00	118-135

Maud Humphrey Bogart Dolls - Unknown

YEAR ISSUE	EDITION LIMIT	YEAR RETD.	ISSUE PRICE	*QUOTE U.S.$
1992 Playing Bridesmaid	Closed	N/A	195.00	225

Maud Humphrey Bogart Doll Collection - M.H. Bogart

YEAR ISSUE	EDITION LIMIT	YEAR RETD.	ISSUE PRICE	*QUOTE U.S.$
1989 Playing Bride	Closed	N/A	135.00	225-250
1990 First Party	Closed	N/A	135.00	150
1990 The First Lesson	Closed	N/A	135.00	149
1991 Seamstress	Closed	N/A	135.00	149
1991 Little Captive	Closed	1996	135.00	135
1992 Kitty's Bath	Closed	1996	135.00	135

Mavis Snyder Dolls - M. Snyder

YEAR ISSUE	EDITION LIMIT	YEAR RETD.	ISSUE PRICE	*QUOTE U.S.$
1994 Tara	Closed	1995	95.00	95

Parker Carousel - B. Parker

YEAR ISSUE	EDITION LIMIT	YEAR RETD.	ISSUE PRICE	*QUOTE U.S.$
1996 Annelise's Musical Ride	Closed	1997	295.00	295

Parker Fairy Tale - B. Parker

YEAR ISSUE	EDITION LIMIT	YEAR RETD.	ISSUE PRICE	*QUOTE U.S.$
1995 Claire	Closed	1997	155.00	155-185
1996 Marissa	Closed	1997	155.00	155-195

Parker Levi Toddlers - B. Parker

YEAR ISSUE	EDITION LIMIT	YEAR RETD.	ISSUE PRICE	*QUOTE U.S.$
1992 Courtney	Closed	1994	135.00	200
1992 Melody	Closed	1994	135.00	135

Parkins Baby - P. Parkins

YEAR ISSUE	EDITION LIMIT	YEAR RETD.	ISSUE PRICE	*QUOTE U.S.$
1995 Baby Alyssa	Closed	1997	225.00	225

Parkins Connisseur - P. Parkins

YEAR ISSUE	EDITION LIMIT	YEAR RETD.	ISSUE PRICE	*QUOTE U.S.$
1993 Faith	Closed	1995	135.00	180

Parkins Portraits - P. Parkins

YEAR ISSUE	EDITION LIMIT	YEAR RETD.	ISSUE PRICE	*QUOTE U.S.$
1993 Lauren	Closed	1995	79.00	110-125
1993 Kelsey	Closed	1997	79.00	79-110
1994 Morgan	Closed	1997	79.00	79-100
1994 Cassidy	Closed	1996	79.00	100

Parkins Toddler Angels - P. Parkins

YEAR ISSUE	EDITION LIMIT	YEAR RETD.	ISSUE PRICE	*QUOTE U.S.$
1996 Celeste	Closed	1997	135.00	135-225
1996 Charity	Closed	1997	135.00	108-135
1996 Charisse	Closed	1997	135.00	135-175
1996 Chantelle	Closed	1997	135.00	135-150

Parkins Treasures - P. Parkins

YEAR ISSUE	EDITION LIMIT	YEAR RETD.	ISSUE PRICE	*QUOTE U.S.$
1992 Tiffany	Closed	1994	55.00	125-135
1992 Dorothy	Closed	1995	55.00	80
1993 Charlotte	Closed	1995	55.00	80-110
1993 Cynthia	Closed	1995	55.00	80

Phyllis Parkins Dolls - P. Parkins

YEAR ISSUE	EDITION LIMIT	YEAR RETD.	ISSUE PRICE	*QUOTE U.S.$
1992 Swan Princess	9,850	1995	195.00	220-250

Phyllis Parkins II Dolls - P. Parkins

YEAR ISSUE	EDITION LIMIT	YEAR RETD.	ISSUE PRICE	*QUOTE U.S.$
1995 Dakota	Closed	1997	135.00	135-160
1996 Kerrie	Closed	1997	135.00	135
1996 Ginny	Closed	1997	135.00	135
1996 Dixie	Closed	1997	135.00	135-150

Picnic In The Park - J. Esteban

YEAR ISSUE	EDITION LIMIT	YEAR RETD.	ISSUE PRICE	*QUOTE U.S.$
1991 Rebecca	Closed	1995	155.00	155-180

YEAR ISSUE	EDITION LIMIT	YEAR RETD.	ISSUE PRICE	*QUOTE U.S.$
1992 Emily	Closed	1995	155.00	155
1992 Victoria	Closed	1995	155.00	155
1993 Benjamin	Closed	1995	155.00	155-180

Pitter Patter Doll Collection - C.W. Derek

YEAR ISSUE	EDITION LIMIT	YEAR RETD.	ISSUE PRICE	*QUOTE U.S.$
1996 Bobbie Jo	Closed	1997	79.00	79-100
1997 Mary Anne	Closed	1997	79.00	79

A Pocket Full of Love Doll Collection - S. Kuck

YEAR ISSUE	EDITION LIMIT	YEAR RETD.	ISSUE PRICE	*QUOTE U.S.$
1997 Gabriella	Closed	1997	29.95	30-55
1998 Tanya	Closed	1997	39.95	40

Precious Moments Christening - S. Butcher

YEAR ISSUE	EDITION LIMIT	YEAR RETD.	ISSUE PRICE	*QUOTE U.S.$
1996 Anna	Closed	1997	95.00	95
1996 Elise	Closed	1997	95.00	95

Proud Indian Nation - R. Swanson

YEAR ISSUE	EDITION LIMIT	YEAR RETD.	ISSUE PRICE	*QUOTE U.S.$
1992 Navajo Little One	Closed	1993	95.00	200-225
1993 Dressed Up For The Pow Wow	Closed	1996	95.00	95-150
1993 Autumn Treat	Closed	1997	95.00	115
1994 Out with Mama's Flock	Closed	1998	95.00	95-115

Rachel Cold Toddlers - R. Cold

YEAR ISSUE	EDITION LIMIT	YEAR RETD.	ISSUE PRICE	*QUOTE U.S.$
1995 Jenny	Closed	1997	95.00	95
1996 Trudy	Closed	1997	95.00	95

The Royal Beauty Dolls - Unknown

YEAR ISSUE	EDITION LIMIT	YEAR RETD.	ISSUE PRICE	*QUOTE U.S.$
1991 Chen Mai	Closed	1994	195.00	195-225

Russian Czarra Dolls - Unknown

YEAR ISSUE	EDITION LIMIT	YEAR RETD.	ISSUE PRICE	*QUOTE U.S.$
1991 Alexandra	Closed	N/A	295.00	350

Sandra Kuck Dolls - S. Kuck

YEAR ISSUE	EDITION LIMIT	YEAR RETD.	ISSUE PRICE	*QUOTE U.S.$
1993 A Kiss Goodnight	Closed	N/A	79.00	79-125
1994 Teaching Teddy	Closed	1997	79.00	79
1995 Reading With Teddy	Closed	1997	79.00	79
1996 Picnic With Teddy	Closed	N/A	79.00	79-95

Santa's Little Helpers - C.W. Derek

YEAR ISSUE	EDITION LIMIT	YEAR RETD.	ISSUE PRICE	*QUOTE U.S.$
1992 Nicholas	Closed	1996	155.00	155-250
1993 Hope	Closed	1996	155.00	155-225

Schmidt Babies - J. Schmidt

YEAR ISSUE	EDITION LIMIT	YEAR RETD.	ISSUE PRICE	*QUOTE U.S.$
1995 Baby	Closed	1997	79.00	79
1996 Snookums	Closed	1997	79.00	79

Schmidt Dolls - J. Schmidt

YEAR ISSUE	EDITION LIMIT	YEAR RETD.	ISSUE PRICE	*QUOTE U.S.$
1994 Kaitlyn	Closed	1995	79.00	120
1995 Kara	Closed	1995	79.00	79
1995 Kathy	Closed	1997	79.00	79
1996 Karla	Closed	1997	79.00	79

Schrubbe Santa Dolls - R. Schrubbe

YEAR ISSUE	EDITION LIMIT	YEAR RETD.	ISSUE PRICE	*QUOTE U.S.$
1994 Jolly Old St. Nick	Closed	1995	135.00	135-150

Sentiments From the Garden - M. Severino

YEAR ISSUE	EDITION LIMIT	YEAR RETD.	ISSUE PRICE	*QUOTE U.S.$
1996 Fairy of Innocence	Closed	1997	59.00	59
1997 Fairy of Loveliness	Closed	1997	59.00	59

Shelton II Doll - V. Shelton

YEAR ISSUE	EDITION LIMIT	YEAR RETD.	ISSUE PRICE	*QUOTE U.S.$
1996 Josie	Closed	1997	79.00	79

Shelton Indians - V. Shelton

YEAR ISSUE	EDITION LIMIT	YEAR RETD.	ISSUE PRICE	*QUOTE U.S.$
1995 Little Cloud	Closed	1997	95.00	120
1996 Little Basketweaver	Closed	1997	95.00	95-135
1996 Little Warrior	Closed	1997	95.00	95-135
1996 Little Skywatcher	Closed	1997	95.00	95-125

Songs of the Seasons Hakata Doll Collection - T. Murakami

YEAR ISSUE	EDITION LIMIT	YEAR RETD.	ISSUE PRICE	*QUOTE U.S.$
1985 Winter Song Maiden	9,800	1991	75.00	75
1985 Spring Song Maiden	9,800	1991	75.00	75
1985 Summer Song Maiden	9,800	1991	75.00	75
1985 Autumn Song Maiden	9,800	1991	75.00	75

Star Trek Doll Collection - E. Daub

YEAR ISSUE	EDITION LIMIT	YEAR RETD.	ISSUE PRICE	*QUOTE U.S.$
1988 Mr. Spock	Closed	N/A	75.00	150
1988 Captain Kirk	Closed	N/A	75.00	120
1989 Dr. Mc Coy	Closed	N/A	75.00	120
1989 Scotty	Closed	N/A	75.00	120
1990 Sulu	Closed	N/A	75.00	120
1990 Chekov	Closed	N/A	75.00	120
1991 Uhura	Closed	N/A	75.00	120

Storybook Dolls - L. Di Leo

YEAR ISSUE	EDITION LIMIT	YEAR RETD.	ISSUE PRICE	*QUOTE U.S.$
1991 Alice in Wonderland	Closed	1996	75.00	75

DOLLS & PLUSH

Through The Eyes of Virginia Turner - V. Turner

YEAR ISSUE	EDITION LIMIT	YEAR RETD.	ISSUE PRICE	*QUOTE U.S.$
1992 Michelle	Closed	1993	95.00	150-180
1992 Danielle	Closed	1997	95.00	113
1993 Wendy	Closed	1995	95.00	125
1994 Dawn	Closed	1996	95.00	95

Toddler Days Doll Collection - D. Schurig

YEAR ISSUE	EDITION LIMIT	YEAR RETD.	ISSUE PRICE	*QUOTE U.S.$
1992 Erica	Closed	1995	95.00	125
1993 Darlene	Closed	1995	95.00	95
1994 Karen	Closed	1995	95.00	95
1995 Penny	Closed	1995	95.00	95

Treasured Toddlers - V. Turner

YEAR ISSUE	EDITION LIMIT	YEAR RETD.	ISSUE PRICE	*QUOTE U.S.$
1992 Whitney	Closed	1996	95.00	200
1993 Natalie	Closed	1996	95.00	150

Vickie Walker 1st's - V. Walker

YEAR ISSUE	EDITION LIMIT	YEAR RETD.	ISSUE PRICE	*QUOTE U.S.$
1995 Leah	Closed	1998	79.00	79
1995 Leslie	Closed	1997	79.00	79
1995 Lily	Closed	1997	79.00	79
1995 Leanna	Closed	1997	79.00	79

Victorian Treasures - C.W. Derek

YEAR ISSUE	EDITION LIMIT	YEAR RETD.	ISSUE PRICE	*QUOTE U.S.$
1992 Katherine	Closed	1996	155.00	155
1993 Madeline	Closed	1996	155.00	155

Virginia Turner Dolls - V. Turner

YEAR ISSUE	EDITION LIMIT	YEAR RETD.	ISSUE PRICE	*QUOTE U.S.$
1995 Amelia	Closed	1997	95.00	95-135
1995 Mckenzie	Closed	1997	95.00	95-135
1996 Grace	Closed	1997	95.00	95-135
1996 Alexis	Closed	1997	95.00	95-135
1997 Felicia	Closed	1997	95.00	95
1997 Courtney	Closed	1997	95.00	95-135
1998 Miranda	Closed	1997	95.00	95

Virginia Turner Little Sisters - V. Turner

YEAR ISSUE	EDITION LIMIT	YEAR RETD.	ISSUE PRICE	*QUOTE U.S.$
1996 Allie	Closed	1997	95.00	95

Wooden Dolls - N/A

YEAR ISSUE	EDITION LIMIT	YEAR RETD.	ISSUE PRICE	*QUOTE U.S.$
1991 Gretchen	9,850	1995	225.00	280
1991 Heidi	9,850	1995	225.00	250

Year Round Fun - D. Schurig

YEAR ISSUE	EDITION LIMIT	YEAR RETD.	ISSUE PRICE	*QUOTE U.S.$
1992 Allison	Closed	1995	95.00	95
1993 Christy	Closed	1995	95.00	95
1993 Paula	Closed	1995	95.00	95
1994 Kaylie	Closed	1995	95.00	125

Zolan Dolls - D. Zolan

YEAR ISSUE	EDITION LIMIT	YEAR RETD.	ISSUE PRICE	*QUOTE U.S.$
1991 A Christmas Prayer	Closed	1993	95.00	250
1992 Winter Angel	Closed	1996	95.00	95-110
1992 Rainy Day Pals	Closed	1996	95.00	125
1992 Quiet Time	Closed	1996	95.00	125
1993 For You	Closed	1996	95.00	125
1993 The Thinker	Closed	1996	95.00	180

Zolan Double Dolls - D. Zolan

YEAR ISSUE	EDITION LIMIT	YEAR RETD.	ISSUE PRICE	*QUOTE U.S.$
1993 First Kiss	Closed	1995	155.00	180-295
1994 New Shoes	Closed	1995	155.00	155

Kurt S. Adler, Inc.

Fleur-dis-Lis Enchanted Garden - J. Mostrom

YEAR ISSUE	EDITION LIMIT	YEAR RETD.	ISSUE PRICE	*QUOTE U.S.$
1997 Alexandra in Plum W3340	Open		20.00	20
1998 Bethany with Flowers W3461	Retrd.	1999	21.00	21
1997 Bonnie in Ribbons W3343	Retrd.	1999	21.00	21
1997 Celeste the Garden Angel W3344	Retrd.	1997	45.00	45
1998 Jennifer Ballerina W3462	Retrd.	2000	18.00	18
1997 Jenny Lind W3336	Retrd.	1999	28.00	28
1997 Lilac Fairy W3342	Retrd.	1999	22.00	22
1997 Lily Fairy W3342	Retrd.	1999	22.00	22
1997 Marissa In Mauve W3340	Open		20.00	20
1997 Melissa in Lace W3343	Retrd.	1999	21.00	21
1998 Michael with Dog W3463	Retrd.	1999	22.00	22
1998 Monica Ballerina W3462	Retrd.	2000	18.00	18
1998 Natalie with Doll W3461	Retrd.	1999	21.00	21
1998 Pauline with Cat W3463	Retrd.	1999	22.00	22
1997 Rose Fairy W3342	Retrd.	1999	22.00	22
1998 Sarah with Present W3461	Retrd.	1999	21.00	21

Fleur-dis-Lis Sugar Plum - J. Mostrom

YEAR ISSUE	EDITION LIMIT	YEAR RETD.	ISSUE PRICE	*QUOTE U.S.$
2000 Bertie in Velvet/Natalie W3877	Retrd.	2000	20.00	20

YEAR ISSUE	EDITION LIMIT	YEAR RETD.	ISSUE PRICE	*QUOTE U.S.$
2000 Etoile with Garland/Cherie with Dove W3878	Retrd.	2000	18.00	18
2000 Sugar Plum Babies W3879	Retrd.	2001	12.50	13

Fleur-dis-Lis Victorian Manor - J. Mostrom

YEAR ISSUE	EDITION LIMIT	YEAR RETD.	ISSUE PRICE	*QUOTE U.S.$
1997 Barbara With Muff W3348	Retrd.	1997	30.00	30
1997 Caroling Jane with Book W3338	Retrd.	1997	22.00	22
1997 Jonathan with Horn W3338	Retrd.	1997	22.00	22
1997 Kathryn with Cape W3338	Retrd.	1997	22.00	22
1997 Rebecca Burgundy Skater Lady W3337	Retrd.	1999	32.00	32

Fleur-dis-Lis Victorian Valentine - J. Mostrom

YEAR ISSUE	EDITION LIMIT	YEAR RETD.	ISSUE PRICE	*QUOTE U.S.$
2000 Jenny with Teapot/Emma with Doll W3867	Retrd.	2000	25.00	25

Fleur-dis-Lis Winter Dreams - J. Mostrom

YEAR ISSUE	EDITION LIMIT	YEAR RETD.	ISSUE PRICE	*QUOTE U.S.$
1997 Charlotte with Hat & Cape W3345	Retrd.	1997	22.00	22
1997 George with Box W3345	Retrd.	1997	22.00	22
1998 Jack Frost W3483	Open		21.00	21
1998 Joshua with Sled W3485	Retrd.	1999	25.00	25
1998 Kristen with Muff W3485	Retrd.	1999	25.00	25
1998 Patricia with Snowflake W3485	Retrd.	1999	25.00	25
1997 Sandra with Box W3345	Retrd.	1997	22.00	22
1998 Snow Fairy W3483	Open		21.00	21
1998 Snowflake Babies W3482	Retrd.	2000	18.00	18

Holly Bearies - H. Adler

YEAR ISSUE	EDITION LIMIT	YEAR RETD.	ISSUE PRICE	*QUOTE U.S.$
1998 Ashton, 10" K2032	Retrd.	1998	40.00	40
1999 Brittany, 24" K2036	Retrd.	2000	67.00	67
1999 Cedric, 20" K2040	Retrd.	2000	40.00	40
1997 Charlie, 6 1/2" H6006	Retrd.	1999	11.00	11
1997 Freemont, 15" K2027	Retrd.	1999	80.00	80
1999 Happy, 17" K2039	Retrd.	2000	33.50	34
1998 Holden, 18" K2031	Retrd.	1999	50.00	50
1999 Katerina, 16" K2038	Retrd.	2000	33.50	34
1998 Merry, Merry Holly Bearie, 12" K2030	Retrd.	1999	35.00	35
1999 Stefan, 20" K2037	Retrd.	2000	50.00	50
1997 Toby, 8" K2025	Retrd.	1999	18.00	18
1999 Tyler, 9 1/2" K2041	Retrd.	2000	27.00	27
1998 Zoe, 10" K2033	Retrd.	1999	28.00	28

Royal Heritage Collection - J. Mostrom

YEAR ISSUE	EDITION LIMIT	YEAR RETD.	ISSUE PRICE	*QUOTE U.S.$
1993 Anastasia J5746	3,000	1996	125.00	125
1993 Good King Wenceslas W2928	2,000	1996	130.00	130
1993 Medieval King of Christmas W2981	2,000	1994	390.00	390
1994 Nicholas on Skates J5750	3,000	1996	120.00	120
1994 Sasha on Skates J5749	3,000	1996	130.00	130

Small Wonders - J. Mostrom

YEAR ISSUE	EDITION LIMIT	YEAR RETD.	ISSUE PRICE	*QUOTE U.S.$
1995 America-Hollie Blue W3162	Retrd.	1999	30.00	30
1995 America-Texas Tyler W3162	Retrd.	1999	30.00	30
1995 Ireland-Cathleen W3082	Retrd.	1997	28.00	28
1995 Ireland-Michael W3082	Retrd.	1997	28.00	28
1995 Kwanzaa-Mufaro W3161	Retrd.	1996	28.00	28
1995 Kwanzaa-Shani W3161	Retrd.	1996	28.00	28

When I Grow Up - J. Mostrom

YEAR ISSUE	EDITION LIMIT	YEAR RETD.	ISSUE PRICE	*QUOTE U.S.$
1995 Dr. Brown W3079	Retrd.	1996	27.00	27
1995 Freddy the Fireman W3163	Open		28.00	28
1995 Melissa the Teacher W3081	Retrd.	1996	28.00	28
1995 Nurse Nancy W3079	Retrd.	1996	27.00	27
1995 Scott the Golfer W3080	Retrd.	1996	28.00	28

Lee Middleton Original Dolls

Our Doll Family - Various

YEAR ISSUE	EDITION LIMIT	YEAR RETD.	ISSUE PRICE	*QUOTE U.S.$
1997 Bye Baby Blessed Homecoming - Lee Middleton	Retrd.	1998	175.00	175-27
1998 Bye Baby To Grandmother's House We Go - Lee Middleton	Retrd.	1999	175.00	175-27
1999 Love & Prayers - R. Schick	Retrd.	1999	190.00	190-27
2000 Dressed For The Holidays - R. Schick	Retrd.	2000	198.00	19
2000 Loving Sisters, set/2 (Convention) - R. Schick	300	2000	249.99	25
2000 Loving Sisters, African/American, set/2 (Convention) - R. Schick	300	2000	249.99	25
2001 Baby's First Tooth (Caucasian) - R. Schick	Retrd.	2001	198.00	19
2001 Baby's First Tooth (African American) - R. Schick	Retrd.	2001	198.00	19
2002 Baby & Me (Light Skin) - R. Schick	Yr.Iss.		198.00	19
2002 Baby & Me (Medium Skin) - R. Schick	Yr.Iss.		198.00	19

YEAR ISSUE	EDITION LIMIT	YEAR RETD.	ISSUE PRICE	*QUOTE U.S.$
Event Series - R. Schick				
2001 Little Mommy	Yr.Iss.	2001	250.00	250
2002 Rock A Bye	Yr.Iss.		198.00	198
Birthday Babies - Lee Middleton				
1992 Winter	Retrd.	1994	180.00	180
1992 Fall	Retrd.	1994	170.00	170
1992 Summer	Retrd.	1994	160.00	160
1992 Spring	3,000	1994	170.00	170
Birthstone Babies - R. Schick				
2002 April	Numbrd.		198.00	198
2001 June	Open		198.00	198
2001 March	Open		198.00	198
2001 October	Open		198.00	198
Bonnets and Bows - R. Schick				
2001 Gingham and Daisies	1,500		188.00	188
2001 Gingham and Stars	500		188.00	188
2001 Pink Gingham	1,500		188.00	188
Charity Piece - Reva Schick				
2000 Precious In His Sight (Baby Face)	Yr.Iss.	2000	170.00	170
2000 Precious In His Sight (Small Wonder)	Yr.Iss.	2000	170.00	170
2001 Young At Heart	Yr.Iss.	2001	198.00	198
Children of the World - R. Schick				
2001 China	1,500	2001	208.00	208
2001 Germany	2,500		208.00	208
2001 India	1,000	2001	198.00	198
2001 Japan	1,500	2001	208.00	208
2002 Kenya	2,000		208.00	208
2002 Peru	2,000		208.00	208
2001 Russia	1,500		208.00	208
2002 Thailand	2,000		208.00	208
Christening Day - Vaious				
2001 Adored - S. Housley	2,000		198.00	198
2001 Blessed - R. Schick	2,000		208.00	208
2001 Cherished - R. Schick	2,000		208.00	208
Christmas Angel Collection - Lee Middleton				
1987 Christmas Angel 1987	4,174	1987	130.00	500-600
1988 Christmas Angel 1988	8,969	1988	130.00	250-300
1989 Christmas Angel 1989	7,500	1991	150.00	225
1990 Christmas Angel 1990	5,000	1991	150.00	200
1991 Christmas Angel 1991	5,000	1992	180.00	225
1992 Christmas Angel 1992	5,000	1995	190.00	200
1993 Christmas Angel 1993-Girl	3,144	1995	190.00	200
1993 Christmas Angel 1993 (set)	1,000	1993	390.00	500
1994 Christmas Angel 1994	5,000	1996	190.00	190
1995 Christmas Angel 1995 (white or black)	3,000	1996	190.00	225
1996 Christmas Angel 1996 (Shall I Play For You)	2,000	1997	250.00	250
Collector Series Vinyl - Lee Middleton				
1999 ABC - Look At Me	2,500	1999	180.00	180
1997 Afternoon Nap-Honey Love - Awake Boy	5,000	1998	170.00	185-200
1997 Afternoon Nap-Honey Love - Awake Dark Boy	2,000	1998	170.00	185-200
1997 Afternoon Nap-Honey Love - Awake Dark Girl	2,000	1997	170.00	185-200
1997 Afternoon Nap-Honey Love - Awake Girl	5,000	1997	170.00	170-210
1997 Afternoon Nap-Honey Love - Dark Sleeping Boy	2,000	1998	170.00	140-170
1997 Afternoon Nap-Honey Love - Dark Sleeping Girl	2,000	1998	170.00	140-170
1997 Afternoon Nap-Honey Love - Sleeping Boy	5,000	1998	170.00	170-175
1997 Afternoon Nap-Honey Love - Sleeping Girl	5,000	1998	170.00	175-185
1998 All Dolled Up	5,000	1999	180.00	180
1987 Amanda - 1st Edition	3,778	1989	140.00	295
1993 Amanda Springtime	612	1994	180.00	225
1985 Angel Face	20,200	1989	90.00	150
1989 Angel Fancy	5,310	1992	120.00	195
1994 Angel Kisses Boy	Retrd.	1997	98.00	98-150
1994 Angel Kisses Girl	Retrd.	1997	98.00	98-150
1995 Angel Kisses-Belly Dancer	1,000	1995	139.00	139-165
1990 Angel Locks	8,140	1992	140.00	150
2000 Baby Beauty	2,000		184.00	184

YEAR ISSUE	EDITION LIMIT	YEAR RETD.	ISSUE PRICE	*QUOTE U.S.$
1991 Baby Grace	4,862	1991	190.00	250
1996 Beloved Bedtime Story	1,500	1997	170.00	170
1996 Beloved Good Friends	1,500	1997	180.00	180-220
1997 Beloved Sunbeams and Flowers	2,500	1997	170.00	170-235
1994 Beloved-Happy Birthday (Blue)	1,000	1995	220.00	250
1994 Beloved-Happy Birthday (Pink)	1,000	1995	220.00	250
1992 Beth	1,414	1997	160.00	160-185
1995 Beth-Flapper	1,000	1995	119.00	140-150
1995 Bethie Bows	1,000	1996	150.00	150
1995 Bethie Buttons	1,000	1996	150.00	150
1996 Bitsy Sister	1,500	1997	130.00	130-145
1998 Bo Peep	2,000	1998	170.00	180-200
1995 The Bride	1,000	1995	250.00	250
1995 The Bride (Ruby Slipper Edition)	1,000	1995	250.00	250
1991 Bubba Batboy	3,925	1994	190.00	190-200
1986 Bubba Chubbs	5,550	1988	100.00	275-350
1996 Bubba Chubbs Bubba The Kid	1,000	1997	196.00	220-250
1988 Bubba Chubbs Railroader	7,925	1994	140.00	170
1999 Bunny Boo Boy	1,500	2001	170.00	170
1999 Bunny Boo Girl	2,500	2000	180.00	180
1997 Bunny Love	5,000	1998	180.00	190-200
1999 Buttercup	2,000	2001	176.00	176
2000 Button Button	2,500	2001	176.00	176
1998 Cat Nap	2,000	1998	170.00	170
1988 Cherish	14,790	1992	160.00	250
1996 Cherish - Hug A Bug	5,000	1999	170.00	170-195
1997 Cherish Little Guy	2,500	1998	170.00	185-220
1997 Christmas Surprise Asleep Red Stocking	Retrd.	1998	180.00	140-185
1997 Christmas Surprise Asleep White Stocking	Retrd.	1998	180.00	180-185
1997 Christmas Surprise Awake Red Stocking	Retrd.	1998	180.00	185-220
1997 Christmas Surprise Awake White Stocking	Retrd.	1998	180.00	185-220
1992 Cottontop Cherish	3,525	1994	180.00	180
1994 Country Boy	Retrd.	1996	118.00	118-140
1994 Country Boy (Dark Flesh)	Retrd.	1996	118.00	118-140
1998 Country Cozy	2,500	1998	170.00	180-200
1994 Country Girl	Retrd.	1996	118.00	118-140
1994 Country Girl (Dark Flesh)	Retrd.	1996	118.00	118-140
2000 Cuddle Time	1,500	2000	184.00	184
2002 Cuddles and Quilts	Numbrd.		198.00	198
1999 Cup of Tea	2,500	1999	176.00	176-190
1986 Dear One - 1st Edition	4,935	1988	90.00	250
1991 Dear One-Sunday Best	1,371	1994	140.00	140
1989 Devan	8,336	1991	170.00	200
1991 Devan Delightful	4,520	1994	170.00	160-295
1997 Devan Happy Birthday	2,500	1998	170.00	170
1993 Echo	Retrd.	1995	180.00	180-220
1996 Echo All Dressed Up	500	1996	180.00	180
1995 Echo Little Eagle	500	1997	180.00	180-250
2000 Faith	1,000		180.00	180
1997 Feelin' Froggy	2,000	1998	180.00	160-195
1997 First Born - Awake Beauty	2,500	1997	180.00	235-250
1997 First Born - Awake Berry Sweet	2,500	1997	170.00	235
1997 First Born - Berry Sweet	2,500	1998	170.00	170
1995 First Born - My Baby Boy	1,500	1995	160.00	160
1995 First Born - Newborn Twin Boy	2,000	1996	160.00	160-180
1995 First Born - Newborn Twin Girl	2,000	1996	160.00	160-180
1996 First Born - So Snuggly	1,000	1996	170.00	190
1996 First Born - Wee One	5,000	1998	170.00	170-185
1998 First Born "Loving Memories" - Lee Middleton	1,000	1998	190.00	190
1996 First Moments - Battenburg Christening	1,000	1997	238.00	238
1995 First Moments - Lullaby Time	1,000	1996	180.00	180
1996 First Moments - Toot Sweet	5,000	1998	170.00	170-200
1990 Forever Cherish	5,000	1991	170.00	200
2000 Garden Party	1,000		180.00	180
1995 Gordon-Growing Up	1,000	1995	220.00	220
1996 Grace Fresh As A Daisy	300	1996	176.00	176-200
1995 Grace-Growing Up	1,000	1995	220.00	220
1992 Gracie Mae (Blond Hair)	3,660	1995	250.00	250
1992 Gracie Mae (Brown Hair)	2,551	1994	250.00	250
1993 Gracie Mae (Red Velvet)	100	1993	250.00	250
1997 Heaven Sent Asleep	7,500	1998	180.00	180
1997 Heaven Sent Awake	7,500	1999	180.00	190-235
1999 Heavenly	Yr.Iss.	1999	200.00	200-235
1997 Hershey's Baker Girl	Retrd.	1997	130.00	130-165
1996 Hershey's Cake Kids Set (2)	Retrd.	1997	220.00	220-235

DOLLS & PLUSH

YEAR ISSUE	EDITION LIMIT	YEAR RETD.	ISSUE PRICE	*QUOTE U.S.$
1996 Hershey's Chocolate Soldier	Retrd.	1997	130.00	130-165
1995 Hershey's Kisses - Gold	Retrd.	1996	99.50	130
1996 Hershey's Kisses - Green	Retrd.	1996	199.00	200
1996 Hershey's Kisses - Red	Retrd.	1996	199.00	200
1994 Hershey's Kisses - Silver	Retrd.	1997	99.50	140-150
1999 I Love You Beary Much	1,000	1999	180.00	180
1996 Joey Go Bye Bye	1,000	1999	190.00	190
1994 Joey-Newborn	1,000	1995	180.00	180
1991 Johanna	1,388	1994	190.00	250
1994 Johanna-Newborn	2,000	1994	180.00	180
1986 Little Angel - 3rd Edition	15,158	1992	90.00	110
1992 Little Angel Boy	Retrd.	1997	130.00	150
1992 Little Angel Girl	Retrd.	1997	130.00	150
1997 Little Angel Wish Finders Star Bright	Retrd.	1997	120.00	120-140
1997 Little Angel Wish Finders Twinkle Twinkle	Retrd.	1997	120.00	120-140
1995 Little Angel-Ballerina	1,000	1995	119.00	119-140
1985 Little Angel-King-2 (Hand Painted)	Retrd.	1985	40.00	200
1981 Little Angel-Kingdom (Hand Painted)	Retrd.	1981	40.00	300
1998 Little Big Guy	2,500	1999	180.00	185-210
2000 Little Blessings	Retrd.	2001	200.00	200
1995 Little Blessings Awake Boy	1,000	1995	180.00	180
1995 Little Blessings Awake Girl	1,000	1995	180.00	180
1995 Little Blessings Blessed Event	1,500	1995	190.00	190
1996 Little Blessings Cuddle Up	1,000	1997	180.00	180-225
1996 Little Blessings Newborn Twins Awake Boy	1,500	1996	180.00	180
1996 Little Blessings Newborn Twins Awake Girl	1,500	1996	180.00	180
1996 Little Blessings Newborn Twins Sleeping Boy	1,000	1996	180.00	180
1996 Little Blessings Newborn Twins Sleeping Girl	1,000	1996	180.00	180
1995 Little Blessings Pretty in Pink	1,500	1997	190.00	190
1997 Little Blessings Ships Ahoy	2,500	1998	170.00	170-175
1995 Little Blessings Sleeping Boy	1,000	1995	180.00	180
1995 Little Blessings Sleeping Girl	1,000	1995	180.00	180
1998 Little Boy Blue	2,000	1999	170.00	170
1999 Little Friends	2,000	2001	180.00	180
1996 Little Love - Cuddle Bumps	5,000	1998	170.00	170-175
1997 Little Love - Peek A Boo Boy	2,500	1998	170.00	170-175
1997 Little Love - Peek A Boo Girl	2,500	1998	170.00	170-175
1996 Little Love - Such A Good Boy	1,000	1996	160.00	190
1995 Little Love - Violets	1,500	1995	160.00	160
1998 Little Patty Cake	2,800	1998	170.00	170
1998 Little Playmate	2,000	1998	170.00	170-180
1999 Loving Memories	1,000	1999	180.00	180
1998 Loving Tribute	Yr.Iss.	1999	220.00	240-250
1997 Lullaby Baby Boy	5,000	1998	180.00	180-200
1997 Lullaby Baby Girl	5,000	1997	180.00	180-200
1998 Mary Mary	2,000	1999	170.00	170-185
1987 Missy	11,855	1991	100.00	120
1991 Missy- Buttercup	4,748	1994	160.00	200
1992 Molly Rose	2,981	1994	196.00	196
1996 Molly Rose Good Friends	1,500	1997	180.00	180-235
1996 My Darling Boy	2,000	1998	170.00	170
1996 My Darling Girl	2,000	1998	170.00	170-185
1989 My Lee	3,794	1991	170.00	275
1991 My Lee Candy Cane	2,240	1994	170.00	295
1993 Patty	4,000	1995	49.00	49
1998 Patty Cake	2,000	1999	170.00	170-185
1997 Picture Perfect	7,500	1999	190.00	190-220
1992 Polly Esther	2,137	1994	160.00	160
1996 Polly Esther - Hershey's Country Girl	Retrd.	1997	130.00	150-165
1995 Polly Esther "Sock Hop"	1,000	1995	119.00	150-165
2000 Pretty As A Rose	1,500		176.00	176
1996 Pretty Baby Sister	1,500	1997	170.00	170-195
1998 Proud Heritage/Boy	2,000	2000	164.00	164
1998 Proud Heritage/Girl	2,000	2000	164.00	164
1998 Quiet As A Mouse	Yr.Iss.	1999	180.00	180
1998 Santa's Little Helper/Boy	Yr.Iss.	1998	180.00	198-220
1998 Santa's Little Helper/Girl	Yr.Iss.	1998	180.00	198-220
1992 Serenity Berries & Bows	458	1993	250.00	250
2000 She's So Pretty	1,500		180.00	180
1988 Sincerity - Limited 1st Ed. - Nettie/Simplicity	3,711	1989	160.00	200-250
1992 Sincerity Petals & Plums	414	1993	250.00	250
1991 Sincerity-Apples n' Spice	1,608	1993	250.00	250
1991 Sincerity-Apricots n' Cream	1,789	1993	250.00	250
1989 Sincerity-Schoolgirl	6,622	1992	180.00	295
1998 Slumber Kisses	1,000	1998	170.00	170

YEAR ISSUE	EDITION LIMIT	YEAR RETD.	ISSUE PRICE	*QUOTE U.S.$
1999 Snow Bunny (African American Boy)	1,000	2000	170.00	170
1999 Snow Bunny (African American Girl)	1,500	2000	170.00	170
1999 Snow Bunny (Caucasian Boy)	2,000	2000	170.00	170
1999 Snow Bunny (Caucasian Girl)	2,000	2000	170.00	170
1998 Softly Sleeping	2,000	1999	164.00	164-175
1998 Starry Night	2,500	1999	170.00	170-175
1997 Summerfun - Asleep Boy	5,000	1998	170.00	170-175
1997 Summerfun - Asleep Dark Boy	2,000	1998	170.00	170-175
1997 Summerfun - Asleep Dark Girl	2,000	1998	170.00	170-175
1997 Summerfun - Asleep Girl	5,000	1999	170.00	170-175
1997 Summerfun - Awake Boy	5,000	1998	170.00	175-185
1997 Summerfun - Awake Dark Boy	2,000	1998	170.00	175-185
1997 Summerfun - Awake Dark Girl	2,000	1999	170.00	180-185
1997 Summerfun - Awake Girl	5,000	1998	170.00	180-190
1999 Sweet Baby Boy	3,000	2000	180.00	180
2000 Sweet Christening	Yr.Iss.	2000	224.00	224
1982 Sweet Dreams	Retrd.	1994	39.00	39
2000 Sweet Memories	Yr.Iss.	2000	220.00	220
1995 Sweetness-Newborn	Retrd.	1995	190.00	190
2000 Tender Moments	1,500		170.00	170
1995 Tenderness French BeBe	1,500	1997	220.00	235-250
1996 Tenderness So Brave	1,500	1997	170.00	190-220
1998 Touch of Velvet	2,500	1999	180.00	180-210
1998 Tough Guy	1,000	1999	170.00	170
1994 Town Boy	Retrd.	1995	118.00	118-140
1994 Town Boy (Dark Flesh)	Retrd.	1995	118.00	118-140
1994 Town Girl	Retrd.	1995	118.00	118-140
1994 Town Girl (Dark Flesh)	Retrd.	1995	118.00	118-140
1997 Treasured Traditions	5,000	1998	170.00	170-195
1998 Warm & Cozy	350	1998	150.00	150
1998 Wee Willie Winkie	2,000	1999	170.00	170-200
1996 Young Lady Bride in White Satin	1,000	1997	250.00	250

Collector Series Vinyl - Reva Schick, unless otherwise noted

YEAR ISSUE	EDITION LIMIT	YEAR RETD.	ISSUE PRICE	*QUOTE U.S.$
2002 Ace	2,000		188.00	188
2001 Adorable	2,500		188.00	188
2000 All Star	1,000	2000	184.00	184
1999 Angel Baby	2,000	2001	180.00	180
2000 Angel Bear (African-American)	1,000	2000	184.00	184
2000 Angel Bear (Caucasian)	2,500	2000	184.00	184
1998 Angel Love	2,000	1998	180.00	185-195
2001 Animal Parade	1-day		198.00	198
1999 Apple Dumpling	3,000	2000	176.00	176
2001 B is for Bear	1,500		188.00	188
2000 Baby Blue	1,000	2000	180.00	180
2001 Baby Boo - E. Helland	1,500	2001	198.00	198
2000 Baby Bows	1,500	2000	170.00	170
1999 Baby Dreams (African American)	2,000		170.00	170
1999 Baby Dreams (Caucasian)	2,000		170.00	170
2000 Baby Girl	1,000	2001	184.00	184
1998 Baby Mine	2,000	1999	164.00	164
1999 Baby Sister	2,500	1999	180.00	180
1999 Baby's First Christmas	1,000	1999	184.00	190-195
2001 Balloons & Bears	1,500		188.00	188
2000 Be My Baby	2,500		184.00	184
1998 Bear Hug/Boy	1,000	1998	180.00	190-210
1998 Bear Hug/Girl	1,000	1998	180.00	190-210
1999 Beary Cute Boy	5,000	2000	180.00	180
1999 Beary Cute Girl	5,000	2000	180.00	180
2000 Beary Precious	1,500	2000	194.00	194
2000 Bedtime Babies Boy	1,500	2000	180.00	180
2000 Bedtime Babies Girl	2,000	2000	180.00	180
2000 Being Good	2,500	2000	190.00	190
2000 Best Buddies	1,000	2000	180.00	180
2001 Best Friend Bear	Yr.Iss.	2001	198.00	198
2000 Bundle of Love	1,000	2000	170.00	170
1998 Bunny Dreams	2,000	1998	180.00	180-200
2000 Bunny Hop	1,500	2000	180.00	180
2000 Butterfly Kisses	Yr.Iss.	2000	190.00	190
2000 By Gone Days Boy	1,000	2000	180.00	180
2000 By Gone Days Girl	1,000	2001	180.00	180
1999 Cat Bird	2,500	2000	180.00	180
1998 Cherry Blossom	2,000	1998	180.00	199-220
2001 Cookies and Milk - S. Housley	2,500		188.00	188
1999 Cotton Candy	5,000	2000	176.00	176
2002 Cotton Tails	Numbrd.		198.00	198
2002 Country Charm	1-week		224.00	224
1998 Cuddle Cub	2,500	2000	190.00	190
2000 Cute As Can Bee	2,500	2000	180.00	180
2000 Cutie Pie	2,000		180.00	180
1999 Daisy Daisy	5,000	2000	180.00	180

*Quotes have been rounded up to nearest dollar

YEAR ISSUE	EDITION LIMIT	YEAR RETD.	ISSUE PRICE	*QUOTE U.S.$
2001 Daisy Time	1,500	2001	198.00	198
1999 Doggone Cute Boy	2,000	1999	184.00	184
1999 Doggone Cute Girl	3,000	2000	184.00	184
2000 Dolly & Me	Yr.Iss.		180.00	180
1998 Fine & Frilly	2,000	1998	174.00	185-220
1998 Forever Friend/Boy	1,500	1999	170.00	170-190
1998 Forever Friend/Girl	2,500	1998	170.00	170
2002 The Forties	2,000		198.00	198
1998 Friends Forever	1,500	1999	160.00	160
1998 Frilly & Fancy	1,000	1998	190.00	190
1999 From The Heart	2,500	1999	180.00	180
2001 Fun At The Zoo	1,500		198.00	198
2000 Fun In The Sun	1,000	2000	180.00	180
2001 Fun on the Slopes	1,500	2001	198.00	198
2000 Fuzzy Wuzzy	2,000	2001	184.00	184
2'1 Garden Time - M. Snyder	1,000		188.00	188
1998 Gimme a Hug	2,000	1998	180.00	180
2001 Going to a Party	1,500	1999	190.00	190
2001 Golden Girl	2,500		198.00	198
1998 Grandmother's Dream	2,500	1999	198.00	198
2000 Growing Up	Retrd.	2000	210.00	210
2002 Happy Birthday Teddy	Numbrd.		208.00	208
1998 Hearts & Flowers	2,000	1999	170.00	170-220
2000 Hearts Desire	2,000		180.00	180
2001 Here Kitty Kitty - S. Housley	2,000		194.00	194
2001 Home Tweet Home - L. Henry	2,500		188.00	188
1999 Honey Pie	3,000	2000	180.00	180
1999 Hugs & Kisses	5,000	2000	180.00	180
1998 Hunny Bunny	2,500	1999	190.00	190
2001 I Love America, Boy	1,500	2001	188.00	188
2001 I Love America, Girl	1,500		198.00	198
2001 I Love Snow	1,500	2000	194.00	194
2001 I Love Violets	2,500		198.00	198
2001 I Love You	2,500		188.00	188
1999 I Love You Beary Much	1,000	1999	180.00	180
1999 I Wanna Play Baseball	2,000	2001	190.00	190
1999 I Wanna Play Basketball	2,000	2001	190.00	190
1999 I Wanna Play Football	2,000	2000	190.00	190
2000 I'm a Big Girl Now	1,500		184.00	184
1999 I'm A Little Angel	2,000	1999	180.00	180-200
1999 I'm So Special	5,000		190.00	190
2000 I'm This Big - M. Snyder	2,000		184.00	184
1998 In The Pink	2,000	1998	180.00	210-225
2001 Irish Eyes - M. Snyder	1,500		198.00	198
2000 Irresistible	1,500	2000	190.00	190
2002 Isn't It Fun?	1-day		198.00	198
1999 Jitterbug	1,500		176.00	176
1999 Just Ducky	3,000	1999	190.00	200-235
2002 Just For Kicks	2,000		188.00	188
2000 Just So Sweet	2,000		180.00	180
2000 Lambie Pie	1,500	2000	194.00	194
2002 Lavender Love	1,000		198.00	198
2001 Leaping Lambs	1,000	2001	188.00	188
1999 Let It Rain Boy	2,000	1999	184.00	184-235
1999 Let It Rain Girl	2,000	1999	184.00	184-235
2000 Let It Snow	1,500	2000	184.00	184
2002 Let's Go Sailing (Light)	1,000		188.00	188
2002 Let's Go Sailing (Medium)	1,000		188.00	188
2001 Let's Play	1,500		198.00	198
2000 Li'l Snowball - M. Snyder	2,000	2000	184.00	184
1999 Lions & Tigers & Bears	2,000	2000	170.00	170
2001 Little Baby Girl - E. Helland	1,500	2001	198.00	198
1999 Little Ballerina, green	1,000	1999	180.00	180
1999 Little Ballerina, pink	1,000	1999	180.00	180
1999 Little Ballerina, yellow	1,500	2000	180.00	180
1999 Little Beauty	2,000	2000	170.00	170
1999 Little Blue Eyes	2,500	1999	180.00	180
1998 Little Chickadee	2,000	1998	180.00	185-225
2001 Little Co-Pilot	1,000		188.00	188
1999 Little Cowboy	1,500	2000	190.00	190
2002 Little Fishies (Light) - E. Helland	1,800		198.00	198
2002 Little Fishies (Medium) - E. Helland	1,000		198.00	198
2002 Little Kitten	2,500		188.00	188
2000 Little Lullaby	1,000		184.00	184
1998 Little Peanut	2,500	1998	180.00	190-225
2001 Little Pilot	1,000	2001	188.00	188
1999 Little Princess (African)	Open		198.00	198
1999 Little Princess (Caucasian)	Open		198.00	198
1999 Little Princess (Hispanic)	Retrd.	2000	198.00	198
2001 Little Rose	2,500		188.00	188
1998 Little Scottie/Boy	1,000	1999	180.00	190-210
1998 Little Scottie/Girl	1,500	1998	180.00	190-210
2001 Little Skater	1,500	2001	188.00	188
2000 Little Sunbeam	2,500	2001	180.00	180
1999 Little Sweetheart	5,000		194.00	194
2000 Little Sweetie	1,500	2001	184.00	184
2000 Little Treasure	2,500		184.00	184
2000 Look What I Found	2,500	2000	180.00	180
1999 Love Bug Boy	1,500	2000	176.00	176
1999 Love Bug Girl	2,500	2000	176.00	176
1999 Love in Bloom	3,000	2000	190.00	190
2002 Love Makes The World Go Round (Dark)	Numbrd.		198.00	198
2002 Love Makes The World Go Round (Light)	Numbrd.		198.00	198
2001 Lovin' Bundle	2,500		198.00	198
1999 Lovin' Gingerbread Boy	3,000		170.00	170
1999 Lovin' Gingerbread Girl	3,000		180.00	180
1999 Lovin' Stuff	2,500	1999	194.00	194
1999 Lucky Ducky	Yr.Iss.	2000	180.00	180
1999 Mittens Mittens	3,000	2000	190.00	190
1999 Mommy's Good Girl	Retrd.	2000	180.00	200
2002 My Little Lamb	2,500		188.00	188
1998 Oops A Daisy	2,000	1999	174.00	195-200
2000 Party Time	1,000	2000	194.00	194
2002 Perfect Baby Girl - E. Helland	Numbrd.		198.00	198
2001 Pigtails and Kites - S. Housley	1,000		198.00	198
1998 Pink & Playful	1,000	1998	190.00	190
1998 Playtime Boy	2,500	1999	140.00	140
1998 Playtime Girl	2,500	1999	140.00	140
2000 Polar Baby	1,500	2000	184.00	184
2000 Pretty as a Picture	1,500		194.00	194
1999 Proud Heritage Boy	1,000	2000	170.00	170
1999 Proud Heritage Girl	1,000	2000	170.00	170
1998 Puppy Love	2,500	1999	190.00	190-200
2002 Puppy Play (Dark)	1,000		180.00	180
2002 Puppy Play (Light)	1,000		188.00	188
2000 Rainy Day Play - S. Housley	1,000	2000	194.00	194
2001 Rattle Time	2,500	2001	188.00	188
2001 Ready for Bed	2,000	2001	198.00	198
2000 Ready To Go	2,000	2000	190.00	190
1999 Ready to Play	3,000	1999	176.00	176
2001 Recital Day	2,500		208.00	208
2000 Ribbons & Lace	1,000		184.00	184
1999 Roses, Lace & Love	3,000	2000	180.00	180
2000 Rosy	2,000	2000	184.00	184
1999 Say Cheese	3,000	2000	190.00	190
1998 Scottie Girl	1,500	1999	180.00	180
2001 She's So Sweet	1-day	2001	198.00	198
2000 Simply Sweet	3,000		184.00	184
1999 Sitting Pretty	2,500		170.00	170
1999 Snips & Snails	1,500		180.00	180
1998 Snoozy Bear	2,500	1999	190.00	190-200
1998 Snow Baby	1,000	1998	170.00	225-235
1998 Soft & Innocent	2,500	1999	180.00	180
2000 Soft & Sweet	1,000	2001	184.00	184
2001 Special Gift - L. Henry	Yr.Iss.	2001	198.00	198
2000 Special Occasion	1,000	2001	200.00	200
1999 Spring Bouquet (green)	1,500		176.00	176
1999 Spring Bouquet (pink)	2,000		176.00	176
1999 Spring Bouquet (white)	3,000	1999	176.00	176-195
1999 Spring Bouquet (yellow)	2,000	2000	176.00	176
2000 Spring in Bloom	1,500	2000	184.00	184
2001 Spring Time Beauty	Yr.Iss.	2001	198.00	198
2001 Springtime	1,000	2001	198.00	198
2000 Springtime Stroll	2,500		184.00	184
1998 Star Struck	2,000	1999	170.00	170
1999 Sugar & Spice	1,500	2000	180.00	180
1998 Sugar Plum	2,000	1999	170.00	180-200
2002 Sunflower - M. Snyder	1,800		188.00	188
1998 Surprise	2,500	2001	180.00	180
2000 Sweet as a Sonnet - S. Housley	1,000		184.00	184
2001 Sweet as Candy	2,000		198.00	198
1998 Sweet Blue Birdie	1,000	2000	184.00	184
2000 Sweet Flower	1,000	2000	184.00	184
1999 Sweet Pea	1,000		188.00	188
2000 Sweet Sis	1,500	2000	170.00	170
1998 Sweetheart Boy	2,500	1999	180.00	180
1998 Sweetheart Girl	2,500	1999	180.00	185-200
1999 Sweetly Sailing, Boy	2,000		170.00	170
1999 Sweetly Sailing, Girl	3,000		170.00	170
1999 Sweetly Sailing, Hispanic Boy	1,500		170.00	170

YEAR ISSUE	EDITION LIMIT	YEAR RETD.	ISSUE PRICE	*QUOTE U.S.$
1999 Sweetly Sailing, Hispanic Girl	2,000		170.00	170
2000 Take Me Home	1,500		194.00	194
2001 Tea Time	1,500		198.00	198
2002 Teddy Bear Tales - L. Henry Boving	1,500		188.00	188
2000 Teddy Poo - S. Housley	2,000	2000	184.00	184
2000 That's My Girl	1,000	2000	180.00	180
2002 The Thirties	2,000		198.00	198
2000 Timeless Beauty	1,000		200.00	200
2000 True Pals	Yr.Iss.	2000	190.00	190
2002 Tulip	1,800		188.00	188
2000 Tumbling Teddies	2,500	2000	184.00	184
2001 Two by Two	2,500	2001	188.00	188
1998 Two Cute/Boy	2,500	1999	180.00	180-235
1998 Two Cute/Girl	2,500	1998	180.00	185-285
2000 Up, Up & Away	2,000		184.00	184
2001 Walk in the Park	1-week	2001	224.00	224
1999 Warm & Cuddly	3,000	2000	190.00	190
2002 Watch Me Go - E. Helland	1,800		196.00	196
2001 Winder Wonder	2,500		188.00	188
2002 Wish Upon a Star (Light)	1,000		188.00	188
2002 Wish Upon a Star (Medium)	1,800		188.00	188
1998 Yesterday's Dream/ Boy	1,500	1998	184.00	184-190
1998 Yesterday's Dream/ Girl	2,500	1999	184.00	184

Collectors' Choice Series - Reva Schick

2002 Our Pride & Joy (Light Skin)	Yr.Iss.		198.00	198
2002 Our Pride & Joy (Medium Skin)	Yr.Iss.		198.00	198

Designer Darlings - R. Schick

2001 Leopard Print	Yr.Iss.	2001	188.00	188
2001 Zebra Print	Yr.Iss.	2001	188.00	188

Elegant Edition Series - Reva Schick, unless otherwise noted

2001 Alexis	750	2001	350.00	350
2002 Alison - E. Helland	750		350.00	350
2000 Chloe	500	2000	350.00	350
2001 Elizabeth	750	2001	350.00	350
2001 Hannah	750	2001	350.00	350
2001 Maia	500	2001	500.00	500
2001 Olivia	750	2001	350.00	350
2001 Rebekah - E. Helland	750	2001	350.00	350
2002 Susannah	750		350.00	350
2002 Tessa	750		350.00	350
2000 Victoria	500	2000	350.00	350

Faces of America - R. Schick

2002 Irish Child	2,000		208.00	208
2002 Italian Girl	1,800		208.00	208
2002 Native American Baby	2,500		208.00	208

Faith, Hope, Love - L. Middleton

2001 Hope	1,000		180.00	180
2001 Love	1,000		180.00	180

FAO Exclusive - Reva Schick

1999 Baby Love	1,000	2000	170.00	170
2000 First Recital	Yr.Iss.	2000	180.00	180
2000 Sweet Angel	1,000	2000	170.00	170
2000 Our Little Sweetie	Yr.Iss.	2000	180.00	180
2001 Baby Soft	1,000		190.00	190
2001 Pretty Girl	1,000		190.00	190

Farmer in the Dell - R. Schick

2001 Duck	1,500		188.00	188
2001 Farmer	1,500		188.00	188
2001 Pig	1,500		188.00	188

Fifties Series - Lee Middleton

1996 Angel Kisses Earth Angel	1,500	1997	130.00	130-140
1996 Angel Kisses Splish Splash	1,500	1997	130.00	130-140
1996 Little Angel Leader of the Pack	1,500	1997	130.00	130-160
1996 Polly Esther Car Hop	1,500	1997	130.00	130-160
1996 Polly Esther Peggy Sue	1,500	1997	130.00	130-150

First Collectibles - Lee Middleton

1990 Sweetest Little Dreamer (Asleep)	Retrd.	1993	40.00	40-59
1990 Day Dreamer (Awake)	Retrd.	1993	42.00	42-59
1991 Day Dreamer Sunshine	Retrd.	1993	49.00	49
1991 Teenie	Retrd.	1993	59.00	59

First Moments Series - Lee Middleton

1984 First Moments (Sleeping)	40,861	1990	69.00	300

YEAR ISSUE	EDITION LIMIT	YEAR RETD.	ISSUE PRICE	*QUOTE U.S.$
1992 First Moments Awake in Blue	1,230	1994	170.00	170-235
1992 First Moments Awake in Pink	856	1994	170.00	170
1986 First Moments Blue Eyes	14,494	1990	120.00	120-150
1987 First Moments Boy	6,075	1989	130.00	130-160
1986 First Moments Brown Eyes	5,324	1989	120.00	120-150
1987 First Moments Christening (Asleep)	9,377	1992	160.00	160-250
1987 First Moments Christening (Awake)	16,384	1992	160.00	160-180
1993 First Moments Heirloom	1,372	1995	190.00	190
1991 First Moments Sweetness	6,323	1995	180.00	180
1990 First Moments Twin Boy	2,971	1991	180.00	180
1990 First Moments Twin Girl	2,544	1991	180.00	180
1994 Sweetness-Newborn	Retrd.	1995	190.00	190

Furry and Fun - R. Schick

2001 Bear	1,500		188.00	188
2001 Kitty	1,500		188.00	188
2001 Lamb	1,500		188.00	188

Home Shopping Network Series - Lee Middleton

1996 Bye Baby Bundle of Joy	2,000	1996	129.00	129
1996 Cherish Ribbons and Bows	2,000	1996	129.00	129
1997 Cherish Sleeping Angels	2,000	1997	129.00	129
1996 First Born Dark Precious Baby Girl	1,000	1996	129.00	129
1997 First Born Dark Snug As A Bug	1,000	1997	129.00	129
1996 First Born Gingham and Lace	2,000	1996	129.00	129
1996 First Born Katie	2,000	1996	129.00	129
1997 First Born Mother's Dream	2,000	1997	129.00	129
1997 First Born Open Eye Bed of Roses	2,000	1997	129.00	129
1997 First Born Open Eye Dark Snug As A Bug	1,000	1997	129.00	129
1997 First Born Open Eye Precious Traditions	2,000	1997	129.00	129
1996 First Moments Open Eye Baseball Boy	2,000	1996	129.00	129
1997 Honey Love Answered Prayer Boy	2,000	1997	129.00	129
1997 Honey Love Answered Prayer Girl	2,000	1997	129.00	129
1997 Honey Love Dark Baby's Sleeping	1,000	1997	129.00	129
1997 Honey Love Open Eye Little Peep	2,000	1997	129.00	129
1996 Little Blessing Awake Grandma's Little Boy	2,000	1996	129.00	129
1997 Little Blessing Open Eye Bundle Up Boy	2,000	1997	129.00	129
1997 Little Blessing Open Eye Bundle Up Girl	2,000	1997	129.00	129
1997 Little Blessing Open Eye Mother's Little Sweetheart (blue)	2,000	1997	129.00	129
1997 Little Blessing Open Eye Mother's Little Sweetheart (pink)	2,000	1997	129.00	129
1997 Little Love Baby Brother	2,000	1997	129.00	129
1997 Little Love Baby Sister	2,000	1997	129.00	129
1996 Little Love Baby's First Book	2,000	1996	129.00	129
1997 Little Love Bunny Surprise	2,000	1997	129.00	129
1996 Little Love Sleepy Time	2,000	1996	129.00	129
2000 Pretty in Pastel Peach, Yellow and Green w/Cuddle Pack, set/3	1,000		300.00	300

I Wanna Play Series - Reva Schick

2000 Peek A Boo	Yr.Iss.	2000	180.00	180
2000 Ring Around the Rosy	Yr.Iss.	2000	170.00	170
2000 Tic Tac Toe	500	2000	170.00	170

J.C. Penney Exclusive - Reva Schick

1999 Baby Bear (My Own Baby)	Open		99.00	99
2001 Gentle Flower	1,000		198.00	198
1999 Rudolph, My Own Baby	Open		120.00	120

J.C. Penney Exclusive Porcelain - Reva Schick

2000 Small Wonder	2,500		204.00	204

J.C. Penney Series - Various

1998 Little Love ABCs - Lee Middleton	Closed	1999	120.00	120

Kewpie Series - R. O'Neill

1997 Almost Angelic	Retrd.	1998	42.00	50-58
1997 Breezy	Retrd.	1998	42.00	50-55
1997 Buddy	Retrd.	1998	52.00	55-65
1997 Rosebud	Retrd.	1998	52.00	55-85

Little League Series - R. Schick

2001 Character	Open		198.00	198
2001 Courage	Open		198.00	198
2001 Loyalty	Open		198.00	198

*Quotes have been rounded up to nearest dollar

YEAR ISSUE	EDITION LIMIT	YEAR RETD.	ISSUE PRICE	*QUOTE U.S.$
Messenger Angels - R. Schick				
2002 Gentleness	1,800		188.00	188
2002 Love	1,800		188.00	188
Millennium Piece - Reva Schick				
2000 Bright New World	Yr.Iss.	2000	220.00	220
Mohair Bear Edition - L. Henry				
1999 Alpha Bear Baby	Yr.Iss.	1999	180.00	180
1999 Ginger Bear Baby	Yr.Iss.	1999	180.00	180
2001 Gingerbread Boy Bear	Retrd.	2001	100.00	100
2001 Gingerbread Girl Bear	Retrd.	2001	100.00	100
1999 Honey Bear Baby Boy	Yr.Iss.	1999	180.00	180
1999 Honey Bear Baby Girl	Yr.Iss.	1999	180.00	180
1999 Hush-A-Bear Baby	Yr.Iss.	1999	180.00	180
1999 Sleep Bear Baby	Yr.Iss.	1999	180.00	180
2001 Warm & Fuzzy Bear Boy	Retrd.	2001	100.00	100
2001 Warm & Fuzzy Bear Girl	Retrd.	2001	100.00	100
My Own Baby Series - Lee Middleton, unless otherwise noted				
2000 Baby Face Boy - R. Schick	Retrd.	2000	99.00	99
2000 Baby Face Girl - R. Schick	Retrd.	2000	99.00	99
2001 Baby Love Toddler - R. Schick	Open		109.99	110
1999 Cuddle Me Boy - R. Schick	Retrd.	2000	99.00	99
2002 Cuddle Me Duck - R. Schick	Open		109.99	110
2002 Cuddle Me Giraffe - R. Schick	Open		109.99	110
1999 Cuddle Me Girl - R. Schick	Open		99.00	99
1996 First Born Asleep My Own Baby Boy	Retrd.	1999	120.00	120-125
1996 First Born Asleep My Own Baby Girl	Retrd.	1999	120.00	120-125
2002 First Born Awake	Open		109.99	110
1997 First Born Awake My Own Baby Boy	Open		120.00	120
1997 First Born Awake My Own Baby Girl	Open		120.00	120
1996 First Born Dark My Own Baby Boy	Retrd.	1998	120.00	120-125
1996 First Born Dark My Own Baby Girl	Retrd.	1998	120.00	120-125
1997 First Moments Awake My Own Baby Boy	Retrd.	1997	120.00	120-125
1997 First Moments Awake My Own Baby Girl	Retrd.	1997	120.00	120-125
1997 First Moments My Own Baby Boy	Retrd.	1997	120.00	120-125
1997 First Moments My Own Baby Girl	Retrd.	1997	120.00	120-125
1998 Honey Love Asleep Boy Dark Skin My Own Baby	Retrd.	1999	120.00	120-125
1998 Honey Love Asleep Boy My Own Baby	Retrd.	2000	120.00	120
1998 Honey Love Asleep Girl Dark Skin My Own Baby	Retrd.	1999	120.00	120-125
1998 Honey Love Asleep Girl My Own Baby	Retrd.	2000	120.00	120
1998 Honey Love Awake Boy African/American My Own Baby	Open		120.00	120
1998 Honey Love Awake Boy My Own Baby	Open		120.00	120
1998 Honey Love Awake Girl My Own Baby	Open		120.00	120
2002 Honey Love Duck (Dark)	Open		109.99	110
2002 Honey Love Duck (Light)	Open		109.99	110
1996 Little Blessings My Own Baby Asleep Boy	Retrd.	1998	120.00	120-125
1996 Little Blessings My Own Baby Asleep Girl	Retrd.	1998	120.00	120-125
1996 Little Blessings My Own Baby Awake Boy	Retrd.	1999	120.00	120-125
1996 Little Blessings My Own Baby Awake Girl	Retrd.	1999	120.00	120-125
1996 Little Love My Own Baby Boy	Open		120.00	120
1996 Little Love My Own Baby Girl	Open		120.00	120
1999 Little One Boy - R. Schick	Retrd.	2000	99.00	99
1999 Little One Girl - R. Schick	Retrd.	2000	99.00	99
1997 Newborn Taylor Bear - L. Henry	Retrd.	1998	120.00	125-155
1999 Small Wonder Boy - R. Schick	Open		99.00	99
2002 Small Wonder Giraffe - R. Schick	Open		109.99	110
1999 Small Wonder Girl - R. Schick	Open		99.00	99
2001 Small Wonder Toddler - R. Schick	Open		109.99	110
1999 Special Delivery - R. Schick	Open		160.00	160
1999 Sweet Cheeks Boy - R. Schick	Retrd.	2000	99.00	99
1999 Sweet Cheeks Girl - R. Schick	Retrd.	2000	99.00	99
NALED Exclusive - Reva Schick				
1999 Forever Yours	1,500	2000	190.00	190
2000 Being Sweet	1,000	2001	150.00	150
Newborn Wonder - R. Schick				
2001 Newborn Wonder, Blue	Open		29.99	30
2001 Newborn Wonder, Mint	Open		29.99	30
2001 Newborn Wonder, Pink	Open		29.99	30
2001 Newborn Wonder, Yellow	Open		29.99	30
Newborns In Need - R. Schick				
2002 Jesus Loves Me (Dark Skin)	Yr.Iss.		198.00	198
2002 Jesus Loves Me (Light Skin)	Yr.Iss.		198.00	198
2001 Young at Heart	Yr.Iss.	2001	198.00	198
Pampers Series - R. Schick				
2000 Gentle Touch Baby (Pampers Series)	Yr.Iss.	2000	190.00	190
2001 Pampers Kid (African American)	Yr.Iss.	2001	198.00	198
2001 Pampers Kid (Asian)	Yr.Iss.	2001	198.00	198
2001 Pampers Kid (Caucasian)	Yr.Iss.	2001	198.00	198
2002 Every Step of the Way	Numbrd.		198.00	198
Play Time Wonder - R. Schick				
2001 Play Time Wonder Blonde Hair/Blue Eyes	Open		99.99	100
2001 Play Time Wonder Brown Hair/Brown Eyes	Open		99.99	100
Please Save the Animals - R. Schick				
2002 Snow Monkey	Numbrd.		208.00	208
2002 Walrus	Numbrd.		208.00	208
2002 White Tiger	Numbrd.		208.00	208
Porcelain Bears & Bunny - Lee Middleton				
1993 Buster Bear	Retrd.	1994	250.00	250
1993 Baby Buster	Retrd.	1994	230.00	230
1993 Bye Baby Bunting	Retrd.	1994	270.00	270
Porcelain Collector Series - Lee Middleton				
1992 Beloved & Bé Bé	362	1994	590.00	600-650
1993 Cherish - Lilac & Lace	141	1994	500.00	500
1992 Sencerity II - Country Fair	253	1994	500.00	500
Porcelain Limited Edition Series - Lee Middleton				
1999 All Dressed Up	2,500	2001	220.00	220
1990 Baby Grace	500	1990	500.00	650-800
1994 Blossom	86	1995	500.00	500
1994 Bride	200	1994	1390.00	1500-2000
1988 Cherish -1st Edition	750	1988	350.00	550
1986 Dear One	750	1988	450.00	450
1989 Devan	543	1991	500.00	500-650
1995 Elise - 1860's Civil War	200	1996	1790.00	1800
1999 Having Fun	2,500	2001	220.00	220
1991 Johanna	381	1992	500.00	500
1999 Just Precious	2,500	2001	180.00	180
1999 Little Dreamer	2,500	1999	180.00	180
1999 Little Sweetheart	2,500	2001	180.00	180
1991 Molly Rose	500	1991	500.00	850
1999 My Beloved	2,500	2001	180.00	180
1989 My Lee	655	1991	500.00	650
1988 Sincerity -1st Edition - Nettie/Simplicity	750	1988	330.00	350-600
1995 Tenderness - Baby Clown	250	1996	590.00	590
1994 Tenderness - Petite Pierrot	250	1995	500.00	500
Porcelain Limited Edition Series - Reva Schick				
1999 Go Bye Bye	2,500	2000	200.00	200
1999 Little Lamb	2,500	2001	200.00	200
1999 Something Special	2,500	2001	200.00	200
1999 Sweet & Petite	2,500	2001	200.00	200
Precious Babies - R. Schick				
2001 Precious in Blue	2,000		208.00	208
2001 Precious in Green	1,500		208.00	208
2001 Precious in Pink	2,000		208.00	208
Romper Series - Lee Middleton				
1996 First Born Dark Romper Boy	2,000	1998	160.00	180-195
1996 First Born Dark Romper Girl	2,000	1997	160.00	180-195
1996 First Born Romper Boy	2,000	1996	160.00	160-180
1996 First Born Romper Girl	2,000	1996	160.00	160-180
1996 Little Love Twin Boy	2,000	1996	160.00	160
1996 Little Love Twin Girl	2,000	1996	160.00	160
Scootles - R. O'Neill				
1997 Scootles	Retrd.	1998	50.00	60-85

Lee Middleton Original Dolls
to Little Gem/Akira Trading Co.

DOLLS & PLUSH

YEAR ISSUE	EDITION LIMIT	YEAR RETD.	ISSUE PRICE	*QUOTE U.S.$
Season of Angels Series - Reva Schick, unless otherwise noted				
2000 Fall Angel	1,500	2000	188.00	188
2001 Spring Angel	2,500		188.00	188
2001 Summer Angel	2,500		188.00	188
2000 Winter Angel	1,500	2000	188.00	188
Show Specials - Various				
1993 Molly Goes to Disneyland - L. Middleton	25	1993	125.00	125
1998 My Best Friend - R. Schick	25	1998	200.00	200
1999 Innocence - R. Schick	100	2000	200.00	200
2000 Love at First Sight - R. Schick	25	2000	200.00	200
2001 Sweet Pea - R. Schick	12	2001	200.00	200
Small Wonder/Life's Little Lessons - Reva Schick				
2002 Baby Is Growing Everyday (Light)	Open		40.00	40
2002 Baby Is Growing Everyday (Medium)	Open		40.00	40
2002 Going to Grandma's (Light)	Open		40.00	40
2002 Going to Grandma's (Medium)	Open		40.00	40
2002 Just Arrived (Light)	Open		40.00	40
2002 Just Arrived (Medium)	Open		40.00	40
2002 Sharing & Giving (Light)	Open		40.00	40
2002 Sharing & Giving (Medium)	Open		40.00	40
Small Wonder/Play Babies - Reva Schick				
2000 Black Hair Girl	Open		49.95	50
2000 Blonde Hair Boy	Open		49.95	50
2000 Blonde Hair Girl	Open		49.95	50
2000 Brown Hair Girl	Open		49.95	50
2002 Bunting Baby (Blonde/Blue)	Open		50.00	50
2002 Bunting Baby (Brown/Brown)	Open		50.00	50
2002 Bunting Baby (Medium Skin Tone)	Open		50.00	50
Someone to Care For - R. Schick				
2002 Someone to Care For (dark skin tone)	Open		109.99	110
2001 Someone to Care For, Green	Open		55.00	55
2001 Someone to Care For, Pink	Open		55.00	55
Special Occasions - R. Schick				
2001 American Beauty	Yr.Iss.	2001	198.00	198
2001 Dainty and Darling	Yr.Iss.	2001	198.00	198
2001 Party Girl	Yr.Iss.	2001	198.00	198
Spiegel Exclusive Limited Edition Series - Reva Schick				
2001 Blushing Hearts	500		110.00	110
2000 Carousel Dreams	Yr.Iss.	2000	108.00	108
2000 Dainty & Sweet	Yr.Iss.	2000	140.00	140
2001 Daisy	Open		110.00	110
1999 Elegance	1,000	2000	149.00	149
2001 Ivy & lace	950		110.00	110
2000 Merry Go Fun	Yr.Iss.	2000	108.00	108
Spiegel MOB Series - Reva Schick				
1999 New Beginnings, pink	Open		100.00	100
1999 New Beginnings, white	Open		100.00	100
1998 Small Wonder	Open		120.00	120
1998 Sweet Cheeks	Open		120.00	120
Spinning Wheel Exclusive - Reva Schick				
2000 Soft and Innocent	200	2000	140.00	140
Toys R Us Exclusive - Reva Schick				
1999 Happy Bear, My Own Baby	Open		100.00	100
1999 Very Good Baby, My Own Baby	Open		100.00	100
Twice as Nice - Various				
2001 Sweet Baby Bear Boy - S. Housley	1,500		188.00	188
2001 Sweet Baby Bear Girl - S. Housley	1,500		188.00	188
2001 Twinkle Star Boy - L. Middleton	1,500		188.00	188
2001 Twinkle Star Girl - L. Middleton	1,500		188.00	188
Wedding Party - R. Schick				
2001 Flower Girl	1,000		198.00	198
2001 Jr. Bridesmaid	1,000		198.00	198
2001 Ring Bearer	1,000		188.00	188
When I Grow Up - Reva Schick, unless otherwise noted				
2001 Firefighter - M. Snyder	Yr.Iss.	2001	198.00	198
2001 Junior Executive	Yr.Iss.	2001	198.00	198
2001 Nurse	Yr.Iss.		198.00	198
2002 Police Officer	1,800		188.00	188
2001 Teacher	Yr.Iss.	2001	198.00	198

YEAR ISSUE	EDITION LIMIT	YEAR RETD.	ISSUE PRICE	*QUOTE U.S.$
Wise Penny Collection - Lee Middleton				
1993 Jennifer (Peach Dress)	Retrd.	1995	140.00	140-185
1993 Jennifer (Print Dress)	Retrd.	1995	140.00	140-185
1993 Molly Jo	Retrd.	1995	140.00	140
1993 Gordon	Retrd.	1995	140.00	140
1993 Ashley (Brown Hair)	Retrd.	1995	120.00	120-195
1993 Merry	Retrd.	1995	140.00	140
1993 Grace	Retrd.	1995	140.00	200
1993 Ashley (Blond Hair)	Retrd.	1995	120.00	120-195
1993 Baby Devan	Retrd.	1995	140.00	140-195

Lenox Collections

YEAR ISSUE	EDITION LIMIT	YEAR RETD.	ISSUE PRICE	*QUOTE U.S.$
Lenox China Dolls - J. Grammer				
1985 Abigail, 20"	Closed	1985	425.00	870
1985 Amanda, 16"	Closed	1985	425.00	770
1985 Amy, 14"	Closed	1985	250.00	650-700
1985 Annabelle, 14"	Closed	1985	250.00	650-700
1985 Elizabeth, 14"	Closed	1985	250.00	650-700
1985 Jennifer, 14"	Closed	1985	250.00	650-700
1985 Jessica, 20"	Closed	1985	475.00	1180
1985 Maggie, 16"	Closed	1985	400.00	770
1985 Mary Anne, 20"	Closed	1985	450.00	1200
1985 Miranda, 14"	Closed	1985	250.00	650-700
1985 Rebecca, 16"	Closed	1985	375.00	770
1985 Samantha, 16"	500	1985	500.00	1400
1985 Sarah, 14"	Closed	1985	250.00	650-700

Little Gem/Akira Trading Co.

YEAR ISSUE	EDITION LIMIT	YEAR RETD.	ISSUE PRICE	*QUOTE U.S.$
Bloosom Bears - L. Mullins				
1999 Daisy	2,000		40.00	40
1999 Lily of the Valley	2,000		40.00	40
1999 Orchid	2,000		40.00	40
1999 Rose Petals	2,000		40.00	40
1999 Violet	2,000		40.00	40
Butterfly Boy - Chu-Ming Wu				
1999 Garden Boy	500	2000	40.00	40
Christmas Collection - L. Lloyd				
1998 Elfie	2,000		40.00	40
1998 Kringle	2,000	2001	40.00	40
Circus Collection - D. Canham				
1999 Bianca	2,000		40.00	40
1999 Boom	2,000		49.00	49
1998 Carrot Top	2,000	2000	40.00	40
1998 Jingle	2,000	2000	40.00	40
1999 Juggler	2,000		49.00	49
1999 Leopold and Larry	2,000		50.00	50
1999 Lulu, Patches and Spots	2,000		60.00	60
1999 Notsosilly	2,000		30.00	30
1998 Pananini	2,000		40.00	40
1998 Plum	2,000	2000	40.00	40
1999 Ringmaster	2,000		40.00	40
Fairy Collection - S. Lambert				
1999 Blossom	2,000		40.00	40
1999 Bugsby	2,000		40.00	40
1999 Dragonfly	2,000		40.00	40
1999 Figis	2,000		40.00	40
1999 Firefly	2,000	2000	40.00	40
Formosa Bear - Chu-Ming Wu				
1998 Formosa Green Bear	1,000	1999	65.00	65
Garden Harvest - L. Mullins, unless otherwise noted				
1999 Berry	2,000		40.00	40
1999 Lemon	2,000		40.00	40
1999 Lime Tart	2,000		40.00	40
1999 Plum Puddin'	2,000	2000	40.00	40
1999 Punkin	2,000		40.00	40
Golfer Collection - Chu-Ming Wu				
1999 Angus	2,000		40.00	40
1999 Master McGreen	2,000		40.00	40
1999 Miss Andrea	2,000		40.00	40
1999 Norman Putt	2,000		40.00	40
Little Gem Teddy Bears - Various				
2000 21st Century Bear - Chu-Ming Wu	2,000	2000	50.00	50

Collectors' Information Bureau   *Quotes have been rounded up to nearest dollar

DOLLS & PLUSH

Little Gem/Akira Trading Co.
to Little Gem/Akira Trading Co.

YEAR ISSUE	EDITION LIMIT	YEAR RETD.	ISSUE PRICE	*QUOTE U.S.$
1998 4th of July Boy - L. Lloyd	500	1999	40.00	40
1998 4th of July Girl - L. Lloyd	500	1999	40.00	40
2002 Albert & Margaret - A. McLean	2,000		40.00	40
1995 Alex - D. Canham	3,000	1997	40.00	55-65
1998 Alex (Open Mouth Bear) - C. Stewart	500	2001	40.00	40
1995 Amelia Baby Blue - D. Canham	3,000	1997	40.00	85-100
2000 Amos - C. Stewart	2,000		40.00	40
1993 Annie - D. Canham	3,000	1995	40.00	45-65
2001 Baby Bloomer - C. Attwood	2,000		40.00	40
1995 Banana & Chip - D. Canham	3,000	1997	40.00	90-140
1998 Bearfoot & Pregnant - L. Spiegel	2,000	1999	40.00	40-50
2001 Belle - D. Canham	2,000		40.00	40
1996 Bilbo & Bruno - D. Canham	2,000		50.00	50
2001 Blue - C. Stewart	2,000		30.00	30
1993 Bonnie - D. Canham	3,000	1995	40.00	50-60
1995 Bosworth & Chichi - D. Canham	3,000	1997	40.00	80-110
2001 Brandy - C. Stewart	2,000		20.00	20
1996 Bumble Bee - D. Canham	3,000	1998	40.00	60-70
2001 Buz Bee - S. Lambert	2,000		40.00	40
1993 Cameo - Chu-Ming Wu	3,000	1996	40.00	90-105
2001 Campbell, McTravish & Mac - A. McLean	2,000		49.00	49
1994 Caramel- Chu-Ming Wu	3,000	1996	40.00	70-80
2001 Chanille - C. Stewart	2,000		30.00	30
1998 Chester I - C. Taylor	2,000		40.00	40
1998 Chester II - C. Taylor	2,000		40.00	40
1994 Chico - D. Canham	3,000	1996	40.00	55-65
1994 Chilly - D. Canham	3,000	1998	40.00	45-75
2000 Chimp - C. Starnes	2,000		30.00	30
1994 Chocolate - Chu-Ming Wu	500	1997	40.00	75-90
1994 Chu-Ming - S. Dotson	3,000	1995	40.00	85-105
2000 Coco - D. Canham	2,000	2000	40.00	40
1994 Cold Weather - Chu-Ming Wu	2,000		30.00	30
2002 Colette - A. McLean	2,000		40.00	40
1993 Connie - Chu-Ming Wu	3,000	1995	40.00	60-65
2000 Court Jester - D. Allen	2,000		40.00	40
1999 Crazy Ike - L. Spiegel	2,000		30.00	30
1996 Cuddles - D. Canham	2,000		40.00	40
1994 Cupid - D. Canham	3,000	1995	40.00	60-65
2001 Daisy - C. Attwood	2,000		40.00	40
2001 Daisy - D. Canham	2,000		25.00	25
1994 Darcy - Chu-Ming Wu	3,000	1997	40.00	40-50
1996 Dizzy - D. Canham	3,000	1998	40.00	40-45
2001 Dotty - C. Attwood	2,000		40.00	40
2002 Eggy - D. Canham	2,000		40.00	40
1999 English Guard - C. Stewart	2,000		48.00	48
1999 Ethan & Edith - L. Lloyd	2,000	2001	50.00	50
2001 Faith - D. Canham	2,000		30.00	30
1998 Fibber - L. Spiegel	2,000	2001	40.00	40
1999 Garden Boy II - Chu-Ming Wu	500	2000	40.00	40
2002 German Celebration - D. Canham	2,000		20.00	20
2001 Gerry - S. Lambert	2,000		40.00	40
1999 Ginger & Snaps - D. Allen	2,000		40.00	40
1998 Gnomes - K. Kilby	2,000		40.00	40
2002 Golly Go - D. Canham	2,000		40.00	40
2001 Gus - S. Lambert	2,000		40.00	40
1999 Harriet & Her Hedgehog - L. Lloyd	2,000		40.00	40
1998 Holland Boy - Lydarys/Gertenback	2,000		40.00	40
2001 Hope - D. Canham	2,000		30.00	30
2000 Huggie - D. Canham	2,000		40.00	40
2001 Issie & Ice - D. Canham	2,000		50.00	50
1998 Jamie Jr. - Chu-Ming Wu	1,000		170.00	170
1994 Jester Blue - D. Canham	3,000	1995	40.00	60-80
1994 Jester Grey - D. Canham	3,000	1995	40.00	60-80
1994 Jester Pink - D. Canham	3,000	1995	40.00	60-70
2002 Johnny on the Pot - L. Spiegel	2,000	2001	40.00	40
2002 Jolly - D. Canham	2,000		40.00	40
1994 Juliet (pin) - D. Canham	3,000	1998	40.00	40-50
1995 Kiki - D. Canham	3,000	1998	40.00	55-65
1996 Lady Bug - D. Canham	3,000	1998	40.00	55-65
2001 Larina - S. Lambert	2,000		40.00	40
1996 Latte - Chu-Ming Wu	3,000	1998	40.00	65-80
1998 Leona - C. Stewart	2,000		40.00	40
1998 Lester Jester - L. Lloyd	2,000		40.00	40
1994 Li-Ling - Chu-Ming Wu	3,000	1996	40.00	40-45
2000 Little Blue - C. Stewart	2,000		30.00	30
1994 Lopsy Blue - D. Canham	3,000	1995	40.00	65-75
1994 Lopsy Plum - D. Canham	3,000	1995	40.00	60-75
1999 Lucky Catch - L. Spiegel	2,000		49.00	49
2001 Lucky Locket - D. Allen	2,000		44.00	44
2001 Lucy - L. Spiegel	2,000		40.00	40
2000 Luv Bug - D. Canham	2,000		40.00	40
2001 Maddie - C. Stewart	2,000		20.00	20
2000 Magical Jester Duo - D. Allen	2,000		40.00	40
2001 Maid Marian - Chu-Ming Wu	2,000		40.00	40
1994 Marcy - Chu-Ming Wu	3,000	1997	40.00	40-45
1998 Mardi Gras - Chu-Ming Wu	2,000	2001	40.00	40
2001 Mary - A. McBean	2,000		40.00	40
1994 Max (Ceylon) - Chu-Ming Wu	3,000	1996	40.00	50-60
2000 Me & Golly - D. Canham	2,000		50.00	50
1994 Mei-Mei - Chu-Ming Wu	3,000	1995	40.00	50-65
1998 Mellie - D. Canham	2,000		40.00	40
1999 Millenium Milton - L. Lloyd	500	2001	40.00	40
1995 Milly & Quackers - D. Canham	3,000	1997	40.00	85-95
2002 Miss Pinky - D. Canham	2,000		30.00	30
2002 Mittens - D. Canham	2,000		40.00	40
1994 Mopsy - Chu-Ming Wu	3,000	1998	40.00	42-55
1999 Mr. Everything - L. Spiegel	2,000		30.00	30
1999 Mr. Golly - L. Lloyd	2,000		40.00	40
2001 Mr. Jingles - S. Lambert	2,000		40.00	40
2001 Muddy - C. Stewart	2,000		20.00	20
1999 Mukaluk & Seal - L. Spiegel	2,000		49.00	49
1998 Nester Jester - L. Lloyd	2,000		40.00	40
1995 Nicholas - D. Canham	3,000	1998	40.00	60-65
1996 No-No (Amber) - Chu-Ming Wu	3,000	1998	40.00	75-85
1998 Old Fashioned - C. Stewart	3,000	2000	40.00	40
1993 Onyx - Chu-Ming Wu	3,000	1995	40.00	90-115
2001 Oscar - C. Attwood	2,000		40.00	40
2001 Paddy and Picadelli - A. McLean	2,000		49.00	49
2001 Peace - D. Canham	2,000		30.00	30
1993 Pearl - Chu-Ming Wu	3,000	1995	40.00	90-115
1996 Perfume Bottle - Chu-Ming Wu	3,000	1998	40.00	80-90
1994 Perky - D. Canham	3,000	1996	40.00	65-80
1999 Pete - L. Lloyd	2,000	2001	49.00	49
1998 Philmore - A. Sison	2,000	2001	40.00	40
2001 Pinky - D. Canham	2,000		40.00	40
2000 Pip - D. Canham	2,000		40.00	40
2001 Pogo & Dolly - A. McLean	2,000		49.00	49
1998 Polar Bear - D. Shaw	2,000	2001	49.00	49
2001 Quacky - D. Canham	2,000		40.00	40
1995 Rags - Chu-Ming Wu	3,000	1998	40.00	45-50
1998 Rainbow - C. Stewart	1,000	1998	40.00	40-45
1998 Rainbow II - C. Stewart	1,000	1999	40.00	40-45
1994 Razz - D. Canham	3,000	1997	40.00	80-90
2002 Remember - A. McLean	2,001		20.00	20
1993 Rex - Chu-Ming Wu	3,000	1997	40.00	60-70
2000 Rex & Rooster - D. Canham	2,000		50.00	50
1995 Rhonda - Chu-Ming Wu	3,000	1997	40.00	55-65
1998 Ripley - A. Sison	2,000		49.00	49
1998 Robin Hood - Chu-Ming Wu	2,000	2000	40.00	40
2001 Rodney and Ned - S. Lambert	2,000		40.00	40
2002 Rollo - D. Canham	2,000		40.00	40
1994 Romeo (pin) - D. Canham	3,000	1998	40.00	40-45
1998 Rosanna - Chu-Ming Wu	2,000		40.00	40
1995 Rosie - Chu-Ming Wu	3,000	1996	40.00	45-50
2001 Rosie - L. Spiegel	2,000		40.00	40
2001 Rough Rider - L. Spiegel	2,000		40.00	40
1994 Rudolph - Chu-Ming Wu	3,000	1997	40.00	80-90
1998 Sailorboy - K. Kilby	2,000	2001	40.00	40
1997 Samantha - S. Dotson	3,000	1997	40.00	95-115
1994 Santa - D. Canham	3,000	1998	40.00	75-80
1995 Saphire (honey) - Chu-Ming Wu	3,000	1996	40.00	45-50
2001 Sassie - L. Spiegel	2,000		40.00	40
2001 Sawyer & Huck - A. McLean	2,000		40.00	. 40
1994 Scottie - D. Canham	3,000	1998	40.00	55-60
2002 Scotty & Wabbit - A. McLean	2,000		30.00	30
1998 See No Evil, Hear No Evil, Speak No Evil - L. Spiegel	2,000	2000	100.00	100
2002 Sgt. Preston Jr. - L. Spiegel	2,000		40.00	40
2002 Shani - C. Starnes	2,000		30.00	30
1995 Sharon - D. Canham	3,000	1997	40.00	50-60
2002 Sinberbear - A. McBean	2,000		40.00	40
2002 Sinter Bear - A. McLean	2,000		40.00	40
2001 Slugs & Snails - C. Attwood	2,000		40.00	40
2001 Snazzy - D. Canham	2,000		40.00	40
2001 Snowball - A. McBean	2,000		40.00	40
1995 Sophie - D. Canham	3,000	1998	40.00	42-60
1998 Spanky - L. Spiegel	2,000	2001	49.00	49
1999 Spencer - L. Spiegel	2,000		40.00	40
2000 Star Bug - D. Canham	2,000		40.00	40
1994 Strawberry (Alpaca) - Chu-Ming Wu	500	1995	40.00	80-100
2001 Stretch - C. Stewart	2,000		30.00	30

DOLLS & PLUSH

YEAR ISSUE	EDITION LIMIT	YEAR RETD.	ISSUE PRICE	*QUOTE U.S.$
2001 Sugar & Snails - L. Attwood	2,000		40.00	40
2001 Sugar & Spice - C. Attwood	2,000		40.00	40
1998 Superteddy - K. Kilby	2,000		40.00	40
1996 Tabatha - D. Canham	3,000	1998	40.00	50-55
1996 Teddy's Bear - L. Mullin	3,000	1998	49.00	75-80
1995 Thai - Chu-Ming Wu	3,000	1996	40.00	65-70
2001 Theodore - L. Spiegel	2,000		40.00	40
1998 Tumbler - L. Mullins	2,000	2001	40.00	40
2002 USA Celebration - D. Canham	2,000		20.00	20
1994 Vanilla - Chu-Ming Wu	500	1995	40.00	70-75
2001 Walter - A. McLean	2,000		40.00	40
2001 Warm Weather - Chu-Ming Wu	2,000		30.00	30
1996 Winter Sprite - D. Canham	3,000	1998	40.00	65-70
1998 Yo Yo Bear - L. Lloyd	2,000		40.00	40
1994 Zack - S. Dotson	3,000	1997	40.00	65-70
1998 Zeke - L. Spiegel	2,000	2001	40.00	40
1994 Zev - Chu-Ming Wu	3,000	1998	40.00	50-55

Mohair Collection - Chu-Ming Wu, unless otherwise noted

YEAR ISSUE	EDITION LIMIT	YEAR RETD.	ISSUE PRICE	*QUOTE U.S.$
1998 Andy D.	1,000	2000	40.00	40
1998 Baby Boo D.	450	1999	40.00	40
1998 Boomer - K. Mahanna	2,000		40.00	40
1998 Candy D.	200	1998	40.00	40-50
1995 Goldie	3,000	1998	40.00	40-50
1998 Midget & Sheep - C. Stewart	2,000		40.00	40
1998 Missy - L. Lloyd	2,000		40.00	40
1995 Priscilla	3,000	1999	40.00	40-50
1998 Stuart - S. Quinn	2,000	2001	40.00	40

Rosemont Special - Chu-Ming Wu

YEAR ISSUE	EDITION LIMIT	YEAR RETD.	ISSUE PRICE	*QUOTE U.S.$
2001 Rodeo	400		40.00	40

Walt Disney World Teddy Bear & Doll Convention - Chu-Ming Wu

YEAR ISSUE	EDITION LIMIT	YEAR RETD.	ISSUE PRICE	*QUOTE U.S.$
1999 Pooh & Bee	750	1999	80.00	80
1998 Winnie the Pooh	500	1998	80.00	175

Original Appalachian Artworks

Collectors Club Editions - X. Roberts

YEAR ISSUE	EDITION LIMIT	YEAR RETD.	ISSUE PRICE	*QUOTE U.S.$
1987 Baby Otis	1,275	1987	250.00	200-300
1989 Anna Ruby	693	1990	250.00	225-300
1990 Lee Ann	468	1991	250.00	250-300
1991 Richard Russell	490	1991	250.00	250-300
1992 Baby Dodd & 'lttle Bitty	354	1993	250.00	250-300
1993 Patti w/ Cabbage Bud Boutonnier	358	1994	280.00	250-300
1994 Mother Cabbage	245	1995	150.00	150
1995 Rosie	322	1996	275.00	230-275
1996 Gabriella (Angel)	Closed	1997	265.00	260-265
1997 Robert London	Closed	1997	275.00	225-275
1998 Dexter (Anniversary)	Yr.Iss.	1998	395.00	395
1999 Harley	Yr.Iss.	1999	345.00	345
2000 Millie	Yr.Iss.	2000	300.00	300
2001 Jillian (Jillie)	Yr.Iss.	2001	325.00	325
2002 Billy	Yr.Iss.		325.00	325

BabyLand Babies - X. Roberts

YEAR ISSUE	EDITION LIMIT	YEAR RETD.	ISSUE PRICE	*QUOTE U.S.$
1991 Newborn	909	1991	195.00	150-195
1991 Reg.	969	1991	190.00	190-240
1992 Newborn	869	1992	195.00	150-195
1992 Engineer -Career Kid	Closed	1992	220.00	250-300
1992 Reg.	770	1992	190.00	190-240
1993 Newborn	1,136	1993	195.00	150-195
1993 Miss BLGH Career 'Kid	240	1993	220.00	220-300
1994 Newborn	1,107	1994	195.00	150-195
1994 Child Star Career 'Kid	241	1994	220.00	260-265
1994 Sweet Sixteen "Casey Ann"	191	1994	260.00	295-500
1994 Reg.	Closed	1994	210.00	210-260
1994 Bald	Closed	1994	210.00	200-250
1994 Preemie	Closed	1994	175.00	150-250
1995 Newborn	1,042	1995	195.00	150-195
1995 Nurse-Career	83	1995	210.00	210-250
1995 Reg.	Closed	1994	210.00	210-260
1995 Preemie	Closed	1995	175.00	150-225
1996 Newborn	1,710	1996	195.00	150-195
1997 Ballerina-Career	Closed	1997	210.00	210
1997 Preemie	Closed	1997	175.00	150-175
1997 Newborn	Closed	1997	195.00	150-195
1998 Newborn	Closed	1998	195.00	150-195
1999 Newborn	Closed	1999	195.00	195
1999 Col. Casey Preemie	Closed	1999	170.00	170
2000 Newborn	Closed	2000	195.00	195

YEAR ISSUE	EDITION LIMIT	YEAR RETD.	ISSUE PRICE	*QUOTE U.S.$
2000 Col. Casey Preemie	Closed	2000	170.00	170
2000 Kellum Valley Preemie (Fall Festival)	200	2000	235.00	235
2001 Newborn	Yr.Iss.	2001	195.00	195
2001 Col. Casey Preemie	Yr.Iss.	2001	170.00	170
2002 Newborn	Yr.Iss.		199.00	199
2002 Col. Casey Preemie	Yr.Iss.		170.00	170

BabyLand General Hospital Convention Baby - X. Roberts

YEAR ISSUE	EDITION LIMIT	YEAR RETD.	ISSUE PRICE	*QUOTE U.S.$
1990 Charlie (Amber)	200	1990	175.00	175-300
1991 Nurse Payne (Garnet)	160	1991	210.00	225-275
1992 Princess Nacoochee (BabyLand)	160	1992	210.00	250
1993 Baby BeBop (BabyLand)	199	1993	210.00	260-300
1994 Norma Jean (BabyLand)	250	1994	225.00	375-500
1995 Delta (BabyLand)	200	1995	230.00	230
1996 Marlene (BabyLand)	200	1996	230.00	230
1997 Hayley (BabyLand)	200	1997	220.00	220
1998 Marisa (BabyLand)	200	1998	250.00	250
1999 Middle Name "Bea"	200	1999	255.00	255
2000 PJ	200	2000	235.00	235

BunnyBees - X. Roberts

YEAR ISSUE	EDITION LIMIT	YEAR RETD.	ISSUE PRICE	*QUOTE U.S.$
1986 Girl	Closed	N/A	13.00	25-50
1986 Boy	Closed	N/A	13.00	25-40
1994 Girl w/Squeaker	Closed	N/A	18.00	18
1994 Boy w/Squeaker	Closed	N/A	18.00	18

Cabbage Patch Kids - X. Roberts

YEAR ISSUE	EDITION LIMIT	YEAR RETD.	ISSUE PRICE	*QUOTE U.S.$
1989 Amber (Reg. & Halloween)	1,356	1990	195.00	135-175
1989 Amber (Halloween, Asian)	654	1989	175.00	135-225
1989 Amber (Toddler)	272	1989	150.00	100-225
1986 Amethyst	9,250	1986	135.00	100-200
1988 Aquamarine	5,000	1988	150.00	150-200
1993 Blackberry Preemie	438	1993	175.00	200
1999 Blue Creek Kid	Closed	1999	255.00	255
1999 Blue Creek (Newborn)	Closed	1999	235.00	235
1999 Blue Creek (Preemie)	Closed	1999	190.00	190
1992 Brass	321	1992	190.00	190
1992 Brass (Flower Girl Toddler)	Closed	1992	175.00	175-225
1992 Brass (Garden Party Girl)	Closed	1992	190.00	190-240
1992 Brass (Hispanic Girl Toddler)	Closed	1992	175.00	175-225
1992 Brass (Ring Bearer Boy Toddler)	Closed	1992	175.00	175-225
1992 Brass (Toddler)	424	1992	175.00	175-225
1995 Bucky (California Collectors Club)	105	1995	220.00	220
1983 Champagne (Andre)	1,000	1983	250.00	250-500
1983 Champagne (Madeira)	1,000	1983	250.00	250-500
1998 Chattahoochee Kid	Closed	1999	255.00	255
1998 Chattahoochee (Newborn)	Closed	1999	195.00	195
1998 Chattahoochee (Preemie)	Closed	1999	185.00	185
1983 Cleveland "Green"	2,000	1983	125.00	400
1991 Copper	241	1991	190.00	190
1991 Copper (Halloween)	273	1991	190.00	190-240
1991 Copper (Toddler)	241	1991	175.00	175-225
1986 Corporate 'Kid	2,000	1986	400.00	150-400
1991 Crystal	176	1991	190.00	190
1991 Crystal (Easter Fashions)	302	1991	190.00	185-210
1991 Crystal (Toddler)	41	1991	175.00	175-225
1991 Crystal (Valentine Fashions)	256	1991	190.00	190-240
1991 Crystal (Valentine Toddler Fashions)	189	1991	175.00	175-225
1984 Daddy's Darlins' (Kitten)	500	1984	300.00	225-400
1984 Daddy's Darlins' (Princess)	500	1984	300.00	225-400
1984 Daddy's Darlins' (Pun'kin)	500	1983	300.00	225-400
1984 Daddy's Darlins' (Tootsie)	500	1984	300.00	225-400
1984 Daddy's Darlins', set/4	2,000	1984	1200.00	1200-2000
2000 Daddy's Lil' Darlin'	Closed	2000	199.00	199
1992 Diamond	360	1993	210.00	210
1992 Diamond (Choir Christmas)	54	1992	210.00	210-260
1992 Diamond (Thanksgiving Indian)	123	1992	210.00	210-260
1992 Diamond (Thanksgiving Toddler Indian)	55	1992	195.00	195-245
1992 Diamond (Toddler)	51	1993	195.00	195-245
2001 Dukes Creek Kid	Yr.Iss.	2001	255.00	255
2001 Dukes Creek (Callie)	Closed	2001	280.00	280
2001 Dukes Creek (Willie)	Closed	2001	235.000	235
2001 Dukes Creek (Preemie)	Yr.Iss.	2001	190.00	190
1985 Emerald	35,000	1985	135.00	100-135
1985 Four Seasons (Autumn)	2,000	1985	160.00	100-160
1985 Four Seasons (Crystal)	2,000	1985	160.00	100-160
1985 Four Seasons (Morton)	2,000	1985	160.00	100-160
1985 Four Seasons (Sunny)	2,000	1985	160.00	100-160
1991 Garnet	376	1991	190.00	200-215
1991 Garnet (Father's Day Toddler)	85	1991	175	250
1991 Garnet (Father's Day)	173	1991	190.00	250

YEAR ISSUE	EDITION LIMIT	YEAR RETD.	ISSUE PRICE	*QUOTE U.S.$
1991 Garnet (Mother's Day Girl)	259	1991	190.00	200
1991 Garnet (Mother's Day Toddler Girl)	364	1991	175.00	200
1991 Garnet (Toddler)	49	1991	175.00	175
1993 Georgia Power (Special Stork Delivery)	288	1993	230.00	250-350
1985 Gold	50,000	1985	135.00	130-135
1995 Graceland Elvis	500	1995	300.00	300
1993 Happily Ever After (Bride)	343	1993	230.00	230-275
1993 Happily Ever After (Groom)	343	1993	230.00	230-275
1994 House of Tyrol (Christina Marie)	1,000	1994	200.00	200
1994 House of Tyrol (Markus Michael)	1,000	1994	200.00	200
1987 Iddy Buds	750	1987	650.00	275-650
1986 Identical Twins, set/2	5,000	1987	150.00	200-350
1985 Ivory	45,000	1985	135.00	130-200
1989 Jade	Closed	1989	150.00	130-150
1989 Jade (4th of July Fashions)	Closed	1989	150.00	150-200
1989 Jade (Mother's Day Fashions)	338	1989	150.00	150-200
1989 Jade (Toddler)	Closed	1989	150.00	150-200
1992 JC Penney 1992 Catalog Exclusive (Cocoa-Girl)	245	1992	200.00	200-215
1992 JC Penney 1992 Catalog Exclusive (Lemon Girl)	248	1992	200.00	200
2000 Kellum Valley Kid	Closed	2000	255.00	255
2000 Kellum Valley (Newborn)	Closed	2000	195.00	195
2000 Kellum Valley (Preemie)	Closed	2000	190.00	190
1983 KP Darker Green	2,000	1983	125.00	195-400
1983 KPB Burgundy	10,000	1983	130.00	185-250
1984 KPF Turquoise	30,000	1984	130.00	130-225
1984 KPZ Bronze	30,000	1984	130.00	130-195
1984 KPG Coral	35,000	1984	130.00	125-135
1983 KPP Purple	20,000	1984	130.00	130-150
1983 KPR Red	2,000	1983	125.00	235-400
1989 Lapis (Swimsuit Fashions)	645	1989	150.00	135-150
1989 Lapis (Swimsuit Fashions-Toddler)	836	1989	150.00	120-150
1993 Little People 27" (Girl)	300	1993	325.00	500-800
1994 Little People 27" (Boy)	300	1994	325.00	300-500
1996 Little People Girls 27"	300	1996	375.00	300-375
1997 Little People 27" (Boy)	300	1997	395.00	395
2000 Little People (Girl)	300	2000	375.00	375
1994 Mt. Laurel (African Inspired Toddler)	Closed	1994	195.00	195
1994 Mt. Laurel (African Inspired) (Reg.)	Closed	1994	210.00	210
1994 Mt. Laurel (Mrs. Pauls)	Closed	1994	198.00	198
1994 Mt. Laurel (Mysterious Barry)	Closed	1994	225.00	225
1994 Mt. Laurel (Northern)	Closed	1995	210.00	210
1994 Mt. Laurel (Twins Baby Sidney & Baby Lanier)	100	1994	390.00	390
1994 Mt. Laurel (Western)	Closed	1994	210.00	210
1994 Mt. Laurel St. Patrick Boys	100	1994	210.00	210
1994 Mt. Laurel St. Patrick Girls	200	1994	210.00	210
1995 Mt. Yonah (Easter)	Closed	1995	215.00	215
1995 Mt. Yonah (Valentine)	Closed	1995	200.00	200-205
1996 Nacoochee Valley (Easter)	Closed	1996	215.00	215
1996 Nacoochee Valley (Halloween)	Closed	1996	210.00	210
1991 Onyx (Thanksgiving Pilgrim)	349	1991	190.00	220-240
1991 Onyx (Toddler)	297	1991	175.00	175-225
1991 Onyx 22"	297	1991	190.00	190
1990 Opal (Easter Toddler Fashions)	751	1989	175.00	125-175
1990 Opal (Garden Fashions)	Closed	1989	175.00	125-175
1990 Opal (Toddler)	Closed	1990	175.00	175
1990 Pearl	542	1990	190.00	190-240
1990 Pearl (Toddler)	226	1990	175.00	175-225
1990 Peridot	680	1990	190.00	170-225
1990 Peridot (Halloween Toddler Fashions)	588	1990	175.00	175-210
1990 Peridot (Toddler)	794	1990	175.00	220-320
1992 Platinum	Closed	1992	210.00	220-320
1992 Platinum (Best Man)	Closed	1992	220.00	320
1992 Platinum (Maid of Honor)	Closed	1992	220.00	320
1992 Platinum (Summertime 'Kids-Watermelon)	Closed	1992	210.00	210
1992 Platinum (Toddler)	19	1992	195.00	195
1985 Preemie (boy)	3,750	1985	150.00	110-145
1985 Preemie (girl)	11,250	1985	150.00	110-145
1985 Preemie Twins, set/2	1,500	1985	600.00	325-600
1990 Quartz (Toddler)	347	1990	175.00	175
1990 Quartz (Valentine Toddler Fashions)	708	1989	175.00	175-225
1992 QVC Exclusive (Janeen Sybil)	200	1992	275.00	275
1993 QVC Exclusive (Lauren Rose)	300	1993	335.00	300-800
1994 QVC Exclusive (Lee Ryan)	300	1994	348.00	600-1000
1992 QVC Exclusive (Preemie) (Celeste Diane)	500	1992	250.00	250

YEAR ISSUE	EDITION LIMIT	YEAR RETD.	ISSUE PRICE	*QUOTE U.S.$
1992 QVC Exclusive (Toddler) (Abigail Sydney)	1,000	1992	225.00	225
1993 QVC Exclusive (Newborn)	187	1993	N/A	200
1985 Rose	40,000	1985	135.00	130-140
1989 Ruby	1,325	1989	150.00	150
1985 Sapphire	35,000	1985	135.00	135
1997 Sautee Valley	Closed	1997	210.00	210
1997 Sautee Valley (Festival Kid)	Closed	1997	220.00	220
2002 Shoal Creek Kid	Yr.Iss.		265.00	265
2002 Shoal Creek (Preemie)	Yr.Iss.		190.00	190
1992 Silver	73	1992	190.00	190
1992 Silver (Asian Toddler)	219	1992	175.00	175-225
1992 Silver (Toddler)	59	1992	175.00	175
1992 Silver (Valentine Toddler)	283	1992	190.00	190-240
1995 Skitts Mountain	192	1995	210.00	210
1986 Southern Belle "Georgiana"	4,000	1990	160.00	120-160
1984 Sweetheart (Beau)	750	1984	150.00	150-300
1984 Sweetheart (Candi)	750	1984	150.00	150-300
1988 Tiger's Eye	3,653	1989	150.00	150-175
1988 Tiger's Eye (Easter)	788	1989	150.00	180-275
1989 Tiger's Eye (Mother's Day)	231	1989	150.00	175-275
1988 Tiger's Eye (Valentine's Day)	328	1989	150.00	175-275
1987 Topaz	5,000	1987	135.00	130-135
1993 Unicoi	Closed	1993	210.00	210
1993 Unicoi (Ballerina Toddler)	Closed	1993	195.00	195-260
1993 Unicoi (Spring Toddler)	Closed	1993	195.00	195-260
1993 Unicoi (Spring)	Closed	1993	210.00	210-260
1993 Unicoi (Summer Dinosaur)	Closed	1993	210.00	210-260
1993 Unicoi (Summer Toddler Dinosaur)	Closed	1993	210.00	210-260
1993 Unicoi (Toddler)	Closed	1993	210.00	210
1993 White Christmas - Regular Kids (only)	223	1993	210.00	210-260
1984 World Class	2,500	1984	150.00	150-400

Cabbage Patch Kids (10 Character Kids) - X. Roberts

YEAR ISSUE	EDITION LIMIT	YEAR RETD.	ISSUE PRICE	*QUOTE U.S.$
1982 Amy L.	206	1982	125.00	500-700
1982 Bobbie J.	314	1982	125.00	450-600
1982 Billy B.	201	1982	125.00	450-600
1982 Dorothy J.	126	1982	125.00	550-700
1982 Gilda R.	105	1982	125.00	700-2500
1982 Marilyn S.	275	1982	125.00	595-800
1982 Otis L.	308	1982	125.00	700
1982 Rebecca R.	301	1982	125.00	500-700
1982 Sybil S.	502	1982	125.00	450-700
1982 Tyler B.	94	1982	125.00	2000-3000

Cabbage Patch Kids Anniversary - X. Roberts

YEAR ISSUE	EDITION LIMIT	YEAR RETD.	ISSUE PRICE	*QUOTE U.S.$
1998 Spring Sass	300		395.00	395
1998 Summer Mischief	300		395.00	395
1998 Autumn Scholar	300		395.00	395
1998 Winter Snuggles	300		395.00	395

Cabbage Patch Kids Baby Character - X. Roberts

YEAR ISSUE	EDITION LIMIT	YEAR RETD.	ISSUE PRICE	*QUOTE U.S.$
1990 Baby Amy Loretta Nursery	509	1990	200.00	130-225
1991 Baby Billy Badd Nursery	306	1991	200.00	130-225
1991 Baby Bobbie Jo Nursery	393	1991	200.00	130-225
1988 Baby Dorothy Jane Nursery	2,000	1992	165.00	130-225
1992 Baby Gilda Roxanne Nursery	351	1992	200.00	130-225
1988 Baby Marilyn Suzanne Nursery	2,000	1992	165.00	130-225
1992 Baby Rebecca Ruby Nursery	373	1992	200.00	130-225
1988 Baby Sybil Sadie Nursery	2,000	1992	165.00	130-225
1988 Baby Tyler Bo Nursery	2,000	1993	165.00	130-225

Cabbage Patch Kids Circus Parade - X. Roberts

YEAR ISSUE	EDITION LIMIT	YEAR RETD.	ISSUE PRICE	*QUOTE U.S.$
1987 Big Top Clown-Baby Cakes	2,000	1987	180.00	225-300
1991 Big Top Tot-Mitzi	1,000	1991	220.00	220-225
1989 Happy Hobo-Bashful Billy	1,000	1989	180.00	250-350
1997 Jingling Jester-Jacqueline	500	1997	275.00	275

Cabbage Patch Kids International - X. Roberts

YEAR ISSUE	EDITION LIMIT	YEAR RETD.	ISSUE PRICE	*QUOTE U.S.$
1983 American Indian/Pair	500	1983	300.00	1000-1200
1984 Bavarian/Pair	500	1984	300.00	350-800
1983 Hispanic/Pair	500	1983	300.00	375-450
1983 Irish/Pair	2,000	1983	320.00	275-320
1983 Oriental/Pair	500	1983	300.00	1000
1987 Polynesian (Lokelina)	1,000	1987	180.00	180
1987 Polynesian (Ohana)	1,000	1987	180.00	180

Cabbage Patch Kids OlympiKids™ - X. Roberts

YEAR ISSUE	EDITION LIMIT	YEAR RETD.	ISSUE PRICE	*QUOTE U.S.$
1996 Baseball Boy	159	1996	275.00	275-280
1996 Basketball Boy & Girl	199	1996	275.00	275
1996 Basketball Girl	302	1996	275.00	275
1996 Cyclist Boy	126	1996	275.00	275

YEAR ISSUE	EDITION LIMIT	YEAR RETD.	ISSUE PRICE	*QUOTE U.S.$
1996 Equestrian Girl	350	1996	275.00	275-350
1995 Gymnastics Boy	241	1996	275.00	275
1995 Rowing Girl	205	1996	275.00	275
1995 Soccer Boy	162	1996	275.00	275
1995 Soccer Girl	262	1996	275.00	275
1996 Softball Girl	140	1996	275.00	275
1995 Track & Field Girl	422	1996	275.00	275
1995 Weight Lifting Boy	158	1996	275.00	275

Cabbage Patch Kids Porcelain - X. Roberts

1994 Porcelain Angel (Angelica)	208	1994	160.00	160
1994 Porcelain Friends (Karen Lee)	59	1994	150.00	150
1994 Porcelain Friends (Kassie Lou)	58	1994	150.00	150
1994 Porcelain Friends (Katie Lyn)	61	1994	150.00	150
1995 Porcelain Peirrot (Sharri Starr)	198	1995	160.00	160

Cabbage Patch Kids Storybook - X. Roberts

1986 Mark Twain (Becky Thatcher)	2,500	1986	160.00	150-170
1986 Mark Twain (Huck Finn)	2,500	1986	160.00	150-170
1986 Mark Twain (Tom Sawyer)	2,500	1986	160.00	150-170
1987 Sleeping Beauty (Prince Charming)	1,250	1991	180.00	150-170
1987 Sleeping Beauty (Sleeping Beauty)	1,250	1991	180.00	150-170

Christmas Collection - X. Roberts

1979 X Christmas	1,000	1979	150.00	3000-5500
1980 Christmas-Nicholas/Noel	500	1980	400.00	900-1000
1982 Christmas-Baby Rudy/Christy Nicole	500	1982	400.00	1000-1600
1983 Christmas-Holly/Berry	1,000	1983	400.00	680-800
1984 Christmas-Carole/Chris	1,000	1984	400.00	425-600
1985 Christmas-Baby Sandy/Claude	2,500	1990	400.00	250-400
1986 Christmas-Hilliary/Nigel	2,000	1990	400.00	400-425
1987 Christmas-Katrina/Misha	2,000	1990	500.00	500
1988 Christmas-Kelly/Kane	2,000	1993	500.00	250-500
1989 Christmas-Joy	500	1989	250.00	300-400
1990 Christmas-Krystina	596	1991	250.00	210-260
1991 Christmas-Nick	700	1991	275.00	275
1992 Christmas-Christy Claus	700	1993	285.00	285
1993 Christmas-Rudolph	500	1993	275.00	275
1994 Christmas-Natalie	500	1994	275.00	225-275
1995 Christmas-Treena	500	1995	275.00	275
1996 Christmas-Sammy The Snowman	500	1996	275.00	245-275
1997 Christmas-Melody	300	1997	295.00	295-400
1998 Christmas-Ginger	300	1998	315.00	245-315
1999 Christmas-Arella	300	1999	320.00	250-320
2000 Christmas-Merry	300	2000	295.00	295
2001 Christmas-December	300	2001	345.00	345

Convention Baby - X. Roberts

1989 Ashley (Jade)	200	1989	250.00	250-500
1990 Bradley (Opal)	200	1990	175.00	300-600
1991 Caroline (Garnet)	200	1991	200.00	300
1992 Duke (Brass)	200	1992	225.00	375-400
1993 Ellen (Unicoi)	200	1993	225.00	300-400
1994 Justin (Mt. Laurel)	200	1994	225.00	300-400
1995 Fifi (Mt. Yonah)	200	1995	250.00	450-700
1996 Gina (Nacoochee Valley)	200	1996	275.00	275
1997 Hannah (Sautee Valley)	200	1997	275.00	300-350
1998 Ian (Chattahoochee)	200	1998	310.00	310-350
1999 Crystal (Blue Creek)	200	1999	255.00	255
2000 Sandy (Kellum Valley)	200	2000	275.00	275
2000 Autumn (Kellum Valley) (Canadian Convention)	Closed	2000	235.00	235
2001 Madison (Dukes Creek)	200	2001	255.00	255
2001 Matthew (Dukes Creek) (Canadian Convention)	Closed	2001	255.00	255

Favorite Memories - X. Roberts

1999 Terrific 30's	200		345.00	345
1999 Fabulous 40's	200		345.00	345
1999 Nifty 50's	200		345.00	345
1999 Super 70's	200		345.00	345

Furskins - X. Roberts

1983 Humphrey Furskin	2,500	1993	75.00	90-100
1985 Boone (no letter)	25,000	1985	55.00	45-75
1985 Farrell (no letter)	25,000	1985	55.00	45-75
1985 Dudley (no letter)	25,000	1985	55.00	45-75
1985 Hattie (no letter)	25,000	1985	55.00	45-75
1985 Boone (A)	25,000	1985	55.00	45-55
1985 Farrell (A)	25,000	1985	55.00	45-55
1985 Dudley (A)	25,000	1985	55.00	45-55
1985 Hattie (A)	25,000	1985	55.00	45-55

YEAR ISSUE	EDITION LIMIT	YEAR RETD.	ISSUE PRICE	*QUOTE U.S.$
1985 Boone (B)	75,000	1985	55.00	45-55
1985 Farrell (B)	75,000	1985	55.00	45-55
1985 Dudley (B)	75,000	1985	55.00	45-55
1985 Hattie (B)	75,000	1985	55.00	45-55
1985 Boone (C)	100,000	1985	55.00	45-55
1985 Farrell (C)	100,000	1985	55.00	45-55
1985 Dudley (C)	100,000	1985	55.00	45-55
1985 Hattie (C)	100,000	1985	55.00	45-55
1985 Boone (D)	125,000	1985	55.00	45-55
1985 Farrell (D)	125,000	1985	55.00	45-55
1985 Dudley (D)	125,000	1985	55.00	45-55
1985 Hattie (D)	125,000	1985	55.00	45-55
1986 Orville T. (no letter)	5,000	1986	55.00	75-125
1986 Jedgar (no letter)	5,000	1986	55.00	75-125
1986 Selma Jean (no letter)	5,000	1986	55.00	75-125
1986 Fannie Fay (no letter)	5,000	1986	55.00	75-125
1986 Orville T. (A)	5,000	1986	55.00	55-100
1986 Jedgar A)	5,000	1986	55.00	55
1986 Selma Jean (A)	5,000	1986	55.00	55
1986 Fannie Fay (A)	5,000	1986	55.00	55
1986 Bubba (licensed)	Closed	1986	30.00	40-45
1986 Cecelia ("CeCe") (licensed)	Closed	1986	30.00	40-45
1986 Hank "Spitball" (licensed)	Closed	1986	30.00	40-45
1986 J. Livingston Clayton ("Scout") (licensed)	Closed	1986	30.00	40-45
1986 Junie Mae (licensed)	Closed	1986	30.00	40-45
1986 Lila Claire (licensed)	Closed	1986	30.00	40-45
1986 Persimmon (licensed)	Closed	1986	30.00	40-45
1986 Thistle (licensed)	Closed	1986	30.00	75-125

Little People - X. Roberts

1978 "A" Blue	1,000	1978	45.00	2000-5000
1978 "B" Red	1,000	1978	80.00	3200-5000
1979 "C" Burgundy	5,000	1979	80.00	1600-2300
1979 "D" Purple	10,000	1979	80.00	500-1000
1979 "E" Bronze	15,000	1980	80.00	450-700
1982 "PE" New 'Ears Preemie	5,000	1982	140.00	225-300
1981 "PR II" Preemie	10,000	1981	130.00	150-250
1980 "SP" Preemie	5,000	1980	100.00	180-400
1982 "U" Unsigned	21,000	1982	125.00	225-300
1982 "U" Unsigned (& 1980)	73,000	1981	125.00	250-300
1980 Celebrity	5,000	1980	200.00	300-400
1980 Grand Edition	1,000	1988	1000.00	700-800
1978 Helen Blue	Closed	1978	30.00	6000-10000
1981 Little People Pals 12"	10,000	N/A	75.00	165-350
1981 New 'Ears	15,000	1981	125.00	130-295
1981 Standing Edition	5,000	1988	300.00	250-300

Mobile Patch Babies - X. Roberts

1992 Garden Party Sprout (Babyland "Miss Eula")	140	1992	250.00	350-500
1992 Garden Party Sprout (Chris' Corner Clown-Daisy)	110	1992	250.00	350-500
1992 Garden Party Sprout (Cottage of Memories Indian Girl)	80	1992	250.00	350-500
1992 Garden Party Sprout (Doll House Sweet Dreams)	82	1992	250.00	350-500
1992 Garden Party Sprout (Hobby City "Tinkerbell")	160	1992	250.00	350-500
1992 Garden Party Sprout (Wee Heather Victorian-Heather)	62	1992	250.00	350-500
1997 Sautee Valley (Mama's Babies & Bears)	Closed	1997	195.00	195
1997 Sautee Valley (Doll & Teddy Bear Expo)	Closed	1997	195.00	195
1997 Sautee Valley (Rainbow's End)	Closed	1997	195.00	195
1997 Sautee Valley (Roxanne's Doll Shoppe)	Closed	1997	195.00	195
1997 Sautee Valley (S.W. Randall Toys & Gifts)	Closed	1997	195.00	195
1997 Sautee Valley (Rainbow Connection)	Closed	1997	195.00	195
1997 Sautee Valley (Heirlooms of Tomorrow)	Closed	1997	195.00	195
1998 Chattahoochee Newborn (Rainbow Connection)	Closed	1998	225.00	225
1998 Chattahoochee Newborn (Hobby City)	Closed	1998	225.00	225
1998 Chattahoochee Newborn (Cape Art Mart)	Closed	1998	225.00	225
1998 Chattahoochee Newborn (Rainbow's End)	Closed	1998	225.00	225
1998 Chattahoochee Newborn (Black Gold Dolls)	Closed	1998	225.00	225

Collectors' Information Bureau   *Quotes have been rounded up to nearest dollar

YEAR ISSUE	EDITION LIMIT	YEAR RETD.	ISSUE PRICE	*QUOTE U.S.$
1998 Chattahoochee Newborn (Mama's Babies & Bears)	Closed	1998	225.00	225
1998 Chattahoochee Newborn (Puppenkinder)	Closed	1998	225.00	225
1998 Chattahoochee Newborn (Doll House)	Closed	1998	225.00	225
1998 Chattahoochee Newborn (Merry Christmas Shoppe)	Closed	1998	225.00	225
1998 Chattahoochee Newborn (Contemporary Dolls)	Closed	1998	225.00	225
1998 Chattahoochee Newborn (Roxanne's Doll Shoppe)	Closed	1998	225.00	225
1998 Chattahoochee Newborn (SW Randall)	Closed	1998	225.00	225
1998 Chattahoochee Newborn (Heirlooms of Tomorrow)	Closed	1998	225.00	225
1999 Blue Creek Newborn	Closed	1999	235.00	235

Show Specials - X. Roberts

YEAR ISSUE	EDITION LIMIT	YEAR RETD.	ISSUE PRICE	*QUOTE U.S.$
1985 Topaz (Iris)	1,500	1985	135.00	450-600
1986 Amethyst (Rusty)	250	1986	135.00	200-300
1986 Amethyst (Tiffy)	500	1986	135.00	200-400
1998 Chattahoochee Preemie (Aimee) (West Coast Expo)	20	1998	225.00	450-600
1998 Chattahoochee Preemie (Abigail) (East Coast Expo)	20	1998	225.00	225
1999 Blue Creek Newborn (Annabelle) (West Coast Booth Baby)	30	1999	225.00	225
1999 Blue Creek Newborn (Amanda) (West Coast Show Baby)	25	1999	225.00	225
2000 Kellum Valley Newborn (Mary Beth) (West Coast Show Baby)	25		225.00	225
2000 Kellum Valley Newborn (Prissy) (East Coast Show Baby)	25		225.00	225
2000 Daddy's Lil' Darlin' (West Coast Show Baby)	Closed	2000	199.00	199
2000 Daddy's Lil' Darlin' (East Coast Show Baby)	Closed	2000	199.00	199

Papel Giftware/Cast Art Industries

Annette Funicello Collectible Bear Co./Angel Collection - Various

YEAR ISSUE	EDITION LIMIT	YEAR RETD.	ISSUE PRICE	*QUOTE U.S.$
2002 Aimee - D. Rife	20,000		81.62	82
2001 Amber - D. Rife	20,000		76.47	77
2001 Angelica - S. Knapp	20,000		49.68	50
2000 Birdie - C. Firmage	20,000		80.00	80
2000 Coral - B. Cardwell	20,000		60.00	60
2000 Danielle - P. Friesen	20,000		85.48	86
2001 Emily - D. Rife	20,000		67.05	68
2000 Felicity - D. Rife	20,000		59.88	60
2000 Melody - L. Scott	2,000		54.25	55
2001 Noelle - J. Antonelli	20,000		44.31	45
2001 Petula - D. Rife	20,000		60.59	70
2002 Sabrina - B. Cardwell	1,500		68.82	70
2002 Twinkle Toes - L. Applebeary	20,000		46.84	47
2000 Twyla - S. Payne	20,000		60.00	60

Annette Funicello Collectible Bear Co./Annettes Favorite - D. Ellis

YEAR ISSUE	EDITION LIMIT	YEAR RETD.	ISSUE PRICE	*QUOTE U.S.$
2002 Violetta	1,000		83.22	84

Annette Funicello Collectible Bear Co./Ballerina Collection - Various

YEAR ISSUE	EDITION LIMIT	YEAR RETD.	ISSUE PRICE	*QUOTE U.S.$
2001 Antoinette - P. Holton	2,500		39.99	40
2002 Tinkerbear - D. Rife	1,500		46.84	47

Annette Funicello Collectible Bear Co./Bear Buddies Collection - Various

YEAR ISSUE	EDITION LIMIT	YEAR RETD.	ISSUE PRICE	*QUOTE U.S.$
2001 Denim & Jean - D. Ellis	3,000		66.25	67
2002 Izza & Bella - A. Dana	1,000		85.48	86
2000 Piggy Bear Ride - D. Rife	3,000		50.00	50
2000 PJ and Snowball - D. Rife	5,000		55.00	55
2001 Some Bunny Loves Me - L. Applebeary	3,000		86.75	87

Annette Funicello Collectible Bear Co./BearScents - T. Hayes

YEAR ISSUE	EDITION LIMIT	YEAR RETD.	ISSUE PRICE	*QUOTE U.S.$
2001 Cinnabear	3,000		86.11	87

Annette Funicello Collectible Bear Co./Beary'licious Collection - L. Applebeary, unless otherwise noted

YEAR ISSUE	EDITION LIMIT	YEAR RETD.	ISSUE PRICE	*QUOTE U.S.$
2001 Bear Ana Nut	10,000		30.00	30
2001 Bubble Cub	10,000		30.00	30
2001 Choc 'O Chip	10,000		30.00	30
2001 Cookies & Milk - K. Millengar	1,500		69.69	70
2001 Creamcicle	10,000		30.00	30
2000 Daisy Mae - K. Ruff	2,500		55.00	55
2001 Ginger Snapp Mates	1,500		129.12	130
2000 Grape Beary Slush - S. Payne	5,000		40.00	40
2001 Gumbeary Drop	5,000		25.15	26
2001 Icebeary Fluff - J. Fox	2,500		59.98	60
2001 Lime Sublime	Open		35.14	36
2000 Peachbeary Fluff - J. Fox	2,500		60.00	60
2001 Raz Mataz	10,000		30.00	30
2001 Strawbeary Cheesecake	10,000		30.00	30

Annette Funicello Collectible Bear Co./Calico Cousins - B. Cardwell

YEAR ISSUE	EDITION LIMIT	YEAR RETD.	ISSUE PRICE	*QUOTE U.S.$
2002 Daisy	2,000		57.15	58
2002 Dixie	2,000		57.15	58
2002 Dolly	2,000		57.15	58

Annette Funicello Collectible Bear Co./Cubcakes - L. Applebeary

YEAR ISSUE	EDITION LIMIT	YEAR RETD.	ISSUE PRICE	*QUOTE U.S.$
2001 Sprinkles	5,000		46.84	47

Annette Funicello Collectible Bear Co./Cute As A Button - M. Talbot

YEAR ISSUE	EDITION LIMIT	YEAR RETD.	ISSUE PRICE	*QUOTE U.S.$
2002 Buttons	2,500		38.25	39

Annette Funicello Collectible Bear Co./Dream Keeper Collection - Various

YEAR ISSUE	EDITION LIMIT	YEAR RETD.	ISSUE PRICE	*QUOTE U.S.$
2000 Gracie - S. Payne	5,000		70.00	70
2000 Pillow Talk - K. Rundlett	5,000		70.00	70
2002 Sasha - L. Medford	2,500		85.45	86
2002 Snoozie Suzy - B. King	2,500		46.84	47

Annette Funicello Collectible Bear Co./Fairy Beary Collection - D. Rife

YEAR ISSUE	EDITION LIMIT	YEAR RETD.	ISSUE PRICE	*QUOTE U.S.$
2001 Tiffany	20,000		39.99	40

Annette Funicello Collectible Bear Co./Fairy Collection - Various

YEAR ISSUE	EDITION LIMIT	YEAR RETD.	ISSUE PRICE	*QUOTE U.S.$
2000 Beary Godmother - K. Ruff	2,500		55.00	55
2002 Flower Fairy - K. Millengar	2,500		67.22	68
2002 Ginny - L. Medford	2,000		62.42	63
2002 Shea - D. Rife	3,000		87.31	88

Annette Funicello Collectible Bear Co./Flavorite Collection - Various

YEAR ISSUE	EDITION LIMIT	YEAR RETD.	ISSUE PRICE	*QUOTE U.S.$
2001 Cocoa - D. Rife	2,000		55.43	56
2000 Razzbeary Truffle - K. Rundlett	2,500		70.00	70
2002 Tangee - M. Talbot	3,000		83.22	84

Annette Funicello Collectible Bear Co./Flower Power Collection - Various

YEAR ISSUE	EDITION LIMIT	YEAR RETD.	ISSUE PRICE	*QUOTE U.S.$
2002 Dalhia - T. Hayes	5,000		85.45	86
2001 Panzee - M. Talbot	5,000		36.50	37

Annette Funicello Collectible Bear Co./Four Seasons Collection - Various

YEAR ISSUE	EDITION LIMIT	YEAR RETD.	ISSUE PRICE	*QUOTE U.S.$
2001 Katrina - D. Rife	1,000		86.11	87
2001 Sunflower Sally - J. Antonelli	2,500		64.22	65
2001 Vanessa - D. Ellis	1,500		60.59	61

Annette Funicello Collectible Bear Co./Hat Box Collection - L. Medford

YEAR ISSUE	EDITION LIMIT	YEAR RETD.	ISSUE PRICE	*QUOTE U.S.$
2000 Olive	2,500		70.00	70
2001 Pearly	2,500		70.00	70

Annette Funicello Collectible Bear Co./High Tea Collection - A. Dana

YEAR ISSUE	EDITION LIMIT	YEAR RETD.	ISSUE PRICE	*QUOTE U.S.$
2001 Dorothy	2,500		59.88	60
2001 Jessica	5,000		59.88	60

Annette Funicello Collectible Bear Co./Holiday Collection - Various

YEAR ISSUE	EDITION LIMIT	YEAR RETD.	ISSUE PRICE	*QUOTE U.S.$
2000 Holly Anna - D. Rife	3,000		70.00	70
2000 Icicle - L. Applebeary	Open		30.00	30
2000 Mr. Snowbear - C. Dana	5,000		80.00	80

Annette Funicello Collectible Bear Co./Ladies Who Lunch - P. Friesen

YEAR ISSUE	EDITION LIMIT	YEAR RETD.	ISSUE PRICE	*QUOTE U.S.$
2001 Pilar	2,500		62.42	63

Annette Funicello Collectible Bear Co./Music Box Collection - L. Scott

YEAR ISSUE	EDITION LIMIT	YEAR RETD.	ISSUE PRICE	*QUOTE U.S.$
2001 Melody	2,000		54.25	55

DOLLS & PLUSH

YEAR ISSUE	EDITION LIMIT	YEAR RETD.	ISSUE PRICE	*QUOTE U.S.$

Annette Funicello Collectible Bear Co./Nostalgia Collection - D. Ellis, unless otherwise noted

YEAR ISSUE	EDITION LIMIT	YEAR RETD.	ISSUE PRICE	*QUOTE U.S.$
2001 Curly Sue - K. Rundlett	1,500		69.47	70
2002 Keylee	1,500		134.44	135
2001 Thoughtful	1,500		140.00	140

Annette Funicello Collectible Bear Co./Rainbow Collection - B. Cardwell

2000 Aura	5,000		55.00	55
2001 Patchwork Heart	5,000		59.00	59

Annette Funicello Collectible Bear Co./Special Collection - Various

2000 Pandamonium - E. Kislingbury	3,000		120.00	120
2000 Sushi - K. Ruff	2,500		50.00	50
2001 Sushi Platter - A. Funicello	10,000		99.97	100
2002 Sweet Pea - M. Talbot	3,000		46.84	47
2002 Wisteria - A. Dana	1,500		86.11	87
2001 Wonton - K. Ruff	1,500		138.82	139

Annette Funicello Collectible Bear Co./Summer Collection - Various

2001 Daisy - E. Kislingbury	1,000		89.67	90
2002 Zoe - M. Talbot	1,500		75.55	76

Annette Funicello Collectible Bear Co./Tea Cup Collection - M. Talbot

2002 Earl Grey	1,500		55.43	56

Annette Funicello Collectible Bear Co./Teddy Tales Collection - L Medford

2001 Frog Princess	1,500		66.25	67

Annette Funicello Collectible Bear Co./Tutti Fruity Collection - A. Dana

2002 Rasbeary	1,500		62.42	63

Annette Funicello Collectible Bear Co./Victorian Collection - Various

2001 Charlotte - L. Applebeary	5,000		38.25	39
2000 Elizabeth Grace - S. Knapp	1,500		99.00	99
2001 Hannah - S. Knapp	5,000		99.75	100
2002 Karla - L. Applebeary	2,000		38.25	39
2002 Katherine - D. Steele	2,000		85.48	86
2002 Natori - A. Dana	1,000		134.44	135
2000 Paluma - A. Dana	1,500		90.00	90
2002 Savanah Rose - J. Fox	3,000		85.45	86

Annette Funicello Collectible Bear Co./Victorian Garden Collection - Various

2001 Arianna - L. Medford	2,500		79.05	45
2000 Katelyn - S. Payne	5,000		45.00	45
2001 Lady Love Bug - P. Vicioso	1,500		109.06	110

Annette Funicello Collectible Bear Co./When I Was Little Collection - D. Rife

2000 Bubbles	5,000		40.00	40
2002 Flutterbye	1,500		51.89	52
2001 Rub a Dub Dub	3,000		50.00	50

Precious Moments/Enesco Group, Inc.

Delicate Blessings Chenille Plush - S. Butcher

2001 Bunny 869570	Open		10.00	10
2001 Elephant 869554	Open		10.00	10
2001 Horse 874450	Open		10.00	10
2001 Lamb 869562	Open		10.00	10
2001 Lion 869546	Open		10.00	10

Fruit Bears Plush - S. Butcher

2001 Grape Bear with Crate 899313	Open		15.00	15
2001 Green Apple Bear with Crate 899305	Open		15.00	15
2001 Lemon Bear with Crate 244155	Open		15.00	15
2001 Orange Bear with Crate 899321	Open		15.00	15
2001 Pear Bear with Crate 899348	Open		15.00	15
2001 Strawberry Bear with Crate 899291	Open		15.00	15

Gentle Bundle Plush - S. Butcher

2001 My Precious Little Lamb 952362	Open		7.00	7

Graduation Plush - S. Butcher

2001 A Trunk Full of Wishes, 12" Elephant 958379	Open		25.00	25

YEAR ISSUE	EDITION LIMIT	YEAR RETD.	ISSUE PRICE	*QUOTE U.S.$
2001 A Trunk Full of Wishes, 6" Elephant 958360	Open		10.00	10

Jack-In-The-Boxes - S. Butcher

1991 You Have Touched So Many Hearts 422282	2-Yr.	1993	175.00	175
1991 May You Have An Old Fashioned Christmas 417777	2-Yr.	1993	200.00	200
1990 The Voice of Spring 408735	2-Yr.	1992	200.00	200
1990 Summer's Joy 408743	2-Yr.	1992	200.00	200
1990 Autumn's Praise 408751	2-Yr.	1992	200.00	200
1990 Winter's Song 408778	2-Yr.	1992	200.00	200

Mom Plush - S. Butcher

2001 Mom Bear 620343	Open		7.00	7

Monthly Bears - Calendar Cuties Plush - S. Butcher

2001 January 600237	Open		7.00	7
2001 February 600288	Open		7.00	7
2001 March 600296	Open		7.00	7
2001 April 600318	Open		7.00	7
2001 May 600326	Open		7.00	7
2001 June 600350	Open		7.00	7
2001 July 600377	Open		7.00	7
2001 August 600474	Open		7.00	7
2001 September 600598	Open		7.00	7
2001 October 600601	Open		7.00	7
2001 November 600806	Open		7.00	7
2001 December 600814	Open		7.00	7

Precious Moments Dolls - S. Butcher

1981 Mikey, 18" E-6214B	Suspd.		150.00	230
1981 Debbie, 18" E-6214G	Suspd.		150.00	260-286
1982 Cubby, 18" E-7267B	5,000		200.00	380
1982 Tammy, 18" E-7267G	5,000		300.00	450-500
1983 Katie Lynne, 16" E-0539	Suspd.		165.00	143-175
1984 Mother Sew Dear, 18" E-2850	Retrd.	1985	350.00	325-350
1984 Kristy, 12" E-2851	Suspd.		150.00	143-170
1984 Timmy, 12" E-5397	Suspd.		125.00	126-150
1985 Aaron, 12" 12424	Suspd.		135.00	160
1985 Bethany, 12" 12432	Suspd.		135.00	160
1985 P.D., 7" 12475	Suspd.		50.00	54-70
1985 Trish, 7" 12483	Suspd.		50.00	68-95
1986 Bong Bong, 13" 100455	12,000		150.00	225-265
1986 Candy, 13" 100463	12,000		150.00	280-300
1986 Connie, 12" 102253	7,500		160.00	203-240
1987 Angie, The Angel of Mercy 12491	12,500		160.00	253-275
1990 The Voice of Spring 408786	2-Yr.	1992	150.00	150
1990 Summer's Joy 408794	2-Yr.	1992	150.00	129-150
1990 Autumn's Praise 408808	2-Yr.	1992	150.00	129-150
1990 Winter's Song 408816	2-Yr.	1992	150.00	129-150
1991 You Have Touched So Many Hearts 427527	2-Yr.	1993	90.00	90
1991 May You Have An Old Fashioned Christmas 417785	2-Yr.	1993	150.00	175
1991 The Eyes Of The Lord Are Upon You (Boy Action Musical) 429570	Suspd.		65.00	75
1991 The Eyes Of The Lord Are Upon You (Girl Action Musical) 429589	Suspd.		65.00	65

Precious Moments Plush - S. Butcher

1999 Friendship Hits The Spot 729167	Retrd.	2001	35.00	35
1999 You Have Touched So Many Hearts 729175	Retrd.	2001	35.00	35
1999 Put On A Happy Face 729183	Retrd.	2001	35.00	35
1999 Lord Keep Me On My Toes 729191	Retrd.	2001	35.00	35
1999 God Loveth A Cheerful Giver 729205	Retrd.	2001	35.00	35
1999 Tell It To Jesus 729221	Retrd.	2001	35.00	35
2000 Make A Joyful Noise 752762	Retrd.	2001	35.00	35
2000 Cheers To The Leader 752835	Retrd.	2001	35.00	35
2000 Jesus Loves Me 752894	Retrd.	2001	35.00	35

Tender Tails A Christmas Tale- S. Butcher

2001 Chloe 890294	6,000		8.99	9
2001 Mouse King 890308	6,000		8.99	9
2001 Mouse Soldier 890383	6,000		8.99	9
2001 Nutcracker 890286	6,000		8.99	9
2001 Snow Queen 890373	6,000		8.99	9
2001 Sugar Plum Fairy 890367	6,000		8.99	9

Tender Tails Dogs - S. Butcher

2000 Beagle 673226	Closed	2001	6.99	7
2000 Cocker Spaniel 704369	Closed	2001	6.99	7

YEAR ISSUE	EDITION LIMIT	YEAR RETD.	ISSUE PRICE	*QUOTE U.S.$
2000 Dachshund 673293	Closed	2001	6.99	7
2000 Dalmation 672742	Closed	2001	6.99	7
2000 Labrador 704342	Closed	2001	6.99	7
2000 Rottweiler 703915	Closed	2001	6.99	7

Tender Tails Internet - Get With The Program - S. Butcher

2001 Crash The Bug 958549	7,500		6.99	7
2001 Holden the Mouse 958514	7,500		6.99	7
2001 Laptop the Dog 958530	7,500		6.99	7
2001 Sam The Ram 958506	7,500		6.99	7
2001 Sky Z Limit the Bear 958522	7,500		6.99	7
2001 Surf the Spider 958492	7,500		6.99	7

Tender Tails Nativity - S. Butcher

2001 Camel 533963	Open		6.99	7
2001 Donkey 533971	Open		6.99	7
2001 Lamb 963151	Open		6.99	7
2001 Mary, Joseph, Jesus 963135	Open		22.49	23
2001 Nativity Cow 540668	Open		6.99	7
2001 Nativity Quilt Backdrop 540676	Open		9.99	10
2001 Palm Tree 963208	Open		9.99	10

Tender Tails Noah's Ark - S. Butcher

2001 Elephants 851140	Yr.Iss.	2001	10.00	10
2001 Llamas 851132	Yr.Iss.	2001	10.00	10
2001 Noah & Wife 851159	Yr.Iss.	2001	20.00	20
2001 Tigers 851124	Yr.Iss.	2001	10.00	10

Tender Tails Once Upon A Tale - S. Butcher

2000 Baby Dragon 749303	Closed	2001	9.99	10
2000 Knight 749273	Closed	2001	9.99	10
2000 Pegasus 749338	Closed	2001	9.99	10
2000 Prince 749265	Closed	2001	9.99	10
2000 Princess 749281	Closed	2001	9.99	10
2000 Unicorn 749311	Closed	2001	9.99	10
2000 White Horse 749346	Closed	2001	9.99	10

Trusting Is Bee-lieving Plush - S. Butcher

2001 12" Bee 927767	Open		15.00	15

R. JOHN WRIGHT DOLLS

The R. JOHN WRIGHT Collectors' Club - R. John Wright

1996 Golliwogg	1,498	1997	535.00	600
1997 Miss Golli	849	1998	535.00	600
1997 Teddy Bear	866	1998	375.00	400
1998 Periwinkle	Closed	1999	385.00	385
1999 Silly Old Bear	Closed	1999	325.00	325

Babes in Toyland Series II - R. John Wright

1984 Lindsay & Michael	250	1985	750.00	1350-2350
1983 Timothy & Rosemary	50	1983	700.00	N/A

Character Dolls - R. John Wright

1979 Bernard	N/A	1981	100.00	N/A
1979 Bridget	N/A	1981	100.00	2400
1979 Elsa	N/A	1981	100.00	N/A
1979 Emma	N/A	1981	100.00	N/A
1979 Erica	N/A	1981	100.00	N/A
1979 Gretchen	N/A	1981	100.00	2400
1979 Guido	N/A	1981	100.00	2400
1979 Jenny	N/A	1981	100.00	N/A
1979 Karl	N/A	1981	100.00	N/A
1979 Kate	N/A	1981	100.00	N/A
1979 Lina	N/A	1981	100.00	N/A
1979 MacTavish	N/A	1981	100.00	2400
1979 Marion	N/A	1981	100.00	N/A
1979 Paddy	N/A	1981	100.00	2400
1979 Seth	N/A	1981	100.00	2400
1979 St. Nicholas	N/A	1981	100.00	3500

Childhood Classics - R. John Wright

1988 Little Red Riding Hood	500	1991	875.00	1200-1600

Children Dolls - R. John Wright

1982 Captain Corey	50	1982	350.00	350
1985 Edward and His Drum	150	1985	425.00	1800
1984 Emily and the Enchanted Doll	150	1984	425.00	3500
1983 The Little Prince	250	1984	375.00	3995
1985 Max and His Pinocchio	150	1984	385.00	1800

Disneyana Convention - R. John Wright

1992 Pinocchio	100	1992	750.00	1000-2000

Little Children - R. John Wright

1981 Becky	250	1985	325.00	1500
1981 Elizabeth	250	1985	325.00	1200
1981 Hannah	250	1985	325.00	325
1981 Jesse	250	1985	325.00	1200
1981 Lillian	250	1985	325.00	900
1985 Lisa	250	1986	325.00	900
1981 Peter	250	1985	325.00	325
1985 Rachel -Sunday Best	250	1986	325.00	1800
1985 Scott	250	1986	325.00	900
1981 Tad	250	1985	325.00	325
1981 William	250	1985	325.00	1000

Pinocchio - R. John Wright

1994 Geppetto & Pinocchio I (marionette)	500	1995	1800.00	2985
1994 Geppetto & Pinocchio II (traditional)	250	1994	1800.00	2750-3125
1992 Pleasure Island Pinocchio	250	1992	725.00	2000

Sewn Felt Dolls - R. John Wright

1978 8" Elfs and Black Imps	N/A	1979	45.00	45

Snow White - R. John Wright

1992 Frightened Dopey	Retrd.	1992	N/A	N/A
1989 Snow White & The Seven Dwarfs (8 pc. matched numbd. set)	1,000	1994	3000.00	2925-4925
1989 Snow White Princess, Snow White in Rags & Seven Dwarfs (matched numbd. set)	250	1994	3500.00	5500-6500
1989 -Snow White in Rags	Retrd.	1994	800.00	800

Winnie-the-Pooh - R. John Wright

1985 Christopher Robin	Retrd.	N/A	595.00	895
1986 Christopher Robin I w/8" Pooh	1,000	1986	595.00	1325-3252
1986 Christopher Robin II Raincoat	500	1987	585.00	1750-3252
1997 Holiday Winnie-the-Pooh	1,000	1997	585.00	750-895
1985 Eeyore 6"	1,000	1988	95.00	450-650
1985 Kanga & Roo 10"	1,000	1988	95.00	695
1987 Lifesize Piglet 9"	1,000	1988	85.00	550
1987 Lifesize Pooh 18"	2,500	1988	190.00	1050-1400
1989 Piglet 10 1/2"	1,000	1989	145.00	675
1997 Party Tigger & Eeyore, set/2	100	N/A	440.00	590
1985 Piglet 5"	1,000	1988	45.00	290-650
1988 Piglet 7" w/Violets	2,500	1989	145.00	650
1985 Tigger 6"	1,000	1988	95.00	295-650
1988 Winnie-the-Pooh 20"	2,500	1988	165.00	1150-2150
1985 Winnie-the-Pooh 8"	1,500	1986	95.00	600-1200
1989 Winnie-the-Pooh and His Favorite Chair 10"	500	1989	595.00	2475
1987 Winnie-the-Pooh with Hunny Pot 14"	5,000	1989	145.00	675-1275

Winnie-the-Pooh Pocket Series - R. John Wright

1997 Christopher Robin	Retrd.	1997	N/A	895
1994 Pocket Eeyore	3,500	N/A	95.00	250-350
1999 Pocket Kanga & Roo	3,500		310.00	310
1999 Pocket Owl	3,500		310.00	310
1994 Pocket Piglet	3,500	1994	135.00	250-350
1993 Pocket Pooh	3,500	1993	285.00	675-875
1996 Pocket Tigger	Retrd.	1996	N/A	295
1996 Wintertime Eeyore (FAO Schwarz Exclusive)	250	1996	725.00	895
1996 -Eeyore's Stickhouse (FAO Schwarz Exclusive)	250	1996	N/A	700-1400
1995 Wintertime Pooh & Piglet (FAO Schwarz Exclusive)	250	1995	725.00	1495-1650

Reco International

Childhood Doll Collection - S. Kuck

1994 A Kiss Goodnight	Retrd.	1995	79.00	79-150
1995 Reading With Teddy	Retrd.	1995	79.00	125-130
1994 Teaching Teddy His Prayers	Retrd.	1997	79.00	125-130
1996 Teddy's Picnic	Retrd.	1997	79.00	79-125

Christmas Doll Collection - S. Kuck

1996 Carol	Retrd.	2000	135.00	135
1997 Kristen	Open		135.00	135

Little Valentina - S. Kuck

1998 Little Valentina	Open		99.00	99

Love Comes on Angel's Wings - S. Kuck

2001 An Angel's Love	Open		70.00	70

DOLLS & PLUSH/FIGURINES

Pocket Full of Love - S. Kuck

YEAR ISSUE	EDITION LIMIT	YEAR RETD.	ISSUE PRICE	*QUOTE U.S.$
1997 Gabriella	Retrd.	2000	30.00	30
1998 Tanya	Open		30.00	30
1999 Victoria	Open		30.00	30
1999 Natasha	Open		30.00	30

Precious Memories of Motherhood - S. Kuck

1993 Bedtime	Retrd.	1994	149.00	90-149
1992 Expectant Moments	Retrd.	1993	149.00	90-149
1990 Loving Steps	Retrd.	1992	125.00	150-195
1991 Lullaby	Retrd.	1995	125.00	125-200

Private Moments - A Wedding Album - S. Kuck

2001 A Vision of Bliss	Open		130.00	130

Wedding Doll - S. Kuck

1997 Jennifer Rose	Open		195.00	195
1998 Audrey & Lindsey	Open		195.00	195

San Francisco Music Box Company

Boyds Bears Musicals-Plush - G. M. Lowenthal

1998 Abbey Ewe	Closed	1999	35.00	35
2000 Adrian Ornament	Open		12.00	12
1999 Alexis Berriman	Closed	1999	70.00	70
1997 Allison Babbit Hare	Closed	1997	24.95	25
1997 Ariel with Heart Ornament	Open		9.95	10
1997 Ashley Hare	Closed	1998	24.95	25
2000 Aubrey Tippietoes	Open		35.00	35
1998 Aunt Becky Boarchild	Closed	1999	50.00	50
1997 Benjamin Honey Bear with Sweater	Closed	1999	24.95	25
1998 Braxton B. Bear	Open		25.00	25
1998 Camomile w/Quilt	Closed	1999	27.00	27
1998 Clarissa Bear	Closed	1999	57.00	57
1997 Cleo P. Pussytoes	Closed	1999	39.95	40
1997 Eugenia Bear	Closed	1998	49.95	50
1998 Fidelity B. Morgan IV Bear	Closed	1999	35.00	35
1997 Guinevere Bear	Closed	1999	24.95	25
1999 Hayes R. Bearington	2,000		125.00	125
1998 Heranamous	Closed	1999	35.00	35
2000 Katie with Welby 12" Doll	Open		50.00	50
1999 Klaus von Fuzzner	Closed	1999	50.00	50
1998 Lady Pembrooke	Closed	1999	25.00	25
1998 Lavina V. Harriweather	Closed	1999	25.00	25
2000 Marissa P. Pussytoes	Open		40.00	40
1998 Momma McBear	Open		30.00	30
2000 Momma McFuzz and Missy	Open		35.00	35
2000 Mrs. Northstar	Open		45.00	45
1999 Mrs. Trumbull	Closed	1999	40.00	40
2000 Poof Puffleberry w/Blankie	Open		30.00	30
1999 Prudence Bearimore	Closed	1999	45.00	45
1997 Rosalind Bear	Closed	1997	39.95	40
1998 Rosalind II Bear	Closed	1998	40.00	40
1998 Rosie O'Pigg	Open		18.00	18
2000 Sally and Annie	Open		30.00	30
2001 Santa Claus Kringlebeary	Open		45.00	45
1997 Smith Witter II	Open		34.95	35
2000 Susan with Malcolm and Beau Bear Collectors	Open		85.00	85
1998 Winnie II in blue Romper	Closed	1999	35.00	35
1998 Winnie II in yellow Romper	Open		38.00	38
1998 Zelda Fitzhare	Closed	1999	35.00	35

Katherine's Collection - W. Kleski

1999 Bubbles Cat Doll Musical	Open		125.00	125
1999 Giggles Cat Doll Musical	Open		125.00	125
1999 Louisa Victorian Baby Doll Musical	Open		150.00	150

Musical Porcelain Dolls - San Francisco Music Box Company

1998 Aerial Angel	2,500	1998	125.00	125
1999 Amanda and Baby Doll	2,500	2000	150.00	150
1997 Angelica Angel	600	1997	200.00	200
1999 Anne Antique	2,500	1999	135.00	135
1999 Ballerina	2,500	1999	100.00	100
1999 Bride	2,500		200.00	200
1999 Brittany II Doll	Closed	2000	85.00	85
1999 Caitlyn Doll	2,500		150.00	150
1997 Christina Ballroom	1,500	1998	200.00	200
2001 Echo Fairy Doll	5,000		125.00	125
1999 Elise Fairy	2,500	1999	200.00	200

1998 Elizabeth Victorian	1,200	1998	200.00	200
1999 Fairy	2,500	2000	200.00	200
1999 Faith Christening Doll	2,500	1999	150.00	150
1999 Genevieve	2,500	1999	99.00	99
1997 Julia Bride	1,600	1998	200.00	200
1998 Michelle with Baby	1,200	2000	200.00	200
1998 Mom & Baby	2,500	1998	150.00	150
1999 Mom & Daughter	2,500	2000	150.00	150
1999 Mom & Toddler	2,500	2000	200.00	200
1999 Nicole w/Rabbit	2,500	1999	150.00	150
1997 Priscilla Bride	600	1997	200.00	200
1999 Rapunzel	2,500	1999	100.00	100
1999 Rose Bride	2,500	2002	200.00	200
1997 Therese Victorian	600	1998	200.00	200
1997 Tiffany Victorian	1,800	1998	200.00	200
1999 Victoria Antique	2,500	1999	135.00	135

Susan Wakeen Doll Co. Inc.

The Littlest Ballet Company - S. Wakeen

1985 Cynthia	375		198.00	350
1987 Elizabeth	250		425.00	1000
1985 Jeanne	375		198.00	800
1985 Jennifer	250		750.00	750
1987 Marie Ann	50		1000.00	1000
1985 Patty	375		198.00	400-500

FIGURINES

Anchor Bay

Great Ships of the World - Staff

2001 110 Island Class	4,000		75.00	75
1997 Lightship "Chesapeake"	Open		155.00	155
1997 Lightship "Chesapeake" (special ed.)	4,000	1997	170.00	170-250
1998 Lightship "Columbia"	4,000		154.00	154
1997 Lightship "Huron"	Retrd.	1998	155.00	155
1997 Lightship "Huron" (special ed.)	4,000		170.00	170
1998 Lightship "Portsmouth"	4,000		170.00	170
1997 Motor Yacht "Kim"	Retrd.	1998	139.00	139
1997 Motor Yacht "Kim" (special ed.)	4,000	1998	154.00	154
1998 Purse Seiner "The Tori Dawn"	4,000		154.00	154
1997 Sardine "Lori"	Retrd.	1998	159.00	159
1997 Sardine "Lori" (special ed.)	4,000		174.00	174
1997 Skipjack "Nancy"	Retrd.	1998	151.00	151
1997 Skipjack "Nancy" (special ed.)	4,000	1998	166.00	149-166
1997 Tugboat "Toledo"	Retrd.	1998	131.00	131
1997 Tugboat "Toledo" (special ed.)	4,000	1998	146.00	146
2002 U.S.C.G. 41 ft. Lifeboat	4,000		65.00	65
1999 U.S.C.G. 44 ft. Lifeboat	4,000		125.00	125
2002 U.S.C.G. 44 ft. Lifeboat (revised)	4,000		70.00	70

Anheuser-Busch, Inc.

Anheuser-Busch Collectible Figurines - A. Busch, Inc., unless otherwise noted

1994 Buddies N4575 - M. Urdahl	7,500	1997	65.00	65
1995 Horseplay F1 - P. Radtke	7,500	2001	65.00	65
1996 "Bud-weis-er Frogs" F4	Retrd.	1999	30.00	30
1996 Something Brewing F3	7,500	2001	65.00	65
1997 "Gone Fishing" F5	7,500	2001	65.00	65
1997 "Boy Meets Girl" Budweiser Frogs F7	Open		30.00	30
1998 "Free Ride" Budweiser Frogs F8	Retrd.	2000	35.00	35
1998 "Louie and Frank" Budweiser Lizards F9	Retrd.	2001	35.00	35
2000 Ferret Takes Center Stage F10	Open		35.00	35

The Clydesdale Collection - A. Busch, Inc.

1998 An Apple For King CLYD5	Open		60.00	60
2001 The Bauernhof at Grant's Farm CLYD16	2,500		250.00	250
1999 Braiding For Parade CLYD9	Open		75.00	75
1998 Clydesdale Football CLYD3	20,000		85.00	85
1999 Five-Horse Hitch CLYD10	20,000		120.00	120
1998 Full Parade Dress CLYD1	Open		50.00	50
1999 Getting Shod CLYD8	Open		80.00	80
2000 Holiday Scene CLYD15	5,000		235.00	235
1998 Mare & Foal CLYD4	Retrd.	2000	70.00	70

Collectors' Information Bureau   *Quotes have been rounded up to nearest dollar

YEAR ISSUE	EDITION LIMIT	YEAR RETD.	ISSUE PRICE	*QUOTE U.S.$
2001 Official Horseshoer CLYD14	Open		70.00	70
1998 Pals CLYD2	Open		65.00	65
2000 Running Free CLYD12	Open		60.00	60
1999 Scottish Farmer CLYD7	Open		60.00	60
2000 Separated At Birth CLYD11	Open		35.00	35
1999 Washington Scene CLYD6	5,000		230.00	230

Armani

G. Armani Society Members Only Figurine - G. Armani

YEAR ISSUE	EDITION LIMIT	YEAR RETD.	ISSUE PRICE	*QUOTE U.S.$
1990 My Fine Feathered Friends (Bonus)122S	Closed	1990	175.00	163-560
1990 Awakening (Members Only) 591C	Closed	1991	137.50	910-1186
1991 Peace & Harmony (Bonus) 824C	7,500	1991	300.00	600-650
1991 Ruffles (Members Only) 745E	Closed	1992	139.00	139-399
1992 Ascent (Members Only) 866C	Closed	1993	195.00	195-274
1992 Julie (Bonus) 293P	Closed	1992	90.00	192-234
1992 Juliette (Bonus) 294P	Closed	1992	90.00	224-260
1993 Venus (Members Only) 881E	Closed	1994	225.00	345-390
1993 Lady Rose (Bonus) 197C	Closed	1993	125.00	125-600
1994 Harlequin 1994 Fifth Anniversary 490C	Closed	1995	300.00	299-495
1994 Flora (Members Only) 212C	Closed	1995	225.00	186-390
1994 Joy Ride (Bonus) 248C	Closed	1994	125.00	156-260
1995 Melody (Members Only) 656C	Closed	1996	250.00	475
1995 Scarlett (Bonus) 698C	Closed	2000	200.00	324-480
1996 Allegra (Members Only) 345C	Closed	1997	250.00	281-350
1996 Arianna (Bonus) 400C	Closed	1996	125.00	125-225
1997 It's Mine (Bonus) 136C	Closed	1997	200.00	160-236
1997 Sabrina (Members Only) 110C	Closed	1998	275.00	250-395
1998 Beth (Bonus) 519C	Closed	1998	115.00	92-150
1998 Lucia (Members Only) 755C	Closed	1999	325.00	260-325
1999 Desiree (Members Only) 303C	Closed	2000	300.00	300-395
2000 Camille (Members Only) 1300C	Closed	2001	300.00	300
2001 Jennifer (Members Only) 1301C	Closed	2001	300.00	300
2002 Belle (Members Only) 1528C	Yr.Iss.		300.00	300

G. Armani Society Member Gift - G. Armani

YEAR ISSUE	EDITION LIMIT	YEAR RETD.	ISSUE PRICE	*QUOTE U.S.$
1993 Petite Maternity 939F	Closed	1993	Gift	60-98
1994 Lady w/Dogs 245F	Closed	1994	Gift	40-100
1995 Lady w/Doves mini 546F	Closed	1995	Gift	44-90
1996 Perfect Match 356F	Closed	1996	Gift	80-100
1997 Quiet Please 446F	Closed	1997	Gift	65-85
1998 Puppy Love 114F	Closed	1998	Gift	65-75
1999 Chantal 361F	Closed	1999	Gift	75
2000 Starr 1326F	Closed	2000	Gift	75
2001 Cherie 1418F	Closed	2001	Gift	100
2002 Tender Friends	Yr.Iss.		Gift	100

G. Armani Society Sponsored Event - G. Armani

YEAR ISSUE	EDITION LIMIT	YEAR RETD.	ISSUE PRICE	*QUOTE U.S.$
1990 Pals (Boy w/ Dog) '90 & '91 409S	Closed	1991	200.00	360-450
1992 Springtime 961C	Closed	1992	250.00	286-390
1993 Loving Arms 880E	Closed	1993	250.00	390-563
1994 Daisy 202E	Closed	1994	250.00	293-450
1995 Iris 628E	Closed	1995	250.00	383-423
1996 Rose 678C	Closed	1996	250.00	250-520
1997 Marianne 135C	Closed	1997	275.00	222-275
1998 Victoria 525C	Closed	1998	275.00	220-275
1999 Heather 428C	Closed	1999	350.00	350
2000 Emma 1330C	Closed	2000	275.00	275

G. Armani Society 10th Anniversary Event - G. Armani

YEAR ISSUE	EDITION LIMIT	YEAR RETD.	ISSUE PRICE	*QUOTE U.S.$
1999 Celebration 1260C	Closed	1999	199.00	210-250

Advantgarde - G. Armani

YEAR ISSUE	EDITION LIMIT	YEAR RETD.	ISSUE PRICE	*QUOTE U.S.$
1999 Born to Dance 1172C	3,000	2001	475.00	475
1999 Joy Ride 1168C	3,000	2001	575.00	575
1999 Lady Wynne 1173C	3,000	2001	475.00	475
1999 On the Road 1169C	3,000	2001	675.00	675
1999 Rosabelle 1171C	3,000	2000	475.00	475
1999 So Pretty 1170C	3,000	2000	475.00	475

Ashley Avery Collection - Armani

YEAR ISSUE	EDITION LIMIT	YEAR RETD.	ISSUE PRICE	*QUOTE U.S.$
1998 Aurora 884M	125		375.00	375
1997 Giselle 681M	100		425.00	425
1997 Juliette 682M	100		425.00	425
1998 Lilacs and Roses 882M	125		375.00	375

Cabaret - G. Armani

YEAR ISSUE	EDITION LIMIT	YEAR RETD.	ISSUE PRICE	*QUOTE U.S.$
2000 Jacqueline 1295C	3,000		850.00	850
2000 Josephine 1294C	3,000		900.00	900

Capodimonte - G. Armani

YEAR ISSUE	EDITION LIMIT	YEAR RETD.	ISSUE PRICE	*QUOTE U.S.$
1985 Boy Reading w/Dog 685C	Retrd.	1999	110.00	240-300
1995 Clear Water 381C	Retrd.	1999	300.00	315
1976 Country Girl (Little Shepherdess) 3153	Closed	1991	47.50	120-150
2002 Forever More 1574C	3,000		1000.00	1000
1997 Gallant Approach 146C	750	2000	1250.00	1250
1985 Girl Reading w/Cat 686C	Retrd.	1999	100.00	240-300
1993 Lady Golfer 911C	Retrd.	1999	325.00	335
1976 Lawyer 414	Retrd.	1986	60.00	48-60
1985 Little Vagabond 328C	Retrd.	1999	55.00	44-55
1977 Napoleon (5464) 464C	Closed	1991	250.00	400-500
1980 Old Drunk (Richard's Night Out) 3243	Closed	1988	130.00	192-240
1978 Organ Grinder 3323	Closed	1989	140.00	280-350
1985 Peasant Group Clock 1115E	Retrd.	1990	320.00	320
1976 The Picture 441B	Retrd.	1983	N/A	N/A
1997 Romance 461C	750	2000	1250.00	1250
2001 Romeo and Juliet 1454C	3,000		1000.00	1000
1976 Shepherd 439	Retrd.	1988	N/A	N/A
1976 Shepherdess 440	Retrd.	1988	N/A	N/A
1977 Swing MIC#7471	Retrd.	1989	275.00	220-275
1980 The Tender Clown 217C	Suspd.		75.00	200-250
2001 Tenderly 1318C	5,000		625.00	625
1984 Two on a Horse 625C	Retrd.	1999	350.00	670
1997 Venetian Night 125C	975		2000.00	2000
1995 Young Hearts 679C	1,500		900.00	1000

Clown Series - G. Armani

YEAR ISSUE	EDITION LIMIT	YEAR RETD.	ISSUE PRICE	*QUOTE U.S.$
1991 Bust of Clown (The Fiddler Clown) 725E	5,000		500.00	575
1984 Clown with Dog 653E	Closed	1991	135.00	100

Commemorative - G. Armani

YEAR ISSUE	EDITION LIMIT	YEAR RETD.	ISSUE PRICE	*QUOTE U.S.$
1992 Discovery of America - Columbus Plaque 867C	2,500	1994	400.00	340-425
1993 Mother's Day Plaque 899C	Closed	1993	100.00	225-293
1994 Mother's Day Plaque-The Swing 254C	Closed	1994	100.00	96-120
1995 Mother's Day Plaque-Love/Peace 538C	Closed	1995	125.00	88-125
1996 Mother's Day Plaque-Mother's Rosebud 341C	Closed	1996	150.00	150-250
1997 Mother's Day Figurine-Mother's Angel 155C	Closed	1997	175.00	123-175
1998 Mother's Day Figurine-Mother's Bouquet 799C	Closed	1998	175.00	100-175
1999 Mother's Day Figurine-Rosette 300C	Closed	1999	100.00	100
2000 Mother's Day Figurine-Babette 1328C	Closed	2000	100.00	100
2001 Mother's Day Figurine-Forget-Me-Not 1435C	Yr.Iss.	2001	95.00	95
2002 Mother's Day Figurine-Blossom Time 1541C	Yr.Iss.		100.00	100

Dance of the Flowers - G. Armani

YEAR ISSUE	EDITION LIMIT	YEAR RETD.	ISSUE PRICE	*QUOTE U.S.$
2000 Innocence 14240	5,000		395.00	395
2000 Love 14220	5,000		395.00	395
2000 Purity 14230	5,000		395.00	395

Disney - G. Armani

YEAR ISSUE	EDITION LIMIT	YEAR RETD.	ISSUE PRICE	*QUOTE U.S.$
2000 Cinderella & Fairy Godmother 1421C	975	2000	1250.00	1250
1999 Eureka 590C	3,000		800.00	800
1997 Fauna 609C	Retrd.	1999	200.00	200
1997 Flora 608C	Retrd.	1999	200.00	200
1995 Jiminy Cricket "Special Backstamp" 379C	1,200	1995	300.00	650-936
1996 Jiminy Cricket 379C	Open		300.00	375
1996 Merryweather 607C	Retrd.	1999	200.00	200
1996 Pinocchio & Figaro 464C	Open		500.00	550
1996 Sleeping Beauty (Briar Rose) 106C	Open		650.00	675
1998 Sorcerer's Apprentice with Commemorative Coin 325C	1,927	1998	650.00	574-650
2000 Sprite 1329C	1,500		675.00	675
1997 Tinkerbell 108C	Open		425.00	425
1993 Snow White 209C	Open		400.00	450
1995 Bashful 916C	Open		150.00	155
1995 Doc 326C	Open		150.00	155
1995 Dopey 200C	Open		105.00	155
1995 Grumpy 917C	Open		145.00	155
1995 Happy 327C	Open		150.00	155
1995 Sleepy 915C	Open		125.00	155
1995 Sneezy 914C	Open		125.00	155
1998 Snow White Kissing Dopey 309C	1,500	1999	875.00	875

FIGURINES

YEAR ISSUE	EDITION LIMIT	YEAR RETD.	ISSUE PRICE	*QUOTE U.S.$

Disneyana - G. Armani

YEAR ISSUE	EDITION LIMIT	YEAR RETD.	ISSUE PRICE	*QUOTE U.S.$
1992 Cinderella '92 783C	500	1992	500.00	4130-4900
1993 Snow White '93 199C	2,000	1993	750.00	825-1550
1994 Ariel (Little Mermaid) '94 505C	1,500	1994	750.00	1200-1750
1995 Beauty and the Beast '95 543C	2,000	1995	975.00	1275-1430
1996 Jasmine & Rajah '96 410C	1,200	1996	800.00	849-1400
1997 Cinderella & Prince 107C	1,000	1997	825.00	825-1658
1998 Geppetto & Pinocchio 490C	1,075	1998	775.00	765-847
1999 Lady & The Tramp 1258C	750	1999	750.00	750-880
2000 Steamboat Willie 1406P	1,000	2000	600.00	600-1100

Etrusca - G. Armani

YEAR ISSUE	EDITION LIMIT	YEAR RETD.	ISSUE PRICE	*QUOTE U.S.$
1993 Lady with Bag 2149E	Retrd.	1996	350.00	263-375

Figurine of the Year - G. Armani

YEAR ISSUE	EDITION LIMIT	YEAR RETD.	ISSUE PRICE	*QUOTE U.S.$
1996 Lady Jane 390C	Yr.Iss.	1996	200.00	350-500
1997 April 121C	Yr.Iss.	1997	250.00	250
1998 Violet 756C	Yr.Iss.	1998	250.00	175-250
1999 Elise 410C	Yr.Iss.	1999	230.00	230-250
2000 Celeste 1302C	Yr.Iss.	2000	295.00	295
2001 Mariah 1407C	Yr.Iss.	2001	250.00	250
2002 Joy of Life 1527C	Yr.Iss.		250.00	250

Florentine Gardens - G. Armani

YEAR ISSUE	EDITION LIMIT	YEAR RETD.	ISSUE PRICE	*QUOTE U.S.$
1992 Abundance 870C	10,000	1996	600.00	540-675
2001 Ares 1448C	3,000		1300.00	1300
2000 Daphne 1353C	4,750		650.00	650
1992 Dawn 874C	10,000	1996	500.00	560-650
2001 Forever 1433C	3,000		750.00	750
2000 Fortuna 1322C	5,000		400.00	400
2000 Fortuna 1322M	250	2001	275.00	275
2001 Free Flight 1450C	3,000		500.00	500
2002 Free Hearts 1563C	5,000		1000.00	1000
2000 Harmonie 1352C	4,750		600.00	600
1999 Heart and Soul 1254C	5,000		400.00	400
2000 Leda 1337C	5,000	2001	400.00	400
2002 Leda 1564C	5,000		650.00	650
2001 The Magic Flute 1449C	3,000		500.00	500
2000 Purity 1338C	5,000	2001	400.00	400
2000 Sky Riders 1324C	3,000		950.00	950
2000 Spring Blossoms 1323C	5,000		400.00	400
2000 Spring Blossoms 1323M	250	2001	275.00	275
2000 Swept Away 1267C	3,000		1000.00	1000
1999 Three Graces 1256C	3,000		800.00	800
1992 Twilight 872C	10,000	1996	560.00	960-1248
1992 Vanity 871C	10,000	1996	585.00	1170-4521
1994 Wisteria 626C	Retrd.	1999	375.00	425-650

Four Seasons - G. Armani

YEAR ISSUE	EDITION LIMIT	YEAR RETD.	ISSUE PRICE	*QUOTE U.S.$
1990 Skating-Winter 542P	Retrd.	1999	355.00	284-450

Galleria Collection - G. Armani

YEAR ISSUE	EDITION LIMIT	YEAR RETD.	ISSUE PRICE	*QUOTE U.S.$
1995 Eros 406T	1,500	1999	750.00	775
1994 Grace 1029T	1,000	2000	465.00	485
1994 Joy 1028T	1,000	2000	465.00	485
1995 Pearl 1019T	1,000	1999	550.00	600
1993 Leda & The Swan 1012T	1,500	1997	550.00	1000-1500
2002 Promenade 1562C	675		2500.00	2500
2002 Pure Love 4123C	500		1000.00	1000
1993 The Sea Wave 1006T	1,500	1994	500.00	506-633
1993 The Sea Wave, signed 1006T	Retrd.	1996	500.00	910-1008
1993 Spring Herald 1009T	1,500	1997	500.00	572-845
1993 Spring Herald, signed 1009T	Retrd.	1996	500.00	600
1993 Spring Water 1007T	1,500	1997	500.00	720-936
1993 Zephyr 1010T	1,500	1997	500.00	600-1200
1993 Set (Sea Wave, Spring Water, Spring Herald, Leda & Swan, Zephyr)	Retrd.	1997	2550.00	3380-5500

Gems Collection - G. Armani

YEAR ISSUE	EDITION LIMIT	YEAR RETD.	ISSUE PRICE	*QUOTE U.S.$
2000 Charme 1317E	250	2000	1000.00	1000
2000 Daphne 1353E	250	2000	875.00	875
2000 Elegance 1180E	250	2000	875.00	875
2000 Enchanting 1181E	250	2000	875.00	875
2000 Harmonie 1352E	250	2000	775.00	775

Golden Age - G. Armani

YEAR ISSUE	EDITION LIMIT	YEAR RETD.	ISSUE PRICE	*QUOTE U.S.$
1995 Fragrance 340C	3,000	2000	500.00	560
1998 In The Mood 164C	5,000		400.00	400
1998 Lacey 645C	3,000		700.00	700
1999 Lady Anne 1159C	Retrd.	2000	375.00	375
1997 Morning Ride 147C	5,000	2000	770.00	770
1995 Promenade 339C	3,000	2000	600.00	650

(continued, right column)

YEAR ISSUE	EDITION LIMIT	YEAR RETD.	ISSUE PRICE	*QUOTE U.S.$
1998 Reverie 646C	3,000	1999	600.00	600
1999 Rosanna 794C	3,000		400.00	400
1995 Soiree 338C	3,000		600.00	630
1995 Spring Morning 337C	3,000	1997	600.00	800-900
1999 Wind Swept 795C	3,000	2001	500.00	500

Gulliver's World - G. Armani

YEAR ISSUE	EDITION LIMIT	YEAR RETD.	ISSUE PRICE	*QUOTE U.S.$
1994 The Barrel 659T	1,000	1998	225.00	255
1981 Boy with Fish 185C	Retrd.	1985	45.00	36-45
1981 Boy with Pistol 191T (original "Cowboy")	Retrd.	1988	45.00	40-50
1981 Children in Shoe 309C	Retrd.	1983	300.00	240-300
1994 Cowboy 657T	1,000	1996	125.00	120-125
1981 Dice Game 305C	Retrd.	1985	265.00	212-265
1994 Getting Clean 661T	1,000	1998	130.00	120-150
1981 Indian Girl w/Dog 262C	Retrd.	1985	60.00	48-60
1994 Ray of Moon 658T	1,000	1998	100.00	80-100
1994 Serenade 660T	1,000	1998	200.00	188-235
1981 Serenade on Barrel 306C	Retrd.	1987	190.00	152-190
1976 Stealing Apples 432C	Retrd.	1989	55.00	44-55
1981 Wine Curriers 199T	Retrd.	1983	130.00	104-130

Impressions - G. Armani

YEAR ISSUE	EDITION LIMIT	YEAR RETD.	ISSUE PRICE	*QUOTE U.S.$
1990 Bittersweet 528C	Retrd.	1993	400.00	910-1040
1990 Bittersweet 528P	Retrd.	1993	275.00	476-595
1990 Masquerade 527C	Retrd.	1993	400.00	344-430
1990 Masquerade 527P	Retrd.	1993	300.00	476-595
1990 Mystery 523C	Retrd.	1993	370.00	296-848
1990 Temptation 522C	Retrd.	1993	400.00	320-400

Masterworks - G. Armani

YEAR ISSUE	EDITION LIMIT	YEAR RETD.	ISSUE PRICE	*QUOTE U.S.$
1995 Aurora 680C	1,500	1997	3500.00	3600-5000
1998 Circle of Joy 760C	1,500		2750.00	2750
2001 The Triumph of Venus 1530C	1,500		2500.00	2500

Moonlight Masquerade - G. Armani

YEAR ISSUE	EDITION LIMIT	YEAR RETD.	ISSUE PRICE	*QUOTE U.S.$
1991 Lady Clown 742C	7,500	1995	390.00	550-650
1991 Lady Clown with Puppet 743C	7,500	1995	410.00	328-585
1991 Lady Harlequin 740C	7,500	1995	450.00	570-695
1991 Lady Pierrot 741C	7,500	1995	390.00	585-780
1991 Queen of Hearts 744C	7,500	1995	450.00	476-595
1991 Set	Retrd.	1995	2090.00	2090

My Fair Ladies™ - G. Armani

YEAR ISSUE	EDITION LIMIT	YEAR RETD.	ISSUE PRICE	*QUOTE U.S.$
1994 At Ease 634C	5,000		650.00	715
1998 Brief Encounter 167C	5,000		350.00	350
1990 Can-Can Dancer 589P	Retrd.	1991	460.00	453-520
1989 Can-Can Dancers 516C	Retrd.	1993	880.00	720-1100
1998 Charm 197C	3,000	2001	850.00	850
1999 Cleo 801C	5,000		500.00	500
2000 Elegance 1180C	4,750		700.00	700
1993 Elegance 195C	5,000		525.00	660
2000 Enchanting 1181C	4,750		700.00	700
1993 Fascination 192C	5,000		500.00	633
1987 Flamenco Dancer 389C	5,000	1996	400.00	579-600
2000 The Flirt 1288C	3,000		400.00	400
1997 Garden Delight 157C	3,000	2000	1000.00	1000
1995 Georgia 414C	5,000		550.00	625
1996 Grace 383C	5,000		475.00	515
1995 In Love 382C	5,000	2001	450.00	500
1994 Isadora 633C	3,000		920.00	1050
2000 Kelly 1290C	3,000		400.00	400
1990 Lady at Piano 449C	Retrd.	1998	370.00	440
1987 Lady with Book 384C	5,000	1999	300.00	475-936
1988 Lady with Chain 411C	Retrd.	1999	125.00	170
1987 Lady with Fan 387C	5,000	1999	300.00	395-514
1988 Lady with Great Dane 429C	5,000	1996	385.00	550-786
1987 Lady with Mirror (Compact) 386C	5,000	1993	300.00	886-1152
1987 Lady with Muff 388C	5,000	1999	250.00	250-390
1988 Lady with Muff 408C	Retrd.	1999	135.00	175
1990 Lady with Parrot 616C	5,000	1995	460.00	1040-1395
1987 Lady with Peacock 385C	5,000	1992	380.00	380-3000
1987 Lady with Peacock 385F	Retrd.	1996	230.00	1675-1880
1987 Lady with Peacock 385P	Retrd.	1996	300.00	1000
1993 Lady with Umbrella-Nellie 196C	5,000		370.00	450
1995 Lara 415C	5,000		450.00	500
1993 Mahogany 194C	5,000	1995	500.00	998-2500
1998 Moonlight 151C	1,500	2001	1250.00	1250
1993 Morning Rose 193C	5,000	2000	450.00	515
2000 Morning Stars 1378C	5,000		600.00	600
1998 Mystical Fountain 159C	3,000	2000	900.00	900
2000 Night Stars 1377C	5,000		825.00	825

*Quotes have been rounded up to nearest dollar

YEAR ISSUE	EDITION LIMIT	YEAR RETD.	ISSUE PRICE	*QUOTE U.S.$
1998 Opal 758C	5,000		450.00	450
1987 The Parrot 393C	Retrd.	1999	175.00	270
1994 Promenade 630C	Retrd.	1999	185.00	215
1999 Samantha 800C	5,000		500.00	500
1998 Starlight 150C	1,500	2001	1250.00	1250
1994 Starry Night 632C	Retrd.	1999	210.00	210
1997 Swans Lake 158C	3,000	2000	900.00	900
1999 Tamara 798C	5,000		500.00	500
1988 The Tango 431F	Retrd.	1993	330.00	264-330
1988 The Tango 441P	Retrd.	1993	550.00	728-910
1999 Tracy 797C	5,000		500.00	500
1989 Two Can-Can Dancers 516C	Retrd.	1993	880.00	1100-2000

Novecento - G. Armani

YEAR ISSUE	EDITION LIMIT	YEAR RETD.	ISSUE PRICE	*QUOTE U.S.$
2001 After Noon 1452C	5,000		500.00	500
2000 Charme 1317C	4,750		600.00	600
2001 Fascination 1412C	3,000		800.00	800
2001 Gentle Breeze 1451C	5,000		500.00	500

Opera - G. Armani

YEAR ISSUE	EDITION LIMIT	YEAR RETD.	ISSUE PRICE	*QUOTE U.S.$
2002 Carmen 1532C	5,000		500.00	500
2002 Madame Butterfly 1533C	5,000		500.00	500
2002 Tosca 1531C	5,000		500.00	500

Pearls Of The Orient - G. Armani

YEAR ISSUE	EDITION LIMIT	YEAR RETD.	ISSUE PRICE	*QUOTE U.S.$
1990 Chu Chu San (Oriental Lady w/Sunshade) 612C	10,000	1995	550.00	572-910
1990 Lotus Blossom (Oriental Lady w/Iris) 613C	10,000	1995	475.00	380-475
1990 Madame Butterfly (Oriental Lady w/Fan) 610C	10,000	1995	500.00	572-910
1990 Turnadot (Oriental Lady w/Parrot) 611C	10,000	1995	500.00	440-660
1990 Set	Retrd.	1995	2025.00	2025

Premiere Ballerinas - G. Armani

YEAR ISSUE	EDITION LIMIT	YEAR RETD.	ISSUE PRICE	*QUOTE U.S.$
1989 Ballerina 508C	10,000	1994	470.00	1326-1658
1989 Ballerina with Drape 504C	10,000	1994	500.00	500-650
1991 Dancer with Peacock 727C	Retrd.	1993	460.00	336-424
1989 Flying Ballerina 503C	10,000	1994	440.00	400-500
1989 Flying Dancers 518C	7,500	1994	780.00	960-1040
1989 Kneeling Ballerina 517C	10,000	1994	340.00	350-429
1989 Two Ballerinas 515C	7,500	1995	670.00	620-775

Religious - G. Armani

YEAR ISSUE	EDITION LIMIT	YEAR RETD.	ISSUE PRICE	*QUOTE U.S.$
1991 Angel with Flowers "Innocence" 772C	Retrd.	1999	135.00	140
1997 Angel with Harp "Heavenly Music" 1033C	Retrd.	1999	600.00	600
1997 Angel with Lute "Raphael" 1031C	Retrd.	1999	600.00	600
1991 Angel with Lyre "Peace 773C	Retrd.	1999	130.00	135
1997 Angel with Trumpet "Gabriel" 1032C	Retrd.	1999	600.00	600
2001 The Annunciation 1502C	3,000		1000.00	1000
1994 The Assumption 697C	5,000		650.00	725
2001 The Child 1189C	3,000		220.00	220
1983 Choir Boys 900	5,000	1996	400.00	660-858
1994 Christ Child (Nativity) 1020C	1,000		175.00	195
1999 Come to Me 783C	5,000		1250.00	1250
1987 Crucifix 1158C	10,000	1990	155.00	650-850
1993 Crucifix 786C	7,500		285.00	315
1987 Crucifix 790C	15,000		160.00	250
1991 Crucifix Plaque 711C	15,000	1996	265.00	265-285
1995 The Crucifixion 780C	5,000		500.00	550
1994 Donkey (Nativity) 1027C	1,000		185.00	210
1995 The Holy Family 788C	5,000		1000.00	1100
1994 La Pieta 802C	5,000	1999	950.00	1100
1994 Madonna (Nativity) 1022C	1,000		365.00	430
2001 Madonna 1188C	3,000		750.00	750
2002 Madonna del Latte 4125C	1,500		825.00	825
1998 Madonna with Jesus Child 766C	750		550.00	550
1994 Magi King Gold (Nativity) 1023C	1,000		600.00	650
1998 Magi King Gold 767C	750		550.00	550
1994 Magi King Incense (Nativity) 1024C	1,000		600.00	650
1998 Magi King Incense 768C	750		410.00	410
1994 Magi King Myrrh (Nativity) 1025C	1,000		450.00	500
1998 Magi King Myrrh 769C	750		530.00	530
1995 Moses 606C	2,500	1997	365.00	400
1999 Moses 785C	5,000		1200.00	1200
1994 Ox (Nativity) 1026C	1,000		300.00	350
1994 Renaissance Crucifix 1017T	5,000		265.00	275
2000 The Sorrow 1325C	5,000		1500.00	1500
1994 St. Joseph (Nativity) 1021C	1,000		500.00	550
2001 St. Joseph 1187C	3,000		1000.00	1000
1998 St. Joseph 765C	750		400.00	400

Renaissance Collection - G. Armani

YEAR ISSUE	EDITION LIMIT	YEAR RETD.	ISSUE PRICE	*QUOTE U.S.$
1994 Ambrosia 482C	5,000	2001	435.00	550
1994 Angelica 484C	5,000	2001	575.00	715
1998 Aprhodite 230C	3,000		1350.00	1350
1997 Artemis 126C	5,000		1750.00	1750
1993 Aurora-Lady With Doves 884C	7,500		370.00	400
1997 Bacchus & Arianna 419C	5,000	1999	1500.00	1500
1995 Ebony 372C	5,000		550.00	600
1994 The Embrace 480C	3,000	1996	1450.00	3000-4000
1998 Flora 173C	5,000		600.00	600
1993 Freedom-Man And Horse 906C	3,000	1996	850.00	1138-1200
1998 Golden Nectar 212C	1,500		2000.00	2000
1993 Liberty-Girl On Horse 903C	5,000	1996	750.00	1105-1268
1993 Lilac & Roses-Girl w/Flowers 882C	7,500		410.00	440
1993 Lovers 191C	3,000	1996	450.00	960-1248
1998 Pomona 174C	5,000	2000	550.00	550
1999 Sea Breeze 864C	5,000		425.00	425
1999 Sea Song 863C	5,000	2001	475.00	475
1994 Summertime-Lady on Swing 485C	5,000		650.00	775
1993 Wind Song-Girl With Sail 904C	5,000		520.00	575

Siena Collection - G. Armani

YEAR ISSUE	EDITION LIMIT	YEAR RETD.	ISSUE PRICE	*QUOTE U.S.$
1993 Back From The Fields 1002T	1,000	1995	400.00	410-550
1994 Country Boy w/Mushrooms 1014T	2,500		135.00	155
1993 Encountering 1003T	1,000	1995	350.00	480-780
1993 Fresh Fruit 1001T	2,500	1995	155.00	332
1993 The Happy Fiddler 1005T	1,000	1997	225.00	239-390
1993 Mother's Hand 1008T	2,500	1998	250.00	228-285
1993 Soft Kiss 1000T	2,500	1995	155.00	332-390
1993 Sound The Trumpet! 1004T	1,000	1995	225.00	280-390
1993 Set of 8	N/A	N/A	1895.00	1895-3200

Skylights - G. Armani

YEAR ISSUE	EDITION LIMIT	YEAR RETD.	ISSUE PRICE	*QUOTE U.S.$
2001 Eclipse 1458C	5,000		600.00	600
2001 Moonlight 1456C	5,000		600.00	600
2001 Sunlight 1457C	5,000		600.00	600

Special Events in a Life - G. Armani

YEAR ISSUE	EDITION LIMIT	YEAR RETD.	ISSUE PRICE	*QUOTE U.S.$
2000 Beloved 1319C	5,000		600.00	600
1994 Black Maternity 502C	3,000	2000	535.00	650
1999 Bliss 386C	5,000		375.00	375
1984 Bride & Groom 641C	Retrd.	1994	125.00	990-1238
1994 Bride with Flower Vase 489C	Retrd.	1998	155.00	165
1993 Carriage Wedding 902C	2,500		1000.00	1100
1986 Enfance (Infant) 694C	Retrd.	1992	380.00	308-380
1991 Just Married 827C	5,000	1998	1000.00	1100-2200
1999 Magic Touch 385C	5,000		500.00	500
1988 Maternity 405C	5,000	1999	415.00	500-570
1999 My Love 238C	5,000		575.00	575
1994 Perfect Love 652C	3,000		1200.00	1250
1999 Pride and Joy 104C	3,000		1000.00	1000
1995 Sweet Smile 366C	Suspd.		420.00	470
1995 Tenderness 418C	5,000		950.00	1000
1995 Tomorrow's Dream 336C	5,000		700.00	730
1991 Wedding Couple At Threshold 813C	7,500	2001	400.00	475
1991 Wedding Couple Kissing 815C	7,500		500.00	575
1991 Wedding Couple With Bicycle 814C	7,500	2001	600.00	665
1994 Wedding Waltz (black) 501C	3,000	2000	750.00	875
1994 Wedding Waltz (white) 493C	3,000		750.00	875

Special Releases - G. Armani

YEAR ISSUE	EDITION LIMIT	YEAR RETD.	ISSUE PRICE	*QUOTE U.S.$
1989 Bust of Eve 590T	1,000	1991	250.00	566-1200
1993 Doctor in Car 848C	2,000	1996	800.00	660-825
1992 Girl in Car 861C	3,000	1995	900.00	740-925
1992 Lady with Dove (Dove Dancer) 858E	1,000	1994	320.00	360-845
1992 Old Couple in Car (Two Hearts Remember) 862C	5,000	1997	1000.00	1000

Spring Melodies - G. Armani

YEAR ISSUE	EDITION LIMIT	YEAR RETD.	ISSUE PRICE	*QUOTE U.S.$
1987 Lady with Wheelbarrow 960C	Retrd.	1999	165.00	230
2000 Spring Bluebell 1333C	3,000		550.00	550
2000 Spring Daisy 1335C	3,000		550.00	550
2000 Spring Iris 1336C	3,000		500.00	500
2000 Spring Rose 1334C	3,000		550.00	550

Starlight-Millennium Collection - G. Armani

YEAR ISSUE	EDITION LIMIT	YEAR RETD.	ISSUE PRICE	*QUOTE U.S.$
1999 Comet-The Future 1275C	5,000		375.00	375
1999 Dawn 1409C	5,000		395.00	395
1999 Silver Moon-The Present 1276C	5,000		375.00	375
1999 Stardust-The Past 1277C	5,000		375.00	375

*Quotes have been rounded up to nearest dollar

FIGURINES

YEAR ISSUE	EDITION LIMIT	YEAR RETD.	ISSUE PRICE	*QUOTE U.S.$
Treasures From Our Past - G. Armani				
2001 Awaiting the Rainbow (25th Anniversary Commemorative) 1501C	5,000		375.00	375
2002 Happy and Free 1602C	5,000		395.00	395
Unforgettable - G. Armani				
2001 I Could Have Danced All Night 1462C	3,000		295.00	295
2001 Moon River 1464C	3,000		350.00	350
2001 Night and Day 1466C	3,000		400.00	295
2001 Some Enchanted Evening 1463C	3,000		350.00	350
2001 Summertime 1465C	3,000		400.00	400
Valentine - G. Armani				
1983 Hoopla 107E	Retrd.	1996	190.00	160-200
1983 Little Nativity 115C	Retrd.	1991	270.00	216-270
1983 Soccer Boy 109C	Retrd.	1994	80.00	64-80
Vanity Fair - G. Armani				
1992 Beauty at the Mirror 850P	Retrd.	1995	300.00	280-350
1992 Beauty w/Perfume 853P	Retrd.	1995	330.00	296-370
Via Veneto - G. Armani				
1994 Alessandra 648C	5,000		355.00	400
1999 Be My Love 1248C	5,000		450.00	450
1997 Black Orchid 444C	5,000		1100.00	1100
1999 Cheek to Cheek 1249C	5,000		500.00	500
1999 Claudia 1193C	5,000		375.00	375
1998 Cuddle Up 322C	3,000		475.00	475
1999 Erika 1192C	5,000		475.00	475
1998 Free Spirit 321C	3,000	2000	825.00	825
1999 Isabella 1190C	5,000		375.00	375
1994 Marina 649C	5,000		450.00	530
1994 Nicole 651C	5,000		500.00	600
1998 Poetry 231C	5,000		600.00	600
1998 Roman Holiday 271C	3,000		1500.00	1500
1999 Silvia 1191C	5,000		450.00	450
1997 Summer Stroll 431C	5,000	1999	650.00	650
1997 Tiger Lily 244C	5,000		1200.00	1200
1994 Valentina 647C	5,000		400.00	440
1997 Whitney 432C	5,000		750.00	750
Wildlife - G. Armani				
1997 Alert (Irish Setters) 550S	975	1999	900.00	900
1998 Back To The Barn 591S	3,000		400.00	400
1989 Bird of Paradise 454S	5,000		475.00	550
1991 Bird of Paradise 718S	5,000	1996	500.00	440-550
2000 Blue Wonder 1359S	1,500		850.00	850
1998 Bonding 744S	3,000	2001	450.00	450
1998 Brilliance 586S	1,500	1999	850.00	850
1982 Cardinal 546C	Retrd.	1989	100.00	80-100
1984 Cat & Kitten 618C	Retrd.	1999	77.50	190
1997 Collie 304S	975	2000	500.00	500
1995 Companions (Two Collies) 302S	3,000	1999	900.00	950
1991 Crane 713S	5,000		430.00	465
1998 Crystal Morning 597S	1,500	2000	900.00	900
1997 Dalmation 552S	975	1999	600.00	600
1998 Descent 604S	3,000		500.00	500
2000 Duck Kiss 1390S	1,500		600.00	600
1998 Early Arrivals 593S	1,500	2001	600.00	600
1997 Early Days (Deer) 557S	975	2000	1200.00	1200
1994 Elegance in Nature (Herons) 226S	3,000	2000	1000.00	1200
1998 Ever Watchful 602S	3,000	1999	450.00	450
1994 The Falconer 224S	3,000	1999	1000.00	1400
1995 Feed Us! (Mother/Baby Owls) 305S	1,500	1998	950.00	800-1000
1997 First Days (Mare & Foal) 564S	1,500		800.00	800
2000 Flaming Feathers 1358S	1,500		900.00	900
1991 Flying Duck 839S	3,000	2000	470.00	530
1993 Galloping Horse 905C	Retrd.	1999	425.00	475
1993 Galloping Horse 905S	7,500		465.00	500
1998 Garden Delight 734S	1,500	1999	500.00	500
1991 Great Argus Pheasant 717S	3,000	1996	625.00	520-650
2001 The Guardian 1379S	1,500		1000.00	1000
1997 High Jump 567S	1,500	1999	850.00	850
1991 Hummingbird 719S	Retrd.	1996	300.00	296-370
1995 The Hunt (Falcon) 290S	3,000	2000	850.00	880
2000 The Hunter 1360S	1,500		1350.00	1350
1991 Large Owl 842S	5,000		520.00	570
1995 Lone Wolf 285S	3,000	2000	550.00	575
1995 Midnight 284S	3,000	2000	600.00	630
2000 Misty Morning 1389S	1,500		600.00	600

YEAR ISSUE	EDITION LIMIT	YEAR RETD.	ISSUE PRICE	*QUOTE U.S.$
1997 Monarch (Stag) 555S	1,500		1200.00	1200
1998 Moon Flight 603S	3,000	2000	600.00	600
1998 Morning Call 742S	3,000	2000	465.00	465
1998 Morning Mist 737S	3,000	2000	335.00	335
1997 Mother's Touch (Elephants) 579S	3,000	2000	700.00	700
1997 Nature's Colors (Pheasant) 582S	1,500	2000	1350.00	1350
1997 Nature's Dance (Herons) 576S	750	1999	1750.00	1750
1995 Night Vigil (Owl) 306S	3,000	1999	650.00	675-1000
1995 Nocturne 976S	1,500	1999	1000.00	1100
1998 On Guard 605S	3,000	2000	475.00	475
1998 On Watch 589S	3,000		400.00	400
1989 Peacock 455S	5,000		620.00	700
1989 Peacock 458S	5,000		650.00	730
1998 Peacock's Pride 733S	1,500	1999	400.00	400
2001 Peacock's Pride1391S	1,500		750.00	750
1997 Please Play (Cocker Spaniels) 312S	975	2000	600.00	600
1997 Pointer 554S	975	1999	700.00	700
2000 Pride 1357C	1,500		1650.00	1650
1995 Proud Watch (Lion) 278S	1,500	1999	700.00	750
1993 Rearing Horse 907C	Retrd.	1999	515.00	530
1993 Rearing Horse 907S	7,500		550.00	585
2000 Regal Splendor 1387S	1,500		750.00	750
1997 Royal Couple (Afghan Hounds) 310S	975	1999	850.00	850
2000 Royal Elegance 1384S	1,500		400.00	400
1994 Running Free (Greyhounds) 972S	3,000		850.00	930
1993 Running Horse 909C	Retrd.	1999	465.00	500
1993 Running Horse 909S	7,500		515.00	550
1997 Shepherd (Dog) 307S	975	2000	450.00	450
2000 Sign of Spring 1356C	1,500		650.00	650
1998 Silent Flight 592S	3,000	2000	450.00	450
2000 Silent Love 1388S	1,500		600.00	600
1995 Silent Watch (Mtn. Lion) 291S	1,500	2001	700.00	750
1997 Sky Watch (Flying Eagle) 559S	3,000		1200.00	1200
1990 Soaring Eagle 970S	5,000	1996	620.00	620-950
1998 Spring Orchestra 584S	975	1999	1250.00	1250
1998 Stallions 572S	1,500		1100.00	1100
1997 Standing Tall (Heron) 577S	1,500		800.00	800
1998 Summer Song 585S	1,500	1999	750.00	750
1991 Swan 714S	5,000		550.00	600
1990 Three Doves 996S	5,000		690.00	750
1998 Tropical Gossip 726S	3,000		450.00	475
1998 Tropical Splendor 288S	1,500		1750.00	1750
1997 Trumpeting (Elephant) 578S	3,000	1999	850.00	850
1983 Unicorn 487C	Retrd.	1999	130.00	250
1995 Vantage Point (Eagle) 270S	3,000		600.00	650
1993 Vase with Doves 204S	3,000	1996	375.00	387-650
1993 Vase with Parrot 736S	3,000	1996	460.00	380-748
1993 Vase with Peacock 735S	3,000		450.00	500
1997 Waiting to Run 550C	975	2000	900.00	900
1998 Wild Colors 727S	3,000	2000	450.00	450
1995 Wild Hearts (Horses) 282S	3,000		2000.00	2100
1997 Wind & Waves 563S	1,500	1999	500.00	500
1998 Winter's End 583S	1,500	1999	900.00	900
1995 Wisdom (Owl) 281S	3,000	2000	1250.00	1300
Zodiac Collection - G. Armani				
1995 Aquarius 427C	5,000		600.00	650
2002 Aries 1554C	5,000		650.00	650
1999 Cancer 1239C	5,000		650.00	650
1998 Capricorn 699C	5,000		650.00	650
1995 Gemini 426C	5,000		600.00	650
1997 Leo 149C	5,000		650.00	650
1999 Libra 1238C	5,000		650.00	650
1997 Pisces 171C	5,000		650.00	650
1998 Sagittarius 698C	5,000		650.00	650
2002 Scorpio 1555C	5,000		650.00	650
1997 Taurus 170C	5,000		650.00	650
1995 Virgo 425C	5,000		600.00	650

Armstrong's

YEAR ISSUE	EDITION LIMIT	YEAR RETD.	ISSUE PRICE	*QUOTE U.S.$
Armstrong's/Ron Lee - R. Skelton				
1984 Captain Freddie	7,500	N/A	85.00	350-450
1984 Freddie the Torchbearer	7,500	N/A	110.00	400-450
Happy Art - W. Lantz				
1982 Woody's Triple Self-Portrait	5,000	N/A	95.00	350
The Red Skelton Collection - R. Skelton				
1981 Clem Kadiddlehopper	Retrd.	N/A	75.00	145-165
1981 Freddie in the Bathtub	5,000	N/A	80.00	85-95

Collectors' Information Bureau   *Quotes have been rounded up to nearest dollar

YEAR ISSUE	EDITION LIMIT	YEAR RETD.	ISSUE PRICE	*QUOTE U.S.$
1981 Freddie on the Green	5,000	1997	80.00	120-125
1981 Freddie the Freeloader	Retrd.	N/A	70.00	150-195
1981 Jr., The Mean Widdle Kid	Retrd.	N/A	75.00	160-175
1981 San Fernando Red	Retrd.	N/A	75.00	125-150
1981 Sheriff Deadeye	Retrd.	N/A	75.00	145-150

Artaffects

Members Only Limited Edition Redemption Offerings - G. Perillo

1983 Apache Brave (Bust)	Closed	N/A	50.00	150-195
1986 Painted Pony	Closed	N/A	125.00	175
1991 Chief Crazy Horse	Closed	N/A	195.00	250-300

Limited Edition Free Gifts to Members - G. Perillo

1986 Dolls	Closed	N/A	Gift	35
1991 Sunbeam	Closed	N/A	Gift	35-49
1992 Little Shadow	Closed	N/A	Gift	35-49

The Chieftains - G. Perillo

1983 Cochise	5,000	N/A	65.00	275
1983 Crazy Horse	5,000	N/A	65.00	200-250
1983 Geronimo	5,000	N/A	65.00	250-300
1983 Joseph	5,000	N/A	65.00	285-300
1983 Red Cloud	5,000	N/A	65.00	275-300
1983 Sitting Bull	5,000	N/A	65.00	200-300

Pride of America's Indians - G. Perillo

1988 Brave and Free	10-day	N/A	50.00	150
1989 Dark Eyed Friends	10-day	N/A	45.00	75
1989 Kindred Spirits	10-day	N/A	45.00	50
1989 Loyal Alliance	10-day	N/A	45.00	75
1989 Noble Companions	10-day	N/A	45.00	50
1989 Peaceful Comrades	10-day	N/A	45.00	50
1989 Small & Wise	10-day	N/A	45.00	50
1989 Winter Scouts	10-day	N/A	45.00	50

Special Issue - G. Perillo

1984 Apache Boy Bust	Closed	N/A	40.00	75-150
1984 Apache Girl Bust	Closed	N/A	40.00	75
1985 Lovers	Closed	N/A	70.00	125
1984 Papoose	325	N/A	500.00	500
1982 The Peaceable Kingdom	950	N/A	750.00	750

The Storybook Collection - G. Perillo

1981 Cinderella	10,000	N/A	65.00	95
1982 Goldilocks & 3 Bears	10,000	N/A	80.00	110
1982 Hansel and Gretel	10,000	N/A	80.00	110
1980 Little Red Ridinghood	10,000	N/A	65.00	95

The Tribal Ponies - G. Perillo

1984 Arapaho	1,500	N/A	65.00	175-200
1984 Comanche	1,500	N/A	65.00	175-200
1984 Crow	1,500	N/A	65.00	175-200

The War Pony - G. Perillo

1983 Apache War Pony	495	N/A	150.00	175-200
1983 Nez Perce War Pony	495	N/A	150.00	175-200
1983 Sioux War Pony	495	N/A	150.00	175-200

Artesania Rinconada Collection/John J. Madison Co. Inc.

Artesania Rinconada Collector's Society - J. & J. Carbajales

1998 White Cat	Closed	1999	Gift	350
1999 Horse	Closed	2000	Gift	N/A
2000 Walking Panda	Closed	2001	Gift	N/A
2000 El Gato (Tabby Cat)	Closed	2001	50.00	50
2001 Tortuga Marina (Sea Turtle)	Closed	2001	50.00	50
2001 Elephant	Closed	2001	Gift	45
2002 La Lechuza Owl	Yr.Iss.		50.00	50
2002 Camel	Yr.Iss.		Gift	N/A

Classic Collection - J. & J. Carbajales

1972 01 Ostrich	Open		12.50	22
1970 2 Musk Ox	Closed	1990	8.00	75
1973 03 Horse	Open		8.00	18
1991 03A Clydesdale Horse	Open		22.00	24
1991 03B Baby Clydesdale	Closed	2000	16.00	19
1970 4 Kangaroo	Closed	1980	11.00	240
1991 04A Circus Elephant Sitting	Closed	2000	14.00	18
1991 04B Circus Elephant Standing	Closed	2000	14.00	18

YEAR ISSUE	EDITION LIMIT	YEAR RETD.	ISSUE PRICE	*QUOTE U.S.$
1991 04C Baby Circus Elephant	Closed	2000	14.00	18
1971 05 Ram	Closed	2000	13.00	23
1972 6 Pig	Open		6.00	12
1986 6A Baby Pig	Open		7.00	14
1986 06B Pig (black)	Open		7.00	16
1995 06BB Baby Pig (black)	Open		8.00	10
1984 06BW Pig (black & white)	Open		7.00	16
1987 6C Pig (White)	Open		7.00	14
1991 06D Pig In Tube	Open		12.00	16
1995 6R Pig (Rust)	Open		14.00	16
1995 06W Pig (white)	Open		14.00	16
1995 06RR Baby Pig (rust)	Open		8.00	10
1995 06WA Baby Pig (black & white)	Open		8.00	10
1995 06WW Baby Pig (white)	Open		8.00	10
1970 7 Large Elephant	Closed	1980	13.00	300-600
1970 7 Large Elephant w/ceramic tusks	Closed	1980	13.00	13
1979 07 Duck	Closed	2000	12.50	19
1993 07A Baby Duck	Closed	2000	14.00	22
1970 08 Middle Elephant	Open		10.00	20
1970 08 Middle Elephant w/ceramic tusks	Closed	N/A	10.00	19
1970 09 Small Elephant	Open		8.50	18
1970 09 Small Elephant w/ceramic tusks	Closed	N/A	8.50	17
1970 10 Rooster	Open		10.00	18
1970 11 Hen	Open		6.00	16
1971 12 Cat	Closed	1980	11.00	600
1980 12 Cat	Open		12.00	20
1990 12A Baby Cat	Closed	2000	13.00	15
1971 13 Gorilla	Closed	1984	13.00	60-80
1987 13 Barn Owl	Closed	2000	17.50	23
1971 14 Baby Gorilla	Closed	1984	5.50	40
1986 14 Baby Barn Owl	Closed	2000	14.00	19
1971 15 Hippo	Open		9.00	18
1971 16 Small Owl	Open		8.00	16
1972 17 Small Lion	Open		8.00	18
1971 18 Parrot	Closed	1987	8.00	60-110
1971 18 Parrot (red & yellow)	Closed	1987	8.00	60-110
1971 19 Llama (1)	Closed	1980	11.00	240
1980 19 Llama (2)	Closed	1984	11.00	150
1987 19 Llama (3)	Open		12.00	18
1989 19A Baby Llama	Closed	2000	5.00	13
1971 20 Baboon	Closed	1984	8.00	140-145
1972 21 Walrus	Closed	2000	10.00	17
1994 21A Baby Walrus	Closed	2000	12.00	14
1994 21B Baby Walrus	Closed	2000	12.00	14
1971 22 Calf	Closed	1984	7.00	60-80
1994 22A Sea Lion	Closed	2000	16.00	19
1994 22B Sea Lion	Closed	2000	16.00	19
1994 22C Sea Lion	Closed	2000	16.00	19
1972 23 Sheep	Closed	1999	7.00	25-45
1972 24 Toucan	Open		12.50	22
1972 25 High Turkey	Closed	1980	12.00	350-500
1979 25 Seal (white)	Closed	1999	11.50	30
1990 25A Seal (brown)	Open		14.50	18
1990 25B Seal (brown)	Closed	1999	14.50	15
1972 26 Flag Dog	Closed	1980	10.00	140-275
1979 26 Baby Seal	Open		9.50	16
1972 27 Fish	Closed	1984	10.00	60-80
1972 28 Whale	Open		10.00	20
1972 29 Rhino	Closed	2000	10.00	19
1972 30 Baby Rhino	Closed	2000	5.50	13
1972 31 Armadillo	Closed	1998	8.00	80-95
1982 31 New Armadillo	Closed	1998	12.50	42-43
1971 32 Tiger	Closed	1998	8.00	45
1987 32A Tiger Baby	Closed	1998	9.50	35
1972 33 Bull W/ Flower	Closed	1984	11.00	83-125
1992 33 Lg. Tiger	Open		18.00	22
1973 34 Turtle	Open		10.00	20
1972 35 Cow	Closed	1984	8.00	68-90
1972 36 Donkey	Closed	1990	8.00	72
1973 37 Goat	Closed	1984	9.00	240
1982 37 Goat	Closed	1999	19.00	19
1973 38 White Rabbit	Closed	1980	10.00	200
1985 38 Rabbit	Open		9.50	18
1972 39 Vicuna	Open		14.50	26
1973 40 Eagle (1)	Closed	1984	14.00	325-1000
1982 40 Eagle (2)	Closed	1987	18.00	165-235
1986 40 Eagle (3)	Open		20.00	24
1973 41 Carpincho	Closed	1980	8.00	240
1974 42 Wild Boar (1)	Closed	1984	10.00	350
1985 42 A Wild Boar (2)	Closed	1990	12.50	85
1971 43 Frog	Open		8.00	18

YEAR ISSUE	EDITION LIMIT	YEAR RETD.	ISSUE PRICE	*QUOTE U.S.$	YEAR ISSUE	EDITION LIMIT	YEAR RETD.	ISSUE PRICE	*QUOTE U.S.$
1972 44 Giraffe	Open		12.50	24	1987 84B Baby Somali Cat	Closed	2000	10.00	13
1973 45 Chimp w/Flowers	Open		10.00	18	1981 85 Cheetah	Closed	1998	12.00	45
1974 46 Chimp w/Bottle	Closed	1999	10.00	25-30	1987 85A Baby Cheetah	Closed	2000	10.00	28
1982 47 Thinking Monkey	Closed	1990	13.00	60	1987 85B Baby Cheetah	Closed	2000	10.00	28
1986 47 Zebra (Male)	Open		15.00	22	1981 86 Wolf	Closed	1984	12.50	110
1972 48 Zebra	Open		10.00	22	1981 87 Tree Frog	Open		11.00	18
1986 48A Baby Zebra	Open		10.00	16	1981 88 American Buffalo	Closed	1990	12.00	80
1993 48B Baby Zebra	Open		13.00	16	1981 88 American Buffalo	Closed	1998	12.00	35
1971 49 Crocodile	Closed	2000	12.50	21	1981 89 African Buffalo	Closed	1995	16.00	80-100
1971 49 Crocodile	Closed	N/A	12.50	21	1981 90 Siamese Cat	Open		12.50	20
1974 50 Dog	Closed	1984	8.00	90	1981 91 Baby Camel	Closed	1984	11.00	100
1993 50A Common Barn Owl	Closed	2000	19.00	21	1982 92 Orca Killer Whale	Closed	2000	16.50	21
1993 50B Common Barn Owl	Closed	2000	16.00	18	1982 93 Quail	Closed	2000	13.50	19
1993 50C Baby Barn Owl in Nest	Closed	2000	17.00	19	1982 94 Goose	Closed	1999	14.00	35-40
1976 51 Moose	Open		10.50	20	1982 94A Baby Goose	Closed	1999	10.00	22-25
1995 51A Moose (Female)	Closed	2000	19.00	20	1987 94B Baby Goose	Closed	2000	10.00	13-22
1974 52 Vampire Bat	Closed	1984	12.50	30-40	1982 95 Middle Owl	Closed	2000	11.50	20-60
1979 52 Coyote Howling	Closed	1998	8.00	40	1982 96 Baby Ostrich	Open		13.00	20
1976 53 Pheasant	Closed	1999	13.50	45	1982 97 Baby Orca	Closed	2000	11.00	15
1976 54 Panda	Closed	1980	10.00	130	1982 98 Baby Gray Fox	Closed	1987	11.00	80
1985 54 Panda Bear	Open		12.50	20	1982 98 Baby Red Fox	Closed	1995	12.00	60-70
1976 55 Brown Bear	Closed	1995	12.50	65	1982 99 Baby Giraffe	Open		12.00	20
1976 56 Dolphin	Open		9.00	20	1982 100 Wild Rabbit	Closed	1995	12.00	100
1976 57 Squirrel	Closed	1987	12.00	60-80	1978 101 Pekingese	Closed	1995	12.50	52
1993 57 Skunk in Cart	Closed	2000	19.00	21	1978 102 Bassethound	Closed	1995	12.00	55
1993 57A Baby Skunk in Cart	Closed	2000	13.00	15	1978 103 Scottish Terrier	Closed	1998	11.00	55
1993 57B Baby Skunk in Cart	Closed	2000	13.00	15	1978 104 Poodle	Closed	1987	17.00	220
1976 58 Large Owl	Closed	1995	16.00	40	1978 105 Bulldog	Closed	1998	11.50	55
1976 59 Penguin	Closed	1984	9.00	75	1979 106 Collie	Closed	1995	12.50	60
1976 60 Racoon	Closed	2000	9.50	17	1979 107 Duchshund	Closed	1998	13.50	55-60
1976 61 Large Lion	Open		12.00	22	1979 108 Husky	Closed	1998	13.50	60
1976 62 Shark	Open		9.50	18	1979 109 German Shephard	Closed	1995	13.50	55-60
1976 63 Papagayo	Closed	2000	9.00	19	1980 110 Boxer	Closed	1995	12.50	50-60
1977 64 Camel	Open		13.50	26	1980 111 Doberman	Closed	1995	13.00	50
1987 64A Baby Camel	Open		12.50	18	1980 112 White Terrier	Closed	1998	12.00	45
1977 65 Okapi	Closed	1980	10.50	150	1980 113 English Sheepdog	Open		13.50	20
1994 65 American Shorthair	Open		17.00	20	1990 113A English Sheepdog Baby	Closed	1999	17.00	25-35
1994 65A Baby American Shorthair	Open		12.00	15	1980 114 Chihuahua	Closed	1998	9.50	10
1994 65B Baby American Shorthair	Open		12.00	15	1980 115 Dalmatian	Closed	1998	11.50	12
1977 66 Pelican	Open		12.00	22	1980 116 Bloodhound	Closed	1990	10.50	30-40
1987 66A Baby Pelican	Open		10.50	14	1992 116 Dalmatian-Female	Closed	2000	17.00	19
1987 66B Baby Pelican	Open		10.50	14	1980 117 Fox Terrrier	Closed	1990	12.50	13
1977 67 Sea Otter	Open		9.50	18	1981 118 St Bernard	Closed	1995	16.50	17
1987 67A Baby Sea Otter	Open		10.50	14	1981 119 Hunting Dog	Closed	1995	12.00	23
1987 67B Baby Sea Otter	Open		10.50	14	1981 120 Spaniel	Open		15.50	20
1977 68 Baby Vicuna	Open		9.50	20	1982 121 Afghan	Closed	1998	15.00	15
1977 69 Baby Turtle	Closed	2000	7.50	15	1984 122 Cocker	Closed	1998	13.00	13
1977 70 Anteater	Closed	1980	10.00	120	1994 123 Bassethound w/Bowl	Closed	2000	18.00	21
1987 70 Canada Goose	Closed	1995	14.00	50	1993 124A Turtle (light green)	Open		15.00	18
1987 70A Baby Canada Goose	Closed	1995	8.50	30-40	1993 124B Turtle (blue)	Open		15.00	18
1977 71 Beaver	Closed	1998	11.00	42	1993 124C Turtle (green)	Open		15.00	18
1994 72 Cats In A Basket	Open		16.00	19	1993 124D Turtle (rose)	Open		15.00	18
1977 72 Condor	Closed	1984	10.00	130-140	1990 125 Galapagos	Closed	1999	20.00	22
1978 73 Mouse	Closed	1999	8.00	40	1990 125A Baby Galapagos Turtle	Closed	2000	16.50	19
1990 73A Mouse On A Book	Open		15.50	20	1990 126 Land Turtle	Closed	1999	15.50	50
1991 73B Mouse w/Photo	Closed	1999	16.00	22	1991 127 Box Turtle	Closed	1999	14.00	35-42
1991 73C Mouse In Santa Boot	Closed	1999	16.00	22	1990 128 Koala w/Baby	Open		22.00	26
1993 73D Mouse In Pumpkin	Closed	1999	18.00	22	1990 128A Baby Koala	Closed	2000	15.00	19
1994 73E Mouse In Cowboy Boot	Closed	1999	16.00	22	1991 129 Lg. Frog	Open		18.00	22
1994 73F Papa Mouse Eating Cheese	Closed	1999	15.00	22	1994 135 Cameo Persian Cat	Closed	1999	15.00	20-35
1994 73G Baby Mouse Asleep	Closed	1999	15.00	35	1994 135A Kitten w/Sock A	Closed	1999	12.00	16-20
1994 73H Baby Mouse Eating Cheese	Closed	1999	15.00	25	1994 135B Kitten w/Sock B	Closed	1999	12.00	16-20
1994 73I Storyteller Mouse	Closed	1999	16.00	22	1982 151 Lemur	Closed	1995	14.50	50-55
1994 73J Baby Mouse	Closed	1999	13.00	22	1982 152 Big Horn Sheep	Closed	1998	16.00	45-50
1994 73K Mice On Bench	Closed	1999	26.00	26-50	1983 153 Tabby Cat	Open		13.50	20
1978 74 Antelope	Closed	1999	11.50	35-40	1983 154 Swan	Closed	1995	16.00	60
1978 75 Orangutan	Closed	1999	11.50	55-145	1983 155 Baby Wild Rabbit	Closed	1999	9.00	30
1978 76 Gray Fox	Closed	1987	11.50	140	1983 156 Sea Turtle	Open		11.50	18
1994 77 Frog On Mushroom	Open		20.00	23	1983 157 Black Bear	Closed	1995	12.50	52
1978 77 Lynx	Closed	1984	10.00	90-120	1983 158 Cockatoo	Closed	1995	14.50	65
1978 78 Koala	Open*		10.50	20	1983 159 Lg. African Elephant	Open		13.00	20
1979 79 Polar Bear	Open		12.00	20	1983 160 Baby African Elephant	Open		9.00	16
1987 79B Polar Bear (Male)	Open		15.00	20	1983 161 Baby Polar Bear	Open		9.50	16
1979 80 Mountain Lion	Closed	1987	12.00	80-120	1987 161B Baby Polar Bear	Open		11.00	16
1987 80 Mountain Lion (2)	Closed	1990	13.50	80	1984 162 Snow Owl	Open		13.50	20
1980 81 Dove	Closed	1987	14.00	85	1987 162A Baby Snow Owl	Closed	1999	10.50	22-23
1980 82 Skunk	Closed	1987	13.00	60-80	1987 162B Baby Snow Owl	Closed	1999	10.50	22-23
1980 83 Persian Cat	Closed	1998	15.00	35	1984 163 Baby Crocodile	Closed	1998	11.00	40
1987 84 Somali Cat	Closed	2000	9.00	19	1984 164 Standing Raccoon	Closed	1999	14.50	30-40
1980 84 Vampire Bat	Closed	1984	12.50	45	1984 165 Kangaroo w/Baby	Open		13.50	20
1987 84A Somali Cat Female	Closed	1995	14.00	35	1983 166 Kangaroo w/Flowers	Closed	1990	9.00	65

Collectors' Information Bureau   *Quotes have been rounded up to nearest dollar

YEAR ISSUE	EDITION LIMIT	YEAR RETD.	ISSUE PRICE	*QUOTE U.S.$
1984 167 Penguin	Closed	2000	12.50	17
1984 168A Baby Penguin	Closed	2000	7.50	13
1984 168B Baby Penguin	Closed	2000	7.50	13
1984 170 Lamb	Closed	2000	9.50	15
1984 171 Tabby Cat Female	Closed	1995	13.50	60
1984 172A Baby Tabby	Closed	2000	8.00	13
1984 172B Baby Tabby	Closed	2000	8.00	13
1984 173 Baby Fish	Closed	1987	8.50	50
1984 174 Flamingo	Open		16.50	22
1995 174A Flamingo Nesting	Closed	2000	20.00	21
1995 174B Flamingo In Nest	Closed	2000	13.00	14
1984 175 Baby Moose	Open		11.00	16
1994 175A Baby Moose	Open		14.00	16
1984 176 Baby Cockatoo	Closed	1995	12.50	40
1984 177 Leopard	Closed	2000	13.50	19
1984 178 Chipmunk	Closed	1998	13.00	30
1984 179 Gorilla	Closed	1998	13.50	35
1984 180 Bull	Closed	1998	13.00	42
1987 180A Baby Bull	Closed	1998	6.00	25
1984 181 Crane	Closed	1990	14.50	60
1984 182 Water Buffalo	Closed	1990	13.50	65
1984 183 Baby Black Bears	Closed	1995	10.00	38
1984 184 Baby Black Bears	Closed	1995	10.00	45
1984 185 Sea Gull	Closed	2000	14.00	19
1985 186 Himlayan	Closed	1999	13.00	25-40
1985 187A Baby Himalayan	Closed	1999	7.50	16
1985 187B Baby Himalayan	Closed	1999	7.50	16
1985 188 Road Runner	Open		13.50	20
1985 189 Langur Monkey	Closed	1990	12.00	72
1985 190 Calico Cat	Open		14.00	20
1985 191A Baby Calico Cat	Open		10.00	14
1985 191B Baby Calico Cat	Open		10.50	14
1985 192 Baby Wild Boar	Closed	1990	8.00	45
1985 193 Burro	Open		14.00	20
1986 194 Cow (Holstein)	Open		13.50	18
1986 194A Baby Holstein Cow	Open		9.00	14
1985 195 Mouse	Closed	1999	10.50	25
1985 196 Baby Standing Racoon	Closed	1999	10.00	22-30
1985 197 Female African Elephant	Closed	1998	13.50	38-40
1986 198 Oriental Cat Male	Closed	1995	14.50	48
1986 199 Oriental Cat Female	Closed	1990	14.50	60
1979 202 Puppy Bassethound	Closed	1995	6.50	35
1979 203 Scottish Puppy	Closed	1998	6.50	35
1980 206 Puppy Colie	Closed	1995	6.50	35
1979 207 Dachshund Puppy	Closed	1998	6.50	42
1979 208 Husky Puppy	Closed	1998	6.50	45
1979 209 Puppy Shephard	Closed	1995	6.50	38-40
1980 210 Puppy Boxer	Closed	1995	6.50	30
1980 211 Puppy Doberman	Closed	1995	6.50	30
1980 212 White Terrier Puppy	Closed	1998	6.50	30
1984 213 English Sheepdog Pup	Open		11.00	12
1980 214 Dalmatian Puppy	Closed	1998	8.00	30
1980 216 Bloodhound Puppy	Closed	1990	7.00	35-38
1992 216A Dalmatian w/Tray	Closed	1999	9.00	30
1992 216B Dalmatian Paw Up	Closed	1999	9.00	30
1992 216C Dalmatian Inclined	Closed	1999	9.00	30
1984 222 Cocker Puppy	Closed	1998	8.00	35
1995 223A Basset Puppy Lying Down	Closed	2000	14.00	15
1995 223B Basset Puppy Standing	Closed	2000	15.00	15
1994 235 Great White Shark	Closed	1999	16.00	30
1994 235A Baby Great White	Closed	1999	15.00	25
1994 236 Bottle-Nosed Dolphin	Open		17.00	20
1994 236A Baby Bottle-Nosed Dolphin	Open		12.00	15
1994 237 Killer Whale	Open		22.00	25
1994 237A Baby Killer Whale	Open		16.00	19
1995 241 Green Toad	Open		17.00	19
1995 244 Monkey With Book	Open		18.00	20
1995 247A Black Mouse	Open		7.00	9
1995 247B Ruby Mouse	Open		7.00	9
1995 247C Yellow Mouse	Open		7.00	9
1984 250A Unicorn (royal blue)	Closed	1999	18.00	23-40
1982 250B Unicorn (green)	Closed	1987	18.00	35-40
1982 250C Unicorn (black)	Closed	1987	18.00	135
1982 250D Unicorn (yellow)	Closed	1987	18.00	100-120
1984 250E Unicorn (maroon)	Closed	1999	18.00	22-40
1984 250F Unicorn (lt. blue)	Closed	1999	18.00	30-45
1984 251 Unicorn Sitting (gold horn)	Closed	1998	15.00	45-55
1983 252 Dragon	Closed	1998	16.00	45
1989 252A Baby Dragon	Closed	1995	12.00	30
1984 253A Baby Unicorn (royal blue)	Closed	1999	12.50	17-25
1983 253B Baby Unicorn (green)	Closed	1987	12.00	25
1983 253C Baby Unicorn (black)	Closed	1987	12.00	65
1983 253D Baby Unicorn (yellow)	Closed	1987	12.00	20
1984 253E Baby Unicorn (maroon)	Closed	1999	12.50	16-25
1984 253F Baby Unicorn (lt. blue)	Closed	1999	12.50	25-30
1989 254 Baby Dragon Pair	Closed	1995	16.00	30-40
1986 255A Pegasus (royal blue)	Closed	1998	11.00	45
1986 255B Pegasus (green)	Closed	1987	18.00	35
1986 255C Pegasus (brown)	Closed	1987	18.00	35
1986 255D Pegasus (yellow)	Closed	1987	18.00	35
1986 255E Pegasus (red)	Closed	1987	18.00	120
1986 255F Pegasus (grey)	Closed	1987	18.00	35
1985 256A Pegasus Female (royal blue)	Closed	1998	11.00	35
1986 256B Pegasus Sitting (green)	Closed	1987	18.00	35-40
1986 256C Pegasus Sitting (brown)	Closed	1987	18.00	40
1986 256D Pegasus Sitting (yellow)	Closed	1987	18.00	40
1986 256E Pegasus Sitting (red)	Closed	1987	18.00	40
1986 256F Pegasus Sitting (grey)	Closed	1987	18.00	40
1986 257A Pegasus Baby Male (royal blue)	Closed	1988	8.00	20
1986 257B Pegasus Baby Male (green)	Closed	1987	13.50	20
1986 257C Pegasus Baby Male (brown)	Closed	1987	13.50	20
1986 257D Pegasus Baby Male (yellow)	Closed	1987	13.50	20
1986 257E Pegasus Baby Male (red)	Closed	1987	13.50	20
1986 257F Pegasus Baby Male (grey)	Closed	1987	13.50	20
1985 258A Baby Pegasus (royal blue)	Closed	1998	8.00	20
1986 258B Pegasus Baby Female (green)	Closed	1987	13.50	20
1986 258C Pegasus Baby Female (brown)	Closed	1987	13.50	20
1986 258D Pegasus Baby Female (yellow)	Closed	1987	13.50	20
1986 258E Pegasus Baby Female (red)	Closed	1987	13.50	20
1986 258F Pegasus Baby Female (grey)	Closed	1987	13.50	20
1985 300 Butterfly Fish	Open		14.50	18
1985 301 Morish Idol Fish	Open		14.00	18
1985 302 Blue Tang Fish	Open		14.00	18
1986 303 Clown Fish (red)	Open		14.50	18
1984 304 Clown Fish (brown)	Closed	1990	14.00	55
1986 305 Clown Fish (orange)	Open		14.50	18
1986 306 Surgeon Fish	Open		14.00	18
1987 307 Long-Nosed Butterfly Fish	Open		15.00	20
1987 308 Butterfly Fish (orange)	Open		14.50	20
1986 310 Panda Male	Open		14.50	20
1986 311 Panda Female	Open		14.50	18
1986 312 Young Panda	Open		12.50	19
1986 313 Baby Panda	Open		11.00	16
1986 314 Persian (black & white)	Closed	1998	15.00	30
1986 315 Baby Persian	Closed	1998	9.50	20
1986 316 Mountain Goat	Closed	1998	15.00	42-44
1986 317 Baby Mountain Goat	Closed	1998	9.50	28-30
1986 318 Dolphin (blue)	Open		14.00	20
1986 318A Baby Dolphin (blue)	Open		9.50	14
1986 318B Baby Dolphin (blue)	Open		9.50	14
1986 319 Green Dolphin	Closed	1990	13.50	60
1986 319A Baby Dolphin (green)	Closed	1990	9.00	30
1986 319B Baby Dolphin (green)	Closed	1990	9.00	30
1986 320 Brown Dolphin	Closed	1990	13.50	60
1986 320A Baby Brown Dolphin	Closed	1990	9.00	30
1986 320B Baby Brown Dolphin	Closed	1990	9.00	30
1986 321 Yellow Dolphin	Closed	1990	13.50	60
1986 321A Baby Yellow Dolphin	Closed	1990	9.00	30
1986 321B Baby Yellow Dolphin	Closed	1990	9.00	30
1986 322 Dolphin (white)	Closed	1999	14.00	45
1986 322A Baby Dolphin	Closed	1999	9.50	25
1986 322B Baby Dolphin	Closed	1999	9.50	25
1987 323 Parrot (blue)	Open		16.00	20
1987 324 Parrot (green)	Open		16.00	20
1987 325 Parrot (red)	Open		16.00	20
1989 327 Baby Bear	Closed	1999	13.00	28-35
1989 327A Bear w/Baby	Closed	1999	16.50	35-45
1989 328A Baby Bear	Closed	1999	10.50	22
1989 328B Baby Bear	Closed	1999	10.50	18
1989 328C Baby Bear	Closed	1999	10.50	18
1989 329 Owl	Closed	1999	16.50	35-40
1989 329A Baby Owl	Closed	1999	12.00	25-32
1992 330A Wise Bear A	Closed	1999	15.00	21-30
1992 330B Wise Bear B	Closed	1999	15.00	21-30
1992 330C Wise Bear C	Closed	1999	15.00	21-30
1993 331 Bear w/Pot Of Honey	Closed	1999	19.00	35
1993 331A Baby Bear w/Honey	Closed	1999	13.00	22
1993 331B Baby Bear w/Lid	Closed	1999	12.00	20
1992 332 Owls On Tree Trunk	Open		20.00	23
1993 333 Kiwi On Egg	Closed	2000	14.00	25
1993 334A Puffin (male)	Open		17.00	20
1993 334B Puffin (female)	Open		17.00	20

YEAR ISSUE	EDITION LIMIT	YEAR RETD.	ISSUE PRICE	*QUOTE U.S.$
1993 335 Blue Persian Cat	Closed	1999	17.00	22
1993 335A Baby Persian On Pillow	Closed	1999	13.00	25
1993 335B Baby Persian (standing)	Closed	1999	10.00	16
1993 335C Baby Persian (sitting)	Closed	1999	10.00	16
1993 336 New Zealand Ram	Closed	1999	20.00	30-45
1993 336A New Zealand Sheep	Closed	1999	18.00	25
1993 336B New Zealand Ram (white)	Closed	1999	16.00	22
1993 336C New Zealand Lamb (black)	Closed	1999	16.00	22
1993 337 Camel (two humped)	Open		23.00	26
1994 337A Female Camel (two humped)	Open		21.00	24
1994 337B Baby Camel (standing)	Open		16.00	19
1994 337C Baby Camel (sitting)	Open		16.00	19
1993 338 Circus Bear (Papa)	Closed	1999	17.00	26
1993 338A Circus Bear (Mama)	Closed	1999	17.00	26
1993 338B Circus Bear (Baby)	Closed	1999	13.00	26
1993 338C Baby Bear On Bike	Closed	1999	13.00	20
1993 339 Hen Nesting in Cart	Open		20.00	23
1993 339A Rooster On Bucket	Open		20.00	23
1994 342 Mama Chimpance w/Baby	Closed	1999	25.00	35-65
1994 343 Baby Chimpance w/Sw.Cl.	Closed	1999	13.00	20-40
1993 344 White Tiger	Open		19.00	22
1993 344A White Tiger Cub	Open		13.00	16
1993 344B White Tiger Cub	Open		13.00	16
1995 350 Ostrich (new)	Open		22.00	24
1995 350A Ostrich (mother)	Open		21.00	23
1995 350B Baby Ostrich (standing)	Open		15.00	17
1995 350C Baby Ostrich In Egg	Open		13.00	15
1995 351 Emperor Penguin	Open		22.00	24
1995 351A Emperor Penguin w/Baby	Open		24.00	26
1995 351B Baby Emperor (sliding)	Open		12.00	14
1995 351C Baby Emperor (standing)	Open		14.00	16

Large Wildlife Collection - J. & J. Carbajales

1986 401 Buffalo	Open		45.00	90
1986 402 Eagle	Open		45.00	100
1985 403 Elephant	Open		70.00	120
1986 404 Horse	Open		88.00	110
1987 405 Peacock	Open		85.00	150
1987 406 Iguana	Open		88.00	140
1987 407 Camel	Open		95.00	140
1990 408 Turtle	Open		96.00	110
1990 409 Tiger Cub	Open		100.00	120
1990 410 Persian Cat	Open		104.00	130
1990 411 Calico Cat	Open		110.00	130
1990 412 Tabby Cat	Open		104.00	120
1990 414 Owl	Open		96.00	130
1991 415 Ram	2,000		150.00	150
1994 416 Moose	3,000		180.00	200
1990 417 Polar Bear	Open		110.00	130
1992 419 Lion	2,500		150.00	180
1993 420 Unicorn	3,000		170.00	200
1993 421 Angora Cat	3,000		140.00	150
1993 424 Zebra	3,000		160.00	170
1994 426 Snowy Owl	3,000		160.00	180
1994 427 Panther	2,000		160.00	180
1994 428 Medieval Horse	2,000		240.00	250
1995 431 Loon	2,000		190.00	200
1994 432 Sea Turtle w/Turtles	3,000		220.00	250
1994 432A Sea Turtle w/Dolphins	3,000		220.00	250

Silver Anniversary Collection - J. & J. Carbajales

1997 700 Ostrich (matte)	Closed	2000	29.00	32-36
2000 700 Ostrich (shiny black)	Closed	2001	29.00	32
1997 701 Ram (black)	Closed	2000	29.00	40-50
2000 701W Ram (white)	Open		29.00	36
1997 703 Duck	Closed	2001	29.00	36
1997 705 Turtle	Open		29.00	36
2000 706 Sea Turtle (blue shell)	Open		29.00	36
1997 706 Sea Turtle (white shell, blue dots)	Closed	2000	29.00	32
1997 707 Moose	Open		32.00	40
2000 708 Hippo (brown)	Open		36.00	40
1998 708 Hippo (purple)	Closed	2000	36.00	36
1997 709 Lion	Open		29.00	36
1997 711 Panther	Open		29.00	36
1997 712 Flamingo	Open		29.00	36
1997 713 Frog	Open		29.00	36
1997 714 Owl	Open		29.00	36
1997 715 Snowy Owl	Open		29.00	36
1997 717 Zebra	Open		29.00	36
1997 718 Camel	Open		32.00	40
1997 719 Elephant	Open		29.00	36

YEAR ISSUE	EDITION LIMIT	YEAR RETD.	ISSUE PRICE	*QUOTE U.S.$
1997 721 Cat	Open		32.00	40
1997 723 Blue Owl	Open		32.00	40
1997 724 Spotted Owl	Open		32.00	40
1997 726 Loon	Open		32.00	40
1997 727 Tiger	Open		36.00	40
1997 728 African Elephant	Open		32.00	40
1998 731 Toad	Open		36.00	40
1998 732 Widgeon	Open		32.00	40
1998 733 Turtle	Open		32.00	40
1998 734 Eagle	Open		32.00	40
1998 735 Dragon	Open		36.00	40
1999 736 Sea Otter	Open		36.00	40
1998 737 Calico Cat	Open		32.00	40
1999 738 Blue Duck	Open		36.00	40
1999 740 Trout	Open		40.00	40
2000 741 Rooster (cream neck)	Open		40.00	40
1999 741 Rooster (dark neck)	Closed	2000	40.00	40
1999 742 Pelican	Open		40.00	40
2000 743 Chicadee	Open		40.00	40
1999 744 Koala	Open		40.00	40
2000 745 Blue Lion	Open		44.00	44
2000 746 Panda	Open		40.00	40
2000 747 Giraffe	Open		40.00	40
2000 748 Dolphin	Open		40.00	40
2000 749 Rhino	Open		40.00	40
2000 751 Manatee	Open		44.00	44
2000 752 Emperor Penguin	Open		44.00	44
2001 754 Peacock	Open		44.00	44
2001 755 Polar Bear	Open		44.00	44
2001 756 Cardinal	Open		44.00	44
2001 757 Persian Cat	Open		44.00	44
2001 760 Siamese Cat	Open		44.00	44
2001 761 Toucan	Open		44.00	44
2001 762 Manatee	1,500		59.00	59

Bing & Grondahl

Centennial Anniversary Commemoratives - F.A. Hallin

1995 Centennial Vase: Behind the Frozen Window	1,250	1995	295.00	295-300

Boyds Collection Ltd.

The Loyal Order of Friends of Boyds ("F.o.B.s" for Short) - G.M. Lowenthal

1996 Raeburn (6" plush bear)	Retrd.	1997	Gift	44
1996 Uncle Elliot Pin	Retrd.	1997	Gift	75
1996 Uncle Elliot...The Head Bean Wants You	Retrd.	1997	Gift	50-90
1996 Velma Q. Berriweather...The Cookie Queen (11" plush)	Retrd.	1997	29.00	50-90
1996 Velma Q. Berriweather...The Cookie Queen (figurine)	Retrd.	1997	19.00	19-32
1998 Eleanor (6" plush bear)	Retrd.	1998	Gift	45
1998 Lady Libearty Patriotic Pin	Retrd.	1998	Gift	17-37
1998 Zelma G. Berriweather (11" plush bear)	Retrd.	1998	32.00	31-38
1998 Ms. Berriweather's Cottage (figurine)	Retrd.	1998	21.00	21-32
1999 Flora Mae Berriweather (6" plush bear)	Retrd.	1999	Gift	42-57
1999 I'm a Bloomin' F.o.B. Bearstone Pin	Retrd.	1999	Gift	N/A
1999 Blossum B. Berriweather...Bloom with Joy!	Retrd.	1999	Gift	38
1999 F.o.B. Mug	Retrd.	1999	7.50	8
1999 Hope, Love and Joy (plush bear)	Retrd.	1999	25.00	25
1999 Sunny and Sally	Retrd.	1999	23.00	23
2000 Caitlin Berriweather (6" plush bear)	Retrd.	2000	Gift	N/A
2000 Catherine & Caitlin Berriweather...Fine Cup of Tea	Retrd.	2000	Gift	N/A
2000 Tea for Three (poem)	Retrd.	2000	Gift	N/A
2000 "Brewin F.o.B." Bearstone Pin	Retrd.	2000	Gift	N/A
2000 Catherine and Caitlin w/Little Scruff	Retrd.	2000	25.00	25
2000 Catherine w/Little Scruff	Retrd.	2000	26.00	26
2000 Mini Tea Set	Retrd.	2000	7.50	8
2000 Noah's Toolbox 2434	Retrd.	2000	12.00	25-47
2001 Gadget 02001-31	Retrd.	2001	Gift	N/A
2001 Gizmoe...Life's A Juggle 02001-21	Retrd.	2001	Gift	N/A
2001 Melvin Sortalion 02001-51	Retrd.	2001	29.50	30
2001 Gussie...Life is a Balancing Act 02001-41	Retrd.	2001	25.00	25

Collectors' Information Bureau   *Quotes have been rounded up to nearest dollar

YEAR ISSUE	EDITION LIMIT	YEAR RETD.	ISSUE PRICE	*QUOTE U.S.$
2001 Gizmoe's Big Top with Giggle McNibble 02001-65	Retrd.	2001	13.00	13
2002 Molly B. Berriweather	Yr.Iss.		Gift	N/A
2002 Morgan B. Berriweather	Yr.Iss.		Gift	N/A
2002 Frolickin' F.O.B. Bearwear Pin	Yr.Iss.		Gift	N/A
2002 Picnic Basket	Yr.Iss.		Gift	N/A
2002 Maggie D. Beariweather	Yr.Iss.		24.95	25
2002 Patti and John Beariweather	Yr.Iss.		19.95	20
2002 Noah's Life Boat	Yr.Iss.		14.95	15

Special Event - G.M. Lowenthal

1997 Prince Hamalot	Retrd.	1997	30.00	50-56
1998 Elizabeth...I am the Queen	Retrd.	1998	34.00	50-62
1999 Victoria Regena Buzzbruin...So Many Flowers, So Little Time 01999-71	Retrd.	1999	26.00	26-46
1999 Matthew Bear (Anniversary Edition) 5000-1	Retrd.	1999	9.50	10-49
2000 Prissie, Sissie and Missie...Fixin' Tea For Three	Retrd.	2000	23.00	23-43
2001 Graffitie...Put on Your Happy Face 0200-71	Retrd.	2001	29.00	29

Barefoot Angels - The Boyds Collection

2001 Addie...Teacher's Inspire 380012	Open		11.00	11
2001 Emmie...Heart & Soul 380011	Open		11.00	11
2001 Miriam...Wish Upon a Star 380014	Open		11.00	11

The Bearstone Collection Nativity™ - G.M. Lowenthal, unless otherwise noted

1997 Ariel & Clarence...As The Pair O' Angels 2411	Retrd.	1999	14.00	35-61
1995 Baldwin...as the Child 2403	Retrd.	1999	14.95	19-55
1997 Bruce...as the Shepherd 2410	Retrd.	1999	15.00	24-38
1998 Caledonia...as the Narrator 2412	Retrd.	1999	16.00	30-41
1997 Essex...as the Donkey 2408	Retrd.	1999	15.00	32-36
1996 Heath as Casper Bearing Frankincense 2405	Retrd.	1999	14.00	23-38
2001 Joseph, Mary The Child, Urns, Creche 2476 - The Boyds Collection	Open		51.00	51
1998 Matthew...as the Drummer 2415	Retrd.	1999	16.00	32-61
1998 Ms. Bruin...as the Teacher 2414	Retrd.	1999	16.00	22-32
1995 Neville...as Joseph 2401	Retrd.	1999	14.95	19-63
1996 Raleigh as Balthasar Bearing Myrrh 2406	Retrd.	1999	14.00	23-37
1998 Serendipity...as the Guardian Angel 2416	Retrd.	1999	16.00	32-38
1995 The Stage...the School Pageant 2425	Retrd.	1999	34.50	30-75
1996 Thatcher & Eden as the Camel 2407	Retrd.	1999	17.00	18-69
1995 Theresa...as Mary 2402	Retrd.	1999	14.95	19-32
2001 The Three Kings, The Shepherd, The Donkey 2477 - The Boyds Collection	Open		14.00	14
1996 Wilson as Melchior Bearing Gold 2404	Retrd.	1999	14.00	37-42
1996 Winkie & Dink as the Lambs 2409	Retrd.	1999	11.00	40-51

The Bearstone Collection™ - G.M. Lowenthal, unless otherwise noted

2001 Abby T. Bearymuch...Yours Truly 227742 - The Boyds Collection	Open		19.00	19
2001 Ace Armstrong...Flyin' High 227752 - The Boyds Collection	Open		20.50	21
2001 Adrienne Monarch...Winged Beauty (waterglobe) 270558 - The Boyds Collection	Open		45.00	45
1994 Agatha & Shelly-'Scardy Cat' 2246	Retrd.	1998	16.25	19-58
2002 Alex & Zach...Great Game 227775 - The Boyds Collection	Open		21.00	21
1999 Alexandra and Belle...Telephone Tied 227720	Retrd.	2001	18.50	19-52
1999 Alexis Bearinsky...The Night Before Christmas 228314	Retrd.	2000	24.50	35-47
2002 Alice Clipensnip with Pita...No Charge 227774	Open		21.00	21
2001 Amanda and Michael...String Section 228366 - The Boyds Collection	Open		30.00	30
2001 Amanda and Michael...Winter Waltzing 270509 - The Boyds Collection	Open		51.00	51
1995 Amelia's Enterprise 'Carrot Juice' 2258	Retrd.	1998	16.25	24-58
2001 Amy B. Bearsdale...Is it Lunchtime Yet? 228364 - The Boyds Collection	Open		25.50	26
1995 Angelica...'the Guardian' 2266	Retrd.	1999	17.95	31-69
1995 Angelica...the Guardian Angel (waterglobe) 2702	Retrd.	1998	37.50	50-69

YEAR ISSUE	EDITION LIMIT	YEAR RETD.	ISSUE PRICE	*QUOTE U.S.$
2001 Arlington's Snow Sculpture...Chip Off the Old Block 27729 - The Boyds Collection	Open		21.00	21
1999 Arnold P. Bomber...The Duffer 227714	Retrd.	2001	21.00	21-40
1993 Arthur...with Red Scarf 2003-03	Retrd.	1994	10.50	88-213
2001 Aspen & Tahoe...Enjoy the Ride 228367 - The Boyds Collection	Open		21.00	21
2001 Aspen & Tahoe...Enjoy the Ride 270508 - The Boyds Collection	Open		46.00	46
2000 Aunt Becky with Zack...Quality Control 228326 - The Boyds Collection	Retrd.	2001	26.00	26-39
2001 Autumn Fallsbeary...Leafy Enterprises 27727 - The Boyds Collection	Open		21.00	21
2002 B.B. Dunker...All Star 227776 . - The Boyds Collection	Open		14.00	14
1997 bailey & becky...the diary 228304	Retrd.	2001	18.50	22-45
1994 Bailey & Emily...'Forever Friends' 2018	Retrd.	1996	34.00	75-110
1994 Bailey & Wixie 'To Have and To Hold' 2017	Retrd.	1998	15.75	29-250
1994 Bailey at the Beach 2020-09	Retrd.	1995	15.75	86-121
1993 Bailey Bear with Suitcase (old version) 2000	Retrd.	1993	14.20	165-575
1993 Bailey Bear with Suitcase (revised version) 2000	Retrd.	2000	14.20	32-81
1996 Bailey...Heart's Desire 2272	Retrd.	2000	15.00	25-98
1993 Bailey...in the Orchard 2006	Retrd.	1996	14.20	52-246
1995 Bailey...'The Baker with Sweetie Pie' 2254	Retrd.	2001	12.50	12-63
1995 Bailey...'The Baker with Sweetie Pie' 2254CL	3,600	1995	15.00	200-259
1995 Bailey...'the Cheerleader' 2268	Retrd.	2001	15.95	27-63
1995 Bailey...'The Honeybear' 2260	Retrd.	2001	15.75	23-98
1997 Bailey..Poor Old Bear 227704	Retrd.	1997	14.00	22-75
1997 Bailey..The Graduate 227701-10	Retrd.	2001	16.50	16-46
2001 Bailey...Swing Time 227756 - The Boyds Collection	Open		19.00	1929
1999 Bailey...The Bride 227712	Open		18.00	18-61
1999 Bailey...The Night Before Christmas (musical) 270501	Retrd.	2001	38.00	37-63
1994 Bailey's Birthday 2014	Retrd.	1999	15.95	15-48
1996 Bailey's Birthday 2763SF	Retrd.	1999	45.00	45
2000 Bear-A-Star 25734 - The Boyds Collection	Retrd.	2001	10.50	11
1998 Beatrice...We are always the Same Age Inside 227802	Yr.Iss.	1998	62.00	52-81
1994 Bessie the Santa Cow 2239	Retrd.	1996	15.75	47-86
2001 Blade Hattrick...He Shoots, He Scores 228357 - The Boyds Collection	Open		18.00	18
2000 Bob C. & Tiny Tim...God Bless Everyone 228334PAW - The Boyds Collection	Retrd.	2001	20.50	21
2000 Bobbit Whiskerdippin' and Jack... Last Chance 228336 - The Boyds Collection	Retrd.	2001	20.50	31-47
2001 Boomer and Toot with Fifi, Squirt & Topper...Let the Show Begin 227808 - The Boyds Collection	N/A		39.00	39-50
2001 Boris Bearloff with Drac...That's a Wrap 228375 - The Boyds Collection	Open		19.00	19
2001 Boxcar Chillie...Starring Roll 2485 - The Boyds Collection	Open		13.00	13
2001 Bradley Boo Bear with Spooks...Tricks? Or Treats? 27607 - The Boyds Collection	Open		23.00	23
2001 Bronson Steadfast...Hangin' Tough 228351 - The Boyds Collection	Open		21.00	21
2002 Bud...This One's For You 82509 - The Boyds Collection	Open		10.50	11
1999 Bumble B. Bee...Sweeter Than Honey 227718	Retrd.	2001	16.00	16-42
2001 Buster and Melonie McRind... Sweet Memories 227749 - The Boyds Collection	Open		23.00	23
1997 Buzz...the flash 227706	Open		18.00	18-55
1993 Byron & Chedda w/Catmint 2010	Retrd.	1994	14.20	75-85
1999 Caren B. Bearlove 227722	Retrd.	1999	13.50	35-38
2001 Casey Whistlestop...All Aboard 2484 - The Boyds Collection	Open		16.00	16
1994 Celeste...'The Angel Rabbit' 2230	Retrd.	1997	16.25	47-59
2001 Chance O' Sullivan...Feelin' Lucky 227743 - The Boyds Collection	Retrd.	2001	17.50	27-34

FIGURINES

YEAR ISSUE	EDITION LIMIT	YEAR RETD.	ISSUE PRICE	*QUOTE U.S.$
1999 Chandler, Mercy Felicity, Constance, Faith, Y.K. and Yew...Light a Candle for a Better World 227805	Retrd.	1999	53.00	75-82
2000 Charity Angelhug and Everychild...Cherish the Children 228343-1 - The Boyds Collection	Retrd.	2001	16.50	17
1994 Charlotte & Bebe...'The Gardeners' 2229	Retrd.	1995	15.75	26-75
2002 Charlotte & Wilbur Hamstein...Blue Ribbon Special 2440 - The Boyds Collection	Open		12.00	12
2000 Chester Birdbreath...purrstone 371006 - The Boyds Collection	Open		17.00	17
2001 Chief Buckley with Jennifer...To the Rescue 227751 - The Boyds Collection	Open		21.00	21
2001 Chopsticks Bearthoven...Tickle the Ivories 227754 - The Boyds Collection	Retrd.	2001	20.50	21
1999 Chrissie...Game, Set, Match 227717	Retrd.	2000	16.50	16-37
1993 Christmas by the Sea 2012	Retrd.	1998	14.20	14-48
1994 Christmas Big Pig, Little Pig BC2256	Retrd.	N/A	N/A	127-173
2001 Cindyrella & Prince Charming...If the Shoe Fits 2454 - The Boyds Collection	Open		25.50	26
1994 Clara...'The Nurse' 2231	Retrd.	1998	16.25	58-360
1999 Clara...the nurse Spoonful of Sugar 2777sf	Open		38.00	38
1999 Clarence & Angelica w/Ariel...Flight Training (votive holder) 27722	Retrd.	2001	27.00	27
1994 Clarence Angel Bear (rust) 2029-11	Retrd.	1995	12.60	70-175
1995 Clarion 2254CL	Retrd.	N/A	13.00	13
2001 Clem Claddiddlebear & Family...Your Most Important Fans 27312 - The Boyds Collection	Open		18.00	18
2001 Clementine...Garden Romance (votive) 27757 - The Boyds Collection	Open		26.00	26
1998 Clestina 25710	Retrd.	1999	10.00	10
2001 Coach Grizberg...Leading the Way 227757 - The Boyds Collection	Open		16.00	16
1998 The Collector (waterglobe) 270551	Retrd.	2001	49.00	49
1998 The Collector 227707	Retrd.	2000	21.00	20-26
2000 Conductor Chugalong w/Little Caboose...Boyds Express 270506 - The Boyds Collection	Retrd.	2001	49.00	49
2001 Constance Twilight...Gentle Dreams 228360 - The Boyds Collection	Open		17.00	17
1995 Cookie Catberg...'Knittin' Kitten' 2250	Retrd.	1997	18.75	32-60
1994 Cookie the Santa Cat 2237	Retrd.	1995	15.25	29-86
1999 Daphne And Eloise (musical) 270553	Open		35.00	35-64
1995 Daphne and Eloise...'Women's Work' 2251	Retrd.	1999	18.00	30-39
1993 Daphne Hare & Maisey Ewe 2011	Retrd.	1995	14.20	42-63
1994 Daphne...The Reader Hare 2226	Retrd.	1998	14.20	14-18
1998 Dean Newbearger 111...the Investor 227715	Retrd.	1998	16.00	32-39
2002 Dolly & Ollie Llama...Pajama-Rama 2441 - The Boyds Collection	Open		12.00	12
2000 Dominique Surfoot w/coach colby 371052 - The Boyds Collection	Open		15.00	15
2000 Dorothy & Company...Off to See the Wizard 227807 - The Boyds Collection	Retrd.	2001	40.00	69-83
1998 Dr. Harrison Griz...m.d., ph.d., b.u.d. 228309	Open		15.00	22-52
1998 Eddie...proud to be a bearamerican 228312	Retrd.	2001	14.00	32-87
2002 Edie & Geri...A Week of Sundaes 227771 - The Boyds Collection	Open		19.00	19
1994 Edmond & Bailey...'Gathering Holly' 2240	Retrd.	2000	24.25	30-121
1997 Edmond...The Graduate 227701-07	Retrd.	2001	16.50	27-44
1998 Edmund the Elf...Christmas Carol 228311	Retrd.	2001	15.00	19-47
2001 Einstein Q. Scaredybear...Take a Load Off 228373 - The Boyds Collection	Open		25.50	26
2002 Eleanore Bearsevelt...God Bless America 227789 - The Boyds Collection	Open		15.00	15
1998 Elgin the Elf Bear 2236	Retrd.	1997	14.20	32-58
1997 Elias The Elf Grizberg 3206	Retrd.	1999	10.00	19-150
1999 Elijah and Joy Believe (musical) 270503	Retrd.	2001	35.00	35
2002 Eliza Doobeary...Flower Petallin' (votive) 27761 - The Boyds Collection	Open		23.00	23
1994 Elliot & Snowbeary 2242	Retrd.	1999	15.25	16-100
1995 Elliot & the Tree (waterglobe) 2704	Retrd.	1997	35.00	35-47
1994 Elliot & The Tree 2241	Retrd.	1999	16.25	17-252
1996 Elliot...the Hero 2280	Retrd.	2000	16.75	25-75
1999 Elliot...The Hero (waterglobe) 2780	Retrd.	2001	38.00	29-32
1998 Elvira & Chauncey Fitzbruin...Shipmates 227708	Hetrd.	2000	19.00	18-62
1999 Elvira and Chauncey Fitzbruin...Shipmates (waterglobe) 270552	Open		37.00	37-58
1996 Emma & Bailey...Afternoon Tea 2277	Retrd.	N/A	18.00	27-75
1995 Emma...'the Witchy Bear' 2269	Open		16.75	17-81
2001 Emmit Kleansweep...Some Jobs are Tougher than Others 227739 - The Boyds Collection	Retrd.	2001	19.00	26-58
2002 Esther Hippydipper...Summer Olympics (waterglobe) 270563 - The Boyds Collection	Open		41.00	41
2002 Esther Hippydipper...Summer Olympics 227786 - The Boyds Collection	Open		18.00	18
1996 Ewell/Walton Manitoba Moosemen BC2228	12,000		24.99	25-78
2002 F.S. Beanster 24100 - The Boyds Collection	Open		10.50	11
2002 Faith...Always Give Thanks (waterglobe) 270565 - The Boyds Collection	Open		40.00	40
2001 Faith...Always Give Thanks 227758 - The Boyds Collection	Retrd.	2001	14.50	15
2001 Fannie Sweetcheeks...Never Enough (votive) 27756 - The Boyds Collection	Open		26.00	26
2001 Fannie Sweetcheeks...Never Enough 227746 - The Boyds Collection	Open		17.50	18-28
1993 Father Chrisbear and Son 2008	Retrd.	1993	15.00	375-546
2001 Father Christmas with Holly & Nick...Holiday Fun 228369 - The Boyds Collection	6,000		16.00	16
1998 Feldman D. Finklebearg & Dooley... "Painless" & The Patient 227710	Retrd.	2000	20.00	21-46
1998 Filbert Q Foghorn 3208	Retrd.	1999	17.00	32-77
1999 Flash McBear and The Sitting 227721	Retrd.	2001	33.00	33-75
2001 Flutter B. Bye...Flights of Fancy 227750 - The Boyds Collection	Open		17.00	17
1997 The Flying Lesson (waterglobe) 270601	Retrd.	1997	62.00	47-144
1997 The Flying Lesson 227801	Yr.Iss.	1997	62.00	37-92
1999 G M Bearenthal...Happy Birthday you ole' bear 228321	Retrd.	2000	18.50	33-39
1999 Gary, Tina, Matt and Bailey...From Our Home to Yours 227804	Open		46.00	46-78
2000 Genevieve Berriman with Brady...Catch a Falling Star 228327 - The Boyds Collection	Retrd.	2001	16.00	16
1996 Gertrude Gerty Grisberg 3201	Retrd.	1998	15.00	15
2000 The Ghost of Christmas Present...It's Not Too Late 228335PAW - The Boyds Collection	Retrd.	2001	18.00	18
2001 Ginny & Jack...Double Shot 27314 - The Boyds Collection	Open		18.00	18
1996 Gladys-Grisberg Shoebox bear 3201-01	Retrd.	1996	15.00	15
2000 Goodfer U. Bear...Way to Go! 227729 - The Boyds Collection	Open		16.00	16-39
1999 Grace & Jonathan...Born to Shop (waterglobe) 270502	Retrd.	2000	37.00	37
1997 Grace & Jonathan...Born to Shop 228306	Retrd.	2000	19.00	22-45
2002 Grace Angelhope...Can You Hear Me? 227777 - The Boyds Collection	Open		13.50	14
2002 Grandpa Bearykins with Molly & Jeff...Just a Kid at Heart 228350 - The Boyds Collection	Open		25.00	25
2001 Grandpa McBruin with Brian...Grandfathers are the Best 228341SYN - The Boyds Collection	Open		18.00	18
2000 Greg McBruin...the Wind Up 227732 - The Boyds Collection	Retrd.	2001	16.00	27-38
1994 Grenville & Beatrice...'Best Friends' 2016	Retrd.	1999	26.25	33-61

YEAR ISSUE	EDITION LIMIT	YEAR RETD.	ISSUE PRICE	*QUOTE U.S.$
1996 Grenville & Beatrice...True Love 2274	Retrd.	2001	36.00	72-109
1995 Grenville & Knute...Football Buddies 2255	Retrd.	1998	19.95	27-41
1993 Grenville & Neville...'The Sign' (prototype) 2099	Retrd.	1993	15.75	17-144
1993 Grenville & Neville...'The Sign' 2099	Retrd.	1998	15.75	16-20
1994 Grenville the Santabear (musical waterball) 2700	Retrd.	1996	35.75	42-73
1994 Grenville the Santabear 2030	Retrd.	1996	14.20	173-281
1996 Grenville with Matthew & Bailey...Sunday Afternoon 2281	Retrd.	2000	34.50	32-75
1994 Grenville...'The Graduate' 2233	Retrd.	1996	16.25	50-63
1995 Grenville...'The Storyteller' 2265	Retrd.	1995	50.00	60-162
1993 Grenville...with Green Scarf 2003-04	Retrd.	1994	10.50	600-660
1993 Grenville...with Red Scarf 2003-08	Retrd.	1995	10.50	70-184
1998 guinevere the angel...love is the master key 228308	Retrd.	2001	15.00	27-29
1998 Gwain...love is the master key 228317	Retrd.	2000	15.00	27-44
2000 Gypsy Rose...Surprise!!! 228332 - The Boyds Collection	Retrd.	2001	26.00	32-36
2002 H.K. Beanster 24102 - The Boyds Collection	Open		10.50	11
2002 Hanna T. Bearsley...Summer Breeze 227788 - The Boyds Collection	Open		19.00	19
2001 Hardley Hasslefree...Chairman of the Bored 228363 - The Boyds Collection	Open		19.00	19
2001 Harry and Millie...Through the Years (waterglobe) 270560 - The Boyds Collection	Open		45.00	45
2001 Harry and Millie...Through the Years 227741 - The Boyds Collection	Open		21.00	21
1998 The Head Bean & Co....Work is Love Made Visible (5th Anniversary) 227803	18,000	1998	61.00	63-94
2000 Henry and Sarah...The Best is Yet to Come 228330 - The Boyds Collection	Retrd.	2001	20.50	25-47
2001 Henry and Sarah's Holiday Moments 3942 - The Boyds Collection	Open		41.00	41
1997 Homer on the Plate (waterglobe) 270550	Retrd.	1999	36.00	42-52
1994 Homer on the Plate 2225	Retrd.	1999	15.75	16-88
1994 Homer on the Plate BC2210			24.99	25-47
1995 Hop-a-Long...'The Deputy' 2247	Retrd.	2000	14.00	28-81
2001 Hope Angelwish and Everychild...Bless Our Children 228361 - The Boyds Collection	Retrd.	2001	18.00	18
2000 Huck w/Mandy, Zoe and Zack...Rollin' along 227727 - The Boyds Collection	Retrd.	2001	22.00	39-42
2002 Hugh Didit...Celebrate! 227784 - The Boyds Collection	Open		14.00	14
1997 Humboldt...the Simple Bear 227703	Retrd.	2001	12.00	24-37
2000 Ima Chillin'...Takin' it Easy 227728 - The Boyds Collection	Open		18.00	18-42
2002 Ima Scholar...Celebrate! 227783 - The Boyds Collection	Open		14.00	14
2002 Ineeda Break....Overworked! 227773 - The Boyds Collection	Open		15.50	16
1997 Ingrid..Be Warm 25651	Retrd.	1998	12.00	12
2001 Irwin & Terri Cropcot...Now Yer Cookin' 2442 - The Boyds Collection	Open		12.00	12
1999 Ivan Mooselbeary 3216	Open		15.00	15
2001 Jackie & Leigh...As Time Rolls By 228346 - The Boyds Collection	Open		20.00	20
2002 Jellie B. Bearypickins...Lil' Patch of Sunshine (waterglobe) 270564 - The Boyds Collection	Open		44.00	44
2002 Jellie B. Bearypickins...Lil' Patch of Sunshine 227779 - The Boyds Collection	Open		14.00	14
2001 Jolly Ol' Saint Snoozen with Jingle, Jangle, Tinker & Shush...Lil' Helpers 228372 - The Boyds Collection	Open		20.00	20
2000 Jonathon C. Tootsenwhistle w/Marjorie Marchalong...one bear band 227806 - The Boyds Collection	Retrd.	2000	25.00	42-52
1997 Judge Griz...Hissonah 228303	Retrd.	1998	18.50	27-58
1994 Juliette Angel Bear (ivory) 2029-10	Retrd.	1995	12.60	50-104
1994 Justina & M. Harrison...'Sweetie Pie' 2015	Retrd.	1999	26.25	25-93
1996 Justina...The Message "Bearer" 2273	Retrd.	2000	16.00	23-24
1999 Justina...the choir singer 228324	Open		18.00	32-37
2000 Kandace Purrshop...hidden treasures 371054 - The Boyds Collection	Retrd.	2000	18.00	18
2002 Karen Gentletouch with Lil' Bearybutt...Kind Heart 227772 - The Boyds Collection	Open		15.00	15
2001 Katie B. Howold...Not Tellin' 228362 - The Boyds Collection	Open		16.00	16
2001 Kimberly Cheerenshout...Got Spirit? 228355 - The Boyds Collection	Open		15.00	15
1994 Knute & The Gridiron 2245	Retrd.	1997	16.25	32-63
1994 Kringle & Bailey with List 2235	Retrd.	1999	14.20	15-120
1996 Kringle And Company 2283	Retrd.	1999	17.45	25-70
2000 Kris Kringle w/Joey....Santa's Secret 270507 - The Boyds Collection	Retrd.	2001	38.00	38
2002 L.T. Beanster 24104 - The Boyds Collection	Open		10.50	11
1995 Lefty...'On the Mound' 2253	Retrd.	2000	15.00	27-94
1995 Lefty...'On the Mound' BC2056	Open		24.99	25-52
2001 Lil' Bear Peep...Got Sheep? 2453	Open		17.50	18
2002 Lil' Miss Muffet...What's in the Bowl? 2455 - The Boyds Collection	Open		20.00	20
1997 Louella and Hedda...The Secret 227705	Retrd.	2000	18.00	27-58
1994 Lucy Big Pig, Little Pig BC2250	Retrd.	1996	24.99	100-150
2002 Lulla B. Hushabye (waterglobe) 270566 - The Boyds Collection	Open		26.00	26
1999 Lydia...Shower of Roses (votive holder) 27755	Retrd.	2001	26.00	26
1996 M. Harrison's Birthday 2275	Retrd.	1999	17.00	32-46
1994 Manheim the 'Eco-Moose' 2243	Retrd.	1999	15.25	35-79
2001 Margaret with Kristen...There Goes the Budget 228354 - The Boyds Collection	Open		30.50	32-50
1998 Margot...The Ballerina 227709	Retrd.	2000	18.00	32-50
2000 Marlowe with Kinsey...Egg Detective 227736 - The Boyds Collection	Retrd.	2000	16.00	16
1999 Marshall and Bill...Give Us Courage (votive holder) 27724	Retrd.	2001	26.00	26
1999 Marshall Toastworthy...Toasty Treats (votive) 27725	Retrd.	2001	20.50	21
2001 Martha Bloomengrow...Thyme to Garden 227748 - The Boyds Collection	Open		27.00	27
2001 Martha Greenthumb...Thyme to Garden (waterglobe) 270557 - The Boyds Collection	Open		45.00	45
1994 Maynard the Santa Moose 2238	Retrd.	1997	15.25	37-104
2001 Meg O'Bytes...Laptop Dancin' 227759 - The Boyds Collection	Open		17.00	17
2001 Melville and Sonny...Mine's Bigger Than Yours 227744 - The Boyds Collection	Open		25.00	25
1998 Miles Grizberg 3209-10	Retrd.	1999	17.00	17
2002 Miss Bearpickins...Berries Today, Jam Tomorrow (votive) 27759 - The Boyds Collection	Open		21.00	21
1995 Miss Bruin & Bailey 'The Lesson' 2259	Open		18.45	19-150
2002 Miss Daisy...He Loves Me! (votive) 27760 - The Boyds Collection	Open		22.00	22
2002 Miss Stopawhyle...Making Time (waterglobe) 270562 - The Boyds Collection	Open		36.00	36
2002 Miss Stopawhyle...Making Time 227781 - The Boyds Collection	Open		14.00	14
1999 Momma & Ellie Grizberg 3211-12	Retrd.	2000	14.00	14
2000 Momma and Poppa McNewbear w/Baby Bundles (musical) 270556 - The Boyds Collection	Retrd.	2001	37.00	37
2000 Momma and Poppa McNewbear w/Baby Bundles 227731 - The Boyds Collection	Open		19.00	19-34
2001 Momma Berriproud with Jamie...Seize the Day 227755 - The Boyds Collection	Open		21.00	21
2002 Momma Guiltrip...Call Your Mom 227780 - The Boyds Collection	Open		18.00	18
1998 Momma Mcbear & Caledonia...Quiet Time 227711	Retrd.	2001	20.00	19-37
1996 Momma Mcbear...Anticipation 2282	Retrd.	2001	14.95	20-73
2001 Momma McBruin and Luke...Baby Love 228349 - The Boyds Collection	Open		15.00	15

YEAR ISSUE	EDITION LIMIT	YEAR RETD.	ISSUE PRICE	*QUOTE U.S.$
2002 Momma McBruin with Munchkin...I Love You (Mother's Day) 82508 - The Boyds Collection	Open		19.00	19
2000 Momma Purrsmore & baby Belle 371053 - The Boyds Collection	Open		19.00	19
2001 Momma with Baby Taylor...Rub-A-Dub Dub 227747 - The Boyds Collection	Open		17.50	18
2002 Momma with Taylor...First Steps 227768 - The Boyds Collection	Open		19.00	19
1993 Moriarty-'The Bear in the Cat Suit' 2005	Retrd.	1995	13.75	86-145
2000 Mother Macabeary with Krista and Cody...Mothers Always Bring Extra Love 227737 - The Boyds Collection	Retrd.	2000	16.00	16-25
2002 Mr. & Mrs. Everlove...From This Day Forward (waterglobe) 270561 - The Boyds Collection	Open		41.00	41
2002 Mr. & Mrs. Everlove...From This Day Forward 227778 - The Boyds Collection	Open		23.00	23
1999 Mr. And Mrs. Noah and Co. (waterglobe) 270505	Retrd.	2001	56.00	56
2002 Mr. Windsor...All Tied Up 227770 - The Boyds Collection	Open		11.00	11
1999 Mrs. Fezziwig w/Marley-Bob & Caroline 371005	Retrd.	1999	27.00	27
1999 Mrs. Tuttle 228315	Retrd.	2001	15.00	32-39
1999 Mrs Friday...take this job 228318	Retrd.	2001	17.00	27-45
2000 Ms. Appleby...It's Elementary 228328 - The Boyds Collection	Open		20.50	21-37
2001 Ms. Appleby's Teaching Center 3941 - The Boyds Collection	Open		41.00	41
1999 Ms. Bruin and Bailey...The Lesson (musical) 270554	Retrd.	2000	38.00	38-125
1996 Ms. Griz...Monday Morning 2276	Retrd.	1999	34.00	32-45
1996 Ms. Griz...Saturday Night GCC 2284	Retrd.	2000	15.00	27-64
2001 Ms. Macintosh...Mulled Spices 27728 - The Boyds Collection	Open		21.00	21
2001 Muriel Angelmuse...Love's Sweet Melody 228347 - The Boyds Collection	Open		13.00	13
2000 Nana Quignapple with Taylor...If Mom Says No 228331 - The Boyds Collection	Open		18.00	18-39
1993 Neville...The 'Bedtime Bear' 2002	Retrd.	1996	14.20	27-65
1997 Neville...compubear 227702	Retrd.	2000	15.50	27-63
2000 Nickleby 25732 - The Boyds Collection	Retrd.	2001	10.50	11
1997 Nickolas Uncle Nick Grizberg 3205	Retrd.	1999	20.00	20
1996 Noah & Co...Ark Builders 2278	Retrd.	1996	61.00	84-195
1996 Noah & Company (waterglobe) 2706	6,000	1996	50.95	88-275
1999 Noah...And the Golden Rule (votive) 27754	Retrd.	2001	26.00	26-57
1999 Noah's Genius at work...table 2429	Retrd.	1999	11.50	37-42
2002 Norman Doinuttin...Sorry Girls, He's Taken 227785 - The Boyds Collection	Open		26.00	26
2000 Ol' Mother McBear...the More the Merrier 227733 - The Boyds Collection	Retrd.	2001	20.50	38-54
2001 Oliver Wendell...Love Letters 227740 - The Boyds Collection	Open		16.00	16
2000 Opie Baithook w/Barney...catch of the day 371051 - The Boyds Collection	Open		19.00	19
1995 Otis...'Taxtime' 2262	Retrd.	1997	18.75	27-66
1995 Otis...'The Fisherman' 2249-06	Retrd.	1998	15.75	17-69
2002 Our American Hero...Strength, Dedication and Courage 227791 - The Boyds Collection	Open		15.00	15
2002 P.S. Beanster 24103 - The Boyds Collection	Open		10.50	11
2001 Paxton's Christmas Blossoms...Holiday Flora 27726 - The Boyds Collection	Open		21.00	21
2001 Peppermint & Spearmint...Sweet Ride 2486 - The Boyds Collection	Open		13.00	13
2001 Pop Pop with Chrissy...Giddy-Up! 228371 - The Boyds Collection	Open		20.50	21
2002 Posey B. Goodcheer...Lookin' Up! 227769 - The Boyds Collection	Open		13.00	13
2002 Potting Shed 2478 - The Boyds Collection	Open		33.00	33
1999 Princess Standingbear 3217	Open		15.00	15
1997 Puck...Slapshot 228305	Open		18.50	18-29
2001 Putter T. Parfore...Birdie This Bogie That 228359 - The Boyds Collection	Open		19.00	19

YEAR ISSUE	EDITION LIMIT	YEAR RETD.	ISSUE PRICE	*QUOTE U.S.$
1998 Ray...Croccodopius (Desk Animals™) 380000	Retrd.	1999	11.00	1
2002 Remembrandt...Eggsellent Work 227790 - The Boyds Collection	Open		17.00	1
2001 Ridley with Riley...Balancing Act (waterglobe) 270559 - The Boyds Collection	Retrd.	2001	40.00	4
1998 Rocky Bruin...Score-Score-Score 228307	Retrd.	2000	19.00	27-65
1999 Rosemarie and Emmie...T.L.C. (musical) 2777	Retrd.	2001	37.50	3
1998 Rosemary...bearhugs 228316	Retrd.	2001	25.00	35-4
2002 Ross with Betsy...Everybody Loves a Parade 227809 - The Boyds Collection	N/A		26.00	2
1999 S. Kringleberry...have a simple x-mas (QVC Exclusive) 228320	Retrd.	1999	15.00	1
2001 S.C. Bearrister and Mr. Picket...The Elfster Claus 228370 - The Boyds Collection	Open		21.00	2
1998 S.C. Northstar & Emmett...lil' helper 228310	Open		25.00	45-50
2001 Sally Quignapple with Annie...Ole Friends are Best (votive) 27758 - The Boyds Collection	Open		22.00	2
2001 Sally Quignapple with Annie...Ole Friends are Best 227760 - The Boyds Collection	Open		15.00	1
2002 Sammy Bearmerican...I Pledge Allegiance 227787 - The Boyds Collection	Open		17.50	1
2000 Scrooge McBear...Bah Humbug 228333PAW - The Boyds Collection	Retrd.	2001	19.00	19
2001 Scrooge McBear...Change of Heart 228374PAW - The Boyds Collection	Open		16.00	1
1994 Sebastian's Prayer 2227	Retrd.	1996	16.25	32-49
1998 Serena 25711	Retrd.	1999	10.00	1
1999 Sergeant Bookum O' Reilly 3214	Open		15.00	1
2001 Sgt. O' Beara with Ali and Friends...Everyday Hero 227745 - The Boyds Collection	Open		19.00	19
1994 Sherlock & Watson-In Disguise 2019	Retrd.	1996	15.75	75-82
1995 Simone & Bailey...'Helping Hands' 2267	Retrd.	1999	25.95	40-55
1996 Simone and Bailey...Helping Hands (waterglobe) 2705	Retrd.	1998	34.80	40-47
1993 Simone De Bearvoire and Her Mom 2001	Retrd.	1996	14.20	173-179
1996 Sir Edmund... Persistence 2279	Retrd.	1999	20.75	39-86
2002 Sir Wilfred & Bertha Blubberton...High Society 2443 - The Boyds Collection	Open		12.00	12
1999 Sissie & Squirt...big helper lil' sipper 228323	Open		21.00	21-49
1999 Sparky & the box 227716	Retrd.	2000	20.00	32-42
2001 Stephanie, John & George...The Family Tree 228348 - The Boyds Collection	Open		21.00	21
1997 Stonewall the Rebel 228302	Retrd.	1999	19.00	36-63
2001 Strike McSpare...9 Outa 10 Ain't Bad 228358 - The Boyds Collection	Open		16.00	16
2001 Sweetie Pie's Cookin' Kitchen 3940 - The Boyds Collection	Open		41.00	41
2001 T.D. Gridiron...Touch Down! 228356 - The Boyds Collection	Open		16.00	16
2001 T.H. Beanster with Ogden...On the Road Again 227765 - The Boyds Collection	Retrd.	2001	28.00	28-38
2002 T.T. Beanster 24 J1 - The Boyds Collection	Open		10.50	11
1998 Tabitha w/Wolsey & Zip...flying high 228319	Retrd.	1999	26.00	26
1994 Ted & Teddy 2223	Retrd.	1997	15.75	27-49
1999 Tessa-Ben & Cissie...T.B.C...a sign of the times 2299	Open		19.00	19-45
1996 Thaddeus Bud Grisberg 3202	Retrd.	1998	10.00	10
2000 Tillie Hopgood...the Eggsitter 227734 - The Boyds Collection	Retrd.	2000	15.00	15-29
1999 Tweedle Bedeedle with Lauren and Company (waterglobe) 270555	Retrd.	2001	38.00	38
2000 Tweedle Bedeedle...Stop and Smell the Roses 227730 - The Boyds Collection	Open		16.00	16-39
1995 Union Jack...'Love Letters' 2263	Retrd.	1998	18.95	31-75

Collectors' Information Bureau   *Quotes have been rounded up to nearest dollar

YEAR ISSUE	EDITION LIMIT	YEAR RETD.	ISSUE PRICE	*QUOTE U.S.$
2001 Victoria Lynn…Great Escapes 227753 - The Boyds Collection	Open		17.50	18-27
1999 Victoria Regina…Home Sweet Hive (waterglobe) 270504	Retrd.	2000	46.00	46
1993 Victoria…'The Lady' 2004	Retrd.	1999	18.40	19-230
1999 Wanda and Gert…A Little Off The Top 227719	Retrd.	2001	18.00	18-42
1996 Wilson 25702	Retrd.	1998	11.00	11
1994 Wilson at the Beach 2020-06	Retrd.	1997	15.75	27-95
1994 Wilson the "Perfesser" 2222	Retrd.	1997	16.25	27-62
1993 Wilson with Love Sonnets 2007	Retrd.	1997	12.60	42-100
1995 Wilson…'the Wonderful Wizard of Wuz' 2261	Retrd.	1999	15.95	27-69
1998 Winnie Hopkins & Bunnylove 3207	Retrd.	2000	20.00	20
2000 Wolfgang 25733 - The Boyds Collection	Retrd.	2001	10.50	11
1994 Xmas Bear Elf with List BC2051	1,865	1994	24.99	1250-1500
2001 Yardley Starboard w/Bouy…Whatever Floats Your Boat 227761 - The Boyds Collection	Open		16.00	16-24
1997 Zoe…Angel of Life (GCC Exclusive) 2286	Retrd.	1997	15.00	27-64

Bearstone Noah's Pageant Series - G.M. Lowenthal, unless otherwise noted

2001 Aurora and Rex…Saving the Family Jewels 2437 - The Boyds Collection	Open		12.00	12
1999 Bernice as Mrs. Noah…the Chief Cook and Bottle Washer 2427	Open		11.00	11-38
2001 Hippolita and Hugo D. Nile…Sink or Swim 2436 - The Boyds Collection	Open		12.00	12
2000 Hsing Hsing & Ling Ling Wongbruin…Carryout 2433 - The Boyds Collection	Open		12.00	12-41
1999 Jeremy as Noah…The Ark Builder 2426	Open		11.00	11-29
2001 Jilli as Noah's Daughter-in-Law… Cruise Director 2438 - The Boyds Collection	Open		12.00	12
2000 Joey & Alice Outback…The Trekkers 2432 - The Boyds Collection	Open		12.00	12-33
2001 Lawrence and Sheherazade O'Sand…One Hump or Two 2435 - The Boyds Collection	Open		12.00	12
2000 Packy & Dermah Trunkspace…Packin' Lite 2431 - The Boyds Collection	Open		12.00	12-41
1999 S.S. Noah…The Ark 2450	Open		34.50	35-76
1999 Stretch and Skye Longnecker…The Lookouts 2428	Open		11.00	11-39
2000 Willie…as Noah's son 2430 - The Boyds Collection	Open		11.00	11-38

The Charming Angels - The Boyds Collection

2002 Ariella and Child…Guardian of Motherhood 28219	Open		25.50	26
2001 Aurora…Guardian of Dreams 28215	Open		25.50	26
2001 Floramella…Guardian of Nature 28216	Open		25.50	26
2002 Gloriana…Guardian of Faith 28221	Open		25.50	26
2001 Guinevere and Felicity…Guardians of Friends 28218	Retrd.	2001	40.00	40
2002 Olivia…Guardian of Flora 28220	Open		25.50	26
2001 Viviana…Guardian of Love 28217	Open		25.50	26

Critic & Co. - The Boyds Collection

2001 Ally & Oops…No Brakes 36520	Open		21.00	21
2000 B.S. Slushfund with Veto…Slippery Platform 36515	Retrd.	2001	16.00	16
1999 Chilly & Millie…Starlights 28106	Retrd.	2001	19.00	19
2001 Cicely & Juneau…Iced Tea Party 36503	Retrd.	2001	15.50	16
2002 Dippy Quackenwaddle…Drops in a Bucket 36606	Open		10.00	10
2000 Farmer McHare 36601 - The Boyds Collection	Retrd.	2001	10.00	10
2000 Flake & Melton…Snow Buddies 28108	Retrd.	2001	20.50	21
1999 Florence and Katerina…Cold Comfort 36511	Retrd.	2000	19.00	19
2000 Graham & Cracker…Makin' S'mores 36514	Retrd.	2001	20.00	20
1999 I.B. Freezin'…Iceberg Lettuce 36508	Retrd.	2000	19.00	19
2001 Jolly Ol' St. Frostnick…It's in the Bag 36518	Open		15.00	15

YEAR ISSUE	EDITION LIMIT	YEAR RETD.	ISSUE PRICE	*QUOTE U.S.$
1999 Ketchum and B. Quick…Got One! 36509	Retrd.	2000	19.00	19
2001 Miss Hopalots with Hop, Skip and Jump…Times Three 36603	Open		10.00	10
2000 Mommie McHopple & babie 36600 - The Boyds Collection	Retrd.	2001	10.00	10
2002 Mrs. Chips with Meg & Nutley…Sunday Stroll 36607	Open		10.00	10
2001 Mrs. G. Clef with Halfnote…Two Part Harmony 36517	Open		20.00	20
1999 Murphy McFrost…Fire & Ice 28105	Retrd.	2000	19.00	19
2000 Pee Wee Buntsalot…Winter League 36516	Retrd.	2001	16.00	16
2001 Skipper Bob…Duck 'n Boom 36604	Open		10.00	10
1997 Slurp and the Snowcone Stand 36500	Retrd.	2000	14.50	15
2002 Thatcher & Margaret…High Tea 36605	Open		10.00	10
2001 Tickles and Prickles…Stuck on You 36602	Open		10.00	10
2001 Wendell P. Jingletoes…Christmas Countdown 36521	Open		15.00	15
2001 Windy and Frostbite…Takes One to Know One 36519	Open		19.00	19
1999 Zip Z. Shovelenhand…Got Snow? 28104	Retrd.	2001	19.00	19

The Crumpletons - The Boyds Collection

2002 Amanda 73108	Open		40.00	40
2001 Clarisse Growsalot 73101	Retrd.	2001	41.00	41
2001 Faith Crumpleton 73105	Open		40.00	40
2001 Grace Z. Beartique 73100	Retrd.	2001	40.00	40
2001 Jacque Downhill Crumpleton 73103	Open		40.00	40
2002 Liddy Pearl 73109	Open		40.00	40
2001 Nicholai S. Crumpleton 73104	Retrd.	2001	40.00	40
2002 Our American Hero…Strength, Dedication and Courage 73110	Open		40.00	40
2001 Patricia Bearsvelt 73102	Retrd.	2001	40.00	40
2001 Tabitha Crumpleton 73106	Open		40.00	40
2002 Watson 73107	Open		40.00	40

The Dollstone Collection™ - G.M. Lowenthal, unless otherwise noted

1995 Betsey & Edmund 3503PE	Retrd.	1995	19.50	27-75
1996 Betsey and Edmund with Union Jack BC35031	Open		24.99	25-82
1995 Katherine, Amanda & Edmund 3505PE	Retrd.	1995	19.50	32-119
1995 Meagan 3504PE	Retrd.	1995	19.50	200-300
1995 Victoria with Samantha 3502PE	Retrd.	1995	19.50	75-90
1995 Set of 4 PE	Retrd.	1995	78.00	312-400
1999 Alyssa With Caroline…A Stitch in Time 3539	Retrd.	2001	18.00	31-38
1997 The Amazing Bailey…'Magic Show' 3518	Yr.Iss.	1997	60.00	45
1998 Amy and Edmund…Momma's Clothes 3529	Retrd.	2000	29.50	38-45
1996 Anne…the Masterpiece 3599	Retrd.	1999	24.25	27-38
1996 Ashley with Chrissie…Dress Up 3506	Retrd.	1998	20.50	28-49
1998 Austin w/Allen…the firechief 3534	Retrd.	1999	20.00	27-45
2000 Barbara Ann w/Jodi and Annie… Stitched w/Love 3554 - The Boyds Collection	Retrd.	2001	23.00	30-47
1997 Benjamin with Mattew…The Speed Trap 3524	Retrd.	2000	30.00	35-57
1996 Betsey with Edmond…The Patriots 3503	Open		20.00	20-47
1999 Butch with Clayton…Eye'n it Up 3562	Retrd.	2001	18.00	26-35
2000 Brooke w/Joshua…Puddle Jumpers 3551 - The Boyds Collection	Open		20.00	20-50
1997 Caitlin with Emma & Edmund…Diapering Baby 3525	Retrd.	1999	20.00	27-50
1999 Calamity with Little Bear…Whoa is Me 3561	Retrd.	2001	19.00	19
1996 Candice with Matthew…Gathering Apples 3514	Retrd.	1999	18.95	31-60
1998 Candice with Matthew…Gathering Apples 25851	Retrd.	1999	10.00	10
2000 Casey w/Baxter…Afternoon Stroll 3557 - The Boyds Collection	120,000	2001	35.00	35-72
2001 Charlotte and Emily…That's What Friends Are For 3572 - The Boyds Collection	Open		20.50	21
1999 Cheryl w/Ashlie…nighty night 3544	Retrd.	2001	20.00	20-39

Boyds Collection Ltd.
to Boyds Collection Ltd.

YEAR ISSUE	EDITION LIMIT	YEAR RETD.	ISSUE PRICE	*QUOTE U.S.$
1996 Christy w/Nicole...Mother's Presence GCC 3516	Open		26.00	26-60
2000 Cindy w/Collier...Dress Up 3555 - The Boyds Collection	Retrd.	2001	14.00	28-31
2001 Claire Marie on Starr...Circus Dreams 3569 - The Boyds Collection	Retrd.	2001	23.50	24
1996 Courtney with Phoebe...over the River and Thru the Woods (waterglobe) 3512	Retrd.	1997	24.25	32-50
2002 Danielle...Sweet Comforts 3577 - The Boyds Collection	Open		21.00	21
1996 Emily with Kathleen & Otis...The Future 3508	Retrd.	2000	30.00	32-100
1998 Emily with Kathleen & Otis...The Future (musical) 272052	Retrd.	2001	37.00	37-60
2001 Felicity with Bennington...Toot Sweet 3568 - The Boyds Collection	Open		15.00	15
2001 Felicity with Bennington...Toot Sweet (votive) 27952 - The Boyds Collection	Open		26.00	26
2001 Georgette with hayden...Filling Momma's Shoes 3570 - The Boyds Collection	Open		25.00	25
1999 Grace and Faith...I Have a Dream (musical) 272054	Retrd.	1999	36.00	36-47
2001 Hannah...Dear Santa 3575 - The Boyds Collection	Open		16.00	16
2001 Heather...Dress Rehearsal 3573 - The Boyds Collection	Open		20.50	21
1999 Heather With Lauren...Bunny Helpers 3538	Retrd.	2001	19.50	35
1998 Jamie and Thomasina...the Last One 3530	Retrd.	2001	20.00	27-37
1996 Jean with Elliot & Debbie...The Bakers 3510	Open		19.50	20-60
1996 Jennifer with Priscilla...The Doll in the Attic 3500	Retrd.	1997	20.50	38-42
1997 Julia with Emmy Lou...Garden Friends 3520	Open		19.00	19-55
1998 Jessica & Timmy...Animal Hospital 3532	72,000	1998	40.00	27-70
1996 Karen & Wilson...Skater's Waltz GCC 3515	Open		26.00	26-33
1997 Karen with Wilson and Eloise...Mother's Present 3515-01	Retrd.	1998	20.00	32-59
1996 Katherine with Amanda & Edmond...Kind Hearts 3505	Retrd.	2001	20.00	32-58
1996 Kelly and Company...The Bear Collector 3542	Open		35.00	35-65
2000 Kelly and Company...The Bear Collector (waterglobe) 272056 - The Boyds Collection	Retrd.	2001	37.00	37
2001 Kendra with Kassidy and Lil' Pete...Garden Friends 3567 - The Boyds Collection	Open		19.50	20
1999 Kimberly with Klaus...Special Delivery 3547	Retrd.	2001	18.00	32-47
1997 Kristi with Nicole...Skater's Waltz 3516	Retrd.	1999	22.00	35
1997 Laura with Jane...First Day of School 3522	Retrd.	2000	23.00	30-60
2001 Lauren...Musical Memories 3574 - The Boyds Collection	Open	2001	20.50	21
1998 Lindsey w/Louise...the recital 3535	Retrd.	2001	18.00	35-43
1999 Lindsey w/Louise...the recital (waterglobe) 272002	Retrd.	2001	48.00	48
2000 Lisa w/Plato...Graduation Day 3550 - The Boyds Collection	Open		18.00	18-38
1999 Lucinda and Dawn...By the Sea (votive) 27951	Retrd.	2000	26.00	26-45
1999 Lucinda and Dawn...By the Sea 3536	Retrd.	2000	18.00	25-38
2002 Madison...Summer's Here 3576 - The Boyds Collection	Open		19.00	19
2002 Maggie...Grandmom's Helper 3578 - The Boyds Collection	N/A		25.00	25
1996 Mallory w/Patsy & J.B....Trick or Treat 3517	Retrd.	1996	27.00	42-68
1999 Mark w/Luke...the prayer 3545	Retrd.	2000	14.00	14
1999 Mary and Laura...Quiet Time 3565	Retrd.		22.00	22
1998 Mary and Paul...The Prayer 3531-01	Retrd.	1998	16.00	36-38
2001 Mary Ann with Braxton...Touch the Sky 3571 - The Boyds Collection	N/A		37.00	37
1996 Megan with Elliot & Annie...Christmas Carol 3504	Retrd.	1997	19.50	27-60
1996 Megan with Elliot...Christmas Carol (waterglobe) 2720	Retrd.	1997	39.45	60-65
1999 Melissa with Katie and Desiree...The Ballet (musical) 272003	Retrd.	2001	36.00	36-48
1999 Melissa with Katie...The Ballet 3537	Retrd.	2001	18.00	34-47
1999 Meredith with Jacqueline...Daisy Chain 3541	Retrd.	1999	18.00	35
1999 Mia...the save 3549	Retrd.	2000	20.00	20-39
2000 Michael and Thayer...Waitin for Grandpa 3552 - The Boyds Collection	Open		24.00	24-35
1996 Michelle with Daisy...Reading is Fun 3511	Retrd.	2000	17.95	23-65
1999 Miranda w/Mary K....pretty as a picture 3548	Retrd.	2001	37.00	50-63
1999 Morgan as Puffasaurus and Merlin...Carver's Delight 3566	Retrd.	2001	25.00	25
1997 Natalie w/Joy...Sunday School 3519	Retrd.	1999	22.00	33-42
1996 Patricia with Molly...Attic Treasures 3501	Retrd.	1998	14.00	17-37
1999 Peter w/James...the prayer (G.M.'s Choice) 3545-06	Retrd.	2000	16.00	16
1998 Rachel w/Barbara & Matthew 3526	Retrd.	1999	23.00	32-50
1996 Rebecca with Elliot...Birthday 3509	Retrd.	2000	20.50	27-65
1999 Ryan and Diane...Love is Forever (waterglobe) 272053	Retrd.	2001	37.00	37-54
2000 Ryan and Diane w/Cory, Wesley and Carly...Love is Forever 3553 - The Boyds Collection	Open		29.00	29-52
1999 Samantha with Conner...Best Friends 3559	Retrd.	2001	20.50	21
1998 sandra claus w/bailey & edmund...christmas morning 3528-1	Open		38.00	38-58
1996 Sara & Heather with Elliot & Amelia...Tea for Four 3507	Retrd.	1997	46.00	37-86
1999 Sarah Anne with Duncan...Icing on the Cake 3560	Retrd.	2001	20.00	20
1998 Shannon & Wilson...waiting for Grandma 3533	Retrd.	2000	34.00	40-58
1998 Shelby...Asleep in Teddy's Arms 3527	Retrd.	2000	15.00	22-40
1999 Stephanie with Jim...School Days (musical) 2783	Retrd.	2001	39.00	39
1999 Stephanie with Jim...School Days 3540	Open		25.00	25-42
1999 Tami w/Doug...half time 3546	Retrd.	2000	20.00	20-39
1999 Taylor with Jumper...Playtime 3563	Open		20.00	20
1998 Teresa and John...The Prayer 3531	Retrd.	2000	14.00	27-37
2001 Tricia...Waiting for Santa 272004 - The Boyds Collection	Open		39.00	39
1996 Victoria with Samantha...Victorian Ladies 3502	Retrd.	1999	20.00	27-43
1997 Wendy...Wash Day 3521	Retrd.	1998	22.00	32-65
1997 Whitney & Wilson...Tea Party 3523	Retrd.	2000	19.00	27-42
1997 Whitney w/Wilson...Tea Party (musical) 272001	Retrd.	2000	37.00	42-58

Faeriessence - G.M. Lowenthal, unless otherwise noted

YEAR ISSUE	EDITION LIMIT	YEAR RETD.	ISSUE PRICE	*QUOTE U.S.$
2000 Amber Faeriedreams...Deep in the Forest 36107 - The Boyds Collection	Open		19.00	19-38
2002 Anastasia Faeriedance 73200 - The Boyds Collection	Open		21.00	21
1997 Angelina - Smidge Angellove 36100	Retrd.	1999	16.00	37-50
1999 Ann & Abby Angelstitch...The Threads That Bind Us 36006	Retrd.	2000	25.00	38-47
1999 Arabella & Oscar...Icy Treats 36510	Retrd.	2000	18.50	19
1999 Autumn L. Fairiefrost...Harvest Time 36005	Retrd.	2001	18.00	35-38
1998 bobby...the defender 36505	Retrd.	1999	19.00	19-27
2001 Boom Boom Magee with Match and Fuse...Thar She Blows! 36403 - The Boyds Collection	Open		30.00	30
1998 Caffeinata "Speedy" Faeriechild...coffee faerie 36304	Retrd.	2000	19.00	34-40
2000 Carrie B. Safe...Call when you get there 36007 - The Boyds Collection	Retrd.	2001	15.00	25-32
1998 cerebella "smarty" faerienoggin 36201	Retrd.	2000	18.00	24-32
1998 cicely & juneau...iced tea party 36503	Retrd.	2001	16.00	16
1999 Confidentia...No tell 36105	Retrd.	2001	18.00	38-40
1997 dentinata "faerielove"...the tooth faerie 36102	Retrd.	1999	16.00	22-40
2002 Echo Faeriebrook...Drifting Along 36116 - The Boyds Collection	Open		20.50	21
1997 electra angelbyte...Angel of Computer Training 36300	Retrd.	2000	18.00	29-52

Collectors' Information Bureau

*Quotes have been rounded up to nearest dollar

FIGURINES

YEAR ISSUE	EDITION LIMIT	YEAR RETD.	ISSUE PRICE	*QUOTE U.S.$
1997 Estudious "cram" faerienoggin...the study faerie 36301	Retrd.	1999	18.00	22-35
2001 Fauna Faeriegaze...Nature's Keeper 36111 - The Boyds Collection	Open		19.50	20
1999 Felicity...angelbliss...The Bride's Angel 36103	Retrd.	2000	18.00	25-36
1996 Fixit...Santa's Faerie 3600	Retrd.	1998	17.45	22-45
1998 flakey...ice sculptor 36504	Retrd.	1999	19.00	29-42
2001 Flora Faeriepetals...Morning Dew 36112 - The Boyds Collection	Open		17.50	18
2001 Flurry Frost...Winter Dusting (waterglobe) 271025 - The Boyds Collection	Open		41.00	41
2001 Flurry Frost...Winter Dusting 36012 - The Boyds Collection	Open		15.00	15
1997 Gabrielle "Gabby" Faeriejabber 36003	Retrd.	1998	18.50	32-40
1999 Grandma Faeriehugs 36106	Open		15.00	15-27
1997 half-pipe...the hotdogger 36502	Retrd.	1999	14.50	22-27
1999 Henry K. Wallstreet...With a Little Bit of Luck 36402	Retrd.	2000	17.00	17-25
2000 Hilda w/Scaredy Cat & Ezra...Witch in Training 36203 - The Boyds Collection	Retrd.	2000	25.50	26
2001 Holly Faerieberry...Holiday Gathering 36014 - The Boyds Collection	Open		14.50	9
1997 Immaculata T Faeriburg...The Cleaning Faerie 36302	Retrd.	2001	18.00	32-40
1998 indulgenia q. bluit...angel of denial 36305	Retrd.	2000	19.00	30-39
1997 Infiniti Faerielove...the Wedding Faerie 36101	Retrd.	1998	16.00	29-49
2002 Irridessa Faerielocket 73202 - The Boyds Collection	Open		21.00	21
2001 Jilian, Piper & Melody...Sugarplum Sonata 36015 - The Boyds Collection	N/A		41.00	41
1997 Kristabell Wee Faerie Frost 36002	Retrd.	1999	17.00	17
1998 mangianata "Nosh" j. faeriechild...The cooking faerie 36303	Retrd.	2000	18.00	29-54
2000 Mary Angelwish...May Your Wishes All Come True 36108 - The Boyds Collection	Open		19.00	19
1999 Ms Pickelsencream...Heaven's Lil' Blessing 36202	Retrd.	2000	18.00	18
2000 Nana Angelbless with Peekins...watching over you 36009 - The Boyds Collection	Open		16.00	16-32
1997 pearl too...the knitter 36501-1	Open		14.50	15-42
1997 pearl...the knitter 36501	Open		14.50	15-27
2000 Polly Pekoe...tee faerie 36109	Open		17.00	17-28
1998 Rememberance Angelflyte...Time Flies 36004	Retrd.	2000	18.00	29-42
2002 Rosemarie Faeriepetal...Morning Dew 36114 - The Boyds Collection	Open		19.00	19-25
2001 Sienna Faerieleaf...Touch of Fall 36011 - The Boyds Collection	Open		16.00	16
2000 Slumber faeriedreams with Nod...Nighty Night 36008 - The Boyds Collection	Open		19.00	19-25
1997 Slurp and the Snowcone stand 36500	Open		14.50	15-32
2002 Sparing Faerieblossom...Morning Mist 36117 - The Boyds Collection	Open		19.00	19
2000 Sudsie Faerisock...Mischief Maker 36306 - The Boyds Collection	Retrd.	2001	19.00	19-27
2002 Summer Faeriesweet...Berry Delight 36115 - The Boyds Collection	Open		17.50	18
1997 t.h. Bean...The Bearmaker Elf 36400	Retrd.	1999	20.00	20-54
1999 Tuxworth P Cummerbund...The Groom's Angel 36104	Retrd.	2001	18.00	25-34
2001 Violetta Faeriegaze...Pause and Reflect (waterglobe) 271052 - The Boyds Collection	Open		53.50	54
2001 Violetta Faeriegaze...Pause and Reflect 36110 - The Boyds Collection	Open		24.00	24
2002 Willow Faerieflutter 73201 - The Boyds Collection	Open		21.00	21

The Folkstone Collection™ - G.M. Lowenthal, unless otherwise noted

YEAR ISSUE	EDITION LIMIT	YEAR RETD.	ISSUE PRICE	*QUOTE U.S.$
1995 Abigail...Peaceable Kingdom (NQGA) 2829	Retrd.	1998	18.95	29-38
1998 Aerobics angel 28244v (GCC)	Retrd.	1999	20.00	20-50
1996 Alvin T. Mac Barker...Dogface 2872	Retrd.	1997	19.00	20-37
1994 Angel of Freedom 2820	Retrd.	1996	16.75	42-58
1994 Angel of Love 2821	Retrd.	1996	16.75	30-94

YEAR ISSUE	EDITION LIMIT	YEAR RETD.	ISSUE PRICE	*QUOTE U.S.$
1994 Angel of Peace 2822	Retrd.	1996	16.75	35-94
1997 Ann & Abby Angelstitch...The Thread That Binds Us 36006	Retrd.	1999	26.00	26-43
2000 Aquarius...The Dawning 28212 - The Boyds Collection	Retrd.	2001	20.50	34-44
1997 Astrid Isinglass...Snow Angel 28206-06	Yr.Iss.	1997	23.50	47-50
1999 Athena...The Wedding Angel 28202	Retrd.	2000	19.00	27-52
1999 Audubon P. Pussywillow...The Birdwatcher (votive) 27803	Retrd.	2000	26.00	27-37
1999 Audubon P. Pussywillow...The Birdwatcher 2868	Retrd.	2000	19.00	19
1998 Auntie Cocoa M. Maximus...Chocolate Angel (NQGA) 28242	Retrd.	2000	20.00	32-68
1998 Barnaby JR...homeward bound 370101	Retrd.	1999	19.00	19-26
1997 Bearly Nick & Buddies 28001	Retrd.	1999	19.50	27-40
1995 Beatrice...the Giftgiver 2836	Retrd.	1999	17.95	28-66
1994 Beatrice...the Birthday Angel (NQGA) 2825	Retrd.	1998	20.00	22-38
1996 Bernie... lgotwaitwanted St. Bernard Santa 2873	Retrd.	1999	17.75	26-35
1996 Betty Biscuit 2870	Retrd.	1999	19.00	19-59
1998 Birdie Holeinone...(NQGA of Golfers) 28245	Retrd.	2000	20.00	25-40
1995 Boowinkle Vonhindenmoose...2831	Open		17.95	18-58
1998 Bridges...Scuba Frog 36751	Retrd.	1999	15.00	15
1997 Bristol...Just sweep in 28101 (GCC)	Retrd.	1997	17.00	40-62
1998 Burt Jr...bundle up 370102	Retrd.	1999	14.00	14
1998 Burt...Bundle Up 370002	Retrd.	1998	20.00	20
1996 Buster Goes A' Courtin' 2844	Retrd.	1998	19.00	22-42
2000 Caffeinata "Speedy" Faeriebean (musical) 271051 - The Boyds Collection	Retrd.	2000	27.00	27
2000 Calliope Clipsalot...Guardian Angel of Pennies 28211 - The Boyds Collection	Retrd.	2001	19.50	20-29
1999 Cantwell Waddlewak & Peek 36802	Open		16.00	16
1998 Charles prince of Tales 36700	Retrd.	1999	13.00	13
1999 Chester Bigheart...Love Much 370053	Retrd.	1999	27.00	27
1999 Chilly & Millie...Starlights 28106	Retrd.	2000	19.00	19
1994 Chilly & Son with Dove 2811	Retrd.	1997	17.75	41-63
1999 Cocoa M. Anglerich & Scoop Musical 271050	Retrd.	2000	28.00	28
1997 Constance & Felicity 28205	14,000	1997	37.50	58-135
1996 Cosmos...The Gardening Angel 28201	Retrd.	2000	19.00	27-59
1998 darby & jasper...knitten' kittens (votive) 27802	Retrd.	1998	26.00	32-42
1994 December 26th 3003	Retrd.	1997	32.00	25-125
1999 Domestica T. Whirlwind...NQGA of Supermoms 28249	Retrd.	2001	20.00	29-39
1999 Dr. R X Mooselberry...making rounds 28301	Retrd.	2000	19.00	30-37
2000 Dusty Rose...Dust Bunnies Can't Hide (waterglobe) 271003 - The Boyds Collection	Retrd.	2001	40.00	40
2000 Dusty Rose...Dust Bunnies Can't Hide 28251 - The Boyds Collection	Retrd.	2001	20.50	21
2000 Edgar w/Allan & Poe...ScreaAway Strawboss 2888 - The Boyds Collection	Retrd.	2000	24.00	24
2002 Edna B. Sungoddess...Life's A Beach 28255 - The Boyds Collection	Open		21.00	21
1996 Egon...the Skier 2837	Retrd.	1999	17.75	32-64
1999 Electronic & Splice ...The Surprise 28004	Retrd.	1999	19.00	30-35
1995 Elmer...been farmin' long? 2851	Retrd.	1998	19.00	19-38
1996 Elmo "Tex" Beefcake...On the Range 2853	Retrd.	1997	19.00	32-57
1995 Ernest Hemmingmoose...the Hunter 2835	Retrd.	1999	17.95	39-58
1995 Esmeralda...the Wonderful Witch 2860	Open		17.95	18-50
1996 Etheral...Angel of Light (G.M.'s Choice)28203-06	7,200	1996	18.25	52-195
1998 Execunick...1st global businessman 28002	Retrd.	1999	21.00	27-40
1999 Fergus Bogey MacDivot 36401	Retrd.	1999	18.00	18
1996 Flora & Amelia...The Gardeners 2843	Retrd.	1999	19.00	26-32
1996 Flora, Amelia & Eloise...The Tea Party 2846	Retrd.	1998	19.00	32-39
1999 Florence and Katerina 36511	Open		19.00	19
1994 Florence...the kitchen angel (NQGA) 2824	Retrd.	1996		46

FIGURINES

YEAR ISSUE	EDITION LIMIT	YEAR RETD.	ISSUE PRICE	*QUOTE U.S.$
2000 Franceska Gentleheart…All Creatures Great & Small 28214 - The Boyds Collection	Retrd.	2001	26.00	26
1998 Francoise & Suzanne…the Spree 2875	Retrd.		20.00	31-56
1998 Frogmorton…fly fishjng 36701	Retrd.	2000	15.00	15
1999 Fuzznick s. Claws & Co. 28003	Retrd.	2000	19.00	19
1999 Gaston Coldfish 36801	Open		16.00	16
1999 Harriet and Punch with Hermine…The Challenge 28402	Retrd.	2000	19.00	25-36
2000 Heather w/Chris…Guardian Angel of Volleyball 28210 - The Boyds Collection	Retrd.	2000	20.00	20-28
1998 Heavenly Sconce 65429	Open		21.00	21
1997 Helga with Ingrid & Anna …Be Warm 2818	Retrd.	1999	19.00	29-31
2001 Herby Highwalker with Tag-A-Long…Day Trippin' 280101 - The Boyds Collection	Open		19.00	19
2001 Hilly and Willy Homegrown…The Politics of Marriage 280102- The Boyds Collection	Open		25.00	25
2000 Honker T. Flatfoot…Send in the Clowns 2887 - The Boyds Collection	Retrd.	2000	19.50	34-39
1998 I.b. coldman…ice is nice 28102	Retrd.	2000	20.00	27-39
1999 I.B. Freezin 36508	Open		19.00	19
1995 Icabod Mooselman…the Pilgrim 2833	Retrd.	1997	17.95	45-95
1994 Ida & Bessie-The Gardeners 2852	Retrd.	1998	19.00	25-47
1996 Illumina…Angel of Light 28203	Retrd.	1999	18.45	29-60
1998 Ingrid & Olaf…Be Warm (votive) 27801	Retrd.	2000	27.00	27
1999 Isabella…Follow Your Heart's Desire 28208	Retrd.	2000	23.00	26-50
2000 Jack Hammer…Hard Hat 2885 - The Boyds Collection	Retrd.	2000	19.00	29-38
1998 Jacques…the wine tester 36702	Retrd.	1998	14.00	14
1996 Jean Claude & Jacque…the Skiers (waterglobe) 2710	Open		37.50	38-55
1995 Jean Claude & Jacques…the Skiers 2815	Retrd.	1999	16.95	29-32
1999 Jeremiah Jellybean Pondhopper 36704	Retrd.	1999	14.00	14
1999 Jester Q. Funnybones 370054	Retrd.	1999	27.00	27
1994 Jill…language of Love 2842	Retrd.	1997	19.00	29-58
1994 Jingle Moose 2830	Retrd.	1996	17.75	62-120
1996 Jingle Nick & Stary Stary (QVC)	Retrd.	1996	N/A	N/A
1994 Jingles & Son with Wreath 2812	Retrd.	1996	17.75	44-52
2001 Jolly Ol' St. Nick…Too Many Cookies 28007 - The Boyds Collection	Open		20.50	21
1999 Ketchem & B. Quick..got one 36509	Open		19.00	19
1997 Krystal Isinglass…Snow Angel 28206	Retrd.	1999	19.00	42-64
1999 Laverne B. Bowler…Strikes and Spares 28248	Retrd.	2000	18.00	27-37
1998 Liddy Pearl…how does your garden grow (waterglobe) 270602	Yr.lss.	1998	51.00	58-104
1998 Liddy Pearl…How Does Your Garden Grow 2881	12,000	1998	40.00	80-99
1994 Lizzie…the Shopping Angel (NQGA) 2827	Retrd.	1998	20.00	23-45
1996 Loretta Moostein…"Yer Cheatin' Heart" 2854	Retrd.	1998	19.00	29-32
1996 Lucky McPlug 2871	Retrd.	1999	19.00	32-50
2000 Ludwig Puffenhuff…Ornament Maker 28005 - The Boyds Collection	Retrd.	2000	20.50	21
1998 Luminette…by the light of the silvery moon (G.M.'s Choice) 28207-06	Retrd.	1999	23.00	23-64
1998 Luna…by the light of the silvery moon 28207	Retrd.	2000	19.00	27-54
2001 Mabel Z. Bargainhunter…What a Deal 280103- The Boyds Collection	Open		25.00	25
1997 Madge…The Magician/Beautician (NQGA) 28243	Retrd.	2001	19.00	29-37
1997 Mercy…Angel of Nurses (NQGA) 28240	Retrd.	2000	19.00	29-37
1998 Milken von hindenmoose…trees company 2832	Retrd.	2000	19.00	35-47
1994 Minerva…the Baseball Angel (NQGA) 2826	Retrd.	1997	20.00	37-52
2001 Miss Biddle…Holdin' It Together 28252 - The Boyds Collection	Open		20.50	21
1998 Miss Prudence P. Carrotjuice…Multiplication 2848	Retrd.	2000	18.50	19

YEAR ISSUE	EDITION LIMIT	YEAR RETD.	ISSUE PRICE	*QUOTE U.S.$
2000 Momma McHutch and Babies…Family Matters 28403 - The Boyds Collection	Retrd.	2000	19.50	20-31
1997 Montague Von Hindenmoose…Surprise! 2839	Open		19.00	19-41
1999 Ms Fries…The Guardian Angel of Waitresses 28246	Retrd.	2000	19.00	32-42
1999 Ms Lilypond…Lesson #1 36705	Retrd.	2001	14.00	14
1999 Ms McFrazzle…Daycare Extraordinaire 2883	Retrd.	2001	20.00	30
1999 Ms McFrazzle…on the job (waterglobe) 271002	Retrd.	2000	39.00	39-49
1997 Ms Patience…Angel of Teachers (NQGA) 28241	Retrd.	1998	19.00	28-37
1999 Ms Pleasant…May I help you? 28250	Retrd.	2001	19.00	19
1998 ms…imin payne (NQGA) 28244	Retrd.	1999	20.00	20
1997 Murphy McFrost…Fire & ice 28105	Retrd.	2000	19.00	19
1999 Myron R. Fishmeister and Billy Bob…Angel of Fish Stories 28247	Retrd.	2001	21.00	29-32
1996 Myrtle…Believe! 2840	Retrd.	1998	20.00	20-38
1998 Nana Mchare…and the Love Gardeners 2849	Open		20.00	20-40
1996 Nanick & Siegfried the Plan 2807	10,000	1996	32.50	115-132
1995 Na-Nick of the North 2804	Retrd.	1999	17.95	32-53
1996 Nanny…the Snowmom 2817	Open		17.95	18-32
1994 Nicholai with Tree 2800	Retrd.	1997	17.75	32-58
1994 Nicholas with Book of lists 2802	Retrd.	1996	17.75	47-50
1994 Nick on Ice (1st ed. GCC) 3001	3,600	1995	49.95	75-86
1994 Nick on Ice 3001	Retrd.	1997	32.95	32-75
1996 Nick, Siegfried…the plan 2807	Yr.lss.	1996	35.00	100-125
1994 Nicknoah…Santa with Ark 2806	Retrd.	1999	17.95	18-47
1994 Niki with Candle 2801	Retrd.	1997	17.75	35-47
1996 No-No Nick…Bad Boy Santa 2805	Retrd.	1998	17.95	27-44
1995 Northbound Wille 2814	Retrd.	1997	16.95	30-47
1994 Oceania….Ocean Angel 2823	Retrd.	1998	16.00	42-60
1997 Olaf…Mogul Meister 2819	Open		16.50	17-39
1998 P.J. McSnoozin with Craxton….Hibearnation 2882	Retrd.	2000	19.00	27-49
1998 Peacenick…the Sixties	Open		20.00	20-32
1998 Peacenick…the sixties santa 2809	Retrd.	1999	20.00	20-40
1994 Peter-The Whopper 2841	Retrd.	1997	19.00	20-32
1997 Polaris & The North Star…on Ice 2880	Open		19.00	19-45
1995 Prudence Moosemaid...the Pilgrim 2834	Retrd.	1997	17.95	50-72
1997 Prudence…Daffodils 2847	Retrd.	2000	18.00	24-42
1998 Purrscilla G. Pussenboots…Mitten Knitters 2865	Open		20.50	21-39
1999 Purrscilla…give thanks 2866	Open		19.00	19-49
1996 Robin…the Snowbird Lover 2816	Retrd.	1999	17.95	27-42
1995 Rufus…Hoedown 2850	Retrd.	1998	19.00	29-37
1998 S.C. Ribbit…Hoppy Christmas 36750	Retrd.	1999	19.00	19
1999 Salem….Give thanks 2867	Retrd.	2000	19.00	23-27
2000 Sam, Libby and Ellis…Fife and Drum 2886 - The Boyds Collection	120,000	2000	40.00	62-78
1998 Santa & the final inspection 370003	Retrd.	1998	50.00	50
1998 Santa in the Nick of time 370000	Retrd.	1998	48.00	48
1998 Santa Jr…nick of time 370100	Retrd.	1999	23.00	23
1998 Santa Jr…quick as a flash 370104	Retrd.	1999	20.00	20
1998 Santa Jr…quick as a flash 370104	Retrd.	1999	20.00	20
1998 Santa Jr…the final inspection 370103	Retrd.	1999	24.00	24
1998 Santa…Quick as a flash 370004	Retrd.	1998	42.00	42
1994 Santa's Challenge (1st ed. GCC) 3002	3,600	1995	49.95	25-65
1994 Santa's Challenge 3002	Retrd.	1997	32.95	37-58
1994 Santa's Flight Plan (1st ed. GCC) 3000	3,600	1995	49.95	37-58
1995 Santa's Flight Plan (waterglobe) 2703	Retrd.	1996	37.00	75-92
1994 Santa's Flight Plan 3000	Retrd.	1997	32.95	25-73
1996 Santa's Hobby 3004	Retrd.	1997	36.00	44-75
1995 Seraphina with Jacob & Rachae l…the Choir Angels (NQGA) 2828	Retrd.	1997	19.95	32-63
1996 Serenity…the Mother's Angel 28204	Retrd.	2000	18.25	40-48
1997 Sgt. Rex & Matt…The Runaway 2874	Retrd.	1999	19.50	23-40
1999 Siegfried and Egon…the Sign 2899	Retrd.		18.95	24-72
1995 Sliknick the Chimney Sweep 2803	Retrd.	1998	17.95	27-52
2000 Soltice Angeldance…Sunlight 28209 - The Boyds Collection	Retrd.	2000	19.00	37-48
1997 St. Nick…the Quest 2808	Retrd.	1999	19.00	34-52
2002 Tilly T. Weedsley…Gardener Extraordinaire 28254 - The Boyds Collection	Open		22.00	22
1996 Too Loose Lapin…The Arte-e-st 2845	Retrd.	1998	19.00	28-40

Collectors' Information Bureau   *Quotes have been rounded up to nearest dollar

YEAR ISSUE	EDITION LIMIT	YEAR RETD.	ISSUE PRICE	*QUOTE U.S.$
1999 Tu Tu C Ribbit...Fog Lake 36703	Retrd.	2001	14.00	14
2002 Uncle Sam...I've Got the April 15th Blues 28253 - The Boyds Collection	Open		19.00	19
1999 Wainwright & Rudy Waddlesworth 36800	Open		16.00	16
1999 Walter T. Goodlife...Live Well 370052	Retrd.		27.00	27
1999 Wendy Willowhare...A Tisket A Tasket 28401	Retrd.	2000	19.50	32-37
1994 Windy with Book 2810	Retrd.	1996	17.75	50
2001 Wrongway Kringle...Darn Those Reindeer 28006 - The Boyds Collection	Open		25.00	25
1997 Yukon, Kodiak & Nanuk...Nome Sweet Home (waterglobe) 271001	Retrd.	1999	38.50	45
1997 Yukon, Kodiak...Nome Sweet Home (votive) 27800	Open		26.00	26
1997 Ziggy...The Duffer 2838	Retrd.	1999	39.50	29-37
1999 Zip Shoveland...Got Snow? 28104	Retrd.	2000	N/A	N/A

Heaven Knows Angels™ - The Boyds Collection

2002 Doris O. Nuttinfits...Nothing to Wear 381000	Open		15.00	15
2002 Fannie B. Teasenfriz...Bad Hair Day 381001	Open		15.00	15
2002 Gladys D. Clutterbag...The Lost Keys 381002	Open		15.00	15

The Hopsalots - The Boyds Collection

2002 Lana Hoppennibble...Jelly Bean Harvest 36711	Open		13.00	13
2002 Mrs. Twigley with Lila & Keefer...'Nap 'Sack 36712	Open		13.00	13
2002 Peter P. Thumperton...Cabbage King 36714	Open		13.00	13

J & T Imaginations - The Boyds Collection

2002 Chef Nicoli...Favorite Recipe 73351	Open		58.00	58
2002 Chef Nicoli...Favorite Recipe 73353	Open		51.00	51
2002 Gardener Nickleby...Hoe, Hoe Hoe 73352	Open		58.00	58
2002 Gardener Nickleby...Hoe, Hoe Hoe 73354	Open		51.00	51
2001 Jolly Ol' St. Nick...Bearing Gifts 73302	Open		80.00	80
2001 Kris Kringle...Yuletide Santa 73300	Open		80.00	80
2001 Nicholas...O' Christmas Tree 73301	Open		80.00	80
2002 Noah & Friends...Two By Two 73350	Open		75.00	75

Moose Troop - The Boyds Collection

2000 Edgar Mooselfluff with Acorn...Moosenap 36902	Retrd.	2001	15.00	15
2000 Hirum Mooselplanter...Friends of the Forest 36901	Retrd.	2001	18.50	19
2000 Jingle Mooselbeary...'Tis the Season 25808	Retrd.	2001	10.50	11
2001 Mattie Frostbuns...Triple Klutz 36904	Open		15.00	15
2001 Mervin & Mattie...Under the Mooseltoe 36903	Open		17.50	18
2000 Milliken Von Hindenmoose...Trees Company 25809	Retrd.	2001	10.50	11
2000 Minty Mooselcane...Hangin' Sweet 25807	Retrd.	2001	10.50	11
2000 Mr. Mocha Java Mooselbean...Doubleshot 36900	Retrd.	2001	17.50	18
2001 Murdock Mufflemoose...Second Thoughts 36905	Open		15.50	16

The Purrstone Collection™ - G.M. Lowenthal, unless otherwise noted

2000 Catarina and Sassy...Purrfect Friends 371011 - The Boyds Collection	Open		23.50	24
2001 Chef Stickypaws and Gingersnap...Roof Repair 371019 - the Boyds Collection	Retrd.	2001	18.00	18
1999 Chester Birdbreath...What Bird? 371006	Retrd.	2001	17.00	17-35
1999 Clawdette Fuzzface and Wuly...Yarn Merchants 371002	Retrd.	2000	15.00	15-28
2000 Darby Fuzzkins...Wound Tight 271800 - The Boyds Collection	Retrd.	2001	10.50	11
2000 Dominique Surefoot with Coach Colby...Practice Makes Purrfect 371052 - The Boyds Collection	Retrd.	2000	15.00	15
1999 Felicity Angelpuss and George...Peace on Earth 371004	Retrd.	2001	15.00	15-28

YEAR ISSUE	EDITION LIMIT	YEAR RETD.	ISSUE PRICE	*QUOTE U.S.$
2000 Fletcher Puckerup...Holiday Kisses 271801 - The Boyds Collection	Retrd.	2001	10.50	11
2001 Florence Whisderfixer with Splint...Feline Better? 371057 - The Boyds Collection	Retrd.	2001	18.00	18
2001 Heranamous Buttintrouble with Tack...Hang in There 371058 - The Boyds Collection	Retrd.	2001	22.00	22
2000 Kandace Purrshop...Hidden Surprises 371054 - The Boyds Collection	Retrd.	2001	18.00	18
2001 Leo Roarsmore with Itty, Bitty and Squish...Split Personality 371056 - The Boyds Collection	Retrd.	2001	28.00	28
1999 Maddie Purrkins with Puddytat...Cat Nap 371001	Retrd.	2001	16.00	16-30
2000 Mama Purrsmore and Baby Belle with Rinky, Dinky and Dew...Once Upon a Time 371053 - The Boyds Collection	Open		18.50	19-30
2000 Mario Fenderbender...1 Down, 8 to go 371009 - The Boyds Collection	Retrd.	2001	16.00	16
2001 Miss Flufficat...Winter Snugglin' 371017 - The Boyds Collection	Open		13.00	13
1999 Momma Craftycat with Lil' Sipper...Got Cream? 371007	Open		18.00	18-35
2000 Momma Purrsley and Claudia...Finishing Touches 371010 - The Boyds Collection	Retrd.	2001	18.00	18-30
2001 Mr. Fuzzywig and Sparky...Holiday Glow 371018 - The Boyds Collection	Open		20.50	21
2001 Mrs. Claws and Suds...Freeze Dried 371020 - The Boyds Collection	N/A		25.00	25
2000 Mrs. Claws w/Topper...Hang in There (waterglobe) 271500 - The Boyds Collection	Retrd.	2001	46.00	46
1999 Mrs. Fezziwig with Marley, Bob and Caroline...Caterwauling 371005	Retrd.	2000	15.00	15-45
2000 Mrs. Partridge...C'mon Get Happy 371012 - The Boyds Collection	Open		15.00	15-20
2000 Opie Baithook with Barney...Catch of the Day 371051 - The Boyds Collection	Retrd.	2001	18.50	19
2000 Patience Purrkins & The Mischief Makers...Christmas Catastrophe 371016 - The Boyds Collection	Retrd.	2001	25.00	25-45
1999 Pawlene Prowler...Spooky Treats 371000	Retrd.	2001	15.00	15-28
2000 Pokie Pawsworthy...bug inspector 371050 - The Boyds Collection	Open		20.50	21-35
2000 Purrcila Prissybuns with Cecil...Ready for My Close-up 371008 - The Boyds Collection	Open		23.00	23-25
1999 Santa Claws and Nibbles...A Purrfect Holiday 371003	Retrd.	2000	15.00	15-30

The Shoe Box Bears™ - The Boyds Collection

2001 Angus Bearger...Quit Your Beafin'! 3230	Open		19.00	19
2000 Bradley Boo Bear...Countin' the Treats 3226	Retrd.	2000	19.00	19
2001 Chicklet Grizberg...A Sprinkle in Time 3220	Retrd.	2001	11.00	11
1999 Chief Sittingbear 3217	Retrd.	2000	17.00	17
2002 Daisie-Mae Petalton...Friends Forever 3233	Open		15.50	16
2001 Giblet McBaste...You Turkey! 3232	Open		19.00	19
1999 Ivan Mooselbeary 3215	Retrd.	2000	19.00	19
1999 Ivy Mooselbeary 3216	Retrd.	2001	15.00	15
2000 Izurs Draggon...Breathe Deeply 3228	Open		19.00	19
2000 N. Mouseking 25726	Retrd.	2000	19.00	19
2000 Nutcracker Princebruin 25727	Retrd.	2000	19.00	19
2000 Paddy O'Beary...Luck of the Irish 3221	Retrd.	2000	14.00	14
2001 Pigadilly Honeyglaze...Don't Pig Out! 3231	Open		18.00	18
2000 Princess Aneeda Knight...Kiss and Tell 3227	Retrd.	2000	19.50	20
1999 Princess Standingbear 3217	Retrd.	2000	15.00	15
2002 Rosie Thornbery...Somebody Loves You 3234	Open		15.50	16
1999 Sergeant Bookum O'Reilly...To Protect & Serve 3214	Retrd.	2000	15.00	15
2000 Sir Oncea Frogh...Hop Nightly 3229	Open		19.00	19
2000 Sugarplum Beary 25725	Retrd.	2000	17.00	17

YEAR ISSUE	EDITION LIMIT	YEAR RETD.	ISSUE PRICE	*QUOTE U.S.$
2000 Webster Grizzberg...Just Duckie 3219	Retrd.	2001	14.00	14
2002 Zinnia Goodwish...Feel Better Soon 3235	Open		15.50	16

The Starlight Children's Foundation Exclusive Pieces - The Boyds Collection

2000 Charity Angelhug and Everychild...Cherish the Children (Boarstone) 228343	Retrd.	2000	14.95	15
2000 Charity Angelhug and Everychild...Cherish the Children pin 26039-1	Retrd.	2000	3.70	4
2001 Vanessa R. Angel (plush) 51111	Retrd.	2001	15.00	15

Wills Creek Collection - The Boyds Collection

2001 Brown Trout 70001	Open		18.00	18
2001 Canada Goose Series No. 6 7007	Open		20.50	21
2001 Canvas Back Drake Series No. 5 7006	Open		20.50	21
2001 Craw-Daddy Series No. 1 70504	Open		20.50	21
2001 Green Wing Teal Drake Series No. 3 7004	Open		20.50	21
2001 Green Wing Teal Hen Series No. 4 7005	Open		20.50	21
2001 Lazy Sal Series No. 1 70502	Open		25.50	26
2001 Leapin' Leopard Series No. 1 70501	Open		25.50	26
2001 Lil' Wobbler Series No. 1 70505	Open		20.50	21
2001 Mallard Drake Series No. 1 7002	Open		20.50	21
2001 Mallard Hen Series No. 2 7003	Open		20.50	21
2001 Perch 70000	Open		20.50	21
2001 Plunker Series No. 1 70506	Open		20.50	21
2001 Winged Dragonfly Series No. 1 70503	Open		25.50	26

Calico Kittens/Enesco Group, Inc.

April Showers - P. Hillman

1996 April Showers 155500	Retrd.	1998	17.50	18
1996 Friendship Grows When Shared 129321	Retrd.	1998	15.00	15
1996 Kite Tails 155497	Retrd.	1998	17.50	18

Birthstone Minis - P. Hillman

2000 January 784788	Open		10.00	10
2000 February 784796	Open		10.00	10
2000 March 784818	Open		10.00	10
2000 April 784826	Open		10.00	10
2000 May 784834	Open		10.00	10
2000 June 784842	Open		10.00	10
2000 July 784850	Open		10.00	10
2000 August 784869	Open		10.00	10
2000 September 784877	Open		10.00	10
2000 October 784893	Open		10.00	10
2000 November 784907	Open		10.00	10
2000 December 784915	Open		10.00	10

Breed Apart Minis - P. Hillman

1999 Calico 642274	Open		9.00	9
1999 Himalayan 642266	Open		9.00	9
1999 Persian 642258	Open		9.00	9
1999 Shorthair 642231	Open		9.00	9
1999 Siamese 642223	Open		9.00	9
1999 Tiffany 642215	Open		9.00	9

Calico Corner - P. Hillman

1995 Buttoned Up with Love 104094	Retrd.	1996	13.50	14
1995 Grandma's Are Sew Full Of Love, set/2 104108	Retrd.	1996	13.50	14
1994 Hand Knitted With Love 626023	Retrd.	1998	13.50	27
1995 Nothing Is Sweeter Than Mom 104086	Retrd.	1996	13.50	14
1994 Our Friendship Is A Quilt Of Love 626015	Retrd.	1998	13.50	14
1994 Sew Happy It's Your Birthday 625965	Retrd.	1998	13.50	14
1994 Tea And You Hit The Spot 625981	Retrd.	1998	13.50	14
1994 You Always Top Off My Days 626007	Retrd.	1998	13.50	14
1994 Your Friendship Is My Silver Lining 625973	Retrd.	1998	13.50	14

Calico Kittens - P. Hillman

1995 3 Asst. Kittens w/Candy Hearts 102199	Retrd.	1997	11.00	11
1994 3 Asst. mini cats 623520	Retrd.	1995	11.00	11
1994 6 Asst. Mini 651117	Retrd.	1997	12.00	12
1995 All About Angels 144215	5,000	1996	25.00	25-47

YEAR ISSUE	EDITION LIMIT	YEAR RETD.	ISSUE PRICE	*QUOTE U.S.$
1998 Bet You're Kit N' Kaboodle We're Five 314579	Yr.Iss.	1998	50.00	50
1994 Blossoms Of Friendship 623555	Retrd.	1995	20.00	20
1999 Chatty Catty 546569	7,500		22.50	23
2000 Countryside Kitty (February Show Exclusive) 720852	Closed	2000	17.50	18
2000 Creature Comforts 720755	Yr.Iss.		17.50	18
1993 Dressed In Our Holiday Best 628190	Retrd.	1996	15.50	16
1994 Ewe Warm My Heart 628182	Retrd.	1996	17.50	18
1994 Extra Special 624624	Retrd.	1998	15.00	15
1999 Feel-ine Fine In The City (January Exclusive) 543500	Closed	1999	17.50	18
1999 Feel-ine Fine In The Country (Spring Flng Exclusive) 543519	Closed	1999	17.50	18
1993 Friends Are Cuddles Of Love 627976	Retrd.	1996	20.00	20
1999 Friends Of A Feather Flock Together (Special Exclusive) 505633	Closed	1999	22.50	23
1994 Friendship Cushions The Fall 651087	Retrd.	1999	18.50	19
1994 Friendship Is A Warm, Close Feeling 623598	Retrd.	1995	25.00	25
1994 Friendship Is The Best O'Luck 623601	Retrd.	1999	13.50	14
1993 A Good Friend Warms The Heart 627984	Retrd.	1996	15.00	15
2000 Handle With Care (Mother's Day) 785024	5,000		25.00	25
2002 Have Yourself a Meow-y Little Christmas 104050	Yr.-Iss.		17.50	18
1996 Hey Diddle Diddle The Cat And The Fiddle 166456	7,500	1996	20.00	20
1994 Home Sweet Home 624705	Retrd.	1998	15.00	15
1993 I'm All Fur You 627968	Retrd.	1996	15.00	15
2002 It Takes A Smart Cookie To Find the Milk 104642	Open		25.00	25
2002 It's Hard To Tame A Wild Heart (Show Special) 101320	Open		20.00	20
1996 I've Been A Good Kitty 178446	Yr.Iss.	1996	17.50	18
1994 Joy To The World "Joy" 625264	Retrd.	1997	22.50	23
2000 Just Hangin Around 720879	7,500		40.00	40
1994 Kitten On Quilt (musical) 620742	Retrd.	1997	40.00	40
1994 Kitten With Signage Plaque 699179	Retrd.	1996	15.00	15
1997 Kitty And Me 203963	Retrd.	1998	20.00	20
2000 Kosmopolitan Kitty (January Show Exclusive) 720844	Closed	2000	20.00	20
1994 Love 624721	Retrd.	1998	15.00	15
1995 Love Pours From My Heart 102210	Retrd.	1998	22.50	23
1994 A Loving Gift "Love" 625272	Retrd.	1997	22.50	25
2002 Mother with Kittens (Mother's Day) 101321	5,000		30.00	30
1998 My Favorite Things 360295	Retrd.	1999	45.00	45
1994 My Heart Belongs To You (lg.) 771201	Retrd.	1996	50.00	50
1994 My Heart Belongs To You (sm.) 771236	Retrd.	1996	25.00	25
1993 Our Friendship Blossomed From The Heart 627887	Retrd.	1996	15.00	15
1997 Our Friendship Is A Magical Spell 274852	Retrd.	1999	13.50	14
1994 Peace On Earth "Peace" 625256	Retrd.	1997	22.50	23
1994 Planting The Seeds Of Friendship 623547	Retrd.	1996	20.00	20
1994 A Pocketful O'Luck For You 623628	Retrd.	1999	13.50	14
1994 Purr-fect Friends 624691	Retrd.	1998	15.00	15
2002 Real Girls Deserve All The Frills (Show Special) 100117	Open		20.00	20
1994 Santa Paws 359653	Yr.Iss.	1998	17.50	18
1995 Stitch In Time Saves Nine 129429	3,000	1995	35.00	35
2000 Surround Yourself With Your Favorite Things 676969	Yr.Iss.		40.00	40
1999 There Are No Ordinary Cats - Expect The Unexpected 686573	Yr.Iss.	1999	17.50	18
1994 There's No Friend Like You 625299	Retrd.	1999	18.50	19
1994 Thinking Of You 624713	Retrd.	1998	15.00	15
1998 Three Little Kittens Who Lost Their Mittens 359785	5,000	1998	25.00	25
1993 Waiting For A Friend Like You - 9" 628662	Retrd.	1998	100.00	100
1993 Waiting For A Friend Like You 627895	Retrd.	1996	30.00	30
1993 We're A Purr-fect Pair 627925	Retrd.	1996	25.00	25
1993 Wrapped In The Warmth Of Friendship 628174	Retrd.	1996	17.50	18
1994 You And Me 624748	Retrd.	1998	15.00	15
1999 Your Friendship Takes The Prize Customer Appreciation 477877	Closed	1999	17.50	18

YEAR ISSUE	EDITION LIMIT	YEAR RETD.	ISSUE PRICE	*QUOTE U.S.$
1993 You're A Friend Fur-ever 628018	Retrd.	1996	20.00	28-34
1994 You're A Special Aunt 651117	Retrd.	1997	12.00	12
1994 You're A Special Friend 651117	Retrd.	1997	12.00	12
1994 You're A Special Grandma 651117	Retrd.	1997	12.00	12
1994 You're A Special Mom 651117	Retrd.	1997	12.00	12
1994 You're A Special Niece 651117	Retrd.	1997	12.00	12
1994 You're A Special Sister 651117	Retrd.	1997	12.00	12
1999 You're the Best Gift of All 543470	Yr.Iss.	1999	20.00	20
1996 You've Earned Your Wings 178454	5,000	1996	35.00	35

Carolling Kitties - P. Hillman

YEAR ISSUE	EDITION LIMIT	YEAR RETD.	ISSUE PRICE	*QUOTE U.S.$
1999 Dance Of The Sugar Plum Fairies 542555	Retrd.	2000	15.00	15
1999 Here Comes Santa Claus 542563	Retrd.	2000	15.00	15
1999 Jingle Bells 542539	Retrd.	2000	15.00	15
1999 O Christmas Tree 542571	Retrd.	2000	15.00	15
1999 Up On The Rooftop 542547	Retrd.	2000	15.00	15
1999 We Three Kings 542598	Retrd.	2000	25.00	25

Cat Astrology Collection - P. Hillman

YEAR ISSUE	EDITION LIMIT	YEAR RETD.	ISSUE PRICE	*QUOTE U.S.$
1999 Leo 542423	Open		12.50	13
1999 Aries 542385	Open		12.50	13
1999 Taurus 542393	Open		12.50	13
1999 Gemini 542407	Open		12.50	13
1999 Cancer 542415	Open		12.50	13
1999 Virgo 542431	Open		12.50	13
1999 Libra 542458	Open		12.50	13
1999 Scorpio 542466	Open		12.50	13
1999 Saguittaruis 542474	Open		12.50	13
1999 Capricorn 542482	Open		12.50	13
1999 Aquarius 542490	Open		12.50	13
1999 Pisces 542504	Open		12.50	13

Cats Do The Darnest Things - P. Hillman

YEAR ISSUE	EDITION LIMIT	YEAR RETD.	ISSUE PRICE	*QUOTE U.S.$
2000 Be Fearless 826014	Open		15.00	15
2000 Dare To Dream 826030	Open		15.00	15
2000 Live On The Edge 826022	Open		15.00	15
2000 Nothing Ventured, Nothing Gained 826006	Open		15.00	15
2000 Reach For The Top 826049	Open		15.00	15
2000 Stretch The Limits 825999	Open		15.00	15

The Cat's Out of the Bag - P. Hillman

YEAR ISSUE	EDITION LIMIT	YEAR RETD.	ISSUE PRICE	*QUOTE U.S.$
1997 Friendship Lets The Cat Out Of The Bag 210544	Retrd.	1999	17.50	18
1997 I'm Sending You A Bag Full Of Love 210587	Retrd.	1999	17.50	18
1997 Our Friendship Is Out Of The Bag 210536	Retrd.	1999	17.50	18

Comfy-Kitties - P. Hillman

YEAR ISSUE	EDITION LIMIT	YEAR RETD.	ISSUE PRICE	*QUOTE U.S.$
2001 Let's Snuggle Up 865826	Open		15.00	15
2001 Love Wraps Us In Warmth 865842	Open		15.00	15
2001 Soft, Fluffy, and Feline 865850	Open		15.00	15
2001 You Warm My Heart 865834	Open		15.00	15

Cozy Kitties - P. Hillman

YEAR ISSUE	EDITION LIMIT	YEAR RETD.	ISSUE PRICE	*QUOTE U.S.$
1997 All Wrapped Up In Warmth 274879	Retrd.	1999	16.50	17
1997 Friendship Covers The Holidays 274887	Retrd.	1999	16.50	17
1997 Hats Off To Friendship 274909	Retrd.	1999	16.50	17
1997 A Purr-fect Fit 274917	Retrd.	1999	16.50	17
1997 You Hold The Strings To My Heart 274895	Retrd.	1999	16.50	17

Curious Kittens - P. Hillman

YEAR ISSUE	EDITION LIMIT	YEAR RETD.	ISSUE PRICE	*QUOTE U.S.$
2001 A Bushel of Laughs 866016	Open		15.00	15
2001 A Harvest of Happiness 866008	Open		15.00	15
2001 A Pile of Smiles 866024	Open		15.00	15

Curl Up With Kitty - P. Hillman

YEAR ISSUE	EDITION LIMIT	YEAR RETD.	ISSUE PRICE	*QUOTE U.S.$
2000 Footwarmer (Maine Coon) 825654	Open		12.50	13
2000 Hopes & Dreams (Tiffany) 825662	Open		12.50	13
2000 Lap of Luxury (Siamese) 825646	Open		12.50	13
2000 Our Friendship Is Tightly Woven (Persian) 825670	Open		12.50	13
2000 Pull Up a Chair (Tabby) 825689	Open		12.50	13
2000 You're My Benchmark (Norwegian Forest) 825697	Open		12.50	13

Different Hats for Different Cats - P. Hillman

YEAR ISSUE	EDITION LIMIT	YEAR RETD.	ISSUE PRICE	*QUOTE U.S.$
2000 The Earth Blossoms For You 720674	Open		17.50	18
2000 Our Friendship Is The Real Deal 720666	Open		15.00	15

YEAR ISSUE	EDITION LIMIT	YEAR RETD.	ISSUE PRICE	*QUOTE U.S.$
2000 Thanks For Guiding Us Towards Our Goal 720631	Open		15.00	15
2000 You Motivate The Rest of Us 720682	Open		15.00	15
2000 You Spice Up My Life 720712	Open		17.50	18
2000 Your Touch Heals Body and Soul 720690	Open		17.50	18

Everything I Know I Learned From My Cat - P. Hillman

YEAR ISSUE	EDITION LIMIT	YEAR RETD.	ISSUE PRICE	*QUOTE U.S.$
1999 Always Land On Your Feet 642320	Open		20.00	20
1999 Meow When You're Hungry 642290	Open		15.00	15
1999 Milk and Treats Are Good For You 642304	Open		15.00	15
1999 Nap Anywhere 642347	Open		17.50	18
1999 Play Hard 642312	Open		15.00	15
1999 Rubbing People the Right Way is a Sign of Affection 642339	Open		17.50	18

For You - P. Hillman

YEAR ISSUE	EDITION LIMIT	YEAR RETD.	ISSUE PRICE	*QUOTE U.S.$
1996 For You 178500	Retrd.	1998	12.50	13
1996 I Love Teacher 178519	Retrd.	1998	12.50	13
1996 Mom 178489	Retrd.	1998	12.50	13
1996 To My Grandma 178497	Retrd.	1998	12.50	13

Gallery of Kittens - P. Hillman

YEAR ISSUE	EDITION LIMIT	YEAR RETD.	ISSUE PRICE	*QUOTE U.S.$
1998 Antiqued Gold 489344	Closed	1999	10.00	10
1998 Black Ebony 489263	Closed	1999	10.00	10
1998 Blue White Porcelain 489271	Closed	1999	10.00	10
1998 Frosted Glass 489336	Closed	1999	10.00	10
1998 Gold Trim 489352	Closed	1999	10.00	10
1998 Granite 489298	Closed	1999	10.00	10
1998 Green Jade 48932	Closed	1999	10.00	10
1998 Ivory 489379	Closed	1999	10.00	10
1998 Marble 489360	Closed	1999	10.00	10
1998 Pewter 489417	Closed	1999	10.00	10
1998 Stitched Cat 489182	Closed	1999	10.00	10
1998 Wood Hand Carved 489190	Closed	1999	10.00	10

Green-Eyed Monsters - P. Hillman

YEAR ISSUE	EDITION LIMIT	YEAR RETD.	ISSUE PRICE	*QUOTE U.S.$
1999 Don't Be A Scaredy Cat 543527	Retrd.	1999	17.50	18
1999 Feel-ine Spooky 543535	Retrd.	1999	15.00	15
1999 Trick or Treat - Preferably Catnip! 543543	Retrd.	1999	17.50	18

Halloween - Feed Me Meow! - P. Hillman

YEAR ISSUE	EDITION LIMIT	YEAR RETD.	ISSUE PRICE	*QUOTE U.S.$
2002 Caught With a Paw in the Pumpkin 104148	Open		15.00	15
2002 Having A Ball! 104149	Open		15.00	15
2002 Still Searching For More Sweets 104147	Open		15.00	15
2002 The Sweet Taste of Victory 104146	Open		15.00	15

Holiday Harmony - P. Hillman

YEAR ISSUE	EDITION LIMIT	YEAR RETD.	ISSUE PRICE	*QUOTE U.S.$
1995 The First Noel 144606	Yr.Iss.	1995	17.50	18
1995 I'll Be Home For Christmas 144614	Retrd.	1998	17.50	18
1995 Jolly Old St. Nicholas 144630	Retrd.	1998	17.50	18
1995 Oh, Tannenbaum 144428	Retrd.	1998	17.50	18
1995 Silent Night 144622	Retrd.	1998	17.50	18

Itty Bitty Christmas Kitties - P. Hillman

YEAR ISSUE	EDITION LIMIT	YEAR RETD.	ISSUE PRICE	*QUOTE U.S.$
1996 Mini Figurines, set/3 178462	Closed	1999	7.00	7

Itty Bitty Garden Kitties - P. Hillman

YEAR ISSUE	EDITION LIMIT	YEAR RETD.	ISSUE PRICE	*QUOTE U.S.$
1997 Mini Figurines, set/3 204048	Closed	1999	7.00	7

Itty Bitty Kitties - P. Hillman

YEAR ISSUE	EDITION LIMIT	YEAR RETD.	ISSUE PRICE	*QUOTE U.S.$
1996 Congratulations 167312	Retrd.	1998	7.50	8
1996 Get Well 167339	Retrd.	1998	7.50	8
1996 Graduation 167347	Retrd.	1998	7.50	8
1996 Happy Birthday 167320	Retrd.	1998	7.50	8
1996 I Love You 167304	Retrd.	1998	7.50	8
1996 Mini Figurines, set/3 155527	Retrd.	1998	7.00	7
1996 Mini Figurines, set/3 155578	Retrd.	1999	7.00	7
1996 New Baby 167355	Retrd.	1998	7.50	8

Itty Bitty Kitties-Cat's Got Your Tongue - P. Hillman

YEAR ISSUE	EDITION LIMIT	YEAR RETD.	ISSUE PRICE	*QUOTE U.S.$
1997 Alley Cat 255122	Retrd.	1998	7.50	8
1997 Cat Baskets, set/3 254924	Retrd.	1999	6.00	6
1997 Cat Tails 255106	Retrd.	1998	7.50	8
1997 Cool Cat 255084	Retrd.	1998	7.50	8
1997 Fat Cat 255076	Retrd.	1998	7.50	8
1997 House Cat 255114	Retrd.	1998	7.50	8
1997 Top Cat 255092	Retrd.	1998	7.50	8

FIGURINES

YEAR ISSUE	EDITION LIMIT	YEAR RETD.	ISSUE PRICE	*QUOTE U.S.$
Itty Bitty...Purr-fect Pairs - P. Hillman				
1997 Best Friends 203629	Retrd.	1999	14.00	14
1997 Mom And Me 204994	Retrd.	1999	14.00	14
1997 True Love 205001	Retrd.	1999	14.00	14
Kitchen Cuddles - P. Hillman				
1999 Calico Kitten in Pitcher 465658	Open		7.50	8
1999 Calico Kitten in Sugar Bowl 465623	Open		7.50	8
1999 Calico Kitten in Teacup 465666	Open		7.50	8
1999 Calico Kitten in Teapot 465615	Open		7.50	8
Kitties Holiday Highlights - P. Hillman				
2001 Christmas-Tree Climbing 865761	Open		20.00	20
2001 Kitty-Wrapping 865737	Open		17.50	18
2001 Poinsettia-Pruning 865788	Open		17.50	18
2001 Ring-Around-The-Kitty 865753	Open		17.50	18
2001 Stuffing-The Stockings 865896	Open		20.00	20
Kitty Capers - P. Hillman				
1996 Hats Off To The Holidays 178381	Retrd.	1999	12.50	13
1996 I'm All Yours 178373	Retrd.	1999	12.50	13
1996 Not Purr-fect, Just Purr-fectly Happy 178403	Retrd.	1999	12.50	13
1996 Wrapped Up In You 178411	Retrd.	1999	15.00	15
1996 You Brighten My Holidays 178365	Retrd.	1999	15.00	15
Life Through A Cat's Eyes - P. Hillman				
1999 A Cat Changes Coming Home To Any Empty House To Coming Home 686565	Open		17.50	18
1999 A Cat Must Be Loved On Its Own Terms 686557	Open		17.50	18
1999 Cats Believe The Best Things In Life Are Free 686603	Open		17.50	18
1999 Cats Like Doors Left Open In Case They Change Their Minds 686581	Open		17.50	18
1999 This House Under Feline Management 686611	Open		17.50	18
A Little Bird Told Me... - P. Hillman				
1997 A Little Bird Told Me You're Tweet 203998	Retrd.	1999	20.00	20
Look What The Cat Dragged In - P. Hillman				
1998 Friends Are a Feast Worth Sharing 360066	Open		15.00	15
1998 It's The Thought That Counts 360074	Retrd.	2000	15.00	15
1999 A Labor of Love 295582	Retrd.	1999	15.00	15
1998 One Look From You Melts My Heart 360120	Retrd.	2000	15.00	15
1998 Sock Full of Love 360090	Retrd.	2000	15.00	15
1999 Some Bunny To Love You 295590	Retrd.	1999	15.00	15
1999 A Splash of Happiness 295566	Retrd.	1999	15.00	15
1999 A Sprinkle of Joy 295574	Retrd.	1999	15.00	15
Mommy's Little Helper - P. Hillman				
1999 Calico w/Kitten 642274	Open		9.00	9
1999 Himalayan w/Kitten 642266	Open		9.00	9
1999 Persian w/Kitten 642258	Open		9.00	9
1999 Shorthair Tabby w/Kitten 642231	Open		9.00	9
1999 Siamese w/Kitten 642223	Open		9.00	9
1999 Tiffany w/Kitten 642215	Open		9.00	9
My Heart Belongs To Kitty - P. Hillman				
1996 Hope All Your Dreams Come True 129356	Retrd.	1998	20.00	20
1996 My Funny Valentine 155454	Retrd.	1998	17.50	18
Nativity - P. Hillman				
1993 Creche 628441	Retrd.	1997	50.00	50
1994 Friends Come From Afar 625248	Retrd.	1997	17.50	18
1993 I'll Bring A Special Gift For You, Friendship Is The Best Gift Of All, Sharing The Gift Of Friendship, set/3 628476	Retrd.	1997	55.00	55
1993 A Purr-fect Angel From Above 628468	Retrd.	1997	15.00	15
1993 Sharing A Special Gift Of Love, Always Watching Over You, set/2 628484	Retrd.	1997	35.00	35
Nine Lives - P. Hillman				
2000 Discover Your World 682993	Open		10.00	10
2000 Fit For Life 683256	Open		9.00	9
2000 The Joy of Your Life 683205	Open		10.00	10
2000 Let Your Beauty Shine 683159	Open		9.00	9
2000 Reach For Your Goals 683167	Open		10.00	1
2000 Recharge Your Batteries 68O3272	Open		10.00	1
2000 Searching For Fulfillment 683213	Open		10.00	1
2000 Soulmates 682993	Open		10.00	1
2000 Treat Yourself 683183	Open		9.00	9
Picks of the Litter - P. Hillman				
1996 Hello, Little One 129410	Retrd.	1999	17.50	1
1996 A Little Litter Of Blessings 168602	Retrd.	1999	15.00	1
1996 New Kit On The Block 903140	Retrd.	1999	12.50	1
1996 Our Friendship Is Squeaky Clean 132713	Retrd.	1999	15.00	1
1996 Tummy Full Of Love For You 132721	Retrd.	1999	12.50	1
1996 Wagon Our Tails For You 172693	Retrd.	1999	17.50	1
Purr-fect Personalities - P. Hillman				
1995 Always Thinking Of You "Solitude" 112437	Retrd.	1998	14.50	
1995 Fishing For A Friend "Mischievous" 112453	Retrd.	1998	14.50	
1995 Good As New "Cleanliness" 113301	Retrd.	1998	14.50	1
1995 I'm Lost Without You "Observant" 112488	Retrd.	1998	14.50	1
1995 My Favorite Companion "Companionship" 112410	Retrd.	1998	14.50	
1995 A Playful Afternoon "Playful" 112429	Retrd.	1998	14.50	1
1995 A Purr-fect Pair "Curiosity" 112445	Retrd.	1998	14.50	1
1995 Sweet Dreams "Catnap" 112461	Retrd.	1998	14.50	1
1995 An Unexpected Treat "Finicky" 112321	Retrd.	1998	14.50	1
Scaredy Cats - P. Hillman				
1997 Carving A Season Of Smiles 274828	Retrd.	1999	13.50	1
1997 Mummy Mischief 274836	Retrd.	1999	13.50	1
1997 Pussy Cat And The Queen 255157	5,000	1998	25.00	2
1997 You Can Always Spot A Friend 274844	Retrd.	1999	13.50	1
Seasonal Scenes - P. Hillman				
2000 Wintery Retreat 785075	Open		30.00	3
2000 Spring Splendors 785040	Open		30.00	3
2001 Summer Breezes 785059	Open		30.00	3
2001 Autumn Harvest 785067	Open		30.00	3
Sophisticats - P. Hillman				
2002 Enjoy Life's Delicate Pleasures 100068	Open		15.00	1
2002 Finally, A Gift Worthy of Me! 100066	Open		15.00	1
2002 It's Not Easy Being The Center of Attention 100063	Open		15.00	1
2002 Life's Little Rewards Are Priceless 100065	Open		15.00	1
2002 The Way To My Heart Is Clear 100067	Open		15.00	1
Sportin' An Attitude - P. Hillman				
1999 Friends Are A Goal Worth Saving 454648	Retrd.	2000	15.00	1
1999 Laughter Drives A Winning Friendship 454664	Retrd.	2000	15.00	1
1999 We're A Perfect Match 454656	Retrd.	2000	15.00	1
1999 You're an All-Star Friend 454621	Retrd.	2000	15.00	1
Springtime Friends - P. Hillman				
1995 3 Asst. Kittens w/eggs 102687	Retrd.	1998	11.00	1
1993 A Bundle Of Love 628433	Retrd.	1997	13.50	14-1
1995 Friendship Is The Best Blessing 102679	Retrd.	1997	20.00	2
1995 Furry And Feathered Friends 102636	Retrd.	1997	20.00	2
1995 Hats Off To A Perfect Friendship 129437	Retrd.	1997	20.00	2
1993 Just Thinking About You (musical) 620742	Retrd.	1997	40.00	4
1993 Just Thinking About You 627917	Retrd.	1997	20.00	2
1995 Love Blooms Fur-Ever 102644	Retrd.	1997	17.50	1
1993 Loves Special Delivery 628425	Retrd.	1997	13.50	1
1994 A Puff-fect Love "True Love" (musical) 622702	Retrd.	1996	60.00	6
1994 A Purr-fect Love Knot 626031	Retrd.	1997	50.00	5
1995 You Make Life Colorful 102601	Retrd.	1995	25.00	2
1993 You'll Always Be Close To My Heart 627909	Retrd.	1997	20.00	2
1995 Your Patchwork Charm Shows Through 129453	Retrd.	1997	17.50	1
1993 You're Always There When I Need You 627992	Retrd.	1997	25.00	2

*Quotes have been rounded up to nearest dollar

YEAR ISSUE	EDITION LIMIT	YEAR RETD.	ISSUE PRICE	*QUOTE U.S.$
Welcome to Whisker Way - P. Hillman				
1995 Blue Without You (Russian Blue) 129615	Retrd.	1998	17.50	18
1995 Friendship Has Many Riches (Persian) 129755	Retrd.	1998	17.50	18
1995 Great Scot, We're The Best Of Friends (Scottish Fold) 129593	Retrd.	1998	17.50	18
1996 I'd Never Desert You (Abyssinian) 903116	Retrd.	1998	17.50	18
1995 It's No Mystery We're Friends (British Shorthair) 129585	Retrd.	1998	17.50	18
1996 Tried And True For The Red, White And Blue (American Shorthair) 903086	Retrd.	1998	17.50	18
1995 We're Insep-purr-able Friends (Siamese) 129577	Retrd.	1998	17.50	18
1995 You're My All American Friend (Tabby) 129607	Retrd.	1998	17.50	18
You're The Cat's Meow - P. Hillman				
1997 A Dash Of Love Makes You Sweeter 276863	Yr.lss.		17.50	18
1998 Friendship Is Heavenly 274968	5,000	1998	20.00	20
1997 White kitten 275891	Yr.lss.	1997	10.00	10
Cast Art Industries				
Dreamsicles Club - K. Haynes				
1993 A Star is Born-CD001	Retrd.	1993	Gift	107-115
1994 Daydream Believer-CD100	Retrd.	1994	29.95	75-85
1994 Join The Fun-CD002	Retrd.	1994	Gift	40-50
1994 Makin' A List-CD101	Retrd.	1994	47.95	65-75
1995 Three Cheers-CD003	Retrd.	1995	Gift	45-60
1995 Town Crier-CD102	Retrd.	1995	24.95	25-45
1995 Snowbound-CD103	Retrd.	1996	24.95	35
1995 Star Shower-CD004	Retrd.	1996	Gift	15-39
1996 Heavenly Flowers-CD104	Retrd.	1997	24.95	25
1996 Bee-Friended-CD105	Retrd.	1999	24.95	25-45
1997 Free Spirit-CD005	Retrd.	1997	Gift	30
1997 Peaceable Kingdom-CD106	Retrd.	1999	14.75	15
1997 First Blush-CD109	12,000	1998	49.95	50
1997 Sweet Tooth (w/cookbook)-CD110	Retrd.	1998	19.95	20
1997 Editor's Choice (Newsletter Participation)-CD107	N/A		Gift	N/A
1997 Golden Halo ("Good Samaritan" award)-CD108	N/A		Gift	N/A
1998 Let's Get Together-CD006	Retrd.	1998	Gift	N/A
1998 Summertime Serenade-CD111	Retrd.	N/A	14.75	15
1998 Above and Beyond (5th Anniversary Piece)-CD112	Retrd.	1999	29.95	30
1999 Share The Magic-CD007	Retrd.	1999	Gift	N/A
1999 Golden Memories-CD113	Retrd.	N/A	20.00	20
1999 Snowflake Angel Hug™ (cherub)-08008	Retrd.	1999	Gift	N/A
1999 Ship of Dreams-CD117	Suspd.		39.95	40
1999 Tic Tac Toe -CD116	Suspd.		29.95	30
2000 Get On Board-CD008	Retrd.	2000	Gift	N/A
2000 Hugged By An Angel-08055	Retrd.	2000	Gift	N/A
2000 Threads of Love-CD128	Retrd.	2000	19.95	20
2001 Dreamsicles Rule CD009	Retrd.	2001	Gift	N/A
2001 Angel Hugs 3 Key Chain	Retrd.	2001	Gift	N/A
2001 Crystal Carousel-CD130	Retrd.	2001	39.95	40
2001 Our Clubhouse-CD131	Retrd.	2001	N/A	N/A
2001 Dreamsicles Lane-CD133	Open		29.95	30
2001 Everything's Just Ducky-CD132	Open		24.95	25
2002 Collecting Memories-CD010	Open			N/A
Dreamsicles - K. Haynes				
2001 10 Years of Smiles 11592 (10th Anniversary Promotional Piece)	Open		3.00	3
2002 Angel in Training-12061	5,000		58.00	58
1997 Anticipation - ICE Commemorative Figurine-SP002	Retrd.	1997	29.95	30
1992 Baby Love-DC147	Retrd.	1995	7.00	10
1995 Best Buddies-DC159	Retrd.	1998	14.00	35
1991 Best Pals-DC103	Retrd.	1994	15.00	40
1992 Bluebird On My Shoulder-DC115	Retrd.	1995	19.00	30-40
1994 Born This Day-DC230	Retrd.	1998	16.00	16
1996 Brotherhood-DC307	Retrd.	1998	20.00	20
1996 Bubble Bath-DC416	Retrd.	1998	22.00	22-35
1992 Bundle of Joy-DC142	Retrd.	1995	7.00	145-295
1993 By the Silvery Moon-DC253	10,000	1994	100.00	150-175

YEAR ISSUE	EDITION LIMIT	YEAR RETD.	ISSUE PRICE	*QUOTE U.S.$
1992 Caroler - Center Scroll-DC216	Retrd.	1995	19.00	28
1992 Caroler - Left Scroll-DC218	Retrd.	1995	19.00	25-28
1992 Caroler - Right Scroll-DC217	Retrd.	1995	19.00	25-28
1996 Carousel Ride-DS283	Retrd.	1998	150.00	150
1994 Carousel-DC174	Suspd.		35.00	35-60
2000 Castle in the Sky-11400	10,000		58.00	58
1993 Catch a Falling Star-DC166	Retrd.	1997	12.00	12-22
1991 Cherub and Child-DC100	Retrd.	1995	15.00	100
1994 Cherub Bowl-Stars-DC161	Suspd.		9.50	50
1992 Cherub For All Seasons-DC114	Retrd.	1995	23.00	45-75
1992 Cherub-DC111	10,000	1992	50.00	105-115
1992 Cherub-DC112	10,000	1993	50.00	200-225
1996 A Child Is Born-DC256	10,000	1996	95.00	95-120
1992 A Child's Prayer-DC145	Retrd.	1995	7.00	7
2000 A Collector's Delight - ICE Commemorative Figurine-SP002	Retrd.	2000	25.00	25
1996 Corona Centennial	Retrd.	1996	Gift	N/A
1996 Crossing Guardian-DC422	Retrd.	1998	40.00	40
1994 Cuddle Blanket-DC153	Retrd.	1995	6.50	7
1996 Cuddle Up DC283	Retrd.	2001	8.00	8
1997 Cutie Pie-10241	12,500	1998	42.00	42
1996 Daffodil Days DC343 (American Cancer Society Figurine)	Retrd.	1998	15.00	30-35
1992 Dance Ballerina Dance-DC140	Retrd.	1995	37.00	42
1998 Daydreamin'-10332	Retrd.	1999	30.00	30
1991 Dimples DA-100	Retrd.		5.50	6
1992 Dream A Little Dream-DC144	Retrd.	1995	7.00	10
1997 Dream Weaver-10159	Retrd.	1999	10.00	10
1997 Dreamboat-10060 (Sp. Ed.)	Retrd.	1998	90.00	90
1997 Dreamin' Of You-10030	Retrd.	1999	10.00	10
1998 Dreamsicles Ark-10564, set/7	Open		100.00	100
1993 Dreamsicles Logo (blue)-DC001	Retrd.	N/A	30.00	30
1993 Dreamsicles Logo (pink)-DC001	Retrd.	N/A	30.00	30
1994 Eager to Please-DC154	Retrd.	1995	6.50	10
1999 Easter Eggspress 10790	Retrd.	2001	38.00	38
1992 Flying Lesson-DC251	10,000	1993	80.00	500-875
1997 Follow Me-10050	Retrd.	1998	28.00	28
1991 Forever Friends-DC102	Retrd.	1994	14.00	35-40
1991 Forever Yours-DC110	Retrd.	1995	44.00	75
1996 Free Kittens-DK038	Retrd.	1998	18.00	18
1996 Free Puppies-DK039	Retrd.	1998	18.00	18
1994 Friendship Cherubs-DC-175	Retrd.	1999	20.00	20
1995 Get Well Soon-DC244	Retrd.	1997	11.00	11-18
2002 God Bless America-12080	5,000		78.00	78
1997 Goodness Me-10160	Retrd.	1999	10.00	10
1998 Handmade With Love-10324	10,000	1998	78.00	78
1997 Happy Landings-10156	5,000	1997	88.00	88
1997 Hear No Evil-10040	Suspd.		18.00	18
1991 Heavenly Dreamer-DC106	Retrd.	1996	11.50	12
1996 Heaven's Gate-DC257 (5th Anniversary piece)	15,000	1996	129.00	129
1999 Help Is Close By 10975	Retrd.	2001	19.50	20
1994 Here's Looking at You-DC172	Retrd.	1995	25.00	24-35
1997 Here's My Hand-10248	Retrd.	1999	20.00	20
N/A Hold Tight (Cracker Barrel Exclusive)-DC123	Retrd.	N/A	N/A	N/A
1991 Honey Bun DA-101	Retrd.	1995	5.50	6
1995 Hugabye Baby-DC701	Retrd.	1997	12.50	13-18
1994 I Can Read-DC151	Retrd.	1995	6.50	10
1992 Ice Dancing-10256	Retrd.	1999	17.00	17
1994 International Collectible Exposition Commemorative Figurine	Retrd.	1995	34.95	116-150
1997 It's Your Day-10220	Retrd.	1998	30.00	30
2001 Just Dreamin'-E0201	5,000		17.50	18
1993 Lg. Candle Holder Boy-DC138	Retrd.	1994	20.00	22
1993 Lg. Candle Holder Girl-DC139	Retrd.	1994	20.00	22
1992 Life Is Good-DC119	Retrd.	1996	10.00	15
1992 Little Darlin'-DC146	Retrd.	1995	7.00	10
1993 Little Dickens-DC127	Retrd.	1995	24.00	25
1992 Littlest Angel-DC143	Retrd.	1995	7.00	10
2000 Live, Love, Laugh-11061	10,000		55.00	55
1993 Long Fellow-DC126	Retrd.	1995	24.00	30-35
2001 Long May It Wave-12073	Open		16.00	16
1995 Lots of Love-DC403	Retrd.	1999	16.00	16
1995 Love Me Do-DC194	Retrd.	1998	15.00	15
1993 Love My Kitty-DC130	Retrd.	1997	14.50	15-18
1993 Love My Puppy-DC131	Retrd.	1997	12.50	13-18
1993 Love My Teddy-DC132	Retrd.	1997	14.50	18-20
1998 Love You Sew-10263	Retrd.	1999	15.00	15
1998 Lullaby and Goodnight-10613 (musical)	Suspd.		45.00	45

YEAR ISSUE	EDITION LIMIT	YEAR RETD.	ISSUE PRICE	*QUOTE U.S.$
1997 Lyrical Lute-10169	Retrd.	1998	29.00	29
2000 A Magical Beginning-11138	10,000		44.00	44
2001 Magical Masterpiece 11925	2,500		198.00	198
2000 Magical Merry Go Round-11481	7,500		150.00	150
1993 Me And My Shadow-DC116	Retrd.	1996	19.00	19-22
1997 Mellow Cello-10170	Retrd.	1998	39.00	39
1991 Mischief Maker-DC105	Retrd.	1996	10.00	10-25
1993 Miss Morningstar-DC141	Retrd.	1996	25.00	35-40
1997 Mom's The Best DC428	Retrd.	2001	10.00	10
1994 Moon Dance-DC210	Retrd.	1997	29.00	29-38
1994 Moon Dance-DC210	Retrd.	1997	29.00	29-38
1991 Musician w/Cymbals-5154	Suspd.		22.00	22
1991 Musician w/Drums-5152	Suspd.		22.00	22
1991 Musician w/Flute-5153	Suspd.		22.00	22-75
1991 Musician w/Trumpet-5151	Suspd.		22.00	22
1992 My Funny Valentine-DC201	Suspd.		17.00	28
1995 Nursery Rhyme-DC229	Suspd.		42.00	50-70
1995 One World-DC306	Retrd.	1998	24.00	24
1993 P.S. I Love You-DC203	Retrd.	1997	7.50	8-18
1999 Passage of Time-10671 (millennium ed.)	Retrd.	1999	40.00	40
1998 Peaceful Dreams-10331	Retrd.	1998	17.00	17
1995 Picture Perfect-DC255	10,000	1995	100.00	89-125
1998 Please Be Mine-10259	Retrd.	1999	14.00	14
1995 Poetry In Motion-DC113 (Sp. Ed.)	Retrd.	1997	80.00	90-115
1996 Pull Toy-DK027	Retrd.	1998	18.00	18
1995 Range Rider-DC305	Retrd.	1998	15.00	15
1994 The Recital-DC254	10,000	1994	135.00	119-240
1998 Relay For Life-10650	Open		21.50	22
1994 See No Evil-10041	Suspd.		18.00	18
1994 Side By Side-DC169	Retrd.	1995	31.50	40-45
1994 The Silvery Moon-DC253	Retrd.	N/A	N/A	N/A
1991 Sitting Pretty-DC101	Retrd.	1996	9.50	12
1996 Sleepover-DC421	Retrd.	1999	18.00	18
2000 Smooth Sailing-11590 (10th Anniversary piece)	10,000		90.00	90
1994 Snowflake-DC117	Suspd.		10.00	14
1996 Snuggle Buddies (GCC Exclusive)-DC017	Retrd.	N/A	N/A	N/A
1997 Speak No Evil-10042	Suspd.		18.00	18
1997 Special Occasions-10167	Retrd.	1999	48.00	48
1997 Special Occasions-10167	Retrd.	1999	45.00	45
1999 Stairway to Heaven-10672	10,000	1999	78.00	78-82
1997 String Serenade-10168	Retrd.	1998	30.00	30
1994 Sucking My Thumb-DC156	Retrd.	1995	6.50	7-10
1996 Sugar 'N Spice-DC327	Retrd.	1999	10.00	10
1994 Sugarfoot-DC167	Retrd.	1998	25.00	25
1994 Surprise Gift-DC152	Retrd.	1998	6.50	10
1993 Sweet Dreams-DC125	Retrd.	1995	29.00	35-45
1996 Swimming For Hope-DC016	Retrd.	1996	75.00	75-100
1997 Taking Aim-DC432	Retrd.	1998	33.00	33
1996 Tea Party-DC015 (GCC event)	Retrd.	1996	19.00	20-40
1993 Teacher's Pet-DC124	Retrd.	1997	11.00	11
2002 Team Spirit-12273	Open		25.00	25
1993 Teeter Tots-DC252	10,000	1993	100.00	90-178
1993 Thinking of You-DC129	Retrd.	1997	42.00	44-55
1993 Tiny Dancer-DC165	Retrd.	1998	14.00	14
1995 Twinkle, Twinkle-DC700	Retrd.	1997	14.50	15
1994 Up All Night-DC155	Retrd.	1995	6.50	10
1998 We Are Winning-10380 (American Cancer Society)	Suspd.		17.00	17
1991 Wild Flower-DC107	Retrd.	1996	10.00	10
1997 Wish You Were Here-10075	Retrd.	1999	14.00	14
1993 Wishin'' On A Star-DC120	Retrd.	1998	10.00	10
1996 Wishing 'N Hoping-DC328	Retrd.	1999	10.00	10
1996 Wishing Well-DC423	Retrd.	1998	35.00	35
1995 Wistful Thinking-DC707	Retrd.	1998	7.00	7-20

Dreamsicles Animals - K. Haynes

YEAR ISSUE	EDITION LIMIT	YEAR RETD.	ISSUE PRICE	*QUOTE U.S.$
1991 Armadillo -5176	Suspd.		13.50	14-25
1992 Beach Baby-DA615	Retrd.	1994	24.00	35
1991 Boo Who?- DA650	Retrd.	1996	10.50	14
1991 Buddy Bear-DA451	Retrd.	1994	6.00	17
1991 Bunny Hop-DA105	Retrd.	1994	6.00	17
1991 Carnation-DA379	Retrd.	1996	16.00	16-30
1993 Country Bear-DA458	Suspd.		14.00	14-29
1991 Dairy Delight-DA381	Retrd.	1995	27.50	30
1992 Dino-DA480	Retrd.	1995	13.00	14
1992 Dodo-DA482	Retrd.	1994	7.50	9
1992 Fat Cat-DA555	Retrd.	1994	27.00	27
1991 Gathering Flowers-DA320	Retrd.	1995	17.50	18

YEAR ISSUE	EDITION LIMIT	YEAR RETD.	ISSUE PRICE	*QUOTE U.S.$
1991 Hambone-DA344	Retrd.	1996	10.75	20-24
1991 Hamlet-DA342	Retrd.	1996	10.75	20-25
1991 Happy Sailing- DA220	Retrd.	1994	15.00	15
1992 Helga-DA112	Retrd.	1995	7.70	8
1994 Henrietta-DA383	Retrd.	1996	27.50	27
1991 Hey Diddle Diddle-DA380	Retrd.	1996	16.00	16-36
1991 Hippity Hop- DA106	Retrd.	1994	31.00	3
1994 Hound Dog-DA568	Retrd.	1994	9.50	1
1991 King Rabbit-DA124	Retrd.	1994	73.00	73-118
1991 Lambie Pie-DA328	Retrd.	1994	7.00	
1992 Mama Bear-DA452	Retrd.	1994	7.00	18-24
1992 Man's Best Friend-DA560	Retrd.	1994	9.50	1
1991 Mr. Bunny-DA107	Retrd.	1994	28.00	28
1991 Mrs. Bunny- DA108	Retrd.	1994	25.00	2
1991 Mutton Chops-DA326	Retrd.	1994	5.50	8
1996 Naptime-DA556	Suspd.		18.00	18
1992 Needlenose-DA610	Suspd.		8.00	8-24
1994 P.J. Mouse-DA476	Retrd.	1994	10.00	10-24
1993 Pal Joey-DA104	Retrd.	1995	13.00	1
1992 Papa Pelican-DA602	Retrd.	1994	22.50	3
1992 Pelican Jr.-DA601	Suspd.		9.00	9-3
1993 Pierre The Bear-DA453	Suspd.		14.00	14-31
1991 Piglet-DA343	Retrd.	1996	10.00	1
1991 Pigmalion-DA340	Retrd.	1995	6.25	20-3
1991 Pigtails-DA341	Retrd.	1995	6.25	1
1992 Pumpkin Harvest-DA322	Retrd.	1994	17.50	1
1992 Puppy Love-DA562	Retrd.	1994	10.00	1
1992 Red Rover-DA566	Retrd.	1994	15.00	1
1992 Rhino-DA481	Retrd.	1994	13.00	1
1991 Ricky Raccoon -5170	Suspd.		28.00	24
1992 Sarge-DA111	Retrd.	1995	8.00	1
1992 Scooter-DA567	Retrd.	1994	9.50	1
1992 Sir Hareold-DA123	Retrd.	1996	41.50	50-64
1991 Soap Box Bunny-DA551	Retrd.	1995	15.00	3
1991 Socrates The Sheep -5029	Suspd.		19.00	1
1993 Splash-DA616	Retrd.	1994	24.00	3
1992 St. Peter Rabbit-DA243	Retrd.	1994	27.00	2
1991 Sweet Cream-DA382	Retrd.	1996	29.00	29-3
1991 Tiny Bunny-DA102	Retrd.	1995	7.00	1
1991 Trick or Treat-DA651	Retrd.	1996	10.50	1
1991 Wooley Bully-DA327	Retrd.	1994	7.75	

Dreamsicles Calendar Collection - K. Haynes

YEAR ISSUE	EDITION LIMIT	YEAR RETD.	ISSUE PRICE	*QUOTE U.S.$
1994 Winter Wonderland (January)-DC180	Retrd.	1995	24.00	30-5
1994 Special Delivery (February)-DC181	Retrd.	1995	24.00	30-5
1994 Ride Like The Wind (March)-DC182	Retrd.	1995	24.00	30-5
1994 Springtime Frolic (April)-DC183	Retrd.	1995	24.00	3
1994 Love In Bloom (May)-DC184	Retrd.	1995	24.00	30-5
1994 Among Friends (June)-DC185	Retrd.	1995	24.00	45-5
1994 Pool Pals (July)-DC186	Retrd.	1995	24.00	30-4
1994 Nature's Bounty August)-DC187	Retrd.	1995	24.00	30-5
1994 School Days (September)-DC188	Retrd.	1995	24.00	30-5
1994 Autumn Leaves (October)-DC189	Retrd.	1995	24.00	30-5
1994 Now Give Thanks (November)-DC190	Retrd.	1995	24.00	3
1994 Holiday Magic (December)-DC191	Retrd.	1995	24.00	30-5

Dreamsicles Christmas - K. Haynes

YEAR ISSUE	EDITION LIMIT	YEAR RETD.	ISSUE PRICE	*QUOTE U.S.$
1998 All Aboard!-10364 (7th Ed.)	Retrd.	1998	78.00	74
1992 Baby Love-DX147	Retrd.	1995	7.00	3
1991 Best Pals-DX103	Retrd.	1995	7.00	3
1992 Bluebird On My Shoulder-DX115	Retrd.	1995	19.00	19-2
1992 Bundle of Joy-DX142	Retrd.	1995	7.00	
1992 Caroler - Center Scroll-DX216	Retrd.	1995	19.00	30-4
1992 Caroler - Left Scroll-DX218	Retrd.	1995	19.00	3
1992 Caroler - Right Scroll-DX217	Retrd.	1995	19.00	30-4
1991 Cherub and Child-DX100	Retrd.	1995	14.00	30-7
1992 A Child's Prayer-DX145	Retrd.	1995	7.00	3
1999 A Christmas Carol-10844	5,000	1999	40.00	4
1998 Christmas Eve-10429	5,000	1998	78.00	7
1999 Dash Away!-10791 (8th Ed.)	Yr.Iss	1999	78.00	7
1992 Dream A Little Dream-DX144	Retrd.	1995	7.00	
1993 Father Christmas-DX246	Suspd.		42.00	4
1993 The Finishing Touches-DX248 (2nd Ed.)	Retrd.	1994	85.00	125-17
1991 Forever Friends-DX102	Retrd.	1995	7.00	3
1991 Forever Yours-DX110	Retrd.	1995	44.00	44-5
1991 Gathering Flowers-DX320	Retrd.	1995	7.00	3
1991 Heavenly Dreamer-DX196	Retrd.	1996	11.00	1
1994 Here's Looking at You-DX172	Retrd.	1995	25.00	35-3
1994 Holiday on Ice-DX249 (3rd Ed.)	Retrd.	1995	85.00	80-17

Collectors' Information Bureau   *Quotes have been rounded up to nearest dollar

YEAR ISSUE	EDITION LIMIT	YEAR RETD.	ISSUE PRICE	*QUOTE U.S.$
1996 Homeward Bound-DX251 (5th Ed.)	Retrd.	1997	80.00	80-100
1995 Hugabye Baby-DX701	Retrd.	1997	12.50	13
1992 Life Is Good-DX119	Retrd.	1996	10.50	12
1992 Little Darlin'-DX146	Retrd.	1995	7.00	10
1993 Little Dickens-DX127	Retrd.	1995	24.00	25-35
1992 Littlest Angel-DX143	Retrd.	1995	7.00	7
1993 Long Fellow-DX126	Retrd.	1995	24.00	25
1996 Mall Santa-DX258	Retrd.	1998	35.00	35
1993 Me And My Shadow-DX116	Retrd.	1996	19.50	20-35
1991 Mischief Maker-DX105	Retrd.	1996	10.50	11-14
1993 Miss Morningstar-DX141	Retrd.	1996	25.50	40-50
1995 Poetry In Motion-DX113 (Sp. Ed.)	Retrd.	1996	80.00	85-105
1991 Santa Bunny-DX203	Retrd.	1994	32.00	32
1992 Santa In Dreamsicle Land-DX247 (1st Ed.)	Retrd.	1993	85.00	300-340
1991 Santa's Elf-DX240	Retrd.	1996	19.00	22
1995 Santa's Kingdom-DX250 (4th Ed.)	Retrd.	1995	80.00	90-100
1991 Santa's Little Helper-DX109	Retrd.	1998	9.50	10
1994 Share The Fun-DX178	Suspd.		14.00	14-25
1994 Side By Side-DX169	Retrd.	1995	31.50	45-50
1991 Sitting Pretty-DX101	Retrd.	1996	10.00	10-15
1997 Sleigh Bells Ring-10187	2,500	1997	48.00	48-95
1994 Stolen Kiss-DX162	Suspd.		12.50	14
1993 Sweet Dreams-DX125	Retrd.	1995	29.00	29
1997 Time To Dash-10184 (6th Ed.)	Retrd.	1998	78.00	78
1998 Tis Better to Give-10421	5,000	1998	38.00	38
1995 Twinkle Twinkle-DX700	Retrd.	1997	14.50	15
1991 Wildflower-DX107	Retrd.	1996	10.50	15
2001 Winter's Flight-11816 (10th Ed.)	Yr.lss.	2001	N/A	N/A

Dreamsicles Day Event - K. Haynes

1995 1995 Dreamsicles Event Figurine-DC075	Retrd.	1995	20.00	39-70
1996 Glad Tidings-DD100	Retrd.	1996	15.95	27-35
1996 Time to Retire-DD103	Retrd.	1996	15.95	30
1997 The Golden Rule-E9701	Retrd.	1997	19.95	30-45
1998 A Day of Fun-E9801	Retrd.	1998	18.00	18
1999 Yours Truly-E9901	Retrd.	1999	20.00	20
2000 With All My Heart-E0001	7,500		18.95	19
2001 10 Treasured Years-E0003	5,000		20.00	20
2001 Aim For The Stars-E0013	5,000		24.95	25

Dreamsicles Golden Halo - K. Haynes

1999 The Flying Lesson Golden Halo Edition-10935	Suspd.		78.00	78
1998 Golden Best Pals-10659	Suspd.		16.00	16
1998 Golden Cherub & Child-10656	Suspd.		15.00	15
1998 Golden Forever Friends-10658	Suspd.		16.00	16
1998 Golden Heavenly Dreamer-10661	Suspd.		12.00	12
1998 Golden Make A Wish-10663	Suspd.		15.00	15
1998 Golden Mischief Maker-10660	Suspd.		12.00	12
1998 Golden Sitting Pretty-10657	Suspd.		12.00	12
1999 Golden Thinking of You-10932	Suspd.		44.00	44
1999 Golden Tiny Dancer-10934	Suspd.		16.00	16
1998 Golden Wildflower-10662	Suspd.		12.00	12

Dreamsicles Heavenly Classics - K. Haynes & S. Hackett

1996 Bundles of Love-HC370	327	1996	80.00	675-700
1995 The Dedication-DC351	10,000	1996	118.00	150-165
1997 Making Memories-10096 (spec. ed.)	Suspd.		100.00	100

Dreamsicles Northern Lights - K. Haynes

1999 Northern Crossing-60013	10,000		38.00	38
1999 Sleddin'-60007	Retrd.	2000	23.00	23

Dreamsicles Nursery Rhymes - K. Haynes

1999 The Frog Prince-10765	Suspd.		17.00	17
1998 Humpty Dumpty-10372	Suspd.		16.50	17
1998 Little Bo Peep-10375	Suspd.		17.50	18
1999 Mary Contrary-10766	Suspd.		17.00	17

Charming Tails/Fitz and Floyd Collectibles

The Leaf & Acorn Club - D. Griff

1997 Thank You 98/700	Closed	1998	Gift	19-35
1997 Maxine's Leaf Collection 98/701	Closed	1998	15.00	30-98
1998 A Growing Friendship 97/12	Closed	1998	17.00	17-28
1998 Sharing a Warm and Cozy Holiday 97/13	Closed	1998	22.00	22-50
1999 You Are My Shining Star 97/11	Closed	1999	Gift	N/A
1999 Nap Time Pin 97/14	Closed	1999	Gift	N/A
1999 Ring Around The Rosie 97/15	Closed	1999	23.00	23-34

YEAR ISSUE	EDITION LIMIT	YEAR RETD.	ISSUE PRICE	*QUOTE U.S.$
1999 A Snowy Trio 97/16	Closed	1999	21.00	30-63
2000 You Hold The Key To My Heart 97/18	Closed	2000	Gift	N/A
2000 This Is The Key 97/20	Closed	2000	Gift	N/A
2000 Peek-A-Boo Bouquet 97/21	Closed	2000	22.00	22-28
2000 Christmas Treasures 97/19	Closed	2000	24.00	24
2001 Lucky Coin Pin	Closed	2001	N/A	N/A
2001 Rich In Friendship 97/25	Closed	2001	N/A	N/A
2001 Holding Onto Luck Incentive Pin	Closed	2001	N/A	N/A
2001 Tweet Dreams 97/26	Closed	2001	22.00	22-31
2001 Stocking Stuffers 97/27	Closed	2001	24.00	24
2001 You're Berry Special Ornament	Closed	2001	12.00	12
2002 Heart Lapel Pin 97/32	Yr.lss.		Gift	N/A
2002 Thank You Pin 98/220	Yr.lss.		Gift	N/A
2002 Friends Both Near & Far 97/31	Yr.lss.		18.00	18
2002 All Packed To Go Pin 97/30	Yr.lss.		6.00	6
2002 Share The Happy News 97/33	Yr.lss.		20.00	20
2002 Sharing The Ride 97/34	Yr.lss.		22.00	22
2002 Holiday Cheer 97/35	Yr.lss.		16.00	16

Charming Tails Event Piece - D. Griff

1996 Take Me Home 87/691	Closed	1997	17.00	25-42
1997 I Picked This For You 98/197	Closed	1997	18.00	40-98
1998 Riding On The Wings of Friendship 98/207	4,500	1998	18.00	34-70
1999 This One Is Yours 98/208	Closed	1999	18.00	18-25
2000 A Treasure of Memories 98/224	Closed	2000	18.00	18-25
2001 Our Love Burns Bright Votive (Retailer Exclusive)	Closed	2001	25.00	25
2001 You're A True Blue Friend (Signing) 98/247	Closed	2001	19.00	18-28
2001 You're A Real Gem (Open House) 98/248	Closed	2001	19.00	18-28
2001 Sailing Away Pin 87/200	Closed	2001	Gift	N/A
2001 Four Seasons Collection 98/291	Closed	2001	100.00	100
2002 Look'in At A Friend (Retailer Exclusive) 98/254	2,000	2002	25.00	25
2002 Showered with Friendship (Signing) 98/205	2,000		20.00	20

Charming Tails Autumn Harvest Figurines - D. Griff

1993 Acorn Built For Two 85/403	Open		10.00	13
2000 Autumn Breezes 85/101	Open		17.00	17
1999 Autumn Harvest Music Box 93/100	Open		40.00	40
1999 Autumn Harvest Picture Frame 93/103	Open		25.00	25
1996 Bag of Tricks...Or Treats 87/436	Closed	2001	15.50	18
2000 Be Thankful For Friends 85/500	Open		20.00	20
1996 Binkey's Acorn Costume 87/429	Closed	2000	11.50	14-41
1998 Boooo! 85/417	Closed	2001	18.00	19
2001 Bubbly Brew 85/102	Open		17.00	17
2001 Building a Pumpkin Man 85/103	Open		17.50	18
1995 Candy Apples 85/611	Closed	1998	16.00	38-48
2001 Candy Corn Caper 85/104	Open		18.00	18
1995 Candy Corn Vampire 85/607	Closed	1997	18.00	25-65
1993 Caps Off to You 85/402	Closed	1996	10.00	35-75
2001 Change Is In The Air 85/502	Open		18.00	18
1996 Chauncey's Pear Costume 87/431	Closed	1998	12.00	13-30
1993 Cornfield Feast 85/399	Closed	1994	15.00	125-150
2002 Enjoy Life's Voyage 85/504	Open		20.00	20
1994 Fall Frolicking (2 pc.) 85/401	Closed	1996	13.00	73-90
2002 Friends Are A Bushel Of Fun 85/505	Open		19.00	19
2002 Friends Are A Rich Harvest 85/506	Open		19.00	19
1994 Frosting Pumpkins 85/511	Closed	1998	16.00	35-65
1995 Garden Naptime 85/615	Closed	1997	18.00	21-57
1997 Ghost Stories 85/703	Closed	2001	18.50	20
1995 Giving Thanks 85/608	Open		16.00	19
1997 The Good Witch 85/704	Closed	2001	18.50	20
1993 Gourd Slide 85/398	Closed	1996	16.00	46-90
1994 Harvest Fruit (2 pc.) 85/507	Closed	1995	16.00	50-163
1999 Harvest Time Honeys 85/882	Open		18.50	19
1999 Haunted Hayride 85/883	Closed	2001	18.50	19
1995 Hocus Pocus 85/880	Open		18.50	19
1995 Horn of Plenty 85/610	Closed	1997	20.00	28-65
1996 Indian Impostor 87/446	Closed	2000	14.00	16
1998 Jack O'Lantern Jalopy 85/410	Closed	2001	18.00	18
1994 Jumpin' Jack O' Lanterns 85/512	Closed	1997	16.00	45-63
1995 Let's Get Cracking 85/776	Closed	1997	20.00	30-65
1996 Look! No Hands 87/428	Closed	1999	15.50	17-35
1999 Mackenzie's Putt-Putt Tractor 85/881	Closed	2001	17.50	18
1996 Maxine's Pumpkin Costume 87/430	Open		12.00	15
1993 Mouse Candleholder (2 pc.) 85/400	Closed	1995	13.00	100-238
1994 Mouse on Leaf Candleholder 87/503	Closed	1995	17.00	110-147
2001 Nuts About Naps 85/503	Open		16.00	16

FIGURINES

YEAR ISSUE	EDITION LIMIT	YEAR RETD.	ISSUE PRICE	*QUOTE U.S.$
1996 Oops, I Missed 87/443	Closed	1998	16.00	20-30
1994 Open Pumpkin 85/508	Closed	1994	15.00	98-125
1994 Painting Leaves 85/514	Closed	1996	16.00	28-82
1994 Pear Candleholder 85/509	Closed	1995	14.00	94-130
1996 Pickin' Time 87/438	Closed	1997	16.00	18-32
1996 Pilgrim's Progress 87/445	Closed	2000	13.50	15
1999 Pumpkin and Squash Votive 93/101	Closed	2001	20.00	20
1995 Pumpkin Pie 85/606	Closed		16.00	63-82
1994 Pumpkin Slide 85/513	Closed	1995	16.00	40-50
2002 Pumpkin Surprise 85/106	Open		16.00	16
1994 Pumpkin Votive 85/510	Closed	1995	13.50	39-74
1998 Pumpkin's First Pumpkin 85/411	Closed	2001	17.00	18
2000 Put On A Happy Face 85/100	Open		17.00	17
1997 Reginald's Gourd Costume 85/701	Closed	2000	12.50	18-38
1995 Reginald's Hideaway 85/777	Closed	1997	14.00	28-32
1998 Stack O'Lanterns 85/416	Open		18.00	18
1997 Stewart's Apple Costume 85/700	Closed	2000	12.50	14
1994 Stump Candleholders (2 pc.) 85/516	Closed	1995	20.00	195-250
2002 There's Something Sweet Between Us 85/107	Open		18.00	18
1997 Turkey Traveller 85/702	Closed	2000	18.50	20
1998 Turkey With Dressing 85/412	Closed	2000	18.00	19-25
2000 What A Hoot! 85/101	Open		17.00	17
2002 You're Boo-tiful 85/108	Open		17.00	17
2001 You're My Princess 85/105	Open		24.00	24
1996 You're Not Scary 87/440	Closed	1998	14.00	15-75
1996 You're Nutty 87/451	Closed	1998	12.00	20-38

Charming Tails Commemorative - D. Griff

YEAR ISSUE	EDITION LIMIT	YEAR RETD.	ISSUE PRICE	*QUOTE U.S.$
2001 Friends Around The World 98/203	5,000		24.00	24
2001 Wear It With Pride Lapel Pin 98/295	10,000		7.00	7
2001 You Make Me Proud 98/297	8,000		19.00	19

Charming Tails Everyday Figurines - D. Griff

YEAR ISSUE	EDITION LIMIT	YEAR RETD.	ISSUE PRICE	*QUOTE U.S.$
1994 After Lunch Snooze 89/558	Closed	1997	15.00	28-42
1996 Ahh-Choo, Get Well Soon 89/624	Closed	2000	12.00	14-21
1999 Along For The Ride 89/100	Open		18.50	19
2000 Apple of My Eye 89/110	Yr.lss.	2000	19.00	19
1996 The Berry Best 87/391	Closed	2000	16.00	18-25
1994 Binkey Growing Carrots 89/605	Closed	1995	15.00	69-94
1993 Binkey in a Lily 89/305	Closed	1996	16.00	30-90
1995 Binkey's First Cake 98/349	Closed	1997	16.00	44-55
1994 Binkey's New Pal 89/586	Closed	1996	14.00	15-31
2001 Bringing Along A Little Love 98/245	Retrd.	2001	17.00	17-28
2000 A Bubbly Personality 89/109	Open		17.00	17
1996 Bunny Buddies 89/619	Closed	2000	20.00	22-41
1994 Bunny w/Carrot Candleholder 89/317	Closed	1995	12.00	57-103
1995 Butterfly Smelling Zinnia 89/606	Closed	1995	15.00	66-122
1994 Can I Keep Him? 89/600	2,500	1994	13.00	300-455
1995 Catchin' Butterflies 87/423	Closed	1998	16.00	33-45
1996 Cattail Catapult 87/448	Closed	1998	16.00	31-40
1995 Charming Tails Display Sign 87/690	Open		20.00	22
1995 The Chase is On 87/386	Closed	1997	16.00	13-17
1994 Chauncey Growing Tomatoes 89/607	Closed	1995	15.00	48-65
1998 A Collection of Friends (Convention Piece) 98/206	7,500	1998	23.00	35-80
2000 Con-Graduations 89/106	Open		17.00	17
2000 Dandelion Wishes 89/107	Open		18.00	18
1994 Duckling Votive 89/315	Closed	1994	12.00	100-175
1998 The Ups And Downs Are Fun 89/705	Closed	2000	16.50	18
1995 Feeding Time 98/417	Closed	1996	16.00	59-100
1999 Floral Candleholder Mackenzie 93/202	Closed	2001	20.00	20
1999 Floral Candleholder Maxine 93/203	Closed	2001	20.00	20
1996 Flower Friends 89/608	Closed	1998	16.00	20-30
1996 Fragile...Handle with Care (no numbers on bottom)	Closed	1997	18.00	250-300
1996 Fragile...Handle with Care 89/601	15,000	1997	18.00	36-163
1996 Fragile...Handle with Love (mismarked) 89/601	Closed	1997	18.00	110-121
2001 Free To Be Friends 89/116	Open		20.00	20
2002 Friendship Is The Best Medicine 89/128	Open		18.00	18
1995 Gardening Break 87/364	Closed	2000	16.00	17-25
1994 Get Well Soon 97/719	Closed	1997	15.00	27-49
1999 A Gift Of Love 89/102	Closed	2001	18.00	18
1994 Good Luck 97/716	Open		15.00	18
1997 Guess What? 89/558	Closed	1999	16.50	17
1997 Hang On (GCC Exclusive) 98/600	Closed	1997	18.00	18
1996 Hangin' Around 89/623	Closed	2001	18.00	20
1994 Happy Birthday 97/715	Open		18.00	18
2001 Happy Birthday Surprise 89/117	Open		17.50	18
1998 Hear, Speak and See No Evil 89/717	Open		17.50	19
1999 Hi Cookie 89/760	Open		17.50	18
1993 Hide and Seek 89/307	Closed	1997	13.50	113-250
1999 The Honeymoon's Over 89/763	Open		20.00	20
1994 Hope You're Feeling Better 97/723	Closed	1997	15.00	30-82
1996 Hoppity Hop 87/425	Closed	1997	16.00	15-42
1994 How Do You Measure Love 98/461	Closed	1996	15.00	25-74
1998 How Many Candles? 89/713	Closed	2001	16.50	18
1996 I Have a Question for You 89/603	Open		16.00	19
1994 I Love You 97/724	Closed	2000	15.00	17
1997 I Love You a Whole Bunch 89/715	Closed	2001	17.00	18
1999 I Miss You Already 89/756	Closed	2001	17.50	18
1996 I See Things Clearly Now 89/626	Closed	2000	14.00	16
2002 I Wish You Weren't So Far Away 89/129	Open		18.00	18
1998 I'm A Winner 89/719	Closed	2001	16.00	17
1998 I'm Here For You 89/706	Open		17.50	19
1994 I'm So Sorry 97/720	Closed	1998	15.00	15-35
1997 I'm Thinking of You 89/701	Closed	1999	15.00	18
1999 In Every Life a Little Rain Must Fall 89/757	Closed	2001	20.00	20
1994 It's Not the Same Without You 97/721	Closed	1997	15.00	23-49
1997 It's Your Move 89/704	Closed	2000	17.00	18
1996 Just Plane Friends 89/627	Closed	2000	19.00	20
2002 Just Weight 89/130	Open		16.00	16
1997 Keeping Our Love Alive 89/710	Closed	2000	19.50	20
1993 King of the Mushroom 89/318	Closed	1996	16.00	30-74
1998 Life is a Bed of Roses (Special Ed. Artist Event) 98/198	7,000	1998	19.00	45-63
2002 Life Is A Bowl Of Cherries 89/135	Open		20.00	20
1998 A Little Birdie Told Me 89/720	Closed	2000	17.00	18-41
1996 Love Blooms (GCC Spring Exclusive) 87/862	Closed	1996	16.00	20-45
1996 Love me-Love Me Not 87/395	Closed	1999	16.00	18
1993 Love Mice 89/314	Closed	1994	15.00	100-150
1994 Mackenzie Growing Beans 89/604	Closed	1995	15.00	38-75
1994 Maxine Goes On-Line 89/702	Closed	2001	17.00	18
1994 Mender of Broken Hearts 98/460	Closed	1996	15.00	50-82
1994 mid-day Snooze 89/617	Closed	1999	19.00	20
2000 Mom Gives The Best Bear Bugs 98/228	Retrd.	2001	17.50	32-63
2000 Morning Hare 89/108			16.00	16
1993 Mouse on a Grasshopper 89/321	Closed	1994	15.00	360-420
1994 New Arrival 97/717	Open		15.00	18
1999 Now I Lay Me Down To Sleep 89/758	Yr.lss.	1999	18.00	20
1999 On The First Day of Christmas 98/210	Yr.lss.	1999	17.50	18-28
1995 One for Me... 87/360	Closed	1997	16.00	26-45
1995 One for You... 87/361	Closed	1997	16.00	32-42
1997 One Mouse Open Sleigh (GCC Spring Exclusive) 98/195	Yr.lss.	1997	17.50	18-98
1999 Party Animals 89/101	Open		22.00	22
2001 Penny For Your Thoughts 89/118	10,000	2001	16.00	16
1998 Picture Perfect 89/712	Closed	2001	18.50	19
1993 Rabbit/Daffodil Candleholder (2 pc.) 89/312	Closed	1995	13.50	180-252
1994 Reach for the Stars 97/718	Open		15.00	19
1999 Rose Votive 93/204	Open		20.00	20
2000 Santa Imposter 98/226	Retrd.	2001	18.00	18-30
2000 Sleepy Head 89/113	Open		19.00	19
1994 Slumber Party 89/560	Closed	1996	16.00	41-55
1993 Spring Flowers (2 pc.) 89/310	Closed	1996	16.00	88-200
1998 Steady Wins The Race 89/716	17,500	1998	20.00	20-30
1995 Surrounded By Friends 87/353	Closed	1997	16.00	16-26
1997 Taggin' Along 87/399	Closed	1997	14.00	12-15
2002 Take Time To Dream 89/131	Open		18.00	18
1996 Take Time To Reflect 87/396	Closed	1997	16.00	16-24
1999 Take Time To Smell The Flowers 89/765	Open		18.00	18
1994 Take Two Aspirin... 89/103	Open		15.00	15
1997 Teacher's Pet 89/700	Closed	1999	19.50	20
1994 Thanks for Being There 89/754	Closed	1996	15.00	18-65
1998 There's No "US" Without "U" 89/703	Closed	2000	19.50	20-27
2002 Tickled Pink 89/132	Open		18.00	18
1999 Together Every Step OF The Way 89/104	Open		18.00	18
1997 Training Wings 87/398	Closed	1997	16.00	25-45
1995 Tuggin' Twosome 87/362	10,000	1997	18.00	20-27
1993 Two Peas in a Pod 89/306	Closed	1994	14.00	40-65
2000 Wash Away Those Worries 89/111	Open		17.00	17
1996 The Waterslide 87/384	Closed	2001	20.00	22
1994 We'll Weather the Storm Together 97/722	Open		15.00	18

*Quotes have been rounded up to nearest dollar

YEAR ISSUE	EDITION LIMIT	YEAR RETD.	ISSUE PRICE	*QUOTE U.S.$
1995 Why, Hello There! 87/357	Closed	1997	14.00	14-25
1999 Wishing You Well 98/930	Closed	2001	20.00	20
2002 Wrapped With Pride 89/139	Open		18.00	18
1999 You Are My Cup of Tea 89/134	Open		19.00	19
1995 You Are Not Alone 98/929	Closed	1996	20.00	35-40
1996 You Couldn't Be Sweeter 89/625	Open		17.00	18
1999 You Quack Me Up 89/105	Open		18.00	18
2001 Your Friendship is Golden 89/119	Open		18.00	18
2001 You're A Very Special Mum 89/120	Open		19.00	19
2001 You're A Very Special Pop-py 89/121	Open		19.00	19
2002 You're Always On Your Toes 89/133	Open		17.00	17
2001 You're Berry Special 89/122	Yr.Iss.	2001	20.00	20
2000 You're Cute as a Button 89/115	Open		18.50	19
2001 You're My Inspiration 89/123	Open		16.00	16
2000 You're Pretty as a Picture 89/112	Open		19.00	19

Charming Tails Family Ties Figurines - D. Griff

YEAR ISSUE	EDITION LIMIT	YEAR RETD.	ISSUE PRICE	*QUOTE U.S.$
2001 Family Portrait 89/124	Open		18.00	18
2002 Grandma, You Bake Me Happy 89/137	Open		18.00	18
2001 Happiness Is Homemade 89/125	Open		20.00	20
2001 Home Is Where The Heart Is 89/126	Open		20.00	20
2002 My Love For You Will Never Grow Old 89/138	Open		19.00	19
2001 You Always Measure Up 89/127	Open		17.00	17
2002 You're The Best Grandpa Hook, Line And Sinker 89/136	Open		20.00	20

Charming Tails Holiday Figurines - D. Griff

YEAR ISSUE	EDITION LIMIT	YEAR RETD.	ISSUE PRICE	*QUOTE U.S.$
1996 Airmail 87/698	Closed	1997	15.00	14-30
1996 All I Can Give You is Me 87/498	Closed	1996	15.00	30-49
1996 All Snug in Their Beds Waterglobe 87/476	Closed	1996	30.00	56-103
1997 All The Trimmings 87/703	Yr.Iss.	1997	15.00	24-53
1996 Angel of Light 87/481	Open		12.00	14
1997 Baby's 1st Christmas 1997 Annual 87/705	Closed	1997	18.50	20-42
1996 Baby's 1st Christmas Waterglobe 87/475	Closed	1996	28.00	36-57
1999 Baby's First Christmas 87/111	Closed	1999	16.50	20-44
2001 Baby's First Christmas 87/115	Yr.Iss.	2001	17.00	17
1997 Bearing Gifts 87/600	Closed	2000	16.00	17-25
1996 Binkey in a Bed of Flowers 87/426	Closed	1996	15.00	34-74
1995 Binkey Snow Shoeing 87/580	Open		14.00	16
1995 Binkey's 1995 Ice Sculpture 87/572	Closed	1995	20.00	20-52
2002 Bringing Home The Tree 87/109	Open		19.00	19
1996 Building a Snowbunny 87/692	Closed	2001	16.00	18
1998 The Building Blocks of Christmas 87/619	Closed	1998	17.00	17-35
2001 Candle Light Kisses 87/116	Open		18.00	18
1995 Charming Choo-Choo and Cabbose 87/579	Closed	1999	35.00	36-70
1997 Chauncey's Choo Choo Ride 87/707	Closed	1999	19.00	20
1996 Chauncey's Noisemakers 87/554	Closed	2000	12.00	14
1995 Christmas Pageant Stage 87/546	Open		30.00	32
1996 Christmas Stroll 87/575	Closed	2000	16.00	18
2002 Christmas Time Is Family Time 87/117	Open		22.00	22
1997 Christmas Trio 87/713	Open		15.50	18
1998 Dashing Through The Snow 87/624	Closed	2001	16.50	18
1997 Decorating Binkey 87/714	Closed	2000	16.00	18-24
1996 Did I Do That? 87/469	Closed	1997	16.00	23-25
2000 Dive Into The Holidays 87/208	Open		22.00	22
1996 The Drum Major 87/556	Closed	2000	12.00	14
1999 Everybody Sing 87/102	Open		26.00	26
1996 Extra! Extra! 87/590	Closed	1997	14.00	17-65
1996 Farmer Mackenzie 87/695	Closed	2000	12.00	14
1996 The Float Driver 87/587	Closed	2000	12.00	14
1995 Flying Leaf Saucer 87/305	Open		16.00	18
1996 Follow in my Footsteps 87/473	Closed	2000	12.00	14
1996 Holiday Trumpeteer 87/555	Closed	2000	12.00	14
1995 Holy Family Players 87/547	Open		20.00	22
2001 Home Sweet Home 87/106	Open		22.00	22
1994 Hot Doggin' 87/993	Closed	1995	20.00	24-46
2002 I Only Have Ice For You 87/122	Open		20.00	20
2001 I'm Stuck on You 87/118	Open		18.00	18
1996 Jingle Bells 87/513	Closed	1997	15.00	23-57
2000 Just The Right Size 87/209	Open		20.00	20
2000 Kiss-Mas Lights 87/205	Yr.Iss.	2000	19.00	19
1994 Lady Bug Express 87/188	Closed	1994	18.00	188-438
1994 Leaf Vine Ornament Hanger 87/519	Closed	1995	25.00	50-63
1996 Lil' Drummer Mouse 87/480	Open		12.00	14
1996 Little Drummer Boy 87/557	Closed	2000	12.00	14
2000 The Littlest Reindeer 87/207	Closed	2001	17.00	17
1994 Mackenzie Building a Snowmouse 87/203	7,500	1994	18.00	107-195
1996 Mackenzie Claus on Parade 87/576	Closed	2000	22.00	24
1998 Mackenzie's Holiday Hat 98/202	Retrd.	1998	17.00	17-42
1998 Mackenzie's Wish List (NALED piece) 98/201	Retrd.	1998	17.00	19-62
1995 Mail Mouse 87/573	Closed	1996	12.00	24-57
1996 Manger Animals 87/482	Open		20.00	22
1994 Maxine and Mackenzie Caroling 87/925	Closed	1995	18.00	27-50
1994 Maxine Making Snow Angels 87/510	Open		20.00	22
1997 Maxine the Snowman (NALED piece) 98/196	Retrd.	1997	16.50	30-63
1999 Maxine's Snowcap (Concepts Direct Exclusive) 98/216	Closed	1999	18.00	35
1996 Maxine's Snowmobile Ride 87/612	Closed	2000	16.00	18
1998 Merry Christmas From Our House To Yours 87/622	Closed	2001	23.00	24
1994 Mouse Candle Climber 87/189	Closed	1995	8.00	25-82
1994 Mouse Card Holder 87/501	Closed	1995	13.00	13-82
1994 Mouse in Tree Hole Candleholder 87/502	Closed	1995	17.00	69-77
1994 Mouse on Basket 87/529	Closed	1995	50.00	60-85
1994 Mouse on Vine Basket 87/506	Closed	1995	55.00	66
1994 Mouse on Vine Candleholder 87/504	Closed	1995	55.00	66-85
1994 Mouse on Vine Wreath 87/505	Closed	1995	55.00	66-150
2002 My Little Angel 87/123	Open		20.00	20
2000 My Little Chick-A-Deer 87/206	Open		18.00	18
1996 My New Toy 87/500	Closed	1997	14.00	18-49
1998 My Spring Bonnet (NALED piece) 98/204	Retrd.	1998	18.50	19-28
1998 Nestled In For The Holidays 87/101	Open		20.00	20
1997 Not a Creature Was Stirring 87/704	Closed	2000	17.00	18
2000 Oh Mackenzie Tree... 87/213	Open		17.00	17
1994 Parade Banner 87/543	Closed	2000	16.00	16
1995 Pear Taxi 87/565	Closed	1996	16.00	20-50
1995 Peeking at Presents 87/527	Closed	1997	13.00	14-40
1998 Please, Just One More... 87/625	Closed	2000	16.50	18
1994 Pyramid with Mice Candleholder 87/509	Closed	1995	40.00	48
1998 Reginald's Choo-Choo Ride 87/620	Closed	1999	19.00	19
1998 Reginald's Newsstand 87/591	Closed	1997	20.00	21-44
1997 The Santa Balloon 87/708	Closed	2000	25.00	26
2001 The Season of Love 87/108	Closed	2001	20.00	20
2001 Secrets For Santa 87/119	Open		18.00	18
1996 Sending A Little Snow Your Way 87/601	Retrd.	1996	15.00	25-45
1997 Shepherd's set 87/710			12.50	14
2000 A Shoveling We Will Go 87/204	Open		18.00	18
2000 Silent Night 98/225	Retrd.	2001	19.50	19-24
1999 Skating Party (NALED piece) 87/103	Closed	2001	21.00	21
2002 Skating Through The Season With You 87/127	Open		19.00	19
2002 Sledding Nut 87/124	Yr.Iss.		17.00	17
1999 Sleigh Ride 87/569	7,500	1995	16.00	45-68
1999 Sleigh Ride Sweeties 87/100	Closed	1999	23.00	25
1996 Snack for the Reindeer 87/512	Closed	1996	13.00	29-40
1996 Snow Plow 87/566	Closed	1996	16.00	18
1995 The Snowball Fight 87/570	Closed	1999	16.00	18
1998 Snowman Float 87/626	Closed	2000	23.00	25
1996 Stewart's Choo Choo Ride 87/694	Closed	1999	17.50	20
1999 The Stockings Were Hung By The Chimney 87/110	Open		18.50	19
1999 Sugar Time Band Float 87/104	Closed	2000	25.00	25
2001 Swinging On A Star 87/107	Open		20.00	20
1999 Tea Party Train Ride 87/105	Closed	1999	26.00	26
1998 Team Igloo 87/623	Closed	1998	23.00	23-45
1995 Teamwork Helps 87/571	Closed	2000	16.00	18-20
1995 Testing the Lights 87/514	Closed	1997	14.00	18-30
1995 Three Wise Mice 87/548	Open		20.00	22
1996 Town Crier 87/696	Closed	2000	14.00	16
1997 Trimming A Tree 87/702	Closed	2001	27.50	28
2002 Visions Of Sugarplums 87/125	Open		20.00	20
2000 Wait For Us! 87/210	Closed	2000	20.00	20-25
1996 Waiting For Christmas 87/496	14,000	1997	16.00	25-36
2002 Waiting For Santa 87/126	Open		19.00	19
2000 A Warm Woolen Mitten 98/234	Retrd.	2001	18.00	18-32
1998 Who Put That Tree There? 87/621	Closed	2000	16.50	18
1996 You Melted My Heart 87/472	Closed	1997	20.00	21-25
2001 You're My Snuggle Bunny 87/120	Open		17.50	18

Charming Tails Holiday Gifts - D. Griff

YEAR ISSUE	EDITION LIMIT	YEAR RETD.	ISSUE PRICE	*QUOTE U.S.$
2001 Pillar Candle Holder 93/503	Open		25.00	25
2001 Stocking Holder 93/504	Open		20.00	20
2001 Votive Candle Holder 93/505	Open		18.00	18

Charming Tails Holly Day Dreams - D. Griff

YEAR ISSUE	EDITION LIMIT	YEAR RETD.	ISSUE PRICE	*QUOTE U.S.$
2001 Candy Jar 93/506	Open		36.00	36
2001 Cookie Jar 93/507	Open		55.00	55
2001 Cookie Plate 93/508	Open		14.00	14
2001 Mug 93/509	Open		14.00	14

Charming Tails Lazy Days of Summer Figurines - D. Griff

YEAR ISSUE	EDITION LIMIT	YEAR RETD.	ISSUE PRICE	*QUOTE U.S.$
2000 Adventure Bound 83/100	Open		20.00	20
2000 Beach Bunnie 83/101	Closed	2001	16.00	16
2001 Binkey's Sand Angel 83/105	Closed	2001	18.00	18
1997 The Blossom Bounce 83/704	Closed	1999	20.00	20-25
1997 Building Castles 83/802	Closed	1999	17.00	17-58
1999 Buried Treasures 83/806	Open		19.00	19
1998 Camping Out 83/703	Closed	2001	18.50	20-53
2000 Catching Fireflies 83/102	Open		18.00	18
1998 Come On In -The Water's Fine! 83/804	Closed	2000	18.00	19
1998 A Day At The Lake 83/803	Closed	2001	18.50	19-26
1999 Friendship is Always a Great Bargain 83/810	Closed	2001	19.50	20
2001 Give Luck a Shot 83/106	Open		18.00	18
1997 Gone Fishin' 83/702	Closed	1999	16.00	14-16
2000 Hang Ten 83/103	Open		19.00	19
2001 Headin' For The Beach 83/107	Open		18.00	18
2002 Just A Hop, Skip And Jump Away 83/110	Open		17.00	17
1997 Life's a Picnic With You 83/701	Closed	1999	18.00	16-18
1999 Mow, Mow, Mow the Lawn 83/809	Open		16.50	17
2000 A Real Lifesaver 83/104	Open		20.00	20
1997 Row Boat Romance 83/801	Open		15.00	17
1998 Stewart's Day In The Sun 83/805	Closed	2000	17.00	18
2002 Sunny Days Are On The Way 83/111	Open		17.00	17
1998 Toasting Marshmallows 83/700	Closed	2000	20.00	21
1999 Triple Delight 83/807	Closed	2001	18.00	18
2002 Wish Upon A Star 83/112	Yr.Iss.		19.00	19
2001 You're My Treasure 83/108	Open		18.00	18

Charming Tails Love Expressions Figurines - D. Griff

YEAR ISSUE	EDITION LIMIT	YEAR RETD.	ISSUE PRICE	*QUOTE U.S.$
1999 An Abundance of Love 84/107	Open		18.00	18
1999 Candy Kisses 84/108	Open		17.00	17
1999 Give Love a Shot! 84/109	Open		15.00	15
2001 Honey Bunnies 84/112	Open		17.00	17
1999 I'd Do It All Over Again 84/106	Closed	2001	17.50	18
2002 I'm Under Your Spell 84/102	Open		19.00	19
1999 I'm Your Love Bunny 84/101	Closed	2001	16.00	16
2002 It Takes Two To Tango 84/105	Open		18.00	18
2001 King of My Heart 84/113	Open		16.00	16
1999 Love Birds 84/110	Closed	2001	20.00	20
1999 Love Is In The Air 84/100	Closed	2001	19.50	20
1999 Our Love Has Blossomed 84/103	Closed	2001	18.00	18
2001 Queen of My Heart 84/114	Open		16.00	16
2002 Romantic At Heart 84/117	Open		18.00	18
2002 Sending All My Love 84/118	Open		19.00	19
2002 Sweetie Pie 84/119	Open		18.00	18
1999 We're a Perfect Fit 84/111	Open		17.00	17
1999 You Can't Run From Love 84/104	Closed	2000	17.50	18
2001 You're a Reflection of My Affection 84/115	Open		14.00	14
2001 You're My Sweet Heart 84/116	Open		17.00	17

Charming Tails Love Is In The Air Gifts - D. Griff

YEAR ISSUE	EDITION LIMIT	YEAR RETD.	ISSUE PRICE	*QUOTE U.S.$
2001 Bud Vase 93/209	Open		29.00	29
2001 Candy Dish 93/210	Open		29.00	29
2000 Dancin' Darlin's Musical 93/208	Open		20.00	20
1999 Heart Picture Frame 93/206	Closed	2001	25.00	25
2000 Love Is In The Air Votive 93/205	Open		20.00	20
2001 Photo Frame 93/205	Open		20.00	20
1999 Thinking of You Picture Frame 93/207	Closed	2001	25.00	25

Charming Tails Moon & Star Nursery Gifts - D. Griff

YEAR ISSUE	EDITION LIMIT	YEAR RETD.	ISSUE PRICE	*QUOTE U.S.$
2000 Musical (pink) 93/601	Closed	2001	39.00	39
2000 Photo Frame (blue) 93/607	Closed	2001	25.00	25
2000 Photo Frame (pink) 93/604	Closed	2001	25.00	25
2000 Waterglobe (blue) 93/602	Closed	2001	45.00	45

Charming Tails Office Gifts - D. Griff

YEAR ISSUE	EDITION LIMIT	YEAR RETD.	ISSUE PRICE	*QUOTE U.S.$
2001 Desk Top Clock 93/300	Open		25.00	25
2001 Lidded Paper Clip Box 93/302	Open		20.00	20
2001 Note Pad Holder 93/301	Open		20.00	20
2001 Pencil Holder 93/303	Open		20.00	20
2001 Photo Frame 93/304	Open		20.00	20
2001 Stapler 93/305	Open		22.00	22

Charming Tails Pumpkin Harvest Gifts - D. Griff

YEAR ISSUE	EDITION LIMIT	YEAR RETD.	ISSUE PRICE	*QUOTE U.S.$
2001 Bud Vase 93/104	Open		29.00	29
2001 Mouse in Taper Candle Holder 93/105	Open		18.00	18
2001 Mouse in Taper Candle Holder 93/106	Open		18.00	18
2001 Picture Frame 93/108	Open		20.00	20
2001 Votive Candle Holder 93/111	Open		20.00	20

Charming Tails Shirt Tails Pins - D. Griff

YEAR ISSUE	EDITION LIMIT	YEAR RETD.	ISSUE PRICE	*QUOTE U.S.$
2002 Acorn Built For Two Little Ones 80/110	Open		7.00	7
2002 Backed By Love 80/105	Open		7.00	7
2002 Brimming With Pride 80/107	Open		7.00	7
2002 Four Seasons Gift Set 80/100	Open		20.00	20
2002 Friends 80/103	Open		7.00	7
2002 Hang On To Your Dreams 80/113	Open		7.00	7
2002 Happy Birthday 80/102	Open		8.00	8
2002 Happy Easter 80/108	Open		7.00	7
2002 Happy Spirit 80/109	Open		7.00	7
2002 It's Friday! 80/112	Open		7.00	7
2002 Spring Garden Gift Set 80/101	Open		20.00	20
2002 Swinging On A Star 80/106	Open		7.00	7
2002 Teachers Rule 80/111	Open		7.00	7
2002 You're All The Luck I Need 80/104	Open		6.00	6

Charming Tails Sports Series - D. Griff

YEAR ISSUE	EDITION LIMIT	YEAR RETD.	ISSUE PRICE	*QUOTE U.S.$
2000 Follow The Bouncing Ball 87/800	8,000		19.00	19
2000 Good Cheer 87/801	10,000		19.00	19
2000 I Get a Kick Out of You 87/802	8,600		19.00	19
2000 Keep Your Eye on the Birdie 87/803	6,600		19.00	19
2000 Ready to Take a Swing at it 87/804	10,000		19.00	19
2000 Spare Me 87/805	6,600		19.00	19
2000 Touchdown 87/806	8,000		19.00	19
2000 Two Love 87/807	6,600		22.00	22

Charming Tails Spring Figurines - D. Griff

YEAR ISSUE	EDITION LIMIT	YEAR RETD.	ISSUE PRICE	*QUOTE U.S.$
1995 After the Hunt 87/372	Closed	2000	18.00	19-26
1993 Animals in Eggs (4 asst.) 89/313	Closed	1996	11.00	140-200
1995 Binkey's Bouncing Bundle 87/422	7,500	1995	18.00	25-74
2000 A Budding Romance 98/212	Closed	2001	20.00	20-60
1994 Bunny Imposter 89/609	Closed	1998	12.00	25-30
1995 Bunny Love 87/424	Closed	2000	18.00	19
1998 Chickie Back Ride 88/700	Closed	2001	15.00	15
2000 Chickie Chariot Ride 88/100	Open		18.00	18
2002 Come Out and Play 88/105	Yr.Iss.		25.00	25
2002 Daisy Bouquet Displayer 88/117	Open		28.00	28
1993 Duckling in Egg with Mouse 89/316	Closed	1994	18.00	158-200
2001 Ducky To Meet You 88/103	Open		17.00	17
1999 Ducky Weather 88/101	Open		18.00	18
2002 Flower Pot Surprise 88/112	Open		18.00	18
1995 Gathering Treats 87/377	Closed	1998	12.00	30-38
2002 Hang'in On To A Good Friend 88/116	Open		10.00	10
2002 Home Tweet Home 88/100	Open		20.00	20
2002 Hoppin' Down The Bunny Trail 88/110	Open		20.00	20
1994 Jelly Bean Feast 89/559	Closed	1996	14.00	28-57
1995 Look Out Below 87/373	Closed	1997	20.00	32-57
1999 Motoring Along 88/703	Closed	2001	16.50	17
1996 No Thanks, I'm Stuffed 88/603	Closed	2000	15.00	16
1998 Paint By Paws 88/701	Closed	2001	16.00	16
1999 Shhh, Don't Make a Peep 88/702	Closed	2001	16.50	17
2001 Sweet Dreams 88/104	Open		17.00	17
2002 Tiny Butterfly Ride 88/114	Open		10.00	10
1994 Wanna Play? 89/561	2,500	1994	15.00	110-125
1995 Want a Bite? 87/379	Closed	1997	18.00	28-38
2002 Water Can Surprise 88/113	Open		18.00	18
1996 What's Hatchin' 88/600	Closed	2001	16.00	17
1999 What's The Buzz 98/212	Closed	2001	18.00	18-35
2002 You Add Color To My World 88/109	Open		20.00	20
2002 You Lifted Me Higher 88/115	Open		10.00	10
2001 You're My Lucky Angel 88/102	Open		17.00	17

Charming Tails Spring Garden Gifts - D. Griff

YEAR ISSUE	EDITION LIMIT	YEAR RETD.	ISSUE PRICE	*QUOTE U.S.$
2002 Birdhouse Votive 93/707	Open		20.00	20
2002 Dancin Darlings 93/208	Open		36.00	36

FIGURINES

Charming Tails/Fitz and Floyd Collectibles
to Cherished Teddies/Enesco Group, Inc.

YEAR ISSUE	EDITION LIMIT	YEAR RETD.	ISSUE PRICE	*QUOTE U.S.$
2002 Flower Row Marker 93/703	Open		14.00	14
2002 Friends Wall Plaque 93/714	Open		20.00	20
2002 Herb Planter 93/710	Open		24.00	24
2002 Herb Row Marker 93/704	Open		14.00	14
2002 Home Tweet Home Wind Chime 93/709	Open		22.00	22
2002 Love Wall Plaque 93/715	Open		20.00	20
2002 Morning Glory Candle Holder 93/708	Open		20.00	20
2002 Morning Glory Vase 93/716	Open		30.00	30
2002 Planter 93/711	Open		18.00	18
2002 Pot Perchers B & C 93/700	Open		18.00	18
2002 Pot Perchers M & S 93/700	Open		18.00	18
2002 Pot Perchers R & S 93/701	Open		18.00	18
2002 Rose Thermometer 93/713	Open		20.00	20
2002 Watering Can 93/712	Open		26.00	26

Charming Tails Teeny Tiny Tails Squashville Country Fair Booths - D. Griff

YEAR ISSUE	EDITION LIMIT	YEAR RETD.	ISSUE PRICE	*QUOTE U.S.$
998 Berry Toss 80/7	Closed	1999	14.00	14-20
998 The Big Winner 80/10	Closed	1999	12.00	12-20
998 Candy Apples 80/3	Closed	1999	12.00	12-27
998 Off to the Fair 80/1	Closed	1999	16.00	16-20
998 Test Your Strength 80/5	Closed	1999	14.00	14-20
998 Ticket Seller Booth 80/2	Closed	1999	16.00	15-18

Charming Tails Teeny Tiny Tails Squashville Country Fair Musical Rides - D. Griff

YEAR ISSUE	EDITION LIMIT	YEAR RETD.	ISSUE PRICE	*QUOTE U.S.$
998 Daffodil Twirl 80/4	Closed	1999	49.50	50-75
998 Mushroom Carousel 80/6	Closed	1999	49.50	50-75
998 Tulip Ferris Wheel 80/8	Closed	1999	49.50	50-75

Charming Tails Travels With Mackenzie - D. Griff

YEAR ISSUE	EDITION LIMIT	YEAR RETD.	ISSUE PRICE	*QUOTE U.S.$
002 The Country Singer w/sticker 82/114	3,000		19.00	19
002 High And Dry w/sticker 82/112	3,000		19.00	19
002 Jackpot w/sticker 82/116	3,000		19.00	19
002 Let Freedom Ring w/sticker 82/110	3,000		19.00	19
002 Little Lady Liberty w/sticker 82/111	3,000		19.00	19
002 Mardi Gras Mouse w/sticker 82/113	3,000		19.00	19
002 Mouse Rushmore w/sticker 82/115	3,000		19.00	19
002 A Star In The Making w/sticker 82/117	3,000		19.00	19
002 What's Shakin w/sticker 82/118	3,000		19.00	19

Charming Tails Wedding Figurines - D. Griff

YEAR ISSUE	EDITION LIMIT	YEAR RETD.	ISSUE PRICE	*QUOTE U.S.$
998 The Altar of Love 82/108	Closed	2000	25.00	25
998 The Best...Bunny 82/103	Closed	2000	16.00	17
998 The Get-Away Car 82/107	Open		22.00	23
998 Here Comes The Bride 82/100	Closed	2000	17.00	18
998 Maid of Honor 82/102	Closed	2000	16.00	17
998 My Heart's All A-Flutter (Groom) 82/101	Closed	2000	17.00	18
998 The Ring Bearer 82/104	Closed	2000	16.00	17
998 Together Forever 82/109	Closed	2001	25.00	26
998 Wedding Day Blossoms 82/105	Closed	2000	16.00	17

Cherished Teddies/Enesco Group, Inc.

Cherished Teddies Club - P. Hillman

YEAR ISSUE	EDITION LIMIT	YEAR RETD.	ISSUE PRICE	*QUOTE U.S.$
995 Cub E. Bear CT001	Yr.Iss.	1995	Gift	37-78
995 Mayor Wilson T. Beary CT951	Yr.Iss.	1995	20.00	37-91
995 Hilary Hugabear CT952	Yr.Iss.	1995	17.50	32-40
996 R. Harrison Hartford-New Membear (yellow pencil) CT002	Yr.Iss.	1996	Gift	25-42
996 R. Harrison Hartford-Charter Membear (red pencil) CT102	Yr.Iss.	1996	Gift	44-69
996 Emily E. Claire CT962	Yr.Iss.	1996	17.50	25-40
996 Kurtis D. Claw CT961	Yr.Iss.	1996	17.50	22-40
996 Town Tattler Building CT953	Yr.Iss.	1996	50.00	40-45
996 Club Glad 901350	Yr.Iss.	1996	20.00	20-40
997 Lloyd, CT Town Railway Conductor-Membership (red suitcase) CT003	Yr.Iss.	1997	Gift	22-38
997 Lloyd, CT Town Railway Conductor-Charter Membear (green suitcase) CT103	Yr.Iss.	1997	Gift	22-38
997 Bernard and Bernice CT972	Yr.Iss.	1997	17.50	27-32
997 Eleanor P. Beary CT971	Yr.Iss.	1997	17.50	22-32
997 Mary Jane "My Favorite Things" 277002 (Cherished Rewards)	Yr.Iss.	1997	Gift	49-110
997 Amelia "You Make Me Smile" 273554 (Cherished Rewards)	Yr.Iss.	1997	Gift	45-76
997 Benny "Let's Ride Through Life Together" 273198 (Cherished Rewards)	Yr.Iss.	1997	Gift	38-60

YEAR ISSUE	EDITION LIMIT	YEAR RETD.	ISSUE PRICE	*QUOTE U.S.$
1997 Blaire Beary (mini figurine) 297550 (Member Get Member)	Yr.Iss.	1997	Gift	32-56
1998 Cherished Teddies Town Accessory Set CT983	Yr.Iss.	1998	17.50	18
1998 Lela Nightingale CT981	Yr.Iss.	1998	15.00	15-32
1998 Wade Weathersbee CT982	Yr.Iss.	1998	13.50	27-44
1998 Cherished Teddies Lithograph CRT608 (Cherished Rewards)	Yr.Iss.	1998	Gift	47-58
1998 Bubbie Waterton (mini figurine) 466808 (Member Get Member)	Yr.Iss.	1998	Gift	35
1998 Dr. Darlene Makebetter (orange bag) CT004	Yr.Iss.	1998	Gift	28
1998 Dr. Darlene Makebetter (pink bag) Charter Membear CT104	Yr.Iss.	1998	Gift	42
1999 Lanny CT005	Yr.Iss.	1999	Gift	32
1999 Lanny (red flag) Charter Membear CT105	Yr.Iss.	1999	Gift	190
1999 Letty CT993 (5th Anniversary)	Yr.Iss.	1999	22.50	23-32
1999 Vivienne CT992	Yr.Iss.	1999	17.50	18-27
1999 Walter CT991	Yr.Iss.	1999	17.50	18-27
2000 Julia Bearon as Gloria Growlette 685747	Yr.Iss.	2000	Gift	40
2000 Brad Wheeler - Troy "Mac McBear" 685976	Yr.Iss.	2000	25.00	25-32
2000 Marco Pawllini 685771	Yr.Iss.	2000	20.00	20-35
2000 Audrey D. Zeiner 685968	Yr.Iss.	2000	22.50	23-37
2001 T. James Bear CT107	Yr.Iss.	2001	Gift	N/A
2001 Deena Wilde CT011	Yr.Iss.	2001	25.00	25
2001 Giacomo Bearcino CT012	Yr.Iss.	2001	15.00	15
2001 Maxine D'Face CT013	Yr.Iss.	2001	25.00	25
2002 Tristan (blue overalls) CT008	Yr.Iss.		Gift	N/A
2002 Tristan (green overalls) Charter Membear CT108	Yr.Iss.		Gift	N/A
2002 Savanah CT021	Yr.Iss.		22.50	23
2002 Dolores CT022	Yr.Iss.		20.00	20
2002 Genevieve CT023	Yr.Iss.		45.00	45

Cherished Teddies - P. Hillman

YEAR ISSUE	EDITION LIMIT	YEAR RETD.	ISSUE PRICE	*QUOTE U.S.$
1993 Abigail "Inside We're All The Same" 900362	Suspd.		16.00	42-104
2000 Abraham "Embrace The Earth" 706876	7,500		45.00	45-270
2002 Aggie "No Celebration Is Complete Without Your Closest Friends" (2002 Fall Adoption Center Event) 104029	10,000		45.00	45
1999 Alex "Cherish The Little Things" (Sculptor Tour Figurine) 368156	Retrd.	1999	17.50	32-57
2000 Alexis (Spring Catalog) 681113	Yr.Iss.	2000	22.50	23
1993 Alice "Cozy Warm Wishes Coming Your Way" (9") 903620	Suspd.		100.00	173-325
1993 Alice "Cozy Warm Wishes Coming Your Way" (Dated 1993) 912875	Yr.Iss.	1993	17.50	176-245
1995 Allison & Alexandria "Two Friends Mean Twice The Love" 127981	Retrd.	1999	25.00	29-52
1999 Alyssa "You Warm My Soul" 533866	Retrd.	2001	15.00	15-24
1995 Amanda "Here's Some Cheer to Last The Year" 141186	Yr.Iss.	1995	17.50	20-78
1993 Amy "Hearts Quilted With Love" 910732	Retrd.	1999	13.50	17-48
2000 Angela "Thanks For Helping Me Get My Wings 706809	Open		50.00	50
1999 "Anxiously Awaiting The Arrival" 476978	Open		15.00	15
1996 Andy "You Have A Special Place In My Heart" 176265	Retrd.	1998	18.50	19-32
1999 Anita "You're A Tulip To Treasure" (1999 Spring Catalog Exclusive) 477915	Yr.Iss.	1999	20.00	20-32
1992 Anna "Hooray For You" 950459	Retrd.	1997	22.50	17-56
1999 Anne "So Glad You're Here To Keep Me Warm 534234	Retrd.	2001	10.00	10
1997 Annie, Brittany, Colby, Danny, Ernie "Strike Up The Band And Give Five Cherished Years A Hand" (5th Anniversary) 205354	Yr.Iss.	1997	75.00	37-99
1999 Anthony "Friendship is a Work of Art" 476528R	Open		20.00	20
1999 Anthony "Friendship is a Work of Art" 476528	Open		20.00	20
1999 Archie "Through Ups and Downs, You're Still The Best Friend Around" 589977	Open		20.00	20
2000 Ariel "Everyone Needs A Little Help Learning To Fly" 706698	Yr.Iss.	2000	17.50	18-28

YEAR ISSUE	EDITION LIMIT	YEAR RETD.	ISSUE PRICE	*QUOTE U.S.$
1999 Arnold "You 'Putt' Me In A Great Mood" 476161	Open		17.50	18-22
2001 Astrid "It's Not The Size Of The Gift, But What's Inside That Counts!" 864218	Yr.Iss.	2001	30.00	30
2001 Austin & Alma "Let Me Call You Sweetheart" (Retailer Exclusive) 789572	Open		45.00	45
2000 Awaiting The Arrival 743801	Open		20.00	20
1994 Baby Boy Jointed (musical -"Schubert's Lullaby") 699314	Suspd.		60.00	60
1994 Baby Girl Jointed (musical -"Schubert's Lullaby") 699322	Suspd.		60.00	60
1993 Baby in Cradle (musical-"Brahms' Lullaby") 914320	Closed	2000	60.00	60
1999 Bailey & Friends 662011	Open		22.50	23
1998 Ballerina in Jewelry Box (musical -"Music Box Dancer") 331473	Open		40.00	40
1997 Barry "I'm Batty Over You" 270016	Open		17.50	18-24
1999 Baxter 644358	Open		22.50	23
1995 Bea " 'Bee' My Friend" 141348	Retrd.	1998	15.00	18-35
1994 Bear as Bunny Jointed (musical -"Here Comes Peter Cottontail") 625302	Retrd.	1996	60.00	69-120
1995 Bear Cupid Girl "Love" "Be Mine" 2 Asst 103640	Suspd.		15.00	17-42
1994 Bear Holding Harp (musical-"Love Makes The World Go Round") 916323	Retrd.	1997	40.00	50-70
1996 Bear In Bunny Outfit Resin Egg Dated 1996 156507	Yr.Iss.	1996	8.50	17-21
1998 Bear in Crib "Tucked in Teddie" (musical-"Brahm's Lullaby") 335797	Closed	1999	75.00	75
1992 Bear on Rocking Reindeer (musical-"Jingle Bells") 950815	Suspd.		60.00	138-196
1998 Bear on Swing in Tree "Picnic in the Park" (musical-"That's What Friends Are For") 335827	Closed	1999	50.00	50
1993 Bear Playing w/Train (musical -"Santa Claus is Coming to Town") 912964	Open		40.00	40
1994 Bear w/Goose (musical-"Wind Beneath My Wings") 627445	Retrd.	1997	45.00	53-63
1994 Bear w/Horse (musical-"My Favorite Things") 628565	Retrd.	1996	150.00	165-174
1994 Bear w/Rocking Reindeer (musical-"Jingle Bells") 629618	Open		165.00	165-169
1994 Bear w/Toy Chest (musical-"My Favorite Things") 627453	Open		60.00	60
1995 Beary Scary Halloween House 152382	Open		20.00	20-30
2000 Beatrice "Honey, You're The Sweetest" 786837	Open		20.00	20
1994 Becky "Springtime Happiness" 916331	Suspd.		20.00	26-65
1992 Benji "Life Is Sweet, Enjoy" 950548	Retrd.	1995	13.50	32-65
2000 Bert "I'm Busy As A Bee Every Day Of The Week 790192	Open		20.00	20
1994 Bessie "Some Bunny Loves You" 916404	Suspd.		15.00	97-163
1995 The Best Is Yet To Come 127949	Open		12.50	14-31
1995 The Best Is Yet To Come 127957	Open		12.50	14-27
1992 Beth & Blossom "Friends Are Never Far Apart" 950564	Retrd.	1997	50.00	44-127
1992 Beth & Blossom "Friends Are Never Far Apart" w/butterfly 950564	Closed	1992	50.00	98-173
1992 Beth "Bear Hugs" 950637	Retrd.	1995	17.50	32-75
1992 Beth "Happy Holidays, Deer Friend" 950807	Suspd.		22.50	39-81
1999 Bette "You Are The Star Of The Show" (1999 Adoption Center Event) 533637	Yr.Iss.	1999	20.00	20-31
1994 Betty "Bubblin' Over With Love" 626066	Open		18.50	20-47
2002 Bev, Bertha & Bethany "Friends Keep Your Spirit On Its Toes" (November Retailer Event) 104632	10,000		50.00	50
2002 Beverly & Lila "We Wish You A Merry Christmas" 104145	Yr.Iss.		25.00	25
1999 Bianca "Sweet Dreams My Little One" 533297	Retrd.	2001	15.00	15-24
1994 Billy "Everyone Needs A Cuddle", Betsey "First Step To Love" Bobbie "A Little Friendship To Share" 624896	Retrd.	1999	12.50	13-37
1994 · Billy "Everyone Needs A Cuddle" 624896	Retrd.	1999	N/A	19-22
1994 · Betsey "First Step To Love" 624896	Retrd.	1999	N/A	22-2
1994 · Bobbie "A Little Friendship To Share" 624896	Retrd.	1999	N/A	19-2
1994 Billie (spelling error) "Everyone Needs A Cuddle", Betsey "First Step To Love" Bobbie "A Little Friendship To Share" 624896	Closed	N/A	12.50	43-4
1998 Bonnie & Harold "Ring in the Holidays with Me" 466301	Retrd.	2001	25.00	25-3
2000 Booker & Fletcher "Together, Wherever We Go" (St. Jude Children's Hospital) 786861	Open		28.50	2
1995 Boy Bear Cupid "Sent With Love" 103551	Suspd.		17.50	28-3
1995 Boy Bear Flying Cupid "Sending You My Heart" 103608	Suspd.		13.00	13-1C
1998 Boy in Train Car (musical-"Toyland") 331465	Open		40.00	5
1993 Boy Praying (musical-"Jesus Loves Me") 914304	Retrd.	1997	37.50	32-7
1994 Boy/Girl in Laundry Basket (musical-"Love Will Keep Us Together") 624926	Open		60.00	60-8
1994 Boy/Girl in Sled (musical-"Oh, What a Merry Christmas Day") 651435	Closed	1998	100.00	100-11
1998 Brandon "Friendship Is My Goal" 354252	Retrd.	2001	20.00	2
1994 Breanna "Pumpkin Patch Pals" 617180	Retrd.	1998	15.00	22-7
2001 Brenna "Nothing Makes Life More Special Than Being Surrounded By Friends" (January Show Exclusive) 864315	Yr.Iss.	2001	45.00	4
1994 Bride/Groom (musical -"Mendelssohn Wedding March") 699349	Open		50.00	5
1998 Brooke "Arriving With Love And Care" 302686	Retrd.	2000	25.00	25-3
2000 Bryce "I Scored A Strike When I Met You" 731870	Open		22.50	3
1993 Buckey & Brenda "How I Love Being Friends With You" 912816	Retrd.	1995	15.00	37-1€
1993 · Brenda "How I Love Being Friends With You" 912816	Retrd.	1995	N/A	44-€
1993 · Buckey "How I Love Being Friends With You" 912816	Retrd.	1995	N/A	34-€
1995 Bunny "Just In Time For Spring" 103802	Retrd.	1998	13.50	15-
1996 Butch "Can I Be Your Football Hero?" 156388	Retrd.	1999	15.00	15-
2000 Caleb & Friends "When One Lacks Vision Another Must Provide Supervision" (Special Event) 661996	Yr.Iss.	2000	Gift	27-
1992 Camille "I'd Be Lost Without You" 950424	Retrd.	1996	20.00	28-
1997 Can't Bear To See You Under The Weather 215856	Open		15.00	15-
1999 Carlin & Janay "When I Count My Blessings, I Count You Twice" 533874	Retrd.	2001	25.00	
2001 Carlton "A Tumble In The Snow Brings Lots of Ho-Ho-Ho's!" 873438	Open		15.00	
1998 Carol "Angels Snow How To Fly" 352969	Retrd.	2000	17.50	18-
2001 Caroline "Like The Stars Of Heaven, I'll Light The Way" 864277	Open		22.50	
1993 Carolyn "Wishing You All Good Things" 912921	Retrd.	1996	22.50	32-
1995 Carrie "The Future 'Beareth' All Things" 141321	Retrd.	1998	18.50	19-
2000 Carter & Friends "Take Time For Others and Others Will Take Time For You" 706817	Open		25.00	25-
2000 Cassandra "Ghostly Greetings" 706779	Open		25.00	
1997 Cathy "An Autumn Breeze Blows Blessings To Please" 269980	Retrd.	2001	25.00	25
2000 Cecilia "You Pull At My Heartstrings" 662445 (Mother's Day Exclusive) 12 pc. 679089	Retrd.	2000	30.00	
1999 Charissa & Ashylynn "Every Journey Begins With One Step" 601578	Open		25.00	
1993 Charity "I Found A Friend In Ewe" 910678	Retrd.	1996	20.00	115-4

Collectors' Information Bureau   *Quotes have been rounded up to nearest doll

YEAR ISSUE	EDITION LIMIT	YEAR RETD.	ISSUE PRICE	*QUOTE U.S.$
1992 Charlie "The Spirit of Friendship Warms The Heart" 950742	Retrd.	1996	22.50	46-58
1993 Chelsea "Good Friends Are A Blessing" 910694	Retrd.	1995	15.00	173-390
1999 Cherish "Reach Out To Someone Around You" 476633	Retrd.	2201	12.50	13
1996 Cheryl & Carl "Wishing You A Cozy Christmas" 141216	Retrd.	1998	25.00	35-39
1995 Christian "My Prayer Is For You" 103837	Retrd.	2001	18.50	19-47
1995 Christine "My Prayer Is For You" 103845	Open		18.50	19-32
1992 Christopher "Old Friends Are The Best Friends" 950483	Open		50.00	50-75
1998 Clown on Ball (musical-"You Are My Sunshine") 336459	Open		40.00	40
2000 Clement & Jodie "Try, Try And Try Again" 706744	Open		20.00	20
1998 Cole "We've Got a Lot To Be Thankful For" (Summer Show Exclusive) 476714	Closed	1998	12.50	36-63
2000 "Collecting Cherished Friends Along The Way" 759511	10,000		50.00	50
1999 Collector Starter Kit CRT675	Open		30.00	30
1993 Connie "You're A Sweet Treat" 912794	Retrd.	1996	15.00	27-52
1999 Corey "I Know How To Take Care of Business" 676942	Open		22.50	23
1992 Couple in Basket/Umbrella Friends Are Never Far Apart (musical-"Let Me Be Your Teddy Bear") 950645	Retrd.	1997	60.00	69-180
1994 Courtney "Springtime Is A Blessing From Above" 916390	Retrd.	1996	15.00	82-132
1999 Crystal "Hang On! We're In For A Wonderful Ride" 589942	Open		20.00	20
1999 Crystal "Hang On! We're In For A Wonderful Ride" 589942R	Open		20.00	20
1995 Cupid Baby on Pillow "Little Bundle of Joy", 2 Asst. 103659	Suspd.		13.50	28-37
1995 Cupid Boy Sitting "From My Heart", "Sealed With Love", 2 Asst. 869074	Suspd.		13.50	25-32
1995 Cupid Boy/Girl Double "Aiming For Your Heart" 103594	Suspd.		25.00	26-50
1995 Cupid Boy/Girl Double "Heart to Heart", "My Love", 2 Asst. 869082	Suspd.		18.50	27-34
2001 Cynthia, Ethel, Nanette. Lola, Opal, & Janel "Love Passes From Generation To Generation" 789585	Open		50.00	50
2000 Dad, Drake & Dustee "You Have A Very Special Way Of Lifting Spirits" 661791	Open		25.00	25
1993 Daisy "Friendship Blossoms With Love" 910651	Retrd.	1996	15.00	313-499
1999 Daisy & Chelsea "Old Friends Always Find Their Way Back" (1999 Reunion Event) 597392	Open		20.00	20-32
1996 Daniel "You're My Little Pumpkin" 176214	Retrd.	1998	22.50	23-45
1997 Danielle, Sabrina, & Tiffany "We're Three Of A Kind" (1997 Adoption Center Only) 265780	Yr.Iss.	1997	35.00	45-98
1996 Debbie "Let's Hear It For Friendship!" 156361	Open		15.00	15-30
2000 Delia "You're The Beary Best Babysitter" 476536	Open		20.00	20
1999 Dennis "You Put The Spice In My Life" (1999 National Event) 510963	Yr.Iss.	1999	17.50	18-29
1999 Design Your Own Double /Raincoats Resin Figurine 726621	Yr.Iss.	1999	30.00	30
2000 Destiny & Kay "You've Never Looked More Beautiful Than You Do Today 789658	Open		25.00	25
2000 Diana "I Cherish Your Bear Hugs" (2000 Adoption Center Exclusive) 786845	Open		15.00	15
2002 Don "Friends Are The Fun Part of Life" (2002 Convention) 104039	Open		15.00	15
1995 Donald "Friends Are Egg-ceptional Blessings" 103799	Retrd.	1998	20.00	27-37
2001 Dora and Ronald "Friends Are There To Comfort Each Other" (St. Jude) 987930	Yr.Iss.	2001	17.50	18
1992 Douglas "Let's Be Friends" 950661	Retrd.	1995	20.00	37-69
2001 Drew "Being Surrounded By My Favorite Things Always Makes Things Better" (Retailer Exclusive) 864234	Open		45.00	45
1995 Earl "Warm Hearted Friends" 131873	Retrd.	1998	17.50	18-47
1999 Ed "There's A Patch In My Heart For You" 466220	Open		20.00	20
2001 Edna "The Leaves of Change Bring Back The Fondest Memories) (2001 Fall Adoption Center Exclusive) 867470	Open		45.00	45
2001 Edna "The Leaves of Change Bring Back The Fondest Memories) (2001 Fall Adoption Center Exclusive) 867470R	Open		45.00	45
1994 Elizabeth & Ashley "My Beary Best Friend" 916277	Retrd.	1996	25.00	42-65
2000 Elmer & Friends "Friends Are The Thread That Holds The Quilt of Life Together" 786691	Open		30.00	30
1994 Eric "Bear Tidings Of Joy" 622796	Retrd.	1998	22.50	25-45
1996 Erica "Friends Are Always Pulling For You" 176028	Retrd.	2000	22.50	23-29
1998 Erin "My Irish Eyes Smile When You're Near" 203068	Open		15.00	15
2000 Ernestine & Regina "I've Never Been More Proud Of You Than I Am Today 789623	Open		25.00	25
2001 Ethan "As Long As The Star Shines, I Shall Follow It" 864293	Open		20.00	20
1998 Evan "May Your Christmas Be Trimmed In Happiness" (Naled Catalog Exclusive) 484822	Open		27.50	28-37
2001 Eve "Everyone Needs Someone To Watch Over Them" 706787	Yr.Iss.	2001	45.00	45
1994 Faith "There's No Bunny Like You" 916412	Suspd.		20.00	30-60
2001 Fay "An Angel's Touch Is Never Far Away" (February Show Exclusive) 867489	Open		22.50	23
2002 Fireman Clark "You're My Hero" 106716	Open		15.00	15
1999 Flossie "I'd Stick My Neck Out For You Anytime" 589950	Open		20.00	20
1998 Frank & Helen "Snow One Like You" (Fall Catalog Exclusive) 352950	Yr.Iss.	1998	22.50	23-47
1993 Freda & Tina "Our Friendship Is A Perfect Blend" 911747	Open		35.00	35-52
1995 Gail "Catching the First Blooms of Friendship" 103772	Retrd.	1998	20.00	27-37
1993 Gary "True Friendships Are Scarce" 912786	Suspd.		18.50	25-55
1995 Girl Bear Cupid "Be My Bow" 103586	Suspd.		15.00	22-30
1995 Girl Bear Flying Cupid "Sending You My Heart" 103616	Suspd.		13.00	29-32
1995 Girl Bear on Ottoman (musical-"Au Clair De La Lune") 128058	Open		55.00	55-69
1998 Girl in Teacup with Saucer (musical -"My Favorite Things") 331457	Open		40.00	45
1993 Girl Praying (musical-"Jesus Loves Me") 914312	Retrd.	1997	37.50	37-75
1999 Glenn "By Land Or By Sea, Let's Go - Just You And Me" 477893	Yr.Iss.	1999	35.00	35
2002 Glenn Thank You Beary Much" (Thank You July Event) 104055	Open		N/A	N/A
2002 Graham "Spread Holiday Cheer To Those You Hold Dear" 104054	Open		45.00	45
1993 Gretel "We Make Magic, Me And You" 912778	Retrd.	1998	18.50	28-39
1998 Growing Better Each Year 302651	Open		22.50	23
2002 Gus & Gerhild "I Cherish Every Moment Spent With You" 105478	Open		45.00	45
2001 Guy "I Come Bearing Gifts For Everyone" 864285	Open		17.50	18
1993 Hans "Friends In Toyland" 912956	Retrd.	1995	20.00	64-111
1999 Harriet "You Make Me Feel Beautiful Inside" 476587	Open		22.50	23
1999 Hazel "I've Got A Notion To Give You A Potion!" 534129	Retrd.	1999	15.00	15-24
2000 Heather & Friends "Remembering The Simple Pleasures Of Childhood (Toys For Tots Figurine) 662038	Open		37.50	38
1993 Heidi & David "Special Friends" 910708	Suspd.		25.00	35-75
1993 Henrietta "A Basketful of Wishes" 910686	Suspd.		22.50	115-202
1994 Henry "Celebrating Spring With You" 916420	Suspd.		20.00	27-75
2002 Home Is Where The Heart Is (GoCollect Exclusive) 728608	15,000		50.00	50

Cherished Teddies/Enesco Group, Inc.
to Cherished Teddies/Enesco Group, Inc.

FIGURINES

YEAR ISSUE	EDITION LIMIT	YEAR RETD.	ISSUE PRICE	*QUOTE U.S.$
1999 Homer & Friends "Adventure Is Just Around The Corner" 662046	Open		35.00	35
1999 Honey "You're A Good Friend That Sticks Like Honey" 534099	Retrd.	1999	16.50	17-25
1995 Hope "Our Love Is Ever-Blooming" 103764	Retrd.	1998	20.00	20-45
1998 Humphrey "Just the Bear Facts, Ma'am" (1998 Regional Event Piece) 352977	Yr.Iss.	1998	15.00	40-82
1998 Hunter "Me Cavebear, You Friend" 354104	Retrd.	1999	15.00	15-26
2000 I Just Called To Say I Love You (2000 Mother's Day) 797170	Open		25.00	25
2002 Ian "Like A Snowflake, You're One-Of-A-Kind" 104141	Yr.Iss.		15.00	15
2000 Isaac, Jeremiah & Temperance "Faith Of Our Fathers" 707031	Open		30.00	30
2000 Irmgard "Your Smile Can Melt Any Heart" 706728	Yr.Iss.	2000	25.00	25
1994 Ingrid "Bundled-Up With Warm Wishes" Dated 1994 617237	Yr.Iss.	1994	20.00	35-78
1999 Irene "Time Leads Us Back To The Things We Love The Most" 476404	Open		20.00	20-27
2001 "It's Moments Like These That Are Meant To Be Cherished (Mother's Day Exclusive) 978841	Retrd.	2001	20.00	20
1999 Ivan "I've Packed My Trunk And I'm Ready To Go" 589969	Open		20.00	20
2001 I've Always Cherished Your Love and Guidance (Father's Day Exclusive) 104889	Retrd.	2001	20.00	20
1992 Jacob "Wishing For Love" 950734	Suspd		22.50	22-46
1996 Jamie & Ashley "I'm All Wrapped Up In Your Love" 141224	Retrd.	1998	25.00	35-45
2000 Jan & Elise "This is The Start of Your Bright and Exciting Future" 789666	Open		17.50	18
1998 Janet "You're Sweet As A Rose" (Avon Exclusive) 336521	Open		9.00	9
2001 Janice "You Suit Me Perfectly" (2001 Regional Event) 661910	Open		15.00	15
1999 Jasmine "A Bouquet Of Blessings For You" (GCC Exclusive) 202940	Open		15.00	15
1992 Jasmine "You Have Touched My Heart" 950475	Suspd.		22.50	27-104
1997 Jean "Cup Full Of Peace" 269859	Retrd.	2000	25.00	25
1994 Jedediah "Giving Thanks For Friends" 617091	Retrd.	1997	17.50	22-46
1996 Jeffrey "Striking Up Another Year" Dated 1996 176044	Yr.Iss.	1996	17.50	18-35
1995 Jennifer "Gathering The Blooms of Friendship" 103810	Retrd.	1998	22.50	23-65
1992 Jeremy "Friends Like You Are Precious And Few" 950521	Retrd.	1995	15.00	25-110
1999 Jerrod "Don't Worry - It's Just Another Little Bump In The Road" 589926	Open		20.00	20
1997 Jessica "A Mother's Heart Is Full of Love" 155438	Retrd.	1997	25.00	27-48
1996 Jessica "A Mother's Heart Is Full of Love" (GCC Early Introduction) 155438A	Retrd.	1996	25.00	46-143
2000 Jessie 2000 National Convention 706655	Yr.Iss.	2000	175.00	175
2002 Jill "I'm Always Good For a Soft Cuddle And A Warm Hug" 199869	Yr.Iss.		50.00	50
1999 Joe "Love Only Gets Better With Age" 476412	Open		15.00	15-30
1999 John & William "When Friends Meet, Hearts Warm" 533858	Retrd.	1999	35.00	35
1993 Jointed Bear Christmas (musical-"Jingle Bells") 903337	Suspd.		60.00	80-110
1998 Joseph "Everyone Has Their 'Old Friends' to Hug" (Palmer Catalog Exclusive) 476471A	Open		25.00	25-43
2002 Josette "You Are The Key To My Heart" (Valentine Gift Set) 805610S	Yr.Iss.		20.00	20
1992 Joshua "Love Repairs All" 950556	Retrd.	1997	20.00	20-31
2000 Jude "Love Is The Beary Best Bedtime Story" (St. Jude Philanthropic begin) 506818	Open		17.50	18
1999 Junior "Everyone Is A Bear's Best Friend" 476641	Retrd.	2001	12.50	13-19
1997 Kara "You're A Honey Of A Friend" Adoption Center (1997 National Event) 265799	Yr.Iss.	1997	15.00	30-50
2001 Karen and Jeff "Sometimes The Road Can Be Bumpy, So Just Keep Pedaling Away" (Scleroderma Research Foundation) 979279	Yr.Iss.	2001	25.00	25
1994 Kathleen "Luck Found Me A Friend In You" 916447	Retrd.	1999	12.50	15-36
1992 Katie "A Friend Always Knows When You Need A Hug" 950440	Retrd.	1997	20.00	29-47
1999 Katie, Renee, Jessica, Matthew "I'm Surrounded By Hugs" 538299	Yr.Iss.	1999	25.00	25-58
2001 Katrina and Forrest - "Each Chapter Brings Us Closer Together" (2001 Adoption Center Exclusive) 101687	Yr.Iss.	2001	17.50	18
2001 Katrina, Fritz & Forrest - Goldilocks and The Three Bears "Friendship Appears In The Most Unlikely Places" (2001 Adoption Center Exclusive) 795607	10,000		35.00	35
1999 Kayla "Big Hearts Come In Small Packages" (January Show Exclusive) 533815	Open		20.00	20-38
1998 Keith & Deborah "The Holidays Are Twice As 'Ice' " 354244	Retrd.	2001	30.00	30-3
1994 Kelly "You're My One And Only" 916307	Suspd.		15.00	45-6
1999 Kent "Officer , I've Got a Warrant Out For Your Heart" 476560	Open		20.00	2
1999 Kent "Officer , I've Got a Warrant Out For Your Heart" 476560R	Open		20.00	2
1995 Kevin "Good Luck To You" 103896	Retrd.	1996	12.50	22-3
2000 Kim "Treat Yourself To Life's Little Pleasures" 661872	Open		17.50	1
1995 Kiss The Hurt And Make It Well 127965	Open		15.00	25-2
1996 Kittie "You Make Wishes Come True" (1996 Adoption Center Event) 131663	Yr.Iss.	1996	17.50	39-6
1995 Kristen "Hugs of Love And Friendship" 141194	Retrd.	1998	20.00	20-4
1998 Kyle "Even Though We're Far Apart, You'll Always Have A Place In My Heart" 476390	Retrd.	2001	15.00	1
1999 Lacey "Cherish the Little Things in Life" (Paint Your Own Resin Figurine) 662453A	Yr.Iss.	1999	25.00	25-3
1998 Lance "Come Fly With Me" (1998 National Event Piece) 337463	Yr.Iss.	1998	20.00	25-4
1997 Larry "You're My Shooting Star" 203440	Retrd.	2001	17.50	18-2
1996 Laura "Friendship Makes It All Better" 156396	Open		15.00	15-2
1997 Lee "You're A Bear's Best Friend" 272167	Yr.Iss.	1997	20.00	25-3
2002 "Let's Celebrate" (2002 Fall Adoption Center Event) 104628	Open		15.00	1
1998 Libby "My Country Tis Of Thee" 305979	Retrd.	1998	20.00	30-4
1997 Lily "Lilies Bloom With Petals of Hope" (Spring Catalog Exclusive) 202959A	Retrd.	2000	15.00	17-3
1996 Linda "ABC And 1-2-3, You're A Friend To Me!" 156426	Open		15.00	15-2
1996 Lindsey & Lyndon "Walking In A Winter Wonderland" (Fall Catalog Exclusive) 141178A	Yr.Iss.	1996	30.00	30-7
1995 Lisa "My Best Is Always You" 103780	Retrd.	1998	20.00	27-4
1998 Lori "Those We Love Should Be Cherished" 476439	Open		17.50	18-2
1998 Lou "Take Me Out To The Ball Game" 203432	Retrd.	2001	15.00	15-2
1999 Lydia "You're the Bees Knees" 661929	Open		27.50	28-4
1997 Lynn "A Handmade Holiday Wish" (Fall Catalog Exclusive) 310735A	Yr.Iss.	1997	25.00	40-7
1998 Lynn "A Handmade Holiday Wish" 310735	Retrd.	2001	25.00	25-4
1995 Madeline "A Cup Full of Friendship" 135593	Retrd.	1999	20.00	2
1992 Mandy "I Love You Just The Way You Are" 950572	Retrd.	1995	15.00	32-5
1999 Marcus "There's Nobody I'd Rather Go 'Round With Than You" 589934	Open		20.00	2
1995 Margaret "A Cup Full of Love" 103667	Retrd.	1999	20.00	20-4
1998 Margy (Avon Exclusive) 475602	Retrd.	1998	19.99	35-4
1993 Marie "Friendship Is A Special Treat" 910767	Retrd.	1999	20.00	20-4

YEAR ISSUE	EDITION LIMIT	YEAR RETD.	ISSUE PRICE	*QUOTE U.S.$
1995 Marilyn "A Cup Full of Cheer" 135682	Retrd.	1999	20.00	27-30
1998 Marlene and Marissa "Good Friends Are Always Beary Near" 368164	Closed	1998	Gift	94-115
1998 Marty "I'll Always Be There For You" (Summer Show Exclusive) 476722	Closed	1998	12.50	36-103
1993 Mary "A Special Friend Warms The Season" 912840	Retrd.	2000	25.00	25-52
1999 Matt And Vicki "Love Is The Best Thing Two Can Share" 476781	Yr.Iss.	1999	35.00	35-49
1995 Maureen "Lucky Friend" 135690	Retrd.	1996	12.50	22-31
1995 Melissa "Every Bunny Needs A Friend" 103829	Retrd.	1998	20.00	22-37
1999 Merideth "You're As Cozy As A Pair of Mittens! 534226	Retrd.	2001	10.00	10
2001 Mermaid Waterglobe (2001 Summer Adoption Center Exclusive) 865079	Open		45.00	45
1993 Michael & Michelle "Friendship Is A Cozy Feeling" 910775	Suspd.		30.00	52-104
1998 Mike "I'm Sweet On You" (1998 Adoption Center Only) 356255	Yr.Iss.	1998	15.00	25-32
1993 Miles "I'm Thankful For A Friend Like You" 912751	Retrd.	1998	17.50	22-45
1995 Millie, Christy, Dorothy "A. Love Me Tender, B. Take Me To Your Heart, C. Love Me True" 128023	Retrd.	1996	37.50	24-69
1995 • Dorothy- "C. Love Me True" 128023	Retrd.	1996	12.50	35-75
1995 • Millie-"A. Love Me Tender 128023	Retrd.	1996	12.50	35-70
1995 • Christy, " B. Take Me To Your Heart 128023	Retrd.	1996	12.50	32-70
1999 Milt & Garrett "A Haunting We Will Go" 534137	Retrd.	1999	20.00	20
1999 Milton "Wishing For A Future As Bright As The Stars" (Millennium Event) 542644	Open		20.00	20
2000 Mimi, Darci and Misty "There's Always Time For Friends and Tea" (Show Exclusive) 786578	Open		50.00	50
1996 Mindy "Friendship Keeps Me On My Toes" 156418	Open		15.00	15
1998 Miranda "No Matter How Blue You Feel, A Hug Can Heal" (Summer Show Exclusive) 476706	Closed	1998	12.50	30-44
1993 Molly "Friendship Softens A Bumpy Ride" 910759	Retrd.	1996	30.00	34-72
1998 Mother Goose and Friends "Friends of a Feather Flock Together" 154016	Open		50.00	50
1994 Nancy "Your Friendship Makes My Heart Sing" 916315	Retrd.	1996	15.00	86-163
1999 Natalie "You Make Me Smile From Ear To Ear" 534110	Retrd.	1999	15.00	15
1998 Nathan "Leave Your Worries Behind" 176222	Retrd.	2001	17.50	18-27
1992 Nathaniel & Nellie "It's Twice As Nice With You" 950513	Retrd.	1996	30.00	27-46
1997 Newton "Ringing In The New Year With Cheer" 272361	Retrd.	2001	15.00	15-25
1999 Nikki "A Cold Winter's Day Won't Keep Me Away" 534218	Retrd.	2001	10.00	10
1994 Nils "Near And Deer For Christmas" 617245	Retrd.	1997	22.50	47-65
1997 Nina "Beary Happy Wishes" (1997 National Event Piece) 215864	Yr.Iss.	1997	17.50	20-27
1999 Norbit & Nyla "A Friend Is Someone Who Reaches For Your Hand And Touches Your Heart 534188	Yr.Iss.	1999	25.00	25-50
1999 Norm "Patience Is A Fisherman's Virtue" 476765	Open		25.00	25-37
2000 Norma (2000 Regional Event Piece) 706639	Yr.Iss.	2000	65.00	65
2002 Northrup "You Make Every Place Merrier" 104139	Yr.Iss.		40.00	40
1996 Olga "Feel The Peace...Hold The Joy...Share The Love" 182966	Yr.Iss.	1996	50.00	32-72
1994 Oliver & Olivia "Will You Be Mine?" 916641	Suspd.		25.00	47-65
1996 Our Hearts Are One (Artist Gallery) 186465	Yr.Iss.	1996	30.00	45
2000 Palmer and Charlene "Clowning Around" 786586	Open		25.00	25
1996 Park Bench w/Bears "Heart to Heart" (1996 National Event Piece) CRT240	Yr.Iss.	1996	12.50	20-39
1995 Paul "Falling For You" 141313	Open		22.50	23-46
1994 Patience "Happiness Is Homemade" 617105	Retrd.	1997	17.50	35-65
1993 Patrice "Thank You For The Sky So Blue" 911429	Retrd.	1999	18.50	24-42
1993 Patrick "Thank You For A Friend That's True" 911410	Retrd.	1999	18.50	25-50
2000 Patty & Peggy "Spending Time With You Is Priceless" 789631	Open		25.00	25
1999 Paul "Good Friends Warm The Heart With Many Blessings" (1999 Adoption Center Exclusive) 466328	Yr.Iss.	1999	22.50	25-40
1998 Penny, Chandler, Boots "We're Inseparable" (1998 Adoption Center Exclusive) 337579	Yr.Iss.	1998	25.00	37-69
1995 Peter "You're Some Bunny Special" 104973	Retrd.	1998	17.50	22-32
1994 Phoebe "A Little Friendship Is A Big Blessing" 617113	Retrd.	1995	13.50	22-39
1993 Priscilla "Love Surrounds Our Friendship" 910724	Retrd.	1997	15.00	27-39
1995 Priscilla & Greta "Our Hearts Belong to You" 128031	Yr.Iss.	1995	50.00	52-109
1993 Prudence "A Friend To Be Thankful For" 912808	Retrd.	1998	17.00	23-31
1996 Pumpkins/Corn Stalk/Scarecrow Mini 3 Asst. 176206	Open		15.00	15-27
1999 Randy "You're Never Alone With Good Friends Around" 476498	Open		22.50	23-35
2000 Ralph "Bring Joy To Those You Hold Dear" 706841	Open		17.50	18
1997 Rex "Our Friendship Will Never Be Extinct" 269999	Open		17.50	18-28
1998 Rich "Always Paws For Holiday Treats" 352721	Yr.Iss.	1998	22.50	34-40
1999 Rita "Wishing You Love Straight From The Heart" (NALED Exclusive) 476617	Open		17.50	18-47
1993 Robbie & Rachel "Love Bears All Things" 911402	Retrd.	1999	27.50	30-48
1996 Robert "Love Keeps Me Afloat" 156272	Retrd.	1999	13.50	14-37
1999 Rodney "I'm Santa's Little Helper" 646504	Yr.Iss.	1999	25.00	25-32
2000 Roberta "Being Your Friend Is My Favorite Pastime" 789615	Open		15.00	15
2000 Ron "Enjoy The Simple Comforts Of Life" (2000 Adoption Center) 706647	25,000		20.00	20-30
2002 Rose, Melinda, Jacki, Christopher and Friends "Reunited For A Day, Together For A Lifetime. 10 Cherished Years" (10th Anniversary) 935077	Open		95.00	95
2000 Rosemarie & Ronald "A Hug Is Worth A Thousand Words, A Friend Is Worth More" 706981	Open		27.50	28-40
2002 Roosevelt "Nothing's Better Than 'A Teddie Bear' Hug (2002 Adoption Center Exclusive) 789755	Yr.Iss.		22.50	23
2002 Rosemary "Colorful Days Are Spent With You" (June Show Exclusive) 811750	Retrd.	2001	22.50	23
1999 Roxie & Shelly "What A Story We Share!" 601586	Open		25.00	25
1998 Roy "I'm Your Country Cowboy" (Special Limited Edition) 466298	Closed	1998	17.50	30-40
1998 Roy "I'm Your Country Cowboy" 466298 & Sierra "You're My Partner" (Special Limited Edtion) 466271, set/2	Closed	1998	25.00	28-30
2000 Russell & Ross "Thanks For Teaching Me About The Real World" 661783	Open		22.50	22
2001 Rusty "Take A Leap of Faith" (Fall Show Special) 100057	Open		35.00	35
1999 Ruth And Gene "Even When We Don't See Eye To Eye We're Always Heart To Heart" 476668	Open		25.00	25
1997 Ryan "I'm Green With Envy For You" 203041	Open		20.00	20-28
1999 Sally And Skip "We Make A Perfect Team" 1999 Adoption Center 510955	25,000	1999	27.50	28-37
1998 Sam "I Want You...To Be My Friend" 302619	Retrd.	1998	17.50	27-40
1992 Sara "LoveYa", Jacki Hugs & Kisses", Karen "Best Buddy" 950432	Open		10.00	27-52

*Quotes have been rounded up to nearest dollar

FIGURINES

YEAR ISSUE	EDITION LIMIT	YEAR RETD.	ISSUE PRICE	*QUOTE U.S.$
1992 • Jacki Hugs & Kisses" 950432	Open		N/A	17-22
1992 • Karen "Best Buddy" 950432	Open		N/A	17-52
1992 • Sara "LoveYa" 950432	Open		N/A	22-52
1999 Sarah "Memories To Wear And Share" 308676	Yr.Iss.	1999	30.00	30-45
1999 Sawyer & Friends "Hold On To The Past, But Look To The Future" 662003	Open		27.50	28
1994 Sean "Luck Found Me A Friend In You" 916439	Retrd.	1999	12.50	20-27
1999 Sedley "We've Turned Over A New Leaf On Our Friendship" 534102	Retrd.	2001	16.50	17-29
1998 Segrid, Justaf, Ingmar "The Spirit of Christmas Grows In Our Hearts" 352799	Yr.Iss.	1998	45.00	45-75
1995 Seth & Sarabeth "We're Beary Good Pals" 128015	Retrd.	1999	25.00	25-50
1998 Shannon "A Figure 8, Our Friendship Is Great!" 354260	Open		20.00	20-30
2002 Shelia "Sometimes You Just Need A Little Peace And Quiet!" (Retailer Exclusive) 851809	Open		45.00	45
1998 Sierra "You're My Partner" (Special Limited Edition) 466271	Closed	1998	17.50	30-45
1999 Simone & Jhodi "I've Always Believed In You" 601551	Open		25.00	25
1998 Sixteen Candles and Many More Wishes 302643	Open		22.50	23
1999 Skylar & Shana "When You Find A Sunbeam, Share The Warmth" 601594	Open		25.00	25
1994 Sonja "Holiday Cuddles" 622818	Retrd.	1998	20.00	26-32
2001 Sonny "A Getting Ready For Santa's Visit" 864307	Open		22.50	23
1999 Spanky "Friendship Can Sometimes Be Bumpy But It's Worth It" (America's Promise) 644382	Open		27.50	28-39
2000 Sparky "Your Cheerful Ways Bring Better Days" 789879	Open		15.00	15
1994 Stacie "You Lift My Spirit" 617148	Retrd.	1998	18.50	24-35
1999 Stanley & Valerie "Togetherness Is The Reason We Have Friends" 476676	Open		35.00	35
1999 Star "Cherish Yesterday, Dream Tomorrow, Live Today" 534250	Yr.Iss.	1999	55.00	55-75
2000 Stella "Touches of Heaven Can Be Found On Earth" 706795	Open		22.50	23
1992 Steven "A Season Filled With Sweetness" 951129	Retrd.	1995	20.00	37-59
2000 Sullivan "The Most Important Truth Is To Be Your True Self" 706760	Open		17.50	18
1997 Sven & Liv "All Paths Lead To Kindness & Friendship" 272159	Yr.Iss.	1997	55.00	50-72
1997 Sylvia "A Picture Perfect Friendship" (Regional Event Piece) 265810	Yr.Iss.	1997	15.00	32-98
1996 Tabitha "You're The Cat's Meow" 176257	Retrd.	1998	15.00	25-30
1999 Tammy "Let's Go To The Hop" (1999 Regional Event) 510947	Yr.Iss.	1999	15.00	52-70
1998 Tanna "When Your Hands Are Full, There's Still Room In Your Heart" (Summer Show Exclusive) 476595	Closed	1998	12.50	44-63
1996 Tasha "In Grandmother's Attic" (1996 Adoption Center Exclusive) 156353	19,960	1996	55.00	93-138
1994 Taylor "Sail The Seas With Me" 617156	Suspd.		15.00	22-45
1999 Teddy "Friends Give You Wings To Fly" 476757	Open		15.00	15-22
1999 Tess & Friends "Things Do Not Change, We Do" 661953	Open		27.50	28
2001 Terry "Always Stay On Track About The True Meaning Of Christmas" 865095	Open		22.50	23
1999 Terry Gift Set 686999	Open		30.00	30
1994 Thanksgiving Quilt 617075	Suspd.		12.00	12-20
1992 Theodore, Samantha & Tyler "Friends Come In All Sizes" 950505	Open		20.00	22-44
1993 Theodore, Samantha & Tyler "Friendship Weathers All Storms" (9") 912883	Suspd.		160.00	160-200
1993 Theodore, Samantha & Tyler "Friendship Weathers All Storms" (musical-"Jingle Bells") 904546	Suspd.		170.00	230-300
1992 Theodore, Samantha & Tyler "Friendship Weathers All Storms" 950769	Retrd.	1997	20.00	38-65
1992 Theodore, Samantha & Tyler (9") "Friends Come In All Sizes" 951196	Retrd.	1999	130.00	130-196
1997 This Calls For A Celebration 215910	Open		15.00	15
1993 Thomas "Chuggin' Along", Jonathan "Sail With Me", Harrison "We're Going Places" 911739	Retrd.	1997	15.00	34-40
1993 • Thomas "Chuggin' Along" 911739	Retrd.	1997	N/A	25-40
1993 • Jonathan "Sail With Me" 911739	Retrd.	1997	N/A	30-39
1993 • Harrison "We're Going Places" 911739	Retrd.	1997	N/A	22-34
1993 Timothy "A Friend Is Forever" 910740	Retrd.	1996	15.00	22-46
2000 Todd & Friend "Share Life's Little Joys With Your Closest Friends" 786683	Open		25.00	25
2001 Tori "Friends Are The Sweetest Part Of Life" 676845	Open		Gift	N/A
1995 Town Tattler Sign (1995 National Event Piece) CRT109	Yr.Iss.	1995	6.00	17-24
1998 Toy Cabinet "My Cherished Treasures" (musical-"My Favorite Things") 335681	Closed	1998	100.00	100
1993 Tracie & Nicole "Side By Side With Friends" 911372	Retrd.	1999	35.00	37-63
1998 Trevor "You Bring Out The Devil In Me" 354112	Retrd.	2001	17.50	18-27
2000 Trina "My Memories of You Are Kept In My Heart" (Paint Your Own Resin Figurine) 676985	Retrd.	2001	30.00	30
2001 Troy "Life's A Beach" (2001 Regional Event) 864366	Open		17.50	18
1995 Tucker & Travis "We're in This Together" 127973	Retrd.	2001	25.00	25-37
1996 Two Boys By Lamp Post (musical-"The First Noel") 141089	Open		50.00	50-58
1995 UK Bears, Bertie "Friends Forever Near or Far" (International Exclusive) 163457	Suspd.		17.50	35-63
1995 UK Bears, Duncan "Your Friendship Is Music To My Ears" (International Exclusive) 163473	Suspd.		17.50	32-63
1995 UK Bears, Gordon "Keepin' A Watchful Eye on You" (International Exclusive) 163465	Suspd.		17.50	32-63
1995 UK Bears, Sherlock "Good Friends Are Hard To Find" (International Exclusive) 163481	Suspd.		17.50	32-125
1995 UK Bears, set/4 (Bertie 163457, Gordon 163465, Duncan 163473, Sherlock 163481)	Suspd.		70.00	104-260
1999 Valentine Watch & Figurine Gift Set 738638	Closed	2000	30.00	30
1998 Veronica "You Make Happiness Bloom" (Spring Catalog Exclusive) 366854	Yr.Iss.	1998	15.00	22-39
1994 Victoria "From My Heart To Yours" 916293	Suspd.		16.50	75-145
1996 Violet "Blessings Bloom When You Are Near" 156280	Retrd.	1999	15.00	17-35
2000 Wanda "A Sprinkling Of Fairy Dust Will Make You Feel Better 786705	Open		20.00	20
2002 Wes "Giddy Up Horsy" (2002 Adoption Center Exclusive) 851523	Yr.Iss.		22.50	23
1999 Wesley, Phillip, Fiona, Renee (1999 I.C.E. piece) 476846	Retrd.	1999	30.00	69
2000 When I Need A Hug, I Run To Dad! 770469	Open		15.00	15
1998 Whitney "We Make A Winning Team" 302678	Open		15.00	22-25
1994 Willie "Bears Of A Feather Stay Together" 617164	Retrd.	1997	15.00	27-32
2000 Willow "Cherished Your Spirit" 661759	Open		35.00	35
1994 Winfield "Anything Is Possible When You Wish On A Star" (Millenium Edition) 476811	Open		50.00	27-58
1994 Winona "Little Fair Feather Friend" 617172	Retrd.	1997	15.00	25-50
1999 Woody "You Hold Everything in Place" 476544	Open		20.00	20
1994 Wyatt "I'm Called Little Running Bear" 629707	Retrd.	1998	15.00	20-45
1994 Wylie "I'm Called Little Friend" 617121	Retrd.	1998	15.00	20-45
2002 Yolanda "You Can Never Disguise A Kind And Loving Heart" (2002 Convention Piece) 104041	Open		15.00	15
1998 You're The Frosting on the Birthday Cake 306398	Open		22.50	23-34

FIGURINES

Cherished Teddies/Enesco Group, Inc.
to Cherished Teddies/Enesco Group, Inc.

YEAR ISSUE	EDITION LIMIT	YEAR RETD.	ISSUE PRICE	*QUOTE U.S.$
1992 Zachary "Yesterday's Memories Are Today's Treasures" 950491	Retrd.	1997	30.00	32-81

Special Limited Edition - P. Hillman

YEAR ISSUE	EDITION LIMIT	YEAR RETD.	ISSUE PRICE	*QUOTE U.S.$
1993 Holding On To Someone Special -Collector Appreciation Fig. 916285	Yr.Iss.	1993	20.00	144-200
1994 Priscilla Ann "There's No One Like Hue" Collectible Exposition Exclusive available only at Secaucus and South Bend in 1994 and at Long Beach in 1995 CRT025	Yr.Iss.	1994	50.00	144-260
1993 Teddy & Roosevelt "The Book of Teddies 1903-1993" (90th Anniversary Commemorative) 624918	Yr.Iss.	1993	20.00	109-215

Across The Seas - P. Hillman

YEAR ISSUE	EDITION LIMIT	YEAR RETD.	ISSUE PRICE	*QUOTE U.S.$
1997 Bazza "I'm Lost Down Under Without You" 276995	Retrd.	1999	17.50	18-24
1996 Bob with Passport "Our Friendship Is From Sea To Shining Sea" 202444P	Retrd.	1999	17.50	23-35
1996 Carlos "I Found An Amigo In You" 202339	Retrd.	1999	17.50	27-49
1996 Claudette "Our Friendship Is Bon Appetit!" 197254	Retrd.	1999	17.50	18-25
1998 Colleen "The Luck Of The Irish To You" 373966	Retrd.	1999	17.50	30-49
1996 Fernando "You Make Everday A Fiesta" 202355	Retrd.	1999	17.50	17-49
1996 Franz "Our Friendship Knows No Boundaries" 202436	Retrd.	1999	17.50	24-30
1996 Katrien "Tulips Blossom With Friendship" 202401	Retrd.	1999	17.50	18-32
1996 Kerstin "You're The Swedish of Them All" 197289	Retrd.	1999	17.50	18-24
1998 Leilani "Tahiti - Sending You Warm And Friendly Island Breezes" 302627	Retrd.	1998	17.50	63
1996 Lian "Our Friendship Spans Many Miles" 202347	Retrd.	1998	17.50	18-35
1996 Lorna "Our Love Is In The Highlands" 202452	Retrd.	1999	17.50	18-24
1996 Machiko "Love Fans A Beautiful Friendship" 202312	Retrd.	1998	17.50	18-30
1996 Nadia "From Russia, With Love" 202320	Retrd.	1999	17.50	18-27
1996 Preston "Riding Across The Great White North" 216739	Retrd.	1998	17.50	18-49
1996 Rajul "You're The Jewel Of My Heart" 202398	Retrd.	1999	17.50	18
1997 Sophia "Like Grapes On The Vine, Our Friendship Is Divine" 276987	Retrd.	1999	17.50	18-27
1996 William "You're a Jolly Ol' Chap!" 202878	Retrd.	1999	17.50	18-21

American Classics Collection - P. Hillman

YEAR ISSUE	EDITION LIMIT	YEAR RETD.	ISSUE PRICE	*QUOTE U.S.$
2001 Colby - "Sometimes Life Needs A Little Push" 778311	Open		20.00	20
2000 Jerald & Mary Ann "What Would Game Night Be Without You" 811742	Open		32.50	33
2001 Johanna - "Hold On To What Life Brings With Both Hands" 845132	Open		20.00	20

American Heroes Collection - P. Hillman

YEAR ISSUE	EDITION LIMIT	YEAR RETD.	ISSUE PRICE	*QUOTE U.S.$
2000 Daniel "You're The Finest Friend in the Forest" 676861	Open		22.50	23
2001 George - "Wishing You Waves Of Discovery In The Future" 545953	Open		17.50	18
2001 Lincoln "Four Score And Seven Years Ago" 281891	Open		17.50	18
2000 Paul "You Can Always Trust Me To Be There" 676888	Open		20.00	20

The Angel Series - P. Hillman

YEAR ISSUE	EDITION LIMIT	YEAR RETD.	ISSUE PRICE	*QUOTE U.S.$
1998 Angela "Peace On Earth And Mercy Mild" 175986	Yr.Iss.	1998	20.00	26-42
1997 Grace "Glory To The Newborn King" 175994	Yr.Iss.	1997	20.00	22-41
1996 Stormi "Hark The Herald Angels Sing" 176001	Yr.Iss.	1996	20.00	32-52

Anniversary Figurines - P. Hillman

YEAR ISSUE	EDITION LIMIT	YEAR RETD.	ISSUE PRICE	*QUOTE U.S.$
1997 You Grow More Dear With Each Passing Year 215880	Open		25.00	25
1998 A Decade of Teddy Bear Love 302694 (10 Yr. Anniversary)	Open		30.00	30-52

YEAR ISSUE	EDITION LIMIT	YEAR RETD.	ISSUE PRICE	*QUOTE U.S.$
1998 25 Years To Treasure Together 302708 (25 Yr. Anniversary)	Open		30.00	30
1998 Forever Yours, Forever True 302716 (40 or 50 Yr. Anniversary)	Open		30.00	30

Antique Toy Minis - P. Hillman

YEAR ISSUE	EDITION LIMIT	YEAR RETD.	ISSUE PRICE	*QUOTE U.S.$
1999 A Big Hug From A Little Friend 537217	Open		12.50	13
1999 Everyone Needs An Occasional Hug 537187	Open		12.50	13
1999 Follow Your Heart Wherever It Takes You 537241	Open		12.50	13
1999 A Friend Is An Answered Prayer 537233	Open		12.50	13
1999 A Journey With You Is One To Remember 537268	Open		12.50	13
1999 Keep Good Friends Close To Your Heart 537195	Open		12.50	13
1999 Our Friendship Is An Adventure 537209	Open		12.50	13
1999 You Have The Biggest Heart of All 537225	Open		12.50	13

Beta Is For Bear - P. Hillman

YEAR ISSUE	EDITION LIMIT	YEAR RETD.	ISSUE PRICE	*QUOTE U.S.$
1998 Alpha 305995	Open		7.50	8
1998 Beta 306002	Open		7.50	8
1998 Gamma 306010	Open		7.50	8
1998 Delta 306037	Open		7.50	8
1998 Epsilon 306045	Open		7.50	8
1998 Zeta 306053	Open		7.50	8
1998 Eta 306088	Open		7.50	8
1998 Theta 306096	Open		7.50	8
1998 Iota 306118	Open		7.50	8
1998 Kappa 306126	Open		7.50	8
1998 Lambda 306134	Open		7.50	8
1998 Mu 306142	Open		7.50	8
1998 Nu 306150	Open		7.50	8
1998 Xi 306185	Open		7.50	8
1998 Omicron 306193	Open		7.50	8
1998 Pi 306207	Open		7.50	8
1998 Rho 306215	Open		7.50	8
1998 Sigma 306223	Open		7.50	8
1998 Tau 306231	Open		7.50	8
1998 Upsilon 306258	Open		7.50	8
1998 Phi 306266	Open		7.50	8
1998 Chi 306274	Open		7.50	8
1998 Psi 306282	Open		7.50	8
1998 Omega 306290	Open		7.50	8

Blossoms of Friendship - P. Hillman

YEAR ISSUE	EDITION LIMIT	YEAR RETD.	ISSUE PRICE	*QUOTE U.S.$
1997 Dahlia "You're The Best Pick of the Bunch" 202932	Retrd.	2000	15.00	15-27
1997 Iris "You're The Iris of My Eye" 202908	Retrd.	2000	15.00	15-27
1998 Lily "Lilies Bloom With Petals Of Hope" 202959	Retrd.	2000	15.00	15
1997 Rose "Everything's Coming Up Roses" 202886	Retrd.	2000	15.00	15-25
1997 Susan "Love Stems From Our Friendship" 202894	Retrd.	2000	15.00	15-25

By The Sea, By The Sea - P. Hillman

YEAR ISSUE	EDITION LIMIT	YEAR RETD.	ISSUE PRICE	*QUOTE U.S.$
1997 Gregg "Everything Pails in Comparison To Friends" 203505	Retrd.	2000	20.00	20-22
1997 Jerry "Ready To Make a Splash" 203475	Retrd.	2000	17.50	18-27
1997 Jim and Joey "Underneath It All We're Forever Friends" 203513	Retrd.	2000	25.00	25-37
1997 Judy "I'm Your Bathing Beauty" 203491	Retrd.	2000	35.00	27-47
1997 Sandy "There's Room In My Sand Castle For You" 203467	Retrd.	2000	20.00	20-32

Carousels - P. Hillman

YEAR ISSUE	EDITION LIMIT	YEAR RETD.	ISSUE PRICE	*QUOTE U.S.$
1999 Archie "Through Ups and Downs, You're Still The Best Friend Around" 589077	Open		20.00	20
1998 Bill "Friends Like You Are Always True Blue" 505552	Retrd.	2000	20.00	20
1998 Cody "I'll Cherish You For Many Moons" 505498	Retrd.	2000	20.00	20
1999 Crystal "Hang On! We're In For a Wonderful Ride" 589942	Open		20.00	20
1999 Flossie "I'd Stick My Neck Out For You Anytime" 589950	Open		20.00	20

FIGURINES

YEAR ISSUE	EDITION LIMIT	YEAR RETD.	ISSUE PRICE	*QUOTE U.S.$
1998 Gina "Where Friends Gather, Magic Blossoms" 502898	Retrd.	2000	20.00	20
1999 Ivan "I've Packed My Trunk And I'm Ready To Go" 589969	Open		20.00	20
1998 Jason "When It Comes To Friendship, You've Really Earned Your Stripes" 506214	Retrd.	2000	20.00	20
1998 Jenelle "A Friend is Somebunny to Cherish Forever" 505579	Retrd.	2000	20.00	20
1999 Jerrod "Don't Worry - It's Just Another Little Bump in the Road" 589926	Open		20.00	20
1999 Marcus "There's Nobody I'd Rather Go 'Round With Than You" 589934	Open		20.00	20
1998 Virginia "It's So Merry Going 'Round With You 506206	Retrd.	2000	20.00	20

Cherished Memories - P. Hillman

YEAR ISSUE	EDITION LIMIT	YEAR RETD.	ISSUE PRICE	*QUOTE U.S.$
2001 Candy - "You Are A Sweetie" 864323	Open		22.50	23
2001 Charlotte And Elaine - "A Woman's Work Is Never Done!" 864226	Open		25.00	25
2001 Judy & Diane "Always Remember I'm Just A Phone Call Away" 864382	Open		25.00	25
2001 Krista - "No Pain, No Gain!" 199389	Open		15.00	15
2001 Lucille - "Friends Like You Are Cherished And Few" 786543	Open		25.00	25
2001 Lucinda - "We'll Always Be, Just You And Me" 199771	Open		25.00	25
2001 May All Your Birthday Wishes Come True 864390	Open		15.00	15
2001 Vince And Connor - "Shooting For Keeps" 789801	Open		25.00	25

The Cherished Seasons - P. Hillman

YEAR ISSUE	EDITION LIMIT	YEAR RETD.	ISSUE PRICE	*QUOTE U.S.$
1997 Megan "Spring Brings A Season Of Beauty" 203300	Retrd.	2001	20.00	20-28
1997 Kimberly "Summer Brings A Season Of Warmth" 203335	Retrd.	2001	22.50	23-28
1997 Hannah "Autumn Brings A Season Of Thanksgiving" 203343	Retrd.	2001	20.00	20-28
1997 Gretchen "Winter Brings A Season Of Joy" 203351	Retrd.	2001	25.00	25-33

Cherished Snowbears - P. Hillman

YEAR ISSUE	EDITION LIMIT	YEAR RETD.	ISSUE PRICE	*QUOTE U.S.$
2002 Adam, Claire & Kristy "From Big To Small, Our Family Has It All 104066	Open		25.00	25
2000 Buddy "And The North Wind Shall Blow" 706892	Open		25.00	25
2001 Delight "I Will Melt Your Heart" 848573	Open		25.00	25
2001 Erika "Remember The Past, Cherish The Years Ahead" 865036	Yr.Iss.	2001	25.00	25
2002 Jillynne "Friends Like You Are Always True" 104630	Open		25.00	25
2000 Merry "In The Meadow We Can Build A Snowman" 706906	Open		25.00	25
2001 Nora "Brrrrr" 848581	Open		25.00	25
2001 Ursula & Bernhard "In The Winter, We Can Build A Snowman" 848603	Open		30.00	30

Childhood Memories - P. Hillman

YEAR ISSUE	EDITION LIMIT	YEAR RETD.	ISSUE PRICE	*QUOTE U.S.$
1999 Albert & Susann "When Life Hands You Lemons, Make Lemonade" 661848	Open		30.00	30
2000 Calvin "Life Is Filled With Ups And Downs" 706965	Open		17.50	18
1999 Dawn "Every Once In A While, There's A Bump In The Road " 661899	Open		17.50	18-24
1999 Fred "You're The Best Thing Since Sliced Bread" 661856	Retrd.	2001	27.50	28
1999 Lorraine "Don't Let It Get You Down" 661880	Open		17.50	18-24
1999 Melinda "I'm Only A Hop, Skip And A Jump Away If You Need Me" 661821	Open		17.50	18

A Christmas Carol - P. Hillman

YEAR ISSUE	EDITION LIMIT	YEAR RETD.	ISSUE PRICE	*QUOTE U.S.$
1994 Bear Cratchit "And A Very Merry Christmas To You Mr. Scrooge" 617326	Suspd.		17.50	26-47
1994 Counting House (Nite-Lite) 622788	Suspd.		75.00	75-115
1994 Cratchit's House (Nite-Lite) 651362	Suspd.		75.00	75-115
1994 Ebearnezer Scrooge "Bah Humbug!" 617296	Suspd.		17.50	25-42
1994 Gloria "I am the Ghost of Christmas Past", Garland "I am the Ghost of Christmas Present", Gabriel "I am the Ghost of Christmas Yet To Come" 614807	Suspd.		55.00	67-88

YEAR ISSUE	EDITION LIMIT	YEAR RETD.	ISSUE PRICE	*QUOTE U.S.$
1994 Jacob Bearly "You Will Be Haunted By Three Spirits" 614785	Suspd.		17.50	18-38
1994 Mrs. Cratchit "A Beary Christmas And Happy New Year!" 617318	Suspd.		18.50	19-47
1994 Tiny Ted-Bear "God Bless Us Every One" 614777	Suspd.		10.00	17-32

Circus Tent - P. Hillman

YEAR ISSUE	EDITION LIMIT	YEAR RETD.	ISSUE PRICE	*QUOTE U.S.$
1996 Bruno "Step Right Up And Smile" 103713	Retrd.	2000	17.50	23
1996 Claudia "You Take Center Ring With Me" 103721	Retrd.	2000	17.50	18-25
1996 Clown on Ball (musical-"Put on a Happy Face") 111430	Open		40.00	40-52
1997 Dudley "Just Clowning Around" 103748	Retrd.	2000	17.50	18-22
1996 Elephant-Trunk Full of Bear Hugs 103977	Retrd.	2000	22.50	23-30
1997 Lion-"You're My Mane Attraction" 203548	Retrd.	2000	12.50	13-18
1997 Logan "Love Is A Bear Necessity" 103756	Retrd.	2000	17.50	18-32
1996 Seal "Seal of Friendship" 137596	Retrd.	2000	10.00	10-18
1997 Shelby "Friendship Keeps You Popping" 203572	Retrd.	2000	17.50	18-32
1997 Tonya "Friends Are Bear Essentials" 103942	Retrd.	2000	20.00	20-22
1996 Wally "You're The Tops With Me" 103934	Retrd.	2000	17.50	18-25

Count on Me - P. Hillman

YEAR ISSUE	EDITION LIMIT	YEAR RETD.	ISSUE PRICE	*QUOTE U.S.$
1998 Bear w/number 0 302945	Open		5.00	5
1998 Bear w/number 1 302821	Open		5.00	5
1998 Bear w/number 2 302848	Open		5.00	5
1998 Bear w/number 3 302856	Open		5.00	5
1998 Bear w/number 4 302864	Open		5.00	5
1998 Bear w/number 5 302872	Open		5.00	5
1998 Bear w/number 6 302899	Open		5.00	5
1998 Bear w/number 7 302902	Open		5.00	5
1998 Bear w/number 8 302910	Open		5.00	5
1998 Bear w/number 9 302929	Open		5.00	5

Days of the Week - P. Hillman

YEAR ISSUE	EDITION LIMIT	YEAR RETD.	ISSUE PRICE	*QUOTE U.S.$
2001 Sunny "The Child That Is Born On Sabbath Day Is Bonny and Blithe An..." 789674	Open		20.00	20
2001 Monica " Monday's Child Is Fair of Face" 789682	Open		20.00	20
2001 Tia "Tuesday's Child Is Full of Grace" 789690	Open		20.00	20
2001 Wendy "Wednesday's Child Is Full of Woe" 789704	Open		20.00	20
2001 Thelma "Thursday's Child Has Far To Go" 789712	Open		20.00	20
2001 Frances "Friday's Child Is Loving And Giving" 789720	Open		20.00	20
2001 Sandra "Saturday's Child Works Hard For A Living" 789739	Open		20.00	20

Down On The Farm - P. Hillman

YEAR ISSUE	EDITION LIMIT	YEAR RETD.	ISSUE PRICE	*QUOTE U.S.$
2001 Chester "Harvest Everything You Can 847275	Open		17.50	18
2001 Deidre, Delilah & Timothy "Ewe Are The Most Wonderful Friend" 847348	Open		27.50	28
2001 Everett "Your Heart Grows The Sweetest Friendship" 101182	Open		20.00	20
2001 MacDonald & Bessie "I'll Always Be There For Moo" 847364	Open		25.00	25
2001 Marsha & Pinky "Hogs and Kisses To My Beary Best Friend" 847356	Open		17.50	18
2001 Susannah "A Warm Heart Hatches The Most Love" 847321	Open		22.50	23

Down Strawberry Lane - P. Hillman

YEAR ISSUE	EDITION LIMIT	YEAR RETD.	ISSUE PRICE	*QUOTE U.S.$
1997 Diane "I Picked The Beary Best For You" 202991	Yr.Iss.	1997	25.00	28-45
1996 Ella "Love Grows in My Heart" 156329	Retrd.	2000	15.00	15-30
1996 Jenna "You're Berry Special To Me" 156337	Retrd.	2000	15.00	15-27
1996 Matthew "A Dash of Love Sweetens Any Day!" 156299	Retrd.	2000	15.00	15-19
1996 Tara "You're My Berry Best Friend!" 156310	Retrd.	2000	15.00	15-27

Collectors' Information Bureau   *Quotes have been rounded up to nearest dollar

FIGURINES

Cherished Teddies/Enesco Group, Inc.

to Cherished Teddies/Enesco Group, Inc.

YEAR ISSUE	EDITION LIMIT	YEAR RETD.	ISSUE PRICE	*QUOTE U.S.$
1996 Thelma "Cozy Tea For Two" 156302	Retrd.	2000	22.50	23-28
1996 Sign/Bunny/Basket of Strawberries Mini 3 Asst. 900931	Open		3.50	4

Easter - P. Hillman
2002 Trudy - "I'm So Hoppy You're My Friend" 726737	Yr.Iss.		20.00	20

Fairy Tales - P. Hillman
1999 Follow The Yellow Brick Road Collector Set: Scott "May Wisdom Follow You Wherever You Go", Tim "A Kind Heart Is The Best Gift", Leo "Courage Comes From Within", Dot "There's No Place Like Home" 476501	Yr.Iss.	1999	75.00	75-105
1999 Pinocchio "You've Got My Heart On A String" 476463	Retrd.	2001	30.00	30-32
1999 Winnie "You're My Perfect Prince" 481696	Retrd.	1999	17.50	18

Follow The Rainbow - P. Hillman
1998 Carter & Elsie "We're Friends Rain Or Shine" 302791	Retrd.	2001	35.00	35
1998 Ellen "You Color My Rainbow" 302775	Retrd.	2001	20.00	20-34
1998 Joyce "Plant A Rainbow And Watch It Grow" 302767	Retrd.	2001	25.00	25-32

Frolic In The Forest - P. Hillman
2002 Hilda "You Know How To Keep My Heart Warm" 104658	Open		15.00	15
2002 Louise "Friends Were Meant For Times Like These" 104657	Open		20.00	20
2002 Marge & Neil "Friends Always Help You Pull Through" 104656	Open		22.50	23

Halloween Harvest - P. Hillman
2001 Dennis & Barb "I Knew I Would Fall For You" 848522	Open		25.00	25
2002 Derek "Count On A Frightful Halloween" 706752	Open		15.00	15
2002 Griselda "Add A Little Hocus Pocus To Every Halloween" 848549	Open		20.00	20
2001 Icabod "Happy Hollow-ween" 848530	Open		20.00	20

Happily Ever After - P. Hillman
1998 Alicia "Through The Looking Glass, I See You!" 302465	Retrd.	2001	22.50	23-30
1998 Brett "Come To Neverland With Me" 302457	Retrd.	2000	22.50	23-27
1998 Christina "I Found My Prince In You" 302473	Retrd.	2001	22.50	23
1998 Harvey & Gigi "Finding The Path To Your Heart" 302481	Retrd.	2000	30.00	30
1998 Kelsie "Be The Apple Of My Eye" 302570	Retrd.	2000	20.00	20
1998 Lois "To Grandmother's House We Go" 302511	Retrd.	2001	22.50	23

Heart Strings - P. Hillman
2000 Best Friends 833290	Open		10.00	10
2000 I Love You 833991	Open		10.00	10
2000 A Kiss Makes Everything Better 833274	Open		10.00	10
2000 You Are My Favorite Friend 833282	Open		10.00	10
2000 You Make My Heart Smile 833983	Open		10.00	10
2000 Your Love Makes My Heart Smile 833320	Open		10.00	10

Holiday Dangling - P. Hillman
1996 Santa Bear 2 asst. "Joy" "Ho Ho" 176168	Retrd.	1999	12.50	13-15
1996 Holden "Catchin' The Holiday Spirit!" 176095	Retrd.	1999	15.00	15-17
1996 Jolene "Dropping You A Holiday Greeting" 176133	Retrd.	1999	20.00	20
1996 Joy "You Always Bring Joy" 176087	Retrd.	1999	15.00	15
1996 Noel "An Old-Fashioned Noel To You" 176109	Retrd.	1999	15.00	15-17
1996 Nolan "A String Of Good Tidings" 176141	Retrd.	1999	20.00	20-29

Just Between Friends - P. Hillman
1998 Forgive Me 303100	Closed	2000	7.50	8
1998 Good Luck 303143	Closed	2000	7.50	8

YEAR ISSUE	EDITION LIMIT	YEAR RETD.	ISSUE PRICE	*QUOTE U.S.$
1998 I Miss You 303127	Closed	2000	7.50	8
1998 I'm Sorry 303097	Closed	2000	7.50	8
1998 Please Smile 303135	Closed	1999	7.50	8
1998 "What A Day!" "Everything's O.K." 303119	Closed	1999	7.50	8

Let Heaven And Nature Sing - P. Hillman
1999 Felicia "Joy to the World" 533890	Yr.Iss.	1999	20.00	20-32
2000 Emma "Let Earth Proclaim It's Peace 533904	Yr.Iss.	2000	20.00	20-27
2001 Rebecca "Let Heaven And Nature Sing" 533912	Yr.Iss.	2001	20.00	20

Lifetime of Memories - P. Hillman
2000 Billie "A Bundle of Joy From Heaven Above" 790206	Open		45.00	45
2000 Dawn "You Don't Have To Search Far To Find Your Rainbow" 739049	Open		20.00	20
2000 Jerald & Mary Ann "What Would Game Night Be Without You?" 811742	Open		32.50	33
2001 Our Journey Has Just Begun 864374	Open		50.00	50
2002 "Home Is Where The Heart Is" (GoCollect Exclusive) 728608	15,000		50.00	50
2002 Kathy & Ken "Charting The Heavens With You" 100055	Open		50.00	50

Little Sparkles - P. Hillman
1997 Bear w/January Birthstone Mini Figurine 239720	Open		7.50	8-10
1997 Bear w/February Birthstone Mini Figurine 239747	Open		7.50	8-10
1997 Bear w/March Birthstone Mini Figurine 239763	Open		7.50	8-10
1997 Bear w/April Birthstone Mini Figurine 239771	Open		7.50	8-10
1997 Bear w/May Birthstone Mini Figurine 239798	Open		7.50	8-10
1997 Bear w/June Birthstone Mini Figurine 239801	Open		7.50	8-10
1997 Bear w/July Birthstone Mini Figurine 239828	Open		7.50	8-10
1997 Bear w/August Birthstone Mini Figurine 239836	Open		7.50	8-10
1997 Bear w/September Birthstone Mini Figurine 239844	Open		7.50	8-10
1997 Bear w/October Birthstone Mini Figurine 239852	Open		7.50	8-10
1997 Bear w/November Birthstone Mini Figurine 239860	Open		7.50	8-10
1997 Bear w/December Birthstone Mini Figurine 239933	Open		7.50	8-10

Love Letters From Teddie Mini - P. Hillman
1997 Bear w/ "I Love Bears" Blocks 902950	Closed	2000	7.50	8-14
1997 Bear w/ "I Love Hugs" Blocks 902969	Closed	2000	7.50	8-14
1997 Bear w/ "I Love You" Blocks 156515	Closed	2000	7.50	8-17
1997 Bear w/Heart Dangling Blocks 203084	Closed	2000	7.50	8-10
1997 Bears w/ "Love" Double 203076	Closed	2000	13.50	14-16

Monthly Friends to Cherish - P. Hillman
1993 Jack January Monthly "A New Year With Old Friends" 914754 (Also available through Hamilton Collection)	Retrd.	1999	15.00	15-25
1993 Phoebe February Monthly "Be Mine" 914762 (Also available through Hamilton Collection)	Retrd.	1999	15.00	15-25
1993 Mark March Monthly "Friendship Is In The Air" 914770 (Also available through Hamilton Collection)	Retrd.	1999	15.00	15-34
1993 Alan April Monthly "Showers of Friendship" 914789 (Also available through Hamilton Collection)	Retrd.	1999	15.00	15-33
1993 May May Monthly "Friendship Is In Bloom" 914797 (Also available through Hamilton Collection)	Retrd.	1999	15.00	15-45
1993 June June Monthly "Planting The Seed of Friendship" 914800 (Also available through Hamilton Collection)	Retrd.	1999	15.00	15-45
1993 Julie July Monthly "A Day in The Park" 914819 (Also available through Hamilton Collection)	Retrd.	1999	15.00	15-25

*Quotes have been rounded up to nearest dollar

Collectors' Information Bureau

137

YEAR ISSUE	EDITION LIMIT	YEAR RETD.	ISSUE PRICE	*QUOTE U.S.$
1993 Arthur August Monthly "Smooth Sailing" 914827 (Also available through Hamilton Collection)	Retrd.	1999	15.00	15-45
1993 Seth September Monthly "School Days" 914835 (Also available through Hamilton Collection)	Retrd.	1999	15.00	15-30
1993 Oscar October Monthly "Sweet Treats" 914843 (Also available through Hamilton Collection)	Retrd.	1999	15.00	15-45
1993 Nicole November Monthly "Thanks For Friends" 914851 (Also available through Hamilton Collection)	Retrd.	1999	15.00	15-25
1993 Denise December Monthly "Happy Holidays, Friend" 914878 (Also available through Hamilton Collection)	Retrd.	1999	15.00	15-25

Nativity - P. Hillman

YEAR ISSUE	EDITION LIMIT	YEAR RETD.	ISSUE PRICE	*QUOTE U.S.$
1993 "Friendship Pulls Us Through" & "Ewe Make Being Friends Special" 912867	Retrd.	2001	13.50	14-24
1992 Angie "I Brought The Star" 951137	Retrd.	2001	15.00	22-49
1995 Celeste "An Angel To Watch Over You" 141267	Retrd.	2001	20.00	20-32
1992 Creche & Quilt 951218	Open		50.00	50
1992 Maria, Baby & Josh "A Baby Is God's Gift of Love" "Everyone Needs a Daddy"- 950688	Retrd.	2001	35.00	35-51
1993 Nativity "Cherish The King" (musical-"O Little Town of Bethlehem") 912859	Suspd.		60.00	120-175
1993 Nativity Camel "Friends Like You Are Precious And True" 904309	Retrd.	1997	30.00	63-86
1994 Nativity Cow "That's What Friends Are For" 651095	Retrd.	1997	22.50	34-81
1993 Nativity Figurine Gift Set w/Creche 916684	Open		100.00	100-115
1996 Nativity Prayer Plaque "The Cherished One" 176362	Closed	2000	13.50	14
1993 Nativity w/ Creche (musical-"Silent Night") 903485	Suspd.		85.00	225-275
1994 Ronnie "I'll Play My Drum For You" 912905	Retrd.	2001	13.50	17-39
1992 Sammy "Little Lambs Are In My Care" 950726	Retrd.	2001	17.50	33-69
1992 Three Kings-Richard "My Gift Is Loving", Edward "My Gift Is Caring", Wilbur "My Gift Is Sharing" 950718	Retrd.	2001	55.00	55-110

Noah's Ark Gift Set - P. Hillman

YEAR ISSUE	EDITION LIMIT	YEAR RETD.	ISSUE PRICE	*QUOTE U.S.$
2001 Noah's Ark Gift Set, set/6 100526	3,500		95.00	95

Nursery Rhyme - P. Hillman

YEAR ISSUE	EDITION LIMIT	YEAR RETD.	ISSUE PRICE	*QUOTE U.S.$
1994 Jack & Jill "Our Friendship Will Never Tumble" 624772	Retrd.	1998	30.00	38-52
1994 Little Bo Peep "Looking For A Friend Like You" 624802	Retrd.	1998	22.50	30-52
1994 Little Jack Horner "I'm Plum Happy You're My Friend" 624780	Retrd.	1998	22.50	30-47
1994 Little Miss Muffet "I'm Never Afraid With You At My Side" 624799	Retrd.	1998	20.00	38-52
1994 Mary, Mary Quite Contrary "Friendship Blooms With Loving Care" 626074	Retrd.	1998	22.50	27-63
1994 Tom, Tom The Piper's Son "Wherever You Go I'll Follow" 624810	Retrd.	1998	20.00	20-27

Nutcracker Suite - P. Hillman

YEAR ISSUE	EDITION LIMIT	YEAR RETD.	ISSUE PRICE	*QUOTE U.S.$
1997 Collector's Set: Mouse King "Sugar Plum Dreams", Herr Drosselmeyer "Making Holiday Wishes Come True", Clara "Our Friendship Is Magical", & Boy Prince "I'll Keep You Beary Safe" 272388	Yr.Iss.	1997	70.00	85-100
1997 Nutcracker Suite Tree (musical -"Dance of the Sugar-Plum Fairy") 292494	Open		45.00	45-58

Old Fashioned Country Christmas - P. Hillman

YEAR ISSUE	EDITION LIMIT	YEAR RETD.	ISSUE PRICE	*QUOTE U.S.$
1999 Annette "Tender Care Given Here" 533769	Retrd.	1999	20.00	20-25
1999 Brian "Look Out Snow! Here We Go!" 533807	Retrd.	1999	22.50	23-25
1999 Justin "We Share Forever, Whatever The Weather" 533793	Retrd.	1999	20.00	20-25

YEAR ISSUE	EDITION LIMIT	YEAR RETD.	ISSUE PRICE	*QUOTE U.S.$
1999 Shirley "These Are The Best Kind of Days" 533777	Retrd.	1999	20.00	20-2
1999 Suzanne "Home Sweet Country Home" 533785	Retrd.	1999	20.00	20-2

Our Cherished Family - P. Hillman

YEAR ISSUE	EDITION LIMIT	YEAR RETD.	ISSUE PRICE	*QUOTE U.S.$
1994 Father "A Father Is The Bearer Of Strength" 624888	Open		13.50	14-2
1999 Fay And Arlene "Thanks For Always Being By My Side" 476684	Open		25.00	22-2
1998 A Gift To Behold (boy) 127922	Open		7.50	
1998 A Gift To Behold (girl) 599352	Open		7.50	8-1
1998 Grandma Is God's Special Gift 127914	Open		17.50	18-2
1998 Grandpa Is God's Special Gift 127906	Open		17.50	18-2
1999 Haley and Logan "Sisters And Hugs Soothe The Soul" 534145	Open		25.00	2
1999 June And Jean "I've Always Wanted To Be Just Like You" 534153	Retrd.	2001	20.00	2
1999 Justine And Janice "Sisters And Friendship Are Crafted With Love" 537810	Open		25.00	2
1994 Mother "A Mother's Love Bears All Things" 624861	Open		20.00	20-3
1994 Older Daughter "Child Of Love" 624845	Open		10.00	10-1
1994 Older Son "Child Of Pride" 624829	Open		10.00	10-2
1994 Young Daughter "Child Of Kindness" 624853	Open		9.00	9-2
1994 Young Son "Child of Hope" 624837	Open		9.00	9-2

Santa - P. Hillman

YEAR ISSUE	EDITION LIMIT	YEAR RETD.	ISSUE PRICE	*QUOTE U.S.$
1995 Nicklaus "You're At The Top Of My List" 141100	Yr.Iss.	1995	20.00	47-59
1996 Klaus "Bearer of Good Tidings" 176036	Yr.Iss.	1996	20.00	24-39
1997 Kris "Up On The Rooftop" 272140	Yr.Iss.	1997	22.50	32
2002 Ricky "Your Wishes Will Come True If You Just Believe" 104144	Yr.Iss.		20.00	20
1998 Santa "A Little Holiday R & R" 352713	Yr.Iss.	1998	22.50	30-35
1999 Sanford "Celebrate Family, Friends & Tradition" 534242	Yr.Iss.	1999	25.00	25-40
2000 Wolfgang "The Spirit of Christmas Is In Us All" 706701	Yr.Iss.	2000	25.00	25
2001 Wendall "Have You Been Naughty of Nice?" 848565	Yr.Iss.	2001	25.00	25

Santa Express - P. Hillman

YEAR ISSUE	EDITION LIMIT	YEAR RETD.	ISSUE PRICE	*QUOTE U.S.$
1996 Car of Toys "Rolling Along With Friends and Smiles" 219096	Retrd.	1998	17.50	18-42
1996 Casey "Friendship Is The Perfect End To The Holidays" 219525	Retrd.	1998	22.50	23-49
1997 Cindy "This Train Is Bound For Holiday Surprises!" 219177	Retrd.	1998	17.50	25-30
1996 Colin "He Knows If You've Been Bad or Good" 219088	Retrd.	1998	17.50	18-35
1997 Kirby "Heading Into The Holidays With Deer Friends" 219118	Retrd.	1998	17.50	25-30
1996 Lionel "All Aboard the Santa Express" 219061	Retrd.	1998	22.50	23-49
1997 Nick "Ho, Ho, Ho — To The Holidays We Go!" 219312	Retrd.	1998	17.50	25-30
1997 Snow Bear 269905	Closed	1999	12.50	13-22
1997 Street Lamp and Bear 269913	Retrd.	1999	15.00	15-22
1996 Tony "A First Class Delivery For You!" 219487	Retrd.	1998	17.50	18-26

Santa's Workshop - P. Hillman

YEAR ISSUE	EDITION LIMIT	YEAR RETD.	ISSUE PRICE	*QUOTE U.S.$
1995 Ginger "Painting Your Holidays With Love" 141127	Retrd.	1998	22.50	23-37
1995 Holly "A Cup of Homemade Love" 141119	Retrd.	1998	18.50	19-32
1995 Meri "Handsewn Holidays" 141135	Retrd.	1998	20.00	20-35
1996 Ornaments/Mailsack/North Pole Sign Mini 3 Asst. 176079	Closed	1999	15.00	15-27
1995 Santa's Workshop Nightlight 141925	Closed	1999	75.00	75
1995 Yule "Building a Sturdy Friendship" 141143	Retrd.	1998	22.50	23-35

Sitting Pretty - P. Hillman

YEAR ISSUE	EDITION LIMIT	YEAR RETD.	ISSUE PRICE	*QUOTE U.S.$
2001 Babs - "A Baby Fills The Empty Space In Every Heart" 611506	Open		27.50	28
2001 Becca - "We Share A Bond That Will Last Forever" 707627	Open		27.50	28

YEAR ISSUE	EDITION LIMIT	YEAR RETD.	ISSUE PRICE	*QUOTE U.S.$
2001 Celia - "You Can always Call My Heart 'Home'" 295264	Open		27.50	28
2001 Ida - "Your Friendship Eases All My Cares Away" 707619	Open		27.50	28
2001 Jenny - "The Bigger The Heart, The More Love It Can Hold" 199877	Open		27.50	28
2001 Lucy - "Rocking Away In My Favorite Reading Chair" 676918	Open		27.50	28

The Springtime Angel Series - P. Hillman

YEAR ISSUE	EDITION LIMIT	YEAR RETD.	ISSUE PRICE	*QUOTE U.S.$
2000 Chantel & Fawn "We're Kindred Spirits" 661740	Yr.Iss.	2000	45.00	45
2001 Daphne "Let Your Spirits Soar" 661767	Open		35.00	35

The Springtime Teddies Collection - P. Hillman

YEAR ISSUE	EDITION LIMIT	YEAR RETD.	ISSUE PRICE	*QUOTE U.S.$
2000 Dawn "You Don't Have To Search Far To Find Your Rainbow" 739049	Open		20.00	20

Sugar & Spice - P. Hillman

YEAR ISSUE	EDITION LIMIT	YEAR RETD.	ISSUE PRICE	*QUOTE U.S.$
1998 Missy, Cookie, Riley "A Special Recipe For Our Friendship" 352586	Retrd.	2000	35.00	35
1998 Pamela & Grayson "A Dash of Love to Warm Your Heart" 352616	Retrd.	2000	22.50	23-27
1998 Sharon "Sweetness Pours From My Heart" 352594	Retrd.	2000	20.00	20
1998 Wayne "Spoonfuls of Sweetness" 352608	Retrd.	2000	20.00	20-29

Sweet Heart Ball - P. Hillman

YEAR ISSUE	EDITION LIMIT	YEAR RETD.	ISSUE PRICE	*QUOTE U.S.$
1996 Craig & Cheri "Sweethearts Forever" 156485	Retrd.	1999	25.00	25-28
1996 Darla "My Heart Wishes For You" 156469	Retrd.	1999	20.00	20-25
1996 Darrel "Love Unveils A Happy Heart" 156450	Retrd.	1999	17.50	18-20
1997 Harry & Katherine "You're The Queen/King Of My Heart" 302732	Yr.Iss.	1997	65.00	65-68
1996 Jilly "Won't You Be My Sweetheart?" 156477	Retrd.	1999	17.50	18-27
1996 Marian "You're The Hero Of My Heart" 156442	Retrd.	1999	20.00	20-32
1996 Robin "You Steal My Heart Away" 156434	Retrd.	1999	17.50	18-27
1997 Sweetheart Collector Set/3, (Balcony displayer), Romeo "There's No Sweeter Rose Than You" & Juliet "Wherefore Art Thou Romeo?" 203114	Yr.Iss.	1997	60.00	75

T Is For Teddies - P. Hillman

YEAR ISSUE	EDITION LIMIT	YEAR RETD.	ISSUE PRICE	*QUOTE U.S.$
1995 Bear w/"A" Block 158488A	Open		5.00	5-9
1995 Bear w/"B" Block 158488B	Open		5.00	5-9
1995 Bear w/"C" Block 158488C	Open		5.00	5-9
1995 Bear w/"D" Block 158488D	Open		5.00	5-7
1995 Bear w/"E" Block 158488E	Open		5.00	5-7
1995 Bear w/"F" Block 158488F	Open		5.00	5-7
1995 Bear w/"G" Block 158488G	Open		5.00	5-7
1995 Bear w/"H" Block 158488H	Open		5.00	5-7
1995 Bear w/"I" Block 158488I	Open		5.00	5-7
1995 Bear w/"J" Block 158488J	Open		5.00	5-9
1995 Bear w/"K" Block 158488K	Open		5.00	5-7
1995 Bear w/"L" Block 158488L	Open		5.00	5-7
1995 Bear w/"M" Block 158488M	Open		5.00	5-7
1995 Bear w/"N" Block 158488N	Open		5.00	5-7
1995 Bear w/"O" Block 158488O	Open		5.00	5-9
1995 Bear w/"P" Block 158488P	Open		5.00	5-7
1995 Bear w/"Q" Block 158488Q	Open		5.00	5-7
1995 Bear w/"R" Block 158488R	Open		5.00	5-7
1995 Bear w/"S" Block 158488S	Open		5.00	5-7
1995 Bear w/"T" Block 158488T	Open		5.00	5-7
1995 Bear w/"U" Block 158488U	Open		5.00	5-7
1995 Bear w/"V" Block 158488V	Open		5.00	5-7
1995 Bear w/"W" Block 158488W	Open		5.00	5-7
1995 Bear w/"X" Block 158488X	Open		5.00	5-7
1995 Bear w/"Y" Block 158488Y	Open		5.00	5-7
1995 Bear w/"Z" Block 158488Z	Open		5.00	5-7

Teddies in Motion - P. Hillman

YEAR ISSUE	EDITION LIMIT	YEAR RETD.	ISSUE PRICE	*QUOTE U.S.$
2000 Andre "The Finish Line is Only a Lap Away" 789836	Open		20.00	20
1999 Chad "With You My Spirits Soar" 477524	Retrd.	2001	20.00	20
1999 Dave "An Oldie But Goodie" 477494	Retrd.	2001	20.00	20
1999 Dustin and Austin "Hold On For The Ride Of Your Life" 477508	Open		30.00	30

YEAR ISSUE	EDITION LIMIT	YEAR RETD.	ISSUE PRICE	*QUOTE U.S.$
2002 Evelyn "A Girl With Style!" 104662	Open		20.00	20
2000 Howard "A Farming We Will Go" 789844	Open		22.50	23
2000 Jan & Elise "This is the Start of Your Bright and Exciting Future" 789666	Open		17.50	18
1999 Ken "You Make My Heart Race" 477559	Retrd.	2001	20.00	20
2002 Rob, Rose, Rita & Rodney "Are We There Yet?" 104664	Open		22.50	23
1999 Roger "You Set My Heart in Motion" 477516	Retrd.	2001	20.00	20
2000 Warren "There is No Limit to How Far You Can Go" 789828	Open		20.00	20

Through The Years - P. Hillman

YEAR ISSUE	EDITION LIMIT	YEAR RETD.	ISSUE PRICE	*QUOTE U.S.$
1993 "Cradled With Love" Baby 911356	Open		16.50	21-30
1993 "Beary Special One" Age 1 911348	Open		13.50	20-30
1993 "Two Sweet Two Bear" Age 2 911321	Open		13.50	20-27
1993 "Three Cheers For You" Age 3 911313	Open		15.00	22-32
1993 "Unfolding Happy Wishes Four You" Age 4 911305	Open		15.00	22-32
1993 "Color Me Five" Age 5 911291	Open		15.00	19-32
1993 "Chalking Up Six Wishes" Age 6 911283	Open		16.50	22-38
1998 "Seven Is As Sweet As Honey" Age 7 466239	Open		16.50	17
1998 "Being Eight Is Really Great!" Age 8 466247	Open		16.50	17
1998 "Being Nine Is Really Fine!" Age 9 466255	Open		16.50	17
1998 "Count To Ten...and Celebrate!" Age 10 466263	Open		16.50	17

U.S. Military Bears - P. Hillman

YEAR ISSUE	EDITION LIMIT	YEAR RETD.	ISSUE PRICE	*QUOTE U.S.$
2000 Air Force 742988	Open		17.50	18
2000 Army 706930	Open		17.50	18
2000 Coast Guard 742961	Open		17.50	18
2000 Marines 706949	Open		17.50	18
2000 Navy 706957	Open		17.50	18

Up In The Attic - P. Hillman

YEAR ISSUE	EDITION LIMIT	YEAR RETD.	ISSUE PRICE	*QUOTE U.S.$
1998 Kaitlyn "Old Treasures, New Memories" 302600	Yr.Iss.	1998	50.00	50-65
2000 Lauren "Cherished Memories Never Fade" 308684	Yr.Iss.	2000	35.00	35-53
1999 Sarah "Memories To Wear And Share"308676	Yr.Iss.	1999	30.00	30-45

Victorian Bonnets & Bows - P. Hillman

YEAR ISSUE	EDITION LIMIT	YEAR RETD.	ISSUE PRICE	*QUOTE U.S.$
1999 Collette "Outer Beauty Is A Reflection Of Inner Beauty" 662518	Retrd.	2001	20.00	20
1999 Teresa "You Have Such Wonderful Grace" 662461	Retrd.	2001	20.00	20
1999 Vanessa "You're My Shelter From The Storm" 662437	Open		22.50	23
1999 Wilfred "A Lifetime Of Friendship...A Trunk Full Of Memories" 662496	Retrd.	2001	25.00	25

We Bear Thanks - P. Hillman

YEAR ISSUE	EDITION LIMIT	YEAR RETD.	ISSUE PRICE	*QUOTE U.S.$
1996 Barbara "Giving Thanks For Our Family" 141305	Retrd.	1997	12.50	13-29
1996 Dina "Bear In Mind, You're Special" 141275	Retrd.	1997	15.00	15-30
1996 John "Bear In Mind, You're Special" 141283	Retrd.	1997	15.00	15-33
1996 Rick "Suited Up For The Holidays" 141291	Retrd.	1997	12.50	22-38
1996 Table With Food / Dog " We Bear Thanks" 141542	Retrd.	1997	30.00	30-47

Wedding - P. Hillman

YEAR ISSUE	EDITION LIMIT	YEAR RETD.	ISSUE PRICE	*QUOTE U.S.$
1999 Bride "Beautiful And Bearly Blushing" 476285	Open		15.00	15-22
1999 Groom "A Beary Special Groom To Be" 476315	Open		15.00	15-22
1999 Bridesmaid "So Glad To Be Part Of Your Special Day" 476323	Open		10.00	10
1999 Groomsman "The Time Has Come For Wedded Bliss" 476366	Open		10.00	10
1999 Ringbearer "I've Got The Most Important Job!" 476382	Open		9.00	9
1999 Flower Girl "Sweet Flowers For The Bride" 476374	Open		9.00	9
1999 Wedding Collectors Set (3 pc.) 510254	Open		50.00	50

Winter Bear Festival - P. Hillman

YEAR ISSUE	EDITION LIMIT	YEAR RETD.	ISSUE PRICE	*QUOTE U.S.$
1997 Adam "It's A Holiday On Ice" 269751	Retrd.	2000	20.00	20-27
1997 Boy Waterball (musical-"White Christmas") 292575	Closed	1999	45.00	20-52
1997 Candace "Skating On Holiday Joy" 269778	Retrd.	2000	20.00	20-27
1997 Girl Waterball (musical-"Let It Snow") 272884	Closed	1998	45.00	45
1997 James "Going My Way For The Holidays" 269786	Retrd.	2000	25.00	25-32
1997 Lindsey & Lyndon "Walking In A Winter Wonderland" 141178	Retrd.	2000	30.00	30-40
1997 Mitch "Friendship Never Melts Away" 269735	Retrd.	2000	30.00	30-42
1997 Spencer "I'm Head Over Skis For You" 269743	Retrd.	2000	20.00	20-28
1997 Ted "Snow Fun When You're Not Around" 269727	Retrd.	2000	18.50	25-30

Dave Grossman Creations

Lladró-Norman Rockwell Collection Series - Rockwell-Inspired

YEAR ISSUE	EDITION LIMIT	YEAR RETD.	ISSUE PRICE	*QUOTE U.S.$
1982 Court Jester RL-405G	5,000	N/A	600.00	990-1250
1982 Daydreamer RL-404G	5,000	N/A	450.00	1100-1500
1982 Lladró Love Letter RL-400G	5,000	N/A	650.00	750-1000
1982 Practice Makes Perfect RL-402G	5,000	N/A	725.00	725-995
1982 Springtime RL-406G	5,000	N/A	450.00	1200-1400
1982 Summer Stock RL-401G	5,000	N/A	750.00	850-900
1982 Young Love RL-403G	5,000	N/A	450.00	1100-1200

Norman Rockwell America Collection - Rockwell-Inspired

YEAR ISSUE	EDITION LIMIT	YEAR RETD.	ISSUE PRICE	*QUOTE U.S.$
1989 Bottom of the Sixth NRC-607	Retrd.	N/A	140.00	140
1981 Breaking Home Ties NRV-300	Retrd.	N/A	2000.00	2300
1989 Doctor and Doll NRP-600	Retrd.	N/A	90.00	60
1989 First Day Home NRC-606	Retrd.	N/A	80.00	80
1989 First Haircut NRC-604	Retrd.	N/A	75.00	100
1989 First Visit NRC-605	Retrd.	N/A	110.00	110
1982 Lincoln NRV-301	Retrd.	N/A	300.00	375
1989 Locomotive NRC-603	Retrd.	N/A	110.00	110-125
1989 Runaway NRP-610	Retrd.	N/A	140.00	190
1982 Thanksgiving NRV-302	Retrd.	N/A	2500.00	2650
1989 Weigh-In NRP-611	Retrd.	N/A	120.00	125-140

Norman Rockwell America Collection-Lg. Ltd. Edition - Rockwell-Inspired

YEAR ISSUE	EDITION LIMIT	YEAR RETD.	ISSUE PRICE	*QUOTE U.S.$
1975 Baseball NR-102	Retrd.	N/A	125.00	450
1989 Bottom of the Sixth NRP-307	Retrd.	N/A	190.00	190
1982 Circus NR-106	Retrd.	N/A	500.00	500-750
1974 Doctor and Doll NR-100	Retrd.	N/A	300.00	1400
1989 Doctor and Doll NRP-300	Retrd.	N/A	150.00	150
1981 Dreams of Long Ago NR-105	Retrd.	N/A	500.00	750
1979 Leapfrog NR-104	Retrd.	N/A	440.00	750
1984 Marble Players NR-107	Retrd.	N/A	500.00	650-750
1975 No Swimming NR-101	Retrd.	N/A	150.00	600-1200
1989 Runaway NRP-310	Retrd.	N/A	190.00	190
1974 See America First NR-103	Retrd.	N/A	100.00	550-1500
1989 Weigh-In NR-311	Retrd.	N/A	160.00	140-175

Norman Rockwell Collection - Rockwell-Inspired

YEAR ISSUE	EDITION LIMIT	YEAR RETD.	ISSUE PRICE	*QUOTE U.S.$
1982 American Mother NRG-42	Retrd.	N/A	100.00	125
1978 At the Doctor NR-29	Retrd.	N/A	108.00	165-195
1979 Back From Camp NR-33	Retrd.	N/A	96.00	145
1973 Back To School NR-02	Retrd.	N/A	20.00	75
1975 Barbershop Quartet NR-23	Retrd.	N/A	100.00	650-1300
1974 Baseball NR-16	Retrd.	N/A	45.00	110-180
1975 Big Moment NR-21	Retrd.	N/A	60.00	130-150
1973 Caroller NR-03	Retrd.	N/A	22.50	75
1975 Circus NR-22	Retrd.	N/A	55.00	145
1983 Country Critic NR-43	Retrd.	N/A	75.00	125
1982 Croquet NR-41	Retrd.	N/A	100.00	150
1973 Daydreamer NR-04	Retrd.	N/A	22.50	45-75
1975 Discovery NR-20	Retrd.	N/A	55.00	170-650
1979 Doctor & Doll NR-12	Retrd.	N/A	65.00	285
1979 Dreams of Long Ago NR-31	Retrd.	N/A	100.00	125-156
1974 Drum For Tommy NRC-24	Retrd.	N/A	40.00	95
1980 Exasperated Nanny NR-35	Retrd.	N/A	96.00	100-160
1978 First Day of School NR-27	Retrd.	N/A	100.00	150-185
1974 Friends In Need NR-13	Retrd.	N/A	45.00	100-115
1983 Graduate NR-44	Retrd.	N/A	30.00	85
1979 Grandpa's Ballerina NR-32	Retrd.	N/A	100.00	130-140
1980 Hankerchief NR-36	Retrd.	N/A	110.00	125-15(
1973 Lazybones NR-08	Retrd.	N/A	30.00	250-45(
1973 Leapfrog NR-09	Retrd.	N/A	50.00	600-104(
1973 Love Letter NR-06	Retrd.	N/A	25.00	85-9(
1973 Lovers NR-07	Retrd.	N/A	45.00	85-11(
1978 Magic Potion NR-28	Retrd.	N/A	84.00	150-20(
1973 Marble Players NR-11	Retrd.	N/A	60.00	390-42(
1973 No Swimming NR-05	Retrd.	N/A	25.00	65-14(
1977 Pals NR-25	Retrd.	N/A	60.00	120-15(
1986 Red Cross NR-47	Retrd.	N/A	67.00	10(
1973 Redhead NR-01	Retrd.	N/A	20.00	21(
1980 Santa's Good Boys NR-37	Retrd.	N/A	90.00	10(
1973 Schoolmaster NR-10	Retrd.	N/A	55.00	225-23(
1984 Scotty's Home Plate NR-46	Retrd.	N/A	30.00	6(
1983 Scotty's Surprise NRS-20	Retrd.	N/A	25.00	60-17(
1974 See America First NR-17	Retrd.	N/A	50.00	15(
1981 Spirit of Education NR-38	Retrd.	N/A	96.00	125-13(
1974 Springtime '33 NR-14	Retrd.	N/A	30.00	75-8(
1977 Springtime '35 NR-19	Retrd.	N/A	50.00	65-7(
1974 Summertime '33 NR-15	Retrd.	N/A	45.00	7(
1974 Take Your Medicine NR-18	Retrd.	N/A	50.00	15(
1979 Teacher's Pet NRA-30	Retrd.	N/A	35.00	10(
1980 The Toss NR-34	Retrd.	N/A	110.00	25(
1982 A Visit With Rockwell NR-40	Retrd.	N/A	120.00	100-12(
1988 Wedding March NR-49	Retrd.	N/A	110.00	17(
1978 Young Doctor NRD-26	Retrd.	N/A	100.00	18(
1987 Young Love NR-48	Retrd.	N/A	70.00	120-15(

Norman Rockwell Collection-Boy Scout Series - Rockwell-Inspired

YEAR ISSUE	EDITION LIMIT	YEAR RETD.	ISSUE PRICE	*QUOTE U.S.$
1981 Can't Wait BSA-01	Retrd.	N/A	30.00	13(
1981 Good Friends BSA-04	Retrd.	N/A	58.00	65-13(
1981 Good Turn BSA-05	Retrd.	N/A	65.00	125-13(
1982 Guiding Hand BSA-07	Retrd.	N/A	58.00	15(
1981 Physically Strong BSA-03	Retrd.	N/A	56.00	150-16(
1981 Scout Is Helpful BSA-02	Retrd.	N/A	38.00	15(
1981 Scout Memories BSA-06	Retrd.	N/A	65.00	10(
1983 Tomorrow's Leader BSA-08	Retrd.	N/A	45.00	55-15(

Norman Rockwell Collection-Country Gentlemen Series - Rockwell-Inspired

YEAR ISSUE	EDITION LIMIT	YEAR RETD.	ISSUE PRICE	*QUOTE U.S.$
1982 Bringing Home the Tree CG-02	Retrd.	N/A	60.00	11(
1982 The Catch CG-04	Retrd.	N/A	50.00	10(
1982 On the Ice CG-05	Retrd.	N/A	50.00	60-7(
1982 Pals CG-03	Retrd.	N/A	36.00	9(
1982 Thin Ice CG-06	Retrd.	N/A	50.00	6(
1982 Turkey Dinner CG-01	Retrd.	N/A	85.00	11(

Norman Rockwell Collection-Huck Finn Series - Rockwell-Inspired

YEAR ISSUE	EDITION LIMIT	YEAR RETD.	ISSUE PRICE	*QUOTE U.S.$
1980 Listening HF-02	Retrd.	N/A	110.00	125-15(
1980 No Kings HF-03	Retrd.	N/A	110.00	15(
1979 The Secret HF-01	Retrd.	N/A	110.00	13(
1980 Snake Escapes HF-04	Retrd.	N/A	110.00	13(

Norman Rockwell Collection-Miniatures - Rockwell-Inspired

YEAR ISSUE	EDITION LIMIT	YEAR RETD.	ISSUE PRICE	*QUOTE U.S.$
1984 At the Doctor's NR-229	Retrd.	N/A	35.00	35(
1979 Back To School NR-202	Retrd.	N/A	18.00	50(
1982 Barbershop Quartet NR-223	Retrd.	N/A	40.00	50-85(
1980 Baseball NR-216	Retrd.	N/A	40.00	50-65(
1982 Big Moment NR-221	Retrd.	N/A	36.00	40(
1979 Caroller NR-203	Retrd.	N/A	20.00	35-50(
1982 Circus NR-222	Retrd.	N/A	35.00	40-75(
1979 Daydreamer NR-204	Retrd.	N/A	20.00	45-60(
1982 Discovery NR-220	Retrd.	N/A	35.00	65(
1979 Doctor and Doll NR-212	Retrd.	N/A	40.00	75(
1999 Doctor and the Doll NRR-610	7,500	2001	30.00	30(
1984 Dreams of Long Ago NR-231	Retrd.	N/A	30.00	30(
1982 Drum For Tommy NRC-224	Retrd.	N/A	25.00	30(
1989 First Day Home MRC-906	Retrd.	N/A	45.00	45(
1984 First Day of School NR-227	Retrd.	N/A	35.00	45(
1989 First Haircut MRC-904	Retrd.	N/A	45.00	45(
1999 Fishing NRR-602	7,500	2001	25.00	25(
1980 Friends In Need NR-213	Retrd.	N/A	30.00	40(
1999 Gramps at the Plate NRR-604	7,500	2001	25.00	25(
1999 Gramps at the Reins (musical) NRR-603M	7,500	2001	40.00	40(
1999 Gramps at the Reins NRR-609	7,500	2001	30.00	30(
1979 Lazybones NR-208	Retrd.	N/A	22.00	45-50(
1979 Leapfrog NR-209	Retrd.	N/A	32.00	45-65(
1979 Love Letter NR-206	Retrd.	N/A	26.00	45-65(
1979 Lovers NR-207	Retrd.	N/A	28.00	60(

YEAR ISSUE	EDITION LIMIT	YEAR RETD.	ISSUE PRICE	*QUOTE U.S.$
1984 Magic Potion NR-228	Retrd.	N/A	30.00	40
2000 Marble Champs NRR-614	7,500	2001	25.00	25
1979 Marble Players NR-211	Retrd.	N/A	36.00	75-80
1999 The Marriage License (musical) NRR-602M	7,500	2001	40.00	40
1999 The Marriage License NRR-607	7,500	2001	30.00	30
1979 No Swimming NR-205	Retrd.	N/A	22.00	60
1984 Pals NR-225	Retrd.	N/A	25.00	25-50
1999 The Pharmacist NRR-606	7,500	2001	30.00	30
1999 Puppy Love NRR-611	7,500	2001	30.00	30
1979 Redhead NR-201	Retrd.	N/A	18.00	50-65
1999 The Runaway NRR-605	7,500	2001	30.00	30
2000 Santa at the Globe NRR-612	7,500	2001	25.00	25
1983 Santa On the Train NR-245	Retrd.	N/A	35.00	55-65
2000 Saturday Night Out NRR-613	7,500	2001	25.00	25
1979 Schoolmaster NR-210	Retrd.	N/A	34.00	45
1980 See America First NR-217	Retrd.	N/A	28.00	55-60
1999 Serenade (musical) NRR-601M	7,500	2001	30.00	30
1999 Serenade NRR-601	7,500	2001	20.00	20
1999 Skaters NRR-600	7,500	2001	20.00	20
1980 Springtime '33 NR-214	Retrd.	N/A	24.00	80
1982 Springtime '35 NR-219	Retrd.	N/A	24.00	30
1999 Stilt Walker NRR-603	7,500	2001	25.00	25
1980 Summertime '33 NR-215	Retrd.	N/A	22.00	50
1980 Take Your Medicine NR-218	Retrd.	N/A	36.00	40-50
1999 Triple Self Portrait NRR-608	7,500	2001	30.00	30
1984 Young Doctor NRD-226	Retrd.	N/A	30.00	50

Norman Rockwell Collection-Pewter Figurines - Rockwell-Inspired

1980 Back to School FP-02	Retrd.	N/A	25.00	25
1980 Barbershop Quartet FP-23	Retrd.	N/A	25.00	25
1980 Big Moment FP-21	Retrd.	N/A	25.00	25
1980 Caroller FP-03	Retrd.	N/A	25.00	25
1980 Circus FP-22	Retrd.	N/A	25.00	25
1980 Doctor and Doll FP-12	Retrd.	N/A	25.00	25
1980 Figurine Display Rack FDR-01	Retrd.	N/A	60.00	60
1980 Grandpa's Ballerina FP-32	Retrd.	N/A	25.00	25
1980 Lovers FP-07	Retrd.	N/A	25.00	25
1980 Magic Potion FP-28	Retrd.	N/A	25.00	25
1980 No Swimming FP-05	Retrd.	N/A	25.00	25
1980 See America First FP-17	Retrd.	N/A	25.00	25
1980 Take Your Medicine FP-18	Retrd.	N/A	25.00	25

Norman Rockwell Collection-Rockwell Club Series - Rockwell-Inspired

1982 Diary RCC-02	Retrd.	N/A	35.00	75
1984 Gone Fishing RCC-04	Retrd.	N/A	30.00	55
1983 Runaway Pants RCC-03	Retrd.	N/A	65.00	75
1981 Young Artist RCC-01	Retrd.	N/A	96.00	130-179

Norman Rockwell Collection-Select Collection, Ltd. - Rockwell-Inspired

1982 Boy & Mother With Puppies SC-1001	Retrd.	N/A	27.50	28
1982 Father With Child SC-1005	Retrd.	N/A	22.00	22
1982 Football Player SC-1004	Retrd.	N/A	22.00	22
1982 Girl Bathing Dog SC-1006	Retrd.	N/A	26.50	27
1982 Girl With Dolls In Crib SC-1002	Retrd.	N/A	26.50	27
1982 Helping Hand SC-1007	Retrd.	N/A	32.00	32
1982 Lemonade Stand SC-1008	Retrd.	N/A	32.00	32
1982 Save Me SC-1010	Retrd.	N/A	35.00	35
1982 Shaving Lesson SC-1009	Retrd.	N/A	30.00	30
1982 Young Couple SC-1003	Retrd.	N/A	27.50	28

Norman Rockwell Collection-Tom Sawyer Miniatures - Rockwell-Inspired

1983 First Smoke TSM-02	Retrd.	N/A	40.00	75
1983 Lost In Cave TSM-05	Retrd.	N/A	40.00	75
1983 Take Your Medicine TSM-04	Retrd.	N/A	40.00	75
1983 Whitewashing the Fence TSM-01	Retrd.	N/A	40.00	75

Norman Rockwell Collection-Tom Sawyer Series - Rockwell-Inspired

1976 First Smoke TS-02	Retrd.	N/A	60.00	235
1978 Lost In Cave TS-04	Retrd.	N/A	70.00	175
1977 Take Your Medicine TS-03	Retrd.	N/A	63.00	235
1975 Whitewashing the Fence TS-01	Retrd.	N/A	60.00	235

Norman Rockwell Saturday Evening Post - Rockwell-Inspired

1992 After the Prom NRP-916	Retrd.	1997	75.00	75
1994 Almost Grown Up NRC-609	Retrd.	2001	75.00	75
1993 Baby's First Step NRC-604	Retrd.	2001	100.00	100
1993 Bed Time NRC-606	Retrd.	1997	100.00	100
1990 Bedside Manner NRP-904	Retrd.	1997	65.00	85
1990 Big Moment NRP-906	Retrd.	N/A	100.00	100
1990 Bottom of the Sixth NRP-908	Retrd.	1997	165.00	165
1993 Bride & Groom NRC-605	Retrd.	2001	100.00	100
1991 Catching The Big One NRP-909	Retrd.	1997	75.00	125
1992 Choosin Up NRP-912	Retrd.	N/A	110.00	130-150
1990 Daydreamer NRP-902	Retrd.	1997	55.00	55
1990 Doctor and Doll NRP-907	Retrd.	N/A	110.00	150
1995 First Down NRC-614	Retrd.	1999	130.00	130
1995 First Haircut NRC-610	Retrd.	1999	85.00	80-85
1994 For A Good Boy NRC-608	Retrd.	1999	100.00	100
1992 Gone Fishing NRP-915	Retrd.	1999	65.00	65
1991 Gramps NRP-910	Retrd.	1999	85.00	85
1994 Little Mother NRC-607	Retrd.	1999	75.00	75
1998 Marriage License NRP-917	Retrd.	1999	65.00	65
1997 Missed NRP-914	Retrd.	1999	110.00	110-130
1995 New Arrival NRC-612	Retrd.	1999	90.00	90
1990 No Swimming NRP-901	Retrd.	N/A	50.00	85
1991 The Pharmacist NRP-911	Retrd.	1997	70.00	70-85
1990 Prom Dress NRP-903	Retrd.	N/A	60.00	60
1990 Runaway NRP-905	Retrd.	1997	130.00	165
1995 Sweet Dreams NRC-611	Retrd.	1999	85.00	70-85
1994 A Visit with Rockwell (100th Aniversary)-NRP-100	1,994	1999	100.00	100

Norman Rockwell Saturday Evening Post-Miniatures - Rockwell-Inspired

1991 A Boy Meets His Dog BMR-01	Retrd.	N/A	35.00	40
1991 Downhill Daring BMR-02	Retrd.	N/A	40.00	40
1991 Flowers in Tender Bloom BMR-03	Retrd.	N/A	32.00	40
1991 Fondly Do We Remember BMR-04	Retrd.	N/A	30.00	30
1991 In His Spirit BMR-05	Retrd.	N/A	30.00	30
1991 Pride of Parenthood BMR-06	Retrd.	N/A	35.00	40
1991 Sweet Serenade BMR-07	Retrd.	N/A	32.00	40-45
1991 Sweet Song So Young BMR-08	Retrd.	N/A	30.00	40-45

Department 56

All Through The House - Department 56

1993 All Snug in Their Bed 9322-0	Closed	1997	48.00	58-69
1992 Aunt Martha With Turkey 9317-3	Closed	1995	27.50	66-70
1993 Away To The Window 9321-1	Closed	1997	42.00	78-88
1995 Carrie Feeds The Cardinals 93339	Closed	1997	18.00	30-32
1994 Children With New Tree 9330-0, set/4	Closed	1997	85.00	84-102
1991 Christmas Tree 9302-5	Closed	1997	25.00	35-55
1992 Christopher Tasting Cookies, Caroline Stringing Cranberries 9310-6, (2 asst.)	Closed	1997	15.00	28-30
1992 Christopher Tasting Cookies 9310-6	Closed	1997	15.00	15-22
1992 Caroline Stringing Cranberries 9310-6	Closed	1997	15.00	16-23
1992 Dinner Table 9313-0	Closed	1995	65.00	88-102
1991 Down the Chimney & Sugar Plum Chair 9300-9, set/2	Closed	1997	96.00	83-132
1993 Elizabeth Spies Santa, Emily Spies Santa 9325-4, (2 asst.)	Closed	1997	16.00	30-32
1993 Elizabeth Spies Santa 9325-4	Closed	1997	16.00	16-36
1993 Emily Spies Santa 9325-4	Closed	1997	16.00	16-20
1994 Fletcher Playing Flute, Kenneth & Katie Singing Carols 9327-0, (3 asst.)	Closed	1997	16.00	16-24
1992 Grandma & Kitchen Table 9308-4, set/2	Closed	1997	55.00	55-90
1994 I Saw Mama Kissing Santa Claus 9332-7, set/2	Closed	1997	45.00	53-90
1993 Johnny Riding His Pony, Judith and Her Jack-In-The-Box 9319-0, (2 asst.)	Closed	1997	15.00	20-30
1993 Johnny Riding His Pony 9319-0	Closed	1997	15.00	15-36
1993 Judith and Her Jack-In-The-Box 9319-0	Closed	1997	15.00	22-25
1991 Jolly Old Elf 9303-3	Closed	1997	25.00	27-36
1992 Kitchen 9307-6	Closed	1997	75.00	74-92
1995 Let's Sing "Here Comes Santa Claus" 93336, set/3	Closed	1997	96.00	90-120
1992 Madeline Making Cookies 9309-2	Closed	1997	24.00	24-35
1992 Mama in Her Kerchief, Papa in His Cap 9304-1	Closed	1997	30.00	30-55
1991 Mary Jo, Billy 9306-8 (2 asst.)	Closed	1997	15.00	32-36
1996 Michael Makes a Snowman 93340	Closed	1997	32.50	22-48
1992 Mr. & Mrs. Bell at Dinner 9314-9, set/2	Closed	1995	40.00	78-98
1992 Nicholas Hanging Coat 9311-4	Closed	1997	22.50	29-32

YEAR ISSUE	EDITION LIMIT	YEAR RETD.	ISSUE PRICE	*QUOTE U.S.$
1992 Nicholas, Natalie, & Spot The Dog 9315-7, set/3	Closed	1995	45.00	34-58
1993 Not A Creature Was Stirring, Not Even a Mouse 9318-1	Closed	1997	37.50	40-54
1993 Pamela & Peter's Pillow Fight 9324-6, (2 asst.)	Closed	1997	16.00	24-32
1993 Pamela's Pillow Fight 9324-6	Closed	1997	16.00	16-46
1993 Peter's Pillow Fight 9324-6	Closed	1997	16.00	16-43
1993 Ruthan & Baby Patrick, Bradley Builds With Blocks 9320-3, (2 asst.)	Closed	1997	16.00	16-62
1991 Sarah Kate & Andy, Sue Ellen 9305-0 (2 asst.)	Closed	1997	28.00	48-55
1991 •Sarah Kate & Andy 9305-0	Closed	1997	16.00	18-22
1991 •Sue Ellen 9305-0	Closed	1997	16.00	9-28
1992 Sideboard 9316-5	Closed	1995	45.00	58-77
1994 Sleigh Full of Toys and St. Nicholas Too 9328-9	Closed	1997	75.00	165-210
1995 Sliding Down The Bannister 9333-5	Closed	1997	70.00	80-96
1994 Snowman with Plexi Sign 9874-4	Closed	1996	25.00	38-44
1991 Staircase 9301-7	Closed	1997	48.00	48-64
1995 Steven Skis on New-Fallen Snow 93338	Closed	1997	15.00	24-28
1995 Suzy and Spencer Making Snowballs 93337, set/2	Closed	1997	30.00	36-46
1992 Theodore Adjusting Time on Grandfather Clock 9312-2, set/2	Closed	1997	32.50	32-44
1994 To His Team Gave a Whistle 9329-7, (2 asst.)	Closed	1997	20.00	62
1996 Uncle John Takes a Family Portrait 93348, set/2	Closed	1997	72.00	72-96
1994 Under The Mistletoe 9331-9	Closed	1997	35.00	46
1994 Up On The Rooftop 9326-2	Closed	1997	85.00	82
1993 Visions of Sugarplums Danced in His Head 9323-8	Closed	1997	24.00	32-40

Bronté Candle Crown - Department 56

YEAR ISSUE	EDITION LIMIT	YEAR RETD.	ISSUE PRICE	*QUOTE U.S.$
1999 Alice in Wonderland Set 50000, set/11 plus book	2,500		4000.00	4000
1999 The Nutcracker Suite 50001, set/10 plus book	2,500		4000.00	4000
1999 The Wizard of Oz 50002, set/9 plus book	2,500		4000.00	4000

Candle Crown Collections - Department 56

YEAR ISSUE	EDITION LIMIT	YEAR RETD.	ISSUE PRICE	*QUOTE U.S.$
2000 Father Time - 2000 50036	Yr.Iss.	2000	50.00	50
2001 Glinda the Good Witch 50045	Open		45.00	45
2001 Halloween Pumpkin 50061	Open		35.00	35
2001 Holiday Tree 50066	Open		40.00	40
2001 Lady Liberty (Anniversary Edition) 50044	5,600		48.00	48
2001 Snowman 50064	Open		35.00	35
2001 Starlight Angel 50065	Open		35.00	35
2001 Thanksgiving Turkey 50063	Open		35.00	35
2001 Wicked Witch of the West 50046	Open		45.00	45

Candle Crown Collections-A Christmas Carol - Department 56

YEAR ISSUE	EDITION LIMIT	YEAR RETD.	ISSUE PRICE	*QUOTE U.S.$
2000 Bob Cratchit & Tiny Tim 50030	Open		45.00	45
2000 Ebenezer Scrooge 50029	Open		40.00	40
2000 Ghost of Christmas Present 50033	Open		40.00	40
2000 Ghost of Jacob Marley 50031	Open		40.00	40
2000 Mr. Fezziwig 50034	Open		40.00	40

Candle Crown Collections-African Safari Animals - Department 56

YEAR ISSUE	EDITION LIMIT	YEAR RETD.	ISSUE PRICE	*QUOTE U.S.$
2000 Enjoying Solitude (Cheetah) 50038	Open		37.50	38
2000 Learning To Play (Elephant) 50041	Open		37.50	38
2000 Loving Touch (Velvet Monkey) 50042	Open		37.50	38
2000 A Quiet Moment (Zebra) 50037	Open		37.50	38

Candle Crown Collections-Alice In Wonderland - Department 56

YEAR ISSUE	EDITION LIMIT	YEAR RETD.	ISSUE PRICE	*QUOTE U.S.$
1999 Alice 50003	Open		35.00	35
1999 Cheshire Cat 50007	Open		40.00	40
1999 King of Hearts 50004	Open		40.00	40
1999 Mad Hatter 50028	Open		40.00	40
1999 Queen of Hearts 50005	Open		40.00	40
1999 White Rabbit 50006	Open		35.00	35

Candle Crown Collections-The Nutcracker - Department 56

YEAR ISSUE	EDITION LIMIT	YEAR RETD.	ISSUE PRICE	*QUOTE U.S.$
1999 Clara & The Nutcracker Doll 50009	Open		45.00	45
1999 Drosselmeyer 50010	Open		40.00	40
1999 Nutcracker Prince 50011	Open		40.00	40
1999 Sugar Plum Fairy 50012	Open		40.00	40

Candle Crown Collections-The Wizard of Oz - Department 56

YEAR ISSUE	EDITION LIMIT	YEAR RETD.	ISSUE PRICE	*QUOTE U.S.$
1999 Cowardly Lion 50026	Open		45.00	45
1999 Dorothy 50025	Open		45.00	45
1999 Scarecrow 50014	Open		45.00	45
1999 Tin Man 50015	Open		45.00	45

Easter Collectibles - Department 56

YEAR ISSUE	EDITION LIMIT	YEAR RETD.	ISSUE PRICE	*QUOTE U.S.$
1991 Bisque Lamb, Large 4" 7392-0	Closed	1991	7.50	29-48
1991 Bisque Lamb, Small 2.5" 7393-8	Closed	1991	5.00	27-69
1991 Bisque Lamb, set	Closed	1991	12.50	39-78
1992 Bisque Rabbit, Large 5" 7498-5	Closed	1992	8.00	20-26
1992 Bisque Rabbit, Small 4" 7499-3	Closed	1992	6.00	18-29
1992 Bisque Rabbit, set	Closed	1992	14.00	42
1993 Bisque Duckling, Large 3.5" 7282-6	Closed	1993	8.50	10-15
1993 Bisque Duckling, Small 2.75" 7281-8	Closed	1993	6.50	10-20
1993 Bisque Duckling, set	Closed	1993	15.00	18-36
1994 Bisque Fledgling in Nest, Large 2.75" 2400-7	Closed	1994	6.00	6-18
1994 Bisque Fledgling in Nest, Small 2.5" 2401-5	Closed	1994	5.00	5-16
1995 Bisque Chick, Large 2464-3	Closed	1996	8.50	7-25
1995 Bisque Chick, Small 2465-1	Closed	1996	6.50	16-25
1995 Bisque Chick, set	Closed	1996	15.00	29
1996 Bisque Rabbit, Large 2765-0	Closed	1996	8.50	12-18
1996 Bisque Rabbit, Small 2764-2	Closed	1996	7.50	12-18
1996 Bisque Rabbit, set	Closed	1996	16.00	29
1997 Bisque Rabbit, large 23700	Closed	1997	8.50	16-20
1997 Bisque Rabbit, small 23701	Closed	1997	7.50	7-15
1998 Bisque Pig, large 23773	Closed	1998	7.50	8
1998 Bisque Pig, small 23774	Closed	1998	6.50	7
1999 Bisque Kitten, large 23862	Closed	1999	7.00	7
1999 Bisque Kitten, small 23861	Closed	1999	6.00	6
2000 Bisque Duck, large 23901	Closed	2000	8.50	9
2000 Bisque Duck, small 23902	Closed	2000	7.50	8
2001 Bisque Squirrel, large 24056	Closed	2001	7.50	8
2001 Bisque Squirrel, small 24097	Closed	2001	6.50	7

Harry Potter - Department 56

YEAR ISSUE	EDITION LIMIT	YEAR RETD.	ISSUE PRICE	*QUOTE U.S.$
2001 Harry Potter Animated Scene 59006	Open		125.00	125
2001 Hogwarts™ School of Witchcraft and Wizardy Lighted Scene 59036	Open		75.00	75
2001 Journey to Hogwarts™ Lighted Scene 59027	Open		75.00	75

Merry Makers - Department 56

YEAR ISSUE	EDITION LIMIT	YEAR RETD.	ISSUE PRICE	*QUOTE U.S.$
1995 Barnaby The Breadman 9361-0	Closed	1996	20.00	18-29
1992 Bartholomew The Baker w/Cart 9366-1	Closed	1996	35.00	60-70
1994 Bremwell The Bell-A-Ringer 9387-4	Closed	1996	22.00	32-36
1995 Brewster The Bird Feeder 93976	Closed	1996	25.00	24-60
1994 Calvin The Candycane Striper 93912	Closed	1996	22.00	24-32
1991 Charles The Cellist 9355-6	Closed	1995	19.00	32-36
1995 Chester The Tester & His Kettle 93972	Closed	1996	27.50	78-86
1993 Clarence the Concertinist (waterglobe/music box) 9377-7	Closed	1996	25.00	42-50
1991 Clarence The Concertinist 9353-0	Closed	1995	19.00	20-32
1991 Frederick The Flutist 9352-1	Closed	1995	19.00	25-32
1993 Garrison The Guzzler 9379-3	Closed	1996	20.00	26-44
1993 Godfrey The Gatherer 9380-7	Closed	1996	20.00	24-29
1995 Halsey The Stocking Hanger 93974	Closed	1996	32.50	28-48
1993 Heavenly Bakery Entrance 9371-8	Closed	1996	20.00	38-56
1991 Horatio The Hornblower 9351-3	Closed	1995	19.00	25-32
1994 Leo The Lamp-A-Lighter 9386-6	Closed	1996	22.00	28-32
1994 Leopold The Lollipopman 9390-4	Closed	1996	22.00	28-30
1994 Lollipop Shop Entrance 9389-0	Closed	1996	35.00	48-60
1993 Martin The Mandolinist (waterglobe/music box) 9377-7	Closed	1996	25.00	37-52
1991 Martin The Mandolinist 9350-5	Closed	1995	19.00	24-32
1993 Maxwell The Mixer at his Table 9372-6, set/8	Closed	1996	50.00	64-68
1994 Merrily We Roll Carolers & Gabriel The Goat 9382-3	Closed	1996	144.00	158-188
1992 Merry Makers Papier-Mache Church 9359-9	Closed	1995	95.00	99-105
1993 Merry Mountain Chapel, lighted 9370-0	Closed	1996	60.00	68-98
1995 Ollie The Optimist 93973	Closed	1996	25.00	46-48
1993 Otto The Ovenman at his Table 9373-4, set/2	Closed	1996	45.00	60
1994 The Peppermint Tree 9394-7	Closed	1996	18.00	24-29
1993 Percival The Puddingman (waterglobe/music box) 9376-9	Closed	1996	30.00	37-52

YEAR ISSUE	EDITION LIMIT	YEAR RETD.	ISSUE PRICE	*QUOTE U.S.$
1992 Percival The Puddingman 9362-9	Closed	1996	20.00	16-29
1994 Percy The Pudding-A-Bringer 9388-2	Closed	1996	22.00	26-32
1994 Peter The Peppermint Maker 9393-9	Closed	1996	22.00	27-38
1993 Porter The Presser & His Press 9378-5, set/2	Closed	1996	65.00	60-74
1993 Samuel the Sampler & Cider Barrel 9381-5, set/3	Closed	1996	27.50	45-58
1992 Sebastian The Snowball Maker 9367-0	Closed	1996	20.00	24-29
1993 Seigfried & The Snowman (waterglobe/music box) 9374-2	Closed	1996	30.00	52-58
1992 Seymore, Seigfried & The Snowman9365-3	Closed	1996	45.00	50-58
1995 Sheridan Thinks Santa 93975, set/2	Closed	1996	27.50	66-76
1991 Sidney The Singer 9354-8	Closed	1995	19.00	24-30
1992 Sigmund The Snowshoer 9358-0	Closed	1996	20.00	24-30
1993 Simon The Pieman (waterglobe/music box) 9376-9	Closed	1996	25.00	37-52
1992 Simon The Pieman 9363-7	Closed	1996	30.00	27-29
1993 Solomon The Sledder (waterglobe/music box) 9385-8	Closed	1996	37.50	44-52
1992 Solomon The Sledder 9356-4	Closed	1996	24.00	28-35
1992 Sweet Treats Tree 9364-5	Closed	1996	18.00	29-32
1992 Thaddeus The Tobogganist (waterglobe/music box) 9375-0	Closed	1996	30.00	38
1993 Thaddeus The Tobogganist 9357-2	Closed	1996	24.00	24-35
1992 Timothy The Taffy Twister 9392-0	Closed	1996	22.00	27-36

Silhouette Santas (Winter Silhouette) - Department 56

YEAR ISSUE	EDITION LIMIT	YEAR RETD.	ISSUE PRICE	*QUOTE U.S.$
1995 Cat Nap Santa & Finishing Touches Santa Bookends/Stocking Hangers 78560, (2 asst.)	Closed	1997	16.50	24-26
1994 Cat Nap Santa 7855-7	Closed	1997	37.50	40-69
1995 Dog's Best Friend Santa 78558, set/2	Closed	1999	37.50	38-69
1995 Finishing Touches Santa 78559	Closed	1997	37.50	39-69
1998 I See You Santa 78553, set/2	Closed	1999	35.00	35
1996 I Spy Santa 78562, set/2	Closed	1999	45.00	45-75
1998 I Wuv You Santa 78554	Closed	1999	30.00	30
1994 Naughty Or Nice? Santa 78565	Closed	1999	37.50	38-65
2002 Santa Ringing Bell 78708	Open		15.00	15
2002 Santa's Gifts 78706	Open		45.00	45
1997 String The Lights Santa 78550	Closed	1999	50.00	50-69
1998 Toys For Tots Santa 78552	Closed	1999	40.00	40
1997 What's New? Santa 78551, set/2	Closed	1999	37.50	38-64
1996 Your Move, Santa 78561, set/2	Closed	1998	37.50	36-64

Silhouette Treasures (Winter Silhouette) - Department 56

YEAR ISSUE	EDITION LIMIT	YEAR RETD.	ISSUE PRICE	*QUOTE U.S.$
1992 Accompanying A Carol 78352, set/2	Closed	1999	55.00	55-87
1995 Advent Tree 78579	Closed	2001	45.00	45
1991 Angel Candle Holder 7794-1	Closed	1997	95.00	104-118
1990 Angel Candle Holder w/Candle 6767-9	Closed	1992	32.50	35-38
2002 Angel of Innocence (votive) 78699, set/4	Open		15.00	15
1999 Angel of Peace 78617	Open		30.00	30
2001 Angel Votive Scene 78677	Open		10.00	10
2002 Angels of Light 78696, set/4	Open		50.00	50
2001 Antique Nativity Angel 78666	Open		95.00	95
2000 Bar Mitzvah 78636	Closed	2001	30.00	30
2000 Bat Mitzvah 78637	Closed	2001	25.00	25
1998 Bedtime Prayers 78601	Open		25.00	25
1991 Bedtime Stories 7792-5	Closed	1997	42.00	46-69
1993 A Bright Star on Christmas Eve 7843-3, set/2	Closed	1997	48.00	48-75
1989 Bringing Home The Tree 7790-9, set/4	Closed	1993	75.00	125-150
2002 Building A Snowman 78701, set/4	Open		37.50	38
1989 Camel w/glass Votive 6766-0	Closed	1993	25.00	50-52
1987 Carolers 7774-7, set/4	Closed	1993	120.00	213-220
1990 Caroling Angel w/Brass Halo & Songbook 6767	Closed	1998	15.00	16-29
1991 Caroling Bells 7798-4, set/3	Closed	1997	60.00	60-85
1992 Carols Around The Spinet 78042, set/4	Closed	2001	100.00	100
1992 Cathedral Façade 78085	Closed	2001	72.00	72
2001 A Child is Born (lighted) 78647	Open		75.00	75
2001 A Child Is Born Nativity 78668, set/10	Open		75.00	75
1998 Child's Play 78610, set/3	Closed	2000	50.00	50
1991 Chimney Sweep 7799-2	Closed	1993	37.50	58-64
1992 A Choir Angel Candle Holder 78034	Closed	1998	13.50	14-33
1992 A Choir of Angels Votive Holder 78026	Closed	1998	18.00	20-28
1994 Christmas Concerto Cellist 78484, set/2	Closed	1998	35.00	18-49
1994 Christmas Concerto Harpist 78468, set/2	Closed	1999	40.00	40-48

YEAR ISSUE	EDITION LIMIT	YEAR RETD.	ISSUE PRICE	*QUOTE U.S.$
1994 Christmas Concerto Violinist 78476	Closed	1998	32.50	18-49
1996 A Christmas Dollhouse Built By Grandfather 78587, set/2	Closed	1999	35.00	35
1993 A Christmas Kiss 7845-0, set/2	Closed	1997	32.50	33-55
2002 The Christmas Pageant 78679	Open		55.00	55
1997 The Christmas Pageant Angels 78593, set/4	Open		45.00	45
1992 Christmas Presents 7805-0, set/2	Closed	1997	35.00	35-64
1995 Christmas Tea 78575, set/3	Closed	1999	40.00	40-52
2000 The Church in the Pines 78644	Open		68.00	68
1997 Clara & The Nutcracker 78594	Closed	2001	20.00	20
2001 Come Dance With Me 78658	Open		40.00	40
1999 Cooking With Grandmother 78623, set/2	Closed	2001	37.50	38
2001 Dash Away All (lighted) 78648	Open		75.00	75
1990 Decorating The Mantel 77917, set/3	Closed	1999	60.00	60-87
1999 Does Santa Really Come Down The Chimney? (lighted) 78625	Open		75.00	75
1995 A Family Tradition 78578	Closed	2000	65.00	65
1989 Father Christmas 7788-7	Closed	1993	50.00	90-104
2001 The First Step 78659	Closed	2001	32.50	33
1998 A Gift For You 78605, set/2	Closed	2000	35.00	35
2001 Glory To the Newborn King 78651	Open		50.00	50
1991 Grandfather Clock 7797-6	Closed	1995	27.50	52-68
2002 Hand in Hand 78685	Open		18.00	18
2000 Happy Anniversary 78640	Closed	2001	45.00	45
1999 Helping Hands 78624, set/6	Closed	2001	45.00	45
2001 Holy Family Votive Scene 78676	Open		48.00	48
2000 Home For Christmas (lighted) 78645	Open		68.00	68
2001 A Hug For Santa 78654	Open		50.00	50
2000 I Believe (boy) 78639	Open		20.00	20
2000 I Believe (girl) 78638	Open		20.00	20
1996 I Spy Santa 78562, set/2	Closed	1998	45.00	36-45
1996 In The Meadow We Can Build A Snowman 78592, set/3	Closed	2000	45.00	45
1992 Jolly St. Nicholas 78018	Closed	2000	30.00	30
1988 Joy To The World "Carolers On Songbooks" 5595-6	Closed	1990	42.00	84-120
1995 Kneeling Angel With Mandolin 78585	Closed	1997	48.00	48-96
2001 The Last Supper (lighted) 78660	Open		75.00	75
2002 Lattice And Lace Elegant Cross 78710	Open		30.00	30
1996 Let It Snow 78591	Closed	2000	70.00	70
2001 Let Me Call You Sweetheart 78667	Open		40.00	40
1997 Letter To Santa 78597	Closed	2000	37.50	38
1990 Lighted Nativity 67695	Closed	2000	37.50	38
1999 Lighting the Menorah 78618	Closed	2001	85.00	85
1997 Little Drummer Boy 78595, set/3	Closed	2001	45.00	45
1998 Little Music Makers 78611, set/4	Closed	2000	45.00	45
2001 Love Birds 78650	Open		15.00	15
2000 Love Is All Around 78643	Closed	2001	15.00	15
2001 A Love Letter 78662	Open		15.00	15
1994 Mantelpiece Santa 7854-9	Closed	1997	55.00	55-92
1992 The Marionette Performance 7807-7, set/3	Closed	1997	75.00	88-110
1998 The Miracle of Christmas 78612, set/3	Closed	2001	70.00	70
2002 Miracle of Christmas Nativity 78687, set/16	Open		150.00	150
1999 Mother and Child 78620	Closed	2001	40.00	40
2002 Nativity Background 78686, set/3	Open		60.00	60
1990 Nativity Scene 67717, set/4	Closed	2001	70.00	70
2002 The New Born King 78694, set/3	Open		150.00	150
1999 O Holy Night Church 78627	Closed	2001	30.00	30
2002 Oh Holy Night 78692	Open		30.00	30
1997 Old World Santa 67725	Closed	1998	50.00	55-87
2002 On This Day Cake Topper 78711	Open		27.50	28
1997 Over The River And Through The Woods 78596, set/2	Closed	2000	65.00	65
1999 Peace and Good Will To All 78616	4,000	1999	200.00	200
2002 The Perfect Tree! 78678	Open		68.00	68
2001 A Pony For Her Birthday 78656	Closed	2001	30.00	30
1989 Putting Up the Tree 7789-5, set/3	Closed	1997	90.00	131-195
2000 Reaching For the Stars 78641	Closed	2001	15.00	15
2001 Ring Around The Christmas Tree 78652	Open		40.00	40
1999 Roses and Lace 78621	Closed	2001	15.00	15
1995 Santa Filling The Stockings (lighted) 78573	Closed	1999	55.00	55-78
1993 Santa Lucia 7844-1	Closed	1997	27.50	28-49
1991 Santa's Reindeer 7796-8, (2 asst.)	Closed	1997	14.00	26-30
1991 Santa's Sleigh & 4 Reindeer 77950, set/5	Closed	1998	125.00	155-184

FIGURINES

YEAR ISSUE	EDITION LIMIT	YEAR RETD.	ISSUE PRICE	*QUOTE U.S.$
2001 A Season For Friends 78653, set/2	Open		37.50	38
1999 The Shepherds Watched 78629, set/2	Closed	2001	50.00	50
1994 Shiny Skates & A Brand New Sled 78522, set/2	Closed	1999	35.00	35-52
1988 Silver Bells Music Box "Corner Carolers" 8271-6	Closed	1990	75.00	135-150
1994 Skater's Waltz 78530, set/2	Closed	1998	42.00	58-63
1988 Skating Children 7773-9, set/2	Closed	1997	33.00	40-58
1988 Skating Couple 7772-0	Closed	1995	35.00	72
2002 Skating Party 78700, set/9	Open		50.00	50
1988 Sleighride 77712	Closed	1998	60.00	65-104
1994 Sliding In The Snow 78492	Closed	2000	37.50	38
1987 Snow Doves 8215-5, set/2	Closed	1992	60.00	68
1992 Snowy White Deer 7837-9, set/2	Closed	1995	55.00	115-135
1998 Some Of My Favorite Things 78602, set/4	Closed	2000	35.00	35
1995 Standing Angel With Horn 78584	Closed	1997	48.00	46-75
2002 Steeple Church (votive) 78693, set/2	Open		20.00	20
1998 Sugar Plum Fairies 78604	Closed	2001	40.00	40
1998 Sugar Plum Fairies Waterglobe 78613	Closed	2001	32.50	33
1997 Tell Us About The Olden Days, Grandpa 78598	Closed	2001	55.00	55
1999 Thank Heaven For Little Girls 78635	Closed	2001	32.50	33
1989 Three Kings Candle Holder 6765-2, set/3	Closed	1992	85.00	172-180
2001 Three Kings Votive Scene 78673	Open		48.00	48
1999 Tidings of Comfort And Joy 78626, set/3	Open		75.00	75
1999 To Have And To Hold 78630	Closed	2001	32.50	33
1999 To Honor Him 78622, set/6	Closed	2001	80.00	80
1991 Town Crier 7800-0	Closed	1994	37.50	58-84
2002 Verdi Votive 78698	Open		12.50	13
1993 A Visit With Santa 78417, set/2	Closed	1999	55.00	55-75
2001 Votive Scenes 78665	Open		15.00	15
2002 Warmth of the Holidays (votive) 78709	Open		15.00	15
1995 We Three Kings 78574, set/3	Closed	2001	250.00	250
2002 We Three Kings 78695, set/3	Open		175.00	175
1996 Winter Nights 78577	Closed	2000	25.00	25
1992 Winter Silhouette Church 78360 (lighted)	Closed	1999	48.00	48
2002 Winter Wonderland (votive) 78704	Open		15.00	15

Snowbabies Collectors' Club - Department 56

YEAR ISSUE	EDITION LIMIT	YEAR RETD.	ISSUE PRICE	*QUOTE U.S.$
1997 You Better Watch Out 68851	Closed	1998	Gift	35-45
1998 Together We Can Make The Season Bright 68852	Closed	1998	75.00	75-110
1998 Baby It's Cold Outside 68889	Closed	1999	Gift	35
1998 Nice To Meet You Little One 68898, set/2	Closed	1999	75.00	75
1999 Friendsdip Charms, set/5	Closed	1999	Gift	N/A
1999 Storytime 68956	Closed	1999	50.00	50
2000 Ready to See The World? 69051	Closed	2001	Gift	N/A
2000 I Think I Can 69052, set/2	Closed	2001	50.00	50
2001 Friendship Clubhouse (5th Anniversary) 69154	Open		45.00	45
2002 I Can Fly 69124, set/4	12/02		40.00	40
2002 Friends On The Frosty Frolic 69127	12/02		45.00	45

Snowbabies - Department 56

YEAR ISSUE	EDITION LIMIT	YEAR RETD.	ISSUE PRICE	*QUOTE U.S.$
2001 Add A Happy Face 69097	Open		35.00	35
1999 All Aboard Star Express 68943, set/4	Closed	2000	55.00	55
2001 All Decked Out And Ready To Go (The Gift of Christmas) 69131	Open		17.50	18
1989 All Fall Down 7984-7, set/4	Closed	1991	36.00	82-98
1997 All We Need Is Love (1998 Mother's Day Event Piece) 68860	Closed	1998	32.50	40-60
1998 ...And That Spells BABY 68923, set/4	Closed	2000	50.00	50
2002 ...And Toto Too? (Snowbabies Guest Collection™) 69921	Open		95.00	95
2001 ...And We've Been Really Good (Holiday Discover 2001) 69915	Closed	2001	65.00	65
1988 Are All These Mine? 7977-4	Closed	1998	10.00	13-23
1995 Are You On My List? 6875-6	Closed	1998	25.00	25-41
2000 As Time Goes By (w/clock) 69053	Yr.Iss.		40.00	40
1999 Batter Up 68957	Closed	1999	16.50	17
1999 Batter Up (Starlight Games™) 69047	Open		16.50	17
2002 Bedtime Prayers 69164	Open		30.00	30
1986 Best Friends 7958-8	Closed	1989	12.00	114-173

YEAR ISSUE	EDITION LIMIT	YEAR RETD.	ISSUE PRICE	*QUOTE U.S.$
1997 Best Little Star 68842	Closed	1999	16.00	16
1997 Bisque Friendship Pin (Event Piece) 68849	Closed	1997	5.00	5-10
2001 Born To Be A Star 69079, set/2	Open		45.00	45
2001 Breakfast in Bed (Discover Department 56® Spring Promotion) 69072	Yr.Iss.	2001	35.00	65
1994 Bringing Starry Pines 6862-4	Closed	1997	35.00	35-50
2001 Burning Up The Lines 69080	Open		35.00	35
1992 Can I Help, Too? 6806-3	18,500	1992	48.00	65-80
1993 Can I Open it Now? (Event Piece) 6838-1	Closed	1994	15.00	45
1997 Candle Light...Season Bright (tree topper) 68863	Closed	1999	20.00	20
1997 Candlelight Trees 68861, set/3	Closed	1999	25.00	25
2001 Catch Me If You Can (The Guest Collection) 69912	Open		50.00	50
1999 Celebrate (1999 Winter Celebration Event Piece) 68941	Closed	1999	60.00	60
1997 Celebrating A Snowbabies Journey, 1987-1997..."Let's Go See Jack Frost" (Event Piece) 68850	Closed	1997	60.00	60-75
2002 Christmas Morning 69160, set/9	Open		75.00	75
2001 The Christmas Pageant (The Gift of Christmas) 69138	Open		125.00	125
2001 Christmas Tree (The Gift of Christmas) 69144	Open		25.00	25
1996 Climb Every Mountain 68816	22,500	1996	75.00	65-188
1986 Climbing on Snowball, Bisque Votive w/Candle 7965-0	Closed	1989	15.00	113-205
1987 Climbing On Tree 7971-5, set/2	Closed	1989	25.00	906-1020
2001 Close Your Eyes and Make a Wish! 69141	Open		17.50	18
2001 Cold Noses, Warm Heart 69074	Open		27.50	27.50
1998 Come Fly With Me 68920	22,500	1999	165.00	165
1999 Come Sail With Me 69019	Closed	2001	60.00	60
2001 Count Your Lucky Stars Candle Jar (Holiday Discover 2001) 69129, set/2	Closed	2001	18.00	18
1993 Crossing Starry Skies 6834-9	Closed	1997	35.00	35-55
2000 Crown Me 69056	Closed	2001	35.00	35
1991 Dancing To a Tune 6808-0, set/3	Closed	1995	30.00	44-88
1987 Don't Fall Off 7968-5	Closed	1990	12.50	79-130
1987 Down The Hill We Go 7960-0	Closed	2000	20.00	23
2000 Dreams Do Come True 69058	Open		22.50	23
2002 Eloise on the Polar Express (Snowbabies Guest Collection™) 69918	Open		50.00	50
1999 Even A Small Light Shines In The Darkness 69017	Open		45.00	45
2002 Everyone Is Beautiful 69168	Open		16.50	17
1999 Falling For You 69035	Closed	2001	18.00	18
1989 Finding Fallen Stars 7985-5	6,000	1990	32.50	188
2000 First To The Finish (Starlight Games™) 69930	Closed	2001	16.50	17
1991 Fishing For Dreams 6809-8	Closed	1994	28.00	44-48
1996 Five-Part Harmony 68824	Closed	1999	32.50	45
2000 Flag (Starlight Games™) 69933	Closed	2001	6.00	6
1999 Follow Me 68944	Closed	2000	17.50	18
1986 Forest Accessory "Frosty Forest" 7963-4, set/2	Open		15.00	20
2002 Forever Friends 69167	Open		27.50	27.50
1988 Frosty Frolic 7981-2	4,800	1989	35.00	975-1095
1989 Frosty Fun 7983-9	Closed	1991	27.50	50-68
1995 Frosty Pines 76687, set/3	Closed	1998	12.50	20
1998 A Gift So Fine From Madeline (1999 Mother's Day Event) (Snowbabies Guest Collection™) 69901	Closed	2001	50.00	50
1986 Give Me A Push 7955-3	Closed	1990	12.00	70-85
2002 Good Sports, Good Friends (Starlight Games™) 69951	Yr.Iss.		18.50	19
2001 Guess! 69087	Open		15.00	15
1986 Hanging Pair (votive) 7966-9	Closed	1989	15.00	132-185
2001 Have A Ball - Cinderella (Snowbabies Guest Collection™) (Anniversary Edition) 69905, set/3	20,000	2001	135.00	135
1997 Heigh-Ho, Heigh-Ho, To Frolic Land We Go! 68853	Closed	2001	48.00	48
1992 Help Me, I'm Stuck 6817-9	Closed	1994	32.50	35-37
1989 Helpful Friends 7982-0	Closed	1993	30.00	45-60
1999 Hit The Mark (Starlight Games™) 69005	Closed	2001	25.00	25
1986 Hold On Tight 7956-1	Closed	1999	12.00	28
2001 Hold That Pose (Starlight Games™) 69944	Open		16.50	17

YEAR ISSUE	EDITION LIMIT	YEAR RETD.	ISSUE PRICE	*QUOTE U.S.$
2001 Hooked On Fishing 69142	Open		30.00	30
1998 How Many Days 'Til Christmas? 68882	Closed	1999	36.00	36-46
2000 I Can Do That, Too! 69012	Closed	2001	37.50	38
1998 I Can Touch My Toes 68927, set/2	Closed	2000	30.00	30
1995 I Can't Find Him 68800	Closed	1998	37.50	38-48
1999 I Caribou You 68942	Open		50.00	50
1995 I Found The Biggest Star of All! 6874-8	Closed	1998	16.00	19-26
1993 I Found Your Mittens 6836-5, set/2	Closed	1996	30.00	30-40
1998 I Have A Feeling We're Not In Kansas Anymore (Snowbabies Guest Collection™) 69900	Closed	2001	50.00	50
1998 I Love You This Much! 68918	Open		16.50	17
1991 I Made This Just For You 6802-0	Closed	1998	15.00	25-38
1992 I Need A Hug 6813-6	Open		20.00	20
1995 I See You! 6878-0, set/2	Closed	1999	27.50	28-33
2001 I Think I Can Train Engine 69153	Open		40.00	40
2001 I'll Be Home For Home For Christmas (Holiday Discover 2001) 69128	Closed	2001	50.00	50
1999 I'll Love You Always (Discover Department 56® Spring Promotion) 69009	Closed	2000	30.00	30
1995 I'll Play A Christmas Tune 68801	Closed	1999	16.00	15-50
1991 I'll Put Up The Tree 6800-4	Closed	1995	24.00	35
1993 I'll Teach You A Trick 6835-7	Closed	1996	24.00	28-34
2000 I'm An Artist 69069, set/3	Closed	2001	22.50	23
2001 I'm A Little Teapot 69088	Open		15.00	15
1993 I'm Making an Ice Sculpture 6842-0	Closed	1996	30.00	42-60
1986 I'm Making Snowballs 7962-6	Closed	1992	12.00	45-69
1994 I'm Right Behind You! 6852-7	Closed	1997	60.00	60-94
1996 I'm So Sleepy 68810	Open	2000	16.00	16-50
1997 I'm The Star Atop Your Tree! (tree topper) 68862	Closed	1999	20.00	20-28
2001 In The Groove (Starlight Games™) 69935	Open		17.50	18
2002 It's A Birdie (Starlight Games™) 69949	Open		18.50	19
1996 It's A Grand Old Flag 68822	Closed	1998	25.00	34-50
2000 It's A Wonderful World 69059	Closed	2001	32.50	33
1996 It's Snowing! 68821	Closed	2001	16.50	17
2001 I've Got Mail 69143	Open		16.00	16
1989 Icy Igloo 7987-1	Closed	2000	37.50	38
1991 Is That For Me 6803-9, set/2	Closed	1993	32.50	48-75
1996 Jack Frost...A Sleighride Through the Stars 68811, set/3	Closed	2000	110.00	110
1999 Jack Frost...Through The Frosty Forest 69020	Open		150.00	150
1994 Jack Frost...A Touch of Winter's Magic 6854-3	Closed	1999	90.00	105-125
1997 Jingle Bell 68855	Closed	2001	16.00	16
1992 Join The Parade 6824-1	Closed	1994	37.50	50-75
1999 Jolly Friends Forevermore 69021, set/11	Open		50.00	50
1998 A Journey For Two By Caribou! 68881	Closed	2001	50.00	50
1999 Jumping For Joy 69036	Closed	2001	18.00	18
1992 Just One Little Candle 6823-3	Closed	1999	15.00	15-25
1999 A Kiss For You and 2000 Too (Snowbabies Guest Collection™) 69902	Closed	2000	50.00	50
2001 Kiss Me (The Gift of Christmas) 69133	Open		25.00	25
1993 Let's All Chime In! 6845-4, set/2	Closed	1995	37.50	52-69
1998 Let's Be Friends (Disney Exclusive) 06850	Closed	1999	N/A	209-263
1994 Let's Go Skating 6860-8	Closed	1998	16.50	20-30
1992 Let's Go Skiing 6815-2	Closed	1999	15.00	20
1994 Lift Me Higher, I Can't Reach 6863-2	Closed	1998	75.00	80-100
1996 A Little Night Light 68823	Closed	1999	32.50	33-41
1996 A Little Night Light (lamp) 68836	Closed	1999	75.00	75
1999 The Littlest Angel 69011	Open		18.00	18
2002 The Littlest Christmas Tree 69165	Open		25.00	25
2002 Look Mom...It's For You! 69158	Open		35.00	35
1992 Look What I Can Do! 6819-5	Closed	1996	16.50	30
1993 Look What I Found 6833-0	Closed	1997	45.00	45-63
2000 Love Is In The Air 69055	Open		18.00	18
1998 Make A Wish 68926	Closed	2001	30.00	30
2002 Make Room For Toto (Snowbabies Guest Collection™) 69922	Open		17.50	18
2001 A Message In My Hands 69081, set/3	Closed	2001	40.00	40

YEAR ISSUE	EDITION LIMIT	YEAR RETD.	ISSUE PRICE	*QUOTE U.S.$
1994 Mickey's New Friend (Disney Exclusive) 714-5	Closed	1995	60.00	540-620
1996 Moonbeams (Night Light) 68835	Closed	1999	20.00	20
2002 Music From Heaven 69166	Open		17.50	18
1999 Music From The Highest 69016, set/3	Closed	2001	45.00	45
1995 Mush 68805	Closed	1999	48.00	48
2001 My Little Star (Starlight Games™) 69946	Open		12.50	13
1998 My Snowbaby Baby Dolls 68919, set/2	Closed	2001	32.50	33
1998 Nice To Meet You Little One 68898, set/2	Closed	1999	75.00	75
1993 Now I Lay Me Down to Sleep 6839-0	Open		13.50	14
1996 Once Upon A Time... (votive candleholder) 68815	Closed	2000	25.00	25
1997 One For You, One For Me 68858	Closed	2001	27.50	28
1992 Over the Milky Way 6828-4	Closed	1995	32.00	38-48
1999 Over the Top (Starlight Games™) 69004	Open		25.00	25
2002 Owl-Ways Watching Over You 69163	Open		22.50	23
1995 Parade of Penguins 68804, set/6	Closed	2000	15.00	15
1989 Penguin Parade 7986-3	Closed	1992	25.00	54-65
1994 Pennies From Heaven 6864-0	Closed	1998	17.50	14-20
2000 Perfect Balance (Starlight Games™) 69932	Open		25.00	25
1990 Playing Games Is Fun 7947-2	Closed	1993	30.00	48-60
1988 Polar Express 7978-2	Closed	1992	22.00	90-98
2001 Pop Goes The Snowman 69076	Open		18.00	18
2002 The Puck Stops Here (Starlight Games™) 69948	Open		17.50	18
2002 Puffin In A Pear Tree (The Gift of Christmas™) 69177	Open		27.50	28
1998 Pull Together 68924	Closed	2001	60.00	60
1999 Reach For The Moon (Avon Exclusive) 66852	Closed	1999	20.00	20
2000 Ready, Set...! (Starlight Games™) 69931	Closed	2001	16.50	17
1990 Read Me a Story! 7945-6	Closed	2000	25.00	25-45
2002 Rejoice (The Gift of Christmas™) 69175	Open		16.50	17
2000 Ride The Wave (Discover Department 56® Holiday Program) 69057	Closed	2000	50.00	50
1995 Ring The Bells...It's Christmas! 6876-4	Closed	2000	40.00	40
1997 Rock-A-Bye Baby (Event Piece) 68848	Closed	1997	15.00	15-20
2001 Rudolph Gets Ready (Snowbabies Guest Collection™) 69906	Open		50.00	50
2002 Scooterbaby (Starlight Games™) 69950	Open		17.50	18
1999 Score (Starlight Games™) 69007	Open		16.50	17
2001 See You On The Slopes (Starlight Games™) 69936	Open		17.50	18
2001 Shh...Don't Tell (The Gift of Christmas) 69132	Open		16.50	17
1999 Shake It Up, Baby 69013	Open		20.00	20
1992 Shall I Play For You? 6820-9	Closed	1998	16.50	20-30
1997 Ship O' Dreams 68859, set/2	Closed	2001	135.00	135
2001 Shoot For The Goal 56937	Open		17.50	18
2002 Sing A Song (The Gift of Christmas™) 69176	Open		35.00	35
2001 Skate With Me 69073, set/11	Open		50.00	50
1998 Slip, Sliding Away (GCC Exclusive) 6808	Closed	1998	28.00	50
1998 Slip, Sliding Away 68934	Closed	2000	28.00	28
2001 A Snow Bird! 69077	Open		22.50	23
1995 Snowbabies Animated Skating Pond 7668-6, set/14	Closed	1998	60.00	60-85
1993 Snowbabies Picture Frame, Baby's First Smile 6846-2	Closed	1998	30.00	30-35
1996 Snowbaby Display Sled 6883-8	Closed	2000	45.00	45
1986 Snowbaby Holding Picture Frame 7970-7, set/2	Closed	1987	15.00	495-842
1986 Snowbaby Nite-Lite 7959-6	Closed	1989	15.00	327
1991 Snowbaby Polar Sign 6804-7	Closed	1996	20.00	40
1997 Snowbaby Shelf Unit 68874	Open		20.00	20
1993 So Much Work To Do 6837-3	Closed	1998	18.00	18-28
1993 Somewhere in Dreamland 6840-3	Closed	1997	85.00	98-115
1994 Somewhere in Dreamland (1 snowflake) 6840-3	Closed	1994	85.00	120-132
1995 Somewhere in Dreamland (2 snowflake) 6840-3	Closed	1995	85.00	95
1996 Somewhere in Dreamland (3 snowflake) 6840-3	Closed	1996	85.00	65-95

YEAR ISSUE	EDITION LIMIT	YEAR RETD.	ISSUE PRICE	*QUOTE U.S.$
1997 Somewhere in Dreamland (4 snowflake) 6840-3	Closed	1997	85.00	95
1990 A Special Delivery 7948-0	Closed	1994	15.00	27-35
1998 Star Gazer's Castle 68925	Closed	2001	40.00	40
1995 Star Gazing (Starter Set) 7800	Open		40.00	40
1995 A Star in the Box (GCC exclusive) 68803	Closed	1996	18.00	38-50
1999 Star On The Top (tree topper) 68952	Closed	2000	12.50	13
1996 Stargazing 68817, set/9	Closed	1998	40.00	40-55
1997 Starlight Serenade 68856	Closed	2000	25.00	25
1999 Starlight, Starbright 69015	Open		25.00	25
1992 Starry Pines 6829-2, set/2	Closed	1998	17.50	25-30
1992 Stars-In-A-Row, Tic-Tac-Toe 6822-5	Closed	1995	32.50	35-45
2001 Star Votive 69149, set/2	Open		12.50	13
1994 Stringing Fallen Stars 6861-6	Closed	1998	25.00	25-35
1998 Stuck In The Snow 68932	Closed	2000	30.00	30
1998 Stuck In The Snow (GCC Exclusive) 6806	Closed	1998	30.00	30-50
2000 Tea For Two (Snowbabies Guest Collection™) 69904, set/2	Closed	2001	50.00	50
2001 Team of Two (Starlight Games™) 69943	Open		32.50	33
2002 Teddy Bear Tea (Snowbabies Guest Collection™) 69923	Open		40.00	40
1997 Thank You 68857	Closed	2001	32.50	33
1994 There's Another One!, 6853-5	Closed	1998	24.00	24-35
1996 There's No Place Like Home 68820	Closed	2000	16.50	17-27
1999 They're Coming From Oz, Oh My! (Snowbabies Guest Collection™) 69010	Open		55.00	55
1991 This Is Where We Live 6805-5	Closed	1994	60.00	50-80
1992 This Will Cheer You Up 6816-0	Closed	1994	30.00	39-49
1998 Three Tiny Trumpeters (1998 Winter Celebration Event Piece) 68888, set/2	Closed	1998	50.00	50-100
2001 Time Out 69075	Open		17.50	18
1988 Tiny Trio 7979-0, set/3	Closed	1990	20.00	168-215
1988 To My Friend 68917	Closed	2001	18.00	18
2001 To The Moon And Beyond 69078	Closed	2001	35.00	35
1999 Tower of Light 69022	Closed	2001	40.00	40
1987 Tumbling In the Snow 7957-0, set/5	Closed	1993	35.00	88-125
1990 Twinkle Little Stars 7942-1, set/2	Closed	1993	37.50	50-60
2001 Twist & Shout (Starlight Games™) 69942	Open		16.50	17
2001 Two Little Angels 69140	Open		34.00	34
1997 Two Little Babies On The Go! 68840	Closed	2001	32.50	33
2000 Under The Midnight Moon With Barbie™ (Snowbabies Guest Collection™) 69903	Closed	2000	60.00	60
2002 Up Into The Stars (Snowbabies Guest Collection™) 69169	15,000		150.00	150
1992 Wait For Me 6812-8	Closed	1994	48.00	38-75
1991 Waiting For Christmas 6807-1	Closed	1993	27.50	50-56
2002 Walk Like A Penguin 69161	Open		27.50	28
1993 We Make a Great Pair 6843-8	Closed	1999	30.00	30
1990 We Will Make it Shine 7946-4	Closed	1992	45.00	50-90
2001 We'll Light The Tree (The Gift of Christmas) 69017	Open		25.00	25
1994 We'll Plant the Starry Pines 6865-9, set/2	Closed	1997	37.50	38-54
1995 We're Building An Icy Igloo 68802	Closed	1997	70.00	90-120
1995 What Shall We Do Today? 6877-2	Closed	1997	32.50	33-48
1996 When the Bough Breaks 68819	Closed	2001	30.00	30
1993 Where Did He Go? 6841-1	Open		35.00	35
1994 Where Did You Come From? 6856-0	Closed	1997	40.00	40-55
1996 Which Way's Up 68812	Closed	1997	30.00	30-45
1997 Whistle While You Work 68854	Closed	1999	32.50	33-41
1990 Who Are You? 7949-9	12,500	1991	32.50	77-130
1991 Why Don't You Talk To Me 6801-2	Open		24.00	24
1993 Will it Snow Today? 6844-6	Closed	1995	45.00	58-65
1992 Winken, Blinken, and Nod 6814-4	Closed	1998	60.00	70-110
1998 Winter Celebration Event Piece rim 68887	Closed	1998	5.00	10-20
1998 Winter Play On A Snowy Day 68880, set/4	Closed	1999	48.00	48
1987 Winter Surprise 7974-0	Closed	1992	15.00	46-58
1997 Wish Upon a Falling Star 68839	Closed	1999	75.00	75-80
1990 Wishing on a Star 7943-0	Closed	1994	22.00	45-50
1997 Wishing You A Merry Christmas 68843	Closed	1998	40.00	40-60
1996 With Hugs & Kisses 68813, set/2	Closed	1998	32.50	35-55
2002 The World Needs Dreamers 69162	Open		18.00	18
2001 You And Me Frame (Discover Department 56® Spring) 69071	Closed	2001	15.00	15

YEAR ISSUE	EDITION LIMIT	YEAR RETD.	ISSUE PRICE	*QUOTE U.S.$
1996 You Are My Lucky Star 68814, set/2	Closed	1999	35.00	35
1999 You Are My Starshine 68945	Closed	2001	17.50	18
1992 You Can't Find Me! 6818-7	Closed	1996	45.00	54-60
1992 You Didn't Forget Me 6821-7	Closed	1999	32.50	33-38
1996 You Need Wings Too! 68818	Closed	2001	25.00	25
1996 You're My Snowbaby (picture frame) 6883-4	Closed	1999	15.00	15
1998 You've Got The Cutest Little Baby Face 68933	Closed	2000	32.50	33
1998 You've Got The Cutest Little Baby Face (GCC Exclusive) 6809	Closed	1998	32.50	33

Snowbabies Babies on the Farm™ - Department 56

YEAR ISSUE	EDITION LIMIT	YEAR RETD.	ISSUE PRICE	*QUOTE U.S.$
2001 Along For The Ride 67500	Open		37.50	38
2002 Babies Best Friend 67525	Open		17.50	18
2001 Baby Sledding Picture Frame 67507	Open		15.00	15
2002 Barn 67524	Open		35.00	35
2001 Barn Picture Frame 67509	Closed	2001	13.00	13
2002 Bobbing For Apples 67518	Open		25.00	25
2002 Farmhouse 67526	Open		35.00	35
2001 Fence 67511	Open		75.00	75
2001 Give A Hoot 67501	Closed	2001	15.00	15
2002 God Bless America 67519	Open		16.50	17
2002 Kitten Courier 67515	Open		25.00	25
2001 Look Out Below! 67504	Open		25.00	25
2001 A Lucky Duck! 67503	Open		15.00	15
2001 Play With Me? (waterglobe) 67513	Open		32.50	33
2001 Pump 67510	Open		10.00	10
2002 Tally Ho 67523	Open		40.00	40
2001 Try It, You'll Like It 67502, set/2	Open		17.50	18
2001 Windmill 67508	Open		17.50	18
2001 You Should Wear A Hat 67507	Open		22.50	23

Snowbabies Let's Pretend™ - Department 56

YEAR ISSUE	EDITION LIMIT	YEAR RETD.	ISSUE PRICE	*QUOTE U.S.$
2002 Dress Up Baby 69188	Open		17.50	18
2002 I Can Feel Your Heartbeat 69185	Open		17.50	18
2002 I'm A Good Witch 69187	Open		17.50	18
2002 Let's Pretend Trunk 69194	Open		17.50	18
2002 Little Liberty 69180	Open		17.50	18
2002 Oh! Pumpkinhead 69186	Open		17.50	18
2002 Save The Day 69182	Open		17.50	18
2002 Teacher's Helper 69184	Open		17.50	18
2002 You're My Prince 69181	Open		17.50	18

Snowbabies Pewter Miniatures - Department 56

YEAR ISSUE	EDITION LIMIT	YEAR RETD.	ISSUE PRICE	*QUOTE U.S.$
1998 All Aboard The Star Express 76739, set/4	Closed	2001	25.00	25
1989 All Fall Down 7617-1, set/4	Closed	1993	25.00	37-75
1998 All We Need Is Love 76722, set/3	Closed	2001	20.00	20
1989 Are All These Mine? 7605-8	Closed	1992	7.00	21-25
1995 Are You On My List? 7669-1, set/2	Closed	1997	9.00	20
1998 Baby, It's Cold Outside 76723, set/2	Closed	2001	8.50	9
2001 Batter Up 76714	Closed	2001	7.00	7
1989 Best Friends 7604-0	Closed	1994	10.00	21-24
1997 Best Little Star 76718	Closed	1999	6.50	7
1994 Bringing Starry Pines 7666-0, set/2	Closed	1997	18.00	18-25
1996 Climb Every Mountain 76702, set/5	Closed	2000	27.50	28
1989 Collector's Sign 76201	Closed	1999	7.00	7
1991 Dancing to a Tune 7630-9, set/3	Closed	1993	18.00	32
1989 Don't Fall Off! 7603-1	Closed	1994	7.00	18-24
1998 Down The Hill We Go! 76066, set/2	Closed	2000	13.50	14
2001 Even A Small Light Shines in the Darkness 76748	Closed	2001	25.00	25
1989 Finding Fallen Stars 7618-0, set/2	Closed	1992	12.50	24-32
1996 Five-Part Harmony 76710, set/2	Closed	1999	22.00	22
1998 Frosty Forest 76720, set/2	Closed	2001	12.00	12
1989 Frosty Frolic 76 3-9, set/4	Closed	1993	24.00	24-46
1998 Frosty Frolic Ice Palace 76729	Closed	2001	95.00	95
1989 Frosty Frolic Land 76198, set/3	Closed	1998	96.00	115-120
1989 Frosty Fun 7611-2, set/2	Closed	1997	13.50	18-20
1989 Give Me a Push! 7601-5	Closed	1994	7.00	18-20
1998 Heigh-Ho, Heigh-Ho, To Frolic Land We Go! 76711	Closed	2001	22.50	23
1992 Help Me, I'm Stuck 7638-4, set/2	Closed	1997	15.00	20
1989 Helpful Friends 7608-2, set/4	Closed	1992	13.50	24-30
2001 Hit The Mark 76744	Closed	2001	12.00	12
1998 Hold On Tight! 76007	Closed	1998	7.00	7-25
1998 How Many Days 'Til Christmas? 76721	Closed	2001	18.00	18
1999 I Can Touch My Toes 76731, set/2	Closed	2001	13.50	14
1995 I Can't Find Him! 76695, set/3	Closed	1998	18.00	20
1995 I Found The Biggest Star Of All! 76690	Closed	1998	7.00	7-15
1998 I Love You This Much 76735	Closed	2001	7.00	7

*Quotes have been rounded up to nearest dollar

YEAR ISSUE	EDITION LIMIT	YEAR RETD.	ISSUE PRICE	*QUOTE U.S.$
1991 I Made This Just for You! 7628-7	Closed	1994	7.00	16-18
1992 I Need A Hug 7640-6	Closed	1997	10.00	10-15
1995 I See You! 76694, set/2	Closed	1999	13.50	14
1989 Icy Igloo, w/tree 7610-4, set/2	Closed	1992	7.50	24-29
2001 I'll Love You Always 76747	Closed	2001	20.00	20
1995 I'll Play A Christmas Tune 76696	Closed	1998	7.50	8-15
1991 I'll Put Up The Tree 7627-9	Closed	1996	9.00	16
1989 I'm Making Snowballs! 76023	Closed	1999	7.00	7
1994 I'm Right Behind You 7662-7, set/5	Closed	1997	27.50	32-35
1996 I'm So Sleepy 76700	Closed	1999	7.00	7
1991 Is That For Me? 7631-7, set/2	Closed	1993	12.50	24-30
1996 It's A Grand Old Flag 76705	Closed	1998	11.00	18-20
1996 It's Snowing 76706	Closed	2001	7.00	7
2001 Jack Frost....A Sleighride Through the Stars 76749	Closed	2001	30.00	30
1997 Jack Frost...A Touch of Winter's Magic 76716, set/3	Closed	2001	27.50	28
1997 Jingle Bell 76713	Closed	2000	7.00	7
1992 Join the Parade 7645-7, set/4	Closed	1995	22.50	30-35
1998 A Journey For Two, By Caribou! 76720	Closed	2001	22.50	23
1992 Just One Little Candle 76449	Closed	1998	7.00	7-15
1993 Let's All Chime In! 76554	Closed	1998	20.00	20-30
1994 Let's Go Skating 76643	Closed	1999	7.00	7
1992 Let's Go Skiing 76368	Closed	1999	7.00	7
1994 Lift Me Highter, I Can't Reach! 7667-8, set/5	Closed	1997	25.00	30-40
2001 The Littlest Angel 76746	Closed	2001	7.00	7
1999 Make A Wish 76733	Closed	2001	15.00	15
1995 Mush 76699, set/2	Closed	2001	25.00	25
1998 My Snowbaby Baby Dolls 76734, set/2	Closed	2001	15.00	15
1998 New Frosty Frolic Land 76728	Closed	2001	50.00	50
1993 Now I Lay Me Down To Sleep 76570	Closed	2001	7.00	7
1998 One For You, One For Me 76724	Closed	2001	13.50	14
2000 Over the Top 76743	Closed	2001	12.00	12
1989 Penguin Parade 7616-3, set/4	Closed	1993	12.50	25-30
1990 Playing Games is Fun! 7623-6, set/2	Closed	1993	13.50	30-58
1989 Polar Express 7609-0, set/2	Closed	1992	13.50	25-45
1998 Pull Together 79740, set/4	Closed	2001	25.00	25
1990 Read Me a Story 7622-8	Closed	1997	11.00	18-20
1995 Ring The Bells...It's Christmas 76692	Closed	2000	20.00	20
2001 Score 76742	Closed	2001	7.00	7
1992 Shall I Play For You? 76422	Closed	1998	7.00	7-15
1998 Ship O' Dreams 76726, set/2	Closed	2001	45.00	45
1998 Slip, Sliding Away 76737	Closed	2001	12.00	12
1993 Somewhere in Dreamland 7656-2, set/5	Closed	1997	30.00	35
1990 A Special Delivery 7624-4	Closed	1993	7.00	18-21
1995 A Star-In-The-Box 76698	Closed	1998	7.50	8-15
1997 Starlight Serenade 76714	Closed	2000	12.00	12
2001 Starlight, Starbright 76745	Closed	2001	7.00	7
1994 Stringing Fallen Stars 76651	Closed	1998	8.00	8-15
1998 Stuck In The Snow 76738	Closed	2001	16.50	17
1997 Thank You 76715, set/3	Closed	2001	20.00	20
1994 There's Another One 7661-9	Closed	1997	10.00	15
1996 There's No Place Like Home 76708	Closed	1998	7.50	8
1992 This Will Cheer You Up 7639-2	Closed	1995	13.75	23
1998 Three Tiny Trumpeters 76725, set/2	Closed	2001	25.00	25
1989 Tiny Trio 7615-5, set/3	Closed	1993	18.00	30-38
1998 To My Friend 76736	Closed	2001	7.50	8
1989 Tumbling in the Snow! 7614-7, set/5	Closed	1992	30.00	75-98
1990 Twinkle Little Stars 7621-0, set/2	Closed	1993	15.00	28-48
1992 Wait For Me! 7641-4, set/4	Closed	1995	22.50	32-35
1991 Waiting for Christmas 7629-5	Closed	1993	12.50	21-24
1993 We Make a Great Pair 7652-0	Closed	1997	13.50	15
1994 We'll Plant The Starry Trees 7663-5, set/4	Closed	1997	22.00	22-25
1995 We're Building An Icy Igloo 76697, set/3	Closed	2001	27.50	28
1995 What Shall We Do Today? 76693, set/2	Closed	1999	17.00	17
1996 When the Bough Breaks 76707	Closed	2001	18.00	18
1993 Where Did He Go? 76546, set/4	Closed	2001	20.00	20
1996 Which Way's Up? 76701, set/2	Closed	2000	13.50	14
1997 Whistle While You Work 76712	Closed	2001	18.00	18
1991 Why Don't You Talk To Me? 76252, set/2	Closed	2001	12.00	12
1993 Will It Snow Today? 76538, set/5	Closed	1998	22.50	23-35
1993 Winken, Blinken & Nod 76589, set/3	Closed	1998	27.50	40
1998 Winter Play On A Snowy Day 76727, set/4	Closed	2001	27.50	28
1989 Winter Surprise! 7607-4	Closed	1994	13.50	26-35
1997 Wish Upon A Falling Star 76717, set/4	Closed	2001	25.00	25
1991 Wishing on a Star 7626-0	Closed	1995	10.00	21-36
1996 With Hugs And Kisses 76704, set/2	Closed	1998	15.00	15
1996 You Are My Lucky Star 76703, set/2	Closed	2000	20.00	20
1999 You Are My Starshine 76732	Closed	2001	7.50	8
1992 You Can't Find Me! 7637-6, set/4	Closed	1996	22.50	35
1992 You Didn't Forget Me! 7643-0, set/3	Closed	1995	17.50	17-20
1996 You Need Wings Too! 76709, set/2	Closed	2000	11.00	11

Snowbabies-Waterglobes - Department 56

YEAR ISSUE	EDITION LIMIT	YEAR RETD.	ISSUE PRICE	*QUOTE U.S.$
1990 All Tired Out 7937-5	Closed	1992	55.00	58-100
1995 Are You On My List? 6879-7	Closed	1997	32.50	40-55
1986 Catch a Falling Star 7967-7	Closed	1987	18.00	528-780
2002 Catch A Keeper (waterglobe) 69250	Open		27.50	28
2001 Catch Me If You Can (Snowbabies Guest Collection™) 69913	Open		32.50	33
1992 Fishing For Dreams 6832-2	Closed	1994	32.50	58
1997 Heigh-Ho 68872	Closed	1999	32.50	33
2001 I Love You Rudolph (Snowbabies Guest Collection™) (musical) 69910	Open		32.50	33
1995 I'll Hug You Goodnight 68798	Open		32.50	33
2001 In The Light of the Moon 69098	Open		32.50	33
1997 Jingle Bell 68871	Closed	1999	32.50	33
1989 Let It Snow 7992-8	Closed	1993	25.00	50-54
1994 Look What I Found 6872-1	Closed	1997	32.50	35
1999 Make A Wish 69040	Closed	2001	32.50	33
1997 Moon Beams 68873	Closed	1999	32.50	33
1996 Now I Lay Me Down To Sleep 6883-1	Open		32.50	33
1991 Peek-A-Boo 7938-3	Closed	1993	50.00	85-100
1994 Planting Starry Pines 6870-5	Closed	1996	32.50	36
1991 Play Me a Tune 7936-7	Closed	1993	50.00	75-100
1996 Practice Makes Perfect 6883-0	Closed	1998	32.50	33-45
1992 Read Me a Story 6831-4	Closed	1996	32.50	60-65
2002 Sculpting With Eloise (Snowbabies Guest Collection™) 69919	Open		32.50	33
1995 Skate With Me 68799	Closed	1998	32.50	35-45
1998 Ship Ahoy 68915	Closed	2001	37.50	38
1999 Ship O' Dreams 69039	Closed	2001	75.00	75
1986 Snowbaby Standing 7964-2	Closed	1987	7.50	313-500
1987 Snowbaby with Wings 7973-1	Closed	1998	20.00	416-675
1993 So Much Work To Do 6849-7	Closed	1995	32.50	24-35
1999 That's What Friends Are For 69041	Open		45.00	45
2000 Time To Dream 69067	Closed	2001	30.00	30
2002 You Didn't Forget Me 6850-0	Closed	1997	32.50	35
1999 You're My Best Partner 68955	Closed	2000	32.50	35
1990 What Are You Doing? 7935-9	Closed	1990	55.00	55
1987 Winter Wonderland 7975-8	Closed	1998	40.00	707-1000

Snowbunnies - Department 56

YEAR ISSUE	EDITION LIMIT	YEAR RETD.	ISSUE PRICE	*QUOTE U.S.$
1999 Afternoon In The Garden 26341	Closed	2002	32.50	33
2000 Airplane Ride 26359	Closed	2002	18.00	18
1997 All The Little Birdies Go Tweet 26288, set/2	Closed	2000	28.00	28
2001 Alleluia Chorus 26392	Closed	2002	36.00	36
1999 Animals On Parade 26326, set/4	Closed	2002	17.50	18
1998 April Brings May Flowers 26308	Closed	2001	35.00	35
1997 Are You My Momma? 26289	Closed	2000	18.00	18
2001 Bee My Baby 26394	Closed	2002	16.50	17
2000 Birch Bench 26384	Closed	2002	15.00	15
1997 Bunny Express 26287	Closed	2000	22.50	23
1999 Bunny Hug 26327	Closed	2002	25.00	25
2001 Bunny Kisses 26414	Open		22.50	23
2001 A Bunny Tale 26393	Open		18.00	18
1999 Butterfly Kisses 26312	Closed	2002	20.00	20
1998 Can You Come Out & Play? 26309	Closed	1999	25.00	25
2000 Captain Of The Seas 26354	Closed	2002	20.00	20
2001 Catch Me If You Can (waterglobe) 26405	Closed	2002	25.00	25
2000 Chick Chat 26352	Closed	2002	16.50	17
2000 Come With Me 26357, set/2	Closed	2001	32.50	33
1996 Counting The Days 'Til Easter 26282	Yr.Iss.	1996	22.50	24-50
1995 Don't Get Lost! 26166	Closed	1998	32.50	35-43
1997 Double Yolk 26293	Yr.Iss.	1997	20.00	20-40
1994 Easter Delivery 26085	Closed	1997	27.50	30-63
1996 Easy Does It 26274, set/2	Closed	1998	30.00	30-40
1999 Ewe Haul 26324	Closed	2002	20.00	20
2001 Fill It Up 26404, set/2	Closed	2002	30.00	30
2000 Flower Basket 26386	Closed	2002	6.00	6
2001 Flower Handle Treat Baskets 26400	Closed	2002	7.50	8
2001 Flower Placecard Easel 26401	Closed	2002	5.00	5
2001 Flower Pot Candles 26409	Closed	2002	7.50	8
2000 For The Birds 26353	Closed	2002	16.50	17

FIGURINES

YEAR ISSUE	EDITION LIMIT	YEAR RETD.	ISSUE PRICE	*QUOTE U.S.$
1999 Full of Blooms 26329, set/6	Closed	2002	15.00	15
1999 Garden Park Bench 26328	Closed	2002	15.00	15
1999 Garden Picket Fence 26340, set/4	Closed	2002	30.00	30
1995 Goosey, Goosey, & Gander 26174, set/2	Closed	1997	30.00	30-41
1999 Guests Are Always Welcome 26325	Yr.Iss.	2000	25.00	25
1996 Happy Birthday To You 26273, set/2	Closed	2001	30.00	30
1994 Help Me Hide The Eggs 26077	Closed	1996	25.00	30-75
2001 Here Smell This 26391	Open		27.50	28
1998 Hop, Skip & A Melody 26301, set/2	Closed	2000	30.00	30
1998 I Can Do It Myself! 26302	Closed	2001	16.50	17
2001 I Need A Little Push, Please 26390	Closed	2002	30.00	30
1995 I'll Color The Easter Egg 26212	Yr.Iss.	1995	20.00	22-50
1995 I'll Love You Forever 26158	Closed	2002	16.00	16
1994 I'll Paint The Top… 26034	Closed	1996	30.00	30-65
2000 I'll Pick You 26355	Closed	2002	16.50	17
2001 I'm All Dressed Up 26395	Closed	2002	16.50	17
1995 I'm Tweeter, You're Totter 26204	Closed	1998	30.00	30-60
1996 Is There Room For Me? 26275	Closed	1999	18.00	16-20
1995 It's Working…We're Going Faster! 26190	Closed	1999	35.00	27-35
1996 I've Got A Brand New Pair of Roller Skates 26272	Closed	1998	25.00	25-50
1994 I've Got A Surprise 26000	Closed	1997	15.00	16-35
1996 Just A Little Off The Top 26278, set/3	Closed	1998	25.00	25-55
1999 Just For You 26323	Closed	2002	16.50	17
1998 Just Start All Over Again 26304	Closed	2000	16.50	17
2000 Kiss Me? 26358, set/2	Closed	2002	28.00	28
2001 Lamb, Chick And Bunny Tea Light 26399	Closed	2002	7.50	8
1996 Let's All Sing Like The Birdies Sing 26276, set/2	Closed	1999	37.50	38-40
1994 Let's Do The Bunny Hop! 26096	Closed	2000	32.50	33
2000 Lily Pad 26365	Closed	2002	7.50	8
2000 Love Grows 26383	Closed	2002	18.00	18
1998 Loves Me, Loves Me Not 26303	Closed	2000	16.50	17
1999 Master Gardener 26321, set/4	Closed	2002	20.00	20
2000 May Day Delivery 26382	Closed	2002	18.00	18
2000 May You Be With You 26381	Closed	2002	18.00	18
1995 My Woodland Wagon, At Dragonfly Hollow 26255	Closed	1997	32.50	34-43
1995 My Woodland Wagon, By Turtle Creek 26239	Closed	1996	32.50	40-65
1995 My Woodland Wagon, Parked In Robins Nest Thicket 26247	Closed	1999	35.00	32-70
1996 On A Trycle Built For Two 26283	17,500	1998	30.00	39-75
2002 On The Fast Track 26389	Yr.Iss.		30.00	30
1994 Oops! I Dropped One! 26018	Closed	1998	16.00	18-35
2001 Oval Flower Frame 26410	Closed	2002	7.50	8
2000 Picture Frames, 3 asst. 26366	Closed	2002	7.50	8
2001 Pink Picket Corner Fence 26408	Open		6.50	7
2000 Puddle Pals 26388	Closed	2002	24.00	24
1997 Rain, Rain, Go Away 26291	Closed	2000	45.00	45
1998 Rock-A-Bye Bunny 26306	Closed	2001	22.50	23
1995 Rub-A-Dub-Dub, 3 Bunnies in a Tub 26115	Closed	1997	32.50	32-65
2000 Showers Brings Flowers (waterglobe) 26368	Closed	2002	20.00	20
1995 Shrubs-In-A-Tub, single 26123, set/4	Closed	1997	12.50	10-13
1995 Shrubs-In-A-Tub, tall 26140, set/2	Closed	1997	9.00	7-10
1995 Shrubs-In-A-Tub, triple 26131	Closed	1997	10.00	7-10
1996 Slow-Moving Vehicle 26280	Closed	1999	45.00	38-45
2001 Snowbunnies Display Ladder 26407	Open		10.00	10
2000 Spring Topiaries, large, 3 asst. 26367	Open		95.00	95
2000 Spring Topiaries, medium, 3 asst. 26386	Closed	2002	30.00	30
2000 Spring Topiaries, small, 3 asst. 26385	Closed	2002	10.00	10
2001 Standing Porcelain Flower 26402	Open		8.50	9
1999 Stop & Smell the Roses 26320, set/2	Closed	2002	20.00	20
1994 Surprise! It's Me! 26042	Closed	1998	25.00	25
2000 Swimming Lessons 26356	Closed	2002	20.00	20
2000 These Are For You 26360	Closed	2002	15.00	15
1998 This One's A Keeper 26307	Closed	2000	16.50	17
1994 A Tisket, A Tasket (waterglobe) 26107	Closed	1998	12.50	15-18
1994 A Tisket, A Tasket 26026	Closed	1996	15.00	20-26
1997 A Tisket, A Tasket Basket 26286	Closed	2002	45.00	45
1996 To Market, To Market, Delivering Eggs! 26281	Closed	1999	65.00	65
1994 Tra-La-La 26069	Closed	1997	37.50	38-50
1999 Trellis in Bloom 26330	Closed	2002	12.50	13
2001 Tulips For My Baby (waterglobe) 26406	Closed	2002	8.50	9

YEAR ISSUE	EDITION LIMIT	YEAR RETD.	ISSUE PRICE	*QUOTE U.S.$
2001 Walk A Mile In My Shoes 26403	Closed	2002	16.50	17
1996 Welcome To The Neighborhood 26277	Closed	1999	25.00	25-50
1995 Wishing You A Happy Easter 26182	Closed	1997	32.50	35-65
1995 You Better Watch Out Or I'll Catch You! 26220	Closed	1999	17.00	18-35
1997 You're Cute As A Bug's Ear 26292	Closed	2000	16.50	17

Disneyana

Disneyana Conventions - Various

YEAR ISSUE	EDITION LIMIT	YEAR RETD.	ISSUE PRICE	*QUOTE U.S.$
1992 1947 Mickey Mouse Plush J20967 - Gund	1,000	1992	50.00	303-360
1992 Big Thunder Mountain A26648 - R. Lee	100	1992	1650.00	2500-2750
1992 Carousel Horse 022482 - PJ's	250	1992	125.00	385-455
1992 Cinderella 022076 - Armani	500	1992	500.00	2600-4400
1992 Cinderella Castle 022077 - John Hine Studios	500	1992	250.00	1100-1593
1992 Cruella DeVil Doll-porcelain 22554 - J. Wolf	25	1992	3000.00	3000-3500
1992 Disneyana Logo Charger - B. White	25	1992	600.00	2800
1992 Medallion	N/A	1992	Gift	121-165
1992 Nifty-Nineties Mickey & Minnie 022503 - House of Laurenz	250	1992	650.00	636-650
1992 Pinocchio - R. Wright	100	1992	750.00	1000-2000
1992 Steamboat Willie-Resin - M. Delle	500	1992	125.00	1452-1500
1992 Tinker Bell 022075 - Lladró	1,500	1992	350.00	2090-3380
1992 Two Merry Wanderers 022074 - Goebel/M.I. Hummel	1,500	1992	250.00	950-1155
1992 Walt's Convertible (Cel) - Disney Art Ed.	500	1992	950.00	2300
1993 1947 Minnie Mouse Plush - Gund	1,000	1993	50.00	98-124
1993 Alice in Wonderland - Malvern	10	1993	8000.00	N/A
1993 Annette Doll - Alexander Doll	1,000	1993	395.00	510-780
1993 The Band Concert "Maestro Mickey" - Disney Art Ed.	275	1993	2950.00	N/A
1993 The Band Concert-Bronze - B. Toma	25	1993	650.00	1815-2420
1993 Bandleader (pewter)	N/A	1993	Gift	110-260
1993 Bandleader-Resin - M. Delle	1,500	1993	125.00	220-424
1993 Family Dinner Figurine - C. Boyer	1,000	1993	600.00	1210-1625
1993 Jumper from King Arthur Carousel - PJ's	250	1993	125.00	275-486
1993 Mickey & Pluto Charger - White/Rhodes	25	1993	850.00	2299-2750
1993 Mickey Mouse, the Bandleader - Arribas Bros.	25	1993	700.00	1568-2145
1993 Mickey's Dreams - R. Lee	250	1993	400.00	605-690
1993 Peter Pan - Lladró	2,000	1993	400.00	726-1200
1993 Sleeping Beauty Castle - John Hine Studios	500	1993	250.00	303-850
1993 Snow White - Armani	2,000	1993	750.00	825-1029
1993 Two Little Drummers - Goebel/M.I. Hummel	1,500	1993	325.00	385-750
1993 Walt's Train Celebration - Disney Art Ed.	950	1993	950.00	1800
1994 Ariel - Armani	1,500	1994	750.00	1056-1560
1994 Cinderella/Godmother - Lladró	2,500	1994	875.00	985-1175
1994 Cinderella's Slipper - Waterford	1,200	1994	250.00	350-550
1994 Euro Disney Castle - John Hine Studios	750	1994	250.00	350-845
1994 Jessica & Roger Charger - White/Rhodes	25	1994	2000.00	2000-2420
1994 Mickey Triple Self Portrait - Goebel Miniatures	500	1994	295.00	787-1235
1994 Minnie Be Patient - Goebel/M.I. Hummel	1,500	1994	395.00	325-450
1994 MM/MN w/House Kinetic - F. Prescott	10	1994	4000.00	N/A
1994 MM/MN/Goofy Limo (Stepin' Out) - Ron Lee	500	1994	500.00	750-1073
1994 Scrooge in Money Bin/Bronze - Carl Barks	100	1994	1800.00	4356-5445
1994 Sleeping Beauty - Malvern	10	1994	5500.00	N/A
1994 Sorcerer Mickey (bronze) - B. Toma	100	1994	1000.00	1815-2200
1994 Sorcerer Mickey (crystal) - Arribas Bros.	50	1994	1700.00	1650-2239
1994 Sorcerer Mickey (pewter)	N/A	1994	Gift	110-260
1994 Sorcerer Mickey (resin) - M. Delle	2,000	1994	125.00	165-390
1995 Ah, Venice - M. Pierson	100	1995	2600.00	2600-3025
1995 Ariel's Dolphin Ride - Wyland	250	1995	2500.00	2500
1995 Barbershop Quartet - Goebel Miniatures	750	1995	300.00	300-600
1995 Beauty and the Beast - Armani	2,000	1995	975.00	1056-1950

YEAR ISSUE	EDITION LIMIT	YEAR RETD.	ISSUE PRICE	*QUOTE U.S.$
1995 Brave Little Tailor Charger - White/Rhodes	15	1995	2000.00	2000-3000
1995 Celebrating-Resin - M. Delle	1,500	1995	125.00	155-182
1995 Donald Duck Gong	N/A	1995	Gift	116
1995 Donald Duck Mini-Charger - White/Rhodes	1,000	1995	75.00	75
1995 Ear Force One - R. Lee	500	1995	600.00	635-1300
1995 Engine No. One - R. Lee	500	1995	650.00	726-765
1995 Fire Station #105 - Lilliput Lane	501	1995	195.00	350-595
1995 For Father - Goebel/M.I. Hummel	1,500	1995	450.00	450-485
1995 Grandpa's Boys - Goebel/M.I. Hummel	1,500	1995	340.00	413-424
1995 Mad Minnie Charger - White/Rhodes	10	1995	2000.00	4000-6050
1995 Memories - B. Toma	200	1995	1200.00	968-1050
1995 Neat & Pretty Mickey (crystal) - Arribas Bros.	50	1995	1700.00	1500-2057
1995 Neat & Pretty Mickey (resin) - M. Delle	2,000	1995	135.00	175-325
1995 Neat & Pretty Music Box	N/A	1994	Gift	110-260
1995 Plane Crazy - Arribas	50	1995	1750.00	1650-1815
1995 The Prince's Kiss - P Gordon	25	1995	250.00	1100-2175
1995 "Proud Pocahontas" Lithogragh - D. Struzan	500	1995	195.00	413
1995 Sheriff of Bullet Valley - Barks/Vought	200	1995	1800.00	2200-2420
1995 Showtime - B. Toma	200	1995	1400.00	1430-1694
1995 Simba - Bolae	200	1995	1500.00	1500
1995 Sleeping Beauty Castle Mirror - P. Gordon	250	1995	1200.00	1200
1995 Sleeping Beauty Dance - Lladró	1,000	1995	1280.00	1210-2275
1995 Sleeping Beauty's Tiara - Waterford	1,500	1995	250.00	374-550
1995 Snow White's Apple - Waterford	1,500	1995	225.00	235-423
1995 "Snow White & Friends" Brooch/Pendant - R. Viramontes	25	1995	1500.00	1500
1995 Thru the Mirror - Barks/Vought	200	1995	2600.00	1925-2420
1995 "Uncle Scrooge" Tile - Barks/Vought	50	1995	900.00	1595-2200
1996 Brave Little Taylor - Arribas Bros.	50	1996	1700.00	1870-2200
1996 Brave Little Taylor (pewter)	N/A	1996	Gift	80-163
1996 Brave Little Taylor (resin) - M. Delle	1,500	1996	125.00	135-325
1996 Brave Little Taylor Clock	N/A	1996	Gift	110-195
1996 Brave Little Taylor Inlaid Leather Box - P. Gordon	25	1996	300.00	300-1100
1996 Breakfast of Tycoons-Scrooge (litho) - C. Barks	295	1996	295.00	385-473
1996 Cinderella's Castle (bronze) - B. Toma	100	1996	1400.00	1870-2057
1996 Flying Dumbo (bronze) - Wolf's Head	N/A	1996	1500.00	2000-3630
1996 Hall of Presidents - Lilliput Lane	500	1996	225.00	396-715
1996 Heigh Ho - R. Lee	350	1996	500.00	605-726
1996 Jasmine & Rajah - Armani	N/A	1996	800.00	895-1430
1996 Mickey - Armani	N/A	1996	Gift	242-350
1996 Jasmine & Rajah w/Mickey - Armani	N/A	1996	800.00	823-1430
1996 Minnie for Mother - Goebel/M.I. Hummel	1,200	1996	470.00	455-470
1996 Proud Pongo (w/backstamp) - Walt Disney Classics	1,200	1996	175.00	160-350
1996 Puppy Love - Goebel Miniatures	750	1996	300.00	384-553
1996 Self Control-Donald Duck (bronze) - C. Barks	150	1996	1800.00	2530-3025
1996 Sorcerer - Waterford	1,200	1996	275.00	440-480
1996 Uncle Scrooge Charger Plate - B. White	25	1996	2000.00	2420-2723
1997 Chernabog Charger - B. White	15	1997	2000.00	3025-3328
1997 Chernabog - Walt Disney Classics	1,500	1997	750.00	1155-1755
1997 Cinderella & Prince - Armani	1,000	1997	825.00	825-1658
1997 Crocodile Clock	N/A	1997	Gift	110-125
1997 Cruella's Car Box - P. Gordon	30	1997	500.00	1155-1555
1997 Disneyland's 40th (pewter)	N/A	1997	Gift	110
1997 Disney Villain Ornament set/6 - Walt Disney Classics	12,000	1997	40.00	94-130
1997 Dragon (Malificent) (pewter)	N/A	1997	Gift	110-228
1997 Grandma's Girl - Goebel/M.I. Hummel	1,000	1997	350.00	350-484
1997 Hands Off My Playthings (bronze) - C. Barks	176	1997	1950.00	2662-2723
1997 Haunted Mansion - Lilliput Lane	500	1997	250.00	605-655
1997 Lonesome Ghost - Arribas Bros.	50	1997	1700.00	1650-1815
1997 Magical Scrooge Serigraph - C. Barks	295	1997	395.00	555-589
1997 Mistletoe Mickey & Minnie - C. Radko	1,500	1997	250.00	275-360
1997 Mickey's 70th (bronze) - B. Toma	100	1997	1400.00	1815
1997 Mickey's 70th Sericel - Disney Art Ed.	1,500	1997	295.00	415
1997 Peg Leg Pete - M. Delle	1,000	1997	125.00	140-300
1997 The Perfect Disguise - Goebel Miniatures	500	1997	300.00	363-456
1997 Scared Mickey Coin - Liberty Mint	500	1997	50.00	50
1997 Tinkerbell - Waterford Crystal	750	1997	250.00	363-425
1997 Walt's Railroad "Lilly Belle" - Visions in Scale	75	1997	1600.00	1600-2294
1998 Ariel (Crystal) - Waterford Crystal	750	1998	275.00	363-396
1998 Bella Note - Goebel Miniatures	500	1998	295.00	400-457
1998 My Best Pal - C. Radko	1,000	1998	70.00	70-185
1998 Best Pals	1,500	1998	Gift	121-220
1998 Casting Call Ornament set/6 - Disney Merchandise	1,500	1998	45.00	45-121
1998 Decades of Reel Memories - P. Gordon	50	1998	750.00	1452-1573
1998 Dopey Charger - B. White	25	1998	2000.00	2000
1998 Dumbo the Clown - Arribas Brothers	50	1998	1700.00	1700-2541
1998 Fond Memories w/Mickey & Friends Sericel - Disney Art Classics	1,998	1998	295.00	295
1998 A Friendly Day Poster - R. Souders	1,000	1998	25.00	25
1998 Friends Forever - Goebel/M.I. Hummel	350	1998	350.00	350-484
1998 Geppetto & Pinocchio - Armani	1,075	1998	775.00	765-1200
1998 Heat Wave Serigraph - C. Barks	195	1998	295.00	295-540
1998 Jiminy Cricket - When Dreams Come True - B. Toma	75	1998	1400.00	2178-2450
1998 Mickey & Pluto (resin) - M. Delle	1,500	1998	125.00	200
1998 Snow White & Prince - Walt Disney Classics	1,650	1998	750.00	605-1000
1998 Tinkerbell Tile - M. Davis	75	1998	495.00	1650
1998 Tribute to Walt Disney Paperweight - Swarovski Crystal	25	1998	495.00	5000
1998 "Magic Kingdom Memories" - Lilliput Lane	500	1998	275.00	400-550
1998 Who's Out There (bronze) - C. Barks	131	1998	1950.00	2844-3200
1999 65 Feisty Years Lithograph - D. Williams	195	1999	195.00	385
1999 Bambi Scene (bronze) - M. Davis	100	1999	1895.00	2200-2500
1999 Bare Necessities Miniature - Goebel Miniatures	500	2000	295.00	295-330
1999 Bella Notte Double Tile - F. Thomas/O. Johnston	75	1999	595.00	1210-1815
1999 Disney Adventure Eggs - J. Levasseur	36	1999	N/A	N/A
1999 Disney Safari Adventure - Liberty Mint Coin	750	1999	75.00	75
1999 Donald & Daisy "Pomp & Circumstance" - Goebel	350	1999	350.00	450-660
1999 Elmer & Tilly (pre registration)	600	1999	Gift	165-300
1999 Jiminy Cricket - Waterford Crystal	1,000	1999	195.00	250-385
1999 Jungle Friends Photomosiac - R. Silvers	250	1999	50.00	125
1999 Kiss The Girl Chargers - E. Gomes	25	1999	750.00	1210
1999 Lady & The Tramp - Armani	750	2000	750.00	750-880
1999 Lion King Ornament, set/7 - Disney	1,000	1999	45.00	110
1999 Main Street Cinema - Lilliput Lane	500	1999	275.00	385-415
1999 Maleficent as Dragon - Walt Disney Classics	1,350	1999	795.00	935-1350
1999 Maleficent Tile - M. Davis	75	1999	495.00	1100-1210
1999 Mickey & Friends Safari Jeep - Swarovski Crystal	50	1999	495.00	1320-2020
1999 Mickey & Pluto w/ compass (check-in sculpture)	1,800	1999	Gift	165
1999 Mickey & The Treasure (pewter) (banquet gift)	2,000	1999	Gift	125
1999 Mickey Meteor Train - M. Trains	300	1999	595.00	635-1000
1999 Phillip & Sampson Miniature - Walt Disney Classics	Closed	2000	100.00	150-1155
1999 Pinocchio (bronze) - B. Toma	50	1999	1600.00	1980-2350
1999 The Pointer (resin) - R. King	1,500	2000	150.00	150-210
1999 Safari Adventure - R. Souders	1,000	1999	25.00	100
1999 Safari Adventure Trunk - P. Gordon	50	1999	895.00	1100-1820
1999 Safari Surprise Sericel - Walt Disney Art. Ed.	1,000	1999	295.00	385
1999 Safari Trading Cards - Disney	250	1999	75.00	125-200
1999 Simba (The Pointer) (crystal) - Arribas Brothers	25	1999	1700.00	1700
1999 Simba Ornament - C. Radko	1,000	1999	70.00	70
1999 Song of the South Charger - B. White	15	1999	2000.00	2750
2000 Apprentice's Dream - D. Williams	195	2000	195.00	195
2000 Bibbidi Bobbidi Boo - Harmony Kingdom	400	2000	200.00	200
2000 Big Trouble - Walt Disney Classics	1,250	2000	750.00	750-1100
2000 Chip N' Dale Bronze - B. Justice	100	2000	1795.00	1795-2525
2000 Cinderella's Castle - P. Gordon	50	2000	980.00	980-1460
2000 Cinderella's Dream - R. Souders	1,000	2000	25.00	25
2000 Dopey - Waterford Crystal	750	2000	225.00	225-380
2000 Evil Queen Lithogragh - A. Lefcourt	200	2000	195.00	195
2000 Fab 5 Sericel "A World of Joy" - Walt Disney Art Editions	500	2000	475.00	475

FIGURINES

YEAR ISSUE	EDITION LIMIT	YEAR RETD.	ISSUE PRICE	*QUOTE U.S.$
2000 "He Honua Pili Kanaka Keia" - D. Kracov	25	2000	1550.00	1550
2000 It's A Small World - E. Gomes	20	2000	850.00	850
2000 It's A Small World Lithograph - C. Fazzino	200	2000	300.00	300
2000 Looking Forward - R. Silvers	250	2000	50.00	50
2000 Marc Davis: Imagineering a Dream - Walt Disney Fine Art	200	2000	395.00	395
2000 Mickey & Doll - (resin)	1,000	2000	220.00	220
2000 Pinocchio & Jiminy Cricket - Lenox Classics	500	2000	125.00	125-330
2000 Pluto Charger - E. Gomes	25	2000	800.00	800
2000 Pluto Jeweled Pin - Swarovski Crystal	200	2000	195.00	195-440
2000 Reel Friends - Goebel/M.I. Hummel	350	2000	450.00	450-650
2000 Scottish Mickey - R. Raikes	100	2000	160.00	160-580
2000 Seven Dwarfs Tile - F. Thomas & O. Johnston	75	2000	975.00	975-1360
2000 Small World - Lilliput Lane	400	2000	325.00	325
2000 Small World Box - Arribas Brothers	250	2000	400.00	400-660
2000 Small World Coin - Great Western Mint	500	2000	75.00	75
2000 Small World Trading Cards - Walt Disney Attractions	250	2000	75.00	75
2000 A Smile Means Friendship - R. King	1,000	2000	150.00	150
2000 Steamboat Willie - Armani	1,000	2000	600.00	600-1100
2000 Tinkerbell on Hook - B. Toma	50	2000	1200.00	1200-1980
2001 2001 Family Reunion Coin - Great Western Mint	500	2001	75.00	75
2001 Adora Belle Mouseketeer Doll - M. Osmond	300	2001	95.00	95-360
2001 All Aboard - Ron Lee	400	2001	150.00	150
2001 Captain Hook & Mr. Smee Bronze - F. Thomas & O. Johnston	50	2001	1950.00	1950-2860
2001 A Concert to Remember - Lenox Classics	500	2001	125.00	125-165
2001 Cruella DeVil - Armani	750	2001	600.00	600-770
2001 Curtain Call Double Tile - F. Thomas & O. Johnston	100	2001	N/A	N/A
2001 Donald's Family Picnic Lithograph - D. Ducky Williams	200	2001	195.00	195
2001 Duck Family Vase - E. Gnomes	20	2001	800.00	800
2001 Dumbo Ride (Pals) - B. Toma	50	2001	1800.00	1800
2001 Family Picnic - Harmony Kingdom	400	2001	200.00	200-525
2001 Family Reunion Bowl - Lenox Classics	250	2001	185.00	185-440
2001 Family Reunion Uncut Trading Cards - Disney Design Group	250	2001	75.00	75
2001 Headed Home - Goebel USA	350	2001	495.00	649-660
2001 Mickey's Best Friend - Waterford Crystal	750	2001	250.00	250-440
2001 Mick-Tych Diptych Lithograph - E. Robinson	250	2001	195.00	195
2001 Monstro the Whale - Walt Disney Classics	750	2001	795.00	795-990
2001 Now Showing Miniature - Olszewski	500	2001	250.00	250-330
2001 Picnic Time - R. King	850	2001	150.00	150-245
2001 Picnic Time With Mickey & Minnie Dolls - R. Raikes	100	2001	275.00	275-685
2001 Sack Race - D. Kracov	50	2001	800.00	800-990
2001 Sleeping Beauty Castle - Paddy Gordon Boxes	50	2001	980.00	980
2001 Sleeping Beauty Castle Jeweled Pin - Swarovski	300	2001	195.00	195-375
2001 Smooches Charger - E. Gnomes	25	2001	75.00	75
2001 Socerer - Arribas Brothers	300	2001	650.00	650
2001 Tinkerbell - R. John Wright	250	2001	999.00	999
2001 Tom Sawyer Island - Lilliput Lane	400	2001	325.00	325-440
2001 Tom Sawyer Island Gicleé - R. Day	150	2001	150.00	150
2001 Walt & Mickey Surprise Charger Plate - Arribas Brothers	100	2001	880.00	880
2001 Walt Disney/Castle Gicleé - P. Ellenshaw	150	2001	750.00	750
2001 Walt Disney's Centennial Carolwood Pacific Caboose - M. Broggie	500	2001	250.00	415
2001 Where the Magic Begins Poster - R. Souders	1,000	2001	25.00	25

Encore

Santa and Snow Buddies™ - Encore

YEAR ISSUE	EDITION LIMIT	YEAR RETD.	ISSUE PRICE	*QUOTE U.S.$
2001 All For Me?	Open		10.00	10
2001 Cookies For Santa?	Open		10.00	10
2002 Crazy Christmas	Open		10.00	10
2001 Deck the Halls	Open		10.00	10
2001 Gingerbread Christmas	Open		10.00	10

YEAR ISSUE	EDITION LIMIT	YEAR RETD.	ISSUE PRICE	*QUOTE U.S.$
1999 Ride 'Em Santa	Closed	2001	15.00	15
2001 Rockin' In The Holidays	Open		10.00	10
2000 Santa, 10" Skiing with Buddies on Back	Closed	2001	30.00	30
1999 Santa, 20" Skiing with Buddies on Back	Closed	2001	78.00	78
2000 Santa, 5" in Sleigh	Closed	2001	15.00	15
2000 Santa, 5" with Buddy and Street Lamp	Closed	2001	15.00	15
2000 Santa, 8" And Two Buddies Skiing	Closed	2001	19.00	19
1999 Santa, 8" at Desk	Closed	2001	30.00	30
2000 Santa, 8" Standing with Buddy On Train	Closed	2001	19.00	19
2000 Santa, 8" with Buddy and Reindeer	Closed	2001	19.00	19
1999 Santa, with Buddy Hanging in Bag	Closed	2001	9.00	9
1999 Santa, with Buddy Holding Tree	Closed	2001	9.00	9
1999 Santa, with Buddy in Bag	Closed	2001	9.00	9
2001 Two Kewl Dudes	Open		10.00	10
2002 Which One Is Mine?	Open		10.00	10

Snow Buddies™ - Encore

YEAR ISSUE	EDITION LIMIT	YEAR RETD.	ISSUE PRICE	*QUOTE U.S.$
1999 Around Tree	Closed	2001	19.00	19
2001 Aunt Crystal, 11"	Open		30.00	30
2001 Aunt Crystal, 20"	Open		78.00	78
2001 Avalanche, 20"	Open		78.00	78
1999 Blizzy 10"	Retrd.	1999	30.00	30
1999 Blizzy Reading	Retrd.	1999	5.00	5
2002 Blizzy with Tray, 30"	Open		390.00	390
1999 Buddies with Reindeer	Retrd.	1999	19.00	19
2001 Cousin Slick, 20"	Open		78.00	78
2001 Cousin Slick, 30"	Open		390.00	390
2000 Crash Landing	Open		19.00	19
2000 Display Sign	Open		9.00	9
2002 Everest with Tray, 30"	Open		390.00	390
2000 Family Portrait	Yr.Iss.	2000	30.00	30
2000 Feeding Time (platinum dealers)	Open		19.00	19
1999 Flurry Walking	Retrd.	1999	5.00	5
2002 Flurry, 20"	Open		78.00	78
2001 Happy Hanukkah	Open		8.00	8
2000 Hill Thrill	Yr.Iss.	2000	9.00	9
2000 Holding Train, 10"	Open		30.00	30
2000 Holding Train, 19 1/2"	Open		78.00	78
1999 Holiday on Ice	Open		15.00	15
2000 The Impersonator	Yr.Iss.	2000	19.00	19
2000 No Dumping (platinum dealers)	Yr.Iss.	2000	19.00	19
2000 On Skis	Yr.Iss.	2000	78.00	78
2000 Penguin Hockey	Open		15.00	15
2000 Polar Tea Party	Yr.Iss.	2000	15.00	15
2001 Powder Puff, 11"	Open		30.00	30
2002 Queen of Everything	Open		9.00	9
2002 Queen of Everything/Throne (musical)	Open		25.00	25
2000 Quiet Time	Yr.Iss.	2000	9.00	9
1999 Ride 'Em Buddies	Open		9.00	9
1999 Santa in Sleigh	Retrd.	1999	30.00	30
1999 Santa w/Powder & Bag	Retrd.	1999	30.00	30
1999 Santa w/Powder & Sign	Retrd.	1999	19.00	19
1999 Santa w/Powder with Tree	Retrd.	1999	19.00	19
2000 Seal of Approval	Open		15.00	15
1999 Secret No Melt	Open		15.00	15
2000 Show Off	Yr.Iss.	2000	15.00	15
2002 Slide Naughty Twin #2, 11"	Open		30.00	30
2002 Slip Naughty Twin #1, 11"	Open		30.00	30
2000 Snow Budds Only!	Open		19.00	19
2001 Snowball, 11"	Open		30.00	30
2002 Snowbelle, 11"	Open		30.00	30
2002 Snowbelle, 20"	Open		78.00	78
1999 Snowboardin'	Open		6.00	6
1999 Special Friend	Open		6.00	6
1999 Tobogganin'	Open		6.00	6
2000 Tons O' Fun (platinum & gold dealers)	Yr.Iss.	2000	19.00	19
1999 Totem with Pipe	Open		9.00	9
1999 Totem without Pipe	Open		9.00	9
2000 The Tree Trimming	Yr.Iss.	2000	30.00	30
2001 Uncle Flake, 11"	Open		30.00	30
2000 Winter On Parade	Yr.Iss.	2000	19.00	19
1999 Yummy	Open		30.00	30

Snow Buddies™ 12 Days of Christmas - Encore

YEAR ISSUE	EDITION LIMIT	YEAR RETD.	ISSUE PRICE	*QUOTE U.S.$
2001 Partridge in a Pear Tree	Closed	2001	8.00	8
2001 Two Turtle Doves	Closed	2001	8.00	8
2001 Three French Hens	Closed	2001	8.00	8
2001 Four Calling Birds	Closed	2001	8.00	8

Collectors' Information Bureau   *Quotes have been rounded up to nearest dollar

YEAR ISSUE	EDITION LIMIT	YEAR RETD.	ISSUE PRICE	*QUOTE U.S.$
2001 Five Golden Rings	Closed	2001	8.00	8
2001 Six Geese a Laying	Closed	2001	8.00	8
2001 Seven Swans a Swimming	Closed	2001	8.00	8
2001 Eight Maids a Milking	Closed	2001	8.00	8
2001 Nine Ladies Dancing	Closed	2001	8.00	8
2001 Ten Lords a Leaping	Closed	2001	8.00	8
2001 Eleven Pipers Piping	Closed	2001	8.00	8
2001 Twelve Drummers Drumming	Closed	2001	8.00	8

Snow Buddies™ All Occasion - Encore

YEAR ISSUE	EDITION LIMIT	YEAR RETD.	ISSUE PRICE	*QUOTE U.S.$
2001 Be Mine	Closed	2001	9.00	9
2001 Bride and Groom	Closed	2001	9.00	9
2001 Congratulations	Closed	2001	9.00	9
2001 Get Well	Closed	2001	9.00	9
2001 Happy Anniversary	Closed	2001	9.00	9
2001 Happy Birthday	Closed	2001	9.00	9
2001 I Love You	Closed	2001	9.00	9
2001 I Miss You	Closed	2001	9.00	9
2001 Thinking of You	Closed	2001	9.00	9

Snow Buddies™ All Seasons Buddies - Encore

YEAR ISSUE	EDITION LIMIT	YEAR RETD.	ISSUE PRICE	*QUOTE U.S.$
2002 January - New Year's	Open		10.00	10
2002 February - Valentine's Day	Open		10.00	10
2002 March - St. Patrick's Day	Open		10.00	10
2002 April - Easter.	Open		10.00	10
2002 May - Mothers Day	Open		10.00	10
2002 June - Graduation	Open		10.00	10
2002 July - 4th of July	Open		10.00	10
2002 August - Vacation Time	Open		10.00	10
2002 September - Back To School	Open		10.00	10
2002 October - Halloween	Open		10.00	10
2002 November - Thanksgiving	Open		10.00	10
2002 December - Christmas	Open		10.00	10
2002 All Season's Display	Open		40.00	40

Snow Buddies™ Avalanche - Encore

YEAR ISSUE	EDITION LIMIT	YEAR RETD.	ISSUE PRICE	*QUOTE U.S.$
2000 Avalanche, 11"	Open		30.00	30
2000 Avalanche, 5"	Closed	2001	9.00	9
2000 Oops!	Open		9.00	9
2000 Remodeling	Open		9.00	9

Snow Buddies™ Baby Buddies - Encore

YEAR ISSUE	EDITION LIMIT	YEAR RETD.	ISSUE PRICE	*QUOTE U.S.$
2001 All Fall Down	Open		8.00	8
2001 Bundle of Joy	Open		8.00	8
2001 Keeping Cool	Open		8.00	8
2001 Life's Little Setbacks	Open		8.00	8
2001 Lullaby Rock	Open		8.00	8
2001 Playing Dress Up	Open		8.00	8
2001 Tall Tales	Open		8.00	8
2001 Baby Buddies Sign	Open		12.00	12
2002 Display	Open		60.00	60

Snow Buddies™ Baby Steps - Encore

YEAR ISSUE	EDITION LIMIT	YEAR RETD.	ISSUE PRICE	*QUOTE U.S.$
2002 Newborn	Open		4.00	4
2002 1 Year	Open		4.00	4
2002 2 Years	Open		4.00	4
2002 3 Years	Open		4.00	4
2002 4 Years	Open		4.00	4
2002 5 Years	Open		4.00	4
2002 6 Years	Open		4.00	4
2002 Display	Open		60.00	60

Snow Buddies™ Blizzy - Encore

YEAR ISSUE	EDITION LIMIT	YEAR RETD.	ISSUE PRICE	*QUOTE U.S.$
2000 #1 Teacher	Open		9.00	9
2000 Blizzy 11"	Open		30.00	30
2000 Blizzy 5"	Closed	2001	9.00	9
2000 Come N' Get It	Open		9.00	9

Snow Buddies™ Boo Buddies - Encore

YEAR ISSUE	EDITION LIMIT	YEAR RETD.	ISSUE PRICE	*QUOTE U.S.$
2001 Bobbin' for Apples	Closed	2001	10.00	10
2000 Boo Buddy Collection Sign	Closed	2001	15.00	15
2001 Fairy Princess	Closed	2001	10.00	10
2001 Ghost Stories	Closed	2001	10.00	10
2001 Ghostly Pranks	Closed	2001	10.00	10
2000 Ghostly Surprise	Closed	2001	5.00	5
2000 Ghostly Trio	Closed	2001	15.00	15
2001 Ghouls, Ghosts & Goblins, Oh My!	Closed	2001	10.00	10
2000 Going Batty	Closed	2001	9.00	9
2001 Going Batty	Closed	2001	10.00	10
2000 The Great Pumpkin	Closed	2001	13.00	13
2000 It's Halloween Time	Closed	2001	5.00	5
2001 Kitty X-ing	Closed	2001	10.00	10

YEAR ISSUE	EDITION LIMIT	YEAR RETD.	ISSUE PRICE	*QUOTE U.S.$
2000 Mummified	Closed	2001	5.00	5
2001 Mummy's Waltz	Closed	2001	10.00	10
2000 My Scary Friend	Closed	2001	5.00	5
2001 No Melt	Closed	2001	10.00	10
2000 Peek-A-Boo	Closed	2001	15.00	15
2000 Pumpkin Fun	Closed	2001	5.00	5
2000 Pumpkin S'Mor	Closed	2001	7.00	7
2001 That's What Friends Are For	Closed	2001	10.00	10
2001 Trick or Treat	Closed	2001	10.00	10
2000 Twin Grins	Closed	2001	9.00	9
2000 Witchly Attired	Closed	2001	5.00	5
2000 Witch-N-Ride	Closed	2001	14.00	14
2000 Woopsie Daisies	Closed	2001	10.00	10

Snow Buddies™ Christmas Pageant - Encore

YEAR ISSUE	EDITION LIMIT	YEAR RETD.	ISSUE PRICE	*QUOTE U.S.$
2001 Christmas Pageant 9 Piece Set	Closed	2001	50.00	50
2001 Avalanche (as Wise Man)	Closed	2001	set	set
2001 Baby in Manger	Closed	2001	set	set
2001 Blizzy (as Mary)	Closed	2001	set	set
2001 Cousin Slick (as Drummer Boy)	Closed	2001	set	set
2001 Grandpa Frostbite (as Wise Man)	Closed	2001	set	set
2001 Powder Puff (as Shepherd)	Closed	2001	set	set
2001 Snowball (as Wise Man)	Closed	2001	set	set
2001 Stable (2 pc. set)	Closed	2001	set	set
2001 Uncle Melty (as Joseph)	Closed	2001	set	set

Snow Buddies™ Circus - Encore

YEAR ISSUE	EDITION LIMIT	YEAR RETD.	ISSUE PRICE	*QUOTE U.S.$
2001 2 Tons of Fun	Closed	2001	10.00	10
2001 Balancing Act	Closed	2001	8.00	8
2001 Fire Ring	Closed	2001	10.00	10
2001 High Wire Act	Closed	2001	10.00	10
2001 The Magician	Closed	2001	8.00	8
2001 Snack Cart	Closed	2001	15.00	15

Snow Buddies™ Cousin Slick - Encore

YEAR ISSUE	EDITION LIMIT	YEAR RETD.	ISSUE PRICE	*QUOTE U.S.$
2000 Cousin Slick, 11"	Open		30.00	30
2000 Cousin Slick, 5"	Open		9.00	9
2000 Doin' An Ollie	Open		9.00	9
2000 Snowboardin'	Open		9.00	9

Snow Buddies™ Dealer Exclusive Events - Encore

YEAR ISSUE	EDITION LIMIT	YEAR RETD.	ISSUE PRICE	*QUOTE U.S.$
2001 Rainy Day Love	Closed	2001	12.00	12
2001 You Melt My Heart	Closed	2001	12.00	12
2002 Buddies Lift Your Spirit	Yr.Iss.		30.00	30
2002 Friends Are Special Treats	Yr.Iss.		5.00	5
2002 It Takes Two For Buddies	Yr.Iss.		10.00	10
2002 Buddies Always Remember	Yr.Iss.		10.00	10

Snow Buddies™ Everest - Encore

YEAR ISSUE	EDITION LIMIT	YEAR RETD.	ISSUE PRICE	*QUOTE U.S.$
2000 Appetizers	Open		9.00	9
2000 Cracking Up	Open		9.00	9
2000 Everest, 11"	Open		30.00	30
2000 Everest, 5"	Closed	2001	9.00	9

Snow Buddies™ Fire Department - Encore

YEAR ISSUE	EDITION LIMIT	YEAR RETD.	ISSUE PRICE	*QUOTE U.S.$
2001 Fire Fighting Buddies	Open		5.00	5
2001 Fire Truck (musical)	Open		20.00	20
2001 Where's the Fire?	Open		4.00	4

Snow Buddies™ For All Seasons - Encore

YEAR ISSUE	EDITION LIMIT	YEAR RETD.	ISSUE PRICE	*QUOTE U.S.$
2001 January - New Year's	Open		10.00	10
2001 February - Valentine's Day	Open		10.00	10
2001 March - St. Patrick's Day	Open		10.00	10
2001 April - Easter	Open		10.00	10
2001 May - Mother's Day	Open		10.00	10
2001 June - Graduation	Open		10.00	10
2001 July - 4th of July	Open		10.00	10
2001 August - Vacation Time	Open		10.00	10
2001 September - Back to School	Open		10.00	10
2001 October - Halloween	Open		10.00	10
2001 November - Thanksgiving	Open		10.00	10
2001 December - Christmas	Open		10.00	10
2001 Snow Buddies For All Seasons Display	Open		40.00	40

Snow Buddies™ Friendship Buddies - Encore

YEAR ISSUE	EDITION LIMIT	YEAR RETD.	ISSUE PRICE	*QUOTE U.S.$
2001 Dream Boat	Open		3.00	3
2001 Flowers For Sale	Open		8.00	8
2001 Guess Who?	Open		8.00	8
2001 Kisses For You	Open		3.00	3
2001 Motherly Love	Open		8.00	8
2001 That's What Friends Are For!	Open		8.00	8
2001 Tundra, Blizzy & Everest (musical)	Open		15.00	15

FIGURINES

YEAR ISSUE	EDITION LIMIT	YEAR RETD.	ISSUE PRICE	*QUOTE U.S.$
2001 You're Cool	Open		3.00	3

Snow Buddies™ Grandpa Frostbite - Encore

2000 Grandpa Frostbite, 11"	Open		30.00	30
2000 Grandpa Frostbite, 5"	Closed	2001	9.00	9
2000 In My Day	Open		9.00	9
2000 U Snooze, U Lose!	Open		9.00	9

Snow Buddies™ Mini Snowballs- Encore

2002 Everest	Open		7.00	7
2002 Flurry	Open		7.00	7
2002 Grandma Cooleen	Open		7.00	7
2002 Slip & Slide	Open		7.00	7
2002 Snowbelle	Open		7.00	7
2002 Snowbrite	Open		7.00	7

Snow Buddies™ Musical Snowballs - Encore

2001 Christmas Morning	Open		37.00	37
2002 Let Me Call You Sweetheart	Open		33.00	33
2001 Material Girl	Open		35.00	35
2001 Nap Time	Open		30.00	30
2002 Over The Rainbow	Open		33.00	33
2002 Rainy Day Love	Open		33.00	33
2001 The Snow Buddies Waltz	Open		33.00	333
2001 Splish Splash	Open		20.00	20
2002 Sweetheart Serenade	Open		33.00	33
2002 Wedding Day	Open		33.00	33
2001 Your Love Comforts Me	Open		35.00	35

Snow Buddies™ Romance Series - Encore

2001 Blizzy Loves Flurry	Closed	2001	12.00	12
2001 I Love You	Closed	2001	12.00	12
2001 I Love You Ice Block	Closed	2001	12.00	12
2001 I Luv You	Closed	2001	12.00	12
2001 I Pledge My Love	Closed	2001	12.00	12
2001 Special Delivery	Closed	2001	12.00	12
2001 Sweetheart Serenade	Closed	2001	12.00	12
2001 Your Love Comforts Me	Closed	2001	12.00	12

Snow Buddies™ Send A Message Buddies - Encore

2002 Aunt Crystal "Happy Birthday"	Open		5.00	5
2002 Blizzy "#1 Mom"	Open		5.00	5
2002 Cousin Slick "My Best Friend"	Open		5.00	5
2002 Everest "Be Mine"	Open		5.00	5
2002 Flurry & Blizzy "Happy Anniversary"	Open		5.00	5
2002 Grandma Cooleen & Powder Puff "I Love Grandma"	Open		5.00	5
2002 Mayor Blustery "Congratulations"	Open		5.00	5
2002 Snowball "WWJD?"	Open		5.00	5
2002 Snowbelle "You're Special"	Open		5.00	5
2002 Snowbrite "Grandma's Little Angel"	Open		5.00	5
2002 Snowbrite "Just Because"	Open		5.00	5
2002 Uncle Flake "I Love You This Much"	Open		5.00	5
2002 Display	Open		60.00	60

Snow Buddies™ Singing and Dancing Buddies - Encore

2002 Aunt Crystal	Open		24.00	24
2001 Cousin Slick	Closed	2001	20.00	20
2001 Everest	Closed	2001	20.00	20
2002 Uncle Flake	Open		24.00	24

Snow Buddies™ Snowballs- Encore

2001 All Aboard	Open		50.00	50
2001 Beach Fun	Open		14.00	14
2000 Buddy Knit Cap Skatin'	Closed	2001	20.00	20
2000 Buddy Knit Cap Skatin'	Closed	2001	45.00	45
2000 Buddy Knit Cap Sleddin'	Closed	2001	20.00	20
2000 Buddy Knit Cap Sleddin', musical	Closed	2001	20.00	20
2000 Buddy Skatin', sm.	Closed	2001	30.00	30
2000 Buddy Skiing, sm.	Closed	2001	30.00	30
2000 Buddy Sleddin', sm.	Closed	2001	30.00	30
2000 Buddy Snowboardin', sm.	Closed	2001	30.00	30
2000 Buddy Top Hat Skiing	Closed	2001	20.00	20
2000 Buddy Top Hat Skiing	Closed	2001	45.00	45
2000 Buddy Top Hat Snowboardin'	Closed	2001	20.00	20
2000 Buddy Top Hat Snowboardin', musical	Open	2001	20.00	20
2001 The Commitment	Open		45.00	45
2001 Dress Up	Open		10.00	10
2001 Happy Birthday	Open		8.00	8
2002 I Love You	Open		15.00	15
2001 Underwater Adventure	Open		16.00	16

Snow Buddies™ Sound - Encore

2001 Aunt Crystal on Harp	Closed	2001	8.00	8
2001 Avalanche on Drums	Closed	2001	8.00	8
2001 Blizzy on Flute	Closed	2001	8.00	8
2001 Cousin Slick on Guitar	Closed	2001	8.00	8
2001 Everest on Triangle	Closed	2001	8.00	8
2001 Flurry as the Conductor	Closed	2001	8.00	8
2001 Grandpa Frostbite on Banjo	Closed	2001	8.00	8
2001 Uncle Flake on Bagpipes	Closed	2001	8.00	8
2001 Snow Buddies Sound Display	Closed	2001	50.00	50

Snow Buddies™ Spring Buddies - Encore

2001 Everest & Powder Puff (musical)	Open		15.00	15
2001 Lunch For All	Open		10.00	10
2001 New Friends	Open		8.00	8
2001 Picnic Pals	Open		10.00	10
2001 Puddle Pals	Open		10.00	10
2001 Spring Cleaning	Open		8.00	8
2001 Spring Has Sprung	Open		3.00	3
2001 Time to Re-Pot	Open		3.00	3
2001 Welcome Spring	Open		3.00	3

Snow Buddies™ Springtime - Encore

2000 Better Hurry	Yr.Iss.	2000	15.00	15
2000 Duckee Weather	Yr.Iss.	2000	15.00	15
2000 Home Improvements	Yr.Iss.	2000	15.00	15
2000 Just For You!	Yr.Iss.	2000	15.00	15
2000 Life Preservers	Yr.Iss.	2000	15.00	15
2000 A Rite of Spring	Yr.Iss.	2000	15.00	15
2000 Spring Cleaning	Yr.Iss.	2000	15.00	15
2000 Spring Harvest	Yr.Iss.	2000	15.00	15
2000 Stayin' Cool	9,500	2001	30.00	30
2000 Team Effort	Yr.Iss.	2000	15.00	15

Snow Buddies™ Sweetheart 2001 - Encore

2001 By Mailbox	Closed	2001	9.00	9
2001 Chain of Hearts	Closed	2001	6.00	6
2001 Cloud 9	Closed	2001	14.00	14
2001 A Heart Garden	Closed	2001	9.00	9
2001 Heart Shaped Cake	Closed	2001	6.00	6
2001 Key To My Heart	Closed	2001	9.00	9
2001 Making Snow Heart	Closed	2001	9.00	9
2001 Painting Red Heart	Closed	2001	9.00	9
2001 Ready To Kiss	Closed	2001	9.00	9
2001 Serenade	Closed	2001	14.00	14
2001 The Suitor	Closed	2001	17.00	17
2001 Tunnel of Love	Closed	2001	9.00	9

Snow Buddies™ Totem Poles - Encore

2002 Cousin Slick, Grandpa Frostbite & Tundra	Open		9.00	9
2002 Powder Puff, Snowball & Blizzy	Open		8.00	8
2002 Snowbelle, Slip & Slide	Open		9.00	9
2002 Snowbrite, Mayor Blustery, Grandma Cooleen & Flurry	Open		9.00	9

Snow Buddies™ Train Set - Encore

2000 Avalanche in Boxcar	Yr.Iss.	2000	9.00	9
2000 Blizzy in Caboose	Yr.Iss.	2000	10.00	10
2000 Cousin Slick in Boxcar with Gifts	Yr.Iss.	2000	10.00	10
2000 Everest in Boxcar with Candy Canes	Yr.Iss.	2000	10.00	10
2000 Mayor Blustery in Engine	Yr.Iss.	2000	10.00	10
2002 Tundra & Slide Boxcar			10.00	10

Snow Buddies™ Uncle Melty - Encore

2000 Slippery When Wet	Open		9.00	9
2000 Splish Splash	Open		9.00	9
2000 Uncle Melty, 11"	Retrd.	2001	30.00	30
2000 Uncle Melty, 5"	Retrd.	2001	9.00	9

Snow Buddies™ Valentine Buddies Melt Your Heart - Encore

2000 Aiming For Your Heart	Closed	2001	5.00	5
2000 Be My Valentine	Closed	2001	9.00	9
2000 Hearts-N-Flowers	Closed	2001	9.00	9
2000 Luv You This Much	Closed	2001	3.00	3
2000 My Love, My Life	Closed	2001	5.00	5
2000 Queen of Hearts	Closed	2001	3.00	3
2000 Sweet Surprise	Closed	2001	3.00	5
2000 Sweets For My Sweet	Closed	2001	9.00	9
2000 Together Forever	Closed	2001	15.00	15
2000 Valentine Display Sign	Closed	2001	15.00	15

Collectors' Information Bureau   *Quotes have been rounded up to nearest dollar

YEAR ISSUE	EDITION LIMIT	YEAR RETD.	ISSUE PRICE	*QUOTE U.S.$
2000 You Melt My Heart	Closed	2001	3.00	3

Snow Buddies™ Valentine's Day - Encore

2001 Cloud 9	Closed	2001	14.00	14
2001 Making Snow Heart	Closed	2001	9.00	9
2001 Painting Red Heart	Closed	2001	9.00	9
2001 Ready to Kiss	Closed	2001	9.00	9
2001 Serenade	Closed	2001	14.00	14
2001 Snow Buddy By Mailbox	Closed	2001	9.00	9
2001 Snow Buddy Holding Key/Holding Heart	Closed	2001	9.00	9
2001 Snow Buddy with Chain of Hearts	Closed	2001	6.00	6
2001 Snow Buddy with Heart Shaped Cake	Closed	2001	6.00	6
2001 The Suitor	Closed	2001	17.00	17
2001 Tunnel of Love	Closed	2001	9.00	9
2001 Watering A Heart Garden	Closed	2001	9.00	9

Snow Buddies™ Vignettes - Encore

2001 Chanteuse Musical	Closed	2001	20.00	20
2001 Charge!	Closed	2001	15.00	15
2001 Display Sign	Closed	2001	15.00	15
2001 Family Reunion	2,500		100.00	100
2001 Fore!	Closed	2001	15.00	15
2001 It's a Goal	Closed	2001	15.00	15
2001 Knit One, Purl Two	Closed	2001	15.00	15
2001 Strike?	Closed	2001	15.00	15
2002 Swingtime in Snowville	2,400		35.00	35
2001 Tight Squeeze	Closed	2001	15.00	15

Snow Buddies™ Water Fountains - Encore

2001 Day on the Slopes	Open		45.00	45
2001 Sunday Morning	Open		45.00	45

Snow Buddies™ Winter Carnival - Encore

2002 1st Prize - Snowball	Open		6.00	6
2002 The Bake Off - Blizzy	Open		15.00	15
2002 The Kissing Booth - Aunt Crystal	Open		10.00	10
2002 Life Is A Banquet - Everest	Open		8.00	8
2002 Mayor Blustery's Address	Open		8.00	8
2002 Picnic Time - Cousin Slick, Flurry & Tundra	Open		15.00	15
2002 The Pie Eating Contest - Everest	Open		15.00	15
2002 Quilts For Sale - Grandma Cooleen	Open		10.00	10
2002 Winter Princess - Powder Puff	Open		6.00	6

Snow Buddies™, 3 1/2" - Encore

2001 Aunt Crystal	Open		6.00	6
2001 Avalanche	Open		6.00	6
2001 Blizzy	Open		6.00	6
2001 Cousin Slick	Open		6.00	6
2001 Everest	Open		6.00	6
2002 Flurry	Open		6.00	6
2002 Grandma Cooleen	Open		6.00	6
2001 Grandpa Frostbite	Open		6.00	6
2001 Mayor Blustery	Open		6.00	6
2001 Powder Puff	Open		6.00	6
2002 Slide Naughty Twin #2	Open		6.00	6
2002 Slip Naughty Twin #1	Open		6.00	6
2001 Snowball	Open		6.00	6
2002 Snowbelle	Open		6.00	6
2002 Snowbrite	Open		6.00	6
2001 Tundra	Open		6.00	6
2001 Uncle Flake	Open		6.00	6
2001 Uncle Melty	Retrd.	2001	6.00	6

Flambro Imports

Emmett Kelly Jr. Members Only Figurine - Undisclosed

1990 Merry-Go-Round	Closed	1990	125.00	313-688
1991 10 Years Of Collecting	Closed	1991	100.00	160-225
1992 All Aboard	Closed	1992	75.00	150-300
1993 Ringmaster	Closed	1993	125.00	154-219
1994 Birthday Mail	Closed	1994	100.00	224-350
1995 Salute To Our Vets	Closed	1995	75.00	195-200
1996 I Love You	Closed	1996	95.00	250-265
1997 Filet of Sole	Closed	1997	130.00	130-160
1998 Autographs	Closed	1998	100.00	100-175
1999 Birthday Bath	Closed	1999	125.00	125
2000 Little Parade	Closed	2000	120.00	120
2001 Hobo Ball	Closed	2001	100.00	100
2002 Chinese New Year	Yr.Iss.		100.00	100

Emmett Kelly Jr. Annual Figurine - Undisclosed

1996 EKJ For President	Retrd.	1996	60.00	60-100
1997 Send in the Clowns	Retrd.	1997	70.00	70
1998 Smile and the World Smiles with You	Retrd.	1998	50.00	50
1999 Our National Treasure	Retrd.	1999	60.00	60
2000 Into The Millenium	Retrd.	2000	55.00	55

EKJ Professionals - Undisclosed

1987 Accountant	Retrd.	1994	50.00	145-175
1991 Barber	Retrd.	1995	50.00	100-195
2000 Biker	Open		70.00	70
1988 Bowler	Retrd.	1994	50.00	115-135
1996 Bowler	Retrd.	2000	55.00	55
1991 Carpenter	Retrd.	1996	50.00	110-145
1991 The Chef	Retrd.	1994	50.00	145-175
1995 Coach	Retrd.	2000	50.00	50
1990 Computer Whiz	Retrd.	1998	50.00	60-100
1997 Computer Whiz (w/garbage can)	Retrd.	2001	55.00	55
2000 Country Western Singer	Open		50.00	50
2001 The Deacon	1,500		60.00	60
1987 Dentist	Retrd.	1995	50.00	110-145
1996 Dentist	Open		55.00	55
1995 Doctor	Retrd.	1998	55.00	55-140
1987 Doctor	Retrd.	1995	50.00	100
1999 Doctor	Open		50.00	50
1987 Engineer	Retrd.	1995	50.00	100
1987 Executive	Retrd.	1998	50.00	52-65
1997 Executive (talking on phone)	Open		55.00	55
1996 Farmer	Retrd.	2000	55.00	55
1999 Fireman	Open		50.00	50
1995 Fireman	Open		55.00	55
1988 Fireman	Retrd.	1994	50.00	100-145
1990 Fisherman	Retrd.	2000	50.00	50
1997 Fisherman (w/fish & dog)	Open		55.00	55
1997 Fitness (runaway weight loss)	Open		55.00	55
1997 Gardener (w/rake)	Open		55.00	55
1999 Golfer	Open		50.00	50
1995 Golfer	Retrd.	2000	55.00	55
1988 Golfer	Retrd.	1996	50.00	100-195
1998 Graduate	Open		60.00	60
1990 Hunter	Open		50.00	50
1997 Hunter (w/orange camouflauge)	Open		55.00	55
1995 Lawyer	Retrd.	1998	55.00	55-120
1987 Lawyer	Retrd.	1995	50.00	120-195
1999 Lawyer	Open		50.00	50
1988 Mailman	Retrd.	1996	50.00	110-145
1996 Mailman	Open		55.00	55
2000 Mime	Open		50.00	50
1993 On Maneuvers	Open		50.00	50
1991 Painter	Retrd.	1998	50.00	50-135
1991 Pharmacist	Retrd.	1995	50.00	50
1990 Photographer	Retrd.	1998	50.00	50-125
1993 Pilot	Retrd.	1998	50.00	50-100
1991 Plumber	Retrd.	1994	50.00	100-110
1995 Policeman	Open		55.00	55
1988 Policeman	Retrd.	1994	50.00	110-135
1999 Policeman	Open		50.00	50
1990 The Putt	Retrd.	1998	50.00	65-100
1998 Race Fan	Retrd.	2001	60.00	60
1993 Realtor	Retrd.	1998	50.00	100-125
1998 Retirement	Retrd.	2001	65.00	65
1998 Salesman	Open		60.00	60
2001 School Crossing Guard	Open		60.00	60
1996 Skier	Open		55.00	55
1988 Skier	Retrd.	1995	50.00	135-150
1987 Stockbrocker	Retrd.	1997	50.00	125-150
1999 Teacher	Open		50.00	50
1987 Teacher	Retrd.	1995	50.00	120-145
2002 The Tourist	Open		70.00	70
2000 Truck Driver	Open		70.00	70
1993 Veterinarian	Retrd.	1997	50.00	100-150

Emmett Kelly Jr. - Undisclosed, unless otherwise noted

1995 20th Anniversary of All Star Circus	5,000	1995	240.00	240-250
1997 25th Anniversary of White House Appearance	5,000		240.00	240
1995 35 Years of Clowning	5,000	1995	240.00	240-250
1989 65th Birthday Commemorative	1,989	1989	300.00	625-969
1993 After The Parade	7,500	1998	190.00	190
1988 Amen	12,000	1991	120.00	282-688
1996 American Circus Extravaganza	5,000		240.00	240

FIGURINES

YEAR ISSUE	EDITION LIMIT	YEAR RETD.	ISSUE PRICE	*QUOTE U.S.$
2002 April in Paris (Block Set)	1,500		300.00	300
1991 Artist At Work	7,500	1997	285.00	300-450
1992 Autumn - D. Rust	Retrd.	1996	60.00	175
1983 The Balancing Act	10,000	1985	75.00	407-1063
1983 Balloons For Sale	10,000	1985	75.00	300-688
1990 Balloons for Sale II	7,500	1998	250.00	250-390
1986 Bedtime	12,000	1991	98.00	125-467
1984 Big Business	9,500	1987	110.00	488-900
1997 Catch of the Day	5,000		240.00	240
2000 Circus Las Vegas	2,000		150.00	150
2000 Circus Parade (Block Set)	1,500		275.00	275
1990 Convention-Bound	7,500	1998	225.00	169-230
1986 Cotton Candy	12,000	1987	98.00	125-469
2001 Couch Potato	1,500		125.00	125
1996 Daredevil Thrill Motor Show	5,000		240.00	240
1988 Dining Out	12,000	1991	120.00	125-563
1984 Eating Cabbage	12,000	1986	75.00	200-594
1998 Economy Class (Block Set)	1,500	1998	275.00	275
2002 Emmett on Ice (Block Set)	1,500		300.00	300
1985 Emmett's Fan	12,000	1986	80.00	225-594
1986 The Entertainers	12,000	1991	120.00	113-250
1986 Fair Game	2,500	1987	450.00	782-1500
1991 Finishing Touch	7,500	1998	230.00	169-307
1991 Follow The Leader	7,500	1998	200.00	150-300
1994 Forest Friends	7,500	1997	190.00	190-325
2002 G'Day Mate	1,500		130.00	130
1983 Hole In The Sole	10,000	1986	75.00	369-594
2001 Home Cooking (Block Set)	1,500		275.00	275
2000 Home For The Holidays (Christmas Ed.)	2,000		150.00	150
2001 Homefires are Burning	1,500		125.00	125
1989 Hurdy-Gurdy Man	9,500	1991	150.00	150-500
1985 In The Spotlight	12,000	1989	103.00	119-438
1993 Kittens For Sale	7,500	1998	190.00	190-200
2000 Kodak's Clown (Hospital Visit)	2,000		130.00	130
2000 Leaving Tombstone	2,000		100.00	100
1994 Let Him Eat Cake	3,500	1995	300.00	300-480
1994 The Lion Tamer	7,500	1997	190.00	200-350
1981 Looking Out To See	12,000	1982	75.00	1040-3500
1986 Making New Friends	9,500	1988	140.00	188-407
1989 Making Up	7,500	1995	200.00	188-563
1985 Man's Best Friend	9,500	1989	98.00	232-750
1990 Misfortune?	3,500	1990	350.00	250-700
2001 Mr. Fix It	1,500		125.00	125
1987 My Favorite Things	9,500	1988	109.00	275-750
1989 No Loitering	7,500	1994	200.00	219-500
1985 No Strings Attached	9,500	1991	98.00	132-300
1992 No Use Crying	7,500	1998	200.00	188-313
1987 On The Road Again	9,500	1991	109.00	200-600
1998 Our Perennial Favorite (Block Set)	1,500	1998	275.00	275
1988 Over a Barrel	9,500	1991	130.00	150-250
1992 Peanut Butter?	7,500	1998	200.00	188-313
1984 Piano Player	9,500	1988	160.00	313-750
1992 Ready-Set-Go	7,500	1998	200.00	150-313
1987 Saturday Night	7,500	1988	153.00	438-875
1983 Spirit of Christmas I	3,500	1984	125.00	2088-3500
1984 Spirit of Christmas II	3,500	1985	270.00	313-688
1985 Spirit of Christmas III	3,500	1989	220.00	407-975
1986 Spirit of Christmas IV	3,500	1989	150.00	187-400
1987 Spirit of Christmas V	2,400	1989	170.00	688-969
1988 Spirit of Christmas VI	2,400	1989	194.00	220-400
1990 Spirit of Christmas VII	3,500	1990	275.00	275-400
1991 Spirit of Christmas VIII	3,500	1992	250.00	294-470
1993 Spirit of Christmas IX	3,500	1998	200.00	250-313
1993 Spirit of Christmas X	3,500	1998	200.00	200-225
1994 Spirit of Christmas XI	3,500	1995	200.00	225-260
1995 Spirit of Christmas XII	3,500	1997	200.00	250-295
1996 Spirit of Christmas XIII	3,500	1998	200.00	200-275
1997 Spirit of Christmas XIV	3,500	1998	200.00	200-275
1998 Spirit of Christmas XV	1,500	1998	250.00	250
1992 Spring - D. Rust	Retrd.	1996	60.00	95
1992 Summer - D. Rust	Retrd.	1996	60.00	250-300
2000 Sweeping Up	2,000		100.00	100
1981 Sweeping Up	12,000	1982	75.00	520-1000
1982 The Thinker	15,000	1986	60.00	657-1032
1987 Toothache	12,000	1995	98.00	75-220
2001 Washday (Block Set)	1,500		275.00	275
1990 Watch the Birdie	9,500	1998	200.00	194-257
1982 Wet Paint	15,000	1983	80.00	369-560
1988 Wheeler Dealer	7,500	1990	160.00	175-500
1982 Why Me?	15,000	1984	65.00	438-750

YEAR ISSUE	EDITION LIMIT	YEAR RETD.	ISSUE PRICE	*QUOTE U.S.$
1992 Winter - D. Rust	Retrd.	1996	60.00	125-150
1983 Wishful Thinking	10,000	1985	65.00	207-750
1993 World Traveler	7,500	1997	190.00	225-300
2000 World's Fair (Block Set)	1,500		275.00	275

Emmett Kelly Jr. A Day At The Fair - Undisclosed

YEAR ISSUE	EDITION LIMIT	YEAR RETD.	ISSUE PRICE	*QUOTE U.S.$
1990 75¢ Please	Retrd.	1994	65.00	150-175
1991 Coin Toss	Retrd.	1994	65.00	125-175
1990 Look At You	Retrd.	1994	65.00	125-175
1991 Popcorn!	Retrd.	1994	65.00	125-175
1990 Ride The Wild Mouse	Retrd.	1994	65.00	95-175
1990 Step Right Up	Retrd.	1994	65.00	165-175
1990 The Stilt Man	Retrd.	1994	65.00	125-175
1990 Thanks Emmett	Retrd.	1994	65.00	125-175
1990 Three For A Dime	Retrd.	1994	65.00	125-175
1991 The Trouble With Hot Dogs	Retrd.	1994	65.00	175
1990 You Can Do It, Emmett	Retrd.	1994	65.00	125-175
1990 You Go First, Emmett	Retrd.	1994	65.00	175

Emmett Kelly Jr. Appearance Figurine - Undisclosed

YEAR ISSUE	EDITION LIMIT	YEAR RETD.	ISSUE PRICE	*QUOTE U.S.$
1992 Now Appearing	Retrd.	1994	100.00	100-188
1993 The Vigilante	Retrd.	1994	75.00	75
1996 Going My Way	Retrd.	1997	90.00	90

Emmett Kelly Jr. Diamond Jubilee Birthday Series - Undisclosed

YEAR ISSUE	EDITION LIMIT	YEAR RETD.	ISSUE PRICE	*QUOTE U.S.$
1999 Big Cake	1,999	1999	100.00	100-103
1999 Birthday Cleanup	1,999	1999	125.00	100-125
1998 Birthday Parade	1,999	1999	150.00	150-200
1999 Jazz (Block Set)	1,500	1999	275.00	275
1999 Oops! Another Birthday (Block Set)	1,500	1999	275.00	275
1999 Surprise	1,999	1999	125.00	125-129

Emmett Kelly Jr. Diamond Jubilee Celebration (Birthday Miniatures) - Undisclosed

YEAR ISSUE	EDITION LIMIT	YEAR RETD.	ISSUE PRICE	*QUOTE U.S.$
1999 Cabbage?	Retrd.	1999	60.00	60
1999 Cake For Two	Retrd.	1999	65.00	65
1999 The Ultimate Gift	Retrd.	1999	60.00	60

Emmett Kelly Jr. Images of Emmett - Undisclosed

YEAR ISSUE	EDITION LIMIT	YEAR RETD.	ISSUE PRICE	*QUOTE U.S.$
1994 Baby's First Christmas	Retrd.	1997	80.00	80-135
1994 Best of Friends	Retrd.	1997	55.00	55-110
1994 Healing Heart	Retrd.	1997	90.00	90-150
1994 Holding The Future	Retrd.	1996	65.00	125-135
1994 Learning Together	Retrd.	1997	85.00	100-135
1994 Tightrope	Retrd.	1997	70.00	85
1994 Why Me, Again?	Retrd.	1997	60.00	60-100

Emmett Kelly Jr. Miniatures - Undisclosed

YEAR ISSUE	EDITION LIMIT	YEAR RETD.	ISSUE PRICE	*QUOTE U.S.$
2002 35 Years of Clowning	Open		60.00	60
1994 65th Birthday	Retrd.	1994	70.00	70-150
1998 All Aboard	Open		30.00	30
1996 Amen	Retrd.	1998	35.00	35-100
1998 Artist at Work	Retrd.	2001	55.00	55
1986 Balancing Act	Retrd.	1992	25.00	125-200
1986 Balloons for Sale	Retrd.	1993	25.00	75-100
1997 Balloons for Sale II	Open		55.00	55
1995 Bedtime	Retrd.	1998	35.00	35-100
1997 Big Boss	Open		55.00	55
1988 Big Business	Retrd.	1995	35.00	75-125
2002 Bon Voyage	Open		60.00	60
2001 Catch of the Day	Open		50.00	50
1997 Convention Bound	Open		55.00	55
1989 Cotton Candy	Retrd.	1991	30.00	135-150
2001 Dining Car	Open		50.00	50
1995 Dining Out	Retrd.	1998	35.00	35-100
1987 Eating Cabbage	Retrd.	1990	30.00	35-90
1987 Emmett's Fan	Retrd.	1994	30.00	135-150
1995 The Entertainers	Retrd.	1998	45.00	45
1994 Fair Game	Open		75.00	75
1999 Forest Friends	Open		55.00	55
1986 Hole in the Sole	Retrd.	1989	25.00	140-150
1995 Hurdy Gurdy Man	Open		40.00	40
1991 In The Spotlight	Retrd.	1996	35.00	90-115
2001 Jazz	Open		50.00	50
2002 Leaving Tombstone	Open		60.00	60
1992 Let Him Eat Cake	Open		65.00	65
1999 Lion Tamer	Open		60.00	60
1986 Looking Out To See	Retrd.	1987	25.00	200-225
1992 Making New Friends	Retrd.	1996	40.00	135-150
1996 Making Up	Retrd.	2000	55.00	55
1989 Man's Best Friend?	Retrd.	1994	35.00	100-130

Collectors' Information Bureau   *Quotes have been rounded up to nearest dollar

YEAR ISSUE	EDITION LIMIT	YEAR RETD.	ISSUE PRICE	*QUOTE U.S.$
1997 Merry Go Round	Open		65.00	65
1996 Misfortune	Open		60.00	60
1990 My Favorite Things	Retrd.	1995	45.00	100-125
1995 No Loitering	Retrd.	2000	50.00	50
1991 No Strings Attached	Retrd.	1996	35.00	125
1992 On the Road Again	Retrd.	1997	35.00	35
2001 Our Perennial Favorite	Open		50.00	50
1994 Over a Barrel	Retrd.	1998	30.00	30-125
2000 Peanut Butter?	Open		50.00	50
1992 Piano Player	Retrd.	1997	50.00	50
2000 Ready Set Go	Open		55.00	55
1999 Ringmaster	Open		60.00	60
1990 Saturday Night	Retrd.	1995	50.00	75-150
1988 Spirit of Christmas I	Retrd.	1990	40.00	100-200
1992 Spirit of Christmas II	Retrd.	1995	50.00	125-160
1990 Spirit of Christmas III	Retrd.	1993	50.00	72-175
1993 Spirit of Christmas IV	Retrd.	1997	40.00	100-115
1994 Spirit of Christmas V	Retrd.	1996	50.00	100-145
1996 Spirit of Christmas VI	Retrd.	1998	55.00	55
1997 Spirit of Christmas VII	Retrd.	1998	50.00	50-100
1998 Spirit of Christmas IX	Open		55.00	55
1986 Sweeping Up	Retrd.	1987	25.00	94-250
1998 Take Good Care of Her	Retrd.	1999	50.00	50
1986 The Thinker	Retrd.	1991	25.00	150-163
1996 The Toothache	Retrd.	2000	35.00	35
1997 Watch the Birdie	Open		55.00	55
1986 Wet Paint	Retrd.	1993	25.00	65-125
1996 Wheeler Dealer	Open		65.00	65
2000 White House Appearance	Open		60.00	60
1986 Why Me?	Retrd.	1989	25.00	57-157
1986 Wishful Thinking	Retrd.	1988	25.00	50-142
1998 World Traveler	Retrd.	2001	55.00	55
2000 World's Fair	Retrd.	2001	55.00	55

Emmett Kelly Jr. Musical Waterglobes - Undisclosed

YEAR ISSUE	EDITION LIMIT	YEAR RETD.	ISSUE PRICE	*QUOTE U.S.$
1997 All Star Circus	Retrd.	2000	35.00	35
1999 EKJ Birthday Mail	Open		50.00	50
1999 EKJ Catch of the Day	Open		55.00	55
1999 EKJ Filet of Sole	Open		50.00	50
1999 EKJ Golfer	Open		40.00	40
1999 EKJ Making New Friends	Open		35.00	35
1999 EKJ Misfortune	Open		40.00	40
1999 EKJ Race Fan	Open		40.00	40
1999 EKJ Teacher	Open		40.00	40
1999 EKJ World Traveler	Open		50.00	50
2000 Liontamer	Retrd.	2000	60.00	60
2000 Send in the Clown	Retrd.	2000	60.00	60

Emmett Kelly Jr. Real Rags Collection - Undisclosed

YEAR ISSUE	EDITION LIMIT	YEAR RETD.	ISSUE PRICE	*QUOTE U.S.$
1993 Big Business II	Retrd.	1996	140.00	200
1993 Checking His List	Closed	N/A	100.00	115-200
1994 Eating Cabbage II	3,000	1997	100.00	100-150
2000 Economy Class (Musical)	Retrd.	2000	120.00	120
1994 A Good Likeness	3,000	1997	120.00	120-175
1993 Looking Out To See II	3,000	1996	100.00	165-200
1994 On in Two	3,000	1996	100.00	135-175
1994 Rudolph Has A Red Nose, Too	3,000	1996	135.00	135-350
1993 Sweeping Up II	3,000	1996	100.00	135-175
1993 Thinker II	3,000	1996	120.00	150-200

Hap Henriksen's Collectors Fellowship - H. Henriksen

YEAR ISSUE	EDITION LIMIT	YEAR RETD.	ISSUE PRICE	*QUOTE U.S.$
XX The Legend (Event Special)	Retrd.	N/A	N/A	N/A
1993 On The Road (Event Special)	Retrd.	1993	N/A	195-255
XX Orbis Terrigena	Retrd.	N/A	88.00	88
XX Phantom	Retrd.	N/A	88.00	88

Hap Henriksen's Dragons - H. Henriksen

YEAR ISSUE	EDITION LIMIT	YEAR RETD.	ISSUE PRICE	*QUOTE U.S.$
1992 Albenon the Forest Dragon	Retrd.	1993	75.00	198
1995 Atnanticus	Retrd.	1996	150.00	175-345
1996 The Awakening	Retrd.	1997	150.00	150-295
1998 Decemurius Dragon of the Frost	750	N/A	441.00	441-525
1991 Drac Terriblius	3,000	N/A	325.00	325-700
1989 Dragon of the Golden Hoard	Retrd.	N/A	N/A	495-775
1989 Guardian of the Keep	Retrd.	N/A	189.00	500
1989 Hatched	Retrd.	N/A	N/A	195
1997 The Hatchling	1,500	N/A	160.00	100-160
1997 Histra Rex	1,500	N/A	295.00	295-350
XX Ice Dragon	Retrd.	N/A	70.00	175-190
1992 Keeper of the Ruin	300	1994	1800.00	3000
1989 Let Sleeping Dragons Lie	3,000	1992	N/A	1100-2000
1989 Leviathan	Retrd.	N/A	N/A	425-650
1992 The Merchant of Dreams	350	1994	1800.00	3000

YEAR ISSUE	EDITION LIMIT	YEAR RETD.	ISSUE PRICE	*QUOTE U.S.$
XX Night & Day	Retrd.	N/A	N/A	320
1998 Rewyne Protector of the Lost World	1,500	N/A	265.00	265-450
1997 Tallonous Wyvernous	1,500		150.00	160
1992 Treasure of the Lost Lands	1,500	1995	N/A	750
1998 World	1,500		265.00	265
1994 Wundor	2,500	N/A	N/A	310-355
1994 Wynd	2,500	1996	N/A	340
1989 Wyvern	1,500	1992	N/A	740
1992 Zornakk the Elder	Retrd.	N/A	N/A	N/A

Hap Henriksen's Jesters - H. Henriksen

YEAR ISSUE	EDITION LIMIT	YEAR RETD.	ISSUE PRICE	*QUOTE U.S.$
1989 His Majesty Bladrick The Incredibly Simple	Retrd.	1990	275.00	275
1989 Jockomo	Retrd.	1990	55.00	55
1989 Jollies Pitchbelly	Retrd.	1990	175.00	175
1989 La DiDa Toogoode	Retrd.	1990	165.00	165
1989 Merry Andrew	Retrd.	1990	125.00	125
1989 Puck	Retrd.	1990	55.00	55
1989 Smack Thickwit	Retrd.	1990	175.00	175-240
1989 Twit Coxcombe	Retrd.	1990	135.00	135
1989 Ursula	Retrd.	1990	90.00	90

Hap Henriksen's Wizards - H. Henriksen

YEAR ISSUE	EDITION LIMIT	YEAR RETD.	ISSUE PRICE	*QUOTE U.S.$
1995 Alkmyne	1,500		135.00	145
1996 Apothes	1,500		195.00	240
1996 Archimedes Lessons	1,500		195.00	240
1994 Astrol	2,500	1996	N/A	250-315
1992 Balador	Retrd.	1993	N/A	500
1990 Balance of Truth	2,500	N/A	220.00	440
1993 Bilanx The Grand Master (Utopian)	3,500	1994	150.00	150
1993 Compriez (S. American)	Retrd.	1994	61.00	61
1995 Confrontation	999		266.00	266
1996 Conversation	1,500		175.00	189
1989 Counter Sign	Retrd.	1991	90.00	250
1997 The Crystal Gazer	1,500		150.00	160
1997 Curiosity	1,500		189.00	189
1997 Dragon Lord	1,500		195.00	195
1991 Dragon Master	1,500	N/A	575.00	695-755
1997 The Elusive Potion	1,500		270.00	270
1994 Farundel The Weary Traveler	2,500	1996	150.00	150-325
1993 Fidem (African)	Retrd.	1994	71.00	71
1989 Foreshadow the Seer	Retrd.	1992	N/A	425-475
1998 Gallianaus	1,500	N/A	136.00	136-175
1993 Hopai (Oriental)	Retrd.	1994	71.00	71
1991 Howland the Wise	2,500	1993	245.00	340-425
1989 Hubble Bubble	Retrd.	1990	75.00	295-450
1992 Journeyman	2,500	1995	240.00	330-440
1993 Karojan (American Indian)	Retrd.	1994	71.00	71
1994 Knowe	2,500	1996	N/A	345-495
1989 Lackey The Apprentice	Retrd.	1990	N/A	130-360
1996 Laidley Worm	1,500		150.00	160
1997 The Magic Sword	1,500		150.00	160
1989 Merlin Wizard Watcher	2,500	1991	N/A	195
1992 Merlinus Ambrosius	2,500	1996	275.00	375-400
1989 Merryweather Sunlighter	3,000	1993	390.00	590-675
1989 Morgan Le Fay	2,500	N/A	150.00	350-450
1989 Moriah	Retrd.	1992	240.00	395-440
1989 Mydwynter	Retrd.	N/A	190.00	390-425
1994 Nateur	2,500	1996	N/A	310-350
1993 Nemesis (Greek)	Retrd.	1994	61.00	61
1994 Noctiluca	2,500	1996	N/A	385-410
1992 Ommiad the Magi	2,500	1995	N/A	350-410
1991 Past, Present and Future	2,500	1996	300.00	350-495
1995 Pelryn	2,500		175.00	199
1991 Pondering the Quest	2,500	1993	210.00	325-410
1995 Rammis	2,500		150.00	160
1989 Repository of Magic	Retrd.	1990	150.00	360-395
1989 Rimbaugh	Retrd.	N/A	N/A	445
1997 Seeking Council	1,500		451.00	451
1993 Smalaz (Russian)	Retrd.	1994	55.00	55
1997 Solaris The Star Seeker	1,500		189.00	189
1993 The Soothsayer	2,500	1996	N/A	385-410
1996 Stormbringer	1,500		150.00	150
1994 Sturm	2,500	1996	N/A	345-410
1998 Taihun, Master of Council	1,500		160.00	300
1989 Thorbauld	Retrd.	N/A	N/A	350
1996 Thorlief Graybeard	1,500		250.00	270
1994 The Travellers	1,500		295.00	295
1993 Troewe (Germanic)	Retrd.	1994	61.00	61
1998 Trouth	1,500	N/A	136.00	136-225
1998 Twiggle Tanglefoot	1,500	N/A	136.00	136-160

YEAR ISSUE	EDITION LIMIT	YEAR RETD.	ISSUE PRICE	*QUOTE U.S.$
1997 Well of Sorrows	1,500		270.00	270
1993 Wroth (Nordic)	Retrd.	1994	61.00	61

Kensington Bears- Bears of Character - Undisclosed

1998 Bear Bell Boy	2,500		75.00	75
1998 Bear Clown	Open		55.00	55
1998 Bear Graduate	Open		35.00	35
1998 Bear Indian	Open		55.00	55
1998 Bear Sewing	Open		35.00	35
1998 Bear With Candle	Open		35.00	35

Kensington Bears- Cute Companions - Undisclosed

1998 Bear	Open		10.00	10
1998 Elephant	Open		10.00	10
1998 Labrador	Open		10.00	10
1998 Rabbit	Open		10.00	10

Kensington Bears- Cute Companions Puppies - Undisclosed

1998 Basset Hound	Open		10.00	10
1998 Boxer	Open		10.00	10
1998 Cocker Spaniel	Open		10.00	10
1998 Rottweiler	Open		10.00	10
1998 Westie Terrier	Open		10.00	10
1998 Yorkshire Terrier	Open		10.00	10

Kensington Bears-Brown Bears - Undisclosed

1998 Baxter	Open		50.00	50
1998 Bobby	Open		30.00	30
1998 Chaplin	Open		30.00	30
1998 Johnny	Open		30.00	30
1998 Louie	Open		50.00	50
1998 Trimble	Open		60.00	60

Kensington Bears-Golden Bears - Undisclosed

1998 Baxter	Open		50.00	50
1998 Bobby	Open		30.00	30
1998 Chaplin	Open		30.00	30
1998 Johnny	Open		30.00	30
1998 Louie	Open		50.00	50
1998 Trimble	Open		60.00	60

Little Emmetts - M. Wu

1998 #1 Teacher	Open		10.00	10
1996 Balancing Act	Retrd.	1998	25.00	25
1996 Balloons for Sale	Retrd.	1998	25.00	25
1994 Birthday Haul	Open		30.00	30
1995 Dance Lessons	Retrd.	1995	50.00	50
1998 Get Well Soon	Open		10.00	10
1998 Happy Birthday	Open		10.00	10
1998 I Love You	Open		10.00	10
1994 Little Artist Picture Frame	Retrd.	1997	22.00	22
1994 Little Emmett Fishing	Retrd.	1997	35.00	35
1995 Little Emmett Noel, Noel	Open		40.00	40
1994 Little Emmett Shadow Show	Retrd.	1997	40.00	40
1995 Little Emmett Someday	Retrd.	1997	50.00	50
1994 Little Emmett w/Blackboard	Retrd.	1997	30.00	30
1994 Little Emmett, Counting Lession (Musical)	Retrd.	1996	30.00	30
1994 Little Emmett, Country Road (Musical)	Retrd.	1996	35.00	35
1994 Little Emmett, Raindrops (Musical)	Retrd.	1995	35.00	35
1994 Little Emmett, You've Got a Friend (Musical)	Retrd.	1996	33.00	33
1996 Long Distance	Open		50.00	50
1995 Looking Back Musical Waterglobe	Retrd.	1997	75.00	75
1995 Looking Forward Musical Waterglobe	Retrd.	1999	75.00	75
1996 Looking Out To See	Retrd.	1998	25.00	25
1998 Miss You	Open		10.00	10
1994 Playful Bookends	Open		40.00	40
1998 Sorry	Open		10.00	10
1996 Sweeping Up	Retrd.	1998	25.00	25
1996 Thinker	Retrd.	1998	25.00	25
1996 Wet Paint	Retrd.	1998	40.00	40
1994 EKJ, Age 1	Open		9.00	9
1994 EKJ, Age2	Open		9.50	10
1994 EKJ, Age 3	Open		12.00	12
1994 EKJ, Age 4	Open		12.00	12
1994 EKJ, Age 5	Open		15.00	15
1994 EKJ, Age 6	Open		15.00	15
1994 EKJ, Age 7	Open		17.00	17
1994 EKJ, Age 8	Open		21.00	21
1994 EKJ, Age 9	Open		22.00	22

YEAR ISSUE	EDITION LIMIT	YEAR RETD.	ISSUE PRICE	*QUOTE U.S.$
1994 EKJ, Age 10	Open		25.00	25
1996 January-New Years	Open		35.00	35
1996 February-Valentine's Day	Open		35.00	35
1996 March-St. Patrick's Day	Open		35.00	35
1996 April-April Showers	Open		35.00	35
1996 May-May Flowers	Open		35.00	35
1996 June-School Is Out	Open		35.00	35
1996 July-Independence Day	Open		35.00	35
1996 August-Summer Picnic	Open		35.00	35
1996 September-School Is In	Open		35.00	35
1996 October-Pumpkins for Fall & Halloween	Open		35.00	35
1996 November-Thanksgiving	Open		35.00	35
1996 December-Snow Sledding w/Friends	Open		35.00	35

Peanuts - Undisclosed

2000 A Day in the Park	1,500		85.00	85
1999 First Day of School	1,500		100.00	100
1999 Heroes	1,500		85.00	85
2000 Hors d' oeuvres	1,500		85.00	85
2000 Joe Cool	1,500		85.00	85
2000 Joe No-Pride	1,500		65.00	65

Fontanini/Roman, Inc.

Fontanini Club Members' Only - E. Simonetti

1990 The Pilgrimage	Closed	1994	24.00	200
1992 She Rescued Me	Yr.Iss.	1992	23.50	150
1993 Christmas Symphony	Yr.Iss.	1993	13.50	85-150
1994 Sweet Harmony	Yr.Iss.	1994	13.50	85-150
1995 Faith: The Fifth Angel	Yr.Iss.	1995	22.50	99-150

Fontanini Club Members' Only Nativity Preview - E. Simonetti

1996 Mara	Yr.Iss.	1996	12.50	55-75
1997 Benjamin	Yr.Iss.	1997	15.00	60
1998 Hannah	Yr.Iss.	1998	15.00	15
1999 Obediah, The Teacher	Yr.Iss.	1999	15.00	15
2000 Jacob	Yr.Iss.	2000	19.50	20
2001 Dinah	Yr.Iss.	2001	19.50	20
2002 Samantha	Yr.Iss.		19.50	20

Fontanini Club Renewal Gift - E. Simonetti

1993 He Comforts Me	Yr.Iss.	1993	Gift	225
1994 I'm Heaven Bound	Yr.Iss.	1994	Gift	150-255
1995 Gift of Joy	Yr.Iss.	1995	Gift	150

Fontanini Club Symbol of Membership - E. Simonetti

1990 I Found Him	Closed	1995	Gift	25-225
1996 Rosannah - Angel of The Roses	Yr.Iss.	1996	Gift	50-75
1997 Leah - Angel of Light	Yr.Iss.	1997	Gift	50
1998 Candace - The Caregiver	Yr.Iss.	1998	Gift	40-45
1999 Lemuel, The Lord's Herald	Yr.Iss.	1999	Gift	N/A
2000 Temira	Yr.Iss.	2000	Gift	N/A
2001 Rayna	Yr.Iss.	2001	Gift	N/A
2002 Aurora			Gift	N/A

Fontanini Special Event - E. Simonetti, unless otherwise noted

1994 Susanna	Yr.Iss.	1994	15.00	30-65
1995 Dominica	Yr.Iss.	1995	15.00	30-60
1996 Sarah	Yr.Iss.	1996	15.00	30-65
1997 Martha	Yr.Iss.	1997	15.00	30-55
1998 Phoebe, Perfume Maker	Yr.Iss.	1998	15.00	18
1999 Herschel, The Carpenter's Apprentice	Yr.Iss.	1999	17.50	18-20
2000 Leora	Yr.Iss.	2000	19.50	20
2001 Lydia - D. Maressa	Yr.Iss.	2001	19.50	20
2002 Uri			19.50	20

Fontanini Personal Tour Exclusive - E. Simonetti

1990 Gideon	Closed	1995	8.00	30-89
1995 Luke	Closed	1998	15.00	30-65
1998 Emanuele, The Founder	Closed	1999	15.00	45

Fontanini 5" Collection - E. Simonetti

1994 Aaron	Open		11.50	12
1967 Aaron	Retrd.	1993	5.50	13
1987 Abraham	Open		7.00	7
1998 Alexander	Open		15.00	15
2001 Amos	Open		19.50	20
1998 Andrew	Open		15.00	15

Collectors' Information Bureau   *Quotes have been rounded up to nearest dollar

YEAR ISSUE	EDITION LIMIT	YEAR RETD.	ISSUE PRICE	*QUOTE U.S.$
1966 Angel, Gloria Angel	Retrd.	1979	3.00	3
1979 Angel, Gloria Angel	Open		7.00	7
1966 Angel, Heraldic Angel	Retrd.	2000	27.50	28
1967 Angel, Kneeling Angel	Retrd.	1994	5.50	13-45
1995 Angel, Kneeling Angel	Open		11.50	12
2001 Angel, Little Shepherd	Open		12.50	13
1967 Angel, Standing Angel	Retrd.	1994	5.50	13-45
1995 Angel, Standing Angel	Open		11.50	12
1998 Anthony	Open		15.00	15
1967 Asa	Retrd.	2000	13.50	14-20
1996 Azzan	Retrd.	1999	15.00	15
1966 Baby Jesus	Retrd.	1991	5.50	12
1992 Baby Jesus	Open		11.50	12
1966 Balthazar	Retrd.	1992	5.50	30
1993 Balthazar	Open		11.50	12
1993 Balthazar on Camel	Open		32.50	33
2000 Benjamin	Open		17.50	18
1998 Birds, Barnyard Birds	Open		29.50	30
1989 Birds, Bethlehem Birds	Open		12.50	13
2000 Birds, Dove Set	Open		9.00	9
1968 Caleb	Open		7.00	7
1993 Camel with Saddle Blanket	Open		17.50	18
1967 Camel, Seated	Open		7.00	7
1967 Camel, Standing	Open		7.00	7
2000 Carmi	Open		19.50	20
2002 Chloe	Open		19.50	20
1996 Cornelius, King's Steward	Open		12.50	13
1968 Daniel	Open		7.00	7
1987 David	Open		7.00	7
1968 Deborah	Open		7.00	7
1967 Dog	Open		2.30	3
1966 Donkey, Seated	Open		7.00	7
1966 Donkey, Standing	Open		6.00	6
1993 Elephant with Saddle Blanket	Open		29.50	30
1987 Eli	Retrd.	2001	7.00	7-15
1996 Elisabeth	Open		12.50	13
1968 Ephraim	Open		7.00	7
1997 Esau	Open		15.00	15
1997 Eva	Open		15.00	15
2002 Ezbon, the Student	Open		17.50	18
1968 Ezra	Retrd.	2001	7.00	7
1997 Flavius	Open		15.00	15
1993 Gabriel	Open		11.50	12
1967 Gabriel	Retrd.	1992	5.50	12-14
1966 Gaspar	Retrd.	1992	5.50	25
1993 Gaspar	Open		11.50	12
1993 Gaspar on Elephant	Open		45.00	45
1996 Gilead, King's Servant	Open		12.50	13
1967 Goat	Open		2.30	3
2001 Hannah	Open		19.50	20
2001 Hiram	Open		19.50	20
1998 Horse, Black with Saddle Blanket	Open		22.50	23
1998 Horse, Brown with Saddle Blanket	Open		22.50	23
1993 Horse, White with Saddle Blanket	Open		17.50	18
1996 Issak	Retrd.	1999	13.50	14
1989 Jareth	Open		12.50	13
1994 Jeremiah	Open		11.50	12
1994 Jethro, Tamar & Saul	Retrd.	2000	24.00	24
1968 Joel	Retrd.	1998	5.50	14-27
1997 John	Open		15.00	15
2002 Jordan, Spice Merchant	Open		19.50	20
1992 Joseph	Open		11.50	12
1966 Joseph	Retrd.	1991	5.50	12-15
1967 Joshua	Retrd.	1999	13.50	14
1997 Joshua	Retrd.	1999	13.50	14
1994 Josiah	Open		11.50	12
1967 Josiah	Retrd.	1993	5.50	12
2002 Journey to Bethlehem	Open		39.50	40
1968 Judith	Retrd.	1998	5.50	13-20
2000 Kenan	Open		22.50	23
1997 Kings on Camels	Open		75.00	75
1978 Kings on Camels	Retrd.	1996	52.00	125
1994 Levi	Open		11.50	12
1967 Levi	Retrd.	1993	5.50	13
1968 Malachi, Camel Driver	Retrd.	2001	7.00	7
1998 Marcus	Open		15.00	15
1997 Mariel	Open		19.50	20
1966 Mary	Retrd.	1991	5.50	12
1992 Mary	Open		11.50	12
1997 Maya	Open		15.00	15
1966 Melchior	Retrd.	1992	5.50	12-25

YEAR ISSUE	EDITION LIMIT	YEAR RETD.	ISSUE PRICE	*QUOTE U.S.$
1993 Melchoir	Open		11.50	12
1993 Melchoir on Horse	Open		32.50	33
1983 Micah	Retrd.	1995	5.50	14
1996 Micah	Open		12.50	13
1968 Michael	Retrd.	1998	5.50	13-17
1967 Miriam	Retrd.	1993	5.50	12
1994 Miriam	Open		11.50	12
1996 Mordecai	Open		12.50	13
1967 Mordecai	Retrd.	1995	5.50	13-29
1996 Naomi	Retrd.	1999	15.00	15
1987 Nathan	Open		7.00	7
2001 Noah	Open		19.50	20
2002 Obediah, the Teacher	Open		17.50	18
2002 Olivia	Open		22.50	23
1966 Ox, Seated	Open		7.00	7
1966 Ox, Standing	Open		6.00	6
1998 Priscilla	Open		15.00	15
1994 Rachel	Open		11.50	12
2000 Rebekah, Aram and Adel	Open		29.50	30
1967 Reuben	Retrd.	1998	5.50	17-29
2001 Ruth	Open		19.50	20
2002 Samson, Caravan Leader	Open		17.50	18
1968 Samuel	Open		7.00	7
1987 Seth	Open		7.00	7
2000 Sharon	Open		19.50	20
1966 Sheep Set, Brown	Open		13.50	14
1998 Sheep Set, White	Open		17.50	18
1990 Shepherd Choir	Open		24.00	24
1995 St. Francis of Assisi	Open		24.00	24
1996 Thaddeus	Open		12.50	13
2001 Timothy	Open		19.50	20
2002 Tobias, Trader	Open		17.50	18
2002 Trumpeting Angels	Open		30.00	30
1966 Zachariah	Open		7.00	7

Fontanini 5" Life of Christ Collection - D. Maressa

YEAR ISSUE	EDITION LIMIT	YEAR RETD.	ISSUE PRICE	*QUOTE U.S.$
2000 Angel at the Resurrection	Open		22.50	23
2002 Children with Palms	Open		22.50	23
2002 Jesus Enters Jerusalem	Open		22.50	23
1999 John, the Apostle	Open		17.50	18
2000 Mary Magdalene	Open		17.50	18
1999 Mary, Mother of Christ	Open		17.50	18
2000 Risen Christ	Open		17.50	18
2001 Wedding at Cana Bride and Groom	Open		35.00	35
2001 Wedding at Cana Jesus	Open		17.50	18

Fontanini Limited Editions - E. Simonetti, unless otherwise noted

YEAR ISSUE	EDITION LIMIT	YEAR RETD.	ISSUE PRICE	*QUOTE U.S.$
1992 Ariel	Closed	1992	29.50	30-89
1993 Jeshua & Adin	Closed	1996	29.50	50-99
1994 Abigail & Peter	Closed	1996	29.50	60-95
1994 14 pc. Golden Edition Heirloom Nativity Set	2,500	1999	375.00	375
1995 Gabriela	25,000	1995	18.00	30-60
1996 Raphael	Closed	1996	18.00	30-60
1997 Judah	Closed	1997	19.50	29-45
1998 Celeste, Angel w/Dove	Yr.Iss.	1998	19.50	20-45
1998 90th Anniversary Nativity Set, (10 pc.), includes Charis, 90th Anniversary Ltd. Ed. Angel	Closed	1999	300.00	300
1998 Charis, 90th Anniversary Angel	Yr.Iss.	1998	29.50	30
1999 Tiras & Lena	Yr.Iss.	1999	27.50	30
2000 Erela	Yr.Iss.	2000	19.50	20
2002 Ednah with Grandchild	2-Yr.		27.50	28
2001 Levana and Barak	2-Yr.		29.50	30

Fontanini Millennium Edition Nativity - E. Simonetti

YEAR ISSUE	EDITION LIMIT	YEAR RETD.	ISSUE PRICE	*QUOTE U.S.$
1999 12 pc. Figure Set	3-Yr.	2001	300.00	300
1999 12 pc. Figure Set with Creche	3-Yr.	2001	475.00	475
1999 3 pc. Angel & Stable Animals Figure Set	3-Yr.	2001	75.00	75
1999 3 pc. Holy Family Figure Set	3-Yr.	2001	75.00	75
1999 3 pc. Holy Family Figure Set with Creche	3-Yr.	2001	250.00	250
1999 3 pc. Shepherds Figure Set	3-Yr.	2001	75.00	75
1999 3 pc. Three Kings Figure Set	3-Yr.	2001	75.00	75
1999 Millennium Edition Nativity Creche	3-Yr.	2001	175.00	175

Fontanini Retired 7.5" Collection - E. Simonetti

YEAR ISSUE	EDITION LIMIT	YEAR RETD.	ISSUE PRICE	*QUOTE U.S.$
1980 Angel, Gloria Angel	Retrd.	2000	27.50	28
1968 Angel, Standing Angel	Retrd.	1995	6.00	25
1968 Baby Jesus	Retrd.	1993	6.00	25

YEAR ISSUE	EDITION LIMIT	YEAR RETD.	ISSUE PRICE	*QUOTE U.S.$
1968 Balthazar	Retrd.	1994	6.00	6
1979 Daniel	Retrd.	1996	13.00	13
1985 Ezra	Retrd.	2001	27.50	28
1979 Gabriel	Retrd.	1993	13.00	25
1968 Gaspar	Retrd.	1994	6.00	6
1985 Isaac	Retrd.	1998	15.00	28-30
1987 Jesse	Retrd.	2001	29.50	30
1968 Joseph	Retrd.	1993	6.00	25
1979 Josiah	Retrd.	1998	13.00	13
1985 Judith	Retrd.	1996	15.00	15
1968 Kneeling Angel	Retrd.	1995	6.00	25
1997 Malachi	Retrd.	2001	27.50	28
1968 Mary	Retrd.	1993	6.00	25
1968 Melchoir	Retrd.	1994	6.00	6
1979 Reuben	Retrd.	1996	13.00	13

Franklin Mint

Joys of Childhood - N. Rockwell

1976 Coasting Along	3,700		120.00	175
1976 Dressing Up	3,700		120.00	175
1976 The Fishing Hole	3,700		120.00	175
1976 Hopscotch	3,700		120.00	175
1976 The Marble Champ	3,700		120.00	175
1976 The Nurse	3,700		120.00	175
1976 Ride 'Em Cowboy	3,700		120.00	175
1976 The Stilt Walker	3,700		120.00	175
1976 Time Out	3,700		120.00	175
1976 Trick or Treat	3,700		120.00	175

G. DeBrekht Artistic Studios/Derévo Collection

Derévo Blessed Angels - G. DeBrekht Artistic Studios

2001 The Messenger angel, 1st in the series 55101	1,200		190.00	190
2002 Muse Angel, 2nd in series #55102	1,200		190.00	190
2003 Blossom Angel, 3rd in series 55103	1,200		190.00	190
2002 The Gift Teddy Guardian Angel 55322	1,200		69.50	70
2002 Angel of Love 55326	1,200		77.50	78
2002 "Bless this Land..." Angel 55327	1,200		69.50	70
2002 Angel of Youth, 4th in series 55401	1,200		99.00	99
2002 "Angel" Votive 55610	1,200		85.00	85
2002 "To watch over you..." Angel Frame 58510	1,200		39.50	40

Derévo Celebration Santa Musicals - G. DeBrekht Artistic Studios

2001 Barrel Snowman 54021	1,200		79.00	79
2002 Bearing Treats Snowman 54024	600		130.00	130
2002 Boyar Santa 51368	1,200		79.00	79
2002 Burgundy Frosted Santa 51369-2	1,200		99.00	99
2001 Celebration Bear 57366	1,200		79.00	79
2002 Celebration Merchant with boy 51791	1,200		99.00	99
2002 Friendship Santa 51365	2-Yr.		85.00	85
2002 Frosted Santa 51369-1	1,200		99.00	99
2002 Frosted Santa 51910	1,200		119.00	119
2001 Golden Majestic Santa 51451	1,200		130.00	130
2002 Golden Santa 51364	1,200		85.00	85
2002 Guardian Angel Santa 51951	1,200		99.00	99
2001 Merchant Santa 51790	1,200	2001	99.00	99
2000 Royal Santa 51367	1,200	2001	79.00	79
2001 Snow Maiden Santa 51510	600		130.00	130
2002 Snowman "Holiday Picnic" 54023	1,200		117.00	117
2001 Time Watcher Snowman 54020	1,200		79.00	79
2002 Villager Father Frost 51909	1,200		119.00	119

Derévo Forest Friends Santa - G. DeBrekht Artistic Studios

2001 Santa with Bear and Owl 51490	600		295.00	295
2001 Santa with Bird 51492	600		190.00	190
2001 Santa with Bird and Squirrel 51491	600		350.00	350

Derévo Gift Givers Little Santa - G. DeBrekht Artistic Studios

2000 Alex Santa 51770-25	Retrd.	2001	35.00	35
2000 Andrej Santa 51770-11	Retrd.	2001	35.00	35
2001 Carrying Santa 51780-2	600		49.00	49
2001 Friendship Santa 51780-3	600		49.00	49
2002 Friendship Santa 51783-1	1,200		49.00	49
2001 Heart Full Santa 51779-2	1,200		39.00	39
2000 Ivan Santa 51770-31	Retrd.	2000	35.00	35
2000 Joseph Santa 51770-21	Retrd.	2001	35.00	35
2002 Jovial Tree Santa 51787	1,200		99.00	99

YEAR ISSUE	EDITION LIMIT	YEAR RETD.	ISSUE PRICE	*QUOTE U.S.$
2001 Klaus Santa 51770-22	1,200		35.00	35
2001 Klaus with Heart Santa #2 51770-22-2	1,200		39.00	39
2000 Klaus with Heart Santa 51770-22-1	1,200	2000	39.00	39
2001 Librarian Santa 51784	1,200		35.00	35
2001 Magic Jovial 51785-1	1,200		35.00	35
2002 Magic Jovial in red Santa 51785-2	1,200		35.00	35
2000 Nicholas Santa 51776-11	Retrd.	2001	35.00	35
2001 Santa's Light 51778-2	600		39.00	39
2002 Schoolboy Santa 51786	1,200		49.00	49
2000 Sergei Santa 51776-12	1,200	2000	35.00	35
2000 Watchful Santa 51779-3	1,200		39.00	39

Derévo Guardian Angels-Musicals - G. DeBrekht Artistic Studios

2002 Angel For All Box 55512	1,200		139.00	139
2002 Angel in the Garden 55511	1,200		85.00	85
2002 Angel of Beauty 55321	1,200		79.50	80
2002 Angel of Gentleness 55325	1,200		79.50	80
2002 Angel of Serenity 55324	1,200		79.50	80
2002 Bless the Child Angel 55501	1,200		130.00	130
2002 Floral Bouquet Angel 55327-22	1,200		79.50	80
2002 Mentor Angel 55323	1,200		79.50	80

Derévo Holiday Home Series - G. DeBrekht Artistic Studios

2002 Coming to Town Santa Lamp 58366-2	600		130.00	130
2002 The Magic Sleigh Box 59020	1,200		79.00	79
2002 Santa's Time Clock 58010	600		130.00	130

Derévo Royal/Regal Santa - G. DeBrekht Artistic Studios

2001 Almost Time Santa 51211	1,500		79.00	79
2002 Mayor Santa #2 51782-2	1,200		49.00	49
2002 Nativity Merchant 51410	1,200		99.00	99
2001 Regal Santa #2 51781-2	1,200	2001	55.00	55

Derévo Russian Fairytale Collection - G. DeBrekht Artistic Studios

2001 Dwarf Clock Watcher 52028	2-Yr.		19.50	20
2001 Dwarf Lamplighter 52029	2-Yr.		19.50	20
2001 Fisherman & Goldfish, 2 pc. Set 52019	2-Yr.		69.00	69
2001 Golden Egg, 2 pc. Set 52017	2-Yr.		69.00	69
2001 Little Bear Accordian 57280	2-Yr.		19.50	20
2001 Little Bear Honey Lover 58282	2-Yr.		19.50	20

Derévo Russian Sleigh Ride - G. DeBrekht Artistic Studios

2001 Balalaika Bear 57281	1,200	2001	49.00	49
2001 Bear with Song 57411	1,200	2001	49.00	49
2002 Bearing Bear Santa 51676-2	1,200		59.00	59
2001 Boundaries Sleigh 51676	1,200		55.00	55
2001 Christmas Song Bear 57413	1,200		49.00	49
2002 Hitchhiking Sleigh Santa 51670-3	600		59.00	59
2001 Pleasure Ride 51673-3	1,200	2001	49.00	49
2001 Sweat Lover Bear 57414	1,200	2001	49.00	49
2001 Winter Wandering 51672-2	1,200		49.00	49

Derévo Wilderness Santa - G. DeBrekht Artistic Studios

2002 Around the World Skiing Santa 51116	600		39.00	39
2002 Jolly Santa 51117	600		49.00	49
2002 Light the Way Santa 51119-1	1,500		19.00	19
2001 Santa's World (blue) 51114-2	1,200		39.00	39
2000 Santa's World (red) 51114-1	1,200		39.00	39
2000 Tree From Santa 51112	Retrd.	2001	35.00	35
2002 Wise world Santa 51118	600		49.00	49

Derévo Working Whimsical Snowman - G. DeBrekht Artistic Studios

2002 The Big Hug 54285	1,200		49.00	49
2000 Happy Snowman 54280	2,500	2001	29.00	29
2000 Joyful Snowman 54271-2	2,500	2001	29.00	29
2002 Little Helper 54313	1,200		29.00	29
2002 Mr. Snowman 54280	1,200		39.00	39
2001 Snowman Cleaner 54013	1,500	2001	59.00	59
2001 Snowman Lamplighter 54010	1,500		59.00	59

G. DeBrekht Artistic Studios/Masterpiece

Masterpiece Angels - G. DeBrekht Artistic Studios

2001 Guardian Angels 25100	10	2002	1900.00	1900
2001 Guardian Children Angel	25	2001	950.00	950
2001 Nativity Angel 25001-1	50		950.00	950
2001 Peasant Angel (sm)	100		335.00	370
2001 Peasant Angel with Flute	50	2001	900.00	950

Masterpiece Children's Santa - G. DeBrekht Artistic Studios

YEAR ISSUE	EDITION LIMIT	YEAR RETD.	ISSUE PRICE	*QUOTE U.S.$
1999 Children on Sleigh	300	2001	270.00	270
1999 Children with Angel	500	2001	270.00	270
1999 Children with Snowman	300	2001	150.00	150-195
1999 Fox and Dwarf	750	2001	150.00	150-195
2001 Gentle "greeting Santa"	100		320.00	350
2001 Gentle "joyful snowman"	75		320.00	350
2001 Gentle "marry Christmas"	100		320.00	350
2001 Gentle "merry musical"	100		320.00	350
2001 Gentle "Santa with deer and children"	100		320.00	350
2001 Gentle "snowmaiden"	100		320.00	350
1998 Girl and Angel SA/03/LG#22	500	2000	270.00	270-300
1999 Girl and Angel SA/03/SM#22	500	2000	150.00	220
1999 Girls with Angel	500	2001	150.00	180
1998 Hunting	250	2000	270.00	270-300
1999 Kids With Snowman	300	2001	270.00	330
1998 Looking for Gifts SA/03-LG#1	150	2000	270.00	330
1998 Looking for Gifts SA/03-SM#1	150	2000	150.00	196
1999 Skiing Children SA/03-LG#7	150	2000	270.00	330
1999 Skiing Children SA/03-SM#7	500	2001	150.00	180
1998 Winter Scene SA/03/LG#9	500	2000	200.00	200-250
1998 Winter Scene SA/03/SM#9	500	2000	130.00	130-150
1998 Winter Scene with Kids	300	2000	270.00	270-300

Masterpiece Collection - G. DeBrekht Artistic Studios

YEAR ISSUE	EDITION LIMIT	YEAR RETD.	ISSUE PRICE	*QUOTE U.S.$
1999 Forest Bear	750	2001	150.00	150-170
1999 Honey Lover Bear	500	2001	390.00	390-450
1998 Hunter	200	2001	390.00	390-450
1999 Hunter with Dog	200		450.00	450
1999 Mushroom Picker Bear	750	2001	450.00	450
1999 Peasant Beauty	250	2000	370.00	370
1999 Peasant Man "Golden Fish", Fairy Tale	150	2001	450.00	450
1998 Samovar Keeper	100	2000	390.00	480
1999 Vacationing Bear	500	2000	390.00	420

Masterpiece Fairy Tale Memories Santa - G. DeBrekht Artistic Studios

YEAR ISSUE	EDITION LIMIT	YEAR RETD.	ISSUE PRICE	*QUOTE U.S.$
1999 Emelya & Pike Santa	2-Yr.	2001	290.00	290
1998 Gossips Santa	2-Yr.	2000	290.00	290
1998 Santa with Couple	2-Yr.	2000	290.00	290
1998 Snow Maiden	2-Yr.	2000	300.00	300

Masterpiece Fairy Tale Santa - G. DeBrekht Artistic Studios

YEAR ISSUE	EDITION LIMIT	YEAR RETD.	ISSUE PRICE	*QUOTE U.S.$
2003 3 bears tails Santa 21370-4	100		196.00	196
2002 Angel with Holiday children 21381-2	100		196.00	196
2002 Angel's day (md) 21390	100		164.00	164
2002 Christmas Bell Santa 21377-1	100		196.00	196
2002 Christmas Diner Santa 21377-2	100		250.00	250
2002 Christmas Night Santa 21379-1	100		250.00	250
2002 Deer Santa 21386	100		196.00	196
2002 Diner time "3 bears tale" 21370-5	100		196.00	196
2001 Forest story with dear Santa	250		195.00	195
2001 Gentle "children on ski"	100	2001	195.00	195
2001 Gentle "father frost"	250		170.00	195
2001 Gentle "playing with snowman"	100	2001	195.00	195
2001 Gentle "Santa with deer"	100		195.00	195
2001 Gentle "snowmaiden with children"	250		170.00	195
2001 Gentle "snowmaiden"	250		170.00	195
2002 Girl w/Cat Santa 21378	100		250.00	250
2002 Music playing Angel Santa 21381-3	100		196.00	196
2002 Night Before Xmas Santa 21379-2	100		250.00	250
2002 Playful snowman 21375	100		196.00	196
2002 Playing snowman tale Santa 21384	100		196.00	196
2002 Skiing children tale Santa 21385	100		196.00	196
2001 Sleighing kids Santa	250		195.00	195
2002 Snowmaiden tale Santa 21383-1	100		196.00	196
2001 Snowmaiden's tale Santa	250		195.00	195
2002 Snowman Sleigh Kids Santa 21376-1	100		196.00	196
2002 Snowman Sleigh Kids Santa 21376-2	100		250.00	250
2001 Snowman's story Santa	250		195.00	195

Masterpiece Forest Bears - G. DeBrekht Artistic Studios

YEAR ISSUE	EDITION LIMIT	YEAR RETD.	ISSUE PRICE	*QUOTE U.S.$
2003 3 bears " tale" 27110-3	100		190.00	190
2002 Diner time "3 bears tale" 27110-2	100		190.00	190
2002 Entertainer bear accordion 27502	50		650.00	650
2002 Honey sleighing bear (lg) 27501	50		650.00	650
2002 Sweet night "3 bears tale" 27110-1	100		190.00	190
2002 Villager bear accordion 27503	50		650.00	650
2002 Walking bear w/stoop (lg) 27009	25		330.00	330

Masterpiece Forest Santa - G. DeBrekht Artistic Studios

YEAR ISSUE	EDITION LIMIT	YEAR RETD.	ISSUE PRICE	*QUOTE U.S.$
2002 Bell-ringer w/stoop (sm) 21155-4	Yr.Iss.		119.00	119

(continued) Masterpiece Forest Santa

YEAR ISSUE	EDITION LIMIT	YEAR RETD.	ISSUE PRICE	*QUOTE U.S.$
2000 Dancing Snow Maiden Santa	75	2001	330.00	330
2002 Fair Santa (xxlg) 21153-2	100		750.00	750
2001 Fair Santa Dancing	50	2001	335.00	350
2000 Forest Santa w/ Bear (xxlg)	10	2001	1300.00	1500
2000 Forest Snow Maiden Santa	150		590.00	590
2000 Forest Snow Maiden Troika	50	2001	690.00	750
2000 Forest Troika Santa	100		750.00	750
2002 Front-bag forest Santa (lg) 21157	100		700.00	700
2000 Happy Honey Bear (20")	75	2001	1895.00	1895
2000 Happy Honey Bear (9")	100		450.00	450
2002 Peasant Santa dressed (md) 21212	100		390.00	390
2002 Playing snow w/ bear 21141	75		550.00	550
2000 Santa is Coming	3-Yr.		150.00	250
2001 Santa is Coming For the Water	2-Yr.		119.00	119
2001 Santa is Coming-Children Sleigh Ride	2-Yr.		119.00	119
2002 Santa Ready Snowmen Santa-bag 21210-3	100		700.00	700
2002 Santa Ready Stick village-bag 21210-4	100		650.00	650
2002 Traditional forest Santa 21149	100		550.00	550
2002 Traditional wilderness 21159	100		550.00	550

Masterpiece Gentle Santa - G. DeBrekht Artistic Studios

YEAR ISSUE	EDITION LIMIT	YEAR RETD.	ISSUE PRICE	*QUOTE U.S.$
2001 Around the World Santa (mid)	100		350.00	390
2002 Around the World Santa (xlg) 21270	100		900.00	900
2001 Guardian Children	100		350.00	425
2002 Holidays on bag musical (lg) 21257	30		790.00	790
2001 Lamplighter Santa with Kids	100		350.00	450
2000 Santa Around the World	25	2001	895.00	895
2000 Santa w/Bear and Owl	25	2001	950.00	1000
2000 Santa w/Bear and Squirrel	25	2001	1100.00	1200

Masterpiece Guardian Angels - G. DeBrekht Artistic Studios

YEAR ISSUE	EDITION LIMIT	YEAR RETD.	ISSUE PRICE	*QUOTE U.S.$
2002 Blessed Christmas angel (lg) 25005	25		1100.00	1100
2002 Christmas night angel (xlg) 25003-2	50		990.00	990
2002 Golden Angel 25105	100		950.00	950
2002 Guardian of world angel (xxlg) 25110	10		3000.00	3000
2002 Guarding winter angel 25104	100		900.00	900
2002 Nativity angel (xlg) 25002-2	100		990.00	990
2002 Night Before Xmas angel (xlg) 25003-1	50		990.00	990
2002 Peasant angel (lg) dressed up 25103	100		900.00	900
2002 Peasant angel (md) dressed up 25102	50		900.00	900
2002 Royal Angel 25106	100		900.00	900
2002 Sleigh Ride angel (lg) 25107	100		900.00	900

Masterpiece Jeweled Santa - G. DeBrekht Artistic Studios

YEAR ISSUE	EDITION LIMIT	YEAR RETD.	ISSUE PRICE	*QUOTE U.S.$
2000 The Golden Santa	150		590.00	590

Masterpiece Kris Kringle Santa - G. DeBrekht Artistic Studios

YEAR ISSUE	EDITION LIMIT	YEAR RETD.	ISSUE PRICE	*QUOTE U.S.$
1998 Children With Angel	750	2000	270.00	330
1998 Girl With Angel	750	2000	270.00	330
1998 Hunter With Dog	500	2000	270.00	270
1998 Looking For Gifts	500	2000	270.00	300
2001 Nativity	150		170.00	170
1998 Peasant Woman	250	2000	370.00	420
1998 Skiing Children	500	2001	270.00	320
1998 Snowmaiden With Squirrel	300	2001	390.00	480
2000 Tree of Light	400	2001	175.00	195
1998 Winter Scene	500	2001	200.00	240

Masterpiece Merchant Santa - G. DeBrekht Artistic Studios

YEAR ISSUE	EDITION LIMIT	YEAR RETD.	ISSUE PRICE	*QUOTE U.S.$
1999 Bag of Happiness	500	2001	390.00	450
1998 Bear of Joy	350		490.00	490
1998 Child of Hope	350	2001	590.00	650
1999 Child of Hope (xlg)	300		695.00	750
2002 Dear w/children merchant (md) 21455	100		490.00	490
2002 Guardian of Children merchant (lg) 21452-2	100		590.00	590
2002 Lamplighter Santa (md) 21457	100		590.00	590
2002 Lamplighter w/kids (lg) 21453	100		700.00	700
2002 Merchant dressed up w/angel 21442	100		590.00	590
1998 Merchant with Children SA/12-LG#3	500	1999	490.00	490
2002 Nativity merchant (md) 21460	100		390.00	390
1998 Night Before Christmas	500	2001	900.00	1150
2002 Nutcracker (lg) skiing kids 21443	100		950.00	950
1999 Santa ...Happy Holiday	750	2000	390.00	390
1998 Santa Christmas Night	500	2000	790.00	790
2001 Santa w/Rooster	75		390.00	390

Masterpiece Natural Series - G. DeBrekht Artistic Studios

YEAR ISSUE	EDITION LIMIT	YEAR RETD.	ISSUE PRICE	*QUOTE U.S.$
2002 Mushroom man w/acorn 22070	10		490.00	490

YEAR ISSUE	EDITION LIMIT	YEAR RETD.	ISSUE PRICE	*QUOTE U.S.$
2002 Mushroom man w/leaf 22071	10		390.00	390
2002 Playing snowman kids 24016	100		190.00	190

Masterpiece Old World Santa - G. DeBrekht Artistic Studios

YEAR ISSUE	EDITION LIMIT	YEAR RETD.	ISSUE PRICE	*QUOTE U.S.$
2000 Bell Ringer	Open		89.00	89
2002 Family Welcome 21046	75		470.00	470
2000 Lamp Lighter	Open		89.00	89
2000 Santa on Stump	3-Yr.		55.00	55
2002 Toy Keeper Santa w/box 21037	2-Yr.		330.00	330

Masterpiece Santa w/Bear - G. DeBrekht Artistic Studios

YEAR ISSUE	EDITION LIMIT	YEAR RETD.	ISSUE PRICE	*QUOTE U.S.$
1998 Night Before Christmas	250	2000	900.00	1150

Masterpiece Santa w/Children - G. DeBrekht Artistic Studios

YEAR ISSUE	EDITION LIMIT	YEAR RETD.	ISSUE PRICE	*QUOTE U.S.$
1998 Christmas Night	750	2001	790.00	950
1998 Nutcracker	750	2001	900.00	950
1998 A Winter Tale	350	1999	650.00	690

Masterpiece Santa's Journey - G. DeBrekht Artistic Studios

YEAR ISSUE	EDITION LIMIT	YEAR RETD.	ISSUE PRICE	*QUOTE U.S.$
2000 The Journey Begins	250		590.00	590
2000 Time to Rest	250		590.00	590

Masterpiece Snowing Santa - G. DeBrekht Artistic Studios

YEAR ISSUE	EDITION LIMIT	YEAR RETD.	ISSUE PRICE	*QUOTE U.S.$
2001 Bell Ringer Santa	2-Yr.		119.00	119
2001 "companions"	75		595.00	595
2001 Forest brown Santa	2-Yr.		130.00	130
2000 Forest Santa	2-Yr.		130.00	130
2001 Magic Lamplighter	3-Yr.		99.00	99
2001 Magic Santa	3-Yr.		90.00	90
2001 Open coat Santa	2-Yr.		90.00	90
2001 "weather Santa"	50		695.00	695
2001 "weather Santa", mini	2-Yr.		59.00	59

Masterpiece Snowmaiden - G. DeBrekht Artistic Studios

YEAR ISSUE	EDITION LIMIT	YEAR RETD.	ISSUE PRICE	*QUOTE U.S.$
1998 Snowmaiden w/Squirrel	300	1999	390.00	390

Masterpiece Storybook Santa - G. DeBrekht Artistic Studios

YEAR ISSUE	EDITION LIMIT	YEAR RETD.	ISSUE PRICE	*QUOTE U.S.$
2001 "12 month" Santa (lg)	50		850.00	950
2001 "12 month" Santa (xlg)	25		1150.00	1150
1999 Christmas Night	100	2001	1895.00	1895-1950
2002 Christmas night Santa (xlg) 21580	100		950.00	950
2002 Christmas night Santa (xxlg) 21580-2	50		1950.00	1950
2002 Hansel & Greta pastel (xlg) 21586-2	250		990.00	990
2000 Hansel & Gretel	250		900.00	950
2002 Nativity merchant (xlg) 21551	50		1150.00	1150
2002 Nativity merchant (xxlg) 21550	50		1900.00	1900
1999 Night Before Christmas	250	2000	950.00	950-1150
2002 Night before Christmas (xlg) 21581	100		900.00	900
2000 Night Before Christmas w/Snowman	25		1890.00	1950
2000 Nutcracker	250		900.00	950
2001 Nutcracker - skiing children (lg)	75	2002	900.00	950
2001 Nutcracker - skiing children (xlg)	50		1150.00	1150
2001 Nutcracker gentle (xlg)	50	2002	1150.00	1150
2002 Nutcracker pastel (xlg) 21595	100		1150.00	1150
2000 Nutcracker Romance	250	2001	950.00	950-1150
2000 Nutcracker Surprise	150		900.00	1150
2002 Royal angels Santa (lg) 21596-2	100		850.00	850
2002 Santa of Children 21599	100		1150.00	1150
2002 Santa of Children 21599-2	100		900.00	900
2000 Snow Queen	250	2002	900.00	950
1999 A Winter Tale	250	2001	900.00	900

Masterpiece Time For Santa - G. DeBrekht Artistic Studios

YEAR ISSUE	EDITION LIMIT	YEAR RETD.	ISSUE PRICE	*QUOTE U.S.$
2000 Almost Home	250		795.00	795
2000 Angel's Blessing	300	2001	595.00	595-650
2000 Bringing Love	300	2001	595.00	595
2001 Gift Giving Bag-bag	50		590.00	590
2000 Santa's Arrival	250		695.00	695
2001 Scomoroch bag-bag	50	2002	395.00	450
2001 Scomoroch bag-on-bag	50		695.00	695

Masterpiece Villager Santa - G. DeBrekht Artistic Studios

YEAR ISSUE	EDITION LIMIT	YEAR RETD.	ISSUE PRICE	*QUOTE U.S.$
2002 First snowfall Santa (lg) 21332	100		290.00	290
2002 Guardian of Playfulness Santa 21349	100		390.00	390
2000 Joyful Snowman	300		325.00	350
2002 Santa & deer w/children 21345	100		350.00	350
2000 Santa's Arrival	300		350.00	350
2000 Santa's Rest	250	2001	350.00	350
2002 Snowmaiden Santa gentle 21346	100		350.00	350
2000 We Wish You A Merry Christmas	300		325.00	350
2000 Winter Troika	300	2001	325.00	350

Masterpiece Wilderness Santa - G. DeBrekht Artistic Studios

YEAR ISSUE	EDITION LIMIT	YEAR RETD.	ISSUE PRICE	*QUOTE U.S.$
2001 Almost there Santa	75		750.00	750
2001 Almost there Santa (md)	250		650.00	650
2002 "Almost There" Troika blue (xlg) 21117-2	100		490.00	490
2001 Boundaries Santa	150		300.00	300
2001 Boundaries Santa #2	100	2001	550.00	550
1999 "easy ride" Santa with troika	Retrd.	2001	650.00	650
2002 "On the Go" Santa Snowman (xlg) 21110-4	150		590.00	590
2002 "On the Go" Santa w/Troika (xlg) 21110-3	150		450.00	450
2000 Santa "on the go"	3-Yr.		450.00	450
2002 Santa Boundaries w/box (xxlg) 21116	100		650.00	650
1999 "Skiing Time" Santa	250	2000	295.00	295
2000 "Skiing Time" w/Troika	50		750.00	750
2001 Time to go Santa	75		495.00	495
2001 Time to go Santa (md)	250		330.00	330
2002 "Time to go" Santa w/clock (lg) 21118-1	100		490.00	490
1999 "Toyland Ride"	150	2001	450.00	450
2002 "Toyland Ride" w/Troika (lg) 21112	100		450.00	450

G. DeBrekht Artistic Studios/Russian Gift & Jewelry

Heritage Floral Fantasy (Eggs) - G. DeBrekht Artistic Studios

YEAR ISSUE	EDITION LIMIT	YEAR RETD.	ISSUE PRICE	*QUOTE U.S.$
1999 Floral Beauty	Retrd.	2000	17.00	17
2001 Floral Beauty #2	3-Yr.		12.50	13
2001 Gift of Spring #2	3-Yr.		35.00	35
1999 Gifts of Spring	Retrd.	2000	35.00	35
2001 Spring Bird Song	3-Yr.		90.00	90
1999 Spring's Sweet Song	Retrd.	2000	39.00	39
2001 Sweet Song	3-Yr.		39.50	40

Heritage Magical Myths (Eggs) - G. DeBrekht Artistic Studios

YEAR ISSUE	EDITION LIMIT	YEAR RETD.	ISSUE PRICE	*QUOTE U.S.$
1998 Alenushka	500	1999	150.00	150
1998 At the Fence	500		150.00	150
1998 Fairy-Tale	2,000		90.00	90
2000 Father Frost Egg	Retrd.	2001	59.00	59
2001 Father Frost Egg #2	3-Yr.		59.00	59
1999 Fire-Bird E/10-MD#1	Open		59.00	59
1999 Fire-Bird E/10-MD#3	Open		59.00	59
1999 For a Water	Open		59.00	59
1999 Humpback Pony	Open		59.00	59
1998 Ivan Princess	150	2000	790.00	790
1998 Lady on Horse	150	1999	790.00	790
1999 Meeting	Retrd.	2001	59.00	59
1999 Morosko E/10-MD#1	Retrd.	2000	59.00	59
1999 Morosko E/10-MD#4	Retrd.	2000	59.00	59
1999 Snow Maiden	Open		59.00	59
2001 Snow Maiden #2	3-Yr.		59.00	59
1999 Summer Scene	Retrd.	2001	59.00	59
1999 Winter Scene	Retrd.	2001	59.00	59

Heritage Symbols of Faith (Wooden Eggs) - G. DeBrekht Artistic Studios

YEAR ISSUE	EDITION LIMIT	YEAR RETD.	ISSUE PRICE	*QUOTE U.S.$
1998 Icon Eggs E21/XLG#1	150	2001	700.00	700
1998 Icon Eggs E21/XLG#2	150	2001	700.00	700
1998 Icon Eggs E21/XLG#3	150	2000	700.00	700
2001 Nativity Box	3-Yr.		99.00	119
2000 Nativity Egg	Retrd.	2002	250.00	250
2001 Nativity Ornaments	3-Yr.		119.00	119

Geo. Zoltan Lefton Company

Child Within - M. Garvin

YEAR ISSUE	EDITION LIMIT	YEAR RETD.	ISSUE PRICE	*QUOTE U.S.$
1998 Apples 11650	Closed	2000	15.00	15
1998 Bee 11641	Closed	2000	13.00	13
1998 Butterfly 11640	Closed	2000	15.00	15
1998 Chick 11638	Closed	2000	15.00	15
1998 Christmas Tree 11630	Closed	2000	15.00	15
1998 Cow 11635	Closed	2000	13.00	13
1998 Elephant 11633	Closed	2000	13.00	13
1998 Frog 11637	Closed	2000	13.00	13
1998 Grape 11631	Closed	2000	15.00	15
1998 Polar Bear 11636	Closed	2000	13.00	13
1998 Rabbit 11639	Closed	2000	13.00	13
1998 Reindeer 11634	Closed	2000	15.00	15

YEAR ISSUE	EDITION LIMIT	YEAR RETD.	ISSUE PRICE	*QUOTE U.S.$
1998 Rose 11629	Closed	2000	15.00	15
1998 Snowman 11628	Closed	2000	15.00	15
1998 Strawberries 11651	Closed	2000	15.00	15
1998 Sunflower 11632	Closed	2000	15.00	15
1998 Watermelons 11649	Closed	2000	15.00	15

Gary Paterson Collections - G. Paterson

YEAR ISSUE	EDITION LIMIT	YEAR RETD.	ISSUE PRICE	*QUOTE U.S.$
1998 #1 Dad 11756	Closed	2000	25.00	25
1998 Art of Casting 11758	Closed	2000	40.00	40
1998 Fully Equiped 11760	Closed	2000	25.00	25
1998 Golf Lover 11759	Closed	2000	25.00	25
1998 It's Only A Game 11763	Closed	2000	40.00	40
1998 Mr. Fix It 11762	Closed	2000	40.00	40
1998 Now What 11752	Closed	2000	25.00	25
1998 Sports Fan 11751	Closed	2000	40.00	40
1998 Super Fan 11764	Closed	2000	25.00	25
1998 Super Mom 11757	Closed	2000	25.00	25
1998 Thrill of Victory 11753	Closed	2000	40.00	40
1998 Tips Up 11755	Closed	2000	25.00	25
1998 Up The Creek 11754	Closed	2000	40.00	40
1998 World's Greatest Golfer 11765	Closed	2000	25.00	25

Regal - Lefton

YEAR ISSUE	EDITION LIMIT	YEAR RETD.	ISSUE PRICE	*QUOTE U.S.$
2001 Ascot Ladys (4 asst.), 10" 14546	Open		45.00	45
2001 Bedtime Child (2 asst.), 7 1/2" 14540	Open		30.00	30
2001 Bedtime Girl (2 asst.), 8" 14555	Open		35.00	35
2001 Constance, 10" 14543	Open		53.00	53
2001 English Rose-Romance (2 asst.), 6" 14529	Open		20.00	20
2001 Faith, Nicole (2 asst.), 10" 14541	Open		45.00	45
2001 Flair (3 asst.), 10" 14558	Open		43.00	43
2001 Girl w/dog (3 asst.), 6" 14549	Open		30.00	30
2001 Giselle (4 asst.), 10" 14551	Open		55.00	55
2001 Grace (3 asst.), 10" 14553	Open		43.00	43
2001 Gypsy Girl (3 asst.), 6" 14547	Open		45.00	45
2001 Juliet, Georgina (2 asst.), 10" 14542	Open		50.00	50
2001 Katie, Sara, Paula (3 asst.), 10" 14537	Open		30.00	30
2001 Lisa, Tessa, 10" 14544	Open		45.00	45
2001 Louise, Janye, Beth, Emma (4 asst.), 8" 14533	Open		25.00	25
2001 Lucy (2 asst.), 8" 14554	Open		35.00	35
2001 Margot, Victoria (2 asst.), 10" 14530	Open		20.00	20
2001 Mother's Love, Happy Days (2 asst.), 10" 14531	Open		65.00	65
2001 Panache (3 asst.), 10" 14557	Open		43.00	43
2001 Peach (2 asst.), 10" 14556	Open		50.00	50
2001 Tenderness, 12" 14532	Open		65.00	65
2001 Valentine English Rose-Romance (3 asst.), 6" 14528	Open		20.00	20

Goebel of North America

Amerikids - H. Holt

YEAR ISSUE	EDITION LIMIT	YEAR RETD.	ISSUE PRICE	*QUOTE U.S.$
1983 Airborne	Closed	N/A	90.00	75-90
1983 Ball One	Closed	N/A	90.00	90
1983 Batter Up	Closed	N/A	90.00	90
1980 Benched	Closed	N/A	115.00	115
1983 Black Belt Champ	Closed	N/A	75.00	75
1980 Cactus Blues	Closed	N/A	100.00	100
1980 Curiosity	Closed	N/A	115.00	100-115
1983 End Run	Closed	N/A	75.00	75
1983 False Start	Closed	N/A	90.00	90
1980 Fish for Two	Closed	N/A	100.00	100
1983 Hot Shot	Closed	N/A	75.00	75
1983 Ice Nymph	Closed	N/A	35.00	35-55
1983 Icicle Treats	Closed	N/A	55.00	55
1980 Mom's Bridal Veil	Closed	N/A	100.00	100
1983 Peewee Dribbler	Closed	N/A	75.00	75
1980 Penny for a Tooth	Closed	N/A	80.00	80
1980 Please	Closed	N/A	80.00	80
1980 Rain Dance	Closed	N/A	115.00	115-125
1983 Ready to Fly	Closed	N/A	85.00	85
1980 Rodeo Cowboy	Closed	N/A	135.00	135
1983 The Signal	Closed	N/A	90.00	90
1983 Strategy	Closed	N/A	90.00	90
1980 The Suitor	Closed	N/A	80.00	75-80
1980 Swimming Hole	Closed	N/A	85.00	85-90
1983 Touchdown Flyer	Closed	N/A	75.00	75
1980 Who's Fish	Closed	N/A	135.00	135

Charlot Byj Blondes - C. Byj

YEAR ISSUE	EDITION LIMIT	YEAR RETD.	ISSUE PRICE	*QUOTE U.S.$
1968 Bless Us All	Closed	1987	6.00	20-55

YEAR ISSUE	EDITION LIMIT	YEAR RETD.	ISSUE PRICE	*QUOTE U.S.$
1968 A Child's Prayer	Closed	1987	6.00	20-78
1968 Evening Prayer	Closed	1986	8.00	30-98
1969 Her Shining Hour	Closed	1988	14.00	60-170
1969 Little Prayers Are Best	Closed	1987	12.00	40-95
1972 Love Bugs	Closed	1986	38.00	130-210
XX Love Bugs (music box)	Closed	1986	80.00	325-400
1968 Madonna of the Doves	Closed	1993	25.00	160-240
1968 Mother Embracing Child	Closed	N/A	12.00	80-160
1968 Rock-A-Bye-Baby	Closed	N/A	7.50	50-130
XX Rock-A-Bye-Baby (music box)	Closed	1985	50.00	250-275
1968 Sitting Pretty	Closed	1983	9.00	50-110
1968 Sleepy Head	Closed	1986	9.00	50-95
1968 Tender Shepherd	Closed	1974	8.00	350-500
1968 The Way To Pray	Closed	1988	8.50	20-100

Charlot Byj Redheads - C. Byj

YEAR ISSUE	EDITION LIMIT	YEAR RETD.	ISSUE PRICE	*QUOTE U.S.$
1982 1-2 Ski-Doo	Closed	1986	75.00	140-150
1985 All Gone	Closed	1988	42.00	70-80
1987 Almost There	Closed	1988	45.00	95-125
1987 Always Fit	Closed	1988	45.00	100-150
1968 Atta Boy	Closed	1984	6.50	65-145
1972 Baby Sitter	Closed	1983	28.00	55-175
1972 Bachelor Degree	Closed	1986	18.00	40-145
1975 Barbeque	Closed	1983	55.00	140-208
1985 Bedtime Boy	Closed	1987	26.00	35-90
1985 Bedtime Girl	Closed	1987	26.00	35-75
1975 Bird Watcher	Closed	1983	48.00	105-170
1971 Bongo Beat	Closed	1980	18.50	60-190
1975 Camera Shy	Closed	1983	48.00	120-165
1984 Captive Audience	Closed	1988	55.00	100-150
1968 Cheer Up	Closed	1988	8.00	50-150
1987 Come Along	Closed	1988	47.50	100-125
1970 Copper Topper	Closed	1986	10.00	110-120
1968 Daisies Won't Tell	Closed	1986	6.00	50-145
1983 A Damper on the Camper	Closed	1986	75.00	160-170
1983 Dating and Skating	Closed	N/A	60.00	80-150
1983 Dear Sirs	Closed	1988	40.00	135-175
1968 Dropping In	Closed	1988	6.00	75-145
1968 E-e-eek	Closed	1986	8.00	50-160
1985 Farm Friends	Closed	1988	46.00	75-120
1987 Figurine Collector	Closed	1988	64.00	250-300
1972 First Degree	Closed	1988	18.00	50-145
1968 Forbidden Fruit	Closed	1978	7.00	50-125
1975 Fore	Closed	1983	48.00	90-150
1983 Four Letter Word For Ouch	Closed	1988	40.00	110-125
1983 A Funny Face From Outer Space	Closed	1987	65.00	170-300
1968 Gangway	Closed	1986	8.50	90-120
1968 Good News	Closed	1988	6.00	50-150
1988 Greetings	Closed	1988	55.00	125-198
1968 Guess Who	Closed	1979	8.50	100-145
1983 Heads or Tails	Closed	1986	60.00	135-175
1968 The Kibitzer	Closed	1983	7.50	50-150
1975 Lazy Day	Closed	1986	55.00	80-200
1969 Let It Rain	Closed	1988	26.00	90-220
1968 Little Miss Coy	Closed	1988	6.00	40-145
1968 Little Prayers Are Best	Closed	1969	13.00	75-91
1969 Little Shopper	Closed	1988	13.00	70-195
1968 Lucky Day	Closed	1986	5.50	50-140
1984 Not Yet a Vet	Closed	1988	65.00	150-175
1983 Nothing Beats a Pizza	Closed	1988	55.00	100-175
1971 The Nurse	Closed	1988	13.00	50-150
1968 Off Key	Closed	1986	7.50	50-155
1968 O'Hair For President	Closed	1983	6.00	50-85
1984 Once Upon a Time	Closed	1988	55.00	130
1984 One Puff's Enough (Yech)	Closed	1988	55.00	156-225
1968 Oops	Closed	1988	8.00	50-120
1987 Please Wait	Closed	1988	47.50	40-145
1968 Plenty of Nothing	Closed	1986	5.50	90
1987 The Practice	Closed	1988	64.00	150-250
1968 Putting on the Dog	Closed	1986	9.00	50-145
1968 The Roving Eye	Closed	1986	6.00	40-140
1972 Say A-a-a-aah	Closed	1986	19.00	60-175
1982 Sea Breeze	Closed	1986	65.00	70-170
1988 Shall We Dance?	Closed	1988	72.50	125-150
1985 Sharing Secrets	Closed	1988	44.00	60-125
1968 Shear Nonsense	Closed	1986	10.00	70-150
1970 Skater's Waltz	Closed	1986	15.00	120-150
XX Skater's Waltz (Musical)	Closed	1986	70.00	275
1983 Something Tells Me	Closed	1987	40.00	75-100
1988 A Special Friend (Black Angel)	Closed	1988	55.00	100-110
1968 Spellbound	Closed	1986	12.00	60-150

FIGURINES

YEAR ISSUE	EDITION LIMIT	YEAR RETD.	ISSUE PRICE	*QUOTE U.S.$
1968 Spring Time	Closed	1983	7.50	50-150
1968 The Stolen Kiss	Closed	1978	13.00	70-165
1968 Strike	Closed	1986	6.00	50-140
1968 Super Service	Closed	1979	9.00	70-150
1985 Sweet Snack	Closed	1988	40.00	60-90
1971 Swinger	Closed	1983	15.00	60-125
1969 Trim Lass	Closed	1978	14.00	80-150
1971 Trouble Shooter (This Won't Hurt)	Closed	1986	13.00	40-148
1975 Wash Day	Closed	1986	55.00	80-200
1984 Yeah Team	Closed	1987	65.00	229-250
1968 A Young Man's Fancy	Closed	1988	10.00	80-150

Co-Boy - G. Skrobek

YEAR ISSUE	EDITION LIMIT	YEAR RETD.	ISSUE PRICE	*QUOTE U.S.$
1981 Al the Trumpet Player	Closed	N/A	45.00	55-120
1987 Bank-Pete the Pirate	Closed	N/A	80.00	225-275
1987 Bank-Utz the Money Bank	Closed	N/A	80.00	120-225
1981 Ben the Blacksmith	Closed	N/A	45.00	63-70
XX Bert the Soccer Player	Closed	N/A	Unkn.	40-120
1971 Bit the Bachelor	Closed	N/A	16.00	30-82
1972 Bob the Bookworm	Closed	N/A	20.00	35-100
1984 Brad the Clockmaker	Closed	N/A	75.00	200-400
1972 Brum the Lawyer	Closed	N/A	20.00	75-120
XX Candy the Baker's Delight	Closed	N/A	Unkn.	45-75
1980 Carl the Chef	Closed	N/A	49.00	63-82
1984 Chris the Shoemaker	Closed	N/A	45.00	88-175
1987 Chuck on His Pig	Closed	N/A	75.00	250-300
1984 Chuck the Chimney Sweep	Closed	N/A	45.00	190-250
1987 Clock-Conny the Watchman	Closed	N/A	125.00	510-700
1987 Clock-Sepp and the Beer Keg	Closed	N/A	125.00	375-400
1972 Co-Boy Plaque (English)	Closed	N/A	20.00	120-200
1972 Co-Boy Plaque (German)	Closed	N/A	N/A	220-275
XX Conny the Night Watchman	Closed	N/A	Unkn.	100-125
1980 Doc the Doctor	Closed	N/A	49.00	75-125
XX Ed the Wine Cellar Steward	Closed	N/A	Unkn.	100-120
1984 Felix the Baker	Closed	N/A	45.00	75-120
1971 Fips the Foxy Fisherman	Closed	N/A	16.00	30-100
1971 Fritz the Happy Boozer	Closed	N/A	16.00	100-120
1981 George the Gourmand	Closed	N/A	45.00	125-150
1980 Gerd the Diver	Closed	N/A	49.00	125
1978 Gil the Goalie	Closed	N/A	34.00	100-120
1981 Greg the Gourmet	Closed	N/A	45.00	100-225
1981 Greta the Happy Housewife	Closed	N/A	45.00	50-75
1980 Herb the Horseman	Closed	N/A	49.00	63-120
1984 Herman the Butcher	Closed	N/A	45.00	45-170
1984 Homer the Driver	Closed	N/A	45.00	120-175
XX Jack the Village Pharmacist	Closed	N/A	Unkn.	35-125
XX Jim the Bowler	Closed	N/A	Unkn.	25-120
XX John the Hawkeye Hunter	Closed	N/A	Unkn.	63-113
1972 Kuni the Painter	Closed	N/A	20.00	35-120
XX Mark-Safety First	Closed	N/A	Unkn.	63-100
1984 Marthe the Nurse	Closed	N/A	45.00	95-250
XX Max the Boxing Champ	Closed	N/A	Unkn.	25-120
1971 Mike the Jam Maker	Closed	N/A	16.00	40-125
1980 Monty the Mountain Climber	Closed	N/A	49.00	75-100
1981 Nick the Nightclub Singer	Closed	N/A	45.00	45-125
1981 Niels the Strummer	Closed	N/A	45.00	55-120
1978 Pat the Pitcher	Closed	N/A	34.00	63-120
1984 Paul the Dentist	Closed	N/A	45.00	100-250
1981 Peter the Accordionist	Closed	N/A	45.00	63-120
XX Petrl the Village Angler	Closed	N/A	Unkn.	60-100
1971 Plum the Pastry Chef	Closed	N/A	16.00	35-100
1972 Porz the Mushroom Muncher	Closed	N/A	20.00	100-150
1984 Rick the Fireman	Closed	N/A	45.00	100-225
1971 Robby the Vegetarian	Closed	N/A	16.00	63-90
1984 Rudy the World Traveler	Closed	N/A	45.00	125-200
1971 Sam the Gourmet	Closed	N/A	16.00	63-110
1972 Sepp the Beer Buddy	Closed	N/A	20.00	63-100
1984 Sid the Vintner	Closed	N/A	45.00	70-120
1980 Ted the Tennis Player	Closed	N/A	49.00	63-90
1971 Tom the Honey Lover	Closed	N/A	16.00	63-100
1978 Tommy Touchdown	Closed	N/A	34.00	63-90
XX Toni the Skier	Closed	N/A	Unkn.	120-125
1972 Utz the Banker	Closed	N/A	20.00	63-120
1981 Walter the Jogger	Closed	N/A	45.00	63-120
1971 Wim the Court Supplier	Closed	N/A	16.00	63-120

Co-Boys-Culinary - Welling/Skrobek

YEAR ISSUE	EDITION LIMIT	YEAR RETD.	ISSUE PRICE	*QUOTE U.S.$
1994 Mike the Jam Maker 301050	Closed	N/A	25.00	30
1994 Plum the Sweets Maker 301052	Closed	N/A	25.00	30
1994 Robby the Vegetarian 301054	Closed	N/A	25.00	30
1994 Sepp the Drunkard 301051	Closed	N/A	25.00	30

YEAR ISSUE	EDITION LIMIT	YEAR RETD.	ISSUE PRICE	*QUOTE U.S.$
1994 Tom the Sweet Tooth 301053	Closed	N/A	25.00	30

Co-Boys-Professionals - Welling/Skrobek

YEAR ISSUE	EDITION LIMIT	YEAR RETD.	ISSUE PRICE	*QUOTE U.S.$
1994 Brum the Lawyer 301060	Closed	N/A	25.00	30
1994 Conny the Nightwatchman 301062	Closed	N/A	25.00	30
1994 Doc the Doctor 301064	Closed	N/A	25.00	30
1994 John the Hunter 301063	Closed	N/A	25.00	30
1994 Utz the Banker 301061	Closed	N/A	25.00	30

Co-Boys-Sports - Welling/Skrobek

YEAR ISSUE	EDITION LIMIT	YEAR RETD.	ISSUE PRICE	*QUOTE U.S.$
1994 Bert the Soccer Player 301059	Closed	N/A	25.00	30
1994 Jim the Bowler 301057	Closed	N/A	25.00	30
1994 Petri the Fisherman 301055	Closed	N/A	25.00	30
1994 Ted the Tennis Player 301058	Closed	N/A	25.00	30
1994 Toni the Skier 301056	Closed	N/A	25.00	30

Fashions on Parade - G. Bochmann, unless otherwise noted

YEAR ISSUE	EDITION LIMIT	YEAR RETD.	ISSUE PRICE	*QUOTE U.S.$
1984 Afternoon Tea	Closed	1988	50.00	75-90
1980 At The Tea Dance	Closed	1988	50.00	75-90
1983 Center Court	Closed	1988	50.00	75-150
1987 Christina	Closed	1988	60.00	60
1980 The Cosmopolitan	Closed	1988	50.00	75-85
1982 Demure Elegance	Closed	1988	50.00	75-90
1986 Diana Viscountess	Closed	1988	55.00	75-90
1981 Edwardian Grace	Closed	1988	50.00	50-90
1987 Eleanor	Closed	1988	60.00	60
1987 Elisabeth	Closed	1988	60.00	60
1984 Equestrian	Closed	1988	50.00	50-75
1983 Fashions on Parade Plaque - K. Sauer	Closed	1988	12.50	13-60
1986 Forever & Always (Bride)	Closed	1988	55.00	55-85
1979 The Garden Fancier	Closed	1988	50.00	75-85
1984 Gentle Breezes	Closed	1988	50.00	75-85
1983 Gentle Moment - A. Gertloff	Closed	1988	50.00	50
1982 Gentle Thoughts	Closed	1988	50.00	75-90
1982 Her Treasured Day	Closed	1988	50.00	75-85
1982 Impatience	Closed	1988	50.00	85
1987 Isabella	Closed	1988	60.00	60-75
1983 A Lazy Day - A. Gertloff	Closed	1988	50.00	50
1987 Marie Antoinette	Closed	1988	60.00	60
1983 On the Fairway	Closed	1988	50.00	75-110
1986 Paris in Fall	Closed	1988	55.00	55-75
1986 Promenade at Nice	Closed	1988	55.00	55-100
1986 The Promise (Groom)	Closed	1988	55.00	55-85
1982 Reflection	Closed	1988	50.00	75-85
1984 River Outing	Closed	1988	50.00	75-90
1986 Say Please	Closed	1988	50.00	95-100
1986 Shepardess' Costume	Closed	1988	55.00	55-75
1986 Silver, Lace & Rhinestones	Closed	1988	55.00	55-95
1983 Skimming Gently	Closed	1988	50.00	75-90
1984 Southern Bell	Closed	1988	50.00	75-95
1980 Strolling On the Avenue	Closed	1988	50.00	75-90
1984 To the Hunt	Closed	1988	50.00	50-75
1979 The Visitor	Closed	1988	50.00	50-90
1982 Waiting For His Love	Closed	1988	50.00	75-85

Goebel Figurines - N. Rockwell

YEAR ISSUE	EDITION LIMIT	YEAR RETD.	ISSUE PRICE	*QUOTE U.S.$
1963 Advertising Plaque 218	Closed	N/A	Unkn.	750-1000
1963 Boyhood Dreams (Adventurers between Adventures) 202	Closed	N/A	12.00	350-400
1963 Buttercup Test (Beguiling Buttercup) 214	Closed	N/A	10.00	350-400
1963 First Love (A Scholarly Pace) 215	Closed	N/A	30.00	350-400
1963 His First Smoke 208	Closed	N/A	9.00	225-275
1963 Home Cure 211	Closed	N/A	16.00	350-400
1963 Little Veterinarian (Mysterious Malady) 201	Closed	N/A	15.00	350-400
1963 Mother's Helper (Pride of Parenthood) 203	Closed	N/A	15.00	350-400
1963 My New Pal (A Boy Meets His Dog) 204	Closed	N/A	12.00	200-365
1963 Patient Anglers (Fisherman's Paradise) 217	Closed	N/A	18.00	350-400
1963 She Loves Me (Day Dreamer) 213	Closed	N/A	8.00	350-400
1963 Timely Assistance (Love Aid) 212	Closed	N/A	16.00	350-400

Looney Tunes Spotlight Collection - Goebel

YEAR ISSUE	EDITION LIMIT	YEAR RETD.	ISSUE PRICE	*QUOTE U.S.$
1998 Accelleratti Incredibus	7,598	2000	175.00	175
1997 And to All a Good Bite	15,098	2000	75.00	75
1997 Bad Hare Day	10,098	2000	110.00	110
1997 Bad Ol' Puddy Tat	5,098	1998	400.00	400-1200
1998 Carnivorous Vulgaris	7,598	2000	175.00	175
1998 Dis Guy's a Pushover	10,098	2000	175.00	175

Collectors' Information Bureau *Quotes have been rounded up to nearest dollar

YEAR ISSUE	EDITION LIMIT	YEAR RETD.	ISSUE PRICE	*QUOTE U.S.$
1997 Duck Dodgers in the 24 1/2 TH Century ("Planet X")	10,098	2000	80.00	80
1997 Gift Wrapped ("Christmas Morning")	10,098	2000	80.00	80
1999 Grand Finale	7,500	2000	195.00	195
1997 Hare-Do	10,098	2000	80.00	80
1999 His Royal Hareness	5,000	2000	70.00	70
1999 I Do?	10,000	2000	175.00	175
1997 In the Name of Mars	10,098	2000	110.00	110
1997 In the Name of the Earth	10,098	2000	110.00	110
1997 Isn't She Wovewe	10,098	2000	185.00	185
1997 Kiss the Little Birdie	10,098	2000	100.00	100
1999 Laughing All The Way	1,200	2000	995.00	995
1997 Looney Tunes Latest News -M.I. Hummel	7,598	2000	320.00	320
1999 Lovelorn Lateral	10,000	2000	100.00	100
1998 Michigan Rag	10,098	2000	160.00	160
1997 Mine, Mine, Mine	7,598	2000	245.00	245
1998 Monster Manicure	10,098	2000	190.00	190
1999 Off Kilt-er	10,000	2000	190.00	190
1999 Oh, Give Me A Home	Closed	1999	50.00	50
1999 The Only Way To Fly	5,000	2000	80.00	80
1999 Paw De Deux	2,500	2000	245.00	245
1997 Rabbit of Seville ("The Barbershop")	10,098	2000	85.00	85
1998 Snowbird (Premier Edition)	Closed	1998	48.00	48-75
1998 That's All Folks!™ (75th Anniversary)	Closed	1999	48.00	48-73
2000 Them's Fightin Words & Yup	2,000	2000	175.00	175
1999 Tweety Wreath	Closed	2000	25.00	25
1997 What a Present!	10,098	2000	70.00	70
1997 Zie Broken Heart of Love	10,098	2000	150.00	150

Miniatures-Americana Series - R. Olszewski

1982 American Bald Eagle 661-B	Closed	1989	45.00	175-285
1986 Americana Display 951-D	Closed	1995	80.00	80-105
1989 Blacksmith 667-P	Closed	1989	55.00	95-150
1986 Carrousel Ride 665-B	Closed	1995	45.00	75-150
1985 Central Park Sunday 664-B	Closed	1995	45.00	95-125
1984 Eyes on the Horizon 663-B	Closed	1995	45.00	75-130
1981 The Plainsman 660-B	Closed	1989	45.00	200-295
1983 She Sounds the Deep 662-B	Closed	1995	45.00	75-150
1987 To The Bandstand 666-B	Closed	1995	45.00	75-125

Miniatures-Bob Timberlake Signature Series - B. Timberlake

1996 Autumn Afternoons Vignette 818061	500		490.00	490

Miniatures-Children's Series - R. Olszewski

1983 Backyard Frolic 633-P	Closed	1995	65.00	100-250
1980 Blumenkinder-Courting 630-P	Closed	1989	55.00	140-395
1990 Building Blocks Castle (large) 968-D	Closed		75.00	100
1987 Carrousel Days (plain base) 637-P	Closed	1989	85.00	815-995
1987 Carrousel Days 637-P	Closed	1995	85.00	250-295
1988 Children's Display (small)	Closed	1995	45.00	60-65
1989 Clowning Around 636-P (new style)	Closed	1995	85.00	175-195
1986 Clowning Around 636-P (old style)	Closed	N/A	85.00	175-200
1984 Grandpa 634-P	Closed	1995	75.00	100-125
1988 Little Ballerina 638-P	Closed	1995	85.00	125-175
1982 Out and About 632-P	Closed	1989	85.00	375-385
1985 Snow Holiday 635-P	Closed	1995	75.00	100-245
1981 Summer Days 631-P	Closed	1989	65.00	300-375

Miniatures-Classic Clocks - Larsen

1995 Alexis 818040	2,500		200.00	200
1995 Blinking Admiral 818042	2,500		200.00	200
1995 Play 818041	2,500		250.00	250

Miniatures-DeGrazia - R. Olszewski

1988 Adobe Display 948D	Closed	N/A	45.00	100-125
1990 Adobe Hacienda (large) Display 958-D	Closed	N/A	85.00	150-200
1989 Beautiful Burden 554-P	Closed	N/A	110.00	110-250
1990 Chapel Display 971-D	Closed	N/A	95.00	100-120
1986 Festival of Lights 507-P	Closed	N/A	85.00	125-250
1985 Flower Boy 502-P	Closed	N/A	85.00	200-225
1985 Flower Girl 501-P	Closed	N/A	85.00	85-230
1986 Little Madonna 552-P	Closed	N/A	93.00	120-225
1989 Merry Little Indian 508-P (new style)	Closed	N/A	110.00	175-200
1987 Merry Little Indian 508-P (old style)	Closed	N/A	95.00	200-300
1991 My Beautiful Rocking Horse 555-P	Closed	N/A	110.00	100-232
1985 My First Horse 503-P	Closed	N/A	85.00	150-165
1986 Pima Drummer Boy 506-P	Closed	N/A	85.00	188-250
1985 Sunflower Boy 551- P	Closed	N/A	93.00	125-282
1985 White Dove 504-P	Closed	N/A	80.00	82-125
1985 Wondering 505-P	Closed	N/A	93.00	175-200

YEAR ISSUE	EDITION LIMIT	YEAR RETD.	ISSUE PRICE	*QUOTE U.S.$

Miniatures-Disneyana Convention - P. Larsen

1994 Mickey Self Portrait	500	1994	295.00	787-1235
1995 Barbershop Quartet	750	1995	300.00	300-600
1996 Puppy Love	750	1996	325.00	400-553
1997 The Perfect Disguise	500	1997	415.00	384-553
1998 Bella Note	500	1998	295.00	400-457
1999 Bare Necessities	500	2000	295.00	295-330

Miniatures-Disney-Cinderella - Disney

1991 Anastasia 172-P	Suspd.		85.00	100-195
1991 Cinderella 176-P	Suspd.		85.00	144-250
1991 Cinderella's Coach Display 978-D	Suspd.		95.00	115-200
1991 Cinderella's Dream Castle 976-D	Suspd.		95.00	120-200
1991 Drizella 174-P	Suspd.		85.00	100-195
1991 Fairy Godmother 180-P	Suspd.		85.00	100-195
1991 Footman 181-P	Suspd.		85.00	100-195
1991 Gus 177-P	Suspd.		80.00	90-175
1991 Jaq 173-P	Suspd.		80.00	90-165
1991 Lucifer 175-P	Suspd.		80.00	90-185
1991 Prince Charming 179-P	Suspd.		85.00	100-225
1991 Stepmother 178-P	Suspd.		85.00	100-175

Miniatures-Disney-Peter Pan - Disney

1994 Captain Hook 188-P	Suspd.		160.00	160-235
1992 John 186-P	Suspd.		90.00	110-195
1994 Lost Boy-Fox 191-P	Suspd.		130.00	130-225
1994 Lost Boy-Rabbit 192-P	Suspd.		130.00	130-225
1992 Michael 187-P	Suspd.		90.00	110-195
1992 Nana 189-P	Suspd.		95.00	110-175
1994 Neverland Display 997-D	Suspd.		150.00	150-215
1992 Peter Pan 184-P	Suspd.		90.00	130-375
1992 Peter Pan's London 986-D	Suspd.		125.00	135-215
1994 Smee 190-P	Suspd.		140.00	125-195
1992 Wendy 185-P	Suspd.		90.00	110-210

Miniatures-Disney-Pinocchio - Disney

1991 Blue Fairy 693-P	Suspd.		95.00	120-135
1990 Geppetto/Figaro 682-P	Suspd.		90.00	110-195
1990 Geppetto's Toy Shop Display 965-D	Suspd.		95.00	120-215
1990 Gideon 683-P	Suspd.		75.00	100-175
1990 J. Worthington Foulfellow 684-P	Suspd.		95.00	115-210
1990 Jiminy Cricket 685-P	Suspd.		75.00	115-185
1991 Little Street Lamp Display 964-D	Suspd.		65.00	80-180
1992 Monstro The Whale 985-D	Suspd.		120.00	135-270
1990 Pinocchio 686-P	Suspd.		75.00	110-205
1991 Stromboli 694-P	Suspd.		95.00	120-185
1991 Stromboli's Street Wagon 979-D	Suspd.		105.00	125-210

Miniatures-Disney-Snow White - Disney

1987 Bashful 165-P	Suspd.		60.00	95-125
1991 Castle Courtyard Display 981-D	Suspd.		105.00	125-155
1987 Cozy Cottage Display 941-D	Suspd.		35.00	300-345
1987 Doc 162-P	Suspd.		60.00	95-135
1987 Dopey 167-P	Suspd.		60.00	110-195
1987 Grumpy 166-P	Suspd.		60.00	95-145
1987 Happy 164-P	Suspd.		60.00	95-135
1988 House In The Woods Display 944-D	Suspd.		60.00	110-145
1992 Path In The Woods 996-D	Suspd.		140.00	150-250
1987 Sleepy 163-P	Suspd.		60.00	95-135
1987 Sneezy 161-P	Suspd.		60.00	95-125
1987 Snow White 168-P	Suspd.		60.00	154-195
1990 Snow White's Prince 170-P	Suspd.		80.00	115-165
1992 Snow White's Queen 182-P	Suspd.		100.00	115-125
1992 Snow White's Witch 183-P	Suspd.		100.00	115-150
1990 The Wishing Well Display 969-D	Suspd.		65.00	85-100

Miniatures-Historical Series - R. Olszewski

1985 Capodimonte 600-P (new style)	Closed	N/A	90.00	425-600
1980 Capodimonte 600-P (old style)	Closed	1987	90.00	355-425
1983 The Cherry Pickers 602-P	Closed	N/A	85.00	295-300
1990 English Country Garden 970-D	Closed	N/A	85.00	110
1989 Farmer w/Doves 607-P	Closed	N/A	85.00	82-169
1984 Floral Bouquet Pompadour 604-P	Closed	N/A	85.00	125-150
1990 Gentleman Fox Hunt 616-P	Closed	N/A	145.00	200-250
1988 Historical Display 943-D	Closed	1996	45.00	60-65
1981 Masquerade-St. Petersburg 601-P	Closed	1989	65.00	125-350
1987 Meissen Parrot 605-P	Closed	N/A	85.00	125-150
1988 Minton Rooster 606-P	7,500		85.00	100
1984 Moor With Spanish Horse 603-P	Closed	1996	85.00	125-300
1992 Poultry Seller 608-G	1,500		200.00	200

FIGURINES

YEAR ISSUE	EDITION LIMIT	YEAR RETD.	ISSUE PRICE	*QUOTE U.S.$
Miniatures-Jack & The Beanstalk - R. Olszewski				
1994 Beanseller 742-P	5,000	N/A	200.00	225-235
1994 Jack & The Beanstalk Display 999-D	5,000	N/A	225.00	260-305
1994 Jack and the Cow 743-P	5,000	N/A	180.00	225-250
1994 Jack's Mom 741-P	5,000	N/A	145.00	180-225
1994 Set of 4	5,000	N/A	750.00	975-1200
Miniatures-Mickey Mouse - Disney				
1990 Fantasia Living Brooms 972-D	Suspd.		85.00	200-400
1990 The Sorcerer's Apprentice 171-P	Suspd.		80.00	157-563
1990 Set	Suspd.		165.00	532-850
Miniatures-Nativity Collection - R. Olszewski				
1992 3 Kings Display 987-D	Closed	1996	85.00	105-125
1992 Balthazar 405-P	Closed	1996	135.00	200
1994 Camel & Tender 819292	Closed	1996	380.00	375-395
1992 Caspar 406-P	Closed	1996	135.00	150-200
1994 Final Nativity Display 991-D	Closed	1996	260.00	275
1994 Guardian Angel 407-P	Closed	1996	200.00	225-295
1991 Holy Family Display 982-D	Closed	1996	85.00	95-100
1991 Joseph 401-P	Closed	1996	95.00	130-150
1991 Joyful Cherubs 403-P	Closed	1996	130.00	165-185
1992 Melchoir 404-P	Closed	1996	135.00	200
1991 Mother/Child 440-P	Closed	1996	120.00	155-165
1994 Sheep & Shepherd 819290	Closed	1996	230.00	240-295
1991 The Stable Donkey 402-P	Closed	1996	95.00	125-150
Miniatures-Night Before Christmas (1st Edition) - R. Olszewski				
1990 Eight Tiny Reindeer 691-P	5,000	N/A	110.00	135-150
1990 Mama & Papa 692-P	5,000	N/A	110.00	140-185
1990 St. Nicholas 690-P	5,000	N/A	95.00	125-165
1990 Sugar Plum Boy 687-P	5,000	N/A	70.00	100-135
1990 Sugar Plum Girl 689-P	5,000	N/A	70.00	100-135
1991 Up To The Housetop 966-D	5,000	N/A	95.00	115-145
1990 Yule Tree 688-P	5,000	N/A	90.00	110-175
Miniatures-Oriental Series - R. Olszewski				
1986 The Blind Men and the Elephant 643-P	Closed	N/A	70.00	150-207
1990 Chinese Temple Lion 646-P	Suspd.		90.00	135-150
1987 Chinese Water Dragon 644-P	Closed	N/A	70.00	150-195
1990 Empress' Garden Display 967-D	Suspd.		95.00	130-135
1982 The Geisha 641-P	Closed	N/A	65.00	128-219
1984 Kuan Yin 640-W (new style)	Closed	N/A	45.00	275
1980 Kuan Yin 640-W (old style)	Closed	1992	40.00	188-375
1987 Oriental Display (small) 945-D	Closed	N/A	45.00	70
1985 Tang Horse 642-P	Closed	N/A	65.00	95-175
1989 Tiger Hunt 645-P	Closed	N/A	85.00	105-125
Miniatures-Pendants - R. Olszewski				
1986 Camper Bialosky 151-P	Closed	1988	95.00	235-375
1991 Chrysanthemum Pendant 222-P	Closed	1996	135.00	155
1991 Daffodil Pendant 221-P	Closed	1996	135.00	100-250
1990 Hummingbird 697-P	Closed	1996	125.00	155-194
1988 Mickey Mouse 169-P	5,000	1989	92.00	265-357
1991 Poinsettia Pendant 223-P	Closed	1996	135.00	155-194
1991 Rose Pendant 220-P	Closed	1996	135.00	155
Miniatures-Portrait of America/Saturday Evening Post - N. Rockwell				
1989 Bottom Drawer 366-P	7,500	1995	85.00	55-95
1988 Bottom of the Sixth 365-P	Closed	1996	85.00	60-195
1988 Check-Up 363-P	Closed	1996	85.00	85-135
1988 The Doctor and the Doll 361-P	Closed	1996	85.00	100-200
1991 Home Coming Vignette -Soldier/Mother 990-D	2,000	1995	190.00	200-300
1988 Marbles Champion (Pewter) 362-P	Closed	1995	85.00	85-135
1988 No Swimming (Pewter) 360-P	Closed	1995	85.00	85-135
1988 Rockwell Display (Pewter) 952-D	Closed	1995	80.00	75-140
1988 Triple Self-Portrait (Pewter) 364-P	Closed	1996	85.00	175-275
Miniatures-Precious Moments Series I - Goebel				
1995 Fields of Friendship-Diorama (display)	Open		135.00	135
1995 God Loveth a Cheerful Giver	Open		70.00	70
1995 His Burden is Light	Open		70.00	70
1995 I'm Sending You a White Christmas	5,000		100.00	100
1995 Love Is Kind	Open		70.00	70
1995 Love One Another	Open		70.00	70
1995 Make a Joyful Noise	Open		70.00	70
1995 Praise the Lord Anyhow	Open		70.00	70
1995 Prayer Changes Things	Open		70.00	70

YEAR ISSUE	EDITION LIMIT	YEAR RETD.	ISSUE PRICE	*QUOTE U.S.$
Miniatures-Precious Moments Series II - Goebel				
1996 Heart & Home-Diorama (display)	Open		150.00	150
1996 Jesus is the Answer	Open		70.00	70
1996 Jesus is the Light	Open		70.00	70
1996 Jesus Loves Me (boy)	Open		70.00	70
1996 Jesus Loves Me (girl)	Open		70.00	70
1996 Merry Christmas Deer	5,000		100.00	100
1996 O, How I Love Jesus	Open		70.00	70
1996 Smile, God Loves You	Open		70.00	70
1996 Unto Us A Child is born	Open		70.00	70
Miniatures-Precious Moments Series III - Goebel				
1997 Come Let Us Adore Him Cameo	Open		70.00	70
1997 God Understands Cameo	Open		70.00	70
1997 He Careth For You Cameo	Open		70.00	70
1997 He Leadeth Me Cameo	Open		70.00	70
1997 Jesus is Born Cameo	Open		70.00	70
1997 Love Lifted Me Cameo	Open		70.00	70
1997 Prayers of Peace Diorama	Open		150.00	150
1997 Process Stick: God Loveth A Cheerful Giver	Open		200.00	200
1997 Tell Me The Story of Jesus	5,000		100.00	100
1997 We Have Seen His Star Cameo	Open		70.00	70
Miniatures-Special Release-Alice in Wonderland - R. Olszewski				
1982 Alice In the Garden 670-P	Closed	1982	60.00	625-835
1984 The Cheshire Cat 672-P	Closed	1984	75.00	395-550
1983 Down the Rabbit Hole 671-P	Closed	1983	75.00	405-540
Miniatures-Special Releases - R. Olszewski				
1994 Dresden Timepiece 450-P	750	N/A	1250.00	1250-1300
1991 Portrait Of The Artist (convention) 658-P	Closed	1991	195.00	525-750
1991 Portrait Of The Artist (promotion) 658-P	Closed	N/A	195.00	210-263
1992 Summer Days Collector Plaque 659-P	Closed	N/A	130.00	160-165
Miniatures-Special Release-Wizard of Oz - R. Olszewski				
1986 The Cowardly Lion 675-P	Closed	1987	85.00	185-438
1992 Dorothy/Glinda 695-P	Closed	1995	135.00	150-194
1992 Good-Bye to Oz Display 980-D	Closed	1996	110.00	200
1988 The Munchkins 677-P	Closed	1995	85.00	113-138
1987 Oz Display 942-D	Closed	1994	45.00	438-550
1984 Scarecrow 673-P	Closed	1985	75.00	395-455
1987 Tinman 674-P	Closed	1986	80.00	300-355
1987 The Wicked Witch 676-P	Closed	1995	85.00	94-150
Miniatures-The American Frontier Collection - Various				
1987 American Frontier Museum Display 947-D - R. Olszewski	Closed	N/A	80.00	100-115
1987 The Bronco Buster 350-B - Remington	Closed	N/A	80.00	110-200
1987 Eight Count 310-B - Pounder	Closed	N/A	75.00	75-100
1987 The End of the Trail 340-B - Frazier	Closed	N/A	80.00	75-125
1987 The First Ride 330-B - Rogers	Closed	N/A	85.00	75-125
1987 Grizzly's Last Stand 320-B - Jonas	Closed	N/A	65.00	75-100
1987 Indian Scout and Buffalo 300-B - Bonheur	Closed	N/A	95.00	100-200
Miniatures-Three Little Pigs - R. Olszewski				
1991 The Hungry Wolf 681-P	7,500	N/A	80.00	80-110
1991 Little Bricks Pig 680-P	7,500	N/A	75.00	80-175
1989 Little Sticks Pig 678-P	7,500	N/A	75.00	80-175
1990 Little Straw Pig 679-P	7,500	N/A	75.00	80-175
1991 Three Little Pigs House 956-D	7,500	N/A	50.00	75-175
Miniatures-Wildlife Series - R. Olszewski				
1985 American Goldfinch 625-P	Closed	N/A	65.00	75-150
1986 Autumn Blue Jay 626-P	Closed	N/A	65.00	195-238
1983 Autumn Blue Jay 626-P (Archive release)	Closed	N/A	125.00	140-195
1980 Chipping Sparrow 620-P	Closed	N/A	55.00	100-520
1987 Country Display (small) 940-D	Closed	N/A	45.00	70
1990 Country Landscape (large) 957-D	Closed	N/A	85.00	115
1989 Hooded Oriole 629-P	Closed	N/A	80.00	125-175
1990 Hummingbird 696-P	Closed	N/A	85.00	175-200
1987 Mallard Duck 627-P	Closed	N/A	75.00	150-200
1981 Owl-Daylight Encounter 621-P	Closed	N/A	65.00	225-1275
1983 Red-Winged Blackbird 623-P	Closed	N/A	65.00	175-185
1988 Spring Robin 628-P	Closed	N/A	75.00	100-232
1982 Western Bluebird 622-P	Closed	N/A	65.00	100-220

*Quotes have been rounded up to nearest dollar

YEAR ISSUE	EDITION LIMIT	YEAR RETD.	ISSUE PRICE	*QUOTE U.S.$
1984 Winter Cardinal 624-P	Closed	N/A	65.00	150-400

Miniatures-Winter Lights - Norrgard

1995 Once Upon a Winter Day	Closed	1996	275.00	275

Miniatures-Women's Series - R. Olszewski

1980 Dresden Dancer 610-P	Closed	1989	55.00	200-550
1985 The Hunt With Hounds (new style) 611-P	Closed	N/A	75.00	225-375
1981 The Hunt With Hounds (old style) 611-P	Closed	1984	75.00	275-532
1986 I Do 615-P	Closed	N/A	85.00	300-425
1983 On The Avenue 613-P	Closed	1995	65.00	120-200
1982 Precious Years 612-P	Closed	N/A	65.00	170-320
1984 Roses 614-P	Closed	1995	65.00	80-150
1989 Women's Display (small) 950-D	Closed	1995	40.00	65-188

Pocket Dragon Land of Legends Collector Club - T. Raine

1988 Sword in the Stone	Retrd.	1989	Gift	250-350

Pocket Dragon Land of Legends Members Only Pieces -Various

1988 Hubble Bubble (LOL) - T. Raine	Retrd.	1989	95.00	275-350
1989 Self Taught (LOL) - H. Henriksen	Retrd.	1990	100.00	325-350
1989 Best Friends (LOL) - H. Henriksen	Retrd.	1990	95.00	205-225

Pocket Dragon Collector Club - R. Musgrave

1989 Take a Chance	Retrd.	1990	Gift	300-350
1991 Collecting Butterflies	Retrd.	1992	Gift	195-205
1992 The Key to My Heart	Retrd.	1993	Gift	195
1993 Want A Bite?	Retrd.	1994	Gift	125-130
1993 Bitsy	Retrd.	1994	Gift	25
1994 Friendship Pin	Retrd.	1994	Gift	85
1994 Blue Ribbon Dragon	Retrd.	1995	Gift	75-125
1995 Making Time For You	Retrd.	1996	Gift	75-100
1996 Good News	Retrd.	1997	Gift	50-95
1997 Lollipop	Retrd.	1998	Gift	59-75
1998 Our Hero	Retrd.	1999	Gift	30-48
1999 Cook's Helper	Retrd.	2000	29.50	30-59
2000 Proud Gardener	Retrd.	2001	29.50	30
2001 Time For Tea	5/02		29.50	30
2002 Reach For The Stars	5/03		N/A	N/A

Pocket Dragon Members Only Pieces - R. Musgrave

1991 Won't You Join Us/A Spot of Tea (set)	Retrd.	1992	75.00	300-361
1991 Wizard's House Limited Print	Retrd.	1993	39.95	80-98
1992 Book Nook	Retrd.	1993	140.00	140-310
1993 Pen Pals	Retrd.	1994	90.00	90-185
1994 Best Seat in the House	Retrd.	1995	75.00	115-193
1995 Party Time	Retrd.	1996	75.00	75-110
1996 Looking For The Right Words	Retrd.	1997	80.00	80-120
1997 Sticking Together	Retrd.	1998	75.00	80-105
1998 The Merry Band	Retrd.	1999	75.00	75-140
1999 Chocolate Strawberry Avalanche Surprise	Retrd.	2000	65.00	65
2000 Gardening Basket	Retrd.	2001	65.00	65
2001 Tea and Gossip	5/02		65.00	65
2002 Rocket Science	5/03		N/A	N/A

Pocket Dragon Annual Christmas Editions - R. Musgrave

1989 Putting Me on the Tree	Retrd.	1990	52.50	98-175
1991 I've Been Very Good	Retrd.	1991	37.50	390-481
1992 A Pocket-Sized Tree	Retrd.	1992	18.95	108-170
1993 Christmas Angel	Retrd.	1993	45.00	95-125
1994 Dear Santa	Retrd.	1995	50.00	65-140
1995 Chasing Snowflakes	Retrd.	1995	35.00	85-120
1996 Christmas Skates	Retrd.	1996	36.00	75-80
1997 Deck The Halls	Retrd.	1997	39.00	50-95
1998 The Littlest Reindeer	Retrd.	1998	40.00	40-45
1999 All Wrapped Up	Retrd.	1999	33.00	33-38
2000 Under The Mistletoe	Retrd.	2000	33.00	33
2001 Sharing	Retrd.	2001	32.00	32
2002 Fa-la-la-la-lah!	Yr.Iss.		32.00	32

Pocket Dragon Event Figurines - R. Musgrave

1993 A Big Hug	Retrd.	1994	35.00	105-115
1994 Packed and Ready	Retrd.	1995	47.00	70-100
1995 Attention to Detail	Retrd.	1996	24.00	40-65
1996 On The Road Again	Retrd.	1997	30.00	30-75
1998 In The Bag	Retrd.	1998	15.00	15-25
1999 Party Hat	Retrd.	1999	16.50	15-17
2000 Slipper Sleeper	Retrd.	2000	18.00	18
2001 Hatbox Hideaway	Retrd.	2001	18.00	18

YEAR ISSUE	EDITION LIMIT	YEAR RETD.	ISSUE PRICE	*QUOTE U.S.$
2002 All Gone	Yr.Iss.		11.25	12

Pocket Dragons - R. Musgrave

1998 And I Won't Be Any Trouble	Retrd.	2001	20.00	20-23
1990 The Apprentice	Retrd.	1994	22.50	70-95
1989 Attack	Retrd.	1992	45.00	150-205
1989 Baby Brother	Retrd.	1992	19.50	58-163
2002 A Balanced Diet	Open		10.50	11
1993 Bath Time	Retrd.	1995	90.00	120-160
2002 Belly Button	Open		7.00	7
2000 Best Friends	Open		28.00	28
1997 Big Heart	Open		21.50	18
2000 Big Splinter...Little Foot	Open		14.00	14
2000 Bird Watcher	Open		24.00	24
1993 The Book End	Retrd.	1996	90.00	93-140
1994 A Book My Size	Retrd.	1998	30.00	30-45
1999 Brave Explorer	Open		18.50	18
1992 Bubbles	Retrd.	1996	55.00	80-120
2001 Bunny Hug	Open		25.00	25
1995 But I am Too Little!	Open		14.50	14
1994 Butterfly Kisses	Retrd.	1999	29.50	30-40
1995 Bye...	Retrd.	2001	15.00	15
1999 Can You Hear Me Now?	Open		16.00	16
1994 Candy Cane	Retrd.	1998	22.50	20-35
2000 Can't Catch Me	Open		14.00	14
1997 A Choice of Ties	Retrd.	1999	38.00	38-44
2000 Christmas Sleigh (waterglobe)	Open		50.00	50
1995 Classical Dragon	Retrd.	1998	80.00	80-90
1997 Clean Hands	Retrd.	2000	28.50	28
1994 Coffee Please	Retrd.	1999	24.00	24-50
2002 Commander Cookie	Open		14.00	14
2000 Cookie Jar (waterglobe)	Open		50.00	50
2002 Cookies for the Queen	Open		28.00	28
1989 Countersign	Retrd.	1991	50.00	375-425
1999 Counting The Days	Open		18.00	18
2002 Cushy	Open		10.50	11
1996 D...Pressing	Retrd.	1999	28.00	30-45
1997 Daisy	Open		17.00	16
1994 Dance Partner	Retrd.	1998	23.00	23-65
2001 Defender of the Universe	Open		37.00	37
2001 Diet Devil	Open		28.00	28
1992 A Different Drummer	Retrd.	1994	32.50	55-63
2001 Dizzy	Open		16.00	16
1989 Do I Have To?	Retrd.	1996	45.00	45-90
1997 Doodles	Retrd.	2001	26.50	24-27
2000 Dr. Dragon	Open		24.00	24
1991 Dragons in the Attic	Retrd.	1995	120.00	125-200
1997 The Driver	Retrd.	2000	27.50	24
1989 Drowsy Dragon	Retrd.	1996	27.50	30-55
2001 An Educated Dragon	Open		25.00	25
1995 Elementary My Dear	Retrd.	1999	35.00	35-49
1999 Fire Brigade	Open		28.00	28
1999 Flannel Nightie	Open		18.00	18
1989 Flowers For You	Retrd.	1992	42.50	125-210
1998 Frequent Flyer	Open		35.00	35
1991 Friends	Retrd.	1997	55.00	57-110
1993 Fuzzy Ears	Retrd.	1997	16.50	17-35
1989 The Gallant Defender	Retrd.	1992	36.50	175-205
1989 Gargoyle Hoping For Raspberry Teacakes	Retrd.	1990	139.50	1800-2500
1994 Gargoyles Just Wanna Have Fun	Retrd.	1997	30.00	30-32
1999 Giggles the Performing Gargoyle	Retrd.	2001	28.00	28
1989 A Good Egg	Retrd.	1991	36.50	200-325
2002 The Green Knight	Open		32.00	32
1998 Grr I'm A Monster	Open		30.00	30
1998 Happy Birthday	Open		30.00	30
1998 Happy Camper	Open		24.00	24
1996 He Ain't Heavy...He's My Puffin	Open	2000	34.00	30-34
1995 Hedgehog's Joke	Open		27.00	28
1995 Hi!	Retrd.	2001	15.00	15
2002 Highly Skeptical	Open		8.00	8
1996 Hopalong Gargoyle	Retrd.	1999	42.00	38-42
1999 Hot! Hot! Hot!	Open		24.00	24
1993 I Ate the Whole Thing	Retrd.	1996	32.50	45-50
1991 I Didn't Mean To	Open		32.50	23
2000 I Don't See a Mess	Open		14.00	14
1995 I Smell Chocolate!	Open		22.50	23
1995 I'll Be The Bride	Open		37.00	37
1995 I'll Be The Groom	Open		37.00	37
2002 I'll Fix It!	Open		23.50	24
1991 I'm A Kitty	Retrd.	1993	37.50	55-155

YEAR ISSUE	EDITION LIMIT	YEAR RETD.	ISSUE PRICE	*QUOTE U.S.$
1999 I'm Cranky	Open		15.00	15
1999 I'm Not Listening	Open		13.00	14
1996 I'm So Pretty	Open		22.50	23
1999 In The Library (waterglobe)	Retrd.	2000	50.00	50
1994 In Trouble Again	Retrd.	1999	35.00	35-40
1995 It's a Present	Retrd.	2001	21.00	18-21
1994 It's Dark Out There	Retrd.	1998	45.00	45
1994 It's Magic	Retrd.	1998	31.00	31-41
1997 It's Me	Retrd.	2001	21.50	18-22
1998 It's Ok To Cry	Open		22.50	23
2001 It's the Law!	Open		20.00	20
1997 I've Had a Hard Day	Open		23.50	23
1994 Jingles	Retrd.	1998	22.50	25-55
1991 A Joyful Noise	Retrd.	1996	16.50	27-45
1992 The Juggler	Retrd.	1997	32.50	33-45
2001 Lady Big Hat	Open		20.00	20
1993 Let's Make Cookies	Retrd.	1996	90.00	93-130
1992 The Library Cat	Retrd.	1994	38.50	75-80
1999 Life Is Good	Open		15.00	15
1993 Little Bit (pin)	Retrd.	1996	12.00	17-45
1993 Little Jewel (brooch)	Retrd.	1994	16.00	20-35
1994 A Little Security	Retrd.	2001	20.00	20
1989 Look at Me	Retrd.	1990	42.50	275-295
2001 Loving Care	Open		22.50	23
2002 Magic Reading Hat	Open		12.00	12
1992 Mitten Toes	Retrd.	1996	16.50	27-30
1994 My Big Cookie	Retrd.	1998	35.00	40-65
1992 Nap Time	Open		15.00	15
2000 Nature Lesson	Open		28.00	28
1997 The Navigator	Retrd.	2000	30.00	30
1989 New Bunny Shoes	Retrd.	1992	28.50	85-155
1989 No Ugly Monsters Allowed	Retrd.	1992	47.50	108-145
1999 Not Fair	Open		14.00	14
1993 Oh Goody!	Retrd.	1997	16.50	20-35
1996 Oh Happy Day	Open		22.00	23
1990 One-Size-Fits-All	Retrd.	1993	16.50	36-65
1992 Oops!	Retrd.	1996	16.50	17-35
1989 Opera Gargoyle	Retrd.	1991	85.00	300-425
1992 Percy	Retrd.	1994	70.00	100-165
1998 Perfect Fit	Open		17.50	18
1991 Pick Me Up	Retrd.	1995	16.50	17-30
1989 Pink 'n' Pretty	Retrd.	1992	23.90	80-155
1994 Playing Dress Up	Retrd.	1997	30.00	30-40
1991 Playing Footsie	Retrd.	1994	16.50	25-45
2001 Playing Princess	Open		20.00	20
1998 Playtime	Retrd.	2001	15.00	16
1997 Pocket Cruise	Retrd.	2000	38.00	37
1989 The Pocket Minstrel	Retrd.	1991	36.50	225-354
2000 Pocket Money (bank)	Open		28.00	28
1996 Pocket Piper	Open		37.00	35
1992 Pocket Posey	Retrd.	1995	16.50	30-40
1993 Pocket Rider (brooch)	Retrd.	1995	19.50	30-45
1991 Practice Makes Perfect	Retrd.	1993	32.50	65-80
1999 Presents (waterglobe)	Retrd.	2000	50.00	50
1997 Pretty Please	Retrd.	2001	17.00	15
1995 Purple	Retrd.	1999	24.00	27-45
2001 Putt Putt	Retrd.	1993	37.50	115
1996 Quartet	Retrd.	2001	80.00	80
2001 Rain, Rain, Go Away	Open		25.00	25
1993 Reading the Good Parts	Retrd.	1997	70.00	100-120
2000 Really I've Grown	Open		25.00	25
1996 Red Ribbon	Retrd.	2001	16.50	16
2002 Royal Cookie Guard	Open		20.00	20
1997 Rub My Tummy?	Open		17.00	15
1991 Scales of Injustice	Retrd.	1997	45.00	50-55
1998 The Scholar	Open		50.00	50
1999 Scooter	Open		33.00	33
1989 Scribbles	Retrd.	1994	32.50	60-65
1989 Sea Dragon	Retrd.	1991	45.00	200-385
1995 Sees All, Knows All	Retrd.	1999	35.00	35-65
2001 Shake Hands	Open		14.00	14
2000 Shy	Open		14.00	14
1989 Sir Nigel Smythebe-Smoke	Retrd.	1993	120.00	240-395
1991 Sleepy Head	Retrd.	1995	37.50	50-70
1999 Smile	Open		30.00	30
1994 Snuggles	Retrd.	1998	35.00	34-52
1997 Spilt Milk	Retrd.	2000	31.50	30-80
1999 Squish!	Open		28.00	28
1989 Stalking the Cookie Jar	Retrd.	1997	27.50	40-45
1997 Stars!	Open		85.00	85
2001 Sugar?	Open		20.00	20

YEAR ISSUE	EDITION LIMIT	YEAR RETD.	ISSUE PRICE	*QUOTE U.S.$
1998 Superstar	Open		18.00	18
1996 Sweetie Pie	Retrd.	2000	28.00	28
2001 System Crash	Open		22.50	23
2002 Ta Ta Ta Tah!	Open		18.00	18
1990 Tag-A-Long	Retrd.	1993	15.00	65-75
1998 Take Your Medicine	Open		15.00	15
2001 Tea For Two	Open		20.00	20
1997 The Teacher	Open		39.00	37
1989 Teddy Magic	Retrd.	1991	85.00	150-170
2001 Tee Hee Hee	Open		14.00	14
1995 Telling Secrets	Retrd.	1998	48.00	48-90
1991 Thimble Foot	Retrd.	1994	38.50	60-75
1991 Tickle	Retrd.	1996	27.50	40-50
1996 Tiny Bit Tired	Retrd.	2001	16.00	15
1989 Toady Goldtrayler	Retrd.	1993	55.00	150-225
1993 Treasure!	Retrd.	1997	90.00	90-110
1995 Tumbly	Retrd.	1999	21.00	19-21
2000 Tummy Ache	Open		14.00	14
1991 Twinkle Toes	Retrd.	1995	16.50	30-40
1997 Varoom!	Open		38.00	37
2000 A Very Good Sign (Countersign)	Open		39.00	39
2001 Very Quiet	Open		14.00	14
1989 Walkies	Retrd.	1992	65.00	250-295
1998 Wash Behind Your Ears	Retrd.	2001	24.00	24
1996 Watcha Doin'?	Open		22.50	23
1995 Watson	Retrd.	1999	22.50	23
1993 We're Very Brave	Retrd.	1996	37.50	65-85
1989 What Cookie?	Retrd.	1997	38.50	60-115
2002 Wheeee...	Open		12.00	12
1998 Why?	Open		15.00	15
2000 Will You Thread My Needle	Open		33.00	33
1999 Winged Messenger	Retrd.	2000	25.00	25-30
1993 You Can't Make Me	Open		15.00	14
1989 Your Paint is Stirred	Retrd.	1991	42.50	175-195
2000 Your Prince is Here	Open		28.00	28
1992 Zoom Zoom	Open		37.50	30

Pocket Dragons Anniversary Special - R. Musgrave

YEAR ISSUE	EDITION LIMIT	YEAR RETD.	ISSUE PRICE	*QUOTE U.S.$
1997 Jaunty	Yr.Iss.	1997	31.00	28-35
1998 Rise & Shine	Yr.Iss.	1998	20.00	18-30
1999 The Winner-10th Anniversary	Yr.Iss.	1999	42.00	42
2000 The Artist	Yr.Iss.	2000	30.00	30

Pocket Dragons Limited Editions - R. Musgrave

YEAR ISSUE	EDITION LIMIT	YEAR RETD.	ISSUE PRICE	*QUOTE U.S.$
1997 Bathing the Gargoyle	3,000	1999	250.00	250-425
1999 Computer Wizard	4,000	2001	375.00	375
2000 Magical Flying Airship	2,500	2001	275.00	275
1996 Pillow Fight	3,500	1996	157.00	157-225
2001 Puddle Jumpers	4,500	2001	125.00	125
1994 Raiding the Cookie Jar	3,500	1995	200.00	250-325
2002 The Royal Collection	2,500		80.00	80
2000 Scary Stories	5,000	2001	175.00	175
1999 Seaside Castle	3,999	2000	165.00	165
1989 Storytime at Wizard's House	3,000	1993	375.00	540-595
2002 Three Tough Dragons From Texas	5,000		35.00	35
1998 Toy Box	3,999	1998	175.00	175-250
1992 Under the Bed	2,500	1995	450.00	575-750
1996 The Volunteer	2,500	1999	350.00	395-475
1989 Wizardry for Fun and Profit	2,500	1992	375.00	375-650
2001 Wee Three Kings	5,000	2001	65.00	65

Goebel/M.I. Hummel

M.I. Hummel Collectors Club Exclusives - M.I. Hummel, unless otherwise noted

YEAR ISSUE	EDITION LIMIT	YEAR RETD.	ISSUE PRICE	*QUOTE U.S.$
1977 Valentine Gift 387	Closed	N/A	45.00	225-995
1978 Smiling Through Plaque 690	Closed	N/A	50.00	35-295
1979 Bust of Sister-M.I.Hummel HU-3 - G. Skrobek	Closed	N/A	75.00	186-350
1980 Valentine Joy 399	Closed	N/A	95.00	130-452
1981 Daisies Don't Tell 380	Closed	N/A	80.00	211-350
1982 It's Cold 421	Closed	N/A	80.00	125-425
1983 What Now? 422	Closed	N/A	90.00	125-267
1983 Valentine Gift Mini Pendant 248-P - R. Olszewski	Closed	N/A	85.00	175-695
1984 Coffee Break 409	Closed	N/A	90.00	142-425
1985 Smiling Through 408/0	Closed	N/A	125.00	185-425
1986 Birthday Candle 440	Closed	N/A	95.00	152-425
1986 What Now? Mini Pendant 249-P - R. Olszewski	Closed	N/A	125.00	136-350
1987 Morning Concert 447	Closed	N/A	98.00	117-350

Collectors' Information Bureau   *Quotes have been rounded up to nearest dollar

YEAR ISSUE	EDITION LIMIT	YEAR RETD.	ISSUE PRICE	*QUOTE U.S.$
1987 Little Cocopah Indian Girl - T. DeGrazia	Closed	N/A	140.00	350-625
1988 The Surprise 431	Closed	N/A	125.00	70-325
1989 Mickey and Minnie - H. Fischer	Closed	N/A	275.00	500-950
1989 Hello World 429	Closed	N/A	130.00	85-350
1989 I Brought You a Gift 479	Closed	N/A	Gift	75-120
1990 I Wonder 486	Closed	N/A	140.00	142-350
1991 Gift From A Friend 485	Closed	N/A	160.00	91-350
1991 Miniature Morning Concert w/ Display 269-P - R. Olszewski	Closed	N/A	175.00	131-175
1991 Two Hands, One Treat 493	Closed	1992	Gift	52-120
1992 My Wish Is Small 463/0	Closed	N/A	170.00	130-295
1992 Cheeky Fellow 554	Closed	N/A	120.00	96-160
1993 I Didn't Do It 626	Closed	1995	175.00	141-250
1993 Sweet As Can Be 541	Closed	1995	125.00	124-160
1994 Little Visitor 563/0	Closed	1996	180.00	180-215
1994 Little Troubadour 558	Closed	1996	130.00	117-160
1994 At Grandpa's 621	10,000	1996	1300.00	1025-1500
1994 Miniature Honey Lover Pendant 247-P	Closed	1996	165.00	125-250
1995 Country Suitor 760	Closed	1997	195.00	150-195
1995 Strum Along 557	Closed	1997	135.00	111-135
1995 A Story From Grandma 620	10,000	1996	1300.00	975-1500
1996 Valentine Gift Plaque 717	Closed	1996	250.00	275
1996 What's New 418	Closed	1997	310.00	240-310
1996 Celebrate with Song 790	Closed	1998	295.00	228-295
1996 One, Two, Three 555	Closed	1998	145.00	116-145
1997 What's That? 488	Closed	1999	150.00	100-157
1997 Playful Blessing 658	Closed	1999	260.00	208-260
1998 Garden Treasures 727	Closed	1999	85.00	75-85
1998 Forever Yours 793	Closed	1999	85.00	75-85
1998 Valentine Gift Doll 524	Closed	1999	200.00	200
1998 At Play 632	Closed	2000	260.00	260
1998 The Poet at the Podium 397/3.0	Closed	2000	150.00	150
1999 Hummele in Bloom (Gift Set) 365	Closed	2000	160.00	160
1999 Lucky Charmer 2071	Closed	2000	90.00	90
1999 Merry Wanderer Plaque 900	Closed	2000	195.00	195
1999 Private Conversation 615	Closed	2000	260.00	260
2000 Wishes Come True 2025A	Closed	2001	695.00	695
2000 Will It Sting? 450/0	Closed	2001	260.00	260
2000 Sharpest Student 2087/A	Closed	2001	95.00	95
2001 Scooter Time 2070	5/02		695.00	695
2001 Looking Around 2089/A	5/02		230.00	230
2001 Puppet Prince 2103/B	5/02		100.00	100
2001 Puppet Princess 2103/A	5/02		Gift	90
2001 Relaxation (25th Anniversary) 316	5/02		390.00	390
2001 Extra! Extra! (25th Anniversary) 2113	5/02		240.00	240
2001 Picture Perfect 2100	5/02		3495.00	3495

Special Edition Anniversary Figurines For 5/10/15/20 Year Membership - M.I. Hummel

1990 Flower Girl 548 (5 year)	Closed	2000	105.00	105-195
1990 The Little Pair 449 (10 year)	Closed	2000	170.00	125-170
1991 Honey Lover 312 (15 year)	Open		190.00	150-210
2000 Behave 339 (20 year)	Open		350.00	320-360
2000 Sunflower Friends 2104 (5 year)	Open		195.00	165-195
2000 Miss Behaving 2105 (10 year)	Open		240.00	205-240

Special Fest Events - M.I. Hummel

1997 Frisky Friends (Fall) 2008	25,000		198.00	198
1998 Tender Love (Spring) 2007	25,000		198.00	198
1998 Playful Pals (Fall) 2053	25,000		198.00	198
1999 Peaceful Offering (Spring) 2066	25,000		198.00	198
1999 Little Farm Hand (Fall) 2085	25,000		198.00	198
2000 Spring Sowing (Spring) 2086	25,000		198.00	198
2000 Bee Hopeful (Fall) 2107/A	25,000		198.00	198
2001 Quilting Bee w/Little Knitter (Collector's Set) (Spring) 2107/B	25,000		198.00	198
2001 Alpine Dancer (Collector's Set) (Fall) 2108/B	25,000		198.00	198
2002 Musik, Please (Collector's Set) (Spring) 2108/A	Open		198.00	198

Special Retailer/Artist Events - M.I. Hummel

1997 Best Wishes 540	25,000		180.00	180-185
1998 Pretzel Girl 2004	25,000		185.00	185
1999 May Dance 791	25,000		199.00	199
2000 Christmas By Candlelight 838	25,000		215.00	215
2001 Generations of Excellence 11/2/0	25,000		200.00	200

Goebel Celebrates 50 Years of Disney Magic - M.I. Hummel

2001 Goebel Celebrates 50 Years of Disney Magic 5-Piece Collector's Set	Open		995.00	995
2001 On The Apple Tree (Collector's Set)	Open		350.00	350
2001 Rainy Times (Collector's Set)	Open		710.00	710
2001 Spring Time (Collector's Set)	Open		350.00	350

M.I. Hummel 60th Anniversary Figurines - M.I. Hummel

1998 Heavenly Protection	Yr.Iss.	1998	495.00	500
1998 Angel Serenade w/Lamb	Yr.Iss.	1998	245.00	250
1998 Brother	Yr.Iss.	1998	230.00	235
1998 For Father	Yr.Iss.	1998	240.00	240-250
1998 Happiness	Yr.Iss.	1998	150.00	116-155
1999 Just Resting 112/I	Yr.Iss.	1999	320.00	310-320
1999 Let's Sing 110/0	Yr.Iss.	1999	149.00	140-149
1999 Let's Sing 110/I	Yr.Iss.	1999	190.00	185-190
1998 Little Cellist	Yr.Iss.	1998	240.00	250
1999 Little Thirtly 118	Yr.Iss.	1999	180.00	135-180
1999 Postman 119/0	Yr.Iss.	1999	230.00	225-230
1998 School Boy	Yr.Iss.	1998	225.00	150-230
1998 School Girl	Yr.Iss.	1998	225.00	162-230
1998 Sister	Yr.Iss.	1998	160.00	120-160
1999 Wayside Harmony 111/I	Yr.Iss.	1999	320.00	310-320
1998 Worship	Yr.Iss.	1998	180.00	150-180

M.I. Hummel Candleholders - M.I. Hummel

XX Angel w/Accordian 1/39/0	Open		60.00	49-70
XX Angel w/Lute 1/38/0	Open		60.00	49-70
XX Angel w/Trumpet 1/40/0	Open		60.00	49-70
XX Boy w/Horse 117	Open		60.00	49-70
XX Girl w/Fir Tree 116	Open		60.00	49-70
XX Girl w/Nosegay 115	Open		60.00	49-70

M.I. Hummel Collectibles Century Collection - M.I. Hummel

1986 Chapel Time 442	Closed	N/A	500.00	800-3500
1987 Pleasant Journey 406	Closed	N/A	500.00	1250-3000
1988 Call to Worship 441	Closed	N/A	600.00	700-1500
1989 Harmony in Four Parts 471	Closed	N/A	850.00	800-2500
1990 Let's Tell the World 487	Closed	N/A	875.00	650-900
1991 We Wish You The Best 600	Closed	N/A	1300.00	719-1550
1992 On Our Way 472	Closed	N/A	950.00	777-1500
1993 Welcome Spring 635	Closed	N/A	1085.00	725-1350
1994 Rock-A-Bye 574	Closed	N/A	1150.00	1100-1300
1995 Strike Up the Band 668	Closed	N/A	1200.00	900-1350
1996 Love's Bounty 751	Yr.Iss.	1996	1200.00	900-1600
1997 Fond Goodbye 660	Yr.Iss.	1997	1450.00	1088-1450
1998 Here's My Heart 766	Yr.Iss.	1998	1375.00	1031-1375
1999 Fanfare 999	Yr.Iss.	1999	1275.00	1275

M.I. Hummel Collectibles Christmas Angels - M.I. Hummel

1993 Angel in Cloud 585	Open		25.00	35-40
1993 Angel with Lute 580	Open		25.00	36-40
1993 Angel with Trumpet 586	Open		25.00	36-40
1993 Celestial Musician 578	Open		25.00	36-40
1993 Festival Harmony with Flute 577	Open		25.00	35-40
1993 Festival Harmony with Mandolin 576	Open		25.00	36-40
1993 Gentle Song 582	Open		25.00	36-40
1993 Heavenly Angel 575	Open		25.00	35-40
1993 Prayer of Thanks 581	Open		25.00	36-40
1993 Song of Praise 579	Open		25.00	36-40

M.I. Hummel Collectibles Figurines - M.I. Hummel

1988 The Accompanist 453	Open		Unkn.	91-130
XX Adoration 23/I	Open		Unkn.	380-570
XX Adventure Bound 347	Open		Unkn.	1800-4200
2001 Afternoon Nap 836	Open		215.00	215
2000 All Aboard (Collector's Set) 2044	Open		250.00	250
1997 All Smiles (Special Event)	25,000		175.00	175
XX Angel Duet 261	Open		Unkn.	208-260
XX Angel Serenade 214/D/I	Open		Unkn.	75-105
XX Angel Serenade with Lamb 83	Open		Unkn.	188-260
XX Angel with Accordion 238/B	Open		Unkn.	55-70
XX Angel with Lute 238/A	Open		Unkn.	45-70
XX Angel With Trumpet 238/C	Open		Unkn.	49-70
2001 Angelic Conductor 2096/A	Open		135.00	135
XX Angelic Song 144	Open		Unkn.	128-180
1995 The Angler 566	Open		Unkn.	270-380
1989 An Apple A Day 403	Open		Unkn.	240-340
XX Apple Tree Boy 142/3/0	Open		Unkn.	124-175
XX Apple Tree Boy 142/I	Open		Unkn.	240-340
XX Apple Tree Boy 142/V	Open		Unkn.	1350-1450
XX Apple Tree Boy 142/X	Open		Unkn.	25750

FIGURINES

YEAR ISSUE	EDITION LIMIT	YEAR RETD.	ISSUE PRICE	*QUOTE U.S.$
XX Apple Tree Girl 141/3/0	Open		Unkn.	124-175
XX Apple Tree Girl 141/I	Open		Unkn.	240-340
XX Apple Tree Girl 141/V	Open		Unkn.	1035-1450
XX Apple Tree Girl 141/X	Open			25750
XX Artist, The 304	Open		Unkn.	210-295
XX Autumn Harvest 355	Open		Unkn.	196-245
2000 Baked With Love 239/A	Open		99.00	99
XX Baker 128	Open		Unkn.	196-245
2001 Baking Time 2116/B	Open		140.00	140
XX Band Leader 129/0	Open		Unkn.	128-181
XX Barnyard Hero 195/2/0	Open		Unkn.	145
XX Bashful 377	Open		Unkn.	150
2002 Bashful Serenade 2133	Open		475.00	475
2001 A Basket of Gifts 618	Open		375.00	375
1990 Bath Time 412	Open		Unkn.	180-520
1999 Be Mine 2050/B	Open		85.00	64-90
XX Be Patient 197/2/0	Open		Unkn.	173-245
2001 Be Patient (50th Anniversary) 197/1	Open		370.00	370
1997 Best Wishes (personalized) 540	Open		180.00	190
2000 Bird Duet (50th Anniversary) 169	Yr.Iss.	2000	175.00	175
XX Bird Duet (personalized)169	Open		Unkn.	165-180
XX Bird Watcher 300	Open		Unkn.	110-260
1994 Birthday Present 341/3/0	Open		140.00	131-175
XX Birthday Serenade 218/2/0	Open		Unkn.	146-205
1996 Blessed Event 333	Open		Unkn.	270-390
XX Blossom Time 608	Open		155.00	120-170
XX Bookworm 8	Open		Unkn.	155-260
XX Bookworm 3/I	Open		Unkn.	259-365
1998 The Botanist 351	Open		Unkn.	200-210
1998 The Botanist w/Vase Sampler 151271	Open		210.00	150-210
XX Boy with Accordion 390	Open		Unkn.	75-100
XX Boy with Horse 239/C	Open		Unkn.	63
XX Boy with Toothache 217	Open		Unkn.	211-245
2001 A Boy's Best Friend 2101/B	Open		140.00	140
XX Brother 95	Open		Unkn.	152-176
XX The Builder 305	Open		Unkn.	210-238
2001 Bumblebee Friend 837	Open		260.00	260
XX Busy Student 367	Open		Unkn.	157-195
XX Call to Glory 739/I	Open		250.00	210-295
2001 Camera Ready 2132	Open		525.00	525
1996 Carefree 490	Open		120.00	94-130
2000 Catch of the Day (Collector's Set) 2031	Open		250.00	250
2001 Celestial Drummer 2096/C	Open		135.00	135
2001 Celestial Musician 188/0	Open		Unkn.	188-260
2001 Celestial Musician (50th Anniversary) 188/I	Open		Unkn.	188-255
2001 Celestial Strings 2096/F	Open		135.00	135
1998 Cheeky Fellow 554	Open		120.00	90-96
XX Chick Girl 57/2/0	Open		Unkn.	128-180
XX Chick Girl 57/0	Open		Unkn.	158-274
XX Chicken-Licken 385/I	Open		Unkn.	330-964
XX Chicken-Licken 385/4/0	Closed	1998	Unkn.	90-125
XX Chimney Sweep 12/2/0	Open		Unkn.	101-116
XX Chimney Sweep 12/I	Open		Unkn.	152-188
1989 Christmas Angel 301	Open		Unkn.	210-300
2001 Christmas Carol 2073/B	Open		140.00	140
1998 Christmas Delivery (Gift Set) 2014/I	Open		485.00	371-510
XX Christmas Delivery 2014/2/0	Open		Unkn.	275
1999 Christmas Gift 2074/A	Open		90.00	90
1996 Christmas Song (mini) 343/4/0	Open		110.00	90-130
XX Christmas Song 343/I	Open		Unkn.	188-260
XX Cinderella 337	Open		Unkn.	160-345
1995 Come Back Soon 545	Open		Unkn.	160-175
2000 Comfort & Care (Collector's Set) 2075	Open		250.00	250
2001 Cowboy Corral 2021	Open		195.00	195
1990 Crossroads (Commemorative) 331	20,000	N/A	360.00	710-725
XX Crossroads (Original) 331	Open		Unkn.	345-588
1998 Cuddles 2049/A	Open		80.00	64-90
XX Culprits 56/A	Open		Unkn.	285-435
2001 Cymbals of Joy 2096	Open		140.00	140
1989 Daddy's Girls 371	Open		Unkn.	191-265
2000 Daydreamer Plaque 827	Open		140.00	145
1998 Dearly Beloved 2003	Open		450.00	345-490
1996 Delicious 435/3/0	Open		155.00	120-170
2001 Divine Drummer 2096/M	Open		135.00	135
XX Doctor 127	Open		Unkn.	129-140
XX Doll Bath 319	Open		Unkn.	276-929
XX Doll Mother 67	Open		Unkn.	105-250
2001 Easter Basket (Gift Set) 2027	Open		240.00	240
XX Easter Time 384	Open		Unkn.	195-238
2000 Easter's Coming (Collectors Set) 2027	5,000		230.00	230
1998 Echoes of Joy (mini) 642/4/0	Open		120.00	94-130
1998 Echoes of Joy 642/0	Open		180.00	139-195
1992 Evening Prayer 495	Open		Unkn.	94-130
2001 Extra! Extra! 2113	Open		240.00	240
2001 Extra! Extra! (personalized) 2113	Open		240.00	240
XX Farm Boy 66	Open		Unkn.	188-233
1996 Fascination 649/0 (Special Event)	25,000	1996	190.00	143-198
XX Feathered Friends 344	Open		Unkn.	150-340
XX Feeding Time 199/0	Open		Unkn.	153-173
XX Feeding Time 199/I	Open		Unkn.	315-325
2000 Fire Fighters (Collectors Set) 2030	Open		250.00	250
2000 First Bloom 2077/A	Open		85.00	90
XX Flower Vendor 381	Open		Unkn.	132-295
2000 A Flower For You 2077/B	Open		85.00	90
1998 For Father (personalized) 87	Open		240.00	250-325
XX For Father 87	Open		Unkn.	188-239
2001 For Me? 2067/B	Open		90.00	90
XX For Mother 257/2/0	Open		Unkn.	105-150
XX For Mother 257/0	Open		Unkn.	124-338
1998 For Mother (Gift Set) 257/2/0	Open		165.00	170-200
1997 A Free Flight (O Canada edition) 469	1,997	1997	210.00	158-210
1996 Free Spirit 564	Open		120.00	94-130
1991 Friend Or Foe 434	Open		Unkn.	189-260
XX Friends 136/I	Open		Unkn.	176-250
1993 Friends Together 662/0 (Commemorative)	Open		260.00	225-350
1993 Friends Together 662/I	25,000		475.00	413-560
1997 From My Garden 795/0	Open		180.00	139-195
1996 From The Heart 761	Open		120.00	94-130
1999 Frosty Friends (Collectors Set) 2035/2036	20,000		598.00	598
2000 Garden Splendor 835	Open		185.00	190
XX Gay Adventure 356	Open		Unkn.	80-238
1995 Gentle Fellowship 628	25,000		550.00	413-560
2000 Gingerbread Lane (Collector's Set) 2067A/B	Open		220.00	220
XX Girl with Doll 239/B	Open		Unkn.	49-70
XX Girl with Fir Tree 239/C	Open		Unkn.	70
XX Girl with Nosegay 239/A	Open		Unkn.	49-70
XX Girl with Sheet Music 389	Open		Unkn.	75-105
2001 A Girl's Best Friend 2101/A	Open		140.00	140
XX Going Home 383	Open		Unkn.	270-380
XX Going to Grandma's 52/0	Open		Unkn.	205-295
XX Good Friends 182	Open		Unkn.	173-299
2001 Good Friends (50th Anniversary) 182	Open		240.00	240
XX Good Hunting 307	Open		Unkn.	110-142
2001 Good Luck Charm 2034	Open		190.00	190
1997 Good News (personalized) 539	Open		180.00	180-208
XX Goose Girl 47/3/0	Open		Unkn.	143-199
XX Goose Girl 47/0	Open		Unkn.	190-200
1997 Goose Girl Sampler 47/3/0	Open		200.00	139-200
XX Grandma's Girl 561	Open		Unkn.	124-175
XX Grandpa's Boy 562	Open		Unkn.	124-175
1991 The Guardian 455	Open		Unkn.	139-195
1991 The Guardian (personalized) 455	Open		Unkn.	180-193
1998 The Guardian (Gift Set) 156017	Open		180.00	139-195
XX Guiding Angel 357	Open		Unkn.	75-105
2000 Halt (Collector's Set) 2039	Open		250.00	250
XX Happiness 86	Open		Unkn.	160-201
XX Happy Birthday 176/0	Open		Unkn.	184-270
XX Happy Days 150/2/0	Open		Unkn.	190-253
XX Happy Traveller 109/0	Open		Unkn.	120-148
XX Hear Ye! Hear Ye! 15/2/0	Open		Unkn.	131-185
1997 Hear Ye! Hear Ye! (Gift Set) 15/2/0	Open		170.00	170-180
XX Hear Ye! Hear Ye! 15/0	Open		Unkn.	173-299
1996 Heart and Soul 559	Open		120.00	94-130
1998 Heart's Delight (w/wooden chair) 698	Open		220.00	169-238
XX Heavenly Angel 21/0	Open		Unkn.	123-158
XX Heavenly Angel 21/0/5	Open		Unkn.	180-260
2001 Heavenly Harmony 2096/L	Open		135.00	135
2001 Heavenly Hornplayer 2096/J	Open		135.00	135
2001 Heavenly Hubbub 2096/P	Open		135.00	135
1999 Heavenly Prayer 815	Open		180.00	135-190
XX Heavenly Protection 88/I	Open		Unkn.	375-528
2001 Heavenly Rhapsody 151637	Open		135.00	135
1997 Holy Child 70	Open		280.00	214-285
XX Home from Market 198/2/0	Open		Unkn.	131-188

YEAR ISSUE	EDITION LIMIT	YEAR RETD.	ISSUE PRICE	*QUOTE U.S.$
2001 Home from Market (50th Anniversary) 198/1	Open		270.00	270
1990 Horse Trainer 423	Open		Unkn.	188-260
1989 Hosanna 480	Open		Unkn.	94-130
2001 Icy Adventure (Collector's Set) 2058A/B	Open		375.00	375
1989 I'll Protect Him 483	Open		Unkn.	75-105
1994 I'm Carefree 633	Open		365.00	420-1040
1989 I'm Here 478	Open		Unkn.	94-135
1989 In D Major 430	Open		Unkn.	169-240
2000 In The Kitchen (Collectors Set) 2038	Open		250.00	250
XX Is It Raining? 420	Open		Unkn.	320-330
XX Joyful 53	Open		Unkn.	145-155
1999 Joyful Noise 643/0	Open		180.00	135-190
1999 Joyful Noise (mini) 643/4/0	Open		120.00	90-130
1995 Just Dozing 451	Open		Unkn.	184-260
XX Just Resting 112/31/0	Open		Unkn.	128-160
2001 Joyful Recital w/base 2096/K	Yr.Iss.	2001	140.00	140
2001 The Kids Club (Collector's Set)	Open		650.00	650
XX The Kindergartner 467	Open		Unkn.	173-240
XX Kiss Me 311	Open		Unkn.	130-300
2001 Kitty Kisses 2033	Open		195.00	195
XX Knit One, Purl One 432	Open		Unkn.	105-150
1991 Land in Sight 530	30,000		1600.00	1092-1800
XX Latest News 184	Open		Unkn.	200-400
XX Latest News (personalized) 184	Open		Unkn.	340-384
1997 Latest News ("Green Bay Wins") - Mader's Exclusive	Closed	1997	650.00	650
1998 Latest News ("Denver Wins")	45-day	1998	320.00	320
1998 Let's Play 2051/B	Open		80.00	64-74
XX Let's Sing 110/0	Open		Unkn.	146-150
XX Let's Sing 110/I	Open		Unkn.	162-205
XX Letter to Santa Claus 340	Open		Unkn.	175-390
2000 Light The Way 715/0	Open		180.00	185
2000 Light The Way (mini) 715/4/0	Open		120.00	130
1993 The Little Architect 410/I	Open		Unkn.	248-355
XX Little Bookkeeper 306	Open		Unkn.	130-345
XX Little Cellist 89/I	Open		Unkn.	255-403
XX Little Drummer 240	Open		Unkn.	128-180
XX Little Fiddler 4	Open		Unkn.	173-245
XX Little Fiddler 2/0	Open		Unkn.	188-325
XX Little Gardener 74	Open		Unkn.	140-175
XX Little Goat Herder 200/0	Open		Unkn.	235-299
2001 Little Goat Herder (50th Anniversary) 200/I	Open		199-370	
XX Little Goat Herder 200/I	Open		Unkn.	199-370
XX Little Guardian 145	Open		Unkn.	128-180
XX Little Helper 73	Open		Unkn.	98-115
XX Little Hiker 16/2/0	Open		Unkn.	115-145
XX Little Nurse 376	Open		Unkn.	190-285
XX Little Pharmacist 322	Open		Unkn.	200-644
XX Little Scholar 80	Open		Unkn.	184-260
2001 Little Scholar 80/2/0	Open		175.00	175
XX Little Shopper 96	Open		Unkn.	60-181
1988 Little Sweeper 171/0	Open		Unkn.	124-260
XX Little Tailor 308	Open		Unkn.	100-295
XX Little Thrifty 118	Open		Unkn.	80-150
1998 Little Troubadour 558	Open		130.00	81-98
XX Lost Stocking 374	Open		Unkn.	105-128
1998 Love In Bloom (w/wooden wagon) 699	Open		220.00	169-235
1995 Lucky Boy (Special Event) 335	25,000	1995	190.00	204-260
2001 Maid To Order (Collector's Set) 2091	Open		250.00	250
XX The Mail is Here 226	Open		Unkn.	450-1000
2001 Make Me Pretty (Collector's Set) 2092	Open		250.00	250
1996 Making New Friends 2002	Open		595.00	446-600
2001 March Winds 43	Open		Unkn.	180-227
2001 March Winds (Progression Set) 43/O	Open		425.00	425
XX Max and Moritz 123	Open		Unkn.	188-260
XX Meditation 13/2/0	Open		Unkn.	124-165
XX Meditation 13/0	Open		Unkn.	213-360
XX Merry Wanderer 11/2/0	Open		Unkn.	124-208
XX Merry Wanderer 11/0	Open		Unkn.	180-299
XX Merry Wanderer 7/0	Open		Unkn.	219-340
XX Merry Wanderer 7/X	Open		Unkn.	25750
1999 Messages of Love 2050/A	Open		85.00	64-90
2000 Millennium Bliss w/base 2096/H	Yr.Iss.	2000	140.00	140
1994 Morning Stroll 375/3/0	Open		170.00	95-210
XX Mother's Helper 133	Open		Unkn.	169-250
XX Mountaineer 315	Open		Unkn.	158-208
1998 My Best Friend 2049/B	Open		80.00	74-90
1991 A Nap 534	Open		Unkn.	60-145
1996 Nimble Fingers w/wooden bench 758	Open		225.00	173-240
1996 No Thank You 535	Open		120.00	90-130
XX Not For You 317	Open		Unkn.	100-381
2001 Nutcracker Sweet (Collector's Set) 2130	10,000		375.00	375
XX On Holiday 350	Open		Unkn.	131-188
XX On Parade 720	Open		Unkn.	142-175
1998 Once Upon A Time 2051/A	Open		80.00	74-90
2000 One Coat or Two? (Collectors Set) 2040	Open		250.00	250
2001 One Cup of Sugar 2116/A	Open		140.00	140
1989 One For You, One For Me 482	Open		Unkn.	94-130
1993 One Plus One 556	Open		Unkn.	113-160
XX Ooh My Tooth 533	Open		Unkn.	130-140
XX Out of Danger 56/B	Open		Unkn.	225-244
2000 Over The Horizon Plaque 828	Open		140.00	145
1993 Parade Of Lights 616	Open		Unkn.	210-295
1999 Pay Attention 426/3/0	Open		170.00	175-185
1999 Peaceful Blessing 814	Open		180.00	180-190
XX The Photographer 178	Open		Unkn.	130-345
1995 Pixie 768	Open		Unkn.	90-135
XX Playmates 58/2/0	Open		Unkn.	128-180
XX Playmates 58/0	Open		Unkn.	120-200
1989 Postman 119/2/0	Open		Unkn.	124-175
XX Postman Sampler 119/2/0	Open		Unkn.	165-175
XX Postman 119/0	Open		Unkn.	152-168
1997 Practice Makes Perfect (w/wooden rocker) 771	Open		250.00	191-270
XX Prayer Before Battle 20	Open		Unkn.	105-247
1996 Pretty Please 489	Open		120.00	90-130
2000 Pretzel Boy (Collectors Set) 2093	Open		185.00	190
1992 The Professor 320/0	Open		Unkn.	173-250
2000 Proud Moments 800	Open		300.00	310
1995 Puppy Love Display Plaque 767	Closed	1995	Unkn.	169-260
2001 Puppy Pause 2032	Open		195.00	195
1997 Rainy Day (Gift Set) 71/2/0	Open		305.00	305
XX Retreat to Safety 201/2/0	Open		Unkn.	139-195
XX Ride into Christmas 396/2/0	Open		Unkn.	199-280
XX Ride into Christmas (Gift Set) 396/I	Open		Unkn.	371-510
2001 Riding Lesson 2020	Open		195.00	195
2001 Ring In the Season 2073/A	Open		140.00	140
XX Ring Around the Rosie 348	Open		Unkn.	2000-2405
1998 Roses Are Red 762	Open		120.00	94-130
XX The Run-A-Way 327	Open		Unkn.	280-300
1997 Ruprecht 473	20,000		450.00	360-470
1992 Scamp 553	Open		Unkn.	94-130
XX School Boy 82/2/0	Open		Unkn.	50-105
XX School Boy 82/0	Open		Unkn.	173-245
XX School Boys 170/I	Open		Unkn.	1013-1440
2002 School Boys 170/III (lg. size)	Open		2750.00	2750
XX School Girl 81/2/0	Open		Unkn.	112-214
XX School Girls 177/I	Open		Unkn.	990-1440
2002 School Girls 177/III (lg. size)	Open		2750.00	2750
1997 School's Out 538	Open		170.00	131-185
XX Sensitive Hunter 6/0	Open		Unkn.	145-173
2001 Seraphim Soprano 2096/R	Open		135.00	135
XX Serenade 85/0	Open		Unkn.	113-150
XX She Loves Me, She Loves Me Not 174	Open		Unkn.	191-250
XX Shepherd's Boy 64	Open		Unkn.	110-351
XX Shining Light 358	Open		Unkn.	75-150
XX Singing Lesson 63	Open		Unkn.	50-182
XX Sister 98/2/0	Open		Unkn.	124-175
1990 Sleep Tight 424	Open		Unkn.	173-460
XX Skier 59	Open		Unkn.	135-260
XX The Smart Little Sister 346	Open		Unkn.	210-758
XX Soloist 135/0	Open		Unkn.	116-200
2001 Soloist 135/III	Open		1500.00	1500
1988 Song of Praise 454	Open		Unkn.	90-130
1988 Sound the Trumpet 457	Open		Unkn.	94-130
1988 Sounds of the Mandolin 438	Open		Unkn.	109-155
XX Spring Dance 353/0	Open		Unkn.	165-380
1997 St. Nicholas' Day 2012	20,000		650.00	650-800
XX Star Gazer 132	Open		Unkn.	200-305
2000 Star Gazer (60th Anniversary) 132	Yr.Iss.	2000	245.00	245
XX Stormy Weather 71/2/0	Open		Unkn.	251-355
XX Stormy Weather 71/I	Open		Unkn.	225-525
1992 Storybook Time 458	Open		Unkn.	348-475
XX Street Singer 131	Open		Unkn.	156-292
2001 String Symphony 2096/D	Open		135.00	135
1998 Strum Along 557	Open		135.00	83-101

FIGURINES

YEAR ISSUE	EDITION LIMIT	YEAR RETD.	ISSUE PRICE	*QUOTE U.S.$
1998 Summertime Surprise 428/3/0	Open		220.00	109-155
1997 Sunshower 634/2/0	10,000		360.00	274-385
XX Surprise 94/3/0	Open		Unkn.	131-185
2000 Swaying Lullaby (Collectors Set) 165	Open		325.00	335
1998 Sweet As Can Be Birthday Sampler 541	Open		150.00	116-165
XX Sweet Greetings 352	Open		Unkn.	150-210
XX Sweet Music 186	Open		Unkn.	173-299
2001 Sweet Music (50th Anniversary) 186/1	Open		240.00	240
2001 Sweet Treats 2067/A	Open		90.00	90
2001 Teacher's Pet 2125	Open		175.00	175
2001 Telling Her Secret 196/0	Open		360.00	360
XX Telling Her Secret (50th Anniversary) 196/0	Open		Unkn.	255-360
1997 Thanksgiving Prayer (mini) 641/4/0	Open		120.00	86-130
1997 Thanksgiving Prayer 641/0	Open		180.00	135-195
XX Thoughtful 415	Open		Unkn.	188-260
XX Timid Little Sister 394	Open		Unkn.	250-510
1995 To Keep You Warm w/ Wooden Chair 759	Open		Unkn.	176-250
XX To Market 49/3/0	Open		Unkn.	185-234
1998 Traveling Trio 787	20,000		490.00	500-675
2001 Treehouse Treats (Collector's Set) 73/554	Open		330.00	330
1997 Trio of Wishes 721	20,000		475.00	356-490
2001 True Friendship 750	365,000		365.00	365
1989 Tuba Player 437	Open		Unkn.	233-330
XX Tuneful Angel 359	Open		Unkn.	75-105
2000 Tuneful Goodnight (Collector's Set) 180	Open		295.00	305
1996 A Tuneful Trio	20,000		450.00	364-485
XX Umbrella Boy 152/A/0	Open		Unkn.	265-695
XX Umbrella Boy 152/A/II	Open		Unkn.	1223-1700
2001 Umbrella Boy 152/A/2/0	Open		300.00	300
XX Umbrella Girl 152/B/0	Open		Unkn.	495-695
XX Umbrella Girl 152/B/II	Open		Unkn.	1650-1775
2001 Umbrella Girl 152/B/2/0	Open		300.00	300
XX Village Boy 51/3/0	Open		Unkn.	130-175
XX Village Boy 51/2/0	Open		Unkn.	145-180
XX Visiting an Invalid 382	Open		Unkn.	100-150
XX Volunteers 50/2/0	Open		Unkn.	188-325
XX Volunteers 50/0	Open		Unkn.	255-442
XX Waiter 154/0	Open		Unkn.	184-260
XX Wash Day 321/I	Open		Unkn.	150-355
XX Watchful Angel 194	Open		Unkn.	298-370
XX Wayside Devotion 28/II	Open		Unkn.	391-968
XX Wayside Harmony 111/3/0	Open		Unkn.	175-221
1993 We Come In Peace (Commemorative) 754	Open		385.00	289-395
XX We Congratulate 214/E/I	Open		Unkn.	139-190
XX We Congratulate 220	Open		Unkn.	129-143
1997 We Congratulate (Gift Set) 220	Open		170.00	131-195
1990 What's New? 418	Open		Unkn.	240-340
1999 Where Are You? 427/3/0	Open		170.00	130-185
XX Which Hand? 258	Open		Unkn.	136-235
2001 Winter Adventure (Collector's Set) 2028	Open		225.00	225
1988 A Winter Song 476	Open		Unkn.	94-140
2001 Wonders of Spring (Collector's Set) 795/0	Open		225.00	225
XX Worship 84/0	Open		Unkn.	157-195

M.I. Hummel Collectibles Figurines Retired - M.I. Hummel

1947 Accordion Boy 185	Closed	1994	Unkn.	169-210
XX Boots 143/0	Closed	1998	Unkn.	216-235
XX Boots 143/I	Closed	1998	Unkn.	225-370
XX Congratulations 17/0	Closed	1999	Unkn.	173-245
1939 Duet 130	Closed	1995	Unkn.	283-330
1937 Farewell 65 TMK1-5	Closed	1993	Unkn.	100-260
1937 Globe Trotter 79 TMK1-7	Closed	1991	Unkn.	188-210
XX Happy Pastime 69	Closed	1996	Unkn.	143-475
1937 Lost Sheep 68/0 TMK1-7	Closed	1992	Unkn.	179-250
1955 Lost Sheep 68/2/0 TMK2-7	Closed	1992	7.50	116-350
XX Mother's Darling 175	Closed	1997	Unkn.	250-300
1935 Puppy Love I TMK1-6	Closed	1988	125.00	325-550
1948 Signs Of Spring 203/2/0 TMK2-6	Closed	1990	120.00	243-400
1948 Signs Of Spring 203/I TMK2-6	Closed	1990	155.00	206-450
1935 Strolling Along 5 TMK1-6	Closed	1989	115.00	320-400
XX Auf Wiedersehen 153/0	Retrd.	2000	Unkn.	295
XX Hello 124/0	Retrd.	2001	Unkn.	113-267

M.I. Hummel Collectibles Madonna Figurines - M.I. Hummel

1996 Flower Madonna, white 10 (Commemorative)	Closed	1996	225.00	169-225
XX Madonna with Halo, color 45/I/6	Open		Unkn.	109-155
2000 Millennium Madonna 855	7,500		495.00	495

M.I. Hummel Collectibles Nativity Components - M.I. Hummel, unless otherwise noted

XX 12-Pc. Set Figs. only, Color, 214/A/M/I, B/I, A/K/I, F/I G/I J/I K/I, L/I, M/I, N/I, O/I, 366/I	Open		Unkn.	1680-1852
XX Angel Serenade 214/D/I	Open		Unkn.	100-150
XX Camel Kneeling - Goebel	Open		Unkn.	206-285
XX Camel Lying - Goebel	Open		Unkn.	206-285
XX Camel Standing - Goebel	Open		Unkn.	206-285
XX Donkey 214/J/0	Open		Unkn.	41-60
XX Donkey 214/J/I	Open		Unkn.	56-85
XX Flying Angel/color 366/I	Open		Unkn.	105-155
XX Good Night 214/C/I	Open		Unkn.	75-105
XX Holy Family, 3 Pcs., Color 214/A/M/0, B/0, A/K/0	Open		Unkn.	250-375
XX Holy Family, 3 Pcs., Color 214/A/M/I, B/I, A/K/I	Open		Unkn.	468-488
1997 Holy Family, 3 Pcs., White 214	Open		200.00	205-215
XX Infant Jesus 214/A/K/0	Open		Unkn.	34-55
XX Infant Jesus 214/A/K/I	Open		Unkn.	53-87
XX King, Kneeling 214/M/I	Open		Unkn.	149-205
XX King, Kneeling 214M/0	Open		Unkn.	120-170
XX King, Kneeling w/ Box 214/N/0	Open		Unkn.	116-165
XX King, Kneeling w/Box 214/N/I	Open		Unkn.	135-190
XX King, Moorish 214/L/0	Open		Unkn.	124-180
XX King, Moorish 214/L/I	Open		Unkn.	150-210
XX Lamb 214/O/0	Open		Unkn.	18-26
XX Lamb 214/O/I	Open		Unkn.	18-26
XX Little Tooter 214/H/I	Open		Unkn.	105-182
XX Little Tooter 214/H/0	Open		Unkn.	83-120
XX Madonna 214/A/M/0	Open		Unkn.	109-160
XX Madonna 214/A/M/I	Open		Unkn.	146-205
XX Ox 214/K/0	Open		Unkn.	42-60
XX Ox 214/K/I	Open		Unkn.	60-85
XX Shepherd Boy 214/G/I	Open		Unkn.	113-145
XX Shepherd Kneeling 214/G/0	Open		Unkn.	98-145
XX Shepherd Standing 214/F/0	Open		Unkn.	124-180
XX Shepherd with Sheep-1 piece 214/F/I	Open		Unkn.	149-205
XX Small Camel Kneeling - Goebel	Open		Unkn.	225-230
XX Small Camel Lying - Goebel	Open		Unkn.	225-230
XX Small Camel Standing - Goebel	Open		Unkn.	225-230
XX St. Joseph 214/B/0	Open		Unkn.	113-160
XX St. Joseph color 214/B/I	Open		Unkn.	146-205
XX Stable only fits 12 or 16-pc. HUM214/II Set	Open		Unkn.	120
XX Stable only, fits 16-piece HUM260 Set	Open		Unkn.	400-465
XX Stable only, fits 3-pc. HUM214 Set	Open		Unkn.	50-83
XX We Congratulate 214/E/I	Open		Unkn.	180-190

M.I. Hummel Disneyana Figurines - M.I. Hummel

1992 Two Merry Wanderers 022074	1,500	1992	250.00	950-1155
1993 Two Little Drummers	1,500	1993	325.00	385-750
1994 Minnie Be Patient	1,500	1994	395.00	325-450
1995 For Father	1,500	1995	450.00	450-450
1995 Grandpa's Boys	1,500	1995	340.00	413-424
1996 Minnie For Mother	1,200	1996	470.00	470
1997 Grandma's Girl	1,000	1998	350.00	350-484
1998 Friends Forever	350	1998	350.00	350-484
1999 Donald & Daisy	350	1999	350.00	450-660
2000 Reel Friends	350	2000	450.00	450-650

M.I. Hummel First Edition Miniatures - M.I. Hummel

1991 Accordion Boy -37225	Suspd.		105.00	169-550
1989 Apple Tree Boy -37219	Suspd.		115.00	130-210
1990 Baker -37222	Suspd.		100.00	130-300
1992 Bavarian Church (Display) -37370	Closed	N/A	60.00	70-75
1988 Bavarian Cottage (Display) -37355	Closed	N/A	60.00	64-95
1990 Bavarian Marketsquare Bridge (Display) -37358	Closed	N/A	110.00	125-130
1988 Bavarian Village (Display) -37356	Closed	N/A	100.00	55-100
1991 Busy Student -37226	Suspd.		105.00	150-300
1990 Cinderella -37223	Suspd.		115.00	125-195
1991 Countryside School (Display) -37365	Closed	N/A	100.00	100-125
1989 Doll Bath -37214	Suspd.		95.00	105-185
1992 Goose Girl -37238	Suspd.		130.00	180-300

Collectors' Information Bureau   *Quotes have been rounded up to nearest dollar

YEAR ISSUE	EDITION LIMIT	YEAR RETD.	ISSUE PRICE	*QUOTE U.S.$
1989 Little Fiddler -37211	Suspd.		90.00	115-250
1989 Little Sweeper -37212	Suspd.		90.00	115-300
1990 Marketsquare Flower Stand (Display) -37360	Closed	N/A	35.00	50-80
1990 Marketsquare Hotel (Display)-37359	Closed	N/A	70.00	90-125
1989 Merry Wanderer -37213	Suspd.		95.00	250-300
1991 Merry Wanderer Dealer Plaque -37229	Closed	N/A	130.00	160-300
1989 Postman -37217	Suspd.		95.00	120-195
1991 Roadside Shrine (Display)-37366	Closed	N/A	60.00	60-85
1992 School Boy -37236	Suspd.		120.00	180-300
1991 Serenade -37228	Suspd.		105.00	120-275
1992 Snow-Covered Mountain (Display)-37371	Closed	N/A	100.00	100-125
1989 Stormy Weather -37215	Suspd.		115.00	150-350
1992 Trees (Display)-37369	Closed	N/A	40.00	50-55
1989 Visiting an Invalid -37218	Suspd.		105.00	130-175
1990 Waiter -37221	Suspd.		100.00	195-300
1992 Wayside Harmony -37237	Suspd.		140.00	180-300
1991 We Congratulate -37227	Suspd.		130.00	150-300

M.I. Hummel Fonts - M.I. Hummel

YEAR ISSUE	EDITION LIMIT	YEAR RETD.	ISSUE PRICE	*QUOTE U.S.$
XX Angel Facing Left 91/A	Open		45.00	38-55
XX Angel Facing Right 91/B	Open		45.00	34-55
XX Angel Shrine 147	Open		55.00	44-65
XX Angel Sitting 22/0	Open		45.00	51-55
XX Angel w/Bird 167	Open		55.00	41-65
XX Child w/Flowers 36/0	Open		45.00	43-55
XX Good Shepherd 35/0	Open		45.00	38-55
XX Heavenly Angel 207	Open		55.00	45-65
XX Holy Family 246	Open		55.00	41-65
XX Madonna & Child 243	Open		55.00	45-65
XX Worship 164	Open		55.00	45-65

M.I. Hummel Hummel Scapes - M.I. Hummel

YEAR ISSUE	EDITION LIMIT	YEAR RETD.	ISSUE PRICE	*QUOTE U.S.$
1997 Around The Town	Open		75.00	56-75
1997 Castle On A Hill	Open		75.00	56-75
1997 Going To Church	Open		75.00	56-75
1996 Heavenly Harmonies	Open		100.00	100
1996 Home Sweet Home	Closed	1997	130.00	75-130
1996 Little Music Makers	Closed	1997	130.00	75-130
1997 Strolling Through The Park	Open		75.00	56-75

M.I. Hummel Millennium Love Series - M.I. Hummel

YEAR ISSUE	EDITION LIMIT	YEAR RETD.	ISSUE PRICE	*QUOTE U.S.$
2001 Little Fiddler (12 1/2") 2/11	Open		1500.00	1500
2001 Soloist (12 1/2") 135/III	Open		1500.00	1500
2001 Sweet Music 186/III	Open		1500.00	1500

M.I. Hummel Pen Pals - M.I. Hummel

YEAR ISSUE	EDITION LIMIT	YEAR RETD.	ISSUE PRICE	*QUOTE U.S.$
1995 For Mother 257/5/0	Open		55.00	41-55
1995 March Winds 43/5/0	Open		55.00	55
1995 One For You, One For Me 482/5/0	Open		55.00	41-55
1995 Sister 98/5/0	Open		55.00	41-55
1995 Soloist 135/5/0	Open		55.00	41-55
1995 Village Boy 151/5/0	Open		55.00	41-55

M.I. Hummel Tree Toppers - M.I. Hummel

YEAR ISSUE	EDITION LIMIT	YEAR RETD.	ISSUE PRICE	*QUOTE U.S.$
1994 Heavenly Angel 755	Suspd.		450.00	375-500

M.I. Hummel Vignettes w/Solitary Domes - M.I. Hummel

YEAR ISSUE	EDITION LIMIT	YEAR RETD.	ISSUE PRICE	*QUOTE U.S.$
1992 Bakery Day w/Baker & Waiter 37726	3,000		225.00	169-230
1992 The Flower Market w/Cinderella 37729	3,000		135.00	101-135
1993 The Mail Is Here Clock Tower 826504	Open		495.00	431-575
1995 Ring Around the Rosie Musical 826101	10,000		675.00	506-675
1992 Winterfest w/Ride Into Christmas 37728	5,000		195.00	146-156

M.I. Hummel/Stieff - M.I. Hummel

YEAR ISSUE	EDITION LIMIT	YEAR RETD.	ISSUE PRICE	*QUOTE U.S.$
1999 Wonder of Christmas Collector's Set 2015	Closed	1999	575.00	463-575
2000 Little Maestro (Collector's Set) 826/I	Open		425.00	425

M.I. Hummel's Temporarily Out of Production (including trademarks) - M.I. Hummel

YEAR ISSUE	EDITION LIMIT	YEAR RETD.	ISSUE PRICE	*QUOTE U.S.$
XX 16-Pc. Set Figs. only, Color, 214/A/M/I, B/I, A/M/I, C/I, D/I, E/I, F/I, G/I, H/I, J/I, K/I, L/I, M/I, N/I, O/I, 366/I	Suspd.		Unkn.	1990
XX 17-Pc. Set Large Color 16 Figs.& Wooden Stable 260 A-R	Suspd.		Unkn.	4540
XX Adoration 23/III	Suspd.		Unkn.	446-510
2000 African Wanderer 2062	Suspd.		250.00	260
2000 American Wanderer 2061	Suspd.		250.00	260

YEAR ISSUE	EDITION LIMIT	YEAR RETD.	ISSUE PRICE	*QUOTE U.S.$
XX Angel Cloud (font) 206	Suspd.		55.00	45-55
XX Angel Duet (candleholder) 193	Suspd.		245.00	188-520
XX Angel Duet (font) 146	Suspd.		55.00	45-65
XX Angel Serenade 260/E	Suspd.		Unkn.	200-300
1935 Angelic Sleep Candleholder 25	Suspd.		Unkn.	139
1962 Apple Tree Boy & Girl Bookend 252A&B	Suspd.		Unkn.	225
XX Apple Tree Boy 142/X	Suspd.		Unkn	15000-25000
XX Apple Tree Girl 141/X	Suspd.		Unkn	15000-25000
1991 Art Critic 318	Suspd.		Unkn.	244-325
2000 Asian Wanderer 2063	Suspd.		250.00	260
XX Auf Wiedersehen 153/I	Suspd.		Unkn.	255-340
2000 Australian Wanderer 2064	Suspd.		250.00	260
XX Baking Day 330	Suspd.		Unkn.	140-195
XX Band Leader 129/4/0	Suspd.		Unkn.	90-245
XX Barnyard Hero 195/I	Suspd.		Unkn.	140-360
XX Be Patient 197/I	Suspd.		Unkn.	140-340
XX Begging His Share 9	Suspd.		Unkn.	242-826
XX Big Housecleaning 363	Suspd.		Unkn.	120-325
1989 Birthday Cake 338	Suspd.		Unkn.	124-175
XX Birthday Serenade 218/0	Suspd.		Unkn.	255-366
XX Blessed Child 78/0	Suspd.		Unkn.	73-179
XX Blessed Child 78/I/83	Suspd.		Unkn.	35-40
XX Blessed Child 78/II/83	Suspd.		Unkn.	41-60
XX Blessed Child 78/III/83	Suspd.		Unkn.	49-75
XX Bookworm 3/II	Suspd.		Unkn.	1100-1350
XX Bookworm 3/III	Suspd.		Unkn.	1500-2000
1946 Boy With Bird, Ashtray 166	Suspd.		Unkn.	98
1988 A Budding Maestro 477	Suspd.		Unkn.	95-135
XX Candlelight (candleholder) 192	Suspd.		255.00	230-473
XX Carnival 328	Suspd.		Unkn.	208-250
1993 Celestial Musician 188/4/0	Suspd.		Unkn.	90-130
XX Celestial Musician 188/I	Suspd.		255.00	221-350
XX Chick Girl 57/I	Suspd.		Unkn.	186-240
XX Child in Bed Plaque 137	Suspd.		Unkn.	56-70
XX Child Jesus (font) 56/0	Suspd.		45.00	38-45
XX Christ Child 18	Suspd.		Unkn.	124-214
XX Close Harmony 336	Suspd.		Unkn.	255-360
XX Confidentially 314	Suspd.		Unkn.	200-423
XX Coquettes 179	Suspd.		Unkn.	190-200
XX Donkey 260/L	Suspd.		Unkn.	101-135
XX Easter Greetings 378	Suspd.		Unkn.	196-270
2000 European Wanderer 2060	Suspd.		250.00	260
XX Eventide 99	Suspd.		Unkn.	299-390
XX A Fair Measure 345	Suspd.		Unkn.	251-753
XX Favorite Pet 361	Suspd.		Unkn.	244-335
XX Festival Harmony, with Flute 173/0	Suspd.		Unkn.	263-360
XX Festival Harmony, with Flute 173/4/0	Suspd.		Unkn.	90-200
XX Festival Harmony, with Flute 173/II	Suspd.		Unkn.	800-1000
XX Festival Harmony, with Mandolin 172/0	Suspd.		Unkn.	360-414
1994 Festival Harmony, with Mandolin 172/4/0	Suspd.		95.00	90-125
XX Festival Harmony, with Mandolin 172/II	Suspd.		Unkn.	800-1000
XX Fitting Butterfly Plaque 139	Suspd.		Unkn.	310
XX Flower Madonna, color 10/I/II	Suspd.		Unkn.	360-462
XX Flower Madonna, color 10/III/II	Suspd.		Unkn.	225-420
XX Flower Madonna, white 10/I/W	Suspd.		Unkn.	420-450
XX Flower Madonna, white 10/III/W	Suspd.		Unkn.	470-750
XX Follow the Leader 369	Suspd.		Unkn.	1350-1560
XX Forest Shrine 183	Suspd.		Unkn.	450-650
1993 A Free Flight 569	Suspd.		Unkn.	150-205
XX Friends 136/V	Suspd.		Unkn.	773-1380
XX A Gentle Glow 439	Suspd.		Unkn.	100-235
XX Girl with Trumpet 391	Suspd.		Unkn.	67-105
XX Going to Grandma's 52/I	Suspd.		Unkn.	300-500
XX Good Night 260/D	Suspd.		Unkn.	105-145
XX Good Shepherd 42	Suspd.		Unkn.	218-377
XX Goose Girl 47/II	Suspd.		Unkn.	315-614
XX Goose Girl 47/IIW	Suspd.		Unkn.	218
XX Guardian Angel 248/0	Suspd.		55.00	41-55
XX Happy Birthday 176/I	Suspd.		Unkn.	255-340
XX Happy Days 150/0	Suspd.		Unkn.	255-442
XX Happy Days 150/I	Suspd.		Unkn.	383-434
XX Happy Traveler 109/II	Suspd.		Unkn.	800-950
XX Hear Ye! Hear Ye! 15/I	Suspd.		Unkn.	131-370
XX Hear Ye! Hear Ye! 15/II	Suspd.		Unkn.	338-500
XX Hear Ye! Hear Ye! 15/IIW	Suspd.		Unkn.	218
XX Heavenly Angel 21/I	Suspd.		Unkn.	221-300
XX Heavenly Angel 21/II	Suspd.		Unkn.	361-500

FIGURINES

YEAR ISSUE		EDITION LIMIT	YEAR RETD.	ISSUE PRICE	*QUOTE U.S.$
XX	Heavenly Angel 21/IIW	Suspd.		Unkn.	218
XX	Heavenly Lullaby 262	Suspd.		Unkn.	183-233
XX	Heavenly Protection 88/II	Suspd.		Unkn.	600-900
1995	Hello (Perpetual Calendar) 788A	Suspd.	295.00		295-310
XX	Hello 124/I	Suspd.		Unkn.	206-275
XX	Holy Child 70	Suspd.		Unkn.	214-285
XX	Home from Market 198/I	Suspd.		Unkn.	184-318
XX	Homeward Bound 334	Suspd.		Unkn.	315-360
XX	Hummel Display Plaque 187	Suspd.		Unkn.	125-175
XX	In The Meadow 459	Suspd.		Unkn.	173-240
XX	In Tune 414	Suspd.		Unkn.	240-310
XX	Infant Jesus 260/C	Suspd.		Unkn.	79-120
XX	Joyous News 27/III	Suspd.		Unkn.	100-250
1985	Jubilee 416 TMK6	Suspd.	200.00		271-495
XX	Just Fishing 373	Suspd.		Unkn.	191-200
XX	Just Resting 112/I	Suspd.		Unkn.	288-340
XX	King, Kneeling 260/P	Suspd.		Unkn.	480
XX	King, Moorish 260/N	Suspd.		Unkn.	430-500
XX	King, Standing 260/O	Suspd.		Unkn.	300-500
XX	Knitting Lesson 256	Suspd.		Unkn.	455-550
XX	Little Band 392	Suspd.		Unkn.	206-234
1968	Little Band Candleholder 388	Suspd.		Unkn.	165-225
1968	Little Band Candleholder on Music Box 388M	Suspd.		Unkn.	248
1968	Little Band on Music Box 392M	Suspd.		Unkn.	270-467
XX	Little Cellist 89/II	Suspd.		Unkn.	270-500
XX	Little Cellist 89/IIW	Suspd.		Unkn.	218
XX	Little Fiddler 2/4/0	Suspd.		Unkn.	90-130
XX	Little Fiddler 2/I	Suspd.		Unkn.	212-340
XX	Little Fiddler 2/II	Suspd.		Unkn.	825-935
XX	Little Fiddler 2/III	Suspd.		Unkn.	900-1099
XX	Little Gabriel 32	Suspd.		Unkn.	92-170
XX	Little Hiker 16/I	Suspd.		Unkn.	188-260
XX	Little Sweeper 171/4/0	Suspd.		Unkn.	90-140
XX	Little Tooter 260/K	Suspd.		Unkn.	128-170
XX	Lullaby 24/I	Suspd.	210.00		158-390
XX	Lullaby 24/III	Suspd.		Unkn.	1000-1200
XX	Madonna 260/A	Suspd.		Unkn.	590
XX	Madonna Holding Child, color 151/II	Suspd.		Unkn.	115-135
XX	Madonna Holding Child, white 151/W	Suspd.		Unkn.	320-350
XX	Madonna Praying, color 46/III/6	Suspd.		Unkn.	400-425
XX	Madonna Praying, white 46/0/W	Suspd.		Unkn.	195-225
XX	Madonna Praying, white 46/I/W	Suspd.		Unkn.	175-185
XX	Madonna w/o Halo, color 46/I/6	Suspd.		Unkn.	300-315
XX	Madonna w/o Halo, white 45/I/W	Suspd.		Unkn.	175-185
XX	Madonna w/o Halo, white 46/I/W	Suspd.		Unkn.	175-185
1989	Make A Wish 475	Suspd.		Unkn.	169-230
XX	Meditation 13/V	Suspd.		Unkn.	1106-1200
XX	Meditation, color 13/II	Suspd.		Unkn.	1200-2500
XX	Merry Christmas Plaque 323	Suspd.		Unkn.	105-119
XX	Merry Wanderer 7/II	Suspd.		Unkn.	825-1250
XX	Merry Wanderer 7/III	Suspd.		Unkn.	975-1300
XX	Merry Wanderer 7/X	Suspd.		Unkn.	12000-20000
XX	Merry Wanderer Stepbase 7/I	Suspd.		Unkn.	319-900
XX	Mischief Maker 342	Suspd.		Unkn.	240-320
XX	On Secret Path 386	Suspd.		Unkn.	110-290
1995	Ooh My Tooth (Special Event) 533	Suspd.		Unkn.	135-175
XX	Ox 260/M	Suspd.		Unkn.	113-135
XX	Playmates 58/I	Suspd.		Unkn.	240-320
1994	The Poet 397/I	Suspd.	220.00		191-270
XX	Retreat to Safety 201/I	Suspd.		Unkn.	194-468
XX	School Boy 82/II	Suspd.		Unkn.	296-510
XX	School Boys 170/III	Suspd.		Unkn.	1365-1850
XX	School Girl 81/0	Suspd.		Unkn.	155-245
XX	School Girls 177/III	Suspd.		Unkn.	1365-1850
XX	Searching Angel Plaque 310	Suspd.		Unkn.	101-135
XX	Sensitive Hunter 6/2/0	Suspd.		Unkn.	124-170
XX	Sensitive Hunter 6/I	Suspd.		Unkn.	137-285
XX	Sensitive Hunter 6/II	Suspd.		Unkn.	195-375
XX	Serenade 85/4/0	Suspd.		Unkn.	90-128
XX	Serenade 85/II	Suspd.		Unkn.	245-510
XX	Sheep (Lying) 260/R	Suspd.		Unkn.	50-100
XX	Sheep (Standing) w/ Lamb 260/H	Suspd.		Unkn.	110
1996	Shepherd Boy 395/0	Suspd.	295.00		225-310
XX	Shepherd Boy, Kneeling 260/J	Suspd.		Unkn.	221-300
XX	Shepherd, Standing 260/G	Suspd.		Unkn.	525
XX	Silent Night 54	Suspd.	360.00		185-370
XX	Sing Along 433	Suspd.		Unkn.	240-330
XX	Sing With Me 405	Suspd.		Unkn.	115-380
1995	Sister (Perpetual Calendar) 788B	Suspd.	295.00		225-310
XX	Sister 98/0	Suspd.		Unkn.	152-176

YEAR ISSUE		EDITION LIMIT	YEAR RETD.	ISSUE PRICE	*QUOTE U.S.$
XX	Soldier Boy 332	Suspd.		Unkn.	168-255
XX	Soloist 135/4/0	Suspd.		Unkn.	90-140
XX	Spring Cheer 72	Suspd.		Unkn.	170-279
XX	Spring Dance 353/I	Suspd.		Unkn.	427-525
XX	St. George 55	Suspd.		Unkn.	263-375
XX	St. Joseph 260/B	Suspd.		Unkn.	390-520
XX	A Stitch in Time 255/4/0	Suspd.		Unkn.	90-193
XX	A Stitch in Time 255/I	Suspd.		Unkn.	181-301
1984	Supreme Protection 364 TMK6	Suspd.	150.00		281-395
XX	Surprise 94/I	Suspd.		Unkn.	325-435
1986	The Tally Plaque 460	Suspd.		Unkn.	116-410
XX	Telling Her Secret 196/I	Suspd.		Unkn.	300-400
XX	To Market 49/0	Suspd.		Unkn.	285-435
XX	To Market 49/I	Suspd.		Unkn.	326-500
XX	Trumpet Boy 97	Suspd.		Unkn.	113-160
XX	Village Boy 51/0	Suspd.		Unkn.	128-300
XX	Village Boy 51/I	Suspd.		Unkn.	138-225
XX	Volunteers 50/I	Suspd.		Unkn.	350-450
XX	Waiter 154/I	Suspd.		Unkn.	251-350
XX	Wayside Devotion 28/III	Suspd.		Unkn.	510-897
XX	Wayside Harmony 111/I	Suspd.		Unkn.	225-340
XX	We Congratulate 260/F	Suspd.		Unkn.	278-400
XX	Weary Wanderer 204	Suspd.		Unkn.	104-370
1992	Whistler's Duet 413	Suspd.		Unkn.	240-340
XX	White Angel 75	Suspd.	45.00		34-45
XX	Whitsuntide 163	Suspd.		Unkn.	248-355
XX	With Loving Greetings 309	Suspd.		Unkn.	169-275
XX	Worship 84/V	Suspd.		Unkn.	825-1125
1989	Wash Day 321/4/0	Suspd.		Unkn.	90-140

Gorham

(Four Seasons) A Boy And His Dog - N. Rockwell

	EDITION LIMIT	YEAR RETD.	ISSUE PRICE	*QUOTE U.S.$
1972 A Boy Meets His Dog	2,500	1980	200.00	1300-1575
1972 Adventurers Between Adventures	2,500	1980	Set	Set
1972 The Mysterious Malady	2,500	1980	Set	Set
1972 Pride of Parenthood	2,500	1980	Set	Set

(Four Seasons) A Helping Hand - N. Rockwell

1980 Year End Court	2,500	1980	650.00	900-1300
1980 Closed For Business	2,500	1980	Set	Set
1980 Swatter's Right	2,500	1980	Set	Set
1980 Coal Seasons Coming	2,500	1980	Set	Set

(Four Seasons) Dad's Boy - N. Rockwell

1981 Ski Skills	2,500	1990	750.00	1000-1300
1981 In His Spirit	2,500	1990	Set	Set
1981 Trout Dinner	2,500	1990	Set	Set
1981 Careful Aim	2,500	1990	Set	Set

(Four Seasons) Four Ages of Love - N. Rockwell

1974 Gaily Sharing Vintage Times	2,500	1980	300.00	600-1250
1974 Sweet Song So Young	2,500	1980	Set	Set
1974 Flowers In Tender Bloom	2,500	1980	Set	Set
1974 Fondly Do We Remember	2,500	1980	Set	Set

(Four Seasons) Going On Sixteen - N. Rockwell

1978 Chilling Chore	2,500	1980	400.00	650-1200
1978 Sweet Serenade	2,500	1980	Set	Set
1978 Shear Agony	2,500	1980	Set	Set
1978 Pilgrimage	2,500	1980	Set	Set

(Four Seasons) Grand Pals - N. Rockwell

1977 Snow Sculpturing	2,500	1980	350.00	1000-1200
1977 Soaring Spirits	2,500	1980	Set	Set
1977 Fish Finders	2,500	1980	Set	Set
1977 Ghostly Gourds	2,500	1980	Set	Set

(Four Seasons) Grandpa and Me - N. Rockwell

1975 Gay Blades	2,500	1980	300.00	800-1000
1975 Day Dreamers	2,500	1980	Set	Set
1975 Goin' Fishing	2,500	1980	Set	Set
1975 Pensive Pals	2,500	1980	Set	Set

(Four Seasons) Life With Father - N. Rockwell

1983 Big Decision	2,500	1990	250.00	250
1983 Blasting Out	2,500	1990	Set	Set
1983 Cheering The Champs	2,500	1990	Set	Set
1983 A Tough One	2,500	1990	Set	Set

(Four Seasons) Me and My Pal - N. Rockwell

1976 A Licking Good Bath	2,500	1980	300.00	1200-1400

YEAR ISSUE	EDITION LIMIT	YEAR RETD.	ISSUE PRICE	*QUOTE U.S.$
1976 Young Man's Fancy	2,500	1980	Set	Set
1976 Fisherman's Paradise	2,500	1980	Set	Set
1976 Disastrous Daring	2,500	1980	Set	Set

(Four Seasons) Old Buddies - N. Rockwell

1984 Shared Success	2,500	1990	250.00	250
1984 Hasty Retreat	2,500	1990	Set	Set
1984 Final Speech	2,500	1990	Set	Set
1984 Endless Debate	2,500	1990	Set	Set

(Four Seasons) Old Timers - N. Rockwell

1982 Canine Solo	2,500	1990	250.00	250
1982 Sweet Surprise	2,500	1990	Set	Set
1982 Lazy Days	2,500	1990	Set	Set
1982 Fancy Footwork	2,500	1990	Set	Set

(Four Seasons) Tender Years - N. Rockwell

1979 New Year Look	2,500	1979	500.00	1200-1400
1979 Spring Tonic	2,500	1979	Set	Set
1979 Cool Aid	2,500	1979	Set	Set
1979 Chilly Reception	2,500	1979	Set	Set

(Four Seasons) Traveling Salesman - N. Rockwell

1985 Horse Trader	2,500	1985	275.00	250-275
1985 Expert Salesman	2,500	1985	Set	Set
1985 Traveling Salesman	2,500	1985	Set	Set
1985 Country Pedlar	2,500	1985	Set	Set

(Four Seasons) Young Love - N. Rockwell

1973 Downhill Daring	2,500	1973	250.00	1100
1973 Beguiling Buttercup	2,500	1973	Set	Set
1973 Flying High	2,500	1973	Set	Set
1973 A Scholarly Pace	2,500	1973	Set	Set

Miniature Christmas Figurines - Various

1979 Tiny Tim - N. Rockwell	Yr.Iss.	1979	15.00	20
1980 Santa Plans His Trip - N. Rockwell	Yr.Iss.	1980	15.00	15
1981 Yuletide Reckoning - N. Rockwell	Yr.Iss.	1981	20.00	20
1982 Checking Good Deeds - N. Rockwell	Yr.Iss.	1982	20.00	20
1983 Santa's Friend - N. Rockwell	Yr.Iss.	1983	20.00	20
1984 Downhill Daring - N. Rockwell	Yr.Iss.	1984	20.00	20
1985 Christmas Santa - T. Nast	Yr.Iss.	1985	20.00	20
1986 Christmas Santa - T. Nast	Yr.Iss.	1986	25.00	25
1987 Annual Thomas Nast Santa - T. Nast	Yr.Iss.	1987	25.00	25

Miniatures - N. Rockwell

1982 The Annual Visit	Closed	1990	50.00	50-75
1981 At the Vets	Closed	1990	27.50	50-75
1987 Babysitter	15,000	1990	75.00	75
1981 Beguiling Buttercup	Closed	1990	45.00	45
1985 Best Friends	Closed	1990	27.50	28
1987 Between The Acts	15,000	1990	60.00	60
1981 Boy Meets His Dog	Closed	1990	37.50	60
1984 Careful Aims	Closed	1990	55.00	55
1987 Cinderella	15,000	1990	70.00	75
1981 Downhill Daring	Closed	1990	45.00	75
1985 Engineer	Closed	1990	55.00	55
1981 Flowers in Tender Bloom	Closed	1990	60.00	60
1986 Football Season	Closed	1990	60.00	60
1981 Gay Blades	Closed	1990	45.00	75
1984 Ghostly Gourds	Closed	1990	60.00	60-80
1984 Goin Fishing	Closed	1990	60.00	60
1986 The Graduate	Closed	1990	30.00	40
1984 In His Spirit	Closed	1990	60.00	60
1984 Independence	Closed	1990	60.00	80-85
1986 Lemonade Stand	Closed	1990	60.00	60
1986 Little Angel	Closed	1990	50.00	60
1985 Little Red Truck	Closed	1990	25.00	25
1982 Marriage License	Closed	1990	60.00	75-125
1987 The Milkmaid	15,000	1990	80.00	85-110
1986 Morning Walk	Closed	1990	60.00	60
1985 Muscle Bound	Closed	1990	30.00	30
1985 New Arrival	Closed	1990	32.50	35-75
1984 The Oculist	Closed	1990	60.00	80
1986 The Old Sign Painter	Closed	1990	70.00	80
1984 Pride of Parenthood	Closed	1990	50.00	50
1987 The Prom Dress	15,000	1990	75.00	75
1982 The Runaway	Closed	1990	50.00	50-80
1984 Shear Agony	Closed	1990	60.00	60
1986 Shoulder Ride	Closed	1990	50.00	65-75
1981 Snow Sculpture	Closed	1990	45.00	70
1985 Spring Checkup	Closed	1990	60.00	60

YEAR ISSUE	EDITION LIMIT	YEAR RETD.	ISSUE PRICE	*QUOTE U.S.$
1987 Springtime	15,000	1990	65.00	75-110
1987 Starstruck	15,000	1990	75.00	80-115
1981 Sweet Serenade	Closed	1990	45.00	45-80
1981 Sweet Song So Young	Closed	1990	55.00	55
1985 To Love & Cherish	Closed	1990	32.50	35
1982 Triple Self Portrait	Closed	1990	60.00	90-175
1983 Trout Dinner	15,000	1990	60.00	60-110
1982 Vintage Times	Closed	1990	50.00	50
1986 Welcome Mat	Closed	1990	70.00	75
1984 Years End Court	Closed	1990	60.00	60
1981 Young Man's Fancy	Closed	1990	55.00	55

Rockwell - N. Rockwell

1983 Antique Dealer RW48	7,500	1990	130.00	200
1982 April Fool's (At The Curiosity Shop) RW39	Closed	1990	55.00	100-110
1974 At The Vets RW4	Closed	1990	25.00	85-125
1974 Batter Up RW6	Closed	1990	40.00	150
1977 Beguiling Buttercup RW-19	Closed	1990	85.00	150
1978 Big Decision RW-25	Closed	1990	55.00	55
1975 Boy And His Dog RW9	Closed	1990	38.00	150
1974 Captain RW8	Closed	1990	45.00	95-130
1984 Card Tricks	7,500	1990	85.00	180
1978 Choosing Up RW24	Closed	1990	85.00	275
1981 Christmas Dancers RW37	7,500	1990	130.00	200-275
1988 Confrontation	15,000	1990	75.00	75
1988 Cramming	15,000	1990	80.00	80
1981 Day in the Life Boy II RW34	Closed	1990	75.00	95-115
1982 A Day in the Life Boy III RW40	Closed	1990	85.00	95
1982 A Day in the Life Girl III RW41	Closed	1990	85.00	115-150
1988 The Diary	15,000	1990	80.00	80-115
1988 Dolores & Eddie NRM59	15,000	1990	75.00	80
1986 Drum For Tommy RW53	Annual	1986	90.00	N/A
1983 Facts of Life RW45	7,500	1990	110.00	180
1974 Fishing RW5	Closed	1990	50.00	175
1977 Gaily Sharing Vintage Time RW-20	Closed	1990	60.00	165
1988 Gary Cooper in Hollywood	15,000	1990	90.00	90
1977 Gay Blades RW-21	Closed	1990	50.00	50-150
1976 God Rest Ye Merry Gentlemen RW13	Closed	1990	50.00	1000-1500
1988 Home for the Holidays	7,500	1990	100.00	100
1976 Independence RW15	Closed	1990	40.00	150
1980 Jolly Coachman RW33	Closed	1990	75.00	200
1982 Marriage License (10 3/4") RW38	5,000	1990	110.00	600
1976 Marriage License (6 1/4") RW16	Closed	1990	50.00	325
1982 Merrie Christmas RW43	7,500	1990	75.00	150
1978 Missed RW23	Closed	1990	85.00	275
1974 Missing Tooth RW2	Closed	1990	30.00	150
1975 No Swimming RW18	Closed	1990	35.00	150-175
1976 The Oculist RW17	Closed	1990	50.00	175
1978 Oh Yeah RW22	Closed	1990	85.00	275
1975 Old Mill Pond RW11	Closed	1990	45.00	145
1985 The Old Sign Painter	7,500	1990	130.00	210
1977 Pride of Parenthood RW18	Closed	1990	50.00	125
1985 Puppet Maker	7,500	1990	130.00	130-200
1987 Santa Planning His Annual Visit	7,500	1990	95.00	95
1984 Santa's Friend	7,500	1990	75.00	160
1976 Saying Grace (5 1/2") RW12	5,000	1990	75.00	265-275
1982 Saying Grace (8") RW42	Closed	1990	110.00	500-600
1984 Serenade	7,500	1990	95.00	165
1974 Skating RW7	Closed	1990	37.50	140
1976 Tackled (Ad Stand)	Closed	1990	35.00	125-150
1982 Tackled (Rockwell Name Signed) RW8662	Closed	1990	45.00	100
1974 Tiny Tim RW3	Closed	1990	30.00	125-135
1980 Triple Self Portrait (10 1/2") RW32	5,000	1990	300.00	600-675
1979 Triple Self Portrait (7 1/2") RW27	Closed	1990	125.00	425
1974 Weighing In RW1	Closed	1990	40.00	150
1981 Wet Sport RW36	Closed	1990	85.00	95-100

Greenwich Workshop

Bronze - Various

1994 Bird Hunters - J. Christensen	50	N/A	4500.00	4500
1990 The Candleman, AP - J. Christensen	100	N/A	2250.00	4500
1991 Comanche Raider - K. McCarthy	100	N/A	812.50	813
1989 The Fish Walker - J. Christensen	100	N/A	3200.00	4500
1999 A Lawyer More Than Adequately Attired in Fine Print - J. Christensen	200		6000.00	6000
1991 Pony Express - K. McCarthy	10	N/A	934.00	934
1994 Thunder of Hooves - K. McCarthy	10	N/A	875.00	875

FIGURINES

YEAR ISSUE	EDITION LIMIT	YEAR RETD.	ISSUE PRICE	*QUOTE U.S.$

The Greenwich Workshop Collection - Various

YEAR ISSUE	EDITION LIMIT	YEAR RETD.	ISSUE PRICE	*QUOTE U.S.$
1998 The Ancient Angel - J. Christensen	1,750		195.00	195
1997 And The Wolf - S. Gustafson	945		350.00	350
1996 And They...Crooked House - J. Christensen	Retrd.	1998	295.00	295-350
1996 Another Fish Act - J. Christensen	2,500		350.00	350
1998 The Artist - W. Bullas	622	1998	95.00	95
1998 Baby Bear - S. Gustafson	1,950		50.00	50
1998 Back Quackers - W. Bullas	1,200		125.00	125
2000 Ballet Parking - W. Bullas	Open		49.95	50
1997 Bassoonist - J. Christensen	1,500		395.00	395
1996 Bed Time Buddies - W. Bullas	Retrd.	1999	75.00	75
1998 Brother Avery - S. Gustafson	5,000		95.00	95
1997 Brother Folio Scrivner - S. Gustafson	2,364		95.00	95
1998 California Stylin - W. Bullas	Open		125.00	125
1996 Candleman - J. Christensen	2,500		295.00	295
2000 The Cat Burglar - W. Bullas	Open		44.95	45
1996 Christmas Angel - W. Bullas	1,996	1996	75.00	75-150
1996 Christmas Elf - W. Bullas	1,996	1996	75.00	150-180
1997 Consultant - W. Bullas	Retrd.	1999	95.00	95
1997 Crooked Cat, Crooked Mouse - J. Christensen	1,724	1998	60.00	60-90
1996 The Dare Devil - W. Bullas	Retrd.	1998	75.00	75-95
2000 Dog Byte - W. Bullas	Open		39.95	40
1998 Dressed for the Holidays - W. Bullas	1,500	N/A	95.00	95
1997 Duck Tape - W. Bullas	600		95.00	95
1996 Ductor - W. Bullas	Retrd.	2001	75.00	75
1997 Dust Bunnies - W. Bullas	500		75.00	75
1997 Fish Walker - J. Christensen	571		350.00	350
1999 The Fish Wizard - J. Christensen	1,500	N/A	160.00	160
1996 Fool and His Bunny - W. Bullas	Open		75.00	75
1998 Fool Moon - W. Bullas	1,750	1998	125.00	125
1997 Forest Fish Rider - J. Christensen	2,500		175.00	175
1998 Fowl Ball - W. Bullas	828		95.00	95
1997 Frog Horn - W. Bullas	2,028		85.00	85
1998 Froggy Goes A-Wooing - S. Gustafson	2,500		125.00	125
2000 Gift of Love - J. Christensen	Retrd.	2000	130.00	130
1999 Gift of Peace - J. Christensen	Retrd.	1999	85.00	85
1998 Goldilocks - S. Gustafson	1,950		130.00	130
1998 The Hare - S. Gustafson	1,950		95.00	95
1996 He Bought a Crooked Cat - J. Christensen	Retrd.	1998	60.00	60-75
1996 Head of the Class - W. Bullas	Retrd.	1998	75.00	75
1997 Hocus Pocus - W. Bullas	547		125.00	125
2001 How Does Your Garden Grow - W. Bullas	Open		44.95	45
1997 How Many Angels Can Fit on Head	536		215.00	215
1997 Humpty Dumpty - S. Gustafson	600		250.00	250
1996 Jack Be Nimble - J. Christensen	Retrd.	1999	295.00	295
1998 Jack Sprat Could Eat No Fat - J. Christensen	1,500	1999	175.00	175
1998 Jack's Wife Could Eat No Lean - J. Christensen	1,500	1999	185.00	185
1996 Jailbirds - W. Bullas	Retrd.	1999	75.00	75
1996 Lawrence Pretended Not to Notice... - J. Christensen	2,500	1998	350.00	350
1996 Levi Levitates a Stone Fish - J. Christensen	2,500		295.00	295
2000 Life of the Party - W. Bullas	Open		49.95	50
1996 Little Angel - W. Bullas	Retrd.	1996	75.00	75
1996 Little Elf - W. Bullas	Retrd.	1996	75.00	75
1999 Little Miss Muffet - S. Gustafson	1,950		245.00	245
1996 Little Red Riding Hood - S. Gustafson	2,500		150.00	150
1998 The Lute Player - J. Christensen	1,500		450.00	450
1998 Mama Bear - S. Gustafson	1,950		175.00	175
1996 Man Who Minds the Moon - J. Christensen	2,500	N/A	295.00	295
1999 Melchior - J. Christensen	Retrd.	1999	80.00	80
1998 The Miniature Artist - J. Christensen	1,500	1998	95.00	95
2001 Monkey Business - W. Bullas	Open		49.95	50
1996 Mother Goose - J. Christensen	Retrd.	1999	275.00	275
1998 Mrs. Claus - J. Christensen	2,500		295.00	295
1999 the mummy strikes! - W. Bullas	Open		95.00	95
1998 The Nurse - W. Bullas	2,500	N/A	95.00	95
2001 The Oath - J. Christensen	950		595.00	595
1995 Olde World Santa - J. Christensen	950	1995	295.00	540-600
1996 The Oldest Angel - J. Christensen	2,500	1998	295.00	295
1998 Ottist - S. Gustafson	1,500	N/A	95.00	95
1998 Owl and the Pussycat - S. Gustafson	2,500		250.00	250
1998 Papa Bear - S. Gustafson	1,950		180.00	180
1999 Pear Balancer - J. Christensen	1,500		160.00	160
1997 Puppy Glove - W. Bullas	Open		95:00	95
1998 Puss in Boots - S. Gustafson	2,500		165.00	165
1998 Responsible Man - J. Christensen	1,950		450.00	450
1996 The Responsible Woman - J. Christensen	2,500		595.00	595
2000 Road Hog - W. Bullas	Open		39.95	40
1997 Rudy - W. Bullas	2,553		125.00	125
1998 Sandtrap Pro - W. Bullas	828		95.00	95
1999 santa gets lit... - W. Bullas	1,500		95.00	95
1998 Santa's Belle - J. Christensen	Retrd.	1998	50.00	59
1998 Santa's Hopper - W. Bullas	1,250		85.00	85
1997 Santa's Other Helpers - J. Christensen	2,500	N/A	295.00	295
1997 The Scholar - J. Christensen	1,700		375.00	375
1999 secret agent - W. Bullas	Open		95.00	95
1998 Snow Buddies - W. Bullas	1,250		125.00	125
1998 Sock Hop - W. Bullas	Open		125.00	125
1999 Sometimes The Spirit Touches Us Through Our Weaknesses w/ graphic After Clouds, Sun - J. Christensen	1,950		275.00	275
1998 Space Cadet - W. Bullas	2,500		95.00	95
1999 superdad... - W. Bullas	Retrd.	N/A	95.00	95
1998 Supermom - W. Bullas	1,228	N/A	95.00	95
1996 There Was a Crooked Man... - J. Christensen	Retrd.	1998	225.00	225-275
1996 Three Blind Mice: Fluffy - J. Christensen	Retrd.	1998	75.00	75-90
1996 Three Blind Mice: Sniffer - J. Christensen	Retrd.	1998	75.00	75-90
1996 Three Blind Mice: Weevil - J. Christensen	Retrd.	1998	75.00	75-90
1997 Tommy Tucker - J. Christensen	1,250	1997	295.00	295
1999 the tooth faerie - W. Bullas	Open		95.00	95
1998 The Tortoise - S. Gustafson	1,950		125.00	125
2001 Total Bull Ship - W. Bullas	Open		44.95	45
1997 The Traveling Fish Salesman - J. Christensen	546	N/A	150.00	150
1996 Trick or Treat - W. Bullas	Retrd.	1998	75.00	75
1996 The Trick Rider - W. Bullas	Retrd.	1999	75.00	75
1996 Tweedle Dee - J. Christensen	1,250	1999	295.00	295
1996 Tweedle Dum - J. Christensen	1,250	1999	295.00	295
2001 Waiting For The Tide - J. Christensen	1,500		250.00	250
1998 Wetland Bird Hunter - J. Christensen	1,950		250.00	250
2002 The Widow's Mite (porcelain) - J. Christensen	650		595.00	595
1996 Wolf - S. Gustafson	2,500		350.00	350
1996 Zippo...the Fire Eater - W. Bullas	Retrd.	1998	75.00	75-95

Pearl Bisque™ - Various

YEAR ISSUE	EDITION LIMIT	YEAR RETD.	ISSUE PRICE	*QUOTE U.S.$
2001 Aquaduck - W. Bullas	Open		39.95	40
2000 bad to the buns - W. Bullas	Open		49.95	50
2000 ballet parking - W. Bullas	Open		24.98	25
2001 Batty - W. Bullas	Open		44.95	45
2000 the cat burglar - W. Bullas	Open		44.95	45
2001 Court of Appeals - W. Bullas	Open		44.95	45
2000 dog byte - W. Bullas	Open		39.95	40
2001 Early Bird Special - W. Bullas	Open		49.95	50
2002 The Eavesdropper - Von Stetina	Open		49.50	50
2001 Faerie Muse - Celeste - J. Christensen	2,500		65.00	65
2001 Faerie Muse - Grace - J. Christensen	2,500		85.00	85
2001 Faerie Muse - Melody - J. Christensen	2,500		75.00	75
2001 Faerie Muse - Poesy - J. Christensen	2,500		95.00	95
2001 First Flight - Von Stetina	Open		49.95	50
2001 Fishing - W. Christensen	950		250.00	250
2001 Fortune's Friend - Von Stetina	Open		24.95	25
2001 The Gift - Von Stetina	Open		24.95	25
2000 hogwash... - W. Bullas	Open		49.95	50
2001 The Jewel Thief - Von Stetina	Open		34.95	35
2001 The Kite Flyer - Von Stetina	Open		19.95	20
2000 life of the party - W. Bullas	Open		49.95	50
2001 Mary, Joseph and Jesus	Open		85.00	85
2001 The Mushroom Dweller - Von Stetina	Open		44.95	45
2000 the nerd dogs... - W. Bullas	Open		49.95	50
2002 O.R. DR. - W. Bullas	Open		35.00	35
2002 O.R.R.N. - W. Bullas	Open		35.00	35
2002 The Optimist - W. Bullas	Open		39.95	40
2000 please bee mine... - W. Bullas	Open		49.95	50
2000 Queen Mab - W. Christensen	1,500		135.00	135
2001 Queen Mab's Fairies-Adeline - W. Christensen	1,500		75.00	75
2001 Queen Mab's Fairies-Cecily - W. Christensen	1,500		75.00	75

YEAR ISSUE	EDITION LIMIT	YEAR RETD.	ISSUE PRICE	*QUOTE U.S.$
2001 Queen Mab's Fairies-Fiona - W. Christensen	1,500		75.00	75
2001 Ring Around The Rosie - Von Stetina	Open		19.95	20
2000 road hog - W. Bullas	Open		39.95	40
2002 Rude Awakening - Von Stetina	Open		35.00	35
2001 Some House Swine - W. Bullas	Open		44.95	45
2001 St. Nicholas - S. Gustafson	Open		75.00	75
2002 St. Schleppina - W. Bullas	Open		39.95	40
2002 Sun Shower - Von Stetina	Open		19.50	20
2001 Sweet Dreams - Von Stetina	Open		44.95	45
2001 Tea Rose Tabby - Von Stetina	Open		24.95	25
2001 Terrestrial Tabby - Von Stetina	Open		34.95	35
2001 Tiger Swallowtale - Von Stetina	Open		29.95	30
2002 Trolling - Von Stetina	Open		39.50	40
2001 Wine-Oceros - W. Bullas	Open		44.95	45
2001 Winter's Magic - Von Stetina	Open		24.95	25

Porcelain Angels - W. Christensen

2001 The Gift of Hope	Open		85.00	85
2000 The Gift of Love	Open		85.00	85
2001 The Gift of Peace	Open		85.00	85

Porcelain Wisemen - W. Christensen

2000 Balthasar	Yr.Iss.	2000	80.00	80
2000 Caspar	Yr.Iss.	2000	80.00	80
2000 Melchoir	Yr.Iss.	2000	80.00	80
2001 The Three Wisemen - The Ages of Man	Open		80.00	80

Hamilton Collection

The Adventures of a Reluctant Penguin - N/A

2000 Friends Never Drift Apart	Open		19.95	20
2000 I'll Brrree Right In	Open		19.95	20
2000 It's Freezing Down There	Open		19.95	20
2000 Life Has Its Ups and Downs	Open		19.95	20

American Garden Flowers - D. Fryer

1987 Azalea	15,000		75.00	75
1988 Calla Lilly	15,000		75.00	75
1987 Camelia	9,800		55.00	75
1988 Day Lily	15,000		75.00	75
1987 Gardenia	15,000		75.00	75
1989 Pansy	15,000		75.00	75
1988 Petunia	15,000		75.00	75
1987 Rose	15,000		75.00	75

American Wildlife Bronze Collection - H./N. Deaton

1980 Beaver	7,500		60.00	65
1979 Bobcat	7,500		60.00	75
1979 Cougar	7,500		60.00	125
1980 Polar Bear	7,500		60.00	65
1980 Sea Otter	7,500		60.00	65
1979 White-Tailed Deer	7,500		60.00	105

Arctic Antics - N/A

1998 Catching a Nap	Open		17.95	18
1998 Cool Slide	Open		17.95	18
1998 Delightful Dreams	Open		17.95	18
1998 Frisky Fun	Open		17.95	18
1998 Ice Fishing	Open		17.95	18
1998 Icy Romp	Open		17.95	18
1998 Strutting Along	Open		17.95	18
1998 Winter Song	Open		17.95	18

Arctic Escapades - N/A

2000 Arctic Lullaby	Open		19.95	20
1998 Come On In	Open		19.95	20
1998 It's Too Cold	Open		19.95	20
1998 A Liitle Nudge	Open		19.95	20
1998 Peek-A-Boo	Open		19.95	20
1998 Sliding Around	Open		19.95	20
1998 Snow Much Trouble	Open		19.95	20
1998 Snuggly Snooze	Open		19.95	20
2000 Splashing for Trouble	Open		19.95	20
2000 Time to Play!	Open		19.95	20
1998 Up We Go	Open		19.95	20
2000 Watch This, Mom!	Open		19.95	20

Arrowhead Spirits - M. Richter

1997 Cry of the Full Moon	28-day		29.95	30
1997 In High Pursuit	28-day		29.95	30
1997 Nature's First Lesson	28-day		29.95	30
1996 Path of the Wolf	28-day		29.95	30
1996 Piercing The Night	28-day		29.95	30
1996 Soul of the Hunter	28-day		29.95	30

Birdhouses in Bloom - L. Yencho

1996 Blackbird's Bower	Open		14.95	15
1996 Blue Jay's Minaret	Open		14.95	15
1996 Cardinal Cottage	Open		14.95	15
1996 Carriage House Perch	Open		14.95	15
1996 Country Morning	Open		14.95	15
1996 Dove Estate	Open		14.95	15
1996 Lilac Landing	Open		14.95	15
1996 Romantic Retreat	Open		14.95	15
1996 Rosebud Cottage	Open		14.95	15
1996 Springtime Victorian	Open		14.95	15
1996 Sweet Nectar Bed & Breakfast	Open		14.95	15
1996 Vineyard Villa	Open		14.95	15

Brrtown Bears - N/A

1997 Brrtown Gliding Glee	Open		14.95	15
1997 Brrtown Journey	Open		14.95	15
1997 Brrtown School Days	Open		14.95	15
1997 The Brrtown Slide	Open		14.95	15
1997 Cool Splash	Open		14.95	15
1997 Fisherbear's Feast	Open		14.95	15
1997 Icy Encounter	Open		14.95	15
1997 Ski Breeze	Open		14.95	15

Camelot Frogs - S. Kerhli

1997 The Aristocratic Actor	Closed	N/A	19.95	20-135
1997 The Country Cook	Closed	N/A	19.95	20-150
1997 Jumping Jester	Closed	N/A	19.95	20-135
1996 King Ribbit	Closed	N/A	19.95	20-135
1997 Knight of The Lily Pad	Closed	N/A	19.95	20-95
1996 Lady of The Lily Pad	Closed	N/A	19.95	20-135
1997 The Noble Artisan	Closed	N/A	19.95	20-135
1997 Queen Ribbit	Closed	N/A	19.95	20-135
1997 The Regal Tailor	Closed	N/A	19.95	20-135
1996 Royal Ribbiteer	Closed	N/A	19.95	20-135
1996 Sir Hop A Lot	Closed	N/A	19.95	20-135
1996 Wizard of Camelot	Closed	N/A	19.95	20-85

A Celebration of Roses - N/A

1989 Brandy	Open		55.00	55
1989 Color Magic	Open		55.00	55
1989 Honor	Open		55.00	55
1989 Miss All-American Beauty	Open		55.00	55
1991 Ole'	Open		55.00	55
1990 Oregold	Open		55.00	55
1991 Paradise	Open		55.00	55
1989 Tiffany	Open		55.00	55

Cherished Teddies Miniature Nativity - P. Hillman

2000 Bearing Good Tidings	Open		29.85	30
2000 A Beary Special Family	Open		29.85	30
2000 Beary Special Guardians	Open		29.85	30
2000 Creche	Open		29.85	30
2000 Wise Men Bearing Gifts	Open		29.85	30

Cherished Teddies Village - P. Hillman

1997 Appletree Schoolhouse	Closed	1999	45.00	45
1997 Camille's Quilt Shop	Open		45.00	45
1995 A Picnic For Two	Open		45.00	45-75
1996 Sweet Treats For Teddie	Closed	1999	45.00	45
1996 Teddie's Boat Shop	Closed	1999	45.00	45-99
1997 Teddies Nursery	Open		45.00	45
1996 Toys For Teddies	Closed	1999	45.00	45-99
1996 The Wedding Gazebo	Closed	1999	45.00	44-99

Chillin' in the Sun - N/A

2001 Fun in the Sun	Open		19.95	20

Chilly's Winter Antics - N/A

2000 A Chilly Companion	Open		19.95	20
2000 It's All Downhill From Here	Open		19.95	20

Chillytown Collection - N/A

2001 Chilly's Fish Camp	Open		24.95	25
2001 Chilly's Sunspot Tanning Salon	Open		24.95	25
2001 Chilly's Warm Up Café	Open		24.95	25
2001 Chilly's Warm Woolen Wear	Open		24.95	25
2001 Northern Lights Theatre	Open		24.95	25

*Quotes have been rounded up to nearest dollar

FIGURINES

YEAR ISSUE	EDITION LIMIT	YEAR RETD.	ISSUE PRICE	*QUOTE U.S.$
Copy Cats - N/A				
1999 Hairdresser	Open		14.95	15
1998 Just A Spoonful	Open		14.95	15
1998 Kitty to the Rescue	Open		14.95	15
1999 Kitty Treats	Open		14.95	15
1998 Kitty's Special Delivery	Open		14.95	15
1999 Teacher's Pet	Open		14.95	15
Coral Reef Beauties - Everhart				
1996 Coral Paradise	Closed	2000	39.95	40
1996 Ocean's Bounty	Closed	2000	39.95	40
1996 Sentinel of the Sea	Closed	2000	39.95	40
Dale Earnhardt Good Ole Bears Figurines - B. Cleaver				
1999 Double Duty	Open		19.95	20
1999 Gassin' Around	Open		19.95	20
1999 The Intimidator	Open		19.95	20
1999 Need A Lift!	Open		19.95	20
1999 Rear Tire Changer	Open		19.95	20
2000 Racin' in Record Time	Open		19.95	20
2000 Ready, Set Go!	Open		19.95	20
2000 Victory Is Sweet	Open		19.95	20
2001 Follow the Sign	Open		19.95	20
2001 Spotting a Winner	Open		19.95	20
Dreamsicles 12 Days of Chrismtas - K. Haynes				
1999 A Partridge in a Pear Tree, Two Turtle Doves, Three French Hens	Open		24.95	25
Dreamsicles Animal Pals - K. Haynes				
1998 African Pals	Open		19.90	20
1998 Frontier Friends	Open		19.90	20
1998 Outback Chums	Open		19.90	20
1998 Striped Companions	Open		19.90	20
1998 Underwater Buddies	Open		19.90	20
1998 Woodland Playmates	Open		19.90	20
Dreamsicles Anniversary Carousel Clock - K. Haynes				
1997 Dreamsicles Anniversary Carousel Clock	Open		95.00	95
Dreamsicles in Bloom - K. Haynes				
2000 Begonia & Marigold	Open		29.90	30
1998 Daisy & Rose	Open		29.90	30
1999 Gardenia & Azalea	Open		29.90	30
1999 Jasmine & Pansy	Open		29.90	30
1998 Sunflower & Poppy	Open		29.90	30
1998 Violet & Lily	Open		29.90	30
Dreamsicles International Friends Collection - K. Haynes				
1998 I'll Always Be Your Amigo	Open		14.95	15
1998 Your Friendship Is Wünderbar	Open		14.95	15
1998 Friendship Spans All Distances	Open		14.95	15
1998 Your Friendship Is A Home Run	Open		14.95	15
Dreamsicles Rainbow Express - K. Haynes				
1998 Full Steam Ahead	Open		14.95	15
1999 Happy Endings	Open		14.95	15
1999 Hearts-A-Plenty	Open		14.95	15
1999 Hold Tight	Open		14.95	15
1999 Moon Dreaming	Open		14.95	15
1999 Pretty Packages	Open		14.95	15
1999 Rainbow Ride	Open		14.95	15
1999 Shining Star	Open		14.95	15
Early Discoveries - Adams-Hart				
1997 Curious Encounters	Open		19.95	20-55
1997 Ducky Discoveries	Closed	1999	19.95	20-55
1996 First Recital	Closed	1999	19.95	20-55
1997 Friendly Encounters	Closed	1999	19.95	20
1997 Friendly Foes	Open		19.95	20
1997 Nature's Scent	Closed	1999	19.95	20
1997 New Explorers	Closed	1999	19.95	20
1996 New Friends	Closed	1999	19.95	20
1997 Peaceful Pals	Closed	1999	19.95	20
1997 Springtime Melodies	Closed	1999	19.95	20-95
1997 Strolling Along	Closed	1999	19.95	20
1996 Sweet Nature	Open		19.95	20
Earnhardt Good Ole Bear Fans - B. Cleaver				
2001 Attitude Is Everything!	Open		19.95	20
2001 Best Seat in the House	Open		19.95	20
2001 Flat Out on Race Day	Open		19.95	20

YEAR ISSUE	EDITION LIMIT	YEAR RETD.	ISSUE PRICE	*QUOTE U.S.$
Elephant Tales - M. Adams				
1998 Cinderella	Open		17.95	18
1998 The Frog & Princess	Open		17.95	18
1998 Rapunzel	Open		17.95	18
1998 Rumpelstilskin	Open		17.95	18
1998 Sleeping Beauty	Open		17.95	18
1998 Snow White	Open		17.95	18
Exploring our Arctic World - N/A				
1998 Icy Rescue	Open		29.95	30
1998 Playful Antics	Open		29.95	30
1998 Frosty Kisses	Open		29.95	30
1998 Polar Playmates	Open		29.95	30
1998 It's Too Chilly	Open		29.95	30
1998 Snuggle Up	Open		29.95	30
1999 First Swim	Open		29.95	30
Family Affair - N/A				
2001 Careful Climb	Open		29.95	30
2001 Safe and Sound	Open		29.95	30
2000 Slippery Slide	Open		29.95	30
2000 Splash Bath	Open		29.95	30
Farm Livin' - N/A				
1999 Hittin' the Hay	Open		17.95	18
1999 A Little Squirt	Open		17.95	18
1998 Squeaky Clean	Open		17.95	18
1999 Tight Squeeze	Open		17.95	18
Farm Livin' Piglets - N/A				
1999 Fun in the Mud	Open		19.95	20
2000 The Great Escape	Open		19.95	20
1999 Hide and Seek	Open		19.95	20
1999 Out of Reach	Open		19.95	20
2000 Pig-nic Time	Open		19.95	20
1999 Scrub-A-Dub-Dub	Open		19.95	20
2001 Time to Play	Open		19.95	20
2001 Tumble Dry	Open		19.95	20
First Loves - N/A				
1999 Bobbin' At The Hop	Open		19.95	20
1998 Our 1st Soda Together	Open		19.95	20
1999 Rainy Day Romance	Open		19.95	20
1998 To My Sweet	Open		19.95	20
First on Race Day Figurine Collection - N/A				
1996 Bill Elliott	Closed	1998	45.00	45
1996 Jeff Gordon	Closed	1998	45.00	45
1996 Sterling Marlin	Closed	1998	45.00	45
Freshwater Challenge - M. Wald				
1992 Prized Catch	Open		75.00	75
1991 Rainbow Lure	Open		75.00	75
1991 The Strike	Open		75.00	75
1991 Sun Catcher	Open		75.00	75
Garden Romances Are Forever - B. Cleaver				
1997 Bundles of Love	Open		14.95	15
1997 Endless Love Songs	Open		14.95	15
1997 Falling In Love	Closed	1999	14.95	15-55
1997 Flowered With Love	Open		14.95	15
1997 Fragrant Love	Open		14.95	15
1997 Fruits of Love	Open		14.95	15
1997 Heartfelt Love	Closed	1999	14.95	15
1997 Humming With Love	Open		14.95	15
1997 Love Buds	Open		14.95	15
1997 Love Has Its Ups and Downs	Open		14.95	15
1996 Love Is In The Air	Closed	1999	14.95	15
1997 Love Pecks	Closed	1999	14.95	15
Gifts of the Ancient Spirits - S. Kerhli				
1996 Talisman of Courage	Open		79.00	79
1996 Talisman of Strength	Closed	1999	79.00	79
1995 Talisman of the Bison	Closed	1999	79.00	79
1996 Talisman of the Buffalo	Open		79.00	79
Gone With The Wind-Porcelain Trading Cards - N/A				
1995 Fire and Passion	28-day	2000	14.95	15
1995 Scarlett and Her Suitors	28-day	2000	14.95	15
1996 Portrait of Scarlett	28-day	2000	14.95	15
1996 Portrait of Rhett	28-day	2000	14.95	15
1996 The Proposal	28-day	2000	14.95	15

Collectors' Information Bureau   *Quotes have been rounded up to nearest dollar

YEAR ISSUE	EDITION LIMIT	YEAR RETD.	ISSUE PRICE	*QUOTE U.S.$
1996 Scarlett and Mammy	28-day	2000	14.95	15
1996 Rhett at Twelve Oaks	28-day	2000	14.95	15
1996 The Bold Entrance	28-day	2000	14.95	15
1996 Sunset Embrace	28-day	2000	14.95	15
1996 The Jail Scene	28-day	2000	14.95	15
1996 The Exodus	28-day	2000	14.95	15
1996 Anger Turns to Passion	28-day	2000	14.95	15
1996 The Reunion	28-day	2000	14.95	15
1997 Belle & Rhett	28-day	2000	14.95	15
1997 Portrait of Ashley	28-day	2000	14.95	15
1997 Rhett & Bonnie	28-day	2000	14.95	15
1997 Scarlett & Ashley	28-day	2000	14.95	15

Guardian of the Heavens - S. Kerhli

1999 Dreamkeeper	Open		69.00	69
1998 Star Shooter	Open		69.00	69

Guardians of Vision - N. Rose

1999 Guardian Spirit	Open		49.95	50
1999 Vision of the White Buffalo	Open		49.95	50

Happy Owlidays - W. Henry

1998 Back to Schoo-owl	Open		17.95	18
1998 Easter Owlebration	Open		17.95	18
1998 Giving Owl Thanks	Open		17.95	18
1998 Happy Owloween	Open		17.95	18
1998 Luck of the Owlrish	Open		17.95	18
1998 Owl Be Home For Christmas	Open		17.95	18
1998 Owl Be Your Valentine	Open		17.95	18
1998 Owl Dependence Day	Open		17.95	18
1998 Owl Lang Syne	Open		17.95	18
1998 Owl What a Beautiful Day	Open		17.95	18
1998 Splashin-Owl Around	Open		17.95	18
1998 Suma Dependence Day	Open		17.95	18

Heart of Nature - S. Kerhli

1999 Song of Devotion	Open		49.95	50
1999 Vision of Beauty	Open		49.95	50

Heavenly Gifts - S. Kuck

1999 Melody	Open		24.95	25

Heaven's Messenger - S. Kerhli

1999 My Spirit Soars	Open		69.95	70

Heroes of Baseball-Porcelain Baseball Cards - N/A

1990 Brooks Robinson	Open		19.50	20
1991 Casey Stengel	Open		19.50	20
1990 Duke Snider	Open		19.50	20
1991 Ernie Banks	Open		19.50	20
1991 Gil Hodges	Open		19.50	20
1991 Jackie Robinson	Open		19.50	20
1991 Mickey Mantle	Open		19.50	20
1990 Roberto Clemente	Open		19.50	20
1991 Satchel Page	Open		19.50	20
1991 Whitey Ford	Open		19.50	20
1990 Willie Mays	Open		19.50	20
1991 Yogi Berra	Open		19.50	20

The Holy Nativity - A. Piñã

2001 A Child is Born	Open		32.92	33

I Love Lucy Figurine Collection - N/A

1999 Lucy's Rhumba	95-day	2000	39.95	40

International Santa - N/A

1995 Alpine Santa	Closed	1999	55.00	55
1993 Belsnickel	Closed	1999	55.00	55
1995 Dedushka Moroz	Closed	1999	55.00	55
1992 Father Christmas	Closed	1999	55.00	55
1992 Grandfather Frost	Closed	1999	55.00	55
1993 Jolly Old St. Nick	Closed	1999	55.00	55
1993 Kris Kringle	Closed	1999	55.00	55
1994 Pére Nöel	Closed	1999	55.00	55
1992 Santa Claus	Closed	1999	55.00	55
1994 Yuletide Santa	Closed	1999	55.00	55

Jeff Gordon Good Ole Bears Figurines - B. Cleaver

1999 Champ	Open		19.95	20
1999 Double Duty	Open		19.95	20
1999 Gassin' Around	Open		19.95	20
1999 Need A Lift!	Open		19.95	20
1999 Rear Tire Changer	Open		19.95	20

Jeweled Carousel - M. Griffin

YEAR ISSUE	EDITION LIMIT	YEAR RETD.	ISSUE PRICE	*QUOTE U.S.$
1996 Amethyst Jumper	Open		55.00	55
1996 Diamond Dancer	Open		55.00	55
1996 Emerald Stander	Open		55.00	55
1996 Ruby Prancer	Open		55.00	55
1995 Sapphire Jumper	Open		55.00	55
1997 Topaz Trotter	Open		55.00	55

Legend of the Rainbow - N/A

2001 Peace	Open		29.95	30

Little Friends of the Arctic - M. Adams

1995 The Young Prince	Open		37.50	38
1995 Princely Fishing	Closed	N/A	37.50	38-75
1996 Playful Prince	Closed	N/A	37.50	38-75
1996 Snoozing Prince	Open		37.50	38
1996 Princely Disguise	Closed	N/A	37.50	50-75
1996 Slippery Prince	Closed	N/A	37.50	38-75
1996 Prince Charming	Closed	N/A	37.50	50
1996 Prince of the Mountain	Closed	N/A	37.50	38-75
1996 Frisky Prince	Closed	N/A	37.50	38
1996 Dreamy Prince	Closed	N/A	37.50	38-75

Little Messengers - P. Parkins

1997 Cleanliness Is Next To Godliness	Closed	N/A	29.95	30-135
1997 Let Your Light Shine Before All	Closed	N/A	29.95	30-125
1997 Love Is Contagious	Closed	N/A	29.95	30-135
1996 Love Is Happiness	Closed	N/A	29.95	30-125
1997 Love Is Harmony	Closed	N/A	29.95	30-150
1996 Love Is Kind	Closed	N/A	29.95	30-135
1997 Love Is Sharing	Closed	N/A	29.95	30-125
1997 Love Knows No Bounds	Closed	N/A	29.95	30-125
1996 Practice Makes Perfect	Closed	N/A	29.95	30-135
1996 Pretty Is As Pretty Does	Closed	N/A	29.95	30-135
1997 Seek And You Shall Find	Closed	N/A	29.95	30-135
1996 Love Is Patient	Closed	N/A	29.95	30-135

Little Messengers Heavenly Gardeners - P. Parkins

1998 Enjoy The Fruits of Your Labors	Open		19.95	20
1997 He Showers Us With Blessings	Open		19.95	20
1998 His Love Gives Life	Open		19.95	20
1998 Plant the Seeds of Love	Open		19.95	20
1998 Sweet Rewards	Open		19.95	20
1998 We Reap What We Sow	Open		19.95	20

Little Night Owls - D.T. Lyttleton

1990 Barn Owl	Open		45.00	45
1991 Barred Owl	Open		45.00	45
1991 Great Grey Owl	Open		45.00	45
1991 Great Horned Owl	Open		45.00	45
1991 Short-Eared Owl	Open		45.00	45
1990 Snowy Owl	Open		45.00	45
1990 Tawny Owl	Open		45.00	45
1991 White-Faced Owl	Open		45.00	45

A Maiden's Path - S. Kerhli

1999 Dreams in the Wind	Open		39.95	40
1999 Gentle Winds of Love	Open		39.95	40
2001 Journey of Peace	Open		39.95	40
2000 Love's Sweet Dream	Open		39.95	40

Makin' A Splash - B. Cleaver

1998 Splashin' Around	N/A		17.95	18
1998 Chill'n Good Time	N/A		17.95	18
1998 Bathin' Time	Open		17.95	18
1998 Frolicin' Fun	Open		17.95	18
1998 Coolin' Off	Open		17.95	18
1998 Singin' in the Snow	Open		17.95	18
1998 A Sprinklin' of Fun	Open		17.95	18
1998 Catchin' A Wave	Open		17.95	18

Masters of the Evening Wilderness - N/A

1994 The Great Snowy Owl	Open		37.50	38
1995 Autumn Barn Owls	Open		37.50	38
1995 Great Grey Owl	Open		37.50	38
1995 Great Horned Owl	Open		37.50	38
1996 Barred Owl	Open		37.50	38
1996 Screech Owl	Open		37.50	38
1996 Burrowing Owl	Open		37.50	38
1996 Eagle Owl	Open		37.50	38

Messenger of the Sky - S. Kerhli

1999 Guardian of Dreams	95-day		49.95	50

FIGURINES

Mickey Mantle Collector's Edition-Porcelain Baseball Cards - N/A

YEAR ISSUE	EDITION LIMIT	YEAR RETD.	ISSUE PRICE	*QUOTE U.S.$
1995 1952 Card #311/1969 Card #500	Open		39.90	40
1996 1956 Card #135/1965 Card #350	Open		39.90	40
1996 1953 Card #82/1964 Card #50	Open		39.90	40
1996 1957 Card #95/1959 Card #10	Open		39.90	40
1996 1958 Card #150/1962 Card #318	Open		39.90	40
1996 1959 Card #564/1961 Card #300	Open		39.90	40

Mickey Mantle Figurine Collection - N/A

YEAR ISSUE	EDITION LIMIT	YEAR RETD.	ISSUE PRICE	*QUOTE U.S.$
1995 Mickey Swings Home	Open		45.00	45-75
1996 The Switch Hitter Connects	Open		45.00	45
1996 The Ultimate Switch Hitter	Open		45.00	45
1996 On Deck	Open		45.00	45
1996 Bunting From the Left	Open		45.00	45

Mickey Mantle Sculpture - N/A

YEAR ISSUE	EDITION LIMIT	YEAR RETD.	ISSUE PRICE	*QUOTE U.S.$
1996 Tribute to a Yankee Legend	Open		195.00	195

Mother's Instinct - W. Henry

YEAR ISSUE	EDITION LIMIT	YEAR RETD.	ISSUE PRICE	*QUOTE U.S.$
1997 Mother's First Born	Closed	1999	17.95	18
1998 Mother's Guidance	Open		17.95	18
1997 Mother's Inspiration	Closed	1999	17.95	18
1998 Mother's Love	Open		17.95	18
1997 Mother's Warmth	Closed	1999	17.95	18
1997 Nourishing Mother	Open		17.95	18
1997 Picked Just For Mother	Closed	1999	17.95	18
1997 A Song For Mother	Closed	1999	17.95	18

Mystic Spirits - S. Douglas

YEAR ISSUE	EDITION LIMIT	YEAR RETD.	ISSUE PRICE	*QUOTE U.S.$
1995 Spirit of the Wolf	Closed	N/A	55.00	55-100
1995 Spirit of the Buffalo	Closed	N/A	55.00	55-100
1995 Spirit of the Golden Eagle	Closed	N/A	55.00	55
1996 Spirit of the Bear	Closed	N/A	55.00	55
1996 Spirit of the Mountain Lion	Closed	N/A	55.00	55-100
1996 Hawk Dancer	Closed	2000	55.00	55
1996 Wolf Scout	Closed	N/A	55.00	55
1996 Spirit of the Deer	Closed	N/A	55.00	55-99

Mystic Wolf Arrowhead - R. Koni

YEAR ISSUE	EDITION LIMIT	YEAR RETD.	ISSUE PRICE	*QUOTE U.S.$
1999 Twilight's Watch	Open		39.95	40
1999 Moonlit Run	Open		39.95	40
1999 Sunset Sentinel	Open		39.95	40
1999 Starlit Song	Open		39.95	40

Mystical Dreams - N/A

YEAR ISSUE	EDITION LIMIT	YEAR RETD.	ISSUE PRICE	*QUOTE U.S.$
1999 Maiden's Dream	Open		39.95	40
1999 Path of Hope	Open		39.95	40
1999 Promise of Love	Open		39.95	40

Nature's Beautiful Bonds - R. Roberts

YEAR ISSUE	EDITION LIMIT	YEAR RETD.	ISSUE PRICE	*QUOTE U.S.$
1996 A Mother's Vigil	Closed	N/A	29.95	30
1996 A Moment's Peace	Closed	N/A	29.95	30
1996 A Warm Embrace	Closed	N/A	29.95	30
1996 Safe By Mother's Side	Closed	N/A	29.95	30
1996 Curious Cub	Closed	N/A	29.95	30
1996 Under Mother's Watchful Eye	Closed	N/A	29.95	30-55
1996 Time To Rest	Closed	N/A	29.95	30
1996 Sheltered From Harm	Closed	N/A	29.95	30

Nature's Little Cherubs - J. Smith

YEAR ISSUE	EDITION LIMIT	YEAR RETD.	ISSUE PRICE	*QUOTE U.S.$
1997 Cherub of the Birds	Open		17.95	18
1997 Cherub of the Creatures	Open		17.95	18
1997 Cherub of the Flowers	Open		17.95	18
1997 Cherub of the Forest	Open		17.95	18
1997 Cherub of the Night	Open		17.95	18
1997 Cherub of the Stars	Open		17.95	18
1997 Cherub of the Sun	Open		17.95	18
1997 Cherub of the Waters	Open		17.95	18

Nature's Majestic Cats - D. Geenty

YEAR ISSUE	EDITION LIMIT	YEAR RETD.	ISSUE PRICE	*QUOTE U.S.$
1995 Tigress and Cubs	Closed	1999	55.00	55-99
1995 White Tiger & Cubs	Closed	1999	55.00	55
1996 Cougar and Cubs	Closed	1999	55.00	55-99
1996 Pride of the Lioness	Closed	1999	55.00	55-99
1996 Bobcat & Cubs	Closed	1999	55.00	55
1996 Jaguar & Cubs	Closed	1999	55.00	55
1996 Cheetah & Cubs	Closed	1999	55.00	55

Nature's Spiritual Realm - S. Kerhli

YEAR ISSUE	EDITION LIMIT	YEAR RETD.	ISSUE PRICE	*QUOTE U.S.$
1998 Spirit of the Earth	Open		69.00	69
1998 Spirit of the Fire	Open		69.00	69
1998 Spirit of the Water	Open		69.00	69
1997 Spirit of the Wind	Open		69.00	69

Nesting Instincts - R. Willis

YEAR ISSUE	EDITION LIMIT	YEAR RETD.	ISSUE PRICE	*QUOTE U.S.$
1995 By Mother's Side	Closed	1999	19.50	20
1995 Learning to Fly	Open		19.50	20
1995 Like Mother, Like Son	Closed	1999	19.50	20
1995 A Mother's Pride	Closed	1999	19.50	20
1997 Out on a Limb	Open		19.50	20
1995 Peaceful Perch	Closed	1999	19.50	20
1995 Safe and Sound	Open		19.50	20
1997 Two of a Kind	Closed	1999	19.50	20
1995 Under Mother's Wings	Closed	1999	19.50	20-55
1995 A Watchful Eye	Closed	1999	19.50	20-55

Noah's Endearing Mates - E. Harris

YEAR ISSUE	EDITION LIMIT	YEAR RETD.	ISSUE PRICE	*QUOTE U.S.$
1997 Chimpanzee Mates	Closed	1999	19.90	20-125
1997 Cow Mates	Closed	1999	19.90	20
1997 Elephant Mates	Open		19.90	20
1997 Giraffe Mates	Open		19.90	20
1997 Lion Mates	Closed	1999	19.90	55
1997 Panda Mates	Closed	1999	19.90	20-125
1997 Penguin Mates	Closed	1999	19.90	20
1997 Pig Mates	Closed	1999	19.90	20
1997 Polar Bear Mates	Closed	1999	19.90	20-125
1997 Tiger Mates	Open		19.90	20
1997 Wolf Mates	Closed	1999	19.90	20
1997 Zebra Mates	Closed	1999	19.90	20

Noble American Indian Women - N/A

YEAR ISSUE	EDITION LIMIT	YEAR RETD.	ISSUE PRICE	*QUOTE U.S.$
1994 Falling Star	Closed	1999	55.00	55
1995 Lily of the Mohawks	Closed	1999	55.00	55
1995 Lozen	Open		55.00	55
1994 Minnehaha	Closed	1999	55.00	55
1994 Pine Leaf	Closed	1999	55.00	55
1995 Pocahontas	Closed	1999	55.00	55
1993 Sacajawea	Closed	1999	55.00	55
1993 White Rose	Closed	1999	55.00	55-95

Noble Destiny - D. Geenty

YEAR ISSUE	EDITION LIMIT	YEAR RETD.	ISSUE PRICE	*QUOTE U.S.$
1999 Noble Destiny	Open		195.00	195

Noble Heritage - N/A

YEAR ISSUE	EDITION LIMIT	YEAR RETD.	ISSUE PRICE	*QUOTE U.S.$
1999 Tribal Guardians	Open		39.95	40

The Noble Swan - G. Granget

YEAR ISSUE	EDITION LIMIT	YEAR RETD.	ISSUE PRICE	*QUOTE U.S.$
1985 The Noble Swan	5,000		295.00	295

Noble Warriors - N/A

YEAR ISSUE	EDITION LIMIT	YEAR RETD.	ISSUE PRICE	*QUOTE U.S.$
1993 Deliverance	Open		135.00	135
1994 Spirit of the Plains	Open		135.00	135
1995 Top Gun	Open		135.00	135
1995 Windrider	Open		135.00	135

The Nolan Ryan Collectors Edition-Porcelain Baseball Cards - N/A

YEAR ISSUE	EDITION LIMIT	YEAR RETD.	ISSUE PRICE	*QUOTE U.S.$
1993 Angels 1972-C #595	Open		19.50	20
1993 Astros 1985-C #7	Open		19.50	20
1993 Mets 1968-C #177	Open		19.50	20
1993 Mets 1969-C #533	Open		19.50	20
1993 Rangers 1990-C #1	Open		19.50	20
1993 Rangers 1992-C #1	Open		19.50	20

North Pole Bear - T. Newsom

YEAR ISSUE	EDITION LIMIT	YEAR RETD.	ISSUE PRICE	*QUOTE U.S.$
1996 All I Want For Christmas	Open		29.95	30
1996 Beary Best Snowman	Open		29.95	30
1996 Beary Started	Open		29.95	30
1996 Papa's Cozy Chair	Open		29.95	30

Ocean Odyssey - W. Youngstrom

YEAR ISSUE	EDITION LIMIT	YEAR RETD.	ISSUE PRICE	*QUOTE U.S.$
1995 Breaching the Waters	Closed	N/A	55.00	55-100
1995 Return to Paradise	Closed	N/A	55.00	55-95
1995 Riding the Waves	Closed	N/A	55.00	55
1996 Baja Bliss	Closed	N/A	55.00	55
1996 Arctic Blue	Closed	N/A	55.00	55
1996 Splashdown	Closed	N/A	55.00	55-95
1996 Free Spirit	Closed	N/A	55.00	55-95
1996 Beluga Belles	Closed	N/A	55.00	55

Owls in Your Big Back Yard - N/A

YEAR ISSUE	EDITION LIMIT	YEAR RETD.	ISSUE PRICE	*QUOTE U.S.$
1998 Autumn Harvest	Closed	2000	17.95	18
1998 Closed for the Season	Closed	2000	17.95	18
1998 Desert Watch	Closed	2000	17.95	18

Collectors' Information Bureau   *Quotes have been rounded up to nearest dollar

YEAR ISSUE	EDITION LIMIT	YEAR RETD.	ISSUE PRICE	*QUOTE U.S.$
1998 Harvest Splendor	Closed	2000	17.95	18
1998 Sandhill Lookout	Closed	2000	17.95	18
1998 Spirit of the Woods	Closed	2000	17.95	18

Pals of the Month - M. Adams

1997 Back to School	Open		14.95	15
1997 Batter Up	Open		14.95	15
1997 Be Mine, Sweet Valentine	Open		14.95	15
1997 Bringing in the New Year	Open		14.95	15
1997 Have Yourself a Merry Xmas	Open		14.95	15
1997 July on Parade	Open		14.95	15
1997 Let's Give Thanks	Open		14.95	15
1997 Making the Grade	Open		14.95	15
1997 Singing in the Rain	Open		14.95	15
1997 Spring is Sprung	Open		14.95	15
1997 Trick or Treat	Open		14.95	15
1997 You're My Lucky Charm	Open		14.95	15

Peacemakers - S. Kerhli

2000 Path of the Bear	Open		39.95	40
1999 Path of the Buffalo	Open		39.95	40
2000 Path of the Eagle	Open		39.95	40
1999 Path of the Wolf	Open		39.95	40

Peanut Pals - T. Newsom

1996 All Aboard!	Open		19.95	20
1997 Feline Frolic	Closed	1999	19.95	20
1996 Having a Ball	Open		19.95	20
1997 The One That Got Away	Closed	1999	19.95	20
1997 Over The Bunny Slopes	Closed	1999	19.95	20
1997 Saturday Night	Closed	1999	19.95	20
1996 Shall I Pour?	Closed	1999	19.95	20-55
1997 Sidewalk Speedster	Open		19.95	20
1997 Sidewalk Surfin'	Closed	1999	19.95	20
1997 A Slice of Fun	Closed	1999	19.95	20
1996 Teeter Totter Fun!	Open		19.95	20

Penguin Polar Playmates - N/A

2000 Back Sliding	Open		14.95	15
1998 Balancing Act	Open		14.95	15
1998 Chilly	Open		14.95	15
1998 Dreaming	Open		14.95	15
2000 Flippy	Open		14.95	15
1998 Look at Me	Open		14.95	15
2000 Look Out Below	Open		14.95	15
2000 Naptime	Open		14.95	15
1998 Peek a Boo	Open		14.95	15
1998 Serenade	Open		14.95	15
1998 Slip Sliding	Open		14.95	15
1998 Splash Down	Open		14.95	15

Polar Playmates - M. Adams

1997 Belly Floppin'	Closed	1999	14.95	15
1997 Dreamin' Away	Closed	1999	14.95	15
1996 Goin' Fishin'	Closed	1999	14.95	15
1997 Hide'n & A Seek'n	Open		14.95	15
1997 Kickin' Back	Open		14.95	15
1996 Look Who's Nappin'	Closed	1999	14.95	15
1997 Lookin' Out	Open		14.95	15
1997 Reachin' for the Stars	Closed	1999	14.95	15-49
1996 Slip'n & Slide'n	Open		14.95	15
1997 Star Gazen'	Closed	1999	14.95	15-49
1997 Strollin' Along	Open		14.95	15
1997 Touchin' Toes	Open		14.95	15

Polar Playmates Playroom - N/A

1998 Just Ducky	Open		17.95	18
1998 Lazy Days	Open		17.95	18
1998 Let's Have a Ball	Open		17.95	18
1998 Play Time	Open		17.95	18
1998 Snack Time	Open		17.95	18
1998 Sweet Rewards	Open		17.95	18
1998 Time Out With Teddy	Open		17.95	18
1998 Up, Up and Away	Open		17.95	18

Portraits of Christ - Inspired by the Art of Warner Saltman

1997 Christ At Dawn	Closed	N/A	49.95	60
1996 His Presence	Closed	N/A	49.95	60-85
1997 Jesus, The Children's Friend	Closed	N/A	49.95	50-85
1997 Jesus, The Light of the World	Closed	N/A	49.95	50-85
1997 The Lord Is My Shepherd	Closed	N/A	49.95	75-99
1997 The Lord's Supper	Closed	N/A	49.95	50-100

Prayer of the Warrior - N/A

YEAR ISSUE	EDITION LIMIT	YEAR RETD.	ISSUE PRICE	*QUOTE U.S.$
1998 Buffalo Prayer	Closed	N/A	75.00	75
1997 Protector of Dreams	Closed	N/A	75.00	75
1997 Proud Dreamer	Closed	N/A	55.00	55
1997 Shield of Courage	Closed	N/A	75.00	75
1998 Victory of Prayer	Closed	N/A	75.00	75

Princess of the Plains - N/A

1995 Mountain Princess	Closed	2000	55.00	55
1995 Nature's Guardian	Closed	2000	55.00	55
1995 Noble Beauty	Closed	2000	55.00	55
1994 Noble Guardian	Closed	2000	55.00	55
1995 Proud Dreamer	Closed	2000	55.00	55
1994 Snow Princess	Closed	2000	55.00	55
1994 Wild Flower	Closed	2000	55.00	55
1995 Winter's Rose	Closed	2000	55.00	55

Protect Nature's Innocents I - R. Manning

1995 African Elephant	Closed	1999	14.95	15
1995 Giant Panda	Closed	1999	14.95	15
1995 Snow Leopard	Closed	1999	14.95	15
1995 Rhinoceros	Open		14.95	15
1996 Orangutan	Open		14.95	15
1996 Key Deer	Open		14.95	15
1996 Bengal Tiger	Closed	1999	14.95	15
1996 Pygmy Hippo	Open		14.95	15
1996 Gray Wolf	Open		14.95	15
1996 Fur Seal	Closed	1999	14.95	15
1996 Gray Kangaroo	Closed	1999	14.95	15
1996 Sea Otter	Closed	1999	14.95	15

Protect Nature's Innocents II - R. Manning

1998 Napping Time	Open		14.95	15
1998 Holding On	Open		14.95	15
1998 Wanna Ride?	Open		14.95	15
1999 Cooling Off	Closed	1999	14.95	15
1999 Butterfly Kisses	Open		14.95	15
1999 Mud Bath	Open		14.95	15

Proud Chieftains - N. Rose

1999 Spirit Quest	Open		39.95	40
1999 Sacred Journey	Open		39.95	40

Puppy Playtime Sculpture Collection - J. Lamb

1991 Cabin Fever	Closed	N/A	29.50	30
1991 Catch of the Day	Closed	N/A	29.50	30
1990 Double Take	Closed	N/A	29.50	30
1991 Fun and Games	Closed	N/A	29.50	30
1991 Getting Acquainted	Closed	N/A	29.50	30
1991 Hanging Out	Closed	N/A	29.50	30
1991 A New Leash on Life	Closed	N/A	29.50	30
1991 Weekend Gardner	Closed	N/A	29.50	30

Rainbow Dreams Lessons in Magic - T. Fabrizio

1999 Flying Lesson	Open		24.95	25
1999 Moonstruck	Open		24.95	25
2000 Morning Sun	Open		24.95	25
2001 A New Day	Open		24.95	25
2001 On My Own	Open		24.95	25
1999 Rising Star	Open		24.95	25
2000 Safe Journey	Open		24.95	25
2000 Your Dreams Come True	Open		24.95	25

Rainbow Dreams Monthly Collection - T. Fabrizio

2000 January	Open		19.95	20
2001 February	Open		19.95	20
2001 March	Open		19.95	20

Rainbow Dreams Sweet Dreams of Inspiration - T. Fabrizio

2001 Happiness	Open		29.95	30
2001 Love	Open		29.95	30
2001 Serenity	Open		29.95	30

Rainbow Dreams Sweethearts - T. Fabrizio

2000 Captive Hearts	Open		29.95	30
1999 The Courtship	Open		29.90	30
2000 Delicate Blossom	Open		31.90	32
1999 First Glance	Open		29.90	30
2000 Forever Yours	Open		29.95	30
2000 The Promise	Open		29.95	30
2000 Season of Love	Open		31.90	32
2000 Season of Romance	Open		29.95	30
1999 Tender Love	Open		31.90	32

FIGURINES

YEAR ISSUE	EDITION LIMIT	YEAR RETD.	ISSUE PRICE	*QUOTE U.S.$
Rainbow Dreams Unicorn - T. Fabrizio				
1998 Butterflies and Rainbow Skies	Open		14.95	15
1998 Where Bluebirds Fly	Open		14.95	15
1998 Meadowland Dreams	Open		14.95	15
1999 Moonbeam Dreams	Open		17.95	18
1999 Dreams Come True	Open		17.95	18
1999 Dreams Take Flight	Open		19.95	20
1999 Field of Dreams	Open		19.95	20
1999 Lazy Day Dreaming	Open		19.95	20
1999 Run with Your Dreams	Open		19.95	20
Rainbow Reef - T. Fabrizio				
1998 Buried Treasure	Open		29.95	30
1999 Castles Under the Sea	Open		29.95	30
1999 Emerald Sea	Open		29.95	30
1999 Fantasy Ride	Open		29.95	30
1998 Friends of the Sea	Open		29.95	30
1999 Splash 'N Around	Open		29.95	30
1999 Twinkling Nights	Open		29.95	30
1999 Undersea Pals	Open		29.95	30
Rainbow Reef Gifts From The Sea - T. Fabrizio				
2001 Blossoms of Happiness	Open		29.95	30
2000 Bounty of Love	Open		29.95	30
Rainbow Reef Treasures of Lost Atlantis - T. Fabrizio				
2000 The Golden Challis	Open		29.95	30
2000 The Royal Discovery	Open		29.95	30
Rainbow Reef Under The Sea - T. Fabrizio				
2000 Catch'n A Ride	Open		29.95	30
2000 Gentle Greeting	Open		29.95	30
2001 Hide 'N Seek Fun	Open		29.95	30
Realm of the Spirits - N/A				
1999 Vision from Above	Open		39.95	40
Ringling Bros. Circus Animals - P. Cozzolino				
1983 Acrobatic Seal	9,800	1999	49.50	50
1983 Baby Elephant	9,800	1999	49.50	55
1983 Miniature Show Horse	9,800	1999	49.50	68-75
1983 Mr. Chimpanzee	9,800	1999	49.50	50
1984 Parade Camel	9,800	1999	49.50	50
1983 Performing Poodles	9,800	1999	49.50	50
1984 Roaring Lion	9,800	1999	49.50	50
1983 Skating Bear	9,800	1999	49.50	50
Sacred Circle of Life - N/A				
2001 Powerful Spirit of the Wolf	Open		29.95	30
2001 Soaring Spirit of the Eagle	Open		29.95	30
Sacred Councils - S. Kerhli				
1999 Sacred Circle of the Wolf	Open		39.95	40
Sacred Crafts - N/A				
1999 Portrait of Power	Closed	2000	39.95	40
Sacred Cultures - S. Kerhli				
1998 Bravery	Open		39.95	40
1998 Courage	Open		39.95	40
1998 Protector	Open		39.95	40
1998 Strength	Open		39.95	40
1998 Vision	Open		39.95	40
1998 Wisdom	Open		39.95	40
Sacred Stones Talisman - N/A				
2000 Brave Bear	Open		19.95	20
2000 Loyal Wolf	Open		19.95	20
2000 Majestic Eagle	Open		19.95	20
2000 Mighty Buffalo	Open		19.95	20
The Sacred Village - S. Kerhli				
2000 Artist's Way	Open		39.95	40
1999 Chieftain's World	Open		39.95	40
1999 Hunter's Realm	Open		39.95	40
2000 Shaman's Secrets	Open		39.95	40
Santa Clothtique - Possible Dreams				
1992 Checking His List	Open		95.00	95
1993 Last Minute Details	Open		95.00	95
1993 Twas the Nap Before Christmas	Open		95.00	95
1994 Upon the Rooftop	Open		95.00	95
1994 O Tannenbaum!	Open		95.00	95

YEAR ISSUE	EDITION LIMIT	YEAR RETD.	ISSUE PRICE	*QUOTE U.S.$
1995 Baking Christmas Cheer	Open		95.00	95
1995 Santa to the Rescue	Open		95.00	95
1996 Toyshop Tally	Open		95.00	95
Seeing Spots - J. Smith				
1997 Spot Finds a Snowman	Open		19.95	20
1997 Spot Gets A Boo-Boo	Open		19.95	20
1997 Spot Gets Caught	Open		19.95	20
1997 Spot Goes Camping	Open		19.95	20
1997 Spot Goes On A Picnic	Open		19.95	20
1997 Spot Goes Sledding	Open		19.95	20
1997 Spot Plays With Fire Truck	Open		19.95	20
1997 Spot Sees A Crab	Open		19.95	20
1996 Spot Takes A Bath	Open		19.95	20
1997 Spot Takes A Nap	Open		19.95	20
1996 Spot Takes A Ride	Open		19.95	20
1997 Spot Visits Friends	Open		19.95	20
Shield of the Mighty Warrior - S. Kerhli				
1995 Spirit of the Grey Wolf	Closed	1999	45.00	45
1996 Spirit of the Bear	Open		45.00	45
1996 Protection of the Cougar	Open		45.00	45
1996 Protection of the Buffalo	Open		45.00	45
1996 Protection of the Bobcat	Open		45.00	45
1996 Protection of the Gray Wolf	Closed	1999	45.00	45
Snuggle - N/A				
1999 A Basket Full of Sweet Snuggles	Open		17.95	18
1999 Cleanliness is Next to Snuggliness	Open		17.95	18
1998 I Want to be Your Snuggle Bear	Open		14.95	15
1998 Peek-a-boo, Snuggle Loves You	Open		14.95	15
1999 Snuggle Hugs	Open		17.95	18
1999 Snuggle Loves Butterfly Kisses	Open		17.95	18
1999 Snuggle's Story Time	Open		17.95	18
1999 Sweet Dreams, Snuggle	Open		17.95	18
Snuggle - The Little Helper - N/A				
2000 A Helping Hand Makes Work a Breeze	Open		19.95	20
2000 A Little Tidiness Brightens the Day	Open		19.95	20
2000 A Little Warmth Goes a Long Way	Open		19.95	20
2000 A Smile Helps Lighten the Load	Open		19.95	20
2000 Smooth Away Life's Little Wrinkles	Open		19.95	20
1999 Wash Away Your Worries	Open		19.95	20
Snuggle Through the Year - N/A				
2001 Autumn Fun	Open		19.95	20
2001 Bear-ing Gifts	Open		19.95	20
2000 Fresh As A Breeze	Open		19.95	20
2000 Sun, Sand and Snuggle	Open		19.95	20
Song of the Four Winds - S. Kerhli				
2000 Ballad of the Southern Breeze	Open		39.95	40
2000 Melody of the Eastern Sky	Open		39.95	40
2000 Music of the Western Wind	Open		39.95	40
2000 Song of the Northern Tundra	Open		39.95	40
Soul of Nature - R. Sun				
2000 Cry of Strength	Open		39.95	40
1999 Eyes of Wisdom	Open		39.95	40
2000 Path of Courage	Open		39.95	40
2001 Time of Reflection	Open		39.95	40
Spirit Messengers - S. Kerhli				
1999 Message of Hope	Open		59.95	60
Spirit of the Eagle - T. Sullivan				
1994 Spirit of Independence	Open		55.00	55
1995 Blazing Majestic Skies	Open		55.00	55
1995 Noble and Free	Open		55.00	55
1995 Proud Symbol of Freedom	Open		55.00	55
1996 Legacy of Freedom	Open		55.00	55
1996 Protector of Liberty	Open		55.00	55
Spirit of the Talisman - J. Pitcher				
1999 Dawn's Majesty	Open		39.95	40
2000 Sacred Flight	Open		39.95	40
2000 Soaring Spirits	Open		39.95	40
2000 Windswept	Open		39.95	40
Spirit Vessels of the Wolf - K. Daniels				
2001 Moonlit Song	Open		29.95	30
2001 Snowswept Hunt	Open		29.95	30
2001 Waterfall Rest	Open		29.95	30

The Spirit Within - N/A

YEAR ISSUE	EDITION LIMIT	YEAR RETD.	ISSUE PRICE	*QUOTE U.S.$
2001 Midnight Call	Open		39.95	40
2001 Moonlit Run	Open		39.95	40
2001 Mystic Reflections	Open		39.95	40
2001 Starlit Song	Open		39.95	40
2001 Sunset Spirit	Open		39.95	40

STAR TREK® : First Contact: The Battle Begins - M.D. Ward

1998 U.S.S. Defiant	Closed	1999	39.95	40
1998 Borg Cube	Closed	1999	39.95	40
1998 U.S.S. Enterprise NCC-1701E	Closed	1999	39.95	40
1998 Borg Sphere	Closed	1999	39.95	40

STAR TREK®: The Next Generation-Porcelain Cards - S. Hillios

1996 Deanna Troi & Data	Closed	1998	39.90	40
1997 Inner Light & All Good Things	Closed	1998	39.90	40
1996 Jean-Luc Picard & Q	Closed	1998	39.90	40
1996 Ship In a Bottle & Best of Both Worlds	Closed	1998	39.90	40
1996 USS Enterprise NCC-1701-D & William T. Riker	Closed	1998	39.90	40
1997 Worf & Klingon Bird-of-Prey	Closed	1998	39.90	40

STAR TREK®: The Voyagers-Porcelain Cards - K. Birdsong

1996 Klingon Bird-of-Prey & Cardassian Galor Warship	28-day	1998	39.90	40
1996 Triple Nacelled USS Enterprise & USS Excelsior	28-day	1998	39.90	40
1996 USS Enterprise NCC-1701 & Klingon Battlecruiser	28-day	1998	39.90	40
1996 USS Enterprise NCC-1701-A & Ferengi Marauder	28-day	1998	39.90	40
1996 USS Enterprise NCC-1701-D & Romulan Warbird	28-day	1998	39.90	40
1996 USS Voyager NCC-74656 & USS Defiant NX-74205	28-day	1998	39.90	40

Star Wars: A New Hope-Porcelain Cards - N/A

1996 Good Versus Evil & Leia's Rescue	28-day	1999	39.90	40
1996 Hiding the Plans & Viewing the Hologram	28-day	1999	39.90	40
1996 In A Tight Spot & Millennium Falcon	28-day	1999	39.90	40
1996 Leia in Detention & Luke Skywalker	28-day	1999	39.90	40
1996 Millennium Falcon Cockpit & Capture of Leia's Ship	28-day	1999	39.90	40
1996 Obi Wan & Luke & A Daring Escape	28-day	1999	39.90	40
1996 Obi-wan Kenobi & C-3PO and R2-D2	28-day	1999	39.90	40
1996 Stormtroopers & X-Wing Attack	28-day	1999	39.90	40-100

Totem Ceremonial Masks - N/A

2001 Spirit of Abundance	Open		29.95	30
2001 Spirit of Courage	Open		29.95	30
2001 Spirit of Freedom	Open		29.95	30
2001 Spirit of Peace	Open		29.95	30
2001 Spirit of Power	Open		29.95	30
2001 Spirit of Strength	Open		29.95	30
2001 Spirit of Vision	Open		29.95	30
2001 Spirit of Wisdom	Open		29.95	30

A Touch of Heaven - S. Kuck

1997 Alexandra	Open		17.95	18
1998 Amanda	Open		17.95	18
1998 Brianna	Open		17.95	18
1998 Cassandra	Open		17.95	18
1998 Katherine	Open		17.95	18
1998 Miranda	Open		17.95	18
1998 Samantha	Open		17.95	18
1997 Victoria	Open		17.95	18

Tropical Treasures - M. Wald

1990 Beaked Coral Butterfly Fish	Open		37.50	38
1990 Blue Girdled Angel Fish	Open		37.50	38
1989 Flag-tail Surgeonfish	Open		37.50	38
1989 Pennant Butterfly Fish	Open		37.50	38
1989 Sail-finned Surgeonfish	Open		37.50	38
1989 Sea Horse	Open		37.50	38
1990 Spotted Angel Fish	Open		37.50	38
1990 Zebra Turkey Fish	Open		37.50	38

Unbridled Spirits - C. DeHaan

1994 Wild Fury	Open		135.00	135

Under The Sea Crystal Shell - R. Koni

1997 Dolphin Dance	Open		29.95	30

1997 Fluid Grace	Open		29.95	30
1997 Manatee Minuet	Open		29.95	30
1997 Orca Ballet	Open		29.95	30
1997 Seahorse Samba	Open		29.95	30
1997 Slow Dance	Open		29.95	30
1997 Soft Serenade	Open		29.95	30
1997 Tropical Twist	Open		29.95	30

Visions of Christmas - M. Griffin

1995 Gifts From St. Nick	Open		135.00	135
1994 Mrs. Claus' Kitchen	Open		135.00	135
1993 Santa's Delivery	Open		135.00	135
1993 Toys in Progress	Open		135.00	135

Warrior's Quest - S. Kerhli

1996 Courage of the Bear	Open		95.00	95
1996 Cry of the Eagle	Open		95.00	95
1996 Power of the Buffalo	Open		95.00	95
1996 Strength of the Wolf	Open		95.00	95

Waterful Ways & Elephant Days - N/A

1997 Back Splash	Closed	1999	17.95	18
1997 The Big Splash!	Open		19.95	20
1997 Catch of the Day	Open		19.95	20
1996 Clean Fun	Closed	1999	14.95	15
1997 How Does Your Garden Grow	Open		19.95	20
1997 Just Splashin' Ducky	Open		14.95	15
1997 Lazy Days	Open		19.95	20
1997 Merrily, Merrily	Open		19.95	20
1997 Rainy Day Splash	Closed	1999	19.95	20-45
1997 Sudsy Fun	Open		19.95	20
1997 Surfer Dude	Open		19.95	20
1997 Water Bathing Beauty	Open		17.95	18

The Way of the Warrior - J. Pyre

1995 One With the Eagle	Open		45.00	45
1996 Star Shooter	Open		45.00	45
1996 Bear Warrior	Open		45.00	45
1996 Beckoning Back the Buffalo	Open		45.00	45
1996 Great Feather Warrior	Open		45.00	45
1996 Calling His Guardian	Open		45.00	45

Wild and Free - C. De Haan

1996 Wild and Free	Open		195.00	195

The Wildlife Nursery - N/A

1997 Go For A Ride, Mommy?	Open		14.95	15
1997 I Love My Doll, Mommy!	Open		14.95	15
1997 I'll Spell, Mommy!	Open		14.95	15
1997 I'm So Pretty, Mommy!	Open		14.95	15
1997 Mommy, Baby Go Boom	Open		14.95	15
1997 Mommy's Little Shaker	Open		14.95	15
1997 More Milk, Mommy	Open		14.95	15
1997 More Please, Mommy!	Open		14.95	15
1997 My Duck, Mommy!	Open		14.95	15
1997 Naptime, Mommy?	Open		14.95	15
1997 Pacify Me, Mommy!	Open		14.95	15
1997 Quiet Time, Mommy	Open		14.95	15

Wolf Spirit Crystal - A. Agnew

1999 Eyes of Nature	Open		35.00	35
2000 Moonlit Cry	Open		35.00	35
2000 Noble Gaze	Open		35.00	35
2000 Bold Spirit	Open		35.00	35

Wolves of the Wilderness - D. Geenty

1995 A Wolf's Pride	Open		55.00	55
1995 Mother's Watch	Open		55.00	55
1996 Time For Play	Open		55.00	55
1996 Morning Romp	Open		55.00	55
1996 First Adventure	Open		55.00	55
1996 Tumbling Twosome	Open		55.00	55
1997 Building Young Bonds	Open		55.00	55
1997 Timid Trio	Open		55.00	55
1997 Winter Hunter	Open		55.00	55

Honeybourne Hollow/Fitz and Floyd Collectibles

Honeybourne Hollow - P. Sebern

1999 B-e-e My Honey 27/108	Open		27.50	28
1999 Building Memories 27/107	Open		25.00	25
1999 Filled With Love 27/110	Open		27.50	28
2000 Filling Daddy's Shoes 27/115	Open		22.50	23

YEAR ISSUE	EDITION LIMIT	YEAR RETD.	ISSUE PRICE	*QUOTE U.S.$
1999 Follow Your Dreams 27/100	5,000		25.00	25
1999 Friendship Keeps Us Warm 27/113	Open		25.00	25
2000 Happy Birthday (Musical) 27/120	Open		49.50	50
2000 Hush-A-Bye 27/117	Open		25.00	25
1999 I'd Follow You Anywhere 27/102	Open		22.50	23
1999 Moms Are Pretty Wonderful 27/103	Open		25.00	25
1999 Old Friends Are The Best Friends 27/106	Open		22.50	23
1999 Sending My Love 27/109	Open		25.00	25
1999 Sharing The Season 27/112	Open		25.00	25
1999 Sharing Warms The Heart 27/105	Open		25.00	25
1999 The Sky's The Limit 27/111	Open		22.50	23
2000 Special Friends Warm The Season 27/118	Open		25.00	25
1999 Time Is Precious (Millennium Ed.) 27/114	2,000		40.00	40
2000 Trick or Treat 27/116	Open		25.00	25
2000 We're Going Places (Musical) 27/119	Open		42.50	43
1999 Where Do We Go From Here? 27/101	Open		25.00	25
1999 You Take The Cake! 27/104	Open		22.50	23

Kiddie Car Classics/Hallmark Keepsake Collections

Kiddie Car Classics - D. Palmiter

YEAR ISSUE	EDITION LIMIT	YEAR RETD.	ISSUE PRICE	*QUOTE U.S.$
2000 1924 Toledo Fire Engine #6 QHG9053	29,500	2000	65.00	65
1999 1926 Speedster QHG9048	29,500	2000	90.00	90
1998 1926 Steelcraft Speedster QHG9045	Retrd.	1998	90.00	90-157
2000 1927 Gillham™ "Honeymoon Special" QHG7111	Numbrd.	2000	60.00	60
2000 1928 Jingle Bell Express QHG9065	14,500	2000	60.00	60
1998 1929 Steelcraft Roadster by Murray® QHG9040	39,500	1998	70.00	70
1998 1930 Custom Biplane QHG7104	Numbrd.	2000	55.00	55
1998 1930 Spirit of Christmas Custom Biplane QHG7105	Retrd.	1998	60.00	60-80
1999 1934 Garton® Chrysler Airflow QHG9056	Retrd.	2000	50.00	50
1999 1934 Garton® Speed Demon QHG9046	Open	2000	55.00	55
2000 1935 American Tandem QHG9058	29,500	2000	100.00	100
2000 1935 American-National Fire Tower QHG9064	14,500	2000	75.00	75
2000 1935 Gillham™ Auburn QHG9059	20,000	2000	90.00	90
2000 1935 Gillham™ Duesenberg QHG7116	14,500	2000	90.00	90
1996 1935 Steelcraft Airplane by Murray® QHG9032	Retrd.	1997	50.00	50-125
1996 1935 Steelcraft by Murray® (Luxury Edition) QHG9029	24,500	1996	65.00	65-130
2000 1935 Timmy Racer QHG7118	14,500	2000	50.00	50
2000 1935 Toledo Duesenberg Racer (5th in Winner's Circle Series) QHG9057	Retrd.	2000	55.00	55
2000 1936 Gillham™ "Birthday" Special QHG7115	14,500	2000	20.00	20
1994 1936 Steelcraft Lincoln Zephyr by Murray® QHG9015	19,500	1996	50.00	60-119
1997 1937 Garton® Ford Luxury QHG9035	Retrd.	1997	65.00	70-145
1999 1937 Steelcraft "Junior" Streamliner QHG9047	39,500	2000	70.00	70
1995 1937 Steelcraft Auburn Luxury Ed. QHG9021	24,500	1996	65.00	94-225
1995 1937 Steelcraft Chrysler Airflow by Murray® QHG9024	24,500	1996	65.00	75-119
2000 1938 American Graham Roadster QHG9060	29,500	2000	75.00	75
1997 1938 Garton® Lincoln Zephyr Luxury Edition QHX9038	Retrd.	1997	65.00	95-125
2000 1938 Toledo Air King Airplane QHG9052	Numbrd.	2000	50.00	50
1997 1939 Garton® Ford Station Wagon QHX9034	Retrd.	1999	55.00	55-100
1998 1940 Custom Roadster with Trailer QHG7106	39,500	2000	75.00	75
1997 1940 Gendron "Red Hot" Roadster, (2nd in Winner's Circle Series) QHX9037	Retrd.	1999	55.00	55-100
1999 1941 Garton® Field Ambulance QHG9049	39,500	2000	65.00	65
1999 1941 Garton® Roadster QHG9050	39,500	2000	70.00	70
1999 1941 Garton® Speed Demon, (4th in Winner's Circle Series) QHG9046	Open	2000	55.00	55
1992 1941 Murray® Airplane QHG9003	14,500	1993	50.00	300-425
1997 1941 Murray® Junior Service Truck QHG9031	Retrd.	1999	55.00	55-82
1998 1941 Steelcraft by Murray® Fire Truck QHG9042	Retrd.	2000	60.00	60
1998 1941 Steelcraft Chrysler by Murray® QHG9044	Retrd.	2000	55.00	55
1997 1941 Steelcraft Oldsmobile by Murray® QHG9036	Retrd.	1999	55.00	55
1994 1941 Steelcraft Spitfire Airplane QHG9009	19,500	1996	50.00	125-150
1995 1948 Murray® Pontiac QHG9026	Retrd.	1998	50.00	55-63
1999 1949 Gillham™ Special QHG7108	Numbrd.	1998	50.00	50
1999 1949 Gillham™ Sport (with golf bag) QHG7109	Retrd.	1998	60.00	60
2000 1949 Gillham™ Sport QHG7109	Numbrd.	1998	50.00	50
1999 1950 Holiday MURRAY® General QHG9054	Yr.Iss.	1999	60.00	60
1999 1950 Murray® General QHG9051	Numbrd.	2000	50.00	50-80
1995 1950 Murray® Torpedo QHG9020	Retrd.	1996	50.00	99-145
1998 1950s Custom Convertible QHG7101	Retrd.	1999	60.00	60
2000 1950s Red Baron Airplane QHG7114	14,500	2000	65.00	65
1992 1953 Murray® Dump Truck QHG9012	14,500	1993	48.00	150-300
1998 1955 Custom Chevy® QHG7103	Retrd.	2000	50.00	50
1992 1955 Murray® Champion QHG9008	14,500	1993	45.00	275-360
1994 1955 Murray® Dump Truck QHG9011	19,500	1996	48.00	75-135
1993 1955 Murray® Fire Chief QHG9006	19,500	1996	45.00	75-145
1992 1955 Murray® Fire Truck QHG9001	14,500	1993	50.00	275-995
1994 1955 Murray® Fire Truck QHG9010	19,500	1996	50.00	225-375
1994 1955 Murray® Ranch Wagon QHG9007	24,500	1996	48.00	75-145
1994 1955 Murray® Red Champion QHG9002	19,500	1996	45.00	80-135
1995 1955 Murray® Royal Deluxe QHG9025	29,500	1999	55.00	55-90
1992 1955 Murray® Tractor and Trailer QHG9004	14,500	1993	55.00	270-375
1994 1956 Garton® Dragnet Police Car QHG9016	24,500	1997	50.00	60-90
1996 1956 Garton® Hot Rod Racer (1st in Winner's Circle Series) QHG9028	Retrd.	1999	50.00	55-75
1994 1956 Garton® Kidillac (Sp. Ed.) QHX9094	Retrd.	1994	50.00	55-100
1996 1956 Garton® Mark V QHG9022	24,500	1997	45.00	45-75
1997 1956 Murray® Golden Eagle QHG9033	29,500	1997	50.00	55-100
2000 1957 Custom Chevy® Bel Air® QHG7117	14,500	2000	55.00	55
2000 1958 Custom Corvette QHG7112	39,500	2000	65.00	65
1994 1958 Murray® Atomic Missile QHG9018	24,500	1997	55.00	45-95
1998 1958 Murray® Champion QHG9041	Retrd.	2000	55.00	55
1995 1959 Garton® Deluxe Kidillac QHG9017	Retrd.	1996	55.00	63-90
1998 1960 Eight Ball Racer (3rd in Winner's Circle Series) QHG9039	Retrd.	2000	55.00	55
1995 1961 Garton® Casey Jones Locomotive QHG9019	Retrd.	1996	55.00	55-110
1994 1961 Murray® Circus Car QHG9014	24,500	1997	48.00	69-100
1994 1961 Murray® Speedway Pace Car QHG9013	24,500	1997	45.00	60-75
1996 1961 Murray® Super Deluxe Tractor w/Trailer QHG9027	Retrd.	1998	55.00	82-90
1995 1962 Murray® Super Deluxe Fire Truck QHG9095	Retrd.	1997	55.00	55-100
1996 1964 1/2 Ford Mustang QHG9030	Retrd.	1999	55.00	55-75
1995 1964 Garton® Tin Lizzie QHG9023	Retrd.	1997	55.00	69-100
1993 1968 Murray® Boat Jolly Roger QHG9005	19,500	1996	50.00	75-135
1998 1998 NASCAR® 50th Anniversary Custom Champion QHG9019	Retrd.	2000	60.00	60
2000 Bill Elliott NASCAR® QHG7113	39,500	2000	65.00	65
2000 Don's Street Rod QHG7102	Retrd.	1999	55.00	55
1998 NASCAR® Custom Murray® Champion QHG7110	Retrd.	2000	60.00	60
2000 Red Baron QHG7144	14,500	2000	65.00	65

Kiddie Car Classics-minis - D. Palmiter

YEAR ISSUE	EDITION LIMIT	YEAR RETD.	ISSUE PRICE	*QUOTE U.S.$
2000 1937 Murray® Steelcraft Auburn QHG2211	14,500	2000	30.00	30
1999 1941 Murray® Pursuit Airplane QHG2203	Numbrd.	2000	25.00	25

YEAR ISSUE	EDITION LIMIT	YEAR RETD.	ISSUE PRICE	*QUOTE U.S.$
2000 1941 Steelcraft Spitfire Airplane QHG2206	Numbrd.	2000	25.00	25
2000 1950 Murray® Torpedo QHG2209	Numbrd.	2000	25.00	25
1999 1953 Murray® Dump Truck QHG2201	Numbrd.	2000	25.00	25
1999 1955 Murray® Champion QHG2202	Numbrd.	2000	25.00	25-50
2000 1955 Murray® Fire Chief QHG2208	Numbrd.	2000	25.00	25
1999 1955 Murray® Fire Truck QHG2204	Numbrd.	2000	25.00	25
1999 1955 Murray® Tractor and Trailer QHG2205	Numbrd.	2000	25.00	25
2000 1956 Garton® Kiddilac QHG2210	Numbrd.	2000	25.00	25
2000 1968 Murray® Boat Jolly Roger QHG2207	Numbrd.	2000	25.00	25

Sidewalk Cruisers - D. Palmiter

YEAR ISSUE	EDITION LIMIT	YEAR RETD.	ISSUE PRICE	*QUOTE U.S.$
1998 1932 Keystone Coast-to-Coast Bus QHG6320	Retrd.	2000	45.00	45
1998 1934 Mickey Mouse Velocipede QHG6316	Retrd.	2000	48.00	48
1996 1935 American Airflow Coaster QHG6310	Retrd.	1998	48.00	48-75
1996 1935 Sky King Velocipede QHG6311	Retrd.	1999	45.00	45-75
1995 1935 Steelcraft Streamline Velocipede by Murray® QHG6306	Retrd.	1999	45.00	45-50
1998 1937 De Luxe Velocipede QHG6319	Retrd.	2000	45.00	45
2000 1937 Mickey Mouse Streamline Express Coaster Wagon QHG6322	24,500	2000	48.00	48
1997 1937 Scamp Wagon QHG6318	Retrd.	2000	48.00	48
1995 1937 Steelcraft Streamline Scooter by Murray® QHG6301	Retrd.	1997	35.00	35-90
1997 1939 American National Pedal Bike QHG6314	Retrd.	2000	38.00	38
1997 1939 Garton® Batwing Scooter QHG6317	Retrd.	2000	38.00	38-45
1995 1939 Mobo Horse QHG6304	Retrd.	1998	45.00	45-63
1995 1940 Garton® Aero Flight Wagon QHG6305	Retrd.	1998	48.00	48-63
1996 1940s (late) Mobo Sulky QHG6308	Retrd.	1999	48.00	48-119
1996 1941 Keystone Locomotive QHG6312	Retrd.	1998	38.00	25-38
1996 1950 Garton® Delivery Cycle QHG6309	Retrd.	1999	38.00	38-50
1999 1951 Hopalong Cassidy Velocipede QHG6325	24,500	2000	48.00	48
1995 1958 Murray® Police Cycle QHG6307	Retrd.	1999	55.00	55-63
1997 1960 Murray® Blaze-O-Jet Tricycle QHG6313	Retrd.	2000	45.00	45
1998 1960s Sealtest Milk Truck QHG6315	Retrd.	2000	40.00	40
1995 1963 Garton® Speedster QHG6303	Retrd.	1999	38.00	38-57
1995 1964 Garton® Super-Sonda QHG6302	Retrd.	1997	45.00	45-60

Kurt S. Adler, Inc.

Angel Darlings - N. Bailey

YEAR ISSUE	EDITION LIMIT	YEAR RETD.	ISSUE PRICE	*QUOTE U.S.$
1996 Almost Fits H4765/1	Retrd.	1998	11.00	11
1996 Bottoms Up H4765/2	Retrd.	1998	11.00	11
1996 Buddies H4765/3	Retrd.	1998	11.00	11
1996 Cuddles H4765/5	Retrd.	1998	11.00	11
1996 Dream Builders H4765/4	Retrd.	1998	11.00	11
1997 For You W7951	Retrd.	1998	21.00	21
1996 Peek-A-Boo H4765/6	Retrd.	1998	11.00	11
1997 The Secret W7950	Retrd.	1999	19.00	19
1997 Sharing W7949	Retrd.	1998	21.00	21

Birthstone Bearies - H. Adler

YEAR ISSUE	EDITION LIMIT	YEAR RETD.	ISSUE PRICE	*QUOTE U.S.$
1998 Bearie w/Heart, 4 1/2" JAN Birthstone W6900/JAN	Retrd.	1999	12.00	12
1998 Bearie w/Heart, 4 1/2" FEB Birthstone W6900/FEB	Retrd.	1999	12.00	12
1998 Bearie w/Heart, 4 1/2" MAR Birthstone W6900/MAR	Retrd.	1999	12.00	12
1998 Bearie w/Heart, 4 1/2" APR Birthstone W6900/APR	Retrd.	1999	12.00	12
1998 Bearie w/Heart, 4 1/2" MAY Birthstone W6900/MAY	Retrd.	1999	12.00	12
1998 Bearie w/Heart, 4 1/2" JUN Birthstone W6900/JUN	Retrd.	1999	12.00	12
1998 Bearie w/Heart, 4 1/2" JUL Birthstone W6900/JUL	Retrd.	1999	12.00	12
1998 Bearie w/Heart, 4 1/2" AUG Birthstone W6900/AUG	Retrd.	1999	12.00	12
1998 Bearie w/Heart, 4 1/2" SEP Birthstone W6900/SEP	Retrd.	1999	12.00	12

YEAR ISSUE	EDITION LIMIT	YEAR RETD.	ISSUE PRICE	*QUOTE U.S.$
1998 Bearie w/Heart, 4 1/2" OCT Birthstone W6900/OCT	Retrd.	1999	12.00	12
1998 Bearie w/Heart, 4 1/2" NOV Birthstone W6900/NOV	Retrd.	1999	12.00	12
1998 Bearie w/Heart, 4 1/2" DEC Birthstone W6900/DEC	Retrd.	1999	12.00	12

Christmas Legends - P.F. Bolinger

YEAR ISSUE	EDITION LIMIT	YEAR RETD.	ISSUE PRICE	*QUOTE U.S.$
1994 Aldwyn of the Greenwood J8196	Retrd.	1996	145.00	145
1994 Berwyn the Grand J8198	Retrd.	1996	175.00	175
1995 Bountiful J8234	Retrd.	1996	164.00	164
1994 Caradoc the Kind J8199	Retrd.	1999	70.00	70
1994 Florian of the Berry Bush J8199	Retrd.	1999	70.00	70
1994 Gustave the Gutsy J8199	Retrd.	1999	70.00	70
1998 Irish Santa J6623	Retrd.	1999	67.00	67
1998 Jolly Old St. Nick J6620	Retrd.	2000	50.00	50
1995 Luminatus J8241	Retrd.	1999	136.00	136
1998 Neptune Santa J3832	Retrd.	1999	60.00	60
1997 Peace Santa J6563	2,500	1999	80.00	80
1994 Silvanus the Cheerful J8197	Retrd.	1996	165.00	165

The Fabriché™ Bear & Friends Series - KSA Design Team

YEAR ISSUE	EDITION LIMIT	YEAR RETD.	ISSUE PRICE	*QUOTE U.S.$
1992 Laughing All The Way J1567	Retrd.	1994	83.00	83
1992 Not A Creature Was Stirring W1534	Retrd.	1996	67.00	67
1993 Teddy Bear Parade W1601	Retrd.	1996	73.00	73

Fabriché™ Angel Series - K.S. Adler

YEAR ISSUE	EDITION LIMIT	YEAR RETD.	ISSUE PRICE	*QUOTE U.S.$
1992 Heavenly Messenger W1584	Retrd.	1994	41.00	41

Fabriché™ Camelot Figure Series - P. Mauk

YEAR ISSUE	EDITION LIMIT	YEAR RETD.	ISSUE PRICE	*QUOTE U.S.$
1994 King Arthur J3372	7,500	1996	110.00	110
1993 Merlin the Magician J7966	7,500	1996	120.00	120
1993 Young Arthur J7967	7,500	1996	120.00	120

Fabriché™ Coca Cola Figurines - Coca-Cola

YEAR ISSUE	EDITION LIMIT	YEAR RETD.	ISSUE PRICE	*QUOTE U.S.$
2000 Coca Cola Santa in Rocking Chair W5862	Retrd.	2002	45.00	45
2001 Santa with Elves W6007	Retrd.	2002	50.00	50

Fabriché™ Holiday Figurines - KSA Design Team, unless otherwise noted

YEAR ISSUE	EDITION LIMIT	YEAR RETD.	ISSUE PRICE	*QUOTE U.S.$
2002 100 Years For Teddy Santa W6151	Open		30.00	30
1998 African American Santa, 10" W1848 - A. Epton	Retrd.	2000	50.00	50
1995 All Aboard For Christmas W1679	Retrd.	1999	56.00	56
1994 All Star Santa W1652	Retrd.	1999	56.00	56
1993 All That Jazz W1640	Retrd.	1994	67.00	67
2002 American Santa in Car W6072	Open		56.00	56
2002 America's Bravest Fireman W6086 - M. Phelps	Open		50.00	50
2002 America's Finest Policeman W6133	Open		50.00	50
2002 Anchor's Away J1703	Open		33.00	33
1992 An Apron Full of Love W1582 - M. Rothenberg	Retrd.	1996	75.00	75
1995 Armchair Quarterback W1693	Retrd.	1996	90.00	90
2002 Astaire Santa W6110 - M. Phelps	Open		56.00	56
2002 At the Helm W6070	Open		50.00	50
2002 Banner Santa W6150	Open		30.00	30
1998 Barbeque Santa W1850 - J. Adams	Retrd.	1999	72.00	72
1994 Basket of Goodies W1650	Retrd.	1996	60.00	60
2001 Beach Day W5886	Open		45.00	45
2002 Beach Patrol Santa W6105	Open		60.00	60
1998 Believe Santa ME156 - M. Engelbreit	Retrd.	2000	56.00	56
2002 Better Bundle Up W6092 - M. Rothenberg	Open		84.00	84
1992 Bringing in the Yule Log W1589 - M. Rothenberg	5,000	1996	200.00	200
1993 Bringing the Gifts W1605	Retrd.	1996	60.00	60
2002 Bundle of Toys - Black Santa W6094	Open		33.00	33
1992 Bundles of Joy W1578	Retrd.	1994	78.00	78
1995 Captain Claus W1680	Retrd.	1996	56.00	56
2000 Captain Santa Holding Boat W5851	Retrd.	2001	30.00	30
2002 Cast A Way J1701	Open		33.00	33
2000 Champion Golf Santa W5850	Open		30.00	30
1994 Checking His List W1643	Retrd.	1996	60.00	65
1993 Checking It Twice W1604	Retrd.	1997	56.00	56
1998 Chef Santa W1903 - J. Adams	Retrd.	2000	56.00	56
2001 Christmas Express W6045	Retrd.	2001	39.00	39
1992 Christmas is in the Air W1590	Retrd.	1995	110.00	125
1997 Christmas Wish List W1773	Retrd.	1999	40.00	40
2002 Coca-Cola Ladder Santa W6087 - Sundblum	Open		56.00	56

FIGURINES

YEAR ISSUE	EDITION LIMIT	YEAR RETD.	ISSUE PRICE	*QUOTE U.S.$
2002 Cool Dude J1720	Open		32.00	32
2002 Dancing Irish Santa W6162 - M. Phelps	Open		50.00	50
1995 Diet Starts Tomorrow W1691	Retrd.	1996	60.00	60
2001 Family Doctor W6033	Retrd.	2002	30.00	30
1997 Fan Mail W1804 - M. Rothenberg	Retrd.	1999	50.00	50
1995 Father Christmas W1687	Retrd.	1996	56.00	56
1994 Firefighting Friends W1654	Retrd.	1996	72.00	72
1997 For the Mrs. W1800 - V. Antonov	Retrd.	1999	42.00	42
1993 Forever Green W1607	Retrd.	1994	56.00	56
1994 Friendship W1642	Retrd.	1996	65.00	65
1997 Frosty Friends W1807	Retrd.	1997	40.00	40
2001 Gepetto Santa w/Pinocchio W5885	Retrd.	2002	45.00	45
1995 Gift From Heaven W1694	Retrd.	1996	60.00	60
1997 Gifts a Plenty W1775	Retrd.	1999	45.00	45
2002 God Bless America Santa W6062	Open		50.00	50
2001 Golfer W6046	Open		29.00	29
2002 Groovin Santa W6093	Open		40.00	40
2002 Happy Birthday Santa W6099	Open		40.00	40
1992 He Did It Again J7944 - T. Rubel	Retrd.	1996	160.00	160
1993 Here Kitty W1618 - M. Rothenberg	Retrd.	1994	90.00	125
1994 Ho, Ho, Ho Santa W1632	Retrd.	1996	56.00	56
1994 Holiday Express W1636	Retrd.	1997	100.00	100
1997 Holiday on Ice W1805 - M. Rothenberg	Retrd.	1999	135.00	135
2001 Holiday Traffic W6044	Retrd.	2002	30.00	30
1992 Homeward Bound W1568	Retrd.	1996	61.00	61
1997 House Calls W1772	Retrd.	2000	40.00	40
1992 Hugs and Kisses W1531	Retrd.	1994	67.00	67
1992 I'm Late, I'm Late J7947 - T. Rubel	Retrd.	1995	100.00	100
2000 Irish Santa "When Irish Eyes Are Smiling" (musical) W5849 - M. Phelps	Open		45.00	45
1992 It's Time To Go J7943 - T. Rubel	Retrd.	1994	150.00	150
2001 Jewelry Maker Santa W6028	Retrd.	2002	56.00	56
2001 Justice For All W6055	Retrd.	2001	33.50	34
1995 Kris Kringle W1685	Retrd.	1996	55.00	55
1997 Labor of Love W1774	Retrd.	1999	45.00	45
2002 Let's Dance W6120	Open		70.00	70
1994 Mail Must Go Through W1667 - KSA/WRG	Retrd.	1996	110.00	110
1997 Making Waves W1806	Retrd.	1999	55.00	55
2002 Merry Caroller W6106	Open		33.00	33
1992 Merry Kissmas W1548 - M. Rothenberg	Retrd.	1993	140.00	140
1995 Merry Memories W1735	Retrd.	1997	56.00	56
1994 Merry St. Nick W1641 - Giordano	Retrd.	2000	90.00	90
2001 Mountain Biker W6047	Open		60.00	60
1995 Mrs. Santa Caroller W1690 - M. Rothenberg	Retrd.	1999	70.00	70
1997 My How You Have Grown W1803 - M. Rothenberg	Retrd.	2000	75.00	75
2002 Nature Walk W6071	Open		40.00	40
1995 Night Before Christmas W1692 - Wood River Gallery	Retrd.	1996	60.00	60
2000 Noah Santa W5856	Retrd.	2001	40.00	40
2002 Noreaster Santa W6069	Open		56.00	56
2001 Northwood Santa W5884	Open		33.50	34
2001 Nutcracker Maker W5883	Open		45.00	45
1994 Officer Claus W1677	Retrd.	2000	56.00	56
1997 One More Story W1796	Retrd.	1999	55.00	55
1997 Paperwork W1776	Retrd.	2000	56.00	56
1993 Par For The Claus W1603	Retrd.	2000	60.00	60
1994 Peace Santa W1631	Retrd.	1996	60.00	60
1995 Pere Noel W1686	Retrd.	1996	55.00	55
1993 Playtime For Santa W1619	Retrd.	1994	67.00	67
2001 Professor Claus W6054	Retrd.	2001	40.00	40
1997 Puppy Love W1808	Retrd.	1999	50.00	50
1994 Santa Calls W1678 - W. Joyce	Retrd.	1996	55.00	55
1995 Santa Caroller W1689 - M. Rothenberg	Retrd.	1999	70.00	70
2000 Santa Chef w/Gingerbread House W5821	Retrd.	2001	37.00	37
1991 Santa Fiddler W1549 - M. Rothenberg	Retrd.	1992	100.00	100
1998 Santa in Police Car W1849	Retrd.	1999	45.00	45
1997 Santa on Line W1799	Retrd.	1999	50.00	50
2001 Santa Size W6032	Open		40.00	40
1992 Santa Steals A Kiss & A Cookie W1581 - M. Rothenberg	Retrd.	1994	150.00	175
1998 Santa w/Cats & Dogs W1853 - Giordano	Retrd.	1999	45.00	45
2000 Santa w/Dog W5823	Open		36.00	36
2001 Santa.com W6042	Open		50.00	50

YEAR ISSUE	EDITION LIMIT	YEAR RETD.	ISSUE PRICE	*QUOTE U.S.$
1992 Santa's Cat Nap W1504 - M. Rothenberg	Retrd.	1992	98.00	110
1994 Santa's Fishtales W1640	Retrd.	1999	60.00	60
1992 Santa's Ice Capades W1588 - M. Rothenberg	Retrd.	1995	110.00	110
2001 Santa's Serve W6043	Open		33.50	34
1994 Schussing Claus W1651	Retrd.	1996	78.00	78
2000 Scottish Santa W5877	Open		37.00	37
2001 Serving Breakfast W6053 - M. Rothenberg	Open		54.00	54
1998 Someone Special W1917 - M. Rothenberg	Retrd.	2000	50.00	50
1992 St. Nicholas The Bishop W1532	Retrd.	1997	78.00	78
1998 St. Nicholas with Tree W1851	Retrd.	2000	50.00	50
2000 St. Patrick Bishop W5822	Retrd.	2000	45.00	45
1994 Star Gazing Santa W1656 - M. Rothenberg	Retrd.	1999	120.00	120
1993 Stocking Stuffer W1622	Retrd.	1994	56.00	56
1995 Strike Up The Band W1681	Retrd.	1996	55.00	55
2001 Sweet Dreams W6051	Open		39.00	39
1998 Tee For Two W1916 - M. Rothenberg	Open		95.00	95
1995 Tee Time W1734	Retrd.	1996	60.00	60
1997 Test Drive W1802	Retrd.	2000	45.00	45
2002 Tisket a Tasket Santa W6091 - M. Rothenberg	Open		50.00	50
2001 To The Rescue W6052	Open		30.00	30
1993 Top Brass W1630	Retrd.	1995	67.00	67
1998 Tourist Santa W1915 - V. Antonov	Retrd.	2000	60.00	60
1997 Up On The Roof W1783 - Giordano	Retrd.	2000	67.00	70
2002 Vacation Time J1700	Open		33.00	33
1997 What a Catch W1801	Retrd.	1997	45.00	45
2001 Winter Games W6031	Open		40.00	40
1993 With All The Trimmings W1616	Retrd.	1999	76.00	76
1995 Woodland Santa W1731 - R. Volpi	Retrd.	1996	67.00	67
2002 Yeah Santa W6108	Open		50.00	50

Fabriché™ International Figurines - KSA Design Team, unless otherwise noted

YEAR ISSUE	EDITION LIMIT	YEAR RETD.	ISSUE PRICE	*QUOTE U.S.$
2001 American Musical Santa W5887	Open		50.00	50
2001 Bavarian Musical Santa W5882	Open		45.00	45
2002 Danny Boy W6104	Open		33.00	33
2002 Dutch Musical Santa W6103	Open		30.00	30
2001 English Father Christmas W5894	Open		50.00	50
2001 French Musical Santa W5890	Open		50.00	50
2002 German Santa W6083	Open		30.00	30
2001 Irish Musical Santa W5892	Open		50.00	50
2001 Italian Musical Santa W5891	Open		50.00	50
2002 Koala Santa W6102	Open		30.00	30
2001 Mexican Musical Santa W5889	Open		50.00	50
2001 Polish Musical Santa W5888	Open		50.00	50
2002 Russian Santa W6081	Open		30.00	30
2002 Scot Santa W6082	Open		30.00	30
2001 Scottish Musical Santa W5893	Open		50.00	50

Fabriché™ Man For All Seasons Santa, 7" - KSA Design Team, unless otherwise noted

YEAR ISSUE	EDITION LIMIT	YEAR RETD.	ISSUE PRICE	*QUOTE U.S.$
2002 Golfing Santa W6107 - Loccisand	Open		37.00	37
2002 Graduate W6080	Open		28.00	28
2002 Here Comes the Sun W6084	Open		39.00	39
2002 Irish Santa W6104	Open		33.00	33
2002 July Fourth Santa W6074	Open		30.00	30
2002 Mr. Pilgrim W6078	Open		28.00	28
2002 Mr. Pilgrim W6135	Open		25.00	25
2002 Snowbound Santa W6098	Open		40.00	40
2002 Spring Santa W6075	Open		28.00	28
2002 Too Many Cookies W6097 - Loccisand	Open		33.00	33
2002 Trick or Treat Santa W6079	Open		28.00	28
2002 Valentine Santa W6098	Open		28.00	28

Fabriché™ Santa at Home Series - M. Rothenberg

YEAR ISSUE	EDITION LIMIT	YEAR RETD.	ISSUE PRICE	*QUOTE U.S.$
1995 Baby Burping Santa W1732	Retrd.	1996	80.00	80
1994 The Christmas Waltz 1635	Retrd.	1996	135.00	135
1995 Family Portrait W1727	Retrd.	1996	140.00	140
1993 Grandpa Santa's Piggyback Ride W1621	7,500	1996	84.00	84
1995 Santa's Horsey Ride W1728	Retrd.	1997	80.00	80
1994 Santa's New Friend W1655	Retrd.	1996	110.00	110

Fabriché™ Santa's Helpers Series - M. Rothenberg

YEAR ISSUE	EDITION LIMIT	YEAR RETD.	ISSUE PRICE	*QUOTE U.S.$
1993 Little Olde Clockmaker W1629	5,000	1996	134.00	134
1992 A Stitch in Time W1591	5,000	1997	135.00	135

*Quotes have been rounded up to nearest dollar

Fabriché™ Smithsonian Museum Series - KSA/Smithsonian

YEAR ISSUE	EDITION LIMIT	YEAR RETD.	ISSUE PRICE	*QUOTE U.S.$
1992 Holiday Drive W1556	Retrd.	1995	155.00	155
1993 Holiday Flight W1617	Retrd.	1995	144.00	144
1992 Peace on Earth Angel Treetop W1583	Retrd.	1995	52.00	52
1992 Peace on Earth Flying Angel W1585	Retrd.	1995	49.00	49
1991 Santa On A Bicycle W1527	Retrd.	1994	150.00	150
1995 Toys For Good Boys and Girls W1696	Retrd.	1996	75.00	75

Fabriché™ Thomas Nast Figurines - KSA Design Team

YEAR ISSUE	EDITION LIMIT	YEAR RETD.	ISSUE PRICE	*QUOTE U.S.$
1992 Caught in the Act W1577	Retrd.	1993	133.00	133
1992 Christmas Sing-A-Long W1576	12,000	1996	110.00	110
1993 Dear Santa W1602	Retrd.	1993	110.00	110
1991 Hello! Little One W1552	12,000	1994	90.00	90

Gallery of Angels - KSA Design Team

YEAR ISSUE	EDITION LIMIT	YEAR RETD.	ISSUE PRICE	*QUOTE U.S.$
1994 Guardian Angel M1099	2,000	1996	150.00	150
1994 Unspoken Word M1100	2,000	1996	150.00	150

Halloween - P.F. Bolinger

YEAR ISSUE	EDITION LIMIT	YEAR RETD.	ISSUE PRICE	*QUOTE U.S.$
1996 Dr. Punkinstein HW535	Retrd.	1999	50.00	50
1996 Eat at Drac's HW493	Retrd.	1999	22.00	22
1996 Pumpkin Grumpkin HW494	Retrd.	1999	18.00	18
1996 Pumpkin Plumpkin HW494	Retrd.	1999	18.00	18
1996 Pumpkins Are Us HW534	Retrd.	1996	17.00	17

Helping Hand Santas - P.F. Bolinger

YEAR ISSUE	EDITION LIMIT	YEAR RETD.	ISSUE PRICE	*QUOTE U.S.$
1996 Harmonious J6509	Retrd.	1999	115.00	115
1996 Noah J6487	Retrd.	1999	56.00	56
1996 Uncle Sam J6488	Retrd.	1996	56.00	56

Ho Ho Ho Gang - P.F. Bolinger

YEAR ISSUE	EDITION LIMIT	YEAR RETD.	ISSUE PRICE	*QUOTE U.S.$
1997 Behavometer J6555	Retrd.	1999	25.00	25
1998 Born To Fish J3812	Retrd.	1999	22.00	22
1996 Box of Chocolate J6510	Retrd.	1997	33.00	33
1997 Boxers or Briefs J6559	Retrd.	1999	25.00	25
1997 Captain Noah J6550	Retrd.	1999	18.00	18
1998 Choo Choo Santa J3806	Retrd.	1999	20.00	20
1994 Christmas Goose J8201	Retrd.	1999	22.00	22
1996 Christmas Shopping Santa J6497	Retrd.	1999	22.00	22
1996 Claus-A-Lounger J6478	Retrd.	1997	33.00	33
1995 Cookie Claus J8286	Retrd.	1996	39.00	39
1995 Do Not Disturb J8233	Retrd.	1996	34.00	34
1996 Fire Department North Pole J6508	Retrd.	1999	50.00	50
1996 Fireman Santa J6476	Retrd.	1999	28.00	28
1997 Golf Heaven J6553	Retrd.	1999	25.00	25
1998 Good Luck Irish J3807	Retrd.	1999	14.00	14
1998 Good Tools J3814	Retrd.	1999	22.00	22
1998 Holy Mackerel J8201	Retrd.	1999	22.00	22
1998 I Clean Chimneys J3809	Retrd.	2000	20.00	20
1998 I Love Chocolate J6628	Retrd.	2000	25.00	25
1997 Java Jumpstart J6554	Retrd.	1999	15.00	15
1996 Joy of Cooking J6496	Retrd.	1999	28.00	28
1998 Joy Rider J3813	Retrd.	2000	23.00	23
1996 Love Santa J6493	Retrd.	1996	18.00	18
1997 Never Say Diet J6578	Retrd.	1997	15.00	15
1995 No Hair Day J8287	Retrd.	1996	50.00	50
1996 Noel Roly Poly J6489	Retrd.	1996	20.00	20
1995 North Pole (large) J8237	Retrd.	1997	56.00	56
1995 North Pole (small) J8238	Retrd.	1997	45.00	45
1997 North Pole Country Club J6557	Retrd.	2000	45.00	45
1996 North Pole Pro-Am J6479	Retrd.	2000	28.00	28
1996 On Strike For More Cookies J6506	Retrd.	1999	33.00	33
1996 Police Department North Pole J6507	Retrd.	1997	50.00	50
1996 Policeman Santa J6475	Retrd.	1999	28.00	28
1996 Psychic Santa J3810	Retrd.	1999	20.00	20
1998 Replace The Divots J3815	Retrd.	1999	22.00	22
1994 Santa Cob J8203	Retrd.	1995	28.00	28
1997 Santa With Bear J6556	Retrd.	1999	8.00	8
1997 Santa's Day Off J6558	Retrd.	1999	25.00	25
1996 Save The Reindeer J6498	Retrd.	1997	28.00	28
1997 Snowmen Are Cool J6551	Retrd.	1997	20.00	20
1996 Some Assembly Required J6477	Retrd.	1997	53.00	53
1997 Spring Sale Snowman J6549	Retrd.	1999	20.00	20
1994 Surprise J8201	Retrd.	1997	22.00	22
1998 Teddy Bear Santa J3816	Retrd.	1999	20.00	20
1998 Things Are Looking Up J3811	Retrd.	1999	14.00	14
1998 Tundra Runners J3808	Retrd.	1999	20.00	20
1998 Whoa Kitty J3805	Retrd.	1999	20.00	20
1998 Will He Make It? J8203	Retrd.	1995	28.00	28
1995 Will Work For Cookies J8235	Retrd.	1999	40.00	40
1997 Winter Fun J6552	Retrd.	1999	25.00	25

YEAR ISSUE	EDITION LIMIT	YEAR RETD.	ISSUE PRICE	*QUOTE U.S.$
1995 Wishful Thinking J8239	Retrd.	1997	32.00	32

Holly Bearies - H. Adler

YEAR ISSUE	EDITION LIMIT	YEAR RETD.	ISSUE PRICE	*QUOTE U.S.$
1996 Angel Bear J7342	Retrd.	1998	14.00	18
1998 Angel Bear, 6 1/4" W6751	Retrd.	1998	19.00	19
1996 Angel Starcatcher (Starlight Foundation) J7222	Retrd.	1996	20.00	20
1997 Angel Starcatcher II (Starlight Foundation) W6457	Retrd.	1997	20.00	20
1998 Angel Starcatcher III (Starlight Foundation) W6912	Retrd.	1998	20.00	20
1999 Angel Starcatcher IV (Starlight Foundation) W7222	Retrd.	1999	23.00	23
1998 Barbeque Bear, 3 1/2" W6933	Retrd.	1999	10.00	10
1998 Bear Angel on Cloud W6935	Retrd.	1998	14.00	15
1998 Bearie in Red Heart Dress, 6" W6754	Retrd.	1998	17.00	17
1998 Bearie in Red PJs Sitting on Box W6787	Retrd.	1998	19.00	19
1997 Bearies Mailing Packages, 5 1/2" W6443	Retrd.	1998	28.00	28
1997 Charlie The Fisherman, 8 1/4" W6448	Yr.Iss.	1997	33.50	34
1998 Father Christmas, 4" W6930	Retrd.	1998	9.00	9
1998 Holly Bearie w/Blanket & Pull Rabbit, 8" W6753	Retrd.	1998	28.00	28
1998 Merry Merry Holly Bearie, 4" W6930	Retrd.	1998	9.00	9
1996 Mother's Day Bear J7318	Retrd.	1996	15.00	16
1997 Sledding Bearies W6445	Retrd.	1998	25.00	26
1996 Teddy Tower J7221	Retrd.	1998	23.00	23
1998 Wedding Couple, 3 1/4" W6926	Retrd.	1999	10.00	10

Holly Bearies Calendar Bears - H. Adler

YEAR ISSUE	EDITION LIMIT	YEAR RETD.	ISSUE PRICE	*QUOTE U.S.$
1996 Fergus & Fritzi's Frosty Frolic, 3 3/4" J7215/Jan	Retrd.	2001	16.00	16
1996 Pinky & Victoria Are Sweeties, 3 7/8" J7215/Feb	Retrd.	2001	16.00	16
1996 Philo's Pot O Gold, 3 3/4" J7215/Mar	Retrd.	2001	16.00	16
1996 Sunshine Catching Raindrops, 3 3/4" J7215/Apr	Retrd.	2001	16.00	16
1996 Petunia & Nathan Plant Posies, 4" J7215/May	Retrd.	2001	16.00	16
1996 Thorndike & Filbert Catch Fish, 4 1/4" J7215/Jun	Retrd.	2001	16.00	16
1996 Clairmont, Dempsey & Pete, 4 1/8" J7215/Jul	Retrd.	2001	16.00	16
1996 Nicole & Nicholas Sun Bearthing, 4 7/8" J7215/Aug	Retrd.	2001	16.00	16
1996 Skeeter & Sigourney Start School, 4 1/4" J7215/Sep	Retrd.	2001	16.00	16
1996 Clara & Carnation The Kitty, 4 1/4" J7215/Oct	Retrd.	2001	16.00	16
1996 Thorndike All Dressed Up, 4 1/4" J7215/Nov	Retrd.	2001	16.00	16
1996 Grandma Gladys, 4 3/8" J7215/Dec	Retrd.	2001	16.00	16

Holly Dearies - H. Adler

YEAR ISSUE	EDITION LIMIT	YEAR RETD.	ISSUE PRICE	*QUOTE U.S.$
1998 Dearie Sliding on Ice (2 asst.) H5447	Retrd.	2000	14.00	14
1997 Santa & Reindeer (Glass Ball) J9905	Retrd.	1998	21.00	21
1997 Santa & Reindeer (Musical Glass Ball) J9906	Retrd.	1998	40.00	40
1997 Santa at the North Pole, 8" H5401	Retrd.	2001	155.00	155

Inspirational - P.F. Bolinger

YEAR ISSUE	EDITION LIMIT	YEAR RETD.	ISSUE PRICE	*QUOTE U.S.$
1997 Angel with Heart J6569	Retrd.	1999	20.00	20
1997 Noah J6487	Retrd.	1997	56.00	56
1997 Saint Francis J6585	Retrd.	1999	56.00	56

Nutcracker Suite - KSA Design Team

YEAR ISSUE	EDITION LIMIT	YEAR RETD.	ISSUE PRICE	*QUOTE U.S.$
1998 Clara w/Nutcracker W1904	Retrd.	2001	45.00	45
1998 Drosselmeir W1905	Retrd.	2001	45.00	45
1998 Mouse King W1907	Retrd.	2001	45.00	45
1998 Nutcracker Prince W1906	Retrd.	2001	45.00	45
1998 Sugar Plum Fairy W1918	Retrd.	1999	45.00	45-50

Old World Santa Series - J. Mostrom

YEAR ISSUE	EDITION LIMIT	YEAR RETD.	ISSUE PRICE	*QUOTE U.S.$
1992 Chelsea Garden Santa W2721	Retrd.	1994	33.50	34
1993 Good King Wenceslas W2928	3,000	1996	134.00	134
1992 Large Black Forest Santa W2717	Retrd.	1994	110.00	110
1992 Large Father Christmas W2719	Retrd.	1994	106.00	106
1993 Medieval King of Christmas W2881	3,000	1994	390.00	390
1992 Mrs. Claus W2714	5,000	1996	37.00	37
1992 Patriotic Santa W2720	3,000	1994	128.00	128
1992 Pere Noel W2723	Retrd.	1994	33.50	34
1992 Small Black Forest Santa W2712	Retrd.	1994	40.00	40

Kurt S. Adler, Inc.
to Legends

FIGURINES

YEAR ISSUE	EDITION LIMIT	YEAR RETD.	ISSUE PRICE	*QUOTE U.S.$
1992 Small Father Christmas W2712	Retrd.	1994	33.50	34
1992 Small Father Frost W2716	Retrd.	1994	43.00	43
1992 Small Grandfather Frost W2718	Retrd.	1994	106.00	106
1992 St. Nicholas W2713	Retrd.	1994	30.00	30
1992 Workshop Santa W2715	5,000	1997	43.00	43

Sesame Street Series - KSA/JHP

1993 Big Bird Fabriche, Figurine J7928	Retrd.	1996	60.00	60
1993 Big Bird Nutcracker H1199	Retrd.	1994	60.00	60

Snow People - P.F. Bolinger

1996 Coola Hula J6430	Retrd.	1996	20.00	20
1996 Snowpoke J6431	Retrd.	1997	28.00	28
1996 Snowy J6429	Retrd.	1997	28.00	28

Snowbearies - H. Adler

1998 Snowbearie Couple Carrying Other Snowbearie, 3 1/4" W6878	Retrd.	1998	11.00	11
1998 Snowbearie Couple Dancing on Ice Block, 3 1/4" W6878	Retrd.	1998	11.00	11
1998 Snowbearie Couple Playing on Ice Block, 3 1/4" W6878	Retrd.	1998	11.00	11
1997 Snowbearie Pair Dancing & Playing Leapfrog W6451	Retrd.	1998	9.00	9
1997 Snowbearie Pair Dancing & Playing Leapfrog W6491	Retrd.	1998	9.00	9
1997 Snowbearie w/Heart, 4 1/2" W6490	Retrd.	1998	18.00	18
1997 Snowbearies at Play W6452	Retrd.	2000	5.50	6
1997 Snowbearies at Play W6492	Retrd.	1998	5.50	6
1997 Snowbearies Hugging, 5 1/4" W6494	Retrd.	1998	20.00	20
1998 Snowbearies on Sled, set/2 W6888	Retrd.	1999	20.00	20
1998 Snowbearies on Sled, set/3 W6887	Retrd.	1999	20.00	20
1998 Snowbearies on Sled, set/4 W6886	Retrd.	1998	21.00	21
1998 Snowbearies on Sled, set/5 W6885	Retrd.	1998	22.50	23
1997 White Bear w/Ribbon & Snowflake, 8 1/2" H5651	Retrd.	1998	10.00	10

Steinbach Camelot Smoking Figure Series - KSA/Steinbach

1994 Chief Sitting Bull Smoker ES834	7,500	1998	150.00	149-190
1993 King Arthur ES832	7,500	1996	175.00	159-175
1992 Merlin The Magician ES830	7,500	1997	150.00	145-150
1994 Sir Lancelot Smoker ES833	7,500	1997	150.00	149-175

Vatican Library Collection - Vatican Library

1999 3 Angels & Baby Jesus V39	Retrd.	2000	35.00	35
1997 Holy Family Set V29	Retrd.	2000	80.00	80
1997 Three Wise Men V30	Retrd.	2000	100.00	100

Visions Of Santa Series - KSA Design Team

1992 Santa Coming Out Of Fireplace J1023	Retrd.	1993	29.00	29
1992 Santa Holding Child J826	Retrd.	1993	24.50	25
1992 Santa Spilling Bag Of Toys J1022	7,500	1994	25.50	26
1992 Santa With Little Girls On Lap J1024	7,500	1996	24.50	25
1992 Santa With Sack Holding Toy J827	7,500	1994	24.50	25
1992 Workshop Santa J825	7,500	1994	27.00	27

Lee Middleton Original Dolls

Times To Cherish - Reva Schick

2000 All Tuckered Out	Open		39.95	40
2000 Blessing of Love	Open		39.95	40
2000 Just Teething	Open		39.95	40
2000 Snuggle Bug	Open		39.95	40
2000 This Little Piggie	Open		39.95	40
2000 What a Big Boy	Open		39.95	40

Legends

Annual Collectors Edition - C. Pardell

1990 The Night Before	500	1991	990.00	1800-2535
1991 Medicine Gift of Manhood	500	1992	990.00	935-1300
1992 Spirit of the Wolf	500	1992	950.00	1073-2000
1993 Tomorrow's Warrior	500	1993	590.00	1200
1994 Guiding Hand	500	1994	590.00	875-1100
1995 Gift of the Sacred Calf	500	1995	650.00	650-900
1996 Spirit and Image	500		750.00	750

Collectors Only - Various

1993 Give Us Peace - C. Pardell	1,250	1993	270.00	350-600
1994 First Born - C. Pardell	1,250	1994	350.00	400-600
1994 River Bandits - K. Cantrell	1,250	1995	350.00	425-514

YEAR ISSUE	EDITION LIMIT	YEAR RETD.	ISSUE PRICE	*QUOTE U.S.$
1995 Sonata - K. Cantrell	1,250	1996	250.00	300-400
1995 Daydreams of Manhood - C. Pardell	2,500	1995	390.00	500
1996 Innocence Remembered - C. Pardell	Retrd.	1996	490.00	490

American Heritage - D. Edwards

1987 Grizz Country (Bronze)	Retrd.	1990	350.00	350
1987 Grizz Country (Pewter)	Retrd.	1990	370.00	370-520
1987 Winter Provisions (Bronze)	Retrd.	1990	340.00	340
1987 Winter Provisions (Pewter)	Retrd.	1990	370.00	370
1987 Wrangler's Dare (Bronze)	Retrd.	1990	630.00	630
1987 Wrangler's Dare (Pewter)	Retrd.	1990	660.00	660

American Indian Dance Premier Edition - C. Pardell

1996 Dancing Ground	750		2500.00	2500
1993 Drum Song	750	1995	2800.00	2000-3950
1994 Footprints of the Butterfly	750	1995	1800.00	1990
1994 Image of the Eagle	750	1997	1900.00	2100
1995 Spirit of the Mountain	750	1999	1750.00	1850

American West Premier Edition - C. Pardell

1992 American Horse	950	1995	1300.00	1300
1992 Defending the People	950	1999	1350.00	1450
1991 First Coup	950	1993	1150.00	1170-1430
1993 Four Bears' Challenge	950	1996	990.00	1050
1994 Season of Victory	950	1997	1500.00	1580
1991 Unexpected Rescuer	950	1991	990.00	1170-1200

The Endangered Wildlife Collection - K. Cantrell

1993 Big Pine Survivor	950	1998	390.00	390
1990 Forest Spirit	950	1991	290.00	1000
1991 Mountain Majesty	950	1997	350.00	390
1991 Old Tusker	950	1997	390.00	390
1992 Plains Monarch	950	1997	350.00	390
1994 Prairie Phantom	950	1997	370.00	390
1990 Savannah Prince	950	1997	290.00	290-350
1993 Silvertip	950	1997	370.00	390
1992 Songs of Autumn	950	1995	390.00	550
1992 Spirit Song	950	1992	350.00	500-700
1994 Twilight	950	1997	290.00	310
1992 Unchallenged	950	1996	350.00	390

Endangered Wildlife Eagle Series - K. Cantrell

1989 Aquila Libre	2,500	1995	280.00	300-400
1993 Defiance	2,500	1999	350.00	350
1992 Food Fight	2,500		650.00	750
1989 Outpost	2,500	1995	280.00	320-350
1989 Sentinel	2,500	1993	280.00	400-500
1993 Spiral Flight	2,500		290.00	300
1992 Sunday Brunch	2,500		550.00	650
1989 Unbounded	2,500	1994	280.00	240-400

Gallery Editions - Various

1994 Center Fire - W. Whitten	350		2500.00	2600
1994 Mountain Family - D. Lemon	150	1996	7900.00	8300
1996 On Wings of Eagles - D. Lemon	250		3700.00	3700
1993 Over the Rainbow - K. Cantrell	600	1995	2900.00	3850-4000
1993 Over the Rainbow AP - K. Cantrell	Retrd.	1996	4000.00	5000
1992 Resolute - C. Pardell	250	1992	7950.00	9100-12000
1993 Visionary - C. Pardell	350		7500.00	9000
1993 The Wanderer - K. Cantrell	350	1999	3500.00	3700
1996 Wind on Still Water - C. Pardell	350	1996	2500.00	4500

Hidden Images Collection - D. Lemon

1994 In Search of Bear Rock	350	1995	1300.00	1500
1995 Sensed, But Unseen	350	1995	990.00	1200
1995 Spirit	350	1997	990.00	990

Indian Arts Collection - C. Pardell

1990 Chief's Blanket	1,500	1992	350.00	600-700
1990 Indian Maiden	1,500	1997	240.00	240
1990 Indian Potter	1,500	1997	260.00	260
1990 Kachina Carver	1,500	1993	270.00	286-400
1990 Story Teller	1,500	1993	290.00	450-550

The Legacies Of The West Premier Edition - C. Pardell

1991 Defiant Comanche	950	1991	1300.00	1000-2210
1993 Eminent Crow	950	1994	1500.00	1400-1755
1994 Enduring	950	1996	1250.00	1350
1992 Esteemed Warrior	950	1992	1750.00	1850-1950
1990 Mystic Vision	950	1990	990.00	1700-2080
1991 No More, Forever	950	1992	1500.00	1690-1800
1992 Rebellious	950	1996	1500.00	1600

Collectors' Information Bureau *Quotes have been rounded up to nearest dollar

YEAR ISSUE	EDITION LIMIT	YEAR RETD.	ISSUE PRICE	*QUOTE U.S.$
1990 Victorious	950	1990	1275.00	1800-2200

The Legendary West Collection - C. Pardell

YEAR ISSUE	EDITION LIMIT	YEAR RETD.	ISSUE PRICE	*QUOTE U.S.$
1992 Beating Bad Odds	2,500		390.00	410
1989 Bustin' A Herd Quitter	2,500	1999	590.00	660
1993 Cliff Hanger	2,500	1996	990.00	1050
1992 Crazy Horse	2,500	1992	390.00	800-1100
1989 Eagle Dancer	2,500	1996	370.00	410
1993 Hunter's Brothers	2,500	1999	590.00	660
1989 Johnson's Last Fight	2,500	1991	590.00	750-1200
1990 Keeper of Eagles	2,500	1997	370.00	410
1987 Pony Express (Bronze)	2,500	N/A	320.00	320-450
1989 Pony Express (Mixed Media)	2,500		390.00	410
1987 Pony Express (Pewter)	2,500	N/A	320.00	320-450
1987 Sacajawea	2,500	1995	380.00	595
1990 Shhh	2,500		390.00	530
1990 Stand of the Sash Wearer	2,500	1996	390.00	295-410
1989 Tables Turned	2,500		680.00	750
1990 Unbridled	2,500	1996	290.00	290
1991 Warning	2,500	1997	390.00	410
1989 White Feather's Vision	2,500	1991	390.00	750

The Legendary West Premier Edition - C. Pardell

YEAR ISSUE	EDITION LIMIT	YEAR RETD.	ISSUE PRICE	*QUOTE U.S.$
1990 Crow Warrior	750	1990	1225.00	1235-2000
1992 The Final Charge	750	1992	1250.00	1300-1500
1989 Pursued	750	1989	750.00	2000-4000
1988 Red Cloud's Coup	750	1988	480.00	5000-5500
1989 Songs of Glory	750	1989	850.00	3500-3900
1991 Triumphant	750	1991	1150.00	2200-2600

Special Commissions - Various

YEAR ISSUE	EDITION LIMIT	YEAR RETD.	ISSUE PRICE	*QUOTE U.S.$
1988 Alpha Pair (Bronze) - C. Pardell	Retrd.	N/A	330.00	330
1988 Alpha Pair (Mixed Media) - C. Pardell	S/O	N/A	390.00	500-750
1988 Alpha Pair (Pewter) - C. Pardell	Retrd.	N/A	330.00	330
1991 American Allegiance - D. Edwards	1,250	1996	570.00	625
1995 Father-The Power Within - D. Medina	350		1500.00	1590
1990 Lakota Love Song - C. Pardell	Retrd.	1990	380.00	1950
1987 Mama's Joy (Bronze) - D. Edwards	Retrd.	N/A	200.00	200
1987 Mama's Joy (Pewter) - D. Edwards	Retrd.	N/A	250.00	250
1996 Proud Heritage - K. Cantrell	2,500		290.00	290
1995 Rapture - W. Whitten	350	1999	1750.00	1850
1995 Scent in the Air - K. Cantrell	750		990.00	1200
1987 Symbols of Freedom - K. Cantrell	2,500		490.00	550
1987 Wild Freedom (Bronze) - D. Edwards	Retrd.	N/A	320.00	320
1987 Wild Freedom (Pewter) - D. Edwards	Retrd.	N/A	330.00	330
1992 Yellowstone Bound - K. Cantrell	600	1994	2500.00	3120-3950

Way of the Cat Collection - K. Cantrell

YEAR ISSUE	EDITION LIMIT	YEAR RETD.	ISSUE PRICE	*QUOTE U.S.$
1996 Cat's Cradle	500	1997	790.00	790
1995 Encounter	500	1995	750.00	1100-1600

Way of the Warrior Collection - C. Pardell

YEAR ISSUE	EDITION LIMIT	YEAR RETD.	ISSUE PRICE	*QUOTE U.S.$
1991 Clan Leader	1,600	1994	170.00	195-225
1991 Elder Chief	1,600	1994	170.00	225
1991 Medicine Dancer	1,600	1994	170.00	195-225
1991 Rite of Manhood	1,600	1994	170.00	189-225
1991 Seeker of Visions	1,600	1994	170.00	195-225
1991 Tribal Defender	1,600	1994	170.00	195-225

Way of the Wolf Collection - K. Cantrell

YEAR ISSUE	EDITION LIMIT	YEAR RETD.	ISSUE PRICE	*QUOTE U.S.$
1993 Courtship	500	1993	590.00	1500
1995 Gossip Column	500	1999	1250.00	1250
1994 Missed by a Hare	500	1994	700.00	850-1100
1994 Renewal	500	1994	700.00	950-1500
1995 Stink Bomb	500	1995	750.00	750-970

Wild Realm Premier Edition - C. Pardell

YEAR ISSUE	EDITION LIMIT	YEAR RETD.	ISSUE PRICE	*QUOTE U.S.$
1989 High Spirit	1,600	1996	870.00	1000
1991 Speed Incarnate	1,600	1996	790.00	790

Lenox Classics

Lenox Classics-China Animal Sculptures - Lenox

YEAR ISSUE	EDITION LIMIT	YEAR RETD.	ISSUE PRICE	*QUOTE U.S.$
1998 Between Sea & Sky (Ivory Dolphins)	Retrd.	2000	136.00	136
1998 Eagle of Freedom (Ivory Eagle)	Retrd.	2000	160.00	160
1999 The Graceful Swan	Open		119.00	119
2002 Lenox Enchantment Cat	Open		45.00	45
1999 The Lenox Ivory Elephant	Retrd.	2002	136.00	136
1998 The Majestic Elephant (Ivory Elephant)	Retrd.	2002	136.00	136
2002 Sweet Devotion	Open		58.50	59

YEAR ISSUE	EDITION LIMIT	YEAR RETD.	ISSUE PRICE	*QUOTE U.S.$
1999 Wave Dancers	Open		119.00	119

Lenox Classics-China Annual Angel - Lenox

YEAR ISSUE	EDITION LIMIT	YEAR RETD.	ISSUE PRICE	*QUOTE U.S.$
1997 Guardian of the Stars	2,500	1999	195.00	195
1998 Guardian of Light	2,500	2000	195.00	195
1999 Guardian of The Millennium	2,000	2000	225.00	225
2000 Guardian of Song	2,500		195.00	195

Lenox Classics-China Annual Santa - Lenox

YEAR ISSUE	EDITION LIMIT	YEAR RETD.	ISSUE PRICE	*QUOTE U.S.$
1997 Santa's Joy (Santa w/Elf & Ornament)	2,500	1999	195.00	195
1998 Santa's Journey	2,500	2000	195.00	195
1999 North Pole Express	2,500	2002	195.00	195
2000 Santa's Route	2,500		195.00	195

Lenox Classics-China Away in a Manger - Lenox

YEAR ISSUE	EDITION LIMIT	YEAR RETD.	ISSUE PRICE	*QUOTE U.S.$
1996 Angel	Retrd.	1998	50.00	50
1997 Gaspar	Retrd.	1998	50.00	50
1997 Heralding Angel	Retrd.	1998	50.00	50
1996 Jesus	Retrd.	1998	40.00	40
1996 Joseph	Retrd.	1998	50.00	50
1996 Mary	Retrd.	1998	50.00	50

Lenox Classics-China Barefoot Blessings - Lenox

YEAR ISSUE	EDITION LIMIT	YEAR RETD.	ISSUE PRICE	*QUOTE U.S.$
1997 Bedtime Prayers (Girl Praying)	Retrd.	1999	60.00	60
1999 A Boy's Best Friend (African-American Boy w/Dog)	Open		60.00	60
1999 Chatterbox (Girl w/Telephone)	Retrd.	2000	60.00	60
1996 Cheerful Giver (Girl w/Vegetables)	Retrd.	1998	60.00	60
1999 First Recital	Retrd.	2000	60.00	60
1998 Friends Forever (Girl w/doll)	Retrd.	2001	60.00	60
1996 Gone Fishing (Boy w/Dog)	Retrd.	2000	60.00	60
1999 The Graduate (Graduation Boy)	Retrd.	2001	60.00	60
1998 Graduation Princess (Girl in cap & gown)	Retrd.	2000	60.00	60
1999 I Love Collecting	3,000	2001	60.00	60
1997 Just Like Mommy (Girl w/Hat)	Retrd.	2000	60.00	60
1999 Little MVP (Soccer Boy)	Retrd.	2000	60.00	60
1997 Making Friends (Girl w/Butterfly)	Retrd.	1999	60.00	60
1996 Morning Chores (Boy w/Cat)	Retrd.	1999	60.00	60
1996 Sharing Secrets (Girl w/Doll)	Retrd.	2000	60.00	60
1996 Spring Surprise (Girl w/Chick)	Retrd.	1998	60.00	60
1997 With This Kiss (Girl Bride & Boy Groom)	Retrd.	2000	145.00	145

Lenox Classics-China Disney Showcase - Lenox

YEAR ISSUE	EDITION LIMIT	YEAR RETD.	ISSUE PRICE	*QUOTE U.S.$
1999 Bashful	Numbrd.		70.00	70
2000 A Blustery Day Adventure	Open		136.00	136
1998 Cinderella	Numbrd.		125.00	125
2001 Dazzling Daisy Duck	Open		136.00	136
2001 Debonair Donald Duck	Open		136.00	136
1999 Doc	Numbrd.		79.00	79
1998 Dopey	Numbrd.		70.00	70
2000 Dumbo	Open		136.00	136
2001 The Empress of Evil	Open		125.00	125
2000 Gentleman Mickey Mouse	Open		136.00	136
2001 Goofy's Grand Evening	Open		136.00	136
1998 Grumpy	Numbrd.		70.00	70
2000 Gus	Numbrd.		79.00	79
1999 Happy	Numbrd.		79.00	79
2000 Jaq	Numbrd.		79.00	79
2001 Jiminy Cricket	Open		76.00	76
2000 Minnie Mouse's Elegant Evening	Open		136.00	136
2001 My Hand, My Heart	Open		145.00	145
2001 My Heart is Yours	Open		125.00	125
2000 The Prince	Numbrd.		125.00	125
2000 Prince Charming	Numbrd.		125.00	125
2000 Sleepy	Numbrd.		79.00	79
2000 Sneezy	Numbrd.		70.00	70
1998 Snow White	Numbrd.		125.00	125
2001 Suzy Mouse	Open		79.00	79
2001 Welcome, Luniere Style	Open		79.00	79

Lenox Classics-China Disneyana Convention - Lenox

YEAR ISSUE	EDITION LIMIT	YEAR RETD.	ISSUE PRICE	*QUOTE U.S.$
2000 Pinocchio & Jiminy Cricket	500	2000	125.00	125

Lenox Classics-China Ethnic - Lenox

YEAR ISSUE	EDITION LIMIT	YEAR RETD.	ISSUE PRICE	*QUOTE U.S.$
1999 Santa's List	2,500	2000	195.00	195

Lenox Classics-China Fantasia 2000 - Lenox

YEAR ISSUE	EDITION LIMIT	YEAR RETD.	ISSUE PRICE	*QUOTE U.S.$
2000 Sorcerer's Apprentice	2,000	2000	225.00	225
2001 While The Sorcerer's Away...	3,500		250.00	250

FIGURINES

YEAR ISSUE	EDITION LIMIT	YEAR RETD.	ISSUE PRICE	*QUOTE U.S.$
Lenox Classics-China Finishing Touches - Lenox				
1997 Checking the List (Elf w/List)	Retrd.	1999	70.00	70
1997 Hush Little Teddy (Elf w/Toy Bag)	Retrd.	1999	70.00	70
1997 Little Jingles (Elf w/Bells)	Retrd.	1999	70.00	70
1997 Loading the Sleigh (Elf w/Pkgs.)	Retrd.	1999	70.00	70
1997 Nap Time (Elf Sleeping)	Retrd.	1999	70.00	70
1997 Painting Stripes (Elf w/Brush)	Retrd.	1999	70.00	70
Lenox Classics-China Gala Fashion Figurines - Lenox				
1999 Belle of the Ball	Open		138.00	138
1999 Evening at the Opera	Open		138.00	138
2000 Ivory Centennial Ball	Open		138.00	138
2000 Ivory Debutante Ball	Open		138.00	138
Lenox Classics-China Holiday/Seasonal - Lenox				
2001 The Gingerbread Gentleman	Open		30.00	30
2001 Rudolph The Red-Nosed Reindeer	Open		50.00	50
Lenox Classics-China Inspirational - Lenox				
2001 The Angels in Adoration	Open		152.00	152
2001 The Angel's Serenade: Angel with Harp	Open		70.00	70
2001 The Angel's Serenade: Angel with Mandolin	Open		70.00	70
1999 The Children's Blessing (Jesus w/Two Children)	Retrd.	2002	136.00	136
2000 Classic Holy Family, set/3	Open		152.00	152
2002 Eternal Love	Open		45.00	45
1998 Footprints (Ivory Footprints sculpt of Jesus w/Child)	Open		152.00	152
2001 The Lenox Classic Three Kings	Open		152.00	152
2001 Nafia, Sweet Angel of Peace	Open		150.00	150
2001 The Spirit of Love	Open		138.00	138
Lenox Classics-China Ivory Garden - Lenox				
2001 Splendor of Spring	Open		45.00	45
2002 Whisper of Spring	Open		45.00	45
Lenox Classics-China Ivory Snowman - Lenox				
2000 Snowy Skier	Open		58.50	59
2001 Snowy Visitor	Open		58.50	59
1999 Special Delivery	Open		58.50	59
Lenox Classics-China Little Graces - Lenox				
1996 Enjoyment (Cherub w/Bell)	5,000	1999	95.00	95
1999 Enlightenment (African-American Cherub w/Torch)	5,000	2001	95.00	95
1998 Faith (Cherub w/ cross & flowers)	5,000	2000	95.00	95
1996 Guidance (Cherub w/Candle)	5,000	1999	95.00	95
1997 Happiness (Cherub Reclining)	5,000	2000	95.00	95
1997 Harmony (Cherub w/ Lg. Harp)	5,000	2001	95.00	95
1996 Hope (Cherub w/Star)	5,000	1999	95.00	95
1996 Innocence (Cherub w/Trumpet)	5,000	2000	95.00	95
1996 Knowledge (Cherub w/Book)	5,000	1999	95.00	95
1997 Love (Cherub w/Heart)	5,000	2000	95.00	95
1996 Peace (Cherub w/Dove)	5,000	2001	95.00	95
1999 Peaceful Messenger	5,000	2001	45.00	45
1996 Tranquility (Cherub w/Harp)	5,000	1999	95.00	95
Lenox Classics-China Moments in Life - Lenox				
2002 An Enchanting Evening	Open		175.00	175
2002 Katia's Celebration of Life	Open		138.00	138
2001 Making Memories	Open		150.00	150
2001 United in Love (Blonde)	Open		150.00	150
2001 United in Love (Brunette)	Open		150.00	150
Lenox Classics-China Mother & Child Sculpture - Lenox				
2000 Mother's Love	Open		138.00	138
2002 Mother's Makeup Artist	Open		175.00	175
2001 Mother's Precious Gift	Open		138.00	138
1999 A Time To Cherish	Open		138.00	138
Lenox Classics-China Santa and Friends - Lenox				
2001 Holding on for the Holidays	Open		150.00	150
Lenox Classics-China Statement Sculptures - Lenox				
1999 Glory of the Millennium	Open		850.00	850
Lenox Classics-China Teddy Bear Collection - Lenox				
2000 First Mate	Open		45.00	45
2000 Sailor Girl	Open		45.00	45

YEAR ISSUE	EDITION LIMIT	YEAR RETD.	ISSUE PRICE	*QUOTE U.S.$
Lenox Classics-China Victorian Ladies of Fashion - Lenox				
1998 Grand Voyage	Retrd.	2000	138.00	138
1998 Morning Promenade	Retrd.	2000	138.00	138
1999 Picnic In The Park (Lady w/Fan)	Retrd.	2000	138.00	138
1999 Shopping on Fifth Avenue	Open		138.00	138
1998 Sunday Stroll	Retrd.	2000	138.00	138
Lenox Classics-Warner Brothers Collection - Lenox				
2002 Lenox Tweety	Open		58.50	59
Lenox Classics-Wood Inspirational - Lenox				
2001 The Lenox Nativity Creche	Open		115.00	115

Lladró

Lladró Collectors Society - Lladró

1985 Little Pals S7600	Closed	1986	95.00	1900-2900
1985 LCS Plaque w/blue writing S7601	Closed	1985	35.00	75-125
1986 Little Traveler S7602	Closed	1987	95.00	999-1550
1987 Spring Bouquets S7603	Closed	1988	125.00	550-780
1988 School Days S7604	Closed	1989	125.00	450-750
1988 Flower Song S7607	Closed	1989	175.00	350-550
1989 My Buddy S7609	Closed	1990	145.00	295-450
1990 Can I Play? S7610	Closed	1991	150.00	320-495
1991 Summer Stroll S7611	Closed	1992	195.00	329-600
1991 Picture Perfect S7612	Closed	1991	350.00	359-525
1992 All Aboard S7619	Closed	1993	165.00	208-350
1992 The Voyage of Columbus LL5847	7,500	1994	1450.00	1450-1550
1993 Best Friend S7620	Closed	1994	195.00	254-320
1993 Jester's Serenade w/base LL5932	3,000	1994	1995.00	2400-2535
1994 Basket of Love S7622	Closed	1995	225.00	279-350
1994 Garden of Dreams 7634	Closed	1996	1250.00	1690-2250
1995 10 Year Society Anniversary - Ten and Growing S7635	Closed	1996	395.00	439-495
1995 Afternoon Promenade S7636	Closed	1996	240.00	275-330
1995 Now and Forever (10 year membership piece) S7642	Closed	2001	395.00	395-550
1996 Innocence In Bloom S7644	Closed	1997	250.00	250-345
1996 Where Love Begins w/base 7649	Closed	1996	895.00	1300-1500
1997 Guardian Angel 6352	Closed	1997	1300.00	1700
1997 Pocket Full of Wishes 7650	Yr.Iss.	1998	360.00	395-450
1998 Dolphins at Play 01007658	Yr.Iss.	1998	21.00	21-65
1998 Heaven and Earth 01001824	5,000	1998	725.00	725-895
1998 It Wasn't Me! 01007672	Yr.Iss.	1998	295.00	320-350
1999 Art Brings Us Together	Yr.Iss.	1999	Gift	N/A
1999 A Wish Come True 7676	Yr.Iss.	1999	340.00	340-380
1999 Scheherazade 7678	1,000	1999	975.00	975-1178
1999 Enchanted Lake 7679	4,000	1999	1225.00	1395-1600
2000 Pals Forever 7686	Yr.Iss.	2000	350.00	350
2000 A Friend For Life 7685	Yr.Iss.	2000	Gift	81
2000 Mystical Garden 6686	5,000	2001	1100.00	1100

Lladró Event Figurines - Lladró

1991 Garden Classic L7617G	Closed	1992	295.00	359-800
1992 Garden Song L7618G	Closed	1993	295.00	349-425
1993 Pick of the Litter L7621G	Closed	1994	350.00	369-450
1994 Little Riders L7623	Closed	1995	250.00	250-425
1995 For A Perfect Performance L7641	Closed	1995	310.00	429-475
1996 Destination Big Top L6245	Closed	1996	225.00	475-650
1997 Tailor Made (Event '97) L6489	Closed	1997	150.00	195-225
1997 Dreams of a Summer's Past (Event '97) L6401	Closed	1997	310.00	310-350
2000 Playing Mom 01006681	Closed	2000	295.00	295

Privilege Annual Collection - Lladró

2001 Prince of the Elves 01007690	Closed	2002	295.00	315
2002 Princess of the Fairies 01007694	Yr.Iss.		315.00	315

Privilege Collection - Lladró

2001 Garden Breeze 01013583	1,500		1800.00	1800
2001 Puppy Parade 01006784	Open		660.00	765
2001 Sincerity 01012422	Open		550.00	595
2001 Thinking of Love 01007693	4,000		1550.00	1550

Capricho - Lladró

1988 Bust w/ Black Veil & base C1538	Open		650.00	1390
1988 Small Bust w/Veil & base C1539	Closed	2001	225.00	750
1987 Orchid Arrangement C1541	Closed	1991	500.00	1700-2100
1987 Iris Arrangement C1542	Closed	1991	500.00	1000-1500
1987 Fan C1546	Closed	1988	675.00	900-1600
1987 Fan C1546.3	Closed	1988	675.00	900-1600
1987 Iris with Vase C1551	Closed	1992	110.00	375

*Quotes have been rounded up to nearest dollar

YEAR ISSUE	EDITION LIMIT	YEAR RETD.	ISSUE PRICE	*QUOTE U.S.$
1987 Flowers Chest C1572	Closed	2001	550.00	1200
1987 Flat Basket with Flowers C1575	Closed	1991	450.00	750-850
1989 White Rosary C1647	Closed	1991	290.00	340-400
1989 Romantic Lady / Black Veil w/base C1666	Closed	1993	420.00	520
1988 White Bust w/ Veil & base C5927	Open		550.00	1150
XX Special Museum Flower Basket C7606	Closed	1991	N/A	450-650

Crystal Sculptures - Lladró

1983 Frosted Bear, Head Up L04502	Closed	1983	200.00	350
1983 Frosted Bear, Head Down L04503	Closed	1983	205.00	350
1983 Frosted Bear, Head Up L04504	Closed	1983	210.00	350
1983 Frosted Bear, Head Straight L04506	Closed	1983	200.00	350
1983 Frosted Angel w/Guitar L04507	Closed	1983	165.00	325-375
1983 Frosted Angel w/Cymbal L04508	Closed	1983	165.00	375
1983 Frosted Angel w/Violin L04509	Closed	1983	165.00	375-450
1983 Frosted Geisha, Praying L04510	Closed	1983	135.00	495
1983 Frosted Geishaw/Fan L04511	Closed	1983	135.00	375
1983 Frosted Geishaw/Flowers L04512	Closed	1983	135.00	375
1983 Clear Bear, Head Straight L04513	Closed	1983	220.00	400-450
1983 Clear Bear, Head Up L04514	Closed	1983	230.00	400-450
1983 Wedding Bell	Closed	1985	35.00	195

Disneyana Limited Edition - Lladró

1992 Tinkerbell LL7518	1,500	1992	350.00	2090-3380
1993 Peter Pan LL7529	3,000	1993	400.00	726-1200
1994 Cinderella and Fairy Godmother LL7553G	2,500	1995	875.00	985-1175
1995 Sleeping Beauty Dance LL7560	1,000	1995	1280.00	1210-2275

Limited Edition - Lladró

1971 Hamlet LL1144	750	1973	125.00	2800-5200
1971 Othello and Desdemona LL1145	750	1973	275.00	2500-3000
1971 Antique Auto LL1146	750	1975	1000.00	4900-6000
1971 Floral LL1184	200	1978	400.00	2200
1971 Floral LL1185	200	1974	475.00	1800
1971 Floral LL1186	200	1976	575.00	2200
1972 Eagles LL1189	750	1978	450.00	3200-4200
1972 Sea Birds with Nest LL1194	500	1975	300.00	2750
1972 Turkey Group LL1196	350	1982	325.00	1800
1972 Peace LL1202	150	1973	550.00	7500-9500
1972 Eagle Owl LL1223	750	1983	225.00	1000-1325
1972 Hansom Carriage LL1225	750	1975	1450.00	9000
1973 Buck Hunters LL1238	800	1976	400.00	3000
1973 Turtle Doves LL1240	850	1976	250.00	2500-3000
1973 The Forest LL1243	500	1976	625.00	3300
1974 Soccer Players LL1266	500	1983	1000.00	7500
1974 Man From LaMancha LL1269	1,500	1977	700.00	3700-4500
1974 Queen Elizabeth II LL1275	250	1985	3650.00	5200
1974 Judge LL1281	1,200	1978	325.00	1650-1800
1974 Partridge LL1290G	800	1974	700.00	1200-2000
1974 The Hunt LL1308	750	1984	4750.00	6900-8300
1974 Ducks at Pond LL1317	1,200	1984	4250.00	6250-6800
1976 Impossible Dream LL1318	1,000	1983	1200.00	4500-5380
1976 Comforting Baby LL1329	750	1978	350.00	1050
1976 Mountain Country Lady LL1330	750	1983	900.00	1700
1976 My Baby LL1331	1,000	1981	275.00	900
1978 Flight of Gazelles LL1352	1,500	1984	1225.00	3100
1978 Car in Trouble LL1375	1,500	1987	3000.00	5500-7000
1978 Fearful Flight LL1377	750		7000.00	21000
1978 Henry VIII LL 1384	1,200	1993	650.00	850-1000
1981 Venus and Cupid LL1392	750	1993	1100.00	1600-2100
1982 First Date w/base LL1393	1,500		3800.00	5900
1982 Columbus LL1432G	1,200	1988	535.00	1100-1300
1983 Venetian Serenade LL1433	750	1989	2600.00	3900-5000
1985 Festival in Valencia w/base LL1457	1,500	1994	1400.00	2350
1985 Camelot LL1458	3,000	1994	950.00	1500
1985 Napoleon Planning Battle w/base LL1459	1,500	1995	825.00	1450
1985 Youthful Beauty w/base LL1461	5,000		750.00	1200
1985 Flock of Birds w/base LL1462	1,500		1060.00	1750
1985 Classic Spring LL1465	1,500	1995	620.00	1100-1300
1985 Classic Fall LL1466	1,500	1995	620.00	975-1300
1985 Valencian Couple on Horse LL1472	3,000		885.00	1550
1985 Coach XVIII Century w/base LL1485	500		14000.00	31000
1986 The New World w/base LL1486	4,000	1997	700.00	750-1350
1986 Fantasia w/base LL1487	1,000		1500.00	2700
1986 Floral Offering w/base LL1490	3,000		2500.00	4450
1986 Oriental Music w/base LL1491	5,000		1350.00	2445
1986 Three Sisters w/base LL1492	3,000		1850.00	3250

YEAR ISSUE	EDITION LIMIT	YEAR RETD.	ISSUE PRICE	*QUOTE U.S.$
1986 At the Stroke of Twelve w/base LL1493	1,500	1993	4250.00	7000-8500
1986 Hawaiian Festival w/base LL1496	4,000	1997	1850.00	3200
1987 A Sunday Drive w/base LL1510	1,000	1999	3400.00	5250
1987 Listen to Don Quixote w/base LL1520	750	1995	1800.00	2900-3200
1987 A Happy Encounter LL1523	1,500		2900.00	4900
1988 Japanese Vase LL1536	750	1989	2600.00	3450-3650
1988 Garden Party w/base LL1578	500	1999	5500.00	7250
1988 Blessed Lady w/base LL1579	1,000	1991	1150.00	3000
1988 Return to La Mancha w/base LL1580	500		6400.00	8350
1989 Southern Tea LL1597	1,000	1995	1775.00	2300-2900
1989 Kitakami w/base LL1605	500	1994	5800.00	7500-9000
1989 Mounted Warriors w/base LL1608	500		2850.00	3450
1989 Circus Parade w/base LL1609	1,000	1998	5200.00	6550
1989 "Jesus the Rock" w/base LL1615	1,000	1994	1175.00	1850-2100
1989 Hopeful Group LL1723	1,000	1993	1825.00	1825
1991 Valencian Cruise LL1731	1,000	1998	2700.00	2950
1991 Venice Vows LL1732	1,500	1998	3755.00	4100
1991 Liberty Eagle LL1738	1,500	1999	1000.00	1100
1991 Heavenly Swing LL1739	1,000		1900.00	2050
1991 Columbus, Two Routes LL1740	1,000	1995	1500.00	1650
1991 Columbus Reflecting LL1741	1,000	1994	1850.00	1995
1991 Onward! LL1742	1,000	1993	2500.00	2750-3100
1991 The Prophet LL1743	300	1997	800.00	950
1991 My Only Friend LL1744	200	1991	1400.00	1475-1700
1991 Dawn LL1745	200	1993	1200.00	2550-2637
1991 Champion LL1746	300	1994	1800.00	1950
1991 Nesting Doves LL1747	300	1994	800.00	875
1991 Comforting News LL1748	300	1997	1200.00	1345
1991 Baggy Pants LL1749	300	1994	1500.00	1650
1991 Circus Show LL1750	300	1994	1400.00	1525
1991 Maggie LL1751	300	1994	900.00	990
1991 Apple Seller LL1752	300	1994	900.00	1000-1075
1991 The Student LL1753	300	1998	1300.00	1425
1991 Tree Climbers LL1754	300	1994	1500.00	1650
1991 The Princess And The Unicorn LL1755	1,500	1994	1750.00	1950-2150
1991 Outing In Seville LL1756	500		23000.00	24500
1992 Hawaiian Ceremony LL1757	1,000		9800.00	10250
1992 Circus Time LL1758	2,500		9200.00	9650
1992 Tea In The Garden LL1759	2,000		9500.00	9750
1993 Paella Valenciano w/base LL1762	500		10000.00	10000
1993 Trusting Friends w/base LL1763	350		1200.00	1200
1993 He's My Brother w/base LL1764	350		1500.00	1500
1993 The Course of Adventure LL1765	250		1625.00	1625
1993 Ties That Bind LL1766	250		1700.00	1700
1993 Motherly Love LL1767	250		1330.00	1330
1993 Travellers' Respite w/base LL1768	250		1825.00	1960
1993 Fruitful Harvest LL1769	350	1996	1300.00	1300
1993 Gypsy Dancers LL1770	250	1995	2250.00	2500-2750
1993 Country Doctor w/base LL1771	250	1998	1475.00	1700
1993 Back To Back LL1772	350	2000	1450.00	1600-1700
1993 Mischevous Musician LL1773	350		975.00	1045
1993 A Treasured Moment w/base LL1774	350		950.00	965
1993 Oriental Garden w/base LL1775	750		22500.00	22500
1994 Conquered by Love w/base LL1776	2,500		2850.00	3000
1994 Farewell Of The Samurai w/base LL1777	2,500		3950.00	3950
1994 Pegasus w/base LL1778	1,500		1950.00	1950
1994 High Speed w/base LL1779	1,500	1998	3830.00	3830
1994 Indian Princess w/base LL1780	3,000		1630.00	1630
1994 Allegory of Time LL1781	5,000	1998	1290.00	1290
1994 Circus Fanfare w/base LL1783	1,500	1998	14240.00	14240
1994 Flower Wagon w/base LL1784	3,000		3290.00	3290
1994 Cinderella's Arrival w/base LL1785	1,500		25950.00	26400
1994 Floral Figure w/base LL1788	300	2000	2198.00	2200
1994 Natural Beauty LL1795	500		650.00	650
1994 Floral Enchantment w/base LL1796	300	1999	2990.00	3080
1995 Enchanted Outing w/base LL1797	3,000		3950.00	3950
1995 Far Away Thoughts LL1798	1,500	1997	3600.00	3600
1995 Immaculate Virgin w/base LL1799	2,000		2250.00	2250
1995 To the Rim w/base LL1800	1,500		2475.00	2475
1995 Love and Marriage w/base LL1802	1,500	2000	2650.00	2650
1995 Vision of Peace w/base LL1803	1,500		1895.00	1895
1995 Portrait of a Family w/base LL1805	2,500		1750.00	1995
1995 A Family of Love w/base LL1806	2,500		1750.00	1995
1995 A Dream of Peace w/base LL1807	2,000	1998	1160.00	1160
1995 Virgin of the Pillar LL1808	3,000	1998	650.00	650
1996 Noah w/base LL1809	1,200	1998	1720.00	1720
1996 Easter Fantasy w/base LL1810	1,000		3500.00	3500

YEAR ISSUE	EDITION LIMIT	YEAR RETD.	ISSUE PRICE	*QUOTE U.S.$
1996 Moses & The Ten Commandments w/base LL1811	1,200		1860.00	1950
1996 La Menina w/base LL1812	1,000		3850.00	3850
1997 Christmas Journey LL1813	1,000	1999	1295.00	1295
1997 Call of the Sea LL1814	500		4250.00	4250
1997 Young Beethoven LL1815	2,500		875.00	875
1997 Venetian Carnival LL1816	1,000		3400.00	3600
1997 The Burial of Christ LL1817	1,250		5300.00	6950
1997 Spring Courtship LL1818	1,500	2000	2350.00	2400
1997 Words of Love LL1819	2,000	2000	475.00	475
1997 Prince of the Sea LL1821	2,500		575.00	575
1997 Loving Couple 01001823	1,000	2000	600.00	700
1998 Pope John Paul II 01001825	2,500		600.00	675
1998 On The Balcony 01001826	1,000		3000.00	3200
1998 A Touch of Holland 01001827	300	2000	1650.00	1750
1998 Flowers of The Marsh 01011828	300	2000	1750.00	1750
1998 Flowers of The Sea 01011829	300	2000	895.00	895
1998 Woodland Treasure 01011830	300	2000	690.00	690
1998 The Poetry of Flowers 01011831	300	2000	830.00	830
1999 A Day With Mom 01011834	1,000		3450.00	3600
2001 Creativity 01011835	2,000		850.00	950
1999 Dance 01011836	2,000		1200.00	1200
1999 Bridal Bouquet 01011837	2,000		875.00	875
1999 The Awakening of Spring 01011838	500	2000	1500.00	1500
2000 Poetry 01011839	2,000		975.00	995
1999 Promises of Love 01011840	1,000		1500.00	1500
1999 Dance of the Nymphs 01001844	1,000		1450.00	1450
1999 Bumblebee Fantasy 01001845	2,000		725.00	725
1999 Butterfly Fantasy 01001846	2,000		725.00	725
1999 Celestial Journey 01001848	1,500		3900.00	3900
1999 The Annunciation 01001849	1,000		1550.00	1550
1999 Fairy of the Butterflies 01001850	1,500	2000	2150.00	2150
2000 Celestial Ascent 01001851	1,500		1300.00	1300
2000 Lozania 01001852	1,500		1900.00	1900
2000 Eros 01001853	1,000		1350.00	1350
2000 Spring's New Arrivals 01001854	1,000		1050.00	1100
2000 Summer in Saint Tropez 01001856	1,500		1250.00	1250
2000 In the Emperor's Forest 01001858	1,000		5350.00	5450
2000 Father Sun 01001859 (Millennium Collection)	500		1750.00	1750
2000 Free as the Wind 01001860	1,500		2900.00	2900
2000 Mother Earth 01001861 (Millennium Collection)	500		5450.00	5450
2000 Love's First Light 01001862	1,500		2100.00	2100
2000 A Heavenly Christmas 01001863	2,500		850.00	850
2001 The Birth of Venus 01001864	1,000		3200.00	3500
2001 Gazebo in Bloom 01001865	2,000		3500.00	3800
2001 River of Dreams 01001866	2,500		1900.00	2200
2002 Flowers of Peace 01001867	4,000		725.00	725
2001 Quiet Conversation 01001868	1,500		1995.00	2200
2002 Gondola of Love 01001870	3,000		4225.00	4225
2002 A Child's Love 01001873	1,000		1725.00	1725
2002 Waiting in the Willow 01001874	1,000		1425.00	1425
2002 Underwater Fantasy 01001875	1,500		1725.00	1725
2002 Floral Serenade 01001877	1,500		1385.00	1385
1970 Girl with Guitar LL2016	750	1982	325.00	1800-2350
1970 Madonna with Child LL2018	300	1974	450.00	1750
1971 Oriental Man LL2021	500	1983	500.00	1850
1971 The Three Graces LL2028	500	1976	950.00	6000
1971 Eve at Tree LL2029	600	1976	450.00	4000
1971 Oriental Horse LL2030	350	1983	1100.00	4000
1971 Lyric Muse LL2031	400	1982	750.00	3000
1971 Madonna and Child LL2043	300	1974	400.00	1500
1973 Peasant Woman LL2049	750	1977	200.00	1300
1973 Passionate Dance LL2051	500	1975	375.00	4500
1977 St. Theresa LL2061	1,200	1987	387.50	1600
1977 Concerto LL2063	1,200	1988	500.00	1235
1977 Flying Partridges LL2064	1,200	1987	1750.00	4300
1987 Christopher Columbus w/base LL2176	1,000	1995	1000.00	1350
1990 Invincible w/base LL2188	300		1100.00	1250
1993 Flight of Fancy w/base LL2243	300	1995	1400.00	1400
1993 The Awakening w/base LL2244	300	2000	1200.00	1200
1993 Inspired Voyage w/base LL2245	1,000	1998	4800.00	4800
1993 Days of Yore w/base LL2248	1,000		1950.00	2050
1993 Holiday Glow w/base LL2249	1,500	1998	750.00	750
1993 Autumn Glow w/base LL2250	1,500	1998	750.00	750
1993 Humble Grace w/base LL2255	2,000		2150.00	2150
2001 Scent of a Flower 01012426	1,000		1100.00	1200
2002 Flowers From Tahiti 01012442	1,000		2295.00	2295
1983 Dawn w/base LL3000	300	1994	325.00	550
1983 Monks w/base LL3001	300	1993	1675.00	2550

YEAR ISSUE	EDITION LIMIT	YEAR RETD.	ISSUE PRICE	*QUOTE U.S.$
1983 Waiting w/base LL3002	125	1990	1550.00	1900
1983 Indolence LL3003	150	1993	1465.00	2100
1983 Venus in the Bath LL3005	200	1991	1175.00	1450
1987 Classic Beauty w/base LL3012	500		1300.00	1900
1987 Youthful Innocence w/base LL3013	500	1998	1300.00	2300
1987 The Nymph w/base LL3014	250		1000.00	1450
1987 Dignity w/base LL3015	150		1400.00	1900
1988 Passion w/base LL3016	750	1998	865.00	1250
1988 Muse w/base LL3017	300	1993	650.00	875
1988 Cellist w/base LL3018	300	1993	650.00	875
1988 True Affection w/base LL3019	300	1998	750.00	1100-1155
1989 Demureness w/base LL3020	300	1993	400.00	700-825
1990 Daydreaming w/base LL3022	500		550.00	775
1990 After The Bath w/base LL3023	300	1991	350.00	975-1450
1990 Discoveries w/Base LL3024	100	1994	1500.00	1750
1991 Resting Nude LL3025	200	1993	650.00	1000-1500
1991 Unadorned Beauty LL3026	200		1700.00	1850
1994 Ebony w/base LL3027	300	1998	1295.00	1295
1994 Modesty w/base LL3028	300		1295.00	1295
1994 Danae LL3029	300		2880.00	3900
1995 Nude Kneeling LL3030	300		975.00	975
1995 Resting LL3031	300	1998	975.00	995
1982 Elk LL3501	500	1987	950.00	1200
1978 Nude with Dove LL3503	1,500	1981	250.00	700-1250
1978 The Rescue LL3504	1,500	1987	2900.00	3500-5000
1978 St. Michael w/base LL3515	1,500	1988	2200.00	4900
1980 Turtle Dove Nest w/base LL3519	1,200	1995	3600.00	6100
1980 Turtle Dove Group w/base LL3520	750	1998	6800.00	11900
1981 Philippine Folklore LL3522	1,500	1995	1450.00	2400
1981 Nest of Eagles w/base LL3523	300	1994	6900.00	11500
1981 Drum Beats/Watusi Queen w/base LL3524	1,500	1994	1875.00	3100
1982 Togetherness LL3527	75	1987	375.00	1100
1982 Wrestling LL3528	50	1987	950.00	1125-1850
1982 Companionship w/base LL3529	65	1995	1000.00	1790
1982 Anxiety w/base LL3530	125	1993	1075.00	1875
1982 Victory LL3531	90	1984	1500.00	1800
1982 Plentitude LL3532	50	1984	1000.00	1375
1982 The Observer w/base LL3533	115	1993	900.00	1700
1982 In the Distance LL3534	75	1986	525.00	1300
1982 Slave LL3535	50	1986	950.00	1200
1982 Relaxation LL3536	100	1983	525.00	1100
1982 Dreaming w/base LL3537	250	1993	475.00	1475
1982 Youth LL3538	250	1988	525.00	1000
1982 Dantiness LL3539	100	1983	1000.00	1400
1982 Pose LL3540	100	1986	1250.00	1450
1982 Tranquility LL3541	75	1983	1000.00	1400
1982 Yoga LL3542	125	1991	650.00	1000
1982 Demure LL3543	100	1986	1250.00	1700
1982 Reflections w/base LL3544	75	1995	650.00	1050
1982 Adoration LL3545	150	1990	1050.00	1600
1982 African Woman LL3546	50	1983	1300.00	3500
1982 Reclining Nude LL3547	75	1983	650.00	975
1982 Serenity w/base LL3548	300	1993	925.00	925-1550
1982 Reposing LL3549	300	1986	425.00	575
1982 Boxer w/base LL3550	300	1993	850.00	1450
1982 Bather LL3551	300	1988	975.00	1300
1982 Blue God LL3552	1,500	1994	900.00	1575
1982 Fire Bird LL3553	1,500	1994	800.00	1350
1982 Desert People w/base LL3555	750	1986	1680.00	3100
1982 Road to Mandalay LL3556	750	1989	1390.00	2100
1982 Jesus in Tiberias w/base LL3557	1,200		2600.00	5450
1992 The Reader LL3560	200	2000	2650.00	2815
1993 Trail Boss LL3561M	1,500	1998	2450.00	2595
1993 Indian Brave LL3562M	1,500	1998	2250.00	2250
1994 Saint James The Apostle w/base LL3563	1,000		950.00	950
1994 Gentle Moment w/base LL3564	1,000		1795.00	1850
1994 At Peace w/base LL3565	1,000		1650.00	1750
1994 Indian Chief w/base LL3566	3,000	1998	1095.00	1095
1994 Trapper w/base LL3567	3,000	1998	950.00	950
1994 American Cowboy w/base LL3568	3,000	1998	950.00	950
1994 A Moment's Pause w/base LL3569	3,500		1495.00	1650
1994 Ethereal Music w/base LL3570	1,000		2450.00	2500
1994 At The Helm w/base LL3571	3,500	1998	1495.00	1495
1994 Proud Warrior w/base LL3572	3,000		995.00	995
1995 Golgotha w/base LL3573	1,000	2000	1650.00	1650
1995 Test of Strength LL3574	1,000		950.00	950
1996 Samurai LL3575	1,000		1725.00	1725
1996 Playing the Blues w/base LL3576	1,000		2160.00	2160
1997 Man of the Sea LL3577	1,000		1850.00	1850

YEAR ISSUE	EDITION LIMIT	YEAR RETD.	ISSUE PRICE	*QUOTE U.S.$
1999 A Soft Refrain LL3578	1,000		1330.00	1400
1999 Sweet Enchantment LL3579	300	2000	890.00	890
1999 Intermezzo LL3580	1,000		1300.00	1330
2000 My Special Garden LL3582	1,000		1900.00	1900
1997 The Journey LL3700	500	2000	700.00	700
1997 In Concert LL3701	350	2000	1050.00	1050
1997 Pensive Journey LL3702	500	2000	700.00	700
1997 Imagination LL3703	500	2000	750.00	750
1985 Napoleon Bonaparte LL5338	5,000	1994	275.00	650
1985 Beethoven w/base LL5339	3,000	1993	760.00	1300
1985 Thoroughbred Horse w/base LL5340	1,000	1993	625.00	1000-1150
1985 I Have Found Thee, Dulcinea LL5341	750	1990	1460.00	3000
1985 Pack of Hunting Dogs w/base LL5342	3,000	1994	925.00	1200-2000
1985 Love Boat w/base LL5343	3,000	1997	825.00	1350
1986 Fox Hunt w/base LL5362	1,000		5200.00	8750
1986 Rey De Copas w/base LL5366	2,000	1993	325.00	600
1986 Rey De Oros w/base LL5367	2,000	1993	325.00	600
1986 Rey De Espadas w/base LL5368	2,000	1993	325.00	600
1986 Rey De Bastos w/base LL5369	2,000	1993	325.00	600
1986 Pastoral Scene w/base LL5386	750	1995	1100.00	2300-2350
1987 Inspiration LL5413	500	1993	1200.00	2100
1987 Carnival Time w/base LL5423	1,000	1993	2400.00	3900
1989 "Pious" LL5541	1,000	1991	1075.00	1560-1700
1989 Freedom LL5602	1,500	1989	875.00	1100-1300
1990 A Ride In The Park LL5718	1,000	1994	3200.00	4500-4700
1991 Youth LL5800	500	1993	650.00	725
1991 Charm LL5801	500	1994	650.00	725
1991 New World Medallion LL5808	5,000	1994	200.00	225
1992 Sorrowful Mother LL5849	1,500	1999	1750.00	925-1850
1992 Justice Eagle LL5863	1,500		1700.00	1875
1992 Maternal Joy LL5864	1,500	1998	1600.00	1700-1750
1992 Motoring In Style LL5884	1,500	1998	3700.00	3850
1992 The Way Of The Cross LL5890	2,000	1998	975.00	1050
1992 Presenting Credentials LL5911	1,500	1999	19500.00	20500
1992 Young Mozart LL5915	2,500	1992	500.00	1495-1575
1993 Infant of Cebu LL5937	1,500	1998	N/A	1390
1993 The Blessing w/base LL5942	2,000		1345.00	1345
1993 Our Lady of Rocio w/base LL5951	2,000		3500.00	3500
1993 Where to Sir? w/base LL5952	1,500	1998	5250.00	5250
1993 Discovery Mug LL5967	1,992	1994	90.00	90-95
1993 Graceful Moment w/base LL6033	3,000		1475.00	1475
1993 The Hand of Justice w/base LL6035	1,000	1998	1250.00	1250-1300
1997 Royal Slumber 01006385	750	2000	1390	1425
1998 Goddess of Youth 01006449	2,500		1150.00	1500
1998 The Pelicans 01006478	1,000	2000	990.00	1200
1998 Melody 01006513	2,000		870.00	950
1999 Ovation 01006614	3,000		525.00	550
2000 Tranquility 01006677	2,000		1340.00	1340
2002 Waiting For A Rainbow 01006803	2,000		1050.00	1050
1995 Abraham Lincoln w/base LL7554	2,500		2190.00	2190
1996 Statue of Liberty w/base LL7563	2,000		1620.00	1620
1997 George Washington LL7575	2,000		1390.00	1390

Lladró - Lladró

YEAR ISSUE	EDITION LIMIT	YEAR RETD.	ISSUE PRICE	*QUOTE U.S.$
1963 Hunting Dog 308.13	Closed	N/A	N/A	2000
1966 Poodle 325.13	Closed	N/A	N/A	2300
1970 Girl with Pigtails L357.13G	Closed	N/A	N/A	1100
1969 Shepherdess with Goats L1001G	Closed	1987	67.50	550-675
1969 Shepherdess with Goats L1001M	Closed	1987	67.50	450
1969 Girl's Head L1003G	Closed	1985	150.00	675
1969 Girl's Head L1003M	Closed	1985	150.00	800
1969 Pan with Cymbals L1006	Closed	1975	45.00	400-550
1969 Pan with Pipes L1007	Closed	1975	45.00	400-700
1969 Satyrs Group L1008G	Closed	1976	N/A	750-1000
1969 Girl With Lamb L1010G	Closed	1993	26.00	202-240
1969 Girl With Pig L1011G	Closed	2001	13.00	97-210
1969 Centaur Girl L1012G	Closed	1989	45.00	455-550
1969 Centaur Girl L1012M	Closed	1989	45.00	400
1969 Centaur Boy L1013G	Closed	1989	45.00	400-425
1973 Christmas Carols L1239G	Closed	1981	125.00	750
1969 Centaur Boy L1013M	Closed	1989	45.00	425-455
1969 Two Women with Water Jugs L1014G	Closed	1985	85.00	550
1969 Dove L1015 G	Closed	1994	21.00	150
1969 Dove L1016 G	Closed	1995	36.00	190-250
1969 Idyl L1017G	Closed	1991	115.00	750
1969 Idyl L1017M	Closed	1991	115.00	625
1969 King Gaspar L1018M	Open		345.00	1895
1969 King Melchior L1019M	Open		345.00	1895
1969 King Baltasar L1020M	Open		345.00	1895
1969 Horse Group L1021G	Open		950.00	2590
1969 Horse Group/All White L1022M	Open		465.00	2150

YEAR ISSUE	EDITION LIMIT	YEAR RETD.	ISSUE PRICE	*QUOTE U.S.$
1969 Flute Player L1025G	Closed	1978	73.00	750
1969 Clown with Concertina L1027G	Closed	1993	95.00	625-800
1969 Girl w/Heart L1028G	Closed	1970	37.50	650
1969 Boy w/Bowler L1029G	Closed	1970	37.50	550
1969 Don Quixote w/Stand L1030G	Open		225.00	1450
1969 Sancho Panza L1031G	Closed	1989	65.00	600
1969 Old Folks L1033G	Closed	1985	140.00	1100-1400
1969 Old Folks L1033M	Closed	1985	140.00	1500
1969 Shepherdess with Dog L1034	Closed	1989	30.00	225-275
1969 Girl with Geese L1035G	Closed	1995	37.50	225-275
1969 Girl With Geese L1035M	Closed	1992	37.50	165
1969 Horseman L1037G	Closed	1970	170.00	2500
1969 Girl with Turkeys L1038G	Closed	1978	95.00	400-550
1969 Violinist and Girl L1039G	Closed	1991	120.00	850-1100
1969 Violinist and Girl L1039M	Closed	1991	120.00	1000
1969 Hen L1041G	Closed	1975	13.00	350
1969 Hen L1042G	Closed	1975	13.00	350
1969 Cock L1043G	Closed	1975	13.00	350
1969 Small Hippo L1045G	Closed	1970	9.50	350-400
1969 Hunters L1048	Closed	1986	115.00	1420
1969 Del Monte (Boy) L1050	Closed	1978	65.00	N/A
1969 Girl with Duck L1052G	Closed	1998	30.00	205-275
1969 Girl with Duck L1052M	Closed	1992	30.00	190
1969 Bird L1053G	Closed	1985	13.00	100
1969 Bird L1054G	Closed	1985	14.00	135-175
1969 Duck L1056G	Closed	1978	19.00	275
1969 Girl with Pheasant L1055G	Closed	1978	105.00	N/A
1969 Panchito L1059	Closed	1980	28.00	100
1969 Bull w/Head Up L1063	Closed	1975	90.00	1100
1969 Deer L1064	Closed	1986	27.50	325-425
1969 Fox and Cub L1065G	Closed	1975	17.50	425
1969 Basset L1066G	Closed	1981	23.50	600
1969 Old Dog L1067G	Closed	1981	40.00	625
1969 Great Dane L1068G	Closed	1989	55.00	500-600
1969 Afghan (sitting) L1069G	Closed	1985	36.00	625
1969 Beagle Puppy L1070G	Closed	1991	16.50	275-350
1969 Beagle Puppy L1071G	Closed	1992	16.50	275-500
1969 Beagle Puppy L1071M	Closed	1992	16.50	250
1969 Beagle Puppy L1072G	Closed	1991	16.50	260-275
1969 Dutch Girl L1077G	Closed	1981	57.50	363-525
1969 Herald L1078G	Closed	1971	110.00	1100
1969 Boy with Lyre L1079M	Closed	1970	20.00	500
1969 Girl with Water Can L1080M	Closed	1970	20.00	500
1969 Girl With Brush L1081G	Closed	1985	14.50	250-325
1969 Girl Manicuring L1082G	Closed	1985	14.50	275-320
1969 Girl With Doll L1083G	Closed	1985	14.50	260-300
1969 Girl with Mother's Shoe L1084G	Closed	1985	14.50	245-320
1969 Musical 19th Century L1085G	Closed	1973	180.00	2500
1969 Pregonero L1086G	Closed	1975	120.00	1500
1969 Little Green-Grocer L1087G	Closed	1981	40.00	385-450
1969 Girl Seated with Flowers L1088G	Closed	1989	45.00	645-750
1971 Lawyer (Face) L1089G	Closed	1973	35.00	850-950
1971 Girl and Gazelle L1091G	Closed	1975	225.00	1200
1971 Satyr with Snail L1092G	Closed	1975	30.00	650
1971 Satyr with Frog L1093G	Closed	1975	50.00	700
1969 Beggar L1094G	Closed	1981	65.00	650-675
1971 Girl with Hens L1103G	Closed	1985	50.00	375-455
1971 Boy With Cornet L1105G	Closed	1973	30.00	350
1971 Byzantine Head L1106G	Closed	1975	105.00	950
1971 Pups in Box L1121G	Closed	1978	33.00	1500-1750
1971 La Tarantela L1123G	Closed	1975	550.00	2250
1971 Pelusa Clown L1125G	Closed	1978	70.00	1000-1700
1971 Pelusa Clown L1125M	Closed	1978	70.00	2250
1971 Clown with Violin L1126G	Closed	1978	71.00	1850
1971 Puppy Love L1127G	Closed	1997	50.00	330-350
1971 Dog in the Basket L1128G	Closed	1985	17.50	425-450
1971 Faun L1131G	Closed	1972	155.00	1500
1971 Carriage of Baccus L1132G	Closed	1972	160.00	2200
1971 Horse L1133G	Closed	1972	115.00	900
1971 Bull L1134G	Closed	1972	130.00	1500
1971 Dog and Snail L1139G	Closed	1972	40.00	845
1971 Girl with Bonnet L1147G	Closed	1985	20.00	260-325
1971 Girl Shampooing L1148G	Closed	1985	20.00	220-310
1971 Dog's Head L1149G	Closed	1981	27.50	450
1971 Elephants (3) L1150G	Open		100.00	795
1971 Elephants (2) L1151G	Closed	1999	45.00	440
1971 Dog Playing Guitar L1152G	Closed	1978	32.50	375-550
1971 Dog Playing Guitar L1153G	Closed	1978	32.50	400-550
1971 Dog Playing Bass Fiddle L1154G	Closed	1978	36.50	400-550
1971 Dog w/Microphone L1155G	Closed	1978	35.00	400-550
1971 Dog Playing Bongos L1156	Closed	1978	32.50	400-550

FIGURINES

YEAR ISSUE	EDITION LIMIT	YEAR RETD.	ISSUE PRICE	*QUOTE U.S.$
1971 Seated Torero L1162G	Closed	1973	35.00	700
1971 Soldier with Gun L1164G	Closed	1978	27.50	400
1971 Soldier with Flag L1165G	Closed	1978	27.50	500
1971 Soldier with Cornet L1166G	Closed	1978	27.50	500
1971 Soldier with Drum L1167G	Closed	1978	27.50	500
1971 Kissing Doves L1169G	Open		32.00	165
1971 Kissing Doves L1169M	Closed	1992	32.00	155
1971 Kissing Doves L1170G	Closed	1988	25.00	250
1971 Girl With Flowers L1172G	Closed	1993	27.00	320-375
1971 Girl With Domino L1175G	Closed	1981	34.00	350
1971 Girl With Dice L1176G	Closed	1981	25.00	300-363
1971 Girl With Ball L1177G	Closed	1981	27.50	450
1971 Girl With Accordian L1178G	Closed	1981	34.00	400
1971 Boy With Concertina L1179G	Closed	1981	34.00	375
1971 Little Girl w/Turkeys L1180G	Closed	1981	55.00	450
1971 Platero and Marcelino L1181G	Closed	1981	50.00	238-455
1971 Girl From Manchuria L1182G	Closed	1975	60.00	750
1972 Little Girl with Cat L1187G	Closed	1989	37.00	315-337
1972 Boy Meets Girl L1188G	Closed	1989	310.00	425
1972 Eskimo L1195G	Open		30.00	140
1972 Horse Resting L1203G	Closed	1981	40.00	600
1972 Attentive Bear, brown L1204G	Closed	1989	16.00	115-125
1972 Good Bear, brown L1205G	Closed	1989	16.00	115-150
1972 Bear Seated, brown L1206G	Closed	1989	16.00	115-125
1972 Attentive Polar Bear, white L1207G	Open		16.00	75
1972 Bear, white L1208G	Open		16.00	75
1972 Bear, white L1209G	Open		16.00	75
1972 Round Fish L1210G	Closed	1981	35.00	650
1972 Girl With Doll L1211G	Closed	1993	72.00	352-440
1972 Woman Carrying Water L1212G	Closed	1983	100.00	475
1972 Little Jug Magno L1222.3G	Closed	1979	35.00	300
1972 Young Harlequin L1229G	Closed	1999	70.00	520
1972 Young Harlequin L1229M	Closed	1991	70.00	550
1972 Friendship L1230G	Closed	1991	68.00	425-475
1972 Friendship L1230M	Closed	1991	68.00	404
1972 Angel with Lute L1231G	Closed	1988	60.00	425-450
1972 Angel with Clarinet L1232G	Closed	1988	60.00	425-475
1972 Angel with Flute L1233G	Closed	1988	60.00	450-475
1972 Little Jesus of Prag L1234G	Closed	1978	70.00	725
1973 Country Flirt L1241G	Closed	1980	110.00	650
1973 Lady at Dressing Table L1242G	Closed	1978	320.00	2500-3650
1973 Fluttering Nightingale L1244G	Closed	1981	44.00	375
1973 The Cart L1245G	Closed	1981	75.00	500-650
1972 Caress and Rest L1246G	Closed	1990	50.00	150-360
1974 Happy Harlequin L1247M	Closed	1983	220.00	1150
1974 Sweety L1248G	Closed	1990	100.00	525-550
1974 The Race L1249G	Closed	1988	450.00	2250
1974 Lovers from Verona L1250G	Closed	1990	330.00	1250
1974 Pony Ride L1251G	Closed	1979	220.00	1400
1974 Shepherd's Rest L1252G	Closed	1981	100.00	500
1974 Sad Chimney Sweep L1253G	Closed	1983	180.00	1200-1250
1974 Hamlet and Yorick L1254G	Closed	1983	325.00	1200-1275
1974 Seesaw L1255G	Closed	1993	110.00	670-847
1974 Mother with Pups L1257G	Closed	1981	50.00	650
1974 Playing Poodles L1258G	Closed	1981	47.50	800
1974 Poodle L1259G	Closed	1985	27.50	488-500
1974 Dalmatian L1260G	Closed	1981	25.00	325-350
1974 Dalmatian L1261G	Closed	1981	25.00	350
1974 Dalmatian L1262G	Closed	1981	25.00	325-350
1974 Flying Duck L1263G	Closed	1998	20.00	77-140
1974 Flying Duck L1264G	Closed	1998	20.00	75-110
1974 Flying Duck L1265G	Closed	1998	20.00	77-110
1974 Girl with Ducks L1267G	Closed	1993	55.00	260-300
1974 Reminiscing L1270G	Closed	1988	975.00	1375
1974 Thoughts L1272G	Closed	1998	87.50	3490
1974 Lovers in the Park L1274G	Closed	1993	450.00	1365-1400
1974 Christmas Seller L1276G	Closed	1981	120.00	700
1974 Feeding Time L1277G	Closed	1994	120.00	323-350
1974 Feeding Time L1277M	Closed	1993	120.00	450
1974 Devotion L1278G	Closed	1990	140.00	380-475
1974 The Wind L1279M	Closed	2001	250.00	850
1974 Child's Play L1280G	Closed	1983	110.00	494-700
1974 Afghan Standing L1282G	Closed	1985	45.00	500
1974 Little Gardener L1283G	Open		250.00	785
1974 "My Flowers" L1284G	Open		200.00	550
1974 "My Goodness" L1285G	Closed	1995	190.00	307-450
1974 Flower Harvest L1286G	Closed	1998	200.00	421-550
1974 Picking Flowers L1287G	Closed	1998	170.00	440-495
1974 Aggressive Duck L1288G	Closed	1995	170.00	489-575
1974 Good Puppy L1289G	Closed	1985	16.60	225-250
1974 Victorian Girl on Swing L1297G	Closed	1990	520.00	1850-1950
1974 Birds Resting L1298G	Closed	1985	235.00	975
1974 Birds in Nest L1299G	Closed	1985	120.00	750
1974 Little Bird L1301G	Closed	1983	72.50	550
1974 Blue Creeper L1302G	Closed	1985	110.00	650
1974 Bird on Cactus L1303G	Closed	1983	150.00	800
1974 Valencian Lady with Flowers L1304G	Open		200.00	625
1974 "On the Farm" L1306G	Closed	1990	130.00	290-425
1974 Ducklings L1307G	Open		47.50	150
1974 Girl with Cats L1309G	Open		120.00	315
1974 Girl with Puppies in Basket L1311G	Closed	1997	120.00	325-375
1974 Exquisite Scent L1313G	Closed	1990	201.00	650
1974 Girl From Scotland L1315G	Closed	1979	450.00	2800
1976 Collie L1316G	Closed	1981	45.00	500
1976 Herons L1319G	Open		1550.00	2625
1977 Angel with Tamborine L1320G	Closed	1985	125.00	450-500
1977 Angel with Lyre L1321G	Closed	1985	125.00	450-475
1977 Angel Recital L1322G	Closed	1985	125.00	475
1977 Angel with Accordian L1323G	Closed	1985	125.00	400
1977 Angel with Violin L1324G	Closed	1985	125.00	400-500
1976 The Helmsman L1325M	Closed	1988	600.00	1220
1976 Playing Cards L1327 M, numbered series	Open		3800.00	6600
1977 Chow Time L1334G	Closed	1981	135.00	625-650
1977 Dove Group L1335G	Closed	1990	950.00	1600
1977 Girl With Watering Can L1339G	Closed	1988	325.00	450-575
1977 Male Jockey L1341G	Closed	1979	120.00	550
1977 Wrath of Don Quixote L1343G	Closed	1990	250.00	875-990
1977 Derby L1344G	Closed	1985	1125.00	2500
1978 Sacristan L1345G	Closed	1979	385.00	2200-2300
1978 Under the Willow L1346G	Closed	1990	1600.00	1950-2150
1978 Mermaid on Wave L1347G	Closed	1983	425.00	1600-1850
1978 Pearl Mermaid L1348G	Closed	1983	225.00	1700-1850
1978 Mermaids Playing L1349G	Closed	1983	425.00	2250-2700
1978 In the Gondola L1350G, numbered series	Open		1850.00	3250
1978 Lady with Girl L1353G	Closed	1985	175.00	575-780
1978 Girl Watering L1354G	Closed	1988	485.00	635
1978 Phyllis L1356G	Closed	1993	75.00	225-275
1978 Shelley L1357G	Closed	1993	75.00	225-250
1978 Beth L1358G	Closed	1993	75.00	205-225
1978 Heather L1359G	Closed	1993	75.00	225
1978 Laura L1360G	Closed	1993	75.00	205-250
1978 Julia L1361G	Closed	1993	75.00	240-275
1978 Girls in the Swing L1366G	Closed	1988	825.00	1425-1900
1978 Playful Dogs L1367	Closed	1982	160.00	710-900
1978 Spring Birds L1368G	Closed	1990	1600.00	2500
1978 Anniversary Waltz L1372G	Open		260.00	570
1978 Chestnut Seller L1373G	Closed	1981	800.00	750-900
1978 Waiting in the Park L1374G	Closed	1993	235.00	450-600
1978 Watering Flowers L1376G	Closed	1990	400.00	748-1150
1978 Suzy and Her Doll L1378G	Closed	1985	215.00	550-650
1978 Debbie and Her Doll L1379G	Closed	1985	215.00	800
1978 Cathy and Her Doll L1380G	Closed	1985	215.00	650
1978 Medieval Girl L1381G	Closed	1985	11.80	400-600
1978 Medieval Boy L1382G	Closed	1985	235.00	700
1978 A Rickshaw Ride L1383G	Open		1500.00	2150
1978 Quixote on Guard L1385G	Closed	1988	350.00	850-975
1981 St. Joseph L1386G	Open		250.00	390
1981 Mary L1387G	Open		240.00	390
1981 Baby Jesus L1388G	Open		85.00	145
1981 Donkey L1389G	Open		95.00	245
1981 Cow L1390G	Open		95.00	245
1982 Holy Mary L1394G, numbered series	Open		1000.00	1475
1982 Full of Mischief L1395G	Closed	1998	420.00	865
1982 Appreciation L1396G	Closed	1998	420.00	584-860
1982 Second Thoughts L1397G	Closed	1998	420.00	880-925
1982 Reverie L1398G	Closed	1998	490.00	970-1075
1982 Dutch Girl L1399G	Closed	1988	750.00	725-775
1982 Valencian Boy L1400G	Closed	1988	298.00	470-560
1982 Butterfly Girl L1401G	Closed	1988	210.00	600-750
1982 Butterfly Girl L1402G	Closed	1988	210.00	595-750
1982 Butterfly Girl L1403G	Closed	1988	210.00	550-750
1982 Matrimony L1404G	Closed	1998	320.00	550-625
1982 Illusion L1413G	Open		115.00	265
1982 Fantasy L1414G	Open		115.00	265
1982 Mirage L1415G	Open		115.00	265
1982 From My Garden L1416G	Closed	1998	140.00	315-365
1982 Nature's Bounty L1417G	Closed	1995	160.00	380-400
1982 Flower Harmony L1418G	Closed	1995	130.00	400
1982 A Barrow of Blossoms L1419G	Open		390.00	675

Collectors' Information Bureau   *Quotes have been rounded up to nearest dollar

YEAR ISSUE	EDITION LIMIT	YEAR RETD.	ISSUE PRICE	*QUOTE U.S.$
1982 Born Free w/base L1420G	Open		1520.00	3300
1982 Mariko w/base L1421G	Closed	1995	860.00	1300-1625
1982 Miss Valencia L1422G	Closed	1998	175.00	415-430
1982 King Melchior L1423G	Open		225.00	440
1982 King Gaspar L1424G	Open		265.00	475
1982 King Balthasar L1425G	Open		315.00	585
1982 Male Tennis Player L1426M	Closed	1988	200.00	300-400
1982 Female Tennis Player L1427M	Closed	1988	200.00	400-475
1982 Afternoon Tea L1428G	Closed	1998	115.00	300-350
1982 Afternoon Tea L1428M	Closed	1998	115.00	300
1982 Winter Wonderland w/base L1429G	Closed	2001	1025.00	2230
1982 High Society L1430G	Closed	1993	305.00	585-695
1982 The Debutante L1431G	Closed	1998	115.00	300-375
1982 The Debutante L1431M	Closed	1998	115.00	300
1983 Vows L1434G	Closed	1991	600.00	425
1983 Blue Moon L1435G	Closed	1988	98.00	355-430
1983 Moon Glow L1436G	Closed	1988	98.00	405-500
1983 Moon Light L1437G	Closed	1988	98.00	450-575
1983 Full Moon L1438G	Closed	1988	115.00	575-675
1983 "How Do You Do!" L1439G	Open		185.00	295
1983 Pleasantries L1440G	Closed	1991	960.00	1700-2300
1983 A Litter of Love L1441G	Open		385.00	645
1983 Kitty Confrontation L1442G	Open		155.00	290
1983 Bearly Love L1443G	Closed	1999	55.00	140-178
1983 Purr-Fect L1444G	Open		350.00	625
1983 Springtime in Japan L1445G	Open		965.00	1800
1983 "Here Comes the Bride" L1446G	Closed	1998	518.00	1000-1145
1983 Michiko L1447G	Open		235.00	515
1983 Yuki L1448G	Closed	1998	285.00	550-625
1983 Mayumi L1449G	Closed	1998	235.00	525-600
1983 Kiyoko L1450G	Closed	1998	235.00	550-575
1983 Teruko L1451G	Open		235.00	550
1983 On the Town L1452G	Closed	1993	220.00	500-595
1983 Golfing Couple L1453G	Open		248.00	545
1983 Flowers of the Season L1454G	Open		1460.00	2550
1983 Reflections of Hamlet L1455G	Closed	1988	1000.00	1650
1983 Cranes w/base L1456G	Open		1000.00	1990
1985 A Boy and His Pony L1460G	Closed	1988	285.00	650-800
1985 Carefree Angel with Flute L1463G	Closed	1988	220.00	650
1985 Carefree Angel with Lyre L1464G	Closed	1988	220.00	650-675
1985 Girl on Carousel Horse L1469G	Closed	2000	470.00	898-945
1985 Boy on Carousel Horse L1470G	Closed	2000	470.00	890-945
1985 Wishing On A Star L1475G	Closed	1988	130.00	495-520
1985 Star Light Star Bright L1476G	Closed	1988	130.00	350-400
1985 Star Gazing L1477G	Closed	1988	130.00	375-400
1985 Hawaiian Dancer/Aloha! L1478G	Open		230.00	440
1985 In a Tropical Garden L1479G	Closed	1995	230.00	450-525
1985 Aroma of the Islands L1480G	Open		260.00	480
1985 Sunning L1481G	Closed	1988	145.00	440-575
1985 Eve L1482	Closed	1988	145.00	600-700
1985 Free As a Butterfly L1483G	Closed	1988	145.00	420-500
1986 Lady of the East w/base L1488G	Closed	1993	625.00	1100-1250
1986 Valencian Children L1489G	Open		700.00	1250
1986 My Wedding Day L1494G	Closed	1998	800.00	1495-1650
1986 A Lady of Taste L1495G	Open		575.00	1025
1986 Don Quixote & The Windmill L1497G	Closed	1997	1100.00	2050-2150
1986 Tahitian Dancing Girls L1498G	Closed	1995	750.00	1450-1550
1986 Blessed Family L1499G	Closed	1998	200.00	395
1986 Ragamuffin L1500G	Closed	1991	125.00	400-425
1986 Ragamuffin L1500M	Closed	1991	125.00	300
1986 Rag Doll L1501G	Closed	1991	125.00	300-310
1986 Rag Doll L1501M	Closed	1991	125.00	300
1986 Forgotten L1502G	Closed	1991	125.00	300-310
1986 Forgotten L1502M	Closed	1991	125.00	300
1986 Neglected L1503G	Closed	1991	125.00	425-550
1986 Neglected L1503M	Closed	1991	125.00	325
1986 The Reception L1504G	Closed	1990	625.00	1040-1100
1986 Nature Boy L1505G	Closed	1991	100.00	230-300
1986 Nature Boy L1505M	Closed	1991	100.00	300
1986 A New Friend L1506G	Closed	1991	110.00	325-350
1986 A New Friend L1506M	Closed	1991	110.00	275
1986 Boy & His Bunny L1507G	Closed	1991	90.00	230-275
1986 Boy & His Bunny L1507M	Closed	1991	90.00	160-275
1986 In the Meadow L1508G	Closed	1991	100.00	195-325
1986 In the Meadow L1508M	Closed	1991	100.00	195-310
1986 Spring Flowers L1509G	Closed	1991	100.00	310
1986 Spring Flowers L1509M	Closed	1991	100.00	295
1987 Cafe De Paris L1511G	Closed	1995	1900.00	2950
1987 Hawaiian Beauty L1512G	Closed	1990	575.00	850-1200
1987 A Flower for My Lady L1513G	Closed	1990	1150.00	1750
1987 Gaspar 's Page L1514G	Closed	1990	275.00	475-550
1987 Melchior's Page L1515G	Closed	1990	290.00	495-550
1987 Balthasar's Page L1516G	Closed	1990	275.00	850
1987 Circus Train L1517G	Closed	1994	2900.00	4350
1987 Valencian Garden L1518G	Closed	1991	1100.00	1795
1987 Stroll in the Park L1519G	Closed	1998	1600.00	2600
1987 The Landau Carriage L1521G	Closed	1998	2500.00	3109-3850
1987 I am Don Quixote! L1522G	Open		2600.00	3950
1987 Valencian Bouquet L1524G	Closed	1991	250.00	380-400
1987 Valencian Dreams L1525G	Closed	1991	240.00	400
1987 Valencian Flowers L1526G	Closed	1991	375.00	550
1987 Tenderness L1527G	Open		260.00	440
1987 I Love You Truly L1528G	Open		375.00	595
1987 Momi L1529G	Closed	1990	275.00	550
1987 Leilani L1530G	Closed	1990	275.00	500-550
1987 Malia L1531G	Closed	1990	275.00	500-550
1987 Lehua L1532G	Closed	1990	275.00	550-600
1987 Not So Fast! L1533G	Closed	1996	175.00	214-325
1988 Little Sister L1534G	Open		180.00	245
1988 Sweet Dreams L1535G	Open		150.00	245
1988 Stepping Out L1537G	Closed	2000	230.00	320-335
1988 Pink Ballet Slippers L1540	Closed	1991	275.00	450-500
1988 White Ballet Slippers L1540.3	Closed	1991	275.00	395-465
1987 Light Blue Spoon L1548G	Closed	1991	70.00	150
1987 Dark Blue Spoon L1548.1	Closed	1991	70.00	140-150
1987 White Spoon L1548.3	Closed	1991	70.00	140-150
1987 Flower Basket L1552	Closed	1991	115.00	213-280
1987 Small Pink Broad Brimmed Hat L1563.3M	Closed	1991	45.00	125
1987 Wild Stallions w/base L1566G	Closed	1993	1100.00	1465
1987 Running Free w/base L1567G	Closed	1998	1500.00	1600
1987 Grand Dame L1568G	Closed	2000	290.00	460-515
1989 Fluttering Crane L1598G	Closed	1998	115.00	128-175
1989 Nesting Crane L1599G	Closed	1998	95.00	98-135
1989 Landing Crane L1600G	Closed	1998	115.00	145-200
1989 Rock Nymph L1601G	Closed	1995	665.00	825-950
1989 Spring Nymph L1602G	Closed	1995	665.00	825-950
1989 Latest Addition L1606G	Open		385.00	480
1989 Flight Into Egypt w/base L1610G	Closed	2000	885.00	1150
1989 Courting Cranes L1611G	Open		565.00	695
1989 Preening Crane L1612G	Closed	1998	385.00	470-525
1989 Bowing Crane L1613G	Closed	1998	385.00	470-485
1989 Dancing Crane L1614G	Closed	2000	385.00	485
1989 Snow Queen Mask No.11 L1645G	Closed	1991	390.00	450
1989 Medieval Cross No.4 L1652G	Closed	1991	250.00	350
1989 Lavender Lady L1667M	Closed	1991	385.00	550
1989 Lacy Butterfly #1 L1673M	Closed	1991	95.00	200
1989 Beautiful Butterfly #2 L1674M	Closed	1991	100.00	195
1989 Black Butterfly #3 L1675M	Closed	1991	120.00	195
1989 Pink & White Butterfly #4 L1676M	Closed	1991	100.00	195
1989 Black & White Butterfly #5 L1677M	Closed	1991	100.00	195
1989 Large Pink Butterfly #6 L1678M	Closed	1991	100.00	175
1989 Pink & Blue Butterfly #7 L1679M	Closed	1991	80.00	150
1989 Small Pink Butterfly #8 L1680M	Closed	1991	72.50	125
1989 Blue Butterfly #9 L1681M	Closed	1991	185.00	275
1989 Pretty Butterfly #10 L1682M	Closed	1991	185.00	275
1989 Spotted Butterfly #11 L1683M	Closed	1991	175.00	260
1989 Leopard Butterfly #12 L1684M	Closed	1991	165.00	200-250
1989 Great Butterfly #13 L1685M	Closed	1991	150.00	180-225
1989 Queen Butterfly #14 L1686M	Closed	1991	125.00	200
1988 Cellist L1700M	Closed	1993	1200.00	1813
1988 Saxophone Player L1701M	Closed	1993	835.00	1840
1988 Boy at the Fair (Decorated) L1708M	Closed	1993	650.00	650
1988 Exodus L1709M	Closed	1993	875.00	875
1988 School Boy L1710M	Closed	1993	750.00	750
1988 School Girl L1711M	Closed	1993	950.00	950
1988 Nanny L1714M	Closed	1993	575.00	700
1988 On Our Way Home (decorated) L1715M	Closed	1993	2000.00	2000
1988 Harlequin with Puppy L1716M	Closed	1993	825.00	1000
1988 Harlequin with Dove L1717M	Closed	1993	900.00	1000
1988 Dress Rehearsal L1718M	Closed	1993	1150.00	1150
1989 Back From the Fair L1719M	Closed	1993	1825.00	1825
1990 Sprite w/base L1720G, numbered series	Open		1200.00	1400
1990 Leprechaun w/base L1721G, numbered series	Open		1200.00	1400
1989 Group Discussion L1722M	Closed	1993	1500.00	1500
1989 Hopeful Group L1723M	Closed	1993	1825.00	1825
1989 Belle Epoque L1724M	Closed	1993	700.00	700
1989 Young Lady with Parasol L1725M	Closed	1993	950.00	950
1989 Young Lady with Fan L1726M	Closed	1993	750.00	750

FIGURINES

YEAR ISSUE	EDITION LIMIT	YEAR RETD.	ISSUE PRICE	*QUOTE U.S.$
1989 Pose L1727M	Closed	1993	725.00	725
1991 Nativity L1730M	Closed	1997	725.00	725
1970 Monkey L2000M	Closed	1975	35.00	500
1970 Cat L2001G	Closed	1975	27.50	625
1970 Gothic King L2002G	Closed	1975	25.00	450
1970 Gothic Queen L2003G	Closed	1975	25.00	450
1970 Shepherdess Sleeping L2005M	Closed	1981	100.00	710
1970 Water Carrier Girl Lamp L2006M	Closed	1975	30.00	600
1970 Mounted Harlequin L2012M	Closed	1981	200	2200
1971 Girl with Dog L2013M	Closed	1975	300.00	2350
1971 Little Eagle Owl L2020M	Closed	1985	15.00	425-618
1971 Boy/Girl Eskimo L2038.3M	Closed	1994	100.00	450
1971 Aida L2039M	Closed	1979	65.00	1200
1974 Setter's Head L2045M	Closed	1981	42.50	550
1974 Magistrates L2052M	Closed	1981	135.00	950-1200
1974 Oriental L2056M	Open		35.00	110
1974 Oriental L2057M	Open		30.00	110
1974 Thailandia L2058M	Open		650.00	1950
1974 Muskateer L2059M	Closed	1981	900.00	2000-3000
1977 Monk L2060M	Closed	1998	60.00	155-195
1977 Day Dream L2062M	Closed	1985	400.00	1300
1977 Chinese Farmer w/Staff L2065M	Closed	1985	340.00	1800
1977 Dogs-Bust L2067M	Closed	1979	280.00	800
1977 Thai Dancers L2069M	Closed	1999	300.00	745
1977 A New Hairdo L2070M	Open		1060.00	1525
1977 Graceful Duo L2073M	Closed	1994	775.00	1650
1977 Nuns L2075M	Closed	2000	90.00	250
1978 Lonely L2076M	Closed	1999	72.50	185
1978 Rain in Spain L2077M	Closed	1990	190.00	475-550
1978 Lola L2078M	Closed	1981	250.00	650
1978 Woman L2080M	Closed	1985	625.00	625
1978 Fisherwoman L2081M	Closed	1985	550.00	1450
1978 Carmen L2083M	Closed	1981	275.00	625
1978 Don Quixote Dreaming L2084M	Closed	1985	550.00	2100
1978 The Little Kiss L2086M	Closed	1985	180.00	500
1978 Girl in Rocking Chair L2089	Closed	1981	235.00	600
1978 Saint Francis L2090	Closed	1981	565.00	765-1400
1978 Holy Virgin L2092M	Closed	1981	260.00	N/A
1978 Girl Waiting L2093M	Closed	1995	90.00	148-210
1978 Tenderness L2094M	Closed	2000	100.00	300
1978 Duck Pulling Pigtail L2095M	Closed	1998	110.00	275-295
1978 Nosy Puppy L2096M	Closed	1993	190.00	349-400
1978 Eskimo Playing L2097M	Open		225.00	465
1978 Laundress and Water Carrier L2109M	Closed	1983	325.00	550-650
1978 Charity L2112M	Closed	1981	360.00	1200-1500
1980 My Little Duckling L2113M	Closed	1993	240.00	295
1980 Kissing Father L2114M	Closed	1981	575.00	575
1980 Mother's Kiss L2115M	Closed	1981	575.00	700
1980 The Whaler L2121M	Closed	1988	820.00	1050
1981 Lost in Thought L2125M	Closed	1990	210.00	300
1983 Indian Chief L2127M	Closed	1988	525.00	700-750
1983 Venus L2128M	Open		650.00	1330
1983 Waiting for Sailor L2129M	Closed	1985	325.00	600
1983 Egyptian Cat L2130M	Closed	1985	75.00	450
1983 Mother & Son L2131M, numbered series	Closed	1998	850.00	1550
1983 Spring Sheperdess L2132M	Closed	1985	450.00	1250
1983 Autumn Sheperdess L2133M	Closed	1985	285.00	1250
1984 Nautical Watch L2134M	Closed	1988	450.00	800
1984 Mystical Joseph L2135M	Closed	1988	428.00	750
1984 The King L2136M	Closed	1988	570.00	710
1984 Fairy Ballerina L2137M	Closed	1988	500.00	1250
1984 Friar Juniper L2138M	Closed	1993	160.00	400-475
1984 Aztec Indian L2139M	Closed	1988	553.00	600
1984 Pepita with Sombrero L2140M	Open		97.50	230
1984 Pedro with Jug L2141M	Open		100.00	230
1984 Sea Harvest L2142M	Closed	1990	535.00	725
1984 Aztec Dancer L2143M	Closed	1988	463.00	650
1984 Leticia L2144M	Closed	1995	100.00	210-225
1984 Gabriela L2145M	Closed	1994	100.00	220-250
1984 Desiree L2146M	Closed	1995	100.00	225
1984 Alida L2147M	Closed	1994	100.00	250
1984 Head of Congolese Woman L2148M	Closed	1988	55.00	695-700
1985 Young Madonna L2149M	Closed	1988	400.00	675
1985 A Tribute to Peace w/base L2150M	Open		470.00	1000
1985 A Bird on Hand L2151M	Closed	1999	118.00	255
1985 Chinese Girl L2152M	Closed	1990	90.00	250-275
1985 Chinese Boy L2153	Closed	1990	90.00	250-275
1985 Hawaiian Flower Vendor L2154M	Closed	2000	245.00	460
1985 Arctic Winter L2156M	Open		75.00	150
1985 Eskimo Girl with Cold Feet L2157M	Open		140.00	300
1985 Pensive Eskimo Girl L2158M	Open		100.00	220
1985 Pensive Eskimo Boy L2159M	Open		100.00	220
1985 Flower Vendor L2160M	Closed	1995	110.00	215
1985 Fruit Vendor L2161M	Closed	1994	120.00	230-315
1985 Fish Vendor L2162M	Closed	1994	110.00	205
1987 Mountain Shepherd L2163M	Closed	1999	120.00	210-235
1987 My Lost Lamb L2164M	Closed	1999	100.00	175
1987 Chiquita L2165M	Closed	1993	100.00	170
1987 Paco L2166M	Closed	1993	100.00	170
1987 Fernando L2167M	Closed	1993	100.00	153-200
1987 Julio L2168M	Closed	1993	100.00	225
1987 Repose L2169M	Open		120.00	215
1987 Spanish Dancer L2170M	Open		190.00	400
1987 Ahoy There L2173M	Open		190.00	350
1987 Andean Flute Player L2174M	Closed	1990	250.00	350
1988 Harvest Helpers L2178M	Open		190.00	290
1988 Sharing the Harvest L2179M	Closed	2001	190.00	280
1988 Dreams of Peace w/base L2180M	Closed	2001	880.00	1450
1988 Bathing Nymph w/base L2181M	Closed	2001	560.00	795-815
1988 Daydreamer w/base L2182M	Open		560.00	795
1989 Wakeup Kitty L2183M	Closed	1993	225.00	285-325
1989 Angel and Friend L2184M	Closed	1994	150.00	185-210
1989 Devoted Reader L2185M	Closed	1994	125.00	195-200
1989 The Greatest Love L2186M	Closed	1998	235.00	310-320
1989 Jealous Friend L2187M	Closed	1995	275.00	365-400
1990 Mother's Pride L2189M	Closed	1999	300.00	375
1990 To The Well L2190M	Closed	2001	250.00	295
1990 Forest Born L2191M	Closed	1991	230.00	300-475
1990 King Of The Forest L2192M	Closed	1992	290.00	325
1990 Heavenly Strings L2194M	Closed	1993	170.00	250
1990 Heavenly Sounds L2195M	Closed	1993	170.00	250
1990 Heavenly Solo L2196M	Closed	1993	170.00	250
1990 Heavenly Song L2197M	Closed	1993	175.00	195-250
1990 A King is Born w/base L2198M	Closed	2001	750.00	895
1990 Devoted Friends w/base L2199M	Closed	1995	700.00	850-895
1990 A Big Hug! L2200M	Open		250.00	310
1990 Our Daily Bread L2201M	Closed	1994	150.00	225-300
1990 A Helping Hand L2202M	Closed	1993	150.00	250
1990 Afternoon Chores L2203M	Closed	1994	150.00	185-250
1990 Farmyard Grace L2204M	Closed	1993	180.00	265-300
1990 Prayerful Stitch L2205M	Closed	1994	160.00	179-250
1990 Sisterly Love L2206M	Open		300.00	375
1990 What A Day! L2207M	Open		550.00	645
1990 Let's Rest L2208M	Open		550.00	675
1991 Long Day L2209M	Open		295.00	340
1991 Lazy Day L2210M	Open		240.00	260
1991 Patrol Leader L2212M	Closed	1993	390.00	425
1991 Nature's Friend L2213M	Closed	1993	390.00	425
1991 Seaside Angel L2214M	Open		150.00	170
1991 Friends in Flight L2215M	Open		165.00	185
1991 Laundry Day L2216M	Open		350.00	400
1991 Gentle Play L2217M	Closed	1993	380.00	425
1991 Costumed Couple L2218M	Closed	1993	680.00	750
1992 Underfoot L2219M	Closed	2001	360.00	425
1992 Free Spirit L2220M	Closed	1994	235.00	245
1992 Spring Beauty L2221M	Closed	1994	285.00	295-350
1992 Tender Moment L2222M	Closed	1999	400.00	450
1992 New Lamb L2223M	Closed	1999	365.00	385
1992 Cherish L2224M	Open		1750.00	1850
1992 Friendly Sparrow L2225M	Open		295.00	325
1992 Boy's Best Friend L2226M	Open		390.00	410
1992 Artic Allies L2227M	Open		585.00	615
1992 Snowy Sunday L2228M	Open		550.00	625
1992 Seasonal Gifts L2229M	Open		450.00	475
1992 Mary's Child L2230M	Closed	1994	525.00	550-640
1992 Afternoon Verse L2231M	Closed	2001	580.00	595
1992 Poor Little Bear L2232M	Open		250.00	265
1992 Guess What I Have L2233M	Closed	2001	340.00	375
1992 Playful Push L2234M	Closed	2000	850.00	875
1993 Adoring Mother L2235M	Closed	1999	405.00	440
1993 Frosty Outing L2236M	Closed	1998	375.00	410
1993 The Old Fishing Hole L2237M	Open		625.00	640
1993 Learning Together L2238M	Closed	1998	500.00	500
1993 Valencian Courtship L2239M	Open		880.00	895
1993 Winged Love L2240M	Closed	1995	285.00	310
1993 Winged Harmony L2241M	Closed	1995	285.00	310-350
1993 Away to School L2242M	Open		465.00	465
1993 Lion Tamer L2246M	Closed	1995	375.00	375-400
1993 Just Us L2247M	Closed	1995	650.00	650
1993 Noella L2251M	Open		405.00	425
1993 Waiting For Father L2252M	Closed	1999	660.00	660

YEAR ISSUE	EDITION LIMIT	YEAR RETD.	ISSUE PRICE	*QUOTE U.S.$
1993 Noisy Friend L2253M	Closed	1998	280.00	280
1993 Step Aside L2254M	Open		280.00	280
1994 Solitude L2256M	Closed	1998	398.00	435
1994 Constant Companions L2257M	Closed	1997	575.00	625
1994 Family Love L2258M	Closed	2000	450.00	485
1994 Little Fisherman L2259M	Closed	1999	298.00	330
1994 Artic Friends L2260M	Closed	1997	345.00	380
1994 Little Sister L2261M	Closed	2001	265.00	268-280
1989 Latest Addition L2262M	Closed	1998	495.00	495
1994 Mother and Child L2263	Closed	1998	285.00	285
1994 Madonna Head L2264	Closed	2000	210.00	220
1994 Don Quixote L2265	Open		225.00	245
1994 Little Friskies L2266	Closed	1998	250.00	260
1994 Dancer L2267	Closed	2001	220.00	240
1994 Playful Kittens L2268	Closed	1998	285.00	300
1994 Eskimo Boy with Pet L2269	Closed	2001	130.00	130-145
1994 Eskimo Riders L2270	Closed	2001	275.00	280
1994 The Wanderer L2271	Closed	1998	245.00	245
1994 My Best Friend L2272	Open		240.00	240
1994 Bashful Bather L2273	Closed	2001	210.00	220
1994 May Flowers L2274	Closed	1998	195.00	195
1994 St. Joseph L2275	Open		270.00	270
1994 Mary L2276	Open		175.00	175
1994 Baby Jesus L2277	Open		85.00	85
1994 King Melchior L2278	Open		290.00	290
1994 King Gaspar L2279	Open		290.00	290
1994 King Balthasar L2280	Open		290.00	290
1994 Ox L2281	Open		185.00	185
1994 Donkey L2282	Open		185.00	185
1994 Lost Lamb L2283	Open		140.00	140
1994 Shepherd Boy L2284	Open		260.00	285
1994 Musical Muse L2285	Closed	1998	465.00	465
1994 Barnyard Scene L2286	Closed	1998	260.00	230-270
1994 Dog's Best Friend L2287	Closed	2000	310.00	310
1994 Carefree L2288	Closed	1998	325.00	325
1994 Dressing The Baby L2289	Closed	1998	325.00	325
1994 Surprise L2290	Closed	2000	335.00	335
1994 The Holy Teacher L2291	Open		375.00	375
1994 World of Fantasy L2292	Closed	1998	325.00	335
1994 Joyful Event L2293	Open		880.00	880
1995 Jesus and Joseph L2294M	Closed	1999	550.00	550
1995 Peaceful Rest L2295M	Closed	1998	390.00	390
1995 Life's Small Wonders L2296M	Open		370.00	370
1995 Elephants L2297M	Closed	2001	875.00	875
1995 Hindu Children L2298M	Closed	2000	450.00	450
1995 Poetic Moment L2299M	Open		465.00	465
1995 Emperor L2300M	Closed	1999	765.00	765
1995 Empress L2301M	Closed	1999	795.00	795
1995 Twilight Years L2302M	Closed	1998	385.00	385-425
1995 Not So Fast L2303M	Closed	1998	350.00	350
1995 Love in Bloom L2304M	Open		420.00	425
1995 Fragrant Bouquet L2305M	Closed	2001	330.00	330
1995 Hurry Now L2306M	Closed	2000	310.00	310
1995 Happy Birthday L2307M	Closed	1998	150.00	150
1995 Let's Make Up L2308M	Closed	1998	265.00	265
1995 Sea Breeze (Windblown Girl) L2309M	Closed	1998	320.00	320
1995 Chit-Chat L2310M	Closed	1998	270.00	270
1995 Good Night L2311M	Closed	1998	280.00	280
1995 Goose Trying to Eat L2312M	Closed	1998	325.00	325
1995 Who's the Fairest L2313M	Closed	1998	230.00	230
1995 Breezy Afternoon L2314M	Closed	1998	220.00	220
1995 On the Green L2315M	Closed	2000	575.00	575
1995 Closing Scene L2316M	Closed	1998	560.00	560
1995 Talk to Me L2317M	Closed	1998	175.00	175
1995 Taking Time L2318M	Closed	1998	175.00	175
1995 A Lesson Shared L2319M	Shared	1997	215.00	215
1995 Cat Nap L2320M	Closed	1999	265.00	265
1995 All Tuckered Out L2321M	Closed	2001	275.00	275
1995 Naptime L2322M	Closed	2001	275.00	275
1995 Water Girl L2323M	Open		245.00	245
1995 A Basket of Fun L2324M	Closed	2001	320.00	320
1995 Spring Splendor L2325M	Closed	2001	440.00	460
1995 Physician L2326M	Closed	1998	350.00	350
1995 Sad Sax L2327M	Closed	2001	225.00	225
1995 Circus Sam L2328M	Closed	2001	225.00	225
1995 Daily Chores L2329M	Closed	1999	345.00	345
1996 The Shepherdess L2330	Closed	1999	410.00	410
1996 Little Peasant Girl (pink) L2331	Open		155.00	160
1996 Little Peasant Girl (blue) L2332	Open		155.00	160
1996 Little Peasant Girl (white) L2333	Open		155.00	160
1996 Asian Melody L2334	Closed	1998	690.00	690
1996 Young Fisherman L2335	Closed	2001	225.00	225
1996 Young Water Girl L2336	Open		315.00	320
1996 Virgin of Montserrat w/base L2337	Open		1000.00	1000
1996 Sultan's Dream L2338	Open		700.00	700
1996 The Sultan L2339	Open		480.00	525
1996 Oriental Fantasy w/bow L2340	Closed	2000	1350.00	1350
1996 Oriental Fantasy w/brooch L2341	Closed	2000	1350.00	1350
1996 Returning From the Well w/base L2342	Closed	2000	1800.00	1800
1996 Care and Tenderness w/base L2343	Closed	1999	860.00	860
1996 Oration L2344	Open		295.00	295
1996 Bedtime Story L2345	Closed	1999	360.00	360
1996 Feeding the Ducks L2346	Closed	1999	305.00	305
1996 Meditation (blue) L2347	Closed	1999	145.00	145
1996 Prayerful Moment (blue) L2348	Closed	1999	145.00	145
1996 Sleigh Ride w/base L2349	Closed	1998	1520.00	1520
1996 Pensive Clown w/base L2350	Closed	1999	680.00	680
1996 Fishing With Gramps w/base L2351	Closed	2001	1025.00	1025
1996 Under My Spell L2352	Closed	1998	225.00	225
1996 Shot on Goal w/base L2353	Closed	1998	935.00	935
1997 Waiting For Spring L2354	Closed	2000	385.00	400
1997 Gabriela L2355	Open		740.00	750
1997 Country Joy L2356	Closed	1999	310.00	310
1997 In Search of Water L2357	Open		410.00	450
1997 I'm Sleepy L2358	Closed	2000	360.00	360
1997 First Crush L2359	Open		945.00	990
1997 Hunting Butterflies L2360	Closed	2000	465.00	465
1997 Cold Weather Companions L2361	Open		380.00	395
1997 Braving The Storm L2362	Closed	1999	470.00	470
1997 Pampered Puppy L2363	Closed	2000	345.00	375
1997 Melodies L2364	Open		590.00	675
1997 Holy Mother L2365	Open		230.00	250
1997 Bread of Life L2366	Open		230.00	250
1997 Pensive Harlequin L2367	Open		560.00	560
1997 Colombina L2368	Closed	1999	585.00	585
1998 Early Awakening 01012369	Open		595.00	725
1997 Intermission 01012370	Open		655.00	775
1998 It's Magic! 01012372	Closed	2000	1045.00	1100
1998 Spring Inspiration 01012374	Open		635.00	750
1998 Emperor 01012375	Closed	2000	695.00	695
1998 Empress 01012376	Closed	2000	735.00	750
1998 Arctic Explorer 01012379	Closed	2000	550.00	580
1998 A Comforting Friend 01012380	Open		330.00	375
1998 Island Beauty 01012382	Open		180.00	195
1998 Pacific Jewel 01012383	Open		170.00	195
1998 What About Me? 01012384	Closed	2000	790.00	925
1998 Tropical Flower 01012385	Open		190.00	195
1998 Low Tide 01012386	Closed	2000	560.00	675
1998 Karina 01012387	Open		390.00	425
1998 Ready To Go 01012388	Open		350.00	375
1998 Time To Go 01012389	Open		330.00	375
1999 Joelia 01012390	Open		1300.00	1400
1998 Loyal Companions 01012391	Open		400.00	495
1998 My Memories 01012392	Open		345.00	425
1998 A Girl in Love 01012393	Open		465.00	550
1999 Island Breeze 01012394	Closed	2001	550.00	550
1999 Serenity 01012395	Open		1450.00	1450
1999 From The Spring 01012396	Open		475.00	475
1999 Little Chief 01012397	Closed	2001	325.00	325
1999 Conversing With Nature 01012398	Closed	2001	370.00	370
1999 Little Brave Resting 01012399	Closed	2001	325.00	325
1999 Waiting at the Beach 01012400	Closed	2000	900.00	900
1999 Little Shepherd 01012401	Closed	2000	275.00	275
1999 Africa 01012402	Open		700.00	750
1999 Pacific Beauty 01012403	Closed	2001	850.00	850
1999 Sunset 01012404	Open		440.00	450
1999 Midday 01012405	Open		535.00	550
1999 Dawn 01012406	Open		550.00	550
2000 Memories of Tuscany 01012407	Open		995.00	995
2000 Deep in Thought 01012408	Open		1325.00	1350
2000 Loving Mother 01012409	Open		1090.00	1100
2000 Poetic Interlude 01012410	Open		460.00	475
2000 In the Country 01012411	Open		525.00	525
2000 Thoughts of Peace 01012412	Open		1000.00	1100
2000 Grace 01012413	Open		250.00	250
2000 Beauty 01012414	Open		250.00	250
2000 Youth 01012415	Open		245.00	245
2000 In Mother's Arms 01012416	Open		990.00	990
2000 Young Mary 01012417	Open		340.00	345
2000 Meditative Moment 01012418	Open		680.00	695
2000 Keep Me Warm 01012419	Open		175.00	195

FIGURINES

YEAR ISSUE	EDITION LIMIT	YEAR RETD.	ISSUE PRICE	*QUOTE U.S.$
2000 Hug Me Tight 01012420	Open		175.00	195
2000 Snuggle Bunny 01012421	Open		175.00	195
2001 After Class 01012423	Open		525.00	550
2001 Dance of Joy 01012424	Open		725.00	775
2001 Cozy Kitties 01012425	Open		325.00	350
2000 A Morning Walk 01012427	Open		285.00	325
2001 An Apron Full of Joy 01012428	Open		380.00	425
2001 Gentle Embrace 01012429	Open		440.00	475
2001 Little Hairdresser 01012430	Open		650.00	675
2001 A Simple Gift 01012431	Open		250.00	275
2001 A Farmyard Friend 01012432	Open		200.00	225
2001 Music From My Heart 01012433	Open		595.00	650
2002 Spirit of the Wind 01012434	Open		740.00	740
2002 Spirit of the Earth 01012436	Open		565.00	565
2002 Reflections of Beauty 01012437	Open		1335.00	1335
2002 Strings of the Heart 01012438	Open		1155.00	1155
2002 Waters of the Oasis 01012439	Open		560.00	560
2002 A Child's Present 01012440	Open		760.00	760
2002 Loving Words 01012443	Open		2050.00	2050
2002 Tropical Wonders 01012445	Open		715.00	715
2002 Loving Words, lamp 01012446	Open		2180.00	2180
1978 Native L3502M	Open		700.00	2450
1978 Letters to Dulcinea L3509M, numbered series	Closed	1998	875.00	2175
1978 Horse Heads L3511M	Closed	1990	260.00	650
1978 Girl With Pails L3512M	Open		140.00	285
1978 A Wintry Day L3513M	Closed	1988	525.00	1100
1978 Pensive w/ base L3514M	Open		500.00	1050
1978 Jesus Christ L3516M	Closed	1988	1050.00	1500
1978 Nude with Rose w/ base L3517M	Open		225.00	790
1980 Lady Macbeth L3518M	Closed	1981	385.00	700-1350
1980 Mother's Love L3521M	Closed	1990	1000.00	1100
1981 Weary w/ base L3525M	Open		360.00	750
1982 Contemplation w/ base L3526M	Open		265.00	650
1982 Stormy Sea w/base L3554M	Open		675.00	1650
1984 Innocence w/base/green L3558M	Closed	1991	960.00	1650
1984 Innocence w/base/red L3558.3M	Closed	1987	960.00	1200
1985 Peace Offering w/base L3559M	Open		397.00	875
1969 Marketing Day L4502G	Closed	1985	40.00	345-400
1969 Girl with Lamb L4505G	Closed	2001	20.00	113-300
1969 Boy with Kid L4506M	Closed	1985	22.50	315-400
1969 Boy with Lambs L4509G	Closed	1981	37.50	275-290
1969 Girl with Parasol and Geese L4510G	Closed	1993	40.00	210-350
1969 Nude L4511M	Closed	1985	45.00	700
1969 Nude L4512G	Closed	1985	44.00	450
1969 Diana L4514G	Closed	1981	65.00	650-750
1969 Man on Horse L4515G	Closed	1985	180.00	1100
1969 Female Equestrian L4516G	Open		170.00	795
1969 Boy Student L4517G	Closed	1978	57.50	475-495
1969 Girl Student L4518G	Closed	1978	57.50	475
1969 Flamenco Dancers L4519G	Closed	1993	150.00	1200-1400
1970 Boy With Dog L4522M	Closed	1992	25.00	170-180
1970 Boy With Dog L4522G	Closed	1998	25.00	180-250
1969 Girl With Slippers L4523G	Closed	1993	17.00	110-125
1969 Girl With Slippers L4523M	Closed	1993	17.00	110-125
1969 Donkey in Love L4524G	Closed	1985	15.00	212-375
1969 Donkey in Love L4524M	Closed	1985	15.00	350
1969 Violinist Lamp L4527G	Closed	1985	75.00	500
1969 Ballet Lamp L4528G	Closed	1985	120.00	750-850
1969 Joseph L4533G	Closed	1996	60.00	110
1969 Joseph L4533M	Closed	1996	60.00	110
1969 Mary L4534G	Open		60.00	90
1969 Mary L4534M	Open		60.00	90
1971 Baby Jesus L4535.3G	Open		60.00	70
1969 Baby Jesus L4535.3M	Open		60.00	70
1969 Angel, Chinese L4536G	Open		45.00	95
1969 Angel, Chinese L4536M	Open		45.00	95
1969 Angel, Black L4537G	Open		13.00	95
1969 Angel, Black L4537M	Open		13.00	95
1969 Angel, Praying L4538G	Open		13.00	95
1969 Angel, Praying L4538M	Open		13.00	95
1969 Angel, Thinking L4539G	Open		13.00	95
1969 Angel, Thinking L4539M	Open		13.00	95
1969 Angel with Horn L4540G	Open		13.00	95
1969 Angel with Horn L4540M	Open		13.00	95
1969 Angel Reclining L4541G	Open		13.00	95
1969 Angel Reclining L4541M	Open		13.00	95
1969 Group of Angels L4542G	Open		31.00	200
1969 Group of Angels L4542M	Open		31.00	200
1969 Troubador L4548G	Closed	1978	67.50	750
1969 Geese Group L4549G	Closed	1997	28.50	245-275
1969 Geese Group L4549M	Closed	1992	28.50	245-275
1969 Flying Dove L4550G	Closed	1998	47.50	265-295
1969 Turtle Dove L4550M	Closed	1992	47.50	265
1969 Ducks, Set/3 asst. L4551-3G	Closed	2001	18.00	140
1969 Shepherd w/Girl & Lamb L4554	Closed	1972	69.00	N/A
1969 Sad Harlequin L4558G	Closed	1993	110.00	600-845
1969 Ballerina L4559G	Closed	1993	110.00	500-550
1970 Llama Group 4561G	Closed	1970	55.00	1600
1969 Couple with Parasol L4563G	Closed	1985	180.00	850-900
1969 Girl with Geese L4568G	Closed	1993	45.00	358-375
1969 Girl With Turkey L4569G	Closed	1981	28.50	375
1969 Shepherd Resting L4571G	Closed	1981	60.00	475
1969 Girl with Piglets L4572G	Closed	1985	70.00	395-425
1969 Girl with Piglets L4572M	Closed	1985	70.00	400
1969 Mother & Child L4575G	Closed	1998	50.00	295-325
1969 New Shepherdess L4576G	Closed	1985	37.50	315
1969 New Shepherd L4577G	Closed	1983	35.00	550
1969 Mardi Gras L4580G	Closed	1975	57.50	1800
1969 Mardi Gras L4580M	Closed	1975	57.50	1800
1969 Setter L4583G	Closed	1981	21.00	600
1969 Girl with Sheep L4584G	Closed	1993	27.00	170-220
1969 Girl with Sheep L4584M	Closed	1993	27.00	190-210
1969 Holy Family L4585G	Open		18.00	135
1969 Holy Family L4585M	Open		18.00	135
1969 Madonna L4586G	Closed	1994	32.50	350
1969 White Cockeral L4588G	Closed	1979	17.50	300
1969 Girl with Pitcher L4590G	Closed	1981	47.50	400
1969 Girl with Cockerel L4591G	Closed	1993	20.00	275
1969 Lady with Greyhound L4594G	Closed	1981	60.00	700-850
1969 Fairy L4595G	Closed	1994	27.50	200-245
1969 Girl With Flower L4596G	Closed	1980	25.00	275
1969 Two Horses L4597	Closed	1990	240.00	1000
1969 Doctor L4602.3G	Closed	1999	33.00	230-295
1969 Nurse-L4603.3G	Closed	N/A	35.00	225
1969 Magic L4605	Closed	1985	160.00	900-1100
1969 Accordian Player L4606	Closed	1978	60.00	650
1969 Cupid L4607G	Closed	1980	15.00	800
1969 Cook in Trouble L4608	Closed	1985	27.50	600-650
1969 Nuns L4611G	Open		37.50	160
1969 Nuns L4611M	Open		37.50	160
1969 Girl Singer L4612G	Closed	1979	14.00	375-450
1969 Boy with Cymbals L4613G	Closed	1979	14.00	400
1969 Boy with Guitar L4614G	Closed	1979	19.50	400
1969 Boy with Double Bass L4615G	Closed	1979	22.50	400-553
1969 Boy with Drum L4616G	Closed	1979	16.50	350
1969 Group of Musicians L4617G	Closed	1979	33.00	500
1969 Clown L4618G	Open		70.00	415
1969 Seminarist L4619G	Closed	1972	18.50	650
1969 Policeman L4620G	Closed	1972	16.00	500
1969 Sea Captain L4621G	Closed	1993	45.00	325-350
1969 Sea Captain L4621M	Closed	1989	42.50	300
1969 Old Man with Violin L4622G	Closed	1982	45.00	700-750
1969 Velazquez Bookend L4626G	Closed	1975	90.00	950
1969 Columbus Bookend L4627G	Closed	1975	90.00	950
1969 Angel with Child L4635G	Open		15.00	135
1969 Honey Peddler L4638G	Closed	1978	60.00	575
1969 Cow with Pig L4640G	Closed	1981	42.50	650-750
1969 Cow with Pig L4640M	Closed	1981	42.50	750
1969 Pekinese L4641G	Closed	1985	20.00	295-450
1969 Dog L4642	Closed	1981	22.50	390-500
1969 Skye Terrier L4643G	Closed	1985	15.00	500
1969 Pierrot w/Mandolin L4646M	Closed	1970	60.00	1950
1969 Andalucians Group L4647G	Closed	1990	412.00	1400
1969 Valencian Couple on Horseback L4648	Closed	1990	900.00	1400
1969 Madonna Head L4649G	Closed	2001	25.00	152-185
1969 Madonna Head L4649M	Closed	2001	25.00	185
1969 Girl with Calla Lillies L4650G	Closed	1998	16.50	155-195
1969 Cellist L4651G	Closed	1978	70.00	600-750
1969 Happy Travelers L4652	Closed	1978	115.00	650
1969 Orchestra Conductor L4653G	Closed	1979	95.00	750-950
1969 The Grandfather L4654G	Closed	1979	75.00	1200
1969 Horses L4655G	Closed	2000	110.00	760
1969 Woodcutter L4656G	Closed	1978	80.00	600
1969 Shepherdess L4660G	Closed	1993	21.00	212-300
1969 Countryman L4664M	Closed	1979	50.00	500
1969 Girl with Basket L4665G	Closed	1979	50.00	450
1969 Girl with Basket L4665M	Closed	1979	50.00	550
1969 Birds L4667G	Closed	1985	25.00	250-750
1969 Maja Head L4668G	Closed	1985	50.00	750-787
1969 Pastoral Couple L4669G	Closed	1978	100.00	850

Collectors' Information Bureau   *Quotes have been rounded up to nearest dollar

YEAR ISSUE	EDITION LIMIT	YEAR RETD.	ISSUE PRICE	*QUOTE U.S.$	YEAR ISSUE	EDITION LIMIT	YEAR RETD.	ISSUE PRICE	*QUOTE U.S.$
1969 Baby Jesus L4670G	Closed	2001	6.00	55	1972 You and Me L4830G	Closed	1979	112.50	1100-1150
1969 Mary L4671G	Closed	2001	70.00	75	1972 Romance L4831G	Closed	1981	175.00	1350-1500
1969 St. Joseph L4672G	Closed	2001	70.50	71-90	1972 Chess Set Pieces L4833.3G	Closed	1985	410	2300
1969 King Melchior L4673G	Closed	2001	11.00	95	1972 Girl w/Lamb L4835G	Closed	1991	42.00	240-350
1969 King Gaspar L4674G	Closed	2001	11.00	95	1973 Clean Up Time L4838G	Closed	1993	36.00	250-295
1969 King Balthasar L4675G	Closed	2001	11.00	77-95	1973 Clean Up Time L4838M	Closed	1992	36.00	250
1969 Shepherd with Lamb L4676G	Closed	2001	14.00	110	1973 Oriental Flower Arranger/Girl L4840G	Closed	1998	90.00	525-600
1969 Shepherd with Lamb L4676M	Closed	N/A	14.00	150	1973 Oriental Flower Arranger/Girl L4840M	Closed	1998	90.00	515-600
1969 Girl with Rooster L4677G	Closed	2001	14.00	80-90	1974 Girl from Valencia L4841G	Open		35.00	240
1969 Girl with Rooster L4677M	Closed	N/A	14.00	150	1973 Viola Lesson L4842G	Closed	1981	66.00	375-450
1969 Shepherdess with Basket L4678G	Closed	2001	13.00	90	1973 Donkey Ride L4843	Closed	1981	86.00	650
1969 Shepherdess with Basket L4678M	Closed	N/A	13.00	150	1973 Pharmacist L4844G	Closed	1985	70.00	1200-1350
1969 Donkey L4679G	Closed	2001	11.50	100	1973 Classic Dance L4847G	Closed	1985	80.00	575-600
1969 Cow L4680G	Closed	2001	12.00	95	1973 Charm L4848G	Closed	1985	45.00	350
1970 Girl with Milkpail L4682G	Closed	1991	28.00	300-375	1973 Feeding The Ducks L4849G	Closed	1995	60.00	300-700
1970 Girl with Milkpail L4682M	Closed	1991	28.00	275	1973 Feeding The Ducks L4849M	Closed	1992	60.00	250
1970 Hebrew Student L4684G	Closed	1985	33.00	585-975	1973 Aesthetic Pose L4850G	Closed	1985	110.00	650
1970 Hebrew Student L4684M	Closed	1985	33.00	620	1973 Lady Golfer L4851M	Closed	1992	70.00	500
1970 Girl's Head w/Cap L4686G	Closed	1984	25.00	750	1973 Gardner in Trouble L4852	Closed	1981	65.00	550
1970 Gothic Queen L4689	Closed	1975	20.00	700	1974 Cobbler L4853G	Closed	1985	100.00	550-600
1970 Troubadour in Love L4699	Closed	1975	60.00	1000	1973 Don Quixote L4854G	Open		40.00	210
1970 Dressmaker L4700G	Closed	1993	45.00	425-488	1983 Death of the Swan L4855G	Closed	2000	45.00	313-330
1970 Mother & Child L4701G	Closed	1998	45.00	295-325	1974 Death of the Swan, white L4855.3	Closed	1987	110.00	250
1970 Girl Jewelry Dish L4713G	Closed	1978	30.00	550	1974 Waltz Time L4856G	Closed	1985	65.00	350-560
1970 Girl Jewelry Dish L4713M	Closed	1978	30.00	550	1974 Dog L4857G	Closed	1979	40.00	550
1970 Boy Jewelry Dish L4714G	Closed	1978	30.00	600	1974 Pleasant Encounter L4858M	Closed	1981	60.00	450
1970 Lady Empire L4719G	Closed	1979	150.00	990-1100	1974 Peddler L4859G	Closed	1985	180.00	750-820
1970 Girl With Tulips L4720G	Closed	1978	65.00	500-600	1974 Dutch Girl L4860G	Closed	1985	45.00	363-425
1970 Girl With Tulips L4720M	Closed	1978	65.00	450	1974 Horse L4861	Closed	1978	55.00	500
1970 Hamlet L4729G	Closed	1980	85.00	700-875	1974 Horse L4862	Closed	1978	55.00	500
1970 Bird Watcher L4730	Closed	1985	35.00	520-1000	1974 Horse L4863	Closed	1978	55.00	400
1970 German Shepherd w/Pup L4731	Closed	1975	40.00	950	1974 Mother L4864G	Closed	1979	190.00	1100
1971 Small Dog L4749	Closed	1985	5.50	190-200	1974 Embroiderer L4865G	Closed	1994	115.00	645-765
1971 Romeo and Juliet L4750G	Open		150.00	1250	1974 Girl with Goose and Dog L4866G	Closed	1993	26.00	205-275
1971 Boy w/Dog L4755G	Closed	1978	50.00	400	1974 Seesaw L4867G	Closed	1997	55.00	375-650
1971 Doncel With Roses L4757G	Closed	1979	35.00	500	1974 Girl with Candle L4868G	Closed	2000	13.00	86-90
1971 Woman L4761G	Closed	1993	60.00	400-500	1974 Girl with Candle L4868M	Closed	1992	13.00	80
1971 Dentist L4762	Closed	1978	36.00	550	1974 Boy Kissing L4869G	Closed	1998	13.00	95-125
1971 Dentist (Reduced) L4762.3G	Closed	1985	30.00	550	1974 Boy Kissing L4869M	Closed	1992	13.00	180
1971 Obstetrician L4763G	Closed	1973	47.50	255-450	1974 Boy Yawning L4870G	Closed	1999	13.00	90-110
1971 Obstetrician L4763.3G	Closed	1973	40.00	300-325	1974 Boy Yawning L4870M	Closed	1992	13.00	180
1971 Obstetrician L4763M	Closed	1998	47.50	255	1974 Girl with Guitar L4871G	Closed	2000	13.00	86-90
1971 Maternal Elephant L4765G	Closed	1975	50.00	700	1974 Girl with Guitar L4871M	Closed	1992	13.00	90
1971 Don Quixote Vase L4770G	Closed	1975	25.00	750	1974 Girl Stretching L4872G	Closed	1992	13.00	90-125
1971 Don Quixote Vase L4770M	Closed	1975	25.00	750	1974 Girl Stretching L4872M	Closed	1992	13.00	90
1971 Rabbit L4772G	Closed	1998	17.50	135-140	1974 Girl Kissing L4873G	Closed	1998	13.00	90-135
1971 Rabbit L4773G	Closed	1998	17.50	130-145	1974 Girl Kissing L4873M	Closed	1992	13.00	90
1971 Dormouse L4774	Closed	1983	30.00	375	1974 Boy & Girl L4874G	Closed	1998	25.00	165-200
1971 Children, Praying L4779G	Closed	1998	36.00	187-260	1974 Boy & Girl L4874M	Closed	1992	25.00	150
1971 Children, Praying L4779M	Closed	1992	36.00	210-225	1974 The Jug Carrier L4875G	Closed	1985	40.00	300
1971 Boy with Goat L4780	Closed	1978	80.00	300-600	1974 Boy Thinking L4876G	Closed	1993	20.00	135-170
1972 Girl Tennis Player L4798	Closed	1981	50.00	400-450	1974 Boy Thinking L4876M	Closed	1992	20.00	120
1972 Japanese Woman L4799	Closed	1975	45.00	425-500	1974 Boy with Flute L4877G	Closed	1981	60.00	450-475
1972 Gypsy with Brother L4800G	Closed	1979	36.00	400-450	1974 Aranjuez Little Lady L4879G	Closed	1997	48.00	295-360
1972 The Teacher L4801G	Closed	1978	45.00	500	1974 Carnival Couple L4882G	Closed	1995	60.00	375-425
1972 Fisherman L4802G	Closed	1979	70.00	550-700	1974 Carnival Couple L4882M	Closed	1991	60.00	280-375
1972 Woman with Umbrella L4805G	Closed	1981	100.00	800	1974 Lady w/ Young Harlequin L4883G	Closed	1975	100.00	1750-2350
1972 Girl with Dog L4806G	Closed	1981	80.00	470-500	1974 Seraph's Head No.1 L4884	Closed	1985	10.00	150-160
1972 Geisha L4807G	Closed	1993	190.00	495-600	1974 Seraph's Head No.2 L4885	Closed	1985	10.00	150-175
1972 Wedding L4808G	Open		50.00	195	1974 Seraph's Head No.3 L4886	Closed	1985	10.00	150
1972 Wedding L4808M	Open		50.00	195	1974 The Kiss L4888G	Closed	1983	150.00	700
1972 Going Fishing L4809G	Closed	2001	33.00	160	1974 Spanish Policeman L4889G	Open		55.00	315
1972 Boy w/Yacht L4810G	Closed	1998	33.00	175-200	1974 Watching the Pigs L4892G	Closed	1978	160.00	1250
1972 Boy w/Yacht L4810M	Closed	1998	33.00	225	1976 "My Dog" L4893G	Open		85.00	250
1972 Dutch Boy L4811	Closed	1988	30.00	289-400	1974 Tennis Player Boy L4894	Closed	1980	75.00	500
1972 Little Girl w/Goat L4812G	Closed	1988	55.00	450-525	1974 Ducks L4895G	Open		45.00	95
1972 Girl with Calf L4813	Closed	1981	50.00	550-650	1974 Ducks L4895M	Closed	1992	45.00	95
1972 Little Girl with Turkey L4814	Closed	1981	45.00	475	1974 Boy with Snails L4896G	Closed	1979	50.00	400-440
1972 Girl with Goose L4815G	Closed	1991	72.00	354-400	1974 Mechanic L4897G	Closed	1985	45.00	325-350
1972 Girl with Goose L4815M	Closed	1991	72.00	295	1974 Boy From Madrid L4898G	Closed	1998	55.00	150-200
1972 Little Shepherd with Goat L4817M	Closed	1981	50.00	475	1974 Boy From Madrid L4898M	Closed	1992	55.00	150
1972 Burro L4821G	Closed	1979	24.00	400-450	1974 Boy with Smoking Jacket L4900	Closed	1983	45.00	200-260
1974 Peruvian Girl with Baby L4822	Closed	1981	65.00	775	1974 Vagabond Dog L4901G	Closed	1979	25.00	300
1974 Legionary L4823	Closed	1978	55.00	500-625	1974 Moping Dog L4902G	Closed	1979	35.00	375
1972 Male Golfer L4824G	Open		66.00	295	1974 Santa Claus L4904G	Closed	1978	100.00	1150
1972 Veterinarian L4825	Closed	1985	48.00	500-550	1974 Admiration/Florinda L4907G	Closed	1985	165.00	650
1972 Rabbit's Food L4826G	Closed	1993	40.00	300-325	1974 Barrister L4908G	Closed	1985	100.00	400-625
1972 Rabbit's Food L4826M	Closed	1993	40.00	225-260	1974 Girl With Dove L4909G	Closed	1982	70.00	425-450
1972 Caressing Calf L4827G	Closed	1981	55.00	475	1974 Girl With Lantern L4910G	Closed	1990	85.00	320-375
1972 Cinderella L4828G	Closed	1998	47.00	235-295	1974 Shepherd L4911G	Closed	1979	175.00	750
1975 Swan L4829G	Closed	1983	16.00	400	1974 Young Lady in Trouble L4912G	Closed	1985	110.00	450-520

FIGURINES

YEAR ISSUE	EDITION LIMIT	YEAR RETD.	ISSUE PRICE	*QUOTE U.S.$
1974 Lesson in the Country L4913G	Closed	1978	240.00	1250
1975 Lady with Shawl L4914G	Closed	1998	220.00	484-800
1975 Girl with Pigeons L4915	Closed	1990	110.00	370-400
1976 Chinese Noblewoman L4916G	Closed	1978	300.00	2000-2145
1974 Dog and Butterfly L4917G	Closed	1981	50.00	800-850
1974 A Girl at the Pond L4918G	Closed	1985	85.00	425
1976 Gypsy Woman L4919G	Closed	1981	165.00	1400-1820
1974 Country Lass with Dog L4920G	Closed	1995	185.00	520-650
1974 Country Lass with Dog L4920M	Closed	1992	185.00	495
1974 Chinese Nobleman L4921G	Closed	1978	325.00	2000-2405
1974 Windblown Girl L4922G	Open		150.00	375
1974 Lanquid Clown L4924G	Closed	1983	200.00	1500
1974 Milk For the Lamb L4926G	Closed	1980	185.00	1300
1974 Medieval Lady L4928G	Closed	1980	275.00	410
1974 Sisters L4930	Closed	1981	250.00	625-650
1974 Children with Fruits L4931G	Closed	1981	210.00	500
1974 Dainty Lady L4934G	Closed	1985	60.00	500
1974 "Closing Scene" L4935G	Closed	1997	180.00	520-546
1983 "Closing Scene"/white L4935.3M	Closed	1987	213.00	275-500
1974 Spring Breeze L4936G	Open		145.00	415
1976 Golden Wedding L4937M	Closed	1981	285.00	600
1976 Baby's Outing L4938G	Closed	2000	250.00	736-775
1976 Milk Maid L4939G	Closed	1981	70.00	371-400
1977 Missy L4951M	Closed	1985	300.00	850
1977 Meditation L4952M	Closed	1979	200.00	1600
1977 Tavern Drinkers L4956G	Closed	1985	1125.00	3500
1977 Attentive Dogs L4957G	Closed	1981	350.00	1750
1977 Cherub, Puzzled L4959G	Open		40.00	140
1977 Cherub, Smiling L4960G	Open		40.00	140
1977 Cherub, Dreaming L4961G	Open		40.00	140
1977 Cherub, Wondering L4962G	Open		40.00	140
1977 Cherub, Wondering L4962M	Closed	1992	40.00	114-195
1977 Infantile Candour L4963G	Closed	1979	285.00	1250
1977 Little Red Riding Hood L4965G	Closed	1983	210.00	480-575
1977 Tennis Player Puppet L4966G	Closed	1985	60.00	525
1977 Soccer Puppet L4967G	Closed	1985	65.00	425
1977 Oympic Puppet L4968	Closed	1983	65.00	800
1977 Sheriff Puppet L4969G	Closed	1985	85.00	600-780
1977 Skier Puppet L4970G	Closed	1983	85.00	500-900
1977 Hunter Puppet L4971G	Closed	1985	95.00	968
1977 Girl with Calla Lillies sitting L4972G	Closed	1998	65.00	190-210
1977 Choir Lesson L4973G	Closed	1981	350.00	1500
1977 Dutch Children L4974G	Closed	1981	375.00	1150
1977 Augustina of Aragon L4976G	Closed	1979	475.00	1500-1800
1977 Harlequin Serenade L4977	Closed	1979	185.00	1250
1977 Milkmaid with Wheelbarrow L4979G	Closed	1981	220.00	950
1978 Ironing Time L4981G	Closed	1985	80.00	375-400
1978 Naughty Dog L4982G	Closed	1995	130.00	275-350
1978 Gossip L4984G	Closed	1985	260.00	1000
1978 Mimi L4985G	Closed	1980	110.00	650
1978 Attentive Lady L4986G	Closed	1981	635.00	2200
1978 Oriental Spring L4988G	Closed	1997	125.00	310-375
1978 Sayonara L4989G	Closed	1997	125.00	300-350
1978 Chrysanthemum L4990G	Closed	1998	125.00	255-375
1978 Butterfly L4991G	Closed	1998	125.00	295-375
1978 Dancers Resting L4992G	Closed	1983	350.00	350-850
1978 Gypsy Venders L4993G	Closed	1985	165.00	475
1978 Ready to Go L4996G	Closed	1981	425.00	1500-1700
1978 Don Quixote & Sancho L4998G	Closed	1983	875.00	2900
1978 Reading L5000G	Open		150.00	285
1978 Elk Family L5001G	Closed	1981	550.00	800-850
1978 Sunny Day L5003G	Closed	1993	193.00	375-425
1978 Eloise L5005G	Closed	1978	175.00	555
1978 Naughty L5006G	Closed	1998	55.00	195-225
1978 Bashful L5007G	Closed	1998	55.00	225-275
1978 Dreamer-Girl w/Straw Hat L5008G	Closed	1999	55.00	155-195
1978 Curious-Girl w/Straw Hat L5009G	Open		55.00	160
1978 Prissy L5010G	Closed	1998	55.00	195-225
1978 Trying on a Straw Hat L5011G	Closed	1998	55.00	195-225
1978 Daughters L5013G	Closed	1991	425.00	990
1978 Genteel L5014G	Closed	1981	725.00	1800-2300
1978 Painful Monkey L5018	Closed	1981	135.00	750-850
1978 Painful Giraffe L5019	Closed	1981	115.00	850
1978 Painful Elephant L5020	Closed	1981	85.00	850
1978 Painful Bear L5021	Closed	1981	75.00	800
1978 Painful Lion L5022G	Closed	1981	95.00	800
1978 Painful Kangaroo L5023G	Closed	1981	150.00	900-950
1978 Woman With Scarf L5024G	Closed	1985	141.00	650-726
1980 A Clean Sweep L5025G	Closed	1985	100.00	350-450
1980 Planning the Day L5026G	Closed	1985	90.00	275
1979 Flower Curtsy L5027G	Open		230.00	475
1980 Flowers in Pot L5028G	Closed	1985	325.00	575-600
1980 The Flower Peddler L5029G	Closed	1985	675.00	1350
1980 Wildflower L5030G	Closed	1994	360.00	591-850
1979 Little Friskies L5032G	Closed	1998	108.00	220-300
1980 Avoiding the Goose L5033G	Closed	1993	160.00	350-600
1980 Goose Trying To Eat L5034G	Closed	1997	135.00	315-350
1980 Act II w/base L5035G	Open		700.00	1425
1979 Jockey with Lass L5036G	Closed	2000	950.00	2590
1980 Sleighride w/base L5037G	Closed	1997	585.00	1050-1300
1979 Girl Bowing L5038G	Closed	1981	185.00	750
1980 Candid L5039G	Closed	1981	145.00	400
1979 Girl Walking L5040G	Closed	1981	150.00	400-1105
1980 Tulips in my Basket L5041G	Closed	1981	160.00	850
1980 Friends L5042G	Closed	1983	385.00	1000
1980 Hind and Baby Deer L5043G	Closed	1981	650.00	2600
1980 Girl with Toy Wagon L5044G	Closed	1998	115.00	249-300
1980 Belinda with Doll L5045G	Closed	1995	115.00	215-250
1980 Organ Grinder L5046G	Closed	1981	328.00	1650
1980 Teacher Woman L5048G	Closed	1981	115.00	600-625
1980 Dancer L5050G	Open		85.00	210
1980 Samson and Delilah L5051G	Closed	1981	350.00	1600
1980 At the Circus L5052G	Closed	1985	525.00	1250
1980 Festival Time L5053G	Closed	1985	250.00	375
1980 Little Senorita L5054G	Closed	1985	235.00	180-400
1980 Apprentice Seaman L5055G	Closed	1985	140.00	450
1980 Boy Clown with Clock L5056G	Closed	1985	290.00	750-850
1980 Clown with Violin L5057G	Closed	1985	270.00	850
1980 Clown with Concertina L5058G	Closed	1985	290.00	600
1980 Clown with Saxaphone L5059G	Closed	1985	320.00	675-700
1980 Clown with Trumpet L5060G	Closed	1985	290.00	500-550
1980 March Wind L5061G	Closed	1983	370.00	600
1980 Kristina L5062G	Closed	1985	225.00	375-400
1980 Margaretta/Dutch Girl With Braids L5063G	Closed	1985	265.00	390-450
1980 Gretel/Dutch Girl, Hands Akimbo L5064G	Closed	1990	255.00	355-425
1980 Ingrid L5065G	Closed	1990	370.00	513-726
1980 Ilsa L5066G	Closed	1990	275.00	360-400
1981 Halloween L5067G	Closed	1983	450.00	1400-1500
1980 Fairy Queen L5068G	Closed	1983	625.00	1250-1600
1980 Napping L5070G	Closed	1983	240.00	850
1980 Nostalgia L5071G	Closed	1993	185.00	355—520
1980 Courtship L5072	Closed	1990	327.00	660-750
1980 Country Flowers L5073	Closed	1985	315.00	500-750
1980 My Hungry Brood L5074G	Closed	1998	295.00	350-400
1980 Little Harlequin "A" L5075G	Closed	1985	217.50	415
1980 Little Harlequin "B" L5076G	Closed	1985	185.00	415
1980 Little Harlequin "C" L5077G	Closed	1985	185.00	500
1980 Teasing the Dog L5078G	Closed	1985	300.00	600
1980 Woman Painting Vase L5079G	Closed	1985	300.00	700-750
1980 Boy Pottery Seller L5080G	Closed	1985	320.00	600-780
1980 Girl Pottery Seller L5081G	Closed	1985	300.00	600-650
1980 Little Flower Seller L5082G	Closed	1985	750.00	2360-2850
1980 Dutch Mother L5083G	Closed	1983	485.00	1100
1980 A Good Book L5084G	Closed	1985	175.00	525
1980 Mother Amabilis L5086G	Closed	1983	275.00	550-580
1980 Roses for My Mom L5088G	Closed	1988	645.00	1150-1350
1980 Scare-Dy Cat/Playful Cat L5091G	Closed	1998	65.00	95-145
1980 After the Dance L5092G	Closed	1983	165.00	350-475
1980 A Dancing Partner L5093G	Closed	1983	165.00	340-500
1980 Ballet First Step L5094G	Closed	1983	165.00	363-400
1980 Ballet Bowing L5095G	Closed	1983	165.00	300-400
1989 Her Ladyship, L5097	Closed	1991	5900.00	6700
1980 Successful Hunt L5098	Closed	1993	5200.00	5200
1982 Playful Tot L5099G	Closed	1985	58.00	250-295
1982 Cry Baby L5100G	Closed	1985	58.00	240-300
1982 Learning to Crawl L5101G	Closed	1985	58.00	275-300
1982 Teething L5102G	Closed	1985	58.00	300
1982 Time for a Nap L5103G	Closed	1985	58.00	250-275
1982 Little Ballet Girl L5105G	Closed	1985	85.00	350-375
1982 Natalia L5106G	Closed	1985	85.00	350
1982 Little Ballet Girl L5108G	Closed	1985	85.00	375-400
1982 Little Ballet Girl L5109G	Closed	1985	85.00	400
1982 Dog Sniffing L5110G	Closed	1985	50.00	625
1982 Timid Dog L5111G	Closed	1985	44.00	600
1982 Play with Me L5112G	Closed	2000	40.00	76-80
1982 Feed Me L5113G	Open		40.00	85
1982 Pet Me L5114G	Closed	1999	40.00	80-110
1982 Little Boy Bullfighter L5115G	Closed	1985	123.00	400
1982 A Victory L5116G	Closed	1985	123.00	400-500
1982 Proud Matador L5117G	Closed	1985	123.00	500

Collectors' Information Bureau   *Quotes have been rounded up to nearest dollar

YEAR ISSUE	EDITION LIMIT	YEAR RETD.	ISSUE PRICE	*QUOTE U.S.$
1982 Girl in Green Dress L5118G	Closed	1985	170.00	650
1982 Girl in Bluish Dress L5119G	Closed	1985	170.00	675
1982 Girl in Pink Dress L5120G	Closed	1985	170.00	585-650
1982 August Moon L5122G	Closed	1993	185.00	350
1982 My Precious Bundle L5123G	Closed	1998	150.00	245-275
1982 Dutch Couple with Tulips L5124G	Closed	1985	310.00	1150-1200
1982 Amparo L5125G	Closed	1990	130.00	350
1982 Sewing A Trousseau L5126G	Closed	1990	185.00	425-600
1982 Marcelina L5127G	Closed	1985	255.00	275
1982 Lost Love L5128G	Closed	1988	400.00	700
1982 Jester w/base L5129G	Closed	2000	220.00	455
1982 Pensive Clown w/base L5130G	Closed	2000	250.00	475
1982 Cervantes L5132G	Closed	1988	925.00	1200-1600
1982 Trophy with Base L5133G	Closed	1983	250.00	650
1982 Girl Soccer Player L5134G	Closed	1983	140.00	440-600
1982 Billy Football Player L5135G	Closed	1983	140.00	600
1982 Billy Skier L5136G	Closed	1983	140.00	800-850
1982 Billy Baseball Player L5137G	Closed	1983	140.00	700
1982 Billy Golfer L5138G	Closed	1983	140.00	750-1000
1982 A New Doll House L5139G	Closed	1983	185.00	850
1982 Feed Her Son L5140G	Closed	1991	170.00	239-340
1982 Balloons for Sale L5141G	Closed	1997	145.00	295
1982 Comforting Daughter L5142G	Closed	1991	195.00	350-560
1982 Scooting L5143G	Closed	1988	575.00	1500-1950
1982 Amy L5145G	Closed	1985	110.00	1400-1500
1982 "E" is for Ellen L5146G	Closed	1985	110.00	1250
1982 Ivez L5147G	Closed	1985	100.00	600
1982 Olivia L5148G	Closed	1985	100.00	400
1982 Ursula L5149G	Closed	1985	100.00	400-425
1982 Girl's Head L5150G	Closed	1983	435.00	1300
1982 Girl's Head L5151G	Closed	1983	380.00	1400
1982 Girl's Head L5152G	Closed	1983	535.00	2000
1982 Girl's Head L5153G	Closed	1983	475.00	1350
1982 First Prize L5154G	Closed	1985	90.00	300
1982 Monks at Prayer L5155M	Open		130.00	325
1982 Susan and the Doves L5156G	Closed	1991	203.00	350-595
1982 Bongo Beat L5157G	Closed	1998	135.00	230-240
1982 A Step In Time L5158G	Closed	1998	90.00	200-250
1982 Harmony L5159G	Closed	1998	270.00	495-550
1982 Rhumba L5160G	Closed	1998	113.00	185-225
1982 Cycling To A Picnic L5161G	Closed	1985	2000.00	2800
1982 Mouse Girl/Mindy L5162G	Closed	1985	125.00	272-500
1982 Bunny Girl/Bunny L5163G	Closed	1985	125.00	442-450
1982 Cat Girl/Kitty L5164G	Closed	1985	125.00	375-510
1982 Sancho with Bottle L5165	Closed	1990	100.00	475
1982 Sea Fever L5166M	Closed	1993	130.00	260-306
1982 Sea Fever L5166G	Closed	1993	130.00	350
1982 Jesus L5167G	Open		130.00	270
1982 King Solomon L5168G	Closed	1985	205.00	950
1982 Abraham L5169G	Closed	1985	155.00	750
1982 Moses L5170G	Closed	2000	175.00	390-410
1982 Madonna with Flowers L5171G	Open		173.00	315
1982 Fish A'Plenty L5172G	Closed	1994	190.00	400-575
1982 Pondering L5173G	Closed	1993	300.00	480-700
1982 Roaring 20's L5174G	Closed	1993	173.00	425-650
1982 Flapper L5175G	Closed	1995	185.00	450-475
1982 Rhapsody in Blue L5176G	Closed	1985	325.00	1450-1850
1982 Dante L5177G	Closed	1983	263.00	750
1982 Stubborn Mule L5178G	Closed	1993	250.00	495-500
1983 Three Pink Roses w/base L5179M	Closed	1990	70.00	300
1983 Dahlia L5180M	Closed	1990	65.00	150-250
1983 Japanese Camelia w/base L5181M	Closed	1990	60.00	100-200
1983 White Peony L5182M	Closed	1990	85.00	150-210
1983 Two Yellow Roses L5183M	Closed	1990	57.50	100-205
1983 White Carnation L5184M	Closed	1990	65.00	100-210
1983 Lactiflora Peony L5185M	Closed	1990	65.00	100-200
1983 Begonia L5186M	Closed	1990	67.50	100-210
1983 Rhododendron L5187M	Closed	1990	67.50	190-205
1983 Miniature Begonia L5188M	Closed	1990	80.00	130-210
1983 Chrysanthemum L5189M	Closed	1990	100.00	150-205
1983 California Poppy L5190M	Closed	1990	97.50	190-210
1985 Predicting the Future L5191G	Closed	1985	135.00	450
1984 Lolita L5192G	Open		80.00	165
1984 Juanita L5193G	Open		80.00	165
1984 Roving Photographer L5194G	Closed	1985	145.00	140-350
1984 Say "Cheese!" L5195G	Closed	1990	170.00	520-600
1983 "Maestro, Music Please!" L5196G	Closed	1988	135.00	395-425
1983 Female Physician L5197	Open		120.00	275
1984 Boy Graduate L5198G	Open		160.00	295
1984 Girl Graduate L5199G	Open		160.00	295
1984 Male Soccer Player L5200G	Closed	1988	155.00	500
1984 Special Male Soccer Player L5200.3G	Closed	1988	150.00	525
1983 Josefa Feeding Duck L5201G	Closed	1991	125.00	295-350
1983 Aracely with Ducks L5202G	Closed	1991	125.00	295-350
1984 Little Jester L5203G	Closed	1993	75.00	350-455
1984 Little Jester L5203M	Closed	1992	75.00	300
1983 Sharpening the Cutlery L5204	Closed	1988	210.00	975
1983 Lamplighter L5205G	Open		170.00	445
1983 Yachtsman L5206G	Closed	1994	110.00	245-384
1983 A Tall Yarn L5207G	Open		260.00	575
1983 Professor L5208G	Closed	1990	205.00	600-650
1983 School Marm L5209G	Closed	1990	205.00	800-850
1984 Jolie L5210G	Open		105.00	270
1984 Angela L5211G	Open		105.00	270
1984 Evita L5212G	Closed	1998	105.00	245-250
1984 Lawyer L5213G	Closed	1998	250.00	620-650
1984 Architect L5214G	Closed	1990	140.00	419-500
1984 Fishing with Gramps w/base L5215G	Closed		410.00	925
1984 On the Lake L5216G	Closed	1988	660.00	1100
1984 Spring L5217G	Open		90.00	220
1984 Spring L5217M	Open		90.00	220
1984 Autumn L5218G	Closed	1999	90.00	200-225
1984 Autumn L5218M	Closed	1999	90.00	200
1984 Summer L5219G	Closed	1999	90.00	185-200
1984 Summer L5219M	Closed	1999	90.00	185-225
1984 Winter L5220G	Closed	2001	90.00	195
1984 Winter L5220M	Closed	2001	90.00	195
1984 Sweet Scent L5221G	Open		80.00	185
1984 Sweet Scent L5221M	Open		80.00	185
1984 Pretty Pickings L5222G	Open		80.00	185
1984 Pretty Pickings L5222M	Open		80.00	185
1984 Spring is Here L5223G	Open		80.00	185
1984 Spring is Here L5223M	Open		80.00	185
1984 The Quest L5224G	Closed	1998	125.00	350-375
1984 Male Candleholder L5226	Closed	1985	660.00	1200
1984 Playful Piglets L5228G	Closed	1998	80.00	165-225
1984 Storytime L5229G	Closed	1990	245.00	850-1100
1984 Graceful Swan L5230G	Open		35.00	150
1984 Swan with Wings Spread L5231G	Open		50.00	150
1984 Playful Kittens L5232G	Open		130.00	300
1984 Charlie the Tramp L5233G	Closed	1991	150.00	850-950
1984 Artistic Endeavor L5234G	Closed	1988	225.00	650
1984 Ballet Trio L5235G	Closed	1998	785.00	1675-1800
1984 Cat and Mouse L5236G	Open		55.00	100
1984 Cat and Mouse L5236M	Closed	1992	55.00	98-130
1984 School Chums L5237G	Closed	1997	225.00	485-550
1984 Eskimo Boy with Pet L5238G	Open		55.00	120
1984 Eskimo Boy with Pet L5238M	Closed	1992	55.00	95
1984 Wine Taster L5239G	Open		190.00	475
1984 Lady from Majorca L5240G	Closed	1990	120.00	475-488
1984 Best Wishes L5244G	Closed	1986	185.00	225-330
1984 A Thought for Today L5245	Closed	1986	180.00	250
1984 St. Cristobal L5246	Closed	1988	265.00	600
1984 Penguin L5247G	Closed	1988	70.00	225-250
1984 Penguin L5248G	Closed	1988	70.00	200-250
1984 Penguin L5249G	Closed	1988	70.00	200-275
1984 Exam Day L5250G	Closed	1994	115.00	165-295
1984 Torch Bearer L5251G	Closed	1988	100.00	400-500
1984 Dancing the Polka L5252G	Closed	1994	205.00	475-525
1984 Cadet L5253G	Closed	1984	150.00	650-700
1984 Making Paella L5254G	Closed	1993	215.00	500-575
1984 Spanish Soldier L5255G	Closed	1988	185.00	475-575
1984 Folk Dancing L5256G	Closed	1990	205.00	525
1984 Vase L5257.30	Closed	1988	55.00	200
1984 Vase L5258.30	Closed	1988	55.00	175
1984 Vase L5261.30	Closed	1988	70.00	150
1984 Vase L5262.30	Closed	1988	70.00	150
1984 Centerpiece-Decorated L5265M	Closed	1990	50.00	175
1985 Bust of Lady from Elche L5269M	Closed	1988	432.00	750
1985 Racing Motor Cyclist L5270G	Closed	1988	360.00	775-850
1985 Gazelle L5271G	Closed	1988	205.00	550
1985 Biking in the Country L5272G	Closed	1990	295.00	795-850
1985 Civil Guard at Attention L5273G	Closed	1988	170.00	440-520
1985 Wedding Day L5274G	Closed	1999	240.00	435
1985 Weary Ballerina L5275G	Closed	1995	175.00	310-375
1985 Weary Ballerina L5275M	Closed	1992	175.00	310
1985 Sailor Serenades His Girl L5276G	Closed	1988	315.00	675-950
1985 Pierrot with Puppy L5277G	Open		95.00	160
1985 Pierrot with Puppy and Ball L5278G	Open		95.00	160
1985 Pierrot with Concertina L5279G	Open		95.00	160
1985 Hiker L5280G	Closed	1988	195.00	385-425
1985 Nativity Scene "Haute Relief" L5281M	Closed	1988	210.00	450

YEAR ISSUE	EDITION LIMIT	YEAR RETD.	ISSUE PRICE	*QUOTE U.S.$
1985 Over the Threshold L5282G	Open		150.00	295
1985 Socialite of the Twenties L5283G	Closed	2001	175.00	350
1985 Glorious Spring L5284G	Open		355.00	750
1985 Summer on the Farm L5285G	Open		235.00	475
1985 Fall Clean-up L5286G	Open		295.00	575
1985 Winter Frost L5287G	Open		270.00	525
1985 Mallard Duck L5288G	Closed	1994	310.00	525-600
1985 Little Leaguer Exercising L5289	Closed	1990	150.00	450-585
1985 Little Leaguer, Catcher L5290	Closed	1990	150.00	475-550
1985 Little Leaguer on Bench L5291	Closed	1990	150.00	450-480
1985 Love in Bloom L5292G	Closed	1998	225.00	420-435
1985 Mother and Child and Lamb L5299G	Closed	1988	180.00	390-750
1985 Medieval Courtship L5300G	Closed	1990	735.00	800
1985 Waiting to Tee Off L5301G	Closed	1999	145.00	295-325
1985 Antelope Drinking L5302	Closed	1988	215.00	550
1985 Playing with Ducks at the Pond L5303G	Closed	1990	425.00	875
1985 Children at Play L5304	Closed	1990	220.00	475-550
1985 A Visit with Granny L5305G	Closed	1993	275.00	550-600
1985 Young Street Musicians L5306G	Closed	1988	300.00	975-1650
1985 Mini Kitten L5307G	Closed	1993	35.00	100-175
1985 Mini Cat L5308G	Closed	1993	35.00	100-150
1985 Mini Cocker Spaniel Pup L5309G	Closed	1993	35.00	125-150
1985 Mini Cocker Spaniel L5310G	Closed	1993	35.00	150
1985 Mini Puppies L5311G	Closed	1990	65.00	225-289
1985 Mini Bison Resting L5312G	Closed	1990	50.00	125-150
1985 Mini Bison Attacking L5313G	Closed	1990	57.50	225
1985 Mini Deer L5314G	Closed	1990	40.00	175
1985 Mini Dromedary L5315G	Closed	1990	45.00	150-175
1985 Mini Giraffe L5316G	Closed	1990	50.00	225-250
1985 Mini Lamb L5317G	Closed	1990	30.00	200
1985 Mini Seal Family L5318G	Closed	1990	77.50	185-280
1985 Wistful Centaur Girl L5319G	Closed	1990	157.00	375-450
1985 Demure Centaur Girl L5320	Closed	1990	157.00	375-425
1985 Parisian Lady L5321G	Closed	1995	193.00	325-350
1985 Viennese Lady L5322G	Closed	1994	160.00	300-370
1985 Milanese Lady L5323G	Closed	1994	180.00	375-400
1985 English Lady L5324G	Closed	1994	225.00	410-495
1985 Ice Cream Vendor L5325G	Closed	1995	380.00	700-750
1985 The Tailor L5326G	Closed	1988	335.00	800-1000
1985 Nippon Lady L5327G	Closed	2000	325.00	565-595
1985 Lady Equestrian L5328G	Closed	1988	160.00	320-475
1985 Gentleman Equestrian L5329G	Closed	1988	160.00	425-525
1985 Concert Violinist L5330G	Closed	1988	220.00	400-450
1985 Gymnast with Ring L5331	Closed	1988	95.00	395
1985 Gymnast Balancing Ball L5332	Closed	1988	95.00	276-375
1985 Gymnast Exercising with Ball L5333G	Closed	1988	95.00	285-350
1985 Aerobics Push-Up L5334G	Closed	1988	110.00	295-425
1985 Aerobics Floor Exercies L5335G	Closed	1988	110.00	250-300
1985 Aerobics Scissor L5336G	Closed	1988	110.00	110-319
1985 "La Giaconda" L5337G	Closed	1988	110.00	400-600
1986 A Stitch in Time L5344G	Closed	1988	425.00	810-850
1986 A New Hat L5345G	Closed	1990	200.00	375
1986 Nature Girl L5346G	Closed	1988	450.00	775
1986 Bedtime L5347G	Closed	1998	300.00	525-600
1986 On The Scent L5348G	Closed	1990	47.50	300
1986 Relaxing L5349G	Closed	1990	47.50	300
1986 On Guard L5350G	Closed	1990	50.00	300
1986 Woe is Me L5351G	Closed	1990	45.00	200
1986 Hindu Children L5352G	Open		250.00	445
1986 Eskimo Riders L5353G	Open		150.00	275
1986 Eskimo Riders L5353M	Open		150.00	275
1986 A Ride in the Country L5354G	Closed	1993	225.00	450-488
1986 Consideration L5355M	Closed	1988	100.00	220-250
1986 Wolf Hound L5356G	Closed	1990	45.00	250
1986 Oration L5357G	Open		170.00	300
1986 Little Sculptor L5358G	Closed	1990	160.00	300-400
1986 El Greco L5359G	Closed	1990	300.00	650-750
1986 Sewing Circle L5360G	Closed	1990	600.00	1200-1400
1986 Try This One L5361G	Closed	1998	225.00	385
1986 Still Life L5363G	Closed	1998	180.00	425-553
1986 Litter of Fun L5364G	Closed	2000	275.00	381-465
1986 Sunday in the Park L5365G	Closed	1997	375.00	625-675
1986 Can Can L5370G	Closed	1990	700.00	1400
1986 Family Roots L5371G	Open		575.00	950
1986 Lolita L5372G	Closed	1993	120.00	250-275
1986 Carmencita L5373G	Closed	1993	120.00	200-275
1986 Pepita L5374G	Closed	1993	120.00	250-275
1986 Teresita L5375G	Closed	1993	120.00	250-275
1986 This One's Mine L5376G	Closed	1995	300.00	300-550
1986 A Touch of Class L5377G	Closed	2000	475.00	708-795
1986 Time for Reflection L5378G	Open		425.00	745
1986 Children's Games L5379G	Closed	1991	325.00	585-750
1986 Sweet Harvest L5380G	Closed	1990	450.00	850-900
1986 Serenade L5381	Closed	1990	450.00	650
1986 Lovers Serenade L5382G	Closed	1990	350.00	850
1986 Petite Maiden L5383	Closed	1990	110.00	265-400
1986 Petite Pair L5384	Closed	1990	225.00	425
1986 Scarecrow & the Lady L5385G	Closed	1997	350.00	680-725
1986 St. Vincent L5387	Closed	1990	190.00	400
1986 Sidewalk Serenade L5388G	Closed	1988	750.00	1300
1986 Deep in Thought L5389G	Closed	1990	170.00	350-450
1986 Spanish Dancer L5390G	Closed	1990	170.00	400-450
1986 A Time to Rest L5391G	Closed	1990	170.00	300-442
1986 Balancing Act L5392G	Closed	1990	35.00	119-200
1986 Curiosity L5393G	Closed	1990	25.00	150
1986 Poor Puppy L5394G	Closed	1990	25.00	250
1986 Valencian Boy L5395G	Closed	1991	200.00	335-400
1986 The Puppet Painter L5396G	Open		500.00	850
1986 The Poet L5397G	Closed	1988	425.00	900
1986 At the Ball L5398G	Closed	1991	375.00	750-910
1987 Time To Rest L5399G	Closed	1993	175.00	295-320
1987 Time To Rest L5399M	Closed	1991	175.00	350
1987 The Wanderer L5400G	Closed	1998	150.00	245-265
1987 My Best Friend L5401G	Closed	1998	150.00	275-312
1987 Desert Tour L5402G	Closed	1990	950.00	1150-1425
1987 The Drummer Boy L5403G	Closed	1990	225.00	400-450
1987 Cadet Captain L5404G	Closed	1990	175.00	360-400
1987 The Flag Bearer L5405G	Closed	1990	200.00	375-450
1987 The Bugler L5406G	Closed	1990	175.00	345-400
1987 At Attention L5407G	Closed	1990	175.00	310-400
1987 Courting Time L5409	Closed	1990	425.00	300-500
1987 Sunday Stroll L5408G	Closed	1990	250.00	455-600
1987 Pilar L5410G	Closed	1990	200.00	400
1987 Teresa L5411G	Closed	1990	225.00	375-430
1987 Isabel L5412G	Closed	1990	225.00	350
1987 Mexican Dancers L5415G	Open		800.00	1195
1987 In the Garden L5416G	Closed	1997	200.00	350
1987 Artist's Model L5417	Closed	1990	425.00	475
1987 Short Eared Owl L5418G	Closed	1990	200.00	280-375
1987 Great Gray Owl L5419G	Closed	1990	190.00	200-230
1987 Horned Owl L5420G	Closed	1990	150.00	230-340
1987 Barn Owl L5421G	Closed	1990	120.00	185-200
1987 Hawk Owl L5422G	Closed	1990	120.00	225-250
1987 Intermezzo L5424	Closed	1990	325.00	410-550
1987 Studying in the Park L5425G	Closed	1990	675.00	950
1987 Studying in the Park L5425M	Closed	1989	675.00	600
1987 One, Two, Three L5426G	Closed	1990	240.00	400
1987 Saint Nicholas L5427G	Closed	1991	425.00	700-795
1987 Feeding the Pigeons L5428	Closed	1990	490.00	568-700
1987 Happy Birthday L5429G	Open		100.00	155
1987 Music Time L5430G	Closed	1990	500.00	675-700
1987 Midwife L5431G	Closed	1990	175.00	650
1987 Midwife L5431M	Closed	1990	175.00	525
1987 Monkey L5432G	Closed	1990	60.00	200
1987 Kangaroo L5433G	Closed	1990	65.00	175-300
1987 Miniature Polar Bear L5434G	Closed	2000	65.00	115
1987 Cougar L5435G	Closed	1990	65.00	250-275
1987 Lion L5436G	Closed	1990	50.00	300
1987 Rhino L5437G	Closed	1990	50.00	175
1987 Elephant L5438G	Closed	1990	50.00	250
1987 The Bride L5439G	Closed	1995	250.00	470-553
1987 Poetry of Love L5442G	Open		500.00	875
1987 Sleepy Trio L5443G	Closed	1997	190.00	350
1987 Will You Marry Me? L5447G	Closed	1994	750.00	1250
1987 Naptime L5448G	Open		135.00	265
1987 Naptime L5448M	Open		135.00	265
1987 Goodnight L5449	Open		225.00	375
1987 I Hope She Does L5450G	Closed	1998	190.00	279-350
1988 Study Buddies L5451G	Open		225.00	295
1988 Masquerade Ball L5452G	Closed	1993	220.00	340-545
1988 Masquerade Ball L5452M	Closed	1992	220.00	350
1988 For You L5453G	Closed	1998	450.00	640-700
1988 For Me? L5454G	Closed	1998	290.00	375-395
1988 Bashful Bather L5455G	Open		150.00	195
1988 Bashful Bather L5455M	Closed	1992	150.00	180
1988 New Playmates L5456G	Open		160.00	260
1988 New Playmates L5456M	Closed	1992	160.00	190
1988 Bedtime Story L5457G	Open		275.00	355
1988 Bedtime Story L5457M	Closed	1992	275.00	330
1988 A Barrow of Fun L5460G	Open		370.00	650
1988 A Barrow of Fun L5460M	Closed	1992	370.00	450

Collectors' Information Bureau   *Quotes have been rounded up to nearest dollar

YEAR ISSUE	EDITION LIMIT	YEAR RETD.	ISSUE PRICE	*QUOTE U.S.$
1988 Koala Love L5461G	Closed	1993	115.00	225-325
1988 Practice Makes Perfect L5462G	Closed	1998	375.00	500-625
1988 Look At Me! L5465G	Open		375.00	530
1988 Look At Me! L5465M	Closed	1992	375.00	455
1988 "Chit-Chat" L5466G	Open		150.00	225
1988 "Chit-Chat" L5466M	Closed	1992	150.00	220
1988 May Flowers L5467G	Open		160.00	245
1988 May Flowers L5467M	Closed	1992	160.00	200
1988 "Who's The Fairest?" L5468G	Closed	2000	150.00	195-205
1988 "Who's The Fairest?" L5468M	Closed	1992	150.00	200
1988 Lambkins L5469G	Closed	1993	150.00	250
1988 Lambkins L5469M	Closed	1989	150.00	200
1988 Tea Time L5470G	Closed	1998	280.00	410-475
1988 Sad Sax L5471G	Open		175.00	210
1988 Circus Sam L5472G	Open		175.00	210
1988 How You've Grown! L5474G	Closed	1998	180.00	270
1988 How You've Grown! L5474M	Closed	1992	180.00	250
1988 A Lesson Shared L5475G	Closed	1998	150.00	195-240
1988 A Lesson Shared L5475M	Closed	1992	150.00	195
1988 St. Joseph L5476G	Open		210.00	295
1988 Mary L5477G	Open		130.00	165
1988 Baby Jesus L5478G	Open		55.00	75
1988 King Melchior L5479G	Open		210.00	265
1988 King Gaspar L5480G	Open		210.00	265
1988 King Balthasar L5481G	Open		210.00	265
1988 Ox L5482G	Open		125.00	180
1988 Donkey L5483G	Open		125.00	180
1988 Lost Lamb L5484G	Open		100.00	145
1988 Shepherd Boy L5485G	Open		140.00	220
1988 Debutantes L5486G	Closed	1998	490.00	650-745
1988 Debutantes L5486M	Closed	1992	490.00	655-695
1988 Ingenue L5487G	Open		110.00	150
1988 Ingenue L5487M	Closed	1992	110.00	150-185
1988 Sandcastles L5488G	Closed	1993	160.00	240-325
1988 Sandcastles L5488M	Closed	1993	160.00	200
1988 Justice L5489G	Closed	1993	675.00	900-950
1988 Flor Maria L5490G	Open		500.00	635
1988 Heavenly Strings L5491G	Closed	1993	140.00	225-250
1988 Heavenly Cellist L5492G	Closed	1993	240.00	325-350
1988 Angel with Lute L5493G	Closed	1993	140.00	150-225
1988 Angel with Clarinet L5494G	Closed	1993	140.00	175-250
1988 Angelic Choir L5495G	Closed	1993	300.00	500-575
1988 Recital L5496G	Open		190.00	295
1988 Dress Rehearsal L5497G	Open		290.00	425
1988 Opening Night L5498G	Open		190.00	295
1988 Pretty Ballerina L5499G	Closed	1998	190.00	274-290
1988 Prayerful Moment (blue) L5500G	Open		90.00	115
1988 Time to Sew (blue) L5501G	Open		90.00	115
1988 Time to Sew (white) L5501.3	Closed	1991	90.00	250-275
1988 Meditation (blue) L5502G	Open		90.00	115
1988 Hurry Now L5503G	Open		180.00	275
1988 Hurry Now L5503M	Closed	1992	180.00	250
1988 Silver Vase No. 20 L5531.4	Closed	1991	135.00	300
1989 Flowers for Sale L5537G	Closed	2000	1200.00	1550
1989 Puppy Dog Tails L5539G	Open		1200.00	1750
1989 An Evening Out L5540G	Closed	1991	350.00	650
1989 Melancholy w/base L5542G	Closed	2000	375.00	437-455
1989 "Hello, Flowers" L5543G	Closed	1993	385.00	485-845
1989 Reaching the Goal L5546G	Closed	1998	215.00	234-375
1989 Only the Beginning L5547G	Closed	1997	215.00	275-300
1989 Pretty Posies L5548G	Closed	1994	425.00	530-575
1989 My New Pet L5549G	Closed	1998	150.00	185-190
1989 Serene Moment (blue) L5550G	Closed	1993	115.00	200-375
1989 Serene Moment (white) L5550.3G	Closed	1991	115.00	250-300
1989 Serene Moment (white) L5550.3M	Closed	1991	115.00	250
1989 Call to Prayer (blue) L5551G	Closed	1993	100.00	200-375
1989 Call to Prayer (white) L5551.3G	Closed	1991	100.00	250-350
1989 Call to Prayer (white) L5551.3M	Closed	1991	100.00	250
1989 Morning Chores (blue) L5552G	Closed	1993	115.00	200-300
1989 Morning Chores (white) L5552G	Closed	1991	115.00	250-300
1989 Wild Goose Chase L5553G	Closed	1998	175.00	196-230
1989 Pretty and Prim L5554G	Closed	1998	215.00	143-320
1989 "Let's Make Up" L5555G	Open		215.00	270
1989 Wide Tulip Vase L5560G	Closed	1990	110.00	300
1989 Green Clover Vase L5561G	Closed	1991	130.00	225
1989 Sad Parting L5583G	Closed	1991	375.00	525
1989 Daddy's Girl/Father's Day L5584G	Closed	1997	175.00	395-450
1989 Fine Melody w/base L5585G	Closed	1993	225.00	325-350
1989 Sad Note w/base L5586G	Closed	1993	185.00	225-325
1989 Wedding Cake L5587G	Closed	1997	595.00	750-850
1989 Blustery Day L5588G	Closed	1993	185.00	230-325
1989 Pretty Pose L5589G	Closed	1993	185.00	230-260
1989 Spring Breeze L5590G	Closed	1993	185.00	230-275
1989 Garden Treasures L5591G	Closed	1993	185.00	230-260
1989 Male Siamese Dancer L5592G	Closed	1993	345.00	449-480
1989 Siamese Dancer L5593G	Closed	1993	345.00	420
1989 Playful Romp L5594G	Closed	1997	215.00	270
1989 Joy in a Basket L5595G	Closed	1998	215.00	230-300
1989 A Gift of Love L5596G	Closed	1998	400.00	495-600
1989 Summer Soiree L5597G	Closed	1998	150.00	180-195
1989 Bridesmaid L5598G	Open		150.00	180
1989 Coquette L5599G	Open		150.00	180
1989 The Blues w/base L5600G	Closed	1993	265.00	365-395
1989 "Ole" L5601G	Open		365.00	465
1989 Close To My Heart L5603G	Closed	1998	125.00	165-215
1989 Spring Token L5604G	Open		175.00	230
1989 Floral Treasures L5605G	Open		195.00	250
1989 Quiet Evening L5606G	Closed	1993	125.00	200-215
1989 Calling A Friend L5607G	Closed	1998	125.00	165-210
1989 Baby Doll L5608G	Open		150.00	180-225
1989 Playful Friends L5609G	Closed	1995	135.00	170
1989 Star Struck w/base L5610G	Closed	1998	335.00	420-450
1989 Sad Clown w/base L5611G	Closed	1998	335.00	336-400
1989 Reflecting w/base L5612G	Closed	1994	335.00	336-420
1989 Sealore Pipe L5613G	Closed	1993	125.00	175-235
1989 Startled L5614G	Closed	1991	265.00	265-425
1989 Bathing Beauty L5615G	Closed	1991	265.00	350-475
1989 Candleholder L5625G	Closed	1990	105.00	125
1989 Candleholder L5626	Closed	1990	90.00	125
1989 Lladró Vase L5631G	Closed	1990	150.00	225-395
1990 Water Dreamer Vase L5633G	Closed	1990	150.00	400
1990 Cat Nap L5640G	Open		125.00	145
1990 The King's Guard w/base L5642G	Closed	1993	950.00	1100
1990 Cathy L5643G	Closed	1998	200.00	190-275
1990 Susan L5644G	Open		190.00	215
1990 Elizabeth L5645G	Closed	1998	190.00	225-250
1990 Cindy L5646G	Closed	1998	190.00	190-225
1990 Sarah L5647G	Closed	1998	200.00	196-250
1990 Courtney L5648G	Open		200.00	230
1990 Nothing To Do L5649G	Closed	1998	190.00	210-220
1990 Anticipation L5650G	Closed	1993	300.00	340-575
1990 Musical Muse L5651G	Closed	1997	375.00	440-500
1990 Marbella Clock L5652	Closed	1994	125.00	132-235
1989 Avila Clock L5653	Closed	1995	135.00	135-185
1990 Venetian Carnival L5658G	Closed	1993	500.00	625
1990 Barnyard Scene L5659G	Closed	1998	200.00	219-245
1990 Sunning In Ipanema L5660G	Closed	1993	370.00	525-600
1990 Traveling Artist L5661G	Closed	1994	250.00	290-300
1990 May Dance L5662G	Open		170.00	215
1990 Spring Dance L5663G	Closed	2000	170.00	203-210
1990 Giddy Up L5664G	Closed	1994	190.00	230-245
1990 Hang On! L5665G	Closed	1995	225.00	285-325
1990 Trino At The Beach L5666G	Closed	1995	390.00	500-550
1990 Valencian Harvest L5668G	Closed	1993	175.00	350-400
1990 Valencian Flowers L5669G	Closed	1993	370.00	375
1990 Valencian Beauty L5670G	Closed	1993	175.00	175-325
1990 Little Dutch Gardener L5671G	Closed	1993	400.00	475
1990 Hi There! L5672G	Closed	1997	450.00	520-570
1990 A Quiet Moment L5673G	Closed	1998	450.00	520-575
1990 A Faun And A Friend L5674G	Closed	1997	450.00	530-550
1990 Tee Time L5675G	Closed	1993	280.00	315
1990 Wandering Minstrel L5676G	Closed	1993	270.00	248-310
1990 Twilight Years L5677G	Closed	1998	370.00	500-550
1990 I Feel Pretty L5678G	Closed	1998	190.00	230
1990 In No Hurry L5679G	Closed	1994	550.00	640-695
1990 Traveling In Style L5680G	Closed	1994	425.00	495-550
1990 On The Road L5681G	Closed	1991	320.00	550
1990 Breezy Afternoon L5682G	Open		180.00	195
1990 Breezy Afternoon L5682M	Open		180.00	195
1990 Beautiful Burro L5683G	Closed	1993	280.00	325-435
1990 Barnyard Reflections L5684G	Closed	1993	460.00	600-650
1990 Promenade L5685G	Closed	1994	275.00	325-375
1990 On The Avenue L5686G	Closed	1994	275.00	325-375
1990 Afternoon Stroll L5687G	Closed	1994	275.00	335-375
1990 Dog's Best Friend L5688G	Open		250.00	310
1990 Can I Help? L5689G	Closed	1998	250.00	335-350
1990 Marshland Mates w/base L5691G	Open		950.00	1200
1990 Street Harmonies w/base L5692G	Closed	1993	3200.00	3750
1990 Circus Serenade L5694G	Closed	1994	300.00	335-375
1990 Concertina L5695G	Closed	1994	300.00	335-360
1990 Mandolin Serenade L5696G	Closed	1994	300.00	360
1990 Over The Clouds L5697G	Open		275.00	310

*Quotes have been rounded up to nearest dollar

Collectors' Information Bureau

FIGURINES

YEAR ISSUE	EDITION LIMIT	YEAR RETD.	ISSUE PRICE	*QUOTE U.S.$	YEAR ISSUE	EDITION LIMIT	YEAR RETD.	ISSUE PRICE	*QUOTE U.S.$
1990 Don't Look Down L5698G	Open		330.00	410	1991 Ocean Beauty L5785G	Open		625.00	665
1990 Sitting Pretty L5699G	Closed	1998	300.00	340	1991 Story Hour L5786G	Closed	1998	550.00	600-625
1990 Southern Charm L5700G	Closed	1998	675.00	1050-1095	1991 Sophisticate L5787G	Closed	1998	185.00	195
1990 Just A Little Kiss L5701G	Closed	1998	320.00	375	1991 Talk Of The Town L5788G	Closed	1998	185.00	195
1990 Back To School L5702G	Closed	1993	350.00	350-445	1991 The Flirt L5789G	Closed	1998	185.00	185-215
1990 Behave! L5703G	Closed	1994	230.00	340-363	1991 Carefree L5790G	Open		300.00	325
1990 Swan Song L5704G	Closed	1995	350.00	410-450	1991 Fairy Godmother L5791G	Closed	1994	375.00	403-600
1990 The Swan And The Princess L5705G	Closed	1994	350.00	410-495	1991 Reverent Moment L5792G	Closed	1994	295.00	320-350
1990 We Can't Play L5706G	Closed	1998	200.00	235-250	1991 Precocious Ballerina L5793G	Closed	1995	575.00	625
1990 After School L5707G	Closed	1993	280.00	315	1991 Precious Cargo L5794G	Closed	1994	460.00	495-550
1990 My First Class L5708G	Closed	1993	280.00	315-360	1991 Floral Getaway L5795G	Closed	1993	625.00	695-745
1990 Between Classes L5709G	Closed	1993	280.00	315	1991 Holy Night L5796G	Closed	1994	330.00	360-400
1990 Fantasy Friend L5710G	Closed	1993	420.00	495-555	1991 Come Out And Play L5797G	Closed	1994	275.00	295-375
1990 A Christmas Wish L5711G	Closed	1998	350.00	349-410	1991 Milkmaid L5798G	Closed	1993	450.00	485-500
1990 Sleepy Kitten L5712G	Open		110.00	130	1991 Shall We Dance? L5799G	Closed	1993	600.00	700-750
1990 The Snow Man L5713G	Open		300.00	350	1991 Elegant Promenade L5802G	Open		775.00	825
1990 First Ballet L5714G	Open		370.00	420	1991 Playing Tag L5804G	Closed	1993	170.00	190-245
1990 Mommy, it's Cold! L5715G	Closed	1994	360.00	450-500	1991 Tumbling L5805G	Closed	1993	130.00	175
1990 Land of The Giants L5716G	Closed	1994	275.00	315-425	1991 Tumbling L5805M	Closed	1992	130.00	140
1990 Rock A Bye Baby L5717G	Closed	1999	300.00	365	1991 Tickling L5806G	Closed	1993	130.00	145
1990 Sharing Secrets L5720G	Closed	1998	290.00	335-375	1991 Tickling L5806M	Closed	1992	130.00	145
1990 Once Upon A Time L5721G	Closed	1998	550.00	670-750	1991 My Puppies L5807G	Closed	1993	325.00	325-360
1990 Follow Me L5722G	Open		140.00	160	1991 Musically Inclined L5810G	Closed	1993	235.00	235-250
1990 Heavenly Chimes L5723G	Open		100.00	120	1991 Littlest Clown L5811G	Open		225.00	240
1990 Angelic Voice L5724G	Open		125.00	145	1991 Tired Friend L5812G	Open		225.00	240
1990 Making A Wish L5725G	Open		125.00	145	1991 Having A Ball L5813G	Open		225.00	240
1990 Sweep Away The Clouds L5726G	Open		125.00	145	1991 Curtain Call L5814G	Closed	1994	490.00	520-825
1990 Angel Care L5727G	Closed	2000	185.00	200-210	1991 Curtain Call L5814M	Closed	1994	490.00	520
1990 Heavenly Dreamer L5728G	Closed	2000	100.00	114-120	1991 In Full Relave L5815G	Closed	1994	490.00	520-825
1991 Carousel Charm L5731G	Closed	1994	1700.00	2100	1991 In Full Relave L5815M	Closed	1994	490.00	520
1991 Carousel Canter L5732G	Closed	1994	1700.00	1482-1850	1991 Prima Ballerina L5816G	Closed	1994	490.00	520
1991 Horticulturist L5733G	Closed	1993	450.00	495	1991 Prima Ballerina L5816M	Closed	1994	490.00	520
1991 Pilgrim Couple L5734G	Closed	1993	490.00	500-525	1991 Backstage Preparation L5817G	Closed	1994	490.00	520-525
1991 Big Sister L5735G	Open		650.00	685	1991 Backstage Preparation L5817M	Closed	1994	490.00	650
1991 Puppet Show L5736G	Closed	1997	280.00	295-375	1991 On Her Toes L5818G	Closed	1994	490.00	490-520
1991 Little Prince L5737G	Closed	1993	295.00	315-330	1991 On Her Toes L5818M	Closed	1994	490.00	520
1991 Best Foot Forward L5738G	Closed	1994	280.00	244-305	1991 Allegory Of Liberty L5819G	Open		1950.00	2100
1991 Lap Full Of Love L5739G	Closed	1995	275.00	295-315	1991 Dance Of Love L5820G	Closed	1993	575.00	625
1991 Alice In Wonderland L5740G	Closed	1997	440.00	495-550	1991 Minstrel's Love L5821G	Closed	1993	525.00	575-595
1991 Dancing Class L5741G	Closed	N/A	340.00	365	1991 Little Unicorn L5826G	Closed	1998	275.00	275-375
1991 Bridal Portrait L5742G	Closed	1995	480.00	560-748	1991 Little Unicorn L5826M	Closed	1998	275.00	295
1991 Don't Forget Me L5743G	Open		150.00	165	1991 I've Got It L5827G	Closed	1995	170.00	180-200
1991 Bull & Donkey L5744G	Closed	1997	250.00	275-295	1991 Next At Bat L5828G	Closed	1998	170.00	180-230
1991 Baby Jesus L5745G	Closed	1997	170.00	185	1991 Heavenly Harpist L5830	Yr.Iss.	1991	135.00	195-250
1991 St. Joseph L5746G	Closed	1997	350.00	375-400	1991 Jazz Horn L5832G	Open		295.00	310
1991 Mary L5747G	Closed	1997	275.00	285-295	1991 Jazz Sax L5833G	Open		295.00	315
1991 Shepherd Girl L5748G	Closed	1997	150.00	165	1991 Jazz Bass L5834G	Open		395.00	425
1991 Shepherd Boy L5749G	Closed	1997	225.00	225-245	1991 I Do L5835G	Open		165.00	195
1991 Little Lamb L5750G	Closed	1997	40.00	42-75	1991 Sharing Sweets L5836G	Closed	1998	220.00	245
1991 Walk With Father L5751G	Closed	1994	375.00	410-440	1991 Sing With Me L5837G	Closed	1998	240.00	250-265
1991 Little Virgin L5752G	Closed	1994	295.00	320-325	1991 On The Move L5838G	Closed	1998	340.00	395
1991 Hold Her Still L5753G	Closed	1993	650.00	695-725	1992 A Quiet Afternoon L5843G	Closed	1995	1050.00	1125
1991 Singapore Dancers L5754G	Closed	1993	950.00	1150-1195	1992 Flirtatious Jester L5844G	Closed	1998	890.00	890-925
1991 Claudette L5755G	Closed	1993	265.00	285-350	1992 Dressing The Baby L5845G	Open		295.00	295
1991 Ashley L5756G	Closed	1993	265.00	275-300	1992 All Tuckered Out L5846G	Open		220.00	265
1991 Beautiful Tresses L5757G	Closed	1993	725.00	760-875	1992 All Tuckered Out L5846M	Open		220.00	265
1991 Sunday Best L5758G	Closed	1998	725.00	620-785	1992 The Loving Family L5848G	Closed	1994	950.00	985-1050
1991 Presto! L5759G	Closed	1993	275.00	325-455	1992 Inspiring Muse L5850G	Closed	1994	1200.00	1250-1650
1991 Interrupted Nap L5760G	Closed	1995	325.00	280-425	1992 Feathered Fantasy L5851G	Closed	1997	1200.00	1200-1250
1991 Out For A Romp L5761G	Closed	1995	375.00	410-533	1992 Easter Bonnets L5852G	Closed	1993	265.00	400
1991 Checking The Time L5762G	Closed	1995	560.00	595-750	1992 Floral Admiration L5853G	Closed	1994	690.00	825
1991 Musical Partners L5763G	Closed	1995	625.00	675	1992 Floral Fantasy L5854G	Closed	1995	690.00	745-890
1991 Seeds Of Laughter L5764G	Closed	1995	525.00	600-695	1992 Afternoon Jaunt L5855G	Closed	1993	420.00	440-500
1991 Hats Off To Fun L5765G	Closed	1995	475.00	510-560	1992 Circus Concert L5856G	Closed	1997	570.00	585-600
1991 Charming Duet L5766G	Closed	1997	575.00	625-725	1992 Grand Entrance L5857G	Closed	1994	265.00	275
1991 First Sampler L5767G	Closed	1995	625.00	680-750	1992 Waiting to Dance L5858G	Closed	1995	295.00	335-345
1991 Academy Days L5768G	Closed	1993	280.00	310-325	1992 At The Ball L5859G	Open		295.00	330
1991 Faithful Steed L5769G	Closed	1994	370.00	375-395	1992 Fairy Garland L5860G	Closed	1995	630.00	750-850
1991 Out For A Spin L5770G	Closed	1995	390.00	420-495	1992 Fairy Flowers L5861G	Closed	1995	630.00	750-850
1991 The Magic Of Laughter L5771G	Closed	1997	950.00	1065-1250	1992 Fragrant Bouquet L5862G	Open		350.00	375
1991 Little Dreamers L5772G	Open		230.00	245	1992 Dressing For The Ballet L5865G	Closed	1995	395.00	415-500
1991 Little Dreamers L5772M	Open		230.00	245	1992 Final Touches L5866G	Closed	1995	395.00	415-500
1991 Graceful Offering L5773G	Closed	1995	850.00	900-1100	1992 Serene Valenciana L5867G	Closed	1994	365.00	385
1991 Nature's Gifts L5774G	Closed	1994	900.00	900-975	1992 Loving Valenciana L5868G	Closed	1994	365.00	385
1991 Gift Of Beauty L5775G	Closed	1994	850.00	900-1100	1992 Fallas Queen L5869G	Closed	1995	420.00	440-535
1991 Lover's Paradise L5779G	Closed	1998	2250.00	2450-2500	1992 Olympic Torch w/Fantasy Logo L5870G	Closed	1994	165.00	145-185
1991 Walking The Fields L5780G	Closed	1993	725.00	795-850	1992 Olympic Champion w/Fantasy Logo L5871G	Closed	1994	165.00	145-250
1991 Not Too Close L5781G	Closed	1995	365.00	365-450	1992 Olympic Pride w/Fantasy Logo L5872G	Closed	1994	165.00	225-495
1991 My Chores L5782G	Closed	1995	325.00	355-400					
1991 Special Delivery L5783G	Closed	1998	525.00	550-650					
1991 A Cradle Of Kittens L5784G	Closed	1998	360.00	360-385					

Collectors' Information Bureau

*Quotes have been rounded up to nearest dollar

YEAR ISSUE	EDITION LIMIT	YEAR RETD.	ISSUE PRICE	*QUOTE U.S.$
1992 Modern Mother L5873G	Closed	1997	325.00	276-375
1992 Off We Go L5874G	Closed	1994	365.00	385
1992 Angelic Cymbalist L5876	Yr.Iss.	1992	140.00	195-250
1992 Guest Of Honor L5877G	Closed	1997	195.00	195-200
1992 Sister's Pride L5878G	Closed	1997	595.00	615-695
1992 Shot On Goal L5879G	Closed	1997	1100.00	1150-1250
1992 Playful Unicorn L5880G	Closed	1998	295.00	320-475
1992 Playful Unicorn L5880M	Closed	1998	295.00	320
1992 Mischievous Mouse L5881G	Closed	1998	285.00	295-345
1992 Restful Mouse L5882G	Closed	1997	285.00	295-325
1992 Loving Mouse L5883G	Closed	1997	285.00	295-325
1992 From This Day Forward L5885G	Open		265.00	290
1992 Hippity Hop L5886G	Closed	1995	95.00	95-125
1992 Washing Up L5887G	Closed	1995	95.00	95-105
1992 That Tickles! L5888G	Closed	1995	95.00	105-165
1992 Snack Time L5889G	Closed	1995	95.00	105-150
1992 The Aviator L5891G	Closed	1998	375.00	450-600
1992 Circus Magic L5892G	Closed	1998	470.00	495
1992 Friendship In Bloom L5893G	Closed	1995	650.00	685
1992 Precious Petals L5894G	Closed	1997	395.00	415
1992 Bouquet of Blossoms L5895G	Closed	1998	295.00	295
1992 The Loaves & Fishes L5896G	Closed	1998	695.00	760-900
1992 Trimming The Tree L5897G	Open		900.00	925
1992 Spring Splendor L5898G	Open		440.00	450
1992 Just One More L5899G	Closed	1998	450.00	495-550
1992 Sleep Tight L5900G	Closed	1998	450.00	500-550
1992 Surprise L5901G	Open		325.00	335
1992 Easter Bunnies L5902G	Closed	1997	240.00	250-265
1992 Down The Aisle L5903G	Closed	1997	295.00	251-345
1992 Sleeping Bunny L5904G	Closed	1998	75.00	75
1992 Attentive Bunny L5905G	Closed	1998	75.00	75-100
1992 Preening Bunny L5906G	Closed	1998	75.00	80-105
1992 Sitting Bunny L5907G	Closed	1998	75.00	80
1992 Just A Little More L5908G	Closed	1998	370.00	323-380
1992 All Dressed Up L5909G	Closed	1998	440.00	450-525
1992 Making A Wish L5910G	Closed	1998	790.00	825-850
1992 Swans Take Flight L5912G	Open		2850.00	2950
1992 Rose Ballet L5919G	Open		210.00	215
1992 Swan Ballet L5920G	Open		210.00	215
1992 Take Your Medicine L5921G	Closed	1998	360.00	370-450
1990 Floral Clock L5924	Closed	1995	N/A	165
1990 Garland Quartz Clock L5926	Closed	1995	195.00	195
1992 Jazz Clarinet L5928G	Open		295.00	295
1992 Jazz Drums L5929G	Open		595.00	610
1992 Jazz Duo L5930G	Open		795.00	900
1993 The Ten Commandments w/Base L5933G	Closed	1997	930.00	930
1993 The Holy Teacher L5934G	Closed	1997	375.00	375-425
1993 Nutcracker Suite L5935G	Closed	1998	620.00	620-675
1993 Little Skipper L5936G	Closed	1997	320.00	289-390
1993 Riding The Waves L5941G	Open	1998	405.00	425-575
1993 World of Fantasy L5943G	Closed	1995	295.00	295-310
1993 The Great Adventurer L5944G	Closed	1994	325.00	325
1993 A Mother's Way L5946G	Closed	1997	1350.00	1350-1400
1993 General Practitioner L5947G	Closed	1998	360.00	315-370
1993 Physician L5948G	Open		360.00	360
1993 Angel Candleholder w/Lyre L5949G	Closed	1998	295.00	315-365
1993 Angel Candleholder w/Tambourine L5950G	Closed	1998	295.00	315-365
1993 Sounds of Summer L5953G	Closed	2001	150.00	150
1993 Sounds of Winter L5954G	Closed	2001	150.00	150
1993 Sounds of Fall L5955G	Closed	2001	150.00	150
1993 Sounds of Spring L5956G	Closed	2001	150.00	150
1993 The Glass Slipper L5957G	Closed	2001	475.00	475
1993 Country Ride w/base L5958G	Open		2850.00	2875
1993 It's Your Turn L5959G	Closed	1997	365.00	365
1993 On Patrol L5960G	Closed	1998	395.00	378-550
1993 The Great Teacher w/base L5961G	Closed	1997	850.00	850
1993 Angelic Melody L5963	Yr.Iss.	1993	145.00	175-275
1993 The Great Voyage L5964G	Open		50.00	50-60
1993 The Clipper Ship w/base L5965M	Closed	1997	240.00	250
1993 Flowers Forever w/base L5966G	Open		4150.00	4150
1993 Honeymoon Ride w/base L5968G	Closed	1995	2750.00	2795
1993 A Special Toy L5971G	Closed	1997	815.00	815-850
1993 Before the Dance w/base L5972G	Open		3550.00	3550
1993 Before the Dance w/base L5972M	Open		3550.00	3550
1993 Family Outing w/base L5974G	Closed	1998	4275.00	4275
1993 Up and Away w/base L5975G	Open		2850.00	2850
1993 The Fireman L5976G	Closed	1998	395.00	465-500
1993 Revelation w/base (white) L5977G	Closed	1995	325.00	325
1993 Revelation w/base (black) L5978M	Closed	1995	325.00	325
1993 Revelation w/base (sand) L5979M	Closed	1995	325.00	325
1993 The Past w/base (white) L5980G	Closed	1995	325.00	325
1993 The Past w/base (black) L5981M	Closed	1995	325.00	325
1993 The Past w/base (sand) L5982M	Closed	1995	325.00	325
1993 Beauty w/base (white) L5983G	Closed	1995	325.00	325
1993 Beauty w/base (black) L5984M	Closed	1995	325.00	325
1993 Beauty w/base (sand) L5985M	Closed	1995	325.00	325
1993 Sunday Sermon L5986G	Open		425.00	425
1993 Talk to Me L5987G	Closed	1998	145.00	175-190
1993 Taking Time L5988G	Closed	1998	145.00	145-175
1993 A Mother's Touch L5989G	Closed	1997	470.00	470
1993 Thoughtful Caress L5990G	Closed	1997	225.00	225
1993 Love Story L5991G	Closed	2000	2800.00	2800
1993 Unicorn and Friend L5993G	Closed	1998	355.00	355-425
1993 Unicorn and Friend L5993M	Closed	1998	355.00	355
1993 Meet My Friend L5994G	Closed	1997	695.00	695
1993 Soft Meow L5995G	Closed	1998	480.00	515-575
1993 Bless the Child L5996G	Closed	1994	465.00	465
1993 One More Try L5997G	Closed	1997	715.00	795-850
1993 My Dad L6001G	Closed	1995	550.00	550-600
1993 Down You Go L6002G	Closed	1998	815.00	815-865
1993 Ready To Learn L6003G	Closed	1999	650.00	650
1993 Bar Mitzvah Day L6004G	Open		395.00	430
1993 Christening Day w/base L6005G	Closed	1995	1425.00	1425
1993 Oriental Colonade w/base L6006G	Closed	1995	1875.00	1875
1993 The Goddess & Unicorn w/base L6007G	Open		1675.00	1675
1993 Joyful Event L6008G	Open		825.00	850
1993 Monday's Child (Boy) L6011G	Closed	1998	245.00	277-352
1993 Monday's Child (Girl) L6012G	Closed	1998	260.00	290-350
1993 Tuesday's Child (Boy) L6013G	Closed	1998	225.00	225-300
1993 Tuesday's Child (Girl) L6014G	Closed	1998	245.00	285-350
1993 Wednesday's Child (Boy) L6015G	Closed	1998	245.00	242-325
1993 Wednesday's Child (Girl) L6016G	Closed	1998	245.00	285-350
1993 Thursday's Child (Boy) L6017G	Closed	1998	225.00	250-300
1993 Thursday's Child (Girl) L6018G	Closed	1998	225.00	250-285
1993 Friday's Child (Boy) L6019G	Closed	1998	225.00	213-320
1993 Friday's Child (Girl) L6020G	Closed	1998	225.00	250-350
1993 Saturday's Child (Boy) L6021G	Closed	1998	245.00	242-285
1993 Saturday's Child (Girl) L6022G	Closed	1998	245.00	285-325
1993 Sunday's Child (Boy) L6023G	Closed	1998	225.00	213-300
1993 Sunday's Child (Girl) L6024G	Closed	1998	225.00	300-325
1993 Barnyard See Saw L6025G	Closed	1998	500.00	425-550
1993 My Turn L6026G	Closed	1998	515.00	475-515
1993 Hanukah Lights L6027G	Closed	1999	345.00	395
1993 Mazel Tov! L6028G	Open		380.00	395
1993 Hebrew Scholar L6029G	Closed	1997	225.00	245-295
1993 On The Go L6031G	Closed	1995	475.00	412-631
1993 On The Green L6032G	Open		645.00	645
1993 Monkey Business L6034G	Closed	1994	745.00	780-850
1993 Young Princess L6036G	Closed	1997	240.00	240
1994 Saint James L6084G	Closed	1998	310.00	310-400
1994 Angelic Harmony L6085G	Closed	1998	495.00	575
1994 Allow Me L6086G	Closed	1998	1625.00	1625
1994 Loving Care L6087G	Closed	1999	250.00	270-295
1994 Communion Prayer (Boy) L6088G	Open		194.00	200
1994 Communion Prayer (Girl) L6089G	Open		198.00	225
1994 Baseball Player L6090G	Closed	1998	295.00	310-400
1994 Basketball Player L6091G	Closed	1998	295.00	310-350
1994 The Prince L6092G	Closed	1998	325.00	325
1994 Songbird L6093G	Closed	2001	395.00	400-425
1994 The Sportsman L6096G	Closed	1998	495.00	540
1994 Sleeping Bunny With Flowers L6097G	Closed	1998	110.00	110-195
1994 Attentive Bunny With Flowers L6098G	Open		140.00	140
1994 Preening Bunny With Flowers L6099G	Closed	1998	140.00	140-175
1994 Sitting Bunny With Flowers L6100G	Open		110.00	115
1994 Follow Us L6101G	Closed	1998	198.00	183-215
1994 Mother's Little Helper L6102G	Closed	1998	275.00	242-325
1994 Beautiful Ballerina L6103G	Closed	1999	250.00	285-325
1994 Finishing Touches L6104	Closed	1999	240.00	250-295
1994 Spring Joy L6106G	Open		795.00	795
1994 Football Player L6107	Closed	1998	295.00	310-375
1994 Hockey Player L6108G	Closed	1998	295.00	310-550
1994 Meal Time L6109G	Closed	2000	495.00	525
1994 Medieval Maiden L6110G	Closed	1997	150.00	175-220
1994 Medieval Soldier L6111G	Closed	1997	225.00	245
1994 Medieval Lord L6112G	Closed	1997	285.00	300
1994 Medieval Lady L6113G	Closed	1997	225.00	225
1994 Medieval Princess L6114G	Closed	1997	245.00	310-350
1994 Medieval Prince L6115G	Closed	1997	295.00	315-325
1994 Medieval Majesty L6116G	Closed	1997	315.00	315-325

FIGURINES

YEAR ISSUE	EDITION LIMIT	YEAR RETD.	ISSUE PRICE	*QUOTE U.S.$
1994 Constance L6117G	Closed	1997	195.00	205
1994 Constance L6117M	Closed	1998	195.00	205-225
1994 Musketeer Portos L6118G	Closed	1997	220.00	230-250
1994 Musketeer Aramis L6119G	Closed	1997	275.00	275-295
1994 Musketeer Dartagnan L6120G	Closed	1997	245.00	242-285
1994 Musketeer Athos L6121G	Closed	1997	245.00	245-290
1994 A Great Adventure L6122	Closed	1998	198.00	183-215
1994 Out For a Stroll L6123G	Closed	1998	198.00	161-250
1994 Travelers Rest L6124G	Closed	1998	275.00	250-295
1994 Angelic Violinist L6126G	Yr.Iss.	1994	150.00	140-250
1994 Sweet Dreamers L6127G	Closed	2001	280.00	290
1994 Christmas Melodies L6128G	Closed	1998	375.00	385
1994 Little Friends L6129G	Closed	1998	225.00	235
1996 Spring Enchantment L6130G	Open		245.00	245
1994 Angel of Peace L6131G	Open		345.00	370
1994 Angel with Garland L6133G	Closed	1999	345.00	315-370
1994 Birthday Party L6134G	Closed	1998	395.00	450-575
1994 Football Star L6135	Closed	1998	295.00	295
1994 Basketball Star L6136G	Closed	1998	295.00	251-295
1994 Baseball Star L6137G	Closed	1998	295.00	221-295
1994 Globe Paperweight L6138M	Closed	1997	95.00	95
1994 Springtime Friends L6140G	Closed	2001	485.00	485
1994 Kitty Cart L6141G	Open		750.00	795
1994 Indian Pose L6142G	Closed	1998	475.00	475-550
1994 Indian Dancer L6143G	Closed	1998	475.00	475
1995 Caribbean Kiss L6144G	Closed	1999	340.00	289-340
1994 Heavenly Prayer L6145	Closed		675.00	695
1994 Spring Angel L6146G	Closed	1998	250.00	265-325
1994 Fall Angel L6147G	Closed	1998	250.00	265-300
1994 Summer Angel L6148G	Closed	1998	220.00	220-295
1994 Winter Angel L6149G	Closed	1998	250.00	265-275
1994 Playing The Flute L6150G	Closed	1999	175.00	190-215
1994 Bearing Flowers L6151G	Closed	1998	175.00	190-220
1994 Flower Gazer L6152G	Closed	1999	175.00	190-220
1994 American Love L6153G	Closed	1998	225.00	235-285
1994 African Love L6154G	Closed	1998	225.00	235-250
1994 European Love L6155G	Closed	1998	225.00	235
1994 Asian Love L6156G	Closed	1998	225.00	235
1994 Polynesian Love L6157G	Closed	1998	225.00	235
1995 Fiesta Dancer L6163G	Closed	1998	285.00	305-345
1994 Wedding Bells L6164G	Open		175.00	195
1995 Pretty Cargo L6165G	Closed	1998	500.00	500
1995 Dear Santa L6166G	Closed	1999	250.00	260
1995 Delicate Bundle L6167G	Closed	1999	275.00	275
1994 The Apollo Landing L6168G	Closed	1995	450.00	525-550
1995 Seesaw Friends L6169G	Closed	2000	795.00	795
1995 Under My Spell L6170G	Closed	1999	195.00	200-250
1995 Magical Moment L6171G	Closed	1999	180.00	200
1995 Coming of Age L6172G	Closed	1998	345.00	345
1995 A Moment's Rest L6173G	Open		130.00	140
1995 Graceful Pose L6174G	Open		195.00	195
1995 Graceful Pose L6174M	Open		195.00	195
1995 White Swan L6175G	Open		90.00	90
1995 Communion Bell L6176G	Closed	2000	85.00	85
1995 Asian Scholar L6177G	Open		315.00	325
1995 Little Matador L6178G	Open		245.00	245
1995 Peaceful Moment L6179G	Open		385.00	385
1995 Sharia L6180G	Open		235.00	240
1995 Velisa L6181G	Open		180.00	185
1996 Wanda L6182	Open		205.00	225
1995 Preparing For The Sabbath L6183G	Closed	1999	385.00	385
1995 For a Better World L6186G	Closed	1998	575.00	489-575
1995 European Boy L6187G	Closed	1998	185.00	185
1995 Asian Boy L6188G	Closed	1998	225.00	225-275
1995 African Boy L6189G	Closed	1998	195.00	195-275
1995 Polynesian Boy L6190G	Closed	1998	250.00	250-275
1995 All American L6191G	Closed	1998	225.00	225-275
1995 American Indian Boy L6192G	Closed	1998	225.00	225-275
1995 Summer Serenade L6193G	Open		375.00	390
1995 Summer Serenade L6193M	Open		375.00	390
1996 Christmas Wishes L6194	Closed	1998	245.00	208-295
1995 Carnival Companions L6195G	Closed	1998	650.00	582-685
1995 Seaside Companions L6196G	Closed	1998	230.00	230
1995 Seaside Serenade L6197G	Closed	1998	275.00	275-285
1995 Soccer Practice L6198G	Open		195.00	195
1995 In The Procession L6199G	Closed	1998	250.00	250-295
1995 In The Procession L6199M	Closed	1998	250.00	250
1995 Bridal Bell L6200G	Closed	2001	125.00	125
1995 Cuddly Kitten L6201G	Closed	1999	270.00	270
1995 Daddy's Little Sweetheart L6202G	Open		595.00	595
1995 Grace and Beauty L6204G	Closed	1998	325.00	276-325

YEAR ISSUE	EDITION LIMIT	YEAR RETD.	ISSUE PRICE	*QUOTE U.S.$
1995 Grace and Beauty L6204M	Closed	1998	325.00	325
1995 Graceful Dance L6205G	Closed	1998	340.00	340-395
1995 Graceful Dance L6205M	Closed	1998	340.00	340-395
1995 Reading the Torah L6208G	Closed	2000	535.00	535
1995 The Rabbi L6209G	Closed	1998	250.00	250-300
1995 Gentle Surprise L6210G	Open		125.00	125
1995 New Friend L6211G	Open		120.00	125
1995 Little Hunter L6212G	Closed	2000	115.00	115
1995 Lady Of Nice L6213G	Closed	1999	198.00	210-220
1995 Lady Of Nice L6213M	Closed	1999	198.00	210
1995 Leo L6214G	Closed	1998	198.00	179-275
1995 Virgo L6215G	Closed	1998	198.00	210-300
1995 Aquarius L6216G	Closed	1998	198.00	210-275
1995 Sagittarius L6217G	Closed	1998	198.00	210-275
1995 Taurus L6218G	Closed	1998	198.00	210-275
1995 Gemini L6219G	Closed	1998	198.00	210-275
1995 Libra L6220G	Closed	1998	198.00	210-300
1995 Aries L6221G	Closed	1998	198.00	210-275
1995 Capricorn L6222G	Closed	1998	198.00	210-275
1995 Pisces L6223G	Closed	1998	198.00	210-275
1995 Cancer L6224G	Closed	1998	198.00	210-300
1995 Scorpio L6225G	Closed	1998	198.00	235-300
1995 Snuggle Up L6226G .	Closed	2000	170.00	170
1995 Trick or Treat L6227G	Closed	1998	250.00	250-300
1995 Special Gift L6228G	Closed	2001	265.00	265
1995 Contented Companion L6229G	Closed	2000	195.00	195
1995 Oriental Dance L6230G	Open		198.00	210
1995 Oriental Lantern L6231G	Open		198.00	210
1995 Oriental Beauty L6232G	Closed	2000	198.00	210
1995 Chef's Apprentice L6233G	Closed	1998	260.00	260-285
1995 Chef's Apprentice L6233M	Closed	1998	260.00	260
1995 The Great Chef L6234G	Closed	1998	195.00	195-225
1995 The Great Chef L6234M	Closed	1998	195.00	195
1995 Dinner is Served L6235G	Closed	1998	185.00	171-225
1995 Dinner is Served L6235M	Closed	1998	185.00	185
1995 Lady of Monaco L6236G	Closed	1999	250.00	260
1995 Lady of Monaco L6236M	Closed	1999	250.00	260-300
1995 The Young Jester-Mandolin L6237G	Closed	1998	235.00	235-275
1995 The Young Jester-Mandolin L6237M	Closed	1998	235.00	235
1995 The Young Jester-Trumpet L6238G	Closed	1998	235.00	235
1995 The Young Jester-Trumpet L6238M	Closed	1998	235.00	235
1995 The Young Jester-Singer L6239G	Closed	1998	235.00	235
1995 The Young Jester-Singer L6239M	Closed	1998	235.00	235
1995 Graceful Ballet L6240G	Closed	1998	795.00	815
1995 Graceful Ballet L6240M	Closed	1998	795.00	815
1995 Allegory of Spring L6241G	Closed	2000	735.00	735
1995 Allegory of Spring L6241M	Closed	2000	735.00	735
1996 Winged Companions L6242G	Closed	1999	270.00	270-300
1996 Winged Companions L6242M	Closed	1999	270.00	270
1996 Sweet Symphony L6243	Open		450.00	450
1996 Pumpkin Ride L6244	Closed	1999	695.00	695
1996 Sunday's Best L6246	Closed	1999	370.00	370
1995 Challenge L6247M	Closed	1997	350.00	350-400
1995 Regatta L6248G	Closed	1997	695.00	695-750
1995 Delphica w/base L6249	Closed	2001	1200.00	1200
1996 Springtime Harvest L6250	Open		760.00	760
1997 Wind of Peace L6251	Closed	1999	310.00	310
1996 Nature's Beauty w/base L6252	Closed	1999	770.00	770
1996 Making Rounds L6256	Open		295.00	295
1996 Pierrot in Preparation L6257	Closed	1999	195.00	166-195
1996 Pierrot in Love L6258	Closed	1999	195.00	166-195
1996 Pierrot Rehearsing L6259	Closed	1999	195.00	166-195
1996 Our Lady "Caridíd Del Cobre" w/base L6268	Closed	1998	1355.00	1355
1996 Diana Goddess of the Hunt w/base L6269	Closed	2000	1550.00	1550
1996 Commencement L6270	Closed	2001	200.00	200
1996 Cap and Gown L6271	Closed	2001	200.00	200
1996 Going Forth L6272	Closed	1999	200.00	200
1996 Pharmacist L6273	Closed	2000	290.00	290
1996 Daisy L6274	Open		150.00	150
1996 Rose L6275	Open		150.00	150
1996 Iris L6276	Open		150.00	150
1996 Young Mandolin Player L6278	Closed	2000	330.00	330
1996 Flowers of Paris L6279	Closed	1999	525.00	525
1996 Paris in Bloom L6280	Closed	1999	525.00	525
1996 Coqueta L6281G	Closed	1998	435.00	435
1996 Coqueta L6281M	Closed	1998	435.00	435
1996 Medic L6282G	Closed	1999	225.00	191-225
1996 Medic L6282M	Closed	1998	225.00	225
1996 Temis L6283G	Closed	1998	435.00	435

*Quotes have been rounded up to nearest dollar

YEAR ISSUE	EDITION LIMIT	YEAR RETD.	ISSUE PRICE	*QUOTE U.S.$
1996 Temis L6283M	Closed	1998	435.00	435
1996 Quione L6284G	Closed	1998	435.00	435
1996 Quione L6284M	Closed	1998	435.00	435
1996 Dreams of Aladdin w/base L6285	Closed	1999	1440.00	1440
1996 Tennis Champion w/base L6286G	Closed	1999	350.00	350-390
1996 Tennis Champion w/base L6286M	Closed	1999	350.00	332-350
1996 Restless Dove L6287G	Closed	1998	105.00	105
1996 Restless Dove L6287M	Closed	1998	105.00	105
1996 Taking Flight L6288G	Closed	1999	150.00	150
1996 Taking Flight L6288M	Closed	1999	150.00	150
1996 Peaceful Dove L6289G	Closed	1999	105.00	105
1996 Peaceful Dove L6289M	Closed	1999	105.00	105
1996 Proud Dove L6290G	Closed	1999	105.00	105
1996 Proud Dove L6290M	Closed	1999	105.00	105
1996 Love Nest L6291G	Open		260.00	290
1996 Love Nest L6291M	Open		260.00	290
1996 Spring Egg L6292	Closed	2001	365.00	365
1997 Summer Egg L6293	Closed	2001	365.00	365
1998 Autumn Egg 01006294	Closed	2001	365.00	365
1999 Winter Egg 01006295	Closed	2001	365.00	365
1996 Sweethearts L6296	Closed	1999	900.00	900
1996 Little Bear L6299	Closed	1999	285.00	285
1996 Rubber Ducky L6300	Closed	1999	285.00	285
1996 Care and Tenderness w/base L6301	Closed	2001	850.00	850
1996 Thena L6302G	Closed	1998	485.00	485
1996 Thena L6302M	Closed	1998	485.00	485
1996 Tuba Player L6303	Closed	1998	315.00	252-375
1996 Bass Drummer L6304	Closed	1998	400.00	340-400
1996 Trumpet Player L6305	Closed	1998	270.00	230-270
1996 Majorette L6306	Closed	1998	310.00	248-310
1996 Young Nurse L6307	Closed	2001	185.00	185
1996 Natural Wonder L6308	Closed	1999	220.00	220-250
1996 Nature's Treasures L6309	Closed	1998	220.00	220
1996 Nature's Song L6310	Closed	1998	230.00	230
1996 Cupid L6311	Closed	2001	200.00	200
1996 The Harpist L6312	Closed	1999	820.00	820
1996 Lost in Dreams L6313	Open		420.00	425
1996 Little Sailor Boy L6314	Closed	1999	225.00	225-245
1996 Dreaming of You L6315	Closed	1999	1280.00	1280
1996 Carnevale L6316	Closed	1998	840.00	840-950
1996 Making House Calls L6317	Closed	1998	260.00	260
1996 Little Distraction L6318	Closed	1999	350.00	298-350
1996 Beautiful Rhapsody L6319	Closed	2001	450.00	450
1996 Architect L6320	Closed	1999	330.00	281-330
1996 Serenading Colombina L6322	Open		415.00	353-415
1996 Stage Presence L6323	Closed	2000	355.00	355
1996 Princess of Peace L6324	Closed	2000	830.00	830
1996 Curtains Up L6325	Closed	1999	255.00	217-255
1996 Virgin of Carmen w/base L6326	Closed	1999	1270.00	1270-1350
1996 Medieval Romance w/base L6327	Closed	1999	2250.00	1645-2250
1996 Venice Festival w/base L6328	Closed	1999	5350.00	5350
1996 Blushing Bride L6329G	Closed	1999	370.00	370
1996 Blushing Bride L6329M	Closed	1999	370.00	370
1996 Refreshing Pause L6330	Open		170.00	170
1996 Bridal Bell L6331	Open		155.00	155
1996 Concerto L6332	Open		490.00	490
1996 Medieval Chess Set L6333	Open		2120.00	2225
1997 Little Fireman L6334	Closed	2000	185.00	185
1997 Home Sweet Home L6336	Closed	1998	85.00	85
1997 Poodle L6337	Closed	2000	150.00	150
1997 I'm Sleepy L6338	Closed	2000	360.00	375
1996 Country Sounds L6339	Closed	1998	750.00	638-750
1996 Sweet Country L6340	Closed	1998	750.00	638-750
1998 Petals of Love 01006346	Open		350.00	370
1997 Little Veterinarian L6348	Closed	1999	210.00	179-210
1997 Little Maestro L6349	Closed	2000	165.00	165
1997 Hunting Butterflies L6350	Closed	2000	425.00	475
1997 Tokens of Love L6351	Closed	2000	385.00	400-425
1997 A World of Love L6353	Open		450.00	450
1997 Attentive Polar Bear w/Flowers L6354	Open		100.00	100
1997 Polar Bear Resting w/Flowers L6355	Closed	2001	100.00	100
1997 Polar Bear Seated w/Flowers L6356	Closed	2001	100.00	100
1997 Kissing Doves w/Flowers L6359	Open		225.00	225
1997 St. Joseph The Carpenter L6363	Closed	1999	1050.00	1050
1997 A Dream Come True L6364	Closed	2000	550.00	550
1997 Spring Flirtation L6365	Open		395.00	395
1998 Summer Infatuation 01006366	Open		325.00	325
1997 Little Policeman L6367	Closed	2000	185.00	185
1997 Little Artist L6368	Closed	2000	175.00	175
1997 Indian Maiden L6369	Closed	1999	600.00	600
1997 Country Chores L6370	Closed	2000	260.00	260
1997 En Pointe L6371	Closed	2000	390.00	390
1997 Palace Dance L6373	Closed	1999	700.00	700
1997 Pas De Deux L6374	Closed	2000	725.00	745
1997 Pierrot's Proposal L6375	Closed	2000	1425.00	1475
1997 Light and Life L6376G	Closed	2000	220.00	220
1997 Light and Life L6376M	Closed	2000	220.00	220
1997 Unity L6377G	Closed	1999	220.00	220-250
1997 Unity L6377M	Closed	1999	220.00	220
1997 Beginning and End L6378G	Closed	1999	220.00	220
1997 Beginning and End L6378M	Closed	1999	220.00	220
1997 Love L6379G	Closed	2000	220.00	220
1997 Love L6379M	Closed	2000	220.00	220
1997 King Gaspar L6380	Closed	1998	75.00	75-90
1997 Little Roadster L6381	Closed	1998	79.00	79-98
1997 New Arrival L6382	Closed	2001	265.00	265
1997 The Ascension L6383	Closed	1999	775.00	775
1997 A Quiet Moment L6384	Closed	1999	270.00	270
1997 Royal Slumber L6385	Open		1390.00	1425
1997 Little Harlequin L6386	Closed	1998	79.00	79-98
1997 A Passionate Dance L6387	Open		890.00	975
1997 Circus Star L6388	Closed	1998	79.00	79-98
1997 The Bouquet L6389	Closed	1998	95.00	95
1997 The Encounter L6391	Closed	1998	150.00	150
1997 The Kiss L6392	Closed	1998	150.00	150-170
1997 Heavenly Flutist L6393	Closed	1998	98.00	98
1997 Seraph with Holly L6394	Closed	1998	79.00	79-98
1997 Through the Park L6395	Open		2350.00	2350
1997 Oriental Forest L6396	Closed	2001	565.00	565
1997 In Neptune's Waves L6397	Closed	1999	1030.00	1030
1997 Morning Delivery L6398	Closed	2001	160.00	160
1997 Generous Gesture L6399	Closed	2000	345.00	345-352
1997 Daydreams L6400	Open		325.00	325
1997 Little Ballerina L6402	Closed	2001	200.00	200
1997 Breathless L6403	Closed	2000	235.00	235-265
1997 Sister w/Sax L6404G	Closed	1999	180.00	180
1997 Sister w/Sax L6404M	Closed	1999	180.00	180
1997 Sister Singing L6405G	Closed	1999	165.00	165
1997 Sister Singing L6405M	Closed	1999	165.00	165
1997 Sister w/Guitar L6406G	Closed	1999	200.00	200-220
1997 Sister w/Guitar L6406M	Closed	1999	200.00	200
1997 Sister w/Tambourine L6407G	Closed	1999	185.00	185
1997 Sister w/Tambourine L6407M	Closed	1999	185.00	185
1997 Sweet Song L6408	Closed	2001	480.00	480
1997 A Surprise Visit L6409	Closed	2000	190.00	190
1997 Would You Be Mine? L6410	Closed	2000	190.00	190
1997 Bath Time L6411	Open		195.00	195
1997 Joy of Life L6412	Closed	2001	215.00	220
1997 Spirit of Youth L6413	Closed	2001	215.00	220
1997 Hello Friend L6414	Closed	2000	235.00	235-248
1997 It's A Boy! L6415	Open		125.00	130
1997 It's A Girl! L6416	Open		125.00	130
1997 Unlikely Friends L6417	Open		125.00	125
1997 So Beautiful! L6418G	Closed	2000	325.00	325
1997 So Beautiful! L6418M	Closed	2000	325.00	325
1997 Arms Full of Love L6419	Open		180.00	180
1997 My Favorite Slippers L6420	Closed	1999	145.00	145-175
1997 Off To Bed L6421	Closed	1999	145.00	145-175
1997 My Chubby Kitty L6422	Open		135.00	145
1997 Precious Papoose L6423	Closed	2000	240.00	240-275
1997 Ceremonial Princess L6424	Closed	2000	240.00	240
1997 Female Attorney L6425	Closed	2000	300.00	320
1997 Male Attorney L6426	Closed	2000	300.00	320
1997 A Flower For You L6427	Closed	2000	320.00	320
1997 My First Step L6428	Closed	2001	165.00	165
1997 Ready To Roll L6429	Closed	2001	165.00	165
1997 Pony Ride L6430	Closed	2000	825.00	825
1997 Little Lawyer L6431	Closed	1999	210.00	210-250
1997 Sea of Love L6432	Closed	2000	1190.00	1290
1997 Cranes in Flight L6433	Closed	2001	1390.00	1460
1997 Pensive Harlequin L6434	Closed	1998	495.00	495
1997 Colombina L6435	Closed	1998	525.00	525
1997 The Dolphins L6436	Open		965.00	1125
1997 Timid Torero L6437	Closed	1999	195.00	195
1997 Young Torero L6438	Closed	2001	240.00	240
1998 Caught In The Act 01006439	Closed	2000	260.00	260
1997 Time For Bed L6440	Closed	1999	160.00	160
1997 Spanish Dance L6444	Closed	2000	445.00	545
1997 Surrounded by Love L6446	Open		315.00	325
1997 Dentist L6450	Closed	2000	225.00	250-268
1997 Little Pilot L6451	Open		170.00	190
1998 Spring Recital 01006452	Open		685.00	750

FIGURINES

YEAR ISSUE	EDITION LIMIT	YEAR RETD.	ISSUE PRICE	*QUOTE U.S.$
1997 German Shepherd with Puppies 01006454	Closed	2000	475.00	510
1997 Collie 01006455	Closed	2000	295.00	300
1997 Dance of the Dolphins 01006456	Open		315.00	385
1997 Bathing Beauties 01006457	Open		240.00	250
1998 Fountain of Love 01006458	Open		395.00	450
1997 Collie with Puppy 01006459	Closed	2000	350.00	355
1997 Lucky Strolling 01006460	Closed	2001	120.00	120
1997 Lucky's Call 01006461	Closed	2001	155.00	155
1997 Lucky In Love 01006462	Open		110.00	115
1997 My Cuddly Puppy 01006463	Open		110.00	120
1997 Who's There? 01006464	Open		115.00	125
1997 Bedtime Prayers 01006465	Open		105.00	115
1998 A Prize Catch 01006466	Closed	2000	340.00	355
1998 A Father's Pride 01006467	Open		475.00	550
2000 A Fishing Lesson 01006468	Open		530.00	545
1997 Our Cozy Home 01006469	Open		195.00	215
1997 A Swimming Lesson 01006470	Open		260.00	275
1997 My Pretty Flowers 01006471	Open		160.00	175
1997 Gardening Buddies 01006472	Open		195.00	200
1998 Sounds of Peace 01006473	Open		98.00	110
1998 Sounds of Love 01006474	Open		98.00	110
1998 Happy Anniversary 01006475	Open		300.00	340
1998 A Symbol of Pride 01006476	Closed	2001	695.00	740
1997 Heavenly Slumber 01006479	Open		185.00	215
1998 A Perfect Day 01006480	Open		495.00	525
1997 Just Resting 01006481	Closed	2000	125.00	145
1997 Just Resting 01016481	Closed	2000	125.00	145
1997 Little Sleepwalker 01006482	Closed	2001	110.00	120
1997 Little Sleepwalker 01016482	Closed	2001	110.00	120
1997 It's Morning Already? 01006483	Closed	2001	105.00	110
1997 It's Morning Already? 01016483	Closed	2001	105.00	110
1998 After the Show 01006484	Closed	2000	350.00	375
1998 In Admiration 01006485	Closed	2000	370.00	400
1998 Posing For a Portrait 01006486	Closed	2000	380.00	410
1998 New Shoes 01006487	Open		150.00	170
1998 Gone Shopping 01006488	Closed	2001	150.00	185
1997 An Angel's Tune 01006490	Open		115.00	115
1997 Heavenly Dreamer 01006491	Open		95.00	95
1998 Your Special Angel 01006492	Open		92.00	95
1998 Filled With Joy 01006493	Open		92.00	95
1998 Onward and Upward 01006494	Open		170.00	175
1998 The Road To Success 01006495	Open		155.00	175
1998 A Child's Prayer 01006496	Open		89.00	95
1998 Sleepy Time 01006497	Open		89.00	95
1998 Heavenly Musician 01006498	Closed	1999	100.00	100
1998 White Swan with Flowers 01006499	Open		110.00	115
1998 Jolly Santa 01006500	Closed	1998	180.00	180-230
1999 Please Come Home! 01006502	Open		695.00	750
1998 My Little Treasure 01006503	Open		295.00	375
1998 Daddy's Blessing 01006504	Open		340.00	375
1998 On The Farm 01006505	Closed	2000	325.00	330-345
1998 Guess Who? 01006506	Closed	2000	430.00	470-490
1998 Pierrot's Proposal 01006508	Closed	2001	1350.00	1600
1998 King Balthasar 01006509	Closed		75.00	75-90
1998 An Unexpected Gift 01006510	Closed	2000	260.00	265
1998 A Birthday Surprise 01006511	Closed	2000	230.00	230
1998 How Skillful! 01006517	Open		390.00	425
1998 A Lovely Thought 01006518	Closed	2000	580.00	580
1998 Love's Tender Tokens 01006521	Open		895.00	950
1998 Through The Clouds 01006522	Closed	2001	440.00	450
1998 Flying High 01006523	Closed		635.00	635
1998 Up And Away 01006524	Closed	2001	560.00	560
1998 Hindu Dancer 01006527	Closed		700.00	795
1998 Little Angel with Lyre 01006528	Open		120.00	125
1998 Little Angel with Violin 01006529	Open		120.00	125
1998 Little Angel with Tambourine 01006530	Open		120.00	125
1998 A New Life 01006531	Closed	2000	490.00	490-530
1998 A Christmas Song 01006532	Closed	2000	198.00	200
1998 The Christmas Caroler 01006533	Closed	2000	175.00	175-190
1998 The Spirit of Christmas 01006534	Closed	2000	198.00	200
1998 Cozy Companions 01006540	Open		195.00	210
1998 Bedtime Buddies 01006541	Open		195.00	210
1998 A Stroll In The Sun 01006542	Closed	2000	450.00	485-500
2002 Summer Breeze 01006543	Open		225.00	225
1998 On Our Way 01006544	Closed	2001	340.00	375
2000 On The Boulevard 01006545	Closed		585.00	585
1998 Baby Boy Lamb 01006546	Closed	2001	105.00	120
1998 Baby Girl Lamb 01006547	Closed	2001	105.00	120
1998 Love Poems 01006548	Closed	2001	470.00	495
1998 Naptime Friends 01006549	Closed	2001	200.00	215
1998 Shhh...They're Sleeping 01006550	Closed	2001	200.00	215
1998 Pretty Posies 01006551	Closed	2001	180.00	180
1998 Pretty Pinwheel 01006552	Closed	2001	145.00	150
1998 Grandparent's Joy 01006553	Closed	2000	645.00	670-700
1999 Treasures of the Heart 01006554	Closed	2001	215.00	215
1999 Springtime Scent 01006555	Closed	2001	255.00	255
1998 Playful Poodle 01006557	Closed	2001	579.00	630
1998 Great Dane 01006558	Closed	2000	890.00	935
1999 A Wish For Love 01006562	Open		1875.00	1875
1999 A Day's Work 01006563	Open		615.00	625
1999 Want A Lift? 01006564	Open		515.00	525
1998 Gabriel The Archangel 01006565	Closed	2000	475.00	475
1998 Secret Spot 01006566	Open		210.00	240
1999 Dreamy Kitten 01006567	Open		250.00	260
1999 Kitten Patrol 01006568	Open		180.00	185
1999 The Milky Way 01006569 (Millennium Collection)	Closed	2000	725.00	750
1999 New Horizons 01006570 (Millennium Collection)	Closed	2000	560.00	560
2000 Rebirth 01006571 (Millennium Collection)	Closed	2000	1270.00	1270
1999 In Touch With Nature 01006572	Open		625.00	625
1998 Parading Donkey 01006573	Closed	2000	220.00	258-275
2000 Take Me Home! 01006574	Open		295.00	295
1998 A Gift From Santa 01006575	Closed	1999	200.00	170-220
1999 Autumn Romance 01006576	Open		345.00	375
2000 Afternoon Snack 01006577	Open		335.00	340
1999 Graceful Tune 01006578	Open		480.00	480
1999 Petals of Peace 01006579	Open		350.00	350
1999 Nightime Blessing 01006581	Open		136.00	165
1998 Bless Us All 01006582	Open		170.00	195
1998 Heaven's Lullabye 01006583	Open		186.00	215
1998 Sunday Prayer 01006584	Closed	2001	200.00	230
1999 Endless Love 01006585	Open		175.00	175
1998 Angelic Light Candleholder 01006586	Closed	2001	198.00	225-258
1998 Morning Calm 01006589	Open		130.00	135
1999 Dinner Trio 01006591	Open		675.00	675
1999 An Expression of Love 01006592	Open		295.00	295
1999 My Bar Mitzvah 01006593	Open		345.00	345
1999 A Night Out 01006594	Closed	2001	135.00	135
1999 On The Runway 01006595	Closed	2001	135.00	135
2000 Cupid's Arrow 01006596	Open		230.00	235
1999 Declaration of Love 01006597	Open		550.00	550
1999 The Enchanted Forest 01006598	Closed	2001	440.00	440
1999 Bosom Buddies 01006599	Open		235.00	240
1999 Like Father, Like Son 01006609	Open		440.00	450
1999 Faithful Companion 01006610	Open		675.00	675
1999 A Flight of Fantasy 01006611	Closed	2001	490.00	490
1999 Heaven's Gift (Boy) 01006612	Open		135.00	135
1999 Heaven's Gift (Boy-blank card) 01006613	Open		135.00	135
1999 Kitty Surprise 01006616	Closed	2001	280.00	280
1999 Puppy Surprise 01006617	Closed	2001	280.00	280
1999 Fawn Surprise 01006618	Closed	2001	280.00	280
1999 Holiday Light Candleholder 01006619	Closed	2001	225.00	250
1999 A Kiss to Remember 01006620	Open		250.00	250
1999 Winter Love 01006621	Open		345.00	345
1999 A Sunny Afternoon 01006622	Open		675.00	675
1999 Bouquet of Love 01016624	Open		150.00	150
1999 The Master Chef 01006625	Closed	2001	240.00	240
1999 Heaven's Gift (Girl) 01006626	Closed	2001	135.00	135
1999 Heaven's Gift (Girl-blank card) 01006627	Open		135.00	135
1999 Adagio 01006628	Open		160.00	165
1999 Allegro 01006629	Open		160.00	165
1999 A Little Romance 01006630	Open		695.00	695
1999 Sweet Mary 01006631	Open		220.00	225
1999 A Birthday Kiss 01006632	Open		575.00	575
1999 Sancho 01006633	Open		255.00	260
1999 A Mother's Love 01006634	Open		335.00	345
1999 My Pretty Puppy 01006635	Open		295.00	295
1999 A Quiet Evening 01006638	Closed	2001	495.00	495
1999 Sunday Stroll 01006639	Open		925.00	950
1999 Little Explorer 01006640	Closed	2000	430.00	430
1999 The Flamingos 01006641	Closed	2001	495.00	495
2000 Little Stowaway 01006642	Open		155.00	160
2000 Lakeside Daydream 01006644	Open		495.00	495
2000 Lillypad Love 01006645	Open		495.00	495
1999 Floral Path 01006646	Open		495.00	495

*Quotes have been rounded up to nearest dollar

YEAR ISSUE	EDITION LIMIT	YEAR RETD.	ISSUE PRICE	*QUOTE U.S.$
1999 Wildflowers 01006647	Open		525.00	525
2000 Flowers in Bloom 01006648	Open		545.00	550
2000 Allegory of Youth 01006649	Open		635.00	675
2000 Quinceañera 01006650	Open		450.00	450
2000 Wings of Fantasy 01006651	Open		775.00	795
2000 Kitty Care 01006652	Open		255.00	265
2000 Elegance on Ice 01006653	Open		365.00	365
2000 On Shore Leave 01006654	Open		285.00	285
2000 On Shore Leave 01016654	Open		285.00	285
2000 Cocktail Party 01006655	Open		265.00	265
2000 Cocktail Party 01016655	Open		265.00	265
2000 Tender Dreams 01006656	Open		150.00	150
2000 Tender Dreams 01016656	Open		150.00	150
2000 Santa's List 01016657	Closed	2000	210.00	210
2000 Morning Song 01006658	Open		885.00	895
2000 Today's Lesson 01006659	Open		265.00	275
2000 Let's Fly Away 01006665	Open		155.00	160
2000 Graceful Landing 01006666	Open		155.00	155
2000 Thank You Santa! 01006674	Open		335.00	340
2000 Dreidel with Dove 01006678	Open		95.00	100
2000 Dreidel 01006679	Open		115.00	120
2000 Ocean Offering 01006682	Closed	2001	470.00	470
2000 Romance 01006683	Open		195.00	195
2000 Dreams 01006684	Open		195.00	195
2000 Happiness 01006685	Open		195.00	195
2000 Sweet Sixteen 01006687	Open		450.00	465
2000 Looking Pretty 0100688	Open		245.00	250
2000 A Perfect Drive 0100689	Open		335.00	345
2000 A Perfect Drive 0101689	Open		335.00	345
2000 Rosy Posey 01006690	Open		300.00	320
2000 Oopsy Daisy 01006991	Open		300.00	320
2000 Computing Companions 01006692	Open		290.00	295
2000 Programming Pals 01006693	Open		290.00	295
2000 Father Time 01006696 (Millennium Collection)	Closed	2000	420.00	420
2000 Petals of Hope 01006701	Open		575.00	575
2000 Nature's Observer 01006702	Open		160.00	165
2000 From Nature's Palette 01006703	Open		140.00	145
2000 Love's Embrace 01006704	Closed	2000	485.00	485
2000 One For You, One For Me 01006705	Open		370.00	375
2000 Menorah 01006706	Open		325.00	325
2000 Peace and Liberty 01006707	Open		1500.00	1750
2000 Serene Moment 01006708	Open		585.00	595
2000 Pensive Traveler 01006709	Closed	2001	400.00	400
2000 Comforting Dreams 01006710	Open		150.00	150
2000 Comforting Dreams 01016710	Open		150.00	150
2000 Lady in Love 01016712	Open		330.00	335
2000 An Embroidery Lesson 01016713	Open		545.00	575
2000 A Christmas Duet 01016714	Open		315.00	325
2000 Dragon with Base 01006715	Open		395.00	395
2000 Underwater Explorers 01006742	Open		655.00	675
2001 A Cozy Fit 01006743	Open		265.00	275
2001 A Well Heeled Puppy 01006744	Open		345.00	365
2001 Arctic Family 01006745	Open		175.00	175
2001 Love's Little Surprises 01006746	Open		395.00	450
2001 Mirror, Mirror... 01006748	Open		395.00	425
2001 Always on the Go 01006749	Open		295.00	295
2001 Evening Light 01016750	Open		1100.00	1100
2001 Morning Dew 01016751	Open		1500.00	1500
2001 On My Way Home 01006752	Open		175.00	395
2001 Traveling Companions 01006753	Open		235.00	250
2001 Sweet and Shy 01006754	Open		175.00	180
2001 A Proper Pose 01006755	Open		180.00	180
2001 Bountiful Blossoms 01006756	Open		290.00	295
2001 First Flowers 01006757	Open		240.00	250
2001 Drifting Through Dreamland 01006758	Open		370.00	375
2001 What a Surprise! 01006759	Open		160.00	165
2001 Walking the Dogs 01006760	Open		365.00	375
2001 Blessed Family 01006761	Open		495.00	525
2001 Underwater Explorer Lamp 01006762	Open		445.00	475
2001 First Performance 01006763	Open		195.00	215
2001 My Debut 01006764	Open		195.00	195
2001 An Afternoon Nap 01006765	Open		485.00	550
2001 A Reading Lesson 01006766	Open		995.00	995
2001 Petals on the Wind 01006767	Open		395.00	425
2001 Reading Companion 01006768	Open		345.00	375
2001 Reading With Daddy 01006770	Open		380.00	395
2001 Someone To Look Up To 01006771	Open		270.00	285
2001 Someone To Look Up To 01016771	Open		270.00	285
2001 Heaven's Harvest 01016772	Open		295.00	325
2001 The Encounter 01006773	Open		775.00	775
2001 Santa's Magic Touch 01006774	Open		225.00	240
2001 A Purr-fect Fit 01006775	Open		335.00	350
2001 Butterfly Treasures 01006777	Open		265.00	275
2001 Butterfly Treasures 01016777	Open		265.00	275
2001 Santa's Busiest Hour 01006779	Yr.Iss.	2001	195.00	195
2001 The Snake 01016780	Open		320.00	325
2001 Sunset in the Country 01016781	Open		325.00	350
2001 Blossom of the Heart 01006782	Open		345.00	375
2001 Winds of Romance 01016783	Open		290.00	325
2001 A Visit to Dreamland 01006786	Open		495.00	495
2000 Dreaming on Dew Drops 01006787	Open		495.00	495
2000 An Angel's Wish 01006788	Open		125.00	130
2000 An Angel's Song 01006789	Open		125.00	130
2001 Counting Sheep 01006790	Open		225.00	225
2001 Taking a Snooze 01006791	Open		225.00	225
2001 A Day with Dad 01006793	Open		395.00	445
2001 Shh...Let Him Sleep 01006794	Open		585.00	650
2001 My Favourite Place 01006795	Open		265.00	275
2001 Majesty of the Seas 01006796	Open		775.00	850
2001 A Fairy Tale Princess 01006797	Open		325.00	350
2001 A Fairy Tale Prince 01006798	Open		325.00	350
2001 Just Like New 01006799	Open		100.00	110
2001 Bundled Bather 01006800	Open		100.00	110
2001 Sleepy Scholar 01006801	Open		325.00	350
2001 Waiting For The Bell 01006802	Open		325.00	350
2002 Romantica 01006805	Open		445.00	445
2001 Delightful 01006806	Open		190.00	195
2001 Peaceful 01006807	Open		180.00	185
2001 Enchanting 01006808	Open		165.00	170
2002 Little School Boy 01006813	Open		300.00	300
2002 Little School Girl 01006814	Open		300.00	300
2002 Childhood Dreams 01006817	Open		775.00	775
2002 A Lover's Dance 01006819	Open		360.00	360
2002 A Poem For My Girl 01006821	Open		565.00	565
2002 Sweet Fragrance 01006822	Open		195.00	195
2002 My Happy Friend 01006824	Open		325.00	325
2002 Hello, Little Squirrel 01006825	Open		415.00	415
2002 You're So Cute! 01006826	Open		330.00	330
2002 The Horse 01006827	Open		395.00	395
2002 Unexpected Visit 01006829	Open		195.00	195
2002 Love Letters 01006830	Open		225.00	225
2001 A New Beginning 01006831	Open		150.00	165
2002 A Sweet Smell 01006832	Open		195.00	195
2002 Petals of Fantasy 01006833	Open		580.00	580
2001 Exploring the Stars 01006839	Open		195.00	195
2001 Dreaming of the Stars 01006840	Open		195.00	195
2002 You're Everything to Me 01006842	Open		590.00	590
2002 Sleep Well, Sweet Baby 01006843	Open		460.00	460
2002 The Perfect Swing 01006845	Open		395.00	395
2002 Aurora 01006847	Open		795.00	795
2002 Alborada 01006848	Open		695.00	695
2002 A Mother's Embrace 01006851	Open		370.00	370
2002 Little Napmates 01006853	Open		460.00	460
2002 By The Seashore 01006855	Open		290.00	290
2002 The Lady of the Rose 01006857	Open		235.00	235
2002 My Little Sweetie 01006858	Open		690.00	690
2002 Pond Dreamer 01006859	Open		195.00	195
2002 Underwater Calm 01006860	Open		195.00	195
2002 An Elegant Touch 01006862	Open		295.00	295
2002 Sweet Sounds of the Morning 01006864	Open		225.00	225
2002 Fragrances and Colors 01006866	Open		550.00	550
2000 A Child's Prayer w/Musical Base 71070036	Open		125.00	125
2000 Heavenly Slumber w/Musical Base 71070037	Open		245.00	245
2000 Heaven's Lullaby w/Musical Base 71070038	Open		245.00	245
1992 Special Torch L7513G	Closed	1997	165.00	175-225
1992 Special Champion L7514G	Closed	1997	165.00	175-196
1992 Special Pride L7515G	Closed	1997	165.00	175-195
1985 Lladró Plaque L7116	Open		17.50	18
1985 Lladró Plaque L7118	Closed	N/A	17.00	18
1993 Courage L7522G	Closed	1997	195.00	235-250
1994 Dr. Martin Luther King, Jr. L7528G	Open		345.00	375
1994 Doc 7533	Closed	1998	195.00	195-375
1995 Dopey 7534	Closed	1998	175.00	175-350
1995 Sneezy 7535	Closed	1998	175.00	225-450
1994 Bashful 7536	Closed	1998	175.00	175-395
1994 Happy 7537	Closed	1998	195.00	295-375
1994 Grumpy 7538	Closed	1998	175.00	250-450

YEAR ISSUE	EDITION LIMIT	YEAR RETD.	ISSUE PRICE	*QUOTE U.S.$
1994 Sleepy 7539	Closed	1998	175.00	175-375
1994 Spike L7543G	Closed	1998	95.00	105-165
1994 Brutus L7544G	Closed	1998	125.00	140-210
1994 Rocky L7545G	Closed	1998	110.00	120-175
1994 Stretch L7546G	Closed	1998	125.00	140-195
1994 Rex L7547G	Closed	1998	125.00	140-210
1995 16th Century Globe Paperweight L7551	Open		105.00	105
1994 Snow White L7555G (Disney-back stamp Theme Park issue)	Closed	N/A	295.00	545-675
1994 Snow White L7555G	Closed	1998	295.00	295-475
1995 Snow White Wishing Well L7558	Closed	1998	1500.00	1500-1800
2000 Christus 01007584	Open		495.00	495
2000 Christus 01017584	Open		495.00	495
2000 Heaven's Gift (Boy-2000 card) 01007586	Closed	2000	140.00	140
2000 Heaven's Gift (It's a Boy) 01007587	Open		140.00	140
2000 Heaven's Gift (Girl-2000 card) 01007588	Closed	2000	140.00	140
2000 Heaven's Gift (It's a Girl) 01007589	Open		140.00	140
1989 Starting Forward/Lolo L7605G	Open		190.00	195
1996 By My Side L7645	Open	1999	250.00	250
1996 Chess Board L8036	Open		145.00	145

Lladró Limited Edition Egg Series - Lladró

YEAR ISSUE	EDITION LIMIT	YEAR RETD.	ISSUE PRICE	*QUOTE U.S.$
1993 1993 Limited Edition Egg L6083M	Closed	1993	145.00	175-300
1994 1994 Limited Edition Egg L7532M	Closed	1994	150.00	150-250
1995 1995 Limited Edition Egg L7548M	Closed	1995	150.00	175-195
1996 1996 Limited Edition Egg L7550M	Closed	1996	155.00	155-175
1997 1997 Limited Edition Egg L7552M	Closed	1997	155.00	155-160
1998 Garden Stroll 01016590	Closed	1998	150.00	150
2000 Parsian Afternoon 01016698	Closed	2000	150.00	150

The Night Before Christmas - Lladró

YEAR ISSUE	EDITION LIMIT	YEAR RETD.	ISSUE PRICE	*QUOTE U.S.$
1999 Visions of Sugarplums 01006667	Closed	2001	260.00	260
1999 Up The Chimney He Rose 01006668	Closed	2001	370.00	370
1999 A Stocking For Kitty 01006669	Closed	2001	235.00	235-255
2000 Christmas is Here! 01006670	Closed	2001	495.00	495
2000 Ringing in the Season 01006671	Closed	2001	245.00	245
2000 I Love Christmas! 01006672	Closed	2001	245.00	245
2001 Christmas Buddies 01006673	Closed	2001	245.00	245
1999 Cookies For Santa 01006675	Closed	2001	325.00	325
2001 Santa Won't Notice 01006676	Closed	2001	175.00	175

Norman Rockwell Collection - Rockwell-Inspired

YEAR ISSUE	EDITION LIMIT	YEAR RETD.	ISSUE PRICE	*QUOTE U.S.$
1982 Lladró Love Letter L1406 (RL-400G)	5,000	N/A	650.00	750-1000
1982 Summer Stock L1407 (RL-401G)	5,000	N/A	750.00	850-900
1982 Practice Makes Perfect L1408 (RL-402G)	5,000	N/A	725.00	725-995
1982 Young Love L1409 (RL-403G)	5,000	N/A	450.00	1100-1500
1982 Daydreamer L1411 (RL-404G)	5,000	N/A	450.00	1100-1500
1982 Court Jester L1405 (RL-405G)	5,000	N/A	600.00	990-1250
1982 Springtime L1410 (RL-406G)	5,000	N/A	450.00	1200-1400

Lucy & Me/Enesco Group, Inc.

Christmas Lucy & Me - L. Riggs

YEAR ISSUE	EDITION LIMIT	YEAR RETD.	ISSUE PRICE	*QUOTE U.S.$
1985 Bear Holding Candle 16845	Retrd.	1989	9.00	39
1979 Bear Holding Candle E-2817	Retrd.	1983	9.00	52
1985 Bear Holding Candy Canes 16845	Retrd.	1989	9.00	27
1984 Bear Holding Doll & Lollipop E-5411	Retrd.	1989	10.00	27
1984 Bear Holding Jack in Box E-5411	Retrd.	1989	10.00	25
1984 Bear Holding Rocking Horse E-5411	Retrd.	1989	10.00	27
1985 Bear Holding Tree 16845	Retrd.	1989	9.00	25
1983 Bear Mailing Letter to Santa E-0555	Retrd.	1986	9.00	63
1983 Boy Bear Pulls Girl Bear on Sled E-0557	Retrd.	1989	15.00	30-63
1987 Boy in Blue Coat Pulling Tree in Wagon 110477	Retrd.	1989	12.00	39
1989 A Christmas Carol - Scrooge 222100	Yr.Iss.	1989	10.00	39
1987 Clown Juggler 110299	Retrd.	1989	10.00	33
1988 Couple Kissing Under the Mistletoe 510319	Retrd.	1989	15.00	31-45
1982 Dad E-5417	Retrd.	1989	9.00	N/A
1986 Dad Sleeping in Chair 105961	Retrd.	1989	10.00	39
1983 Girl Holding Teddy and Package E-0556	Retrd.	1986	10.00	25-27
1987 Girl in Nightgown Holds Stocking 110337	Retrd.	1989	10.00	30
1985 Girl Kneeling Next to Doll House 16675	Retrd.	1989	12.00	39
1987 Girl w/ Nightie and Cap 110310	Retrd.	1989	9.00	33

YEAR ISSUE	EDITION LIMIT	YEAR RETD.	ISSUE PRICE	*QUOTE U.S.$
1989 Gnome Skiing 222062	Retrd.	1990	9.00	27
1982 Grandma E-5417	Retrd.	1989	9.00	39
1982 Grandpa E-5417	Retrd.	1989	9.00	34
1982 Mom E-5417	Retrd.	1989	9.00	N/A
1987 Mrs. Bear Strings Cranberry Garland 110957	Retrd.	1989	N/A	27
1988 Nutcracker Clara 510246	Retrd.	1989	11.00	39
1990 Red Skier 228141	Retrd.	1994	12.00	33
1985 Santa w/List of Good Girls and Boys 16640	Retrd.	1989	10.00	30-39
1987 Shoemaker Repairs Shoes 110485	Retrd.	1988	50.00	33-39
1989 Skier in Yellow & Blue Outfit 222038	Retrd.	1990	10.00	20
1986 Three Bears on a Toboggan 104981	Retrd.	N/A	20.00	57
1985 Tumbling Santa Claus (3 poses) 16039	Retrd.	1989	10.00	39-45
1987 Two Bears Dressed as Reindeer, set/2 110639	Retrd.	1990	10.00	33

Lucy & Me - L. Riggs

YEAR ISSUE	EDITION LIMIT	YEAR RETD.	ISSUE PRICE	*QUOTE U.S.$
1986 Angel Kissing 105767	Retrd.	1989	20.00	27
1985 Baby Boy Nap on Pillow 102156	Retrd.	1989	9.00	30
1988 Baby on Goose 114081	Retrd.	1988	9.50	33
1982 Baby w/Bear E-9341	Retrd.	1990	10.00	25
1987 Bear Dressed as Bunny with Carrot 111619	Retrd.	1990	11.00	39
1979 Bear in Bunny Ears w/blue Basket E-4731	Retrd.	1985	N/A	39
1985 Bear in Duck Inner Tube 101575	Retrd.	1989	8.00	45
1984 Bear in Red and White Clown Jester Suit 10170	Retrd.	1989	11.00	39
1981 Bear on Rocking Horse E-7135	Retrd.	1987	15.00	153
1986 Bear on Sandpile 107107	Retrd.	1989	9.50	39
1987 Bear Sitting w/honey Pot 112992	Retrd.	1989	8.00	20
1984 Bear w/Broken Leg 101621	Retrd.	1988	9.00	39
1985 Boy as Easter Egg 101370	Retrd.	1990	13.00	27
1983 Boy Bowler E-3079	Retrd.	1990	10.50	33
1979 Boy Gardener in Blue E4727	Retrd.	1985	2.30	27
1986 Boy w/Geese 106585	Retrd.	1989	9.50	39
1986 Boy w/Pail & Shovel 107107	Retrd.	1989	9.50	39
1987 Boy with Pacifier 114227	Retrd.	1991	9.50	33
1987 Canadian Bear as a Mountie 510491	Retrd.	1991	9.50	29
1990 Cavebears, Boy & Girl, set/2 228184	Retrd.	N/A	10.00	40
1985 Cookie Cutter Bear Skating 19618	Retrd.	1987	N/A	65
1989 Cow 224596	Retrd.	1992	10.00	15
1986 Dad and Son Fishing 104337	Retrd.	1989	10.00	33
1985 Dad w/Cub on Shoulders 101613	Retrd.	1991	15.00	30-39
1985 Dancing Bears in Irish Outfits 102032	Retrd.	1989	7.50	45
1986 Devil Kissing 105767	Retrd.	1989	20.00	27
1990 Elf Hammering Toy 568635	Retrd.	1992	33.30	69
1986 Family Going to Church (set/4) 106267	Retrd.	1992	11.00	65
1984 Fireman 11940	Retrd.	1989	11.00	20
1984 Four Seated Bears & Picnic Basket, set/6 12912	Retrd.	1988	N/A	123
1988 Gardener w/Cart 509353	Retrd.	1991	15.00	27
1987 Gardener w/Rake 111856	Retrd.	1990	11.00	39
1989 Gardner (w/o Flower Pot) 223659	Retrd.	1992	N/A	15
1987 German Bear w/ Bear Stein 510505	Retrd.	1991	9.50	23-33
1983 Get Well Bear E-3079	Retrd.	1990	10.50	33
1986 Girl Getting Ready For Bed 106941	Retrd.	1989	9.50	39
1984 Girl Pilgrim E-5414	Retrd.	1989	N/A	33
1986 Girl w/Coffee Pot 111635	Retrd.	1989	8.00	39
1986 Girl w/Yellow Dress w/Steno Pad 106968	Retrd.	1989	8.00	23
1987 Girl with Pacifier 114227	Retrd.	1991	9.50	27
1988 Graduate on School Books 106038	Retrd.	1991	10.00	25
1981 Hairdresser E-7137	Retrd.	1985	10.00	160
1981 Hugging Couple w/Valentine Hearts E-4729	Retrd.	1988	8.92	45-57
1987 John Hancock Bear 109681	Retrd.	1989	9.50	27
1987 Kissing Couple E-3197	Retrd.	1985	N/A	45
1989 Lamaze Couple, set/2 224537	Retrd.	N/A	20.00	45
1987 Little Red Riding Hood 510971	Retrd.	1989	9.50	30-39
1987 Mexican Bear in Sombrero Serape 510513	Retrd.	1991	9.50	33
1988 Mom w/Baby Diaper and Bag 114057	Retrd.	1988	10.00	39
1987 Mother and Child Carrying Laundry 111619	Retrd.	1989	11.00	39
1987 Party Animal 113018	Retrd.	1989	8.00	27
1986 Pilot with Plane 101019	Retrd.	1988	9.50	20-27
1985 Pregnant Mom (yellow) w/Baby Care Book (3 pc.) 101605	Retrd.	1992	12.00	27

YEAR ISSUE	EDITION LIMIT	YEAR RETD.	ISSUE PRICE	*QUOTE U.S.$
1988 Queen of Hearts With Tarts 111791	Retrd.	1992	12.00	18
1988 Roller-skating Waitress 510602	Retrd.	1990	10.00	30-39
1979 Sailor Bear E3128	Retrd.	1989	9.00	27
1984 Sailor Bear w/Lollipop 11886	Retrd.	1988	10.50	33
1988 Sitting Bear w/Daisy 111953	Retrd.	1988	20.00	45
1984 Sitting Bear w/Heart 10715	Retrd.	1988	12.50	27
1986 Teddy Bear University 109541	Retrd.	1992	9.50	33
1982 Tennis Girl E-9342	Retrd.	1989	10.50	33
1983 Thank You Bear E-3079	Retrd.	1990	10.50	33
1982 Three Easter Bears E-9345	Retrd.	1990	N/A	75-93
1988 Turkey 510327	Retrd.	N/A	10.00	15
1985 Two Bears Playing Hearts, set/2 111538	Retrd.	1989	11.00	25-35
1986 Two Clowns Juggling Hearts 105775	Retrd.	1991	12.00	33
1979 Two Moms Hugging Cubs E-4733	Retrd.	1988	15.00	30-39
1982 Two Tumbling Bears E-8676	Retrd.	1990	10.00	45
1986 Vampire 103438	Retrd.	1989	10.00	25-33
1979 Wedding Couple E-4728	Retrd.	N/A	14.00	27
1986 Woman Holding Baby, set/2 105988	Retrd.	1988	10.00	66

Lucy & Me "Childs" - L. Riggs

YEAR ISSUE	EDITION LIMIT	YEAR RETD.	ISSUE PRICE	*QUOTE U.S.$
1986 Sunday's Child - Girl Goes to Church 107824	Retrd.	1989	11.00	40
1986 Monday's Child - Girl in Long Dress & Hat 107751	Retrd.	1989	11.00	N/A
1986 Tuesday's Child - Girl Ballerina 107778	Retrd.	1989	11.00	40
1986 Wednesday's Child - Girl w/ Handkerchief 107786	Retrd.	1989	11.00	40
1986 Thursday's Child - Girl Dressed in Hat/Coat 107794	Retrd.	1989	11.00	27
1986 Friday's Child - Bear Girl Holding Baby 107808	Retrd.	1989	11.00	40
1986 Saturday's Child - Girl as Nurse 107816	Retrd.	1989	11.00	27

Lucy & Me Alice in Wonderland - L. Riggs

YEAR ISSUE	EDITION LIMIT	YEAR RETD.	ISSUE PRICE	*QUOTE U.S.$
1988 Alice in Wonderland w/White Rabbit 510661	Retrd.	1990	35.00	123
1987 Alice in Wonderland Bear 111473	Retrd.	1989	9.00	25
1987 Mad Hatter Bear 111481	Retrd.	1989	9.00	25
1987 Tweedle-dee Bear 111503	Retrd.	1989	9.00	25
1987 Tweedle-dum Bear 111503	Retrd.	1989	9.00	25
1987 White Rabbit 111511	Retrd.	1989	9.50	25
1987 Two Bears Playing Cards 111538	Retrd.	1989	11.00	25-31
1987 March Hare 111545	Retrd.	1989	11.50	25

Lucy & Me Goldilocks - L. Riggs

YEAR ISSUE	EDITION LIMIT	YEAR RETD.	ISSUE PRICE	*QUOTE U.S.$
1986 Lucylocks Sleeping in Baby Bear's Cradle 107840	Retrd.	1989	40.00	123
1986 Lucylocks - Bear as Goldilocks 106976	Retrd.	1989	9.50	27
1986 3 Bears -Mama, Papa, Baby Table/Porridge, set/4 107034	Retrd.	1989	30.00	N/A
1986 3 Bears -Mama 107034	Retrd.	1989	30.00	27
1986 3 Bears -Papa 107034	Retrd.	1989	30.00	27
1986 3 Bears -Table 107034	Retrd.	1989	30.00	27
1986 3 Bears -Baby 107034	Retrd.	1989	30.00	27
1986 Lucylocks in Baby Bear's Chair 107875	Retrd.	1989	13.50	27
1986 Lucylocks in Mama Bear's Chair 107883	Retrd.	1989	16.50	27
1986 Lucylocks in Papa Bear's Chair 107891	Retrd.	1989	16.50	27

Maud Humphrey Bogart/Enesco Group, Inc.

Maud Humphrey Bogart Collectors' Club Members Only - M. Humphrey

YEAR ISSUE	EDITION LIMIT	YEAR RETD.	ISSUE PRICE	*QUOTE U.S.$
1991 Friends For Life MH911	Closed	N/A	60.00	63-130
1992 Nature's Little Helper MH921	Closed	N/A	65.00	82-94
1993 Sitting Pretty MH931	Closed	N/A	60.00	60-78

Maud Humphrey Bogart - Symbol Of Membership Figurines - M. Humphrey

YEAR ISSUE	EDITION LIMIT	YEAR RETD.	ISSUE PRICE	*QUOTE U.S.$
1991 A Flower For You H5596	Closed	N/A	Unkn.	35-65
1992 Sunday Best M0002	Closed	N/A	Unkn.	57-75
1993 Playful Companions M0003	Closed	N/A	Unkn.	57-91

Maud Humphrey Bogart - M. Humphrey

YEAR ISSUE	EDITION LIMIT	YEAR RETD.	ISSUE PRICE	*QUOTE U.S.$
1991 All Bundled Up -910015	19,500	N/A	85.00	75-80
1990 Autumn Days H1348	24,500	N/A	45.00	38-65
1992 Autumn's Child 910260	24,500	N/A	50.00	50-63
1989 The Bride-Porcelain H1388	15,000	N/A	125.00	119-125

YEAR ISSUE	EDITION LIMIT	YEAR RETD.	ISSUE PRICE	*QUOTE U.S.$
1990 A Chance Acquaintance H5589	19,500	N/A	70.00	75-143
1992 The Christmas Carol 915823	24,500	N/A	75.00	69-75
1988 Cleaning House H1303	Retrd.	N/A	60.00	44-90
1991 Doubles -910023	19,500	N/A	70.00	82
1993 The Entertainer 910562	19,500	N/A	60.00	75-82
1993 Flying Lessons 910139	15,000	N/A	50.00	63-69
1988 Gift Of Love H1319	Retrd.	N/A	65.00	38-65
1994 Good As New 914924	5,000	N/A	100.00	88
1991 The Graduate H5559	19,500	N/A	75.00	219-225
1994 A Hidden Treasure - 914940	5,000	N/A	60.00	94
1990 Holiday Surprise H5551	24,500	N/A	50.00	30-75
1991 Hush A Bye Baby H5695	19,500	N/A	62.00	73-82
1989 In The Orchard H1373	24,500	N/A	33.00	32-44
1990 Kitty's Bath H1384	19,500	N/A	103.00	125-144
1989 Kitty's Lunch H1355	19,500	N/A	60.00	30-69
1989 Little Bo Peep H1382	Retrd.	N/A	45.00	32-55
1989 The Little Captive H1374	19,500	N/A	55.00	32-75
1988 Little Chickadees H1306	Retrd.	N/A	65.00	32-50
1989 Little Red Riding Hood H1381	24,500	N/A	42.50	57-65
1990 A Little Robin H1347	19,500	N/A	55.00	55-69
1994 Love To Last A Lifetime - 655627	5,000	N/A	45.00	50-63
1993 Love's First Bloom 910120	15,000	N/A	50.00	63-69
1988 The Magic Kitten H1308	Retrd.	N/A	66.00	38-85
1994 Marie-Childhood Memories 869619	5,000	N/A	35.00	35-44
1988 My 1st Birthday H1320	Retrd.	N/A	47.00	57-65
1988 My First Dance H1311	Retrd.	N/A	60.00	150-188
1990 My Winter Hat H5554	24,500	N/A	40.00	69
1989 No More Tears H1351	24,500	N/A	44.00	38-88
1991 The Pinwheel H5600	24,500	N/A	45.00	50
1989 Playing Bridesmaid H5500	19,500	N/A	125.00	120-125
1993 Playing Mama 5th Anniv. Figurine 915963	Retrd.	N/A	80.00	140-160
1993 Playing Mama Event Figurine 915963R	Retrd.	N/A	80.00	110-120
1988 A Pleasure To Meet You H1310	Retrd.	N/A	65.00	78-91
1988 Sarah H1312	Retrd.	N/A	60.00	188-358
1988 School Days H1318	Retrd.	N/A	42.50	46-50
1990 School Lesson H1356	19,500	N/A	77.00	77-188
1988 Sealed With A Kiss H1316	Retrd.	N/A	45.00	44-50
1988 Seamstress H1309	Retrd.	N/A	66.00	90-195
1988 Special Friends H1317	Retrd.	N/A	66.00	52-82
1990 A Special Gift H5550	19,500	N/A	70.00	63-88
1989 Springtime Gathering H1385	7,500	N/A	295.00	295
1992 Stars and Stripes Forever 910201	Retrd.	N/A	75.00	90-113
1992 Summer's Child 910252	24,500	N/A	50.00	50-57
1989 A Sunday Outing H1386	15,000	N/A	135.00	75-119
1988 Susanna H1305	Retrd.	N/A	60.00	132-144
1988 Tea And Gossip H1301	Retrd.	N/A	65.00	75-104
1989 Winter Fun H1354	Retrd.	N/A	46.00	46-75
1991 Winter Ride 910066	Retrd.	N/A	60.00	60-65

Maud Humphrey Bogart Gallery Figurines - M. Humphrey

YEAR ISSUE	EDITION LIMIT	YEAR RETD.	ISSUE PRICE	*QUOTE U.S.$
1991 Mother's Treasures H5619	15,000	N/A	118.00	88-118

Maud Humphrey Bogart Linen and Lace - M. Humphrey

YEAR ISSUE	EDITION LIMIT	YEAR RETD.	ISSUE PRICE	*QUOTE U.S.$
1994 Artist of Her Time 916722	2,500	N/A	60.00	60-69
1994 Capture the Moment 912654	2,500	N/A	125.00	125

Melody in Motion/MMC LLC

Melody In Motion/Collector's Society - S. Nakane, unless otherwise noted

YEAR ISSUE	EDITION LIMIT	YEAR RETD.	ISSUE PRICE	*QUOTE U.S.$
1992 Amazing Willie the One-Man Band 07152	Retrd.	1994	130.00	300-400
1992 Willie The Conductor	Retrd.	1994	Gift	150
1993 Charmed Bunnies	Retrd.	1993	Gift	40-45
1993 Willie The Collector 07170	Retrd.	1995	200.00	200-250
1994 Springtime	Retrd.	1994	Gift	30-50
1995 Best Friends	Retrd.	1995	Gift	30-50
1996 Willie The Entertainer 07199	Retrd.	1996	200.00	300-350
1996 '86 Santa Replica - K. Maeda	Retrd.	1997	Gift	50-80
1997 Willie on Parade/Drum 07214 - K. Maeda	Retrd.	1997	220.00	200-220
1997 Willie Sr.- K. Maeda	Retrd.	1997	Gift	28-40
1998 Willie & Jumbo 07224 - K. Maeda	Retrd.	1998	180.00	180-200
1998 Purr-Fect Harmony 07307 - L. Miquez	Retrd.	1998	Gift	28-40
1999 Cheers 07240 - K. Maeda	Retrd.	1999	170.00	170
1999 Nocturne 07308 - T. Nomura	Retrd.	1999	Gift	45
2000 Y2K Willie 07309 - T. Nomura	Retrd.	2000	Gift	N/A
2001 Glazed Policeman Clock 07251 - K. Maeda	Retrd.	2001	260.00	260
2001 Willie The Rider 07310 - T. Nomura	Retrd.	2001	Gift	N/A

FIGURINES

YEAR ISSUE	EDITION LIMIT	YEAR RETD.	ISSUE PRICE	*QUOTE U.S.$
2002 Railroad Station Willie 2002 - T. Nomura	Yr.Iss.		Gift	N/A

Melody In Motion - S. Nakane, unless otherwise noted

YEAR ISSUE	EDITION LIMIT	YEAR RETD.	ISSUE PRICE	*QUOTE U.S.$
1985 Willie The Trumpeter 07000	Retrd.	2000	90.00	175-300
1985 Willie The Hobo (Memories) 07001	2,500	1985	90.00	175-195
1985 Willie The Hobo (Show Me...) 07001	Retrd.	1996	90.00	200-275
1985 Willie The Whistler (Show Me...) 07002	2,500	1985	90.00	200-225
1985 Willie The Whistler (Memories) 07002	Retrd.	1998	90.00	200-250
1985 Salty 'N' Pepper 07010	Retrd.	1992	90.00	300-450
1986 The Cellist 07011	Retrd.	1995	100.00	200-400
1986 Santa Claus 1986 07012	20,000	1986	100.00	1800-2500
1986 The Guitarist 07013	Retrd.	1994	100.00	200-250
1986 The Fiddler 07014	Retrd.	1995	100.00	200-250
1987 Lamppost Willie 07051	Open		85.00	150
1987 The Organ Grinder 07053	Retrd.	1994	85.00	200-300
1987 Violin Clown 07055	Retrd.	1992	85.00	200-250
1987 Clarinet Clown 07056	Retrd.	1991	85.00	175-200
1987 Saxophone Clown 07057	Retrd.	1991	85.00	175-200
1987 Accordion Clown 07058	Retrd.	1991	85.00	175-200
1987 Santa Claus 1987 07060	16,000	1987	110.00	600-1200
1987 Balloon Clown 07061	Retrd.	2000	85.00	150-160
1987 The Carousel (1st Edition) 07065	Retrd.	1993	190.00	200-350
1987 Madame Violin 07075	Retrd.	1991	130.00	200-350
1987 Madame Mandolin 07076	Retrd.	1994	130.00	200-400
1987 Madame Cello 07077	Retrd.	1991	130.00	200-350
1987 Madame Flute 07078	Retrd.	1992	130.00	200-400
1987 Madame Harpsichord 07080	Retrd.	1991	130.00	200-400
1987 Madame Lyre 07081	Retrd.	1994	130.00	150-300
1988 Madame Harp 07079	Retrd.	1998	130.00	150-250
1988 Spotlight Clown Cornet 07082	Retrd.	1992	120	150-200
1988 Spotlight Clown Banjo 07083	Retrd.	1992	120.00	150-250
1988 Spotlight Clown Trombone 07084	Retrd.	1992	120.00	150-200
1988 Spotlight Clown Bingo 07085	Retrd.	1996	130.00	150
1988 Spotlight Clown Tuba 07086	Retrd.	1992	120	150-250
1988 Spotlight Clown Bass 07087	Retrd.	1994	130.00	200-275
1988 Peanut Vendor 07088	Retrd.	1994	140.00	200-300
1988 Ice Cream Vendor 07089	Retrd.	1994	140.00	200-250
1988 Santa Claus 1988 07090	12,000	1988	130.00	700-1000
1989 Clockpost Willie 07091	Open		150.00	230
1989 Santa Claus 1989 (Willie) 07092	12,000	1989	130.00	400-600
1989 Lull'aby Willie 07093	Retrd.	1992	170.00	400-500
1989 The Grand Carousel 07094	Retrd.	1995	3000.00	3000-4000
1989 Grandfather's Clock 07096	Retrd.	1994	200.00	220-325
1990 Santa Claus 1990 07097	12,000	1990	150.00	300-325
1990 Shoemaker 07130	3,700	1993	110.00	150-210
1990 Blacksmith 07131	3,700	1993	110.00	150-200
1990 Woodchopper 07132	3,700	1993	110.00	150-200
1990 Accordion Boy 07133	4,100	1992	120.00	150-200
1990 Hunter 07134	Retrd.	1994	110.00	150-250
1990 Robin Hood 07135 - C. Johnson	2,000	1991	180.00	300-400
1990 Little John 07136 - C. Johnson	2,000	1992	180.00	250-300
1990 Clockpost Willie II (European) 07140	Retrd.	1990	N/A	2000
1990 Clockpost Clown 07141	Retrd.	1999	220.00	220
1990 Lull' A Bye Willie II (European) 07142	Retrd.	1990	N/A	250-450
1991 The Carousel (2nd Edition) 07065	Retrd.	1995	240.00	300-400
1991 Victoria Park Carousel 07143	Retrd.	1999	300.00	360
1991 Hunter Timepiece 07144	Retrd.	1994	250.00	200-350
1991 Santa Claus 1991 07146	7,000	1991	150.00	300-400
1991 Willie The Fisherman 07148	Retrd.	1998	150.00	200
1992 King of Clowns Carousel 07149	Retrd.	1998	740.00	800-1200
1992 Golden Mountain Clock 07150	Retrd.	1995	250.00	250-300
1992 Santa Claus 1992 07151	11,000	1992	160.00	150-200
1992 Dockside Willie 07153	Retrd.	1998	160.00	150-250
1992 Wall Street Willie 07147	Retrd.	2000	180.00	250
1993 Wild West Willie 07154	Retrd.	1995	175.00	200-250
1993 Alarm Clock Post 07155 (Willie European)	Retrd.	1996	240.00	350-450
1993 Lamplight Willie 07156	Retrd.	1996	220.00	200-350
1993 Madame Cello Player, glaze 07157	200	1993	170.00	400
1993 Madame Flute, glaze 07158	200	1993	170.00	400
1993 Madame Harpsichord, glaze	200	1993	170.00	400
1993 Madame Harp, glaze	150	1993	190.00	400
1993 Santa Claus 1993 Coke 07161	6,000	1993	180.00	250-475
1993 Wall Street (Japanese) 07162	Retrd.	1993	N/A	350-450
1993 Santa Claus 1993 (European) 07163	1,000	1993	N/A	375-450
1993 When I Grow Up 07171	Retrd.	1996	200.00	200-400
1993 Willie The Golfer - Alarm 07164	Retrd.	1995	240.00	200-240
1993 The Artist 07165	Retrd.		200.00	200-240
1993 Heartbreak Willie 07166	Retrd.	1998	180.00	190-300
1993 South of the Border 07167	Retrd.	1996	180.00	200-250
1994 Low Pressure Job-Alarm 07168	Retrd.	1995	240.00	240-325
1994 Day's End-Alarm 07169	Retrd.	1996	240.00	200-300
1994 Santa '94 Coca-Cola 07174	9,000	1994	190.00	200-250
1994 Smooth Sailing 07175	Retrd.	1996	200.00	250-300
1994 Santa Claus 1994 (European) 07176	700	1994	N/A	300-400
1994 The Longest Drive 07177	Open		150.00	160
1994 Happy Birthday Willie 07178	Retrd.	2001	170.00	170
1994 Chattanooga Choo Choo 07179	Open		180.00	200
1994 Jackpot Willie 07182	Open		180.00	200
1994 Caroler Boy 07189	10,000	1998	172.00	172-190
1994 Caroler Girl 07190	10,000	1998	172.00	100-172
1994 Day's End-Clock 07269	Retrd.	1997	240.00	200-240
1994 Willie the Yodeler 07192	Open		158.00	170
1994 Willie the Golfer- Clock 07264	Open		240.00	255
1995 Blue Danube Carousel 07173	Retrd.	2000	280.00	315
1995 Campfire Cowboy 07172	Retrd.	1995	180.00	200-300
1995 Coca-Cola Norman Rockwell 07194	Retrd.	1998	194.00	200
1995 Santa Claus '95 07195	6,000	1995	190.00	175-250
1995 Gaslight Willie 07197	Retrd.	2000	170.00	190
1995 Low Pressure Job-Clock 07268	Retrd.	1997	240.00	170-250
1995 Coca Cola Polar Bear 07198	6,000	1998	180.00	180-190
1995 Willie the Conductor (10th Anniversary) 07181	10,000	1999	220.00	220-300
1995 Willie The Fireman 07271	1,500	1996	200.00	200-300
1996 The Candy Factory-I Love Lucy 07203 - Willingham/Maeda	Retrd.	1998	250.00	200-250
1996 Willie On The Road 07204 - K. Maeda	Open		180.00	190
1996 Marionette Clown 07205 - K. Maeda	Open		200.00	210
1996 Willie the Racer 07206 - K. Maeda	Open		180.00	210
1996 Willie the Organ Grinder 07207	3,000	2000	200.00	210
1996 Santa Claus '96 07208 - K. Maeda	7,000	1999	220.00	220
1996 Willie the Champion 07209 - K. Maeda	Open		180.00	190
1996 Willie the Photographer 07211 - K. Maeda	Retrd.	1999	220.00	220-235
1997 Willie on Parade/Trumpet 07212 - K. Maeda	Open		220.00	220
1997 Willie on Parade/Sousaphone 07213 - K. Maeda	Open		220.00	220
1997 Willie on Parade/Trombone 07215 - K. Maeda	Open		220.00	220
1997 I Love Lucy/Vitameatavegamin 07216 - K. Maeda	4,000	1998	220.00	150-250
1997 Santa Claus 1997 07217 - K. Maeda	4,000	1997	220.00	150-255
1997 Side Street Circus/Balancing Dog 07230	Closed	1998	110.00	50-110
1997 Side Street Circus/Juggling 07231	Closed	1998	110.00	50-110
1997 Side Street Circus/Accordian 07232	Closed	1998	110.00	50-110
1997 Side Street Circus/Clarinet 07233	Closed	1998	110.00	50-110
1997 Side Street Circus/Plate Spinning 07234	Closed	1998	110.00	50-110
1998 Coca Cola Santa Claus Clock 07223 - K. Maeda	3,000	1998	250.00	250-350
1998 Wedding Couple, white 07220 - K. Maeda	Open		196.00	210
1998 Willie The Wanderer 07221 - K. Maeda	Open		170.00	180
1998 Santa Claus 1998 07222 - K. Maeda	4,000	1998	220.00	220-300
1999 Balloon Clown (Europe) 07062 - K. Maeda	Open		150.00	160
1999 Willie The Entertainer ("As Time Goes By") 07199	360	1999	200.00	210-300
1999 Just For You (Europe) 07239	Retrd.	1999	170.00	170
1999 Wedding Couple, colors 07220 - K. Maeda	300	1999	196.00	200
1999 Willie the Hunter (Europe) 07241 - K. Maeda	Open		170.00	180
1999 Clock Post Clown (Europe) 07242 - K. Maeda	Retrd.	1999	200.00	200-240
1999 Santa Claus 1999 07243 - K. Maeda	3,000	1999	220.00	220
2000 Santa Claus 2000 07244 - K. Maeda	3,000	2000	250.00	250
2000 Santa Claus Clock 07245 - K. Maeda	600	2000	260.00	260
2000 Rail Road Cart Willie 07246	Open		200.00	200
2001 Willie The Policeman Clock 07248 - K. Maeda	Open		260.00	260
2001 DX Carousel 07249 - K. Maeda	Open		440.00	440
2001 DX Carousel 07250 - K. Maeda	Open		440.00	440
2001 Fireman Willie 07252 - K. Maeda	Open		220.00	220
2001 Santa Claus 2001 07253 - K. Maeda	3,000	2001	250.00	250
2002 Chattanooga Choo Choo Clock 07254 - K. Maeda	Open		260.00	260
2002 Santa Claus 2002 07255 - K. Maeda	2,500		240.00	240

Collectors' Information Bureau

*Quotes have been rounded up to nearest dollar

YEAR ISSUE	EDITION LIMIT	YEAR RETD.	ISSUE PRICE	*QUOTE U.S.$
Memories of Yesterday/Enesco Group, Inc.				
Memories of Yesterday Society Figurines - M. Attwell				
1991 Welcome To Your New Home MY911	Yr.Iss.	1991	30.00	48
1992 I Love My Friends MY921	Yr.Iss.	1992	32.50	35
1993 Now I'm The Fairest Of Them All MY931	Yr.Iss.	1993	35.00	35
1993 A Little Love Song for You MY941	Yr.Iss.	1993	35.00	35
1994 Wot's All This Talk About Love MY942	Yr.Iss.	1994	27.50	28-40
1995 Sharing the Common Thread of Love MY951	Yr.Iss.	1995	100.00	100
1995 A Song For You From One That's True MY952	Yr.Iss.	1995	37.50	38
1996 You've Got My Vote MY961	Yr.Iss.	1996	40.00	40
1996 Peace, Heavenly Peace MY962	Yr.Iss.	1996	30.00	30
1997 We Take Care of One Another MY971	Yr.Iss.	1997	45.00	45
1997 You Mean the World to Me MY972	Yr.Iss.	1997	40.00	40
1998 A Little Caring Makes Everything Better MY981	Yr.Iss.	1998	45.00	45
1998 No Worries Here MY982	Yr.Iss.	1998	40.00	40
1999 She Loves Me MY991	Yr.Iss.	1999	30.00	55
Memories of Yesterday Exclusive Membership Figurine - M. Attwell				
1991 We Belong Together S0001	Yr.Iss.	1991	Gift	37
1992 Waiting For The Sunshine S0002	Yr.Iss.	1992	Gift	25-35
1993 I'm The Girl For You S0003	Yr.Iss.	1993	Gift	40-50
1994 Blowing a Kiss to a Dear I Miss S0004	Yr.Iss.	1994	Gift	N/A
1995 Time to Celebrate S0005	Yr.Iss.	1995	Gift	N/A
1996 Forget-Me-Not! S0006	Yr.Iss.	1996	Gift	N/A
1997 Holding On To Childhood Memories S0007	Yr.Iss.	1997	Gift	N/A
1998 I'll Never Leave Your Side S0008	Yr.Iss.	1998	Gift	N/A
1999 He Loves Me S0009	Yr.Iss.	1999	Gift	50
Memories of Yesterday Exclusive Charter Membership Figurine - M. Attwell				
1992 Waiting For The Sunshine S0102	Yr.Iss.	1992	Gift	N/A
1993 I'm The Girl For You S0103	Yr.Iss.	1993	Gift	N/A
1994 Blowing a Kiss to a Dear I Miss S0104	Yr.Iss.	1994	Gift	N/A
1995 Time to Celebrate S0105	Yr.Iss.	1995	Gift	N/A
1996 Forget-Me-Not! S0106	Yr.Iss.	1996	Gift	N/A
1997 Holding On To Childhood Memories S0107	Yr.Iss.	1997	Gift	N/A
1998 I'll Never Leave Your Side S0108	Yr.Iss.	1998	Gift	N/A
Memories of Yesterday 10th Anniversary Celebration - M. Attwell				
1997 Meeting Friends Along The Way Figurine 270407	Yr.Iss.	1997	85.00	85
1997 Meeting Friends Along The Way Covered Box 277746	Yr.Iss.	1997	14.00	14
Memories of Yesterday - M. Attwell				
1995 A Friend Like You Is Hard To Find 101176	Retrd.	1999	45.00	45-55
1995 A Helping Hand For You 101192	Retrd.	1997	40.00	40
1998 Good Morning Sunshine 115258	5,000	1999	30.00	30
1998 Have A Little Christmas Cheer 134856	Retrd.	1999	30.00	30-45
1995 Won't You Skate With Me? 134864	5,000	1999	35.00	35
1995 Dear Old Dear, Wish You Were Here 134872	5,000	1999	37.50	38
1998 Make a Little Garden 137618	5,000	1999	40.00	40
1995 You're My Sunshine On A Rainy Day 137626	Retrd.	1998	37.50	38
1995 Boo-Boo's Band Set/5 137758	Retrd.	1999	25.00	25
1996 We're In Trouble Now! 162299	7,500	1999	37.50	38
1998 Daddy's Little Shaver 162507	5,000	1999	30.00	30
1998 Night, Night Dollie 162566	Retrd.	1999	35.00	35
1996 A Basket Full of Love 162582	Retrd.	1999	50.00	50
1997 You're My Bouquet of Blessings 162604	5,000	1999	30.00	30
1996 Just Longing To See You 162620	7,500	1999	27.50	28
1996 We Are All His Children 162639	Retrd.	1999	30.00	30
1998 I'm A Little Lady 162655	5,000	1999	30.00	30
1996 Just Like Daddy 162698	7,500	1999	27.50	28
1998 Wishin You A Jolly Holiday 162736	Retrd.	1999	35.00	35
1998 Over The River And Through The Woods 162752	Retrd.	1999	65.00	65-85
1998 This Is The Life 162817	5,000	1999	32.50	33
1998 Hard Work Reaps Many Blessings 162841	5,000	1999	40.00	40

YEAR ISSUE	EDITION LIMIT	YEAR RETD.	ISSUE PRICE	*QUOTE U.S.$
1996 How Good of God To Make Us All 164135	5,000	1999	50.00	50
1997 I Know You Can Do It 209821	5,000	1999	35.00	35
1997 In the Hands of a Guardian Angel 209856	5,000	1999	50.00	50
1997 There's Always a Rainbow 209864	5,000	1999	37.50	38
1997 Bringing Gifts of Friendship To Share 209872	5,000	1999	37.50	38
1997 Let Me Be Your Guardian Angel 279722	Retrd.	1999	25.00	25
1997 How 'Bout a Little Kiss 279730	Retrd.	1999	25.00	25
1997 Hoping To See You Soon 279706	Retrd.	1999	25.00	25
1997 I Pray Thee Lord My Soul To Keep 279714	Retrd.	1999	25.00	25
1997 Now I Lay Me Down To Sleep 279749	Retrd.	1999	25.00	25
1997 Time For Bed 279765	Retrd.	1999	25.00	25
1998 Fit For A Day 306509	5,000	1999	30.00	30
1990 Collection Sign 513156	Closed	1993	7.00	7
1989 Blow Wind, Blow 520012	Retrd.	1997	40.00	40
1990 Hold It! You're Just Swell 520020	Retrd.	1999	50.00	50
1990 Kiss The Place And Make It Well 520039	Retrd.	1999	50.00	50
1989 Let's Be Nice Like We Was Before 520047	Retrd.	1999	50.00	35-50
1991 Who Ever Told Mother To Order Twins? 520063	Retrd.	1999	33.50	34
1989 I'se Spoken For 520071	Retrd.	1991	30.00	30-50
1993 You Do Make Me Happy 520098	Retrd.	1999	27.50	28
1990 Where's Muvver? 520101	Retrd.	1994	30.00	30
1990 Here Comes The Bride And Groom God Bless 'Em! (musical) 520136	Retrd.	1999	80.00	80
1989 Daddy, I Can Never Fill Your Shoes 520187	Retrd.	1997	30.00	30
1989 This One's For You, Dear 520195	Retrd.	1999	50.00	50
1989 Should I . . . ? 520209	Retrd.	1999	50.00	50
1990 Luck At Last! He Loves Me 520217	Retrd.	1992	35.00	36-58
1989 Here Comes The Bride-God Bless Her! 520527	Retrd.	1999	95.00	60-95
1989 We's Happy! How's Yourself? (musical) 520616	Retrd.	1991	70.00	85-150
1989 Here Comes The Bride & Groom (musical) God Bless 'Em 520896	Retrd.	1999	50.00	50
1989 The Long and Short of It 522384	Retrd.	1994	32.50	33
1989 As Good As His Mother Ever Made 522392	Retrd.	1997	32.50	32-40
1989 Must Feed Them Over Christmas 522406	Retrd.	1996	38.50	39
1989 Knitting You A Warm & Cozy Winter 522414	Retrd.	1999	37.50	38
1989 Joy To You At Christmas 522449	Retrd.	1996	45.00	45
1989 For Fido And Me (musical) 522457	Retrd.	1999	70.00	70
1991 Wishful Thinking 522597	Retrd.	1999	45.00	45
1991 Why Don't You Sing Along? 522600	Retrd.	1995	55.00	55
1995 You Brighten My Day With A Smile 522627	Retrd.	1998	30.00	30
1991 I Must Be Somebody's Darling 522635	Retrd.	1993	30.00	30
1991 Tying The Knot 522678	Retrd.	1998	60.00	60
1991 Wherever I Am, I'm Dreaming of You 522686	Retrd.	1999	40.00	40
1993 Will You Be Mine? 522694	Retrd.	1997	30.00	30
1991 Sitting Pretty 522708	Retrd.	1993	40.00	50
1993 Here's A Little Song From Me To You (musical) 522716	Retrd.	1999	70.00	70
1992 A Whole Bunch of Love For You 522732	Retrd.	1996	40.00	40
1992 I'se Such A Good Little Girl Sometimes 522759	Retrd.	1999	30.00	30
1992 Things Are Rather Upside Down 522775	Retrd.	1999	30.00	30
1991 Pull Yourselves Together Girls, Waists Are In 522783	Retrd.	1999	30.00	30
1993 Bringing Good Luck To You 522791	Retrd.	1996	30.00	30
1995 I Comfort Fido And Fido Comforts Me 522813	5,000	1999	50.00	50
1992 A Kiss From Fido 523119	Retrd.	1999	35.00	35
1994 Bless 'Em! 523217	Retrd.	1998	35.00	35
1994 Bless 'Em 523232	Retrd.	1998	35.00	35
1990 I'm Not As Backwards As I Looks 523240	Retrd.	1997	32.50	33
1990 I Pray The Lord My Soul To Keep 523259	Retrd.	1999	25.00	25
1990 He Hasn't Forgotten Me 523267	Retrd.	1999	30.00	30
1990 Time For Bed 9" 523275	Yr.Iss.	1991	95.00	73-125

FIGURINES

YEAR ISSUE	EDITION LIMIT	YEAR RETD.	ISSUE PRICE	*QUOTE U.S.$
1991 Just Thinking 'bout You (musical) 523461	Retrd.	1999	70.00	70
1992 Now Be A Good Dog Fido 524581	Retrd.	1997	45.00	45
1991 Them Dishes Nearly Done 524611	Retrd.	1999	50.00	50
1995 Join Me For A Little Song 524654	5,000	1999	37.50	38
1990 Let Me Be Your Guardian Angel 524670	Retrd.	1999	32.50	33
1990 A Lapful Of Luck 524689	Retrd.	1999	30.00	30
1990 Not A Creature Was Stirrin' 524697	Retrd.	1999	45.00	45
1990 I'se Been Painting 524700	Retrd.	1999	37.50	38
1992 The Future-God Bless "Em! 524719	Retrd.	1998	37.50	38
1990 A Dash of Something With Something For the Pot 524727	Retrd.	1997	55.00	55
1991 Opening Presents Is Much Fun! 524735	Retrd.	1999	37.50	38
1992 You'll Always Be My Hero 524743	Retrd.	1997	50.00	50
1990 Got To Get Home For The Holidays (musical) 524751	Retrd.	1994	100.00	100
1990 Hush-A-Bye Baby (musical) 524778	Retrd.	1997	80.00	80
1990 The Greatest Treasure The World Can Hold 524808	Retrd.	1997	50.00	50
1994 With A Heart That's True, I'll Wait For You 524816	Retrd.	1996	50.00	50
1990 Hoping To See You Soon 524824	Retrd.	1999	30.00	30
1991 We All Loves A Cuddle 524832	Retrd.	1992	30.00	35
1991 He Loves Me 9" 525022	Retrd.	1992	100.00	50-100
1993 Now I Lay Me Down To Sleep (musical) 525413	Retrd.	1999	65.00	65
1992 Making Something Special For You 525472	Retrd.	1999	45.00	45
1991 I'm As Comfy As Can Be 525480	Retrd.	1999	50.00	50
1992 I'm Hopin' You're Missing Me Too 525499	Retrd.	1999	55.00	55
1992 A Friendly Chat & A Cup of Tea 525510	Yr.Iss.	1992	50.00	69-75
1993 The Jolly Ole Sun Will Shine Again 525502	Retrd.	1994	55.00	55
1997 May I Have This Dance? 525529	5,000	1999	50.00	50
1991 Friendship Has No Boundaries (Special Understamp) 525545	Yr.Iss.	1991	30.00	30-50
1992 Home's A Grand Place To Get Back To (musical) 525553	Retrd.	1995	100.00	100
1991 Give It Your Best Shot 525561	Retrd.	1999	35.00	35
1992 I Pray the Lord My Soul To Keep (musical) 525596	Retrd.	1999	65.00	65
1991 Could You Love Me For Myself Alone? 525618	Retrd.	1994	30.00	30
1996 Whenever I Get A Moment-I Think of You 526626	7,500	1999	37.50	38
1992 Good Night and God Bless You In Every Way! 525634	Retrd.	1999	50.00	50
1992 Five Years Of Memories (Five Year Anniversary Figurine) 525669	Yr.Iss.	1992	50.00	50-65
1992 Five Years Of Memories Celebrating Our Five Years 1992 525669A	Yr.Iss.	1992	N/A	N/A
1996 Loving You One Stitch At A Time 525677	5,000	1999	50.00	50
1993 May Your Flowers Be Even Better Than The Pictures On The Packets 525685	Retrd.	1997	37.50	38
1995 Let's Sail Away Together 525707	Retrd.	1999	32.50	33
1993 You Won't Catch Me Being A Golf Widow 525715	Retrd.	1998	30.00	30
1995 Good Friends Are Great Gifts 525723	Retrd.	1999	50.00	50
1994 Taking After Mother 525731	Retrd.	1999	40.00	40
1994 Too Shy For Words 525758	Retrd.	1996	50.00	50
1991 Good Morning, Little Boo-Boo 525766	Retrd.	1996	40.00	40
1997 Dreams Are Sweeter With Friends 525774	5,000	1999	37.50	38
1992 Hurry Up For the Last Train to Fairyland 525863	Retrd.	1999	40.00	40
1992 I'se So Happy You Called 9" 526401	Yr.Iss.	1993	100.00	100
1994 Pleasant Dreams and Sweet Repose-(musical) 526592	Retrd.	1999	80.00	80
1998 Always Getting Stronger 526606	5,000	1999	35.00	35
1998 Just A Ring To Say Hello 526975	5,000	1999	30.00	30
1996 Put Your Best Foot Forward 526983	5,000	1999	50.00	50
1994 Bobbed 526991	Retrd.	1995	32.50	33
1996 Can I Keep Her, Mommy? 527025	Retrd.	1999	13.50	14
1992 Time For Bed 527076	Retrd.	1999	30.00	30
1991 S'no Use Lookin' Back Now! 527203	Yr.Iss.	1991	75.00	75
1992 Collection Sign 527300	Retrd.	1999	30.00	30
1993 Having A Wash And Brush Up 527424	Retrd.	1999	35.00	35
1994 Having a Good Ole Laugh 527432	Retrd.	1999	50.00	50

YEAR ISSUE	EDITION LIMIT	YEAR RETD.	ISSUE PRICE	*QUOTE U.S.$
1993 A Bit Tied Up Just Now-But Cheerio 527467	Retrd.	1999	45.00	45
1992 Send All Life's Little Worries Skipping 527505	Retrd.	1997	30.00	30
1994 Don't Wait For Wishes to Come True-Go Get Them! 527645	Retrd.	1999	37.50	38
1993 Hullo! Did You Come By Underground? 527653	Yr.Iss.	1993	40.00	40
1993 Hullo! Did You Come By Underground? Commemorative Issue: 1913 1993 527653A	500	1999	N/A	N/A
1993 Look Out-Something Good Is Coming Your Way! 528781	Retrd.	1999	37.50	38-50
1992 Merry Christmas, Little Boo-Boo 528803	Retrd.	1999	37.50	38
1994 Do Be Friends With Me 529117	Retrd.	1999	40.00	40
1994 Good Morning From One Cheery Soul To Another 529141	Retrd.	1999	30.00	30
1994 May Your Birthday Be Bright And Happy 529575	Retrd.	1998	35.00	35
1996 God Bless Our Future 529583	5,000	1999	45.00	45
1993 Strikes Me, I'm Your Match 529656	Retrd.	1999	27.50	28
1993 Wot's All This Talk About Love? 9" 529737	Yr.Iss.	1994	100.00	100
1994 Thank God For Fido 9" 529753	Yr.Iss.	1994	100.00	100
1994 Making the Right Connection 529907	Yr.Iss.	1994	32.50	33
1994 Still Going Strong 530344	Retrd.	1998	27.50	28
1997 Let Your Light Shine 530360	5,000	1999	30.00	30
1993 Do You Know The Way To Fairyland? 530379	Retrd.	1996	50.00	50-75
1996 We'd Do Anything For You, Dear 530905	5,000	1999	50.00	50
1994 Comforting Thoughts 531367	Retrd.	1998	32.50	33
1995 Love To You Always 602752	Retrd.	1999	30.00	30
1995 Wherever You Go, I'll Keep In Touch 602760	Retrd.	1996	30.00	30
1995 Love Begins With Friendship 602914	Retrd.	1997	50.00	50
1994 The Nativity Pageant 602945	Retrd.	1999	90.00	90
1995 May You Have A Big Smile For A Long While 602965	Retrd.	1999	45.00	45
1995 Love To You Today 602973	Retrd.	1999	30.00	30
1998 Did I Hear You Say You Like Me 602981	5,000	1999	30.00	30
1996 You Warm My Heart 603007	7,500	1999	35.00	35

Memories of Yesterday Charter 1988 - M. Attwell

YEAR ISSUE	EDITION LIMIT	YEAR RETD.	ISSUE PRICE	*QUOTE U.S.$
1988 Mommy, I Teared It 114480	Retrd.	1999	27.50	40-143
1988 Now I Lay Me Down To Sleep 114499	Retrd.	1999	25.00	25-65
1988 We's Happy! How's Yourself? 114502	Retrd.	1996	45.00	33-60
1988 Hang On To Your Luck! 114510	Retrd.	1999	27.50	27-70
1988 How Do You Spell S-O-R-R-Y? 114529	Retrd.	1990	27.50	40-50
1988 What Will I Grow Up To Be? 114537	Retrd.	1999	45.00	45
1988 Can I Keep Her Mommy? 114545	Retrd.	1995	27.50	27-70
1988 Hush! 114553	Retrd.	1990	50.00	80-125
1988 It Hurts When Fido Hurts 114561	Retrd.	1992	32.50	32-75
1988 Anyway, Fido Loves Me 114588	Retrd.	1999	32.50	32-75
1988 If You Can't Be Good, Be Careful 114596	Retrd.	1993	55.00	55-90
1988 Welcome Santa 114960	Retrd.	1999	50.00	50-100
1988 Special Delivery 114979	Retrd.	1991	32.50	32-70
1988 How 'bout A Little Kiss? 114987	Retrd.	1995	27.50	75-85
1988 Waiting For Santa 114995	Retrd.	1999	45.00	32-50
1988 Dear Santa. . . 115002	Retrd.	1999	55.00	50-150
1988 I Hope Santa Is Home . . . 115010	Retrd.	1999	32.50	30-45
1988 It's The Thought That Counts 115029	Retrd.	1999	27.50	29-75
1988 Is It Really Santa? 115347	Retrd.	1996	55.00	55-60
1988 He Knows If You've Been Bad Or Good 115355	Retrd.	1999	45.00	45-75
1988 Now He Can Be Your Friend, Too! 115363	Retrd.	1999	50.00	50-70
1988 We Wish You A Merry Christmas 115371 (musical)	Retrd.	1999	75.00	75
1988 Good Morning Mr. Snowman 115401	Retrd.	1992	80.50	80-170
1988 Mommy, I Teared It, 9" 115924	Yr.Iss.	1990	95.00	125

Memories of Yesterday Event Item Only - M. Attwell

YEAR ISSUE	EDITION LIMIT	YEAR RETD.	ISSUE PRICE	*QUOTE U.S.$
1994 I'll Always Be Your Truly Friend 525693	Yr.Iss.	1994	30.00	30
1995 Wrapped In Love And Happiness 602930	Yr.Iss.	1995	35.00	35
1996 A Sweet Treat For You 115126	Yr.Iss.	1996	30.00	30
1997 Mommy, I Teared It 114480A	Yr.Iss.	1997	27.50	28
1998 A Circle of Friends 525030	Yr.Iss.	1998	30.00	30

YEAR ISSUE	EDITION LIMIT	YEAR RETD.	ISSUE PRICE	*QUOTE U.S.$
Alice in Wonderland - M. Attwell				
1997 Alice in Wonderland Collector Set 255254	3,000	1999	150.00	150
Cinderella - M. Attwell				
1998 Cinderella Collector Set 314854	3,000	1999	150.00	150
Comforting Thoughts - M. Attwell				
1997 You Make My Heart Feel Glad 209880	5,000	1999	30.00	30
Exclusive Heritage Dealer Figurine - M. Attwell				
1991 A Friendly Chat and a Cup of Tea 525510	Yr.Iss.	1991	50.00	69-100
1993 I'm Always Looking Out For You 527440	Yr.Iss.	1993	55.00	55
1994 Loving Each Other Is The Nicest Thing We've Got 522430	Yr.Iss.	1994	60.00	60
1995 A Little Help From Fairyland 529133	1,995	1995	55.00	55
1995 Friendship Is Meant To Be Shared 602922	Yr.Iss.	1995	50.00	50
1995 Bedtime Tales-set 153400	2,000	1996	60.00	60
1996 Tucking My Dears All Safe Away 130095	Yr.Iss.	1996	50.00	50
1996 I Do Like My Holiday Crews 522805	1,996	1999	100.00	100
1996 Peter Pan Collector's Set 174564	1,000	1999	150.00	150
1997 Every Stitch is Sewn With Kindness 209910	Yr.Iss.	1997	50.00	50
1997 We're Going to Be Great Friends 525537	1,997	1999	50.00	50
Friendship - M. Attwell				
1996 I'll Miss You 179183	Retrd.	1999	20.00	25
1996 I Love You This Much! 179191	Retrd.	1999	20.00	25
1996 Thinking of You 179213	Retrd.	1999	20.00	25
1996 You And Me 179205	Retrd.	1999	20.00	25
Holiday Snapshots - M. Attwell				
1995 I'll Help You Mommy 144673	Retrd.	1999	20.00	25
1995 Isn't She Pretty? 144681	Retrd.	1999	20.00	25
1995 I Didn't Mean To Do It 144703	Retrd.	1999	20.00	25
1995 Can I Open Just One? 144711	Retrd.	1999	20.00	25
A Loving Wish For You - M. Attwell				
1995 Happiness Is Our Wedding Wish 135178	Retrd.	1999	20.00	25
1995 A Blessed Day For You 135186	Retrd.	1999	20.00	25
1995 Wishing You A Bright Future 135194	Retrd.	1999	20.00	25
1995 An Anniversary Is Love 135208	Retrd.	1999	25.00	25
1995 A Birthday Wish For You 135216	Retrd.	1999	20.00	25
1995 Bless You, Little One 135224	Retrd.	1999	20.00	25
1996 You Are My Shining Star 164585	Retrd.	1999	20.00	25
1996 You Brighten My Days 164615	Retrd.	1999	20.00	25
Memories Of A Special Day - M. Attwell				
1994 Monday's Child... 531421	Retrd.	1999	35.00	35
1994 Tuesday's Child... 531448	Retrd.	1999	35.00	35
1994 Wednesday's Child... 531405	Retrd.	1999	35.00	35
1994 Thursday's Child... 531413	Retrd.	1999	35.00	35
1994 Friday's Child... 531391	Retrd.	1999	35.00	35
1994 Saturday's Child... 531383	Retrd.	1999	35.00	35
1994 Sunday's Child... 531480	Retrd.	1999	35.00	35
1994 Collector's Commemorative Edition Set of 7, Hand-numbered 528056	1,994	1994	250.00	250
Nativity - M. Attwell				
1994 Nativity Set of 4 602949	Retrd.	1999	90.00	90
1995 Innkeeper 602892	Retrd.	1999	27.50	28
1996 Shepherd 602906	Retrd.	1999	27.50	28
Once Upon A Fairy Tale™... - M. Attwell				
1992 Mother Goose 526428	18,000	1999	50.00	50
1993 Mary, Mary Quite Contrary 526436	18,000	1999	45.00	45
1993 Little Miss Muffett 526444	18,000	1999	50.00	50
1992 Simple Simon 526452	18,000	1999	35.00	35
1992 Mary Had A Little Lamb 526479	18,000	1999	45.00	45
1994 Tweedle Dum & Tweedle Dee 526460	10,000	1999	50.00	50
A Penny For Your Thoughts - M. Attwell				
1997 You're Nice 204722	Retrd.	1999	20.00	20
1997 Now Do You Love Me Or Do You Don't 204730	Retrd.	1999	20.00	20

YEAR ISSUE	EDITION LIMIT	YEAR RETD.	ISSUE PRICE	*QUOTE U.S.$
1997 Roses Are Red, Violets Are Blue -Violets Are Sweet, An' So Are You 204757	Retrd.	1999	20.00	20
Peter Pan - M. Attwell				
1996 John 165441	Retrd.	1999	20.00	25
1996 Michael and Nana 165425	Retrd.	1999	25.00	30
1996 Peter Pan 164666	Retrd.	1999	20.00	25
1996 Wendy 164674	Retrd.	1999	20.00	25
Special Edition - M. Attwell				
1989 As Good As His Mother Ever Made 523925	Yr.Iss.	1989	32.50	44-150
1988 Mommy, I Teared It 523488	Yr.Iss.	1988	25.00	175-325
1990 A Lapful of Luck 525014	Yr.Iss.	1990	30.00	32-180
1990 Set of Three	N/A		87.50	735
When I Grow Up - M. Attwell				
1995 When I Grow Up, I Want To Be A Doctor 102997	Retrd.	1999	20.00	25
1995 When I Grow Up, I Want To Be A Mother 103195	Retrd.	1999	20.00	25
1995 When I Grow Up, I Want To Be A Ballerina 103209	Retrd.	1999	20.00	25
1995 When I Grow Up, I Want To Be A Teacher 103357	Retrd.	1999	20.00	25
1995 When I Grow Up, I Want To Be A Fireman 103462	Retrd.	1999	20.00	25
1995 When I Grow Up, I Want To Be A Nurse 103535	Retrd.	1999	20.00	25
1996 When I Grow Up, I Want To Be A Businessman 164623	Retrd.	1999	20.00	25
1996 When I Grow Up, I Want To Be A Businesswoman 164631	Retrd.	1999	20.00	25

Miss Martha's Collection/Enesco Group, Inc.

YEAR ISSUE	EDITION LIMIT	YEAR RETD.	ISSUE PRICE	*QUOTE U.S.$
Miss Martha's Collection - M. Root				
1993 Erin-Don't Worry Santa Won't Forget Us 307246	Retrd.	1994	55.00	110
1993 Amber-Mr. Snowman! (waterglobe) 310476	Closed	1994	50.00	100-115
1993 Kekisha-Heavenly Peace Musical 310484	Closed	1994	60.00	120
1993 Whitney-Let's Have Another Party 321559	Closed	1994	45.00	85-90
1993 Megan-My Birthday Cake! 321567	Closed	1994	60.00	115-120
1993 Doug-I'm Not Showin' Off 321575	Closed	1994	40.00	75-80
1993 Francie-Such A Precious Gift! 321583	Closed	1994	50.00	95-100
1993 Alicia-A Blessing From God 321591	Closed	1994	40.00	75-80
1993 Anita-It's For You, Mama! 321605	Closed	1994	45.00	85-90
1994 Jeffrey-Bein' A Fireman Sure Is Hot & Thirsty Work 350206	Closed	1994	40.00	80
1993 Jess-I Can Fly 350516	Retrd.	1994	45.00	80
1993 Ruth-Littlest Angel Figurine 350524	Closed	1994	40.00	80
1993 Stephen-I'll Be The Best Shepherd In The World! 350540	Closed	1994	40.00	80
1993 Jonathon-Maybe I Can Be Like Santa 350559	Closed	1994	40.00	90
1994 Charlotte-You Can Be Whatever You Dream 353191	Closed	1994	40.00	80
1992 Lillie-Christmas Dinner! 369373	Retrd.	1993	55.00	105-110
1992 Eddie-What A Nice Surprise! 369381	Retrd.	1994	50.00	95-100
1992 Kekisha-Heavenly Peace 421456	Closed	1994	40.00	75-80
1992 Angela-I Have Wings 421464	Closed	1994	45.00	90
1992 Amber-Mr. Snowman 421472	Retrd.	1993	60.00	120
1992 Mar/Jsh/Christopher-Hush Baby! It's Your B-day! Musical 431362	Closed	1994	80.00	105-160
1992 Carrie-God Bless America 440035	Closed	1994	45.00	90
1993 Hallie-Sing Praises To The Lord 443166	Retrd.	1993	60.00	120
1991 Jana-Plant With Love 443174	Closed	1994	40.00	80
1993 Hallie-Sing Praises To The Lord 443182	Closed	1994	37.50	75
1992 Belle-Maize-Not Now, Muffin 443204	Retrd.	1993	50.00	100
1991 Sammy/Leisha-Sister's First Day Of School 443190	Closed	1994	55.00	110
1991 Nate-Hope You Hear My Prayer, Lord 443212	Closed	1994	17.50	55
1991 Sadie-They Can't Find Us Here 443220	Retrd.	1993	45.00	90
1992 Patsy-Clean Clothes For Dolly 443239	Retrd.	1993	50.00	100
1991 Dawn-Pretty Please, Mama 443247	Closed	1994	40.00	80
1991 Tonya-Hush, Puppy Dear 443255	Closed	1994	50.00	100

FIGURINES

YEAR ISSUE	EDITION LIMIT	YEAR RETD.	ISSUE PRICE	*QUOTE U.S.$
1991 Jenny/Jeremiah-Birthday Biscuits, With Love... 443263	Retrd.	1993	60.00	150
1991 Suzi-Mama, Watch Me! 443271	Retrd.	1993	35.00	70
1992 Mattie-Sweet Child 443298	Retrd.	1993	30.00	60
1992 Sara Lou-Here, Lammie 443301	Retrd.	1993	50.00	100
1992 Angel Tree Topper 446521	Closed	1994	80.00	155-250
1992 Mar/Jsh/Christopher-Hush, Baby! It's Your B-day Figurine 448354	Closed	1994	55.00	110

Museum Collections, Inc.

American Family I - N. Rockwell

YEAR ISSUE	EDITION LIMIT	YEAR RETD.	ISSUE PRICE	*QUOTE U.S.$
1979 Baby's First Step	22,500	N/A	90.00	195-225
1980 Birthday Party	22,500	N/A	110.00	150
1981 Bride and Groom	22,500	N/A	110.00	125
1980 First Haircut	22,500	N/A	90.00	150-175
1980 First Prom	22,500	N/A	90.00	110-150
1980 Happy Birthday, Dear Mother	22,500	N/A	90.00	135
1980 Little Mother	22,500	N/A	110.00	125
1981 Mother's Little Helpers	22,500	N/A	110.00	135
1980 The Student	22,500	N/A	110.00	125-175
1980 Sweet Sixteen	22,500	N/A	90.00	125-175
1980 Washing Our Dog	22,500	N/A	110.00	125-150
1980 Wrapping Christmas Presents	22,500	N/A	90.00	125-130

Christmas - N. Rockwell

YEAR ISSUE	EDITION LIMIT	YEAR RETD.	ISSUE PRICE	*QUOTE U.S.$
1980 Checking His List	Yr.Iss.	1980	65.00	110
1983 High Hopes	Yr.Iss.	1983	95.00	175
1981 Ringing in Good Cheer	Yr.Iss.	1981	95.00	100
1984 Space Age Santa	Yr.Iss.	1984	65.00	100-110
1982 Waiting for Santa	Yr.Iss.	1982	95.00	110

Classic - N. Rockwell

YEAR ISSUE	EDITION LIMIT	YEAR RETD.	ISSUE PRICE	*QUOTE U.S.$
1984 All Wrapped Up	Closed	N/A	65.00	100
1984 Bedtime	Closed	N/A	65.00	125-150
1984 The Big Race	Closed	N/A	65.00	90-95
1983 Bored of Education	Closed	N/A	65.00	95-110
1983 Braving the Storm	Closed	N/A	65.00	135-150
1980 The Cobbler	Closed	N/A	65.00	95-125
1982 The Country Doctor	Closed	N/A	65.00	95-125
1981 A Dollhouse for Sis	Closed	N/A	65.00	90-95
1983 Dreams in the Antique Shop	Closed	N/A	65.00	90-95
1983 A Final Touch	Closed	N/A	65.00	90-95
1980 For A Good Boy	Closed	N/A	65.00	145-200
1984 Goin' Fishin'	Closed	N/A	65.00	90-95
1983 High Stepping	Closed	N/A	65.00	100-115
1982 The Kite Maker	Closed	N/A	65.00	100-110
1980 Lighthouse Keeper's Daughter	Closed	N/A	65.00	110-135
1980 Memories	Closed	N/A	65.00	110-150
1981 The Music Lesson	Closed	N/A	65.00	125-135
1981 Music Master	Closed	N/A	65.00	125
1981 Off to School	Closed	N/A	65.00	95-125
1981 Puppy Love	Closed	N/A	65.00	90-95
1984 Saturday's Hero	Closed	N/A	65.00	95-115
1983 A Special Treat	Closed	N/A	65.00	90-95
1982 Spring Fever	Closed	N/A	65.00	90-95
1980 The Toymaker	Closed	N/A	65.00	110-125
1981 While The Audience Waits	Closed	N/A	65.00	100-110
1983 Winter Fun	Closed	N/A	65.00	90-95
1982 Words of Wisdom	Closed	N/A	65.00	110-125

Commemorative - N. Rockwell

YEAR ISSUE	EDITION LIMIT	YEAR RETD.	ISSUE PRICE	*QUOTE U.S.$
1985 Another Masterpiece by Norman Rockwell	5,000	N/A	125.00	250-275
1981 Norman Rockwell Display	5,000	N/A	125.00	200-250
1983 Norman Rockwell, America's Artist	5,000	N/A	125.00	225
1984 Outward Bound	5,000	N/A	125.00	225-250
1986 The Painter and the Pups	5,000	N/A	125.00	250
1982 Spirit of America	5,000	N/A	125.00	225-275

Original Appalachian Artworks

Extra Special - X. Roberts

YEAR ISSUE	EDITION LIMIT	YEAR RETD.	ISSUE PRICE	*QUOTE U.S.$
1985 Baby's First Step	Closed	N/A	18.00	40
1984 Bedtime Story	Closed	N/A	15.00	25
1984 Birthday Party	Closed	N/A	26.50	40-45
1984 The Building Block	Closed	N/A	8.00	12
1985 Carousel (musical)	Closed	N/A	90.00	200
1984 CPK Clubhouse	Closed	N/A	26.50	45-50
1984 Daydreams	Closed	N/A	8.00	15
1984 Deer Friends	Closed	N/A	26.50	45
1984 Discovering New Life	Closed	N/A	16.00	25
1985 The Entertainers	30,000	N/A	50.00	85-100
1984 Getting Acquainted	Closed	N/A	20.00	40
1984 I Can Do It	Closed	N/A	8.00	15
1984 Just Being Silly	Closed	N/A	8.00	15
1984 The Little Drummer	Closed	N/A	8.00	15
1985 Lovely Ladies	Closed	N/A	26.50	50-60
1984 Noel, Noel	Closed	N/A	20.00	40-45
1984 Playtime	Closed	N/A	8.00	25
1985 Rainbow Sweetheart	Closed	N/A	15.00	15
1984 Sandcastles	Closed	N/A	26.50	45-55
1984 Sharing a Soda Cream	Closed	N/A	15.00	30
1984 Sleigh Ride	Closed	N/A	18.50	30
1985 Special Delivery	25,000	N/A	50.00	100
1985 A Special Gift	Closed	N/A	15.00	35
1984 Tea For Two	Closed	N/A	16.50	30
1984 Waiting Patiently	Closed	N/A	8.00	15

Extra Special Easter Collection - X. Roberts

YEAR ISSUE	EDITION LIMIT	YEAR RETD.	ISSUE PRICE	*QUOTE U.S.$
1985 Easter Artists	Closed	N/A	40.00	50-55
1985 Findin' Easter Treats	Closed	N/A	26.50	50-55
1985 In Your Easter Bonnet	Closed	N/A	8.00	15
1985 Our Easter Bunny	Closed	N/A	8.00	15

Extra Special Valentine Collection - X. Roberts

YEAR ISSUE	EDITION LIMIT	YEAR RETD.	ISSUE PRICE	*QUOTE U.S.$
1985 Hugs and Kisses	Closed	N/A	18.00	30
1985 I Love You	Closed	N/A	14.50	30
1985 Rainbow Sweetheart	Closed	N/A	15.00	30

Papel Giftware/Cast Art Industries

The Windsor Bears of Cranbury Commons - Team

YEAR ISSUE	EDITION LIMIT	YEAR RETD.	ISSUE PRICE	*QUOTE U.S.$
1998 Alexander "I'll Be There"	Retrd.	2001	22.50	23
1998 Alyssa "Time to Hit the Slopes"	Retrd.	2001	18.50	19
2000 Amanda "Building Your Dreams"	Retrd.	2001	22.50	23
1996 Amanda "Sew Happy"	Retrd.	1997	14.50	15
1998 Amber "Thinking of You"	Retrd.	2000	16.50	17
1997 Amy "Roses are Red"	Retrd.	1999	16.00	16
2000 Andrea "The Maid of Honor"	Retrd.	2001	16.50	17
1997 Andrew & Allison "Love Is In the Air"	Retrd.	2001	30.00	30
1998 Andy "Reach for the Stars"	Retrd.	2001	22.50	23
1997 Angela "My Lil' Angel"	Retrd.	2000	16.00	16
1998 Ann & Me "And the Stockings Were Hung By the Chimney with Care"	Retrd.	2001	30.00	30
1997 Arnold "Breakin' Par"	Retrd.	2001	18.00	18
1996 Ashley & Tyler "Skater's Waltz"	Retrd.	1997	25.00	25
1998 Becky "I'm Sweet on You"	Retrd.	2001	18.00	18
2000 Beth & Ben "America on Parade"	Retrd.	2001	30.00	30
1997 Betsy "Stars and Stripes Forever"	Retrd.	2000	16.00	16
1996 Brandon "Soft Landing"	Retrd.	1997	17.50	18
2000 Brannon "Hang In There"	Retrd.	2001	22.50	23
1999 Brett "Thinking of You at Christmas"	Retrd.	2000	22.50	23
2000 Brianna "My Favorite Time of Year"	Retrd.	2001	22.50	23
1996 Brittany "All Things Grow With Love"	Retrd.	1997	14.50	15
2000 Bruce "Just Put Your Mind to It"	Retrd.	2001	16.50	17
2000 Caitlin "Your Secret Pal"	Retrd.	2001	18.00	18
1998 Cameron "Soccer Star"	Retrd.	2001	16.50	17
1999 Carey "Congratulations"	Retrd.	2001	18.00	18
1998 Casey "Welcome to Cranbury Commons"	Retrd.	2001	16.50	17
2000 Charles "The Best Man"	Retrd.	2001	16.50	17
1997 Charlie "The Littlest Christmas Tree"	Retrd.	2001	20.00	20
1998 Chris & Cody "We Made It!"	Retrd.	2001	30.00	30
1996 Christopher "Sweet Surprise"	Retrd.	1997	14.50	15
1996 Coleen "Luck O' the Irish"	Retrd.	1997	16.00	16
1998 Connor "Follow Your Dreams"	Retrd.	2001	22.50	23
1997 Courtney "How Does Your Garden Grow?"	Retrd.	1999	16.00	16
1998 Dad & Cory "Dad, How much Longer?"	Retrd.	2001	16.50	17
1996 Daddy & Junior "Once Upon A Time"	Retrd.	1997	14.50	15
1998 Daddy & Steven "Daddy, Can I Do It?"	Retrd.	2001	30.00	30
2000 Daddy and Me "Don't Worry, I Got You"	Retrd.	2001	27.50	28
2000 Daisy "How Do I Love Thee...?"	Retrd.	2001	18.00	18
1998 Dan "Let's Play"	Retrd.	2001	16.50	17
1998 Danielle & Derek "Sunday's Best"	Retrd.	2001	32.50	33
1997 David "Graduation Day"	Retrd.	2001	14.50	15
1999 Dennis & Doug "A Friend Is Always There In A Time of Need"	Retrd.	2001	30.00	30
1997 Dora & Her Little Sister "Halloween Surprise"	Retrd.	1999	16.00	16

Collectors' Information Bureau   *Quotes have been rounded up to nearest dollar

YEAR ISSUE	EDITION LIMIT	YEAR RETD.	ISSUE PRICE	*QUOTE U.S.$
1998 Dr. Jonathon Windsor "TLC…Tender Loving Care"	Retrd.	2001	16.50	17
2000 Dr. Windsor & Me "Smile"	Retrd.	2001	25.00	25
1998 Elizabeth & Evan "Hugs & Kisses"	Retrd.	2001	30.00	30
1996 Emily "Sleepy Head"	Retrd.	1997	14.50	15
1997 Eric "Bloomin' With Love"	Retrd.	1999	16.50	17
2000 Erica "Planting Seeds of Happiness"	Retrd.	2001	22.50	23
2000 Erin "The Sweetest Sounds of Harmony"	Retrd.	2001	18.00	18
2000 Ethan "Learning New Things Everyday"	Retrd.	2001	22.50	23
1997 Florence "Feeling Better?"	Retrd.	2001	14.50	15
1999 George "We Are Grateful"	Retrd.	2000	18.00	18
1999 Grace "We are Grateful"	Retrd.	2000	18.00	18
1998 Grandma & Timothy "Can I Lick the Spoon?"	Retrd.	2001	30.00	30
1999 Grandpa & Me "Grandpa, Can You Teach Me"	Retrd.	2001	27.50	28
1998 Greg "Wow, Look At All these Treats"	Retrd.	2001	22.50	23
2000 Heather "A Brush of Happiness"	Retrd.	2000	25.00	25
1997 Jack "It's Time for Pumpkin Pickin'"	Retrd.	2001	16.00	16
2000 James "My Favorite Present"	Retrd.	2001	22.50	23
1998 Jamie "Baby's First Christmas"	Retrd.	2001	22.50	23
1999 Jason "It's Not the Same Without You"	Retrd.	2001	20.00	20
1999 Jean "Congratulations"	Retrd.	2001	18.00	18
1999 Jenna & Debbie "Our Friendship is the Best Bargain"	Retrd.	2001	30.00	30
1998 Jennifer "Happy Birthday"	Retrd.	2001	16.50	17
1999 Jeremy "The Ring Bearer"	Retrd.	2001	12.50	13
1996 Jessica "Homework Helper"	Retrd.	1997	14.50	15
2000 Jessica "Now I Lay Me Down to Sleep"	Retrd.	2001	30.00	30
1999 Jessie "Baby's 1st Birthday"	Retrd.	2001	12.50	13
1997 Jimmy "Fool for Love"	Retrd.	1999	16.00	16
2000 Joe "Leading the Team to Excellence"	Retrd.	2001	16.50	17
1998 John "Happy Birthday"	Retrd.	2001	16.50	17
2000 Jordan "Don't Worry, Be Happy"	Retrd.	2001	16.50	17
1996 Jordan "First Day"	Retrd.	1997	14.50	15
1997 Justin "Still Life with Flowers"	Retrd.	1999	22.50	23
1998 Kathleen & Me "Spending Time With You"	Retrd.	2000	27.50	28
1996 Katie & Dolly "Best Friends"	Retrd.	1997	14.50	15
1998 Kelly "Love, Loyalty, & Friendship"	Retrd.	2001	18.00	18
2000 Keri "You Can Do It"	Retrd.	2001	16.50	17
1998 Kevin & Nicole "Will You Marry Me?"	Retrd.	2001	30.00	30
1997 Kimberly "Graduation Day"	Retrd.	2000	14.50	15
2000 Kristen "Everything Is Under Control"	Retrd.	2001	25.00	25
1997 Kyle "Look What Santa Brought Me"	Retrd.	2001	22.50	23
2000 Laura "A Caring Heart"	Retrd.	2001	18.00	18
1996 Lauren "Homemade with Love"	Retrd.	1997	14.50	15
1999 Lindsay & Louis "Childhood Sweethearts"	Retrd.	2001	30.00	30
1999 Lisa "Get Well Soon"	Retrd.	2001	18.00	18
1999 Lynn "You're As Sweet As Pie"	Retrd.	2001	25.00	25
2000 Maria & Nick "Bon Voyage"	Retrd.	2001	30.00	30
2000 Mark "Go For the Goal"	Retrd.	2001	18.00	18
1998 Mary "Miracle of Love"	Retrd.	2001	16.50	17
1997 Matthew "Bringing Home the Tree"	Retrd.	1997	16.50	17
1997 Maureen & Sean "Top O' the Morning"	Retrd.	2001	30.00	30
1997 Meghan & Daniel "Forever Yours"	Retrd.	2001	30.00	30
1997 Melissa "My Egg-stra Special Day"	Retrd.	2000	16.50	17
2000 Michael "Go For It"	Retrd.	2001	18.00	18
1997 Michael & Stephanie "Bee Mine"	Retrd.	1999	30.00	30
1999 Michelle "Have I Told You Lately"	Retrd.	2000	18.00	18
1999 Michelle & Todd "Together We Can Go Anywhere"	Retrd.	2001	30.00	30
1997 Mickey "Play Ball"	Retrd.	2001	16.00	16
1998 Miss Windsor & Brian "School Days"	Retrd.	2001	27.50	28
1998 Mommy & Me "Bundle of Joy"	Retrd.	2001	20.00	20
1999 Mommy & Me "You Always See the Best in Me"	Retrd.	2001	25.00	25
1998 Mommy, Daddy, & Me "Baby's First Step"	Retrd.	2000	32.50	33
2000 Monica "Tennis Anyone?"	Retrd.	2001	20.00	20
1999 Mr. & Mrs. Windsor "The Anniversary Waltz" Happy 50th Anniversary	Retrd.	2001	25.00	25
1999 Mr. & Mrs. Windsor "Through the Years" Happy 25th Anniversary	Retrd.	2001	25.00	25
1998 Mr. Thomas "World Class Teacher"	Retrd.	2001	16.50	17
2000 Mrs. Windsor and Dad "The First Dance"	Retrd.	2001	25.00	25

YEAR ISSUE	EDITION LIMIT	YEAR RETD.	ISSUE PRICE	*QUOTE U.S.$
1997 Nancy "Fore"	Retrd.	2001	18.00	18
1999 The New Mr. & Mrs. Windsor "And the Bride Cuts the Cake"	Retrd.	2001	30.00	30
1997 The New Mr. & Mrs. Windsor "Dearly Beloved"	Retrd.	2001	25.00	25
1998 The New Mr. & Mrs. Windsor "Over the Theshold"	Retrd.	2001	25.00	25
1996 Nicholas "Santa's Little Helper"	Retrd.	1999	16.50	17
1999 Officer Bob "To Serve and Protect"	Retrd.	2001	20.00	20
2000 Officer Windsor and Me "Welcome Home"	Retrd.	2001	20.00	20
1996 Patrick "At the End of the Rainbow"	Retrd.	1997	16.00	16
1998 Paul "Just For You"	Retrd.	2001	18.00	18
1997 Peter "Where Did They Go?"	Retrd.	2000	16.50	17
1999 Rachel "The Flower Girl"	Retrd.	2001	12.50	13
1999 Randy "All Bundled Up"	Retrd.	2001	18.00	18
1999 Rebecca "Thank You"	Retrd.	2001	16.50	17
1999 Redd "Courageous Hero"	Retrd.	2001	20.00	20
1998 Richard "Gone Fishing"	Retrd.	2001	22.50	23
1998 Riley "Kiss Me I'm Irish"	Retrd.	2001	18.00	18
1996 Robert "Sunny Morning"	Retrd.	1997	16.50	17
1997 Ryan "Watch Your Step"	Retrd.	2001	20.00	20
1997 Sam "Yankee Doodle Dandy"	Retrd.	2001	16.00	16
2000 Samantha "Prima Ballerina"	Retrd.	2000	16.50	17
1999 Sammy "Take Me Out to the Ball Game"	Retrd.	2001	50.00	50
1997 Sarah "Uh Oh!"	Retrd.	2001	22.50	23
1998 Scott "Halloween Traditions"	Retrd.	2001	16.50	17
1999 Tiffany "I'm Cheering for You"	Retrd.	2000	16.50	17
1998 Tyler "Lil' Conductor"	Retrd.	2001	18.00	18
1997 William "Lil' Drummer Bear"	Retrd.	2001	20.00	20
1998 The Windsor Family "A Time to Remember"	Retrd.	2001	100.00	100
2000 The Windsor Family "Christmas Morning"	Retrd.	2001	75.00	75
1999 The Windsor Family "Sweet Dreams"	Retrd.	2001	75.00	75
1997 Zachary "Winter Buddies"	Retrd.	2001	25.00	25

The Windsor Bears of Cranbury Commons Accessories - Team

YEAR ISSUE	EDITION LIMIT	YEAR RETD.	ISSUE PRICE	*QUOTE U.S.$
1999 Decorated Christmas Tree	Retrd.	2001	16.00	16
1999 Holiday Fireplace	Retrd.	2001	14.50	15
1999 Snowy Tree, lg.	Retrd.	2001	12.50	13
1999 Snowy Tree, med.	Retrd.	2001	10.00	10
1999 Snowy Tree, sm.	Retrd.	2001	7.50	8

PenDelfin

PenDelfin Family Circle Collectors' Club - J. Heap, unless otherwise noted

YEAR ISSUE	EDITION LIMIT	YEAR RETD.	ISSUE PRICE	*QUOTE U.S.$
1993 Herald	Closed	1993	Gift	249-290
1993 Bosun PD600	Closed	1993	50.00	120-200
1994 Buttons	Closed	1994	Gift	80-160
1994 Puffer PD601	Closed	1995	85.00	210-250
1995 Bellman PD502	Closed	1995	Gift	100-231
1995 Georgie and the Dragon PD602	Closed	1995	125.00	175
1996 Newsie PD534	Closed	1996	Gift	60-120
1996 Delia PD536	Closed	1996	125.00	125-210
1997 Little Tom PD556	Closed	1997	Gift	75-120
1997 Woody PD556	Closed	1997	125.00	125-165
1998 Tidy Patch PD574	Closed	1998	Gift	70-113
1998 Gramps PD576	Closed	1998	125.00	125
1999 Trove PD596	Closed	1999	Gift	75
1999 Treasure PD598 - D. Roberts	Closed	1999	130.00	130
2000 Little Hero PD618	Closed	2000	Gift	N/A
2000 Gran PD620	Closed	2000	120.00	120
2001 Peggy PD631	Closed	2001	Gift	N/A
2001 Sudsy PD632 - D. Roberts	Closed	2001	135.00	135
2002 Gift	Yr.Iss.		Gift	N/A
2002 The Gaffer PD644 - W. Heap			140.00	140

40th Anniversary Piece - PenDelfin

YEAR ISSUE	EDITION LIMIT	YEAR RETD.	ISSUE PRICE	*QUOTE U.S.$
1994 Aunt Ruby PD700	10,000	2001	275.00	351

Event Piece - J. Heap, unless otherwise noted

YEAR ISSUE	EDITION LIMIT	YEAR RETD.	ISSUE PRICE	*QUOTE U.S.$
1994 Walmsley PD252	Retrd.	1995	75.00	149-250
1995 Runaway PD254	Retrd.	1995	90.00	90-125
1996 Bodgit PD544	Retrd.	1996	85.00	98-188
1997 Sylvana PD564 - D. Roberts	Retrd.	1997	85.00	75-224
1998 Rockafella PD584	Retrd.	1998	85.00	85-90
1999 Gentleman Jack PD610	Retrd.	1999	85.00	85-90
2000 Event Piece PD624	Retrd.	2000	100.00	100

YEAR ISSUE	EDITION LIMIT	YEAR RETD.	ISSUE PRICE	*QUOTE U.S.$
2001 Event Piece PD636	Retrd.	2001	100.00	100

Nursery Rhymes - Various

1956 Little Bo Peep - J. Heap	Retrd.	1959	2.00	N/A
1956 Little Jack Horner - J. Heap	Retrd.	1959	2.00	N/A
1956 Mary Mary Quite Contrary - J. Heap	Retrd.	1959	2.00	N/A
1956 Miss Muffet - J. Heap	Retrd.	1959	2.00	N/A
1956 Tom Tom the Piper's Son - J. Heap	Retrd.	1959	2.00	N/A
1956 Wee Willie Winkie - J. Heap	Retrd.	1959	2.00	N/A

Retired Figurines - Various

1990 Angelo - J. Heap	Retrd.	2000	90.00	97
1985 Apple Barrel - J. Heap	Retrd.	1992	N/A	20-83
1963 Aunt Agatha - J. Heap	Retrd.	1965	N/A	1400-3000
1982 Balcony's Scene - D. Roberts	Retrd.	1998	200.00	200
1955 Balloon Woman - J. Heap	Retrd.	1956	1.00	798-1200
1964 Bandstand (mold 1) - J. Heap	Retrd.	1973	70.00	495
1968 Barrow Boy - J. Heap	Retrd.	2001	35.00	55
1967 The Bath Tub - J. Heap	Retrd.	1975	4.50	83-125
1955 Bell Man - J. Heap	Retrd.	1956	1.00	800-1200
1996 Big Spender - D. Roberts	Retrd.	2000	53.00	53
1984 Blossom - D. Roberts	Retrd.	1989	35.00	85-205
1955 Bobbin Woman - J. Heap	2	1959	N/A	5000
1964 Bongo - D. Roberts	Retrd.	1987	31.00	115-150
1966 Cakestand - J. Heap	Retrd.	1972	2.00	495-595
1993 Campfire - D. Roberts	Retrd.	1999	39.00	35-38
1982 Casanova - J. Heap	Retrd.	1998	44.00	44-73
1968 Castle Tavern - D. Roberts	Retrd.	2001	120.00	160
1953 Cauldron Witch - J. Heap	Retrd.	1959	3.50	1014-2000
1959 Cha Cha - J. Heap	Retrd.	1961	N/A	1485-2000
1990 Charlotte - D. Roberts	Retrd.	1992	25.00	96-205
1996 Cheeky - D. Roberts	Retrd.	1998	53.00	53
1989 Chirpy - D. Roberts	Retrd.	1992	31.50	85-125
1996 Christmas Island - J. Heap	Retrd.	2001	200.00	200
1985 Christmas Set - D. Roberts	2,000	1986	N/A	550-1150
1983 Clanger - J. Heap	Retrd.	1998	44.00	44-87
1983 Clinger - J. Heap	Retrd.	1997	38.00	38
1967 Cobble Cottage - D. Roberts	Retrd.	2001	80.00	105
1962 Cornish Prayer (Corny) - J. Heap	Retrd.	1965	N/A	990-1200
1993 Cousin Beau - D. Roberts	Retrd.	1999	55.00	55
1980 Crocker - D. Roberts	Retrd.	1989	20.00	126-164
1963 Cyril Squirrel - J. Heap	Retrd.	1965	N/A	1300-2000
1955 Daisy Duck - J. Heap	Retrd.	1958	N/A	1650-2500
1955 Desmond Duck - J. Heap	Retrd.	1958	2.50	1650-2500
1964 Dodger - J. Heap	Retrd.	1996	24.00	42-95
1955 Dungaree Father - N/A	Retrd.	1960	N/A	1073-1240
1955 Elf - J. Heap	Retrd.	1956	1.00	990
1953 The Fairy Shop - J. Heap	Retrd.	1958	N/A	1000-3000
1961 Father Mouse (grey) - J. Heap	Retrd.	1966	N/A	372-743
1958 Father/Mother Book Ends - N/A	Retrd.	1965	N/A	824
1955 Flying Witch - J. Heap	Retrd.	1956	1.00	825
1993 Forty Winks - D. Roberts	Retrd.	1996	57.00	99-206
1968 Fruit Shop - J. Heap	Retrd.	2001	125.00	170
1969 Gallery Pieface - J. Heap	Retrd.	1971	N/A	575
1969 The Gallery Series: Wakey, Pieface, Poppet, Robert, Dodger - J. Heap	Retrd.	1971	N/A	400-600
1961 Grand Stand (mold 1) - J. Heap	Retrd.	1969	35.00	660-775
1992 Grand Stand (mold 2)- J. Heap	Retrd.	1996	150.00	108-150
1960 Gussie - J. Heap	Retrd.	1968	N/A	454-800
1989 Honey - D. Roberts	Retrd.	1993	40.00	115-132
1988 Humphrey Go-Kart - J. Heap	Retrd.	1994	70.00	120-165
1986 Jim-Lad - D. Roberts	Retrd.	1992	22.50	144-230
1985 Jingle - D. Roberts	Retrd.	1992	11.25	125-165
1960 Kipper Tie Father - N/A	Retrd.	1970	N/A	506-660
1986 Little Mo - D. Roberts	Retrd.	1994	35.00	85-150
1961 Lollipop (grey) (Mouse) - J. Heap	Retrd.	1966	N/A	700-825
1960 Lucy Pocket - J. Heap	Retrd.	1967	4.20	109-300
1956 Manx Kitten - J. Heap	Retrd.	1958	2.00	33
1955 Margot - J. Heap	Retrd.	1961	2.00	254-500
1967 Maud - J. Heap	Retrd.	1970	N/A	289-400
1961 Megan - J. Heap	Retrd.	1967	3.00	361-800
1956 Midge (Replaced by Picnic Midge) - J. Heap	Retrd.	1965	2.00	254-800
1966 Milk Jug Stand - J. Heap	Retrd.	1972	2.00	500-910
1999 Millennium Queen	Retrd.	2001	500.00	500
1960 Model Stand - J. Heap	Retrd.	1964	4.00	371-750
1961 Mother Mouse (grey) - J. Heap	Retrd.	1966	N/A	655-800
1965 Mouse House (bronze) - J. Heap	Retrd.	1969	N/A	288-400
1965 Mouse House (stoneware) - J. Heap	N/A	N/A	N/A	700-990
1965 Muncher - J. Heap	Retrd.	1983	26.00	73-200

YEAR ISSUE	EDITION LIMIT	YEAR RETD.	ISSUE PRICE	*QUOTE U.S.$
1990 New Boy - D. Roberts	Retrd.	1999	55.00	55-66
1981 Nipper - D. Roberts	Retrd.	1989	20.50	116-210
1999 The Nursery	Retrd.	2001	550.00	550
1955 Old Adam - J. Heap	Retrd.	1956	4.00	1980
1955 Old Father (remodeled)- J. Heap	Retrd.	1970	50.	700-1000
1957 Old Mother - J. Heap	Retrd.	1978	6.25	330-400
1956 Old Mother (thin neck) - J. Heap	Retrd.	1956	6.25	361-410
1984 Oliver - D. Roberts	Retrd.	1995	25.00	99-132
1955 Original Father - J. Heap	Retrd.	1960	50.00	750-1450
1956 Original Robert - J. Heap	Retrd.	1967	2.50	200-454
1953 Pendle Witch (stoneware) - J. Heap	Retrd.	1957	4.00	1645-1980
1995 Pepper - D. Roberts	Retrd.	2001	49.00	49
1967 Phumf - J. Heap	Retrd.	1985	24.00	99-160
1955 Phynnodderee (Commissioned -Exclusive) - J. Heap	Retrd.	1956	1.00	990
1966 Picnic Basket - J. Heap	Retrd.	1968	2.00	400-495
1996 Picnic Midge - J. Heap	Retrd.	1999	25.00	22-40
1965 Picnic Stand - J. Heap	Retrd.	1985	62.50	132-245
1967 Picnic Table - J. Heap	Retrd.	1972	N/A	250-600
1966 Pieface - D. Roberts	Retrd.	1987	31.00	66-100
1994 Pipkin - J. Heap	Retrd.	2001	50.00	50
1965 Pixie Bods - J. Heap	Retrd.	1987	N/A	400-506
1953 Pixie House - J. Heap	Retrd.	1958	N/A	N/A
1962 Pooch - D. Roberts	Retrd.	1987	24.50	73-125
1958 Rabbit Book Ends - J. Heap	Retrd.	1965	10.00	1500-2000
1983 The Raft - J. Heap	Retrd.	1997	70.00	60-132
1954 Rhinegold Lamp - J. Heap	Retrd.	1956	21.00	N/A
1967 Robert w/lollipop - D. Roberts	Retrd.	1979	12.00	132-400
1985 Robin's Cave - D. Roberts	Retrd.	1999	285.00	240-285
1959 Rocky - J. Heap	Retrd.	1978	32.00	50-100
1978 Rocky (mold 2) - J. Heap	Retrd.	1997	37.50	22-50
1959 Rolly - J. Heap	Retrd.	1997	17.50	22-66
1957 Romeo & Juliet - J. Heap	Retrd.	1959	11.00	N/A
1982 Rosa - J. Heap	Retrd.	1997	40.00	100-413
1991 Scoffer - D. Roberts	Retrd.	2002	55.00	57
1985 Scrumpy - J. Heap	Retrd.	2000	35.00	47
1960 Shiner w/black eye - J. Heap	Retrd.	1967	2.50	400-578
1981 Shrimp Stand - D. Roberts	Retrd.	1994	70.00	125-165
1985 Solo - D. Roberts	Retrd.	1993	40.00	99-125
1960 Squeezy - J. Heap	Retrd.	1970	2.50	299-495
1980 Sun Flower Plinth - N/A	Retrd.	1985	N/A	224-249
1977 Tammy - D. Roberts	Retrd.	1987	24.50	75-100
1987 Tennyson - D. Roberts	Retrd.	1994	35.00	113-132
1996 Tiddler - N/A	Retrd.	2002	57.00	57
1956 Timber Stand - J. Heap	Retrd.	1982	35.00	132-165
1995 Tippit - J. Heap	Retrd.	2000	55.00	55
1953 Tipsy Witch - J. Heap	Retrd.	1959	3.50	N/A
1955 Toper - J. Heap	Retrd.	1956	1.00	N/A
1971 Totty - J. Heap	Retrd.	1981	21.00	75-150
1997 Uncle Henry - J. Heap	Retrd.	2001	300.00	300
1959 Uncle Soames - J. Heap	Retrd.	1985	105.00	224-500
1959 Uncle Soames (brown trousers) - J. Heap	Retrd.	1985	105.00	105
1991 Wordsworth - D. Roberts	Retrd.	1993	60.00	119-200

Possible Dreams

Santa Claus Network® Collectors Club - Staff

1992 The Gift Giver 805001	Retrd.	1993	Gift	40
1993 Santa's Special Friend 805050	Retrd.	1994	59.00	59
1993 Special Delivery 805002	Retrd.	1994	Gift	N/A
1994 On a Winter's Eve 805051	Retrd.	1994	65.00	65
1994 Jolly St. Nick 805003	Retrd.	1995	Gift	N/A
1995 Marionette Santa 805052	Retrd.	1995	50.00	50
1995 Checking His List 805004	Retrd.	1996	Gift	40
1995 A Frosty Friend 805053	Retrd.	1996	48.00	48
1996 A Tree For the Children 805054	Retrd.	1996	40.00	40-48
1996 A Cookie From Santa 805005	Retrd.	1996	Gift	25
1997 Santa's Rocking Horse 805055	Retrd.	1997	40.00	48
1997 Santa's Handiwork 805006	Retrd.	1997	Gift	25
1998 Cross Country Crinkle	Retrd.	1998	18.50	19
1998 Wish Upon a Star 805056	Retrd.	1998	Gift	44-54
1999 North Pole Nanny 805057	Retrd.	1999	45.00	45
1999 Santa & Friends 805008	Retrd.	1999	Gift	25-48
1999 Right on Time 805053	Retrd.	1999	Gift	N/A
1999 A Child's Delight 713200 (Special Event Piece)	Retrd.	2000	40.00	40
2000 Fuzzy Friends 805009	Retrd.	2000	Gift	N/A
2000 Santa Express 805058	Retrd.	2000	65.00	65
2000 Holiday Treasures 713259 (Special Event Piece)	Retrd.	2000	50.00	50

Collectors' Information Bureau   *Quotes have been rounded up to nearest dollar

YEAR ISSUE	EDITION LIMIT	YEAR RETD.	ISSUE PRICE	*QUOTE U.S.$
2001 Santa's Slolam 805010	Retrd.	2001	Gift	N/A
2001 A Decade of Delight 805059	Retrd.	2001	55.00	55
2001 December Disc Jockey 713255 (Special Event Piece)	Retrd.	2001	44.00	44
2001 Out For A Ride 713242 (Shining Star Dealer)	Retrd.	2001	62.00	62
2001 Apple of His Eye 713290 (Evergreen & Shining Star Dealers)	Retrd.	2001	38.00	38
2001 Jolly to the Core 713279 (Evergreen & Shining Star Dealers)	Retrd.	2001	42.00	42
2002 Star Spangled Santa 805011	Yr.Iss.		Gift	N/A
2002 A Midnight Mug 805060	Yr.Iss.		40.00	40
2002 Sweetening The Deal 713517 (Special Event Piece)	Yr.Iss.		35.00	35

African Spirit® - W. Still

YEAR ISSUE	EDITION LIMIT	YEAR RETD.	ISSUE PRICE	*QUOTE U.S.$
1997 Bororo Man 347003	Open		119.50	120
1998 Bushman and Son 347008	Open		139.60	140
1997 Fulani Woman 347004	Open		100.00	100
1997 Hausa Man 347001	Open		100.00	100
1997 Maasai Warrior 347005	Open		115.00	115
1997 Peul Woman 347002	Open		100.00	100
1998 Rendille Woman & Child 347007	Open		136.00	136

The Citizens of Londonshire® - Unknown

YEAR ISSUE	EDITION LIMIT	YEAR RETD.	ISSUE PRICE	*QUOTE U.S.$
1990 Admiral Waldo 713407	Open		65.00	68
1992 Albert 713426	Retrd.	1994	65.00	68
1991 Bernie 713414	Open		68.00	71
1992 Beth 713417	Open		35.00	37
1992 Christopher 713418	Open		35.00	37
1992 Countess of Hamlett 713419	Open		65.00	68
1992 David 713423	Open		37.50	39
1992 Debbie 713422	Open		37.50	39
1990 Dianne 713413	Open		33.00	35
1992 Dr. Isaac 713409	Retrd.	1995	65.00	68
1989 Earl of Hamlett 713400	Retrd.	1994	65.00	68
1992 Jean Claude 713421	Open		35.00	37
1989 Lady Ashley 713405	Open		65.00	68
1989 Lord Nicholas 713402	Open		72.00	76
1989 Lord Winston of Riverside 713403	Retrd.	1994	65.00	68
1994 Maggie 713428	Retrd.	1994	57.00	57
1990 Margaret of Foxcroft 713408	Open		65.00	68
1992 Nicole 713420	Open		35.00	37
1993 Nigel As Santa 713427	Open		53.50	56
1990 Officer Kevin 713406	Retrd.	1994	65.00	68
1990 Phillip 713412	Open		33.00	35
1992 Rebecca 713424	Open		35.00	37
1992 Richard 713425	Open		35.00	37
1989 Rodney 713404	Open		65.00	68
1991 Sir Red 713415	Retrd.	1994	72.00	76
1989 Sir Robert 713401	Open		65.00	68
1992 Tiffany Sorbet 713416	Open		65.00	68
1990 Walter 713410	Retrd.	1994	33.00	35
1990 Wendy 713411	Retrd.	1994	33.00	35

Clothtique® American Artist Collection™ - Various

YEAR ISSUE	EDITION LIMIT	YEAR RETD.	ISSUE PRICE	*QUOTE U.S.$
1996 The 12 Days of Christmas 15052 - M. Monterio	Retrd.	1997	48.00	58
2002 12 Days of Christmas 15116 - J. Cleveland	Open		58.00	58
2001 25 Across 15111 - J. Hargate	Open		60.00	60
1991 Alpine Christmas 15003 - J. Brett	Retrd.	1994	129.00	120-135
1992 An Angel's Kiss 15008 - J. Griffith	Retrd.	1995	85.00	125
1993 A Beacon of Light 15022 - J. Vaillancourt	Retrd.	1996	60.00	65
2001 Bearly Christmas 15104 - T. Browning	Open		46.00	46
2002 Beloved Wayfarer 15119 - M. Monteiro	Open		40.00	40
2002 Blown-Glass Miracles 15107 - T. Browning	Open		45.00	45
1998 Bone Appetit! 15067 - G. Benvenuti	Retrd.	2001	53.50	54
2002 Bountiful Santa Treetopper 713308 - P. Toole	Open		60.00	60
2000 Bourbon Street Santa 15096 - J. Beury	Retrd.	2001	72.00	72
1993 A Brighter Day 15024 - J. St. Denis	Retrd.	1997	67.50	70
2001 Candy Claus 15101 - A. Mistretta	Open		49.00	49
1994 Captain Claus 15030 - M. Monteiro	Retrd.	1996	77.00	77
1999 Celtic Father Christmas 15089	Retrd.	2000	46.70	47
1995 Christmas Caller 15035 - J. Vaillancourt	Retrd.	1999	57.50	58
1992 Christmas Company 15011 - T. Browning	Open		77.00	125
2001 Christmas Glow 15103 - T. Browning	Retrd.	2001	50.00	50
1996 Christmas Light 15055 - D. Wenzel	Retrd.	1997	53.50	54

YEAR ISSUE	EDITION LIMIT	YEAR RETD.	ISSUE PRICE	*QUOTE U.S.$
1996 Christmas Stories 15054 - T. Browning	Retrd.	2001	63.50	64
1994 Christmas Surprise 15033 - M. Alvin	Retrd.	1997	88.00	88
1998 Clean Sweep 15071 - M. Humphries	Retrd.	2000	47.00	47
2000 A Coastline Christmas 15200 - B. Stebleton	Open		38.00	38
1999 Cookie Break 15081 - L. Fletcher	Retrd.	2000	49.00	49
1997 Cookie Maker 15063 - T. Browning	Retrd.	1998	55.00	55-65
1995 Country Sounds 15042 - M. Monteiro	Retrd.	1998	74.00	74
2000 Crystal Christmas 15093 - D. Selter	Retrd.	2001	50.00	50
1999 December 26th 15079 - L. Fletcher	Retrd.	2001	46.00	46
1997 Downhill Thrills 15058 - T. Browning	Retrd.	1998	49.00	49
1998 Dreams Come True 15065 - T. Browning	Open		69.00	69
1998 Dress Rehearsal 15075 - L. Fletcher	Retrd.	2000	50.00	50
1996 Dressed For the Holidays 15050 - J. Vaillancourt	Retrd.	2000	27.00	27
1993 Easy Putt 15018 - T. Browning	Retrd.	1996	110.00	115-135
1991 Father Christmas 15007 - J. Vaillancourt	Retrd.	1995	59.50	75-90
1993 Father Earth 15017 - M. Monteiro	Open		77.00	80
1998 Felice Natale! 15068 - G. Benvenuti	Retrd.	2000	45.90	46
2002 Fine Feathered Friends 15118 - L. Fletcher	Open		60.00	60
1995 Fresh From The Oven 15051 - M. Alvin	Retrd.	1997	49.00	49
1991 A Friendly Visit 15005 - T. Browning	Retrd.	1994	99.50	105
2000 Frontier Cheer 15090 - L. Fletcher	Retrd.	2001	70.00	70
1997 The Fun Seekers 15064 - T. Browning	Retrd.	1998	48.00	48-54
1994 The Gentle Craftsman 15031 - J. Griffith	Retrd.	1996	81.00	99
1994 Gifts from the Garden 15032 - J. Griffith	Retrd.	1996	77.00	92
1995 Giving Thanks 15045 - M. Alvin	Open		45.50	46
2001 Golden Gifts 15102 - J. Vaillancourt	Open		46.00	46
1995 A Good Round 15041 - T. Browning	Retrd.	1997	73.00	73
1992 Heralding the Way 15014 - J. Griffith	Retrd.	1995	72.00	75
2001 Hide and Seek 15106 - L. Fletcher	Open		56.00	56
1999 Holiday Hiker 15085 - J. Beury	Retrd.	2000	53.00	53
1993 Ice Capers 15025 - T. Browning	Retrd.	1996	99.50	129
2001 Ice Sculpture 15110 - T. Browning	Open		60.00	60
2001 Jingle If Your Love Jesus 15108 - L. Fletcher	Retrd.	2001	50.00	50
2001 Jingle Journey 15105 - J. Beury	Open		40.00	40
1999 Journey to Christmas 15083 - J. Vaillancourt	Open		44.00	44
1993 Just Scooting Along 15023 - J. Vaillancourt	Retrd.	1998	79.50	83
2000 Lamplighter Santa 15097 - J. Beury	Open		42.00	42
1997 Last Minute Prep 15060 - D. Wenzel	Retrd.	1998	52.50	53
1992 Lighting the Way 15012 - L. Bywaters	Retrd.	1996	85.00	106
1991 The Magic of Christmas 15001 - L. Bywaters	Retrd.	1994	132.00	139
2000 A Merry Musician 15094 - T. Browning	Open		58.00	58
2001 Model Maker 15112	Open		70.00	70
1997 Morning Brew 15056 - J. Cleveland	Retrd.	1998	44.50	45
1992 Music Makers 15010 - T. Browning	Retrd.	1995	135.00	155
1993 Nature's Love 15016 - M. Alvin	Retrd.	1996	75.00	75-79
1998 New Arrival 15069 - S. Rusinko	Retrd.	2000	48.00	48
1995 A New Suit For Santa 15053 - T. Browning	Retrd.	1998	90.00	90
1997 North Country Weather 15057 - J. Cleveland	Retrd.	2001	40.00	40
2002 North Woods 15100 - J. Vaillancourt	Open		40.00	40
1996 Not a Creature Was Stirring 15046 - J. Cleveland	Retrd.	1998	44.00	55
1992 Out of the Forest 15013 - J. Vaillancourt	Retrd.	1995	60.00	68
1995 Patchwork Santa 15039 - J. Cleveland	Retrd.	1999	67.50	68
2000 Peace 15092 - D. Selter	Open		43.00	43
1992 Peace on Earth 15009 - M. Alvin	Retrd.	1995	87.50	92
1997 Peaceable Kingdom 15061 - J. Griffith	Retrd.	2000	78.80	79
1991 A Peaceful Eve 15002 - L. Bywaters	Retrd.	1994	99.50	100-105
1999 Pedal Power 15088 - T. Browning	Open		84.00	84
2002 The Perfect Tree 15102 - J. Beury	Open		45.00	45
1999 A Pinch of Cheer 15084 - T. Browning	Retrd.	2000	70.80	71
1998 Playing Through 15066 - T. Browning	Open		49.30	50
2002 Rainy Day Cheer 15117 - T. Browning	Open		56.00	56
1995 Ready For Christmas 15049 - T. Browning	Retrd.	1997	95.00	99
1995 Refuge From The Storm 15047 - M. Monterio	Retrd.	1997	49.00	49
1995 Riding High 15040 - L. Nillson	Retrd.	1997	115.00	115-125

FIGURINES

YEAR ISSUE	EDITION LIMIT	YEAR RETD.	ISSUE PRICE	*QUOTE U.S.$
2002 A Sack Full of Wishes 15082 - J. Vaillancourt	Open		49.00	49
1994 Santa and Feathered Friend 15026 - D. Wenzel	Retrd.	1999	84.00	84
1995 Santa and the Ark 15038 - J. Griffith	Retrd.	1997	71.50	75
1999 Santa Be Good 15086 - L. Fletcher	Retrd.	2001	54.00	54
1992 Santa in Rocking Chair 713090 - M. Monteiro	Retrd.	1995	85.00	100
1997 Santa on the Green 15062 - T. Browning	Open		41.00	41
2001 Santa's Coattails 15115 - E. Benvenuti	Open		65.00	65
1991 Santa's Cuisine 15006 - T. Browning	Retrd.	1994	138.00	148
2001 Santa's Letters 15114	Open		70.00	70
1998 Santa's On A Roll 15072 - W. Still	Open		41.80	42
2000 Santa's Vineyard 15095 - T. Browning	Open		55.00	55
2001 Santa's Wish List 15113	Open		80.00	80
1998 Scandinavian Father Christmas 15078 - J. Vaillancourt	Open		40.00	40
1995 Southwest Santa 15043 - V. Wiseman	Retrd.	1996	65.00	89
1999 Speeding Through the Snow 15087 - J. Beury	Retrd.	2001	58.00	58
1994 Spirit of Christmas Past 15036 - J. Vaillancourt	Retrd.	2000	79.00	79
1994 Spirit of Santa 15028 - T. Browning	Retrd.	1996	68.00	75
2002 Spirit of the Forest 15701 - J. Vaillancourt	Open		40.00	40
1995 The Storyteller 15029 - T. Browning	Retrd.	2000	76.00	76
1993 Strumming the Lute 15015 - M. Alvin	Retrd.	1998	79.00	83
1999 Sun, Surf & Santa 15080 - T. Browning	Open		36.00	36
1995 Sunflower Santa 15044 - J. Griffith	Retrd.	1997	75.00	75
1994 Tea Time 15034 - M. Alvin	Retrd.	1997	90.00	90
1994 Teddy Love 15037 - J. Griffith	Retrd.	1999	89.00	89
1994 A Touch of Magic 15027 - T. Browning	Retrd.	1998	95.00	64-95
1991 Traditions 15004 - T. Blackshear	Retrd.	1994	50.00	75
1998 Trailside Prayer 15074 - L. Fletcher	Retrd.	2001	59.80	60
1993 The Tree Planter 15020 - J. Griffith	Retrd.	2000	79.50	84
2000 Unbearably Delicious 15098 - D. Wenzel	Open		44.00	44
1995 Visions of Sugar Plums 15048 - J. Griffith	Retrd.	1997	50.00	50
2000 Winter Green 15091 - L. Fletcher	Open		52.00	52
2001 Wired for Christmas 15109 - L. Fletcher	Open		50.00	50
1998 The Woman Behind Christmas 15073 - L. Fletcher	Retrd.	2000	57.70	58
1993 The Workshop 15019 - T. Browning	Retrd.	1995	140.00	175
2002 Yule Pool 15121 - T. Browning	Open		38.00	38
1997 Yuletide Gardner 15059 - J. Griffith	Retrd.	2000	50.00	50
1998 Yuletide Round Up 15070 - J. Sorenson	Retrd.	2001	43.00	43

Clothtique® Angels-Elves

YEAR ISSUE	EDITION LIMIT	YEAR RETD.	ISSUE PRICE	*QUOTE U.S.$
1997 Irish Angel 714167	Open		29.30	30
1997 Irish Lass 713677	Open		26.80	27

Clothtique® Champion Collection - Staff, unless otherwise noted

YEAR ISSUE	EDITION LIMIT	YEAR RETD.	ISSUE PRICE	*QUOTE U.S.$
2001 Adult Basketball Player 711153	Open		45.00	45
2001 Adult Football Player 711154	Open		44.00	44
2001 Adult Soccer Player 711155	Open		44.00	44
2001 Business Boy 711158	Open		23.00	23
2001 Construction Boy 711156	Open		23.00	23
2000 Female Basketball Player 711113	Open		24.00	24
2000 Female Soccer Player 711111	Open		24.00	24
2000 Female Softball Player 711112	Open		24.00	24
2001 Fireman Boy 711157	Open		23.00	23
2001 Fisherman Boy 711160	Open		23.00	23
2001 Golfer Boy 711159	Open		23.00	23
2001 Golfer Boy 711163	Open		23.00	23
2000 Male Baseball Player 711114	Open		24.00	24
2000 Male Football Player 711115	Open		24.00	24
2000 Male Hockey Player 711117	Open		24.00	24
2000 Male Soccer Player 711116	Open		24.00	24
2001 Medical Girl 711164	Open		23.00	23
2001 Nurse Girl 711161	Open		23.00	23

Clothtique® Couture Collection - Staff, unless otherwise noted

YEAR ISSUE	EDITION LIMIT	YEAR RETD.	ISSUE PRICE	*QUOTE U.S.$
2000 Alice, Circa 1910 711123	Open		40.00	40
2000 Diane, Circa 1920 711124	Open		36.00	36
2000 Dorothy, Circa 1950 711127	Open		40.00	40
2000 Irene, Circa 1930 711125	Open		38.00	38
2000 Joanne, Circa 1960 711128	Open		36.00	36
2000 Lauren, Circa 1970 711129	Open		36.00	36
2000 Margaret, Circa 1940 711126	Open		38.00	38
2000 Victoria, Circa 1900 711122	Open		40.00	40

Clothtique® Fine Arts Collection - Staff

YEAR ISSUE	EDITION LIMIT	YEAR RETD.	ISSUE PRICE	*QUOTE U.S.$
2000 Best Friends 711132	Open		70.00	70
2000 Mademoiselle 711133	Open		54.00	54
2000 Mother & Child 711131	Open		72.00	72
2000 Romance 711134	Open		80.00	80
2000 Sisters 711130	Open		65.00	65

Clothtique® Garfield® Collection - Staff

YEAR ISSUE	EDITION LIMIT	YEAR RETD.	ISSUE PRICE	*QUOTE U.S.$
1997 Countdown to Christmas 275003	Open		41.60	42
1996 Love Me, Love My Teddy Bear 275002	Open		51.60	52
1997 Private Stash 275004	Open		50.20	51
1996 Return to Sender 275001	Open		58.00	58

Clothtique® Historical Collection - Staff

YEAR ISSUE	EDITION LIMIT	YEAR RETD.	ISSUE PRICE	*QUOTE U.S.$
2000 Catherine the Great (Russia) 711120	Open		72.00	72
2000 Elizabeth (England) 711118	Open		84.00	84
2001 Florence Nightingale 711152	Open		52.00	52
2000 Mary Queen of Scots (Scotland) 711119	Open		68.00	68
2000 Queen Isabella (Spain) 711121	Open		56.00	56

Clothtique® Limited Edition Santas - Unknown

YEAR ISSUE	EDITION LIMIT	YEAR RETD.	ISSUE PRICE	*QUOTE U.S.$
1988 Father Christmas 3001	10,000	1993	240.00	550-650
1988 Kris Kringle 3002	10,000	1992	240.00	550-650
1988 Patriotic Santa 3000	10,000	1994	240.00	550-650
1989 Traditional Santa 40's 3003	10,000	1994	240.00	550-650

Clothtique® Looney Tunes® Collection - Staff

YEAR ISSUE	EDITION LIMIT	YEAR RETD.	ISSUE PRICE	*QUOTE U.S.$
1995 Bugs Bunny's 14 Carot Santa 3402	Open		57.50	58
1996 Merry Master of Ceremonies 3404	Open		55.40	56
1996 Pepe's Christmas Serenade 3406	Open		42.80	43
1996 Selfish Elfish Daffy Duck 3405	Open		46.90	47
1995 Sylvester's Holiday High Jinks 3403	Open		65.00	65
1996 Tasmanian Rhapsody 3407	Open		47.30	48
1995 Yosemite Sam's Rootin' Tootin' Christmas 3401	Open		59.00	59

Clothtique® Santas Collection - Staff, unless otherwise noted

YEAR ISSUE	EDITION LIMIT	YEAR RETD.	ISSUE PRICE	*QUOTE U.S.$
1992 1940's Traditional Santa 713049	Retrd.	1994	44.00	65
1992 African American Santa 713056	Retrd.	1995	65.00	68
1993 African-American Santa w/ Doll 713102	Open		40.00	42
2001 Afternoon Break 713307	Open		175.00	175
2002 American Hero 713361	Open		50.00	50
1998 Angel w/Tree Topper 713678	Open		24.00	24
2002 Arctic Artisan 713440	Open		50.00	50
1997 Autograph For a Fan 713143	Retrd.	2000	39.00	39
2002 Away in a Manger 713473	Open		45.00	45
1989 Baby's First Christmas 713042	Retrd.	1992	42.00	46
1995 Baby's First Noel 713120	Retrd.	1997	62.00	65
1998 Baseball Santa 713682	Retrd.	2001	19.80	20
1998 Basketball Santa 713681	Retrd.	2001	19.80	20
2001 Beach Santa 713358	Open		50.00	50
2002 Bishop of Myra Circa 1350 (musical) 713681	Open		40.00	40
2000 Bringing Home the Tree 713230	Open		64.00	64
2002 Candlelight Vigil 713692	Open		25.00	25
2002 Candy Cane Carry-On 713475	Open		45.00	45
2001 Candy Cane Cuts 713372	Open		30.00	30
1988 Carpenter Santa 713033	Retrd.	1992	38.00	44
2001 Catch The Spirit 713356	Open		36.00	36
1999 Catching Some Zs 713197	Retrd.	2001	40.50	41
2001 Celtic Companions 713395	Retrd.	2001	96.00	96
1997 Celtic Sounds 713162	Retrd.	2000	46.00	46
2001 Checking It Twice 713365	Open		50.00	50
2000 Christmas 101 713232	Open		36.00	36
2002 Christmas Carousel 713311	Open		90.00	90
1994 Christmas Cheer 713109	Retrd.	1997	58.00	58
2001 Christmas Chocolatier 713280	Open		42.00	42
2002 Christmas Clock Maker 713354	Open		60.00	60
2002 Christmas Cookout 713507	Open		56.00	56
2001 Christmas Cowboy 713364	Open		38.00	38
1999 A Christmas Dance 713211	Retrd.	2001	42.00	42
1994 Christmas Guest 713112	Retrd.	1997	79.00	79
1998 Christmas in the Alps 713171	Retrd.	2000	48.00	48
1994 Christmas is for Children 713115	Retrd.	2001	62.00	62
2002 Christmas Kahuna 713504	Open		40.00	40

YEAR ISSUE	EDITION LIMIT	YEAR RETD.	ISSUE PRICE	*QUOTE U.S.$
1986 Christmas Man 713027	Retrd.	1989	34.50	35
2000 Christmas on the Farm 713245	Open		62.00	62
1999 Christmas Orbit 713202	Retrd.	2001	38.80	39
2000 Christmas Piper 713226	Open		48.00	48
1998 Christmas Spruce 713172	Retrd.	2001	42.00	42
2001 Colonial Christmas 713324	Open		38.00	38
1987 Colonial Santa 713032	Retrd.	1990	38.00	40
2000 Cross Country Santa 713250	Open		24.00	24
2001 Culling The Catch 713277	Open		52.00	52
2001 A Decade Of Delight 805059	Open		55.00	55
1999 December Descent 713188	Retrd.	2000	47.50	48
1997 Deck The Halls 713161	Retrd.	1998	39.70	38
1997 Doctor Claus 713157	Retrd.	1999	35.00	39
1995 Down Hill Santa 713123	Retrd.	1999	66.50	67
1997 Down the Chimney He Came 713154	Retrd.	2000	42.50	43
2000 Dressed for Success 713246	Open		38.00	38
1997 Easy Ridin' Santa 713159	Retrd.	2000	37.50	38
2002 Emerald Islander 730006	2,000		75.00	75
1992 Engineer Santa 713057	Retrd.	1995	130.00	137
1993 European Santa 713095	Retrd.	1996	53.00	48-69
2002 Even Fishes Have Wishes 713492	Open		50.00	50
2001 Evergreen Traveler (musical) 713237	Open		85.00	85
1989 Exhausted Santa 713043	Retrd.	1992	60.00	65
2002 Eye on the Ball 713391	Open		50.00	50
1991 Father Christmas 713087	Retrd.	1993	43.00	47
2002 Father Christmas Circa 1836 (musical) 713690	Open		40.00	40
1995 Finishing Touch 713121	Retrd.	1998	54.70	55
1993 Fireman & Child 713106	Retrd.	1998	55.00	55-60
1992 Fireman Santa 713053	Retrd.	1996	60.00	70
2002 First Swing 713510	Open		44.00	44
2002 Football Santa 713679	Open		19.80	20
1998 For A Special Little Girl 713179	Retrd.	2001	44.00	44
1996 For Someone Special 713142	Retrd.	1998	39.00	39
2002 Friend on the Mend 713445	Open		50.00	50
1995 Frisky Friend 713130	Retrd.	1997	45.50	55
1988 Frontier Santa 713034	Retrd.	1991	40.00	42
2002 A Generous Gent (Toys For Tots piece) 713397	Open		40.00	40
1999 Getting in Shape 713201	Retrd.	2000	34.80	35
2002 A Gift of Green 713313	Open		34.00	34
1999 Gift of Hope 713206	Open		53.00	53
1999 A Gifted Fellow 713199	Retrd.	2001	41.00	41
1995 Ginger Bread Baker 713135	Retrd.	1997	35.00	35
2002 Gingerbread Artchitect 713378	Open		50.00	50
2000 Glassworks 713218	Open		64.00	64
1998 Gloria In Cielo 713674 - G. Benvenuti	Open		33.80	34
2002 God Bless America 713509	Open		44.00	44
2001 Going For The Gold 713292	Open		50.00	50
1994 Good Tidings 713107	Retrd.	1996	51.00	60
1997 Grampa Claus 713146	Retrd.	1998	41.40	42
2000 Greeting The Millennium 713213	Retrd.	2000	48.00	48
2001 Greetings By Post 713371	Open		39.00	39
2002 Hanging the Pickle 713312	Open		34.00	34
2002 Happy Huladays 713284	Open		30.00	30
2002 Harlem Santa 713046	Retrd.	1994	46.00	55
2000 Hawaii or Bust 713241	Open		37.50	38
1995 Heaven Sent 713138	Retrd.	1997	50.00	50-56
2001 Highland Heritage 730004	Retrd.	2001	80.00	80
1998 Highland Santa 713169	Retrd.	2000	42.50	43
1993 His Favorite Color 713098	Retrd.	1996	48.00	50
1995 His Littlest Fan 713195	Open		60.00	60
1999 Ho: Ho-Hole in One 713131	Retrd.	1999	43.00	48
2000 Hockey Holiday 713251	Open		24.00	24
2002 Holiday Banquet 713494	Open		60.00	60
1999 A Holiday Built for Two 713212	Retrd.	2000	56.00	56
1994 Holiday Friend 713110	Retrd.	1998	104.00	104
1997 Holiday Gourmet 713147	Retrd.	1999	39.10	45
1999 Holiday Hero 713198	Open		36.50	37
2000 Holiday Hoopster 713262	Open		44.00	44
2002 Holiday Hygiene 713346	Open		45.00	45
2001 Holiday Memories 730003	Retrd.	2001	80.00	80
1999 Holiday Thunder 713190	Open		50.00	50
1997 Holiday Traffic 713148	Retrd.	1998	47.50	50
2001 Home From The Station 713398	Open		44.00	44
1995 Home Spun Holidays 713128	Retrd.	1998	49.50	50
2001 Home Tweet Home 713299	Open		48.00	48
2000 Homerun For The Holidays 713260	Open		44.00	44
1995 Hook Line and Santa 713129	Retrd.	1998	49.70	50-55
2001 Hooked On Christmas 713293	Open		40.00	40
2002 Hungarian Rhapsody 713243	Open		50.00	50
1999 An Irish Gentleman 713185	Retrd.	2001	45.00	45-47
2000 Irish Melody Maker 713240	Retrd.	2001	42.00	42
1999 Irish Santa 713185	Open		45.00	45
2000 An Irish Toast 713254	Open		38.00	38
1998 Italian Angel Tree Topper 713673 - G. Benvenuti	Open		33.30	34
2001 I've Been Good 713357	Open		54.00	54
1999 A Jolly Old Saint 713191	Retrd.	2001	38.50	39
2002 Jolly Volley 713508	Open		44.00	44
2002 Jultomten Circa 1900 (musical) 713687	Open		40.00	40
1996 Jumping Jack Santa 713139	Retrd.	1998	45.50	46
2002 Kerstman Circa 1920 (musical) 713688	Open		40.00	40
2001 King Wenceslaus 730001	Open		75.00	75
1991 Kris Kringle 713088	Retrd.	1993	43.00	48
2002 Kris Kringle Circa 1850 (musical) 713684	Open		40.00	40
1998 Landing Beacon 713181	Retrd.	2001	43.40	44
2000 Leading the Way 713258	Retrd.	2001	55.00	55-57
1997 Leprechaun 713153	Open		18.50	19
2002 Let It Glow 713379	Open		50.00	50
1999 Letters From Santa 713192	Open		37.20	38
2001 The Light Keeper 713373	Open		65.00	65
2000 A Long Drive 713231	Open		38.00	38
1993 A Long Trip 713105	Retrd.	2000	95.00	100
1998 Mariachi Santa 713174	Open		48.80	49
1996 Master Toy Maker 713141	Retrd.	1998	44.80	45
1993 May Your Wishes Come True 713096	Retrd.	1996	59.00	65
2002 Merry Kissmas 713316	Open		50.00	50
2002 Merry Mountaineer 713490	Open		48.00	48
2000 Millennium Angel 714228	Open		38.00	38
2002 Mistletoe Merriment 713314	Open		34.00	34
1993 The Modern Shopper 713103	Retrd.	1996	40.00	42
1995 A Modern Skier 713123	Retrd.	1998	59.50	60
1994 A Most Welcome Visitor 713113	Retrd.	1999	63.00	63
2001 Mousing Around 713360	Open		60.00	60
1994 Mrs. Claus 713118	Retrd.	1997	58.00	58
1991 Mrs. Claus in Coat 713078	Retrd.	1995	47.00	71
1989 Mrs. Claus w/doll 713041	Retrd.	1992	42.00	43
2000 Mrs. O' Claus 713257	Retrd.	2001	42.00	42
1992 Nicholas 713052	Retrd.	1994	57.50	60
2002 Nicholas of the North 713383	Open		50.00	50
2001 Night Before Christmas 713323	Open		50.00	50
1999 No. Pole Nanny 805057	Open		36.90	37
1998 North Pole 500 713180	Retrd.	2001	38.80	39
2002 North Pole Duet 713486	Open		45.00	45
1998 North Pole Party Line 713167	Retrd.	2000	44.90	45
1999 North Pole Patrol 713196	Retrd.	2000	44.50	55
2000 North Pole Pizza 713219	Open		50.00	50
1997 North Pole Polka 713163	Retrd.	1998	46.00	48
1997 North Pole Prescription 713164	Retrd.	1998	65.60	66
2000 North Pole Volunteer 713247	Open		56.00	56
1998 Officer Claus 713119	Retrd.	1999	37.80	38
1997 On Christmas Pond 713156	Retrd.	2001	52.30	52
1994 Our Hero 713116	Retrd.	1999	62.00	62
2000 Out For a Ride 713242	Open		62.00	62
2002 Paging Dr. Claus 713310	Open		25.00	25
2002 Passion For Powder 713491	Open		48.00	48
2000 A Peaceful Prayer 713274	Open		50.00	50
2002 Pearl of a Girl 713454	Open		50.00	50
1989 Pelze Nichol 713039	Retrd.	1993	40.00	47
2000 Peppermint Twist 713217	Retrd.	2001	56.00	56
2002 Pere Noel Circa 1840 (musical) 713689	Open		40.00	40
2000 Picture Perfect Christmas 713204	Retrd.	2000	52.00	52
1994 Playmates 713111	Retrd.	1996	104.00	104
2002 Plotting the Course 713287	Open		70.00	70
2002 Pondering The Putt 713456	Open		35.00	35
2000 Pray For Peace 713272	Retrd.	2001	50.00	50
1994 Puppy Love 713117	Retrd.	1997	62.00	62
1998 A Purry Friend 713168	Open		42.50	43
2000 Reel Good Time 713249	Open		56.00	56
2002 Ring in the New 713483	Open		50.00	50
2001 Rock-A-Bye Kitty 713285	Open		55.00	55
2002 Rooftop Delivery 713479	Open		55.00	55
1995 Rooftop Santa 659006	Retrd.	1998	28.50	29
2000 Rub-A-Dub Santa 713248	Open		47.00	47
1988 Russian St. Nicholas 713036	Retrd.	1996	40.00	43
2001 Russian Treasure 713228	Open		49.00	49

YEAR ISSUE	EDITION LIMIT	YEAR RETD.	ISSUE PRICE	*QUOTE U.S.$
2000 Salty Claus 713244	Open		35.00	35
1990 Santa "Please Stop Here" 713045	Retrd.	1992	63.00	72
2002 Santa Claus Circa 1926 (musical) 713685	Open		40.00	40
1991 Santa Decorating Christmas Tree 713079	Retrd.	1992	60.00	60
2000 Santa Express 713253	Open		64.00	64
1991 Santa in Bed 713076	Retrd.	1994	76.00	139
1997 Santa O' Claus 713165	Retrd.	2000	41.50	175
1992 Santa on Motorbike 713054	Retrd.	1994	115.00	130-135
1992 Santa on Reindeer 713058	Retrd.	1995	75.00	83
1992 Santa on Sled 713050	Retrd.	1994	75.00	79
1992 Santa on Sleigh 713091	Retrd.	1995	79.00	83
1997 Santa Online 713151	Retrd.	1998	55.20	56
1991 Santa Shelf Sitter 713089	Retrd.	1995	55.50	60
1999 Santa Strikes Again 713205	Open		36.00	36
2000 Santa 'The IceBox' Claus 713261	Open		44.00	44
1990 Santa w/Blue Robe 713048	Retrd.	1992	46.00	69
1989 Santa w/Embroidered Coat 713040	Retrd.	1991	43.00	43
1993 Santa w/Groceries 713099	Retrd.	1996	47.50	50
1997 Santa w/Nativity 713150	Retrd.	1999	36.00	36
1986 Santa w/Pack 713026	Retrd.	1989	34.50	35
1993 Santa with Doll 713102	Open		40.00	40
1998 Santa with Tree 713183	Open		38.50	39
1997 Santa's Better Half 713155	Retrd.	2000	35.80	36
1998 Santa's Check Up 713175	Retrd.	2001	37.00	37
1999 Santa's Favorite Pastime 713194	Open		37.60	38
1998 Santa's Flying Machines 713176	Retrd.	2000	39.60	37-40
1997 Santa's Grab Bag 713158	Retrd.	2000	47.50	48
1998 Santa's New List 713178	Retrd.	2000	44.90	45
1995 Santa's Pet Project 713134 - L. Craven	Retrd.	1999	37.00	37
2000 Santa's Shillelagh 713236	Open		44.00	44
2000 Santa's Snow Day 713256	Open		48.00	48
2002 Santa's Spa 713366	Open		50.00	50
2000 Santa's Toy 713229	Open		47.00	47
1998 Santa's Tree 713182	Retrd.	2000	36.40	37
2001 Santa's Tree Farm 713289	Open		46.00	46
2001 Schanachie 713275	Open		45.00	45
2002 Seasonings Greetings 28013	Open		70.00	70
1996 Shamrock Santa 713140	Open		41.50	42
1991 Siberian Santa 713077	Retrd.	1993	49.00	96
2000 Skating Lesson 713227	Open		56.00	56
1990 Skiing Santa 713047	Retrd.	1993	62.00	65
2001 Slam Dunk 713296	Open		46.00	46
2001 S'mores For Santa 713282	Open		48.00	48
1998 A Snack For Santa 713177	Retrd.	2000	37.00	37
2001 Snow King 713297	Open		47.00	47
2001 Snow Light, Snow Bright	Open		400.00	400
2002 Snowball Buddies 713480	Open		70.00	70
1998 Soccer Santa 713683	Open		19.80	20
2002 Something For Everyone 713399	Open		45.00	45
2002 A Song in His Heart 713472	Open		40.00	40
1995 Sounds of Christmas 713127	Retrd.	1996	57.50	58
1999 A Special Place 713207	Retrd.	2000	36.90	37-40
1995 A Special Treat 713122	Retrd.	1998	50.50	51
1988 St. Nicholas 713035	Retrd.	1991	40.00	170
2002 St. Nicholas Circa 1700 (musical) 713686	Open		40.00	40
1999 Stargazer 713186	Open		44.90	45
1995 The Stockings Were Hung 713126	Retrd.	1997	N/A	65
1999 Tee-Ball Instructor 713210	Retrd.	2000	44.00	44
1998 Tennis Santa 713680	Open		19.80	20
1997 Test Ride 713149	Open		47.10	48
1995 Three Alarm Santa 713137	Retrd.	2001	42.50	43
2002 Three Little Kittens 713315	Open		34.00	34
2001 Time For A Trim 713355	Open		60.00	60
1998 Top O' The Mornin' 713173	Retrd.	2000	41.50	42
1987 Traditional Deluxe Santa 713030	Retrd.	1990	38.00	38
1986 Traditional Santa 713028	Retrd.	1989	34.50	125
1989 Traditional Santa 713038	Retrd.	1992	42.00	43
2001 Trail To Tipperary 713276	Open		56.00	56
1991 The True Spirit of Christmas 713075	Retrd.	1992	97.00	97
1987 Ukko 713031	Retrd.	1990	38.00	38
2002 Ukrainian Christmas 713515	Open		44.00	44
1995 Victorian Evergreen 713125	Retrd.	1998	49.00	49
1995 Victorian Puppeteer 713124	Retrd.	1997	51.50	52
1993 Victorian Santa 713097	Retrd.	1996	55.50	58
2001 Victorian Traveler 713300	Open		44.00	44
2000 Vincent Van Claus 713264	Open		55.00	55
1998 Visitor From The North 713170	Retrd.	2000	39.50	40

YEAR ISSUE	EDITION LIMIT	YEAR RETD.	ISSUE PRICE	*QUOTE U.S.$
2002 Wading For Supper 713489	Open		35.00	35
2002 Wee Wooly One 713432	Open		50.00	50
1988 Weihnachtsman 713037	Retrd.	1991	40.00	43
2000 Welcome 2000 713263	Retrd.	2000	48.00	48
1994 A Welcome Visit 713114	Retrd.	1996	62.00	65
2002 Wheels O' Green 713433	Open		45.00	45
1999 While Santa's Away 713203	Open		36.00	36
2000 Winter Pals 713216	Open		50.00	50
1997 Winter Wanderer 713152	Retrd.	1998	56.90	57-64
2002 Winter Wetland 713493	Open		35.00	35
2001 Wishful Thinking 713368	Open		50.00	50
2002 Woodland Waterfall (musical) 713430	Open		82.00	82
1990 Workbench Santa 713044	Retrd.	1993	72.00	95
2002 Working Late 713506	Open		50.00	50
1999 Yankee Doodle Santa 713193	Retrd.	2000	39.00	39
2001 Yuletide Dude 713298	Open		58.00	58
2001 Yuletide Goal 713209	Open		34.00	34
1994 Yuletide Journey 713108	Retrd.	1998	58.00	58
1999 Yuletide Nibble 713208	Retrd.	2001	36.90	37-49
2002 Yuletide Tune-Up 713309	Open		55.00	55

Clothtique® Saturday Evening Post J. C. Leyendecker - J. Leyendecker

YEAR ISSUE	EDITION LIMIT	YEAR RETD.	ISSUE PRICE	*QUOTE U.S.$
1991 Hugging Santa 3599	Retrd.	1994	129.00	150
1996 Hugging Santa 3650 (smaller re-issue)	Retrd.	1998	52.50	53-65
1992 Santa on Ladder 3598	Retrd.	1995	135.00	150
1996 Santa on Ladder 3651 (smaller re-issue)	Retrd.	1998	59.00	59-65
1991 Traditional Santa 3600	Retrd.	1992	100.00	125
1996 Traditional Santa 3652 (smaller re-issue)	Retrd.	1997	66.00	66

Clothtique® Saturday Evening Post J. F. Kernan - J. F. Kernan

YEAR ISSUE	EDITION LIMIT	YEAR RETD.	ISSUE PRICE	*QUOTE U.S.$
2001 Model Maker 15112	Open		70.00	70

Clothtique® Saturday Evening Post Norman Rockwell - N. Rockwell

YEAR ISSUE	EDITION LIMIT	YEAR RETD.	ISSUE PRICE	*QUOTE U.S.$
1992 Balancing the Budget 3064	Retrd.	1998	120.00	126
1989 Christmas "Dear Santa" 3102	Retrd.	1992	160.00	180
1996 Christmas "Dear Santa" 3050 (smaller re-issue)	Retrd.	1998	70.50	71
1989 Christmas "Santa with Globe" 3051	Retrd.	1992	154.00	184
1996 Santa With Globe 3101 (smaller re-issue)	Retrd.	1998	73.00	73
1991 Doctor and Doll 3055	Retrd.	1995	196.00	206
1991 The Gift 3057	Retrd.	1996	160.00	160-195
1991 Gone Fishing 3054	Retrd.	1995	250.00	263
1997 Gone Fishing 3104 (smaller re-issue)	Open		67.70	68
1991 Gramps at the Reins 3058	Open		290.00	305
1990 Hobo 3052	Open		159.00	167
1990 Love Letters 3053	Open		172.00	180
1991 Man with Geese 3059	Open		120.00	126
1992 Marriage License 3062	Open		195.00	205
1996 Not a Creature was Stirring (smaller re-issue)	Open		44.00	44
1991 Santa Plotting His Course 3060	Retrd.	1998	160.00	168
1992 Santa's Helpers 3063	Retrd.	1994	170.00	179
1997 Santa's Helpers 3103 (smaller re-issue)	Retrd.	1998	64.90	65
2001 Santa's Letters 15114	Open		70.00	70
2001 Santa's Wish List 15113	Open		80.00	80
1991 Springtime 3056	Retrd.	1996	130.00	137
1992 Triple Self Portrait 3061	Retrd.	1995	230.00	250
1997 Triple Self Portrait 3105 (smaller re-issue)	Open		65.70	66

Clothtique® Signature Series® - Stanley/Chang

YEAR ISSUE	EDITION LIMIT	YEAR RETD.	ISSUE PRICE	*QUOTE U.S.$
1995 Department Store Santa, USA/Circa 1940s 721001	Retrd.	1995	108.00	108
1995 Father Christmas, England/Circa 1890s 721002	Retrd.	2000	90.00	90
1996 St. Nicholas, Myra/Circa 1300s 721004	Retrd.	1996	99.00	99
1996 Kriss Kringle, USA/Circa 1840s 721005	Retrd.	2000	99.00	99
1997 Union Santa, USA/Circa 1863 721007	Retrd.	1998	79.00	79-100
1998 Romanov Santa, Russia/Circa 1890s 721008	Retrd.	1998	83.50	84

Collectors' Information Bureau

*Quotes have been rounded up to nearest dollar

Possible Dreams
to Possible Dreams

YEAR ISSUE	EDITION LIMIT	YEAR RETD.	ISSUE PRICE	*QUOTE U.S.$
Clothtique® Snowfolk - Staff				
2002 Admiral Iceberger 718037	Open		16.00	16
2002 Amanda Blizzardo 23708	Open		32.00	32
2002 Angelica Alto 718071	Open		20.50	21
2002 Bartholemew Baritone 718072	Open		20.00	20
2002 Bronco Hailstorm 718033	Open		16.00	16
2002 Chief Chattertooth 718034	Open		16.00	16
2002 Cupey Frozetti 718068	Open		16.00	16
2002 Danny McFrost 713353	Open		32.00	32
2002 Darren O'Deepfreeze 715055	Open		16.00	16
2002 Derek Avalanchetti 718050	Open		34.00	34
2002 Felicity Frozetti 718069	Open		16.00	16
2002 Hearty Hail, M.D. 718040	Open		16.00	16
2002 Koko Snowflake 22904	Open		16.20	17
2002 Mama Frozetti 718062	Open		16.00	16
2002 Max Mailer 718031	Open		16.00	16
2002 Morley Blizzardo 22902	Open		32.00	32
2002 Nurse Snowdrift 718039	Open		16.00	16
2002 Officer Frigeratus 718030	Open		16.00	16
2002 Oly Doodledrum 718053	Open		30.00	30
2002 Pete Sweetser 718060	Open		32.00	32
2002 Pierre Alpine 718036	Open		16.00	16
2002 Pilgrim Frozetti 718066	Open		16.00	16
2002 Rebecca Avalanchetti 718052	Open		20.00	20
2002 Scooter Avalanchetti 718051	Open		17.00	17
2002 Scotty McGlaze 22215	Open		24.00	24
2002 Snovik Blowzell 718073	Open		34.00	34
2002 Witchy Frozetti 718061	Open		16.00	16
Clothtique® TLC Collection - Staff				
2000 The Good Doctor 711139	Open		40.00	40
2000 Loving Sisters 711143	Open		40.00	40
2000 Officer Friendly 711136	Open		40.00	40
2000 Save The Day 711137	Open		40.00	40
2000 Sew Sweet 711141	Open		50.00	50
2000 Special Delivery 711140	Open		48.00	48
2000 Take Care Bear 711138	Open		40.00	40
2000 Warm Hearts 711135	Open		44.00	44
Coca-Cola Brand Clothtique® Santas - H. Sundblom				
1998 Busy Man's Pause 468002	Retrd.	1999	49.00	49
1999 Greetings From Coca-Cola 468004	Retrd.	2000	62.80	63
1997 Hospitality 468001	Retrd.	1999	50.00	50
1999 It Will Refresh You Too 468007	Retrd.	1999	69.00	69
1998 Santa's Greetings 468005	Retrd.	1999	46.00	46
1999 Santa's Pause 468008	Retrd.	1999	47.00	47
1998 Step Up To Refreshment 468006	Retrd.	1999	47.00	47
1998 Thanks For the Pause That Refreshes 468003	Retrd.	1999	47.00	47
Crinkle Angels - Staff				
1996 Crinkle Angel w/Candle 659405	Open		19.80	20
1996 Crinkle Angel w/Dove 659403	Open		19.80	20
1996 Crinkle Angel w/Harp 659402	Open		19.80	20
1996 Crinkle Angel w/Lamb 659401	Open		19.80	20
1996 Crinkle Angel w/Lantern 659400	Open		19.80	20
1996 Crinkle Angel w/Mandolin 659404	Open		19.80	20
Crinkle Carousel - Staff				
1999 American Eagle 659816	Open		14.30	15
1999 Black Mane Crinkle 659819	Open		14.30	15
1998 Checkmate Crinkle 659807	Open		9.00	9
1998 Crinkle Antlers 659814	Open		16.00	16
1998 Crinkle Champion 659803	Open		10.50	11
1999 Crinkle Champion 659820	Open		14.30	15
1998 Crinkle Doodle-Doo 659810	Open		15.00	15
1998 Crinkle Filly 659801	Open		16.00	16
1998 Crinkle Pony (musical) Waterdome 659881	Open		40.00	40
1998 Crinkle Stallion (musical) Waterdome 659880	Open		40.00	40
1998 Frisky Crinkle 659806	Open		12.00	12
1998 Galloping Crinkle 659804	Open		16.00	16
1999 Golden Mane Crinkle 659815	Open		14.30	15
1998 Happy Hog Crinkle 659808	Open		15.00	15
1998 Hippity-Hop Crinkle 659811	Open		15.00	15
1998 Honey Bear Crinkle 659809	Open		15.00	15
1998 Laughing Lion Crinkle 659812	Open		15.40	16
1999 Leopard Spot Crinkle 659820	Open		14.30	15
1998 Merry-Go Crinkle (lighted) 659860	Open		34.00	34
1998 Pachyderm Crinkle 659813	Open		16.00	16
1998 Parosol Crinkle 659805	Open		13.30	14
1998 Prancing Crinkle (mucial) 659850	Open		30.00	30
1999 Purple Palomino Crinkle 659817	Open		14.30	15
1998 Surf Rider Crinkle 659802	Open		16.00	16
1999 Three Ring Crinkle 659818	Open		14.30	15
Crinkle Claus - Staff				
1995 American Santa 657224	Retrd.	1998	15.50	16-20
1997 Appalachian Light 659030	Open		8.30	9
1995 Arctic Santa 659107	Retrd.	1998	15.70	16
1999 Arriving by Ram 659918	5,000		18.30	19
1995 Austrian Santa 659103	Retrd.	1998	15.80	16
1997 Bavarian Crinkle 659029	Open		8.30	9
1998 Bavarian Om-Pah Crinkle (musical) 659605	Open		38.80	39
1997 Bedtime Story 659910	Open		31.40	32
1995 Bell Shape Santa 659008	Retrd.	1996	23.50	25
1996 Bishop of Maya 659111	Open		19.90	20
1996 Bishop of Maya Plaque 659306	Open		19.90	20
1996 Black Forest Gift Giver 659114	Open		19.90	20
1996 Black Forest Gift Giver Plaque 659302	Open		19.90	20
1997 Blarney Stone Crinkle 659125	Open		13.40	14
1999 Bobbing Bell Crinkle 659154	Open		17.00	17
1999 Bobbing Tree Crinkle 659155	Open		18.90	19
1998 Bottle Crinkle 659052	Open		15.90	16
1997 Brazilian Fiesta 659028	Open		8.30	9
1997 British Jubilee 659027	Open		8.30	9
1996 Buckets of Fruit for Good Girls & Boys 659903	5,000	1997	45.00	45
1997 Buckingham Crinkle 659126	Open		13.40	14
1995 Candle Stick Santa 659121	Open		15.80	16
1999 Candy Cane Crinkle 659136	Open		13.60	14
1999 Candy Cane Crinkle 659150	Open		13.60	14
1996 Carrying The Torch	Open		19.80	20
1999 Cartwheel Crinkle 659161	Open		13.50	14
2000 Catch O' The Day Crinkle 659174	Open		14.00	14
1996 Catch of The Day 659504	Open		19.90	20
2000 Celtic Keepsake Crinkle 659172	Open		14.00	14
1996 Celtic Santa 659110	Retrd.	1997	19.90	20
1996 Celtic Santa Plaque 659305	Retrd.	1997	19.90	20
1996 Choo-Choo For The Children 659904	5,000		25.00	25
1998 Christmas Expedition 659914	5,000		26.90	27
1997 Christmas King Crinkle 659123	Open		13.40	14
1999 Christmas Tree Crinkle 659036	Open		16.30	17
1995 Christmas Tree Santa 659117	Open		19.90	20
1997 Christmas Wilderness Waterdome 659603	Retrd.	1998	46.80	47
1998 Clickety-Clack Crinkle 659044	Open		17.20	18
1995 Crescent Moon Santa 659119	Retrd.	1998	19.00	20
1997 Crinkle Ark (lighted) 660301	Open		57.00	57
1997 Crinkle Bears 660303	Open		14.90	15
1999 Crinkle Candle 659139	Open		10.50	11
1998 Crinkle Cello 659054	Open		14.80	15
1999 Crinkle Celtic Golfer 659163	Open		13.10	14
1998 Crinkle Christmas Eve 659252	Open		28.50	29
1999 Crinkle Claddaugh 659166	Open		12.50	13
1998 Crinkle Claus Cruise 659055	Open		17.20	18
1995 Crinkle Claus w/Dome-German Santa 659601	Retrd.	1998	45.00	45
1996 Crinkle Claus w/Dome-Santa/Chimney 659600	Retrd.	1998	45.00	45
1996 Crinkle Claus w/Dome-St. Nicholas 659602	Retrd.	1998	45.00	45
1999 Crinkle Clocker 659153	Open		12.20	13
1999 Crinkle Cone Santa 659148	Open		12.80	13
1998 Crinkle Cross 659053	Open		15.00	15
2001 Crinkle Doctor Santa 659944	Open		14.00	14
1999 Crinkle Elephants 660308	Open		14.50	15
1998 Crinkle Elf Carpenter 659060	Open		8.50	9
1998 Crinkle Elf Chef 659059	Open		8.50	9
1998 Crinkle Elf Fireman 659062	Open		8.50	9
1998 Crinkle Elf Postman 659056	Open		8.50	9
1998 Crinkle Elf Toymaker 659058	Open		8.50	9
1998 Crinkle Elf w/Jester 659063	Open		8.50	9
1998 Crinkle Elf w/Snowman 659061	Open		8.50	9
1998 Crinkle Elf w/Teddy 659057	Open		8.50	9
2000 Crinkle Engineer 659173	Open		20.00	20
1998 Crinkle Flag Bearer 659049	Open		12.40	13
1999 Crinkle Giraffes 660310	Open		12.40	13
1997 Crinkle Horses 660305	Open		13.30	14
1999 Crinkle House 659142	Open		13.50	14
1999 Crinkle Lions 660309	Open		11.90	12
1997 Crinkle Locomotive & Coal Car 660201	Open		42.00	42

FIGURINES

YEAR ISSUE	EDITION LIMIT	YEAR RETD.	ISSUE PRICE	*QUOTE U.S.$
1998 Crinkle Lyre 659051	Open		16.70	17
1998 Crinkle Mail Car 660202	Open		18.80	19
2001 Crinkle Motorcycle Santa 659946	Open		14.00	14
1997 Crinkle Noah 660302	Open		10.30	11
1999 Crinkle on the Green 659162	Open		13.10	14
1999 Crinkle Pitcher 659137	Open		14.00	14
1999 Crinkle Pot O' Gold 659168	Open		13.70	14
1997 Crinkle Reindeer 660306	Open		13.30	14
1997 Crinkle Sheep 660304	Open		10.80	11
1998 Crinkle Spirit of Giving 659253	Open		23.50	24
1999 Crinkle Tall Tales 659169	Open		13.70	14
2001 Crinkle Teacher Santa 659945	Open		14.00	14
1998 Crinkle Uncle Sam 659045	Open		13.50	14
1999 Crinkle Zebras 660307	Open		12.00	12
1996 A Crown of Antlers	Open		19.70	20
1996 Dashing Through The Snow 659902	5,000	1997	45.00	45
1998 Department Store Crinkle 659250	Open		23.50	24
1998 Ding Dong Crinkle 659046	Open		16.60	17
1996 Display Figurine-965003	Open		11.00	11
1997 Down The Chimney 659911	Open		31.10	32
1998 Dutch Treat Crinkle (musical) 659604	Open		38.80	39
1998 Emerald Isle Crinkle 659040	Open		13.40	14
1998 English Crinkle at Westminster Abbey 659355	Open		28.50	29
1995 English Santa 659100	Retrd.	1998	15.80	16
1999 Fairway Crinkle 659164	Open		13.10	14
1996 Feeding His Forest Friends 659905	5,000	1997	27.50	30-35
1998 Fine Feathered Friends 659915	5,000		25.40	26
1998 Firecracker Crinkle 659047	Open		14.60	15
1997 Fjord Crinkle 659124	Open		13.40	14
1997 Flickering Crinkle 659035	Open		14.00	14
1995 Forest Santa 657225	Open		15.50	16
1999 Four Leaf Crinkle 659165	Open		13.10	14
1995 French Santa 659108	Retrd.	1998	15.70	16
1998 German Crinkle at Rothenburg 659352	Open		28.50	29
1995 German Santa 659105	Retrd.	1998	15.80	16
1999 Gift Giver Crinkle 659143	Open		17.80	18
1999 Gravy Boat Crinkle 659138	Open		14.00	14
1998 Grizzly Bear Helper 659912	5,000		25.90	26
1999 Handstand Crinkle 659159	Open		13.50	14
1995 Hard Boiled Santa 659115	Retrd.	1997	13.70	17
1998 High Flying Crinkle 659251	Open		32.50	33
1995 High Hat Santa 657134	Retrd.	1998	13.40	14-17
1997 High Ho 659025	Open		13.20	14
1997 High Note 659023	Open		13.20	14
1997 Highland Piper 659026	Open		8.30	9
1997 Holiday Cane Crinkle 659034	Open		14.00	14
1999 Holiday Spokes-Man 659916	5,000		19.10	20
1995 Hour Glass Santa 659118	Open		15.00	15
2000 I Love The Irish 659175	Open		14.00	14
1996 Iceland Visitor 659112	Open		19.90	20
1996 Iceland Visitor Plaque 659303	Open		19.90	20
1998 Irish Crinkle at St. Patrick's Cathedral 659354	Open		28.50	29
2001 Irish Crinkle Claus Santa 659947	Open		10.00	10
2001 Irish Golfer Santa 659943	Open		14.00	14
2001 Irish Policeman Santa 659940	Open		14.00	14
2001 Irish Santa Fireman 659941	Open		14.00	14
2001 Irish Santa Postman 659942	Open		14.00	14
1995 Italian Santa 659106	Retrd.	1998	15.70	16
1995 Jolly St. Nick 659012	Retrd.	1998	15.00	15
1997 Kelly Crinkle 659132	Open		16.00	16
1997 Kelly Crinkle 659712	Open		7.80	8
2000 Kilted Crinkle 659171	Open		14.00	14
1998 Kremlin Crinkle (musical) 659606	Open		38.80	39
1996 Learned Gentleman	Open		19.80	20
1998 Liberty Crinkle 659048	Open		12.40	13
1996 Lighting The Way	Open		19.80	20
1997 Lisbon Traveler 659033	Open		8.30	9
1996 Low & Behold	Open		13.90	14
1999 Lucky Crinkle 659170	Open		10.60	11
1997 Madrid Crinkle 659131	Open		16.00	16
1997 Madrid Crinkle 659708	Open		7.80	8
1997 Mediterranean Treasure 659032	Open		8.30	9
1996 Merry Old England 659113	Retrd.	1997	19.90	20
1996 Merry Old England Plaque 659301	Open		19.90	20
1997 Moscow Crinkle 659128	Retrd.	1998	16.00	16
1997 Moscow Crinkle 659711	Retrd.	1998	7.80	10
1997 Munich Crinkle 659130	Retrd.	1998	16.00	16
1997 Munich Crinkle 659710	Open		7.80	8

YEAR ISSUE	EDITION LIMIT	YEAR RETD.	ISSUE PRICE	*QUOTE U.S.$
1996 The Music Man	Open		19.80	20
1995 Netherlands Santa 659102	Retrd.	1998	15.70	16
1997 North Pole Artisan 659907	Open		30.00	30
1999 North Pole Caboose 660203	Open		19.30	20
1996 Northland Santa 659109	Retrd.	1998	19.90	20
1996 Northland Santa Plaque 659304	Open		19.90	20
1998 A Nutty Noel 659913	5,000		25.90	26
1998 Old Glory Crinkle 659050	Open		12.40	13
1997 Pamplona Crinkle 659122	Open		13.40	14
1997 Paris Crinkle 659129	Retrd.	1998	7.80	10-16
1995 Pine Cone Santa 657226	Retrd.	1997	15.50	16
1999 Pipe Dream Crinkle 659144	Open		14.10	15
2000 Pour on the Luck 659176	Open		16.00	16
1996 Rag/Doll Delivery 659906	5,000	1997	34.50	35-45
1997 Rocking Crinkle 659039	Open		17.60	18
1995 Roly Poly Santa 3.5" 657138	Retrd.	1996	12.50	18-22
1995 Roly Poly Santa 4" 659009	Retrd.	1996	23.00	23-27
1995 Rooftop Santa 659006	Retrd.	1998	28.50	29
1998 Royal Crinkle (musical) 659607	Open		38.80	39
1996 Running Down The List 659901	5,000	1997	33.00	35-45
1998 Russian Crinkle at St. Basil's 659353	Open		28.50	29
1995 Russian Santa 3.5" 659101	Retrd.	1998	15.70	16
1995 Russian Santa 4" 657228	Retrd.	1996	15.50	16
1995 Santa on Bag 657508	Open		15.00	15
1995 Santa Sitting Pretty 659116	Open		13.90	14
1995 Santa w/Book 659010	Retrd.	1997	13.80	14
1995 Santa w/Candy Cane 4.5" 657139	Retrd.	1996	13.00	13
1996 Santa w/Candy Cane 5" 657142	Retrd.	1996	27.00	27
1996 Santa w/Candy Cane 6.5" 657135	Retrd.	1996	17.50	18
1995 Santa w/Cane & Bag 657230	Retrd.	1996	12.00	12
1995 Santa w/Gifts 657143	Retrd.	1996	27.00	27-32
1995 Santa w/Lantern & Bag 657229	Retrd.	1996	15.50	16
1995 Santa w/Lantern 5" 657136	Retrd.	1996	12.50	13
1995 Santa w/Lantern 5" 657144	Retrd.	1996	27.00	27
1995 Santa w/Noah's Ark 657227	Retrd.	1998	15.50	16
1995 Santa w/Patchwork Bag 657232	Retrd.	1997	19.00	19
1995 Santa w/Stars 657140	Retrd.	1996	14.00	14
1995 Santa w/Teddy Bear 657231	Retrd.	1997	16.00	16
1995 Santa w/Tree 659011	Retrd.	1996	14.20	15
1995 Santa w/Wreath 657141	Retrd.	1996	16.30	19
1995 Santa's Candy Surprise	Open		27.00	27
1999 Santas Polar Delivery 659917	5,000		21.20	22
1995 Scandinavian Santa 659104	Retrd.	1998	15.80	17
1998 Scottish Crinkle at Glamis 659350	Open		28.50	29
1998 Shamrock Crinkle 659041	Open		13.40	14
1999 Sit-Down Crinkle 659156	Open		13.50	14
1997 Slavic Crinkle 659133	Open		16.00	16
1997 Slavic Crinkle 659713	Open		7.80	8
1997 Sled Filled With Joy 659908	Open		31.00	31
1995 Slimline Santa 657137	Retrd.	1996	12.00	18
1999 Somersault Crinkle 659160	Open		13.50	14
1997 Something For Everyone 659909	Open		31.10	32
1999 Special Postcard 659167	Open		13.10	14
1999 Stand-up Crinkle 659158	Open		13.50	14
1997 Starburst Crinkle 659038	Open		14.20	15
1995 Tall Santa	Open		17.50	18
1999 Tassel Top Crinkle 659147	Open		12.80	13
1999 Teapot Crinkle 659146	Open		10.50	11
1998 Teddy Beefeater Crinkle 659072	Open		20.00	20
1998 Teddy Crinkle Italiano 659071	Open		20.00	20
1998 Teddy Dutch Crinkle 659070	Open		20.00	20
1998 Teddy Mc Crinkle 659076	Open		24.80	25
1998 Teddy O' Crinkle 659075	Open		24.80	25
1998 Teddy Russian Crinkle 659073	Open		20.00	20
1998 Teddy Von Crinkle 659074	Open		20.00	20
1995 Tick Tock Santa 659120	Retrd.	1998	15.00	15-17
1995 Tip Top Santa 659007	Retrd.	1996	23.50	26
1999 Tippity Top Crinkle 659149	Open		13.60	14
1996 To The Rescue	Open		19.90	20
1997 Top of the List 659022	Open		13.20	14
1997 Top of the Tree 659024	Open		13.20	14
1997 Top Spin Crinkle 659037	Retrd.	1998	13.70	14
1999 Topsy Turvy Crinkle 659157	Open		13.50	14
1999 Toychest Crinkle 659152	Open		12.60	13
1998 US Crinkle at The Capitol 659351	Open		28.50	29
1997 Vatican Crinkle 659127	Open		13.40	14
1996 Well Rounded Santa	Open		13.70	14
1997 West Coast Beat 659031	Open		8.30	9

Crinkle Claus Agriclaus - Staff

YEAR ISSUE	EDITION LIMIT	YEAR RETD.	ISSUE PRICE	*QUOTE U.S.$
2000 Santa at Water Pump 659181	Open		16.00	16

FIGURINES

Possible Dreams
to Possible Dreams

YEAR ISSUE	EDITION LIMIT	YEAR RETD.	ISSUE PRICE	*QUOTE U.S.$
2000 Santa on Tractor 659179	Open		24.00	24
2000 Santa with Cow 659178	Open		16.00	16
2000 Santa with Rooster 659182	Open		16.00	16
2000 Santa with Sheep and Pig 659180	Open		16.00	16
2000 Santa with Wheelbarrow 659177	Open		18.00	18

Crinkle Claus Candle Cuffs - Staff
2000 Santa at Fireplace 22438	Open		24.50	25
2000 Santa in Sleigh 22415	Open		29.10	30
2000 Santa on Sled 22414	Open		29.10	30

Crinkle Cousins - Staff
1995 Crinkle Cousin w/Clock 659002	Retrd.	1997	15.50	16
1995 Crinkle Cousin w/Clown 659004	Retrd.	1997	15.50	16
1995 Crinkle Cousin w/Dolls 659003	Retrd.	1997	15.50	16
1995 Crinkle Cousin w/Lantern 659001	Retrd.	1997	15.50	16
1995 Crinkle Cousin w/Teddy 659005	Retrd.	1997	15.50	16

Crinkle Crackers - Staff
1995 Admiral Crinkle Cracker 659212	Retrd.	1997	18.50	19
1995 Captain Crinkle Cracker 659211	Retrd.	1996	13.00	13
1995 Corporal Crinkle Cracker 659214	Retrd.	1996	14.60	15
1995 French Crinkle Cracker 659203	Open		22.00	22
1995 French Lieutenant Crinkle Cracker 659205	Open		13.50	14
1995 General Crinkle Cracker 659213	Retrd.	1996	15.50	16
1995 Lieutenant Crinkle Cracker 659209	Open		26.50	27
1995 Major Crinkle Cracker 659215	Open		14.50	15
1995 Private Crinkle Cracker 659210	Retrd.	1996	15.00	15
1995 Roly Poly French Crinkle Cracker 659204	Open		13.90	14
1995 Roly Poly Russian Crinkle Cracker 659207	Open		13.50	14
1995 Roly Poly Sergeant Crinkle Cracker 659216	Open		13.50	14
1995 Roly Poly U.S. Crinkle Cracker 659201	Open		13.90	14
1995 Russian Crinkle Cracker 4" 659208	Open		13.50	14
1995 Russian Crinkle Cracker 7.75" 659206	Open		29.50	30
1995 U.S. Crinkle Cracker 3.75" 659202	Open		13.50	14
1995 U.S.Crinkle Cracker 7.5" 659200	Open		29.00	29

Crinkle Professionals - Staff
1996 Baseball Player 659507	Retrd.	1998	19.50	22-25
1996 Doctor 659500	Retrd.	1998	19.50	22-25
1996 Fireman 659503	Retrd.	1998	19.50	22-25
1996 Fisherman 659504	Retrd.	1998	19.50	22-25
1996 Football Player 659506	Retrd.	1997	19.50	22-25
1996 Golfer 659505	Open		19.50	20
1996 Hockey Player 659508	Retrd.	1997	19.50	22
1997 Lawyer 659511	Open		19.50	20
1996 Policeman 659502	Open		19.50	20
1996 Postman 659501	Open		19.50	20
1996 Soccer Player 659509	Retrd.	1997	19.50	20-25
1997 Teacher 659510	Retrd.	1998	19.50	22
1997 Tennis Player 659512	Retrd.	1998	19.50	22

Crystol Claus - Staff
2001 Bear w/Stocking Hat 659971	Open		10.00	10
2001 Christmas Tree, 4" 659953	Open		7.00	7
2001 Christmas Tree, 5.5" 659954	Open		7.00	7
2001 Christmas Tree, 7" 659981	Open		15.00	15
2001 Irish Santa Egg/Pot'O'Gold 659985	Open		14.00	14
2001 Irish Santa w/Pot'O'Gold 659973	Open		15.00	15
2001 Irish Snowman w/Cane & Tam Hat 659983	Open		14.00	14
2001 Irish Snowman w/Top Hat & Pot'O'Gold 659955	Open		14.00	14
2001 Patriotic Santa 659963	Open		15.00	15
2001 Santa 659947	Open		20.00	20
2001 Santa w/Drums 659969	Open		15.00	15
2001 Santa w/Flute 659970	Open		15.00	15
2001 Santa w/Horn 659968	Open		15.00	15
2001 Snowman w/Harp 659984	Open		14.00	14
2001 Snowman w/Top Hat 659951	Open		14.00	14

Floristine Angels® - B. Sargent
1996 Angel of Happiness 668002	Open		100.00	100
1996 An Angel's Prayer 668003	Open		98.00	98
1997 Blissful Ballet 668008	Open		72.40	73
1996 Celestial Garden 668001	Open		98.00	98
1996 Heavenly Harmony 668006	Open		100.00	100

YEAR ISSUE	EDITION LIMIT	YEAR RETD.	ISSUE PRICE	*QUOTE U.S.$
1996 Lessons From Above 668005	Open		100.00	100
1996 My Guardian Angel 668004	Open		112.00	112
1997 My Inspiration 668007	Open		37.70	38
1997 Sacred Virgil 668009	Open		47.10	48

Ingrid's Clowns - I. White
1998 Bobo 317003	Open		11.80	12
1998 Carrot Top 317004	Open		11.80	12
1998 Harley 317001	Open		11.80	12
1998 Jester 317006	Open		11.80	12
1998 Pinky 317002	Open		11.80	12
1998 Popcorn 317005	Open		11.80	12
1998 Slapstick 317007	Open		11.80	12

McDonald's Santa - Staff
1999 Down the Chimney, Down the Hatch 132003	Retrd.	2000	57.00	57
1998 Happy Holiday 132002	Retrd.	2000	50.00	50
1998 Midnight Break 132001	Retrd.	2000	54.00	54
1999 Working Up An Appetite 132004	Retrd.	2000	46.00	46

Poultry Power - B. Stebleton
2000 Cheep! Cheep! Cheap! 194150	Open		20.00	20
2000 Ham & Eggs 194148	Open		18.00	18
2000 Motherhood is Exhausting 194146	Open		18.00	18
2000 A Mother's Work is Never Done 194149	Open		24.00	24
2000 Which Came First 194147	Open		13.00	13

Spanglers Realm® - R. Spangler
1997 Bath Time 191019	Open		15.50	16
1997 Best Friends 191020	Open		18.10	19
1997 Cherish The Small Wonders of Life 191005	Open		15.00	15
1997 Chocolate Treat 191018	Open		17.30	18
1998 Christmas Cookie Express 191004	Open		27.80	28
1997 Christmas Treasures 191021	Open		18.10	19
1997 Delicious Discovery 191001	Open		35.70	36
1997 Downhill Racer 191013	Open		18.90	19
1997 Draggin' In The Morning 191009	Open		21.90	22
1998 Dragling on the Scale 191007	Open		35.60	36
1997 A Dragon's Work Is Never Done 191006	Open		19.80	20
1997 Equal Partners Stocking Holder 191150	Open		25.20	26
1997 Fishin' Chips 191017	Open		16.30	17
1997 A Flour Just For You 191016	Open		18.10	19
1997 From Dagmar, To Dewey 191015	Open		18.30	19
1997 Guardian Angel 191010	Open		15.40	16
1997 Hole In One 191014	Open		18.50	19
1997 Home Is Where The Magic Is 191101	Open		144.50	145
1998 No Smoking Sign 191002	Open		31.30	32
1998 Santa's Surprise 191008	Open		17.10	18
1998 Sleepy Time 191022	Open		18.50	19
1997 Story Time 191012	Open		21.20	22
1997 To The Rescue 191011	Open		15.90	16
1997 'Twas The Night Before 191003	Open		19.90	20

Stebleton Folk Art - B. Stebleton
1998 Bearly Balanced 194050	Open		25.20	26
2001 Cat Teapot 194214	Open		50.00	50
1999 Celestial Santa (lg.) 194053	Open		34.00	34
1999 Celestial Santa (sm.) 194054	Open		19.00	19
2001 Group Hug 194215	Open		35.00	35
1998 Jolly Jurassic Christmas 194051	Open		32.00	32
2001 Morse Toad 194182	Open		50.00	50
2001 Ornament Hanger 194186	Open		20.00	20
2001 Rooster Teapot 194213	Open		50.00	50
2001 Santa with Tree 194185	Open		34.00	34
1998 Scuba Claus 194052	Open		39.00	39
2001 Spin Kitty 194180	Open		50.50	51
2001 Spin Kitty Jr. 194181	Open		18.50	19

Stebleton's Cagey Critters - B. Stebleton
2001 60 Watt 194206	Open		38.00	38
2000 Angel Kitty 194140	Open		26.00	26
2001 Ball Gone It 194205	Open		25.00	25
1998 Beach Belly 194106	Open		15.60	16
2001 Bug Eyes 194201	Open		25.00	25
2000 Cleared for Take-Off 194139	Open		24.00	24
1999 Curly-Q 194113	Open		15.40	16
1999 Derby Day Duo 194117	Open		15.40	16
2000 Devil's Food Feline 194138	Open		25.00	25

YEAR ISSUE	EDITION LIMIT	YEAR RETD.	ISSUE PRICE	*QUOTE U.S.$
1999 Dream Team 194114	Open		15.40	16
1998 Finger Food 194105	Open		14.00	14
1999 Furry Yellow Fellow 194115	Open		15.50	16
2001 Hypnotic Hound 194202	Open		25.00	25
1999 Kitty Court Jester 194116	Open		15.80	16
2001 Kitty Hawk 465073	Open		46.00	46
1998 Liberty Kitty 194103	Open		15.60	16
1998 Lunch is on Me 194107	Open		17.70	18
2001 Mutt Point 194204	Open		28.00	28
2000 Pool Pals 194142	Open		25.00	25
1998 Randolph The Red Nose Cat 194108	Open		17.50	18
2001 Rollover Rover 194203	Open		25.00	25
1998 Simply Red 194101	Open		11.30	12
1999 Skateboard Buddies 194118	Open		17.20	18
2000 Sun Tan Tabby 194141	Open		20.00	20
1998 Sushi Cat 194102	Open		14.00	14
2000 Welcoming Committee 194144	Open		25.00	25
1998 Yokes on You 194104	Open		17.90	18
2001 Yuletide Ride 194136	Open		41.00	41

The Thickets at Sweetbriar® - B. Ross

YEAR ISSUE	EDITION LIMIT	YEAR RETD.	ISSUE PRICE	*QUOTE U.S.$
1997 Amber Twinkle 350140	Open		26.80	27
1995 Angel Dear 350123	Open		32.00	32
1996 Autumn Peppergrass 350135	Open		31.00	31
1997 Berty Cosgrove 350137	Open		27.50	28
1993 The Bride-Emily Feathers 350112	Open		30.00	30
1995 Buttercup 350121	Open		32.00	32
1995 Cecily Pickwick 350125	Open		32.00	32
1998 Celeste 350146	Open		26.40	27
1998 Chip Weezley 350148	Open		10.50	11
1995 Clem Jingles 350130	Open		37.00	37
1993 Clovis Buttons 350101	Retrd.	1996	24.15	25
1996 Dainty Whiskers 350136	Open		30.00	30
1997 Divinity 350142	Open		27.30	28
1998 Dottie Crispin 350149	Open		26.80	27
1998 Erin Penny 350145	Open		25.50	26
1996 Goody Pringle 350134	Open		31.00	31
1993 The Groom-Oliver Doone 350111	Retrd.	1996	30.00	30
1997 Herman Noodles 350141	Open		27.50	28
1993 Jewel Blossom 350106	Open		36.75	37
1995 Katy Hollyberry 350124	Retrd.	1996	35.00	35
1997 Kitty Glitter 350143	Open		27.50	28
1995 Kris Krinkle 350414	Open		12.50	13
1994 Lady Slipper 350116	Open		20.00	20
1996 Lily Blossom (musical) 350201	Retrd.	1996	59.50	60
1993 Lily Blossom 350105	Retrd.	1996	36.75	37
1998 Marie Periwinkle 350148	Open		25.50	26
1997 Mary Pawpins 350138	Open		26.80	27
1993 Maude Tweedy 350100	Retrd.	1994	26.25	27
1998 Maybelle Pudding 350144	Open		25.90	26
1996 Merry Heart 350131	Open		30.00	30
1994 Morning Dew 350113	Open		30.00	30
1993 Morning Glory 350104	Open		30.45	31
1993 Mr. Claws 350109	Retrd.	1996	34.00	34
1993 Mrs. Claws 350110	Retrd.	1996	34.00	34
1993 Orchid Beasley 350103	Retrd.	1996	26.25	27
1995 Parsley Divine 350129	Open		37.00	37
1996 Patience Finney 350132	Open		31.00	31
1993 Peablossom Thorndike 350102	Retrd.	1994	26.25	27
1995 Penny Pringle 350128	Open		32.00	32
1995 Pittypat 350122	Open		32.00	32
1994 Precious Petals 350115	Open		34.00	34
1993 Raindrop 350122	Retrd.	1996	47.25	48
1995 Riley Pickens 350127	Open		32.00	32
1993 Rose Blossom 350107	Open		36.75	37
1998 Samuel Goodley 350147	Open		21.00	21
1997 Smokey Longwood 350139	Open		27.50	28
1994 Sunshine 350118	Open		33.00	33
1994 Sweetie Flowers 350114	Retrd.	1996	33.00	33
1995 Tillie Lilly 350120	Open		32.00	32
1995 Timmy Evergreen 350126	Open		29.00	29
1996 Velvet Winterberry 350132	Open		30.00	30
1995 Violet Wiggles 350119	Open		32.00	32

Precious Moments/Enesco Group, Inc.

Precious Moments Collectors Club Welcome Gift - S. Butcher

YEAR ISSUE	EDITION LIMIT	YEAR RETD.	ISSUE PRICE	*QUOTE U.S.$
1982 But Love Goes On Forever-Plaque E-0202	Yr.Iss.	1982	N/A	45-102
1983 Let Us Call the Club to Order E-0303	Yr.Iss.	1983	N/A	39-60

YEAR ISSUE	EDITION LIMIT	YEAR RETD.	ISSUE PRICE	*QUOTE U.S.$
1984 Join in on the Blessings E-0404	Yr.Iss.	1984	N/A	27-111
1985 Seek and Ye Shall Find E-0005	Yr.Iss.	1985	N/A	21-41
1986 Birds of a Feather Collect Together E-0006	Yr.Iss.	1986	N/A	21-46
1987 Sharing Is Universal E-0007	Yr.Iss.	1987	N/A	22-30
1988 A Growing Love E-0008	Yr.Iss.	1988	N/A	22-50
1989 Always Room For One More C-0009	Yr.Iss.	1989	N/A	21-40
1990 My Happiness C-0010	Yr.Iss.	1990	N/A	16-50
1991 Sharing the Good News Together C-0011	Yr.Iss.	1991	N/A	21-29
1992 The Club That's Out Of This World C-0012	Yr.Iss.	1992	N/A	23-36
1993 Loving, Caring, and Sharing Along the Way C-0013	Yr.Iss.	1993	N/A	20-30
1994 You Are the End of My Rainbow C-0014	Yr.Iss.	1994	N/A	23-30
1995 You're The Sweetest Cookie In The Batch C-0015	Yr.Iss.	1995	N/A	16-22
1996 You're As Pretty As A Picture C-0016	Yr.Iss.	1996	N/A	19-37
1997 A Special Toast To Precious Moments C-0017	Yr.Iss.	1997	N/A	10-35
1998 Focusing In On Those Precious Moments C-0018	Yr.Iss.	1998	N/A	19-35
1999 Wishing You a World of Peace C-0019	Yr.Iss.	1999	N/A	N/A
2000 Thanks A Bunch C-0020	Yr.Iss.	2000	N/A	N/A
2001 Friends Write From The Start C-0021	Yr.Iss.	2001	N/A	N/A
2002 It's Time to Bless Your Own Day C-0022	Yr.Iss.		N/A	N/A

Precious Moments Inscribed Charter Member Renewal Gift - S. Butcher

YEAR ISSUE	EDITION LIMIT	YEAR RETD.	ISSUE PRICE	*QUOTE U.S.$
1981 But Love Goes on Forever E-0001	Yr.Iss.	1981	N/A	98-130
1982 But Love Goes on Forever-Plaque E-0102	Yr.Iss.	1982	N/A	24-72
1983 Let Us Call the Club to Order E-0103	Yr.Iss.	1983	N/A	39-65
1984 Join in on the Blessings E-0104	Yr.Iss.	1984	N/A	32-50
1985 Seek and Ye Shall Find E-0105	Yr.Iss.	1985	N/A	33-45
1986 Birds of a Feather Collect Together E-0106	Yr.Iss.	1986	N/A	26-48
1987 Sharing Is Universal E-0107	Yr.Iss.	1987	N/A	20-40
1988 A Growing Love E-0108	Yr.Iss.	1988	N/A	23-35
1989 Always Room For One More C-0109	Yr.Iss.	1989	N/A	35-45
1990 My Happiness C-0110	Yr.Iss.	1990	N/A	23-40
1991 Sharing The Good News Together C-0111	Yr.Iss.	1991	N/A	35-50
1992 The Club That's Out Of This World C-0112	Yr.Iss.	1992	N/A	23-40
1993 Loving, Caring, and Sharing Along the Way C-0113	Yr.Iss.	1993	N/A	35-40
1994 You Are the End of My Rainbow C-0114	Yr.Iss.	1994	N/A	15-26
1995 You're The Sweetest Cookie In The Batch C-0115	Yr.Iss.	1995	N/A	26-35
1996 You're As Pretty As A Picture C-0116	Yr.Iss.	1996	N/A	33-35
1997 A Special Toast To Precious Moments C-0117	Yr.Iss.	1997	N/A	35
1998 Focusing In On Those Precious Moments C-0118	Yr.Iss.	1998	N/A	39
1999 Wishing You a World of Peace C-0119	Yr.Iss.	1999	N/A	N/A
2000 Thanks A Bunch C-0120	Yr.Iss.	2000	N/A	N/A
2001 Friends Write From The Start C-0121	Yr.Iss.	2001	N/A	N/A

Precious Moments Special Edition Members' Only - S. Butcher

YEAR ISSUE	EDITION LIMIT	YEAR RETD.	ISSUE PRICE	*QUOTE U.S.$
1981 Hello, Lord, It's Me Again PM-811	Yr.Iss.	1981	25.00	275-520
1982 Smile, God Loves You PM-821	Yr.Iss.	1982	25.00	95-260
1983 Put on a Happy Face PM-822	Yr.Iss.	1983	25.00	129-221
1983 Dawn's Early Light PM-831	Yr.Iss.	1983	27.50	48-70
1984 God's Ray of Mercy PM-841	Yr.Iss.	1984	25.00	38-95
1984 Trust in the Lord to the Finish PM-842	Yr.Iss.	1984	25.00	40-68
1985 The Lord is My Shepherd PM-851	Yr.Iss.	1985	25.00	53-70
1985 I Love to Tell the Story PM-852	Yr.Iss.	1985	27.50	35-65
1986 Grandma's Prayer PM-861	Yr.Iss.	1986	25.00	43-90
1986 I'm Following Jesus PM-862	Yr.Iss.	1986	25.00	48-68
1987 Feed My Sheep PM-871	Yr.Iss.	1987	25.00	45-92
1987 In His Time PM-872	Yr.Iss.	1987	25.00	30-58
1987 Loving You Dear Valentine PM-873	Yr.Iss.	1987	25.00	30-45
1987 Loving You Dear Valentine PM-874	Yr.Iss.	1987	25.00	30-49
1988 God Bless You for Touching My Life PM-881	Yr.Iss.	1988	27.50	34-67
1988 You Just Can't Chuck A Good Friendship PM-882	Yr.Iss.	1988	27.50	27-54

FIGURINES

Precious Moments/Enesco Group, Inc.
to Precious Moments/Enesco Group, Inc.

YEAR ISSUE	EDITION LIMIT	YEAR RETD.	ISSUE PRICE	*QUOTE U.S.$
1989 You Will Always Be My Choice PM-891	Yr.Iss.	1989	27.50	30-52
1989 Mow Power To Ya PM-892	Yr.Iss.	1989	27.50	35-72
1990 Ten Years And Still Going Strong PM-901	Yr.Iss.	1990	30.00	33-52
1990 You Are A Blessing To Me PM-902	Yr.Iss.	1990	30.00	27-58
1991 One Step At A Time PM-911	Yr.Iss.	1991	33.00	36-55
1991 Lord, Keep Me In TeePee Top Shape PM-912	Yr.Iss.	1991	33.00	45-58
1992 Only Love Can Make A Home PM-921	Yr.Iss.	1992	30.00	49-60
1992 Sowing The Seeds of Love PM-922	Yr.Iss.	1992	30.00	26-39
1993 His Little Treasure PM-931	Yr.Iss.	1993	30.00	32-48
1993 Loving PM-932	Yr.Iss.	1993	30.00	45-80
1994 Caring PM-941	Yr.Iss.	1994	35.00	38-43
1994 Sharing PM-942	Yr.Iss.	1994	35.00	30-40
1995 You Fill The Pages of My Life (figurine/book)	Yr.Iss.	1994	37.50	50-76
1995 You're One In A Million To Me PM-951	Yr.Iss.	1995	35.00	28-35
1995 Always Take Time To Pray PM-952	Yr.Iss.	1995	35.00	35-57
1996 Teach Us To Love One Another PM-961	Yr.Iss.	1996	40.00	43-57
1996 Our Club Is Soda-licious PM-962	Yr.Iss.	1996	35.00	42-58
1997 You Will Always Be A Treasure To Me PM-971	Yr.Iss.	1997	50.00	50-55
1997 Blessed Are The Merciful PM-972	Yr.Iss.	1997	40.00	35-48
1998 Happy Trails PM-981	Yr.Iss.	1998	50.00	50
1998 Lord Please Don't Put Me On Hold PM-982	Yr.Iss.	1998	40.00	40
1998 How Can Two Work Together Except They Agree PM-983	Yr.Iss.	1998	125.00	125
1999 Jumping For Joy PM-991	Yr.Iss.	1999	30.00	30-40
1999 God Speed PM-992	Yr.Iss.	1999	30.00	30-50
1999 He Watches Over Us All PM-993	Yr.Iss.	1999	225.00	225
2000 My Collection PM001	Yr.Iss.	2000	20.00	20
2000 Collecting Friends Along The Way PM002	Yr.Iss.	2000	100.00	100
2001 Calling To Say You're Special PM0011	Yr.Iss.	2001	50.00	50
2001 You're A Computie Cutie PM0012	Yr.Iss.	2001	35.00	35
2001 Thank You For Your Membership (5th Club Anniversary) 635243	Yr.Iss.	2001	35.00	35
2001 Thank You For Your Membership (10th Club Anniversary) 635251	Yr.Iss.	2001	40.00	40
2001 Thank You For Your Membership (15th Club Anniversary) 635278	Yr.Iss.	2001	50.00	50
2001 Thank You For Your Membership (20th Club Anniversary) 635286	Yr.Iss.	2001	60.00	60
2002 You Are My In-SPA-ration PM0021	Yr.Iss.		45.00	45
2002 You Are My Favorite Pastime PM0022	Yr.Iss.		40.00	40
2002 Bubble Your Troubles Away 101730	Yr.Iss.		29.99	30
2002 I'm So Glad You Sled Into My Life 101731	Yr.Iss.		19.99	20
2002 Tender Tails Gwen The Penguin with Momma Penguin FC022	Yr.Iss.		9.00	9

Precious Moments Club 5th Anniversary Commemorative Edition - S. Butcher

1985 God Bless Our Years Together 12440	Yr.Iss.	1985	175.00	247-300

Precious Moments Club 10th Anniversary Commemorative Edition - S. Butcher

1988 The Good Lord Has Blessed Us Tenfold 114022	Yr.Iss.	1988	90.00	100-188

Precious Moments Club 15th Anniversary Commemorative Edition - S. Butcher

1993 15 Happy Years Together: What A Tweet 530786	Yr.Iss.	1993	100.00	100-274
1995 A Perfect Display of 15 Happy Years 127817	Yr.Iss.	1995	100.00	100-150

Precious Moments Club 20th Anniversary Commemorative Edition - S. Butcher

1998 20 Years And The Vision's Still The Same 306843	Yr.Iss.	1998	55.00	45-55

Precious Moments - S. Butcher

1983 Sharing Our Season Together E-0501	Suspd.		50.00	112-128
1983 Jesus is the Light that Shines E-0502	Suspd.		23.00	44-50
1983 Blessings from My House to Yours E-0503	Suspd.		27.00	60-73
1983 Christmastime Is for Sharing E-0504	Retrd.	1989	37.00	63-80
1983 Surrounded with Joy E-0506	Retrd.	1987	21.00	50-104
1983 God Sent His Son E-0507	Suspd.		32.50	58-80

YEAR ISSUE	EDITION LIMIT	YEAR RETD.	ISSUE PRICE	*QUOTE U.S.$
1983 Prepare Ye the Way of the Lord E-0508	Suspd.		75.00	122-138
1983 Bringing God's Blessing to You E-0509	Suspd.		35.00	54-90
1983 Tubby's First Christmas E-0511	Suspd.		12.00	15-26
1983 It's a Perfect Boy E-0512	Suspd.		18.50	19-47
1983 Onward Christian Soldiers E-0523	Open		24.00	28-65
1983 You Can't Run Away from God E-0525	Retrd.	1989	28.50	50-175
1983 He Upholdeth Those Who Fall E-0526	Suspd.		35.00	68-112
1987 His Eye Is On The Sparrow E-0530	Retrd.	1987	28.50	70-120
1979 Jesus Loves Me E-1372B	Retrd.	1998	7.00	30-130
1979 Jesus Loves Me E-1372G	Open		7.00	21-39
1979 Smile, God Loves You E-1373B	Retrd.	1984	7.00	38-72
1979 Jesus is the Light E-1373G	Retrd.	1988	7.00	33-104
1979 Praise the Lord Anyhow E-1374B	Retrd.	1982	8.00	40-106
1979 Make a Joyful Noise E-1374G	Retrd.	2000	8.00	30-106
1979 Love Lifted Me E-1375A	Retrd.	1993	11.00	35-175
1979 Prayer Changes Things E-1375B	Suspd.		11.00	80-126
1979 Love One Another E-1376	Open		10.00	30-98
1979 He Leadeth Me E-1377A	Suspd.		9.00	40-135
1979 He Careth For You E-1377B	Suspd.		9.00	75-140
1979 God Loveth a Cheerful Giver E-1378	Retrd.	1981	11.00	625-975
1979 Love is Kind E-1379A	Suspd.		8.00	15-80
1979 God Understands E-1379B	Suspd.		8.00	72-135
1979 O, How I Love Jesus E-1380B	Retrd.	1984	8.00	70-175
1979 His Burden Is Light E-1380G	Retrd.	1984	8.00	40-175
1979 Jesus is the Answer E-1381	Suspd.		11.50	90-170
1992 Jesus is the Answer E-1381R	Retrd.	1996	55.00	46-130
1979 We Have Seen His Star E-2010	Suspd.		8.00	50-120
1979 Come Let Us Adore Him E-2011	Retrd.	1981	10.00	143-290
1979 Jesus is Born E-2012	Suspd.		12.00	85-260
1979 Unto Us a Child is Born E-2013	Suspd.		12.00	32-111
1982 May Your Christmas Be Cozy E-2345	Suspd.		23.00	51-100
1982 May Your Christmas Be Warm E-2348	Suspd.		30.00	80-149
1983 Tell Me the Story of Jesus E-2349	Suspd.		30.00	75-150
1982 Dropping in for Christmas E-2350	Suspd.		18.00	42-115
1982 Holy Smokes E-2351	Retrd.	1987	27.00	52-120
1983 O Come All Ye Faithful E-2353	Retrd.	1986	27.50	45-101
1982 I'll Play My Drum for Him E-2356	Suspd.		30.00	39-115
1982 I'll Play My Drum for Him E-2360	Retrd.	2001	16.00	28-48
1982 Christmas Joy from Head to Toe E-2361	Suspd.		25.00	44-80
1982 Camel Figurine E-2363	Open		20.00	35-42
1982 Goat Figurine E-2364	Suspd.		10.00	45-80
1982 The First Noel E-2365	Suspd.		16.00	40-80
1982 The First Noel E-2366	Suspd.		16.00	44-100
1982 Bundles of Joy E-2374	Retrd.	1993	27.50	49-133
1982 Dropping Over for Christmas E-2375	Retrd.	1991	30.00	45-133
1982 Our First Christmas Together E-2377	Suspd.		35.00	49-100
1982 3 Mini Nativity Houses & Palm Tree E-2387	Open		45.00	75-78
1982 Come Let Us Adore Him E-2395 (11pc. set)	Open		80.00	104-224
1980 Come Let Us Adore Him E-2800 (9 pc. set)	Open		70.00	110-175
1980 Jesus is Born E-2801	Suspd.		37.00	227-293
1980 Christmas is a Time to Share E-2802	Suspd.		20.00	53-110
1980 Crown Him Lord of All E-2803	Suspd.		20.00	41-120
1980 Peace on Earth E-2804	Suspd.		20.00	104-155
1980 Wishing You a Season Filled w/ Joy E-2805	Retrd.	1985	20.00	61-115
1984 You Have Touched So Many Hearts E-2821	Suspd.		25.00	33-90
1984 This is Your Day to Shine E-2822	Retrd.	1988	37.50	56-84
1984 To God Be the Glory E-2823	Suspd.		40.00	58-155
1984 To a Very Special Mom E-2824	Open		27.50	35-62
1984 To a Very Special Sister E-2825	Retrd.	2001	37.50	50-75
1984 May Your Birthday Be a Blessing E-2826	Suspd.		37.50	38-150
1984 I Get a Kick Out of You E-2827	Suspd.		50.00	149-205
1984 Precious Memories E-2828	Retrd.	1999	45.00	43-115
1984 I'm Sending You a White Christmas E-2829	Retrd.	2000	37.50	41-77
1984 God Bless the Bride E-2832	Open		35.00	42-60
1986 Sharing Our Joy Together E-2834	Suspd.		30.00	34-85
1984 Baby Figurines (set of 6) E-2852	Closed	N/A	16.00	63-140
1984 Boy Standing E-2852A	Suspd.		13.50	17-27
1984 Girl Standing E-2852B	Suspd.		13.50	19-22
1984 Boy & Girl Standing, set E-2852A&B	Suspd.		27.00	125-228
1984 Boy Sitting Up E-2852C	Suspd.		13.50	17-32
1984 Girl Sitting Clapping E-2852D	Suspd.		13.50	17-30
1984 Boy Crawling E-2852E	Suspd.		13.50	14-30

FIGURINES

YEAR ISSUE	EDITION LIMIT	YEAR RETD.	ISSUE PRICE	*QUOTE U.S.$
1984 Girl Laying Down E-2852F	Suspd.		13.50	27-36
1980 Blessed Are the Pure in Heart E-3104	Suspd.		9.00	21-60
1980 He Watches Over Us All E-3105	Suspd.		11.00	39-84
1980 Mother Sew Dear E-3106	Open		13.00	33-80
1980 Blessed are the Peacemakers E-3107	Retrd.	1985	13.00	49-96
1980 The Hand that Rocks the Future E-3108	Suspd.		13.00	45-78
1980 The Purr-fect Grandma E-3109	Open		13.00	33-59
1980 Loving is Sharing E-3110B	Retrd.	1993	13.00	55-145
1980 Loving is Sharing E-3110G	Open		13.00	33-105
1980 Be Not Weary In Well Doing E-3111	Retrd.	1985	14.00	52-100
1980 God's Speed E-3112	Retrd.	1983	14.00	33-90
1980 Thou Art Mine E-3113	Open		16.00	32-90
1980 The Lord Bless You and Keep You E-3114	Open		16.00	38-95
1980 But Love Goes on Forever E-3115	Open		16.50	40-100
1980 Thee I Love E-3116	Retrd.	1994	16.50	40-145
1980 Walking By Faith E-3117	Suspd.	2000	35.00	64-130
1980 Eggs Over Easy E-3118	Retrd.	1983	12.00	50-125
1980 It's What's Inside that Counts E-3119	Suspd.		13.00	80-130
1980 To Thee With Love E-3120	Suspd.		13.00	43-75
1981 The Lord Bless You and Keep You E-4720	Suspd.		14.00	34-38
1981 The Lord Bless You and Keep You E-4721	Open		14.00	35-115
2000 The Lord Bless You and Keep You E-4721B	Open		37.00	37
2000 The Lord Bless You and Keep You E-4721DB	Open		37.00	37
1981 Love Cannot Break a True Friendship E-4722	Suspd.		22.50	79-125
1981 Peace Amid the Storm E-4723	Suspd.		22.50	56-84
1981 Rejoicing with You E-4724	Open		25.00	34-67
1981 Peace on Earth E-4725	Suspd.		25.00	49-84
1981 Love Lifted Me E-5201	Suspd.		25.00	48-110
1981 Thank You for Coming to My Ade E-5202	Suspd.		22.50	84-125
1981 Let Not the Sun Go Down Upon Your Wrath E-5203	Suspd.		22.50	86-160
1981 To A Special Dad E-5212	Suspd.		20.00	33-75
1981 God is Love E-5213	Suspd.		17.00	38-100
1981 Prayer Changes Things E-5214	Suspd.		35.00	80-220
1984 May Your Christmas Be Blessed E-5376	Suspd.		37.50	56-80
1984 Love is Kind E-5377	Retrd.	1987	27.50	62-85
1984 Joy to the World E-5378	Suspd.		18.00	34-42
1984 Isn't He Precious? E-5379	Retrd.	2000	20.00	21-33
1984 A Monarch is Born E-5380	Suspd.		33.00	56-80
1984 His Name is Jesus E-5381	Suspd.		45.00	75-104
1984 For God So Loved the World E-5382	Suspd.		70.00	104-110
1984 Wishing You a Merry Christmas E-5383	Yr.Iss.	1984	17.00	29-45
1984 I'll Play My Drum for Him E-5384	Open		10.00	15-35
1984 Oh Worship the Lord (B) E-5385	Suspd.		10.00	36-46
1984 Oh Worship the Lord (G) E-5386	Suspd.		10.00	40-70
1981 Come Let Us Adore Him E-5619	Suspd.		13.00	13-33
1981 Donkey Figurine E-5621	Open		6.00	15-25
1981 They Followed the Star E-5624	Open		130.00	161-275
1981 We Three Kings E-5635	Open		40.00	40-78
1981 Rejoice O Earth E-5636	Retrd.	1999	15.00	26-78
1981 The Heavenly Light E-5637	Retrd.	2001	15.00	30-76
1981 Cow with Bell Figurine E-5638	Open		16.00	36-40
1981 Isn't He Wonderful (B) E-5639	Suspd.		12.00	35-50
1981 Isn't He Wonderful (G) E-5640	Suspd.		12.00	56-100
1981 They Followed the Star E-5641	Suspd.		75.00	144-180
1981 Nativity Wall (2 pc. set) E-5644	Open		60.00	84-160
1984 God Sends the Gift of His Love E-6613	Suspd.		22.50	50-70
1982 God is Love, Dear Valentine E-7153	Suspd.		16.00	22-65
1982 God is Love, Dear Valentine E-7154	Suspd.		16.00	17-65
1982 Thanking Him for You E-7155	Suspd.		16.00	26-60
1982 I Believe in Miracles E-7156	Suspd.		17.00	56-175
1988 I Believe in Miracles E-7156R	Retrd.	1992	22.50	44-156
1982 There is Joy in Serving Jesus E-7157	Retrd.	1986	17.00	30-67
1982 Love Beareth All Things E-7158	Open		25.00	36-46
1982 Lord Give Me Patience E-7159	Suspd.		25.00	27-65
1982 The Perfect Grandpa E-7160	Suspd.		25.00	48-71
1982 His Sheep Am I E-7161	Suspd.		25.00	52-85
1982 Love is Sharing E-7162	Suspd.		25.00	125-170
1982 God is Watching Over You E-7163	Suspd.		27.50	68-80
1982 Bless This House E-7164	Suspd.		45.00	130-250
1982 Let the Whole World Know E-7165	Suspd.		45.00	82-165
1981 The Lord Bless You And Keep You E-7167	Suspd.		25.00	25-48
1983 Love is Patient E-9251	Suspd.		35.00	64-100
1983 Forgiving is Forgetting E-9252	Suspd.		37.50	58-110
1983 The End is in Sight E-9253	Suspd.		25.00	43-100
1983 Praise the Lord Anyhow E-9254	Retrd.	1994	35.00	40-152
1983 Bless You Two E-9255	Open		21.00	42-55
1983 We are God's Workmanship E-9258	Retrd.	2001	19.00	30-58
1983 We're In It Together E-9259	Suspd.		24.00	43-104
1983 God's Promises are Sure E-9260	Suspd.		30.00	57-105
1983 Seek Ye the Lord E-9261	Suspd.		21.00	36-52
1983 Seek Ye the Lord E-9262	Suspd.		21.00	48-70
1983 How Can Two Walk Together Except They Agree E-9263	Suspd.		35.00	119-200
1983 Press On E-9265	Retrd.	1999	40.00	53-70
1983 I'm Falling For Some Bunny/Our Love Is Heaven-scent E-9266	Suspd.		18.50	19-22
1983 Animal Collection, Teddy Bear E-9267A	Suspd.		6.50	15-28
1983 Animal Collection, Dog W/ Slippers E-9267B	Suspd.		6.50	15-28
1983 Animal Collection, Bunny W/ Carrot E-9267C	Suspd.		6.50	15-22
1983 Animal Collection, Kitty With Bow E-9267D	Suspd.		6.50	15-22
1983 Animal Collection, Lamb With Bird E-9267E	Suspd.		6.50	12-28
1983 Animal Collection, Pig W/ Patches E-9267F	Suspd.		6.50	12-28
1983 Nobody's Perfect E-9268	Retrd.	1990	21.00	50-93
1983 Nobody's Perfect (smiling) E-9268	Retrd.	1990	21.00	398
1983 Let Love Reign E-9273	Retrd.	1987	27.50	53-110
1983 Taste and See that the Lord is Good E-9274	Retrd.	1986	22.50	45-75
1983 Jesus Loves Me E-9278	Retrd.	1998	9.00	16-31
1983 Jesus Loves Me E-9279	Retrd.	2000	9.00	17-33
1983 To Some Bunny Special E-9282A	Suspd.		8.00	15-34
1983 You're Worth Your Weight In Gold E-9282B	Suspd.		8.00	15-34
1983 Especially For Ewe E-9282C	Suspd.		8.00	22-48
1983 Set of Three Animals E-9282A,B,C	Suspd.		24.00	41-72
1983 If God Be for Us, Who Can Be Against Us E-9285	Suspd.		27.50	68-98
1983 Peace on Earth E-9287	Suspd.		37.50	108-200
1997 And A Child Shall Lead Them E-9287R	Open		50.00	45-55
1983 Sending You a Rainbow E-9288	Suspd.		22.50	68-120
1983 Trust in the Lord E-9289	Suspd.		21.00	53-100
1985 Love Covers All 12009	Suspd.		27.50	45-68
1985 Part of Me Wants to be Good 12149	Suspd.		19.00	48-110
1987 This Is The Day Which The Lord Has Made 12157	Suspd.		20.00	30-60
1985 Get into the Habit of Prayer 12203	Suspd.		19.00	24-52
1985 Miniature Clown 12238A	Suspd.		13.50	29-49
1985 Miniature Clown 12238B	Suspd.		13.50	20-59
1985 Miniature Clown 12238C	Suspd.		13.50	29-49
1985 Miniature Clown 12238D	Suspd.		13.50	21-49
1985 It is Better to Give than to Receive 12297	Suspd.		19.00	95-178
1985 Love Never Fails 12300	Retrd.	2000	25.00	34-70
1985 God Bless Our Home 12319	Retrd.	1998	40.00	48-69
1986 You Can Fly 12335	Suspd.		25.00	52-60
1985 Jesus is Coming Soon 12343	Suspd.		22.50	34-45
1985 Halo, and Merry Christmas 12351	Suspd.		40.00	149-195
1985 May Your Christmas Be Delightful 15482	Suspd.		25.00	33-55
1985 Honk if You Love Jesus 15490	Retrd.	2001	13.00	18-30
1985 Baby's First Christmas 15539	Yr.Iss.	1985	13.00	23-38
1985 Baby's First Christmas 15547	Yr.Iss.	1985	13.00	18-38
1985 God Sent His Love 15881	Yr.Iss.	1985	17.00	24-45
1985 God Bless You With Rainbows 16020	Suspd.		57.50	115
1986 To My Favorite Paw 100021	Suspd.		22.50	25-60
1986 To My Deer Friend 100048	Open		33.00	42-70
1986 Sending My Love 100056	Suspd.		22.50	36-51
1986 O Worship the Lord 100064	Open		24.00	34-55
1986 To My Forever Friend 100072	Open		33.00	46-70
1987 He's The Healer Of Broken Hearts 100080	Retrd.	1999	33.00	42-62
1987 Make Me A Blessing 100102	Retrd.	1990	35.00	43-82
1986 Lord I'm Coming Home 100110	Open		22.50	30-50

Collectors' Information Bureau *Quotes have been rounded up to nearest dollar

YEAR ISSUE	EDITION LIMIT	YEAR RETD.	ISSUE PRICE	*QUOTE U.S.$
1986 Lord, Keep Me On My Toes 100129	Retrd.	1988	22.50	56-85
1986 The Joy of the Lord is My Strength 100137	Open		35.00	46-125
1986 God Bless the Day We Found You 100145	Suspd.		37.50	62-120
1995 God Bless the Day We Found You (Girl) 100145R	Open		60.00	60-80
1986 God Bless the Day We Found You 100153	Suspd.		37.50	55-115
1995 God Bless the Day We Found You (Boy) 100153R	Open		60.00	51-60
1986 Serving the Lord 100161	Suspd.		19.00	46-82
1986 I'm a Possibility 100188	Retrd.	1993	21.00	44-68
1987 The Spirit Is Willing But The Flesh Is Weak 100226	Retrd.	1991	19.00	38-85
1987 The Lord Giveth & the Lord Taketh Away 100226	Retrd.	1995	33.50	50-85
1986 Friends Never Drift Apart 100250	Retrd.	2000	35.00	49-65
1986 Help, Lord, I'm In a Spot 100269	Retrd.	1989	18.50	47-70
1986 He Cleansed My Soul 100277	Open		24.00	34-50
1986 Serving the Lord 100293	Suspd.		19.00	26-62
1987 Scent From Above 100528	Retrd.	1991	19.00	48-64
1987 I Picked A Very Special Mom 100536	Yr.Iss.	1987	40.00	50-75
1986 Brotherly Love 100544	Open		37.00	65-78
2002 You're An All Star Graduate - Blonde 101498	Open		25.00	25
2002 You're An All Star Graduate - Brunette 101499	Open		25.00	25
2002 Love Spills Over For You Mom 101513	Open		35.00	35
2002 Loads of Love For My Mommy 101514	Open		35.00	35
2002 Planting the Seeds of Love (Century Circle) 101548	7,500		100.00	100
2002 Precious Moments in Paradise (Century Circle Event) 101549	Open		45.00	45
1987 No Tears Past The Gate 101826	Open		40.00	59-95
1987 Smile Along The Way 101842	Retrd.	1991	30.00	131-150
1987 Lord, Help Us Keep Our Act Together 101850	Retrd.	1991	35.00	85-148
1986 O Worship the Lord 102229	Open		24.00	34-40
1986 Shepherd of Love 102261	Open		10.00	15-32
1986 Three Mini Animals 102296	Suspd.		13.50	21-25
1986 Wishing You a Cozy Christmas 102342	Yr.Iss.	1986	17.00	30-48
1986 Love Rescued Me 102393	Retrd.	1999	21.00	32-40
1986 Angel of Mercy 102482	Open		19.00	26-33
1986 Sharing our Christmas Together 102490	Suspd.		35.00	60-80
1987 We Are All Precious In His Sight 102903	Yr.Iss.	1987	30.00	60-80
1986 God Bless America 102938	Yr.Iss.	1986	30.00	35-91
2002 God Bless America 102938R	Open		40.00	40
1986 It's the Birthday of a King 102962	Suspd.		18.50	32-57
1987 I Would Be Sunk Without You 102970	Open		15.00	18-28
1986 We Belong To The Lord 103004	Retrd.	1986	50.00	169-215
1987 My Love Will Never Let You Go 103497	Open		25.00	34-42
1986 I Believe in the Old Rugged Cross 103632	Open		25.00	30-55
1986 Come Let Us Adore Him 104000 (9 pc. set w/cassette)	Open		95.00	110-140
1987 With this Ring I... 104019	Open		40.00	55-80
1987 Love Is The Glue That Mends 104027	Suspd.		33.50	49-68
1987 Cheers To The Leader 104035	Retrd.	1997	22.50	28-75
2002 May Your Holidays Sparkle With Joy 104202	Yr.Iss.		35.00	35
2002 Jesus Is Born-Nativity 104210	Yr.Iss.		40.00	40
2002 Hark The Harold Angels Sing-Mini-Nativity 104211	Yr.Iss.		20.00	20
2002 You Are My Christmas Special 104215	Yr.Iss.		100.00	100
2002 Merry Christ-miss 104218	Open		35.00	35
2002 Friends Share A Special Bond 104219	Open		45.00	45
2002 You're O.K. Buy Me 104267	Open		37.50	38
1987 Happy Days Are Here Again 104396	Suspd.		25.00	47-82
1986 Come Let Us Adore Him 9 pc. 104523	Suspd.		350.00	350-550
1987 A Tub Full of Love 104817	Suspd.		22.50	23-35
1987 Sitting Pretty 104825	Suspd.		22.50	42-68
1987 Have I Got News For You 105635	Suspd.		22.50	39-52

YEAR ISSUE	EDITION LIMIT	YEAR RETD.	ISSUE PRICE	*QUOTE U.S.$
1988 Something's Missing When You're Not Around 105643	Suspd.		32.50	50-75
1987 To Tell The Tooth You're Special 105813	Suspd.		38.50	140-275
1988 Hallelujah Country 105821	Retrd.	2000	35.00	38-163
1987 We're Pulling For You 106151	Suspd.		40.00	46-59
1987 God Bless You Graduate 106194	Open		20.00	30-55
1987 Congratulations Princess 106208	Open		20.00	30-65
1987 Lord Help Me Make the Grade 106216	Suspd.		25.00	43-50
2002 God Shed His Grace On Thee (Special Issue) 106632	Open		60.00	60
2002 Stand Beside Her and Guide Her 106671	Open		40.00	40
1988 Heaven Bless Your Togetherness 106755	Retrd.	1999	65.00	77-100
1988 Precious Memories 106763	Open		37.50	45-75
1988 Puppy Love Is From Above 106798	Retrd.	1995	45.00	45-70
1988 Happy Birthday Poppy 106836	Suspd.		27.50	33-72
1988 Sew In Love 106844	Retrd.	1997	45.00	52-110
1987 They Followed The Star 108243	Open		75.00	96-144
1987 The Greatest Gift Is A Friend 109231	Retrd.	1999	30.00	33-55
1988 Believe the Impossible 109487	Suspd.		35.00	36-88
1988 Happiness Divine 109584	Retrd.	1992	25.00	33-82
1987 Wishing You A Yummy Christmas 109754	Suspd.		35.00	42-75
1987 We Gather Together To Ask The Lord's Blessing 109762	Retrd.	1995	130.00	250-345
1988 Meowie Christmas 109804	Retrd.	2000	30.00	30-53
1987 Oh What Fun It Is To Ride 109819	Retrd.	1998	85.00	92-117
1988 Wishing You A Happy Easter 109886	Retrd.	1999	23.00	30-37
1988 Wishing You A Basket Full Of Blessings 109924	Retrd.	1999	23.00	30-38
1988 Sending You My Love 109967	Retrd.	2000	38.00	38-45
1988 Mommy, I Love You 109975	Open		22.50	26-30
1987 Love Is The Best Gift of All 110930	Yr.Iss.	1987	22.50	30-42
1988 Faith Takes The Plunge 111155	Suspd.		27.50	28-38
1988 Tis the Season 111163	Suspd.		27.50	35-80
1987 O Come Let Us Adore Him (4 pc. 9" Nativity) 111333	Suspd.		200.00	176-234
1988 Mommy, I Love You 112143	Retrd.	2001	22.50	26-45
1987 A Tub Full of Love 112313	Open		22.50	28-33
1988 This Too Shall Pass 114014	Retrd.	1999	23.00	26-38
1988 Some Bunny's Sleeping 115274	Suspd.		15.00	16-23
1988 Our First Christmas Together 115290	Suspd.		50.00	64-72
1988 Time to Wish You a Merry Christmas 115339	Yr.Iss.	1988	24.00	24-42
1995 Love Blooms Eternal 127019 (1st in dated cross series)	Yr.Iss.	1995	35.00	30-60
2000 He Shall Lead The Children Into the 21st Century (Millennium Event) 127930A	Open		160.00	160
2000 He Shall Lead The Children Into the 21st Century (Millennium Event) 127930	Open		160.00	160
1995 Dreams Really Do Come True 128309	Open		37.50	40
1995 Another Year More Grey Hares 128686	Open		17.50	17-19
1995 Happy Hula Days 128694	Open		30.00	26-35
1995 I Give You My Love Forever True 129100	Open		70.00	59-85
1997 Love Letters in The Sand 129488	Open		35.00	30-35
2000 He Is My Salvation (Salvation Army) 135984	Yr.Iss.	2000	45.00	45
1995 Love Makes The World Go 'Round 139475	15,000		200.00	360-438
1995 He Covers The Earth With His Beauty 142654	Yr.Iss.	1995	30.00	26-30
1995 Come Let Us Adore Him 142743-Large Nativity	Open		50.00	50-55
1995 Come Let Us Adore Him 142743-Small Nativity	Open		35.00	35
1995 Making A Trail to Bethlehem 142751	Retrd.	1998	30.00	25-35
1995 I'll Give Him My Heart 150088	Retrd.	1998	40.00	32-48
1995 Scoot Yourself To A Merry Christmas 150096	Retrd.	1999	30.00	30-37
1995 Making Spirits Bright 150118	Retrd.	1998	37.50	28-40
1998 Even The Heavens Shall Praise Him 150312	15,000		125.00	125
1999 Blessed Are They With A Caring Heart (Century Circle) 163724	Open		55.00	55
1996 Standing In The Presence Of The Lord 163732 (2nd in dated cross series)	Yr.Iss.	1996	37.50	32-60

FIGURINES

YEAR ISSUE	EDITION LIMIT	YEAR RETD.	ISSUE PRICE	*QUOTE U.S.$
1996 Take It To The Lord In Prayer 163767	Retrd.	2001	30.00	26-30
1996 The Sun Is Always Shining Somewhere 163775	Retrd.	1999	37.50	33-40
1996 Sowing Seeds of Kindness 163856 (1st in Growing In God's Garden Of Love Series)	Open		37.50	33-38
1996 It May Be Greener, But It's Just As Hard to Cut 163899	Retrd.	2001	37.50	33-38
1996 God's Love Is Reflected In You 175277	15,000		150.00	163-267
1996 Some Plant, Some Water, But God Giveth The Increase 176958 (2nd in Growing In God's Garden Of Love Series)	Open		37.50	38-40
1996 Peace On Earth...Anyway 183342	Yr.Iss.	1996	32.50	35-50
1996 Angels On Earth-Boy Making Snow Angel 183776	Retrd.	2001	40.00	38-45
1996 Snowbunny Loves You Like I Do 183792	Retrd.	2001	18.50	17-19
1997 The Most Precious Gift of All 183814	Retrd.	2001	37.50	40-46
1996 Sing In Excelsis Deo Tree Topper 183830	Retrd.	1999	125.00	125
1997 You're Just Too Sweet To Be Scary 183849	Open		55.00	55
1996 Color Your World With Thanksgiving 183857	Retrd.	1998	50.00	42-65
1996 Shepard/Standing White Lamb/Sitting Black Lamb 3pc. Nativity set 183954	Open		40.00	33-40
1997 Shepard with Lambs 3pc. Nativity set 183962	Open		40.00	34-40
1996 Making a Trail to Bethlehem-Mini Nativity 184004	Open		18.50	19-34
1996 All Sing His Praises-Large Nativity 184012	Open		32.50	29-42
1996 Love Makes The World Go 'Round 184209	Yr.Iss.	1996	22.50	42
1997 A Bouquet From God's Garden Of Love 184268 (3rd in God's Garden of Love series)	Retrd.	2001	37.50	40
1997 You're A Life Saver To Me 204854	Retrd.	2000	35.00	30-35
1996 Shepherd with Sheep-Mini Nativity 2-pc. 213616	Open		22.50	23
1996 Wee Three Kings-Mini Nativity set 213624	Open		55.00	47-55
1997 Lead Me To Calvary 260916 (3rd in dated cross series)	Yr.Iss.	1997	37.50	33-40
1997 Friends From The Very Beginning 261068	Retrd.	2000	50.00	45-55
1997 You Have Touched So Many Hearts 261084	Open		37.50	40
2001 You Have Touched So Many Hearts 261084B	Open		40.00	40
1997 Lettuce Pray 261122	Retrd.	1999	17.50	12-18
1997 Have You Any Room For Jesus 261130	Retrd.	2001	35.00	30-35
1997 Say I Do 261149	Open		35.00	48-60
1997 We All Have Our Bad Hair Days 261157	Open		35.00	35
1997 The Lord Is the Hope Of Our Future 261564	Open		40.00	34-40
2000 The Lord Is the Hope Of Our Future 261564B	Open		42.00	42
2000 The Lord Is the Hope Of Our Future 261564G	Open		42.00	42
1998 In God's Beautiful Garden Of Love 261629	15,000		150.00	150-197
1997 Happy Birthday Jesus 272523	Open		35.00	30-35
1997 Sharing The Light of Love 272531	Open		35.00	30-35
1997 I Think You're Just Divine 272558	Retrd.	2001	40.00	34-40
1997 Nativity Enhancement Set 4pc. 272582	Open		60.00	51-60
1997 I'm Dreaming Of A White Christmas 272590	Open		25.00	22-25
1997 Cane You Join Us For A Merry Christmas 272671	Open		30.00	26-30
1997 And You Shall See a Star-Large Nativity 272787	Retrd.	2001	32.50	35
1998 My Love Will Keep You Warm 272957	Open		37.50	33-38
1997 Animal Additions-Mini Nativity 3-pc. 279323	Open		30.00	30
1997 Lighted Inn-Large Nativity 283428	Open		100.00	80-100
1997 Mini- Nativity Wall 283436	Open		40.00	34-40
1997 For An Angel You're So Down To Earth-Mini Nativity 283444	Open		17.50	18
1997 Cats With Kittens Mini-Nativity 291293	Open		18.50	17-19
1997 Wishing Well 292753	Retrd.	2001	30.00	26-30
1998 He Shall Cover You With His Wings 306935	Yr.Iss.	1998	37.50	38
1998 For The Sweetest Tu-Lips In Town 306959	Open		30.00	27-33
2001 For The Sweetest Tu-Lips In Town 306959B	Open		35.00	35
1998 You Are Always On My Mind 306967	Retrd.	2000	37.50	34-40
1998 Missum You 306991	Retrd.	2001	45.00	38-50
1997 Charity Begins In The Heart 307009	Retrd.	1998	50.00	40-60
2001 Wait Patiently On The Lord 325279	Open		30.00	30
1998 Only One Life To Offer 325309	Retrd.	2001	35.00	33-35
1998 The Good Lord Will Always Uphold Us 325325	Retrd.	2001	50.00	42-50
2000 By Grace We Have Communion With God 325333C	Open		75.00	75
1998 There Are Two Sides To Every Story 325368	Retrd.	2001	15.00	15
1999 Mom, You're My Special-Tea 325473	Retrd.	1999	25.00	25-28
1998 Marvelous Grace 325503	Yr.Iss.	1998	50.00	50-60
1998 Well, Blow Me Down It's Yer Birthday 325538	Retrd.	2001	50.00	42-50
1998 I'm Sending You a Merry Christmas 455601	Yr.Iss.	1998	30.00	26-30
1998 Mornin' Pumpkin 455687	Retrd.	1999	45.00	37-45
1998 Praise God From Whom All Blessings Flow 455695	Retrd.	2001	40.00	33-40
1998 Praise The Lord And Dosie-Do 455733	Open		50.00	41-50
1998 Peas On Earth 455768	Retrd.	2001	32.50	35
1998 Alaska Once More, How's Yer Christmas? 455784	Open		35.00	35
1998 You Can Always Fudge A Little During the Season 455792	Open		35.00	35
2000 Wishing You An Old Fashioned Christmas 455806	Open		45.00	45
1998 Wishing You A Yummy Christmas 455814	Retrd.	2001	30.00	30-53
1998 I Saw Mommy Kissing Santa Claus 455822	Open		65.00	53-65
1999 Warmest Wishes For The Holidays 455830	Retrd.	2001	50.00	50
1998 Time For A Holy Holiday 455849	Retrd.	2001	35.00	29-35
1998 Have A Cozy Country Christmas 455873	Open		50.00	41-50
1998 Friends Are Forever, Sew Bee It 455903	Open		60.00	50-60
1998 I Now Pronounce You Man And Wife 455938	Open		30.00	26-30
1998 The Light Of The World Is Jesus-Large Nativity 455954	Open		30.00	30
1998 Hang On To That Holiday Feeling-Mini Nativity 455962	Retrd.	2001	17.50	15-18
1999 Sharing Our Time Is So Precious (Century Circle) 456349	Open		110.00	110
1999 My Universe Is You 487902	Retrd.	1999	45.00	37-48
1999 Believe It Or Knot I Luv You 487910	Open		35.00	35
1999 You're My Honey Bee 487929	Retrd.	2001	20.00	17-20
1999 Jesus Is My Lighthouse (January Show) 487945	Open		75.00	64-75
1999 You Can Always Count On Me 487953	Open		35.00	29-35
1999 What Better To Give Than Yourself 487988	Open		30.00	25-30
1999 Mom, You've Given Me So Much 488046	Open		35.00	29-35
1999 You Just Can't Replace A Good Friendship 488054	Open		35.00	35
2000 He'll Carry Me Through 488089	Open		45.00	45
1999 Confirmed In The Lord 488178	Open		30.00	25-30
1999 A Very Special Bond 488240	Open		70.00	70
2000 You'll Always Be Daddy's Little Girl 488224	Open		50.00	50
1998 Victorian Girlw/Umbrella (1998 Summer Show Exclusive) 488259	Yr.Iss.	1998	70.00	58-70
1999 You Can't Take It With You 488321	Open		25.00	21-25
1999 Always Listen To Your Heart 488356	Open		25.00	21-25
1999 You Count 488372	Open		25.00	21-25
1999 You Always Stand Behind Me 492140	Open		50.00	41-50
2000 Have Faith in God 505153	Open		50.00	50
1988 Rejoice O Earth 520268	Open		13.00	19-30

228   Collectors' Information Bureau   *Quotes have been rounded up to nearest dollar

Precious Moments/Enesco Group, Inc.

to Precious Moments/Enesco Group, Inc.

YEAR ISSUE	EDITION LIMIT	YEAR RETD.	ISSUE PRICE	*QUOTE U.S.$
1988 Jesus the Savior Is Born 520357	Suspd.		25.00	36-65
1992 The Lord Turned My Life Around 520535	Suspd.		35.00	25-50
1991 In The Spotlight Of His Grace 520543	Suspd.		35.00	33-40
1990 Lord, Turn My Life Around 520551	Suspd.		35.00	24-75
1992 You Deserve An Ovation 520578	Open		35.00	33-38
1989 My Heart Is Exposed With Love 520624	Retrd.	1999	45.00	42-78
1989 A Friend Is Someone Who Cares 520632	Retrd.	1995	30.00	44-75
1989 I'm So Glad You Fluttered Into My Life 520640	Retrd.	1991	40.00	149-395
1989 Eggspecially For You 520667	Retrd.	1999	45.00	38-65
1989 Puppy Love 520764	Retrd.	1999	12.50	14-24
1989 Your Love Is So Uplifting 520675	Retrd.	1998	60.00	57-75
1989 Sending You Showers Of Blessings 520683	Retrd.	1992	32.50	45-85
1989 Just A Line To Wish You A Happy Day 520721	Suspd.		65.00	70-93
1989 Friendship Hits The Spot 520748	Retrd.	2000	55.00	59-90
1989 Jesus Is The Only Way 520756	Suspd.		40.00	42-75
1989 Many Moons In Same Canoe, Blessum You 520772	Retrd.	1990	50.00	200-361
1989 Wishing You Roads Of Happiness 520780	Open		60.00	68-93
1989 Someday My Love 520799	Retrd.	1992	40.00	40-88
1989 My Days Are Blue Without You 520802	Suspd.		65.00	71-100
1989 We Need A Good Friend Through The Ruff Times 520810	Suspd.		35.00	40-56
1989 You Are My Number One 520829	Suspd.		25.00	30-37
1989 The Lord Is Your Light To Happiness 520837	Open		50.00	52-72
1989 Wishing You A Perfect Choice 520845	Open		55.00	56-70
1989 I Belong To The Lord 520853	Suspd.		25.00	27-48
1990 Heaven Bless You 520934	Retrd.	2001	35.00	30-42
1989 There Is No Greater Treasure Than To Have A Friend Like You 521000	Retrd.	1998	30.00	26-40
1990 That's What Friends Are For 521183	Retrd.	2000	45.00	42-62
1997 Lord, Spare Me 521191	Retrd.	2001	37.50	40-58
1990 Hope You're Up And OnThe Trail Again 521205	Suspd.		35.00	40-65
1993 The Fruit of the Spirit is Love 521213	Retrd.	1999	30.00	28-35
1996 Enter His Court With Thanksgiving 521202	Open		35.00	30-40
1991 Take Heed When You Stand 521272	Suspd.		55.00	51-65
1990 Happy Trip 521280	Suspd.		35.00	40-80
1991 Hug One Another 521299	Retrd.	1995	45.00	42-100
1998 Yield Not To Temptation 521310	Suspd.		27.50	30-55
1998 Heaven Must Have Sent You 521388	Retrd.	2001	60.00	65
1990 Faith Is A Victory 521396	Retrd.	1993	25.00	110-136
1990 I'll Never Stop Loving You 521418	Retrd.	1996	37.50	42
1991 To A Very Special Mom & Dad 521434	Suspd.		35.00	37-50
1990 Lord, Help Me Stick To My Job 521450	Retrd.	1997	30.00	28-85
2000 I'll Wait For You 521469	Open		30.00	30
1989 Tell It To Jesus 521477	Open		35.00	35-78
1991 There's A Light At The End Of The Tunnel 521485	Suspd.		55.00	53-85
1991 A Special Delivery 521493	Open		30.00	28-38
1990 Water-Melancholy Day Without You 521515	Open		35.00	30-35
1991 Thumb-body Loves You 521698	Suspd.		55.00	51-100
1996 My Love Blooms For You 521728	Open		50.00	42-55
1990 Sweep All Your Worries Away 521779	Retrd.	1996	40.00	34-150
1990 Good Friends Are Forever 521817	Open		50.00	46-70
1990 Love Is From Above 521841	Suspd.		45.00	53-100
1989 The Greatest of These Is Love 521868	Suspd.		27.50	34-39
1997 Pizza On Earth 521884	Retrd.	2001	55.00	46-55
1989 Easter's On Its Way 521892	Retrd.	1999	60.00	55-85
1991 Hoppy Easter Friend 521906	Retrd.	1999	40.00	40-43
1994 Perfect Harmony 521914	Retrd.	1999	55.00	55-58
1993 Safe In The Arms Of Jesus 521922	Open		30.00	30-35
1989 Wishing You A Cozy Season 521949	Suspd.		42.50	48-68
1990 High Hopes 521957	Suspd.		30.00	30-55
1991 To A Special Mum 521965	Retrd.	1999	30.00	28-45
1999 Caught Up In Sweet Thoughts Of You 521973	Open		30.00	25-30
1996 Marching To The Beat of Freedom's Drum 521981	Open		35.00	30-35
1993 To The Apple Of God's Eye 522015	Retrd.	1999	32.50	35-37
1989 May Your Life Be Blessed With Touchdowns 522023	Retrd.	1998	45.00	40-60
1989 Thank You Lord For Everything 522031	Suspd.		55.00	48-95
1994 Now I Lay Me Down To Sleep 522058	Retrd.	1997	30.00	32-70
1991 May Your World Be Trimmed With Joy 522082	Suspd.		55.00	53-95
1990 There Shall Be Showers Of Blessings 522090	Retrd.	1999	60.00	49-80
1992 It's No Yolk When I Say I Love You 522104	Suspd.		60.00	65-92
1989 Don't Let the Holidays Get You Down 522112	Retrd.	1993	42.50	60-100
1989 Wishing You A Very Successful Season 522120	Retrd.	1999	60.00	60-74
1989 Bon Voyage! 522201	Suspd.		75.00	110-157
1989 He Is The Star Of The Morning 522252	Suspd.		55.00	60-88
1989 To Be With You Is Uplifting 522260	Retrd.	1994	20.00	24-60
1991 A Reflection Of His Love 522279	Retrd.	1999	50.00	41-53
1990 Thinking Of You Is What I Really Like To Do 522287	Suspd.		30.00	34-40
1989 Merry Christmas Deer 522317	Retrd.	1997	50.00	41-120
1996 Sweeter As The Years Go By 522333	Retrd.	1998	60.00	60-70
1989 Oh Holy Night 522546	Yr.Iss.	1989	25.00	28-45
1995 Just A Line To Say You're Special 522864	Retrd.	1999	50.00	50-60
1997 On My Way To A Perfect Day 522872	Open		45.00	38-45
1989 Isn't He Precious 522988	Suspd.		15.00	19-27
1990 Some Bunny's Sleeping 522996	Suspd.		12.00	27-36
1989 Jesus Is The Sweetest Name I Know 523097	Suspd.		22.50	30-40
1991 Joy On Arrival 523178	Open		50.00	46-60
1990 The Good Lord Always Delivers 523453	Open		27.50	30
2001 The Good Lord Always Delivers 523453B	Open		30.00	30
1990 This Day Has Been Made In Heaven 523496	Open		30.00	30-42
1990 God Is Love Dear Valentine 523518	Retrd.	1999	27.50	30-32
1991 I Will Cherish The Old Rugged Cross 523534	Yr.Iss.	1991	27.50	24-39
1992 You Are The Type I Love 523542	Open		40.00	38-50
2001 I Will Always Love You (Spring Catalog) 523569	Open		45.00	45
1993 The Lord Will Provide 523593	Yr.Iss.	1993	40.00	40-75
1991 Good News Is So Uplifting 523615	Retrd.	1999	60.00	59-74
1992 I'm So Glad That God Has Blessed Me With A Friend Like You 523623	Retrd.	1995	50.00	50-135
1994 I Will Always Be Thinking Of You 523631	Retrd.	1996	45.00	48-90
1990 Time Heals 523739	Retrd.	2000	37.50	34-40
1990 Blessings From Above 523747	Retrd.	1994	45.00	63-72
1994 Just Poppin' In To Say Halo 523755	Retrd.	1999	45.00	45-48
1991 I Can't Spell Success Without You 523763	Suspd.		40.00	44-150
1990 Once Upon A Holy Night 523836	Yr.Iss.	1990	25.00	27-45
1996 Love Never Leaves A Mother's Arms 523941	Open		40.00	40
2002 You're The Best Friend On The Block 524018	Open		50.00	50
1992 My Warmest Thoughts Are You 524085	Retrd.	1996	55.00	51-95
2001 Missing You (GCC Exclusive) 524107	Open		40.00	40
1991 Good Friends Are For Always 524123	Retrd.	1999	27.50	28-40
1994 Lord Teach Us to Pray 524158	Yr.Iss.	1994	35.00	30-40
1991 May Your Christmas Be Merry 524166	Yr.Iss.	1991	27.50	28-35
1995 Walk In The Sonshine 524212	Retrd.	2001	35.00	30-37
1991 He Loves Me 524263	Yr.Iss.	1991	35.00	30-50
1992 Friendship Grows When You Plant A Seed 524271	Retrd.	1994	40.00	78-120
1993 May Your Every Wish Come True 524298	Open		50.00	42-50
1991 May Your Birthday Be A Blessing 524301	Open		30.00	30-35
2001 May Your Birthday Be A Blessing 524301B	Open		35.00	35

*Quotes have been rounded up to nearest dollar

YEAR ISSUE	EDITION LIMIT	YEAR RETD.	ISSUE PRICE	*QUOTE U.S.$
1992 Our Friendship Is Soda-Licious 524336	Retrd.	1999	70.00	70
1992 What The World Needs Now 524352	Retrd.	1997	50.00	42-100
1997 Something Precious From Above 524360	Open		50.00	45-55
1993 You Are Such A Purr-fect Friend 524395	Open		35.00	30-53
1991 May Only Good Things Come Your Way 524425	Retrd.	1998	30.00	33-48
1993 Sealed With A Kiss 524441	Retrd.	1996	50.00	45-100
1993 A Special Chime For Jesus 524468	Retrd.	1997	32.50	35-70
1994 God Cared Enough To Send His Best 524476	Retrd.	1996	50.00	42-125
1990 Happy Birthday Dear Jesus 524875	Suspd.		13.50	20-30
1992 It's So Uplifting To Have A Friend Like You 524905	Retrd.	1999	40.00	38-45
1990 We're Going To Miss You 524913	Retrd.	2001	50.00	48-69
1991 Angels We Have Heard On High 524921	Retrd.	1996	60.00	60-74
1992 Tubby's First Christmas 525278	Retrd.	1999	10.00	10-15
1991 It's A Perfect Boy 525286	Retrd.	1999	16.50	19-28
1993 May Your Future Be Blessed 525316	Open		35.00	34-40
1992 Ring Those Christmas Bells 525898	Retrd.	1996	95.00	111-117
2002 We All Need A Friend Through The Ruff Times 525901	Open		45.00	45
1998 Let's Put The Pieces Together 525928	Open		60.00	51-60
2001 All About Heaven-Mini Nativity 525952	Open		20.00	20
1992 Going Home 525979	Open		60.00	60
1996 A Prince Of A Guy 526037	Retrd.	2000	35.00	24-35
1996 Pretty As A Princess 526053	Open		35.00	30-40
1998 The Pearl Of A Great Price 526061	Open		50.00	50-65
2001 I'm Completely Suspended With Love 526096	Retrd.	2001	28.50	29
1992 I Would Be Lost Without You 526142	Retrd.	1999	27.50	21-100
1993 Friends To The Very End 526150	Retrd.	1997	45.00	48-56
1992 You Are My Happiness 526185	Yr.Iss.	1992	37.50	45-85
1994 You Suit Me to a Tee 526193	Retrd.	1999	35.00	30-36
1994 Sharing Sweet Moments Together 526487	Retrd.	1999	45.00	45-62
1996 The Lord Is With You 526835	Retrd.	1999	27.50	24-28
1991 We Have Come From Afar 526959	Suspd.		17.50	18-25
1993 Bless-Um You 527335	Retrd.	1998	35.00	30-40
1992 You Are My Favorite Star 527378	Retrd.	1997	55.00	66-90
1992 Bring The Little Ones To Jesus 527556	Open		90.00	85-90
1992 God Bless The U.S.A. 527564	Yr.Iss.	1992	32.50	28-42
1993 Tied Up For The Holidays 527580	Suspd.		40.00	34-75
1993 Bringing You A Merry Christmas 527599	Retrd.	1995	45.00	60-77
1992 Wishing You A Ho Ho Ho 527629	Retrd.	2001	40.00	45-50
2000 Waiting For A Merry Christmas (April Shows) 527637	Retrd.	2000	65.00	65
1991 You Have Touched So Many Hearts w/personalization kit 527661	Suspd.		37.50	33-44
1992 But The Greatest of These Is Love 527688	Yr.Iss.	1992	27.50	28-35
1992 Wishing You A Comfy Christmas 527750	Retrd.	1999	30.00	30-35
1993 I Only Have Arms For You 527769	Retrd.	1998	15.00	14-25
1992 This Land Is Our Land 527777	Yr.Iss.	1992	35.00	30-70
1994 Nativity Cart 528072	Retrd.	2001	16.00	19
1999 He Came As The Gift Of God's Love 528129	Open		30.00	30
1994 I Got News For You 528137	Retrd.	1999	16.00	14-19
1994 To a Very Special Sister 528633	Open		60.00	52-65
1993 America You're Beautiful 528862	Yr.Iss.	1993	35.00	33-100
2002 America You're Beautiful 528862R	Open		35.00	35
1996 My True Love Gave To Me 529273	Open		40.00	34-40
1993 Happiness Is At Our Fingertips (Spring Catalog) 529931	Open		35.00	35-47
1993 Ring Out The Good News 529966	Retrd.	1997	27.50	30-80
1999 Wishes For The World (Millennium Event) 530018	Open		35.00	35
1993 Wishing You the Sweetest Christmas 530166	Yr.Iss.	1993	27.50	30-45
1994 You're As Pretty As A Christmas Tree 530425	Yr.Iss.	1994	27.50	27-40
1994 Serenity Prayer Girl 530697	Open		35.00	33-38
1994 Serenity Prayer Boy 530700	Open		35.00	33-40
1995 We Have Come From Afar 530913	Retrd.	2001	12.00	12-15
1995 I Only Have Ice For You 530956	Retrd.	1999	27.50	40-100

YEAR ISSUE	EDITION LIMIT	YEAR RETD.	ISSUE PRICE	*QUOTE U.S.$
1997 Sometimes You're Next To Impossible 530964	Open		50.00	50
1998 My World's Upside Down Without You 531014	Open		15.00	15
1997 Potty Time 531022	Retrd.	2001	25.00	22-25
1998 You Are My Once In A Lifetime 531030	Retrd.	2000	45.00	45
1995 What The World Needs Is Love 531065	Retrd.	1999	45.00	38-53
1994 Money's Not The Only Green Thing Worth Saving 531073	Retrd.	1996	50.00	54-64
1996 What A Difference You've Made In My Life 531138	Retrd.	2001	50.00	42-55
1995 Vaya Con Dios (To Go With God) 531146	Open		32.50	30-40
1995 Bless Your Soul 531162	Retrd.	2001	25.00	24-42
2002 Our Friendship Goes A Long Way 531626	Open		60.00	60
1997 Who's Gonna Fill You're Shoes 531634	Open		37.50	38-42
1996 You Deserve a Halo—Thank You 531693	Retrd.	1998	55.00	46-60
1994 The Lord Is Counting on You 531707	Open		32.50	30-35
1994 Sharing Our Christmas Together 531944	Open		35.00	30-35
1994 Dropping In For The Holidays 531952	Retrd.	1998	40.00	40-45
1999 Lord Speak To Me 531987	Open		45.00	37-45
1995 Hallelujah For The Cross 532002	Retrd.	1999	35.00	30-37
1995 Sending You Oceans Of Love 532010	Retrd.	1996	35.00	37-75
1995 I Can't Bear To Let You Go 532037	Retrd.	1999	50.00	53-58
1998 Who's Gonna Fill Your Shoes 532061	Open		37.50	40
1995 Lord Help Me To Stay On Course 532096	Retrd.	2001	35.00	35-59
1994 The Lord Bless You and Keep You 532118	Open		40.00	42-50
1994 The Lord Bless You and Keep You 532126	Open		30.00	30-35
1994 The Lord Bless You and Keep You 532134	Open		30.00	30-35
1994 Luke 2:10 11 532916	Retrd.	1999	35.00	25-40
2001 It's Almost Time For Santa 532932	Yr.Iss.	2001	70.00	70
1999 Lord, Police Protect Us 539953	Open		45.00	36-45
1999 Sharing Our Winter Wonderland 539988	Open		75.00	75
1991 May Your World Be Trimmed... 552082	Suspd.		55.00	55-68
1999 Slide Into The Next Millenium With Joy 587761	Open		35.00	35
1999 Witch Way Do You Spell Love? 587869	Open		25.00	20-25
1999 May Your Seasons Be Jelly And Bright 587885	Open		37.50	30-38
1999 My Life Is A Vacuum Without You 587907	Open		37.50	30-38
1999 RV Haven' Fun Or What 587915	Open		45.00	36-45
1999 Thank You Sew Much 587923	Open		25.00	20-25
1999 Behold The Lamb of God 588164	Open		45.00	36-45
1994 Nothing Can Dampen The Spirit of Caring 603864	Open		35.00	30-35
1997 May Your Christmas Be Delightful 604135	Open		40.00	34-40
1995 A Poppy For You 604208	Suspd.		35.00	25-45
2001 Life's Beary Precious With You 642673	Open		25.00	25
2001 Giving My Heart Freely 650013	Open		40.00	40
1999 I Will Love You Always 679701S	Retrd.	2000	26.00	26
2000 Life Is Worth Fighting For 680982 (NABCO)	Open		30.00	30
2001 Life Is Worth Fighting For 680982B (NABCO)	Open		30.00	30
2000 God Gives Us Memories So That We Might Have Roses In December (Compassionate Friends) 680990	Open		45.00	45
2000 Precious Moments Will Last Forever (Gene Freedman World Tour) 681008	Open		35.00	35
2000 Let Freedom Ring 681059E	Open		45.00	45
1999 Alleluia, He Is Risen 692409	Open		30.00	30
2000 The Future Is In Our Hands 730068	Yr.Iss.	2000	30.00	30
2000 We're A Family That Sticks Together (Spring Fling) 730114	Retrd.	2000	40.00	40
2000 There's Sno-boredom With You 730122	Open		45.00	45
2000 Raisin' Cane On The Holidays 730130	Open		35.00	35

Collectors' Information Bureau   *Quotes have been rounded up to nearest dollar

FIGURINES

Precious Moments/Enesco Group, Inc.
to Precious Moments/Enesco Group, Inc.

YEAR ISSUE	EDITION LIMIT	YEAR RETD.	ISSUE PRICE	*QUOTE U.S.$
001 Everything Is Beautiful In It's Own Way 730149	Open		25.00	25
000 Home Made of Love 730211	Open		45.00	45
000 The Fun Is Being Together (Century Circle Exclusive) 730262	Open		200.00	200
000 Squeaky Clean (Century Circle Event) 731048	Open		45.00	45
001 Take Thyme For Yourself 731064	Open		32.50	33
001 I'll Never Let You Down 731065	Open		45.00	45
000 Grandma I'll Never Outgrow You 731587	Open		25.00	25
000 Grandpa I'll Never Outgrow You 731595	Open		25.00	25
000 Fall Festival 732494	Open		150.00	150
000 You Should Be As Proud As A Peacock-Congratulations 733008	Open		27.50	28
000 You Have A Special Place In My Heart (June Show) 737534	Retrd.	2000	55.00	55
000 Cradle Large Nativity 737607	Open		25.00	25
000 Auntie, You Make Beauty Blossom 737623	Open		40.00	40
002 You're A Real Barbe-cutie 742872	Open		35.00	35
001 To The Sweetest Girl In The Cast 742880	Open		35.00	35
000 Collection of Precious Moments 745510	Open		27.00	27
000 Eat Turkey 763225	Open		25.00	25
000 You Are Always In My Heart (boy) 768952 (Pre-Show 2001)	Open		40.00	40
000 You Are Always In My Heart (girl) 768987 (Pre-Show 2001)	Open		40.00	40
000 May All Your Days Be Rosy (Mother's Day) 781770C	Open		30.00	30
000 Your Love Keeps Me Toasty Warm (GCC Catalog Exclusive) 788031	Open		37.50	38
000 May All Your Days Be Rosy (CCR 2000 Only) 781770	Open		30.00	30
001 You Are The Queen Of Hearts 795151	Yr.Iss.		50.00	50
001 You Will Always Be Mine 795186	Open		45.00	45
001 You Can't Hide From God 795194	Open		18.50	19
001 The Lord Can Dew Anything 795208	Open		35.00	35
001 You're A Dandy Mom, And I'm Not Lion 795232V	Retrd.	2001	27.50	28
001 It's A Banner Day-Congratulations 795259	Open		25.00	25
001 You Are The Wind Beneath My Wings 795267	Open		35.00	35
001 You're As Sweet As Apple Pie 795275	Open		35.00	35
001 You're A Honey 795283	Open		32.50	33
001 O' Fish-Aly Friends For A Lifetime 795305	Open		50.00	50
001 Wishing You A Birthday Full of Surprises 795313	Open		40.00	40
002 No Bones About It - You're Grrr-eat 795321	Open		40.00	40
000 I Give You My Heart 801313C	Open		30.00	30
000 I Give You My Heart 801313 (CCR 2001 Only)	Open		30.00	30
000 A Winning Spirit Comes From Within (Special Olympics) 813044	Open		35.00	35
000 I Will Make My Country Proud (Canadian Exclusive) 820423	Open		37.50	38
001 May Your Christmas Begins With A Bang! 877433	Yr.Iss.	2001	30.00	30
001 On A Scale From 1 To 10 You Are The Deerest 878944	Open		30.00	30
001 Celebrating His Arrival 878952	Open		40.00	40
001 The Royal Budge Is Good For The Soul-Large Nativity 878987	Open		45.00	45
001 Life Is So Uplifting 878995	Open		35.00	35
001 Roll Away, Roll Away, Roll Away 879002	Open		35.00	35
001 Lord Let Our Friendship Bloom 879126	Open		37.50	38-40
001 Our Friendship Was Made To Order 879134	Open		35.00	35
001 Up To Our Ears In A White Christmas (January Show) 879185	Open		55.00	55
001 Count Your Many Blessings (Spring Fling) 879274	Open		50.00	50
001 O Holy Night (Nativity Set) 879428	3,000		375.00	375
002 Let Love Reign 890596	Yr.Iss.		60.00	60

YEAR ISSUE	EDITION LIMIT	YEAR RETD.	ISSUE PRICE	*QUOTE U.S.$
2002 You Have A Heart Of Gold 890626	Open		25.00	25
2002 Nearer To the Heart of God 890731	Open		40.00	40
2002 God's Love Has No Measure 890871	Open		25.00	25
2002 You Are The Cat's Meow 890952	Open		25.00	25
2002 Just A Happy Note 890960	Open		25.00	25
2002 Best Friends Share The Same Heart 890987	Open		50.00	50
2002 Daddy's Little Girl 891045	Open		40.00	40
2002 You Are My Gift From Above 891738	Open		50.00	50
2002 Healing Begins With Forgiveness 892157	Open		45.00	45
2002 Ewe Are So Precious To Me 892726	Open		45.00	45
2001 Loving, Caring And Shearing (Summer Show) 898414	10,000		60.00	60
2002 You Are My Favorite Dish 898457	Open		25.00	25
2002 We've Got The Right Plan 937282	Open		80.00	80
2002 Our Heroes In The Sky - Female Flight Attendant 958832	Open		35.00	35
2002 Our Heroes In The Sky - Male Flight Attendant/Pilot 958840	Open		35.00	35
2002 I See Bright Hope In Your Future (Fall Show Exclusive) 973912	Open		50.00	50

Animal Affections - S. Butcher

YEAR ISSUE	EDITION LIMIT	YEAR RETD.	ISSUE PRICE	*QUOTE U.S.$
2002 So You Finally Met Your Match, Congratulations 101493	Open		20.00	20
2002 You Are A Real Cool Mommy 101495	Open		20.00	20
2002 Rats, I Missed Your Birthday 101496	Open		20.00	20
2002 We're Behind You All The Way 994863	Open		20.00	20
2002 Miracles Can Happen 994871	Open		20.00	20
2002 Holy Mackerel It's Your Birthday 994898	Open		20.00	20

Anniversary Figurines - S. Butcher

YEAR ISSUE	EDITION LIMIT	YEAR RETD.	ISSUE PRICE	*QUOTE U.S.$
1984 God Blessed Our Years Together With So Much Love And Happiness E-2853	Open		35.00	42-66
1984 God Blessed Our Year Together With So Much Love And Happiness (1st) E-2854	Retrd.	2000	35.00	42-65
1984 God Blessed Our Years Together With So Much Love And Happiness (5th) E-2855	Suspd.		35.00	60-75
1984 God Blessed Our Years Together With So Much Love And Happiness (10th) E-2856	Suspd.		35.00	67-78
1984 God Blessed Our Years Together With So Much Love And Happiness (25th) E-2857	Retrd.	2001	35.00	50-65
1984 God Blessed Our Years Together With So Much Love And Happiness (40th) E-2859	Suspd.		35.00	42-80
1984 God Blessed Our Years Together With So Much Love And Happiness (50th) E-2860	Retrd.	2001	35.00	50-78
1994 I Still Do 530999	Open		30.00	30-50
1994 I Still Do 531006	Open		30.00	30-50

Baby Classics - S. Butcher

YEAR ISSUE	EDITION LIMIT	YEAR RETD.	ISSUE PRICE	*QUOTE U.S.$
1997 Good Friends Are Forever 272422	Open		30.00	26-30
1997 Make A Joyful Noise 272450	Open		30.00	26-30
1997 We Are God's Workmanship 272434	Open		25.00	22-25
1997 I Believe In Miracles 272469	Open		25.00	22-25
1997 God Loveth A Cheerful Giver 272477	Retrd.	1998	25.00	25-27
1997 Love Is Sharing 272493	Open		25.00	22-25
1997 You Have Touched So Many Hearts 272485	Open		25.00	22-25
1997 Love One Another 272507	Open		30.00	24-30
1998 Friendship Hits The Spot 306916	Open		30.00	30
1998 Loving You Dear Valentine 306932	Open		25.00	22-25
1998 He Cleansed My Soul 306940	Open		25.00	25

Baby's First - S. Butcher

YEAR ISSUE	EDITION LIMIT	YEAR RETD.	ISSUE PRICE	*QUOTE U.S.$
1984 Baby's First Step E-2840	Suspd.		35.00	60-105
1984 Baby's First Picture E-2841	Retrd.	1986	45.00	129-175
1985 Baby's First Haircut 12211	Suspd.		32.50	117-198
1986 Baby's First Trip 16012	Suspd.		32.50	195-275
1989 Baby's First Pet 520705	Suspd.		45.00	45-68
1990 Baby's First Meal 524077	Retrd.	1999	35.00	25-45
1992 Baby's First Word 527238	Retrd.	1999	24.00	21-35
1993 Baby's First Birthday 524069	Open		25.00	25-35

FIGURINES

YEAR ISSUE	EDITION LIMIT	YEAR RETD.	ISSUE PRICE	*QUOTE U.S.$

Birthday Club Figurines - S. Butcher

YEAR ISSUE	EDITION LIMIT	YEAR RETD.	ISSUE PRICE	*QUOTE U.S.$
1986 Fishing For Friends BC-861	Yr.Iss.	1986	10.00	94-130
1987 Hi Sugar BC-871	Yr.Iss.	1987	11.00	65-100
1988 Somebunny Cares BC-881	Yr.Iss.	1988	13.50	35-80
1989 Can't Bee Hive Myself Without You BC-891	Yr.Iss.	1989	13.50	35-55
1990 Collecting Makes Good Scents BC-901	Yr.Iss.	1990	15.00	29-35
1990 I'm Nuts Over My Collection BC-902	Yr.Iss.	1990	15.00	26-35
1991 Love Pacifies BC-911	Yr.Iss.	1991	15.00	24-36
1991 True Blue Friends BC-912	Yr.Iss.	1991	15.00	24-73
1992 Every Man's Home Is His Castle BC-921	Yr.Iss.	1992	16.50	14-30
1992 I Got You Under My Skin BC-922	Yr.Iss.	1992	16.00	30-35
1993 Put a Little Punch In Your Birthday BC-931	Yr.Iss.	1993	15.00	17-24
1993 Owl Always Be Your Friend BC-932	Yr.Iss.	1993	16.00	24-30
1994 God Bless Our Home BC-941	Yr.Iss.	1994	16.00	26-36
1994 Yer A Pel-I-Can Count On BC-942	Yr.Iss.	1994	16.00	17-26
1995 Making A Point To Say You're Special BC-951	Yr.Iss.	1995	15.00	21-32
1995 10 Wonderful Years Of Wishes BC-952	Yr.Iss.	1995	50.00	50-58
1996 There's A Spot In My Heart For You BC-961	Yr.Iss.	1996	15.00	15-30
1996 You're First In My Heart BC-962	Yr.Iss.	1996	15.00	19-28
1997 Hare's To The Birthday Club BC-971	Yr.Iss.	1997	16.00	16-20
1998 Holy Tweet BC-972	Yr.Iss.	1997	18.50	19-23
1998 Slide Into The Celebration BC-981	Yr.Iss.	1998	15.00	15-18

Birthday Club Inscribed Charter Membership Renewal Gift - S. Butcher

YEAR ISSUE	EDITION LIMIT	YEAR RETD.	ISSUE PRICE	*QUOTE U.S.$
1987 A Smile's the Cymbal of Joy B-0102	Yr.Iss.	1987	Unkn.	53-80
1988 The Sweetest Club Around B-0103	Yr.Iss.	1988	Unkn.	30-50
1989 Have A Beary Special Birthday B-0104	Yr.Iss.	1989	Unkn.	26-55
1990 Our Club Is A Tough Act To Follow B-0105	Yr.Iss.	1990	Unkn.	26-38
1991 Jest To Let You Know You're Tops B-0106	Yr.Iss.	1991	Unkn.	24-40
1992 All Aboard For Birthday Club Fun B-0107	Yr.Iss.	1992	Unkn.	25-35
1993 Happiness is Belonging B-0108	Yr.Iss.	1993	Unkn.	17-34
1994 Can't Get Enough of Our Club B-0109	Yr.Iss.	1994	Unkn.	19-25
1995 Hoppy Birthday B-0110	Yr.Iss.	1995	Unkn.	14-35
1996 Scootin' By Just To Say Hi! B-0111	Yr.Iss.	1996	Unkn.	21-32
1997 The Fun Starts Here B-0112	Yr.Iss.	1997	Unkn.	21-25

Birthday Club Welcome Gift - S. Butcher

YEAR ISSUE	EDITION LIMIT	YEAR RETD.	ISSUE PRICE	*QUOTE U.S.$
1986 Our Club Can't Be Beat B-0001	Yr.Iss.	1986	Unkn.	64-90
1987 A Smile's The Cymbal of Joy B-0002	Yr.Iss.	1987	Unkn.	44-70
1988 The Sweetest Club Around B-0003	Yr.Iss.	1988	Unkn.	32-50
1989 Have A Beary Special Birthday B-0004	Yr.Iss.	1989	Unkn.	21-35
1990 Our Club Is A Tough Act To Follow B-0005	Yr.Iss.	1990	Unkn.	25-35
1991 Jest To Let You Know You're Tops B-0006	Yr.Iss.	1991	Unkn.	20-32
1992 All Aboard For Birthday Club Fun B-0007	Yr.Iss.	1992	Unkn.	23-30
1993 Happiness Is Belonging B-0008	Yr.Iss.	1993	Unkn.	16-24
1994 Can't Get Enough of Our Club B-0009	Yr.Iss.	1994	Unkn.	16-25
1995 Hoppy Birthday B-0010	Yr.Iss.	1995	Unkn.	14-28
1996 Scootin' By Just To Say Hi! B-0011	Yr.Iss.	1996	Unkn.	16-28
1997 The Fun Starts Here B-0012	Closed	1998	Unkn.	16

Birthday Series - S. Butcher

YEAR ISSUE	EDITION LIMIT	YEAR RETD.	ISSUE PRICE	*QUOTE U.S.$
1988 Friends To The End 104418	Suspd.		15.00	18-32
1987 Showers Of Blessings 105945	Retrd.	1993	16.00	21-47
1987 Brighten Someone's Day 105953	Suspd.		12.50	15-34
1990 To My Favorite Fan 521043	Suspd.		16.00	21-43
1989 Hello World! 521175	Retrd.	1999	13.50	16-21
1993 Hope You're Over The Hump 521671	Suspd.		16.00	17-30
1990 Not A Creature Was Stirring 524484	Suspd.		17.00	17-25
1991 Can't Be Without You 524492	Retrd.	1999	16.00	18
1991 How Can I Ever Forget You 526924	Retrd.	2001	15.00	16-18
1992 Let's Be Friends 527270	Retrd.	1996	15.00	18-35
1992 Happy Birdie 527343	Suspd.		8.00	18-30
1993 Happy Birthday Jesus 530492	Retrd.	1999	20.00	16-25
1994 Oinky Birthday 524506	Retrd.	1999	13.50	14-18
1995 Wishing You A Happy Bear Hug 520659	Suspd.		27.50	29-45

YEAR ISSUE	EDITION LIMIT	YEAR RETD.	ISSUE PRICE	*QUOTE U.S.$
1996 I Haven't Seen Much of You Lately 531057	Open		13.50	12-
1997 From The First Time I Spotted You I Knew We'd Be Friends 260940	Retrd.	2000	18.50	18-5
2001 Wishing You A Blow Out Birthday 680184	Open		30.00	3

Birthday Train Figurines - S. Butcher

YEAR ISSUE	EDITION LIMIT	YEAR RETD.	ISSUE PRICE	*QUOTE U.S.$
1985 Bless The Days Of Our Youth 16004	Open		15.00	20-4
1985 May Your Birthday Be Warm 15938	Open		10.00	14-1
1985 Happy Birthday Little Lamb 15946	Open		10.00	14-
1985 God Bless You On Your Birthday 15962	Open		11.00	16-4
1985 Heaven Bless Your Special Day 15954	Open		11.00	16-3
1985 May Your Birthday Be Gigantic 15970	Open		12.50	18-3
1985 This Day Is Something To Roar About 15989	Open		13.50	20-2
1985 Keep Looking Up 15997	Open		13.50	20-4
1988 Wishing You Grr-eatness 109479	Open		18.50	19-3
1988 Isn't Eight Just Great 109460	Open		18.50	19-2
1998 May Your Christmas Be Warm 470279	Open		15.00	13-1
1991 Being Nine Is Just Divine 521833	Open		25.00	23-3
1991 May Your Birthday Be Mammoth 521825	Open		25.00	23-2
1999 Take Your Time It's Your Birthday 488003	Open		25.00	2
2000 Give A Grin & Let The Fun Begin 488011	Open		25.00	2
2000 You Mean The Moose To Me 488038	Open		25.00	2

Bless Those Who Serve Their Country - S. Butcher

YEAR ISSUE	EDITION LIMIT	YEAR RETD.	ISSUE PRICE	*QUOTE U.S.$
1991 Bless Those Who Serve Their Country (Navy) 526568	Suspd.		32.50	95-16
1991 Bless Those Who Serve Their Country (Army) 526576	Suspd.		32.50	40-8
1991 Bless Those Who Serve Their Country (Air Force) 526584	Suspd.		32.50	38-6
1991 Bless Those Who Serve Their Country (Girl Soldier) 527289	Suspd.		32.50	34-4
1991 Bless Those Who Serve Their Country (Soldier) 527297	Suspd.		32.50	32-4
1991 Bless Those Who Serve Their Country (Marine) 527521	Suspd.		32.50	37-9
1995 You Will Always Be Our Hero 136271	Yr.Iss.	1995	40.00	34-4

Boys & Girls Club - S. Butcher

YEAR ISSUE	EDITION LIMIT	YEAR RETD.	ISSUE PRICE	*QUOTE U.S.$
1996 Shoot For The Stars And You'll Never Strike Out 521701	Open		60.00	51-6
1997 He Is Our Shelter From The Storm 523550	Open		75.00	63-7
1998 Love Is Color Blind 524204	Open		60.00	50-6
1999 I Couldn't Make It Without You 635030	Open		60.00	6
2000 You Tug On My Heart Strings 795526	Open		60.00	6
2001 Building Special Friendships 879029	Open		80.00	8

Bridal Party - S. Butcher

YEAR ISSUE	EDITION LIMIT	YEAR RETD.	ISSUE PRICE	*QUOTE U.S.$
1984 Bridesmaid E-2831	Open		13.50	22-3
1985 Ringbearer E-2833	Open		11.00	17-2
1985 Flower Girl E-2835	Open		11.00	17-2
1984 Best Man E-2836	Open		13.50	22-3
1986 Groom E-2837	Open		13.50	24-3
1987 This is the Day That the Lord Hath Made E-2838	Yr.Iss.	1987	185.00	181-22
1985 Junior Bridesmaid E-2845	Open		12.50	20-2
1987 Bride E-2846	Open		18.00	24-3
1987 God Bless Our Family (Parents of the Groom) 100498	Retrd.	1999	35.00	42-5
1987 God Bless Our Family (Parents of the Bride) 100501	Retrd.	1999	35.00	42-5
1987 Wedding Arch 102369	Suspd.		22.50	26-4
2001 Our Love Will Flow Eternal 588059	Open		90.00	9
2001 African-American Bride 795364	Open		27.50	2
2001 African-American Groom 795372	Open		27.50	2
2001 Hispanic Bride 795380	Open		27.50	2
2001 Hispanic Groom 795399	Open		27.50	2
2001 Asian Bride 795402	Open		27.50	2
2001 Asian Groom 795410	Open		27.50	2
2001 Caucasian Bride - Brunette 874485	Open		27.50	2
2001 Caucasian Groom - Brunette 874493	Open		27.50	2
2001 I Give You My Love Forever True (musical) 876143	Open		125.00	12

Collectors' Information Bureau   *Quotes have been rounded up to nearest dollar

FIGURINES

Precious Moments/Enesco Group, Inc.
to Precious Moments/Enesco Group, Inc.

YEAR ISSUE	EDITION LIMIT	YEAR RETD.	ISSUE PRICE	*QUOTE U.S.$
2001 Bridal Arch (musical) 876151	Open		50.00	50
2001 Latino Best Man 901563	Open		25.00	25
2001 Latino Maid Of Honor 901571	Open		25.00	25
2001 African-American Best Man 902020	Open		25.00	25
2001 African-American Maid Of Honor 902039	Open		25.00	25
2001 Asian Best Man 902047	Open		25.00	25
2001 Asian Maid Of Honor 902055	Open		25.00	25

Calendar Girl - S. Butcher

1988 January 109983	Open		37.50	38-45
1988 February 109991	Open		27.50	33-50
1988 March 110019	Open		27.50	34-40
1988 April 110027	Open		30.00	34-110
1988 May 110035	Open		25.00	25-35
1988 June 110043	Open		40.00	55-62
1988 July 110051	Open		35.00	40-45
1988 August 110078	Open		40.00	40-55
1988 September 110086	Open		27.50	33-52
1988 October 110094	Open		35.00	35-52
1988 November 110108	Open		32.50	33-52
1988 December 110116	Open		27.50	30-45
1997 Garnet-Color of Boldness January 335533	Open		25.00	25
1997 Amethyst-Color of Faith February 335541	Open		25.00	25
1997 Aquamarine-Color of Kindness March 335568	Open		25.00	25
1997 Diamond-Color of Purity April 335576	Open		25.00	25
1997 Emerald-Color of Patience May 335584	Open		25.00	25
1997 Pearl-Color of Love June 335592	Open		25.00	25
1997 Ruby-Color of Joy July 335606	Open		25.00	25
1997 Peridot-Color of Pride August 335614	Open		25.00	25
1997 Sapphire-Color of Confidence September 335622	Open		25.00	25
1997 Opal-Color of Happiness October 335657	Open		25.00	25
1997 Topaz-Color of Truth November 335665	Open		25.00	25
1997 Turquoise-Color of Loyalty December 335673	Open		25.00	25
2002 January - Snowdrop-Pure and Gentle 101515	Open		40.00	40
2002 February - Carnation-Bold and Brave 101517	Open		40.00	40
2002 March - Violet-Modest 101518	Open		40.00	40
2002 April - Lily-Virtuous 101519	Open		40.00	40
2002 May - Hawthone-Bright and Hopeful 101520	Open		40.00	40
2002 June - Rose-Beautiful 101521	Open		40.00	40
2002 July - Daisy-Wide-eyed and Innocent 101522	Open		40.00	40
2002 August - Poppy-Peaceful 101523	Open		40.00	40
2002 September - Morning Glory-Easily Contended 101525	Open		40.00	40
2002 October - Cosmos-Ambitious 101526	Open		40.00	40
2002 November - Chrysanthemum-Sassy and Cheerful 101527	Open		40.00	40
2002 December - Holly-Full of Foresight 101528	Open		40.00	40

Care-A-Van Tour - S. Butcher

1998 Have a Heavenly Journey 12416R	Yr.Iss.	1998	25.00	19-35
1998 How Can Two Work Together Except They Agree (ornament) 456268	Yr.Iss.	1998	25.00	18-25
1999 Scootin Your Way To A Perfect Day 634999	Yr.Iss.	1999	25.00	19-25
2000 Believe the Impossible 109487R	Yr.Iss.	2000	45.00	45
2000 Care-Van 2000 Die Cast Truck 817546	Yr.Iss.	2000	30.00	30

Chapel Exclusives - S. Butcher

1996 His Presence Is Felt In The Chapel 163872	Retrd.	1998	25.00	25
1995 Lighting The Way To A Happy Holiday 129267	Retrd.	1998	30.00	23-30
1989 There's A Christian Welcome Here 523011	Suspd.		45.00	47-144
1991 He Is My Inspiration 523038	Retrd.	N/A	60.00	60-87

YEAR ISSUE	EDITION LIMIT	YEAR RETD.	ISSUE PRICE	*QUOTE U.S.$
1991 Blessed Are...Shall Obtain Mercy 523291	Retrd.	N/A	55.00	55-59
1991 Blessed Are The Meek, They Shall Inherit The Earth 523313	Retrd.	N/A	55.00	55-59
1991 Blessed Are They That Hunger... 523321	Retrd.	N/A	55.00	55-59
1991 Blessed Are The Poor In Spirit... 523347	Retrd.	N/A	55.00	55-100
1991 Blessed Are The Peacemakers... 523348	Retrd.	N/A	55.00	55-152
1991 Blessed Are They That Mourn... 523380	Retrd.	N/A	55.00	55-59
1991 Blessed Are The Pure in Heart... 523399	Retrd.	N/A	55.00	55

Christmas Remembered - S. Butcher

2000 Sure Good Use Less Hustle & Bustle 737550	Open		37.50	38
2001 May Your Days Be Merry And Bright 878901	Open		45.00	45
2002 ...And To All A Good Night 104217	Open		55.00	55

Clown - S. Butcher

1985 I Get a Bang Out of You 12262	Retrd.	1997	30.00	33-65
1986 Lord Keep Me On the Ball 12270	Suspd.		30.00	38-45
1985 Waddle I Do Without You 12459	Retrd.	1989	30.00	48-95
1986 The Lord Will Carry You Through 12467	Retrd.	1988	30.00	55-72

Clown Series - S. Butcher

2002 Love Is On Its Way 101544	Open		30.00	30
2002 Lord Help Me Clean Up My Act 101545	Open		30.00	30
2002 Life Never Smelled So Sweet 101547	Open		35.00	35
2002 Our Love Is Heaven Scent 101546	Open		35.00	35
2002 Friends Are Never Far Behind 101543	Open		45.00	45

Commemorative 500th Columbus Anniversary - S. Butcher

1992 This Land Is Our Land 527386	Yr.Iss.	1992	350.00	318-375

Commemorative Easter Seal - S. Butcher

1988 Jesus Loves Me 9" fig. 104531	1,000		500.00	1400-1750
1987 He Walks With Me 107999	Yr.Iss.	1987	25.00	30-45
1988 Blessed Are They That Overcome 115479	Yr.Iss.	1988	27.50	25-32
1989 Make A Joyful Noise 9" fig. 520322	1,500		N/A	745-937
1989 His Love Will Shine On You 522376	Yr.Iss.	1989	30.00	37-55
1990 You Have Touched So Many Hearts 9" fig. 523283	2,000		500.00	561-775
1991 We Are God's Workmanship 9" fig. 523879	2,000		N/A	683-725
1990 Always In His Care 524522	Yr.Iss.	1990	30.00	29-40
1992 You Are Such A Purr-fect Friend 9" fig. 526010	2,000		N/A	582-700
1991 Sharing A Gift Of Love 527114	Yr.Iss.	1991	30.00	43-50
1992 A Universal Love 527173	Yr.Iss.	1992	32.50	75-105
1993 Gather Your Dreams 9" fig. 529680	2,000		500.00	575-625
1993 You're My Number One Friend 530026	Yr.Iss.	1993	30.00	34-55
1994 It's Not Secret What God Can Do 531111	Yr.Iss.	1994	30.00	30-50
1994 You Are The Rose of His Creation 9" fig. 531243	2,000		N/A	500-555
1995 Take Time To Smell the Flowers 524387	Yr.Iss.	1995	30.00	26-48
1995 He's Got The Whole World In His Hands 9" fig. 526886	Yr.Iss.	1995	500.00	N/A
1996 He Loves Me 9" fig. 152277	2,000		500.00	N/A
1996 You Can Always Count on Me 526827	Yr.Iss.	1996	30.00	28-38
1997 Love Is Universal 9" fig. 192376	2,000		N/A	446-560
1997 Give Ability A Chance 192368	Yr.Iss.	1997	30.00	26-30
1998 Love Grows Here 9" fig. 272981	2,000		N/A	N/A
1998 Somebody Cares 522325	Yr.Iss.	1998	40.00	32-45
1999 We Are All Precious In His Sight 475068	1,500		N/A	N/A
1999 Heaven Bless You Easter Seal 456314	Yr.Iss.	1999	35.00	29-35
2000 Jesus Loves Me 9" ES2000	1,500		500.00	500
2000 Give Your Whole Heart 490245	Yr.Iss.	2000	30.00	30
2000 Love One Another 9" LE2001	1,500		500.00	500
2001 You Have The Beary Best Heart 730254	Yr.Iss.	2001	35.00	35
2001 Loving, Caring, Sharing 822159	Yr.Iss.	2001	14.99	15

FIGURINES

YEAR ISSUE	EDITION LIMIT	YEAR RETD.	ISSUE PRICE	*QUOTE U.S.$
Country Lane - S. Butcher				
1999 Hogs & Kisses 261106	Open		50.00	41-50
1998 You're Just As Sweet As Pie 307017	Retrd.	2001	45.00	37-45
1998 Oh Taste And See That The Lord Is Good 307025	Retrd.	2001	55.00	45-55
1998 Fork Over Those Blessings 307033	Open		45.00	37-45
1998 Nobody Likes To Be Dumped 307041	Retrd.	1999	65.00	65
1998 I'll Never Tire of You 307068	Retrd.	1999	50.00	41-50
1998 Peas Pass The Carrots 307076	Retrd.	2000	35.00	29-35
1998 Bringing In The Sheaves (Musical) 307084	Yr.Iss.	1998	90.00	90-250
1999 Moo-ie Christmas 455856	Open		60.00	48-60
1999 Shear Happiness and Hare Cuts 539910	Open		40.00	32-40
1999 Eat Ham 587842	Open		25.00	20-25
1999 You Brighten My Field of Dreams 587850	Open		55.00	44-55
1999 Dear Jon, I Will Never Leave You-JESUS 588091	Open		50.00	40-50
2001 Life Would Be the Pits Without Friends 795356	Open		40.00	40
2001 Oh, What A Wonder-Fall Day 879096	Open		37.50	38
2001 Overalls, I Think You're Special 898147	Open		45.00	45
Cruise - S. Butcher				
1993 15 Year Tweet Music Together (15th Anniversary Collection Convention Medallion) 529087	Yr.Iss.	1993	Gift	58-86
1993 Friends Never Drift Apart (15th Anniversary Cruise Medallion) 529079	Yr.Iss.	1993	Gift	N/A
1995 Sailabration (15th Anniversary Collectors Club Cruise Figurine) 150061	Yr.Iss.	1995	Gift	507
1998 Our Future Is Looking Much Brighter (20th Anniversary Collection Cruise Figurine) 325511	Yr.Iss.	1998	Gift	N/A
2000 Whale Have Oceans Of Fun 748412	Yr.Iss.	2000	Gift	N/A
Events Figurines - S. Butcher				
1988 You Are My Main Event 115231	Yr.Iss.	1988	30.00	36-72
1989 Sharing Begins In The Heart 520861	Yr.Iss.	1989	25.00	30-80
1990 I'm A Precious Moments Fan 523526	Yr.Iss.	1990	25.00	23-48
1990 Good Friends Are Forever 525049	Yr.Iss.	1990	25.00	550-625
1991 You Can Always Bring A Friend 527122	Yr.Iss.	1991	27.50	28-55
1992 An Event Worth Wading For 527319	Yr.Iss.	1992	32.50	28-62
1993 An Event For All Seasons 530158	Yr.Iss.	1993	30.00	31-62
1994 Memories Are Made of This 529982	Yr.Iss.	1994	30.00	34-45
1995 Follow Your Heart 528080	Yr.Iss.	1995	30.00	36-55
1996 Hallelujah Hoedown 163864	Yr.Iss.	1996	32.50	33-58
1996 May The Sun Always Shine On You 184217	Yr.Iss.	1996	37.50	58-68
1997 We're So Hoppy You're Here 261351	Yr.Iss.	1997	32.50	28-35
1998 Love Is Kind E1379R	Yr.Iss.	1998	8.00	8-17
1999 You Oughta Be in Pictures 490327	Yr.Iss.	1999	32.50	26-38
1999 You Color Our World With Loving, Caring and Sharing 644463 (September Event)	Retrd.	1999	19.00	19
1999 He Leadeth Me E1377R	Yr.Iss.	1999	19.00	19
2000 Scoopin' Up Some Love 635049	Retrd.	2000	35.00	35
2000 Mr. Fujioka 781851	Retrd.	2000	Gift	N/A
2000 To God Be the Glory E-2823R	Retrd.	2000	45.00	45-69
2001 A Penny A Kiss, a Penny A Hug (March Event) 101234	Retrd.	2002	35.01	36
2001 Let's Have A Ball Together (July Event) 889849	Retrd.	2001	35.00	35
2001 God Understands (Sept. Event) E1379BR	Retrd.	2001	19.00	19
2001 The Peace That Passes Understanding (Nov. Event) 730173	10,000		125.00	125
2002 A Penny Saved Is A Penny Earned (March Event) 730173	10,000		35.01	36
2002 Hugs Can Tame The Wildest Hearts (July Event) 104282	8,500		35.00	35
2002 Koala Bear-Tender Tails (July Event) 106043	5,000		6.99	7
2002 Carry A Song in your Heart (Sept. Event) 104281	8,500		35.00	35
2002 A Horse Of A Different Color -Tender Tails (Sept. Event) 103778	5,000		6.99	7
2002 The True Spirit of Christmas Guides the Way (Nov. Event) 104784	5,000		125.00	125
2002 Merry Kiss-Mass-Tender Tails (July Event) 103770	5,000		9.99	10
Family - S. Butcher				
2002 The Sweetest Baby Boy - Blonde 101500	Open		17.50	18
2002 The Sweetest Baby Girl - Blonde 101501	Open		17.50	18
2002 I'm A Big Sister - Blonde 101502	Open		20.00	20
2002 I'm A Big Brother - Blonde 101503	Open		20.00	20
2002 Precious Grandma - Blonde 101504	Open		25.00	25
2002 Precious Grandpa - Blonde 101505	Open		25.00	25
2002 Your Love Is Just So Comforting 104268	Open		35.00	35
2002 I'm So Lucky To Have You As A Daughter 104269	Open		35.00	35
Family Christmas Scene - S. Butcher				
1985 May You Have the Sweetest Christmas 15776	Suspd.		17.00	27-60
1985 The Story of God's Love 15784	Suspd.		22.50	33-60
1985 Tell Me a Story 15792	Suspd.		10.00	27-35
1985 God Gave His Best 15806	Suspd.		13.00	23-50
1985 Silent Night 15814	Suspd.		37.50	63-87
1986 Sharing Our Christmas Together 102490	Suspd.		40.00	50-90
1989 Have A Beary Merry Christmas 522856	Suspd.		15.00	18-45
1990 Christmas Fireplace 524883	Suspd.		37.50	37-62
1999 Wishing You An Old Fashioned Christmas 634778	Yr.Iss.	1999	175.00	140-170
Four Seasons - S. Butcher				
1985 The Voice of Spring 12068	Yr.Iss.	1985	30.00	150-400
1985 Summer's Joy 12076	Yr.Iss.	1985	30.00	78-95
1986 Autumn's Praise 12084	Yr.Iss.	1986	30.00	44-75
1986 Winter's Song 12092	Yr.Iss.	1986	30.00	92-108
1986 Set	Yr.Iss.	1986	120.00	250-550
1999 He Graces The Earth With Abundance (Fall) 129119	Open		50.00	50
1999 He Covers The Earth With His Glory (Winter) 129135	Open		50.00	50
1999 The Beauty Of God Blooms Forever (Spring) 129143	Open		50.00	50
1999 Beside The Still Waters (Summer) 129127	Open		50.00	50
Fun Club - S. Butcher				
1999 You Are My Mane Inspiration B-0014	Yr.Iss.	1999	Gift	18
1999 Chester BC-992	Yr.Iss.	1999	6.99	7
1999 Ewe Are So Special to Me (Buttercup) BC-993	Yr.Iss.	1999	15.00	15
2000 Hold On To The Moment FC003	Yr.Iss.	2000	6.99	7
2000 Reed The Centipede FC001	Yr.Iss.	2000	6.99	7
2000 Don't Fret, We'll Get You There Yet (Charter) F0012	Yr.Iss.	2000	16.49	N/A
2000 Don't Fret, We'll Get You There Yet F0002	Yr.Iss.	2000	Gift	N/A
2000 Ronnie The Rhino FC002	Yr.Iss.	2000	25.00	25
2001 True Friendship Is A Precious Treasure (Charter) F0103	Yr.Iss.	2001	Gift	N/A
2001 True Friendship Is A Precious Treasure F0003	Yr.Iss.	2001	Gift	N/A
2001 Chris The Crocodile FC012	Yr.Iss.	2001	6.99	7
2001 I'm Always Happy When You're A-Long FC011	Yr.Iss.	2001	18.50	19
2001 Monty The Mandrill FC013	Yr.Iss.	2001	6.99	7
2002 Seal-ed With A Kiss F0004	Yr.Iss.		Gift	N/A
2002 You Are The Coolest Friend FC021	Yr.Iss.		30.00	30
2002 You're So Bear-y Cool FC022	Yr.Iss.		20.00	20
Girl Sports - S. Butcher				
2002 I Trust In the Lord For My Strength (Karate) 104798	Open		25.00	25
2002 I'd Jump Through Hoops For You (Basketball) 104799	Open		25.00	25
2002 You're A Perfect 10 (Gymnast) 104800	Open		25.00	25
2002 We're A Perfect Match (Tennis) 104801	Open		25.00	25

Collectors' Information Bureau

*Quotes have been rounded up to nearest dollar

YEAR ISSUE	EDITION LIMIT	YEAR RETD.	ISSUE PRICE	*QUOTE U.S.$
2002 Your Spirit Is An Inspiration (Cheerleader) 104802	Open		25.00	25
2002 Serving Up Fun (Volleyball) 104803	Open		25.00	25

Growing In Grace - S. Butcher

YEAR ISSUE	EDITION LIMIT	YEAR RETD.	ISSUE PRICE	*QUOTE U.S.$
1995 Infant Angel With Newspaper 136204	Open		22.50	21-28
2001 It's A Girl Baby Angel 136204B	Open		22.50	23
1995 Age 1 Baby With Cake 136190	Open		25.00	22-25
2001 Age 1 Baby With Cake 136190B	Open		25.00	25
1995 Age 2 Girl With Blocks 136212	Open		25.00	22-25
2001 Age 2 Girl With Blocks 136212B	Open		25.00	25
1995 Age 3 Girl With Flowers 136220	Open		25.00	22-28
2001 Age 3 Girl With Flowers 136220B	Open		25.00	25
1995 Age 4 Girl With Doll 136239	Open		27.50	24-28
2001 Age 4 Girl With Doll 136239B	Open		30.00	30
1995 Age 5 Girl With Lunch Box 136247	Open		27.50	28-33
2001 Age 5 Girl With Lunch Box 136247B	Open		30.00	30
1995 Age 6 Girl On Bicycle 136255	Open		30.00	26-30
2002 Age 6 Girl On Bicycle 136255B	Open		30.00	30
1996 Age 7 Girl Dressed As Nurse 163740	Open		32.50	28-33
2002 Age 7 Girl Dressed As Nurse 163740B	Open		32.50	33
1996 Age 8 Girl Shooting Marbles 163759	Open		32.50	28-33
2002 Age 8 Girl Shooting Marbles 163759B	Open		32.50	33
1996 Age 9 Girl With Charm Bracelet 183865	Open		30.00	26-30
2002 Age 9 Girl With Charm Bracelet 183865B	Open		30.00	33
1996 Age 10 Girl Bowling 183873	Open		37.50	38-40
2002 Age 10 Girl Bowling 183873B	Open		37.50	38
1997 Age 11 Girl With Ice Cream Cone 260924	Open		37.50	33-38
2002 Age 11 Girl With Ice Cream Cone 260924B	Open		37.50	38
1997 Age 12 Girl/Puppy Holding Clock 260932	Open		37.50	33-38
2002 Age 12 Girl/Puppy Holding Clock 260932B	Open		37.50	38
1997 Age 13 Girl/Turtle Race 272647	Open		40.00	34-40
2002 Age 13 Girl/Turtle Race 272647B	Open		40.00	40
1997 Age 14 Girl With Diary 272655	Open		35.00	30-35
2002 Age 14 Girl With Diary 272655B	Open		35.00	35
1997 Age 15 Girl With List 272663	Open		40.00	34-40
2002 Age 15 Girl With List 272663B	Open		40.00	40
1995 Age 16 Sweet Sixteen Girl Holding Sixteen Roses 136263	Open		45.00	38-52
2002 Age 16 Sweet Sixteen Girl Holding Sixteen Roses 136263B	Open		45.00	45

Heavenly Daze - S. Butcher

YEAR ISSUE	EDITION LIMIT	YEAR RETD.	ISSUE PRICE	*QUOTE U.S.$
2001 Starsmith, set/3 879568	Open		100.00	100
2002 Halo Maker, set/3 879576	Open		85.00	85
2002 Golden Town Seamstress, set/6 879606	Open		85.00	85

Inspirational - S. Butcher

YEAR ISSUE	EDITION LIMIT	YEAR RETD.	ISSUE PRICE	*QUOTE U.S.$
2001 Blessed With A Loving Godmother 795348	Open		40.00	40
2001 A Godchild Close To My Heart (baby) 804096	Open		25.00	25
2001 A Godchild Close To My Heart (girl) 811807	Open		35.00	35
2001 A Godchild Close To My Heart (boy) 811815	Open		35.00	35
2002 It's What Inside That Counts 101497	Open		35.00	35

Japanese Figurines Exclusives - S. Butcher

YEAR ISSUE	EDITION LIMIT	YEAR RETD.	ISSUE PRICE	*QUOTE U.S.$
2000 On Our Way To A Special Day - Kindergarten Boy 481602	Open		17.50	18
2000 On Our Way To A Special Day - Kindergarten Girl 481610	Open		17.50	18
2000 Shiny New And Ready For School - Elem. Girl 481629	Open		20.00	20
2000 Shiny New And Ready For School - Elem. Boy 481637	Open		20.00	20
2000 Growing In Wisdom - Jr. High Boy 481645	Open		22.50	23
2000 Growing In Wisdom - Jr. High Girl 481653	Open		22.50	23
2000 All Girls Are Beautiful - set/4 Girls Festival 481661	Open		55.00	55
2000 Make Me Strong - set/4 Boys Festival 481688	Open		55.00	55-60

YEAR ISSUE	EDITION LIMIT	YEAR RETD.	ISSUE PRICE	*QUOTE U.S.$
2000 Everybody Has A Part - set/3 Summer Festival 731625	Open		50.00	50
2000 Good Fortune 731633	Open		17.50	18
2000 Girl Festival Additions - set/3 791113	Open		60.00	60
2000 Boy & Girl Dance Of The Lion 791121	Open		60.00	60
2001 Different Beats Can Still Come Together (set/3) 791148	Open		55.00	55
2000 Hisssterricaly Sweet 821969	Open		16.00	16

Jesus Loves Me - S. Butcher

YEAR ISSUE	EDITION LIMIT	YEAR RETD.	ISSUE PRICE	*QUOTE U.S.$
2001 Jesus Loves Me - Latino Boy 899526	Open		20.00	20
2001 Jesus Loves Me - Latino Girl 899542	Open		20.00	20
2001 Jesus Loves Me - African American Boy 899771	Open		20.00	20
2001 Jesus Loves Me - African American Boy 899879	Open		20.00	20
2001 Jesus Loves Me - Asian Boy 900575	Open		20.00	20
2001 Jesus Loves Me -Asian Boy 901555	Open		20.00	20

Latino Series - S. Butcher

YEAR ISSUE	EDITION LIMIT	YEAR RETD.	ISSUE PRICE	*QUOTE U.S.$
2001 Mi Pequeño Amor (My Little Sweetheart) 928461	Open		30.00	30
2001 Preparado Con Amor (Prepared With Love) 928445	Open		35.00	35
2001 Seguro En Los Brazos de Padrinos (Safe In The Arms Of Godparents) 928453	Open		50.00	50
2001 Un Dia Muy Especial (A Very Special Day) 902098	Open		30.00	30
2001 Una Bendición del Cielo (A Blessing From Heaven) 928488	Open		37.50	38
2001 Una Madre Es el Corazón de la Familia (A Mother Is The Heart Of The Family) 902101	Open		30.00	30

Little Angel Series - S. Butcher

YEAR ISSUE	EDITION LIMIT	YEAR RETD.	ISSUE PRICE	*QUOTE U.S.$
2001 Daddy's Little Angel - Brunette Girl 887935	Open		25.00	25
2001 Daddy's Little Angel - Blonde Girl 887951	Open		25.00	25
2001 Grandma's Little Angel - Blonde Girl 887900	Open		25.00	25
2001 Grandma's Little Angel - Brunette Girl 887927	Open		25.00	25
2001 Grandma's Little Angel - Blonde Boy 887978	Open		25.00	25
2001 Grandma's Little Angel - Brunette Boy 887986	Open		25.00	25
2001 Mommy's Little Angel - Blonde Boy 887994	Open		25.00	25
2001 Mommy's Little Angel - Brunette Boy 888001	Open		25.00	25

Little Moments - S. Butcher

YEAR ISSUE	EDITION LIMIT	YEAR RETD.	ISSUE PRICE	*QUOTE U.S.$
2002 Nurses Are Blessed With Patients 101554	Open		20.00	20
1996 Where Would I Be Without You 139491	Open		20.00	20
1996 All Things Grow With Love 139505	Open		20.00	20
1996 You're The Berry Best 139513	Open		20.00	20
1996 You Make The World A Sweeter Place 139521	Open		20.00	20
1996 You're Forever In My Heart 139548	Open		20.00	20-25
1996 Birthday Wishes With Hugs & Kisses 139556	Open		20.00	20
1996 You Make My Spirit Soar 139564	Open		20.00	20
2000 Winter Wishes Warm The Heart 184241	Open		8.50	9
2000 Winter Wishes Warm The Heart (CCR 2000 Only) 184241	Open		8.50	9
1997 Bless Your Little Tutu 261173	Open		20.00	20
1997 January 261203	Open		20.00	20
1997 February 261246	Open		20.00	20
1997 April 261300	Open		20.00	20
1997 March 261270	Open		20.00	20
1997 May 261211	Open		20.00	20
1997 June 261254	Open		20.00	20
1997 July 261289	Open		20.00	20
1997 August 261319	Open		20.00	20
1997 September 261238	Open		20.00	20
1997 October 261262	Open		20.00	20
1997 November 261297	Open		20.00	20
1997 December 261327	Open		20.00	20

YEAR ISSUE	EDITION LIMIT	YEAR RETD.	ISSUE PRICE	*QUOTE U.S.$
1997 You Will Always Be A Winner To Me (Boy) 272612	Open		20.00	20
1997 It's Ruff To Always Be Cheery 272639	Open		20.00	20
1997 You Will Always Be A Winner To Me (Girl) 283460	Open		20.00	20
1997 Holiday Wishes Sweetie Pie 312444	Open		20.00	20
1997 You're Just Perfect In My Book 320560	Open		25.00	20-22
1997 Loving Is Caring 320579	Open		20.00	20
1997 Loving Is Caring 320595	Open		20.00	18-20
1997 You Set My Heart Ablaze 320625	Open		20.00	20
1997 Just The Facts...You're Terrific 320668	Open		20.00	20
1997 You Have Such A Special Way Of Caring Each And Every Day 320706	Open		25.00	25
1997 What Would I Do Without You? 320714	Open		25.00	25
1998 Thank You For The Time We Share (Avon Exclusive) 384836	Retrd.	1998	19.99	25
1999 World's Greatest Student (Boy) 491586	Open		20.00	20
1999 World's Greatest Student (Girl) 491616	Open		25.00	25
1999 World's Sweetest Girl 491594	Open		25.00	25
1999 World's Best Helper (Girl) 491608	Open		25.00	25
1999 You're No. 1 (Girl) 491624	Open		25.00	25
1999 You're No. 1 (Boy) 491640	Open		25.00	25
2000 Life's Filled With Little Surprises 524034	Open		22.50	23
2001 I Pray The Lord My Soul To Keep, set/2 Boy (National Children's Day) 553867	Open		22.50	23
2001 I Pray The Lord My Soul To Keep, set/2 Girl (National Children's Day) 553875	Open		22.50	23
2001 Sharing The Season With You (Hallmark Gold Crown Exclusive) 702862	Open		22.50	23
2000 Sharing Sweet Moments Together 731579	Open		20.00	20-48
2001 A Mother's Job Is Never Done (Avon Exclusive) 829269	Open		19.99	20
2001 You Decorate My Life (GCC Exclusive) 881147	Open		20.00	20
2001 You Decorate My Life (Winter Catalog) 881139	Open		35.00	35
2001 Hug Me Before I Melt (Avon) 883875	Open		19.99	20

Little Moments Bible Stories - S. Butcher

1999 Jonah And The Whale 488283	Open		25.00	25
1999 Daniel And The Lion's Den 488291	Open		25.00	25
1999 Joseph's Special Coat 488305	Open		25.00	25
1999 Baby Moses 649953	Open		25.00	25
2001 Ruth And Naomi 649961	Open		25.00	25
1999 The Good Samaritan 649988	Open		25.00	25
1999 The Great Pearl 649996	Open		20.00	20
2001 The Sower And The Seed 650005	Open		20.00	20
2001 David And Goliath 650064	Open		20.00	20

Little Moments Build A Family - S. Butcher

2001 Blonde Dad 848743	Open		20.00	20
2001 Blonde Infant Daughter 848808	Open		12.50	13
2001 Blonde Infant Son 848816	Open		12.50	13
2001 Blonde Mom 848735	Open		20.00	20
2001 Blonde Teen Daughter 848751	Open		17.50	18
2001 Blonde Teen Son 848778	Open		17.50	18
2001 Blonde Toddler Daughter 848786	Open		15.00	15
2001 Blonde Toddler Son 848794	Open		15.00	15
2001 Brunette Dad 880841	Open		20.00	20
2001 Brunette Infant Daughter 880906	Open		12.50	13
2001 Brunette Infant Son 880914	Open		12.50	13
2001 Brunette Mom 880833	Open		20.00	20
2001 Brunette Teen Daughter 880868	Open		17.50	18
2001 Brunette Teen Son 880876	Open		17.50	18
2001 Brunette Toddler Daughter 880884	Open		15.00	15
2001 Brunette Toddler Son 880892	Open		15.00	15
2001 Family Cat 848832	Open		10.00	10
2001 Family Dog 848824	Open		10.00	10

Little Moments Days of the Week - S. Butcher

2000 The Child That's Born On The Sabbath Day...692077	Open		20.00	20

YEAR ISSUE	EDITION LIMIT	YEAR RETD.	ISSUE PRICE	*QUOTE U.S.$
2000 Monday's Child Is Fair Of Face 692085	Open		20.00	20
2000 Tueday's Child Is Full Of Grace 692093	Open		20.00	20
2000 Wednesday's Child Is Full Of Woe 692107	Open		20.00	20
2000 Thursday's Child Has Far To Go 692115	Open		20.00	20
2000 Friday's Child Is Loving And Giving 692123	Open		20.00	20
2000 Saturday's Child Works Hard For A Living 692131	Open		20.00	20

Little Moments Highway To Happiness - S. Butcher

1999 Cross Walk 649511	Open		20.00	20
1999 Go 4 It 649438	Open		20.00	20
1999 God's Children At Play 649481	Open		20.00	20
1999 Highway To Happiness 649457	Open		20.00	20
1999 I'll Never Stop Loving You 649465	Open		20.00	20
1999 There's No Wrong Way With You 649473	Open		20.00	20

Little Moments Internationals - S. Butcher

1998 You Are A Dutch-ess To Me 456373	Open		20.00	20
1998 Life Is A Fiesta 456381	Open		20.00	20
1998 Don't Rome Too Far From Home 456403	Open		20.00	20
1998 You Can't Beat The Red, White And Blue 456411	Open		20.00	20
1998 Love's Russian Into My Heart 456446	Open		20.00	20
1998 Hola, Amigo 456454	Open		20.00	20
1998 Afri-can Be There For You, Then I Will Be 456462	Open		20.00	20
1998 I'd Travel The Highlands To Be With You 456470	Open		20.00	20
1998 Sure Would Love To Squeeze You 456896	Open		20.00	20
1998 You Are My Amour 456918	Open		20.00	20
1998 Our Friendship Is Always In Bloom 456926	Open		20.00	20
1998 My Love Will Stand Guard Over You 456934	Open		20.00	20

Military - S. Butcher

1999 Army Boy-Caucasian "I'm Proud To Be An American" 588105	Open		32.50	33
1999 Marine Boy-Caucasian "I'm Proud To Be An American" 588113	Open		32.50	33
1999 Navy Boy-Caucasian "I'm Proud To Be An American" 588121	Open		32.50	33
1999 Coast Guard Boy-Caucasian "I'm Proud To Be An American" 588148	Open		32.50	33
1999 Air Force Boy-Caucasian "I'm Proud To Be An American" 588156	Open		32.50	33
1999 Army Girl-Caucasian "I'm Proud To Be An American" 729876	Open		32.50	33
1999 Marine Girl-Caucasian "I'm Proud To Be An American" 729884	Open		32.50	33
1999 Navy Girl-Caucasian "I'm Proud To Be An American" 729892	Open		32.50	33
1999 Coast Guard Girl-Caucasian "I'm Proud To Be An American" 729906	Open		32.50	33
1999 Air Force Girl-Caucasian "I'm Proud To Be An American" 729914	Open		32.50	33
1999 Army Boy-African American "I'm Proud To Be An American" 729973	Open		32.50	33
1999 Marine Boy-African American "I'm Proud To Be An American" 730009	Open		32.50	33
1999 Navy Boy-African American "I'm Proud To Be An American" 730017	Open		32.50	33
1999 Coast Guard Boy-African American "I'm Proud To Be An American" 730025	Open		32.50	33
1999 Air Force Boy-African American "I'm Proud To Be An American" 730033	Open		32.50	33
1999 Army Girl-African American "I'm Proud To Be An American" 729922	Open		32.50	33
1999 Marine Girl-African American "I'm Proud To Be An American" 729930	Open		32.50	33
1999 Navy Girl-African American "I'm Proud To Be An American" 729949	Open		32.50	33
1999 Coast Guard Girl-African American "I'm Proud To Be An American" 729957	Open		32.50	33

*Quotes have been rounded up to nearest dollar

YEAR ISSUE	EDITION LIMIT	YEAR RETD.	ISSUE PRICE	*QUOTE U.S.$
1999 Air Force Girl-African American "I'm Proud To Be An American" 729965	Open		32.50	33

Motherhood Elongated - S. Butcher

YEAR ISSUE	EDITION LIMIT	YEAR RETD.	ISSUE PRICE	*QUOTE U.S.$
1999 A Love Like No Other 681075	Open		45.00	45
2001 Cherish Each Step 795224	Open		50.00	50
2002 Cherishing Each Special Moment 101233	Open		50.00	50

Musical Figurines - S. Butcher

YEAR ISSUE	EDITION LIMIT	YEAR RETD.	ISSUE PRICE	*QUOTE U.S.$
1983 Sharing Our Season Together E-0519	Retrd.	1986	70.00	112-138
1983 Wee Three Kings E-0520	Suspd.		60.00	108-138
1983 Let Heaven And Nature Sing E-2346	Suspd.		55.00	100-170
1982 O Come All Ye Faithful E-2352	Suspd.		50.00	124-152
1982 I'll Play My Drum For Him E-2355	Suspd.		45.00	136-205
1980 Christmas Is A Time To Share E-2806	Retrd.	1984	35.00	90-180
1980 Crown Him Lord Of All E-2807	Suspd.		35.00	80-130
1980 Unto Us A Child Is Born E-2808	Suspd.		35.00	84-140
1980 Jesus Is Born E-2809	Suspd.		35.00	96-170
1980 Come Let Us Adore Him E-2810	Suspd.		45.00	83-155
1980 Peace On Earth E-4726	Suspd.		45.00	100-137
1981 The Hand That Rocks The Future E-5204	Retrd.	2001	30.00	54-100
1981 My Guardian Angel E-5205	Suspd.		22.50	88-118
1981 My Guardian Angel E-5206	Suspd.		22.50	64-110
1984 Wishing You A Merry Christmas E-5394	Suspd.		55.00	88-120
1981 Silent Knight E-5642	Suspd.		45.00	268-475
1981 Rejoice O Earth E-5645	Retrd.	1988	35.00	64-130
1982 The Lord Bless You And Keep You E-7180	Retrd.	2001	55.00	85-135
1982 Mother Sew Dear E-7182	Retrd.	2001	35.00	65-100
1982 The Purr-fect Grandma E-7184	Suspd.		35.00	53-98
1982 Love Is Sharing E-7185	Retrd.	1985	40.00	122-175
1982 Let the Whole World Know E-7186	Suspd.		60.00	96-165
1985 Lord Keep My Life In Tune (B) (2/set) 12165	Suspd.		50.00	94-266
1985 We Saw A Star 12408	Suspd.		50.00	75-104
1987 Lord Keep My Life In Tune (G) (2/set) 12580	Suspd.		50.00	218-285
1985 God Sent You Just In Time 15504	Retrd.	1989	60.00	81-138
1986 Heaven Bless You 100285	Suspd.		45.00	57-75
1986 Our 1st Christmas Together 101702	Retrd.	1992	50.00	70-100
1986 Let's Keep In Touch 102520	Retrd.	1999	85.00	72-96
1988 Peace On Earth 109746	Suspd.		120.00	116-130
1987 I'm Sending You A White Christmas 112402	Retrd.	1993	55.00	82-150
1988 You Have Touched So Many Hearts 112577	Suspd.		50.00	52-65
1991 Lord Keep My Life In Balance 520691	Suspd.		60.00	55-88
1989 The Light Of The World Is Jesus 521507	Retrd.	1999	65.00	59-74
1992 Do Not Open Till Christmas 522244	Suspd.		75.00	70-85
1992 This Day Has Been Made In Heaven 523682	Open		60.00	55-65
1993 Wishing You Were Here 526916	Suspd.		100.00	83-100

Rejoice in the Lord - S. Butcher

YEAR ISSUE	EDITION LIMIT	YEAR RETD.	ISSUE PRICE	*QUOTE U.S.$
1985 There's a Song In My Heart 12173	Suspd.		11.00	34-58
1985 Happiness is the Lord 12378	Suspd.		15.00	30-54
1985 Lord Give Me a Song 12386	Suspd.		15.00	34-54
1985 He is My Song 12394	Suspd.		17.50	33-50

Salvation Army - S. Butcher

YEAR ISSUE	EDITION LIMIT	YEAR RETD.	ISSUE PRICE	*QUOTE U.S.$
2000 He Is My Salvation 135984	Open		45.00	45

Sammy's Circus - S. Butcher

YEAR ISSUE	EDITION LIMIT	YEAR RETD.	ISSUE PRICE	*QUOTE U.S.$
1994 Markie 528099	Suspd.		18.50	15-19
1994 Dusty 529176	Suspd.		22.50	19-24
1994 Katie 529184	Suspd.		17.00	17-22
1994 Tippy 529192	Suspd.		12.00	12-15
1994 Collin 529214	Suspd.		20.00	20-25
1994 Sammy 529222	Yr.Iss.	1994	20.00	20-45
1994 Circus Tent 528196 (Nite-Lite)	Suspd.		90.00	45-90
1995 Jordan 529168	Suspd.		20.00	20-26
1996 Jennifer 163708	Suspd.		20.00	20-30

Spring Catalog - S. Butcher

YEAR ISSUE	EDITION LIMIT	YEAR RETD.	ISSUE PRICE	*QUOTE U.S.$
1993 Happiness Is At Our Fingertips 529931	Yr.Iss.	1993	35.00	42-90
1994 So Glad I Picked You As A Friend 524379	Yr.Iss.	1994	40.00	45-53
1995 Sending My Love Your Way 528609	Yr.Iss.	1995	40.00	40-62

YEAR ISSUE	EDITION LIMIT	YEAR RETD.	ISSUE PRICE	*QUOTE U.S.$
1996 Have I Toad You Lately I Love You 521329	Yr.Iss.	1996	30.00	30-45
1997 Happiness To The Core 261378	Yr.Iss.	1997	37.50	38-50
1998 Mom, You Always Make Our House A Home 325465	Yr.Iss.	1998	37.50	38

Sugartown - S. Butcher

YEAR ISSUE	EDITION LIMIT	YEAR RETD.	ISSUE PRICE	*QUOTE U.S.$
1992 Chapel Night Light 529621	Retrd.	1994	85.00	89-160
1992 Christmas Tree 528684	Retrd.	1994	15.00	25-35
1992 Grandfather 529516	Retrd.	1994	15.00	25-36
1992 Nativity 529508	Retrd.	1994	20.00	41-55
1992 Philip 529494	Retrd.	1994	17.00	19-27
1992 Aunt Ruth & Aunt Dorothy 529486	Retrd.	1994	20.00	20-43
1992 Sam Butcher 529567 (1st sign)	Yr.Iss.	1992	22.50	100-169
1993 7 pc. Sam's House Collector's Set 531774	Retrd.	1997	189.00	189-254
1993 Sam's House Night Light 529605	Retrd.	1997	80.00	71-85
1993 Fence 529796	Retrd.	1997	10.00	10-18
1993 Sammy 528668	Retrd.	1997	17.00	16-28
1993 Katy Lynne 529524	Retrd.	1997	20.00	20-42
1993 Sam Butcher 529842 (2nd sign)	Yr.Iss.	1993	22.50	35-70
1993 Dusty 529435	Retrd.	1997	17.00	17-34
1993 Sam's Car 529443	Retrd.	1997	22.50	24-35
1994 Dr. Sam Sugar 529850	Retrd.	1997	17.00	17-34
1994 Doctor's Office Night Light 529869	Retrd.	1997	80.00	69-85
1994 Sam's House 530468	Yr.Iss.	1994	17.50	18-75
1994 Jan 529826	Retrd.	1997	17.00	17-20
1994 Sugar & Her Dog House 533165	Retrd.	1997	20.00	20-32
1994 Stork With Baby Sam 529788	Yr.Iss.	1994	22.50	18-48
1994 Free Christmas Puppies 528064	Retrd.	1997	18.50	11-23
1994 7 pc. Doctor's Office Collectors Set 529281	Yr.Iss.	1994	189.00	167-221
1994 Leon & Evelyn Mae 529818	Retrd.	1997	20.00	20-30
1995 Sam the Conductor 150169	Retrd.	1995	20.00	20-45
1995 Train Station Night Light 150150	Retrd.	1997	50.00	58-125
1995 Railroad Crossing Sign 150177	Retrd.	1997	12.00	12-20
1995 Tammy and Debbie 531812	Retrd.	1997	22.50	20-25
1995 Donny 531871	Retrd.	1997	22.50	18-25
1995 Luggage Cart With Kitten And Tag 150185	Retrd.	1997	13.00	12-23
1995 6 pc. Train Station Collector Set 750193	Yr.Iss.	1995	190.00	156-209
1996 Sugar Town Skating Sign 184020	Yr.Iss.	1996	15.00	12-26
1996 Skating Pond 184047	Retrd.	1997	40.00	34-45
1996 Mazie 184055	Retrd.	1997	18.50	19-32
1996 Cocoa 184063	Retrd.	1997	7.50	8-15
1996 Leroy 184071	Retrd.	1997	18.50	19-25
1996 Hank and Sharon 184098	Retrd.	1997	25.00	19-33
1996 Lighted Warming Hut 192341	Retrd.	1997	60.00	60
1997 Lighted Schoolhouse 272795	Retrd.	1997	80.00	80-100
1997 Chuck 272809	Retrd.	1997	22.50	20-30
1997 Aunt Cleo 272817	Retrd.	1997	18.50	17-21
1997 Aunt Bulah & Uncle Sam 272825	Retrd.	1997	22.50	20-23
1997 Heather 272833	Retrd.	1997	20.00	18-24
1997 Merry-Go-Round 272841	Retrd.	1997	20.00	18-20
1997 Schoolhouse Collector's Set-6-pc. 272876	Retrd.	1997	183.50	153-184
1997 Sugar Town Accessories 212725	Retrd.	1997	20.00	20
1997 Sugar Town Train Cargo Car 273007	Yr.Iss.	1997	27.50	28
1998 Post Office Collector's Set 456217	Yr.Iss.	1998	250.00	199-250

Sugartown Enhancements - S. Butcher

YEAR ISSUE	EDITION LIMIT	YEAR RETD.	ISSUE PRICE	*QUOTE U.S.$
1995 Bus Stop 150207	Retrd.	1997	8.50	8-13
1995 Fire Hydrant 150215	Retrd.	1997	5.00	5-9
1995 Bird Bath 150223	Retrd.	1997	8.50	8-13
1995 Sugartown Enhancement Pack, set/5 152269	Retrd.	1997	45.00	38-79
1996 Tree Night Light 184039	Retrd.	1997	45.00	45-75
1996 Flag Pole w/Kitten 184136	Retrd.	1997	15.00	18-20
1996 Wooden Barrel Hot Cocoa Stand 184144	Retrd.	1997	15.00	15
1997 Bonfire with Bunnies 184152	Retrd.	1997	10.00	9-17
1997 Bike Rack 272906	Retrd.	1997	15.00	15
1997 Garbage Can 272914	Retrd.	1997	20.00	18-20
1997 Enhancements 3-pc. 273015	Retrd.	1997	43.50	37-44
1995 Dog And Kitten On Park Bench 529540	Retrd.	1997	13.00	13-21
1994 Lamp Post 529559	Retrd.	1997	8.00	8-13
1994 Bunnies Caroling 531804	Retrd.	1997	10.00	10
1994 Mailbox 531847	Retrd.	1997	8.00	8-12
1995 Street Sign 532185	Retrd.	1997	5.00	10-18

FIGURINES

YEAR ISSUE	EDITION LIMIT	YEAR RETRD.	ISSUE PRICE	*QUOTE U.S.$
1994 Village Town Hall Clock 532908	Retrd.	1997	80.00	85
1994 Curved Sidewalk 533149	Retrd.	1997	10.00	10-15
1994 Straight Sidewalk 533157	Retrd.	1997	10.00	10-15
1994 Single Tree 533173	Retrd.	1997	10.00	10-23
1994 Double Tree 533181	Retrd.	1997	10.00	10-23
1994 Cobble Stone Bridge 533203	Retrd.	1997	17.00	17-25

Tender Tails Internet-Get With The Program - S. Butcher

2002 Crash the Bug 958549	Open		6.99	7
2002 Holden the Mouse 958514	Open		6.99	7
2002 Laptop the Dog 958530	Open		6.99	7
2002 Sam the Ram 958506	Open		6.99	7
2002 Sky Z Limit the Bear 958522	Open		6.99	7
2002 Surf The Spider 958492	Open		6.99	7

To Have And To Hold - S. Butcher

1996 Love Vows To Always Bloom 1st Anniversary Couple With Flowers 129097	Open		70.00	70-75
1996 A Year Of Blessings-1st Anniversary Couple With Cake 163783	Open		70.00	70-75
1996 Each Hour Is Precious With You-5th Anniversary Couple With Clock 163791	Open		70.00	70-75
1996 Ten Years Heart To Heart-10th Anniversary Couple With Pillow 163805	Open		70.00	70-75
1996 A Silver Celebration To Share-25th Anniversary Couple With Silver Platter 163813	Open		70.00	70-75
1996 Sharing The Gift of 40 Precious Years-40th Anniversary Couple With Gift Box 163821	Open		70.00	70-75
1996 Precious Moments To Remember-50th Anniversary Couple With Photo Album 163848	Open		70.00	70-75

Trusting Is Bee-living - S. Butcher

2002 I Am A Bee-liever 928534	Open		30.00	30
2002 Precious Friends 928542	Open		40.00	40
2002 The Lord Is Always Bee-side Us 928550	Open		37.50	38

Two By Two - S. Butcher

1993 Noah, Noah's Wife, & Noah's Ark (lighted) 530042	Open		125.00	125-150
1993 Sheep (mini double fig.) 530077	Open		10.00	13-25
1993 Pigs (mini double fig.) 530085	Open		12.00	12-18
1993 Giraffes (mini double fig.) 530115	Open		16.00	16-22
1993 Bunnies (mini double fig.) 530123	Open		9.00	9-15
1993 Elephants (mini double fig.) 530131	Open		18.00	18-25
1993 Eight Piece Collector's Set 530948	Open		190.00	190
1994 Llamas 531375	Open		15.00	15-20
1995 Congratulations You Earned Your Stripes 127809	Open		15.00	15
1996 I'd Goat Anywhere With You 163694	Open		10.00	10-15

You Are Always There For Me - S. Butcher

1996 Mother Kissing Daughter's Owie 163600	Open		50.00	55-57
1996 Father Helping Son Bat 163627	Open		50.00	50
1996 Sister Consoling Sister 163635	Open		50.00	50
1997 Mother Kissing Son's Owie 163619	Open		50.00	55
1997 Father Bandaging Daughter's Doll 163597	Open		50.00	50-53

Prizm, Inc./Pipka

Pipka's Memories of Christmas Collector's Club - Pipka

1998 1998/99 Club Kit 13707	3,950	1999	40.00	N/A
1998 Knock, Knock Santa Figurine 13923	3,300	1999	95.00	95-335
1998 Knock, Knock Santa Ornament 11418	3,950	1999	Gift	20-150
1999 Knock, Knock Santa Door 13702	1,651	1999	75.00	75-150
1999 Knock, Knock Small Door 13703	3,950	1999	Gift	25-75
2000 2000 Club Kit 13721	Yr.lss.	2000	40.00	40-50
2000 Christmas Ark 13941	3,300	2000	95.00	95-175
2000 Christmas Ark Ornament 11433	Yr.lss.	2000	Gift	N/A
2000 Ark Pin 13733	Closed	2001	Gift	N/A
2000 Two by Two Santa 11330	Yr.lss.	2000	Gift	N/A
2001 2001 Club Kit 13739	Yr.lss.	2001	40.00	40-45
2001 Collector Santa 13942	Yr.lss.	2001	105.00	105

YEAR ISSUE	EDITION LIMIT	YEAR RETRD.	ISSUE PRICE	*QUOTE U.S.$
2001 St. Nicholas 11338	Yr.lss.	2001	Gift	N/A
2001 Collector's Santa Ornament 11439	Yr.lss.	2001	Gift	N/A
2002 Santa's List 13953	Yr.lss.		95.00	95
2002 Tiny & Clyde 40019	Yr.lss.		22.50	23
2002 Decorative Keepsake Box	Yr.lss.		Gift	N/A
2002 Santa's Mailbag 6" Figurine 11345	Yr.lss.		Gift	N/A
2002 Santa's List Ornament 11446	Yr.lss.		Gift	N/A

Display Trees - Pipka

2000 Oh Christmas Tree 13731	Open		30.00	30
2002 Tree of Bows 13769	Open		30.00	30
2002 Tree of Lights 13770	Open		30.00	30
2000 Winter Bird Tree 13730	900	2002	30.00	30
2000 Woodland Tree 13732	600	2001	25.00	25

The First Christmas by Pipka - Pipka

2000 Angel Children 30002	Open		18.00	18
2000 Animal Set on Grass 30003	Open		40.00	40
2000 Animal Set on Snow 30004	Open		40.00	40
2000 6 pc. Basket Set 30006	Open		20.00	40
2000 6 pc. Pottery Set 30005	Open		12.00	40
2000 Evergreen Tree, large 30007	Open		35.00	40
2000 Evergreen Tree, medium 30008	Open		30.00	40
2000 Evergreen Tree, small 30009	Open		25.00	40
2000 Palm Tree, large 30010	Open		35.00	40
2000 Palm Tree, medium 30011	Open		32.50	40
2000 Holy Night Manger 30012	Open		195.00	195
2000 The Holy Family Set 30001	Open		110.00	110
2000 Holy Night Manger Set/12 30014	Open		485.00	485
2000 Stable of Bethlehem 30013	Closed	2001	195.00	195
2000 Stable of Bethlehem Set/12 30015	Open		462.50	463
2001 Daniel, The Kneeling Shepherd 30016	Open		40.00	40
2001 Shepherd Boy 30017	Open		25.00	25
2001 Drummer Boy 30018	Open		20.00	20
2001 Jacob, The Older Shepherd 30020	Open		40.00	40
2001 Set of Sheep 30019	Open		18.00	18
2001 Good Tidings Angel 30021	Open		35.00	35

Merry Mice by Pipka - Pipka

2002 Billy (Mouse sledding) 40018	Open		12.00	12
2002 Emma (Mouse Lady w/tree) 40017	Open		25.00	25
2002 Mabel and Millie (Lady mice talking) 40020	Open		22.50	23
2002 Mouse House 40015	Open		45.00	45
2002 Ollie and Pip (Mouse reading w/tree) 40022	Open		32.00	32
2002 Sam the Mailmouse 40020	Open		10.00	10
2002 Santa Mouse 40016	Open		15.00	15

Midnight Visitor Collection - Pipka

2002 Midnight Visitor 11615	400		425.00	425

Patriotic Collection - Pipka

2001 Patriotic Santa 11645	Open		45.00	45
2001 Patriotic Santa 13950	Retrd.	2001	110.00	110-125
2001 Patriotic Santa Miniature 11646	Open		9.00	9

Pipka's Artist Choice Santa - Pipka

1999 Laplander Santa 13922	6,216	2000	130.00	130-150
2000 Chef Claus 13938	Closed	2001	110.00	110-120
2001 Sinter Klaas 13948	Closed	2001	120.00	120-150
2001 Black Peter 13735	Closed	2001	27.00	27
2001 Hans & Katrina 13736	6/02		40.00	40
2002 Advent Santa 13962	6/03		120.00	120

Pipka's Boot Figurines - Pipka

2002 Czechoslovakian Boot Container 40027	Open		19.50	20
2002 Dear Santa Boot Container 40028	Open		19.50	20
2002 Santa's Boot Container 40029	Open		19.50	20
2002 Starcoat Santa Boot Container 40025	Open		19.50	20
2002 Teddy Bear Santa Boot Container 40026	Open		19.50	20
2002 Where's Rudolph? Boot Container 40024	Open		19.50	20

Pipka's Charity Piece - Pipka

2000 The Caring Santa 13949	Closed	2001	105.00	105
2001 Rudolph & Friends 13747	600	2002	55.00	55

Pipka's Displays - Pipka

2000 Angel Garden Backdrop 13725	Open		20.00	20
2000 German Village Backdrop 13724	Open		20.00	20

Collectors' Information Bureau   *Quotes have been rounded up to nearest dollar

YEAR ISSUE	EDITION LIMIT	YEAR RETD.	ISSUE PRICE	*QUOTE U.S.$

Pipka's Earth Angels, 7" - Pipka

YEAR ISSUE	EDITION LIMIT	YEAR RETD.	ISSUE PRICE	*QUOTE U.S.$
2001 Alexandra, Dutch Angel 11714	2,500		40.00	40
2000 Angel of Hearts 11701	2,500		40.00	40
2000 Angel of Joy 11708	2,500		40.00	40
2000 Angel of Roses 11704	2,500		40.00	40
2001 Carolyn, Angel of Contemplation 11713	2,500		50.00	50
2000 Celestial Angel 11707	2,500		40.00	40
2000 Elizabeth & Mikaela 11703	2,500		50.00	50
2000 The Giving Angel 11706	2,500		40.00	40
2000 Guardian Angel 11702	2,500		50.00	50
2001 Michele, The Snow Angel 11710	2,500		50.00	50
2001 Sang, The Teddy Bear Angel 11711	2,500		40.00	40
2001 Sylvia, The Song Angel 11712	2,500		40.00	40
2001 Victorian Angel 11709	2,500		40.00	40
2000 Whitney, The Wedding Angel 11705	2,500		40.00	40

Pipka's Earth Angels, 9" - Pipka

YEAR ISSUE	EDITION LIMIT	YEAR RETD.	ISSUE PRICE	*QUOTE U.S.$
2001 Alexandra-Dutch Angel 13825	2,500		65.00	65
1996 Angel of Hearts 13801	3,400	1999	85.00	85-90
1997 Angel of Roses 13804	2,840	2001	85.00	85
2000 Carolyn- Angel of Contemplation 13820	2,500		65.00	65
1998 Celeste-Angel of Stars 13807	5,400		90.00	90
1998 Christine-The Christmas Angel 13808	5,400		90.00	90
1996 Cottage Angel 13800	3,400	2001	85.00	85
1998 Elizabeth-Forget-Me-Not Angel 13809	1,800	2002	90.00	90
2000 Eric- The Leader Angel 13821	2,500		30.00	30
1996 Gardening Angel 13802	3,400	2001	85.00	90
1997 Guardian Angel 13805	5,400	2000	85.00	85
2001 Heaven's Angel 13826	2,500		65.00	65
2000 Jessica- The Bell Ringer 13822	2,500		35.00	35
1999 Kim & Lee-Baby Angel 13816	1,000	2000	40.00	40
2000 Lindsey- The Baby Angel 13823	1,000	2001	20.00	20
1997 Messenger Angel 13803	2,840	2002	85.00	85
1999 Michele-The Snow Angel 13813	1,000	2000	95.00	95
1998 Mikaela-Angel of Innocence 13810	1,800	2002	40.00	40
2000 Pauline- The Poinsettia Angel 13819	2,500		65.00	65
1998 Samantha-The Playful Angel 13811	5,400		40.00	40
1999 Sang-The Teddy Bear Angel 13815	1,000	2000	90.00	90
1998 Sarah-The Littlest Angel 13812	1,800	2002	40.00	40
1999 Sissy-The Little Helper 13814	1,000	2000	40.00	40
1999 Sylvia-The Song Angel 13817	1,000	2000	95.00	95
2001 Victorian Angel 13824	2,500		65.00	65
2000 Whitney- The Wedding Angel 13818	812	2002	65.00	65

Pipka's Fifth Year Anniversary Santa - Pipka

YEAR ISSUE	EDITION LIMIT	YEAR RETD.	ISSUE PRICE	*QUOTE U.S.$
1999 Irish Santa 13926	7,180	2000	100.00	100-175

Pipka's Gallery Collection - Pipka

YEAR ISSUE	EDITION LIMIT	YEAR RETD.	ISSUE PRICE	*QUOTE U.S.$
2002 Babbo Natale (Italian Santa) 13945	Yr.Iss.		105.00	105
2002 Befana 13755			70.00	70
2000 Caribbean Santa 13934	Yr.Iss.	2000	105.00	105-200
2001 The Christmas Preacher 13947	12/02		105.00	105
2002 Italian Angel 13749	Yr.Iss.		60.00	60
2001 Jasmine, Guiding Light Angel 13744	600	2002	30.00	30
2000 Julbock 13712	Open		30.00	30
2000 Jul-Tomte 13713	Open		20.00	20
2000 Little Helper - Jul-To 13714	Open		20.00	20
2001 MacKenzie, The Scottish Angel 13743	6/03		60.00	60
2002 Our Lady of Loreto (Italian Madonna) 12005	Yr.Iss.		60.00	60
2001 Scottish Santa 13946	6/03		110.00	110
2002 Shoemaker Santa 13959	Yr.Iss.		115.00	115
2000 St. Lucia 13711	Open		45.00	45
2000 Starlight Angel 13729	Closed	2001	15.00	15
2000 Starlight Santa 13932	2-Yr.		100.00	100
2000 Starlight Sleigh 13710	Open		45.00	45
2000 Swedish Father Christmas 13931	Yr.Iss.	2000	110.00	110-150
2001 Wee Lass 13734	6/03		30.00	30

Pipka's Kinder Christmas - Pipka

YEAR ISSUE	EDITION LIMIT	YEAR RETD.	ISSUE PRICE	*QUOTE U.S.$
2000 Best Friends 13717	1,260	2001	40.00	40
2001 His Christmas Treasures 13746	6,500		30.00	30
2000 His New Train 13718	6,500		40.00	40
1999 Jakub's Tree 13700	6,500		55.00	55
2000 Muffy's Tea Party 13719	6,500		45.00	45
1999 Playful Pals 13701	6,500		55.00	55
2000 Snow Gentleman 13716	6,500		50.00	50

YEAR ISSUE	EDITION LIMIT	YEAR RETD.	ISSUE PRICE	*QUOTE U.S.$
2001 Special Christmas Errand 13745	6,500		40.00	40

Pipka's Madonna Collection - Pipka

YEAR ISSUE	EDITION LIMIT	YEAR RETD.	ISSUE PRICE	*QUOTE U.S.$
2000 Black Wooden Display Base 13737	Closed	2001	10.00	10
1998 Decorative Displayer 12001	1,000	1999	30.00	30
2001 Madonna of Peace 12003	600	2001	60.00	60
2000 Mary, Mother of All Children 12004	1,212	2001	110.00	110
1998 Queen of Roses 12000	3,000	2002	90.00	90
1999 Renaissance Madonna 12002	1,600	2000	90.00	90

Pipka's Memories of Christmas - Pipka

YEAR ISSUE	EDITION LIMIT	YEAR RETD.	ISSUE PRICE	*QUOTE U.S.$
1995 Czechoslovakian Santa 13905	3,600	1996	85.00	350-540
1995 Gingerbread Santa 13903	3,600	1997	85.00	200-275
1995 Midnight Visitor 13902	3,600	1996	85.00	550-1200
1995 Santa's Ark 13901	3,600	1997	85.00	200-310
1995 Star Catcher Santa 13904	3,600	1996	85.00	275-475
1995 Starcoat Santa 13900	3,600	1996	85.00	350-500
1995 Set of 1995 Santas (13900-13905)	Closed	N/A	510.00	1000-2400
1996 Aussie Santa & Boomer 13906	3,600	1997	85.00	200-380
1996 Good News Santa 13908	3,600	1997	85.00	250-325
1996 Storytime Santa 13909	3,600	1997	85.00	125-223
1996 Ukrainian Santa 13907	3,600	1997	85.00	223-285
1997 Norwegian/Julenisse Santa 13911	3,600	1997	90.00	219-275
1997 Polish Father Christmas 13917	3,600	1997	90.00	150-250
1997 Russian Santa 13916	3,600	1998	90.00	115-150
1997 Santa's Spotted Grey 13914	3,600	1998	90.00	125-225
1997 St. Nicholas 13912	3,600	1998	90.00	145-239
1997 Where's Rudolph? 13915	3,600	1997	90.00	260-375
1998 Father Christmas 13919	3,600	1998	95.00	150-300
1998 Peace Maker 13918	3,600	1998	95.00	110-160
1998 San Nicolas 13921	3,600	1998	95.00	95-225
1998 Teddy Bear Santa 13920	3,600	1998	95.00	280-450
1999 Door County Santa 13924	4,500	1999	110.00	110-250
1999 Yes Virginia 13925	4,500	1999	105.00	105-139
1999 Winterman 13927	4,500	1999	95.00	95-225
1999 German St. Nick 13928	4,500	1999	100.00	100-125
1999 Santa & His Snow Friend 13929	4,500	2000	95.00	95-100
1999 The Christmas Traveler 13930	4,500	2000	95.00	95-100
2000 Old Father Christmas 13939	4,500	2001	95.00	95
2000 Santa with Toys 13940	4,500		95.00	95
2000 St. Nicholas and the Christkind 13937	4,500	2002	150.00	150-200
2000 Victorian Father Christmas 13933	4,500		100.00	100
2001 Poinsettia Santa 13935	4,500		105.00	105
2001 Tyrolean Santa 13944	4,500		105.00	105
2001 Woodland Santa 13954	4,500		105.00	105
2001 Alaskan Santa 13943	4,500		115.00	115
2002 Candy Cane Santa 13952	4,500		90.00	90
2002 Pere Noel (French Santa) 13954	4,500		105.00	105
2002 Nicole, French Girl 13748	Open		22.50	23
2002 The Cottage Santa 13955	4,500		100.00	100
2002 Christmas Cottage Angel 13750	Open		60.00	60
2002 Snowflake Santa 13958	4,500		100.00	100

Pipka's Millennium Santa - Pipka

YEAR ISSUE	EDITION LIMIT	YEAR RETD.	ISSUE PRICE	*QUOTE U.S.$
2000 Carpenter Santa 13936	5,616	2000	100.00	100

Pipka's Miniature Collection - Pipka

YEAR ISSUE	EDITION LIMIT	YEAR RETD.	ISSUE PRICE	*QUOTE U.S.$
2002 Cottage Santa 13762	Open		9.00	9
2002 Czechoslovakian Santa 13761	Open		9.00	9
2002 Door County Santa 13758	Open		9.00	9
2002 German St. Nick 13765	Open		9.00	9
2002 Midnight Visitor 13756	Open		9.00	9
2002 Star Catcher Santa 13764	Open		9.00	9
2002 Teddy Bear Santa 13759	Open		9.00	9
2002 The Winterman 13757	Open		9.00	9

Pipka's Reflections of Christmas - Pipka

YEAR ISSUE	EDITION LIMIT	YEAR RETD.	ISSUE PRICE	*QUOTE U.S.$
2002 Alaskan Santa 11343	9,700		40.00	40
1997 Amish Country Santa 11305	4,330	1999	40.00	40-45
1998 Aussie Santa & Boomer 11306	3,760	2000	40.00	40
1997 Better Watch Out Santa 11304	4,330	1999	40.00	40-55
2002 Caribbean Santa 11340	9,700		40.00	40
2001 Carpenter Santa 11335	9,700		40.00	40
2001 Chef Claus 11333	9,700		45.00	45
2002 A Christmas Journey 11346	9,700		40.00	40
2000 The Christmas Traveler 11327	9,700		40.00	40
1997 Czechoslovakian Santa 11301	4,330	1999	40.00	40-45
1998 Dear Santa 11311	4,960	2001	40.00	40
2000 The Door County Santa 11324	4,016	2002	40.00	40
1999 Father Christmas 11319	9,700		40.00	40
2002 Feathered Friends 11347	9,700		40.00	40
1999 German St. Nick 11321	4,500	2001	40.00	40

FIGURINES

YEAR ISSUE	EDITION LIMIT	YEAR RETD.	ISSUE PRICE	*QUOTE U.S.$
1998 Gingerbread Santa 11309	4,960		40.00	40
1998 Good News Santa 11307	3,760	2000	40.00	40
1999 Irish Santa 11320	7,800	2001	40.00	40
2001 Laplander Santa 11334	9,700		45.00	45
1997 Midnight Visitor 11300	4,330	1999	40.00	40-50
1998 Norwegian Julenisse 11313	5,200	2001	40.00	40-60
2001 Old Father Christmas 11336	2,216	2002	40.00	40
1999 Peace Maker 11322	3,000	2000	40.00	40
1998 Polish Father Christmas 11312	5,800	2002	40.00	40
1999 Russian Santa 11317	4,000		40.00	40
2000 Santa & Snow Friend 11326	3,116	2002	40.00	40
2001 Santa With Toys 11337	9,700		40.00	40
1999 Santa's Spotted Grey 11316	4,000		40.00	40
2002 Scottish Santa 11341	9,700		40.00	40
2002 St. Nicholas & The Christkind 11342	9,700		40.00	40
1999 St. Nicholas 11314	4,600		40.00	40
1997 Star Catcher Santa 11303	4,330	1999	40.00	40-45
1997 Starcoat Santa 11302	4,330	1999	40.00	40-50
2000 Starlight Santa 11329	9,700		40.00	40
2000 Starlight Sleigh 11331	Open		30.00	30
1998 Storytime Santa 11308	3,360	2000	40.00	40
2000 Swedish Father Christmas 11328	9,700		40.00	40
1998 Teddy Bear Santa 11318	9,700		40.00	40
1998 Ukrainian Santa 11310	3,360	2000	40.00	40-60
2001 Victorian Father Christmas 11332	9,700		40.00	40
1998 Where's Rudolph? 11315	5,820	2002	40.00	40
2000 The Winterman 11325	9,700		40.00	40
1999 Yes Virginia 11323	3,000	2001	40.00	40

Pipka's Signs - Pipka

1996 Angel's Gate 13806	1,600		35.00	35
1996 Memories Sign 13910	2,100	2000	35.00	35

Reco International

Fancy Footwork - J. Everett

1999 Everything's Coming Up Rosy	Retrd.	2000	20.00	20
1999 Family Ties	Retrd.	2000	20.00	20
1999 Head Over Heals	Retrd.	2000	20.00	20
1999 Hook Shot	Retrd.	2000	20.00	20
1999 Just Desserts	Retrd.	2000	20.00	20
1999 Life's a Beach	Retrd.	2000	20.00	20
1999 Ski Bunnies	Retrd.	2000	20.00	20
1999 Splish, Splash	Retrd.	2000	20.00	20
1999 This Boot Is Made For Working	Retrd.	2000	20.00	20

Forever In His Love - G. Olsen

2000 Alpha & Omega	Open		60.00	60
2000 Be Not Afraid	Open		75.00	75
2000 Forever and Ever	Open		60.00	60
2000 The Good Shepherd	Open		65.00	65
2001 In His Constant Care	Open		60.00	60
2001 In His Light	Open		60.00	60

Legends of The Old West (bookends) - G. Perillo

1999 Crazy Horse & George Armstrong Custer	900		80.00	80
1999 Indian Brave & Pony Express	900		90.00	90

Masquerade - Lakeland Studios, unless otherwise noted

1998 Aviator	Open		30.00	30
1998 Chef	Open		30.00	30
1998 Conductor	Open		30.00	30
1998 Drover	Open		30.00	30
1998 Engineer	Open		30.00	30
1998 Fireman	Open		30.00	30
1998 Fish Merchant - A. Brindley	Open		30.00	30
1998 Fisherman	Open		30.00	30
1998 Josephine - A. Brindley	Open		30.00	30
1998 Lifeboatman	Open		30.00	30
1998 Long Shoreman	Open		30.00	30
1998 Miner	Open		30.00	30
1998 Napoleon - A. Brindley	Open		30.00	30
1998 Nurse	Open		30.00	30
1998 Pharmacist	Open		30.00	30
1998 Policeman	Open		30.00	30
1998 Sailor - A. Brindley	Open		30.00	30
1998 Sea Captain	Open		30.00	30
1998 Seamen - A. Brindley	Open		30.00	30
1998 Sherlock Holmes - A. Brindley	Open		30.00	30
1998 Skipper - A. Brindley	Open		30.00	30
1998 Trainer	Open		30.00	30

YEAR ISSUE	EDITION LIMIT	YEAR RETD.	ISSUE PRICE	*QUOTE U.S.$
1998 Trawlerman - A. Brindley	Open		30.00	30
1998 Yachtsman - A. Brindley	Open		30.00	30

Pure Potential - J. Claybrooks

1999 Chocolate Drop	Open		17.50	18
1999 Gospel Truth	Open		19.00	19
1999 More Bubbles	Open		22.50	23
1999 Pure Potential	Open		19.00	19

Reco Creche Collection - J. McClelland

1988 Cow	Retrd.	2000	15.00	15
1988 Donkey	Retrd.	2000	16.50	17
1987 Holy Family (3 Pieces)	Retrd.	2000	49.00	49
1988 King/Frankincense	Retrd.	2000	22.50	23
1988 King/Gold	Retrd.	2000	22.50	23
1988 King/Myrrh	Retrd.	2000	22.50	23
1987 Lamb	Retrd.	2000	9.50	10
1987 Shepherd-Kneeling	Retrd.	2000	22.50	23
1987 Shepherd-Standing	Retrd.	2000	22.50	23

The Roaring Adventures of Rip Squeak™ - L. Filgate

2000 Balancing Act	Open		30.00	30
2000 Harmony	Open		70.00	70
2000 The Hug	Open		20.00	20
2000 Sports Fan	Open		25.00	25
2000 Storyteller	Open		30.00	30
2000 Sweet Dreams	Open		39.00	39

Sandra Kuck's Treasures - S. Kuck

1997 Baby Bunnies	Open		20.00	20
1997 Be Good	Open		20.00	20
2000 Birthday Wishes	Open		25.00	25
1998 Bridge of Love	Open		27.50	28
1999 Bundle of Joy	Open		25.00	25
1999 Cherub Fountain	Open		35.00	35
1997 Christmas Morning	1,200		Gift	N/A
1997 Fishin' Buddies	Open		25.00	25
1997 For Mom	Open		20.00	20
1998 Friendship & Sharing	Open		50.00	50
1998 Gift of Love	Open		30.00	30
1998 Giving Thanks	Open		30.00	30
1999 Grandma's Trunk	Open		30.00	30
1998 Happy Birthday	Open		25.00	25
2000 Happy Bubbles	Open		20.00	20
1999 Kitty Did It	Open		20.00	20
2000 Little Blessings	Open		25.00	25
1998 Little Cowboy	Open		27.50	28
1999 Little Miss Sunshine	Open		30.00	30
2000 Look What I Found	Open		20.00	20
1998 Lost & Found	Open		20.00	20
1997 Love and Kisses	Open		20.00	20
1998 Make Believe	Open		30.00	30
1999 Morning Prayers	Open		30.00	30
2000 My New Friend	Open		25.00	25
1997 Playful Kitten	Open		20.00	20
1998 Pretty Kitty	Open		30.00	30
1999 Rose Gazebo	Open		50.00	50
1998 Schooldays	Open		25.00	25
1998 Sisters	Open		30.00	30
1999 Storybook Dreams	Open		20.00	20
1997 Sunday Stroll	Open		20.00	20
1998 Sweet Dreams	Open		20.00	20
1997 Swing For Two	Open		25.00	25
1997 Tea With Kitty	Open		20.00	20
1997 Teacher's Pet	Open		20.00	20
1997 Teddy & Me	Open		20.00	20
1998 Thank You So Much	Open		20.00	20
1999 To Grandma's House	Open		30.00	30
1997 Victoria's Garden	Open		20.00	20
1998 Winter Fun	Open		30.00	30

St. Isidore - Reco

2001 St. Isidore Figurine	Open		45.00	45
2001 St. Isidore PC Protector Figurine	Open		20.00	20

Victorian Home Collection - S. Kuck

1999 Gift of Knowledge Bookends	Open		85.00	85
1999 Gift of Peace Candlestick	Open		40.00	40
1999 Unity Candlestick	Open		40.00	40

YEAR ISSUE	EDITION LIMIT	YEAR RETD.	ISSUE PRICE	*QUOTE U.S.$
River Shore				
Rockwell Single Issues - N. Rockwell				
1982 Grandpa's Guardian	9,500	N/A	125.00	195
1981 Looking Out To Sea	9,500	N/A	85.00	195
Roman, Inc.				
Animal Kingdom - D. Griff				
1994 Cat w/Mice Inside Waterball	Closed	N/A	19.50	20
1994 Cat w/Mouse on Tail	Closed	N/A	15.00	15
1994 Chipmunk w/Mice Musical	Closed	N/A	35.00	35
1995 Glitterdome Musical	Closed	N/A	45.00	45
1994 Lounging Cat on Pillow	Closed	N/A	13.50	14
1994 Two Kittens in Basket	Closed	N/A	15.00	15
1995 Yawning Chipmunks Waterglobe	Closed	N/A	45.00	45
Bouncing Baby Bunnies - D. Griff				
1996 Bunnies on Block	Closed	N/A	7.00	7
1996 Bunnies on Carrot	Closed	N/A	6.50	7
1996 Bunnies on Flowers	Closed	N/A	6.00	6
1996 Bunnies w/Carrot Slippers	Closed	N/A	6.00	6
1996 Bunnies w/Crayons	Closed	N/A	4.00	4
1996 Bunnies w/White Diapers	Closed	N/A	4.50	5
1996 Bunny Bubble Bath in Teacup	Closed	N/A	10.00	10
1996 Bunny Bubble Bath in Teacup Musical	Closed	N/A	27.50	28
1996 Bunny Cowboy	Closed	N/A	8.00	8
1996 Bunny Doctor	Closed	N/A	7.00	7
1996 Bunny Fireman	Closed	N/A	7.00	7
1996 Bunny Policeman	Closed	N/A	8.00	8
1996 Bunny Sliding on Easter Egg	Closed	N/A	7.50	8
1996 Ring-Around-The-Rosie	Closed	N/A	10.00	10
1996 Three Bunnies in an Easter Basket	Closed	N/A	9.00	9
1996 Two Bunnies w/egg Cup	Closed	N/A	9.00	9
A Child's World 1st Edition - F. Hook				
1980 Beach Buddies, signed	15,000	N/A	29.00	600
1980 Beach Buddies, unsigned	15,000	N/A	29.00	450
1980 Helping Hands	Closed	N/A	45.00	85
1980 Kiss Me Good Night	15,000	N/A	29.00	40
1980 My Big Brother	Closed	N/A	39.00	200
1980 Nighttime Thoughts	Closed	N/A	25.00	65
1980 Sounds of the Sea	15,000	N/A	45.00	150
A Child's World 2nd Edition - F. Hook				
1981 All Dressed Up	15,000	N/A	36.00	70
1981 Cat Nap	15,000	N/A	42.00	125
1981 I'll Be Good	15,000	N/A	36.00	80
1981 Making Friends	15,000	N/A	42.00	46
1981 The Sea and Me	15,000	N/A	39.00	80
1981 Sunday School	15,000	N/A	39.00	70
A Child's World 3rd Edition - F. Hook				
1981 Bear Hug	15,000	N/A	42.00	45
1981 Pathway to Dreams	15,000	N/A	47.00	50
1981 Road to Adventure	15,000	N/A	47.00	50
1981 Sisters	15,000	N/A	64.00	75
1981 Spring Breeze	15,000	N/A	37.50	50
1981 Youth	15,000	N/A	37.50	40
A Child's World 4th Edition - F. Hook				
1982 All Bundled Up	15,000	N/A	37.50	40
1982 Bedtime	15,000	N/A	35.00	38
1982 Birdie	15,000	N/A	37.50	40
1982 Flower Girl	15,000	N/A	42.00	45
1982 My Dolly!	15,000	N/A	39.00	40
1982 Ring Bearer	15,000	N/A	39.00	40
A Child's World 5th Edition - F. Hook				
1983 Brothers	15,000	N/A	64.00	70
1983 Finish Line	15,000	N/A	39.00	42
1983 Handful of Happiness	15,000	N/A	36.00	40
1983 He Loves Me...	15,000	N/A	49.00	55
1983 Puppy's Pal	15,000	N/A	39.00	42
1983 Ring Around the Rosie	15,000	N/A	99.00	105
A Child's World 6th Edition - F. Hook				
1984 Can I Help?	15,000	N/A	37.50	40
1984 Future Artist	15,000	N/A	42.00	45
1984 Good Doggie	15,000	N/A	47.00	50
1984 Let's Play Catch	15,000	N/A	33.00	35

YEAR ISSUE	EDITION LIMIT	YEAR RETD.	ISSUE PRICE	*QUOTE U.S.$
1984 Nature's Wonders	15,000	N/A	29.00	31
1984 Sand Castles	15,000	N/A	37.50	40
A Child's World 7th Edition - F. Hook				
1985 Art Class	15,000	N/A	99.00	105
1985 Don't Tell Anyone	15,000	N/A	49.00	50
1985 Look at Me!	15,000	N/A	42.00	45
1985 Mother's Helper	15,000	N/A	45.00	50
1985 Please Hear Me	15,000	N/A	29.00	30
1985 Yummm!	15,000	N/A	36.00	39
A Child's World 8th Edition - F. Hook				
1985 Chance of Showers	15,000	N/A	33.00	35
1985 Dress Rehearsal	15,000	N/A	33.00	35
1985 Engine	15,000	N/A	36.00	40
1985 Just Stopped By	15,000	N/A	36.00	40
1985 Private Ocean	15,000	N/A	29.00	31
1985 Puzzling	15,000	N/A	36.00	40
A Child's World 9th Edition - F. Hook				
1987 Hopscotch	15,000	N/A	67.50	70
1987 Li'l Brother	15,000	N/A	60.00	65
Classic Brides of the Century - E. Williams				
1989 1900-Flora	5,000	N/A	175.00	175
1989 1910-Elizabeth Grace	5,000	N/A	175.00	175
1989 1920-Mary Claire	5,000	N/A	175.00	175
1989 1930-Kathleen	5,000	N/A	175.00	175
1989 1940-Margaret	5,000	N/A	175.00	175
1989 1950-Barbara Ann	5,000	N/A	175.00	175
1989 1960-Dianne	5,000	N/A	175.00	175
1989 1970-Heather	5,000	N/A	175.00	175
1989 1980-Jennifer	5,000	N/A	175.00	175
1992 1990-Stephanie Helen	5,000	N/A	175.00	175-199
The Dennis Franzen Collection - D. Franzen				
2001 Bobcat	Open		30.00	30
2001 Caribou	Open		110.00	110
1998 Cougar, "Character is what you know you are..."	Open		120.00	120
2001 Deer	Open		30.00	30
2000 Deer, "Be still..."	Open		95.00	95
2001 Eagle	Open		30.00	30
1998 Eagle, "In the shadow of your wings..."	Open		95.00	95
2000 Fox, "If we pull together..."	Open		39.50	40
1999 Horse, "Draw near to God..."	Open		120.00	120
2001 Horse, "If we pull together..." Waterglobe	Open		27.50	30
2000 Horse, "Live each day..."	Open		39.50	40
2001 Jaguar	Open		90.00	90
2000 Lion, "Have the courage to do what is right."	Open		39.50	40
2001 Lion, "Have the courage to do what is right." Waterglobe	Open		27.50	28
1998 Lion, "He gives strength to the weary..."	Open		95.00	95
1998 Otter, "Alone we can do so little.."	Open		120.00	120
2000 Owl, "A man's wisdom..."	Open		90.00	90
2000 Panda, "No act of kindness, however small..."	Open		39.50	40
2000 Panther, "Always keep your goal in sight."	Open		39.50	40
2000 Tiger, "In all thy ways acknowledge Him..."	Open		90.00	90
2001 Wolf, "Alone we can do so little.." Waterglobe	Open		27.50	28
1999 Wolf, "Be strong and of good courage..."	Open		95.00	95
2000 Wolf, "Keep your priorities in mind at all times."	Open		39.50	40
Frances Hook - F. Hook				
1986 Carpenter Bust	Retrd.	1986	95.00	95
1986 Carpenter Bust-Heirloom Edition	Retrd.	1986	95.00	95
1987 Little Children, Come to Me	15,000	N/A	45.00	45
1987 Madonna and Child	15,000	N/A	39.50	40
1982 Sailor Mates	2,000	N/A	290.00	315
1982 Sun Shy	2,000	N/A	290.00	315
Frances Hook's Four Seasons - F. Hook				
1984 Winter	12,500	N/A	95.00	100
1985 Spring	12,500	N/A	95.00	100
1985 Summer	12,500	N/A	95.00	100

YEAR ISSUE	EDITION LIMIT	YEAR RETD.	ISSUE PRICE	*QUOTE U.S.$
1985 Fall	12,500	N/A	95.00	100

Magic of Christmas™ - D. Morgan

YEAR ISSUE	EDITION LIMIT	YEAR RETD.	ISSUE PRICE	*QUOTE U.S.$
2001 Christmas Future	Open		50.00	50
2001 Christmas Future Musical Glitterdome	Retrd.	2001	45.00	45
2000 Christmas Past	Retrd.	2001	65.00	65
2001 Christmas Past Musical Glitterdome	Open		47.50	48
2000 Christmas Present	Retrd.	2001	65.00	65
2001 Christmas Present Musical Glitterdome	Open		47.50	48
1999 Magic of Christmas	Retrd.	2001	65.00	65
2000 Magic of Christmas Musical Glitterdome	Retrd.	2001	47.50	48
1999 Magic of Giving	Retrd.	2001	65.00	65
2001 Magic of Giving Musical Glitterdome	Open		47.50	48
1999 Santa's Magic	Retrd.	2001	65.00	65
2001 Santa's Magic Musical Glitterdome	Open		47.50	48
2001 Yes Virginia, There is a Santa Claus	Retrd.	2001	50.00	50
2001 Yes Virginia, There is a Santa Claus Musical Glitterdome	Retrd.	2001	35.00	35

The Millenium® Collection - G. Ho

YEAR ISSUE	EDITION LIMIT	YEAR RETD.	ISSUE PRICE	*QUOTE U.S.$
1998 Boy in Prayer Figure	Open		19.50	20
1998 Boy in Prayer Musical	Open		25.00	25
2002 Christening Angel	Open		45.00	45
2001 Comfort of Heaven	Open		25.00	25
2001 Comfort of Mother and Child	Open		55.00	55
1998 Girl in Prayer Figure	Open		19.50	20
1998 Girl in Prayer Musical	Open		25.00	25
1999 Guardian Angel, First in Series	Open		35.00	35
2000 Guardian Angel, Second in Series	Open		37.50	38
2001 Guardian Angel, Third in Series	Open		35.00	35
2002 Guardian Angel, Fourth in Series	Open		45.00	45
1999 Infinite Peace	Open		39.50	40
1999 J-O-Y	Open		35.00	35
2002 Love Never Ends, Boy	Open		45.00	45
2002 Love Never Ends, Girl	Open		45.00	45
2001 Mary and Her Son	Open		59.50	60
2002 Millenium Crucifix	Open		45.00	45
2001 N-O-E-L	Open		49.50	50
2002 P-E-A-C-E	Open		59.00	59
2001 Peace on Earth	Open		35.00	35
2002 Sent from Above	Open		35.00	35
1999 Serenity	Open		50.00	50
2002 Spirit of Hope	Open		45.00	45

The Millenium® Collection - Sr. Mary Jean Dorcy

YEAR ISSUE	EDITION LIMIT	YEAR RETD.	ISSUE PRICE	*QUOTE U.S.$
1996 The Annunciation	Open		29.50	35
1999 The Annunciation Musical	Retrd.	2001	49.50	60
1996 Cause of Our Joy (5.5")	Open		29.50	30
1998 Cause of Our Joy 10" with wooden base	Retrd.	2001	65.00	65
1997 Cause of Our Joy 7" Musical	Retrd.	2001	49.50	50
1997 Gentle Love	Open		29.50	35
1999 Heaven's Blessing	Open		29.50	35
1999 Joyful Promise	Open		29.50	45
1996 Peace on Earth	Open		35.00	35
1996 Prince of Peace	Retrd.	1998	29.50	30-50
1998 Rejoice	Open		29.50	35
1996 Silent Night	Open		29.50	35
1998 Silent Night Musical	Open		55.00	55

The Millenium® Nativity - G. Ho

YEAR ISSUE	EDITION LIMIT	YEAR RETD.	ISSUE PRICE	*QUOTE U.S.$
2002 Gloria Angel	Open		15.00	15
2000 Have You Heard the News	Open		15.00	15
2000 Holy Family (four piece set)	Open		35.00	35
1998 Holy Family Figure	Open		39.50	40
2000 Lift Up Your Hearts	Open		15.00	15
2000 A Newborn King to See	Open		15.00	15
2001 O Come Let Us Adore Him	Open		17.50	18
2000 Our Finest Gifts We Bring	Open		17.50	18
2000 Shall I Play for You?	Open		12.00	12
2000 Stable - Double Arch Design	Open		35.00	35
2002 Stable - Traditional Design	Open		49.50	50
2002 Three Kings	Open		45.00	45
2001 We Have Heard on High	Open		17.50	18

The Museum Collection by Angela Tripi - A. Tripi

YEAR ISSUE	EDITION LIMIT	YEAR RETD.	ISSUE PRICE	*QUOTE U.S.$
1994 The Batter	1,000	N/A	95.00	95
1993 Be a Clown	1,000	N/A	95.00	95
1994 Blackfoot Woman with Baby	1,000	N/A	95.00	95

YEAR ISSUE	EDITION LIMIT	YEAR RETD.	ISSUE PRICE	*QUOTE U.S.$
1990 The Caddie	1,000	N/A	135.00	135
1992 Checking It Twice	2,500	N/A	95.00	95
1990 Christopher Columbus	1,000	N/A	250.00	250
1994 Crow Warrior	1,000	N/A	195.00	195
1990 The Fiddler	1,000	N/A	175.00	176
1992 Flying Ace	1,000	N/A	95.00	95
1993 For My Next Trick	1,000	N/A	95.00	95
1992 Fore!	1,000	N/A	175.00	175
1992 The Fur Trapper	1,000	N/A	175.00	175
1991 A Gentleman's Game	1,000	N/A	175.00	175
1992 The Gift Giver	2,500	N/A	95.00	95
1994 Iroquois Warrior	1,000	N/A	95.00	95
1994 Jesus in Gethsemane	1,000	N/A	75.00	75
1993 Jesus, The Good Shepherd	1,000	N/A	95.00	95
1992 Justice for All	1,000	N/A	95.00	95
1992 Ladies' Day	1,000	N/A	175.00	175
1992 Ladies' Tee	1,000	N/A	250.00	250
1990 The Mentor	1,000	N/A	290.00	291
1993 Native American Woman-Cherokee Maiden	1,000	N/A	110.00	110
1992 Nativity Set-8 pc.	2,500	N/A	425.00	425
1994 Nurse	1,000	N/A	95.00	95
1993 One Man Band Clown	1,000	N/A	95.00	95
1992 Our Family Doctor	1,000	N/A	95.00	95
1994 The Pitcher	1,000	N/A	95.00	95
1993 Preacher of Peace	1,000	N/A	175.00	175
1992 Prince of the Plains	1,000	N/A	175.00	175
1993 Public Protector	1,000	N/A	95.00	95
1993 Rhapsody	1,000	N/A	95.00	95
1993 Right on Schedule	1,000	N/A	95.00	95
1993 Road Show	1,000	N/A	95.00	95
1995 The Runner	1,000	N/A	95.00	95
1993 Serenade	1,000	N/A	95.00	95
1995 Sioux Chief	1,000	N/A	95.00	95
1993 Sonata	1,000	N/A	95.00	95
1990 St. Francis of Assisi	1,000	N/A	175.00	175
1992 The Tannenbaum Santa	2,500	N/A	95.00	95
1992 The Tap In	1,000	N/A	175.00	175
1994 Teacher	1,000	N/A	95.00	95
1990 Tee Time at St. Andrew's	1,000	N/A	175.00	175
1992 This Way, Santa	2,500	N/A	95.00	95
1992 To Serve and Protect	1,000	N/A	150.00	150
1993 Tripi Crucifix-Large	Open		59.00	59
1993 Tripi Crucifix-Medium	Open		35.00	35
1993 Tripi Crucifix-Small	Open		27.50	28

On Angel's Wings - G.G. Santiago

YEAR ISSUE	EDITION LIMIT	YEAR RETD.	ISSUE PRICE	*QUOTE U.S.$
1999 Angel of Dance	Open		65.00	65
1999 Angel of Dreams	Open		65.00	65
1999 Angel of Joy	Open		65.00	65
1999 Angel of Knowledge	Open		65.00	65
1999 Angel of Love	Open		65.00	65
1999 Angel of Music	Open		65.00	65
1999 Angel of Peace	Open		65.00	65
1999 Angel of Song	Open		65.00	65

Remember When by Frances Hook - F. Hook

YEAR ISSUE	EDITION LIMIT	YEAR RETD.	ISSUE PRICE	*QUOTE U.S.$
1999 Beach Buddies	Open		30.00	30
1999 Bear Hug	Open		30.00	30
1999 Can I Help?	Open		30.00	30
1999 Finish Line	Open		30.00	30
1999 Handful of Happiness	Open		30.00	30
1999 Sand Castles	Open		30.00	30
1999 The Sea and Me	Open		30.00	30
1999 Sounds of the Sea	Open		30.00	30

Valencia, Blessings for Baby - G. Ho

YEAR ISSUE	EDITION LIMIT	YEAR RETD.	ISSUE PRICE	*QUOTE U.S.$
2002 Baby Boy in Bassinet Musical	Open		27.50	28
2002 Baby Girl in Bassinet Musical	Open		27.50	28

Valencia, Blissful Moments - G. Ho

YEAR ISSUE	EDITION LIMIT	YEAR RETD.	ISSUE PRICE	*QUOTE U.S.$
2002 Ballerina - As the music ends	Open		30.00	30
2002 Ballerina - Just Before Curtain	Open		25.00	25
2002 Compassion's Champion - Doctor	Open		39.50	40
2002 Compassion's Champion - Nurse	Open		39.50	40
2002 A Glance Over My Shoulder	Open		59.50	60
2002 Ladies Day on the Links	Open		49.50	50
2002 Victorian Stroll	Open		59.50	60

Valencia, Celebrations of Life - G. Ho

YEAR ISSUE	EDITION LIMIT	YEAR RETD.	ISSUE PRICE	*QUOTE U.S.$
2002 Dance of Joy	Open		59.50	60
2002 Feeding the Geese	Open		49.50	50

YEAR ISSUE	EDITION LIMIT	YEAR RETD.	ISSUE PRICE	*QUOTE U.S.$
2002 Gathering Blossoms	Open		29.50	30
2000 Gentle Lullabies	Open		45.00	45
2002 Graces In the Garden	Open		250.00	250
2002 Joy of Celebration	Open		59.50	60
2002 A New Family	Open		100.00	100
2000 Pride and Joy	Open		45.00	45
2002 Reading Stories	Open		45.00	45
2002 Spring In the Garden	Open		29.50	30
2002 Summertime Fun	Open		29.50	30
2002 Tender Memories	Open		45.00	45
2002 Times of Fun	Open		45.00	45
2000 With All My Heart	Open		45.00	45

Valencia, Children's Prayers - G. Ho

YEAR ISSUE	EDITION LIMIT	YEAR RETD.	ISSUE PRICE	*QUOTE U.S.$
1983 In the Palm of His Hand, Boy	Open		15.00	15
1983 In the Palm of His Hand, Girl	Open		15.00	15
1983 Kneeling Boy	Open		13.50	14
1983 Kneeling Girl	Open		13.50	14
2002 My First Communion - Fruit of the Field & Vineyard Musical, Boy	Open		30.00	30
2002 My First Communion - Fruit of the Field & Vineyard Musical, Girl	Open		30.00	30
2002 My First Communion - Fruit of the Field & Vineyard, Boy	Open		15.00	15
2002 My First Communion - Fruit of the Field & Vineyard, Girl	Open		15.00	15
1997 My Guardian Angel, Boy	Open		49.50	50
1997 My Guardian Angel, Girl	Open		49.50	50

Valencia, Flora & Fauna - G. Ho

YEAR ISSUE	EDITION LIMIT	YEAR RETD.	ISSUE PRICE	*QUOTE U.S.$
2002 Butterfly & Day Lily	Open		17.50	18
2002 Butterfly & Impatiens	Open		17.50	18
2002 Hummingbird & Fucshia	Open		22.50	23
2002 Hummingbird & Iris	Open		22.50	23
2002 Nature's Mothers, Doe & Fawn	Open		29.50	30
2002 Nature's Mothers, Dolphins	Open		29.50	30
2002 Nature's Mothers, Lioness & Cub	Open		29.50	30
2002 Nature's Mothers, Mare & Foal	Open		29.50	30
2002 Nature's Mothers, Polar Bear & Cub	Open		29.50	30

Valencia, Our Unforgettable Day - G. Ho

YEAR ISSUE	EDITION LIMIT	YEAR RETD.	ISSUE PRICE	*QUOTE U.S.$
2002 Calla Lily Couple Caketopper	Open		20.00	20
2001 Wedding Couple Caketopper	Open		20.00	20
2001 Wedding Couple Musical	Open		49.50	50

Valencia, Sacred Portraits - G. Ho

YEAR ISSUE	EDITION LIMIT	YEAR RETD.	ISSUE PRICE	*QUOTE U.S.$
1997 Angel with Dove	Retrd.	2001	49.50	50
2002 Lippi Maddona	Open		39.50	40
1997 Madonna with Rose	Open		39.50	40
2001 Moses	Open		59.50	60
2001 Noah	Open		49.50	50
1997 St. Francis	Open		39.50	40

Valencia, Story of Jesus - G. Ho

YEAR ISSUE	EDITION LIMIT	YEAR RETD.	ISSUE PRICE	*QUOTE U.S.$
1998 The Annunciation	Open		59.50	60
1998 Crucifix	Open		39.50	40
1998 Flight into Egypt	Open		90.00	90
1998 Gethsemane	Open		45.00	45
1998 The Good Shepherd	Open		45.00	45
2001 Holy Family, Joseph Watches Over Mary & Jesus, 12"	Open		225.00	225
1997 Holy Family, Joseph Watches Over Mary & Jesus, 8"	Open		59.50	60
2000 Humble Master	Open		35.00	35
1997 Jesus	Open		39.50	40
1998 Jesus with Children, 5.5"	Open		45.00	45
2002 Jesus with Children, 8.5"	Open		125.00	125
1997 Joseph w/the Baby Jesus	Open		39.50	40
1997 Last Supper	Open		125.00	125
2001 Nativity-Camel	Open		20.00	20
1999 Nativity-Holy Family, 3 pc. Set	Open		50.00	50
1999 Nativity-Kneeling Gloria Angel	Open		17.50	18
2001 Nativity-Sheep Set (2 pc.)	Open		15.00	15
1999 Nativity-Shepherd, Ox & Donkey	Open		59.59	60
1999 Nativity-Shepherd	Open		90.00	90
2001 Nativity-Standing Gloria Angel	Open		27.50	28
1999 Nativity-Wise Men	Open		68.00	68
2001 Risen Christ	Open		59.50	60
1997 Seated Madonna and Child	Open		39.50	40
1997 Standing Madonna and Child	Open		39.50	40
1998 Way of the Cross	Open		59.50	60

Royal Copenhagen

Santa Figurines - S. Vestergaard

YEAR ISSUE	EDITION LIMIT	YEAR RETD.	ISSUE PRICE	*QUOTE U.S.$
2001 Santa Goes Skiing	Annual		65.00	65

Royal Doulton

Royal Doulton International Collectors' Club - Various

YEAR ISSUE	EDITION LIMIT	YEAR RETD.	ISSUE PRICE	*QUOTE U.S.$
1980 John Doulton Jug (8 O'Clock) D6656 - E. Griffiths	Yr.Iss.	1981	70.00	350-369
1981 Sleepy Darling Figure HN2953 - P. Parsons	Yr.Iss.	1982	100.00	195-250
1982 Dog of Fo-Flambe - N/A	Yr.Iss.	1983	50.00	175
1982 Prized Possessions Figure HN2942 - R. Tabbenor	Yr.Iss.	1983	125.00	450-555
1983 Loving Cup - N/A	Yr.Iss.	1984	75.00	350-395
1983 Springtime HN3033 - A. Hughes	Yr.Iss.	1984	125.00	325-450
1984 Sir Henry Doulton Jug D6703 - E. Griffiths	Yr.Iss.	1985	50.00	200-300
1984 Pride & Joy Figure HN2945 - R. Tabbenor	Yr.Iss.	1985	125.00	350-400
1985 Top of the Hill HN2126 - P. Gee	Yr.Iss.	1986	35.00	175-300
1985 Wintertime Figure HN3060 - A. Hughes	Yr.Iss.	1986	125.00	250-465
1986 Albert Sagger Toby Jug - W. Harper	Yr.Iss.	1987	35.00	85
1986 Auctioneer Figure HN2988 - R. Tabbenor	Yr.Iss.	1987	150.00	400-500
1987 Collector Bunnykins DB54 - D. Lyttleton	Yr.Iss.	1988	40.00	653-1400
1987 Summertime Figurine HN3137 - P. Parsons	Yr.Iss.	1988	140.00	300-450
1988 Top of the Hill Miniature Figurine HN2126 - P. Gee	Yr.Iss.	1989	95.00	125-225
1988 Beefeater Tiny Jug - R. Tabbenor	Yr.Iss.	1989	25.00	125-225
1988 Old Salt Tea Pot - N/A	Yr.Iss.	1989	135.00	200-275
1989 Geisha Flambe Figure HN3229 - P. Parsons	Yr.Iss.	1990	195.00	195
1989 Flower Sellers Children Plate - N/A	Yr.Iss.	1990	65.00	70-100
1990 Autumntime Figure HN3231 - P. Parsons	Yr.Iss.	1991	190.00	224-450
1990 Jester Mini Figure HN3335 - C.J. Noke	Yr.Iss.	1991	115.00	115
1990 Old King Cole Tiny Jug - H. Fenton	Yr.Iss.	1991	35.00	100-125
1991 Bunny's Bedtime Figure HN3370 - N. Pedley	9,500	1992	195.00	200-260
1991 Charles Dickens Jug D6901 - W. Harper	Yr.Iss.	1992	100.00	140-150
1991 L'Ambiteuse Figure (Tissot Lady) HN3359 - V. Annand	5,000	1992	295.00	350-375
1991 Christopher Columbus Jug D6911 - S. Taylor	Yr.Iss.	1992	95.00	125-175
1992 Discovery Figure HN3428 - A. Munslow	Yr.Iss.	1993	160.00	100
1992 King Edward Jug D6923 - W. Harper	Yr.Iss.	1993	250.00	295-310
1992 Master Potter Bunnykins DB131 - W. Platt	Yr.Iss.	1993	50.00	190-275
1992 Eliza Farren Prestige Figure HN3442 - N/A	Yr.Iss.	1993	335.00	325-400
1993 Barbara Figure - N/A	Yr.Iss.	1994	285.00	510-586
1993 Lord Mountbatten L/S Jug - S. Taylor	5,000	1994	225.00	225-269
1993 Punch & Judy Double Sided Jug - S. Taylor	2,500	1994	400.00	465-475
1993 Flambe Dragon HN3552 - N/A	Retrd.	1994	260.00	260-415
1994 Diane HN3604 - N/A	Retrd.	1995	250.00	300-400
1995 Le Bal HN3702 - N/A	Retrd.	1996	350.00	350
1995 George Tinworth Jug, sm. D7000 - W. Harper	Retrd.	1996	99.00	125-175
1995 Partners in Collecting Bunnykins DB151	Retrd.	1996	45.00	85-150
1996 Special Delivery Plate - N/A	Retrd.	1996	45.00	60-100
1996 Welcome - N/A	Retrd.	1996	80.00	121-150
1996 Pamela HN3756 - T. Potts	Retrd.	1996	275.00	293-310
1996 Mr. Pickwick Jug, sm. D7025 - M. Alcock	Retrd.	1996	138.00	150-250
1996 Winter's Day HN3769 - N. Pedley	Retrd.	1997	325.00	325-450
1996 Gifts For All plate - N. Pedley	Retrd.	1997	40.00	40
1997 Susan HN3871 - N. Pedley	Retrd.	1997	345.00	345-400
1997 Joy - (1997 membership gift) - N. Pedley	Retrd.	1997	85.00	85-140
1997 Sir Henry Doulton S/S - W. Harper	Retrd.	1997	157.50	165
1997 Janet Figure HN4042 - V. Annand	Retrd.	1998	275.00	275-375
1998 Richard III Jug - R. Tabbenor	Retrd.	1998	275.00	275-450

YEAR ISSUE	EDITION LIMIT	YEAR RETD.	ISSUE PRICE	*QUOTE U.S.$
1998 Bunnykins Builds a Snowman plate - N/A	Retrd.	1998	60.00	60
1999 Nicole HN4112 - N. Pedley	Yr.lss.	1999	295.00	295
1999 Melody HN4117 - N. Pedley	Yr.lss.	1999	50.00	50
1999 Judge Bunnykins DB188 - S. Ridge	Yr.lss.	1999	50.00	68-75
1999 Tourist Bunnykin DB190 - M. Alcock	Yr.lss.	1999	50.00	50-75
1999 King John - R. Tabbenor	Yr.lss.	1999	310.00	310
1999 The Moor - Colorway - C. Noke	99	1999	5865.00	5865
2000 Lawyer Bunnykins DB214 - M. Alcock	Yr.lss.	2000	50.00	55-75
2000 Sightseer Bunnykins DB215 - M. Alcock	Yr.lss.	2000	50.00	50-82
2000 The Collector D7147 - R. Tabbenor	Yr.lss.	2000	145.00	145
2000 Sweet Lilac HN3792 - J. Bromley	Yr.lss.	2000	295.00	295
2000 Greetings HN4250 - A. Maslankowski	Yr.lss.	2000	50.00	50
2000 Lido Lady HN4247 - N. Pedley	Yr.lss.	2000	395.00	395
2001 Embrace HN4258 - A. Maslankowski	Yr.lss.	2001	50.00	50
2001 Choir Singer Bunnykin DB223 - M. Alcock	Yr.lss.	2001	50.00	50
2001 Jacqueline HN4309 - N. Pedley	Yr.lss.	2001	295.00	295
2001 The Figure Collector D7156 - R. Tabbenor	Yr.lss.	2001	145.00	145
2001 Cherished Memories HN4265	6/02		245.00	245
2002 Cherish Figurine HN4442 - A. Maslankowski			50.00	50
2002 Vicar Bunnykins DB254 - S. Ridge	Yr.lss.		50.00	50
2002 Applause HN4328 - V. Annand	Yr.lss.		270.00	270

Age of Innocence - N. Pedley

1991 Feeding Time HN3373	9,500	1994	245.00	300-400
1992 First Outing HN3377	9,500	1994	275.00	300-390
1991 Making Friends HN3372	9,500	1994	270.00	250-325
1991 Puppy Love HN3371	9,500	1994	270.00	300-390

Angels Of Harmony - Royal Doulton

1998 Angel of Autumn	Retrd.	1999	80.00	80
1998 Angel of Friendship	Retrd.	1999	80.00	80
1998 Angel of Love	Retrd.	1999	80.00	80
1998 Angel of Peace	Retrd.	1999	80.00	80
1998 Angel of Spring	Retrd.	1999	80.00	80
1998 Angel of Summer	Retrd.	1999	80.00	80
1998 Angel of Winter	Retrd.	1999	80.00	80
1998 Guardian Angel	Retrd.	1999	80.00	80

Archive Collection - A. Maslankowski

2000 Artemis HN4081	250	2001	1465.00	1465
2000 Aurora HN4078	250	2001	2935.00	2935
2000 Ceres HN4080	250	2001	1465.00	1465
2000 Erato HN4082	250	2001	1465.00	1465
2000 Hebe HN4079	250	2001	1465.00	1465

Archive Noke Collection - R. Tabbenor

2001 Polar Bear and Cub	200		1595.00	1595

Art Deco - T. Potts

2000 Destiny HN4164	500	2001	1160.00	1160
2000 Ecstasy HN4163	500	2001	1160.00	1160
2000 Optimism HN4165	500	2001	1160.00	1160
2000 Wisdom HN4166	500	2001	1160.00	1160

Art Is Life - A. Maslankowski

2000 Ballerina AIL9	1,250	2001	430.00	430
2000 Ballet Dancer AIL10	1,250	2001	430.00	430
2000 Eagle AIL5	1,500	2000	340.00	340
2000 Girl on Rock AIL8	2,000	2001	245.00	245
2000 Girl Stretching AIL6	2,000	2001	305.00	305
2000 Girl w/Ponytail AIL7	2,000	2001	305.00	305
2000 Horses AIL4	1,500	2001	340.00	340
2000 Kiss AIL1	950	2001	380.00	380
2001 Lions AIL11	950	2001	380.00	380
2000 Love AIL2	950	2001	380.00	380
2001 Polar Bear AIL12	950	2001	360.00	360
2000 Wolves AIL3	1,500	2001	360.00	360

Beatrix Potter Figures - Various

1967 Amiable Guinea Pig P2061 - A. Hallam	Retrd.	1983	29.95	315-450
2000 Amiable Guinea Pig P4031 - W. Platt	Open		48.00	48
1992 And This Pig Had None P3319 - M. Alcock	Retrd.	1998	29.95	38-60
1963 Anna Maria P1851 - A. Hallam	Retrd.	1983	29.95	395-450
1971 Appley Dapply P2333 - A. Hallam	Open		29.95	36
1970 Aunt Pettitoes P2276 - A. Hallam	Retrd.	1993	29.95	75-115

YEAR ISSUE	EDITION LIMIT	YEAR RETD.	ISSUE PRICE	*QUOTE U.S.$
1989 Babbity Bumble P2971 - W. Platt	Retrd.	1993	29.95	145-165
1992 Benjamin Ate a Lettuce Leaf P3317 - M. Alcock	Retrd.	1998	29.95	36-58
1948 Benjamin Bunny P1105 - A. Gredington	Retrd.	1997	29.95	36-300
1983 Benjamin Bunny Sat on a Bank P2803 - D. Lyttleton	Retrd.	1997	29.95	55-145
1975 Benjamin Bunny with Peter Rabbit P2509 - A. Maslankowski	Retrd.	1995	39.95	95
1995 Benjamin Bunny, lg. P3403 - M. Alcock	Retrd.	1997	65.00	75
1991 Benjamin Wakes Up P3234 - A. Hughes-Lubeck	Retrd.	1997	29.95	35-50
1965 Cecily Parsley P1941 - A. Gredington	Retrd.	1993	29.95	125-217
1979 Chippy Hackee P2627 - D. Lyttleton	Retrd.	1993	29.95	55-65
1991 Christmas Stocking P3257 - M. Alcock	Retrd.	1994	65.00	180-195
1985 Cottontail at Lunchtime P2878 - D. Lyttleton	Retrd.	1996	29.95	65-80
1970 Cousin Ribby P2284 - A. Hallam	Retrd.	1993	29.95	49-75
1982 Diggory Diggory Delvet P2713 - D. Lyttleton	Retrd.	1997	29.95	40-75
1955 Dutchess w/Pie P1355 - G. Orwell	Retrd.	1967	29.95	200-350
1995 F.W. Gent, lg. P3450 - M. Alcock	Retrd.	1997	65.00	73
2000 Farmer Potatoes P4014 - S. Ridge	Open		60.00	60
1977 Fierce Bad Rabbit P2586 - D. Lyttleton	Retrd.	1997	29.95	35-100
1954 Flopsy Mopsy and Cottontail P1274 - A. Gredington	Retrd.	1997	29.95	45-100
1990 Foxy Reading Country News P3219 - A. Hughes-Lubeck	Retrd.	1997	49.95	58-75
1954 Foxy Whiskered Gentleman P1277 - A. Gredington	Open		29.95	36
1990 Gentleman Mouse Made a Bow P3200 - T. Chawner	Retrd.	1996	29.95	33-45
1976 Ginger P2559 - D. Lyttleton	Retrd.	1982	29.95	550-695
1986 Goody and Timmy Tiptoes P2957 - D. Lyttleton	Retrd.	1996	49.95	65-90
1961 Goody Tiptoes P1675 - A. Gredington	Retrd.	1997	29.95	50-75
1998 Hiding From the Cat P3766 - G. Tongue	3,500	1998	195.00	195-205
1951 Hunca Munca P1198 - A. Gredington	Retrd.	2000	29.95	35-76
1992 Hunca Munca Spills the Beads P3288 - M. Alcock	Retrd.	1996	29.95	50-95
1977 Hunca Munca Sweeping P2584 - D. Lyttleton	Retrd.	2000	29.95	40-100
2001 Hunca Munca with Pan P4074 - S. Ridge	Open		60.00	60
1990 Jemima Puddleduck-Foxy Whiskered Gentleman P3193 - T. Chawner	Retrd.	1999	55.00	60-80
1998 Jemima Puddleduck and her Ducklings P3786 - M. Alcock	Open		60.00	60
1983 Jemima Puddleduck Made a Feather Nest-P2823 - D. Lyttleton	Retrd.	1997	29.95	45-75
1948 Jemima Puddleduck P1092 - A. Gredington	Open		29.95	36
1993 Jemima Puddleduck, lg. P3373 - M. Alcock	Retrd.	1997	49.95	75-95
1999 Jeremy Fisher Catches A Fish P3919 - M. Alcock	Open		37.00	72
1988 Jeremy Fisher Digging P3090 - T. Chawner	Retrd.	1994	50.00	175-275
1995 Jeremy Fisher lg. P3372 - M. Alcock	Retrd.	1997	65.00	75-112
1950 Jeremy Fisher P1157 - A. Gredington	Retrd.	2000	29.95	40-122
1990 John Joiner P2965 - G. Tongue	Retrd.	1997	29.95	55
2000 Johnny Townmouse Holding Corn P3931 - M. Alcock	Open		48.00	48
1954 Johnny Townmouse P1276 - A. Gredington	Retrd.	1993	29.95	75-90
1988 Johnny Townmouse w/Bag P3094 - T. Chawner	Retrd.	1994	50.00	135-350
1990 Lady Mouse Made a Curtsy P3220 - A. Hughes-Lubeck	Retrd.	1997	29.95	40-65
1950 Lady Mouse P1183 - A. Gredington	Retrd.	2000	29.95	35-85
1977 Little Black Rabbit P2585 - D. Lyttleton	Retrd.	1997	29.95	36-65
1987 Little Pig Robinson Spying P3031 - T. Chawner	Retrd.	1993	29.95	150-275
1991 Miss Dormouse P3251 - M. Alcock	Retrd.	1995	29.95	75-95
1978 Miss Moppet P1275 - A. Gredington	Open		32.50	36
1990 Mittens & Moppet P3197 - T. Chawner	Retrd.	1994	50.00	100-175
1999 Mittens, Tom Kitten & Moppet (Tableau) P3792 - A. Hughes-Lubeck	Yr.lss.	1999	205.00	205-250

Collectors' Information Bureau

*Quotes have been rounded up to nearest dollar

YEAR ISSUE	EDITION LIMIT	YEAR RETD.	ISSUE PRICE	*QUOTE U.S.$
1989 Mother Ladybird P2966 - W. Platt	Retrd.	1996	29.95	55-75
1973 Mr. Alderman Ptolemy P2424 - G. Tongue	Retrd.	1997	29.95	55-176
1965 Mr. Benjamin Bunny P1940 - A. Gredington	Retrd.	2000	29.95	40-85
1979 Mr. Drake Puddleduck P2628 - D. Lyttleton	Retrd.	2000	29.95	35-75
1974 Mr. Jackson P2453 - A. Hallam	Retrd.	1997	29.95	36-75
1995 Mr. McGregor P3506 - M. Alcock	Open		42.50	60
1988 Mr. Tod P3091 - T. Chawner	Retrd.	1993	29.95	130-160
1965 Mrs. Flopsy Bunny P1942 - A. Gredington	Retrd.	1999	29.95	48-65
1997 Mrs. Rabbit and Peter P3646 - W. Platt	Retrd.	2000	67.50	68
1997 Mrs. Rabbit and the Four Bunnies P3672 - S. Ridge	1,997	1997	275.00	290-395
1992 Mrs. Rabbit Cooking P3278 - M. Alcock	Retrd.	1999	29.95	36-51
1951 Mrs. Rabbit P1200 - A. Gredington	Retrd.	2000	29.95	33-60
1976 Mrs. Rabbit with Bunnies P2543 - D. Lyttleton	Retrd.	1997	29.95	55-85
1995 Mrs. Rabbit, lg. P3398 - M. Alcock	Retrd.	1997	65.00	75-79
1951 Mrs. Ribby P1199 - A. Gredington	Retrd.	2000	29.95	39-90
2000 Mrs. Tiggy-winkle P2877 - D. Lyttleton	Open		36.00	36
1998 Mrs. Tiggy-winkle Washing P3789 - W. Platt	Retrd.	2000	38.00	38
1997 Mrs. Tiggywinkle, lg. P3437 - M. Alcock	Retrd.	1997	75.00	75-275
1948 Mrs. Tittlemouse P1103 - A. Gredington	Retrd.	1993	29.95	50-195
2000 Mrs. Tittlemouse P4015 - S. Ridge	Open		48.00	48
1992 No More Twist P3325 - M. Alcock	Retrd.	1997	29.95	60-65
1986 Old Mr. Bouncer P2956 - D. Lyttleton	Retrd.	1995	29.95	55
1963 Old Mr. Brown P1796 - A. Hallam	Retrd.	1999	29.95	36-163
1983 Old Mr. Pricklepin P2767 - D. Lyttleton	Retrd.	1982	29.95	95-195
1959 Old Woman Who Lived in a Shoe P1545 - C. Melbourne	Retrd.	1997	29.95	50-225
1983 Old Woman Who Lived in a Shoe, Knitting P2804 - D. Lyttleton	Open		29.95	36
2000 Peter & Benjamin Picking Onions P3930 - M. Alcock	3,000	2000	215.00	215
1991 Peter & The Red Handkerchief P3242 - M. Alcock	Retrd.	1997	39.95	35-48
1995 Peter in Bed P3473 - M. Alcock	Open		39.95	60
1999 Peter in the Watering Can P3940 - W. Platt	Open		39.00	60
2001 Peter Rabbit Digging P4075 - M. Alcock	Open		60.00	60
1989 Peter Rabbit in the Gooseberry Net P3157 - D. Lyttleton	Retrd.	1995	39.95	60-75
1948 Peter Rabbit P1098 - A. Gredington	Open		29.95	36
1993 Peter Rabbit, lg. P3356 - M. Alcock	Retrd.	1997	65.00	65-75
1996 Peter with Daffodils P3597 - A. Hughes-Lubeck	Retrd.	2000	42.50	48-60
1996 Peter with Postbag P3591 - A. Hughes-Lubeck	Retrd.	1999	42.50	45-60
1996 Peter with Red Pocket Handkerchief, lg. P3592 - A. Hughes-Lubeck	Retrd.	1999	75.00	75
1971 Pickles P2334 - A. Hallam	Retrd.	1982	29.95	298-500
1948 Pig Robinson P1104 - A. Gredington	Retrd.	1999	29.95	36
1972 Pig Wig P2381 - A. Hallam	Retrd.	1982	29.95	450-500
1955 Pigling Bland P1365 - G. Orwell	Retrd.	1999	29.95	48-55
1991 Pigling Eats Porridge P3252 - M. Alcock	Retrd.	1994	50.00	95-150
1976 Poorly Peter Rabbit P2560 - D. Lyttleton	Retrd.	1997	29.95	64-104
1981 Rebeccah Puddleduck P2647 - D. Lyttleton	Retrd.	2000	29.95	32-65
1992 Ribby and the Patty Pan P3280 - M. Alcock	Retrd.	1998	29.95	36-65
1974 Sally Henry Penney P2452 - A. Hallam	Retrd.	1993	29.95	65-125
1948 Samuel Whiskers P1106 - A. Gredington	Retrd.	1995	29.95	45-95
1975 Simpkin P2508 - A. Maslankowski	Retrd.	1983	29.95	660-690
1973 Sir Isaac Newton P2425 - G. Tongue	Retrd.	1984	29.95	456-525
1948 Squirrel Nutkin P1102 - A. Gredington	Retrd.	2000	29.95	45-275
1961 Tabitha Twitchitt P1676 - A. Gredington	Retrd.	1995	29.95	60-88
1976 Tabitha Twitchitt with Miss Moppett P2544 - D. Lyttleton	Retrd.	1993	29.95	130-225
1949 Tailor of Gloucester P1108 - A. Gredington	Open		29.95	36
1995 Tailor of Gloucester, lg. P3449 - M. Alcock	Retrd.	1997	65.00	75
1948 Tiggy Winkle P1107 - A. Gredington	Retrd.	2000	29.95	36-51
1985 Tiggy Winkle Takes Tea P2877 - D. Lyttleton	Open		29.95	36
1948 Timmy Tiptoes P1101 - A. Gredington	Retrd.	1997	29.95	60-163
2000 Timmy Willie Fetching Milk P3976 - W. Platt	Open		36.00	48
1949 Timmy Willie P1109 - A. Gredington	Retrd.	1993	29.95	65-88
1986 Timmy Willie Sleeping P2996 - G. Tongue	Retrd.	1996	29.95	55-95
1998 Tom Kitten in the Rockery P3719 - W. Platt	Retrd.	2000	36.00	36
1948 Tom Kitten P1100 - A. Gredington	Retrd.	1999	29.95	36
1995 Tom Kitten, lg. P3405 - M. Alcock	Retrd.	1997	65.00	75-90
1987 Tom Kitten and Butterfly P3030 - T. Chawner	Retrd.	1994	50.00	295-350
1987 Tom Thumb P2989 - W. Platt	Retrd.	1997	29.95	55-165
1955 Tommy Brock P1348 - G. Orwell	Open		29.95	36
2000 Yock Yock in Tub P3946 - W. Platt	Open		60.00	60

Birthday Figure of the Year - N. Pedley

YEAR ISSUE	EDITION LIMIT	YEAR RETD.	ISSUE PRICE	*QUOTE U.S.$
2000 Happy Birthday 2000 HN4215	Yr.Iss.		195.00	195
2001 Happy Birthday 2001 NH4308	Yr.Iss.	2001	195.00	195
2002 Happy Birthday 2002 HN4393	Yr.Iss.		175.00	175

Brambly Hedge - Various

YEAR ISSUE	EDITION LIMIT	YEAR RETD.	ISSUE PRICE	*QUOTE U.S.$
2002 Basil Woodmouse DBH38 - S. Ridge	Open		75.00	75
2002 The Bride & Groom (Dusty and Poppy) DBH44 - M. Alcock	Open		150.00	150
2002 Dusty Dogwood DBH37 - M. Alcock	Open		75.00	75
2002 Happy Birthday Wilfred DBH45 - M. Alcock	3,000		235.00	235
2000 Ice Ball DBH30 - S. Ridge	3,000		240.00	240
2000 Lady Woodmouse DBH32 - W. Platt	Open		80.00	80
2000 Lord Woodmouse DBH31 - S. Ridge	Open		80.00	80
2001 Mr. Saltapple DBH39 - S. Ridge	Open		80.00	80
2001 Mrs. Saltapple DBH40 - M. Alcock	Open		80.00	80
2001 Pebble DBH41 - M. Alcock	Open		60.00	60
2002 Poppy Eyebright DBH36 - W. Platt	Open		75.00	75
2000 Primrose Woodmouse DBH33 - S. Ridge	Open		60.00	60
2001 Shell DBH42 - W. Platt	Open		60.00	60
2001 Shrimp DBH43 - W. Platt	Open		60.00	60
2000 Toy Chest Moneybox - M. Alcock	Open		100.00	145
2000 Wilfred Toadflax DBH34 - S. Ridge	Open		60.00	60
2002 Wilfred's Brithday Tableau DBH45	3,000		235.00	235

British Sporting Heritage - V. Annand

YEAR ISSUE	EDITION LIMIT	YEAR RETD.	ISSUE PRICE	*QUOTE U.S.$
1994 Ascot HN3471	5,000	1997	475.00	475-497
1996 Croquet HN3470	5,000	1997	475.00	475-497
1993 Henley HN3367	5,000	1997	475.00	475-497
1995 Wimbledon HN3366	5,000	1997	475.00	475-497

Bunnykins - Various

YEAR ISSUE	EDITION LIMIT	YEAR RETD.	ISSUE PRICE	*QUOTE U.S.$
1999 Airman DB199 - M. Alcock	5,000	2000	60.00	85-135
1999 Angel DB196 - M. Alcock	Open		39.00	42
2000 Ballerina DB176 - G. Tongue	Open		49.00	49
1995 Bathtime DB148 - M. Alcock	Retrd.	1997	40.00	48-65
1987 Be Prepared DB56 - D. Lyttleton	Retrd.	1995	40.00	40-75
1987 Bed Time DB55 - D. Lyttleton	Retrd.	1998	40.00	40-55
1995 Boy Skater DB152 - M. Alcock	Retrd.	1998	40.00	42-68
1991 Bride DB101 - A. Hughes	Retrd.	2001	40.00	45-55
1987 Brownie DB61 - W. Platt	Retrd.	1993	39.00	75-95
2001 Bunnykins Bath Night DB241 - M. Alcock	5,000		140.00	140
1999 Businessman DB203 - M. Alcock	5,000	2000	60.00	60-116
1994 Christmas Surprise DB146 - W. Platt	Retrd.	2000	50.00	53-65
1990 Cook DB85 - W. Platt	Retrd.	1994	35.00	75-85
1998 Doctor Bunnykins DB181 - M. Alcock	Retrd.	2000	45.00	49-55
1984 Drummer Bunnykins (Golden Jubilee) DB26A	Yr.Iss.	1984	N/A	163-175
1995 Easter Greetings - M. Alcock	Retrd.	1999	50.00	55
1996 Father Bunnykin DB154 - M. Alcock	Retrd.	1996	50.00	75-95
1988 Father, Mother, Victoria DB68 - M. Alcock	Retrd.	1995	40.00	60-86
1989 Fireman DB75 - M. Alcock	Open		40.00	42
1998 Fisherman - S. Ridge	Retrd.	2000	52.50	65-90
1990 Fisherman DB84 - W. Platt	Retrd.	1993	39.00	125-140
2000 Fortune Teller DB218 - W. Platt	Retrd.	2000	60.00	62-70
2001 Friar Tuck DB246 - M. Alcock	Open		60.00	60
1996 Gardener DB156 - W. Platt	Retrd.	1998	40.00	50-80
1995 Girl Skater DB153 - M. Alcock	Retrd.	1997	40.00	50-65

YEAR ISSUE	EDITION LIMIT	YEAR RETD.	ISSUE PRICE	*QUOTE U.S.$
1995 Goodnight DB157 - S. Ridge	Retrd.	1999	40.00	42-50
1991 Groom DB102 - M. Alcock	Retrd.	2001	40.00	45-55
1993 Halloween Bunnykin DB132 - M. Alcock	Retrd.	1997	50.00	50-125
1983 Happy Birthday DB21 - G. Tongue	Retrd.	1997	40.00	45-50
1988 Harry DB73 - M. Alcock	Retrd.	1993	34.00	55-95
1972 Helping Mother DB2 - A. Hallam	Retrd.	1993	34.00	75-95
1986 Home Run DB43 - D. Lyttleton	Retrd.	1993	39.00	100-130
1990 Ice Cream DB82 - W. Platt	Retrd.	1993	39.00	95-190
2000 Jack and Jill DB222 - M. Alcock	Open		120.00	120
2000 Little Bo Peep DB220 - M. Alcock	Open		60.00	60
2002 Little Boy Blue DB239 - S. Ridge	Open		60.00	60
2000 Little Jack Horner DB221 - M. Alcock	Open		60.00	60
2001 Little John DB243 - M. Alcock	Open		60.00	60
2002 Little Miss Muffet DB240 - W. Platt	Open		60.00	60
2001 Maid Marian DB245 - M. Alcock	Open		60.00	60
2002 Mary Mary Quite Contrary DB247 - S. Ridge	Open		60.00	60
1997 Mother and Baby DB167 - S. Ridge	Open		42.00	49
1996 Mother's Day DB155 - S. Ridge	Retrd.	2000	42.00	55
1986 Mr. Bunnykins "At The Easter Parade" (maroon jacket) DB51 - D. Lyttleton	Yr.Iss.	1986	40.00	1100-1800
1982 Mr. Bunnykins "At The Easter Parade" (red jacket) DB18 - G. Tongue	Retrd.	1993	39.00	85-100
1982 Mrs. Bunnykins "At The Easter Parade" (blue dress) DB19 - D. Lyttleton	Retrd.	1993	40.00	60-103
1982 Mrs. Bunnykins "At The Easter Parade" (pink dress) DB52 - D. Lyttleton	Yr.Iss.	1986	40.00	700-1500
1999 Mystic DB197 - M. Alcock	Yr.Iss.	2000	59.00	60-79
1995 New Baby DB158 - G. Tongue	Retrd.	1999	40.00	43-70
1989 Nurse DB74 - M. Alcock	Retrd.	2000	35.00	45-55
1989 Paper Boy DB77 - M. Alcock	Retrd.	1993	39.00	100-150
1972 Playtime DB8 - A. Hallam	Retrd.	1993	34.00	55-75
1988 Policeman DB69 - M. Alcock	Retrd.	2000	40.00	45
1988 Polly DB71 - M. Alcock	Retrd.	1993	34.00	60-85
1995 Rainy Day DB147 - M. Alcock	Retrd.	1997	40.00	40-60
2001 Robin Hood DB244 - M. Alcock	Open		60.00	60
1997 Sailor Bunnykins DB166 - S. Ridge	Yr.Iss.	1997	52.50	59-70
2002 Sandcastle Money Box (30th Anniversary) DB228 - W. Platt	Yr.Iss.		225.00	225
1981 Santa Bunnykins DB17 - D. Lyttleton	Retrd.	1995	40.00	50-125
1987 School Days DB57 - D. Lyttleton	Retrd.	1994	40.00	75-80
1982 School Master DB60 - W. Platt	Retrd.	1995	40.00	60-80
1974 Sleepytime DB15 - A. Maslankowski	Retrd.	1993	39.00	55-95
1972 Sleigh Ride DB4 - A. Hallam	Retrd.	1997	40.00	50-85
1972 Story Time DB9 - A. Hallam	Retrd.	1997	35.00	40-70
1988 Susan DB70 - M. Alcock	Retrd.	1993	34.00	75-80
1992 Sweetheart Bunnykin DB130 - W. Platt	Retrd.	1997	40.00	45-65
1988 Tom DB72 - M. Alcock	Retrd.	1993	34.00	75-100
1986 Uncle Sam DB50 - D. Lyttleton	Retrd.	2001	40.00	45-113
1988 William DB69 - M. Alcock	Retrd.	1993	34.00	75-150

Bunnykins-Event - Various

2000 Morris Dancer DB204 - S. Ridge	Yr.Iss.	2000	70.00	70-105
2001 Tyrolean Dancer DB242 - S. Ridge	Yr.Iss.	2001	70.00	70
2002 Flamenco Dancer DB256 - S. Ridge	Yr.Iss.		70.00	70

Bunnykins-Figure of the Year - M. Alcock

1998 Seaside Bunnykins	Yr.Iss.	1998	55.00	59-75
1999 Mother Bunnykins DB189	Yr.Iss.	1999	42.50	43-55
2000 Sundial DB213 - W. Platt	Yr.Iss.	2000	50.00	52-60
2001 Sands of Time DB229	Yr.Iss.	2001	60.00	60
2002 Stopwatch DB253 - M. Alcock	Yr.Iss.		60.00	60

Character Sculptures - Various

1984 Balloon Lady HN2935 - P. Gee	Open		235.00	245
1940 Balloon Man HN1954 - L. Harradine	Open		345.00	360
1938 Biddy Penning Farthing HN1843 - L. Harradine	Open		345.00	360
1996 Bill Sikes HN3785 - A. Dobson	Retrd.	1996	306.25	307
1996 Bowls Player HN3780 - J. Jones	Retrd.	1996	137.50	138
1993 Captain Hook - R. Tabbenor	Retrd.	1996	250.00	270-325
1995 Cyrano de Bergerac HN3751 - D. Biggs	Retrd.	1996	268.75	269
1994 D' Artagnan - R. Tabbenor	Retrd.	1996	260.00	269
1993 Dick Turpin - R. Tabbenor	Retrd.	1996	250.00	269
2001 Doctor HN4286 - A. Hughes	Open		395.00	395
1995 Fagin HN3752 - A. Dobson	Retrd.	1996	268.75	269

YEAR ISSUE	EDITION LIMIT	YEAR RETD.	ISSUE PRICE	*QUOTE U.S.$
2002 Fireman HN4411 - A. Hughes	Open		350.00	350
1995 Gulliver - D. Biggs	Retrd.	1996	285.00	307
2002 Judge HN4412 - A. Hughes	Open		395.00	395
2001 Lawyer HN4289 - A. Hughes	Open		330.00	330
1993 Long John Silver - A. Maslankowski	Retrd.	1996	250.00	269
2001 Nurse HN4287 - A. Hughes	Open		395.00	395
1996 Oliver Twist and Artful Dodger HN3786 - A. Dobson	Retrd.	1996	275.00	275
1994 Pied Piper - A. Maslankowski	Retrd.	1996	260.00	269
2001 Policeman HN4410 - A. Hughes	Open		330.00	330
1995 Richard The Lionheart HN3675 - P. Parsons	Retrd.	2001	615.00	640
1993 Robin Hood - A. Maslankowski	Retrd.	1996	250.00	269
2000 Santa Claus HN4175 - R. Tabbenor	Open		340.00	340
1995 Sherlock Holmes HN3639 - R. Tabbenor	Retrd.	1996	268.75	269
1996 Sir Francis Drake HN3770 - D. Biggs	Retrd.	1996	275.00	275
1985 Sir Winston Churchill HN3057 - A. Hughes	Open		345.00	360
2000 Sorcerer HN4252 - A. Maslankowski	Open		450.00	495
2000 Sorceress HN4253 - A. Maslankowski	Open		395.00	395
1995 Wizard HN3722 - A. Maslankowski	Retrd.	1996	306.25	330-405

Charity Figure of the Year - N. Pedley

1998 Hope	Yr.Iss.	1998	225.00	225-315
1999 Faith HN4151	Yr.Iss.	1999	235.00	235
2000 Charity HN4243	Retrd.	2001	235.00	235
2001 New Dawn HN4314	6/02		235.00	235

Chelsea - V. Annand

2001 Becky HN4322	Open		175.00	175
2001 Bethany HN4326	Open		175.00	175
1997 Kathryn HN4040	Retrd.	2001	165.00	185
2001 Kaitlin HN4323	Open		175.00	175
2000 Melinda HN4209	Open		165.00	185
1997 Olivia HN3717	Retrd.	2001	165.00	185
2000 Zoe HN4208	Open		165.00	185

Children - A. Maslankowski

1996 Ballet Class HN3731	Retrd.	2001	90.00	95
1992 Little Ballerina HN3395	Open		90.00	95
1997 Stage Struck HN3951	Retrd.	2001	85.00	95
1997 Star Performer HN3950	Retrd.	2001	85.00	95

Christmas Figure of the Year - N. Pedley

1999 Christmas Day HN4214	Yr.Iss.	1999	295.00	295
2000 Christmas Day 2000 HN4242	Yr.Iss.	2000	295.00	295
2001 Christmas Day 2001 HN4315	Yr.Iss.	2001	295.00	295

Classique - Royal Doulton, unless otherwise noted

1999 Anyone For Tennis CL4007 - T. Potts	Retrd.	2001	185.00	185
2001 At The Races CL4014 - T. Potts	Retrd.	2001	195.00	195
1999 Bernadette CL4005 - T. Potts	Retrd.	2001	245.00	245
2000 Celebration CL4011- T. Potts	Retrd.	2001	195.00	195
1998 Christina	Retrd.	2000	195.00	195
2000 Elizabeth CL4009 - T. Potts	Retrd.	2001	195.00	195
1999 Eve CL4002 - T. Potts	Retrd.	2001	195.00	195
1998 Faye CL3984	Retrd.	2000	175.00	175
1998 Felicity CL3986	Retrd.	1999	175.00	175
1998 From This Day Forth CL3990	Retrd.	1999	175.00	175
2000 Gabrielle CL4012- T. Potts	Retrd.	2001	185.00	185
1998 Helena	Retrd.	2000	175.00	175
1998 Isobel CL3890	Retrd.	1999	175.00	175
1997 Lorna CL3997 - T. Potts	Retrd.	2000	175.00	175
1998 Lucinda CL3983	Retrd.	2000	175.00	175
1998 Naomi	Retrd.	2000	225.00	225
1999 Nicola CL4000 - T. Potts	Retrd.	2001	175.00	175
2000 Philippa CL4010 - T. Potts	Retrd.	2001	185.00	185
1999 Simone CL4004 - T. Potts	Retrd.	2001	175.00	225
2001 Taking The Reins CL4013 - T. Potts	Retrd.	2001	195.00	195
1999 Tanya CL4006 - T. Potts	Retrd.	2001	195.00	195
1999 To Love and Cherish CL4003 - T. Potts	Retrd.	2000	175.00	175
1999 To The Fairway CL4008 - T. Potts	Retrd.	2001	245.00	245
1998 Vanessa CL3989	Retrd.	2001	175.00	175
2001 Victoria	Retrd.	2001	245.00	245

Country Maid Collection - N. Pedley

2000 Dairy Maid HN4249	Retrd.	2001	225.00	225
2000 Fair Maid HN4222	Retrd.	2001	225.00	225
2001 Maid of the Meadow HN4316	Open		225.00	225
2001 Milk Maid HN4305	Retrd.	2001	225.00	225

YEAR ISSUE	EDITION LIMIT	YEAR RETD.	ISSUE PRICE	*QUOTE U.S.$
Diamond Anniversary Tinies - Various				
1994 John Barleycorn - C. Noke	2,500	1994	350.00	450-500
1994 Simon The Cellarer - Noke/Fenton	2,500	1994	set	Set
1994 Dick Turpin - W. Harper	2,500	1994	set	Set
1994 Granny - W. Harper	2,500	1994	set	Set
1994 Jester - C. Noke	2,500	1994	set	Set
1994 Parson Brown - W. Harper	2,500	1994	set	Set
Femmes Fatales - P. Davies				
1979 Cleopatra HN2868	750	1995	750.00	1350
1984 Eve HN2466	750	1995	1250.00	1300-1500
1981 Helen of Troy HN2387	750	1993	1250.00	1400-1600
1985 Lucrezia Borgia HN2342	750	1993	1250.00	1300-1500
1982 Queen of Sheba HN2328	750	1996	1250.00	1300-1600
1983 Tz'u-Hsi HN2391	750	1996	1250.00	1300-1500
Figure of the Year - Various				
1991 Amy HN3316 - P. Gee	Closed	1991	195.00	695
1992 Mary HN3375 - P. Gee	Closed	1992	225.00	470-495
1993 Patricia HN3365 - V. Annand	Closed	1993	250.00	322-470
1994 Jennifer HN3447 - P. Gee	Closed	1994	250.00	300-400
1995 Deborah - HN3644 - N. Pedley	Closed	1995	225.00	225-276
1996 Belle HN3703 - V. Annand	Closed	1996	231.25	235
1997 Jessica HN3850 - N. Pedley	Closed	1997	245.00	245-400
1998 Rebecca HN4041 - V. Annand	Closed	1998	195.00	195-315
1999 Lauren HN3975 - D. Hughes	Yr.Iss.	1999	215.00	224-293
2000 Rachel HN3976 - D. Hughes	Yr.Iss.	2000	215.00	215
2001 Melissa HN3977 - D. Hughes	Yr.Iss.	2001	215.00	215
2002 Sarah HN3978 - D. Hughes	Yr.Iss.		215.00	215
The Four Seasons - V. Annand				
1993 Springtime HN3477	Retrd.	1996	325.00	395-445
1994 Summertime HN3478	Retrd.	1996	325.00	350-465
1993 Autumntime HN3621	Retrd.	1996	325.00	350
1993 Wintertime HN3622	Retrd.	1996	325.00	350
Gainsborough Ladies - P. Gee				
1991 Countess of Sefton HN3010	5,000	1996	650.00	700
1991 Hon Frances Duncombe HN3009	5,000	1996	650.00	700
1991 Lady Sheffield HN3008	5,000	1996	650.00	700
1990 Mary, Countess Howe HN3007	5,000	1996	650.00	700
Great Lovers - R. Jefferson				
1995 Antony and Cleopatra HN3114	150	1997	5250.00	5250
1996 Lancelot and Guinevere HN3112	150	1997	5250.00	5250
1994 Robin Hood and Maid Marian HN3111	150	1997	5250.00	5250
1993 Romeo and Juliet HN3113	150	1997	5250.00	5250
Image of the Year - Various				
1998 Best Friends HN4026 - D. Tootle	Yr.Iss.	1998	125.00	125
1999 The Promise HN4033 - D. Tootle	Yr.Iss.	1999	150.00	150-205
2000 Kindred Spirits HN4077 - R. Tabbenor	Yr.Iss.	2000	145.00	145
2001 Special Friends HN4257 - A. Maslankowski	Yr.Iss.	2001	145.00	145
2002 Keep in Touch HN4377 - A. Maslankowski	Yr.Iss.		135.00	135
Images - Various				
1997 Amen HN4021 - D. Tootle	Retrd.	2001	55.00	63
1997 Angel HN3940 - A. Maslankowski	Retrd.	1999	125.00	125
1997 The Ballerina HN3828 - D. Tootle	Retrd.	2000	95.00	95
1998 The Ballet Dancer HN4027 - D. Tootle	Retrd.	2000	110.00	110
1998 Ballet Lesson HN4028 - D. Tootle	Retrd.	2000	110.00	110
1991 Bride & Groom HN3281 - R. Tabbenor	Retrd.	2000	85.00	99
1991 Bridesmaid HN3280 - R. Tabbenor	Retrd.	1999	85.00	99
1998 Bridesmaid HN4373 - A. Maslankowski	Open		65.00	65
1993 Brother & Sister HN3460 - A. Hughes	Retrd.	2001	52.50	125
1991 Brothers HN3191 - E. Griffiths	Retrd.	2001	90.00	125
1991 Congratulations HN3351 - P. Gee	Open		187.50	188
1998 The Dance HN4025 - D. Tootle	Retrd.	2001	120.00	120
1981 Family HN2720 - E. Griffiths	Retrd.	2001	187.50	240
2001 First Lesson HN4358 - A. Maslankowski	Retrd.	2001	70.00	70
1988 First Love HN2747 - D. Tootle	Retrd.	1997	170.00	215
1991 First Steps HN3282 - R. Tabbenor	Retrd.	2000	142.00	215
1993 Gift of Freedom HN3443 - P. Gee	Retrd.	2001	90.00	125
1997 Graduation HN3942 - A. Maslankowski	Retrd.	2001	125.00	140
1989 Happy Anniversary HN3254 - D. Tootle	Open		187.50	240
1997 Happy Birthday HN3829 - D. Tootle	Retrd.	2001	95.00	99
1998 The Kiss Boy HN4064 - A. Maslankowski	Retrd.	2001	62.50	63
1998 The Kiss Girl HN4065 - A. Maslankowski	Retrd.	2001	62.50	63
1999 Leap Frog HN4030 - D. Tootle	Retrd.	2000	150.00	150
2000 Love Everlasting HN4280 - A. Hughes	Open		90.00	90
1981 Lovers HN2762 - D. Tootle	Retrd.	1997	187.50	215-346
1997 The Messiah HN3952	Retrd.	1999	145.00	145
1980 Mother & Daughter HN2841 - E. Griffiths	Retrd.	1997	187.50	215
1997 Mother and Child HN3938 - A. Maslankowski	Open		125.00	140
1998 Night Watch (Owls) HN3895 - R. Tabbenor	Retrd.	2000	70.00	70
1993 Our First Christmas HN3452 - N/A	Retrd.	1998	185.00	215
1989 Over the Threshold HN3274 - R. Tabbenor	Retrd.	1998	187.50	215
2001 Page Boy HN4374 - A. Maslankowski	Open		65.00	65
2001 Perfect Pose HN4357 - A. Maslankowski	Retrd.	2001	70.00	70
1997 The Performance HN3827 - D. Tootle	Retrd.	2000	235.00	235
2002 Prayers HN4378 - A. Maslankowski	Open		62.50	63
2001 Sister and Brother HN4356 - A. Maslankowski	Retrd.	2001	99.00	99
1983 Sisters HN3018 - P. Parson	Retrd.	2001	90.00	125
2002 Sleepyhead HN4413 - A. Hughes	Open		62.50	63
2001 Surprise HN4376 - A. Maslankowski	Open		65.00	65
2000 Sweetheart Boy HN4351 - A. Maslankowski	Retrd.	2001	70.00	70
2000 Sweetheart Girl HN4352 - A. Maslankowski	Retrd.	2001	70.00	70
1995 Tommorrow's Dreams HN3665 - P. Gee	Open		70.00	70
1987 Wedding Day HN2748 - D. Tootle	Open		187.50	240
Images of Nature - R. Tabbenor, unless otherwise noted				
1993 Always and Forever (Doves) HN3550 - A. Hughes	Open		85.00	85
1982 Courtship HN3525 - R. Willis	Open		250.00	250
2000 Dedication (Polar Bears) HN4173 - A. Hughes	Retrd.	2001	145.00	145
1996 Devotion (Doves) HN3467 - A. Hughes	Retrd.	2001	80.00	80
2002 Endless Love (Swans) HN4440 - A. Maslankowski	Open		135.00	135
2001 Majestic HN4177	Open		175.00	175
2000 Running Wild (Cheetahs) HN4172	Retrd.	2001	99.00	165
1998 Sleepyhead (Cats) HN3894	Retrd.	2001	145.00	145
2000 Soaring High (Eagles) HN4087	Retrd.	2001	99.00	165
2000 Standing Tall (Giraffes) HN3898	Retrd.	2001	99.00	165
2001 Tumbling Waters HN4359 - A. Maslankowski	1,000	2001	1450.00	1450
1999 Running Free HN3896	Retrd.	2000	99.00	99
Impressions - P. Parsons, unless otherwise noted				
2000 Daybreak HN4196	Retrd.	2001	245.00	245
2000 In Loving Arms HN4262	Retrd.	2001	265.00	265
2000 Secret Thoughts HN4197	Retrd.	2001	245.00	245
2000 Summer Blooms HN4194	Retrd.	2001	245.00	245
2000 Summer Fragrance HN4195	Retrd.	2001	245.00	245
2000 Sunrise HN4199	Retrd.	2001	245.00	245
2000 Sunset HN4198	Retrd.	2001	245.00	245
2000 Sweet Dreams HN4193	Retrd.	2001	245.00	245
2000 Tender Greetings HN4261	Retrd.	2001	265.00	265
2000 Tender Moment HN4192 - A. Maslankowski	Retrd.	2001	245.00	245
In Vogue Collection - V. Annand				
1998 Abigail HN4044	Retrd.	2001	195.00	195
2001 The Bride HN4324	Open		195.00	195
2000 Claudia HN4230	Open		195.00	195
1997 Emma HN3714	Open		195.00	195
2002 Finishing Touch HN4329	Open		195.00	195
2000 Joanne HN4202	Open		225.00	225
2000 Rebecca HN4203	Open	2001	225.00	225
Jody's Dreamkeepers - J. Bergsma				
1998 The Best Thing About Mom Is Everything	Retrd.	1999	20.00	20
1998 Happiness Is Made To Be Shared	Retrd.	1999	25.00	25
1998 Home Is Where The Heart Is	Retrd.	1999	30.00	30

FIGURINES

YEAR ISSUE	EDITION LIMIT	YEAR RETD.	ISSUE PRICE	*QUOTE U.S.$
1998 A Home Without A Dog Is Just A House	Retrd.	1999	15.00	15
1998 Life Is Best...Just Putting Around!	Retrd.	1999	20.00	20
1998 May All Our Hearts Beat As One	Retrd.	1999	35.00	35
1998 May Your Heart Be Filled With Simple Joys	Retrd.	1999	20.00	20
1998 The Memories Of Christmas	Retrd.	1999	40.00	40
1998 Never Let Go Of Your Dreams	Retrd.	1999	20.00	20
1998 Of All The Treasures In Life, Friendship Is The Greatest	Retrd.	1999	30.00	30
1998 The Purpose Of Life Is To Celebrate Living	Retrd.	1999	50.00	50
1998 Reach Out For The Impossible	Retrd.	1999	75.00	75
1998 Simple Pleasures Are The Treasures Of Life	Retrd.	1999	20.00	20
1998 There Are Very Few...As Special As You	Retrd.	1999	30.00	30
1998 To Be A Child Is To Know The Joy Of Living	Retrd.	1999	50.00	50
1998 We Are Always On Our Way To A Miracle	Retrd.	1999	20.00	20
1998 We Never Outgrow Our Need For Hugs	Retrd.	1999	15.00	15
1998 When I Count My Blessings, I Count You Twice	Retrd.	1999	20.00	20
1998 When You Need A Friend You Can Count On Me	Retrd.	1999	25.00	25
1998 The Work Is Hard, But The Reward Is Great	Retrd.	1999	15.00	15

Limited Edition Figurines - Various

YEAR ISSUE	EDITION LIMIT	YEAR RETD.	ISSUE PRICE	*QUOTE U.S.$
2000 The Bather HN4244 - N. Pedley	2,000		440.00	440
1992 Christopher Columbus HN3392 - A. Maslankowski	1,492	1995	1950.00	1950
1993 Duke of Wellington HN3432 - A. Maslankowski	1,500	1998	1750.00	1750
1996 Eastern Grace Flambe HN3683 - P. Parsons	2,500	1996	493.75	520
1994 Field Marshal Montgomery HN3405 - N/A	1,944	1996	1100.00	1100
1993 General Robert E. Lee HN3404 - R. Tabbenor	5,000	1995	1175.00	1175
2002 George VI and Queen Mother Pair HN4420/4421 - V. Annand	1,000		715.00	715
2000 HM Queen Elizabeth (Queen Mother) HN4086 - A. Maslankowski	2,000	2001	395.00	395
1997 HM Queen Elizabeth, The Queen Mother HN3944 - A. Maslankowski	5,000	1998	635.00	635
1993 Lt. General Ulysses S. Grant HN3403 - R. Tabbenor	5,000	1995	1175.00	1175
1992 Napoleon at Waterloo HN3429 - A. Maslankowski	1,500	1994	1900.00	1900
2002 Princess Badoura, sm HN4179 - R. Tabbenor	500		995.00	995
2002 Queen Elizabeth II HN4372 - A. Maslankowski	1,500		445.00	445
1992 Samurai Warrior HN3402 - R. Tabbenor	950	1995	500.00	500-600
1997 Sir Henry Doulton HN3891 - R. Tabbenor	1,997	1997	430.00	450
2000 Sunshine Girl HN4245 - N. Pedley	2,000		440.00	440
2000 The Swimmer HN4246 - N. Pedley	2,000		440.00	440
1997 Top o' the Hill Blue HN 3735 - L. Harradine	3,500	1997	370.00	370
1993 Vice Admiral Lord Nelson HN3489 - A. Maslankowski	950	1996	1750.00	1750
1993 Winston S. Churchill HN3433 - A. Maslankowski	5,000	1994	595.00	595-650

Literary Heroines - P. Parsons

YEAR ISSUE	EDITION LIMIT	YEAR RETD.	ISSUE PRICE	*QUOTE U.S.$
1998 Elizabeth Bennet	3,500	1999	350.00	350
1998 Emma	3,500	1999	375.00	375
1998 Jane Eyre	3,500	1999	375.00	375
1999 Moll Flanders HN3849	3,500	2001	395.00	395
1998 Tess of the D'Urbervilles	3,500	1999	350.00	350

Literary Loves - A. Maslankowski

YEAR ISSUE	EDITION LIMIT	YEAR RETD.	ISSUE PRICE	*QUOTE U.S.$
1999 Heathcliff and Cathy HN4071	750	2001	1275.00	1275

Michael Doulton Event Figure - Various

YEAR ISSUE	EDITION LIMIT	YEAR RETD.	ISSUE PRICE	*QUOTE U.S.$
2000 Susan HN4230 - J. Bromley	Yr.Iss.	2000	255.00	255
2001 Christine HN4307 - N. Pedley	Yr.Iss.	2001	255.00	255
2001 Old Salt Colourway D7153 - G. Sharpe	Yr.Iss.	2001	110.00	110
2002 Linda HN4450 - N. Pedley	Yr.Iss.		235.00	235

Movie Classics - V. Annand

YEAR ISSUE	EDITION LIMIT	YEAR RETD.	ISSUE PRICE	*QUOTE U.S.$
2000 Scarlett O' Hara (Gone With The Wind) HN4200	Retrd.	2000	350.00	350

Myths & Maidens - R. Jefferson

YEAR ISSUE	EDITION LIMIT	YEAR RETD.	ISSUE PRICE	*QUOTE U.S.$
1986 Diana The Huntress HN2829	300	1990	2950.00	3000
1985 Europa & Bull HN2828	300	1990	2950.00	3000
1984 Juno & Peacock HN2827	300	1990	2950.00	3000
1982 Lady & Unicorn HN2825	300	1990	2500.00	2500
1983 Leda & Swan HN2826	300	1990	2950.00	3000

Old Bear And Friends - J. Hissey

YEAR ISSUE	EDITION LIMIT	YEAR RETD.	ISSUE PRICE	*QUOTE U.S.$
1998 Bramwell Brown Has a Good Idea	Retrd.	1999	20.00	20
1998 Don't Worry Rabbit	Retrd.	1999	20.00	20
1998 Long Red Scarf	Retrd.	1999	29.00	29
1998 Old Bear	Retrd.	1999	15.00	15
1998 Ruff's Price	Retrd.	1999	21.50	22
1998 Snowflake Biscuits	Retrd.	1999	29.00	29
1998 Time For A Cuddle, Hug Me Tight	Retrd.	1999	20.00	20
1998 Time For Bed	Retrd.	1999	25.00	25
1998 Waiting For Snow	Retrd.	1999	25.00	25
1998 Welcome Home, Old Bear	Retrd.	1999	21.50	22

Prestige Figures - Various

YEAR ISSUE	EDITION LIMIT	YEAR RETD.	ISSUE PRICE	*QUOTE U.S.$
1996 Charge of the Light Brigade HN3718 - A. Maslankowski	Retrd.	2001	17500.00	19250
1982 Columbine HN2738 - D. Tootle	Retrd.	1999	1250.00	1375
1982 Harlequin HN2737 - D. Tootle	Retrd.	1999	1250.00	1375
1997 Henry V at Agincourt HN3947 - A. Maslankowski	Open		18300.00	18300
1964 Indian Brave HN2376 - M. Davis	500	1993	2500.00	5500
1952 Jack Point HN2080 - C.J. Noke	Retrd.	2001	2900.00	3750
1950 King Charles HN2084 - C.J. Noke	Retrd.	1992	2500.00	2500
1964 Matador and Bull HN2324 - M. Davis	Open		21500.00	27845
1952 The Moor HN2082 - C.J. Noke	Retrd.	1998	2500.00	3000
1964 The Palio HN2428 - M. Davis	500	1993	2500.00	6500
1952 Princess Badoura HN2081 - H. Stanton	Open		28000.00	36400
1999 Romeo & Juliet HN4057 - D. Tootle	300	2000	2900.00	2900
1978 St George and Dragon HN2856 - W.K. Harper	Retrd.	1999	13600.00	14500
2001 St. George HN4371 - A. Maslankowski	50		17950.00	17950

Pretty Ladies - N. Pedley, unless otherwise noted

YEAR ISSUE	EDITION LIMIT	YEAR RETD.	ISSUE PRICE	*QUOTE U.S.$
2002 Angela HN4405	Open		195.00	195
2001 Belle HN4235 - J. Bromley	Open		360.00	360
2001 Bells Across the Valley HN4300	Open		275.00	275
1999 Beth HN4156	Open		215.00	215
2000 Camilla HN4220	Open		235.00	235
2001 Catherine HN4304	Retrd.	2001	225.00	225
1998 Charlotte HN4092	Retrd.	2001	185.00	185
2000 Ellen HN4231 - J. Bromley	Open		285.00	285
1998 Emily HN4093	Open		205.00	205
2000 Flowers of Scotland HN4240	Open		225.00	225
2001 Gentle Breeze HN4317	Open		235.00	235
2002 Gillian HN4404	Open		195.00	195
1999 Hannah HN4052 - V. Annand	Retrd.	2000	245.00	245
2002 Hannah HN4407	Open		195.00	195
1993 Helen Blue HN3601	Open		260.00	260
2001 Janet HN4310	Retrd.	2001	225.00	225
2000 Jennifer HN4248	Open		235.00	235
2000 Josephine HN4223	Open		175.00	175
2002 Julia HN4390	Open		235.00	235
2002 Just For You HN4236 - J. Bromley	Open		315.00	315
1999 Kelly HN4157	Open		185.00	185
2000 Lorraine HN4301	Open		185.00	185
2001 Loving Thougts HN4318	Open		225.00	225
1999 Lynne HN4155	Retrd.	2001	225.00	225
1999 Madeline HN4152	Retrd.	2001	225.00	225
1999 Marianne HN4153	Retrd.	2001	235.00	235
1999 Mary HN4114	Retrd.	2001	230.00	230
1999 Michelle HN4158	Open		185.00	185
1999 Natasha HN4154	Retrd.	2000	225.00	225
1999 The Open Road HN4161 - T. Potts	Retrd.	2000	245.00	245
1998 Rosie HN4094	Open		205.00	205
2002 Samantha HN4403	Open		195.00	195
2002 Scarlett HN4408	Open		295.00	295
2001 Special Celebration HN4234 - J. Bromley	Open		335.00	335
2002 Special Moments HN4430 - C. Froud	Open		235.00	235
1998 Special Occasion HN4100	Open		240.00	240

YEAR ISSUE	EDITION LIMIT	YEAR RETD.	ISSUE PRICE	*QUOTE U.S.$
2000 Specially For You HN4232 - J. Bromley	Open		315.00	335
2002 Summer Stroll HN4406	Open		195.00	195
2000 Susannah HN4221	Retrd.	2001	225.00	225
2001 Sweet Music HN4302	Open		195.00	195
1999 Sweet Poetry HN4113	Open		205.00	205
2001 Sweetheart HN4319	Open		245.00	245
1937 Top 'O' The Hill HN1834 - L. Harradine	Open		395.00	410
Queens of Realm - P. Parsons				
1989 Mary, Queen of Scots HN3142	S/O	1992	550.00	850-900
1988 Queen Anne HN3141	S/O	1992	525.00	600-800
1986 Queen Elizabeth I HN3099	S/O	1992	495.00	650-1100
1987 Queen Victoria HN3125	S/O	1992	495.00	1500-1750
1987 Set of 4	S/O	1992	2065.00	3000-3450
Reynolds Collection - P. Gee				
1992 Countess Harrington HN3317	5,000	1995	550.00	595
1993 Countess Spencer HN3320	5,000	1995	595.00	550-595
1991 Lady Worsley HN3318	5,000	1995	550.00	595
1992 Mrs. Hugh Bonfoy HN3319	5,000	1995	550.00	595
Royal Doulton Figurines - Various				
1989 The Balloon Seller (mini) HN2130 - L. Harradine	Retrd.	1992	140.00	149
1933 Beethoven HN1778 - R. Garbe	25	1935	N/A	6500
1975 The Jersey Milkmaid HN2057A - L. Harradine	Closed	1981	N/A	225
1987 Life Boatman HN2764 - W. Harper	Closed	1991	N/A	350-400
1986 The Newsvendor HN2891 - W.K. Harper	2,500	N/A	225.00	349
1929 Old Balloon Seller HN1315 - L. Harradine	Retrd.	1998	250.00	270-299
1924 Tony Weller HN684 - C. Noke	Closed	1938	N/A	1800
Royalty - Various				
1986 Duchess Of York HN3086 - E. Griffiths	1,500	1987	495.00	650
1981 Duke Of Edinburgh HN2386 - P. Davis	750	1982	395.00	450
1982 Lady Diana Spencer HN2885 - E. Griffiths	1,500	1982	395.00	2000-2300
1981 Prince Of Wales HN2883 - E. Griffiths	1,500	1982	395.00	450-650
1981 Prince Of Wales HN2884 - E. Griffiths	1,500	1982	750.00	1000
1982 Princess Of Wales HN2887 - E. Griffiths	1,500	1982	750.00	1700-2650
1997 Queen Elizabeth II & Duke of Edinburgh HN3836 - P. Parsons	750	1997	650.00	650
1973 Queen Elizabeth II HN2502 - P. Davis	750	1975	N/A	1800
1982 Queen Elizabeth II HN2878 - E. Griffiths	2,500	1984	N/A	450-800
1992 Queen Elizabeth II, 2nd. Version HN3440 - P. Gee	3,500	1994	460.00	460
1989 Queen Elizabeth, the Queen Mother as the Duchess of York HN3230 - P. Parsons	9,500	1990	N/A	450
1990 Queen Elizabeth, the Queen Mother HN3189 - E. Griffiths	2,500	1992	N/A	450-700
1980 Queen Mother HN2882 - E. Griffiths	1,500	1983	650.00	1250
Sentiments - A. Maslankowski				
2000 Forget Me Not HN3388	Retrd.	2001	95.00	95
2000 Friendship HN3491	Retrd.	2001	95.00	95
1999 Good Luck HN4070	Retrd.	2001	82.50	85
2000 Happy Anniversary HN4068	Retrd.	2001	95.00	95
2000 Happy Christmas HN4255	Retrd.	2001	85.00	85
2000 Loving You HN3389	Retrd.	2001	95.00	95
2000 Many Happy Returns HN4254	Retrd.	2001	85.00	85
1999 Missing You HN4076	Retrd.	2001	80.00	85
2000 Remembering You HN4085	Retrd.	2001	85.00	85
2000 Thank You HN3390	Retrd.	2001	95.00	95
2000 With Love HN3393	Retrd.	2001	95.00	95
Triumphs Of The Heart - J. Griffin				
1998 Forever Yours	Retrd.	1999	150.00	150
1998 Love Conquers All	Retrd.	1999	150.00	150
1998 Loveswept	Retrd.	1999	150.00	150
1998 My Beloved	Retrd.	1999	150.00	150
1998 Only You	Retrd.	1999	150.00	150

YEAR ISSUE	EDITION LIMIT	YEAR RETD.	ISSUE PRICE	*QUOTE U.S.$
1998 Sweet Embrace	Retrd.	1999	150.00	150
Vanity Fair - N. Pedley				
2001 Anna HN4391	Open		175.00	175
2000 Josephine HN4223	Open		175.00	175
2001 Margaret HN4311	Open		175.00	175

Seraphim Classics®/Roman, Inc.

Seraphim Classics® Club Members' Only - G. Ho				
1998 Lillian - Nurturing Life	Yr.Iss.	1998	65.00	125-275
1999 Josephine-Celebration of Peace	Yr.Iss.	1999	65.00	65-225
1999 Heavenly Reflections Club Set	Yr.Iss.	1999	500.00	500
2000 Sierra - Nature's Haven	Yr.Iss.	2000	75.00	75
2000 Jacquelyn - Happiness Abounds	Yr.Iss.	2000	175.00	175
2000 Garden of Angels Club Set	Retrd.	2001	500.00	500
2001 Abigail - Precious Gift	Yr.Iss.	2001	85.00	85
2001 Abigail - Precious Gift Musical Glitterdome®	Yr.Iss.	2001	50.00	50
2002 Malanie - Love Everlasting	Yr.Iss.		65.00	65

Seraphim Classics® Club Symbol of Membership - G. Ho				
1997 Tess - Tender One	Yr.Iss.	1998	55.00	85-175
1999 Eve-Tender Heart	Yr.Iss.	1999	59.50	65-100
2000 Cassidy - Blessings From Above	Yr.Iss.	2000	59.50	60-65
2001 Claire - Angel Friend	Yr.Iss.	2001	65.00	65
2002 Phoebe - Heart's Content	Yr.Iss.		75.00	75

Seraphim Classics® Special Event - G. Ho				
1996 Dawn - Sunshine's Guardian Angel	Closed	1997	55.00	115-295
1997 Monica - Under Love's Wing	Closed	1997	55.00	55-150
1998 Alexandra - Endless Dreams	Closed	1998	65.00	85-94
1999 Rebecca-Beautiful Dreamer	Yr.Iss.	1999	125.00	125-150
1999 Hope - Light in the Distance Musical	Yr.Iss.	1999	50.00	50
2000 Amanda - Sharing The Spirit	Yr.Iss.	2000	65.00	65

Seraphim Classics® 4" - G. Ho				
2001 April - Spring's Blossom	Open		19.50	20
2001 Arianna - Winter's Warmth	Open		19.50	20
2001 Caring Touch - Medical Professional Angel	Open		26.00	26
1999 Celine - The Morning Star	Open		19.50	20
2001 Chelsea - Summer's Delight	Open		-19.50	20
1995 Cymbeline - Peacemaker	Retrd.	1999	19.50	20-125
2002 Diana - Heaven's Rose	Open		19.50	20
1995 Evangeline - Angel of Mercy	Retrd.	1999	19.50	20-50
2000 Faith - The Easter Angel	Open		19.50	20
1995 Felicia - Adoring Maiden	Retrd.	1999	19.50	20-100
1999 Gabriel - Celestial Messenger	Open		19.50	20
2002 Grace - Born Anew	Open		19.50	20
2000 Harmony - Love's Guardian	Open		19.50	20
2001 Heather - Autumn Beauty	Open		19.50	20
1995 Iris - Rainbow's End	Retrd.	1999	19.50	20-50
1995 Isabel - Gentle Spirit	Retrd.	1999	19.50	20-57
1995 Laurice - Wisdom's Child	Retrd.	1999	19.50	20
1995 Lydia - Winged Poet	Retrd.	1999	19.50	20-60
2000 Mariah - Heavenly Joy	Open		19.50	20
2000 Melody - Heaven's Song	Open		19.50	20
2002 Michael - Victorious	Open		19.50	20
1995 Ophelia - Heart Seeker	Retrd.	1999	19.50	20-65
2001 Practice Makes Perfect, Delicate Balance	Open		25.00	25
2001 Practice Makes Perfect, Finishing Touch	Open		25.00	25
2001 Practice Makes Perfect, Prepare to Dance	Open		25.00	25
2001 Practice Makes Perfect, Reaching New Heights	Open		25.00	25
2001 Practice Makes Perfect, Reaching New Heights Musical Glitterdome	Open		50.00	50
2001 Practice Makes Perfect, Sweet Surprise	Open		25.00	25
1995 Priscilla - Benevolent Guide	Retrd.	1999	19.50	20
2000 Rachel - Children's Joy	Open		19.50	20
1999 Rosalie - Nature's Delight	Open		19.50	20
2002 Samantha - Blessed at Birth	Open		19.50	20
1995 Seraphina - Heaven's Helper	Retrd.	1999	19.50	20-119
1999 Serena - Angel of Peace	Open		19.50	20
2001 Victoria - Embrace Life	Open		19.50	20

Seraphim Classics® 4" Angels of the Month - G. Ho				
2001 January-Angel of the Month	Open		19.50	20
2001 February-Angel of the Month	Open		19.50	20

YEAR ISSUE	EDITION LIMIT	YEAR RETD.	ISSUE PRICE	*QUOTE U.S.$
2001 March-Angel of the Month	Open		19.50	20
2001 April-Angel of the Month	Open		19.50	20
2001 May-Angel of the Month	Open		19.50	20
2001 June-Angel of the Month	Open		19.50	20
2001 July-Angel of the Month	Open		19.50	20
2001 August-Angel of the Month	Open		19.50	20
2001 September-Angel of the Month	Open		19.50	20
2001 October-Angel of the Month	Open		19.50	20
2001 November-Angel of the Month	Open		19.50	20
2001 December-Angel of the Month	Open		19.50	20

Seraphim Classics® 7" - G. Ho

YEAR ISSUE	EDITION LIMIT	YEAR RETD.	ISSUE PRICE	*QUOTE U.S.$
1998 Amelia - Eternal Bloom	Yr.Iss.	1998	65.00	65-76
2001 America the Beautiful Freedom Angel Musical	Open		39.50	40
2000 Amy - Paradise Found	Retrd.	2001	125.00	125
2001 Andrea - Creation Praise	Retrd.	2001	65.00	65
2002 Angela - Heaven's Grace	Open		65.00	65
1998 Angels' Touch - The Dedication Angel	Retrd.	2000	59.50	60
1999 Angel's Touch - The Dedication Angel Musical	Open		75.00	75
2001 Anna - Tranquil Heart	Open		85.00	85
1998 Annabella - Announcement of Joy	Yr.Iss.	1998	59.50	60-125
1999 April - Spring's Blossom	Retrd.	2001	59.50	60
1999 Arianna - Winter's Warmth	Retrd.	2000	59.50	60
1999 Audra - Embraced By Love	Retrd.	2000	59.50	60
2000 Bethany - Lighting the Way	Retrd.	2001	59.50	60
2001 Blessed at Birth - Happy Birthday Glitterdome® Musical	Open		50.00	50
2002 Brooke - Peaceful Soul			59.50	60
2001 Caring Touch - Angel with Fireman	Open		87.50	88
2000 Caring Touch - Angel with Medical Professional	Open		87.50	60
2001 Caring Touch - Angel with Nurse	Open		87.50	88
2001 Caring Touch - Angel with Policeman	Open		95.00	95
1999 Caroline-Garden Song	Retrd.	2000	75.00	75
1999 Cassandra - Heavenly Beauty, 5th Anniversary Figurine	Yr.Iss.	1999	100.00	100-120
2001 Cecilia - Gift From the Heart	Open		59.50	60
2001 Cecilia - Gift From the Heart Musical Glitterdome®	Open		50.00	50
2000 Celebration - Rejoice in Life	Retrd.	2001	100.00	100
2002 Celebration Angel, Angel of Faith	Yr.Iss.		65.00	65
2002 Celebration Angel, Angel of Hope	Yr.Iss.		65.00	65
2002 Celebration Angel, Angel of Love	Yr.Iss.		65.00	65
2001 Celebration Angel, Daisy - Celebrate Friendship	Yr.Iss.	2001	65.00	65
2001 Celebration Angel, Lily - Celebrate Motherhood	Yr.Iss.	2001	65.00	65
2001 Celebration Angel, Pansy - Celebrate the Season	Yr.Iss.	2001	65.00	65
2001 Celebration Angel, Rose - Celebrate Your Love for Her	Yr.Iss.	2001	65.00	65
2000 Celeste - Light of the World	Retrd.	2001	65.00	65
1996 Celine - The Morning Star	Retrd.	2000	55.00	55
1999 Charisse-Bloom From Heaven	Retrd.	2000	65.00	65
1997 Chelsea - Summer's Delight	Retrd.	2000	55.00	55-65
2002 Christine - The Footprints Angel	Open		59.50	60
1999 Clarissa-Celestial Sounds	2-Yr.	2000	65.00	125-225
1996 Constance-Gentle Keeper	Closed	1997	55.00	153-225
1994 Cymbeline - Peacemaker	Retrd.	1997	49.50	75-100
1999 Danielle - Messenger of Love	Retrd.	2001	75.00	75
1998 Diana - Heaven's Rose	Retrd.	2000	59.50	60
2000 Dominique - Simple Pleasures	Retrd.	2001	65.00	65
2001 Dreams Come True - The Graduation Angel	Open		59.50	60
1999 Eden - Beautiful Haven Fountain	Retrd.	2001	175.00	175
1999 Elizabeth - Heaven's Victory	Retrd.	2001	59.50	60
1999 Erin - Irish Blessing	Retrd.	2001	59.50	60
2001 Eternal Love - The Wedding Angel	Open		100.00	100
1994 Evangeline - Angel of Mercy	Retrd.	2000	49.50	55-69
1998 Evangeline - Angel of Mercy Musical	Open		75.00	75
1996 Faith - The Easter Angel	Retrd.	1999	55.00	55-94
1995 Felicia - Adoring Maiden	Retrd.	1998	49.50	67-195
2001 Frances - Gentle Guide	Open		65.00	65
1996 Francesca - Loving Guardian	Retrd.	1998	65.00	65
1994 Francesca - Loving Guardian Musical	Retrd.	1998	75.00	75-80
1995 Francesca - Loving Guardian-Glitterdome® Musical	Open		50.00	50
1996 Gabriel - Celestial Messenger	Retrd.	2000	59.50	60-88

YEAR ISSUE	EDITION LIMIT	YEAR RETD.	ISSUE PRICE	*QUOTE U.S.$
2002 Glad Tidings - The Annunciation Angel	Open		59.50	60
1997 Grace - Born Anew	Retrd.	2000	55.00	55-75
2001 Haley - Joyful Soul	Retrd.	2001	125.00	125
1997 Hannah - Always Near	Retrd.	2000	55.00	55-60
2000 Hannah - Always Near Musical	Open		59.50	60
2002 Happy Anniversary - 25 Years of Love	Open		59.50	60
2002 Happy Anniversary - 50 Years of Love	Open		59.50	60
1997 Harmony - Love's Guardian	Retrd.	2000	55.00	55-65
1999 Harmony - Love's Guardian Musical	Open		75.00	60
1997 Heather - Autumn Beauty	Retrd.	2000	55.00	55-69
2001 Heavenly Carousel, Blythe - Heavenly Dreams	Open		65.00	65
2001 Heavenly Carousel, Emily - Heaven's Spirit	Open		65.00	65
2001 Heavenly Carousel, Stephanie - Joyful Paradise	Open		65.00	65
2001 Heavenly Carousel, Taylor - Day Dreamer	Open		65.00	65
2001 Heavenly Circle - Joined In Friendship	Open		100.00	100
2002 Heavenly Concert - Angel Trio Musical	Open		75.00	75
2001 Heavenly Dance - The Ballerina	Open		65.00	65
2001 Heavenly Friends, Forever Friends	120-day		65.00	65
2002 Heavenly Friends, Gift of Kindness	Open		65.00	65
2002 Heavenly Friends, Heavenly Gift	Open		65.00	65
2002 Heavenly Friends, Heavenly Slumber	Open		65.00	65
2002 Heavenly Friends, Song of Friendship	Open		65.00	65
2002 Heavenly Friends, Treasured Friends	Yr.Iss.		65.00	65
1999 Heavenly Guardian with Little Boy Musical	Open		49.50	50
1999 Heavenly Guardian with Little Girl Musical	Open		49.50	50
2001 I Said a Prayer for You - The Praying Angel	Open		59.50	60
2001 In Appreciation - The Thank You Angel	Open		59.50	60
2001 In God's Care - Memorial Angel	Open		59.50	60
1994 Iris - Rainbow's End	Retrd.	1999	49.50	55-69
1996 Iris - Rainbow's End Musical	Open		65.00	65
1997 Iris - Rainbow's End-Glitterdome® Musical	Open		50.00	50
1994 Isabel - Gentle Spirit	Retrd.	2000	49.50	55-65
2001 Jenna-Unconditional Love	Yr.Iss.	2001	59.50	60
2001 Jessica - Grateful Heart	Open		29.95	30
1999 Joelle - Nature's Spirit	Yr.Iss.	1999	59.50	75
2002 Jordan - Thoughtful Reflection	Open		135.00	135
1999 Joy-Gift of Heaven	Retrd.	2000	65.00	65
1999 Juliette - Music's Gift	2-Yr.	2000	65.00	65
2001 Kimberly - Abundant Blessings	Open		59.50	60
1999 Kristina - Song of Joy	2-Yr.	2000	85.00	85
1999 Laurel-Nature's Harmony	Retrd.	2000	65.00	65
1995 Laurice - Wisdom's Child	Retrd.	1997	49.50	55-75
2000 Leah - Bless Our Home	Yr.Iss.	2000	59.50	60
2001 Loving Arms - Angel with Mother and Child	Open		95.00	95
2001 Loving Arms - Angel with Father and Child	Open		95.00	95
1994 Lydia - Winged Poet	Retrd.	1997	49.50	54-70
2002 Maria - Guided by Faith	Open		59.50	60
1996 Mariah - Heavenly Joy	Retrd.	2000	59.50	59-70
1998 Mariah-Heavenly Joy Musical	Retrd.	2001	80.00	80
2001 May God Bless You - First Communion Angel w/Boy	Open		39.50	40
2001 May God Bless You - First Communion Angel w/Girl	Open		39.50	40
2002 Maya - True Believer	Open		59.50	60
2002 Melissa - Peaceful Moments	120-day		65.00	65
1997 Melody - Heaven's Song	Retrd.	2000	55.00	55-65
1999 Michael - Victorious	Retrd.	2000	59.50	60-65
2002 Michelle - Hope Blooms	Open		65.00	65
1999 Naomi - Nurturing Spirit	Retrd.	2000	59.50	60
2002 Natalie - Joy to the World	Open		59.50	60
1998 Noelle - Giving Spirit	Retrd.	1999	59.50	59-75
1999 Olivia-Loving Heart	Retrd.	2000	65.00	65
1994 Ophelia - Heart Seeker	Retrd.	1996	49.50	115-125

*Quotes have been rounded up to nearest dollar

Seraphim Classics®/Roman, Inc.
to United Design Corp.

YEAR ISSUE	EDITION LIMIT	YEAR RETD.	ISSUE PRICE	*QUOTE U.S.$
1999 Patrice-Delight in the Day	Yr.Iss.	1999	59.50	60-90
1995 Priscilla - Benevolent Guide	Retrd.	1998	49.50	55-69
1997 Rachel - Children's Joy	Retrd.	1999	55.00	55-65
2001 Raphael - In Heaven's Care	Open		59.50	60
2001 Renee - Celebrate Life	Open		59.50	60
1996 Rosalie - Nature's Delight	Retrd.	2000	55.00	55-65
1995 Sabrina - Eternal Guide	Yr.Iss.	1997	55.00	54-65
1998 Samantha - Blessed At Birth	Retrd.	2000	59.50	60
2000 Sarah - Peaceful Reflections	Retrd.	2001	59.50	60
1995 Seraphina - Heaven's Helper	Retrd.	1996	49.50	116-120
1996 Serena - Angel of Peace	Retrd.	2000	65.00	65
1999 Serena-Angel of Peace Glitterdome® Musical	Open		50.00	50
1999 Serenity - Trusting Soul	Retrd.	2001	65.00	65
2001 Serenity - Trusting Soul Musical	Open		59.50	60
1998 Simone - Nature's Own	Retrd.	2000	100.00	100-135
1999 Sisters-Heart and Soul	Retrd.	2000	115.00	115
2001 Song Of Praise	Open		125.00	125
2001 Song Of Praise Musical Glitterdome®	Open		75.00	75
1997 Tamara - Blessed Guardian	Retrd.	2000	65.00	65
2001 Thy Will Be Done - Jesus in Gethsemane	Open		125.00	125
2000 Victoria - Embrace Life	Open		65.00	65

Seraphim Classics® 4" Nativity - G. Ho

2002 Holy Family	Open		40.00	40
2002 Shepherds and Animals	Open		50.00	50
2002 Stable and Palm Trees	Open		50.00	50
2002 Three Kings	Open		50.00	50

Seraphim Classics® 7" Nativity - G. Ho

2000 Camel	Retrd.	2001	25.00	25
1998 Gloria Angel	Retrd.	2001	59.50	60
1996 Holy Family & Lambs - 5 pc. Set	Retrd.	2001	125.00	125
2000 Holy Family Musical Glitterdome	Retrd.	2001	55.00	55
2000 Ox & Donkey - 2 pc. Set	Retrd.	2001	40.00	40
1998 Shepherds - 2 pc. Set	Retrd.	2001	65.00	65
2000 Stable	Retrd.	2001	50.00	50
1997 Three Kings - 3 pc. set	Retrd.	2001	125.00	125

Seraphim Classics® 12" - G. Ho

1995 Alyssa - Nature's Angel	Yr.Iss.	1995	145.00	1200-1895
1996 Vanessa - Heavenly Maiden	Yr.Iss.	1996	150.00	162-325
1997 Chloe - Nature's Gift	Yr.Iss.	1997	159.00	162-213
1997 Ariel - Heaven's Shining Star	Yr.Iss.	1997	159.00	159-249
1998 Hope - Light in the Distance	Closed	1999	175.00	175-200
1998 Avalon - Free Spirit	Yr.Iss.	1998	175.00	175-212
1998 Annalisa - Celebrating The Millennium	2-Yr.	2000	175.00	175
1999 Nina-Heavenly Harvest	Yr.Iss.	1999	175.00	175
2000 Jillian - Cherish The Day	Yr.Iss.	2000	195.00	195
2000 Jacquelyn - Happiness Abounds	Yr.Iss.	2000	175.00	175
2001 Nicole - Endless Possibilities	Yr.Iss.	2001	175.00	175
2001 Valerie - Heaven's Treasure	Yr.Iss.	2001	175.00	175
2001 Madeline - Faithful One	Yr.Iss.	2001	135.00	135
2002 O Holy Night	Open		400.00	400
2002 Ashley with the Bluebird of Happiness	Yr.Iss.		175.00	175

Seraphim Classics® 20+" - G. Ho

2000 Alyssa - Nature's Angel	Retrd.	2001	750.00	750
2001 Shannon - Heavenly Guide	Open		600.00	600

Seraphim Classics® Angels To Watch Over Me - G. Ho

1996 Newborn - Blonde	Open		39.50	40
1996 Newborn - Brunette	Open		39.50	40
1996 First Year - Girl	Open		39.50	40
1996 Second Year - Girl	Open		39.50	40
1996 Third Year - Girl	Open		39.50	40
1996 Fourth Year - Girl	Open		39.50	40
1996 Fifth Year - Girl	Open		39.50	40
1997 Sixth Year - Girl	Open		39.50	40
1997 Seventh Year - Girl	Open		39.50	40
1998 Eighth Year - Girl	Open		45.00	45
1999 Ninth Year - Girl	Open		45.00	45
1999 Tenth Year - Girl	Open		45.00	45
1999 Sixteenth Year - Girl	Open		50.00	50
1997 First Year - Boy	Open		39.50	40
1997 Second Year - Boy	Open		39.50	40
1997 Third Year - Boy	Open		39.50	40
1997 Fourth Year - Boy	Open		39.50	40
1997 Fifth Year - Boy	Open		39.50	40

YEAR ISSUE	EDITION LIMIT	YEAR RETD.	ISSUE PRICE	*QUOTE U.S.$
1997 Sixth Year - Boy	Open		39.50	40
1998 Seventh Year - Boy	Open		45.00	45

Seraphim Classics® Heaven Sent - Seraphim Studios

1997 Hope Eternal Musical	Retrd.	2000	37.50	38-65
1997 Loving Spirit Musical	Retrd.	2000	37.50	38
1998 Peaceful Embrace Musical	Retrd.	2001	85.00	85
1997 Pure At Heart Musical	Retrd.	2000	37.50	38

Sports Impressions/Enesco Group, Inc.

Collectors' Club Members Only - Various

1990 The Mick-Mickey Mantle 5000-1	Yr.Iss.	N/A	75.00	40-75
1991 Rickey Henderson-Born to Run 5001-11	Yr.Iss.	N/A	49.95	50
1991 Nolan Ryan-300 Wins 5002-01	Yr.Iss.	N/A	125.00	125
1991 Willie, Mickey & Duke plate 5003-04	Yr.Iss.	N/A	39.95	50
1992 Babe Ruth 5006-11	Yr.Iss.	N/A	40.00	38-40
1992 Walter Payton 5015-01	Yr.Iss.	N/A	50.00	38-50
1993 The 1927 Yankees plate - R.Tanenbaum	Yr.Iss.	N/A	60.00	35-60

Collectors' Club Symbol of Membership - Sports Impressions

1991 Mick/7 plate 5001-02	Yr.Iss.	N/A	Gift	25-50
1992 USA Basketball team plate 5008-30	Yr.Iss.	N/A	Gift	25
1993 Nolan Ryan porcelain card	Yr.Iss.	N/A	Gift	25

Baseball Superstar Figurines - Sports Impressions

1988 Al Kaline	2,500	N/A	90.00	90
1988 Andre Dawson	2,500	N/A	90.00	50-100
1988 Bob Feller	2,500	N/A	90.00	50-100
1992 Cubs Ryne Sandberg Home (signed) 1118-23	975	1993	150.00	250
1987 Don Mattingly	Closed	N/A	90.00	225-250
1987 Don Mattingly (Franklin glove variation)	Closed	N/A	90.00	350-600
1989 Duke Snider	2,500	N/A	90.00	50-100
1994 Giants Barry Bonds (signed) 1160-46	975	1995	150.00	100-150
1992 Johnny Bench (hand signed) 1126-23	975	1994	150.00	225
1987 Jose Canseco	Closed	N/A	90.00	50-100
1987 Keith Hernandez	2,500	N/A	90.00	50-100
1989 Kirk Gibson	Closed	N/A	90.00	50-100
1991 Mark McGwire 10" (Oakland As) 1039-12	1,900	N/A	295.00	295
1987 Mickey Mantle	Closed	N/A	90.00	150-195
1996 Mickey Mantle "The Greatest Switch Hitter" (hand signed) 1228-46 - T. Treadway	975	1995	395.00	495-600
1992 Nolan Ryan Figurine/plate/stand 1134-31	500	1994	260.00	260
1990 Nolan Ryan Kings of K	Closed	N/A	125.00	89-125
1990 Nolan Ryan Mini	Closed	N/A	50.00	50
1990 Nolan Ryan Supersize	Closed	N/A	250.00	225-250
1993 Oakland A's Reggie Jackson (signed) 1048-46	975	1994	150.00	150-275
1993 Rangers Nolan Ryan (signed) 1127-46	975	1994	175.00	225-250
1994 Rangers Nolan Ryan (signed) Farewell 1161-49	975	1994	150.00	225-250
1990 Ted Williams	Closed	N/A	90.00	90-125
1994 Tom Glavine (signed) 1163-46	975	N/A	150.00	90-150
1990 Wade Boggs	Closed	N/A	90.00	50-100
1989 Will Clark	Closed	N/A	90.00	50-100
1993 Yankees Mickey Mantle (signed) 1038-46	975	1993	195.00	350

Basketball Superstar Figurines - Sports Impressions

1993 Julius Erving 76ers (hand signed) 4102-46	975	1994	150.00	150-250
1995 Larry Bird (hand signed) 4086-46	975	N/A	195.00	150-250

United Design Corp.

Angels Collection - D. Newburn, unless otherwise noted

1999 Angel in Flight AA-178 - G.G. Santiago	5,000		N/A	N/A
1993 Angel of Flight AA-032 - K. Memoli	10,000	2001	100.00	110
1993 Angel w/ Birds AA-034	10,000	1995	75.00	75
1994 Angel w/ Book AA-058	10,000	1998	84.00	90
1994 Angel w/ Christ Child AA-061 - K. Memoli	10,000	2001	84.00	90
1993 Angel w/ Lilies AA-033	10,000	1998	80.00	84

YEAR ISSUE	EDITION LIMIT	YEAR RETD.	ISSUE PRICE	*QUOTE U.S.$
1993 Angel w/ Lilies, Crimson AA-040	10,000	1996	80.00	80
1992 Angel, Lamb & Critters AA-021 - S. Bradford	10,000	1998	90.00	95
1996 Angel, Lion & Fawn AA-093 - K. Memoli	20,000		280.00	280
1992 Angel, Lion & Lamb AA-020 - K. Memoli	10,000	1994	135.00	195-300
1994 Angel, Roses and Bluebirds AA-054	10,000	2000	65.00	84
1996 Angels, Roses & Doves AA-112	10,000	1999	75.00	84
2000 Archangel w/Lion & Lamb AA-184 - J. Beasley	7,500		70.00	70
2002 Archangel Michael w/Lion & Lamb AA-210 - A. Tsalikhin	3,500		75.00	75
1993 Autumn Angel AA-035	10,000	1996	70.00	70-80
1993 Autumn Angel, Emerald AA-041	10,000	1996	70.00	70
1995 Celestial Guardian Angel AA-069 - S. Bradford	10,000	1997	120.00	120
1991 Christmas Angel AA-003 - S. Bradford	10,000	1994	125.00	125
2001 Classic Angel AA-194 - B. Tortolani	7,500		50.00	50
2002 Classic Angel w/Lamb AA-211 - B. Tortolani	7,500		40.00	40
1991 Classical Angel AA-005 - S. Bradford	10,000	1998	79.00	79
1994 Dreaming of Angels AA-060 - K. Memoli	10,000	2000	120.00	130
1996 Dreaming of Angels, pastel AA-111 - K. Memoli	10,000		120.00	130
1994 Earth Angel AA-059 - S. Bradford	10,000	1997	84.00	84
1997 Eyes Toward Heaven AA-132 - K. Memoli	10,000	1999	130.00	130
2002 Faith AA-213 - V. Oldham	7,500		43.00	43
1991 The Gift AA-009 - S. Bradford	2,500	1991	135.00	550-665
1992 The Gift '92 AA-018 - S. Bradford	3,500	1992	140.00	325-350
1993 The Gift '93 AA-037 - S. Bradford	3,500	1993	120.00	225-235
1994 The Gift '94 AA-057	5,000	1994	140.00	165-175
1995 The Gift '95 AA-067	5,000	1995	140.00	140-180
1996 The Gift '96 AA-094	5,000	1996	140.00	140
1997 The Gift '97 AA-128 - P.J. Jonas	7,500	1997	150.00	150
1998 The Gift '98 AA-147 - P.J. Jonas-Pendergast	5,000	1998	150.00	150
1999 The Gift '99 AA-176 - K. Memoli	5,000	1999	N/A	N/A
2000 The Gift 2000 AA-187 - C. Smith	7,500	2000	75.00	75
2001 The Gift 2001 AA-191 - V. Oldham	7,500	2001	78.00	78
2002 The Gift 2002 AA-212 - B. Tortolani	7,500		75.00	75
1995 Guardian Angel, Lion & Lamb AA-083 - S. Bradford	10,000	1998	165.00	170-195
1995 Guardian Angel, Lion & Lamb, lt. AA-068 - S. Bradford	10,000	2000	165.00	170
1994 Harvest Angel AA-063 - S. Bradford	10,000	1997	84.00	84
1991 Heavenly Shepherdess AA-008 - S. Bradford	10,000	1999	99.00	99
2001 Hope AA-205 - V. Oldham	7,500		43.00	43
2001 Joy AA-207 - V. Oldham	7,500		43.00	43
1992 Joy To The World AA-016	10,000	1996	90.00	95
1995 A Little Closer to Heaven AA-081 - K. Memoli	10,000	1998	230.00	245
1995 A Little Closer to Heaven, lt. AA-085 - K. Memoli	10,000		230.00	230
2001 Love AA-208 - V. Oldham	7,500		43.00	43
1993 Madonna AA-031 - K. Memoli	10,000	1999	100.00	100
1991 Messenger of Peace AA-006 - S. Bradford	10,000	1997	75.00	79
1999 Musical Motion AA-174 - P.J. Couch	5,000		55.00	55
2001 Peace AA-206 - V. Oldham	7,500		43.00	43
1992 Peaceful Encounter AA-017	10,000	2000	100.00	100
1997 Rejoice AA-130 - K. Memoli	10,000	2001	90.00	90
1997 Rejoice, silver AA-143 - K. Memoli	10,000	1997	90.00	90
1997 Serenity AA-131 - K. Memoli	10,000	1997	90.00	90
1997 Serenity, silver AA-144 - K. Memoli	10,000	1997	90.00	90
1998 Spirit of Autumn AA-158 - G.G. Santiago	15,000		200.00	200
1998 Spirit of Spring AA-146 - G.G. Santiago	15,000		200.00	200
1999 Spirit of Summer AA-170 - G.G. Santiago	15,000		200.00	200
1997 Spirit of Winter AA-142 - G.G. Santiago	15,000		200.00	200
1995 Starlight Starbright AA-066	10,000	1998	70.00	80
1991 Trumpeter Angel AA-004 - S. Bradford	10,000	1997	99.00	99
1992 Winter Angel AA-019	10,000	2000	75.00	75
2000 Winter Flight AA-183 - P.J. Couch	2,000		250.00	250

YEAR ISSUE	EDITION LIMIT	YEAR RETD.	ISSUE PRICE	*QUOTE U.S.$
1991 Winter Rose Angel AA-007 - S. Bradford	10,000	1994	65.00	65

Backyard Birds™ - Various

YEAR ISSUE	EDITION LIMIT	YEAR RETD.	ISSUE PRICE	*QUOTE U.S.$
1994 Allen's on Pink Flowers BB-044 - P.J. Jonas	Retrd.	1999	22.00	22
1994 Allen's on Purple Morning Glory BB-051 - P.J. Jonas	Retrd.	1999	22.00	22
1989 Baltimore Oriole BB-024 - S. Bradford	Retrd.	1996	19.50	22
1989 Blue Jay BB-026 - S. Bradford	Retrd.	2001	19.50	22
1989 Blue Jay, Baby BB-027 - S. Bradford	Retrd.	1996	15.00	15
1990 Bluebird (Upright) BB-031 - S. Bradford	Retrd.	1997	20.00	20
1988 Bluebird BB-009 - S. Bradford	Open		15.00	21
1988 Bluebird Hanging BB-017 - S. Bradford	Retrd.	1990	11.00	12
1988 Bluebird, Small BB-001 - S. Bradford	Retrd.	1999	10.00	11
1994 Broadbill on Blue Morning Glory BB-053 - P.J. Jonas	Retrd.	1999	22.00	22
1994 Broadbill on Trumpet Vine BB-043 - P.J. Jonas	Retrd.	1999	22.00	22
1994 Broadbill on Yellow Fuscia BB-055 - P.J. Jonas	Retrd.	1997	22.00	22
1994 Broadbill Pair on Yellow Flowers BB-048 - P.J. Jonas	Retrd.	1997	30.00	30
1988 Cardinal Hanging BB-018 - S. Bradford	Retrd.	1990	11.00	11
1988 Cardinal, Female BB-011 - S. Bradford	Retrd.	1999	15.00	17
1988 Cardinal, Male BB-013 - S. Bradford	Open		15.00	18
1988 Cardinal, Small BB-002 - S. Bradford	Retrd.	2001	10.00	11
1990 Cedar Waxwing Babies BB-033 - S. Bradford	Retrd.	1996	22.00	22
1990 Cedar Waxwing BB-032 - S. Bradford	Retrd.	1996	20.00	20
1988 Chickadee BB-010 - S. Bradford	Retrd.	1999	15.00	18
1988 Chickadee Hanging BB-019 - S. Bradford	Retrd.	1990	11.00	11
1988 Chickadee, Small BB-003 - S. Bradford	Retrd.	1999	10.00	11
1990 Evening Grosbeak BB-034 - S. Bradford	Retrd.	1996	22.00	22
1989 Goldfinch BB-028 - S. Bradford	Retrd.	2001	16.50	20
1989 Hoot Owl BB-025 - S. Bradford	Retrd.	1997	15.00	20
1988 Humingbird BB-012 - S. Bradford	Open		15.00	18
1988 Hummingbird Female, Small BB-005 - S. Bradford	Retrd.	1991	10.00	10
1988 Hummingbird Flying, Small BB-004 - S. Bradford	Retrd.	1999	10.00	11
1988 Hummingbird Sm., Hanging BB-022	Retrd.	1990	11.00	11
1988 Hummingbird, Lg., Hanging BB-023	Retrd.	1990	15.00	15
1990 Indigo Bunting BB-036 - S. Bradford	Retrd.	1996	20.00	20
1990 Indigo Bunting, Female BB-039 - S. Bradford	Retrd.	1996	20.00	20
1994 Magnificent Pair on Trumpet Vine BB-046 - P.J. Jonas	Retrd.	1997	30.00	30
1990 Nuthatch, White-throated BB-037 - S. Bradford	Retrd.	1996	20.00	20
1990 Painted Bunting BB-040 - S. Bradford	Retrd.	1996	20.00	20
1990 Painted Bunting, Female BB-041 - S. Bradford	Retrd.	1996	20.00	20
1990 Purple Finch BB-038 - S. Bradford	Retrd.	1996	20.00	20
1988 Red-winged Blackbird BB-014 - S. Bradford	Retrd.	1991	15.00	17
1988 Robin Babies BB-008 - S. Bradford	Retrd.	1999	15.00	19
1988 Robin Baby, Small BB-006 - S. Bradford	Retrd.	1999	10.00	11
1988 Robin BB-015 - S. Bradford	Open		15.00	21
1988 Robin Hanging BB-020 - S. Bradford	Retrd.	1990	11.00	11
1990 Rose Breasted Grosbeak BB-042 - S. Bradford	Retrd.	1996	20.00	20
1994 Rubythroat on Pink Fuscia BB-054 - P.J. Jonas	Retrd.	1997	22.00	22
1994 Rubythroat on Red Morning Glory BB-052 - P.J. Jonas	Retrd.	2001	22.00	22
1994 Rubythroat on Thistle BB-049 - P.J. Jonas	Retrd.	2001	16.50	17

FIGURINES

YEAR ISSUE	EDITION LIMIT	YEAR RETD.	ISSUE PRICE	*QUOTE U.S.$
1994 Rubythroat on Yellow Flowers BB-045 - P.J. Jonas	Retrd.	1997	22.00	22
1994 Rubythroat Pair on Pink Flowers BB-047 - P.J. Jonas	Retrd.	1999	30.00	30
1989 Saw-Whet Owl BB-029 - S. Bradford	Retrd.	1999	15.00	18
1988 Sparrow BB-016 - S. Bradford	Retrd.	2001	15.00	17
1988 Sparrow Hanging BB-021 - S. Bradford	Retrd.	1990	11.00	11
1988 Sparrow, Small BB-007 - S. Bradford	Retrd.	1996	10.00	11
1989 Woodpecker BB-030 - S. Bradford	Retrd.	1997	16.50	20

Easter Bunny Family™ - D. Kennicutt

1994 All Hidden SEC-045	Retrd.	1996	24.50	25
1989 Auntie Bunny SEC-008	Retrd.	1992	20.00	23
1992 Auntie Bunny w/Cake SEC-033R	Retrd.	1994	20.00	22
1991 Baby in Buggy, Boy SEC-027R	Retrd.	1994	20.00	22
1991 Baby in Buggy, Girl SEC-029R	Retrd.	1994	20.00	22
1994 Babysitter SEC-049	Retrd.	1996	24.50	25
1999 Baseball Buddies SEC-075	Retrd.	2001	18.00	18
1999 Baskets to Fill SEC-074	Retrd.	2001	18.00	18
1994 Bath Time SEC-044	Retrd.	1997	24.50	25
1995 Bed Time SEC-057	Retrd.	1999	24.00	24
2001 Blue Ribbon Prize - SEC-081	Retrd.	2001	20.00	20
1992 Boy Bunny w/Large Egg SEC-034R	Retrd.	1994	20.00	22
1991 Bubba in Wheelbarrow SEC-021	Retrd.	1993	20.00	20
1990 Bubba w/Wagon SEC-016	Retrd.	1993	16.50	18
1988 Bunnies, Basket Of SEC-001	Retrd.	1991	13.00	18
1991 Bunny Boy w/Basket SEC-025	Retrd.	1993	20.00	20
1988 Bunny Boy w/Duck SEC-002	Retrd.	1991	13.00	18
1997 Bunny Express SEC-070	Retrd.	2001	27.00	27
1988 Bunny Girl w/Hen SEC-004	Retrd.	1991	13.00	18
2000 Bunny Tea Party - SEC-079	Retrd.	2000	20.00	20
1989 Bunny w/Prize Egg SEC-010	Retrd.	1993	19.50	22
1988 Bunny, Easter SEC-003	Retrd.	1991	15.00	18
1993 Christening Day SEC-040	Retrd.	1995	20.00	20
1998 Doll Buggy, 1998 SEC-071	Yr.lss.	1999	15.00	15
1989 Ducky w/Bonnet, Blue SEC-015	Retrd.	1992	10.00	12
1989 Ducky w/Bonnet, Pink SEC-014	Retrd.	1992	10.00	12
1996 Easter Bunny In Evening Clothes-SEC-064	Retrd.	1998	20.00	20
1992 Easter Bunny w/Back Pack SEC-030	Retrd.	1999	20.00	22
1990 Easter Bunny w/Crystal SEC-017	Retrd.	1995	23.00	25
1993 Easter Bunny, Chocolate Egg SEC-041	Retrd.	1996	23.00	25
1995 Easter Cookies SEC-052	Retrd.	2001	24.00	25
1997 Easter Dress SEC-067	Retrd.	1999	22.00	22
1989 Easter Egg Hunt SEC-012	Retrd.	1995	16.50	22
1996 Easter Pageant - SEC-059	Retrd.	1999	17.00	17
1996 Easter Parade - SEC-063	Retrd.	1998	25.00	25
1998 Egg Paint Design SEC-072	Retrd.	2001	18.00	18
1993 Egg Roll SEC-036	Retrd.	2001	23.00	25
2002 Eggs-spert Painters - SEC-083	Yr. Iss.		20.00	20
1991 Fancy Find SEC-028	Retrd.	1995	20.00	20
1996 First Kiss - SEC-061	Retrd.	2000	20.00	20
1995 First Outing SEC-054	Retrd.	1998	19.00	20
1994 First Steps SEC-048	Retrd.	1998	24.50	25
1997 Friendship, 1997 SEC-068	Yr.lss.	1997	22.00	22
1997 The Gardener SEC-069	Retrd.	2000	22.00	22
1994 Gift Carrot SEC-046	Retrd.	2000	22.00	22
1993 Girl Bunny w/Basket SEC-039	Retrd.	1999	20.00	22
1992 Girl Bunny w/Large Egg SEC-035R	Retrd.	1994	20.00	22
1993 Grandma & Quilt SEC-037	Retrd.	1997	23.00	25
1992 Grandma w/ Bible SEC-031	Retrd.	1996	20.00	22
1996 Grandma's Dress Makers Form-1996-SEC-066	Yr.lss.	1996	25.00	25
1992 Grandpa w/Carrots SEC-032R	Retrd.	1994	20.00	22
1996 Grandpa w/Sunflowers - SEC-065	Retrd.	1999	20.00	20
1999 Happy Spring SEC-077	Retrd.	2001	18.00	18
1990 Hen w/Chick SEC-018	Retrd.	1992	13.00	23
1994 Large Prize Egg SEC-047	Retrd.	1999	22.00	22
1989 Little Sis w/Lolly SEC-009	Retrd.	1992	14.50	18
1993 Lop Ear Dying Eggs SEC-042	Retrd.	1997	23.00	25
1996 Lop Girl w/Bit Box - SEC-060	Retrd.	1999	20.00	20
1991 Lop-Ear w/Crystal SEC-022	Retrd.	1999	23.00	25
1993 Mom Storytime SEC-043	Retrd.	1999	20.00	22
1996 Mom w/Chocolate Egg - SEC-062	Retrd.	1998	25.00	25
1990 Momma Making Basket SEC-019	Retrd.	1992	23.00	23
1990 Mother Goose SEC-020	Retrd.	1992	16.50	22
1991 Nest of Bunny Eggs SEC-023	Retrd.	1998	17.50	22
1995 Painting Lessons SEC-053	Retrd.	1998	19.00	20
2000 Potter's Bench - SEC-080	Yr. Iss.	2000	25.00	25
1995 Quality Inspector SEC-055	Retrd.	1998	19.00	20
1988 Rabbit, Grandma SEC-005	Retrd.	1991	15.00	20

1988 Rabbit, Grandpa SEC-006	Retrd.	1991	15.00	20
1988 Rabbit, Momma w/Bonnet SEC-007	Retrd.	1991	15.00	20
1989 Rock-A-Bye Bunny SEC-013	Retrd.	1995	20.00	25
1993 Rocking Horse SEC-038	Retrd.	1996	20.00	22
2001 Rural Delivery - SEC-082	Yr. Iss.	2001	20.00	20
1989 Sis & Bubba Sharing SEC-011	Retrd.	1996	22.50	25
2000 Slam Dunk Hares - SEC-078	Retrd.	2000	25.00	25
1999 Smile (1999 Coll. Piece) SEC-076	Yr.lss.	1999	18.00	18
1998 Spring Break SEC-073	Retrd.	2001	15.00	15
1995 Spring Flying SEC-058	Retrd.	1997	19.00	19
1995 Team Work SEC-051	Retrd.	2001	24.00	24
1995 Two in a Basket SEC-056	Retrd.	1997	24.00	25
1991 Victorian Auntie Bunny SEC-026	Retrd.	1993	20.00	20
1991 Victorian Momma SEC-024	Retrd.	1993	20.00	20
1994 Wheelbarrow Full SEC-050	Retrd.	2000	24.50	25

Easter Bunny Family™ Babies - D. Kennicutt

1995 Baby in Basket SEC-815	Retrd.	2001	8.00	8
1994 Baby on Blanket, Naptime SEC-807	Retrd.	1999	6.50	7
1996 Baby w/Diaper & Bottle, Blue - SEC-825	Retrd.	1999	8.00	8
1996 Baby w/Diaper & Bottle, Pink - SEC-817	Retrd.	1999	8.00	8
1996 Baby w/Diaper & Bottle, Yellow - SEC-824	Retrd.	1999	8.00	8
1995 Basket of Carrots SEC-812	Retrd.	2001	8.00	8
1994 Boy Baby w/Blocks SEC-805	Retrd.	1999	6.50	7
1994 Boy w/Baseball Bat SEC-801	Retrd.	2001	6.50	7
1994 Boy w/Baseball Mitt - SEC-822	Retrd.	2001	8.00	8
1994 Boy w/Basket and Egg SEC-802	Retrd.	2001	6.50	7
1996 Boy w/Big Teddy - SEC-819	Retrd.	1999	8.00	8
1995 Boy w/Butterfly SEC-814	Retrd.	2001	8.00	8
1994 Boy w/Stick Horse SEC-803	Retrd.	2001	6.50	7
1996 Boy w/Train Engine - SEC-816	Retrd.	1999	8.00	8
1997 Bubble Bath SEC-828	Retrd.	1999	8.50	9
1998 Bunny & Birdhouse SEC-831	Retrd.	2001	8.50	9
1996 Dress Up Girl - SEC-821	Retrd.	1999	8.00	8
1996 Egg Delivery - SEC-823	Retrd.	1999	8.00	8
1995 Gift Egg SEC-808	Retrd.	1999	8.00	8
1996 Girl w/Apron Full - SEC-820	Retrd.	2001	8.00	8
1994 Girl w/Big Egg SEC-806	Retrd.	2001	6.50	7
1994 Girl w/Blanket SEC-800	Retrd.	1999	6.50	7
1996 Girl w/Book - SEC-818	Retrd.	1999	8.00	8
1994 Girl w/Toy Rabbit SEC-804	Retrd.	1999	6.50	7
1999 Grandma's Girl SEC-833	Retrd.	2001	8.50	9
1997 Grandpa's Boy SEC-826	Retrd.	2001	8.50	9
1999 H.M.S. Springtime SEC-835	Retrd.	2001	8.00	8
1995 Hostess SEC-810	Retrd.	1999	8.00	8
1995 Lop Ear & Flower Pot SEC-809	Retrd.	1999	8.00	8
1999 Mary's Lamb SEC-834	Retrd.	2001	8.50	9
1998 The Rocking Chair SEC-832	Retrd.	2001	8.50	9
1997 Soccer Player SEC-829	Retrd.	2001	8.50	9
1999 Special Delivery SEC-836	Retrd.	2001	8.50	9
1995 Spring Flowers SEC-813	Retrd.	1999	8.00	8
1998 Spring Showers SEC-830	Retrd.	2001	8.00	8
1995 Tea Party SEC-811	Retrd.	2001	8.00	8
1997 Thank You SEC-827	Retrd.	1999	8.50	9

Kooky Cats™ - D. Wentzel

2000 Kooky Cat Chef ND-0092	2,500		90.00	90
2000 Kooky Basket Case ND-0091	2,500		90.00	90
2000 Kooky Cupholder ND-0093	2,500		90.00	90
2000 Kooky Mouse Slide ND-0094	2,500		140.00	140
2000 Kooky Waiter ND-0095	2,500		90.00	90

Legend of Santa Claus™ - L. Miller, unless otherwise noted

2001 Alpine Santa CF-089 - B. Stross	7,500	2001	75.00	75
1992 Arctic Santa CF-035 - S. Bradford	7,500	1997	90.00	110-165
1988 Assembly Required CF-017	7,500	1994	79.00	115-130
2002 Bear Essentials CF-100 - D. Moore	7,500		75.00	75
1997 Bells of Christmas Morn CF-074 - K. Memoli	7,500	2000	190.00	190
1997 Bells of Christmas Morn, Victorian CF-075 - K. Memoli	7,500	2000	190.00	190
1991 Blessed Flight CF-032 - K. Memoli	7,500	1994	159.00	325-350
1989 Blessing Santa CF-066 - K. Memoli	10,000		160.00	170
1987 Checking His List CF-009	15,000	1994	75.00	105-170
1997 A Christmas Galleon CF-073 - K. Memoli	7,500	2000	150.00	150
1989 Christmas Harmony CF-020 - S. Bradford	7,500	1992	85.00	119-130

FIGURINES

YEAR ISSUE	EDITION LIMIT	YEAR RETD.	ISSUE PRICE	*QUOTE U.S.$
1998 Christmas Sharing CF-080 - K. Memoli	10,000	2001	150.00	150
1992 The Christmas Tree CF-038	7,500	1995	90.00	95-165
2001 Classic Santa with Elf CF-090 - J. Thomson	7,500	2001	45.00	45
2001 Classic Santa with Tree CF-091 - B. Tortolani	7,500	2001	40.00	40
2000 Come An' Get It Cowboy Santa CF-086 - J. Littlejohn	7,500		130.00	130
1993 Dear Santa CF-046 - K. Memoli	7,500	1996	170.00	180-230
1995 Dear Santa, Vict. C-063	10,000	2000	170.00	180
1987 Dreaming Of Santa CF-008 - S. Bradford	15,000	1988	65.00	325
1998 Drifts & Gifts CF-079 - K. Memoli	10,000	2000	140.00	140
1992 Earth Home Santa CF-040 - S. Bradford	7,500	1997	135.00	140-150
1986 Elf Pair CF-005	10,000	1992	60.00	80-151
1988 Father Christmas CF-018 - S. Bradford	7,500	1993	75.00	110-135
1991 For Santa CF-029	7,500	1997	99.00	160
1990 Forest Friends CF-025	7,500	1993	90.00	110-125
1998 Friends of the North Santa CF-077 - J. Littlejohn	10,000	2000	100.00	100
2001 The Geography Lesson CF-087 - P. Di Pasquali	7,500	2001	65.00	65
1995 Getting Santa Ready CF-056	10,000	1998	170.00	140-190
1996 High Country Santa CF-064	15,000		190.00	200
1989 Hitching Up CF-021	7,500	1993	90.00	100-110
1995 Into the Wind CF-061	10,000		140.00	150
1995 Into the Wind, Vict. CF-062	10,000	2001	140.00	150
1993 Jolly St. Nick CF-045 - K. Memoli	7,500	1999	130.00	140
1993 Jolly St. Nick, Victorian CF-050 - K. Memoli	7,500	1999	120.00	140
1986 Kris Kringle CF-002	10,000	1991	60.00	155-160
1992 Letters to Santa CF-036	7,500	1995	125.00	130-210
1997 A Light on the Roof CF-072 - K. Memoli	7,500	2000	160.00	160
1997 A Light on the Roof, Victorian CF-076 - K. Memoli	7,500	2000	160.00	160
1988 Load 'Em Up CF-016 - S. Bradford	7,500	1990	79.00	350-450
1987 Loading Santa's Sleigh CF-010	15,000	1993	100.00	90-110
1992 Loads of Happiness CF-041 - K. Memoli	7,500	1996	100.00	135-165
1994 Long Stocking Dilemma, Victorian CF-055 - K. Memoli	7,500	1999	170.00	190
1994 Longstocking Dilemma CF-052 - K. Memoli	7,500	2001	170.00	190
2001 Loving Send Off CF-096 - J. Littlejohn	7,500		45.00	45
1987 Mrs. Santa CF-006 - S. Bradford	15,000	1991	60.00	235
1993 The Night Before Christmas CF-043	7,500	1996	100.00	110-165
1993 Northwoods Santa CF-047 - S. Bradford	7,500	1996	100.00	100-110
1987 On Santa's Knee-CF007 - S. Bradford	15,000	1994	65.00	95-135
1996 Pause For a Tale CF-065	10,000	2000	190.00	200
1996 Pause For a Tale, Victorian CF-069 - K. Memoli	10,000	2000	190.00	200
2002 Paws for Christmas CF-101 - K. Johnson	7,500		50.00	50
2002 Pony Express CF-099 - J. Littlejohn	7,500		90.00	90
1998 Prince of Giving CF-078 - K. Memoli	10,000	2000	180.00	180
1998 Prince of Giving, Victorian CF-082 - K. Memoli	10,000	2000	180.00	180
1990 Puppy Love CF-024	7,500	1994	100.00	135-220
1989 A Purr-Fect Christmas CF-019 - S. Bradford	7,500	1994	95.00	115-135
1991 Reindeer Walk CF-031 - K. Memoli	7,500	1997	150.00	170
1995 The Ride CF-058	10,000	1998	130.00	140
1986 Rooftop Santa CF-004 - S. Bradford	10,000	1991	65.00	200-225
1990 Safe Arrival CF-027 - Memoli/Jonas	7,500	1996	150.00	175-200
1996 Santa & Blitzen CF-067 - K. Memoli	10,000		140.00	190
1996 Santa & Blitzen, Victorian CF-070 - K. Memoli	10,000	2001	140.00	190
1992 Santa and Comet CF-037	7,500	1995	110.00	115-165
1992 Santa and Mrs. Claus CF-039 - K. Memoli	7,500	2001	150.00	160
1992 Santa and Mrs. Claus, Victorian CF-042 - K. Memoli	7,500	2001	135.00	160
1986 Santa At Rest CF-001	10,000	1988	70.00	600
1991 Santa At Work CF-030	7,500	1999	99.00	95-175
1987 Santa On Horseback CF-011 - S. Bradford	15,000	1990	75.00	115-350
1994 Santa Riding Dove CF-053	7,500	1998	120.00	130-140

YEAR ISSUE	EDITION LIMIT	YEAR RETD.	ISSUE PRICE	*QUOTE U.S.$
1986 Santa With Pups CF-003	10,000	1988	65.00	570-575
1995 Santa, Dusk & Dawn CF-060	10,000	2001	150.00	160
1993 Santa's Friends CF-044	7,500	1996	100.00	100-110
1988 St. Nicholas CF-015	7,500	1992	75.00	90-135
1994 Star Santa w/ Polar Bear CF-054 - S. Bradford	7,500	1998	130.00	140
1995 Starlight Express CF-059	10,000	1999	170.00	180
1994 The Story of Christmas CF-051 - K. Memoli	10,000	1996	180.00	190-300
1996 The Story of Christmas, Victorian CF-068 - K. Memoli	10,000		180.00	190
1998 Totem Gathering CF-081 - J. Littlejohn	10,000	2000	120.00	120
1999 Up on the Rooftop CF-083 - J. Littlejohn	5,000		190.00	190
1993 Victorian Lion & Lamb Santa CF-048 - S. Bradford	7,500	1997	100.00	110-120
1990 Victorian Santa CF-028 - S. Bradford	7,500	1992	125.00	295-325
1991 Victorian Santa w/ Teddy CF-033 - S. Bradford	7,500	1997	150.00	160-170
1990 Waiting For Santa CF-026 - S. Bradford	7,500	1995	100.00	225-250
1999 Warm & Fuzzy Christmas CF-084 - K. Memoli	5,000		150.00	150
1999 Wilderness Santa CF-071	10,000	2001	300.00	300
1999 Woodland Santa CF-085 - D. Vaughan	7,500	2000	120.00	120

Legend Of The Little People™ - L. Miller

YEAR ISSUE	EDITION LIMIT	YEAR RETD.	ISSUE PRICE	*QUOTE U.S.$
1989 Adventure Bound LL-002	Retrd.	1993	35.00	50
1989 Caddy's Helper LL-007	Retrd.	1993	35.00	50
1991 The Easter Bunny's Cart LL-020	Retrd.	1994	45.00	50
1991 Fire it Up LL-023	Retrd.	1994	50.00	55
1990 Fishin' Hole LL-012	Retrd.	1994	35.00	50
1989 A Friendly Toast LL-003	Retrd.	1993	35.00	50
1990 Gathering Acorns LL-014	Retrd.	1994	100.00	100
1991 Got It LL-021	Retrd.	1994	45.00	50
1990 Hedgehog In Harness LL-010	Retrd.	1994	45.00	50
1990 Husking Acorns LL-008	Retrd.	1994	60.00	65
1991 It's About Time LL-022	Retrd.	1994	55.00	60
1990 A Little Jig LL-018	Retrd.	1994	40.00	50
1990 A Look Through The Spyglass LL-015	Retrd.	1994	45.00	50
1989 Magical Discovery LL-005	Retrd.	1993	45.00	50
1990 Ministral Magic LL-017	Retrd.	1994	45.00	50
1990 A Proclamation LL-013	Retrd.	1994	45.00	55
1989 Spring Water Scrub LL-006	Retrd.	1993	35.00	50
1990 Traveling Fast LL-009	Retrd.	1994	45.00	50
1989 Treasure Hunt LL-004	Retrd.	1993	45.00	50
1991 Viking LL-019	Retrd.	1994	45.00	50
1989 Woodland Cache LL-001	Retrd.	1993	35.00	50
1990 Woodland Scout LL-011	Retrd.	1994	40.00	50
1990 Writing The Legend LL-016	Retrd.	1994	35.00	65

Lil' Doll™ - Various

YEAR ISSUE	EDITION LIMIT	YEAR RETD.	ISSUE PRICE	*QUOTE U.S.$
1992 Clara & The Nutcracker LD-017 - D. Newburn	Retrd.	1994	35.00	35
1991 The Nutcracker LD-006 - P.J. Jonas	Retrd.	1994	35.00	35

Music Makers™ - Various

YEAR ISSUE	EDITION LIMIT	YEAR RETD.	ISSUE PRICE	*QUOTE U.S.$
1991 A Christmas Gift MM-015 - D. Kennicutt	Retrd.	1993	59.00	59
1991 Crystal Angel MM-017 - D. Kennicutt	Retrd.	1993	59.00	59
1991 Dashing Through The Snow MM-013 - D. Kennicutt	Retrd.	1993	59.00	59
1989 Evening Carolers MM-005 - D. Kennicutt	Retrd.	1993	69.00	69
1989 Herald Angel MM-011 - S. Bradford	Retrd.	1993	79.00	79
1991 Nutcracker MM-024 - P.J. Jonas	Retrd.	1994	69.00	69
1991 Peace Descending MM-025 - P.J. Jonas	Retrd.	1993	69.00	69
1991 Renaissance Angel MM-028 - P.J. Jonas	Retrd.	1994	69.00	69
1989 Santa's Sleigh MM-004 - L. Miller	Retrd.	1993	69.00	69
1991 Teddy Bear Band #2 MM-023 - D. Kennicutt	Retrd.	1994	90.00	90
1989 Teddy Bear Band MM-012 - S. Bradford	Retrd.	1993	99.00	100
1989 Teddy Drummers MM-009 - D. Kennicutt	Retrd.	1993	69.00	69
1991 Teddy Soldiers MM-018 - D. Kennicutt	Retrd.	1994	69.00	84
1991 Victorian Santa MM-026 - L. Miller	Retrd.	1993	69.00	69

Collectors' Information Bureau

*Quotes have been rounded up to nearest dollar

Party Animals™ - L. Miller, unless otherwise noted

YEAR ISSUE	EDITION LIMIT	YEAR RETD.	ISSUE PRICE	*QUOTE U.S.$
1984 Democratic Donkey ('84) - D. Kennicutt		1986	14.50	16
1986 Democratic Donkey ('86)	Retrd.	1988	14.50	15
1988 Democratic Donkey ('88)	Retrd.	1990	14.50	16
1990 Democratic Donkey ('90) - D. Kennicutt	Retrd.	1992	16.00	16
1992 Democratic Donkey ('92) - K. Memoli	Retrd.	1994	20.00	20
1984 GOP Elephant ('84)		1986	14.50	16
1986 GOP Elephant ('86)		1988	14.50	15
1988 GOP Elephant ('88)		1990	14.50	16
1990 GOP Elephant ('90) - D. Kennicutt	Retrd.	1992	16.00	16
1992 GOP Elephant ('92) - K. Memoli	Retrd.	1994	20.00	20

PenniBears™ - P.J. Jonas

YEAR ISSUE	EDITION LIMIT	YEAR RETD.	ISSUE PRICE	*QUOTE U.S.$
1992 After Every Meal PB-058	Retrd.	1994	22.00	22
1992 Apple For Teacher PB-069	Retrd.	1994	24.00	24
1989 Attic Fun PB-019	Retrd.	1992	20.00	40
1989 Baby Hugs PB-007	Retrd.	1992	20.00	35
1991 Baking Goodies PB-043	Retrd.	1993	26.00	30
1989 Bathtime Buddies PB-023	Retrd.	1992	20.00	25
1992 Batter Up PB-066	Retrd.	1994	22.00	22
1991 Bear Footin' it PB-037	Retrd.	1993	24.00	24
1992 Bear-Capade PB-073	Retrd.	1994	22.00	22
1991 Bearly Awake PB-033	Retrd.	1993	22.00	25
1989 Beautiful Bride PB-004	Retrd.	1992	20.00	35
1993 Big Chief Little Bear PB-088	Retrd.	1996	28.00	28
1989 Birthday Bear PB-018	Retrd.	1992	20.00	40
1991 Boo Hoo Bear PB-050	Retrd.	1994	22.00	22
1990 Boooo Bear PB-025	Retrd.	1993	20.00	22
1991 Bountiful Harvest PB-045	Retrd.	1994	24.00	24
1989 Bouquet Boy PB-003	Retrd.	1992	20.00	45
1989 Bouquet Girl PB-001	Retrd.	1992	20.00	45
1991 Bump-bear-Crop PB-035	Retrd.	1993	26.00	30
1991 Bunny Buddies PB-042	Retrd.	1993	22.00	25
1989 Butterfly Bear PB-005	Retrd.	1992	20.00	45-50
1990 Buttons & Bows PB-012	Retrd.	1992	20.00	45
1992 Christmas Cookies PB-075	Retrd.	1994	22.00	22
1991 Christmas Reinbear PB-046	Retrd.	1994	28.00	28
1992 Cinderella PB-056	Retrd.	1994	22.00	22
1992 Clowning Around PB-065	Retrd.	1994	22.00	22
1989 Cookie Bandit PB-006	Retrd.	1992	20.00	30
1990 Count Bearacula PB-027	Retrd.	1993	22.00	24
1991 Country Lullabye PB-036	Retrd.	1993	24.00	25
1990 Country Quilter PB-030	Retrd.	1993	22.00	30
1990 Country Spring PB-013	Retrd.	1992	20.00	45
1991 Curtain Call PB-049	Retrd.	1994	24.00	24
1992 Decorating The Wreath PB-076	Retrd.	1994	22.00	22
1989 Doctor Bear PB-008	Retrd.	1992	20.00	30
1992 Downhill Thrills PB-070	Retrd.	1994	24.00	24
1990 Dress Up Fun PB-028	Retrd.	1993	22.00	30
1992 Dust Bunny Roundup PB-062	Retrd.	1994	22.00	22
1992 First Prom PB-064	Retrd.	1994	22.00	22
1990 Garden Path PB-014	Retrd.	1992	20.00	45-50
1993 Getting 'Round On My Own PB-085	Retrd.	1996	26.00	26
1990 Giddiap Teddy PB-011	Retrd.	1992	20.00	35
1991 Goodnight Little Prince PB-041	Retrd.	1993	26.00	26
1991 Goodnight Sweet Princess PB-040	Retrd.	1993	26.00	30
1993 Gotta Try Again PB-082	Retrd.	1996	24.00	24
1989 Handsome Groom PB-015	Retrd.	1992	20.00	40
1993 Happy Birthday PB-084	Retrd.	1996	26.00	26
1993 A Happy Camper PB-077	Retrd.	1996	28.00	28
1991 Happy Hobo PB-051	Retrd.	1994	26.00	26
1989 Honey Bear PB-002	Retrd.	1992	20.00	45
1992 I Made It Boy PB-061	Retrd.	1994	22.00	22
1992 I Made It Girl PB-060	Retrd.	1994	22.00	22
1989 Lazy Days PB-009	Retrd.	1992	20.00	25
1992 Lil' Devil PB-071	Retrd.	1994	24.00	24
1991 Lil' Mer-teddy PB-034	Retrd.	1993	24.00	24
1992 Lil' Sis Makes Up PB-074	Retrd.	1994	22.00	22
1993 Little Bear Peep PB-083	Retrd.	1996	24.00	24
1993 Making It Better PB-087	Retrd.	1996	24.00	24
1993 May Joy Be Yours PB-080	Retrd.	1996	24.00	24
1993 My Forever Love PB-078	Retrd.	1996	28.00	28
1989 Nap Time PB-016	Retrd.	1992	20.00	22
1989 Nurse Bear PB-017	Retrd.	1992	20.00	35
1992 On Your Toes PB-068	Retrd.	1994	24.00	24
1989 Petite Mademoiselle PB-010	Retrd.	1992	20.00	40
1991 Pilgrim Provider PB-047	Retrd.	1994	32.00	32
1992 Pot O' Gold PB-059	Retrd.	1994	22.00	22
1992 Puddle Jumper PB-057	Retrd.	1994	24.00	24
1989 Puppy Bath PB-020	Retrd.	1992	20.00	25
1989 Puppy Love PB-021	Retrd.	1992	20.00	25
1993 Rest Stop PB-079	Retrd.	1996	24.00	24
1992 Sandbox Fun PB-063	Retrd.	1994	22.00	22
1990 Santa Bear-ing Gifts PB-031	Retrd.	1993	24.00	30
1993 Santa's Helper PB-081	Retrd.	1996	28.00	28
1990 Scarecrow Teddy PB-029	Retrd.	1993	24.00	25
1992 Smokey's Nephew PB-055	Retrd.	1994	22.00	22
1990 Sneaky Snowball PB-026	Retrd.	1993	20.00	25
1989 Southern Belle PB-024	Retrd.	1992	20.00	35
1992 Spanish Rose PB-053	Retrd.	1994	24.00	24
1990 Stocking Surprise PB-032	Retrd.	1993	22.00	26
1993 Summer Belle PB-086	Retrd.	1996	24.00	24
1991 Summer Sailing PB-039	Retrd.	1993	26.00	30
1991 Sweet Lil 'Sis PB-048	Retrd.	1994	22.00	22
1991 Sweetheart Bears PB-044	Retrd.	1993	28.00	30
1992 Tally Ho! PB-054	Retrd.	1994	22.00	22
1992 Touchdown PB-072	Retrd.	1994	22.00	22
1989 Tubby Teddy PB-022	Retrd.	1992	20.00	22
1991 A Wild Ride PB-052	Retrd.	1994	26.00	26
1992 Will You Be Mine? PB-067	Retrd.	1994	22.00	22
1991 Windy Day PB-038	Retrd.	1993	24.00	24

PenniBears™ Collector's Club Members Only Editions - P.J. Jonas

YEAR ISSUE	EDITION LIMIT	YEAR RETD.	ISSUE PRICE	*QUOTE U.S.$
1990 1990 First Collection PB-C90	Retrd.	1990	26.00	125
1991 1991 Collecting Makes Cents PB-C91	Retrd.	1991	26.00	150
1992 1992 Today's Treasures, Tomorrow's Treasures PB-C92	Retrd.	1992	26.00	100
1993 1993 Chalkin Up Another Year PB-C93	Retrd.	1993	26.00	35
1994 1994 Artist's Touch-Collector's Treasure PB-C94	Retrd.	1994	26.00	26

Reasons to Believe Santas™ - D. Brown/S. Schultz

YEAR ISSUE	EDITION LIMIT	YEAR RETD.	ISSUE PRICE	*QUOTE U.S.$
2000 Captain Claus CF-402	Retrd.	2001	47.50	48
2000 Christmas Dance CF-405	3,500		35.00	35
2000 High Country Excursion CF-410	3,500		39.50	40
2000 Making Dreams Come True CF-407	Retrd.	2001	47.50	48
2000 North Pole Aviary CF-401	3,500		42.50	43
2000 Polar Express CF-409	3,500		145.00	145
2000 Santa In Toyland CF-404	3,500		32.50	33
2000 Santa's Chair CF-400	Retrd.	2001	62.50	63
2000 Seaside Santa CF-411	Retrd.	2001	47.50	48
2000 Southwest Santa CF-406	Retrd.	2001	60.00	60
2000 Sweet Talkin' Santa CF-403	Retrd.	2001	27.50	28
2000 Windswept Santa CF-408	3,500		37.50	38

Storytime Rhymes & Tales - H. Henriksen

YEAR ISSUE	EDITION LIMIT	YEAR RETD.	ISSUE PRICE	*QUOTE U.S.$
1991 Humpty Dumpty SL-008	Retrd.	1993	64.00	64
1991 Little Jack Horner SL-007	Retrd.	1993	50.00	50
1991 Little Miss Muffet SL-006	Retrd.	1993	64.00	64
1991 Mistress Mary SL-002	Retrd.	1993	64.00	64
1991 Mother Goose SL-001	Retrd.	1993	64.00	64
1991 Owl & Pussy Cat SL-004	Retrd.	1993	100.00	100
1991 Simple Simon SL-003	Retrd.	1993	90.00	90
1991 Three Little Pigs SL-005	Retrd.	1993	100.00	100

Teddy Angels™ - P.J. Jonas

YEAR ISSUE	EDITION LIMIT	YEAR RETD.	ISSUE PRICE	*QUOTE U.S.$
1995 Bruin & Bluebirds "Nurture nature." BA-013	Retrd.	2000	19.00	19
1995 Bruin Making Valentines "Holidays start within the heart." BA-012	Retrd.	2000	15.00	15
1995 Bruin With Harp Seal "Make your corner of the world a little warmer." BA-021	Retrd.	2000	15.00	15
1995 Bunny's Picnic "Make a feast of friendship." BA-007	Retrd.	2000	19.00	19
1995 Casey & Honey Reading "Friends are the best recipe for relaxation." BA-023	Retrd.	2000	15.00	15
1995 Casey Tucking Honey In "There is magic in the simplest things we do." BA-005	Retrd.	2000	15.00	15
1995 Cowboy Murray "Have a Doo Da Day." BA-002	Retrd.	2000	19.00	19
1995 Honey "Love gives our hearts wings." BA-014	Retrd.	2000	13.00	13
1995 Ivy & Blankie "Nothing is as comfortable as an old friend." BA-003	Retrd.	2000	13.00	13
1995 Ivy In Garden "Celebrate the little things." BA-009	Retrd.	2000	15.00	15

FIGURINES

YEAR ISSUE	EDITION LIMIT	YEAR RETD.	ISSUE PRICE	*QUOTE U.S.$
1995 Ivy With Locket "You're always close at heart." BA-028	Retrd.	2000	13.00	13
1995 Murray & Little Bit "Imagination can take you anywhere." BA-004	Retrd.	2000	19.00	19
1995 Murray Mending Bruin "Everybody needs a helping hand." BA-005	Retrd.	2000	15.00	15
1995 Murray With Angel "I believe in you, too." BA-022	Retrd.	2000	22.00	22
1995 Nicholas With Stars "Dreams are never too far away to catch." BA-024	Retrd.	2000	15.00	15
1995 Old Bear "Always remember your way home." BA-011	Retrd.	2000	19.00	19
1995 Old Bear & Little Bit Gardening "The well-watered garden produces a great harvest." BA-026	Retrd.	2000	15.00	15
1995 Old Bear & Little Bit Reading "Love to learn and learn to love." BA-006	Retrd.	2000	15.00	15
1995 Rufus Helps Bird "We could all use a little lift." BA-027	Retrd.	2000	15.00	15
1995 Sweetie "Come tell me all about it." BA-001	Retrd.	2000	15.00	15
1995 Sweetie With Kitty Cats "Always close-knit." BA-025	Retrd.	2000	15.00	15
1995 Tilli & Murray "Friendship is a bridge between hearts." BA-010	Retrd.	2000	15.00	15

Teddy Angels™ Christmas - P.J. Jonas

YEAR ISSUE	EDITION LIMIT	YEAR RETD.	ISSUE PRICE	*QUOTE U.S.$
1997 Angel & Sweetie BA-029	Retrd.	2000	22.00	22
1995 Casey "You're a bright & shining star." BA-019	Retrd.	2000	13.00	13
1995 Ivy "Enchantment glows in winter snows." BA-020	Retrd.	2000	13.00	13
1995 Sweetie & Santa Bear "Tis the season of surprises." BA-016	Retrd.	2000	22.00	22
1995 Tilli & Doves "A wreath is a circle of love." BA-015	Retrd.	2000	19.00	19

Tyber Katz™ - P. & P. Tyber

YEAR ISSUE	EDITION LIMIT	YEAR RETD.	ISSUE PRICE	*QUOTE U.S.$
2000 Cha Cha & Rumba TK-4004	2,500		45.00	45
1999 Fanbelt & Squeaky TK-2001	2,500	2000	45.00	45
1999 Fuzzhead & Friend TK-2000	2,500		45.00	45
2000 Hoochie & Koochie TK-4003	2,500		45.00	45
2000 Hugs & Kisses TK-4005	2,500		45.00	45
2000 Kit & Caboodle TK-4006	2,500	2000	45.00	45
1999 Kozmo & Blue Willow TK-3002	2,500		42.00	42
1999 Kozmo & Indigo TK-2005	2,500		45.00	45
2000 Lovey & Dovey TK-4001	2,500		45.00	45
1999 Lying 'Round TK-1002	2,500		29.00	29
1999 Mr. Dude & Chirper TK-2004	2,500		45.00	45
1999 Mr. Dude & Majolica TK-3001	2,500	2000	42.00	42
1999 Pooker & Flutterby TK-2003	2,500		45.00	45
2000 Rhythm & Blue TK-2006	2,500		45.00	45
2000 Rock & Roll TK-2007	2,500		45.00	45
1999 Sitting Pretty TK-1000	2,500	2000	29.00	29
2000 Smoochie & Woochie TK-4002	2,500		45.00	45
2000 Stanley & Livingstone TK-4007	2,500		45.00	45
1999 Tasha & Blue Jasper TK-3000	2,500	2000	42.00	42
2000 Tiki & Squeaky TK-4005	2,500		45.00	45
1999 Tux & Redhead TK-2002	2,500		45.00	45

Wacky Dogs™ - D. Wentzel

YEAR ISSUE	EDITION LIMIT	YEAR RETD.	ISSUE PRICE	*QUOTE U.S.$
1999 Senor Wacky ND-0022	Retrd.	2000	100.00	100
2000 Senor Wacky, Small ND-0053	Retrd.	2000	65.00	65
1999 Wacky Chef ND-0021	Open		100.00	100
2000 Wacky Chef, Small ND-0052	Open		50.00	50
1999 Wacky Floral Friend ND-0019	Retrd.	2000	100.00	100
2000 Wacky Floral Friend, Small ND-0050	Open		50.00	50
1999 Wacky Go-Getter ND-0020	Open		120.00	120
2000 Wacky Go-Getter, Small ND-0051	Retrd.	2000	60.00	60
2000 Wacky Hipster ND-0061	2,500		100.00	100
2000 Wacky Lantern Holder ND-0054	2,500		120.00	120
1999 Wacky Lightbearer ND-0017	Open		100.00	100
2000 Wacky Racer ND-0060	2,500		100.00	100
1999 Wacky Retriever, Small ND-0048	Retrd.	2000	50.00	50
1999 Wacky Thoroughbred ND-0018	Retrd.	2000	120.00	120
1999 Wacky Thoroughbred, Small ND-0049	Open		60.00	60
2000 Wacky Timekeeper ND-0055	2,500		120.00	120

United Treasures

Angels of Inspiration - K. Stafford

YEAR ISSUE	EDITION LIMIT	YEAR RETD.	ISSUE PRICE	*QUOTE U.S.$
2000 Faith 71001	Open		29.95	30
2000 Happiness 71006	Open		29.95	30
2000 Joy 71000	Open		29.95	30
2000 Kente Claus® 72000	Open		39.95	40
2000 Love 71002	Open		29.95	30
2000 Mercy 71005	Open		29.95	30
2000 Peace 71003	Open		29.95	30
2000 Unity 71004	Open		29.95	30

Billy Dee Williams Romance - B. D. Williams

YEAR ISSUE	EDITION LIMIT	YEAR RETD.	ISSUE PRICE	*QUOTE U.S.$
1999 Dancers 68002	5,000		125.00	125
1999 Gardenia 68001	5,000		95.00	95
1999 Passion 68000	5,000		95.00	95

Black Legend Series - N. Hughes

YEAR ISSUE	EDITION LIMIT	YEAR RETD.	ISSUE PRICE	*QUOTE U.S.$
1994 Bill Pickett 60404	Open		50.00	50
1994 George Washington Carver 60405	Open		50.00	50
1994 Ida B. Wells 60402	Open		60.00	60
1994 Mahalia Jackson 60401	Open		50.00	50

Classic Positive Image - N. Hughes

YEAR ISSUE	EDITION LIMIT	YEAR RETD.	ISSUE PRICE	*QUOTE U.S.$
1991 Boy in Chair 60301	Open		25.00	25
1992 Buffalo Soldier 60311	Open		50.00	50
1996 Civil War Soldier 60310	Open		50.00	50
1991 Girl in Chair 60302	Open		25.00	25
XX Madonna With Child 60600	Open		75.00	75
XX Old Fashion Santa 61201	Open		50.00	50
1997 Praying Slave 60328	Open		75.00	75
1994 Sailor Going Home On Leave 60326	Open		50.00	50
XX Santa's Treat 61202	Open		75.00	75
1992 Tuskegee Airman 60323	Open		50.00	50
1996 Tuskegee Bust 60601	Open		75.00	75
1995 Vietnam Field Nurse 60330	Open		50.00	50
1995 Vietnam Soldier 60329	Open		50.00	50

Emma Jane's Babies - E.J. Watkins

YEAR ISSUE	EDITION LIMIT	YEAR RETD.	ISSUE PRICE	*QUOTE U.S.$
1999 Baby Bertie May Watched Over Little Hattie 62100	Open		25.00	25
1999 Baby Booker Found the Lost Puppy Under the Old Barn 62102	Open		25.00	25
2001 Baby Calbert Had a Crush 62110	Open		25.00	25
1999 Baby Calvin Held His Momma's Picture Close to His Heart 62106	Open		25.00	25
1999 Baby Chloe Gave Her Momma a Rose for Christmas 62104	Open		25.00	25
1999 Baby Cissie Didn't Want Her Picture Taken "No Way, No How" 62103	Open		25.00	25
2001 Baby Clara posed on the back porch 62114	Open		25.00	25
1999 Baby Eubie Just Stood There and Grinned 62101	Open		25.00	25
1999 Baby Lexie Wore Her First "Sunday Go To Meeting Dress" 62108	Open		25.00	25
2001 Baby Lily loved her new tutu 62113	Open		25.00	25
1999 Baby Maizie Daydreamed About her Boyfriend All Afternoon 62107	Open		25.00	25
1999 Baby Nate's Pa Took Him to His First Day of School 62105	Open		25.00	25
2001 Baby Pearl brought her first Christmas present to Grandma 62112	Open		25.00	25
2001 Baby Ruby Caught 3 Blue Gills 62109	Open		25.00	25
2001 Baby Silas Taking a Bath 62111	Open		25.00	25

Emma Jane's Children - E.J. Watkins

YEAR ISSUE	EDITION LIMIT	YEAR RETD.	ISSUE PRICE	*QUOTE U.S.$
1997 Baby Lexie Wore Her First "Sunday Go To Meeting Dress" 62000	5,000		75.00	75
1997 Bertie May Watched Over Little Hattie 62000	5,000		95.00	95
1997 Booker Found the Lost Puppy Under the Old Barn 62002	5,000		75.00	75
2000 Calbert's dreamin' 'bout Maizie	5,000		75.00	75
1997 Calvin Held His Momma's Picture Close to His Heart 62006	5,000		75.00	75
1997 Chloe Gave Her Momma a Rose for Christmas 62004	5,000		75.00	75
1997 Cissie Didn't Want Her Picture Taken "No Way, No How" 62003	5,000		75.00	75
1997 Eubie Just Stood There and Grinned 62001	5,000		75.00	75
1997 Maizie Daydreamed About her Boyfriend All Afternoon 62007	5,000		75.00	75
1997 Nate's Pa Took Him to His First Day of School 62005	5,000		75.00	75

YEAR ISSUE	EDITION LIMIT	YEAR RETD.	ISSUE PRICE	*QUOTE U.S.$
Keith Mallet Collection - K. Mallet				
2002 Family Circle 73001	5,000		65.00	65
2002 Griot 73003	5,000		75.00	75
2002 Spring 73000	5,000		75.00	75
2002 Tree of Life 73002	5,000		75.00	75
Rolling Round Heaven - N. Hughes				
1994 Daydreamer Susie 60507	Open		15.00	15
1994 Dress Up Angel Desiree 60502	Open		15.00	15
1994 Praying Angel Leroy 60505	Open		15.00	15
1994 Reach For A Star Mary 60504	Open		15.00	15
1994 Rolling Round Heaven Display Piece 60500	Open		15.00	15
1994 Why Me Lord Buster 60506	Open		15.00	15
Sankofa - N. Hughes				
1998 Akoko Nan "Mother and Child" 60703	5,000		60.00	60
1998 Akomo Ntoaso "The Family" 60701	5,000		85.00	85
1998 Donno Ntoaso "The Drummer" 60709	5,000		95.00	95
1998 Dono "The Dancer" 60707	5,000		85.00	85
1998 Fie Kwan "Lovers" 60708	5,000		95.00	95
1998 Nyame Dua "Joy" 60710	5,000		100.00	100
1998 Se Ne Tekrema "Father and Son" 60702	5,000		85.00	85
1998 Sun Sum "Woman with Bucket" 60704	5,000		60.00	60
1998 Wo Soro "Woman with Gourd" 60706	5,000		75.00	75
Shades of Africa - N. Hughes				
2002 Angel of Justice 60803	3,000		75.00	75
2001 Mother and Child 60801	3,000		50.00	50
2002 Offerings 60802	3,000		75.00	75
2001 The Young Prince 60800	3,000		75.00	75

Walt Disney

Walt Disney Collectors Society - Disney Studios

YEAR ISSUE	EDITION LIMIT	YEAR RETD.	ISSUE PRICE	*QUOTE U.S.$
1993 Jiminy Cricket Members Only Gift Piece (Kit)	Closed	1993	Gift	150-275
1993 Jiminy Cricket 4"	Closed	1993	Gift.	125-204
1993 Brave Little Tailor 7 1/4" "I Let em' Have It!" 41048 (Animator's Choice)	Closed	1994	160.00	135-275
1994 Cheshire Cat 4 3/4"	Closed	1994	Gift	95-145
1994 Pecos Bill and Widowmaker 9 1/2" (American Folk Heros)	Closed	1994	650.00	550-840
1994 Admiral Duck 6 1/4" (Animator's Choice)	Closed	1995	165.00	175-190
1995 Dumbo	Closed	1995	Gift	95-135
1995 Cruella De Vil 10 1/4" "Anita, Daahling" (Animator's Choice)	Closed	1995	250.00	250-410
1995 Dumbo Ornament "Simply Adorable"	Closed	1995	20.00	40
1995 Slue Foot Sue 41075 (American Folk Heros)	Closed	1995	695.00	350-750
1996 Winnie the Pooh "Time for something sweet" 41091	Closed	1996	Gift	80-90
1996 Winnie the Pooh Ornament "Time for something sweet" 41096	Closed	1996	25.00	25-55
1996 Princess Minnie 41095 (Animator's Choice)	Closed	1996	165.00	138-200
1996 Casey at the Bat 41107 (American Folk Heros)	Closed	1996	395.00	190-395
1997 Magician Mickey "On with the show" 41134	Closed	1997	Gift	50-75
1997 Magician Mickey "On with the show" Ornament 41135	Closed	1997	25.00	25-75
1997 Mickey's Debut (Steamboat Willie) (5th Anniversary) (Charter member backstamp) 41136	Closed	1997	175.00	175-325
1997 Mickey's Debut (Steamboat Willie) (5th Anniversary) (Non-Charter member) 41255	Open		175.00	175
1997 Goofy-Moving Day "Oh The World Owes Me A Livin." 41138 (Animator's Choice)	Yr.Iss.	1997	185.00	154-240
1997 Maleficent: "The Mistress of all Evil" 41177 (Disney Villians)	Closed	1997	450.00	350-545
1997 Chernabog: Night on Bald Mountain, A/P	25	1997	750.00	1120-1265
1998 Timon: "Luau!" 41197	Closed	1998	Gift	50-75
1998 Timon: "Luau!" Ornament 41262	Closed	1998	25.00	25
1998 Timothy Mouse: "Friendship Offering" Ornament 41179	Closed	1998	55.00	55-60
1998 Autumn Fairy: The Touch of an Autumn Fairy 41281	Closed	1998	495.00	495-568
1998 Pluto: Sticky Situation 41199 (Animator's Choice)	Closed	1998	150.00	150-170
1998 Jafar: "Oh Mighty Evil One" 41280 (Disney Villians)	Closed	1998	395.00	395-450
1998 Snow White and Prince, A/P "A Kiss Brings Love Anew"	75	1998	750.00	795-1000
1999 Lady: A Perfectly Beautiful Little Lady	Closed	1999	Gift	50-70
1999 White Rabbit Figural Ornament "No Time to Say Hello-Goodbye" 41373	Closed	1999	59.00	59
1999 "Tinker Bell Pauses to Reflect" 41366 (Animator's Choice)	Closed	1999	240.00	240-275
1999 Cruella in Bed "It's That De Vil Woman" 41405 (Disney Villians)	Closed	1999	450.00	450
1999 Pumbaa & Timon: "Double Trouble" 41416	Closed	1999	135.00	135
2000 Footman: Presenting The Glass Slipper 1204011	Closed	2001	125.00	125
2000 Millennium Midway: "On Top of the World"	Closed	2000	50.00	50-75
2000 Pinocchio: "I'll Never Lie Again" 1202881 (Animator's Choice)	Closed	2001	240.00	240
2000 Fantasia Fairy: "Pretty in Pink" Ornament 1202880	Open		59.00	59
2000 Headless Horseman & Ichabod Crane: Haunted Horseman & Terrified Teacher 1214124	3,500		695.00	695
2000 Evil Queen: "Enthroned Evil" 1205544 (Disney Villians)	Open		395.00	395
2001 Peter Pan: Nana, Faithful Nursemaid 1214730	Open		95.00	95
2001 Tinker Bell: Little Charmer 1214731	Closed	2001	Gift	N/A
2001 Tinker Bell Base 1214882	Closed	2001	45.00	45
2001 ...It Was All Started by a Mouse: Walt & Mickey 1213091	Closed	2001	250.00	250
2001 Dumbo: Baby Mine 1215512 (Animator's Choice)	Closed	2001	195.00	195
2001 Pinocchio: Cleo & Figaro Purrfect Kiss Ornament 1210007	Closed	2001	59.00	59
2001 Scar: "Life Isnt' Fair Is It?" 1215530 (Disney Villians)	Closed	2001	225.00	225
2002 Snow White: "Won't You Smile for Me?"	Yr.Iss.		Gift	N/A
2002 Pedro the Mailplane: "Cleared for Take-Off" 1212443	Yr.Iss.		75.00	75
2002 Flower & Miss Skunk 1217961 (Scene Completer)	Yr.Iss.		125.00	125
2002 Baloo & Mowgli 1214732 (Animator's Choice)	Yr.Iss.		195.00	195
2002 Stromboli 1218013 (Disney Villians)	Yr.Iss.		395.00	395
2002 Mad Hatter & March Hare 1217955	2,500		450.00	450

Walt Disney Classics Collection-Special Event - Disney Studios

YEAR ISSUE	EDITION LIMIT	YEAR RETD.	ISSUE PRICE	*QUOTE U.S.$
1993 Flight of Fancy 3" 41051	Closed	1994	35.00	60-95
1994 Mr. Smee 5" "Oh, dear, dear, dear."41062	Closed	1995	90.00	100-150
1994 Mr. Smee 5" 41062 (teal stamp)	Closed	1995	90.00	95-110
1995 Lucky 41080	Closed	1995	40.00	50-65
1995 Wicked Witch "Take the apple, dearie." 41084	Closed	1996	130.00	200-500
1996 Tinkerbell Ornament	Closed	1996	50.00	50-85
1996 Fairy Godmother "Bibbidi, Bobbidi, Boo" 41108	Closed	1996	125.00	125-160
1997 Evil Queen "Bring back her heart...." 41165	Closed	1997	150.00	145-275
1997 Winnie the Pooh Ornament 41176	Closed	1997	59.00	59-95
1997 Hercules and Pegasus: A gift from the Gods Ornament 41167	Closed	1997	55.00	55
1997 Blue Fairy: Making Dreams Come True 41139	Closed	1997	150.00	120-190
1998 Shere Khan: Everyone Runs From Shere Kahn 41254	Closed	1998	145.00	146-182
1998 Ursula: "We Made a Deal" 41285	Closed	1998	165.00	165-195
1999 Dopey/Sneezy in Coat: Dancing Partner 1028787	Closed	1999	150.00	150
2000 Bambi & Mother: My Little Bambi 1204799	Closed	2000	195.00	195
2000 Jiminy Cricket: "Let Your Conscience Be Your Guide" 1210986	Closed	2000	85.00	85-100
2000 Chef Donald 1217772	5,000	2001	85.00	85

FIGURINES

YEAR ISSUE	EDITION LIMIT	YEAR RETD.	ISSUE PRICE	*QUOTE U.S.$
2001 Beauty and Beast Fountain Accessory 1210978	Open		50.00	50
2001 Belle in Blue Dress: Dreaming of a Great Wide Somewhere 1210979	Closed	2001	150.00	150

Disneyana - Disney Studios

1996 Proud Pongo (w/backstamp)	1,200	1996	175.00	226-358
1997 Chernabog: Night on Bald Mountain	1,500	1997	750.00	1160-1755
1997 Disney Villain Ornament, set/6	12,000	1997	40.00	94-130
1998 Snow White & Prince	1,650	1998	750.00	750-1000
1999 Lion King Ornament, set/7	1,000	1999	45.00	110
1999 Maleficent as Dragon	1,350	1999	795.00	935-1350
1999 Phillip and Sampson Miniature	Closed	2000	95.00	95-150
2000 Willie the Giant: Big Trouble	506	2000	1015.00	1015
2001 Monstro's Revenge with Mini Geppetto Boat 1217771	750	2001	795.00	795-990

DisneyDuo - Disney Studios

2002 Si & Am Siamese Cats 1217953	Yr.Iss.		195.00	195
2000 Toby Tortoise and Max Hare, set/2 1207737	Closed	2000	195.00	195
2000 • Toby Tortoise: Slow But Sure	Closed	2000	set	set
2000 • Max Hare: The Blue Streak	Closed	2000	set	set
2001 Tweedledee & Tweedledum: Riddles 'n' Rhymes; Puzzles 'n' Poems 1204379	Yr.Iss.	2001	195.00	195

Disney's Enchanted Places - Disney Studios

1998 Alice in Wonderland: A Tea Party in Wonderland 41295	4,500		395.00	395
1997 Ariel's Secret Grotto: The Little Mermaid 41235	Open		175.00	175-215
1996 The Beast's Castle: Beauty & The Beast 41225	Retrd.	2001	245.00	245-470
1997 A Castle For Cinderella: Cinderella	Retrd.	1997	225.00	225-300
1997 Cruella's Car: 101 Dalmatians 41230	Retrd.	1999	165.00	165
1996 An Elegant Coach For Cinderella: Cinderella 41208	Retrd.	1999	265.00	265
1996 Fiddler Pig's Stick House: Three Little Pigs 41204	Retrd.	1998	85.00	85-90
1996 Fifer Pig's Straw House: Three Little Pigs 41205	Retrd.	1998	85.00	85-90
1998 Geppettos Toy Creation: Pinocchio 41315	4,000	1998	125.00	125-195
1996 Geppetto's Toy Shop: Pinocchio 41207	Retrd.	1998	150.00	150-180
1996 Grandpa's House: Peter & The Wolf 41221	Closed	1996	125.00	125
1997 Hade's Chariot: Hercules 41246	Retrd.	1997	125.00	125
1996 The Jolly Roger: Peter Pan 41209	10,000		475.00	475-495
1997 King Louie's Temple: Jungle Book	Yr.Iss.	1997	125.00	125
1997 Pastoral Setting: Fantasia 41232	3,000	1997	195.00	195-210
1997 Pooh Bear's House: Winnie the Pooh & The Honey Tree 41231	Retrd.	2001	150.00	150
1996 Practical Pig's Brick House: Three Little Pigs 41206	Retrd.	1998	115.00	85-115
1999 Rose and Table: The Enchanted Rose: Beauty & The Beast 41343	Open		100.00	100-140
1995 Seven Dwarf's Cottage: Snow White 41200	Retrd.	2000	180.00	180
1995 Seven Dwarf's Jewel Mine: Snow White 41203	Retrd.	2000	190.00	190
1998 Sleeping Beauty's Castle 41263	Retrd.	2001	225.00	225-385
1997 Snow White's Wishing Well: Snow White 41248	Retrd.	2000	160.00	160-250
2000 Spinning Wheel: Spinning an Evil Spell: Sleeping Beauty 1214729	Open		65.00	65
1998 Steamboat Willie's Steamboat 41264	Closed	1998	160.00	160
1995 White Rabbit's House: Alice in Wonderland 41202	Retrd.	1999	175.00	175
1995 Woodcutter's Cottage: Sleeping Beauty 41201	Retrd.	1999	170.00	170-195

Disney's Enchanted Places Miniatures - Disney Studios

1997 Ariel 41240	Retrd.	1999	50.00	50
1998 Bashful 41273	Retrd.	2000	50.00	50
1996 Briar Rose 41214	Retrd.	1999	50.00	50
1996 Captain Hook 41219	Retrd.	1998	50.00	50
1998 Doc 41271	Retrd.	2000	50.00	50
1996 Dopey 41215	Retrd.	2000	50.00	50
1999 Eeyore 41319	Retrd.	2001	50.00	50
1996 Fiddler Pig 41224	Retrd.	1998	50.00	50
1996 Fifer Pig 41223	Retrd.	1998	50.00	50

YEAR ISSUE	EDITION LIMIT	YEAR RETD.	ISSUE PRICE	*QUOTE U.S.$
1997 Grumpy 41239	Retrd.	2000	50.00	50
1996 Gus 41218	Retrd.	1999	50.00	50
1998 Happy 41272	Retrd.	2000	50.00	50
1996 Jaq 41242	Retrd.	1999	50.00	50
1998 Jiminy Cricket 41335	Closed	1998	50.00	50
1999 Kanga & Roo 1201838	Retrd.	2001	50.00	50
1998 Mickey Mouse 41265	Closed	1998	50.00	50
1997 Pain 41247	Retrd.	1997	50.00	50-70
1997 Panic 41250	Retrd.	1997	50.00	50-75
1996 Peter 41221	Closed	1996	50.00	50
1999 Piglet 41337	Retrd.	2001	50.00	50
1996 Pinocchio 41217	Retrd.	1998	50.00	50
1996 Practical Pig 41216	Retrd.	1998	50.00	50
1999 Sleepy 41411	Retrd.	2000	50.00	50
1998 Sneezy 41338	Retrd.	2000	50.00	50
1996 Snow White 41212	Retrd.	2000	50.00	50
1998 Tigger 41274	Retrd.	2001	50.00	50
1997 Unicorn 41237	Retrd.	1998	50.00	50-60
1996 White Rabbit 41213	Retrd.	1999	50.00	50-85
1997 Winnie the Pooh 41238	Retrd.	2001	50.00	50-65
1999 Witch 1201785	Retrd.	2000	50.00	50

Signature Series - Disney Studios

2001 Cinderella's Coach 1215509	1,000		2250.00	2250
2000 Snow White and the Seven Dwarfs: Soup's On! 1210013	1,937	2000	1975.00	1975

Walt Disney Classics Collection-101 Dalmatians - Disney Studios

1996 "Go get him thunder!" Two Puppies on Newspaper 41129	Retrd.	1999	120.00	120-143
1996 Lucky and Television "Come on Lucky..." 41131	Retrd.	1999	150.00	135-150
1996 Patient Perdita Perdita with Patch and Puppy 41133	Retrd.	1999	175.00	140-175
1996 Proud Pongo Pongo with Pepper and Penny 41132	Retrd.	1999	175.00	175-190
1996 Rolly "I'm hungry, Mother" 41130	Retrd.	1999	65.00	65-77
1996 Opening Title 41169	Open		29.00	29

Walt Disney Classics Collection-Aladdin - Disney Studios

2002 Aladdin & Jasmine: "A Whole New World" 1217933 (Gold Circle Exclusive)	1,992		395.00	395
1998 Genie: "I'm Losing to a Rug" 41269	12,500		450.00	450
2002 Opening Title 1217936	Open		29.00	29

Walt Disney Classics Collection-Alice in Wonderland - Disney Studios

1999 Alice: "Yes, Your Majesty" 41375	Retrd.	2001	145.00	145
1999 Card Player: "Playing Card" 41414	Retrd.	2001	120.00	120
1999 King of Hearts: "...and the King" 41419	Retrd.	2001	90.00	90
1999 Queen of Hearts "Let the Game Begin!" 41413	Closed	1999	175.00	175
1999 Opening Title 41378	Open		29.00	29

Walt Disney Classics Collection-Aristocats - Disney Studios

2000 Berlioz: Little Rascal 1210006	Open		55.00	55
2000 Duchess: Fetching Feline 1210008	Open		90.00	90
2000 Marie: Coquettish Kitty 1210011	Open		55.00	55
2000 Thomas O'Malley: O'Malley the Alley Cat 1210014	Open		95.00	95
2000 Toulose: Little Tiger 1210015	Open		55.00	55
2000 Aristocats Base - Sofa 1210004	Open		100.00	100
2000 Opening Title 1210005	Open		29.00	29

Walt Disney Classics Collection-Atlantis - Disney Studios

2001 Kida 1215505	2,001		225.00	225

Walt Disney Classics Collection-Bambi - Disney Studios

1992 Bambi "Purty Flower" 6" 41033	Retrd.	1998	195.00	195-350
2002 Bambi "Weak in the Knees" 1217957	Open		175.00	175
1992 Bambi & Flower "He can call me a flower if he wants to" 6" 41010	10,000	1992	298.00	358-700
2002 Faline: "Light as a Feather" 1217958	Open		175.00	175
1992 Field Mouse-not touching "Little April Shower" 5 3/5" 41012	Closed	1993	195.00	950-1200
1992 Field Mouse-touching "Little April Shower" 5 3/5" 41012	Closed	1993	195.00	900-1200
1992 Flower "Oh...gosh!" 3" 41034	Retrd.	1998	78.00	85-140

YEAR ISSUE	EDITION LIMIT	YEAR RETD.	ISSUE PRICE	*QUOTE U.S.$
1992 Friend Owl "What's going on around here?" 8 3/5" 41011	Retrd.	1998	195.00	195-215
1992 Thumper "Hee! Hee! Hee!" 3" 41013	Retrd.	1998	55.00	75-105
2002 Thumper & Miss Bunny: "Twitterpated in the Springtime" 1217960	Open		135.00	135
1992 Thumper's Sisters "Hello, hello there!" 3 3/5" 41014	Retrd.	1998	69.00	70-130
1992 Opening Title 41015	Retrd.	1998	29.00	25-35

Walt Disney Classics Collection-Beauty & The Beast - Disney Studios

YEAR ISSUE	EDITION LIMIT	YEAR RETD.	ISSUE PRICE	*QUOTE U.S.$
2002 Babette: "Ooh-la-la" 1204800	Open		65.00	65
2000 Belle and Beast: "She Didn't Shudder at My Paw" (2000 Gold Circle Exclusive) 1209684	1,991		395.00	395
2001 Gaston 1210983	Open		175.00	175
2001 Le Fou 1215520	Open		110.00	110
1997 Lumiere: Vive L'amour! 41181	Open		115.00	115
1997 Cogsworth: Just in Time 41182	Open		120.00	120
1997 Mrs. Potts and Chip: "Good Night, Luv" 41183	Open		125.00	125
1997 Tale as Old as Time-Belle and the Beast Dancing 41156	Open		295.00	295
2002 Wardrobe: "You'll Look Ravishing in This One" 1217939	Open		150.00	150
1997 Opening Title 41189	Open		29	29

Walt Disney Classics Collection-Brave Little Tailor - Disney Studios

YEAR ISSUE	EDITION LIMIT	YEAR RETD.	ISSUE PRICE	*QUOTE U.S.$
2000 Opening Title 1204010	Retrd.	2001	29.00	29

Walt Disney Classics Collection-Canine Caddy - Disney Studios

YEAR ISSUE	EDITION LIMIT	YEAR RETD.	ISSUE PRICE	*QUOTE U.S.$
1997 Mickey Mouse: "What a swell day for a game of golf!" 41149	Open		150.00	150
1999 Pluto: A Golfer's Best Friend 41314	Open		125.00	125
1997 Canine Caddy Base 41423	Open		40.00	40
1999 Opening Title 41417	Open		29.00	29

Walt Disney Classics Collection-Cinderella - Disney Studios

YEAR ISSUE	EDITION LIMIT	YEAR RETD.	ISSUE PRICE	*QUOTE U.S.$
1993 A Lovely Dress For Cinderelly 41030/ wheel & clef	5,000	1993	800.00	1375-2239
2000 Anastasia: Awful Anastasia 1202883	Open		145.00	145
1993 Birds "We'll tie a sash around it" 6 2/5" 41005	Retrd.	1994	149.00	90-198
1992 Bruno "Just learn to like cats" 4 2/5" 41002	Retrd.	1993	69.00	75-195
1992 Chalk Mouse "No time for dilly-dally" 3 2/5" 41006	Retrd.	1994	65.00	75-150
1992 Cinderella "They can't stop me from dreaming" 6" 41000	Retrd.	1992	195.00	360-450
2000 Cinderella: Fit For a Princess 1202882	Open		225.00	225
1995 Cinderella & Prince Charming "So this is love" 41079	Open		275.00	275
1998 Cinderella & Prince Wedding Sculpture: Fairy Tale Wedding 41267	Retrd.	2001	195.00	195-305
2000 Drizella: Dreadful Drizella 1202885	Open		145.00	145
2000 Grand Duke: Royal Fitting 1202884	Open		150.00	150
1992 Gus "You go get some trimmin'" 3 2/5" 41007	Retrd.	1994	65.00	110-195
1992 Jaq "You go get some trimmin'" 4 1/5" 41008	Retrd.	1994	65.00	75-150
2000 Lady Termaine: Spiteful Stepmother 1204798	Open		165.00	165
1992 Lucifer "Meany, sneaky, roos-a-fee" 2 3/5" 41001	Retrd.	1993	69.00	75-195
1992 Needle Mouse "Hey, we can do it!" 5 4/5" 41004	Retrd.	1994	69.00	98-180
1992 Sewing Book 41003	Retrd.	1994	69.00	45-90
1992 Opening Title 41009	Open		29.00	29-45
1992 Opening Title-Technicolor 41009	Closed	1993	29.00	25-80

Walt Disney Classics Collection-Delivery Boy - Disney Studios

YEAR ISSUE	EDITION LIMIT	YEAR RETD.	ISSUE PRICE	*QUOTE U.S.$
1992 Mickey "Hey Minnie, wanna go steppin?" 6" 41020	Retrd.	1997	125.00	105-295
1992 Minnie "I'm a Jazz Baby" 6" 41021	Retrd.	1996	125.00	135-160
1992 Pluto Dynamite Dog 3 3/5" 41022	Retrd.	1993	125.00	125-250
1992 Pluto Dynamite Dog- 1st version (raised letters) 3 3/5" 41022/ wheel	Closed	1993	125.00	270-402
1992 Opening Title 41019	Retrd.	1993	29.00	20-35

Walt Disney Classics Collection-Dognapper - Disney Studios

YEAR ISSUE	EDITION LIMIT	YEAR RETD.	ISSUE PRICE	*QUOTE U.S.$
2002 Mickey Policeman: On Patrol 1217266	Open		135.00	135

Walt Disney Classics Collection-Don Donald - Disney Studios

YEAR ISSUE	EDITION LIMIT	YEAR RETD.	ISSUE PRICE	*QUOTE U.S.$
1999 Daisy Duck: Daisy's Debut (Gold Circle Dealer's Exclusive) 1028770	Closed	1999	130.00	130

Walt Disney Classics Collection-Donald's Better Self - Disney Studios

YEAR ISSUE	EDITION LIMIT	YEAR RETD.	ISSUE PRICE	*QUOTE U.S.$
1998 Donald Duck: Donald's Decision 41296	Retrd.	1999	145.00	110-145
1998 Donald Duck: Little Devil 41309	Retrd.	1999	145.00	145-180
1998 Donald Duck: What An Angel 41297	Retrd.	1999	145.00	145-180
1998 Opening Title 41298	Retrd.	1999	29.00	29

Walt Disney Classics Collection-Double Dribble - Disney Studios

YEAR ISSUE	EDITION LIMIT	YEAR RETD.	ISSUE PRICE	*QUOTE U.S.$
1999 Goofy Basketball: Dribbling Down Court 41404	Retrd.	2001	175.00	175

Walt Disney Classics Collection-Dumbo - Disney Studios

YEAR ISSUE	EDITION LIMIT	YEAR RETD.	ISSUE PRICE	*QUOTE U.S.$
1997 Bundle of Joy (Dumbo and Stork) 41153	Open		125.00	125
2002 Casey Jr. Train: "All Aboard! Let's go!" 1210980	Open		75.00	75

Walt Disney Classics Collection-Fantasia - Disney Studios

YEAR ISSUE	EDITION LIMIT	YEAR RETD.	ISSUE PRICE	*QUOTE U.S.$
1993 Blue Centaurette-Beauty in Bloom 7 1/2" 41041	Retrd.	1995	195.00	100-215
1992 Broom, Bucket Brigade 5 4/5" 41017	Retrd.	1995	75.00	90-150
1992 Broom, Bucket Brigade w/water spots 5 4/5" 41017/ wheel	Retrd.	1992	75.00	190-220
1996 Ben Ali Gator 7 1/2" 41118	Retrd.	1999	185.00	160-192
2001 Diana: "The Pastoral Symphony" (Gold Circle Dealer's Exclusive) 1214870	1,940		295.00	295
1996 Hyacinth Hippo 5 1/2" 41117	Retrd.	1999	195.00	200-225
1993 Love's Little Helpers Cupids 8" 41042	Retrd.	1995	290.00	140-290
1994 Small Mushroom: Hop Low 41067	Retrd.	1999	35.00	35-40
1994 Mushroom Dancer-Medium 4 1/4" 41068	Retrd.	1999	50.00	60
1994 Mushroom Dancer-Large 4 3/4" 41058	Retrd.	1999	60.00	70-90
1993 Pink Centaurette-Romantic Reflections 7 1/2" 41040	Retrd.	1995	175.00	175-210
1992 Mickey Mouse: Mischievous Apprentice 5 1/8" 41016	Retrd.	1993	195.00	200-275
1997 Mademoiselle Upanova: Prima Ballerina 41178	Retrd.	1999	165.00	165
1992 Opening Title 41018	Open		29.00	29-50
1992 Opening Title-Technicolor 41018	Closed	1993	29.00	25-35

Walt Disney Classics Collection-Fantasia 2000 - Disney Studios

YEAR ISSUE	EDITION LIMIT	YEAR RETD.	ISSUE PRICE	*QUOTE U.S.$
2000 Donald & Daisy: Looks Like Rain 1201846	Closed	2000	325.00	325
2000 Duke: Drumming Up a Dream 1210009	2,000		225.00	225
2000 Elk: Magnificence in the Forest 1214872	2,000		250.00	250-265
2001 Firebird w/miniature Sprite: Volcanic Fury 1210982	2,000		650.00	650
1999 Flamingo: Flamingo Fling 1201841	2,000		195.00	195-385
2001 Jack-in-the-Box w/miniature Tin Soldier & Ballerina: Jealous Jack 1217314	2,000		395.00	395
1999 Sprite: Spirit of Spring 1201845	2,000		650.00	650
1999 Tin Soldier & Ballerina: From the Heart 1201842	2,000		345.00	345-360
1999 Whales: Soaring in the Clouds 1201840	2,000		395.00	395
2000 Yen Sid & Mickey: Oops... 1201839	Closed	2000	295.00	295
2000 Opening Title 1205734	Open		29.00	29

Walt Disney Classics Collection-First Aiders - Disney Studios

YEAR ISSUE	EDITION LIMIT	YEAR RETD.	ISSUE PRICE	*QUOTE U.S.$
1999 Figaro: First Aid Fiasco 1201780	Open		85.00	85
1999 Minnie: Student Nurse 1201778	Open		110.00	110
1999 Pluto: Perfect Patient 1201779	Open		95.00	95
1999 First Aiders Base 1206162	Open		75.00	75

YEAR ISSUE	EDITION LIMIT	YEAR RETD.	ISSUE PRICE	*QUOTE U.S.$
1999 Opening Title 1201781	Open		29.00	29

Walt Disney Classics Collection-Holiday Series - Disney Studios

YEAR ISSUE	EDITION LIMIT	YEAR RETD.	ISSUE PRICE	*QUOTE U.S.$
1995 Mickey Mouse: "Presents For My Pals" 41086	Closed	1995	150.00	150-195
1996 Pluto: Pluto Helps Decorate 41112	Closed	1996	150.00	70-170
1997 Chip 'n Dale: Little Mischief Makers 41163	Closed	1997	150.00	90-150
1997 Holiday Base 41140	Closed	1997	25.00	25
1997 Santa Candle 41172	Closed	1997	40.00	40
1998 Minnie Mouse: Caroler Minnie 41308	Closed	1998	150.00	150
1999 Goofy: "Tis the Season to Be Jolly" 41367	Closed	1999	175.00	175
2000 Donald Duck: "Fa La La..." 1207741	Closed	2000	150.00	150
2000 Lampost Base Lighted 1209688	Open		100.00	100
2000 Opening Title 1205736	Open		29.00	29

Walt Disney Classics Collection-How To Play Baseball - Disney Studios

YEAR ISSUE	EDITION LIMIT	YEAR RETD.	ISSUE PRICE	*QUOTE U.S.$
1998 Goofy Baseball: Batter Up 1028732	Retrd.	2001	175.00	175

Walt Disney Classics Collection-Jungle Book - Disney Studios

YEAR ISSUE	EDITION LIMIT	YEAR RETD.	ISSUE PRICE	*QUOTE U.S.$
1997 King of the Swingers (King Louie) 41158	Retrd.	1999	175.00	175-195
1997 Monkeying Around (Flunky Monkey) 41159	Closed	1997	135.00	135-175
1997 Hula Baloo (Baloo) 41160	Retrd.	1999	185.00	185
1997 Mancub (Mowgli) 41161	Retrd.	1999	115.00	115-135
1997 Bagheera: Mowgli's Protector 41162	Retrd.	1999	135.00	135
1997 Opening Title 41171	Open		29.00	29

Walt Disney Classics Collection-Lady and The Tramp - Disney Studios

YEAR ISSUE	EDITION LIMIT	YEAR RETD.	ISSUE PRICE	*QUOTE U.S.$
1996 Lady: Lady in Love 4 1/2" 41089	Retrd.	1997	120.00	135-195
1996 Tramp: Tramp in Love 5 1/2" 41090	Retrd.	1996	100.00	140-200
1998 Lady and Tramp: Spaghetti Scene Base 41403	Open		75.00	75
1998 Lady and Tramp: "Bella Notte" (Matched Numbered - 3 Sculpture Set) 41284	5,000	1999	795.00	795-864
1996 Opening Title 41099	Open		29.00	29-35

Walt Disney Classics Collection-Lady and The Tramp Christmas Series - Disney Studios

YEAR ISSUE	EDITION LIMIT	YEAR RETD.	ISSUE PRICE	*QUOTE U.S.$
2001 Tramp & Tree 1217797	Yr.Iss.		195.00	195

Walt Disney Classics Collection-Lion King - Disney Studios

YEAR ISSUE	EDITION LIMIT	YEAR RETD.	ISSUE PRICE	*QUOTE U.S.$
1999 Nala: Nala's Joy 41359	Open		165.00	165
1999 Rafiki with Cub: The Circle Continues 41358	Open		150.00	150
1999 Simba: Simba's Pride 41357	Open		175.00	175
1999 Zazu: Major Domo 41360	Closed	1999	75.00	75
1999 Opening Title 41356	Open		29.00	29

Walt Disney Classics Collection-Little Mermaid - Disney Studios

YEAR ISSUE	EDITION LIMIT	YEAR RETD.	ISSUE PRICE	*QUOTE U.S.$
1997 Ariel: Seahorse Surprise 41184	Retrd.	1999	275.00	275
1997 Ariel: Seahorse Surprise-1st version (Bandstand) 41184	Closed	1997	275.00	305-380
1997 Blackfish: Deep Sea Diva 41195	Retrd.	1999	95.00	95-110
1998 Carp: Classic Carp (Gold Circle Dealer's Exclusive) 41194	Closed	1998	150.00	150-175
2001 Eric & Ariel: "Kiss the Girl" (Gold Circle Dealer's Exclusive) 1214733	2,500		425.00	425
1997 Flounder: Flounder's Fandango 41198	Retrd.	1999	150.00	150
1998 Fluke: The Duke of Soul 41191	Retrd.	1999	120.00	120
1998 Newt: Newt's Nautical Note 41193	Retrd.	1999	135.00	135-200
1998 Sebastian: Calypso Crustacean 41187	Retrd.	1999	130.00	130
1998 Snails: Sing-Along Snails 41196	Retrd.	1999	135.00	135-160
1997 Turtle: Twistin' Turtle 41192	Retrd.	1999	85.00	85
1997 Opening Title 41188	Retrd.	1999	29.00	29

Walt Disney Classics Collection-Little Whirlwind - Disney Studios

YEAR ISSUE	EDITION LIMIT	YEAR RETD.	ISSUE PRICE	*QUOTE U.S.$
1999 Minnie Mouse: For My Sweetie 1200907	Retrd.	2001	95.00	95

Walt Disney Classics Collection-Love Bug - Disney Studios

YEAR ISSUE	EDITION LIMIT	YEAR RETD.	ISSUE PRICE	*QUOTE U.S.$
2000 Herbie the Love Bug: Rarin' to Race 1210984 (Disney Store Exclusive)	2,500		150.00	150

Walt Disney Classics Collection-Mary Poppins - Disney Studios

YEAR ISSUE	EDITION LIMIT	YEAR RETD.	ISSUE PRICE	*QUOTE U.S.$
2001 Bert: "Feeling Grand" 1214869	Open		175.00	175
2001 Mary: "It's a Jolly Holiday With Mary" 1214874	Open		185.00	185
2001 Mary Poppins Special Backstamp Set (Gold Circle Dealer's Exclusive) 1213025	600		560.00	560
2001 Single Penguin: "You're Our Favorite Person" 1214880	Open		55.00	55
2001 Trio Penguin: "Anything for You, Mary Poppins" 1214879	Open		145.00	145
2001 Table and Chairs Accessory 1214876	Open		85.00	85
2001 Opening Title 1214875	Open		29.00	29

Walt Disney Classics Collection-Melody Time - Disney Studios

YEAR ISSUE	EDITION LIMIT	YEAR RETD.	ISSUE PRICE	*QUOTE U.S.$
2002 Little Toot Tugboat: Tugging and Tooting 1212445	Open		75.00	75

Walt Disney Classics Collection-Mickey Cuts Up - Disney Studios

YEAR ISSUE	EDITION LIMIT	YEAR RETD.	ISSUE PRICE	*QUOTE U.S.$
1999 Minnie Mouse: Minnie's Garden 1208793	Retrd.	2001	120.00	120
1999 Mickey Mouse: "A Little Off the Top" 1203578 (Parkwest Exclusive)	3,500		150.00	150
1999 Opening Title 1203580	Retrd.	2001	29.00	29

Walt Disney Classics Collection-Mickey Through The Years - Disney Studios

YEAR ISSUE	EDITION LIMIT	YEAR RETD.	ISSUE PRICE	*QUOTE U.S.$
1998 Mickey Mouse (The Band Concert): From The Top 41277	Retrd.	2001	100.00	100
1998 Mickey Mouse (Fantasia): Summoning The Stars 41278	Retrd.	2001	100.00	100
1998 Mickey Mouse (Plane Crazy): How To Fly 41268	Retrd.	2001	100.00	100
1998 Mickey Mouse (The Prince and the Pauper): Long Live The King 41279	Retrd.	2001	100.00	100
1998 Bases set of 4, 41301	Closed	1998	30.00	30

Walt Disney Classics Collection-Mickey's Birthday Party - Disney Studios

YEAR ISSUE	EDITION LIMIT	YEAR RETD.	ISSUE PRICE	*QUOTE U.S.$
1997 Mickey Mouse: "Happy Birthday" 1028648	Open		95.00	95

Walt Disney Classics Collection-Mickey's Fire Brigade - Disney Studios

YEAR ISSUE	EDITION LIMIT	YEAR RETD.	ISSUE PRICE	*QUOTE U.S.$
2002 Donald Fireman: Duck! A Fire! 1217975	Open		125.00	125
2000 Mickey Mouse: Fireman To The Rescue 1204801	Open		125.00	125

Walt Disney Classics Collection-Mickey's Orphans - Disney Studios

YEAR ISSUE	EDITION LIMIT	YEAR RETD.	ISSUE PRICE	*QUOTE U.S.$
2000 Mickey Holiday: "Hooray for the Holidays" 1210012	5,000		375.00	375

Walt Disney Classics Collection-Mickey's Revue - Disney Studios

YEAR ISSUE	EDITION LIMIT	YEAR RETD.	ISSUE PRICE	*QUOTE U.S.$
2000 Dippy Dawg: Goofy's Debut (Gold Circle Dealer's Exclusive) 1205237	5,000		165.00	165

Walt Disney Classics Collection-Mr. Duck Steps Out - Disney Studios

YEAR ISSUE	EDITION LIMIT	YEAR RETD.	ISSUE PRICE	*QUOTE U.S.$
1993 Donald & Daisy "Oh boy, what a jitterbug!" 6 3/5" 41024	5,000	1996	295.00	340-600
1994 Donald Duck: "With love from Daisy" 6 1/4" 41060	Retrd.	1996	180.00	180
1993 Dewey: "I got somethin for ya" 4" 41025	Retrd.	1996	65.00	65
1993 Huey: Tag-Along Trouble 4" 41049	Retrd.	1996	65.00	65
1993 Nephew Duck-Louie 4" 41050	Retrd.	1994	65.00	65
1993 Opening Title 41023	Retrd.	1996	29.00	29-38

Walt Disney Classics Collection-Nifty Nineties - Disney Studios

YEAR ISSUE	EDITION LIMIT	YEAR RETD.	ISSUE PRICE	*QUOTE U.S.$
2001 Mickey Nifty Nineties: A Perfect Gent! 1214877	Yr.Iss.	2001	95.00	95
2002 Minnie: A Lovely Lady 1214878	Yr.Iss.		95.00	95

Walt Disney Classics Collection-Nightmare Before Christmas - Disney Studios

YEAR ISSUE	EDITION LIMIT	YEAR RETD.	ISSUE PRICE	*QUOTE U.S.$
2001 Barrel 1215506	Open		55.00	55
2000 Jack: "My Christmas is Filled with Laughter and Joy..." 1204384	Open		160.00	160

Collectors' Information Bureau   *Quotes have been rounded up to nearest dollar

YEAR ISSUE	EDITION LIMIT	YEAR RETD.	ISSUE PRICE	*QUOTE U.S.$
2001 Lock 1215523	Open		55.00	55
2001 Mayor 1215526	Open		155.00	155
2000 Sally: The Sandy Claws Seamstress 1204383	Open		150.00	150
2001 Shock 1215532	Open		55.00	55
2000 Zero: Spirited Companion 1204382	Open		75.00	75
2001 Opening Title 1204381	Open		29.00	29

Walt Disney Classics Collection-On Ice - Disney Studios

1999 Donald: Away We Go! 1200936	Retrd.	2000	150.00	150
1997 Minnie Mouse: "Whee!" 1028633	Retrd.	2000	165.00	165
1998 Mickey Mouse: "Watch Me!" 1028736	Retrd.	2000	165.00	165
1998 Ice Pond Base 1200944	Retrd.	2000	50.00	50
1998 Opening Title 1028727	Retrd.	2000	29.00	29

Walt Disney Classics Collection-Peter Pan - Disney Studios

1993 Captain Hook: "I've got you this time!" 8" 41044	Retrd.	2000	275.00	290-470
1993 Crocodile: "Tick-tock, tick-tock" 6 1/4" 41054	Retrd.	2000	315.00	315-360
1993 Peter Pan: "Nobody calls Pan a coward!" 7 1/2" 41043	Retrd.	2000	165.00	175-200
1993 Tinkerbell: A firefly! A pixie! Amazing!" 5" 41045	12,500	1993	215.00	300-350
1993 Opening Title 41047	Retrd.	2000	29.00	22-35

Walt Disney Classics Collection-Peter Pan Nursery Scene - Disney Studios

2000 John: "You'll Never Leave This Ship Alive!" 1211845	Open		115.00	115
2000 Michael: "Back, You Villian!" 1211847	Open		80.00	80
2002 Peter: "Off to Never Land!" 1211849	Open		135.00	135
2000 Wendy: True Believer 1211852	Open		120.00	120
2000 Bed Base 1214881	Open		85.00	85
2002 Window Accessory with Tinker Bell miniature 1217950	Open		95.00	95

Walt Disney Classics Collection-Pinocchio - Disney Studios

1996 Figaro "Say hello to Figaro" 41111	Retrd.	1998	55.00	55-80
1996 Geppetto "Good-bye, Son" 41114	Retrd.	1998	145.00	155-170
1996 Jiminy Cricket "Wait for me, Pinoke!" Retrd. 41109	Retrd.	1998	85.00	85-115
2000 Jiminy: "Let Your Conscience Be Your Guide" 1210986	Retrd.	2000	85.00	85
1996 Pinocchio "Good-bye Father" 41110	Retrd.	1998	125.00	140-195
1996 Opening Title 41116	Retrd.	1998	29.00	29

Walt Disney Classics Collection-Puppy Love - Disney Studios

1998 Mickey Mouse: "Brought You Something" 41324	Retrd.	2000	135.00	135
1998 Minnie Mouse: "Oh, It's Swell!" 41325	Retrd.	2000	135.00	135
1998 Fifi: Flirtatious Fifi 41336	Retrd.	2000	95.00	95
1998 Opening Title 41326	Retrd.	2000	29.00	29

Walt Disney Classics Collection-Reluctant Dragon - Disney Studios

1996 The Reluctant Dragon "The more the merrier" 7" 41072	7,500	1996	695.00	489-695

Walt Disney Classics Collection-Scrooge McDuck and the Money - Disney Studios

1997 Money! Money! Money! Scrooge McDuck 41152	2,000	2001	175.00	175

Walt Disney Classics Collection-Simple Things - Disney Studios

1999 Mickey Mouse: Somethin' Fishy 41363	Retrd.	2001	150.00	150

Walt Disney Classics Collection-Sleeping Beauty - Disney Studios

1997 Briar Rose: "Once upon a dream" 41157	12,500		345.00	345-415
1998 Aurora & Phillip: A Dance in the Clouds 1028723 (blue dress)	Open		295.00	295
1998 Aurora & Phillip: A Dance in the Clouds 1028581 (pink dress)	2,000	1998	295.00	750-850
1998 Fauna: A Little Bit of Both 41259	Open		100.00	100
1998 Flora: A Little Bit of Pink 41258	Open		100.00	100
1998 Merryweather: A Little Bit of Blue 41260	Open		95.00	95
2002 Sleeping Beauty Kiss: Love's First Kiss 1217923 (Gold Circle Exclusive)	1,959		450.00	450

YEAR ISSUE	EDITION LIMIT	YEAR RETD.	ISSUE PRICE	*QUOTE U.S.$
1998 Opening Title 41275	Open		29.00	29

Walt Disney Classics Collection-Snow White - Disney Studios

1994 Snow White: The Fairest One of All 8 1/4" 1028550	Open		175.00	165-310
1995 Bashful "Aw, shucks" 5" 1028558	Open		90.00	90
1995 Doc: Cheerful Leader 5 1/4" 1028560	Open		100.00	100
1995 Dopey: Dopey 5" 1028563	Open		105.00	105
1995 Grumpy with Pipe Organ "Humph!" 7 3/4" 1028552	Open		180.00	180-198
1995 Happy "Happy, that's me!" 5 1/2" 1028551	Open		125.00	125-155
1995 Sleepy "zzzzzzz" 3 1/4" 1028555	Open		95.00	95
1995 Sneezy "Ah-Choo!" 4 1/2" 1028562	Open		95.00	95
2002 The Dwarfs' Hearth 1217064	Open		95.00	95
1999 Snow White and Prince: "I'm Wishing For The One I Love" 1028797	Retrd.	2000	295.00	295
1995 Opening Title 1028572	Open		29.00	29

Walt Disney Classics Collection-Song of the South - Disney Studios

1996 Brer Bear: "Duh" 7 1/2" 41112	Retrd.	1997	175.00	125-238
1996 Brer Fox: "I got cha, Brer Rabbit" 4" 41101	Retrd.	1997	120.00	110-194
1996 Brer Rabbit: Born and Bred in a Briar Patch 4 3/4" 41103	Retrd.	1997	150.00	150-250
1996 Opening Title 41104	Retrd.	1997	29.00	29-60

Walt Disney Classics Collection-Susie the Little Blue Coupe - Disney Studios

2002 Susie, The Little Blue Coupe: Isn't She a Beauty? 1212444	Open		75.00	75

Walt Disney Classics Collection-Symphony Hour - Disney Studios

1993 Clarabelle Cow: Clarabella's Crescendo 6 4/5" 41027/ wheel	Retrd.	1993	198.00	198-204
1994 Clara Cluck: Bravo Bravissimo 41061	Retrd.	1997	185.00	90-185
1996 Donald Duck: Donald's Drum Beat 8 1/4" 41105/ hat	Retrd.	1996	225.00	250-430
1993 Goofy: Goofy's Grace Notes 6 4/5" 41026/wheel	Retrd.	1993	198.00	1150-2700
1993 Goofy: Goofy's Grace Notes 6 4/5" 41026	Retrd.	1997	198.00	125-260
1993 Horace Horsecollar: Horace's High Notes 6 4/5" 41028	Retrd.	1997	198.00	105-215
1996 Donald Duck: Donald's Drum Beat 8 1/4" 41105	Retrd.	1997	225.00	375-407
1993 Mickey Mouse Conductor: Maestro Michael Mouse 7 3/8" 41029	Retrd.	1997	185.00	121-230
1996 Sylvester Macaroni 41106	12,500	1997	395.00	395
1993 Opening Title 41031	Retrd.	1997	29.00	29

Walt Disney Classics Collection-Tarzan - Disney Studios

1999 Jane: Miss Jane Porter 41428	Retrd.	1999	150.00	150
1999 Tarzan: Tarzan of the Jungle 41427	Retrd.	1999	165.00	165
1999 Terk: Jungle Rhythm 41429	Retrd.	1999	225.00	225
1999 Opening Title 41426	Open		29.00	29

Walt Disney Classics Collection-Theme Park - Disney Studios

2000 Main Street Electrical Parade: Cinderella's Coach 1207513	Yr.Iss.	2000	135.00	135
1998 Main Street Electrical Parade: Goofy's Train 41289	Retrd.	2000	145.00	145
1998 Main Street Electrical Parade: Lightening Bug 41291	Retrd.	2000	85.00	85
1998 Main Street Electrical Parade: Mickey's Drum 41290	Retrd.	2000	145.00	145
2000 Main Street Electrical Parade: Musical Accessory 1210010	Retrd.	2000	50.00	50
1999 Main Street Electrical Parade: Pete's Dragon 41384	Retrd.	2000	165.00	165-200
1999 Main Street Electrical Parade: Twinkling Turtle 41385	Retrd.	2000	85.00	85

Walt Disney Classics Collection-Theme Park Convention Exclusive - Disney Studios

1999 Haunted Mansion: "Beware of Hitchhiking Ghosts" 1207739	1,500	1999	395.00	395-660

YEAR ISSUE	EDITION LIMIT	YEAR RETD.	ISSUE PRICE	*QUOTE U.S.$
2000 Pirates of the Caribbean: "A Pirate's Life for Me" 1207739	1,500	2000	495.00	495-670
2000 Mr. Toad: Blue Boy (Disneyland Exclusive)	1,500	2000	175.00	175
2000 Mr. Toad: Pinkie (Disneyland Exclusive)	1,500	2000	175.00	175
2001 Fantasyland Sculpture; Mad Hatter 1217634, Timothy 1217336, Dormouse 121341	750	2001	450.00	450
2001 Fantasyland Sculpture Base 1217361	750		70.00	70

Walt Disney Classics Collection-Three Caballeros - Disney Studios

1995 Amigo Donald 7" 41076	Retrd.	1996	180.00	180
1995 Amigo Jose 7" 41077	Retrd.	1996	180.00	180
1995 Amigo Panchito 7" 41078	Retrd.	1996	180.00	180
1995 Opening Title 41070	Retrd.	1996	29.00	15-33

Walt Disney Classics Collection-Three Little Pigs - Disney Studios

1993 Big Bad Wolf "Who's afraid of the Big Bad Wolf?" 41039 (short straight teeth/cone base) 1st version	S/O	1993	295.00	695-794
1993 Big Bad Wolf "Who's afraid of the Big Bad Wolf?" 41039 (short straight teeth/flat base) 2nd version	S/O	1994	295.00	380-495
1993 Big Bad Wolf "Who's afraid of the Big Bad Wolf?" 41039 (long/short curved teeth) 3rd version	S/O	1994	295.00	373-895
1996 Big Bad Wolf "I'm a poor little sheep..." 41094	Retrd.	1998	225.00	225-245
1993 Fiddler Pig "Hey diddle, diddle, I play my fiddle" 4 1/2" 41038	Retrd.	1998	75.00	75-111
1993 Fifer Pig " I toot my flute, I don't give a hoot" 4 1/2" 41037	Retrd.	1998	75.00	75-111
1993 Practical Pig "Work and play don't mix" 4 1/2" 41036	Retrd.	1998	75.00	75-111
1993 Opening Title 41046	Retrd.	1998	29.00	28-46

Walt Disney Classics Collection-Touchdown Mickey - Disney Studios

1998 Mickey Mouse: "Rah, Rah, Mickey!" 41252	Retrd.	2001	150.00	150

Walt Disney Classics Collection-Toy Story - Disney Studios

1998 Bo Peep: "I Found My Moving Buddy" 41320	Open		150.00	150
1998 Buzz 41304	Open		175.00	175
1998 Hamm: "It's Showtime" 41321	Open		90.00	90
1999 Mr. Potato Head: "That's Mr. Potato Head To You" 1201782	Open		115.00	115
1999 Rex: "I'm So Glad You're Not a Dinosaur" 41334	Closed	1999	140.00	140-165
1998 Woody 41305	Open		175.00	175
1998 Opening Title 41306	Open		29.00	29

Walt Disney Classics Collection-Toy Story 2 - Disney Studios

2002 Jessie & Bullseye: "Yeee-ha!" and "Ride Like the Wind" 1215519	Open		250.00	250
2002 Record Player Base 1217951	Open		95.00	95
2002 Opening Title 1217917	Open		29.00	29

Walt Disney Classics Collection-Tribute Series - Disney Studios

1995 Simba & Mufasa: Pals Forever 41085	Closed	1995	175.00	175-295
1996 Pocahontas "Listen With Your Heart" 6 1/2" 41098	Closed	1996	225.00	225-275
1997 Quasimodo and Esmeralda "Not a single monster line" 41143	Closed	1997	195.00	195-210
1998 Hercules: "From Zero To Hero" 41253	Closed	1998	250.00	250-286
1999 Mulan: Honorable Decision 41374	Closed	1999	175.00	175-225

Walt Disney Classics Collection-Trick or Treat - Disney Studios

2001 Dewey Devil 1215535	Open		55.00	55
2001 Halloween Base 1215534	Open		50.00	50
2001 Huey Ghost 1215510	Open		55.00	55
2001 Louie Witch 1215536	Open		55.00	55
2001 Witch Hazel 1218015	Open		75.00	75
2001 Opening Title 1215533	Open		29.00	29

YEAR ISSUE	EDITION LIMIT	YEAR RETD.	ISSUE PRICE	*QUOTE U.S.$

Walt Disney Classics Collection-Who Framed Roger Rabbit - Disney Studios

1998 Roger and Jessica: "Dear Jessica, How Do I Love Thee?" 41322	7,500		295.00	295

Walt Disney Classics Collection-Winnie the Pooh & the Blustery Day - Disney Studios

2001 Pooh's Hero Party: "Hip! Hip! Pooh-ray!" 1216842	1,968		225.00	225

Walt Disney Classics Collection-Wise Little Hen - Disney Studios

1997 Donald Duck: Donald's Debut (Gold Circle Dealer's Exclusive) 41175	Closed	1997	110.00	110-200

Willitts Designs

Just The Right Club - Raine

1999 Ribeting	Retrd.	2000	16.00	16
1999 The Wave	Retrd.	2000	20.00	20
1999 Touch of Lace	Retrd.	2000	20.00	20
2001 Society Slide	Retrd.	2001	20.00	20
2001 Late For A Date	Retrd.	2001	20.00	20
2002 Water (Elements)	Yr.Iss.		40.00	40
2002 Fire (Elements)	Yr.Iss.		40.00	40

Just The Right Shoe Event - Raine

2001 Flight of Fancy	Retrd.	2001	16.50	17

Just The Right Shoe/Accessories - Raine

1999 All That Glitters (purse Musical)	Open		30.00	30
1999 Arabesque (musical)	Open		37.50	38
1999 Bayou (purse Musical)	Open		28.00	28
2000 Carved Heel (purse)	Retrd.	2001	13.50	14
1999 Chic Plastique (purse box)	Open		16.00	16
1999 Cotillion (purse)	Open		15.50	16
1999 Devoted to You (musical)	Open		35.00	35
1999 Fanfare (hat box)	Open		17.50	18
1999 Feather Flair (hat box)	Open		17.50	18
1999 Fedora (hat box)	Open		17.50	18
1999 From the Sea (purse box)	Open		16.00	16
1999 Frosted Fantasy (purse box)	Open		23.50	24
1999 Girl's Best Friend (musical)	Open		40.00	40
1999 I Do (box)	Open		27.50	28
2000 In Scale (purse)	Open		12.00	12
1999 Ingenue (box)	Open		15.50	16
1999 Majestic (purse)	Retrd.	2002	16.50	17
2000 Midnight Promises (purse)	Retrd.	2002	14.50	15
1999 Minuet (musical)	Open		37.50	38
1999 Pas de Deux (shoe Musical)	Open		37.50	38
1999 Pink Frost (hat w/mannequin)	Open		28.50	29
1999 Raine (purse box)	Open		14.00	14
1999 Sea of Pearls (hat w/mannequin)	Open		29.50	30
1999 Seregeti (purse box)	Open		15.50	16
1999 Silver Kitten (musical)	Open		37.50	38
1999 Sweet Surprise (box)	Retrd.	2001	16.50	17
1999 Tapestry (purse box)	Open		17.50	18
1999 Traveler (purse box)	Open		13.00	13
1999 Tweed (hat box)	Open		17.50	18
1999 Velvet Crush (purse Musical)	Open		28.00	28
2000 You Animal You (purse)	Retrd.	2002	16.00	16

Just The Right Shoe/Children - Raine

1999 Baby Quilt (shoe musical)	Open		35.00	35
1999 Beach Time (box)	Open		16.50	17
1999 Blue Lullabye (box)	Open		14.00	14
1999 Mary Jane (box)	Open		14.50	15
1999 Pink Lullabye (box)	Open		14.00	14
1999 Rough 'n Tumble (box)	Open		14.00	14
1999 Sleepy Time (shoe musical)	Open		38.50	39

Just The Right Shoe/Classic Collection - Raine

2001 Afternoon Stroll	Open		15.00	15
2001 Afternoon Tea	Open		24.00	24
1999 Aladdin's Delight	Retrd.	2001	16.00	16
2000 Aristocrat	Retrd.	2001	15.50	16
2000 Baroness	Open		16.00	16
1999 Blush	Retrd.	1999	13.50	20-35
2001 Bobby Soxer	Open		13.00	13
1999 Bordeaux	Retrd.	1999	16.00	20-38
1999 Bovine Bliss	Retrd.	2001	14.00	14
2000 Brave Warrior	Open		12.00	12

Collectors' Information Bureau   *Quotes have been rounded up to nearest dollar

YEAR ISSUE	EDITION LIMIT	YEAR RETD.	ISSUE PRICE	*QUOTE U.S.$
1998 Brocade Court	Retrd.	1999	16.00	23-38
2000 Calla Lily	Retrd.	2001	16.50	17
2001 Carolynn	Open		18.00	18
2000 Carved Heel	Retrd.	2001	13.00	13
2000 Check It Out!	Open		15.00	15
2000 Cork Wedge	Retrd.	2002	14.00	14
2001 Countess	Open		16.00	16
1998 Deco Boot	Retrd.	1999	25.00	25-38
2001 Denim Blues	Open		14.00	14
2001 Dressed to Impress	Open		12.00	12
1999 Edwardian Grace	Retrd.	2001	18.00	18
2001 Elizabeth	Open		13.00	13
1998 The Empress	Retrd.	2000	18.00	18-35
1998 En Pointe	Open		17.50	18
2001 Figure Eight	Open		20.00	20
2001 French Velvet	Open		14.00	14
1998 Frosted Fantasy	Open		20.00	20
1999 Geometrika	Retrd.	2001	12.50	13
2000 Golden Leaf	Retrd.	2001	15.00	15
2001 Grand Marquise	Open		14.00	14
1999 High-Buttoned Boot	Open		17.50	18
2000 Home on the Range	Retrd.	2001	15.00	15
1999 I Do	Open		16.00	16
2000 In Scale	Open		13.00	13
1999 Ingenue	Retrd.	2001	14.50	15
1998 Italian Racer	Retrd.	1999	13.50	20-31
1998 Jeweled Heel Pump	Retrd.	2001	24.00	24-32
2000 Lavish Tapestry	Retrd.	2001	14.50	15
1998 Leopard Stiletto	Retrd.	2002	15.00	15-32
1999 Magnetic Allure	Retrd.	2001	14.00	14-32
1999 Majestic	Retrd.	2002	17.50	18
2000 Midori	Open		20.00	20
1999 New Heights	Retrd.	2000	12.00	12
1998 Opera Boot	Retrd.	2001	25.00	25
2001 Parisian Nights	Open		20.00	20
1998 Pavé	Retrd.	2000	22.00	22-35
1998 Pearl Mule	Retrd.	2000	17.00	17-32
1998 Promenade	Open		20.00	20
2001 Pump It Up	Open		14.50	15
1999 Purple Dream	Retrd.	2001	15.00	15
1998 Ravishing Red	Retrd.	2000	12.00	12-32
2001 Red Hot	Open		20.00	20
2001 Retroactive	Open		13.00	13
1998 Rose Court	Retrd.	2000	15.00	15-32
2001 Seduction	Open		17.00	17
1999 Serengeti	Retrd.	2001	15.00	15-32
1999 Shimmering Night	Open		16.00	16
1999 Shower of Flowers	Retrd.	2001	14.00	14
2001 Silken Wrap	Open		13.50	14
1998 Silver Cloud	Retrd.	1999	14.50	15-35
1999 Sneaking By	Retrd.	2002	15.00	15
2000 Spectate This	Retrd.	2002	13.00	13
1998 Sumptuous Quilt	Retrd.	1999	13.50	18-35
2000 Sunray	Retrd.	2001	13.50	14
2000 Tassles	Retrd.	2001	17.50	18
1998 Teetering Court	Retrd.	1999	18.00	21-38
2001 Toe Tapper	Open		15.00	15
2000 Treads	Retrd.	2001	12.50	13
2000 Truffles	Retrd.	2001	12.50	13
1998 Tying the Knot	Retrd.	2001	15.00	15
2001 Untamed	Open		18.00	18
1999 Va-Va-Voom	Open		14.50	15
1999 Versailles	Retrd.	1999	15.00	15
2000 Victorian Ankle Boot	Retrd.	2001	17.50	18
2000 Victorian Wedding Boot	Open		16.00	16
2000 You Animal You!	Retrd.	2002	17.00	17

Just The Right Shoe/Designer Collection - Raine

YEAR ISSUE	EDITION LIMIT	YEAR RETD.	ISSUE PRICE	*QUOTE U.S.$
2001 Aloha	Open		14.00	14
2001 Apres	Open		17.00	17
2000 Bow Me	Open		14.50	15
2001 Canton	Open		17.00	17
2001 Diamonds	Open		22.50	23
2000 Espadrille "Pacha"	Open		17.00	17
2000 Fruity	Open		14.50	15
2000 Fruity Purse	Open		15.50	16
2001 Jewels Shoes	Retrd.	2002	18.00	18
2000 La Rosa	Open		18.50	19
2000 Mostly Matisse	Open		17.50	18
2000 Queen of Hearts	Open		14.00	14
2000 Queen of Hearts Purse	Open		16.00	16

YEAR ISSUE	EDITION LIMIT	YEAR RETD.	ISSUE PRICE	*QUOTE U.S.$
2001 Rosie Toes	Open		13.00	13
2000 Sparkle Purse	Open		15.50	16
2000 Sparkle Shoe	Open		15.50	16

Just The Right Shoe/Exclusives - Raine

YEAR ISSUE	EDITION LIMIT	YEAR RETD.	ISSUE PRICE	*QUOTE U.S.$
2000 Celebration (Exclusive Color) (Parkwest)	Open		13.00	13
2001 Cork Wedge, Tangerine (Carlton Cards)	Open		16.20	17
2000 Denim Blues (GCC)	Open		14.00	14
2001 Forever Yours, Blue (GCC)	Open		20.50	21
1999 Frosted Fantasy (Exclusive Color)	Open		20.00	20
2001 Mary Jane, Red (Parkwest, NALED)	Open		10.00	10
2000 Opulent Purse (QVC)	Open		20.00	20
1998 Opulent Shoe (QVC)	Open		20.00	20
2001 Spring Raine, Lavendar (GoCollect.com)	Open		16.50	17
1999 Tuxedo (Exclusive Color) (GCC)	Open		16.50	17
1999 Victoria (Exclusive Color) (QVC)	Open		18.00	18
1998 Victorious (Exclusive Color) (POG)	Open		17.00	17

Just The Right Shoe/Men's Collection - Raine

YEAR ISSUE	EDITION LIMIT	YEAR RETD.	ISSUE PRICE	*QUOTE U.S.$
1999 Cowboy Boot	Retrd.	2002	14.00	14
1999 Golf Shoe	Open		12.50	13
1999 Military Boot	Open		13.00	13
1999 Motorcycle Boot	Open		14.00	14
1999 Penny Loafer	Retrd.	2002	12.00	12
1999 Tassie Loafer	Retrd.	2002	12.00	12

Just The Right Shoe/Museum-Biltmore Estate Collection - Raine

YEAR ISSUE	EDITION LIMIT	YEAR RETD.	ISSUE PRICE	*QUOTE U.S.$
2000 Brogue Ballyhoo	Open		13.00	13
2000 Charisma	Open		15.00	15
2000 Something Blue	Open		16.00	16
2000 Starry Night	Open		15.50	16
2000 Sweet Elegance	Open		14.00	14

Just The Right Shoe/Museum-Mt. Vernon Collection - Raine

YEAR ISSUE	EDITION LIMIT	YEAR RETD.	ISSUE PRICE	*QUOTE U.S.$
2000 First Lady Slipper	Open		13.00	13
2000 George Washington Dress Shoe	Open		13.00	13
2000 George Washington Riding Boot	Open		17.00	17
2000 Martha Washington Dress Shoe	Open		14.00	14
2000 Martha Washington Wedding Shoe	Open		15.00	15

Just The Right Shoe/Raine Originals - Raine

YEAR ISSUE	EDITION LIMIT	YEAR RETD.	ISSUE PRICE	*QUOTE U.S.$
2002 Air (Elements)	Open		20.00	20
2000 Autumn	Retrd.	2001	13.00	13
2001 Bahama Mama	Open		16.00	16
2001 Cloaked in Mystery	Open		14.00	14
2000 Courageous Rose	Retrd.	2002	17.00	17
2000 Crocus	Retrd.	2002	14.50	15
2001 Custom Made	Open		17.50	18
2002 Dazzle	Open		16.00	16
2002 Earth (Elements)	Open		14.00	14
2002 Electric	Open		16.00	16
2002 Emerald Luna	Open		18.00	18
2002 En Vogue	Open		17.00	17
2002 Enchanted	Open		18.50	19
2002 Enlisted	Open		17.00	17
2002 Evening Emerald	Open		17.00	17
2002 Eye of the Tiger	Open		17.00	17
2002 Felicity	Open		16.50	17
2000 Forever Yours	Open		20.00	20
2000 Groovy Baby	Open		24.50	25
2001 Kutsuya	Open		15.50	16
2002 Lace It Up	Open		18.50	19
2000 Later Gator	Open		13.50	14
2001 Lone Star	Open		16.00	16
2002 Love Hurts	Open		14.00	14
2001 Luminous	Open		17.50	18
2002 Madagascar Comet	Open		20.00	20
2002 Mahalo	Open		14.00	14
2000 Mardi Gras	Open		22.50	23
2002 Maricopa	Open		14.00	14
2000 Midnight Promises	Retrd.	2002	16.00	16
2001 Passion's Flame	Open		18.00	18
2002 Patricia in Plum	Open		16.00	16
2002 Perfect Game	Open		13.50	14
2001 Perfectly Python	Open		20.00	20
2002 Picnic	Open		17.00	17
2002 Pretty in Pink	Open		17.00	17

FIGURINES

YEAR ISSUE	EDITION LIMIT	YEAR RETD.	ISSUE PRICE	*QUOTE U.S.$
2000 Pretty Penny	Open		13.50	14
2002 Raine Runner	Open		16.00	16
2000 Red Devil	Open		18.50	19
2001 Rendezvous	Open		15.50	16
2000 Rio	Open		15.00	15
2000 Sea of Pearls	Open		20.00	20
2000 Snake Skin Wrap	Retrd.	2001	16.00	16
2002 Snakes Alive	Open		17.00	17
2001 Solaris	Open		16.00	16
2000 Spring Raine	Open		16.00	16
2001 Stardust Memories	Open		25.00	25
2001 Summer Buzz	Open		18.00	18
2000 Tuxedo	Retrd.	2002	16.50	17
2000 Venus in Pearls	Retrd.	2001	15.00	15
2001 Wrap It Up	Open		18.50	19
2000 Zap	Retrd.	2002	14.50	15
2002 Zapata	Open		16.50	17

Just The Right Shoe/Rainedrops - Raine

YEAR ISSUE	EDITION LIMIT	YEAR RETD.	ISSUE PRICE	*QUOTE U.S.$
2001 Beach Baby	Open		8.00	8
2001 First Step	Open		8.00	8
2001 High Button Baby	Open		8.00	8
2001 It's a Boy	Open		8.00	8
2001 It's a Girl	Open		8.00	8
2001 Little Sneaker	Open		8.00	8
2001 Mary Jane	Open		8.00	8
2001 Peaches N' Cream	Open		8.00	8

Just The Right Shoe/Raineforest - Raine

YEAR ISSUE	EDITION LIMIT	YEAR RETD.	ISSUE PRICE	*QUOTE U.S.$
2001 Bamboo Bear	Open		16.00	16
2001 Lone Wolf	Open		15.00	15
2001 Northwoods Owls	Open		17.50	18
2001 On The Prowl	Open		14.50	15

Just The Right Shoe/Shoes of the Century - Raine

YEAR ISSUE	EDITION LIMIT	YEAR RETD.	ISSUE PRICE	*QUOTE U.S.$
1999 Class Act	Retrd.	2001	13.00	13
1999 Courtly Riches	Retrd.	2001	14.00	14
1999 Elegant Affair	Retrd.	2001	14.00	14
1999 Golden Stiletto	Retrd.	2001	15.00	15
1999 Ladylike	Retrd.	2001	12.50	13
1999 Pastiche	Retrd.	2001	13.00	13
1999 Patently Perfect	Retrd.	2001	13.00	13
1999 Rising Star	Retrd.	2001	16.00	16
1999 Struttin'	Retrd.	2001	13.50	14
1999 Suffrogette	Retrd.	2001	15.00	15

The Latest Thing/After Dark - S. Bayne

YEAR ISSUE	EDITION LIMIT	YEAR RETD.	ISSUE PRICE	*QUOTE U.S.$
2000 After Eight	Open		29.50	30
2000 Debutante	Open		29.50	30
2000 Eastern Promise	Open		29.50	30
2000 Glitz and Glamour	Open		29.50	30
2000 Hollywood Nights	Open		29.50	30
2000 Midnight Desire	Open		29.50	30
2000 Moonstruck	Open		29.50	30
2000 Premiere	Open		29.50	30
2000 Putting on the Ritz	Open		29.50	30
2000 Rendezvous	Open		29.50	30
2000 Sheer Elegance	Open		29.50	30
2000 Soiree	Open		29.50	30

The Latest Thing/Fashion Showcase - S. Bayne

YEAR ISSUE	EDITION LIMIT	YEAR RETD.	ISSUE PRICE	*QUOTE U.S.$
2000 All the Rage	Open		17.50	18
2000 Contemporary Grace	Open		26.50	27
2000 Dress for Success	Open		22.50	23
2000 Fabulous Folds	Open		26.50	27
2000 Girl Power	Open		17.50	18
2000 Happy Days	Open		20.00	20
2000 High Society	Open		22.50	23
2000 Illusion	Open		22.50	23
2000 Silver Lady	Open		22.50	23
2000 Tailored to Perfection	Open		26.50	27

The Latest Thing/Silhouettes - S. Bayne

YEAR ISSUE	EDITION LIMIT	YEAR RETD.	ISSUE PRICE	*QUOTE U.S.$
2000 Black Magic	Open		20.00	20
2000 Breathless	Open		22.50	23
2000 Groovy Baby	Open		16.50	17
2000 In Full Bloom	Open		26.50	27
2000 Satin and Lace	Open		17.50	18
2000 Scarlet Fever	Open		16.50	17
2000 Second Skin	Open		16.50	17
2000 Soft to the Touch	Open		17.50	18
2000 Taboo	Open		20.00	20

YEAR ISSUE	EDITION LIMIT	YEAR RETD.	ISSUE PRICE	*QUOTE U.S.$
2000 Vital Statistics	Open		17.50	18
2000 Welcome Home	Open		20.00	20
2000 What a Waist!	Open		17.50	18

The Latest Thing/Style Sensations - S. Bayne

YEAR ISSUE	EDITION LIMIT	YEAR RETD.	ISSUE PRICE	*QUOTE U.S.$
2000 Afternoon Stroll	Open		26.50	27
2000 Animal Instinct	Open		17.50	18
2000 Bathing Belle	Open		22.50	23
2000 Decadence	Open		26.50	27
2000 Decked Out	Open		22.50	23
2000 Diva	Open		20.00	20
2000 Dolce Vida	Open		22.50	23
2000 Dolly Bird	Open		17.50	18
2000 Drama!	Open		20.00	20
2000 English Rose	Open		26.50	27
2000 The Eyes Have It	Open		17.50	18
2000 Feel the Vibe	Open		20.00	20
2000 High Impact	Open		17.50	18
2000 Hot to Go	Open		15.00	15
2000 In the Swim	Open		17.50	18
2000 Jazzing it Up	Open		22.50	23
2000 Liberation	Open		22.50	23
2000 Living Doll	Open		30.00	30
2000 Making a Splash	Open		15.00	15
2000 Mix and Match	Open		20.00	20
2000 On Parade	Open		23.50	24
2000 On the Fairway	Open		22.50	23
2000 Opulence	Open		29.50	30
2000 Out of this World	Open		15.00	15
2000 Perfect Skin	Open		15.00	15
2000 Slender Lines	Open		23.50	24
2000 Socialite	Open		25.50	26
2000 Suitably Sophisticated	Open		22.50	23
2000 Summer of Love	Open		20.00	20
2000 Sweet Dreams	Open		20.00	20
2000 Taking the Plunge	Open		17.50	18
2000 That Certain Something	Open		23.50	24
2000 Unashamed Luxury	Open		29.50	30

Maasai - S. Bayne

YEAR ISSUE	EDITION LIMIT	YEAR RETD.	ISSUE PRICE	*QUOTE U.S.$
2001 Age of Privilege	3,500		225.00	225
2001 Dark Beauty	9,000		165.00	165
2001 Daughter of Africa	4,500	2001	100.00	100
2001 Days of Reflection	3,500		225.00	225
2001 Fearless Sentinel	3,500	2002	225.00	225
2001 Full of Song	3,500	2002	160.00	160
2001 Gentle Ruler	3,500		225.00	225
2001 The Gift	1,000		575.00	575
2001 The Gift of Love	9,000		200.00	200
2001 Heartfelt Offering	9,000		165.00	165
2001 Holder of Dreams	9,000		125.00	125
2001 Jewel of the Tribe	9,000		100.00	100
2001 Keeper of Fortune	3,500	2002	90.00	90
2001 Loving Father	9,000		200.00	200
2002 Mother's Embrace	9,000		225.00	225
2001 Mother's Love	3,500	2001	225.00	225
2001 Mothers Touch	4,500		185.00	185
2001 On This Festive Day	3,500		175.00	175
2002 Princess of the Plains	9,000		90.00	90
2002 Sacred Vows	9,000		165.00	165
2002 Sister's Offering	9,000		120.00	120
2001 Strength of the Family	9,000		225.00	225
2001 Visionary	3,500		200.00	200
2001 Youthful Days	3,500	2001	90.00	90

Maasai/Children of the Maasai - S. Bayne

YEAR ISSUE	EDITION LIMIT	YEAR RETD.	ISSUE PRICE	*QUOTE U.S.$
2002 Beautiful One	Open		35.00	35
2002 The Cattle Game, set/4	Open		75.00	75
2001 God's Gift	Open		40.00	40
2001 Little Creation	Open		30.00	30
2001 Loving One	Open		50.00	50
2001 Njeri & Nafula	Open		50.00	50
2001 Quiet Warrior	Open		55.00	55
2001 She is Trustworthy	Open		55.00	55

MasterPeace Collection - Various

YEAR ISSUE	EDITION LIMIT	YEAR RETD.	ISSUE PRICE	*QUOTE U.S.$
1999 Coat of Many Colors - T. Blackshear	Open		180.00	180
1999 Coat of Many Colors A/P - T. Blackshear	25		216.00	216
1998 Forgiven - T. Blackshear	Open		200.00	200
1998 Forgiven A/P - T. Blackshear	100		240.00	240
1998 The Invitation - M. Weistling	Retrd.	1999	250.00	250

*Quotes have been rounded up to nearest dollar

YEAR ISSUE	EDITION LIMIT	YEAR RETD.	ISSUE PRICE	*QUOTE U.S.$
1998 The Invitation A/P - M. Weistling	100	1999	300.00	300
1998 Victorious Lion of Judah - M. Dudash	Retrd.	1999	175.00	175
1998 Victorious Lion of Judah A/P - M. Dudash	100	1999	210.00	210
1998 Watchers in the Night - T. Blackshear	Retrd.	1999	300.00	300-600
1998 Watchers in the Night A/P - T. Blackshear	100	1999	360.00	360

Our Song - B. Joysmith

1999 Barefoot Dreams	Open		25.00	25
1999 Bedtime Story	Retrd.	2001	75.00	75
2000 Big Brother	Open		40.00	40
1999 Bumpin'	Open		42.50	43
1999 Country Mouse	Retrd.	2000	32.50	33
2000 Delta Girls's	Open		90.00	90
2000 Developing a Winner	7,500		150.00	150
2001 Doll Play	Open		65.00	65
2000 Dreaming	Open		55.00	55
2001 Dress Up	Open		30.00	30
1999 He's My Brother	Retrd.	2000	35.00	35-48
2000 Joyful Noise	Open		60.00	60
2001 The Lesson	Open		30.00	30
1999 Men of the Bench	7,500		225.00	225
2000 Mother and Child	Open		47.50	48
1999 Open Gate	Open		37.50	38
2000 Part of Growing	Retrd.	2001	60.00	60
2000 Roses and Sunshine	Open		45.00	45
2001 Sally Walker	4,500		125.00	125
2001 Sanctuary	Open		80.00	80
2001 Shoe Laces	Open		47.50	48
1999 Sisters & Secrets	Retrd.	2000	47.50	48
2001 Still Raining	Open		35.00	35
2000 Summer Dress	Open		40.00	40
2000 Summer's Song	Open		35.00	35
2000 Tricycle	Open		50.00	50

Rainbow Babies - A. Blackshear

1998 Beloved	Retrd.	1999	31.50	45-195
1997 Bright Eyes	Retrd.	1999	27.50	28-35
1998 Cuddles	Retrd.	1999	39.50	49-175
1998 Lil' Blossom	Retrd.	1999	34.50	35
1999 Lil' Wonder	Retrd.	1999	28.00	28
1998 Peek-A-Boo Pals	Retrd.	1999	47.50	48-59
1997 Peewee & Peeper	Retrd.	1999	39.50	40-49
1997 Pookie	Retrd.	1999	24.50	25-35
1997 Precious	Retrd.	1999	29.50	30-59
1999 Sleepyhead	Retrd.	1999	34.50	35-39
1999 SnuggleBunnies	Retrd.	1999	35.00	35
1997 Sunshine	Retrd.	1999	32.50	33

Sandy's Closet-Claudette Collection - S. Clough

2000 Candle	Open		17.50	18
2000 Hat	Open		14.50	15
2000 Hatbox	Open		14.50	15
2000 Mug	Open		7.00	7
2000 Parasol	Open		12.00	12
2000 Photo Frame	Open		20.00	20
2000 Shoe	Open		10.00	10
2000 Water Globe	Open		10.00	10

Sandy's Closet-Frames - S. Clough

2000 Sandy's Closet Frame	Open		20.00	20

Sandy's Closet-Gloria Collection - S. Clough

2000 Candle	Open		17.50	18
2000 Hatbox	Open		14.50	15
2000 Mug	Open		7.00	7
2000 Parasol	Open		12.00	12
2000 Photo Frame	Open		20.00	20
2000 Shoe	Open		10.00	10
2000 Water Globe	Open		10.00	10

Sandy's Closet-Laura Collection - S. Clough

2000 Hatbox	Open		14.50	15
2000 Mug	Open		7.00	7
2000 Parasol	Open		12.00	12
2000 Photo Frame	Open		20.00	20
2000 Shoe	Open		10.00	10

Sandy's Closet-Lillian Collection - S. Clough

2000 Candle	Open		17.50	18
2000 Hat	Open		14.50	15

YEAR ISSUE	EDITION LIMIT	YEAR RETD.	ISSUE PRICE	*QUOTE U.S.$
2000 Hatbox	Open		14.50	15
2000 Mug	Open		7.00	7
2000 Parasol	Open		12.00	12
2000 Photo Frame	Open		20.00	20
2000 Shoe	Open		10.00	10
2000 Water Globe	Open		10.00	10

Sandy's Closet-Ruby Collection - S. Clough

2000 Hat	Open		14.50	15
2000 Hatbox	Open		14.50	15
2000 Mug	Open		7.00	7
2000 Parasol	Open		12.00	12
2000 Photo Frame	Open		20.00	20
2000 Shoe	Open		10.00	10

Sandy's Closet-Suzette Collection - S. Clough

2000 Candle	Open		17.50	18
2000 Hat	Open		14.50	15
2000 Hatbox	Open		14.50	15
2000 Mug	Open		7.00	7
2000 Parasol	Open		12.00	12
2000 Photo Frame	Open		20.00	20
2000 Shoe	Open		10.00	10
2000 Water Globe	Open		10.00	10

Take A Seat - Raine

2000 Adirondack	Open		11.00	11
2000 Art Nouveau	Open		11.50	12
2001 Beach Chair	Open		17.50	18
2000 Billiard Room	Open		15.00	15
2000 Corner	Open		13.00	13
2000 Cow	Open		13.00	13
2001 Director's Chair	Open		17.50	18
2000 Folkloric	Open		13.00	13
2000 Form & Function	Open		12.00	12
2001 Garden Bench	Open		18.50	19
2000 Giltwood Rococo	Open		12.00	12
2000 Graphite	Open		17.00	17
2000 Leather & Chrome	Open		14.00	14
2000 Leather Recliner w/Ottoman	Open		12.50	13
2000 Longhorn	Open		13.00	13
2000 Louis XVI	Open		13.50	14
2000 Mexican Leather	Open		12.00	12
2000 Mission Style	Open		14.00	14
2000 Mr. Vanderbilt's	Open		16.00	16
2000 Mrs. Vanderbilt's	Open		15.00	15
2000 Music Room	Open		16.00	16
2001 On Deck	Open		18.50	19
2000 Pati	Open		13.00	13
2001 Peacock Splendor	Open		14.50	15
2000 Pearwood	Open		12.00	12
2000 Red Heart	Open		12.00	12
2000 Regency Leopard	Open		14.00	14
2000 Ribbon	Open		12.00	12
2000 San Demas	Open		15.00	15
2000 Screaming Red	Open		13.50	14
2000 Slipper	Open		14.50	15
2000 Slope Wingback	Open		13.00	13
2000 Stenciled	Open		14.50	15
2000 Viridian	Open		13.00	13
2000 Wicker w/Ottoman	Open		13.00	13
2001 Willow Rocker	Open		15.00	15
2000 Zebra	Open		16.00	16

Take A Seat Event - Raine

2001 Stardust Memories (chair & shoe)	Retrd.	2001	15.00	15

The Blackshear Circle Collector Club - T. Blackshear

1997 A Child Shall Lead Them	5,900	1998	225.00	695-895
1999 Spring	6,250	1999	150.00	565-895
2000 Summer	Yr.Iss.	2000	140.00	350-500
2001 Autumn	Yr.Iss.	2001	165.00	165-205
2001 A Child Shall Lead Them (Renewal Plate)	Yr.Iss.	2001	50.00	50-100
2002 Winter	Yr.Iss.		160.00	160

The Blackshear Jamboree Parade - T. Blackshear

2001 Birdy	Open		70.00	70
2001 Birdy A/P	50		84.00	84
2001 Birdy G/P	50		91.00	91
2000 Gypsy	Open		60.00	60
2000 Gypsy A/P	50		72.00	72

FIGURINES

YEAR ISSUE	EDITION LIMIT	YEAR RETD.	ISSUE PRICE	*QUOTE U.S.$
2000 Gypsy G/P	50		78.00	78
2000 Jay Jay and Cluck	Open		60.00	60
2000 Jay Jay and Cluck A/P	50		72.00	72
2000 Jay Jay and Cluck G/P	50		78.00	78
2001 K9 And Monkeyshine	Open		50.00	50
2001 K9 And Monkeyshine A/P	50		60.00	60
2001 K9 And Monkeyshine G/P	50		65.00	65
2000 Skeeter	Open		65.00	65
2000 Skeeter A/P	50		78.00	78
2000 Skeeter G/P	50		84.50	85
2002 Tami Tambourine	Open		50.00	50
2002 Tami Tambourine A/P	50		60.00	60
2002 Tami Tambourine G/P	50		65.00	65
2000 Tootie	Open		60.00	60
2000 Tootie A/P	50		72.00	72
2000 Tootie G/P	50		78.00	78

Thomas Blackshear Jamboree Parade Event Pieces - T. Blackshear

YEAR ISSUE	EDITION LIMIT	YEAR RETD.	ISSUE PRICE	*QUOTE U.S.$
2000 Rudy Toot	Yr.Iss.	2000	50.00	50-100
2001 Kitty	Yr.Iss.	2001	50.00	50-120

Thomas Blackshear's Ebony Visions - T. Blackshear

YEAR ISSUE	EDITION LIMIT	YEAR RETD.	ISSUE PRICE	*QUOTE U.S.$
2000 Bundle of Joy	Open		175.00	175
2000 Bundle of Joy A/P	50		210.00	210
2000 Bundle of Joy G/P	50		227.50	228
1998 Catching The Eye	Retrd.	1999	235.00	235-475
1997 Catching The Eye (Parkwest/NALED exclusive)	1,000	1997	225.00	225
1998 Catching The Eye A/P	50	1999	282.00	282-350
1998 Catching The Eye G/P	50	1999	305.50	325-350
1999 Cherished	Open		160.00	160
1999 Cherished A/P	50		192.00	192
1999 Cherished G/P	50		208.00	208
1998 The Comforter	Open		250.00	250
1998 The Comforter A/P	50		300.00	300
1998 The Comforter G/P	50		325.00	325
2000 Commitment	Open		190.00	190
2000 Commitment A/P	50		228.00	228
2000 Commitment G/P	50		247.00	247
1999 Daddy's Girl	Retrd.	2001	160.00	160
1999 Daddy's Girl A/P	50		192.00	192
1999 Daddy's Girl G/P	50		208.00	208
2001 Devoted Love	Open		185.00	185
2001 Devoted Love A/P	50		210.00	210
2001 Devoted Love G/P	50		227.50	228
2002 Double Hug	Open		100.00	100
2002 Double Hug A/P	50		120.00	120
2002 Double Hug G/P	50		130.00	130
1996 The Dreamer	11,500	1997	135.00	135-250
1996 The Dreamer A/P	50	1997	162.00	225-399
1996 The Dreamer G/P	50	1997	175.50	176-399
1997 Ebony Visions in Bas Relief	4,000	1998	150.00	150-199
1997 Ebony Visions in Bas Relief A/P	50	1998	180.00	180-250
1997 Ebony Visions in Bas Relief G/P	50	1998	195.00	200-250
1997 The Family	11,200	1999	225.00	225-299
1997 The Family A/P	50	1999	270.00	270-399
1997 The Family G/P	50	1999	292.50	300-399
1999 First Step	Retrd.	2002	150.00	150
1999 First Step A/P	50		180.00	180
1999 First Step G/P	50		195.00	195
1997 The Flower Girl	12,350	2000	100.00	100-250
1997 The Flower Girl A/P	50	2000	120.00	120
1997 The Flower Girl G/P	50	2000	130.00	130
1999 Forever Friends	Retrd.	2001	100.00	100
1999 Forever Friends A/P	50		120.00	120
1999 Forever Friends G/P	50		130.00	130
1998 The Fruits of Friendship	7,960	2000	115.00	115-150
1998 The Fruits of Friendship A/P	50	2000	138.00	138
1998 The Fruits of Friendship G/P	50	2000	149.50	150
1999 Grandmama	Retrd.	2002	175.00	175
1999 Grandmama A/P	50		210.00	210
1999 Grandmama G/P	50		227.00	227
1996 The Guardian	25,600	1999	300.00	950-1200
1996 The Guardian A/P	50	1999	360.00	360
1996 The Guardian G/P	50	1999	390.00	390
2001 He Hears Our Prayer	Open		225.00	225
2001 He Hears Our Prayer A/P	50		270.00	270
2001 He Hears Our Prayer G/P	50		292.50	293
1997 The Heirs	13,175	1999	125.00	125-145
1997 The Heirs A/P	50	1999	150.00	150
1997 The Heirs G/P	50	1999	162.50	195
1998 Hero	Retrd.	2001	200.00	200-299
1998 Hero A/P	50		240.00	240
1998 Hero G/P	50		260.00	260
1997 Hopes & Dreams	2,500	1997	225.00	400-500
1997 Hopes & Dreams A/P	50	1997	270.00	270-399
1997 Hopes & Dreams G/P	50	1997	292.50	325-399
2000 Intimacy	Open		165.00	165
2000 Intimacy A/P	50		198.00	198
2000 Intimacy G/P	50		214.50	215
1998 Joyful Noise	Retrd.	2001	150.00	150-190
1998 Joyful Noise A/P	50	2001	180.00	180
1998 Joyful Noise G/P	50	2001	195.00	195
1997 The Kiss	9,100	1999	225.00	325-475
1997 The Kiss A/P	50	1999	270.00	270-550
1997 The Kiss G/P	50	1999	292.50	293-520
1999 Leap of Faith	Retrd.	2002	170.00	170
1999 Leap of Faith A/P	50		204.00	204
1999 Leap of Faith G/P	50		221.00	221
1995 The Madonna	13,325	1997	160.00	600-755
1995 The Madonna A/P	50	1997	192.00	192-230
1995 The Madonna G/P	50	1997	208.00	208
2000 Message to God	Open		90.00	90
2000 Message to God A/P	50		108.00	108
2000 Message to God G/P	50		117.00	117
1997 Midnight	9,825	2000	250.00	250-390
1997 Midnight A/P	50	2000	300.00	300-399
1997 Midnight G/P	50	2000	325.00	325-399
1996 The Music Maker	12,375	1998	195.00	365-450
1996 The Music Maker A/P	50	1998	234.00	250-450
1996 The Music Maker G/P	50	1998	253.50	295-400
1998 Night in Day	Retrd.	2001	225.00	225-350
1998 Night in Day A/P	50		270.00	270
1998 Night in Day G/P	50		292.50	293
1995 The Nurturer	16,923	1998	160.00	500-899
1995 The Nurturer A/P	50	1998	192.00	192-290
1995 The Nurturer G/P	50	1998	208.00	208
2000 Oh No She Didn't	4,500	2000	300.00	300-1000
2000 Oh No She Didn't A/P	50		36.00	360
2000 Oh No She Didn't G/P	50		390.00	390
2001 Oh Yes She Did!	Open		150.00	150
2001 Oh Yes She Did! A/P	50		180.00	180
2001 Oh Yes She Did! G/P	50		195.00	195
2002 Planting A Kiss	Open		180.00	180
2002 Planting A Kiss A/P	50		216.00	216
2002 Planting A Kiss G/P	50		234.00	234
2002 Praise	Open		300.00	300
2002 Praise A/P	50		360.00	360
2002 Praise G/P	50		390.00	390
1997 The Prayer	15,025	2000	150.00	150-295
1997 The Prayer A/P	50	2000	180.00	180
1997 The Prayer G/P	50	2000	195.00	195
1995 The Protector	7,900	1996	195.00	1450-1600
1995 The Protector A/P	50	1996	234.00	600-995
1995 The Protector G/P	50	1996	253.50	600-650
2001 Riding High	Retrd.	2002	150.00	150
2001 Riding High A/P	50		180.00	180
2001 Riding High G/P	50		195.00	195
2000 Rite of Passage	5,500	2000	400.00	550-1300
2000 Rite of Passage A/P	50	2000	480.00	480-995
2000 Rite of Passage G/P	50	2000	520.00	520-995
1999 Serenity	Retrd.	2002	190.00	190
1999 Serenity A/P	50		228.00	228
1999 Serenity G/P	50		247.00	247
1995 Siblings	8,800	1996	120.00	645-795
1995 Siblings A/P	50	1996	144.00	275-490
1995 Siblings G/P	50	1996	156.00	345-395
1998 Sisters Forever: In Childhood	Retrd.	2001	140.00	140-349
1998 Sisters Forever: In Childhood A/P	50		168.00	168
1998 Sisters Forever: In Childhood G/P	50		182.00	182
2001 Sisters G/P	50		227.50	228
2001 Sisters: A Time To Share	Open		175.00	175
2001 Sisters: A Time To Share A/P	50		210.00	210
2001 Sisters: A Time To Share G/P	50		227.50	228
1995 The Storyteller	2,500	1996	410.00	4000-4900
1995 The Storyteller A/P	50	1996	492.00	2900
2001 Surprise	Open		140.00	140
2001 Surprise A/P	50		168.00	168
2001 Surprise G/P	50		182.00	182
1995 The Tender Touch	16,900	1997	185.00	575-695
1995 The Tender Touch A/P	50	1997	222.00	222-595

YEAR ISSUE	EDITION LIMIT	YEAR RETD.	ISSUE PRICE	*QUOTE U.S.$
1995 The Tender Touch G/P	50	1997	240.50	280-595
1996 A Time To Dream	10,500	1997	120.00	120-290
1996 A Time To Dream A/P	50	1997	144.00	150-290
1996 A Time To Dream G/P	50	1997	156.00	195-290

Legends Edition - T. Blackshear

YEAR ISSUE	EDITION LIMIT	YEAR RETD.	ISSUE PRICE	*QUOTE U.S.$
2000 The Guardian	300	2001	2200.00	2200-3900
2000 The Guardian - Walter Payton Tribute	34	2001	3400.00	3400-4500
2000 The Guardian A/P	50	2001	2640.00	2640-2999
2000 The Guardian G/P	50	2001	2860.00	2860-2960
2002 Little Blue Wings	750	2002	400.00	400
2002 Little Blue Wings A/P	50	2002	480.00	480
2002 Little Blue Wings G/P	50	2002	520.00	520
1998 The Madonna	550	1999	1075.00	1075-1900
1998 The Madonna A/P	50	1999	1290.00	1290-2400
1998 The Madonna G/P	50	1999	1397.50	1398-2400
2001 On Wings of Praise	750	2002	600.00	600
2001 On Wings of Praise A/P	50	2002	720.00	720
2001 On Wings of Praise G/P	50	2002	780.00	780
1997 The Protector	950	2001	1450.00	1450-1800
1997 The Protector A/P	50	2001	1740.00	1740-2800
1997 The Protector G/P	50	2001	1885.00	1885-2900
1996 The Storyteller	650	1996	1900.00	1900-2900
1996 The Storyteller A/P	50	1996	2300.00	2300-3400
1996 The Storyteller G/P	50	1996	2470.00	2470-3400
2001 Tender Touch	350	2002	2200.00	2200
2001 Tender Touch A/P	50	2002	2640.00	2640
2001 Tender Touch G/P	50	2002	2860.00	2860

GRAPHICS

Anheuser-Busch, Inc.

Anheuser-Busch - H. Droog

1994 Gray Wolf Mirror N4570	2,500	1999	135.00	125-160

Endangered Species Fine Art Prints - B. Kemper

1996 Bald Eagle Print, framed N9995	2,500	1997	159.00	135-159
1996 Bald Eagle, unframed N9995U	2,500	1997	79.00	79
1996 Cougar Print, framed N9993	2,500	1997	159.00	135-159
1996 Cougar Print, unframed N9993U	2,500	1997	79.00	79
1996 Gray Wolf Print, framed N9992	2,500	1997	159.00	135-159
1996 Gray Wolf Print, unframed N9992U	2,500	1997	79.00	79
1996 Panda Print, framed N9994	2,500	1997	159.00	135-159
1996 Panda Print, unframed N9994U	2,500	1997	79.00	79

Armani

Canvas Repligraphs - G. Armani

1995 Abiding Love 105A	675		475.00	475
1995 Aurora Lady with Dove 112A	300		650.00	650
1995 Cinderella (Disney Exclusive) 100AD	300	1995	475.00	475
1995 The Embrace 103A	675	1997	475.00	475
1995 La Pieta 102A	675	1999	475.00	475
1995 Lady with Mirror 101A	675	1999	475.00	475
1995 Lady with Peacock 100A	675	1999	475.00	475
1997 Lilacs and Roses 113A	300		650.00	650
1995 Wind Song 104A	675	1998	475.00	475

Arts Uniq', Inc.

Fincher - K. Andrews Fincher

1996 The Angel's Promise (lg.)	2,950		30.00	30
1996 The Best Gift (lg.)	2,950		35.00	35
1998 The Blessing	Open		22.00	22
1997 Butterflies	Open		20.00	20
1997 Charm School (lg.)	2,950		40.00	40
1995 The Children's Table (lg.) A/P	195	1998	48.00	48
1995 The Children's Table (lg.) A/P	1,950		28.00	28
1997 Doin' Chores	2,950		30.00	30
1997 Firefly	2,950		30.00	30
1995 First Look (lg.)	1,950		28.00	28
1995 First Look (lg.) A/P	195	1998	28.00	28
1995 Glimpse Of Glory I	1,950		60.00	60
1995 Glimpse Of Glory I A/P	195	1998	80.00	80
1995 Glimpse Of Glory II	1,950		60.00	60
1995 Glimpse Of Glory II A/P	195	1998	80.00	80

YEAR ISSUE	EDITION LIMIT	YEAR RETD.	ISSUE PRICE	*QUOTE U.S.$
1999 God's Treasure	Open		15.00	15
1999 God's Treasure (Mini)	Open		2.40	3
1997 Grandma's Treasures	Closed	2000	15.00	15
1997 Howdy Partner	Open		15.00	15
1994 If Time Could Stand Still	950	2000	65.00	65
1993 Ladybug (lg.)	1,950		45.00	45
1997 Light On Learning	Open		20.00	20
1994 Lightplay	1,950		25.00	25
1996 Look Into My World (lg.)	2,950		30.00	30
1996 Mom Said Share (lg.)	2,950		35.00	35
1995 Mom Will Be Proud	1,950	1997	55.00	55
1997 Mom Will Be Proud	Open		28.00	28
1995 Mom Will Be Proud A/P	195	1997	75.00	75
1993 Mom Won't Mind	1,950	1995	55.00	55
1996 Mom Won't Mind (sm.)	Open		24.00	24
1995 Mom Won't Mind A/P	Closed	1996	55.00	55
1994 A Morning Visit	1,950	1997	45.00	45
1993 My Moment, My Child	1,950		45.00	45
1993 Path To The Meadow	1,950		45.00	45
1993 A Place To Dream	1,950	2000	45.00	45
1993 Seasons Of Color	1,950		40.00	40
1994 Seek And Find	1,950		40.00	40
1997 Shucks	2,950		30.00	30
1993 Siblings	1,950		55.00	55
1993 This Moment Is Mine	1,950		65.00	65
1997 Three Wishes	2,950		35.00	35
1997 Time Out	Open		28.00	28
1999 Together We Build	Open		15.00	15
1993 Together We'll See The World	950		65.00	65
1994 When You Get Big Like Me	1,950		12.00	12
1993 Where Dreams Begin	1,950		35.00	35
1997 Wings	Closed	1999	15.00	15

Talbott-Boassy - G. Talbott-Boassy

1998 Among My Favorite Memories	Open		22.00	22
1998 Angelic Innocence	Open		20.00	20
1997 Angels In The Garden	Closed	1999	15.00	15
XX Attic Angel	1,000		25.00	25
XX Attic Beauties	Closed	1995	25.00	25
1993 Best Wishes - Mother	Open		15.00	15
1993 Best Wishes - Sister	Open		15.00	15
2000 Breath Of Romance	Open		9.00	9
1999 Clean And Neat	Open		4.80	5
1999 Clean and Neat	Open		4.80	5
1994 Curl Up With A Book	Open		12.00	12
XX Dresses I	Closed	1995	11.00	11
1999 Earth And Flowers	Open		4.80	5
1991 Empty Nest	1,950		18.00	18
1993 First Christmas	Open		12.00	12
1992 Free As A Melody	Closed	N/A	12.00	12
1996 A Garden Wedding	Open		12.00	12
2000 Green Glide	Open		4.80	5
1995 Heaven's Treasures	Closed	2000	22.00	22
1990 Her Guardian Angel	1,950	1997	30.00	30
1991 His Favorite Season	1,950	2000	25.00	25
XX I Sing	1,950	1996	35.00	35
2000 I Will Honor Christmas	Open		9.00	9
XX In Service Of Our Country (lg.)	Open		15.00	15
1990 Keepsakes	Closed	1998	22.00	22
1991 Letters Of Love	1,950	1997	28.00	28
1995 Love Me Tender	Closed	2000	15.00	15
1990 Me And Mommy	1,950		30.00	30
XX Mi' Ladies	1,950		25.00	25
1999 Misty Early Morning	Open		9.00	9
1991 Mother's Love	Open		12.00	12
1999 Nice Clean Fun	Open		2.40	3
2000 An Old Flame	Open		4.80	5
1999 Paradise On Earth	Open		9.00	9
1997 Peanut Butter Picnic	Open		22.00	22
1997 Poetry Bouquet	Open		15.00	15
1995 Precious Gifts	Open		22.00	22
1995 Pretty As A Pitcher	1,950		35.00	35
1995 Pretty As A Pitcher A/P	195	1998	50.00	50
2000 Red Racer	Open		4.80	5
1999 Relaxing In Your Tub	Open		2.40	3
XX Remember Me	1,950	1999	25.00	25
2000 Santa	Open		15.00	15
2000 Santa (mini)	Open		2.40	3
XX Scarlet Ribbons	1,950		28.00	28
1997 Shared Moments	Closed	2000	28.00	28
1997 Shared Moments - Sister	Closed	1999	28.00	28

YEAR ISSUE	EDITION LIMIT	YEAR RETD.	ISSUE PRICE	*QUOTE U.S.$
1999 A Shovel And A Hose	Open		4.80	5
1990 Sincerely Yours - Single Rose	Closed	1996	12.00	12
XX Sincerely Yours-Best Friend	Closed	1995	12.00	12
1999 Sunny Hours	Open		9.00	9
1990 Sweet Dreams	1,950	1997	25.00	25
XX Tea Party	Closed	1995	26.00	26
1990 Tea Party	Open		22.00	22
1997 Tea Party - Ethnic	Open		22.00	22
1995 Teacups And Tassels	Open		15.00	15
1994 They Had Wings	Open		24.00	24
XX Those Who Have Suffered	Open		12.00	12
XX Three Sisters	1,000		20.00	20
1992 Timeless Treasures	Open		12.00	12
2000 True Blue	Open		4.80	5
1997 Waiting In The Attic (sm.)	Open		15.00	15
1995 Waiting In The Attic A/P	1,950		35.00	35
1995 Waiting In The Attic A/P	175	1998	45.00	45
XX When The Party Is Over	1,950		18.00	18
XX Wilt Thou Go	Closed	1998	12.00	12
1990 Your Love Keeps Me Warm	Closed	1998	24.00	24

Terry - J. Terry

2000 Courtyard Fountain	Open		28.00	28
2000 Courtyard Garden	Open		28.00	28
2000 Duck Hunter's Dream	Open		28.00	28
2001 Flowers For The Misses	Open		175.00	175
2001 A Grand View	950		175.00	175
2001 A Grand View (Hand Embellished)	750		775.00	775
2001 Guadalupe Crossing	950		150.00	150
2001 Here Comes The Rain	950		150.00	150
2000 Misty Trail	950		150.00	150
2001 A New Day	Open		28.00	28
2001 Out on the Trail	950		150.00	150
2001 Out on the Trail (Hand Embellished)	500		500.00	500
2001 Sierra Sunrise	950		150.00	150
2000 Spring Bouquet I	Open		28.00	28
2000 Spring Bouquet II	Open		28.00	28
2000 Tranquil Refuge	Open		28.00	28
2001 Undampened Spirits	Open		28.00	28
2001 Where Friendships Form	Open		20.00	20
2000 Winter Home	Open		28.00	28

Wright - C. Shores

1996 Anna's Hummingbird With Roses I	Open		12.00	12
1994 Anna's Hummingbird With Salvia	Open		12.00	12
1994 Anna's With Azaleas	Open		12.00	12
1999 Anna's With Trumpet Vine	Open		4.80	5
XX Apartments	Open		12.00	12
2001 April Love	Open		4.80	5
2001 Autumn	Open		4.80	5
XX Backyard Chef	Closed	1995	14.00	14
1997 Barn Swallows With Dawn Flowers	Open		15.00	15
2001 Be My Love	Open		4.80	5
2001 Because of You	Open		4.80	5
1995 Berry Hill Fruit I	Closed	1998	12.00	12
1995 Berry Hill Fruit II	Closed	N/A	12.00	12
1995 Birdhouse Row	Open		12.00	12
1994 Birdhouse With Bluebirds	Open		12.00	12
1994 Birdhouse With Chickadee	Open		12.00	12
1996 Birdhouse With Roses	Open		12.00	12
1994 Birdhouse With Wren	Open		12.00	12
1994 Birdhouse With Yellow Throats	Open		12.00	12
1990 Bits And Pieces	1,950		12.00	12
XX Box Of Bunnies	Closed	1995	12.00	12
XX Break Point	1,950	1995	15.00	15
XX Briarpatch Bunny	1,000	1995	15.00	15
1999 Broad-Billed with Salvia	Open		4.80	5
XX Bunny Band	1,000	1995	15.00	15
1995 Butterfly Inn I	Open		12.00	12
1995 Butterfly Inn II	Open		12.00	12
1999 Calliope and Chorisia	Open		4.80	5
1990 Cardinal Female	Open		11.00	11
1994 Cardinal On A Flowering Branch	2,950		38.00	38
1999 Carnival I	Open		15.00	15
1999 Carnival II	Open		15.00	15
1992 Cascade	950	1995	45.00	45
1991 Cherries	Open		11.00	11
1994 Cherub Choir	Open		12.00	12
1993 Chickadee And Fledglings	1,950	1996	15.00	15
1997 Chickadees And Dogwood	Open		12.00	12
2001 Chives	Open		4.80	5

YEAR ISSUE	EDITION LIMIT	YEAR RETD.	ISSUE PRICE	*QUOTE U.S.$
1992 Classic	950	1995	45.00	45
2000 Cookies with a Friend	Open		4.80	5
XX Cuddled Pair	1,950	2001	10.00	10
1993 The Day's Catch (Premat)	Open		12.00	12
1994 Dynasty	Open		12.00	12
1992 Eastern Bluebirds	1,950	1999	38.00	38
1994 Embassy	Open		12.00	12
1995 Emperor	Open		12.00	12
1993 Evening Stroll	950		15.00	15
1995 Exotic Blooms I (Deckled)	Open		13.00	13
1995 Exotic Blooms II (Deckled)	Open		13.00	13
1996 Exotic Blooms III (Deckled)	Open		13.00	13
1996 Exotic Blooms IV (Deckled)	Open		13.00	13
1994 Fancy Flight	2,950		38.00	38
XX Farm House	Closed	1995	12.00	12
XX Father's Pride	1,950	1995	12.00	12
1990 Featherdo	1,950		12.00	12
XX Feeding Time-N/S	500		14.00	14
1999 Festival	Open		34.00	34
1989 Five Of A Kind A/P	1,950	1998	15.00	15
1992 Flowering Season I	950		15.00	15
1992 Flowering Season II	950		15.00	15
1992 Flowering Season III	950		15.00	15
XX Four Little Birds	1,950	1995	15.00	15
XX Friends	Closed	1995	12.00	12
1995 Fruit Fiesta	Closed	2000	15.00	15
1994 Garden Cherub	Open		12.00	12
1994 Geranium (lg.)	Open		12.00	12
1997 Goldfinch And Apple Blossoms	Open		12.00	12
1996 Goldfinch And Clematis	Open		12.00	12
XX Grandmother I	1,000		15.00	15
XX Grandmother II	1,000		15.00	15
1989 Grandmother's Darlings	1,950		15.00	15
1993 Grandmother's Little Man	950		15.00	15
1999 Harvest Home	Open		2.40	3
2000 He Will Shield You	Open		4.80	5
XX High Fashion	Closed	1995	15.00	15
1989 Holiday Cruise	1,950	1999	12.00	12
1999 Holly House	Open		2.40	3
2000 A House Made by God	Open		4.80	5
XX Hula Hoop	1,950		12.00	12
1994 Impromptu	Closed	1998	12.00	12
1995 Ivy Topiary I	Open		15.00	15
1995 Ivy Topiary II	Open		15.00	15
XX Joyful I	1,950	1997	15.00	15
XX Just A Swingin'	1,950		15.00	15
2001 Lavender	Open		4.80	5
1991 Lavender Blue	1,950	1995	20.00	20
1998 Lemon Tree	Open		15.00	15
1992 Little Hummer IV	2,950	1995	20.00	20
1995 Little Hummer IX	9,950	1998	20.00	20
1993 Little Hummer V	2,950	1995	20.00	20
1993 Little Hummer VI	2,950	1995	20.00	20
1993 Little Hummer VII	9,950		20.00	20
XX Little Hummer VII A/P	Closed	1998	30.00	30
1993 Little Hummer VIII	9,950	1995	20.00	20
XX Little Hummer VIII A/P	Closed	1995	30.00	30
1995 Little Hummer X	9,950		20.00	20
1998 Little Hummer XI	9,950		20.00	20
1998 Little Hummer XII	9,950		20.00	20
1994 A Little Sun I	Open		12.00	12
1994 A Little Sun II	Open		12.00	12
2000 Love	Open		4.80	5
2000 Love One Another	Open		4.80	5
2001 Lyrical Garden	Open		4.80	5
1996 Magnolia Memory (Deckled)	Open		25.00	25
1997 Magnolia Topiary I	Open		15.00	15
1997 Magnolia Topiary II	Open		15.00	15
2000 Making Music	Open		4.80	5
XX Mama's Bunch	Closed	1995	15.00	15
1995 May Day	Open		12.00	12
2001 Mint	Open		4.80	5
1999 Moon Shell with Border	Closed	1999	4.80	5
XX Mother's Joy	1,950	1995	12.00	12
1989 Nature's Harmony	1,950		35.00	35
1999 Nature's Sampler I	Open		20.00	20
1999 Nature's Sampler II	Open		20.00	20
1999 Nature's Sampler III	Open		20.00	20
2000 A New Song	Open		4.80	5
2001 No Other Love	Open		4.80	5
1994 Noah's Boat	Open		12.00	12

*Quotes have been rounded up to nearest dollar

YEAR ISSUE	EDITION LIMIT	YEAR RETD.	ISSUE PRICE	*QUOTE U.S.$
1997 Nuthatches With Morning Glories	Closed	2001	12.00	12
1999 Operetta Plate with Border	Closed	1999	9.00	9
1998 Orange Tree	Open		15.00	15
XX Out To Lunch	1,000		12.00	12
1999 Pacific Scallop Shell with Border	Closed	1999	4.80	5
XX Pals	Closed	1995	12.00	12
1997 Pansy Morning	Open		15.00	15
1993 Paurla Warblers	1,950	1996	15.00	15
1992 Peonies	1,950	1995	25.00	25
1990 Petals And Patches	1,950		12.00	12
1994 Petunia	Open		12.00	12
2001 Poetic Garden	Open		4.80	5
1997 Porch Visitor I	Open		20.00	20
1997 Porch Visitor II	Open		20.00	20
1997 Portrait	Open		15.00	15
2000 Precious Place	Open		4.80	5
1994 Princess	Closed	1998	12.00	12
1992 Promises Ii	2,950		12.00	12
1997 Purple Martin With Trumpet Vine	Open		15.00	15
1994 Quilt Patterns I	Open		12.00	12
1996 Radiant Blooms I (Deckled)	Open		13.00	13
1996 Radiant Blooms II (Deckled)	Open		13.00	13
1989 Retirement Benefits	1,950		15.00	15
1994 Romance	Open		12.00	12
1994 Rose Basket Cherubs	Open		12.00	12
1993 Rose Parade (Premat)	Open		20.00	20
2001 Rosemary	Open		4.80	5
1995 Rosemont	Open		12.00	12
XX Round Ball	Closed	1995	15.00	15
2001 Royal Garden	Open		4.80	5
1996 Ruby Throated Humingbird W/Roses II	Open		12.00	12
1994 Ruby Throated With Geranium	Open		12.00	12
1994 Ruby Throated With Hibiscus	Open		12.00	12
2001 Sage	Open		4.80	5
1990 Sampler I	Open		15.00	15
1990 Sampler II	Open		15.00	15
1990 Sampler III	Open		15.00	15
1990 Sampler IV	Closed	1998	15.00	15
1999 Scallop Shell with Border	Open		4.80	5
1997 Scarlet Finches With Mock Orange	Open		12.00	12
XX Set Point	1,950	1995	15.00	15
2000 Sharing a Dream	Open		4.80	5
2000 Sisters Share	Open		4.80	5
XX Soft Feathers	1,950		10.00	10
1993 A Special Friend	950		15.00	15
XX Spring Fantasy (lg.)	1,950	1995	40.00	40
2001 Spring Garden	Open		4.80	5
XX Spring Magic II	Closed	1995	20.00	20
XX Spring Song	Closed	1995	12.00	12
1995 St Nicholas II A/P	195	1998	36.00	36
1995 St. Nicholas I	1,950		16.00	16
1995 St. Nicholas I A/P	195	1998	36.00	36
1995 St. Nicholas II	1,950		16.00	16
1991 Strawberries	Open		11.00	11
1993 Sugarplums (Premat)	Open		15.00	15
2000 Summer Time I	Open		4.80	5
2000 Summer Time II	Open		4.80	5
2000 Sweetest Memories	Open		4.80	5
1992 Sweethearts	1,950	1995	15.00	15
1990 Tabby Tangle	Open		14.00	14
1998 Tapestry	Open		28.00	28
XX Tea Party	Open		12.00	12
1997 Three Owls	Open		15.00	15
2001 Thyme	Open		4.80	5
1996 Timeless	2,950		48.00	48
1999 Top Shell with Border	Closed	1999	4.80	5
1994 Topiary I	Open		15.00	15
1994 Topiary II	Closed	1999	15.00	15
1993 Touch Of Blue (Premat)	1,950		20.00	20
2001 Trophy Rooster I	Open		15.00	15
2001 Trophy Rooster II	Open		15.00	15
2000 A True Friend	Open		4.80	5
2000 Tuscan Companion I	Open		15.00	15
2000 Tuscan Companion II	Open		15.00	15
2000 Tuscan Orchids	Open		28.00	28
XX Two Step	Closed	1995	12.00	12
1989 Warbler's Spring	1,950	1996	40.00	40
1993 Western Still Life	Open		15.00	15
1999 White-Eared with Freshia	Open		4.80	5
2001 Wild Flowers I	Open		15.00	15

YEAR ISSUE	EDITION LIMIT	YEAR RETD.	ISSUE PRICE	*QUOTE U.S.$
2001 Wild Flowers II	Open		15.00	15
2001 Winter	Open		4.80	5
1993 Winter Rural	Open		11.00	11
1997 Winter Rural (S)	Open		15.00	15

Circle Fine Art

Rockwell - N. Rockwell

YEAR ISSUE	EDITION LIMIT	YEAR RETD.	ISSUE PRICE	*QUOTE U.S.$
XX American Family Folio	200		Unkn.	17500
XX The Artist at Work	130		Unkn.	3500
XX At the Barber	200		Unkn.	4900
XX Autumn	200		Unkn.	3500
XX Autumn/Japon	25		Unkn.	3600
XX Aviary	200		Unkn.	4200
XX Barbershop Quartet	200		Unkn.	4200
XX Baseball	200		Unkn.	3600
XX Ben Franklin's Philadelphia	200		Unkn.	3600
XX Ben's Belles	200		Unkn.	3500
XX The Big Day	200		Unkn.	3400
XX The Big Top	148		Unkn.	2800
XX Blacksmith Shop	200		Unkn.	6300
XX Bookseller	200		Unkn.	2700
XX Bookseller/Japon	25		Unkn.	2750
XX The Bridge	200		Unkn.	3100
XX Cat	200		Unkn.	3400
XX Cat/Collotype	200		Unkn.	4000
XX Cheering	200		Unkn.	3600
XX Children at Window	200		Unkn.	3600
XX Church	200		Unkn.	3400
XX Church/Collotype	200		Unkn.	4000
XX Circus	200		Unkn.	2650
XX County Agricultural Agent	200		Unkn.	3900
XX The Critic	200		Unkn.	4650
XX Day in the Life of a Boy	200		Unkn.	6200
XX Day in the Life of a Boy/Japon	25		Unkn.	6500
XX Debut	200		Unkn.	3600
XX Discovery	200		Unkn.	5900
XX Doctor and Boy	200		Unkn.	9400
XX Doctor and Doll-Signed	200		Unkn.	11900
XX Dressing Up/Ink	60		Unkn.	4400
XX Dressing Up/Pencil	200		Unkn.	3700
XX The Drunkard	200		Unkn.	3600
XX The Expected and Unexpected	200		Unkn.	3700
XX Family Tree	200		Unkn.	5900
XX Fido's House	200		Unkn.	3600
XX Football Mascot	200		Unkn.	3700
XX Four Seasons Folio	200		Unkn.	13500
XX Four Seasons Folio/Japon	25		Unkn.	14000
XX Freedom from Fear-Signed	200		Unkn.	6400
XX Freedom from Want-Signed	200		Unkn.	6400
XX Freedom of Religion-Signed	200		Unkn.	6400
XX Freedom of Speech-Signed	200		Unkn.	6400
XX Gaiety Dance Team	200		Unkn.	4300
XX Girl at Mirror-Signed	200		Unkn.	8400
XX The Golden Age	200		Unkn.	3500
XX Golden Rule-Signed	200		Unkn.	4400
XX Golf	200		Unkn.	3600
XX Gossips	200		Unkn.	5000
XX Gossips/Japon	25		Unkn.	5100
XX Grotto	200		Unkn.	3400
XX Grotto/Collotype	200		Unkn.	4000
XX High Dive	200		Unkn.	3400
XX The Homecoming	200		Unkn.	3700
XX The House	200		Unkn.	3700
XX Huck Finn Folio	200		Unkn.	35000
XX Ichabod Crane	200		Unkn.	6700
XX The Inventor	200		Unkn.	4100
XX Jerry	200		Unkn.	4700
XX Jim Got Down on His Knees	200		Unkn.	4500
XX Lincoln	200		Unkn.	11400
XX Lobsterman	200		Unkn.	5500
XX Lobsterman/Japon	25		Unkn.	5750
XX Marriage License	200		Unkn.	6900
XX Medicine	200		Unkn.	3400
XX Medicine/Color Litho	200		Unkn.	4000
XX Miss Mary Jane	200		Unkn.	4500
XX Moving Day	200		Unkn.	3900
XX Music Hath Charms	200		Unkn.	4200
XX My Hand Shook	200		Unkn.	4500
XX Out the Window	200		Unkn.	3400
XX Out the Window/ Collotype	200		Unkn.	4000

GRAPHICS

YEAR ISSUE	EDITION LIMIT	YEAR RETD.	ISSUE PRICE	*QUOTE U.S.$
XX Outward Bound-Signed	200		Unkn.	7900
XX Poor Richard's Almanac	200		Unkn.	24000
XX Prescription	200		Unkn.	4900
XX Prescription/Japon	25		Unkn.	5000
XX The Problem We All Live With	200		Unkn.	4500
XX Puppies	200		Unkn.	3700
XX Raliegh the Dog	200		Unkn.	3900
XX Rocket Ship	200		Unkn.	3650
XX The Royal Crown	200		Unkn.	3500
XX Runaway	200		Unkn.	3800
XX Runaway/Japon	200		Unkn.	5700
XX Safe and Sound	200		Unkn.	3800
XX Saturday People	200		Unkn.	3300
XX Save Me	200		Unkn.	3600
XX Saying Grace-Signed	200		Unkn.	7400
XX School Days Folio	200		Unkn.	14000
XX Schoolhouse	200		Unkn.	4500
XX Schoolhouse/Japon	25		Unkn.	4650
XX See America First	200		Unkn.	5650
XX See America First/Japon	25		Unkn.	6100
XX Settling In	200		Unkn.	3600
XX Shuffelton's Barbershop	200		Unkn.	7400
XX Smoking	200		Unkn.	3400
XX Smoking/Collotype	200		Unkn.	4000
XX Spanking	200		Unkn.	3400
XX Spanking/ Collotype	200		Unkn.	4000
XX Spelling Bee	200		Unkn.	6500
XX Spring	200		Unkn.	3500
XX Spring Flowers	200		Unkn.	5200
XX Spring/Japon	25		Unkn.	3600
XX Study for the Doctor's Office	200		Unkn.	6000
XX Studying	200		Unkn.	3600
XX Summer	200		Unkn.	3500
XX Summer Stock	200		Unkn.	4900
XX Summer Stock/Japon	25		Unkn.	5000
XX Summer/Japon	25		Unkn.	3600
XX The Teacher	200		Unkn.	3400
XX The Teacher/Japon	25		Unkn.	3500
XX Teacher's Pet	200		Unkn.	3600
XX The Texan	200		Unkn.	3700
XX Then For Three Minutes	200		Unkn.	4500
XX Then Miss Watson	200		Unkn.	4500
XX There Warn't No Harm	200		Unkn.	4500
XX Three Farmers	200		Unkn.	3600
XX Ticketseller	200		Unkn.	4200
XX Ticketseller/Japon	25		Unkn.	4400
XX Tom Sawyer Color Suite	200		Unkn.	30000
XX Tom Sawyer Folio	200		Unkn.	26500
XX Top of the World	200		Unkn.	4200
XX Trumpeter	200		Unkn.	3900
XX Trumpeter/Japon	25		Unkn.	4100
XX Two O'Clock Feeding	200		Unkn.	3600
XX The Village Smithy	200		Unkn.	3500
XX Welcome	200		Unkn.	3500
XX Wet Paint	200		Unkn.	3800
XX When I Lit My Candle	200		Unkn.	4500
XX White Washing	200		Unkn.	3400
XX Whitewashing the Fence/Collotype	200		Unkn.	4000
XX Window Washer	200		Unkn.	4800
XX Winter	200		Unkn.	3500
XX Winter/Japon	25		Unkn.	3600
XX Ye Old Print Shoppe	200		Unkn.	3500
XX Your Eyes is Lookin'	200		Unkn.	4500

Flambro Imports

Emmett Kelly Jr. Lithographs - B. Leighton-Jones

YEAR ISSUE	EDITION LIMIT	YEAR RETD.	ISSUE PRICE	*QUOTE U.S.$
1995 All Star Circus	2 Yr.	1997	150.00	150
1994 EKJ 70th Birthday Commemorative	1,994	1997	150.00	150
1994 I Love You	2 Yr.	1996	90.00	90-150
1994 Joyful Noise	2 Yr.	1996	90.00	90-150
1994 Picture Worth 1,000 Words	2 Yr.	1996	90.00	90-150

Greenwich Workshop

Austin - C. Austin

YEAR ISSUE	EDITION LIMIT	YEAR RETD.	ISSUE PRICE	*QUOTE U.S.$
1997 Saturday Near Sunset	850		150.00	150
1996 The Storm	850		165.00	165
1996 Wheat Field	850		125.00	125

Ballantyne - Ballantyne

YEAR ISSUE	EDITION LIMIT	YEAR RETD.	ISSUE PRICE	*QUOTE U.S.$
1995 John's New Pup	850		150.00	150
1995 Kate and Her Fiddle	850		150.00	150
1996 Partners	850		150.00	150

Bama - J. Bama

YEAR ISSUE	EDITION LIMIT	YEAR RETD.	ISSUE PRICE	*QUOTE U.S.$
1993 Art of James Bama Book with Chester Medicine Crow Fathers Flag Print	2,500	N/A	345.00	351-375
1981 At a Mountain Man Wedding	1,500	N/A	145.00	145-200
1981 At Burial Gallager and Blind Bill	1,650	N/A	135.00	150-350
1988 Bittin' Up-Rimrock Ranch	1,250	N/A	195.00	630-1290
1992 Blackfeet War Robe	1,000		195.00	195
1995 Blackfoot Ceremonial Headdress (Iris Print)	200		850.00	850
1987 Buck Norris-Crossed Sabres Ranch	1,000	N/A	195.00	790-1023
1990 Buffalo Bill	1,250	N/A	210.00	165-210
1993 The Buffalo Dance	1,000		195.00	195
1991 Ceremonial Lance	1,000		225.00	225
1996 Cheyene Split Horn Headdress (Iris Print)	200		850.00	850
1994 Cheyenne Dog Soldier	1,000		225.00	225
1991 Chuck Wagon	1,000		225.00	225
1975 Chuck Wagon in the Snow	1,000	N/A	50.00	1200-1520
1992 Coming' Round the Bend	1,000		195.00	195
1978 Contemporary Sioux Indian	1,000	N/A	75.00	1450-1600
1995 A Cowboy Named Anne	1,000		185.00	185
1992 Crow Cavalry Scout	1,000		195.00	195
1977 A Crow Indian	1,000	N/A	65.00	243-468
1982 Crow Indian Dancer	1,250		150.00	150
1988 Crow Indian From Lodge Grass	1,250		225.00	225
1988 Dan-Mountain Man	1,250	N/A	195.00	195-211
1983 The Davilla Brothers-Bronc Riders	1,250		145.00	145
1983 Don Walker-Bareback Rider	1,250	N/A	85.00	126-175
1991 The Drift on Skull Creek Pass	1,500		225.00	225
1979 Heritage	1,500	N/A	75.00	274-425
1978 Indian at Crow Fair	1,500	N/A	75.00	118-125
1988 Indian Wearing War Medicine Bonnet	1,000	N/A	225.00	225
1980 Ken Blackbird	1,500	N/A	95.00	125-150
1974 Ken Hunder, Working Cowboy	1,000	N/A	55.00	695-1105
1989 Little Fawn-Cree Indian Girl	1,250	N/A	195.00	165-195
1979 Little Star	1,500	N/A	80.00	1325-1650
1993 Magua-"The Last of the Mohicans"	1,000		225.00	225
1993 Making Horse Medicine	1,000		225.00	225
1978 Mountain Man	1,000	N/A	75.00	350-469
1980 Mountain Man 1820-1840 Period	1,500	N/A	115.00	395-808
1979 Mountain Man and His Fox	1,500	N/A	90.00	350-457
1982 Mountain Man with Rifle	1,250	N/A	135.00	195-200
1978 A Mountain Ute	1,000	N/A	75.00	700-787
1992 Northern Cheyenne Wolf Scout	1,000		195.00	195
1981 Old Arapaho Story-Teller	1,500	N/A	135.00	135-175
1980 Old Saddle in the Snow	1,500	N/A	75.00	525-638
1980 Old Sod House	1,500	N/A	80.00	425-551
1981 Oldest Living Crow Indian	1,500	N/A	135.00	135-150
1990 On the North Fork of the Shoshoni	1,000		195.00	195
1990 Paul Newman as Butch Cassidy & Video	2,000		250.00	250
1981 Portrait of a Sioux	1,500	N/A	135.00	135-150
1979 Pre-Columbian Indian with Atlatl	1,500	N/A	75.00	165-195
1991 Ready to Rendezvous	1,000		225.00	225
1995 Ready to Ride	1,000		185.00	185
1990 Ridin' the Rims	1,250	N/A	210.00	215-281
1991 Riding the High Country	1,250		225.00	225
1978 Rookie Bronc Rider	1,000	N/A	75.00	188-315
1976 Sage Grinder	1,000	N/A	65.00	995-1397
1980 Sheep Skull in Drift	1,500	N/A	75.00	116-160
1974 Shoshone Chief	1,000	N/A	65.00	1200-1272
1982 Sioux Indian with Eagle Feather	1,250	N/A	150.00	150
1992 Sioux Subchief	1,000		195.00	195
1994 Slim Warren, The Old Cowboy	1,000		125.00	125
1983 Southwest Indian Father & Son	1,250		145.00	145
1977 Timber Jack Joe	1,000	N/A	65.00	975-1357
1988 The Volunteer	1,500		225.00	225
1996 The Warrior (Iris Print)	200		550.00	550
1987 Winter on Trout Creek	1,000	N/A	150.00	300-490
1981 Winter Trapping	1,500	N/A	150.00	595-779
1980 Young Plains Indian	1,500	N/A	125.00	1500-1992
1990 Young Sheepherder	1,500		225.00	225

Collectors' Information Bureau   *Quotes have been rounded up to nearest dollar

YEAR ISSUE	EDITION LIMIT	YEAR RETD.	ISSUE PRICE	*QUOTE U.S.$
Bastin - M. Bastin				
1997 Autumn Celebration	1,950		95.00	95
1997 Dinner Guests	2,500	1998	95.00	195-215
1997 Dinner Guests (framed)	34		277.00	277
1998 Garden Party	1,950		110.00	110
Bean - A. Bean				
1998 Apollo: An Eyewitness Account & Kissing the Earth	650	N/A	345.00	345
1993 Conrad Gordon and Bean:The Fantasy	1,000		385.00	385-500
2000 The Hammer and the Feather	650		315.00	315
1997 Heavenly Reflections	850		275.00	275
1987 Helping Hands	850	N/A	150.00	150
1998 Homeward Bound	550		215.00	215
1995 Houston, We Have a Problem	1,000	1998	500.00	500
1988 How It Felt to Walk on the Moon	850	N/A	150.00	150
1992 In Flight	850	1998	385.00	385
1994 In The Beginning Apollo 25 C/S	1,000	N/A	450.00	550
2000 Lone Star	250		850.00	850
1999 Moon Rovers	550		215.00	215
1997 Reaching For the Stars (canvas)	1,500		2200.00	2200
2001 Right Stuff Field Geologists	550		495.00	495
1999 Straightening Our Stripes	550		195.00	195
Beecham - G. Beecham				
1999 The Boys of December	550		185.00	185
1998 Bustin' Through	750		150.00	150
2000 The Cascades (Giclée on canvas)	75		795.00	795
1998 Ferdinand	750		150.00	150
2001 Lift	550		160.00	160
2001 Lift (canvas)	100		495.00	495
1999 Mystic Warrior	550		185.00	185
2000 Polar Attraction	550		185.00	185
1999 Step Into The Light	550		185.00	185
1998 Tag Team	750		150.00	150
2000 Top of the World (Giclée on canvas)	75		1350.00	1350
Blackshear - T. Blackshear				
1994 Beauty and the Beast	1,000	1998	225.00	575-595
2000 Coat of Many Colors	Open		125.00	125
1996 Dance of the Wind & Storm	850		195.00	195
1996 Golden Breeze	850		225.00	225
1993 Hero Frederick Douglass	746		20.00	20
1993 Hero Harriet Tubman	753		20.00	20
1993 Hero Martin Luther King, Jr.	762		20.00	20
1993 Heroes of Our Heritage Portfolio	5,000	N/A	35.00	35
1995 Intimacy	550		850.00	1200
1995 Night in Day	850	N/A	195.00	975-1095
1994 Swansong	1,000		175.00	175
2001 Watchers in the Night	2,500		495.00	495
Blake - B. Blake				
1995 The Old Double Diamond	850		175.00	175
1994 West of the Moon	650		195.00	195
Blish - C. Blish				
1997 A Change in the Air w/book	950		195.00	195
1998 Father The Hour Has Come (framed)	559		95.00	95
1998 Father The Hour Has Come (gold frame)	621		150.00	150
1998 Father The Hour Has Come (unframed)	4,186		70.00	70
1997 Gathering Sea Oats	550		135.00	135
1998 He Stills the Sea (cherry frame)	Open		150.00	150
1998 He Stills the Sea (gold frame)	Open		150.00	150
1998 He Stills the Sea (unframed)	Open		110.00	110
1997 Island Church (framed)	149		95.00	95
1997 Jennifer (framed)	150		95.00	95
1997 Skywatcher (framed)	148		95.00	95
1997 The Swan (framed)	149		95.00	95
1997 Trinity (framed)	148		95.00	95
1997 Windswept Headlands (framed)	144		95.00	95
Blossom - C. Blossom				
1987 After the Last Drift	950	N/A	145.00	145
1984 Ah Your Majesty (poster)	N/A	N/A	45.00	45
1985 Allerton on the East River	650	N/A	145.00	145
1996 Arthur James Heading Out	850		150.00	150
1988 Black Rock	950	N/A	150.00	150
1984 December Moonrise	650	N/A	135.00	135-150
1984 December Moonrise, remarque	25	N/A	175.00	175
1990 Ebb Tide	950	N/A	175.00	175
1983 First Out	450	N/A	90.00	600-750
1983 First Out, remarque	25	N/A	190.00	800-1000
1987 Gloucester Mackeral Seiners	950	N/A	145.00	145
1998 Gold Rush Twilight	450		195.00	195
1998 Gold Rush Twilight, remarque	100		395.00	395
1989 Harbor Light	950	N/A	165.00	165
1988 Heading Home	950	N/A	150.00	250
1998 Morning Set	450		195.00	195
1985 Off Palmer Land	850	N/A	145.00	145
1995 Onshore Breeze	850		175.00	175
1992 Port of Call	850		175.00	175
1986 Potomac By Moonlight	950	N/A	145.00	145
1987 San Francisco-Eve of the Gold Rush	950	N/A	150.00	150
1992 Silhouette	850		175.00	175
1986 Southport @ Twilight	950	N/A	145.00	145
1985 Tranquil Dawn	650	N/A	95.00	95
1994 Traveling in Company	850		175.00	175
1994 Traveling in Company, Remarque	100		415.00	415
1992 Windward	950		175.00	175
1986 Winter Dawn @ Boston Wharf	850	N/A	85.00	85
Boren - N. Boren				
1999 "She Love Me...?"	150		850.00	850
1999 Cowboy Romance	350		295.00	295
2000 Saddle Straps	550		175.00	175
1999 Sittin' Pretty	450		345.00	345
Bralds - B. Bralds				
1997 Abyssinian	175		195.00	195
1998 American Shorthair	175	N/A	195.00	195
1995 Bag Ladies	2,500	1995	150.00	675-725
1996 Basket Cases	2,500	1996	150.00	175-225
2000 Boucat	950		165.00	165
2000 Boucat (canvas)	150		595.00	595
1997 British Blue Short Hair (Nine Lives)	175		195.00	195
1999 A Bushel and a Peck	1,250		145.00	145
1996 Cabinet Meeting	2,000	1996	150.00	195-225
2000 Cat-as-trophy	1,500	N/A	165.00	165
1996 Cheese	2,000		150.00	150
1997 Chocolate Point Siamese	175	N/A	195.00	195
1997 Cinnamon Tabby Maine Coon	175		195.00	195
1999 Diane's Broken Heart	1,500		125.00	125
2000 Heart to Heart	950		135.00	135
1998 Miss Kitty	2,500		125.00	125
1998 A Mixed Bag	2,500		125.00	125
1997 Nine Lives Suite - (Brit., Snowshoe, Persian)	1,750		150.00	150
1998 Nine Lives Suite - (Sho/Bur/Tabby)	1,750		150.00	150
1997 Nine Lives Suite - (Siamese, Abyssinian, Coon)	1,750		150.00	150
1997 Persian (Nine Lives)	175		195.00	195
1999 Rainbow Whiskers	1,250		155.00	155
2000 Rock Star	1,500		165.00	165
1997 Siamese Twins	2,250		150.00	150
1997 Snowshoe (Nine Lives)	175		195.00	195
1998 Table Manners	1,950		175.00	175
Bullas - W. Bullas				
2000 the bad doggies...	750		135.00	135
1999 bad to the bun	750		95.00	95
1998 Ballet Parking	750		110.00	110
2000 ballet parking....	Open		49.95	50
2001 The Bar Exam	1,250		125.00	125
2001 The Bar Exam (canvas)	150		395.00	395
1995 The Big Game	1,500		95.00	95
1993 Billy the Pig	850		95.00	95
2000 the cat burglar....	450		95.00	95
1997 A Chick Off The Old Block (framed)	57		125.00	125
2000 a chick with brains....	450		95.00	95
1995 The Chimp Shot	1,000		95.00	95
1994 Clucks Unlimited	850		95.00	95
1995 The Consultant	1,000	N/A	95.00	95
1994 Court of Appeals	850	1995	95.00	275-395
1995 Dog Byte	1,000	1998	95.00	175-195
1997 Duck Tape (framed)	296	1998	125.00	125
1994 Ductor	850	1998	95.00	95
1997 Federal Duck Stump	1,250		95.00	95
1998 A Fool And His Bunny	950		95.00	95
1998 A Fool And His Bunny (framed)	Open		150.00	150
1998 A Fool Moon Collectors' Edition Book & Porcelain	900	1998	165.00	165

GRAPHICS

YEAR ISSUE	EDITION LIMIT	YEAR RETD.	ISSUE PRICE	*QUOTE U.S.$
1995 fowl ball...	1,500		95.00	95
1994 Fridays After Five	850		95.00	95
1998 The House Swine	950		125.00	125
2000 how does your garden grow....	450		95.00	95
1998 Jingle This....	950		125.00	125
1995 Legal Eagles	1,000		95.00	95
2000 life of the party....	450		95.00	95
1999 a little sangria	750		110.00	110
2000 monkey business....	450		95.00	95
1993 Mr. Harry Buns	850	N/A	95.00	95
1996 The Nerd Dogs	1,500		95.00	95
1997 No Assembly Required	99		125.00	125
2000 the nutcracker....	450		95.00	95
1993 Our Ladies of the Front Lawn	850		95.00	95
1997 Our of the Woods (framed)	320		125.00	125
1993 The Pale Prince	850		110.00	110
2000 please bee mine....	450		95.00	95
1993 Sand Trap Pro	850	1998	95.00	95-195
1997 Sock Hop (framed)	211	N/A	125.00	125
1993 Some Set of Buns	850		95.00	95
2000 space cadet....	450		95.00	95
1997 Supermom (framed)	100		125.00	125
1995 tennis, anyone?	1,000		95.00	95
1993 Wine-Oceros	850	1998	95.00	595
1993 You Rang, Madam?	850		95.00	114
1996 Zippo...The Fire Eater	850		95.00	95

Buxton - J. Buxton

2001 A. Lincoln (19" x 40") (print)	100		695.00	695
2001 A. Lincoln (40" x 85") (print)	20		2500.00	2500
1999 God's Gift	550		165.00	165
2001 He Returns Victorious - 1783 (canvas)	100		595.00	595
2000 High Place	550		135.00	135

Carey - J. Carey

2001 Greenwood Cove	550		175.00	175
2001 Greenwood Cove (canvas)	100		595.00	595
2001 The Mission Courtyard	550		175.00	175
2001 The Mission Courtyard (canvas)	150		695.00	695
2001 Vigna Del Sole	550		175.00	175
2001 Vigna Del Sole (canvas)	100		750.00	750

Christensen - J. Christensen

2000 All The World's a Stage	3,000		225.00	225
1989 The Annunciation	850	N/A	175.00	210-325
1995 Balancing Act	3,500	N/A	185.00	195-215
1996 The Bassonist	2,500		125.00	125
1996 The Believer's Etching Edition	1,000		795.00	795
1998 Benediction	950	N/A	150.00	150
1990 The Burden of the Responsible Man	850	N/A	145.00	1650-2950
1991 The Candleman	850	N/A	160.00	350-375
2000 A Christensen Character Cleverly Camouflaged in a Doolittle Landscape	3,500		135.00	135
1993 College of Magical Knowledge	4,500	N/A	185.00	325-675
1993 College of Magical Knowledge, remarque	500	N/A	252.50	500-650
1996 Court of the Faeries	3,500	N/A	245.00	245-500
1991 Diggery Diggery Dare-Etching	75	N/A	210.00	600-1100
1994 Evening Angels	4,000	N/A	195.00	195
1994 Evening Angels w/Art Furnishings Frame	200	N/A	800.00	800
1989 Fantasies of the Sea-poster	Open		35.00	35
1995 Fishing	2,500	N/A	145.00	150-190
1999 Flight of the Fablemaker	2,500		195.00	195
1998 Gerome Spent His Free Time Daydreaming of Being Reincarnated as a Snake	1,250		295.00	295
1998 Gethsemane	Open		125.00	125
1993 Getting it Right	4,000	N/A	185.00	100-185
1985 The Gift For Mrs. Claus	3,500	N/A	80.00	550-600
1998 The Great Garibaldi (serigraph)	450		800.00	800
1999 Icarus Bound	950		135.00	135
1991 Jack Be Nimble-Etching	75	N/A	210.00	975-1425
1986 Jonah	850	N/A	95.00	375-395
1991 Lawrence and a Bear	850	N/A	145.00	400-600
1998 Lawyer More Than Adequately Attired	950	1998	150.00	150-425
1998 Levi Levitates a Stonefish (serigraph)	450		800.00	800
1987 Low Tech-Poster	Open		35.00	35

YEAR ISSUE	EDITION LIMIT	YEAR RETD.	ISSUE PRICE	*QUOTE U.S.$
1999 A Man and His Dog	950	N/A	225.00	225
1991 Man in the Moon-Etching	75	N/A	210.00	650-700
1988 The Man Who Minds the Moon	850	N/A	145.00	600-650
1991 Mother Goose-Etching	75	N/A	210.00	875-1200
2000 The Oath	2,950		160.00	160
1987 Old Man with a Lot on His Mind	850	N/A	85.00	575-725
1986 Olde World Santa	3,500	N/A	80.00	650-695
1992 The Oldest Angel	850	N/A	125.00	1000-1250
1992 The Oldest Angel-Etching	75	N/A	210.00	1275-1550
1991 Once Upon a Time	1,500	N/A	175.00	1100-1650
1991 Once Upon a Time, remarque	500	N/A	220.00	1550-1600
1996 One Light	1,500		125.00	125
1999 Parables	1,500	N/A	150.00	150
1991 Pelican King	850	N/A	115.00	350-600
2001 The Pelican King And The Prince	750		135.00	135
2001 The Pelican King And The Prince (canvas)	250		295.00	295
1991 Peter Peter Pumpkin Eater-Etching	75	N/A	210.00	600-1100
1995 Piscatorial Percussionist	3,000	N/A	125.00	125
2000 The Princess and the Puffins	250		750.00	750
2000 Queen Mab in the Ruins	1,950	N/A	185.00	185-265
1992 The Reponsible Woman	2,500	N/A	175.00	600-875
1990 Rhymes & Reasons w/Booklet	Open		150.00	150
1990 Rhymes & Reasons w/Booklet, remarque	500	N/A	208.00	350-595
1993 The Royal Music Barque	2,750	N/A	375.00	375
1992 The Royal Processional	1,500	N/A	185.00	450-575
1992 The Royal Processional, remarque	500	N/A	252.50	475-595
1997 Santa's Other Helpers	1,950		125.00	125
1993 The Scholar	3,250	N/A	125.00	125-215
1995 Serenade For an Orange Cat	3,000	N/A	125.00	125-150
1987 The Shakespearean Poster	Open		35.00	35
2001 Sharing Our Light	650		165.00	165
2001 Sharing Our Light (canvas)	450		595.00	595
1995 Sisters of the Sea	2,000	N/A	195.00	195-325
1994 Six Bird Hunters-Full Camouflage 3	4,662	N/A	165.00	195
1994 Sometimes the Spirit Touches w/book	3,600	N/A	195.00	280-450
1998 Superstitious w/Booket/Key	2,500	1998	195.00	195-350
1998 Superstitious, remarque	200	1998	395.00	450
1991 Three Blind Mice-Etching	75	N/A	210.00	3000
1991 Three Wise Men of Gotham-Etching	75	N/A	210.00	990
1991 Tweedle Dee & Tweedle Dum-Etching	75	N/A	210.00	990
1994 Two Angels Discussing Botticelli	2,950	N/A	145.00	125-150
2001 Two Men in Conversation Attempting To Put Things Into Proper Perspective	475		495.00	495
1990 Two Sisters	650	N/A	325.00	325-700
1996 The Voyage of the Basset Collector's Edition Book & The Oldest Professor	2,500		195.00	195
1987 Voyage of the Basset w/Journal	850	N/A	225.00	1100-1250
1993 Waiting for the Tide	2,250	N/A	150.00	185-270
1997 Wendall Realized He Had A Dilemma	950	1998	125.00	125
1988 The Widows Mite	850	N/A	145.00	2900-3400
1986 Your Place, or Mine?	850	N/A	125.00	250-375

Clifton - R. Clifton

2000 Afternoon Mallards	550		150.00	150
2000 October Morning	550		150.00	150
2001 Widgeon - Out Front	550		150.00	150

Combes - S. Combes

1992 African Oasis	650	N/A	375.00	795-850
2001 Afterglow	550		165.00	165
2001 Afterglow (canvas)	50		595.00	595
1981 Alert	1,000	N/A	95.00	95
1987 The Angry One	850	N/A	95.00	95
1988 Bushwhacker	850	N/A	145.00	145
1983 Chui	275	N/A	250.00	250
1988 Confrontation	850	N/A	145.00	145
1988 The Crossing	1,250	N/A	245.00	245
1994 Disdain	850		110.00	110
2000 Drinks All Around (Giclée on canvas)	75		1750.00	1750
1999 Drought, Dust and Danger (canvas)	75		1700.00	1700
1998 Facing the Wind	1,500	N/A	75.00	75-125
1993 Fearful Symmetry	850	N/A	110.00	110-215
1997 From The Shadows (canvas)	250		395.00	395
1995 Golden Silhouette	950		175.00	175

*Quotes have been rounded up to nearest dollar

YEAR ISSUE	EDITION LIMIT	YEAR RETD.	ISSUE PRICE	*QUOTE U.S.$
1994 Great Cats Masterwork & 9 prints with Journals	500		1900.000	1900
1998 Great Cats: Stories & Art From A World Traveler & Prowler	450		195.00	195
1990 The Guardian (Silverback)	1,000	N/A	185.00	185
1997 Heavy Drinkers	550		425.00	425
1999 Hot Lions	250		795.00	795
1992 The Hypnotist	1,250		145.00	145
1999 Imminent Pursuit	550		150.00	150
1994 Indian Summer	950		175.00	175
1980 Interlude	1,500	N/A	85.00	95-115
1995 Jungle Phantom	950		175.00	175
2001 Keeping Distance (canvas)	75		1750.00	1750
1991 Kilimanjaro Morning	850	N/A	185.00	185
1981 Leopard Cubs	1,000	N/A	95.00	315
1992 Lookout	1,250		95.00	95
1980 Manyara Afternoon	1,500	N/A	75.00	325-425
1989 Masai-Longonot, Kenya	850		145.00	145
1992 Midday Sun (Lioness & Cubs)	850	N/A	125.00	125
1989 Mountain Gorillas	550	N/A	135.00	135-150
1995 Mountain Myth	950		175.00	175
1995 Pride	950		175.00	175
1998 Sentinels	550		125.00	125
1980 Serengeti Monarch	1,500	N/A	85.00	275
1995 Serious Intent	950		175.00	175
1995 Siberian Winter	950		175.00	175
1996 The Siberians	850		175.00	175
1988 Simba	850	1998	125.00	125
1997 Snow Pack	550		175.00	175
1995 Snow Tracker	950		175.00	175
1980 Solitary Hunter	1,500	N/A	75.00	75
1990 Standoff	850	N/A	375.00	550-695
1991 Study in Concentration	850	N/A	185.00	395
1987 Tall Shadows	850	N/A	150.00	450-825
1985 Tension at Dawn	825	N/A	145.00	900-1100
1985 Tension at Dawn, remarque	25	N/A	275.00	1150-1295
1998 There Was A Time, One of Two	250		975.00	975
1998 There Was A Time, Two of Two	250		975.00	975
1989 The Watering Hole	850	N/A	225.00	225
1986 The Wildebeest Migration	450	N/A	350.00	1500-2150

Coronato - B. Coronato

YEAR ISSUE	EDITION LIMIT	YEAR RETD.	ISSUE PRICE	*QUOTE U.S.$
2000 Them's abuch-abrone stomp'n...	550		195.00	195

Crowley - D. Crowley

YEAR ISSUE	EDITION LIMIT	YEAR RETD.	ISSUE PRICE	*QUOTE U.S.$
1981 Afterglow	1,500	N/A	110.00	110
1992 Anna Thorne	650	N/A	160.00	160
1980 Apache in White	1,500	N/A	85.00	85-125
1979 Arizona Mountain Man	1,500	N/A	85.00	85-125
1980 Beauty and the Beast	1,500	N/A	85.00	85-135
1992 Colors of the Sunset	650		175.00	175
1979 Desert Sunset	1,500	N/A	75.00	75-125
1978 Dorena	1,000	N/A	75.00	75-115
1995 The Dreamer	650		150.00	150
1981 Eagle Feathers	1,500	N/A	95.00	95-125
1988 Ermine and Beads	550	N/A	85.00	215
1989 The Gunfighters	3,000	N/A	35.00	35
1981 The Heirloom	1,000	N/A	125.00	125
1982 Hopi Butterfly	275	N/A	350.00	350
1978 Hudson's Bay Blanket	1,000	N/A	75.00	75-125
1980 The Littlest Apache	275	N/A	325.00	325-850
1997 Morning Fire (Canvas)	650		495.00	495
1994 Plumes and Ribbons	650		160.00	160
1979 Security Blanket	1,500	N/A	65.00	65-175
1981 Shannandoah	275	N/A	325.00	275-325
1978 The Starquilt	1,000	N/A	65.00	500-525
1986 The Trapper	550	N/A	75.00	75
1997 Water in the Draw	550		160.00	160

Daly - J. Daly

YEAR ISSUE	EDITION LIMIT	YEAR RETD.	ISSUE PRICE	*QUOTE U.S.$
2001 Bedtime Story	550		150.00	150
2001 Fastball	550		175.00	175

Dawson - J. Dawson

YEAR ISSUE	EDITION LIMIT	YEAR RETD.	ISSUE PRICE	*QUOTE U.S.$
1992 The Attack (Cougars)	850		175.00	175
1993 Berry Contented	850		150.00	150
1993 Berry Contented, remarque	100		235.00	235
1994 The Face Off (Right & Left Panel)	850		150.00	150
1993 Looking Back	850		110.00	110
1993 Otter Wise	850		150.00	150
1993 Taking a Break	850	N/A	150.00	150

Doolittle - B. Doolittle

YEAR ISSUE	EDITION LIMIT	YEAR RETD.	ISSUE PRICE	*QUOTE U.S.$
1983 Art of Camouflage, signed	2,000	1983	55.00	395-450
2000 Blue Mesa (poster)	Open		30.00	30
1980 Bugged Bear	1,000	1980	85.00	3700-3950
1987 Calling the Buffalo	8,500	1987	245.00	975
1983 Christmas Day, Give or Take a Week	4,581	1983	80.00	1975
1988 Doubled Back	15,000	1988	245.00	1575
1996 Drawn From the Heart-Etching Suite	349	1996	750.00	1775-2100
1992 Eagle Heart	48,000	1992	285.00	225-285
1982 Eagle's Flight	1,500	1982	185.00	3600-3975
1999 The Earth Is My Mother Collector's Ed. Book w/print	12,500		295.00	295
1983 Escape by a Hare	1,500	1983	80.00	595-850
1984 The Forest Has Eyes	8,544	1984	175.00	2950-4200
2000 Fox Haven	Open		35.00	35
1980 Good Omen, The	1,000	1980	85.00	1650-3000
1987 Guardian Spirits	13,238	1987	295.00	595-862
1990 Hide and Seek (Composite & Video)	25,000	1990	1200.00	850-900
1984 Let My Spirit Soar	1,500	1984	195.00	4000-4800
2000 Mesa Ruins	Open		35.00	35
1997 Music in the Wind	43,500	1998	330.00	850-1350
1998 No Respect	25,000		195.00	195
2000 Painted Ladies	Open		35.00	35
1979 Pintos	1,000	1979	65.00	2295-7300
1993 Prayer for the Wild Things	65,000	1993	325.00	1650-1775
1983 Runs With Thunder	1,500	1983	150.00	795-1095
1983 Rushing War Eagle	1,500	1983	150.00	975-1075
1991 Sacred Circle (Print & Video)	40,192	1991	325.00	2350
1989 Sacred Ground	69,996	1989	265.00	700-750
1987 Season of the Eagle	36,548	1987	245.00	650-675
1991 The Sentinel	35,000	1991	275.00	550
1981 Spirit of the Grizzly	1,500	1981	150.00	650-3950
1995 Spirit Takes Flight	48,000		225.00	225
1996 Three More for Breakfast	20,000	1996	245.00	1650-1775
1986 Two Bears of the Blackfeet	2,650	1986	225.00	1650-1775
1985 Two Indian Horses	12,253	1985	225.00	1700-3650
1995 Two More Indian Horses	48,000	1995	225.00	1650-1775
1981 Unknown Presence	1,500	1981	135.00	1775-1990
1992 Walk Softly (Chapbook)	40,192	1992	225.00	225-295
2000 West Fork Pintos	Open		35.00	35
1994 When The Wind Had Wings	57,500		325.00	325
1986 Where Silence Speaks, Doolittle The Art of Bev Doolittle	3,500	1986	650.00	1200-2600
1980 Whoo !?	1,000	1980	75.00	1295-1950
1993 Wilderness? Wilderness!	50,000		65.00	65
1985 Wolves of the Crow	2,650	1985	225.00	1100-1650
1981 Woodland Encounter	1,500	1981	145.00	1775-6950

Dubowski - E. Dubowski

YEAR ISSUE	EDITION LIMIT	YEAR RETD.	ISSUE PRICE	*QUOTE U.S.$
1996 Aspen Flowers	850		145.00	145
1998 The Errand	550		125.00	125
1996 Fresh From the Garden	850		145.00	145
1998 Open For Business	550		125.00	125
1998 The Readers	550		125.00	125
1997 Reflections	850		175.00	175

Dudash - C.M. Dudash

YEAR ISSUE	EDITION LIMIT	YEAR RETD.	ISSUE PRICE	*QUOTE U.S.$
2000 He Shall Hear My Voice	Open		125.00	125

Entz - L. Entz

YEAR ISSUE	EDITION LIMIT	YEAR RETD.	ISSUE PRICE	*QUOTE U.S.$
1996 Apple Pie	850		150.00	150
1995 Life's a Dance	850		150.00	150
1996 New Shoes	850		150.00	150
1997 A Plot of Her Own	650		175.00	175

Ferris - K. Ferris

YEAR ISSUE	EDITION LIMIT	YEAR RETD.	ISSUE PRICE	*QUOTE U.S.$
1990 The Circus Outbound	1,000		225.00	225
1991 Farmer's Nightmare	850		185.00	185
1991 Linebacker in the Buff	1,000		225.00	225
1983 Little Willie Coming Home	1,000	N/A	145.00	1750-1850
1994 Real Trouble	1,000		195.00	195
1995 Schweinfurt Again	1,000		195.00	195
1982 Sunrise Encounter	1,000	N/A	145.00	145-195
1993 A Test of Courage	850		185.00	185
1991 Too Little, Too Late w/Video	1,000		245.00	245

Frazier - L. Frazier

YEAR ISSUE	EDITION LIMIT	YEAR RETD.	ISSUE PRICE	*QUOTE U.S.$
1999 Bows on the String	550		170.00	170
1998 The Concubine	750		150.00	150
1998 Constant Traveler	750		150.00	150
1998 The Nomad	750		150.00	150
1997 Pay Dirt	450		425.00	425

*Quotes have been rounded up to nearest dollar

Collectors' Information Bureau

YEAR ISSUE	EDITION LIMIT	YEAR RETD.	ISSUE PRICE	*QUOTE U.S.$
1997 Royal Escort	450		395.00	395
1999 Search For Oneself	550		185.00	185
2000 Slack Water Buddies (canvas)	150		650.00	650
2000 Unconquerable (Giclée on canvas)	75		1350.00	1350

Frederick - R. Frederick

YEAR ISSUE	EDITION LIMIT	YEAR RETD.	ISSUE PRICE	*QUOTE U.S.$
1990 Autumn Leaves	1,250	N/A	175.00	125-175
1996 Autumn Trail	850		195.00	195
1989 Barely Spring	1,500		165.00	165
1994 Beeline (C)	1,000		195.00	195
1987 Before the Storm (Diptych)	550	N/A	350.00	550-675
1991 Breaking the Ice	2,750	N/A	235.00	195-235
1997 Cascade Gold	650		175.00	175
1989 Colors of Home	1,500	N/A	165.00	295-425
1995 Drifters	850		175.00	175
1985 Early Evening Gathering	475	N/A	325.00	435-495
1992 An Early Light Breakfast	1,750	N/A	235.00	295-300
1990 Echoes of Sunset	1,750	N/A	235.00	725-775
1987 Evening Shadows (White-Tail Deer)	1,500	N/A	125.00	95-125
1992 Fast Break	2,250		235.00	235
1992 Fire and Ice (Suite of 2)	1,750		175.00	175
1984 First Moments of Gold	825	N/A	145.00	225
1984 First Moments of Gold, remarque	25	N/A	172.50	265
1984 From Timber's Edge	850	N/A	125.00	140-165
1996 Geyser Basin	850		175.00	175
1989 Gifts of the Land #2	500	N/A	150.00	150
1988 Gifts of the Land w/Wine & Wine Label	500	N/A	150.00	150
1988 Glimmer of Solitude	1,500	N/A	145.00	145
1993 Glory Days	1,750		115.00	115
1986 Great Horned Owl	1,250	N/A	115.00	135
1995 High Country Harem	1,000		185.00	185
1985 High Society	950	N/A	115.00	425
1995 Jaywalkers	850		175.00	175
1991 The Long Run	1,750	N/A	235.00	250-295
1991 The Long Run, AP	200	N/A	167.50	495
1985 Los Colores De Chiapas	950	N/A	85.00	85
1994 The Lost World	1,000		175.00	175
1985 Misty Morning Lookout	950	N/A	145.00	145
1984 Misty Morning Sentinel	850	N/A	125.00	145
1989 Monarch of the North	2,000		150.00	150
1990 Morning Surprise	1,750	N/A	165.00	165
1991 Morning Thunder	1,750	N/A	185.00	200
1988 The Nesting Call	2,500	N/A	150.00	150
1988 The Nesting Call, remarque	1,000	N/A	165.00	165
1993 New Heights	1,950		195.00	195
1987 Northern Light	1,500	N/A	165.00	165
1986 Out on a Limb	1,250	N/A	145.00	300-375
1993 Point of View	1,000		235.00	235
1992 Rain Forest Rendezvous	1,500	N/A	225.00	225
1988 Rim Walk	1,500	N/A	90.00	90
1988 Shadows of Dusk	1,500	N/A	165.00	165
1990 Silent Watch (High Desert Museum)	2,000	N/A	35.00	35
1994 Snow Pack	1,000		175.00	175
1992 Snowstorm	1,750		195.00	195
1990 Snowy Reflections (Snowy Egret)	1,500	N/A	150.00	150
1986 Sounds of Twilight	1,500	N/A	135.00	250-295
1991 Summer's Song (Triptych)	2,500		225.00	225
1993 Temple of the Jaguar	1,500		225.00	225
1988 Timber Ghost w/Mini Wine Label	3,000	N/A	150.00	150
1994 Tropic Moon	850		165.00	165
1987 Tundra Watch (Snowy Owl)	1,500	N/A	145.00	145
1994 Way of the Caribou	1,235		235.00	235
1987 Winter's Brilliance (Cardinal)	1,500	N/A	135.00	135
1986 Winter's Call	1,250	N/A	165.00	550
1986 Winter's Call Raptor, AP	100	N/A	165.00	600
1987 Woodland Crossing (Caribou)	1,500	N/A	145.00	145
1988 World of White	2,500	N/A	150.00	150

Grace - R. Grace

YEAR ISSUE	EDITION LIMIT	YEAR RETD.	ISSUE PRICE	*QUOTE U.S.$
2000 The Great Shepard	Open		125.00	125

Gurney - J. Gurney

YEAR ISSUE	EDITION LIMIT	YEAR RETD.	ISSUE PRICE	*QUOTE U.S.$
1992 Birthday Pageant	2,500	N/A	60.00	60
1992 Birthday Pageant, remarque	300	N/A	275.00	250-295
1991 Dinosaur Boulevard	2,000	N/A	125.00	125-150
1991 Dinosaur Boulevard, remarque	250	N/A	196.00	425
1990 Dinosaur Parade	1,995	1995	125.00	125-175
1990 Dinosaur Parade, remarque	150	N/A	130.00	2500-2800
1992 Dream Canyon	N/A	N/A	125.00	125
1992 Dream Canyon, remarque	150	N/A	196.00	395
1993 The Excursion	3,500		175.00	175

YEAR ISSUE	EDITION LIMIT	YEAR RETD.	ISSUE PRICE	*QUOTE U.S.$
1993 Garden of Hope	3,500		175.00	175
1990 Morning in Treetown	1,500	N/A	175.00	275-325
1993 Palace in the Clouds	3,500	N/A	175.00	175
1993 Ring Riders	2,500	N/A	175.00	175
1995 Rumble & Mist	2,500		175.00	175
1995 Santa Claus	2,000		95.00	95
1990 Seaside Romp	1,000	N/A	175.00	395
1992 Skybook Print w/Dinotopia Book	3,500	N/A	295.00	295
1994 Small Wonder	3,299	N/A	75.00	75
1994 Steep Street	3,500		95.00	95
1995 Twilight in Bonaba	3,000		195.00	195
1991 Waterfall City	3,000	N/A	125.00	125
1991 Waterfall City, remarque	250	N/A	186.00	395
1995 The World Beneath Collectors' Book w/print	3,000		195.00	195

Gustafson - S. Gustafson

YEAR ISSUE	EDITION LIMIT	YEAR RETD.	ISSUE PRICE	*QUOTE U.S.$
1995 The Alice in Wonderland Suite	4,000		195.00	195
1999 Don Quixote	950		150.00	150
1994 Frog Prince	3,500	1994	125.00	150
1993 Goldilocks and the Three Bears	3,500	1993	125.00	300-400
1995 Hansel & Gretel	3,000		125.00	125
1993 Humpty Dumpty	3,500	1993	125.00	125
1995 Jack in the Beanstalk	3,500		125.00	125
2000 The Journey Begins	2,000		145.00	145
1998 Little Bo Peep	950		125.00	125
1998 Little Miss Muffet	950		125.00	125
1993 Little Red Riding Hood	3,500	1993	125.00	125
2000 The Maiden and the Unicorn	1,250		185.00	185
1999 Mary, Mary, Quite Contrary	950		125.00	125
1998 Merlin and Arthur	1,250	N/A	185.00	185
1996 Old King Cole	2,750		125.00	125
1997 The Owl and the Pussycat	950		125.00	125
1994 Pat-A-Cake	4,000	1998	125.00	100-125
1997 Peter Peter Pumpkin Eater	950		125.00	125
1996 Puss in Boots	2,750		145.00	145
1995 Rumplestiltskin	2,750		125.00	125
1993 Snow White and the Seven Dwarfs	3,500	1993	165.00	225
1997 Tom Thumb	950	1998	125.00	125
1995 Touched by Magic	4,000		185.00	185
1999 The Wizard of Oz	2,000		185.00	185

Hartough - L. Hartough

YEAR ISSUE	EDITION LIMIT	YEAR RETD.	ISSUE PRICE	*QUOTE U.S.$
2000 3rd Hole, Brookline, MA	850		225.00	225
2000 5th Hole, Pebble Beach	Open		45.00	45
1995 7th Hole, Pebble Beach Golf Links	850	1998	225.00	225
2000 7th Hole, Pebble Beach	950		650.00	650
2000 The 8th Hole, Pebble Beach	350		950.00	950
1996 Postage Stamp 8th Royal Troon	154	N/A	210.00	210
2000 9th Hole, The Country Club, MA (poster)	Open		40.00	40
2000 10th Hole, Mamaroneck, NY	1,250		210.00	210
1996 10th Hole, West Course Winged Foot	657	N/A	210.00	210
2000 11th Hole, Pebble Beach	950		650.00	650
1996 11th Hole, "White Dogwood", Augusta National Golf Club	850	1998	225.00	225
1995 The 13th Hole, "Azalea"	25	N/A	225.00	225
1996 13th Hole, Augusta National	430	N/A	225.00	225
1999 14th and 4th Holes, Carnoustie Golf Links	850		225.00	225
2000 14th Hole, Carnoustie	950		650.00	650
1995 14th Hole, St. Ar rews	850	1995	225.00	225
2000 14th Hole, St. An rews, Scotland	950		650.00	650
2000 15th Hole, Daufusk J, SC	850		210.00	210
1996 15th Hole, "Firethr n", Augusta National Golf Cl J	850	N/A	325.00	325
1996 15th Hole, Haig Point Rees Jones	226		210.00	210
2000 15th Hole, Pebble Beach	950		650.00	650
1996 17th Hole Clubhouse, Royal Troon	522		165.00	165
1996 17th Hole, Royal Dornoch	86	N/A	210.00	210
1996 17th Hole, Royal St. George, 1993 Bristish Open	153		225.00	225
2000 17th Hole, St. Andrews, Scotland	950		650.00	650
1996 The Ultimate 18th Eden Royal H.K.	634		210.00	210
2000 18th Hole, Dublin, OH	1,250		210.00	210
1997 18th Hole, Harbourtown Links	850	N/A	250.00	250
2000 18th Hole, Hilton Head	950		650.00	650
1996 18th Hole, Muirfield Village	780		210.00	210
2000 18th Hole, Pebble Beach	Open		45.00	45
1996 18th Hole, Royal Birkdale, 1991 British Open	245		210.00	210

Collectors' Information Bureau   *Quotes have been rounded up to nearest dollar

YEAR ISSUE	EDITION LIMIT	YEAR RETD.	ISSUE PRICE	*QUOTE U.S.$
1996 18th Hole, Royal Lytham & St. Annes Golf Club	850	N/A	225.00	225
1997 18th Hole, 1997 Royal Troon	345		225.00	225
Holm - J. Holm				
1998 Five Persians	550		130.00	130
1997 I Spy Summer	850		95.00	95
1998 The Sentry	550		125.00	125
1996 Slipper Thief	850		95.00	95
Howell-Sickles - D. Howell-Sickles				
1997 Cowgirl Rising w/And the Cowgirl Jumped Over the Moon print	1,000		245.00	245
1999 A Family Tradition	650		295.00	295
1998 Legends	650		295.00	295
Hurley - W. Hurley				
1998 Late Summer Sunset	550		225.00	225
1998 The Utah Suite - Monument Valley	550		1495.00	1495
1998 The Wyoming Suite (center panel 1/3)	550		500.00	500
1998 The Wyoming Suite (left panel 2/3)	550		500.00	500
1998 The Wyoming Suite (right panel 3/3)	550		495.00	495
Johnson - J. Johnson				
1994 Moose River	650		175.00	175
1994 Sea Treasures	650		125.00	125
1994 Winter Thaw	650		150.00	150
1993 Wolf Creek	550	N/A	165.00	200
Kennedy - S. Kennedy				
1988 After Dinner Music	2,500	N/A	175.00	230
1995 Alaskan Malamute	1,000		125.00	125
1992 Aurora	2,250	N/A	195.00	195
1991 A Breed Apart	2,750	N/A	225.00	225
1992 Cabin Fever	2,250		175.00	175
1995 Cliff Dwellers	850		175.00	175
1998 Crossing Over	750		135.00	135
1997 Curious Encounter & New Generation	850		125.00	125
1988 Distant Relations	950	N/A	200.00	300
1988 Eager to Run	950	N/A	200.00	1400-1790
1990 Fish Tales	5,500	N/A	225.00	225
1997 Fishing Buddies	1,000		165.00	165
1991 In Training	3,350	N/A	165.00	150-295
1991 In Training, remarque	150	N/A	215.50	345
1996 Keeping Watch	850		150.00	150
1995 The Lesson	1,000		125.00	125
1996 Looking For Trouble	850		125.00	125
1993 Midnight Eyes	1,750		125.00	125
1997 Miracle Mile	750		145.00	145
1993 Never Alone	2,250		225.00	225
1993 Never Alone, remarque	250	N/A	272.50	273
1997 The New Kitten	850		125.00	125
1990 On the Edge	4,000		225.00	225
1995 On the Heights	850		175.00	175
1994 Quiet Time Companions-Samoyed	1,000	1998	125.00	125
1994 Quiet Time Companions-Siberian Husky	1,000	N/A	125.00	125
1998 Rocky Mountain Gold	550		175.00	175
1998 Samoyed Pup	1,250		95.00	95
1998 Scouting the Trail	750		150.00	150
1994 Silent Observers	1,250	N/A	165.00	165
1996 Snow Buddies	850		125.00	125
1989 Snowshoes	4,000	N/A	185.00	185
1994 Spruce and Fur	1,500		165.00	165
1995 Standing Watch	850		175.00	175
1993 The Touch	1,500		115.00	115
1989 Up a Creek	2,500	N/A	185.00	185
1997 White Christmas	750		95.00	95
Kodera - C. Kodera				
1986 The A Team (K10)	850	N/A	145.00	145
1995 A.M. Sortie	1,000		225.00	225
1996 Canyon Starliner	850		185.00	185
1991 Darkness Visible (Stealth)	2,671	N/A	40.00	40
1987 Fifty Years a Lady	550	N/A	150.00	450-500
1988 The Great Greenwich Balloon Race	1,000		145.00	145
1990 Green Light-Jump!	650	N/A	145.00	200
1992 Halsey's Surprise	850		95.00	95
1997 Hitting the Kwai w/Artifact	850		265.00	265
1994 Last to Fight	1,000		225.00	225
1995 Lonely Flight to Destiny	1,000	1995	347.00	895-1000
1992 Looking For Nagumo	1,000		225.00	225
1996 The Lost Squadron	850		275.00	275
1992 Memphis Belle/Dauntless Dotty	1,250		245.00	245
1990 A Moment's Peace	1,250	N/A	150.00	150
1988 Moonlight Intruders	1,000	N/A	125.00	125
1995 Only One Survived	1,000		245.00	245
1989 Springtime Flying in the Rockies	550	N/A	95.00	95
1996 Stratojet Shakedown	1,000		265.00	265
1992 Thirty Seconds Over Tokyo	1,000	N/A	275.00	275
1991 This is No Drill w/Video	1,000		225.00	225
1994 This is No Time to Lose an Engine	850		150.00	150
1994 Tiger's Bite	850		150.00	150
1987 Voyager: The Skies Yield	1,500	N/A	225.00	225
Landry - P. Landry				
1996 Afternoon Tea (canvas)	450	1996	495.00	495
1993 The Antique Shop	1,250	N/A	125.00	125
1992 Apple Orchard	1,250		150.00	150
1999 Apple Valley Orchard	850		165.00	165
1992 Aunt Martha's Country Farm	1,500	N/A	185.00	300
1996 Autumn Hayride	550		165.00	165
1995 Autumn Market	1,000	N/A	185.00	185
1987 Bluenose Country	550	N/A	115.00	175
1992 Boardwalk Promenade	1,250		175.00	175
1989 A Canadian Christmas	1,250	N/A	125.00	125
1989 Cape Cod Welcome Cameo	850	N/A	75.00	275
1990 The Captain's Garden	1,000	N/A	165.00	425
2000 Cecilia's Garden	550		165.00	165
2000 Cecilia's Garden (canvas)	100		595.00	595
1993 Christmas at Mystic Seaport	2,000		125.00	125
1992 Christmas at the Flower Market	2,500		125.00	125
1994 Christmas Carousel Pony	2,000		125.00	125
1997 Christmas Door	850		95.00	95
1997 Christmas Door, remarque	S/O	N/A	95.00	95
1998 A Christmas Morning	550		145.00	145
1990 Christmas Treasures	2,500	N/A	165.00	165
2000 A Christmas Wish	950		95.00	95
2000 A Christmas Wish (canvas)	200		275.00	275
1992 Cottage Garden	1,250	N/A	160.00	160
1995 Cottage Reflections	850		135.00	135
1998 Country Garden	850		185.00	185
1994 An English Cottage	850		150.00	150
2001 Evening at the Flower Market	550		175.00	175
2001 Evening at the Flower Market (canvas)	250		695.00	695
1994 Flower Barn	1,000	N/A	175.00	175
1988 Flower Boxes	550	N/A	75.00	250
1991 Flower Market	1,500	N/A	185.00	1000
1990 Flower Wagon	1,500	N/A	165.00	165
1994 Flowers For Mary Hope	1,250		165.00	165
1999 Garden Suite - Climbing Roses	Open		30.00	30
1999 Garden Suite - Memories	Open		30.00	30
1999 Garden Suite - Nestled In	Open		30.00	30
1997 A Gardener's Pride	950		95.00	95
1995 Harbor Garden	1,000		160.00	160
1993 Hometown Parade	1,250		165.00	165
1996 It's a Wonderful Christmas	1,250		165.00	165
1996 Joseph's Corner (canvas)	450		495.00	495
1996 Joseph's Corner, Artist Touch (canvas)	100		795.00	795
1995 Lantern Skaters	1,500		135.00	135
2000 Moonlight and Roses	850	N/A	110.00	110
1990 Morning Papers	1,250	N/A	135.00	145
1994 Morning Walk	850		135.00	135
1998 Mother's Day (Watercolor Sketch)	200		180.00	180
1991 Nantucket Colors	1,500		150.00	150
1998 New England Classic	850		150.00	150
1993 Paper Boy	1,500		150.00	150
1993 A Place in the Park	1,500		185.00	185
1984 Regatta	500	N/A	75.00	150
1984 Regatta, remarque	50	N/A	97.50	145
2000 A Schooner's Return (canvas)	250		295.00	295
1990 Seaside Carousel	1,500	N/A	165.00	200
1988 Seaside Cottage	550	N/A	125.00	125
1986 Seaside Mist	450	N/A	85.00	200
1985 The Skaters	500	N/A	75.00	75
1985 The Skaters, remarque	50	N/A	97.50	98
1998 Southport (mixed media)	350		600.00	600
1995 Spring Song	2,500		145.00	145
1997 Springtime Garden	850		185.00	185
1994 Summer Buddies	950		135.00	135
1991 Summer Concert	1,500		195.00	195
1989 Summer Garden	850	N/A	125.00	400

*Quotes have been rounded up to nearest dollar

YEAR ISSUE	EDITION LIMIT	YEAR RETD.	ISSUE PRICE	*QUOTE U.S.$
1997 Summer Hill	850		165.00	165
1995 Summer Mist (Fine Art Original Lithograph)	550		750.00	850
1998 Summer Potpourri (mixed media)	350		600.00	600
1992 Sunflowers	1,250	N/A	125.00	125
1991 The Toymaker	1,500	N/A	165.00	165
1999 Verandah (canvas)	450		450.00	450
1991 Victorian Memories	1,500	N/A	150.00	150
1996 Winter Memories w/The Captain's Garden Collector's Edition Book	2,000		195.00	195

Larson - J. Larson

YEAR ISSUE	EDITION LIMIT	YEAR RETD.	ISSUE PRICE	*QUOTE U.S.$
2001 Kinship	2,500		245.00	245
2001 Kinship (canvas)	250		650.00	650
2000 Medicine Crow	2,500		245.00	245
2000 Medicine Crow (canvas)	250		595.00	595
2001 The Survivors	1,000		245.00	245
2001 The Survivors (canvas)	150		650.00	650

Lovell - T. Lovell

YEAR ISSUE	EDITION LIMIT	YEAR RETD.	ISSUE PRICE	*QUOTE U.S.$
1988 The Battle of the Crater	1,500	N/A	225.00	225
1988 Berdan's Sharpshooters -Gettysburg	1,500		225.00	225
1986 Blackfeet Wall	450	N/A	325.00	1195-1500
1981 Carson's Boatyard	1,000		150.00	150
1985 Chiricahua Scout	650		90.00	90
1981 The Deceiver	1,000		150.00	150
1990 Dry Goods and Molasses	1,000		225.00	225
1981 Fires Along the Oregon Trail	1,000	N/A	150.00	295
1993 The Handwarmer	1,000		225.00	225
1988 The Hunter	1,000		150.00	150
1982 Invitation to Trade	1,000	N/A	150.00	150
1989 The Lost Rag Doll	1,000		225.00	225
1988 Mr. Bodmer's Music Box	5,000		40.00	40
1975 The Mud Owl's Warning	1,000	N/A	150.00	175-250
1988 North Country Rider	2,500		95.00	95
1976 Quicksand at Horsehead	1,000		150.00	150
1976 Shotgun Toll	1,000		150.00	150
1983 Sugar in The Coffee	650	N/A	165.00	165
1987 Surrender at Appomattox	1,000	N/A	225.00	1695
1992 Target Practice	2,000		25.00	25
1976 Time of Cold-Maker	1,000		150.00	150
1989 Union Fleet Passing Vicksburg	1,500		225.00	225
1982 Walking Coyote & Buffalo Orphans	650	N/A	165.00	195-225
1982 The Wheelsoakers	1,000		150.00	150
1984 Winter Holiday	850		95.00	95
1989 Youth's Hour of Glory	1,500		175.00	175

Lyman - S. Lyman

YEAR ISSUE	EDITION LIMIT	YEAR RETD.	ISSUE PRICE	*QUOTE U.S.$
1997 Ahwahnee-The Deep Grassy Valley	1,500	1998	225.00	225-450
1990 Among The Wild Brambles	1,750	1990	185.00	600-625
1985 Autumn Gathering	850	N/A	115.00	850-1350
1996 Beach Bonfire	6,500	1996	225.00	175-225
1985 Bear & Blossoms (C)	850	N/A	75.00	600-665
1987 Canadian Autumn	1,500	1987	165.00	275-350
1995 Cathedral Snow	4,000	1996	245.00	245-265
2001 Changing of the Guard	550		245.00	245
1989 Color In The Snow (Pheasant)	1,500	N/A	165.00	350-500
1996 The Crossing	2,500	1996	195.00	215-225
1991 Dance of Cloud and Cliff	1,500	1991	225.00	495
1991 Dance of Water and Light	3,000	1991	225.00	225-245
1983 Early Winter In The Mountains	850	N/A	95.00	695-750
1987 An Elegant Couple (Wood Ducks)	1,000	N/A	125.00	295
1991 Embers at Dawn	3,500	1991	225.00	1500-1800
1983 End Of The Ridge	850	N/A	95.00	575-695
1990 Evening Light	2,250	1990	225.00	3000-3200
1995 Evening Star w/collector's edition book	9,500	1995	195.00	225-245
1993 Fire Dance	8,500	1993	235.00	540-600
1984 Free Flight	850	N/A	70.00	150
1999 Handsome (canvas)	1,250		295.00	295
2001 The Heart of Alaska	550		245.00	245
2001 The Heart of Alaska (canvas)	75		745.00	745
1987 High Creek Crossing	1,000	N/A	165.00	1350-1400
1989 High Light	1,250	1989	165.00	475-550
1986 High Trail At Sunset	1,000	N/A	125.00	700-750
1988 The Intruder	1,500	N/A	150.00	250
1993 Lake of the Shining Rocks	2,250	1993	235.00	400-625
1992 Lantern Light Print w Firelight Chapbook	10,000	1993	195.00	195
1989 Last Light of Winter	1,500	1989	175.00	1050-1250
1998 Last Touch of Light	975		595.00	595

YEAR ISSUE	EDITION LIMIT	YEAR RETD.	ISSUE PRICE	*QUOTE U.S.$
1999 A Light in the Wilderness (A Limited Ed. Lieuve de Luxe)	2,250		750.00	750
2000 The Long Autumn	950		270.00	270
1995 Midnight Fire	8,500	1996	245.00	195-225
1994 Moon Fire	7,500	1994	245.00	500-895
1987 Moon Shadows	1,500	N/A	135.00	150-185
1998 Moonbear Listens to the Earth	1,250	N/A	175.00	175
1994 Moonlit Flight on Christmas Night	2,750	1994	165.00	195
1996 Morning Light	8,000	1996	245.00	450-475
1986 Morning Solitude	850	N/A	115.00	595-700
1990 A Mountain Campfire	1,500	1990	195.00	3100-3200
1994 New Kid on the Rock	2,250	1996	185.00	215-225
1987 New Territory (Grizzly & Cubs)	1,000	N/A	135.00	495-550
1984 Noisy Neighbors	675	N/A	95.00	1395-1450
1984 Noisy Neighbors, remarque	25	N/A	127.50	1800
1994 North Country Shores	3,000	1994	225.00	325-525
1999 October Flight	950	N/A	195.00	195
1983 The Pass	850	N/A	95.00	750-1000
1989 Quiet Rain	1,500	N/A	165.00	900-995
1988 The Raptor's Watch	1,500	N/A	150.00	600-1000
1988 Return Of The Falcon	1,500	N/A	150.00	300-450
1993 Riparian Riches	2,500	1993	235.00	215-235
1992 River of Light (Geese)	2,950	N/A	225.00	225-235
1991 Secret Watch (Lynx)	2,250	N/A	150.00	150-165
1997 Sentinel of the Grove	450		195.00	195
1990 Silent Snows	1,750	N/A	210.00	400-450
1988 Snow Hunter	1,500	N/A	135.00	195-400
1986 Snowy Throne (C)	850	N/A	85.00	575-795
2000 Sounds of Sunset (canvas)	250		695.00	695
1993 The Spirit of Christmas	2,750	1993	165.00	495-550
1998 Steller Autumn	1,250	N/A	225.00	225
2000 Storm Over Tenaya Canyon	850		235.00	235
2000 Storm Over Tenaya Canyon (canvas)	125		895.00	895
1998 Sunrise in the Wallowas	950	1998	450.00	575-675
1996 Sunset Fire (PC)	N/A	1996	245.00	215-300
1995 Thunderbolt	7,000	N/A	235.00	695
1987 Twilight Snow (C)	950	N/A	85.00	450-600
1988 Uzumati: Great Bear of Yosemite	1,750	N/A	150.00	250
1992 Warmed by the View	8,500	1992	235.00	395-425
1992 Wilderness Welcome	8,500	N/A	235.00	800-1200
1992 Wildflower Suite (Hummingbird)	2,250	N/A	175.00	225-325
1997 Winter Shadows	2,500	1997	225.00	195-225
1992 Woodland Haven	2,500	N/A	195.00	240-250
1999 Yosemite Alpenglow	950		270.00	270

Marris - B. Marris

YEAR ISSUE	EDITION LIMIT	YEAR RETD.	ISSUE PRICE	*QUOTE U.S.$
1987 Above the Glacier	850	N/A	145.00	145
1986 Best Friends	850	N/A	85.00	235-295
1994 Big Gray's Barn and Bistro	1,000		125.00	125
1989 Bittersweet	1,000	N/A	135.00	135
2001 Black Magic	550		165.00	165
2001 Black Magic (canvas)	100		595.00	595
1990 Bugles and Trumpets!	1,000	N/A	175.00	175
1996 Catch The Wind	850		165.00	165
1992 The Comeback	1,250		175.00	175
1991 Cops & Robbers	1,000	N/A	165.00	165
1988 Courtship	850	N/A	145.00	145
1995 Dairy Queens	1,000		125.00	125
1995 The Dartmoor Ponies	1,000		165.00	165
1987 Desperados	850	N/A	135.00	135
1996 Dog Days	1,000	N/A	165.00	165
1991 End of the Season	1,000	1998	165.00	165
1985 The Fishing Lesson	1,000		145.00	145
1997 For the Love of Pete	950		130.00	130
1995 The Gift	1,000		125.00	125
2000 The Gifts of Spring (canvas)	150		695.00	695
1999 The Gold Thread	550		150.00	150
1987 Honey Creek Whitetales	850	N/A	145.00	145
1985 Kenai Dusk	1,000	N/A	145.00	800
1994 Lady Marmalade's Bed & Breakfast	1,000	N/A	125.00	125
1996 A Little Pig with a Big Heart	1,000	1996	95.00	95
1990 Mom's Shadow	1,000	N/A	165.00	165
1994 Moonshine	1,000		95.00	95
1989 New Beginnings	1,000	N/A	175.00	375
1990 Of Myth and Magic	1,500	N/A	175.00	175
1998 Old Faithful	750		125.00	125
1996 Other Footsteps	950	N/A	75.00	75
1989 The Playground Showoff	850	N/A	165.00	165
1992 Security Blanket	1,250		175.00	175
2001 Showdown	550		175.00	175

*Quotes have been rounded up to nearest dollar

YEAR ISSUE	EDITION LIMIT	YEAR RETD.	ISSUE PRICE	*QUOTE U.S.$
2001 Showdown (canvas)	50		595.00	595
1993 Spring Fever	1,000		165.00	165
1991 The Stillness (Grizzzly & Cubs)	1,000	N/A	165.00	165
1992 Sun Bath	1,000		95.00	95
1997 Sun Splashed	750		130.00	130
1992 To Stand and Endure	1,000	N/A	195.00	275-395
1991 Under the Morning Star	1,500		175.00	175
1998 Undercover	750		145.00	145
1988 Waiting For the Freeze	1,000	N/A	125.00	125
1995 Where Best Friends Are Welcome	850	1996	95.00	195
1999 Wolfsong	550		165.00	165

McCarthy - F. McCarthy

YEAR ISSUE	EDITION LIMIT	YEAR RETD.	ISSUE PRICE	*QUOTE U.S.$
1996 After the Council	1,000		195.00	195
1996 After the Council	550		850.00	850
1984 After the Dust Storm	1,000	N/A	145.00	295
1982 Alert	1,000	N/A	135.00	135
1984 Along the West Fork	1,000	N/A	175.00	225
1998 Ambush	750		195.00	195
1995 Ambush at the Ancient Rocks	1,000	1998	225.00	225
1978 Ambush, The	1,000	N/A	125.00	300
1982 Apache Scout	1,000	N/A	165.00	165
1988 Apache Trackers (C)	1,000	N/A	95.00	95
1992 The Art of Frank McCarthy	10,418	N/A	60.00	60
1982 Attack on the Wagon Train	1,400	N/A	150.00	150
1977 The Beaver Men	1,000	N/A	75.00	350
1980 Before the Charge	1,000	N/A	115.00	150
1978 Before the Norther	1,000	N/A	90.00	325
1990 Below The Breaking Dawn	1,250	N/A	225.00	225
1994 Beneath the Cliff (Petraglyphs)	1,500		295.00	295
1989 Big Medicine	1,000	N/A	225.00	350
1983 Blackfeet Raiders	1,000	N/A	90.00	200
1992 Breaking the Moonlit Silence	650	N/A	375.00	375
1986 The Buffalo Runners	1,000	N/A	195.00	170
1997 Buffalo Soldier Advance	1,500		225.00	225
1980 Burning the Way Station	1,000	N/A	125.00	250
1993 By the Ancient Trails They Passed	1,000	N/A	245.00	245
1989 Canyon Lands	1,250	N/A	225.00	225
1982 The Challenge	1,000	N/A	175.00	275-450
1995 Charge of the Buffalo Soldiers	1,000	1995	195.00	285
1985 Charging the Challenger	1,000	N/A	150.00	425
1991 The Chase	1,000		225.00	225
1986 Children of the Raven	1,000	N/A	185.00	550
1987 Chiricahua Raiders	1,000	N/A	165.00	225
1977 Comanche Moon	1,000	N/A	75.00	235
1992 Comanche Raider-Bronze	100		812.50	813
1986 Comanche War Trail	1,000	N/A	165.00	170
1989 The Coming Of The Iron Horse	1,500	N/A	225.00	225
1989 The Coming Of The Iron Horse (Print/Pewter Train Special Pub. Ed.)	100	N/A	1500.00	1600-2150
1981 The Coup	1,000	N/A	125.00	500
1998 The Crossing	850		185.00	185
1981 Crossing the Divide (The Old West)	1,500	N/A	850.00	450-750
1984 The Decoys	450	N/A	325.00	500
1977 Distant Thunder	1,500	N/A	75.00	500
1989 Down From The Mountains	1,500	N/A	245.00	245
1986 The Drive (C)	1,000	N/A	95.00	95-175
1977 Dust Stained Posse	1,000	N/A	75.00	650
1985 The Fireboat	1,000	N/A	175.00	175
1994 Flashes of Lighting-Thunder of Hooves	550		435.00	435
1987 Following the Herds	1,000	N/A	195.00	265-475
1980 Forbidden Land	1,000	N/A	125.00	125
1978 The Fording	1,000		75.00	250
1987 From the Rim	1,000	N/A	225.00	225
1981 Headed North	1,000	N/A	150.00	275
1992 Heading Back	1,000		225.00	225
1995 His Wealth	850		225.00	225
1990 Hoka Hey: Sioux War Cry	1,250	N/A	225.00	225
1987 The Hostile Land	1,000	N/A	225.00	235
1976 The Hostiles	1,000	N/A	75.00	475
1984 Hostiles, signed	1,000	N/A	55.00	55
1974 The Hunt	1,000	N/A	75.00	450
1988 In Pursuit of the White Buffalo	1,500	N/A	225.00	425-525
1992 In the Land of the Ancient Ones	1,250	N/A	245.00	265
1983 In The Land Of The Sparrow Hawk People	1,000	N/A	165.00	175
1987 In The Land Of The Winter Hawk	1,000	N/A	225.00	300
1978 In The Pass	1,500	N/A	90.00	265
1997 In The Shallows	1,000		185.00	185
1985 The Last Crossing	550	N/A	350.00	350
1989 The Last Stand: Little Big Horn	1,500	N/A	225.00	225
1984 Leading the Charge, signed	1,000	N/A	55.00	80
1974 Lone Sentinel	1,000	N/A	55.00	1100
1979 The Loner	1,000	N/A	75.00	225
1974 Long Column	1,000	N/A	75.00	400
1985 The Long Knives	1,000	N/A	175.00	350
1989 Los Diablos	1,250	N/A	225.00	225
1995 Medicine Man	850	1996	165.00	165
1983 Moonlit Trail	1,000	N/A	90.00	295
1992 Navajo Ponies Comanchie Warriors	1,000		225.00	225
1978 Night Crossing	1,000	N/A	75.00	200
1974 The Night They Needed a Good Ribbon Man	1,000	N/A	65.00	300
1977 An Old Time Mountain Man	1,000	N/A	65.00	200
1990 On the Old North Trail (Triptych)	650	N/A	550.00	675
1979 On the Warpath	1,000	N/A	75.00	150-175
1983 Out Of The Mist They Came	1,000	N/A	165.00	235
1990 Out Of The Windswept Ramparts	1,250	N/A	225.00	225
1976 Packing In	1,000	N/A	65.00	400
1998 Patrol at Broken Finger	750		165.00	165
1991 Pony Express	1,000		225.00	225
1979 The Prayer	1,500	N/A	90.00	450
1991 The Pursuit	650	N/A	550.00	550
1981 Race with the Hostiles	1,000	N/A	135.00	135
1987 Red Bull's War Party	1,000	N/A	165.00	165
1979 Retreat to Higher Ground	2,000	N/A	90.00	240-360
1975 Returning Raiders	1,000	N/A	75.00	300
1997 The Roar of the Falls	950		195.00	195
1980 Roar of the Norther	1,000	N/A	90.00	200
1977 Robe Signal	850	N/A	60.00	375
1988 Saber Charge	2,250	N/A	225.00	225-250
1984 The Savage Taunt	1,000	N/A	225.00	275
1985 Scouting The Long Knives	1,400	N/A	195.00	270
1993 Shadows of Warriors (3 Print Suite)	1,000		225.00	225
1994 Show of Defiance	1,000		195.00	195
1993 Sighting the Intruders	1,000		225.00	225
1978 Single File	1,000	N/A	75.00	850
1976 Sioux Warriors	650	N/A	55.00	250
1975 Smoke Was Their Ally	1,000	N/A	75.00	225
1980 Snow Moon	1,000	N/A	115.00	225
1995 Splitting the Herd	550		465.00	465
1986 Spooked	1,400	N/A	195.00	195
1981 Surrounded	1,000	N/A	150.00	350-395
1975 The Survivor	1,000	N/A	65.00	275
1980 A Time Of Decision	1,150	N/A	125.00	225
1978 To Battle	1,000	N/A	75.00	350-400
1985 The Traders	1,000	N/A	195.00	195
1996 The Trek	850		175.00	175
1980 The Trooper	1,000	N/A	90.00	165
1988 Turning The Leaders	1,500	N/A	225.00	225
1983 Under Attack	5,676	N/A	125.00	375-500
1981 Under Hostile Fire	1,000	N/A	150.00	160
1975 Waiting for the Escort	1,000	N/A	75.00	100
1976 The Warrior	650	N/A	55.00	350
1982 The Warriors	1,000	N/A	150.00	150
1984 Watching the Wagons	1,400	N/A	175.00	750
1995 The Way of the Ancient Migrations	1,250		245.00	245
1987 When Omens Turn Bad	1,000	N/A	165.00	425-500
1992 When the Land Was Theirs	1,000		225.00	225
1992 Where Ancient Ones Had Hunted	1,000	N/A	245.00	245
1992 Where Others Had Passed	1,000	N/A	245.00	245
1986 Where Tracks Will Be Lost	550	N/A	350.00	350
1982 Whirling He Raced to Meet the Challenge	1,000	N/A	175.00	400-525
1991 The Wild Ones	1,000	N/A	225.00	225
1990 Winter Trail	1,500	N/A	235.00	235
1993 With Pistols Drawn	1,000		195.00	195

Mitchell - D. Mitchell

YEAR ISSUE	EDITION LIMIT	YEAR RETD.	ISSUE PRICE	*QUOTE U.S.$
1994 Bonding Years	550		175.00	175
1993 Country Church	550		175.00	175
1997 Fort Scott Soldier	850	N/A	150.00	150
1995 Innocence	1,000		150.00	150
1995 Let Us Pray	850		175.00	175
1993 Psalms 4:1	550	N/A	195.00	195
1996 Return For Honor	850		150.00	150
1992 Rowena	550	N/A	195.00	300

Mo Da-Feng - M. Da-Feng

YEAR ISSUE	EDITION LIMIT	YEAR RETD.	ISSUE PRICE	*QUOTE U.S.$
1990 Family Boat	888		235.00	235
1993 First Journey	650		150.00	150

GRAPHICS

YEAR ISSUE	EDITION LIMIT	YEAR RETD.	ISSUE PRICE	*QUOTE U.S.$
1989 Fishing Hut	888		235.00	235
1994 Ocean Mist	850		150.00	150
Morrissey - D. Morrissey				
2000 Father Christmas	2,000		125.00	125
2000 Father Christmas (canvas)	100		495.00	495
2000 The Magic Door	950		175.00	175
2001 The Weathermill	550		175.00	175
2001 The Weathermill (canvas)	75		695.00	695
Palmore - T. Palmore				
2001 The Duchess of Wister (canvas)	75		225.00	225
2001 Sheeba (canvas)	75		1495.00	1495
Parker, Ed. - E. Parker				
1996 Acadia Tea and Tennis Society	850		135.00	135
1995 The Glorious 4th	850		150.00	150
1996 St. Duffer's Golf Club	850		135.00	135
1995 A Visit From St. Nicholas	850		125.00	125
1997 Windjammer Days	850		125.00	125
Parker, Ron. - R. Parker				
1995 The Breakfast Club	850		125.00	125
1995 Coastal Morning	850		195.00	195
1995 Evening Solitude	850		195.00	195
1994 Forest Flight	850		195.00	195
1997 Gliding Swan	650		145.00	145
1994 Grizzlies at the Falls	850		225.00	225
1994 Morning Flight	4,000		20.00	20
1996 Summer Memories	850		125.00	125
1996 Summer Reading	850		125.00	125
1995 Tea For Two	850		125.00	125
Phillips - W. Phillips				
2001 Accompaniment to the Symphony of Spring	750		175.00	175
2001 Accompaniment to the Symphony of Spring (canvas)	550		695.00	695
1982 Advantage Eagle	1,000	N/A	135.00	300
1992 Alone No More	850		195.00	195
1988 America on the Move	1,500	N/A	185.00	150-185
1994 Among the Columns of Thor	1,000		295.00	295
1993 And Now the Trap	850		175.00	175
1999 And The Light Shall Prevail	950		195.00	195
1998 The Beginning of the End	1,000		365.00	365
1999 Cape Neddick Dawn	950	N/A	195.00	195
1997 Caping the Tico	950		275.00	275
1986 Changing of the Guard	500	N/A	100.00	100
1993 Chasing the Daylight	850	N/A	185.00	185
1994 Christmas Leave When Dreams Come True	1,500	N/A	185.00	185-220
1996 Clipper at the Gate	850		185.00	185
1986 Confrontation at Beachy Head	1,000	N/A	150.00	150
1999 Courtyard	950		165.00	165
1991 Dauntless Against a Rising Sun	850	N/A	195.00	195
1995 Dawn The World Forever Changed	1,000	1996	347.50	348
1998 December of '45	1,500		195.00	195
1995 The Dream Fulfilled	1,750	N/A	195.00	200
1998 Dust Off: Angels of Mercy Book	1,450		265.00	265
1997 Early Morning Visitors	1,250		195.00	195
1999 Evening Song (canvas)	550	N/A	595.00	595-1400
1991 Fifty Miles Out	1,000		175.00	175
1983 The Giant Begins to Stir	1,250	N/A	185.00	1100-1400
1990 Going in Hot w/Book	1,500		250.00	250
1985 Heading For Trouble	1,000	N/A	125.00	250
1984 Hellfire Corner	1,225	N/A	185.00	600
1984 Hellfire Corner, remarque	25	N/A	225.80	800
1998 Hill Country Homecoming	1,250		195.00	195
2001 Home Is The Hunter	550		195.00	195
2001 Home Is The Hunter (canvas)	75		795.00	795
1990 Hunter Becomes the Hunted w/video	1,500	N/A	265.00	265
1992 I Could Never Be So Lucky Again	850	N/A	295.00	750
1993 If Only in My Dreams	1,000	N/A	175.00	750-1000
1984 Into the Teeth of the Tiger	975	N/A	135.00	925
1984 Into the Teeth of the Tiger, remarque	25	N/A	167.50	2000
1994 Into the Throne Room of God w/book "The Glory of Flight"	750	N/A	195.00	600
1991 Intruder Outbound	1,000		225.00	225
1991 Last Chance	1,000	N/A	165.00	350
1985 Lest We Forget	1,250	N/A	195.00	250
1994 Lethal Encounter	1,000		225.00	225

YEAR ISSUE	EDITION LIMIT	YEAR RETD.	ISSUE PRICE	*QUOTE U.S.$
1996 The Lightkeepers Gift	1,000	N/A	175.00	175
1988 The Long Green Line	3,500	N/A	185.00	185
1992 The Long Ride Home (P-51D)	850	N/A	195.00	195
1991 Low Pass For the Home Folks, BP	1,000	N/A	175.00	175
1996 The Moonwatchers	1,750	1998	185.00	185-400
1986 Next Time Get 'Em All	1,500	N/A	225.00	275
1989 No Empty Bunks Tonight	1,500	N/A	165.00	165
1989 No Flying Today	1,500		185.00	185
1999 On Wings and a Prayer	950		175.00	175
1989 Over the Top	1,000		165.00	165
1985 The Phantoms and the Wizard	850	N/A	145.00	800
1992 Ploesti: Into the Fire and Fury	850		195.00	195
2000 Point Bonita: Last Light	950		185.00	185
1987 Range Wars	1,000	N/A	160.00	160
2000 Rejoice	750		175.00	175
2000 Rejoice (canvas)	550		695.00	695
1996 Return of the Red Gremlin	1,000		350.00	350
1987 Shore Birds at Point Lobos	1,250	N/A	175.00	175
1989 Sierra Hotel	1,250	N/A	175.00	175
1997 Spring Fling	1,250		195.00	195
1998 The Storm Watchers	1,250		195.00	195
1995 Summer of '45	1,750	1998	195.00	1000
1998 Sunset Sentinels	550		695.00	695
1987 Sunward We Climb	1,000	N/A	175.00	175
1983 Those Clouds Won't Help You Now	625	N/A	135.00	500
1983 Those Clouds Won't Help You Now, remarque	25	N/A	275.00	675
1987 Those Last Critical Moments	1,250	N/A	185.00	300
1993 Threading the Eye of the Needle	1,000		195.00	195
1996 Thunder and Lightning	850		185.00	185
1996 Thunder in the Canyon	1,000	N/A	165.00	600
1990 A Time of Eagles	1,250	1996	245.00	245
1989 Time to Head Home	1,500	N/A	165.00	165
1986 Top Cover for the Straggler	1,000	N/A	145.00	325
1983 Two Down, One to Go	3,000	N/A	15.00	15
2000 Victory Pass	550		175.00	175
1982 Welcome Home Yank	1,000	N/A	135.00	800
1993 When Prayers Are Answered	850		245.00	245
1991 When You See Zeros, Fight Em'	1,500	N/A	245.00	245
2000 Wintering Over	750		175.00	175
2000 Wintering Over (canvas)	550		695.00	695
Pomm - Pomm				
1999 Above It All	150		395.00	395
2000 Courtyard Romance	450		200.00	200
1999 A Perfect Moment	450		200.00	200
Poskas - P. Poskas				
1997 Island Sea	650		175.00	175
1996 Yellow Moon Rising	850		175.00	175
Presse - H. Presse				
1998 Dance of the Sun	550		125.00	125
2000 Dressed In Ribbon's Fair	550		150.00	150
1999 The Flower Girl	550		145.00	145
1999 The Gardeners	550		150.00	150
2001 In Full Bloom	550		160.00	160
1998 Oliver's Porch	550		125.00	125
1998 Stay This Moment	550		125.00	125
2001 Sunlight	550		150.00	150
1998 The Victorian	550		125.00	125
Prosek - J. Prosek				
1996 Alaskan Rainbow Trout	1,000		125.00	125
1996 Brook Trout	1,000		125.00	125
1997 Yellowstone Cutthroat Trout	1,000		125.00	125
Reynolds - J. Reynolds				
1994 Arizona Cowboys	850	N/A	195.00	245
1994 Cold Country, Hot Coffee	1,000		185.00	185
1994 The Henry	850	N/A	195.00	195
1995 Mystic of the Plains	1,000		195.00	195
1994 Quiet Place	1,000	N/A	185.00	195
1994 Spring Showers	1,000		225.00	225
1996 A Strange Sign (canvas)	550		750.00	750
1996 The Summit	950		195.00	195
1998 Swing Shift	450		495.00	495
Riddick - R. Riddick				
1999 Early to Bed, Early to Rise	550		185.00	185
1998 The Muddy Arbuckle Café	550		185.00	185
1998 Prelude to the Dance	550		185.00	185

Collectors' Information Bureau   *Quotes have been rounded up to nearest dollar

Riley - K. Riley

YEAR ISSUE	EDITION LIMIT	YEAR RETD.	ISSUE PRICE	*QUOTE U.S.$
1997 As One (Canvas print)	550		395.00	395
1997 Ceremonial Regalia	550		495.00	495
1999 Crow Fair	550		185.00	185
1998 Legend of the Mandan (serlith)	250		750.00	750
1998 The Red Flute (serlith)	250		750.00	750
1998 Split Horn Bonnet	550		425.00	425

Simpkins - J. Simpkins

YEAR ISSUE	EDITION LIMIT	YEAR RETD.	ISSUE PRICE	*QUOTE U.S.$
1994 All My Love	850		125.00	125
1993 Angels	850		225.00	225
1994 Gold Falls	1,750		195.00	195
1995 Mrs. Tenderhart	1,000		175.00	175
1995 Pavane in Gold	2,500		175.00	175
1996 Pavane von Khint	1,000		195.00	195
1994 Reverence For Life w/border & card	750	N/A	175.00	335
1994 Reverence For Life w/frame	100	N/A	600.00	600
1995 Where Love Resides (Premiere Ed.)	1,000		450.00	450
1995 Where Love Resides (Studio Ed.)	1,000		225.00	225

Smith - T. Smith

YEAR ISSUE	EDITION LIMIT	YEAR RETD.	ISSUE PRICE	*QUOTE U.S.$
1992 The Challenger	1,300		185.00	185
1995 The Refuge	1,000		245.00	245

Solberg - M. Solberg

YEAR ISSUE	EDITION LIMIT	YEAR RETD.	ISSUE PRICE	*QUOTE U.S.$
1997 Rufous and Roses	550		150.00	150

Spirin - G. Spirin

YEAR ISSUE	EDITION LIMIT	YEAR RETD.	ISSUE PRICE	*QUOTE U.S.$
1997 Carnival in Venice (Inkjet)	200		395.00	395
1997 Tournament of Honor	200		395.00	395

Swindle - L. Swindle

YEAR ISSUE	EDITION LIMIT	YEAR RETD.	ISSUE PRICE	*QUOTE U.S.$
2000 Be It Unto Me	950	N/A	135.00	135-195
2000 Hold on Tight	1,500		95.00	95
2000 The Lamb of God	950		135.00	135
2000 The Lamb of God (canvas)	350		595.00	595

Terpning - H. Terpning

YEAR ISSUE	EDITION LIMIT	YEAR RETD.	ISSUE PRICE	*QUOTE U.S.$
1992 Against the Coldmaker	1,000	1992	195.00	195
1993 The Apache Fire Makers	1,000	1993	235.00	235
1993 Army Regulations	1,000		235.00	235
1997 Before the Little Big Horn	1,000		195.00	195
1987 Blackfeet Among the Aspen	1,000	1987	225.00	250
1985 Blackfeet Spectators	475	1985	350.00	1200-2250
2001 Blessing From The Medicine Man (canvas)	N/A		950.00	950
1988 Blood Man	1,250	1988	95.00	300
2001 The Bonnet Game (canvas)	650		750.00	750
1982 CA Set Pony Soldiers/Warriors	1,000	1982	200.00	450-650
1985 The Cache	1,000	N/A	175.00	175
1992 Capture of the Horse Bundle	1,250	1998	235.00	395
2000 Cheyenne Mother (canvas)	600		695.00	695
1982 Chief Joseph Rides to Surrender	1,000	1982	150.00	2600-3000
1996 Color of Sun	1,000	1998	175.00	175-350
1986 Comanche Spoilers	1,000	N/A	195.00	195
2000 Council of Chiefs (canvas)	950		850.00	850
1990 Cree Finery	1,000	1998	225.00	375
1996 Crossing Below the Falls	1,000	1996	245.00	245
1983 Crossing Medicine Lodge Creek	1,000	1983	150.00	200-300
1994 Crow Camp, 1864	1,000	1994	235.00	235
1997 Crow Pipe Ceremony	975	1998	895.00	895-2200
1984 Crow Pipe Holder	1,000	N/A	150.00	150
1991 Digging in at Sappa Creek MW	650	1991	375.00	375
1994 The Feast	1,850	1994	245.00	285
1992 Four Sacred Drummers	1,000	1992	225.00	225
1997 Gold Seekers to the Black Hills'	1,000	1997	245.00	245
1999 Grandfather Speaks (canvas)	975		875.00	875
1998 Holy Man of the Blackfoot	975	1998	895.00	800-895
1988 Hope Springs Eternal-Ghost Dance	2,250	N/A	225.00	475-800
1998 Horse Feathers	975		495.00	495
1994 Isdzan-Apache Woman	1,000	1994	175.00	195
1991 The Last Buffalo	1,000		225.00	225
1991 Leader of Men	1,250	1991	235.00	300-500
1984 The Long Shot, signed	1,000	1984	55.00	75
1984 Medicine Man of the Cheyene	450	1984	350.00	2895-3195
1993 Medicine Pipe	1,000	1993	150.00	185
1999 Offerings to the Little People	975		875.00	875
2000 On The Edge of the World	850		225.00	225
1985 One Man's Castle	1,000	N/A	150.00	150
1995 Opening the Sacred Bundle (canvas)	550	1995	850.00	2295-3000
1983 Paints	1,000	1983	140.00	200
1992 Passing Into Womanhood	650	1992	375.00	400-1950
1987 The Ploy	1,000	1987	195.00	600-695
1992 Prairie Knights	1,000	1992	225.00	225
1996 Prairie Shade	1,000		225.00	225
1987 Preparing for the Sun Dance	1,000	1987	175.00	300-375
1988 Pride of the Cheyene	1,250	N/A	195.00	195
1993 Profile of Wisdom	1,000		175.00	175
1985 The Scouts of General Crook	1,000	1985	175.00	250-275
1989 Scout's Report	1,250	N/A	225.00	225
1988 Search For the Pass	1,000	1988	225.00	250
1982 Search For the Renegades	1,000	1982	150.00	195
1989 Shepherd of the Plains Cameo	1,250	N/A	125.00	125
1982 Shield of Her Husband	1,000	1982	150.00	600-900
1983 Shoshonis	1,250	1983	85.00	200-225
1985 The Signal	1,250	1985	90.00	400-600
1999 Signals in the Wind	750		225.00	225
1981 Sioux Flag Carrier	1,000	1981	125.00	165
1981 Small Comfort	1,000	1981	135.00	400-450
1993 Soldier Hat	1,000	N/A	235.00	235
1981 The Spectators	1,000	1981	135.00	195-295
2001 Spirit of the Plains People	950		295.00	295
1994 Spirit of the Rainmaker	1,500		235.00	235
1983 Staff Carrier	1,250	1983	90.00	550
1986 Status Symbols	1,000	1986	185.00	1250-1600
1981 Stones that Speak	1,000	1981	150.00	950-1200
1989 The Storyteller w/Video & Book	1,500	1989	950.00	1150-1500
1992 The Strength of Eagles	1,250	N/A	235.00	235
1988 Sunday Best	1,250	N/A	195.00	195
1995 Talking Robe	1,250		235.00	235
1990 Telling of the Legends	1,250	1990	225.00	900-1200
1986 Thunderpipe and the Holy Man	550	1986	350.00	500-800
1997 To Capture Enemy Horses	950		225.00	225
1995 Trading Post at Chadron Creek	1,000		225.00	225
1991 Transferring the Medicine Shield	850	1991	375.00	1300-1800
1996 The Trophy (canvas)	1,000	N/A	925.00	925
1981 The Victors	1,000	1981	150.00	825-1100
1985 The Warning	1,650	1985	175.00	550-750
1986 Watching the Column	1,250	1986	90.00	400
1998 The Weather Dancer Dream	1,000		225.00	225
1990 When Careless Spelled Disaster	1,000	1990	225.00	350
1987 Winter Coat	1,250	1987	95.00	175
1996 With Mother Earth	1,250	N/A	245.00	245
1984 Woman of the Sioux	1,000	1984	165.00	925-1200

Townsend - B. Townsend

YEAR ISSUE	EDITION LIMIT	YEAR RETD.	ISSUE PRICE	*QUOTE U.S.$
1994 Autumn Hillside	1,000		175.00	175
1993 Dusk	1,250		195.00	195
1995 Gathering of the Herd	1,000		195.00	195
1993 Hailstorm Creek	1,250		195.00	195
1994 Mountain Light	1,000		195.00	195
1992 Open Ridge	1,500	N/A	225.00	179-225
1993 Out of the Shadows	1,500	1998	195.00	195
1996 Out of the Valley	850		185.00	185
1992 Riverbend	1,000	N/A	185.00	300

Weiss - J. Weiss

YEAR ISSUE	EDITION LIMIT	YEAR RETD.	ISSUE PRICE	*QUOTE U.S.$
1995 All Is Well	1,250		165.00	165
1984 Basset Hound Puppies	1,000	N/A	65.00	200-300
2001 Before the Tempest	550		165.00	165
2001 Before the Tempest (canvas)	100		550.00	550
1988 Black Labrador Head Study Cameo	1,000		90.00	90
1984 Cocker Spaniel Puppies	1,000	N/A	75.00	200-295
1999 Cold Nose, Warm Heart	950		125.00	125
1992 Cuddle Time	850		95.00	95
1998 Double Trouble	1,450		95.00	95
2000 Evening Companions	950		165.00	165
2000 Evening Companions (canvas)	100		495.00	495
1999 Facing The Storm Together	950		125.00	125
1993 A Feeling of Warmth	1,000	N/A	165.00	475
1994 Forever Friends	1,000	1994	95.00	255
1998 Golden Moments	750		125.00	125
1983 Golden Retriever Puppies	1,000	N/A	65.00	900
1988 Goldens at the Shore	850	N/A	145.00	525-725
1997 Good As Gold	1,250	1998	95.00	95-150
1995 I Didn't Do It	1,250	1998	125.00	125
1982 Lab Puppies	1,000	N/A	65.00	195-250
1996 New Friends	1,000		125.00	195
1992 No Swimming Lessons Today	1,000	1998	140.00	140
1984 Old English Sheepdog Puppies	1,000	N/A	65.00	200-250
1993 Old Friends	1,000	1993	95.00	700-800
1986 One Morning in October	850	N/A	125.00	525-650
2000 Our Favorite Place	950		165.00	165

GRAPHICS

YEAR ISSUE	EDITION LIMIT	YEAR RETD.	ISSUE PRICE	*QUOTE U.S.$
2000 Our Favorite Place (canvas)	100		495.00	495
1985 Persian Kitten	1,000	N/A	65.00	80-95
1999 Pick of the Litter	1,250		95.00	95
1982 Rebel & Soda	1,000	N/A	45.00	135
1999 Retrievers	950		110.00	110
1997 Storytime	850		95.00	95
1998 Three's Company	1,250		95.00	95
2001 True Companions	550		165.00	165
2001 True Companions (canvas)	100		550.00	550
1991 Wake Up Call	850		165.00	165
1988 Yellow Labrador Head Study Cameo	1,000		90.00	90

Weistling - M. Weistling

2000 The Invitation	Open		125.00	125

Williams - B.D. Williams

1993 Avant Garde S&N	500	N/A	60.00	60
1993 Avant Garde unsigned	2,603	N/A	30.00	30

Wootton - F. Wootton

1990 Adlertag, 15 August 1940 & Video	1,500	N/A	245.00	245
1993 April Morning:France, 1918	850		245.00	245
1983 The Battle of Britain	850	N/A	150.00	300
1988 Encounter with the Red Baron	850	N/A	165.00	200
1985 Huntsmen and Hounds	650		115.00	115
1982 Knights of the Sky	850	N/A	165.00	375
1993 Last Combat of the Red Baron	850		185.00	185
1992 The Last of the First F. Wooten	850		235.00	235
1994 Peenemunde	850		245.00	245
1986 The Spitfire Legend	850	N/A	195.00	195

Wysocki - C. Wysocki

1988 The Americana Bowl	3,500		295.00	295
1983 Amish Neighbors	1,000		150.00	1100-1200
1989 Another Year At Sea	2,500		175.00	450-900
1983 Applebutter Makers	1,000		135.00	1200-1350
1987 Bach's Magnificat in D Minor	2,250	N/A	150.00	800-825
1991 Beauty And The Beast	2,000	N/A	125.00	125-175
1990 Belly Warmers	2,500		150.00	195
1984 Bird House Cameo	1,000	N/A	85.00	275-295
1985 Birds of a Feather	1,250		145.00	950-1150
1989 Bostonians And Beans (PC)	6,711	N/A	225.00	625-650
1979 Butternut Farms	1,000		75.00	1350-1450
1980 Caleb's Buggy Barn	1,000	N/A	80.00	395-435
1984 Cape Cod Cold Fish Party	1,000	N/A	150.00	150-195
1986 Carnival Capers	620	N/A	200.00	200
1981 Carver Coggins	1,000	N/A	145.00	1050-1150
1989 Christmas Greeting	11,000	N/A	125.00	100-125
1982 Christmas Print, 1982	2,000	N/A	80.00	500
1984 Chumbuddies, signed	1,000		55.00	55
1985 Clammers at Hodge's Horn	1,000	N/A	150.00	1200-1250
1983 Commemorative Print, 1983	2,000	N/A	55.00	55
1983 Commemorative Print, 1984	2,000		55.00	55
1984 Commemorative Print, 1985	2,000		55.00	55
1985 Commemorative Print, 1986	2,000		55.00	55
1984 Cotton Country	1,000	N/A	150.00	350-375
1983 Country Race	1,000	N/A	150.00	235-350
1997 Cow (framed)	150		135.00	135
1986 Daddy's Coming Home	1,250	N/A	150.00	875-895
1987 Dahalia Dinalhaven Makes a Dory Deal	2,250	N/A	150.00	425-475
1986 Dancing Pheasant Farms	1,750	N/A	165.00	405-525
1980 Derby Square	1,000	N/A	90.00	1000-1100
1986 Devilbelly Bay	1,000	N/A	145.00	250-395
1986 Devilstone Harbor/An American Celebration (Print & Book)	3,500	N/A	195.00	375-400
1989 Dreamers	3,000	N/A	175.00	425-450
1992 Ethel the Gourmet	10,179	N/A	150.00	500-700
1979 Fairhaven by the Sea	1,000	N/A	75.00	700-750
1988 Feathered Critics	2,500	N/A	150.00	150
1997 Fox Hill Farms (framed)	150		135.00	135
1979 Fox Run	1,000	N/A	75.00	950-1100
1984 The Foxy Fox Outfoxes the Fox Hunters	1,500	N/A	150.00	395-425
1992 Frederick the Literate	6,500	N/A	150.00	2500
1989 Fun Lovin' Silly Folks	3,000	N/A	185.00	475-495
1984 The Gang's All Here	Open		65.00	65
1984 The Gang's All Here, remarque	250		90.00	90
1992 Gay Head Light	2,500		165.00	165
1997 Hawk River Hollow (framed)	150		135.00	135
1986 Hickory Haven Canal	1,500	N/A	165.00	650-900
1988 Home Is My Sailor	2,500	N/A	150.00	150

YEAR ISSUE	EDITION LIMIT	YEAR RETD.	ISSUE PRICE	*QUOTE U.S.$
1985 I Love America	2,000		20.00	20
1990 Jingle Bell Teddy and Friends	5,000		125.00	125
1980 Jolly Hill Farms	1,000	N/A	75.00	650-850
1997 Kitty Treat (framed)	150		135.00	135
1986 Lady Liberty's Independence Day Enterprising Immigrants	1,500	N/A	140.00	375-525
1992 Love Letter From Laramie	1,500		150.00	150
1989 The Memory Maker	2,500	1998	165.00	165-195
1985 Merrymakers Serenade	1,250	N/A	135.00	135-175
1986 Mr. Swallobark	2,000	N/A	145.00	1300-1550
1982 The Nantucket	1,000	N/A	145.00	275
1997 Nantucket Winds (framed)	150		135.00	135
1981 Olde America	1,500	N/A	125.00	450-500
1981 Page's Bake Shoppe	1,000	N/A	115.00	275-350
1997 Peppercricket Farms (framed)	150		135.00	135
1997 Pickwick Cottage (framed)	150		135.00	135
1983 Plum Island Sound, signed	1,000	N/A	55.00	675
1983 Plum Island Sound, unsigned	Open	N/A	40.00	40
1981 Prairie Wind Flowers	1,000	N/A	125.00	1375-1495
1992 Proud Little Angler	2,750	N/A	150.00	200
1994 Remington w/Book-Heartland	15,000	1998	195.00	250-300
1990 Robin Hood	2,000		165.00	165
1991 Rockland Breakwater Light	2,500	N/A	165.00	165-235
1985 Salty Witch Bay	475	N/A	350.00	2400
1991 Sea Captain's Wife Abiding	1,500	N/A	150.00	150-165
1979 Shall We?	1,000	N/A	75.00	1175-1450
1982 Sleepy Town West	1,500	N/A	150.00	575-650
1984 Storin' Up	450	N/A	325.00	750-1900
1982 Sunset Hills, Texas Wildcatters	1,000	N/A	125.00	150-195
1984 Sweetheart Chessmate	1,000	N/A	95.00	575-1200
1983 Tea by the Sea	1,000	N/A	145.00	950-1350
1997 Teddy Bear Express (framed)	150		135.00	135
1993 The Three Sisters of Nauset, 1880	2,500	N/A	165.00	165-325
1987 'Twas the Twilight Before Christmas	7,500	N/A	95.00	150-195
1984 A Warm Christmas Love	3,951	N/A	80.00	200-375
1990 Wednesday Night Checkers	2,500	1998	175.00	200-295
1991 West Quoddy Head Light, Maine	2,500	1998	165.00	165-240
1990 Where The Bouys Are	2,750	N/A	175.00	175-195
1991 Whistle Stop Christmas	5,000		125.00	125
1980 Yankee Wink Hollow	1,000	N/A	95.00	1000-1350
1987 Yearning For My Captain	2,000	N/A	150.00	325-1350
1987 You've Been So Long at Sea, Horatio	2,500	N/A	150.00	215-295

Young - C. Young

1999 Japanese Apples	550		145.00	145
2000 Tuscan Cloud	550		175.00	175
1999 Tuscan Primrose	550		145.00	145
2000 Tuscan Villa	550		270.00	270

Hadley House

Agnew - A. Agnew

1997 American Odyssey	750		125.00	125
2000 A Bend in the Road	999		150.00	150
1997 Birds of a Feather	999		50.00	50
1997 Quick Silver	999	1998	75.00	235
1997 Time Well Spent	999		150.00	150

Barnhouse - D. Barnhouse

1997 Every Boys' Dream	1,950		150.00	150
1997 A Finishing Touch	1,950		150.00	150
1997 Horsepower	1,950		150.00	150
2000 Indian Summer	1,950		150.00	150
1997 Spring Cleaning	1,950	1997	150.00	220-265
1997 Sunset Strip	1,950		150.00	150
2000 Taking the Back Roads	1,250		100.00	100
1997 The Warmth of Home	1,950		150.00	150

Bogle - C. Bogle

1997 The Colors of Autumn	999	1997	75.00	75
1997 Crossing Paths	999		125.00	125
1997 A Golden Moment	999	1998	100.00	350

Bush - D. Bush

1997 Cabin Fever	1,250		125.00	125
1997 Evening Run	999	1997	125.00	125-295
1997 Legends of The Lake	1,250	1998	125.00	125
1994 Moondance	999	1995	125.00	220-315
2000 Morning Run	1,250		150.00	150
1997 Once in a Life Time	999		125.00	125
2000 Silent Shores	1,250		125.00	125
1996 Still of the Night	1,250	1997	125.00	195-215

*Quotes have been rounded up to nearest dollar

YEAR ISSUE	EDITION LIMIT	YEAR RETD.	ISSUE PRICE	*QUOTE U.S.$
1997 Time Flies	1,250		125.00	125
1997 Winter Colors	Open		35.00	35

Capser - M. Capser

YEAR ISSUE	EDITION LIMIT	YEAR RETD.	ISSUE PRICE	*QUOTE U.S.$
2000 Autumn Blush	999		75.00	75
1997 Blossoms and Promises	999		100.00	100
1993 Briar and Brambles	999	1996	100.00	100
1992 Comes the Dawn	600		100.00	100
1994 Dashing Through the Snow	999		100.00	100
1994 Down the Lane	Retrd.	1998	30.00	30
1995 Enchanted Waters	999		100.00	100
1997 Grandma's Garden	999	1999	100.00	100
1995 Grapevine Estates	999	1998	100.00	100
1997 Guiding The Sails	999	1998	100.00	100
1994 The Lifting Fog	Retrd.	1997	30.00	30
1995 Mariner's Point	999	1996	100.00	100
1994 Nappin'	999		100.00	100
1994 A Night's Quiet	999		100.00	100
1995 On Gentle Wings	999		100.00	100
1993 Pickets & Vines	999	1994	100.00	100
2000 A Place of Peace	999		125.00	125
1992 Reflections	600	1993	100.00	100
1993 Rock Creek Spring	999		80.00	80
1994 September Blush	999	1996	100.00	100
1992 Silence Unbroken	600	1996	100.00	100
1993 Skyline Serenade	600	1993	100.00	100
1995 Spring Creek Fever	999	1996	100.00	100
2000 Standing Through Time	999		125.00	125
1993 A Summer's Glow	999	1997	60.00	60
1997 Sunrise Symphony	999		100.00	100
1994 A Time For Us	999		125.00	125
1994 To Search Again	Open		30.00	30
1992 The Watch	600	1993	100.00	150-517
1994 The Way Home	Retrd.	1998	30.00	30
1993 Whispering Wings	1,500	1994	100.00	100
1997 Woodland Warmth	999		125.00	125

Franca - O. Franca

YEAR ISSUE	EDITION LIMIT	YEAR RETD.	ISSUE PRICE	*QUOTE U.S.$
1988 The Apache	950	1990	70.00	175
1990 Blue Navajo	1,500	1991	125.00	179-319
1990 Blue Tranquility	999	1990	100.00	450-776
1988 Cacique	950	1990	70.00	150-216
1990 Cecy	1,500	1992	125.00	225-305
1990 Destiny	999	1990	100.00	100-345
1991 Early Morning	3,600	1994	125.00	225
1993 Evening In Taos	4,000	1994	80.00	80
1988 Feathered Hair Ties	600	1988	80.00	1198-1595
1990 Feathered Hair Ties II	999	1990	100.00	259-300
1991 The Lovers	2,400	1991	125.00	1224-1800
1991 The Model	1,500	1991	125.00	469-495
1992 Navajo Daydream	3,600	1993	175.00	450-480
1989 Navajo Fantasy	999	1989	80.00	150-302
1992 Navajo Meditating	4,000	1994	80.00	125
1992 Navajo Reflection	4,000	1992	80.00	100-225
1990 Navajo Summer	999	1988	100.00	175-345
1991 Olympia	1,500	1991	125.00	390
1989 Pink Navajo	999	1989	80.00	250-345
1988 The Red Shawl	600	1990	80.00	300
1991 Red Wolf	1,500	1991	125.00	125-130
1990 Santa Fe	1,500	1991	125.00	150-300
1988 Sitting Bull	950	1990	70.00	200-259
1988 Slow Bull	950	1990	70.00	200
1990 Turqoise Necklace	999	1990	100.00	200-317
1990 Wind Song	999	1990	100.00	195-345
1992 Wind Song II	4,000	1992	80.00	150-175
1989 Winter	999	1989	80.00	175
1989 Young Warrior	999	1989	80.00	450-560

Hanks - S. Hanks

YEAR ISSUE	EDITION LIMIT	YEAR RETD.	ISSUE PRICE	*QUOTE U.S.$
1994 All Gone Awry	2,000		150.00	150
1994 All In a Row	2,000	1994	150.00	164-200
1997 Being Perfect Angels	1,500	1997	150.00	150-175
1995 A Captive Audience	1,500	1997	150.00	150
1993 Catching The Sun	999	1993	150.00	495
1995 Cat's Lair	1,500		150.00	150
1992 Conferring With the Sea	999	1993	125.00	495
1990 Contemplation	999	1997	100.00	150
1995 Country Comfort	999	1997	100.00	100
1995 Drip Castles	4,000		30.00	30
1991 Duet	999	1993	150.00	150-600
1990 Emotional Appeal	999	1998	150.00	225

YEAR ISSUE	EDITION LIMIT	YEAR RETD.	ISSUE PRICE	*QUOTE U.S.$
1993 Gathering Thoughts	1,500	1995	150.00	345
1996 Her Side	1,500	1997	100.00	100
1992 An Innocent View	999	1992	150.00	315-450
1994 The Journey Is The Goal	1,500	1995	150.00	495
1995 Kali	Open		25.00	25
1996 Little Angels	999	1996	125.00	250-395
1993 Little Black Crow	1,500		150.00	150
1994 Michaela and Friends/Book	2,500		200.00	200
2000 A Moment For Reflection	1,250		150.00	150
1997 The Music Room	1,500	1997	150.00	150
1993 The New Arrival	1,500	1995	150.00	150-200
1995 Pacific Sanctuary	1,500	1998	150.00	275
1993 Peeking Out	Open		40.00	40
1993 Places I Remember	1,500		150.00	150
1990 Quiet Rapport	999	1997	150.00	300
1996 Sending Flowers	1,500	1997	150.00	180-225
1993 A Sense of Belonging	1,500	1997	150.00	150
1995 Small Miracle	1,500		125.00	125
1992 Sometimes It's the Little Things	999	1995	125.00	225
1994 Southwestern Bedroom	999	1997	150.00	180-225
1992 Stepping Stones	999	1993	150.00	295
1991 Sunday Afternoon	Open		40.00	40
1997 Sunshine Across The Sheets	1,500	1998	100.00	100
1992 Things Worth Keeping	999	1991	125.00	1100-1450
1993 The Thinkers	1,500		150.00	150
1994 Water Lilies In Bloom	750		295.00	295
1993 When Her Blue Eyes Close	999		100.00	100
2000 Where The Healing Begins	1,650		165.00	165
1994 Where The Light Shines Brightest	1,500		150.00	150
1991 A World For Our Children	999	1992	125.00	1595

Hulings - C. Hulings

YEAR ISSUE	EDITION LIMIT	YEAR RETD.	ISSUE PRICE	*QUOTE U.S.$
1990 Ancient French Farmhouse	999		150.00	225
1989 Chechaquene-Morocco Market Square	999	1993	150.00	250
1992 Cuernavaca Flower Market	580		225.00	225
1988 Ile de la Cite-Paris	580	1990	150.00	225
1990 The Lonely Man	999	1993	150.00	150
1988 Onteniente	580	1989	150.00	425-457
1991 Place des Ternes	580	1991	195.00	700
1989 Portuguese Vegetable Woman	999	1993	85.00	216
1994 The Red Raincoat	580		225.00	225
1990 Spanish Shawl	999	1994	125.00	125-169
1993 Spring Flowers	580		225.00	225
1992 Sunday Afternoon	580		195.00	275
1988 Three Cats on a Grapevine	580	1989	65.00	225
1993 Washday In Provence	580		225.00	225

Redlin - T. Redlin

YEAR ISSUE	EDITION LIMIT	YEAR RETD.	ISSUE PRICE	*QUOTE U.S.$
1981 1981 MN Duck Stamp Print	7,800	1981	125.00	150
1982 1982 MN Trout Stamp Print	960	1982	125.00	600
1983 1983 ND Duck Stamp Print	3,438	1983	135.00	150
1984 1984 Quail Conservation	1,500	1984	135.00	135
1985 1985 MN Duck Stamp	4,385	1985	135.00	135
1985 Afternoon Glow	960	1985	150.00	1095-1475
1979 Ageing Shoreline	960	1979	40.00	395-733
1981 All Clear	960	1981	150.00	395
1994 America, America	29,500		250.00	250
1994 And Crown Thy Good w/Brotherhood	29,500		250.00	250
1977 Apple River Mallards	Retrd.	1977	10.00	100
1981 April Snow	960	1981	100.00	595-776
1989 Aroma of Fall	6,800	1989	200.00	1700-1800
1987 Autumn Afternoon	4,800	1987	100.00	795
1993 Autumn Evening	29,500		250.00	250
2000 Autumn Evening	29,500		250.00	250
1980 Autumn Run	960	1980	60.00	375-575
1983 Autumn Shoreline	Retrd.	1983	50.00	150-450
1997 Autumn Traditions	1,950		275.00	275
1978 Back from the Fields	720	1978	40.00	250-375
1985 Back to the Sanctuary	960	1986	150.00	475-625
1978 Backwater Mallards	720	1978	40.00	945-1125
1983 Backwoods Cabin	960	1983	150.00	965
1990 Best Friends (AP)	570	1993	1000.00	1895
1982 The Birch Line	960	1982	100.00	1295-1681
1984 Bluebill Point (AP)	240	1984	300.00	785-790
1988 Boulder Ridge	4,800		150.00	150
1997 Bountiful Harvest	19,500		275.00	275
1980 Breaking Away	960	1980	60.00	430
1985 Breaking Cover	960	1985	150.00	400-862
1981 Broken Covey	960	1981	100.00	525-700

GRAPHICS

YEAR ISSUE	EDITION LIMIT	YEAR RETD.	ISSUE PRICE	*QUOTE U.S.$
1985 Brousing	960	1985	150.00	895
1994 Campfire Tales	29,500		250.00	250
1988 Catching the Scent	2,400		200.00	200
1986 Changing Seasons-Autumn	960	1986	150.00	450-503
1987 Changing Seasons-Spring	960	1987	200.00	475-595
1984 Changing Seasons-Summer	960	1984	150.00	1400
1986 Changing Seasons-Winter	960	1986	200.00	600-1100
1985 Clear View	1,500	1985	150.00	950-1195
1980 Clearing the Rail	960	1980	60.00	850-1034
1984 Closed for the Season	960	1984	150.00	450-495
1979 Colorful Trio	960	1979	40.00	700-800
1991 Comforts of Home	22,900	N/A	175.00	300-400
1986 Coming Home	2,400	1986	100.00	1195-2400
1992 The Conservationists	29,500		175.00	175
1988 Country Neighbors	4,800	1988	150.00	375-600
1980 Country Road	960	1980	60.00	650-745
1987 Deer Crossing	2,400	1987	200.00	950-1200
1985 Delayed Departure	1,500	1985	150.00	500-1000
1980 Drifting	960	1980	60.00	400
1987 Evening Chores (print & book)	2,400	1988	400.00	1000-1121
1985 Evening Company	960	1985	150.00	500-1300
1983 Evening Glow	960	1983	150.00	2250
1987 Evening Harvest	960	1987	200.00	1350-1950
2000 Evening Rendezvous	9,500		275.00	275
1982 Evening Retreat (AP)	300	1982	400.00	3000
1990 Evening Solitude	9,500	1990	200.00	600-1450
1983 Evening Surprise	960	1983	150.00	1000-2500
1990 Evening With Friends	19,500	1991	225.00	1500-1700
1990 Family Traditions	Retrd.	1993	80.00	240-250
1979 Fighting a Headwind	960	1979	30.00	350-450
1991 Flying Free	14,500		200.00	200
1993 For Amber Waves of Grain	29,500		250.00	250
1993 For Purple Mountains Majesty	29,500		250.00	250
1995 From Sea to Shining Sea	29,500		250.00	250
1994 God Shed His Grace on Thee	29,500		250.00	250
1987 Golden Retreat (AP)	500	1986	800.00	2000
1995 Harvest Moon Ball	9,500	1995	275.00	350-695
1986 Hazy Afternoon	2,560	1986	200.00	850-1125
1990 Heading Home	Retrd.	1993	80.00	135-200
1997 A Helping Hand	9,500		275.00	275
1983 Hidden Point	960	1983	150.00	600-1250
1981 High Country	960	1981	100.00	600-1150
1981 Hightailing	960	1981	75.00	350-650
1980 The Homestead	960	1980	60.00	640-675
1988 Homeward Bound	Retrd.	1993	70.00	150
1989 Homeward Bound	Retrd.	1994	80.00	250
1988 House Call	6,800	1990	175.00	1000-1350
1991 Hunter's Haven (A/P)	1,000	N/A	175.00	1000
1989 Indian Summer	4,800	1989	200.00	725-905
1980 Intruders	960	1980	60.00	320
1982 The Landing	Retrd.	1982	30.00	80
1981 The Landmark	960	1981	100.00	400-575
1984 Leaving the Sanctuary	960	1984	150.00	475
1994 Lifetime Companions	29,500		250.00	250
1988 Lights of Home	9,500	1988	125.00	650-775
1979 The Loner	960	1979	40.00	300
1990 Master of the Valley	6,800		200.00	200
1988 The Master's Domain	2,400	1988	225.00	800-850
1988 Moonlight Retreat (A/P)	530	N/A	1000.00	1600
1979 Morning Chores	960	1979	40.00	1350
1984 Morning Glow	960	1984	150.00	1400-1879
1981 Morning Retreat (AP)	240	N/A	400.00	3000
1989 Morning Rounds	6,800	1992	175.00	450-595
1991 Morning Solitude	12,107	1991	250.00	400-760
1984 Night Harvest	960	1984	150.00	1550-1795
1985 Night Light	1,500	1985	300.00	1195-1350
1986 Night Mapling	960	1986	200.00	1000-2550
1995 A Night on the Town	29,500		150.00	150
1980 Night Watch	2,400	1980	60.00	1000
1984 Nightflight (AP)	360	1984	600.00	2200
1982 October Evening	960	1982	100.00	1000
1989 Office Hours	6,800	1991	175.00	948
1992 Oh Beautiful for Spacious Skies	29,500		250.00	250
1978 Old Loggers Trail	720	1978	40.00	950-1200
1983 On the Alert	960	1983	125.00	400
1977 Over the Blowdown	Retrd.	1977	20.00	400-690
1978 Over the Rushes	720	1978	40.00	450
1981 Passing Through	960	1981	100.00	225
1983 Peaceful Evening	960	1983	100.00	1150-1595
1991 Pleasures of Winter	24,500	1992	150.00	245-325
1986 Prairie Monuments	960	1986	200.00	795-1200

YEAR ISSUE	EDITION LIMIT	YEAR RETD.	ISSUE PRICE	*QUOTE U.S.$
1988 Prairie Morning	4,800	1988	150.00	450-550
1984 Prairie Skyline	960	1984	150.00	2328
1983 Prairie Springs	960	1983	150.00	525-595
1987 Prepared for the Season	Retrd.	1994	70.00	160
1990 Pure Contentment	9,500	1989	150.00	475-500
1978 Quiet Afternoon	720	1978	40.00	695
1988 Quiet of the Evening	4,800	1988	150.00	595-800
1982 Reflections	960	1982	100.00	600-725
1985 Riverside Pond	960	1985	150.00	525-1070
1984 Rural Route	960	1984	150.00	395
1983 Rushing Rapids	960	1983	125.00	750
1980 Rusty Refuge I	960	1980	60.00	295-495
1981 Rusty Refuge II	960	1980	100.00	495-525
1984 Rusty Refuge III	960	1984	150.00	595-950
1985 Rusty Refuge IV	960	1985	150.00	695-900
1980 Secluded Pond	960	1980	60.00	295-350
1982 Seed Hunters	960	1982	100.00	575-670
1985 Sharing Season I	Retrd.	1993	60.00	150-225
1986 Sharing Season II	Retrd.	1993	60.00	200-240
1981 Sharing the Bounty	960	1981	100.00	1500
1994 Sharing the Evening	29,500		175.00	175
1987 Sharing the Solitude	2,400	1987	125.00	800-850
1986 Silent Flight	960	1986	150.00	400-600
1980 Silent Sunset	960	1980	60.00	780-1121
1984 Silent Wings Suite (set of 4)	960	1984	200.00	750-975
1981 Soft Shadows	960	1984	100.00	325-395
1989 Special Memories (AP)	570		1000.00	1000
1982 Spring Mapling	960	1982	100.00	975
1981 Spring Run-Off	1,700	1981	125.00	695-991
1980 Spring Thaw	960	1980	60.00	460-585
1980 Squall Line	960	1980	60.00	300
1978 Startled	720	1978	30.00	995-1336
1986 Stormy Weather	1,500	1986	200.00	550-1050
1992 Summertime	24,900	1999	225.00	225-350
1997 Sunday Morning	9,500		275.00	275
1984 Sundown	960	1984	300.00	575-1100
1986 Sunlit Trail	960	1986	150.00	200-500
1984 Sunny Afternoon	960	1984	150.00	700-1100
1987 That Special Time	2,400	1987	125.00	850-900
1987 Together for the Season	Open		70.00	100
1995 Total Comfort	9,500	1995	275.00	275-375
1986 Twilight Glow	960	1986	200.00	1500-2100
1988 Wednesday Afternoon	6,800	1989	175.00	900
1990 Welcome to Paradise	14,500	1990	150.00	700-974
1985 Whistle Stop	960	1985	150.00	785-900
1979 Whitecaps	960	1979	40.00	425-445
1982 Whitewater	960	1982	100.00	400-870
1982 Winter Haven	500	1982	85.00	800
1977 Winter Snows	Retrd.	1977	20.00	595-690
1984 Winter Windbreak	960	1984	150.00	750
1992 Winter Wonderland	29,500	1993	150.00	250

Hamilton Collection

Grateful Dead Autographed Prints - S. Mouse

YEAR ISSUE	EDITION LIMIT	YEAR RETD.	ISSUE PRICE	*QUOTE U.S.$
1999 Family Album	Open		49.95	50
1999 Icecream Kid	Open		49.95	50
1999 Mars Hotel	Open		49.95	50
1999 One More Saturday Night	Open		49.95	50
1999 Skelton and Roses	Open		49.95	50
1999 Workingman's Dead	Open		49.95	50

Mickey Mantle - R. Tanenbaum

1996 An All American Legend-The Mick	Open		95.00	95

Imperial Graphics, Ltd.

Chang - L. Chang

1988 Egrets with Lotus S/N	1,950		10.00	10
1988 Flamingos with Catail S/N	1,950		10.00	10

Irvine - G. Irvine

1995 Pansies	Open		8.00	8
1995 Violets	Open		8.00	8

Lee - H.C. Lee

1988 Blue Bird of Paradise S/N	950	1999	35.00	35
1988 Cat & Callas S/N	1,950	1999	30.00	30
1990 Double Red Hibiscus S/N	1,950	1999	16.00	16
1988 Hummingbird I S/N	1,950	1999	16.00	16
1988 Hummingbird II S/N	1,950	1999	16.00	16

YEAR ISSUE	EDITION LIMIT	YEAR RETD.	ISSUE PRICE	*QUOTE U.S.$
1990 Maroon & Mauve Peonies S/N	950	1999	60.00	60
1990 Maroon & Peach Peonies S/N	950	1999	60.00	60
1990 Maroon Peony S/N	2,950		20.00	20
1990 Peacock w/Tulip & Peony S/N	1,950		105.00	105
1990 Peonies & Butterflies S/N	2,950		40.00	40
1990 Pink Peony S/N	2,950		20.00	20
1990 Single Red Hibiscus S/N	1,950		16.00	16
1988 White Bird of Paradise S/N	950	1999	35.00	35
1988 White Peacocks w/Peonies S/N	950	1999	65.00	65

Liu - Angels Among Us - L. Liu

YEAR ISSUE	EDITION LIMIT	YEAR RETD.	ISSUE PRICE	*QUOTE U.S.$
1997 Angel of Light S/N	3,500		125.00	125
1997 Angel of Love S/N	3,500		80.00	80
1996 Angel with Harp S/N	5,500		40.00	40
1996 Angel with Trumpet S/N	5,500		40.00	40
1996 Guardian Angel S/N	5,500		125.00	125
1997 Urn with Irises S/N	3,500	2000	45.00	45
1997 Urn with Tulips S/N	3,500	2000	45.00	45

Liu - Cats & Dogs - L. Liu

YEAR ISSUE	EDITION LIMIT	YEAR RETD.	ISSUE PRICE	*QUOTE U.S.$
2001 Blue	950		25.00	25
2001 Happy	950		25.00	25
2001 Hope	950		25.00	25
2001 Lacy	950		25.00	25

Liu - Celestial Symphony Series - L. Liu

YEAR ISSUE	EDITION LIMIT	YEAR RETD.	ISSUE PRICE	*QUOTE U.S.$
1995 Flute Interlude S/N	5,500		40.00	40
1995 French Horn Melody S/N	5,500		40.00	40
1995 Piano Sonata S/N	5,500		40.00	40
1995 Violin Concerto S/N	5,500		40.00	40

Liu - Dance & Music Series - L. Liu

YEAR ISSUE	EDITION LIMIT	YEAR RETD.	ISSUE PRICE	*QUOTE U.S.$
2001 Ballet	2,500		35.00	35
2001 Big Band	2,500		45.00	45
2001 Chamber Music	2,500		45.00	45
2001 Dance Ensemble	2,500		50.00	50
2001 Flamenco	2,500		35.00	35
2001 Tango	2,500		35.00	35
2001 Waltz	2,500		35.00	35

Liu - Garden of Paradise - L. Liu

YEAR ISSUE	EDITION LIMIT	YEAR RETD.	ISSUE PRICE	*QUOTE U.S.$
1999 Majestic Peacock	2,950		135.00	135
1999 Majestic Peacock - Canvas	300		395.00	395
1999 Royal Peahen	2,950		135.00	135
1999 Royal Peahen - Canvas	300		395.00	395
1999 Swan Duet	2,950		135.00	135
1999 Swan Duet - Canvas	300		395.00	395

Liu - L. Liu

YEAR ISSUE	EDITION LIMIT	YEAR RETD.	ISSUE PRICE	*QUOTE U.S.$
1989 Abundance of Lilies (poster)	Closed	1993	25.00	30
1998 Abundant Blessings S/N	3,500		125.00	125
XX Afternoon Nap S/N	1,000		45.00	45
1994 Allen's Hummingbird w/Columbine S/N	3,300	1994	30.00	70-90
1987 Amaryllis S/N	1,950	N/A	16.00	60
2000 Angel of Purity S/N	2,500		50.00	50
2000 Angel of Wishes S/N	2,500		50.00	50
1993 Anna's Hummingbird w/Fuchsia S/N	3,300	1993	30.00	30
1998 Autumn Glory S/N	2,950		145.00	145
1989 Autumn Melody S/N	1,950	1993	45.00	45
1990 Azalea Path S/N	2,500	N/A	85.00	85
1990 Azalea w/Dogwood S/N	2,500	N/A	55.00	55
1988 Baby Bluebirds S/N	1,950	N/A	18.00	30
1990 Baby Bluebirds w/Plum Tree S/N	2,500	N/A	18.00	90-100
1988 Baby Chickadees S/N	1,950	N/A	16.00	215
1990 Baby Chickadees w/Pine Tree S/N	2,500	N/A	18.00	70-90
1999 Bamboo (9 x 15)	3,300		28.00	28
XX Basket of Begonias S/N	2,500	N/A	40.00	40
1993 Basket of Calla Lilies S/N	3,300	1994	50.00	88-100
1991 Basket of Grapes & Raspberries S/N	2,500	N/A	25.00	30
1993 Basket of Hydrangra S/N	3,300	1995	50.00	93-116
1989 Basket of Irises & Lilacs S/N	1,950	N/A	45.00	45
1993 Basket of Magnolias S/N	3,300	1993	50.00	100-235
1993 Basket of Orchids S/N	3,300	N/A	50.00	72-90
1992 Basket of Pansies & Lilacs S/N	2,950	N/A	50.00	50
1991 Basket of Pansies S/N	2,500	N/A	40.00	40
1991 Basket of Peonies S/N	2,500	N/A	40.00	40
1992 Basket of Roses & Hydrangeas S/N	2,950	N/A	50.00	50
1991 Basket of Roses S/N	2,500	N/A	40.00	40
1991 Basket of Strawberries & Grapes S/N	2,500	N/A	25.00	50-70
1991 Basket of Sweet Peas S/N	2,500	N/A	25.00	50-75
1989 Basket of Tulips & Lilacs S/N	1,950	N/A	45.00	45

YEAR ISSUE	EDITION LIMIT	YEAR RETD.	ISSUE PRICE	*QUOTE U.S.$
1991 Basket of Wild Roses S/N	2,500	N/A	25.00	75-120
1991 Baskets of Primroses S/N	2,500	N/A	25.00	50-75
1986 Bearded Irises S/N	1,950	N/A	45.00	45
1994 Berries & Cherries S/N	3,500	1998	30.00	100-150
1990 Bluebirds & Dandelion S/N	2,500	N/A	40.00	64-80
1986 Bluebirds w/Plum Blossoms S/N	1,950	N/A	35.00	35
1988 Bluebirds w/Rhododendrons S/N	1,950	N/A	40.00	144-180
1990 Bouquet of Peonies S/N	2,500	N/A	50.00	50
1990 Bouquet of Poppies S/N	2,500	N/A	50.00	50
1992 Bouquet of Roses S/N	2,950	1994	20.00	20
1992 Breath of Spring S/N	2,950	N/A	135.00	135-165
1993 Broad-Billed HB w/Petunias S/N	3,300	N/A	30.00	64-80
1995 Burgundy Irises w/Foxgloves S/N	5,500	N/A	60.00	91-114
1995 Butterfly Garden I S/N	5,500		50.00	50
1995 Butterfly Garden II S/N	5,500		50.00	50
1994 Butterfly Kisses S/N	3,500	1998	50.00	67-125
1998 Butterfly Paradise S/N	3,500	N/A	80.00	80
1990 Butterfly w/Clematis S/N	2,500	1994	40.00	165-225
1990 Butterfly w/Wild Rose S/N	2,500	1993	40.00	50
1987 Calla Lily S/N	1,950	N/A	35.00	35
1994 Calliope Hummingbird w/Trumpet Vine S/N	3,300	N/A	30.00	64-80
1999 Camellia (12 x 12) S/N	2,950		28.00	28
1990 Cardinal & Queen Anne's Lace S/N	2,500	1994	40.00	225
XX Cat & Hummer S/N	1,000		45.00	45
1989 Cherries & Summer Bouquet S/N	2,500	N/A	45.00	45
1993 Cherub Orchestra S/N	3,300	1994	80.00	123-300
1991 Cherubim w/Ivy S/N	2,500	1993	20.00	20
1988 Chickadees w/Cherry Blossoms S/N	1,950	N/A	40.00	144-180
2000 The Chirp Inn S/N	2,500		45.00	45
1992 Conservatory S/N	2,950	1994	80.00	235-250
1999 Cymbidium w/White Butterfly S/N	1,950		40.00	40
1987 Daylily S/N	1,950	N/A	35.00	35
1989 Daylily w/Hummingbird S/N	2,500	N/A	18.00	18
1998 The Delights of Spring S/N	3,500		80.00	80
1987 Dogwood S/N	1,950	N/A	30.00	30
1986 The Dreamer S/N	950		65.00	65
1991 Dried-Floral Bouquet S/N	2,500	N/A	25.00	40-50
1991 The Drying Room S/N	2,500	N/A	75.00	112-140
1992 Early Spring S/N	2,950	1993	85.00	85
1988 Eastern Black Swallowtail w/Milkweed S/N	1,950	N/A	45.00	80-100
1991 Egret's w/Queen Anne's Lace S/N	2,500	1995	60.00	80-100
1992 Entryway S/N	2,950		40.00	40
1997 Evening Reflections S/N	5,500		135.00	135
1993 Fairy Ballet S/N	3,300	N/A	80.00	80
1986 Fall S/N	950	N/A	35.00	35
1988 Feathered Harmony S/N	1,950	N/A	60.00	295
1991 Field of Irises S/N	2,500	1994	85.00	120-150
1999 Fireside Solitude S/N	1,950		105.00	105
1989 First Landing S/N	1,950	N/A	16.00	25
1991 Floral Arch S/N	2,500	1996	25.00	25
1988 Floral Symphony S/N	1,950	N/A	95.00	95
1990 Forest Azalea S/N	2,500	N/A	55.00	225-250
1992 Forest Stream S/N	2,950	1995	85.00	218-261
1992 Fountain S/N	2,950		40.00	40
1986 Free Flight I -Rust Butterfly S/N	950		60.00	60
1986 Free Flight II -Pink Butterfly S/N	950		60.00	60
1989 Fritillaries w/ Violet S/N	2,500		18.00	18
1989 Fruit & Spring Basket S/N	1,500	N/A	45.00	225-250
1988 Garden Blossoms I S/N	1,950	N/A	35.00	35
1988 Garden Blossoms II S/N	1,950	N/A	35.00	35
1997 Garden Gate S/N	5,500		80.00	80
1991 Garden Peonies S/N	2,500	1997	60.00	88-110
1997 Garden Pleasure S/N	5,500		80.00	80
1986 Garden Poppies S/N	2,000	N/A	45.00	88-110
1991 Garden Poppies S/N	2,500	N/A	60.00	60
1992 Garden Seat S/N	2,950		40.00	40
1991 The Gathering S/N	2,500	N/A	75.00	75
1988 Harmonious Flight S/N	1,950	N/A	50.00	100-150
1994 Heavenly Tulips S/N	3,300	1994	80.00	250
1987 Herons & Irises S/N	1,950	N/A	65.00	130-150
1987 Hibiscus & Hummer S/N	1,950	1995	45.00	45
1988 Hummingbird & Hollyhock S/N	1,950	N/A	40.00	40
1989 Hummingbird & Floral I S/N	2,500	1994	35.00	35
1989 Hummingbird & Floral II S/N	2,500	1994	35.00	2500
2000 Hummingbird Paradise S/N	2,950		105.00	105
1996 Hummingbird with Lilac S/N	5,500	2000	50.00	50
1988 Hummingbirds & Iris S/N	1,950	N/A	40.00	40
2000 Hummingbirds with Azaleas S/N	2,500		40.00	40
1996 Hummingbirds with Fuchsia S/N	5,500		50.00	50

Imperial Graphics, Ltd.
to Imperial Graphics, Ltd.

GRAPHICS

YEAR ISSUE	EDITION LIMIT	YEAR RETD.	ISSUE PRICE	*QUOTE U.S.$
2000 Hummingbirds with Roses S/N	2,500		40.00	40
1999 Hydrangea (12 x 12) S/N	2,950		28.00	28
1989 Hydrangea Bouquet S/N	2,500	N/A	30.00	96-120
1989 Innocents S/N	1,950	N/A	16.00	50-75
1993 Iris Garden II S/N	3,300	1994	105.00	400-510
2000 Iris Jubilee (Giclée)	150		950.00	950
2000 Iris Jubilee S/N	950		125.00	125
1989 Iris Profusion (poster)	Closed	1995	30.00	60-80
1987 Iris S/N	1,950	N/A	16.00	16
1991 Irises in Bloom S/N	2,500	N/A	85.00	85
1992 Ivy & Fragrant Flowers S/N	3,300	1993	60.00	225-250
1992 Ivy & Honeysuckle S/N	3,300	1993	50.00	75
1992 Ivy & Sweetpea S/N	3,300	1994	50.00	75
1988 Kingfisher & Iris S/N	1,950	N/A	45.00	67-84
1986 Kingfisher S/N	950	1998	35.00	35
2001 L 'innocence S/N	950		30.00	30
2001 La célébration S/N	950		30.00	30
2001 La cour S/N	950		30.00	30
2001 Les fleurs d'amour S/N	950		135.00	135
1999 Lilac (12 x 12) S/N	2,950		28.00	28
1995 Lilac Breezes S/N	5,500		80.00	80
1986 Lily Pond S/N	950	1998	35.00	35
1987 Lily S/N	1,950	N/A	16.00	16
1999 Magnolia (12 x 12) S/N	2,950		28.00	28
1998 Magnolia Bouquet S/N	3,500	N/A	50.00	80-100
1995 Magnolia Path S/N	5,500		135.00	135
1987 Magnolia S/N	1,950	N/A	30.00	30
1999 Magnolia Serenade S/N	1,950		105.00	105
1995 Magnolias & Day Lilies S/N	5,500		80.00	80
1995 Magnolias & Hydrangeas S/N	5,500		80.00	80
2000 The Manor House S/N	2,500		45.00	45
1986 Mauve Veiltail S/N	1,000	N/A	35.00	35
1994 Mermaid Callas S/N	5,500	N/A	80.00	194-232
1996 Messengers of Love S/N	5,500		60.00	60
XX Misty Valley S/N	1,950	N/A	45.00	45
1990 Mixed Irises I S/N	2,500	N/A	50.00	50
1990 Mixed Irises II S/N	2,500	N/A	50.00	50
1988 Moonlight Splendor S/N	1,950	N/A	60.00	60
1987 Morning Glories & Hummer S/N	1,950	N/A	45.00	45
1989 The Morning Room S/N	2,500	N/A	95.00	325-395
1987 Motherlove S/N	1,950	N/A	45.00	265
1987 Motif Orientale S/N	1,950	N/A	95.00	95
1994 Mystic Bouquet S/N	3,300	N/A	80.00	120-150
1995 Nature's Retreat S/N	5,500	N/A	145.00	210-375
1998 Nature's Tranquility S/N	2,950		125.00	125
1986 Nuthatch w/Dogwood S/N	1,950	N/A	35.00	35
1992 Old Stone House S/N	2,950	1996	50.00	72-90
1986 Opera Lady S/N	950	N/A	95.00	95
1989 Orange Tip & Blossoms S/N	2,500		18.00	18
2000 Orchid Oasis S/N	2,950		105.00	105
1989 Oriental Screen S/N	2,500	N/A	95.00	350-375
1996 Oriental Splendor S/N	5,500	1999	145.00	210-252
1988 Painted Lady w/Thistle S/N	1,950	N/A	45.00	88-110
1988 Pair of Finches S/N	1,950	N/A	35.00	35
1992 Palladian Windows S/N	2,950	1993	80.00	80
1990 Pansies & Ivy S/N	2,500	N/A	18.00	18
1992 Pansies & Lilies of the Valley S/N	2,950	1993	20.00	20
1991 Pansies in a Basket S/N	2,500	N/A	25.00	25
1993 Pansies w/Blue Stardrift S/N	2,950	1995	25.00	40-50
1993 Pansies w/Daisies S/N	2,950	N/A	25.00	34-46
1992 Pansies w/Sweet Peas S/N	2,950	1994	20.00	20
1991 Pansies w/Violets S/N	2,500	N/A	16.00	16
1987 Parenthood S/N	1,950	N/A	45.00	45
1992 Patio S/N	2,950		40.00	40
1993 Peach & Purple Irises S/N	3,300	1994	50.00	50-100
1993 Peach & Yellow Roses S/N	3,300	N/A	50.00	50-80
1986 Peach Veiltail S/N	1,000	1998	35.00	35
1994 Peaches & Fruits S/N	3,500	N/A	30.00	80-110
1991 Peacock Duet-Serigraph S/N	325		550.00	550
1987 Peacock Fantasy S/N	950	N/A	65.00	65
1991 Peacock Solo-Serigraph S/N	325		550.00	550
1988 Peonies & Azaleas S/N	1,950	N/A	35.00	35
1988 Peonies & Forsythia S/N	1,950	N/A	35.00	35
1988 Peonies & Waterfall S/N	1,950	N/A	65.00	65
1993 Peonies S/N	3,300	1995	30.00	140
2000 Peony Enchantment (Giclée)	150		950.00	950
2000 Peony Enchantment S/N	950		125.00	125
2000 Peony Rhapsody S/N	2,950		135.00	135
1990 Petunias & Ivy S/N	2,500	N/A	18.00	18
1999 Phalaenopsis w/Blue Butterflies S/N	1,950		40.00	40
1989 Phlox w/Hummingbird S/N	2,500	N/A	18.00	18
1999 Poetic Melody S/N	1,950		150.00	150
1990 Potted Beauties S/N	2,500	1997	105.00	152-190
1996 Potted Pansies S/N	5,500	N/A	40.00	64-80
1996 Potted Petunias S/N	5,500		40.00	40
1996 Protectors of Peace S/N	5,500		60.00	60
1995 Purple Irises w/Foxgloves S/N	5,500		60.00	60
1991 Putti w/Column S/N	2,500	N/A	20.00	20
1990 Quiet Moment S/N	2,500	N/A	105.00	450-525
1998 Rhapsody in Yellow & Blue S/N	3,500		45.00	45
1989 Romantic Abundance S/N	1,950	N/A	95.00	95
1989 Romantic Garden (poster)	Open		35.00	35
1994 Romantic Reflection S/N	5,950	1996	145.00	399-485
1998 Romantic Reverie S/N	3,500		45.00	45
1997 Rose Arbor S/N	5,500		80.00	80
1993 Rose Bouquet w/Tassel S/N	3,300	1995	25.00	25
1994 Rose Fairies S/N	5,500	1996	80.00	195
1996 Rose Memories S/N	5,500		80.00	80
1989 Roses & Lilacs S/N	2,500	N/A	30.00	96-120
1992 Roses & Violets S/N	2,950	1993	20.00	40-50
1999 Roses (14 x 14) S/N	2,950		36.00	36
2000 Roses from Monet's Garden S/N	950		95.00	95
1993 Roses in Bloom S/N	3,300	1995	105.00	210-250
1990 Royal Garden S/N	1,950		95.00	95
1990 Royal Retreat S/N	1,950	N/A	95.00	450
1995 Ruby Throated Hummingbird w/Hibiscus S/N	5,800		40.00	40
1993 Rufous Hummingbird w/Foxgloves S/N	3,300	1993	30.00	30
1998 Seasonal Flowers I	Open		20.00	20
1998 Seasonal Flowers II	Open		20.00	20
1998 Seasonal Flowers III	Open		20.00	20
1998 Seasonal Flowers IV	Open		20.00	20
1988 Snapdragon S/N	1,950	N/A	16.00	16
1987 Solitude S/N	1,950	N/A	60.00	295
1993 Southern Magnolia S/N	3,300	1995	30.00	65-85
1987 Spring Blossoms I S/N	1,950	N/A	45.00	45
1987 Spring Blossoms II S/N	1,950	N/A	45.00	45
1989 Spring Bouquet (poster)	Open		30.00	30
1989 Spring Bouquet (poster-signed)	Open		45.00	45
1996 Spring Bulbs S/N	5,500		50.00	50
1994 Spring Conservatory S/N	3,300		105.00	105
1986 Spring Fairy S/N	950	1998	35.00	35
1990 Spring Floral S/N	2,500	N/A	105.00	105
1995 Spring Garden S/N	5,500		125.00	125
1986 Spring S/N	950		35.00	35
1987 Spring Song S/N	1,950		60.00	120-140
1986 Spring Tulips S/N	1,950		45.00	45
1989 Spring Tulips S/N	2,500		45.00	45
1987 Stream w/Blossoms S/N	1,950	N/A	45.00	90-120
1992 Study for a Breath of Spring S/N	2,950	N/A	105.00	105
1996 Summer Bouquet S/N	5,500		50.00	50
1986 Summer Glads S/N	1,950	N/A	45.00	45
1988 Summer Lace w/Blue Chicory S/N	1,950	1991	45.00	45
1987 Summer Lace w/Chicadees S/N	950	N/A	65.00	170
1988 Summer Lace w/Chickadees II S/N	1,950	1991	65.00	65
1988 Summer Lace w/Daisies S/N	1,950	1991	45.00	45
1987 Summer Lace w/Dragon Fly S/N	950	N/A	45.00	45
1987 Summer Lace w/Lady Bug S/N	950	N/A	45.00	45
1989 Summer Rose S/N	2,500	N/A	45.00	45
1986 Summer S/N	950	N/A	35.00	35
1998 Sunflower Bouquet S/N	3,500		50.00	50
1987 Swans & Callas S/N	1,950	1994	65.00	65
1991 Swans w/Daylilies S/N	2,500	1993	60.00	60
1989 Swans w/Dogwood S/N	1,950	N/A	65.00	65
1995 Sweet Bounty S/N	5,500		80.00	80
1994 Sweet Delight S/N	3,500	1998	50.00	80-110
1988 Sweet Pea Floral S/N	1,950	N/A	16.00	16
1986 Three Little Deer S/N	950	1998	35.00	35
1997 Togetherness S/N	1,950	N/A	60.00	60
2000 Transformation I - Roses S/N	950		75.00	75
1988 Trio of Sparrows S/N	1,950	N/A	35.00	35
1993 Tulip Bouquet w/Tassel S/N	3,300	1995	25.00	30
1999 Tulips (14 x 14) S/N	2,950		36.00	36
1987 Tulips S/N	1,950	N/A	16.00	16
1993 Two Burgundy Irises S/N	3,300	1994	50.00	50
1990 Two White Irises S/N	2,500	N/A	40.00	40
1977 Urn with Irises S/N	3,500	2000	45.00	45
1977 Urn with Tulips S/N	3,500	2000	45.00	45
1992 Victorian Pavilion S/N	2,950	N/A	50.00	80-100
1992 Vintage Bouquet S/N	2,950	1994	135.00	250-265

Collectors' Information Bureau   *Quotes have been rounded up to nearest dollar

YEAR ISSUE	EDITION LIMIT	YEAR RETD.	ISSUE PRICE	*QUOTE U.S.$
1993 Violet Crowned HB w/Morning Glories S/N	3,300	1996	30.00	46-60
1989 Waterfall w/Dogwood S/N	1,950	N/A	45.00	45
1989 Waterfall w/White & Pink Dogwood S/N	1,950	N/A	45.00	45
1990 White & Blue Irises S/N	2,500	N/A	40.00	40
1993 White & Burgundy Roses S/N	3,300	1995	50.00	64-80
1995 White Eared Hummingbird w/Hydrangea S/N	5,800		40.00	40
1991 Wild Flowers w/Single Butterfly S/N	2,500	1998	50.00	80-100
1991 Wild Flowers w/Two Butterflies S/N	2,500	1998	50.00	80-100
1986 Winter S/N	950	N/A	35.00	35
1996 Wisteria Dreams S/N	5,500		80.00	80
1993 Woodland Path S/N	3,300	1994	135.00	325-450
1993 Woodland Steps S/N	3,300	1995	85.00	85
1993 Woodland View S/N	3,300	1995	85.00	160-180
1995 Wreath of Lilies S/N	5,500		55.00	55
1995 Wreath of Pansies S/N	5,500		55.00	55
1994 Wreath of Peonies S/N	3,500	1998	55.00	80-100
1994 Wreath of Roses S/N	3,500	1995	55.00	210-252

Liu - The Music Room - L. Liu

1994 Clarinet Ensemble S/N	5,500		115.00	115
1996 Concerto with Guitar S/N	5,500		45.00	45
1996 Concerto with Violin S/N	5,500		45.00	45
1994 Fancy Fiddle S/N	5,500	1994	80.00	114-142
1996 Harmonic Duet S/N	5,500		55.00	55
1999 Homage to Beethoven-Symphony No. 9 S/N	2,950		80.00	80
1999 Homage to Mozart-The Marriage of Figaro S/N	2,950		80.00	80
1994 Love Notes S/N	5,500	1994	80.00	120-150
1991 The Music Room I S/N	2,500	1992	135.00	2300-2400
1994 The Music Room III-Composer's Retreat S/N	5,500	1994	145.00	358-435
1992 The Music Room II-Nutcracker S/N	4,500	1993	200.00	627-762
1995 The Music Room IV-Swan Melody S/N	6,500	1997	150.00	206-247
1999 The Music Room VII-Afternoon Repose S/N	5,500		150.00	150
1997 The Music Room VI-Romantic Overture S/N	5,500		150.00	150
1996 The Music Room V-Morning Serenade S/N	5,500		145.00	145
1996 Musical Trio S/N	5,500		55.00	55

Liu - Unframed Canvas Transfers - L. Liu

1998 Abundant Blessings S/N	300		395.00	395
2000 Angel of Purity S/N	300		195.00	195
2000 Angel of Wishes S/N	300		195.00	195
1996 Angel with Harp S/N	300		145.00	145
1996 Angel with Trumpet S/N	300		145.00	145
1998 Autumn Glory S/N	300		395.00	395
1993 Basket of Calla Lilies S/N	300	1995	195.00	195
1993 Basket of Magnolias S/N	300	1997	195.00	195
1998 Butterfly Paradise S/N	300		295.00	295
1999 Camellia (12 x 12) S/N	300		125.00	125
1993 Cherub Orchestra S/N	300	1995	295.00	400-550
2000 The Chip Inn S/N	300		195.00	195
1992 Conservatory S/N	300	1995	295.00	295
1999 Cymbidium w/White Butterfly S/N	300		145.00	145
1998 The Delights of Spring S/N	300		295.00	295
1997 Evening Reflections S/N	300		395.00	395
1993 Fairy Ballet S/N	300	1997	295.00	295
1994 Fancy Fiddle S/N	300		295.00	295
1999 Fireside Solitude S/N	300		365.00	365
1997 Garden Gate S/N	300		295.00	295
1997 Garden Pleasure S/N	300		295.00	295
2000 Hummingbird Paradise S/N	300		345.00	345
1996 Hummingbird with Fuchsia S/N	300		195.00	195
1996 Hummingbird with Lilac S/N	300		195.00	195
1999 Hydrangea (12 x 12) S/N	300		125.00	125
1993 Iris Garden II S/N	300	1995	395.00	395-475
2000 Iris Jubilee S/N	300		345.00	345
2001 L 'innocence S/N	300		125.00	125
2001 La célébration S/N	300		125.00	125
2001 La cour S/N	300		125.00	125
2001 Les fleurs d'amour S/N	300		395.00	395
1999 Lilac (12 x 12) S/N	300		125.00	125
1995 Lilac Breezes S/N	300		295.00	295
1994 Love Notes S/N	300		295.00	295
1999 Magnolia (12 x 12) S/N	300		125.00	125

1998 Magnolia Bouquet S/N	300		195.00	195
1995 Magnolia Path S/N	300	1996	395.00	395
1999 Magnolia Serenade S/N	300		365.00	365
2000 The Manor House S/N	300		195.00	195
1994 Mermaid Callas S/N	300	1997	295.00	295-450
1999 Nature's Retreat S/N	300	1999	395.00	395
1998 Nature's Tranquility S/N	300		365.00	365
1992 Old Stone House S/N	300	1997	195.00	195
2000 Orchid Oasis S/N	300		345.00	345
1996 Oriental Splendor S/N	300	1998	395.00	395
1992 Palladian Windows S/N	300	1995	295.00	295-395
2000 Peony Enchantment S/N	300		345.00	345
2000 Peony Rhapsody S/N	300		345.00	345
1999 Phalaenopsis w/Blue Butterflies S/N	300		145.00	145
1999 Poetic Melody S/N	300		425.00	425
1996 Potted Pansies S/N	300		145.00	145
1996 Potted Petunias S/N	300		145.00	145
1998 Rhaposdy in Yellow & Blue S/N	300		195.00	195
1994 Romantic Reflection S/N	300	1997	395.00	395-450
1998 Romantic Reverie S/N	300		195.00	195
1997 Rose Arbor S/N	300		295.00	295
1994 Rose Fairies S/N	300	1997	295.00	295
1996 Rose Memories S/N	300		295.00	295
1999 Roses (13 x 13) S/N	300		145.00	145
2000 Roses from Monet's Garden S/N	300		295.00	295
1993 Roses in Bloom S/N	300	1995	395.00	395
1996 Spring Bulbs S/N	300		195.00	195
1994 Spring Conservatory S/N	300	1997	395.00	395
1995 Spring Garden S/N	300		395.00	395
2000 Summer Bouquet S/N	300		195.00	195
1998 Sunflower Bouquet S/N	300		195.00	195
1995 Sweet Bounty S/N	300		295.00	295
1999 Tulips (13 x 13) S/N	300		145.00	145
1992 Victorian Pavillion S/N	300	1997	195.00	195
2000 Vintage Bouquet S/N	300	1995	395.00	395
1996 Wisteria Dreams S/N	300		295.00	295
1993 Woodland Path S/N	300		495.00	495

Liu - Unframed Canvas Transfers Angels Among Us - L. Liu

1997 Angel of Light S/N	300		395.00	395
1997 Angel of Love S/N	300		395.00	395
1996 Guardian Angel S/N	300		395.00	395
1996 Messengers of Love S/N	300		250.00	250
1996 Protectors of Peace S/N	300		250.00	250

Liu - Unframed Canvas Transfers Celestial Symphony Series - L. Liu

1995 Flute Interlude S/N	300		145.00	145
1995 French Horn Melody S/N	300		145.00	145
1995 Piano Sonata S/N	300		145.00	145
1995 Violin Concerto S/N	300	1998	145.00	76-145

Liu - Unframed Canvas Transfers Dance & Music Series - L. Liu

2001 Ballet	300		125.00	125
2001 Big Band	300		145.00	145
2001 Chamber Music	300		145.00	145
2001 Flamenco	300		125.00	125
2001 Tango	300		125.00	125
2001 Waltz	300		125.00	125

Liu - Unframed Canvas Transfers The Music Room Series - L. Liu

1991 The Music Room S/N	300	1992	395.00	700-900
1992 The Music Room II-Nutcracker S/N	300	1993	395.00	600
1994 The Music Room III-Composer's Retreat S/N	300	1994	395.00	500
1995 The Music Room IV-Swan Melody S/N	300		425.00	425
1996 The Music Room V-Morning Serenade S/N	300		395.00	395
1999 Homage to Beethoven-Symphony No. 9 S/N	300		205.00	205
1999 Homage to Mozart-The Marriage of Figaro S/N	300		295.00	295
1999 The Music Room VII-Afternoon Repose S/N	300		425.00	425
1997 The Music Room VI-Romantic Overture S/N	300		425.00	425
1997 Clarinet Ensemble S/N	300		395.00	395
1996 Harmonic Duet S/N	300		195.00	195
1996 Musical Trio S/N	300		195.00	195

YEAR ISSUE	EDITION LIMIT	YEAR RETD.	ISSUE PRICE	*QUOTE U.S.$
Liu - Unframed Limited Edition Art Tiles - L. Liu				
2001 Anna's Hummingbird with Fuchsia	5,500		30.00	30
2001 Guardian Angel	5,500		30.00	30
2001 Hummingbird with Trumpet Vine Art	5,500		30.00	30
2001 Hydrangea Bouquet	5,500		30.00	30
2001 Iris Bouquet	5,500		30.00	30
2001 Motif Orientale	5,500		35.00	35
McDonald - M. McDonald				
1988 Amaryllis Dancer S/N	1,000	1999	55.00	55
1988 Lily Queen S/N	1,000	1999	55.00	55
Lightpost Publishing				
Kinkade Member's Only Collectors' Society - T. Kinkade				
1992 Skater's Pond	Closed	N/A	295.00	995-1035
1992 Morning Lane	Closed	N/A	Gift	595
1994 Collector's Cottage I	Closed	1995	315.00	550-825
1994 Painter of Light Book	Closed	1995	Gift	100-125
1995 Lochavan Cottage	Closed	1995	295.00	595-895
1995 Gardens Beyond Autumn Gate-pencil sketch	Closed	1995	Gift	110-125
1996 Julianne's Cottage-Keepsake Box	Closed	1996	Gift	50-69
1996 Skater's Pond Sketch Portfolio Edition	Closed	1997	75.00	894
1996 Julianne's Cottage Library Print	Closed	1997	50.00	75-95
1996 Meadowood Cottage (canvas framed)	4,950	1997	375.00	650-825
1996 Meadowood Cottage (paper unframed)	950	1997	150.00	225-390
1997 Simpler Times are Better Times	Closed	1997	Gift	50
1997 The Village Inn Library Print	Closed	1998	65.00	95
1997 Collectors' Cottages Portfolio Edition	Closed	1998	175.00	195-275
1997 Home is Where the Heart Is	Closed	1998	295.00	500-1000
1998 Let Your Light Shine	Closed	1998	Gift	50
1998 A Light In The Storm	Closed	1998	295.00	295
1998 Clearing Storms	Closed	1998	49.50	50
1999 Open Gate, Sussex	Closed	1999	Gift	N/A
1999 Teacup Cottage	Closed	1999	95.00	95
1999 Olde Porterfield Tea Room	Closed	1999	295.00	295
2000 Pye Corner Cottage	Closed	2000	Gift	N/A
2000 Teacup Cottage Classic (9 x 12)	Closed	2000	199.00	199
2000 Teacup Cottage Classic (12 x 16)	Closed	2000	299.00	299
2000 Teacup Cottage Teapot	2,950		100.00	100
2000 Beacon of Hope	Closed	2000	49.50	50
2000 The Sea of Tranquility	Closed	2000	49.50	50
2000 Light In The Storm	Closed	2000	49.50	50
2000 Pye Corner Cottage (1st Time Members)	Closed	2001	Gift	N/A
2001 Lochaven Cottage	Closed	2001	Gift	N/A
2001 Victorian Garden II (12 x 16)	Closed	2001	299.00	299
2001 Teacup Cottage Cup and Saucer	Closed	2001	29.95	30
2001 Creamer and Sugar Set	Closed	2001	39.95	40
2001 Lit Sculpted Meadowood Cottage	Closed	2001	44.95	45
2001 Lit Sculpted Lochaven Cottage	Closed	2001	44.95	45
2001 Lit Sculpted Open Gate Sussex	Closed	2001	44.95	45
2001 Wishing Well Village Diorama Base	Closed	2001	62.95	63
Kinkade-Event Pieces - T. Kinkade				
1996 Candlelight Cottage (canvas framed)	Closed	1997	375.00	525-855
1996 Candlelight Cottage (canvas unframed)	Closed	1997	275.00	395-415
1996 Candlelight Cottage (paper framed)	Closed	1997	325.00	325-445
1996 Candlelight Cottage (paper unframed)	Closed	1997	150.00	150-245
1996 Lamplight Village	Closed	1997	Gift	80-125
1996 We Wish You a Merry Christmas	Closed	1997	70.00	70-125
1997 Chandler's Cottage Inspirational Print (Mother's Day Event)	Closed	1997	80.00	75-125
Kinkade-Archival Paper/Canvas-Combined Edition-Framed - T. Kinkade				
1989 Blue Cottage (Paper)	Retrd.	1993	125.00	295-845
1989 Blue Cottage (Canvas)	Retrd.	1993	495.00	1695-1930
1990 Moonlit Village (Paper)	Closed	1992	225.00	695-1755
1990 Moonlit Village (Canvas)	Closed	1992	595.00	2950-5065
1986 New York, 1932 (Paper)	Closed	N/A	225.00	750-2235
1986 New York, 1932 (Canvas)	Closed	N/A	595.00	2950-5395
1989 Skating in the Park (Paper) S/N	750	1994	225.00	1295-1850
1989 Skating in the Park (Canvas) S/N	750	1994	595.00	3595-3845

YEAR ISSUE	EDITION LIMIT	YEAR RETD.	ISSUE PRICE	*QUOTE U.S.$
Kinkade-Canvas Editions-Framed - T. Kinkade				
1991 Afternoon Light, Dogwood A/P	98	1991	615.00	2350-3525
1991 Afternoon Light, Dogwood P/P	100	N/A	795.00	795-3595
1991 Afternoon Light, Dogwood R/P	200	N/A	N/A	3525-3775
1991 Afternoon Light, Dogwood S/N	980	N/A	515.00	1500-3225
1992 Amber Afternoon A/P	200	1992	715.00	2625-3250
1992 Amber Afternoon G/P	200	1992	765.00	1795-2725
1992 Amber Afternoon P/P	100	1992	815.00	2350-2925
1992 Amber Afternoon S/N	980	N/A	615.00	2425-2895
2001 The Aspen Chapel A/P (18 x 27)	590		1090.00	1090
2001 The Aspen Chapel A/P (24 x 36)	590		1645.00	1645
2001 The Aspen Chapel G/P (18 x 27)	1,100		1090.00	1090
2001 The Aspen Chapel G/P (24 x 36)	1,100		1645.00	1645
2001 The Aspen Chapel P/P (18 x 27)	530		1140.00	1140
2001 The Aspen Chapel P/P (24 x 36)	530		1695.00	1695
2001 The Aspen Chapel R/E (24 x 36)	240		4485.00	4485
2001 The Aspen Chapel S/N (18 x 27)	2,950		940.00	940
2001 The Aspen Chapel S/N (24 x 36)	2,950		1495.00	1495
2001 The Aspen Chapel S/P (18 x 27)	120		4275.00	4700
2001 The Aspen Chapel S/P (24 x 36)	120		7475.00	7475
1994 Autumn at Ashley's Cottage A/P	395	1999	590.00	695-785
1994 Autumn at Ashley's Cottage G/P	990		590.00	785
1994 Autumn at Ashley's Cottage P/P	315		640.00	835
1994 Autumn at Ashley's Cottage S/N	3,950		440.00	635
1991 The Autumn Gate A/P	200	N/A	695.00	3995-5675
1991 The Autumn Gate P/P	100	N/A	795.00	5765-6175
1991 The Autumn Gate R/E	Closed	1992	695.00	4000-5000
1991 The Autumn Gate R/P	200	N/A	N/A	6105-6775
1991 The Autumn Gate S/N	980	N/A	595.00	3995-5375
1995 Autumn Lane A/P	295	1998	800.00	775-1090
1995 Autumn Lane G/P	740	2000	750.00	1005-1125
1995 Autumn Lane P/P	240	2000	850.00	1140
1995 Autumn Lane S/N	2,950		650.00	940
2000 Autumn Snow A/P	390		1645.00	1645
2000 Autumn Snow G/P	700		1645.00	1645
2000 Autumn Snow P/P	350		1695.00	1695
2000 Autumn Snow S/N	1,950		1495.00	1495
1994 Beacon of Hope A/P	275	1994	765.00	1450-2315
1994 Beacon of Hope G/P	685	1994	765.00	1893-2315
1994 Beacon of Hope P/P	220	N/A	815.00	1945-2365
1994 Beacon of Hope S/N	2,750	1994	615.00	1545-2115
1996 Beginning of a Perfect Day A/P	295	1996	1240.00	2095-2625
1996 Beginning of a Perfect Day G/P	740	1998	1240.00	2075-2625
1996 Beginning of a Perfect Day P/P	240	1999	1290.00	1860-2675
1996 Beginning of a Perfect Day S/N	2,950	1998	1090.00	1850-2475
1996 Beginning of a Perfect Day S/P	95		3270.00	9450-13550
1993 Beside Still Waters A/P	400	N/A	615.00	3495-4015
1993 Beside Still Waters G/P	490	N/A	665.00	3350-4015
1993 Beside Still Waters P/P	100	N/A	715.00	3295-4215
1993 Beside Still Waters S/N	980	N/A	515.00	3195-4000
1995 Beside Still Waters S/P	95	N/A	2325.00	8900-10500
1993 Beyond Autumn Gate A/P	600	1993	915.00	2640-5415
1993 Beyond Autumn Gate G/P	500	N/A	965.00	2695-5615
1995 Beyond Autumn Gate P/P	100	N/A	1045.00	3400-5945
1993 Beyond Autumn Gate S/N	1,750	N/A	815.00	2190-5115
1995 Beyond Autumn Gate S/P	95	N/A	N/A	8000-14850
1997 Beyond Spring Gate A/P	345	1997	1300.00	3850-5115
1997 Beyond Spring Gate G/P	865	1997	1300.00	3850-5115
1997 Beyond Spring Gate P/P	280	1997	1350.00	3995-5315
1997 Beyond Spring Gate S/N	3,450	1997	1150.00	3250-4915
1997 Beyond Spring Gate S/P	95	1997	3450.00	6995-15350
2001 Beyond Summer Gate A/P (12 x 18)	590		840.00	840
2001 Beyond Summer Gate A/P (18 x 27)	590		1090.00	1090
2001 Beyond Summer Gate A/P (24 x 36)	590		1645.00	1645
2001 Beyond Summer Gate G/P (12 x 18)	1,100		840.00	840
2001 Beyond Summer Gate G/P (18 x 27)	1,100		1090.00	1090
2001 Beyond Summer Gate G/P (24 x 36)	1,100		1645.00	1645
2001 Beyond Summer Gate P/P (12 x 18)	530		890.00	890
2001 Beyond Summer Gate P/P (18 x 27)	530		1140.00	1140
2001 Beyond Summer Gate P/P (24 x 36)	530		1695.00	1695
2001 Beyond Summer Gate R/E (18 x 27)	240		2250.00	2565
2001 Beyond Summer Gate R/E (24 x 36)	240		4485.00	4485
2001 Beyond Summer Gate S/N (12 x 18)	2,950		690.00	690
2001 Beyond Summer Gate S/N (18 x 27)	2,950		940.00	940
2001 Beyond Summer Gate S/N (24 x 36)	120		7475.00	7475
2001 Beyond Summer Gate S/N (24 x 36)	2,950		1495.00	1495
1993 The Blessings of Autumn A/P	300	1994	715.00	2295-2725
1993 The Blessings of Autumn G/P	250	1994	765.00	1495-2925
1993 The Blessings of Autumn P/P	100	1994	815.00	2150-3175
1993 The Blessings of Autumn S/N	1,250	1994	615.00	2195-2625

YEAR ISSUE	EDITION LIMIT	YEAR RETD.	ISSUE PRICE	*QUOTE U.S.$
1993 The Blessings of Autumn S/P	95	1999	3750.00	5500-7550
1994 The Blessings of Spring A/P	275	1994	665.00	1210-1280
1994 The Blessings of Spring G/P	685	2000	665.00	995-1280
1994 The Blessings of Spring P/P	220		715.00	1375
1994 The Blessings of Spring S/N	2,750	1994	515.00	675-1125
1995 Blessings of Summer A/P	495		1015.00	1395
1995 Blessings of Summer G/P	1,240		965.00	1395
1995 Blessings of Summer P/P	400		1065.00	1445
1995 Blessings of Summer S/N	4,950		865.00	1245
1998 Block Island A/P (12 x 18)	490		775.00	840
1998 Block Island A/P (18 x 27)	490		940.00	1090
1998 Block Island G/P (12 x 18)	860		775.00	840
1998 Block Island G/P (18 x 27)	860		940.00	1090
1998 Block Island P/P (12 x 18)	300		825.00	890
1998 Block Island P/P (18 x 27)	300		990.00	1140
1998 Block Island R/E (12 x 18)	200		1800.00	1950
1998 Block Island R/E (18 x 27)	200		2250.00	2565
1998 Block Island S/N (12 x 18)	2,450		625.00	690
1998 Block Island S/N (18 x 27)	2,450		790.00	940
1998 Block Island S/P (18 x 27)	100		3750.00	4275
1995 Blossom Bridge A/P	295		730.00	910
1995 Blossom Bridge G/P	740		680.00	910
1995 Blossom Bridge P/P	240		780.00	960
1995 Blossom Bridge S/N	2,950		580.00	760
1995 Blossom Bridge S/P	95		1740.00	3800
1992 Blossom Hill Church A/P	200	1994	715.00	2455-2790
1992 Blossom Hill Church P/P	100	1999	815.00	2890-2950
1992 Blossom Hill Church R/E	Closed	1993	695.00	1600-2495
1992 Blossom Hill Church R/P	Closed	1993	N/A	2905-3390
1992 Blossom Hill Church S/N	980	1994	615.00	1650-2595
1991 Boston A/P	50	N/A	615.00	2095-4495
1991 Boston P/P	25	N/A	715.00	2495-4795
1991 Boston S/N	550	N/A	515.00	2995-3795
1999 Boulevard Lights, Paris A/P (18 x 27)	590		1005.00	1090
1999 Boulevard Lights, Paris A/P (24 x 36)	590		1510.00	1645
1999 Boulevard Lights, Paris G/P (18 x 27)	1,100		1005.00	1090
1999 Boulevard Lights, Paris G/P (24 x 36)	1,100		1510.00	1645
1999 Boulevard Lights, Paris P/P (18 x 27)	530		1055.00	1140
1999 Boulevard Lights, Paris P/P (24 x 36)	530		1560.00	1695
1999 Boulevard Lights, Paris R/E (18 x 27)	240		2565.00	2820
1999 Boulevard Lights, Paris R/E (24 x 36)	240		4080.00	4485
1999 Boulevard Lights, Paris S/N (18 x 27)	2,950		855.00	940
1999 Boulevard Lights, Paris S/N (24 x 36)	2,950		1360.00	1495
1999 Boulevard Lights, Paris S/P (18 x 27)	120		4275.00	4700
1999 Boulevard Lights, Paris S/P (24 x 36)	120		6800.00	7475
1997 Bridge of Faith A/P	395	1997	1300.00	3795-4795
1997 Bridge of Faith G/P	990	1997	1300.00	3895-5165
1997 Bridge of Faith P/P	320	1997	1350.00	3555-4845
1997 Bridge of Faith S/N	3,950	1997	1150.00	3000-4595
1997 Bridge of Faith S/P	95	1997	3450.00	6000-16550
1992 Broadwater Bridge A/P	200	N/A	615.00	1950-3825
1992 Broadwater Bridge G/P	200	N/A	665.00	2350-3975
1992 Broadwater Bridge P/P	100	N/A	715.00	3795-4325
1992 Broadwater Bridge S/N	980	N/A	495.00	1795-3625
1995 Brookside Hideaway A/P	395	1995	695.00	1050-1745
1995 Brookside Hideaway G/P	990	1998	695.00	1395-1745
1995 Brookside Hideaway P/P	320		745.00	1945
1995 Brookside Hideaway S/N	3,950	1996	545.00	895-1545
1991 Carmel, Dolores Street and the Tuck Box Tea Room A/P	200	1992	745.00	2950-3495
1991 Carmel, Dolores Street and the Tuck Box Tea Room P/P	100	1992	845.00	4805-5105
1991 Carmel, Dolores Street and the Tuck Box Tea Room R/P	Closed	1992	745.00	3750-3950
1991 Carmel, Dolores Street and the Tuck Box Tea Room S/N	980	1992	645.00	2525-4445
1989 Carmel, Ocean Avenue A/P	50	N/A	795.00	4200-7415
1989 Carmel, Ocean Avenue P/P	25	N/A	N/A	6825-7715
1989 Carmel, Ocean Avenue S/N	935	N/A	595.00	5222-5995
1999 Carmel, Sunset on Ocean Ave. A/P (18 x 27)	990		940.00	1090
1999 Carmel, Sunset on Ocean Ave. A/P (24 x 36)	990	2001	1410.00	1645
1999 Carmel, Sunset on Ocean Ave. A/P (28 x 42)	990		2100.00	2225
1999 Carmel, Sunset on Ocean Ave. E/P (24 x 36)	980	1999	1410.00	1410-1645
1999 Carmel, Sunset on Ocean Ave. G/P (18 x 27)	1,750	2001	940.00	1090
1999 Carmel, Sunset on Ocean Ave. G/P (24 x 36)	1,750	2000	1410.00	1645
1999 Carmel, Sunset on Ocean Ave. G/P (28 x 42)	1,750		2100.00	2225
1999 Carmel, Sunset on Ocean Ave. P/P (18 x 27)	900		990.00	1140
1999 Carmel, Sunset on Ocean Ave. P/P (24 x 36)	900	2001	1460.00	1695
1999 Carmel, Sunset on Ocean Ave. P/P (28 x 42)	900		2150.00	2275
1999 Carmel, Sunset on Ocean Ave. R/E (18 x 27)	400		2250.00	2820
1999 Carmel, Sunset on Ocean Ave. R/E (24 x 36)	400		3600.00	4485
1999 Carmel, Sunset on Ocean Ave. R/E (28 x 42)	400		5850.00	6225
1999 Carmel, Sunset on Ocean Ave. S/N (18 x 27)	4,950		790.00	940
1999 Carmel, Sunset on Ocean Ave. S/N (24 x 36)	4,950		1260.00	1495
1999 Carmel, Sunset on Ocean Ave. S/N (28 x 42)	4,950		1950.00	2075
1999 Carmel, Sunset on Ocean Ave. S/P (18 x 27)	200	2000	3750.00	4275
1999 Carmel, Sunset on Ocean Ave. S/P (24 x 36)	200	2000	6000.00	6450-7475
1999 Carmel, Sunset on Ocean Ave. S/P (28 x 42)	200		9750.00	10375
2001 Catalina Marina A/P	190		650.00	650
2001 Catalina Marina G/P	335		650.00	650
2001 Catalina Marina P/P	175		700.00	700
2001 Catalina Marina S/N	950		500.00	500
1991 Cedar Nook Cottage A/P	200	1991	315.00	595-1225
1991 Cedar Nook Cottage P/P	100	1991	515.00	945-1350
1991 Cedar Nook Cottage R/E	200	1991	315.00	700-1015
1991 Cedar Nook Cottage R/P	Closed	1991	N/A	1045-1425
1991 Cedar Nook Cottage S/N	1,960	1991	195.00	625-1075
1990 Chandler's Cottage A/P	100	N/A	N/A	2675-5115
1990 Chandler's Cottage P/P	50	N/A	N/A	4895-5415
1990 Chandler's Cottage S/N	550	N/A	495.00	2295-4815
1992 Christmas At the Ahwahnee A/P	200	1999	615.00	885-1250
1992 Christmas At the Ahwahnee G/P	200	1998	665.00	880-1235
1992 Christmas At the Ahwahnee P/P	100	N/A	715.00	985-1888
1992 Christmas At the Ahwahnee S/N	980	1999	515.00	745-1065
XX Christmas at the Courthouse S/N	2,950	N/A	N/A	2445-3500
1990 Christmas Cottage 1990 A/P	100	N/A	295.00	1595-3485
1990 Christmas Cottage 1990 P/P	50	N/A	N/A	3145-3745
1990 Christmas Cottage 1990 S/N	550	N/A	N/A	1825-3185
1991 Christmas Eve A/P	200	1991	515.00	1350-2995
1991 Christmas Eve P/P	100	1991	615.00	2545-3250
1991 Christmas Eve R/E	Retrd.	1991	495.00	2186-2595
1991 Christmas Eve R/P	Closed	1991	N/A	2645-3350
1991 Christmas Eve S/N	980	N/A	415.00	1235-2695
1994 Christmas Memories A/P	345	1996	695.00	895-1200
1994 Christmas Memories G/P	860		695.00	1180
1994 Christmas Memories P/P	275		745.00	1280
1994 Christmas Memories S/N	3,450	1995	545.00	550-1050
1994 Christmas Tree Cottage A/P	395		590.00	785
1994 Christmas Tree Cottage G/P	990		590.00	785
1994 Christmas Tree Cottage P/P	315		640.00	835
1994 Christmas Tree Cottage S/N	3,950		440.00	635
1996 A Christmas Welcome A/P	295	1996	675.00	785-1250
1996 A Christmas Welcome G/P	740		675.00	785
1996 A Christmas Welcome P/P	240		725.00	835
1996 A Christmas Welcome S/N	2,950		525.00	635
1996 A Christmas Welcome S/P	95		2750.00	3175
1997 Clearing Storms A/P (18 x 27)	590	1998	875.00	1695-2275
1997 Clearing Storms A/P (24 x 36)	590	1998	1300.00	1975-2945
1997 Clearing Storms G/P (18 x 27)	740	1998	875.00	1495-2145
1997 Clearing Storms G/P (24 x 36)	740	1998	1300.00	1995-2945
1997 Clearing Storms P/P (18 x 27)	360	1999	925.00	1705-2195
1997 Clearing Storms P/P (24 x 36)	360	1998	1350.00	1895-2995
1997 Clearing Storms R/E (18 x 27)	240	1998	2175.00	2895-3915
1997 Clearing Storms R/E (24 x 36)	240	1998	3450.00	3895-5950
1997 Clearing Storms S/N (18 x 27)	2,950	1998	725.00	1395-1995
1997 Clearing Storms S/N (24 x 36)	2,950	1998	1150.00	1875-2795
1997 Clearing Storms S/P (18 x 27)	120	N/A	3625.00	5200-8350
1997 Clearing Storms S/P (24 x 36)	120	N/A	5750.00	6000-12950
2001 Clocktower Cottage A/P (18 x 27)	790		1090.00	1090
2001 Clocktower Cottage A/P (24 x 36)	790		1645.00	1645
2001 Clocktower Cottage G/P (18 x 27)	1,400		1090.00	1090
2001 Clocktower Cottage G/P (24 x 36)	1,400	2001	1645.00	1645
2001 Clocktower Cottage P/P (18 x 27)	710		1140.00	1140
2001 Clocktower Cottage P/P (24 x 36)	710		1695.00	1695

YEAR ISSUE	EDITION LIMIT	YEAR RETD.	ISSUE PRICE	*QUOTE U.S.$
2001 Clocktower Cottage R/E (24 x 36)	320		4485.00	4485
2001 Clocktower Cottage S/N (18 x 27)	3,950		940.00	940
2001 Clocktower Cottage S/N (24 x 36)	3,950		1495.00	1495
2001 Clocktower Cottage S/P (18 x 27)	120		5250.00	5715
2001 Clocktower Cottage S/P (24 x 36)	160		7475.00	7475
2000 Cobblestone Bridge A/P (18 x 27)	990	2001	1090.00	1440-1775
2000 Cobblestone Bridge A/P (24 x 36)	590	2001	1645.00	1550-2225
2000 Cobblestone Bridge A/P (28 x 42)	590		2225.00	2225
2000 Cobblestone Bridge G/P (18 x 27)	1,750	2001	1090.00	1440-1775
2000 Cobblestone Bridge G/P (24 x 36)	1,100	2000	1645.00	1995-2225
2000 Cobblestone Bridge G/P (28 x 42)	1,100		2225.00	2225
2000 Cobblestone Bridge P/P (18 x 27)	900	2001	1140.00	1490-1825
2000 Cobblestone Bridge P/P (24 x 36)	530	2001	1695.00	2045-3500
2000 Cobblestone Bridge P/P (28 x 42)	530	2001	2275.00	2275
2000 Cobblestone Bridge R/E (18 x 27)	240	2001	3270.00	3590-3850
2000 Cobblestone Bridge R/E (24 x 36)	240	2001	4485.00	4935-5550
2000 Cobblestone Bridge S/N (18 x 27)	2,950	2001	940.00	1100-1625
2000 Cobblestone Bridge S/N (24 x 36)	2,950	2001	1495.00	1650-2075
2000 Cobblestone Bridge S/N (28 x 42)	2,950		2075.00	2075
2000 Cobblestone Bridge S/P (18 x 27)	120	2001	5715.00	5995
2000 Cobblestone Bridge S/P (24 x 36)	120	2001	7475.00	8125-8995
1997 Cobblestone Brooke A/P	495	1998	1300.00	1495-2435
1997 Cobblestone Brooke G/P	1,240	1998	1300.00	1495-2435
1997 Cobblestone Brooke P/P	400	1997	1350.00	1510-2485
1997 Cobblestone Brooke S/N	4,950	1997	1150.00	1360-2285
1997 Cobblestone Brooke S/P	95	1998	3450.00	6500-12350
1996 Cobblestone Lane A/P	295	1996	1125.00	2295-4295
1996 Cobblestone Lane G/P	740	1996	1125.00	2395-4295
1996 Cobblestone Lane P/P	240	1996	1175.00	2350-4595
1996 Cobblestone Lane S/N	2,950	1996	975.00	1940-4095
1996 Cobblestone Lane S/P	95	1996	2925.00	7900-15450
1998 Cobblestone Village A/P (18 x 24)	1,190		940.00	1090
1998 Cobblestone Village A/P (25 1/2 x 34)	1,190		1410.00	1645
1998 Cobblestone Village A/P (30 x 40)	990		2100.00	2225
1998 Cobblestone Village G/P (18 x 24)	2,100		940.00	1090
1998 Cobblestone Village G/P (25 1/2 x 34)	2,100		1410.00	1645
1998 Cobblestone Village G/P (30 x 40)	1,750		2100.00	2225
1998 Cobblestone Village P/P (18 x 24)	1,100		990.00	1140
1998 Cobblestone Village P/P (25 1/2 x 34)	1,100		1460.00	1695
1998 Cobblestone Village P/P (30 x 40)	900		2150.00	2275
1998 Cobblestone Village R/E (18 x 24)	480		2250.00	2820
1998 Cobblestone Village R/E (25 1/2 x 34)	480		3600.00	4485
1998 Cobblestone Village R/E (30 x 40)	400		5850.00	6225
1998 Cobblestone Village S/N (18 x 24)	5,950		790.00	940
1998 Cobblestone Village S/N (25 1/2 x 34)	5,950		1260.00	1495
1998 Cobblestone Village S/N (30 x 40)	4,950		1950.00	2075
1998 Cobblestone Village S/P (18 x 24)	240		3750.00	4700
1998 Cobblestone Village S/P (25 1/2 x 34)	240		6000.00	7475
1998 Cobblestone Village S/P (30 x 40)	200		9750.00	10375
1999 Conquering the Storms A/P (18 x 27)	590	2000	940.00	1295-1395
1999 Conquering the Storms A/P (24 x 36)	590	2000	1410.00	1800-1945
1999 Conquering the Storms A/P (28 x 42)	590		2100.00	2225
1999 Conquering the Storms E/P (24 x 36)	Closed	1999	1410.00	1550-1945
1999 Conquering the Storms G/P (18 x 27)	1,100	2000	940.00	1295-1395
1999 Conquering the Storms G/P (24 x 36)	1,100	1999	1410.00	1410-1945
1999 Conquering the Storms G/P (28 x 42)	1,100		2100.00	2225
1999 Conquering the Storms P/P (18 x 27)	530	2000	990.00	1345-1445
1999 Conquering the Storms P/P (24 x 36)	530	2000	1460.00	1920-1995
1999 Conquering the Storms P/P (28 x 42)	530		2150.00	2275
1999 Conquering the Storms R/E (18 x 27)	240		2250.00	2995
1999 Conquering the Storms R/E (24 x 36)	240		3600.00	4795
1999 Conquering the Storms R/E (28 x 42)	240		5850.00	6225
1999 Conquering the Storms S/N (18 x 27)	2,950	2000	790.00	775-1550
1999 Conquering the Storms S/N (24 x 36)	2,950	2000	1260.00	1360-1895
1999 Conquering the Storms S/N (28 x 42)	2,950		1950.00	2075
1999 Conquering the Storms S/P (18 x 27)	120	2001	3750.00	4935-5095
1999 Conquering the Storms S/P (24 x 36)	120		6000.00	6000-7995
1999 Conquering the Storms S/P (28 x 42)	120		9750.00	10375
1992 Cottage-By-The-Sea A/P	200	1992	715.00	2395-3315
1992 Cottage-By-The-Sea G/P	200	N/A	765.00	1950-3465
1992 Cottage-By-The-Sea P/P	100	1992	815.00	3345-3765
1992 Cottage-By-The-Sea S/N	980	N/A	615.00	2150-3115
1992 Country Memories A/P	200	1992	515.00	1395-1815
1992 Country Memories G/P	200	1997	565.00	1295-1915
1992 Country Memories P/P	100	1999	615.00	1600-2050
1992 Country Memories S/N	980	1994	395.00	1230-1615
1994 Creekside Trail A/P	198	1999	840.00	985-1090
1994 Creekside Trail G/P	500	1999	840.00	965-1090
1994 Creekside Trail P/P	160	2000	890.00	1015-1140
1994 Creekside Trail S/N	1,984		690.00	940
1994 Days of Peace A/P	198	1999	840.00	940-1090
1994 Days of Peace G/P	496	1999	840.00	940-1090
1994 Days of Peace P/P	160	2000	890.00	1055-1140
1994 Days of Peace S/N	1,984		690.00	940
1995 Deer Creek Cottage A/P	295	1996	615.00	800-1220
1995 Deer Creek Cottage G/P	740	1999	565.00	800-1350
1995 Deer Creek Cottage P/P	240	1999	665.00	950-1495
1995 Deer Creek Cottage S/N	2,950	1998	465.00	975-1250
1995 Deer Creek Cottage S/P	95	1999	1395.00	3000-4545
1994 Dusk in the Valley A/P	198		840.00	1090
1994 Dusk in the Valley G/P	500		840.00	1090
1994 Dusk in the Valley P/P	160		890.00	1140
1994 Dusk in the Valley S/N	1,984		690.00	940
1994 Emerald Isle Cottage A/P	275	1994	665.00	995-1445
1994 Emerald Isle Cottage G/P	685	1998	665.00	1195-1445
1994 Emerald Isle Cottage P/P	220	2000	715.00	1295-1595
1994 Emerald Isle Cottage S/N	2,750	1998	515.00	1125-1295
1993 End of a Perfect Day I A/P	400	1994	615.00	2495-3365
1993 End of a Perfect Day I G/P	300	N/A	665.00	2695-3865
1993 End of a Perfect Day I P/P	100	N/A	715.00	2800-4165
1993 End of a Perfect Day I S/N	1,250	1994	515.00	2245-3365
1995 End of a Perfect Day I S/P	95	1996	2325	8800-14295
1994 End of a Perfect Day II A/P	495	1994	965.00	2450-4295
1994 End of a Perfect Day II G/P	1,240	1994	965.00	2750-4295
1994 End of a Perfect Day II P/P	400	N/A	1015.00	4105-4545
1994 End of a Perfect Day II S/N	4,950	1995	815.00	2165-4045
1995 End of a Perfect Day III A/P	495	1995	1145.00	1825-2805
1995 End of a Perfect Day III G/P	1,240	1998	1145.00	2100-2955
1995 End of a Perfect Day III P/P	400	N/A	1195.00	2095-3055
1995 End of a Perfect Day III S/N	4,950	1996	995.00	1695-2755
1989 Entrance to the Manor House A/P	50	1996	595.00	1875-2505
1989 Entrance to the Manor House P/P	25	N/A		2495-2805
1989 Entrance to the Manor House S/N	550	N/A	495.00	2305-3500
1989 Evening at Merritt's Cottage A/P	50	N/A	595.00	2495-4475
1989 Evening at Merritt's Cottage P/P	25	N/A		4350-4675
1989 Evening at Merritt's Cottage S/N	Closed	N/A	495.00	1095-3975
1992 Evening at Swanbrooke Cottage Thomashire A/P	200	N/A	715.00	2650-4095
1992 Evening at Swanbrooke Cottage Thomashire P/P	200	N/A	765.00	2650-4195
1992 Evening at Swanbrooke Cottage Thomashire P/P	100	N/A	815.00	4330-4395
1992 Evening at Swanbrooke Cottage Thomashire S/N	980	N/A	615.00	2435-3795
1992 Evening Carolers A/P	200	1999	415.00	580-615
1992 Evening Carolers G/P	200	1998	465.00	570-615
1992 Evening Carolers P/P	100	2000	515.00	630-665
1992 Evening Carolers S/N	1,960		315.00	465
1999 Evening Glow A/P (12 x 16)	590		750.00	785
1999 Evening Glow A/P (16 x 20)	590		865.00	910
1999 Evening Glow G/P (12 x 16)	1,110		750.00	785
1999 Evening Glow G/P (16 x 20)	1,110		865.00	910
1999 Evening Glow P/P (12 x 16)	530		800.00	835
1999 Evening Glow P/P (16 x 20)	530		915.00	960
1999 Evening Glow R/E (12 x 16)	240		1650.00	1905
1999 Evening Glow R/E (16 X 20)	240		2145.00	2280
1999 Evening Glow S/N (12 x 16)	2,950		600.00	635
1999 Evening Glow S/N (16 x 20)	2,950		715.00	760
1999 Evening Glow S/P (12 x 16)	120		3000.00	3175
1999 Evening Glow S/P (16 x 20)	120		3575.00	3800
1995 Evening in the Forest A/P	495		695.00	910
1995 Evening in the Forest G/P	1,240		645.00	910
1995 Evening in the Forest P/P	400		745.00	960
1995 Evening in the Forest S/N	4,950		545.00	760
1999 Evening Majesty A/P (18 x 27)	990		1005.00	1090
1999 Evening Majesty A/P (24 x 36)	990		1510.00	1645
1999 Evening Majesty A/P (28 x 42)	990		2145.00	2225
1999 Evening Majesty G/P (18 x 27)	1,750	2001	1005.00	1090
1999 Evening Majesty G/P (24 x 36)	1,750	2000	1510.00	1645
1999 Evening Majesty G/P (28 x 42)	1,750		2145.00	2225
1999 Evening Majesty P/P (18 x 27)	900		1055.00	1140
1999 Evening Majesty P/P (24 x 36)	900	2000	1560.00	1695
1999 Evening Majesty P/P (28 x 42)	900		2195.00	2275
1999 Evening Majesty R/E (18 x 27)	400		2565.00	2820
1999 Evening Majesty R/E (24 x 36)	400		4080.00	4485
1999 Evening Majesty R/E (28 x 42)	400		5985.00	6225
1999 Evening Majesty S/N (18 x 27)	4,950		855.00	940
1999 Evening Majesty S/N (24 x 36)	4,950		1360.00	1495
1999 Evening Majesty S/N (28 x 42)	4,950		1995.00	2075
1999 Evening Majesty S/P (18 x 27)	200		4275.00	4700
1999 Evening Majesty S/P (24 x 36)	200		6800.00	7475
1999 Evening Majesty S/P (28 x 42)	200		9975.00	10375

YEAR ISSUE	EDITION LIMIT	YEAR RETD.	ISSUE PRICE	*QUOTE U.S.$
1998 Everett's Cottage A/P (16 x 20)	1,190		800.00	910
1998 Everett's Cottage A/P (20 x 24)	1,190		900.00	1090
1998 Everett's Cottage A/P (24 x 30)	990		1150.00	1395
1998 Everett's Cottage G/P (16 x 20)	2,100		835.00	910
1998 Everett's Cottage G/P (20 x 24)	2,100		940.00	1090
1998 Everett's Cottage G/P (24 x 30)	1,750		1200.00	1395
1998 Everett's Cottage P/P (16 x 20)	1,100		885.00	960
1998 Everett's Cottage P/P (20 x 24)	1,100		990.00	1140
1998 Everett's Cottage P/P (24 x 30)	600		1250.00	1445
1998 Everett's Cottage R/E (16 x 20)	480		1950.00	2280
1998 Everett's Cottage R/E (20 x 24)	480		2250.00	2820
1998 Everett's Cottage R/E (24 x 30)	400		3000.00	3735
1998 Everett's Cottage S/N (16 x 20)	5,950		650.00	760
1998 Everett's Cottage S/N (20 x 24)	5,950		750.00	940
1998 Everett's Cottage S/N (24 x 30)	4,950		1000.00	1245
1998 Everett's Cottage S/P (16 x 20)	240		3260.00	3800
1998 Everett's Cottage S/P (20 x 24)	240		3750.00	4700
1998 Everett's Cottage S/P (24 x 30)	200		5000.00	6225
1993 Fisherman's Wharf San Francisco A/P	275	1993	1065.00	1750-2520
1993 Fisherman's Wharf San Francisco G/P	550	N/A	1115.00	1410-2520
1993 Fisherman's Wharf San Francisco P/P	230	1998	1165.00	2000-2295
1993 Fisherman's Wharf San Francisco S/N	2,750	1995	965.00	1145-1595
1991 Flags Over The Capitol A/P	200	1999	715.00	1500-1695
1991 Flags Over The Capitol P/P	100	1999	815.00	1195-1745
1991 Flags Over The Capitol R/E	Retrd.	N/A	695.00	1000-1345
1991 Flags Over The Capitol R/P	200	N/A	N/A	1395-2110
1991 Flags Over The Capitol S/N	980	1998	615.00	1195-1695
1999 The Forest Chapel A/P (20 x 24)	590	2000	940.00	1205-1945
1999 The Forest Chapel A/P (24 x 30)	590	2000	1200.00	1700-2295
1999 The Forest Chapel G/P (20 x 24)	1,100	1999	940.00	1455-1945
1999 The Forest Chapel G/P (24 x 30)	1,100	1999	1200.00	1735-2295
1999 The Forest Chapel P/P (20 x 24)	530	2000	990.00	1505-1995
1999 The Forest Chapel P/P (24 x 30)	530	2000	1250.00	1785-2345
1999 The Forest Chapel R/E (20 x 24)	240	2000	2250.00	3215-4050
1999 The Forest Chapel R/E (24 x 30)	240	2000	3000.00	3495-5100
1999 The Forest Chapel S/N (20 x 24)	2,950	1999	790.00	1055-1795
1999 The Forest Chapel S/N (24 x 30)	2,950	1999	1050.00	1525-2145
1999 The Forest Chapel S/P (20 x 24)	120	2000	3750.00	4500-6250
1999 The Forest Chapel S/P (24 x 30)	120	2000	5000.00	5600-8080
1999 Foxglove Cottage A/P (16 x 20)	790		835.00	910
1999 Foxglove Cottage A/P (20 x 24)	790		940.00	1090
1999 Foxglove Cottage A/P (24 x 30)	790		1200.00	1395
1999 Foxglove Cottage G/P (16 x 20)	1,400		835.00	910
1999 Foxglove Cottage G/P (20 x 24)	1,400		940.00	1090
1999 Foxglove Cottage G/P (24 x 30)	1,400		1200.00	1395
1999 Foxglove Cottage P/P (16 x 20)	710		885.00	960
1999 Foxglove Cottage P/P (20 x 24)	710		990.00	1140
1999 Foxglove Cottage P/P (24 x 30)	710		1250.00	1445
1999 Foxglove Cottage R/E (16 x 20)	320		1950.00	2280
1999 Foxglove Cottage R/E (20 x 24)	320		2250.00	2820
1999 Foxglove Cottage R/E (24 x 30)	320		3000.00	3735
1999 Foxglove Cottage S/N (16 x 20)	3,950		685.00	760
1999 Foxglove Cottage S/N (20 x 24)	3,950		790.00	940
1999 Foxglove Cottage S/N (24 x 30)	3,950		1050.00	1245
1999 Foxglove Cottage S/P (16 x 20)	160		3250.00	3800
1999 Foxglove Cottage S/P (20 x 24)	160		3750.00	4700
1999 Foxglove Cottage S/P (24 x 30)	160		5000.00	6225
2001 Front Street, Lahaina G/P	260		785.00	785
2001 Front Street, Lahaina S/N	750		635.00	635
1997 Garden of Prayer A/P (18 x 24)	990	1998	900.00	1795-2845
1997 Garden of Prayer A/P (25 1/2 x 34)	990	1998	1350.00	2595-3995
1997 Garden of Prayer A/P (30 x 40)	790	1999	2100.00	2995-4200
1997 Garden of Prayer G/P (18 x 24)	1,750	1998	900.00	1140-2845
1997 Garden of Prayer G/P (25 1/2 x 34)	1,750	1998	1350.00	2595-3995
1997 Garden of Prayer G/P (30 x 40)	1,400	1999	2100.00	2895-4195
1997 Garden of Prayer P/P (18 x 24)	600	1999	950.00	1190-2895
1997 Garden of Prayer P/P (25 1/2 x 34)	600	1998	1400.00	1710-4045
1997 Garden of Prayer P/P (30 x 40)	480	1999	2150.00	2350-4245
1997 Garden of Prayer R/E (18 x 24)	400	1999	2250.00	3295-5500
1997 Garden of Prayer R/E (25 1/2 x 34)	400	1999	3600.00	5950-8975
1997 Garden of Prayer R/E (30 x 40)	320	1999	5850.00	6250-9950
1997 Garden of Prayer S/N (18 x 24)	4,950	1998	750.00	1495-2645
1997 Garden of Prayer S/N (25 1/2 x 34)	4,950	1998	1200.00	2350-3795
1997 Garden of Prayer S/N (30 x 40)	3,950	1999	1950.00	2595-3995
1997 Garden of Prayer S/P (18 x 24)	200	1998	3750.00	5690-9000
1997 Garden of Prayer S/P (25 1/2 x 34)	200	1998	6000.00	9400-14450
1997 Garden of Prayer S/P (30 x 40)	160	1999	9750.00	9750-16250
1993 The Garden of Promise A/P	400	N/A	715.00	2695-3815
1993 The Garden of Promise G/P	300	N/A	765.00	2795-3915
1993 The Garden of Promise P/P	100	N/A	815.00	3495-4115
1993 The Garden of Promise S/N	1,250	1994	615.00	2700-3515
1993 The Garden of Promise S/P	95	N/A	2800.00	8600-15250
1992 The Garden Party A/P	200		615.00	910
1992 The Garden Party G/P	200	1999	665.00	695-910
1992 The Garden Party P/P	100	2000	715.00	960
1992 The Garden Party S/N	980		515.00	760
1994 Gardens Beyond Autumn Gate S/N	5,193	1996	1025.00	1750-3295
1998 Gardens Beyond Spring Gate A/P (18 x 24)	1,190	2000	900.00	940-1255
1998 Gardens Beyond Spring Gate A/P (25 1/2 x 34)	1,190	1999	1350.00	1495-2295
1998 Gardens Beyond Spring Gate A/P (30 x 40)	1,190		2100.00	2225
1998 Gardens Beyond Spring Gate G/P (18 x 24)	2,100	2000	900.00	1190-1255
1998 Gardens Beyond Spring Gate G/P (25 1/2 x 34)	2,100	1999	1350.00	1525-2295
1998 Gardens Beyond Spring Gate G/P (30 x 40)	2,100		2100.00	2225
1998 Gardens Beyond Spring Gate P/P (18 x 24)	710	2001	950.00	1285-1305
1998 Gardens Beyond Spring Gate P/P (25 1/2 x 34)	710	1999	1400.00	1875-2345
1998 Gardens Beyond Spring Gate P/P (30 x 40)	710		2150.00	2275
1998 Gardens Beyond Spring Gate R/E (18 x 24)	480		2250.00	2855
1998 Gardens Beyond Spring Gate R/E (25 1/2 x 34)	480		3600.00	4645
1998 Gardens Beyond Spring Gate R/E (30 x 40)	480		5850.00	6225
1998 Gardens Beyond Spring Gate S/N (18 x 24)	5,950		750.00	1040
1998 Gardens Beyond Spring Gate S/N (25 1/2 x 34)	5,950	1998	1200.00	1250-2115
1998 Gardens Beyond Spring Gate S/N (30 x 40)	5,950		1950.00	2075
1998 Gardens Beyond Spring Gate S/P (18 x 24)	240		3750.00	4795
1998 Gardens Beyond Spring Gate S/P (25 1/2 x 34)	240		6000.00	8150
1998 Gardens Beyond Spring Gate S/P (30 x 40)	240		9750.00	10375
1993 Glory of Evening A/P	400	1993	365.00	900-2535
1993 Glory of Evening G/P	490	N/A	365.00	695-2635
1993 Glory of Evening P/P	100	1994	830.00	1300-2835
1993 Glory of Evening S/N	1,980	1994	315.00	1215-2235
1993 Glory of Evening S/P	95	1994	2000.00	4000-9500
1993 Glory of Morning A/P	400	1993	365.00	730-2535
1993 Glory of Morning G/P	490	1993	365.00	875-2635
1993 Glory of Morning P/P	100	1993	830.00	1300-2835
1993 Glory of Morning S/N	1,980	1994	315.00	1850-2235
1993 Glory of Morning S/P	95	1993	2000.00	4000-9500
1993 Glory of Winter A/P	300		715.00	1090
1993 Glory of Winter G/P	250	1999	715.00	695-1005
1993 Glory of Winter P/P	175		815.00	1140
1993 Glory of Winter S/N	1,250		615.00	940
1995 Golden Gate Bridge, San Francisco A/P	395	1996	1240.00	2495-2620
1995 Golden Gate Bridge, San Francisco G/P	990	N/A	1190.00	1995-2620
1995 Golden Gate Bridge, San Francisco P/P	320	1996	1290.00	2395-2845
1995 Golden Gate Bridge, San Francisco S/N	3,950	1996	1090.00	1795-2500
1995 Golden Gate Bridge, San Francisco S/P	95	1996	3270.00	7995-13950
2001 The Good Shepherd's Cottage A/P (18 x 24)	590		1090.00	1090
2001 The Good Shepherd's Cottage A/P (25 1/2 x 34)	590		1645.00	1645
2001 The Good Shepherd's Cottage G/P (18 x 24)	1,100		1090.00	1090
2001 The Good Shepherd's Cottage G/P (25 1/2 x 34)	1,100		1645.00	1645
2001 The Good Shepherd's Cottage P/P (18 x 24)	530		1140.00	1140
2001 The Good Shepherd's Cottage P/P (25 1/2 x 34)	530		1695.00	1695
2001 The Good Shepherd's Cottage S/N (18 x 24)	2,950		940.00	940

YEAR ISSUE	EDITION LIMIT	YEAR RETD.	ISSUE PRICE	*QUOTE U.S.$
2001 The Good Shepherd's Cottage S/N (25 1/2 x 34)	2,950		1495.00	1495
1994 Guardian Castle A/P	475		1015.00	1395
1994 Guardian Castle G/P	1,190		1015.00	1395
1994 Guardian Castle P/P	380		1065.00	1445
1994 Guardian Castle S/N	4,750		865.00	1245
1993 Heather's Hutch A/P	400	1993	515.00	900-1545
1993 Heather's Hutch G/P	300	N/A	565.00	995-1645
1993 Heather's Hutch P/P	100	1999	615.00	1600-1795
1993 Heather's Hutch S/N	1,250	N/A	415.00	775-1395
1993 Heather's Hutch S/P	95		N/A	3950
1994 Hidden Arbor A/P	375	2000	665.00	910-1145
1994 Hidden Arbor G/P	940		665.00	910
1994 Hidden Arbor P/P	300		715.00	960
1994 Hidden Arbor S/N	3,750		515.00	760
1990 Hidden Cottage I A/P	100	N/A	595.00	1275-5225
1990 Hidden Cottage I P/P	50	N/A	N/A	2295-5825
1990 Hidden Cottage I S/N	550	N/A	495.00	1975-4725
1993 Hidden Cottage II A/P	400	1993	615.00	1050-1825
1993 Hidden Cottage II G/P	400	1995	665.00	995-1950
1993 Hidden Cottage II P/P	100	1995	715.00	1695-2075
1993 Hidden Cottage II S/N	1,480	1994	515.00	875-1625
1993 Hidden Cottage II S/P	95	1995	3250.00	4025-8150
1994 Hidden Gazebo A/P	240	1994	665.00	1150-1775
1994 Hidden Gazebo G/P	600	1994	665.00	1025-1775
1994 Hidden Gazebo P/P	190	1999	715.00	1725-2100
1994 Hidden Gazebo S/N	2,400	1994	515.00	950-1495
1998 A Holiday Gathering A/P (12 x 16)	1,390		725.00	785
1998 A Holiday Gathering A/P (18 x 24)	1,390		940.00	1090
1998 A Holiday Gathering A/P (25 1/2 x 34)	1,390		1410.00	1645
1998 A Holiday Gathering G/P (12 x 16)	2,450		725.00	785
1998 A Holiday Gathering G/P (18 x 24)	2,450	2000	940.00	1090
1998 A Holiday Gathering G/P (25 1/2 x 34)	2,450		1410.00	1645
1998 A Holiday Gathering P/P (12 x 16)	1,250		775.00	835
1998 A Holiday Gathering P/P (18 x 24)	1,250		990.00	1140
1998 A Holiday Gathering P/P (25 1/2 x 34)	1,250		1460.00	1695
1998 A Holiday Gathering R/E (12 x 16)	550		1650.00	1905
1998 A Holiday Gathering R/E (18 x 24)	550		2250.00	2820
1998 A Holiday Gathering R/E (25 1/2 x 34)	550		3600.00	4485
1998 A Holiday Gathering S/N (12 x 16)	6,950		575.00	635
1998 A Holiday Gathering S/N (18 x 24)	6,950		790.00	940
1998 A Holiday Gathering S/N (25 1/2 x 34)	6,950		1260.00	1495
1998 A Holiday Gathering S/P (12 x 16)	280		2750.00	3175
1998 A Holiday Gathering S/P (18 x 24)	280		3750.00	4700
1998 A Holiday Gathering S/P (25 1/2 x 34)	280		6000.00	7475
1996 Hollyhock House A/P	395	1999	730.00	835-910
1996 Hollyhock House G/P	990		730.00	910
1996 Hollyhock House P/P	320		780.00	960
1996 Hollyhock House S/N	3,950		580.00	760
1996 Hollyhock House S/P	95	1998	1740.00	4400-5970
1991 Home For The Evening A/P	200	1994	315.00	875-1345
1991 Home For The Evening P/P	100	N/A	415.00	1485-1645
1991 Home For The Evening S/N	980	N/A	215.00	850-1115
1991 Home For The Holidays A/P	200	1991	715.00	2495-4265
1991 Home For The Holidays P/P	100	1991	815.00	4195-4565
1991 Home For The Holidays R/E	N/A	1991	695.00	3995-4195
1991 Home For The Holidays S/N	980	N/A	615.00	1995-3765
1992 Home is Where the Heart Is I A/P	200	N/A	715.00	2050-3745
1992 Home is Where the Heart Is I G/P	200	N/A	765.00	1165-3845
1992 Home is Where the Heart Is I P/P	100	N/A	815.00	2695-4045
1992 Home is Where the Heart Is I S/N	980	N/A	615.00	1995-3445
1996 Home is Where the Heart Is II A/P	495	1997	840.00	1050-1245
1996 Home is Where the Heart Is II G/P	1,240		840.00	1245
1996 Home is Where the Heart Is II P/P	400		890.00	1285
1996 Home is Where the Heart Is II S/N	Closed	1997	690.00	940-1175
1996 Home is Where the Heart Is II S/P	95	1997	2070.00	5570-7295
1993 Homestead House A/P	300	1996	715.00	940-7495
1993 Homestead House G/P	250	N/A	765.00	1100-1995
1993 Homestead House P/P	100	1999	815.00	1895-2095
1993 Homestead House S/N	1,250	1996	615.00	995-1695
1998 Hometown Bridge A/P (18 x 27)	1,190		940.00	1090
1998 Hometown Bridge A/P (24 x 36)	1,190		1410.00	1645
1998 Hometown Bridge A/P (28 x 42)	990		2100.00	2225
1998 Hometown Bridge G/P (18 x 27)	2,100		940.00	1090
1998 Hometown Bridge G/P (24 x 36)	2,100		1410.00	1645
1998 Hometown Bridge G/P (28 x 42)	1,750		2100.00	2225
1998 Hometown Bridge P/P (18 x 27)	1,100		990.00	1140
1998 Hometown Bridge P/P (24 x 36)	1,100		1460.00	1695
1998 Hometown Bridge P/P (28 x 42)	900		2150.00	2275
1998 Hometown Bridge R/E (18 x 27)	480		2250.00	2820
1998 Hometown Bridge R/E (24 x 36)	480		3600.00	4485
1998 Hometown Bridge R/E (28 x 42)	400		5850.00	6225
1998 Hometown Bridge S/N (18 x 27)	5,950		790.00	940
1998 Hometown Bridge S/N (24 x 36)	5,950		1260.00	1495
1998 Hometown Bridge S/N (28 x 42)	4,950		1950.00	2075
1998 Hometown Bridge S/P (18 x 27)	240		3750.00	4700
1998 Hometown Bridge S/P (24 x 36)	240		6000.00	7475
1998 Hometown Bridge S/P (28 x 42)	200		9750.00	10375
1995 Hometown Chapel A/P	495	1999	1045.00	1285-1395
1995 Hometown Chapel G/P	1,240	1999	995.00	1200-1285
1995 Hometown Chapel P/P	400		1095.00	1445
1995 Hometown Chapel S/N	4,950		895.00	1245
1996 Hometown Evening A/P	295	1996	1070.00	2550-4065
1996 Hometown Evening G/P	740	1996	1070.00	2895-4065
1996 Hometown Evening P/P	240	1996	1120.00	3455-4265
1996 Hometown Evening S/N	2,950	1996	920.00	1950-3765
1997 Hometown Lake A/P	495	1998	1125.00	2550-3545
1997 Hometown Lake G/P	1,240	1998	1125.00	2625-3545
1997 Hometown Lake P/P	400	1998	1175.00	2405-3695
1997 Hometown Lake S/N	4,950	1998	975.00	2250-3295
1997 Hometown Lake S/P	125	1998	3900.00	8800-14200
1995 Hometown Memories I A/P	495	1995	1015.00	2395-3515
1995 Hometown Memories I G/P	1,240	N/A	1015.00	2450-3525
1995 Hometown Memories I P/P	400	N/A	1065.00	2850-3850
1995 Hometown Memories I S/N	4,950	1996	865.00	1895-3215
2000 Hometown Morning A/P (24 x 30)	790	2001	1285.00	1395-1425
2000 Hometown Morning A/P (25 1/2 x 34)	790		1510.00	1645
2000 Hometown Morning A/P (30 x 40)	790		2145.00	2225
2000 Hometown Morning G/P (24 x 30)	1,400	2000	1285.00	1395
2000 Hometown Morning G/P (25 1/2 x 34)	1,400		1510.00	1645
2000 Hometown Morning G/P (30 x 40)	1,400		2145.00	2225
2000 Hometown Morning P/P (24 x 30)	710		1335.00	1445
2000 Hometown Morning P/P (25 1/2 x 34)	710	2001	1560.00	1695
2000 Hometown Morning P/P (30 x 40)	710		2195.00	2275
2000 Hometown Morning R/E (25 1/2 x 34)	320		4080.00	4485
2000 Hometown Morning S/N (24 x 30)	3,950		1135.00	1245
2000 Hometown Morning S/N (25 1/2 x 34)	3,950		1360.00	1495
2000 Hometown Morning S/N (30 x 40)	3,950		1995.00	2075
2000 Hometown Morning S/P (25 1/2 x 34)	160		6800.00	7475
1996 Hyde Street and the Bay, SF A/P	395	1996	1125.00	2695-3650
1996 Hyde Street and the Bay, SF G/P	980	1996	1125.00	2595-3750
1996 Hyde Street and the Bay, SF P/P	320	1996	1175.00	2705-3495
1996 Hyde Street and the Bay, SF S/N	3,950	1996	975.00	2495-3795
1996 Hyde Street and the Bay, SF S/P	95	1996	2925.00	5250-15500
2001 Island Afternoon, Greece G/P	260		785.00	785
2001 Island Afternoon, Greece S/N	750		635.00	635
2001 It Doesn't Get Much Better A/P (18 x 24)	690		1090.00	1090
2001 It Doesn't Get Much Better A/P (25 1/2 x 34)	690		1645.00	1645
2001 It Doesn't Get Much Better G/P (18 x 24)	1,200		1090.00	1090
2001 It Doesn't Get Much Better G/P (25 1/2 x 34)	1,200		1645.00	1645
2001 It Doesn't Get Much Better P/P (18 x 24)	620		1140.00	1140
2001 It Doesn't Get Much Better P/P (25 1/2 x 34)	620		1695.00	1695
2001 It Doesn't Get Much Better R/E (25 1/2 x 34)	280		4255.00	4255
2001 It Doesn't Get Much Better S/N (18 x 24)	3,450		940.00	940
2001 It Doesn't Get Much Better S/N (25 1/2 x 34)	3,450		1495.00	1495
2001 It Doesn't Get Much Better S/P (25 1/2 x 34)	140		7245.00	7245
1992 Julianne's Cottage A/P	200	N/A	515.00	2600-3565
1992 Julianne's Cottage G/P	200	N/A	565.00	2400-3765
1992 Julianne's Cottage P/P	100	N/A	615.00	3595-4065
1992 Julianne's Cottage S/N	980	N/A	415.00	2250-3165
1999 Lakeside Hideaway A/P (12 x 16)	590		725.00	785
1999 Lakeside Hideaway A/P (16 x 20)	590		835.00	910
1999 Lakeside Hideaway A/P (18 x 24)	590		940.00	1090
1999 Lakeside Hideaway G/P (12 x 16)	1,100		725.00	785
1999 Lakeside Hideaway G/P (16 x 20)	1,100		835.00	910
1999 Lakeside Hideaway G/P (18 x 24)	1,100		940.00	1090
1999 Lakeside Hideaway P/P (12 x 16)	530		775.00	835
1999 Lakeside Hideaway P/P (16 x 20)	530		885.00	960
1999 Lakeside Hideaway P/P (18 x 24)	530		990.00	1140
1999 Lakeside Hideaway R/E (12 x 16)	240		1650.00	1905
1999 Lakeside Hideaway R/E (16 x 20)	240		1950.00	2280
1999 Lakeside Hideaway R/E (18 x 24)	240		2250.00	2820

Lightpost Publishing
to Lightpost Publishing

YEAR ISSUE	EDITION LIMIT	YEAR RETD.	ISSUE PRICE	*QUOTE U.S.$
1999 Lakeside Hideaway S/N (12 x 16)	2,950		575.00	635
1999 Lakeside Hideaway S/N (16 x 20)	2,950		685.00	760
1999 Lakeside Hideaway S/N (18 x 24)	2,950		790.00	940
1999 Lakeside Hideaway S/P (12 x 16)	120		2750.00	3175
1999 Lakeside Hideaway S/P (16 x 20)	120		3250.00	3800
1999 Lakeside Hideaway S/P (18 x 24)	120		3750.00	4700
1996 Lamplight Bridge A/P	295	1996	730.00	950-1595
1996 Lamplight Bridge G/P	740	N/A	730.00	1395-1600
1996 Lamplight Bridge P/P	240	1999	780.00	1495-1775
1996 Lamplight Bridge S/N	2,950	1996	580.00	850-1395
1996 Lamplight Bridge S/P	95	1996	1740.00	3250-7500
1993 Lamplight Brooke A/P	400	1994	715.00	1095-3585
1993 Lamplight Brooke G/P	330	1994	765.00	1850-3735
1993 Lamplight Brooke P/P	230	1999	815.00	3555-4100
1993 Lamplight Brooke S/N	1,650	1994	615.00	1650-3285
1994 Lamplight Inn A/P	275	1994	765.00	940-1740
1994 Lamplight Inn G/P	685	1998	765.00	940-1895
1994 Lamplight Inn P/P	220	1999	815.00	1055-1840
1994 Lamplight Inn S/N	2,750	1994	615.00	650-1535
1993 Lamplight Lane A/P	200	N/A	715.00	2995-5215
1993 Lamplight Lane G/P	200	1994	765.00	3295-5315
1995 Lamplight Lane P/P	100	N/A	815.00	2995-5515
1993 Lamplight Lane S/N	980	N/A	615.00	2290-4915
1995 Lamplight Lane S/P	Closed	N/A	N/A	9000-15150
2000 Lamplight Manor A/P (18 x 27)	990		1005.00	1090
2000 Lamplight Manor A/P (24 x 36)	990		1510.00	1645
2000 Lamplight Manor A/P (28 x 42)	990		2145.00	2225
2000 Lamplight Manor G/P (18 x 27)	1,750		1005.00	1090
2000 Lamplight Manor G/P (24 x 36)	1,750		1510.00	1645
2000 Lamplight Manor G/P (28 x 42)	1,750		2145.00	2225
2000 Lamplight Manor P/P (18 x 27)	900		1055.00	1140
2000 Lamplight Manor P/P (24 x 36)	900		1560.00	1695
2000 Lamplight Manor P/P (28 x 42)	900		2195.00	2275
2000 Lamplight Manor R/E (24 x 36)	400		4080.00	4485
2000 Lamplight Manor S/N (18 x 27)	4,950		855.00	940
2000 Lamplight Manor S/N (24 x 36)	4,950		1360.00	1495
2000 Lamplight Manor S/N (28 x 42)	4,950		1995.00	2075
2000 Lamplight Manor S/P (24 x 36)	200		6800.00	7475
1995 Lamplight Village A/P	495	1995	800.00	1266-2215
1995 Lamplight Village G/P	1,210	N/A	800.00	1381-2295
1995 Lamplight Village P/P	400	1999	850.00	1496-2415
1995 Lamplight Village S/N	4,950	1995	650.00	1390-2015
1995 A Light in the Storm A/P	395	1995	800.00	1295-1845
1995 A Light in the Storm G/P	990	1998	750.00	1095-1845
1995 A Light in the Storm P/P	320	1999	850.00	1325-1945
1995 A Light in the Storm S/N	3,950	1996	650.00	940-1645
1995 A Light in the Storm S/P	95	N/A	2070.00	6400-11445
1996 The Light of Peace A/P	345	1996	1300.00	3855-4995
1996 The Light of Peace G/P	865	1996	1300.00	3855-4995
1996 The Light of Peace P/P	280	1996	1350.00	3500-5145
1996 The Light of Peace S/N	3,450	1996	1150.00	3595-4595
1996 The Light of Peace S/P	95	1996	3450.00	12500 15500
1995 The Lights of Home S/N (8 x 10)	2,500	N/A	195.00	625-1020
2000 The Lights of Liberty A/P (12 x 16)	400		750.00	785
2000 The Lights of Liberty A/P (16 x 20)	400		865.00	910
2000 The Lights of Liberty A/P (20 x 24)	400		1005.00	1090
2000 The Lights of Liberty G/P (12 x 16)	700		750.00	785
2000 The Lights of Liberty G/P (16 x 20)	700		865.00	910
2000 The Lights of Liberty G/P (20 x 24)	700		1005.00	1090
2000 The Lights of Liberty P/P (12 x 16)	360		800.00	835
2000 The Lights of Liberty P/P (16 x 20)	360		915.00	960
2000 The Lights of Liberty P/P (20 x 24)	360		1055.00	1140
2000 The Lights of Liberty R/E (16 x 20)	160		2145.00	2280
2000 The Lights of Liberty S/N (12 x 16)	2,000		600.00	635
2000 The Lights of Liberty S/N (16 x 20)	2,000		715.00	760
2000 The Lights of Liberty S/N (20 x 24)	2,000		855.00	940
2000 The Lights of Liberty S/P (16 x 20)	80		3575.00	3800
1996 Lilac Gazebo A/P	295	1997	615.00	725-785
1996 Lilac Gazebo G/P	740		615.00	785
1996 Lilac Gazebo P/P	240		665.00	835
1996 Lilac Gazebo S/N	2,950		465.00	635
1996 Lilac Gazebo S/P	95	1998	1395.00	2750-3530
1998 Lingering Dusk A/P (16 x 20)	790		800.00	910
1998 Lingering Dusk A/P (20 x 24)	790		900.00	1090
1998 Lingering Dusk G/P (16 x 20)	1,400		800.00	910
1998 Lingering Dusk G/P (20 x 24)	1,400		900.00	1090
1998 Lingering Dusk P/P (16 x 20)	480		850.00	960
1998 Lingering Dusk P/P (20 x 24))	480		950.00	1140
1998 Lingering Dusk R/E (16 x 20)	320		1950.00	2145
1998 Lingering Dusk R/E (20 x 24)	320		2250.00	2565
1998 Lingering Dusk S/N (16 x 20)	3,950		650.00	760
1998 Lingering Dusk S/N (20 x 24)	3,950		750.00	940
1998 Lingering Dusk S/P (16 x 20)	160		3250.00	3575
1998 Lingering Dusk S/P (20 x 24)	160		3750.00	4275
1991 The Lit Path A/P	200	1991	315.00	475-1090
1991 The Lit Path P/P	100	1998	415.00	895-1140
1991 The Lit Path R/E	Closed	1991	395.00	495-1095
1991 The Lit Path S/N	1,960	1994	215.00	525-875
1995 Main Street Celebration A/P	125		800.00	1090
1995 Main Street Celebration P/P	400		850.00	1140
1995 Main Street Celebration S/N	1,250		650.00	940
1995 Main Street Courthouse A/P	125		800.00	1090
1995 Main Street Courthouse P/P	400		850.00	1140
1995 Main Street Courthouse S/N	1,250		650.00	940
1995 Main Street Matinee A/P	125		800.00	1090
1995 Main Street Matinee P/P	400		850.00	1140
1995 Main Street Matinee S/N	1,250		650.00	940
1995 Main Street Trolley A/P	125		800.00	1090
1995 Main Street Trolley P/P	400		850.00	1140
1995 Main Street Trolley S/N	1,250		650.00	940
1991 McKenna's Cottage A/P	200	N/A	615.00	835-1505
1991 McKenna's Cottage P/P	100	1998	715.00	1395-1515
1991 McKenna's Cottage R/E	200	N/A	615.00	700-2045
1991 McKenna's Cottage S/N	980	1995	515.00	750-1255
2001 Memories of Christmas A/P (12 x 16)	590		785.00	785
2001 Memories of Christmas A/P (18 x 24)	590		1090.00	1090
2001 Memories of Christmas G/P (12 x 16)	1,100		785.00	785
2001 Memories of Christmas G/P (18 x 24)	1,100		1090.00	1090
2001 Memories of Christmas P/P (12 x 16)	530		835.00	835
2001 Memories of Christmas P/P (18 x 24)	530		1140.00	1140
2001 Memories of Christmas R/E (18 x 24)	240		2820.00	2820
2001 Memories of Christmas S/N (12 x 16)	2,950		635.00	635
2001 Memories of Christmas S/N (18 x 24)	2,950		940.00	940
2001 Memories of Christmas S/P (18 x 24)	120		4700.00	4700
1992 Miller's Cottage, Thomashire A/P	200	N/A	615.00	2250-2615
1992 Miller's Cottage, Thomashire G/P	200	N/A	665.00	1495-2715
1992 Miller's Cottage, Thomashire P/P	100	1998	715.00	2645-2915
1992 Miller's Cottage, Thomashire S/N	980	1994	515.00	1950-2315
2001 Monterey Marina G/P	260		785.00	785
2001 Monterey Marina S/N	750		635.00	635
2001 Moonlight Cottage A/P (16 x 20)	590		910.00	910
2001 Moonlight Cottage A/P (24 x 30)	590		1395.00	1395
2001 Moonlight Cottage G/P (16 x 20)	1,100		910.00	910
2001 Moonlight Cottage G/P (24 x 30)	1,100		1395.00	1395
2001 Moonlight Cottage P/P (16 x 20)	530		960.00	960
2001 Moonlight Cottage P/P (20 x 24)	530		1140.00	1140
2001 Moonlight Cottage P/P (24 x 30)	530		1445.00	1445
2001 Moonlight Cottage R/E (24 x 30)	240		3705.00	3735
2001 Moonlight Cottage S/N (16 x 20)	2,950		760.00	760
2001 Moonlight Cottage S/N (20 x 24)	2,950		940.00	940
2001 Moonlight Cottage S/N (24 x 30)	2,950		1245.00	1245
2001 Moonlight Cottage S/P (24 x 30)	120		6195.00	6195
1994 Moonlight Lane I A/P	240	1995	665.00	695-1115
1994 Moonlight Lane I G/P	600	1999	665.00	835-1210
1994 Moonlight Lane I P/P	190		715.00	1165
1994 Moonlight Lane I S/N	2,400	1998	515.00	625-965
1985 Moonlight on the Riverfront S/N	260	N/A	715.00	1250-2695
1992 Moonlit Sleigh Ride A/P	200	1995	415.00	850-1225
1992 Moonlit Sleigh Ride G/P	200	1995	465.00	590-1400
1992 Moonlit Sleigh Ride P/P	100	2000	515.00	795-1325
1992 Moonlit Sleigh Ride S/N	1,960	1995	315.00	625-1015
1995 Morning Dogwood A/P	495	1999	645.00	800-840
1995 Morning Dogwood G/P	1,240		645.00	840
1995 Morning Dogwood P/P	400		695.00	890
1995 Morning Dogwood S/N	4,950		495.00	690
1995 Morning Glory Cottage A/P	495	1997	695.00	795-1275
1995 Morning Glory Cottage G/P	1,240	1999	645.00	895-1275
1995 Morning Glory Cottage P/P	400	2000	745.00	1260-1325
1995 Morning Glory Cottage S/N	4,950	1998	545.00	715-1075
1992 Morning Lane I A/P	Closed		N/A	2095-2135
1990 Morning Light A/P	N/A	N/A	695.00	2095-2895
1998 Mountain Chapel A/P (16 x 20)	1,190		800.00	910
1998 Mountain Chapel A/P (24 x 30)	1,190		1150.00	1395
1998 Mountain Chapel A/P (32 x 40)	990		2100.00	2225
1998 Mountain Chapel G/P (16 x 20)	2,100		835.00	910
1998 Mountain Chapel G/P (24 x 30)	2,100	2000	1200.00	1285
1998 Mountain Chapel G/P (32 x 40)	1,750		2100.00	2225
1998 Mountain Chapel P/P (16 x 20)	1,100		885.00	960
1998 Mountain Chapel P/P (24 x 30)	1,100		1250.00	1445

YEAR ISSUE	EDITION LIMIT	YEAR RETD.	ISSUE PRICE	*QUOTE U.S.$
1998 Mountain Chapel P/P (32 x 40)	900		2150.00	2275
1998 Mountain Chapel R/E (16 x 20)	480		1950.00	2280
1998 Mountain Chapel R/E (24 x 30)	480		3000.00	3735
1998 Mountain Chapel R/E (32 x 40)	400		5850.00	6225
1998 Mountain Chapel S/N (16 x 20)	5,950		650.00	760
1998 Mountain Chapel S/N (24 x 30)	5,950		1000.00	1245
1998 Mountain Chapel S/N (32 x 40)	4,950		1950.00	2075
1998 Mountain Chapel S/P (16 x 20)	240		3250.00	3800
1998 Mountain Chapel S/P (24 x 30)	240		5000.00	6225
1998 Mountain Chapel S/P (32 x 40)	200		9750.00	10375
1998 Mountain Majesty A/P (18 x 24)	790	2001	990.00	1145
1998 Mountain Majesty A/P (25 1/2 x 34)	790	1999	1460.00	1510-2160
1998 Mountain Majesty A/P (30 x 40)	790		2100.00	2225
1998 Mountain Majesty G/P (18 x 24)	1,400	2000	990.00	1040-1145
1998 Mountain Majesty G/P (25 1/2 x 34)	1,400	1999	1460.00	1510-2005
1998 Mountain Majesty S/P (30 x 40)	1,400		2100.00	2225
1998 Mountain Majesty P/P (18 x 24)	710		1040.00	1195
1998 Mountain Majesty P/P (25 1/2 x 34)	710	2000	1510.00	1560-2055
1998 Mountain Majesty P/P (30 x 40)	710		2150.00	2275
1998 Mountain Majesty R/E (18 x 24)	320		2250.00	2820
1998 Mountain Majesty R/E (25 1/2 x 34)	320		3600.00	4870
1998 Mountain Majesty R/E (30 x 40)	320		5850.00	6225
1998 Mountain Majesty S/N (18 x 24)	3,950	2000	840.00	775-995
1998 Mountain Majesty S/N (25 1/2 x 34)	3,950	1999	1310.00	1190-1855
1998 Mountain Majesty S/N (30 x 40)	3,950		1950.00	2075
1998 Mountain Majesty S/P (18 x 24)	160		3750.00	4850
1998 Mountain Majesty S/P (25 1/2 x 34)	160	1999	6000.00	5800-8750
1998 Mountain Majesty S/P (30 x 40)	160		9750.00	10375
2000 The Mountains Declare His Glory A/P (20 x 24)	590		1005.00	1090
2000 The Mountains Declare His Glory A/P (24 x 30)	590		1285.00	1395
2000 The Mountains Declare His Glory A/P (32 x 40)	390		2145.00	2225
2000 The Mountains Declare His Glory G/P (20 x 24)	1,100		1005.00	1090
2000 The Mountains Declare His Glory G/P (24 x 30)	1,100		1285.00	1395
2000 The Mountains Declare His Glory G/P (32 x 40)	700		2145.00	2225
2000 The Mountains Declare His Glory P/P (20 x 24)	530		1055.00	1140
2000 The Mountains Declare His Glory P/P (24 x 30)	530		1335.00	1445
2000 The Mountains Declare His Glory P/P (32 x 40)	350		2195.00	2275
2000 The Mountains Declare His Glory R/E (24 x 30)	240		3405.00	3735
2000 The Mountains Declare His Glory S/N (20 x 24)	2,950		855.00	940
2000 The Mountains Declare His Glory S/N (24 x 30)	2,950		1135.00	1245
2000 The Mountains Declare His Glory S/N (32 x 40)	1,950		1995.00	2075
2000 The Mountains Declare His Glory S/P (24 x 30)	120		5675.00	6225
1997 A New Day Dawning A/P	395	1997	1300.00	2405-3915
1997 A New Day Dawning G/P	990	1997	1300.00	3495-3915
1997 A New Day Dawning P/P	320	1998	1350.00	3495-4015
1997 A New Day Dawning S/N	3,950	1998	1150.00	2895-3990
1997 A New Day Dawning S/P	95	1997	3450.00	8250-13995
1992 Olde Porterfield Gift Shoppe A/P	200	1995	615.00	895-1465
1992 Olde Porterfield Gift Shoppe G/P	200	N/A	665.00	1150-1515
1992 Olde Porterfield Gift Shoppe P/P	100	2000	715.00	1445-1615
1992 Olde Porterfield Gift Shoppe S/N	980	1994	515.00	850-1265
1991 Olde Porterfield Tea Room A/P	200	N/A	615.00	1495-2595
1991 Olde Porterfield Tea Room P/P	100	1998	715.00	2395-2795
1991 Olde Porterfield Tea Room R/E	Closed	1991	595.00	1500-2695
1991 Olde Porterfield Tea Room S/N	980	N/A	515.00	1250-2445
2001 Olympic Mountain Evening S/N (16 x 20)	2,002	2001	760.00	760-1295
1999 Open Gate A/P (12 x 16)	790		725.00	785
1999 Open Gate A/P (16 x 20)	790		835.00	910
1999 Open Gate A/P (18 x 24)	790		940.00	1090
1999 Open Gate G/P (12 x 16)	1,400		725.00	785
1999 Open Gate G/P (16 x 20)	1,400		835.00	910
1999 Open Gate G/P (18 x 24)	1,400		940.00	1090
1999 Open Gate P/P (12 x 16)	710		775.00	835
1999 Open Gate P/P (16 x 20)	710		885.00	960
1999 Open Gate P/P (18 x 24)	710		990.00	1140
1999 Open Gate R/E (12 x 16)	320		1650.00	1905
1999 Open Gate R/E (16 x 20)	320		1950.00	2280
1999 Open Gate R/E (18 x 24)	320		2250.00	2820
1999 Open Gate S/N (12 x 16)	3,950		575.00	635
1999 Open Gate S/N (16 x 20)	3,950		685.00	760
1999 Open Gate S/N (18 x 24)	3,950		790.00	940
1999 Open Gate S/P (12 x 16)	160		2750.00	3175
1999 Open Gate S/P (16 x 20)	160		3250.00	3800
1999 Open Gate S/P (18 x 24)	160		3750.00	4700
1991 Open Gate, Sussex A/P	100	1994	315.00	750-1165
1991 Open Gate, Sussex P/P	100	1994	415.00	1105-1215
1991 Open Gate, Sussex R/E	Closed	1992	295.00	595-1175
1991 Open Gate, Sussex S/N	980	1994	215.00	625-975
1993 Paris, City of Lights A/P	600	1994	715.00	2395-4025
1993 Paris, City of Lights G/P	600	N/A	765.00	2695-4125
1993 Paris, City of Lights P/P	200	1994	815.00	2895-4375
1993 Paris, City of Lights S/N	1,980	N/A	615.00	2150-3775
1993 Paris, City of Lights S/P	190	1994	3750.00	6500-11000
1994 Paris, Eiffel Tower A/P	275	1994	945.00	1395-2565
1994 Paris, Eiffel Tower G/P	685	1995	945.00	1625-2565
1994 Paris, Eiffel Tower P/P	220	1998	995.00	1525-2815
1994 Paris, Eiffel Tower S/N	2,750	1994	795.00	1495-2215
2000 A Peaceful Time A/P (12 x 16)	590		750.00	785
2000 A Peaceful Time A/P (16 x 20)	590		865.00	910
2000 A Peaceful Time A/P (18 x 24)	590		1005.00	1090
2000 A Peaceful Time G/P (12 x 16)	1,110		750.00	785
2000 A Peaceful Time G/P (16 x 20)	1,110		865.00	910
2000 A Peaceful Time G/P (18 x 24)	1,110		1005.00	1090
2000 A Peaceful Time P/P (12 x 16)	530		800.00	835
2000 A Peaceful Time P/P (16 x 20)	530		915.00	960
2000 A Peaceful Time P/P (18 x 24)	530		1055.00	1140
2000 A Peaceful Time R/E (18 x 24)	240		2565.00	2820
2000 A Peaceful Time S/N (12 x 16)	2,950		600.00	635
2000 A Peaceful Time S/N (16 x 20)	2,950		715.00	760
2000 A Peaceful Time S/N (18 x 24)	2,950		855.00	940
2000 A Peaceful Time S/P (18 x 24)	120		4275.00	4700
2001 The Perfect Red Rose A/P (12 x 16)	590		785.00	785
2001 The Perfect Red Rose G/P (12 x 16)	1,100		785.00	785
2001 The Perfect Red Rose P/P (12 x 16)	530		835.00	835
2001 The Perfect Red Rose R/E (12 x 16)	240		1905.00	1905
2001 The Perfect Red Rose S/N (12 x 16)	2,950		635.00	635
2001 The Perfect Red Rose S/P (12 x 16)	120		3175.00	3175
2001 A Perfect Summer Day A/P (18 x 27)	590		1090.00	1090
2001 A Perfect Summer Day A/P (24 x 36)	590		1645.00	1645
2001 A Perfect Summer Day G/P (18 x 27)	1,100		1090.00	1090
2001 A Perfect Summer Day G/P (24 x 36)	1,100		1645.00	1645
2001 A Perfect Summer Day P/P (18 x 27)	530		1140.00	1140
2001 A Perfect Summer Day P/P (24 x 36)	530		1695.00	1695
2001 A Perfect Summer Day R/E (24 x 36)	240		4485.00	4485
2001 A Perfect Summer Day S/N (18 x 27)	2,950		940.00	940
2001 A Perfect Summer Day S/N (24 x 36)	2,950		1495.00	1495
2001 A Perfect Summer Day S/P (24 x 36)	120		7475.00	7475
2001 The Perfect Yellow Rose A/P (12 x 16)	590		785.00	785
2001 The Perfect Yellow Rose G/P (12 x 16)	1,100		785.00	785
2001 The Perfect Yellow Rose P/P (12 x 16)	530		835.00	835
2001 The Perfect Yellow Rose R/E (12 x 16)	240		1905.00	1905
2001 The Perfect Yellow Rose S/N (12 x 16)	2,950		635.00	635
2001 The Perfect Yellow Rose S/P (12 x 16)	120		3175.00	3175
2000 Perseverance A/P (18 x 27)	590		1005.00	1090
2000 Perseverance A/P (24 x 36)	590		1510.00	1645
2000 Perseverance G/P (24 x 36)	1,100		1005.00	1090
2000 Perseverance G/P (24 x 36)	1,100	2001	1510.00	1645
2000 Perseverance P/P (18 x 27)	530		1055.00	1140
2000 Perseverance P/P (24 x 36)	530	2001	1560.00	1695
2000 Perseverance R/E (24 x 36)	240		4080.00	4485
2000 Perseverance S/N (18 x 27)	2,950		855.00	940
2000 Perseverance S/N (24 x 36)	2,950		1360.00	1495
2000 Perseverance S/P (24 x 36)	120		6800.00	7475
1995 Petals of Hope A/P	395	1998	730.00	855-1255
1995 Petals of Hope G/P	990	1998	680.00	1015-1255
1995 Petals of Hope P/P	320	1999	780.00	1325-3575
1995 Petals of Hope S/N	3,950	1999	580.00	795-1150
1995 Petals of Hope S/P	95		1740.00	4350
1996 Pine Cove Cottage A/P	495		840.00	1090
1996 Pine Cove Cottage G/P	1,240		840.00	1090
1996 Pine Cove Cottage P/P	400		890.00	1140
1996 Pine Cove Cottage S/N	4,950		690.00	940
1996 Pine Cove Cottage S/P	95		2070.00	4700
1999 Pools of Serenity A/P (20 x 24)	990		1005.00	1090
1999 Pools of Serenity A/P (24 x 30)	990		1285.00	1395
1999 Pools of Serenity A/P (32 x 40)	990		2145.00	2225
1999 Pools of Serenity G/P (20 x 24)	1,750		1005.00	1090
1999 Pools of Serenity G/P (24 x 30)	1,750	2001	1285.00	1395

Collectors' Information Bureau

*Quotes have been rounded up to nearest dollar

YEAR ISSUE	EDITION LIMIT	YEAR RETD.	ISSUE PRICE	*QUOTE U.S.$
1999 Pools of Serenity G/P (32 x 40)	1,750		2145.00	2225
1999 Pools of Serenity P/P (20 x 24)	900		1055.00	1140
1999 Pools of Serenity P/P (24 x 30)	900		1335.00	1445
1999 Pools of Serenity P/P (32 x 40)	900		2195.00	2275
1999 Pools of Serenity R/E (20 x 24)	400		2565.00	2820
1999 Pools of Serenity R/E (24 x 30)	400		3405.00	3735
1999 Pools of Serenity R/E (32 x 40)	400		5985.00	6225
1999 Pools of Serenity S/N (20 x 24)	4,950		855.00	940
1999 Pools of Serenity S/N (24 x 30)	4,950		1135.00	1245
1999 Pools of Serenity S/N (32 x 40)	4,950		1995.00	2075
1999 Pools of Serenity S/P (20 x 24)	200		4275.00	4700
1999 Pools of Serenity S/P (24 x 30)	200		5675.00	6225
1999 Pools of Serenity S/P (32 x 40)	200		9975.00	10375
1994 The Power & The Majesty A/P	275		765.00	1090
1994 The Power & The Majesty G/P	685		765.00	1090
1994 The Power & The Majesty P/P	220 ·		815.00	1140
1994 The Power & The Majesty S/N	2,750		615.00	940
1999 Prince of Peace A/P (18 x 24)	390	2000	800.00	800-1825
1999 Prince of Peace G/P (18 x 24)	700	1999	800.00	800-1575
1999 Prince of Peace P/P (18 x 24)	350	2000	850.00	850-1450
1999 Prince of Peace S/N (18 x 24)	1,950	1999	650.00	1055-1595
1991 Pye Corner Cottage A/P	200	N/A	315.00	595-985
1991 Pye Corner Cottage P/P	100	1999	415.00	910-1085
1991 Pye Corner Cottage R/E	Closed	N/A	295.00	695-1045
1991 Pye Corner Cottage R/P	200	N/A	N/A	1110-1285
1991 Pye Corner Cottage S/N	1,960	1996	215.00	485-785
1998 Quiet Evening A/P (16 x 20)	790	2001	835.00	1010-1150
1998 Quiet Evening A/P (20 x 24)	790	2001	940.00	1425-1850
1998 Quiet Evening A/P (24 x 30)	790	2000	1200.00	1695-2145
1998 Quiet Evening G/P (16 x 20)	1,400	2000	835.00	1010-1150
1998 Quiet Evening G/P (20 x 24)	1,400	1999	940.00	790-1830
1998 Quiet Evening G/P (24 x 30)	1,400	1999	1200.00	1050-2145
1998 Quiet Evening P/P (16 x 20)	710	2001	885.00	1095-1200
1998 Quiet Evening P/P (20 x 24)	710	2001	990.00	1595-1900
1998 Quiet Evening P/P (24 x 30)	710	2000	1250.00	1745-2195
1998 Quiet Evening R/E (16 x 20)	320		1950.00	2650
1998 Quiet Evening R/E (20 x 24)	320	2000	2250.00	3395-3795
1998 Quiet Evening R/E (24 x 30)	320	2000	3000.00	3700-4550
1998 Quiet Evening S/N (16 x 20)	3,950	2000	685.00	860-1000
1998 Quiet Evening S/N (20 x 24)	3,950	2000	790.00	855-1700
1998 Quiet Evening S/N (24 x 30)	3,950	2001	1050.00	1135-1995
1998 Quiet Evening S/P (16 x 20)	160		3250.00	4250
1998 Quiet Evening S/P (20 x 24)	160	2000	3750.00	3650-5950
1998 Quiet Evening S/P (24 x 30)	160		5000.00	7150
2000 Radiant Surf G/P	200		910.00	910
2000 Radiant Surf R/E	45		2280.00	2280
2000 Radiant Surf S/N	550		760.00	760
2001 Rock of Salvation A/P (18 x 27)	590		1090.00	1090
2001 Rock of Salvation A/P (24 x 36)	590		1645.00	1645
2001 Rock of Salvation G/P (18 x 27)	1,100		1090.00	1090
2001 Rock of Salvation G/P (24 x 36)	1,100		1645.00	1645
2001 Rock of Salvation P/P (18 x 27)	530		1140.00	1140
2001 Rock of Salvation P/P (24 x 36)	530		1695.00	1695
2001 Rock of Salvation R/E (24 x 36)	240		4485.00	4485
2001 Rock of Salvation S/N (18 x 27)	2,950		940.00	940
2001 Rock of Salvation S/N (24 x 36)	2,950		1495.00	1495
2001 Rock of Salvation S/P (24 x 36)	120		7475.00	7475
1988 Room with a View S/N	N/A	N/A	795.00	995-2325
1990 The Rose Arbor Cottage A/P	98	N/A	595.00	2100-2795
1990 The Rose Arbor Cottage S/N	935	N/A	495.00	1975-2495
2000 The Rose Garden A/P (20 x 24)	590		1005.00	1090
2000 The Rose Garden A/P (24 x 30)	590		1285.00	1395
2000 The Rose Garden A/P (32 x 40)	590		2145.00	2225
2000 The Rose Garden G/P (20 x 24)	1,100		1005.00	1090
2000 The Rose Garden G/P (24 x 30)	1,100		1285.00	1395
2000 The Rose Garden G/P (32 x 40)	1,100		2145.00	2225
2000 The Rose Garden P/P (20 x 24)	530		1055.00	1140
2000 The Rose Garden P/P (24 x 30)	530		1335.00	1445
2000 The Rose Garden P/P (32 x 40)	530		2195.00	2275
2000 The Rose Garden R/E (24 x 30)	400		3405.00	3735
2000 The Rose Garden R/E (32 x 40)	240		5985.00	6225
2000 The Rose Garden S/N (20 x 24)	2,950		855.00	940
2000 The Rose Garden S/N (24 x 30)	2,950		1135.00	1245
2000 The Rose Garden S/N (32 x 40)	2,850		1995.00	2075
2000 The Rose Garden S/P (24 x 30)	120		5675.00	6225
2000 The Rose Garden S/P (32 x 40)	120		9975.00	10375
1996 Rose Gate A/P	295	1996	615.00	725-840
1996 Rose Gate G/P	740		615.00	840
1996 Rose Gate P/P	230		665.00	890
1996 Rose Gate S/N	2,950		465.00	690
1996 Rose Gate S/P	95	1998	1395.00	2750-4715

YEAR ISSUE	EDITION LIMIT	YEAR RETD.	ISSUE PRICE	*QUOTE U.S.$
1994 San Francisco Market Street A/P	750		945.00	1090
1994 San Francisco Market Street G/P	1,875		945.00	1090
1994 San Francisco Market Street P/P	600		995.00	1140
1994 San Francisco Market Street S/N	7,500		795.00	940
2001 San Francisco, Lombard Street A/P (18 x 24)	690		1090.00	1090
2001 San Francisco, Lombard Street A/P (25 1/2 x 34)	690		1645.00	1645
2001 San Francisco, Lombard Street A/P (30 x 40)	690		2225.00	2225
2001 San Francisco, Lombard Street G/P (18 x 24)	1,200		1090.00	1090
2001 San Francisco, Lombard Street G/P (25 1/2 x 34)	1,200		1645.00	1645
2001 San Francisco, Lombard Street G/P (30 x 40)	1,200		2225.00	2225
2001 San Francisco, Lombard Street P/P (18 x 24)	620		1140.00	1140
2001 San Francisco, Lombard Street P/P (25 1/2 x 34)	620		1695.00	1695
2001 San Francisco, Lombard Street P/P (30 x 40)	620		2275.00	2275
2001 San Francisco, Lombard Street R/E (25 1/2 x 34)	280		4485.00	4485
2001 San Francisco, Lombard Street S/N (18 x 24)	3,450		940.00	940
2001 San Francisco, Lombard Street S/N (25 1/2 x 34)	3,450		1495.00	1495
2001 San Francisco, Lombard Street S/N (30 x 40)	3,450		2075.00	2075
2001 San Francisco, Lombard Street S/P (25 1/2 x 34)	140		7475.00	7475
1992 San Francisco, Nob Hill (California St.) A/P	Closed	N/A	715.00	6200-7645
1992 San Francisco, Nob Hill (California St.) G/P	200	N/A	765.00	5275-7945
1992 San Francisco, Nob Hill (California St.) P/P	100	N/A	815.00	5700-8495
1992 San Francisco, Nob Hill (California St.) S/N	980	N/A	615.00	4895-6995
1989 San Francisco, Union Square A/P	50	N/A	795.00	4500-7545
1989 San Francisco, Union Square P/P	25	N/A	N/A	7705-8005
1989 San Francisco, Union Square S/N	935	N/A	595.00	4000-6605
1998 The Sea of Tranquility A/P (18 x 27)	1,190		940.00	1090
1998 The Sea of Tranquility A/P (24 x 36)	1,190		1410.00	1645
1998 The Sea of Tranquility A/P (28 x 42)	1,190		2100.00	2225
1998 The Sea of Tranquility G/P (18 x 27)	2,100		940.00	1090
1998 The Sea of Tranquility G/P (24 x 36)	2,100		1410.00	1645
1998 The Sea of Tranquility G/P (28 x 42)	2,100		2100.00	2225
1998 The Sea of Tranquility P/P (18 x 27)	1,100		990.00	1140
1998 The Sea of Tranquility P/P (24 x 36)	1,100		1460.00	1695
1998 The Sea of Tranquility P/P (28 x 42)	1,100		2150.00	2275
1998 The Sea of Tranquility R/E (24 x 36)	480		2250.00	2820
1998 The Sea of Tranquility R/E (24 x 36)	480		3600.00	4485
1998 The Sea of Tranquility R/E (28 x 42)	480		5850.00	6225
1998 The Sea of Tranquility S/N (18 x 27)	5,950	2001	790.00	940
1998 The Sea of Tranquility S/N (24 x 36)	5,950		1260.00	1495
1998 The Sea of Tranquility S/N (28 x 42)	5,950		1950.00	2075
1998 The Sea of Tranquility S/P (18 x 27)	240		3750.00	4700
1998 The Sea of Tranquility S/P (24 x 36)	240		6000.00	7475
1998 The Sea of Tranquility S/P (28 x 42)	200		9750.00	10375
2000 Seaside Village A/P (18 x 24)	400		1005.00	1090
2000 Seaside Village A/P (24 x 30)	400		1285.00	1395
2000 Seaside Village G/P (18 x 24)	700		1005.00	1090
2000 Seaside Village G/P (24 x 30)	700		1285.00	1395
2000 Seaside Village P/P (18 x 24)	360		1055.00	1140
2000 Seaside Village P/P (24 x 30)	360		1335.00	1445
2000 Seaside Village S/N (18 x 24)	2,000		855.00	940
2000 Seaside Village S/N (24 x 30)	2,000		1135.00	1245
1992 Silent Night A/P	200	N/A	515.00	1495-2395
1992 Silent Night G/P	200	N/A	565.00	1495-2445
1992 Silent Night P/P	100	N/A	615.00	1750-2545
1992 Silent Night S/N	980	N/A	415.00	1850-2350
2000 Silver and Gold G/P	200		785.00	785
2000 Silver and Gold R/E	45		1905.00	1905
2000 Silver and Gold S/N	550		635.00	635
1995 Simpler Times I A/P	345	1998	840.00	940-1090
1995 Simpler Times I G/P	870		790.00	1090
1995 Simpler Times I P/P	280		890.00	1140
1995 Simpler Times I S/N	3,450		690.00	940
1995 Simpler Times I S/P	95		2070.00	4700
2001 Split Rock Light A/P (16 x 20)	490		910.00	910
2001 Split Rock Light A/P (20 x 24)	490		1090.00	1090

GRAPHICS

YEAR ISSUE	EDITION LIMIT	YEAR RETD.	ISSUE PRICE	*QUOTE U.S.$
2001 Split Rock Light G/P (16 x 20)	860		910.00	910
2001 Split Rock Light G/P (20 x 24)	860		1090.00	1090
2001 Split Rock Light P/P (16 x 20)	300		960.00	960
2001 Split Rock Light P/P (20 x 24)	300		1140.00	1140
2001 Split Rock Light R/E (20 x 24)	200		2820.00	2820
2001 Split Rock Light S/N (16 x 20)	2,450		760.00	760
2001 Split Rock Light S/N (20 x 24)	2,450		940.00	940
2001 Split Rock Light S/P (20 x 24)	100		4700.00	4700
1990 Spring At Stonegate A/P	100	N/A	515.00	1150-1515
1990 Spring At Stonegate P/P	50	N/A	615.00	1345-1615
1990 Spring At Stonegate S/N	550	1995	415.00	725-1265
1996 Spring Gate A/P	395	1997	1240.00	2495-3485
1996 Spring Gate G/P	990	1998	1240.00	2195-3585
1996 Spring Gate P/P	320	1997	1290.00	2645-3885
1996 Spring Gate S/N	3,950	1998	1090.00	2395-3245
1996 Spring Gate S/P	95	1997	3270.00	6000-14450
1994 Spring in the Alps A/P	198		725.00	910
1994 Spring in the Alps G/P	500		725.00	910
1994 Spring in the Alps P/P	160		775.00	960
1994 Spring in the Alps S/N	1,984		575.00	760
1993 St. Nicholas Circle A/P	420	1995	715.00	1795-2570
1993 St. Nicholas Circle G/P	350	1995	765.00	2125-2720
1993 St. Nicholas Circle P/P	100	1995	815.00	2145-2945
1993 St. Nicholas Circle S/N	1,750	1994	615.00	1850-2500
1993 St. Nicholas Circle S/P	95	1999	3750.00	5250-11450
1998 Stairway to Paradise A/P (18 x 24)	790	2001	940.00	995-1695
1998 Stairway to Paradise A/P (25 1/2 x 34)	790	2000	1410.00	1520-2225
1998 Stairway to Paradise A/P (30 x 40)	790		2100.00	2225
1998 Stairway to Paradise G/P (18 x 24)	1,400	1999	940.00	940-1365
1998 Stairway to Paradise G/P (25 1/2 x 34)	1,400	1999	1410.00	1410-2225
1998 Stairway to Paradise G/P (30 x 40)	1,400		2100.00	2225
1998 Stairway to Paradise P/P (18 x 24)	710	2001	990.00	1240-1415
1998 Stairway to Paradise P/P (25 1/2 x 34)	710	2000	1460.00	1895-2275
1998 Stairway to Paradise P/P (30 x 40)	710		2150.00	2275
1998 Stairway to Paradise R/E (18 x 24)	320		2250.00	3025
1998 Stairway to Paradise R/E (25 1/2 x 34)	320	2000	3600.00	4595-5050
1998 Stairway to Paradise R/E (30 x 40)	320		5850.00	6225
1998 Stairway to Paradise S/N (18 x 24)	3,950	2000	790.00	855-1215
1998 Stairway to Paradise S/N (25 1/2 x 34)	3,950	2000	1260.00	1360-2075
1998 Stairway to Paradise S/N (30 x 40)	3,950		1950.00	2075
1998 Stairway to Paradise S/P (18 x 24)	160	2001	3750.00	4900-5250
1998 Stairway to Paradise S/P (25 1/2 x 34)	160	2000	6000.00	5800-7975
1998 Stairway to Paradise S/P (30 x 40)	N/A		9750.00	10375
1995 Stepping Stone Cottage A/P	295	1996	840.00	1245-1775
1995 Stepping Stone Cottage G/P	740	1998	790.00	1245-1555
1995 Stepping Stone Cottage P/P	240	2000	890.00	1345-1655
1995 Stepping Stone Cottage S/N	2,950	1996	690.00	1195-1495
1995 Stepping Stone Cottage S/P	95	1998	2070.00	5295-8150
1998 Stillwater Bridge A/P (12 x 16)	990		700.00	785
1998 Stillwater Bridge A/P (18 x 24)	790		900.00	1090
1998 Stillwater Bridge G/P (12 x 16)	1,750		700.00	785
1998 Stillwater Bridge G/P (18 x 24)	1,400	2000	900.00	1090
1998 Stillwater Bridge P/P (12 x 16)	600		750.00	835
1998 Stillwater Bridge P/P (18 x 24)	480		950.00	1140
1998 Stillwater Bridge R/E (12 x 16)	400		1650.00	1905
1998 Stillwater Bridge R/E (18 x 24)	320		2250.00	2820
1998 Stillwater Bridge S/N (12 x 16)	4,950		550.00	635
1998 Stillwater Bridge S/N (18 x 24)	3,950	2000	750.00	940
1998 Stillwater Bridge S/P (12 x 16)	200		2750.00	3175
1998 Stillwater Bridge S/P (18 x 24)	160	2001	3750.00	4700
1993 Stonehearth Hutch A/P	400	N/A	515.00	995-1815
1993 Stonehearth Hutch G/P	300	1994	565.00	1300-1885
1993 Stonehearth Hutch P/P	150	1999	615.00	1425-1965
1993 Stonehearth Hutch S/N	1,650		415.00	995-1515
1993 Stonehearth Hutch S/P	95	1999	2750.00	3750-4895
2000 Streams of Living Water A/P (18 x 24)	590		1090.00	1090
2000 Streams of Living Water A/P (25 1/2 x 34)	590	2001	1645.00	1645
2000 Streams of Living Water A/P (30 x 40)	590		2225.00	2225
2000 Streams of Living Water G/P (18 x 24)	1,100		1090.00	1090
2000 Streams of Living Water G/P (25 1/2 x 34)	1,100	2001	1645.00	1645
2000 Streams of Living Water G/P (30 x 40)	1,100		2225.00	2225
2000 Streams of Living Water P/P (18 x 24)	530		1140.00	1140
2000 Streams of Living Water P/P (25 1/2 x 34)	530	2001	1695.00	1695
2000 Streams of Living Water P/P (30 x 40)	530		2275.00	2275
2000 Streams of Living Water R/E (25 1/2 x 34)	240		4485.00	4485
2000 Streams of Living Water R/E (25 1/2 x 34)	240		4485.00	4485
2000 Streams of Living Water S/N (18 x 24)	2,950		940.00	940
2000 Streams of Living Water S/N (25 1/2 x 34)	2,950		1495.00	1495
2000 Streams of Living Water S/N (30 x 40)	2,950		2075.00	2075
2000 Streams of Living Water S/P (25 1/2 x 34)	120		7475.00	7475
1993 Studio in the Garden A/P	400	1998	515.00	950-1335
1993 Studio in the Garden G/P	600	1999	565.00	725-1335
1993 Studio in the Garden P/P	100	1998	615.00	950-1585
1993 Studio in the Garden S/N	1,480	1996	415.00	825-1235
1993 Studio in the Garden S/P	95		N/A	3650
1999 Summer Gate A/P (18 x 24)	1,190		940.00	1090
1999 Summer Gate A/P (25 1/2 x 34)	1,190		1410.00	1645
1999 Summer Gate A/P (30 x 40)	1,190		2100.00	2225
1999 Summer Gate G/P (18 x 24)	2,100		940.00	1090
1999 Summer Gate G/P (25 1/2 x 34)	2,100		1410.00	1645
1999 Summer Gate G/P (30 x 40)	2,100		2100.00	2225
1999 Summer Gate P/P (18 x 24)	1,100		990.00	1140
1999 Summer Gate P/P (25 1/2 x 34)	1,100		1460.00	1695
1999 Summer Gate P/P (30 x 40)	1,100		2150.00	2275
1999 Summer Gate R/E (18 x 24)	480		2250.00	2820
1999 Summer Gate R/E (25 1/2 x 34)	480		3600.00	4485
1999 Summer Gate R/E (30 x 40)	480		5850.00	6225
1999 Summer Gate S/N (18 x 24)	5,950		790.00	940
1999 Summer Gate S/N (25 1/2 x 34)	5,950		1260.00	1495
1999 Summer Gate S/N (30 x 40)	5,950		1950.00	2075
1999 Summer Gate S/P (18 x 24)	240		3750.00	4700
1999 Summer Gate S/P (25 1/2 x 34)	240		6000.00	7475
1999 Summer Gate S/P (30 x 40)	240		9750.00	10375
2000 Sunday Afternoon G/P	260		1090.00	1090
2000 Sunday Afternoon R/E	60		2820.00	2820
2000 Sunday Afternoon S/N	750		940.00	940
1992 Sunday at Apple Hill A/P	200	1993	615.00	1650-2545
1992 Sunday at Apple Hill G/P	200	N/A	665.00	1895-2615
1992 Sunday at Apple Hill P/P	100	N/A	715.00	2095-2875
1992 Sunday at Apple Hill S/N	980	1993	515.00	1495-2295
1996 Sunday Evening Sleigh Ride A/P	298	1996	875.00	1295-2495
1996 Sunday Evening Sleigh Ride G/P	740	1998	875.00	1595-2145
1996 Sunday Evening Sleigh Ride P/P	240	2000	925.00	1405
1996 Sunday Evening Sleigh Ride S/N	2,950	1997	725.00	1945-2450
1996 Sunday Evening Sleigh Ride S/P	95	1998	2175.00	3760-7775
1993 Sunday Outing A/P	200	N/A	615.00	1795-2705
1993 Sunday Outing G/P	200	N/A	665.00	1595-2805
1993 Sunday Outing P/P	100	N/A	715.00	2345-2935
1993 Sunday Outing S/N	980	N/A	515.00	1850-2550
1993 Sunday Outing S/P	95	N/A	3250.00	6000-9695
1999 Sunrise A/P (20 x 24)	590		1005.00	1090
1999 Sunrise A/P (24 x 30)	590		1285.00	1395
1999 Sunrise A/P (32 x 40)	400		2145.00	2225
1999 Sunrise G/P (20 x 24)	1,110	2001	1005.00	1090
1999 Sunrise G/P (24 x 30)	1,110	2001	1285.00	1395
1999 Sunrise G/P (32 x 40)	700		2145.00	2225
1999 Sunrise P/P (20 x 24)	530		1005.00	1140
1999 Sunrise P/P (24 x 30)	530		1335.00	1445
1999 Sunrise P/P (32 x 40)	360		2195.00	2275
1999 Sunrise R/E (24 x 30)	240		2565.00	2820
1999 Sunrise R/E (24 x 30)	240		3405.00	3405
1999 Sunrise R/E (32 x 40)	160		5985.00	5985
1999 Sunrise S/N (20 x 24)	2,950		855.00	940
1999 Sunrise S/N (24 x 30)	2,950		1135.00	1245
1999 Sunrise S/N (32 x 40)	2,000		1995.00	2075
1999 Sunrise S/P (20 x 24)	120		4275.00	4700
1999 Sunrise S/P (24 x 30)	120		5675.00	5675
1999 Sunrise S/P (32 x 40)	80		9975.00	9975
1996 Sunset on Riverbend Farm A/P	495	1998	840.00	940-1090
1996 Sunset on Riverbend Farm G/P	1,240		840.00	1090
1996 Sunset on Riverbend Farm P/P	400		890.00	1140
1996 Sunset on Riverbend Farm S/N	4,950		690.00	940
1996 Sunset on Riverbend Farm S/P	95	1998	2070.00	4250-5990
1992 Sweetheart Cottage I A/P	200	1992	615.00	1595-2205
1992 Sweetheart Cottage I G/P	200	N/A	665.00	1435-2205
1992 Sweetheart Cottage I P/P	100	2000	715.00	1495-2265
1992 Sweetheart Cottage I S/N	980	N/A	515.00	1250-1905
1993 Sweetheart Cottage II A/P	400	1993	515.00	2195-3335
1993 Sweetheart Cottage II G/P	490	N/A	665.00	2750-3350
1993 Sweetheart Cottage II P/P	100	N/A	715.00	1995-3465
1993 Sweetheart Cottage II S/N	980	N/A	515.00	2495-3005
1993 Sweetheart Cottage II S/P	95	N/A	3250.00	8500-12150
1994 Sweetheart Cottage III A/P	165	1994	765.00	1005-1715
1994 Sweetheart Cottage III G/P	410	1998	765.00	940-1715
1994 Sweetheart Cottage III P/P	130	2000	815.00	1195-1825

Collectors' Information Bureau

*Quotes have been rounded up to nearest dollar

YEAR ISSUE	EDITION LIMIT	YEAR RETD.	ISSUE PRICE	*QUOTE U.S.$
1994 Sweetheart Cottage III S/N	1,650	1994	615.00	695-1455
1996 Teacup Cottage A/P	295	1997	875.00	1140-1675
1996 Teacup Cottage G/P	740	1998	875.00	1140-1675
1996 Teacup Cottage P/P	240	1999	925.00	1395-1775
1996 Teacup Cottage S/N	2,950	1998	725.00	1025-1495
1999 Town Square A/P (18 x 27)	790		940.00	1090
1999 Town Square G/P (18 x 27)	1,400		940.00	1090
1999 Town Square P/P (18 x 27)	710		990.00	1140
1999 Town Square S/N (18 x 27)	3,950		790.00	940
1997 Twilight Cottage A/P	495	1998	N/A	860-1725
1997 Twilight Cottage G/P	1,240	1999	N/A	1115-1725
1997 Twilight Cottage P/P	400	1999	775.00	1195-1805
1997 Twilight Cottage S/N	4,950	1999	625.00	945-1990
1997 Twilight Cottage S/P	95	1997	3250.00	3700-5950
1999 Twilight Vista A/P (24 x 36)	790		1410.00	1680
1999 Twilight Vista G/P (24 x 36)	1,400		1410.00	1680
1999 Twilight Vista P/P (24 x 36)	480		1460.00	1730
1999 Twilight Vista R/E (24 x 36)	320		3600.00	4080
1999 Twilight Vista S/N (24 x 36)	3,950		1260.00	1530
1999 Twilight Vista S/P (24 x 36)	160		6000.00	6800
1997 Valley of Peace A/P	395	1997	1300.00	3695-4315
1997 Valley of Peace G/P	990	1997	1300.00	2655-4315
1997 Valley of Peace P/P	320	1998	1350.00	2855-4515
1997 Valley of Peace S/N	3,950	1998	1150.00	3045-4150
1997 Valley of Peace S/P	95	1997	3450.00	6000-15950
1996 Venice A/P	495		1240.00	1645
1996 Venice G/P	1,240		1240.00	1645
1996 Venice P/P	400		1290.00	1695
1996 Venice S/N	4,950		1090.00	1495
1996 Venice S/P	95		3270.00	7475
1992 Victorian Christmas I A/P	200	1992	715.00	3150-4695
1992 Victorian Christmas I G/P	200	1992	765.00	3095-4795
1992 Victorian Christmas I P/P	100	1992	815.00	4145-5020
1992 Victorian Christmas I S/N	980	1992	615.00	2895-4165
1993 Victorian Christmas II A/P	400	1994	715.00	2095-3975
1993 Victorian Christmas II G/P	300	1994	765.00	2095-3975
1993 Victorian Christmas II P/P	150	1994	815.00	3295-4305
1993 Victorian Christmas II S/N	980	1994	615.00	2595-3645
1993 Victorian Christmas II S/P	95	1994	3750.00	8200-13700
1994 Victorian Christmas III A/P	395	1994	800.00	940-1825
1994 Victorian Christmas III G/P	990	1998	800.00	1195-1295
1994 Victorian Christmas III P/P	300	1999	850.00	1150-1995
1994 Victorian Christmas III S/N	3,950	1997	650.00	855-1595
1995 Victorian Christmas IV S/N	2,330	1995	650.00	850-1545
1991 Victorian Evening A/P	200	1993	N/A	1795-2050
1991 Victorian Evening P/P	100	1993	N/A	1995-2250
1991 Victorian Evening S/N	980	1993	495.00	1125-1895
1992 Victorian Garden I A/P	200	1993	915.00	3195-4145
1992 Victorian Garden I G/P	200	1993	965.00	2345-4245
1992 Victorian Garden I P/P	100	1993	1015.00	3845-4425
1992 Victorian Garden I S/N	980	1993	815.00	2195-3715
1997 Victorian Garden II A/P	395	1998	875.00	950-1090
1997 Victorian Garden II G/P	990	2000	875.00	950-1090
1997 Victorian Garden II P/P	320	2000	925.00	1140
1997 Victorian Garden II S/N	3,950		725.00	750-940
1997 Victorian Garden II S/P	95	N/A	2175.00	4250-6990
2000 Victorian Lights A/P (16 x 20)	590		865.00	910
2000 Victorian Lights A/P (18 x 24)	590		1005.00	1090
2000 Victorian Lights A/P (24 x 30)	590		1285.00	1395
2000 Victorian Lights G/P (16 x 20)	1,100		865.00	910
2000 Victorian Lights G/P (18 x 24)	1,100		1005.00	1090
2000 Victorian Lights G/P (24 x 30)	1,100		1285.00	1395
2000 Victorian Lights P/P (18 x 24)	530		915.00	960
2000 Victorian Lights P/P (18 x 24)	530		1055.00	1140
2000 Victorian Lights P/P (24 x 30)	530		1335.00	1445
2000 Victorian Lights S/N (16 x 20)	2,950		715.00	760
2000 Victorian Lights S/N (18 x 24)	2,950		855.00	940
2000 Victorian Lights S/N (24 x 30)	2,950		1135.00	1245
1997 Village Christmas A/P (18 x 24)	990	2000	900.00	1270-1620
1997 Village Christmas A/P (25 1/2 x 34)	390	1998	1350.00	1585-2425
1997 Village Christmas G/P (18 x 24)	1,240	1999	900.00	1065-1620
1997 Village Christmas G/P (25 1/2 x 34)	490	1998	1350.00	1585-2425
1997 Village Christmas P/P (18 x 24)	600	2000	950.00	1250-1695
1997 Village Christmas P/P (25 1/2 x 34)	240	1999	1400.00	1660-2600
1997 Village Christmas R/E (18 x 24)	325	1999	2250.00	2750-4000
1997 Village Christmas R/E (25 1/2 x 34)	150	1999	3600.00	3600-5400
1997 Village Christmas S/N (12 x 16)	2,450	1999	630.00	575-855
1997 Village Christmas S/N (18 x 24)	4,950	1999	750.00	925-1445
1997 Village Christmas S/N (25 1/2 x 34)	1,950	1999	1200.00	1495-2245
1997 Village Christmas S/P (18 x 24)	155		3750.00	7400
1997 Village Christmas S/P (25 1/2 x 34)	80	1998	6000.00	6000-14350

YEAR ISSUE	EDITION LIMIT	YEAR RETD.	ISSUE PRICE	*QUOTE U.S.$
1993 Village Inn A/P	400	1996	615.00	1050-1485
1993 Village Inn G/P	400	N/A	665.00	995-1535
1993 Village Inn P/P	100	1999	715.00	1300-1660
1993 Village Inn S/N	1,200	1994	515.00	765-1255
1994 The Warmth of Home A/P	345		590.00	785
1994 The Warmth of Home G/P	860		590.00	785
1994 The Warmth of Home P/P	275		640.00	835
1994 The Warmth of Home S/N	3,450		440.00	635
1992 Weathervane Hutch A/P	200	1995	515.00	895-1205
1992 Weathervane Hutch G/P	200	N/A	565.00	615-1285
1992 Weathervane Hutch P/P	100	1999	615.00	1295-1550
1992 Weathervane Hutch S/N	1,960	1995	415.00	795-1130
1998 The Wind of the Spirit A/P (18 x 27)	1,190		940.00	1090
1998 The Wind of the Spirit A/P (24 x 36)	1,190		1410.00	1645
1998 The Wind of the Spirit A/P (28 x 42)	990		2100.00	2225
1998 The Wind of the Spirit G/P (18 x 27)	2,100		940.00	1090
1998 The Wind of the Spirit G/P (24 x 36)	2,100		1410.00	1645
1998 The Wind of the Spirit G/P (28 x 42)	1,750		2100.00	2225
1998 The Wind of the Spirit P/P (18 x 27)	1,100		990.00	1140
1998 The Wind of the Spirit P/P (24 x 36)	1,100		1460.00	1695
1998 The Wind of the Spirit P/P (28 x 42)	900		2150.00	2275
1998 The Wind of the Spirit R/E (18 x 27)	480		2250.00	2820
1998 The Wind of the Spirit R/E (24 x 36)	480		3600.00	4485
1998 The Wind of the Spirit R/E (28 x 42)	400		5850.00	6225
1998 The Wind of the Spirit S/N (18 x 27)	5,950		790.00	940
1998 The Wind of the Spirit S/N (24 x 36)	5,950		1260.00	1495
1998 The Wind of the Spirit S/N (28 x 42)	4,950		1950.00	2075
1998 The Wind of the Spirit S/P (18 x 27)	240		3750.00	4700
1998 The Wind of the Spirit S/P (24 x 36)	240		6000.00	7475
1998 The Wind of the Spirit S/P (28 x 42)	200		9750.00	10375
1996 Winsor Manor A/P	395		1070.00	1395
1996 Winsor Manor G/P	990		1070.00	1395
1996 Winsor Manor P/P	320		1120.00	1445
1996 Winsor Manor S/N	3,950		920.00	1245
1996 Winsor Manor S/P	95		2760.00	6225
1999 Winter Chapel A/P (12 x 18)	590		775.00	840
1999 Winter Chapel A/P (18 x 27)	790		940.00	1090
1999 Winter Chapel G/P (12 x 18)	1,100		775.00	840
1999 Winter Chapel G/P (18 x 27)	1,400		940.00	1090
1999 Winter Chapel P/P (12 x 18)	530		825.00	890
1999 Winter Chapel P/P (18 x 27)	710		990.00	1140
1999 Winter Chapel R/E (12 x 18)	320		1800.00	1950
1999 Winter Chapel R/E (18 x 27)	240		2250.00	2565
1999 Winter Chapel S/N (12 x 18)	2,950		625.00	690
1999 Winter Chapel S/N (18 x 27)	3,950		790.00	940
1999 Winter Chapel S/P (12 x 18)	160		3000.00	3250
1999 Winter Chapel S/P (18 x 27)	120		3750.00	4275
1999 Winter Glen A/P (24 x 36)	390		1510	1645
1999 Winter Glen G/P (24 x 36)	700		1510.00	1645
1999 Winter Glen P/P (24 x 36)	350		1560.00	1695
1999 Winter Glen S/N (24 x 36)	1,950		1360.00	1495
1993 Winter's End A/P	400	1999	715.00	995-1455
1993 Winter's End G/P	490	1999	765.00	995-1455
1993 Winter's End P/P	100	1998	815.00	975-1515
1993 Winter's End S/N	1,450	1999	615.00	895-1425
1991 Woodman's Thatch A/P	200	1995	315.00	850-1005
1991 Woodman's Thatch P/P	100	1995	415.00	650-1405
1991 Woodman's Thatch R/E	200	N/A	295.00	695-1105
1991 Woodman's Thatch S/N	1,960	1994	215.00	450-845
1992 Yosemite A/P	200	1998	715.00	1775-2645
1992 Yosemite G/P	200	1998	765.00	1395-2695
1992 Yosemite P/P	100	1998	815.00	1295-3045
1992 Yosemite S/N	980	1997	615.00	1625-2245
2001 Yosemite Valley A/P	120		865.00	910
2001 Yosemite Valley G/P	210		865.00	910
2001 Yosemite Valley P/P	110		915.00	960
2001 Yosemite Valley S/N	595		715.00	760

Kinkade-Premium Paper-Unframed - T. Kinkade

YEAR ISSUE	EDITION LIMIT	YEAR RETD.	ISSUE PRICE	*QUOTE U.S.$
1991 Afternoon Light, Dogwood A/P	98	N/A	295.00	1825-2200
1991 Afternoon Light, Dogwood S/N	980	N/A	185.00	495-1325
1992 Amber Afternoon	980	1998	225.00	450-1005
2001 The Aspen Chapel A/P (24 x 36)	570		345.00	345
2001 The Aspen Chapel S/N (24 x 36)	2,850		295.00	295
1994 Autumn at Ashley's Cottage A/P	245		335.00	225
1994 Autumn at Ashley's Cottage S/N	2,450		185.00	175
1991 The Autumn Gate S/N	980	1994	225.00	1785-2225
1995 Autumn Lane A/P	285		400.00	280
1995 Autumn Lane S/N	2,850		250.00	230
1994 Beacon of Hope A/P	275		385	280
1994 Beacon of Hope S/N	2,750	1999	235.00	310-650

YEAR ISSUE	EDITION LIMIT	YEAR RETD.	ISSUE PRICE	*QUOTE U.S.$
1996 Beginning of a Perfect Day A/P	285		475.00	345
1996 Beginning of a Perfect Day S/N	2,850		325.00	295
1993 Beside Still Waters S/N	980	1994	185.00	1036-1675
1993 Beyond Autumn Gate S/N	1,750	1994	285.00	495-1775
1997 Beyond Spring Gate A/P	335		475.00	345
1997 Beyond Spring Gate S/N	3,350	1999	325.00	400-495
2001 Beyond Summer Gate A/P (18 x 27)	295		435.00	435
2001 Beyond Summer Gate A/P (24 X 36)	2,000		295.00	295
2001 Beyond Summer Gate S/N (18 x 27)	1,475		285.00	285
1985 Birth of a City S/N	750	N/A	150.00	250-295
1993 The Blessings of Autumn S/N	1,250		235.00	230
1994 The Blessings of Spring A/P	275		345.00	280
1994 The Blessings of Spring S/N	2,750		195.00	230
1995 Blessings of Summer A/P	485		450.00	330
1995 Blessings of Summer S/N	4,850		300.00	280
1998 Block Island A/P (12 x 18)	470		380.00	225
1998 Block Island A/P (18 x 27)	470		435.00	280
1998 Block Island S/N (12 x 18)	2,350		230.00	175
1998 Block Island S/N (18 x 27)	2,350		285.00	230
1995 Blossom Bridge A/P	285		355.00	280
1995 Blossom Bridge S/N	2,850		205.00	230
1992 Blossom Hill Church S/N	980		225.00	230
1991 Boston A/P	100	N/A	245.00	1845-2110
1991 Boston S/N	550	1994	175.00	1295-1760
1999 Boulevard Lights, Paris S/N (24 x 36)	2,850		400.00	295
1997 Bridge of Faith A/P	385		475.00	345
1997 Bridge of Faith S/N	3,850		325.00	295
1992 Broadwater Bridge S/N	980	1994	225.00	450-1305
1995 Brookside Hideaway A/P	385		355.00	280
1995 Brookside Hideaway S/N	3,850		205.00	230
1996 Candlelight Cottage S/N	Closed	1997	150.00	195-340
1991 Carmel, Delores Street and the Tuck Box Tea Room S/N	980	1994	275.00	685-2195
1989 Carmel, Ocean Avenue S/N	935	N/A	225.00	1550-2885
1999 Carmel, Sunset on Ocean Ave. A/P (18 x 27)	970		435.00	280
1999 Carmel, Sunset on Ocean Ave. A/P (24 x 36)	970		520.00	345
1999 Carmel, Sunset on Ocean Ave. A/P (28 x 42)	970		650.00	425
1999 Carmel, Sunset on Ocean Ave. S/N (18 x 27)	4,850		285.00	230
1999 Carmel, Sunset on Ocean Ave. S/N (24 x 36)	4,850		370.00	295
1999 Carmel, Sunset on Ocean Ave. S/N (28 x 42)	4,850		500.00	375
1990 Chandler's Cottage S/N	550	N/A	125.00	1415-1665
1992 Christmas At the Ahwahnee S/N	980		175.00	230
XX Christmas At the Courthouse S/N	Closed	N/A	N/A	595-635
1990 Christmas Cottage 1990 S/N	550	N/A	95.00	595-1535
1991 Christmas Eve S/N	980		125.00	825
1994 Christmas Memories A/P	245		355.00	280
1994 Christmas Memories S/N	2,450		205.00	230
1994 Christmas Tree Cottage A/P	295		335.00	225
1994 Christmas Tree Cottage S/N	2,950		185.00	175
1996 A Christmas Welcome A/P	285		350.00	225
1996 A Christmas Welcome S/N	2,850		200.00	175
1997 Clearing Storms A/P (18 x 27)	570		400.00	280
1997 Clearing Storms A/P (24 x 36)	570		475.00	345
1997 Clearing Storms S/N (18 x 27)	2,850		250.00	230
1997 Clearing Storms S/N (24 x 36)	2,850		325.00	295
2001 Clocktower Cottage A/P (24 x 36)	770		565.00	345
2001 Clocktower Cottage S/N (24 x 36)	3,850		415.00	295
2000 Cobblestone Bridge A/P (24 x 36)	570		550.00	345
2000 Cobblestone Bridge S/N (24 x 36)	2,850		400.00	295
1997 Cobblestone Brooke A/P	485		475.00	345
1997 Cobblestone Brooke S/N	4,850		325.00	295
1996 Cobblestone Lane A/P	285		450.00	330
1996 Cobblestone Lane S/N	2,850		300.00	280
1998 Cobblestone Village A/P (18 x 24)	1,170		435.00	280
1998 Cobblestone Village A/P (25 1/2 x 34)	1,170		520.00	345
1998 Cobblestone Village A/P (30 x 40)	970		650.00	425
1998 Cobblestone Village S/N (18 x 24)	5,850		285.00	230
1998 Cobblestone Village S/N (25 1/2 x 34)	5,850		370.00	295
1998 Cobblestone Village S/N (30 x 40)	4,850		500.00	375
1999 Conquering The Storms A/P (18 x 27)	570		435.00	435
1999 Conquering The Storms A/P (24 x 36)	570		520.00	345
1999 Conquering The Storms A/P (28 x 42)	570		650.00	650
1999 Conquering The Storms S/N (18 x 27)	2,850		285.00	285
1999 Conquering The Storms S/N (24 x 36)	2,850		370.00	295
1999 Conquering The Storms S/N (28 x 42)	2,850		500.00	500

YEAR ISSUE	EDITION LIMIT	YEAR RETD.	ISSUE PRICE	*QUOTE U.S.$
1992 Cottage-By-The-Sea S/N	980	N/A	250.00	450-1325
1992 Country Memories A/P	200		N/A	225
1992 Country Memories S/N	980	1999	185.00	295-515
1994 Creekside Trail A/P	198		425.00	280
1994 Creekside Trail S/N	1,984		275.00	230
1984 Dawson S/N	750	N/A	150.00	750-2900
1994 Days of Peace A/P	198		425.00	280
1994 Days of Peace S/N	1,984		275.00	230
1995 Deer Creek Cottage A/P	285		335.00	225
1995 Deer Creek Cottage S/N	2,850		185.00	175
1994 Dusk in the Valley A/P	198		425.00	280
1994 Dusk in the Valley S/N	1,984		275.00	230
1994 Emerald Isle Cottage A/P	275		345.00	280
1994 Emerald Isle Cottage S/N	2,750		195.00	230
1993 End of a Perfect Day I S/N	1,250	1994	195.00	495-1495
1994 End of a Perfect Day II A/P	275	1998	385.00	550-1125
1994 End of a Perfect Day II S/N	2,750	1996	235.00	500-895
1995 End of a Perfect Day III A/P	485		475.00	345
1995 End of a Perfect Day III S/N	4,850		325.00	295
1989 Entrance to the Manor House S/N	550	N/A	125.00	750-1395
1989 Evening at Merritt's Cottage S/N	N/A	N/A	125.00	1095-1700
1992 Evening at Swanbrooke Cottage S/N	980	1994	250.00	475-1495
1999 Evening Glow A/P (16 X 20)	570		400.00	280
1999 Evening Glow S/N (16 X 20)	2,850		250.00	230
1995 Evening in the Forest A/P	485		355.00	280
1995 Evening in the Forest S/N	4,850		205.00	230
1999 Evening Majesty A/P (24 x 36)	970		550.00	345
1999 Evening Majesty S/N (24 x 36)	4,850		400.00	295
1985 Evening Service S/N	Closed	N/A	90.00	390-450
1998 Everett's Cottage A/P (16 x 20)	1,170		390.00	280
1998 Everett's Cottage A/P (20 x 24)	1,170		420.00	280
1998 Everett's Cottage A/P (24 x 30)	970		480.00	520
1998 Everett's Cottage S/N (16 x 20)	5,850		240.00	230
1998 Everett's Cottage S/N (20 x 24)	5,850		270.00	230
1998 Everett's Cottage S/N (24 x 30)	4,850		330.00	280
1993 Fisherman's Wharf, San Francisco S/N	2,750		325.00	295
1991 Flags Over The Capitol S/N	980		195.00	230
1999 The Forest Chapel A/P (24 x 30)	570		500.00	540
1999 The Forest Chapel S/N (24 x 30)	2,850		350.00	280
1999 Foxglove Cottage A/P (16 x 20)	770		400.00	280
1999 Foxglove Cottage A/P (20 x 24)	770		435.00	280
1999 Foxglove Cottage A/P (24 x 30)	770		500.00	330
1999 Foxglove Cottage S/N (16 x 20)	3,850		250.00	230
1999 Foxglove Cottage S/N (20 x 24)	3,850		285.00	230
1999 Foxglove Cottage S/N (24 x 30)	3,850		350.00	280
1997 Garden of Prayer A/P (18 x 24)	970		420.00	280
1997 Garden of Prayer A/P (25 1/2 x 34)	970		500.00	345
1997 Garden of Prayer A/P (30 x 40)	770		650.00	425
1997 Garden of Prayer S/N (18 x 24)	4,850		270.00	230
1997 Garden of Prayer S/N (25 1/2 x 34)	4,850		350.00	295
1997 Garden of Prayer S/N (30 x 40)	3,850		500.00	375
1993 The Garden of Promise S/N	1,250	1994	235.00	1065-2995
1992 The Garden Party S/N	980		175.00	230
1994 Gardens Beyond Autumn Gate S/N	789	1996	325.00	700-1195
1998 Gardens Beyond Spring Gate A/P (18 x 24)	1,170		435.00	280
1998 Gardens Beyond Spring Gate A/P (25 1/2 x 34)	1,170		520.00	345
1998 Gardens Beyond Spring Gate A/P (30 x 40)	1,170		650.00	425
1998 Gardens Beyond Spring Gate S/N (18 x 24)	5,850		270.00	230
1998 Gardens Beyond Spring Gate S/N (25 1/2 x 34)	5,850		350.00	295
1998 Gardens Beyond Spring Gate S/N (30 x 40)	5,850		500.00	375
1993 Glory of Winter S/N	1,250		235.00	230
1995 Golden Gate Bridge, San Francisco A/P	385		475.00	345
1995 Golden Gate Bridge, San Francisco S/N	3,850		325.00	295
2001 The Good Shepherd's Cottage A/P (25 1/2 x 34)	570		565.00	345
2001 The Good Shepherd's Cottage S/N (25 1/2 x 34)	2,850		415.00	295
1994 Guardian Castle A/P	275		450.00	330
1994 Guardian Castle S/N	2,750		300.00	280
1993 Heather's Hutch S/N	1,250	1999	175.00	230-545
1994 Hidden Arbor A/P	375		345.00	280
1994 Hidden Arbor S/N	2,750		195.00	230
1990 Hidden Cottage I S/N	550	N/A	125.00	1000-1840
1993 Hidden Cottage II S/N	1,480	1998	195.00	395-695

GRAPHICS

YEAR ISSUE	EDITION LIMIT	YEAR RETD.	ISSUE PRICE	*QUOTE U.S.$
1994 Hidden Gazebo A/P	240		345.00	280
1994 Hidden Gazebo, S/N	2,400	1998	195.00	250-575
1998 A Holiday Gathering A/P (12 x 16)	1,370		380.00	225
1998 A Holiday Gathering A/P (18 x 24)	1,370		435.00	280
1998 A Holiday Gathering A/P (25 1/2 x 34)	1,370		520.00	345
1998 A Holiday Gathering S/N (12 x 16)	6,850		230.00	175
1998 A Holiday Gathering S/N (18 x 24)	6,850		285.00	230
1998 A Holiday Gathering S/N (25 1/2 x 34)	6,850		370.00	295
1996 Hollyhock House A/P	385		355.00	280
1996 Hollyhock House S/N	3,850		205.00	230
1991 Home For The Evening S/N	980	N/A	100.00	195-545
1991 Home For The Holidays S/N	980	1994	225.00	495-1395
1992 Home is Where the Heart Is I S/N	980	1994	225.00	750-1285
1996 Home is Where the Heart Is II A/P	485		400.00	440
1996 Home is Where the Heart Is II S/N	Closed	1997	250.00	285-655
1993 Homestead House S/N	1,250		235.00	230
1998 Hometown Bridge A/P (18 x 27)	1,170		435.00	280
1998 Hometown Bridge A/P (24 x 36)	1,170		520.00	345
1998 Hometown Bridge A/P (28 x 42)	970		650.00	425
1998 Hometown Bridge S/N (18 x 27)	5,850		285.00	230
1998 Hometown Bridge S/N (24 x 36)	5,850		370.00	295
1998 Hometown Bridge S/N (28 x 42)	4,850		500.00	395
1996 Hometown Evening A/P	285		450.00	330
1996 Hometown Evening S/N	2,850		300.00	280
1997 Hometown Lake A/P	485		450.00	330
1997 Hometown Lake S/N	4,850		300.00	280
1995 Hometown Memories I A/P	485		450.00	330
1995 Hometown Memories I S/N	4,850		300.00	280
2000 Hometown Morning A/P (25 1/2 x 34)	770		550.00	345
2000 Hometown Morning S/N (25 1/2 x 34)	3,850		400.00	295
1996 Hyde Street and the Bay A/P	385		450.00	330
1996 Hyde Street and the Bay S/N	3,850		300.00	280
2001 It Doesn't Get Much Better A/P (25 1/2 x 34)	670		565.00	345
2001 It Doesn't Get Much Better S/N (25 1/2 x 34)	3,350		415.00	295
1992 Julianne's Cottage S/N	980	N/A	185.00	500-1015
1999 Lakeside Hideaway A/P (12 x 16)	570		380.00	225
1999 Lakeside Hideaway A/P (16 x 20)	570		400.00	280
1999 Lakeside Hideaway A/P (18 x 24)	570		435.00	280
1999 Lakeside Hideaway S/N (12 x 16)	2,850		230.00	175
1999 Lakeside Hideaway S/N (16 x 20)	2,850		250.00	230
1999 Lakeside Hideaway S/N (18 x 24)	2,850		285.00	230
1996 Lamplight Bridge A/P	285		335.00	280
1996 Lamplight Bridge S/N	2,850		205.00	230
1993 Lamplight Brooke S/N	1,650	1995	235.00	395-1205
1994 Lamplight Inn A/P	275		385.00	280
1994 Lamplight Inn S/N	2,750		235.00	230
1993 Lamplight Lane S/N	980	N/A	225.00	695-1755
2000 Lamplight Manor A/P (24 x 36)	970		550.00	345
2000 Lamplight Manor S/N (24 x 36)	4,850		400.00	295
1995 Lamplight Village A/P	485		400.00	280
1995 Lamplight Village S/N	4,850		250.00	230
1995 A Light in the Storm A/P	385		400.00	280
1995 A Light in the Storm S/N	3,850		250.00	230
1996 The Light of Peace A/P	335		475.00	345
1996 The Light of Peace S/N	3,350	2000	325.00	400-495
1995 The Lights of Home A/P	250	1996	225.00	250-380
1996 Lilac Gazebo A/P	285		335.00	225
1996 Lilac Gazebo S/N	2,850		185.00	175
1998 Lingering Dusk A/P (16 x 20)	770		390.00	280
1998 Lingering Dusk A/P (20 x 24)	770		420.00	280
1998 Lingering Dusk S/N (16 x 20)	3,850		240.00	230
1998 Lingering Dusk S/N (20 x 24)	3,850		270.00	230
1995 Main Street Celebration A/P	195		400.00	280
1995 Main Street Celebration S/N	1,950		250.00	230
1995 Main Street Courthouse A/P	195		400.00	280
1995 Main Street Courthouse S/N	1,950		250.00	230
1995 Main Street Matinee A/P	195		400.00	280
1995 Main Street Matinee S/N	1,950		250.00	230
1995 Main Street Trolley A/P	195		400.00	280
1995 Main Street Trolley S/N	1,950		250.00	230
1991 McKenna's Cottage S/N	980	1999	150.00	325-725
2001 Memories of Christmas A/P (18 x 24)	570		280.00	280
2001 Memories of Christmas S/N (18 x 24)	2,850		230.00	230
1992 Miller's Cottage S/N	980	1995	175.00	495-795
1994 Moonlight Lane I A/P	240		345.00	280
1994 Moonlight Lane I S/N	2,400		195.00	230
1985 Moonlight on the Riverfront S/N	260	N/A	150.00	295-795
1995 Morning Dogwood A/P	485		345.00	225
1995 Morning Dogwood S/N	4,850		195.00	175
1995 Morning Glory Cottage A/P	485		355.00	280
1995 Morning Glory Cottage S/N	4,850		205.00	230
1992 Morning Lane S/N	Closed	N/A	N/A	285-400
1998 Mountain Chapel A/P (16 x 20)	1,170		400.00	280
1998 Mountain Chapel A/P (24 x 30)	1,170		500.00	330
1998 Mountain Chapel A/P (32 x 40)	970		650.00	425
1998 Mountain Chapel S/N (16 x 20)	5,850		250.00	230
1998 Mountain Chapel S/N (24 x 30)	5,850		350.00	280
1998 Mountain Chapel S/N (32 x 40)	4,850		500.00	375
1998 Mountain Majesty A/P (18 x 24)	770		435.00	280
1998 Mountain Majesty A/P (25 1/2 x 34)	770		520.00	345
1998 Mountain Majesty A/P (30 x 40)	770		650.00	425
1998 Mountain Majesty S/N (18 x 24)	3,850		285.00	230
1998 Mountain Majesty S/N (25 1/2 x 34)	3,850		370.00	295
1998 Mountain Majesty S/N (30 x 40)	3,850		500.00	375
1997 A New Day Dawning A/P	385		475.00	345
1997 A New Day Dawning S/N	3,850		325.00	295
1986 New York, 6th Avenue S/N	950	N/A	150.00	1500-2820
1992 Olde Porterfield Gift Shoppe S/N	980		175.00	310
1991 Olde Porterfield Tea Room S/N	980	1998	150.00	395-955
1999 Open Gate A/P (12 x 16)	770		380.00	225
1999 Open Gate A/P (16 x 20)	770		400.00	280
1999 Open Gate A/P (18 x 24)	770		435.00	280
1999 Open Gate S/N (12 x 16)	3,850		230.00	175
1999 Open Gate S/N (16 x 20)	3,850		250.00	230
1999 Open Gate S/N (18 x 24)	3,850		285.00	230
1991 Open Gate, Sussex S/N	980		100.00	190
1993 Paris, City of Lights S/N	1,980		250.00	230
1994 Paris, Eiffel Tower A/P	275		445.00	280
1994 Paris, Eiffel Tower S/N	2,750		295.00	230
2000 A Peaceful Time A/P (16 x 20)	570		400.00	280
2000 A Peaceful Time S/N (16 x 20)	2,850		250.00	230
2001 The Perfect Red Rose A/P (12 x 16)	570		395.00	225
2001 The Perfect Red Rose S/N (12 x 16)	2,850		245.00	175
2001 A Perfect Summer Day A/P (24 x 30)	570		345.00	345
2001 A Perfect Summer Day S/N (24 x 30)	2,850		295.00	295
2001 The Perfect Yellow Rose A/P (12 x 16)	570		395.00	225
2001 The Perfect Yellow Rose S/N (12 x 16)	2,850		245.00	175
2000 Perseverance A/P (24 x 36)	570		550.00	345
2000 Perseverance S/N (24 x 36)	2,850		400.00	295
1995 Petals of Hope A/P	385		355.00	280
1995 Petals of Hope S/N	3,850		205.00	230
1996 Pine Cove Cottage A/P	485		400.00	280
1996 Pine Cove Cottage S/N	4,850		250.00	230
1984 Placerville, 1916 S/N	950	N/A	90.00	2495-3325
1999 Pools of Serenity A/P (24 x 30)	N/A		530.00	330
1999 Pools of Serenity S/N (24 x 30)	4,850		380.00	280
1994 The Power & The Majesty A/P	275		385.00	280
1994 The Power & The Majesty S/N	2,750		235.00	230
1999 Prince of Peace A/P	370		670.00	670
1999 Prince of Peace S/N	1,850		520.00	520
1998 Quiet Evening A/P (16 x 20)	770		400.00	280
1998 Quiet Evening A/P (20 x 24)	770		435.00	280
1998 Quiet Evening A/P (24 x 30)	770		500.00	330
1998 Quiet Evening S/N (16 x 20)	3,850		250.00	230
1998 Quiet Evening S/N (20 x 24)	3,850		285.00	230
1998 Quiet Evening S/N (24 x 30)	3,850		350.00	280
2001 Rock of Salvation A/P (24 x 36)	570		565.00	345
2001 Rock of Salvation S/N (24 x 36)	2,850		415.00	295
1988 Room with a View S/N	N/A	N/A	150.00	550-1395
1990 Rose Arbor S/N	935	1994	125.00	750-1495
2000 The Rose Garden A/P (24 x 30)	570		530.00	330
2000 The Rose Garden S/N (24 x 30)	2,850		380.00	280
1996 Rose Gate A/P	285		335.00	225
1996 Rose Gate S/N	2,850		185.00	175
1994 San Francisco Market Street A/P	750		250	320
1994 San Francisco Market Street S/N	7,500		375.00	470
1986 San Francisco, 1909 S/N	950	N/A	150.00	1800-2735
2001 San Francisco, Lombard Street A/P (25 1/2 x 34)	345		345.00	345
2001 San Francisco, Lombard Street S/N (25 1/2 x 34)	1,725		295.00	295
1992 San Francisco, Nob Hill (California St.) S/N	980	N/A	275.00	1275-3135
1989 San Francisco, Union Square S/N	Closed	N/A	225.00	1950-3060
1998 The Sea of Tranquility A/P (18 x 27)	1,170		420.00	280
1998 The Sea of Tranquility A/P (24 x 36)	1,170		500.00	345
1998 The Sea of Tranquility A/P (28 x 42)	1,170		650.00	425
1998 The Sea of Tranquility S/N (18 x 27)	5,850		275.00	230
1998 The Sea of Tranquility S/N (24 x 36)	5,850		350.00	295
1998 The Sea of Tranquility S/N (28 x 42)	5,850		500.00	375

*Quotes have been rounded up to nearest dollar

GRAPHICS

YEAR ISSUE	EDITION LIMIT	YEAR RETD.	ISSUE PRICE	*QUOTE U.S.$
1992 Silent Night S/N	980	1999	175.00	350-735
1995 Simpler Times I A/P	335		400.00	280
1995 Simpler Times I S/N	3,895		250.00	230
2001 Split Rock Light S/N (16 x 20)	2,350		190.00	190
2001 Split Rock Light S/N (20 x 24)	470		280.00	280
2001 Split Rock Light S/N (20 x 24)	2,350		230.00	230
1990 Spring At Stonegate S/N	550	1996	200.00	265-865
1996 Spring Gate A/P	385		475.00	345
1996 Spring Gate S/N	3,850		325.00	295
1994 Spring in the Alps A/P	198		375.00	280
1994 Spring in the Alps S/N	1,984		225.00	230
1993 St. Nicholas Circle S/N	1,750		235.00	230
1998 Stairway to Paradise A/P (18 x 24)	770		435.00	280
1998 Stairway to Paradise A/P (25 1/2 x 34)	770		520.00	345
1998 Stairway to Paradise A/P (30 x 40)	770		650.00	425
1998 Stairway to Paradise S/N (18 x 24)	3,850		285.00	230
1998 Stairway to Paradise S/N (25 1/2 x 34)	3,850		370.00	295
1998 Stairway to Paradise S/N (30 x 40)	3,850		500.00	375
1995 Stepping Stone Cottage A/P	285		400.00	280
1995 Stepping Stone Cottage S/N	2,850		250.00	230
1998 Stillwater Bridge A/P (12 x 16)	570		370.00	225
1998 Stillwater Bridge A/P (18 x 24)	770		420.00	280
1998 Stillwater Bridge S/N (12 x 16)	2,850		220.00	175
1998 Stillwater Bridge S/N (18 x 24)	3,850		270.00	230
1993 Stonehearth Hutch S/N	1,650		175.00	175
2000 Streams of Living Water A/P (25 1/2 x 34)	1,170		565.00	345
2000 Streams of Living Water S/N (25 1/2 x 34)	2,850		415.00	295
1993 Studio in the Garden S/N	980	1995	175.00	230-535
1999 Summer Gate A/P (18 x 24)	1,170		435.00	280
1999 Summer Gate A/P (25 1/2 x 34)	1,170		520.00	345
1999 Summer Gate A/P (30 x 40)	1,170		650.00	650
1999 Summer Gate S/N (18 x 24)	5,850		285.00	230
1999 Summer Gate S/N (25 1/2 x 34)	5,850		370.00	295
1999 Summer Gate S/N (30 x 40)	5,850		500.00	500
1992 Sunday At Apple Hill S/N	980	1994	175.00	395-805
1996 Sunday Evening Sleigh Ride A/P	285		400.00	280
1996 Sunday Evening Sleigh Ride S/N	2,850		250.00	230
1993 Sunday Outing S/N	980	1995	175.00	375-695
1999 Sunrise A/P (24 x 30)	570		530.00	330
1999 Sunrise S/N (24 x 30)	2,850		380.00	280
1996 Sunset at Riverbend Farm A/P	485		400.00	280
1996 Sunset at Riverbend Farm S/N	4,850		250.00	230
1992 Sweetheart Cottage I S/N	980	1995	150.00	310-695
1993 Sweetheart Cottage II S/N	980	1994	150.00	690-795
1993 Sweetheart Cottage III A/P	165		385.00	280
1993 Sweetheart Cottage III S/N	1,650		235.00	230
1996 Teacup Cottage A/P	285		400.00	280
1996 Teacup Cottage S/N	2,850		250.00	230
1999 Town Square A/P	770		435.00	280
1999 Town Square S/N	3,850		285.00	230
1997 Twilight Cottage A/P	395		375.00	280
1997 Twilight Cottage S/N	3,950		225.00	230
1999 Twilight Vista A/P	770		500.00	345
1999 Twilight Vista S/N	3,850		350.00	295
1997 Valley of Peace A/P	385		475.00	345
1997 Valley of Peace S/N	3,850		325.00	295
1996 Venice A/P	485		475.00	345
1996 Venice S/N	4,850		325.00	295
1992 Victorian Christmas I S/N	980	N/A	235.00	750-1545
1993 Victorian Christmas II S/N	1,650	1996	235.00	345-695
1994 Victorian Christmas III A/P	295		400.00	280
1994 Victorian Christmas III S/N	2,950		250.00	230
1995 Victorian Christmas IV S/N	756	1995	250.00	300-715
1991 Victorian Evening S/N	980	1993	150.00	500-1025
1992 Victorian Garden I S/N	980	1994	275.00	750-1695
1997 Victorian Garden II A/P	385		400.00	280
1997 Victorian Garden II S/N	3,850		250.00	230
2000 Victorian Light A/P (24 x 30)	570		530.00	330
2000 Victorian Light S/N (24 x 30)	2,850		380.00	280
1997 Village Christmas A/P (18 x 24)	970		420.00	280
1997 Village Christmas A/P (25 1/2 x 34)	370		500.00	345
1997 Village Christmas S/N (18 x 24)	4,850		270.00	230
1997 Village Christmas S/N (25 1/2 x 34)	1,850		350.00	295
1993 Village Inn S/N	1,200	2000	195.00	295-425
1994 The Warmth of Home A/P	245		335.00	225
1994 The Warmth of Home S/N	2,450		185.00	175
1998 The Wind of the Spirit A/P (18 x 27)	1,170		420.00	280
1998 The Wind of the Spirit A/P (24 x 36)	1,170		500.00	345
1998 The Wind of the Spirit A/P (28 x 42)	970		650.00	425
1998 The Wind of the Spirit S/N (18 x 27)	5,850		270.00	230
1998 The Wind of the Spirit S/N (24 x 36)	5,850		350.00	295
1998 The Wind of the Spirit S/N (28 x 42)	4,850		500.00	375
1996 Winsor Manor A/P	385		450.00	330
1996 Winsor Manor S/N	3,850		300.00	280
1999 Winter Chapel A/P (12 x 18)	570		380.00	225
1999 Winter Chapel A/P (18 x 27)	770		435.00	280
1999 Winter Chapel S/N (12 x 18)	2,850		230.00	175
1999 Winter Chapel S/N (18 x 27)	3,850		285.00	230
1993 Winter's End S/N	875	2000	235.00	320-495
1992 Yosemite S/N	980	1996	225.00	685-1795

Lightpost Publishing/Recollections by Lightpost

American Heroes Collection-Framed - Recollections

YEAR ISSUE	EDITION LIMIT	YEAR RETD.	ISSUE PRICE	*QUOTE U.S.$
1992 Abraham Lincoln	7,500	1997	150.00	150
1993 Babe Ruth	2,250	1996	95.00	95
1993 Ben Franklin	1,000	1997	95.00	95-125
1994 Dwight D. Eisenhower	Closed	1997	30.00	30
1994 Eternal Love (Civil War)	1,861	1997	195.00	195
1994 Franklin D. Roosevelt	Closed	1997	30.00	30
1992 George Washington	7,500	1997	150.00	150-225
1994 George Washington	Closed	1997	30.00	30
1994 John F. Kennedy	Closed	1997	30.00	30
1992 John F. Kennedy	7,500	1997	150.00	150
1992 Mark Twain	7,500	1997	150.00	150
1994 A Nation Divided	1,000	1997	150.00	150
1993 A Nation United	1,000	1997	150.00	150

Cinema Classics Collection - Recollections

YEAR ISSUE	EDITION LIMIT	YEAR RETD.	ISSUE PRICE	*QUOTE U.S.$
1993 As God As My Witness Classic Clip	Closed	1995	40.00	40
1994 Attempted Deception Classic Clip	Closed	1997	30.00	30
1994 A Chance Meeting Classic Clip	Closed	1997	30.00	30
1993 A Dream Remembered Classic Clip	Closed	1995	40.00	40
1993 The Emerald City Classic Clip	Closed	1995	40.00	40
1993 Follow the Yellow Brick Road Classic Clip	Closed	1995	40.00	40
1993 Frankly My Dear Classic Clip	Closed	1995	40.00	40
1994 The Gift Classic Clip	Closed	1997	30.00	30
1993 Gone With the Wind-Movie Ticket Classic Clip	2,000	1997	40.00	40
1994 If I Only Had a Brain Classic Clip	Closed	1997	30.00	30
1994 If I Only Had a Heart Classic Clip	Closed	1997	30.00	30
1994 If I Only Had the Nerve Classic Clip	Closed	1997	30.00	30
1993 The Kiss Classic Clip	Closed	1995	40.00	40
1993 Not A Marrying Man	12,500	1997	150.00	150
1993 Over The Rainbow	7,500	1997	150.00	150
1994 The Proposal Classic Clip	Closed	1997	30.00	30
1993 The Ruby Slippers Classic Clip	Closed	1995	40.00	40
1993 Scarlett & Her Beaux	12,500	1997	150.00	150
1994 There's No Place Like Home Classic Clip	Closed	1997	30.00	30
1993 We're Off to See the Wizard Classic Clip	Closed	1995	40.00	40
1993 You Do Waltz Divinely	12,500	1997	195.00	195
1993 You Need Kissing	12,500	1997	195.00	195

The Elvis Collection - Recollections

YEAR ISSUE	EDITION LIMIT	YEAR RETD.	ISSUE PRICE	*QUOTE U.S.$
1994 Celebrity Soldier/Regular G.I.	Closed	1997	30.00	30
1994 Dreams Remembered/Dreams Realized	Closed	1997	30.00	30
1994 Elvis the King	2,750	1997	195.00	195
1994 Elvis the Pelvis	2,750	1997	195.00	195
1994 The King/The Servant	Closed	1997	30.00	30
1994 Lavish Spender/Generous Giver	Closed	1997	30.00	30
1994 Professional Artist/Practical Joker	Closed	1997	30.00	30
1994 Public Image/Private Man	Closed	1997	30.00	30
1994 Sex Symbol/Boy Next Door	Closed	1997	30.00	30
1994 To Elvis with Love	2,750	1997	195.00	195
1994 Vulgar Showman/Serious Musician	Closed	1997	30.00	30

Gone With the Wind - Recollections

YEAR ISSUE	EDITION LIMIT	YEAR RETD.	ISSUE PRICE	*QUOTE U.S.$
1995 Final Parting Classic Clip	Closed	1997	30.00	30
1995 A Parting Kiss Classic Clip	Closed	1997	30.00	30
1995 The Red Dress Classic Clip	Closed	1997	30.00	30
1995 Sweet Revenge Classic Clip	Closed	1997	30.00	30

The Wizard of Oz - Recollections

YEAR ISSUE	EDITION LIMIT	YEAR RETD.	ISSUE PRICE	*QUOTE U.S.$
1995 Glinda the Good Witch	Closed	1997	30.00	30
1995 Toto	Closed	1997	30.00	30
1995 The Wicked Witch	Closed	1997	30.00	30
1995 The Wizard	Closed	1997	30.00	30

Collectors' Information Bureau   *Quotes have been rounded up to nearest dollar

YEAR ISSUE	EDITION LIMIT	YEAR RETD.	ISSUE PRICE	*QUOTE U.S.$
Little Angel Publishing				
Dona's Christmas Classics - Framed Canvas - D. Gelsinger				
2001 Footprints (12 x 16)	Open		242.00	242
2001 Footprints (5 x 7)	Open		99.00	99
2001 A Long Winter Nap (8 x 10)	Open		135.00	135
2001 Silent Night, Gentle Light (12 x16)	Open		242.00	242
2001 Silent Night, Gentle Light (5 x 7)	Open		99.00	99
Dona's Christmas Classics -Unframed Paper - D. Gelsinger				
2001 A Long Winter Nap (13 x 17)	Open		36.00	36
2001 A Long Winter Nap (6 x 8)	Open		16.00	16
2001 Silent Night, Gentle Light (13 x17)	Open		36.00	36
2001 Silent Night, Gentle Light (6 x 8)	Open		16.00	16
Gelsinger - Framed Canvas - D. Gelsinger				
1995 Alexandria's Teddy (12 x 16) A/P	25		352.50	353
1995 Alexandria's Teddy (12 x 16) S/N	250		295.00	295
1997 An Angel's Touch (8 x 10) A/P	50		169.00	169
1997 An Angel's Touch (8 x 10) S/N	500		137.50	138
1997 The Boardwalk (18 x 24) A/P	5	1997	660.00	660-950
1997 The Boardwalk (18 x 24) S/N	45		560.00	560
1997 Farewell Bend (20 x 24) A/P	5	1997	675.00	675-950
1997 Farewell Bend (20 x 24) S/N	40	2001	575.00	575-800
1995 Fire Light (20 x 24) A/P	30	1996	595.00	595-650
1995 Fire Light (20 x 24) S/N	300		520.00	520
1994 A Flower For Baby (20 x 24) A/P	25		585.00	585
1994 A Flower For Baby (20 x 24) S/N	250		510.00	510
1997 Gentle Guidance (8 x 10) A/P	50		169.00	169
1997 Gentle Guidance (8 x 10) S/N	500		137.50	138
1995 Golden Gate (24 X 36) A/P	20		795.00	795
1995 Golden Gate (24 x 36) S/N	200		695.00	695
1998 Heceta Head Lighthouse (18 x 24) A/P	20		699.00	699
1998 Heceta Head Lighthouse (18 x 24) S/N	200		599.00	599
1998 Heceta Head Lighthouse (8 x 10) A/P	20		238.00	238
1998 Heceta Head Lighthouse (8 x 10) S/N	200		188.00	188
1997 A Joyous Feast (11 x 14) A/P	6	1998	370.00	370-470
1997 A Joyous Feast (11 x 14) S/N	54	1998	290.00	290-390
1995 Life's Little Tangles (20 x 24) A/P	35	1996	595.00	595-650
1995 Life's Little Tangles (20 x 24) S/N	350		520.00	520
1996 The Lighthouse Keeper (16 x 20) A/P	10	1997	625.00	625-1150
1996 The Lighthouse Keeper (16 x 20) S/N	50	1997	525.00	525-900
1995 Motherly Love (16 x 20) A/P	30		525.00	525
1995 Motherly Love (16 x 20) S/N	300		450.00	450
1995 The Perfect Tree (12 x 16) A/P	25		352.50	353
1995 The Perfect Tree (12 x 16) S/N	250		295.00	295
1996 Sugar & Spice (12 x 16) A/P	20		352.50	353
1996 Sugar & Spice (12 x 16) S/N	200		295.00	295
1998 Tender Love (18 x 24) A/P	50		699.00	699
1998 Tender Love (18 x 24) S/N	500		599.00	599
1994 The Toy Box (16 x 20) A/P	25		525.00	525
1994 The Toy Box (16 x 20) S/N	250		450.00	450
Gelsinger - Unframed Paper - D. Gelsinger				
1995 Alexandria's Teddy A/P	15		120.00	120
1995 Alexandria's Teddy S/N	150		80.00	80
1997 An Angel's Touch A/P	30		87.00	87
1997 An Angel's Touch S/N	300		57.00	57
1995 Fire Light A/P	15		200.00	200
1995 Fire Light S/N	150		150.00	150
1994 A Flower For Baby A/P	15		190.00	190
1994 A Flower For Baby S/N	150		140.00	140
1997 Gentle Guidance A/P	30		87.00	87
1997 Gentle Guidance S/N	300		57.00	57
1995 Golden Gate A/P	10		230.00	230
1995 Golden Gate S/N	100		180.00	180
1998 Heceta Head Lighthouse (18 x 24) A/P	20		200.00	200
1998 Heceta Head Lighthouse (18 x 24) S/N	200		150.00	150
1998 Heceta Head Lighthouse (8 x 10) A/P	20		87.00	87
1998 Heceta Head Lighthouse (8 x 10) S/N	200		57.00	57
1995 Life's Little Tangles (20 x 24) A/P	15		200.00	200
1995 Life's Little Tangles(20 x 24) S/N	150	2001	150.00	150
1995 Motherly Love A/P	15		170.00	170
1995 Motherly Love S/N	150		120.00	120
1995 The Perfect Tree A/P	15		120.00	120
1995 The Perfect Tree S/N	150		80.00	80
1996 Sugar & Spice A/P	5		120.00	120
1996 Sugar & Spice S/N	50		80.00	80
1998 Tender Love A/P	50		200.00	200

YEAR ISSUE	EDITION LIMIT	YEAR RETD.	ISSUE PRICE	*QUOTE U.S.$
1998 Tender Love S/N	500		150.00	150
1994 The Toy Box A/P	15		170.00	170
1994 The Toy Box S/N	150		120.00	120
Heaven's Little Angels - Framed Canvas - D. Gelsinger				
2001 An Angel's Blessing (8 x 10)	Open		135.00	135
2001 An Angel's Care (12 x 16)	Open		242.00	242
2001 An Angel's Care (5 x 7)	Open		99.00	99
2001 An Angel's Charity (8 x 10)	Open		135.00	135
2001 An Angel's Gift (12 x 16)	Open		242.00	242
2001 An Angel's Gift (5 x 7)	Open		99.00	99
2001 An Angel's Guidance (12 x 16)	Open		242.00	242
2001 An Angel's Guidance (5 x 7)	Open		99.00	99
2001 An Angel's Spirit (12 x 16)	Open		242.00	242
2001 An Angel's Spirit (5 x 7)	Open		99.00	99
1999 Garden Miracle (5 x 7)	Open		99.00	99
1999 Gentle Guardian (5 x 7)	Open		99.00	99
2000 Heavenly Blessings (8 x 10)	Open		135.00	135
2000 Heavenly Gifts (8 x 10)	Open		135.00	135
2001 Joyful Hope (12 x 16)	Open		242.00	242
2001 Joyful Hope (5 x 7)	Open		99.00	99
2001 Joyful Prayer (12 x 16)	Open		242.00	242
2001 Joyful Prayer (5 x 7)	Open		99.00	99
1999 A Little Faith (12 x 16)	Open		242.00	242
1999 A Little Faith (5 x 7)	Open		99.00	99
1999 A Little Hope (12 x 16)	Open		242.00	242
1999 A Little Hope (5 x 7)	Open		99.00	99
2000 A Little Joy (12 x 16)	Open		242.00	242
2000 A Little Joy (5 x 7)	Open		99.00	99
2000 A Little Tenderness (12 x 16)	Open		242.00	242
2000 A Little Tenderness (5x7)	Open		99.00	99
2001 Simple Faith (12 x 16)	Open		242.00	242
2001 Simple Faith (5 x 7)	Open		99.00	99
Heaven's Little Angels - Unframed Paper - D. Gelsinger				
2001 An Angel's Blessing (9x11)	Open		20.00	20
2001 An Angel's Care (13 x 17)	Open		36.00	36
2001 An Angel's Care (6 x 8)	Open		16.00	16
2001 An Angel's Charity (6 x 8)	Open		16.00	16
2001 An Angel's Gift (13 x 17)	Open		36.00	36
2001 An Angel's Gift (6 x 8)	Open		16.00	16
2001 An Angel's Guidance (13 x 17)	Open		36.00	36
2001 An Angel's Guidance (6 x 8)	Open		16.00	16
2001 An Angel's Spirit (13 x 17)	Open		36.00	36
2001 An Angel's Spirit (6 x 8)	Open		16.00	16
1999 Garden Miracle (5 x 7)	Open		16.00	16
1999 Gentle Guardian (5 x 7)	Open		16.00	16
2000 Heavenly Blessings (8 x 10)	Open		20.00	20
2000 Heavenly Gifts (8 x 10)	Open		20.00	20
2001 Joyful Hope (13 x 17)	Open		36.00	36
2001 Joyful Hope (6 x 8)	Open		16.00	16
2001 Joyful Prayer (13 x 17)	Open		36.00	36
2001 Joyful Prayer (6 x 8)	Open		16.00	16
1999 A Little Faith (12 x 16)	Open		36.00	36
1999 A Little Faith (5 x 7)	Open		16.00	16
1999 A Little Hope (12 x 16)	Open		36.00	36
1999 A Little Hope (5 x 7)	Open		16.00	16
1999 A Little Hope (9x11)	Open		26.00	26
2000 A Little Joy (12 x 16)	Open		36.00	36
2000 A Little Joy (5 x 7)	Open		16.00	16
2000 A Little Tenderness (12 x 16)	Open		36.00	36
2000 A Little Tenderness (5 x 7)	Open		16.00	16
2001 Simple Faith (13 x 17)	Open		36.00	36
2001 Simple Faith (6 x 8)	Open		16.00	16
The Seasons of Angels - Framed Canvas - D. Gelsinger				
1996 Spring Angel (8 x 10) A/P	12	1999	234.00	234
1996 Spring Angel (8 x 10) S/N	125		184.00	184
1996 Winter Angel (8 x 10) A/P	12	1999	234.00	234
1996 Winter Angel (8 x 10) S/N	125		184.00	184
The Seasons of Angels - Unframed Paper - D. Gelsinger				
1996 Spring Angel A/P	12		87.00	87
1996 Spring Angel S/N	125		57.00	57
1996 Winter Angel A/P	12		87.00	87
1996 Winter Angel S/N	125		57.00	57
Mill Pond Press				
Bateman - R. Bateman				
1982 Above the River-Trumpeter Swans	950	1984	200.00	850-1035
1984 Across the Sky-Snow Geese	950	1985	220.00	800-905

GRAPHICS

YEAR ISSUE	EDITION LIMIT	YEAR RETD.	ISSUE PRICE	*QUOTE U.S.$
1980 African Amber-Lioness Pair	950	1980	175.00	475
1979 Afternoon Glow-Snowy Owl	950	1979	125.00	525-603
1990 Air, The Forest and The Watch	42,558	N/A	325.00	325-681
1984 Along the Ridge-Grizzly Bears	950	1984	200.00	700-900
1984 American Goldfinch-Winter Dress	950	1984	75.00	165-207
1979 Among the Leaves-Cottontail Rabbit	950	1980	75.00	1000
1980 Antarctic Elements	950	1980	125.00	160-216
1995 Approach-Bald Eagle	N/A		1295.00	1295
1991 Arctic Cliff-White Wolves	13,000	1991	325.00	600
1982 Arctic Evening-White Wolf	950	1982	185.00	1050-1700
1980 Arctic Family-Polar Bears	950	1980	150.00	1150-2200
1992 Arctic Landscape-Polar Bear	5,000	N/A	345.00	195
1992 Arctic Landscape-Polar Bear-Premier Ed.	450	1992	800.00	800
1982 Arctic Portrait-White Gyrfalcon	950	1982	175.00	325
1985 Arctic Tern Pair	950	1985	175.00	185
1981 Artist and His Dog	950	1983	150.00	550
1980 Asleep on Hemlock-Screech Owl	950	1980	125.00	575-825
1991 At the Cliff-Bobcat	12,500	1991	325.00	300-325
1992 At the Feeder-Cardinal	950	1992	125.00	200-475
1987 At the Nest-Secretary Birds	950	1987	290.00	290
1982 At the Roadside-Red-Tailed Hawk	950	1984	185.00	875
1980 Autumn Overture-Moose	950	1980	245.00	2000
1980 Awesome Land-American Elk	950	1980	245.00	2350
1989 Backlight-Mute Swan	950	1989	275.00	450
1983 Bald Eagle Portrait	950	1983	185.00	300-390
2000 Bank of Swans	950		225.00	225
1982 Baobab Tree and Impala	950	1986	245.00	300
1980 Barn Owl in the Churchyard	950	1981	125.00	690-800
1989 Barn Swallow and Horse Collar	950	N/A	225.00	225
1982 Barn Swallows in August	950	N/A	245.00	350
1992 Beach Grass and Tree Frog	1,250		345.00	345
1985 Beaver Pond Reflections	950	1985	185.00	265
1984 Big Country, Pronghorn Antelope	950	1985	185.00	185
1986 Black Eagle	950	1986	200.00	200-250
1993 Black Jaguar-Premier Edition	450	N/A	850.00	1000
1986 Blacksmith Plover	950	1986	185.00	185
1986 Black-Tailed Deer in the Olympics	950	1986	245.00	245
1991 Bluebird and Blossoms	4,500		235.00	235
1991 Bluebird and Blossoms-Prestige Ed.	450		625.00	625
1980 Blushing Bull-African Elephant	950	1981	135.00	1100-1450
1981 Bright Day-Atlantic Puffins	950	1985	175.00	875-1300
1989 Broad-Tailed Hummingbird Pair	950	1989	225.00	225
1980 Brown Pelican and Pilings	950	1980	165.00	550
1979 Bull Moose	950	1979	125.00	650
2000 By The River	950		275.00	275
1978 By the Tracks-Killdeer	950	1980	75.00	825-1025
1983 Call of the Wild-Bald Eagle	950	1983	200.00	200-250
1985 Canada Geese Family(stone lithograph)	260	1985	350.00	795-895
1985 Canada Geese Over the Escarpment	950	1985	135.00	225
1986 Canada Geese With Young	950	1986	195.00	200-265
1981 Canada Geese-Nesting	950	1981	295.00	1395-1595
1993 Cardinal and Sumac	2,510	N/A	235.00	235
1988 Cardinal and Wild Apples	12,183	1988	235.00	235
1989 Catching The Light-Barn Owl	2,000	1990	295.00	295
1988 Cattails, Fireweed and Yellowthroat	950	1988	235.00	275
1989 Centennial Farm	950	1989	295.00	295
1988 The Challenge-Bull Moose	10,671	1989	325.00	325
1980 Chapel Doors	950	1985	135.00	700-850
1986 Charging Rhino	950	1986	325.00	475-575
1982 Cheetah Profile	950	1985	245.00	365
1978 Cheetah With Cubs	950	1980	95.00	365
1988 Cherrywood with Juncos	950	1988	245.00	245
1990 Chinstrap Penguin	810	1991	150.00	150
1992 Clan of the Raven	950	1992	235.00	345-425
1981 Clear Night-Wolves	950	1981	245.00	4400-4600
1988 Colonial Garden	950	1988	245.00	400-525
1987 Continuing Generations-Spotted Owls	950	1987	525.00	475-550
1991 Cottage Lane-Red Fox	950	1991	285.00	250
1984 Cougar Portrait	950	1984	95.00	290
1979 Country Lane-Pheasants	950	1981	85.00	600
1981 Courting Pair-Whistling Swans	950	1981	245.00	275
1981 Courtship Display-Wild Turkey	950	1981	175.00	225
1980 Coyote in Winter Sage	950	1980	245.00	2250-2500
1992 Cries of Courtship-Red Crowned Cranes	950	1992	350.00	395-550
1980 Curious Glance-Red Fox	950	1980	135.00	995-1450
1986 Dark Gyrfalcon	950	1986	225.00	300
1993 Day Lilies and Dragonflies	1,250		345.00	345
1982 Dipper By the Waterfall	950	1985	165.00	475-48
1989 Dispute Over Prey	950		325.00	32
1989 Distant Danger-Raccoon	1,600	1989	225.00	22
1984 Down for a Drink-Morning Dove	950	1985	135.00	26
1978 Downy Woodpecker on Goldenrod Gall	950	1979	50.00	1000-130
1988 Dozing Lynx	950	1988	335.00	1300-150
1986 Driftwood Perch-Striped Swallows	950	1986	195.00	19
1983 Early Snowfall-Ruffed Grouse	950	1985	195.00	195-22
1983 Early Spring-Bluebird	950	1984	185.00	625-75
1981 Edge of the Ice-Ermine	950	1981	175.00	40
1982 Edge of the Woods-Whitetail Deer, w/Book	950	1983	745.00	925-107
1991 Elephant Cow and Calf	950	1991	300.00	40
1982 Elephant Herd and Grouse	950	1986	235.00	32
1991 Encounter in the Bush-African Lions	950	1991	295.00	34
1987 End of Season-Grizzly	950	1987	325.00	595-62
1991 Endangered Spaces-Grizzly	4,008	1991	325.00	32
1985 Entering the Water-Common Gulls	950	1986	195.00	19
1986 European Robin and Hydrangeas	950	1986	130.00	200-299
1989 Evening Call-Common Loon	950	1989	235.00	495-625
1980 Evening Grosbeak	950	1980	125.00	695
1983 Evening Idyll-Mute Swans	950	1984	245.00	675
1981 Evening Light-White Gyrfalcon	950	1981	245.00	775-975
1979 Evening Snowfall-American Elk	950	1980	150.00	950-1150
1987 Everglades	950	1987	360.00	360
1980 Fallen Willow-Snowy Owl	950	1980	200.00	515-600
1987 Farm Lane and Blue Jays	950	1987	225.00	300-400
1987 Fence Post and Burdock	950	1987	130.00	275
1991 Fluid Power-Orca	290		2500.00	2500
1980 Flying High-Golden Eagle	950	1980	150.00	1000
1982 Fox at the Granary	950	1985	165.00	300
1982 Frosty Morning-Blue Jay	950	1982	185.00	800-900
1982 Gallinule Family	950		135.00	135
1981 Galloping Herd-Giraffes	950	1981	175.00	950-1200
1985 Gambel's Quail Pair	950	1985	95.00	325
1982 Gentoo Penguins and Whale Bones	950	1986	205.00	550-600
1983 Ghost of the North-Great Gray Owl	950	1983	200.00	1700-3950
1982 Golden Crowned Kinglet and Rhododendron	950	1982	150.00	1800-2700
1979 Golden Eagle	950	1981	150.00	250
1985 Golden Eagle Portrait	950	1987	115.00	175
1989 Goldfinch In the Meadow	1,600	1989	150.00	250
1983 Goshawk and Ruffed Grouse	950	1984	185.00	500
1988 Grassy Bank-Great Blue Heron	950	1988	285.00	225
1981 Gray Squirrel	950	1981	180.00	685-1015
1979 Great Blue Heron	950	1987	125.00	800-1400
1988 Great Blue Heron in Flight	950	1987	295.00	295-395
1988 Great Crested Grebe	950	1988	135.00	135
1987 Great Egret Preening	950	1987	315.00	600-725
1983 Great Horned Owl in the White Pine	950	1983	225.00	450
1987 Greater Kudu Bull	950	1987	145.00	145
1993 Grizzly and Cubs	2,250	1993	335.00	400
1991 Gulls on Pilings	1,950	N/A	265.00	265
1988 Hardwood Forest-White-Tailed Buck	630	1988	300.00	1600-1950
1988 Harlequin Duck-Bull Kelp-Executive Ed.	623	1988	550.00	550
1988 Harlequin Duck-Bull Kelp-Gold Plated	950	1988	300.00	300
1980 Heron on the Rocks	950	1980	75.00	500-800
1981 High Camp at Dusk	950	1985	245.00	465-1100
1979 High Country-Stone Sheep	950	1982	125.00	600-900
1987 High Kingdom-Snow Leopard	950	1987	325.00	550-800
2001 Hindu Temple - Tiger	950		235.00	235
1990 Homage to Ahmed	290	N/A	3300.00	3500
1984 Hooded Mergansers in Winter	950	1984	210.00	400-500
1984 House Finch and Yucca	950	1984	95.00	195
1986 House Sparrow	950	1986	125.00	160-225
1987 House Sparrows and Bittersweet	950	1987	220.00	300-370
1986 Hummingbird Pair Diptych	950	1986	330.00	550-625
1987 Hurricane Lake-Wood Ducks	950	1987	135.00	200
1981 In for the Evening	950	1981	150.00	1750-2500
1994 In His Prime-Mallard	950	N/A	195.00	250-295
1984 In the Brier Patch-Cottontail	950	1984	165.00	350-400
1986 In the Grass-Lioness	950	1986	245.00	245
1985 In the Highlands-Golden Eagle	950	1985	235.00	350
1985 In the Mountains-Osprey	950	1987	95.00	200
1992 Intrusion-Mountain Gorilla	2,250	1996	325.00	325-550
1990 Ireland House	950	1990	265.00	265-295
2001 Irish Church and Barn Owl	950		235.00	235
1985 Irish Cottage and Wagtail	950	1990	175.00	200-300

Collectors' Information Bureau

*Quotes have been rounded up to nearest dollar

YEAR ISSUE	EDITION LIMIT	YEAR RETD.	ISSUE PRICE	*QUOTE U.S.$
1992 Junco in Winter	1,250	1992	185.00	215-280
1990 Keeper of the Land	290		3300.00	3300
1993 Kestrel and Grasshopper	1,250		335.00	335
1979 King of the Realm	950	1979	125.00	575-690
1987 King Penguins	950	1987	130.00	140-195
1981 Kingfisher and Aspen	950	1981	225.00	855-900
1980 Kingfisher in Winter	950	1981	175.00	825-1000
1980 Kittiwake Greeting	950	1980	75.00	365
1981 Last Look-Bighorn Sheep	950	1986	195.00	129-225
1987 Late Winter-Black Squirrel	950	1987	165.00	165
1981 Laughing Gull and Horseshoe Crab	950	1981	125.00	125
1982 Leopard Ambush	950	1986	245.00	395-625
1988 Leopard and Thomson Gazelle Kill	950	1988	275.00	275
1985 Leopard at Seronera	950	1985	175.00	290
1980 Leopard in a Sausage Tree	950	1980	150.00	1695-2195
1984 Lily Pads and Loon	950	1984	200.00	1250-1716
1987 Lion and Wildebeest	950	1987	265.00	265
1980 Lion at Tsavo	950	1983	150.00	350
1978 Lion Cubs	950	1981	125.00	259
1987 Lioness at Serengeti	950	1987	325.00	325
1985 Lions in the Grass	950	1985	265.00	700-825
1981 Little Blue Heron	950	1981	95.00	225
1982 Lively Pair-Chickadees	950	1982	160.00	362
1983 Loon Family	950	1983	200.00	850
1990 Lunging Heron	1,250	1990	225.00	225
1978 Majesty on the Wing-Bald Eagle	950	1979	150.00	2500-3395
1988 Mallard Family at Sunset	950	1988	235.00	235
1986 Mallard Family-Misty Marsh	950	1986	130.00	130
1986 Mallard Pair-Early Winter	41,740	1986	135.00	200
1985 Mallard Pair-Early Winter 24K Gold	950	1986	1650.00	2000
1986 Mallard Pair-Early Winter Gold Plated	7,691	1986	250.00	375
1989 Mangrove Morning-Roseate Spoonbills	2,000	1989	325.00	414
1991 Mangrove Shadow-Common Egret	1,250		285.00	285
1993 Marbled Murrelet	55	1993	1200.00	1200-1900
1986 Marginal Meadow	950	1986	220.00	220-250
1979 Master of the Herd-African Buffalo	950	1980	150.00	1895-3150
1984 May Maple-Scarlet Tanager	950	1984	175.00	625-725
1982 Meadow's Edge-Mallard	950	1982	175.00	600
1982 Merganser Family in Hiding	950	1982	200.00	575
1994 Meru Dusk-Lesser Kudu	950		135.00	135
1989 Midnight-Black Wolf	25,352	1989	325.00	1395-1983
1980 Mischief on the Prowl-Raccoon	950	1980	85.00	150-195
1980 Misty Coast-Gulls	950	1980	135.00	420
1984 Misty Lake-Osprey	950	1985	95.00	150-225
1981 Misty Morning-Loons	950	1981	150.00	1100-1300
1986 Moose at Water's Edge	950	1986	130.00	285
1990 Morning Cove-Common Loon	950	1990	165.00	185
1985 Morning Dew-Roe Deer	950	1985	175.00	175-230
1983 Morning on the Flats-Bison	950	1983	200.00	300
1984 Morning on the River-Trumpeter Swans	950	1984	185.00	320
1990 Mossy Branches-Spotted Owl	4,500	1990	300.00	475-700
1990 Mowed Meadow	950	1990	190.00	190
1986 Mule Deer in Aspen	950	1986	175.00	175
1983 Mule Deer in Winter	950	1983	200.00	275
1988 Muskoka Lake-Common Loons	2,500	1988	265.00	300-500
1989 Near Glenburnie	950		265.00	265
1983 New Season-American Robin	950	1983	200.00	325
1986 Northern Reflections-Loon Family	8,631	1986	255.00	1897-2550
1985 Old Whaling Base and Fur Seals	950	1985	195.00	300
1987 Old Willow and Mallards	950	1987	325.00	325
1980 On the Alert-Chipmunk	950	1980	60.00	390
1993 On the Brink-River Otters	1,250	1994	345.00	345-500
1985 On the Garden Wall	950	1985	115.00	300
2001 On The Move - Red Fox	950		145.00	145
1985 Orca Procession	950	1985	245.00	2475-4000
1981 Osprey Family	950	1981	245.00	245
1983 Osprey in the Rain	950	1983	110.00	500-600
1987 Otter Study	950	1987	235.00	360-475
1981 Pair of Skimmers	950	1981	150.00	195-220
1988 Panda's At Play (stone lithograph)	160		400.00	1200-1379
1994 Path of the Panther	1,950	1997	295.00	295
1984 Peregrine and Ruddy Turnstones	950	1985	200.00	425-500
1985 Peregrine Falcon and White-Throated Swifts	950	1985	245.00	765-850
1987 Peregrine Falcon on the Cliff-Stone Litho	525	1988	350.00	780-1300
1983 Pheasant in Cornfield	950	1983	200.00	325
1988 Pheasants at Dusk	950	1988	325.00	550-724
1982 Pileated Woodpecker on Beech Tree	950	1982	175.00	825-900

YEAR ISSUE	EDITION LIMIT	YEAR RETD.	ISSUE PRICE	*QUOTE U.S.$
1990 Pintails in Spring	9,651	1989	135.00	300
1982 Pioneer Memories-Magpie Pair	950	1982	175.00	175
1987 Plowed Field-Snowy Owl	950	1987	145.00	280-300
1990 Polar Bear	290	1990	3300.00	3300
1982 Polar Bear Profile	950	1982	210.00	1900-2586
1982 Polar Bears at Bafin Island	950	1982	245.00	875-1300
1990 Power Play-Rhinoceros	950	1990	320.00	320-500
1980 Prairie Evening-Short-Eared Owl	950	1983	150.00	293-325
1994 Predator Portfolio/Black Bear	950		475.00	475
1992 Predator Portfolio/Cougar	950		465.00	465
1993 Predator Portfolio/Grizzly	950		475.00	475
1993 Predator Portfolio/Polar Bear	950		485.00	485
1993 Predator Portfolio/Wolf	950		475.00	475
1994 Predator Portfolio/Wolverine	950		275.00	275
1988 Preening Pair-Canada Geese	950	1988	235.00	235
1987 Pride of Autumn-Canada Goose	15,294	1987	135.00	245-325
2000 Prothonotary Warbler	950		95.00	95
1986 Proud Swimmer-Snow Goose	950	1986	185.00	185
1989 Pumpkin Time	950		195.00	195
1982 Queen Anne's Lace and American Goldfinch	950	1982	150.00	700-900
1984 Ready for Flight-Peregrine Falcon	950	1984	185.00	470
1982 Ready for the Hunt-Snowy Owl	950	1982	245.00	650-770
1993 Reclining Snow Leopard	1,250		335.00	335
1988 Red Crossbills	950	1988	125.00	175
1984 Red Fox on the Prowl	950	1984	245.00	665-938
1982 Red Squirrel	950	1982	175.00	325
1986 Red Wolf	950	1986	250.00	275-395
1981 Red-Tailed Hawk by the Cliff	950	1981	245.00	425-655
1981 Red-Winged Blackbird and Rail Fence	950	1981	195.00	315
1984 Reeds	950	1984	185.00	388-415
1986 A Resting Place-Cape Buffalo	950	1986	265.00	265
1987 Rhino at Ngoro Ngoro	950	1988	325.00	171-325
1993 River Otter-North American Wilderness	350	N/A	325.00	800
1993 River Otters	290		1500.00	1500
2000 Roadside Tapestry	950		135.00	135
1986 Robins at the Nest	950	1986	185.00	138-195
2000 Rockface Descent	450		345.00	345
1987 Rocky Point-October	950	1987	195.00	420
1990 Rocky Wilderness-Cougar	950	1990	175.00	975-1600
1990 Rolling Waves-Greater Scaup	3,330	N/A	125.00	135
1993 Rose-breasted Grosbeak	290		450.00	450
1981 Rough-Legged Hawk in the Elm	950	1991	175.00	175-200
1981 Royal Family-Mute Swans	950	1981	245.00	715-950
1983 Ruby Throat and Columbine	950	1983	150.00	2000
1987 Ruddy Turnstones	950	1987	175.00	175
1994 Salt Spring Sheep	1,250		235.00	235
1981 Sarah E. with Gulls	950	1981	245.00	2500-5500
1993 Saw Whet Owl and Wild Grapes	950	N/A	185.00	185
1991 The Scolding-Chickadees & Screech Owl	12,500	1992	235.00	235
1991 Sea Otter Study	950	1991	150.00	245
1993 Shadow of the Rain Forest	9,000	1993	345.00	475-825
1981 Sheer Drop-Mountain Goats	950	1981	245.00	1900
1988 Shelter	950	1988	325.00	750-875
1992 Siberian Tiger	4,500	1992	325.00	325
1984 Smallwood	950	1985	200.00	700-925
1990 Snow Leopard	290	1990	2500.00	2200-2600
1985 Snowy Hemlock-Barred Owl	950	1985	245.00	245
1994 Snowy Nap-Tiger	950	1994	185.00	1034-1825
1994 Snowy Owl	150	N/A	265.00	600-750
1987 Snowy Owl and Milkweed	950	1987	235.00	575-845
1983 Snowy Owl on Driftwood	950	1983	245.00	650
1983 Spirits of the Forest	950	1984	170.00	2000
1986 Split Rails-Snow Buntings	950	1986	220.00	220
1980 Spring Cardinal	950	1980	125.00	512-625
1982 Spring Marsh-Pintail Pair	950	1982	200.00	302
1980 Spring Thaw-Killdeer	950	1980	85.00	121-245
1982 Still Morning-Herring Gulls	950	1982	200.00	200
1987 Stone Sheep Ram	950	1987	175.00	175
1985 Stream Bank June	950	1986	160.00	175
1984 Stretching-Canada Goose	950	1984	225.00	2300-4000
1985 Strutting-Ring-Necked Pheasant	950	1985	225.00	450-575
1985 Sudden Blizzard-Red-Tailed Hawk	950	1985	245.00	400-645
1990 Summer Morning Pasture	950	1990	175.00	175
1984 Summer Morning-Loon	950	1984	185.00	1000-1500
1986 Summertime-Polar Bears	950	1986	225.00	225
1979 Surf and Sanderlings	950	1980	65.00	1600-2000
1981 Swift Fox	950	1981	175.00	175-259
1986 Swift Fox Study	950	1986	115.00	200
1987 Sylvan Stream-Mute Swans	950	1987	125.00	175

GRAPHICS

YEAR ISSUE	EDITION LIMIT	YEAR RETD.	ISSUE PRICE	*QUOTE U.S.$
1984 Tadpole Time	950	1985	135.00	400-500
1988 Tawny Owl In Beech	950	1988	325.00	325
1992 Tembo (African Elephant)	1,550	1992	350.00	350
2001 Thinking Like A Mountain	950		110.00	110
1984 Tiger at Dawn	950	1984	225.00	1700-2600
1983 Tiger Portrait	950	1983	130.00	425-625
1988 Tree Swallow over Pond	950	1988	290.00	150-290
1991 Trumpeter Swan Family	290		2500.00	2500
1985 Trumpeter Swans and Aspen	950	1985	245.00	450-500
2000 Twilight - Siberian Tiger	1,350		245.00	245
2001 Up A Tree - Lion Cub	950		95.00	95
1979 Up in the Pine-Great Horned Owl	950	1981	150.00	675-795
1980 Vantage Point	950	1980	245.00	795-1121
1993 Vigilance	9,500		330.00	330
1989 Vulture And Wildebeest	550		295.00	295
1981 Watchful Repose-Black Bear	950	1981	245.00	475
1985 Weathered Branch-Bald Eagle	950	1985	115.00	300
1991 Whistling Swan-Lake Erie	1,950		325.00	375
1980 White Encounter-Polar Bear	950	1980	245.00	2950-4300
1990 White on White-Snowshoe Hare	950	1990	195.00	425
1982 White World-Dall Sheep	950	1982	200.00	600
1985 White-Breasted Nuthatch on a Beech Tree	950	1985	175.00	300
1980 White-Footed Mouse in Wintergreen	950	1980	60.00	650
1982 White-Footed Mouse on Aspen	950	1983	90.00	150-225
1992 White-Tailed Deer Through the Birches	10,000		335.00	335
1984 White-Throated Sparrow and Pussy Willow	950	1984	150.00	575-645
1991 Wide Horizon-Tundra Swans	2,862	1991	325.00	350
1991 Wide Horizon-Tundra Swans Companion	2,862		325.00	325
1986 Wildbeest	950		185.00	185
1982 Willet on the Shore	950	N/A	125.00	195-280
1979 Wily and Wary-Red Fox	950	1979	125.00	1075
1984 Window into Ontario	950	1984	265.00	1275
1983 Winter Barn	950	1984	170.00	420
1979 Winter Cardinal	950	1979	75.00	2250
1992 Winter Coat	1,250		245.00	575
1985 Winter Companion	950	1985	175.00	895
1980 Winter Elm-American Kestrel	950	1980	135.00	800-1000
1986 Winter in the Mountains-Raven	950	1987	200.00	200
1981 Winter Mist-Great Horned Owl	950	1981	245.00	500-722
1980 Winter Song-Chickadees	950	1980	95.00	550-776
1984 Winter Sunset-Moose	950	1984	245.00	1600
1992 Winter Trackers	4,500	1992	335.00	335
1981 Winter Wren	950	1981	135.00	450
1983 Winter-Lady Cardinal	950	1983	200.00	1025
1979 Winter-Snowshoe Hare	950	1980	95.00	1100-2300
1987 Wise One, The	950	1987	325.00	1800
1979 Wolf Pack in Moonlight	950	1979	95.00	1552-2150
1994 Wolf Pair in Winter	290	1994	795.00	1600
1983 Wolves on the Trail	950	1983	225.00	425-488
1985 Wood Bison Portrait	950	1985	165.00	225
1983 Woodland Drummer-Ruffed Grouse	950	1984	185.00	235
1981 Wrangler's Campsite-Gray Jay	950	1981	195.00	725
1979 Yellow-Rumped Warbler	950	1980	50.00	435
2000 Yeti	950		85.00	85
1978 Young Barn Swallow	950	1979	75.00	575-700
1983 Young Elf Owl-Old Saguaro	950	1983	95.00	325
1991 Young Giraffe	290	1997	850.00	2500
1989 Young Kittiwake	950		195.00	195
1988 Young Sandhill-Cranes	950	1988	325.00	325
1989 Young Snowy Owl	950	1990	195.00	112-195

Brenders - C. Brenders

YEAR ISSUE	EDITION LIMIT	YEAR RETD.	ISSUE PRICE	*QUOTE U.S.$
1986 The Acrobat's Meal-Red Squirrel	950	1989	65.00	475-603
1996 Amber Gaze-Snowy Owl	1,950		175.00	175
1988 Apple Harvest	950	1989	115.00	525
1989 The Apple Lover	1,500	1990	125.00	250
1987 Autumn Lady	950	1989	150.00	825-1207
1991 The Balance of Nature	1,950		225.00	225
1993 Black Sphinx	950		235.00	235
1986 Black-Capped Chickadees	950	1989	40.00	625-931
1990 Blond Beauty	1,950	1990	185.00	185
1986 Bluebirds	950	1989	40.00	150-250
1988 California Quail	950	1989	95.00	462-600
1991 Calm Before the Challenge-Moose	1,950	1991	225.00	225
1987 Close to Mom	950	1988	150.00	1095-2150
1993 Collectors Group (Butterfly Collections)	290		375.00	375
1986 Colorful Playground-Cottontails	950	1989	75.00	625-819
1989 The Companions	18,036	1989	200.00	525-600
1994 Dall Sheep Portrait	950		115.00	115
1992 Den Mother-Pencil Sketch	2,500	1992	135.00	135
1992 Den Mother-Wolf Family	25,000	1992	250.00	250-350
1986 Disturbed Daydreams	950	1989	95.00	425
1987 Double Trouble-Raccoons	950	1988	120.00	700-1550
1993 European Group (Butterfly Collections)	290		375.00	375
1993 Exotic Group (Butterfly Collections)	290		375.00	375
2001 Flash of Sapphire - Blue Jay	2,500		75.00	75
1989 Forager's Reward-Red Squirrel	1,250	1989	135.00	135
1988 Forest Sentinel-Bobcat	950	1988	135.00	425-550
1990 Full House-Fox Family	20,106	1990	235.00	500
2001 Gleam of Gold - Goldfinch	2,500		75.00	75
1986 Golden Season-Gray Squirrel	950	1987	85.00	600-700
1986 Harvest Time-Chipmunk	950	1989	65.00	216
1988 Hidden In the Pines-Immature Great Hor	950	1988	175.00	1000-1125
1988 High Adventure-Black Bear Cubs	950	1989	105.00	415-860
1988 A Hunter's Dream	950	1988	165.00	1000
1993 In Northern Hunting Grounds	1,750		375.00	375
1992 Island Shores-Snowy Egret	2,500		250.00	250
1987 Ivory-Billed Woodpecker	950	1989	95.00	775
2001 The Loner	3,500		195.00	195
1988 Long Distance Hunters	950	1988	175.00	895-1095
1989 Lord of the Marshes	1,250	1989	135.00	175-447
1989 Meadowlark	950	1989	40.00	170-285
1989 Merlins at the Nest	1,250	1989	165.00	235-300
1985 Mighty Intruder	950	1989	95.00	265
1989 Migration Fever-Barn Swallows	950	1989	150.00	465-776
1990 The Monarch is Alive	4,071	1990	265.00	295
1993 Mother of Pearls	5,000		275.00	275
1990 Mountain Baby-Bighorn Sheep	1,950		165.00	195
1987 Mysterious Visitor-Barn Owl	950	1989	150.00	325-500
1993 Narrow Escape-Chipmunk	1,750		150.00	150
1991 The Nesting Season-House Sparrow	1,950	1991	195.00	200-295
1989 Northern Cousins-Black Squirrels	950	1989	150.00	290
2000 On A Mission	1,500		195.00	195
1984 On the Alert-Red Fox	950	1986	95.00	350-397
1990 On the Old Farm Door	1,500	1990	225.00	225
1991 One to One-Gray Wolf	10,000	1991	245.00	425-662
1992 Pathfinder-Red Fox	5,000	1992	245.00	245-300
2000 Picnic Perch	950		110.00	110
1987 Playful Pair-Chipmunks	950	1987	60.00	628-695
1994 Power and Grace	2,500	1994	265.00	600
1989 The Predator's Walk	1,250	1989	150.00	175-293
1992 Red Fox Study	1,250	1992	125.00	125
1994 Riverbank Kestrel	2,500	1995	225.00	300-350
1988 Roaming the Plains-Pronghorns	950	1989	150.00	195
1986 Robins	950	1989	40.00	175-431
1993 Rocky Camp-Cougar Family	5,000	1995	275.00	350
1993 Rocky Camp-Cubs	950		225.00	225
1992 Rocky Kingdom-Bighorn Sheep	1,750	1997	255.00	255-300
1991 Shadows in the Grass-Young Cougars	1,950	1991	235.00	235
1990 Shoreline Quartet-White Ibis	1,950	1995	265.00	265-340
1984 Silent Hunter-Great Horned Owl	950	1987	95.00	450-560
1988 Silent Passage	950	1988	150.00	350-475
1990 Small Talk	1,500	1990	125.00	140
1992 Snow Leopard Portrait	1,750	1993	150.00	150-172
2000 Sovereign Gold	950		195.00	195
2001 Spark of Ruby - Cardinal	2,500		75.00	75
1990 Spring Fawn	1,500	1990	125.00	275
1990 Squirrel's Dish	1,950		110.00	110
1989 Steller's Jay	1,250	1989	135.00	150-175
1993 Summer Roses-Winter Wren	1,500	1993	250.00	595-690
1989 The Survivors-Canada Geese	1,500	1989	225.00	400
1994 Take Five-Canadian Lynx	1,500	N/A	245.00	475-500
1988 Talk on the Old Fence	950	1988	165.00	825-975
1990 A Threatened Symbol	1,950	1990	145.00	160-175
1994 Tundra Summit-Arctic Wolves	6,061	1994	265.00	432-450
1984 Waterside Encounter	950	1987	95.00	1000-1500
1987 White Elegance-Trumpeter Swans	950	1989	115.00	500
1988 Witness of a Past-Bison	950	1990	110.00	95-135
1992 Wolf Scout #1	2,500	1992	105.00	78-150
1992 Wolf Scout #2	2,500	1992	105.00	135-160
1991 Wolf Study	950	1991	125.00	75-150
1987 Yellow-Bellied Marmot	950	1989	95.00	335-595
2000 Yin and Yang	2,500		185.00	185
1989 A Young Generation	1,250	1989	165.00	175-295

Calle - P. Calle

YEAR ISSUE	EDITION LIMIT	YEAR RETD.	ISSUE PRICE	*QUOTE U.S.$
1981 Almost Home	950	1981	150.00	150
1991 Almost There	950	1991	165.00	165
1989 And A Good Book For Company	950	1990	135.00	435
1993 And A Grizzly Claw Necklace	750		150.00	150
1981 And Still Miles to Go	950	1981	245.00	400
1981 Andrew At The Falls	950	1981	150.00	150
1989 The Beaver Men	950		125.00	125
2000 Bound For Rendevous	950		195.00	195
1984 A Brace for the Spit	950	1985	110.00	275-300
1980 Caring for the Herd	950	1981	110.00	110
1985 The Carrying Place	950	1990	195.00	195
1984 Chance Encounter	950	1986	225.00	325
1981 Chief High Pipe (Color)	950	1981	265.00	265
1980 Chief High Pipe (Pencil)	950	1980	75.00	175
1980 Chief Joseph-Man of Peace	950	1980	135.00	165
1990 Children of Walpi	350		160.00	160
1990 The Doll Maker	950		95.00	95
1982 Emerging from the Woods	950	1987	110.00	110
1981 End of a Long Day	950	1981	150.00	225
1984 Fate of the Late Migrant	950	1985	110.00	375
1983 Free Spirits	950	1985	195.00	475
1983 Free Trapper Study	550	1985	75.00	125-300
1981 Fresh Tracks	950	1981	150.00	150
1981 Friend or Foe	950		125.00	125
1981 Friends	950	1987	150.00	150
1985 The Frontier Blacksmith	950		245.00	245
1989 The Fur Trapper	550		75.00	175
1982 Generations in the Valley	950	1987	245.00	245
1985 The Grandmother	950	1987	400.00	400
1989 The Great Moment	950		350.00	350
1992 Hunter of Geese	950		125.00	125
1993 I Call Him Friend	950		235.00	235
1983 In Search of Beaver	950	1983	225.00	600
1991 In the Beginning . . . Friends	1,250	1993	250.00	275
1987 In the Land of the Giants	950	1988	245.00	900
1990 Interrupted Journey	1,750	1991	265.00	265
1990 Interrupted Journey-Prestige Ed.	290	1991	465.00	465
1987 Into the Great Alone	950	1988	245.00	700-850
1981 Just Over the Ridge	950	1982	245.00	245
1980 Landmark Tree	950	1980	125.00	225
1991 Man of the Fur Trade	550		110.00	110
1984 Mountain Man	550	1988	95.00	225-395
1993 Mountain Man-North American Wilderness Portfolio	350		325.00	N/A
1989 The Mountain Men	300	1989	400.00	400
1989 Navajo Madonna	650		95.00	95
1988 A New Day	950		150.00	150
1981 One With The Land	950	1981	245.00	250
1992 Out of the Silence	2,500		265.00	265
1992 Out of the Silence-Prestige	290		465.00	465
1981 Pause at the Lower Falls	950	1981	110.00	250
1980 Prayer to the Great Mystery	950	1980	245.00	245
1982 Return to Camp	950	1982	245.00	500
1991 The Silenced Honkers	1,250	1993	250.00	250
1980 Sioux Chief	950	1980	85.00	140
1986 Snow Hunter	950	1988	150.00	225
1980 Something for the Pot	950	1980	175.00	1100
1990 Son of Sitting Bull	950		95.00	675
1985 Storyteller of the Mountains	950	1985	225.00	675-960
1983 Strays From the Flyway	950	1983	195.00	225
1981 Teton Friends	950	1981	150.00	225
1991 They Call Me Matthew	950		125.00	125
1992 Through the Tall Grass	950		175.00	175
1988 Trapper at Rest	550		95.00	95
2001 The Trapper's Feast (2-piece set)	250		950.00	950
1982 Two from the Flock	950	1982	245.00	500
1980 View from the Heights	950	1980	245.00	245
1988 Voyageurs and Waterfowl...Constant	950	1988	265.00	700-900
1980 When Snow Came Early	950	1980	85.00	250-340
1984 When Trails Cross	950	1984	245.00	750
1991 When Trails Grow Cold	2,500		265.00	265
1991 When Trails Grow Cold-Prestige Ed.	290	1991	465.00	465
1994 When Trappers Meet	750		165.00	165
1989 Where Eagles Fly	1,250	1990	265.00	350-570
1989 A Winter Feast	1,250	1989	265.00	375
1989 A Winter Feast-Prestige Ed.	290	1989	465.00	465
1981 Winter Hunter (Color)	950	1981	245.00	800
1980 Winter Hunter (Pencil)	950	1980	65.00	450
1983 A Winter Surprise	950	1984	195.00	500

Cross - T. Cross

YEAR ISSUE	EDITION LIMIT	YEAR RETD.	ISSUE PRICE	*QUOTE U.S.$
1994 April	750		55.00	55
1994 August	750		55.00	55
1993 Ever Green	750		135.00	135
1993 Flame Catcher	750	1993	185.00	185
1993 Flicker, Flash and Twirl	525		165.00	165
1994 July	750		55.00	55
1994 June	750		55.00	55
1994 March	750		55.00	55
1994 May	750		55.00	55
1992 Shell Caster	750	1993	150.00	150-391
1993 Sheperds of Magic	750	N/A	135.00	135
1993 Spellbound	750	N/A	85.00	85-115
1994 Spring Forth	750		145.00	145
1992 Star Weaver	750	1993	150.00	150-195
1994 Summer Musings	750		145.00	145
1993 The Summons...And Then They Are One	750	1993	195.00	195
1994 When Water Takes to Air	750		135.00	135
1993 Wind Sifter	750	1993	150.00	515

Daly - J. Daly

YEAR ISSUE	EDITION LIMIT	YEAR RETD.	ISSUE PRICE	*QUOTE U.S.$
1994 All Aboard	950		145.00	145
1990 The Big Moment	1,500		125.00	125
1994 Catch of My Dreams	4,500		45.00	45
1991 Cat's Cradle-Prestige Ed.	950		450.00	450
1994 Childhood Friends	950	1997	110.00	110-270
1990 Confrontation	1,500	1992	85.00	97-150
1990 Contentment	1,500	1990	95.00	275-450
1992 Dominoes	1,500		155.00	155
1992 Favorite Gift	2,500	1992	175.00	175
1987 Favorite Reader	950	1990	85.00	130-250
1986 Flying High	950	1988	50.00	525-603
1992 The Flying Horse	950		325.00	325
1993 Good Company	1,500		155.00	155
1992 Her Secret Place	1,500	1992	135.00	200-509
1991 Home Team: Zero	1,500	1998	150.00	150
1991 Homemade	1,500	1992	125.00	125
1990 Honor and Allegiance	1,500	1993	110.00	110
1990 The Ice Man	1,500	1992	125.00	135-265
1992 The Immigrant Spirit	5,000		125.00	125
1992 The Immigrant Spirit-Prestige Ed.	950		125.00	125
1989 In the Doghouse	1,500	1990	75.00	425-589
1990 It's That Time Again	1,500		120.00	120
1992 Left Out	1,500		110.00	110
1989 Let's Play Ball	1,500	1991	75.00	125-135
1990 Make Believe	1,500	1990	75.00	400-457
1994 Mud Mates	950		150.00	150
1994 My Best Friends	950	1995	85.00	365-450
1991 A New Beginning	5,000		125.00	125
1993 The New Citizen	5,000		125.00	125
1993 The New Citizen-Prestige Ed.	950		125.00	125
1987 Odd Man Out	950	1988	85.00	85
1988 On Thin Ice	950	1993	95.00	345-389
1991 Pillars of a Nation-Charter Ed.	20,000		175.00	175
1992 Playmates	1,500	1992	155.00	395-595
1990 Radio Daze	1,500		150.00	150
1983 Saturday Night	950	1985	85.00	1125
1990 The Scholar	1,500	N/A	110.00	112
1993 Secret Admirer	1,500		150.00	150
1994 Slugger	950		75.00	75
1982 Spring Fever	950	1988	85.00	600-759
1993 Sunday Afternoon	1,500		150.00	150
1988 Territorial Rights	950	1990	85.00	350
1989 The Thief	1,500	1990	95.00	250-379
1989 The Thorn	1,500	1990	125.00	350-688
1988 Tie Breaker	950	1990	95.00	293-350
1991 Time-Out	1,500	1993	125.00	125
1993 To All a Good Night	1,500		160.00	160
1992 Walking the Rails	1,500		175.00	175
1993 When I Grow Up	1,500		175.00	175
1994 The Wind-Up	950	1998	75.00	75-119
1988 Wiped Out	1,250	1990	125.00	500-579

Morrissey - D. Morrissey

YEAR ISSUE	EDITION LIMIT	YEAR RETD.	ISSUE PRICE	*QUOTE U.S.$
1994 The Amazing Time Elevator	950	1994	195.00	195
1993 Charting the Skies	1,250	1993	195.00	195-219
1993 Charting the Skies-Caprice Edition	550	1993	375.00	375
1993 Draft of a Dream	175	1993	250.00	195-250
1994 The Dreamer's Trunk	1,500	1997	195.00	195-276
1993 Drifting Closer	1,250		175.00	175

GRAPHICS

YEAR ISSUE	EDITION LIMIT	YEAR RETD.	ISSUE PRICE	*QUOTE U.S.$
1994 Father Time Flying Past	450		195.00	195
1993 The Mystic Mariner	750	1993	150.00	150-175
1993 The Redd Rocket	1,250	1993	175.00	375-400
1994 The Redd Rocket-Pre-Flight	950	1993	110.00	110-155
1992 The Sandman's Ship of Dreams	750	1993	150.00	300-340
1994 Sighting off the Stern	950		135.00	135
1993 Sleeper Flight	1,250	1993	195.00	175-195
1993 The Telescope of Time	5,000		195.00	195

Olsen - G. Olsen

YEAR ISSUE	EDITION LIMIT	YEAR RETD.	ISSUE PRICE	*QUOTE U.S.$
1993 Airship Adventures	750		150.00	150
1993 Angels of Christmas	750	1993	135.00	135
2000 Bon Voyage	2,500		185.00	185
2000 Daddy's Little Girl	950		230.00	230
1993 Dress Rehearseal	750	1993	165.00	2600
1993 The Fraternity Tree	750		195.00	195
2001 Heavenly Hands	650		150.00	150
2000 King of Kings	650		185.00	185
1994 Little Girls Will Mothers Be	750	N/A	135.00	135
1994 Mother's Love	750	1994	165.00	165
1995 O Jerusalem	5,000	N/A	165.00	1250-2700
1994 Summerhouse	750	N/A	165.00	165

Seerey-Lester - J. Seerey-Lester

YEAR ISSUE	EDITION LIMIT	YEAR RETD.	ISSUE PRICE	*QUOTE U.S.$
1994 Abandoned	950		175.00	175
1986 Above the Treeline-Cougar	950	1986	130.00	130
1986 After the Fire-Grizzly	950	1990	95.00	95
1986 Along the Ice Floe-Polar Bears	950		200.00	200
1987 Alpenglow-Artic Wolf	950	1987	200.00	200
1987 Amboseli Child-African Elephant	950		160.00	160
1984 Among the Cattails-Canada Geese	950	1985	130.00	375
1984 Artic Procession-Willow Ptarmigan	950	1988	220.00	500-789
1990 Artic Wolf Pups	290		500.00	500
1987 Autumn Mist-Barred Owl	950	1987	160.00	160
1987 Autumn Thunder-Muskoxen	950		150.00	150
1985 Awakening Meadow-Cottontail	950		50.00	50
1992 Banyan Ambush- Black Panther	950	1992	235.00	235-300
1984 Basking-Brown Pelicans	950	1988	115.00	125
1988 Bathing-Blue Jay	950		95.00	95
1987 Bathing-Mute Swan	950	1992	175.00	275-299
1989 Before The Freeze-Beaver	950		165.00	165
1990 Bittersweet Winter-Cardinal	1,250	1990	150.00	175-186
1992 Black Jade	1,950	1992	275.00	350
1992 Black Magic-Panther	750	1992	195.00	225-579
1984 Breaking Cover-Black Bear	950	N/A	130.00	150-200
1987 Canyon Creek-Cougar	950	1987	135.00	435-965
2000 Celebrating Hua Mei	950		95.00	95
1992 The Chase-Snow Leopard	950		200.00	200
1994 Child of the Outback	950		175.00	175
1985 Children of the Forest-Red Fox Kits	950	1985	110.00	325
1985 Children of the Tundra-Artic Wolf Pup	950	1985	110.00	325-395
1988 Cliff Hanger-Bobcat	950		200.00	200
1984 Close Encounter-Bobcat	950	1989	130.00	130
1988 Coastal Clique-Harbor Seals	950		160.00	160
1986 Conflict at Dawn-Heron and Osprey	950	1989	130.00	325
1983 Cool Retreat-Lynx	950	1988	85.00	125-200
1986 Cottonwood Gold-Baltimore Oriole	950		85.00	85
1985 Cougar Head Study	950		60.00	60
1989 Cougar Run	950	1989	185.00	225
1994 The Courtship	950		175.00	175
2000 The Courtship	950		175.00	175
1993 Dark Encounter	3,500	N/A	200.00	200-365
1990 Dawn Majesty	1,250	1991	185.00	225-275
1987 Dawn on the Marsh-Coyote	950		200.00	200
1985 Daybreak-Moose	950		135.00	135
2001 Denali Encounter - Grizzly, Cub and Raven	650		135.00	135
1991 Denali Family-Grizzly Bear	950	1991	195.00	235-550
1986 Early Arrivals-Snow Buntings	950		75.00	75
1983 Early Windfall-Gray Squirrels	950		85.00	85
1988 Edge of the Forest-Timber Wolves	950	1988	500.00	500-700
1989 Evening Duet-Snowy Egrets	1,250		185.00	185
1991 Evening Encounter-Grizzly & Wolf	1,250		185.00	185
1988 Evening Meadow-American Goldfinch	950		150.00	150
1991 Face to Face	1,250		200.00	200
1985 Fallen Birch-Chipmunk	950	1985	60.00	375-415
1985 First Light-Gray Jays	950	1985	130.00	175
1983 First Snow-Grizzly Bears	950	1984	95.00	325-395
1987 First Tracks-Cougar	950		150.00	150
1989 Fluke Sighting-Humback Whales	950	1989	185.00	185
1993 Freedom I	350		500.00	500

YEAR ISSUE	EDITION LIMIT	YEAR RETD.	ISSUE PRICE	*QUOTE U.S.$
1993 Frozen Moonlight	2,500	1993	225.00	200-215
1985 Gathering-Gray Wolves, The	950	1987	165.00	250
1989 Gorilla	290	1989	400.00	450
1993 Grizzly Impact	950	N/A	225.00	300-385
1990 Grizzly Litho	290	1990	400.00	400-600
1989 Heavy Going-Grizzly	950	1989	175.00	240
1986 Hidden Admirer-Moose	950	1986	165.00	275
1988 Hiding Place-Saw-Whet Owl	950		95.00	95
1989 High and Mighty-Gorilla	950	1989	185.00	185
1986 High Country Champion-Grizzly	950	1986	175.00	375-465
1984 High Ground-Wolves	950	1984	130.00	225
1987 High Refuge-Red Squirrel	950		120.00	120
1984 Icy Outcrop-White Gyrfalcon	950	1986	115.00	200
1987 In Deep-Black Bear Cub	950		135.00	135
1990 In Their Presence	1,250		200.00	200
1985 Island Sanctuary-Mallards	950	1987	95.00	150-315
1986 Kenyan Family-Cheetahs	950		130.00	130
1986 Lakeside Family-Canada Geese	950		75.00	75
1988 Last Sanctuary-Florida Panther	950	1993	175.00	350
1983 Lone Fisherman-Great Blue Heron	950	1985	85.00	375
2000 Loonlight	1,500		225.00	225
1993 Loonlight	1,500		225.00	225
1986 Low Tide-Bald Eagles	950		130.00	130
1987 Lying in Wait-Arctic Fox	950		175.00	175
1984 Lying Low-Cougar	950	1986	85.00	550
1991 Monsoon-White Tiger	950	1994	195.00	195-345
1991 Moonlight Chase-Cougar	1,250		195.00	195
1988 Moonlight Fishermen-Raccoons	950	1990	175.00	175-305
1988 Moose Hair	950	N/A	165.00	225-385
1988 Morning Display-Common Loons	3,395	1988	135.00	135
1986 Morning Forage-Ground Squirrel	950		75.00	75
1993 Morning Glory-Bald Eagle	1,250		225.00	225
1984 Morning Mist-Snowy Owl	950	1988	95.00	180-225
1990 Mountain Cradle	1,250	N/A	200.00	200
1988 Night Moves-African Elephants	950		150.00	150
1990 Night Run-Artic Wolves	1,250	1990	200.00	200-415
1993 Night Specter	1,250		195.00	195
1986 Northwoods Family-Moose	950		75.00	75
1987 Out of the Blizzard-Timber Wolves	950	1987	215.00	450-500
1992 Out of the Darkness	290		200.00	200
1987 Out of the Mist-Grizzly	950	1990	200.00	375
1991 Out on a Limb-Young Barred Owl	950		185.00	185
1991 Panda Trilogy	950	N/A	375.00	375
1993 Phantoms of the Tundra	950		235.00	235
1984 Plains Hunter-Prairie Falcon	950		95.00	95
1990 The Plunge-Northern Sea Lions	1,250		200.00	200
1986 Racing the Storm-Artic Wolves	950	1986	200.00	300
1987 Rain Watch-Belted Kingfisher	950		125.00	125
1993 The Rains-Tiger	950		225.00	225
1992 Ranthambhore Rush	950		225.00	225
1983 The Refuge-Raccoon	950	1983	85.00	275
1992 Regal Majesty	290		200.00	200
1985 Return to Winter-Pintails	950	1990	135.00	200-229
1983 River Watch-Peregrine Falcon	950		85.00	85
1988 Savana Siesta-African Lions	950		165.00	165
1990 Seasonal Greeting-Cardinal	1,250	1993	150.00	150-250
1993 Seeking Attention	950		200.00	200
1991 Sisters-Artic Wolves	1,250		185.00	185
2000 Sneak Peak	950		185.00	185
1989 Sneak Peak	950		185.00	185
1986 Snowy Excursion-Red Squirrel	950		75.00	75
1988 Snowy Watch-Great Gray Owl	950		175.00	175
1989 Softly, Softly-White Tiger	950	1989	220.00	395-450
1991 Something Stirred (Bengal Tiger)	950		195.00	195
1988 Spanish Mist-Young Barred-Owl	950		175.00	175
1984 Spirit of the North-White Wolf	950	1986	130.00	185
1990 Spout	290		500.00	500
1989 Spring Flurry-Adelie Penguins	950		185.00	185
1986 Spring Mist-Chickadees	950	1986	105.00	1160
1990 Suitors-Wood Ducks	3,313	1989	135.00	135-160
1990 Summer Rain-Common Loons	4,500	1990	200.00	200
1990 Summer Rain-Common Loons (Prestige)	450		425.00	425
1987 Sundown Alert-Bobcat	950	N/A	150.00	195
1985 Sundown Reflections-Wood Ducks	950		85.00	85
1990 Their First Season	1,250	1990	200.00	200
1990 Togetherness	1,250		125.00	185
2000 Togetherness	1,250		125.00	125
1986 Treading Thin Ice-Chipmunk	950		75.00	75
1988 Tundra Family-Artic Wolves	950		200.00	200
1985 Under the Pines-Bobcat	950	1986	95.00	275-318

YEAR ISSUE	EDITION LIMIT	YEAR RETD.	ISSUE PRICE	*QUOTE U.S.$
1989 Water Sport-Bobcat	950	1989	185.00	185-219
1990 Whitetail Spring	1,250	1990	185.00	185
1988 Winter Grazing-Bison	950		185.00	185
1986 Winter Hiding-Cottontail	950		75.00	75
1983 Winter Lookout-Cougar	950	1985	85.00	600-700
1986 Winter Perch-Cardinal	950	1986	85.00	150
1985 Winter Rendezvous-Coyotes	950	1985	140.00	140
1988 Winter Spirit-Gray Wolf	950		200.00	200
1987 Winter Vigil-Great Horned Owl	950	1990	175.00	175
1993 Wolong Whiteout	950		225.00	225
1986 The Young Explorer-Red Fox Kit	950	N/A	75.00	95
1992 Young Predator-Leopard	950		200.00	200

Smith - D. Smith

YEAR ISSUE	EDITION LIMIT	YEAR RETD.	ISSUE PRICE	*QUOTE U.S.$
1993 African Ebony-Black Leopard	1,250	1994	195.00	195
1997 Ancient Mariner	950		165.00	165
1992 Armada	950	N/A	195.00	195
2000 Ascending Song	950		95.00	95
1998 Brother Wolf	950	1998	125.00	249
1993 Catching the Scent-Polar Bear	950	1993	175.00	175
1994 Curious Presence-Whitetail Deer	950	1996	195.00	195-300
1991 Dawn's Early Light-Bald Eagles	950	1997	185.00	185
2000 Early Snow	950		165.00	165
1993 Echo Bay-Loon Family	1,150	1993	185.00	185-400
1992 Eyes of the North	2,500	1996	225.00	225
1994 Forest Veil-Cougar	950	1994	195.00	376
1993 Guardians of the Den	1,500	N/A	195.00	195
2000 High Rollers	950		175.00	175
1991 Icy Reflections-Pintails	500		250.00	250
2000 Into The Stillness	950		135.00	135
1992 Night Moves-Cougar	950	1994	185.00	185
2000 Out of the Silence	1,500		85.00	85
1994 Parting Reflections	950		185.00	185
2000 Sacred Heights	2,500		75.00	75
1993 Shrouded Forest-Bald Eagle	950	N/A	150.00	650-1100
2000 Silent Pursuit	650		185.00	185
2001 Testing The Waters	950		185.00	185
1991 Twilight's Calling-Common Loons	950	1991	175.00	250
1993 What's Bruin	1,750	1993	185.00	185-349
2001 When Paths Cross	950		175.00	175
2001 Wings of Gold	950		185.00	185

New Masters Publishing

Bannister - P. Bannister

YEAR ISSUE	EDITION LIMIT	YEAR RETD.	ISSUE PRICE	*QUOTE U.S.$
1982 Amaryllis	500	N/A	285.00	2000
1988 Apples and Oranges	485	N/A	265.00	650-675
1982 April	300	N/A	200.00	1200
1984 April Light	950	N/A	150.00	650-675
1987 Autumn Fields	950	N/A	150.00	300-350
1978 Bandstand	250	N/A	75.00	600-625
1992 Bed of Roses	663	N/A	265.00	525-575
1995 Bridesmaids	950	N/A	265.00	530-600
1991 Celebration	662	N/A	350.00	800-825
1989 Chapter One	485	N/A	265.00	1700-1875
1982 Cinderella	500	N/A	285.00	580-620
1991 Crossroads	485	N/A	295.00	600-625
1993 Crowning Glory	485	N/A	265.00	600-650
1981 Crystal	300	N/A	300.00	3000
1992 Crystal Bowl	485	N/A	265.00	600-675
1989 Daydreams	485	N/A	265.00	625
1993 Deja Vu	663	N/A	265.00	1400-1500
1983 The Duchess	500	N/A	250.00	2000
1980 Dust of Autumn	200	N/A	200.00	1225
1981 Easter	300	N/A	260.00	1200
1982 Emily	500	N/A	285.00	1200-1225
1980 Faded Glory	200	N/A	200.00	1225
1984 The Fan Window	950	N/A	195.00	600-675
1987 First Prize	950	N/A	115.00	275-350
1988 Floribunda	485	N/A	265.00	675-750
1994 Fountain	485	N/A	265.00	600-725
1994 From Russia With Love	950	N/A	165.00	400-550
1980 Gift of Happiness	200	N/A	200.00	2050
1980 Girl on the Beach	200	N/A	200.00	1400-1500
1990 Good Friends	485	N/A	265.00	750-825
1988 Guinevere	485	N/A	265.00	1300-1375
1993 Into The Woods	485	N/A	265.00	500-600
1982 Ivy	500	N/A	285.00	750-800
1982 Jasmine	500	N/A	285.00	725-775
1981 Juliet	300	N/A	260.00	5050
1990 Lavender Hill	485	N/A	265.00	775-800

YEAR ISSUE	EDITION LIMIT	YEAR RETD.	ISSUE PRICE	*QUOTE U.S.$
1992 Love Letters	485	N/A	265.00	550-650
1988 Love Seat	485	N/A	230.00	500-525
1989 Low Tide	485	N/A	265.00	650
1995 Magnolias	950	N/A	265.00	1000-1200
1982 Mail Order Brides	500	N/A	325.00	2400
1984 Make Believe	950	N/A	150.00	775-800
1989 March Winds	485	N/A	265.00	530-550
1983 Mementos	950	N/A	150.00	1500
1982 Memories	500	N/A	235.00	500-575
1992 Morning Mist	485	N/A	265.00	500-600
1981 My Special Place	300	N/A	260.00	2150
1995 Now and Then	950	N/A	265.00	265-550
1982 Nuance	500	N/A	235.00	500-580
1994 Once Upon A Time	950	N/A	265.00	600-700
1983 Ophelia	950	N/A	150.00	700-750
1996 Paradise Cove	950	N/A	265.00	865-950
1989 Peace	485	N/A	265.00	1200-1300
1981 Porcelain Rose	300	N/A	260.00	2100
1982 The Present	500	N/A	260.00	950
1986 Pride & Joy	950	N/A	150.00	325
1991 Puddings & Pies	485	N/A	265.00	500-575
1987 Quiet Corner	950	N/A	115.00	625-675
1989 The Quilt	485	N/A	265.00	950-975
1993 Rambling Rose	485	N/A	265.00	500-575
1981 Rehearsal	300	N/A	260.00	1950
1990 Rendezvous	485	N/A	265.00	650
1984 Scarlet Ribbons	950	N/A	150.00	350
1980 Sea Haven	300	N/A	260.00	1200-1350
1990 Seascapes	485	N/A	265.00	550
1987 September Harvest	950	N/A	150.00	400-500
1980 The Silver Bell	200	N/A	200.00	2000-2200
1990 Sisters	485	N/A	265.00	1250
1990 Songbird	485	N/A	265.00	550
1996 Southern Belle	950	N/A	265.00	850-950
1991 String of Pearls	485	N/A	265.00	850
1988 Summer Choices	300	N/A	250.00	850-900
1991 Teatime	485	N/A	295.00	650-700
1980 Titania	350	N/A	260.00	950-1125
1991 Wildflowers	485	N/A	295.00	725
1983 Window Seat	950	N/A	150.00	700-800

Past Impressions

Limited Edition Canvas Transfers - A. Maley

YEAR ISSUE	EDITION LIMIT	YEAR RETD.	ISSUE PRICE	*QUOTE U.S.$
1990 Cafe Royale	100	N/A	665.00	665
1992 Circle of Love	250	N/A	445.00	550-850
1992 An Elegant Affair	250	N/A	595.00	1095
1992 Evening Performance	100	N/A	295.00	1050
1990 Festive Occasion	100	N/A	595.00	250-300
1990 Gracious Era	100	N/A	645.00	1500-1700
1995 The Letter	250	N/A	465.00	600
1987 Love Letter	75	N/A	445.00	1250
1994 New Years Eve	250	N/A	445.00	600-800
1994 Parisian Beauties	250	N/A	645.00	750
1993 Rags and Riches	250	N/A	445.00	550-625
1993 The Recital	250	N/A	595.00	900-1400
1990 Romantic Engagement	100	N/A	445.00	1225
1993 Sleigh Bells	250	N/A	595.00	600
1991 Summer Carousel	250	N/A	345.00	500-600
1994 Summer Elegance	250	N/A	595.00	950
1995 Summer Romance	250	N/A	465.00	575-750
1993 Visiting The Nursery	250	N/A	445.00	1400
1992 A Walk in the Park	250	N/A	595.00	650-1000
1989 Winter Impressions	100	N/A	595.00	775-1100

Limited Edition Paper Prints - A. Maley

YEAR ISSUE	EDITION LIMIT	YEAR RETD.	ISSUE PRICE	*QUOTE U.S.$
1989 Alexandra	750	1994	125.00	125
1989 Beth	750	1994	125.00	125
1988 The Boardwalk	500	N/A	250.00	395
1989 Catherine	750	1994	125.00	200
1987 Day Dreams	500	N/A	200.00	325
1989 English Rose	750	N/A	250.00	400
1990 Festive Occasion	750	N/A	250.00	500-900
1984 Glorious Summer	350	N/A	150.00	600
1989 In Harmony	750	1995	250.00	250
1988 Joys of Childhood	500	N/A	250.00	320
1987 Love Letter	450	N/A	200.00	200
1988 Opening Night	500	N/A	250.00	2000
1985 Passing Elegance	350	N/A	150.00	900
1987 The Promise	450	N/A	200.00	525
1984 Secluded Garden	350	N/A	150.00	970

GRAPHICS

YEAR ISSUE	EDITION LIMIT	YEAR RETD.	ISSUE PRICE	*QUOTE U.S.$
1985 Secret Thoughts	350	N/A	150.00	850
1990 Summer Pastime	750	N/A	250.00	375
1986 Tell Me	450	N/A	150.00	800
1988 Tranquil Moment	500	N/A	250.00	325
1989 Victoria	750	1994	125.00	125
1988 Victorian Trio	500	N/A	250.00	325-350
1986 Winter Romance	450	N/A	150.00	1000

Pemberton & Oakes

Membership-Miniature Lithographs - D. Zolan

1992 Brotherly Love	Retrd.	1992	18.00	59
1993 New Shoes	Retrd.	1993	18.00	28-42
1993 Country Walk	Retrd.	1993	22.00	20-39
1994 Enchanted Forest	Retrd.	1994	22.00	35-40

Zolan's Children-Lithographs - D. Zolan

1989 Almost Home	Retrd.	1989	98.00	135-150
1991 Autumn Leaves	Retrd.	1991	98.00	115-120
1993 The Big Catch	Retrd.	1993	98.00	98-130
1989 Brotherly Love	Retrd.	1989	98.00	295
1982 By Myself	Retrd.	1982	98.00	230
1989 Christmas Prayer	Retrd.	1989	98.00	100-145
1990 Colors of Spring	Retrd.	1990	98.00	200-375
1990 Crystal's Creek	Retrd.	1990	98.00	175-225
1989 Daddy's Home	Retrd.	1989	98.00	292-310
1988 Day Dreamer	Retrd.	1988	35.00	130
1992 Enchanted Forest	Retrd.	1992	98.00	110-125
1982 Erik and the Dandelion	Retrd.	1982	98.00	350-400
1990 First Kiss	Retrd.	1990	98.00	229-249
1991 Flowers for Mother	Retrd.	1991	98.00	160-195
1993 Grandma's Garden	Retrd.	1993	98.00	100-135
1989 Grandma's Mirror	Retrd.	1989	98.00	175
1990 Laurie and the Creche	Retrd.	1990	98.00	95-115
1989 Mother's Angels	Retrd.	1989	98.00	295-349
1992 New Shoes	Retrd.	1992	98.00	150-175
1989 Rodeo Girl	Retrd.	1989	98.00	125-225
1984 Sabina in the Grass	Retrd.	1984	98.00	625
1988 Small Wonder	Retrd.	1988	98.00	250
1989 Snowy Adventure	Retrd.	1989	98.00	205-225
1991 Summer Suds	Retrd.	1991	98.00	140-175
1989 Summer's Child	Retrd.	1989	98.00	90-165
1986 Tender Moment	Retrd.	1986	98.00	275
1988 Tiny Treasures	Retrd.	1988	150.00	215
1987 Touching the Sky	Retrd.	1987	98.00	225-245
1988 Waiting to Play	Retrd.	1988	35.00	135
1988 Winter Angel	Retrd.	1988	98.00	230-300

Prizm, Inc./Pipka

Pipka Collectibles - Pipka

1999 Christmas Ark 10004 (framed)	578	2001	240.00	240
1999 Christmas Ark 10006 (unframed)	Retrd.	2001	60	60
1999 Gardening Angel Print 10003 (framed)	229	2001	240.00	240
1999 Gardening Angel Print 10005 (unframed)	Retrd.	2001	60.00	60
1998 Knock, Knock Santa Print 10001 (framed)	750	1999	180.00	180-300
1998 Knock, Knock Santa Print 10002 (unframed)	—	1999	50.00	50

Reco International

Fine Art Canvas Reproduction - J. McClelland

1990 Beach Play	350	1998	80.00	80
1991 Flower Swing	350	1998	100.00	100
1991 Summer Conversation	350	1998	80.00	80

Limited Edition Print - S. Kuck

1986 Ashley	500	1998	85.00	150
1985 Heather	Retrd.	1987	75.00	150
1984 Jessica	Retrd.	1986	60.00	400

McClelland - J. McClelland

XX I Love Tammy	500	1998	75.00	100
XX Just for You	300	1998	155.00	155
XX Olivia	300	1998	175.00	175
XX Reverie	300	1998	110.00	110
XX Sweet Dreams	300	1998	145.00	145

Roman, Inc.

Frances Hook - F. Hook

YEAR ISSUE	EDITION LIMIT	YEAR RETD.	ISSUE PRICE	*QUOTE U.S.$
1982 Bouquet	Closed	1994	70.00	350
1981 The Carpenter	Closed	1981	100.00	1000
1981 The Carpenter (remarque)	Closed	1981	100.00	3000
1982 Frolicking	Closed	1994	60.00	350
1982 Gathering	Closed	1994	60.00	350-450
1982 Little Children, Come to Me	Closed	1994	50.00	500
1982 Little Children, Come to Me, remarque	50	N/A	100.00	500
1982 Posing	Closed	1987	70.00	350
1982 Poulets	Closed	1994	60.00	350
1982 Surprise	Closed	1988	50.00	350

Portraits of Love - F. Hook

1988 Expectation	Closed	1991	25.00	25
1988 In Mother's Arms	Closed	1990	25.00	25
1988 My Kitty	Closed	1992	25.00	25
1988 Remember When...	Closed	1991	25.00	25
1988 Sharing	Closed	1991	25.00	25
1988 Sunkissed Afternoon	Closed	1991	25.00	25

V.F. Fine Arts

Kuck - S. Kuck

1994 '95 Angel Collection, S/N	750	1995	198.00	198
1995 '96 Angel Collection, S/N	750		198.00	198
1997 '98 Angel Collection	750		135.00	135
1997 '98 Angel Collection, canvas	150		330.00	330
1998 Afternoon Tea	1,250		95.00	95
1998 Afternoon Tea. Canvas	395		240.00	240
1993 Best Friend, proof	250	N/A	175.00	225
1993 Best Friends, canvas transfer	250	N/A	500.00	600
1993 Best Friends, S/N	2,500	N/A	145.00	150
1994 Best of Days, S/N	750	1994	160.00	175
1989 Bundle of Joy, S/N	1,000	1989	125.00	250
1993 Buttons & Bows, proof	95	N/A	125.00	150
1993 Buttons & Bows, S/N	950	N/A	95.00	125
1990 Chopsticks, proof	150	1991	120.00	150
1990 Chopsticks, remarque	25	1991	160.00	200
1990 Chopsticks, S/N	1,500	1990	80.00	95
1995 Christmas Magic, S/N	950		80.00	80
1987 The Daisy, proof	90	1988	40.00	175
1987 The Daisy, S/N	900	1988	30.00	125
1989 Day Dreaming, proof	90	1989	225.00	250
1989 Day Dreaming, remarque	50	1989	300.00	395
1989 Day Dreaming, S/N	900	1989	150.00	200
1994 Dear Santa, S/N	950	1994	95.00	125-225
1992 Duet, canvas framed	500	1994	255.00	325
1992 Duet, proof	95	N/A	175.00	200
1992 Duet, S/N	950	N/A	125.00	135
1998 Enchanted Garden	950		95.00	95
1998 Enchanted Garden, canvas	295		240.00	240
1988 First Recital, proof	25	1988	250.00	750
1988 First Recital, remarque	25	1988	400.00	1000
1988 First Recital, S/N	150	1988	200.00	500
1990 First Snow, proof	50	1990	150.00	250
1990 First Snow, remarque	25	1990	200.00	350
1990 First Snow, S/N	500	1990	95.00	150
1987 The Flower Girl, proof	90	1987	50.00	125
1987 The Flower Girl, S/N	900	1987	40.00	95
1994 Garden Memories canvas transfer	250	N/A	500.00	500
1994 Garden Memories, S/N	2,500	N/A	145.00	175
1997 Gift From Angel	950		74.50	75
1997 Gift From Angel, AP	95		82.00	82
1997 Gift From Angel, canvas	295		119.50	120
1991 God's Gift, proof	150	N/A	150.00	175
1991 God's Gift, S/N	1,500	1993	95.00	125
1997 Golden Days	950		75.00	75
1997 Golden Days, canvas	295		120.00	120
1997 Gone Fishing	950		75.00	75
1997 Gone Fishing, canvas	495		120.00	120
1993 Good Morning, canvas	250	1993	500.00	500
1993 Good Morning, proof	50	N/A	175.00	200
1993 Good Morning, S/N	2,500	N/A	145.00	165
1997 Heavenly Whisper	950		74.50	75
1997 Heavenly Whisper, AP	95		82.00	82
1997 Heavenly Whisper, canvas	295		119.50	120
1996 Hidden Garden, canvas transfer	395		379.00	379

Collectors' Information Bureau

*Quotes have been rounded up to nearest dollar

YEAR ISSUE	EDITION LIMIT	YEAR RETD.	ISSUE PRICE	*QUOTE U.S.$
1996 Hidden Garden, S/N	950	1996	95.00	95
1995 Homecoming, proof	95	1995	172.50	173
1995 Homecoming, S/N	1,150	1995	125.00	125
1989 Innocence, proof	90	1989	225.00	275
1989 Innocence, remarque	50	1989	300.00	395
1989 Innocence, S/N	900	1989	150.00	220
1997 Interlude	500	1997	145.00	145
1997 Interlude, AP	50		175.00	175
1997 Interlude, canvas	200		300.00	300
1992 Joyous Day, canvas transfer	250	N/A	250.00	295
1992 Joyous Day, proof	120	N/A	175.00	200
1992 Joyous Day, S/N	1,200	1993	125.00	150
1997 Kate & Oliver	3,000		80.00	80
1997 Kate & Oliver, canvas	1,000		90.00	90
1997 Kitten Tails	950		75.00	75
1997 Kitten Tails, canvas	495		120.00	120
1988 The Kitten, proof	50	1988	150.00	1000
1988 The Kitten, remarque	25	1988	250.00	1200
1988 The Kitten, S/N	350	1988	120.00	1000
1990 Le Beau, proof	150	1990	120.00	225
1990 Le Beau, remarque	25	1990	160.00	275
1990 Le Beau, S/N	1,500	1990	80.00	175
1987 Le Papillon, proof	35	1990	110.00	175
1987 Le Papillon, remarque	7	1990	150.00	250
1987 Le Papillon, S/N	350	1990	90.00	150
1990 Lilly Pond, color remarque	125	1990	500.00	500
1990 Lilly Pond, proof	75	1990	200.00	200
1990 Lilly Pond, S/N	750	1990	150.00	150
1997 Lilly Pond, canvas	295		135.00	135
1988 Little Ballerina, proof	25	1988	150.00	350
1988 Little Ballerina, remarque	25	1988	225.00	450
1988 Little Ballerina, S/N	150	1988	110.00	275
1987 The Loveseat, proof	90	1987	40.00	150
1987 The Loveseat, S/N	900	1987	30.00	100
1991 Memories, S/N	5,000	1991	195.00	250
1997 Merry Christmas	950		95.00	95
1997 Merry Christmas, canvas	495		240.00	240
1987 Mother's Love, proof	12	1987	225.00	1200
1987 Mother's Love, S/N	150	1987	195.00	750
1988 My Dearest, proof	50	1988	200.00	900
1988 My Dearest, remarque	25	1988	325.00	1200
1988 My Dearest, S/N	350	1988	160.00	700
1995 Night Before Christmas, S/N	1,150		95.00	95
1995 Playful Kitten	950	1995	95.00	95
1997 Precious	950		95.00	95
1997 Precious, canvas	395		265.00	265
1997 Puppy Love	950	1997	75.00	75
1997 Puppy Love, canvas	495	1997	120	120
1989 Puppy, proof	50	1989	180.00	500
1989 Puppy, remarque	50	1989	240.00	750
1989 Puppy, S/N	500	1989	120.00	400
1997 Quiet Garden	950		109.00	109
1997 Quiet Garden, AP	95		139.00	139
1997 Quiet Garden, canvas	295		249.00	249
1987 A Quiet Time, proof	90	1987	50.00	100
1987 A Quiet Time, S/N	900	1987	40.00	75
1987 The Reading Lesson, proof	90	1987	70.00	150
1987 The Reading Lesson, S/N	900	1987	60.00	150
1997 Rehearsal	950	1998	75.00	75
1997 Rehearsal, canvas	495		120.00	120
1995 Rhapsody & Lace	1,150		95.00	100
1989 Rose Garden, proof	50	1989	150.00	400
1989 Rose Garden, remarque	50	1989	200.00	500
1989 Rose Garden, S/N	500	1989	95.00	390
1986 Silhouette, proof	25	1987	90.00	250
1986 Silhouette, S/N	250	1987	80.00	200
1997 Sisters	950		75.00	75
1997 Sisters, canvas	495		120.00	120
1989 Sisters, proof	90	1989	150.00	550
1989 Sisters, remarque	50	1989	200.00	650
1989 Sisters, S/N	900	1988	95.00	300
1989 Sonatina, proof	90	1989	225.00	700
1989 Sonatina, remarque	50	1989	300.00	850
1989 Sonatina, S/N	900	1989	150.00	400
1986 Summer Reflections, proof	90	1987	70.00	300
1986 Summer Reflections, S/N	900	1987	60.00	250
1997 Take Me Home	950		125.00	125
1997 Take Me Home, canvas	295		295.00	295
1997 Tea With Kitty	950		80.00	80
1997 Tea With Kitty, canvas	295		200.00	200
1986 Tender Moments, proof	50	1986	80.00	300

YEAR ISSUE	EDITION LIMIT	YEAR RETD.	ISSUE PRICE	*QUOTE U.S.$
1986 Tender Moments, S/N	500	1986	70.00	200
1993 Thinking of You, canvas transfer	250	1993	500.00	500
1993 Thinking of You, S/N	2,500	N/A	145.00	175
1988 Wild Flowers, proof	50	1988	175.00	300
1988 Wild Flowers, remarque	25	1988	250.00	400
1988 Wild Flowers, S/N	350	1988	160.00	250
1992 Yesterday, canvas framed	550	N/A	195.00	200
1992 Yesterday, proof	95	N/A	150.00	150
1992 Yesterday, S/N	950	N/A	95.00	95

Walt Disney

Disney Store Exclusive Portrait Series - Disney Studios

2001 Beauty and Beast Set 1212078	Yr.Iss.	2001	85.00	85

Willitts Designs

Cooperstown Film Cels - Willitts Designs

1997 Babe Ruth	Retrd.	1999	25.00	25
1997 Hank Aaron	Retrd.	1999	25.00	25
1997 Lou Gehrig	Retrd.	1999	25.00	25
1997 Ted Williams	Retrd.	1999	25.00	25

Cooperstown Lithograph w/Lighted Film Cel - Willitts Designs

1997 Babe Ruth/Lou Gehrig	700	1999	250.00	250
1997 Hank Aaron	2,500	1999	200.00	200
1997 Jackie Robinson	2,500	1999	200.00	200
1998 Mickey Mantle	2,500	1999	200.00	200
1997 Ted Williams	2,500	1999	200.00	200

Cooperstown Motion Cels - Willitts Designs

1997 Babe Ruth	14,500	1999	25.00	25
1997 Hank Aaron	14,500	1999	25.00	25
1997 Jackie Robinson	14,500	1999	25.00	25
1997 Lou Gehrig	14,500	1999	25.00	25
1997 Stan Musial	14,500	1999	25.00	25
1997 Ted Williams	14,500	1999	25.00	25

Disney Showcase Collection Film Cels - Willitts Designs

1998 Beauty and the Beast: Beast	Retrd.	1999	25.00	25
1998 Beauty and the Beast: Belle	Retrd.	1999	25.00	25
1998 Beauty and the Beast: Enchanted Objects	Retrd.	1999	25.00	25
1998 Beauty and the Beast: Gaston	Retrd.	1999	25.00	25
1998 Cinderella	Retrd.	1999	25.00	25
1998 Cinderella: Menagerie	Retrd.	1999	25.00	25
1998 Cinderella: Royals	Retrd.	1999	25.00	25
1998 Cinderella: Stepfamily	Retrd.	1999	25.00	25
1998 Magician Mickey	Retrd.	1999	25.00	25
1998 Mickey Mouse: Brave Little Tailor	Retrd.	1999	25.00	25
1998 Mickey Mouse: Prince and the Pauper	Retrd.	1999	25.00	25
1998 Mickey Mouse: Runaway Brain	Retrd.	1999	25.00	25
1998 Peter Pan	Retrd.	1999	25.00	25
1998 Peter Pan: Captain Hook	Retrd.	1999	25.00	25
1998 Peter Pan: Citizens of Neverland	Retrd.	1999	25.00	25
1998 Peter Pan: Tinkerbell	Retrd.	1999	25.00	25
1998 Peter Pan: Wendy, Michael, John	Retrd.	1999	25.00	25
1998 Snow White	Retrd.	1999	25.00	25
1998 Snow White Commemorative	Retrd.	1999	25.00	25
1998 Snow White: Seven Dwarfs	Retrd.	1999	25.00	25
1998 Snow White: Wicked Queen	Retrd.	1999	25.00	25

Disney Showcase Collection Motion Cels - Willitts Designs

1998 Beauty and the Beast	Retrd.	1999	25.00	25
1998 Cinderella	Retrd.	1999	25.00	25
1998 Mickey Mouse (Brave Little Tailor)	Retrd.	1999	25.00	25
1998 Peter Pan	Retrd.	1999	25.00	25
1998 Snow White	Retrd.	1999	25.00	25

Disney Showcase Lithograph w/Lighted Film Cel - Willitts Designs

1998 Beauty & the Beast	2,500	1999	200.00	200
1998 Cinderella	2,500	1999	200.00	200
1998 Mickey Mouse	5,000	1999	200.00	200
1998 Peter Pan	2,500	1999	200.00	200
1998 Snow White	2,500	1999	200.00	200

MasterPeace Collection - Various

1998 Forgiven - T. Blackshear	Retrd.	1999	40.00	40
1998 The Invitation - M. Weistling	Retrd.	1999	99.00	99
1998 Victorious Lion of Judah - M. Dudash	Retrd.	1999	99.00	99

YEAR ISSUE	EDITION LIMIT	YEAR RETD.	ISSUE PRICE	*QUOTE U.S.$
1998 Watchers in the Night - T. Blackshear	Retrd.	1999	50.00	50

Thomas Blackshear's Ebony Visions - T. Blackshear

1997 Ebony Visions-Canvas Transfer (framed)	950	1998	575.00	575
1997 Ebony Visions-Canvas Transfer A/P (framed)	100	1998	690.00	690
1997 Ebony Visions-Canvas Transfer G/P (framed)	100	1998	747.50	748
1998 Ebony Visions-Lithograph (framed)	1,950	2000	275.00	275
1998 Ebony Visions-Lithograph A/P (framed)	50	2000	330.00	330
1998 Ebony Visions-Lithograph G/P (framed)	50	2000	357.00	357

Titanic Film Cels - Willitts Designs

1998 Cal and Love Joy	Retrd.	1999	25.00	25
1998 Crew	Retrd.	1999	25.00	25
1998 Eternal Romance	2,500	1999	25.00	25
1998 Jack & Rose	Retrd.	1999	25.00	25
1998 Jack Dawson	Retrd.	1999	25.00	25
1998 Passengers	Retrd.	1999	25.00	25
1998 Rose DeWitt Bukater	Retrd.	1999	25.00	25
1998 Titanic	Retrd.	1999	25.00	25

Titanic Lithograph w/Lighted Film Cel - Willitts Designs

1998 Domestic	5,000	1999	200	200
1998 I'm Flying	5,000	1999	200	200
1998 International	2,500	1999	200	200
1998 Titanic	2,500	1999	200	200

NUTCRACKERS

Christian Ulbricht USA

Christian Ulbricht Collectors' Club - C. Ulbricht

1998 Lantern Child Smoker	Retrd.	1999	Gift	45-50
1998 SnowKing 000501	Retrd.	1999	154.00	200-300
1999 Arabian Knight Smoker	Retrd.	2000	Gift	N/A
1999 Teddybear King 000505	Retrd.	2000	154.00	154
2000 Bird Seller Smoker 35-210	Retrd.	2001	Gift	N/A
2000 Frog King 000508	Retrd.	2001	154.00	154
2002 Mushroom Man Smoker	Yr.Iss.		Gift	N/A
2002 Elf King	Yr.Iss.		154.00	154

Christian Ulbricht Event - C. Ulbricht

1997 Woodpecker 32-450	2,500	1997	49.95	125-150
1998 Penguin 32-451	Yr.Iss.	1998	49.95	65-100
1999 Bluebird 32-453	Yr.Iss.	1999	65.00	65-100
2000 Cardinal 32-455	Yr.Iss.	2000	49.95	50
2001 Hummingbird 32-455	Yr.Iss.	2001	59.50	60

American Folk Hero/Midwest© - C. Ulbricht

1994 Davy Crockett 12960-9	1,500	1996	160.00	170-229
1994 Johnny Appleseed 12959-3	1,500	1996	160.00	200-229
1995 Paul Bunyan 12800-8	1,500	1996	170.00	170-199
1996 Sacajawea 17018-2	1,000	1996	200.00	185-200
1996 Wyatt Earp 17019-9	1,000	1996	200.00	200-225

Artists of the World - C. Ulbricht

2002 Cezanne 000421	3,000		240.00	240
2001 Vincent van Gogh 000409	3,000		236.00	236

A Christmas Carol - C. Ulbricht

1997 Bob Cratchit & Tiny Tim 000145	5,000		236.00	236
1994 Bob Cratchit and Tiny Tim/Midwest© 09577-5	2,500	1996	210.00	275
1996 Ghost of Christmas Past/Midwest© 18299-4	1,500	1996	200.00	275-350
2001 Ghost of Christmas Present 000404	5,000		236.00	236
1992 Ghost of Christmas Present/Midwest© 12041-5	1,500	1996	170.00	179-300
2000 Ghost of Christmas Yet to Come 000180	5,000		236.00	236
1996 Ghost of Christmas Yet to Come/Midwest© 17021-2	1,500	1996	190.00	199-300
1999 Marley's Ghost 000170	5,000		236.00	236
1998 Mrs. Cratchit 000149	5,000		230.00	230
1996 Scrooge 000123	5,000		228.00	228
1993 Scrooge/Midwest© 09584-3	2,500	1996	200.00	250

Don Quixote - C. Ulbricht

2000 Don Quixote 000188	5,000		236.00	236
2000 Sancho Pansa 000189	5,000		236.00	236

Great American Inventors - C. Ulbricht

1998 Alexander Graham Bell 000148	1,500	2000	250.00	250-270
1997 Henry Ford 000146	1,500	2000	260.00	260-270
1996 Thomas Edison 000129	1,500	2000	270.00	270

Great Inventors - C. Ulbricht

2001 Johnanes Gutenberg 000408	1,500		240.00	240

Limited Edition Nutcrackers - C. Ulbricht

1998 Angel 000147	2,500	2000	230.00	230
2000 Artist 000187	2,500		230.00	230
2002 Bavarian Santa 000418	3,000		236.00	236
1997 Biker Lady 000124	5,000	1999	198.00	210-220
2001 Christmas Snowman 000402	3,000		142.00	142
2001 Cold Bringing Woman 000403	3,000		236.00	236
2000 Country Santa 000183	2,500	2002	230.00	230
2002 Cycle Santa 000419	2,500		230.00	230
1997 Doc Holiday 000137	3,000	2000	222.00	222-229
1999 Dottie Doolittle 000172	5,000		230.00	230
1996 Elf on Reindeer 000128	5,000	1999	180.00	180
2000 Father Christmas 000184	2,500	2002	230.00	230
2000 Father Time 000191	2,500	2001	236.00	236
2001 Father Time 000199	1,500	2001	236.00	236
2002 Forest Santa 000424	2,500		236.00	236
2001 Frogking Prince 000412	3,000		236.00	236
2001 Frogking Princess 000411	3,000		230.00	230
1997 Frosty 000143	3,000	2000	117.00	117-119
2000 Hans the Clockmaker 000186	2,500		236.00	236
1997 Jack the Hacker 000135	3,000	2000	240.00	240
2000 James the Golfer 000185	2,500		222.00	222
1999 King Henry VIII 000168	5,000		230.00	230
2001 King Solomon 000407	3,000		236.00	236
2001 Kris Kringle 000400	3,000		230.00	230
1998 Lawyer 000149	2,500		222.00	222
2002 Leprechaun 000417	2,500		230.00	230
1996 Lone Wolf 000107	5,000	2000	209.00	209
2000 Millenium 000200	2,500	2001	236.00	236
1996 Moon & Star Santa 000112	5,000	2000	219.00	219
1994 Mr. Santa Claus/Midwest© 9588-1	2,500	1996	160.00	190-200
1998 Mr. Snowman 000154	2,500	1996	154.00	154-160
1994 Mrs. Santa Claus/Midwest© 9587-4	2,500	1996	160.00	190-200
1998 Mrs. Snowman 000155	2,500	2000	154.00	154-160
1997 Nic Taylor 000134	3,000	2000	240.00	240
1999 Oliver Pickwick 000171	5,000		230.00	230
1998 Santa in Canoe 000163	2,500	2000	230.00	230
1996 Santa in Chimney 000131	5,000	2001	219.00	219
1999 Santa in the Alps 000175	2,500	2002	222.00	222
1997 Santa MacNic 000133	3,000	2000	230.00	230
1997 Santa O'Claus 000132	3,000	2000	230.00	230
1996 Santa on Reindeer 000127	5,000	1999	180.00	180
1998 Santa w/ Long Robe 000161	2,500	2001	222.00	222
1998 Santa w/ Short Robe 000152	2,500	2001	222.00	222
1997 Santa Winterwonderland 000140	3,000	2000	230.00	230
1997 Santa's Ark 000139	3,000	2000	230.00	230
1999 Santa's Coffeetime 000169	2,500		230.00	230
2002 Shepherd 000428	3,000		230.00	230
2001 St. Nicholas 000401	3,000		230.00	230
1997 Stars & Stripes Forever 000138	3,000	2001	222.00	222
2002 Stars and Stripes 000415	3,000		230.00	230
2002 Steiff Teddy Roosevelt (Steiff Exclusive) 000420	2,500		490.00	490
1998 Summer Wonderland 000153	3,000	2000	230.00	218-230
2001 Teddybear Maker (Steiff Exclusive) 000414	1,500	2002	350.00	350
1996 Teddybear Maker 000109	500	1996	270.00	600-650
1996 Teddybear Santa 000111	5,000	1998	200.00	225-229
2000 V. Two Sam 000182	2,500		230.00	230
2002 Victorian Santa 000425	2,500		236.00	236
1996 White Feather 000108	5,000	2000	209.00	209
2001 Woodland Santa 000410	3,000		236.00	236
2002 Zorro 000416	2,500		236.00	236

Native American Kachina - C. Ulbricht

1997 Eagle Dancer 000144	3,000	2000	240.00	240
2002 Eagle Kachina 000426	5,000		240.00	240
1999 Sun Face 000174	3,000		240.00	240
1998 White Buffalo 000157	3,000	2002	240.00	240

YEAR ISSUE	EDITION LIMIT	YEAR RETD.	ISSUE PRICE	*QUOTE U.S.$
Nutcracker Ballet - C. Ulbricht				
1996 Clara 000121	5,000		219.00	219
1996 Herr Drosselmeyer 000119	5,000		228.00	228
1996 Mouse King 000120	5,000		228.00	228
1996 Prince 000122	5,000		219.00	219
2000 Sugar Plum Fairy w/Music 000190	5,000		270.00	270
1998 Toy Soldier 000165	5,000		238.00	238
Nutcracker Ballet/Midwest© - C. Ulbricht				
1991 Clara 03657-0	Retrd.	1996	124.00	200-220
1991 Herr Drosselmeyer 03656-3	Retrd.	1996	160.00	229-250
1991 Mouse King 04510-7	Retrd.	1996	160.00	225-229
1991 Prince 03665-5	Retrd.	1996	154.00	154-220
1991 Toy Soldier 03666-2	Retrd.	1996	154.00	154-238
Nutcrackers - C. Ulbricht				
1993 Red Riding Hood	Retrd.	1996	120.00	165-250
Peter Pan© Disney - C. Ulbricht				
1998 Captain Hook 000500	2,500	2001	275.00	275
1999 Peter Pan 000502	2,500	2001	190.00	190
1999 Tinker Bell 000504	2,500	2001	160.00	160
Plays of Shakespeare - C. Ulbricht				
1999 Hamlet 000166	5,000	2001	236.00	236
1997 Juliet 000136	5,000	2001	230.00	230
1998 Romeo 000156	5,000	2001	236.00	236
1997 Shakespeare 000142	5,000	2001	236.00	236
Santa Claus/Midwest© - C. Ulbricht				
1992 Father Christmas (1st) 07094-9	2,500	1995	210.00	239-350
1993 Toymaker (2nd) 09531-7	2,500	1996	210.00	210-250
1994 Victorian Santa (3rd) 2961-6	2,500	1996	210.00	250
1995 King of Christmas (4th) 13665-2	2,500	1996	210.00	500-750
Snow White© Disney - C. Ulbricht				
1999 Bashful 000517	2,500	2001	170.00	170
1999 Doc 000511	2,500	2001	170.00	170
1999 Dopey 000516	2,500	2001	170.00	170
1999 Grumpy 000512	2,500	2001	170.00	170
1999 Happy 000514	2,500	2001	170.00	170
1999 Sleepy 000515	2,500	2001	170.00	170
1999 Sneezy 000513	2,500	2001	170.00	170
1999 Snow White 000510	2,500	2001	209.00	209
Three Musketeers - C. Ulbricht				
1996 Portos 000114	5,000	2001	200.00	200
Three Wisemen - C. Ulbricht				
2001 Balthasar 000406	3,000		230.00	230
1996 Caspar 000115	5,000	2002	209.00	209
1999 Melchior 000176	5,000	2002	209.00	209
Wizard of Oz - C. Ulbricht				
1998 Cowardly Lion 000151	5,000		240.00	240
1998 Dorothy 000150	5,000		230.00	230
2001 Good Witch Glinda 000405	5,000		230.00	230
1999 Scarecrow 000167	5,000		230.00	230
1997 Tin Woodsman 000141	5,000		230.00	230
1999 Wicked Witch 000173	5,000		236.00	236
2000 Wizard of Oz 000181	5,000		236.00	236

Christopher Radko

YEAR ISSUE	EDITION LIMIT	YEAR RETD.	ISSUE PRICE	*QUOTE U.S.$
Nutcrackers - C. Radko				
1997 The Bishop 97-K01-00	5,000		485.00	485
1997 Candy Stripe 97-K03-00	5,000		445.00	445
1997 Snow Gent 97-K04-00	5,000		445.00	445
1997 Winter Dream 97-K02-00	5,000		485.00	485

G. DeBrekht Artistic Studios/Masterpiece

YEAR ISSUE	EDITION LIMIT	YEAR RETD.	ISSUE PRICE	*QUOTE U.S.$
Masterpiece Nutcrackers - G. DeBrekht Artistic Studios				
2002 Nutcracker "holiday surprise" (md) 26021	100		550.00	550
2002 Nutcracker "Sword men" (md) 26022	100		550.00	550
2002 Nutcracker (xxlg) 26010	25		1950.00	1950

Kurt S. Adler, Inc.

YEAR ISSUE	EDITION LIMIT	YEAR RETD.	ISSUE PRICE	*QUOTE U.S.$
Jim Henson's Muppet Nutcrackers - KSA/JHP				
1993 Kermit The Frog H1223	Retrd.	1995	90.00	90

YEAR ISSUE	EDITION LIMIT	YEAR RETD.	ISSUE PRICE	*QUOTE U.S.$
Steinbach Nutcracker Collectors' Club - KSA/Steinbach				
1995 Mini Town Crier	Retrd.	1997	Gift	100
1995 King Wenceslaus ES900	Retrd.	1997	225.00	550-650
1997 Mini Chimney Sweep	Retrd.	1998	Gift	55-75
1997 Marek The Royal Guardsman ES856	Retrd.	1998	225.00	400-450
1998 Mini Forester	Retrd.	1999	Gift	50-55
1998 Gustav The Royal Cook ES1824	Retrd.	1999	225.00	420-450
1999 Bavarian Beer Drinker	Retrd.	2000	Gift	N/A
1999 Otto, The Royal Drummer ES1828	Retrd.	2000	250.00	250
2000 Black Forest Clockmaker	Retrd.	2001	Gift	N/A
2000 Reginald the Beefeater	Retrd.	2001	250.00	250
2001 Little King	Retrd.	2002	Gift	N/A
2001 Guido, Captain of the Swiss Guard ES1831	Retrd.	2002	250.00	250
2002 Gardener	Open		Gift	N/A
2002 Night Watchman ES1832	Open		260.00	260
Steinbach Nutcracker American Inventor Series - KSA/Steinbach				
1993 Ben Franklin ES635	12,000	1996	225.00	450-500
Steinbach Nutcracker American Presidents Series - KSA/Steinbach				
1992 Abraham Lincoln ES622	12,000	1995	195.00	450-600
1992 George Washington ES623	12,000	1994	195.00	450-750
1993 Teddy Roosevelt ES644	10,000	1997	225.00	450-750
1996 Thomas Jefferson ES866	7,500	1997	260.00	450-495
Steinbach Nutcracker Biblical - KSA/Steinbach				
2002 Jonah ES1812	7,500		275.00	275
1998 Joseph and the Dreamcoat ES1810	7,500		255.00	255
2000 King Solomon ES1811	7,500		275.00	275
1997 Moses ES894	10,000		250.00	250
1996 Noah ES893	10,000	1999	260.00	375-450
Steinbach Nutcracker Camelot Series - KSA/Steinbach				
1992 King Arthur ES621	7,500	1993	195.00	750-1500
1991 Merlin The Magician ES610	7,500	1991	185.00	3500-5000
1995 Queen Guenevere ES869	10,000	1997	245.00	295-400
1994 Sir Galahad ES862	12,000	1997	225.00	225-500
1993 Sir Lancelot ES638	12,000	1997	225.00	225-500
Steinbach Nutcracker Christmas Carol Series - KSA/Steinbach				
1998 Bob Cratchit and Tiny Tim ES1820	7,500		265.00	265
1997 Ebenezer Scrooge ES896	7,500		250.00	275
2001 Ghost of Christmas Present ES1817	7,500		275.00	275
1999 Marley's Ghost ES1819	7,500		265.00	265
2002 Scrooge in Nightclothes ES1804	7,500		275.00	275
Steinbach Nutcracker Christmas Legends Series - KSA/Steinbach				
1995 1930s Santa Claus ES891	7,500	2000	245.00	245 505
1999 Bavarian Santa ES1827	7,500		270.00	270
2000 Duncan Scottish Santa ES1829	7,500		275.00	275
1993 Father Christmas ES645	7,500	1996	225.00	250-800
1997 Grandfather Frost ES895	7,500	1999	250.00	350-750
2001 Patrick O' Santa ES1835	7,500		275.00	275
1998 Père Noel ES1822	7,500	2000	250.00	250-450
2002 Polish Santa ES1834	7,500		275.00	275
1994 St. Nicholas, The Bishop ES865	7,500	1995	225.00	275-1000
Steinbach Nutcracker Collection - KSA/Steinbach				
1991 Columbus ES697	Retrd.	1992	194.00	229-260
1992 Happy Santa ES601	Retrd.	1998	190.00	199-220
1984 Oil Sheik	Retrd.	1985	100.00	1500-1750
Steinbach Nutcracker Famous Chieftains Series - KSA/Steinbach				
1995 Black Hawk ES889	7,500	1996	245.00	375-450
1993 Chief Sitting Bull ES637	8,500	1995	225.00	500-600
1994 Red Cloud ES864	8,500	1996	225.00	229-350
Steinbach Nutcracker Famous Royalty Series - KSA/Steinbach				
1998 King Henry ES1823	7,500		255.00	255
2001 Louis XIV ES1801	7,500		275.00	275
Steinbach Nutcracker Looney Tunes Series - KSA/Warner Brothers				
2000 Bugs Bunny ES962	Retrd.	2001	275.00	275

YEAR ISSUE	EDITION LIMIT	YEAR RETD.	ISSUE PRICE	*QUOTE U.S.$

Steinbach Nutcracker Mini Series - KSA/Steinbach

YEAR ISSUE	EDITION LIMIT	YEAR RETD.	ISSUE PRICE	*QUOTE U.S.$
2002 Bavarian ES292	7,500		65.00	65
2000 Bavarian Santa ES355	7,500		65.00	65
1999 Bob Cratchit ES358	10,000	2001	66.00	66
2001 Duncan the Scottish Santa ES363	7,500		65.00	65
2002 Ghost of Christmas Present ES250	7,500		65.00	65
1998 Grandfather Frost ES343	10,000	2000	60.00	55-75
2002 Irish Santa ES255	7,500		65.00	65
2000 Joseph ES353	7,500		65.00	65
1997 King Arthur ES337	15,000	2001	50.00	50
2000 Marley's Ghost ES362	7,500		65.00	65
1996 Merlin ES335	15,000	1999	50.00	55-75
1999 Moses ES359	10,000	2001	66.00	66
1997 Noah and His Ark ES339	10,000		50.00	50
1999 Père Noel ES357	10,000	2001	66.00	66
1996 Robin Hood ES336	10,000		50.00	50
1998 Scrooge ES342	10,000		60.00	60
1999 Sir Galahad ES356	10,000	2001	66.00	66
1998 Sir Lancelot ES344	10,000	2001	60.00	60
1997 St. Nicholas ES338	15,000	2001	50.00	50
2001 Wise King Solomon ES352	7,500		65.00	65

Steinbach Nutcracker Peter Pan Series - KSA/Steinbach

1999 Captain Hook ES1826	7,500		270.00	270
2000 Crocodile ES1818	5,000	2001	265.00	265
2001 Peter Pan with Tinkerbell ES1816	5,000		275.00	275

Steinbach Nutcracker Tales of Sherwood Forest - KSA/Steinbach

1995 Friar Tuck ES890	7,500	1997	245.00	350-600
1997 King Richard the Lion-Hearted ES897	7,500	1999	250.00	265-450
1999 Maid Marion ES1825	5,000	2001	260.00	260-450
1992 Robin Hood ES863	7,500	1996	225.00	275-850
1996 Sherif of Nottingham ES892	7,500	1999	260.00	260-450

Steinbach Nutcracker Three Musketeers - KSA/Steinbach

1996 Aramis ES722	7,500	1997	130.00	145-175
1998 Athos ES1821	7,500		125.00	125
2001 D' Artaghan ES1814	7,500		165.00	165
2000 Porthos ES1815	7,500		180.00	180

Steinbach Nutcracker Wizard of Oz Series - KSA/Warner Brothers

2001 Cowardly Lion ES1805	Open		275.00	275
2002 Dorothy ES1806	Open		275.00	275
1999 Scarecrow ES961	Open		270.00	270
2000 Tin Man ES960	Open		275.00	275

Steinbach Special Limited Edition Nutcracker - KSA/Steinbach

2002 Firefighter ES1785	5,000		275.00	275
2002 The Last Deutshe Mark ES1699	6,000		225.00	225
2002 Swiss Yodeler (musical) ES1696	Open		295.00	295
2001 Uncle Sam (musical) ES1800	3,000		275.00	275
2002 Uncle Sam ES1784	5,000		275.00	275

Zuber Nutcracker Series - KSA/Zuber

1992 The Annapolis Midshipman EK7	5,000	1994	125.00	125
1992 The Bavarian EK16	5,000	1994	130.00	130-139
1992 Bronco Billy The Cowboy EK1	5,000	1994	125.00	125-140
1992 The Chimney Sweep EK6	5,000	1993	125.00	125
1992 The Country Singer EK19	5,000	1993	125.00	125
1992 The Fisherman EK17	5,000	1996	125.00	130-140
1994 The Gardner EK26	2,500	1996	150.00	150
1992 Gepetto, The Toymaker EK9	5,000	1994	125.00	125-139
1992 The Gold Prospector EK18	5,000	1994	125.00	125
1992 The Golfer EK5	5,000	1994	125.00	125-130
1993 Herr Drosselmeir Nutcracker EK21	5,000	1996	150.00	1000-2500
1993 The Ice Cream Vendor EK24	5,000	1996	150.00	150
1992 The Indian EK15	5,000	1994	135.00	135
1994 Jazz Player EK25	2,500	1999	145.00	140-145
1994 Kurt the Traveling Salesman EK28	2,500	1999	155.00	155-159
1994 Mouse King EK31	2,500	2000	150.00	150
1993 Napoleon Bonaparte EK23	5,000	1994	150.00	150
1992 The Nor' Easter Sea Captain EK3	5,000	1994	125.00	125-140
1992 Paul Bunyan The Lumberjack EK2	5,000	1993	125.00	125
1994 Peter Pan EK28	2,500	2000	145.00	145
1992 The Pilgrim EK14	5,000	1994	125.00	125
1993 The Pizzamaker EK22	5,000	1999	150.00	150
1994 Scuba Diver EK27	2,500	1999	150.00	150

1994 Soccer Player EK30	2,500	1999	145.00	145
1992 TheTyrolean EK4	5,000	1994	125.00	125
1992 The West Point Cadet With Canon EK8	5,000	1994	130.00	130-135

San Francisco Music Box Company

Nutcrackers - San Francisco Music Box Company

1998 Alexander the Great	10,000	1998	35.00	35
1999 Father Christmas	10,000	1999	45.00	45
1998 Jolly Ol' St. Nick	10,000	1998	35.00	35
1998 King Arthur	10,000	1998	35.00	35
1999 Prince Charming	10,000	1999	45.00	45
1999 Puss n' Boots	10,000	1999	45.00	45
1999 Sir Galahad	10,000	1999	45.00	45

ORNAMENTS

Anheuser-Busch, Inc.

A & Eagle Collector Ornament Series - A.-Busch, Inc.

1991 Budweiser Girl-Circa 1890's N3178	Retrd.	N/A	15.00	15-20
1992 1893 Columbian Exposition N3649	Retrd.	N/A	15.00	15-20
1993 Greatest Triumph N4089	Retrd.	N/A	15.00	15-20

Christmas Ornaments - Various

1992 Clydesdales 3 Mini Plate Ornament N3650 - S. Sampson	Retrd.	N/A	23.00	20-28
1993 Budweiser Six-Pack Mini Plate Ornament N4220 - M. Urdahl	Retrd.	1994	10.00	15-30

Armani

Christmas - G. Armani

1991 Christmas Ornament 779A	Retrd.	1991	11.50	39-175
1992 Christmas Ornament 788F	Retrd.	1992	23.50	39-150
1993 Christmas Ornament 892P	Retrd.	1993	25.00	39-125
1994 Christmas Ornament-Christmas 801P	Retrd.	1994	25.00	34-68
1995 Christmas Ornament-Gifts & Snow 640P	Retrd.	1995	30.00	39-100
1996 Christmas Ornament-A Sweet Christmas 355P	Retrd.	1996	30.00	100
1997 Christmas Ornament-Christmas Snow 137F	Retrd.	1998	37.50	38-50
1998 Christmas Ornament-Christmas Eve 123F	Retrd.	1998	35.00	70
1999 Christmas Ornament-Cappy 355F	Retrd.	1999	37.50	38-50
2000 Christmas Ornament-Frosty 1327F	Retrd.	2000	35.00	35
2001 Christmas Ornament-Christmas Melody 1472F	Retrd.	2001	35.00	35
2002 Christmas Ornament-Christmas Star 1490F	Yr.Iss.		35.00	35

Bing & Grondahl

Christmas - Various

1985 Christmas Eve at the Farmhouse - E. Jensen	Closed	1985	19.50	30
1986 Silent Night, Holy Night - E. Jensen	Closed	1986	19.50	30
1987 The Snowman's Christmas Eve - E. Jensen	Closed	1987	22.50	23-28
1988 In the King's Garden - E. Jensen	Closed	1988	25.00	27-30
1989 Christmas Anchorage - E. Jensen	Closed	1989	27.00	27-30
1990 Changing of the Guards - E. Jensen	Closed	1990	32.50	33-35
1991 Copenhagen Stock Exchange - E. Jensen	Closed	1991	34.50	35
1992 Christmas at the Rectory - J. Steensen	Closed	1992	36.50	37-39
1993 Father Christmas in Copenhagen - J. Nielsen	Closed	1993	36.50	37
1994 A Day at the Deer Park - J. Nielsen	Closed	1994	36.50	38
1995 The Towers of Copenhagen - J. Nielsen	Closed	1995	37.50	45
1996 Winter at the Old Mill - J. Nielsen	Closed	1996	37.50	32-45
1997 Country Christmas - J. Nielsen	Closed	1998	37.50	32-38
1998 Santa the Storyteller - J. Nielsen	Closed	1998	37.50	32-38
1999 Around the Christmas Tree - J. Nielsen	Closed	1999	39.50	32-40
2000 Ringing at the Bell Tower - J. Nielsen	Closed	2000	39.50	40
2001 Playing in the Snow - J. Nielsen	Annual		39.50	40

YEAR ISSUE	EDITION LIMIT	YEAR RETD.	ISSUE PRICE	*QUOTE U.S.$
Christmas Around the World - H. Hansen				
1995 Santa in Greenland	Yr.Iss.	1995	25.00	29-45
1996 Santa in Orient	Yr.Iss.	1996	25.00	30
1997 Santa in Russia	Yr.Iss.	1997	25.00	30
1998 Santa in Australia	Yr.Iss.	1998	25.00	25-29
1999 Santa in Europe	Yr.Iss.	1999	27.50	20-28
2000 Santa in America	Yr.Iss.	2000	27.50	23-28
Christmas In America - J. Woodson				
1986 Christmas Eve in Williamsburg	Closed	1986	12.50	126
1987 Christmas Eve at the White House	Closed	1987	15.00	10-21
1988 Christmas Eve at Rockefeller Center	Closed	1988	18.50	10-21
1989 Christmas Eve in New England	Closed	1989	20.00	10-21
1990 Christmas Eve at the Capitol	Closed	1990	20.00	10-45
1991 Independence Hall	Closed	1991	23.50	10-30
1992 Christmas in San Francisco	Closed	1992	25.00	10-30
1993 Coming Home For Christmas	Closed	1993	25.00	10-30
1994 Christmas Eve in Alaska	Closed	1994	25.00	10-30
1995 Christmas Eve in Mississippi	Closed	1995	25.00	10-30
Santa Claus - H. Hansen				
1989 Santa's Workshop	Yr.Iss.	1989	20.00	49-54
1990 Santa's Sleigh	Yr.Iss.	1990	20.00	49-75
1991 The Journey	Yr.Iss.	1991	24.00	51-54
1992 Santa's Arrival	Yr.Iss.	1992	25.00	49
1993 Santa's Gifts	Yr.Iss.	1993	25.00	25-49
1994 Christmas Stories	Yr.Iss.	1994	25.00	30-49
The Snow Fairies - K. Seeberg				
2001 The Snow Fairies	Annual		28.00	28
2001 The Snow Fairies Figurine Ornament	Annual		37.00	37

Boyds Collection Ltd.

The Bearstone Collection™ - G.M. Lowenthal, unless otherwise noted

	EDITION LIMIT	YEAR RETD.	ISSUE PRICE	*QUOTE U.S.$
2000 Angelbrite 25731 - The Boyds Collection	Retrd.	2001	10.50	11
1998 Baby's Christmas 25954	Retrd.	1998	13.00	13
1998 bailey...home sweet home 25708	Open		11.00	11
2001 Belle with Dolly...Bow Perfect 25751 - The Boyds Collection	Open		10.50	11
2001 Big Ben...Victory Lap 25745 - The Boyds Collection	Open		10.50	11
2001 Casey's Siren Ride...Where's the Fire? 25743 - The Boyds Collection	Open		10.50	11
1998 Celestina...peace angel 25710	Retrd.	1999	10.00	10
1999 Chandler, Constance & Felicity ...A Brighter World 25723	Retrd.	2000	21.00	21
1994 'Charity' 2502, 'Faith' 2500, 'Hope' 2501, set/3	Retrd.	1996	28.35	60-94
1994 'Charity'-Angel Bear with Star 2502	Retrd.	1996	9.45	38
1996 Clair w/gingerbread man 25701	Retrd.	1998	11.00	11-20
1999 Doc Buzzby...Bee Healthy 25716	Retrd.	2001	10.00	10
1995 'Edmund'...Believe 2505	Retrd.	1998	11.00	11
1995 'Edmund'...Believe 2505	Retrd.	1997	9.45	38
1996 Edmund-Clair-Winston 25700-25701-25702	Retrd.	1998	11.00	11-20
1995 'Elliot with Tree' 2507	Retrd.	1997	9.45	38
2001 Elmer's Chugalong...On the Right Track 25744 - The Boyds Collection	Open		10.50	11
1994 'Faith'-Angel Bear with Trumpet 2500	Retrd.	1996	9.45	38
1998 george & gracie...forever 25707	Open		11.00	11
2001 Ginger's Holiday Garland...Baker's Delight 25747 - The Boyds Collection	Open		10.50	11
1999 Grenville & Beatrice...Our Christmas 25722	Retrd.	2000	13.00	13
2000 Hansel 25730 - The Boyds Collection	Retrd.	2001	10.50	11
1994 'Hope'-Angel Bear with Wreath 2501	Retrd.	1996	9.45	38
2001 Hy Hoopster...Jump For It 25739 - The Boyds Collection	Open		10.50	11
2001 Jingles...Ring in the Cheer 25750 - The Boyds Collection	Open		10.50	11
1998 Juliette...love angel 25712	Retrd.	1999	10.00	10
1998 Knute...half time 25705	Retrd.	1999	11.00	13-15
2001 Kyle Beariman...Spicy Treat 25748 - The Boyds Collection	Open		10.50	11
1998 Larry...Nutin But Net 25706	Retrd.	1999	11.00	11-15
1995 'Manheim' the Moose with Wreath 2506	Retrd.	1997	9.45	44

YEAR ISSUE	EDITION LIMIT	YEAR RETD.	ISSUE PRICE	*QUOTE U.S.$
1999 Mario..Hat Trick 25718	Retrd.	2000	11.00	11-13
1997 Matthew with Kip (Baby's 1st Christmas) 2508	Retrd.	1997	9.45	22-27
1999 McDuffer...The 19th Hole 25719	Retrd.	2000	11.00	11
1999 McGwire...it's out of here 25717	Retrd.	2001	11.00	11-18
2001 Miss Macintosh...Teacher's Rule 25740 - The Boyds Collection	Open		10.50	11
2001 Mr. Baybeary...2001 Wishes 25752 - The Boyds Collection	Retrd.	2001	10.50	11
2001 Mysteri Bearlove...Special Wishes 25742 - The Boyds Collection	Open		10.50	11
2001 Naomi Chart Keeper...Nurses Have Patience 25741 - The Boyds Collection	Open		10.50	11
1998 Noel Bruinski...da electrician 25953	Retrd.	1998	13.00	13-49
2001 Pendleton Goalscore...Let's Play 25738 - The Boyds Collection	Open		10.50	11
2001 Putter T. Parfore...Birdie This Bogie That 25736 - The Boyds Collection	Open		10.00	10
1998 Regina d. ferrisdavel...I AM the queen 25709	Retrd.	1999	11.00	11-22
1998 rocky...score, score, score 25704	Open		11.00	11-15
1999 Sage Buzzby...Bee Wis 25715	Retrd.	2001	10.00	10
1998 Serendipity "Peace" to all 25955	Retrd.	1998	21.00	21-35
2001 Simon...Icing Touches 25746 - The Boyds Collection	Open		10.50	11
2000 Snowbearski 25729 - The Boyds Collection	Retrd.	2001	10.50	11
2001 T.D. Gridiron...Touch Down! 25737 - The Boyds Collection	Open		10.50	11
2001 Tinker...A Few Little Taps 25749 - The Boyds Collection	Open		10.50	11
1996 Wilson w/shooting star 25702	Retrd.	1998	11.00	11-20
1997 Zoe Starlight Christmas (GCC Exclusive) 25951	Retrd.	1997	21.50	32

The Charming Angels - The Boyds Collection

	EDITION LIMIT	YEAR RETD.	ISSUE PRICE	*QUOTE U.S.$
2001 Aurora...Guardian of Dreams 25101	Open		14.00	14
2001 Floramella...Guardian of Nature 25102	Open		14.00	14
2001 Viviana...Guardian of Love 25103	Open		14.00	14

The Dollstone Collection™ - G.M. Lowenthal, unless otherwise noted

	EDITION LIMIT	YEAR RETD.	ISSUE PRICE	*QUOTE U.S.$
1999 Amy & Sam...Baby's First Christmas 25857	Retrd.	2000	12.00	25-38
1999 Betsey...the Patriot 25854	Retrd.	2000	11.00	22-41
2000 Calamity...Whoa is Me 25860 - The Boyds Collection	Retrd.	2000	11.00	11
1998 Jean with elliot...the bakers 25852	Retrd.	1999	10.00	10
1999 Katerine...Kind Heart 25853	Retrd.	2000	11.00	11-24
2000 Lara...Moscow at Midnight 25859	Retrd.	2000	10.50	11
1998 Megan with elliot...christmas carol 25850	Retrd.	1999	10.00	10-23
1999 Michelle...Reading is Fun 25855	Retrd.	1999	11.00	11-24
1999 Ryan and Diane...Love is Forever 25856	Retrd.	1999	12.00	12-25
2000 Samantha w/Conner...Best Friends 25861 - The Boyds Collection	Retrd.	2000	10.50	11
1999 Shannon...Christmas at Grandma's 25858	Retrd.	1999	12.00	12-25

Faeriessence - G.M. Lowenthal, unless otherwise noted

	EDITION LIMIT	YEAR RETD.	ISSUE PRICE	*QUOTE U.S.$
2001 Flurry Frost...Winter Dusting 25811 - The Boyds Collection	Open		11.00	11
2000 giselle 25803 - The Boyds Collection	Retrd.	2001	11.00	11-27
2001 Holly Faerieberry...Holiday Gathering 25810 - The Boyds Collection	Open		11.00	11
2000 margot 25802 - The Boyds Collection	Retrd.	2001	11.00	11-27
1998 olivia...wishing you peace 25800	Retrd.	1999	12.00	14-35
2001 Sienna Faerieleaf...Touch of Fall 25812 - The Boyds Collection	Open		11.00	11
2000 twila 25801 - The Boyds Collection	Retrd.	2001	11.00	11-27

The Folkstone Collection™ - G.M. Lowenthal, unless otherwise noted

	EDITION LIMIT	YEAR RETD.	ISSUE PRICE	*QUOTE U.S.$
1997 axel...thou shalt not melt! 25652	Retrd.	1998	12.00	14-35
1998 Barnaby...homeward bound 370001	Open		10.00	10
1999 Birdie...fore! 25661	Retrd.	1999	11.00	15-22
1998 Bjorn w/Nils & Sven 25654	Retrd.	2000	12.00	16-32
1998 Burt...Bundle Up 370202	Open		10.00	10
1996 Chilly with wreath 2564	Retrd.	1998	10.00	10
1995 Father Christmas 2553	Retrd.	1997	9.45	10-25
1997 Ingrid... be warm 25651	Retrd.	1998	12.00	12

YEAR ISSUE	EDITION LIMIT	YEAR RETD.	ISSUE PRICE	*QUOTE U.S.$
1997 Jacques...Starlight Skier 25950	Retrd.	1997	21.00	21-45
1995 Jean Claude & Jacque...the Skiers 2561	Retrd.	1997	9.45	32
1995 Jingles the Snowman with Wreath 2562	Retrd.	1997	9.45	32
1998 Lars...ski, ski, ski 25653	Retrd.	2000	12.00	15-26
1999 Laverne...On Strike 25659	Retrd.	2000	11.00	15-21
1999 Madge....Magic Scissors 25658	Retrd.	2000	11.00	11
1999 Mercy...Night Shift Nurse 25656	Retrd.	2000	11.00	11
1997 Mistletoe & Holly Snowball 25900	Retrd.	1997	14.00	14
1999 Ms Patience...Inspiration Teacher 25657	Retrd.	2000	11.00	11-15
1999 Myron...the Angler 25660	Retrd.	1999	11.00	11-15
1998 Nanuk...winter wonderland 25956	Yr.Iss.		21.00	22
1995 Nicholai with Tree 2550	Retrd.	1997	9.45	38
1995 Nicholas the Giftgiver 2551	Retrd.	1997	9.45	32
1995 Olaf...Let it Snow 2560	Retrd.	1997	9.45	38
1997 Olaf...let it snow 25650	Retrd.	1998	12.00	12
1998 robin...peace on earth 25655	Retrd.	1998	12.00	12-15
1998 Santa & the final inspection 370203	Open		10.00	10
1998 Santa in the Nick of time 370200	Open		10.00	10
1998 Santa...Quick as a flash 370204	Open		10.00	10
1995 Sliknick in the Chimney 2552	Retrd.	1997	9.45	32
1996 Willy with broom 2565	Retrd.	1998	10.00	10
1996 Windy with Tree 2563	Retrd.	1998	10.00	10

Moose Troop - The Boyds Collection

2001 Dale and Ilona...Under the Mooseltoe 25002	Open		10.50	11
2001 Mattie Frostbuns...Triple Klutz 25001	Open		10.50	11
2001 Murdock Mufflemoose...Second Thoughts 25003	Open		10.50	11

The Purrstone Collection™ - The Boyds Collection

2001 Caterina's Stockin' Up...Yummy Catch 271803	Open		10.50	11
2000 Felicity Angelpuss...Peace on Earth 271802	Retrd.	2001	10.50	11
2001 Fuzzywig's Round Up...Strike a Merry Cord 271804	Open		10.50	11
2001 Penny Copperpuss...A New Suit 271805	Open		10.50	11

Snow Dooodes - The Boyds Collection

2001 Frostbite...One Flake 25052	Open		10.50	11
2001 Hillary Smoothrider...Easy Slopes 25050	Open		10.50	11
2001 Willy B. Speedy...Winged Friends 25051	Open		10.50	11

Calico Kittens/Enesco Group, Inc.

Calico Kittens - P. Hillman

1993 Baby's First Christmas (Boy) 628204	Retrd.	1997	16.00	16
1993 Baby's First Christmas (Girl) 628255	Retrd.	1997	16.00	16
1995 Cat in stocking wearing a red Santa's hat 144304	Yr.Iss.	1995	16.00	16
1993 Cat With Blue Hat 623814	Retrd.	1997	11.00	11
1993 Cat With Green Hat 623814	Retrd.	1997	11.00	11
1993 Cat With Red Hat 623814	Retrd.	1997	11.00	11
2000 Dated Ornament 720771	Yr.Iss.	2000	10.00	10
1994 First Christmas Together 651346	Yr.Iss.	1997	15.00	15
1994 Grey Kitten as Santa 625280	Yr.Iss.	1994	12.50	13
2002 Have Yourself a Meow-y Little Christmas 104052	Yr.Iss.		10.00	10
1994 Joy To The World 651354	Retrd.	1997	13.50	14
1998 Kitten in Knitted Mitten 359645	Yr.Iss.	1998	10.00	10
1999 Kitten in Shoe 543489	Yr.Iss.	1999	10.00	10
1996 Kitten in Wreath 178551	Yr.Iss.	1996	10.00	10
1996 Kitty And Me 178543	Retrd.	1996	17.50	18
1996 My Spoiled Kitty 178535	Retrd.	1996	17.50	18
1995 Our First Christmas Together 144282	Retrd.	1999	13.50	14
1994 Peace On Earth 651354	Retrd.	1997	13.50	14
1993 Tan Angel Kitten Reading to a Mouse 627534	Retrd.	1998	12.50	13
1993 White Girl Kitten w/Sewing Basket 628220	Yr.Iss.	1993	12.50	13

Cat in the Act - P. Hillman

1999 Domestic Shorthair 543438	Closed	1999	8.50	9
1999 Himalayan 543373	Closed	1999	8.50	9
1999 Ragdoll 543411	Closed	1999	8.50	9
1999 Scottish Fold 543365	Closed	1999	8.50	9

YEAR ISSUE	EDITION LIMIT	YEAR RETD.	ISSUE PRICE	*QUOTE U.S.$
1999 Siamese 543357	Closed	1999	8.50	9
1999 White Persian 543314	Closed	1999	8.50	9

Festive Felines - P. Hillman

2002 Christmas With Mew Baby 104085	Open		7.50	8
2002 Favorite Teacher 104084	Open		7.50	8
2002 Our First Christmas Together 104088	Open		7.50	8
2002 Welcome To Our New Home 104087	Open		7.50	8

I Love My Kitty - P. Hillman

1995 Bird-Seed From Kitty 144355	Retrd.	1998	11.00	11
1995 I Love My Cat 144320	Retrd.	1998	11.00	11
1995 To My Cat 144398	Retrd.	1998	11.00	11
1995 To My Kitty 144274	Retrd.	1998	11.00	11

Itty Bitty Kitties - P. Hillman

1998 3 Asst. Itty Bitty Kitty 360260	Retrd.	1999	7.50	8

Kittie's Christmas - P. Hillman

2001 3 Asst. Kittie's Christmas 360260	Open		6.00	6

Charming Tails/Fitz and Floyd Collectibles

Blown Glass Ornaments - D. Griff

2001 By The Light Of The Moon 95/107	Open		19.00	19
2001 Caps Off To You 95/113	3,000	2001	15.00	15
2001 Christmas Stocking Surprise 95/109	Open		19.00	19
2001 Close Knit Friends 95/108	Open		20.00	20
2002 Coo Coo For Christmas 95/128	Open		18.00	18
2002 Fluttery Friends 95/135	Open		18.00	18
2001 Holdin On 95/105	Open		19.00	19
2001 Holiday Ribbon 95/117	3,000	2001	15.00	15
2001 Holiday Trimmings 95/118	3,000	2001	15.00	15
2001 Holly-Days 95/114	3,000	2001	15.00	15
2001 King Of My Heart (lg.) 95/102	3,000	2001	26.00	26
2001 King Of My Heart (sm.) 95/100	3,000	2001	18.00	18
2001 A Love For All Seasons 95/110	Open		20.00	20
2001 Lucky Lydia 95/120	3,000	2001	15.00	15
2001 My Shining Star 95/106	Open		19.00	19
2001 Nutty For The Holidays 95/111	Open		19.00	19
2001 Queen Of My Heart (lg.) 95/103	3,000	2001	26.00	26
2001 Queen Of My Heart (sm.) 95/101	3,000	2001	18.00	18
2001 Ringing In The Season 95/116	3,000	2001	15.00	15
2002 Rubber Ducky 95/134	Open		18.00	18
2002 Santa-Mouse Sleigh 95/130	Open		20.00	20
2001 Sidney's Special Gift 95/121	3,000	2001	15.00	15
2002 Snow-Mouse 95/125	Open		18.00	18
2002 Stacks Of Joy 95/123	Open		18.00	18
2001 Star Bright 95/115	3,000	2001	15.00	15
2002 A Star To Guide You 95/126	Open		18.00	18
2002 You're The Perfect Gift 95/104	Open		19.00	19

Charming Tails Everyday Ornaments - D. Griff

1994 Binkey in the Berry Patch 89/752	Closed	1996	12.00	32-44
1995 Hello, Sweet Pea 87/367	Closed	1997	12.00	13-42
1995 I Am Full 87/365	Closed	1997	15.00	15-30
1994 Maxine Pick Strawberries 89/562	Closed	1997	15.00	18-35
1993 Maxine's Butterfly Ride 89/190	Open		16.50	18
1993 Mouse on a Bee 89/191	Closed	1994	16.50	225-360
1993 Mouse on a Dragonfly 89/320	Closed	1994	16.50	400-960
1995 Picking Peppers 87/369	Closed	1997	12.00	13-18
1994 Springtime Showers (3 pc.) 89/563	Closed	1996	10.00	25-36
1995 This Is Hot! 87/366	Closed	1997	15.00	16-20

Charming Tails Spring - D. Griff

1994 Easter Parade 89/615	Closed	1996	10.00	10-27
1994 Peek-a-boo 89/753	Closed	1996	12.00	12-40

Charming Tails Trim a Tree - D. Griff

1991 Sticky Situations (2 pc.) 87/991	Closed	1995	16.00	60
1992 Catching ZZZ's 86/785	Closed	1995	12.00	32-52
1992 Chickadees on Ball 86/787	Closed	1995	13.50	110-150
1992 The Drifters (2 pc.) 86/784	Closed	1996	12.00	35-88
1992 Fresh Fruit (3 pc.) 86/789	Closed	1995	12.00	12-90
1992 Mice/Rabbit Ball (2 pc.) 86/788	Closed	1995	12.00	85-150
1992 Mice in Leaf Sleigh 86/786	Closed	1995	26.00	300-360
1993 Bunny & Mouse Bell (2 pc.) 87/038	Closed	1995	10.50	81
1993 Chick with Bead Garland 86/791	Closed	1995	17.50	86-250
1993 Hang in There (3 pc.) 87/941	Closed	1996	10.00	35
1993 Holiday Wreath (2 pc.) 87/939	Closed	1995	12.00	45-80
1993 Mackenzie Napping 87/940	Closed	1995	12.00	27-45

ORNAMENTS

Charming Tails/Fitz and Floyd Collectibles
to Cherished Teddies/Enesco Group, Inc.

YEAR ISSUE	EDITION LIMIT	YEAR RETD.	ISSUE PRICE	*QUOTE U.S.$
1993 Maxine Lights a Candle 87/942	Closed	1995	11.00	25-42
1993 Mouse on Snowflake (lighted) 87/037	Closed	1995	11.00	35-47
1993 Mouse w/Apple Candleholder (2 pc.) 87/044	Closed	1995	13.00	160-188
1993 Porcelain Mouse Bell 87/036	Closed	1995	5.00	5
1994 Baby's First Christmas 87/184	Closed	1994	12.00	25-41
1994 Binkey & Reginald on Ice (2 pc.) 87/924	Closed	1994	10.00	88-95
1994 Friends in Flight 87/971	Closed	1994	18.00	126
1994 The Grape Escape (grape) 87/186	Closed	1995	18.00	53-88
1994 The Grape Escape (green) 87/186	Closed	1995	18.00	58-75
1994 High Flying Mackenzie 87/992	Closed	1997	20.00	21-65
1994 Holiday Lights 87/969	Closed	1995	10.00	45-88
1994 Horsin' Around 87/202	Closed	1996	18.00	25-65
1994 Mackenzie and Binkey's Snack (cherry & plum) 87/187	Closed	1994	12.00	120-150
1994 Mackenzie Blowing Bubbles 87/191	Closed	1994	12.00	40-107
1994 Mackenzie on Ice 87/970	Closed	1996	10.00	33-40
1994 Mackenzie's Bubble Ride 87/192	Closed	1996	13.00	35-52
1994 Mackenzie's Snowball (dated) 87/994	Closed	1994	12.00	88-114
1994 Maxine and Mackenzie (2 pc.) 87/185	Closed	1996	12.00	29-88
1994 Reginald's Bubble Ride 87/199	Closed	1994	12.00	41
1994 Reginald On Ice 87/924	Closed	1994	10.00	88
1994 Apple House (lighted) 87/032	Closed	1995	13.00	55-100
1994 Pear House (lighted) 87/027	Closed	1995	13.00	68-100
1994 Mouse on Yellow Bulb (lighted) 87/045	Closed	1995	10.00	88-110
1994 Mouse Star Treetop 87/958	Closed	1995	10.00	50-82
1995 1995 Annual 87/306	Closed	1995	16.00	16-32
1995 Binkey's Poinsettia 87/303	Closed	1997	12.00	13-42
1995 Christmas Cookies (3 pc.) 87/301	Closed	1999	10.00	20-42
1995 Christmas Flowers 87/304	Closed	2000	12.00	13
1995 Holiday Balloon Ride 87/299	Closed	1996	16.00	30-38
1995 Mackenzie's Whirligig 87/300	Closed	1997	20.00	20-44
1995 Peppermint Party (2 pc.) 87/314	Closed	1997	10.00	11-25
1995 Reginald in Leaves (2 pc.) 87/302	Closed	1997	10.00	11-25
1995 Stewart at Play 87/308	Closed	1995	12.00	30-36
1995 Stewart's Winter Fun (2 pc.) 87/307	Closed	1995	10.00	24-36
1996 1996 Annual-All Wrapped Up 87/471	Closed	1996	12.00	20-31
1996 Baby's First Christmas 87/850	Closed	1996	13.00	20-25
1996 Christmas Stamps 87/485	Closed	1997	12.00	13-30
1996 Our First Christmas (dated) 87/532	Closed	1996	18.00	32-38
1996 Fallen Angel 87/492	Closed	1997	12.00	13-42
1996 Flights of Fancy 87/490	Closed	1997	12.00	13-25
1996 Frequent Flyer 87/491	Closed	1997	12.00	13-33
1996 Letter to Santa 87/486	Closed	1997	12.00	13-37
1996 Stamp Dispenser 87/483	Closed	2000	12.00	13
1996 Weeeeee! 87/493	Closed	1997	12.00	13-25
1997 All Lit Up (lighted) 86/660	Open		11.00	13
1997 Chauncey's First Christmas 86/710	Closed	1997	9.00	9-20
1997 Mackenzie In Mitten 86/704	Closed	2000	9.00	8-11
1997 Our First Christmas (dated) 86/708	Closed	1997	18.00	32-38
1997 1997 Annual-Mackenzie's Jack in the Box 86/709	Closed	1997	10.00	10
1997 Maxine's Angel 86/701	Closed	2000	9.00	8-11
1997 Our First Christmas 86/708	Closed	1997	12.50	12-16
1997 A Special Delivery 86/707	Closed	2000	9.00	8-10
1998 Air Mail To Santa 86/652	Closed	2000	13.00	13-20
1998 Our First Christmas Together 86/653	Closed	1998	12.00	12-15
1998 Bundle of Joy - Baby's First Christmas 86/655	Closed	1998	12.00	12-20
1998 Heading For The Slopes 86/656	Closed	2001	13.00	13
1998 Ski Jumper 86/657	Closed	2000	13.00	13
1998 Tricycle Built From Treats 86/658	Closed	1998	13.00	13
1998 Pine Cone Predicament 86/659	Closed	1998	11.00	11-20
1999 Baby's First Christmas 86/792	Closed	1999	11.50	12-49
1999 Binkey's Candy Cane Flyer 86/793	Open		11.50	12
1999 A Cup of Christmas Cheer 86/796	Open		11.50	12
1999 Snowbird 86/797	Closed	1999	11.50	12
2000 2000 Annual Snowflakes 86/100	Yr.Iss.	2000	11.50	12
2000 Baby's First (Bootie Baby) 86/101	Closed	2000	11.50	12
2000 Holiday Baking (Mother & Son) 86/102	Open		11.50	12
2000 Our First Christmas 86/103	Open		11.50	12
2000 Teacher 86/104	Closed	2000	11.50	12
2000 Weeee...Three Kings! 86/105	Open		11.50	12
2001 Candy Cane, Two Pack Gift Set 86/106	Open		18.50	19
2001 Christmas Carousel 86/107	Yr.Iss.	2001	11.50	12
2001 Christmas Is a Ball With You 86/108	Yr.Iss.	2001	12.00	12

YEAR ISSUE	EDITION LIMIT	YEAR RETD.	ISSUE PRICE	*QUOTE U.S.$
2001 Fa La La 86/109	Open		12.00	12
2001 Holiday Wreath 86/110	Yr.Iss.	2001	11.50	12
2001 Stringing Popcorn 86/111	Open		11.50	12
2001 You're Just "Write" For Me 86/112	Yr.Iss.	2001	11.50	12
2002 A World Of Learning 86/114	Open		12.00	12
2001 Yuded Tied Sweetie 86/113	Open		12.00	12
2002 Four Calling Birds 86/4	Open		12.00	12
2002 Is It Christmas Yet 86/117	Open		14.00	14
2002 Flying In For The Holidays 86/122	Open		12.00	12
2002 Candy Cane Bunnies 86/116	Open		18.50	19
2002 Holdin' Tight For The Holly-Day 86/123	Open		12.00	12
2002 Holly Ornament Stand 93/502	Open		16.00	16
2002 Jingle Bell Baby 86/115	Yr.Iss.		12.00	12
2002 Key To The Holidays 86/118	Open		12.00	12
2002 MacKenzie Marionette 86/119	Open		12.00	12
2002 Our First Christmas 86/120	Yr.Iss.		12.00	12
2002 A Partridge In A Pear Tree 86/1	Open		12.00	12
2002 Snow Cone 86/121	Yr.Iss.		12.00	12
2002 Three French Hens 86/3	Open		12.00	12
2002 Two Turtle Doves 86/2	Open		12.00	12

Cherished Teddies/Enesco Group, Inc.

Across The Seas - P. Hillman

1998 American Boy 451010	Closed	1999	10.00	10
1998 Australian Boy 464120	Closed	1999	10.00	10
1998 Canadian Boy 451053	Closed	1999	10.00	10
1998 Chinese Boy 450960	Closed	1999	10.00	10
1998 Dutch Girl 450995	Closed	1999	10.00	10
1998 English Boy 451045	Closed	1999	10.00	10
1998 French Girl "Joyeux Noel!" 450901	Closed	1999	10.00	10
1998 German Boy 451002	Closed	1999	10.00	10
1998 Indian Girl 450987	Closed	1999	10.00	10
1998 Italian Girl 464112	Closed	1999	10.00	10
1998 Japanese Girl 450936	Closed	1999	10.00	10
1998 Mexican Boy 450952	Closed	1999	10.00	10
1998 Russian Girl 450944	Closed	1999	10.00	10
1998 Scottish Girl 451029	Closed	1999	10.00	10
1998 Spanish Boy 450979	Closed	1999	10.00	10
1998 Swedish Girl 450928	Closed	1999	10.00	10

Cherished Snowbears - P. Hillman

2001 Snowman 865044	Yr.Iss.	2001	12.00	12

Cherished Teddies - P. Hillman

1992 Angel 950777	Suspd.		12.50	39-69
1992 Bear In Stocking (dated) 950653	Yr.Iss.	1992	16.00	25-46
1992 Beth On Rocking Reindeer 950793	Suspd.		20.00	38-64
1992 Christmas Sister Bears, 3 asst. 951226	Suspd.		12.50	19-34
1993 Angel, 3 Asst. 912980	Suspd.		12.50	17-60
1993 Baby Boy (dated) 913014	Yr.Iss.	1993	12.50	22-39
1993 Baby Girl (dated) 913006	Yr.Iss.	1993	12.50	25-39
1993 Girl w/Muff (Alice) (dated) 912832	Yr.Iss.	1993	13.50	50-75
1993 Jointed Teddy Bear 914894	Suspd.		12.50	21-39
1994 Baby in Basket (dated) 617253	Yr.Iss.	1994	15.00	30-39
1994 Bundled Up For The Holidays "Our First Christmas" (dated) 617229	Yr.Iss.	1994	15.00	28-32
1994 Drummer Boy (dated) 912891	Yr.Iss.	1994	10.00	25-30
1995 Baby Angel on Cloud "Baby's First Christmas" 141240	Open		13.50	14-22
1995 Elf Bear W/Doll 625434	Suspd.		12.50	13-27
1995 Boy Bear Flying Cupid "Sending You My Heart" 103608	Suspd.		13.00	25-38
1995 Boy/Girl with Banner "Our First Christmas" 141259	Open		13.50	14-40
1995 Elf Bear W/Stuffed Reindeer 625442	Suspd.		12.50	13-27
1995 Elf Bears/Candy Cane 651389	Suspd.		12.50	13-27
1995 Girl Bear Flying Cupid "Sending You My Heart" 103616	Suspd.		13.00	13-30
1995 Mrs Claus Xmas Holding Tray/Cookies 625426	Suspd.		12.50	13-32
1995 Teddies Santa Bear 651370	Open		12.50	13
1995 Teddy with Ice Skates (dated) 141232	Yr.Iss.	1995	12.50	15-34
1996 Bear w/Dangling Mittens 177768	Open		12.50	13-26
1996 Toy Soldier (dated) 176052	Yr.Iss.	1996	12.50	20-22
1997 Dangling Snowflake (dated) 272175	Yr.Iss.	1997	12.50	22-25
1998 Bear in Picnic Basket 406627	Closed	1999	12.50	13
1998 Bear in Wagon 400793	Closed	1999	12.50	13-17

ORNAMENTS

YEAR ISSUE	EDITION LIMIT	YEAR RETRD.	ISSUE PRICE	*QUOTE U.S.$
1998 Bear on Kitchen Hutch 406481 (Special Limited Editon)	Closed	1998	12.50	13
1998 Bear on Train 401196	Closed	1999	12.50	13
1998 Bears on Sled 406635	Closed	1999	12.50	13
1998 Gingerbread Bear 352748	Yr.Iss.	1998	12.50	13-24
1998 Two Bears w/Teacup & Saucer 406473	Closed	1999	12.50	13-17
1999 Eskimo Holding Fish (dated 1999) 534161	Yr.Iss.	1999	25.00	25-32
1999 Teddy Bear/Drum 546550	Retrd.	1999	Gift	N/A
2000 Eskimo Holding Fish (dated 2000) 536377	Yr.Iss.	2000	25.00	25-32
2000 Dated Ornament 706663	Yr.Iss.	2000	12.50	13
2001 Baby Wrapped In Blanket 864242	Yr.Iss.	2001	10.00	10
2001 Two Bears Hugging in Heart 865001	Yr.Iss.	2001	10.00	10
2001 Plush Bear Ornament 867292	Open		15.00	15
2002 Jack Frost 104142	Yr.Iss.		12.00	12
2002 Baby's First Christmas 865028	Yr.Iss.		12.00	12

Christopher Radko

Christopher Radko Family of Collectors - C. Radko

YEAR ISSUE	EDITION LIMIT	YEAR RETRD.	ISSUE PRICE	*QUOTE U.S.$
1993 Angels We Have Heard on High SP1	Retrd.	1993	50.00	188-600
1994 Starbuck Santa SP3	Retrd.	1994	75.00	250-350
1995 Dash Away All SP7	Retrd.	1995	34.00	40-84
1995 Purrfect Present SP8	Retrd.	1995	Gift	36-85
1996 Christmas Magic SP13	Retrd.	1996	50.00	82-192
1996 Frosty Weather SP14	Retrd.	1996	Gift	45-54
1997 Enchanted Evening SP20	Retrd.	1997	55.00	40-70
1997 Li'l Miss Angel SP21	Retrd.	1997	Gift	50
1998 Candy Castle SP36	Retrd.	1998	70.00	70-82
1998 Mouse Wrap SP32	Retrd.	1998	Gift	N/A
1999 No Time Like The Present 99SP54	Yr.Iss.	1999	Gift	N/A
2000 Starlight Guardian 00-SP-69	Yr.Iss.	2000	Gift	N/A
2001 Starlight Express 01-0184	Yr.Iss.	2001	Gift	N/A

10 Year Anniversary - C. Radko

YEAR ISSUE	EDITION LIMIT	YEAR RETRD.	ISSUE PRICE	*QUOTE U.S.$
1995 On Top of the World SP6	Yr.Iss.	1995	32.00	75-85

Event Only - C. Radko

YEAR ISSUE	EDITION LIMIT	YEAR RETRD.	ISSUE PRICE	*QUOTE U.S.$
1993 Littlest Snowman 347S (store & C. Radko event)	Retrd.	1993	15.00	33
1994 Roly Poly 94125E (store & C. Radko event)	Retrd.	1994	22.00	29-65
1995 Forever Lucy 91075E (store & C. Radko event)	Retrd.	1995	32.00	43-60
1996 Poinsettia Elegance 287E (store event)	Retrd.	1996	32.00	32-79
1996 A Job Well Done SP18 (C. Radko event)	Retrd.	1996	30.00	35-60
1997 Little Golden Hood 97-261E (store event)	Retrd.	1997	39.00	39-90
1997 Merry Travelers SP27 (C. Radko event)	Retrd.	1997	44.00	44
1998 Elf Secrets 98-306E (store event)	Retrd.	1998	47.00	47
1999 Mrs. Iceberg 99SP52 (spring event)	Yr.Iss.	1999	30.00	30
1999 Mr. Iceberg 99SP51 (fall event)	Yr.Iss.	1999	30.00	30
2000 Billy Bunny Goes Shopping 00-SP-74 (national rep. Event)	Yr.Iss.	2000	38.00	38
2000 Flower Power 00-SP-67 (spring event)	Yr.Iss.	2000	47.00	47
2000 Santa Suits Billy Bunny 00-1264-0 (national rep. Event - autumn)	Yr.Iss.	2000	36.00	36
2000 Greenhouse Greetings 00-SP-68 (autumn event)	Yr.Iss.	2000	36.00	36
2000 Mary Mischief 00-MC-01 (national rep. training director event)	Yr.Iss.	2000	33.00	33
2000 Skiin' Steve 00-SDB-01 (corporate promotional rep. event)	Yr.Iss.	2000	32.00	32
2001 Spring Chillin' 01-SP-85 (spring event)	Yr.Iss.	2001	34.00	34
2001 Chillin' Treats 01-SP-86 (fall event)	Yr.Iss.	2001	36.00	36
2001 Hilly Billy Bunny 01-SP-07 (national rep. Event - spring)	Yr.Iss.	2001	36.00	36
2001 Chilly Billy 01-SP-88 (national rep. Event - fall)	Yr.Iss.	2001	35.00	35
2002 Billy Doodle Dandy 02-SP-92 (national rep. Event - spring)	Yr.Iss.		38.00	38
2002 Forest Flutter 02-SP-98 (store event)	Yr.Iss.		48.00	48

1986 Holiday Collection - C. Radko

YEAR ISSUE	EDITION LIMIT	YEAR RETRD.	ISSUE PRICE	*QUOTE U.S.$
1986 Alpine Flowers 40-0	Retrd.	N/A	16.00	60-125
1986 Big Top 48-1	Retrd.	1988	15.00	75-150
1986 Deep Sea 41-1	Retrd.	N/A	N/A	32-96

YEAR ISSUE	EDITION LIMIT	YEAR RETRD.	ISSUE PRICE	*QUOTE U.S.$
1986 Emerald City 17	Retrd.	N/A	N/A	33-90
1986 Golden Alpine 86-040-1	Retrd.	N/A	N/A	48
1986 Long Icicle (red) 6	Retrd.	N/A	N/A	90-174
1986 Midas Touch 49	Retrd.	N/A	N/A	114-120
1986 Roses 115	Retrd.	1988	16.00	125-140
1986 Santa's Cane (pink) 5-1	Retrd.	N/A	N/A	90
1986 Siberian Sleighride 110-1	Retrd.	N/A	N/A	40-48
1986 Three Ribbon Oval 44-0	Retrd.	N/A	N/A	125-150
1986 Three Wise Swans 12	Retrd.	N/A	N/A	72-150

1987 Holiday Collection - C. Radko

YEAR ISSUE	EDITION LIMIT	YEAR RETRD.	ISSUE PRICE	*QUOTE U.S.$
1987 Baby Balloons 44	Retrd.	1988	6.00	95
1987 Celestial (red) 21-1	Retrd.	N/A	N/A	48-96
1987 Double Royal Star Reflector 79	Retrd.	N/A	N/A	150
1987 Faberge Ball 34	Retrd.	N/A	N/A	32-84
1987 Four Tier Pendant 50	Retrd.	N/A	N/A	45-50
1987 Granny's Reflector (red)	Retrd.	N/A	N/A	150
1987 Grecian Column (red/gold) 520	Retrd.	N/A	N/A	90-125
1987 Grecian Column (silver) 520	Retrd.	N/A	N/A	125
1987 Kat Koncert 88-067	Retrd.	1994	16.00	49-95
1987 Memphis 18	Retrd.	N/A	15.00	48-95
1987 Neopolitan Angels 14	Retrd.	N/A	N/A	60-72
1987 Ruby Scarlet 10	Retrd.	N/A	N/A	34-48
1987 Serpents 38	Retrd.	N/A	N/A	23-30
1987 Twin Finial 800	Retrd.	N/A	N/A	135
1987 Victorian Lamp 63	Retrd.	N/A	N/A	90

1988 Holiday Collection - C. Radko

YEAR ISSUE	EDITION LIMIT	YEAR RETRD.	ISSUE PRICE	*QUOTE U.S.$
1988 Alpine Flowers 8822	Retrd.	N/A	16.00	85-110
1988 Baby Balloon 8832	Retrd.	N/A	7.95	75-110
1988 Birdhouse 8873	Retrd.	1987	10.00	95-120
1988 Blue Rainbow 8863	Retrd.	N/A	16.00	60-150
1988 Buds in Bloom (pink) 8824	Retrd.	N/A	16.00	95-125
1988 Celestial (blue) 884	Retrd.	N/A	15.00	38-65
1988 Celestial 884	Retrd.	N/A	15.00	75
1988 Christmas Fanfare 8850	Retrd.	1988	15.00	72-125
1988 Circle of Santas 11	Retrd.	N/A	14.50	15-50
1988 Circle of Santas 8811	Retrd.	N/A	16.95	54-95
1988 Circus Spikes 75	Retrd.	N/A	9.00	240
1988 Cornucopia/Pear Branch 8839	Retrd.	N/A	15.00	360
1988 Crescent Moon Santa 881	Retrd.	N/A	15.00	95-125
1988 Crown Jewels 8874	Retrd.	1993	15.00	45-60
1988 Double Royal Star 8856	Retrd.	1991	23.00	125
1988 Exclamation Flask 8871	Retrd.	N/A	7.50	25-120
1988 Faberge Oval 883	Retrd.	N/A	15.00	75-110
1988 French Regency 17	Retrd.	N/A	N/A	60-155
1988 Gilded Leaves 8813	Retrd.	N/A	16.00	95-110
1988 Grecian Column 8842	Retrd.	1990	9.95	95
1988 Harlequin 26	Retrd.	N/A	N/A	36-55
1988 Hot Air Balloon 885	Retrd.	N/A	15.00	125-150
1988 Jumbo Nautilus (gold) 102-1	Retrd.	N/A	N/A	30-36
1988 Kat Koncert 8867	Retrd.	N/A	14.50	48-72
1988 Large Nautilus (gold) 102	Retrd.	N/A	N/A	20-30
1988 Lilac Sparkle 1814	Retrd.	N/A	15.00	140-150
1988 Medium Nautilus 101	Retrd.	N/A	N/A	10-19
1988 Merry Christmas Maiden 52	Retrd.	N/A	14.50	72
1988 Mushroom in Winter 8862	Retrd.	1993	12.00	45-85
1988 Neopolitan Angel 870141	Retrd.	1995	16.00	125-150
1988 Oz Balloon 872	Retrd.	N/A	18.00	78-160
1988 Ripples on Oval 8844	Retrd.	1987	6.00	38-65
1988 Royal Crest Oval 18	Retrd.	N/A	14.50	102
1988 Royal Diadem 8860	Retrd.	1987	25.00	135-240
1988 Royal Porcelain 8812	Retrd.	1991	16.00	125-180
1988 Royal Rooster 70	Retrd.	N/A	14.50	66
1988 Russian St. Nick 8823	Retrd.	N/A	15.00	30-90
1988 Satin Scepter 8847	Retrd.	1987	8.95	50-110
1988 Shiny-Brite 8843	Retrd.	N/A	5.00	36-50
1988 Simply Cartiere 8817	Retrd.	N/A	16.95	65-96
1988 Squiggles 889	Retrd.	N/A	15.00	95-120
1988 Stained Glass 8816	Retrd.	1990	16.00	90-125
1988 Striped Balloon 8877	Retrd.	N/A	16.95	40-96
1988 Tiger 886	Retrd.	N/A	15.00	150-375
1988 Tree on Ball 8864	Retrd.	N/A	9.00	50-125
1988 Twin Finial 8857	Retrd.	N/A	23.50	100-135
1988 Vienna 1900 37	Retrd.	N/A	16.00	96
1988 Zebra 886	Retrd.	N/A	15.00	150

1989 Holiday Collection - C. Radko

YEAR ISSUE	EDITION LIMIT	YEAR RETRD.	ISSUE PRICE	*QUOTE U.S.$
1989 Alpine Flowers 9-43	Retrd.	N/A	17.00	30
1989 Baroque Angel 9-11	Retrd.	1989	17.00	95-150
1989 Carmen Miranda 9-40	Retrd.	N/A	17.00	67-95

Collectors' Information Bureau   *Quotes have been rounded up to nearest dollar

ORNAMENTS

Christopher Radko
to Christopher Radko

YEAR ISSUE	EDITION LIMIT	YEAR RETD.	ISSUE PRICE	*QUOTE U.S.$
1989 Charlie Chaplin (blue hat) 9-55	Retrd.	1990	8.50	25-30
1989 Circle of Santas 9-32	Retrd.	1991	17.00	90-95
1989 Clown Snake 60	Retrd.	N/A	9.00	40-95
1989 Clown Snake 60 (signed)	Retrd.	N/A	9.00	96
1989 Double Top 9-71	Retrd.	1989	7.00	40
1989 Drop Reflector 88	Retrd.	N/A	23.00	90
1989 Elf on Ball (matte) 9-62	Retrd.	1990	9.50	50-85
1989 Faberge Finial 106	Retrd.	N/A	36.00	96-116
1989 Fisher Frog 9-65	Retrd.	1991	7.00	75
1989 Fleurs de Provence 30	Retrd.	N/A	17.00	96
1989 Fluted Column (gold) 86	Retrd.	N/A	10.00	120
1989 Friendly Visitor 9-97	Retrd.	N/A	11.00	175
1989 Grecian Urn 9-69	Retrd.	1989	9.00	35
1989 Harlequin Finial (tree topper) 107	Retrd.	N/A	22.00	142-186
1989 Hi-Fi Pink 20	Retrd.	N/A	17.00	240
1989 Hi Boy Elroy 9-104	Retrd.	1991	8.00	120
1989 The Holly 9-49	Retrd.	N/A	17.00	40-90
1989 Hurricane Lamp 9-67	Retrd.	1989	7.00	45
1989 The Ivy 9-47	Retrd.	N/A	16.50	120
1989 Jester 41	Retrd.	N/A	16.50	120
1989 Joey Clown (light pink) 9-58	Retrd.	1992	9.00	50-96
1989 Kim Ono 9-57	Retrd.	1990	6.50	50-60
1989 King Arthur (Lt. Blue) 9-103	Retrd.	1991	12.00	50-72
1989 Kite Face 64	Retrd.	N/A	8.50	95
1989 Lilac Sparkle 9-7	Retrd.	1989	17.00	75-125
1989 Lucky Fish 9-73	Retrd.	1989	6.50	20-55
1989 Miranda 40	Retrd.	N/A	17.00	48-162
1989 Parachute 9-68	Retrd.	1989	6.50	75-96
1989 Pastel Harlequin 22	Retrd.	N/A	17.00	66
1989 Patchwork 52	Retrd.	N/A	16.50	108
1989 Peppermint Stripes 89	Retrd.	N/A	29.00	300
1989 Royal Rooster 9-18	Retrd.	1993	17.00	95
1989 Royal Star Tree Finial 108	Retrd.	N/A	42.00	95
1989 Santa Claus 15	Retrd.	N/A	16.00	90
1989 Scepter 105	Retrd.	N/A	25.00	144
1989 Seahorse 9-54	Retrd.	1992	10.00	72-150
1989 Serpent 9-72	Retrd.	N/A	7.00	30
1989 Shy Kitten 9-66	Retrd.	N/A	7.00	54-96
1989 Shy Rabbit 9-61	Retrd.	N/A	7.00	48-90
1989 Small Reflector 9-76	Retrd.	N/A	7.50	23-32
1989 Smiling Sun 9-59	Retrd.	N/A	7.00	60
1989 Song Birds 21	Retrd.	N/A	17.50	138-240
1989 Starlight Santa 56	Retrd.	N/A	6.00	190
1989 Tiffany 44	Retrd.	N/A	17.00	500-650
1989 Vineyard 9-51	Retrd.	N/A	17.00	115-200
1989 Walrus 9-63	Retrd.	1990	8.00	120-150
1989 Zebra 9-75	Retrd.	1991	17.50	110

1990 Holiday Collection - C. Radko

YEAR ISSUE	EDITION LIMIT	YEAR RETD.	ISSUE PRICE	*QUOTE U.S.$
1990 Angel on Harp 46	Retrd.	1990	9.00	45-85
1990 Atomic Age 27	Retrd.	N/A	18.00	60
1990 Ballooning Santa 85	Retrd.	1991	20.00	175-200
1990 Bathing Baby 70	Retrd.	N/A	11.00	48-54
1990 Bolero 67	Retrd.	N/A	7.25	72
1990 Boy Clown on Reflector 82	Retrd.	N/A	18.00	53-150
1990 Calla Lilly 38	Retrd.	N/A	7.00	30-119
1990 Candy Trumpet Man (blue) 85-1	Retrd.	N/A	28.00	35-48
1990 Candy Trumpet Man 85-1	Retrd.	N/A	28.00	35-84
1990 Carmen Miranda 18	Retrd.	1991	19.00	95-125
1990 Chimney Sweep Bell 179	Retrd.	N/A	27.00	75-150
1990 Christmas Cardinals 16	Retrd.	1992	18.00	42-90
1990 Classic Column 63	Retrd.	N/A	8.00	90
1990 Comet Reflector 31	Retrd.	N/A	16.00	60
1990 Conch Shell 65	Retrd.	1991	9.00	48-90
1990 Country Church 37	Retrd.	N/A	12.00	36
1990 Crowned Prince 56	Retrd.	1990	14.00	55-64
1990 Deco Floral 29	Retrd.	N/A	19.00	110-120
1990 Double Royal Star Reflector 104	Retrd.	N/A	30.00	150
1990 Dublin Pipe 40	Retrd.	1990	14.00	50
1990 Eagle Medallion 67	Retrd.	1990	9.00	40-60
1990 Early Winter 24	Retrd.	1990	10.00	28-40
1990 Elephant on Ball 94	Retrd.	N/A	20.00	110
1990 Emerald City 92	Retrd.	1990	7.50	33-65
1990 Fat Lady 35	Retrd.	N/A	7.00	36
1990 Father Christmas 76	Retrd.	N/A	7.00	45
1990 Frog Under Balloon 58	Retrd.	1991	14.00	32-60
1990 Frosty 62	Retrd.	N/A	14.00	36-72
1990 Golden Puppy 53	Retrd.	1990	8.00	90-120
1990 Google Eyes 44	Retrd.	1990	9.00	95-100
1990 Gypsy Queen 54	Retrd.	N/A	11.50	54-69
1990 Happy Gnome 77	Retrd.	1991	8.00	60-75

YEAR ISSUE	EDITION LIMIT	YEAR RETD.	ISSUE PRICE	*QUOTE U.S.$
1990 Hearts & Flowers (ball) 15	Retrd.	N/A	19.00	50-90
1990 Heritage Santa 9075-2	Retrd.	N/A	24.00	24-36
1990 Holly Ball 4	Retrd.	N/A	19.00	125
1990 Honey Bear 167	Retrd.	N/A	14.00	55
1990 Jester 41	Retrd.	N/A	16.50	120
1990 Joey Clown (red striped) 55	Retrd.	N/A	14.00	28-60
1990 Kim Ono 79	Retrd.	1990	6.00	35-55
1990 King Arthur (Red) 72	Retrd.	N/A	16.00	95-110
1990 Lullaby 47	Retrd.	1990	9.00	25-63
1990 Maracca 94	Retrd.	1990	9.00	45-125
1990 Mediterranean Sunshine 140	Retrd.	N/A	27.00	34-49
1990 Mission Ball 26	Retrd.	N/A	18.00	32-48
1990 Mother Goose (blue bonnet/pink shawl) 52	Retrd.	N/A	10.00	32-58
1990 Nativity 36	Retrd.	1990	6.00	19-50
1990 Olympiad 7	Retrd.	N/A	18.00	48
1990 Peacock (on snowball) 74	Retrd.	N/A	18.00	75-100
1990 Pierre Le Berry	Retrd.	N/A	10.00	48-54
1990 Polish Folk Dance 13	Retrd.	N/A	19.00	120-150
1990 Praying Angel 37	Retrd.	N/A	5.00	27-75
1990 Proud Peacock 74	Retrd.	N/A	18.00	46-84
1990 Pudgy Clown 39	Retrd.	N/A	6.50	25-60
1990 Roly Poly Santa (Red bottom) 69	Retrd.	N/A	13.00	24-72
1990 Rose Lamp 96	Retrd.	1990	14.00	70-180
1990 Santa on Ball 80	Retrd.	1991	16.00	40-59
1990 Silent Movie (black hat) 75	Retrd.	1990	8.50	25-60
1990 Small Nautilus Shell 78	Retrd.	N/A	7.00	22
1990 Smiling Kite 63	Retrd.	1990	14.00	40-85
1990 Snowball Tree 71	Retrd.	1990	17.00	65-114
1990 Snowman on Ball 45	Retrd.	1990	14.00	49-72
1990 Songbirds 6	Retrd.	N/A	19.00	101
1990 Southwest Indian Ball 19	Retrd.	N/A	19.00	240
1990 Spin Top 90	Retrd.	N/A	11.00	36-48
1990 Summer Parasol 88	Retrd.	N/A	7.00	132-156
1990 Sunburst Fish (green/yellow) 68	Retrd.	N/A	13.00	50
1990 Swami 41	Retrd.	N/A	8.00	66
1990 Tabby 42	Retrd.	N/A	7.00	30-45
1990 Tropical Fish 74	Retrd.	N/A	24.00	28-48
1990 Trumpet Player 83	Retrd.	N/A	18.00	100
1990 Tuxedo Penquin 57	Retrd.	1990	8.00	150-250
1990 Walrus 59	Retrd.	1990	8.50	120
1990 Yarn Fight 23	Retrd.	N/A	17.00	75-150

1991 Holiday Collection - C. Radko

YEAR ISSUE	EDITION LIMIT	YEAR RETD.	ISSUE PRICE	*QUOTE U.S.$
1991 All Weather Santa 137	Retrd.	1992	32.00	135-230
1991 Alladin 29	Retrd.	N/A	14.00	28-72
1991 Altar Boy 18	Retrd.	1992	16.00	36-66
1991 Anchor America 65	Retrd.	1992	21.50	52-65
1991 Apache 42	Retrd.	N/A	8.50	22-54
1991 Aspen 76	Retrd.	1992	20.50	60-120
1991 Astro Top (light blue) 168	Retrd.	N/A	11.50	75-168
1991 Aztec 141	Retrd.	1991	21.50	50-104
1991 Aztec Bird 41	Retrd.	1992	20.00	65-162
1991 Ballooning Santa 110	Retrd.	1991	23.00	150-208
1991 Barnum Clown 56	Retrd.	1991	15.00	55-95
1991 Bishop 22	Retrd.	N/A	15.00	30-54
1991 Black Forest Cone 97	Retrd.	N/A	8.00	42
1991 Blue Rainbow 136	Retrd.	1992	21.50	95-100
1991 Bowery Kid 50	Retrd.	1991	14.50	29-48
1991 Butterfly Bouquet 142	Retrd.	N/A	21.50	54-65
1991 By the Nile 124	Retrd.	1992	21.50	65-72
1991 Cardinal Richelieu 109	Retrd.	N/A	15.50	23-90
1991 Carnival (cloudy) 123	Retrd.	N/A	20.00	15-50
1991 Carousel Stripes 132	Retrd.	N/A	20.50	50
1991 Chance Encounter 104	Retrd.	1992	13.50	60
1991 Chief Sitting Bull 107	Retrd.	1992	16.00	43-90
1991 Chimney Santa 12	Retrd.	N/A	14.50	60-107
1991 Christmas Trim 128	Retrd.	N/A	21.50	75
1991 Clown Drum 33	Retrd.	1991	14.00	10-54
1991 Comet 52	Retrd.	1991	9.00	18-60
1991 Cosette 16	Retrd.	1991	16.00	45-60
1991 Cottage Garden 84	Retrd.	N/A	21.00	60
1991 Country Quilt 140	Retrd.	N/A	21.00	30-60
1991 Cowboy Santa 106	Retrd.	N/A	15.50	32-69
1991 Dapper Shoe 89	Retrd.	1991	10.00	35-42
1991 Dawn & Dusk 34	Retrd.	N/A	14.00	30-36
1991 Deco Floral 133	Retrd.	1991	22.00	75-125
1991 Deco Sparkle 134	Retrd.	1992	21.00	66-96
1991 Deep Sea (pale green, signed) 72	Retrd.	N/A	21.50	72
1991 Dutch Boy 27	Retrd.	1991	11.00	30-55
1991 Dutch Girl 28	Retrd.	1991	11.00	55-75

YEAR ISSUE	EDITION LIMIT	YEAR RETD.	ISSUE PRICE	*QUOTE U.S.$
1991 Edwardian Lace 82	Retrd.	1991	21.50	125
1991 Einstein Kite 98	Retrd.	N/A	20.00	90-125
1991 Elephant on Ball (gold) 115	Retrd.	N/A	23.00	500
1991 Elephant on Ball (striped) 115	Retrd.	N/A	23.00	450-500
1991 Elf Reflector 135	Retrd.	1992	23.00	75-169
1991 Evening Santa 20	Retrd.	N/A	14.50	90
1991 Fanfare 126	Retrd.	1992	21.50	72-98
1991 Fisher Frog 44	Retrd.	1991	11.00	75
1991 Florentine 83	Retrd.	N/A	22.00	66-100
1991 Flower Child 90	Retrd.	1991	13.00	30-40
1991 Forest Santa Reflector 151	Retrd.	N/A	34.50	120-150
1991 Frog Under Balloon 53	Retrd.	N/A	16.00	72
1991 Froggy Child 26	Retrd.	N/A	9.00	18-27
1991 Fruit in Balloon 40	Retrd.	N/A	22.00	95-144
1991 Fu Manchu 11	Retrd.	N/A	15.00	29-75
1991 Galaxy 120	Retrd.	1991	21.50	60-72
1991 Grapefruit Tree 113	Retrd.	N/A	23.00	150-240
1991 Harvest 3	Retrd.	N/A	13.50	22-50
1991 Hatching Duck 35	Retrd.	1991	14.00	40-50
1991 Hearts & Flowers Finial 158	Retrd.	1993	53.00	150-156
1991 Her Majesty 39	Retrd.	1991	21.00	50-96
1991 Her Purse 88	Retrd.	N/A	10.00	20-60
1991 Holly Ball 156	Retrd.	N/A	22.00	49-60
1991 Holly Ribbons Finial 153	Retrd.	N/A	54.00	120
1991 Irish Laddie 10	Retrd.	1991	12.00	55-65
1991 Jemima's Child 111	Retrd.	1991	16.00	45-60
1991 King Arthur (Blue) 95	Retrd.	N/A	18.50	55-85
1991 Lion's Head 31	Retrd.	N/A	16.00	26-79
1991 Lucy's Favorite (gold) 75-1	Retrd.	N/A	10.50	45-60
1991 Lucy's Favorite (signed) 75	Retrd.	N/A	10.50	42-60
1991 Madeleine's Puppy 25	Retrd.	N/A	11.00	27-36
1991 Madonna & Child 103	Retrd.	N/A	15.00	49-125
1991 Melon Slice 99	Retrd.	N/A	18.00	30-50
1991 Mother Goose 57	Retrd.	N/A	11.00	40
1991 Ms. Maus 94	Retrd.	N/A	14.00	35-100
1991 Munchkin 91	Retrd.	N/A	8.00	36
1991 Olympiad 125	Retrd.	1992	22.00	43-125
1991 Patrick's Bunny 24	Retrd.	N/A	11.00	35-59
1991 Peruvian 74	Retrd.	1991	21.50	60-100
1991 Pierre Le Berry 2	Retrd.	1993	14.00	66-125
1991 Pink Clown on Ball 32	Retrd.	N/A	14.00	41-60
1991 Pink Elephants 70	Retrd.	N/A	21.50	60-72
1991 Pipe Man 93	Retrd.	N/A	20.00	54-90
1991 Pipe Smoking Monkey 54	Retrd.	1991	11.00	30-48
1991 Polish Folk Art 116	Retrd.	N/A	20.50	48-75
1991 Prince on Ball (pink/blue/green) 51	Retrd.	1991	15.00	36-80
1991 Prince Umbrella 21	Retrd.	1991	15.00	28-65
1991 Proud Peacock 37	Retrd.	N/A	23.00	72-150
1991 Puss N Boots 23	Retrd.	N/A	11.00	19-35
1991 Rainbow Bird 92	Retrd.	1991	16.00	48
1991 Rainbow Cone 105	Retrd.	N/A	10.00	48-84
1991 Rainbow Trout 17	Retrd.	N/A	14.50	22-54
1991 Raspberry & Lime 96	Retrd.	1991	12.00	55-96
1991 Red Star 129	Retrd.	1992	21.50	42-72
1991 Royal Porcelain 71	Retrd.	N/A	21.50	72
1991 Russian Santa (coral) 112-4	Retrd.	N/A	22.00	60-130
1991 Russian Santa (striped) 112	Retrd.	N/A	22.00	59-72
1991 Russian Santa (white) 112	Retrd.	N/A	22.00	36-72
1991 Sally Ann 43	Retrd.	1991	8.00	15-46
1991 Santa Bootie (blue) 55	Retrd.	N/A	10.00	60
1991 Santa Bootie 55	Retrd.	1993	10.00	30-36
1991 Santa in Winter White (red) 112-2	Retrd.	N/A	22.00	110-200
1991 Santa in Winter White (silver) 112-1	Retrd.	N/A	22.00	50-175
1991 Ship To Shore 122	Retrd.	N/A	20.50	84
1991 Shirley 15	Retrd.	1991	16.00	60-75
1991 Shy Elf 1	Retrd.	1991	10.00	27-60
1991 Silver Bells (signed) 73	Retrd.	N/A	20.50	96
1991 Sitting Bull 107	Retrd.	N/A	16.00	65-240
1991 Sleepy Time Santa (cobalt store exclusive) 52	Retrd.	N/A	15.00	48
1991 Sleepy Time Santa 52	Retrd.	N/A	15.00	59-144
1991 Smitty 9	Retrd.	N/A	15.00	45-60
1991 Snowman Reflector 13	Retrd.	N/A	16.00	66
1991 Star Quilt 139	Retrd.	1991	21.50	66-75
1991 Sunburst Fish 108	Retrd.	N/A	15.00	120
1991 Sunshine 67	Retrd.	N/A	22.00	40-60
1991 Tabby 46	Retrd.	1991	8.00	30-50
1991 Talking Pipe 93	Retrd.	N/A	20.00	84
1991 Tiffany 68	Retrd.	1991	22.00	50
1991 Tiger 5	Retrd.	N/A	15.00	42-69
1991 Timepiece 30	Retrd.	N/A	8.00	42
1991 Trigger 114	Retrd.	1991	15.00	60-102
1991 Tropical Flower (lavender) 61	Retrd.	N/A	14.00	72
1991 Trumpet Man 100	Retrd.	1992	21.00	72
1991 Tulip Fairy 63	Retrd.	1992	16.00	46-72
1991 Vienna 1901 127	Retrd.	1992	21.50	46-72
1991 Villandry 87	Retrd.	1991	21.00	50-75
1991 Winking St. Nick 102	Retrd.	N/A	16.00	96
1991 Woodland Santa 38	Retrd.	N/A	14.00	55-84
1991 Zebra (glittered) 79	Retrd.	1991	22.00	400-500

1992 Holiday Collection - C. Radko

YEAR ISSUE	EDITION LIMIT	YEAR RETD.	ISSUE PRICE	*QUOTE U.S.$
1992 Alpine Flowers-Tiffany 162	Retrd.	1992	28.00	50-60
1992 Alpine Village 105	Retrd.	N/A	24.00	45-125
1992 Aspen 120	Retrd.	1992	26.00	50
1992 Barbie's Mom 69	Retrd.	1992	18.00	63
1992 Benjamin's Nutcrackers (pr.) 185	Retrd.	N/A	58.00	150-188
1992 Binkie the Clown 168	Retrd.	N/A	12.00	36-60
1992 Blue Santa 65	Retrd.	N/A	18.00	25-48
1992 Butterfly Bouquet 119	Retrd.	1992	26.50	60-125
1992 By the Nile 139	Retrd.	1992	27.00	50-75
1992 Cabaret-Tiffany (see-through) 159	Retrd.	1993	28.00	60
1992 Candy Trumpet Men (pink/blue) 98	Retrd.	N/A	27.00	33-75
1992 Candy Trumpet Men (red) w/ white glitter 98	Retrd.	1992	27.00	33-80
1992 Candy Trumpet Men (red) w/o white glitter 98	Retrd.	N/A	27.00	33-48
1992 Celestial 129	Retrd.	N/A	26.00	100
1992 Cheerful Sun 50	Retrd.	N/A	18.00	40-60
1992 Chevron 160	Retrd.	1992	28.00	40
1992 Chevron-Tiffany 160	Retrd.	N/A	28.00	98
1992 Chimney Sweep Bell 179	Retrd.	N/A	27.00	78-184
1992 Choir Boy 114	Retrd.	1992	24.00	36-50
1992 Christmas Cardinals 123	Retrd.	1992	26.00	42-58
1992 Christmas Rose 143	Retrd.	1992	25.50	48-60
1992 Christmas Spider 212	Retrd.	N/A	22.00	35
1992 Cinderella's Bluebirds 240	Retrd.	N/A	26.00	54
1992 Circus Lady 54	Retrd.	1992	12.00	27
1992 Clown Snake 62	Retrd.	N/A	22.00	22-55
1992 Country Scene 169	Retrd.	N/A	12.00	40-54
1992 Country Star Quilt 176	Retrd.	N/A	12.00	50-100
1992 Cowboy Santa 94	Retrd.	N/A	24.00	48-100
1992 Crescent Moons 189	Retrd.	N/A	26.00	60-72
1992 Dawn & Dusk 96	Retrd.	N/A	19.00	36-48
1992 Delft Design 124	Retrd.	1992	26.50	60-173
1992 Diva 73	Retrd.	1992	17.00	19-65
1992 Dolly Madison 115	Retrd.	1992	17.00	60-75
1992 Down The Chimney 191	Retrd.	N/A	16.50	40-60
1992 Downhill Racer 76	Retrd.	1992	34.00	125-140
1992 Elephant on Parade 141	Retrd.	N/A	26.00	70-85
1992 Elephant Reflector 181	Retrd.	N/A	17.00	48-66
1992 Elf Reflectors 136	Retrd.	N/A	28.00	48-96
1992 Eveningstar Santa 186	Retrd.	N/A	60.00	144-156
1992 Extravagance Garland 227	Retrd.	N/A	64.00	96
1992 Faberge (pink/lavender) 148	Retrd.	N/A	26.50	45-55
1992 Faith, Hope & Love 183	Retrd.	1992	12.00	17-36
1992 Festive Smitty	Retrd.	N/A	28.95	33-45
1992 Floral Cascade Finial 173	Retrd.	N/A	68.00	102
1992 Floral Cascade Tier Drop 175	Retrd.	N/A	64.00	125-400
1992 Florentine 131	Retrd.	N/A	27.00	45-75
1992 Flutter By's 201(Set/4)	Retrd.	1992	11.00	48-65
1992 Folk Art Set 95	Retrd.	1992	10.00	13
1992 Forest Friends 103	Retrd.	N/A	14.00	20-54
1992 French Country 121	Retrd.	N/A	26.00	48-60
1992 Fruit in Balloon 83	Retrd.	N/A	28.00	60-125
1992 Gallant's Trumpets 188	Retrd.	N/A	20.00	25
1992 Harlequin Ball 196	Retrd.	N/A	27.00	27-48
1992 Harlequin Finial (tree topper) 199	Retrd.	N/A	70.00	120-136
1992 Harlequin Tier Drop 74	Retrd.	1992	36.00	60-90
1992 Harold Lloyd Reflector 218	Retrd.	1992	70.00	200-450
1992 Her Purse 43	Retrd.	N/A	20.00	36-60
1992 Her Slipper 56	Retrd.	1992	17.00	25
1992 Holly Finial 200	Retrd.	N/A	70.00	83
1992 Honey Bear 167	Retrd.	N/A	14.00	34-42
1992 Ice Pear 241	Retrd.	N/A	20.00	36-60
1992 Ice Poppies 127	Retrd.	1992	26.00	48-60
1992 Jester Ball 151	Retrd.	N/A	25.50	66
1992 Jumbo 99	Retrd.	N/A	31.00	45-48
1992 Just Like Grandma's 164	Retrd.	N/A	10.00	25-30l
1992 Kewpie 51	Retrd.	N/A	18.00	38-60l
1992 King of Prussia 149	Retrd.	1992	27.00	38-48
1992 Kitty Rattle 166	Retrd.	1993	18.00	32-95

YEAR ISSUE	EDITION LIMIT	YEAR RETD.	ISSUE PRICE	*QUOTE U.S.$
1992 Little Eskimo 38	Retrd.	N/A	14.00	27-48
1992 Little League 53	Retrd.	1992	20.00	65-75
1992 The Littlest Snowman (red hat) 67	Retrd.	N/A	14.00	29-36
1992 Littlest Snowman 67	Retrd.	N/A	14.00	42-60
1992 Locomotive Garland 216	Retrd.	N/A	60.00	75-150
1992 Madeline's Puppy 49	Retrd.	N/A	18.00	69
1992 Majestic Reflector 187	Retrd.	N/A	70.00	120
1992 Mediterranean Sunshine 140	Retrd.	N/A	17.00	34-40
1992 Melon Slice 91	Retrd.	N/A	26.00	26-48
1992 Merlin Santa 75	Retrd.	N/A	32.00	75-84
1992 Merry Christmas Maiden 137	Retrd.	1992	26.00	40-48
1992 Mission Ball 153	Retrd.	N/A	27.00	27-48
1992 Mother Goose 37	Retrd.	N/A	15.00	25-48
1992 Mr. & Mrs. Claus 59	Retrd.	N/A	18.00	150-200
1992 Mushroom Elf 87	Retrd.	N/A	18.00	36-60
1992 Neopolitan Angels 152 (Set/3)	Retrd.	1992	27.00	144-300
1992 Norweigian Princess 170	Retrd.	1992	15.00	66
1992 Olympiad 132	Retrd.	N/A	26.00	80
1992 Palace Guard 60	Retrd.	N/A	17.00	26-54
1992 Pierre Winterberry 64	Retrd.	1993	17.00	30-75
1992 Pink Lace Ball (See Through) 158	Retrd.	1992	28.00	60-100
1992 Polar Bear 184	Retrd.	N/A	16.00	22-48
1992 Primary Colors 108	Retrd.	1992	30.00	85-150
1992 Quilted Hearts (Old Salem Museum) 194	Retrd.	N/A	27.50	42-51
1992 Rainbow Parasol 90	Retrd.	1992	18.00	60-100
1992 Royal Scepter 77	Retrd.	1992	36.00	75-175
1992 Ruby Scarlet Finial 198	Retrd.	N/A	70.00	95-156
1992 Russian Imperial 112	Retrd.	1992	25.00	50
1992 Russian Jewel Hearts 146	Retrd.	N/A	27.00	48-100
1992 Russian Star 130	Retrd.	1992	26.00	32-40
1992 Sail Away 215	Retrd.	N/A	22.00	50
1992 Santa Claus Garland 220	Retrd.	N/A	66.00	96-120
1992 Santa in Winter White 106	Retrd.	N/A	28.00	60-65
1992 Santa's Helper 78	Retrd.	N/A	17.00	36-72
1992 Scallop Shell 150	Retrd.	N/A	27.00	30-38
1992 Seafaring Santa 71	Retrd.	N/A	18.00	36-66
1992 Seahorse (pink) 92	Retrd.	1992	20.00	72-86
1992 Serpents of Paradise 97	Retrd.	N/A	13.00	30
1992 Shy Rabbit 40	Retrd.	N/A	14.00	36-72
1992 Siberian Sleigh Ride (pink) 154	Retrd.	N/A	27.00	45-85
1992 Silver Icicle 89	Retrd.	N/A	12.00	48-60
1992 Sitting Bull 93	Retrd.	1992	26.00	43-60
1992 Sleepytime Santa (pink) 81	Retrd.	N/A	18.00	60-95
1992 Sloopy Snowman 328	Retrd.	N/A	19.90	54
1992 Snake Prince 171	Retrd.	N/A	19.00	30
1992 Snowflakes 209	Retrd.	N/A	10.00	30-40
1992 Southern Colonial 142	Retrd.	N/A	27.00	60
1992 Sputniks 134	Retrd.	1992	25.50	72-100
1992 St. Nickcicle 107	Retrd.	N/A	26.00	30-72
1992 Star of Wonder 177	Retrd.	1992	27.00	35-50
1992 Starbursts 214	Retrd.	N/A	12.00	30-48
1992 Stardust Joey 110	Retrd.	1992	16.00	54-150
1992 Starlight Santa (powder blue) 180	Retrd.	N/A	18.00	50
1992 Sterling Silver Garland 204	Retrd.	N/A	12.00	60
1992 Talking Pipe (black stem) 104	Retrd.	N/A	26.00	110
1992 Thunderbolt 178	Retrd.	1993	60.00	186-222
1992 Tiffany Bright Harlequin 161	Retrd.	1992	28.00	48-114
1992 Tiffany Pastel Harlequin 163	Retrd.	N/A	28.00	48-114
1992 Tiffany Pine Lace 158	Retrd.	N/A	28.00	85
1992 To Grandma's House 239	Retrd.	N/A	20.00	58-84
1992 Topiary 117	Retrd.	N/A	30.00	120-250
1992 Tropical Fish 109	Retrd.	N/A	17.00	60
1992 Tulip Fairy 57	Retrd.	1992	18.00	22-45
1992 Tuxedo Santa 88	Retrd.	1993	22.00	25-125
1992 Two Sided Santa Reflector 102	Retrd.	1992	28.00	75
1992 Umbrella Santa 182	Retrd.	N/A	60.00	140-150
1992 Victorian Santa & Angel Balloon 122	Retrd.	1992	68.00	225-600
1992 Vienna 1901 128	Retrd.	1992	27.00	45-150
1992 Village Carolers 172	Retrd.	N/A	17.00	21-66
1992 Virgin Mary 46	Retrd.	1992	20.00	28-63
1992 Wacko's Brother, Doofus 55	Retrd.	N/A	20.00	36-66
1992 Water Lilies 133	Retrd.	1992	26.00	90-100
1992 Wedding Bells 217	Retrd.	N/A	40.00	165-225
1992 Winking St. Nick 70	Retrd.	N/A	22.00	22-48
1992 Winter Kiss 82	Retrd.	N/A	18.00	48-60
1992 Winter Tree 101	Retrd.	N/A	28.00	33-84
1992 Winter Wonderland 156	Retrd.	1992	26.00	42-96
1992 Woodland Santa 111	Retrd.	N/A	20.00	39-55
1992 Ziegfeld Follies 126	Retrd.	1992	27.00	100-130

1993 Holiday Collection - C. Radko

YEAR ISSUE	EDITION LIMIT	YEAR RETD.	ISSUE PRICE	*QUOTE U.S.$
1993 1939 World's Fair 149	Retrd.	N/A	26.80	60-100
1993 Accordian Elf 189	Retrd.	N/A	21.00	32-42
1993 Aladdin's Lamp 237	Retrd.	N/A	20.00	39-72
1993 Allegro 179	Retrd.	N/A	26.80	65-108
1993 Alpine Village 420	Retrd.	1993	23.80	125
1993 Alpine Wings 86	Retrd.	N/A	58.00	96
1993 Anassazi 172	Retrd.	N/A	26.60	65-75
1993 Anchor Santa 407	Retrd.	N/A	32.00	54-90
1993 Angel Light 256	Retrd.	N/A	16.00	16-48
1993 Angel of Peace 132	Retrd.	1993	17.00	22-54
1993 Apache 357	Retrd.	1993	13.90	54-75
1993 Auld Lang Syne 246	Retrd.	N/A	15.00	27-60
1993 Away in a Manger 379	Retrd.	N/A	24.00	28-55
1993 Bavarian Santa 335	Retrd.	N/A	23.00	45-66
1993 Beauregard 296	Retrd.	N/A	24.00	25-60
1993 Bedtime Buddy 239	Retrd.	N/A	29.00	102-114
1993 Bell House Boy 291	Retrd.	1993	21.00	48
1993 Bells Are Ringing 268	Retrd.	N/A	18.00	24-36
1993 Bells-Tiffany 334	Retrd.	N/A	8.80	36-45
1993 Beyond the Stars 108	Retrd.	1993	18.50	35-70
1993 Bishop of Myra 327	Retrd.	1993	19.90	25-50
1993 Bishops Cross Garland 79	Retrd.	N/A	48.90	90
1993 Black Forest Clock 360	Retrd.	N/A	20.00	32-48
1993 Blue Top 114	Retrd.	1993	16.00	30-75
1993 Bowzer 228	Retrd.	N/A	22.80	65-125
1993 By Jiminy 285	Retrd.	N/A	16.40	48
1993 Calla Lilly 314	Retrd.	N/A	12.90	15-25
1993 Candied Citrus 278	Retrd.	N/A	9.00	25-42
1993 Candlelight 118	Retrd.	N/A	16.00	22-36
1993 Carnival Rides 303	Retrd.	N/A	18.00	65-75
1993 Cathedral Bells 343	Retrd.	N/A	8.20	54
1993 Celeste 271	Retrd.	N/A	26.00	33-39
1993 Celestial Peacock 197	Retrd.	N/A	27.90	30-75
1993 Celestial Peacock Finial 322	Retrd.	N/A	69.00	200-295
1993 Center Ring (Exclusive) 192	Retrd.	1993	30.80	48-150
1993 Centurian 224	Retrd.	1993	25.50	65-150
1993 Chimney Sweep Bell 294	Retrd.	1993	26.00	180
1993 Christmas Express (Garland) 394	Retrd.	N/A	58.00	42-80
1993 Christmas Goose 129	Retrd.	N/A	14.80	42
1993 Christmas Stars 342	Retrd.	N/A	14.00	20-36
1993 Church Bell 295	Retrd.	N/A	24.00	42-45
1993 Cinderella's Bluebirds 145	Retrd.	1993	25.90	54-120
1993 Circle of Santas Finial 413	Retrd.	N/A	69.00	100
1993 Circus Seal 249	Retrd.	1993	28.00	65-132
1993 Circus Star 358	Retrd.	N/A	24.00	48-90
1993 Class Clown 332	Retrd.	N/A	21.00	66-132
1993 Classic Christmas 408	Retrd.	N/A	29.00	60-126
1993 Cloud Nine 369	Retrd.	N/A	25.00	42-72
1993 Clowning Around 84	Retrd.	N/A	42.50	50-68
1993 Cool Cat 184	Retrd.	N/A	21.00	100
1993 Copenhagen 166	Retrd.	1993	26.80	100-190
1993 Country Flowers 205	Retrd.	N/A	16.00	30-40
1993 Country Scene 204	Retrd.	N/A	11.90	36-48
1993 Crescent Moons Finial 397	Retrd.	N/A	69.00	69-108
1993 Crocus Blossoms 283	Retrd.	N/A	16.00	24-54
1993 Crowned Passion 299	Retrd.	1993	23.00	36-48
1993 Crystal Fountain 243	Retrd.	N/A	34.00	114
1993 Crystal Rainbow 308	Retrd.	N/A	29.90	200-300
1993 Dancing Harlequin 232	Retrd.	N/A	36.00	45-84
1993 Daniel Star 211	Retrd.	N/A	26.00	30-54
1993 Dawn & Dusk 318	Retrd.	N/A	18.90	19-36
1993 Deco Snowfall 147	Retrd.	1993	26.80	42-48
1993 Deco Tree Garland 60	Retrd.	N/A	42.00	86-105
1993 Deer Drop 304	Retrd.	N/A	34.00	36-110
1993 Del Monte 219	Retrd.	N/A	23.50	24-54
1993 Devotion 203	Retrd.	N/A	17.00	24-36
1993 Don't Hold Your Breath 92-1	Retrd.	N/A	11.00	50
1993 Downhill Racer 195	Retrd.	1993	30.00	60-108
1993 Dynasty Garland 55	Retrd.	N/A	49.00	78
1993 Eggman 241	Retrd.	N/A	22.50	48-72
1993 Elf Bell 125	Retrd.	N/A	18.00	28-42
1993 Emerald Wizard 279	Retrd.	N/A	18.00	28-51
1993 Emperor's Pet 253	Retrd.	1993	22.00	60-126
1993 Enchanted Gardens 341	Retrd.	1993	5.50	13
1993 English Kitchen 234	Retrd.	1993	26.00	54-60
1993 Epiphany 421	Retrd.	N/A	29.00	48-90
1993 Eskimo Elves Garland 72	Retrd.	N/A	39.20	78
1993 Eskimo Kitty 281	Retrd.	N/A	14.50	20-36

ORNAMENTS

YEAR ISSUE	EDITION LIMIT	YEAR RETD.	ISSUE PRICE	*QUOTE U.S.$
1993 Evening Star Santa 409	Retrd.	1993	59.00	95-182
1993 Extravagance Garland 87	Retrd.	N/A	53.00	90
1993 Faberge Egg 257	Retrd.	N/A	17.50	42-45
1993 Fantastia 143	Retrd.	N/A	24.00	55-130
1993 Fantasy Cone 324	Retrd.	N/A	17.90	30-36
1993 Fantasy Garland II 88	Retrd.	N/A	40.40	84
1993 Far Out Santa 138	Retrd.	N/A	39.00	120-150
1993 Fiesta Ball 316	Retrd.	N/A	26.40	48
1993 First Snow 365	Retrd.	N/A	10.00	36
1993 Fleurice 282	Retrd.	N/A	23.50	54-125
1993 Flora Dora 255	Retrd.	N/A	25.00	45-60
1993 Fly Boy 235	Retrd.	N/A	33.00	60-95
1993 Forest Bells 136	Retrd.	N/A	25.00	48-54
1993 Forest Friends 250	Retrd.	1993	28.00	35-100
1993 French Regency Balloon 161	Retrd.	N/A	29.00	47-110
1993 French Rose 152	Retrd.	1993	26.60	48-60
1993 Fruit in Balloon 115	Retrd.	N/A	27.90	80
1993 Geisha Girls 261	Retrd.	1993	11.90	25-60
1993 Georgian Santa 292	Retrd.	N/A	30.00	38-65
1993 Gerard 252	Retrd.	N/A	26.00	48-96
1993 Gilded Cage 406	Retrd.	N/A	44.00	48-108
1993 Glory on High 116	Retrd.	N/A	17.00	25-72
1993 Gold Fish 158	Retrd.	1993	25.80	75-100
1993 Golden Crescendo Finial 381-1	Retrd.	N/A	50.00	600
1993 Goofy Fruits 367	Retrd.	N/A	14.00	36-66
1993 Goofy Garden (Pickle) 191	Retrd.	N/A	15.00	48
1993 Goofy Garden (Set/4) 191	Retrd.	N/A	60.00	100-150
1993 Grand Monarch 306	Retrd.	N/A	16.00	48-175
1993 Grandpa Bear 260	Retrd.	1993	12.80	30
1993 Grecian Urn 231	Retrd.	1993	23.00	50-60
1993 Guardian Angel 124	Retrd.	N/A	36.00	84-132
1993 Gypsy Girl 371	Retrd.	1993	16.00	16-35
1993 Hansel & Gretel 100	Retrd.	N/A	24.00	25-54
1993 Harvest 354	Retrd.	N/A	19.90	48
1993 Holiday Inn 137	Retrd.	N/A	21.00	54
1993 Holiday Sparkle 144	Retrd.	N/A	16.80	144
1993 Holiday Spice 422	Retrd.	N/A	24.00	36-48
1993 Holly Ribbons 415	Retrd.	N/A	24.80	24-36
1993 Honey Bear 352	Retrd.	1993	13.90	20-55
1993 Ice Bear 284	Retrd.	N/A	17.50	36-48
1993 Ice Star Santa 405	Retrd.	1993	38.00	250-300
1993 Injun Joe 102	Retrd.	N/A	24.00	24-48
1993 It's A Small World 96	Retrd.	N/A	17.00	25-42
1993 Jack Frost (blue) 333	Retrd.	N/A	23.00	29-48
1993 Jaques Le Berry 356	Retrd.	N/A	16.90	100-150
1993 Jewel Box 213	Retrd.	N/A	12.00	20-36
1993 Jingle Bells 61	Retrd.	N/A	64.00	145
1993 Joey B. Clown 135	Retrd.	N/A	26.00	45-91
1993 Jumbo Spintops 302	Retrd.	N/A	27.00	45-132
1993 Just Like Grandma's Lg. 200	Retrd.	N/A	7.20	25-50
1993 Just Like Grandma's Sm. 200	Retrd.	N/A	7.20	25-30
1993 King's Ransom 449	Retrd.	N/A	49.00	75
1993 Kissing Cousins (Pair) 245	Retrd.	N/A	30.00	85-180
1993 Kitty Rattle 374	Retrd.	1993	17.80	90
1993 Lamp Light 251	Retrd.	N/A	22.50	45-60
1993 Letter to Santa 188	Retrd.	N/A	22.00	42-48
1993 Light in the Windows 229	Retrd.	1994	24.50	45-55
1993 Little Boy Blue 361	Retrd.	N/A	25.90	60-78
1993 Little Doggie 180	Retrd.	1993	7.00	30-36
1993 Little Eskimo 355	Retrd.	N/A	13.90	22
1993 Little Slugger 187	Retrd.	N/A	22.00	22-36
1993 Lucky Shoe 346	Retrd.	N/A	16.00	54
1993 Majestic Reflector 312	Retrd.	1993	70.00	100
1993 Maxine 240	Retrd.	N/A	10.00	35-84
1993 Mediterranean Sunshine 156	Retrd.	N/A	26.90	75
1993 Midas Touch 142	Retrd.	N/A	27.80	68
1993 Monkey Business 126	Retrd.	N/A	14.80	20-54
1993 Monkey Man 97	Retrd.	N/A	16.00	27-42
1993 Monterey 290	Retrd.	1993	15.00	25-36
1993 Moon Dust 128	Retrd.	N/A	15.00	36-78
1993 Moon Jump 423	Retrd.	N/A	29.00	84-120
1993 Mooning Over You 106	Retrd.	N/A	17.00	24
1993 Mountain Christmas 384	Retrd.	N/A	25.50	28-78
1993 Mr. & Mrs. Claus 121	Retrd.	1993	17.90	80-125
1993 Mushroom Elf 267	Retrd.	N/A	17.90	38
1993 Mushroom Santa 212	Retrd.	N/A	28.00	125-156
1993 Nellie (Italian ornament) 225	Retrd.	1993	27.50	60-200
1993 Nesting Stork Finial (red or gold) 380	Retrd.	N/A	50.00	150
1993 Nesting Stork Finial 380	Retrd.	N/A	50.00	216-220
1993 North Woods 317	Retrd.	1993	26.80	49-120
1993 Northwind 266	Retrd.	N/A	17.00	22-48
1993 Nuts & Berries (signed) 64	Retrd.	N/A	58.00	120
1993 Nuts & Berries 64	Retrd.	N/A	58.00	50-80
1993 One Small Leap 222	Retrd.	N/A	26.00	95-175
1993 Pagoda 258	Retrd.	1993	8.00	15-30
1993 Pennsylvania Dutch 146	Retrd.	1993	26.80	42-65
1993 Piggly Wiggly 101	Retrd.	N/A	11.00	54
1993 Pineapple Quilt 150	Retrd.	N/A	26.80	54-65
1993 Pineapple Slice 376	Retrd.	N/A	14.00	15-54
1993 Pinecone Santa 142	Retrd.	N/A	24.00	36-49
1993 Pinocchio 248	Retrd.	N/A	26.00	60-95
1993 Pisces Garland 59	Retrd.	N/A	37.00	72-78
1993 Pixie Santa 186	Retrd.	N/A	16.00	42
1993 Plum 185	Retrd.	N/A	6.40	20
1993 Poinsetta Santa 269	Retrd.	N/A	19.80	65-76
1993 Polar Bears 112A	Retrd.	1993	15.50	16
1993 Pompadour 344	Retrd.	1993	8.80	10-24
1993 President Taft 92	Retrd.	N/A	15.00	24-60
1993 Prince Albert 263	Retrd.	N/A	23.00	45-65
1993 Purse 389	Retrd.	1993	15.60	16
1993 Quartet 392	Retrd.	1993	3.60	11
1993 Radio Monkey 104	Retrd.	N/A	16.20	48
1993 Rainbow Beads 78	Retrd.	N/A	44.00	72-96
1993 Rainbow Reflector 154	Retrd.	1993	26.60	48-96
1993 Rainbow Shark 277	Retrd.	N/A	18.00	65-70
1993 Rainy Day Friend 206	Retrd.	N/A	22.00	45-65
1993 Rambling Rose 148	Retrd.	N/A	16.60	32-52
1993 Regal Rooster 177	Retrd.	N/A	25.80	45-75
1993 Remembrance 151	Retrd.	N/A	16.60	54-72
1993 Rose Pointe Finial 323	Retrd.	1993	34.00	40
1993 Russian Santa (red) 209	Retrd.	N/A	27.90	50
1993 Sail by Starlight 339	Retrd.	1993	11.80	14-19
1993 Sailor Man 238	Retrd.	N/A	22.00	66-95
1993 Santa Baby 112	Retrd.	N/A	18.00	24-36
1993 Santa Hearts Garland 76	Retrd.	N/A	58.00	42-84
1993 Santa in Space 127	Retrd.	N/A	39.00	120-125
1993 Santa in Winter White 300	Retrd.	N/A	27.90	65
1993 Santa Tree 320	Retrd.	N/A	66.00	250-300
1993 Santa's Helper 329	Retrd.	N/A	16.90	20-60
1993 Saraband 140	Retrd.	1993	27.80	65-150
1993 Scotch Pine 167	Retrd.	N/A	26.80	38-48
1993 Serenade Pink 157	Retrd.	1993	26.80	48-60
1993 Shy Rabbit 280	Retrd.	N/A	14.00	75-90
1993 Siberian Sleigh Ride 403	Retrd.	N/A	16.80	60-78
1993 Siegfried 227	Retrd.	1996	25.00	55-90
1993 Silent Night (blue hat) 120	Retrd.	N/A	18.00	75
1993 Silent Night 120	Retrd.	N/A	18.00	48-60
1993 Silver Bells 52	Retrd.	N/A	27.00	90
1993 The Skating Bettinas 242	Retrd.	N/A	29.00	162-200
1993 Ski Baby 99	Retrd.	N/A	21.00	54-100
1993 Sloopy Snowman 328	Retrd.	1993	19.90	37-54
1993 Smitty 378	Retrd.	N/A	17.90	75-90
1993 Snow Dance 247	Retrd.	N/A	29.00	90
1993 Snowday Santa 98	Retrd.	1993	20.00	60-72
1993 Snowman by Candlelight 155	Retrd.	N/A	26.50	42-116
1993 Southern Colonial 171	Retrd.	N/A	26.90	85-135
1993 Special Delivery 91	Retrd.	N/A	17.00	26-36
1993 Spider & the Fly 393	Retrd.	1993	6.40	30
1993 Spintop Santa 288	Retrd.	N/A	22.80	46-75
1993 Sporty 345	Retrd.	N/A	20.00	36-42
1993 St. Nickcicle 298	Retrd.	N/A	25.90	90
1993 St. Nick's Pipe 330	Retrd.	N/A	4.40	42-54
1993 Star Children 208	Retrd.	1993	18.00	36-60
1993 Star Fire 175	Retrd.	N/A	26.80	40-90
1993 Star Ribbons 377	Retrd.	N/A	16.00	24-102
1993 Starlight Santa 348	Retrd.	N/A	11.90	19
1993 Sterling Reindeer 21	Retrd.	N/A	113.00	540
1993 Stocking Stuffers 236	Retrd.	1993	16.00	30-50
1993 Sugar Plum 185	Retrd.	N/A	6.40	42
1993 Sugar Shack 368	Retrd.	N/A	22.00	32-54
1993 Sunny Side Up 103	Retrd.	N/A	22.00	48-55
1993 Sweetheart 202	Retrd.	1993	16.00	28-60
1993 Talking Pipe 373	Retrd.	N/A	26.00	55
1993 Tannenbaum 243	Retrd.	N/A	24.00	30
1993 Tea & Sympathy 244	Retrd.	N/A	20.00	38-63
1993 Teenage Mermaid 226	Retrd.	N/A	27.50	48
1993 Texas Star 338	Retrd.	1993	7.50	8-15
1993 Thomas Nast Santa 217	Retrd.	N/A	23.00	35-72
1993 Tiffany Bells (cobalt) 334	Retrd.	N/A	9.00	24
1993 Tiger 90	Retrd.	N/A	23.90	24-44
1993 Time Piece 259	Retrd.	N/A	16.50	25-36
1993 Time Will Tell 349	Retrd.	N/A	22.00	30-42

Collectors' Information Bureau

*Quotes have been rounded up to nearest dollar

YEAR ISSUE	EDITION LIMIT	YEAR RETD.	ISSUE PRICE	*QUOTE U.S.$
1993 Tutti Fruitti (Carrot) 221	Retrd.	N/A	26.80	78-210
1993 Tuxedo Santa 117	Retrd.	1993	21.90	125-150
1993 Tweeter 94	Retrd.	1993	3.20	12-36
1993 Twinkle Toes 233	Retrd.	N/A	28.00	52-60
1993 Twinkle Tree 254	Retrd.	N/A	15.50	35-42
1993 Twister 214	Retrd.	N/A	16.80	45-75
1993 U-Boat 353	Retrd.	1993	15.50	34-48
1993 V.I.P. 230	Retrd.	1993	23.00	85-200
1993 Versaille Balloon 176	Retrd.	N/A	29.00	68-90
1993 Victorian Santa Reflector 198	Retrd.	N/A	28.00	55-180
1993 Vintage 67	Retrd.	N/A	49.00	90
1993 Wacko 272	Retrd.	N/A	24.00	35-48
1993 Waddles 95	Retrd.	1993	3.80	30
1993 Wally 223	Retrd.	N/A	26.00	60-75
1993 Will 181	Retrd.	N/A	23.00	30-42
1993 Wings & A Prayer 123	Retrd.	N/A	12.00	18-25
1993 Winter Birds (cloudy) 164	Retrd.	N/A	26.80	38-42
1993 Winterbirds (pr.) 164	Retrd.	1993	26.80	42-100
1994 Holiday Collection - C. Radko				
1994 Accordion Elf 127	Retrd.	N/A	23.00	65
1994 Airplane 315	Retrd.	N/A	56.00	76-150
1994 All Wrapped Up 161	Retrd.	N/A	26.00	28-78
1994 Andy Gump 48	Retrd.	N/A	18.00	36-42
1994 Angel Bounty 208	Retrd.	N/A	44.00	48-60
1994 Angel on Board 310	Retrd.	N/A	37.00	56-228
1994 Angel Song 141	Retrd.	N/A	45.60	40-90
1994 Angel Star 428	Retrd.	N/A	25.00	54-96
1994 Angelique 135	Retrd.	1996	33.30	52-84
1994 Aunt Kitty 183	Retrd.	N/A	26.00	26-42
1994 Autumn Tapestry 203	Retrd.	N/A	29.00	36-66
1994 Baby Booties (pink) 236	Retrd.	N/A	17.00	30-35
1994 Bag of Goodies 56	Retrd.	N/A	26.00	27-78
1994 Batter Up 397	Retrd.	N/A	13.00	25-36
1994 Berry Stripe 454	Retrd.	N/A	48.00	69-95
1994 Bird Bath 272	Retrd.	N/A	76.00	228
1994 Bird Brain 254	Retrd.	N/A	33.00	42-90
1994 Black Berry 340	Retrd.	N/A	14.00	13-27
1994 Bloomers 354	Retrd.	N/A	18.80	19-48
1994 Blue Satin 200	Retrd.	N/A	29.00	48
1994 Bobo 308	Retrd.	N/A	31.00	96
1994 Bow Ties 364	Retrd.	N/A	12.00	15-22
1994 Brazilia 302	Retrd.	N/A	38.00	48-90
1994 Bright Heavens Above 136	Retrd.	N/A	56.00	75-96
1994 Bubbles 267	Retrd.	N/A	42.00	42-72
1994 Bubbly 258	Retrd.	1994	43.00	48-84
1994 Buon Natale 266	Retrd.	N/A	36.00	95
1994 Cabernet 285	Retrd.	N/A	24.00	29-84
1994 Camille 212	Retrd.	N/A	29.00	35-48
1994 Candelabra 303	Retrd.	N/A	33.00	85
1994 Captain 260	Retrd.	N/A	47.20	84-108
1994 Carousel Willie 126	Retrd.	N/A	74.00	74-102
1994 Castanetta 321	Retrd.	N/A	37.00	50-60
1994 Celestial (blue) 408	Retrd.	N/A	28.80	50-63
1994 Checking It Twice 373	Retrd.	N/A	25.90	40-60
1994 Cheeky Santa 311	Retrd.	N/A	22.00	46
1994 Chianti 268	Retrd.	N/A	26.00	46-78
1994 Chic of Araby 220	Retrd.	N/A	17.00	24-30
1994 Chop Suey, set/2 329	Retrd.	N/A	34.00	65-150
1994 Christmas Express 437	Retrd.	N/A	72.00	72-90
1994 Christmas Harlequin 216	Retrd.	N/A	29.00	42-49
1994 Christmas in Camelot 113	Retrd.	N/A	27.00	45-48
1994 Chubbs & Slim 255	Retrd.	N/A	28.50	120-132
1994 Circus Band 92	Retrd.	1994	33.30	36-60
1994 Circus Delight 446	Retrd.	N/A	64.00	64-90
1994 Circus Star Balloon 201	Retrd.	N/A	29.00	60-90
1994 Classic Christmas 415	Retrd.	N/A	33.90	72-96
1994 Conchita 271	Retrd.	N/A	37.00	48
1994 Concord 342	Retrd.	N/A	16.00	22-31
1994 Cool Cat 219	Retrd.	N/A	26.00	36-100
1994 Corn Husk 336	Retrd.	N/A	13.00	20-36
1994 Cow Poke 284	Retrd.	N/A	42.00	56-84
1994 Crescent Moon Santa 398	Retrd.	N/A	29.00	96
1994 Crescent Moons 195	Retrd.	N/A	29.00	40-75
1994 Crock O'Dile 291	Retrd.	N/A	33.00	65-102
1994 Crown of Thorns 222	Retrd.	N/A	26.00	42-55
1994 Crowned Peacocks 377	Retrd.	N/A	15.00	15-22
1994 Damask Rose 429	Retrd.	N/A	29.00	29-60
1994 Dear-Ring 225	Retrd.	N/A	16.00	46
1994 Deep Sea 425	Retrd.	N/A	29.00	40-55
1994 Deercicle 291	Retrd.	N/A	29.00	48-96

YEAR ISSUE	EDITION LIMIT	YEAR RETD.	ISSUE PRICE	*QUOTE U.S.$
1994 Del Monte 348	Retrd.	N/A	31.00	31-36
1994 Dolly 283	Retrd.	N/A	42.00	60-84
1994 Dolly 283 & Cowpoke 284	Retrd.	N/A	84.00	147
1994 Dutch Maiden 38	Retrd.	N/A	44.00	30-44
1994 Egg Head 166	Retrd.	N/A	19.00	22
1994 Einstein's Kite 375	Retrd.	N/A	29.90	45
1994 Elephant Prince 170	Retrd.	N/A	14.50	25-60
1994 English Santa 55	Retrd.	N/A	26.00	34-78
1994 Epiphany Ball 211	Retrd.	N/A	29.00	48-66
1994 Faberge Finial 417	Retrd.	N/A	78.00	100-142
1994 Fido 50	Retrd.	N/A	20.00	34-42
1994 First Snow 355	Retrd.	N/A	15.00	15-24
1994 Fleet's In 281	Retrd.	N/A	38.00	65-78
1994 Florentine 190	Retrd.	N/A	29.00	48
1994 Forest Holiday 445	Retrd.	N/A	64.00	85-150
1994 Forget Your Troubles 146	Retrd.	N/A	17.00	22-42
1994 Frat Brothers 96	Retrd.	N/A	22.00	66
1994 French Country 192	Retrd.	N/A	29.00	65-95
1994 French Regency Balloon 393	Retrd.	N/A	32.50	35-60
1994 French Regency Finial 388	Retrd.	N/A	78.00	135-156
1994 From a Distance 322	Retrd.	N/A	32.00	60-75
1994 Gilded Cage 350	Retrd.	N/A	48.00	60-144
1994 Glad Tidings 430	Retrd.	N/A	44.00	114
1994 Glow Worm 275	Retrd.	N/A	32.00	65-78
1994 Golden Alpine 204	Retrd.	N/A	29.00	29-36
1994 Golden Crescendo Finial 384	Retrd.	N/A	42.00	125
1994 Grape Buzz 19	Retrd.	N/A	19.00	19-30
1994 Gretel 500	Retrd.	N/A	70.00	175
1994 H. Dumpty 46	Retrd.	N/A	19.00	24-46
1994 Hansel 501	Retrd.	N/A	70.00	175
1994 Harvest Home 414	Retrd.	N/A	28.80	54-95
1994 Harvest Moon 23	Retrd.	N/A	19.00	35-40
1994 Heavens Above 42	Retrd.	N/A	76.00	150-180
1994 Hieroglyph 194	Retrd.	N/A	29.00	29-54
1994 Holiday Sparkle 426	Retrd.	N/A	29.00	48-95
1994 Holly Heart 402	Retrd.	N/A	24.00	30
1994 Holly Jolly 399	Retrd.	N/A	40.00	54-72
1994 Holly Ribbons Finial 407	Retrd.	N/A	78.00	100
1994 Honey Belle 156	Retrd.	N/A	74.00	90-150
1994 Horse of a Different Color 309	Retrd.	N/A	28.00	60-102
1994 House Sitting Santa 240	Retrd.	N/A	26.00	26
1994 Ice House 98	Retrd.	N/A	14.00	17-23
1994 Ice Man Cometh 63	Retrd.	N/A	22.00	42
1994 Jack Clown 68	Retrd.	N/A	22.00	50
1994 Jean Claude 323	Retrd.	N/A	31.00	44-102
1994 Jockey Pipe 51	Retrd.	N/A	36.00	66-84
1994 Jolly Stripes 210	Retrd.	N/A	28.00	35-120
1994 Jubilee Finial 383-1	Retrd.	N/A	44.00	180
1994 Jumbo Harlequin 379	Retrd.	N/A	48.00	78-85
1994 Just Like Us 324	Retrd.	N/A	29.50	125-192
1994 Kaiser Pipe 134	Retrd.	N/A	32.00	34-60
1994 Kayo 165	Retrd.	N/A	14.00	20-42
1994 Kewpie 292	Retrd.	N/A	22.00	20-40
1994 King of Kings 18	Retrd.	N/A	22.00	22-75
1994 King's Guard 253	Retrd.	N/A	44.00	95
1994 Kissing Cousins (pair) 249	Retrd.	N/A	28.00	200
1994 Kitty Tamer 331	Retrd.	N/A	65.00	234-250
1994 Kosher Dill 338	Retrd.	N/A	12.00	20
1994 Lantern Lights 442	Retrd.	N/A	64.00	84
1994 Leader of the Band 94-915D (wh pants) - signed	Retrd.	1994	25.00	45-100
1994 Leader of the Band 94-915D (wh pants) - unsigned	Retrd.	1994	25.00	50-95
1994 Lemon Twist 28	Retrd.	N/A	14.00	40
1994 Letter to Santa 77	Retrd.	N/A	31.00	55-60
1994 Liberty Ball 172	Retrd.	N/A	26.00	36-66
1994 Liberty Bell 145	Retrd.	N/A	22.00	35-54
1994 Lil' Bo Peep 62	Retrd.	N/A	22.00	39
1994 Little Orphan 47	Retrd.	N/A	18.00	36-42
1994 Little Slugger 95	Retrd.	N/A	26.00	26-48
1994 Lola Ginabridgida 290	Retrd.	N/A	44.00	69-72
1994 The Los Angeles 155	Retrd.	N/A	26.00	54-75
1994 Madonna & Child 177	Retrd.	N/A	24.00	30-35
1994 Major Duck 327	Retrd.	N/A	58.00	198
1994 Mama's Little Angel 175	Retrd.	N/A	23.00	36
1994 Mandolin Angel 76	Retrd.	N/A	46.00	46-66
1994 Martian Holiday 326	Retrd.	N/A	42.00	168
1994 Masquerade 45	Retrd.	N/A	16.00	25-28
1994 Medium Nautilus (gold) 103	Retrd.	N/A	16.00	13-25
1994 Messiah 221	Retrd.	N/A	22.00	48
1994 Metamorphisis 174	Retrd.	N/A	16.00	36-42

ORNAMENTS

YEAR ISSUE	EDITION LIMIT	YEAR RETD.	ISSUE PRICE	*QUOTE U.S.$
1994 Mexican Hat Dance 307	Retrd.	N/A	32.00	96
1994 Midnight Mass 913	Retrd.	N/A	N/A	34-45
1994 Mission Ball (tree topper) 389	Retrd.	N/A	78.00	78-136
1994 Misty 97	Retrd.	N/A	19.00	25
1994 Mittens For Kittens 21	Retrd.	1994	22.00	35-40
1994 Moon Dust 133	Retrd.	N/A	18.00	36-40
1994 Moon Martian 298	Retrd.	N/A	26.00	140-144
1994 Moon Mullins 230	Retrd.	N/A	18.00	22-28
1994 Moon Ride 60	Retrd.	N/A	28.00	31-46
1994 Mother and Child 83	Retrd.	N/A	28.50	48-78
1994 Mountain Church 86	Retrd.	N/A	42.00	72-126
1994 Mr. Longneck 288	Retrd.	N/A	26.00	84
1994 Mr. Moto 280	Retrd.	N/A	35.60	58-102
1994 Mr. Smedley Drysdale 37	Retrd.	N/A	44.00	108-120
1994 My Darling 385	Retrd.	N/A	22.00	22-30
1994 My What Big Teeth	Retrd.	N/A	29.00	100-150
1994 New Year's Babe 239	Retrd.	N/A	21.00	48-66
1994 Nicky 316	Retrd.	N/A	24.00	20-60
1994 Nighty Night 299	Retrd.	N/A	36.00	90-120
1994 Oh My Stars 101	Retrd.	N/A	12.00	15-27
1994 Old Sour Puss 256	Retrd.	N/A	34.00	96
1994 Ollie 269	Retrd.	1996	49.50	74-150
1994 On The Run (Spoon/left side) 247	Retrd.	N/A	45.00	175-180
1994 One Small Step 314	Retrd.	N/A	58.00	76-95
1994 Over The Waves 261	Retrd.	N/A	38.00	90
1994 Owl Reflector 40	Retrd.	N/A	54.00	90-96
1994 Papa's Jamboree 427	Retrd.	N/A	29.00	30-45
1994 Partridge Pear Garland 435	Retrd.	N/A	68.00	72-150
1994 Party Hopper 274	Retrd.	N/A	37.00	115-195
1994 Party Time 902	Retrd.	N/A	24.00	24-36
1994 Peas on Earth 227	Retrd.	N/A	16.00	20-22
1994 Peking Santa 102	Retrd.	N/A	18.00	54
1994 Perky Pete 64	Retrd.	N/A	30.00	40-49
1994 Pickled 317	Retrd.	N/A	26.00	46-60
1994 Piggly Wiggly 169	Retrd.	N/A	14.00	40
1994 Piglet 294	Retrd.	N/A	13.00	42-45
1994 Pinecone Santa 118	Retrd.	N/A	29.50	50-100
1994 Pinocchio Gets Hitched 250	Retrd.	N/A	29.50	30-84
1994 Pixie Santa 218	Retrd.	N/A	20.00	28-35
1994 President Taft 74	Retrd.	N/A	18.00	50
1994 Pretty Bird 112	Retrd.	N/A	26.00	39-48
1994 Prince Philip 909	Retrd.	N/A	20.00	150
1994 Princess 286	Retrd.	N/A	18.00	22
1994 Private Eye 163	Retrd.	N/A	18.00	34-48
1994 Purple Plum 347	Retrd.	N/A	15.00	18-48
1994 Queen's Hare 44	Retrd.	N/A	22.00	60
1994 Quick Draw 330	Retrd.	N/A	65.00	220-250
1994 Radiant Birth 75	Retrd.	N/A	76.00	86-144
1994 Rain Dance 282	Retrd.	N/A	34.00	75
1994 Rainbow Snow 361	Retrd.	N/A	15.00	16-36
1994 Rainy Day Smile 54	Retrd.	N/A	22.00	20-30
1994 Rajah 25	Retrd.	N/A	19.00	22-42
1994 Raspberry 339	Retrd.	N/A	12.00	22
1994 Razzle Dazzle 372	Retrd.	N/A	37.90	45-102
1994 Red Cap 24	Retrd.	1996	22.00	33-72
1994 Ring Master 61	Retrd.	N/A	22.00	36-48
1994 Ring Twice 151	Retrd.	N/A	21.00	47-55
1994 Ringing Red Boots 114	Retrd.	N/A	46.00	60-72
1994 Rising Stars 121	Retrd.	N/A	12.90	18
1994 Roly Poly Angel 58	Retrd.	N/A	22.00	28-36
1994 Roly Poly Clown 173	Retrd.	N/A	19.40	45-75
1994 Roly Poly Pinocchio 328	Retrd.	N/A	54.00	110
1994 Rose Cone 31	Retrd.	N/A	25.00	34-36
1994 Rosy Lovebirds 89	Retrd.	N/A	48.00	72-90
1994 Royale Finial 382	Retrd.	N/A	64.00	95
1994 Ruby Reflector 352	Retrd.	N/A	26.00	42-102
1994 Santa Copter 306	Retrd.	N/A	47.00	125-216
1994 Santa Hearts 461	Retrd.	N/A	66.00	96-120
1994 Santa Reflector Finial 381	Retrd.	N/A	92.00	120
1994 Santa's Helper 131	Retrd.	N/A	19.90	35-40
1994 Saturn Rings 458	Retrd.	N/A	64.00	64-72
1994 School's Out 29	Retrd.	N/A	19.00	40-48
1994 Scotch Pine Finial 419	Retrd.	N/A	78.00	110-144
1994 Season's Greetings 41	Retrd.	N/A	42.00	45-60
1994 Serenity 196	Retrd.	N/A	44.00	60-78
1994 Sex Appeal 238	Retrd.	N/A	22.00	78-85
1994 Ships Ahoy 263	Retrd.	N/A	38.00	54
1994 Shivers 262	Retrd.	N/A	25.00	90-150
1994 Shooting The Moon 33	Retrd.	N/A	28.00	96
1994 Siberian Bear 392	Retrd.	N/A	23.90	42-59
1994 Silent Night 129	Retrd.	N/A	27.00	55
1994 Smiley 52	Retrd.	N/A	16.00	60
1994 Snow Bell 237	Retrd.	N/A	13.00	42-48
1994 Snow Dancing 91	Retrd.	N/A	29.00	72-95
1994 Snowy 313	Retrd.	N/A	26.00	50
1994 Soldier Boy 142	Retrd.	N/A	19.00	24-66
1994 Spring Chick 30	Retrd.	1996	27.00	46-84
1994 Squash Man 67	Retrd.	N/A	28.00	28-70
1994 Squiggles 157	Retrd.	N/A	29.90	55
1994 Squirreling Away 39	Retrd.	N/A	26.00	50-54
1994 St. Nick 65	Retrd.	N/A	18.00	30-36
1994 St. Nick's Pipe 235	Retrd.	N/A	12.00	36-42
1994 Stafford Floral 205	Retrd.	N/A	29.00	36-48
1994 Starfire Finial 418	Retrd.	N/A	84.00	92-114
1994 Starry Night 300	Retrd.	N/A	31.00	46-114
1994 Stocking Full 159	Retrd.	N/A	24.00	32-54
1994 Stocking Sam 108	Retrd.	N/A	23.00	42-72
1994 Strawberry 333	Retrd.	N/A	12.00	18-21
1994 Sugar Berry 341	Retrd.	N/A	12.00	13-22
1994 Sugar Cone 413	Retrd.	N/A	46.50	86-120
1994 Sugar Pear 335	Retrd.	N/A	13.00	19
1994 Surf's Up 325	Retrd.	N/A	36.00	84-102
1994 Swami 128	Retrd.	N/A	18.00	25
1994 Swan Fountain 278	Retrd.	N/A	44.00	174
1994 Swan Lake 911	Retrd.	N/A	16.00	65
1994 Sweet Gherkin 343	Retrd.	N/A	12.00	15-18
1994 Sweet Pear 59	Retrd.	N/A	24.00	24-72
1994 Tangerine 332	Retrd.	N/A	12.00	30
1994 Teddy Roosevelt 232	Retrd.	N/A	22.00	22-40
1994 Tee Time 167	Retrd.	N/A	16.00	35
1994 Teenage Mermaid 270	Retrd.	N/A	33.00	58
1994 Terrance 53	Retrd.	N/A	16.00	42-45
1994 Time to Spare 78	Retrd.	N/A	29.00	32-60
1994 Tiny Nautilus (gold) 100	Retrd.	N/A	12.00	15-40
1994 Tiny Ted 49	Retrd.	N/A	15.00	15-21
1994 Tiny Tunes 36	Retrd.	N/A	22.00	72
1994 Tomba 279	Retrd.	N/A	34.00	90
1994 Top Cat 206	Retrd.	N/A	29.00	42-48
1994 Topo 318	Retrd.	N/A	33.00	42-84
1994 Tuxedo Carousel 245	Retrd.	N/A	52.00	70-150
1994 Twinkle Star 360	Retrd.	N/A	13.00	13-36
1994 Uncle Max 66	Retrd.	1994	26.00	42-60
1994 Valcourt 213	Retrd.	N/A	29.00	60-100
1994 Vaudeville Sam 57	Retrd.	N/A	18.00	27-66
1994 Waldo 17	Retrd.	N/A	22.00	28-54
1994 Walnut 337	Retrd.	N/A	11.00	22
1994 Wedded Bliss 94	Retrd.	N/A	88.00	195-216
1994 Wednesday 120	Retrd.	N/A	42.00	45-70
1994 What a Donkey 277	Retrd.	N/A	34.00	55-90
1994 White Nights 197	Retrd.	N/A	26.00	36-48
1994 White Tiger 223	Retrd.	N/A	25.90	45
1994 Wind Swept 188	Retrd.	N/A	28.80	32
1994 Wings and a Snail 301	Retrd.	N/A	32.00	75-110
1994 Wings of Peace 69	Retrd.	N/A	22.00	36-60
1994 Winter Frolic 287	Retrd.	N/A	18.00	36-48
1994 Xenon 304	Retrd.	N/A	38.00	120-195
1994 Yuletide Bells 148	Retrd.	N/A	12.00	66

1995 Holiday Collection - C. Radko

YEAR ISSUE	EDITION LIMIT	YEAR RETD.	ISSUE PRICE	*QUOTE U.S.$
1995 10, 9, 8 139	Retrd.	N/A	22.00	22-36
1995 Al Pine 161	Retrd.	N/A	24.00	30
1995 Aloisius Beer 194	Retrd.	N/A	75.00	125
1995 American Pride 105	Retrd.	N/A	24.00	34
1995 Andrew Jacksons, pair 208	Retrd.	1995	68.00	300-350
1995 Annie 2	Retrd.	N/A	26.00	26-30
1995 Another Fine Mess 160	Retrd.	N/A	16.00	72-80
1995 Aqualina 293	Retrd.	1996	26.00	41-90
1995 Autumn Oak King 23	Retrd.	N/A	28.00	28-38
1995 Away We Go 173	Retrd.	N/A	24.00	28-42
1995 Bailey 283	Retrd.	N/A	46.00	100
1995 Banana Split 246	Retrd.	N/A	24.00	24-27
1995 Be It Ever So Humble 53	Retrd.	N/A	22.00	24-30
1995 Bear Mail 38	Retrd.	1996	28.00	40-107
1995 Bearly Mooning 7	Retrd.	N/A	26.00	30
1995 Beezlebub 94	Retrd.	N/A	14.00	66
1995 Best Friends 130	Retrd.	N/A	22.00	22-65
1995 Bishop (original coloration) 127	Retrd.	N/A	74.00	110-180
1995 Blue Dolphin 238	Retrd.	N/A	22.00	36-48
1995 Blue Lucy Finial 309	Retrd.	N/A	90.00	121-153
1995 Bordeaux 901	Retrd.	N/A	N/A	24-45
1995 Bringing Home the Bacon 204	Retrd.	N/A	26.00	48-110
1995 Buford T 63	Retrd.	N/A	14.00	30

Collectors' Information Bureau

*Quotes have been rounded up to nearest dollar

ORNAMENTS

YEAR ISSUE	EDITION LIMIT	YEAR RETD.	ISSUE PRICE	*QUOTE U.S.$
1995 Bundle of Toys 70	Retrd.	N/A	34.00	34-48
1995 Butcher Sam 190	Retrd.	N/A	22.00	36
1995 Buttons 21	Retrd.	N/A	36.00	34-45
1995 Caribbean Constable 11	Retrd.	N/A	24.00	100-138
1995 Carousel Santa 133	Retrd.	N/A	36.00	36-75
1995 Catch O' Day 93	Retrd.	N/A	13.50	20
1995 Celeste 262	Retrd.	N/A	52.00	72
1995 Cheeky St. Nick 274	Retrd.	N/A	32.00	32-75
1995 Christmas Cake 35	Retrd.	N/A	24.00	33-49
1995 Christmas Joy 33	Retrd.	N/A	42.00	45-60
1995 Christmas Morning 141	Retrd.	N/A	24.00	25-38
1995 Christmas Pie 135	Retrd.	N/A	54.00	55-78
1995 Chubby Decker 3	Retrd.	N/A	36.00	36-54
1995 Claudette 95-017-0	Retrd.	1995	22.00	54-95
1995 Climbing Higher 146	Retrd.	N/A	26.00	30
1995 Clown Rattle 230	Retrd.	N/A	16.00	44-100
1995 Clown Spin 151-1	Retrd.	N/A	38.00	39-60
1995 Cock O' Doodle 91	Retrd.	N/A	19.00	24
1995 Cockle Bell 175	Retrd.	N/A	38.00	34-50
1995 Creole Dancer 275	Retrd.	N/A	52.00	52-90
1995 Curlycue Santa 219	Retrd.	N/A	30.00	35-48
1995 David 56	Retrd.	N/A	28.00	30
1995 Decker 3	Retrd.	N/A	36.00	47
1995 Della Robbia Garland 308	Retrd.	N/A	34.00	68-100
1995 Department Store Santa 131	Retrd.	N/A	36.00	60-213
1995 Dolly For Susie 101	Retrd.	N/A	25.00	42
1995 Drum Major 66	Retrd.	N/A	24.00	33-69
1995 Drummer Santa 149	Retrd.	N/A	38.00	40-48
1995 Dutch Dolls 136	Retrd.	N/A	22.00	36-95
1995 Eagle Eye 104	Retrd.	N/A	26.00	35
1995 Elfin 903	Retrd.	N/A	N/A	24-60
1995 Evening Owl 193	Retrd.	N/A	36.00	36-45
1995 Fairy Dust 253	Retrd.	N/A	72.00	72-110
1995 Farmer Boy 108	Retrd.	N/A	28.00	48-150
1995 Flying High 8	Retrd.	N/A	22.00	50-57
1995 Forest Cabin 179	Retrd.	N/A	15.00	28-48
1995 French Lace 134	Retrd.	N/A	24.00	24-42
1995 Frog Lady 26	Retrd.	N/A	24.00	48-125
1995 Frosted Santa 143	Retrd.	N/A	25.00	38-62
1995 Fruit Basket 181	Retrd.	N/A	14.00	24
1995 Fruit Kan Chu 267	Retrd.	1995	50.00	60
1995 Fruit Nuts 213	Retrd.	N/A	14.00	20-28
1995 Garden Elves (pink hat) 207	Retrd.	N/A	56.00	56-72
1995 Garden Girls (pair) 39	Retrd.	N/A	18.00	90-108
1995 Gay Blades 272	Retrd.	1996	46.00	46-85
1995 Glad Tidings To All 115	Retrd.	N/A	44.00	44-72
1995 Glorianna 263	Retrd.	N/A	56.00	56-72
1995 Gobbles 203	Retrd.	N/A	52.00	85
1995 Grandpa Jones 144	Retrd.	N/A	22.00	40-95
1995 Gunther 233	Retrd.	N/A	32.00	108-175
1995 Gypsy Bear 908	Retrd.	N/A	N/A	26-30
1995 Having a Ball 126	Retrd.	N/A	26.00	27-47
1995 Heavy Load 19	Retrd.	N/A	42.00	55-96
1995 Helmut's Bells 28	Retrd.	N/A	18.00	35
1995 Henrietta 217	Retrd.	N/A	24.00	24-40
1995 Here Boy 222	Retrd.	N/A	12.00	35-150
1995 Hi Ho 97	Retrd.	N/A	56.00	56-96
1995 High Flying 8	Retrd.	N/A	22.00	54-95
1995 Ho Ho Ho 78	Retrd.	N/A	18.00	20-36
1995 Holiday Star Santa 27	Retrd.	N/A	16.00	19-125
1995 Holly Santa 123	Retrd.	N/A	18.00	19-25
1995 Hooty Hoot 24	Retrd.	1996	26.00	39-42
1995 Hot Head 221	Retrd.	N/A	18.00	45
1995 Hubbard's the Name 206	Retrd.	N/A	26.00	84-125
1995 I'm Late, I'm Late 291	Retrd.	N/A	48.00	48-65
1995 Imperial Helmet 240	Retrd.	N/A	22.00	42-95
1995 Jazz Santa 196	Retrd.	N/A	28.00	30-45
1995 Jingles 46	Retrd.	N/A	26.00	39-48
1995 Joy To The World 42	Retrd.	N/A	68.00	40-63
1995 JT Cricket 137	Retrd.	N/A	22.00	22-36
1995 Jumbo Walnut 249	Retrd.	N/A	18.00	48-80
1995 Just A Kiss Away 228	Retrd.	N/A	24.00	63
1995 Kaleidoscope Cone 25	Retrd.	N/A	44.00	48-60
1995 Kitty Claus 225	Retrd.	N/A	22.00	22-40
1995 Kitty Vittles 79	Retrd.	N/A	18.00	18-50
1995 Laugh Til You Cry 236	Retrd.	N/A	24.00	28-45
1995 Lavender Berry Garland 307	Retrd.	N/A	42.00	72
1995 Lavender Light 157	Retrd.	N/A	28.00	28-75
1995 Lean & Lanky 95	Retrd.	N/A	23.00	23-35
1995 Little Dreamer 159	Retrd.	N/A	16.00	36-51
1995 Little Drummer Bear 37	Retrd.	N/A	22.00	22-30
1995 Little Prince 6	Retrd.	N/A	39.00	125
1995 Little Red 214	Retrd.	N/A	22.00	40-95
1995 Little Toy Maker 167	Retrd.	N/A	26.00	48-100
1995 Midnight Mass 913	Retrd.	N/A	N/A	45-78
1995 Miss Mamie 110	Retrd.	N/A	34.00	45
1995 Mother Mary 98	Retrd.	N/A	24.00	42
1995 Mugsy 183	Retrd.	N/A	22.00	48-100
1995 My Bonnie Lass 170	Retrd.	N/A	24.00	35
1995 My Favorite Chimp 148	Retrd.	N/A	26.00	38-55
1995 My What Big Eyes 910	Retrd.	N/A	N/A	28
1995 Neptune's Charge 113	Retrd.	N/A	36.00	66-90
1995 Nesting Stork 198	Retrd.	N/A	24.00	60-66
1995 Nibbles 18	Retrd.	N/A	24.00	40-42
1995 O Holy Night 260	Retrd.	N/A	52.00	75-77
1995 Off to Market 223	Retrd.	N/A	24.00	48-100
1995 Officer Joe 122	Retrd.	N/A	22.00	60-95
1995 On the Court 45	Retrd.	N/A	26.00	26-30
1995 Papa Bear Reflector 292	Retrd.	N/A	52.00	52-56
1995 Party Time 902	Retrd.	N/A	N/A	24.00
1995 Pecky Woodpecker 288	Retrd.	N/A	36.00	36-66
1995 Peek A Boo 212	Retrd.	N/A	18.00	48
1995 Pencil Santa 232	Retrd.	N/A	18.00	18-33
1995 Penelope 197	Retrd.	N/A	26.00	36-110
1995 Percussion 255	Retrd.	N/A	50.00	50-110
1995 Pere Noel 41	Retrd.	N/A	44.00	33-46
1995 Personal Delivery 116	Retrd.	N/A	36.00	48-150
1995 Pine Tree Santa 912	Retrd.	N/A	N/A	26-46
1995 Pirate Ship 250	Retrd.	N/A	44.00	168-198
1995 Polar Express 76	Retrd.	N/A	24.00	45-59
1995 Pork Chop 231	Retrd.	N/A	22.00	22-40
1995 Prince of Thieves 44	Retrd.	N/A	28.00	40
1995 Punch 172	Retrd.	N/A	22.00	36
1995 Quakers 261	Retrd.	1996	24.00	24-35
1995 Quilted Santa 187	Retrd.	N/A	68.00	40-68
1995 Rainbow Scallop (gold) 9	Retrd.	N/A	16.00	15-42
1995 Rakish Charm 142	Retrd.	N/A	22.00	45
1995 Reflecto 281	Retrd.	N/A	46.00	46-96
1995 Ricky Raccoon 138	Retrd.	N/A	24.00	42
1995 Rockateer 284	Retrd.	N/A	44.00	65
1995 Round About Santa 5	Retrd.	N/A	42.00	42-60
1995 Round Up 1	Retrd.	N/A	26.00	26-30
1995 Royal Tiger 34	Retrd.	N/A	36.00	72
1995 Rummy Tum Tum 168	Retrd.	N/A	44.00	65-72
1995 Santa Fantasy 20	Retrd.	N/A	44.00	95
1995 Santa Maria 286	Retrd.	N/A	64.00	140
1995 Shy Elephant 282	Retrd.	N/A	32.00	85
1995 Siamese Slippers 264	Retrd.	1995	16.00	55
1995 Sister Act-set 140	Retrd.	N/A	18.00	48-160
1995 Skater's Waltz 12	Retrd.	N/A	28.00	38-65
1995 Slim Pickins 114	Retrd.	N/A	22.00	22-55
1995 Snow Ball 100	Retrd.	N/A	28.00	120-240
1995 Snow Song 40	Retrd.	N/A	18.00	20-30
1995 Spellbound 128	Retrd.	N/A	26.00	48
1995 Spring Arrival 82	Retrd.	N/A	44.00	50-65
1995 Springtime Sparrow 119	Retrd.	N/A	14.00	25
1995 St. Peter's Keys 298	Retrd.	N/A	8.00	18
1995 Stork Lantern 241	Retrd.	N/A	18.00	22
1995 Storytime Santa 22	Retrd.	N/A	44.00	44-60
1995 Swan Lake 911	Retrd.	N/A	36.00	58
1995 Sweet Carrot 248	Retrd.	N/A	22.00	29-42
1995 Sweet Dreams 258	Retrd.	N/A	28.00	40-48
1995 Sweet Madame 192	Retrd.	N/A	48.00	150-180
1995 Sweethearts 99	Retrd.	N/A	26.00	34
1995 Swinging on a Star 183	Retrd.	N/A	44.00	50
1995 Teddy's Tree 156	Retrd.	N/A	22.00	22-45
1995 Tennis Anyone? 14	Retrd.	N/A	18.00	18-36
1995 Time For A Bite 251	Retrd.	N/A	62.00	62-110
1995 Trick or Treat 13	Retrd.	N/A	23.00	30-36
1995 Turtle Bird 121	Retrd.	N/A	22.00	35-35
1995 Very Berry 92	Retrd.	N/A	11.00	15-42
1995 Warm Wishes 112	Retrd.	N/A	22.00	22-36
1995 Washington's (Martha & George) 103	Retrd.	N/A	28.00	72-116
1995 Westminster Santa 189	Retrd.	N/A	24.00	26-48
1995 White Dove 88	Retrd.	N/A	32.00	32-48
1995 Wiggle Men 89	Retrd.	N/A	10.00	15-22
1995 Winter Pooch 163	Retrd.	N/A	22.00	33-35
1995 Winter Sun 145	Retrd.	N/A	31.00	45
1995 Youthful Madonna 259	Retrd.	N/A	28.00	29-42

1996 Holiday Collection - C. Radko

YEAR ISSUE	EDITION LIMIT	YEAR RETD.	ISSUE PRICE	*QUOTE U.S.$
1996 Angel Prayer 135	Retrd.	N/A	22.00	24-36

ORNAMENTS

YEAR ISSUE	EDITION LIMIT	YEAR RETD.	ISSUE PRICE	*QUOTE U.S.$
1996 Astro Pup 36	Retrd.	1996	32.00	30-45
1996 Baby Angel 3	Retrd.	N/A	22.00	22-30
1996 Baby Elephants 277	Retrd.	1996	18.00	30
1996 Bella D. Snowball 160	Retrd.	N/A	26.00	30-38
1996 Billy Bunny 97	Retrd.	N/A	26.00	27-36
1996 Bottoms Up 148	Retrd.	N/A	26.00	27-40
1996 By The Shore 15	Retrd.	N/A	16.00	16-30
1996 Candy Swirl 299	Retrd.	N/A	24.00	45-50
1996 Caroline 152	Retrd.	N/A	24.00	28-48
1996 Casey 107	Retrd.	N/A	18.00	24-27
1996 Catavarius 84	Retrd.	N/A	38.00	72
1996 Charlie Horse 4	Retrd.	N/A	20.00	21-30
1996 Checkered Past 63	Retrd.	N/A	50.00	50-75
1996 Christmas King 147	Retrd.	N/A	46.00	54-57
1996 Christmas Past 223	Retrd.	N/A	18.00	18-22
1996 Church Window 301	Retrd.	N/A	16.00	16-24
1996 Circus Seal 141	Retrd.	N/A	22.00	33
1996 The Clauses 159	Retrd.	N/A	26.00	38-54
1996 Cookin' Up Christmas 129	Retrd.	N/A	18.00	48
1996 Count Dimitri 145	Retrd.	N/A	24.00	36
1996 Crescent Kringle 40	Retrd.	N/A	36.00	36-67
1996 Croc Cutie 241	Retrd.	N/A	22.00	54
1996 Cycle Santa 114	Retrd.	N/A	26.00	30-35
1996 Czech Express 104	Retrd.	N/A	36.00	39-42
1996 Davey 55	Retrd.	N/A	48.00	48-54
1996 Dreamy 12	Retrd.	N/A	17.00	17-30
1996 Elfcycle 14	Retrd.	N/A	28.00	36-42
1996 English Garden 199	Retrd.	N/A	36.00	54
1996 Eskimo Cheer 157	Retrd.	1996	22.00	30
1996 Every Bead Of My Heart 246	Retrd.	N/A	22.00	32
1996 Festiva (gold) 212	Retrd.	N/A	36.00	44-48
1996 Field Blossom 64	Retrd.	N/A	46.00	48-60
1996 Flying High 257	Retrd.	N/A	42.00	60
1996 For Clara 86	Retrd.	N/A	32.00	39-48
1996 Frosty Cardinal 215	Retrd.	N/A	32.00	36-45
1996 Frosty Pepper 234	Retrd.	N/A	12.00	28
1996 Full of Joy 134	Retrd.	N/A	12.00	20-25
1996 Gilded Wings (red) 8	Retrd.	N/A	16.00	30
1996 Grape Bouquet 61	Retrd.	N/A	33.00	38-54
1996 Great Gobbles 207	Retrd.	N/A	38.00	48
1996 Heavenly Triumph 185	Retrd.	N/A	22.00	26-36
1996 Hi Ho Trio 56	Retrd.	N/A	47.00	47-60
1996 His Goil 67	Retrd.	N/A	40.00	40-95
1996 His Wizardry 255	Retrd.	N/A	22.00	25-36
1996 Hot n' Frosty 225	Retrd.	N/A	10.00	18
1996 Incantation 105	Retrd.	N/A	24.00	35-70
1996 Lancer 13	Retrd.	N/A	29.00	30-35
1996 Lemon Guard 233	Retrd.	N/A	22.00	22-28
1996 Lilac Angel 51	Retrd.	N/A	44.00	44-54
1996 Lilac Winter 50	Retrd.	1996	44.00	48
1996 Londonberry 193	Retrd.	N/A	44.00	55-60
1996 Love and Valor (purple) 72	Retrd.	N/A	14.50	24
1996 Love Is In The Air 183	Retrd.	N/A	22.00	24-30
1996 Lucinda 204	Retrd.	N/A	38.00	49
1996 Magic Munchkin 240	Retrd.	N/A	32.00	36-46
1996 Merry Matador 189	Retrd.	N/A	23.95	25-42
1996 Midnight Orchid 285	Retrd.	N/A	32.00	54
1996 Midnight Ride 169	Retrd.	1996	51.00	72-76
1996 Minuet 167	Retrd.	1996	54.00	54-65
1996 Miss Flurry 94	Retrd.	N/A	38.00	150
1996 Monte Carlo 27	Retrd.	1996	52.00	65
1996 Ms. Peanut 42	Retrd.	1996	30.00	100
1996 Night Magic 2	Retrd.	N/A	26.00	26-36
1996 Ocean Call 245	Retrd.	N/A	18.00	18-34
1996 Oh Christmas Tree! 156	Retrd.	N/A	42.00	43-80
1996 Persia 237	Retrd.	N/A	18.00	35
1996 Pineapple Frost 112	Retrd.	N/A	14.00	28
1996 Poinsettia Snow 216	Retrd.	N/A	32.00	36-48
1996 Polar Nights 208	Retrd.	N/A	32.00	32-54
1996 Pookie 187	Retrd.	N/A	16.00	24
1996 Professor Hare 144	Retrd.	N/A	26.00	32-36
1996 Puff 69	Retrd.	N/A	48.00	57
1996 Pumpkin Eater 203	Retrd.	N/A	34.00	40
1996 Punkin Patch 5	Retrd.	N/A	26.00	42
1996 Ragamuffins 52	Retrd.	N/A	39.00	40-47
1996 Rainbow Drops (set/3) 123	Retrd.	N/A	14.00	72
1996 Rainbow-Tiffany 302	Retrd.	N/A	26.00	26-50
1996 Reach For a Star 209	Retrd.	N/A	32.00	36
1996 Return Engagement 151	Retrd.	N/A	38.00	39-43
1996 Rocket Santa 38	Retrd.	N/A	48.00	65-84
1996 Rosy Cheek Santa 10	Retrd.	N/A	20.00	21-48
1996 Round Midnight 274	Retrd.	1996	30.00	40
1996 Roxanne 33	Retrd.	N/A	40.00	40-60
1996 Russian Knight 21	Retrd.	N/A	100.00	150
1996 Sapphire Santa 158	Retrd.	N/A	34.00	35-48
1996 Shimmy Down 253	Retrd.	N/A	42.00	51-64
1996 Shining Armour 188	Retrd.	1996	22.00	22
1996 Shoe Shack 140	Retrd.	N/A	44.00	48
1996 Sing We Now 176	Retrd.	N/A	22.00	22-29
1996 Sleighfull 150	Retrd.	N/A	34.00	46-65
1996 Slim Wizard 115	Retrd.	N/A	18.00	40
1996 Snow Castle 139	Retrd.	1996	12.00	18
1996 Snow Hare 73	Retrd.	N/A	14.00	15-24
1996 Snow Kitties 125	Retrd.	N/A	26.00	32-36
1996 Snowballing 146	Retrd.	N/A	26.00	30-42
1996 Snowday 192	Retrd.	N/A	19.00	24
1996 Snowtem Pole 155	Retrd.	N/A	32.00	42-44
1996 Speed Racer Garland 1	Retrd.	N/A	66.00	67-195
1996 Star Shot 249	Retrd.	N/A	32.00	32-48
1996 Starscape Santa 143	Retrd.	N/A	44.00	50-85
1996 Starship 113	Retrd.	N/A	28.00	43-60
1996 Strong To The Finish 66	Retrd.	N/A	48.00	50
1996 Sweet Tomato 224	Retrd.	N/A	14.00	34
1996 Tiffany Rainbow 302	Retrd.	N/A	26.00	50
1996 Time Flies 314	Retrd.	1996	28.00	32-46
1996 Topolina 288	Retrd.	1996	42.00	60
1996 Toys For All 153	Retrd.	N/A	44.00	39-44
1996 Twilight Santa Reflector 289	Retrd.	N/A	48.00	79
1996 Under The Sea 313	Retrd.	N/A	17.00	24
1996 Up And Away 286	Retrd.	N/A	42.00	50-60
1996 Village Santa 99	Retrd.	N/A	30.00	36-42
1996 Vintage Classics 222	Retrd.	N/A	24.00	30
1996 Winter Blossom 284	Retrd.	N/A	46.00	46-59
1996 Winter Dream 250	Retrd.	N/A	42.00	40-51
1996 Winter Holiday 62	Retrd.	N/A	44.00	78
1996 Winter Wind 121	Retrd.	N/A	24.00	28-36
1996 Yankee Doodle Santa 251	Retrd.	N/A	34.00	40-52
1996 Yo Ho Ho 53	Retrd.	N/A	48.00	48-50

1997 Holiday Collection - C. Radko

YEAR ISSUE	EDITION LIMIT	YEAR RETD.	ISSUE PRICE	*QUOTE U.S.$
1997 Angel on High 11	Retrd.	N/A	31.00	33-60
1997 Carnivale Garland 453	Retrd.	N/A	68.00	78
1997 Christmas Cloudhoppers 90	Retrd.	N/A	65.00	72-120
1997 Crystal Frost 428	Retrd.	N/A	68.00	73
1997 Dutch Date 137	Retrd.	N/A	56.00	90
1997 Enough For All 209	Retrd.	N/A	76.00	78-85
1997 Galaxy Frost 59	Retrd.	N/A	65.00	108
1997 Gardening Angels 121	Retrd.	N/A	34.00	60
1997 General Cracker 95	Retrd.	N/A	34.00	41-48
1997 Goodnight Prayer 171	Retrd.	N/A	42.00	45-49
1997 Holly Frost 135	Retrd.	N/A	24.00	28
1997 Huggy Bear 161	Retrd.	N/A	50.00	54-60
1997 Humperdink 328	Retrd.	N/A	24.00	53
1997 Jolly Elf 148	Retrd.	N/A	40.00	49
1997 Making A List 222	Retrd.	N/A	40.00	42-47
1997 Monster Mash 20	Retrd.	N/A	32.00	34-44
1997 Nick of Time 289	Retrd.	N/A	70.00	75
1997 Off The Wall Jumbo 356	Retrd.	N/A	60.00	64-84
1997 Old World Angel 114	Retrd.	N/A	26.00	34
1997 Pepper's Frost 107	Retrd.	N/A	15.00	21
1997 Rainbow Iris 71	Retrd.	N/A	38.00	66
1997 Roy Rabbit 724	Retrd.	N/A	42.00	44-49
1997 Royal Game 433	Retrd.	N/A	76.00	80
1997 Santa Tree Finial 96	Retrd.	N/A	70.00	96
1997 Sleepy Hollowhead 226	Retrd.	N/A	48.00	52
1997 Star Gazing Finial 81	Retrd.	N/A	100.00	150
1997 White Winter Blossom Finial 288	Retrd.	N/A	105.00	145
1997 Willy Wobble 132	Retrd.	N/A	50.00	53-66
1997 Winter Birds 123	Retrd.	N/A	22.00	30
1997 Winter Skate 341	Retrd.	N/A	54.00	67
1997 Woodland Frost Garland 26	Retrd.	N/A	60.00	96

1998 Holiday Collection - C. Radko

YEAR ISSUE	EDITION LIMIT	YEAR RETD.	ISSUE PRICE	*QUOTE U.S.$
1998 Blizzard Baron 822	Retrd.	N/A	42.00	47
1998 Deer Friends Wreath 815	Retrd.	N/A	39.00	44
1998 Stardust Snowflake 816	Retrd.	N/A	47.00	52
1998 Surrounded by Friends 819	Retrd.	N/A	49.00	54

1999 Holiday Collection - C. Radko

YEAR ISSUE	EDITION LIMIT	YEAR RETD.	ISSUE PRICE	*QUOTE U.S.$
1999 Beefeater Bear 172	Retrd.	N/A	42.00	48
1999 Blue Amazon 174	Retrd.	N/A	38.00	43
1999 Eggstatic Garland 235	Retrd.	N/A	38.00	66

Collectors' Information Bureau

*Quotes have been rounded up to nearest dollar

YEAR ISSUE	EDITION LIMIT	YEAR RETD.	ISSUE PRICE	*QUOTE U.S.$
1999 Elegant Evergreen 413	Retrd.	N/A	74.00	79
1999 Every Bead of My Heart Garland 151	Retrd.	N/A	38.00	48
1999 Hickory Dickory Dock 160	Retrd.	N/A	32.00	38
1999 Holiday Reunion 228	Retrd.	N/A	38.00	43
1999 Love You This Much 31	Retrd.	N/A	33.00	38
1999 Millennium Puppy 291	Retrd.	N/A	33.00	55
1999 Peaceful Season 200	Retrd.	N/A	32.00	37
1999 Persian Elegance 329	Retrd.	N/A	46.00	50
1999 Romanza 332	Retrd.	N/A	65.00	70
1999 Rose Garden 336	Retrd.	N/A	45.00	50
1999 Royal Roadster 85	Retrd.	N/A	69.00	74
1999 Royal Russian Holiday 209	Retrd.	N/A	33.00	39
1999 Royal Tapestry 337	Retrd.	N/A	46.00	50
1999 Saint Patrick 288	Retrd.	N/A	38.00	46
1999 Teacher Santa 118	Retrd.	N/A	34.00	38
1999 Wedding Day 406	Retrd.	N/A	125.00	130

2001 Ornament of the Month Continuity Program - C. Radko

2001 April Eggstra Plenty 01-0419-0	Yr.Iss.	2001	46.00	46
2001 May Love in Bloom 01-0532-0	Yr.Iss.	2001	34.00	34
2001 June Bluebird Suite 01-0091-0	Yr.Iss.	2001	42.00	42
2001 July Freedom's Wings 01-0307-0	Yr.Iss.	2001	38.00	38
2001 August Hawaiian Holiday 01-0218-0	Yr.Iss.	2001	39.00	39
2001 September Wreath of Good Cheer 01-0171-0	Yr.Iss.	2001	37.00	37
2001 October The Patchworthies 01-0518-0	Yr.Iss.	2001	39.00	39
2001 November Thanksgiving Spread 01-0150-0	Yr.Iss.	2001	35.00	35
2001 December Santa in Tree-pose 01-0438-0	Yr.Iss.	2001	48.00	48
2002 January Happy Snow Year 021-0104-0	Yr.Iss.	2002	42.00	42
2002 February Cupid's Surprise 02-0105-0	Yr.Iss.	2002	39.00	39
2002 March Nicholas O' Reilly 02-0106-0	Yr.Iss.	2002	44.00	44

2002 Ornament of the Month Continuity Program - C. Radko

2002 April Shower Me With Love 02-0499-0	Yr.Iss.		54.00	54
2002 May My Honey's Home 02-0088-0	Yr.Iss.		42.00	42
2002 June Wedded Dove Chime 02-0101-0	Yr.Iss.		62.00	62
2002 July Freedom Rings Forever 02-0606-0	Yr.Iss.		42.00	42
2002 August Shine On Santa 02-0529-0	Yr.Iss.		54.00	54
2002 September School Daze 02-0296-0	Yr.Iss.		52.00	52
2002 October Wigglesworth 02-0050-0	Yr.Iss.		56.00	56
2002 November Hats Off To Tom! 02-0297-0	Yr.Iss.		47.00	47
2002 December Special Invitation 02-0021-0	Yr.Iss.		58.00	58
2003 January New Year's Blow Out 03-0001-0	Yr.Iss.		45.00	58
2003 February Tweet Love 03-0002-0	Yr.Iss.		46.00	46
2003 March Snuggle Swing 03-0003-0	Yr.Iss.		66.00	66

Aids Awareness - C. Radko

1993 A Shy Rabbit's Heart 462	Retrd.	1993	15.00	50-94
1994 Frosty Cares SP5	Retrd.	1994	25.00	50-95
1995 On Wings of Hope SP10	Retrd.	1995	30.00	45-65
1996 A Winter Bear's Heart SP15	Retrd.	1996	34.00	40-55
1997 A Caring Clown 97-SP-22	Retrd.	1997	36.00	38-50
1998 Sugar Holiday (Elizabeth Taylor Aids Foundation) 98-SP-29	Retrd.	1998	38.00	38-50
1999 Cubby's Rainbow 99-SP-45	Retrd.	1999	36.00	36-40
2000 Sir Elton Claus (Elton John Aids Foundation) 00-SP-59	Yr.Iss.	2000	37.00	37
2001 A Little Pop Music 01-SP-79	Retrd.	2001	34.00	34
2002 Heartfelt Joy 02-SP-93	Yr.Iss.		39.00	39

Alvin And The Chipmunks - C. Radko

1998 Downhill Racer 98-CHP-01	Retrd.	1999	26.00	26
1998 Oh Tannenbaum 98-CHP-02	Retrd.	1999	27.00	27
1998 Winter Fun 98-CHP-03	Retrd.	1999	27.00	27

The American Red Cross of Greater New York - C. Radko

2001 Brave Heart 01-0594-0	Open		34.00	37

Animal Related Charities - C. Radko

2000 Pet Pals 00-SP-61	Retrd.	2000	37.00	37
2001 Charlie 01-SP-81	Retrd.	2001	34.00	34
2002 Festive Furry Friends 02-SP-95	Yr.Iss.		38.00	38

Breast Cancer Research - C. Radko

1998 Felina's Heart 98-SP-31	Retrd.	1998	32.00	32-35

YEAR ISSUE	EDITION LIMIT	YEAR RETD.	ISSUE PRICE	*QUOTE U.S.$
1999 Bonny Maureen 99-SP-47	Retrd.	1999	32.00	32-40
2000 Bonny Spring 00-SP-60	Yr.Iss.	2000	34.00	35
2001 Wings of Love 01-SP-82	Yr.Iss.	2001	35.00	35
2002 Pretty Petals 02-SP-89	Yr.Iss.		39.00	39

Carson Pirie Scott - C. Radko

1997 Carson Snowman 97-CPS-01	Retrd.	1997	44.00	44

CBS and Desilu's "I Love Lucy" - C. Radko

1997 Candy Maker 97-LCY-07	Retrd.	1999	42.00	42
1998 Ethel and Fred Heart 98-LCY-03	Open		19.00	19
1997 Ethel's Christmas & Fred's Christmas (pair) 97-LCY-02	Open		80.00	80
1999 Fortune Teller 99-LCY-01	Retrd.	2000	32.00	32
2000 Grape Stomping Lucy 00-LCY-03	Retrd.	2001	33.00	33
2000 Hollywood Showgirl Lucy 00-LCY-02	Retrd.	2001	33.00	33
1997 I Love Lucy Heart 97-LCY-08	Open		36.00	36
1997 Lucy and Ricky's Christmas 97-LCY-01	Retrd.	1999	45.00	45
1998 Lucy Heart 98-LCY-02	Retrd.	1999	19.00	19
2000 Lucy Loves Christmas 00-LCY-01	Retrd.	2001	30.00	30
2000 Lucy Ole! 99-LCY-02	Retrd.	2000	32.00	32
2000 Petite Fortune Teller 00-LCY-05	Retrd.	2001	24.00	24
2000 Petite Lucy Ole! 00-LCY-04	Retrd.	2001	24.00	24
2000 Pink Lucy Heart 00-LCY-06	Retrd.	2001	22.00	22
1998 Vitametavegaimin 98-LCY-01	Retrd.	1999	29.00	29

Charlie Chaplin - C. Radko

1997 Charlie Chaplin 97-CAR-01	Open		39.00	39
1999 Modern Times Chaplin 99-CAR-01	Retrd.	1999	34.00	34
1999 Charlie Chaplin Candy Cane 99-CAR-02	Retrd.	1999	28.00	28

A Christmas Carol - C. Radko

1998 Scrooge 98-ACC-1	10,000	1998	62.00	62
1999 Ghost of Christmas Present 99-ACC-2	10,000	1999	62.00	62-65
2000 Bob Cratchit & Tiny Tim 00-ACC-3	10,000	2000	49.00	49
2001 Ghost of Christmas Future 01-ACC-4	10,000	2001	42.00	42
2002 Christmas Past Spirit 02-ACC-5	10,000		58.00	58

The Christopher Radko Foundation for Children Designs - C. Radko

1998 Cozykins 98-SP-28	Retrd.	1998	34.00	34-43
1999 Little Chipper 99-SP-50	Retrd.	1999	34.00	34
2000 Squeakles 00-SP-56	Retrd.	2000	34.00	34
2001 Warm Hearted Wonder 01-SP-83	Retrd.	2001	39.00	39
2002 Chilly Tunes Trio 02-SP-96	Yr.Iss.		42.00	42

Clara's Beaux - C. Radko

1998 Clara's Beaux 98-NCR-1	10,000	1998	135.00	135
1999 Cracker King 99-NCR-2	10,000	1999	75.00	75
2000 St. Cracker Claus 00-NCR-3	10,000	2000	74.00	74
2001 Band Stand Brigade 01-NCR-4	10,000	2001	74.00	74
2002 A Stride with Pride 02-NCR-5	10,000		76.00	76

Dave Thomas Foundation for Adoption - C. Radko

2000 Celebrating Adoption 00-DTF-01	Open		38.00	38

Disney - C. Radko

2000 Sorcerer Mickey Wreath 2000 00-DIS-11	Open		32.00	32

Disney Art Classics: Hercules - C. Radko

1997 Hercules 97-DIS-79	Retrd.	1998	39.00	39
1997 Pegasus 97-DIS-91	Retrd.	1998	42.00	42

Disney Art Classics: Peter Pan - C. Radko

1998 Captain Hook 98-DIS-20	Retrd.	1999	32.00	32
1998 The Darling Children 98-DIS-19	Retrd.	1999	32.00	32
1998 Peter Pan 98-DIS-18	Retrd.	1999	28.00	28-38
1998 Peter Pan Boxed Set (includes Pirate Ship 98-DIS-22) 98-DIS-44	Retrd.	1999	149.00	149
1998 Tinker Bell 98-DIS-21	Retrd.	1999	28.00	28

Disney Art Classics: Snow White & the Seven Dwarfs - C. Radko

1997 Snow White 97-DIS-31	Retrd.	1998	46.00	47-84
1997 Bashful 97-DIS-24	Retrd.	1998	38.00	39
1997 Doc 97-DIS-28	Retrd.	1998	38.00	38-45
1997 Dopey 97-DIS-25	Retrd.	1998	38.00	38-45
1997 Grumpy 97-DIS-26	Retrd.	1998	38.00	38-45
1997 Happy 97-DIS-30	Retrd.	1998	38.00	38
1997 Sleepy 97-DIS-27	Retrd.	1998	38.00	38
1997 Sneezy 97-DIS-29	Retrd.	1998	38.00	38
1997 Snow White Boxed Set 98-SW-0	Retrd.	1998	390.00	525-600

ORNAMENTS

YEAR ISSUE	EDITION LIMIT	YEAR RETD.	ISSUE PRICE	*QUOTE U.S.$
1998 The Hag 98-DIS-13	Retrd.	1999	34.00	34
1998 The Queen 98-DIS-14	Retrd.	1999	34.00	34
1998 Snow White Boxed Set (includes Mirror, Mirror 98-DIS-16) 98-DIS-43	Retrd.	1999	94.00	94

Disney Art Classics: The Little Mermaid - C. Radko

YEAR ISSUE	EDITION LIMIT	YEAR RETD.	ISSUE PRICE	*QUOTE U.S.$
1997 Ariel 97-DIS-82	Retrd.	1998	42.00	42-45
1997 Flounder 97-DIS-84	Retrd.	1998	42.00	42
1997 Sebastian 97-DIS-85	Retrd.	1998	42.00	42
1997 Ursula 97-DIS-83	Retrd.	1998	42.00	42

The Disney Catalog - C. Radko

YEAR ISSUE	EDITION LIMIT	YEAR RETD.	ISSUE PRICE	*QUOTE U.S.$
1997 4th of July Pooh 97-DIS-44	Retrd.	1997	42.00	60-75
1998 Chip and Dale 98-DIS-34	3,500		26.00	26
1997 Christmas Pooh 97-DIS-47	Retrd.	1997	42.00	42
1997 Easter Pooh 97-DIS-16	Retrd.	1997	50.00	50-79
2001 Goofy Wreath 2001 01-DIS-10	Open		32.00	32
1997 Halloween Pooh 97-DIS-45	Retrd.	1998	42.00	42
1998 Lady and the Tramp 98-DIS-39	3,500		30.00	30
1998 Mickey and Minnie Wedding 98-DIS-30	Open		39.00	39
1999 Petite Snow White & Dwarfs Set 99-DIS-30	Open		250.00	250
1998 Pooh Snowman 98-DIS-31	Open		30.00	30
1997 Thanksgiving Pooh 97-DIS-46	Retrd.	1998	42.00	42
1997 Toy Soldier Mickey 97-DIS-77	Open		40.00	40
1997 Toy Soldier Minnie 97-DIS-78	Open		40.00	40
1997 Valentine's Day Pooh 97-DIS-15	Retrd.	1997	45.00	46-65
2000 White Rabbit 01-DIS-51	Open		36.00	36
2001 Winnie the Pooh 01-DIS-26	Open		36.00	36

Disney Theme Parks - C. Radko

YEAR ISSUE	EDITION LIMIT	YEAR RETD.	ISSUE PRICE	*QUOTE U.S.$
2000 100 Acre Wood Pooh Finial 00-DIS-06	Open		90.00	90
2001 30th Anniv.Magic KindomSet/3 01-DIS-25	Open		110.00	110
2001 Brooms of Cheer 01-DIS-16	Open		32.00	32
1999 Cleo & Figaro 99-DIS-37	Open		29.00	29
2001 Cruisin' Mickey 01-DIS-07	Open		34.00	34
2001 Cruisin' Minnie 01-DIS-08	Open		34.00	34
2001 Downhill Pooh 01-DIS-22	Open		38.00	38
2000 Mad Party Teacup 00-DIS-08	Open		34.00	34
2001 Mickey Bell 01-DIS-03	Open		44.00	44
2001 Minnie Bell 01-DIS-04	Open		44.00	44
2001 Perfect Chime 01-DIS-20	Open		44.00	44
2000 Pet. Beauty & the Beast 00-DIS-09	Open		36.00	36
2001 Pooh Bell 01-DIS-18	Open		44.00	44
2001 Rollin' Mickey 01-DIS-05	Open		38.00	38
2001 Rollin' Minnie 01-DIS-06	Open		38.00	38
2001 Rollin' Pooh 01-DIS-11	Open		38.00	38
2001 Rollin' Tigger 01-DIS-12	Open		38.00	38
2000 Sleeping Beauty Fairies, set/3 00-DIS-48	Open		31.50	32
2001 Snuggled Up Piglet 01-DIS-15	Open		30.00	30
2001 Snuggled Up Pooh 01-DIS-13	Open		30.00	30
2001 Snuggled Up Tigger 01-DIS-14	Open		30.00	30
2001 Sorcerer Mickey's World 01-DIS-09	Open		36.00	36
2001 Tigger Bell 01-DIS-19	Open		44.00	44
2001 Tigger's Downhill Thrill 01-DIS-21	Open		38.00	38

Disney World Exclusives - C. Radko

YEAR ISSUE	EDITION LIMIT	YEAR RETD.	ISSUE PRICE	*QUOTE U.S.$
2000 Baby's First 00-DIS-40	Open		24.00	24
2000 Chip n' Dale Christmas 00-DIS-39	Open		32.00	32
1998 Cinderella Castle 98-DIS-42	Open		39.00	39
2000 Disney World Postcard 00-DIS-50	Open		38.00	38
1999 Lumberjack Mickey 99-DIS-15	Open		26.00	26
1999 Winter Minnie 99-DIS-16	Open		28.00	28

Disney World, Stores & Catalog Exclusives - C. Radko

YEAR ISSUE	EDITION LIMIT	YEAR RETD.	ISSUE PRICE	*QUOTE U.S.$
1999 Petite Snow White Set 99-DIS-30	Open		251.00	251

Disneyana - C. Radko

YEAR ISSUE	EDITION LIMIT	YEAR RETD.	ISSUE PRICE	*QUOTE U.S.$
1997 Mistletoe Mickey & Minnie 97-DIS-65	1,500	1997	250.00	275-360
1998 My Best Pal 98-DIS-40	1,000	1998	70.00	121-215
1999 Simba	1,000	1999	50.00	50

Disneyland Exclusive - C. Radko

YEAR ISSUE	EDITION LIMIT	YEAR RETD.	ISSUE PRICE	*QUOTE U.S.$
2000 Cheshire Cat 00-DIS-47	Open		24.00	24
2000 Disneyland Postcard 00-DIS-45	Open		38.00	38
2000 Jewel Daisy Snowball 00-DIS-35	Open		24.00	24
2000 Jewel Donald Snowball 00-DIS-36	Open		24.00	24
2000 Jewel Goofy Snowball 00-DIS-37	Open		24.00	24
2000 Jewel Mickey Snowball 00-DIS-33	Open		24.00	24
2000 Jewel Minnie Snowball 00-DIS-34	Open		24.00	24

YEAR ISSUE	EDITION LIMIT	YEAR RETD.	ISSUE PRICE	*QUOTE U.S.$
2000 Jewel Pluto Snowball 00-DIS-38	Open		24.00	24
2000 Maleficent 00-DIS-46	Open		34.00	34
2001 Mickey and Minnie Wedding 01-DIS-27	Open		37.00	37
2000 Pooh & Friends 00-DIS-41	Open		36.00	36
2000 Snowman Pooh Finial 00-DIS-49	Open		75.00	75

Disney's Mickey & Co. - C. Radko

YEAR ISSUE	EDITION LIMIT	YEAR RETD.	ISSUE PRICE	*QUOTE U.S.$
1998 Caroler Daisy Duck 98-DIS-09	Retrd.	1999	24.00	24
1999 Caroler Mickey 99-DIS-06	Retrd.	1999	24.00	24
1998 Caroler Minnie Mouse 98-DIS-08	Retrd.	1999	24.00	24
1999 Caroler Pluto 99-DIS-07	Retrd.	1999	24.00	24
1997 Daisy Duck 97-DIS-20	Retrd.	1997	38.00	24-38
1998 Daisy Duck Stocking 98-DIS-06	Retrd.	1999	22.00	22
1999 Disney Petite Set 99-DIS-41	Retrd.	1999	98.00	98
1998 Donald & Daisy Block 98-DIS-11	Open		18.00	18
1998 Down the Chimney 98-DIS-23	Retrd.	1999	28.00	28-39
1997 Downhill Mickey (Starlight Exclusive) 97-DIS-42	Retrd.	1997	42.00	42
1998 Downhill Minnie 98-DIS-04	Retrd.	1999	26.00	26
1997 Goofy Tree 97-DIS-23	Retrd.	1997	38.00	38
1998 Happy New Year Mickey 98-DIS-01	Open		22.00	22
1998 Happy New Year Pluto 98-DIS-02	Open		22.00	22
1999 Hockey Goofy 99-DIS-12	Retrd.	1999	28.00	28
1998 Mickey & Minnie Block 98-DIS-10	Open		18.00	18
1997 Mickey & Minnie Christmas 97-DIS-34	Retrd.	1997	42.00	42
1998 Mickey Mouse Wreath 98-DIS-03	Retrd.	1999	19.00	19
1998 Mickey Stocking 98-DIS-05	Retrd.	1999	22.00	22
1997 Mickey's Sleigh Ride (Roger's Exclusive) 97-DIS-93	Retrd.	1997	48.00	48
1999 Minnie Mouse Wreath 99-DIS-33	Retrd.	1999	19.00	19
1997 Noel Minnie 97-DIS-21	Retrd.	1997	38.00	38
1998 Pluto & Goofy Block 98-DIS-12	Open		18.00	18
1998 Pluto Stocking 98-DIS-07	Open		22.00	22
1997 Pluto Wreath (Starlight Exclusive) 97-DIS-73	Retrd.	1997	36.00	36-39
1997 Pluto's Dog House 97-DIS-57	Open		39.00	39
1997 Pluto's Snowman 99-DIS-13	Retrd.	1999	29.00	29
1997 Rooftop Mickey 97-DIS-32	Retrd.	1999	40.00	40
1999 Skiing Mickey 99-DIS-08	Retrd.	1999	29.00	29
1999 Skiing Minnie 99-DIS-09	Retrd.	1999	29.00	29
1997 Three Cheers For Mickey 97-DIS-33	Retrd.	1999	44.00	44
1999 Winter Romance 99-DIS-28	Retrd.	1999	33.00	33

Egyptian Series - C. Radko

YEAR ISSUE	EDITION LIMIT	YEAR RETD.	ISSUE PRICE	*QUOTE U.S.$
1997 Ramses 97-EGY-1	15,000	1997	50.00	55-59
1998 Cheops 98-EGY-2	15,000	1998	55.00	55
1999 Eternal Mystery 99-EGY-3	15,000	1999	34.00	34

Event Ornaments - C. Radko

YEAR ISSUE	EDITION LIMIT	YEAR RETD.	ISSUE PRICE	*QUOTE U.S.$
1999 Mr. Iceberg (Fall) 99-SP-51	Retrd.	1999	30.00	30
1999 Mrs. Iceberg (Spring) 99-SP-52	Retrd.	1999	30.00	30

FAO Schwarz - C. Radko

YEAR ISSUE	EDITION LIMIT	YEAR RETD.	ISSUE PRICE	*QUOTE U.S.$
1997 1920 Santa 97-FAO-03	3,000	1997	42.00	42
1998 1929 FAO Santa 98-FAO-02	3,600		38.00	38
1998 FAO Clock Tower 98-FAO-01	5,000		40.00	40
1997 Toy Block Bear 97-FAO-04	3,000	1997	52.00	60-119

Harley-Davidson - C. Radko

YEAR ISSUE	EDITION LIMIT	YEAR RETD.	ISSUE PRICE	*QUOTE U.S.$
1998 Bar & Shield 98-HAR-03	Retrd.	2001	19.00	19
2001 Bar & Shield X-mas 01-HAR-05	Open		30.00	30
1997 Biker Boot 97-HAR-04	Retrd.	1999	36.00	45-49
2000 Chilly Rider 00-HAR-01	Retrd.	2001	36.00	36-49
2000 Christmas Crusin' 00-HAR-03	Retrd.	2001	36.00	36
1999 Fat Boy 99-HAR-04	Retrd.	2001	38.00	38
2002 Fat Boy-Red 02-HAR-04	Open		43.00	43
1998 Fill-r-up 98-HAR-02	Retrd.	1999	29.00	29
1997 Free Wheeling Santa 97-HAR-01	Retrd.	1999	46.00	46-49
2001 Happy Harley Days 01-HAR-01	Retrd.	2001	39.00	39
2002 Harley Bell 02-HAR-01	Open		45.00	45
2000 Harley Leather Jacket 00-HAR-02	Open		32.00	32
1998 Harley Santa 98-HAR-01	Retrd.	2001	32.00	32
2001 Harley Stocking 01-HAR-04	Open		33.00	33
2002 Harley-Davidson Bear Family 02-HAR-02	Open		44.00	44
2001 Man of Steel 01-HAR-03	Open		37.00	37
1999 Mrs. Harley Claus 99-HAR-01	Retrd.	2001	32.00	32
2000 Petite Biker Boot 00-HAR-06	Retrd.	2001	24.00	24
2000 Petite Free Wheelin' Santa 00-HAR-05	Retrd.	2001	33.00	33
2001 Petite Harley Santa 01-HAR-07	Open		30.00	30
2002 Petite Mrs. Harley Claus 02-HAR-03	Open		29.00	29
2001 Rising High 01-HAR-02	Open		45.00	45

Collectors' Information Bureau

*Quotes have been rounded up to nearest dollar

YEAR ISSUE	EDITION LIMIT	YEAR RETD.	ISSUE PRICE	*QUOTE U.S.$
1999 Sidecar Harley Santa 99-HAR-03	Retrd.	2001	38.00	38
2000 South Pole Bikers 00-HAR-04	Retrd.	2001	35.00	35
1999 Special Delivery Mrs. Claus 99-HAR-02	Retrd.	2001	38.00	38

Harold LLoyd - C. Radko

YEAR ISSUE	EDITION LIMIT	YEAR RETD.	ISSUE PRICE	*QUOTE U.S.$
1997 Harold Lloyd 97-LYD-01	Open		42.00	42
1998 Holiday Reflections 98-LYD-01	Open		75.00	75
1999 Holiday Bounty 99-LYD-02	Retrd.	1999	40.00	40-45
1999 Millennium Clock 99-LYD-01	Open		40.00	40

Hasbro's Monopoly - C. Radko

YEAR ISSUE	EDITION LIMIT	YEAR RETD.	ISSUE PRICE	*QUOTE U.S.$
1998 Dice Uncle 98-MON-02	Retrd.	1999	26.00	26
1998 High Roller 98-MON-02	Open		26.00	26
1998 Holiday Cheer 98-MON-01	Retrd.	1999	26.00	26
1997 Monopoly Wreath 97-MON-04	Retrd.	1999	36.00	36
1997 Roadster Rich Uncle Pennybags 97-MON-03	Retrd.	1999	39.00	39

Hasbro's Mr. Potato Head - C. Radko

YEAR ISSUE	EDITION LIMIT	YEAR RETD.	ISSUE PRICE	*QUOTE U.S.$
1997 Mr. Potato Head 97-PQT-02	Open		39.00	39
1998 Mr. Potato Head Lumberjack 98-POT-01	Open		26.00	26
1997 Mr. Potato Head Santa 97-POT-01	Open		39.00	39
1997 Mrs. Potato Head Santa 97-POT-04	Open		39.00	39
1998 Soldier Potato 98-POT-02	Open		26.00	26

Homes For The Holidays - C. Radko

YEAR ISSUE	EDITION LIMIT	YEAR RETD.	ISSUE PRICE	*QUOTE U.S.$
1997 Sugar Hill 97-HOU-1	10,000	1997	140.00	150-152
1998 Sugar Hill II 98-HOU-2	10,000	1998	190.00	190-200
1999 Candy Land Corner 99-HOU-3	10,000	1999	99.00	99

The Huntington - C. Radko

YEAR ISSUE	EDITION LIMIT	YEAR RETD.	ISSUE PRICE	*QUOTE U.S.$
1997 The Blue Boy 97-HUN-01	5,000		38.00	38
1997 Pinky 97-HUN-02	5,000		38.00	38

International Children's Charity - C. Radko

YEAR ISSUE	EDITION LIMIT	YEAR RETD.	ISSUE PRICE	*QUOTE U.S.$
1999 United We Stand 99-SP-53	Open		44.00	44

It's a Wonder Life - C. Radko

YEAR ISSUE	EDITION LIMIT	YEAR RETD.	ISSUE PRICE	*QUOTE U.S.$
1997 Jimmy Stewart 97-WON-01	Retrd.	1999	42.00	42-65

Jim Henson's Muppets - C. Radko

YEAR ISSUE	EDITION LIMIT	YEAR RETD.	ISSUE PRICE	*QUOTE U.S.$
1997 Bah Humbug Block 97-MPT-02	Retrd.	2000	38.00	38
1997 Checking It Twice 97-MPT-01	Retrd.	1999	39.00	39-49
1997 Christmas with Miss Piggy 97-MPT-06	Retrd.	1999	42.00	42-55
1997 Fozzie & Gonzo Block 97-MPT-04	Retrd.	2000	38.00	38
1997 Fozzie Bear Baker 97-MPT-05	Retrd.	2000	39.00	39
1997 Home For The Holidays 99-MPT-02	Retrd.	1999	32.00	32
1997 Kermit and Miss Piggy Block 97-MPT-03	Retrd.	2000	38.00	38
1998 Kermit and Piggy Snowball 98-MPT-01	Retrd.	1999	30.00	30-39
1998 Mistletoe Miss Piggy 98-MPT-02	Retrd.	1999	28.00	28
1997 Muppet Bobsled 99-MPT-01	Retrd.	1999	28.00	28
1997 Muppet Totem 97-MPT-09	Retrd.	1999	42.00	42
1997 Nutcracker 98-MPT-03	Retrd.	1999	26.00	26
1997 Play It Again Santa 97-MPT-07	Retrd.	1999	38.00	38
1997 Wocka Wocka Christmas 97-MPT-08	Retrd.	1999	46.00	46

The Kennedy Center - C. Radko

YEAR ISSUE	EDITION LIMIT	YEAR RETD.	ISSUE PRICE	*QUOTE U.S.$
1997 Kennedy Center Honors 97-JFK-03	3,000		36.00	36

Laurel & Hardy - C. Radko

YEAR ISSUE	EDITION LIMIT	YEAR RETD.	ISSUE PRICE	*QUOTE U.S.$
1997 Laurel & Hardy 97-LAH-01	Retrd.	1999	78.00	78-82
1999 Exit Stage Right 99-LAH-01	Retrd.	1999	34.00	34

Limited Edition Ornaments - C. Radko

YEAR ISSUE	EDITION LIMIT	YEAR RETD.	ISSUE PRICE	*QUOTE U.S.$
1995 And Snowy Makes Eight (set of 8)	15,000	1996	125.00	125
1996 Russian Rhapsody RUS (Set/6)	7,500	1996	150.00	150-225
1997 Yippy Yi Yo SP-25	7,000	1997	70.00	70-77
2002 Christmas Planner 02-SP-91	10,000		82.00	82
1998 Cookbook Santas 98-SP-35	10,000		152.00	152
1998 Forest Angel 98-SP-33	7,500	1999	125.00	125
1998 Spring Maidens 98-SP-34	5,000	1999	95.00	95
1998 Sugar Shack Extravaganza 98-SP-37	5,000	1998	178.00	178-210
1999 Peace on Earth 99-SP-41	5,000	1999	58.00	58-60
2000 Holiday Hideaway 00-1259-0	2,000		34.00	34
2000 Frosty Carousel 00-SP-75	2,500		180.00	180
2000 N*O*E*L* (set/4) 00-SP-65	7,000		125.00	125
2000 North Pole Express 00-SP-70	10,000	2001	87.00	87
2000 Ring in the Holiday 00-SP-71	7,500	2000	78.00	78
2001 Hang On 'til Christmas 01-SP-78	10,000		110.00	110

YEAR ISSUE	EDITION LIMIT	YEAR RETD.	ISSUE PRICE	*QUOTE U.S.$
2001 Jolly Good Fellow 01-SP-76	7,500		64.00	64

Lucasfilm's Star Wars - C. Radko

YEAR ISSUE	EDITION LIMIT	YEAR RETD.	ISSUE PRICE	*QUOTE U.S.$
1999 C-3PO & R2D2 99-STW-01	Open		28.00	28
1998 C-3PO 98-STW-03	Open		18.00	18
1998 Chewbacca 98-STW-04	Open		20.00	20
1998 Darth Vader 98-STW-01	Open		20.00	20
1999 Darth Vader 99-STW-02	Open		26.00	26
1999 Darth Vader-The Duel 99-STW-05	7,500		38.00	38
1999 Ewoks 99-STW-06	Open		28.00	28
1998 Storm Tropper 98-STW-05	Open		20.00	20
1998 Yoda 98-STW-02	Open		18.00	18

Make-A-Wish Foundation Charity Design - C. Radko

YEAR ISSUE	EDITION LIMIT	YEAR RETD.	ISSUE PRICE	*QUOTE U.S.$
1997 Well Wishes 97-MAW-01	5,000		64.00	64

Marshall Fields - C. Radko

YEAR ISSUE	EDITION LIMIT	YEAR RETD.	ISSUE PRICE	*QUOTE U.S.$
1997 Marshall Fields Clock 97-MAR-01	Retrd.	1997	38.00	38
1998 Marshall Fields Clock 98-MAR-01	5,000		38.00	38

Matt Berry Memorial Soccer Fund - C. Radko

YEAR ISSUE	EDITION LIMIT	YEAR RETD.	ISSUE PRICE	*QUOTE U.S.$
1995 Matthew's Game 158-0	Open		12.00	12

Mattel's Barbie - C. Radko

YEAR ISSUE	EDITION LIMIT	YEAR RETD.	ISSUE PRICE	*QUOTE U.S.$
1997 Alpine Blush Barbie 97-BAR-03	Retrd.	1999	44.00	44
1998 Barbie Heart 98-BAR-03	Retrd.	1999	15.00	15
1998 Barbie Stocking 98-BAR-02	Open		19.00	19
1998 Elegant Holiday 98-BAR-01	Retrd.	1999	32.00	32-59
1997 Holiday Barbie 97-BAR-01	Retrd.	1999	50.00	50

Moscow Circus Series - C. Radko

YEAR ISSUE	EDITION LIMIT	YEAR RETD.	ISSUE PRICE	*QUOTE U.S.$
1997 Ivan & Misha 97-CIR-01	10,000	1997	90.00	90-97
1998 Grand Ring Master 98-CIR-02	10,000	1998	90.00	90-100
1999 Brutus 99-CIR-03	10,000	1999	45.00	45
2000 The Greatest Show on Earth 00-CIR-4	10,000		69.00	69
2002 Russian Ring Master 02-CIR-5	10,000		48.00	48

Musicians Series - C. Radko

YEAR ISSUE	EDITION LIMIT	YEAR RETD.	ISSUE PRICE	*QUOTE U.S.$
1998 Hooked on Classics 98-COM-1	5,000	1998	108.00	108

Nativity Series - C. Radko

YEAR ISSUE	EDITION LIMIT	YEAR RETD.	ISSUE PRICE	*QUOTE U.S.$
1995 Three Wise Men WM (Set/3)	15,000	1996	90.00	125-196
1996 Holy Family HF (Set/3)	15,000	1996	70.00	90-95
1997 Shepherd's Prayer, Gloria 97-NAT-3	15,000	1997	90.00	90

Neiman Marcus - C. Radko

YEAR ISSUE	EDITION LIMIT	YEAR RETD.	ISSUE PRICE	*QUOTE U.S.$
1997 The Original Store 97-NM-01	Retrd.	1997	48.00	48

North American Bears' Muffy Vanderbear - C. Radko

YEAR ISSUE	EDITION LIMIT	YEAR RETD.	ISSUE PRICE	*QUOTE U.S.$
2000 A Christmas Carol: Bearly in Tune Hoppy 00-NAB-02	Yr.Iss.	2000	34.00	34
2000 A Christmas Carol: Bearly in Tune Muffy 00-NAB-01	Yr.Iss.	2000	34.00	34
2001 Christmas Caroling 01-NAB-03	Retrd.	2001	39.00	39
2002 Cirque De La Lune 02-NAB-05	Open		36.00	36
2002 Countess Muffula 02-NAB-02	Open		39.00	39
2000 Czarina Muffina 00-NAB-03	Retrd.	2001	34.00	34
1999 Grand VanderBall Hoppy VanderBear 99-NAB-02	Retrd.	2001	29.00	29
1999 Grand VanderBall Muffy VanderBear 99-NAB-01	Retrd.	2001	29.00	29
1999 Hearts & Flowers Muffy VanderBear 99-NAB-04	Retrd.	2001	29.00	29
2001 Highland Fling Hoppy 01-NAB-10	Open		35.00	35
2001 Highland Fling Muffy 01-NAB-09	Open		35.00	35
1999 Messenger of Love Hoppy VanderBear 99-NAB-03	Retrd.	2001	29.00	29
2001 Muffy Angel Finial 01-NAB-12	Open		110.00	110
1998 Muffy Candy C'angel (Roger's Garden Exclusive) 98-NAB-01	Retrd.	2001	29.00	29
1998 Muffy Ginger Bear 98-NAB-02	Retrd.	1999	29.00	29
2001 Muffy Little Fir Tree 01-NAB-08	Open		37.00	37
1998 Muffy Plum Fairy 98-NAB-03	Retrd.	1999	29.00	29
2002 Muffy Snowflake 02-NAB-01	Open		39.00	39
2002 Muffy the Red-Nose Reindeer 02-NAB-03	Open		39.00	39
2000 Muffy Winter Princess 00-NAB-13	Open		34.00	40
2001 Petite Candy C'Angel Muffy 01-NAB-01	Open		24.00	24
2001 Petite Gingerbear muffy 00-NAB-07	Yr.Iss.	2000	24.00	24
2001 Petite Hearts and Flowers Muffy 01-NAB-06	Retrd.	2001	28.00	28
2001 Petite Plum Fairy 01-NAB-02	Open		28.00	28
2000 Petite Portrait in Black & White 00-NAB-06	Yr.Iss.	2000	24.00	24

ORNAMENTS

YEAR ISSUE	EDITION LIMIT	YEAR RETD.	ISSUE PRICE	*QUOTE U.S.$
2001 Petite VanderBall Hoppy 01-NAB-05	Retrd.	2001	26.00	26
2001 Petite VanderBall Muffy 01-NAB-04	Retrd.	2001	28.00	28
1999 Pickin' Posies Muffy 99-NAB-05	Retrd.	2001	29.00	29
1997 Portrait in Black and White 97-NAB-02	Retrd.	1999	38.00	38-45
2000 Santa's Workshop Hoppy 00-NAB-05	Yr.Iss.	2000	34.00	34
2000 Santa's Workshop Muffy 00-NAB-04	Yr.Iss.	2000	34.00	34
2002 Sleddin' and Skidaddlin' 02-NAB-04	Open		39.00	39
1997 Sleddin' and Skidadlin' 97-NAB-01	Retrd.	1999	38.00	38-45

Nutcracker Series - C. Radko

YEAR ISSUE	EDITION LIMIT	YEAR RETD.	ISSUE PRICE	*QUOTE U.S.$
1995 Nutcracker Suite I NC1 (Set/3)	15,000	1996	90.00	90-150
1996 Nutcracker Suite II NC2 (Set/3)	15,000	1997	90.00	90-110
1997 Nutcracker Suite III NC3 (Set/3)	15,000	1997	90.00	90-110

Parkwest - C. Radko

YEAR ISSUE	EDITION LIMIT	YEAR RETD.	ISSUE PRICE	*QUOTE U.S.$
1998 Special Charity Set 98-PW-SPE	Open		140.00	140

Patriots Series - C. Radko

YEAR ISSUE	EDITION LIMIT	YEAR RETD.	ISSUE PRICE	*QUOTE U.S.$
1997 LaFayette 97-PAT-1	7,500	1997	34.00	34-38
1998 Alexander Hamilton 98-PAT-2	7,500	1998	40.00	40-43
1999 Paul Revere 99-PAT-3	7,500	1999	28.00	28
2000 Thomas Jefferson 00-PAT-4	7,500	2000	37.00	37
2001 Benjamin Franklin 01-PAT-5	7,500	2001	32.00	32
2002 Proud Patriot 02-PAT-6	7,500		44.00	44

Pediatrics Cancer Research - C. Radko

YEAR ISSUE	EDITION LIMIT	YEAR RETD.	ISSUE PRICE	*QUOTE U.S.$
1994 A Gifted Santa 70	Retrd.	1994	25.00	25-81
1995 Christmas Puppy Love SP11	Retrd.	1995	30.00	38-65
1996 Bearly Awake SP16	Retrd.	1996	34.00	40-60
1997 Kitty Cares 97-SP-23	Retrd.	1997	30.00	30-32
1998 Elfin Magic 98-SP-30	Retrd.	1998	32.00	32
1999 Dear To My Heart 99-SP-46	Retrd.	1999	28.00	28
2000 Gift of Health 00-SP-73	Retrd.	2000	36.00	36
2001 Onesie Twosome 01-SP-80	Retrd.	2001	36.00	36
2002 Gift of Giving 02-SP-94	Yr.Iss.		39.00	39

Polish Children's Home Fund - C. Radko

YEAR ISSUE	EDITION LIMIT	YEAR RETD.	ISSUE PRICE	*QUOTE U.S.$
1997 Watch Over Me 97-SP-26	Retrd.	1997	28.00	28-35

Rosemont Special - C. Radko

YEAR ISSUE	EDITION LIMIT	YEAR RETD.	ISSUE PRICE	*QUOTE U.S.$
1997 Blue Caroline 96-1521	Retrd.	1997	26.00	44-65

Saks Fifth Avenue - C. Radko

YEAR ISSUE	EDITION LIMIT	YEAR RETD.	ISSUE PRICE	*QUOTE U.S.$
1995 Saks Santa SAK01	2,500	1997	48.00	120-230
1996 Saks Calls 95SAK02	Retrd.	1996	56.00	288-460
1997 Saks Nutcraker 97-SAK-03	5,000	1997	40.00	40-125
1998 Saks International Santa 98-SAK-01	3,000		36.00	36

South Bend Special - C. Radko

YEAR ISSUE	EDITION LIMIT	YEAR RETD.	ISSUE PRICE	*QUOTE U.S.$
1995 Polar Express (lilac) 95-076SB	Retrd.	1995	24.95	75-85

Special Color Variations - C. Radko

YEAR ISSUE	EDITION LIMIT	YEAR RETD.	ISSUE PRICE	*QUOTE U.S.$
1996 Snowtem Pole (Glass Pheasant) 96155G	Retrd.	1996	33.00	90-100
1996 White Dolphin (Four Seasons) 96238F	Retrd.	1996	25.00	75

Starlight and Rising Star Store Exclusives - C. Radko

YEAR ISSUE	EDITION LIMIT	YEAR RETD.	ISSUE PRICE	*QUOTE U.S.$
1998 Sterling Rider 98-SP-39	2,500	1998	175.00	175
1999 Carousel of Dreams 99-SP-49	2,500	1999	190.00	190
1999 Santa's Shroom 994960	Open		65.00	65
2000 Supreme Santa Finial 00-SP-62	Yr.Iss.	2000	250.00	250

Starlight and Rising Star Store Exclusives/St. Nick Portrait Series - C. Radko

YEAR ISSUE	EDITION LIMIT	YEAR RETD.	ISSUE PRICE	*QUOTE U.S.$
1996 Esquire Santa 96-SP-17	750	1996	150.00	650-1000
1997 Regency Santa 97-SP-24	2,500		180.00	180
1998 Moondream 98-SP-38	2,500	1998	186.00	186

Starlight and Rising Star Store Special Colorations - C. Radko

YEAR ISSUE	EDITION LIMIT	YEAR RETD.	ISSUE PRICE	*QUOTE U.S.$
1996 Baby Bear (Christmas Dove) 322-0	N/A		30.00	30
1996 Far Away Places (Christmas Village) 321-0	N/A		40.00	40
1996 Frosty Bear (Christmas House) 326-0	N/A		30.00	30
1996 Kitty Christmas (Tuck's) 323-0	N/A		30.00	30
1996 Little St. Mick (Roger's Gardens) DIS7	N/A	1996	45.00	50-85
1996 On His Way (Geary's) 319-0	N/A		30.00	30
1996 Ruffles (Christmas Attic) 320-0	N/A		30.00	30
1996 Snow Fun (Vinny's) 324-0	N/A		30.00	30
1996 Tweedle Dee (Glass Pheasant) 325-0	N/A		40.00	40
1998 Bergdorf Star (Bergdorf Goodman) 98-BG-01	N/A		90.00	90

YEAR ISSUE	EDITION LIMIT	YEAR RETD.	ISSUE PRICE	*QUOTE U.S.$
1998 Best of Times (Loot N Boot) 98-194-BO	N/A		42.00	42
1998 Bunny Express (FAO Schwarz) 98-378-FA	N/A		50.00	50
1998 Candy Santa (Pine Creek Collectibles) 98-301-PC	N/A		52.00	52
1998 Circle of Cheer (Four Seasons Christmas Shoppe) 98-222-F	N/A		52.00	52
1998 Derby Rocker (Bloomingdales) 98-365-BM	N/A		43.50	44
1998 Ginger Cracker (Christmas Attic) 98-162-CA	N/A		48.00	48
1998 June Buggy (Chatsworth Florist) 98-102-CF	N/A		60.00	60
1998 Lucky Laddie (Borsheim's Jewelry) 98-458-B	N/A		48.00	48
1998 Sleddin' Snowman (Carson Pirie Scott) 98-CPS-01	N/A		44.00	44
1998 Slim Traveler (Margo's Gift Shop) 98-120-M	N/A		38.00	38
1998 Snow Star (Curio Cabinet) 98-129-CC	N/A		36.00	36
1998 Spring Romance (R. Blooms) 98-321-RB	N/A		46.00	46
1998 Stuffings Full (Glass Pheasant) 98-159-GP	N/A		44.00	44
1998 Summertime Santa 98-RG-01	3,000		70.00	70
1998 Teddy Tunes (Christmas Store) 98-256-CS	N/A		42.00	42
1998 Triple Nick (Story Book Kids) 98-150-SK	N/A		36.00	36
1996 Winter Kitten (Margo's) 327-0	N/A		30.00	30
1998 Woodcut Santa (Botanicals on the Park) 98-214-BP	N/A		44.00	44

Sterling Silver Collection - C. Radko

YEAR ISSUE	EDITION LIMIT	YEAR RETD.	ISSUE PRICE	*QUOTE U.S.$
1997 Winter Spirit 97-J01-00	5,000		175.00	175
1998 Regal Reindeer 98-J02-00	5,000		150.00	150

Sunday Brunch - C. Radko

YEAR ISSUE	EDITION LIMIT	YEAR RETD.	ISSUE PRICE	*QUOTE U.S.$
1996 Hansel & Gretel and Witch HG01	7,500	1996	50.00	50
1997 Nibble Nibble 97-HG-02	7,500	1997	58.00	58-8

The Three Stooges - C. Radko

YEAR ISSUE	EDITION LIMIT	YEAR RETD.	ISSUE PRICE	*QUOTE U.S.$
1999 Restless Knights 99-STO-01	Retrd.	2000	28.00	2

Twelve Days of Christmas - C. Radko

YEAR ISSUE	EDITION LIMIT	YEAR RETD.	ISSUE PRICE	*QUOTE U.S.$
1993 Partridge in a Pear Tree SP2	5,000	1993	35.00	96
1994 Two Turtle Doves SP4	10,000	1994	28.00	95-175
1995 Three French Hens SP9	10,000	1995	34.00	140-22
1995 Three French Hens (signed) SP9	Retrd.	1995	34.00	100-17
1996 Four Calling Birds SP12	10,000	1996	44.00	75-12
1997 Five Gold Rings SP19	10,000	1997	60.00	125-15
1998 Six Geese a Laying SP40	10,000	1998	68.00	68-9
1999 Seven Swans a Swimming SP42	10,000	1999	50.00	50-6
2000 Eight Maids a'Milking 00-SP-58	10,000	2000	54.00	5
2001 Nine Ladies Dancing 01-SP-77	10,000		58.00	5
2002 No. 10 Downing Street 02-SP-97	10,000		64.00	6

The Twin Towers Fund - C. Radko

YEAR ISSUE	EDITION LIMIT	YEAR RETD.	ISSUE PRICE	*QUOTE U.S.$
2001 Heros All 01-1099-0	Open		34.00	3

The United Way - C. Radko

YEAR ISSUE	EDITION LIMIT	YEAR RETD.	ISSUE PRICE	*QUOTE U.S.$
2001 United For Freedom Ribbon 01-1021-0	Open		29.00	29

Universal Studios:Universal and Steven Speilberg's Lost World - C. Radko

YEAR ISSUE	EDITION LIMIT	YEAR RETD.	ISSUE PRICE	*QUOTE U.S.$
1997 Baby T-REX 97-UNI-12	Retrd.	1999	38.00	3
1997 Baby Trike 97-UNI-11	Retrd.	1999	38.00	3
1997 Stegosaurus 97-UNI-15	Open		42.00	4
1997 T-REX 97-UNI-14	Retrd.	1999	42.00	4

Universal Studios:Universal Monsters - C. Radko

YEAR ISSUE	EDITION LIMIT	YEAR RETD.	ISSUE PRICE	*QUOTE U.S.$
1997 Bride of Frankenstein 97-UNI-17	Open		42.00	4
1998 Creature From the Black Lagoon 98-MST-03	Retrd.	1999	22.00	2
1997 Dracula 97-UNI-02	Open		42.00	4
1997 Frankenstein 97-UNI-03	Retrd.	1999	42.00	42-5
1998 The Mummy 98-MST-01	Retrd.	1999	21.00	2
1999 Shrunken Heads 99-MST-01	Retrd.	1999	17.00	1
1998 Wolfman 98-MST-02	Open		22.00	2

Universal Studios:Universal's Rocky, Bullwinkle and Friends - C. Radko

YEAR ISSUE	EDITION LIMIT	YEAR RETD.	ISSUE PRICE	*QUOTE U.S.$
1998 Boris & Natasha Block 98-RAB-01	Open		19.00	1

YEAR ISSUE	EDITION LIMIT	YEAR RETD.	ISSUE PRICE	*QUOTE U.S.$
1997 Bullwinkle's Wreath 97-UNI-09	Retrd.	1999	36.00	36-45
1997 Rocky & Bullwinkle Block 97-UNI-06	Open		38.00	38
1997 Rocky's Wreath 97-UNI-08	Retrd.	1999	36.00	36
1998 Sleigh Ride 98-RAB-02	Open		27.00	27
1998 Totem Trouble 98-RAB-03	Retrd.	1999	26.00	26

Virginia Diner Exclusive - C. Radko

YEAR ISSUE	EDITION LIMIT	YEAR RETD.	ISSUE PRICE	*QUOTE U.S.$
1998 Virginia Diner Peanut 98-VAD-01	Open		12.00	12

The Walt Disney Gallery - C. Radko

YEAR ISSUE	EDITION LIMIT	YEAR RETD.	ISSUE PRICE	*QUOTE U.S.$
1997 Bambi 97-DIS-74	5,000		44.00	44
1997 Bambi, set/4 (signed) 97-DIS-99	1,000		180.00	180
1997 Bambi's Winter Forest (for special boxed set, 4 pc.) 96-273-DG	2,500		N/A	N/A
1996 Best Friends DIS10	10,000	1996	60.00	60-72
1996 By Jiminy DIS11	7,500	1996	38.00	54-78
1996 Cruella De Vil DIS13	10,000	1996	55.00	57-110
1998 Disney's Beast 97-DIS-96	5,000		N/A	N/A
1998 Disney's Belle 97-DIS-95	5,000		N/A	N/A
1997 Eeyore 97-DIS-19	5,000		44.00	44
1997 Flower 97-DIS-75	5,000		44.00	44
1996 A Goofy Surprise DIS5	2,500	1996	38.00	50-110
1996 Holiday Skaters DIS8	Retrd.	1996	42.00	69-72
1997 Huey, Louie and Dewey 97-DIS-32	2,500		34.00	34
1996 Lucky DIS14	Retrd.	1996	45.00	72-95
1997 Mickey's Birthday Set, set/5 97-DIS-48	750		N/A	N/A
1995 Mickey's Tree DIS1	2,500	1995	45.00	125-180
1997 Minnie Statue of Liberty (NY City Gallery Only) 97-DIS-94	2,500		38.00	38
1996 Noel Pluto DIS3	2,500	1996	37.00	48-50
1997 Piglet 97-DIS-98	5,000		38.00	38
1996 Pinocchio DIS9	5,000	1996	45.00	60-144
1995 Pooh's Favorite Gift (signed) DIS2	Retrd.	1995	45.00	135-300
1995 Pooh's Favorite Gift DIS2	2,500	1995	45.00	106-180
1997 Puppy Pole 97-DIS-17	2,500		44.00	44
1996 Ready For Sea DIS4	2,500	1996	38.00	44-150
1997 Scrooge McDuck 97-DIS-97	5,000		44.00	44
1997 Snow White Set w/Apple (leather box) 97-DIS-92	500		500.00	500
1997 Thumper 97-DIS-76	5,000		44.00	44
1997 Tigger 97-DIS-18	5,000		42.00	42
1997 Tinker Bell DIS12	10,000	1997	55.00	65-125
1997 Winnie the Pooh 97-DIS-88	5,000		42.00	42
1996 Xmas Eve Mickey DIS06	Retrd.	1996	45.00	40-88

The Walt Disney Gallery & Parks Exclusives - C. Radko

YEAR ISSUE	EDITION LIMIT	YEAR RETD.	ISSUE PRICE	*QUOTE U.S.$
2000 100 Acre Wood Pooh Tree Topper 00-DIS-06	Open		75.00	75

Warner Brothers Studio Store Gallery Exclusive - C. Radko

YEAR ISSUE	EDITION LIMIT	YEAR RETD.	ISSUE PRICE	*QUOTE U.S.$
2000 Motorcycle Taz 00-WB-03	Open		32.00	32
2000 Petite Ruby Slippers 00-WB-04	Open		26.00	26
2000 Superman Logo 00-WB-05	Open		22.00	22
2000 Tweety Snowman 00-WB-01	Open		30.00	30
2000 Willie Coyote and Roadrunner Sleigh 00-WB-02	Open		32.00	32

Warner Brothers Studio Stores - C. Radko

YEAR ISSUE	EDITION LIMIT	YEAR RETD.	ISSUE PRICE	*QUOTE U.S.$
1997 Alicia Silverstone as Batgirl 97-WB-22	3,000		44.00	44
1997 Arnold Schwarznegger as Mr. Freeze 97-WB-21	3,000		44.00	44
1999 Batman 99-WB-05	Retrd.	N/A	28.00	69
1999 Bugs Bunny Santa 99-WB-13	Retrd.	N/A	28.00	49
1998 Bugs Bunny Sprite 98-WB-02	5,000		46.00	46
1998 Faberge Tweety 98-WB-01	5,000		38.00	38
1998 George Clooney as Batman 97-WB-20	3,000		44.00	44
1998 Glenda the Good Witch 98-WB-03	10,000		44.00	44
1997 Gossamer 97-WB-17	5,000		44.00	44
1998 Je t'aime Heart 98-WB-04	5,000		36.00	36
1998 K-9 (Warner Bros. Collector's Guild Exclusive) 98-WB-05	2,500		42.00	42
1996 Little Angel Tweety WB10	5,000	1996	45.00	75-96
1997 Marvin the Martian 97-WB-12	5,000		42.00	42
1995 Santa's Bugs Bunny WB1	Retrd.	1995	45.00	38-75
1997 Scooby Doo 97-WB-11	5,000		42.00	42
1998 Scooby Doo Wreath 98-WB-06	5,000		36.00	36
1996 Superman WB7	7,500	1996	48.00	69-94
1997 Sylvester & Tweety Stockings 97-WB-15	5,000		58.00	58
1999 Sylvester and Tweety Snowman 99-WB-14	Retrd.	N/A	29.00	49

YEAR ISSUE	EDITION LIMIT	YEAR RETD.	ISSUE PRICE	*QUOTE U.S.$
1996 Sylvester Sprite WB9	5,000	1996	45.00	69-88
1996 Taz & Bugs Stockings WB4	5,000	1996	65.00	50-100
1995 Taz Angel WB2	Retrd.	1995	40.00	75-120
1997 Taz Sprite WB13	5,000		46.00	46
1996 Trio Tree Topper 96-WB8	5,000	1997	78.00	180-195
1995 Tweety's Sprite WB3	Retrd.	1995	45.00	75-125
1999 Twinkle Twinkle Tweety Star 99-WB-12	Retrd.	N/A	32.00	49
1997 Wizard of Oz Dorothy 97-WB-18	10,000		45.00	45
1998 Wizard of Oz Lion 98-WB-09	10,000		44.00	44
1997 Wizard of Oz Ruby Slippers 97-WB-19	10,000		44.00	44
1998 Wizard of Oz Scarecrow 98-WB-08	10,000		44.00	44
1997 Wizard of Oz Tin Man 97-WB-14	10,000		46.00	46
1999 Yosemite Sam 99-WB-15	Retrd.	N/A	29.00	49

White Christmas - C. Radko

YEAR ISSUE	EDITION LIMIT	YEAR RETD.	ISSUE PRICE	*QUOTE U.S.$
1999 Bing Crosby as Bob Wallace 99-WHT-03	Retrd.	2000	24.00	24
1999 Danny Kaye as Phil Davis 99-WHT-03	Retrd.	2000	24.00	24
1999 Rosemary Clooney as Betty Haynes 99-WHT-02	Retrd.	2000	24.00	24
1999 Vera-Ellen as Judy Haynes 99-WHT-01	Retrd.	2000	24.00	24
1999 White Christmas, boxed set/4 99-WHT-05	Retrd.	2000	98.00	98

The Wubbulous World of Dr. Seuss - C. Radko

YEAR ISSUE	EDITION LIMIT	YEAR RETD.	ISSUE PRICE	*QUOTE U.S.$
1998 Cat in the Hat and Whozits 98-SUS-01	Retrd.	1999	26.00	26
1997 The Cat-In-The-Hat Wreath 97-SUS-03	Retrd.	1999	36.00	36
1997 The Grinch and Whozits 97-SUS-05	Retrd.	1999	44.00	44
1998 Thidwick and Whozits 98-SUS-03	Open		30.00	30
1998 Up On The Rooftop 98-SUS-02	Retrd.	1999	28.00	28

Crystal World

Disney Showcase Collection - Various

YEAR ISSUE	EDITION LIMIT	YEAR RETD.	ISSUE PRICE	*QUOTE U.S.$
1999 Tinker Bell - R. Nakai	Yr.Iss.	1999	58.00	58
2000 Sorcerer Mickey - Team	Yr.Iss.	2000	58.00	58

Dave Grossman Creations

Rockwell Collection-Annual Rockwell Ball - Rockwell-Inspired

YEAR ISSUE	EDITION LIMIT	YEAR RETD.	ISSUE PRICE	*QUOTE U.S.$
1975 Santa with Feather Quill NRO-01	Retrd.	N/A	3.50	25-35
1976 Santa at Globe NRO-02	Retrd.	N/A	4.00	25-35
1977 Grandpa on Rocking Horse NRO-03	Retrd.	N/A	4.00	12-20
1978 Santa with Map NRO-04	Retrd.	N/A	4.50	12-20
1979 Santa at Desk with Mail Bag NRO-05	Retrd.	N/A	5.00	12-20
1980 Santa Asleep with Toys NRO-06	Retrd.	N/A	5.00	10-18
1981 Santa with Boy on Finger NRO-07	Retrd.	N/A	5.00	10
1982 Santa Face on Winter Scene NRO-08	Retrd.	N/A	5.00	10
1983 Coachman with Whip NRO-9	Retrd.	N/A	5.00	10
1984 Christmas Bounty Man NRO-10	Retrd.	N/A	5.00	10-18
1985 Old English Trio NRO-11	Retrd.	N/A	5.00	10-15
1986 Tiny Tim on Shoulder NRO-12	Retrd.	N/A	5.00	10
1987 Skating Lesson NRO-13	Retrd.	N/A	5.00	10
1988 Big Moment NRO-14	Retrd.	N/A	5.50	10
1989 Discovery NRO-15	Retrd.	N/A	6.00	10-15
1990 Bringing Home The Tree NRO-16	Retrd.	N/A	6.00	10-15
1991 Downhill Daring NRO-17	Retrd.	N/A	6.00	10-15
1992 On The Ice NRO-18	Retrd.	N/A	6.00	10
1993 Gramps NRO-19	Retrd.	N/A	6.00	10-15
1994 Triple Self Portrait-Commemorative NRO-20	Retrd.	1994	6.00	10
1994 Merry Christmas NRO-94	Retrd.	1994	6.00	7
1995 Young Love NRO-21	Retrd.	N/A	6.00	7
1996 Christmas Feast NRO-22	Retrd.	1996	6.00	7
1997 Lovers NRO-23	Yr.Iss.	1997	6.00	7-11
1998 Merry Christmas NRO-24	Yr.Iss.	1998	6.00	6
1999 Bedside Manner NRO-25	Yr.Iss.	1999	6.00	6
2000 Homecoming NRO-26	Yr.Iss.	2000	6.00	6
2001 See America First NRO-27	Yr.Iss.		6.00	6

Rockwell Collection-Annual Rockwell Figurine Ornaments - Rockwell-Inspired

YEAR ISSUE	EDITION LIMIT	YEAR RETD.	ISSUE PRICE	*QUOTE U.S.$
1978 Caroler NRX-03	Retrd.	N/A	15.00	45
1979 Drum for Tommy NRX-24	Retrd.	N/A	20.00	30-40
1980 Santa's Good Boys NRX-37	Retrd.	N/A	20.00	30-55
1981 Letters to Santa NRX-39	Retrd.	N/A	20.00	55
1982 Cornettist NRX-32	Retrd.	N/A	20.00	30-40
1983 Fiddler NRX-83	Retrd.	N/A	20.00	40

ORNAMENTS

YEAR ISSUE	EDITION LIMIT	YEAR RETD.	ISSUE PRICE	*QUOTE U.S.$
1984 Christmas Bounty NRX-84	Retrd.	N/A	20.00	30-40
1985 Jolly Coachman NRX-85	Retrd.	N/A	20.00	35
1986 Grandpa on Rocking Horse NRX-86	Retrd.	N/A	20.00	35-45
1987 Skating Lesson NRX-87	Retrd.	N/A	20.00	35
1988 Big Moment NRX-88	Retrd.	N/A	20.00	30
1989 Discovery NRX-89	Retrd.	N/A	20.00	30-45
1990 Bringing Home The Tree NRX-90	Retrd.	N/A	20.00	10-30
1991 Downhill Daring B NRX-91	Retrd.	N/A	20.00	30-45
1992 On The Ice	Retrd.	N/A	20.00	30-40
1993 Granps NRX-93	Retrd.	N/A	24.00	10-30
1993 Marriage License First Christmas Together NRX-m1	Retrd.	N/A	30.00	30-50
1994 Merry Christmas NRX-94	Retrd.	N/A	24.00	24
1994 Triple Self-Portrait NRX-TS	Retrd.	N/A	30.00	30-50
1995 Young Love NRX-95	Retrd.	1995	24.00	45-65
1996 Christmas Feast NRX-96	Retrd.	1996	24.00	24-32
1997 Lovers NRX-97	Retrd.	1997	24.00	24
1998 Tiny Tim NRX-98	Retrd.	1998	24.00	24
1999 Bedside Manner NRX-99	Retrd.	1999	24.00	7-24
2000 Homecoming NRX-00	Yr.Iss.	2000	24.00	24
2001 See America First NRX-01	Yr.Iss.		24.00	24

Department 56

Bisque Light-Up, Clip-on Ornaments - Department 56

YEAR ISSUE	EDITION LIMIT	YEAR RETD.	ISSUE PRICE	*QUOTE U.S.$
1986 Angelic Lite-up 8260-0	Closed	1998	4.00	6
1987 Anniversary Love Birds, (pair) w/brass ribbon 8353-4	Closed	1988	4.00	42
1986 Dessert, 4 asst. 3803-4	Closed	1987	5.00	40-96
1990 Owl w/clip 8344-5	Closed	1994	5.00	15-18
1986 Plum Pudding 3803-5	Closed	1987	4.50	42-45
1989 Pond-Frog w/clip 8347-0	Closed	1991	5.00	36-42
1989 Pond-Snail w/clip 8347-0	Closed	1991	5.00	36-58
1988 Rabbit w/clip 8350-0	Closed	1998	4.00	4
1987 Shells 8349-6, set/4	Closed	1991	14.00	132-150
1986 Shooting Star 7106-4	Closed	1987	5.50	36-48
1985 Snowbirds 8358-5, set/8	Closed	1988	20.00	20
1985 Snowbirds 8367-4, set/6	Closed	1988	15.00	15-21
1985 Snowbirds, (pair) w/clip 8357-7	Open		5.00	6
1985 Snowmen, 3 asst. 8360-7	Closed	1988	10.50	11
1986 Teddy Bear w/clip 8262-7	Closed	1991	5.00	22
1986 Truffles Sampler 7102-1, set/4	Closed	1989	17.50	42-96
1986 Winged Snowbird 8261-9	Closed	1988	2.50	3-58
1989 Woodland-Field Mouse w/clip 8348-8	Closed	1991	5.00	30-36
1989 Woodland-Squirrel w/clip 8348-8	Closed	1991	5.00	36-40

CCP Ornaments-Flat - Department 56

YEAR ISSUE	EDITION LIMIT	YEAR RETD.	ISSUE PRICE	*QUOTE U.S.$
1986 Christmas Carol Houses (6504-8), set/3	Closed	1989	13.00	35-42
1986 • The Cottage of Bob Cratchit & Tiny Tim	Closed	1989	4.35	7-30
1986 • Fezziwig's Warehouse	Closed	1989	4.35	6-20
1986 • Scrooge and Marley Countinghouse	Closed	1989	4.35	8-20
1986 New England Village (6536-6), set/7	Closed	1989	25.00	300
1986 • Apothecary Shop	Closed	1989	3.50	10-25
1986 • Brick Town Hall	Closed	1989	3.50	20-30
1986 • General Store	Closed	1989	3.50	20-55
1986 • Livery Stable & Boot Shop	Closed	1989	3.50	10-20
1986 • Nathaniel Bingham Fabrics	Closed	1989	3.50	10-25
1986 • Red Schoolhouse	Closed	1989	3.50	30-55
1986 • Steeple Church	Closed	1989	3.50	100-150

Christmas Carol Character Ornaments-Flat - Department 56

YEAR ISSUE	EDITION LIMIT	YEAR RETD.	ISSUE PRICE	*QUOTE U.S.$
1986 Christmas Carol Characters (6505-6), set/3	Closed	1987	13.00	36-42
1986 • Bob Cratchit & Tiny Tim	Closed	1987	4.35	20
1986 • Poulterer	Closed	1987	4.35	20
1986 • Scrooge	Closed	1987	4.35	20-30

Christmas Carol Ornaments-Face - Department 56

YEAR ISSUE	EDITION LIMIT	YEAR RETD.	ISSUE PRICE	*QUOTE U.S.$
1988 Bob & Mrs. Crachit 5914-5	Closed	1989	18.00	32
1988 Scrooge's Head 5912-9	Closed	1989	12.95	32
1988 Tiny Tim's Head 5913-7	Closed	1989	10.00	24-32

Classic Ornament Series-Christmas in the City - Department 56

YEAR ISSUE	EDITION LIMIT	YEAR RETD.	ISSUE PRICE	*QUOTE U.S.$
1998 Cathedral Church of St. Mark 98759	Closed	2000	20.00	20
1998 City Hall 98741	Closed	1998	15.00	15
1998 City Hall 98771	Closed	2000	20.00	20

YEAR ISSUE	EDITION LIMIT	YEAR RETD.	ISSUE PRICE	*QUOTE U.S.$
1998 Dorothy's Dress Shop 98740	Closed	1998	15.00	1
1998 Dorothy's Dress Shop 98770	Closed	1999	20.00	18-2
1999 Hollydale's Department Store (1991-1997) 98782	Closed	2000	20.00	2
1998 Red Brick Fire Station 98758	Closed	2000	20.00	2

Classic Ornament Series-Dickens' Village - Department 56

YEAR ISSUE	EDITION LIMIT	YEAR RETD.	ISSUE PRICE	*QUOTE U.S.$
1998 Christmas Carol Cottages 98745, set/3	Closed	2000	50.00	5
1998 Dickens' Village Church 98737	Closed	1998	15.00	1
1998 Dickens' Village Church 98767	Closed	2000	20.00	2
1997 Dickens' Village Mill 98733	Closed	1998	15.00	1
1998 Dickens' Village Mill 98766	Closed	2000	22.50	2
1999 Dickens' Village Victorian Station (1989-1998) 98780	Closed	2000	22.50	2
1998 The Old Curiosity Shop 98738	Closed	1998	15.00	1
1998 The Old Curiosity Shop 98768	Closed	2000	20.00	2

Classic Ornament Series-Heritage Village - Department 56

YEAR ISSUE	EDITION LIMIT	YEAR RETD.	ISSUE PRICE	*QUOTE U.S.$
1999 The Times Tower 98775	Closed	2000	25.00	25-2

Classic Ornament Series-New England - Department 56

YEAR ISSUE	EDITION LIMIT	YEAR RETD.	ISSUE PRICE	*QUOTE U.S.$
1998 Captain's Cottage 98756	Closed	2000	20.00	2
1998 Craggy Cove Lighthouse 98739	Closed	1998	15.00	1
1998 Craggy Cove Lighthouse 98769	Closed	2000	20.00	2
1998 Steeple Church 98757	Closed	2000	20.00	2

Classic Ornament Series-North Pole - Department 56

YEAR ISSUE	EDITION LIMIT	YEAR RETD.	ISSUE PRICE	*QUOTE U.S.$
1998 Elf Bunkhouse 98763	Closed	2000	20.00	2
1997 North Pole Santa's Workshop 98734	Closed	1998	16.50	1
1999 Real Plastic Snow Factory (1998-current) 98781	Closed	2000	20.00	2
1998 Reindeer Barn 98762	Closed	2000	20.00	2
1998 Santa's Lookout Tower 98742	Closed	1998	15.00	1
1998 Santa's Lookout Tower 98773	Closed	2000	20.00	2
1998 Santa's Workshop 98772	Closed	2000	20.00	2

Classic Ornament Series-The Original Snow Village - Department 56

YEAR ISSUE	EDITION LIMIT	YEAR RETD.	ISSUE PRICE	*QUOTE U.S.$
1998 J. Young's Granary 98632	Closed	1998	15.00	1
1998 J. Young's Granary 98644	Closed	2000	20.00	2
1999 Jingle Belle Houseboat (1989-1991) 98648	Closed	2000	20.00	2
1998 Lighthouse 98635	Closed	2000	20.00	2
1998 Nantucket 98630	Closed	1998	15.00	1
1998 Nantucket 98642	Closed	2000	20.00	2
1998 Pinewood Log Cabin (lighted) 98637	Closed	2000	20.00	2
1999 Queen Anne Victorian (1990-1996) 98646	Closed	2000	20.00	2
1998 Steepled Church 98631	Closed	1998	15.00	1
1998 Steepled Church 98643	Closed	2000	20.00	2
1999 Street Car (1982-1984) 98645	Closed	2000	20.00	2

Clip On Lite-Up Ornaments - Department 56

YEAR ISSUE	EDITION LIMIT	YEAR RETD.	ISSUE PRICE	*QUOTE U.S.$
1989 Field Mouse 8348-8	Closed	1991	4.50	4
1989 Frog 8347-0	Closed	1991	4.50	5
1990 Owl 8344-5	Closed	1994	5.00	15-1
1989 Snail 8347-0	Closed	1991	4.50	35-5
1989 Squirrel 8348-8	Closed	1991	4.50	48-5

Dickens' Village Signature Series Ornaments - Department 56

YEAR ISSUE	EDITION LIMIT	YEAR RETD.	ISSUE PRICE	*QUOTE U.S.$
1994 Dickens Village Dedlock Arms 9872-8, (porcelain, gift boxed)	Closed	1994	12.50	17-2
1995 Sir John Falstaff 9870-1 (Charles Dickens' Signature Series)	Closed	1995	15.00	19-2
1996 The Grapes Inn 98729	Yr.Iss.	1996	15.00	24-2
1996 Crown & Cricket Inn 98730	Yr.Iss.	1996	15.00	28-4
1996 The Pied Bull Inn 98731	Yr.Iss.	1996	15.00	10-4
1997 Gad's Hill Place 98732	Yr.Iss.	1997	15.00	25-3

Discover Department 56 - Department 56

YEAR ISSUE	EDITION LIMIT	YEAR RETD.	ISSUE PRICE	*QUOTE U.S.$
1999 Ronald McDonald House 98774	Closed	1999	16.50	1
2000 1955 Pink Cadillac 98791	Yr.Iss.	2000	10.00	
2000 Elvis Presley's Graceland 98790	Yr.Iss.	2000	15.00	

Home For The Holidays - Department 56

YEAR ISSUE	EDITION LIMIT	YEAR RETD.	ISSUE PRICE	*QUOTE U.S.$
1997 Ronald McDonald House® 8961	Yr.Iss.	1997	7.50	4
1999 The First House That Love Built (25th Anniversary) 98774	Yr.Iss.	1999	16.50	8-1

Merry Makers - Department 56

YEAR ISSUE	EDITION LIMIT	YEAR RETD.	ISSUE PRICE	*QUOTE U.S.$
1994 Burgess The Bell Ringer 9368-8	Closed	1996	13.50	14-1
1993 Horatio The Hornblower 9383-1	Closed	1996	13.50	14-1

YEAR ISSUE	EDITION LIMIT	YEAR RETD.	ISSUE PRICE	*QUOTE U.S.$
1993 Martin The Mandolinist 9383-1	Closed	1996	13.50	14-25
1993 Merry Mountain Chapel 9384-0	Closed	1996	7.50	7-18
1994 Percival/Puddingman, Leopold /Lollipopman, 2 asst. 9396-3	Closed	1996	13.50	14-18
1994 Potter/Peppermint Make, Calvin /Candy Striper, 2 asst. 9397-1	Closed	1996	13.50	14-23
1993 Sinclair The Singer 9383-1	Closed	1996	13.50	19-28
1995 Stanislav The Skier 93977	Closed	1996	13.50	14-24
1995 Stuart The Skater 93978	Closed	1996	13.50	14-24
1992 Tolland The Toller 9369-6	Closed	1995	11.00	8-17

Miscellaneous Ornaments - Department 56

1992 Silver/Gold Ice Skate Ornament 84255	Closed	1992	2.50	20
1983 Snow Village Wood Ornaments 5099-7, set/6	Closed	1984	30.00	N/A
1983 · Carriage House	Closed	1984	5.00	20-40
1983 · Centennial House	Closed	1984	5.00	30-50
1983 · Countryside Church	Closed	1984	5.00	30-50
1983 · Gabled House	Closed	1984	5.00	50-75
1983 · Pioneer Church	Closed	1984	5.00	50-75
1983 · Swiss Chalet	Closed	1984	5.00	50-75
1984 Dickens 2-sided Tin Ornaments 6522-6, set/6	Closed	1985	12.00	440
1984 · Abel Beesley Butcher	Closed	1985	2.00	55
1984 · Bean and Son Smithy Shop	Closed	1985	2.00	55
1984 · Crowntree Inn	Closed	1985	2.00	55
1984 · Golden Swan Baker	Closed	1985	2.00	55
1984 · Green Grocer	Closed	1985	2.00	55
1984 · Jones & Co. Brush & Basket Shop	Closed	1985	2.00	55
1986 Cherub on Brass Ribbon, 8248-1	Closed	1988	8.00	72-75
1986 Teddy Bear on Brass Ribbon 8263-5	Closed	1988	7.00	72-94
1988 Balsam Bell Brass Dickens' Candlestick 6244-8	Closed	1989	3.00	15
1988 Christmas Carol- Bob & Mrs. Cratchit 5914-5	Closed	1989	18.00	30-36
1988 Christmas Carol- Scrooge's Head 5912-9	Closed	1989	12.95	25-33
1988 Christmas Carol- Tiny Tim's Head 5913-7	Closed	1989	10.00	20-33

Silhouette Treasures (Winter Silhouette) - Department 56

1995 Angel with Open Arms 78586	Closed	1998	25.00	25-44
1996 Cherub, large 85839	Closed	1998	16.50	17-30
1996 Cherub, small 85820	Closed	1998	8.50	9
1995 Chiming Bell Ornaments 78582, set/3	Closed	1998	36.00	18-36
1999 Christmas Angel 78634	Closed	2001	15.00	15
2001 A Christmas Bouquet 78663	Open		15.00	15
1999 Christmas Drummer 78632	Closed	2001	15.00	15
1999 Christmas Skater 78633	Closed	2001	15.00	15
2001 A Christmas Story 78664	Open		15.00	15
1999 Clara & The Nutcracker 78631	Closed	2001	15.00	15
2001 First Christmas Together 78650	Open		17.50	18
2002 Holiday Stocking 78725	Open		10.00	10
2002 The Holy Familiy 78689, set/3	Open		25.00	25
2002 Jingle Jingle Bell 78724	Open		10.00	10
1998 O Holy Light-Ups 78614	Closed	2001	15.00	15
2001 Pierced Lighted Ornaments 78674	Closed	2001	12.50	13
2002 Ringing with Joy 78723	Yr.Iss.		10.00	10
2002 St. Nick 78705	Yr.Iss.		12.50	13

Snowbabies Bootiebaby Bisque Ornaments - Department 56

1997 One, Two High Button Shoe 68844	Closed	2001	12.50	13
1997 Three, Four, No Room For One More 68845	Closed	2001	12.50	13
1998 Five, Six, A Drum With Sticks 68865	Closed	2001	13.50	14-22
1998 Seven, Eight, Time To Skate 68886	Closed	2001	12.50	13-21
1998 Nine, Ten, You're My Best Friend 68900	Closed	2001	12.50	13

Snowbabies Mercury Glass Ornaments - Department 56

1997 Snowbaby Atop a Glittered Green Tree 68992	Closed	1998	22.50	23-30
1997 Snowbaby Atop a Glittered Silver Drum 68993	Closed	1998	22.50	23-30
1996 Snowbaby Drummer The Night Before Christmas 68983	Closed	1998	18.00	18-24
1996 Snowbaby in Package The Night Before Christmas 68986	Closed	1998	18.00	18-24
1996 Snowbaby Jinglebaby The Night Before Christmas 68989	Closed	1998	20.00	20-24
1996 Snowbaby on Moon The Night Before Christmas 68988	Closed	1998	18.00	18-24

YEAR ISSUE	EDITION LIMIT	YEAR RETD.	ISSUE PRICE	*QUOTE U.S.$
1996 Snowbaby on Package The Night Before Christmas 68981	Closed	1998	18.00	18-24
1996 Snowbaby on Snowball The Night Before Christmas 68984	Closed	1998	20.00	20-69
1996 Snowbaby Soldier The Night Before Christmas 68982	Closed	1998	18.00	18-24
1996 Snowbaby With Bell The Night Before Christmas 68987	Closed	1998	18.00	18-24
1996 Snowbaby With Sisal Tree The Night Before Christmas 68990	Closed	1998	20.00	20-24
1996 Snowbaby With Star The Night Before Christmas 68991	Closed	1998	18.00	18-24
1996 Snowbaby With Wreath The Night Before Christmas 68980	Closed	1998	18.00	18-24

Snowbabies Miniature Ornaments - Department 56

2001 Batter Up 69517	Open		12.50	13
1999 Best Friends 69038	Open		12.50	13
1998 Celebrate 68902	Closed	2001	12.50	13
1998 Give Me A Push 68910	Closed	2001	12.50	13
1998 Give Someone A Hug 68905	Open		12.50	13
2002 Hold That Pose 69524	Open		12.50	13
1998 I Love You 68901	Open		12.50	13
1998 I'll Read You A Story 68907	Closed	2001	12.50	13
2001 In The Groove (Starlight Games™) 69520	Open		12.50	13
2002 Jump For Joy 69525	Open		12.50	13
1998 Let It Snow 68912	Closed	2001	12.50	13
1998 Let's Go Skiing 68911	Closed	2000	12.50	13
1998 My Gift To You 68909	Closed	2000	12.50	13
2000 Pretty As A Picture 69065	Closed	2001	12.50	13
2001 Ready, Set...! 69519	Open		12.50	13
1998 Rock-A-Bye-Baby 68908	Closed	2001	12.50	13
2001 See You On The Slopes (Starlight Games™) 69521	Open		12.50	13
2001 Send A Message 69145	Open		12.50	13
1998 Shall I Play For You? 68904	Closed	2000	12.50	13
2001 Shoot For The Goal 69522	Open		12.50	13
2001 Score 69518	Open		12.50	13
1998 Starlight Serenade 68906	Closed	2000	12.50	13
1998 Sweet Dreams 68903	Open		12.50	13
1999 They Call Me Joyful 69037	Closed	2001	12.50	13
1998 Display Tree 68936	Open		30.00	30

Snowbabies Ornaments - Department 56

2001 1st Birthday 69091	Closed	2001	16.50	17
2001 2nd Birthday 69092	Closed	2001	16.50	17
2001 3rd Birthday 69093	Closed	2001	16.50	17
2002 Air Mail 69523	Open		12.50	13
1998 Baby's 1st Photo 68913	Closed	2000	7.50	9
1996 Baby's 1st Rattle 68828	Closed	1998	15.00	15-30
1994 Be My Baby 6866-7	Closed	1998	15.00	20-30
1998 Candle Light...Season Bright, Clip-On 68918	Closed	2000	13.50	14
1986 Crawling, Lite-Up, Clip-On, 7953-7	Closed	1992	7.00	18-35
1994 First Star Jinglebaby, 6858-6	Closed	1997	10.00	8-20
1998 Fly Me To The Moon 68885	Closed	2001	16.50	17
2002 From God 69200	Yr.Iss.		15.00	15
1998 Frosty Frolic Friends 68879 (1998 Winter Celebration Event Piece)	Closed	1998	15.00	15-30
1999 Frosty Frolic Friends (1999 Winter Celebration Event Piece) 68950	Closed	1999	15.00	15-27
2000 Frosty Frolic Friends (2000 Winter Celebration Event Piece) 69054	Closed	2000	15.00	15
1994 Gathering Stars in the Sky, 6855-1	Closed	1997	12.50	20-25
2001 Guiding The Sleigh (Snowbabies Guest Collection™) 69907	Open		15.00	15
1996 Jinglebell Jinglebaby 68826	Closed	1998	11.00	15-20
2001 Jolly & Happy With You (The Guest Collection) 66914	Open		15.00	15
1995 Joy 68007, set/3	Closed	1999	32.50	33-35
1996 Joy to the World 68829	Closed	1998	16.50	17-25
1994 Juggling Stars in the Sky 6867-5	Closed	1998	15.00	20-30
1994 Just For You Jinglebaby 6869-1	Closed	1998	11.00	9-26
1994 Little Drummer Jinglebaby, 6859-4	Closed	1997	11.00	14-20
1987 Mini, Winged Pair, Lite-Up, Clip-On, 7976-6	Closed	1999	9.00	12
1987 Moon Beams, 7951-0	Closed	1999	7.50	10
1999 Moondreams & Hangin' On 69032	Open		15.00	15
1991 My First Star, 6811-0	Closed	1998	7.00	8-23
1989 Noel, 7988-0	Closed	1998	7.50	8-14
1995 One Little Candle Jinglebaby 68806	Closed	1998	11.00	11-26

YEAR ISSUE	EDITION LIMIT	YEAR RETD.	ISSUE PRICE	*QUOTE U.S.$
1995 Overnight Delivery, 759-5 (Event Piece)	Closed	1995	10.00	35-40
1995 Overnight Delivery, 68808	Closed	2001	10.00	10
1990 Penguin, Lite-Up, Clip-On, 7940-5	Closed	1992	5.00	14-30
1990 Polar Bear, Lite-Up, Clip-On, 7941-3	Closed	1992	5.00	18-30
1998 Reach For The Moon 68914, set/2	Closed	2000	15.00	15
2001 The Red-Nosed Reindeer (Snowbabies Guest Collection™) 69908	Open		17.50	18
1990 Rock-A-Bye Baby, 7939-1	Closed	1995	7.00	10-27
1999 Royal Bootiebaby 68951	Closed	2001	13.50	14
1986 Sitting, Lite-Up, Clip-On, 7952-9	Closed	1990	7.00	34-58
2000 Sealed With A Kiss 69062	Open		13.50	14
1992 Snowbunnies Icicle With Star, 6825-0	Closed	1995	16.00	18-34
1987 Snowbaby Adrift Lite-Up, Clip-On, 7969-3	Closed	1990	8.50	37-157
1996 Snowbaby in my Stocking 68827	Closed	2000	10.00	10
1986 Snowbaby on Brass Ribbon, 7961-8	Closed	1989	8.00	147-200
1993 Sprinkling Stars in the Sky, 6848-9	Closed	1997	12.50	15-25
1989 Star Bright, 7990-1	Closed	1999	7.50	9
1996 Starry Pine Jinglebaby 68825	Closed	1998	11.00	12-26
1992 Starry, Starry Night, 6830-6	Closed	2001	12.50	13
1994 Stars in My Stocking Jinglebaby 6868-3	Closed	1998	11.00	9-21
1989 Surprise, 7989-8	Closed	1994	12.00	14-42
2002 Swinging On the Moon with Eloise (Snowbabies Guest Collection™) 69920	Open		17.50	18
1991 Swinging On a Star, 6810-1	Closed	2001	9.50	10
2001 Tooth Fairy Hinged Box Ornament 69095	Closed	2001	17.50	18
1988 Twinkle Little Star, 7980-4	Closed	1990	7.00	69-188
1993 Wee...This is Fun!, 6847-0	Closed	1997	13.50	15-20
2002 We See Eye To Eye (Snowbabies Guest Collection™) 69924	Open		15.00	15
1986 Winged, Lite-Up, Clip-On, 7954-5	Closed	1990	7.00	50-65

Snowbunnies Ornaments - Department 56

2001 Easter Egg Photo Frame 26397	Closed	2002	5.00	5
2000 Mini Ornaments, 6 asst. 26335	Closed	2002	7.50	8
2000 Ornament Display Tree 26367	Closed	2002	25.00	25

Village Light-Up Ornaments - Department 56

1987 Christmas Carol Cottages (6513-7), set/3	Closed	1989	17.00	30-72
1987 • The Cottage of Bob Cratchit & Tiny Tim	Closed	1989	6.00	10-30
1987 • Fezziwig's Warehouse	Closed	1989	6.00	10-30
1987 • Scrooge & Marley Countinghouse	Closed	1989	6.00	10-30
1987 Dickens' Village (6521-8, 6520-), set/14	Closed	1989	84.00	400-495
1987 Dickens' Village (6520-0), set/6	Closed	1989	36.00	100-150
1987 • Barley Bree Farmhouse	Closed	1989	6.00	10-35
1987 • Blythe Pond Mill House	Closed	1989	6.00	25-40
1987 • Brick Abbey	Closed	1989	6.00	35-75
1987 • Chesterton Manor House	Closed	1989	6.00	35-56
1987 • Kenilworth Castle	Closed	1989	6.00	33-48
1987 • The Old Curiosity Shop	Closed	1989	6.00	32-50
1985 Dickens' Village (6521-8), set/8	Closed	1989	48.00	181-200
1985 • Abel Beesley Butcher	Closed	1989	6.00	10-25
1985 • Bean and Son Smithy Shop	Closed	1989	6.00	10-35
1985 • Candle Shop	Closed	1989	6.00	15-30
1985 • Crowntree Inn	Closed	1989	6.00	20-45
1985 • Dickens' Village Church	Closed	1989	6.00	48-50
1985 • Golden Swan Baker	Closed	1989	6.00	10-20
1985 • Green Grocer	Closed	1989	6.00	10-35
1985 • Jones & Co. Brush & Basket Shop	Closed	1989	6.00	20-35
1987 New England Village (6533-1, 6534-0), set/13	Closed	1989	78.00	700-750
1987 New England Village (6534-0), set/6	Closed	1989	36.00	200-275
1987 • Craggy Cove Lighthouse	Closed	1989	6.00	65-148
1987 • Jacob Adams Barn	Closed	1989	6.00	20-50
1987 • Jacob Adams Farmhouse	Closed	1989	6.00	20-50
1987 • Smythe Woolen Mill	Closed	1989	6.00	25-115
1987 • Timber Knoll Log Cabin	Closed	1989	6.00	25-105
1987 • Weston Train Station	Closed	1989	6.00	25-65
1986 New England Village (6533-1), set/7	Closed	1989	42.00	281-325
1986 • Apothecary Shop	Closed	1989	6.00	10-25
1986 • Brick Town Hall	Closed	1989	6.00	10-40
1986 • General Store	Closed	1989	6.00	10-45
1986 • Livery Stable & Boot Shop	Closed	1989	6.00	10-35
1986 • Nathaniel Bingham Fabrics	Closed	1989	6.00	10-35

YEAR ISSUE	EDITION LIMIT	YEAR RETD.	ISSUE PRICE	*QUOTE U.S.$
1986 • Red Schoolhouse	Closed	1989	6.00	25-90
1986 • Steeple Church	Closed	1989	6.00	65-165

Encore

Santa and Snow Buddies™ - Encore

2000 Santa at Desk	Closed	2001	4.00	4
2000 Santa in Sleigh	Closed	2001	4.00	4
2000 Santa Skiing with Buddies on Back	Closed	2001	4.00	4

Snow Buddies™ - Encore

2002 Annual Ornament 2002	Yr.Iss.		2.50	3
2002 Baby's First Christmas	Yr.Iss.		3.00	3
2001 Baby's First Christmas 2001	Yr.Iss.	2001	3.00	3
2000 Blizzy with Box Car	Open		2.50	3
2001 Bowl of Snowflakes 2001	Yr.Iss.		3.00	3
2000 Flurry with Engine	Open		2.50	3
2000 Holding Joy Sign	Open		2.50	3
2000 In Stocking	Open		2.50	3
2000 Knit Cap with 2000 Candy Cane	Yr.Iss.	2000	2.50	3
2000 Knit Cap with 2000 Snowflake	Yr.Iss.	2000	2.50	3
2000 On Candy Cane	Open		2.50	3
2001 Our First Christmas Together 2001	Yr.Iss.	2001	6.00	6
2002 Our First Christmas Together 2002	Yr.Iss.		3.00	3
2000 Powder with Caboose	Open		2.50	3
1999 Powder with Harp	Retrd.	1999	2.50	3
1999 Powder with Sign	Retrd.	1999	2.50	3
1999 Powder with Tree	Retrd.	1999	2.50	3
1999 Santa & Powder Walking	Retrd.	1999	5.00	5
1999 Santa Holding Powder	Retrd.	1999	5.00	5
1999 Santa with Powder Sitting	Retrd.	1999	5.00	5
2000 Skatin'	Open		2.50	3
1999 The Skier	Open		2.50	3
2000 Sleddin'	Open		2.50	3
2000 Snowboardin'	Open		2.50	3
1999 Special Friend	Open		2.50	3
2000 Tobogganin'	Open		2.50	3
2000 Top Hat with 2000 Sign	Yr.Iss.	2000	2.50	3
2000 Top Hat with 2000 Snowflake	Yr.Iss.	2000	2.50	3

Snow Buddies™ Character Ornaments - Encore

2001 Aunt Crystal	Open		2.50	3
2000 Avalanche	Open		2.50	3
2000 Blizzy	Open		2.50	3
2000 Cousin Slick	Open		2.50	3
2000 Everest	Open		2.50	3
2002 Flurry	Open		2.50	3
2002 Grandma Cooleen	Open		2.50	3
2002 Grandpa Frostbite	Open		2.50	3
2001 Mayor Blustery	Open		2.50	3
2001 Powder Puff	Open		2.50	3
2002 Slide	Open		2.50	3
2002 Slip	Open		2.50	3
2001 Snowball	Open		2.50	3
2002 Snowbelle	Open		2.50	3
2002 Snowbrite	Open		2.50	3
2001 Tundra	Open		2.50	3
2001 Uncle Flake	Open		2.50	3
2000 Uncle Melty	Retrd.	2001	2.50	3

Snow Buddies™ Swing Ornaments - Encore

2001 Avalanche	Open		3.00	3
2001 Cousin Slick	Open		3.00	3
2001 Everest	Open		3.00	3
2001 Grandpa Frostbite	Open		3.00	3
2001 Powder Puff	Open		3.00	3
2000 Uncle Melty	Retrd.	2001	3.00	3

Snow Buddies™ Wreath Ornaments - Encore

2002 Aunt Crystal	Open		5.00	5
2002 Avalanche	Open		5.00	5
2002 Blizzy	Open		5.00	5
2002 Cousin Slick	Open		5.00	5
2002 Everest	Open		5.00	5
2002 Flurry	Open		5.00	5
2002 Grandma Cooleen	Open		5.00	5
2002 Grandpa Frostbite	Open		5.00	5
2002 Mayor Blustery	Open		5.00	5
2002 Powder Puff	Open		5.00	5
2002 Slip & Slide	Open		5.00	5
2002 Snowball	Open		5.00	5
2002 Snowbelle	Open		5.00	5

YEAR ISSUE	EDITION LIMIT	YEAR RETD.	ISSUE PRICE	*QUOTE U.S.$
2002 Snowbrite	Open		5.00	5
2002 Tundra	Open		5.00	5
2002 Uncle Flake	Open		5.00	5

Fenton Art Glass Company

Christmas Limited Edition - M. Reynolds

1996 Golden Winged Angel, Hndpt. 3 1/2"	2,000	1996	27.50	28-45
1999 Angel, 4 1/2"	Closed	1999	49.00	49

Flambro Imports

Emmett Kelly Jr. Christmas Ornaments - Undisclosed

1989 65th Birthday	Yr.Iss.	1989	24.00	200
1990 30 Years Of Clowning	Yr.Iss.	1990	30.00	75-160
1991 EKJ With Stocking And Toys	Yr.Iss.	1991	24.00	26-50
1992 Home For Christmas	Yr.Iss.	1992	24.00	30-75
1993 Christmas Mail	Yr.Iss.	1993	25.00	30-75
1994 '70 Birthday Commemorative	Yr.Iss.	1994	24.00	70-90
1995 20th Anniversary All Star Circus	Yr.Iss.	1995	25.00	50-70
1996 Christmas Pageant	Yr.Iss.	1996	29.00	75
1997 1997 Dated Ornament	Yr.Iss.	1997	30.00	30
1998 1998 Dated Ornament	Yr.Iss.	1998	20.00	20
1999 1999 Dated Ornament	Yr.Iss.	1999	35.00	35
2000 2000 Dated Ornament	Yr.Iss.	2000	35.00	35
2001 2001 Dated Ornament	Yr.Iss.	2001	30.00	30
2002 2002 Dated Ornament	Yr.Iss.		30.00	30

Little Emmett Ornaments - M. Wu

1995 Little Emmett Christmas Wrap	Open		11.50	12
1995 Little Emmett Deck the Neck	Open		11.50	12
1996 Little Emmett Singing Carols	Open		13.00	13
1996 Little Emmett Your Present	Open		13.00	13
1996 Little Emmett Baby 1st Christmas	Open		13.00	13
1996 Little Emmett on Rocking Horse	Open		25.00	25

Fontanini/Roman, Inc.

Fontanini Limited Edition Ornaments - E. Simonetti

1995 The Annunciation	20,000	N/A	20.00	20
1996 Journey to Bethlehem	20,000	N/A	20.00	20
1997 Gloria Angel	Yr.Iss.	1997	20.00	20-40

Fontanini Tour Exclusive - E. Simonetti

2000 2000 Fontanini Tour Ornament	Yr.Iss.	2000	20.00	20
2001 2001 Fontanini Tour Ornament	Yr.Iss.	2001	22.50	23
2002 2002 Fontanini Tour Ornament	Yr.Iss.		22.50	23

G. DeBrekht Artistic Studios/Derévo Collection

Derévo Guardian Angels Ornaments - G. DeBrekht Artistic Studios

2002 Angel Herald 55311	1,200		57.50	58
2002 Angel of Peace 55312	1,200		57.50	58
2002 Angel of Hope 55313	1,200		57.50	58

Derévo House of Romanoff Ornaments - G. DeBrekht Artistic Studios

2002 Peter the Great 53511	1,500		59.00	59
2002 Catherine the Great 53512	1,500		59.00	59

Derévo Nutcracker Ornaments - G. DeBrekht Artistic Studios

2001 Nutcrackers (set/4) 53310	1,200		195.00	195
2002 Nutcrackers (set/4) 53311	1,200		195.00	195

G. DeBrekht Artistic Studios/Russian Gift & Jewelry

Heritage Russkiye Fantasy and Fairytales - G. DeBrekht Artistic Studios

2001 As If By Magic Bell	3-Yr.		69.00	69
2001 Country Dancing	2-Yr.		59.00	59
2000 Father Frost	2-Yr.		59.00	59
2001 Father Frost #2	3-Yr.		59.00	59
1999 Fire Bird	Open		59.00	59
2000 Fire Bird Bell	3-Yr.		69.00	69
1999 Girl-Friends	Retrd.	2000	59.00	59
2000 Love	2-Yr.		59.00	59
2000 Magic Pike	3-Yr.		59.00	59
1999 Meeting	Retrd.	2001	59.00	59
2000 Morozko	2-Yr.		59.00	59

YEAR ISSUE	EDITION LIMIT	YEAR RETD.	ISSUE PRICE	*QUOTE U.S.$
2001 Morozko #2	3-Yr.		59.00	59
1999 Snow Maiden EO/FT#4	Retrd.	2000	59.00	59
1999 Snow Maiden EO/FT#8	Open		59.00	59
2000 Swan Princes Bell	3-Yr.		69.00	69
1999 Tea Party	Open		59.00	59
1999 Troika	Open		59.00	59
2001 Winter Romance	3-Yr.		59.00	59

Heritage Russkiye Floral Fantasy - G. DeBrekht Artistic Studios

2000 Floral Balls Ornament	Open		39.00	39
2001 Floral Bells Ornament	Open		39.00	39
2001 Floral Drop Ornament	Open		39.00	39
2001 Floral Teardrop Ornament	Open		39.00	39
2000 Floral Tree Topper	Open		59.50	60
1999 Flowers	Open		35.00	35
2001 Gold-ball Ornament	3-Yr.		35.00	35
2001 Gold-bell Ornament	3-Yr.		49.00	49

Russkiye Bells - G. DeBrekht Artistic Studios

1999 Angel	Open		19.50	20
1998 Girl	Open		19.50	20
1999 Santa	Open		19.50	20

Russkiye Holiday Traditions - G. DeBrekht Artistic Studios

1998 Boyar Ornament	Open		17.00	17
1998 Cat Fisherman	Retrd.	1999	20.00	20
1998 Czar	Retrd.	1999	39.00	39
1998 Knight"	Open		20.00	20
1998 Ladies #1	Retrd.	2000	20.00	20
1998 Ladies #2	Retrd.	2001	20.00	20
1998 Ladies #3	Open		30.00	30
1998 Ladies #3 with Icons	Retrd.	2000	30.00	30
1998 Peasant Man	Open		20.00	20
1998 Peasant Man Flat	Retrd.	2001	11.00	11
1998 Peasant Musical	Open		20.00	20
1998 Peasant Woman 5PW	Retrd.	2000	20.00	20
1998 Peasant Women 5PW/LE	Open		39.00	39
1998 Priest	Open		27.00	27
1998 Snow Maiden	Retrd.	2000	20.00	20
1998 Soldiers 5NS	Retrd.	2001	20.00	20
1998 Soldiers 5VK	Open		20.00	20

Russkiye Roly-Poly - G. DeBrekht Artistic Studios

1998 Angel	Retrd.	2001	20.00	20
1998 Boy RO/B	Retrd.	2000	19.00	19
1998 Bunny	Open		19.00	19
1998 Czar & Czaritsa, set/2	Retrd.	2001	90.00	90
1998 Girl RB/G	Retrd.	2000	20.00	20
1998 Girl RO/G	Retrd.	2001	19.00	19
1998 Santa RB/S	Retrd.	2001	20.00	20
1998 Santa RO/S	Retrd.	2001	19.00	19
1998 Snowmen	Retrd.	2000	35.00	35

Russkiye Santa & Friends - G. DeBrekht Artistic Studios

1998 Bear Ornament	Retrd.	1999	15.00	15
1998 Santa 6ST/2	Retrd.	2000	27.00	27
1998 Santa #1	Open		16.00	16
1998 Santa 6SES	Retrd.	2000	10.00	10
1998 Santa CO/ST	Open		25.00	25
1998 Santa Flat 6ST/F	Open		10.00	10
1998 Santa on Sleigh	Retrd.	2000	20.00	20
1998 Santa with Bag 6ST/3	Open		27.00	27
1998 Santa with Paintings	Open		35.00	35
1998 Santa with Tree	Retrd.	2001	25.00	25
1998 Santa-Bell	Retrd.	2001	15.00	15
1998 Snow Maiden 6SEM	Retrd.	2001	10.00	10
1998 Snow Maiden 6SM/LE	Retrd.	2001	35.00	35
1998 Snow Maiden Flat 6SM/F	Open		10.00	10
1998 Snowman 6SN/2	Open		20.00	20
1998 Snowman S/50MD	Retrd.	1999	50.00	50
1998 Snowman with Bell	Retrd.	1999	16.00	16

Geo. Zoltan Lefton Company

Colonial Village Ornaments - Lefton

1987 Charity Chapel	Closed	1990	6.00	18
1987 Church of the Golden Rule	Closed	1990	6.00	18
1987 Lil Red School House	Closed	1990	6.00	18
1987 Nelson House	Closed	1990	6.00	18
1987 Old Stone Church	Closed	1990	6.00	18
1987 Penny House	Closed	1990	6.00	18

ORNAMENTS

YEAR ISSUE	EDITION LIMIT	YEAR RETD.	ISSUE PRICE	*QUOTE U.S.$
Goebel of North America				
Angel Bell 3" - Goebel				
1994 Angel w/Clarinet - Red	Closed	1994	17.50	18
1995 Angel w/Harp - Blue	Closed	1995	17.50	18-20
1996 Angel w/Mandolin - Champagne	Closed	1996	18.00	18-20
1997 Angel w/Accordian - Rose	Closed	1997	18.00	18-20
1998 Angel w/Bell - Blue	Closed	1998	20.00	20
1999 Angel w/Violin - Green	Closed	1999	20.00	20
2001 Angel w/Tamborine	Closed	2001	20.00	20
2002 Angel w/Triangle	Yr.Iss.		20.00	20
Angel Bells - 3 Asst. Colors - Goebel				
1976 Angel Bell w/Clarinet (3 colors)	Closed	1976	8.00	65
1976 Angel Bell w/Clarinet (white bisque)	Closed	1976	6.00	25-50
1977 Angel Bell w/Mandolin (3 colors)	Closed	1977	8.50	55-60
1977 Angel Bell w/Mandolin (white bisque)	Closed	1977	6.50	40-50
1978 Angel Bell w/Harp (3 colors)	Closed	1978	9.00	25-65
1978 Angel Bell w/Harp (white bisque)	Closed	1978	7.00	40-50
1979 Angel Bell w/Accordion (3 colors)	Closed	1979	9.50	55-65
1979 Angel Bell w/Accordion (white bisque)	Closed	1979	7.50	40-50
1980 Angel Bell w/Saxaphone (3 colors)	Closed	1980	10.00	55-65
1980 Angel Bell w/Saxaphone (white bisque)	Closed	1980	8.00	20-50
1981 Angel Bell w/Music (3 colors)	Closed	1981	11.00	55-65
1981 Angel Bell w/Music (white bisque)	Closed	1981	9.00	20-50
1982 Angel Bell w/French Horn (3 colors)	Closed	1982	11.75	55-65
1982 Angel Bell w/French Horn (white bisque)	Closed	1982	9.75	20-50
1983 Angel Bell w/Flute (3 colors)	Closed	1983	12.50	55-65
1983 Angel Bell w/Flute (white bisque)	Closed	1983	10.50	20-50
1984 Angel Bell w/Drum (3 colors)	Closed	1984	14.00	55-65
1984 Angel Bell w/Drum (white bisque)	Closed	1984	12.00	20-50
1985 Angel Bell w/Trumpet (3 colors)	Closed	1985	14.00	20-65
1985 Angel Bell w/Trumpet (white bisque)	Closed	1985	12.00	20-50
1986 Angel Bell w/Bells (3 colors)	Closed	1986	15.00	55-65
1986 Angel Bell w/Bells (white bisque)	Closed	1986	12.50	20-50
1987 Angel Bell w/Conductor (3 colors)	Closed	1987	16.50	55-65
1987 Angel Bell w/Conductor (white bisque)	Closed	1987	13.50	20-50
1988 Angel Bell w/Candle (3 colors)	Closed	1988	17.50	55-65
1988 Angel Bell w/Candle (white bisque)	Closed	1988	15.00	22-50
1989 Angel Bell w/Star (3 colors)	Closed	1989	20.00	55-65
1989 Angel Bell w/Star (white bisque)	Closed	1989	17.50	20-50
1990 Angel Bell w/Lantern (3 colors)	Closed	1990	22.50	55-65
1990 Angel Bell w/Lantern (white bisque)	Closed	1990	20.00	25-50
1991 Angel Bell w/Teddy (3 colors)	Closed	1991	25.00	55-65
1991 Angel Bell w/Teddy (white bisque)	Closed	1991	22.50	40-50
1992 Angel Bell w/Doll (3 colors)	Closed	1992	27.50	55-65
1992 Angel Bell w/Doll (white bisque)	Closed	1992	25.00	40-50
1993 Angel Bell w/Rocking Horse (3 colors)	Closed	1993	30.00	55-65
1993 Angel Bell w/Rocking Horse (white bisque)	Closed	1993	27.50	40-50
1994 Angel Bell w/Clown (3 colors)	Closed	1994	34.50	55-65
1994 Angel Bell w/Clown (white bisque)	Closed	1994	29.50	40-50
1995 Angel Bell w/Train (3 colors)	Closed	1995	37.00	55-65
1995 Angel Bell w/Train (white bisque)	Closed	1995	30.50	31-50
1996 Angel Bell w/Puppy (3 colors)	Closed	1996	40.00	55-65
1996 Angel Bell w/Puppy (white bisque)	Closed	1996	32.00	40-50
1997 Angel Bell w/Kitten (3 colors)	Closed	1997	42.50	55-65
1997 Angel Bell w/Kitten (white bisque)	Closed	1997	32.50	40-50
1998 Angel Bell w/Lamb (3 colors)	Closed	1998	45.00	55-65
1998 Angel Bell w/Lamb (white bisque)	Closed	1998	34.00	40-50
1999 Angel Bell w/Rabbit (3 colors)	Closed	1999	45.00	45
1999 Angel Bell w/Rabbit (white bisque)	Closed	1999	35.00	35
2001 Angel Bell w/Gingerbread Man (3 colors)	Closed	2001	45.00	45
2001 Angel Bell w/Gingerbread Man (white bisque)	Closed	2001	35.00	35
2002 Angel Bell w/Candy Cane (3 colors)	Yr.Iss.		45.00	45
2002 Angel Bell w/Candy Cane (white bisque)	Yr.Iss.		35.00	35
Pocket Dragons - R. Musgrave				
2001 All Wrapped Up	Open		15.00	15
2001 Chasing Snowflakes	Open		15.00	15
2001 Christmas Angel	Open		15.00	15
2001 Christmas Skates	Open		15.00	15
2001 Dear Santa	Open		15.00	15
2001 Deck The Halls	Open		15.00	15
2001 I've Been Very Good	Open		15.00	15
2001 The Littlest Reindeer	Open		15.00	15

YEAR ISSUE	EDITION LIMIT	YEAR RETD.	ISSUE PRICE	*QUOTE U.S.$
2001 A Pocket-Sized Tree	Open		15.00	15
2001 Putting Me On The Tree	Open		15.00	15
2001 Sharing	Yr.Iss.	2001	15.00	15
2001 The Twelve Years of Christmas Limited Edition Boxed Set	2,000	2001	160.00	160
2001 Under The Mistletoe	Open		15.00	15
Goebel/M.I. Hummel				
M.I. Hummel Annual Figurine Ornaments - M.I. Hummel				
1988 Flying High 452	Closed	N/A	75.00	104-300
1989 Love From Above 481	Closed	N/A	75.00	120-156
1990 Peace on Earth 484	Closed	N/A	80.00	65-130
1991 Angelic Guide 571	Closed	N/A	95.00	125-155
1992 Light Up The Night 622	Closed	N/A	100.00	75-135
1993 Herald on High 623	Closed	N/A	155.00	150-200
1997 Boy with Horse 239/C/O	Open		60.00	65-70
1997 Girl with Nosegay 239/A/O	Open		60.00	65-70
1997 Girl with Doll 239/B/O	Open		60.00	65-70
1997 Girl with Fir Tree 239/D/O	10,000		60.00	65-70
2000 Cuddles 2049/A/O	Open		80.00	80
2000 First Bloom 2077/A/O	Open		80.00	80
2000 A Flower For You 2077/B/O	Open		80.00	80
2000 My Best Friend 2049/B/O	Open		80.00	80
2001 For Me? 2067/B/O	Open		80.00	80
M.I. Hummel Ball Ornaments - M.I. Hummel				
2001 Angel Duet 930014	Open		49.00	49
2001 Angel Serenade 930015	Open		49.00	49
2001 Celestial Musician 930011	Open		49.00	49
2001 Christmas Angel 930013	Open		49.00	49
2001 Christmas Song 930016	Open		49.00	49
2001 Festival Harmony with Flute 930017	Open		49.00	49
2001 Festival Harmony with Mandolin 930018	Open		49.00	49
2001 Heavenly Angel 930019	Open		49.00	49
M.I. Hummel Bas Relief Ornaments - M.I. Hummel				
2000 Christmas Delivery Star 2110/A	Open		20.00	20
2000 Heavenly Angel Bell 876/A	Open		20.00	20
2000 Making New Friends 2111/A	Open		20.00	20
2000 Millennium Bliss Star 2098/A	Open		20.00	20
2000 Ride Into Christmas Tree 877/A	Open		20.00	20
2001 Joyful Recital Star 2098/B	Open		20.00	20
2001 Sleep Tight Ball 878/A	Open		20.00	20
2001 St. Nicholas' Day Boot 2099/A	Open		20.00	20
M.I. Hummel Collectibles Christmas Bell Ornaments - M.I. Hummel				
1989 Ride Into Christmas 775	Closed	1989	35.00	60-195
1990 Letter to Santa Claus 776	Closed	1990	37.50	60-100
1991 Hear Ye, Hear Ye 777	Closed	1991	40.00	60-100
1992 Harmony in Four Parts 778	Closed	1992	50.00	60-80
1993 Celestial Musician 779	Closed	1993	50.00	60-70
1994 Festival Harmony w/Mandolin 780	Closed	1994	50.00	60-70
1995 Festival Harmony w/Flute 781	Closed	1995	55.00	55-70
1996 Christmas Song 782	Closed	1996	65.00	70-75
1997 Thanksgiving Prayer 783	Closed	1997	68.00	70-139
1998 Echoes of Joy 784	Yr.Iss.	1998	70.00	70
1999 Joyful Noise 785	Yr.Iss.	1999	70.00	70
2000 Light The Way 786	Yr.Iss.	2000	70.00	70
M.I. Hummel Collectibles Miniature Ornaments - M.I. Hummel				
1993 Celestial Musician 646	Closed	1993	90.00	125-130
1994 Festival Harmony w/Mandolin 647	Closed	1994	95.00	125-130
1995 Festival Harmony w/Flute 648	Closed	1995	100.00	125-130
1996 Christmas Song 645	Closed	1996	115.00	125-130
1997 Thanksgiving Prayer 642	Closed	1997	120.00	125-130
1998 Echoes of Joy 597	Yr.Iss.	1998	120.00	125-130
1999 Joyful Noise 598	Yr.Iss.	1999	120.00	125-130
2000 Light The Way 599	Yr.Iss.	2000	120.00	125-130
Greenwich Workshop				
Elves - S. Gustafson				
2001 Åårikka	Open		15.00	15
2001 Cruquius Sgrooten	Open		15.00	15
2001 Eena	Open		15.00	15
2001 Post Master Bündel	Open		15.00	15
2001 Spriggs	Open		15.00	15
2001 Sweetie	Open		15.00	15

Collectors' Information Bureau

*Quotes have been rounded up to nearest dollar

YEAR ISSUE	EDITION LIMIT	YEAR RETD.	ISSUE PRICE	*QUOTE U.S.$
2001 Trenkle	Open		15.00	15
2001 Welvin	Open		15.00	15

The Greenwich Workshop Collection - J. Christensen

1995 The Angel's Gift	Yr.Iss.	1995	50.00	95
1996 A Gift of Light	7,500	1996	75.00	75
1997 A Gift of Music	7,500	1997	75.00	75

Pearl Bisque™ - Various

2000 Ancient Angel - J. Christensen	Open		7.50	8
2000 bearing gifts - W. Bullas	Open		6.25	7
2001 Benediction - J. Christensen	Open		15.00	15
2001 Chimp Shot - W. Bullas	Open		10.95	11
2000 The Christmas Angel - J. Christensen	Open		7.50	8
2001 Cool Yule - W. Bullas	Open		12.50	13
2000 duck tape - W. Bullas	Open		6.25	7
2001 Dust Bunnies - W. Bullas	Open		10.95	11
2000 The Fish Walker - J. Christensen	Open		7.50	8
2000 the fool - W. Bullas	Open		6.25	7
2001 Fool Moon - W. Bullas	Open		12.50	13
2000 The Forest Fishrider - J. Christensen	Open		7.50	8
2001 Gift Ahoy - J. Christensen	Open		15.00	15
2001 The Horn Blower - J. Christensen	Open		15.00	15
2000 jingle this - W. Bullas	Open		6.25	7
2000 The Lute Player - J. Christensen	Open		7.50	8
2000 mistle toad - W. Bullas	Open		6.25	7
2001 Nutcracker - W. Bullas	Open		9.50	10
2000 Olde World Santa - J. Christensen	Open		7.50	8
2001 Puppy Lover - W. Bullas	Open		29.95	30
2001 The Responsible Man - J. Christensen	Open		19.95	20
2001 The Responsible Woman - J. Christensen	Open		19.95	20
2001 Santa on a Fish - J. Christensen	Open		15.00	15
2000 snow bunny - W. Bullas	Open		6.25	7
2001 The Tooth Fairy - W. Bullas	Open		12.50	13

Hallmark Keepsake Ornaments

1973 Hallmark Keepsake Bell Ornaments - Keepsake

1973 Betsey Clark (1st Ed.) XHD110-2	Yr.Iss.	1973	2.50	61-112
1973 Betsey Clark XHD100-2	Yr.Iss.	1973	2.50	77-85
1973 Christmas Is Love XHD106-2	Yr.Iss.	1973	2.50	64-80
1973 Elves XHD103-5	Yr.Iss.	1973	2.50	60-99
1973 Manger Scene XHD102-2	Yr.Iss.	1973	2.50	95-120
1973 Santa with Elves XHD101-5	Yr.Iss.	1973	2.50	68-85

1973 Keepsake Yarn Ornaments - Keepsake

1973 Angel XHD78-5	Yr.Iss.	1973	1.25	15-23
1973 Blue Girl XHD85-2	Yr.Iss.	1973	1.25	15-23
1973 Boy Caroler XHD83-2	Yr.Iss.	1973	1.25	24-30
1973 Choir Boy XHD80-5	Yr.Iss.	1973	1.25	17-28
1973 Elf XHD79-2	Yr.Iss.	1973	1.25	15-25
1973 Green Girl XHD84-5	Yr.Iss.	1973	1.25	15-21
1973 Little Girl XHD82-5	Yr.Iss.	1973	1.25	15-25
1973 Mr. Santa XHD74-5	Yr.Iss.	1973	1.25	15-25
1973 Mr. Snowman XHD76-5	Yr.Iss.	1973	1.25	15-25
1973 Mrs. Santa XHD75-2	Yr.Iss.	1973	1.25	15-25
1973 Mrs. Snowman XHD77-2	Yr.Iss.	1973	1.25	15-23
1973 Soldier XHD81-2	Yr.Iss.	1973	1.00	15-24

1974 Hallmark Keepsake Bell Ornaments - Keepsake

1974 Angel QX110-1	Yr.Iss.	1974	2.50	28-75
1974 Betsey Clark (2nd Ed.) QX108-1	Yr.Iss.	1974	2.50	47-85
1974 Buttons & Bo (Set/2) QX113-1	Yr.Iss.	1974	3.50	40-50
1974 Charmers QX109-1	Yr.Iss.	1974	2.50	26-45
1974 Currier & Ives (Set/2) QX112-1	Yr.Iss.	1974	3.50	43-55
1974 Little Miracles (Set/4) QX115-1	Yr.Iss.	1974	4.50	44-55
1974 Norman Rockwell QX106-1	Yr.Iss.	1974	2.50	46-95
1974 Norman Rockwell QX111-1	Yr.Iss.	1974	2.50	68-95
1974 Raggedy Ann and Andy (4/set) QX114-1	Yr.Iss.	1974	4.50	60-75
1974 Snowgoose QX107-1	Yr.Iss.	1974	2.50	50-75

1974 Keepsake Yarn Ornaments - Keepsake

1974 Angel QX103-1	Yr.Iss.	1974	1.50	17-28
1974 Elf QX101-1	Yr.Iss.	1974	1.50	15-23
1974 Mrs. Santa QX100-1	Yr.Iss.	1974	1.50	15-25
1974 Santa QX105-1	Yr.Iss.	1974	1.50	15-25
1974 Snowman QX104-1	Yr.Iss.	1974	1.50	15-23
1974 Soldier QX102-1	Yr.Iss.	1974	1.50	15-23

YEAR ISSUE	EDITION LIMIT	YEAR RETD.	ISSUE PRICE	*QUOTE U.S.$

1975 Handcrafted Ornaments: Adorable - Keepsake

1975 Betsey Clark QX157-1	Yr.Iss.	1975	2.50	180-225
1975 Drummer Boy QX161-1	Yr.Iss.	1975	2.50	180-300
1975 Mrs. Santa QX156-1	Yr.Iss.	1975	2.50	220-275
1975 Raggedy Andy QX160-1	Yr.Iss.	1975	2.50	300-375
1975 Raggedy Ann QX159-1	Yr.Iss.	1975	2.50	236-295
1975 Santa QX155-1	Yr.Iss.	1975	2.50	200-250

1975 Handcrafted Ornaments: Nostalgia - Keepsake

1975 Drummer Boy QX130-1	Yr.Iss.	1975	3.50	92-175
1975 Joy QX132-1	Yr.Iss.	1975	3.50	100-150
1975 Locomotive (dated) QX127-1	Yr.Iss.	1975	3.50	100-175
1975 Peace on Earth (dated) QX131-1	Yr.Iss.	1975	3.50	80-165
1975 Rocking Horse QX128-1	Yr.Iss.	1975	3.50	100-175
1975 Santa & Sleigh QX129-1	Yr.Iss.	1975	3.50	100-125

1975 Keepsake Property Ornaments - Keepsake

1975 Betsey Clark (3rd Ed.) QX133-1	Yr.Iss.	1975	2.50	31-75
1975 Betsey Clark (Set/2) QX167-1	Yr.Iss.	1975	3.50	25-45
1975 Betsey Clark (Set/4) QX168-1	Yr.Iss.	1975	4.50	14-50
1975 Betsey Clark QX163-1	Yr.Iss.	1975	2.50	32-43
1975 Buttons & Bo (Set/4) QX139-1	Yr.Iss.	1975	5.00	40-50
1975 Charmers QX135-1	Yr.Iss.	1975	3.00	24-31
1975 Currier & Ives (Set/2) QX137-1	Yr.Iss.	1975	4.00	32-40
1975 Currier & Ives (Set/2) QX164-1	Yr.Iss.	1975	2.50	28-55
1975 Little Miracles (Set/4) QX140-1	Yr.Iss.	1975	5.00	32-40
1975 Marty Links QX136-1	Yr.Iss.	1975	3.00	48-60
1975 Norman Rockwell QX134-1	Yr.Iss.	1975	3.00	38
1975 Norman Rockwell QX166-1	Yr.Iss.	1975	2.50	45-55
1975 Raggedy Ann and Andy (2/set) QX138-1	Yr.Iss.	1975	4.00	52-65
1975 Raggedy Ann QX165-1	Yr.Iss.	1975	2.50	50-65

1975 Keepsake Yarn Ornaments - Keepsake

1975 Drummer Boy QX123-1	Yr.Iss.	1975	1.75	14-25
1975 Little Girl QX126-1	Yr.Iss.	1975	1.75	14-23
1975 Mrs. Santa QX125-1	Yr.Iss.	1975	1.75	15-22
1975 Raggedy Andy QX122-1	Yr.Iss.	1975	1.75	21-57
1975 Raggedy Ann QX121-1	Yr.Iss.	1975	1.75	18-55
1975 Santa QX124-1	Yr.Iss.	1975	1.75	15-25

1976 Bicentennial Commemoratives - Keepsake

1976 Bicentennial '76 Commemorative QX211-1	Yr.Iss.	1976	2.50	54-60
1976 Bicentennial Charmers QX198-1	Yr.Iss.	1976	3.00	60-95
1976 Colonial Children (Set/2) 4 QX208-1	Yr.Iss.	1976	4.00	52-95

1976 Decorative Ball Ornaments - Keepsake

1976 Cardinals QX205-1	Yr.Iss.	1976	2.30	36-85
1976 Chickadees QX204-1	Yr.Iss.	1976	2.30	40-65

1976 First Commemorative Ornament - Keepsake

1976 Baby's First Christmas QX211-1	Yr.Iss.	1976	2.50	120-150

1976 Handcrafted Ornaments: Nostalgia - Keepsake

1976 Drummer Boy QX130-1	Yr.Iss.	1976	3.50	128-175
1976 Locomotive QX222-1	Yr.Iss.	1976	3.50	160
1976 Peace on Earth QX223-1	Yr.Iss.	1976	3.50	76-175
1976 Rocking Horse QX128-1	Yr.Iss.	1976	3.50	132-165

1976 Handcrafted Ornaments: Tree Treats - Keepsake

1976 Angel QX176-1	Yr.Iss.	1976	3.00	120-195
1976 Reindeer QX 178-1	Yr.Iss.	1976	3.00	92-115
1976 Santa QX177-1	Yr.Iss.	1976	3.00	156-275
1976 Shepherd QX175-1	Yr.Iss.	1976	3.00	115-125

1976 Handcrafted Ornaments: Twirl-Abouts - Keepsake

1976 Angel QX171-1	Yr.Iss.	1976	4.50	69-136
1976 Partridge QX174-1	Yr.Iss.	1976	4.50	156-195
1976 Santa QX172-1	Yr.Iss.	1976	4.50	80-103
1976 Soldier QX173-1	Yr.Iss.	1976	4.50	79-95

1976 Handcrafted Ornaments: Yesteryears - Keepsake

1976 Drummer Boy QX184-1	Yr.Iss.	1976	5.00	98-121
1976 Partridge QX183-1	Yr.Iss.	1976	5.00	83-115
1976 Santa QX182-1	Yr.Iss.	1976	5.00	77-165
1976 Train QX181-1	Yr.Iss.	1976	5.00	100-160

1976 Property Ornaments - Keepsake

1976 Betsey Clark (4th Ed.) QX195-1	Yr.Iss.	1976	3.00	36-125
1976 Betsey Clark (Set/3) QX218-1	Yr.Iss.	1976	4.50	45-65
1976 Betsey Clark QX210-1	Yr.Iss.	1976	2.50	30-68
1976 Charmers (Set/2) QX215-1	Yr.Iss.	1976	3.50	52-95

YEAR ISSUE	EDITION LIMIT	YEAR RETD.	ISSUE PRICE	*QUOTE U.S.$
1976 Currier & Ives QX197-1	Yr.Iss.	1976	3.00	40-50
1976 Currier & Ives QX209-1	Yr.Iss.	1976	2.50	40-50
1976 Happy the Snowman (Set/2) QX216-1	Yr.Iss.	1976	3.50	44-55
1976 Marty Links (Set/2) QX207-1	Yr.Iss.	1976	4.00	36-65
1976 Norman Rockwell QX196-1	Yr.Iss.	1976	3.00	28-85
1976 Raggedy Ann QX212-1	Yr.Iss.	1976	2.50	52-65
1976 Rudolph and Santa QX213-1	Yr.Iss.	1976	2.50	60-95

1976 Yarn Ornaments - Keepsake

1976 Caroler QX126-1	Yr.Iss.	1976	1.75	17-28
1976 Drummer Boy QX123-1	Yr.Iss.	1976	1.75	15-23
1976 Mrs. Santa QX125-1	Yr.Iss.	1976	1.75	15-22
1976 Raggedy Andy QX122-1	Yr.Iss.	1976	1.75	25-40
1976 Raggedy Ann QX121-1	Yr.Iss.	1976	1.75	22-35
1976 Santa QX124-1	Yr.Iss.	1976	1.75	16-24

1977 Christmas Expressions Collection - Keepsake

1977 Bell QX154-2	Yr.Iss.	1977	3.50	28-35
1977 Mandolin QX157-5	Yr.Iss.	1977	3.50	52-65
1977 Ornaments QX155-5	Yr.Iss.	1977	3.50	52-65
1977 Wreath QX156-2	Yr.Iss.	1977	3.50	52-65

1977 Cloth Doll Ornaments - Keepsake

1977 Angel QX220-2	Yr.Iss.	1977	1.75	32-50
1977 Santa QX221-5	Yr.Iss.	1977	1.75	40-80

1977 Colors of Christmas - Keepsake

1977 Bell QX200-2	Yr.Iss.	1977	3.50	36-45
1977 Candle QX203-5	Yr.Iss.	1977	3.50	44-55
1977 Joy QX201-5	Yr.Iss.	1977	3.50	36-45
1977 Wreath QX202-2	Yr.Iss.	1977	3.50	36-65

1977 Commemoratives - Keepsake

1977 Baby's First Christmas QX131-5	Yr.Iss.	1977	3.50	39-75
1977 First Christmas Together QX132-2	Yr.Iss.	1977	3.50	22-45
1977 For Your New Home QX263-5	Yr.Iss.	1977	3.50	96-120
1977 Granddaughter QX208-2	Yr.Iss.	1977	3.50	120-150
1977 Grandmother QX260-2	Yr.Iss.	1977	3.50	120-150
1977 Grandson QX209-5	Yr.Iss.	1977	3.50	120-150
1977 Love QX262-2	Yr.Iss.	1977	3.50	76-95
1977 Mother QX261-5	Yr.Iss.	1977	3.50	60-75

1977 Decorative Ball Ornaments - Keepsake

1977 Christmas Mouse QX134-2	Yr.Iss.	1977	3.50	52-65
1977 Rabbit QX139-5	Yr.Iss.	1977	2.50	76-95
1977 Squirrel QX138-2	Yr.Iss.	1977	2.50	76-95
1977 Stained Glass QX152-2	Yr.Iss.	1977	3.50	32-70

1977 Holiday Highlights - Keepsake

1977 Drummer Boy QX312-2	Yr.Iss.	1977	3.50	30-65
1977 Joy QX310-2	Yr.Iss.	1977	3.50	36-45
1977 Peace on Earth QX311-5	Yr.Iss.	1977	3.50	52-65
1977 Star QX313-5	Yr.Iss.	1977	3.50	40-50

1977 Metal Ornaments - Keepsake

1977 Snowflake Collection (Set/4) QX210-2	Yr.Iss.	1977	5.00	76-95

1977 Nostalgia Collection - Keepsake

1977 Angel QX182-2	Yr.Iss.	1977	5.00	72-125
1977 Antique Car QX180-2	Yr.Iss.	1977	5.00	50-65
1977 Nativity QX181-5	Yr.Iss.	1977	5.00	108-165
1977 Toys QX183-5	Yr.Iss.	1977	5.00	112-155

1977 Peanuts Collection - Keepsake

1977 Peanuts (Set/2) QX163-5	Yr.Iss.	1977	4.00	75
1977 Peanuts QX135-5	Yr.Iss.	1977	3.50	60
1977 Peanuts QX162-2	Yr.Iss.	1977	2.50	40-60

1977 Property Ornaments - Keepsake

1977 Betsey Clark (5th Ed.) QX264-2	Yr.Iss.	1977	3.50	350-460
1977 Charmers QX153-5	Yr.Iss.	1977	3.50	50-65
1977 Currier & Ives QX130-2	Yr.Iss.	1977	3.50	55
1977 Disney (Set/2) QX137-5	Yr.Iss.	1977	4.00	75
1977 Disney QX133-5	Yr.Iss.	1977	3.50	45-75
1977 Grandma Moses QX150-2	Yr.Iss.	1977	3.50	100-175
1977 Norman Rockwell QX151-5	Yr.Iss.	1977	3.50	35-70

1977 The Beauty of America Collection - Keepsake

1977 Desert QX159-5	Yr.Iss.	1977	2.50	20-25
1977 Mountains QX158-2	Yr.Iss.	1977	2.50	12-15
1977 Seashore QX160-2	Yr.Iss.	1977	2.50	40-50
1977 Wharf QX161-5	Yr.Iss.	1977	2.50	24-50

1977 Twirl-About Collection - Keepsake

1977 Bellringer QX192-2	Yr.Iss.	1977	6.00	45-55
1977 Della Robia Wreath QX193-5	Yr.Iss.	1977	4.50	93-125
1977 Snowman QX190-2	Yr.Iss.	1977	4.50	50-75
1977 Weather House QX191-5	Yr.Iss.	1977	6.00	75-95

1977 Yesteryears Collection - Keepsake

1977 Angel QX172-2	Yr.Iss.	1977	6.00	85-135
1977 House QX170-2	Yr.Iss.	1977	6.00	100-125
1977 Jack-in-the-Box QX171-5	Yr.Iss.	1977	6.00	100-125
1977 Reindeer QX173-5	Yr.Iss.	1977	6.00	106-140

1978 Colors of Christmas - Keepsake

1978 Angel QX354-3	Yr.Iss.	1978	3.50	32-43
1978 Candle QX357-6	Yr.Iss.	1978	3.50	68-85
1978 Locomotive QX356-3	Yr.Iss.	1978	3.50	40-60
1978 Merry Christmas QX355-6	Yr.Iss.	1978	3.50	40-50

1978 Commemoratives - Keepsake

1978 25th Christmas Together QX269-3	Yr.Iss.	1978	3.50	28-35
1978 Baby's First Christmas QX200-3	Yr.Iss.	1978	3.50	52-85
1978 First Christmas Together QX218-3	Yr.Iss.	1978	3.50	36-55
1978 For Your New Home QX217-6	Yr.Iss.	1978	3.50	60-75
1978 Granddaughter QX216-3	Yr.Iss.	1978	3.50	44-55
1978 Grandmother QX267-6	Yr.Iss.	1978	3.50	40-50
1978 Grandson QX215-6	Yr.Iss.	1978	3.50	36-45
1978 Love QX268-3	Yr.Iss.	1978	3.50	44-55
1978 Mother QX266-3	Yr.Iss.	1978	3.50	20-40

1978 Decorative Ball Ornaments - Keepsake

1978 Drummer Boy QX252-3	Yr.Iss.	1978	3.50	28-35
1978 Hallmark's Antique Card Collection QX220-3	Yr.Iss.	1978	3.50	32-40
1978 Joy QX254-3	Yr.Iss.	1978	3.50	24-45
1978 Merry Christmas (Santa) QX202-3	Yr.Iss.	1978	3.50	36-55
1978 Nativity QX253-6	Yr.Iss.	1978	3.50	36-150
1978 The Quail QX251-6	Yr.Iss.	1978	3.50	45
1978 Yesterday's Toys QX250-3	Yr.Iss.	1978	3.50	44-55

1978 Handcrafted Ornaments - Keepsake

1978 Angel QX139-6	Yr.Iss.	1981	4.50	68-95
1978 Angels QX150-3	Yr.Iss.	1978	8.00	276-345
1978 Animal Home QX149-6	Yr.Iss.	1978	6.00	113-175
1978 Calico Mouse QX137-6	Yr.Iss.	1978	4.50	91-150
1978 Carrousel Series (1st Ed.) QX146-3	Yr.Iss.	1978	6.00	150-300
1978 Dough Angel QX139-6	Yr.Iss.	1981	5.50	92-95
1978 Dove QX190-3	Yr.Iss.	1978	4.50	62-85
1978 Holly and Poinsettia Ball QX147-6	Yr.Iss.	1978	6.00	68-85
1978 Joy QX138-3	Yr.Iss.	1978	4.50	73-85
1978 Panorama Ball QX145-6	Yr.Iss.	1978	6.00	108-135
1978 Red Cardinal QX144-3	Yr.Iss.	1978	4.50	122-175
1978 Rocking Horse QX148-3	Yr.Iss.	1978	6.00	68-85
1978 Schneeberg Bell QX152-3	Yr.Iss.	1978	8.00	120-190
1978 Skating Raccoon QX142-3	Yr.Iss.	1978	6.00	34-95

1978 Holiday Chimes - Keepsake

1978 Reindeer Chimes QX320-3	Yr.Iss.	1980	4.50	48-60

1978 Holiday Highlights - Keepsake

1978 Dove QX310-3	Yr.Iss.	1978	3.50	77-100
1978 Nativity QX309-6	Yr.Iss.	1978	3.50	28-70
1978 Santa QX307-6	Yr.Iss.	1978	3.50	60-90
1978 Snowflake QX308-3	Yr.Iss.	1978	3.50	52-65

1978 Little Trimmers - Keepsake

1978 Drummer Boy QX136-3	Yr.Iss.	1978	2.50	55-59
1978 Praying Angel QX134-3	Yr.Iss.	1978	2.50	90
1978 Santa QX135-6	Yr.Iss.	1978	2.50	50-59
1978 Set/4 - QX355-6	Yr.Iss.	1978	10.00	400-450
1978 Thimble Series (Mouse) (1st Ed.) QX133-6	Yr.Iss.	1978	2.50	195-295

1978 Peanuts Collection - Keepsake

1978 Peanuts QX203-6	Yr.Iss.	1978	2.50	50
1978 Peanuts QX204-3	Yr.Iss.	1978	2.50	60
1978 Peanuts QX205-6	Yr.Iss.	1978	3.50	65
1978 Peanuts QX206-3	Yr.Iss.	1978	3.50	50

1978 Property Ornaments - Keepsake

1978 Betsey Clark (6th Ed.) QX201-6	Yr.Iss.	1978	3.50	60
1978 Disney QX207-6	Yr.Iss.	1978	3.50	125-150
1978 Joan Walsh Anglund QX221-6	Yr.Iss.	1978	3.50	65
1978 Spencer Sparrow QX219-6	Yr.Iss.	1978	3.50	50

ORNAMENTS

YEAR ISSUE	EDITION LIMIT	YEAR RETD.	ISSUE PRICE	*QUOTE U.S.$
1978 Yarn Collection - Keepsake				
1978 Green Boy QX123-1	Yr.Iss.	1979	2.00	27
1978 Green Girl QX126-1	Yr.Iss.	1979	2.00	20
1978 Mr. Claus QX340-3	Yr.Iss.	1979	2.00	25
1978 Mrs.Claus QX125-1	Yr.Iss.	1979	2.00	20-22
1979 Collectible Series - Keepsake				
1979 Bellringer (1st Ed.) QX147-9	Yr.Iss.	1979	10.00	199-400
1979 Carousel (2nd Ed.) QX146-7	Yr.Iss.	1979	6.50	150-180
1979 Here Comes Santa (1st Ed.) QX155-9	Yr.Iss.	1979	9.00	340-560
1979 Snoopy and Friends QX141-9	Yr.Iss.	1979	8.00	90-165
1979 Thimble (2nd Ed.) QX131-9	Yr.Iss.	1980	3.00	148-160
1979 Colors of Christmas - Keepsake				
1979 Holiday Wreath QX353-9	Yr.Iss.	1979	3.50	29-45
1979 Partridge in a Pear Tree QX351-9	Yr.Iss.	1979	3.50	36-45
1979 Star Over Bethlehem QX352-7	Yr.Iss.	1979	3.50	60-85
1979 Words of Christmas QX350-7	Yr.Iss.	1979	3.50	68-85
1979 Commemoratives - Keepsake				
1979 Baby's First Christmas QX154-7	Yr.Iss.	1979	8.00	175
1979 Baby's First Christmas QX208-7	Yr.Iss.	1979	3.50	24-30
1979 Friendship QX203-9	Yr.Iss.	1979	3.50	18
1979 Granddaughter QX211-9	Yr.Iss.	1979	3.50	24-35
1979 Grandmother QX252-7	Yr.Iss.	1979	3.50	10-40
1979 Grandson QX210-7	Yr.Iss.	1979	3.50	29-35
1979 Love QX258-7	Yr.Iss.	1979	3.50	18-40
1979 Mother QX251-9	Yr.Iss.	1979	3.50	23
1979 New Home QX212-7	Yr.Iss.	1979	3.50	45
1979 Our First Christmas Together QX209-9	Yr.Iss.	1979	3.50	65
1979 Our Twenty-Fifth Anniversary QX250-7	Yr.Iss.	1979	3.50	17-29
1979 Teacher QX213-9	Yr.Iss.	1979	3.50	8-15
1979 Decorative Ball Ornaments - Keepsake				
1979 Behold the Star QX255-9	Yr.Iss.	1979	3.50	32-40
1979 Black Angel QX207-9	Yr.Iss.	1979	3.50	20-25
1979 Christmas Chickadees QX204-7	Yr.Iss.	1979	3.50	15-30
1979 Christmas Collage QX257-9	Yr.Iss.	1979	3.50	23-40
1979 Christmas Traditions QX253-9	Yr.Iss.	1979	3.50	28-35
1979 The Light of Christmas QX256-7	Yr.Iss.	1979	3.50	14-30
1979 Night Before Christmas QX214-7	Yr.Iss.	1979	3.50	32-40
1979 Handcrafted Ornaments - Keepsake				
1979 Christmas Eve Surprise QX157-9	Yr.Iss.	1979	6.50	52-65
1979 Christmas Heart QX140-7	Yr.Iss.	1979	6.50	104-115
1979 Christmas is for Children QX135-9	Yr.Iss.	1980	5.00	73-75
1979 A Christmas Treat QX134-7	Yr.Iss.	1980	5.00	68-85
1979 The Downhill Run QX145-9	Yr.Iss.	1979	6.50	59-175
1979 The Drummer Boy QX143-9	Yr.Iss.	1979	8.00	90-125
1979 Holiday Scrimshaw QX152-7	Yr.Iss.	1979	4.00	200-270
1979 Outdoor Fun QX150-7	Yr.Iss.	1979	8.00	100-125
1979 Raccoon QX142-3	Yr.Iss.	1979	6.50	68-85
1979 Ready for Christmas QX133-9	Yr.Iss.	1979	6.50	96
1979 Santa's Here QX138-7	Yr.Iss.	1979	5.00	54-75
1979 The Skating Snowman QX139-9	Yr.Iss.	1980	5.00	50-66
1979 Holiday Chimes - Keepsake				
1979 Reindeer Chimes QX320-3	Yr.Iss.	1980	4.50	75
1979 Star Chimes QX137-9	Yr.Iss.	1979	4.50	80-86
1979 Holiday Highlights - Keepsake				
1979 Christmas Angel QX300-7	Yr.Iss.	1979	3.50	95-150
1979 Christmas Cheer QX303-9	Yr.Iss.	1979	3.50	95
1979 Christmas Tree QX302-7	Yr.Iss.	1979	3.50	34-75
1979 Love QX304-7	Yr.Iss.	1979	3.50	80-88
1979 Snowflake QX301-9	Yr.Iss.	1979	3.50	40-45
1979 Little Trimmer Collection - Keepsake				
1979 Angel Delight QX130-7	Yr.Iss.	1979	3.00	80-95
1979 A Matchless Christmas QX132-7	Yr.Iss.	1979	4.00	67-85
1979 Santa QX135-6	Yr.Iss.	1979	3.00	55
1979 Thimble Series-Mouse QX133-6	Yr.Iss.	1979	3.00	104-225
1979 Property Ornaments - Keepsake				
1979 Betsey Clark (7th Ed.) QX201-9	Yr.Iss.	1979	3.50	33-40
1979 Joan Walsh Anglund QX205-9	Yr.Iss.	1979	3.50	35
1979 Mary Hamilton QX254-7	Yr.Iss.	1979	3.50	14-25
1979 Peanuts (Time to Trim) QX202-7	Yr.Iss.	1979	3.50	40
1979 Spencer Sparrow QX200-7	Yr.Iss.	1979	3.50	25-40
1979 Winnie-the-Pooh QX206-7	Yr.Iss.	1979	3.50	40-50
1979 Sewn Trimmers - Keepsake				
1979 Angel Music QX343-9	Yr.Iss.	1980	2.00	20
1979 Merry Santa QX342-7	Yr.Iss.	1980	2.00	20
1979 The Rocking Horse QX340-7	Yr.Iss.	1980	2.00	23
1979 Stuffed Full Stocking QX341-9	Yr.Iss.	1980	2.00	18-25
1979 Yarn Collection - Keepsake				
1979 Green Boy QX123-1	Yr.Iss.	1979	2.00	20
1979 Green Girl QX126-1	Yr.Iss.	1979	2.00	18
1979 Mr.Claus QX340-3	Yr.Iss.	1979	2.00	20
1979 Mrs.Claus QX125-1	Yr.Iss.	1979	2.00	20
1980 Collectible Series - Keepsake				
1980 The Bellringers (2nd Ed.) QX157-4	Yr.Iss.	1980	15.00	50-61
1980 Carrousel (3rd Ed.) QX141-4	Yr.Iss.	1980	7.50	99-165
1980 Frosty Friends (1st Ed.) QX137-4	Yr.Iss.	1980	6.50	345-560
1980 Here Comes Santa (2nd Ed.) QX143-4	Yr.Iss.	1980	12.00	143-169
1980 Norman Rockwell (1st Ed.) QX306-1	Yr.Iss.	1980	6.50	210
1980 Snoopy & Friends (2nd Ed.) QX154-1	Yr.Iss.	1980	9.00	115-175
1980 Thimble (3rd Ed.) QX132-1	Yr.Iss.	1980	4.00	175-195
1980 Colors of Christmas - Keepsake				
1980 Joy QX350-1	Yr.Iss.	1980	4.00	23
1980 Commemoratives - Keepsake				
1980 25th Christmas Together QX206-1	Yr.Iss.	1980	4.00	11-22
1980 Baby's First Christmas QX156-1	Yr.Iss.	1980	12.00	40-50
1980 Baby's First Christmas QX200-1	Yr.Iss.	1980	4.00	26-30
1980 Beauty of Friendship QX303-4	Yr.Iss.	1980	4.00	48-65
1980 Black Baby's First Christmas QX229-4	Yr.Iss.	1980	4.00	24-35
1980 Christmas at Home QX210-1	Yr.Iss.	1980	4.00	28-38
1980 Christmas Love QX207-4	Yr.Iss.	1980	4.00	32-40
1980 Dad QX214-1	Yr.Iss.	1980	4.00	7-9
1980 Daughter QX212-1	Yr.Iss.	1980	4.00	24-40
1980 First Christmas Together QX205-4	Yr.Iss.	1980	4.00	30-45
1980 First Christmas Together QX305-4	Yr.Iss.	1980	4.00	24-55
1980 Friendship QX208-1	Yr.Iss.	1980	4.00	10-20
1980 Granddaughter QX202-1	Yr.Iss.	1980	4.00	28-35
1980 Grandfather QX231-4	Yr.Iss.	1980	4.00	8-20
1980 Grandmother QX204-1	Yr.Iss.	1980	4.00	16-20
1980 Grandparents QX213-4	Yr.Iss.	1980	4.00	19-40
1980 Grandson QX201-4	Yr.Iss.	1980	4.00	18-35
1980 Love QX302-1	Yr.Iss.	1980	4.00	52-65
1980 Mother and Dad QX230-1	Yr.Iss.	1980	4.00	11-23
1980 Mother QX203-4	Yr.Iss.	1980	4.00	12-22
1980 Mother QX304-1	Yr.Iss.	1980	4.00	28-35
1980 Son QX211-4	Yr.Iss.	1980	4.00	29-35
1980 Teacher QX209-4	Yr.Iss.	1980	4.00	11-20
1980 Decorative Ball Ornaments - Keepsake				
1980 Christmas Cardinals QX224-1	Yr.Iss.	1980	4.00	28-35
1980 Christmas Choir QX228-1	Yr.Iss.	1980	4.00	68-149
1980 Christmas Time QX226-1	Yr.Iss.	1980	4.00	24-30
1980 Happy Christmas QX222-1	Yr.Iss.	1980	4.00	24-30
1980 Jolly Santa QX227-4	Yr.Iss.	1980	4.00	24-30
1980 Nativity QX225-4	Yr.Iss.	1980	4.00	100-125
1980 Santa's Workshop QX223-4	Yr.Iss.	1980	4.00	12-30
1980 Frosted Images - Keepsake				
1980 Dove QX308-1	Yr.Iss.	1980	4.00	25-40
1980 Drummer Boy QX309-4	Yr.Iss.	1980	4.00	20-25
1980 Santa QX310-1	Yr.Iss.	1980	4.00	15-25
1980 Handcrafted Ornaments - Keepsake				
1980 The Animals' Christmas QX150-1	Yr.Iss.	1980	8.00	62
1980 Caroling Bear QX140-1	Yr.Iss.	1980	7.50	100-113
1980 Christmas is for Children QX135-9	Yr.Iss.	1980	5.50	95
1980 A Christmas Treat QX134-7	Yr.Iss.	1980	5.50	75
1980 A Christmas Vigil QX144-1	Yr.Iss.	1980	9.00	95-185
1980 Drummer Boy QX147-4	Yr.Iss.	1980	5.50	50-85
1980 Elfin Antics QX142-1	Yr.Iss.	1980	9.00	175-210
1980 A Heavenly Nap QX139-4	Yr.Iss.	1981	6.50	41-55
1980 Heavenly Sounds QX152-1	Yr.Iss.	1980	7.50	72-95
1980 Santa 1980 QX146-1	Yr.Iss.	1980	5.50	86
1980 Santa's Flight QX138-1	Yr.Iss.	1980	5.50	99-115
1980 Skating Snowman QX139-9	Yr.Iss.	1980	5.50	80
1980 The Snowflake Swing QX133-4	Yr.Iss.	1980	4.00	41-45
1980 A Spot of Christmas Cheer QX153-4	Yr.Iss.	1980	8.00	149-155
1980 Holiday Chimes - Keepsake				
1980 Reindeer Chimes QX320-3	Yr.Iss.	1980	5.50	25
1980 Santa Mobile QX136-1	Yr.Iss.	1981	5.50	25-50

ORNAMENTS

YEAR ISSUE	EDITION LIMIT	YEAR RETD.	ISSUE PRICE	*QUOTE U.S.$
1980 Snowflake Chimes QX165-4	Yr.Iss.	1981	5.50	32

1980 Holiday Highlights - Keepsake

1980 Three Wise Men QX300-1	Yr.Iss.	1980	4.00	30
1980 Wreath QX301-4	Yr.Iss.	1980	4.00	34-85

1980 Little Trimmers - Keepsake

1980 Christmas Owl QX131-4	Yr.Iss.	1982	4.00	25-40
1980 Christmas Teddy QX135-4	Yr.Iss.	1980	2.50	82-135
1980 Clothespin Soldier QX134-1	Yr.Iss.	1980	3.50	40
1980 Merry Redbird QX160-1	Yr.Iss.	1980	3.50	51-65
1980 Swingin' on a Star QX130-1	Yr.Iss.	1980	4.00	65-85
1980 Thimble Series-A Christmas Salute QX131-9	Yr.Iss.	1980	4.00	175

1980 Old-Fashioned Christmas Collection - Keepsake

1980 In a Nutshell QX469-7	Yr.Iss.	1988	5.50	24-33

1980 Property Ornaments - Keepsake

1980 Betsey Clark (8th Ed.) QX215-4	Yr.Iss.	1980	4.00	25-30
1980 Betsey Clark QX307-4	Yr.Iss.	1980	6.50	54-60
1980 Betsey Clark's Christmas QX194-4	Yr.Iss.	1980	7.50	17-35
1980 Disney QX218-1	Yr.Iss.	1980	4.00	30
1980 Joan Walsh Anglund QX217-4	Yr.Iss.	1980	4.00	20-24
1980 Marty Links QX221-4	Yr.Iss.	1980	4.00	11-23
1980 Mary Hamilton QX219-4	Yr.Iss.	1980	4.00	18-23
1980 Muppets QX220-1	Yr.Iss.	1980	4.00	30-40
1980 Peanuts QX216-1	Yr.Iss.	1980	4.00	40

1980 Sewn Trimmers - Keepsake

1980 Angel Music QX343-9	Yr.Iss.	1980	2.00	20
1980 Merry Santa QX342-7	Yr.Iss.	1980	2.00	20
1980 The Rocking Horse QX340-7	Yr.Iss.	1980	2.00	22
1980 Stuffed Full Stocking QX341-9	Yr.Iss.	1980	2.00	25

1980 Special Editions - Keepsake

1980 Checking it Twice QX158-4	Yr.Iss.	1981	20.00	176
1980 Heavenly Minstrel QX156-7	Yr.Iss.	1980	15.00	325-345

1980 Yarn Ornaments - Keepsake

1980 Angel QX162-1	Yr.Iss.	1981	3.00	10
1980 Santa QX161-4	Yr.Iss.	1981	3.00	9
1980 Snowman QX163-4	Yr.Iss.	1981	3.00	9
1980 Soldier QX164-1	Yr.Iss.	1981	3.00	9

1981 Collectible Series - Keepsake

1981 Bellringer (3rd Ed.) QX441-5	Yr.Iss.	1981	15.00	50-72
1981 Carrousel (4th Ed.) QX427-5	Yr.Iss.	1981	9.00	50-80
1981 Frosty Friends (2nd Ed.) QX433-5	Yr.Iss.	1981	8.00	297-416
1981 Here Comes Santa (3rd Ed.) QX438-2	Yr.Iss.	1981	13.00	219-265
1981 Norman Rockwell (2nd Ed.) QX511-5	Yr.Iss.	1981	8.50	35-50
1981 Rocking Horse (1st Ed.) QX422-2	Yr.Iss.	1981	9.00	549-630
1981 Snoopy and Friends (3rd Ed.) QX436-2	Yr.Iss.	1981	12.00	100-125
1981 Thimble (4th Ed.) QX413-5	Yr.Iss.	1981	4.50	150-155

1981 Commemoratives - Keepsake

1981 25th Christmas Together QX504-2	Yr.Iss.	1981	5.50	10-22
1981 25th Christmas Together QX707-5	Yr.Iss.	1981	4.50	10-22
1981 50th Christmas QX708-2	Yr.Iss.	1981	4.50	6-20
1981 Baby's First Christmas QX440-2	Yr.Iss.	1981	13.00	39-50
1981 Baby's First Christmas QX513-5	Yr.Iss.	1981	8.50	11-20
1981 Baby's First Christmas QX516-2	Yr.Iss.	1981	5.50	24-30
1981 Baby's First Christmas-Black QX602-2	Yr.Iss.	1981	4.50	28
1981 Baby's First Christmas-Boy QX601-5	Yr.Iss.	1981	4.50	20-25
1981 Baby's First Christmas-Girl QX600-2	Yr.Iss.	1981	4.50	15-20
1981 Daughter QX607-5	Yr.Iss.	1981	4.50	21-40
1981 Father QX609-5	Yr.Iss.	1981	4.50	8-20
1981 First Christmas Together QX505-5	Yr.Iss.	1981	5.50	13-25
1981 First Christmas Together QX706-2	Yr.Iss.	1981	4.50	22-33
1981 Friendship QX503-5	Yr.Iss.	1981	5.50	17-30
1981 Friendship QX704-2	Yr.Iss.	1981	4.50	13-30
1981 The Gift of Love QX705-5	Yr.Iss.	1981	4.50	14-25
1981 Godchild QX603-5	Yr.Iss.	1981	4.50	17-23
1981 Granddaughter QX605-5	Yr.Iss.	1981	4.50	13-33
1981 Grandfather QX701-5	Yr.Iss.	1981	4.50	16-20
1981 Grandmother QX702-2	Yr.Iss.	1981	4.50	11-25
1981 Grandparents QX703-5	Yr.Iss.	1981	4.50	11-22
1981 Grandson QX604-2	Yr.Iss.	1981	4.50	13-30
1981 Home QX709-5	Yr.Iss.	1981	4.50	16-20
1981 Love QX502-2	Yr.Iss.	1981	5.50	34-50
1981 Mother and Dad QX700-2	Yr.Iss.	1981	4.50	12-20
1981 Mother QX608-2	Yr.Iss.	1981	4.50	10-20

1981 Son QX606-2	Yr.Iss.	1981	4.50	14-20
1981 Teacher QX800-2	Yr.Iss.	1981	4.50	7-15

1981 Crown Classics - Keepsake

1981 Angel QX507-5	Yr.Iss.	1981	4.50	11-25
1981 Tree Photoholder QX515-5	Yr.Iss.	1981	5.50	17-30
1981 Unicorn QX516-5	Yr.Iss.	1981	8.50	16-28

1981 Decorative Ball Ornaments - Keepsake

1981 Christmas 1981 QX809-5	Yr.Iss.	1981	4.50	9-25
1981 Christmas in the Forest QX813-5	Yr.Iss.	1981	4.50	116-145
1981 Christmas Magic QX810-2	Yr.Iss.	1981	4.50	15-25
1981 Let Us Adore Him QX811-5	Yr.Iss.	1981	4.50	28
1981 Merry Christmas QX814-2	Yr.Iss.	1981	4.50	15-25
1981 Santa's Coming QX812-2	Yr.Iss.	1981	4.50	13-30
1981 Santa's Surprise QX815-5	Yr.Iss.	1981	4.50	14-25
1981 Traditional (Black Santa) QX801-5	Yr.Iss.	1981	4.50	46

1981 Fabric Ornaments - Keepsake

1981 Calico Kitty QX403-5	Yr.Iss.	1981	3.00	20
1981 Cardinal Cutie QX400-2	Yr.Iss.	1981	3.00	9-23
1981 Gingham Dog QX402-2	Yr.Iss.	1981	3.00	15-20
1981 Peppermint Mouse QX401-5	Yr.Iss.	1981	3.00	38

1981 Frosted Images - Keepsake

1981 Angel QX509-5	Yr.Iss.	1981	4.00	50-65
1981 Mouse QX508-2	Yr.Iss.	1981	4.00	28
1981 Snowman QX510-2	Yr.Iss.	1981	4.00	25

1981 Hand Crafted Ornaments - Keepsake

1981 Candyville Express QX418-2	Yr.Iss.	1981	7.50	55-95
1981 Checking It Twice QX158-4	Yr.Iss.	1981	23.00	195
1981 Christmas Dreams QX437-5	Yr.Iss.	1981	12.00	192-200
1981 Christmas Fantasy QX155-4	Yr.Iss.	1982	13.00	59-85
1981 Dough Angel QX139-6	Yr.Iss.	1981	5.50	36-80
1981 Drummer Boy QX148-1	Yr.Iss.	1981	2.50	36
1981 The Friendly Fiddler QX434-2	Yr.Iss.	1981	8.00	72
1981 A Heavenly Nap QX139-4	Yr.Iss.	1981	6.50	50-80
1981 Ice Fairy QX431-5	Yr.Iss.	1981	6.50	85-100
1981 The Ice Sculptor QX432-2	Yr.Iss.	1982	8.00	70-99
1981 Love and Joy QX425-2	Yr.Iss.	1981	9.00	75-95
1981 Mr. & Mrs. Claus QX448-5	Yr.Iss.	1981	12.00	110-135
1981 Sailing Santa QX439-5	Yr.Iss.	1981	13.00	226-295
1981 Space Santa QX430-2	Yr.Iss.	1981	6.50	88
1981 St. Nicholas QX446-2	Yr.Iss.	1981	5.50	40-50
1981 Star Swing QX421-5	Yr.Iss.	1981	5.50	24-60
1981 Topsy-Turvy Tunes QX429-5	Yr.Iss.	1981	7.50	67
1981 A Well-Stocked Stocking QX154-7	Yr.Iss.	1981	9.00	65-85

1981 Holiday Chimes - Keepsake

1981 Santa Mobile QX136-1	Yr.Iss.	1981	5.50	40
1981 Snowflake Chimes QX165-4	Yr.Iss.	1981	5.50	25
1981 Snowman Chimes QX445-5	Yr.Iss.	1981	5.50	25-30

1981 Holiday Highlights - Keepsake

1981 Christmas Star QX501-5	Yr.Iss.	1981	5.50	17-30
1981 Shepherd Scene QX500-2	Yr.Iss.	1981	5.50	16-30

1981 Little Trimmers - Keepsake

1981 Clothespin Drummer Boy QX408-2	Yr.Iss.	1981	4.50	25-45
1981 Jolly Snowman QX407-5	Yr.Iss.	1981	3.50	45
1981 Perky Penguin QX409-5	Yr.Iss.	1982	3.50	43
1981 Puppy Love QX406-2	Yr.Iss.	1981	3.50	20-25
1981 The Stocking Mouse QX412-2	Yr.Iss.	1981	4.50	65-82

1981 Plush Animals - Keepsake

1981 Christmas Teddy QX404-2	Yr.Iss.	1981	5.50	24
1981 Raccoon Tunes QX405-5	Yr.Iss.	1981	5.50	15-25

1981 Property Ornaments - Keepsake

1981 Betsey Clark (9th Ed.)QX 802-2	Yr.Iss.	1981	4.50	23-35
1981 Betsey Clark Cameo QX512-2	Yr.Iss.	1981	8.50	20-30
1981 Betsey Clark QX423-5	Yr.Iss.	1981	9.00	40-45
1981 Disney QX805-5	Yr.Iss.	1981	4.50	13-15
1981 The Divine Miss Piggy QX425-5	Yr.Iss.	1982	12.00	75-95
1981 Joan Walsh Anglund QX804-2	Yr.Iss.	1981	4.50	18-30
1981 Kermit the Frog QX424-2	Yr.Iss.	1981	9.00	78-85
1981 Marty Links QX808-2	Yr.Iss.	1981	4.50	19-25
1981 Mary Hamilton QX806-2	Yr.Iss.	1981	4.50	14-24
1981 Muppets QX807-5	Yr.Iss.	1981	4.50	15-35
1981 Peanuts QX803-5	Yr.Iss.	1981	4.50	23-40

Collectors' Information Bureau   *Quotes have been rounded up to nearest dollar

YEAR ISSUE	EDITION LIMIT	YEAR RETD.	ISSUE PRICE	*QUOTE U.S.$
1982 Brass Ornaments - Keepsake				
1982 Brass Bell QX460-6	Yr.Iss.	1982	12.00	18-25
1982 Santa and Reindeer QX467-6	Yr.Iss.	1982	9.00	40-50
1982 Santa's Sleigh QX478-6	Yr.Iss.	1982	9.00	14-35
1982 Collectible Series - Keepsake				
1982 The Bellringer (4th Ed.) QX455-6	Yr.Iss.	1982	15.00	60
1982 Carrousel Series (5th Ed.) QX478-3	Yr.Iss.	1982	10.00	50-95
1982 Clothespin Soldier (1st Ed.) QX458-3	Yr.Iss.	1982	5.00	79-121
1982 Frosty Friends (3rd Ed.) QX452-3	Yr.Iss.	1982	8.00	95-225
1982 Here Comes Santa (4th Ed.) QX464-3	Yr.Iss.	1982	15.00	102-150
1982 Holiday Wildlife (1st Ed.) QX313-3	Yr.Iss.	1982	7.00	239-375
1982 Rocking Horse (2nd Ed.) QX 502-3	Yr.Iss.	1982	10.00	300-450
1982 Snoopy and Friends (4th Ed.) QX478-3	Yr.Iss.	1982	13.00	125-135
1982 Thimble (5th Ed.) QX451-3	Yr.Iss.	1982	5.00	50-62
1982 Tin Locomotive (1st Ed.) QX460-3	Yr.Iss.	1982	13.00	575-600
1982 Colors of Christmas - Keepsake				
1982 Nativity QX308-3	Yr.Iss.	1982	4.50	53
1982 Santa's Flight QX308-6	Yr.Iss.	1982	4.50	50
1982 Commemoratives - Keepsake				
1982 25th Christmas Together QX211-6	Yr.Iss.	1982	4.50	6-20
1982 50th Christmas Together QX212-3	Yr.Iss.	1982	4.50	6-20
1982 Baby's First Christmas (Boy) QX 216-3	Yr.Iss.	1982	4.50	16-21
1982 Baby's First Christmas (Girl) QX 207-3	Yr.Iss.	1982	4.50	16-22
1982 Baby's First Christmas QX302-3	Yr.Iss.	1982	5.50	19-40
1982 Baby's First Christmas QX455-3	Yr.Iss.	1982	13.00	29-50
1982 Baby's First Christmas-Photoholder QX312-6	Yr.Iss.	1982	6.50	23
1982 Christmas Memories QX311-6	Yr.Iss.	1982	6.50	16-20
1982 Daughter QX204-6	Yr.Iss.	1982	4.50	22
1982 Father QX205-6	Yr.Iss.	1982	4.50	8-20
1982 First Christmas Together QX211-3	Yr.Iss.	1982	4.50	31-39
1982 First Christmas Together QX302-6	Yr.Iss.	1982	5.50	9-23
1982 First Christmas Together QX306-6	Yr.Iss.	1982	8.50	15-45
1982 First Christmas Together-Locket QX456-3	Yr.Iss.	1982	15.00	25-40
1982 Friendship QX208-6	Yr.Iss.	1982	4.50	8-20
1982 Friendship QX304-6	Yr.Iss.	1982	5.50	15-25
1982 Godchild QX222-6	Yr.Iss.	1982	4.50	13-23
1982 Granddaughter QX224-3	Yr.Iss.	1982	4.50	12-30
1982 Grandfather QX207-6	Yr.Iss.	1982	4.50	8-20
1982 Grandmother QX200-3	Yr.Iss.	1982	4.50	8-18
1982 Grandparents QX214-6	Yr.Iss.	1982	4.50	12-18
1982 Grandson QX224-6	Yr.Iss.	1982	4.50	12-30
1982 Love QX209-6	Yr.Iss.	1982	4.50	9-20
1982 Love QX304-3	Yr.Iss.	1982	5.50	16-30
1982 Moments of Love QX209-3	Yr.Iss.	1982	4.50	5-18
1982 Mother and Dad QX222-3	Yr.Iss.	1982	4.50	7-17
1982 Mother QX205-3	Yr.Iss.	1982	4.50	9-19
1982 New Home QX212-6	Yr.Iss.	1982	4.50	10-23
1982 Sister QX208-3	Yr.Iss.	1982	4.50	17-30
1982 Son QX204-3	Yr.Iss.	1982	4.50	14-30
1982 Teacher QX214-3	Yr.Iss.	1982	4.50	8-15
1982 Teacher QX312-3	Yr.Iss.	1982	6.50	11-18
1982 Teacher-Apple QX301-6	Yr.Iss.	1982	5.50	8-14
1982 Decorative Ball Ornaments - Keepsake				
1982 Christmas Angel QX220-6	Yr.Iss.	1982	4.50	11-25
1982 Currier & Ives QX201-3	Yr.Iss.	1982	4.50	10-25
1982 Santa QX221-6	Yr.Iss.	1982	4.50	13-20
1982 Season for Caring QX221-3	Yr.Iss.	1982	4.50	18-25
1982 Designer Keepsakes - Keepsake				
1982 Merry Christmas QX225-6	Yr.Iss.	1982	4.50	23
1982 Old Fashioned Christmas QX227-6	Yr.Iss.	1982	4.50	59
1982 Old World Angels QX226-3	Yr.Iss.	1982	4.50	25
1982 Patterns of Christmas QX226-6	Yr.Iss.	1982	4.50	15-22
1982 Stained Glass QX228-3	Yr.Iss.	1982	4.50	12-25
1982 Twelve Days of Christmas QX203-6	Yr.Iss.	1982	4.50	30
1982 Handcrafted Ornaments - Keepsake				
1982 Baroque Angel QX456-6	Yr.Iss.	1982	15.00	175
1982 Christmas Fantasy QX155-4	Yr.Iss.	1982	13.00	59
1982 Cloisonne Angel QX145-4	Yr.Iss.	1982	12.00	95
1982 Cowboy Snowman QX480-6	Yr.Iss.	1982	8.00	50-55
1982 Cycling Santa QX435-5	Yr.Iss.	1983	20.00	100
1982 Elfin Artist QX457-3	Yr.Iss.	1982	9.00	25-42
1982 Embroidered Tree QX494-6	Yr.Iss.	1982	6.50	40
1982 Ice Sculptor QX432-2	Yr.Iss.	1982	8.00	75
1982 Jogging Santa QX457-6	Yr.Iss.	1982	8.00	32-50
1982 Jolly Christmas Tree QX465-3	Yr.Iss.	1982	6.50	80
1982 Peeking Elf QX419-5	Yr.Iss.	1982	6.50	25-40
1982 Pinecone Home QX461-3	Yr.Iss.	1982	8.00	89-170
1982 Raccoon Surprises QX479-3	Yr.Iss.	1982	9.00	89-130
1982 Santa Bell QX148-7	Yr.Iss.	1982	15.00	59
1982 Santa's Workshop QX450-3	Yr.Iss.	1983	10.00	50-80
1982 The Spirit of Christmas QX452-6	Yr.Iss.	1982	10.00	107-125
1982 Three Kings QX307-3	Yr.Iss.	1982	8.50	17-27
1982 Tin Soldier QX483-6	Yr.Iss.	1982	6.50	33-50
1982 Holiday Chimes - Keepsake				
1982 Bell Chimes QX494-3	Yr.Iss.	1982	5.50	21-30
1982 Tree Chimes QX484-6	Yr.Iss.	1982	5.50	50
1982 Holiday Highlights - Keepsake				
1982 Angel QX309-6	Yr.Iss.	1982	5.50	16-35
1982 Christmas Magic QX311-3	Yr.Iss.	1982	5.50	22-30
1982 Christmas Sleigh QX309-3	Yr.Iss.	1982	5.50	40-75
1982 Ice Sculptures - Keepsake				
1982 Arctic Penguin QX300-3	Yr.Iss.	1982	4.00	10-20
1982 Snowy Seal QX300-6	Yr.Iss.	1982	4.00	14-20
1982 Little Trimmers - Keepsake				
1982 Christmas Kitten QX454-3	Yr.Iss.	1983	4.00	34-38
1982 Christmas Owl QX131-4	Yr.Iss.	1982	4.50	35
1982 Cookie Mouse QX454-6	Yr.Iss.	1982	4.50	35-50
1982 Dove Love QX462-3	Yr.Iss.	1982	4.50	32-47
1982 Jingling Teddy QX477-6	Yr.Iss.	1982	4.00	20-23
1982 Merry Moose QX415-5	Yr.Iss.	1982	5.50	50-60
1982 Musical Angel QX459-6	Yr.Iss.	1982	5.50	112-125
1982 Perky Penguin QX409-5	Yr.Iss.	1982	4.00	35
1982 Property Ornaments - Keepsake				
1982 Betsey Clark (10th Ed.) QX215-6	Yr.Iss.	1982	4.50	24-34
1982 Betsey Clark QX305-6	Yr.Iss.	1982	8.50	17-25
1982 Disney QX217-3	Yr.Iss.	1982	4.50	22-35
1982 The Divine Miss Piggy QX425-5	Yr.Iss.	1982	12.00	125
1982 Joan Walsh Anglund QX219-3	Yr.Iss.	1982	4.50	10-23
1982 Kermit the Frog QX495-6	Yr.Iss.	1982	11.00	62-95
1982 Mary Hamilton QX217-6	Yr.Iss.	1982	4.50	14-23
1982 Miss Piggy and Kermit QX218-3	Yr.Iss.	1982	4.50	29-35
1982 Muppets Party QX218-6	Yr.Iss.	1982	4.50	31-40
1982 Norman Rockwell (3rd Ed.) QX305-3	Yr.Iss.	1982	8.50	23-26
1982 Norman Rockwell QX202-3	Yr.Iss.	1982	4.50	11-28
1982 Peanuts QX200-6	Yr.Iss.	1982	4.50	22-40
1983 Collectible Series - Keepsake				
1983 The Bellringer (5th Ed.) QX 403-9	Yr.Iss.	1983	15.00	80-125
1983 Carrousel (6th Ed.) QX401-9	Yr.Iss.	1983	11.00	35-50
1983 Clothespin Soldier (2nd Ed.) QX402-9	Yr.Iss.	1983	5.00	35-43
1983 Frosty Friends (4th Ed.) QX400-7	Yr.Iss.	1983	8.00	208-313
1983 Here Comes Santa (5th Ed.) QX403-7	Yr.Iss.	1983	13.00	239-295
1983 Holiday Wildlife (2nd Ed.) QX309-9	Yr.Iss.	1983	7.00	50-53
1983 Porcelain Bear (1st Ed.) QX428-9	Yr.Iss.	1983	7.00	50-74
1983 Rocking Horse (3rd Ed.) QX417-7	Yr.Iss.	1983	10.00	155-281
1983 Snoopy and Friends (5th Ed.) QX416-9	Yr.Iss.	1983	13.00	95
1983 Thimble (6th Ed.) QX401-7	Yr.Iss.	1983	5.00	29-39
1983 Tin Locomotive (2nd Ed.) QX404-9	Yr.Iss.	1983	13.00	200-276
1983 Commemoratives - Keepsake				
1983 25th Christmas Together QX224-7	Yr.Iss.	1983	4.50	8-20
1983 Baby's First Christmas QX200-7	Yr.Iss.	1983	4.50	19-30
1983 Baby's First Christmas QX200-9	Yr.Iss.	1983	4.50	24
1983 Baby's First Christmas QX301-9	Yr.Iss.	1983	7.50	9-18
1983 Baby's First Christmas QX302-9	Yr.Iss.	1983	7.00	5-25
1983 Baby's First Christmas QX402-7	Yr.Iss.	1983	14.00	31-40
1983 Baby's Second Christmas QX226-7	Yr.Iss.	1983	4.50	16-35
1983 Child's Third Christmas QX226-9	Yr.Iss.	1983	4.50	20-25
1983 Daughter QX203-7	Yr.Iss.	1983	4.50	20-49
1983 First Christmas Together QX208-9	Yr.Iss.	1983	4.50	17-35
1983 First Christmas Together QX301-7	Yr.Iss.	1983	7.50	9-25
1983 First Christmas Together QX306-9	Yr.Iss.	1983	6.00	17-23
1983 First Christmas Together QX310-7	Yr.Iss.	1983	6.00	31-40
1983 First Christmas Together-Brass Locket QX432-9	Yr.Iss.	1983	15.00	20-40
1983 Friendship QX207-7	Yr.Iss.	1983	4.50	8-15
1983 Friendship QX305-9	Yr.Iss.	1983	6.00	6-20
1983 Godchild QX201-7	Yr.Iss.	1983	4.50	19-23

YEAR ISSUE	EDITION LIMIT	YEAR RETD.	ISSUE PRICE	*QUOTE U.S.$
1983 Grandchild's First Christmas QX312-9	Yr.Iss.	1983	6.00	19-25
1983 Grandchild's First Christmas QX430-9	Yr.Iss.	1983	14.00	21-30
1983 Granddaughter QX202-7	Yr.Iss.	1983	4.50	24-30
1983 Grandmother QX205-7	Yr.Iss.	1983	4.50	10-24
1983 Grandparents QX429-9	Yr.Iss.	1983	6.50	11-22
1983 Grandson QX201-9	Yr.Iss.	1983	4.50	12-30
1983 Love Is a Song QX223-9	Yr.Iss.	1983	4.50	8-30
1983 Love QX207-9	Yr.Iss.	1983	4.50	34-70
1983 Love QX305-7	Yr.Iss.	1983	6.00	10-20
1983 Love QX310-9	Yr.Iss.	1983	6.00	32-40
1983 Love QX422-7	Yr.Iss.	1983	13.00	12-40
1983 Mom and Dad QX429-7	Yr.Iss.	1983	6.50	14-24
1983 Mother QX306-7	Yr.Iss.	1983	6.00	12-20
1983 New Home QX210-7	Yr.Iss.	1983	4.50	12-32
1983 Sister QX206-9	Yr.Iss.	1983	4.50	16-23
1983 Son QX202-9	Yr.Iss.	1983	4.50	32-40
1983 Teacher QX224-9	Yr.Iss.	1983	4.50	8-17
1983 Teacher QX304-9	Yr.Iss.	1983	6.00	11-15
1983 Tenth Christmas Together QX430-7	Yr.Iss.	1983	6.50	12-24

1983 Crown Classics - Keepsake

1983 Enameled Christmas Wreath QX311-9	Yr.Iss.	1983	9.00	8-15
1983 Memories to Treasure QX303-7	Yr.Iss.	1983	7.00	19-40
1983 Mother and Child QX302-7	Yr.Iss.	1983	7.50	18-30

1983 Decorative Ball Ornaments - Keepsake

1983 QX220-9	Yr.Iss.	1983	4.50	13-30
1983 Angels QX219-7	Yr.Iss.	1983	5.00	17-24
1983 The Annunciation QX216-7	Yr.Iss.	1983	4.50	24-30
1983 Christmas Joy QX216-9	Yr.Iss.	1983	4.50	12-30
1983 Christmas Wonderland QX221-9	Yr.Iss.	1983	4.50	76-125
1983 Currier & Ives QX215-9	Yr.Iss.	1983	4.50	6-25
1983 Here Comes Santa QX217-7	Yr.Iss.	1983	4.50	30-43
1983 An Old Fashioned Christmas QX2217-9	Yr.Iss.	1983	4.50	29-35
1983 Oriental Butterflies QX218-7	Yr.Iss.	1983	4.50	24-30
1983 Season's Greeting QX219-9	Yr.Iss.	1983	4.50	10-22
1983 The Wise Men QX220-7	Yr.Iss.	1983	4.50	43-59

1983 Handcrafted Ornaments - Keepsake

1983 Angel Messenger QX408-7	Yr.Iss.	1983	6.50	89-95
1983 Baroque Angels QX422-9	Yr.Iss.	1983	13.00	130
1983 Bell Wreath QX420-9	Yr.Iss.	1983	6.50	35
1983 Brass Santa QX423-9	Yr.Iss.	1983	9.00	23
1983 Caroling Owl QX411-7	Yr.Iss.	1983	4.50	25
1983 Christmas Kitten QX454-3	Yr.Iss.	1983	4.00	35
1983 Christmas Koala QX419-9	Yr.Iss.	1983	4.00	20-33
1983 Cycling Santa QX435-5	Yr.Iss.	1983	20.00	195
1983 Embroidered Heart QX421-7	Yr.Iss.	1983	6.50	19-25
1983 Embroidered Stocking QX479-6	Yr.Iss.	1983	6.50	9-27
1983 Hitchhiking Santa QX424-7	Yr.Iss.	1983	8.00	33-40
1983 Holiday Puppy QX412-7	Yr.Iss.	1983	3.50	16
1983 Jack Frost QX407-9	Yr.Iss.	1983	9.00	60
1983 Jolly Santa QX425-9	Yr.Iss.	1983	3.50	21-25
1983 Madonna and Child QX428-7	Yr.Iss.	1983	12.00	27-45
1983 Mailbox Kitten QX415-7	Yr.Iss.	1983	6.50	40
1983 Mountain Climbing Santa QX407-7	Yr.Iss.	1984	6.50	15-23
1983 Mouse in Bell QX419-7	Yr.Iss.	1983	10.00	30-65
1983 Mouse on Cheese QX413-7	Yr.Iss.	1983	6.50	25-45
1983 Old-Fashioned Santa QX409-9	Yr.Iss.	1983	11.00	42-65
1983 Peppermint Penguin QX408-9	Yr.Iss.	1983	6.50	20-29
1983 Porcelain Doll, Diana QX423-7	Yr.Iss.	1983	9.00	18-30
1983 Rainbow Angel QX416-7	Yr.Iss.	1983	5.50	69-113
1983 Santa's Many Faces QX311-6	Yr.Iss.	1983	6.00	30
1983 Santa's on His Way QX426-9	Yr.Iss.	1983	10.00	20-35
1983 Santa's Workshop QX450-3	Yr.Iss.	1983	10.00	60
1983 Scrimshaw Reindeer QX424-9	Yr.Iss.	1983	8.00	17-35
1983 Skating Rabbit QX409-7	Yr.Iss.	1983	8.00	47-55
1983 Ski Lift Santa QX418-7	Yr.Iss.	1983	8.00	60
1983 Skiing Fox QX420-7	Yr.Iss.	1983	8.00	31-40
1983 Sneaker Mouse QX400-9	Yr.Iss.	1983	4.50	20-24
1983 Tin Rocking Horse QX414-9	Yr.Iss.	1983	6.50	45-59
1983 Unicorn QX426-7	Yr.Iss.	1983	10.00	55

1983 Holiday Highlights - Keepsake

1983 Christmas Stocking QX303-9	Yr.Iss.	1983	6.00	14
1983 Star of Peace QX304-7	Yr.Iss.	1983	6.00	15-20
1983 Time for Sharing QX307-7	Yr.Iss.	1983	6.00	40

YEAR ISSUE	EDITION LIMIT	YEAR RETD.	ISSUE PRICE	*QUOTE U.S.$
1983 Holiday Sculptures - Keepsake				
1983 Heart QX307-9	Yr.Iss.	1983	4.00	45-50
1983 Santa QX308-7	Yr.Iss.	1983	4.00	17-35

1983 Property Ornaments - Keepsake

1983 Betsey Clark (11th Ed.) QX211-9	Yr.Iss.	1983	4.50	33
1983 Betsey Clark QX404-7	Yr.Iss.	1983	6.50	31-35
1983 Betsey Clark QX440-1	Yr.Iss.	1983	9.00	31-35
1983 Disney QX212-9	Yr.Iss.	1983	4.50	45-95
1983 Kermit the Frog QX495-6	Yr.Iss.	1983	11.00	35
1983 Mary Hamilton QX213-7	Yr.Iss.	1983	4.50	68-75
1983 Miss Piggy QX405-7	Yr.Iss.	1983	13.00	225
1983 The Muppets QX214-7	Yr.Iss.	1983	4.50	39-50
1983 Norman Rockwell (4th Ed.) QX300-7	Yr.Iss.	1983	7.50	35
1983 Norman Rockwell QX215-7	Yr.Iss.	1983	4.50	32-50
1983 Peanuts QX212-7	Yr.Iss.	1983	4.50	24-40
1983 Shirt Tales QX214-9	Yr.Iss.	1983	4.50	25

1984 Collectible Series - Keepsake

1984 Art Masterpiece (1st Ed.) QX349-4	Yr.Iss.	1984	6.50	18
1984 The Bellringer (6th & Final Ed.) QX438-4	Yr.Iss.	1984	15.00	29-50
1984 Betsey Clark (12th Ed.) QX249-4	Yr.Iss.	1984	5.00	25-33
1984 Clothespin Soldier (3rd Ed.) QX447-1	Yr.Iss.	1984	5.00	22-30
1984 Frosty Friends (5th Ed.) QX437-1	Yr.Iss.	1984	8.00	62-92
1984 Here Comes Santa (6th Ed.) QX438-4	Yr.Iss.	1984	13.00	63-90
1984 Holiday Wildlife (3rd Ed.) QX347-4	Yr.Iss.	1984	7.25	21
1984 Norman Rockwell (5th Ed.) QX341-1	Yr.Iss.	1984	7.50	24-35
1984 Nostalgic Houses and Shops (1st Ed.) QX448-1	Yr.Iss.	1984	13.00	133-215
1984 Porcelain Bear (2nd Ed.) QX454-1	Yr.Iss.	1984	7.00	34-50
1984 Rocking Horse (4th Ed.) QX435-4	Yr.Iss.	1984	10.00	50-100
1984 Thimble (7th Ed.) QX430-4	Yr.Iss.	1984	5.00	42-60
1984 Tin Locomotive (3rd Ed.) QX440-4	Yr.Iss.	1984	14.00	65-75
1984 The Twelve Days of Christmas (1st Ed.) QX3484	Yr.Iss.	1984	6.00	200-260
1984 Wood Childhood Ornaments (1st Ed.) QX439-4	Yr.Iss.	1984	6.50	25-41

1984 Commemoratives - Keepsake

1984 Baby's First Christmas QX300-1	Yr.Iss.	1984	7.00	9-20
1984 Baby's First Christmas QX340-1	Yr.Iss.	1984	6.00	24-40
1984 Baby's First Christmas QX438-1	Yr.Iss.	1984	14.00	29-50
1984 Baby's First Christmas QX904-1	Yr.Iss.	1984	16.00	40-50
1984 Baby's First Christmas-Boy QX240-4	Yr.Iss.	1984	4.50	12-23
1984 Baby's First Christmas-Girl QX340-1	Yr.Iss.	1984	4.50	21
1984 Baby's Second Christmas QX241-1	Yr.Iss.	1984	4.50	17-44
1984 Baby-sitter QX253-1	Yr.Iss.	1984	4.50	6-14
1984 Child's Third Christmas QX261-1	Yr.Iss.	1984	4.50	15-25
1984 Daughter QX244-4	Yr.Iss.	1984	4.50	20-33
1984 Father QX257-1	Yr.Iss.	1984	6.00	15-20
1984 First Christmas Together QX245-1	Yr.Iss.	1984	4.50	13-30
1984 First Christmas Together QX340-4	Yr.Iss.	1984	7.50	12-30
1984 First Christmas Together QX342-1	Yr.Iss.	1984	6.00	11-23
1984 First Christmas Together QX436-4	Yr.Iss.	1984	15.00	12-40
1984 First Christmas Together QX904-4	Yr.Iss.	1984	16.00	32-41
1984 Friendship QX248-1	Yr.Iss.	1984	4.50	14-23
1984 From Our Home to Yours QX248-4	Yr.Iss.	1984	4.50	40-50
1984 The Fun of Friendship QX343-1	Yr.Iss.	1984	6.00	8-35
1984 A Gift of Friendship QX260-4	Yr.Iss.	1984	4.50	19-25
1984 Godchild QX242-1	Yr.Iss.	1984	4.50	20-25
1984 Grandchild's First Christmas QX257-4	Yr.Iss.	1984	4.50	7-17
1984 Grandchild's First Christmas QX460-1	Yr.Iss.	1984	11.00	20-30
1984 Granddaughter QX243-1	Yr.Iss.	1984	4.50	24-30
1984 Grandmother QX244-1	Yr.Iss.	1984	4.50	13-23
1984 Grandparents QX256-1	Yr.Iss.	1984	4.50	14-20
1984 Grandson QX242-4	Yr.Iss.	1984	4.50	18-30
1984 Gratitude QX344-4	Yr.Iss.	1984	6.00	8-12
1984 Heartful of Love QX443-4	Yr.Iss.	1984	10.00	36-45
1984 Love QX255-4	Yr.Iss.	1984	4.50	16-25
1984 Love...the Spirit of Christmas QX247-4	Yr.Iss.	1984	4.50	15-43
1984 The Miracle of Love QX342-4	Yr.Iss.	1984	6.00	25-33
1984 Mother and Dad QX258-1	Yr.Iss.	1984	6.50	13-25
1984 Mother QX343-4	Yr.Iss.	1984	6.00	14-18
1984 New Home QX245-4	Yr.Iss.	1984	4.50	59-85
1984 Sister QX259-4	Yr.Iss.	1984	6.50	20-32
1984 Son QX243-4	Yr.Iss.	1984	4.50	8-30
1984 Teacher QX249-1	Yr.Iss.	1984	4.50	13

Collectors' Information Bureau   *Quotes have been rounded up to nearest dollar

YEAR ISSUE	EDITION LIMIT	YEAR RETD.	ISSUE PRICE	*QUOTE U.S.$
1984 Ten Years Together QX258-4	Yr.Iss.	1984	6.50	11-25
1984 Twenty-Five Years Together QX259-1	Yr.Iss.	1984	6.50	15-20

1984 Holiday Humor - Keepsake

YEAR ISSUE	EDITION LIMIT	YEAR RETD.	ISSUE PRICE	*QUOTE U.S.$
1984 Bell Ringer Squirrel QX443-1	Yr.Iss.	1984	10.00	20-40
1984 Christmas Owl QX444-1	Yr.Iss.	1984	6.00	20-33
1984 A Christmas Prayer QX246-1	Yr.Iss.	1984	4.50	24
1984 Flights of Fantasy QX256-4	Yr.Iss.	1984	4.50	20
1984 Fortune Cookie Elf QX452-4	Yr.Iss.	1984	4.50	28-36
1984 Frisbee Puppy QX444-4	Yr.Iss.	1984	5.00	45-50
1984 Marathon Santa QX456-4	Yr.Iss.	1984	8.00	39-43
1984 Mountain Climbing Santa QX407-7	Yr.Iss.	1984	6.50	35
1984 Musical Angel QX434-4	Yr.Iss.	1984	5.50	70
1984 Napping Mouse QX435-1	Yr.Iss.	1984	5.50	38-50
1984 Peppermint 1984 QX452-1	Yr.Iss.	1984	4.50	45
1984 Polar Bear Drummer QX430-1	Yr.Iss.	1984	4.50	19-30
1984 Raccoon's Christmas QX447-7	Yr.Iss.	1984	9.00	30-36
1984 Reindeer Racetrack QX254-4	Yr.Iss.	1984	4.50	10-25
1984 Roller Skating Rabbit QX457-1	Yr.Iss.	1985	5.00	18-30
1984 Santa Mouse QX433-4	Yr.Iss.	1984	4.50	40-50
1984 Santa Star QX450-4	Yr.Iss.	1984	5.50	33-40
1984 Snowmobile Santa QX431-4	Yr.Iss.	1984	6.50	36-40
1984 Snowshoe Penguin QX453-1	Yr.Iss.	1984	6.50	50-61
1984 Snowy Seal QX450-1	Yr.Iss.	1985	4.00	13-24
1984 Three Kittens in a Mitten QX431-1	Yr.Iss.	1985	5.00	32-60

1984 Keepsake Magic Ornaments - Keepsake

YEAR ISSUE	EDITION LIMIT	YEAR RETD.	ISSUE PRICE	*QUOTE U.S.$
1984 All Are Precious QLX704-1	Yr.Iss.	1985	8.00	10-25
1984 Brass Carrousel QLX707-1	Yr.Iss.	1984	9.00	69-95
1984 Christmas in the Forest QLX703-4	Yr.Iss.	1984	8.00	12-20
1984 City Lights QLX701-4	Yr.Iss.	1984	10.00	34-54
1984 Nativity QLX700-1	Yr.Iss.	1985	12.00	20-30
1984 Santa's Arrival QLX702-4	Yr.Iss.	1984	13.00	47-65
1984 Santa's Workshop QLX700-4	Yr.Iss.	1985	13.00	47-62
1984 Stained Glass QLX703-1	Yr.Iss.	1984	8.00	16-20
1984 Sugarplum Cottage QLX701-1	Yr.Iss.	1986	11.00	36-45
1984 Village Church QLX702-1	Yr.Iss.	1985	15.00	37-45

1984 Limited Edition - Keepsake

YEAR ISSUE	EDITION LIMIT	YEAR RETD.	ISSUE PRICE	*QUOTE U.S.$
1984 Classical Angel QX459-1	Yr.Iss.	1984	28.00	50-61

1984 Property Ornaments - Keepsake

YEAR ISSUE	EDITION LIMIT	YEAR RETD.	ISSUE PRICE	*QUOTE U.S.$
1984 Betsey Clark Angel QX462-4	Yr.Iss.	1984	9.00	19-35
1984 Currier & Ives QX250-1	Yr.Iss.	1984	4.50	23
1984 Disney QX250-4	Yr.Iss.	1984	4.50	23-43
1984 Katybeth QX463-1	Yr.Iss.	1984	9.00	17-33
1984 Kit QX453-4	Yr.Iss.	1984	5.50	19-28
1984 Muffin QX442-1	Yr.Iss.	1984	5.50	19-33
1984 The Muppets QX251-4	Yr.Iss.	1984	4.50	20-35
1984 Norman Rockwell QX251-1	Yr.Iss.	1984	4.50	35
1984 Peanuts QX252-1	Yr.Iss.	1984	4.50	33-40
1984 Shirt Tales QX252-4	Yr.Iss.	1984	4.50	8-20
1984 Snoopy and Woodstock QX439-1	Yr.Iss.	1984	7.50	95

1984 Traditional Ornaments - Keepsake

YEAR ISSUE	EDITION LIMIT	YEAR RETD.	ISSUE PRICE	*QUOTE U.S.$
1984 Alpine Elf QX452-1	Yr.Iss.	1984	6.00	32-40
1984 Amanda QX432-1	Yr.Iss.	1984	9.00	14-25
1984 Chickadee QX451-4	Yr.Iss.	1984	6.00	33-40
1984 Christmas Memories Photoholder QX300-4	Yr.Iss.	1984	6.50	25
1984 Cuckoo Clock QX455-1	Yr.Iss.	1984	10.00	45
1984 Gift of Music QX451-1	Yr.Iss.	1984	15.00	63-95
1984 Holiday Friendship QX445-1	Yr.Iss.	1984	13.00	20-30
1984 Holiday Jester QX437-4	Yr.Iss.	1984	11.00	20-30
1984 Holiday Starburst QX253-4	Yr.Iss.	1984	5.00	25
1984 Madonna and Child QX344-1	Yr.Iss.	1984	6.00	50
1984 Needlepoint Wreath QX459-4	Yr.Iss.	1984	6.50	5-15
1984 Nostalgic Sled QX442-4	Yr.Iss.	1984	6.00	13-19
1984 Old Fashioned Rocking Horse QX346-4	Yr.Iss.	1984	7.50	10-20
1984 Peace on Earth QX341-4	Yr.Iss.	1984	7.50	10-30
1984 Santa QX458-4	Yr.Iss.	1984	7.50	9-20
1984 Santa Sulky Driver QX436-1	Yr.Iss.	1984	9.00	18-35
1984 A Savior is Born QX254-1	Yr.Iss.	1984	4.50	33
1984 Twelve Days of Christmas QX415-9	Yr.Iss.	1984	15.00	100-125
1984 Uncle Sam QX449-1	Yr.Iss.	1984	6.00	42-50
1984 White Christmas QX905-1	Yr.Iss.	1984	16.00	71-95

1985 Collectible Series - Keepsake

YEAR ISSUE	EDITION LIMIT	YEAR RETD.	ISSUE PRICE	*QUOTE U.S.$
1985 Art Masterpiece (2nd Ed.) QX377-2	Yr.Iss.	1985	6.75	12-16
1985 Betsey Clark (13th & final Ed.) QX263-2	Yr.Iss.	1985	5.00	24-50

YEAR ISSUE	EDITION LIMIT	YEAR RETD.	ISSUE PRICE	*QUOTE U.S.$
1985 Clothespin Soldier (4th Ed.) QX471-5	Yr.Iss.	1985	5.50	21-30
1985 Frosty Friends (6th Ed.) QX482-2	Yr.Iss.	1985	8.50	51-69
1985 Here Comes Santa (7th Ed.) QX496-5	Yr.Iss.	1985	14.00	45-59
1985 Holiday Wildlife (4th Ed.) QX376-5	Yr.Iss.	1985	7.50	19-30
1985 Miniature Creche (1st Ed.) QX482-5	Yr.Iss.	1985	8.75	20-35
1985 Norman Rockwell (6th Ed.) QX374-5	Yr.Iss.	1985	7.50	22-30
1985 Nostalgic Houses and Shops (2nd Ed.) QX497-5	Yr.Iss.	1985	13.75	99-165
1985 Porcelain Bear (3rd Ed.) QX479-2	Yr.Iss.	1985	7.50	36-60
1985 Rocking Horse (5th Ed.) QX493-2	Yr.Iss.	1985	10.75	59-95
1985 Thimble (8th Ed.) QX472-5	Yr.Iss.	1985	5.50	20-33
1985 Tin Locomotive (4th Ed.) QX497-2	Yr.Iss.	1985	14.75	58-80
1985 Twelve Days of Christmas (2nd Ed.) QX371-2	Yr.Iss.	1985	6.50	53-70
1985 Windows of the World (1st Ed.) QX490-2	Yr.Iss.	1985	9.75	74-110
1985 Wood Childhood Ornaments (2nd Ed.) QX472-2	Yr.Iss.	1985	7.00	30-34

1985 Commemoratives - Keepsake

YEAR ISSUE	EDITION LIMIT	YEAR RETD.	ISSUE PRICE	*QUOTE U.S.$
1985 Baby Locket QX401-2	Yr.Iss.	1985	16.00	15-30
1985 Baby's First Christmas QX260-2	Yr.Iss.	1985	5.00	20-25
1985 Baby's First Christmas QX370-2	Yr.Iss.	1985	5.75	12-22
1985 Baby's First Christmas QX478-2	Yr.Iss.	1985	7.00	5-18
1985 Baby's First Christmas QX499-2	Yr.Iss.	1985	15.00	45-49
1985 Baby's First Christmas QX499-5	Yr.Iss.	1985	16.00	23-45
1985 Baby's Second Christmas QX478-5	Yr.Iss.	1985	6.00	24-37
1985 Baby-sitter QX264-2	Yr.Iss.	1985	4.75	5-13
1985 Child's Third Christmas QX475-5	Yr.Iss.	1985	6.00	25-33
1985 Daughter QX503-2	Yr.Iss.	1985	5.50	21-30
1985 Father QX376-2	Yr.Iss.	1985	6.50	3-13
1985 First Christmas Together QX261-2	Yr.Iss.	1985	4.75	13-25
1985 First Christmas Together QX370-5	Yr.Iss.	1985	6.75	4-20
1985 First Christmas Together QX400-5	Yr.Iss.	1985	16.75	7-30
1985 First Christmas Together QX493-5	Yr.Iss.	1985	13.00	15-26
1985 First Christmas Together QX507-2	Yr.Iss.	1985	8.00	4-18
1985 Friendship QX378-5	Yr.Iss.	1985	6.75	12-20
1985 Friendship QX506-2	Yr.Iss.	1985	7.75	3-15
1985 From Our House to Yours QX520-2	Yr.Iss.	1985	7.75	12-15
1985 Godchild QX380-2	Yr.Iss.	1985	6.75	12-25
1985 Good Friends QX265-2	Yr.Iss.	1985	4.75	15-30
1985 Grandchild's First Christmas QX260-5	Yr.Iss.	1985	5.00	12-15
1985 Grandchild's First Christmas QX495-5	Yr.Iss.	1985	11.00	11-24
1985 Granddaughter QX263-5	Yr.Iss.	1985	4.75	24-30
1985 Grandmother QX262-5	Yr.Iss.	1985	4.75	12-20
1985 Grandparents QX380-5	Yr.Iss.	1985	7.00	7-15
1985 Grandson QX262-2	Yr.Iss.	1985	4.75	27-30
1985 Heart Full of Love QX378-2	Yr.Iss.	1985	6.75	5-20
1985 Holiday Heart QX498-2	Yr.Iss.	1985	8.00	18-29
1985 Love at Christmas QX371-5	Yr.Iss.	1985	5.75	20-40
1985 Mother and Dad QX509-2	Yr.Iss.	1985	7.75	10-25
1985 Mother QX372-2	Yr.Iss.	1985	6.75	3-5
1985 New Home QX269-5	Yr.Iss.	1985	4.75	24-39
1985 Niece QX520-5	Yr.Iss.	1985	5.75	7-11
1985 Sister QX506-5	Yr.Iss.	1985	7.25	7-25
1985 Son QX502-5	Yr.Iss.	1985	5.50	36-50
1985 Special Friends QX372-5	Yr.Iss.	1985	5.75	7-10
1985 Teacher QX505-2	Yr.Iss.	1985	6.00	8-20
1985 Twenty-Five Years Together QX500-5	Yr.Iss.	1985	8.00	5-20
1985 With Appreciation QX375-2	Yr.Iss.	1985	6.75	7-10

1985 Country Christmas Collection - Keepsake

YEAR ISSUE	EDITION LIMIT	YEAR RETD.	ISSUE PRICE	*QUOTE U.S.$
1985 Country Goose QX518-5	Yr.Iss.	1985	7.75	4-14
1985 Old-Fashioned Doll QX519-5	Yr.Iss.	1985	15.00	40
1985 Rocking Horse Memories QX518-2	Yr.Iss.	1985	10.00	6-15
1985 Sheep at Christmas QX517-5	Yr.Iss.	1985	8.25	14-29
1985 Whirligig Santa QX519-2	Yr.Iss.	1985	13.00	13-30

1985 Heirloom Christmas Collection - Keepsake

YEAR ISSUE	EDITION LIMIT	YEAR RETD.	ISSUE PRICE	*QUOTE U.S.$
1985 Charming Angel QX512-5	Yr.Iss.	1985	9.75	6-25
1985 Keepsake Basket QX514-5	Yr.Iss.	1985	15.00	14-20
1985 Lacy Heart QX511-2	Yr.Iss.	1985	8.75	24-27
1985 Snowflake QX510-5	Yr.Iss.	1985	6.50	7-23
1985 Victorian Lady QX513-2	Yr.Iss.	1985	9.50	25

1985 Holiday Humor - Keepsake

YEAR ISSUE	EDITION LIMIT	YEAR RETD.	ISSUE PRICE	*QUOTE U.S.$
1985 Baker Elf QX491-2	Yr.Iss.	1985	5.75	24-30
1985 Beary Smooth Ride QX480-5	Yr.Iss.	1986	6.50	13-25
1985 Bottlecap Fun Bunnies QX481-5	Yr.Iss.	1985	7.75	12-24
1985 Candy Apple Mouse QX470-5	Yr.Iss.	1985	6.50	65
1985 Children in the Shoe QX490-5	Yr.Iss.	1985	9.50	33-50

YEAR ISSUE	EDITION LIMIT	YEAR RETD.	ISSUE PRICE	*QUOTE U.S.$
1985 Dapper Penguin QX477-2	Yr.lss.	1985	5.00	17-30
1985 Do Not Disturb Bear QX481-2	Yr.lss.	1986	7.75	16-30
1985 Doggy in a Stocking QX474-2	Yr.lss.	1985	5.50	24-40
1985 Engineering Mouse QX473-5	Yr.lss.	1985	5.50	15-25
1985 Ice-Skating Owl QX476-5	Yr.lss.	1985	5.00	17-25
1985 Kitty Mischief QX474-5	Yr.lss.	1986	5.00	14-25
1985 Lamb in Legwarmers QX480-2	Yr.lss.	1985	7.00	14-25
1985 Merry Mouse QX403-2	Yr.lss.	1986	4.50	18-30
1985 Mouse Wagon QX476-2	Yr.lss.	1985	5.75	38-58
1985 Nativity Scene QX264-5	Yr.lss.	1985	4.75	30
1985 Night Before Christmas QX449-4	Yr.lss.	1985	13.00	14-45
1985 Roller Skating Rabbit QX457-1	Yr.lss.	1985	5.00	19
1985 Santa's Ski Trip QX496-2	Yr.lss.	1985	12.00	43-60
1985 Skateboard Raccoon QX473-2	Yr.lss.	1986	6.50	25-43
1985 Snow-Pitching Snowman QX470-2	Yr.lss.	1985	4.50	21-25
1985 Snowy Seal QX450-1	Yr.lss.	1985	4.00	16
1985 Soccer Beaver QX477-5	Yr.lss.	1986	6.50	10-14
1985 Stardust Angel QX475-2	Yr.lss.	1985	5.75	22-27
1985 Sun and Fun Santa QX492-2	Yr.lss.	1985	7.75	29-40
1985 Swinging Angel Bell QX492-5	Yr.lss.	1985	11.00	17-40
1985 Three Kittens in a Mitten QX431-1	Yr.lss.	1985	8.00	35
1985 Trumpet Panda QX471-2	Yr.lss.	1985	4.50	13-25

1985 Keepsake Magic Ornaments - Keepsake

1985 All Are Precious QLX704-1	Yr.lss.	1985	8.00	25-30
1985 Baby's First Christmas QLX700-5	Yr.lss.	1985	17.00	25-40
1985 Chris Mouse-1st Ed.) QLX703-2	Yr.lss.	1985	13.00	59-89
1985 Christmas Eve Visit QLX710-5	Yr.lss.	1985	12.00	26-33
1985 Katybeth QLX710-2	Yr.lss.	1985	10.75	30-43
1985 Little Red Schoolhouse QLX711-2	Yr.lss.	1985	15.75	71-95
1985 Love Wreath QLX702-5	Yr.lss.	1985	8.50	19-30
1985 Mr. and Mrs. Santa QLX705-2	Yr.lss.	1986	15.00	55-68
1985 Nativity QLX700-1	Yr.lss.	1985	12.00	18-30
1985 Santa's Workshop QLX700-4	Yr.lss.	1985	13.00	58
1985 Season of Beauty QLX712-2	Yr.lss.	1985	8.00	19-36
1985 Sugarplum Cottage QLX701-1	Yr.lss.	1985	11.00	45
1985 Swiss Cheese Lane QLX706-5	Yr.lss.	1985	13.00	34-50
1985 Village Church QLX702-1	Yr.lss.	1985	15.00	35-50

1985 Limited Edition - Keepsake

1985 Heavenly Trumpeter QX405-2	Yr.lss.	1985	28.00	69-75

1985 Property Ornaments - Keepsake

1985 Betsey Clark QX508-5	Yr.lss.	1985	8.50	30
1985 A Disney Christmas QX271-2	Yr.lss.	1985	4.75	30
1985 Fraggle Rock Holiday QX265-5	Yr.lss.	1985	4.75	23-30
1985 Hugga Bunch QX271-5	Yr.lss.	1985	5.00	15-30
1985 Kit the Shepherd QX484-5	Yr.lss.	1985	5.75	24
1985 Merry Shirt Tales QX267-2	Yr.lss.	1985	4.75	20
1985 Muffin the Angel QX483-5	Yr.lss.	1985	5.75	24
1985 Norman Rockwell QX266-2	Yr.lss.	1985	4.75	28
1985 Peanuts QX266-5	Yr.lss.	1985	4.75	36
1985 Rainbow Brite and Friends QX268-2	Yr.lss.	1985	4.75	25
1985 Snoopy and Woodstock QX491-5	Yr.lss.	1985	7.50	65-80

1985 Traditional Ornaments - Keepsake

1985 Candle Cameo QX374-2	Yr.lss.	1985	6.75	15
1985 Christmas Treats QX507-5	Yr.lss.	1985	5.50	18
1985 Nostalgic Sled QX442-4	Yr.lss.	1985	6.00	20
1985 Old-Fashioned Wreath QX373-5	Yr.lss.	1985	7.50	25
1985 Peaceful Kingdom QX373-2	Yr.lss.	1985	5.75	20-30
1985 Porcelain Bird QX479-5	Yr.lss.	1985	6.50	25-40
1985 Santa Pipe QX494-2	Yr.lss.	1985	9.50	10-15
1985 Sewn Photoholder QX379-5	Yr.lss.	1985	7.00	25-35
1985 The Spirit of Santa Claus (Special Ed.) QX498-5	Yr.lss.	1985	23.00	72-95

1986 Christmas Medley Collection - Keepsake

1986 Christmas Guitar QX512-6	Yr.lss.	1986	7.00	13-25
1986 Favorite Tin Drum QX514-3	Yr.lss.	1986	8.50	30
1986 Festive Treble Clef QX513-3	Yr.lss.	1986	8.75	9-28
1986 Holiday Horn QX514-6	Yr.lss.	1986	8.00	17-33
1986 Joyful Carolers QX513-6	Yr.lss.	1986	9.75	21-36

1986 Collectible Series - Keepsake

1986 Art Masterpiece (3rd & Final Ed.) QX350-6	Yr.lss.	1986	6.75	20-32
1986 Betsey Clark: Home for Christmas (1st Ed.) QX277-6	Yr.lss.	1986	5.00	32-35
1986 Clothespin Soldier (5th Ed.) QX406-3	Yr.lss.	1986	5.50	21-29
1986 Frosty Friends (7th Ed.) QX405-3	Yr.lss.	1986	8.50	46-75
1986 Here Comes Santa (8th Ed.) QX404-3	Yr.lss.	1986	14.00	50-75
1986 Holiday Wildlife (5th Ed.) QX321-6	Yr.lss.	1986	7.50	21-30

YEAR ISSUE	EDITION LIMIT	YEAR RETD.	ISSUE PRICE	*QUOTE U.S.$
1986 Miniature Creche (2nd Ed.) QX407-6	Yr.lss.	1986	9.00	45-59
1986 Mr. and Mrs. Claus (1st Ed.) QX402-6	Yr.lss.	1986	13.00	79-110
1986 Norman Rockwell (7th Ed.) QX321-3	Yr.lss.	1986	7.75	20-30
1986 Nostalgic Houses and Shops (3rd Ed.) QX403-3	Yr.lss.	1986	13.75	294-320
1986 Porcelain Bear (4th Ed.) QX405-6	Yr.lss.	1986	7.75	28-45
1986 Reindeer Champs (1st Ed.) QX422-3	Yr.lss.	1986	7.50	99-155
1986 Rocking Horse (6th Ed.) QX401-6	Yr.lss.	1986	10.75	57-90
1986 Thimble (9th Ed.) QX406-6	Yr.lss.	1986	5.75	20-30
1986 Tin Locomotive (5th Ed.) QX403-6	Yr.lss.	1986	14.75	54-80
1986 Twelve Days of Christmas (3rd Ed.) QX378-6	Yr.lss.	1986	6.50	35-45
1986 Windows of the World (2nd Ed.) QX408-3	Yr.lss.	1986	10.00	23-41
1986 Wood Childhood Ornaments (3rd Ed.) QX407-3	Yr.lss.	1986	7.50	21-30

1986 Commemoratives - Keepsake

1986 Baby Locket QX412-3	Yr.lss.	1986	16.00	24-27
1986 Baby's First Christmas Photoholder QX379-2	Yr.lss.	1986	8.00	14-25
1986 Baby's First Christmas QX271-3	Yr.lss.	1986	5.50	20-30
1986 Baby's First Christmas QX380-3	Yr.lss.	1986	6.00	16-25
1986 Baby's First Christmas QX412-6	Yr.lss.	1986	9.00	31-40
1986 Baby's Second Christmas QX413-3	Yr.lss.	1986	6.50	23-30
1986 Baby-Sitter QX275-6	Yr.lss.	1986	4.75	7-12
1986 Child's Third Christmas QX413-6	Yr.lss.	1986	6.50	20-27
1986 Daughter QX430-6	Yr.lss.	1986	5.75	28-49
1986 Father QX431-3	Yr.lss.	1986	6.50	5-15
1986 Fifty Years Together QX400-6	Yr.lss.	1986	10.00	5-16
1986 First Christmas Together QX270-3	Yr.lss.	1986	4.75	12-30
1986 First Christmas Together QX379-3	Yr.lss.	1986	7.00	17-35
1986 First Christmas Together QX400-3	Yr.lss.	1986	16.00	12-17
1986 First Christmas Together QX409-6	Yr.lss.	1986	12.00	32-38
1986 Friends Are Fun QX272-3	Yr.lss.	1986	4.75	32-40
1986 Friendship Greeting QX427-3	Yr.lss.	1986	8.00	5-15
1986 Friendship's Gift QX381-6	Yr.lss.	1986	6.00	12-15
1986 From Our Home to Yours QX383-3	Yr.lss.	1986	6.00	10-15
1986 Godchild QX271-6	Yr.lss.	1986	4.75	12-20
1986 Grandchild's First Christmas QX411-6	Yr.lss.	1986	10.00	7
1986 Granddaughter QX273-6	Yr.lss.	1986	4.75	20-33
1986 Grandmother QX274-3	Yr.lss.	1986	4.75	8-16
1986 Grandparents QX432-3	Yr.lss.	1986	7.50	9-25
1986 Grandson QX273-3	Yr.lss.	1986	4.75	20-40
1986 Gratitude QX432-6	Yr.lss.	1986	6.00	9-12
1986 Husband QX383-6	Yr.lss.	1986	8.00	10-20
1986 Joy of Friends QX382-3	Yr.lss.	1986	6.75	14-18
1986 Loving Memories QX409-3	Yr.lss.	1986	9.00	15-35
1986 Mother and Dad QX431-6	Yr.lss.	1986	7.50	12-28
1986 Mother QX382-6	Yr.lss.	1986	7.00	11-25
1986 Nephew QX381-3	Yr.lss.	1986	6.25	12-15
1986 New Home QX274-6	Yr.lss.	1986	4.75	34-65
1986 Niece QX426-6	Yr.lss.	1986	6.00	7-11
1986 Season of the Heart QX270-6	Yr.lss.	1986	4.75	6-18
1986 Sister QX380-6	Yr.lss.	1986	6.75	14
1986 Son QX430-3	Yr.lss.	1986	5.75	16-39
1986 Sweetheart QX408-6	Yr.lss.	1986	11.00	39-70
1986 Teacher QX275-3	Yr.lss.	1986	4.75	5-12
1986 Ten Years Together QX401-3	Yr.lss.	1986	7.50	20-25
1986 Timeless Love QX379-6	Yr.lss.	1986	6.00	17-40
1986 Twenty-Five Years Together QX410-3	Yr.lss.	1986	8.00	20-25

1986 Country Treasures Collection - Keepsake

1986 Country Sleigh QX511-3	Yr.lss.	1986	10.00	14-29
1986 Little Drummers QX511-6	Yr.lss.	1986	12.50	17-35
1986 Nutcracker Santa QX512-3	Yr.lss.	1986	10.00	25-50
1986 Remembering Christmas QX510-6	Yr.lss.	1986	8.75	30
1986 Welcome, Christmas QX510-3	Yr.lss.	1986	8.25	20-35

1986 Holiday Humor - Keepsake

1986 Acorn Inn QX424-3	Yr.lss.	1986	8.50	25-30
1986 Beary Smooth Ride QX480-5	Yr.lss.	1986	6.50	20
1986 Chatty Penguin QX417-6	Yr.lss.	1986	5.75	13-25
1986 Cookies for Santa QX414-6	Yr.lss.	1986	4.50	19-30
1986 Do Not Disturb Bear QX481-2	Yr.lss.	1986	7.75	15-32
1986 Happy Christmas to Owl QX418-3	Yr.lss.	1986	6.00	14-25
1986 Heavenly Dreamer QX417-3	Yr.lss.	1986	5.75	22-35
1986 Jolly Hiker QX483-2	Yr.lss.	1987	5.00	16-30
1986 Kitty Mischief QX474-5	Yr.lss.	1986	5.00	25
1986 Li'l Jingler QX419-3	Yr.lss.	1987	6.75	19-40
1986 Merry Koala QX415-3	Yr.lss.	1987	5.00	17-23

YEAR ISSUE	EDITION LIMIT	YEAR RETD.	ISSUE PRICE	*QUOTE U.S.$
1986 Merry Mouse QX403-2	Yr.Iss.	1986	4.50	22
1986 Mouse in the Moon QX416-6	Yr.Iss.	1987	5.50	30
1986 Open Me First QX422-6	Yr.Iss.	1986	7.25	35
1986 Playful Possum QX425-3	Yr.Iss.	1986	11.00	35
1986 Popcorn Mouse QX421-3	Yr.Iss.	1986	6.75	42-53
1986 Puppy's Best Friend QX420-3	Yr.Iss.	1986	6.50	17-30
1986 Rah Rah Rabbit QX421-6	Yr.Iss.	1986	7.00	40
1986 Santa's Hot Tub QX426-3	Yr.Iss.	1986	12.00	55-60
1986 Skateboard Raccoon QX473-2	Yr.Iss.	1986	6.50	40
1986 Ski Tripper QX420-6	Yr.Iss.	1986	6.75	12-22
1986 Snow Buddies QX423-6	Yr.Iss.	1986	8.00	38
1986 Snow-Pitching Snowman QX470-2	Yr.Iss.	1986	4.50	23
1986 Soccer Beaver QX477-5	Yr.Iss.	1986	6.50	25
1986 Special Delivery QX415-6	Yr.Iss.	1986	5.00	17-30
1986 Tipping the Scales QX418-6	Yr.Iss.	1986	6.75	15-30
1986 Touchdown Santa QX423-3	Yr.Iss.	1986	8.00	42
1986 Treetop Trio QX424-6	Yr.Iss.	1987	11.00	18-33
1986 Walnut Shell Rider QX419-6	Yr.Iss.	1987	6.00	17-30
1986 Wynken, Blynken and Nod QX424-6	Yr.Iss.	1986	9.75	20-39

1986 Lighted Ornament Collection - Keepsake

YEAR ISSUE	EDITION LIMIT	YEAR RETD.	ISSUE PRICE	*QUOTE U.S.$
1986 Baby's First Christmas QLX710-3	Yr.Iss.	1986	19.50	45
1986 Chris Mouse (2nd Ed.) QLX705-6	Yr.Iss.	1986	13.00	66-80
1986 Christmas Classics (1st Ed.) QLX704-3	Yr.Iss.	1986	17.50	65-80
1986 Christmas Sleigh Ride QLX701-2	Yr.Iss.	1986	24.50	120-145
1986 First Christmas Together QLX707-3	Yr.Iss.	1986	14.00	29-43
1986 General Store QLX705-3	Yr.Iss.	1986	15.75	43-60
1986 Gentle Blessings QLX708-3	Yr.Iss.	1986	15.00	110-175
1986 Keep on Glowin' QLX707-6	Yr.Iss.	1987	10.00	37-50
1986 Merry Christmas Bell QLX709-3	Yr.Iss.	1986	8.50	10-16
1986 Mr. and Mrs. Santa QLX705-2	Yr.Iss.	1986	14.50	83-100
1986 Santa and Sparky (1st Ed.) QLX703-3	Yr.Iss.	1986	22.00	97
1986 Santa's On His Way QLX711-5	Yr.Iss.	1986	15.00	63-75
1986 Santa's Snack QLX706-6	Yr.Iss.	1986	10.00	58
1986 Sharing Friendship QLX706-3	Yr.Iss.	1986	8.50	15-20
1986 Sugarplum Cottage QLX701-1	Yr.Iss.	1986	11.00	45
1986 Village Express QLX707-2	Yr.Iss.	1987	24.50	54-125

1986 Limited Edition - Keepsake

YEAR ISSUE	EDITION LIMIT	YEAR RETD.	ISSUE PRICE	*QUOTE U.S.$
1986 Magical Unicorn QX429-3	Yr.Iss.	1986	27.50	75

1986 Property Ornaments - Keepsake

YEAR ISSUE	EDITION LIMIT	YEAR RETD.	ISSUE PRICE	*QUOTE U.S.$
1986 Heathcliff QX436-3	Yr.Iss.	1986	7.50	21-33
1986 Katybeth QX435-3	Yr.Iss.	1986	7.00	25
1986 Norman Rockwell QX276-3	Yr.Iss.	1986	4.75	30
1986 Paddington Bear QX435-6	Yr.Iss.	1986	6.00	38-40
1986 Peanuts QX276-6	Yr.Iss.	1986	4.75	30
1986 Shirt Tales Parade QX277-3	Yr.Iss.	1986	4.75	18
1986 Snoopy and Woodstock QX434-6	Yr.Iss.	1986	8.00	55-60
1986 The Statue of Liberty QX384-3	Yr.Iss.	1986	6.00	8-26

1986 Special Edition - Keepsake

YEAR ISSUE	EDITION LIMIT	YEAR RETD.	ISSUE PRICE	*QUOTE U.S.$
1986 Jolly St. Nick QX429-6	Yr.Iss.	1986	22.50	48-75

1986 Traditional Ornaments - Keepsake

YEAR ISSUE	EDITION LIMIT	YEAR RETD.	ISSUE PRICE	*QUOTE U.S.$
1986 Bluebird QX428-3	Yr.Iss.	1986	7.25	54
1986 Christmas Beauty QX322-3	Yr.Iss.	1986	6.00	3-10
1986 Glowing Christmas Tree QX428-6	Yr.Iss.	1986	7.00	15
1986 Heirloom Snowflake QX515-3	Yr.Iss.	1986	6.75	32-47
1986 Holiday Jingle Bell QX404-6	Yr.Iss.	1986	16.00	32-55
1986 The Magi QX272-6	Yr.Iss.	1986	4.75	23
1986 Mary Emmerling:American Country Collection QX275-2	Yr.Iss.	1986	7.95	25
1986 Memories to Cherish QX427-6	Yr.Iss.	1986	7.50	25
1986 Star Brighteners QX322-6	Yr.Iss.	1986	6.00	20

1987 Artists' Favorites - Keepsake

YEAR ISSUE	EDITION LIMIT	YEAR RETD.	ISSUE PRICE	*QUOTE U.S.$
1987 Beary Special QX455-7	Yr.Iss.	1987	4.75	16-30
1987 December Showers QX448-7	Yr.Iss.	1987	5.50	24-38
1987 Three Men in a Tub QX454-7	Yr.Iss.	1987	8.00	8-28
1987 Wee Chimney Sweep QX451-9	Yr.Iss.	1987	6.25	16-25

1987 Christmas Pizzazz Collection - Keepsake

YEAR ISSUE	EDITION LIMIT	YEAR RETD.	ISSUE PRICE	*QUOTE U.S.$
1987 Christmas Fun Puzzle QX467-9	Yr.Iss.	1987	8.00	30
1987 Doc Holiday QX467-7	Yr.Iss.	1987	8.00	43
1987 Happy Holidata QX471-7	Yr.Iss.	1988	6.50	15-30
1987 Holiday Hourglass QX470-7	Yr.Iss.	1987	8.00	23-25
1987 Jolly Follies QX466-9	Yr.Iss.	1987	8.50	35
1987 Mistletoad QX468-7	Yr.Iss.	1988	7.00	23-30
1987 St. Louie Nick QX453-9	Yr.Iss.	1988	7.75	17-30

1987 Collectible Series - Keepsake

YEAR ISSUE	EDITION LIMIT	YEAR RETD.	ISSUE PRICE	*QUOTE U.S.$
1987 Betsey Clark:Home for Christmas (2nd Ed.) QX272-7	Yr.Iss.	1987	5.00	17-25
1987 Clothespin Soldier (6th & Final Ed.) QX480-7	Yr.Iss.	1987	5.50	20-30
1987 Collector's Plate (1st Ed.) QX481-7	Yr.Iss.	1987	8.00	39-79
1987 Frosty Friends (8th Ed.) QX440-9	Yr.Iss.	1987	8.50	45-60
1987 Here Comes Santa (9th Ed.) QX484-7	Yr.Iss.	1987	14.00	63-95
1987 Holiday Heirloom (1st Ed./limited Ed.) QX485-7	Yr.Iss.	1987	25.00	25-48
1987 Holiday Wildlife (6th Ed.) QX371-7	Yr.Iss.	1987	7.50	18-27
1987 Miniature Creche (3rd Ed.) QX481-9	Yr.Iss.	1987	9.00	25-40
1987 Mr. and Mrs. Claus (2nd Ed.) QX483-7	Yr.Iss.	1987	13.25	39-69
1987 Norman Rockwell (8th Ed.) QX370-7	Yr.Iss.	1987	7.75	16-25
1987 Nostalgic Houses and Shops (4th Ed.) QX483-9	Yr.Iss.	1987	14.00	62-80
1987 Porcelain Bear (5th Ed.) QX442-7	Yr.Iss.	1987	7.75	26-40
1987 Porcelain Bear (5th Ed.) QX442-7	Yr.Iss.	1987	7.75	26-35
1987 Reindeer Champs (2nd Ed.) QX480-9	Yr.Iss.	1987	7.50	29-55
1987 Rocking Horse (7th Ed.) QX482-9	Yr.Iss.	1987	10.75	58-80
1987 Thimble (10th Ed.) QX441-9	Yr.Iss.	1987	5.75	21-30
1987 Tin Locomotive (6th Ed.) QX484-9	Yr.Iss.	1987	14.75	48-65
1987 Twelve Days of Christmas (4th Ed.) QX370-9	Yr.Iss.	1987	6.50	28-40
1987 Windows of the World (3rd Ed.) QX482-7	Yr.Iss.	1987	10.00	26-30
1987 Wood Childhood Ornaments (4th Ed.) QX441-7	Yr.Iss.	1987	7.50	18-27

1987 Commemoratives - Keepsake

YEAR ISSUE	EDITION LIMIT	YEAR RETD.	ISSUE PRICE	*QUOTE U.S.$
1987 Baby Locket QX461-7	Yr.Iss.	1987	15.00	24-30
1987 Baby's First Christmas Photoholder QX4661-9	Yr.Iss.	1987	7.50	24-30
1987 Baby's First Christmas QX372-9	Yr.Iss.	1987	6.00	20-25
1987 Baby's First Christmas QX411-3	Yr.Iss.	1987	9.75	23-30
1987 Baby's First Christmas-Baby Boy QX274-9	Yr.Iss.	1987	4.75	20-30
1987 Baby's First Christmas-Baby Girl QX274-7	Yr.Iss.	1987	4.75	20-28
1987 Baby's Second Christmas QX460-7	Yr.Iss.	1987	5.75	27-33
1987 Babysitter QX279-7	Yr.Iss.	1987	4.75	12-20
1987 Child's Third Christmas QX459-9	Yr.Iss.	1987	5.75	23-30
1987 Dad QX462-9	Yr.Iss.	1987	6.00	29-40
1987 Daughter QX463-7	Yr.Iss.	1987	5.75	21-36
1987 Fifty Years Together QX443-7	Yr.Iss.	1987	8.00	20-25
1987 First Christmas Together QX272-9	Yr.Iss.	1987	4.75	21-30
1987 First Christmas Together QX371-9	Yr.Iss.	1987	6.50	6-20
1987 First Christmas Together QX445-9	Yr.Iss.	1987	8.00	19-38
1987 First Christmas Together QX446-7	Yr.Iss.	1987	9.50	19-30
1987 First Christmas Together QX446-9	Yr.Iss.	1987	15.00	24-30
1987 From Our Home to Yours QX279-9	Yr.Iss.	1987	4.75	40-50
1987 Godchild QX276-7	Yr.Iss.	1987	4.75	16-25
1987 Grandchild's First Christmas QX460-9	Yr.Iss.	1987	9.00	16-28
1987 Granddaughter QX374-7	Yr.Iss.	1987	6.00	23-27
1987 Grandmother QX277-9	Yr.Iss.	1987	4.75	12-18
1987 Grandparents QX277-7	Yr.Iss.	1987	4.75	15-20
1987 Grandson QX276-9	Yr.Iss.	1987	4.75	24-30
1987 Heart in Blossom QX372-7	Yr.Iss.	1987	6.00	20-25
1987 Holiday Greetings QX375-7	Yr.Iss.	1987	6.00	5-13
1987 Husband QX373-9	Yr.Iss.	1987	7.00	9-12
1987 Love is Everywhere QX278-7	Yr.Iss.	1987	4.75	25-28
1987 Mother and Dad QX462-7	Yr.Iss.	1987	7.00	20-25
1987 Mother QX373-7	Yr.Iss.	1987	6.50	16-20
1987 New Home QX376-7	Yr.Iss.	1987	6.00	24-30
1987 Niece QX275-9	Yr.Iss.	1987	4.75	9-13
1987 Sister QX474-7	Yr.Iss.	1987	6.00	12-15
1987 Son QX463-9	Yr.Iss.	1987	5.75	12-45
1987 Sweetheart QX447-9	Yr.Iss.	1987	11.00	18-30
1987 Teacher QX466-7	Yr.Iss.	1987	5.75	16-21
1987 Ten Years Together QX444-7	Yr.Iss.	1987	7.00	20-25
1987 Time for Friends QX280-7	Yr.Iss.	1987	4.75	18-22
1987 Twenty-Five Years Together QX443-9	Yr.Iss.	1987	7.50	6-30
1987 Warmth of Friendship QX375-9	Yr.Iss.	1987	6.00	9-12
1987 Word of Love QX447-7	Yr.Iss.	1987	8.00	8-25

1987 Holiday Humor - Keepsake

YEAR ISSUE	EDITION LIMIT	YEAR RETD.	ISSUE PRICE	*QUOTE U.S.$
1987 Bright Christmas Dreams QX440-7	Yr.Iss.	1987	7.25	27-80
1987 Chocolate Chipmunk QX456-7	Yr.Iss.	1987	6.00	46-50
1987 Christmas Cuddle QX453-7	Yr.Iss.	1987	5.75	19-35

*Quotes have been rounded up to nearest dollar

ORNAMENTS

YEAR ISSUE	EDITION LIMIT	YEAR RETD.	ISSUE PRICE	*QUOTE U.S.$
1987 Dr. Seuss:The Grinch's Christmas QX278-3	Yr.Iss.	1987	4.75	95
1987 Fudge Forever QX449-7	Yr.Iss.	1987	5.00	23-40
1987 Happy Santa QX456-9	Yr.Iss.	1987	4.75	28-30
1987 Hot Dogger QX471-9	Yr.Iss.	1987	6.50	21-30
1987 Icy Treat QX450-9	Yr.Iss.	1987	4.50	21-30
1987 Jack Frosting QX449-9	Yr.Iss.	1987	7.00	29-50
1987 Jammie Pies QX283-9	Yr.Iss.	1987	4.75	16-18
1987 Jogging Through the Snow QX457-7	Yr.Iss.	1987	7.25	22-40
1987 Jolly Hiker QX483-2	Yr.Iss.	1987	5.00	18
1987 Joy Ride QX440-7	Yr.Iss.	1987	11.50	56-75
1987 Let It Snow QX458-9	Yr.Iss.	1987	6.50	12-30
1987 Li'l Jingler QX419-3	Yr.Iss.	1987	6.75	22-36
1987 Merry Koala QX415-3	Yr.Iss.	1987	5.00	17
1987 Mouse in the Moon QX416-6	Yr.Iss.	1987	5.50	21
1987 Nature's Decorations QX273-9	Yr.Iss.	1987	4.75	24-35
1987 Night Before Christmas QX451-7	Yr.Iss.	1988	6.50	20-33
1987 Owliday Wish QX455-9	Yr.Iss.	1988	6.50	14-25
1987 Peanuts QX281-9	Yr.Iss.	1987	4.75	28-40
1987 Pretty Kitten QX448-9	Yr.Iss.	1987	11.00	25-35
1987 Raccoon Biker QX458-7	Yr.Iss.	1987	7.00	16-30
1987 Reindoggy QX452-7	Yr.Iss.	1987	5.75	20-35
1987 Santa at the Bat QX457-9	Yr.Iss.	1987	7.75	19-30
1987 Seasoned Greetings QX454-9	Yr.Iss.	1987	6.25	16-30
1987 Sleepy Santa QX450-7	Yr.Iss.	1987	6.25	19-30
1987 Snoopy and Woodstock QX472-9	Yr.Iss.	1987	7.25	45-50
1987 Spots 'n Stripes QX452-9	Yr.Iss.	1987	5.50	25
1987 Treetop Dreams QX459-7	Yr.Iss.	1988	6.75	16-30
1987 Treetop Trio QX425-6	Yr.Iss.	1987	11.00	25
1987 Walnut Shell Rider QX419-6	Yr.Iss.	1987	6.00	18-24

1987 Keepsake Collector's Club - Keepsake

1987 Carousel Reindeer QXC580-7	Yr.Iss.	1987	8.00	43-56
1987 Wreath of Memories QXC580-9	Yr.Iss.	1988	Gift	25-48

1987 Keepsake Magic Ornaments - Keepsake

1987 Angelic Messengers QLX711-3	Yr.Iss.	1987	18.75	42-65
1987 Baby's First Christmas QLX704-9	Yr.Iss.	1987	13.50	30-40
1987 Bright Noel QLX705-9	Yr.Iss.	1987	7.00	18-33
1987 Chris Mouse (3rd Ed.) QLX705-7	Yr.Iss.	1987	11.00	48-60
1987 Christmas Classics (2nd Ed.) QLX702-9	Yr.Iss.	1987	16.00	40-75
1987 Christmas Morning QLX701-3	Yr.Iss.	1988	24.50	35-50
1987 First Christmas Together QLX708-7	Yr.Iss.	1987	11.50	40-50
1987 Good Cheer Blimp QLX704-6	Yr.Iss.	1987	16.00	48-59
1987 Keeping Cozy QLX704-7	Yr.Iss.	1987	11.75	24-37
1987 Lacy Brass Snowflake QLX709-7	Yr.Iss.	1987	11.50	16-30
1987 Loving Holiday QLX701-6	Yr.Iss.	1987	22.00	38-55
1987 Memories are Forever Photoholder QLX706-7	Yr.Iss.	1987	8.50	33-42
1987 Meowy Christmas QLX708-9	Yr.Iss.	1987	10.00	39-63
1987 Santa and Sparky (2nd Ed.) QLX701-9	Yr.Iss.	1987	19.50	65-75
1987 Season for Friendship QLX706-9	Yr.Iss.	1987	8.50	16-20
1987 Train Station QLX703-9	Yr.Iss.	1987	12.75	40-50

1987 Lighted Ornament Collection - Keepsake

1987 Keep on Glowin' QLX707-6	Yr.Iss.	1987	10.00	37
1987 Village Express QLX707-2	Yr.Iss.	1987	24.50	87-120

1987 Limited Edition - Keepsake

1987 Christmas is Gentle QX444-9	Yr.Iss.	1987	17.50	58-75
1987 Christmas Time Mime QX442-9	Yr.Iss.	1987	27.50	40-46

1987 Old-Fashioned Christmas Collection - Keepsake

1987 Country Wreath QX470-9	Yr.Iss.	1987	5.75	30
1987 Folk Art Santa QX474-9	Yr.Iss.	1987	5.25	20-35
1987 In a Nutshell QX469-9	Yr.Iss.	1988	5.50	20-35
1987 Little Whittler QX469-9	Yr.Iss.	1987	6.00	25-33
1987 Nostalgic Rocker QX468-9	Yr.Iss.	1987	6.50	27-33

1987 Special Edition - Keepsake

1987 Favorite Santa QX445-7	Yr.Iss.	1987	22.50	32-45

1987 Traditional Ornaments - Keepsake

1987 Christmas Keys QX473-9	Yr.Iss.	1987	5.75	30
1987 Currier & Ives: American Farm Scene QX282-9	Yr.Iss.	1987	4.75	30
1987 Goldfinch QX464-9	Yr.Iss.	1987	7.00	46-61
1987 Heavenly Harmony QX465-9	Yr.Iss.	1987	15.00	20-35
1987 I Remember Santa QX278-9	Yr.Iss.	1987	4.75	33
1987 Joyous Angels QX465-7	Yr.Iss.	1987	7.75	22-25

YEAR ISSUE	EDITION LIMIT	YEAR RETD.	ISSUE PRICE	*QUOTE U.S.$
1987 Norman Rockwell:Christmas Scenes QX282-7	Yr.Iss.	1987	4.75	30
1987 Promise of Peace QX374-9	Yr.Iss.	1987	6.50	25
1987 Special Memories Photoholder QX464-7	Yr.Iss.	1987	6.75	27

1988 Artist Favorites - Keepsake

1988 Baby Redbird QX410-1	Yr.Iss.	1988	5.00	18-20
1988 Cymbals of Christmas QX411-1	Yr.Iss.	1988	5.50	18-30
1988 Little Jack Horner QX408-1	Yr.Iss.	1988	8.00	16-25
1988 Merry-Mint Unicorn QX423-4	Yr.Iss.	1988	8.50	12-23
1988 Midnight Snack QX410-4	Yr.Iss.	1988	6.00	21-23
1988 Very Strawbeary QX409-1	Yr.Iss.	1988	4.75	14-23

1988 Christmas Pizzazz Collection - Keepsake

1988 Happy Holidata QX471-7	Yr.Iss.	1988	6.50	15-30
1988 Mistletoad QX468-7	Yr.Iss.	1988	7.00	22-30
1988 St. Louie Nick QX453-9	Yr.Iss.	1988	7.75	17-22

1988 Collectible Series - Keepsake

1988 Betsey Clark: Home for Christmas (3rd Ed.) QX271-4	Yr.Iss.	1988	5.00	18-25
1988 Collector's Plate (2nd Ed.) QX406-1	Yr.Iss.	1988	8.00	35-50
1988 Five Golden Rings (5th Ed.) QX371-4	Yr.Iss.	1988	6.50	18-30
1988 Frosty Friends (9th Ed.) QX403-1	Yr.Iss.	1988	8.75	45-65
1988 Here Comes Santa (10th Ed.) QX400-1	Yr.Iss.	1988	14.00	34-50
1988 Holiday Heirloom (2nd Ed.) QX406-4	Yr.Iss.	1988	25.00	24-30
1988 Holiday Wildlife (7th Ed.) QX371-1	Yr.Iss.	1988	7.75	18-30
1988 Mary's Angels (1st Ed.) QX407-4	Yr.Iss.	1988	5.00	39-75
1988 Miniature Creche (4th Ed.) QX403-4	Yr.Iss.	1988	8.50	22-35
1988 Mr. and Mrs. Claus (3rd Ed.) QX401-1	Yr.Iss.	1988	13.00	43-58
1988 Norman Rockwell (9th Ed.) QX370-4	Yr.Iss.	1988	7.75	14-23
1988 Nostalgic Houses and Shops (5th Ed.) QX401-4	Yr.Iss.	1988	14.50	44-65
1988 Porcelain Bear (6th Ed.) QX404-4	Yr.Iss.	1988	8.00	26-40
1988 Reindeer Champs (3rd Ed.) QX405-1	Yr.Iss.	1988	7.50	28-40
1988 Rocking Horse (8th Ed.) QX402-4	Yr.Iss.	1988	10.75	56-70
1988 Thimble (11th Ed.) QX405-4	Yr.Iss.	1988	5.75	18-25
1988 Tin Locomotive (7th Ed.) QX400-4	Yr.Iss.	1988	14.75	40-60
1988 Windows of the World (4th Ed.) QX402-1	Yr.Iss.	1988	10.00	22-30
1988 Wood Childhood (5th Ed.) QX404-1	Yr.Iss.	1988	7.50	20-23

1988 Commemoratives - Keepsake

1988 Baby's First Christmas (Boy) QX272-1	Yr.Iss.	1988	4.75	20-25
1988 Baby's First Christmas (Girl) QX272-4	Yr.Iss.	1988	4.75	16-30
1988 Baby's First Christmas QX372-1	Yr.Iss.	1988	6.00	16-23
1988 Baby's First Christmas QX470-1	Yr.Iss.	1988	9.75	29-40
1988 Baby's First Christmas QX470-4	Yr.Iss.	1988	7.50	24-30
1988 Baby's Second Christmas QX471-1	Yr.Iss.	1988	6.00	20-33
1988 Babysitter QX279-1	Yr.Iss.	1988	4.75	5-11
1988 Child's Third Christmas QX471-4	Yr.Iss.	1988	6.00	20-30
1988 Dad QX414-1	Yr.Iss.	1988	7.00	20-25
1988 Daughter QX415-1	Yr.Iss.	1988	5.75	52-65
1988 Fifty Years Together QX374-1	Yr.Iss.	1988	6.75	8-20
1988 First Christmas Together QX274-1	Yr.Iss.	1988	4.75	22-28
1988 First Christmas Together QX373-1	Yr.Iss.	1988	6.75	12-23
1988 First Christmas Together QX489-4	Yr.Iss.	1988	9.00	22-40
1988 Five Years Together QX274-4	Yr.Iss.	1988	4.75	7-23
1988 From Our Home to Yours QX279-4	Yr.Iss.	1988	4.75	14-18
1988 Godchild QX278-4	Yr.Iss.	1988	4.75	16-20
1988 Granddaughter QX277-4	Yr.Iss.	1988	4.75	19-50
1988 Grandmother QX276-4	Yr.Iss.	1988	4.75	16-23
1988 Grandparents QX277-1	Yr.Iss.	1988	4.75	16-20
1988 Grandson QX278-1	Yr.Iss.	1988	4.75	20-40
1988 Gratitude QX375-4	Yr.Iss.	1988	6.00	9-12
1988 Love Fills the Heart QX374-4	Yr.Iss.	1988	6.00	18-25
1988 Love Grows QX275-4	Yr.Iss.	1988	4.75	26-32
1988 Mother and Dad QX414-4	Yr.Iss.	1988	8.00	20-25
1988 Mother QX375-1	Yr.Iss.	1988	6.50	16-23
1988 New Home QX376-1	Yr.Iss.	1988	6.00	20-25
1988 Sister QX499-4	Yr.Iss.	1988	8.00	26-33
1988 Son QX415-4	Yr.Iss.	1988	5.75	33-40
1988 Spirit of Christmas QX276-1	Yr.Iss.	1988	4.75	18-23
1988 Sweetheart QX490-1	Yr.Iss.	1988	9.75	14-30
1988 Teacher QX417-1	Yr.Iss.	1988	6.25	14-30
1988 Ten Years Together QX275-1	Yr.Iss.	1988	4.75	9-23

*Quotes have been rounded up to nearest dollar

YEAR ISSUE	EDITION LIMIT	YEAR RETD.	ISSUE PRICE	*QUOTE U.S.$
1988 Twenty-Five Years Together QX373-4	Yr.Iss.	1988	6.75	4-19
1988 Year to Remember QX416-4	Yr.Iss.	1988	7.00	20-25

1988 Hallmark Handcrafted Ornaments - Keepsake

YEAR ISSUE	EDITION LIMIT	YEAR RETD.	ISSUE PRICE	*QUOTE U.S.$
1988 Americana Drum QX488-1	Yr.Iss.	1988	7.75	19-34
1988 Arctic Tenor QX472-1	Yr.Iss.	1988	4.00	11-19
1988 Christmas Cardinal QX494-1	Yr.Iss.	1988	4.75	9-20
1988 Christmas Cuckoo QX480-1	Yr.Iss.	1988	8.00	40
1988 Christmas Memories QX372-4	Yr.Iss.	1988	6.50	25
1988 Christmas Scenes QX273-1	Yr.Iss.	1988	4.75	24
1988 Cool Juggler QX487-4	Yr.Iss.	1988	6.50	20
1988 Feliz Navidad QX416-1	Yr.Iss.	1988	6.75	22-29
1988 Filled with Fudge QX419-1	Yr.Iss.	1988	4.75	18-33
1988 Glowing Wreath QX492-1	Yr.Iss.	1988	6.00	14
1988 Go For The Gold QX417-4	Yr.Iss.	1988	8.00	17-30
1988 Goin' Cross-Country QX476-4	Yr.Iss.	1988	8.50	14-29
1988 Gone Fishing QX479-4	Yr.Iss.	1989	5.00	16-19
1988 Hoe-Hoe-Hoe QX422-1	Yr.Iss.	1988	5.00	11-20
1988 Holiday Hero QX423-1	Yr.Iss.	1988	5.00	20
1988 Jingle Bell Clown QX477-4	Yr.Iss.	1988	15.00	21-30
1988 Jolly Walrus QX473-1	Yr.Iss.	1988	4.50	24-30
1988 Kiss from Santa QX482-1	Yr.Iss.	1989	4.50	10-30
1988 Kiss the Claus QX486-1	Yr.Iss.	1988	5.00	10-19
1988 Kringle Moon QX495-1	Yr.Iss.	1988	5.00	35
1988 Kringle Portrait QX496-1	Yr.Iss.	1988	7.50	22-40
1988 Kringle Tree QX495-4	Yr.Iss.	1988	6.50	21-40
1988 Love Santa QX486-4	Yr.Iss.	1988	5.00	20
1988 Loving Bear QX493-4	Yr.Iss.	1988	4.75	10-20
1988 Nick the Kick QX422-4	Yr.Iss.	1988	5.00	25
1988 Noah's Ark QX490-4	Yr.Iss.	1988	8.50	40
1988 Old-Fashioned Church QX498-1	Yr.Iss.	1988	4.00	25
1988 Old-Fashioned School House QX497-1	Yr.Iss.	1988	4.00	23
1988 Oreo QX481-4	Yr.Iss.	1989	4.00	13-20
1988 Par for Santa QX479-1	Yr.Iss.	1988	5.00	20
1988 Party Line QX476-1	Yr.Iss.	1989	8.75	22-30
1988 Peanuts QX280-1	Yr.Iss.	1988	4.75	50
1988 Peek-a-boo Kittens QX487-1	Yr.Iss.	1989	7.50	23
1988 Polar Bowler QX478-4	Yr.Iss.	1989	5.00	11-20
1988 Purrfect Snuggle QX474-4	Yr.Iss.	1988	6.25	16-30
1988 Sailing! Sailing! QX491-1	Yr.Iss.	1988	8.50	20-25
1988 Santa Flamingo QX483-4	Yr.Iss.	1988	4.75	25-31
1988 Shiny Sleigh QX492-4	Yr.Iss.	1988	5.75	20
1988 Slipper Spaniel QX472-4	Yr.Iss.	1988	4.50	11-20
1988 Snoopy and Woodstock QX474-1	Yr.Iss.	1988	6.00	35-49
1988 Soft Landing QX475-1	Yr.Iss.	1988	7.00	13-25
1988 Sparkling Tree QX483-1	Yr.Iss.	1988	6.00	19
1988 Squeaky Clean QX475-4	Yr.Iss.	1988	6.75	13-25
1988 Starry Angel QX494-4	Yr.Iss.	1988	4.75	20
1988 Sweet Star QX418-4	Yr.Iss.	1988	5.00	21-33
1988 Teeny Taster QX418-1	Yr.Iss.	1989	4.75	25-30
1988 The Town Crier QX473-4	Yr.Iss.	1988	5.50	14-20
1988 Travels with Santa QX477-1	Yr.Iss.	1988	10.00	27-40
1988 Uncle Sam Nutcracker QX488-4	Yr.Iss.	1988	7.00	27-30
1988 Winter Fun QX478-1	Yr.Iss.	1988	8.50	17-25

1988 Hallmark Keepsake Ornament Collector's Club - Keepsake

YEAR ISSUE	EDITION LIMIT	YEAR RETD.	ISSUE PRICE	*QUOTE U.S.$
1988 Angelic Minstrel QXC408-4	Yr.Iss.	1988	27.50	40-53
1988 Christmas is Sharing QXC407-1	Yr.Iss.	1988	17.50	31-50
1988 Hold on Tight QXC570-4	Yr.Iss.	1988	Gift	30-77
1988 Holiday Heirloom (2nd Ed.) QXC406-4	Yr.Iss.	1988	25.00	24
1988 Our Clubhouse QXC580-4	Yr.Iss.	1988	Gift	20-33
1988 Sleighful of Dreams QC580-1	Yr.Iss.	1988	8.00	28-55

1988 Holiday Humor - Keepsake

YEAR ISSUE	EDITION LIMIT	YEAR RETD.	ISSUE PRICE	*QUOTE U.S.$
1988 Night Before Christmas QX451-7	Yr.Iss.	1988	6.50	31-44
1988 Owliday Wish QX455-9	Yr.Iss.	1988	6.50	14-25
1988 Reindoggy QX452-7	Yr.Iss.	1988	5.75	20-25
1988 Treetop Dreams QX459-7	Yr.Iss.	1988	6.75	15-25

1988 Keepsake Magic Ornaments - Keepsake

YEAR ISSUE	EDITION LIMIT	YEAR RETD.	ISSUE PRICE	*QUOTE U.S.$
1988 Baby's First Christmas QLX718-4	Yr.Iss.	1988	24.00	45-60
1988 Bearly Reaching QLX715-1	Yr.Iss.	1988	9.50	26-41
1988 Chris Mouse (4th Ed.) QLX715-4	Yr.Iss.	1988	8.75	43-60
1988 Christmas Classics (3rd Ed.) QLX716-1	Yr.Iss.	1988	15.00	31-45
1988 Christmas is Magic QLX717-1	Yr.Iss.	1988	12.00	35-55
1988 Christmas Morning QLX701-3	Yr.Iss.	1988	24.50	33-50
1988 Circling the Globe QLX712-4	Yr.Iss.	1988	10.50	36-47
1988 Country Express QLX721-1	Yr.Iss.	1988	24.50	40-75
1988 Festive Feeder QLX720-4	Yr.Iss.	1988	11.50	44-50
1988 First Christmas Together QLX702-7	Yr.Iss.	1988	12.00	37-40
1988 Heavenly Glow QLX711-4	Yr.Iss.	1988	11.75	19-30
1988 Kitty Capers QLX716-4	Yr.Iss.	1988	13.00	36-40
1988 Kringle's Toy Shop QLX701-7	Yr.Iss.	1988	25.00	32-39
1988 Last-Minute Hug QLX718-1	Yr.Iss.	1988	19.50	16-49
1988 Moonlit Nap QLX713-4	Yr.Iss.	1988	8.75	22-30
1988 Parade of the Toys QLX719-4	Yr.Iss.	1988	22.00	37-52
1988 Radiant Tree QLX712-1	Yr.Iss.	1988	11.75	22-28
1988 Santa and Sparky (3rd Ed.) QLX719-1	Yr.Iss.	1988	19.50	31-43
1988 Skater's Waltz QLX720-1	Yr.Iss.	1988	19.50	38-63
1988 Song of Christmas QLX711-1	Yr.Iss.	1988	8.50	14-30
1988 Tree of Friendship QLX710-4	Yr.Iss.	1988	8.50	20-25

1988 Keepsake Miniature Ornaments - Keepsake

YEAR ISSUE	EDITION LIMIT	YEAR RETD.	ISSUE PRICE	*QUOTE U.S.$
1988 Baby's First Christmas	Yr.Iss.	1988	6.00	12
1988 Brass Angel	Yr.Iss.	1988	1.50	13
1988 Brass Star	Yr.Iss.	1988	1.50	13
1988 Brass Tree	Yr.Iss.	1988	1.50	9-19
1988 Candy Cane Elf	Yr.Iss.	1988	3.00	10-21
1988 Country Wreath	Yr.Iss.	1988	4.00	12
1988 Family Home (1st Ed.)	Yr.Iss.	1988	8.50	11-31
1988 First Christmas Together	Yr.Iss.	1988	4.00	9-25
1988 Folk Art Lamb	Yr.Iss.	1988	2.50	14-23
1988 Folk Art Reindeer	Yr.Iss.	1988	2.50	14-20
1988 Friends Share Joy	Yr.Iss.	1988	2.00	10-16
1988 Gentle Angel	Yr.Iss.	1988	2.00	16-20
1988 Happy Santa	Yr.Iss.	1988	4.50	19-21
1988 Holy Family	Yr.Iss.	1988	8.50	12
1988 Jolly St. Nick	Yr.Iss.	1988	8.00	14-31
1988 Joyous Heart	Yr.Iss.	1988	3.50	24-30
1988 Kittens in Toyland (1st Ed.)	Yr.Iss.	1988	5.00	19-26
1988 Little Drummer Boy	Yr.Iss.	1988	4.50	21-27
1988 Love is Forever	Yr.Iss.	1988	2.00	15
1988 Mother	Yr.Iss.	1988	3.00	14
1988 Penguin Pal (1st Ed.)	Yr.Iss.	1988	3.75	16-28
1988 Rocking Horse (1st Ed.)	Yr.Iss.	1988	4.50	24-45
1988 Skater's Waltz	Yr.Iss.	1988	7.00	15
1988 Sneaker Mouse	Yr.Iss.	1988	4.00	14-20
1988 Snuggly Skater	Yr.Iss.	1988	4.50	29
1988 Sweet Dreams	Yr.Iss.	1988	7.00	16-23
1988 Three Little Kitties	Yr.Iss.	1988	6.00	13-19

1988 Old Fashioned Christmas Collection - Keepsake

YEAR ISSUE	EDITION LIMIT	YEAR RETD.	ISSUE PRICE	*QUOTE U.S.$
1988 In A Nutshell QX469-7	Yr.Iss.	1988	5.50	24-33

1988 Special Edition - Keepsake

YEAR ISSUE	EDITION LIMIT	YEAR RETD.	ISSUE PRICE	*QUOTE U.S.$
1988 The Wonderful Santacycle QX411-4	Yr.Iss.	1988	22.50	37-40

1989 Artists' Favorites - Keepsake

YEAR ISSUE	EDITION LIMIT	YEAR RETD.	ISSUE PRICE	*QUOTE U.S.$
1989 Baby Partridge QX452-5	Yr.Iss.	1989	6.75	10-15
1989 Bear-i-Tone QX454-2	Yr.Iss.	1989	4.75	11-20
1989 Carousel Zebra QX451-5	Yr.Iss.	1989	9.25	16-31
1989 Cherry Jubilee QX453-2	Yr.Iss.	1989	5.00	16-20
1989 Mail Call QX452-2	Yr.Iss.	1989	8.75	16-20
1989 Merry-Go-Round Unicorn QX447-2	Yr.Iss.	1989	10.75	16-25
1989 Playful Angel QX453-5	Yr.Iss.	1989	6.75	17-25

1989 Collectible Series - Keepsake

YEAR ISSUE	EDITION LIMIT	YEAR RETD.	ISSUE PRICE	*QUOTE U.S.$
1989 Betsey Clark:Home for Christmas (4th Ed.) QX230-2	Yr.Iss.	1989	5.00	19-29
1989 Christmas Kitty (1st Ed.) QX544-5	Yr.Iss.	1989	14.75	15-26
1989 Collector's Plate (3rd Ed.) QX461-2	Yr.Iss.	1989	8.25	19-32
1989 Crayola Crayon (1st Ed.) QX435-2	Yr.Iss.	1989	8.75	30-69
1989 Frosty Friends (10th Ed.) QX457-2	Yr.Iss.	1989	9.25	39-70
1989 The Gift Bringers (1st Ed.) QX279-5	Yr.Iss.	1989	5.00	21-25
1989 Hark! It's Herald (1st Ed.) QX455-5	Yr.Iss.	1989	6.75	16-25
1989 Here Comes Santa (11th Ed.) QX458-5	Yr.Iss.	1989	14.75	34-49
1989 Mary's Angels (2nd Ed.) QX454-5	Yr.Iss.	1989	5.75	90-125
1989 Miniature Creche (5th Ed.) QX459-2	Yr.Iss.	1989	9.25	15-23
1989 Mr. and Mrs. Claus (4th Ed.) QX457-5	Yr.Iss.	1989	13.25	33-60
1989 Nostalgic Houses and Shops (6th Ed.) QX458-2	Yr.Iss.	1989	14.25	49-70
1989 Porcelain Bear (7th Ed.) QX461-5	Yr.Iss.	1989	8.75	21-40
1989 Reindeer Champs (4th Ed.) QX456-2	Yr.Iss.	1989	7.75	8-25
1989 Rocking Horse (9th Ed.) QX462-2	Yr.Iss.	1989	10.75	54-70
1989 Thimble (12th Ed.) QX455-2	Yr.Iss.	1989	5.75	18-27
1989 Tin Locomotive (8th Ed.) QX460-2	Yr.Iss.	1989	14.75	33-60
1989 Twelve Days of Christmas (6th Ed.) QX381-2	Yr.Iss.	1989	6.75	18-28
1989 Windows of the World (5th Ed.) QX462-5	Yr.Iss.	1989	10.75	22-30

YEAR ISSUE	EDITION LIMIT	YEAR RETD.	ISSUE PRICE	*QUOTE U.S.$
1989 Winter Surprise (1st Ed.) QX427-2	Yr.Iss.	1989	10.75	27
1989 Wood Childhood Ornaments (6th Ed.) QX459-5	Yr.Iss.	1989	7.75	15-20

1989 Commemoratives - Keepsake

YEAR ISSUE	EDITION LIMIT	YEAR RETD.	ISSUE PRICE	*QUOTE U.S.$
1989 Baby's Fifth Christmas QX543-5	Yr.Iss.	1989	6.75	13-20
1989 Baby's First Christmas Photoholder QX468-2	Yr.Iss.	1989	6.25	40-50
1989 Baby's First Christmas QX381-5	Yr.Iss.	1989	6.75	10-18
1989 Baby's First Christmas QX449-2	Yr.Iss.	1989	7.25	66-85
1989 Baby's First Christmas-Baby Boy QX272-5	Yr.Iss.	1989	4.75	17-23
1989 Baby's First Christmas-Baby Girl QX272-2	Yr.Iss.	1989	4.75	20-65
1989 Baby's Fourth Christmas QX543-2	Yr.Iss.	1989	6.75	13-21
1989 Baby's Second Christmas QX449-5	Yr.Iss.	1989	6.75	26-35
1989 Baby's Third Christmas QX469-5	Yr.Iss.	1989	6.75	13-28
1989 Brother QX445-2	Yr.Iss.	1989	6.25	18-23
1989 Dad QX442-5	Yr.Iss.	1989	7.25	12-15
1989 Daughter QX443-2	Yr.Iss.	1989	6.25	18-33
1989 Festive Year QX384-2	Yr.Iss.	1989	7.75	10-25
1989 Fifty Years Together Photoholder QX486-2	Yr.Iss.	1989	8.75	13-20
1989 First Christmas Together QX273-2	Yr.Iss.	1989	4.75	25-30
1989 First Christmas Together QX383-2	Yr.Iss.	1989	6.75	18-25
1989 First Christmas Together QX485-2	Yr.Iss.	1989	9.75	18-25
1989 Five Years Together QX273-5	Yr.Iss.	1989	4.75	18-23
1989 Forty Years Together Photoholder QX545-2	Yr.Iss.	1989	8.75	12-18
1989 Friendship Time QX413-2	Yr.Iss.	1989	9.75	19-33
1989 From Our Home to Yours QX384-5	Yr.Iss.	1989	6.25	12-15
1989 Godchild QX311-2	Yr.Iss.	1989	6.25	14-20
1989 Granddaughter QX278	Yr.Iss.	1989	4.75	7-27
1989 Granddaughter's First Christmas QX382-2	Yr.Iss.	1989	6.75	7-9
1989 Grandmother QX277-5	Yr.Iss.	1989	4.75	16-20
1989 Grandparents QX277-2	Yr.Iss.	1989	4.75	14-20
1989 Grandson QX278-5	Yr.Iss.	1989	4.75	15-25
1989 Grandson's First Christmas QX382-5	Yr.Iss.	1989	6.75	9-18
1989 Gratitude QX385-2	Yr.Iss.	1989	6.75	11-14
1989 Language of Love QX383-5	Yr.Iss.	1989	6.25	20-25
1989 Mom and Dad QX442-5	Yr.Iss.	1989	9.75	19-24
1989 Mother QX440-5	Yr.Iss.	1989	9.75	28-30
1989 New Home QX275-5	Yr.Iss.	1989	4.75	16-20
1989 Sister QX279-2	Yr.Iss.	1989	4.75	16-20
1989 Son QX444-5	Yr.Iss.	1989	6.25	20-35
1989 Sweetheart QX486-5	Yr.Iss.	1989	9.75	22-33
1989 Teacher QX412-5	Yr.Iss.	1989	5.75	14-25
1989 Ten Years Together QX274-2	Yr.Iss.	1989	4.75	24-30
1989 Twenty-five Years Together Photoholder QX485-5	Yr.Iss.	1989	8.75	14-18
1989 World of Love QX274-5	Yr.Iss.	1989	4.75	28-35

1989 Hallmark Handcrafted Ornaments - Keepsake

YEAR ISSUE	EDITION LIMIT	YEAR RETD.	ISSUE PRICE	*QUOTE U.S.$
1989 Peek-a-boo Kittens QX487-1	Yr.Iss.	1989	7.50	21

1989 Hallmark Keepsake Ornament Collector's Club - Keepsake

YEAR ISSUE	EDITION LIMIT	YEAR RETD.	ISSUE PRICE	*QUOTE U.S.$
1989 Christmas is Peaceful QXC451-2	Yr.Iss.	1989	18.50	30-45
1989 Collect a Dream QXC428-5	Yr.Iss.	1989	9.00	44-59
1989 Holiday Heirloom (3rd Ed.) QXC460-5	Yr.Iss.	1989	25.00	29-35
1989 Noelle QXC448-3	Yr.Iss.	1989	19.75	39-50
1989 Sitting Purrty QXC581-2	Yr.Iss.	1989	Gift	15-44
1989 Visit from Santa QXC580-2	Yr.Iss.	1989	Gift	39

1989 Holiday Traditions - Keepsake

YEAR ISSUE	EDITION LIMIT	YEAR RETD.	ISSUE PRICE	*QUOTE U.S.$
1989 Camera Claus QX546-5	Yr.Iss.	1989	5.75	13-23
1989 A Charlie Brown Christmas QX276-5	Yr.Iss.	1989	4.75	35-40
1989 Cranberry Bunny QX426-2	Yr.Iss.	1989	5.75	11-18
1989 Deer Disguise QX426-5	Yr.Iss.	1989	5.75	17-25
1989 Feliz Navidad QX439-2	Yr.Iss.	1989	6.75	20-39
1989 The First Christmas QX547-5	Yr.Iss.	1989	7.75	14-18
1989 Gentle Fawn QX548-5	Yr.Iss.	1989	7.75	15-20
1989 George Washington Bicentennial QX386-2	Yr.Iss.	1989	6.75	9-20
1989 Gone Fishing QX479-4	Yr.Iss.	1989	5.75	17
1989 Gym Dandy QX418-5	Yr.Iss.	1989	5.75	12-20
1989 Hang in There QX430-5	Yr.Iss.	1989	5.25	23-27
1989 Here's the Pitch QX545-5	Yr.Iss.	1989	5.75	12-20
1989 Hoppy Holidays QX469-2	Yr.Iss.	1989	7.75	14-25
1989 Joyful Trio QX437-2	Yr.Iss.	1989	9.75	15-20
1989 A Kiss™ from Santa QX482-1	Yr.Iss.	1989	4.50	20
1989 Kristy Claus QX424-5	Yr.Iss.	1989	5.75	10-15

YEAR ISSUE	EDITION LIMIT	YEAR RETD.	ISSUE PRICE	*QUOTE U.S.$
1989 Norman Rockwell QX276-2	Yr.Iss.	1989	4.75	20-25
1989 North Pole Jogger QX546-2	Yr.Iss.	1989	5.75	12-23
1989 Old-World Gnome QX434-5	Yr.Iss.	1989	7.75	16-30
1989 On the Links QX419-2	Yr.Iss.	1989	5.75	16-23
1989 Oreo® Chocolate Sandwich Cookies QX481-4	Yr.Iss.	1989	4.00	15-18
1989 Owliday Greetings QX436-5	Yr.Iss.	1989	4.00	13-23
1989 Paddington Bear QX429-2	Yr.Iss.	1989	5.75	16-27
1989 Party Line QX476-1	Yr.Iss.	1989	8.75	27
1989 Peek-a-Boo Kitties QX487-1	Yr.Iss.	1989	7.50	16-22
1989 Polar Bowler QX478-4	Yr.Iss.	1989	5.75	17
1989 Sea Santa QX415-2	Yr.Iss.	1989	5.75	14-30
1989 Snoopy and Woodstock QX433-2	Yr.Iss.	1989	6.75	16-29
1989 Snowplow Santa QX420-5	Yr.Iss.	1989	5.75	12-23
1989 Special Delivery QX432-5	Yr.Iss.	1989	5.25	13-25
1989 Spencer Sparrow, Esq. QX431-2	Yr.Iss.	1990	6.75	16-28
1989 Stocking Kitten QX456-5	Yr.Iss.	1990	6.75	13-23
1989 Sweet Memories Photoholder QX438-5	Yr.Iss.	1989	6.75	25
1989 Teeny Taster QX418-1	Yr.Iss.	1989	4.75	17

1989 Keepsake Magic Collection - Keepsake

YEAR ISSUE	EDITION LIMIT	YEAR RETD.	ISSUE PRICE	*QUOTE U.S.$
1989 Angel Melody QLX720-2	Yr.Iss.	1989	9.50	20-25
1989 The Animals Speak QLX723-2	Yr.Iss.	1989	13.50	78-125
1989 Baby's First Christmas QLX727-2	Yr.Iss.	1989	30.00	47-65
1989 Backstage Bear QLX721-5	Yr.Iss.	1989	13.50	15-35
1989 Busy Beaver QLX724-5	Yr.Iss.	1989	17.50	36-55
1989 Chris Mouse (5th Ed.) QLX722-5	Yr.Iss.	1989	9.50	40-58
1989 Christmas Classics (4th Ed.) QLX724-2	Yr.Iss.	1989	13.50	27-43
1989 First Christmas Together QLX734-2	Yr.Iss.	1989	17.50	33-45
1989 Forest Frolics (1st Ed.) QLX728-2	Yr.Iss.	1989	24.50	83-95
1989 Holiday Bell QLX722-2	Yr.Iss.	1989	17.50	20-35
1989 Joyous Carolers QLX729-5	Yr.Iss.	1989	30.00	47-70
1989 Kringle's Toy Shop QLX701-7	Yr.Iss.	1989	24.50	60
1989 Loving Spoonful QLX726-2	Yr.Iss.	1989	19.50	32-38
1989 Metro Express QLX725-5	Yr.Iss.	1989	28.00	35-80
1989 Moonlit Nap QLX713-4	Yr.Iss.	1989	8.75	30-80
1989 Rudolph the Red-Nosed Reindeer QLX725-2	Yr.Iss.	1989	19.50	63-70
1989 Spirit of St. Nick QLX728-5	Yr.Iss.	1989	24.50	39-75
1989 Tiny Tinker QLX717-4	Yr.Iss.	1989	19.50	52-60
1989 Unicorn Fantasy QLX723-5	Yr.Iss.	1989	9.50	13-17

1989 Keepsake Miniature Ornaments - Keepsake

YEAR ISSUE	EDITION LIMIT	YEAR RETD.	ISSUE PRICE	*QUOTE U.S.$
1989 Acorn Squirrel QXM568-2	Yr.Iss.	1989	4.50	9
1989 Baby's First Christmas QXM573-2	Yr.Iss.	1989	6.00	8-12
1989 Brass Partridge QXM572-5	Yr.Iss.	1989	3.00	10-12
1989 Brass Snowflake QXM570-2	Yr.Iss.	1989	4.50	14
1989 Bunny Hug QXM577-5	Yr.Iss.	1989	3.00	8-11
1989 Country Wreath QXM573-1	Yr.Iss.	1989	4.50	12
1989 Cozy Skater QXM573-5	Yr.Iss.	1989	4.50	12-18
1989 First Christmas Together QXM564-2	Yr.Iss.	1989	8.50	8-12
1989 Folk Art Bunny QXM569-2	Yr.Iss.	1989	4.50	10
1989 Happy Bluebird QXM566-2	Yr.Iss.	1989	4.50	12-15
1989 Holiday Deer QXM577-2	Yr.Iss.	1989	3.00	12
1989 Holy Family QXM561-1	Yr.Iss.	1989	8.50	15
1989 Kittens in Toyland (2nd Ed.) QXM561-2	Yr.Iss.	1989	4.50	15-20
1989 Kitty Cart QXM572-2	Yr.Iss.	1989	3.00	7
1989 The Kringles (1st Ed.) QXM562-2	Yr.Iss.	1989	6.00	20-26
1989 Little Soldier QXM567-5	Yr.Iss.	1989	4.50	9-24
1989 Little Star Bringer QXM562-2	Yr.Iss.	1989	6.00	17-27
1989 Load of Cheer QXM574-5	Yr.Iss.	1989	6.00	12-20
1989 Lovebirds QXM563-5	Yr.Iss.	1989	6.00	10-14
1989 Merry Seal QXM575-5	Yr.Iss.	1989	6.00	13-15
1989 Mother QXM564-5	Yr.Iss.	1989	6.00	9-15
1989 Noel R.R. (1st Ed.) QXM576-2	Yr.Iss.	1989	8.50	29-37
1989 Old English Village (2nd Ed.) QXM561-5	Yr.Iss.	1989	8.50	19-29
1989 Old-World Santa QXM569-5	Yr.Iss.	1989	3.00	7-16
1989 Penguin Pal (2nd Ed.) QXM560-2	Yr.Iss.	1989	4.50	16-20
1989 Pinecone Basket QXM573-4	Yr.Iss.	1989	4.50	7-10
1989 Puppy Cart QXM571-5	Yr.Iss.	1989	3.00	7-22
1989 Rejoice QXM578-2	Yr.Iss.	1989	6.00	10
1989 Rocking Horse (2nd Ed.) QXM560-5	Yr.Iss.	1989	4.50	24-28
1989 Roly-Poly Pig QXM571-2	Yr.Iss.	1989	3.00	13-18
1989 Roly-Poly Ram QXM570-5	Yr.Iss.	1989	3.00	13-18
1989 Santa's Magic Ride QXM563-2	Yr.Iss.	1989	8.50	17-20
1989 Santa's Roadster QXM566-5	Yr.Iss.	1989	6.00	12-18
1989 Scrimshaw Reindeer QXM568-5	Yr.Iss.	1989	4.50	7-10
1989 Sharing a Ride QXM576-5	Yr.Iss.	1989	8.50	12-17

YEAR ISSUE	EDITION LIMIT	YEAR RETD.	ISSUE PRICE	*QUOTE U.S.$
1989 Slow Motion QXM575-2	Yr.Iss.	1989	6.00	13-17
1989 Special Friend QXM565-2	Yr.Iss.	1989	4.50	12-14
1989 Starlit Mouse QXM565-5	Yr.Iss.	1989	4.50	12-16
1989 Stocking Pal QXM567-2	Yr.Iss.	1989	4.50	11
1989 Strollin' Snowman QXM574-2	Yr.Iss.	1989	4.50	13-18
1989 Three Little Kitties QXM569-4	Yr.Iss.	1989	6.00	19

1989 New Attractions - Keepsake

YEAR ISSUE	EDITION LIMIT	YEAR RETD.	ISSUE PRICE	*QUOTE U.S.$
1989 Balancing Elf QX489-5	Yr.Iss.	1989	6.75	21-25
1989 Cactus Cowboy QX411-2	Yr.Iss.	1989	6.75	29-45
1989 Claus Construction QX488-5	Yr.Iss.	1990	7.75	19-40
1989 Cool Swing QX487-5	Yr.Iss.	1989	6.25	24-35
1989 Country Cat QX467-2	Yr.Iss.	1989	6.25	16-20
1989 Festive Angel QX463-5	Yr.Iss.	1989	6.75	13-27
1989 Goin' South QX410-5	Yr.Iss.	1989	4.25	18-20
1989 Graceful Swan QX464-2	Yr.Iss.	1989	6.75	16-20
1989 Horse Weathervane QX463-2	Yr.Iss.	1989	5.75	16-18
1989 Let's Play QX488-2	Yr.Iss.	1989	7.25	27-30
1989 Nostalgic Lamb QX466-5	Yr.Iss.	1989	6.75	10-20
1989 Nutshell Dreams QX465-5	Yr.Iss.	1989	5.75	14-23
1989 Nutshell Holiday QX465-2	Yr.Iss.	1989	5.75	17-27
1989 Nutshell Workshop QX487-2	Yr.Iss.	1989	5.75	23
1989 Peppermint Clown QX450-5	Yr.Iss.	1989	24.75	23-35
1989 Rodney Reindeer QX407-2	Yr.Iss.	1989	6.75	10-15
1989 Rooster Weathervane QX467-5	Yr.Iss.	1989	5.75	16-25
1989 Sparkling Snowflake QX547-2	Yr.Iss.	1989	7.75	14-25
1989 TV Break QX409-2	Yr.Iss.	1989	6.25	16-20
1989 Wiggly Snowman QX489-2	Yr.Iss.	1989	6.75	21-36

1989 Special Edition - Keepsake

YEAR ISSUE	EDITION LIMIT	YEAR RETD.	ISSUE PRICE	*QUOTE U.S.$
1989 The Ornament Express QX580-5	Yr.Iss.	1989	22.00	35-50

1990 Artists' Favorites - Keepsake

YEAR ISSUE	EDITION LIMIT	YEAR RETD.	ISSUE PRICE	*QUOTE U.S.$
1990 Angel Kitty QX4746	Yr.Iss.	1990	8.75	19-28
1990 Donder's Diner QX4823	Yr.Iss.	1990	13.75	11-23
1990 Gentle Dreamers QX4756	Yr.Iss.	1990	8.75	21-30
1990 Happy Woodcutter QX4763	Yr.Iss.	1990	9.75	18-23
1990 Mouseboat QX4753	Yr.Iss.	1990	7.75	13-20
1990 Welcome, Santa QX4773	Yr.Iss.	1990	11.75	19-34

1990 Collectible Series - Keepsake

YEAR ISSUE	EDITION LIMIT	YEAR RETD.	ISSUE PRICE	*QUOTE U.S.$
1990 Betsey Clark: Home for Christmas (5th Ed.) QX2033	Yr.Iss.	1990	5.00	16-25
1990 Christmas Kitty (2nd Ed.) QX4506	Yr.Iss.	1990	14.75	18-22
1990 Cinnamon Bear (8th Ed.) QX4426	Yr.Iss.	1990	8.75	22-35
1990 Cookies for Santa (4th Ed.) QX4436	Yr.Iss.	1990	8.75	22-35
1990 CRAYOLA Crayon-Bright Moving Colors (2nd Ed.) QX4586	Yr.Iss.	1990	8.75	40-50
1990 Fabulous Decade (1st Ed.) QX4466	Yr.Iss.	1990	7.75	20-40
1990 Festive Surrey (12th Ed.) QX4923	Yr.Iss.	1990	14.75	32-43
1990 Frosty Friends (11th Ed.) QX4396	Yr.Iss.	1990	9.75	24-42
1990 The Gift Bringers-St. Lucia (2nd Ed.) QX2803	Yr.Iss.	1990	5.00	15-25
1990 Greatest Story (1st Ed.) QX4656	Yr.Iss.	1990	12.75	20-26
1990 Hark! It's Herald (2nd Ed.) QX4463	Yr.Iss.	1990	6.75	10-24
1990 Heart of Christmas (1st Ed.) QX4726	Yr.Iss.	1990	13.75	65-80
1990 Holiday Home (7th Ed.) QX4696	Yr.Iss.	1990	14.75	62-78
1990 Irish (6th Ed.) QX4636	Yr.Iss.	1990	10.75	21
1990 Mary's Angels-Rosebud (3rd Ed.) QX4423	Yr.Iss.	1990	5.75	29-40
1990 Merry Olde Santa (1st Ed.) QX4736	Yr.Iss.	1990	14.75	50-73
1990 Popcorn Party (5th Ed.) QX4393	Yr.Iss.	1990	13.75	38-58
1990 Reindeer Champs-Comet (5th Ed.) QX4433	Yr.Iss.	1990	7.75	22-30
1990 Rocking Horse (10th Ed.) QX4646	Yr.Iss.	1990	10.75	79-100
1990 Seven Swans A-Swimming (7th Ed.) QX3033	Yr.Iss.	1990	6.75	21-33
1990 Winter Surprise (2nd Ed.) QX4443	Yr.Iss.	1990	10.75	19

1990 Commemoratives - Keepsake

YEAR ISSUE	EDITION LIMIT	YEAR RETD.	ISSUE PRICE	*QUOTE U.S.$
1990 Across The Miles QX3173	Yr.Iss.	1990	6.75	14-18
1990 Baby's First Christmas QX3036	Yr.Iss.	1990	6.75	11-23
1990 Baby's First Christmas QX4853	Yr.Iss.	1990	9.75	10-19
1990 Baby's First Christmas QX4856	Yr.Iss.	1990	7.75	33-40
1990 Baby's First Christmas-Baby Boy QX2063	Yr.Iss.	1990	4.75	16-20
1990 Baby's First Christmas-Baby Girl QX2066	Yr.Iss.	1990	4.75	16-19
1990 Baby's First Christmas-Photo Holder QX4843	Yr.Iss.	1990	7.75	21-30
1990 Baby's Second Christmas QX4683	Yr.Iss.	1990	6.75	27-34
1990 Brother QX4493	Yr.Iss.	1990	5.75	10-15
1990 Child Care Giver QX3166	Yr.Iss.	1990	6.75	11-14

YEAR ISSUE	EDITION LIMIT	YEAR RETD.	ISSUE PRICE	*QUOTE U.S.$
1990 Child's Fifth Christmas QX4876	Yr.Iss.	1990	6.75	13-20
1990 Child's Fourth Christmas QX4873	Yr.Iss.	1990	6.75	13-25
1990 Child's Third Christmas QX4866	Yr.Iss.	1990	6.75	19-30
1990 Copy of Cheer QX4486	Yr.Iss.	1990	7.75	16-20
1990 Dad QX4533	Yr.Iss.	1990	6.75	11-18
1990 Dad-to-Be QX4913	Yr.Iss.	1990	5.75	17-23
1990 Daughter QX4496	Yr.Iss.	1990	5.75	14-25
1990 Fifty Years Together QX4906	Yr.Iss.	1990	9.75	10-20
1990 Five Years Together QX2103	Yr.Iss.	1990	4.75	18-25
1990 Forty Years Together QX4903	Yr.Iss.	1990	9.75	16-20
1990 Friendship Kitten QX4142	Yr.Iss.	1990	6.75	17-23
1990 From Our Home to Yours QX2166	Yr.Iss.	1990	4.75	9-20
1990 Godchild QX3167	Yr.Iss.	1990	6.75	11-20
1990 Granddaughter QX2286	Yr.Iss.	1990	4.75	16-30
1990 Granddaughter's First Christmas QX3106	Yr.Iss.	1990	6.75	18-23
1990 Grandmother QX2236	Yr.Iss.	1990	4.75	16-20
1990 Grandparents QX2253	Yr.Iss.	1990	4.75	16-20
1990 Grandson QX2293	Yr.Iss.	1990	4.75	21-28
1990 Grandson's First Christmas QX3063	Yr.Iss.	1990	6.75	17-20
1990 Jesus Loves Me QX3156	Yr.Iss.	1990	6.75	11-14
1990 Mom and Dad QX4593	Yr.Iss.	1990	8.75	17-30
1990 Mom-to-Be QX4916	Yr.Iss.	1990	5.75	25-33
1990 Mother QX4536	Yr.Iss.	1990	8.75	24-30
1990 New Home QX4343	Yr.Iss.	1990	6.75	26-30
1990 Our First Christmas Together QX2136	Yr.Iss.	1990	4.75	20-27
1990 Our First Christmas Together QX3146	Yr.Iss.	1990	6.75	13-25
1990 Our First Christmas Together QX4883	Yr.Iss.	1990	9.75	16-30
1990 Our First Christmas Together-Photo Holder Ornament QX4886	Yr.Iss.	1990	7.75	16-20
1990 Peaceful Kingdom QX2106	Yr.Iss.	1990	4.75	18-23
1990 Sister QX2273	Yr.Iss.	1990	4.75	14-23
1990 Son QX4516	Yr.Iss.	1990	5.75	16-23
1990 Sweetheart QX4893	Yr.Iss.	1990	11.75	12-30
1990 Teacher QX4483	Yr.Iss.	1990	7.75	14-17
1990 Ten Years Together QX2153	Yr.Iss.	1990	4.75	18-23
1990 Time for Love QX2133	Yr.Iss.	1990	4.75	20-25
1990 Twenty-Five Years Together QX4896	Yr.Iss.	1990	9.75	13-24

1990 Holiday Traditions - Keepsake

YEAR ISSUE	EDITION LIMIT	YEAR RETD.	ISSUE PRICE	*QUOTE U.S.$
1990 Spencer Sparrow, Esq. QX431-2	Yr.Iss.	1990	6.75	12-15
1990 Stocking Kitten QX456-5	Yr.Iss.	1990	6.75	8-15

1990 Keepsake Collector's Club - Keepsake

YEAR ISSUE	EDITION LIMIT	YEAR RETD.	ISSUE PRICE	*QUOTE U.S.$
1990 Armful of Joy QXC445-3	Yr.Iss.	1990	8.00	20-41
1990 Christmas Limited 1975 QXC476-6	38,700	1990	19.75	75-100
1990 Club Hollow QXC445-6	Yr.Iss.	1990	Gift	20-36
1990 Crown Prince QXC560-3	Yr.Iss.	1990	Gift	10-39
1990 Dove of Peace QXC447-6	25,400	1990	24.75	50-65
1990 Sugar Plum Fairy QXC447-3	25,400	1990	27.75	35-50

1990 Keepsake Magic Ornaments - Keepsake

YEAR ISSUE	EDITION LIMIT	YEAR RETD.	ISSUE PRICE	*QUOTE U.S.$
1990 Baby's First Christmas QLX7246	Yr.Iss.	1990	28.00	34-65
1990 Beary Short Nap QLX7326	Yr.Iss.	1990	10.00	24-33
1990 Blessings of Love QLX7363	Yr.Iss.	1990	14.00	44-50
1990 Children's Express QLX7243	Yr.Iss.	1990	28.00	44-70
1990 Chris Mouse Wreath QLX7296	Yr.Iss.	1990	10.00	29-45
1990 Christmas Memories QLX7276	Yr.Iss.	1990	25.00	38-95
1990 Deer Crossing QLX7213	Yr.Iss.	1990	18.00	41-50
1990 Elf of the Year QLX7356	Yr.Iss.	1990	10.00	16-25
1990 Elfin Whittler QLX7265	Yr.Iss.	1990	20.00	37-55
1990 Forest Frolics QLX7236	Yr.Iss.	1990	25.00	49-70
1990 Holiday Flash QLX7333	Yr.Iss.	1990	18.00	26-40
1990 Hop 'N Pop Popper QLX7353	Yr.Iss.	1990	20.00	79-100
1990 Letter to Santa QLX7226	Yr.Iss.	1990	14.00	28-40
1990 The Littlest Angel QLX7303	Yr.Iss.	1990	14.00	31-50
1990 Mrs. Santa's Kitchen QLX7263	Yr.Iss.	1990	25.00	65-90
1990 Our First Christmas Together QLX7255	Yr.Iss.	1990	18.00	30-50
1990 Partridges in a Pear QLX7212	Yr.Iss.	1990	14.00	22-35
1990 Santa's Ho-Ho-Hoedown QLX7256	Yr.Iss.	1990	25.00	50-90
1990 Song and Dance QLX7253	Yr.Iss.	1990	20.00	59-95
1990 Starlight Angel QLX7306	Yr.Iss.	1990	14.00	27-38
1990 Starship Christmas QLX7336	Yr.Iss.	1990	18.00	38-55

1990 Keepsake Miniature Ornaments - Keepsake

YEAR ISSUE	EDITION LIMIT	YEAR RETD.	ISSUE PRICE	*QUOTE U.S.$
1990 Acorn Wreath QXM5686	Yr.Iss.	1990	6.00	9-12
1990 Air Santa QXM5656	Yr.Iss.	1990	4.50	10-13

YEAR ISSUE	EDITION LIMIT	YEAR RETD.	ISSUE PRICE	*QUOTE U.S.$
1990 Baby's First Christmas QXM5703	Yr.Iss.	1990	8.50	15-20
1990 Basket Buddy QXM5696	Yr.Iss.	1990	6.00	9-12
1990 Bear Hug QXM5633	Yr.Iss.	1990	6.00	10-14
1990 Brass Bouquet 600QMX5776	Yr.Iss.	1990	6.00	5-7
1990 Brass Horn QXM5793	Yr.Iss.	1990	3.00	5-10
1990 Brass Peace QXM5796	Yr.Iss.	1990	3.00	5-10
1990 Brass Santa QXM5786	Yr.Iss.	1990	3.00	6-9
1990 Brass Year QXM5833	Yr.Iss.	1990	3.00	5-8
1990 Busy Carver QXM5673	Yr.Iss.	1990	4.50	10
1990 Christmas Dove QXM5636	Yr.Iss.	1990	4.50	13
1990 Cloisonne Poinsettia QMX5533	Yr.Iss.	1990	10.75	13-25
1990 Coal Car QXM5756	Yr.Iss.	1990	8.50	21-28
1990 Country Heart QXM5693	Yr.Iss.	1990	4.50	6-9
1990 First Christmas Together QXM5536	Yr.Iss.	1990	6.00	11-15
1990 Going Sledding QXM5683	Yr.Iss.	1990	4.50	11-15
1990 Grandchild's First Christmas QXM5723	Yr.Iss.	1990	6.00	6-12
1990 Holiday Cardinal QXM5526	Yr.Iss.	1990	3.00	8-11
1990 Kittens in Toyland QXM5736	Yr.Iss.	1990	4.50	12-17
1990 The Kringles (2nd Ed.) QXM5753	Yr.Iss.	1990	6.00	12-24
1990 Lion and Lamb QXM5676	Yr.Iss.	1990	4.50	7-12
1990 Loving Hearts QXM5523	Yr.Iss.	1990	3.00	8-10
1990 Madonna and Child QXM5643	Yr.Iss.	1990	6.00	11
1990 Mother QXM5716	Yr.Iss.	1990	4.50	9-13
1990 Nativity QXM5706	Yr.Iss.	1990	4.50	9-14
1990 Nature's Angels QMX5733	Yr.Iss.	1990	4.50	16-28
1990 Panda's Surprise QXM5616	Yr.Iss.	1990	4.50	11
1990 Penguin Pal QXM5746	Yr.Iss.	1990	4.50	14-20
1990 Perfect Fit QXM5516	Yr.Iss.	1990	4.50	10-13
1990 Puppy Love QXM5666	Yr.Iss.	1990	6.00	11-15
1990 Rocking Horse QXM5743	Yr.Iss.	1990	4.50	21-24
1990 Ruby Reindeer QXM5816	Yr.Iss.	1990	6.00	10-12
1990 Santa's Journey QXM5826	Yr.Iss.	1990	8.50	13-18
1990 Santa's Streetcar QXM5766	Yr.Iss.	1990	8.50	13-20
1990 School QXM5763	Yr.Iss.	1990	8.50	19-21
1990 Snow Angel QXM5773	Yr.Iss.	1990	6.00	11-15
1990 Special Friends QXM5726	Yr.Iss.	1990	6.00	11-13
1990 Stamp Collector QXM5623	Yr.Iss.	1990	4.50	8
1990 Stringing Along QXM5606	Yr.Iss.	1990	8.50	15-18
1990 Sweet Slumber QXM5663	Yr.Iss.	1990	4.50	11
1990 Teacher QXM5653	Yr.Iss.	1990	4.50	5-7
1990 Thimble Bells QXM5543	Yr.Iss.	1990	6.00	15-20
1990 Type of Joy QXM5646	Yr.Iss.	1990	4.50	7-10
1990 Warm Memories QXM5713	Yr.Iss.	1990	4.50	9
1990 Wee Nutcracker QXM5843	Yr.Iss.	1990	8.50	12-15

1990 New Attractions - Keepsake

1990 Baby Unicorn QX5486	Yr.Iss.	1990	9.75	12-25
1990 Bearback Rider QX5483	Yr.Iss.	1990	9.75	13-32
1990 Beary Good Deal QX4733	Yr.Iss.	1990	6.75	8-17
1990 Billboard Bunny QX5196	Yr.Iss.	1990	7.75	13-20
1990 Born to Dance QX5043	Yr.Iss.	1990	7.75	15-25
1990 Chiming In QX4366	Yr.Iss.	1990	9.75	20-25
1990 Christmas Croc QX4373	Yr.Iss.	1990	7.75	13-28
1990 Christmas Partridge QX5246	Yr.Iss.	1990	7.75	10-23
1990 Claus Construction QX4885	Yr.Iss.	1990	7.75	12-20
1990 Country Angel QX5046	Yr.Iss.	1990	6.75	76
1990 Coyote Carols QX4993	Yr.Iss.	1990	8.75	17-20
1990 Cozy Goose QX4966	Yr.Iss.	1990	5.75	10-14
1990 Feliz Navidad QX5173	Yr.Iss.	1990	6.75	18-30
1990 Garfield QX2303	Yr.Iss.	1990	4.75	13-25
1990 Gingerbread Elf QX5033	Yr.Iss.	1990	5.75	15-23
1990 Goose Cart QX5236	Yr.Iss.	1990	7.75	14-18
1990 Hang in There QX4713	Yr.Iss.	1990	6.75	15-23
1990 Happy Voices QX4645	Yr.Iss.	1990	6.75	14-18
1990 Holiday Cardinals QX5243	Yr.Iss.	1990	7.75	16-23
1990 Home for the Owlidays QX5183	Yr.Iss.	1990	6.75	11-18
1990 Hot Dogger QX4976	Yr.Iss.	1990	7.75	15-20
1990 Jolly Dolphin QX4683	Yr.Iss.	1990	6.75	16-21
1990 Joy is in the Air QX5503	Yr.Iss.	1990	7.75	15-20
1990 King Klaus QX4106	Yr.Iss.	1990	7.75	13-25
1990 Kitty's Best Pal QX4716	Yr.Iss.	1990	6.75	16-20
1990 Little Drummer Boy QX5233	Yr.Iss.	1990	7.75	19-30
1990 Long Winter's Nap QX4703	Yr.Iss.	1990	6.75	15-25
1990 Lovable Dears QX5476	Yr.Iss.	1990	8.75	14-19
1990 Meow Mart QX4446	Yr.Iss.	1990	7.75	17-30
1990 Mooy Christmas QX4933	Yr.Iss.	1990	6.75	26-33
1990 Norman Rockwell Art QX2296	Yr.Iss.	1990	4.75	10-25
1990 Nutshell Chat QX5193	Yr.Iss.	1990	6.75	16-258
1990 Nutshell Holiday QX465-2	Yr.Iss.	1990	5.75	13-28
1990 Peanuts QX2233	Yr.Iss.	1990	4.75	27-30

YEAR ISSUE	EDITION LIMIT	YEAR RETD.	ISSUE PRICE	*QUOTE U.S.$
1990 Pepperoni Mouse QX4973	Yr.Iss.	1990	6.75	14-20
1990 Perfect Catch QX4693	Yr.Iss.	1990	7.75	12-20
1990 Polar Jogger QX4666	Yr.Iss.	1990	5.75	9-20
1990 Polar Pair QX4626	Yr.Iss.	1990	5.75	15-30
1990 Polar Sport QX5156	Yr.Iss.	1990	7.75	12-25
1990 Polar TV QX5166	Yr.Iss.	1990	7.75	12-20
1990 Polar V.I.P. QX4663	Yr.Iss.	1990	5.75	12-20
1990 Polar Video QX4633	Yr.Iss.	1990	5.75	9-24
1990 Poolside Walrus QX4986	Yr.Iss.	1990	7.75	14-30
1990 S. Claus Taxi QX4686	Yr.Iss.	1990	11.75	25-30
1990 Santa Schnoz QX4983	Yr.Iss.	1990	6.75	32-40
1990 Snoopy and Woodstock QX4723	Yr.Iss.	1990	6.75	28-43
1990 Spoon Rider QX5496	Yr.Iss.	1990	9.75	10-19
1990 Stitches of Joy QX5186	Yr.Iss.	1990	7.75	16-23
1990 Stocking Kitten QX456-5	Yr.Iss.	1990	6.75	7
1990 Stocking Pals QX5493	Yr.Iss.	1990	10.75	20-25
1990 Three Little Piggies QX4996	Yr.Iss.	1990	7.75	15-25
1990 Two Peas in a Pod QX4926	Yr.Iss.	1990	4.75	23-29

1990 Special Edition - Keepsake

1990 Dickens Caroler Bell-Mr. Ashbourne QX5056	Yr.Iss.	1990	21.75	42-55

1991 Artists' Favorites - Keepsake

1991 Fiddlin' Around QX4387	Yr.Iss.	1991	7.75	16-20
1991 Hooked on Santa QX4109	Yr.Iss.	1991	7.75	20-25
1991 Noah's Ark QX4867	Yr.Iss.	1991	13.75	28-50
1991 Polar Circus Wagon QX4399	Yr.Iss.	1991	13.75	25-30
1991 Santa Sailor QX4389	Yr.Iss.	1991	9.75	19-27
1991 Tramp and Laddie QX4397	Yr.Iss.	1991	7.75	21-50

1991 Club Limited Editions - Keepsake

1991 Galloping Into Christmas QXC4779	28,400	1991	19.75	99-101
1991 Secrets for Santa QXC4797	28,700	1991	23.75	50

1991 Collectible Series - Keepsake

1991 1957 Corvette (1st Ed.) QX4319	Yr.Iss.	1991	12.75	135-210
1991 Betsey Clark: Home for Christmas (6th Ed.) QX2109	Yr.Iss.	1991	5.00	19-30
1991 Checking His List (6th Ed.) QX4339	Yr.Iss.	1991	13.75	31-50
1991 Christmas Kitty (3rd Ed.) QX4377	Yr.Iss.	1991	14.75	17-27
1991 CRAYOLA CRAYON-Bright Vibrant Carols (3rd Ed.) QX4219	Yr.Iss.	1991	9.75	29-40
1991 Eight Maids A-Milking (8th Ed.) QX3089	Yr.Iss.	1991	6.75	20-30
1991 Fabulous Decade (2nd Ed.) QX4119	Yr.Iss.	1991	7.75	19-42
1991 Fire Station (8th Ed.) QX4139	Yr.Iss.	1991	14.75	44-70
1991 Frosty Friends (12th Ed.) QX4327	Yr.Iss.	1991	9.75	30-40
1991 The Gift Bringers-Christkind (3rd Ed.) QX2117	Yr.Iss.	1991	5.00	20-25
1991 Greatest Story (2nd Ed.) QX4129	Yr.Iss.	1991	12.75	24-30
1991 Hark! It's Herald (3rd Ed.) QX4379	Yr.Iss.	1991	6.75	19-24
1991 Heart of Christmas (2nd Ed.) QX4357	Yr.Iss.	1991	13.75	27-30
1991 Heavenly Angels (1st Ed.) QX4367	Yr.Iss.	1991	7.75	10-30
1991 Let It Snow! (5th Ed.) QX4369	Yr.Iss.	1991	8.75	19-30
1991 Mary's Angels-Iris (4th Ed.) QX4279	Yr.Iss.	1991	6.75	29-50
1991 Merry Olde Santa (2nd Ed.) QX4359	Yr.Iss.	1991	14.75	54-83
1991 Peace on Earth-Italy (1st Ed.) QX5129	Yr.Iss.	1991	11.75	12-27
1991 Puppy Love (1st Ed.) QX5379	Yr.Iss.	1991	7.75	60-69
1991 Reindeer Champ-Cupid (6th Ed.) QX4347	Yr.Iss.	1991	7.75	20-30
1991 Rocking Horse (11th Ed.) QX4147	Yr.Iss.	1991	10.75	38-60
1991 Santa's Antique Car (13th Ed.) QX4349	Yr.Iss.	1991	14.75	40-60
1991 Winter Surprise (3rd Ed.) QX4277	Yr.Iss.	1991	10.75	18-23

1991 Commemoratives - Keepsake

1991 Across the Miles QX3157	Yr.Iss.	1991	6.75	13-15
1991 Baby's First Christmas QX4889	Yr.Iss.	1991	7.75	10-34
1991 Baby's First Christmas QX5107	Yr.Iss.	1991	17.75	33-45
1991 Baby's First Christmas-Baby Boy QX2217	Yr.Iss.	1991	4.75	12-20
1991 Baby's First Christmas-Baby Girl QX2227	Yr.Iss.	1991	4.75	12-20
1991 Baby's First Christmas-Photo Holder QX4869	Yr.Iss.	1991	7.75	22
1991 Baby's Second Christmas QX4897	Yr.Iss.	1991	6.75	25-31
1991 The Big Cheese QX5327	Yr.Iss.	1991	6.75	18-20
1991 Brother QX5479	Yr.Iss.	1991	6.75	11-18
1991 A Child's Christmas QX4887	Yr.Iss.	1991	9.75	14-18
1991 Child's Fifth Christmas QX4909	Yr.Iss.	1991	6.75	15-20
1991 Child's Fourth Christmas QX4907	Yr.Iss.	1991	6.75	16-25

Collectors' Information Bureau   *Quotes have been rounded up to nearest dollar

YEAR ISSUE	EDITION LIMIT	YEAR RETD.	ISSUE PRICE	*QUOTE U.S.$	YEAR ISSUE	EDITION LIMIT	YEAR RETD.	ISSUE PRICE	*QUOTE U.S.$
1991 Child's Third Christmas QX4899	Yr.Iss.	1991	6.75	21-26	1991 Cool 'n' Sweet QXM5867		1991	4.50	25
1991 Dad QX5127	Yr.Iss.	1991	7.75	19	1991 Country Sleigh QXM5999	Yr.Iss.	1991	4.50	13-15
1991 Dad-to-Be QX4879	Yr.Iss.	1991	5.75	13-18	1991 Courier Turtle QXM5857	Yr.Iss.	1991	4.50	14
1991 Daughter QX5477	Yr.Iss.	1991	5.75	16-50	1991 Fancy Wreath QXM5917	Yr.Iss.	1991	4.50	13
1991 Extra-Special Friends QX2279	Yr.Iss.	1991	4.75	12-18	1991 Feliz Navidad QXM5887	Yr.Iss.	1991	6.00	14-22
1991 Fifty Years Together QX4947	Yr.Iss.	1991	8.75	18	1991 Fly By QXM5859	Yr.Iss.	1991	4.50	13-18
1991 Five Years Together QX4927	Yr.Iss.	1991	7.75	12-16	1991 Friendly Fawn QXM5947	Yr.Iss.	1991	6.00	13-17
1991 Forty Years Together QX4939	Yr.Iss.	1991	7.75	18	1991 Grandchild's First Christmas QXM5697	Yr.Iss.	1991	4.50	13
1991 Friends Are Fun QX5289	Yr.Iss.	1991	9.75	18-23					
1991 From Our Home to Yours QX2287	Yr.Iss.	1991	4.75	15-23	1991 Heavenly Minstrel QXM5687	Yr.Iss.	1991	9.75	19-22
1991 Gift of Joy QX5319	Yr.Iss.	1991	8.75	19-25	1991 Holiday Snowflake QXM5997	Yr.Iss.	1991	3.00	12
1991 Godchild QX5489	Yr.Iss.	1991	6.75	18-20	1991 Inn (4th Ed.) QXM5627	Yr.Iss.	1991	8.50	23-30
1991 Granddaughter QX2299	Yr.Iss.	1991	4.75	25-30	1991 Key to Love QXM5689	Yr.Iss.	1991	4.50	17
1991 Granddaughter's First Christmas QX5119	Yr.Iss.	1991	6.75	15-25	1991 Kittens in Toyland (4th Ed.) QXM5639	Yr.Iss.	1991	4.50	15-20
1991 Grandmother QX2307	Yr.Iss.	1991	4.75	16-20	1991 Kitty in a Mitty QXM5879	Yr.Iss.	1991	4.50	14
1991 Grandparents QX2309	Yr.Iss.	1991	4.75	14-17	1991 The Kringles (3rd Ed.) QXM5647	Yr.Iss.	1991	6.00	6-24
1991 Grandson QX2297	Yr.Iss.	1991	4.75	19-25	1991 Li'l Popper QXM5897	Yr.Iss.	1991	4.50	14-17
1991 Grandson's First Christmas QX5117	Yr.Iss.	1991	6.75	14-27	1991 Love Is Born QXM5959	Yr.Iss.	1991	6.00	18
1991 Jesus Loves Me QX3147	Yr.Iss.	1991	7.75	14	1991 Lulu & Family QXM5677	Yr.Iss.	1991	6.00	21
1991 Mom and Dad QX5467	Yr.Iss.	1991	9.75	13-22	1991 Mom QXM5699	Yr.Iss.	1991	6.00	18
1991 Mom-to-Be QX4877	Yr.Iss.	1991	5.75	10-27	1991 N. Pole Buddy QXM5927	Yr.Iss.	1991	4.50	14-18
1991 Mother QX5457	Yr.Iss.	1991	9.75	25-33	1991 Nature's Angels (2nd Ed.) QXM5657	Yr.Iss.	1991	4.50	13-21
1991 New Home QX5449	Yr.Iss.	1991	6.75	20-30	1991 Noel QXM5989	Yr.Iss.	1991	3.00	12
1991 Our First Christmas Together QX2229	Yr.Iss.	1991	4.75	14-20	1991 Our First Christmas Together QXM5819	Yr.Iss.	1991	6.00	17
1991 Our First Christmas Together QX3139	Yr.Iss.	1991	6.75	20-30	1991 Passenger Car (3rd Ed.) QXM5649	Yr.Iss.	1991	8.50	38-50
1991 Our First Christmas Together QX4919	Yr.Iss.	1991	8.75	18-28	1991 Penguin Pal (4th Ed.) QXM5629	Yr.Iss.	1991	4.50	16
					1991 Ring-A-Ding Elf QXM5669	Yr.Iss.	1991	8.50	18
1991 Our First Christmas Together-Photo Holder QX4917	Yr.Iss.	1991	8.75	24-30	1991 Rocking Horse (4th Ed.) QXM5637	Yr.Iss.	1991	4.50	19-26
					1991 Seaside Otter QXM5909	Yr.Iss.	1991	4.50	15
1991 Sister QX5487	Yr.Iss.	1991	6.75	16-20	1991 Silvery Santa QXM5679	Yr.Iss.	1991	9.75	22
1991 Son QX5469	Yr.Iss.	1991	5.75	16-23	1991 Special Friends QXM5797	Yr.Iss.	1991	8.50	18
1991 Sweetheart QX4957	Yr.Iss.	1991	9.75	18-25	1991 Thimble Bells (2nd Ed.) QXM5659	Yr.Iss.	1991	6.00	10-14
1991 Teacher QX2289	Yr.Iss.	1991	4.75	9-12	1991 Tiny Tea Party (set/6) QXM5827	Yr.Iss.	1991	29.00	145-165
1991 Ten Years Together QX4929	Yr.Iss.	1991	7.75	15-23	1991 Top Hatter QXM5889	Yr.Iss.	1991	6.00	11-16
1991 Terrific Teacher QX5309	Yr.Iss.	1991	6.75	13-15	1991 Treeland Trio QXM5899	Yr.Iss.	1991	8.50	16
1991 Twenty -Five Years Together QX4937	Yr.Iss.	1991	8.75	10-20	1991 Upbeat Bear QXM5907	Yr.Iss.	1991	6.00	14-16
					1991 Vision of Santa QXM5937	Yr.Iss.	1991	4.50	13
1991 Under the Mistletoe QX4949	Yr.Iss.	1991	8.75	19	1991 Wee Toymaker QXM5967	Yr.Iss.	1991	8.50	6-16
					1991 Woodland Babies QXM5667	Yr.Iss.	1991	6.00	6-24

1991 Keepsake Collector's Club - Keepsake

1991 Beary Artistic QXC7259		1991	10.00	32-40	**1991 New Attractions - Keepsake**				
1991 Hidden Treasure/Li'l Keeper QXC4769	Yr.Iss.	1991	15.00	37-40	1991 All-Star QX5329	Yr.Iss.	1991	6.75	17-23
					1991 Basket Bell Players QX5377	Yr.Iss.	1991	7.75	21-28

1991 Keepsake Magic Ornaments - Keepsake

					1991 Bob Cratchit QX4997	Yr.Iss.	1991	13.75	22-35
1991 Angel of Light QLT7239	Yr.Iss.	1991	30.00	48-60	1991 Chilly Chap QX5339	Yr.Iss.	1991	6.75	14-17
1991 Arctic Dome QLX7117	Yr.Iss.	1991	25.00	39-55	1991 Christmas Welcome QX5299	Yr.Iss.	1991	9.75	21-25
1991 Baby's First Christmas QLX7247	Yr.Iss.	1991	30.00	69-99	1991 Christopher Robin QX5579	Yr.Iss.	1991	9.75	26-38
1991 Bringing Home the Tree-QLX7249	Yr.Iss.	1991	28.00	39-58	1991 Cuddly Lamb QX5199	Yr.Iss.	1991	6.75	16-20
1991 Chris Mouse Mail QLX7207	Yr.Iss.	1991	10.00	25-40	1991 Dinoclaus QX5277	Yr.Iss.	1991	7.75	17-27
1991 Elfin Engineer QLX7209	Yr.Iss.	1991	10.00	20-25	1991 Ebenezer Scrooge QX4989	Yr.Iss.	1991	13.75	28-45
1991 Father Christmas QLX7147	Yr.Iss.	1991	14.00	26-45	1991 Evergreen Inn QX5389	Yr.Iss.	1991	8.75	15-18
1991 Festive Brass Church QLX7179	Yr.Iss.	1991	14.00	26-33	1991 Fanfare Bear QX5337	Yr.Iss.	1991	8.75	18
1991 Forest Frolics QLX7219	Yr.Iss.	1991	25.00	56-70	1991 Feliz Navidad QX5279	Yr.Iss.	1991	6.75	16-28
1991 Friendship Tree QLX7169	Yr.Iss.	1991	10.00	23-25	1991 Folk Art Reindeer QX5359	Yr.Iss.	1991	8.75	14-20
1991 Holiday Glow QLX7177	Yr.Iss.	1991	14.00	24-30	1991 GARFIELD QX5177	Yr.Iss.	1991	7.75	22-30
1991 It's A Wonderful Life QLX7237	Yr.Iss.	1991	20.00	62-75	1991 Glee Club Bears QX4969	Yr.Iss.	1991	8.75	12-18
1991 Jingle Bears QLX7323	Yr.Iss.	1991	25.00	45-58	1991 Holiday Cafe QX5399	Yr.Iss.	1991	8.75	10-14
1991 Kringles's Bumper Cars-QLX7119	Yr.Iss.	1991	25.00	38-55	1991 Jolly Wolly Santa QX5419	Yr.Iss.	1991	7.75	10-23
1991 Mole Family Home QLX7149	Yr.Iss.	1991	20.00	29-50	1991 Jolly Wolly Snowman QX5427	Yr.Iss.	1991	7.75	10-21
1991 Our First Christmas Together QXL7137	Yr.Iss.	1991	25.00	29-60	1991 Jolly Wolly Soldier QX5429'	Yr.Iss.	1991	7.75	18-20
					1991 Joyous Memories-Photoholder QX5369	Yr.Iss.	1991	6.75	16-28
1991 PEANUTS QLX7229	Yr.Iss.	1991	18.00	32-75					
1991 Salvation Army Band QLX7273	Yr.Iss.	1991	30.00	50-80	1991 Kanga and Roo QX5617	Yr.Iss.	1991	9.75	35-48
1991 Santa Special QLX7167	Yr.Iss.	1992	40.00	57-80	1991 Look Out Below QX4959	Yr.Iss.	1991	8.75	18-20
1991 Santa's Hot Line QLX7159	Yr.Iss.	1991	18.00	29-45	1991 Loving Stitches QX4987	Yr.Iss.	1991	8.75	23-29
1991 Ski Trip QLX7266	Yr.Iss.	1991	28.00	50-60	1991 Mary Engelbreit QX2237	Yr.Iss.	1991	4.75	22-27
1991 Sparkling Angel QLX7157	Yr.Iss.	1991	18.00	27-38	1991 Merry Carolers QX4799	Yr.Iss.	1991	29.75	62-95
1991 Toyland Tower QLX7129	Yr.Iss.	1991	20.00	37-45	1991 Mrs. Cratchit QX4999	Yr.Iss.	1991	13.75	23-33
					1991 Night Before Christmas QX5307	Yr.Iss.	1991	9.75	13-25

1991 Keepsake Miniature Ornaments - Keepsake

					1991 Norman Rockwell Art QX2259	Yr.Iss.	1991	5.00	10-30
1991 All Aboard QXM5869	Yr.Iss.	1991	4.50	17	1991 Notes of Cheer QX5357	Yr.Iss.	1991	5.75	12-14
1991 Baby's First Christmas QXM5799	Yr.Iss.	1991	6.00	18-23	1991 Nutshell Nativity QX5176	Yr.Iss.	1991	6.75	19-27
1991 Brass Church QXM5979	Yr.Iss.	1991	3.00	9	1991 Nutty Squirrel QX4833	Yr.Iss.	1991	5.75	10-13
1991 Brass Soldier QXM5987	Yr.Iss.	1991	3.00	9	1991 Old-Fashioned Sled QX4317	Yr.Iss.	1991	8.75	16-20
1991 Bright Boxers QXM5877	Yr.Iss.	1991	4.50	6-16	1991 On a Roll QX5347	Yr.Iss.	1991	6.75	16-22
1991 Busy Bear QXM5939	Yr.Iss.	1991	4.50	12	1991 Partridge in a Pear Tree QX5297	Yr.Iss.	1991	9.75	10-18
1991 Cardinal Cameo QXM5957	Yr.Iss.	1991	6.00	17	1991 PEANUTS QX2257	Yr.Iss.	1991	5.00	14-29
1991 Caring Shepherd QXM5949	Yr.Iss.	1991	6.00	14-18	1991 Piglet and Eeyore QX5577	Yr.Iss.	1991	9.75	30-50
					1991 Plum Delightful QX4977	Yr.Iss.	1991	8.75	18-22

ORNAMENTS

YEAR ISSUE	EDITION LIMIT	YEAR RETD.	ISSUE PRICE	*QUOTE U.S.$
1991 Polar Classic QX5287	Yr.Iss.	1991	6.75	15-23
1991 Rabbit QX5607	Yr.Iss.	1991	9.75	25-33
1991 Santa's Studio QX5397	Yr.Iss.	1991	8.75	14-20
1991 Ski Lift Bunny QX5447	Yr.Iss.	1991	6.75	14-23
1991 Snoopy and Woodstock QX5197	Yr.Iss.	1991	6.75	28-40
1991 Snow Twins QX4979	Yr.Iss.	1991	8.75	11-20
1991 Snowy Owl QX5269	Yr.Iss.	1991	7.75	18
1991 Sweet Talk QX5367	Yr.Iss.	1991	8.75	14-18
1991 Tigger QX5609	Yr.Iss.	1991	9.75	76-130
1991 Tiny Tim QX5037	Yr.Iss.	1991	10.75	24-40
1991 Up 'N'Down Journey QX5047	Yr.Iss.	1991	9.75	22-28
1991 Winnie-the Pooh QX5569	Yr.Iss.	1991	9.75	40-55
1991 Yule Logger QX4967	Yr.Iss.	1991	8.75	19-22

1991 Special Edition - Keepsake

YEAR ISSUE	EDITION LIMIT	YEAR RETD.	ISSUE PRICE	*QUOTE U.S.$
1991 Dickens Caroler Bell-Mrs. Beaumont QX5039	Yr.Iss.	1991	21.75	28-43
1991 Starship Enterprise QLX7199	Yr.Iss.	1991	20.00	195-389

1992 Artists' Favorites - Keepsake

YEAR ISSUE	EDITION LIMIT	YEAR RETD.	ISSUE PRICE	*QUOTE U.S.$
1992 Elfin Marionette QX5931	Yr.Iss.	1992	11.75	22-25
1992 Mother Goose QX4984	Yr.Iss.	1992	13.75	27-30
1992 Polar Post QX4914	Yr.Iss.	1992	8.75	20
1992 Stocked With Joy QX5934	Yr.Iss.	1992	7.75	12-17
1992 Turtle Dreams QX4991	Yr.Iss.	1992	8.75	20-28
1992 Uncle Art's Ice Cream QX5001	Yr.Iss.	1992	8.75	12-23

1992 Collectible Series - Keepsake

YEAR ISSUE	EDITION LIMIT	YEAR RETD.	ISSUE PRICE	*QUOTE U.S.$
1992 1966 Mustang (2nd Ed.) QX4284	Yr.Iss.	1992	12.75	25-55
1992 Betsey's Country Christmas (1st Ed.) QX2104	Yr.Iss.	1992	5.00	19-30
1992 CRAYOLA CRAYON-Bright Colors (4th Ed.) QX4264	Yr.Iss.	1992	9.75	25-34
1992 Fabulous Decade (3rd Ed.) QX4244	Yr.Iss.	1992	7.75	31-50
1992 Five-and-Ten-Cent Store (9th Ed.) QX4254	Yr.Iss.	1992	14.75	29-45
1992 Frosty Friends (13th Ed.) QX4291	Yr.Iss.	1992	9.75	29-35
1992 The Gift Bringers-Kolyada (4th Ed.) QX2124	Yr.Iss.	1992	5.00	14-23
1992 Gift Exchange (7th Ed.) QX4294	Yr.Iss.	1992	14.75	30-45
1992 Greatest Story (3rd Ed.) QX4251	Yr.Iss.	1992	12.75	15-25
1992 Hark! It's Herald (4th Ed.) QX4464	Yr.Iss.	1992	7.75	18-20
1992 Heart of Christmas (3rd Ed.) QX4411	Yr.Iss.	1992	13.75	16-31
1992 Heavenly Angels (2nd Ed.) QX4454	Yr.Iss.	1992	7.75	21-30
1992 Kringle Tours (14th Ed.) QX4341	Yr.Iss.	1992	14.75	28-39
1992 Mary's Angels-Lily (5th Ed.) QX4274	Yr.Iss.	1992	6.75	41-60
1992 Merry Olde Santa (3rd Ed.) QX4414	Yr.Iss.	1992	14.75	24-40
1992 Nine Ladies Dancing (9th Ed.) QX3031	Yr.Iss.	1992	6.75	19-25
1992 Owliver (1st Ed.) QX4544	Yr.Iss.	1992	7.75	14-19
1992 Peace On Earth-Spain (2nd Ed.) QX5174	Yr.Iss.	1992	11.75	10-21
1992 Puppy Love (2nd Ed.) QX4484	Yr.Iss.	1992	7.75	25-44
1992 Reindeer Champs-Donder (7th Ed.) QX5284	Yr.Iss.	1992	8.75	21-35
1992 Rocking Horse (12th Ed.) QX4261	Yr.Iss.	1992	10.75	24-50
1992 Sweet Holiday Harmony (6th Ed.) QX4461	Yr.Iss.	1992	8.75	19-25
1992 Tobin Fraley Carousel (1st Ed.) QX4891	Yr.Iss.	1992	28.00	20-62
1992 Winter Surprise (4th Ed.) QX4271	Yr.Iss.	1992	11.75	22-27

1992 Collectors' Club - Keepsake

YEAR ISSUE	EDITION LIMIT	YEAR RETD.	ISSUE PRICE	*QUOTE U.S.$
1992 Chipmunk Parcel Service QXC5194	Yr.Iss.	1992	6.75	21
1992 Rodney Takes Flight QXC5081	Yr.Iss.	1992	9.75	15-21
1992 Santa's Club List QXC7291	Yr.Iss.	1992	15.00	29-40

1992 Commemoratives - Keepsake

YEAR ISSUE	EDITION LIMIT	YEAR RETD.	ISSUE PRICE	*QUOTE U.S.$
1992 Across the Miles QX3044	Yr.Iss.	1992	6.75	10-14
1992 Anniversary Year QX4851	Yr.Iss.	1992	9.75	10-27
1992 Baby's First Christmas QX4641	Yr.Iss.	1992	7.75	20-25
1992 Baby's First Christmas QX4644	Yr.Iss.	1992	7.75	20-30
1992 Baby's First Christmas-Baby Boy QX2191	Yr.Iss.	1992	4.75	16-20
1992 Baby's First Christmas-Baby Girl QX2204	Yr.Iss.	1992	4.75	16-25
1992 Baby's First ChristmasQX4581	Yr.Iss.	1992	18.75	29-40
1992 Baby's Second Christmas QX4651	Yr.Iss.	1992	6.75	21-23
1992 Brother QX4684	Yr.Iss.	1992	6.75	13-16
1992 A Child's Christmas QX4574	Yr.Iss.	1992	9.75	19
1992 Child's Fifth Christmas QX4664	Yr.Iss.	1992	6.75	13-23
1992 Child's Fourth Christmas QX4661	Yr.Iss.	1992	6.75	15-25

YEAR ISSUE	EDITION LIMIT	YEAR RETD.	ISSUE PRICE	*QUOTE U.S.$
1992 Child's Third Christmas QX4654	Yr.Iss.	1992	6.75	20-25
1992 Dad QX4674	Yr.Iss.	1992	7.75	18-23
1992 Dad-to-Be QX4611	Yr.Iss.	1992	6.75	10-17
1992 Daughter QX5031	Yr.Iss.	1992	6.75	8-20
1992 For My Grandma QX5184	Yr.Iss.	1992	7.75	10-14
1992 For The One I Love QX4884	Yr.Iss.	1992	9.75	20
1992 Friendly Greetings QX5041	Yr.Iss.	1992	7.75	10-14
1992 Friendship Line QX5034	Yr.Iss.	1992	9.75	19-29
1992 From Our Home To Yours QX2131	Yr.Iss.	1992	4.75	13-17
1992 Godchild QX5941	Yr.Iss.	1992	6.75	19
1992 Granddaughter QX5604	Yr.Iss.	1992	6.75	13-25
1992 Granddaughter's First Christmas QX4634	Yr.Iss.	1992	6.75	14-20
1992 Grandmother QX2011	Yr.Iss.	1992	4.75	16-20
1992 Grandparents QX2004	Yr.Iss.	1992	4.75	13-17
1992 Grandson QX5611	Yr.Iss.	1992	6.75	19-25
1992 Grandson's First Christmas QX4621	Yr.Iss.	1992	6.75	16-23
1992 Holiday Memo QX5044	Yr.Iss.	1992	7.75	15-17
1992 Love To Skate QX4841	Yr.Iss.	1992	8.75	10-20
1992 Mom and Dad QX4671	Yr.Iss.	1992	9.75	21-37
1992 Mom QX5164	Yr.Iss.	1992	7.75	19
1992 Mom-to-Be QX4614	Yr.Iss.	1992	6.75	16-20
1992 New Home QX5191	Yr.Iss.	1992	8.75	12-20
1992 Our First Christmas Together QX4694	Yr.Iss.	1992	8.75	20-25
1992 Our First Christmas Together QX3011	Yr.Iss.	1992	6.75	17
1992 Our First Christmas Together QX5061	Yr.Iss.	1992	9.75	19
1992 Secret Pal QX5424	Yr.Iss.	1992	7.75	14
1992 Sister QX4681	Yr.Iss.	1992	6.75	14
1992 Son QX5024	Yr.Iss.	1992	6.75	16-27
1992 Special Cat QX5414	Yr.Iss.	1992	7.75	14-17
1992 Special Dog QX5421	Yr.Iss.	1992	7.75	10-30
1992 Teacher QX2264	Yr.Iss.	1992	4.75	5-17
1992 V. P. of Important Stuff QX5051	Yr.Iss.	1992	6.75	12-15
1992 World-Class Teacher QX5054	Yr.Iss.	1992	6.75	10-20

1992 Easter Ornaments - Keepsake

YEAR ISSUE	EDITION LIMIT	YEAR RETD.	ISSUE PRICE	*QUOTE U.S.$
1992 Easter Parade (1st Ed.) 675QEO8301	Yr.Iss.	1992	6.75	19-26
1992 Egg in Sports (1st Ed.) 675QEO9341	Yr.Iss.	1992	6.75	24-35

1992 Limited Edition Ornaments - Keepsake

YEAR ISSUE	EDITION LIMIT	YEAR RETD.	ISSUE PRICE	*QUOTE U.S.$
1992 Christmas Treasures QXC5464	15,500	1992	22.00	110-122
1992 Victorian Skater (w/ base) QXC4067	14,700	1992	25.00	50-75

1992 Magic Ornaments - Keepsake

YEAR ISSUE	EDITION LIMIT	YEAR RETD.	ISSUE PRICE	*QUOTE U.S.$
1992 Angel Of Light QLT7239	Yr.Iss.	1992	30.00	30
1992 Baby's First Christmas QLX7281	Yr.Iss.	1992	22.00	72-110
1992 Chris Mouse Tales (8th Ed.) QLX7074	Yr.Iss.	1992	12.00	18-25
1992 Christmas Parade QLX7271	Yr.Iss.	1992	30.00	55-60
1992 Continental Express QLX7264	Yr.Iss.	1992	32.00	61-75
1992 The Dancing Nutcracker QLX7261	Yr.Iss.	1992	30.00	54-60
1992 Enchanted Clock QLX7274	Yr.Iss.	1992	30.00	48-60
1992 Feathered Friends QLX7091	Yr.Iss.	1992	14.00	28-30
1992 Forest Frolics (4th Ed.) QLX7254	Yr.Iss.	1992	28.00	52-65
1992 Good Sledding Ahead QLX7244	Yr.Iss.	1992	28.00	42-58
1992 Lighting the Way QLX7231	Yr.Iss.	1992	18.00	31-50
1992 Look! It's Santa QLX7094	Yr.Iss.	1992	14.00	30-50
1992 Nut Sweet Nut QLX7081	Yr.Iss.	1992	10.00	21
1992 Out First Christmas Together QLX7221	Yr.Iss.	1992	20.00	39-45
1992 PEANUTS (2nd Ed.) QLX7214	Yr.Iss.	1992	18.00	49-64
1992 Santa Special QLX7167	Yr.Iss.	1992	40.00	80
1992 Santa Sub QLX7321	Yr.Iss.	1992	18.00	34-40
1992 Santa's Answering Machine QLX7241	Yr.Iss.	1992	22.00	41-44
1992 Under Construction QLX7324	Yr.Iss.	1992	18.00	36-40
1992 Watch Owls QLX7084	Yr.Iss.	1992	12.00	25-30
1992 Yuletide Rider QLX7314	Yr.Iss.	1992	28.00	53-60

1992 Miniature Ornaments - Keepsake

YEAR ISSUE	EDITION LIMIT	YEAR RETD.	ISSUE PRICE	*QUOTE U.S.$
1992 A+ Teacher QXM5511	Yr.Iss.	1992	3.75	5-8
1992 Angelic Harpist QXM5524	Yr.Iss.	1992	4.50	12-15
1992 Baby's First Christmas QXM5494	Yr.Iss.	1992	4.50	17-20
1992 The Bearymores(1st Ed.) QXM5544	Yr.Iss.	1992	5.75	10-18
1992 Black-Capped Chickadee QXM5484	Yr.Iss.	1992	3.00	12-15
1992 Box Car (4th Ed.) Noel R.R. QXM5441	Yr.Iss.	1992	7.00	14-24
1992 Bright Stringers QXM5841	Yr.Iss.	1992	3.75	12-15
1992 Buck-A-Roo QXM5814	Yr.Iss.	1992	4.50	6-11
1992 Christmas Bonus QXM5811	Yr.Iss.	1992	3.00	5-8

Collectors' Information Bureau   *Quotes have been rounded up to nearest dollar

YEAR ISSUE	EDITION LIMIT	YEAR RETD.	ISSUE PRICE	*QUOTE U.S.$
1992 Christmas Copter QXM5844	Yr.Iss.	1992	5.75	14
1992 Church (5th Ed.) Old English V. QXM5384	Yr.Iss.	1992	7.00	24-35
1992 Coca-Cola Santa QXM5884	Yr.Iss.	1992	5.75	7-17
1992 Cool Uncle Sam QXM5561	Yr.Iss.	1992	3.00	15-18
1992 Cozy Kayak QXM5551	Yr.Iss.	1992	3.75	10-14
1992 Fast Finish QXM5301	Yr.Iss.	1992	3.75	12
1992 Feeding Time QXM5481	Yr.Iss.	1992	5.75	12-15
1992 Friendly Tin Soldier QXM5874	Yr.Iss.	1992	4.50	14-18
1992 Friends Are Tops QXM5521	Yr.Iss.	1992	4.50	10-12
1992 Gerbil Inc. QXM5924	Yr.Iss.	1992	3.75	8-11
1992 Going Places QXM5871	Yr.Iss.	1992	3.75	9
1992 Grandchild's First Christmas QXM5501	Yr.Iss.	1992	5.75	12-15
1992 Grandma QXM5514	Yr.Iss.	1992	4.50	3-15
1992 Harmony Trio-Set/3 QXM5471	Yr.Iss.	1992	11.75	12-21
1992 Hickory, Dickory, Dock QXM5861	Yr.Iss.	1992	3.75	13-15
1992 Holiday Holly QXM5364	Yr.Iss.	1992	9.75	15-21
1992 Holiday Splash QXM5834	Yr.Iss.	1992	5.75	12
1992 Hoop It Up QXM5831	Yr.Iss.	1992	4.50	5-13
1992 Inside Story QXM5881	Yr.Iss.	1992	7.25	14-19
1992 Kittens in Toyland (5th Ed.) QXM5391	Yr.Iss.	1992	4.50	14-18
1992 The Kringles (4th Ed.) QXM5381	Yr.Iss.	1992	6.00	16-19
1992 Little Town of Bethlehem QXM5864	Yr.Iss.	1992	3.00	17-23
1992 Minted for Santa QXM5854	Yr.Iss.	1992	3.75	12-15
1992 Mom QXM5504	Yr.Iss.	1992	4.50	12-15
1992 Nature's Angels (3rd Ed.) QXM5451	Yr.Iss.	1992	4.50	13-20
1992 The Night Before Christmas QXM5541	Yr.Iss.	1992	13.75	15-28
1992 Perfect Balance QXM5571	Yr.Iss.	1992	3.00	10-14
1992 Polar Polka QXM5534	Yr.Iss.	1992	4.50	14
1992 Puppet Show QXM5574	Yr.Iss.	1992	3.00	10-13
1992 Rocking Horse (5th Ed.) QXM5454	Yr.Iss.	1992	4.50	16-24
1992 Sew Sew Tiny (set/6) QXM5794	Yr.Iss.	1992	29.00	35-65
1992 Ski For Two QXM5821	Yr.Iss.	1992	4.50	10-15
1992 Snowshoe Bunny QXM5564	Yr.Iss.	1992	3.75	8-13
1992 Snug Kitty QXM5554	Yr.Iss.	1992	3.75	5-14
1992 Spunky Monkey QXM5921	Yr.Iss.	1992	3.00	12-15
1992 Thimble Bells (3rd Ed.) QXM5461	Yr.Iss.	1992	6.00	15-18
1992 Visions Of Acorns QXM5851	Yr.Iss.	1992	4.50	12-15
1992 Wee Three Kings QXM5531	Yr.Iss.	1992	5.75	17-23
1992 Woodland Babies (2nd Ed.) QXM5444	Yr.Iss.	1992	6.00	16

1992 New Attractions - Keepsake

YEAR ISSUE	EDITION LIMIT	YEAR RETD.	ISSUE PRICE	*QUOTE U.S.$
1992 Bear Bell Champ QX5071	Yr.Iss.	1992	7.75	16-30
1992 Caboose QX5321	Yr.Iss.	1992	9.75	8-29
1992 Cheerful Santa QX5154	Yr.Iss.	1992	9.75	8-29
1992 Coal Car QX5401	Yr.Iss.	1992	9.75	14-19
1992 Cool Fliers QX5474	Yr.Iss.	1992	10.75	20-25
1992 Deck the Hogs QX5204	Yr.Iss.	1992	8.75	17-22
1992 Down-Under Holiday QX5144	Yr.Iss.	1992	7.75	18-23
1992 Egg Nog Nest QX5121	Yr.Iss.	1992	7.75	14-18
1992 Eric the Baker QX5244	Yr.Iss.	1992	8.75	8-18
1992 Feliz Navidad QX5181	Yr.Iss.	1992	6.75	17-23
1992 Franz the Artist QX5261	Yr.Iss.	1992	8.75	19-25
1992 Freida the Animals' Friend QX5264	Yr.Iss.	1992	8.75	8-19
1992 Fun on a Big Scale QX5134	Yr.Iss.	1992	10.75	14-24
1992 GARFIELD QX5374	Yr.Iss.	1992	7.75	15-25
1992 Genius at Work QX5371	Yr.Iss.	1992	10.75	20-22
1992 Golf's a Ball QX5984	Yr.Iss.	1992	6.75	14-30
1992 Gone Wishin' QX5171	Yr.Iss.	1992	8.75	19
1992 Green Thumb Santa QX5101	Yr.Iss.	1992	7.75	15-18
1992 Hello-Ho-Ho QX5141	Yr.Iss.	1992	9.75	17-23
1992 Holiday Teatime QX5431	Yr.Iss.	1992	14.75	27-30
1992 Holiday Wishes QX5131	Yr.Iss.	1992	7.75	8-17
1992 Honest George QX5064	Yr.Iss.	1992	7.75	12-16
1992 Jesus Loves Me QX3024	Yr.Iss.	1992	7.75	12-14
1992 Locomotive QX5311	Yr.Iss.	1992	9.75	25-40
1992 Loving Shepherd QX5151	Yr.Iss.	1992	7.75	14-17
1992 Ludwig the Musician QX5281	Yr.Iss.	1992	8.75	14-23
1992 Mary Engelbreit Santa Jolly Wolly QX5224	Yr.Iss.	1992	7.75	5-8
1992 Max the Tailor QX5251	Yr.Iss.	1992	8.75	20-23
1992 Memories to Cherish QX5161	Yr.Iss.	1992	10.75	20
1992 Merry "Swiss" Mouse QX5114	Yr.Iss.	1992	7.75	14-16
1992 Norman Rockwell Art QX2224	Yr.Iss.	1992	5.00	17-25
1992 North Pole Fire Fighter QX5104	Yr.Iss.	1992	9.75	21
1992 Otto the Carpenter QX5254	Yr.Iss.	1992	8.75	19-23
1992 Owl QX5614	Yr.Iss.	1992	9.75	15-28
1992 Partridge In a Pear Tree QX5234	Yr.Iss.	1992	8.75	18-29
1992 PEANUTS® QX2244	Yr.Iss.	1992	5.00	10-23

YEAR ISSUE	EDITION LIMIT	YEAR RETD.	ISSUE PRICE	*QUOTE U.S.$
1992 Please Pause Here QX5291	Yr.Iss.	1992	14.75	20-32
1992 Rapid Delivery QX5094	Yr.Iss.	1992	8.75	20-25
1992 A Santa-Full! QX5991		1992	9.75	32-40
1992 Santa's Hook Shot QX5434	Yr.Iss.	1992	12.75	19-28
1992 Santa's Roundup QX5084	Yr.Iss.	1992	8.75	20-25
1992 Silver Star QX5324	Yr.Iss.	1992	28.00	55-68
1992 Skiing 'Round QX5214	Yr.Iss.	1992	8.75	15-19
1992 SNOOPY®and WOODSTOCK QX5954	Yr.Iss.	1992	8.75	16-50
1992 Spirit of Christmas Stress QX5231	Yr.Iss.	1992	8.75	10-18
1992 Stock Car QX5314	Yr.Iss.	1992	9.75	19-25
1992 Tasty Christmas QX5994	Yr.Iss.	1992	9.75	19-25
1992 Toboggan Tail QX5459	Yr.Iss.	1992	7.75	15-20
1992 Tread Bear QX5091	Yr.Iss.	1992	8.75	12-25

1992 Special Edition - Keepsake

YEAR ISSUE	EDITION LIMIT	YEAR RETD.	ISSUE PRICE	*QUOTE U.S.$
1992 Dickens Caroler Bell-Lord Chadwick (3rd Ed.) QX4554	Yr.Iss.	1992	21.75	38-45

1992 Special Issues - Keepsake

YEAR ISSUE	EDITION LIMIT	YEAR RETD.	ISSUE PRICE	*QUOTE U.S.$
1992 Elvis QX562-4	Yr.Iss.	1992	14.75	15-31
1992 Santa Maria QX5074	Yr.Iss.	1992	12.75	10-27
1992 Shuttlecraft Galileo 2400QLX733-1	Yr.Iss.	1992	24.00	31-51

1993 Anniversary Edition - Keepsake

YEAR ISSUE	EDITION LIMIT	YEAR RETD.	ISSUE PRICE	*QUOTE U.S.$
1993 Frosty Friends QX5682	Yr.Iss.	1993	20.00	28-47
1993 Glowing Pewter Wreath QX5302	Yr.Iss.	1993	18.75	22-31
1993 Shopping With Santa QX5675	Yr.Iss.	1993	24.00	32-45
1993 Tannenbaum's Dept. Store QX5612	Yr.Iss.	1993	26.00	25-55

1993 Artists' Favorites - Keepsake

YEAR ISSUE	EDITION LIMIT	YEAR RETD.	ISSUE PRICE	*QUOTE U.S.$
1993 Bird Watcher QX5252	Yr.Iss.	1993	9.75	12-20
1993 Howling Good Time QX5255	Yr.Iss.	1993	9.75	19-23
1993 On Her Toes QX5265	Yr.Iss.	1993	8.75	18
1993 Peek-a-Boo Tree QX5245	Yr.Iss.	1993	10.75	19-22
1993 Wake-Up Call QX5262	Yr.Iss.	1993	8.75	8-22

1993 Collectible Series - Keepsake

YEAR ISSUE	EDITION LIMIT	YEAR RETD.	ISSUE PRICE	*QUOTE U.S.$
1993 1956 Ford Thunderbird (3rd Ed.) QX5275	Yr.Iss.	1993	12.75	20-40
1993 Betsey's Country Christmas (2nd Ed.) QX2062	Yr.Iss.	1993	5.00	15-21
1993 Cozy Home (10th Ed.) QX4175	Yr.Iss.	1993	14.75	34-53
1993 CRAYOLA CRAYON-Bright Shining Castle (5th Ed.) QX4422	Yr.Iss.	1993	11.00	19-33
1993 Fabulous Decade (4th Ed.) QX4475	Yr.Iss.	1993	7.75	8-17
1993 A Fitting Moment (8th Ed.) QX4202	Yr.Iss.	1993	14.75	28-45
1993 Frosty Friends (14th Ed.) QX4142	Yr.Iss.	1993	9.75	26-40
1993 The Gift Bringers-The Magi (5th Ed.) QX2065	Yr.Iss.	1993	5.00	17-20
1993 Happy Haul-idays (15th Ed.) QX4102	Yr.Iss.	1993	14.75	19-40
1993 Heart Of Christmas (4th Ed.) QX4482	Yr.Iss.	1993	14.75	19-30
1993 Heavenly Angels (3rd Ed.) QX4945	Yr.Iss.	1993	7.75	15-18
1993 Humpty-Dumpty (1st Ed.) QX5282	Yr.Iss.	1993	13.75	28-54
1993 Mary's Angels-Ivy (6th Ed.) QX4282	Yr.Iss.	1993	6.75	14-30
1993 Merry Olde Santa (4th Ed.) QX4842	Yr.Iss.	1993	14.75	28-40
1993 Owliver (2nd Ed.) QX5425	Yr.Iss.	1993	7.75	5-16
1993 Peace On Earth-Poland (3rd Ed.) QX5242	Yr.Iss.	1993	11.75	14-25
1993 Peanuts (1st Ed.) QX5315	Yr.Iss.	1993	9.75	30-63
1993 Puppy Love (3rd Ed.) QX5045	Yr.Iss.	1993	7.75	14-40
1993 Reindeer Champs-Blitzen (8th Ed.) QX4331	Yr.Iss.	1993	8.75	21-30
1993 Rocking Horse (13th Ed.) QX4162	Yr.Iss.	1993	10.75	41-50
1993 Ten Lords A-Leaping (10th Ed.) QX3012	Yr.Iss.	1993	6.75	15-25
1993 Tobin Fraley Carousel (2nd Ed.) QX5502	Yr.Iss.	1993	28.00	15-35
1993 U.S. Christmas Stamps (1st Ed.) QX5292	Yr.Iss.	1993	10.75	29-44

1993 Commemoratives - Keepsake

YEAR ISSUE	EDITION LIMIT	YEAR RETD.	ISSUE PRICE	*QUOTE U.S.$
1993 Across the Miles QX5912	Yr.Iss.	1993	8.75	16-20
1993 Anniversary Year QX5972	Yr.Iss.	1993	9.75	18
1993 Apple for Teacher QX5902	Yr.Iss.	1993	7.75	12-16
1993 Baby's First Christmas QX5512	Yr.Iss.	1993	18.75	36-40
1993 Baby's First Christmas QX5515	Yr.Iss.	1993	10.75	21-23
1993 Baby's First Christmas QX5522	Yr.Iss.	1993	7.75	20-25
1993 Baby's First Christmas QX5525	Yr.Iss.	1993	7.75	26-32
1993 Baby's First Christmas-Baby Boy QX2105	Yr.Iss.	1993	4.75	16-20
1993 Baby's First Christmas-Baby Girl QX2092	Yr.Iss.	1993	4.75	12-16
1993 Baby's Second Christmas QX5992	Yr.Iss.	1993	6.75	21-23

YEAR ISSUE	EDITION LIMIT	YEAR RETD.	ISSUE PRICE	*QUOTE U.S.$
1993 Brother QX5542	Yr.Iss.	1993	6.75	13
1993 A Child's Christmas QX5882	Yr.Iss.	1993	9.75	10-20
1993 Child's Fifth Christmas QX5222	Yr.Iss.	1993	6.75	18-20
1993 Child's Fourth Christmas QX5215	Yr.Iss.	1993	6.75	15-20
1993 Child's Third Christmas QX5995	Yr.Iss.	1993	6.75	17-20
1993 Coach QX5935	Yr.Iss.	1993	6.75	14
1993 Dad QX5855	Yr.Iss.	1993	7.75	10-17
1993 Dad-to-Be QX5532	Yr.Iss.	1993	6.75	5-16
1993 Daughter QX5872	Yr.Iss.	1993	6.75	9-21
1993 Godchild QX5875	Yr.Iss.	1993	8.75	5-18
1993 Grandchild's First Christmas QX5552	Yr.Iss.	1993	6.75	13
1993 Granddaughter QX5635	Yr.Iss.	1993	6.75	18-23
1993 Grandmother QX5665	Yr.Iss.	1993	6.75	13-20
1993 Grandparents QX2085	Yr.Iss.	1993	4.75	10-18
1993 Grandson QX5632	Yr.Iss.	1993	6.75	19-22
1993 Mom and Dad QX5845	Yr.Iss.	1993	9.75	18
1993 Mom QX5852	Yr.Iss.	1993	7.75	17-20
1993 Mom-to-Be QX5535	Yr.Iss.	1993	6.75	15-18
1993 Nephew QX5735	Yr.Iss.	1993	6.75	13
1993 New Home QX5905	Yr.Iss.	1993	7.75	40-50
1993 Niece QX5732	Yr.Iss.	1993	6.75	13
1993 Our Christmas Together QX5942	Yr.Iss.	1993	10.75	12-23
1993 Our Family QX5892	Yr.Iss.	1993	7.75	17-20
1993 Our First Christmas Together QX3015	Yr.Iss.	1993	6.75	17
1993 Our First Christmas Together QX5642	Yr.Iss.	1993	9.75	15-25
1993 Our First Christmas Together QX5952	Yr.Iss.	1993	8.75	16-25
1993 Our First Christmas Together QX5955	Yr.Iss.	1993	18.75	34-38
1993 People Friendly QX5932	Yr.Iss.	1993	8.75	16-18
1993 Sister QX5545	Yr.Iss.	1993	6.75	19-25
1993 Sister to Sister QX5885	Yr.Iss.	1993	9.75	29-54
1993 Son QX5865	Yr.Iss.	1993	6.75	9-18
1993 Special Cat QX5235	Yr.Iss.	1993	7.75	14
1993 Special Dog QX5962	Yr.Iss.	1993	7.75	15-18
1993 Star Teacher QX5645	Yr.Iss.	1993	5.75	13
1993 Strange and Wonderful Love QX5965	Yr.Iss.	1993	8.75	5-16
1993 To My Grandma QX5555	Yr.Iss.	1993	7.75	10-16
1993 Top Banana QX5925	Yr.Iss.	1993	7.75	18-20
1993 Warm and Special Friends QX5895	Yr.Iss.	1993	10.75	16-23

1993 Easter Ornaments - Keepsake

YEAR ISSUE	EDITION LIMIT	YEAR RETD.	ISSUE PRICE	*QUOTE U.S.$
1993 Easter Parade (2nd Ed.) QEO8325	Yr.Iss.	1993	6.75	10-17
1993 Egg in Sports (2nd Ed.) QEO8332	Yr.Iss.	1993	6.75	6-18
1993 Springtime Bonnets (1st Ed.) QEO8322	Yr.Iss.	1993	7.75	16-26

1993 Keepsake Collector's Club - Keepsake

YEAR ISSUE	EDITION LIMIT	YEAR RETD.	ISSUE PRICE	*QUOTE U.S.$
1993 It's In The Mail QXC5272	Yr.Iss.	1993	10.00	12-21
1993 Trimmed With Memories QXC5432	Yr.Iss.	1993	12.00	30-38

1993 Keepsake Magic Ornaments - Keepsake

YEAR ISSUE	EDITION LIMIT	YEAR RETD.	ISSUE PRICE	*QUOTE U.S.$
1993 Baby's First Christmas QLX7365	Yr.Iss.	1993	22.00	22-45
1993 Bells Are Ringing QLX7402	Yr.Iss.	1993	28.00	33-65
1993 Chris Mouse Flight (9th Ed.) QLX7152	Yr.Iss.	1993	12.00	15-38
1993 Dog's Best Friend QLX7172	Yr.Iss.	1993	12.00	15-25
1993 Dollhouse Dreams QLX7372	Yr.Iss.	1993	22.00	35-50
1993 Forest Frolics (5th Ed.) QLX7165	Yr.Iss.	1993	25.00	29-53
1993 Home On The Range QLX7395	Yr.Iss.	1993	32.00	39-75
1993 The Lamplighter QLX7192	Yr.Iss.	1993	18.00	36-43
1993 Last-Minute Shopping QLX7385	Yr.Iss.	1993	28.00	41-60
1993 North Pole Merrython QLX7392	Yr.Iss.	1993	25.00	46-50
1993 Our First Christmas Together QLX7355	Yr.Iss.	1993	20.00	39-43
1993 PEANUTS (3rd Ed.) QLX7155	Yr.Iss.	1993	18.00	40-50
1993 Radio News Flash QLX7362	Yr.Iss.	1993	22.00	31-50
1993 Raiding The Fridge QLX7185	Yr.Iss.	1993	16.00	28-41
1993 Road Runner and Wile E. Coyote QLX7415	Yr.Iss.	1993	30.00	49-68
1993 Santa's Snow-Getter QLX7352	Yr.Iss.	1993	18.00	29-39
1993 Santa's Workshop QLX7375	Yr.Iss.	1993	28.00	34-60
1993 Song Of The Chimes QLX7405	Yr.Iss.	1993	25.00	50-55
1993 Winnie The Pooh QLX7422	Yr.Iss.	1993	24.00	23-51

1993 Limited Edition Ornaments - Keepsake

YEAR ISSUE	EDITION LIMIT	YEAR RETD.	ISSUE PRICE	*QUOTE U.S.$
1993 Gentle Tidings QXC5442	17,500	1993	25.00	40-47
1993 Sharing Christmas QXC5435	16,500	1993	20.00	30-41

1993 Miniature Ornaments - Keepsake

YEAR ISSUE	EDITION LIMIT	YEAR RETD.	ISSUE PRICE	*QUOTE U.S.$
1993 Baby's First Christmas QXM5145	Yr.Iss.	1993	5.75	10-15
1993 The Bearymores (2nd Ed.) QXM5125	Yr.Iss.	1993	5.75	14-17
1993 Cheese Please QXM4072	Yr.Iss.	1993	3.75	8
1993 Christmas Castle QXM4085	Yr.Iss.	1993	5.75	9-13
1993 Cloisonne Snowflake QXM4012	Yr.Iss.	1993	9.75	15-20
1993 Country Fiddling QXM4062	Yr.Iss.	1993	3.75	10
1993 Crystal Angel QXM4015	Yr.Iss.	1993	9.75	30-54
1993 Ears To Pals QXM4075	Yr.Iss.	1993	3.75	7-9
1993 Flatbed Car (5th Ed.) QXM5105	Yr.Iss.	1993	7.00	20-25
1993 Grandma QXM5162	Yr.Iss.	1993	4.50	10-13
1993 I Dream Of Santa QXM4055	Yr.Iss.	1993	3.75	6-11
1993 Into The Woods QXM4045	Yr.Iss.	1993	3.75	6-8
1993 The Kringles (5th Ed.) QXM5135	Yr.Iss.	1993	5.75	8-14
1993 Learning To Skate QXM4122	Yr.Iss.	1993	3.00	8-11
1993 Lighting A Path QXM4115	Yr.Iss.	1993	3.00	7-9
1993 March Of The Teddy Bears (1st Ed.) QXM2403	Yr.Iss.	1993	4.50	13-15
1993 Merry Mascot QXM4042	Yr.Iss.	1993	3.75	7-9
1993 Mom QXM5155	Yr.Iss.	1993	4.50	5-11
1993 Monkey Melody QXM4092	Yr.Iss.	1993	5.75	13
1993 Nature's Angels (4th Ed.) QXM5122	Yr.Iss.	1993	4.50	14-20
1993 The Night Before Christmas (2nd Ed.) QXM5115	Yr.Iss.	1993	4.50	8-16
1993 North Pole Fire Truck QXM4105	Yr.Iss.	1993	4.75	6-11
1993 On The Road (1st Ed.) QXM4002	Yr.Iss.	1993	5.75	10-18
1993 Pear-Shaped Tones QXM4052	Yr.Iss.	1993	3.75	5-8
1993 Pull Out A Plum QXM4095	Yr.Iss.	1993	5.75	10-13
1993 Refreshing Flight QXM4112	Yr.Iss.	1993	5.75	13
1993 Rocking Horse (6th Ed.) QXM5112	Yr.Iss.	1993	4.50	10-14
1993 'Round The Mountain QXM4025	Yr.Iss.	1993	7.25	11-17
1993 Secret Pals QXM5172	Yr.Iss.	1993	3.75	8-10
1993 Snuggle Birds QXM5182	Yr.Iss.	1993	5.75	10-14
1993 Special Friends QXM5165	Yr.Iss.	1993	4.50	9-14
1993 Thimble Bells (4th Ed.) QXM5142	Yr.Iss.	1993	5.75	10-54
1993 Tiny Green Thumbs, set/6, QXM4032	Yr.Iss.	1993	29.00	32-54
1993 Toy Shop (6th Ed.) QXM5132	Yr.Iss.	1993	7.00	16-22
1993 Visions Of Sugarplums QXM4022	Yr.Iss.	1993	7.25	9-15
1993 Woodland Babies (3rd Ed.) QXM5102	Yr.Iss.	1993	5.75	6-14

1993 New Attractions - Keepsake

YEAR ISSUE	EDITION LIMIT	YEAR RETD.	ISSUE PRICE	*QUOTE U.S.$
1993 Beary Gifted QX5762	Yr.Iss.	1993	7.75	15-18
1993 Big on Gardening QX5842	Yr.Iss.	1993	9.75	18
1993 Big Roller QX5352	Yr.Iss.	1993	8.75	16-19
1993 Bowling For ZZZ's QX5565	Yr.Iss.	1993	7.75	8-18
1993 Bugs Bunny QX5412	Yr.Iss.	1993	8.75	15-24
1993 Caring Nurse QX5785	Yr.Iss.	1993	6.75	12-18
1993 Christmas Break QX5825	Yr.Iss.	1993	7.75	18-25
1993 Clever Cookie QX5662	Yr.Iss.	1993	7.75	16-30
1993 Curly 'n' Kingly QX5285	Yr.Iss.	1993	10.75	20-25
1993 Dunkin' Roo QX5575	Yr.Iss.	1993	7.75	8-15
1993 Eeyore QX5712	Yr.Iss.	1993	9.75	18-21
1993 Elmer Fudd QX5495	Yr.Iss.	1993	8.75	12-19
1993 Faithful Fire Fighter QX5782	Yr.Iss.	1993	7.75	8-20
1993 Feliz Navidad QX5365	Yr.Iss.	1993	9.75	17-25
1993 Fills the Bill QX5572	Yr.Iss.	1993	8.75	10-18
1993 Great Connections QX5402	Yr.Iss.	1993	10.75	18-23
1993 He Is Born QX5362	Yr.Iss.	1993	9.75	24-40
1993 High Top-Purr QX5332	Yr.Iss.	1993	8.75	12-24
1993 Home For Christmas QX5562	Yr.Iss.	1993	7.75	15-18
1993 Icicle Bicycle QX5835	Yr.Iss.	1993	9.75	15-18
1993 Kanga and Roo QX5672	Yr.Iss.	1993	9.75	13-23
1993 Little Drummer Boy QX5372	Yr.Iss.	1993	8.75	12-24
1993 Look For Wonder QX5685	Yr.Iss.	1993	12.75	16-28
1993 Lou Rankin Polar Bear QX5745	Yr.Iss.	1993	9.75	15-22
1993 Makin' Music QX5325	Yr.Iss.	1993	9.75	15-18
1993 Making Waves QX5775	Yr.Iss.	1993	9.75	22-27
1993 Mary Engelbreit QX2075	Yr.Iss.	1993	5.00	14-18
1993 Maxine QX5385	Yr.Iss.	1993	8.75	16-33
1993 One-Elf Marching Band QX5342	Yr.Iss.	1993	12.75	25-28
1993 Owl QX5695	Yr.Iss.	1993	9.75	13-23
1993 PEANUTS QX2072	Yr.Iss.	1993	5.00	15-30
1993 Peep Inside QX5322	Yr.Iss.	1993	13.75	25-30
1993 Perfect Match QX5772	Yr.Iss.	1993	8.75	5-18
1993 The Pink Panther QX5755	Yr.Iss.	1993	12.75	16-29
1993 Playful Pals QX5742	Yr.Iss.	1993	14.75	20-30
1993 Popping Good Times QX5392	Yr.Iss.	1993	14.75	27-30
1993 Porky Pig QX5652	Yr.Iss.	1993	8.75	12-20
1993 Putt-Putt Penguin QX5795	Yr.Iss.	1993	9.75	12-24
1993 Quick As A Fox QX5792	Yr.Iss.	1993	8.75	10-19

YEAR ISSUE	EDITION LIMIT	YEAR RETD.	ISSUE PRICE	*QUOTE U.S.$
1993 Rabbit QX5702	Yr.Iss.	1993	9.75	13-20
1993 Ready For Fun QX5124	Yr.Iss.	1993	7.75	16-20
1993 Room For One More QX5382	Yr.Iss.	1993	8.75	27-53
1993 Silvery Noel QX5305	Yr.Iss.	1993	12.75	15-36
1993 Smile! It's Christmas QX5335	Yr.Iss.	1993	9.75	18
1993 Snow Bear Angel QX5355	Yr.Iss.	1993	7.75	16
1993 Snowbird QX5765	Yr.Iss.	1993	7.75	5-17
1993 Snowy Hideaway QX5312	Yr.Iss.	1993	9.75	18
1993 Star Of Wonder QX5982	Yr.Iss.	1993	6.75	19-32
1993 Superman QX5752	Yr.Iss.	1993	12.75	19-47
1993 The Swat Team QX5395	Yr.Iss.	1993	12.75	22-30
1993 Sylvester and Tweety QX5405	Yr.Iss.	1993	9.75	25-34
1993 That's Entertainment QX5345	Yr.Iss.	1993	8.75	12-21
1993 Tigger and Piglet QX5705	Yr.Iss.	1993	9.75	16-52
1993 Tin Airplane QX5622	Yr.Iss.	1993	7.75	18-30
1993 Tin Blimp QX5625	Yr.Iss.	1993	7.75	12-16
1993 Tin Hot Air Balloon QX5615	Yr.Iss.	1993	7.75	17-25
1993 Water Bed Snooze QX5375	Yr.Iss.	1993	9.75	15-21
1993 Winnie the Pooh QX5715	Yr.Iss.	1993	9.75	16-33

1993 Showcase Folk Art Americana - Keepsake

1993 Angel in Flight QK1052	Yr.Iss.	1993	15.75	15-50
1993 Polar Bear Adventure QK1055	Yr.Iss.	1993	15.00	50-65
1993 Riding in the Woods QK1065	Yr.Iss.	1993	15.75	60-75
1993 Riding the Wind QK1045	Yr.Iss.	1993	15.75	39-65
1993 Santa Claus QK1072	Yr.Iss.	1993	16.75	145-225

1993 Showcase Holiday Enchantment - Keepsake

1993 Angelic Messengers QK1032	Yr.Iss.	1993	13.75	16-30
1993 Bringing Home the Tree QK1042	Yr.Iss.	1993	13.75	16-25
1993 Journey to the Forest QK1012	Yr.Iss.	1993	13.75	16-33
1993 The Magi QK1025	Yr.Iss.	1993	13.75	16-30
1993 Visions of Sugarplums QK1005	Yr.Iss.	1993	13.75	16-35

1993 Showcase Old-World Silver - Keepsake

1993 Silver Dove of Peace QK1075	Yr.Iss.	1993	24.75	25-35
1993 Silver Santa QK1092	Yr.Iss.	1993	24.75	25-50
1993 Silver Sleigh QK1082	Yr.Iss.	1993	24.75	32-60
1993 Silver Stars and Holly QK1085	Yr.Iss.	1993	24.75	22-35

1993 Showcase Portraits in Bisque - Keepsake

1993 Christmas Feast QK1152	Yr.Iss.	1993	15.75	25-31
1993 Joy of Sharing QK1142	Yr.Iss.	1993	15.75	25-32
1993 Mistletoe Kiss QK1145	Yr.Iss.	1993	15.75	20-30
1993 Norman Rockwell-Filling the Stockings QK1155	Yr.Iss.	1993	15.75	27-35
1993 Norman Rockwell-Jolly Postman QK1142	Yr.Iss.	1993	15.75	27-33

1993 Special Editions - Keepsake

1993 Dickens Caroler Bell-Lady Daphne (4th Ed.) QX5505	Yr.Iss.	1993	21.75	32-41
1993 Julianne and Teddy QX5295	Yr.Iss.	1993	21.75	45-55

1993 Special Issues - Keepsake

1993 Holiday Barbie (1st Ed.) QX572-5	Yr.Iss.	1993	14.75	95-180
1993 Messages of Christmas QLX747-6	Yr.Iss.	1993	35.00	46-58
1993 Star Trek® The Next Generation QLX741-2	Yr.Iss.	1993	24.00	29-65

1994 Artists' Favorites - Keepsake

1994 Cock-a-Doodle Christmas QX5396	Yr.Iss.	1994	8.95	10-30
1994 Happy Birthday Jesus QX5423	Yr.Iss.	1994	12.95	16-20
1994 Keep on Mowin' QX5413	Yr.Iss.	1994	8.95	15-30
1994 Kitty's Catamaran QX5416	Yr.Iss.	1994	10.95	17-24
1994 Making It Bright QX5403	Yr.Iss.	1994	8.95	14-20

1994 Collectible Series - Keepsake

1994 1957 Chevy (4th Ed.) QX5422	Yr.Iss.	1994	12.95	13-33
1994 Baseball Heroes-Babe Ruth (1st Ed.) QX5323	Yr.Iss.	1994	12.95	19-60
1994 Betsey's Country Christmas (3rd Ed.) QX2403	Yr.Iss.	1994	5.00	13-17
1994 Cat Naps (1st Ed.) QX5313	Yr.Iss.	1994	7.95	15-50
1994 CRAYOLA CRAYON-Bright Playful Colors (6th Ed.) QX5273	Yr.Iss.	1994	10.95	24-30
1994 Fabulous Decade (5th Ed.) QX5263	Yr.Iss.	1994	7.95	11-24
1994 Frosty Friends (15th Ed.) QX5293	Yr.Iss.	1994	9.95	14-40
1994 Handwarming Present (9th Ed.) QX5283	Yr.Iss.	1994	14.95	19-40
1994 Heart of Christmas (5th Ed.) QX5266	Yr.Iss.	1994	14.95	15-30
1994 Hey Diddle Diddle (2nd Ed.) QX5213	Yr.Iss.	1994	13.95	20-47
1994 Makin' Tractor Tracks (16th Ed.) QX5296	Yr.Iss.	1994	14.95	36-55

YEAR ISSUE	EDITION LIMIT	YEAR RETD.	ISSUE PRICE	*QUOTE U.S.$
1994 Mary's Angels-Jasmine (7th Ed.) QX5276	Yr.Iss.	1994	6.95	12-25
1994 Merry Olde Santa (5th Ed.) QX5256	Yr.Iss.	1994	14.95	24-35
1994 Murray Blue Champion (1st Ed.) QX5426	Yr.Iss.	1994	13.95	29-66
1994 Neighborhood Drugstore (11th Ed.) QX5286	Yr.Iss.	1994	14.95	24-40
1994 Owliver (3rd Ed.) QX5226	Yr.Iss.	1994	7.95	14-18
1994 PEANUTS-Lucy (2nd Ed.) QX5203	Yr.Iss.	1994	9.95	10-30
1994 Pipers Piping (11th Ed.) QX3183	Yr.Iss.	1994	6.95	16-23
1994 Puppy Love (4th Ed.) QX5253	Yr.Iss.	1994	7.95	12-25
1994 Rocking Horse (14th Ed.) QX5016	Yr.Iss.	1994	10.95	19-35
1994 Tobin Fraley Carousel (3rd Ed.) QX5223	Yr.Iss.	1994	28.00	28-60
1994 Xmas Stamp (2nd Ed.) QX5206	Yr.Iss.	1994	10.95	10-23
1994 Yuletide Central (1st Ed.) QX5316	Yr.Iss.	1994	18.95	24-36

1994 Commemoratives - Keepsake

1994 Across the Miles QX5656	Yr.Iss.	1994	8.95	17
1994 Anniversary Year QX5683	Yr.Iss.	1994	10.95	16-20
1994 Baby's First Christmas Photo QX5636	Yr.Iss.	1994	7.95	16-19
1994 Baby's First Christmas QX5633	Yr.Iss.	1994	18.95	25-40
1994 Baby's First Christmas QX5713	Yr.Iss.	1994	7.95	21-28
1994 Baby's First Christmas QX5743	Yr.Iss.	1994	12.95	17-27
1994 Baby's First Christmas-Baby Boy QX2436	Yr.Iss.	1994	5.00	13
1994 Baby's First Christmas-Baby Girl QX2433	Yr.Iss.	1994	5.00	12-14
1994 Baby's Second Christmas QX5716	Yr.Iss.	1994	7.95	16-21
1994 Brother QX5516	Yr.Iss.	1994	6.95	15
1994 Child's Fifth Christmas QX5733	Yr.Iss.	1994	6.95	17-22
1994 Child's Fourth Christmas QX5726	Yr.Iss.	1994	6.95	17-23
1994 Child's Third Christmas QX5723	Yr.Iss.	1994	6.95	17-21
1994 Dad QX5463	Yr.Iss.	1994	7.95	17
1994 Dad-To-Be QX5473	Yr.Iss.	1994	7.95	10-20
1994 Daughter QX5623	Yr.Iss.	1994	6.95	10-16
1994 Friendly Push QX5686	Yr.Iss.	1994	8.95	14-18
1994 Godchild QX4453	Yr.Iss.	1994	8.95	14-25
1994 Godparents QX2423	Yr.Iss.	1994	5.00	16-23
1994 Grandchild's First Christmas QX5676	Yr.Iss.	1994	7.95	13-18
1994 Granddaughter QX5523	Yr.Iss.	1994	6.95	18-22
1994 Grandma Photo QX5613	Yr.Iss.	1994	6.95	15
1994 Grandmother QX5673	Yr.Iss.	1994	7.95	18-20
1994 Grandpa QX5616	Yr.Iss.	1994	7.95	17-20
1994 Grandparents QX2426	Yr.Iss.	1994	5.00	12-17
1994 Grandson QX5526	Yr.Iss.	1994	6.95	17-22
1994 Mom and Dad QX5666	Yr.Iss.	1994	9.95	19-25
1994 Mom QX5466	Yr.Iss.	1994	7.95	12-17
1994 Mom-To-Be QX5506	Yr.Iss.	1994	7.95	14-18
1994 Nephew QX5546	Yr.Iss.	1994	7.95	15-17
1994 New Home QX5663	Yr.Iss.	1994	8.95	18-20
1994 Niece QX5543	Yr.Iss.	1994	7.95	12-16
1994 Our Family QX5576	Yr.Iss.	1994	7.95	16-20
1994 Our First Christmas Together Photo QX5653	Yr.Iss.	1994	8.95	18-20
1994 Our First Christmas Together QX3186	Yr.Iss.	1994	6.95	13-17
1994 Our First Christmas Together QX4816	Yr.Iss.	1994	9.95	18-20
1994 Our First Christmas Together QX5643	Yr.Iss.	1994	9.95	18-25
1994 Our First Christmas Together QX5706	Yr.Iss.	1994	18.95	21-40
1994 Secret Santa QX5736	Yr.Iss.	1994	7.95	8-18
1994 Sister QX5513	Yr.Iss.	1994	6.95	16-20
1994 Sister to Sister QX5533	Yr.Iss.	1994	9.95	16-25
1994 Son QX5626	Yr.Iss.	1994	6.95	15-18
1994 Special Cat QX5606	Yr.Iss.	1994	7.95	12-16
1994 Special Dog QX5603	Yr.Iss.	1994	7.95	7-16
1994 Thick 'N' Thin QX5693	Yr.Iss.	1994	10.95	13-23
1994 Tou Can Love QX5646	Yr.Iss.	1994	8.95	14-18

1994 Easter Ornaments - Keepsake

1994 Baby's First Easter QEO8153	Yr.Iss.	1994	6.75	8-18
1994 Carrot Trimmers QEO8226	Yr.Iss.	1994	5.00	5-20
1994 CRAYOLA CRAYON-Colorful Spring QEO8166	Yr.Iss.	1994	7.75	18-28
1994 Daughter QEO8156	Yr.Iss.	1994	5.75	6-15
1994 Divine Duet QEO8183	Yr.Iss.	1994	6.75	16
1994 Easter Art Show QEO8193	Yr.Iss.	1994	7.75	17
1994 Egg Car (1st Ed.) QEO8093	Yr.Iss.	1994	7.75	24-35
1994 Golf (3rd Ed.) QEO8133	Yr.Iss.	1994	6.75	15-19

ORNAMENTS

YEAR ISSUE	EDITION LIMIT	YEAR RETD.	ISSUE PRICE	*QUOTE U.S.$
1994 Horn (3rd Ed.) QEO8136	Yr.Iss.	1994	6.75	14-19
1994 Joyful Lamb QEO8206	Yr.Iss.	1994	5.75	15
1994 PEANUTS QEO8176	Yr.Iss.	1994	7.75	20-50
1994 Peeping Out QEO8203	Yr.Iss.	1994	6.75	16
1994 Riding a Breeze QEO8213	Yr.Iss.	1994	5.75	15
1994 Son QEO8163	Yr.Iss.	1994	5.75	6-14
1994 Springtime Bonnets (2nd Ed.) QEO8096	Yr.Iss.	1994	7.75	15-25
1994 Sunny Bunny Garden, (Set/3) QEO8146	Yr.Iss.	1994	15.00	15-28
1994 Sweet as Sugar QEO8086	Yr.Iss.	1994	8.75	8-20
1994 Sweet Easter Wishes Tender Touches QEO8196	Yr.Iss.	1994	8.75	19-25
1994 Treetop Cottage QEO8186	Yr.Iss.	1994	9.75	19
1994 Yummy Recipe QEO8143	Yr.Iss.	1994	7.75	6-19

1994 Keepsake Collector's Club - Keepsake

YEAR ISSUE	EDITION LIMIT	YEAR RETD.	ISSUE PRICE	*QUOTE U.S.$
1994 First Hello QXC4846	Yr.Iss.	1994	5.00	22-69
1994 Happy Collecting QXC4803	Yr.Iss.	1994	3.00	20-25
1994 Holiday Pursuit QXC4823	Yr.Iss.	1994	11.75	12-22
1994 Mrs. Claus' Cupboard QXC4843	Yr.Iss.	1994	55.00	100-210
1994 On Cloud Nine QXC4853	Yr.Iss.	1994	12.00	17-27
1994 Sweet Bouquet QXC4806	Yr.Iss.	1994	8.50	12-22
1994 Tilling Time QXC8256	Yr.Iss.	1994	5.00	20-68

1994 Keepsake Magic Ornaments - Keepsake

YEAR ISSUE	EDITION LIMIT	YEAR RETD.	ISSUE PRICE	*QUOTE U.S.$
1994 Away in a Manager QLX7383	Yr.Iss.	1994	16.00	29-40
1994 Baby's First Christmas QLX7466	Yr.Iss.	1994	20.00	24-45
1994 Candy Cane Lookout QLX7376	Yr.Iss.	1994	18.00	60-95
1994 Chris Mouse Jelly (10th Ed.) QLX7393	Yr.Iss.	1994	12.00	10-24
1994 Conversations With Santa QLX7426	Yr.Iss.	1994	28.00	15-28
1994 Country Showtime QLX7416	Yr.Iss.	1994	22.00	28-45
1994 The Eagle Has Landed QLX7486	Yr.Iss.	1994	24.00	29-46
1994 Feliz Navidad QLX7433	Yr.Iss.	1994	28.00	39-75
1994 Forest Frolics (6th Ed.) QLX7436	Yr.Iss.	1994	28.00	39-60
1994 Gingerbread Fantasy (Sp. Ed.) QLX7382	Yr.Iss.	1994	44.00	45-97
1994 Kringle Trolley QLX7413	Yr.Iss.	1994	20.00	20-48
1994 Maxine QLX7503	Yr.Iss.	1994	20.00	42-50
1994 PEANUTS (4th Ed.) QLX7406	Yr.Iss.	1994	20.00	40-43
1994 Peekaboo Pup QLX7423	Yr.Iss.	1994	20.00	34-43
1994 Rock Candy Miner QLX7403	Yr.Iss.	1994	20.00	10-36
1994 Santa's Sing-Along QLX7473	Yr.Iss.	1994	24.00	34-59
1994 Tobin Fraley (1st Ed.) QLX7496	Yr.Iss.	1994	32.00	48-75
1994 Very Merry Minutes QLX7443	Yr.Iss.	1994	24.00	43-48
1994 White Christmas QLX7463	Yr.Iss.	1994	28.00	54-75
1994 Winnie the Pooh Parade QLX7493	Yr.Iss.	1994	32.00	45-65

1994 Limited Editions - Keepsake

YEAR ISSUE	EDITION LIMIT	YEAR RETD.	ISSUE PRICE	*QUOTE U.S.$
1994 Jolly Holly Santa QXC4833	N/A	1994	22.00	35-45
1994 Majestic Deer QXC4836	N/A	1994	25.00	35-45

1994 Miniature Ornaments - Keepsake

YEAR ISSUE	EDITION LIMIT	YEAR RETD.	ISSUE PRICE	*QUOTE U.S.$
1994 Babs Bunny QXM4116	Yr.Iss.	1994	5.75	5-12
1994 Baby's First Christmas QXM4003	Yr.Iss.	1994	5.75	5-13
1994 Baking Tiny Treats, (Set/6) QXM4033	Yr.Iss.	1994	29.00	44-60
1994 Beary Perfect Tree QXM4076	Yr.Iss.	1994	4.75	9
1994 The Bearymores (3rd Ed.) QXM5133	Yr.Iss.	1994	5.75	13-17
1994 Buster Bunny QXM5163	Yr.Iss.	1994	5.75	6-12
1994 Centuries of Santa (1st Ed.) QXM5153	Yr.Iss.	1994	6.00	22-25
1994 Corny Elf QXM4063	Yr.Iss.	1994	4.50	6-9
1994 Cute as a Button QXM4103	Yr.Iss.	1994	3.75	12-15
1994 Dazzling Reindeer (Pr. Ed.) QXM4026	Yr.Iss.	1994	9.75	18
1994 Dizzy Devil QXM4133	Yr.Iss.	1994	5.75	5-13
1994 Friends Need Hugs QXM4016	Yr.Iss.	1994	4.50	13-15
1994 Graceful Carousel QXM4056	Yr.Iss.	1994	7.75	10-17
1994 Hamton QXM4126	Yr.Iss.	1994	5.75	9-12
1994 Hat Shop (7th Ed.) QXM5143	Yr.Iss.	1994	7.00	7-17
1994 Have a Cookie QXM5166	Yr.Iss.	1994	5.75	12-20
1994 Hearts A-Sail QXM4006	Yr.Iss.	1994	5.75	10-13
1994 Jolly Visitor QXM4053	Yr.Iss.	1994	5.75	8-16
1994 Jolly Wolly Snowman QXM4093	Yr.Iss.	1994	3.75	12-15
1994 Journey to Bethlehem QXM4036	Yr.Iss.	1994	5.75	14-18
1994 Just My Size QXM4086	Yr.Iss.	1994	3.75	9-12
1994 Love Was Born QXM4043	Yr.Iss.	1994	4.50	9-13
1994 March of the Teddy Bears (2nd Ed.) QXM5106	Yr.Iss.	1994	4.50	13-14
1994 Melodic Cherub QXM4066	Yr.Iss.	1994	3.75	6-10
1994 A Merry Flight QXM4073	Yr.Iss.	1994	5.75	6-12
1994 Mom QXM4013	Yr.Iss.	1994	4.50	5-9
1994 Nature's Angels (5th Ed.) QXM5126	Yr.Iss.	1994	4.50	6-12

YEAR ISSUE	EDITION LIMIT	YEAR RETD.	ISSUE PRICE	*QUOTE U.S.$
1994 Night Before Christmas (3rd Ed.) QXM5123	Yr.Iss.	1994	4.50	7-13
1994 Noah's Ark (Sp. Ed.) QXM4106	Yr.Iss.	1994	24.50	39-56
1994 Nutcracker Guild (1st Ed.) QXM5146	Yr.Iss.	1994	5.75	10-23
1994 On the Road (2nd Ed.) QXM5103	Yr.Iss.	1994	5.75	6-14
1994 Plucky Duck QXM4123	Yr.Iss.	1994	5.75	5-12
1994 Pour Some More QXM5156	Yr.Iss.	1994	5.75	6-12
1994 Rocking Horse (7th Ed.) QXM5116	Yr.Iss.	1994	4.50	12
1994 Scooting Along QXM5173	Yr.Iss.	1994	6.75	5-14
1994 Stock Car (6th Ed.) QXM5113	Yr.Iss.	1994	7.00	17-22
1994 Sweet Dreams QXM4096	Yr.Iss.	1994	3.00	9-13
1994 Tea With Teddy QXM4046	Yr.Iss.	1994	7.25	8-15

1994 New Attractions - Keepsake

YEAR ISSUE	EDITION LIMIT	YEAR RETD.	ISSUE PRICE	*QUOTE U.S.$
1994 All Pumped Up QX5923	Yr.Iss.	1994	8.95	18
1994 Angel Hare QX5896	Yr.Iss.	1994	8.95	12-27
1994 Batman QX5853	Yr.Iss.	1994	12.95	15-35
1994 Beatles Gift Set QX5373	Yr.Iss.	1994	48.00	40-100
1994 BEATRIX POTTER The Tale of Peter Rabbit QX2443	Yr.Iss.	1994	5.00	16-23
1994 Big Shot QX5873	Yr.Iss.	1994	7.95	17
1994 Busy Batter QX5876	Yr.Iss.	1994	7.95	8-20
1994 Candy Caper QX5776	Yr.Iss.	1994	8.95	12-19
1994 Caring Doctor QX5823	Yr.Iss.	1994	8.95	5-18
1994 Champion Teacher QX5836	Yr.Iss.	1994	6.95	13-16
1994 Cheers to You! QX5796	Yr.Iss.	1994	10.95	15-23
1994 Cheery Cyclists QX5786	Yr.Iss.	1994	12.95	15-27
1994 Child Care Giver QX5906	Yr.Iss.	1994	7.95	8-18
1994 Coach QX5933	Yr.Iss.	1994	7.95	16
1994 Colors of Joy QX5893	Yr.Iss.	1994	7.95	10-18
1994 Cowardly Lion QX5446	Yr.Iss.	1994	9.95	38-55
1994 Daffy Duck QX5415	Yr.Iss.	1994	8.95	16-19
1994 Daisy Days QX5986	Yr.Iss.	1994	9.95	5-16
1994 Deer Santa Mouse (2) QX5806	Yr.Iss.	1994	14.95	27-30
1994 Dorothy and Toto QX5433	Yr.Iss.	1994	10.95	68-85
1994 Extra-Special Delivery QX5833	Yr.Iss.	1994	7.95	13-17
1994 Feelin' Groovy QX5953	Yr.Iss.	1994	7.95	14-21
1994 A Feline of Christmas QX5816	Yr.Iss.	1994	8.95	10-30
1994 Feliz Navidad QX5793	Yr.Iss.	1994	8.95	19-23
1994 Follow the Sun QX5846	Yr.Iss.	1994	8.95	9-18
1994 Fred and Barney QX5003	Yr.Iss.	1994	14.95	15-29
1994 Friendship Sundae QX4766	Yr.Iss.	1994	10.95	19-29
1994 GARFIELD QX5753	Yr.Iss.	1994	12.95	15-30
1994 Gentle Nurse QX5973	Yr.Iss.	1994	6.95	18-20
1994 Harvest Joy QX5993	Yr.Iss.	1994	9.95	17-25
1994 Hearts in Harmony QX4406	Yr.Iss.	1994	10.95	21-23
1994 Helpful Shepherd QX5536	Yr.Iss.	1994	8.95	10-20
1994 Holiday Patrol QX5826	Yr.Iss.	1994	8.95	18-20
1994 Ice Show QX5946	Yr.Iss.	1994	7.95	5-17
1994 In the Pink QX5763	Yr.Iss.	1994	9.95	8-21
1994 It's a Strike QX5883	Yr.Iss.	1994	8.95	18-20
1994 Jingle Bell Band QX5783	Yr.Iss.	1994	10.95	15-30
1994 Joyous Song QX4473	Yr.Iss.	1994	8.95	18-20
1994 Jump-along Jackalope QX5756	Yr.Iss.	1994	9.95	9-23
1994 Kickin' Roo QX5916	Yr.Iss.	1994	7.95	16-20
1994 Kringle's Kayak QX5886	Yr.Iss.	1994	7.95	17-22
1994 LEGO'S QX5453	Yr.Iss.	1994	10.95	12-23
1994 Lou Rankin Seal QX5456	Yr.Iss.	1994	9.95	16-21
1994 Magic Carpet Ride QX5883	Yr.Iss.	1994	7.95	17-25
1994 Mary Engelbreit QX2416	Yr.Iss.	1994	5.00	14-24
1994 Merry Fishmas QX5513	Yr.Iss.	1994	8.95	12-23
1994 Mistletoe Surprise (2)QX5996	Yr.Iss.	1994	12.95	26-33
1994 Norman Rockwell QX2413	Yr.Iss.	1994	5.00	13-20
1994 Open-and-Shut Holiday QX5696	Yr.Iss.	1994	9.95	20-22
1994 Out of This World Teacher QX5766	Yr.Iss.	1994	7.95	14-19
1994 Practice Makes Perfect QX5863	Yr.Iss.	1994	7.95	17-20
1994 Red Hot Holiday QX5843	Yr.Iss.	1994	7.95	8-20
1994 Reindeer Pro QX5926	Yr.Iss.	1994	9.95	8-20
1994 Relaxing Moment QX5356	Yr.Iss.	1994	14.95	15-30
1994 Road Runner and Wile E. Coyote QX5602	Yr.Iss.	1994	12.95	15-30
1994 Scarecrow QX5436	Yr.Iss.	1994	9.95	44-60
1994 A Sharp Flat QX5773	Yr.Iss.	1994	10.95	14-25
1994 Speedy Gonzales QX5343	Yr.Iss.	1994	8.95	10-21
1994 Stamp of Approval QX5703	Yr.Iss.	1994	7.95	16-18
1994 Sweet Greeting (2) QX5803	Yr.Iss.	1994	10.95	21-23
1994 Tasmanian Devil QX5605	Yr.Iss.	1994	8.95	25-64
1994 Thrill a Minute QX5866	Yr.Iss.	1994	8.95	14-20
1994 Time of Peace QX5813	Yr.Iss.	1994	7.95	5-15
1994 Tin Man QX5443	Yr.Iss.	1994	9.95	49-55
1994 Tulip Time QX5983	Yr.Iss.	1994	9.95	16-25

*Quotes have been rounded up to nearest dollar

YEAR ISSUE	EDITION LIMIT	YEAR RETD.	ISSUE PRICE	*QUOTE U.S.$
1994 Winnie the Pooh/Tigger QX5746	Yr.Iss.	1994	12.95	16-30
1994 Yosemite Sam QX5346	Yr.Iss.	1994	8.95	12-21
1994 Yuletide Cheer QX5976	Yr.Iss.	1994	9.95	16-25

1994 Personalized Ornaments - Keepsake

1994 Baby Block QP6035	Yr.Iss.	1994	14.95	12-15
1994 Computer Cat 'N' Mouse QP6046	Yr.Iss.	1994	12.95	9-13
1994 Cookie Time QP6073	Yr.Iss.	1994	12.95	9-13
1994 Etch-A-Sketch QP6006	Yr.Iss.	1994	12.95	9-13
1994 Festive Album QP6025	Yr.Iss.	1994	12.95	9-26
1994 From the Heart QP6036	Yr.Iss.	1994	14.95	10-15
1994 Goin' Fishin' QP6023	Yr.Iss.	1994	14.95	10-15
1994 Goin' Golfin' QP6012	Yr.Iss.	1994	12.95	9-13
1994 Holiday Hello QXR6116	Yr.Iss.	1994	24.95	17-25
1994 Mailbox Delivery QP6015	Yr.Iss.	1994	14.95	10-15
1994 Novel Idea QP6066	Yr.Iss.	1994	12.95	9-13
1994 On the Billboard QP6022	Yr.Iss.	1994	12.95	9-13
1994 Playing Ball QP6032	Yr.Iss.	1994	12.95	9-13
1994 Reindeer Rooters QP6056	Yr.Iss.	1994	12.95	9-13
1994 Santa Says QP6005	Yr.Iss.	1994	14.95	10-15

1994 Premiere Event - Keepsake

1994 Eager for Christmas QX5336	Yr.Iss.	1994	15.00	12-28

1994 Showcase Christmas Lights - Keepsake

1994 Home for the Holidays QK1123	Yr.Iss.	1994	15.75	25-32
1994 Moonbeams QK1116	Yr.Iss.	1994	15.75	13-16
1994 Mother and Child QK1126	Yr.Iss.	1994	15.75	13-16
1994 Peaceful Village QK1106	Yr.Iss.	1994	15.75	13-20

1994 Showcase Folk Art Americana Collection - Keepsake

1994 Catching 40 Winks QK1183	Yr.Iss.	1994	16.75	19-38
1994 Going to Town QK1166	Yr.Iss.	1994	15.75	19-35
1994 Racing Through the Snow QK1173	Yr.Iss.	1994	15.75	24-50
1994 Rarin' to Go QK1193	Yr.Iss.	1994	15.75	19-38
1994 Roundup Time QK1176	Yr.Iss.	1994	16.75	19-43

1994 Showcase Holiday Favorites - Keepsake

1994 Dapper Snowman QK1053	Yr.Iss.	1994	13.75	11-14
1994 Graceful Fawn QK1033	Yr.Iss.	1994	11.75	19-24
1994 Jolly Santa QK1046	Yr.Iss.	1994	13.75	12-28
1994 Joyful Lamb QK1036	Yr.Iss.	1994	11.75	9-24
1994 Peaceful Dove QK1043	Yr.Iss.	1994	11.75	19-24

1994 Showcase Old World Silver Collection - Keepsake

1994 Silver Bells QK1026	Yr.Iss.	1994	24.75	32-40
1994 Silver Bows QK1023	Yr.Iss.	1994	24.75	32-40
1994 Silver Poinsettias QK1006	Yr.Iss.	1994	24.75	32-40
1994 Silver Snowflakes QK1016	Yr.Iss.	1994	24.75	32-40

1994 Special Edition - Keepsake

1994 Lucinda and Teddy QX4813	Yr.Iss.	1994	21.75	18-29

1994 Special Issues - Keepsake

1994 Barney QLX7506	Yr.Iss.	1994	24.00	45-50
1994 Barney QX5966	Yr.Iss.	1994	9.95	22-25
1994 Holiday Barbie™ (2nd Ed.) QX5216	Yr.Iss.	1994	14.95	24-58
1994 Klingon Bird of Prey™ QLX7386	Yr.Iss.	1994	24.00	29-45
1994 Mufasa/Simba-Lion King QX5406	Yr.Iss.	1994	14.95	12-32
1994 Nostalgic-Barbie™ (1st Ed.) QX5006	Yr.Iss.	1994	14.95	19-48
1994 Simba/Nala-Lion King (2) QX5303	Yr.Iss.	1994	12.95	15-32
1994 Simba/Sarabi/Mufasa The Lion King QLX7513	Yr.Iss.	1994	20.00	51-75
1994 Simba/Sarabi/Mufasa The Lion King QLX7513	Yr.Iss.	1994	32.00	41-52
1994 Timon/Pumbaa-Lion King QX5366	Yr.Iss.	1994	8.95	15-27

1995 Anniversary Edition - Keepsake

1995 Pewter Rocking Horse QX6167	Yr.Iss.	1995	20.00	29-46

1995 Artists' Favorite - Keepsake

1995 Barrel-Back Rider QX5189	Yr.Iss.	1995	9.95	25-30
1995 Our Little Blessings QX5209	Yr.Iss.	1995	12.95	19-36

1995 Collectible Series - Keepsake

1995 1956 Ford Truck (1st Ed.) QX5527	Yr.Iss.	1995	13.95	20-35
1995 1969 Chevrolet Camaro (5th Ed.) QX5239	Yr.Iss.	1995	12.95	18-23
1995 Bright 'n' Sunny Tepee (7th Ed.) QX5247	Yr.Iss.	1995	10.95	15-35
1995 Camellia - Mary's Angels (8th Ed.) QX5149	Yr.Iss.	1995	6.95	17-23
1995 Cat Naps (2nd Ed.) QX5097	Yr.Iss.	1995	7.95	14-30

YEAR ISSUE	EDITION LIMIT	YEAR RETD.	ISSUE PRICE	*QUOTE U.S.$
1995 A Celebration of Angels (1st Ed.) QX5077	Yr.Iss.	1995	12.95	10-23
1995 Christmas Eve Kiss (10th Ed.) QX5157	Yr.Iss.	1995	14.95	27-33
1995 Fabulous Decade (6th Ed.) QX5147	Yr.Iss.	1995	7.95	10-22
1995 Frosty Friends (16th Ed.) QX5169	Yr.Iss.	1995	10.95	15-30
1995 Jack and Jill (3rd Ed.) QX5099	Yr.Iss.	1995	13.95	19-30
1995 Lou Gehrig (2nd Ed.) QX5029	Yr.Iss.	1995	12.95	13-27
1995 Merry Olde Santa (6th Ed.) QX5139	Yr.Iss.	1995	14.95	10-20
1995 Murray® Fire Truck (2nd Ed.) QX5027	Yr.Iss.	1995	13.95	14-30
1995 The PEANUTS® Gang (3rd Ed.) QX5059	Yr.Iss.	1995	9.95	15-22
1995 Puppy Love (5th Ed.) QX5137	Yr.Iss.	1995	7.95	14-25
1995 Rocking Horse (15th Ed.) QX5167	Yr.Iss.	1995	10.95	19-30
1995 Santa's Roadster (17th Ed.) QX5179	Yr.Iss.	1995	14.95	18-25
1995 St. Nicholas (1st Ed.) QX5087	Yr.Iss.	1995	14.95	15-21
1995 Tobin Fraley Carousel (4th Ed.) QX5069	Yr.Iss.	1995	28.00	28-36
1995 Town Church (12th Ed.) QX5159	Yr.Iss.	1995	14.95	20-39
1995 Twelve Drummers Drumming (12th Ed.) QX3009	Yr.Iss.	1995	6.95	7-18
1995 U.S. Christmas Stamps (3rd Ed.) QX5067	Yr.Iss.	1995	10.95	10-22
1995 Yuletide Central (2nd Ed.) QX5079	Yr.Iss.	1995	18.95	19-40

1995 Commemoratives - Keepsake

1995 Across the Miles QX5847	Yr.Iss.	1995	8.95	14-20
1995 Air Express QX5977	Yr.Iss.	1995	7.95	12-18
1995 Anniversary Year QX5819	Yr.Iss.	1995	8.95	14-20
1995 Baby's First Christmas QX5547	Yr.Iss.	1995	18.95	17-32
1995 Baby's First Christmas QX5549	Yr.Iss.	1995	7.95	16-21
1995 Baby's First Christmas QX5557	Yr.Iss.	1995	9.95	13-20
1995 Baby's First Christmas QX5559	Yr.Iss.	1995	7.95	19-28
1995 Baby's First Christmas-Baby Boy QX2319	Yr.Iss.	1995	5.00	12-45
1995 Baby's First Christmas-Baby Girl QX2317	Yr.Iss.	1995	5.00	14-16
1995 Baby's Second Christmas QX5567	Yr.Iss.	1995	7.95	16-25
1995 Brother QX5679	Yr.Iss.	1995	6.95	13
1995 Child's Fifth Christmas QX5637	Yr.Iss.	1995	6.95	15-18
1995 Child's Fourth Christmas QX5629	Yr.Iss.	1995	6.95	16-19
1995 Child's Third Christmas QX5627	Yr.Iss.	1995	7.95	15-22
1995 Christmas Fever QX5967	Yr.Iss.	1995	7.95	16-20
1995 Christmas Patrol QX5959	Yr.Iss.	1995	7.95	17-20
1995 Dad QX5649	Yr.Iss.	1995	7.95	10-18
1995 Dad-to-Be QX5667	Yr.Iss.	1995	7.95	10-16
1995 Daughter QX5677	Yr.Iss.	1995	6.95	10-19
1995 For My Grandma QX5729	Yr.Iss.	1995	6.95	14-16
1995 Friendly Boost QX5827	Yr.Iss.	1995	8.95	17-22
1995 Godchild QX5707	Yr.Iss.	1995	7.95	14-25
1995 Godparent QX2417	Yr.Iss.	1995	5.00	10-17
1995 Grandchild's First Christmas QX5777	Yr.Iss.	1995	7.95	9-15
1995 Granddaughter QX5779	Yr.Iss.	1995	6.95	18-20
1995 Grandmother QX5767	Yr.Iss.	1995	7.95	14-28
1995 Grandpa QX5769	Yr.Iss.	1995	8.95	12-16
1995 Grandparents QX2419	Yr.Iss.	1995	5.00	9-13
1995 Grandson QX5787	Yr.Iss.	1995	6.95	12-17
1995 Important Memo QX5947	Yr.Iss.	1995	8.95	18-20
1995 In a Heartbeat QX5817	Yr.Iss.	1995	8.95	18-23
1995 Mom and Dad QX5657	Yr.Iss.	1995	9.95	17-23
1995 Mom QX5647	Yr.Iss.	1995	7.95	14-19
1995 Mom-to-Be QX5659	Yr.Iss.	1995	7.95	12-15
1995 New Home QX5839	Yr.Iss.	1995	8.95	13-17
1995 North Pole 911 QX5957	Yr.Iss.	1995	10.95	22-25
1995 Number One Teacher QX5949	Yr.Iss.	1995	7.95	16
1995 Our Christmas Together QX5809	Yr.Iss.	1995	9.95	16-20
1995 Our Family QX5709	Yr.Iss.	1995	7.95	16-19
1995 Our First Christmas Together QX3177	Yr.Iss.	1995	6.95	12-20
1995 Our First Christmas Together QX5797	Yr.Iss.	1995	16.95	24-35
1995 Our First Christmas Together QX5799	Yr.Iss.	1995	8.95	18-20
1995 Our First Christmas Together QX5807	Yr.Iss.	1995	8.95	18-20
1995 Packed With Memories QX5639	Yr.Iss.	1995	7.95	17-20
1995 Sister QX5687	Yr.Iss.	1995	6.95	10-13
1995 Sister to Sister QX5689	Yr.Iss.	1995	8.95	18-20
1995 Son QX5669	Yr.Iss.	1995	6.95	10-16
1995 Special Cat QX5717	Yr.Iss.	1995	7.95	13-17
1995 Special Dog QX5719	Yr.Iss.	1995	7.95	13-17

YEAR ISSUE	EDITION LIMIT	YEAR RETD.	ISSUE PRICE	*QUOTE U.S.$
1995 Two for Tea QX5829	Yr.Iss.	1995	9.95	14-32

1995 Easter Ornaments - Keepsake

YEAR ISSUE	EDITION LIMIT	YEAR RETD.	ISSUE PRICE	*QUOTE U.S.$
1995 3 Flowerpot Friends 1495QEO8229	Yr.Iss.	1995	14.95	16-23
1995 Baby's First Easter QEO8237	Yr.Iss.	1995	7.95	13-17
1995 Bugs Bunny (Looney Tunes) QEO8279	Yr.Iss.	1995	8.95	14-19
1995 Bunny w/Crayons (Crayola) QEO8249	Yr.Iss.	1995	7.95	18-22
1995 Bunny w/Seed Packets (Tender Touches) QEO8259	Yr.Iss.	1995	8.95	14-22
1995 Bunny w/Water Bucket QEO8253	Yr.Iss.	1995	6.95	10-13
1995 Collector's Plate (2nd Ed.) QEO8219	Yr.Iss.	1995	7.95	12-19
1995 Daughter Duck QEO8239	Yr.Iss.	1995	5.95	9-12
1995 Easter Beagle (Peanuts) QEO8257	Yr.Iss.	1995	7.95	15-20
1995 Easter Egg Cottages (1st Ed.) QEO8207	Yr.Iss.	1995	8.95	12-25
1995 Garden Club (1st Ed.) QEO8209	Yr.Iss.	1995	7.95	11-19
1995 Ham n Eggs QEO8277	Yr.Iss.	1995	7.95	11-15
1995 Here Comes Easter (2nd Ed.) QEO8217	Yr.Iss.	1995	7.95	12-20
1995 Lily (Religious) QEO8267	Yr.Iss.	1995	6.95	8-12
1995 Miniature Train QEO8269	Yr.Iss.	1995	4.95	13-15
1995 Son Duck QEO8247	Yr.Iss.	1995	5.95	9-18
1995 Springtime Barbie™ (1st Ed.) QEO8069	Yr.Iss.	1995	12.95	14-38
1995 Springtime Bonnets (3rd Ed.) QEO8227	Yr.Iss.	1995	7.95	18-23

1995 Keepsake Collector's Club - Keepsake

YEAR ISSUE	EDITION LIMIT	YEAR RETD.	ISSUE PRICE	*QUOTE U.S.$
1995 1958 Ford Edsel Citation Convertible QXC4167	Yr.Iss.	1995	12.95	39-65
1995 Brunette Debut-1959 QXC5397	Yr.Iss.	1995	14.95	35-68
1995 Christmas Eve Bake-Off QXC4049	Yr.Iss.	1995	55.00	170
1995 Cinderella's Stepsisters QXC4159	Yr.Iss.	1995	3.75	4-29
1995 Collecting Memories QXC4117	Yr.Iss.	1995	12.00	10-32
1995 Cool Santa QXC4457	Yr.Iss.	1995	5.75	8-13
1995 Cozy Christmas QXC4119	Yr.Iss.	1995	8.50	15
1995 Fishing for Fun QXC5207	Yr.Iss.	1995	10.95	8-17
1995 A Gift From Rodney QXC4129	Yr.Iss.	1995	5.00	8-10
1995 Home From the Woods QXC1059	Yr.Iss.	1995	15.95	16-41
1995 May Flower QXC8246	Yr.Iss.	1995	4.95	25-47

1995 Keepsake Magic Ornaments - Keepsake

YEAR ISSUE	EDITION LIMIT	YEAR RETD.	ISSUE PRICE	*QUOTE U.S.$
1995 Baby's First Christmas QLX7317	Yr.Iss.	1995	22.00	16-42
1995 Chris Mouse Tree (11th Ed.) QLX7307	Yr.Iss.	1995	12.50	24-30
1995 Coming to See Santa QLX7369	Yr.Iss.	1995	32.00	49-65
1995 Forest Frolics (7th Ed.) QLX7299	Yr.Iss.	1995	28.00	29-56
1995 Fred and Dino QLX7289	Yr.Iss.	1995	28.00	48-60
1995 Friends Share Fun QLX7349	Yr.Iss.	1995	16.50	19-38
1995 Goody Gumballs! QLX7367	Yr.Iss.	1995	12.50	30-33
1995 Headin' Home QLX7327	Yr.Iss.	1995	22.00	39-50
1995 Holiday Swim QLX7319	Yr.Iss.	1995	18.50	19-35
1995 Jukebox Party QLX7339	Yr.Iss.	1995	24.50	18-25
1995 Jumping for Joy QLX7347	Yr.Iss.	1995	28.00	39-60
1995 My First HOT WHEELS™ QLX7279	Yr.Iss.	1995	28.00	25-60
1995 PEANUTS® (5th Ed.) QLX7277	Yr.Iss.	1995	24.50	18-50
1995 Santa's Diner QLX7337	Yr.Iss.	1995	24.50	24-35
1995 Space Shuttle QLX7396	Yr.Iss.	1995	24.50	29-65
1995 Superman™ QLX7309	Yr.Iss.	1995	28.00	31-50
1995 Tobin Fraley Holiday Carousel (2nd Ed.) QLX7269	Yr.Iss.	1995	32.00	32-60
1995 Victorian Toy Box (Special Ed.) QLX7357	Yr.Iss.	1995	42.00	39-67
1995 Wee Little Christmas QLX7329	Yr.Iss.	1995	22.00	34-43
1995 Winnie the Pooh Too Much Hunny QLX7297	Yr.Iss.	1995	24.50	40-50

1995 Miniature Ornaments - Keepsake

YEAR ISSUE	EDITION LIMIT	YEAR RETD.	ISSUE PRICE	*QUOTE U.S.$
1995 Alice in Wonderland (1st Ed.) QXM4777	Yr.Iss.	1995	6.75	9-13
1995 Baby's First Christmas QXM4027	Yr.Iss.	1995	4.75	8-14
1995 Calamity Coyote QXM4467	Yr.Iss.	1995	6.75	12-16
1995 Centuries of Santa (2nd Ed.) QXM4789	Yr.Iss.	1995	5.75	8-15
1995 Christmas Bells (1st Ed.) QXM4007	Yr.Iss.	1995	4.75	12-26
1995 Christmas Wishes QXM4087	Yr.Iss.	1995	3.75	5-14
1995 Cloisonne Partridge QXM4017	Yr.Iss.	1995	9.75	10-18
1995 Downhill Double QXM4837	Yr.Iss.	1995	4.75	12
1995 Friendship Duet QXM4019	Yr.Iss.	1995	4.75	8-13
1995 Furrball QXM4459	Yr.Iss.	1995	5.75	12-16
1995 Grandpa's Gift QXM4829	Yr.Iss.	1995	5.75	10-13
1995 Heavenly Praises QXM4037	Yr.Iss.	1995	5.75	10-15
1995 Joyful Santa QXM4089	Yr.Iss.	1995	4.75	11-13
1995 Little Beeper QXM4469	Yr.Iss.	1995	5.75	12-16
1995 March of the Teddy Bears (3rd Ed.) QXM4799	Yr.Iss.	1995	4.75	10-13
1995 Merry Walruses QXM4057	Yr.Iss.	1995	5.75	12-19
1995 Milk Tank Car (7th Ed.) QXM4817	Yr.Iss.	1995	6.75	10-19
1995 Miniature Clothespin Soldier (1st Ed.) QXM4097	Yr.Iss.	1995	3.75	9-14
1995 A Moustershire Christmas QXM4839	Yr.Iss.	1995	24.50	28-44
1995 Murray® "Champion" (1st Ed.) QXM4079	Yr.Iss.	1995	5.75	7-20
1995 Nature's Angels (6th Ed.) QXM4809	Yr.Iss.	1995	4.75	8-20
1995 The Night Before Christmas (4th Ed.) QXM4807	Yr.Iss.	1995	4.75	12-18
1995 Nutcracker Guild (2nd Ed.) QXM4787	Yr.Iss.	1995	5.75	8-16
1995 On the Road (3rd Ed.) QXM4797	Yr.Iss.	1995	5.75	14-17
1995 Pebbles and Bamm-Bamm QXM4757	Yr.Iss.	1995	9.75	14-22
1995 Playful Penguins QXM4059	Yr.Iss.	1995	5.75	10-23
1995 Precious Creations QXM4077	Yr.Iss.	1995	9.75	10-20
1995 Rocking Horse (8th Ed.) QXM4827	Yr.Iss.	1995	4.75	11-14
1995 Santa's Little Big Top (1st Ed.) QXM4779	Yr.Iss.	1995	6.75	15-20
1995 Santa's Visit QXM4047	Yr.Iss.	1995	7.75	16-18
1995 Starlit Nativity QXM4039	Yr.Iss.	1995	7.75	18-20
1995 Sugarplum Dreams QXM4099	Yr.Iss.	1995	4.75	10-15
1995 Tiny Treasures (set of 6) QXM4009	Yr.Iss.	1995	29.00	28-45
1995 Tudor House- (8th Ed.) QXM4819	Yr.Iss.	1995	6.75	15-25
1995 Tunnel of Love QXM4029	Yr.Iss.	1995	4.75	8-12

1995 New Attractions - Keepsake

YEAR ISSUE	EDITION LIMIT	YEAR RETD.	ISSUE PRICE	*QUOTE U.S.$
1995 Acorn 500 QX5929	Yr.Iss.	1995	10.95	18-20
1995 Batmobile QX5739	Yr.Iss.	1995	14.95	15-30
1995 Betty and Wilma QX5417	Yr.Iss.	1995	14.95	12-27
1995 Bingo Bear QX5919	Yr.Iss.	1995	7.95	18-20
1995 Bobbin' Along QX5879	Yr.Iss.	1995	8.95	19-40
1995 Bugs Bunny QX5019	Yr.Iss.	1995	8.95	12-16
1995 Catch the Spirit QX5899	Yr.Iss.	1995	7.95	10-20
1995 Christmas Morning QX5997	Yr.Iss.	1995	10.95	12-16
1995 Colorful World QX5519	Yr.Iss.	1995	10.95	20-23
1995 Cows of Bali QX5999	Yr.Iss.	1995	8.95	18-20
1995 Delivering Kisses QX4107	Yr.Iss.	1995	10.95	15-23
1995 Dream On QX6007	Yr.Iss.	1995	10.95	21-24
1995 Dudley the Dragon QX6209	Yr.Iss.	1995	10.95	16-23
1995 Faithful Fan QX5897	Yr.Iss.	1995	8.95	9-18
1995 Feliz Navidad QX5869	Yr.Iss.	1995	7.95	8-19
1995 Forever Friends Bear QX5258	Yr.Iss.	1995	8.95	10-21
1995 GARFIELD QX5007	Yr.Iss.	1995	10.95	15-25
1995 Glinda, Witch of the North QX5749	Yr.Iss.	1995	13.95	25-32
1995 Gopher Fun QX5887	Yr.Iss.	1995	9.95	20-25
1995 Happy Wrappers QX6037	Yr.Iss.	1995	10.95	20-23
1995 Heaven's Gift QX6057	Yr.Iss.	1995	20.00	24-50
1995 Hockey Pup QX5917	Yr.Iss.	1995	9.95	18-23
1995 In Time With Christmas QX6049	Yr.Iss.	1995	12.95	14-30
1995 Joy to the World QX5867	Yr.Iss.	1995	8.95	19
1995 LEGO® Fireplace With Santa QX4769	Yr.Iss.	1995	10.95	15-23
1995 Lou Rankin Bear QX4069	Yr.Iss.	1995	9.95	19-23
1995 The Magic School Bus™ QX5849	Yr.Iss.	1995	10.95	15-22
1995 Mary Engelbreit QX2409	Yr.Iss.	1995	5.00	12-18
1995 Merry RV QX6027	Yr.Iss.	1995	12.95	25-30
1995 Muletide Greetings QX6009	Yr.Iss.	1995	7.95	8-16
1995 The Olympic Spirit QX3169	Yr.Iss.	1995	7.95	10-20
1995 On the Ice QX6047	Yr.Iss.	1995	7.95	10-23
1995 Perfect Balance QX5927	Yr.Iss.	1995	7.95	16-18
1995 PEZ® Santa QX5267	Yr.Iss.	1995	7.95	8-22
1995 Polar Coaster QX6117	Yr.Iss.	1995	8.95	22-30
1995 Popeye® QX5257	Yr.Iss.	1995	10.95	12-23
1995 Refreshing Gift QX4067	Yr.Iss.	1995	14.95	22-29
1995 Rejoice! QX5987	Yr.Iss.	1995	10.95	15-23
1995 Roller Whiz QX5937	Yr.Iss.	1995	7.95	17-20
1995 Santa in Paris QX5877	Yr.Iss.	1995	8.95	24-30
1995 Santa's Serenade QX6017	Yr.Iss.	1995	8.95	18-20
1995 Santa's Visitors QX2407	Yr.Iss.	1995	5.00	14-20
1995 Simba, Pumbaa and Timon QX6159	Yr.Iss.	1995	12.95	15-20
1995 Ski Hound QX5909	Yr.Iss.	1995	8.95	18-20
1995 Surfin' Santa QX6019	Yr.Iss.	1995	9.95	15-28
1995 Sylvester and Tweety QX5017	Yr.Iss.	1995	13.95	18-27
1995 Takin' a Hike QX6029	Yr.Iss.	1995	7.95	18-20
1995 Tennis, Anyone? QX5907	Yr.Iss.	1995	7.95	18-20

Collectors' Information Bureau · *Quotes have been rounded up to nearest dollar

YEAR ISSUE	EDITION LIMIT	YEAR RETD.	ISSUE PRICE	*QUOTE U.S.$
1995 Thomas the Tank Engine-No. 1 QX5857	Yr.Iss.	1995	9.95	24-35
1995 Three Wishes QX5979	Yr.Iss.	1995	7.95	18-20
1995 Vera the Mouse QX5537	Yr.Iss.	1995	8.95	17-19
1995 Waiting Up for Santa QX6106	Yr.Iss.	1995	8.95	18-20
1995 Water Sports QX6039	Yr.Iss.	1995	14.95	29-35
1995 Wheel of Fortune® QX6187	Yr.Iss.	1995	12.95	12-21
1995 Winnie the Pooh and Tigger QX5009	Yr.Iss.	1995	12.95	23-31
1995 The Winning Play QX5889	Yr.Iss.	1995	7.95	18-23

1995 Personalized Ornaments - Keepsake

1995 Baby Bear QP6157	Yr.Iss.	1995	12.95	9-13
1995 The Champ QP6127	Yr.Iss.	1995	12.95	9-13
1995 Computer Cat 'n' Mouse QP6046	Yr.Iss.	1995	12.95	9-13
1995 Cookie Time QP6073	Yr.Iss.	1995	12.95	9-27
1995 Etch-A-Sketch® QP6006	Yr.Iss.	1995	12.95	9-13
1995 From the Heart QP6036	Yr.Iss.	1995	14.95	10-15
1995 Key Note QP6149	Yr.Iss.	1995	12.95	9-13
1995 Mailbox Delivery QP6015	Yr.Iss.	1995	12.95	9-13
1995 Novel Idea QP6066	Yr.Iss.	1995	12.95	9-13
1995 On the Billboard QP6022	Yr.Iss.	1995	12.95	9-13
1995 Playing Ball QP6032	Yr.Iss.	1995	12.95	9-13
1995 Reindeer Rooters QP6056	Yr.Iss.	1995	14.95	10-15

1995 Premiere Event - Keepsake

1995 Wish List QX5859	Yr.Iss.	1995	15.00	15-30

1995 Showcase All Is Bright Collection - Keepsake

1995 Angel of Light QK1159	Yr.Iss.	1995	11.95	15-23
1995 Gentle Lullaby QK1157	Yr.Iss.	1995	11.95	15-23

1995 Showcase Angel Bells Collection - Keepsake

1995 Carole QK1147	Yr.Iss.	1995	12.95	24
1995 Joy QK1137	Yr.Iss.	1995	12.95	22-25
1995 Noelle QK1139	Yr.Iss.	1995	12.95	24

1995 Showcase Folk Art Americana Collection - Keepsake

1995 Fetching the Firewood QK1057	Yr.Iss.	1995	15.95	24-32
1995 Fishing Party QK1039	Yr.Iss.	1995	15.95	24-32
1995 Guiding Santa QK1037	Yr.Iss.	1995	18.95	33-44
1995 Learning to Skate QK1047	Yr.Iss.	1995	14.95	25-35

1995 Showcase Holiday Enchantment Collection - Keepsake

1995 Away in a Manger QK1097	Yr.Iss.	1995	13.95	19-25
1995 Following the Star QK1099	Yr.Iss.	1995	13.95	19-25

1995 Showcase Invitation to Tea Collection - Keepsake

1995 Cozy Cottage Teapot QK1127	Yr.Iss.	1995	15.95	24-30
1995 European Castle Teapot QK1129	Yr.Iss.	1995	15.95	24-30
1995 Victorian Home Teapot QK1119	Yr.Iss.	1995	15.95	24-32

1995 Showcase Nature's Sketchbook Collection - Keepsake

1995 Backyard Orchard QK1069	Yr.Iss.	1995	18.95	24-30
1995 Christmas Cardinal QK1077	Yr.Iss.	1995	18.95	32-41
1995 Raising a Family QK1067	Yr.Iss.	1995	18.95	24-31
1995 Snowy Garden QX8284	Yr.Iss.	1995	13.95	30
1995 Violets and Butterflies QK1079	Yr.Iss.	1995	16.95	24-31

1995 Showcase Symbols of Christmas Collection - Keepsake

1995 Jolly Santa QK1087	Yr.Iss.	1995	15.95	16-28
1995 Sweet Song QK1089	Yr.Iss.	1995	15.95	16-28

1995 Showcase Turn-of-the-Century Parade - Keepsake

1995 The Fireman QK1027	Yr.Iss.	1995	16.95	19-40

1995 Special Edition - Keepsake

1995 Beverly and Teddy QX5259	Yr.Iss.	1995	21.75	25-29

1995 Special Issues - Keepsake

1995 Captain James T. Kirk QXI5539	Yr.Iss.	1995	13.95	21-25
1995 Captain Jean-Luc Picard QXI5737	Yr.Iss.	1995	13.95	14-25
1995 Captain John Smith and Meeko QXI6169	Yr.Iss.	1995	12.95	15-23
1995 Holiday Barbie™ (3rd Ed.) QXI5057	Yr.Iss.	1995	14.95	15-40
1995 Hoop Stars (1st Ed.) QXI5517	Yr.Iss.	1995	14.95	15-55
1995 Joe Montana (1st Ed.) QXI5759	Yr.Iss.	1995	14.95	15-35
1995 Percy, Flit and Meeko QXI6179	Yr.Iss.	1995	9.95	17
1995 Pocahontas and Captain John Smith QXI6197	Yr.Iss.	1995	14.95	23
1995 Pocahontas QX6177	Yr.Iss.	1995	12.95	16-20
1995 Romulan Warbird™ QXI7267	Yr.Iss.	1995	24.00	24-40
1995 The Ships of Star Trek® QXI4109	Yr.Iss.	1995	19.95	20-23

YEAR ISSUE	EDITION LIMIT	YEAR RETD.	ISSUE PRICE	*QUOTE U.S.$
1995 Solo in the Spotlight-Barbie™ (2nd Ed.) QXI5049	Yr.Iss.	1995	14.95	15-33

1995 Special Offer - Keepsake

1995 Charlie Brown QRP4207	Yr.Iss.	1995	3.95	19-36
1995 Linus QRP4217	Yr.Iss.	1995	3.95	8-25
1995 Lucy QRP4209	Yr.Iss.	1995	3.95	8-25
1995 SNOOPY QRP4219	Yr.Iss.	1995	3.95	19-35
1995 Snow Scene QRP4227	Yr.Iss.	1995	3.95	8-25
1995 5-Pc. Set		1995	19.95	50-72

1996 Collectible Series - Keepsake

1996 1955 Chevrolet Camero (2nd Ed.) QX5241	Yr.Iss.	1996	13.95	15-30
1996 1959 Cadillac De Ville (6th Ed.) QX5384	Yr.Iss.	1996	12.95	15-28
1996 700E Hudson Steam Locomotive (1st Ed.) QX5531	Yr.Iss.	1996	18.95	22-100
1996 Bright Flying Colors (8th Ed.) QX5391	Yr.Iss.	1996	10.95	15-25
1996 Cat Naps (3rd Ed.) QX5641	Yr.Iss.	1996	7.95	14-22
1996 A Celebration of Angels (2nd Ed.) QX5634	Yr.Iss.	1996	12.95	13-30
1996 Christkind (2nd Ed.) QX5631	Yr.Iss.	1996	14.95	12-27
1996 Christy-All God's Children-Martha Holcombe (1st Ed.) QX5564	Yr.Iss.	1996	12.95	15-28
1996 Cinderella-1995 (1st Ed.) QX6311	Yr.Iss.	1996	14.95	26-46
1996 Evergreen Santa (Special Ed.) QX5714	Yr.Iss.	1996	22.00	36-44
1996 Fabulous Decade (7th Ed.) QX5661	Yr.Iss.	1996	7.95	10-20
1996 Frosty Friends (17th Ed.) QX5681	Yr.Iss.	1996	10.95	12-30
1996 Mary Had a Little Lamb (4th Ed.) QX5644	Yr.Iss.	1996	13.95	10-25
1996 Merry Olde Santa (7th Ed.) QX5654	Yr.Iss.	1996	14.95	15-30
1996 Murray Airplane (3rd Ed.) QX5364	Yr.Iss.	1996	13.95	12-26
1996 Native American Barbie™ (1st Ed.) QX5561	Yr.Iss.	1996	14.95	15-32
1996 The PEANUTS Gang (4th Ed.) QX5381	Yr.Iss.	1996	9.95	10-21
1996 Puppy Love (6th Ed.) QX5651	Yr.Iss.	1996	7.95	10-19
1996 Rocking Horse (16th Ed.) QX5674	Yr.Iss.	1996	10.95	19-34
1996 Santa's 4X4 (18th Ed.) QX5684	Yr.Iss.	1996	14.95	15-33
1996 Satchel Paige (3rd Ed.) QX5304	Yr.Iss.	1996	12.95	8-23
1996 Victorian Painted Lady (13th Ed.) QX5671	Yr.Iss.	1996	14.95	15-30
1996 Violet-Mary's Angels (9th Ed.) QX5664	Yr.Iss.	1996	6.95	12-20
1996 Yuletide Central (3rd Ed.) QX5011	Yr.Iss.	1996	18.95	19-40

1996 Commemoratives - Keepsake

1996 Baby's First Christmas QX5754	Yr.Iss.	1996	9.95	10-17
1996 Baby's First Christmas-Beatrix Potter QX5744	Yr.Iss.	1996	18.95	22-29
1996 Baby's First Christmas-Bessie Pease Gutmann QX5751	Yr.Iss.	1996	10.95	13-25
1996 Baby's First Christmas-Child's Age Collection QX5764	Yr.Iss.	1996	7.95	19-35
1996 Baby's First Christmas-Photo Holder QX5761	Yr.Iss.	1996	7.95	14-25
1996 Baby's Second Christmas-Child's Age Collection QX5771	Yr.Iss.	1996	7.95	14-22
1996 Child's Fifth Christmas-Child's Age Collection QX5784	Yr.Iss.	1996	6.95	10-18
1996 Child's Fourth Christmas-Child's Age Collection QX5781	Yr.Iss.	1996	7.95	10-19
1996 Child's Third Christmas-Child's Age Collection QX5774	Yr.Iss.	1996	7.95	10-20
1996 Close-Knit Friends QX5874	Yr.Iss.	1996	9.95	7-20
1996 Dad QX5831	Yr.Iss.	1996	7.95	10-17
1996 Daughter QX6077	Yr.Iss.	1996	8.95	14-19
1996 Godchild QX5841	Yr.Iss.	1996	8.95	10-20
1996 Granddaughter QX5697	Yr.Iss.	1996	7.95	15-20
1996 Grandma QX5844	Yr.Iss.	1996	8.95	7-23
1996 Grandpa QX5851	Yr.Iss.	1996	8.95	7-18
1996 Grandson QX5699	Yr.Iss.	1996	7.95	12-19
1996 Hearts Full of Love QX5814	Yr.Iss.	1996	9.95	16-19
1996 Mom and Dad QX5821	Yr.Iss.	1996	9.95	10-30
1996 Mom QX5824	Yr.Iss.	1996	7.95	10-20
1996 Mom-to-Be QX5791	Yr.Iss.	1996	7.95	10-20
1996 New Home QX5881	Yr.Iss.	1996	8.95	14-20
1996 On My Way-Photo Holder QX5861	Yr.Iss.	1996	7.95	12-15
1996 Our Christmas Together QX5794	Yr.Iss.	1996	18.95	20-40
1996 Our Christmas Together-Photo Holder QX5804	Yr.Iss.	1996	8.95	10-28

YEAR ISSUE	EDITION LIMIT	YEAR RETD.	ISSUE PRICE	*QUOTE U.S.$
1996 Our First Christmas Together QX5811	Yr.Iss.	1996	9.95	12-20
1996 Our First Christmas Together -Acrylic QX3051	Yr.Iss.	1996	6.95	10-21
1996 Our First Christmas Together-Collector's Plate QX5801	Yr.Iss.	1996	10.95	8-21
1996 Sister to Sister QX5834	Yr.Iss.	1996	9.95	15-19
1996 Son QX6079	Yr.Iss.	1996	8.95	7-18
1996 Special Dog Photo Holder QX5864	Yr.Iss.	1996	7.95	8-19
1996 Thank You, Santa-Photo Holder QX5854	Yr.Iss.	1996	7.95	6-18

1996 Keepsake Collector's Club - Keepsake

YEAR ISSUE	EDITION LIMIT	YEAR RETD.	ISSUE PRICE	*QUOTE U.S.$
1996 1937 Steelcraft Auburn by Murray® QXC4174	Yr.Iss.	1996	15.95	19-56
1996 1988 Happy Holidays® Barbie™ Doll QXC4181	Yr.Iss.	1996	14.95	29-77
1996 Airmail for Santa QXC4194	Yr.Iss.	1996	8.95	15-19
1996 Rudolph the Red-Nosed Reindeer® QXC7341	Yr.Iss.	1996	N/A	5-29
1996 Rudolph®'s Helper QXC4171	Yr.Iss.	1996	N/A	8-13
1996 Santa QXC4164	Yr.Iss.	1996	N/A	10-20
1996 Santa's Club Soda #4 QXC4191	Yr.Iss.	1996	8.50	12-15
1996 Santa's Toy Shop QXC4201	Yr.Iss.	1996	60.00	50-125
1996 The Wizard of Oz QXC4161	Yr.Iss.	1996	12.95	35-67

1996 Keepsake Magic Ornaments - Keepsake

YEAR ISSUE	EDITION LIMIT	YEAR RETD.	ISSUE PRICE	*QUOTE U.S.$
1996 Baby's First Christmas QLX7404	Yr.Iss.	1996	22.00	22-45
1996 Chicken Coop Chorus QLX7491	Yr.Iss.	1996	24.50	25-41
1996 Chris Mouse Inn (12th Ed.) QLX7371	Yr.Iss.	1996	14.50	19-30
1996 Father Time QLX7391	Yr.Iss.	1996	24.50	29-50
1996 Freedom 7 (1st Ed.) QLX7524	Yr.Iss.	1996	24.00	49-65
1996 THE JETSONS QLX7411	Yr.Iss.	1996	28.00	38-57
1996 Jukebox Party QLX7339	Yr.Iss.	1996	24.50	34-59
1996 Let Us Adore Him QLX7381	Yr.Iss.	1996	16.50	27-45
1996 North Pole Volunteers (Special Ed.) QLX7471	Yr.Iss.	1996	42.00	52-91
1996 Over the Rooftops QLX7374	Yr.Iss.	1996	14.50	10-30
1996 PEANUTS-Lucy and Schroeder QLX7394	Yr.Iss.	1996	18.50	28-36
1996 Pinball Wonder QLX7451	Yr.Iss.	1996	28.00	20-60
1996 Sharing a Soda QLX7424	Yr.Iss.	1996	24.50	28-49
1996 Slippery Day QLX7414	Yr.Iss.	1996	24.50	39-50
1996 STAR WARS-Millennium Falcon QLX7474	Yr.Iss.	1996	24.00	29-61
1996 The Statue of Liberty QLX7421	Yr.Iss.	1996	24.50	28-50
1996 Tobin Fraley Holiday Carousel (3rd Ed.) QLX7461	Yr.Iss.	1996	32.00	32-57
1996 Treasured Memories QLX7384	Yr.Iss.	1996	18.50	24-40
1996 Video Party QLX7431	Yr.Iss.	1996	28.00	20-59
1996 THE WIZARD OF OZ-Emerald City QLX7454	Yr.Iss.	1996	32.00	40-65

1996 Miniature Ornaments - Keepsake

YEAR ISSUE	EDITION LIMIT	YEAR RETD.	ISSUE PRICE	*QUOTE U.S.$
1996 African Elephants QXM4224	Yr.Iss.	1996	5.75	10-35
1996 Centuries of Santa (3rd Ed.) QXM4091	Yr.Iss.	1996	5.75	8-15
1996 A Child's Gifts QXM4234	Yr.Iss.	1996	6.75	9-13
1996 Christmas Bear QXM4241	Yr.Iss.	1996	4.75	8-14
1996 Christmas Bells (2nd Ed.) QXM4071	Yr.Iss.	1996	4.75	13-15
1996 Cookie Car (8th Ed.) QXM4114	Yr.Iss.	1996	6.75	10-18
1996 Cool Delivery Coca-Cola QXM4021	Yr.Iss.	1996	5.75	14
1996 GONE WITH THE WIND QXM4211	Yr.Iss.	1996	19.95	20-29
1996 Hattie Chapeau QXM4251	Yr.Iss.	1996	4.75	6-12
1996 Joyous Angel QXM4231	Yr.Iss.	1996	4.75	9-14
1996 Long Winter's Nap QXM4244	Yr.Iss.	1996	5.75	12-14
1996 Loony Tunes Lovables Baby Sylvester QXM4154	Yr.Iss.	1996	5.75	9-14
1996 Loony Tunes Lovables Baby Tweety QXM4014	Yr.Iss.	1996	5.75	14-23
1996 Mad Hatter (2nd Ed.) QXM4074	Yr.Iss.	1996	6.75	12-17
1996 March of the Teddy Bears (4th Ed.) QXM4094	Yr.Iss.	1996	4.75	9-12
1996 Message for Santa QXM4254	Yr.Iss.	1996	6.75	10-16
1996 Miniature Clothespin Soldier (2nd Ed.) QXM4144	Yr.Iss.	1996	4.75	7-13
1996 Murray "Fire Truck" (2nd Ed.) QXM4031	Yr.Iss.	1996	6.75	8-19
1996 Nature's Angels (7th Ed.) QXM4111	Yr.Iss.	1996	4.75	6-12
1996 The Night Before Christmas (5th Ed.) QXM4104	Yr.Iss.	1996	5.75	10-13
1996 The Nutcracker Ballet (1st Ed.) QXM4034	Yr.Iss.	1996	14.75	15-27
1996 Nutcracker Guild (3rd Ed.) QXM4084	Yr.Iss.	1996	5.75	10-17
1996 O Holy Night (Special Ed.) QXM4204	Yr.Iss.	1996	24.50	24-36
1996 On the Road (4th Ed.) QXM4101	Yr.Iss.	1996	5.75	7-13
1996 Peaceful Christmas QXM4214	Yr.Iss.	1996	4.75	7-15
1996 Rocking Horse (9th Ed.) QXM4121	Yr.Iss.	1996	4.75	9-15
1996 Santa's Little Big Top (2nd Ed.) QXM4081	Yr.Iss.	1996	6.75	8-15
1996 Sparkling Crystal Angel (Precious Ed.) QXM4264	Yr.Iss.	1996	9.75	10-24
1996 Tiny Christmas Helpers QXM4261	Yr.Iss.	1996	29.00	29-58
1996 A Tree for WOODSTOCK QXM4767	Yr.Iss.	1996	5.75	10-15
1996 The Vehicles of STAR WARS QXM4024	Yr.Iss.	1996	19.95	20-40
1996 Village Mill (9th Ed.) QXM4124	Yr.Iss.	1996	6.75	10-15
1996 Winnie the Pooh and Tigger QXM4044	Yr.Iss.	1996	5.75	12-21

1996 New Attractions - Keepsake

YEAR ISSUE	EDITION LIMIT	YEAR RETD.	ISSUE PRICE	*QUOTE U.S.$
1996 Antlers Aweigh! QX5901	Yr.Iss.	1996	9.95	10-24
1996 Apple for Teacher QX6121	Yr.Iss.	1996	7.95	6-16
1996 Bounce Pass QX6031	Yr.Iss.	1996	7.95	10-18
1996 Bowl 'em Over QX6014	Yr.Iss.	1996	7.95	13-20
1996 BOY SCOUTS OF AMERICA Growth of a Leader QX5541	Yr.Iss.	1996	9.95	7-24
1996 Child Care Giver QX6071	Yr.Iss.	1996	8.95	7-15
1996 Christmas Joy QX6421	Yr.Iss.	1996	14.95	15-30
1996 Christmas Snowman QX6214	Yr.Iss.	1996	9.95	15-23
1996 Come All Ye Faithful QX6244	Yr.Iss.	1996	12.95	19-28
1996 Fan-tastic Season QX5924	Yr.Iss.	1996	9.95	7-20
1996 Feliz Navidad QX6304	Yr.Iss.	1996	9.95	10-18
1996 Glad Tidings QX6231	Yr.Iss.	1996	14.95	15-30
1996 Goal Line Glory QX6001	Yr.Iss.	1996	12.95	15-33
1996 Happy Holi-doze QX5904	Yr.Iss.	1996	9.95	7-20
1996 High Style QX6064	Yr.Iss.	1996	8.95	10-19
1996 Hillside Express QX6134	Yr.Iss.	1996	12.95	19-28
1996 Holiday Haul QX6201	Yr.Iss.	1996	14.95	15-35
1996 Hurrying Downstairs QX6074	Yr.Iss.	1996	8.95	10-17
1996 I Dig Golf QX5891	Yr.Iss.	1996	10.95	15-24
1996 Jackpot Jingle QX5911	Yr.Iss.	1996	9.95	12-20
1996 Jolly Wolly Ark QX6221	Yr.Iss.	1996	12.95	13-23
1996 Kindly Shepherd QX6274	Yr.Iss.	1996	12.95	15-30
1996 Lighting the Way QX6124	Yr.Iss.	1996	12.95	10-30
1996 A Little Song and Dance QX6211	Yr.Iss.	1996	9.95	7-20
1996 Little Spooners QX5504	Yr.Iss.	1996	12.95	13-27
1996 LOONEY TUNES Foghorn Leghorn and Henery Hawk QX5444	Yr.Iss.	1996	13.95	12-26
1996 LOONEY TUNES Marvin the Martian QX5451	Yr.Iss.	1996	10.95	21-25
1996 Madonna & Child QX6324	Yr.Iss.	1996	12.95	13-24
1996 Making His Rounds QX6271	Yr.Iss.	1996	14.95	11-30
1996 Matchless Memories QX6061	Yr.Iss.	1996	9.95	7-20
1996 Maxine QX6224	Yr.Iss.	1996	9.95	15-29
1996 Merry Carpoolers QX5884	Yr.Iss.	1996	14.95	15-27
1996 Olive Oyl and Swee' Pea QX5481	Yr.Iss.	1996	10.95	11-22
1996 Peppermint Surprise QX6234	Yr.Iss.	1996	7.95	8-16
1996 Percy the Small Engine-No. 6 QX6314	Yr.Iss.	1996	9.95	18-20
1996 PEZ® Snowman QX6534	Yr.Iss.	1996	7.95	12-19
1996 Polar Cycle QX6034	Yr.Iss.	1996	12.95	12-27
1996 Prayer for Peace QX6261	Yr.Iss.	1996	7.95	14-16
1996 Precious Child QX6251	Yr.Iss.	1996	8.95	6-18
1996 Pup-Tenting QX6011	Yr.Iss.	1996	7.95	8-18
1996 Regal Cardinal QX6204	Yr.Iss.	1996	9.95	15-23
1996 Sew Sweet QX5921	Yr.Iss.	1996	8.95	10-20
1996 SPIDER-MAN QX5757	Yr.Iss.	1996	12.95	15-30
1996 Star of the Show QX6004	Yr.Iss.	1996	8.95	16-20
1996 Tamika QX6301	Yr.Iss.	1996	7.95	10-15
1996 Tender Lovin' Care QX6114	Yr.Iss.	1996	7.95	10-15
1996 This Big! QX5914	Yr.Iss.	1996	9.95	15-20
1996 Time for a Treat QX5464	Yr.Iss.	1996	11.95	10-22
1996 Tonka Mighty Dump Truck QX6321	Yr.Iss.	1996	13.95	12-35
1996 A Tree for SNOOPY QX5507	Yr.Iss.	1996	8.95	12-22
1996 Welcome Guest QX5394	Yr.Iss.	1996	14.95	11-30
1996 Welcome Him QX6264	Yr.Iss.	1996	8.95	9-18
1996 Winnie the Pooh and Piglet QX5454	Yr.Iss.	1996	12.95	16-25
1996 THE WIZARD OF OZ Witch of the West QX5554	Yr.Iss.	1996	13.95	20-30
1996 WONDER WOMAN QX5941	Yr.Iss.	1996	12.95	15-27
1996 Woodland Santa QX6131	Yr.Iss.	1996	12.95	10-24
1996 Yogi Bear and Boo Boo QX5521	Yr.Iss.	1996	12.95	15-27
1996 Yuletide Cheer QX6054	Yr.Iss.	1996	7.95	6-18
1996 Ziggy QX6524	Yr.Iss.	1996	9.95	15-25

YEAR ISSUE	EDITION LIMIT	YEAR RETD.	ISSUE PRICE	*QUOTE U.S.$
1996 NFL Ornaments - Keepsake				
1996 Arizona Cardinals QSR6484	Yr.Iss.	1996	9.95	14
1996 Atlanta Falcons QSR6364	Yr.Iss.	1996	9.95	14
1996 Browns QSR6391	Yr.Iss.	1996	9.95	10-20
1996 Buffalo Bills QSR6371	Yr.Iss.	1996	9.95	10-14
1996 Carolina Panthers QSR6374	Yr.Iss.	1996	9.95	10-20
1996 Chicago Bears QSR6381	Yr.Iss.	1996	9.95	14
1996 Cincinnati Bengals QSR6384	Yr.Iss.	1996	9.95	14-20
1996 Dallas Cowboys QSR6394	Yr.Iss.	1996	9.95	14-20
1996 Denver Broncos QSR6411	Yr.Iss.	1996	9.95	14
1996 Detroit Lions QSR6414	Yr.Iss.	1996	9.95	14-20
1996 Green Bay Packers QSR6421	Yr.Iss.	1996	9.95	29-50
1996 Indianapolis Colts QSR6431	Yr.Iss.	1996	9.95	14
1996 Jacksonville Jaguars QSR6434	Yr.Iss.	1996	9.95	14-20
1996 Kansas City Chiefs QSR6361	Yr.Iss.	1996	9.95	14
1996 Miami Dolphins QSR6451	Yr.Iss.	1996	9.95	10-20
1996 Minnesota Vikings QSR6454	Yr.Iss.	1996	9.95	10-20
1996 New England Patriots QSR6461	Yr.Iss.	1996	9.95	15-23
1996 New Orleans Saints QSR6464	Yr.Iss.	1996	9.95	14-20
1996 New York Giants QSR6471	Yr.Iss.	1996	9.95	14-20
1996 New York Jets QSR6474	Yr.Iss.	1996	9.95	14-20
1996 Oakland Raiders QSR6441	Yr.Iss.	1996	9.95	10
1996 Oilers QSR6424	Yr.Iss.	1996	9.95	14
1996 Philadelphi Eagles QSR6481	Yr.Iss.	1996	9.95	14-20
1996 Pittsburgh Steelers QSR6491	Yr.Iss.	1996	9.95	10-29
1996 San Diego Chargers QSR6494	Yr.Iss.	1996	9.95	14
1996 San Francisco 49ers QSR6501	Yr.Iss.	1996	9.95	14-20
1996 Seattle Seahawks QSR6504	Yr.Iss.	1996	9.95	14-20
1996 St.Louis Rams QSR6444	Yr.Iss.	1996	9.95	10-15
1996 Tampa Bay Buccaneers QSR6511	Yr.Iss.	1996	9.95	14
1996 Washington Redskins QSR6514	Yr.Iss.	1996	9.95	10-20
1996 Premiere Event - Keepsake				
1996 Bashful Mistletoe-Merry Minatures QFM8054	Yr.Iss.	1996	12.95	9-13
1996 Welcome Sign-Tender Touches QX6331	Yr.Iss.	1996	15.00	10-30
1996 Showcase Cookie Jar Friends Collection - Keepsake				
1996 Carmen QK1164	Yr.Iss.	1996	15.95	20-30
1996 Clyde QK1161	Yr.Iss.	1996	15.95	20-27
1996 Showcase Folk Art Americana Collection - Keepsake				
1996 Caroling Angel QK1134	Yr.Iss.	1996	16.95	19-30
1996 Mrs. Claus QK1204	Yr.Iss.	1996	18.95	23-30
1996 Santa's Gifts QK1124	Yr.Iss.	1996	18.95	24-40
1996 Showcase Magi Bells Collection - Keepsake				
1996 Balthasar (Frankincense) QK1174	Yr.Iss.	1996	13.95	14-26
1996 Caspar (Myrrh) QK1184	Yr.Iss.	1996	13.95	14-26
1996 Melchior (Gold) QK1181	Yr.Iss.	1996	13.95	14-26
1996 Showcase Nature's Sketchbook Collection - Keepsake				
1996 The Birds' Christmas Tree QK1114	Yr.Iss.	1996	18.95	35-45
1996 Christmas Bunny QK1104	Yr.Iss.	1996	18.95	30
1996 The Holly Basket QK1094	Yr.Iss.	1996	18.95	19-30
1996 Showcase Sacred Masterworks Collection - Keepsake				
1996 Madonna and Child QK1144	Yr.Iss.	1996	15.95	16-30
1996 Praying Madonna QK1154	Yr.Iss.	1996	15.95	16-30
1996 Showcase The Language of Flowers Collection - Keepsake				
1996 Pansy (1st Ed.) QK1171	Yr.Iss.	1996	15.95	29-55
1996 Showcase Turn-of-the-Century Parade Collection - Keepsake				
1996 Uncle Sam (2nd Ed.) QK1084	Yr.Iss.	1996	16.95	17-32
1996 Special Issues - Keepsake				
1996 101 Dalmatians-Collector's Plate QXI6544	Yr.Iss.	1996	12.95	9-24
1996 Featuring the Enchanted Evening -Barbie™ Doll (3rd Ed.) QXI6541	Yr.Iss.	1996	14.95	15-31
1996 Holiday Barbie™ (4th Ed.) QXI5371	Yr.Iss.	1996	14.95	15-38
1996 HUNCHBACK OF NOTRE DAME -Esmeralda and Djali QXI6351	Yr.Iss.	1996	14.95	18-27
1996 HUNCHBACK OF NOTRE DAME -Laverne, Victor and Hugo QXI6354	Yr.Iss.	1996	12.95	13-26
1996 THE HUNCHBACK OF NOTRE DAME-Quasimodo QXI6341	Yr.Iss.	1996	9.95	13-19
1996 It's A Wonderful Life™ (Anniversary Ed.) QXI6531	Yr.Iss.	1996	14.95	29-40

YEAR ISSUE	EDITION LIMIT	YEAR RETD.	ISSUE PRICE	*QUOTE U.S.$
1996 Larry Bird-Hoop Stars (2nd Ed.) QXI5014	Yr.Iss.	1996	14.95	15-38
1996 Nolan Ryan-At the Ballpark (1st Ed.) QXI5711	Yr.Iss.	1996	14.95	15-37
1996 OLYMPIC-Parade of Nations -Collector's Plate QXE5741	Yr.Iss.	1996	10.95	7-11
1996 OLYMPIC-Cloisonne Medallion QXE4041	Yr.Iss.	1996	9.75	7-20
1996 OLYMPIC-Invitation to the Games QXE5511	Yr.Iss.	1996	14.95	24-29
1996 OLYMPIC-IZZY-The Mascot QXE5724	Yr.Iss.	1996	9.95	7-20
1996 OLYMPIC-Lighting the Flame QXE7444	Yr.Iss.	1996	28.00	20-55
1996 OLYMPIC-Olympic Triumph QXE5731	Yr.Iss.	1996	10.95	10-22
1996 STAR TREK® THE NEXT GENERATION-Commander William T. Riker QXI5551	Yr.Iss.	1996	14.95	15-33
1996 STAR TREK®-30 Years QXI7534	Yr.Iss.	1996	45.00	50-77
1996 STAR TREK®-Mr. Spock QXI5544	Yr.Iss.	1996	14.95	15-33
1996 STAR TREK®-U.S.S.Voyager QXI7544	Yr.Iss.	1996	24.00	36-47
1996 Troy Aikman-Football Legends (2nd Ed.) QXI5021	Yr.Iss.	1996	14.95	15-27
1996 Spring Ornaments - Keepsake				
1996 Apple Blossom Lane QEO8084	Yr.Iss.	1996	8.95	12-16
1996 Collector's Plate QEO8221	Yr.Iss.	1996	7.95	15-18
1996 Daffy Duck, LOONEY TUNES QEO8154	Yr.Iss.	1996	8.95	11-16
1996 Easter Morning QEO8164	Yr.Iss.	1996	7.95	14-17
1996 Eggstra Special Surprise, Tender Touches QEO8161	Yr.Iss.	1996	8.95	13-18
1996 Garden Club QEO8091	Yr.Iss.	1996	7.95	11-17
1996 Here Comes Easter QEO8094	Yr.Iss.	1996	7.95	10-17
1996 Hippity-Hop Delivery, CRAYOLA® Crayon QEO8144	Yr.Iss.	1996	7.95	13-17
1996 Joyful Angels QEO8184	Yr.Iss.	1996	9.95	13-30
1996 Locomotive, Cottontail Express QEO8074	Yr.Iss.	1996	8.95	15-43
1996 Look What I Found! QEO8181	Yr.Iss.	1996	7.95	13-15
1996 Parade Pals, PEANUTS® QEO8151	Yr.Iss.	1996	7.95	16-19
1996 Peter Rabbit™ Beatrix Potter™ QEO8071	Yr.Iss.	1996	8.95	49-85
1996 Pork 'n Beans QEO8174	Yr.Iss.	1996	7.95	9-14
1996 Springtime Barbie™ QEO8081	Yr.Iss.	1996	12.95	19-30
1996 Springtime Bonnets QEO8134	Yr.Iss.	1996	7.95	19-30
1996 Strawberry Patch QEO8171	Yr.Iss.	1996	6.95	11-14
1996 Strike Up the Band! QEO8141	Yr.Iss.	1996	14.95	20-23
1997 Collectible Series - Keepsake				
1997 1950 Santa Fe F3 Diesel Locomotive (2nd Ed.) QX6145	Yr.Iss.	1997	18.95	25-43
1997 1953 GMC (3rd Ed.) QX6105	Yr.Iss.	1997	13.95	14-27
1997 1969 Hurst Oldsmobile 442 (7th Ed.) QX6102	Yr.Iss.	1997	13.95	14-28
1997 Bright Rocking Colors (8th Ed.) QX6235	Yr.Iss.	1997	12.95	15-44
1997 Cafe (14th Ed.) QX6245	Yr.Iss.	1997	16.95	17-35
1997 Cat Naps (4th Ed.) QX6205	Yr.Iss.	1997	8.95	16-19
1997 A Celebration of Angels (3rd Ed.) QX6175	Yr.Iss.	1997	13.95	15-30
1997 Chinese Barbie™ (2nd Ed.) QX6162	Yr.Iss.	1997	14.95	15-32
1997 The Clauses on Vacation (1st Ed.) QX6112	Yr.Iss.	1997	14.95	15-41
1997 The Claus-Mobile (19th Ed.) QX6262	Yr.Iss.	1997	14.95	18-27
1997 Daisy-Mary's Angels (10th Ed.) QX6242	Yr.Iss.	1997	7.95	8-16
1997 Fabulous Decade (8th Ed.) QX6232	Yr.Iss.	1997	7.95	10-16
1997 The Flight at Kitty Hawk (1st Ed.) QX5574	Yr.Iss.	1997	14.95	19-32
1997 Frosty Friends (18th Ed.) QX6255	Yr.Iss.	1997	10.95	11-20
1997 Jackie Robinson (4th Ed.) QX6202	Yr.Iss.	1997	12.95	15-28
1997 Kolyada (3rd Ed.) QX6172	Yr.Iss.	1997	14.95	10-27
1997 Little Boy Blue (5th Ed.) QX6215	Yr.Iss.	1997	13.95	14-30
1997 Little Red Riding Hood-1991 (2nd Ed.) QX6155	Yr.Iss.	1997	14.95	22-33
1997 Marilyn Monroe (1st Ed.) QX5704	Yr.Iss.	1997	14.95	15-30
1997 Merry Olde Santa (8th Ed.) QX6225	Yr.Iss.	1997	14.95	18-28
1997 Murray Dump Truck (4th Ed.) QX6195	Yr.Iss.	1997	13.95	15-25
1997 Nikki-All God's Children®-Martha Root (2nd Ed.) QX6142	Yr.Iss.	1997	12.95	24-26
1997 Puppy Love (7th Ed.) QX6222	Yr.Iss.	1997	7.95	10-23

YEAR ISSUE	EDITION LIMIT	YEAR RETD.	ISSUE PRICE	*QUOTE U.S.$
1997 Scarlett O'Hara (1st Ed.) QX6125	Yr.Iss.	1997	14.95	15-36
1997 Snowshoe Rabbits in Winter-Mark Newman (1st Ed.) QX5694	Yr.Iss.	1997	12.95	23-30
1997 Yuletide Central (4th Ed.) QX5812	Yr.Iss.	1997	18.95	20-36

1997 Commemoratives - Keepsake

1997 Baby's First Christmas QX6485	Yr.Iss.	1997	9.95	16-32
1997 Baby's First Christmas QX6492	Yr.Iss.	1997	9.95	5-21
1997 Baby's First Christmas QX6495	Yr.Iss.	1997	7.95	12-20
1997 Baby's First Christmas QX6535	Yr.Iss.	1997	14.95	18-25
1997 Baby's First Christmas-Photo Holder QX6482	Yr.Iss.	1997	7.95	16-27
1997 Baby's Second Christmas QX6502	Yr.Iss.	1997	7.95	10-16
1997 Book of the Year-Photo Holder QX6645	Yr.Iss.	1997	7.95	8-20
1997 Child's Fifth Christmas QX6515	Yr.Iss.	1997	7.95	12-20
1997 Child's Fourth Christmas QX6512	Yr.Iss.	1997	7.95	5-18
1997 Child's Third Christmas QX6505	Yr.Iss.	1997	7.95	16-20
1997 Dad QX6532	Yr.Iss.	1997	8.95	7-16
1997 Daughter QX6612	Yr.Iss.	1997	7.95	16
1997 Friendship Blend QX6655	Yr.Iss.	1997	9.95	19
1997 Godchild QX6662	Yr.Iss.	1997	7.95	15-17
1997 Granddaughter QX6622	Yr.Iss.	1997	7.95	17-20
1997 Grandma QX6625	Yr.Iss.	1997	8.95	7-20
1997 Grandson QX6615	Yr.Iss.	1997	7.95	6-16
1997 Mom and Dad QX6522	Yr.Iss.	1997	9.95	10-22
1997 Mom QX6525	Yr.Iss.	1997	8.95	10-19
1997 New Home QX6652	Yr.Iss.	1997	8.95	3-19
1997 Our Christmas Together QX6475	Yr.Iss.	1997	16.95	5-32
1997 Our First Christmas Together QX6465	Yr.Iss.	1997	10.95	5-20
1997 Our First Christmas Together-Acrylic QX3182	Yr.Iss.	1997	7.95	5-15
1997 Our First Christmas Together-Photo Holder QX6472	Yr.Iss.	1997	8.95	17-25
1997 Sister to Sister QX6635	Yr.Iss.	1997	9.95	7-21
1997 Son QX6605	Yr.Iss.	1997	7.95	10-20
1997 Special Dog-Photo Holder QX6632	Yr.Iss.	1997	7.95	8-17

1997 Disney Ornaments - Keepsake

1997 Ariel QX14072	Yr.Iss.	1997	12.95	14-23
1997 Bandleader Mickey (1st Ed.) QXD4022	Yr.Iss.	1997	13.95	12-24
1997 Cinderella (1st Ed.) QXD4045	Yr.Iss.	1997	14.95	18-30
1997 Donald's Surprising Gift (1st Ed.) QXD4025	Yr.Iss.	1997	12.95	12-40
1997 Esmeralda & Phoebus QXD6344	Yr.Iss.	1997	14.95	8-24
1997 Goofy's Ski Adventure QXD4042	Yr.Iss.	1997	12.95	13-24
1997 Gus & Jaq QXD4052	Yr.Iss.	1997	12.95	13-30
1997 Hercules QXI4005	Yr.Iss.	1997	12.95	10-26
1997 Honey of a Gift (Miniature) QXD4255	Yr.Iss.	1997	6.95	7-15
1997 Jasmine & Aladdin QXD4062	Yr.Iss.	1997	14.95	15-27
1997 Megara and Pegasus QXI4012	Yr.Iss.	1997	16.95	31-34
1997 Mickey Snow Angel QXD4035	Yr.Iss.	1997	9.95	8-18
1997 Mickey's Long Shot QXD6412	Yr.Iss.	1997	10.95	7-28
1997 New Pair of Skates QXD4032	Yr.Iss.	1997	13.95	14-28
1997 Snow White (Anniversary Ed.) QXD4055	Yr.Iss.	1997	16.95	16-31
1997 Timon & Pumbaa QXD4065	Yr.Iss.	1997	12.95	13-26
1997 Two Tone QXD4015	Yr.Iss.	1997	9.95	10-18
1997 Waitin' on Santa QXD6365	Yr.Iss.	1997	12.95	15-26
1997 Winnie the Pooh Plate QXE6835	Yr.Iss.	1997	12.95	13-24

1997 Keepsake Collector's Club - Keepsake

1997 1937 Steelcraft Airflow by Murray® QXC5185	Yr.Iss.	1997	15.95	19-50
1997 1989 Happy Holidays® Barbie™ Doll QXC5162	Yr.Iss.	1997	15.95	25-52
1997 Away to the Window QXC5135	Yr.Iss.	1997	N/A	7-14
1997 Farmer's Market, Tender Touches QXC5182	Yr.Iss.	1997	15.00	20-36
1997 Happy Christmas to All! QXC5132	Yr.Iss.	1997	N/A	9-18
1997 Jolly Old Santa QXC5145	Yr.Iss.	1997	N/A	9-14
1997 Mrs. Claus (Artist on Tour) QXC5192	Yr.Iss.	1997	14.95	10-26
1997 Ready for Santa QXC5142	Yr.Iss.	1997	N/A	9-12
1997 Trimming Santa's Tree (Artist on Tour) QXC5175	Yr.Iss.	1997	60.00	40-76

1997 Keepsake Magic Ornaments - Keepsake

1997 Chris Mouse Luminaria (13th Ed.) QLX7525	Yr.Iss.	1997	14.95	15-30

YEAR ISSUE	EDITION LIMIT	YEAR RETD.	ISSUE PRICE	*QUOTE U.S.$
1997 Decorator Taz QLX7502	Yr.Iss.	1997	30.00	20-60
1997 Friendship 7 (2nd Ed.) QLX7532	Yr.Iss.	1997	24.00	18-51
1997 Glowing Angel QLX7435	Yr.Iss.	1997	18.95	14-39
1997 Holiday Serenade QLX7485	Yr.Iss.	1997	24.00	43-48
1997 Joy to the World QLX7512	Yr.Iss.	1997	14.95	12-30
1997 Lighthouse Greetings (1st Ed.) QLX7442	Yr.Iss.	1997	24.00	45-99
1997 The Lincoln Memorial QLX7522	Yr.Iss.	1997	24.00	29-48
1997 Madonna & Child QLX7425	Yr.Iss.	1997	19.95	24-50
1997 Motorcycle Chums QLX7495	Yr.Iss.	1997	24.00	29-45
1997 Santa's Secret Gift QLX7455	Yr.Iss.	1997	24.00	29-48
1997 Santa's Showboat (Special Ed.) QLX7465	Yr.Iss.	1997	42.00	59-85
1997 SNOOPY Plays Santa QLX7475	Yr.Iss.	1997	22.00	16-44
1997 Teapot Party QLX7482	Yr.Iss.	1997	18.95	19-38

1997 Miniature Ornaments - Keepsake

1997 Antique Tractors (1st Ed.) QXM4185	Yr.Iss.	1997	6.95	10-28
1997 Candy Car (9th Ed.) QXM4175	Yr.Iss.	1997	6.95	7-15
1997 Casablanca, set/3 QXM4272	Yr.Iss.	1997	19.95	18-36
1997 Centuries of Santa (4th Ed.) QXM4295	Yr.Iss.	1997	5.95	8-12
1997 Christmas Bells (3rd Ed.) QXM4162	Yr.Iss.	1997	4.95	9-20
1997 Clothespin Soldier (3rd Ed.) QXM4155	Yr.Iss.	1997	4.95	4-11
1997 Future Star QXM4232	Yr.Iss.	1997	5.95	4-12
1997 Gentle Giraffes QXM4221	Yr.Iss.	1997	5.95	6-15
1997 He Is Born QXM4235	Yr.Iss.	1997	7.95	6-15
1997 Heavenly Music QXM4292	Yr.Iss.	1997	5.95	4-12
1997 Herr Drosselmeyer (2nd Ed.) QXM4135	Yr.Iss.	1997	5.95	12-15
1997 Home Sweet Home QXM4222	Yr.Iss.	1997	5.95	5-13
1997 Ice Cold Coca-Cola® QXM4252	Yr.Iss.	1997	6.95	14-34
1997 King of the Forest QXM4262	Yr.Iss.	1997	24.00	25-45
1997 Murray "Pursuit" Airplane (3rd Ed.) QXM4132	Yr.Iss.	1997	6.95	6-14
1997 Nutcracker Guild (4th Ed.) QXM4165	Yr.Iss.	1997	6.95	6-16
1997 On The Road (5th Ed.) QXM4172	Yr.Iss.	1997	5.95	5-12
1997 Our Lady of Guadalupe (Precious Ed.) QXM4275	Yr.Iss.	1997	8.95	9-19
1997 Peppermint Painter QXM4312	Yr.Iss.	1997	4.95	5-12
1997 Polar Buddies QXM4332	Yr.Iss.	1997	4.95	5-12
1997 Rocking Horse (10th Ed.) QXM4302	Yr.Iss.	1997	4.95	5-15
1997 Santa's Little Big Top (3rd Ed.) QXM4152	Yr.Iss.	1997	6.95	6-14
1997 Seeds of Joy QXM4242	Yr.Iss.	1997	6.95	5-14
1997 Sew Talented QXM4195	Yr.Iss.	1997	5.95	5-14
1997 Shutterbug QXM4212	Yr.Iss.	1997	5.95	5-14
1997 Snowboard Bunny QXM4315	Yr.Iss.	1997	4.95	4-12
1997 Snowflake Ballet (1st Ed.) QXM4192	Yr.Iss.	1997	5.95	6-14
1997 Teddy-Bear Style (1st Ed.) QXM4215	Yr.Iss.	1997	5.95	3-15
1997 Tiny Home Improvers,set/6 QXM4282	Yr.Iss.	1997	29.00	31-44
1997 Victorian Skater QXM4305	Yr.Iss.	1997	5.95	4-12
1997 Village Depot (10th Ed.) QXM4182	Yr.Iss.	1997	6.95	7-15
1997 Welcome Friends, set/4 (1st Ed.) QXM4205	Yr.Iss.	1997	6.95	9-20
1997 White Rabbit (3rd Ed.) QXM4142	Yr.Iss.	1997	6.95	8-17

1997 NBA Collection - Keepsake

1997 Charlotte Hornets QSR1222	Yr.Iss.	1997	9.95	10
1997 Chicago Bulls QSR1232	Yr.Iss.	1997	9.95	15-20
1997 Detroit Pistons QSR1242	Yr.Iss.	1997	9.95	10
1997 Houston Rockets QSR1245	Yr.Iss.	1997	9.95	10
1997 Indiana Pacers QSR1252	Yr.Iss.	1997	9.95	18-20
1997 Los Angeles Lakers QSR1262	Yr.Iss.	1997	9.95	10
1997 New York Knickerbockers QSR1272	Yr.Iss.	1997	9.95	10
1997 Orlando Magic QSR1282	Yr.Iss.	1997	9.95	10
1997 Phoenix Suns QSR1292	Yr.Iss.	1997	9.95	10
1997 Seattle Supersonics QSR1295	Yr.Iss.	1997	9.95	10

1997 New Attractions - Keepsake

1997 All-Round Sports Fan QX6392	Yr.Iss.	1997	8.95	9-30
1997 All-Weather Walker QX6415	Yr.Iss.	1997	8.95	10-18
1997 Angel Friend (Archive Collection) QX6762	Yr.Iss.	1997	14.95	19-32
1997 Biking Buddies QX6682	Yr.Iss.	1997	12.95	5-23
1997 Breezin' Along QX6722	Yr.Iss.	1997	8.95	6-17
1997 Bucket Brigade QX6382	Yr.Iss.	1997	8.95	5-16
1997 Catch of the Day QX6712	Yr.Iss.	1997	9.95	5-18
1997 Christmas Checkup QX6385	Yr.Iss.	1997	7.95	8-16
1997 Classic Cross QX6805	Yr.Iss.	1997	13.95	14-19
1997 Clever Camper QX6445	Yr.Iss.	1997	7.95	8-15
1997 Cycling Santa QX6425	Yr.Iss.	1997	14.95	19-30

YEAR ISSUE	EDITION LIMIT	YEAR RETD.	ISSUE PRICE	*QUOTE U.S.$
1997 Downhill Run QX6705	Yr.lss.	1997	9.95	18-20
1997 Elegance on Ice QX6432	Yr.lss.	1997	9.95	19-21
1997 Expressly for Teacher QX6375	Yr.lss.	1997	7.95	8-16
1997 Feliz Navidad QX6665	Yr.lss.	1997	8.95	28-30
1997 God's Gift of Love QX6792	Yr.lss.	1997	16.95	19-34
1997 Heavenly Song (Archive Collection) QX6795	Yr.lss.	1997	12.95	15-26
1997 Howdy Doody (Anniversary Ed.) QX6272	Yr.lss.	1997	12.95	13-24
1997 The Incredible Hulk QX5471	Yr.lss.	1997	12.95	20-26
1997 Jingle Bell Jester QX6695	Yr.lss.	1997	9.95	18-20
1997 Juggling Stars QX6595	Yr.lss.	1997	9.95	6-20
1997 King Noor-First King QX6552	Yr.lss.	1997	12.95	29-45
1997 Lion and Lamb QX6602	Yr.lss.	1997	7.95	10-18
1997 The Lone Ranger QX6265	Yr.lss.	1997	12.95	20-38
1997 Love to Sew QX6435	Yr.lss.	1997	7.95	8-17
1997 Madonna del Rosario QX6545	Yr.lss.	1997	12.95	24-26
1997 Marbles Champion QX6342	Yr.lss.	1997	10.95	4-22
1997 Meadow Snowman QX6715	Yr.lss.	1997	12.95	19-33
1997 Michigan J. Frog QX6332	Yr.lss.	1997	9.95	10-20
1997 Miss Gulch QX6372	Yr.lss.	1997	13.95	28-30
1997 Mr. Potato Head QX6335	Yr.lss.	1997	10.95	19-24
1997 Nativity Tree QX6575	Yr.lss.	1997	14.95	17-32
1997 The Night Before Christmas -Collector's Choice QX5721	Yr.lss.	1997	24.00	24-55
1997 Playful Shepherd QX6592	Yr.lss.	1997	9.95	12-20
1997 Porcelain Hinged Box QX6772	Yr.lss.	1997	14.95	15-27
1997 Praise Him QX6512	Yr.lss.	1997	8.95	9-18
1997 Prize Topiary QX6675	Yr.lss.	1997	14.95	15-30
1997 Sailor Bear QX6765	Yr.lss.	1997	14.95	15-30
1997 Santa Mail QX6702	Yr.lss.	1997	10.95	11-29
1997 Santa's Friend QX6685	Yr.lss.	1997	12.95	15-27
1997 Santa's Magical Sleigh QX6672	Yr.lss.	1997	24.00	29-48
1997 Santa's Polar Friend (Archive Collection) QX6755	Yr.lss.	1997	16.95	19-35
1997 Santa's Ski Adventure QX6422	Yr.lss.	1997	12.95	13-27
1997 Snow Bowling QX6395	Yr.lss.	1997	6.95	7-15
1997 Snow Girl QX6562	Yr.lss.	1997	7.95	4-17
1997 The Spirit of Christmas-Collector's Plate QX6585	Yr.lss.	1997	9.95	27-34
1997 Stealing a Kiss QX6555	Yr.lss.	1997	14.95	15-30
1997 Sweet Discovery QX6325	Yr.lss.	1997	11.95	13-24
1997 Sweet Dreamer QX6732	Yr.lss.	1997	6.95	7-15
1997 Swinging in the Snow QX6775	Yr.lss.	1997	12.95	13-26
1997 Taking a Break QX6305	Yr.lss.	1997	14.95	19-30
1997 Tomorrow's Leader QX6452	Yr.lss.	1997	9.95	10-14
1997 Tonka® Mighty Front Loader QX6362	Yr.lss.	1997	13.95	20-30
1997 What a Deal! QX6442	Yr.lss.	1997	8.95	5-18

1997 NFL Ornaments - Keepsake

1997 Arizona Cardinals QSR5505	Yr.lss.	1997	9.95	10
1997 Atlanta Falcons QSR5305	Yr.lss.	1997	9.95	10
1997 Baltimore Ravens QSR5352	Yr.lss.	1997	9.95	10-20
1997 Buffalo Bills QSR5312	Yr.lss.	1997	9.95	10
1997 Carolina Panthers QSR5315	Yr.lss.	1997	9.95	10-20
1997 Chicago Bears QSR5322	Yr.lss.	1997	9.95	10-20
1997 Cincinnati Bengals QSR5325	Yr.lss.	1997	9.95	10
1997 Dallas Cowboys QSR5355	Yr.lss.	1997	9.95	10-20
1997 Denver Broncos QSR5362	Yr.lss.	1997	9.95	10-30
1997 Detroit Lions QSR5365	Yr.lss.	1997	9.95	10
1997 Green Bay Packers QSR5372	Yr.lss.	1997	9.95	22-25
1997 Houston Oilers QSR5375	Yr.lss.	1997	9.95	10-18
1997 Indianapolis Colts QSR5411	Yr.lss.	1997	9.95	10
1997 Jacksonville Jaquars QSR5415	Yr.lss.	1997	9.95	10-20
1997 Kansas City Chiefs QSR5502	Yr.lss.	1997	9.95	10-20
1997 Miami Dolphins QSR5472	Yr.lss.	1997	9.95	10-20
1997 Minnesota Vikings QSR5475	Yr.lss.	1997	9.95	10-18
1997 New England Patriots QSR5482	Yr.lss.	1997	9.95	10-18
1997 New Orleans Saints QSR5485	Yr.lss.	1997	9.95	10
1997 New York Giants QSR5492	Yr.lss.	1997	9.95	10
1997 New York Jets QSR5495	Yr.lss.	1997	9.95	10
1997 Oakland Raiders QSR5422	Yr.lss.	1997	9.95	10-20
1997 Philadelphia Eagles QSR5502	Yr.lss.	1997	9.95	10
1997 Pittsburgh Steelers QSR5512	Yr.lss.	1997	9.95	10-20
1997 San Diego Chargers QSR5515	Yr.lss.	1997	9.95	4-20
1997 San Francisco 49ers QSR5522	Yr.lss.	1997	9.95	10
1997 Seattle Seahawks QSR5525	Yr.lss.	1997	9.95	10
1997 St. Louis Rams QSR5425	Yr.lss.	1997	9.95	10
1997 Tampa Bay Buccaneers QSR5532	Yr.lss.	1997	9.95	10
1997 Washington Redskins QSR5535	Yr.lss.	1997	9.95	10

1997 Premiere Event - Keepsake

1997 The Perfect Tree-Tender Touches QX6572	Yr.lss.	1997	15.00	19-30

1997 Showcase Folk Art Americana Collection - Keepsake

1997 Leading the Way QX6782	Yr.lss.	1997	16.95	17-35
1997 Santa's Merry Path QX6785	Yr.lss.	1997	16.95	24-36

1997 Showcase Nature's Sketchbook Collection - Keepsake

1997 Garden Bouquet QX6752	Yr.lss.	1997	14.95	15-30
1997 Garden Bunnies QEO8702	Yr.lss.	1997	14.95	18-30
1997 Honored Guest QX6745	Yr.lss.	1997	14.95	30-33

1997 Showcase The Language of Flowers Collection - Keepsake

1997 Snowdrop Angel (2nd Ed.) QX1095	Yr.lss.	1997	15.95	15-31

1997 Showcase Turn-of-the-Century Parade Collection - Keepsake

1997 Santa Claus (3rd Ed.) QX1215	Yr.lss.	1997	16.95	15-31

1997 Special Issues - Keepsake

1997 1997 Corvette Miniature QXI4322	Yr.lss.	1997	6.95	8-14
1997 1997 Corvette QXI6455	Yr.lss.	1997	13.95	15-25
1997 Ariel QXI4072	Yr.lss.	1997	12.95	18-26
1997 Barbie™ And Ken Wedding Day QXI6815	Yr.lss.	1997	35.00	35-55
1997 Barbie™ Wedding Day-1959-1962 (4th Ed.) QXI6812	Yr.lss.	1997	15.95	20-35
1997 C-3PO & R2-D2 QXI4265	Yr.lss.	1997	12.95	13-28
1997 Commander Data QXI6345	Yr.lss.	1997	14.95	21-30
1997 Darth Vader QXI7531	Yr.lss.	1997	24.00	24-48
1997 Dr. Leonard H. McCoy QXI6352	Yr.lss.	1997	14.95	19-32
1997 Hank Aaron (2nd Ed.) QXI6152	Yr.lss.	1997	14.95	15-27
1997 Holiday Barbie™(5th Ed.) QXI6212	Yr.lss.	1997	15.95	29-32
1997 Jeff Gordon (1st Ed.) QXI6165	Yr.lss.	1997	15.95	19-50
1997 Joe Namath (3rd Ed.) QXI6182	Yr.lss.	1997	14.95	15-28
1997 Luke Skywalker (1st Ed.) QXI5484	Yr.lss.	1997	13.95	20-32
1997 Magic Johnson (3rd Ed.) QXI6832	Yr.lss.	1997	14.95	15-27
1997 U.S.S. Defiant QXI7481	Yr.lss.	1997	24.00	38-48
1997 Victorian Christmas-Thomas Kinkade (1st Ed.) QXI6135	Yr.lss.	1997	10.95	26-30
1997 The Warmth of Home QXI7545	Yr.lss.	1997	18.95	20-37
1997 Wayne Gretzky (1st Ed.) QXI6275	Yr.lss.	1997	15.95	19-33
1997 Yoda QXI6355	Yr.lss.	1997	9.95	20-40

1997 Spring Ornaments - Keepsake

1997 1935 Steelcraft Streamline Velocipede by Murray® (1st Ed.) QEO8632	Yr.lss.	1997	12.95	16-29
1997 Apple Blossom Lane QEO8662	Yr.lss.	1997	8.95	11-16
1997 Barbie™ as Rapunzel Doll (1st Ed.) QEO8635	Yr.lss.	1997	14.95	9-32
1997 Bumper Crop, Tender Touches QEO8735	Yr.lss.	1997	14.95	18-27
1997 Collector's Plate QEO8675	Yr.lss.	1997	7.95	8-15
1997 Colorful Coal Car (2nd Ed.) QEO8652	Yr.lss.	1997	8.95	12-18
1997 Digging In QEO8712	Yr.lss.	1997	7.95	10-18
1997 Eggs-pert Artist QEO8695	Yr.lss.	1997	8.95	14-19
1997 Garden Club QEO8665	Yr.lss.	1997	7.95	10-18
1997 Gentle Guardian QEO8732	Yr.lss.	1997	6.95	14-16
1997 Here Comes Easter QEO8682	Yr.lss.	1997	7.95	15-18
1997 Jemima Puddle-Duck (2nd Ed.) QEO8645	Yr.lss.	1997	8.95	10-26
1997 Joyful Angels QEO8655	Yr.lss.	1997	10.95	15-22
1997 A Purr-fect Princess QEO8715	Yr.lss.	1997	7.95	11-16
1997 Springtime Barbie™ QEO8642	Yr.lss.	1997	12.95	14-25
1997 Springtime Bonnets QEO8672	Yr.lss.	1997	7.95	16-18
1997 Swing-Time QEO8705	Yr.lss.	1997	7.95	15-17
1997 Victorian Cross QEO8725	Yr.lss.	1997	8.95	11-19

1998 25th Anniversary - Keepsake

1998 Angelic Flight QXI4146	25,000	1998	85.00	85-125
1998 Halls Station QX6833	Yr.lss.	1998	25.00	25-50
1998 Joyful Messenger QXI4146	Yr.lss.	1998	18.95	24-40
1998 Tin Locomotive QX6826	Yr.lss.	1998	25.00	45-50

1998 Collectible Series - Keepsake

1998 1917 Curtiss JN-4D "Jenny" (2nd Ed.) QX6286	Yr.lss.	1998	14.95	21-28
1998 1937 Ford V-8 (4th Ed.) QX6263	Yr.lss.	1998	13.95	18-24
1998 1955 Murray® Tractor and Trailer (5th Ed.) QX6376	Yr.lss.	1998	16.95	20-26

ORNAMENTS

YEAR ISSUE	EDITION LIMIT	YEAR RETD.	ISSUE PRICE	*QUOTE U.S.$
1998 1970 Plymouth Hemi 'Cuda (8th Ed.) QX6256	Yr.Iss.	1998	13.95	18-27
1998 Bright Sledding Colors (10th Ed.) QX6166	Yr.Iss.	1998	12.95	12-23
1998 Cat Naps (5th Ed.) QX6383	Yr.Iss.	1998	8.95	12-18
1998 A Celebration of Angels (4th Ed.) QX6366	Yr.Iss.	1998	13.95	14-26
1998 The Clauses on Vacation (2nd Ed.) QX6276	Yr.Iss.	1998	14.95	18-20
1998 Daphne-Mary's Angels (11th Ed.) QX6153	Yr.Iss.	1998	7.95	12-16
1998 Fabulous Decade (9th Ed.) QX6393	Yr.Iss.	1998	7.95	20-30
1998 Frosty Friends (19th Ed.) QX6226	Yr.Iss.	1998	10.95	15-33
1998 Glorious Angel (1st Ed.) QX6493	Yr.Iss.	1998	14.95	18-27
1998 Grocery Store (15th Ed.) QX6266	Yr.Iss.	1998	16.95	27-30
1998 Joe Cool (1st Ed.) QX6453	Yr.Iss.	1998	9.95	20-22
1998 Marilyn Monroe (2nd Ed.) QX6333	Yr.Iss.	1998	14.95	15-27
1998 Merry Olde Santa (9th Ed.) QX6386	Yr.Iss.	1998	15.95	16-30
1998 Mexican Barbie™ (3rd Ed.) QX6356	Yr.Iss.	1998	14.95	18-30
1998 Mop Top Wendy (3rd Ed.) QX6353	Yr.Iss.	1998	14.95	20-25
1998 Pennsylvania GG-1 Locomotive (3rd Ed.) QX6346	Yr.Iss.	1998	18.95	28-35
1998 Pony Express Rider (1st Ed.) QX6323	Yr.Iss.	1998	13.95	20-27
1998 A Pony for Christmas (1st Ed.) QX6316	Yr.Iss.	1998	10.95	14-30
1998 Puppy Love (8th Ed.) QX6163	Yr.Iss.	1998	7.95	12-15
1998 Ricky-All God's Children®-Martha Root (3rd Ed.) QX6363	Yr.Iss.	1998	12.95	15-23
1998 Santa's Bumper Car (20th Ed.) QX6283	Yr.Iss.	1998	14.95	27-30
1998 Scarlett O'Hara (2nd Ed.) QX6336	Yr.Iss.	1998	14.95	21-27
1998 Snow Buddies (1st Ed.) QX6853	Yr.Iss.	1998	7.95	20-35
1998 Timber Wolves at Play-Mark Newman (2nd Ed.) QX6273	Yr.Iss.	1998	12.95	15-28
1998 A Visit From Piglet (1st Ed.) QXD4086	Yr.Iss.	1998	13.95	14-28
1998 Yuletide Central (5th Ed.) QX6373	Yr.Iss.	1998	18.95	23-50

1998 Collegiate Ornaments - Keepsake

YEAR ISSUE	EDITION LIMIT	YEAR RETD.	ISSUE PRICE	*QUOTE U.S.$
1998 Florida State Seminoles™ QSR2316	Yr.Iss.	1998	9.95	10
1998 Michigan Wolverines™ QSR2323	Yr.Iss.	1998	9.95	10
1998 North Carolina Tar Heels™ QSR2333	Yr.Iss.	1998	9.95	10
1998 Notre Dame® Fighting Irish™ QSR2313	Yr.Iss.	1998	9.95	10-14
1998 Penn State Nittany Lions™ QSR2326	Yr.Iss.	1998	9.95	10

1998 Commemoratives - Keepsake

YEAR ISSUE	EDITION LIMIT	YEAR RETD.	ISSUE PRICE	*QUOTE U.S.$
1998 #1 Student QX6646	Yr.Iss.	1998	7.95	6-17
1998 Baby's Fifth Christmas QX6623	Yr.Iss.	1998	7.95	10-16
1998 Baby's First Christmas QX6233	Yr.Iss.	1998	9.95	14-20
1998 Baby's First Christmas QX6586	Yr.Iss.	1998	9.95	14-19
1998 Baby's First Christmas QX6596	Yr.Iss.	1998	8.95	10-20
1998 Baby's First Christmas QX6603	Yr.Iss.	1998	7.95	16-25
1998 Baby's Fourth Christmas QX6616	Yr.Iss.	1998	7.95	10-21
1998 Baby's Second Christmas QX6606	Yr.Iss.	1998	7.95	10-20
1998 Baby's Third Christmas QX6613	Yr.Iss.	1998	7.95	10-20
1998 Chatty Chipmunk QX6716	Yr.Iss.	1998	9.95	8-22
1998 Dad QX6663	Yr.Iss.	1998	8.95	10-17
1998 Daughter QX6673	Yr.Iss.	1998	8.95	10-16
1998 Forever Friends Bear QX6303	Yr.Iss.	1998	8.95	16-18
1998 Friend of My Heart QX6723	Yr.Iss.	1998	14.95	15-30
1998 Godchild QX6703	Yr.Iss.	1998	7.95	6-17
1998 Granddaughter QX6683	Yr.Iss.	1998	7.95	14-16
1998 Grandma's Memories QX6686	Yr.Iss.	1998	8.95	7-18
1998 Grandson QX6676	Yr.Iss.	1998	7.95	10-15
1998 Mom and Dad QX6653	Yr.Iss.	1998	9.95	8-20
1998 Mom QX6656	Yr.Iss.	1998	8.95	10-17
1998 Mother and Daughter QX6696	Yr.Iss.	1998	8.95	7-25
1998 New Arrival QX6306	Yr.Iss.	1998	18.95	14-30
1998 New Home QX6713	Yr.Iss.	1998	9.95	8-23
1998 Our First Christmas Together QX3193	Yr.Iss.	1998	7.95	15-20
1998 Our First Christmas Together QX6636	Yr.Iss.	1998	8.95	7-20
1998 Our First Christmas Together QX6643	Yr.Iss.	1998	18.95	16-36
1998 A Perfect Match QX6633	Yr.Iss.	1998	10.95	8-22
1998 Sister to Sister QX6693	Yr.Iss.	1998	8.95	10-17
1998 Son QX6666	Yr.Iss.	1998	8.95	13-16
1998 Special Dog QX6606	Yr.Iss.	1998	7.95	6-16

1998 Crown Reflections - Keepsake

YEAR ISSUE	EDITION LIMIT	YEAR RETD.	ISSUE PRICE	*QUOTE U.S.$
1998 1955 Murray® Fire Truck QBG6909	Yr.Iss.	1998	35.00	41-48
1998 Festive Locomotive QBG6903	Yr.Iss.	1998	35.00	29-32
1998 Frankincense QBG6896	2-Yr.		22.00	22
1998 Frosty Friends, set/2 QBG6907	Yr.Iss.	1998	48.00	55-60
1998 Gold QBG6836	2-Yr.		22.00	22
1998 Myrrh QBG6893	2-Yr.		22.00	22
1998 Pink Poinsettias QBG6926	Yr.Iss.	1998	25.00	32-35
1998 Red Poinsettias (1st) QBG6906	Yr.Iss.	1998	35.00	43-48
1998 Sugarplum Cottage QBG6917	Yr.Iss.	1998	35.00	41-45
1998 Sweet Memories, set/8 QBG6933	Yr.Iss.	1998	45.00	45-60
1998 White Poinsettias QBG6923	Yr.Iss.	1998	25.00	32-35

1998 Disney Ornaments - Keepsake

YEAR ISSUE	EDITION LIMIT	YEAR RETD.	ISSUE PRICE	*QUOTE U.S.$
1998 Bouncy Baby-sitter QXD4096	Yr.Iss.	1998	12.95	14-24
1998 Building a Snowman QXD4133	Yr.Iss.	1998	14.95	16-28
1998 Buzz Lightyear QXD4066	Yr.Iss.	1998	14.95	29
1998 Cinderella's Coach QXD4083	Yr.Iss.	1998	14.95	21-28
1998 Cruella de Vil (1st Ed.) QXD4063	Yr.Iss.	1998	14.95	18-24
1998 Daydreams QXD4136	Yr.Iss.	1998	13.95	27-30
1998 Donald and Daisy in Venice (1st Ed.) QXD4103	Yr.Iss.	1998	14.95	18-26
1998 Flik QXD4153	Yr.Iss.	1998	12.95	27-30
1998 Goofy Soccer Star QXD4123	Yr.Iss.	1998	10.95	21-23
1998 Iago, Abu amd the Genie QXD4076	Yr.Iss.	1998	12.95	28
1998 Make-Believe Boat QXD4113	Yr.Iss.	1998	12.95	13-28
1998 The Mickey and Minnie Handcar QXD4116	Yr.Iss.	1998	14.95	22-26
1998 Mickey's Favorite Reindeer QXD4013	Yr.Iss.	1998	13.95	25-28
1998 Minnie Plays the Flute (2nd Ed.) QXD4106	Yr.Iss.	1998	13.95	14-22
1998 Mulan, Mushu and Cri-Kee QXD4156	Yr.Iss.	1998	14.95	29
1998 Princess Aurora QXD4126	Yr.Iss.	1998	12.95	15-27
1998 Ready For Christmas (2nd Ed.) QXD4006	Yr.Iss.	1998	12.95	15-23
1998 Runaway Toboggan QXD4003	Yr.Iss.	1998	16.95	17-33
1998 Simba & Nala QXD4073	Yr.Iss.	1998	13.95	14-28
1998 Tree Trimmin' Time,set/3 QXD4236	Yr.Iss.	1998	19.95	20-39
1998 A Visit From Piglet QXD4086	Yr.Iss.	1998	13.95	16-24
1998 Walt Disney's Snow White (2nd Ed.) QXD4056	Yr.Iss.	1998	14.95	17-26
1998 Woody the Sheriff QXD4163	Yr.Iss.	1998	14.95	18-27

1998 Holiday Traditions - Keepsake

YEAR ISSUE	EDITION LIMIT	YEAR RETD.	ISSUE PRICE	*QUOTE U.S.$
1998 A Child Is Born QX6176	Yr.Iss.	1998	12.95	13-25
1998 A Christmas Eve Story QX6873	Yr.Iss.	1998	13.95	14-24
1998 Christmas Request QX6193	Yr.Iss.	1998	14.95	15-2?
1998 Christmas Sleigh Ride QX6556	Yr.Iss.	1998	12.95	13-26
1998 Cross of Peace QX6856	Yr.Iss.	1998	9.95	10-20
1998 Cruising Into Christmas QX6196	Yr.Iss.	1998	16.95	30-33
1998 Fancy Footwork QX6536	Yr.Iss.	1998	8.95	13-16
1998 Feliz Navidad QX6173	Yr.Iss.	1998	8.95	10-1?
1998 Guardian Friend QX6543	Yr.Iss.	1998	8.95	9-18
1998 Heavenly Melody (Archive Collection) QX6576	Yr.Iss.	1998	18.95	19-40
1998 Holiday Decorator QX6566	Yr.Iss.	1998	13.95	14-2?
1998 The Holy Family, set/3 QX6523	3-Yr.		25.00	2?
1998 Journey To Bethlehem (Collector's Choice) QX6223	Yr.Iss.	1998	16.95	27-30
1998 King Kharoof-Second King QX6186	Yr.Iss.	1998	12.95	15-2?
1998 Madonna and Child QX6516	Yr.Iss.	1998	12.95	15-2?
1998 Memories of Christmas QX2406	Yr.Iss.	1998	5.95	12-1?
1998 Merry Chime QX6692	Yr.Iss.	1998	9.95	14-2?
1998 Miracle in Bethlehem QX6513	Yr.Iss.	1998	12.95	23-34
1998 Mistletoe Fairy QX6216	Yr.Iss.	1998	12.95	22-2?
1998 Nick's Wish List QX6863	Yr.Iss.	1998	8.95	9-1?
1998 Night Watch QX6725	Yr.Iss.	1998	9.95	10-2?
1998 Our Song QX6183	Yr.Iss.	1998	9.95	10-2?
1998 Peekaboo Bears QX6563	Yr.Iss.	1998	12.95	15-2?
1998 Purr-fect Little Deer QX6526	Yr.Iss.	1998	7.95	8-1?
1998 Santa's Deer Friend QX6583	Yr.Iss.	1998	24.00	24-5?
1998 Santa's Flying Machine QX6573	Yr.Iss.	1998	16.95	15-3?
1998 Santa's Hidden Surprise QX6913	Yr.Iss.	1998	14.95	27-3?
1998 Sweet Rememberings QX6876	Yr.Iss.	1998	8.95	9-1?
1998 Treetop Choir QX6506	Yr.Iss.	1998	7.95	10-2?
1998 Warm and Cozy QX6866	Yr.Iss.	1998	8.95	9-1
1998 Watchful Shepherd QX6499	Yr.Iss.	1998	8.95	10-1?
1998 Writing to Santa QX6533	Yr.Iss.	1998	7.95	8-1?

1998 Keepsake Collector's Club - Keepsake

YEAR ISSUE	EDITION LIMIT	YEAR RETD.	ISSUE PRICE	*QUOTE U.S.$
1998 1935 Steelcraft by Murray®	Yr.Iss.	1998	15.95	25-5?
1998 1990 Happy Holidays® Barbie™ Doll	Yr.Iss.	1998	15.95	25-3?
1998 Follow The Leader, set/2	Yr.Iss.	1998	16.95	3?
1998 Kringle Bells	Yr.Iss.	1998	N/A	9-1?
1998 Making His Way	Yr.Iss.	1998	N/A	2?

YEAR ISSUE	EDITION LIMIT	YEAR RETD.	ISSUE PRICE	*QUOTE U.S.$
1998 New Christmas Friend	Yr.Iss.	1998	N/A	14-19

1998 Keepsake Magic Ornaments - Keepsake

YEAR ISSUE	EDITION LIMIT	YEAR RETD.	ISSUE PRICE	*QUOTE U.S.$
1998 1998 Corvette® QLX7605	Yr.Iss.	1998	24.00	29-47
1998 Apollo Lunar Module (3rd Ed.) QLX7543	Yr.Iss.	1998	24.00	30-49
1998 Cinderella at the Ball QXD7576	Yr.Iss.	1998	24.00	19-52
1998 Lighthouse Greetings (2nd Ed.) QLX7536	Yr.Iss.	1998	24.00	25-50
1998 Mickey's Comet QXD7586	Yr.Iss.	1998	24.00	24-48
1998 Santa's Show 'n' Tell QLX7566	Yr.Iss.	1998	18.95	19-40
1998 Santa's Spin Top QLX7573	Yr.Iss.	1998	22.00	27-43
1998 St. Nicholas Circle QXI7556	Yr.Iss.	1998	18.95	28-40
1998 The Stone Church (1st Ed.) QLX7636	Yr.Iss.	1998	18.95	19-48
1998 U.S.S. Enterprise™ NCC-1701-E QXI7633	Yr.Iss.	1998	24.00	36-45
1998 The Washington Monument QLX7553	Yr.Iss.	1998	24.00	25-45
1998 X-wing Starfighter™ QXI7596	Yr.Iss.	1998	24.00	23-39

1998 Lifestyles & Occupations - Keepsake

YEAR ISSUE	EDITION LIMIT	YEAR RETD.	ISSUE PRICE	*QUOTE U.S.$
1998 Catch of the Season QX6786	Yr.Iss.	1998	14.95	15-30
1998 Checking Santa's Files QX6806	Yr.Iss.	1998	8.95	9-18
1998 Compact Skater QX6766	Yr.Iss.	1998	9.95	12-21
1998 Downhill Dash QX6776	Yr.Iss.	1998	13.95	14-30
1998 Future Ballerina QX6756	Yr.Iss.	1998	7.95	8-16
1998 Gifted Gardener QX6736	Yr.Iss.	1998	7.95	10-16
1998 Good Luck Dice QX6813	Yr.Iss.	1998	9.95	10-20
1998 Holiday Camper QX6783	Yr.Iss.	1998	12.95	13-25
1998 National Salute QX6293	Yr.Iss.	1998	8.95	9-16
1998 North Pole Reserve QX6803	Yr.Iss.	1998	10.95	14-20
1998 Polar Bowler QX6746	Yr.Iss.	1998	7.95	8-16
1998 Puttin' Around QX6763	Yr.Iss.	1998	9.95	10-17
1998 Rocket to Success QX6793	Yr.Iss.	1998	8.95	9-18
1998 Sew Gifted QX6743	Yr.Iss.	1998	7.95	13-20
1998 Spoonful of Love QX6796	Yr.Iss.	1998	8.95	16-18
1998 Surprise Catch QX6753	Yr.Iss.	1998	7.95	10-15

1998 Miniature Ornaments - Keepsake

YEAR ISSUE	EDITION LIMIT	YEAR RETD.	ISSUE PRICE	*QUOTE U.S.$
1998 1937 Steelcraft Auburn (1st Ed.) QXM4143	Yr.Iss.	1998	6.95	9-20
1998 Angel Chime (Precious Ed.) QXM4283	Yr.Iss.	1998	8.95	14-18
1998 Antique Tractors (2nd Ed.) QXM4166	Yr.Iss.	1998	6.95	9-18
1998 Betsey's Prayer QXM4263	Yr.Iss.	1998	4.95	10
1998 Caboose (10th Ed.) QXM4216	Yr.Iss.	1998	6.95	10-14
1998 Centuries of Santa (5th Ed.) QXM4206	Yr.Iss.	1998	5.95	6-12
1998 Cheshire Cat (4th Ed.) QXM4186	Yr.Iss.	1998	6.95	8-13
1998 Christmas Bells (4th Ed.) QXM4196	Yr.Iss.	1998	4.95	7-12
1998 Coca-Cola Time QXM4296	Yr.Iss.	1998	6.95	7-15
1998 Fishy Surprise QXM4276	Yr.Iss.	1998	6.95	7-14
1998 Glinda, The Good Witch™, The Wicked Witch of the West™ QXM4233	Yr.Iss.	1998	14.95	20-28
1998 Holly-Jolly Jig QXM4266	Yr.Iss.	1998	6.95	8-13
1998 Miniature Clothespin Soldier (4th Ed.) QXM4193	Yr.Iss.	1998	4.95	9
1998 Murray Inc.® Dump Truck (4th Ed.) QXM4183	Yr.Iss.	1998	6.95	8-12
1998 The Nativity (1st Ed.) QXM4156	Yr.Iss.	1998	9.95	13-39
1998 Noel R.R. Locomotive (Anniversary Ed.)1989-1998 QXM4286	Yr.Iss.	1998	10.95	15-18
1998 Nutcracker (3rd Ed.) QXM4146	Yr.Iss.	1998	5.95	14-20
1998 Nutcracker Guild (5th Ed.) QXM4203	Yr.Iss.	1998	6.95	9-14
1998 On the Road (6th Ed.) QXM4213	Yr.Iss.	1998	5.95	10
1998 Peaceful Pandas QXM4253	Yr.Iss.	1998	5.95	10
1998 Pixie Parachute QXM4256	Yr.Iss.	1998	4.95	5-9
1998 Sharing Joy QXM4273	Yr.Iss.	1998	4.95	10
1998 Singin' in the Rain™ QXM4303	Yr.Iss.	1998	10.95	11-20
1998 Snowflake Ballet (2nd Ed.) QXM4173	Yr.Iss.	1998	5.95	9-12
1998 SUPERMAN™ QXM4313	Yr.Iss.	1998	10.95	16-20
1998 Teddy-Bear Style (2nd Ed.) QXM4176	Yr.Iss.	1998	5.95	8-11
1998 Welcome Friends (2nd Ed.) QXM4153	Yr.Iss.	1998	6.95	11-15
1998 Winter Fun With SNOOPY® (1st Ed.) QXM4243	Yr.Iss.	1998	6.95	10-14

1998 NBA Ornaments - Keepsake

YEAR ISSUE	EDITION LIMIT	YEAR RETD.	ISSUE PRICE	*QUOTE U.S.$
1998 Charlotte Hornets QSR1033	Yr.Iss.	1998	9.95	10
1998 Chicago Bulls QSR1036	Yr.Iss.	1998	9.95	18
1998 Detroit Pistons QSR1043	Yr.Iss.	1998	9.95	10
1998 Houston Rockets QSR1046	Yr.Iss.	1998	9.95	10
1998 Indiana Pacers QSR1053	Yr.Iss.	1998	9.95	18
1998 Los Angeles Lakers QSR1056	Yr.Iss.	1998	9.95	10
1998 New York Knickerbockers QSR1063	Yr.Iss.	1998	9.95	10
1998 Orlando Magic QSR1066	Yr.Iss.	1998	9.95	10
1998 Seattle Supersonics QSR1076	Yr.Iss.	1998	9.95	10

YEAR ISSUE	EDITION LIMIT	YEAR RETD.	ISSUE PRICE	*QUOTE U.S.$
1998 Utah Jazz QSR1083	Yr.Iss.	1998	9.95	10

1998 NFL Ornaments - Keepsake

YEAR ISSUE	EDITION LIMIT	YEAR RETD.	ISSUE PRICE	*QUOTE U.S.$
1998 Carolina Panthers™ QSR5026	Yr.Iss.	1998	9.95	10-18
1998 Chicago Bears™ QSR5033	Yr.Iss.	1998	9.95	10-18
1998 Dallas Cowboys™ QSR5046	Yr.Iss.	1998	9.95	14
1998 Denver Broncos™ QSR5053	Yr.Iss.	1998	9.95	23-30
1998 Green Bay Packers™ QSR5063	Yr.Iss.	1998	9.95	14-18
1998 Kansas City Chiefs™ QSR5013	Yr.Iss.	1998	9.95	10-18
1998 Miami Dolphins™ QSR5096	Yr.Iss.	1998	9.95	10
1998 Minnesota Vikings™ QSR5126	Yr.Iss.	1998	9.95	10-20
1998 New York Giants™ QSR5143	Yr.Iss.	1998	9.95	10-13
1998 Oakland Raiders™ QSR5086	Yr.Iss.	1998	9.95	10-18
1998 Philadelphia Eagles™ QSR5153	Yr.Iss.	1998	9.95	10-18
1998 Pittsburgh Steelers™ QSR5163	Yr.Iss.	1998	9.95	10
1998 San Francisco 49ers™ QSR5173	Yr.Iss.	1998	9.95	10
1998 St. Louis Rams™ QSR5093	Yr.Iss.	1998	9.95	10-18
1998 Washington Redskins™ QSR5186	Yr.Iss.	1998	9.95	13-18

1998 Pop Culture Icons - Keepsake

YEAR ISSUE	EDITION LIMIT	YEAR RETD.	ISSUE PRICE	*QUOTE U.S.$
1998 1998 Corvette® Convertible QX6416	Yr.Iss.	1998	13.95	14-26
1998 Bugs Bunny-LOONEY TUNES QX6443	Yr.Iss.	1998	13.95	14-24
1998 Decorating Maxine-Style	Yr.Iss.	1998	10.95	10-22
1998 Hot Wheels™ QX6436	Yr.Iss.	1998	13.95	25-28
1998 Larry, Moe, and Curly-The Three Stooges™ QX6503	Yr.Iss.	1998	27.00	34-73
1998 Maxine QX6446	Yr.Iss.	1998	9.95	10-21
1998 Mrs. Potato Head® QX6886	Yr.Iss.	1998	10.95	14-23
1998 Munchkinland™ Mayor and Cornoner QX6463	Yr.Iss.	1998	13.95	15-28
1998 Superman™ QX6423	Yr.Iss.	1998	12.95	14-24
1998 Sweet Treat HERSHEY'S™ QX6433	Yr.Iss.	1998	10.95	20-35
1998 Tonka® Road Grader QX6483	Yr.Iss.	1998	13.95	13-27

1998 Premiere Event - Keepsake

YEAR ISSUE	EDITION LIMIT	YEAR RETD.	ISSUE PRICE	*QUOTE U.S.$
1998 Santa's Merry Workshop QX6816	Yr.Iss.	1998	32.00	32-56

1998 Showcase Folk Art Americana Collection - Keepsake

YEAR ISSUE	EDITION LIMIT	YEAR RETD.	ISSUE PRICE	*QUOTE U.S.$
1998 Soaring With Angels QX6213	Yr.Iss.	1998	16.95	19-39

1998 Showcase Nature's Sketchbook Collection - Keepsake

YEAR ISSUE	EDITION LIMIT	YEAR RETD.	ISSUE PRICE	*QUOTE U.S.$
1998 Country Home QX5172	Yr.Iss.	1998	10.95	17-22

1998 Showcase The Language of Flowers Collection - Keepsake

YEAR ISSUE	EDITION LIMIT	YEAR RETD.	ISSUE PRICE	*QUOTE U.S.$
1998 Iris Angel (3rd Ed.) QX6156	Yr.Iss.	1998	15.95	24-27

1998 Special Issues - Keepsake

YEAR ISSUE	EDITION LIMIT	YEAR RETD.	ISSUE PRICE	*QUOTE U.S.$
1998 Barbie™Silken Flame (5th Ed.) QXI4043	Yr.Iss.	1998	15.95	14-27
1998 Boba Fett™ QXI4053	Yr.Iss.	1998	14.95	16-32
1998 Cal Ripken Jr. (3rd) QXI4033	Yr.Iss.	1998	14.95	20-27
1998 Captain Kathryn Janeway™ QXI4046	Yr.Iss.	1998	14.95	27-30
1998 Emmitt Smith (4th) QXI4036	Yr.Iss.	1998	14.95	20-27
1998 Ewoks™ QXI4223	Yr.Iss.	1998	16.95	27-31
1998 Grant Hill (4th) QXI6846	Yr.Iss.	1998	14.95	15-28
1998 The Grinch QXI6466	Yr.Iss.	1998	13.95	50-65
1998 Holiday Barbie™- African American (1st Ed.) QX6936	Yr.Iss.	1998	15.95	16-30
1998 Holiday Barbie™(6th Ed.) QXI4023	Yr.Iss.	1998	15.95	19-34
1998 Joe Montana-Notre Dame QXI6843	Yr.Iss.	1998	14.95	24-26
1998 Mario Lemieux (2nd) QXI6476	Yr.Iss.	1998	15.95	15-27
1998 Princess Leia™ (2nd Ed.) QXI4026	Yr.Iss.	1998	13.95	14-28
1998 Richard Petty (2nd) QXI4143	Yr.Iss.	1998	15.95	18-27
1998 Victorian Christmas II-Thomas Kinkade (2nd Ed.) QX6343	Yr.Iss.	1998	10.95	14-25

1998 Spring Ornaments - Keepsake

YEAR ISSUE	EDITION LIMIT	YEAR RETD.	ISSUE PRICE	*QUOTE U.S.$
1998 1931 Ford Model A Roadster (1st Ed.) QEO8416	Yr.Iss.	1998	14.95	17-27
1998 1939 Mobo Horse (2nd Ed.) QEO8393	Yr.Iss.	1998	12.95	12-29
1998 Barbie™ as Little Bo Peep Doll (2nd Ed.) QEO8373	Yr.Iss.	1998	14.95	17-27
1998 Bashful Gift QEO8446	Yr.Iss.	1998	11.95	12-24
1998 Benjamin Bunny™ Beatrix Potter™ (3rd Ed.) QEO8383	Yr.Iss.	1998	8.95	8-20
1998 Bouquet of Memories QEO8456	Yr.Iss.	1998	7.95	9-15
1998 Forever Friends QEO8423	Yr.Iss.	1998	9.95	10-20
1998 Garden Club (4th Ed.)	Yr.Iss.	1998	7.95	8-17
1998 The Garden of Piglet and Pooh QEO8396	Yr.Iss.	1998	10.95	13-24

YEAR ISSUE	EDITION LIMIT	YEAR RETD.	ISSUE PRICE	*QUOTE U.S.$
1998 Going Up? Charlie Brown-PEANUTS® QEO8433	Yr.Iss.	1998	9.95	10-21
1998 Happy Diploma Day! QEO8476	Yr.Iss.	1998	7.95	8
1998 Joyful Angels (3rd Ed.) QEO8386	Yr.Iss.	1998	10.95	13-22
1998 Midge™-35th Anniversary QEO8413	Yr.Iss.	1998	14.95	15-27
1998 Passenger Car (3rd Ed.) QEO8376	Yr.Iss.	1998	9.95	10-23
1998 Practice Swing-Donald Duck QEO8396	Yr.Iss.	1998	10.95	11-21
1998 Precious Baby QEO8463	Yr.Iss.	1998	9.95	10-18
1998 Special Friends QEO8523	Yr.Iss.	1998	12.95	13
1998 Star Wars™ QEO8406	Yr.Iss.	1998	12.95	18-100
1998 Sweet Birthday QEO8473	Yr.Iss.	1998	7.95	8-15
1998 Tigger in the Garden QEO8436	Closed	1998	9.95	10-18
1998 Victorian Cross QEO8453	Yr.Iss.	1998	8.95	9-18
1998 Wedding Memories QEO8466	Yr.Iss.	1998	9.95	10
1998 What's Your Name QEO8443	Yr.Iss.	1998	7.95	8-16

1999 Collectible Series - Keepsake

YEAR ISSUE	EDITION LIMIT	YEAR RETD.	ISSUE PRICE	*QUOTE U.S.$
1999 1955 Chevrolet® Nomad® Wagon (9th Ed.) QX6367	Yr.Iss.	1999	13.95	17-40
1999 1957 Dodge® Sweptside D100 (5th Ed.) QX6269	Yr.Iss.	1999	13.95	15-21
1999 1968 Murray® Jolly Roger Flagship (6th Ed.) QX6279	Yr.Iss.	1999	13.95	16-20
1999 746 Norfolk and Western Steam Locomotive (4th Ed.) QX6377	Yr.Iss.	1999	18.95	25-32
1999 Angel of the Nativity (2nd Ed.) QX6419	Yr.Iss.	1999	14.95	17-30
1999 Bill Elliott (3rd Ed.) QXI4039	Yr.Iss.	1999	15.95	15-44
1999 The Cat in the Hat (1st Ed.) QXI6457	Yr.Iss.	1999	14.95	20-41
1999 The Clauses on Vacation (3rd Ed.) QX6399	Yr.Iss.	1999	14.95	15
1999 Colonial Church (2nd Ed.) QLX7387	Yr.Iss.	1999	18.95	19-39
1999 Curious Raccoons (3rd Ed.) QX6287	Yr.Iss.	1999	12.95	15-26
1999 Curtiss R3C-2 Seaplane (3rd Ed.) QX6387	Yr.Iss.	1999	14.95	16-24
1999 Dan Marino (5th Ed.) QXI4029	Yr.Iss.	1999	14.95	15
1999 David and Goliath (1st Ed.) QX6447	Yr.Iss.	1999	13.95	15-25
1999 Donald Plays the Cymbals (3rd Ed.) QXD4057	Yr.Iss.	1999	13.95	14
1999 Fabulous Decade (10th Ed.) QX6357	Yr.Iss.	1999	7.95	25
1999 Famous Flying Ace (2nd Ed.) QX6409	Yr.Iss.	1999	9.95	11-18
1999 Farm House (1st Ed.) QX6439	Yr.Iss.	1999	15.95	19-39
1999 Frosty Friends (20th Ed.) QX6297	Yr.Iss.	1999	12.95	25-33
1999 Gay Parisienne™ (6th Ed.) QXI5301	Yr.Iss.	1999	15.95	21-32
1999 Gift Bearers (1st Ed.) QX6437	Yr.Iss.	1999	12.95	16-23
1999 Gordie Howe® (3rd Ed.) QXI4047	Yr.Iss.	1999	15.95	16
1999 Han Solo™ (3rd Ed.) QXI4007	Yr.Iss.	1999	13.95	15-26
1999 Heather - Mary's Angels (12th Ed.) QX6329	Yr.Iss.	1999	7.95	10-16
1999 Heritage Springer® (1st Ed.) QXI8007	Yr.Iss.	1999	14.95	18-30
1999 Honey Time (2nd Ed.) QXD4129	Yr.Iss.	1999	13.95	14
1999 House on Holly Lane (16th Ed.) QX6349	Yr.Iss.	1999	16.95	17-29
1999 Joyful Santa (1st Ed.) QX6949	Yr.Iss.	1999	14.95	15-29
1999 Ken Griffey Jr. (4th Ed.) QXI4037	Yr.Iss.	1999	14.95	15-25
1999 Lighthouse Greetings (3rd Ed.) QLX7379	Yr.Iss.	1999	24.00	24-89
1999 Lunar Rover Vehicle (4th Ed.) QLX7377	Yr.Iss.	1999	24.00	24-35
1999 Marilyn Monroe (3rd Ed.) QX6389	Yr.Iss.	1999	14.95	16-26
1999 Merry Olde Santa (10th Ed.) QX6359	Yr.Iss.	1999	15.95	16-29
1999 Mickey and Minnie in Paradise (2nd Ed.) QXD4049	Yr.Iss.	1999	14.95	15
1999 Minnie Trims the Tree (3rd Ed.) QXD4059	Yr.Iss.	1999	12.95	13
1999 Mischievous Kittens (1st Ed.) QX6427	Yr.Iss.	1999	9.95	20-24
1999 Playing With Pooh (1st Ed.) QXD4147	Yr.Iss.	1999	13.95	14-17
1999 A Pony for Christmas (2nd Ed.) QX6299	Yr.Iss.	1999	10.95	11-22
1999 Prospector (2nd Ed.) QX6317	Yr.Iss.	1999	13.95	14-27
1999 Puppy Love (9th Ed.) QX6327	Yr.Iss.	1999	7.95	12-17
1999 Red Queen - Alice in Wonderland (4th Ed.) QX6379	Yr.Iss.	1999	14.95	15-18
1999 Rose Angel (4th Ed.) QX6289	Yr.Iss.	1999	15.95	16
1999 Russian BARBIE™ (4th Ed.) QX6369	Yr.Iss.	1999	14.95	21-28
1999 Santa's Golf Cart (21st Ed.) QX6337	Yr.Iss.	1999	14.95	15-29
1999 Scarlett O'Hara™ (3rd Ed.) QX6397	Yr.Iss.	1999	14.95	15-27
1999 Scottie Pippen (5th Ed.) QXI4177	Yr.Iss.	1999	14.95	15-18
1999 Snow Buddies (2nd Ed.) QX6319	Yr.Iss.	1999	7.95	12-18
1999 Snow White's Jealous Queen (2nd Ed.) QXD4089	Yr.Iss.	1999	14.95	15-28

YEAR ISSUE	EDITION LIMIT	YEAR RETD.	ISSUE PRICE	*QUOTE U.S.$
1999 Victorian Christmas III (3rd Ed.) QX6407	Yr.Iss.	1999	10.95	11-20
1999 Walt Disney's Sleeping Beauty (3rd Ed.) QXD4097	Yr.Iss.	1999	14.95	15-21

1999 Collegiate Ornaments - Keepsake

YEAR ISSUE	EDITION LIMIT	YEAR RETD.	ISSUE PRICE	*QUOTE U.S.$
1999 Arizona Wildcats QSR2429	Yr.Iss.	1999	9.95	10
1999 Duke Blue Devils QSR2437	Yr.Iss.	1999	9.95	10
1999 Florida State® Seminoles® QSR2439	Yr.Iss.	1999	9.95	10
1999 Georgetown Hoyas QSR2447	Yr.Iss.	1999	9.95	10
1999 Kentucky Wildcats QSR2449	Yr.Iss.	1999	9.95	10
1999 Michigan Wolverines QSR2457	Yr.Iss.	1999	9.95	10
1999 Nebraska Cornhuskers QSR2459	Yr.Iss.	1999	9.95	10
1999 North Carolina Tar Heels® QSR2467	Yr.Iss.	1999	9.95	10
1999 Notre Dame® Fighting Irish® QSR2427	Yr.Iss.	1999	9.95	10
1999 Penn State® Nittany Lions® QSR2469	Yr.Iss.	1999	9.95	10

1999 Commemoratives - Keepsake

YEAR ISSUE	EDITION LIMIT	YEAR RETD.	ISSUE PRICE	*QUOTE U.S.$
1999 Baby's First Christmas QX6647	Yr.Iss.	1999	18.95	19-38
1999 Baby's First Christmas QX6649	Yr.Iss.	1999	7.95	8-20
1999 Baby's First Christmas QX6657	Yr.Iss.	1999	8.95	9-17
1999 Baby's First Christmas QX6659	Yr.Iss.	1999	9.95	10-14
1999 Baby's First Christmas QX6667	Yr.Iss.	1999	7.95	16-22
1999 Baby's Second Christmas QX6669	Yr.Iss.	1999	7.95	16-18
1999 Child's Fifth Christmas QX6679	Yr.Iss.	1999	7.95	16
1999 Child's Fourth Christmas QX6687	Yr.Iss.	1999	7.95	8-21
1999 Child's Third Christmas QX6677	Yr.Iss.	1999	7.95	8-16
1999 Counting on Success QX6707	Yr.Iss.	1999	7.95	8
1999 Dad QX6719	Yr.Iss.	1999	8.95	12-17
1999 Daughter QX6729	Yr.Iss.	1999	8.95	16-21
1999 For My Grandma QX6747	Yr.Iss.	1999	8.95	9
1999 Godchild QX6759	Yr.Iss.	1999	7.95	8-16
1999 Granddaughter QX6739	Yr.Iss.	1999	8.95	9-15
1999 Grandson QX6737	Yr.Iss.	1999	8.95	9-19
1999 Handled With Care QX6769	Yr.Iss.	1999	8.95	9-16
1999 Hello, Hello QX6777	Yr.Iss.	1999	14.95	15-20
1999 Mom and Dad QX6709	Yr.Iss.	1999	9.95	10-20
1999 Mom QX6717	Yr.Iss.	1999	8.95	9-18
1999 Mother and Daugher QX6757	Yr.Iss.	1999	9.95	10-24
1999 My Sister, My Friend QX6749	Yr.Iss.	1999	7.95	8-21
1999 New Home QX6347	Yr.Iss.	1999	9.95	10-19
1999 Our Christmas Together QX6689	Yr.Iss.	1999	9.95	10
1999 Our First Christmas Together QX3207	Yr.Iss.	1999	7.95	8-17
1999 Our First Christmas Together QX6697	Yr.Iss.	1999	8.95	9-12
1999 Our First Christmas Together QX6699	Yr.Iss.	1999	22.00	22
1999 Son QX6727	Yr.Iss.	1999	8.95	9-16
1999 Special Dog QX6767	Yr.Iss.	1999	7.95	8-11
1999 Sweet Friendship QX6779	Yr.Iss.	1999	9.95	10-12

1999 Crown Reflections - Keepsake

YEAR ISSUE	EDITION LIMIT	YEAR RETD.	ISSUE PRICE	*QUOTE U.S.$
1999 1950 LIONEL® Santa Fe F3 Diesel Locomotive QBG6119	Yr.Iss.	1999	35.00	45-48
1999 1955 Murray® Ranch Wagon QBG6077	Yr.Iss.	1999	35.00	35-38
1999 Childhood Treasures QBG4237	Yr.Iss.	1999	30.00	30
1999 Festival of Fruit (2nd Ed.) QBG6069	Yr.Iss.	1999	35.00	35
1999 Frosty Friends QBG6067	Yr.Iss.	1999	35.00	35-58
1999 Harvest of Grapes QBG6047	Yr.Iss.	1999	25.00	25
1999 The Holy Family QBG6127	Yr.Iss.	1999	30.00	30
1999 Jolly Snowman QBG6059	Yr.Iss.	1999	20.00	20
1999 U.S.S. Enterprise™ NCC-1701 QBG6117	Yr.Iss.	1999	25.00	36-59
1999 Village Church QBG6057	Yr.Iss.	1999	30.00	30
1999 Yummy Memories QBG6049	Yr.Iss.	1999	45.00	45-58

1999 Disney Ornaments - Keepsake

YEAR ISSUE	EDITION LIMIT	YEAR RETD.	ISSUE PRICE	*QUOTE U.S.$
1999 Baby Mickey's Sweet Dreams QXD4087	Yr.Iss.	1999	10.95	11-14
1999 Donald Plays the Cymbals (3rd Ed.) QXD4057	Yr.Iss.	1999	13.95	14-20
1999 Dumbo's First Flight QXD4117	Yr.Iss.	1999	13.95	16-27
1999 The Family Portrait QXD4149	Yr.Iss.	1999	14.95	15-28
1999 Girl Talk QXD4069	Yr.Iss.	1999	12.95	8-13
1999 Goofy As Santa's Helper QXD4079	Yr.Iss.	1999	12.95	13-23
1999 Honey Time (2nd Ed.) QXD4129	Yr.Iss.	1999	13.95	15-27
1999 Mickey and Minnie in Paradise (2nd Ed.) QXD4049	Yr.Iss.	1999	14.95	20-28

YEAR ISSUE	EDITION LIMIT	YEAR RETD.	ISSUE PRICE	*QUOTE U.S.$
1999 Minnie Trims the Tree (3rd Ed.) QXD4059	Yr.Iss.	1999	12.95	13-15
1999 Piano Player Mickey QXD7389	Yr.Iss.	1999	24.00	24-34
1999 Pinocchio and Geppetto QXD4107	Yr.Iss.	1999	16.95	17-30
1999 Playing With Pooh QXD4197	Yr.Iss.	1999	13.95	15-28
1999 Presents From Pooh QXD4093	Yr.Iss.	1999	14.95	15-18
1999 Skating With Pooh QXD4127	Yr.Iss.	1999	6.95	7
1999 Snow White's Jealous Queen (2nd Ed.) QXD4089	Yr.Iss.	1999	14.95	18-28
1999 Tigger Plays Soccer QXD4119	Yr.Iss.	1999	10.95	11-19
1999 Walt Disney's Sleeping Beauty (3rd Ed.) QXD4097	Yr.Iss.	1999	14.95	15-18
1999 Woody's Roundup Walt Disney's Toy Story 2	Yr.Iss.	1999	13.95	17-27

1999 Holiday Traditions - Keepsake

YEAR ISSUE	EDITION LIMIT	YEAR RETD.	ISSUE PRICE	*QUOTE U.S.$
1999 All Sooted Up QX6837	Yr.Iss.	1999	9.95	10-19
1999 Angel of Hope QXI6339	Yr.Iss.	1999	14.95	15-28
1999 Angel Song QX6939	Yr.Iss.	1999	18.95	19
1999 Balthasar-The Magi QX8037	2-Yr.	2001	12.95	13-15
1999 Best Pals QX6879	2-Yr.	2001	18.95	19
1999 Caspar-The Magi QX8039	2-Yr.	2001	12.95	13-15
1999 Child of Wonder QX6817	Yr.Iss.	1999	14.95	15-29
1999 The Christmas Story QX6897	Yr.Iss.	1999	22.00	22-29
1999 Cross of Hope QX6557	Yr.Iss.	1999	9.95	10-14
1999 Feliz Navidad - Santa QX6999	Yr.Iss.	1999	8.95	9-17
1999 Forecast for Fun QX6869	Yr.Iss.	1999	14.95	15-18
1999 In The Workshop QX6979	Yr.Iss.	1999	9.95	10
1999 Jazzy Jalopy QX6549	Yr.Iss.	1999	24.00	24-40
1999 Jolly Locomotive QX6859	Yr.Iss.	1999	14.95	15-28
1999 Joyous Angel QX6787	Yr.Iss.	1999	8.95	9-12
1999 A Joyous Christmas QX6827	Yr.Iss.	1999	5.95	6-18
1999 King Malh-Third King QX6797	Yr.Iss.	1999	13.95	14-27
1999 Kringle's Whirligig QX6847	Yr.Iss.	1999	12.95	13-25
1999 Let It Snow! QLX7427	Yr.Iss.	1999	18.95	19-31
1999 Little Cloud Keeper QX6877	Yr.Iss.	1999	16.95	17-25
1999 Mary's Bears QX5569	Yr.Iss.	1999	12.95	13-26
1999 Melchior-The Magi QX6819	2-Yr.	2001	12.95	13
1999 Milk 'n' Cookies Express QX6839	Yr.Iss.	1999	8.95	9-15
1999 Millennium Snowman QX8059	Yr.Iss.	1999	8.95	39-75
1999 Noah's Ark QX6809	Yr.Iss.	1999	12.95	12-28
1999 Playful Snowman QX6867	Yr.Iss.	1999	12.95	13-18
1999 Praise the Day QX6799	Yr.Iss.	1999	14.95	15-27
1999 Red Barn QX6947	Yr.Iss.	1999	15.95	16-24
1999 Sleddin' Buddies QX6849	Yr.Iss.	1999	9.95	10
1999 Snowmen of Mitford QXI8587	Yr.Iss.	1999	15.95	24-39
1999 Spellin' Santa QX6857	Yr.Iss.	1999	9.95	10-16
1999 A Time of Peace QX6807	Yr.Iss.	1999	8.95	9-11
1999 Warm Welcome QLX7417	Yr.Iss.	1999	16.95	17
1999 Welcome to 2000 QX6829	Yr.Iss.	1999	10.95	25-94
1999 Wintertime Treat QX6989	Yr.Iss.	1999	12.95	13-25

1999 Keepsake Collector's Club - Keepsake

YEAR ISSUE	EDITION LIMIT	YEAR RETD.	ISSUE PRICE	*QUOTE U.S.$
1999 1939 GARTON® Ford Station Wagon QXC4509	Yr.Iss.	1999	15.95	16-29
1999 1991 Happy Holidays® BARBIE® Doll QXC4507	Yr.Iss.	1999	15.95	35-41
1999 Arctic Artist QXC4527A	Yr.Iss.	1999	N/A	7
1999 Hollow Log Café QXC4667A	Yr.Iss.	1999	14.95	15
1999 Noel R.R.-gold plated	Yr.Iss.	1999	10.95	11
1999 North Pole Pond QXC4677A	Yr.Iss.	1999	40.00	40
1999 Snowy Days-PEANUTS® QXC4517	Yr.Iss.	1999	18.95	19-34
1999 Snowy Plaza QXC4669A	Yr.Iss.	1999	35.00	35
1999 Snowy Surprise QXC4529A	Yr.Iss.	1999	N/A	7
1999 The Toymaker's Gift QXC4519A	Yr.Iss.	1999	N/A	14
1999 Waiting for a Hug QXC4537A	Yr.Iss.	1999	N/A	19

1999 Laser Creations - Keepsake

YEAR ISSUE	EDITION LIMIT	YEAR RETD.	ISSUE PRICE	*QUOTE U.S.$
1999 Angelic Messenger QLZ4287	Yr.Iss.	1999	7.95	8-12
1999 Christmas in Bloom QLZ4257	Yr.Iss.	1999	8.95	9-11
1999 Don't Open Till 2000 QLZ4289	Yr.Iss.	1999	8.95	9-18
1999 Inside Santa's Workshop QLZ4239	Yr.Iss.	1999	8.95	9-13
1999 Ringing in Christmas QLZ4277	Yr.Iss.	1999	6.95	7-10
1999 A Visit From St. Nicholas QLZ4229	Yr.Iss.	1999	5.95	6-17
1999 A Wish for Peace QLZ4249	Yr.Iss.	1999	6.95	7-11
1999 Yuletide Charm QLZ4269	Yr.Iss.	1999	5.95	6

1999 Lifestyles & Occupations - Keepsake

YEAR ISSUE	EDITION LIMIT	YEAR RETD.	ISSUE PRICE	*QUOTE U.S.$
1999 Adding the Best Part QX6569	Yr.Iss.	1999	7.95	8-11
1999 Angel in Disguise QX6629	Yr.Iss.	1999	8.95	9-13
1999 Bowling's a Ball QX6577	Yr.Iss.	1999	7.95	8
1999 Dance for the Season QX6587	Yr.Iss.	1999	9.95	10-14

YEAR ISSUE	EDITION LIMIT	YEAR RETD.	ISSUE PRICE	*QUOTE U.S.$
1999 Flame-Fighting Friends QX6619	Yr.Iss.	1999	14.95	15-23
1999 Merry Motorcycle QX6637	Yr.Iss.	1999	8.95	9-18
1999 Military on Parade QX6639	Yr.Iss.	1999	10.95	11-22
1999 A Musician of Note QX6567	Yr.Iss.	1999	7.95	8-16
1999 North Pole Star QX6589	Yr.Iss.	1999	8.95	9-11
1999 Outstanding Teacher QX6627	Yr.Iss.	1999	8.95	9
1999 Reel Fun QX6609	Yr.Iss.	1999	10.95	11-19
1999 Sew Handy QX6597	Yr.Iss.	1999	8.95	9-26
1999 Sprinkling Stars QX6599	Yr.Iss.	1999	9.95	10-14
1999 Sundae Golfer QX6617	Yr.Iss.	1999	12.95	13-19
1999 Surfin' the Net QX6607	Yr.Iss.	1999	9.95	10-19
1999 Sweet Skater QX6579	Yr.Iss.	1999	7.95	8-11

1999 Miniature Ornaments - Keepsake

YEAR ISSUE	EDITION LIMIT	YEAR RETD.	ISSUE PRICE	*QUOTE U.S.$
1999 1937 Steelcraft Airflow by Murray® (2nd Ed.) QXM4477	Yr.Iss.	1999	6.95	7-16
1999 1955 Murray® Tractor and Trailer (5th Ed.) QXM4479	Yr.Iss.	1999	6.95	7-15
1999 Antique Tractors (3rd Ed.) QXM4567	Yr.Iss.	1999	6.95	8-14
1999 Betsey's Perfect 10 QXM4609	Yr.Iss.	1999	4.95	5-12
1999 Celestial Kitty QXM4639	Yr.Iss.	1999	6.95	7
1999 Centuries of Santa (6th Ed.) QXM4589	Yr.Iss.	1999	5.95	6-13
1999 Christmas Bells (5th Ed.) QXM4489	Yr.Iss.	1999	4.95	5-8
1999 Classic Batman™ and Robin™ QXM4659	Yr.Iss.	1999	12.95	19-25
1999 Crystal Claus QXM4637	Yr.Iss.	1999	9.95	13-19
1999 Dorothy's Ruby Slippers (1st Ed.) QXM4599	Yr.Iss.	1999	5.95	25-35
1999 Electric Glide (2nd Ed.) QXI6137	Yr.Iss.	1999	7.95	10-16
1999 Holiday Flurries (1st Ed.) QXM4547	Yr.Iss.	1999	6.95	7-15
1999 Locomotive and Tender (1st Ed.) QXM4549	Yr.Iss.	1999	10.95	15-25
1999 Love to Share QXM4557	Yr.Iss.	1999	6.95	7
1999 Marvin The Martian QXM4657	Yr.Iss.	1999	8.95	9-10
1999 Merry Grinch-mas! QXI4627	Yr.Iss.	1999	19.95	25-35
1999 Miniature Clothespin Soldier (5th Ed.) QXM4579	Yr.Iss.	1999	4.95	5-10
1999 Mouse King (4th Ed.) QXM4487	Yr.Iss.	1999	5.95	6-13
1999 The Nativity (2nd Ed.) QXM4497	Yr.Iss.	1999	9.95	10-18
1999 Nutcracker Guild (6th Ed.) QXM4587	Yr.Iss.	1999	6.95	7-12
1999 Roll-a-Bear QXM4629	Yr.Iss.	1999	6.95	7-9
1999 Santa Time QXM4647	Yr.Iss.	1999	7.95	8
1999 Seaside Scenes (1st Ed.) QXM4649	Yr.Iss.	1999	7.95	8-17
1999 Snowflake Ballet (3rd Ed.) QXM4569	Yr.Iss.	1999	5.95	6-12
1999 Taz and the She-Devil QXM4619	Yr.Iss.	1999	8.95	10-18
1999 Teddy-Bear Style (3rd Ed.) QXM4499	Yr.Iss.	1999	5.95	6-12
1999 Trusty Reindeer QXM4617	Yr.Iss.	1999	5.95	8-13
1999 Welcome Friends (3rd Ed.) QXM4577	Yr.Iss.	1999	6.95	7-15
1999 Winter Fun With SNOOPY® (2nd Ed.) QXM4559	Yr.Iss.	1999	6.95	10-19

1999 NBA Ornaments - Keepsake

YEAR ISSUE	EDITION LIMIT	YEAR RETD.	ISSUE PRICE	*QUOTE U.S.$
1999 Charlotte Hornets™ QSR1057	Yr.Iss.	1999	10.95	11
1999 Chicago Bulls™ QSR1019	Yr.Iss.	1999	10.95	11
1999 Detroit Pistons™ QSR1027	Yr.Iss.	1999	10.95	11
1999 Houston Rockets™ QSR1029	Yr.Iss.	1999	10.95	11
1999 Indiana Pacers™ QSR1037	Yr.Iss.	1999	10.95	11
1999 Los Angeles Lakers™ QSR1039	Yr.Iss.	1999	10.95	11
1999 New York Knicks™ QSR1047	Yr.Iss.	1999	10.95	11
1999 Orlando Magic™ QSR1059	Yr.Iss.	1999	10.95	11
1999 Seattle Supersonics™ QSR1067	Yr.Iss.	1999	10.95	11
1999 Utah Jazz™ QSR1069	Yr.Iss.	1999	10.95	11

1999 NFL Ornaments - Keepsake

YEAR ISSUE	EDITION LIMIT	YEAR RETD.	ISSUE PRICE	*QUOTE U.S.$
1999 Carolina Panthers™ QSR5217	Yr.Iss.	1999	10.95	11
1999 Chicago Bears™ QSR5219	Yr.Iss.	1999	10.95	11
1999 Cleveland Browns™	Yr.Iss.	1999	10.95	11
1999 Dallas Cowboys™ QSR5227	Yr.Iss.	1999	10.95	11
1999 Denver Broncos™ QSR5229	Yr.Iss.	1999	10.95	11
1999 Green Bay Packers™ QSR5237	Yr.Iss.	1999	10.95	11
1999 Kansas City Chiefs™ QSR5197	Yr.Iss.	1999	10.95	11
1999 Miami Dolphins™ QSR5239	Yr.Iss.	1999	10.95	11
1999 Minnesota Vikings™ QSR5247	Yr.Iss.	1999	10.95	11-15
1999 New England Patriots™ QSR5279	Yr.Iss.	1999	10.95	11
1999 New York Giants™ QSR5249	Yr.Iss.	1999	10.95	11
1999 Oakland Raiders™ QSR5257	Yr.Iss.	1999	10.95	11
1999 Philadelphia Eagles™ QSR5259	Yr.Iss.	1999	10.95	11
1999 Pittsburgh Steelers™ QSR5267	Yr.Iss.	1999	10.95	11
1999 San Francisco 49ers™ QSR5269	Yr.Iss.	1999	10.95	11
1999 Washington Redskins™ QSR5277	Yr.Iss.	1999	10.95	11

YEAR ISSUE	EDITION LIMIT	YEAR RETD.	ISSUE PRICE	*QUOTE U.S.$

1999 Pop Culture Icons - Keepsake

1999 1949 Cadillac® Coupe deVille QX6429	Yr.Iss.	1999	14.95	18-29
1999 Clownin' Around QX6487	Yr.Iss.	1999	10.95	11-20
1999 Cocoa Break HERSHEY'S™ QX8009	Yr.Iss.	1999	10.95	11-20
1999 Dorothy and Glinda, The Good Witch™ QX6509	Yr.Iss.	1999	24.00	30-40
1999 The Flash™ QX6469	Yr.Iss.	1999	12.95	15-20
1999 G.I. Joe®, Action Soldier™ QX6537	Yr.Iss.	1999	13.95	14-26
1999 Howdy Doody™ QX6519	Yr.Iss.	1999	14.95	18-23
1999 Jet Threat™ Car With Case QX6527	Yr.Iss.	1999	12.95	16-22
1999 Larry, Moe, and Curly QX6499	Yr.Iss.	1999	30.00	33-56
1999 The Lollipop Guild™ QX8029	Yr.Iss.	1999	19.95	23-34
1999 Lucy Gets in Pictures QX6547	Yr.Iss.	1999	13.95	18-26
1999 North Pole Mr. Potato Head™ QX8027	Yr.Iss.	1999	10.95	11-17
1999 On Thin Ice QX6489	Yr.Iss.	1999	10.95	11-20
1999 Pepé Le Pew and Penelope QX6507	Yr.Iss.	1999	12.95	15-24
1999 The Poky Little Puppy QX6479	Yr.Iss.	1999	11.95	16-23
1999 Rhett Butler™ QX6467	Yr.Iss.	1999	12.95	17-23
1999 Scooby Doo™ QX6997	Yr.Iss.	1999	14.95	20-24
1999 The Tender QX6497	Yr.Iss.	1999	14.95	18-29
1999 Tonka® 1956 Suburban Pumper No. 5 QX6459	Yr.Iss.	1999	13.95	22-25

1999 Premiere Event - Keepsake

1999 Zebra Fantasy QX6559	Yr.Iss.	1999	14.95	20-31

1999 Special Issues - Keepsake

1999 40th Anniversary Barbie™ QXI8049	Yr.Iss.	1999	15.95	16-45
1999 African-American Millennium Princess Barbie™ QXI6449	Yr.Iss.	1999	15.95	16-38
1999 Barbie™ Gay Parisienne (6th Ed.) QXI5301	Yr.Iss.	1999	14.95	16-26
1999 Chewbacca™ QXI4009	Yr.Iss.	1999	14.95	16-43
1999 Darth Vader's TIE Fighter QXI7399	Yr.Iss.	1999	24.00	26-36
1999 Dream House® Playhouse QXI8047	Yr.Iss.	1999	14.95	15-30
1999 Han Solo™ (3rd Ed.) QXI4007	Yr.Iss.	1999	13.95	14-17
1999 Lieutenant Commander Worf™ QXI4139	Yr.Iss.	1999	14.95	16-28
1999 Max Rebo Band™ QXI4597	Yr.Iss.	1999	19.95	20-30
1999 Millennium Princess Barbie™ QXI4019	Yr.Iss.	1999	15.95	23-45
1999 Muhammad Ali QXI4147	Yr.Iss.	1999	14.95	15-25
1999 Runabout-U.S.S. Rio Grande QXI7593	Yr.Iss.	1999	24.00	23-35
1999 Star Wars Figural-Star Wars™ QXI4187	Yr.Iss.	1999	14.95	15-28
1999 Starship-Star Wars™ QXI7613	Yr.Iss.	1999	18.95	20-50
1999 Travel Case and Barbie™ QXI6129	Yr.Iss.	1999	12.95	13

1999 Spring Ornaments - Keepsake

1999 1932 Chevrolet Standard Sports Roadster (2nd Ed.) QEO8379	Yr.Iss.	1999	14.95	15-27
1999 1950 GARTON® Delivery Cycle (3rd Ed.) QEO8367	Yr.Iss.	1999	12.95	13-23
1999 1956 GARTON® Hot Rod Racer QEO8479	Yr.Iss.	1999	13.95	14-26
1999 Barbie® as Cinderella Doll (3rd Ed.) QEO8327	Yr.Iss.	1999	14.95	15-27
1999 Barbie™ Anniversary Edition QEO8399	Yr.Iss.	1999	12.95	13-23
1999 Batter Up! QEO8389	Yr.Iss.	1999	12.95	13-23
1999 Birthday Celebration QEO8409	Yr.Iss.	1999	8.95	9
1999 Cross of Faith QEO8467	Yr.Iss.	1999	13.95	14
1999 Easter Egg Nest QEO8427	Yr.Iss.	1999	7.95	8
1999 Easter Egg Surprise QEO8377	Yr.Iss.	1999	14.95	15
1999 Eastern Bluebird (1st) QEO8451	Yr.Iss.	1999	9.95	10
1999 Final Putt - Minnie Mouse QEO8349	Yr.Iss.	1999	10.95	11
1999 Flatbed Car (4th Ed.) QEO8387	Yr.Iss.	1999	9.95	10
1999 Friendly Delivery - Mary's Bears QEO8419	Yr.Iss.	1999	12.95	13-22
1999 Happy Bubble Blower QEO8437	Yr.Iss.	1999	7.95	8
1999 Happy Diploma Day! QEO8357	Yr.Iss.	1999	10.95	11
1999 Inspirational Angel QEO8347	Yr.Iss.	1999	12.95	13
1999 Mop Top Billy, Madame Alexander® QEO8337	Yr.Iss.	1999	14.95	16-29
1999 Precious Baby QEO8417	Yr.Iss.	1999	9.95	10
1999 Spring Chick QEO8469	Yr.Iss.	1999	22.00	22
1999 Springtime Harvest QEO8429	Yr.Iss.	1999	7.95	8
1999 Strawberry QEO8369	Yr.Iss.	1999	9.95	12-18

YEAR ISSUE	EDITION LIMIT	YEAR RETD.	ISSUE PRICE	*QUOTE U.S.$
1999 The Tale of Peter Rabbit™- Beatrix Potter™ QEO8397	Yr.Iss.	1999	19.95	19-36
1999 Tiggerific Easter Delivery QEO8359	Yr.Iss.	1999	10.95	12-20
1999 Tom Kitton™ (4th Ed.) QEO8329	Yr.Iss.	1999	8.95	10-18
1999 Wedding Memories QEO8407	Yr.Iss.	1999	9.95	10

2000 American Spirit Medallion Collection - Keepsake

2000 Connecticut Medallion QMP9404	Yr.Iss.	2000	12.95	13
2000 Delaware Medallion QMP9400	Yr.Iss.	2000	12.95	13
2000 Georgia Medallion QMP9403	Yr.Iss.	2000	12.95	13
2000 Maryland Medallion QMP9426	Yr.Iss.	2000	14.95	15
2000 Massachusetts Medallion QMP9423	Yr.Iss.	2000	12.95	13
2000 New Hampshire Medallion QMP9432	Yr.Iss.	2000	14.95	15
2000 New Jersey Medallion QMP9402	Yr.Iss.	2000	12.95	13
2000 Pennsylvania Medallion QMP9401	Yr.Iss.	2000	12.95	13
2000 Sacagaweta Medallion	Yr.Iss.	2000	19.95	20
2000 South Carolina Medallion QMP9429	Yr.Iss.	2000	14.95	15
2000 Virginia Medallion	Yr.Iss.	2000	14.95	15

2000 Collectible Series - Keepsake

2000 1924 Toledo Fire Engine #6 (7th Ed.) QX6691	Yr.Iss.	2000	13.95	14-17
2000 1969 Pontiac® GTO™-The Judge™ (10th Ed.) QX6584	Yr.Iss.	2000	13.95	14-17
2000 1978 Dodge® Li'l Red Express Truck (6th Ed.) QX6581	Yr.Iss.	2000	13.95	14-23
2000 Adobe Church (3rd Ed.) LX7334	Yr.Iss.	2000	18.95	19
2000 Bait Shop With Boat (2nd Ed.) QX6631	Yr.Iss.	2000	15.95	16-20
2000 Baton Twirler Daisy (4th Ed.) QXD4034	Yr.Iss.	2000	13.95	14
2000 A Blustery Day (3rd Ed.) QXD4021	Yr.Iss.	2000	13.95	14
2000 Christmas Holly (5th Ed.) QX6611	Yr.Iss.	2000	14.95	15-19
2000 Commuter Set™ (7th Ed.) QX6814	Yr.Iss.	2000	15.95	16-20
2000 Cool Decade QX6764	Yr.Iss.	2000	7.95	8
2000 The Detective (5th Ed.) QX6564	Yr.Iss.	2000	9.95	10
2000 Donald & Daisy at Lover's Lodge (3rd Ed.) QXD4031	Yr.Iss.	2000	14.95	15
2000 Eric Lindros (4th Ed.) QXI6801	Yr.Iss.	2000	15.95	16
2000 Fashion Afoot QX8341	Yr.Iss.	2000	14.95	15-18
2000 Fat Boy® (2nd Ed.) QXI6774	Yr.Iss.	2000	14.95	15
2000 Foxes in the Forest (4th Ed.) QX6794	Yr.Iss.	2000	12.95	13
2000 Frosty Friends (21st Ed.) QX6601	Yr.Iss.	2000	10.95	11-14
2000 Gift Bearers (2nd Ed.) QX6651	Yr.Iss.	2000	12.95	13
2000 John Elway (6th Ed.) QXI6811	Yr.Iss.	2000	14.95	15
2000 Jonah and the Great Fish (2nd Ed.) QX6701	Yr.Iss.	2000	13.95	14-18
2000 Joyful Santa (2nd Ed.) QX6784	Yr.Iss.	2000	14.95	15
2000 Karl Malone (6th Ed.) QXI6901	Yr.Iss.	2000	14.95	15-18
2000 Lighthouse Greetings (4th Ed.) QLX7344	Yr.Iss.	2000	24.00	24-35
2000 LIONEL® General Steam Locomotive (5th Ed.) QX6684	Yr.Iss.	2000	18.95	19-23
2000 Marguerite-Mary's Angels (13th Ed.) QX6571	Yr.Iss.	2000	7.95	8-10
2000 Mark McGwire (5th Ed.) QXI5361	Yr.Iss.	2000	14.95	15
2000 Mischievous Kittens (2nd Ed.) QX6641	Yr.Iss.	2000	9.95	10-20
2000 Mountain Man (3rd Ed.) QX6594	Yr.Iss.	2000	15.95	16
2000 Obi-Wan Kenobi™ (4th Ed.) QXI6704	Yr.Iss.	2000	14.95	15
2000 One Fish Two Fish Red Fish Blue Fish™ (2nd Ed.) QX6781	Yr.Iss.	2000	14.95	15-19
2000 A Pony for Christmas (3rd Ed.) QX6624	Yr.Iss.	2000	12.95	13
2000 Puppy Love (10th Ed.) QX6554	Yr.Iss.	2000	7.95	8
2000 Robot Parade QX6771	Yr.Iss.	2000	14.95	15
2000 Scarlett O'Hara™ (4th Ed.) QX6671	Yr.Iss.	2000	14.95	15
2000 Schoolhouse (3rd Ed.) QX6591	Yr.Iss.	2000	14.95	15-25
2000 Sleeping Beauty's Maleficent (3rd Ed.) QXD4001	Yr.Iss.	2000	14.95	15-22
2000 Sleigh X-2000 (22nd Ed.) QX6824	Yr.Iss.	2000	14.95	15
2000 Snow Buddies (3rd Ed.) QX6654	Yr.Iss.	2000	7.95	8-15
2000 Spirit of St. Louis (4th Ed.) QX6634	Yr.Iss.	2000	14.95	15
2000 Story Time With Pooh (2nd Ed.) QXD4024	Yr.Iss.	2000	13.95	14
2000 Toymaker Santa QX6751	Yr.Iss.	2000	14.95	15-21
2000 Twilight Angel (3rd Ed.) QX6614	Yr.Iss.	2000	14.95	15-34

2000 Collegiate Ornaments - Keepsake

2000 Alabama® Crimson Tide® QSR2344	Yr.Iss.	2000	9.95	10-14
2000 Florida Gators® QSR2324	Yr.Iss.	2000	9.95	10-14

Collectors' Information Bureau   *Quotes have been rounded up to nearest dollar

YEAR ISSUE	EDITION LIMIT	YEAR RETD.	ISSUE PRICE	*QUOTE U.S.$
2000 Florida State® Seminoles® QSR2341	Yr.Iss.	2000	9.95	10-14
2000 Michigan Wolverines™ QSR2271	Yr.Iss.	2000	9.95	10-14
2000 Nebraska Cornhuskers QSR2321	Yr.Iss.	2000	9.95	10-14
2000 North Carolina® Tar Heels® QSR2304	Yr.Iss.	2000	9.95	10-14
2000 Notre Dame® Fighting Irish™ QSR2284	Yr.Iss.	2000	9.95	10-14
2000 Penn State® Nittany Lions® QSR2311	Yr.Iss.	2000	9.95	10-14
2000 Tennessee Volunteers® QSR2334	Yr.Iss.	2000	9.95	10-14
2000 The University Of Kentucky® Wildcats™ QSR2291	Yr.Iss.	2000	9.95	10-14

2000 Commemoratives - Keepsake

YEAR ISSUE	EDITION LIMIT	YEAR RETD.	ISSUE PRICE	*QUOTE U.S.$
2000 Baby's First Christmas QX6914	Yr.Iss.	2000	7.95	8
2000 Baby's First Christmas QX8031	Yr.Iss.	2000	8.95	9-11
2000 Baby's First Christmas QX8034	Yr.Iss.	2000	10.95	11-14
2000 Baby's First Christmas QX8041	Yr.Iss.	2000	18.95	19-23
2000 Baby's Second Christmas QX6921	Yr.Iss.	2000	7.95	8
2000 Child's Fifth Christmas QX6934	Yr.Iss.	2000	7.95	8
2000 Child's Fourth Christmas QX6931	Yr.Iss.	2000	7.95	8
2000 Child's Third Christmas QX6924	Yr.Iss.	2000	7.95	8
2000 A Class Act QX8074	Yr.Iss.	2000	7.95	8
2000 Close-Knit Friends QX8204	Yr.Iss.	2000	14.95	15-18
2000 Dad QX8071	Yr.Iss.	2000	8.95	9
2000 Daughter QX8081	Yr.Iss.	2000	8.95	9
2000 Friendly Greeting QX8174	Yr.Iss.	2000	9.95	10-13
2000 Godchild QX8161	Yr.Iss.	2000	7.95	8
2000 Granddaughter QX8091	Yr.Iss.	2000	8.95	9
2000 Grandma's House QX8141	Yr.Iss.	2000	10.95	11
2000 Grandson QX8094	Yr.Iss.	2000	8.95	9
2000 Mom and Dad QX8061	Yr.Iss.	2000	9.95	10
2000 Mom QX8064	Yr.Iss.	2000	8.95	9
2000 Mother and Daughter QX8154	Yr.Iss.	2000	9.95	10
2000 New Home QX8171	Yr.Iss.	2000	8.95	9
2000 New Millennium Baby QX8581	Yr.Iss.	2000	10.95	11
2000 Our Christmas Together QX8054	Yr.Iss.	2000	9.95	10
2000 Our Family QX8211	Yr.Iss.	2000	7.95	8
2000 Our First Christmas Together QX3104	Yr.Iss.	2000	7.95	8
2000 Our First Christmas Together QX8051	Yr.Iss.	2000	8.95	9
2000 Our First Christmas Together QX8701	Yr.Iss.	2000	10.95	11-14
2000 Sister to Sister QX8144	Yr.Iss.	2000	12.95	13
2000 Son QX8084	Yr.Iss.	2000	8.95	9

2000 Crown Reflections - Keepsake

YEAR ISSUE	EDITION LIMIT	YEAR RETD.	ISSUE PRICE	*QUOTE U.S.$
2000 1955 Murray® Dump Truck QBG4081	Yr.Iss.	2000	35.00	35
2000 Backpack Bear QBG4071	Yr.Iss.	2000	30.00	30-34
2000 Christmas Rose QBG4054	Yr.Iss.	2000	35.00	35-39
2000 Frosty Friends QBG4094	Yr.Iss.	2000	40.00	40-44
2000 Li'l Apple QBG4261	Yr.Iss.	2000	7.95	8
2000 Li'l Cascade-Red (Tri-Color) QBG4241	Yr.Iss.	2000	7.95	8
2000 Li'l Cascade-White (Tri-Color) QBG4244	Yr.Iss.	2000	7.95	8
2000 Li'l Christmas Tree QBG4361	Yr.Iss.	2000	7.95	8
2000 Li'l Gift-Green Bow QBG4344	Yr.Iss.	2000	7.95	8
2000 Li'l Gift-Red Bow QBG4341	Yr.Iss.	2000	7.95	8
2000 Li'l Grapes QBG4254	Yr.Iss.	2000	7.95	8
2000 Li'l Jack-in-the-Box QBG4274	Yr.Iss.	2000	7.95	8
2000 Li'l Mr. Claus QBG4364	Yr.Iss.	2000	7.95	8
2000 Li'l Mrs. Claus QBG4371	Yr.Iss.	2000	7.95	8
2000 Li'l Partridge QBG4374	Yr.Iss.	2000	7.95	8
2000 Li'l Pear QBG4254	Yr.Iss.	2000	7.95	8
2000 Li'l Robot QBG4271	Yr.Iss.	2000	7.95	8
2000 Li'l Roly-Poly Penguin QBG4281	Yr.Iss.	2000	7.95	8
2000 Li'l Roly-Poly Santa QBG4161	Yr.Iss.	2000	7.95	8
2000 Li'l Roly-Poly Snowman QBG4284	Yr.Iss.	2000	7.95	8
2000 Li'l Santa-Traditional QBG4354	Yr.Iss.	2000	7.95	8
2000 Li'l Snowman-Traditional QBG4351	Yr.Iss.	2000	7.95	8
2000 Li'l Stars-Metallic Look QBG4221	Yr.Iss.	2000	9.95	10
2000 Li'l Stars-Patriotic QBG4214	Yr.Iss.	2000	9.95	10
2000 Li'l Stars-Traditional QBG4224	Yr.Iss.	2000	9.95	10
2000 Li'l Swirl-Green QBG4234	Yr.Iss.	2000	7.95	8
2000 Li'l Swirl-Red QBG4231	Yr.Iss.	2000	7.95	8
2000 Li'l Teddy Bear QBG4264	Yr.Iss.	2000	7.95	8
2000 Lieutenant Commander Worf™ QBG4064	Yr.Iss.	2000	30.00	30
2000 Li'l Pineapple QBG4251	Yr.Iss.	2000	7.95	8

YEAR ISSUE	EDITION LIMIT	YEAR RETD.	ISSUE PRICE	*QUOTE U.S.$
2000 LIONEL® 4501 Southern Mikado Steam Locomotive QBG4074	Yr.Iss.	2000	35.00	35-39
2000 Thimble Soldier QBG4061	Yr.Iss.	2000	22.00	22

2000 Disney Ornaments - Keepsake

YEAR ISSUE	EDITION LIMIT	YEAR RETD.	ISSUE PRICE	*QUOTE U.S.$
2000 Alice Meets the Cheshire Cat QXD4011	Yr.Iss.	2000	14.95	15
2000 Baton Twirler Daisy (4th) QXD4034	Yr.Iss.	2000	13.95	14
2000 A Blustery Day (3rd Ed.) QXD4021	Yr.Iss.	2000	13.95	14
2000 Dog Dish Dilemma QXD4044	Yr.Iss.	2000	12.95	13
2000 Donald and Daisy at Lovers' Lodge (3rd Ed.) QXD4031	Yr.Iss.	2000	14.95	15
2000 Dressing Cinderella QXD4109	Yr.Iss.	2000	12.95	13-17
2000 Mickey and Minnie Mouse QXD4041	Yr.Iss.	2000	12.95	13
2000 Mickey's Bedtime Reading QXD4077	Yr.Iss.	2000	10.95	11
2000 Mickey's Sky Rider QXD4159	Yr.Iss.	2000	18.95	19-23
2000 The Newborn Prince QXD4194	Yr.Iss.	2000	13.95	14-17
2000 Off To Neverland! QXD4004	Yr.Iss.	2000	12.95	13
2000 Piglet's Jack-in-the-Box QXD4187	Yr.Iss.	2000	14.95	15
2000 Pooh Chooses the Tree QXD4157	Yr.Iss.	2000	12.95	13
2000 Sleeping Beauty's Maleficent (3rd Ed.) QXD4001	Yr.Iss.	2000	14.95	15
2000 Story Time With Pooh (2nd Ed.) QXD4024	Yr.Iss.	2000	13.95	14
2000 Tigger-ific Tidings to Pooh QXD4014	Yr.Iss.	2000	8.95	9

2000 Holiday Traditions - Keepsake

YEAR ISSUE	EDITION LIMIT	YEAR RETD.	ISSUE PRICE	*QUOTE U.S.$
2000 All Things Beautiful QX8351	Yr.Iss.	2000	13.95	14
2000 Angel-Blessed Tree QX8241	Yr.Iss.	2000	8.95	9
2000 Angelic Trio QX8234	Yr.Iss.	2000	10.95	11-14
2000 Blue Glass Angel QX8381	Yr.Iss.	2000	7.95	8
2000 Bringing Her Gift QX8334	Yr.Iss.	2000	10.95	11-14
2000 Caroler's Best Friend QX8354	Yr.Iss.	2000	12.95	13
2000 Celebrate His Birth! QX2464	Yr.Iss.	2000	6.95	7
2000 The Christmas Belle QX8311	Yr.Iss.	2000	10.95	11-14
2000 Christmas Tree Surprise QX8321	Yr.Iss.	2000	16.95	17
2000 Cool Character QX8271	Yr.Iss.	2000	12.95	13
2000 Feliz Navidad QX8214	Yr.Iss.	2000	8.95	9
2000 Gingerbread Church QX8244	Yr.Iss.	2000	9.95	10
2000 The Good Book QX8254	Yr.Iss.	2000	13.95	14
2000 Graceful Glory QX8304	Yr.Iss.	2000	18.95	19-23
2000 A Holiday Gathering QX8561	Yr.Iss.	2000	10.95	11
2000 Holly Berry Bell QX8291	Yr.Iss.	2000	14.95	15
2000 The Holy Family QX6523	Yr.Iss.	2000	25.00	25
2000 Hooray for the U.S.A. QX8281	Yr.Iss.	2000	9.95	10-13
2000 Max QX8584	Yr.Iss.	2000	7.95	8
2000 Memories of Christmas QX8264	Yr.Iss.	2000	12.95	13
2000 Merry Ballooning QX8384	Yr.Iss.	2000	16.95	17
2000 Millennium Time Capsule QX8044	Yr.Iss.	2000	10.95	11
2000 Northern Art Bear QX8294	Yr.Iss.	2000	8.95	9-14
2000 Our Lady of Guadalupe QX8231	Yr.Iss.	2000	12.95	13
2000 Safe in Noah's Ark QX8514	Yr.Iss.	2000	10.95	11
2000 Santa's Chair QX8314	Yr.Iss.	2000	12.95	13
2000 The Shepherds QX8361	Yr.Iss.	2000	25.00	25-39
2000 Snow Girl QX8274	Yr.Iss.	2000	9.95	10
2000 Toy Shop Serenade QX8301	Yr.Iss.	2000	16.95	17
2000 A Visit From St. Nicholas QX8344	Yr.Iss.	2000	10.95	11
2000 Warmed by Candleglow QX2471	Yr.Iss.	2000	6.95	7
2000 Winterberry Santa QXI4331	Yr.Iss.	2000	14.95	15

2000 Keepsake Collector's Club - Keepsake

YEAR ISSUE	EDITION LIMIT	YEAR RETD.	ISSUE PRICE	*QUOTE U.S.$
2000 1938 GARTON® Lincoln Zephyr QXC4501	Yr.Iss.	2000	15.95	16-28
2000 1992 Happy Holidays® BARBIE® Doll QXC4494	Yr.Iss.	2000	15.95	16-28
2000 Angelic Bell QXC4504	Yr.Iss.	2000	16.95	17
2000 Bell-Bearing Elf QXC4514A	Yr.Iss.	2000	N/A	8
2000 A Friend Chimes In QXC4491A	Yr.Iss.	2000	N/A	5
2000 Jingle Bell Kringle QXC4481A	Yr.Iss.	2000	N/A	9
2000 Ringing Reindeer QXC4484A	Yr.Iss.	2000	N/A	6

2000 Keepsake Magic Ornaments - Keepsake

YEAR ISSUE	EDITION LIMIT	YEAR RETD.	ISSUE PRICE	*QUOTE U.S.$
2000 Angels Over Bethlehem QLX7563	Yr.Iss.	2000	18.95	19-23
2000 The Blessed Family QLX7564	Yr.Iss.	2000	18.95	19-21
2000 Mary's Angels QLX7561	Yr.Iss.	2000	18.95	19-22
2000 Millennium Express QLX7364	Yr.Iss.	2000	42.00	42-79
2000 Time for Joy QX6904	Yr.Iss.	2000	24.00	24-28

2000 Laser Ornaments - Keepsake

YEAR ISSUE	EDITION LIMIT	YEAR RETD.	ISSUE PRICE	*QUOTE U.S.$
2000 Angel Light QLZ4311	Yr.Iss.	2000	7.95	8-11
2000 Dove QLZ4294	Yr.Iss.	2000	7.95	8
2000 Fun-Stuffed Stocking QLZ4291	Yr.Iss.	2000	5.95	6
2000 Heavenly Peace QLZ4314	Yr.Iss.	2000	6.95	7-12

YEAR ISSUE	EDITION LIMIT	YEAR RETD.	ISSUE PRICE	*QUOTE U.S.$
2000 Jack-in-the-Box QLZ4321	Yr.Iss.	2000	8.95	9
2000 Nativity QLZ4301	Yr.Iss.	2000	8.95	9-14
2000 The Nutcracker QLZ4284	Yr.Iss.	2000	5.95	6-11
2000 Window View into a Home QI 74281	Yr.Iss.	2000	8.95	9-11

2000 Lifestyles & Occupations - Keepsake

2000 Busy Bee Shopper QX6964	Yr.Iss.	2000	7.95	8-11
2000 Dancin' In Christmas QX6971	Yr.Iss.	2000	7.95	8
2000 Dousin' Dalmatian QX8024	Yr.Iss.	2000	9.95	10
2000 The Fishing Hole QX6984	Yr.Iss.	2000	12.95	13
2000 Friends in Harmony QX8001	Yr.Iss.	2000	9.95	10-13
2000 Gold-Star Teacher QX6951	Yr.Iss.	2000	7.95	8
2000 Golfer Supreme QX6991	Yr.Iss.	2000	10.95	11
2000 Kris "Cross-Country" Kringle QX6954	Yr.Iss.	2000	12.95	13
2000 Loggin' On to Santa QX8224	Yr.Iss.	2000	8.95	9-11
2000 Mrs. Claus's Holiday QX8011	Yr.Iss.	2000	9.95	10
2000 North Pole Network QX6994	Yr.Iss.	2000	10.95	11-17
2000 A Reader to the Core QX6974	Yr.Iss.	2000	9.95	10
2000 Stroll Round the Pole QX8164	Yr.Iss.	2000	10.95	11
2000 Tending Her Topiary QX8004	Yr.Iss.	2000	9.95	10
2000 Together We Serve QX8021	Yr.Iss.	2000	9.95	10
2000 Tree Guy QX6961	Yr.Iss.	2000	8.95	9
2000 Warm Kindness QX8014	Yr.Iss.	2000	8.95	9-14
2000 Yule Tide Runner QX6981	Yr.Iss.	2000	9.95	10

2000 Miniature Ornaments - Keepsake

2000 1935 Steelcraft by Murray® (3rd Ed.) QXM5951	Yr.Iss.	2000	6.95	7
2000 1968 Murray® Jolly Roger Flagship (6th Ed.) QXM5944	Yr.Iss.	2000	6.95	7
2000 Antique Tractors (4th Ed.) QXM5994	Yr.Iss.	2000	6.95	7-15
2000 Bugs Bunny and Elmer Fudd QXM5934	Yr.Iss.	2000	9.95	10
2000 Catwoman QXM6021	Yr.Iss.	2000	9.95	10
2000 Celestial Bunny QXM6641	Yr.Iss.	2000	6.95	7
2000 Christmas Bells (6th Ed.) QXM5964	Yr.Iss.	2000	4.95	5-9
2000 Devoted Donkey QXM6044	Yr.Iss.	2000	6.95	7
2000 Green Eggs and Ham™ Dr. Seuss™ set/3 QXM6034	Yr.Iss.	2000	19.95	20
2000 Holiday Flurries (2nd Ed.) QXM5311	Yr.Iss.	2000	6.95	7-10
2000 Horse Car and Milk Car (2nd Ed.) QXM5971	Yr.Iss.	2000	12.95	13
2000 Ice Block Buddies (1st Ed.) QXM6011	Yr.Iss.	2000	5.95	6
2000 Kindly Lions QXM5314	Yr.Iss.	2000	5.95	6
2000 Loyal Elephant QXM6041	Yr.Iss.	2000	6.95	7
2000 Mr. Potato Head™ QXM6014	Yr.Iss.	2000	5.95	6
2000 The Nativity (3rd Ed.) QXM5961	Yr.Iss.	2000	9.95	10-13
2000 Nutcracker Guild (7th Ed.) QXM5991	Yr.Iss.	2000	6.95	7
2000 Precious Penguin (Precious Ed.) QXM6104	Yr.Iss.	2000	9.95	10
2000 Sack of Money (1st Ed.) QXM5341	Yr.Iss.	2000	8.95	9-12
2000 Sailor (6th Ed.) QXM5334	Yr.Iss.	2000	4.95	5-8
2000 Santa's Journey Begins QXM6004	Yr.Iss.	2000	9.95	10
2000 Seaside Scenes (2nd Ed.) QXM5974	Yr.Iss.	2000	7.95	8-12
2000 Silken Flame™ BARBIE™ Ornament and Travel Case QXM6031	Yr.Iss.	2000	12.95	13
2000 Star Fairy QXM6101	Yr.Iss.	2000	4.95	5-9
2000 Sugarplum Fairy (5th Ed.) QXM5984	Yr.Iss.	2000	5.95	6
2000 Teddy-Bear Style (4th Ed.) QXM5954	Yr.Iss.	2000	5.95	6
2000 The Tin Man's Heart (2nd Ed.) QXM5981	Yr.Iss.	2000	5.95	6
2000 Welcoming Angel QXM5321	Yr.Iss.	2000	5.95	6
2000 Winter Fun With SNOOPY® (3rd Ed.) QXM5324	Yr.Iss.	2000	6.95	7

2000 Nature's Sketchbook - Keepsake

2000 Snowy Garden QX8284	Yr.Iss.	2000	13.95	14

2000 NFL Ornaments - Keepsake

2000 Cleveland Browns QSR5161	Yr.Iss.	2000	9.95	10
2000 Dallas Cowboys QSR5121	Yr.Iss.	2000	9.95	10
2000 Denver Broncos QSR5111	Yr.Iss.	2000	9.95	10
2000 Green Bay Packers QSR5114	Yr.Iss.	2000	9.95	10
2000 Kansas City Chiefs QSR5131	Yr.Iss.	2000	9.95	10
2000 Miami Dolphins QSR5144	Yr.Iss.	2000	9.95	10
2000 Minnesota Vikings QSR5164	Yr.Iss.	2000	9.95	10
2000 Pittsburgh Steelers QSR5124	Yr.Iss.	2000	9.95	10
2000 San Francisco 49ers QSR5134	Yr.Iss.	2000	9.95	10
2000 Washington Redskins QSR5151	Yr.Iss.	2000	9.95	10

2000 Pop Culture Icons - Keepsake

2000 1962 BARBIE™ Hatbox Doll Case QX6791	Yr.Iss.	2000	9.95	10-13

YEAR ISSUE	EDITION LIMIT	YEAR RETD.	ISSUE PRICE	*QUOTE U.S.$
2000 1968 DEORA™ QXI6891	Yr.Iss.	2000	14.95	15-18
2000 Blue's Clues QXI8391	Yr.Iss.	2000	10.95	11-13
2000 Bob the Tomato™ and Larry the Cucumber™ QXI4334	Yr.Iss.	2000	9.95	10
2000 Borg™ Cube QLX7354	Yr.Iss.	2000	24.00	24-35
2000 Bugs Bunny and Gossamer QX6574	Yr.Iss.	2000	12.95	13
2000 G.I. Joe® Action Pilot QX6734	Yr.Iss.	2000	13.95	14-17
2000 The Great Oz QLX7361	Yr.Iss.	2000	32.00	32
2000 Hopalong Cassidy™ QX6714	Yr.Iss.	2000	14.95	15-18
2000 I Love Lucy™ "Lucy Is Enciente" QX6884	Yr.Iss.	2000	15.95	16
2000 Jeannie the Genie QXI8564	Yr.Iss.	2000	14.95	15
2000 King of the Ring QX6864	Yr.Iss.	2000	10.95	11
2000 Larry, Moe & Curly QX6851	Yr.Iss.	2000	30.00	30-62
2000 The Lone Ranger™ QX6941	Yr.Iss.	2000	15.95	16
2000 The Lullabye League QX6604	Yr.Iss.	2000	19.95	20
2000 Mr. Monopoly™ QX8101	Yr.Iss.	2000	10.95	11-14
2000 Rhett Butler™ QX6674	Yr.Iss.	2000	12.95	13
2000 Scooby-Doo™ QXI8394	Yr.Iss.	2000	12.95	13
2000 Scuffy The Tugboat QX6871	Yr.Iss.	2000	11.95	12
2000 Self-Portrait Maxine QX6644	Yr.Iss.	2000	10.95	11
2000 Seven of Nine™ QX6844	Yr.Iss.	2000	14.95	15
2000 Super Friends™ QX6724	Yr.Iss.	2000	14.95	15
2000 The Tender Shepherd QX6834	Yr.Iss.	2000	13.95	14
2000 Tonka Dump Truck® QX6681	Yr.Iss.	2000	13.95	14-28
2000 The Yellow Submarine QXI6841	Yr.Iss.	2000	13.95	14-17
2000 Tonka Dump Truck® QX6681	Yr.Iss.	2000	13.95	14-28
2000 The Yellow Submarine QXI6841	Yr.Iss.	2000	13.95	14-17

2000 Premiere Event - Keepsake

2000 Frosty Friends QX6534	Yr.Iss.	2000	18.95	19
2000 Little Red Riding Hood – 1991 QFM7062	Yr.Iss.	2000	6.95	7

2000 Snoopy Christmas - Keepsake

2000 Charlie Brown QRP4191	Yr.Iss.	2000	4.95	5-10
2000 Linus QRP4204	Yr.Iss.	2000	4.95	5-10
2000 Lucy QRP4174	Yr.Iss.	2000	4.95	5-10
2000 Snoopy QRP4184	Yr.Iss.	2000	4.95	5-10
2000 Woodstock on Doghouse QRP4211	Yr.Iss.	2000	4.95	5-10

2000 Special Issues - Keepsake

2000 102 Dalmatians QXI5231	Yr.Iss.	2000	12.95	13
2000 1962 Duo-Glide™ (2nd Ed.) QXI6001	Yr.Iss.	2000	7.95	8
2000 Angel of Promise QXI4144	Yr.Iss.	2000	14.95	15
2000 Arnold Palmer QXI4324	Yr.Iss.	2000	14.95	15
2000 BARBIE™ Angel of Joy™ QXI6861	Yr.Iss.	2000	14.95	15
2000 BARBIE™ QXI6821	Yr.Iss.	2000	15.95	16
2000 Big Twin Evolution® Engine Harley-Davidson® Motorcycles QXI7571	Yr.Iss.	2000	24.00	24
2000 Dale Earnhardt QXI6754	Yr.Iss.	2000	14.95	15-39
2000 Darth Maul™ QXI6885	Yr.Iss.	2000	14.95	15
2000 Eric Lindros (4th Ed.) QXI6801	Yr.Iss.	2000	15.95	16-18
2000 Fat Boy® (2nd Ed.) QXI6774	Yr.Iss.	2000	14.95	15
2000 THE GRINCH QXI5344	Yr.Iss.	2000	12.95	13
2000 Gungan™ Submarine QXI7351	Yr.Iss.	2000	24.00	24
2000 Harley-Davidson® BARBIE™ QXI8554	Yr.Iss.	2000	14.95	15-20
2000 Imperial Stormtrooper™ QXI6711	Yr.Iss.	2000	14.95	15
2000 Jedi Council Members: Saesee Tinn, Yoda and Ki-Ad-Mundi QXI6744	Yr.Iss.	2000	19.95	20
2000 John Elway (6th Ed.) QXI6811	Yr.Iss.	2000	14.95	15
2000 Karl Malone (6th Ed.) QXI6901	Yr.Iss.	2000	14.95	15
2000 Kristi Yamaguchi QXI6854	Yr.Iss.	2000	13.95	14
2000 Mark McGwire (5th Ed.) QXI5361	Yr.Iss.	2000	14.95	15
2000 Obi-Wan Kenobi™ (4th Ed.) QXI6704	Yr.Iss.	2000	14.95	15
2000 Qui-Gon Jinn™ QXI6741	Yr.Iss.	2000	14.95	15
2000 Toy Story I-Space Ranger QXI5234	Yr.Iss.	2000	14.95	15
2000 Winter Fun With BARBIE™ and KELLY™ QXI6561	Yr.Iss.	2000	15.95	16

2000 Spring Ornaments - Keepsake

2000 1935 Auburn Speedster (3rd Ed.) QEO8401	Yr.Iss.	2000	14.95	15-18
2000 1940 GARTON® "Red Hot" Roadster (2nd in Winner's Circle) QEO8401	Yr.Iss.	2000	13.95	14
2000 Alice in Wonderland QEO8421	Yr.Iss.	2000	14.95	15
2000 Ballerina Barbie™ QEO8471	Yr.Iss.	2000	12.95	13
2000 Bar and Shield QEO8444	Yr.Iss.	2000	13.95	14-17
2000 Blueberry (2nd) QEO8454	Yr.Iss.	2000	9.95	10
2000 Bugs Bunny QEO8524	Yr.Iss.	2000	10.95	11

YEAR ISSUE	EDITION LIMIT	YEAR RETD.	ISSUE PRICE	*QUOTE U.S.$
2000 Caboose (5th Ed.) QEO8464	Yr.Iss.	2000	9.95	10
2000 Eastern Bluebird QEO8485	Yr.Iss.	2000	9.95	10
2000 Frolicking Friends Bambi, Thumper, and Flower QEO8434	Yr.Iss.	2000	14.95	15
2000 Happy Diploma Day! QEO8431	Yr.Iss.	2000	10.95	11
2000 Hopalong Cassidy™ Velocipede (4th Ed.) QEO8411	Yr.Iss.	2000	12.95	13
2000 Mr. Jeremy Fisher™ Beatrix Potter™ (5th Ed.) QEO8441	Yr.Iss.	2000	8.95	9-12
2000 Peanuts® QEO8444	Yr.Iss.	2000	14.95	15-18
2000 Rabbit (2nd Ed.) QEO8461	Yr.Iss.	2000	14.95	15
2000 A Snug Hug QEO8424	Yr.Iss.	2000	9.95	10
2000 A Swing With Friends QEO8414	Yr.Iss.	2000	14.95	15
2000 Time in the Garden QEO8511	Yr.Iss.	2000	10.95	11

2001 American Spirit Medallion Collection - Keepsake

2001 Kentucky Medallion QMP	Yr.Iss.	2001	14.95	15
2001 New York Medallion QMP	Yr.Iss.	2001	14.95	15
2001 North Carolina Medallion QMP	Yr.Iss.	2001	14.95	15
2001 Rhode Island Medallion QMP	Yr.Iss.	2001	14.95	15
2001 Vermont Medallion QMP	Yr.Iss.	2001	14.95	15

2001 Barbie Ornaments - Keepsake

2001 1950s BARBIE™ QXI8882	Yr.Iss.	2001	14.95	15
2001 1961 BARBIE™ Hatbox Case QX6922	Yr.Iss.	2001	9.95	10
2001 BARBIE™ and KELLY™ on the ice QXI6915	Yr.Iss.	2001	15.95	16
2001 BARBIE™ Angel™ QXI6925	Yr.Iss.	2001	15.95	16
2001 BARBIE™ as the Sugar Plum Princess QXI6132	Yr.Iss.	2001	15.95	16
2001 BARBIE™ in Busy Gal™ Fashion (8th) QX6965	Yr.Iss.	2001	15.95	16
2001 Celebration BARBIE™ QXI5202	Yr.Iss.	2001	15.95	16
2001 Harley-Davidson® BARBIE™ QXI8885	Yr.Iss.	2001	15.95	16
2001 Victorian BARBIE™ with Cedric Bear™ QXI6952	Yr.Iss.	2001	15.95	16

2001 Collectible Series - Keepsake

2001 1930 Custom Biplane (8th Ed.) QX6975	Yr.Iss.	2001	13.95	14
2001 1953 Buick® Roadmaster™ Skylark™ (11th Ed.) QX6872	Yr.Iss.	2001	13.95	14
2001 1959 Chevrolet® El Camino™ (7th Ed.) QX6072	Yr.Iss.	2001	13.95	14
2001 Beaglescout (4th Ed.) QX6085	Yr.Iss.	2001	9.95	10
2001 Cool Decade (2nd Ed.) QX6992	Yr.Iss.	2001	7.95	8
2001 Daniel in the Lion's Den (3rd Ed.) QX8122	Yr.Iss.	2001	13.95	14
2001 Fashion Afoot (2nd Ed.) QX8105	Yr.Iss.	2001	14.95	15
2001 Fire Station No. 1 (3rd Ed.) QX8052	Yr.Iss.	2001	15.95	16
2001 Frosty Friends (22nd Ed.) QX8012	Yr.Iss.	2001	10.95	11
2001 Gee Bee R-1 Super Sportster (5th Ed.) QX8005	Yr.Iss.	2001	14.95	15
2001 Gift Bearers (3rd Ed.) QX8115	Yr.Iss.	2001	12.95	13
2001 Horton Hatches the Egg™ (3rd Ed.) QX6282	Yr.Iss.	2001	14.95	15
2001 Joyful Santa (3rd Ed.) QX8152	Yr.Iss.	2001	14.95	15
2001 Kris and the Kringles QX8112	Yr.Iss.	2001	24.00	24
2001 LIONEL® Chessie Steam Special Locomotive (6th Ed.) QX6092	Yr.Iss.	2001	18.95	19
2001 A Little Nap QX8072	Yr.Iss.	2001	7.95	8
2001 Margaret "Meg" March QX6315	Yr.Iss.	2001	15.95	16
2001 Mary's Angels-Chrysantha (14th Ed.) QX6985	Yr.Iss.	2001	7.95	8
2001 Mischievous Kittens (3rd Ed.) QX8025	Yr.Iss.	2001	9.95	10
2001 Mistletoe Miss QX8092	Yr.Iss.	2001	14.95	15
2001 A Pony For Christmas (4th Ed.) QX6995	Yr.Iss.	2001	12.95	13
2001 Puppy Love (11th Ed.) QX6982	Yr.Iss.	2001	7.95	8
2001 Robot Parade (2nd Ed.) QX8162	Yr.Iss.	2001	14.95	15
2001 Safe and Snug QX8342	Yr.Iss.	2001	12.95	13
2001 Santa's Snowplow (23rd Ed.) QX8065	Yr.Iss.	2001	14.95	15
2001 Service Station (18th Ed.) QX8045	Yr.Iss.	2001	14.95	15
2001 Snow Buddies (4th Ed.) QX6972	Yr.Iss.	2001	7.95	8
2001 Tender-LIONEL® Chessie Steam Special QX6285	Yr.Iss.	2001	13.95	14
2001 Toymaker Santa (2nd Ed.) QX8032	Yr.Iss.	2001	14.95	15
2001 Victorian Christmas (6th Ed.) QX6855	Yr.Iss.	2001	14.95	15

2001 Collegiate Ornaments - Keepsake

2001 Alabama® Crimson Tide® QSR2132	Yr.Iss.	2001	9.95	10
2001 Florida Gators® QSR2165	Yr.Iss.	2001	9.95	10
2001 Florida State® Seminoles® QSR2162	Yr.Iss.	2001	9.95	10
2001 Michigan Wolverines™ QSR2142	Yr.Iss.	2001	9.95	10
2001 Nebraska Cornhuskers™ QSR2135	Yr.Iss.	2001	9.95	10
2001 North Carolina® Tar Heels® QSR2155	Yr.Iss.	2001	9.95	10
2001 Notre Dame® Fighting Irish™ QSR2145	Yr.Iss.	2001	9.95	10
2001 Penn State® Nittany Lions® QSR2122	Yr.Iss.	2001	9.95	10
2001 Tennessee Volunteers® QSR2125	Yr.Iss.	2001	9.95	10
2001 The University Of Kentucky® Wildcats™ QSR2152	Yr.Iss.	2001	9.95	10

2001 Disney Classic Movies - Keepsake

2001 Bambi Discovers Winter QXD7541	Yr.Iss.	2001	24.00	24
2001 Cinderella's Castle QXD4172	Yr.Iss.	2001	18.00	18
2001 The Glass Slipper QXD4182	Yr.Iss.	2001	7.95	8
2001 Hello, Dumbo! QXD4162	Yr.Iss.	2001	12.95	13
2001 Jiminy Cricket QXD4185	Yr.Iss.	2001	7.95	8
2001 A Magical Dress for Briar Rose QXD4202	Yr.Iss.	2001	14.95	15
2001 Monsters, Inc. QXI6145	Yr.Iss.	2001	14.95	15
2001 Mrs. Potts and Chip QXD4165	Yr.Iss.	2001	12.95	13
2001 Thomas O'Malley and Duchess QXD4175	Yr.Iss.	2001	14.95	15

2001 Friends and Family - Keepsake

2001 2001 Time Capsule QX2802	Yr.Iss.	2001	9.95	10
2001 2001 Vacation QX2822	Yr.Iss.	2001	9.95	10
2001 All-Sport Santa QX8332	Yr.Iss.	2001	9.95	10
2001 All-Star Kid QX2805	Yr.Iss.	2001	9.95	10
2001 America for Me! QX2882	Yr.Iss.	2001	9.95	10
2001 Baby Boy's First Christmas QX8365	Yr.Iss.	2001	8.95	9
2001 Baby Girl's First Christmas QX8372	Yr.Iss.	2001	8.95	9
2001 Baby's First Christmas QX8355	Yr.Iss.	2001	8.95	9
2001 Baby's First Christmas QX8362	Yr.Iss.	2001	8.95	9
2001 Baby's First Christmas QX8375	Yr.Iss.	2001	7.95	8
2001 Baby's First Christmas QX8482	Yr.Iss.	2001	9.95	10
2001 Baby's Second Christmas QX8382	Yr.Iss.	2001	7.95	8
2001 Beginning Ballet QX2875	Yr.Iss.	2001	12.95	13
2001 Child's Fifth Christmas QX8395	Yr.Iss.	2001	7.95	8
2001 Child's Fourth Christmas QX8392	Yr.Iss.	2001	7.95	8
2001 Childs' Third Christmas QX8385	Yr.Iss.	2001	7.95	8
2001 Cozy Home QX8965	Yr.Iss.	2001	9.95	10
2001 A Cup of Friendship QX8472	Yr.Iss.	2001	8.95	9
2001 Dad QX8425	Yr.Iss.	2001	8.95	9
2001 Daughter QX8425	Yr.Iss.	2001	8.95	9
2001 Four-Alarm Friends QX8325	Yr.Iss.	2001	9.95	10
2001 Friendly Elves QX8805	Yr.Iss.	2001	14.95	15
2001 Godchild QX8452	Yr.Iss.	2001	7.95	8
2001 Gouda Reading QX2855	Yr.Iss.	2001	9.95	10
2001 Grandchild's First Christmas QX8485	Yr.Iss.	2001	8.95	9
2001 Granddaughter QX8435	Yr.Iss.	2001	8.95	9
2001 Grandmother QX8445	Yr.Iss.	2001	9.95	10
2001 Grandson QX8442	Yr.Iss.	2001	8.95	9
2001 Guiding Star QX8962	Yr.Iss.	2001	9.95	10
2001 I Love My Dog QX8802	Yr.Iss.	2001	7.95	8
2001 It Had To Be You QX2815	Yr.Iss.	2001	9.95	10
2001 Kiss The Cook QX2852	Yr.Iss.	2001	9.95	10
2001 Laptop Santa QX8972	Yr.Iss.	2001	7.95	8
2001 Lazy Afternoon QX8335	Yr.Iss.	2001	9.95	10
2001 Mom and Dad QX8462	Yr.Iss.	2001	9.95	10
2001 Mom QX8415	Yr.Iss.	2001	8.95	9
2001 Mother and Daughter Locket QX6962	Yr.Iss.	2001	9.95	10
2001 No. 1 Teacher QX2865	Yr.Iss.	2001	9.95	10
2001 Our Christmas Together QX3162	Yr.Iss.	2001	7.95	8
2001 Our Christmas Together QX8412	Yr.Iss.	2001	19.95	20
2001 Our Family QX8995	Yr.Iss.	2001	8.95	9
2001 Our First Christmas Together QX6012	Yr.Iss.	2001	8.95	9
2001 Our First Christmas Together QX8405	Yr.Iss.	2001	9.95	10
2001 Pat The Bunny QX8582	Yr.Iss.	2001	9.95	10
2001 A Perfect Blend QX8985	Yr.Iss.	2001	9.95	10
2001 Santa's Day Off QX2872	Yr.Iss.	2001	9.95	10
2001 Santa's Workshop QX2812	Yr.Iss.	2001	9.95	10
2001 Sew Sweet Angel QX2862	Yr.Iss.	2001	9.95	10
2001 Sisters QX8455	Yr.Iss.	2001	8.95	9
2001 Son QX8432	Yr.Iss.	2001	8.95	9

YEAR ISSUE	EDITION LIMIT	YEAR RETD.	ISSUE PRICE	*QUOTE U.S.$
2001 Winter Friends QX2242	Yr.Iss.	2001	6.95	7

2001 Frostlight Faeries - Keepsake

YEAR ISSUE	EDITION LIMIT	YEAR RETD.	ISSUE PRICE	*QUOTE U.S.$
2001 Faerie Brilliana QP1672	Yr.Iss.	2001	14.95	15
2001 Faerie Candessa QP1665	Yr.Iss.	2001	14.95	15
2001 Faerie Delandra QP1685	Yr.Iss.	2001	14.95	15
2001 Faerie Estrella QP1695	Yr.Icc.	2001	14.05	15
2001 Faerie Floriella QP1692	Yr.Iss.	2001	14.95	15
2001 Queen Aurora Tree Topper QP1662	Yr.Iss.	2001	35.00	35

2001 Harry Potter Ornaments - Keepsake

YEAR ISSUE	EDITION LIMIT	YEAR RETD.	ISSUE PRICE	*QUOTE U.S.$
2001 Fluffy on Guard QXE4415	Yr.Iss.	2001	12.95	13
2001 Hagrid and Norbert the Dragon QXE4412	Yr.Iss.	2001	15.95	16
2001 Harry Potter Lunch Box QXE8832	Yr.Iss.	2001	10.95	11
2001 Harry Potter QXE4402	Yr.Iss.	2001	12.95	13
2001 Hermoine's Granger's Trunk QXE4422	Yr.Iss.	2001	14.95	15
2001 Hogwarts School Crests QXE4452	Yr.Iss.	2001	12.95	13
2001 The Mirror of Erised QXI8645	Yr.Iss.	2001	15.95	16
2001 The Potions Master QXI8652	Yr.Iss.	2001	14.95	15
2001 Ron Weasley and Scabbers QXE4405	Yr.Iss.	2001	12.95	13

2001 Holiday Traditions - Keepsake

YEAR ISSUE	EDITION LIMIT	YEAR RETD.	ISSUE PRICE	*QUOTE U.S.$
2001 Angel of Faith QXI5375	Yr.Iss.	2001	14.95	15
2001 Angel's Whisper QX8852	Yr.Iss.	2001	9.95	10
2001 Beautiful Cross QX8825	Yr.Iss.	2001	9.95	10
2001 Carving Santa QX8265	Yr.Iss.	2001	12.95	13
2001 Christmas Brings Us Together QX8285	Yr.Iss.	2001	9.95	10
2001 The Christmas Cone QX8875	Yr.Iss.	2001	8.95	9
2001 Christmas Parrot QX8175	Yr.Iss.	2001	8.95	9
2001 Creative Cutter-Cooking For Christmas QX8865	Yr.Iss.	2001	9.95	10
2001 Eye of God-Feliz Navidad QX8185	Yr.Iss.	2001	9.95	10
2001 The Flight at Kitty Hawk QXM5215	Yr.Iss.	2001	6.95	7
2001 Flying School Airplane Hanger QX8172	Yr.Iss.	2001	15.95	16
2001 Graceful Angel Bell QX8182	Yr.Iss.	2001	9.95	10
2001 Graceful Reindeer QX8912	Yr.Iss.	2001	15.95	16
2001 Happy Snowman QX8942	Yr.Iss.	2001	8.95	9
2001 Jolly Santa Bells QX8915	Yr.Iss.	2001	19.95	20
2001 Jolly Visitor QX2235	Yr.Iss.	2001	6.95	7
2001 Journey to Bethlehem Bell QX8386	Yr.Iss.	2001	14.95	15
2001 The Land of Christmastime QX8282	Yr.Iss.	2001	12.95	13
2001 Mary and Joseph QX8195	Yr.Iss.	2001	18.95	20
2001 Mary Hamilton Angel Chorus QX2232	Yr.Iss.	2001	6.95	7
2001 Mitford Snowman Jubilee QX2825	Yr.Iss.	2001	19.95	20
2001 Moose's Merry Christmas QX8835	Yr.Iss.	2001	12.95	13
2001 Mrs. Claus's Chair QX6955	Yr.Iss.	2001	12.95	13
2001 My First Snowman-Nature's Sketchbook QX4442	Yr.Iss.	2001	9.95	10
2001 Noah's Ark QX2835	Yr.Iss.	2001	12.95	13
2001 Noche de Paz QX8192	Yr.Iss.	2001	12.95	13
2001 Old-World Santa QX8975	Yr.Iss.	2001	9.95	10
2001 One Little Angel QX8935	Yr.Iss.	2001	8.95	9
2001 A Partridge in a Pear Tree QX8215	Yr.Iss.	2001	12.95	13
2001 Peanuts® Pageant QX2832	Yr.Iss.	2001	14.95	15
2001 Peek-a-Boo Present QX8302	Yr.Iss.	2001	9.95	10
2001 Penguins at Play QX8982	Yr.Iss.	2001	9.95	10
2001 Ready Reindeer QX8295	Yr.Iss.	2001	13.95	14
2001 Ready Teddy QX8842	Yr.Iss.	2001	9.95	10
2001 Rocking Reindeer QX8261	Yr.Iss.	2001	12.95	13
2001 Santa Sneaks a Sweet-Cooking For Christmas QX8862	Yr.Iss.	2001	15.95	16
2001 Santa's Sweet Surprise QX8275	Yr.Iss.	2001	14.95	15
2001 Sharing Santa's Snacks QX8212	Yr.Iss.	2001	8.95	9
2001 Skating Sugar Bear Bell QX6005	Yr.Iss.	2001	9.95	10
2001 Snoozing Santa QX8165	Yr.Iss.	2001	18.95	19
2001 Snow Blossom QX8494	Yr.Iss.	2001	9.95	10
2001 Snuggly Sugar Bear Bell QX8922	Yr.Iss.	2001	9.95	10
2001 Springing Santa QX8085	Yr.Iss.	2001	7.95	8
2001 Victorian Christmas Memories, Thomas Kinkade, Painter of Light QX8292	Yr.Iss.	2001	14.95	15
2001 Victorian Sleigh QX8855	Yr.Iss.	2001	12.95	13
2001 Waddles QX8952	Yr.Iss.	2001	8.95	9
2001 Waggles QX8945	Yr.Iss.	2001	8.95	9
2001 Wiggles QX8955	Yr.Iss.	2001	8.95	9
2001 A Wise Follower QX8202	Yr.Iss.	2001	8.95	9
2001 Wreath of Evergreens QX8832	Yr.Iss.	2001	8.95	9

2001 Keepsake Collector's Club - Keepsake

YEAR ISSUE	EDITION LIMIT	YEAR RETD.	ISSUE PRICE	*QUOTE U.S.$
2001 1958 Custom Corvette QXC4505	Yr.Iss.	2001	17.95	18
2001 Lettera, Globus & Mrs. Claus, set/3 QXC2001A	Yr.Iss.	2001	N/A	N/A
2001 Nesting Nativity QXC4502	Yr.Iss.	2001	23.50	24
2001 Ready for Delivery QXC4552A	Yr.Iss.	2001	N/A	N/A
2001 Santa Claus Marionette QXC4525	Yr.Iss.	2001	13.95	14
2001 Santa Claus, set/2 QXI5395	Yr.Iss.	2001	18.95	19
2001 Santa's Desk QXC4562A	Yr.Iss.	2001	N/A	N/A
2001 Santa's Sleigh, set/2 QX8872	Yr.Iss.	2001	18.95	19
2001 Santa's Toy Box, set/4 QXI5392	Yr.Iss.	2001	12.95	13
2001 With Help From Pup QXC4565A	Yr.Iss.	2001	N/A	N/A

2001 Keepsake Magic Ornaments - Keepsake

YEAR ISSUE	EDITION LIMIT	YEAR RETD.	ISSUE PRICE	*QUOTE U.S.$
2001 Candlelight Services (4th Ed.) QX7552	Yr.Iss.	2001	18.95	19
2001 Farewell Scene-Gone With the Wind QXL7562	Yr.Iss.	2001	24.00	24
2001 Lighthouse Greetings (5th Ed.) QX7572	Yr.Iss.	2001	24.00	24
2001 Poppy Field-The Wizard of Oz QXL7565	Yr.Iss.	2001	24.00	24
2001 Up on the Housetop QLX7575	Yr.Iss.	2001	42.00	42

2001 Mickey & Co. - Keepsake

YEAR ISSUE	EDITION LIMIT	YEAR RETD.	ISSUE PRICE	*QUOTE U.S.$
2001 Bell Ringing Santa QXD4125	Yr.Iss.	2001	9.95	10
2001 Disney's School Bus QXD4115	Yr.Iss.	2001	14.95	15
2001 Donald Goes Motoring QXD4122	Yr.Iss.	2001	12.95	13
2001 Merry Carolers QXD7585	Yr.Iss.	2001	24.00	24
2001 Mickey's Sweetheart QXD4192	Yr.Iss.	2001	9.95	10
2001 Minnie's Sweetheart QXD4195	Yr.Iss.	2001	9.95	10
2001 Pluto Plays Triangle QXD4112	Yr.Iss.	2001	13.95	14

2001 Miniature Ornaments - Keepsake

YEAR ISSUE	EDITION LIMIT	YEAR RETD.	ISSUE PRICE	*QUOTE U.S.$
2001 1924 Toledo Fire Truck #6 (7th Ed.) QXM5192	Yr.Iss.	2001	6.95	7
2001 1937 Garton® Ford (4th Ed.) QXM5195	Yr.Iss.	2001	6.95	7
2001 1947 Servi-Car (3rd Ed.) QXI5282	Yr.Iss.	2001	7.95	8
2001 1947 Servi-Car™ (3rd Ed.) QXI5282	Yr.Iss.	2001	7.95	8
2001 Antique Tractors (5th Ed.) QXM5252	Yr.Iss.	2001	6.95	7
2001 Battle of Naboo QXM5212	Yr.Iss.	2001	14.95	15
2001 Bouncy Kangaroos QXM5332	Yr.Iss.	2001	5.95	6
2001 Car Carrier and Caboose (3rd Ed.) QXM5265	Yr.Iss.	2001	12.95	13
2001 Christmas Bells (7th Ed.) QXM5245	Yr.Iss.	2001	4.95	5
2001 Dashing Through The Snow QXM5335	Yr.Iss.	2001	6.95	7
2001 The Flight at Kitty Hawk QXM5215	Yr.Iss.	2001	6.95	7
2001 Gearing Up for Christmas QXM5352	Yr.Iss.	2001	6.95	7
2001 The Glass Slipper QXD4182	Yr.Iss.	2001	7.95	8
2001 Graceful Angel-Tree Topper QXM5385	Yr.Iss.	2001	12.95	13
2001 Holiday Flurries (3rd Ed.) QXM5272	Yr.Iss.	2001	6.95	7
2001 Holiday Shoe QXM5365	Yr.Iss.	2001	4.95	5
2001 Ice Block Buddies (2nd Ed.) QXM5295	Yr.Iss.	2001	5.95	6
2001 Jiminy Cricket QXD4185	Yr.Iss.	2001	7.95	8
2001 The Nativity (4th Ed.) QXM5255	Yr.Iss.	2001	9.95	10
2001 Race Car (2nd Ed.) QXM5292	Yr.Iss.	2001	8.95	9
2001 Radiant Christmas QXM5342	Yr.Iss.	2001	7.95	8
2001 Ready for a Ride QXM5302	Yr.Iss.	2001	6.95	7
2001 Santa-in-a-Box QXM355	Yr.Iss.	2001	6.95	7
2001 Scooby-Doo™ QXM5322	Yr.Iss.	2001	6.95	7
2001 Seaside Scenes (3rd Ed.) QXM5275	Yr.Iss.	2001	7.95	8
2001 Solo in the Spotlight™ Case and BARBIE™ QXM5312	Yr.Iss.	2001	12.95	13
2001 Solo in the Spotlight™ QXM5265	Yr.Iss.	2001	12.95	13
2001 Starfleet Legends QXM5325	Yr.Iss.	2001	14.95	15
2001 Sweet Contribution-Cooking For Christmas QXM4492	Yr.Iss.	2001	4.95	5
2001 Sweet Slipper Dream QXM5345	Yr.Iss.	2001	4.95	5
2001 Thing One and Thing Two™! QXM5315	Yr.Iss.	2001	14.95	15
2001 Toto (3rd Ed.) QXM5285	Yr.Iss.	2001	5.95	6
2001 Tweety QXM5305	Yr.Iss.	2001	6.95	7
2001 Winter Fun With Snoopy® (4th Ed.) QXM5262	Yr.Iss.	2001	6.95	7

2001 NFL Ornaments - Keepsake

YEAR ISSUE	EDITION LIMIT	YEAR RETD.	ISSUE PRICE	*QUOTE U.S.$
2001 Cleveland Browns QSR5572	Yr.Iss.	2001	9.95	10
2001 Dallas Cowboys QSR5622	Yr.Iss.	2001	9.95	10
2001 Denver Broncos QSR5545	Yr.Iss.	2001	9.95	10

YEAR ISSUE	EDITION LIMIT	YEAR RETD.	ISSUE PRICE	*QUOTE U.S.$
2001 Green Bay Packers QSR5625	Yr.Iss.	2001	9.95	10
2001 Kansas City Chiefs QSR5542	Yr.Iss.	2001	9.95	10
2001 Miami Dolphins QSR5555	Yr.Iss.	2001	9.95	10
2001 Minnesota Vikings QSR5575	Yr.Iss.	2001	9.95	10
2001 Pittsburgh Steelers QSR5565	Yr.Iss.	2001	9.95	10
2001 San Francisco 49ers QSR5562	Yr.Iss.	2001	9.95	10
2001 Washington Redskins QSR5552	Yr.Iss.	2001	9.95	10

2001 Pop Culture Icons - Keepsake

YEAR ISSUE	EDITION LIMIT	YEAR RETD.	ISSUE PRICE	*QUOTE U.S.$
2001 1957 XL Sportster® (3rd Ed.) QXI8125	Yr.Iss.	2001	14.95	15
2001 1968 Silhouette™ and Case-Hot Wheels QX6605	Yr.Iss.	2001	14.95	15
2001 2000 Oscar Mayer Wienermobile™ QX6935	Yr.Iss.	2001	12.95	13
2001 2001 Jeep™ Sport Wrangler QXI6362	Yr.Iss.	2001	14.95	15
2001 Anakin Skywalker™ QX6942	Yr.Iss.	2001	14.95	15
2001 Blue and Periwinkle QXI6142	Yr.Iss.	2001	9.95	10
2001 Captain Benjamin Sisko™-Star Trek:Deep Space Nine QX6865	Yr.Iss.	2001	14.95	15
2001 Color Crew Chief QX6185	Yr.Iss.	2001	10.95	11
2001 G.I.Joe® Fighter Pilot QX6045	Yr.Iss.	2001	13.95	14
2001 Jar Jar Binks™ QX6882	Yr.Iss.	2001	14.95	15
2001 LIONEL® 1-400E Blue Comet Locomotive QBG4355	Yr.Iss.	2001	35.00	35
2001 Lionel™ Plays With Words QXI6902	Yr.Iss.	2001	14.95	15
2001 Lucy Does a TV Commercial QX6862	Yr.Iss.	2001	15.95	16
2001 Naboo Royal Starship QX8475	Yr.Iss.	2001	18.95	19
2001 A Perfect Christmas! QXI6895	Yr.Iss.	2001	12.95	13
2001 Q™ Star Trek: The Next Generation™ QBG4345	Yr.Iss.	2001	24.00	24
2001 R-2-D2™ (5th) QX6875	Yr.Iss.	2001	14.95	15
2001 Raggedy Andy QX8574	Yr.Iss.	2001	10.95	11
2001 Raggedy Ann QX8571	Yr.Iss.	2001	10.95	11
2001 Samantha "Sam" Stevens QXI6892	Yr.Iss.	2001	14.95	15
2001 Space Station Deep Space 9-Star Trek:Deep Space Nine QX6065	Yr.Iss.	2001	32.00	32
2001 Starfleet Legends - Star Trek™ QXM5325	Yr.Iss.	2001	14.95	15
2001 TONKA® 1955 Steam Shovel QX6292	Yr.Iss.	2001	13.95	14
2001 Tootle the Train QX6052	Yr.Iss.	2001	11.95	12
2001 Waiting for Santa Larry the Cucumber™ and Bob the Tomato™ Veggie Tales® QXI6932	Yr.Iss.	2001	12.95	13
2001 What a Grinchy Trick! QXI6405	Yr.Iss.	2001	14.95	15

2001 Sports - Keepsake

YEAR ISSUE	EDITION LIMIT	YEAR RETD.	ISSUE PRICE	*QUOTE U.S.$
2001 Brett Favre (7th) QXI5232	Yr.Iss.	2001	14.95	15
2001 Dale Jarrett QXI5205	Yr.Iss.	2001	14.95	15
2001 Jaromir Jagr (5th) QXI6852	Yr.Iss.	2001	15.95	16
2001 Mickey Mantle-New York Yankees QXI6804	Yr.Iss.	2001	14.95	15
2001 Peggy Fleming QXI6845	Yr.Iss.	2001	14.95	15
2001 Sammy Sosa (6th) QXI6375	Yr.Iss.	2001	14.95	15
2001 Steve Young-San Francisco 49ers QXI6305	Yr.Iss.	2001	14.95	15
2001 Tim Duncan (7th) QXI5235	Yr.Iss.	2001	14.95	15

2001 Warner Bros. - Keepsake

YEAR ISSUE	EDITION LIMIT	YEAR RETD.	ISSUE PRICE	*QUOTE U.S.$
2001 Holiday Spa-Tweety QX6945	Yr.Iss.	2001	9.95	10
2001 The Jetsons™ QX6312	Yr.Iss.	2001	14.95	15
2001 The Mystery Machine™ -Scooby-Doo QX6295	Yr.Iss.	2001	13.95	14
2001 Portrait of Scarlett™ QX2885	Yr.Iss.	2001	15.95	16
2001 SCOOBY-DOO™ QXM5322	Yr.Iss.	2001	6.95	7
2001 Sylvester's Bang-Up Gift -Looney Tunes QX6912	Yr.Iss.	2001	12.95	13
2001 Toto (3rd) QXM5285	Yr.Iss.	2001	5.95	6
2001 Tweety-Looney Tunes QXM5305	Yr.Iss.	2001	6.95	7

2001 Winnie the Pooh - Keepsake

YEAR ISSUE	EDITION LIMIT	YEAR RETD.	ISSUE PRICE	*QUOTE U.S.$
2001 Eeyore Helps Out QXD4145	Yr.Iss.	2001	12.95	13
2001 A Familiar Face QXD4152	Yr.Iss.	2001	12.95	13
2001 Just What They Wanted! QXD4142	Yr.Iss.	2001	12.95	13
2001 A Story For Pooh (3rd) QXD4135	Yr.Iss.	2001	13.95	14
2001 Tracking the Jagular (4th) QXD4132	Yr.Iss.	2001	13.95	14

Hamilton Collection

Christmas Angels - S. Kuck

YEAR ISSUE	EDITION LIMIT	YEAR RETD.	ISSUE PRICE	*QUOTE U.S.$
1994 Angel of Charity	Open		19.50	20
1995 Angel of Joy	Open		19.50	20
1995 Angel of Grace	Open		19.50	20
1995 Angel of Faith	Open		19.50	20
1995 Angel of Patience	Open		19.50	20
1995 Angel of Glory	Open		19.50	20
1996 Angel of Gladness	Open		19.50	20
1996 Angel of Innocence	Open		19.50	20
1996 Angel of Beauty	Open		19.50	20
1996 Angel of Purity	Open		19.50	20
1996 Angel of Charm	Open		19.50	20
1996 Angel of Kindness	Open		19.50	20

Derek Darlings - N/A

YEAR ISSUE	EDITION LIMIT	YEAR RETD.	ISSUE PRICE	*QUOTE U.S.$
1995 Jessica, Sara, Chelsea (set)	Open		29.85	30

Dreamsicles Joy of Christmas Suncatcher - N/A

YEAR ISSUE	EDITION LIMIT	YEAR RETD.	ISSUE PRICE	*QUOTE U.S.$
1997 Bearing Gifts	Open		14.95	15
1997 Open Me First	Open		14.95	15
1997 Snowflake Magic	Open		14.95	15
1997 Under The Mistletoe	Open		14.95	15

Dreamsicles Suncatchers - K. Haynes

YEAR ISSUE	EDITION LIMIT	YEAR RETD.	ISSUE PRICE	*QUOTE U.S.$
1996 Stolen Kiss	Open		19.95	20
1996 Sharing Hearts	Open		19.95	20
1996 Love Letters	Open		19.95	20
1996 I Love You	Open		19.95	20
1996 Daisies and Dreamsicles	Open		19.95	20
1997 First Love	Open		19.95	20
1997 Perfect Match	Open		19.95	20
1997 Hand in Hand	Open		19.95	20

Earnhardt Holiday Ornaments - N/A

YEAR ISSUE	EDITION LIMIT	YEAR RETD.	ISSUE PRICE	*QUOTE U.S.$
2001 That Holiday Attitude	Open		12.95	13
2001 Ready to Ride	Open		12.95	13
2001 Takin' Off for the Holidays	Open		12.95	13
2001 Last Lap Delivery	Open		12.95	13
2001 Hooked on #3	Open		12.95	13
2001 Deck the Walls	Open		12.95	13

Earnhardt Ornaments - S. Bass

YEAR ISSUE	EDITION LIMIT	YEAR RETD.	ISSUE PRICE	*QUOTE U.S.$
2000 Black Attack	Open		12.95	13
2000 Champion's Choice!	Open		12.95	13
2000 Fade To Black!	Open		12.95	13
2000 Finally First!	Open		12.95	13
2000 Hooked Up!	Open		12.95	13
2000 The Intimidator!	Open		12.95	13
1999 Look of a Winner	Open		12.95	13
2000 The Magnificent Seven!	Open		12.95	13
1999 Man On A Mission!	Open		12.95	13
1999 Ready!	Open		12.95	13
2000 Rising Son!	Open		12.95	13
2000 Silver Select!	Open		12.95	13

Little Messengers - P. Parkins

YEAR ISSUE	EDITION LIMIT	YEAR RETD.	ISSUE PRICE	*QUOTE U.S.$
1997 Ice Skater, Christmas Lights, Gingerbreadman, set/3	Open		29.90	30
1997 Shining Star, Candle, Mistletoe, set/3	Open		29.90	30
1997 Snowflake, Wreath, Choirbook, set/3	Open		29.90	30
1997 Stocking, Harp, Kitten, set/3	Open		29.90	30

Harbour Lights

Christmas Ornaments - Harbour Lights

YEAR ISSUE	EDITION LIMIT	YEAR RETD.	ISSUE PRICE	*QUOTE U.S.$
1996 Big Bay Pt. MI 7040	Closed	1996	15.00	14-30
1996 Burrows Island WA 7043	Closed	1996	15.00	14-30
1996 Holland MI 7041	Closed	1999	15.00	14-15
1996 Sand Island WI 7042	Closed	1996	15.00	14-30
1996 Set of 4 702	Closed	1999	60.00	60
1996 30 Mile Pt. NY 7044	Closed	1996	15.00	14-30
1996 Cape Neddick ME 7047	Closed	1999	15.00	14-15
1996 New London Ledge CT 7046	Closed	1999	15.00	15
1996 S.E. Block Island RI 7045	Closed	1999	15.00	14-15
1996 Set of 4 703	Closed	1999	60.00	56-60
1997 Cape Hatteras NC 7048	Closed	1999	15.00	14-15
1997 Saugerties NY 7049	Closed	1999	15.00	14-15
1997 Thomas Point MD 7050	Closed	1999	15.00	14-15
1997 Colchester Reef VT 7051	Closed	1999	15.00	15

ORNAMENTS

YEAR ISSUE	EDITION LIMIT	YEAR RETD.	ISSUE PRICE	*QUOTE U.S.$
1997 Set of 4 705	Closed	1999	60.00	60
1998 Montauk NY 7052	Open		15.00	15
1998 Middle Bay AL 7053	Open		15.00	15
1998 White Shoal MI 7054	Open		15.00	15
1998 Alcatraz CA 7055	Open		15.00	15
1998 Set of 4 706	Open		60.00	60
1000 Barnegat NJ 7056	Open		15.00	15
1999 Gay Head MA 7057	Open		15.00	15
1999 West Quoddy ME 7058	Open		15.00	15
1999 Old Field NY 7059	Open		15.00	15
1999 Set of 4 709	Open		60.00	60
2000 Old Mackinac MI 7060	Open		15.00	15
2000 Cape Elizabeth ME 7061	Open		15.00	15
2000 Hudson-Athens NY 7062	Open		15.00	15
2000 East Quoddy Canada 7063	Open		15.00	15
2000 Set of 4 711	Open		60.00	60
2001 Dunkirk NY 7064	Open		15.00	15
2001 Ship John Shoal DE 7065	Open		15.00	15
2001 Rockland Breakwater ME 7066	Open		15.00	15
2001 Hereford Inlet NJ 7067	Open		15.00	15
2001 Set of 4 713	Open		60.00	60

Kurt S. Adler, Inc.

Children's Hour - J. Mostrom

1995 Alice in Wonderland J5751	Retrd.	1996	22.50	23
1995 Bow Peep J5753	Retrd.	1997	27.00	27
1995 Cinderella J5752	Retrd.	1996	28.00	28
1995 Little Boy Blue J5755	Retrd.	1995	18.00	18
1995 Miss Muffet J5753	Retrd.	1997	27.00	27
1995 Mother Goose J5754	Retrd.	1996	27.00	27
1995 Red Riding Hood J5751	Retrd.	1996	22.50	23

Christmas in Chelsea Collection - J. Mostrom

1994 Alice, Marguerite W2973	Retrd.	1996	28.00	28
1992 Allison Sitting in Chair W2812	Retrd.	1994	25.50	26
1992 Allison W2729	Retrd.	1993	21.00	21
1992 Amanda W2709	Retrd.	1994	21.00	21
1992 Amy W2729	Retrd.	1994	21.00	21
1992 Christina W2812	Retrd.	1994	25.50	26
1992 Christopher W2709	Retrd.	1994	21.00	21
1992 Delphinium W2728	Retrd.	1997	20.00	20
1995 Edmond With Violin W3078	Retrd.	1996	32.00	32
1994 Guardian Angel With Baby W2974	Retrd.	1995	31.00	31
1992 Holly Hock W2728	Retrd.	1997	20.00	20
1992 Holly W2709	Retrd.	1994	21.00	21
1995 Jose With Violin W3078	Retrd.	1996	32.00	32
1995 Pauline With Violin W3078	Retrd.	1996	32.00	32
1992 Peony W2728	Retrd.	1997	20.00	20
1992 Rose W2728	Retrd.	1997	20.00	20

Cornhusk Mice Ornament Series - M. Rothenberg

1994 3" Father Christmas W2976	Retrd.	1998	18.00	18
1994 9" Father Christmas W2982	Retrd.	1997	25.00	25
1995 Angel Mice W3088	Retrd.	1997	10.00	10
1995 Baby's First Mouse W3087	Retrd.	1998	10.00	10
1993 Ballerina Cornhusk Mice W2700	Retrd.	1994	13.50	14
1994 Clara, Prince W2948	Retrd.	1997	16.00	16
1994 Cowboy W2951	Retrd.	1996	18.00	18
1994 Drosselmeir Fairy, Mouse King W2950	Retrd.	1997	16.00	16
1994 Little Pocahontas, Indian Brave W2950	Retrd.	1997	18.00	18
1995 Miss Tammie Mouse W3086	Retrd.	1996	17.00	17
1995 Mr. Jamie Mouse W3086	Retrd.	1996	17.00	17
1995 Mrs. Mollie Mouse W3086	Retrd.	1996	17.00	17
1993 Nutcracker Suite Fantasy Cornhusk Mice W2885	Retrd.	1994	15.50	16

Fabriché™ Ornament Series - KS. Adler, unless otherwise noted

1994 All Star Santa W1665	Retrd.	1996	27.00	27
1992 An Apron Full of Love W1594 - M. Rothenberg	Retrd.	1996	27.00	27
1995 Captain Claus W1711	Retrd.	1998	25.00	25
1994 Checking His List W1634	Retrd.	1996	23.50	24
1992 Christmas in the Air W1593	Retrd.	1996	35.50	36
1994 Cookies For Santa W1639	Retrd.	1996	28.00	28
1994 Firefighting Friends W1668	Retrd.	1996	28.00	28
1992 Hello Little One! W1561	Retrd.	1996	22.00	22
1994 Holiday Flight W1637 - Smithsonian	Retrd.	1996	40.00	40
1993 Homeward Bound W1596	Retrd.	1996	27.00	27

YEAR ISSUE	EDITION LIMIT	YEAR RETD.	ISSUE PRICE	*QUOTE U.S.$
1992 Hugs and Kisses W1560	Retrd.	1996	22.00	22
1993 Master Toymaker W1595	Retrd.	1996	27.00	27
1992 Merry Chrismouse W1565	Retrd.	1994	10.00	10
1992 Not a Creature Was Stirring W1563	Retrd.	1996	22.00	22
1993 Par For the Claus W1625	Retrd.	1997	27.00	27
1993 Santa With List W1510	Retrd.	1996	20.00	20
1994 Santa's Fishtales W1666	Retrd.	1997	29.00	29
1995 Strike Up The Band W1710	Retrd.	1996	25.00	25

Fabriché™ Vatican Library Collection - Vatican Library

1998 Vatican Angels in Flight (2 asst.) V34/A	Retrd.	1999	29.00	29
1998 Vatican Angels in Flight (gold) V34/GO	Retrd.	1999	29.00	29

International Christmas - J. Mostrom

1994 Cathy, Johnny W2945	Retrd.	1996	24.00	24
1994 Eskimo-Atom, Ukpik W2967	Retrd.	1996	28.00	28
1994 Germany-Katerina, Hans W2969	Retrd.	1996	27.00	27
1994 Native American-White Dove, Little Wolf W2970	Retrd.	1994	28.00	28
1994 Poland-Marissa, Hedwig W2965	Retrd.	1997	27.00	27
1994 Scotland-Bonnie, Douglas W2966	Retrd.	1997	27.00	27
1994 Spain-Maria, Miguel W2968	Retrd.	1997	27.00	27

Little Dickens - J. Mostrom

1994 Little Bob Crachit W2961	Retrd.	1996	30.00	30
1994 Little Marley's Ghost W2964	Retrd.	1996	33.50	34
1994 Little Mrs. Crachit W2962	Retrd.	1997	27.00	27
1994 Little Scrooge in Bathrobe W2959	Retrd.	1997	30.00	30
1994 Little Scrooge in Overcoat W2960	Retrd.	1997	30.00	30
1994 Little Tiny Tim W2963	Retrd.	1997	22.50	23

Polonaise™ - KSA/Komozja, unless otherwise noted

2002 1920's Flapper AP1499	Open		30.00	30
2000 2000 Global Santa AP1144	Retrd.	2000	30.00	30
1999 2000 Ornament AP1119	Retrd.	2000	17.95	18
1994 Acorn AP342	Retrd.	1995	11.00	60-150
2002 Acrobatical AP1526	Open		25.00	25
1999 Adoring Santa, 6 1/2" AP955 - I. Wiszniewska	Retrd.	1999	39.95	40-45
1995 African-American Santa AP389/A	Retrd.	1998	22.50	28
2002 Alamo AP1538	Open		30.00	30
1995 Alarm Clock AP452	Retrd.	1996	25.00	25
1997 Alice Collection 4 pc set AP548	Retrd.	2001	150.00	150
1997 Alice Collection 5 pc set AP547	7,500	1998	175.00	175-190
1997 Alice in Wonderland AP692	Retrd.	2001	29.95	30
1997 Alice in Wonderland, 4 asst. AP692/356	Retrd.	2001	29.95	30
1994 Angel AP309	Retrd.	1996	18.00	20
1999 Angel Tree Top AP1042	Retrd.	1999	80.00	80
1994 Angel w/Bear AP396	Retrd.	1995	20.00	30-45
2002 Anheuser-Busch Antique Truck AP1517	Open		35.00	35
1998 Ann & Andy on the Moon AP887	Retrd.	1999	39.95	40
1999 Annunciation Box (Artist Series) AP201	Retrd.	2000	70.00	70
1996 Antique Cars boxed set AP522	Retrd.	1999	120.00	120-135
2002 Antique Cars, 3 asst. AP1437A3	Open		33.00	33
1995 Antique Cars, 4 asst. AP429	Retrd.	1998	22.50	23
2002 Antique Roadster, 2 asst. AP1436A2	Open		30.00	30
1994 Apple AP339	Retrd.	1995	11.00	15-30
1999 Arabian Nights 3 pc. AP582	Retrd.	2001	120.00	120
1999 Arabian Nights 3, \sst, 6 1/2" AP982/34	Retrd.	2001	34.95	35
2001 Arctic Wind Santa ^P1316 - Stefan	Retrd.	2001	33.00	33
1997 Babar Elephant, F AP817 - Clifford Ross/Nelrana	Retrd.	1999	37.50	40
1998 Babe Ruth AP914	Retrd.	1999	39.95	40
2000 Babe Ruth Bust AP1203	Retrd.	2001	36.00	36
2002 Baby Pram AP1524	Open		20.00	20
1999 Baby's 1st Christmas AP985/BF	Retrd.	2000	24.95	25
2000 Baby's First Christmas "Sweet Lullaby" AP1293	Retrd.	2001	28.00	28
2000 Baby's First Christmas Elephant AP1200	Retrd.	2001	22.50	23
2002 Barney Basset AP1557	Open		20.00	20
2002 Batman AP1537	Open		40.00	40
2000 Bear and Bull AP1231	Retrd.	2001	33.00	33
2000 Bear in Stocking AP1096	Retrd.	2001	35.00	35
2000 Beefeater AP1258	Retrd.	2001	33.00	33
1994 Beer Glass AP366	Retrd.	1999	15.95	18

Collectors' Information Bureau   *Quotes have been rounded up to nearest dollar

ORNAMENTS

Kurt S. Adler, Inc.

to Kurt S. Adler, Inc.

YEAR ISSUE	EDITION LIMIT	YEAR RETD.	ISSUE PRICE	*QUOTE U.S.$
1999 Behold, the Lamb of God AP971 - I. Wiszniewska	Retrd.	1999	34.95	35-40
1998 Believe Santa AP890 - M. Engelbreit	Retrd.	2000	37.50	38
1999 Best Friends Cat and Dog, 4 1/2" AP980	Retrd.	2000	29.95	30
1999 Betty Boop "2000" AP1165	Retrd.	2000	37.50	38
2001 Betty Boop "Little Betty" (Petite Noels) AP1276	Retrd.	2001	22.50	23
1996 Betty Boop AP624 - King Features	Retrd.	1999	34.95	35-45
1998 Betty Boop as Mae West AP876	Retrd.	2000	39.95	40-45
2002 Betty Boop Bewitched AP1474	Open		35.00	35
1999 Betty Boop in Bubble Bath AP1038	Retrd.	2000	39.95	40-45
2000 Betty Boop w/Toys AP1253	Retrd.	2001	40.00	40-45
1997 The Bible AP841 - I. Wiszniewska	Retrd.	2001	34.95	35
1997 Big Bird AP699	Retrd.	1999	34.95	36-42
2001 Big Tops, 3 asst. 1302	Retrd.	2001	22.50	23
1998 Bi-Plane, green AP896	Retrd.	2000	45.00	45
1999 Bi-Plane, red AP896/2R	Retrd.	2001	45.00	45
1998 Bishop AP856	Retrd.	2000	34.95	35
2000 Black Holly Bearie AP827/BLK - H. Adler	Retrd.	2001	29.95	30
2002 Black Magic AP1481	Open		30.00	30
1999 Black Piano, AP1018 BLK	Retrd.	2001	29.95	30
1995 Blessed Mother AP413	Retrd.	1997	19.95	25
1998 Bob Cratchit w/Tiny Tim AP885	Retrd.	2000	39.95	40
1994 Boot w/Gifts AP375	Retrd.	1999	19.95	20
2002 Bountiful Betty AP1543	Open		35.00	35
2002 Bringing Joy AP1533	Open		33.00	33
2001 Bud Clydesdale 3 pc boxed set AP239	Open		150.00	150
2001 Bud on Ice AP1342	Open		25.00	25
2002 Bundle of Fun AP1534	Open		20.00	20
2001 Cactus Pete AP1241	Retrd.	2001	25.00	25
1995 Caesar AP422	Retrd.	1998	19.95	20-25
1997 Calvary, Gunner, Drummer AP645	Retrd.	2001	29.95	30
2000 Campbell Chicken Soup AP877/CH	Retrd.		33.00	33
1998 Campbell Soup Can-Tomato AP877	Retrd.	2001	34.95	35
1999 Campbell Soup Kid, 6 1/2" AP975	Retrd.	2000	29.95	30
2000 Campbell Soup Kids AP1187	Retrd.	2001	40.00	40
1996 Candleholder AP450	Retrd.	1997	17.95	20
2002 Candy Cane Frolic AP1520	Open		20.00	20
2002 Candy Cane Prince AP1392	Open		35.00	35
1995 Cardinal AP473 - Stefan	Retrd.	1999	29.95	30-33
1994 Cardinal on Pine Cone AP420	Retrd.	1995	18.00	35
2002 Cardinal's Cottage AP1458	Open		30.00	30
1999 Carousel, 5 1/2" AP998	Retrd.	2000	34.50	35
1999 Casablanca 3 pc. boxed set AP589	Retrd.	2001	170.00	170
1999 Casablanca Disc AP1065	Retrd.	2001	39.95	40
1995 Cat in Boot AP478 - Rothenberg	Retrd.	1999	29.95	30-33
1994 Cat w/Ball AP390	Retrd.	1995	18.00	50
1995 Cat w/Bow AP443	Retrd.	1999	22.50	24
2000 Celebrate Millennium 3 pc. Set AP230	Retrd.	2000	120.00	120
2001 Celestial Santa AP1262 - Stefan	Open		38.00	38
2000 Charlie Brown as Santa AP1212	Open		36.00	36
1997 Charlie Brown Peanuts, 5 1/2" AP824	Retrd.	1999	34.95	35-40
1998 Charlie Brown with Gifts AP917	Retrd.	2000	39.95	40-45
2001 Checking It Twice AP1346 - J. Thompson	Retrd.	2001	28.00	28
1998 Cherubs AP845/67	Retrd.	1999	19.95	20
2000 Chimney Sweeper AP1111	Retrd.	2000	25.00	25
1995 Christ Child AP414	Retrd.	1997	17.95	20
1999 Christmas Carol Book, 6 1/2" AP973 - I. Wiszniewska	Retrd.	2000	34.95	35
1998 Christmas Carol, 4 asst. AP832/4	Retrd.	2001	37.50	38
2002 Christmas Cheer 3 pc. boxed set AP0263	Open		135.00	135
2001 Christmas in Paris AP1322	Open		30.00	30
2002 Christmas in Pisa AP1569	Open		25.00	25
1997 Christmas in Poland 4pc set AP534	Retrd.	1999	150.00	150-165
1995 Christmas Tree AP461	Retrd.	1999	24.95	25-45
1994 Church AP369	Retrd.	1997	15.95	20
1999 Cigar Store Indian AP1026	Retrd.	2001	29.95	30
1996 Cinderella 4 pc boxed set AP512	Retrd.	1998	130.00	135
1996 Cinderella 6 pc boxed set AP511	7,500	1996	190.00	190-250
1996 Cinderella AP488	Retrd.	1998	27.50	28-31
1996 Cinderella Coach AP487	Retrd.	1999	34.95	37-40
1997 Circus Collection 5 pc set AP545	Retrd.	2000	180.00	180-188
1997 Circus Ring Master AP691	Retrd.	2001	32.50	35
1997 Circus Salt AP688	Retrd.	2000	29.95	30
1997 Circus Strongman AP690	Retrd.	2001	32.50	35
2002 Clara AP1396	Open		35.00	35
1995 Clara AP408	Retrd.	2000	19.95	20
2000 Cleopatra's Boat-Egyptian Boat AP1084	Retrd.	2001	35.00	35
1999 Climbing Santa, 5 1/2" AP1004	Retrd.	1999	34.95	36
1994 Clown 4" AP301	Retrd.	1995	13.50	45
1994 Clown 6" AP303	Retrd.	1995	22.50	40
1995 Clown Head 4.5" AP640	Retrd.	1997	22.50	30-40
1994 Clown on Ball 6.5" AP302	Retrd.	1995	22.50	35
2000 Clown, 4 asst. AP1126	Retrd.	2001	30.00	30
1997 Clowns 3 asst. AP682	Retrd.	1999	34.95	35
1997 Coca-Cola 3 pc AP553	Retrd.	2001	130.00	130
1995 Coca-Cola 4 pc boxed set AP517	Retrd.	1998	135.00	135
1997 Coca-Cola 6 Pack AP803	Retrd.	1999	34.95	40-45
1999 Coca-Cola 8 Wheeler, 8" AP1040	Retrd.	2000	37.50	38
1996 Coca-Cola Bear AP630	Retrd.	1999	34.95	37-50
1998 Coca-Cola Bear in Balloon AP939	Retrd.	2000	45.00	45
1995 Coca-Cola Bear Skiing AP801	Retrd.	2000	34.95	35-40
1997 Coca-Cola Bear Snowmobile AP802	Retrd.	2000	34.95	35-40
1997 Coca-Cola Bottle (golden) AP800	Retrd.	1999	34.95	35-40
1996 Coca-Cola Bottle AP631	Retrd.	1999	29.95	35-40
1996 Coca-Cola Bottle Cap AP633	Retrd.	1999	24.95	27-30
2000 Coca-Cola Bottle, green AP631/GB	Retrd.	2001	32.50	33
1998 Coca-Cola Bottles 4 pc. AP567	Retrd.	1999	150.00	150
2000 Coca-Cola Can, 4" AP1014	Open		34.95	35
2000 Coca-Cola Carousel Bear AP1239	Retrd.	2001	40.00	40
2001 Coca-Cola Diner AP1362	Retrd.	2001	45.00	45
1996 Coca-Cola Disk AP632	Retrd.	1998	24.95	40-45
1998 Coca-Cola Disk w/Santa Hat AP842	Retrd.	2000	29.95	30
2002 Coca-Cola Elves AP1523	Open		25.00	25
1999 Coca-Cola Ho-Ho-Ho 2 pc. boxed set AP585	Retrd.	2000	120.00	120
2001 Coca-Cola Juke Box AP1364	Open		40.00	40
2000 Coca-Cola Millenium Bear AP1238	Retrd.	2000	40.00	40
1997 Coca-Cola Old Delivery Truck AP804	Retrd.	2000	37.50	38-40
1997 Coca-Cola Roly Poly Santa AP867	Open		45.00	45
2000 Coca-Cola Sign AP1221	Retrd.	2001	33.00	33
2001 Coca-Cola Snowman AP1365	Retrd.	2001	39.00	39
2001 Coca-Cola Soda Fountain AP1076	Retrd.	2001	34.95	35
1997 Coca-Cola Train 4 pc AP572	Retrd.	1999	110.00	110
1996 Coca-Cola Vending Machine AP634	Retrd.	1999	34.95	36-51
2001 Coca-Cola Vintage Coke Santa AP1357	Open		40.00	40
2002 Cock-A-Doodle AP1529	Open		25.00	25
2002 Coke Arctica AP1543	Open		35.00	35
2002 Coke Can-Diet AP1014DC	Open		33.00	33
1999 Coke Locomotive AP444	Retrd.	1999	25.00	25
1999 Coke Signature Ball AP1064	Retrd.	2000	29.95	30
1999 Columbus Flotillia 3 asst. AP1051/23	Retrd.	2000	32.50	33
1999 Columbus Flotillia 3 pc. boxed set AP587	Retrd.	2000	130.00	130
2000 Confederate Soldier AP1122	Retrd.	2001	27.50	28
1998 Cookie Monster AP923	Retrd.	2001	37.50	38
2002 Coral Splendor 4 pc. boxed set AP0259	Open		120.00	120
2002 Coral Splendor, 4 asst. AP1125A4	Open		22.50	23
2002 Coral Tropics, 3 asst. AP1371/03	Open		20.00	20
1996 Cossack AP604	Retrd.	1998	34.95	35-39
1999 Couch Cat AP1045 - Stefan	Retrd.	2001	37.50	38
2002 Country Chapel AP1434	Open		33.00	33
2002 Country Fair AP1518	Open		30.00	30
2002 Cow Over the Moon AP1233 - Stefan	Retrd.	2001	30.00	37
1999 Cow, 5 1/2" AP961	Retrd.	2000	27.50	28
2002 Cowardly Lion - Wizard of Oz AP1498	Open		35.00	35
2002 Cowardly Lion AP1401	Open		25.00	25
1998 Cowboy Head AP462	Retrd.	1998	29.95	33-45
1998 Cowboy Head, black hat AP462/BH	Retrd.	1998	29.95	30
2000 Cracker Jack Bear AP1204	Retrd.	2000	36.00	36
2000 Cracker Jack Box AP1020	Retrd.	2000	39.95	40
1995 Creche AP458 - Stefan	Retrd.	1999	27.50	28
1996 Crocodile AP468	Retrd.	1996	28.00	30
2001 Crystal Palace AP1354	Open		40.00	40
2002 Dancing on Ice AP1527	Open		25.00	25
2002 Debonaire Bear AP1489	Open		33.00	33
1999 Dec. 1999 & Jan. 2000 Calendars, 2 asst. AP1140/1	Retrd.	1999	20.00	20
2002 Delivering Coke AP1568	Open		35.00	35
1995 Dice boxed set AP509	Retrd.	1997	55.00	60
1994 Dinosaurs 2 asst. green AP397	Retrd.	1996	22.50	24-60
1995 Dinosaurs-brown AP397	Retrd.	1995	22.50	55-60
2000 Divine Love AP1250 - I. Wiszniewska	Retrd.	2001	39.00	39
1999 Dog in Tub, 5" AP981	Retrd.	1999	29.95	30
1994 Doll AP377	Retrd.	1995	13.50	35

Kurt S. Adler, Inc.
to Kurt S. Adler, Inc.

ORNAMENTS

YEAR ISSUE	EDITION LIMIT	YEAR RETD.	ISSUE PRICE	*QUOTE U.S.$
1999 Doll, 5 1/2" AP1003	Retrd.	2000	17.95	18
2000 Don Quixote 3 pc. boxed set AP215	Retrd.	2000	130.00	130
2002 Dorothy & Toto - Wizard of Oz AP1496	Open		35.00	35
2002 Dorothy AP1403	Open		25.00	25
2000 Dorothy w/Rainbow-Oz AP1214	Retrd.	2001	30.00	30
1999 Dorothy-Full Body AP1060	Retrd.	2001	39.95	40
1995 Dove on Ball AP472 - Stefan	Retrd.	1996	29.95	32
1998 Down the Chimney Santa AP860	Retrd.	2000	29.95	30
2001 Downhill Wonder AP1256 - I. Wiszniewska	Retrd.	2001	38.00	38
1997 Dr. Watson AP813	Retrd.	1999	29.95	30-36
1998 Dragonflies, 3 asst. AP883	Open		45.00	45
2001 Dreidel AP1288	Open		22.50	22
2002 Drink Coca-Cola 3 pc. boxed set AP0268	Open		140.00	140
2002 Drosselmeir AP1395	Open		35.00	35
2000 Drum "Beating The Drums" AP1108	Retrd.	2000	25.00	25
1995 Eagle AP453	Retrd.	1999	29.95	30
1998 Ebenezer Scrooge AP832	Retrd.	2001	37.50	38
2001 Egyptian - mini (boxed set) AP243	Retrd.	2001	110.00	110
1994 Egyptian (12 pc boxed set) AP500	Retrd.	1995	214.00	214-360
2002 Egyptian 3 pc. asst. AP1507A3	Open		30.00	30
1997 Egyptian 4 pc set AP515	Retrd.	1999	150.00	150
2000 Egyptian Architecture AP1083	Retrd.	2001	34.95	35
1996 Egyptian Cat AP351	Retrd.	2001	27.50	30
1996 Egyptian II boxed set AP510	Retrd.	1999	150.00	150-170
2002 Egyptian Mummy AP1508	Open		30.00	30
1996 Egyptian Princess AP482	Retrd.	1999	34.95	33-35
1995 Egyptian set 4 pc. boxed AP500/4	Retrd.	1997	100.00	110-120
2002 Egyptian Sphinx AP1507	Open		30.00	30
2002 Egyptian Treasures, 3 asst. AP1463A8	Open		33.00	33
2001 Eight Maids A Milking (12 Days of Christmas) AP1268 - Stefan	Open		45.00	45
1998 Elegant Santa, burgundy AP857/BURG	Retrd.	2000	32.50	33
1998 Elegant Santa, gold AP857/GD	Retrd.	1999	32.50	33
1998 Elegant Santa, purple AP857/PURP	Retrd.	1999	32.50	33
1998 Elegant Santa, white AP857/W	Retrd.	1999	32.50	33
1998 Elegant Santa, 4 asst. AP857	Retrd.	2000	32.50	33
1995 Elephant AP 464	Retrd.	1999	27.50	25-28
2000 Elephant AP1219 - WWF	Retrd.	2001	30.00	30
2002 Eleven Pipers (12 Days of Christmas) AP1383	Open		33.00	33
1997 Elmo AP843	Retrd.	1999	37.50	38
1996 Elves AP611/23	Retrd.	1999	29.95	30
2000 Elvis Name AP1205	Retrd.	2001	36.00	36
2000 Elvis with Guitar AP1207	Open		50.00	50
1996 Emerald City AP623	Retrd.	1998	29.95	30-37
2001 Emerald City of Oz AP1336	Open		40.00	40
1998 English Barrister AP831	Retrd.	2000	29.95	30
1997 English Bobbie AP814	Retrd.	1999	29.95	30-36
1999 Ermine Santa, 6 1/2" AP945	Retrd.	2000	34.95	35
1999 Ernie AP1049	Retrd.	2001	37.50	38
2002 Evergreen Gifts AP1461	Open		30.00	30
1997 The Evolution of Polonaise™ Kit (boxed set) AP564	Retrd.	2000	50.00	50
2001 Fair Feather Friend AP1345 - J. Thompson	Retrd.	2001	28.00	28
2000 Farm Horse "Stable Mate" AP1112	Retrd.	2001	25.00	25
2001 Fearful Lion AP1063	Retrd.	2001	39.95	40
2001 Fire Chief Santa AP1331	Retrd.	2001	39.00	39
2000 Fire Engine "To The Rescue" AP1197	Retrd.	2001	35.00	35
1996 Fire Engine AP605	Retrd.	1999	29.95	30-40
1995 Fish 4 pc. boxed AP506	Retrd.	1998	110.00	120-125
2000 Fish, 4 asst. AP1125	Retrd.	2001	22.50	23
2002 Fishing Holiday AP1554	Open		30.00	30
2000 Five Golden Rings (12 Days of Christmas) AP899 - Stefan	Open		37.50	38
1999 Flight Into Egypt (Artist Series) AP597	Retrd.	2000	70.00	70
2002 Flower Fairies, 4 asst. AP1500A4	Open		33.00	33
2002 Fluttering Friends, 3 asst. AP1439A3	Open		30.00	30
1998 Flying Angels, 3 asst. AP881	Retrd.	2001	45.00	45
2000 Flying Man "Up & Away" AP1085	Retrd.	2000	37.50	38
1999 Flying Monkey-Oz AP1054	Retrd.		39.95	40
1998 Ford Mustang, red AP929	Retrd.	2001	39.95	40
1999 Ford Station Wagon AP1044	Retrd.	2001	45.00	45
1998 Ford Truck w/Christmas Tree AP937	Retrd.	2001	39.95	40
2002 Forever Remembered AP1495	Yr.Iss.		30.00	30
1997 Four Calling Birds (12 Days of Christmas) AP828	Open		37.50	38
1999 French Boots AP1115 - L. Nicole	Retrd.	2001	29.95	30
1998 Friendly Ghost AP834	Hetrd.	1999	29.95	25-30
1999 Frog King, 7" AP1000	Retrd.	2001	37.50	38
2002 Frog with Lily Pad AP1536	Open		25.00	25
2002 Frolicking Penguin AP1503	Open		25.00	25
2002 Furry Friends AP1407	Open		35.00	35
1998 Garfield AP891	Retrd.	2000	37.50	38-40
1999 Garfield Santa w/Gifts AP1073	Retrd.	2001	37.50	38
2000 Gentleman Golfer AP1232	Retrd.	2001	37.00	37
1999 Gepetto, 7 1/2" AP947	Retrd.	2001	37.50	38
2002 Giddy Ap! AP1539	Open		33.00	33
1996 Gift Boxes AP614	Retrd.	1999	24.95	25
2002 Gift Express AP1419R	Open		35.00	35
2002 Gift Mouse AP1469	Open		27.00	27
2002 Gingerbread House AP1460	Open		33.00	33
1997 Gingerbread House AP664	Retrd.	1999	29.95	30-36
2000 Giraffe-World Wild Fund AP1130	Retrd.	2001	25.00	25
1999 Girl with Bear, 6 1/2" AP989	Retrd.	1999	24.95	25
1995 Glinda Good Witch-Oz AP621	Retrd.	1998	34.95	35-40
1998 Glinda the Good Witch AP920	Open		39.95	40
2001 Glinda The Good Witch of Oz AP1311	Open		30.00	30
2000 Glinda The Good Witch-Oz AP1189	Open		37.50	38
1994 Gnome AP347	Retrd.	1995	18.00	35
1994 Golden Cherub Head AP372	Retrd.	1994	18.00	60-75
1994 Golden Rocking Horse AP355	Retrd.	1994	22.50	60-65
1999 Gone With The Wind 2 pc. boxed set AP590	Retrd.	2000	135.00	135
1997 Gone With The Wind 3 pc boxed set AP557	Retrd.	1999	150.00	150-175
1998 Gone With The Wind boxed set AP574	Retrd.	2001	165.00	165
1998 Gone With the Wind Heart AP925	Retrd.	1999	39.95	40
1997 Gone With The Wind Rhett Butler AP815	Retrd.	1999	37.50	38-45
1997 Gone With The Wind Scarlett O'Hara AP805	Retrd.	1999	39.95	40-45
1997 Gone With The Wind Tara AP816	Retrd.	2001	37.50	38
1999 Good Humor Truck AP1068	Retrd.	2000	39.95	40
1995 Goose w/Wreath AP475 - Stefan	Retrd.	1999	29.95	30-33
2001 Gooseberry AP1333 - J. Thompson	Retrd.	2001	33.00	33
2001 Gossamer Wings AP1313	Retrd.	2001	39.00	39
1996 Gramophone AP446	Retrd.	1996	22.50	23
1997 Grand Father Frost AP810COL	Retrd.	1999	50.00	50
2002 Guardian Angel, 2 asst. AP1425A2	Open		35.00	35
2000 Halloween Cat AP1223	Retrd.	2001	25.00	25
1999 Handyman Teddy Bear, 6" AP958	Retrd.	1999	34.95	35
1997 Hansel & Gretel AP662	Retrd.	2000	29.95	30
1997 Hansel/Gretel 4 pc set AP538	Retrd.	2000	150.00	135-150
1999 Happy Easter Snoopy AP1164	Retrd.	2001	35.00	35
2000 Happy Holiday 2000/2001 Ball AP1227	Retrd.	2000	30.00	30
2002 Harlequin Frog AP1480	Open		33.00	33
2000 Harry Potter 2 pc boxed set AP245	Open		120.00	120
2001 Harry Potter 4 pc boxed set AP238	Open		170.00	170
2001 Harry Potter Harry & Hedwig AP1266	Open		50.00	50
2001 Harry Potter Harry Playing Quidditch AP1263	Open		65.00	65
2001 Harry Potter Hermione with Book AP1265	Retrd.	2001	50.00	50
2001 Harry Potter Ron with Scabbers AP1264	Retrd.	2001	50.00	50
2002 Harry Potter™ and Sorcerer's Stone AP1369	Open		45.00	45
2002 Harry Potter™ in Potions Class AP1414	Open		40.00	40
1997 Hat Boxes AP620	Retrd.	1999	27.50	28
2001 Haulin' Bud AP1308	Open		45.00	45
2002 Heavenly Betty Boop AP1487	Open		35.00	35
1997 Herald Rabbit AP693	Retrd.	2001	32.50	35
1995 Herr Drosselmeier AP465 - Rothenberg	Retrd.	1999	29.95	30-35
2002 He's Got Rhythmn AP1528	3,500		40.00	40
2001 His Lordship AP1289	Retrd.	2001	33.00	33
1999 Hockey Player, 6" AP1013	Retrd.	2000	34.95	35
2002 Holiday Jazz AP1555	Open		35.00	35
1997 Holly Show Bearie AP827	Open		29.95	35-38
2000 The Holy Family 1 pc. boxed set AP200	Retrd.	2000	70.00	70
1995 Holy Family 3 pc. AP504	Retrd.	1997	80.00	60-84
1998 Holy Family 3 pc. boxed set AP576	Retrd.	2001	100.00	100

YEAR ISSUE	EDITION LIMIT	YEAR RETD.	ISSUE PRICE	*QUOTE U.S.$
000 The Holy Family AP1148	Retrd.	2001	27.50	28
002 Holy Family AP1432	Open		30.00	30
994 Holy Family AP371	Retrd.	1998	27.50	28-30
998 Holy Family AP898	Retrd.	1999	37.50	38
998 Holy Family, 3 asst. AP861/23	Retrd.	2000	29.95	30
998 Honey Bear AP900	Retrd.	1999	29.95	30
000 Honey Bee & Wasp, 2 asst. AP1080/81	Retrd.	2001	27.50	28
001 Honeymooners Escape AP1376	Open		25.00	25
002 Horus AP1509	Open		30.00	30
996 Horus AP484	Retrd.	1998	34.95	30-35
995 Houses (2 asst.) AP455	Retrd.	1996	25.00	30
999 Howdy Doody AP968	Retrd.	2001	39.95	40
998 Hummingbirds, 2 asst. AP893	Retrd.	2001	37.50	38
999 Humphrey Bogart AP1048	Retrd.	2001	39.95	40
002 Humpty Dumpty AP1468	Open		33.00	33
995 Humpty Dumpty AP477 - Stefan	Retrd.	1999	29.95	30-33
997 Hunter AP667	Retrd.	2001	29.95	30
995 Icicle Santa AP474 - Stefan	Retrd.	1995	25.00	40-45
995 Indian Chief AP463	Retrd.	1999	29.95	30-33
998 Indian Motorcycle AP940	Retrd.	2000	39.95	40
999 Ingrid Bergman AP1047	Retrd.	2001	39.95	40
999 Isis AP1041	Retrd.	2001	32.50	33
998 It's a Wonderful Life AP910	Retrd.	2001	45.00	45
000 Jack O'Lantern AP897/NW	Retrd.	2001	19.95	20
999 James Dean, 7" AP995	Retrd.	2001	39.95	40
998 Jazz Band 4 pc. AP569	Retrd.	1999	150.00	150
998 Jazz Musicians, 4 asst. AP851/04	Retrd.	1999	29.95	30
997 Jewelry Boxes AP637	Retrd.	1999	15.95	16
002 Jewels of the Nile 4 pc. boxed set AP0260	Open		160.00	160
001 Jingle Bear AP1344	Retrd.	2001	23.00	23
998 Joseph AP862	Retrd.	2001	29.95	30
000 Journey to Egypt 3 pc. boxed set AP208	Retrd.	2001	120.00	120
002 Joyful Santa, set/3 AP1504	2,500		60.00	60
002 Just Married 2 pc. boxed set AP0267	Open		100.00	100
999 Just Married 2 pc. boxed set AP584	Retrd.	2001	90.00	90
997 Just Married AP829	Open		22.50	22
996 King Balthazar AP607	Retrd.	1997	29.95	31
998 King Kong AP918	Retrd.	2000	39.95	40
000 King Kong II AP1183	Retrd.	2001	37.50	38
997 King Neptune AP496	Retrd.	1999	34.95	35
000 King Richard-Shakespearean Collection AP1185	Retrd.	2001	35.00	35
001 King Tut & Cleopatra (Petite Noels) AP1294/97	Open		22.50	22
002 Kings Bearing Gifts, 3 asst. AP1446A3	Open		33.00	33
002 Kitten Friends AP1441A2	Open		27.00	27
994 Knight's Helmet AP304	Retrd.	1995	18.00	22-26
998 Knight's Horse AP640	Retrd.	1999	34.95	35
002 Kozy Kitten, 2 asst. AP1530A2	Open		20.00	20
997 Krakow Castle AP670	Retrd.	1999	34.95	33-35
997 Krakow Man AP674	Retrd.	1999	29.95	30-38
002 Lady Liberty AP1422	Open		33.00	33
998 Large Churches, 3 asst. AP880/03	Retrd.	2000	29.95	30
998 Let It Rain AP901	Retrd.	2000	29.95	30
996 Light Bulb AP449	Retrd.	1996	20.00	20
002 Lil' Poinsettia Tree AP1513	Open		20.00	20
002 Lil' Witch AP1484	Open		30.00	30
001 Ling Panda WWI AP1286	Open		30.00	30
001 Ling Panda-World Wild Fund AP1286	Retrd.	2001	33.00	33
000 Lion-Oz AP1215	Retrd.	2001	30.00	30
998 Little Elfers AP935	Retrd.	1999	37.50	38-44
001 Little Engine (Petite Noels) AP1318	Open		25.00	25
995 The Little Mermaid 5 pc. boxed set AP513	Retrd.	1998	165.00	165-175
996 Little Mermaid AP492	Retrd.	1997	27.50	28-31
998 Little Mermaid, 2 asst. AP492/NW	Retrd.	1999	27.50	28
997 Little Red Riding Hood 3 pc. AP544	Retrd.	1999	110.00	110
997 Little Red Riding Hood 4 pc set AP539	Yr.Iss.	1997	140.00	135-150
997 Little Red Riding Hood 5 1/2" AP665	Retrd.	2001	29.95	30
001 Little Tops, 3 asst. (Petite Noels) AP1301	Open		20.00	20
994 Locomotive AP353	Retrd.	1998	19.95	20-24
995 Locomotive AP447	Retrd.	1999	27.50	28-30
998 London Bus AP686	Retrd.	2000	29.95	30
998 London Phone Booth AP698	Retrd.	2000	27.50	28
001 Loon Lake AP1361	Retrd.	2001	28.00	28

YEAR ISSUE	EDITION LIMIT	YEAR RETD.	ISSUE PRICE	*QUOTE U.S.$
2002 Lovey Dovey AP1522	Open		30.00	30
2002 Luck of the Irish AP1483	Open		30.00	30
1997 Lucy Peanuts AP825	Retrd.	1999	34.95	35
2001 M & M Blue "I'm Blue" AP1324	Open		33.00	33
2001 M & M Red "Red Hot" AP1325	Open		33.00	33
2001 M & M Yellow "Yellow Fever" AP1326	Open		33.00	33
2002 M & M's boxed set AP0262	Open		150.00	150
2002 M & M's I'm Green AP1475	Open		30.00	30
2002 M & M's Tobogganing AP1516	Open		40.00	40
1997 Mad Hatter AP696	Retrd.	2001	32.50	35
1998 Madeline AP922	Retrd.	2001	37.50	38
1999 Madeline by Eiffel Tower AP1069	Retrd.	2000	39.95	40
2001 Madeline-In-Waiting AP1273	Retrd.	2001	40.00	40
1998 Madonna & Child AP861	Retrd.	2001	29.95	30
1994 Madonna w/Child AP370	Retrd.	1997	22.50	25-27
1999 Magic Fish, 4" AP963	Retrd.	2001	17.95	18
1997 Magician's Hat AP689	Retrd.	1999	34.95	35-39
2002 Make a Joyful Noise AP1491	Open		45.00	45
1998 Mammy-GWW AP924	Retrd.	2001	39.95	40
2000 Man of the Hour AP1175 - M. Engelbreit	Retrd.	2001	40.00	40
2002 Marilyn Monroe AP1550	Open		40.00	40
1997 Marilyn Monroe AP818	Retrd.	2000	37.50	38
2000 Marilyn Monroe Bust AP1210 - CMG	Retrd.	2001	39.00	39
1999 Marilyn Monroe II, 7" AP992	Retrd.	2001	37.50	38
1998 Marley's Ghost AP886	Retrd.	2001	34.95	35
1996 Medieval boxed set AP519	Retrd.	1998	150.00	100-170
1996 Medieval Dragon AP642	Retrd.	1999	34.95	35
1996 Medieval Knight AP641	Retrd.	1999	34.95	35
1996 Medieval Lady AP643	Retrd.	1998	34.95	35
2002 Menorah AP1488	Open		30.00	30
1994 Merlin AP373	Retrd.	1995	20.00	30-42
2000 Merlin The Magician AP1194	Retrd.	2001	30.00	30
2002 Merry Crescent AP1552	Open		40.00	40
1997 MGM Cowardly Lion AP821	Retrd.	2001	39.95	40
1997 MGM Dorothy AP819	Retrd.	2001	39.95	40
1997 MGM Scarecrow AP822	Retrd.	2001	39.95	40
1997 MGM Tin Man AP820	Retrd.	2001	39.95	40
1997 MGM Wizard of Oz 4 pc. boxed set AP555	Retrd.	2001	180.00	180
1995 Mickey Mouse AP392	Retrd.	1995	33.00	30-100
1995 Mickey Mouse AP392 & Minnie Mouse (pr.) AP391,set	Retrd.	1995	66.00	90-135
1999 Millenium 3 pc. boxed set AP595	Retrd.	1999	100.00	100
2000 Millenium Tree AP1235	Retrd.	2000	22.50	23
1995 Millenium Village AP391	Retrd.	1995	33.00	36-82
1999 Miss Chiquita Banana AP1037	Retrd.	2000	37.50	38
2001 Miss Lily Ponds AP1314	Retrd.	2001	39.00	39
1999 Monk with Cask, 5 1/2" AP986	Retrd.	2000	27.50	28
1999 Motorcycles 2 asst., 6 1/2" AP993/4	Retrd.	2001	34.50	35
2002 Mouse King AP1397	Open		35.00	35
1994 Mouse King AP406	Retrd.	1999	19.95	20-25
1999 Mr. & Mrs. Claus Decorating 2 pc. AP580/DN	Retrd.	1999	100.00	100
1999 Mr. & Mrs. Claus-Chair 2 asst., 7" AP1010/1	Retrd.	1999	37.50	38
2002 Mr. & Mrs. Hoppity, 2 asst. AP1493A2	Open		30.00	30
2000 Mr. Peanut "Everybody Loves Nut" AP1188	Retrd.	2000	37.50	38
1998 Mr. Peanut AP938	Retrd.	2001	37.50	38
1998 Mrs. Cratchit AP884	Retrd.	1999	34.95	35
1996 Mummy AP483	Retrd.	1999	34.95	30-35
2000 The Munchkin Mayor-Oz AP1191	Retrd.	2001	25.00	25
2000 Mushroom with Elf AP1095	Retrd.	2000	25.00	25
2000 Musical Quartet 4 pc. boxed set AP214	Retrd.	2001	130.00	130
1999 Musketeers 4 pc. boxed set AP579	7,500	2001	150.00	150
2000 Mustang Convertible, white AP929/W	Retrd.	2001	39.95	40
1997 Napoleonic Soldier AP543	Retrd.	2000	150.00	150
2001 Nativity 5 pc boxed set AP251	Open		150.00	150
2000 Nativity Ball AP1173 - Stefan	Retrd.	2001	35.00	35
2002 Nativity Creche 5 pc. boxed set AP0261	Open		170.00	170
1996 Nefertiti 96 AP485	Retrd.	2001	34.95	35
1994 Nefertiti AP349	Retrd.	1996	24.95	40-45
1999 New Christmas Tree, 6" AP997	Retrd.	2001	45.00	45
1999 New Locomotive, 6" AP1032	Retrd.	2001	34.95	35
1998 New Scarlett AP928	Retrd.	1999	39.95	40

ORNAMENTS

YEAR ISSUE	EDITION LIMIT	YEAR RETD.	ISSUE PRICE	*QUOTE U.S.$
2002 Newborn King AP1449	Open		33.00	33
1994 Night & Day AP307	Retrd.	1997	19.95	20-23
2000 Night Before Christmas Book AP1225 - I. Wiszniewska	Retrd.	2001	36.00	36
2001 Nine Ladies Dancing (12 Days of Christmas) AP1334 - Stefan	Open		39.00	39
2000 Noah And His Ark AP1196	Retrd.	2001	35.00	35
1995 Noah's Ark AP469	Retrd.	2000	27.50	30-35
2000 North & South 4 pc. boxed set AP596	Retrd.	2000	120.00	120
1999 North Pole Express 3 pc. boxed set AP586	Retrd.	2000	110.00	110
1999 North Star Santa, 10 1/2" AP1039	Retrd.	2000	37.50	38
2002 Northpole Snoopy AP1511	Open		40.00	40
1998 Northwind Santa AP878 - Stefan	Retrd.	2001	29.95	30
1994 Nutcracker AP404	Retrd.	1999	19.95	20-22
2002 Nutcracker Prince AP1394	Open		35.00	35
1995 Nutcracker Suite 4 pc. boxed AP507	Retrd.	1999	125.00	120-125
2002 Nutcracker Suite 4 pc. boxed set AP0254	Open		180.00	180
2002 Nutcracker Suite, 4 asst. AP1394A	Open		30.00	30
1997 NY Ball 5/asst. AP677	Retrd.	2000	27.50	28
2002 O' Holy Night AP1473	Open		30.00	30
1994 Old Fashioned Car AP380	Retrd.	1999	22.50	25-29
2000 The Old West 2 pc. boxed set AP578	Retrd.	2001	90.00	90
2000 Ole' King Cole AP1149 - Stefan	Retrd.	2001	35.00	35
1998 Oma & Opa AP870/1	Retrd.	2000	27.50	28
2001 One More Delivery AP1315 - Giordano	Retrd.	2001	45.00	45
2001 Osiris & Isis, 2 asst. (Petite Noels) AP1295/96	Open		22.50	23
1998 Our New Home AP933	Retrd.	1999	29.95	30
1995 Owl (gold) AP328	Retrd.	1999	17.50	18-20
1994 Owl AP328	Retrd.	1998	17.50	23
1998 Paddington Bear AP915	Retrd.	1999	37.50	38-40
2000 Paddington Bear AP915/BL	Retrd.	2001	34.50	35
1998 Paddington Bear, red coat AP915/R	Retrd.	2001	37.50	38
2001 Pancho AP1240	Retrd.	2001	30.00	30
2000 Parrot "Jungle Fever" AP1091	Retrd.	2001	25.00	25
1994 Parrot AP332	Retrd.	1995	15.50	40-48
1995 Partridge in a Pear Tree (12 Days of Christmas) AP467 - Stefan	Open		34.95	40-45
2000 Party Elephant "Party Time" AP1113	Retrd.	2000	27.50	28
1998 Peace on Angel AP888	Retrd.	1999	39.95	40-45
2000 Peace on Earth 2 pc. boxed set (dealers only) AP232 - KSA/Wiszniewska	Retrd.	2001	100.00	100
2002 Peace on Earth AP1462	Open		30.00	30
1994 Peacock 5" AP324	Retrd.	1996	18.00	25
1994 Peacock on Ball 7.5" AP323	Retrd.	1996	28.00	28
2001 Peanuts "Flying Ace" Snoopy AP1341	Open		27.00	27
1997 Peanuts 3 pc boxed set AP556	Retrd.	2000	135.00	135
1998 Peanuts 3 pc. boxed set AP575	Retrd.	1999	150.00	150
2000 Peanuts 50th Anniversary AP1177	Retrd.	2001	40.00	40
2000 Peanuts Ball AP1211	Retrd.	2001	37.00	37
1999 Peanuts Gang on Toboggan AP1027	Retrd.	2001	39.95	40
2001 Peanuts Joe Cool AP1277	Open		38.00	38
1998 Peanuts, 3 asst. AP879/79	Retrd.	2000	39.95	40
2000 Penguin "Dressed To The Nines" AP1128	Retrd.	2001	22.50	23
1995 Peter Pan 4 pc. boxed set AP503	Retrd.	1997	125.00	94-125
1995 Peter Pan AP419	Retrd.	1998	19.95	23
2000 Phantom of the Opera AP1179	Retrd.	2001	35.00	35
1999 Phantom of the Opera, 6" AP1016	Retrd.	2001	39.95	40
1996 Pharaoh AP481	Retrd.	1999	34.95	32-35
2001 Piero II (Petite Noels) AP1303	Retrd.	2001	20.00	20
1994 Pierrot Clown AP405	Retrd.	1995	18.00	35-40
2002 Pile of Pumpkins AP1545	Open		35.00	35
1998 Pillsbury Doughboy AP916	Retrd.	1999	37.50	38
2000 Pillsbury Doughboy w/Candy Cane AP1171	Open		37.50	38
1998 Pink Panther AP889	Retrd.	2000	39.95	40
1999 Pinocchio 3 pc. AP583	Retrd.	2001	140.00	140
1999 Pinocchio, 6 1/2" AP946	Retrd.	2001	34.95	35
2002 Play It! Santa AP1393	Open		35.00	35
2002 Playful Raggedy Andy AP1514	Open		25.00	25
2002 Playful Raggedy Ann AP1512	Open		25.00	25

YEAR ISSUE	EDITION LIMIT	YEAR RETD.	ISSUE PRICE	*QUOTE U.S.$
2000 Playtime Santa-Swinging Santa AP944	Retrd.	2000	34.95	3
2001 Polar Express AP1242	Retrd.	2001	40.00	4
1997 Polish Mountain Man AP675	Retrd.	1999	29.95	30-3
1999 Pony 3 asst. AP985/123	Retrd.	2000	24.95	2
1998 Popeye the Sailor AP907	Retrd.	2000	37.50	3
1996 Prince Charming AP489	Retrd.	1997	27.50	28-3
1998 Pumpkin AP897	Retrd.	2000	22.50	23-2
2002 Pumpkin Patch AP1388	Open		25.00	2
1999 Puppeteer, 7" AP948	Retrd.	2000	39.95	4
1994 Puppy (gold) AP333	Retrd.	1994	13.50	3
2000 Puss 'N Boots AP1151 - Stefan	Retrd.	2001	35.00	3
1998 Pyramid AP352	Retrd.	1998	21.95	2
2000 Queen Elizabeth Shakespearean Collection AP1186	Retrd.	2001	35.00	3
1997 Queen of Hearts AP695	Retrd.	2001	32.50	3
2002 Radio Flyer Wagon AP1548	Open		40.00	4
2001 Raggedy Andy AP1338	Open		30.00	3
1997 Raggedy Andy AP322	Retrd.	2000	24.95	25-3
2000 Raggedy Ann & Andy on Rocking Horse AP1213	Retrd.	2001	40.00	4
2002 Raggedy Ann & Andy Valentine AP1515	Open		40.00	4
2001 Raggedy Ann AP1337	Open		30.00	3
1996 Raggedy Ann AP321	Retrd.	2000	27.50	28-3
1999 Raggedy Ann on Cushion, 5 1/2" AP1024	Retrd.	2000	37.50	3
1997 Raggedy Ann/Andy AP550	Retrd.	2000	80.00	8
1998 Red & White Santa AP858	Retrd.	1999	24.95	2
1995 Red Dice AP363/R	Retrd.	1999	17.50	14-
2000 Rhett and Scarlett Embraced AP1209	Retrd.	2001	36.00	3
1999 Rhett Butler Bust AP1067	Retrd.	2001	39.95	4
2002 Ride Em Freezy AP1390	Open		27.00	2
1998 Riverboat AP855	Retrd.	2000	29.95	3
2000 Rocking Horse "Holiday Rocker" AP1136	Retrd.	2001	25.00	3
1994 Rocking Horse 5" AP356	Retrd.	1999	22.50	3
1999 Rocking Pony 3/Asst, 4 1/2" AP985/123	Retrd.	2000	24.95	3
1994 Roly-Poly Santa AP317	Retrd.	1999	21.95	3
1995 Roman 4 pc. boxed set AP502/4	Retrd.	1995	110.00	140-19
1995 Roman 7 pc. boxed set AP502	Retrd.	1995	164.00	165-19
1998 Roman Centurion AP427	Retrd.	1998	19.95	2
2001 Roses & Lace AP1358	Retrd.	2001	28.00	2
1997 Royal Suite 4 pc set AP552	Retrd.	1999	140.00	140-14
1997 Royal Suite 4/asst. AP806	Retrd.	2001	29.95	3
1998 Ruby Slippers-Oz AP838	Open		29.95	3
1996 Russian 5 pc boxed set AP514	Retrd.	1998	180.00	19
1996 Russian Bishop AP603	Retrd.	1998	34.95	35-
1998 Russian Woman AP602	Retrd.	1998	34.95	35-
2002 S.S. Santa AP1540	Open		40.00	4
1998 Sabrina Snow Girl AP859/BL	Retrd.	1999	19.95	2
1995 Sailing Ship AP415	Retrd.	1999	29.95	3
1994 Saint Nick AP316	Retrd.	1998	24.95	2
1998 San Francisco Ball AP927/SF	Retrd.	2001	29.95	3
1998 San Francisco Trolley Car AP911/SF	Open		34.95	3
2002 Santa Americana AP1531	Open		30.00	3
1995 Santa AP317	Retrd.	1999	22.50	24-
1995 Santa AP389	Retrd.	1998	22.50	25-
2001 Santa Banana AP1329 - Stefan	Retrd.	2001	30.00	3
2000 Santa Bringing Gifts AP1201	Retrd.	2001	35.00	3
2000 Santa Bringing Toys AP1174 - Giordano	Retrd.	2001	40.00	4
1999 Santa Cowboy, 5 1/2" AP1023	Retrd.	2001	29.95	3
2000 Santa Dollar Bill "On the Dollar" AP1087	Retrd.	2000	27.50	2
1999 Santa Drinking Coke, 6 1/2" AP1031	Retrd.	2000	37.50	3
1999 Santa Golfer, 6 1/2" AP1025	Retrd.	2001	29.95	3
1994 Santa Head 4" AP315	Retrd.	1995	13.50	1
1994 Santa Head 4.5" AP374	Retrd.	1996	19.00	2
2000 Santa Head w/Wreath AP1226	Retrd.	2001	30.00	3
1997 Santa Heart AP811	Retrd.	1999	22.50	2
1996 Santa in Airplane AP365	Retrd.	1999	34.95	40-
2000 Santa in Car AP1228	Retrd.	2001	33.00	3
1996 Santa in Car AP367	Retrd.	2000	34.95	30-
2002 Santa Kong AP1423	Open		33.00	3
1995 Santa Moon AP454 - Stefan	Retrd.	1999	27.50	28-
2000 Santa of the Month-December Santa AP1178	Retrd.	2001	37.50	3
2001 Santa of the Month-February Santa "Holiday Kisses" AP1347	Retrd.	2001	28.00	2

YEAR ISSUE	EDITION LIMIT	YEAR RETD.	ISSUE PRICE	*QUOTE U.S.$
2000 Santa of the Month-Irish Santa AP1193	Retrd.	2001	35.00	35
2001 Santa of the Month-July Santa "Fireworks" AP1257 - J. Thompson	Retrd.	2001	37.00	37
1999 Santa of the Month-Millennium Santa on Moon, 6 1/2" AP1012	Retrd.	2000	37.50	38
1995 Santa on Goose on Sled AP479	Retrd.	1999	29.95	30-32
2000 Santa on Locomotive AP1229	Retrd.	2001	33.00	33
1998 Santa on Motorcycle AP931	Retrd.	1999	34.95	35
2000 Santa on Skateboard AP1202	Retrd.	2001	30.00	30
2000 Santa on Spaceship AP1230	Retrd.	2001	33.00	33
1999 Santa Sleeping Under Tree, 5 1/2" AP943	Retrd.	1999	34.95	35
2001 Santa Surprise AP1310	Retrd.	2001	39.00	39
2002 Santa Teddy AP1377	Open		22.50	23
2002 Santa to the Rescue AP1454	Open		33.00	33
2000 Santa Turtle "Slow Poke" AP1134	Retrd.	2000	22.50	23
1995 Santa w/Puppy AP442	Retrd.	1999	22.50	25-28
2002 Santa's Visit AP1430	Open		65.00	65
2002 Santa's World AP1542	Open		45.00	45
2002 Scarecrow - Wizard of Oz AP1519	Open		35.00	35
2002 Scarecrow AP1402	Open		25.00	25
1999 Scarecrow Leaning on Fence AP1062	Retrd.	2001	39.95	40
2001 Scarecrow w/Diploma AP1216	Retrd.	2001	30.00	30
2000 Scarlett O'Hara "Riches to Rags" AP1195	Retrd.	2001	35.00	35
1999 Scarlett O'Hara Bust AP1066	Retrd.	2001	39.95	40
2000 Scrooge "Bah Humbug!" AP1180	Retrd.	2001	35.00	35
1996 Sea Horse AP494	Retrd.	1998	24.95	25-38
2001 Secret Moments AP1348	Retrd.	2001	39.00	39
2002 Serving Up Coke AP1565	Open		35.00	35
1997 Seven Dwarfs AP611	Retrd.	2000	29.95	30-38
2000 Seven Swans Swimming (12 Days of Christmas) AP1167 - Stefan	Open		35.00	35
2000 Shakespeare 3 pc. boxed set AP599	1,000		135.00	135
2002 Shall We Dance AP1553	Open		33.00	33
1995 Shark AP417	Retrd.	1996	18.00	25
1998 Shepherd AP863	Retrd.	2000	29.95	30
1997 Sherlock Holmes 3 pc set AP551	Retrd.	1999	125.00	125-135
1997 Sherlock Holmes AP812	Retrd.	1999	29.95	30-36
2002 Shopping Spree AP1384	Open		33.00	33
1999 Singing in the Rain AP1070	Retrd.	2001	37.50	38
1999 Sir Bones, 6 1/2" AP934	Retrd.	2001	27.50	28
1998 Sir Hogmas AP902	Retrd.	1999	24.95	25
1999 Six Geese (12 Days of Christmas) AP1075 - Stefan	Open		39.95	40
2001 Slalom, 3 asst. (Petite Noels) AP1291	Retrd.	2001	22.50	23
2001 Sleighbells AP1290 - L. Nichole	Open		39.00	39
1996 Slipper AP490	Retrd.	1997	19.95	20-25
1997 Smithsonian Astronaut AP826	Retrd.	1999	34.95	35
2000 Smithsonian Locomotive Phantom AP1181	Retrd.	2001	40.00	40
1998 Smithsonian Montgolfier Balloon AP908	Retrd.	1999	39.95	40
2000 Smithsonian Santa in Hot Air Balloon AP1237	Retrd.	2001	33.00	33
1997 Smithsonian Space Capsule AP839	Retrd.	1999	34.95	35
1999 Smokey Bear, 6 1/2" AP1007	Retrd.	2000	37.50	38
2002 Snap Shot Santa AP1455	Open		33.00	33
1999 Snoopy Dracula on Pumpkin AP1057	Retrd.	2001	37.50	38
2001 Snoopy Flying Ace AP1341	Open		30.00	30
1998 Snoopy on the Doghouse AP879	Retrd.	2001	39.95	40-45
1997 Snoopy Peanuts AP823	Retrd.	1999	34.95	35-40
1999 Snoopy Santa AP1046	Retrd.	2001	37.50	38-45
1998 Snow Bearie AP827/S	Retrd.	1999	29.95	30
2002 Snow Star AP1497	Open		20.00	20
1997 Snow White & 7 Dwarfs 8 pc boxed set AP558	Retrd.	2000	290.00	290
1997 Snow White AP660	Retrd.	1999	29.95	30
2002 Snowbound Snoopy AP1451	Open		35.00	35
2001 Snowday Memories AP1284 - M. Engelbreit	Retrd.	2001	45.00	45
1998 Snowgirl AP859/BL	Retrd.	1999	19.50	20
1999 Snowman Family AP1077	Retrd.	2001	34.95	35
2002 Snowman Finial AP1417	Open		33.00	33
1999 Snowman w/Coke Bottle, 6 1/2" AP1028	Retrd.	2000	39.95	40
1994 Snowman w/Parcel AP313	Retrd.	1999	21.95	22
1994 Snowman w/Specs AP312	Retrd.	1995	20.00	35
1999 Snowman, 6" AP991	Retrd.	2000	19.95	20
2002 Snowman's Treasure AP1470	Open		30.00	30

YEAR ISSUE	EDITION LIMIT	YEAR RETD.	ISSUE PRICE	*QUOTE U.S.$
2000 Snowtown Snowman AP1078 - M. Stoebner	Retrd.	2001	27.50	28
2001 Snowy Friends AP1283 - J. Thompson	Open		40.00	40
2001 Snowy Thinker (Petite Noels) AP1328 - J. Thompson	Retrd.	2001	22.50	23
2002 Soaring Santa AP1431	Open		35.00	35
1994 Soldier AP407	Retrd.	1995	15.50	175
1998 Songbirds AP894	Retrd.	1999	34.95	35-38
1994 Sparrow AP329	Retrd.	1995	15.50	20
1994 Sphinx AP350	Retrd.	1995	22.50	60-65
1996 Sphinx AP480	Retrd.	1999	29.95	30
1994 Spinner Top AP359	Retrd.	1995	9.00	28
2001 A Spot of Tea AP1274 - M. Engelbreit	Open		45.00	45
2001 Springs Jack-In-Box, 2 asst. (Petite Noels) AP1300	Retrd.	2001	18.00	18
1996 St. Basils Cathedral AP600	Retrd.	1999	34.95	35-39
1995 St. Joseph AP412	Retrd.	1996	22.50	23
2000 St. Nick on Horseback AP1154 - Stefan	Retrd.	2001	35.00	35
2002 Stack of Gifts AP1453	Open		30.00	30
1998 Standing Angels, 3 asst. AP882	Retrd.	1999	55.00	55
1997 Star 3/asst. AP671	Retrd.	1999	19.95	20
1997 Star Boy AP676	Retrd.	2000	34.95	35
2002 Star of David AP1476	Open		25.00	25
1995 Star Santa AP470 - Stefan	Retrd.	1999	27.50	30-35
1997 Star Santa, blue AP470/BL - Stefan	Retrd.	1999	27.50	28
1997 Star Snowman AP625 - Stefan	Retrd.	1999	29.95	33-45
1997 Star Snowman AP625/BL - Stefan	Retrd.	1999	29.95	30-35
1999 Starlight Angel AP1092	Retrd.	2000	35.00	35
2002 Stars & Stripes AP1479	Open		25.00	25
1998 Statue of Liberty AP942	Open		39.95	40
1998 Statue of Liberty Ball AP677/SL	Retrd.	2001	27.50	28
1996 Sting Ray AP495	Retrd.	1996	28.00	28-44
2002 Stocking Stuffer AP1457	Open		30.00	30
2001 Sunday Parade AP1317	Retrd.	2001	33.00	33
2001 Sunday's Best, 2 asst. AP1304	Retrd.	2001	28.00	28
1999 Sunface, 4 1/2" AP967	Retrd.	1999	19.95	20
2001 Sunflowers Van Gogh (Artist Series) AP235	Retrd.	2001	80.00	80
2002 Superman AP1549	Open		40.00	40
1994 Swan AP325	Retrd.	1997	17.50	20
2001 Swan Lake AP1292	Retrd.	2001	28.00	28
2002 Sweet Angels, 3 asst. AP1405A3	Open		33.00	33
2002 Sweet Dreams AP1103A2	Open		30.00	30
2002 Swirl Santa AP1525	Open		20.00	20
2002 Taking A Break AP1486	Open		33.00	33
1997 Tatar Prince AP672	Retrd.	1999	34.95	35
2002 Tea Party AP1478	Open		40.00	40
2000 Teapot "Tea For Two" AP1169 - M. Engelbreit	Retrd.	2001	40.00	40
1999 Teapot AP1043 - M. Engelbreit	Retrd.	2001	44.95	45
1994 Teddy Bear (gold) AP338	Retrd.	1994	13.50	25-40
1999 Teddy Bear in Chair, 6" AP959	Retrd.	2000	34.95	35-37
1999 Teddy Bear with Balloons, 6 1/2" AP987	Retrd.	1999	24.95	25
2002 Teddy's ABC AP1535	Open		20.00	20
2001 Tee Time AP1299	Retrd.	2001	33.00	33
1995 Telephone AP448	Retrd.	1996	25.00	25
2001 Ten Lords-A-Leaping (12 Days of Christmas) AP1343 - Stefan	Open		40.00	40
1999 Texaco Pump, 6 1/2" AP1030	Retrd.	2001	34.95	35
2001 Texaco Truck AP1298	Open		45.00	45
1996 Three French Hens (12 Days of Christmas) AP626 - Stefan	Open		36.00	36
2001 Three Kings - mini (boxed set) AP246	Open		110.00	110
2001 Three Kings (Petite Noels) AP1305/67	Open		30.00	30
2000 Three Kings Ball AP1166 - Stefan	Retrd.	2001	35.00	35
1996 Three Kings boxed set AP516	Retrd.	2000	125.00	144
1995 Three Kings, 3 asst. AP609	Retrd.	1999	29.95	35
1999 Three Musketeers 3/Asst, 6 1/2" AP950/12	Retrd.	2001	37.50	38
2000 Thunderbird, red AP930/R	Retrd.	2001	39.95	40
2001 Thunderbird, yellow AP1339	Retrd.	2001	40.00	40
2000 Tiger-World Wild Fund AP1131	Retrd.	2001	25.00	25
2002 Tin Man - Wizard of Oz AP1502	Open		35.00	35
2002 Tin Man AP1404	Open		25.00	25
1999 Tin Man Sitting on Stump AP1061	Retrd.	2001	39.95	40
2000 Tin Man w/Heart AP1217	Retrd.	2001	30.00	30
1998 Titanic AP941	Retrd.	2000	45.00	45

YEAR ISSUE	EDITION LIMIT	YEAR RETD.	ISSUE PRICE	*QUOTE U.S.$
2002 To My Sweetheart AP1556	Open		35.00	35
2002 Together Forever AP1485	Open		30.00	30
1999 Toucan, 7" AP1009	Retrd.	1999	19.95	20-22
2001 Train - mini (boxed set) AP244	Open		125.00	125
2002 Train boxed set AP0266	Open		140.00	140
1994 Train Coaches AP354	Retrd.	1999	14.95	15
1994 Train Set (boxed) AP501	Retrd.	1999	100.00	100-110
1995 Treasure Chest AP416	Retrd.	1996	20.00	20
1998 Trolley Car AP911	Retrd.	2000	34.95	35
1994 Tropical Fish (4 asst.) AP409	Retrd.	1997	22.50	25-35
2000 Tropical Fish 4 pc. boxed set AP598	Retrd.	2001	120.00	120
1997 Tropical Fish AP410	Retrd.	1999	22.50	28
1997 Tropical Fish AP554	Retrd.	1999	110.00	110
1994 Tropical Fish boxed set AP506	Retrd.	1997	110.00	110-115
1996 Tsar Ivan AP601	Retrd.	1998	34.95	39
2001 Tugboat Santa AP1330	Retrd.	2001	39.00	39
1994 Turkey AP326	Retrd.	1996	20.00	20
1996 Tutenkhamen #2 AP476	Retrd.	2001	32.50	35
1994 Tutenkhamen AP348	Retrd.	1996	28.00	33
2002 Twelve Drummers (12 Days of Christmas) AP1408	Open		33.00	33
1999 Two Little Pigs, 4" AP962	Retrd.	2000	24.95	25
1995 Two Turtle Doves (12 Days of Christmas) AP471 - Stefan	Open		34.95	
1998 Uncle Sam AP869	Retrd.	2000	34.95	35
2000 Union Soldier AP1121	Retrd.	2001	27.50	28
2000 United States of Santa 3 pc. boxed set AP210	Retrd.	2000	100.00	100
2002 Upon A Cloud, 2 asst. AP1482A2	Open		33.00	33
2002 Vintage Coke Sign AP1573	Open		40.00	40
1998 Vintage Ford 3 asst. AP937/09	Retrd.	1999	39.95	40
2002 Viva Elvis AP1490	Open		40.00	40
2000 Wedding Cake AP1199	Open		35.00	35
1998 Wedding Couple AP868	Retrd.	2001	34.95	35
1999 Wheel of Fortune AP1071	Retrd.	2000	29.95	30
2002 Whirlybird AP1419	Open		35.00	35
2002 White Christmas AP1409	Open		33.00	33
1994 White Dice (original-square) AP363	Retrd.	1994	18.00	42-66
1999 White Piano AP1018/W	Retrd.	1999	29.95	33-40
1996 Wicked Witch AP606	Retrd.	2001	29.95	30
2001 Wicked Witch of Oz AP1312	Open		30.00	30
2000 The Wicked Witch of the West-Oz AP1190	Retrd.	2001	37.50	38
1998 Wicked Witch-Oz AP921	Retrd.	2001	39.95	40
1996 Winter Boy AP615	Retrd.	1998	19.95	20-22
1996 Winter Girl AP615	Retrd.	1998	19.95	20-22
2001 Winter Jam AP1349	Retrd.	2001	30.00	30
2001 Wise Ole Owl AP1351	Retrd.	2001	30.00	30
2002 Wish Upon A Star (Starlight Foundation) AP1452	Open		33.00	33
1997 Witch-Hanzel & Gretel, 7" AP661	Retrd.	1999	34.95	36-38
1996 Wizard in Balloon AP622	Retrd.	2000	34.95	35
1998 Wizard of Oz 3 pc. boxed set AP573	Retrd.	2000	150.00	150
1999 Wizard of Oz 4 asst. AP1060/123	Retrd.	2001	39.95	40
1995 Wizard of Oz 4 pc. boxed set AP505	Retrd.	2000	125.00	125
1999 Wizard of Oz 4 pc. boxed set AP591	Retrd.	2000	190.00	190
1995 Wizard of Oz 6 pc. boxed set AP508	5,000	1995	170.00	120-180
2001 Wizard of Oz AP1335	Open		35.00	35
1999 Wizard of Oz Book AP1050	Retrd.	2000	37.50	38
1995 Wizard of Oz Cowardly Lion AP433	Retrd.	2000	22.50	23
1995 Wizard of Oz Dorothy AP434	Retrd.	2000	22.50	25
2001 Wizard of Oz Glinda The Good Witch AP1311	Open		33.00	33
1996 Wizard of Oz II boxed set AP518	Retrd.	2000	150.00	164
1995 Wizard of Oz Scarecrow AP435	Retrd.	2000	22.50	23
1995 Wizard of Oz Tinman AP436	Retrd.	2000	22.50	23
1999 Wizard of Oz Under Rainbow AP1074	Open		44.95	45
2001 Wizard of Oz Wicked Witch AP1312	Open		33.00	33
2002 Wizard of Oz, 4 asst. AP1401A	Open		25.00	25
2002 Wizard of Oz, 4 asst. AP1496A4	Open		35.00	35
1997 Wizard of Oz, 4 asst. AP819/4	Retrd.	2001	39.95	40
1997 Wolf AP666	Retrd.	2001	32.50	35
1998 Woodstock on Candy Cane AP919	Retrd.	2000	37.50	38-45
2001 Woodstock w/Candy Cane AP1368	Open		25.00	25
1998 Yellow Taxi Cab AP909	Retrd.	2001	34.95	35
2000 Zebra-World Wild Fund AP1129	Retrd.	2001	25.00	25
1998 Zeppelin Dirigible AP913	Retrd.	1999	27.50	28
1994 Zodiac Sun AP381	Retrd.	1995	22.50	52-55

The Polonaise™ Collector's Guild - KSA/Komozja, unless otherwise noted

YEAR ISSUE	EDITION LIMIT	YEAR RETD.	ISSUE PRICE	*QUOTE U.S.$
1997 Grandfather Frost AP810/COL	Retrd.	1998	Gift	60
1999 Carousel Horse AP972/COL	Retrd.	1999	Gift	
2000 Peace Angel AP1224/CLB	Retrd.	2000	Gift	N
2001 Blizzard Snowman AP2001/COL	Yr.Iss.	2001	Gift	N
2002 Heavenly Rest AP2002/COL			Gift	N

Polonaise™ Event Signing Collection - KSA/Komozja

YEAR ISSUE	EDITION LIMIT	YEAR RETD.	ISSUE PRICE	*QUOTE U.S.$
1996 Szlachcic AP673/SIG	Yr.Iss.	1996	35.50	35
1997 Szlachcianka AP840	Yr.Iss.	1997	34.95	
1998 Patriarch Alexis AP926/SIG	Yr.Iss.	1998	35.95	36
1999 Just In Time Santa AP1035/SIG	Yr.Iss.	1999	35.95	36
2000 Coming Down The Chimney AP1234/SIG	Yr.Iss.	2000	35.00	
2001 Tuckered Out AP1287/SIG	Yr.Iss.	2001	34.95	
2002 Toy Stop (dealer signing) AP1532	Open		40.00	

Polonaise™ Pedestals - KSA/Komozja, unless otherwis noted

YEAR ISSUE	EDITION LIMIT	YEAR RETD.	ISSUE PRICE	*QUOTE U.S.$
2000 Angel APD882	Retrd.	2001	60.00	
2000 Babe Ruth APD914	Retrd.	2001	45.00	
2000 Baby's 1st Christmas APD1200	Retrd.	2001	27.00	
2000 Believe Santa APD890 - M. Engelbreit	Retrd.	2001	45.00	
2000 Betty Boop APD876	Retrd.	2001	45.00	
2000 Black Piano APD1018/BLK	Retrd.	2001	45.00	
2000 Christmas Tree II APD997	Retrd.	2001	50.00	
2000 English Barrister APD831	Retrd.	2001	45.00	
2000 Garfield APD891	Retrd.	2001	45.00	
2000 Just Married APD829	Retrd.	2001	30.00	
2000 King Kong APD918	Retrd.	2001	45.00	
2000 Madonna & Child APD653	Retrd.	2001	40.00	
2000 Nativity APD458	Retrd.	2001	33.00	
2000 Phantom of the Opera APD1016	Retrd.	2001	50.00	
2000 Raggedy Ann APD321	Retrd.	2001	33.00	
2000 Santa Bringing Gifts APD1201	Retrd.	2001	45.00	
2000 Smithsonian Astronaut APD826	Retrd.	2001	40.00	
2000 Snoopy Easter Beagle APD1164/E	Retrd.	2001	40.00	
2000 Statue of Liberty APD942	Retrd.	2001	40.00	
2000 Titanic APD941	Retrd.	2001	45.00	
2000 Trolley APD911	Retrd.	2001	36.00	
2000 Tutentkhamen APD476	Retrd.	2001	36.00	
2000 Wedding Cake APD1199	Retrd.	2001	40.00	
2000 Wedding Couple APD868	Retrd.	2001	40.00	
2000 Yellow Cab Taxi APD909	Retrd.	2000	40.00	

Polonaise™ Vatican Library Collection - Vatican Librar

YEAR ISSUE	EDITION LIMIT	YEAR RETD.	ISSUE PRICE	*QUOTE U.S.$
1995 Cherub AP650	Retrd.	1999	37.50	38
1996 Cherub Bust Glass AP651	Retrd.	1999	34.95	
1996 Cherubum boxed set, AP 521	Retrd.	1999	150.00	160-1
1996 Dancing Cherubs on Ball AP652	Retrd.	1998	34.95	
1995 Eggs AP656	Retrd.	1999	29.50	
1996 Full Body Cherub AP 650	Retrd.	1999	34.95	
1996 Garden of Mary boxed set, AP 520	Retrd.	1998	135.00	1
1996 Lily Glass AP655	Retrd.	1998	34.95	35
1996 Madonna & Child AP653	Retrd.	1999	34.95	35
1996 Rose Glass Pink/Ivory Rose AP654/PIV	Retrd.	1999	34.95	
1996 Rose Glass Red Rose AP654/R	Retrd.	1999	34.95	
1999 Vatican Angels AP1058	Retrd.	2000	39.95	
1996 Vatican Cross w/Jewels AP1059	Retrd.	1999	40.00	40
1995 Vatican Egg "Noel" AP658	Retrd.	2000	32.50	
1995 Vatican Egg-Cherub AP657	Retrd.	2000	32.00	
2000 Vatican Madonna Foligno AP1245	Retrd.	2001	39.00	
1997 Vatican Madonna w/Child Egg AP830	Retrd.	1998	37.50	

Royal Heritage Collection - J. Mostrom

YEAR ISSUE	EDITION LIMIT	YEAR RETD.	ISSUE PRICE	*QUOTE U.S.$
1993 Anastasia W2922	Retrd.	1994	28.00	
1996 Angelique Angel Baby W3278	Retrd.	1996	25.00	
1995 Benjamin J5756	Retrd.	1996	24.50	
1995 Blythe J5756	Retrd.	1996	24.50	
1996 Brianna Ivory W7663	Retrd.	1999	25.00	
1996 Brianna Pink W7663	Retrd.	1999	25.00	
1993 Caroline W2924	Retrd.	1995	25.50	
1993 Charles W2924	Retrd.	1995	25.50	
1993 Elizabeth W2924	Retrd.	1995	25.50	
1996 Etoile Angel Baby W3278	Retrd.	1996	25.00	
1996 Francis Winter Boy W3279	Retrd.	1997	28.00	
1996 Gabrielle in Pink Coat W3276	Retrd.	1999	28.00	

YEAR ISSUE	EDITION LIMIT	YEAR RETD.	ISSUE PRICE	*QUOTE U.S.$
1996 Giselle w/Bow W3277	Retrd.	1997	28.00	28
1996 Giselle Winter Girl w/Package W3279	Retrd.	1997	28.00	28
1994 Ice Fairy, Winter Fairy W2972	Retrd.	1996	25.50	26
1993 Joella W2979	Retrd.	1993	27.00	27
1993 Kelly W2979	Retrd.	1993	27.00	27
1996 Lady Colette in Sled W3301	Retrd.	1997	32.00	32
1996 Laurielle Lady Skater W3281	Retrd.	1997	36.00	36
1996 Miniotte w/Muff W3279	Retrd.	1997	28.00	28
1996 Monique w/Hat Box W3277	Retrd.	1999	28.00	28
1993 Nicholas W2923	Retrd.	1996	25.50	26
1996 Nicole w/Balloon W3277	Retrd.	1999	28.00	28
1993 Patina W2923	Retrd.	1996	25.50	26
1996 Rene Victorian Lady W3280	Retrd.	1997	36.00	36
1993 Sasha W2923	Retrd.	1996	25.50	26
1994 Snow Princess W2971	Retrd.	1996	28.00	28

Smithsonian Museum Carousel - KSA/Smithsonian

1987 Antique Bunny S3027/2	Retrd.	1992	14.50	15-22
1992 Antique Camel S3027/12	Retrd.	1996	15.00	15-22
1989 Antique Cat S3027/6	Retrd.	1995	14.50	15
1992 Antique Elephant S3027/11	Retrd.	1996	14.50	15-22
1995 Antique Frog S3027/18	Retrd.	1999	15.50	16
1988 Antique Giraffe S3027/4	Retrd.	1993	14.50	15
1987 Antique Goat S3027/1	Retrd.	1992	14.50	15
1991 Antique Horse S3027/10	Retrd.	1996	14.50	15-22
1993 Antique Horse S3027/14	Retrd.	1998	15.00	15-22
1988 Antique Horse S3027/3	Retrd.	1993	14.50	15
1989 Antique Lion S3027/5	Retrd.	1994	14.50	15
1994 Antique Pig S3027/16	Retrd.	1998	15.50	16-22
1994 Antique Reindeer S3027/15	Retrd.	1999	15.50	16
1991 Antique Rooster S3027/9	Retrd.	1994	14.50	15
1990 Antique Seahorse S3027/8	Retrd.	1999	14.50	15

Lenox China

Annual Ornaments - Lenox

1982 1982 Ball	Yr.Iss.	1983	30.00	55-70
1983 1983 Teardrop Shape	Yr.Iss.	1984	35.00	75
1984 1984 Starburst	Yr.Iss.	1985	38.00	65
1985 1985 Bell	Yr.Iss.	1986	37.50	60
1986 1986 The Three Magi	Yr.Iss.	1987	38.50	50
1987 1987 Dickens Village	Yr.Iss.	1988	39.00	40-45
1988 1988 Ball	Yr.Iss.	1989	39.00	45
1989 1989 Faberge Egg	Yr.Iss.	1990	39.00	39
1990 1990 Bell	Yr.Iss.	1991	42.00	42
1991 1991 Ornament	Yr.Iss.	1992	39.00	39
1992 1992 Ball	Yr.Iss.	1993	42.00	42
1993 1993 Lantern	Yr.Iss.	1994	45.00	45
1994 1994 Star	Yr.Iss.	1995	39.00	39
1995 1995 Santa	Yr.Iss.	1996	46.50	47
1996 1996 Traditional Ball	Yr.Iss.	1996	46.50	47

Yuletide - Lenox

1994 Cat	Open		19.50	20
1995 Candle	Open		19.95	20
1996 Christmas Angel™	Open		21.00	21

Lenox Classics

Lenox Classics-China Disney Showcase - Lenox

2001 A Dopey Kind of Holiday	Open		30.00	30
2001 From Grumpy, with Love	Open		30.00	30
2001 A Honey of a Holiday	Retrd.	2002	25.00	25

Lenox Classics-China Ivory Snowman - Lenox

2000 Joyful Tidings	Retrd.	2001	25.00	25

Lenox Classics-China Ornaments - Lenox

2000 Millennium Drummer	Closed	2000	25.00	25
2000 Santa's Special Delivery	Closed	2000	25.00	25
2000 Teddy's Millennium Wish	Closed	2000	25.00	25
2001 Ho-Ho-Ho From Above	Open		30.00	30
2001 Santa's Downhill Delivery	Retrd.	2002	25.00	25
2001 An Angel All My Own	Open		25.00	25
2001 Chilly Chap	Retrd.	2002	25.00	25
2001 Sledding Snowpals	Retrd.	2002	25.00	25
2001 The Jeweled Christmas Tree	Retrd.	2002	25.00	25

Lenox Classics-Crystal Ornaments - Lenox

1999 Heavenly Messenger (Angel)	Retrd.	2002	45.00	45
1999 Eternal Peace (Dove)	Retrd.	2001	60.00	60

YEAR ISSUE	EDITION LIMIT	YEAR RETD.	ISSUE PRICE	*QUOTE U.S.$

Lenox Classics-Little Graces - Lenox

1997 Little Surprise	5,000	2001	45.00	45
1998 Little Hope (Cherub wStar)	5,000	1999	45.00	45
2000 Little Trumpeter	5,000	2001	45.00	45

Little Angel Publishing

An Angel's Touch Sculptural Ornament Collection - D. Gelsinger

2000 Nature's Beauty, Gentle Embrace, Garden Miracles	95-day		29.97	30
2000 An Angel's Guidance, Heavenly Blessings, Precious Moments	95-day		29.97	30
2000 Gentle Guardian, An Angel's Caring, Delicate Blessings	95-day		29.97	30
2000 Heavenly Hugs, An Angel's Love, Loving Kindness	95-day		29.97	30
2000 Nature's Guardians, An Angel's Tenderness, An Angel's Prayer	95-day		29.97	30
2000 An Angel's Kindness, Perpetual Embrace, An Angel's Hope	95-day		29.97	30

Delicate Blessings - D. Gelsinger

1999 Tree Topper	Open		39.95	40

Heavenly Messengers Heirloom Porcelain Collection - D. Gelsinger

2000 Angel's Guidance, Angel's Love, Angel's Blessings	95-day		29.97	30
2000 Angel's Touch, Angel's Prayer, Angel's Kindness	95-day		29.97	30
2000 Angel's Tenderness, Angel's Caring, Angel's Warmth	95-day		29.97	30
2000 Angel's Spirit, Angel's Comfort, Angel's Faith	95-day		29.97	30
2000 Angel's Wonder, Angel's Joy, Angel's Devotion	95-day		29.97	30
2000 Angel's Grace, Angel's Happiness, Angel's Beauty	95-day		29.97	30

Heaven's Little Angels - D. Gelsinger

1998 Gentle Guardian, Gentle Miracle, Loving Kindness	95-day		29.97	30
1998 Nature's Blessings, Garden Beauty, Gentle Hugs	95-day		29.97	30
1999 Angel's Guidance, Angel's Tenderness, Nature's Guardian	95-day		29.97	30
1999 Nature's Beauty, Divine Guardian, Heavenly Innocence	95-day		29.97	30
1999 Precious Devotion, Angel's Spirit, Delicate Blessings	95-day		29.97	30
1999 Angel's Warmth, Loving Gift, Precious Playmates	95-day		29.97	30
1999 Tender Touch, Perpetual Embrace, Angel's Grace	95-day		29.97	30
1999 Angel's Hope, Heaven Sent, Tender Moments	95-day		29.97	30
1999 Heavenly Hugs, Angel's Kindness, Angel's Caring	95-day		29.97	30
1999 Angel's Joy, Angel's Prayer, Angel's Love	95-day		29.97	30
1999 Devoted Guardian, Angel's Heart, Reverent Joy	95-day		29.97	30
1999 Innocent Wonder, Loving Touch, Angel's Faith	95-day		29.97	30
1999 Gentle Kindness, Devoted Spirit, Nature's Joy	95-day		29.97	30
1999 Loving Guardian, Delicate Embrace, Precious Blessings	95-day		29.97	30
1999 Gentle Beauty, Angel's Comfort, Heavenly Faith	95-day		29.97	30

Lladró

Angels - Lladró

1994 Joyful Offering L6125G	Yr.Iss.	1994	245.00	245-300
1995 Angel of the Stars L6132G	Yr.Iss.	1995	195.00	195-250
1996 Rejoice L6321G	Yr.Iss.	1996	220.00	220-240

Annual Ornaments - Lladró

1988 Christmas Ball-L1603M	Yr.Iss.	1988	60.00	75-104
1989 Christmas Ball-L5656M	Yr.Iss.	1989	65.00	45-75
1990 Christmas Ball-L5730M	Yr.Iss.	1990	70.00	75-100
1991 Christmas Ball-L5829M	Yr.Iss.	1991	52.00	40-52

ORNAMENTS

YEAR ISSUE	EDITION LIMIT	YEAR RETD.	ISSUE PRICE	*QUOTE U.S.$
1992 Christmas Ball-L5914M	Yr.Iss.	1992	52.00	45-52
1993 Christmas Ball-L6009M	Yr.Iss.	1993	54.00	54-78
1994 Christmas Ball-L6105M	Yr.Iss.	1994	55.00	55
1995 Christmas Ball-L6207M	Yr.Iss.	1995	55.00	45-55
1996 Christmas Ball-L6298M	Yr.Iss.	1996	55.00	55-65
1997 Christmas Ball-L6442M	Yr.Iss.	1997	55.00	55-65
1998 Christmas Ball-01016561	Yr.Iss.	1998	55.00	55-60
1999 Christmas Ball-01016637	Yr.Iss.	1999	55.00	55-60
2000 Christmas Ball-01016699	Yr.Iss.	2000	60.00	60
2001 Christmas Ball-01016717	Yr.Iss.	2001	55.00	55

Miniature Ornaments - Lladró

1988 Miniature Angels-L1604G, Set/3	Yr.Iss.	1988	75.00	200-225
1989 Holy Family-L5657G, Set/3	Yr.Iss.	1990	79.50	143-225
1990 Three Kings-L5729G, Set/3	Yr.Iss.	1991	87.50	125-145
1991 Holy Shepherds-L5809G	Yr.Iss.	1991	97.50	110-175
1993 Nativity Trio-L6095G	Yr.Iss.	1993	115.00	175-260

Ornaments - Lladró

1995 Christmas Tree L6261G	Open		75.00	75
1995 Landing Dove L6266G	Closed	1998	49.00	43-50
1995 Surprised Cherub L6253G	Closed	1998	120.00	120-160
1995 Flying Dove L6267G	Closed	1998	49.00	43-50
1995 Playing Cherub L6254G	Closed	1998	120.00	102-120
1995 Rocking Horse L6262G	Closed	1998	69.00	75-80
1995 Doll L6263G	Closed	1998	69.00	69
1995 Thinking Cherub L6255G	Closed	1998	120.00	102-120
1995 Train L6264G	Closed	1998	69.00	65-87
1991 Our First-1991-L5840G	Closed	1991	50.00	65-75
1992 Snowman-L5841G	Closed	1994	55.00	79-125
1992 Santa-L5842G	Closed	1992	55.00	60-95
1992 Baby's First-1992-L5922G	Closed	1992	55.00	55
1992 Our First-1992-L5923G	Closed	1992	50.00	52-59
1992 Elf Ornament-L5938G	Closed	1994	50.00	79-300
1992 Mrs. Claus-L5939G	Closed	1994	55.00	45-59
1992 Christmas Morning-L5940G	Closed	1992	97.50	125-200
1993 Nativity Lamb-L5969G	Closed	1994	85.00	85
1993 Baby's First 1993-L6037G	Closed	1993	57.00	57
1993 Our First-L6038G	Closed	1993	52.00	57-75
1996 Santa's Journey-L6265	Closed	1997	49.00	49
1996 Welcome Home-L6335	Closed	1998	85.00	85-100
1996 King Melchior-L6341	Closed	1998	75.00	75-90
1996 Seraph With Bells-L6342	Closed	1998	79.00	79
1996 Little Aviator-L6343	Closed	1998	79.00	79
1996 Teddy Bear-L6344	Closed	1998	67.00	67
1996 Toy Soldier-L6345	Closed	1998	90.00	90-95
1996 Heavenly Tenor-L6372	Closed	1998	98.00	98-105
1998 Seraph with Bow-01006445	Closed	1999	79.00	80
1998 Heavenly Musician-01006498	Closed	1999	98.00	98-100
1998 King Balthaser-01006509	Closed	1999	75.00	75-89
1998 Our Winter Home-01006519	Closed	1999	85.00	85
1998 Baby's First Christmas-1998 01016588	Closed	1998	55.00	55-65
1999 Baby's First Christmas-1999 01016694	Closed	1999	55.00	55
2000 Baby's First Christmas-2000 01016697	Closed	2000	65.00	65
2000 Our First Christmas-2000 01016716	Closed	2000	65.00	65
2001 Baby's First Christmas-2001 01016719	Closed	2001	65.00	65
2001 Baby's First Christmas-2001 01016720	Closed	2001	65.00	65
2001 Our First Christmas-2001 01016721	Closed	2001	65.00	65

Tree Topper Ornaments - Lladró

1990 Angel Tree Topper-L5719G-Blue	Yr.Iss.	1990	100.00	200-325
1991 Angel Tree Topper-L5831G-Pink	Yr.Iss.	1991	115.00	175-195
1992 Angel Tree Topper-L5875G-Green	Yr.Iss.	1992	120.00	160-195
1993 Angel Tree Topper -L5962G-Lavender	Yr.Iss.	1993	125.00	143-195
1997 Angel of Light-01006501	Closed	1997	175.00	149-175
1998 Message of Peace-01006587	Closed	1998	150.00	125-150
1999 Message of Love-01006643	Yr.Iss.	1999	150.00	150
2000 A Celestial Christmas-01006747	Yr.Iss.	2000	270.00	270
2001 Heavenly Melodies-01006835	Yr.Iss.	2001	150.00	150
2001 Star of the Heavens-01006792	Yr.Iss.	2001	150.00	150

YEAR ISSUE	EDITION LIMIT	YEAR RETD.	ISSUE PRICE	*QUOTE U.S.$

Memories of Yesterday/Enesco Group, Inc.

Memories of Yesterday Society Member's Only - M. Attwell

1992 With Luck And A Friend, I's In Heaven MY922	Yr.Iss.	1992	16.00	20
1993 I'm Bringing Good Luck-Wherever You Are	Yr.Iss.	1993	16.00	22

Memories of Yesterday - M. Attwell

1997 Angel w/Holder 264709	Retrd.	1999	17.50	18
1997 Sharing Gingerbread Blessings 271721	Yr.Iss.	1999	17.50	18-39
1988 Baby's First Christmas 1988 520373	Yr.Iss.	1988	13.50	40-60
1988 Special Delivery! 1988 520381	Yr.Iss.	1988	13.50	25-35
1989 Baby's First Christmas 522465	Retrd.	1996	15.00	15-20
1989 A Surprise for Santa 522473 (1989)	Yr.Iss.	1989	13.50	15-28
1989 Christmas Together 522562	Retrd.	1999	15.00	15-25
1995 Happy Landings (Dated 1995) 522619	Yr.Iss.	1995	16.00	16
1990 Time For Bed 524638	Yr.Iss.	1990	15.00	15-30
1990 New Moon 524646	Retrd.	1999	15.00	15-25
1994 Just Dreaming of You 524786	Retrd.	1999	16.00	16
1990 Moonstruck 524794	Retrd.	1992	15.00	25
1991 Just Watchin' Over You 525421	Retrd.	1994	17.50	25
1991 Lucky Me 525448	Retrd.	1993	16.00	22
1993 Wish I Could Fly To You 525790 (dated)	Yr.Iss.	1993	16.00	16
1992 I'll Fly Along To See You Soon 525804 (1992 Dated Bisque)	Yr.Iss.	1992	16.00	16-25
1991 Star Fishin' 525820	Retrd.	1999	16.00	16
1991 Lucky You 525847	Retrd.	1993	16.00	16
1995 Now I Lay Me Down to Sleep 527009	Retrd.	1999	15.00	15
1995 I Pray the Lord My Soul to Keep 527017	Retrd.	1999	15.00	15
1992 Mommy, I Teared It 527041 (Five Year Anniversary Limited Edition)	Yr.Iss.	1992	15.00	20
1991 S'no Use Lookin' Back Now! 527181(dated)	Yr.Iss.	1991	15.00	28
1992 Merry Christmas, Little Boo-Boo 528803	Retrd.	1999	37.50	38
1993 May All Your Finest Dreams Come True 528811	Retrd.	1999	16.00	16
1992 Star Light, Star Bright 528838	Retrd.	1999	16.00	16
1994 Give Yourself a Hug From Me! 529109 ('94 Dated)	Yr. Iss.	1994	17.50	18
1998 God Bless And Merry Christmas! 531731 ('98 Dated)	Yr. Iss.	1998	17.50	18
1992 Swinging Together 580481(1992 Dated Artplas)	Yr.Iss.	1992	17.50	22
1992 Sailin' With My Friends 587575 (Artplas)	Retrd.	1999	25.00	25
1993 Bringing Good Wishes Your Way 592846 (Artplas)	Retrd.	1999	25.00	25
1994 Bout Time I Came Along to See You 592854 (Artplas)	Retrd.	1999	17.50	18

Event Item Only - Enesco

1993 How 'Bout A Little Kiss? 527068	Closed	1993	16.50	50
1996 Hoping To See You Soon 527033	Yr.Iss.	1996	15.00	15

Friendship - Enesco

1996 I Love You This Much! 185809	Retrd.	1999	13.50	14

Peter Pan - Enesco

1996 Tinkerbell 164682	Retrd.	1999	17.50	20

Miss Martha's Collection/Enesco Group, Inc.

Miss Martha's Collection - M. Holcombe

1993 Caroline - Always Someone Watching Over Me 350532	Closed	1994	25.00	50
1993 Arianna - Heavenly Sounds 350567	Closed	1994	25.00	50-55
1992 Baby in Basket 369454	Closed	1994	25.00	50-75
1992 Baby in Swing 421480	Retrd.	1993	25.00	50-75
1992 Girl Holding Stocking DTD 1992 421499	Closed	1994	25.00	45-55
1992 Girl/Bell In Hand 421502	Retrd.	1993	25.00	50

Collectors' Information Bureau   *Quotes have been rounded up to nearest dollar

YEAR ISSUE	EDITION LIMIT	YEAR RETD.	ISSUE PRICE	*QUOTE U.S.$

Possible Dreams

Clothtique Ornaments - Staff

YEAR ISSUE	EDITION LIMIT	YEAR RETD.	ISSUE PRICE	*QUOTE U.S.$
2001 Celebrate Love 715069	Open		25.00	25
2002 Christmas Stories 718093	Open		15.00	15
2001 Fireman Santa 714013	Retrd.	2001	19.50	20
2002 A Friendly Visit 718098	Open		15.00	15
2002 Friends Forever 718101	Open		15.00	15
2001 German Santa 715067	Open		15.00	15
2001 Happy Angler Santa 715075	Open		15.00	15
2002 Ice Capers 718097	Open		15.00	15
2001 Irish Santa 714126	Open		15.00	15
2001 Mexican Santa 715065	Open		15.00	15
2001 Mrs. Claus 714102	Open		14.00	14
2001 Mrs. Claus Grandma 715063	Open		15.00	15
2001 New Home Santa 715070	Open		15.00	15
2002 A New Suit For Santa 718096	Open		25.00	25
2001 Patriotic Santa 715076	Open		15.00	15
2002 Playing Through 718090	Open		15.00	15
2001 Polish Santa 715068	Open		15.00	15
2001 Purrfect Pet Santa 715064	Open		25.00	25
2001 Russian Santa 715066	Open		15.00	15
2001 Santa 714101	Open		14.00	14
2002 Santa on the Green 718091	Open		15.00	15
2001 Santa With Newborn 715074	Open		15.00	15
2002 Santa With Shamrocks 715077	Open		15.00	15
2002 Santa's Cuisine 718100	Open		15.00	15
2001 Santa's Shillelagh 714129	Open		15.00	15
2001 Scottish Santa 714125	Open		15.00	15
2001 Special Daughter Santa 715072	Open		15.00	15
2001 Special Mom Santa 715062	Open		15.00	15
2001 Special Son Santa 715073	Open		15.00	15
2002 Spirit of Santa 718099	Open		15.00	15
2002 Sun, Surf & Santa 718092	Open		15.00	15
2002 A Touch of Magic 718094	Open		15.00	15
2002 Workshop 718095	Open		15.00	15
2001 Workshop Santa 715071	Open		15.00	15
2002 World's Greatest Teacher 715078	Open		15.00	15

Crinkle Claus - Staff

YEAR ISSUE	EDITION LIMIT	YEAR RETD.	ISSUE PRICE	*QUOTE U.S.$
1996 Bishop of Maya-659702	Retrd.	1998	7.80	8
1996 Black Forest Santa-659706	Open		7.80	8
1999 Blazing Crinkle 659720	Open		9.20	10
1999 Cardinal Crinkle 659730	Open		9.20	10
1999 Choo-Choo Crinkle 659719	Open		6.90	7
1999 Christmas Crinkle 659718	Open		6.90	7
1999 Crinkle Jester 659725	Open		9.40	10
1999 Crinkle on the Chimney 659717	Open		6.90	7
1999 Crinkle on the Links 659722	Open		9.40	10
1999 Crinkle on the Moon 659723	Open		9.20	10
1999 Crinkle Star 659727	Open		9.20	10
1999 Crinkle Tree 659715	Open		6.90	7
2000 Crinkle World Peace 659733	Open		16.00	16
1999 Crinkle Wreath 659721	Open		9.40	10
1999 Diamond Crinkle 659724	Open		9.20	10
1996 Father Christmas-659703	Open		7.80	8
1999 Fire Fighting Crinkle 659728	Open		9.20	10
1996 German Santa-659701	Retrd.	1998	7.80	8
1999 Irish Crinkle Shepherd 659732	Open		8.00	8
1999 Leaping Crinkle 659729	Open		9.20	10
1996 Pere Noel Santa-659705	Open		7.80	8
1999 Quarter Moon Crinkle 659716	Open		6.90	7
1999 Red Bow Crinkle 659726	Open		9.20	10
1999 Slavic Crinkle 659713	Retrd.	1998	7.80	10
1996 St. Nicholas-659704	Retrd.	1998	7.80	8
1999 Traveling Crinkle 659731	Open		9.20	10

Garfield® Ornaments - Staff

YEAR ISSUE	EDITION LIMIT	YEAR RETD.	ISSUE PRICE	*QUOTE U.S.$
1997 Frostbite Feline 275103	Open		20.50	21
1997 Here Comes Santa Paws 275102	Open		25.50	26
1997 Wake Me When It's Christmas 275101	Open		25.50	26

Splanglers Realm® - R. Splangler

YEAR ISSUE	EDITION LIMIT	YEAR RETD.	ISSUE PRICE	*QUOTE U.S.$
1997 The Stowaway 191052	Open		8.40	9
1997 Tied To Perfection 191051	Open		9.30	10
1997 Twinkle, Twinkle, Little Dragon 191050	Open		7.90	8

Stebleton Folk Art - B. Stebleton

YEAR ISSUE	EDITION LIMIT	YEAR RETD.	ISSUE PRICE	*QUOTE U.S.$
1998 Ball & Cone Shaped Santa 194012	Open		6.80	7
1998 Bell Shaped Santa 194007	Open		6.30	7
1998 Big Ball Shaped Santa 194009	Open		6.30	7
1998 Big Top Shaped Santa 194010	Open		5.90	6
1998 Candle Shaped 194011	Open		4.40	5
1998 Egg Shaped Santa 194003	Open		5.90	6
1998 Funnel Shaped Santa 194006	Open		7.00	7
1998 Oval Shaped Santa 194002	Open		5.20	6
1998 Pear Shaped Santa 194013	Open		6.30	7
1998 Pencil Shaped Santa 194008	Open		5.90	6
1998 Santas, bell shaped, wood, set/6 194001	Open		19.50	20
1998 Tall Cone Shaped Santa 194004	Open		6.90	7
1998 Tiny Top Shaped Santa 194005	Open		4.80	5

Stebleton's Cagey Critters - B. Stebleton

YEAR ISSUE	EDITION LIMIT	YEAR RETD.	ISSUE PRICE	*QUOTE U.S.$
2000 Beach Belly 194510	Open		9.00	9
2000 Curly Q 194500	Open		8.00	8
2000 Derby Day Duo 194508	Open		10.00	10
2000 Dream Team 194507	Open		9.00	9
2000 Finger Food 194501	Open		10.00	10
2000 Furry Yellow Fellow 194502	Open		8.00	8
2000 Hearts and Whiskers 194145	Open		16.00	16
2000 Kitty Court Jester 194512	Open		9.00	9
2000 Lunch is on Me 194505	Open		9.00	9
2000 Randolph the Red Nose 194509	Open		9.00	9
2000 Simply Red 194506	Open		8.00	8
2000 Skateboard Buddies 194503	Open		10.00	10
2000 Sushi Cat 194511	Open		10.00	10
2000 Yokes on You 194504	Open		10.00	10

The Thickets at Sweetbriar® - B. Ross

YEAR ISSUE	EDITION LIMIT	YEAR RETD.	ISSUE PRICE	*QUOTE U.S.$
1995 Christmas Whiskers 350400	Retrd.	1996	11.50	12
1995 Jingle Bells 350407	Retrd.	1996	12.00	12
1996 Snuggles 350416	Open		11.70	12
2000 Nibbley-Do 350415	Open		10.50	11
2000 Twinkle Tails 350415	Retrd.	1996	11.50	12

Precious Moments/Enesco Group, Inc.

Precious Moments - S. Butcher

YEAR ISSUE	EDITION LIMIT	YEAR RETD.	ISSUE PRICE	*QUOTE U.S.$
1983 Surround Us With Joy E-0513	Yr.Iss.	1983	9.00	50-88
1983 Mother Sew Dear E-0514	Open		9.00	16-38
1983 To A Special Dad E-0515	Suspd.		9.00	46-82
1983 The Purr-fect Grandma E-0516	Open		9.00	16-50
1983 The Perfect Grandpa E-0517	Open		9.00	39-50
1983 Blessed Are The Pure In Heart E-0518	Yr.Iss.	1983	9.00	25-50
1983 O Come All Ye Faithful E-0531	Suspd.		10.00	40-69
1983 Let Heaven And Nature Sing E-0532	Retrd.	1986	9.00	28-35
1983 Tell Me The Story Of Jesus E-0533	Suspd.		9.00	36-47
1983 To Thee With Love E-0534	Retrd.	1989	9.00	28-37
1984 Love Is Patient E-0535	Suspd.		9.00	40-92
1984 Love Is Patient E-0536	Suspd.		9.00	35-55
1983 Jesus Is The Light That Shines E-0537	Suspd.		9.00	62-75
1982 Joy To The World E-2343	Suspd.		9.00	38-60
1982 I'll Play My Drum For Him E-2359	Yr.Iss.	1982	9.00	57-119
1982 Baby's First Christmas E-2362	Suspd.		9.00	50-57
1982 The First Noel E-2367	Suspd.		9.00	12-78
1982 The First Noel E-2368	Retrd.	1984	9.00	25-80
1982 Dropping In For Christmas E-2369	Retrd.	1986	9.00	27-70
1982 Unicorn E-2371	Retrd.	1988	10.00	32-63
1982 Baby's First Christmas E-2372	Suspd.		9.00	20-57
1982 Dropping Over For Christmas E-2376	Retrd.	1985	9.00	29-55
1982 Mouse With Cheese E-2381	Suspd.		9.00	92-130
1982 Our First Christmas Together E-2385	Suspd.		10.00	20-56
1982 Camel, Donkey & Cow (3 pc. set) E-2386	Suspd.		25.00	69-95
1984 Wishing You A Merry Christmas E-5387	Yr.Iss.	1984	10.00	28-40
1984 Joy To The World E-5388	Retrd.	1987	10.00	26-60
1984 Peace On Earth E-5389	Suspd.		10.00	35-52
1984 May God Bless You With A Perfect Holiday Season E-5390	Suspd.		10.00	22-50
1984 Love Is Kind E-5391	Suspd.		10.00	29-48
1984 Blessed Are The Pure In Heart E-5392	Yr.Iss.	1984	10.00	14-36
1981 But Love Goes On Forever E-5627	Suspd.		6.00	94-132
1981 But Love Goes On Forever E-5628	Suspd.		6.00	72-115
1981 Let The Heavens Rejoice E-5629	Yr.Iss.	1981	6.00	232-288
1981 Unto Us A Child Is Born E-5630	Suspd.		6.00	39-75
1981 Baby's First Christmas E-5631	Suspd.		6.00	50-68
1981 Baby's First Christmas E-5632	Suspd.		6.00	48-68

Precious Moments/Enesco Group, Inc.

ORNAMENTS

to Precious Moments/Enesco Group, Inc.

YEAR ISSUE	EDITION LIMIT	YEAR RETD.	ISSUE PRICE	*QUOTE U.S.$
1981 Come Let Us Adore Him (4pc. set) E-5633	Suspd.		22.00	145-182
1981 Wee Three Kings (3pc. set) E-5634	Suspd.		19.00	113-175
1981 We Have Seen His Star E-6120	Retrd.	1984	6.00	25-75
1991 Sharing The Good News Together PM-37	Retrd.	1991	N/A	64-95
1986 Birds Of A Feather Collect Together PM-864	Retrd.	1986	N/A	113-200
1990 My Happiness PM-904	Retrd.	1990	N/A	68-95
1985 Have A Heavenly Christmas 12416	Suspd.		12.00	17-34
1985 God Sent His Love 15768	Suspd.		10.00	23-40
1985 May Your Christmas Be Happy 15822	Suspd.		10.00	28-40
1985 Happiness Is The Lord 15830	Suspd.		10.00	20-34
1985 May Your Christmas Be Delightful 15849	Suspd.		10.00	22-38
1999 May Your Christmas Be Delightful 15849R	Open		20.00	15-20
1985 Honk If You Love Jesus 15857	Suspd.		10.00	23-35
1985 Baby's First Christmas 15903	Yr.Iss.	1985	10.00	25-38
1985 Baby's First Christmas 15911	Yr.Iss.	1985	10.00	30-40
2002 A Beary Warm Aloha (Century Circle) 101550	Yr.Iss.		15.00	15
1986 Shepherd of Love 102288	Suspd.		10.00	18-48
1986 Wishing You A Cozy Christmas 102326	Yr.Iss.	1986	10.00	30-42
1986 Our First Christmas Together 102350	Yr.Iss.	1986	10.00	18-40
1986 Trust And Obey 102377	Retrd.	2001	10.00	19-35
1986 Love Rescued Me 102385	Retrd.	2001	10.00	19-32
1986 Angel Of Mercy 102407	Open		10.00	16-35
1986 It's A Perfect Boy 102415	Suspd.		10.00	19-43
1986 Lord Keep Me On My Toes 102423	Retrd.	1990	10.00	23-48
1986 Serve With A Smile 102431	Suspd.		10.00	17-40
1986 Serve With A Smile 102458	Suspd.		10.00	26-40
1986 Reindeer 102466	Yr.Iss.	1986	11.00	125-185
1986 Rocking Horse 102474	Suspd.		10.00	14-35
1986 Baby's First Christmas 102504	Yr.Iss.	1986	10.00	19-40
1986 Baby's First Christmas 102512	Yr.Iss.	1986	10.00	17-35
2002 Baby's First Christmas (boy) 104204	Yr.Iss.		20.00	20
2002 Baby's First Christmas (girl) 104206	Yr.Iss.		20.00	20
2002 Our First Christmas Together 104207	Yr.Iss.		25.00	25
2002 Home Sweet Home 104208	Yr.Iss.		30.00	30
2002 There's Sno-One Like You 104209	Yr.Iss.		19.00	19
1987 Bear The Good News Of Christmas 104515	Yr.Iss.	1987	12.50	18-24
2002 There's Sno-One Quite Like You-Little Moments 104781	Open		25.00	25
1987 Baby's First Christmas 109401	Yr.Iss.	1987	12.00	37-63
1987 Baby's First Christmas 109428	Yr.Iss.	1987	12.00	30-60
1987 Love Is The Best Gift Of All 109770	Yr.Iss.	1987	11.00	32-63
1987 I'm A Possibility 111120	Suspd.		11.00	27-48
1987 You Have Touched So Many Hearts 112356	Retrd.	1996	11.00	20-42
1987 Waddle I Do Without You 112364	Retrd.	1999	11.00	20-30
1987 I'm Sending You A White Christmas 112372	Suspd.		11.00	20-36
1987 He Cleansed My Soul 112980	Retrd.	1999	12.00	16-30
1987 Our First Christmas Together 112399	Yr.Iss.	1987	11.00	21-47
1988 To My Forever Friend 113956	Retrd.	1999	16.00	17-38
1988 Smile Along The Way 113964	Suspd.		15.00	21-45
1988 God Sent You Just In Time 113972	Suspd.		13.50	30-40
1988 Rejoice O Earth 113980	Retrd.	1991	13.50	19-45
1988 Cheers To The Leader 113999	Suspd.		13.50	23-45
1988 My Love Will Never Let You Go 114006	Suspd.		13.50	27-35
1988 Baby's First Christmas 115282	Yr.Iss.	1988	15.00	28-31
1988 Time To Wish You A Merry Christmas 115320	Yr.Iss.	1988	13.00	27-42
1996 Owl Be Home For Christmas 128708	Yr.Iss.	1996	18.50	16-25
1995 Lighting The Way To A Happy Holiday (Chapel Exclusive) 129275	Open		20.00	20
1995 He Covers The Earth With His Beauty 142662	Yr.Iss.	1995	17.00	20-45
1995 He Covers The Earth With His Beauty (ball) 142689	Yr.Iss.	1995	30.00	26-40
1995 Our First Christmas Together 142700	Yr.Iss.	1995	18.50	17-20
1995 Baby's First Christmas 142719	Yr.Iss.	1995	17.50	16-20
1995 Baby's First Christmas 142727	Yr.Iss.	1995	17.50	16-24
1995 Joy From Head To Mistletoe 150126	Open		18.50	15-19
1995 You're "A" Number One In My Book, Teacher 150142	Open		18.50	15-22
1995 Personalized House 150231	Open		19.95	20-68
1995 Joy To The World (trumpet) 150320	Retrd.	1999	20.00	21-25
1996 Joy To The World (flute) 153338	Retrd.	1999	20.00	18-20
1995 Peace On Earth (Century Circle) 177091	15,000	1995	25.00	26-38
1996 Peace On Earth...Anyway (Ball) 183350	Yr.Iss.	1996	30.00	26-30
1996 Peace On Earth...Anyway 183369	Yr.Iss.	1996	18.50	17-30
1996 God's Precious Gift 183881	Open		20.00	18-20
1996 When The Skating's Ruff, Try Prayer 183903	Open		18.50	17-19
1996 Our First Christmas Together 183911	Yr.Iss.	1996	22.50	21-33
1996 Baby's First Christmas 183938	Yr.Iss.	1996	17.50	16-25
1996 Baby's First Christmas 183946	Yr.Iss.	1996	17.50	16-20
1996 Your Precious Spirit Comes Shining Through 212563	Yr.Iss.	1996	30.00	122
1998 In God's Beautiful Garden Of Love 261599	Open		50.00	50-73
1997 Joy To The World (harp) 272566	Retrd.	1999	20.00	18-20
1997 Cane You Join Us For A Merry Christmas 272671	Yr.Iss.	1997	18.50	17-32
1997 Cane You Join Us For A Merry Christmas 272728	Yr.Iss.	1997	18.50	26-30
1997 Our First Christmas Together 272736	Yr.Iss.	1997	20.00	20-25
1997 Baby's First Christmas (Girl) 272744	Yr.Iss.	1997	18.50	19-22
1997 Baby's First Christmas (Boy) 272752	Yr.Iss.	1997	18.50	17-19
1997 Slow Down For The Holidays 272760	Yr.Iss.	1997	18.50	19-25
1997 Puppies With Sled 272892	Open		18.50	17-19
1997 My Love/Keep You 272965	Retrd.	N/A	20.00	16-22
1998 I'm Sending You A Merry Christmas 455628	Yr.Iss.	1998	18.50	19-25
1998 Our First Christmas Together 455636	Yr.Iss.	1998	25.00	25-28
1998 Baby's First Christmas (Girl) 455644	Yr.Iss.	1998	18.50	18-22
1998 Baby's First Christmas (Boy) 455652	Yr.Iss.	1998	18.50	16-22
1998 I'll Be Dog-ged It's That Season Again 455660	Yr.Iss.	1998	18.50	16-19
1998 I'm Just Nutty About The Holidays 455776	Open		17.50	17-19
1988 Our First Christmas Together 520233	Yr.Iss.	1988	13.00	13-35
1988 Baby's First Christmas 520241	Yr.Iss.	1988	15.00	20-38
1988 You Are My Gift Come True 520276	Yr.Iss.	1988	12.50	15-29
1988 Hang On For The Holly Days 520292	Yr.Iss.	1988	13.00	21-33
1988 A Growing Love 520349	Yr.Iss.	1988	N/A	68
1992 I'm Nuts About You 520411	Yr.Iss.	1992	15.00	15-32
1995 Hippo Holy Days 520403	Yr.Iss.	1995	17.00	26-40
1991 Sno-Bunny Falls For You Like I Do 520438	Yr.Iss.	1991	15.00	25-31
2001 Sno-Ball Without You 520446	Yr.Iss.	2001		18
1998 Happy Holi-daze 520454	Open		17.50	17-19
1989 Christmas is Ruff Without You 520462	Yr.Iss.	1989	13.00	28-36
1993 Slow Down & Enjoy The Holidays 520489	Yr.Iss.	1993	16.00	28-36
1990 Wishing You A Purr-fect Holiday 520497	Yr.Iss.	1990	15.00	25-40
1989 May All Your Christmases Be White 521302 (dated)	Suspd.		15.00	20-50
1999 May All Your Christmases Be White 521302R	Open		20.00	16-20
1989 Our First Christmas Together 521558	Yr.Iss.	1989	17.50	25-30
1990 Glide Through the Holidays 521566	Retrd.	1992	13.50	20-40
1990 Dashing Through the Snow 521574	Suspd.		15.00	20-35
1990 Don't Let the Holidays Get You Down 521590	Retrd.	1994	15.00	20-32
1989 Oh Holy Night 522804	Yr.Iss.	1989	13.50	21-30
1989 Make A Joyful Noise 522910	Suspd.		15.00	16-31
1989 Love One Another 522929	Retrd.	2001	17.50	20-25
1990 Friends Never Drift Apart 522937	Retrd.	1995	17.50	27-53
1991 Our First Christmas Together 522945	Yr.Iss.	1991	17.50	17-28

Collectors' Information Bureau   *Quotes have been rounded up to nearest dollar

ORNAMENTS

Precious Moments/Enesco Group, Inc.
to Precious Moments/Enesco Group, Inc.

YEAR ISSUE	EDITION LIMIT	YEAR RETD.	ISSUE PRICE	*QUOTE U.S.$
1989 I Believe In The Old Rugged Cross 522953	Suspd.		15.00	18-53
1989 Always Room For One More 522961	Retrd.	1989	N/A	83
1989 Peace On Earth 523062	Yr.Iss.	1989	25.00	39-69
1989 Baby's First Christmas 523194	Yr.Iss.	1989	15.00	19-35
1989 Baby's First Christmas 523208	Yr.Iss.	1989	15.00	19-25
1991 Happy Trails Is Trusting Jesus 523224	Suspd.		15.00	18-45
1990 May Your Christmas Be A Happy Home 523704	Yr.Iss.	1990	27.50	26-45
1990 Baby's First Christmas 523798	Yr.Iss.	1990	15.00	14-35
1990 Baby's First Christmas 523771	Yr.Iss.	1990	15.00	14-35
1990 Once Upon A Holy Night 523852	Yr.Iss.	1990	15.00	17-30
1992 Good Friends Are For Always 524131	Retrd.	1996	15.00	28-50
1991 May Your Christmas Be Merry 524174	Yr.Iss.	1991	15.00	28-38
1990 Bundles of Joy 525057	Yr.Iss.	1990	15.00	24-31
1990 Our First Christmas Together 525068	Yr.Iss.	1990	17.50	16-35
1993 Lord, Keep Me On My Toes 525332	Retrd.	2001	15.00	19-50
1991 May Your Christmas Be Merry (on Base) 526940	Yr.Iss.	1991	30.00	30-45
1991 Baby's First Christmas (Boy) 527084	Yr.Iss.	1991	15.00	15-30
1991 Baby's First Christmas (Girl) 527092	Yr.Iss.	1991	15.00	15-40
1991 The Good Lord Always Delivers 527165	Suspd.		15.00	26-42
1993 Share in The Warmth of Christmas 527211	Retrd.	2001	15.00	16-19
1994 Onward Christmas Soldiers 527327	Retrd.	2001	16.00	15-19
1992 Baby's First Christmas 527475	Yr.Iss.	1992	15.00	30-39
1992 Baby's First Christmas 527483	Yr.Iss.	1992	15.00	25-40
1992 But The Greatest of These Is Love 527696	Yr.Iss.	1992	15.00	25-45
1992 But The Greatest of These Is Love 527734 (on Base)	Yr.Iss.	1992	30.00	19-50
1992 There's A Christian Welcome Here (Chapel Exclusive) 528021	Open		22.50	15-31
1994 Sending You A White Christmas 528218	Retrd.	2001	16.00	19-35
1994 Bringing You A Merry Christmas 528226	Retrd.	1998	16.00	15-20
1993 It's So Uplifting to Have a Friend Like You 528846	Retrd.	1999	16.00	16-30
1992 Our First Christmas Together 528870	Yr.Iss.	1992	17.50	30-40
1994 Our 1st Christmas Together 529206	Yr.Iss.	1994	18.50	30-35
1993 Wishing You the Sweetest Christmas 530190	Yr.Iss.	1993	30.00	40-63
1993 Wishing You the Sweetest Christmas 530212	Yr.Iss.	1993	15.00	35-45
1994 Baby's First Christmas 530255	Yr.Iss.	1994	16.00	15-78
1994 Baby's First Christmas 530263	Yr.Iss.	1994	16.00	19-36
1994 You're As Pretty As A Christmas Tree 530387	Yr.Iss.	1994	30.00	37-57
1994 You're As Pretty As A Christmas Tree 530395	Yr.Iss.	1994	16.00	30-50
1993 Our First Christmas Together 530506	Yr.Iss.	1993	17.50	25-36
1993 Baby's First Christmas 530859	Yr.Iss.	1993	15.00	14-25
1993 Baby's First Christmas 530867	Yr.Iss.	1993	15.00	14-30
1994 You Are Always In My Heart 530972	Yr.Iss.	1994	16.00	25-35
1993 Surrounded With Joy 531685	Open		17.50	18-30
1994 Death Can't Keep Him In The Ground (Chapel Exclusive) 531928	Open		30.00	30-36
1994 You Are Always In My Heart (Chapel Exclusive) 532088	Retrd.	1995	17.50	29
1999 Slide Into The Next Millenium with Joy 587788	Open		20.00	20
1999 Our First Christmas Together 587796	Open		25.00	20-25
1999 May Your Wishes For Peace Take Wing 587818	Open		20.00	20
1999 Baby's First Christmas 587826	Yr.Iss.	1999	18.50	15-19
1999 Baby's First Christmas 587834	Yr.Iss.	1999	18.50	19
1999 May Your Christmas Be Delightful 587931	Open		20.00	16-20
1999 Pretty As A Princess 587958	Open		20.00	16-20
1999 The Future Is In Our Hands 730076	Yr.Iss.	1999	19.00	19
2000 Our First Christmas Together 730084	Yr.Iss.	2000	25.00	25
2000 Baby's First Christmas 730092	Yr.Iss.	2000	19.00	19
2000 Baby's First Christmas 730106	Yr.Iss.	2000	19.00	19
2000 One Good Turn Deserves Another 737569	Open		20.00	20
2000 Your Love Keeps Me Toasty Warm (GCC Catalog Exclusive) 795577	Open		25.00	25
2000 Your Love Keeps Me Toasty Warm (GCC Catalog Exclusive) 800813	Yr.Iss.	2000	30.00	30
2000 Let's Keep Our Eyes On The Goal (Canadian Exclusive) 802557	Open		20.00	20
2001 May Your Christmas Begin With A Bang! 877441	Yr.Iss.	2001	19.00	19
2001 Baby's First Christmas 877506	Yr.Iss.	2001	19.00	19
2001 Baby's First Christmas 877514	Yr.Iss.	2001	19.00	19
2001 Our First Christmas Together 878855	Yr.Iss.	2001	25.00	25
2001 You Decorate My Life (GCC Winter Exclusive) 881147	Open		20.00	20
2001 Baby's First Christmas (Avon Exclusive) (Boy) 934038	Yr.Iss.	2001	7.99	8
2001 Baby's First Christmas (Avon Exclusive) (Girl) 934046	Yr.Iss.	2001	7.99	8
2001 Angel Icicle (Avon Exclusive) 952338	Yr.Iss.	2001	7.99	8

Precious Moments Club 15th Anniversary Commemorative Edition - S. Butcher

YEAR ISSUE	EDITION LIMIT	YEAR RETD.	ISSUE PRICE	*QUOTE U.S.$
1993 15 Years Tweet Music Together 530840	Yr.Iss.	1993	15.00	24-40

Precious Moments Club 20th Anniversary Commemorative Edition - S. Butcher

YEAR ISSUE	EDITION LIMIT	YEAR RETD.	ISSUE PRICE	*QUOTE U.S.$
1998 20 Years And The Vision's Still The Same 451312	Yr.Iss.	1998	22.50	19-23
1998 How Can Two Work Together Except They Agree 466268	Yr.Iss.	1998	25.00	25

Christmas Remembered - S. Butcher

YEAR ISSUE	EDITION LIMIT	YEAR RETD.	ISSUE PRICE	*QUOTE U.S.$
2000 One Good Turn Deserves Another 737569	Open		20.00	20

DSR Open House Weekend Ornaments - S. Butcher

YEAR ISSUE	EDITION LIMIT	YEAR RETD.	ISSUE PRICE	*QUOTE U.S.$
1992 The Magic Starts With You 529648	Yr.Iss.	1992	16.00	15-35
1993 An Event For All Seasons 529974	Yr.Iss.	1993	15.00	14-40
1994 Take A Bow Cuz You're My Christmas Star 520470	Yr.Iss.	1994	16.00	15-42
1995 Merry Chrismoose 150134	Yr.Iss.	1995	17.00	20-45
1996 Wishing You a Bearie Merry Christmas 531200	Yr.Iss.	1996	17.50	16-30
1997 Pack Your Trunk For The Holidays 272949	Yr.Iss.	1997	20.00	18-25
1999 Merry Giftness 532223	Yr.Iss.	1999	20.00	16-20

Easter Seal Commemorative Ornaments - S. Butcher

YEAR ISSUE	EDITION LIMIT	YEAR RETD.	ISSUE PRICE	*QUOTE U.S.$
1990 Always In His Care 225290	Yr.Iss.	1990	8.00	7
1991 Sharing A Gift Of Love 233196	Yr.Iss.	1991	8.00	7
1994 It's No Secret What God Can Do 244570	Yr.Iss.	1994	6.50	7
1995 Take Time To Smell The Flowers 128899	Yr.Iss.	1995	7.50	8
1996 You Can Always Count on Me 152579	Yr.Iss.	1996	6.50	7-29
1997 Give Ability A Chance 192384	Yr.Iss.	1997	6.50	7
1998 Somebody Cares 272922	Yr.Iss.	1998	6.50	7
1999 Heaven Bless You 475076	Yr.Iss.	1999	6.50	7
2000 Give Your Whole Heart 634751	Yr.Iss.	2000	9.50	10

Family Ornament Program - S. Butcher

YEAR ISSUE	EDITION LIMIT	YEAR RETD.	ISSUE PRICE	*QUOTE U.S.$
2002 Bringing Bouquets of Love - Daughter 104790	Open		18.50	19
2002 Delivering Lots of Love - Grandpa 104789	Open		18.50	19
2002 Hanging Out For The Holidays - Cat 104795	Open		16.50	17
2002 Holiday Surprises Come In All Sizes - Toddler Son 104793	Open		18.50	19
2002 Hooked On The Holidays - Dog 104791	Open		16.50	17
2002 Making The Holidays Special - Grandma 104788	Open		18.50	19
2002 On One's Sweeter Than You - Mom 104785	Open		18.50	19
2002 Overflowing With Holiday Joy - Toddler Daughter 104792	Open		18.50	19
2002 Packed With Love - Son 104791	Open		18.50	19
2002 Papa's Make The Season Bright - Dad 104786	Open		18.50	19

ORNAMENTS

YEAR ISSUE	EDITION LIMIT	YEAR RETD.	ISSUE PRICE	*QUOTE U.S.$
Members' Only - S. Butcher				
1992 The Club That's Out Of This World PM-38	Yr.Iss.	1992	N/A	60-84
1990 Blessed Are The Poor In Spirit, For Theirs Is The Kingdom of Heaven PM-190	Yr.Iss.	1990	15.00	15
1990 Blessed Are They That Mourn, For They Shall Be Comforted PM-290	Yr.Iss.	1990	15.00	15
1990 Blessed Are The Meek, For They Shall Inherit The Earth PM-390	Yr.Iss.	1990	15.00	15
1990 Blessed Are They That Hunger And Thirst, For They Shall Be Filled PM-490	Yr.Iss.	1990	15.00	15
1990 Blessed Are The Merciful, For They Shall Obtain Mercy PM-590	Yr.Iss.	1990	15.00	15
1990 Blessed Are The Pure In Heart, For They Shall See God PM-690	Yr.Iss.	1990	15.00	15
1990 Blessed Are The Peacemakers, For They Shall Be Called Sons of God PM-790	Yr.Iss.	1990	15.00	15
1990 Set of 7 PM-890	Yr.Iss.	1990	105.00	88-105
Special Edition Members' Only - S. Butcher				
1993 Loving, Caring And Sharing Along The Way PM-040 (Club Appreciation)	Yr.Iss.	1993	12.50	25-35
1994 You Are The End of My Rainbow PM-041	Yr.Iss.	1994	15.00	22-35
Sugartown - S. Butcher				
1993 Sugartown Chapel Ornament 530484	Yr.Iss.	1993	17.50	18-35
1994 Sam's House 530468	Yr.Iss.	1994	17.50	20-38
1995 Dr. Sugar's Office 530441	Yr.Iss.	1995	17.50	16-30
1996 Train Station 18a101	Yr.Iss.	1996	18.50	17-35
Twelve Days Of Christmas - S. Butcher				
1998 My True Love Gave To Me - Day 1 455989	Yr.Iss.	1998	20.00	20
1998 We're Two' Of A Kind - Day 2 455997	Yr.Iss.	1998	20.00	20
1998 Saying 'Oui' To Our Love - Day 3 456004	Yr.Iss.	1998	20.00	20-24
1998 Ringing In The Season - Day 4 456012	Yr.Iss.	1998	20.00	20
1999 The Golden Rings of Friendship - Day 5 456020	Yr.Iss.	1999	20.00	20
1999 Hatching The Perfect Holiday - Day 6 456039	Yr.Iss.	1999	20.00	20
1999 Swimming Into Your Heart - Day 7 456047	Yr.Iss.	1999	20.00	20
1999 Eight Mice A Milking - Day 8 456055	Yr.Iss.	1999	20.00	20
2000 Nine Ladies Dancing w/Joy - Day 9 456063	Yr.Iss.	2000	20.00	20
2000 Leaping Into The Holidays - Day 10 456071	Yr.Iss.	2000	20.00	20
2000 Piping in Perfect Harmony - Day 11 456098	Yr.Iss.	2000	20.00	20
2000 Twelve Drummers Drumming Fun - Day 12 456101	Yr.Iss.	2000	20.00	20

Prizm, Inc./Pipka

YEAR ISSUE	EDITION LIMIT	YEAR RETD.	ISSUE PRICE	*QUOTE U.S.$
Hand Blown Polish Glass Ornaments - Pipka				
2002 Door County Santa 40070	Open		40.00	40
2002 Irish Santa 40066	Open		40.00	40
2002 Old Father Christmas 40072	Open		40.00	40
2002 Polish Father Christmas 40065	Open		40.00	40
2002 Santa & His Snow Friend 40068	Open		40.00	40
2002 St. Nicholas 40067	Open		40.00	40
2002 Teddy Bear Santa 40069	Open		40.00	40
2002 The Winterman 40071	Open		40.00	40
Midnight Visitor Collection - Pipka				
2002 Midnight Visitor 11617	Open		18.00	18
Paint Brush Ornaments - Pipka				
2001 Christmas Ark Santa 40009	Open		10.00	10
2001 Door County Santa 40012	Open		10.00	10
2001 The Irish Santa 40010	Open		10.00	10
2001 Polish Father Christmas 40014	Open		10.00	10
2001 Scottish Santa 40011	Open		10.00	10
2001 Storytime Santa 40008	Open		10.00	10
2001 Teddy Bear Santa 40007	Open		10.00	10

YEAR ISSUE	EDITION LIMIT	YEAR RETD.	ISSUE PRICE	*QUOTE U.S.$
2001 The Winterman 40013	Open		10.00	10
Patriotic Collection - Pipka				
2001 Patriotic Santa 11647	Open		9.00	9
Pipka's Boot Ornaments - Pipka				
2002 Dear Santa Boot Ornament 40040	Open		9.00	9
2002 Polish Father Christmas Boot Ornament 40039	Open		9.00	9
2002 Santa's Boot Ornament 40035	Open		9.00	9
2002 Starcoat Santa Boot Ornament 40037	Open		9.00	9
2002 Teddy Bear Santa Boot Ornament 40038	Open		9.00	9
2002 Where's Rudolph? Boot Ornament 40036	Open		9.00	9
Pipka's Earth Angel Ornaments - Pipka				
1999 Angel of Hearts 11500	Open		15.00	15
1999 Angel of Roses 11502	Open		15.00	15
2001 Carolyn-Angel of Contemplation 11515	Open		15.00	15
1999 Celeste-Angel of Stars 11505	Open		15.00	15
2001 Celestial Angel 11517	Open		15.00	15
1999 Christine-The Christmas Angel 11504	Open		15.00	15
2000 Cottage Angel 11508	Open		15.00	15
2001 Dutch Angel 11518	Open		15.00	15
1999 Elizabeth-Forget-Me-Not Angel 11506	Open		15.00	15
1999 Gardening Angel 11507	Open		15.00	15
2001 The Giving Angel 11516	Open		15.00	15
1999 Guardian Angel 11503	Open		15.00	15
1999 Messenger Angel 11501	Open		15.00	15
2000 Michele The Snow Angel 11509	Open		15.00	15
2000 Pauline-The Poinsettia Angel 11513	Open		15.00	15
2000 Sang-The Teddy Bear Angel 11510	Open		15.00	15
2000 Sylvia-The Song Angel 11511	Open		15.00	15
2001 Victorian Angel 11514	Open		15.00	15
2000 Whitney-The Wedding Angel 11512	Open		15.00	15
Pipka's Stories of Christmas - Pipka				
2002 Alaskan Santa 11444	Open		15.00	15
1999 Amish County Santa 11416	4,024		15.00	15
2001 Aussie Santa (white) 40005	950		8.00	8
1997 Aussie Santa 11404	4,000	1999	15.00	15
1999 Better Watch Out 11420	Open		15.00	15
2002 Caribbean Santa 11441	Open		15.00	15
2001 Carpenter Santa 11435	Open		15.00	15
2001 Chef Claus 11432	Open		15.00	15
2002 A Christmas Journey 11447	Open		15.00	15
2000 The Christmas Traveler 11429	Open		15.00	15
2001 Czechoslovakian Santa (white) 40002	1,000		8.00	8
1997 Czechoslovakian Santa 11401	4,000	1999	15.00	15
2000 Dear Santa 11426	Open		15.00	15
2000 The Door County Santa 11427	4,440	2002	15.00	15
1998 Father Christmas 11412	Open		15.00	15
2002 Feathered Friends 11448	Open		15.00	15
1999 German St. Nick 11424	4,800	2001	15.00	15
1999 Gingerbread Santa 11422	Open		15.00	15
1999 Good News Santa 11417	3,880		15.00	15
1999 Irish Santa 11423	7,320	2001	15.00	15
2001 Laplander Santa 11434	Open		15.00	15
2001 Midnight Visitor (white) 40001	950		8.00	8
1997 Midnight Visitor 11400	4,000	1999	15.00	15
1998 Norwegian/Julenisse Santa 11407	3,680	2000	15.00	15
2001 Old Father Christmas 11436	Open		15.00	15
1998 Peace Maker 11413	3,680	2000	15.00	15
1998 Polish Father Christmas 11408	5,840	2001	15.00	15
1999 Russian Santa 11421	3,880	2001	15.00	15
1998 San Nicolas 11415	3,560		15.00	15
2000 Santa & Snow Friend 11430	Open		15.00	15
2001 Santa With Toys 11437	Open		15.00	15
1998 Santa's Spotted Grey 11411	3,680	2000	15.00	15
2002 Scottish Santa 11442	Open		15.00	15
2002 St. Nicholas & The Christkind 11443	Open		15.00	15
1998 St. Nicholas 11409	5,246	2001	15.00	15
2001 Star Catcher Santa (white) 40004	910		8.00	8
1997 Star Catcher Santa 11403	4,000	1999	15.00	15
2001 Starcoat Santa (white) 40003	950		8.00	8
1997 Starcoat Santa 11402	4,000	1999	15.00	15
1998 Storytime Santa 11410	3,680	2000	15.00	15

YEAR ISSUE	EDITION LIMIT	YEAR RETD.	ISSUE PRICE	*QUOTE U.S.$
2000 Swedish Father Christmas 11431	Open		15.00	15
1998 Teddy Bear Santa 11414	Open		15.00	15
2001 Ukrainian Santa (white) 40006	1,000		8.00	8
1997 Ukrainian Santa 11405	4,000	1999	15.00	15
2001 Victorian Father Christmas 11438	Open		15.00	15
1998 Where's Rudolph? 11406	5,246		15.00	15
2000 The Winterman 11428	Open		15.00	15
1999 Yes Virginia 11425	3,580		15.00	15

Reco International

Heaven Sent - S. Kuck

1999 Angelic Moments	95-day		9.99	10
1999 Dreamy Days	95-day		9.99	10
1999 Heavenly Thoughts	95-day		9.99	10
2000 Heavens Blossom	95-day		9.99	10
2000 Gracious Blessing	95-day		9.99	10
2000 Precious Wonder	95-day		9.99	10
2000 Innocent Spirit	95-day		9.99	10
2000 Sweetest Devotion	95-day		9.99	10
2000 Graceful Touch	95-day		9.99	10
2000 Littlest Miracle	95-day		9.99	10
2000 Sweet Starlight	95-day		9.99	10
2000 Daisy Delight	95-day		9.99	10
2000 Beautiful Bouquet	95-day		9.99	10
2000 Softest Hush	95-day		9.99	10
2000 Heavenly Surprise	95-day		9.99	10
2000 Sunshine Girl	95-day		9.99	10
2001 Always Faithful	95-day		9.99	10
2001 Angelic Promise	95-day		9.99	10
2001 Celestial Hope	95-day		9.99	10
2001 Gentle Breeze	95-day		9.99	10
2001 Gracious Giver	95-day		9.99	10
2001 Happy Harmony	95-day		9.99	10
2001 Heavenly Comfort	95-day		9.99	10
2000 Sweet Laughter	95-day		9.99	10

Sugar & Spice - S. Kuck

1999 Best Friends	95-day		9.99	10
1999 Special Day	95-day		9.99	10
1999 Tea Party	95-day		9.99	10
2000 Storybook Memories	95-day		9.99	10
2000 Cats Cradle	95-day		9.99	10
2000 How Precious	95-day		9.99	10
2001 Morning Prayers	95-day		9.99	10
2001 Teddy Bear Tales	95-day		9.99	10
2001 Morning Visitor	95-day		9.99	10
2001 Going To Town	95-day		9.99	10
2001 Pretty Girl	95-day		9.99	10
2001 Garden Beauty	95-day		9.99	10

Reed & Barton

12 Days of Christmas Sterling and Lead Crystal - Reed & Barton

1988 Partridge in a Pear Tree	Yr.Iss.	1988	25.00	30-40
1989 Two Turtle Doves	Yr.Iss.	1989	25.00	30-40
1990 Three French Hens	Yr.Iss.	1990	27.50	30-40
1991 Four Colly birds	Yr.Iss.	1991	27.50	30-40
1992 Five Golden Rings	Yr.Iss.	1992	27.50	30-40
1993 Six Geese A Laying	Yr.Iss.	1993	27.50	30-40
1994 Seven Swans A 'Swimming	Yr.Iss.	1994	27.50	30-40
1995 Eight Maids A Milking	Yr.Iss.	1995	30.00	30-40
1996 Nine Ladies Dancing	Yr.Iss.	1996	30.00	30-40
1997 Ten Lords a-Leaping	Yr.Iss.	1997	32.50	33-40
1998 Eleven Pipers Piping	Yr.Iss.	1998	32.50	33-40
1999 Twelve Drummers Drumming	Yr.Iss.		35.00	35

Christmas Cross - Reed & Barton

1971 Sterling Silver-1971	Closed	1971	10.00	150-175
1971 24Kt. Gold over Sterling-V1971	Closed	1971	17.50	120-300
1972 Sterling Silver-1972	Closed	1972	10.00	60-125
1972 24Kt. Gold over Sterling-V1972	Closed	1972	17.50	75
1973 Sterling Silver-1973	Closed	1973	10.00	60-85
1973 24Kt. Gold over Sterling-V1973	Closed	1973	17.50	60-85
1974 Sterling Silver-1974	Closed	1974	12.95	75-90
1974 24Kt. Gold over Sterling-V1974	Closed	1974	20.00	60
1975 Sterling Silver-1975	Closed	1975	12.95	35-75
1975 24Kt. Gold over Sterling-V1975	Closed	1975	20.00	50-60
1976 Sterling Silver-1976	Closed	1976	13.95	60
1976 24Kt. Gold over Sterling-V1976	Closed	1976	19.95	45-50

YEAR ISSUE	EDITION LIMIT	YEAR RETD.	ISSUE PRICE	*QUOTE U.S.$
1977 Sterling Silver-1977	Closed	1977	15.00	60
1977 24Kt. Gold over Sterling-V1977	Closed	1977	18.50	45-50
1978 Sterling Silver-1978	Closed	1978	16.00	60
1978 24Kt. Gold over Sterling-V1978	Closed	1978	20.00	50
1979 Sterling Silver-1979	Closed	1979	20.00	50-60
1979 24Kt. Gold over Sterling-V1979	Closed	1979	24.00	45
1980 Sterling Silver-1980	Closed	1980	35.00	50-60
1980 24Kt. Gold over Sterling-V1980	Closed	1980	40.00	45-50
1981 Sterling Silver-1981	Closed	1981	35.00	45-60
1981 24Kt. Gold over Sterling-V1981	Closed	1981	40.00	45-50
1982 Sterling Silver-1982	Closed	1982	35.00	60-65
1982 24Kt. Gold over Sterling-V1982	Closed	1982	40.00	45-50
1983 Sterling Silver-1983	Closed	1983	35.00	60
1983 24Kt. Gold over Sterling-V1983	Closed	1983	40.00	45-50
1984 Sterling Silver-1984	Closed	1984	35.00	45-60
1984 24Kt. Gold over Sterling-V1984	Closed	1984	45.00	50
1985 Sterling Silver-1985	Closed	1985	35.00	60-80
1985 24Kt. Gold over Sterling-V1985	Closed	1985	40.00	40-50
1986 Sterling Silver-1986	Closed	1986	38.50	45-60
1986 24Kt. Gold over Sterling-V1986	Closed	1986	40.00	40-50
1987 Sterling Silver-1987	Closed	1987	35.00	60
1987 24Kt. Gold over Sterling-V1987	Closed	1987	40.00	40-50
1988 Sterling Silver-1988	Closed	1988	35.00	60
1988 24Kt. Gold over Sterling-V1988	Closed	1988	40.00	40-50
1989 Sterling Silver-1989	Closed	1989	35.00	45-50
1989 24Kt. Gold over Sterling-V1989	Closed	1989	40.00	40
1990 Sterling Silver-1990	Closed	1990	40.00	50
1990 24Kt. Gold over Sterling-1990	Closed	1990	45.00	40-45
1991 Sterling Silver-1991	Closed	1991	40.00	50
1991 24Kt. Gold over Sterling-1991	Closed	1991	45.00	40-45
1992 Sterling Silver-1992	Closed	1992	40.00	40-50
1992 24Kt. Gold over Sterling-1992	Closed	1992	45.00	40-45
1993 Sterling Silver-1993	Closed	1993	40.00	40
1993 24Kt. Gold over Sterling-1993	Closed	1993	45.00	35-45
1994 Sterling Silver-1994	Closed	1994	40.00	40
1994 24Kt. Gold over Sterling-1994	Closed	1994	45.00	35-45
1995 Sterling Silver-1995	Closed	1995	40.00	40-45
1995 24Kt. Gold over Sterling-1995	Closed	1995	45.00	35-45
1996 Sterling Silver-1996	Closed	1996	40.00	35-45
1996 Gold Vermiel-1996	Closed	1996	45.00	35-45
1997 Sterling Silver-1997	Closed	1997	40.00	35-40
1997 24Kt. Gold over Sterling-1997	Closed	1997	45.00	30-45
1998 Sterling Silver-1998	Closed	1998	40.00	30-40
1998 24Kt. Gold over Sterling-1998	Closed	1998	45.00	35-45
1999 Sterling Silver-1999	Closed	1999	40.00	40
1999 Vermeil-1999	Closed	1999	45.00	45
2000 Sterling Silver-2000	Yr.Iss.		45.00	45
2000 24 Kt. Vermeil-2000	Yr.Iss.		50.00	50

Holly Ball/Bell - Reed & Barton

1976 1976 Ball	Closed	1976	14.00	26-40
1977 1977 Ball	Closed	1977	15.00	15-26
1978 1978 Ball	Closed	1978	15.00	15-26
1979 1979 Ball	Closed	1979	15.00	15-26
1980 1980 Ball	Closed	1980	22.50	26-35
1980 Bell, gold plate, V1980	Closed	1980	25.00	26-45
1981 1981 Bell	Closed	1981	22.50	26-30
1981 Bell, gold plate, V1981	Closed	1981	27.50	26-35
1982 1982 Bell	Closed	1982	22.50	26-35
1982 Bell, gold plate, V1982	Closed	1982	27.50	26-50
1983 1983 Bell	Closed	1983	23.50	26-45
1983 Bell, gold plate, V1983	Closed	1983	30.00	26-30
1984 1984 Bell	Closed	1984	25.00	26-35
1984 Bell, gold plate, V1984	Closed	1984	28.50	26-50
1985 1985 Bell	Closed	1985	25.00	26-80
1985 Bell, gold plate, V1985	Closed	1985	28.50	26-50
1986 1986 Bell	Closed	1986	25.00	26-75
1986 Bell, gold plate, V1986	Closed	1986	28.50	26-50
1987 1987 Bell	Closed	1987	27.50	26-70
1987 Bell, gold plate, V1987	Closed	1987	30.00	26-50
1988 1988 Bell	Closed	1988	27.50	26-40
1988 Bell, gold plate, V1988	Closed	1988	30.00	26-30
1989 1989 Bell	Closed	1989	27.50	26-55
1989 Bell, gold plate, V1989	Closed	1989	30.00	26-30
1990 Bell, gold plate, V1990	Closed	1990	30.00	26-30
1990 1990 Bell	Closed	1990	27.50	26-55
1991 Bell, gold plate, V1991	Closed	1991	30.00	26-30
1991 1991 Bell	Closed	1991	27.50	26-50
1992 Bell, gold plate, V1992	Closed	1992	30.00	26-30
1992 Bell, silver plate, 1992	Closed	1992	27.50	26-50
1993 Bell, gold plate, V1993	Closed	1993	27.50	28

YEAR ISSUE	EDITION LIMIT	YEAR RETD.	ISSUE PRICE	*QUOTE U.S.$
1993 Bell, silver plate, 1993	Closed	1993	30.00	26-50
1994 Bell, gold plate, 1994	Closed	1994	30.00	26-30
1994 Bell, silver plate, 1994	Closed	1994	27.50	26-30
1995 Bell, gold plate, 1995	Closed	1995	30.00	26-30
1995 Bell, silver plate, 1995	Closed	1995	27.50	26-30
1996 Bell, gold plate, 1996	Closed	1996	35.00	26-35
1996 Bell, silver plate, 1996	Closed	1996	30.00	26-35
1997 Bell, 24Kt. gold plate, 1997	Closed	1997	35.00	26-35
1997 Bell, silver plate, 1997	Closed	1997	30.00	26-30
1998 Bell, 24Kt. gold plate, 1998	Closed	1998	35.00	26-35
1998 Bell, silver plate, 1998	Closed	1998	30.00	26-30
1999 Bell, Sterling, 1999	Closed	1999	50.00	50
1999 Bell, Engraved, 1999	Closed	1999	55.00	55

Roman, Inc.

Animal Kingdom - D. Griff

YEAR ISSUE	EDITION LIMIT	YEAR RETD.	ISSUE PRICE	*QUOTE U.S.$
1994 3 Kittens Sleeping in Basket	Closed	N/A	9.00	9
1994 Bear Cub on Ball	Closed	N/A	10.00	10
1994 Bear Juggling Ball	Closed	N/A	8.00	8
1994 Bear Taking Bath	Closed	N/A	13.50	14
1994 Bear with Bubble on Nose	Closed	N/A	6.50	7
1994 Cat Holding on Ball	Closed	N/A	12.00	12
1994 Cat in Bubbles Jar	Closed	N/A	8.00	8
1994 Cat on Bubble Wand	Closed	N/A	10.00	10
1994 Cat w/Dangling Bubbles	Closed	N/A	9.00	9
1994 Cat w/Mouse on Tail	Closed	N/A	13.50	14
1994 Cat w/Paw on Bubble	Closed	N/A	9.00	9
1994 Chipmunk Blowing Bubble	Closed	N/A	9.50	10
1994 Chipmunk Hangs From Bubble	Closed	N/A	9.00	9
1994 Chipmunk w/Bubble	Closed	N/A	6.50	7
1994 Lounging Cat	Closed	N/A	9.00	10
1994 Mice on Bubble	Closed	N/A	4.00	4
1994 Raccoon Opens Walnut	Closed	N/A	9.00	9
1995 Skunk with Bubble on Tail	Closed	N/A	7.00	7
1995 Squirrel with Bubble	Closed	N/A	4.00	4
1995 Two Chickadees w/Metal Bow	Closed	N/A	17.50	18

Magic of Christmas - D. Morgan

YEAR ISSUE	EDITION LIMIT	YEAR RETD.	ISSUE PRICE	*QUOTE U.S.$
2001 Christmas Future Figural	Open		13.50	14
2001 Christmas Past Figural	Retrd.	2001	13.50	14
2001 Christmas Past Miniature Musical Glitterdome	Retrd.	2001	16.00	16
2001 Christmas Present Figural	Retrd.	2001	13.50	14
2001 Christmas Present Miniature Musical Glitterdome	Retrd.	2001	16.00	16
2000 Magic of Christmas Figural	Retrd.	2001	18.00	18
2000 Magic of Christmas glass ball	Retrd.	2001	40.00	40
2001 Magic of Christmas Miniature Musical Glitterdome	Retrd.	2001	16.00	16
2000 Magic of Giving Figural	Retrd.	2001	18.00	18
2000 Magic of Giving glass ball	Retrd.	2001	40.00	40
2001 Magic of Giving Miniature Musical Glitterdome	Retrd.	2001	16.00	16
2000 Santa's Magic Figural	Retrd.	2001	18.00	18
2000 Santa's Magic glass ball	Retrd.	2001	40.00	40
2001 Santa's Magic Miniature Musical Glitterdome	Retrd.	2001	16.00	16
2001 Yes Virginia, There Is A Santa Claus Figural	Retrd.	2001	13.50	14
2001 Yes Virginia, There Is A Santa Claus Miniature Musical Glitterdome	Retrd.	2001	16.00	16

The Millenium® Collection - G. Ho

YEAR ISSUE	EDITION LIMIT	YEAR RETD.	ISSUE PRICE	*QUOTE U.S.$
2001 Asleep in a Manger	Open		17.50	18
2001 Heaven On Earth	Open		17.50	18
2000 Mary & Jesus Poinsettia Wreath	Open		15.00	15
2001 Peace on Earth	Open		17.50	18
2002 Sent From Above	Open		17.50	18

The Millenium® Collection - Sr. Mary Jean Dorcy

YEAR ISSUE	EDITION LIMIT	YEAR RETD.	ISSUE PRICE	*QUOTE U.S.$
1994 The Annunciation	20,000	1994	20.00	20-75
1995 Cause of Our Joy	20,000	1995	20.00	20
1997 Gentle Love	Yr.Iss.	1997	20.00	20
1999 Heaven's Blessing	Yr.Iss.	1999	20.00	20
1999 Joyful Promise	2-Yr.	2000	20.00	20
1994 Peace On Earth	20,000	1994	20.00	20-66
1996 Prince of Peace	30,000	1994	20.00	20-55
1998 Rejoice	Yr.Iss.	1998	20.00	20
1994 Silent Night	20,000	1994	20.00	20-100

Valencia, Story of Jesus - G. Ho

YEAR ISSUE	EDITION LIMIT	YEAR RETD.	ISSUE PRICE	*QUOTE U.S.$
2000 Holy Family Ornament	Retrd.	2001	12.00	12

Wenceslaus Crowne Ornament Collection - Roman, Inc.

YEAR ISSUE	EDITION LIMIT	YEAR RETD.	ISSUE PRICE	*QUOTE U.S.$
2001 Angel	Open		25.00	25
2001 Ball Ornament	Open		35.00	35
2001 Bell	Open		25.00	25
2001 Candy Cane	Open		30.00	30
2002 Cardinal	Open		25.00	25
2001 Christmas Tree	Yr.Iss.	2001	25.00	25
2002 Christmas Tree, Red & Green	Open		30.00	30
2002 Cross	Open		30.00	30
2002 Holiday Gift	Open		30.00	30
2001 Joyful Heart	Open		20.00	20
2001 Shooting Star	Open		20.00	20
2002 Snowflake	Open		35.00	35
2001 Snowflake with Blue Crystal Accents	Open		25.00	25
2001 Snowman	Open		35.00	35
2002 Star of Bethlehem	Open		20.00	20
2002 Star-Halo Angel	Yr.Iss.		30.00	30
2002 Tear Drop Ornament	Open		30.00	30

Royal Doulton

Bunnykins - Royal Doulton, unless otherwise noted

YEAR ISSUE	EDITION LIMIT	YEAR RETD.	ISSUE PRICE	*QUOTE U.S.$
1991 Santa Bunny - D. Lyttleton	Yr.Iss.	1991	19.00	19
1992 Caroling - D. Lyttleton	Yr.Iss.	1992	19.00	19
1994 Trimming the Tree	Yr.Iss.	1994	20.00	20
1995 Fun in the Snow	Yr.Iss.	1995	20.00	20
1996 Christmas Morn	Yr.Iss.	1996	20.00	20
1997 Home for the Holidays	Yr.Iss.	1997	20.00	20

Christmas Ornaments - Various

YEAR ISSUE	EDITION LIMIT	YEAR RETD.	ISSUE PRICE	*QUOTE U.S.$
1993 Royal Doulton-Together For Christmas - J. James	Yr.Iss.	1993	20.00	20
1993 Royal Albert-Sleighride - N/A	Yr.Iss.	1993	20.00	20
1994 Royal Doulton-Home For Christmas - J. James	Yr.Iss.	1994	20.00	20
1994 Royal Albert-Coaching Inn - N/A	Yr.Iss.	1994	20.00	20
1995 Royal Doulton-Season's Greetings - J. James	Yr.Iss.	1995	20.00	20
1995 Royal Albert-Skating Pond - N/A	Yr.Iss.	1995	20.00	20
1996 Royal Doulton-Night Before Christmas - J. James	Yr.Iss.	1996	20.00	20
1996 Royal Albert-Gathering Winter Fuel - N/A	Yr.Iss.	1996	20.00	20

Merry Wreath Ornaments - Royal Doulton

YEAR ISSUE	EDITION LIMIT	YEAR RETD.	ISSUE PRICE	*QUOTE U.S.$
1998 Angels	Retrd.	1998	17.50	18
1998 Candy Cane	Retrd.	1998	17.50	18
1998 Toyland	Retrd.	1998	17.50	18
1998 Winter Wonderland	Retrd.	1998	17.50	18

Santa Bell Ornaments - V. Heilbron

YEAR ISSUE	EDITION LIMIT	YEAR RETD.	ISSUE PRICE	*QUOTE U.S.$
1998 Father Christmas	Retrd.	1998	25.00	25
1998 Pere Noel	Retrd.	1998	25.00	25
1998 Santa Claus	Retrd.	1998	25.00	25
1998 St. Nicholas	Retrd.	1998	25.00	25

Victorian Card Ornaments - Royal Doulton

YEAR ISSUE	EDITION LIMIT	YEAR RETD.	ISSUE PRICE	*QUOTE U.S.$
1998 Joy	Retrd.	1998	15.00	15
1998 Merry Christmas	Retrd.	1998	15.00	15
1998 Noel	Retrd.	1998	15.00	15
1998 Peace on Earth	Retrd.	1998	15.00	15

San Francisco Music Box Company

Boyds Bears Musical Bearstone - G.M. Lowenthal

YEAR ISSUE	EDITION LIMIT	YEAR RETD.	ISSUE PRICE	*QUOTE U.S.$
1999 Home Sweet Home	Closed	1999	18.00	18
1999 Peace on Earth	Open		18.00	18
1999 Two Hearts	Open		18.00	18

Boyds Bears Musicals-Plush - G. M. Lowenthal

YEAR ISSUE	EDITION LIMIT	YEAR RETD.	ISSUE PRICE	*QUOTE U.S.$
1999 Angelina Cat	Open		10.00	10
1999 Galaxy Bear	Closed	1999	15.00	15
1998 Juliette Bear	Open		10.00	10

Cloissone - San Francisco Music Box Company

YEAR ISSUE	EDITION LIMIT	YEAR RETD.	ISSUE PRICE	*QUOTE U.S.$
1999 Bell	2,500	1999	35.00	35
2000 Bell	Open		40.00	40

YEAR ISSUE	EDITION LIMIT	YEAR RETD.	ISSUE PRICE	*QUOTE U.S.$
Crystal Vision - M. Sarnat				
2001 Dragon with Sphere	Open		16.00	16
Santa - Harley Davidson				
1998 King of the Road Santa	10,000		25.00	25
Wizard of Oz™ - San Francisco Music Box Company				
2001 Cowardly Lion	Closed	2002	22.00	22
2001 Dorothy & Toto	Closed	2002	22.00	22
2001 Glinda	Closed	2002	22.00	22
2001 Scarecrow	Closed	2002	22.00	22
2001 Tinman	Closed	2002	22.00	22
2001 Wicked Witch	Closed	2002	22.00	22

Seraphim Classics®/Roman, Inc.

Seraphim Classics® Club Exclusive Dimensional Ornaments - G. Ho

YEAR ISSUE	EDITION LIMIT	YEAR RETD.	ISSUE PRICE	*QUOTE U.S.$
2000 Cassidy - Blessings From Above	Yr.Iss.	2000	Gift	20
2001 Claire - Angel Friend	Yr.Iss.	2001	Gift	N/A
2002 Phoebe - Heart's Content	Yr.Iss.		Gift	N/A

Seraphim Classics® Tour Exclusive Ornaments - G. Ho

2000 Laurel - Nature's Harmony	Yr.Iss.	2000	15.00	15

Seraphim Classics® Dimensional Ornaments - G. Ho

YEAR ISSUE	EDITION LIMIT	YEAR RETD.	ISSUE PRICE	*QUOTE U.S.$
1999 Annalisa - Celebrating The Millennium	2-Yr.	2001	20.00	20
2001 Cecilia - Gift From the Heart	Open		19.50	20
2000 Celeste - Light of the World	Open		19.50	20
2002 Emily - Heaven's Praise	Open		19.50	20
2001 Holy Family	Open		15.00	15
1999 Hope-Light in the Distance	Closed	2000	20.00	20
1999 Joy-Gift of Heaven	Open		19.50	20
2002 Natalie - Joy to the World	Open		19.50	20
1998 Noelle - Giving Spirit	Open		19.50	20
2002 Taylor - Day Dreamer	Open		19.50	20

Seraphim Classics® Faro Collection - Faro Studios

YEAR ISSUE	EDITION LIMIT	YEAR RETD.	ISSUE PRICE	*QUOTE U.S.$
1994 Rosalyn, Rarest of Heaven	20,000	1994	25.00	25-125
1995 Helena, Heaven's Herald	20,000	1995	25.00	25-70
1996 Flora, Flower of Heaven	20,000	1996	25.00	25-60
1997 Emily, Heaven's Treasure	Yr.Iss.	1997	25.00	25-55
1998 Elise - Heaven's Glory	Yr.Iss.	1998	25.00	25-55
1999 Gwydolyn-Heaven's Triumph	Yr.Iss.	1999	25.00	25-65

Seraphim Classics® Heaven Sent Collection - Seraphim Studios

YEAR ISSUE	EDITION LIMIT	YEAR RETD.	ISSUE PRICE	*QUOTE U.S.$
1997 Hope Eternal	Retrd.	2001	30.00	30
1997 Loving Spirit	Retrd.	2001	30.00	30
1997 Pure At Heart	Retrd.	2001	30.00	30

Seraphim Classics® Wafer Ornaments - G. Ho

YEAR ISSUE	EDITION LIMIT	YEAR RETD.	ISSUE PRICE	*QUOTE U.S.$
2000 Audra - Embraced by Love	Open		15.00	15
1997 Celine - The Morning Star	Retrd.	2001	15.00	15
1998 Chelsea - Summer's Delight	Retrd.	2000	15.00	15
1996 Cymbeline - Peacemaker	Retrd.	1998	15.00	15-20
1999 Diana-Heaven's Rose	Retrd.	2000	15.00	15
1996 Evangeline - Angel of Mercy	Retrd.	1998	15.00	15-20
1996 Felicia - Adoring Maiden	Retrd.	1998	15.00	15-20
1997 Francesca - Loving Guardian	Open		15.00	15
1997 Gabriel - Celestial Messenger	Retrd.	2000	15.00	15
1999 Grace-Born Anew	Retrd.	2001	15.00	15
1999 Hannah-Always Near	Open		15.00	15
1998 Harmony - Love's Guardian	Retrd.	2000	15.00	15
1999 Heather-Autumn Beauty	Retrd.	2000	15.00	15
1995 Iris - Rainbow's End	Retrd.	2000	15.00	15
1995 Isabel - Gentle Spirit	Retrd.	1999	15.00	15
1996 Laurice - Wisdom's Child	Retrd.	1998	15.00	15-20
1996 Lydia - Winged Poet	Retrd.	1998	15.00	15-55
1997 Mariah - Heavenly Joy	Retrd.	2000	15.00	15
1998 Melody - Heaven's Song	Retrd.	2001	15.00	15
2000 Naomi - Nurturing Spirit	Open		15.00	15
1996 Ophelia - Heart Seeker	Retrd.	1998	15.00	15-20
1996 Priscilla - Benevolent Guide	Retrd.	1998	15.00	15-20
1998 Rachel - Children's Joy	Open		15.00	15
1997 Rosalie - Nature's Delight	Open		15.00	15
1999 Samantha-Blessed at Birth	Open		15.00	15
1998 Seraphina - Heaven's Helper	Retrd.	1998	15.00	15
1997 Serena - Angel of Peace	Retrd.	2000	15.00	15
1998 Tamara - Blessed Guardian	Retrd.	2000	15.00	15

Slavic Treasures

Treasure Hunters Club - G. Lewis

YEAR ISSUE	EDITION LIMIT	YEAR RETD.	ISSUE PRICE	*QUOTE U.S.$
2000 2000 Treasures 00-CLUB	Yr.Iss.	2000	45.00	45
2001 Americana Santa 01-CLUB	Yr.Iss.	2001	45.00	45
2002 Springtime Santa 02-CLUB	Yr.Iss.		45.00	45

Event - G. Lewis

2001 Blooming Brightly (Poinsettia Disk)	Yr.Iss.	2001	24.00	24
2002 Holiday Treasure	Yr.Iss.		27.00	27

Charity Designs - G. Lewis

2001 Shambala Logo SHA-01	Yr.Iss.	2001	30.00	30

1998 Animal Collages - G. Lewis

YEAR ISSUE	EDITION LIMIT	YEAR RETD.	ISSUE PRICE	*QUOTE U.S.$
1998 Elephant Ball PG-088	Closed	1998	34.00	35
1998 Kitten Ball PG-087	Closed	1998	34.00	34
1998 Rabbit Ball PG-086	Closed	1998	34.00	35

1998 Christmas Icons - G. Lewis

1998 Bunches O' Santa Ball PG-092	Closed	1998	34.00	35
1998 Christmas Candy Ball PG-093	Closed	1998	34.00	35
1998 Holiday Fancy Ball PG-094	Closed	1998	34.00	35

1998 Christmas Nostalgia - G. Lewis

1998 Ania's Dollhouse PG-030	Closed	1998	32.00	33
1998 Aunt Betty's Cookies PG-032	Closed	1998	33.00	34
1998 Deck the Halls PG-031	Closed	1998	33.00	33-46
1998 Tomek's Train PG-029	Closed	1998	32.00	33

1998 Classic Christmas - G. Lewis

YEAR ISSUE	EDITION LIMIT	YEAR RETD.	ISSUE PRICE	*QUOTE U.S.$
1998 Cheerful Cherubs PG-011	Closed	1998	33.00	34
1998 Chest O' Fun PG-072	Closed	1998	31.00	31
1998 Four Hands Required PG-013	Closed	1998	33.00	33-42
1998 Fresh Delivery PG-012	Closed	1998	33.00	33-38
1998 Heavenly Harpist PG-010	Closed	1998	31.00	31-38
1998 Heavenly Light PG-059	Closed	1998	31.00	32
1998 Heavenly Package PG-058	Closed	1998	31.00	31
1998 Heavenly Prayer PG-009	Closed	1998	31.00	31
1998 Heavenly Star-catcher PG-057	Closed	1998	31.00	32
1998 Holiday Hard Drive PG-074	Closed	1998	32.00	32
1998 Hot Doggin' PG-054	Closed	1998	35.00	36-50
1998 King with Frankincense PG-006	Closed	1998	31.00	31
1998 King with Gold PG-005	Closed	1998	31.00	31
1998 King with Myrrh PG-007	Closed	1998	31.00	31
1998 Oh, Tannenbaum PG-008	Closed	1998	31.00	31
1998 Stately Dazzler PG-055	Closed	1998	33.00	33
1998 Totem Elf Cane PG-061	Closed	1998	40.00	40
1998 Totem Santa Cane PG-075	Closed	1998	40.00	40
1998 Totem Santa Icicle PG-076	Closed	1998	40.00	40
1998 Toy Soldier Cane PG-062	Closed	1998	40.00	40
1998 Wrap Me Up PG-014	Closed	1998	32.00	32

1998 Elegant Birds - G. Lewis

1998 Feather-Crown Jewel Peacock FB-016	Closed	1998	37.00	37-48
1998 Fine Feathers - Blue Band FB-029	Closed	1998	37.00	37-56
1998 Fine Feathers - Feather Top FB-027	Closed	1998	37.00	37
1998 Fine Feathers - Gold Band FB-030	Closed	1998	37.00	37
1998 Fine Feathers - White Band FB-028	Closed	1998	37.00	37
1998 Rainbow Peacock FB-026	Closed	1998	37.00	37
1998 Winter Peacock FB-015	Closed	1998	37.00	37

1998 Fresh Fruits - G. Lewis

1998 Fruit and Leaves Ball PG-089	Closed	1998	34.00	34-40
1998 Fruit Bowl Ball PG-090	Closed	1998	34.00	34
1998 Fruit Slice Ball PG-091	Closed	1998	34.00	34

1998 Frog Ballet/Orchestra Series - G. Lewis

YEAR ISSUE	EDITION LIMIT	YEAR RETD.	ISSUE PRICE	*QUOTE U.S.$
1998 Bow-Tie Bullfrog FB-007	Closed	1998	37.00	37
1998 Frog Astaire FB-006	Closed	1998	37.00	38
1998 Frog King FB-008	Closed	1998	37.00	37-42
1998 Green Kelley FB-014	Closed	1998	37.00	37
1998 Maestro FB-009	Closed	1998	37.00	38
1998 Pretty Prancer FB-013	Closed	1998	37.00	37
1998 Tutu Toad FB-005	Closed	1998	37.00	38
1998 Twinkle Toes FB-004	Closed	1998	37.00	37

1998 Full Bloom Series - G. Lewis

1998 Full Bloom Daisies PG-080	Closed	1998	32.00	33
1998 Full Bloom Irises PG-081	Closed	1998	32.00	33
1998 Full Bloom Mixed Roses PG-085	Closed	1998	32.00	33
1998 Full Bloom Red Roses PG-084	Closed	1998	32.00	33

YEAR ISSUE	EDITION LIMIT	YEAR RETD.	ISSUE PRICE	*QUOTE U.S.$
1998 Full Bloom Sunflowers PG-082	Closed	1998	32.00	33
1998 Full Bloom Tiger Lillies PG-083	Closed	1998	32.00	33

1998 Holiday Critters - G. Lewis

1998 Acrobatic Tree-trimmers PG-017	Closed	1998	32.00	33
1998 Beary Much Love PG-018	Closed	1998	32.00	32
1998 Geoffrey Giraffe PG-020	Closed	1998	33.00	33-38
1998 It's YOU, Daddy! PG-015	Closed	1998	33.00	33-38
1998 Kelly Kitty PG-019	Closed	1998	33.00	33
1998 Mama's Safe Arms PG-016	Closed	1998	32.00	32
1998 Zeke Zebra PG-021	Closed	1998	33.00	33-39

1998 Jolly Roger Pirates - G. Lewis

1998 Captain Christmas PG-038	Closed	1998	32.00	32
1998 Jolly Roger PG-041	Closed	1998	32.00	32
1998 Lucky's Loot PG-040	Closed	1998	32.00	32
1998 One-Eyed Pete PG-039	Closed	1998	32.00	32

1998 Lamps - G. Lewis

1998 Orange Ball Tiffany FB-021	Closed	1998	33.00	33
1998 Pink Ridge Tiffany FB-022	Closed	1998	33.00	33
1998 White Point Tiffany FB-023	Closed	1998	33.00	33

1998 Modern Art - G. Lewis

1998 Cocoon PG-065	Closed	1998	32.00	32
1998 Infinity PG-064	Closed	1998	32.00	32

1998 Officially Licensed Grateful Dead Designs - G. Lewis

1998 At The Show GG-001	Closed	2001	25.00	27
1998 Bearly Dancin' GG-005	Closed	2001	25.00	27
1998 Bearly Jammin' GG-007	Closed	2001	25.00	27
1998 Bearly Shufflin' GG-006	Closed	2001	25.00	27
1998 Chorus Line GG-002	Closed	2001	25.00	27
1998 Love Our Earth GG-008	Closed	2001	25.00	27
1998 Skull and Roses GG-009	Closed	2001	25.00	27
1998 Steal Your Face GG-003	Closed	2001	25.00	27
1998 Steal Your Tree GG-004	Closed	2001	25.00	27

1998 Old McDonald - G. Lewis

1998 ... There Was A Dog PG-035	Closed	1998	32.00	33
1998 ... There Was A Horse PG-034	Closed	1998	32.00	33
1998 ... There Was A Pig PG-036	Closed	1998	30.00	30-32
1998 ... There Was A Sheep PG-037	Closed	1998	30.00	30-32
1998 Old McDonald PG-033	Closed	1998	33.00	33

1998 Retailer Designs - G. Lewis

1998 Gleam Team I - Diamond RT-03	500	1998	34.00	34
1998 Gleam Team I - Emerald RT-01	500	1998	34.00	34
1998 Gleam Team I - Ruby RT-02	500	1998	34.00	34

1998 Saint Nicholas - G. Lewis

1998 Blue-bell Santa PG-004	Closed	1998	33.00	34
1998 Classic Claus PG-005	Closed	1998	28.50	29-34
1998 Golden Santa PG-003	Closed	1998	33.00	33-42
1998 Regal Santa PG-002	Closed	1998	33.00	34-40
1998 Santa in the Hood PG-006	Closed	1998	33.00	29-33
1998 Toy Bundle PG-001	Closed	1998	33.00	33-39

1998 SETS - Grecian, Urns, and Neptune - G. Lewis

1998 Black and White Urns FB-033	Closed	1998	60.00	60
1998 Grecian Tabletop FB-032	Closed	1998	96.00	96
1998 Neptune Set - 5 pcs. FB-034	Closed	1998	56.00	56

1998 Singing Moons - G. Lewis

1998 Crescent Crooner FB-036	Closed	1998	37.00	37
1998 Moonlight Melody FB-035	Closed	1998	37.00	37
1998 Moonlight Serenade FB-024	Closed	1998	37.00	37

1998 Small Wonders - G. Lewis

1998 Angel of Peace PG-049	Closed	1998	13.00	13
1998 Bonzo PG-050	Closed	1998	10.50	11
1998 Cross-legged Kringle PG-044	Closed	1998	14.00	14
1998 Gold Fish - "Make A Wish" PG-053	Closed	1998	10.50	11
1998 Gold Star Santa PG-063	Closed	1998	12.50	13
1998 Harold Bear PG-067	Closed	1998	12.50	13
1998 King's Court Clown PG-051	Closed	1998	10.50	11
1998 Load of Goodies PG-042	Closed	1998	15.50	16
1998 Madonna and Child PG-048	Closed	1998	13.00	13
1998 The Santa Express PG-043	Closed	1998	14.00	14-20
1998 Smiling Moon PG-066	Closed	1998	10.50	11
1998 Teddy Loves Presents PG-046	Closed	1998	12.50	13
1998 Teddy's Ice Cream PG-073	Closed	1998	12.50	13
1998 Teddy's Toy PG-045	Closed	1998	12.50	13

YEAR ISSUE	EDITION LIMIT	YEAR RETD.	ISSUE PRICE	*QUOTE U.S.$
1998 Winter Bunny PG-052	Closed	1998	10.50	11
1998 Winter Warm-up PG-047	Closed	1998	13.00	13

1998 Special Event/Commemorative Designs - G. Lewis

1998 Autumn Antics SE-003	250	1998	34.00	34-38
1998 Beach-Bum Santa SE-004	150	1998	34.00	34
1998 First Year Fanfare SE-001	1,500	1998	34.00	34
1998 Hawaiian Holiday SE-010	15	1998	Gift	40
1998 Lobster Limbo SE-008	250	1998	34.00	34
1998 Patriotic Santa SE-007	250	1998	34.00	34-42
1998 Peach Pal SE-002	250	1998	34.00	34
1998 Reardon Hearts SE-009	350	1998	25.00	25
1998 Regal Santa in Green SE-006	250	1998	34.00	34
1998 Seaside Santa SE-005	250	1998	34.00	34-38
1998 Six-Shootin' Santa SE-011	15	1998	Gift	40-45

1998 The L.E. Phant Family - G. Lewis

1998 Junior FB-003	Closed	1998	37.00	37
1998 Momma's Girl FB-025	Closed	1998	37.00	37
1998 Mr. L.E. Phant FB-001	Closed	1998	37.00	37-150
1998 Mrs. Phant FB-002	Closed	1998	37.00	37

1998 Tree-toppers and Coordinating Balls - G. Lewis

1998 Holiday Reflections PG-095	Closed	1998	31.00	31
1998 Holiday Reflections Dazzler PG-096	Closed	1998	33.00	33
1998 Holiday Reflections Tree-Topper TT-001	Closed	1998	56.00	56

1998 Vases - G. Lewis

1998 Black Vase FB-019	Closed	1998	33.00	33
1998 Blue Vase FB-018	Closed	1998	33.00	33
1998 Coffee Mug FB-020	Closed	1998	26.00	26
1998 White Vase FB-017	Closed	1998	33.00	33

1998 Way-Out Bugs and Such - G. Lewis

1998 Gentleman Ant FB-011	Closed	1998	37.00	37
1998 Green "Kootie" FB-013	Closed	1998	37.00	37
1998 Jeepers Creepers FB-010	Closed	1998	37.00	37
1998 Queen Bee FB-012	Closed	1998	37.00	37

1998 World Wildlife Series - G. Lewis

1998 African Elephant PG-023	Closed	1998	33.00	33-42
1998 Bengal Tiger PG-024	Closed	1998	32.00	32-42
1998 Black Rhino PG-025	Closed	1998	33.00	33-42
1998 Lion PG-026	Closed	1998	32.00	32-40
1998 Monkey PG-027	Closed	1998	32.00	33
1998 Zebra PG-028	Closed	1998	32.00	32-40

1999 Aliens - G. Lewis

1999 Star-Belly 99-159-A-FB	300	1999	48.00	49

1999 Allyson's Corner - Limited Edition Sculpted Orbs - B. Lewis

1999 Butterfly Ball 99-086-A	1,000	1999	85.00	86
1999 Fantasy Bird Ball 99-089-A	1,000	1999	68.00	68
1999 Fish and Coral Ball 99-090-A	1,000	1999	74.00	74
1999 Flamingo Ball 99-088-A	1,000	1999	68.00	68
1999 Hummingbird Ball 99-087-A	1,000	1999	85.00	86
1999 Winter Cardinal Ball 99-091-A	1,000	1999	68.00	69

1999 Angel Series - G. Lewis

1999 Heavenly Light - Glitter '99 98-059-B	Closed	1999	38.00	38
1999 Millennium Angel 99-033-A	Closed	1999	38.00	38

1999 Animal Collage Series - G. Lewis

1999 Elephant Ball 98-088-B	Closed	1999	42.00	35-43
1999 Jurassic Ball 99-074-A	Closed	2001	42.00	42
1999 Kitten Ball 98-087-B	Closed	1999	42.00	43
1999 Puppy Ball 99-073-A	Closed	1999	42.00	43
1999 Rabbit Ball 98-086-B	Closed	2001	42.00	42

1999 Beary Merry Christmas - G. Lewis

1999 It's YOU, Daddy! 98-015-B	Closed	1999	38.00	39
1999 Mama's Safe Arms 98-016-B	Closed	1999	36.00	36-37
1999 Roll Away (With You) 99-036-A	Closed	1999	36.00	36-37

1999 Bugs - G. Lewis

1999 Fly Guy 99-155-A-FB	300	1999	85.00	85
1999 Gentleman Ant - Glitter '99 98-111-B-FB	600	1999	48.00	48
1999 Goldstinger 99-156-A-FB	150	1999	135.00	135-300
1999 Jeepers Baby 99-153-A-FB	600	1999	48.00	48
1999 Jeepers Daddy - '99 98-110-D-FB	600	1999	48.00	49

YEAR ISSUE	EDITION LIMIT	YEAR RETD.	ISSUE PRICE	*QUOTE U.S.$
1999 Jeepers Momma 99-152-A-FB	600	1999	48.00	49
1999 The Lady's A Bug 99-157-A-FB	1,000	2001	48.00	48-50
1999 Rainbow "Kootie" - '99 98-113-B-FB	600	1999	48.00	49
1999 Whopper Hopper 99-154-A-FB	1,000	2001	44.00	44

1999 By The Seashore - G. Lewis

1999 Seashell Cluster I - Sanddollar 99-043-A	Open		40.00	40
1999 Seashell Cluster II - Conch 99-044-A	Open		40.00	40

1999 Cat Breeds - G. Lewis

1999 Flame-Point Himalayan 99-063-A	Open		38.00	40
1999 Tin Roof Prowler 99-062-A	Open		38.00	40

1999 Christmas At The Zoo Series - G. Lewis

1999 Charlie Chimp 99-046-A	Closed	2001	38.00	38
1999 Emily Elephant 99-045-A	Closed	2001	38.00	38
1999 Geoffrey Giraffe - Glitter '99 98-020-B	Closed	2001	38.00	38
1999 Zeke Zebra - Glitter '99 98-021-B	Closed	2001	38.00	38

1999 Christmas Canes - G. Lewis

1999 Fruit Cane 99-114-A	Closed	1999	56.00	57
1999 Kitten Cane 99-113-A	Closed	1999	56.00	56
1999 Totem Santa Cane Glitter 98-075-C	Closed	1999	56.00	57

1999 Christmas Icon Series - G. Lewis

1999 Bunches O' Santa Ball 98-092-B	Closed	1999	40.00	40
1999 Christmas Candy Ball 98-093-B	Closed	1999	40.00	40
1999 Holiday Fancy Ball 98-094-B	Closed	1999	40.00	40

1999 Classic Christmas Series - G. Lewis

1999 Best Friends 99-025-A	Closed	2001	32.00	34-36
1999 Gift-Wrapped 99-026-A	Open		38.00	40
1999 Hear Them Ring 99-028-A	Closed	1999	32.00	33
1999 Hot Doggin' - Glitter 98-054-C	Closed	1999	48.00	48-50
1999 Polar Pals 99-024-A	Closed	2001	36.00	36-38
1999 Ski Bear 99-023-A	Closed	1999	48.00	48
1999 Tannenbaum 98-008-B	Closed	1999	36.00	37
1999 Two of a Feather 99-177-A	Closed	2001	38.00	40
1999 Woody 99-027-A	Closed	2001	38.00	40

1999 Cosmic Collection - G. Lewis

1999 Big Head and Spot 99-082-A	Closed	2001	40.00	40-42
1999 Big's Cruiser 99-083-A	Closed	2001	36.00	36
1999 Rocket Ride 99-081-A	Closed	2001	38.00	38
1999 Space Cadet 99-080-A	Closed	2001	42.00	42

1999 Crystal Kringles - Series I - G. Lewis

1999 Amber Santa 99-013-A	Open		47.00	47
1999 Amethyst Santa 99-014-A	Open		47.00	47
1999 Malachite Santa 99-015-A	Open		47.00	47
1999 Rose Quartz Santa 99-016-A	Open		47.00	47

1999 Dog Breeds - G. Lewis

1999 Black Lab 99-060-A	Open		38.00	40
1999 Dalmation 99-059-A	Open		40.00	42
1999 English Bulldog 99-058-A	Open		38.00	40
1999 Yellow Lab 99-061-A	Open		38.00	40
1999 Yorkshire Terrier 99-057-A	Open		36.00	38

1999 Easter Designs - G. Lewis

1999 Goose Party 99-128-A	Closed	2001	40.00	40
1999 Just Hatched 99-124-A	Closed	2001	32.00	32
1999 Robert Rabbit 99-125-A	Closed	2001	34.00	34
1999 Rose and Roxy Rabbit 99-126-A	Closed	2001	34.00	34-40
1999 Spring Parade 99-127-A	Closed	2001	38.00	34-39

1999 Elegant Birds - G. Lewis

1999 Feather-Crown Jewel Peacock 98-116-B-FB	300	2001	48.00	48
1999 Fine Feathers - Blue Band 98-129-B-FB	300	1999	56.00	56

1999 Floral Elegance - G. Lewis

1999 Flower Cluster I 99-072-A	Open		38.00	40
1999 Full Bloom Irises 98-081-B	Closed	2001	40.00	40-42
1999 Full Bloom Poinsettias 99-071-A	Open		40.00	42
1999 Full Bloom Red Roses 98-084-B	Closed	2001	40.00	40-42
1999 Full Bloom Sunflowers 98-082-B	Closed	2001	40.00	40-42
1999 Sugar Magnolia - Blossoms Bloomin' 99-070-A	Closed	1999	40.00	40-42

YEAR ISSUE	EDITION LIMIT	YEAR RETD.	ISSUE PRICE	*QUOTE U.S.$

1999 Frog Series - 1st in Series of 3 - G. Lewis

1999 Mr. Saxy 99-151-A-FB	150	1999	90.00	90
1999 Number 3 99-150-A-FB	300	1999	56.00	56

1999 Frogs - G. Lewis

1999 Frog Astaire - Glitter Boy 99 98-106-B-FB	600	1999	48.00	49
1999 Frog King - Purple Robe 99 98-108-B-FB	600	1999	48.00	49
1999 Maestro - White Tux 99 98-109-B-FB	600	1999	48.00	49
1999 Mr. Happy Hoppy 99-146-A-FB	1,000	1999	44.00	45
1999 Mrs. Happy Hoppy 99-147-A-FB	1,000	1999	44.00	44
1999 Pea Green - The Spotted Toad 99-148-A-FB	150	1999	48.00	48

1999 Fruit and Vegetable "Clusters" Series - G. Lewis

1999 Fruit and Leaves Ball 98-089-B	Closed	2001	40.00	40
1999 Fruit Cluster I - Watermelon 99-037-A	Closed	2001	38.00	38
1999 Fruit Cluster II - Banana 99-038-A	Closed	2001	38.00	38
1999 Pairs of Pears 99-039-A	Closed	2001	38.00	38
1999 Sun Kissed 99-040-A	Closed	2001	38.00	38
1999 Veggie Cluster I - Corn 99-041-A	Closed	2001	38.00	38
1999 Veggie Cluster II - Tomato 99-042-A	Closed	2001	38.00	38

1999 Garlands - G. Lewis

1999 Halloween Collection Garland I 99-120-A	Closed	1999	115.00	116
1999 Holiday Travel Garland 99-119-A	Closed	1999	115.00	115
1999 Santa and Packages Garland 99-118-A	Closed	1999	115.00	116
1999 Santa Bell Garland 99-117-A	Closed	1999	115.00	115

1999 Ghosts - G. Lewis

1999 Polter Gal 99-164-A-FB	600	2001	48.00	48
1999 Polter Guy 99-165-A-FB	600	2001	48.00	48
1999 Pumpkin Haid 99-166-A-FB	150	2001	135.00	135

1999 Halloween Harvest Goodies - G. Lewis

1999 The A. P. Reeshun Family 99-138-A	Closed	1999	38.00	38-40
1999 Blue Boo 99-134-A	Closed	1999	36.00	37
1999 Funny Phantom 99-135-A	Closed	2001	36.00	36
1999 Perry Normal 99-140-A	Closed	2001	40.00	40
1999 Pinkie Poltergeist 99-133-A	Closed	1999	36.00	37
1999 Scary Airy 99-137-A	Closed	2001	36.00	36
1999 Skeleton Sam 99-141-A	Closed	1999	34.00	35
1999 Spooky Specter 99-136-A	Closed	2001	36.00	36
1999 Witchy's Kitty 99-139-A	Closed	2001	40.00	40-42

1999 Just For Fun - G. Lewis

1999 America's Cup 99-084-A	Closed	1999	38.00	39
1999 Holiday Hard-drive 98-074-B	Closed	1999	38.00	38
1999 Sour Grapes 99-085-A	Closed	2001	42.00	42

1999 Nostalgia Series - G. Lewis

1999 Ania's Dollhouse 98-030-B	Closed	1999	38.00	39
1999 Deck the Halls - Glitter 98-031-B	Closed	2001	46.00	46
1999 Happy First 99-035-A	Closed	1999	44.00	45
1994 A Teddy From Mama 99-034-A	Closed	1999	44.00	45

1999 Pedestal Designs - Annealed Glass Stands - G. Lewis

1999 Royal Crown Egg 99-170-A-PD	150	1999	135.00	136
1999 Santa Sleigh Egg 99-169-A-PD	150	1999	135.00	136
1999 Standing Figurine - Amber Santa 99-173-A-PD	300	1999	135.00	136
1999 Standing Figurine - Deck The Halls 99-171-A-PD	300	1999	110.00	111
1999 Standing Figurine - White Whistler 99-176-A-PD	300	1999	110.00	111
1999 Standing Figurine - Woodland Santa 99-172-A-PD	300	1999	110.00	111

1999 Retailer Designs - G. Lewis

1999 Gleam Team II - Elf with Diamond 99-180-C	600	2000	38.00	38
1999 Gleam Team II - Elf with Emerald 99-180-A	600	2000	38.00	38
1999 Gleam Team II - Elf with Ruby 99-180-B	600	2000	38.00	38

1999 Saint Nicholas - G. Lewis

1999 Beach-Bum Santa 99-010-B	Closed	1999	38.00	39
1999 Checking It Twice 99-001-A	Closed	1999	38.00	39
1999 Christmas Carp 99-005-A	Closed	1999	40.00	40

ORNAMENTS

YEAR ISSUE	EDITION LIMIT	YEAR RETD.	ISSUE PRICE	*QUOTE U.S.$
1999 Classic Claus in Red 98-056-B	Closed	2001	32.00	32
1999 Ebony Santa 99-006-A	Closed	2001	38.00	40
1999 Golden Flame Santa 98-003-B	Closed	2001	40.00	40
1999 Leader of the Band 99-008-A	Closed	2001	38.00	38-40
1999 Patriotic Santa 99-009-B	Closed	2001	42.00	44-47
1999 Pause For St. Nick 99-003-A	Closed	2001	40.00	40-42
1999 Regal Santa in Red 98-002-C	Closed	2001	38.00	38
1999 Santa's Secret (Behind His Back) 99-002-A	Closed	2001	42.00	42-44
1999 Seaside Santa 99-011-B	Closed	2001	40.00	40
1999 Silver-bell Santa in Blue 98-004-B	Closed	1999	38.00	39
1999 Six-Shootin' Santa 99-012-C	Closed	2001	40.00	42
1999 Toy Bundle 98-001-B	Closed	1999	38.00	39
1999 Winter Winks - cobalt blue 99-007-B	Closed	1999	32.00	32-34
1999 Winter Winks - purple 99-007-C	Closed	1999	32.00	32-34
1999 Winter Winks - red 99-007-A	Closed	2001	32.00	34
1999 Woodland Santa 99-004-A	Closed	2001	42.00	42-44

1999 Santa's Elves - G. Lewis

1999 Autumn Antics 99-018-C	Closed	2001	38.00	38-40
1999 Four Hands Required 98-013-B	Closed	1999	42.00	42
1999 Fresh Delivered Ornament 98-012-B	Closed	1999	38.00	39
1999 Hangin' On 99-022-A	Open		42.00	42
1999 Joyful Noises 99-020-A	Open		32.00	34
1999 Peach Pal 99-017-C	Closed	1999	38.00	38
1999 Pepper Meant Elf 99-021-A	Closed	2001	30.00	30-32
1999 Pining For Christmas 99-019-B	Closed	2001	40.00	42

1999 Seasonal Egg Designs - G. Lewis

1999 Autumn Egg - Harvest 99-132-A	Closed	2001	36.00	38
1999 Spring Egg - Blossom 99-131-A	Closed	2001	36.00	38
1999 Summer Egg - Fire 99-129-A	Closed	2001	36.00	38
1999 Winter Egg - Ice 99-130-A	Closed	2001	36.00	38

1999 Small Wonders Series (Smaller Size) - G. Lewis

1999 Bats-'n-Spiders Santa 99-107-A	Closed	1999	24.00	25
1999 Chilly Charlie 99-092-A	Closed	2001	25.00	25
1999 Christmas Morn Surprise 99-099-A	Open		28.00	28
1999 Cobalt Santa Head 99-100-A	Closed	1999	24.00	25
1999 Enchantress 99-105-A	Closed	2001	26.00	26
1999 Fruit Cluster - Mini 99-104-A	Closed	1999	26.00	27
1999 Hall Decker 99-101-A	Closed	1999	30.00	30
1999 Harold Bear - Glitter 98-067-B	Closed	1999	20.00	20
1999 Ice Rink Cutie 99-093-A	Closed	1999	28.00	29
1999 Lion Head - Mini 99-103-A	Open		30.00	30
1999 Little Nicholas 99-096-A	Closed	2001	25.00	25
1999 Littlest Golf Pro 99-097-A	Closed	2001	25.00	25
1999 Pint-Size Specter 99-108-A	Closed	2001	22.00	22
1999 Purple Fish 98-053-B	Closed	1999	20.00	20
1999 Rock-A-Billy 99-098-A	Closed	2001	25.00	25
1999 Ski Boy 99-094-A	Closed	2001	25.00	25
1999 Super Kid 99-106-A	Closed	2001	26.00	26
1999 Sweet Susie 99-095-A	Closed	2001	25.00	25
1999 Tiger Head - Mini 99-102-A	Open		30.00	30

1999 Small-Size Santas - G. Lewis

1999 Lighten Your Holiday 99-110-A	Closed	2001	30.00	30
1999 North Wind Santa 99-111-A	Closed	2001	30.00	30-32
1999 Old World Wanderer 99-112-A	Closed	2001	30.00	30-32
1999 Santa's Tree 99-109-A	Closed	2001	30.00	30-32

1999 Snowmen/Snowwomen - G. Lewis

1999 Polar Postage 99-032-A	Open		38.00	40
1999 Snowman Santa 99-030-A	Open		38.00	40
1999 White Whistler 99-029-A	Open		38.00	40
1999 Wintry Woman 99-031-A	Closed	1999	38.00	38-39

1999 Special Event/Commemorative Designs - G. Lewis

1999 Second Year Santa 99-144-A	1,500	1999	40.00	40

1999 St. Patrick's - G. Lewis

1999 Catch Lucky! 99-123-A	Closed	2001	36.00	36

1999 Stocking Stuffers - G. Lewis

1999 Kyle Kitty 98-019-B	Closed	1999	38.00	38-39
1999 Paulie Puppy 99-047-A	Closed	1999	38.00	38-39
1999 Peggy Pig 99-048-A	Closed	1999	38.00	38

1999 Thanksgiving Designs - G. Lewis

1999 Giving Thanks 99-143-A	Closed	2001	40.00	40
1999 Pilgrim's Bounty 99-142-A	Closed	2001	38.00	38-40

YEAR ISSUE	EDITION LIMIT	YEAR RETD.	ISSUE PRICE	*QUOTE U.S.$
1999 The Night Before Christmas - (Boxed, Numbered, Tagged Set) First In Series - G. Lewis				
1999 Night Before Christmas I (Santa Driver, Dasher, Dancer), set/3 99-145-A	2,800	1999	280.00	280
1999 Tree-Toppers - G. Lewis				
1999 Heading For Christmas 99-115-A	Closed	2001	76.00	76
1999 Two Better Than One 99-116-A	Closed	2001	76.00	76
1999 Tropical Fish - G. Lewis				
1999 Deep Sea I - Blue/Navy/Yellow 99-064-A	Open		38.00	38
1999 Deep Sea II - Black/White 99-065-A	Open		38.00	38
1999 Deep Sea III - Orange/White 99-066-A	Open		38.00	38
1999 Deep Sea IV - Blue/Orange 99-067-A	Open		38.00	38
1999 Deep Sea V - Black 99-068-A	Open		38.00	38
1999 Deep Sea VI - Pearl 99-069-A	Open		38.00	38
1999 Veterans Memorial - G. Lewis				
1999 All You Can Be 99-075-A	Closed	2001	40.00	40
1999 Anchors Aweigh 99-077-A	Closed	2001	40.00	40-42
1999 The Few and Proud 99-076-A	Closed	2001	40.00	40
1999 High-Flying Hero 99-078-A	Closed	2001	40.00	40-42
1999 M*A*S*H Nurse 99-079-A	Closed	2001	40.00	40-42
1999 Wedded Bliss - G. Lewis				
1999 Across The Threshold 99-122-A	Open		36.00	38
1999 Just Married 99-121-A	Closed	2001	36.00	40
1999 World Wildlife Series - G. Lewis				
1999 African Elephant 98-023-A	Closed	1999	42.00	43
1999 Bengal Tiger 98-024-B	Closed	1999	38.00	38-40
1999 Black Rhino 98-025-B	Closed	1999	42.00	43
1999 Cheetah 99-049-A	Open		40.00	42
1999 Chimpanzee (Monkey - '99) 98-027-B	Open		40.00	42
1999 Giraffe 99-053-A	Open		42.00	44
1999 Gorilla 99-051-A	Open		38.00	40
1999 Hippo 99-054-A	Open		38.00	40
1999 Lion 98-026-B	Open		38.00	40
1999 Panda 99-050-A	Open		38.00	40
1999 Parrot - Blue Macaw 99-052-A	Closed	1999	42.00	42-44
1999 Polar Bear 99-055-A	Open		38.00	40
1999 White-Tail Deer 99-056-A	150	1999	48.00	48-250
1999 Zebra 98-028-B	Open		38.00	40
2000 Allyson's Corner - G. Lewis				
2000 Butterfly Ball - 2000 99-086-B	1,000	2001	85.00	85
2000 Flamingo Ball - 2000 99-088-B	1,000	2001	68.00	68
2000 Hummingbird Ball - 2000 99-087-B	1,000	2001	85.00	85
2000 Winter Cardinal Ball - 2000 99-091-B	1,000	2001	68.00	68
2000 American Pride - G. Lewis				
2000 Fireworks Santa 00-228-A	Closed	2001	38.00	38
2000 Angel Series - G. Lewis				
2000 Angelic Mandolin 00-246-A	Open		38.00	38
2000 Heard on High 00-245-A	Open		38.00	38
2000 Millennium Angel 99-033-B	Closed	2001	38.00	38
2000 Animal Characters - G. Lewis				
2000 Gift For A Friend 00-238-A	Open		38.00	38
2000 Hound-dog Holiday 00-239-A	Open		34.00	34
2000 Kitty Christmas 00-240-A	Open		34.00	34
2000 Season's Greetings 00-236-A	Open		34.00	34
2000 Together We Shine 00-237-A	Open		40.00	40
2000 Animal Collage Series - G. Lewis				
2000 Kitten Ball 98-087-C	Closed	2001	42.00	42
2000 Puppy Ball 99-073-B	Closed	2001	42.00	42-48
2000 Animal Theme - G. Lewis				
2000 Cheetah Pattern 00-305-A	Closed	2001	28.00	28
2000 Dalmation Pattern 00-310-A	Closed	2001	28.00	28
2000 Elephant Pattern 00-308-A	Closed	2001	28.00	28
2000 Giraffe Pattern 00-309-A	Closed	2001	28.00	28
2000 Tiger Pattern 00-306-A	Closed	2001	28.00	28
2000 Zebra Pattern 00-307-A	Closed	2001	28.00	28
2000 Bugs - G. Lewis				
2000 Bloodsucker 00-407-A-FB	450	2001	48.00	48

Collectors' Information Bureau   *Quotes have been rounded up to nearest dollar

ORNAMENTS

YEAR ISSUE	EDITION LIMIT	YEAR RETD.	ISSUE PRICE	*QUOTE U.S.$
2000 Flying Dragon 00-409-A-FB	150	2001	77.00	77
2000 The Lady's A Bug 99-157-B-FB	750	2001	48.00	48
2000 Lightning Flasher 00-412-A-FB	225	2001	48.00	48
2000 Mantis Man 00-410-A-FB	225	2001	64.00	64
2000 Nat the Gnat 00-411-A-FB	750	2001	40.00	40-42
2000 Web Weaver 00-408-A-FB	450	2001	56.00	56
2000 Whopper Hopper 99-154-B-FB	750	2001	44.00	44

2000 By The Seashore - G. Lewis
2000 Beach Party 00-218-A	Open		42.00	42
2000 Octopus' Garden 00-217-A	Open		42.00	42

2000 Cat Breeds - G. Lewis
2000 Midnite 00-207-A	Open		40.00	40
2000 Patches 00-208-A	Open		40.00	40
2000 Salt and Pepper 00-206-A	Open		40.00	40
2000 Siamese 00-205-A	Open		40.00	40

2000 Chess Set - G. Lewis
2000 Bishop 00-265-A	Open		40.00	40
2000 King 00-267-A	Open		42.00	42
2000 Knight 00-264-A	Open		38.00	38
2000 Pawn 00-262-A	Open		36.00	36
2000 Queen 00-266-A	Open		40.00	40
2000 Rook 00-263-A	Open		38.00	38

2000 Christmas Canes - G. Lewis
2000 Kitten Cane 99-113-A	300	2001	56.00	56

2000 Christmas Icon Series - G. Lewis
2000 Bunches O' Santa Ball 98-092-C	150	2001	70.00	70
2000 Christmas Candy Ball 98-093-C	150	2001	70.00	70

2000 Christmas Memory Balls - G. Lewis
2000 Double Dazzle 00-333-A	Closed	2001	33.00	33
2000 Ice Drop 00-332-A	Closed	2001	33.00	33
2000 Party Ball 00-334-A	Closed	2001	30.00	30
2000 Snow Blanket 00-331-A	Closed	2001	30.00	30
2000 Star Bright 00-335-A	Closed	2001	30.00	30
2000 Winter Woods Walk 00-330-A	Closed	2001	30.00	30

2000 Classic Christmas Series - G. Lewis
2000 Christmas is for Lovers 00-233-A	Open		34.00	34
2000 Ginger Boy 00-234-A	Open		40.00	40
2000 Ginger Girl 00-235-A	Open		40.00	40

2000 Crystal Kringles - Series I - G. Lewis
2000 Agate Santa 00-230-A	Open		47.00	47
2000 Citrine Santa 00-231-A	Open		47.00	47

2000 Dog Breeds - G. Lewis
2000 Chocolate Lab 00-288-A	Open		40.00	40
2000 Cocker Spaniel 00-200-A	Open		40.00	40
2000 Golden Retriever 00-204-A	Open		40.00	40
2000 Pekinese 00-203-A	Open		38.00	38
2000 Saint Bernhard 00-199-A	Open		42.00	42
2000 Shar-pei 00-202-A	Open		42.00	42
2000 Sheepdog 00-201-A	Open		42.00	42

2000 Floral Elegance - G. Lewis
2000 Flower Cluster II 00-188-A	Open		40.00	40
2000 Sugar Magnolia - Blossoms Bloomin' 99-070-B	Open		42.00	42

2000 Flower Balls - G. Lewis
2000 Gerbers 00-313-A	Closed	2001	28.00	28
2000 Hydrangea 00-315-A	Closed	2001	28.00	28
2000 Irises 00-311-A	Closed	2001	28.00	28
2000 Pansies 00-316-A	Closed	2001	28.00	28
2000 Roses 00-312-A	Closed	2001	28.00	28
2000 Tulips 00-314-A	Closed	2001	28.00	28

2000 Frog Series - 2nd in Series of 3 - G. Lewis
2000 Number 5 00-405-A-FB	225	2001	56.00	56
2000 Tune Jumper 00-406-A-FB	150	2001	72.00	72

2000 Frogs - G. Lewis
2000 Chief Big Croak 00-401-A-FB	750	2001	48.00	48
2000 Flambe Froggy 00-404-A-FB	750	2001	48.00	48
2000 High-Wire Honey 00-403-A-FB	750	2001	48.00	48
2000 Jumping Jester 00-402-A-FB	750	2001	48.00	48
2000 Mr. Happy Hoppy 99-146-A-FB	750	2001	44.00	44
2000 Mrs. Happy Hoppy 99-147-E-FB	750	2001	44.00	44
2000 Rootin' Tootin' Toad 00-400-A-FB	450	2001	48.00	48

2000 Garlands - G. Lewis
2000 Halloween Collection Garland 99-120-A	125	2001	115.00	115
2000 Santa and Packages Garland 99-118-A	125	2001	115.00	115
2000 Santa Bell Garland 99-117-A	125	2001	115.00	115

2000 Ghosts - G. Lewis
2000 Pumpkin Daid 99-165-B-FB	150	2001	135.00	135

2000 Glitter Balls - G. Lewis
2000 Burgundy Glitter 00-318-A	Closed	2001	15.00	15
2000 Gold Glitter 00-320-A	Closed	2001	15.00	15
2000 Opal Glitter 00-323-A	Closed	2001	15.00	15
2000 Orange Glitter 00-322-A	Closed	2001	15.00	15
2000 Pink/Salmon Glitter 00-321-A	Closed	2001	15.00	15
2000 Purple Glitter 00-319-A	Closed	2001	15.00	15
2000 Red & Gold Glitter Mix 00-324-A	Closed	2001	15.00	15
2000 Red Glitter 00-317-A	Closed	2001	15.00	15

2000 Glitter Swirls - G. Lewis
2000 Blue & White 00-336-A	Closed	2001	19.00	19
2000 Purple & Gold 00-340-A	Closed	2001	19.00	19
2000 Purple & Orange 00-339-A	Closed	2001	19.00	19
2000 Red & Gold 00-337-A	Closed	2001	19.00	19
2000 Red & White 00-338-A	Closed	2001	19.00	19

2000 Halloween Harvest Goodies - G. Lewis
2000 (I've Got My) Eye On You 00-271-A	Open		40.00	40
2000 Bone Pile 00-277-A	Open		40.00	40
2000 Count Pumpkula 00-275-A	Open		24.00	24
2000 Howling Goblin 00-269-A	Open		24.00	24
2000 Jack's Bat 00-270-A	Open		38.00	38
2000 Moonlight Goblin 00-268-A	Open		28.00	28
2000 Scare D. Cat 00-274-A	Open		40.00	40
2000 Spiderella 00-276-A	Open		38.00	38
2000 Who's Afraid? 00-273-A	Open		38.00	38
2000 Zelda and the Raven 00-272-A	Open		40.00	40

2000 Hermitage Museum Series - G. Lewis
2000 Amber Ball 00-304-A	Closed	2001	37.00	37
2000 Burgundy Court Ball 00-302-A	Closed	2001	37.00	37
2000 Burgundy Court Icicle 00-303-A	Closed	2001	42.00	42
2000 Enamel Motif Ball 00-325-A	Closed	2001	37.00	37
2000 Enamel Motif Double Orb 00-326-A	Closed	2001	52.00	52
2000 Gilded Facet Ball 00-327-A	Closed	2001	37.00	37
2000 Regal Green Ball 00-301-A	Closed	2001	37.00	37
2000 Royal Blue Ball 00-300-A	Closed	2001	37.00	37

2000 Just For Fun - G. Lewis
2000 Formerly Known As Prince 00-278-A	Closed	2001	34.00	34-36
2000 Green With Envy 00-280-A	Closed	2001	42.00	42
2000 Holiday Cheer 00-279-A	Closed	2001	42.00	42

2000 Nostalgia Series - G. Lewis
2000 Newborn Miracle 00-248-A	Open		38.00	38
2000 Terrific Twos 00-247-A	Closed	2001	42.00	42

2000 Officially Licensed Bozo The Clown - G. Lewis
2000 Bozo Santa BZ-001	Closed	2001	29.00	29
2000 Here's Bozo! BZ-003	Closed	2001	29.00	29
2000 Top Hat Bozo BZ-002	Closed	2001	29.00	29

2000 Officially Licensed Nancy & Sluggo - G. Lewis
2000 Nancy UM-001	Closed	2001	29.00	29
2000 Sluggo UM-002	Closed	2001	29.00	29

2000 Officially Licensed Ziggy & Friends - G. Lewis
2000 Purr-fect Pets UM-005	Closed	2001	29.00	29
2000 Ziggy Santa UM-003	Closed	2001	29.00	29
2000 Ziggy's Best Friend UM-004	Closed	2001	29.00	29

2000 Other Holiday and Events - G. Lewis
2000 Bunny Boy 00-184-A	Open		38.00	38
2000 Crusin' For Chicks 00-185-A	Open		42.00	42
2000 Easter Morning 00-187-A	Open		40.00	40
2000 Eggspressive 00-183-A	Open		38.00	38
2000 Gift For Dad 00-191-A	Open		40.00	40
2000 Golden Clover 00-182-A	Open		38.00	38
2000 Miss Stars-N'-Stripes 00-189-A	Open		40.00	40
2000 Mom's Bouquet 00-190-A	Open		40.00	40
2000 Puppy Love 00-181-A	Open		40.00	40
2000 Topper 00-186-A	Open		38.00	38

ORNAMENTS

YEAR ISSUE	EDITION LIMIT	YEAR RETD.	ISSUE PRICE	*QUOTE U.S.$
2000 Retailer Designs - G. Lewis				
2000 Gleam Santa - Diamond 00-286-A	600	2001	42.00	42
2000 Gleam Santa - Emerald 00-284-A	600	2001	42.00	42
2000 Gleam Santa - Ruby 00-285-A	600	2001	42.00	42
2000 Saint Nicholas - G. Lewis				
2000 Christmas for Rover 00-223-A	Open		38.00	38
2000 Flight Plan 00-224-A	Open		40.00	40
2000 Frosty Holiday 00-225-A	Open		38.00	38
2000 Golden Holly Santa 98-003-C	Closed	2001	42.00	42
2000 Holiday Heart Santa 00-227-A	Open		38.00	38
2000 Jolly Old Elf 00-292-A	Open		44.00	44
2000 Patriotic Santa 99-009-B	Closed	2001	44.00	44
2000 Regal Santa in Red 98-002-C	Closed	2001	40.00	40
2000 Reindeer Wreath 00-221-A	Open		38.00	38
2000 Santa's Secret (Behind His Back) 99-002-B	Closed	2001	44.00	44
2000 Satchel Santa 00-261-A	Open		28.00	28
2000 Seaside Santa 99-011-B	Closed	2001	40.00	40
2000 Six-Shootin' Santa 99-012-C	Closed	2001	42.00	42
2000 Toy Maker Santa 00-222-A	Open		40.00	40
2000 Twist-Top Santa 00-226-A	Open		34.00	34
2000 Winter Winks - green 00-229-A	Open		34.00	34
2000 Santa's Elves - G. Lewis				
2000 Lobster Limbo 00-232-B	Open		40.00	40
2000 Small Wonders Series (Smaller Size) - G. Lewis				
2000 Captain Jack 00-260-A	Open		24.00	24
2000 Childlike Glow 00-254-A	Open		24.00	24
2000 Christmas Moon 00-252-A	Open		24.00	24
2000 Downhill Dasher 00-253-A	Open		24.00	24
2000 Little Engineer 00-259-A	Open		24.00	24
2000 Panda Head - Mini 00-290-A	Open		28.00	28
2000 Polar Bear Head - Mini 00-291-A	Open		28.00	28
2000 Snow Bunny 00-249-A	Open		17.00	17
2000 Snowball Attack! 00-258-A	Open		24.00	24
2000 Snowfort Architect 00-257-A	Open		24.00	24
2000 Snowman Planned 00-256-A	Open		24.00	24
2000 Summer - Winter 00-251-A	Open		24.00	24
2000 Thanksgiving Catch 00-255-A	Open		21.00	21
2000 Twinkle, Twinkle, set/3 00-250-A	Open		33.00	33
2000 Snowmen/Snowwomen - G. Lewis				
2000 Blizzard Boomer 00-244-A	Open		24.00	24
2000 Cool Rhythm 00-242-A	Open		24.00	24
2000 Deep Freeze Diva 00-241-A	Open		24.00	24
2000 Squeezebox Snowdude 00-243-A	Open		24.00	24
2000 Special Event/Commemorative Designs - G. Lewis				
2000 Third Year Thrills 00-287-A	1,500	2001	42.00	42
2000 Twisted Toads SP-01-A/B/C/D	350	2001	30.00	30
2000 Sporting Goods - G. Lewis				
2000 Catch of the Day 00-219-A	Open		42.00	42
2000 Santa's Golf Bag 00-220-A	Open		42.00	42
2000 Sports Nut 00-216-A	Open		42.00	42
2000 Stocking Stuffers - G. Lewis				
2000 Kevin Kitty 98-019-C	Closed	2001	38.00	38
2000 Peter Puppy 99-047-B	Closed	2001	38.00	38
2000 The Night Before Christmas II - G. Lewis				
2000 Night Before Christmas II (I In My Cap, Snug In Their Beds, Sugar Plum Visions), set/3 00-281-A	2,800	2001	120.00	120
2000 Woodland Animals - G. Lewis				
2000 Black Bear 00-193-A	Open		42.00	42
2000 Falcon 00-198-A	Open		40.00	40
2000 Gray Squirrel 00-194-A	Open		38.00	38
2000 Owl 00-197-A	Open		38.00	38
2000 Raccoon 00-196-A	Open		38.00	38
2000 Skunk 00-195-A	Open		38.00	38
2000 Timber Wolf 00-192-A	Open		40.00	40
2000 Tree Frog 00-278-A	Open		30.00	30
2000 World Wildlife - G. Lewis				
2000 African Elephant II 00-289-A	Open		40.00	40
2000 Bald Eagle 00-215-A	Open		42.00	42
2000 Bengal Tiger - white 98-024-C	Open		40.00	40
2000 Emperor Penguin 00-213-A	Open		40.00	40
2000 Kangaroo 00-209-A	Open		38.00	38

YEAR ISSUE	EDITION LIMIT	YEAR RETD.	ISSUE PRICE	*QUOTE U.S.$
2000 Koala 00-210-A	Open		38.00	38
2000 Lioness 00-211-A	Open		40.00	40
2000 Lynx 00-212-A	Open		42.00	42
2000 Parrot - Scarlet Macaw 99-052-B	Open		44.00	44
2000 Walrus 00-214-A	Open		42.00	42
2001 Aliens Among Us - G. Lewis				
2001 Cosmo Chiq 01-511-A	2,001		38.00	38
2001 TuFace 01-510-A	2,001		38.00	38
2001 U-812 01-512-A	2,001		38.00	38
2001 AniBalls - G. Lewis				
2001 AniBalls - Alligator 01-413-A	Open		27.00	27
2001 AniBalls - Bear 01-414-A	Open		27.00	27
2001 AniBalls - Chimp 01-415-A	Open		27.00	27
2001 AniBalls - Elephant 01-416-A	Open		27.00	27
2001 AniBalls - Frog 01-417-A	Open		27.00	27
2001 AniBalls - Lion 01-418-A	Open		27.00	27
2001 AniBalls - Tiger 01-419-A	Open		27.00	27
2001 AniBalls - Zebra 01-420-A	Open		27.00	27
2001 Animal Characters - G. Lewis				
2001 Christmas Moose 01-485-A	Open		32.00	32
2001 Animal Figures - G. Lewis				
2001 Cheetah Figure 01-421-A	Open		36.00	36
2001 Elephant Figure 01-422-A	Open		36.00	36
2001 Giraffe Figure 01-423-A	Open		36.00	36
2001 Lion Figure 01-424-A	Open		36.00	36
2001 Panda Figure 01-425-A	Open		36.00	36
2001 Polar Bear Figure 01-426-A	Open		36.00	36
2001 Tiger Figure 01-427-A	Open		36.00	36
2001 Zebra Figure 01-428-A	Open		36.00	36
2001 By The Seashore - G. Lewis				
2001 At The Beach 01-468-A	Open		30.00	30
2001 Keeping Watch 01-466-A	Open		28.00	28
2001 Seashell Cluster III 01-467-A	Open		32.00	32
2001 Clip-On Birds - G. Lewis				
2001 Bluebird 01-440-A	Open		20.00	20
2001 Cardinal 01-439-A	Open		20.00	20
2001 Swallow 01-441-A	Open		20.00	20
2001 Clowning Around - G. Lewis				
2001 Barney - Guitar 01-465-A	Open		28.00	28
2001 Clarence - Xylophone 01-463-A	Open		28.00	28
2001 Jason - Trumpet 01-464-A	Open		28.00	28
2001 Dog Breeds - G. Lewis				
2001 Dachshund Head 01-437-A	Open		32.00	32
2001 Poodle Head 01-438-A	Open		32.00	32
2001 Fancy Footwork - G. Lewis				
2001 Dapper Dude 01-454-A	Open		20.00	20
2001 Eleganza 01-453-A	Open		20.00	20
2001 Spanish Steps 01-450-A	Open		20.00	20
2001 Steppin' Out 01-452-A	Open		20.00	20
2001 Truckin' 01-451-A	Open		20.00	20
2001 Floral Elegance - G. Lewis				
2001 Blooming Heart 01-492-A	Open		24.00	24
2001 Don't Bug Me 01-496-A	Open		28.00	28
2001 Gerber Fervor 01-493-A	Open		28.00	28
2001 Majestic 01-495-A	Open		28.00	28
2001 Natural Beauty 01-491-A	Open		34.00	34
2001 Serene 01-494-A	Open		28.00	28
2001 Frog Frolic - G. Lewis				
2001 Buckingham Toad 01-506-A	2,001	2001	46.00	46
2001 The Godfrogger 01-508-A	2,001	2001	42.00	42
2001 Harry A. Frog 01-507-A	2,001	2001	42.00	42
2001 On The Hunt 01-505-A	2,001	2001	42.00	42
2001 Pucker Up 01-504-A	2,001	2001	42.00	42
2001 Touchdown Toad 01-509-A	2,001	2001	46.00	46
2001 Halloween Harvest Goodies - G. Lewis				
2001 Baneful Bill 01-448-A	Open		28.00	28
2001 Carving Crone 01-446-A	Open		32.00	32
2001 Cat O' Lantern 01-445-A	Open		28.00	28
2001 The Count 01-443-A	Open		34.00	34
2001 Creepy Cruiser 01-444-A	Open		22.00	22
2001 Ghastly Gilbert 01-449-A	Open		28.00	28
2001 Midnight Rider 01-442-A	Open		34.00	34

Collectors' Information Bureau   *Quotes have been rounded up to nearest dollar

YEAR ISSUE	EDITION LIMIT	YEAR RETD.	ISSUE PRICE	*QUOTE U.S.$
2001 Odious Otis 01-447-A	Open		28.00	28

2001 Horse Breeds - G. Lewis

2001 Arabian 01-435-A	Open		34.00	34
2001 Pygmy Horse 01-436-A	Open		30.00	30
2001 Thoroughbred 01-434-A	Open		34.00	34

2001 Know Your Reindeer - G. Lewis

2001 Blitzen 01-462-A	Open		38.00	38
2001 Comet 01-459-A	Open		38.00	38
2001 Cupid 01-460-A	Open		38.00	38
2001 Dancer 01-456-A	Open		38.00	38
2001 Dasher 01-455-A	Open		38.00	38
2001 Donner 01-461-A	Open		38.00	38
2001 Prancer 01-457-A	Open		38.00	38
2001 Vixen 01-458-A	Open		38.00	38

2001 Night Before Christmas III - G. Lewis

2001 ...Not Even A Mouse, By The Chimney With Care, Ma In Her Kerchief, set/3 01-474	2,800		100.00	100

2001 Nostalgia Series - G. Lewis

2001 Bath Wrap 01-490-A	Open		23.00	23
2001 Strolling Along 01-489-A	Open		32.00	32

2001 Sign of the Cross - G. Lewis

2001 Jeweled Cross 01-486-A	Open		32.00	32
2001 Petal Cross 01-488-A	Open		32.00	32
2001 Quadrant Cross 01-487-A	Open		32.00	32

2001 Small Wonders - G. Lewis

2001 Mellow Moon 01-470-A	Open		22.00	22
2001 Tranquil Sun 01-469-A	Open		22.00	22

2001 Special Issues - G. Lewis

2001 (I've Got Your) Eye In Me D-20m-07	150	2001	110.00	110
2001 Blue Hopper D-20m-01	150	2001	110.00	110
2001 CAT! D-20m-02	150	2001	70.00	70
2001 Cross- Country Snowman D-20m-03	150	2001	90.00	90
2001 Demon Mouse D-20m-04	150	2001	90.00	90
2001 Happy Baby D-20m-05	150	2001	90.00	90
2001 Humpty Dumpty D-20m-06	150	2001	70.00	70
2001 Ice Cream Headache D-20m-20	150	2001	110.00	110
2001 Jack On Jack D-20m-08	150	2001	90.00	90
2001 Jester and Lester D-20m-09	150	2001	120.00	120
2001 Jingle Bears - 2001 Dated Santa 01-475-A	Yr.Iss.	2001	36.00	36
2001 Lost My Head D-20m-10	150	2001	90.00	90
2001 Monday Morning D-20m-11	150	2001	45.00	45
2001 Moon Man "2001" D-20m-12	150	2001	90.00	90
2001 My Favorite Martian D-20m-13	150	2001	110.00	110
2001 Reindeer Santa Snowman D-20m-14	150	2001	110.00	110
2001 Sailor Boy D-20m-15	150	2001	90.00	90
2001 Snow Ho Ho D-20m-17	150	2001	110.00	110
2001 SnowBelly D-20m-18	150	2001	110.00	110
2001 Snowmerica D-20m-16	150	2001	90.00	90
2001 Viking Devil D-20m-19	150	2001	110.00	110

2001 St. Nicholas - G. Lewis

2001 Autumn Rake 01-481-A	Open		34.00	34
2001 Christmas Cookies 01-473-A	Open		32.00	32
2001 City Santa 01-478-A	Open		34.00	34
2001 Country Santa 01-479-A	Open		34.00	34
2001 Dolphin Ride 01-477-A	Open		36.00	36
2001 Forest Santa 01-480-A	Open		34.00	34
2001 Springtime Bloomers 01-483-A	Open		34.00	34
2001 Summer Cut 01-482-A	Open		34.00	34
2001 Surfin' Santa 01-476-A	Open		36.00	36
2001 Winter Dash 01-484-A	Open		34.00	34

2001 Tiny Treasures - G. Lewis

2001 3 Baubles - Set 1 - Set of 3 pcs 01-543-A	Open		16.00	16
2001 3 Baubles - Set 2 - Set of 3 pcs 01-544-A	Open		16.00	16
2001 Bearly Stocking 01-540-A	Open		16.00	16
2001 Big Top 01-527-A	Open		16.00	16
2001 Bugle Corps 01-538-A	Open		16.00	16
2001 Bunny Nick 01-532-A	Open		16.00	16
2001 Canine Christmas 01-541-A	Open		16.00	16
2001 Drum Corps 01-537-A	Open		16.00	16
2001 Funny Flag 01-528-A	Open		16.00	16
2001 Heart Angel 01-523-A	Open		16.00	16
2001 Jingle Nick 01-530-A	Open		16.00	16
2001 Kitty Cover 01-542-A	Open		16.00	16
2001 Lyre Angel 01-526-A	Open		16.00	16
2001 Muffy 01-533-A	Open		16.00	16
2001 Peace Angel 01-524-A	Open		16.00	16
2001 Plaid Nick 01-529-A	Open		16.00	16
2001 Postal Nick 01-531-A	Open		16.00	16
2001 Pray Angel 01-525-A	Open		16.00	16
2001 Pudge 01-536-A	Open		16.00	16
2001 Sweepy 01-534-A	Open		16.00	16
2001 Tree Gripper 01-534-A	Open		16.00	16
2001 Winter Guard 01-539-A	Open		16.00	16

2001 Twist and Shout - G. Lewis

2001 Twisted Clown 01-519-A	2,001	2001	30.00	30
2001 Twisted Elephant 01-517-A	2,001	2001	30.00	30
2001 Twisted Elf 01-520-A	2,001	2001	30.00	30
2001 Twisted Lion 01-516-A	2,001	2001	30.00	30
2001 Twisted Mrs. Claus 01-514-A	2,001	2001	30.00	30
2001 Twisted Pumpkin 01-522-A	2,001	2001	30.00	30
2001 Twisted Santa 01-513-A	2,001	2001	30.00	30
2001 Twisted Snowman 01-515-A	2,001	2001	30.00	30
2001 Twisted Tiger 01-518-A	2,001	2001	30.00	30
2001 Twisted Vampire 01-521-A	2,001	2001	30.00	30

2001 Way Out Bugs - G. Lewis

2001 Clara - Lady(bug) with a Fan 01-499-A	2,001	2001	38.00	38
2001 Fly Boy 01-502-A	2,001	2001	38.00	38
2001 Hop-A-Long 01-501-A	2,001	2001	42.00	42
2001 Lawrence Larva 01-497-A	2,001	2001	46.00	46
2001 Rudy Roach 01-500-A	2,001	2001	42.00	42
2001 Sir Glass-A lot 01-498-A	2,001	2001	42.00	42

2001 Women Through The Ages - G. Lewis

2001 Gatsby Girl 01-471-A	Open		34.00	34
2001 Turn Of The Century Girl 01-472-A	Open		34.00	34

2001 World Wildlife - G. Lewis

2001 Camel Head 01-430-A	Open		34.00	34
2001 Jaguar Head 01-431-A	Open		34.00	34
2001 Mandrill Head 01-432-A	Open		34.00	34
2001 Seal Head 01-433-A	Open		30.00	30
2001 Wild Boar Head 01-429-A	Open		30.00	30

2002 12 Days of Christmas - G. Lewis

2002 12 Days - Partridge on Pear 02-674	Open		22.00	22
2002 12 Days - Turtle Doves 02-736	Open		22.00	22
2002 12 Days - French Hen 02-737	Open		22.00	22
2002 12 Days - Calling Bird 02-675	Open		19.00	19
2002 12 Days - Five Gold Rings 02-676	Open		19.00	19
2002 12 Days - Geese Laying 02-677	Open		22.00	22
2002 12 Days - Swan Swimming 02-678	Open		22.00	22
2002 12 Days - Maid Milking 02-734	Open		25.00	25
2002 12 Days - Ladies Dancing 02-672	Open		25.00	25
2002 12 Days - Lord Leaping 02-673	Open		25.00	25
2002 12 Days - Pipers Piping 02-670	Open		25.00	25
2002 12 Days - Drummers Drumming	Open		25.00	25

2002 American Pride - G. Lewis

2002 Betsy's Stitch 02-756	Open		19.00	19
2002 Colonial Claus 02-1035	Open		29.00	29
2002 Family United - Patriotic 02-637	Open		27.00	27
2002 Freedom Santa 02-747	Open		29.00	29
2002 Funky Sam 02-839	Open		19.00	19
2002 Gallant Santa - Patriotic 02-636	Open		29.00	29
2002 God Bless America Santa 02-990	Open		27.00	27
2002 The Heart of America 02-1084	Open		19.00	19
2002 Ice Slice - Patriotic 02-958	Open		27.00	27
2002 Journeyman Santa - Patriotic 02-862	Open		29.00	29
2002 Out For A Stroll - Patriotic 02-609	Open		27.00	27
2002 Patriotic Pair 02-743	Open		27.00	27
2002 Prestige Santa - Patriotic 02-660	Open		19.00	19
2002 Rally Round The Flag 02-1036	Open		23.00	23
2002 Roly Poly Angel - Patriotic 02-771	Open		27.00	27
2002 Roly Poly Elephant - Patriotic 02-765	Open		27.00	27
2002 Roly Poly Pixie - Patriotic 02-766	Open		27.00	27
2002 Roly Poly Santa - Patriotic 02-709	Open		27.00	27

ORNAMENTS

YEAR ISSUE	EDITION LIMIT	YEAR RETD.	ISSUE PRICE	*QUOTE U.S.$
2002 Roly Poly Snowman - Patriotic 02-868	Open		27.00	27
2002 Santa - United States 02-998	Open		27.00	27
2002 Skating Away - Patriotic 02-597	Open		23.00	23
2002 Star-Spangled Glory 02-1085	Open		23.00	23
2002 Unfurling Honor 02-999	Open		27.00	27
2002 Victorian Giving - Patriotic 02-773	Open		19.00	19

2002 Angel Series - G. Lewis

2002 Angel - Beholder 02-664	Open		23.00	23
2002 Angel - Harp 02-667	Open		23.00	23
2002 Angel - Mandolin 02-668	Open		23.00	23
2002 Angel - Noel 02-662	Open		23.00	23
2002 Angel - Pray 02-663	Open		23.00	23
2002 Angel - Proclaimer 02-666	Open		23.00	23
2002 Angel - Protector 02-665	Open		23.00	23
2002 Rainbow Flying Angel - Red 02-700	Open		23.00	23
2002 Special Delivery - Red 02-1040	Open		27.00	27

2002 AniBalls - G. Lewis

2002 Aniball - Ladybug 02-559	Open		25.00	25
2002 AniBall Cat - Gray and White Stripe 02-563	Open		25.00	25
2002 AniBall Cat - Red 02-562	Open		25.00	25
2002 AniBall Cat - White and Black 02-561	Open		25.00	25
2002 AniBall Dog - Black Lab 02-568	Open		25.00	25
2002 AniBall Dog - Bulldog 02-565	Open		25.00	25
2002 AniBall Dog - Chocolate Lab 02-566	Open		25.00	25
2002 AniBall Dog - Dalmation 02-564	Open		25.00	25
2002 AniBall Dog - Yellow Lab 02-567	Open		25.00	25
2002 AniBall Dragon - Blue 02-689	Open		25.00	25
2002 AniBall Dragon - Red 02-688	Open		25.00	25

2002 Animal Characters - G. Lewis

2002 Apple For Teacher 02-598	Open		25.00	25
2002 Apron Strings 02-631	Open		25.00	25
2002 Balancing Act 02-649	Open		27.00	27
2002 Billy Bull 02-595	Open		25.00	25
2002 Black Bear Fisherman 02-600	Open		25.00	25
2002 Brown Bear Santa 02-657	Open		25.00	25
2002 Dr. Tiger 02-571	Open		25.00	25
2002 Duck Hunter 02-558	Open		25.00	25
2002 Helping Paws 02-920	Open		27.00	27
2002 Lion Santa 02-654	Open		25.00	25
2002 Miss Milker 02-594	Open		25.00	25
2002 Moose Hunter 02-572	Open		25.00	25
2002 Owl Lawyer 02-669	Open		25.00	25
2002 Racoon Santa 02-656	Open		25.00	25
2002 Reindeer Santa 02-942	Open		27.00	27
2002 Ringmaster 02-648	Open		27.00	27
2002 Rock-A-Bye, Mousey 02-629	Open		25.00	25
2002 Roly Poly Elephant - Red 02-697	Open		27.00	27
2002 Roly Poly Giraffe 02-714	Open		27.00	27
2002 Roly Poly Reindeer 02-716	Open		27.00	27
2002 Roly Poly Zebra 02-715	Open		27.00	27
2002 Santa Paws 02-570	Open		25.00	25
2002 Sargeant Woofer 02-616	Open		25.00	25
2002 Trapese Trip 02-650	Open		27.00	27
2002 Trout Fisherman 02-655	Open		25.00	25
2002 Turkey Hunter 02-577	Open		25.00	25
2002 Wall Street Toad 02-555	Open		25.00	25

2002 Cat Full Figures - G. Lewis

2002 Ceramic Cat - Black & Red 02-876	Open		22.00	22
2002 Ceramic Cat - Blue & White 02-993	Open		22.00	22
2002 Electric Cat 02-996	Open		19.00	19
2002 Long Hair Cat - Brown 02-626	Open		19.00	19
2002 Long Hair Cat - Gray & White Stripes 02-627	Open		19.00	19
2002 Long Hair Cat - Red 02-992	Open		19.00	19
2002 Short Hair Cat - Gray & White Stripes 02-625	Open		19.00	19
2002 Short Hair Cat - Red 02-991	Open		19.00	19
2002 Tucked Cat - Black and White 02-579	Open		19.00	19
2002 Tucked Cat - Brown and White 02-580	Open		19.00	19
2002 Tucked Cat - White 02-578	Open		19.00	19

2002 Classic Christmas Series - G. Lewis

2002 Bear-In-The-Box 02-556	Open		23.00	23
2002 Christmas Tree - Green 02-588	Open		20.00	20
2002 Christmas Tree - White 02-587	Open		20.00	20
2002 Light Me Up 02-1009	Open		27.00	27
2002 Little Tree 02-1030	Open		17.00	17
2002 Miss Giftbox 02-725	Open		15.00	15
2002 Mr. Package 02-726	Open		15.00	15
2002 Old Fashioned Christmas 02-740	Open		27.00	27
2002 Package Pile-up 02-735	Open		19.00	19
2002 Snowflake - Blue/Gold 02-802	Open		13.00	13
2002 Snowflake - Green/Gold 02-940	Open		13.00	13
2002 Snowflake - Red/Gold 02-941	Open		13.00	13
2002 Stately Stocking - Burgundy 02-1028	Open		15.00	15
2002 Stately Stocking - Gold 02-1029	Open		15.00	15

2002 Designs For Baby - G. Lewis

2002 Baby Blocks 02-772	Open		25.00	25
2002 Baby's 1st Christmas 02-843	Open		28.00	28
2002 It's A Boy 02-842	Open		28.00	28
2002 It's A Girl 02-841	Open		28.00	28
2002 Newborn Boy 02-791	Open		25.00	25
2002 Newborn Girl 02-792	Open		25.00	25

2002 Dog Breeds - G. Lewis

2002 Beagle 02-617	Open		28.00	28
2002 German Shepherd 02-620	Open		28.00	28
2002 Siberian Husky 02-619	Open		28.00	28

2002 Dog Full Figures - G. Lewis

2002 Afghan Hound - Brown 02-624	Open		23.00	23
2002 Afghan Hound - White 02-623	Open		23.00	23
2002 Black Lab 02-581	Open		23.00	23
2002 Border Collie 02-622	Open		23.00	23
2002 Ceramic Dog - Black & Red 02-875	Open		25.00	25
2002 Ceramic Dog - Blue & White 02-994	Open		25.00	25
2002 Collie 02-621	Open		23.00	23
2002 German Shepherd 02-574	Open		23.00	23
2002 Yellow Lab 02-582	Open		23.00	23

2002 Fairies and Pixies - G. Lewis

2002 Enchanted Meeting - Gold 02-861	Open		20.00	20
2002 Enchanted Meeting - Green 02-758	Open		20.00	20
2002 Enchanted Meeting - Mint Green 02-643	Open		20.00	20
2002 Enchanted Meeting - Purple 02-728	Open		20.00	20
2002 Enchanted Meeting - Red & White 02-759	Open		20.00	20
2002 Enchanted Meeting - Red 02-757	Open		20.00	20
2002 Flower Fairy - Blue 02-684	Open		20.00	20
2002 Flower Fairy - Forest Green 02-685	Open		20.00	20
2002 Flower Fairy - Gold 02-687	Open		20.00	20
2002 Flower Fairy - Green/Gold 02-683	Open		20.00	20
2002 Flower Fairy - Orange 02-844	Open		20.00	20
2002 Flower Fairy - Pink 02-682	Open		20.00	20
2002 Flower Fairy - Purple 02-686	Open		20.00	20
2002 Flower Fairy - Red 02-845	Open		20.00	20
2002 Flower Fairy - Silver/Light Blue 02-1042	Open		20.00	20
2002 Rainbow Flying Fairy - Blue 02-869	Open		20.00	20
2002 Rainbow Flying Fairy - Red 02-691	Open		20.00	20
2002 Roly Poly Pixie - Gold/Green 02-713	Open		27.00	27
2002 Roly Poly Pixie - Pink 02-704	Open		27.00	27
2002 Roly Poly Pixie - Pink/Apple Blossom 02-769	Open		27.00	27
2002 Roly Poly Pixie - Purple/Flower 02-767	Open		27.00	27
2002 Roly Poly Pixie - Red 02-705	Open		27.00	27
2002 Roly Poly Pixie - Red/Strawberry 02-768	Open		27.00	27
2002 Roly Poly Pixie - Springtime Green 02-706	Open		27.00	27

2002 Frog Frolic - G. Lewis

2002 Amphibious Fiddle D-02-1102	Open		68.00	6
2002 Horny Hopper D-02-1101	Open		68.00	6
2002 Javelin Jumper D-02-1117	Open		64.00	6
2002 Number 8 D-02-1116	Open		64.00	6
2002 Strummin' Croaker D-02-1103	Open		68.00	6
2002 Timpani Toad D-02-1104	Open		68.00	6

2002 Gold Theme - G. Lewis

2002 Bringing The Fun 02-746	Open		22.00	2
2002 Corkscrew Santa 02-1017	Open		27.00	2

YEAR ISSUE	EDITION LIMIT	YEAR RETD.	ISSUE PRICE	*QUOTE U.S.$
2002 Frosty Filling 02-1026	Open		25.00	25
2002 Frosty Friends 02-711	Open		19.00	19
2002 Having A Ball 02-722	Open		22.00	22
2002 Holiday Treat 02-694	Open		19.00	19
2002 Jolly Ringer 02-763	Open		22.00	22
2002 Lamplighter Santa 02-762	Open		22.00	22
2002 List Keeper 02-955	Open		23.00	23
2002 Nocturnal Patron 02-789	Open		29.00	29
2002 Polar Packages 02-1004	Open		27.00	27
2002 Polar Pouch 02-602	Open		19.00	19
2002 Rainbow Flying Angel 02-698	Open		23.00	23
2002 Rainbow Flying Santa 02-870	Open		23.00	23
2002 Rainbow Flying Snowman 02-703	Open		23.00	23
2002 Ready To Go 02-960	Open		24.00	24
2002 Roly Poly Angel 02-738	Open		27.00	27
2002 Sashay Snowman 02-719	Open		20.00	20
2002 Shovelin' Along 02-712	Open		19.00	19
2002 Sled and Slide 02-717	Open		22.00	22
2002 Snow Nick 02-873	Open		23.00	23
2002 Special Delivery 02-1000	Open		27.00	27
2002 Svelte Santa 02-1020	Open		23.00	23
2002 Winter Friends 02-613	Open		22.00	22
2002 Winter Roll Up 02-638	Open		23.00	23

2002 Halloween Harvest Goodies - G. Lewis

YEAR ISSUE	EDITION LIMIT	YEAR RETD.	ISSUE PRICE	*QUOTE U.S.$
2002 All Wrapped Up 02-1071	Open		23.00	23
2002 Beasty Pumpkin 02-549	Open		27.00	27
2002 Bonehead 02-1067	Open		17.00	17
2002 Cabbage Roost 02-1077	Open		27.00	27
2002 Cat-Eyed Gourd 02-826	Open		19.00	19
2002 Curly Pumpkin 02-552	Open		27.00	27
2002 Curly Watermelon 02-814	Open		27.00	27
2002 Demon Gourd 02-1076	Open		23.00	23
2002 Devilish Goblin 02-551	Open		18.00	18
2002 Don't Talk With Your Mouth Full 02-835	Open		25.00	25
2002 Frankie 02-1068	Open		25.00	25
2002 Fright Friends 02-1074	Open		25.00	25
2002 Frightful Fruit 02-985	Open		27.00	27
2002 Ghostly Blue 02-806	Open		17.00	17
2002 Ghostly White 02-977	Open		16.00	16
2002 Giddy Gourd 02-836	Open		19.00	19
2002 Gruesome Grin 02-825	Open		19.00	19
2002 Halloween Kitty - Standing 02-997	Open		23.00	23
2002 Halloween Kitty - Tucked 02-995	Open		23.00	23
2002 Halloween Sneer 02-833	Open		19.00	19
2002 I'm Stuck In Here 02-986	Open		25.00	25
2002 Jughead Imp 02-554	Open		18.00	18
2002 Kitty's Costume 02-1070	Open		25.00	25
2002 Looking for Spooks 02-823	Open		16.00	16
2002 Mum's The Word 02-1072	Open		23.00	23
2002 Oh Fine! 02-834	Open		16.00	16
2002 Patch My Bones - Red 02-1078	Open		27.00	27
2002 Patch My Bones - White 02-984	Open		27.00	27
2002 Phantom Feline 02-831	Open		18.00	18
2002 Pint-sized Pumpkin 02-1066	Open		13.00	13
2002 Pumpkin snowman 02-827	Open		27.00	27
2002 SCERRY Christmas! 02-1073	Open		17.00	17
2002 Shake Your Bones 02-1075	Open		25.00	25
2002 Tongue-lashing Goblin 02-829	Open		18.00	18
2002 Too Much Candy 02-832	Open		18.00	18
2002 Wacky Warlock 02-838	Open		18.00	18
2002 Watermelon Man 02-553	Open		27.00	27
2002 Wee Witch 02-1069	Open		27.00	27
2002 What The Cat Drug In... 02-837	Open		16.00	16
2002 Wide Snide 02-830	Open		19.00	19

2002 Heritage Santas - G. Lewis

YEAR ISSUE	EDITION LIMIT	YEAR RETD.	ISSUE PRICE	*QUOTE U.S.$
2002 Santa - England 02-855	Open		27.00	27
2002 Santa - France 02-858	Open		27.00	27
2002 Santa - Germany 02-860	Open		27.00	27
2002 Santa - Holland 02-854	Open		27.00	27
2002 Santa - Ireland 02-856	Open		27.00	27
2002 Santa - Italy 02-857	Open		27.00	27
2002 Santa - Mexico 02-965	Open		27.00	27
2002 Santa - Scotland 02-859	Open		27.00	27
2002 Santa - Slavic 02-951	Open		27.00	27

2002 Nativity Series - G. Lewis

YEAR ISSUE	EDITION LIMIT	YEAR RETD.	ISSUE PRICE	*QUOTE U.S.$
2002 Baby Jesus 02-1060	Open		17.00	17
2002 Joseph 02-1062	Open		25.00	25
2002 King with Chest 02-1063	Open		27.00	27

YEAR ISSUE	EDITION LIMIT	YEAR RETD.	ISSUE PRICE	*QUOTE U.S.$
2002 King with Incense 02-1064	Open		27.00	27
2002 King with Pitcher 02-1065	Open		27.00	27
2002 Mother Mary 02-1061	Open		25.00	25

2002 Night Before Christmas IV - G. Lewis

YEAR ISSUE	EDITION LIMIT	YEAR RETD.	ISSUE PRICE	*QUOTE U.S.$
2002 What's All The Clatter?, Prancer Reindeer, set/2 02-1086	2,800		108.00	108

2002 Nostalgia Series - G. Lewis

YEAR ISSUE	EDITION LIMIT	YEAR RETD.	ISSUE PRICE	*QUOTE U.S.$
2002 All Aboard! 02-796	Open		20.00	20
2002 Christmas Monkey 02-727	Open		15.00	15
2002 Clown Bear - Hot Pink and Purple 02-557	Open		17.00	17
2002 Clown Bear - Red and Gold 02-874	Open		17.00	17
2002 Funny Phone - Blue 02-605	Open		15.00	15
2002 Funny Phone - Pink 02-606	Open		15.00	15
2002 Funny Phone - White 02-604	Open		15.00	15
2002 Rubber Ducky 02-658	Open		10.00	10

2002 Other Holiday and Events - G. Lewis

YEAR ISSUE	EDITION LIMIT	YEAR RETD.	ISSUE PRICE	*QUOTE U.S.$
2002 Be Mine, Valentine 02-807	Open		18.00	18
2002 For You, Valentine 02-853	Open		18.00	18
2002 Grand Gobbler 02-733	Open		20.00	20
2002 New Year Countdown 02-809	Open		23.00	23
2002 Valentine Jester - Red Hearts 02-851	Open		18.00	18
2002 Valentine Jester - White Hearts 02-735	Open		18.00	18

2002 Pastel Theme - G. Lewis

YEAR ISSUE	EDITION LIMIT	YEAR RETD.	ISSUE PRICE	*QUOTE U.S.$
2002 Bringing The Fun 02-954	Open		22.00	22
2002 Cardinal Calm 02-1022	Open		27.00	27
2002 Clown Bear 02-744	Open		17.00	17
2002 Corkscrew Santa 02-1016	Open		23.00	23
2002 Frosty Filling 02-1025	Open		25.00	25
2002 Frosty Friends 02-608	Open		19.00	19
2002 Having A Ball 02-721	Open		23.00	23
2002 Holiday Treat 02-695	Open		19.00	19
2002 Jolly Ringer 02-953	Open		22.00	22
2002 Lamplighter Santa 02-956	Open		22.00	22
2002 Let It Snow! 02-1006	Open		27.00	27
2002 List Keeper 02-615	Open		22.00	22
2002 Polar Packages 02-1005	Open		27.00	27
2002 Polar Pouch 02-603	Open		19.00	19
2002 Rainbow Flying Angel 02-699	Open		23.00	23
2002 Rainbow Flying Santa 02-729	Open		23.00	23
2002 Rainbow Flying Snowman 02-702	Open		23.00	23
2002 Ready To Go 02-959	Open		24.00	24
2002 Roly Poly Angel 02-651	Open		17.00	17
2002 Sashay Snowman 02-718	Open		20.00	20
2002 Shovelin' Along 02-635	Open		19.00	19
2002 Sled and Slide 02-720	Open		22.00	22
2002 Snow Nick 02-808	Open		23.00	23
2002 Special Delivery 02-1001	Open		27.00	27
2002 Svelte Santa 02-1019	Open		23.00	23
2002 Taking A Break 02-646	Open		25.00	25
2002 Winter Friends 02-952	Open		22.00	22
2002 Winter Roll Up 02-817	Open		23.00	23

2002 Santa's Elves - G. Lewis

YEAR ISSUE	EDITION LIMIT	YEAR RETD.	ISSUE PRICE	*QUOTE U.S.$
2002 Elfin Thoughts 02-633	Open		27.00	27
2002 Package Stack - Gold 02-1098	Open		27.00	27
2002 Package Stack - Red 02-1041	Open		27.00	27
2002 Rollin' Along 02-550	Open		27.00	27
2002 Stumpy Elf 02-546	Open		23.00	23

2002 Small Wonders Series (Smaller Size) - G. Lewis

YEAR ISSUE	EDITION LIMIT	YEAR RETD.	ISSUE PRICE	*QUOTE U.S.$
2002 Astral Elf - Blue 02-724	Open		23.00	23
2002 Astral Elf - Gold 02-723	Open		23.00	23
2002 For My Love 02-969	Open		17.00	17
2002 Happy Star - Blue 02-895	Open		10.00	10
2002 Happy Star - Christmas 02-891	Open		13.00	13
2002 Happy Star - Gold 02-898	Open		10.00	10
2002 Happy Star - Lime Green 02-892	Open		10.00	10
2002 Happy Star - Orange 02-896	Open		10.00	10
2002 Happy Star - USA 02-887	Open		13.00	13
2002 Holiday Girl 02-589	Open		17.00	17
2002 Moonlight Santa - Gold 02-871	Open		23.00	23
2002 Moonlight Santa - Red 02-872	Open		23.00	23
2002 The One I Adore 02-801	Open		17.00	17
2002 Star Lamp - Blue 02-1008	Open		19.00	19
2002 Star Lamp - Gold 02-1007	Open		19.00	19
2002 Sun Santa 02-731	Open		13.00	13

YEAR ISSUE	EDITION LIMIT	YEAR RETD.	ISSUE PRICE	*QUOTE U.S.$
2002 Victorian Giving 02-647	Open		17.00	17

2002 Snowmen/Snowwomen - G. Lewis

YEAR ISSUE	EDITION LIMIT	YEAR RETD.	ISSUE PRICE	*QUOTE U.S.$
2002 Apple Snowman 02-1031	Open		25.00	25
2002 Buddy Building 02-661	Open		27.00	27
2002 Cheerful Snowman 02-1033	Open		25.00	25
2002 Dapper Snowman - Blue 02-584	Open		23.00	23
2002 Dapper Snowman - Red 02-585	Open		23.00	23
2002 Frosty Filling - Red 02-1024	Open		25.00	25
2002 Frosty Friends - Red 02-607	Open		19.00	19
2002 Frosty Ski Jump 02-548	Open		29.00	29
2002 Having A Ball - Red 02-790	Open		23.00	23
2002 Holiday Treat - Red 02-693	Open		19.00	19
2002 Ice Slice - Hot Pink 02-573	Open		25.00	25
2002 Imposter Snowman 02-1032	Open		25.00	25
2002 Jolly Snowman 02-1034	Open		25.00	25
2002 Out For A Stroll 02-610	Open		27.00	27
2002 Polar Packages - Red 02-1039	Open		27.00	27
2002 Polar Pouch - Red 02-710	Open		19.00	19
2002 Rainbow Flying Snowman - Red 02-701	Open		23.00	23
2002 Roly Poly Snowman - Red 02-640	Open		27.00	27
2002 Sashay Snowman - Red 02-569	Open		20.00	20
2002 Shovelin' Along - Red 02-634	Open		19.00	19
2002 Sled and Slide - Red 02-690	Open		22.00	22
2002 Snow Dancer 02-547	Open		27.00	27
2002 Snow Nick - Red 02-653	Open		23.00	23
2002 Winter Roll Up - Red Plaid 02-639	Open		23.00	23

2002 Special Issues - G. Lewis

YEAR ISSUE	EDITION LIMIT	YEAR RETD.	ISSUE PRICE	*QUOTE U.S.$
2002 American Eagle D-02-1114	150		64.00	64
2002 The Buckeye Brothers - 2 pcs. D-02-1107	150		70.00	70
2002 Chief Of The Elves D-02-1109	150		70.00	70
2002 Clearing The Way - 2002 Dated Santa 02-1087	Yr.Iss.		29.00	29
2002 Darling Daughter (Allyson) D-02-1125	150		70.00	70
2002 Deep Sea Diver D-02-1108	150		80.00	80
2002 Elefantasy D-02-1122	150		82.00	82
2002 Fancy Meeting You Here! D-02-1121	150		100.00	100
2002 Giant Giraffe D-02-1115	150		84.00	84
2002 Here Comes Santa Claus D-02-1105	150		80.00	80
2002 I Am The Walrus D-02-1106	150		64.00	64
2002 Paciderm Performer D-02-1123	150		82.00	82
2002 Pinochio D-02-1118	150		80.00	80
2002 Pretty Pigtails (Nicole) D-02-1126	150		70.00	70
2002 Shroomer Man D-02-1120	150		70.00	70
2002 Snowman Band - Conductor D-02-1111	150		90.00	90
2002 Snowman Band - Saxaphone D-02-1113	150		90.00	90
2002 Snowman Band - Trumpet D-02-1112	150		90.00	90
2002 Sweep Me Away D-02-1110	150		100.00	100
2002 Weird Wizard D-02-1124	150		70.00	70
2002 Wobblin' Goblin D-02-1119	150		56.00	56

2002 Sporting Goods - G. Lewis

YEAR ISSUE	EDITION LIMIT	YEAR RETD.	ISSUE PRICE	*QUOTE U.S.$
2002 Baseball Boy 02-1091	Open		20.00	20
2002 Baseball Girl 02-1090	Open		20.00	20
2002 Basketball Boy 02-1093	Open		20.00	20
2002 Basketball Girl 02-1092	Open		20.00	20
2002 Football Boy 02-1097	Open		20.00	20
2002 Gymnast Girl 02-1096	Open		20.00	20
2002 Soccer Boy 02-1089	Open		20.00	20
2002 Soccer Girl 02-1088	Open		20.00	20
2002 Swimmer Boy 02-1095	Open		20.00	20
2002 Swimmer Girl 02-1094	Open		20.00	20
2002 Time For Tee 02-971	Open		27.00	27

2002 St. Nicholas - G. Lewis

YEAR ISSUE	EDITION LIMIT	YEAR RETD.	ISSUE PRICE	*QUOTE U.S.$
2002 Airplane Santa 02-866	Open		29.00	29
2002 All I Want For Christmas... 02-1010	Open		29.00	29
2002 Alluring Friend - Green 02-750	Open		32.00	32
2002 Alluring Friend - Rose 02-974	Open		32.00	32
2002 Bear Hug 02-1037	Open		23.00	23
2002 Bringing The Fun - Red 02-764	Open		23.00	23
2002 Car Santa 02-936	Open		29.00	29
2002 Cardinal Calm - Red 02-1021	Open		27.00	27
2002 Checkered Chum 02-642	Open		25.00	25
2002 Choo-Choo Santa 02-863	Open		29.00	29

YEAR ISSUE	EDITION LIMIT	YEAR RETD.	ISSUE PRICE	*QUOTE U.S.$
2002 Corkscrew Santa - Red 02-1015	Open		23.00	23
2002 Creature Comforter 02-755	Open		32.00	32
2002 Double Claus 02-583	Open		20.00	20
2002 Gallant Santa - Gold 02-576	Open		29.00	29
2002 Gallant Santa - Silver 02-575	Open		29.00	29
2002 Gangway! - Red 02-754	Open		32.00	32
2002 Gangway! - White 02-966	Open		32.00	32
2002 Gracious Voyage - Red 02-751	Open		32.00	32
2002 Gracious Voyage - White 02-752	Open		32.00	32
2002 Holiday Heap 02-1038	Open		27.00	27
2002 Jolly Ringer - Red 02-645	Open		23.00	23
2002 Lamplighter Santa - Green 02-644	Open		23.00	23
2002 List Keeper - Red 02-614	Open		23.00	23
2002 Midnight Santa 02-934	Open		29.00	29
2002 Nocturnal Patron - Red 02-775	Open		32.00	32
2002 Nocturnal Patron - White 02-776	Open		32.00	32
2002 Over The Top - Brown 02-774	Open		27.00	27
2002 Over The Top 02-659	Open		27.00	27
2002 Rainbow Flying Santa - Red 02-770	Open		23.00	23
2002 Ready To Go - Red 02-592	Open		27.00	27
2002 Ready To Go - White 02-591	Open		27.00	27
2002 Roly Poly Santa - Red 02-708	Open		27.00	27
2002 Sailboat Santa 02-865	Open		29.00	29
2002 Santa Pop-Up 02-1023	Open		25.00	25
2002 Santa the Sailor 02-681	Open		23.00	23
2002 Santa's Saunter 02-749	Open		32.00	32
2002 Serene Santa - Blue Snowflake 02-1013	Open		25.00	25
2002 Serene Santa - Green Snowflake 02-1012	Open		25.00	25
2002 Serene Santa - Purple Snowflake 02-1014	Open		25.00	25
2002 Serene Santa - Red 02-1011	Open		25.00	25
2002 Skating Away - Pear Sled 02-596	Open		23.00	23
2002 Skating Away - Rainbow 02-560	Open		23.00	23
2002 Skating Away - White 02-761	Open		23.00	23
2002 Svelte Santa - Red 02-1018	Open		23.00	23
2002 Taking A Break - Crème 02-760	Open		25.00	25
2002 Taking A Break - Red 02-732	Open		25.00	25
2002 Up, Up, and Away Santa! 02-798	Open		48.00	48
2002 Verdant Santa 02-739	Open		27.00	27
2002 Winter Friends - Red 02-612	Open		23.00	23
2002 Working Away 02-928	Open		27.00	27

2002 Tropical Fish - G. Lewis

YEAR ISSUE	EDITION LIMIT	YEAR RETD.	ISSUE PRICE	*QUOTE U.S.$
2002 Koi Fish - Black/White 02-1083	Open		29.00	29
2002 Koi Fish - Gold/White 02-1082	Open		29.00	29

2002 Twist and Shout - G. Lewis

YEAR ISSUE	EDITION LIMIT	YEAR RETD.	ISSUE PRICE	*QUOTE U.S.$
2002 Coiled Cane 1 - Ring In The Holidays D-02-1127	500		48.00	48
2002 Coiled Cane 2 - Ring In The Holidays D-02-1128	500		48.00	48
2002 Coiled Cane 3 - Tree Trekker D-02-1129	500		48.00	48
2002 Coiled Cane 4 - Tree Trekker D-02-1130	500		48.00	48
2002 Coiled Cane 5 - Lighting The Way D-02-1131	500		48.00	48
2002 Coiled Cane 6 - Lighting The Way D-02-1132	500		48.00	48

2002 Wacky Fruits and Veggies - G. Lewis

YEAR ISSUE	EDITION LIMIT	YEAR RETD.	ISSUE PRICE	*QUOTE U.S.$
2002 Abnormal Apple 02-1054	Open		17.00	17
2002 Bizarre Banana 02-1057	Open		17.00	17
2002 Bogus Blackberries 02-1059	Open		17.00	17
2002 Braindead Broccoli 02-1048	Open		15.00	15
2002 Careless Carrot 02-1056	Open		17.00	17
2002 Challenged Chili 02-1046	Open		15.00	15
2002 Cheesy Cherries 02-1050	Open		17.00	17
2002 Crazy Corn 02-1043	Open		15.00	15
2002 Eccentric Eggplant 02-1049	Open		17.00	17
2002 Kooky Cucumber 02-1044	Open		17.00	17
2002 Ludicrous Lemon 02-1052	Open		17.00	17
2002 Odd Orange 02-1058	Open		17.00	17
2002 Peculiar Pineapple 02-1045	Open		17.00	17
2002 Perky Pear 02-1051	Open		17.00	17
2002 Puzzled Peas 02-1047	Open		17.00	17
2002 Silly Strawberry 02-1055	Open		17.00	17
2002 Tasteless Tomato 02-1053	Open		17.00	17

2002 Way Out Bugs - G. Lewis

YEAR ISSUE	EDITION LIMIT	YEAR RETD.	ISSUE PRICE	*QUOTE U.S.$
2002 Soaring Colors D-02-1100	500		56.00	56

Collectors' Information Bureau   *Quotes have been rounded up to nearest dollar

YEAR ISSUE	EDITION LIMIT	YEAR RETD.	ISSUE PRICE	*QUOTE U.S.$
2002 Wedding - G. Lewis				
2002 Auburn Bride 02-963	Open		25.00	25
2002 Blonde Bride 02-962	Open		25.00	25
2002 Brunette Bride 02-964	Open		25.00	25
2002 Groom's Greetings - Black 02-884	Open		25.00	25
2002 Groom's Greetings - Silver 02-886	Open		25.00	25
2002 The Happy Couple - Black 02-878	Open		28.00	28
2002 The Happy Couple - Dark Gray 02-879	Open		28.00	28
2002 The Happy Couple - Silver 02-811	Open		28.00	28
2002 Just Married 02-967	Open		27.00	27
2002 Seniorita 02-880	Open		28.00	28
2002 Wedding Dance 02-883	Open		28.00	28
2002 Woodland Animals - G. Lewis				
2002 Mountain Lion Head 02-1079	Open		28.00	28
2002 World Wildlife - G. Lewis				
2002 Bengal Tiger Head III 02-1133	Open		28.00	28
2002 Black Jaguar Head 02-1081	Open		28.00	28
2002 Ostrich Head 02-1080	Open		23.00	23
2002 Zodiac Signs - G. Lewis				
2002 Zodiac - Aquarius 02-780	Open		20.00	20
2002 Zodiac - Aries 02-778	Open		20.00	20
2002 Zodiac - Cancer 02-785	Open		20.00	20
2002 Zodiac - Capricorn 02-779	Open		20.00	20
2002 Zodiac - Gemini 02-782	Open		20.00	20
2002 Zodiac - Leo 02-787	Open		20.00	20
2002 Zodiac - Libra 02-786	Open		20.00	20
2002 Zodiac - Pisces 02-781	Open		20.00	20
2002 Zodiac - Sagittarius 02-788	Open		20.00	20
2002 Zodiac - Scorpio 02-784	Open		20.00	20
2002 Zodiac - Taurus 02-777	Open		20.00	20
2002 Zodiac - Virgo 02-783	Open		20.00	20
Glasscots University Mascots-Atlantic Coast Conference - G. Lewis				
1999 Clemson Tiger - Full Figure GM-090	Open		25.00	29
2002 Clemson Tigers - Treetopper GMTT-005	Open		39.00	39
1998 Clemson Tigers GM-001	Open		25.00	25
2000 Duke Blue Devils - Basketball GM-127	Open		29.00	29
2002 Duke Blue Devils - Figure/Disk GM-150	Open		20.00	20
1999 Duke Blue Devils - Full Figure GM-003	Closed	2001	25.00	33
1999 Duke Blue Devils - Head Only GM-002	Closed	2001	25.00	29
2002 Duke Blue Devils - LOGO Disk GM-151	Open		17.00	17
2002 Florida State Seminoles - Double Logo Disk GM-154	Open		20.00	20
2002 Florida State Seminoles - Treetopper GMTT-008	Open		34.00	34
1998 Florida State Seminoles GM-004	Open		25.00	29
2002 Georgia Tech Yellow Jackets Buzz Figure #2 GM-157	Open		20.00	20
1998 Georgia Tech Yellow Jackets GM-005	Open		25.00	29
1998 Maryland Terrapins GM-006	Open		25.00	29
1998 NCSU Wolfpack - Full Figure GM-054	Open		25.00	29
1998 NCSU Wolfpack - Head Only GM-053	Closed	2001	25.00	29
2002 NCSU Wolfpack - Treetopper GMTT-020	Open		34.00	34
2002 NCSU Wolfpack - Wolf Head #2 GM-166	Open		20.00	20
2000 North Carolina Tar Heels - Basketball GM-131	Open		33.00	33
1998 North Carolina Tar Heels - Full Figure GM-008	Open		25.00	29
1998 North Carolina Tar Heels - Head Only GM-007	Closed	2001	25.00	29
2002 North Carolina Tar Heels - Logo Disk GM-167	Open		20.00	20
2002 North Carolina Tar Heels - Treetopper GMTT-019	Open		34.00	34
1999 Virginia Cavaliers - Cav Head GM-091	Open		25.00	29
1998 Virginia Cavaliers GM-055	Open		25.00	29
1999 Wake Forest Deacons - Full Figure GM-057	Open		25.00	29

YEAR ISSUE	EDITION LIMIT	YEAR RETD.	ISSUE PRICE	*QUOTE U.S.$
1998 Wake Forest Deacons - Head Only GM-056	Open		25.00	29
Glasscots University Mascots-Big 10 Conference - G. Lewis				
1998 Illinois Fighting Illini GM-022	Open		25.00	29
1998 Indiana Hoosiers GM-023	Open		25.00	25
1998 Iowa Hawkeyes GM-024	Open		25.00	25
2000 Michigan State Spartans - Basketball GM-130	Open		33.00	33
2002 Michigan State Spartans - Sparky GM-162	Open		20.00	20
1998 Michigan State Spartans GM-075	Open		27.00	29
2000 Michigan Wolverines Block "M" GM-123	Open		25.00	25
1998 Michigan Wolverines GM-025	Open		27.00	29
1998 Minnesota Gophers GM-026	Open		25.00	29
1998 Northwestern Wildcats GM-027	Open		25.00	25
2000 Ohio State Buckeyes - Basketball GM-132	Open		33.00	33
1998 Ohio State Buckeyes GM-028	Open		25.00	29
2002 Ohio State Buckeyes Treetopper GMTT-021	Open		34.00	34
2002 Penn State Nittany Lions - Fig/Disk GM-170	Open		20.00	20
1998 Penn State Nittany Lions GM-029	Open		27.00	29
2002 Purdue Boilermakers - Purdue Pete GM-171	Open		20.00	20
1998 Purdue Boilermakers GM-030	Open		27.00	29
2002 Wisconsin Badgers - Fig/Disk GM-182	Open		20.00	20
1998 Wisconsin Badgers GM-031	Open		25.00	29
Glasscots University Mascots-Big East Conference - G. Lewis				
1998 Boston College Eagles GM-061	Open		25.00	29
2000 Connecticut Huskies - Basketball GM-125	Open		33.00	33
2002 Connecticut Huskies - Fig/Disk GM-148	Open		20.00	20
1998 Connecticut Huskies GM-043	Closed	2001	25.00	29
1998 Georgetown Hoyas GM-044	Open		25.00	29
1999 Miami Hurricanes GM-045	Closed	2001	27.00	29
2002 Pittsburgh Panthers - Figure GM-186	Open		20.00	20
1998 Pittsburgh Panthers GM-047	Open		25.00	29
1999 St. John's Red Storm GM-100	Open		25.00	29
1998 Syracuse University Orangemen GM-086	Open		25.00	29
1998 Temple University Owls GM-074	Open		25.00	29
1998 Villanova Wildcats GM-058	Open		25.00	29
2002 Virginia Tech Hokies - Fig/Disk GM-181	Open		20.00	20
1998 Virginia Tech Hokies GM-049	Open		25.00	25
1998 West Virginia Mountaineers GM-048	Open		25.00	25
2000 West Virginia Mountaineers GM-119	Open		29.00	29
Glasscots University Mascots-Big Twelve Conference - G. Lewis				
1998 Baylor Bears GM-078	Open		27.00	29
2002 Colorado Buffaloes Fig/Disk GM-146	Open		20.00	20
1998 Colorado Buffs GM-077	Open		25.00	29
1998 Iowa State Cyclones GM-079	Open		25.00	29
2000 Kansas Jayhawks - Basketball GM-128	Open		33.00	33
1998 Kansas Jayhawks GM-041	Open		27.00	29
2000 Kansas State - "Power Cat" GM-124	Open		29.00	29
2002 Kansas State Wildcats - Figurine GM-159	Open		20.00	20
1998 Kansas State Wildcats GM-040	Open		25.00	29
2002 Missouri Tigers Fig/Disk GM-164	Open		20.00	20
1998 Missouri Tigers GM-080	Open		25.00	29
2002 Nebraska Cornhuskers - Lil' Red Figure GM-165	Open		17.00	17
1999 Nebraska Cornhuskers GM-038	Open		25.00	29
1998 Oklahoma Sooners GM-081	Open		27.00	29
2002 Oklahoma Sooners Treetopper GMTT-022	Open		34.00	34
1998 Oklahoma State Cowboys GM-039	Open		25.00	29
2002 Oklahoma State Cowboys Treetopper GMTT-023	Open		34.00	34
1999 Texas - Football Figure GM-099	Open		27.00	29
2002 Texas A&M Aggies - Sarge Figure GM-174	Open		20.00	20
1998 Texas A&M Aggies GM-082	Open		27.00	29

ORNAMENTS

YEAR ISSUE	EDITION LIMIT	YEAR RETD.	ISSUE PRICE	*QUOTE U.S.$
1998 Texas Longhorns GM-042	Open		25.00	25
2002 Texas Longhorns Longhorn Head GM-175	Open		25.00	25
2002 Texas Longhorns Treetopper GMTT-028	Open		34.00	34
2002 Texas Tech Red Raiders - Raider Figure GM-176	Open		20.00	20
1998 Texas Tech Red Raiders GM-083	Open		25.00	29

Glasscots University Mascots-Conference USA - G. Lewis

YEAR ISSUE	EDITION LIMIT	YEAR RETD.	ISSUE PRICE	*QUOTE U.S.$
1999 Army Black Knights GM-101	Open		25.00	29
2002 Charlotte 49er's - Fig/Disk GM-179	Open		20.00	20
2000 Cincinnati Bearcats - Basketball GM-126	Open		33.00	33
2002 Cincinnati Bearcats - Fig/Disk GM-145	Open		20.00	20
1998 Cincinnati Bearcats GM-050	Closed	2001	25.00	29
2002 East Carolina Pirates - Fig/Disk GM-152	Open		20.00	20
1998 East Carolina Pirates GM-051	Closed	2001	25.00	29
2002 Louisville Cardinals - Figure GM-185	Open		20.00	20
2002 Memphis Tigers - Figure GM-184	Open		20.00	20
1998 Memphis Tigers GM-066	Open		25.00	29
2002 Southern Mississippi Eagles - Figure GM-118	Open		20.00	20
2002 Tulane Green Wave - Pelican Figure GM-177	Open		20.00	20
2002 UAB Blazers - Fig/Disk GM-178	Open		20.00	20
1998 Univ. of Ala. at Birmingham Blazers GM-060	Closed	2001	27.00	29

Glasscots University Mascots-Independents & Miscellaneous - G. Lewis

YEAR ISSUE	EDITION LIMIT	YEAR RETD.	ISSUE PRICE	*QUOTE U.S.$
2002 Appalachian State Mountaineers - Figure GM-137	Open		20.00	20
1998 Boston University Terriers GM-062	Open		25.00	29
2002 Central Florida Golden Knights - Figure GM-144	Open		20.00	20
2000 The Citadel Bulldogs GM-116	Open		29.00	29
2002 College of Charleston Cougars - Figure GM-138	Open		20.00	20
2002 Cornell Bears - Figure GM-149	Open		20.00	20
1999 Delaware Fightin' Blue Hens GM-102	Open		25.00	29
2002 Furman Paladins - Logo Disk GM-139	Open		17.00	17
2000 Harvard GM-121	Open		29.00	29
1998 James Madison University - JMU GM-073	Open		25.00	29
1998 Maine Black Bears GM-072	Open		25.00	29
1999 Marshall Thundering Herd GM-059	Open		27.00	29
1999 Naval Academy Midshipmen - (Navy) GM-103	Open		25.00	29
1998 North Dakota Fighting Sioux GM-070	Open		25.00	25
2002 Notre Dame - Logo Disk GM-046	Open		17.00	17
1999 Rhode Island Rams GM-104	Open		25.00	29
2000 SMS - Southwest Missouri State GM-120	Open		29.00	29
2000 Southern Mississippi GM-118	Open		29.00	29
2002 Tulsa Hurricane - Figure GM-183	Open		20.00	20
2002 William and Mary Tribe -Logo Disk GM-140	Open		17.00	17
2000 Yale Bulldogs GM-122	Open		29.00	29

Glasscots University Mascots-Mountain West Conference - G. Lewis

YEAR ISSUE	EDITION LIMIT	YEAR RETD.	ISSUE PRICE	*QUOTE U.S.$
1999 Air Force Academy Falcons GM-095	Open		25.00	29
2002 Brigham Young Cougars - Figure GM-143	Open		20.00	20
1998 Brigham Young Cougars GM-065	Closed	2001	25.00	29
2002 Colorado State Rams - Fig/Disk GM-147	Open		20.00	20
1998 Colorado State Rams GM-067	Closed	2001	25.00	29

Glasscots University Mascots-Pacific Ten Conference - G. Lewis

YEAR ISSUE	EDITION LIMIT	YEAR RETD.	ISSUE PRICE	*QUOTE U.S.$
1998 Arizona State Sun Devils GM-089	Open		25.00	29
1998 Arizona Wildcats GM-032	Open		25.00	29
1998 California Bears GM-033	Open		25.00	29
1998 Oregon Ducks GM-087	Open		25.00	25
1998 Oregon State Beavers GM-088	Open		25.00	29
1998 Stanford University Cardinal GM-085	Open		25.00	29
1998 UCLA Bruins GM-034	Open		27.00	29

YEAR ISSUE	EDITION LIMIT	YEAR RETD.	ISSUE PRICE	*QUOTE U.S.$
1998 USC Trojans - Disk Logo GM-035	Open		25.00	29
1998 Washington Huskies GM-036	Open		25.00	29
1998 Washington State Cougars GM-037	Open		25.00	29

Glasscots University Mascots-Southeastern Conference - G. Lewis

YEAR ISSUE	EDITION LIMIT	YEAR RETD.	ISSUE PRICE	*QUOTE U.S.$
1999 Alabama - Elephant Figure GM-092	Open		27.00	29
2002 Alabama Crimson Tide - Treetopper GMTT-001	Open		34.00	34
1998 Alabama Crimson Tide GM-009	Open		25.00	29
2002 Arkansas Razorbacks - Running Boar GM-142	Open		20.00	20
2002 Arkansas Razorbacks - Treetopper GMTT-002	Open		34.00	34
1998 Arkansas Razorbacks GM-010	Open		25.00	29
1999 Auburn Disk - Tiger Eyes GM-093	Open		25.00	29
2002 Auburn Tigers - Treetopper GMTT-003	Open		34.00	34
1998 Auburn Tigers GM-011	Open		25.00	29
1998 Florida Gators - Disk Logo GM-012	Open		25.00	29
2002 Florida Gators - Figure/Disk GM-153	Open		20.00	20
1998 Florida Gators - Gator Full Figure GM-076	Open		27.00	29
2002 Florida Gators - Treetopper GMTT-007	Open		34.00	34
2000 Georgia "Uga" with Football GM-117	Open		29.00	29
2002 Georgia Bulldogs - Classic Head #2 GM-155	Open		20.00	20
1998 Georgia Bulldogs - Full Figure GM-014	Closed	2001	25.00	29
2002 Georgia Bulldogs - Hairy #2 GM-156	Open		20.00	20
1998 Georgia Bulldogs - Head Only GM-013	Closed	2001	25.00	29
2002 Georgia Bulldogs - Treetopper GMTT-009	Open		34.00	34
2000 Kentucky Wildcats - Basketball GM-129	Open		33.00	33
2002 Kentucky Wildcats - Figure GM-160	Open		20.00	20
1998 Kentucky Wildcats GM-015	Closed	2001	25.00	29
2002 Louisiana State Tigers - Tiger Head GM-161	Open		20.00	20
2002 Louisiana State Tigers - Treetopper GMTT-013	Open		34.00	34
1998 Louisianna State Tigers GM-016	Open		25.00	29
2002 Mississippi State Bulldogs Fig/Disk GM-163	Open		20.00	20
1998 Mississippi State Bulldogs GM-017	Open		25.00	29
2002 Mississippi State Bulldogs Treetopper GMTT-016	Open		34.00	34
2002 Ole Miss Rebels Fig/Disk GM-168	Open		20.00	20
1999 Ole Miss Rebels GM-018	Open		25.00	29
2002 Ole Miss Rebels Treetopper GMTT-024	Open		34.00	34
2002 South Carolina Gamecocks - Cocky Figure GM-172	Open		20.00	20
1998 South Carolina Gamecocks GM-019	Open		25.00	29
2002 South Carolina Gamecocks Treetopper GMTT-053	Open		34.00	34
1999 Tennessee - Smokey with Football GM-094	Open		27.00	29
2002 Tennessee Volunteers - T Vols Fig/Disk GM-173	Open		17.00	17
1998 Tennessee Volunteers GM-020	Open		25.00	29
2002 Tennessee Volunteers Treetopper GMTT-026	Open		34.00	34
1999 Vanderbilt Commodores GM-021	Open		25.00	29

Glasscots University Mascots-Western Athletic Conference - G. Lewis

YEAR ISSUE	EDITION LIMIT	YEAR RETD.	ISSUE PRICE	*QUOTE U.S.$
1998 New Mexico Lobos GM-068	Open		25.00	29
1999 San Diego State Aztecs GM-096	Open		25.00	29
1999 Southern Methodist Mustangs GM-097	Open		27.00	29
1999 Texas Christian Horned Frogs GM-098	Open		25.00	29
1999 UNLV Rebels GM-052	Open		25.00	29
1998 Utah Utes GM-063	Open		25.00	29
2002 UTEP Miners - Fig/Disk GM-180	Open		20.00	20

Glasscots University Santas-Atlantic Coast Conference - G. Lewis

YEAR ISSUE	EDITION LIMIT	YEAR RETD.	ISSUE PRICE	*QUOTE U.S.$
2002 Clemson Tigers - University Santa GMS-005	Open		25.00	25

YEAR ISSUE	EDITION LIMIT	YEAR RETD.	ISSUE PRICE	*QUOTE U.S.$
2002 Duke Blue Devils - University Santa GMS-006	Open		25.00	25
2002 Florida State Seminoles - University Santa GM-008	Open		25.00	25
2002 Georgia Tech Yellow Jackets - University Santa GMS-010	Open		25.00	25
2002 Maryland Terrapins - University Santa GMS-025	Open		25.00	25
2002 NCSU Wolfpack - University Santa GMS-020	Open		25.00	25
2002 North Carolina Tar Heels - University Santa GMS-019	Open		25.00	25
2002 Virginia Cavaliers - University Santa GMS-061	Open		25.00	25
2002 Wake Forest Deacons - University Santa GMS-063	Open		25.00	25

Glasscots University Santas-Big 10 Conference - G. Lewis

YEAR ISSUE	EDITION LIMIT	YEAR RETD.	ISSUE PRICE	*QUOTE U.S.$
2002 Illinois Fighting Illini University Santa GMS-041	Open		25.00	25
2002 Indiana Hoosiers University Santa GMS-042	Open		25.00	25
2002 Iowa Hawkeyes University Santa GMS-043	Open		25.00	25
2002 Michigan State Spartans University Santa GMS-015	Open		25.00	25
2002 Michigan Wolverines University Santa GMS-014	Open		25.00	25
2002 Minnesota Gophers University Santa GMS-048	Open		25.00	25
2002 Ohio State Buckeyes University Santa GMS-021	Open		25.00	25
2002 Penn State Nittany Lions University Santa GMS-052	Open		25.00	25
2002 Purdue Boilermakers University Santa GMS-025	Open		25.00	25
2002 Wisconsin Badgers University Santa GMS-030	Open		25.00	25

Glasscots University Santas-Big East Conference - G. Lewis

YEAR ISSUE	EDITION LIMIT	YEAR RETD.	ISSUE PRICE	*QUOTE U.S.$
2002 Boston College Eagles University Santa GMS-072	Open		25.00	25
2002 Connecticut Huskies University Santa GMS-038	Open		25.00	25
2002 Georgetown Hoyas University Santa GMS-040	Open		25.00	25
2002 Miami Hurricanes University Santa GMS-047	Open		25.00	25
2002 Pittsburgh Panthers University Santa GMS-070	Open		25.00	25
2002 Syracuse Orangemen University Santa GMS-056	Open		25.00	25
2002 Virginia Tech Hokies University Santa GMS-062	Open		25.00	25
2002 West Virginia Mountaineers University Santa GMS-065	Open		25.00	25

Glasscots University Santas-Big Twelve Conference - G. Lewis

YEAR ISSUE	EDITION LIMIT	YEAR RETD.	ISSUE PRICE	*QUOTE U.S.$
2002 Baylor Bears University Santa GMS-004	Open		25.00	25
2002 Colorado Buffaloes University Santa GMS-037	Open		25.00	25
2002 Iowa State Cyclones University Santa GMS-044	Open		25.00	25
2002 Kansas Jayhawks University Santa GMS-011	Open		25.00	25
2002 Kansas State Wildcats University Santa GMS-045	Open		25.00	25
2002 Missouri Tigers University Santa GMS-017	Open		25.00	25
2002 Nebraska Cornhuskers University Santa GMS-018	Open		25.00	25
2002 Oklahoma Sooners University Santa GMS-022	Open		25.00	25
2002 Oklahoma State Cowboys University Santa GMS-023	Open		25.00	25
2002 Texas A&M Aggies University Santa GMS-027	Open		25.00	25
2002 Texas Longhorns University Santa GMS-028	Open		25.00	25
2002 Texas Tech Red Raiders University Santa GMS-058	Open		25.00	25

Glasscots University Santas-Conference USA - G. Lewis

YEAR ISSUE	EDITION LIMIT	YEAR RETD.	ISSUE PRICE	*QUOTE U.S.$
2002 Army Black Knights University Santa GMS-034	Open		25.00	25
2002 Charlotte 49er's University Santa GMS-076	Open		25.00	25
2002 Cincinnati Bearcats University Santa GMS-036	Open		25.00	25
2002 East Carolina Pirates University Santa GMS-039	Open		25.00	25
2002 Louisville Cardinals University Santa GMS-078	Open		25.00	25
2002 Memphis Tigers University Santa GMS-066	Open		25.00	25
2002 Southern Mississippi Eagles University Santa GMS-068	Open		25.00	25
2002 Tulane Green Wave University Santa GMS-077	Open		25.00	25

Glasscots University Santas-Independents & Miscellaneous - G. Lewis

YEAR ISSUE	EDITION LIMIT	YEAR RETD.	ISSUE PRICE	*QUOTE U.S.$
2002 Marshall Thundering Herd University Santa GMS-075	Open		25.00	25
2002 Naval Academy Midshipmen University Santa GMS-049	Open		25.00	25
2002 Notre Dame University Santa GMS-073	Open		25.00	25
2002 Tulsa Hurricane University Santa GMS-071	Open		25.00	25

Glasscots University Santas-Mountain West Conference - G. Lewis

YEAR ISSUE	EDITION LIMIT	YEAR RETD.	ISSUE PRICE	*QUOTE U.S.$
2002 Air Force Academy Falcons University Santa GMS-031	Open		25.00	25
2002 Brigham Young Cougars University Santa GMS-069	Open		25.00	25

Glasscots University Santas-Pacific Ten Conference - G. Lewis

YEAR ISSUE	EDITION LIMIT	YEAR RETD.	ISSUE PRICE	*QUOTE U.S.$
2002 Arizona State Sun Devils University Santa GMS-033	Open		25.00	25
2002 Arizona Wildcats University Santa GMS-032	Open		25.00	25
2002 California Bears University Santa GMS-035	Open		25.00	25
2002 Oregon Ducks University Santa GMS-050	Open		25.00	25
2002 Oregon State Beavers University Santa GMS-051	Open		25.00	25
2002 Southern California Trojans University Santa GMS-054	Open		25.00	25
2002 Stanford University Cardinal University Santa GMS-067	Open		25.00	25
2002 UCLA Bruins University Santa GMS-059	Open		25.00	25
2002 Washington Huskies University Santa GMS-064	Open		25.00	25
2002 Washington State Cougars University Santa GMS-074	Open		25.00	25

Glasscots University Santas-Southeastern Conference - G. Lewis

YEAR ISSUE	EDITION LIMIT	YEAR RETD.	ISSUE PRICE	*QUOTE U.S.$
2002 Alabama Crimson Tide - University Santa GMS-001	Open		25.00	25
2002 Arkansas Razorbacks - University Santa GMS-002	Open		25.00	25
2002 Auburn Tigers - University Santa GMS-003	Open		25.00	25
2002 Florida Gators - University Santa GMS-007	Open		25.00	25
2002 Georgia Bulldogs - University Santa GMS-009	Open		25.00	25
2002 Kentucky Wildcats - University Santa GMS-012	Open		25.00	25
2002 Louisiana State Tigers - Unversity Santa GMS-013	Open		25.00	25
2002 Mississippi State Bulldogs University Santa GMS-016	Open		25.00	25
2002 Ole Miss Rebels University Santa GMS-024	Open		25.00	25
2002 South Carolina Gamecocks University Santa GMS-053	Open		25.00	25
2002 Tennessee Volunteers University Santa GMS-026	Open		25.00	25
2002 Vandebilt Commodores University Santa GMS-029	Open		25.00	25

ORNAMENTS

YEAR ISSUE	EDITION LIMIT	YEAR RETD.	ISSUE PRICE	*QUOTE U.S.$
Glasscots University Santas-Western Athletic Conference - G. Lewis				
2002 Southern Methodist Mustangs University Santa GMS-055	Open		25.00	25
2002 Texas Christian Horned Frogs University Santa GMS-057	Open		25.00	25
National Hockey League - G. Lewis				
2002 NHL Logo Disk NHL-001	Open		15.00	15
2002 Boston Bruins - Logo Disk NHL-002	Open		17.00	17
2002 Buffalo Sabres - Logo Disk NHL-003	Open		17.00	17
2002 Chicago Blackhawks - Logo Disk NHL-004	Open		17.00	17
2002 Colorado Avalanche - Logo Disk NHL-005	Open		17.00	17
2002 Dallas Stars - Logo Disk NHL-006	Open		17.00	17
2002 Detroit Red Wings - Logo Disk NHL-007	Open		17.00	17
2002 Edmonton Oilers - Logo Disk NHL-008	Open		17.00	17
2002 Los Angeles Kings - Logo Disk NHL-021	Open		17.00	17
2002 Mighty Ducks of Anaheim - Logo Disk NHL-009	Open		17.00	17
2002 Minnesota Wild - Logo Disk NHL-010	Open		17.00	17
2002 Montreal Canadiens - Logo Disk NHL-011	Open		17.00	17
2002 New Jersey Devils - Logo Disk NHL-012	Open		17.00	17
2002 New York Islanders - Logo Disk NHL-013	Open		17.00	17
2002 New York Rangers - Logo Disk NHL-014	Open		17.00	17
2002 Philadelphia Flyers - Logo Disk NHL-015	Open		17.00	17
2002 Pittsburgh Penguins - Logo Disk NHL-016	Open		17.00	17
2002 San Jose Sharks - Logo Disk NHL-017	Open		17.00	17
2002 St. Louis Blues - Logo Disk NHL-018	Open		17.00	17
2002 Toronto Maple Leafs - Logo Disk NHL-019	Open		17.00	17
2002 Washington Capitals - Logo Disk NHL-020	Open		17.00	17
Santa Football Helmets - G. Lewis				
1999 Alabama Crimson Tide GM-105	1,000	2201	40.00	40
1999 Arkansas Razorbacks GM-106	1,000	2001	40.00	40
1999 Clemson Tigers GM-107	1,000	2001	40.00	40
1999 Florida State Seminoles GM-108	1,000	2001	40.00	40
2000 Michigan State Spartans GM-136	1,000	2001	40.00	40
1999 Michigan Wolverines GM-109	1,000	2001	40.00	40
1999 Nebraska Cornhuskers GM-110	1,000	2001	40.00	40
1999 Ohio State Buckeyes GM-111	1,000	2001	40.00	40
1999 Penn State Nittany Lions GM-112	1,000	2001	40.00	40
1999 Syracuse Orangemen GM-113	1,000	2001	40.00	40
1999 Tennessee Volunteers GM-114	1,000	2001	40.00	40
2000 Texas Longhorns GM-134	1,000	2001	40.00	40
1999 UCLA Bruins GM-115	1,000	2001	40.00	40
1999 USC Trojans - Santa Wearing Helmet GM-084	1,000	2001	40.00	40
2000 Washington Huskies GM-135	1,000	2001	40.00	40
2000 Wisconsin Badgers GM-133	1,000	2001	40.00	40

Swarovski Consumer Goods Ltd.

YEAR ISSUE	EDITION LIMIT	YEAR RETD.	ISSUE PRICE	*QUOTE U.S.$
Christmas Ornaments - Swarovski				
1981 1981 Snowflake 7563NR35	Yr.Iss.	1981	30.00	422-500
1986 1986 Holiday Ornament 92086	Yr.Iss.	1986	N/A	170-429
1987 1987 Holiday Etching-Candle	Yr.Iss.	1987	20.00	210-360
1988 1988 Holiday Etching-Wreath	Yr.Iss.	1988	25.00	100-124
1989 1989 Holiday Etching-Dove	Yr.Iss.	1989	35.00	219-415
1990 1990 Holiday Etching-Merry Christmas	Yr.Iss.	1990	25.00	175-250
1991 1991 Holiday Ornament-Star (U.S. Version, silver cap)	Yr.Iss.	1991	35.00	375-438
1991 1991 Holiday Ornament-Star (European Version, gold cap)	Yr.Iss.	1991	35.00	375-488
1992 1992 Holiday Ornament-Star	Yr.Iss.	1992	37.50	188-240
1993 1993 Holiday Ornament-Star	Yr.Iss.	1993	37.50	350-385
1993 1993 Holiday Ornament-Season's Greetings 94004	Yr.Iss.	1993	25.00	155-175
1994 1994 Holiday Ornament-Star	Yr.Iss.	1994	37.50	138-250

YEAR ISSUE	EDITION LIMIT	YEAR RETD.	ISSUE PRICE	*QUOTE U.S.$
1995 1995 Holiday Ornament-Star	Yr.Iss.	1995	40.00	104-139
1996 1996 Holiday Ornament-Snowflake	Yr.Iss.	1996	45.00	60-115
1997 1997 Holiday Ornament-Star	Yr.Iss.	1997	45.00	65-139
1998 1998 Christmas Ornament - Snowflake	Yr.Iss.	1998	49.50	65-113
1999 1999 Christmas Ornament	Yr.Iss.	1999	55.00	85-138
2000 2000 Christmas Ornament	Yr.Iss.	2000	65.00	65-100
2001 2001 Christmas Ornament	Yr.Iss.	2001	55.00	55-80
2002 2002 Christmas Ornament	Yr.Iss.		55.00	55
Swarovski Crystal Moments Ornaments				
2000 Angel	Open		95.00	95
1996 Bells	Open		45.00	50
1996 Boot	Open		45.00	50
1997 Candy Cane	Open		45.00	50
1998 Christmas Tree	Open		45.00	50
1999 Drum	Open		45.00	50
1998 Gingerbread House	Open		45.00	50
1999 Harp	Open		55.00	50
1996 Holly	Open		45.00	50
1997 Icicles	Retrd.	2000	45.00	50
1998 Locomotive	Open		45.00	50
1996 Moon	Retrd.	2000	45.00	50
1997 Pine Cone	Open		45.00	50
1996 Sun	Open		45.00	50
1999 Violin	Open		45.00	50
1996 Wreath 9443000005	Retrd.	2000	45.00	50
Swarovski Crystal Moments-Annual Edition Angels				
1996 1996 Annual Edition Angel 9443NR960001	Retrd.	1996	75.00	75-240
1997 1997 Annual Edition Angel 9443NR970001	Retrd.	1997	75.00	73-215
1998 1998 Annual Edition Angel 9443NR980001	Retrd.	1998	75.00	45-96
1999 1999 Annual Edition Angel 9443NR990001	Retrd.	1999	75.00	85-95

Towle Silversmiths

YEAR ISSUE	EDITION LIMIT	YEAR RETD.	ISSUE PRICE	*QUOTE U.S.$
Christmas Angel Medallions - Towle				
1991 1991 Angel	Closed	1991	45.00	70
1992 1992 Angel	Closed	1992	45.00	70
1993 1993 Angel	Closed	1993	45.00	55-70
1994 1994 Angel	Closed	1994	50.00	50-60
1995 1995 Angel	Closed	1995	50.00	50-55
1996 1996 Angel	Closed	1996	50.00	40-50
1997 1997 Angel	Closed	1997	50.00	50
1998 1998 Angel	Closed	1998	50.00	50
1999 1999 Angel	Closed	1999	50.00	50
Christmas Star - Towle				
1997 1997 Star	Closed	1997	50.00	50
1998 1998 Star	Closed	1998	50.00	50
1999 1999 Star	Closed	1999	50.00	50
Millennium 2000 Ornament - Towle				
1999 Millennium Ornament	Closed	1999	45.00	45
Remembrance Collection - Towle				
1990 1990 - Old Master Snowflake	Closed	1990	40.00	70
1991 1991 - Old Master Snowflake	Closed	1991	40.00	60
1992 1992 - Old Master Snowflake	Closed	1992	40.00	40-60
1993 1993 - Old Master Snowflake	Closed	1993	40.00	45-60
1994 1994 - Old Master Snowflake	Closed	1994	50.00	60
1995 1995 - Old Master Snowflake	Closed	1995	50.00	40-60
1996 1996 - Old Master Snowflake	Closed	1996	50.00	40-60
1997 1997 - Old Master Snowflake	Closed	1997	50.00	35-50
1998 1998 - Old Master Snowflake	Closed	1998	50.00	50
1999 1999 - Old Master Snowflake	Closed	1999	50.00	50
Songs of Christmas Medallions - Towle				
1978 Silent Night Medallion	Closed	1978	35.00	60
1979 Deck The Halls	Closed	1979	35.00	60
1980 Jingle Bells	Closed	1980	53.00	60
1981 Hark the Hearld Angels Sing	Closed	1981	53.00	60-125
1982 O Christmas Tree	Closed	1982	35.00	60-100
1983 Silver Bells	Closed	1983	40.00	60-65
1984 Let It Snow	Closed	1984	30.00	60
1985 Chestnuts Roasting on Open Fire	Closed	1985	35.00	60-70
1986 It Came Upon a Midnight Clear	Closed	1986	35.00	60-70
1987 White Christmas	Closed	1987	35.00	60-100

Collectors' Information Bureau   *Quotes have been rounded up to nearest dollar

Sterling Cross - Towle

YEAR ISSUE	EDITION LIMIT	YEAR RETD.	ISSUE PRICE	*QUOTE U.S.$
1994 Sterling Cross	Closed	1994	50.00	60
1995 Christmas Cross	Closed	1995	50.00	40-60
1996 1996 Cross	Closed	1996	50.00	40-50
1997 1997 Cross	Closed	1997	50.00	40-50
1998 1998 Cross	Closed	1998	50.00	50
1999 1999 Cross	Closed	1999	50.00	50

Sterling Floral Medallions - Towle

YEAR ISSUE	EDITION LIMIT	YEAR RETD.	ISSUE PRICE	*QUOTE U.S.$
1983 Christmas Rose	Closed	1983	40.00	40
1984 Hawthorn/Glastonbury Thorn	Closed	1984	40.00	40
1985 Poinsettia	Closed	1985	35.00	40-50
1986 Laurel Bay	Closed	1986	35.00	40-45
1987 Mistletoe	Closed	1987	35.00	40-45
1988 Holly	Closed	1988	40.00	50-95
1989 Ivy	Closed	1989	35.00	50-95
1990 Christmas Cactus	Closed	1990	40.00	50-95
1991 Chrysanthemum	Closed	1991	40.00	40-55
1992 Star of Bethlehem	Closed	1992	40.00	40-50

Sterling Nativity Medallions - Towle

YEAR ISSUE	EDITION LIMIT	YEAR RETD.	ISSUE PRICE	*QUOTE U.S.$
1988 The Angel Appeared	Closed	1988	40.00	60
1989 The Journey	Closed	1989	40.00	60
1990 No Room at the Inn	Closed	1990	40.00	60
1991 Tidings of Joy	Closed	1991	40.00	60
1992 Star of Bethlehem	Closed	1992	40.00	60
1993 Mother and Child	Closed	1993	40.00	60
1994 Three Wisemen	Closed	1994	40.00	50
1995 Newborn King	Closed	1995	40.00	50

Sterling Twelve Days of Christmas Medallions - Towle

YEAR ISSUE	EDITION LIMIT	YEAR RETD.	ISSUE PRICE	*QUOTE U.S.$
1971 Partridge in A Pear Tree	Closed	1971	10.00	300
1972 Two Turtle Doves	Closed	1972	10.00	125-250
1973 Three French Hens	Closed	1973	10.00	75
1974 Four Colly Birds	Closed	1974	30.00	75-90
1975 Five Gold Rings	Closed	1975	30.00	60
1975 Five Gold Rings (vermeil)	Closed	1975	30.00	60
1976 Six Geese-a-Laying	Closed	1976	30.00	60
1977 Seven Swans-a-Swimming	Closed	1977	35.00	60
1977 Seven Swans-a-Swimming (turquoise)	Closed	1977	35.00	50
1978 Eight Maids-a-Milking	Closed	1978	37.00	60
1979 Nine Ladies Dancing	Closed	1979	37.00	60
1980 Ten Lords-a-Leaping	Closed	1980	76.00	60
1981 Eleven Pipers Piping	Closed	1981	50.00	60
1982 Twelve Drummers Drumming	Closed	1982	35.00	60

Twelve Days of Christmas - Towle

YEAR ISSUE	EDITION LIMIT	YEAR RETD.	ISSUE PRICE	*QUOTE U.S.$
1991 Partridge in A Pear Tree In A Wreath	Closed	1991	50.00	55-75
1992 Two Turtle Doves In A Wreath	Closed	1992	50.00	50-60
1993 Three French Hens In A Wreath	Closed	1993	50.00	40-50
1994 Four Colly Birds In A Wreath	Closed	1995	50.00	40-60
1996 Five Gold Rings In A Wreath	Closed	1996	50.00	40-50
1996 Six Geese A Laying In A Wreath	Closed	1996	50.00	40-50
1997 Seven Swans A Swimming	Closed	1997	50.00	35-50
1998 Eight Maids-a-Milking	Closed	1998	50.00	50
1999 Nine Ladies Dancing	Closed	1999	50.00	50

Treasury Masterpiece Editions/Enesco Group, Inc.

Treasury Ornaments Collectors' Club (formerly known as Enesco Treasury of Christmas Ornaments Collectors' Club) - Enesco, unless otherwise noted

YEAR ISSUE	EDITION LIMIT	YEAR RETD.	ISSUE PRICE	*QUOTE U.S.$
1993 The Treasury Card T0001 - Gilmore	Yr.Iss.	1993	Gift	20
1993 Together We Can Shoot For The Stars TR931 - Hahn	Yr.Iss.	1993	17.50	35
1993 Can't Weights For The Holidays TR932	Yr.Iss.	1993	18.50	35
1994 Seedlings Greetings TR933 - Hahn	Yr.Iss.	1994	22.50	23
1994 Spry Fry (Club) TR934	Yr.Iss.	1994	15.00	15
1995 You're the Perfect Fit T0002 - Hahn	Yr.Iss.	1995	Gift	20
1995 You're the Perfect Fit T0102 (Charter Members) - Hahn	Yr.Iss.	1995	Gift	20
1995 Things Go Better With Coke™ TR951	Yr.Iss.	1995	15.00	15-30
1995 Buttoning Up Our Holiday Best TR952 - Gilmore	Yr.Iss.	1995	22.50	23
1995 Holiday High-Light TR953 - Gilmore	Yr.Iss.	1995	15.00	15
1995 First Class Christmas TR954 - Gilmore	Yr.Iss.	1995	22.50	23-25
1996 Yo Ho Holidays T0003	Yr.Iss.	1996	Gift	20
1996 Yo Ho Holidays T0103 (Charter Members)	Yr.Iss.	1996	Gift	20
1996 Coca Cola® Choo Choo TR961	Yr.Iss.	1996	35.00	35

YEAR ISSUE	EDITION LIMIT	YEAR RETD.	ISSUE PRICE	*QUOTE U.S.$
1996 Friends Are Tea-riffic TR962	Yr.Iss.	1996	25.00	25
1996 On Track With Coke™ TR963	Yr.Iss.	1996	25.00	25
1996 Riding High TR964 - Hahn	Yr.Iss.	1996	20.00	20
1997 Advent-ures In Ornament Collecting T0004 - Hahn	Yr.Iss.	1997	Gift	N/A
1997 Advent-ures In Ornament Collecting T0104 (Charter Members) - Hahn	Yr.Iss.	1997	Gift	N/A
1997 Coca Cola® Caboose TR971	Yr.Iss.	1997	25.00	25-59
1997 The Sweetest Nativity TR972 - Hahn	Yr.Iss.	1997	20.00	20

Treasury Masterpiece Editions (formerly known as Enesco Treasury of Christmas Ornaments) - Enesco, unless otherwise noted

YEAR ISSUE	EDITION LIMIT	YEAR RETD.	ISSUE PRICE	*QUOTE U.S.$
1983 Wide Open Throttle E-0242	3-Yr.	1985	12.00	35
1983 Baby's First Christmas E-0271	Yr.Iss.	1983	6.00	N/A
1983 Grandchild's First Christmas E-0272	Yr.Iss.	1983	5.00	N/A
1983 Baby's First Christmas E-0273	3-Yr.	1985	9.00	N/A
1983 Toy Drum Teddy E-0274	4-Yr.	1986	9.00	N/A
1983 Watching At The Window E-0275	3-Yr.	1985	13.00	N/A
1983 To A Special Teacher E-0276	7-Yr.	1989	5.00	15
1983 Toy Shop E-0277	7-Yr.	1989	8.00	20-50
1983 Merry Christmas Carousel Horse E-0278	7-Yr.	1989	9.00	20
1981 Look Out Below E-6135	2-Yr.	1982	6.00	N/A
1982 Flyin' Santa Christmas Special 1982 E-6136	Yr.Iss.	1982	9.00	75
1981 Flyin' Santa Christmas Special 1981 E-6136	Yr.Iss.	1981	9.00	N/A
1981 Sawin' Elf Helper E-6138	2-Yr.	1982	6.00	40
1981 Snow Shoe-In Santa E-6139	2-Yr.	1982	6.00	35
1981 Baby's First Christmas 1981 E-6145	Yr.Iss.	1981	6.00	N/A
1981 Our Hero E-6146	2-Yr.	1982	4.00	N/A
1981 Whoops E-6147	2-Yr.	1982	3.50	N/A
1981 Whoops, It's 1981 E-6148	Yr.Iss.	1981	7.50	75
1981 Not A Creature Was Stirring E-6149	2-Yr.	1982	4.00	25
1984 Joy To The World E-6209	2-Yr.	1985	9.00	35
1984 Letter To Santa E-6210	2-Yr.	1985	5.00	30
1984 Lucy & Me Someone Special Photo Frame E-6211	3-Yr.	1986	5.00	N/A
1984 Lucy & Me Special Friend Photo Frame E-6211	3-Yr.	1986	5.00	N/A
1984 Lucy & Me Teacher Photo Frame E-6211	3-Yr.	1986	5.00	N/A
1984 Lucy & Me Grandma Photo Frame E-6211	3-Yr.	1986	5.00	N/A
1984 Lucy & Me For Baby Photo Frame E-6211	3-Yr.	1986	5.00	N/A
1984 Lucy & Me Grandpa Photo Frame E-6211	3-Yr.	1986	5.00	N/A
1984 Baby's First Christmas 1984 E-6212 - Gilmore	Yr.Iss.	1984	10.00	30
1984 Merry Christmas Mother E-6213	3-Yr.	1986	10.00	30
1984 Baby's First Christmas 1984 E-6215	Yr.Iss.	1984	6.00	N/A
1984 Ferris Wheel Mice E-6216	2-Yr.	1985	9.00	30
1984 Cuckoo Clock E-6217	2-Yr.	1985	8.00	40
1984 Muppet Babies Baby's First Christmas E-6222 - J. Henson	Yr.Iss.	1984	10.00	45
1984 Muppet Babies Baby's First Christmas E-6223 -J. Henson	Yr.Iss.	1984	10.00	45
1984 Garfield Hark! The Herald Angel E-6224 - J. Davis	2-Yr.	1985	7.50	35
1984 Fun in Santa's Sleigh E-6225 - J. Davis	2-Yr.	1985	12.00	35
1984 Deer! Odie E-6226 -J. Davis	2-Yr.	1985	6.00	30
1984 Garfield The Snow Cat E-6227 - J. Davis	2-Yr.	1985	12.00	35
1984 Peek-A-Bear Baby's First Christmas E-6228	3-Yr.	1986	8.00	N/A
1984 Peek-A-Bear Baby's First Christmas E-6229	3-Yr.	1986	9.00	N/A
1984 Owl Be Home For Christmas E-6230	2-Yr.	1985	8.00	23
1984 Santa's Trolley E-6231	3-Yr.	1986	11.00	50
1984 Holiday Penguin E-6240	3-Yr.	1986	1.50	15-20
1984 Little Drummer E-6241	5-Yr.	1988	2.00	N/A
1984 Happy Holidays E-6248	2-Yr.	1985	2.00	5
1984 Christmas Nest E-6249	2-Yr.	1985	3.00	25
1984 Bunny's Christmas Stocking E-6251	Yr.Iss.	1984	2.00	15
1984 Santa On Ice E-6252	3-Yr.	1986	2.50	25
1984 Treasured Memories The New Sled E-6256	2-Yr.	1985	7.00	N/A
1984 Penguins On Ice E-6280	2-Yr.	1985	7.50	N/A
1984 Up On The House Top E-6281	6-Yr.	1989	9.00	N/A

YEAR ISSUE	EDITION LIMIT	YEAR RETD.	ISSUE PRICE	*QUOTE U.S.$
1984 Grandchild's First Christmas (pink) 1984 E-6286	Yr.Iss.	1984	5.00	N/A
1984 Grandchild's First Christmas (blue) 1984 E-6286	Yr.Iss.	1984	5.00	N/A
1984 Godchild's First Christmas E-6287	3-Yr.	1986	7.00	N/A
1984 Santa In The Box E-6292	2-Yr.	1985	6.00	N/A
1984 Carousel Horse E-6913	2-Yr.	1985	1.50	N/A
1983 Arctic Charmer E-6945	2-Yr.	1984	7.00	N/A
1982 Victorian Sleigh E-6946	4-Yr.	1985	9.00	15
1983 Wing-A-Ding Angel E-6948	3-Yr.	1985	7.00	50
1982 A Saviour Is Born This Day E-6949	8-Yr.	1989	4.00	18
1982 Crescent Santa E-6950 - Gilmore	4-Yr.	1985	10.00	50
1982 Baby's First Christmas 1982 E-6952	Yr.Iss.	1982	10.00	N/A
1982 Polar Bear Fun Whoops, It's 1982 E-6953	Yr.Iss.	1982	10.00	75
1982 Holiday Skier E-6954 - J. Davis	5-Yr.	1986	7.00	N/A
1982 Toy Soldier 1982 E-6957	Yr.Iss.	1982	6.50	N/A
1982 Carousel Horses E-6958	3-Yr.	1984	8.00	20-40
1982 Dear Santa E-6959 - Gilmore	8-Yr.	1989	10.00	25
1982 Merry Christmas Grandma E-6975	3-Yr.	1984	5.00	N/A
1982 Penguin Power E-6977	2-Yr.	1983	6.00	15
1982 Bunny Winter Playground 1982 E-6978	Yr.Iss.	1982	10.00	N/A
1982 Baby's First Christmas 1982 E-6979	Yr.Iss.	1982	10.00	N/A
1983 Carousel Horse E-6980	4-Yr.	1986	8.00	N/A
1982 Grandchild's First Christmas 1982 E-6983	Yr.Iss.	1982	5.00	73
1982 Merry Christmas Teacher E-6984	4-Yr.	1985	7.00	N/A
1983 Garfield Cuts The Ice E-8771 - J. Davis	3-Yr.	1985	6.00	45
1984 A Stocking Full For 1984 E-8773 - J. Davis	Yr.Iss.	1984	6.00	N/A
1983 Stocking Full For 1983 E-8773 - J. Davis	Yr.Iss.	1983	6.00	N/A
1985 Santa Claus Balloon 55794	Yr.Iss.	1985	8.50	20-40
1985 Carousel Reindeer 55808	4-Yr.	1988	12.00	33
1985 Angel In Flight 55816	4-Yr.	1988	8.00	23
1985 Christmas Penguin 55824	4-Yr.	1988	7.50	43
1985 Merry Christmas Godchild 55832 - Gilmore	5-Yr.	1989	8.00	N/A
1985 Baby's First Christmas 55840	2-Yr.	1986	15.00	N/A
1985 Old Fashioned Rocking Horse 55859	2-Yr.	1986	10.00	15
1985 Child's Second Christmas 55867	5-Yr.	1989	11.00	N/A
1985 Fishing For Stars 55875	5-Yr.	1989	9.00	25
1985 Baby Blocks 55883	2-Yr.	1986	12.00	N/A
1985 Christmas Toy Chest 55891	5-Yr.	1989	10.00	10-25
1985 Grandchild's First Christmas 55921	5-Yr.	1989	7.00	30
1985 Joy Photo Frame 55956	Yr.Iss.	1985	6.00	N/A
1985 We Three Kings 55964	Yr.Iss.	1985	4.50	20
1985 The Night Before Christmas 55972	2-Yr.	1986	5.00	N/A
1985 Baby's First Christmas 55980	Yr.Iss.	1985	6.00	N/A
1985 Baby Rattle Photo Frame 56006	2-Yr.	1986	5.00	N/A
1985 Baby's First Christmas 1985 56014 - Gilmore	Yr.Iss.	1985	10.00	N/A
1985 Christmas Plane Ride 56049 - L. Rigg	6-Yr.	1990	10.00	N/A
1985 Scottie Celebrating Christmas 56065	5-Yr.	1989	7.50	25
1985 North Pole Native 56073	2-Yr.	1986	9.00	N/A
1985 Skating Walrus 56081	2-Yr.	1986	9.00	20
1985 Ski Time 56111 - J. Davis	Yr.Iss.	1985	13.00	N/A
1985 North Pole Express 56138 - J. Davis	Yr.Iss.	1985	12.00	N/A
1985 Merry Christmas Mother 56146 - J. Davis	Yr.Iss.	1985	8.50	N/A
1985 Hoppy Christmas 56154 - J. Davis	Yr.Iss.	1985	8.50	N/A
1985 Merry Christmas Teacher 56170 - J. Davis	Yr.Iss.	1985	6.00	N/A
1985 Garfield-In-The-Box 56189 - J. Davis	Yr.Iss.	1985	6.50	25
1985 Merry Christmas Grandma 56197	Yr.Iss.	1985	7.00	N/A
1985 Christmas Lights 56200	2-Yr.	1986	8.00	N/A
1985 Victorian Doll House 56251	Yr.Iss.	1985	13.00	40
1985 Tobaoggan Ride 56286	4-Yr.	1988	6.00	15
1985 St. Nicholas Circa 1910 56359	5-Yr.	1989	6.00	15
1985 Look Out Below 56375	Yr.Iss.	1985	8.50	40
1985 Flying Santa Christmas Special 56383	2-Yr.	1986	10.00	N/A
1985 Sawin Elf Helper 56391	Yr.Iss.	1985	8.00	N/A
1985 Snow Shoe-In Santa 56405	Yr.Iss.	1985	8.00	50
1985 Our Hero 56413	Yr.Iss.	1985	5.50	N/A
1985 Not A Creature Was Stirring 56421	2-Yr.	1986	4.00	N/A
1985 Merry Christmas Teacher 56448	Yr.Iss.	1985	9.00	N/A
1985 A Stocking Full For 1985 56444 - J. Davis	Yr.Iss.	1985	6.00	25
1985 Christmas Tree Photo Frame 56871	4-Yr.	1988	10.00	N/A
1995 How...Do I Love Thee 104949	Yr.Iss.	1995	22.50	23
1995 Swishing You Sweet Greetings 105201	Yr.Iss.	1995	20.00	20
1995 Planely Delicious 109665	Yr.Iss.	1996	20.00	20
1996 Spice Up The Season 111724	Yr. Iss.	1996	20.00	20
1995 Home For The Howl-i-days 111732	Yr.Iss.	1995	20.00	20
1995 Time For Refreshment 111872	Yr.Iss.	1995	20.00	20
1995 Holiday Bike Hike 111937	Yr.Iss.	1995	20.00	20
1996 Santa's Sacks 111945 - Hahn	Yr. Iss.	1996	15.00	18
1995 Ho, Ho, Hole in One! 111953	Yr.Iss.	1995	20.00	20
1995 No Time To Spare at Christmas 111961	Yr.Iss.	1995	20.00	20
1995 Hustling Up Some Cheer 112038	Yr.Iss.	1995	20.00	20
1995 Scoring Big at Christmas 112046	Yr.Iss.	1995	20.00	20
1995 Serving Up the Best 112054	Yr.Iss.	1995	17.50	18
1995 Sea-sons Greetings, Teacher 112070 - Gilmore	Yr.Iss.	1996	17.50	18
1995 Siesta Santa 112089 - Gilmore	Yr.Iss.	1995	25.00	25
1995 We've Shared Sew Much 112097 - Gilmore	Yr.Iss.	1995	25.00	25
1995 Toys To Treasure 112119	Yr.Iss.	1995	20.00	20-24
1995 To Santa, Post Haste 112151 - Gilmore	Yr.Iss.	1995	15.00	15
1995 Yule Logon For Christmas Cheer 122513	Yr.Iss.	1995	20.00	20
1995 Pretty Up For The Holidays 125830 - Butcher	Yr.Iss.	1995	20.00	20
1995 You Bring The Love to Christmas 125849 - Butcher	Yr.Iss.	1995	15.00	15
1995 Happy Birthday Jesus 125857 - Butcher	Yr.Iss.	1995	15.00	15
1995 Let's Snuggle Together For Christmas 125865 - Butcher	Yr.Iss.	1995	15.00	15
1995 I'm In A Spin Over You 125873 - Butcher	Yr.Iss.	1995	15.00	15
1995 Our First Christmas Together 125881 - Butcher	Yr.Iss.	1995	22.50	23
1995 Twinkle, Twinkle Christmas Star 125903 - Butcher	Yr.Iss.	1995	17.50	18
1995 Bringing Holiday Wishes To You 125911 - Butcher	Yr.Iss.	1995	22.50	23
1995 You Pull The Strings To My Heart 125938 - Butcher	Yr.Iss.	1995	20.00	20
1995 Baby's First Christmas 125946 - Butcher	Yr.Iss.	1995	15.00	15
1995 Baby's First Christmas 125954 - Butcher	Yr.Iss.	1995	15.00	15
1995 Friends Are The Greatest Treasure 125962 - Butcher	20,000	1995	25.00	25
1995 4-Alarm Christmas 128767 - Gilmore	Yr.Iss.	1995	17.50	18
1995 Truckin'/1956 Ford F-100 Truck 128813	Yr.Iss.	1995	25.00	20-25
1995 1955 Red Ford Thunderbird 128821	19,550	1995	20.00	28-40
1995 57 HVN/1957 Chevy Bel Air 128848	Yr.Iss.	1995	20.00	20-29
1995 1965 Chevrolet Corvette Stingray 128856	Yr.Iss.	1995	20.00	20
1995 Mom's Taxi/Dodge Caravan 128872	Yr.Iss.	1995	25.00	25
1995 Choc Full of Wishes 128945	Yr.Iss.	1995	20.00	20
1995 Have a Coke and a Smile™ 128953	Yr.Iss.	1995	22.50	23
1995 Trunk Full of Treasures 128961	20,000	1995	25.00	25-30
1995 Make Mine a Coke™ 128988	Yr.Iss.	1995	25.00	25
1995 Dashing Through the Snow 128996	Yr.Iss.	1995	20.00	20
1995 Happy Yuleglide 129003	Yr.Iss.	1995	17.50	18
1995 Santa's Speedway 129011	Yr.Iss.	1995	20.00	20
1995 You're My Cup of Tea 129038	Yr.Iss.	1996	20.00	20
1995 Crackin' a Smile 129046	Yr.Iss.	1995	17.50	18
1995 Rx:Mas Greetings 129054	Yr.Iss.	1995	17.50	18
1996 Special Bear-Livery 129062	Yr.Iss.	1996	15.00	15
1995 Merry McMeal 129070	Yr.Iss.	1995	17.50	18
1995 Above the Crowd 129089	Yr.Iss.	1995	20.00	20
1995 Mickey at the Helm 132063	Yr.Iss.	1995	17.50	18-30
1995 1959 Cadillac Eldorado 132705	Yr.Iss.	1995	20.00	20
1996 Catch Of The Holiday 132888 - Hahn	Yr.Iss.	1996	20.00	20
1995 Jackpot Joy! 132896 - Hahn	Yr.Iss.	1996	17.50	18
1995 Get in the Spirit...Recycle 132918 - Hahn	Yr.Iss.	1996	17.50	18
1995 Miss Merry's Secret 132934 - Hahn	Yr.Iss.	1995	20.00	20-24
1995 ...Good Will Toward Men 132942 - Hahn	19,450	1995	25.00	25

YEAR ISSUE	EDITION LIMIT	YEAR RETD.	ISSUE PRICE	*QUOTE U.S.$	YEAR ISSUE	EDITION LIMIT	YEAR RETD.	ISSUE PRICE	*QUOTE U.S.$
1995 Friendships Bloom Through All Seasons 132950 - Hahn	Yr.Iss.	1995	22.50	23	1996 #1 Coach 168440	Yr.Iss.	1996	9.00	9
1995 Merry Monopoly 132969	Yr.Iss.	1996	22.50	23	1996 Goin' Fishin' 168459	Yr.Iss.	1996	22.50	23-25
1995 The Night B 4 Christmas 134848	Yr.Iss.	1995	20.00	20	1996 Gifts From Mickey 168467	Yr.Iss.	1996	20.00	20
- Hahn					1996 All Fired Up For Christmas 168475	Yr.Iss.	1996	25.00	25
1996 A Cup Of Cheer 135070 - Gilmore	Yr.Iss.	1996	25.00	25	1996 Minnie's Mall Haul 168491	Yr.Iss.	1996	25.00	25
1995 Bubblin' With Joy 136581	Yr.Iss.	1995	15.00	15-40	1996 A Magic Moment 172197	Yr.Iss.	1996	17.50	18
1996 Steppin' With Minnie 136603	Yr.Iss.	1996	13.50	14	1996 Happy's Holiday 172200	Yr.Iss.	1996	17.50	18
1995 Minnie's Merry Christmas 136611	Yr.Iss.	1995	20.00	20-22	1996 Sitting Pretty 172219	Yr.Iss.	1996	17.50	18
1996 Motorcycle Mickey 136654	Yr.Iss.	1996	25.00	25	1996 Life's Sweet Choices 172634	Yr.Iss.	1996	25.00	25
1995 Makin' Tracks With Mickey 136662	Yr.Iss.	1995	20.00	20	1996 Holiday In Bloom 172669	Yr.Iss.	1996	25.00	25
1995 Mickey's Airmail 136670	Yr.Iss.	1996	20.00	20	1996 Have A Cracker Jack Christmas 172979	Yr.Iss.	1996	25.00	20
1995 Holiday Bound 136689	Yr.Iss.	1996	20.00	20	1996 Hair's The Place 173029 - Hahn	Yr.Iss.	1996	25.00	25
1995 Goofed-Up! 136697	Yr.Iss.	1996	20.00	20	1996 Merry Manicure 173339 - Hahn	Yr.Iss.	1996	25.00	25
1995 On The Ball At Christmas 136700	Yr.Iss.	1995	15.00	15	1996 100 Years...And Still On A Roll	19,960	1996	17.50	18
1995 Sweet on You 136719	Yr.Iss.	1995	22.50	23-30	173770				
1995 Nutty About Christmas 137030	Yr.Iss.	1995	22.50	23-25	1996 Tracking Reindeer Pause 173789	Yr.Iss.	1996	25.00	25
1995 Tinkertoy Joy 137049	Yr.Iss.	1996	20.00	20	- Hahn				
1995 Starring Roll At Christmas 137057	Yr.Iss.	1996	17.50	18-24	1996 Holiday Dreams Of Green 173797	Yr.Iss.	1996	15.00	15
1995 A Thimble of the Season 137243	Yr.Iss.	1996	22.50	23	- Hahn				
- Gilmore					1996 1965 Ford Mustang 173800	Yr.Iss.	1996	22.50	23
1995 A Little Something Extra...Extra	10,000	1995	25.00	25	1996 Toyland, Joyland 173878	Yr.Iss.	1996	20.00	20-25
137251					1996 Tobin's Debut Dancer 173886	20,000	1996	20.00	20-24
1995 The Maze Of Our Lives 139599	Yr.Iss.	1995	17.50	18	- Fraley				
- Hahn					1996 Thou Art My Lamp, O Lord 173894	Yr.Iss.	1996	25.00	25
1995 A Sip For Good Measure 139610	Yr.Iss.	1995	17.50	18	173770				
1995 Christmas Fishes, Dad 139629 - Hahn	Yr.Iss.	1996	17.50	18-20	1996 'Tis The Season To Be Nutty 175234	Yr.Iss.	1996	17.50	18-23
1995 Christmas Is In The Bag 139645	Yr.Iss.	1995	17.50	18	1996 1956 Chevy Corvette 175269	19,560	1996	22.50	23
1995 Gotta Have a Clue 139653	Yr.Iss.	1995	20.00	20	1996 A World Of Good Taste 175420	18,600	1996	20.00	20
1995 Fun In Hand 139661	Yr.Iss.	1995	17.50	18	1996 It's Time For Christmas 175455	Yr.Iss.	1996	25.00	25
1995 Christmas Cuddle 139688	Yr.Iss.	1996	20.00	20	1996 15 Years Of Hits 175463	10,000	1996	25.00	25-30
1995 Dreaming Of The One I Love 139696	Yr.Iss.	1996	25.00	25	1996 Sew Darn Cute 176761 - Hahn	Yr.Iss.	1996	25.00	25
1995 Sneaking a Peek 139718	Yr.Iss.	1996	22.50	23	1996 Decked Out For Christmas 176796 -	Yr.Iss.	1996	25.00	10-25
1995 Christmas Eve Mischief 139726	Yr.Iss.	1995	17.50	18	Hahn				
1995 All Tucked In 139734	Yr.Iss.	1995	15.00	15-25	1996 Campaign For Christmas 176818	19,960	1996	17.50	15-18
1995 Merry Christmas To Me 139742	Yr.Iss.	1995	17.50	18	1996 Delivering Holiday Cheers 177318	Yr.Iss.	1996	25.00	25
1995 Looking Our Holiday Best 139750	Yr.Iss.	1995	20.00	20	1996 A Splash Of Cool Yule 213713	Yr.Iss.	1996	20.00	20
1995 Christmas Vacation 142158	Yr.Iss.	1996	20.00	20	1997 100 Years of Soup-erb Good Taste!	Yr.Iss.	1997	20.00	20
1995 Just Fore Christmas 142174	Yr.Iss.	1996	15.00	15	265586				
1995 Christmas Belle 142182	Yr.Iss.	1996	20.00	20	1997 Tobin's Graceful Steed 265594	Yr.Iss.	1997	20.00	20
1995 Tail Waggin' Wishes 142190	Yr.Iss.	1995	17.50	18	- Fraley				
1995 Holiday Ride 142204	Yr.Iss.	1995	17.50	18	1997 Movin' And Groovin' 270482	Yr.Iss.	1997	22.50	23
1995 A Carousel For Ariel 142212	Yr.Iss.	1995	17.50	18	1997 Twist And Shout, "Have A Coke!"	Yr.Iss.	1997	25.00	25
1995 On The Move At Christmas 142220	Yr.Iss.	1995	17.50	18	277398				
- Hahn					1997 Cracker Jack...The Home Run	Yr.Iss.	1997	25.00	25
1995 T-Bird 146838	Yr.Iss.	1995	20.00	20	Snack 277401				
1996 Swinging On A Star 166642	Yr.Iss.	1996	20.00	20	1997 I'm So Glad I Fondue As A Friend	Yr.Iss.	1997	20.00	20
1996 A-Joy Matie, Throw Me A Lifesavers	Yr.Iss.	1996	20.00	20	277428 - Hahn				
166677					1997 Workin' 'Round The Clock 277436	Yr.Iss.	1997	22.50	23
1996 It's Plane To See...Coke Is It	Yr.Iss.	1996	25.00	25	1997 WWW.HappyHolidays!.Com 277444	Yr.Iss.	1997	25.00	25
166723					1997 Always Cool With Coke 277967	Yr.Iss.	1997	22.50	23
1996 A Century Of Good Taste 166774	Yr.Iss.	1996	25.00	25-28	1997 The Forecast Calls For Coke 277983	Yr.Iss.	1997	20.00	20
1996 Servin' Up Joy 166847	Yr.Iss.	1996	20.00	20	1997 Stockin' Up For The Holidays	Yr.Iss.	1997	22.50	23
1996 In-Line To Help Santa 166855	Yr.Iss.	1996	20.00	10-20	277991				
1996 I Love My Daughter 166863	Yr.Iss.	1996	9.00	9	1997 Home Sweet Home 278017	Yr.Iss.	1997	25.00	25
1996 I Love Grandma 166898	Yr.Iss.	1996	9.00	9	1997 Ordering Up A Merry Christmas	Yr.Iss.	1997	25.00	25
1996 I Love Dad 166901	Yr.Iss.	1996	9.00	9	278068				
1996 I Love Mom 166928	Yr.Iss.	1996	9.00	9	1997 Best Bet's A 'Vette 278092	Yr.Iss.	1997	22.50	23
1996 I Love My Godchild 166936	Yr.Iss.	1996	9.00	9	1997 Deere Made Christmas 278106	Yr.Iss.	1997	25.00	25
1996 Baby's 1st Christmas 166944	Yr.Iss.	1996	9.00	9	1997 On Track With Santa 278114	Yr.Iss.	1997	20.00	20
1996 A Boot Full Of Cheer 166952	Yr.Iss.	1996	20.00	20	1997 Prepare For Battle 278122	Yr.Iss.	1997	25.00	25
1996 Summons For A Merry Christmas	Yr.Iss.	1996	22.50	23	1997 Have Your Cake & Bake It, Too	Yr.Iss.	1997	20.00	20
166960					278130				
1996 An Appointment With Santa 166979	Yr.Iss.	1996	20.00	20	1997 G.I. Joe Loves Christmas 278149	Yr.Iss.	1997	20.00	20
1996 Play It Again, Nick 166987	Yr.Iss.	1996	17.50	18	1997 Priming Iron 278165 - Hahn	Yr.Iss.	1997	20.00	20
1996 Holiday Tinkertoy Tree 166995	Yr.Iss.	1996	17.50	18	1997 On Course With Santa 278304	Yr.Iss.	1997	20.00	20
1996 A Picture Perfect Pair 167002	Yr.Iss.	1996	25.00	25	- Hahn				
1996 Santa's On The Line 167037	Yr.Iss.	1996	25.00	18-25	1997 Ice Cream Of The Crop 278408	Yr.Iss.	1997	20.00	20
1996 Downhill Delivery 167053	Yr.Iss.	1996	25.00	25	1997 50 Years Of Miracles 278432	Yr.Iss.	1997	20.00	20
1996 On A Roll With Diet Coke 167061	Yr.Iss.	1996	20.00	20	1997 Beep Me Up! 278440	Yr.Iss.	1997	20.00	20
1996 Hold On, Santa! 167088	Yr.Iss.	1996	25.00	25	1997 Bubbling With Cheer 278467 - Hahn	Yr.Iss.	1997	20.00	20
1996 There's A Friendship Brewing	Yr.Iss.	1996	25.00	25	1997 Fired Up For Christmas 278491	Yr.Iss.	1997	22.50	23-25
167096 - Hahn					- Hahn				
1996 Tails A' Waggin' 167126	Yr.Iss.	1996	20.00	20	1997 Spare Time For Christmas Fun	Yr.Iss.	1997	25.00	25
1996 In Store For More 167134	15,000	1996	25.00	25-35	280291 - Hahn				
1996 Jeep Grand Cherokee 167215	Yr.Iss.	1996	22.50	15-23	1997 Everyone Knows It's Slinky 280992	Yr.Iss.	1997	22.50	23
1996 Chevy Blazer 167223	Yr.Iss.	1996	22.50	23	1997 Cherish The Joy 281263 - Hillman	Yr.Iss.	1997	25.00	25-30
1996 Ford Explorer 167231	Yr.Iss.	1996	22.50	23	1997 Ho, Ho, Ho, A Grilling We Will Go!	Yr.Iss.	1997	25.00	25
1996 Dodge Ram Truck 167258	Yr.Iss.	1996	22.50	23	281301				
1996 Trees To Please 168378	Yr.Iss.	1996	25.00	25	1997 Hula Hoop Holidays 281336	Yr.Iss.	1997	20.00	20
1996 Plane Crazy 168386	Yr.Iss.	1996	22.50	23	1997 Howl-A-Day Pet Shoppe 286192	Yr.Iss.	1997	25.00	25
1996 I Love My Son 168432	Yr.Iss.	1996	9.00	9	- Hahn				

YEAR ISSUE	EDITION LIMIT	YEAR RETD.	ISSUE PRICE	*QUOTE U.S.$
1997 Heading 4-Wheel Merry Christmas 287059	Yr.Iss.	1997	22.50	23
1997 For All You Do, Merry Christmas To You 290858	Yr.Iss.	1997	25.00	25
1997 Play It Again, Santa 295256	Yr.Iss.	1997	20.00	20-22
1988 Making A Point 489212 - G.G. Santiago	3-Yr.	1990	10.00	N/A
1988 Mouse Upon A Pipe 489220 - G.G. Santiago	2-Yr.	1989	10.00	12
1988 North Pole Deadline 489387	3-Yr.	1990	13.50	25
1988 Christmas Pin-Up 489409	2-Yr.	1989	11.00	30
1988 Airmail For Teacher 489425 - Gilmore	3-Yr.	1990	13.50	N/A
1994 Sending You A Season's Greetings 550140 - Butcher	Yr.Iss.	1994	25.00	25
1994 Goofy Delivery 550639	Yr.Iss.	1994	22.50	23
1994 Happy Howl-idays 550647	Yr.Iss.	1994	22.50	23-25
1994 Christmas Crusin' 550655	Yr.Iss.	1994	22.50	23
1994 Holiday Honeys 550663	Yr.Iss.	1994	20.00	20
1994 May Your Holiday Be Brightened With Love 550698 - Butcher	Yr.Iss.	1994	15.00	15
1994 May All Your Wishes Come True 550701 - Butcher	Yr.Iss.	1994	20.00	20
1994 Baby's First Christmas 550728 - Butcher	Yr.Iss.	1994	20.00	20
1994 Baby's First Christmas 550736 - Butcher	Yr.Iss.	1994	20.00	20
1994 Our First Christmas Together 550744 - Butcher	Yr.Iss.	1994	25.00	25
1994 Drumming Up A Season Of Joy 550752 - Butcher	Yr.Iss.	1994	18.50	19
1994 Friendships Warm The Holidays 550760 - Butcher	Yr.Iss.	1994	20.00	20
1994 Dropping In For The Holidays 550779 - Butcher	Yr.Iss.	1994	20.00	20
1994 Ringing Up Holiday Wishes 550787 - Butcher	Yr.Iss.	1994	18.50	19
1994 A Child Is Born 550795 - Butcher	Yr.Iss.	1995	25.00	25
1994 Tis The Season To Go Shopping 550811 - Butcher	Yr.Iss.	1994	22.50	23
1994 The Way To A Mouse's Heart 550922	Yr.Iss.	1994	15.00	15
1994 Teed-Off Donald 550930	Yr.Iss.	1994	15.00	15
1994 Holiday Show-Stopper 550949	Yr.Iss.	1995	15.00	15
1994 Answering Christmas Wishes 551023	Yr.Iss.	1994	17.50	18-25
1994 Pure Christmas Pleasure 551066	Yr.Iss.	1995	20.00	20
1986 First Christmas Together 1986 551171	Yr.Iss.	1986	9.00	15-35
1986 Elf Stringing Popcorn 551198	4-Yr.	1989	10.00	20-30
1986 Christmas Scottie 551201	4-Yr.	1989	7.00	15-30
1986 Santa and Child 551236	4-Yr.	1989	13.50	25-50
1986 The Christmas Angel 551244	4-Yr.	1989	22.50	75
1986 Peace, Love, Joy Carousel Unicorn 551252 - Gilmore	4-Yr.	1989	12.00	38
1986 Have a Heavenly Holiday 551260	4-Yr.	1989	9.00	N/A
1986 Siamese Kitten 551279	4-Yr.	1989	9.00	36
1986 Old Fashioned Doll House 551287	4-Yr.	1989	15.00	N/A
1986 Holiday Fisherman 551309	3-Yr.	1988	8.00	40
1986 Antique Toy 551317	3-Yr.	1988	9.00	10
1986 Time For Christmas 551325 - Gilmore	4-Yr.	1989	13.00	13-20
1986 Christmas Calendar 551333	2-Yr.	1987	7.00	12-16
1994 Good Tidings, Tidings, Tidings, Tidings 551333	Yr.Iss.	1995	20.00	15-20
1994 Merry Christmas 551341 - Gilmore	3-Yr.	1988	8.00	40-50
1994 From Our House To Yours 551384 - Gilmore	Yr.Iss.	1994	25.00	25
1994 Sugar 'N' Spice For Someone Nice 551406 - Gilmore	Yr.Iss.	1994	30.00	30
1994 Picture Perfect Christmas 551465	Yr.Iss.	1994	15.00	15
1994 Toodles 551503 - Zimnicki	Yr.Iss.	1994	25.00	25
1994 A Bough For Belle! 551554	Yr.Iss.	1994	18.50	15-19
1986 The Santa Claus Shoppe Circa 1905 551562 - J. Grossman	4-Yr.	1989	8.00	15
1994 Ariel's Christmas Surprise! 551570	Yr.Iss.	1994	20.00	20
1994 Merry Little Two-Step 551589	Yr.Iss.	1995	12.50	13
1994 Sweets For My Sweetie 551600	Yr.Iss.	1994	15.00	15
1994 Friends Are The Spice of Life 551619 - Hahn	Yr.Iss.	1995	20.00	20
1994 Cool Cruise/1964 1/2 Ford Mustang 551635	19,640	1994	20.00	20
1986 Baby Bear Sleigh 551651 - Gilmore	3-Yr.	1988	9.00	30
1994 Special Delivery 561657	Yr.Iss.	1994	20.00	20
1986 Baby's First Christmas 1986 551678 - Gilmore	Yr.Iss.	1986	10.00	20
1986 First Christmas Together 551708	3-Yr.	1988	6.00	10
1986 Baby's First Christmas 551716	3-Yr.	1988	5.50	10
1986 Baby's First Christmas 1986 551724	Yr.Iss.	1986	6.50	30
1994 A Christmas Tail 551759	Yr.Iss.	1995	20.00	20
1994 Merry Mischief- 551767	Yr.Iss.	1994	15.00	15
1994 L'il Stocking Stuffer 551791	Yr.Iss.	1994	17.50	18
1994 Once Upon A Time 551805	Yr.Iss.	1994	15.00	15
1994 Wishing Upon A Star 551813	Yr.Iss.	1994	18.50	19
1994 A Real Boy For Christmas 551821	Yr.Iss.	1994	15.00	15-20
1986 Peek-A-Bear Grandchild's First Christmas	Yr.Iss.	1986	6.00	23
1986 Peek-A-Bear in Stocking Present 552089	4-Yr.	1989	2.50	N/A
1986 Peek-A-Bear in Box Present 552089	4-Yr.	1989	2.50	N/A
1986 Peek-A-Bear in Shopping Bag Present 552089	4-Yr.	1989	2.50	N/A
1986 Peek-A-Bear in Cloth Bag Present 552089	4-Yr.	1989	2.50	N/A
1986 Merry Christmas (Boy) 552186 - L. Rigg	Yr.Iss.	1986	8.00	N/A
1994 Minnie's Holiday Treasure 552216	Yr.Iss.	1994	12.00	12
1994 Sweet Holidays 552259 - Butcher	Yr.Iss.	1994	12.00	12
1986 Merry Christmas (Girl) 552534 - L. Rigg	Yr.Iss.	1986	8.00	N/A
1986 Lucy & Me Christmas Tree 552542 - L. Rigg	3-Yr.	1988	7.00	25
1986 Santa's Helpers 552607	3-Yr.	1988	2.50	N/A
1986 My Special Friend 552615	3-Yr.	1988	6.00	10
1986 Christmas Wishes From Panda 552623	3-Yr.	1988	6.00	N/A
1986 Lucy & Me Ski Time 552658 - L. Rigg	2-Yr.	1987	6.50	30
1986 Merry Christmas Teacher 552666	3-Yr.	1988	6.50	N/A
1986 Country Cousins Merry Christmas, Mom (Girl on Skates) 552704	3-Yr.	1988	7.00	23
1986 Country Cousins Merry Christmas, Dad (Girl on Skates) 552704	3-Yr.	1988	7.00	23
1986 Country Cousins Merry Christmas, Mom (Boy w/Kite) 552712	4-Yr.	1989	7.00	23
1986 Country Cousins Merry Christmas, Dad (Boy w/Kite) 552712	4-Yr.	1989	7.00	25
1986 Grandmother's Little Angel 552747	4-Yr.	1989	8.00	N/A
1988 Puppy's 1st Christmas 552909	Yr.Iss.	1988	4.00	N/A
1988 Kitty's 1st Christmas 552917	Yr.Iss.	1988	4.00	25
1988 Kitty's 1st Christmas 552917	Yr.Iss.	1988	4.00	25
1988 Merry Christmas Puppy 552925	Yr.Iss.	1988	3.50	N/A
1988 Merry Christmas Kitty 552933	Yr.Iss.	1988	3.50	N/A
1986 I Love My Grandparents 553263	Yr.Iss.	1986	6.00	N/A
1986 Merry Christmas Mom & Dad 553271	Yr.Iss.	1986	6.00	N/A
1986 Hollycopter 553344	4-Yr.	1989	13.50	35
1986 From Our House To Your House 553360	3-Yr.	1988	15.00	40
1986 Christmas Rattle 553379	3-Yr.	1988	8.00	35
1986 Bah, Humbug! 553387	4-Yr.	1989	9.00	N/A
1986 God Bless Us Everyone 553395	4-Yr.	1989	10.00	15
1987 Carousel Mobile 553409	3-Yr.	1989	15.00	50
1986 Holiday Train 553417	4-Yr.	1989	10.00	N/A
1986 Lighten Up! 553603 - J. Davis	5-Yr.	1990	10.00	10-36
1986 Gift Wrap Odie 553611 - J. Davis	Yr.Iss.	1986	7.00	20
1987 M.V.B. (Most Valuable Bear) Golfing 554219	2-Yr.	1988	3.00	N/A
1987 M.V.B. (Most Valuable Bear) Ice Hockey 554219	2-Yr.	1988	3.00	N/A
1987 M.V.B. (Most Valuable Bear) Skiing 554219	2-Yr.	1988	3.00	N/A
1987 M.V.B. (Most Valuable Bear) Bowling 554219	2-Yr.	1988	3.00	N/A
1988 1st Christmas Together 554537 - Gilmore	3-Yr.	1990	15.00	N/A
1988 An Eye On Christmas 554545 - Gilmore	3-Yr.	1990	22.50	60
1988 A Mouse Check 554553 - Gilmore	3-Yr.	1990	13.50	45
1988 Merry Christmas Engine 554561	2-Yr.	1989	22.50	35
1988 Sardine Express 554588 - Gilmore	2-Yr.	1990	17.50	30
1988 1st Christmas Together 1988 554596	Yr.Iss.	1988	10.00	N/A
1988 Forever Friends 554626 - Gilmore	2-Yr.	1989	12.00	27
1988 Santa's Survey 554642	2-Yr.	1989	35.00	75-100
1989 Old Town Church 554871 - Gilmore	2-Yr.	1990	17.50	20
1988 Christmas Is Coming 554901	3-Yr.	1990	12.00	12
1988 Baby's First Christmas 1988 554928	Yr.Iss.	1988	7.50	N/A
1988 Baby's First Christmas 1988 554936 - Gilmore	Yr.Iss.	1988	10.00	25
1988 The Christmas Train 554944	3-Yr.	1990	15.00	N/A
1988 Li'l Drummer Bear 554952 - Gilmore	3-Yr.	1990	12.00	12
1987 Baby's First Christmas 555061	3-Yr.	1989	12.00	N/A

YEAR ISSUE	EDITION LIMIT	YEAR RETD.	ISSUE PRICE	*QUOTE U.S.$
1987 Baby's First Christmas 555088	3-Yr.	1989	7.50	N/A
1987 Baby's First Christmas 555118	3-Yr.	1989	6.00	N/A
1988 Sugar Plum Bearies 555193	Yr.Iss.	1988	4.50	N/A
1987 Garfield Merry Kissmas 555215 - J. Davis	3-Yr.	1989	8.50	30-35
1988 Sleigh Away 555401	2-Yr.	1989	12.00	N/A
1987 Merry Christmas (Boy) 555428 - L. Rigg	Yr.Iss.	1987	8.00	N/A
1987 Merry Christmas (Girl) 555436 - L. Rigg	Yr.Iss.	1987	8.00	N/A
1987 Lucy & Me Storybook Bear 555444 - L. Rigg	3-Yr.	1989	6.50	N/A
1987 Time For Christmas 555452 - L. Rigg	3-Yr.	1989	12.00	20
1987 Lucy & Me Angel On A Cloud 555487 - L. Rigg	3-Yr.	1989	8.00	35
1987 Teddy's Stocking 555940 - Gilmore	3-Yr.	1989	10.00	N/A
1987 Kitty's Jack-In-The-Box 555959	3-Yr.	1989	11.00	30
1987 Merry Christmas Teacher 555967	3-Yr.	1989	7.50	N/A
1987 Mouse In A Mitten 555975	3-Yr.	1989	7.50	N/A
1987 Boy On A Rocking Horse 555983	3-Yr.	1989	12.00	18
1987 Peek-A-Bear Letter To Santa 555991	2-Yr.	1988	8.00	30
1987 Garfield Sugar Plum Fairy 556009 - J. Davis	3-Yr.	1989	8.50	12-23
1987 Garfield The Nutcracker 556017 - J. Davis	4-Yr.	1990	8.50	10-20
1987 Joy To The World Carousel Lion 556025 - Gilmore	3-Yr.	1989	12.00	25
1988 Home Sweet Home 556033 - Gilmore	2-Yr.	1989	15.00	40
1988 Baby's First Christmas 556041	3-Yr.	1990	10.00	20
1988 Little Sailor Elf 556068	2-Yr.	1989	10.00	12-20
1987 Carousel Goose 556076	3-Yr.	1989	17.00	40
1988 Night Caps Mom 556084	Yr.Iss.	1988	5.50	N/A
1988 Night Caps Dad 556084	Yr.Iss.	1988	5.50	N/A
1988 Night Caps Grandpa 556084	Yr.Iss.	1988	5.50	N/A
1988 Night Caps Grandma 556084	Yr.Iss.	1988	5.50	N/A
1988 Rocking Horse Past Joys 556157	2-Yr.	1989	10.00	20
1987 Partridge In A Pear Tree 556173 - Gilmore	3-Yr.	1989	9.00	25-35
1987 Skating Santa 1987 556211	Yr.Iss.	1987	13.50	75
1987 Baby's First Christmas 1987 556238 - Gilmore	Yr.Iss.	1987	10.00	25
1987 Baby's First Christmas 1987 556254	Yr.Iss.	1987	7.00	25
1988 Teddy's Suspenders 556262	3-Yr.	1990	8.50	22
1987 Baby's First Christmas (boy) 1987 556297	Yr.Iss.	1987	2.00	N/A
1987 Baby's First Christmas (girl) 1987 556297	Yr.Iss.	1987	2.00	N/A
1987 Beary Christmas Family (Grandma) 556300	2-Yr.	1988	2.00	N/A
1987 Beary Christmas Family (Grandpa) 556300	2-Yr.	1988	2.00	N/A
1987 Beary Christmas Family (Mom) 556300	2-Yr.	1988	2.00	N/A
1987 Beary Christmas Family (Dad) 556300	2-Yr.	1988	2.00	N/A
1988 Beary Christmas Family (Brother) 556300	2-Yr.	1988	2.00	N/A
1987 Beary Christmas Family (Sister)556300	2-Yr.	1988	2.00	N/A
1987 Merry Christmas Teacher (Boy) 556319	2-Yr.	1988	2.00	N/A
1987 Merry Christmas Teacher (Girl) 556319	2-Yr.	1988	2.00	N/A
1987 1st Christmas Together 1987 556335	Yr.Iss.	1987	9.00	18
1987 Katie Goes Ice Skating 556378	3-Yr.	1989	8.00	30
1987 Scooter Snowman 556386	3-Yr.	1989	8.00	30
1987 Santa's List 556394	3-Yr.	1989	7.00	23
1988 Kitty's Bed 556408	3-Yr.	1989	12.00	30
1988 Grandchild's First Christmas 556416	2-Yr.	1989	10.00	N/A
1987 Two Turtledoves 556432 - Gilmore	3-Yr.	1989	9.00	30
1987 Three French Hens 556440 - Gilmore	3-Yr.	1989	9.00	30
1988 Four Calling Birds 556459 - Gilmore	3-Yr.	1990	11.00	30
1988 Teddy Takes A Spin 556467	3-Yr.	1990	13.00	35
1987 Tiny Toy Thimble Mobile 556475	2-Yr.	1988	12.00	35
1987 Bucket O'Love (Puppy's 1st Christmas) 556491	2-Yr.	1988	2.50	N/A
1987 Bucket O'Love (Kitty's 1st Christmas) 556491	2-Yr.	1988	2.50	N/A
1987 Bucket O'Love (Christmas Kitty) 556491	2-Yr.	1988	2.50	N/A
1987 Bucket O'Love (Christmas Puppy) 556491	2-Yr.	1988	2.50	N/A
1987 Puppy Love 556505	3-Yr.	1989	6.00	N/A
1987 Peek-A-Bear My Special Friend 556513	4-Yr.	1990	6.00	30
1987 Our First Christmas Together 556548	3-Yr.	1989	13.00	20
1987 Three Little Bears 556556	3-Yr.	1989	7.50	15
1988 Lucy & Me Mailbox Bear 556564 - L. Rigg	3-Yr.	1990	3.00	N/A
1987 Twinkle Bear 556572 - Gilmore	3-Yr.	1989	8.00	N/A
1988 I'm Dreaming Of A Bright Christmas 556602	Yr.Iss.	1988	2.50	N/A
1988 Christmas Train 557196	2-Yr.	1989	10.00	N/A
1988 Dairy Christmas 557501 - M. Cook	2-Yr.	1989	10.00	22-30
1988 Merry Christmas (Boy) 557595 - L. Rigg	Yr.Iss.	1988	10.00	N/A
1988 Merry Christmas (Girl) 557609 - L. Rigg	Yr.Iss.	1988	10.00	N/A
1988 Toy Chest Keepsake 558206 - L. Rigg	3-Yr.	1990	12.50	30
1988 Teddy Bear Greetings 558214 - L. Rigg	3-Yr.	1990	8.00	30
1988 Jester Bear 558222 - L. Rigg	2-Yr.	1989	8.00	N/A
1988 Night-Watch Cat 558362 - J. Davis	3-Yr.	1990	13.00	35
1988 Christmas Thim-bell Mouse 558389	Yr.Iss.	1988	4.00	30
1988 Christmas Thim-bell Snowman 558389	Yr.Iss.	1988	4.00	N/A
1988 Christmas Thim-bell Bear 558389	Yr.Iss.	1988	4.00	N/A
1988 Christmas Thim-bell Santa 558389	Yr.Iss.	1988	4.00	N/A
1988 Baby's First Christmas 558397 - D. Parker	3-Yr.	1990	16.00	30
1988 Christmas Tradition 558400 - Gilmore	3-Yr.	1990	10.00	25
1988 Stocking Story 558419 - G.G. Santiago	3-Yr.	1990	10.00	23
1988 Winter Tale 558427 - G.G. Santiago	2-Yr.	1989	6.00	N/A
1988 Party Mouse 558435 - G.G. Santiago	3-Yr.	1990	12.00	30
1988 Christmas Watch 558443 - G.G. Santiago	2-Yr.	1989	11.00	32
1988 Christmas Vacation 558451 - G.G. Santiago	3-Yr.	1990	10.00	23
1988 Sweet Cherub 558478 - G.G. Santiago	3-Yr.	1990	7.00	8
1988 Time Out 558486 - G.G. Santiago	2-Yr.	1989	11.00	N/A
1988 The Ice Fairy 558516 - G.G. Santiago	3-Yr.	1990	23.00	35-55
1988 Santa Turtle 558559	2-Yr.	1989	10.00	35
1988 The Teddy Bear Ball 558567	3-Yr.	1990	10.00	25
1988 Turtle Greetings 558583	2-Yr.	1989	8.50	25
1988 Happy Howladays 558605	Yr.Iss.	1988	7.00	15
1988 Special Delivery 558699 - J. Davis	3-Yr.	1990	9.00	30
1988 Deer Garfield 558702 - J. Davis	3-Yr.	1990	12.00	30
1988 Garfield Bags O' Fun 558761 - J. Davis	Yr.Iss.	1988	3.30	N/A
1988 Gramophone Keepsake 558818	2-Yr.	1989	13.00	20
1988 North Pole Lineman 558834 - Gilmore	2-Yr.	1989	10.00	50
1988 Five Golden Rings 559121 - Gilmore	3-Yr.	1990	11.00	25
1988 Six Geese A-Laying 559148 - Gilmore	3-Yr.	1990	11.00	25
1988 Pretty Baby 559156 - R. Morehead	3-Yr.	1990	12.50	25
1988 Old Fashioned Angel 559164 - R. Morehead	3-Yr.	1990	12.50	20
1988 Two For Tea 559776 - Gilmore	3-Yr.	1990	20.00	35-40
1988 Merry Christmas Grandpa 560065	3-Yr.	1990	8.00	N/A
1990 Reeling In The Holidays 560405 - M. Cook	3-Yr.	1991	8.00	15
1991 Walkin' With My Baby 561029 - M. Cook	2-Yr.	1992	10.00	N/A
1989 Scrub-A-Dub Chipmunk 561037 - M. Cook	2-Yr.	1990	8.00	10-20
1989 Christmas Cook-Out 561045 - M. Cook	2-Yr.	1990	9.00	12-20
1989 Bunkie 561835 - S. Zimnicki	3-Yr.	1991	22.50	25-30
1989 Sparkles 561843 - S. Zimnicki	3-Yr.	1991	17.50	25-28
1992 Sparky & Buffer 561851 - S. Zimnicki	3-Yr.	1994	25.00	25
1989 Popper 561878 - S. Zimnicki	3-Yr.	1991	12.00	25
1989 Seven Swans A-Swimming 562742 - Gilmore	3-Yr.	1991	12.00	23
1989 Eight Maids A-Milking 562750 - Gilmore	3-Yr.	1991	12.00	23
1989 Nine Ladies Dancing 562769 - Gilmore	3-Yr.	1991	15.00	23
1989 Baby's First Christmas 1989 562807	Yr.Iss.	1989	8.00	20
1989 Baby's First Christmas 1989 562815 - Gilmore	Yr.Iss.	1989	10.00	N/A
1989 First Christmas Together 1989 562823	Yr.Iss.	1989	11.00	N/A
1989 Travelin' Trike 562882 - Gilmore	3-Yr.	1991	15.00	15

YEAR ISSUE	EDITION LIMIT	YEAR RETD.	ISSUE PRICE	*QUOTE U.S.$
1989 Victorian Sleigh Ride 562890	3-Yr.	1991	22.50	23
1991 Santa Delivers Love 562904 - Gilmore	2-Yr.	1992	17.50	18
1989 Chestnut Roastin' 562912 - Gilmore	2-Yr.	1990	13.00	13
1990 Th-Ink-In' Of You 562920 - Gilmore	2-Yr.	1991	20.00	30
1989 Ye Olde Puppet Show 562939	2-Yr.	1990	17.50	20-34
1989 Static In The Attic 562947	2-Yr.	1990	13.00	25
1989 Mistle-Toast 1989 562963 - Gilmore	Yr.Iss.	1989	15.00	25
1989 Merry Christmas Pops 562971 - Gilmore	3-Yr.	1991	12.00	12
1990 North Pole Or Bust 562998 - Gilmore	2-Yr.	1991	25.00	20-25
1989 By The Light Of The Moon 563005 - Gilmore	3-Yr.	1991	12.00	24
1989 Stickin' To It 563013 - Gilmore	2-Yr.	1990	10.00	12
1989 Christmas Cookin' 563048 - Gilmore	3-Yr.	1991	22.50	25
1989 All Set For Santa 563080 -Gilmore	3-Yr.	1991	17.50	20-25
1990 Santa's Sweets 563196 - Gilmore	2-Yr.	1991	20.00	20
1990 Purr-Fect Pals 563218	2-Yr.	1991	8.00	8
1989 The Pause That Refreshes 563226	3-Yr.	1991	15.00	45-75
1989 Ho-Ho Holiday Scrooge 563234 - J. Davis	3-Yr.	1991	13.50	30
1989 God Bless Us Everyone 563242 - J. Davis	3-Yr.	1991	13.50	20
1989 Scrooge With The Spirit 563250 - J. Davis	3-Yr.	1991	13.50	30
1989 A Chains Of Pace For Odie 563269 - J. Davis	3-Yr.	1991	12.00	25
1990 Jingle Bell Rock 1990 563390 - G. Armgardt	Yr.Iss.	1990	13.50	25-30
1989 Joy Ridin' 563463 - J. Davis	2-Yr.	1990	15.00	30
1989 Just What I Wanted 563668 - M. Peters	3-Yr.	1991	13.50	14
1990 Pucker Up! 563676 - M. Peters	3-Yr.	1992	11.00	11
1989 What's The Bright Idea 563684 - M. Peters	3-Yr.	1991	13.50	14
1990 Fleas Navidad 563978 - M. Peters	3-Yr.	1992	13.50	25
1990 Tweet Greetings 564044 - J. Davis	2-Yr.	1991	15.00	12-20
1990 Trouble On 3 Wheels 564052 - J. Davis	3-Yr.	1992	20.00	25
1989 Mine, All Mine! 564079 - J. Davis	Yr.Iss.	1989	15.00	25
1989 Star of Stars 564389 - J. Jonik	3-Yr.	1991	9.00	15
1990 Hang Onto Your Hat 564397 - J. Jonik	3-Yr.	1992	8.00	15
1990 Fireplace Frolic 564435 - N. Teiber	2-Yr.	1991	25.00	25-32
1994 Merry Miss Merry 564508 - Hahn	Yr.Iss.	1994	12.00	12
1994 Santa Delivers 564567	Yr.Iss.	1994	12.00	12
1989 Hoe! Hoe! Hoe! 564761	2-Yr.	1989	20.00	25-35
1991 Double Scoop Snowmouse 564796 - M. Cook	3-Yr.	1993	13.50	14
1990 Christmas Is Magic 564826 - M. Cook	2-Yr.	1991	10.00	10
1990 Lighting Up Christmas 564834 - M. Cook	2-Yr.	1991	10.00	10
1989 Feliz Navidad! 1989 564842 - M. Cook	Yr.Iss.	1989	11.00	40
1989 Spreading Christmas Joy 564850 - M. Cook	3-Yr.	1991	10.00	10
1989 Yuletide Tree House 564915 - J. Jonik	3-Yr.	1991	20.00	20
1990 Brewing Warm Wishes 564974	2-Yr.	1991	10.00	10
1990 Yippie-I-Yuletide 564982 - Hahn	3-Yr.	1992	15.00	15
1990 Coffee Break 564990 - Hahn	3-Yr.	1992	15.00	15
1990 You're Sew Special 565008 - Hahn	Yr.Iss.	1990	20.00	35
1989 Full House Mouse 565016 - Hahn	3-Yr.	1990	13.50	30-75
1989 I Feel Pretty 565024 - Hahn	3-Yr.	1991	20.00	30-40
1990 Warmest Wishes 565032 - Hahn	3-Yr.	1992	15.00	15-25
1990 Baby's Christmas Feast 565040 - Hahn	3-Yr.	1992	13.50	14
1990 Bumper Car Santa 565083 - G.G. Santiago	Yr.Iss.	1990	20.00	22-40
1989 Special Delivery (Proof Ed.) 565091 - G.G. Santiago	Yr.Iss.	1989	12.00	15
1990 Ho! Ho! Yo-Yo! (Proof Ed.) 565105 - G.G. Santiago	Yr.Iss.	1990	12.00	15
1989 Weightin' For Santa 565148 - G.G. Santiago	3-Yr.	1991	7.50	8
1989 Holly Fairy 565199 - C.M. Baker	Yr.Iss.	1989	15.00	45
1990 The Christmas Tree Fairy 565202 - C.M. Baker	Yr.Iss.	1990	15.00	40
1989 Merry Christmas (Boy) 565210 - L. Rigg	Yr.Iss.	1989	12.00	38
1989 Top Of The Class 565237 - L. Rigg	3-Yr.	1991	11.00	11
1989 Deck The Hogs 565490 - M. Cook	2-Yr.	1991	12.00	14
1989 Pinata Ridin' 565504 - M. Cook	2-Yr.	1990	11.00	N/A
1989 Hangin' In There 1989 565598 - K. Wise	Yr.Iss.	1989	10.00	20
1990 Meow-y Christmas 1990 565601 - K. Wise	Yr.Iss.	1990	10.00	25
1990 Seaman's Greetings 566047	2-Yr.	1991	11.00	24
1990 Hang In There 566055	3-Yr.	1992	13.50	14
1990 Deck The Halls 566063	3-Yr.	1992	12.50	N/A
1991 Pedal Pushin' Santa 566071	Yr.Iss.	1991	20.00	20-30
1990 Merry Christmas Teacher 566098	2-Yr.	1991	11.00	11
1990 Festive Flight 566101	2-Yr.	1991	11.00	11-15
1993 I'm Dreaming of a White-Out Christmas 566144	2-Yr.	1994	22.50	23
1990 Santa's Suitcase 566160	3-Yr.	1992	25.00	25
1989 The Purr-Fect Fit! 566462	3-Yr.	1991	15.00	15-35
1990 Tumbles 1990 566519 - S. Zimnicki	Yr.Iss.	1990	16.00	25
1990 Twiddles 566551 - S. Zimnicki	3-Yr.	1992	15.00	30
1991 Snuffy 566578 - S. Zimnicki	3-Yr.	1993	17.50	18
1990 All Aboard 567671 - Gilmore	2-Yr.	1991	17.50	18-20
1990 Gone With The Wind 567698	Yr.Iss.	1989	13.50	30
1989 Dorothy 567760	Yr.Iss.	1989	12.00	35
1989 The Tin Man 567779	Yr.Iss.	1989	12.00	12
1989 The Cowardly Lion 567787	Yr.Iss.	1989	12.00	12
1989 The Scarecrow 567795	Yr.Iss.	1989	12.00	12
1990 Happy Holiday Readings 568104	2-Yr.	1991	8.00	8
1989 Merry Christmas (Girl) 568325 - L. Rigg	Yr.Iss.	1989	12.00	N/A
1991 Holidays Ahoy 568368	2-Yr.	1992	12.50	13-15
1990 Christmas Countdown 568376	3-Yr.	1992	20.00	20
1989 Clara 568406	Yr.Iss.	1989	12.50	20
1990 The Nutcracker 568414	Yr.Iss.	1990	12.50	30
1991 Clara's Prince 568422	2-Yr.	1991	12.50	18
1989 Santa's Little Reindeer 568430	2-Yr.	1991	15.00	25
1991 Tuba Totin' Teddy 568449	3-Yr.	1993	15.00	15
1990 A Calling Home At Christmas 568457	2-Yr.	1991	15.00	15
1991 Love Is The Secret Ingredient 568562 - L. Rigg	2-Yr.	1992	15.00	15
1990 A Spoonful of Love 568570 - L. Rigg	2-Yr.	1991	10.00	10
1990 Merry Christmas (Boy) 568597 - L. Rigg	Yr.Iss.	1990	13.00	N/A
1990 Merry Christmas (Girl) 568600 - L. Rigg	Yr.Iss.	1990	13.00	N/A
1990 Bearing Holiday Wishes 568619 - L. Rigg	3-Yr.	1992	22.50	23
1992 Moonlight Swing 568627 - L. Rigg	3-Yr.	1994	15.00	15
1992 Smitch 570184 - S. Zimnicki	3-Yr.	1992	22.50	23
1992 Carver 570192 - S. Zimnicki	Yr.Iss.	1992	17.50	18
1991 Twinkle & Sprinkle 570206 - S. Zimnicki	3-Yr.	1993	22.50	23
1990 Blinkie 570214 - S. Zimnicki	3-Yr.	1992	15.00	15
1990 Have A Coke And A Smile™ 571512	3-Yr.	1992	15.00	20-55
1990 Fleece Navidad 571903 - M. Cook	2-Yr.	1991	13.50	25
1990 Have a Navaho-Ho-Ho 1990 571970 - M. Cook	Yr.Iss.	1990	15.00	24-35
1990 Cheers 1990 572411 - T. Wilson	Yr.Iss.	1990	13.50	22
1990 A Night Before Christmas 572438 - T. Wilson	2-Yr.	1991	17.50	18
1990 Merry Kissmas 572446 - T. Wilson	2-Yr.	1991	10.00	30
1992 A Rockin' GARFIELD Christmas 572527 - J. Davis	2-Yr.	1993	17.50	18
1991 Here Comes Santa Paws 572535 - J. Davis	3-Yr.	1993	20.00	20-25
1990 Frosty Garfield 1990 572551 - J. Davis	Yr.Iss.	1990	13.50	35
1990 Pop Goes The Odie 572578 - J. Davis	2-Yr.	1991	15.00	30
1992 Sweet Beams 572586 - J. Davis	2-Yr.	1993	13.50	14
1990 An Apple A Day 572594 - J. Davis	2-Yr.	1991	12.00	12
1990 Dear Santa 572608 - J. Davis	3-Yr.	1992	17.00	17
1991 Have A Ball This Christmas 572616 - J. Davis	Yr.Iss.	1991	15.00	15-30
1990 Oh Shoosh! 572624 - J. Davis	3-Yr.	1992	17.00	17-20
1990 Little Red Riding Cat 572632 - J. Davis	Yr.Iss.	1990	13.50	33
1991 All Decked Out 572659 - J. Davis	2-Yr.	1993	13.50	14
1990 Over The Rooftops 572721 - J. Davis	2-Yr.	1991	17.50	28-35
1990 Garfield NFL Los Angeles Rams 572764 - J. Davis	2-Yr.	1991	12.50	13
1993 Born To Shop 572942	Yr.Iss.	1993	26.50	35
1990 Garfield NFL Cincinnati Bengals 573000 - J. Davis	2-Yr.	1991	12.50	13
1990 Garfield NFL Cleveland Browns 573019 - J. Davis	2-Yr.	1991	12.50	13
1990 Garfield NFL Houston Oiliers 573027 - J. Davis	2-Yr.	1991	12.50	13

Collectors' Information Bureau   *Quotes have been rounded up to nearest dollar

YEAR ISSUE	EDITION LIMIT	YEAR RETD.	ISSUE PRICE	*QUOTE U.S.$
1990 Garfield NFL Pittsburg Steelers 573035 - J. Davis	2-Yr.	1991	12.50	13
1990 Garfield NFL Denver Broncos 573043 - J. Davis	2-Yr.	1991	12.50	13
1990 Garfield NFL Kansas City Chiefs 573051 - J. Davis	2-Yr.	1991	12.50	13
1990 Garfield NFL Los Angeles Raiders 573078 - J. Davis	2-Yr.	1991	12.50	13
1990 Garfield NFL San Diego Chargers 573086 - J. Davis	2-Yr.	1991	12.50	13
1990 Garfield NFL Seattle Seahawks 573094 - J. Davis	2-Yr.	1991	12.50	13
1990 Garfield NFL Buffalo Bills 573108 - J. Davis	2-Yr.	1991	12.50	13
1990 Garfield NFL Indianapolis Colts 573116 - J. Davis	2-Yr.	1991	12.50	13
1990 Garfield NFL Miami Dolphins 573124 - J. Davis	2-Yr.	1991	12.50	13
1990 Garfield NFL New England Patriots 573132 - J. Davis	2-Yr.	1991	12.50	13
1990 Garfield NFL New York Jets 573140 - J. Davis	2-Yr.	1991	12.50	13
1990 Garfield NFL Atlanta Falcons 573159 - J. Davis	2-Yr.	1991	12.50	13
1990 Garfield NFL New Orleans Saints 573167 - J. Davis	2-Yr.	1991	12.50	13
1990 Garfield NFL San Francisco 49ers 573175 - J. Davis	2-Yr.	1991	12.50	13
1990 Garfield NFL Dallas Cowboys 573183 - J. Davis	2-Yr.	1991	12.50	13
1990 Garfield NFL New York Giants 573191 - J. Davis	2-Yr.	1991	12.50	13
1990 Garfield NFL Philadelphia Eagles 573205 - J. Davis	2-Yr.	1991	12.50	13
1990 Garfield NFL Phoenix Cardinals 573213 - J. Davis	2-Yr.	1991	12.50	13
1990 Garfield NFL Washington Redskins 573221 - J. Davis	2-Yr.	1991	12.50	13
1990 Garfield NFL Chicago Bears 573248 - J. Davis	2-Yr.	1991	12.50	13
1990 Garfield NFL Detroit Lions 573256 - J. Davis	2-Yr.	1991	12.50	13
1990 Garfield NFL Green Bay Packers 573264 - J. Davis	2-Yr.	1991	12.50	13
1990 Garfield NFL Minnesota Vikings 573272 - J. Davis	2-Yr.	1991	12.50	13
1990 Garfield NFL Tampa Bay Buccaneers 573280 - J. Davis	2-Yr.	1991	12.50	13
1991 Tea For Two 573299 - Hahn	3-Yr.	1993	30.00	50
1991 Hot Stuff Santa 573523	Yr.Iss.	1991	25.00	30
1990 Merry Moustronauts 573558 - M. Cook	3-Yr.	1992	20.00	20-40
1991 Santa Wings It 573612 - J. Jonik	3-Yr.	1993	13.00	13-15
1990 All Eye Want For Christmas 573647 - Gilmore	3-Yr.	1992	27.50	32
1991 Stuck On You 573655 - Gilmore	2-Yr.	1992	12.50	13
1990 Professor Michael Bear, The One Bear Band 573663 - Gilmore	3-Yr.	1992	22.50	28
1990 A Caroling Wee Go 573671 - Gilmore	3-Yr.	1992	12.00	12
1990 Merry Mailman 573698 - Gilmore	2-Yr.	1991	15.00	30
1990 Deck The Halls 573701 - Gilmore	3-Yr.	1992	22.50	30
1992 Sundae Ride 583707	2-Yr.	1993	20.00	20
1990 You're Wheel Special 573728 - Gilmore	3-Yr.	1992	15.00	15
1991 Come Let Us Adore Him 573736 - Gilmore	2-Yr.	1992	9.00	9-15
1991 Moon Beam Dreams 573760 - Gilmore	3-Yr.	1993	12.00	12
1991 A Song For Santa 573779 - Gilmore	3-Yr.	1993	25.00	25
1991 Warmest Wishes 573825 - Gilmore	Yr.Iss.	1990	17.50	25
1991 Kurious Kitty 573868 - Gilmore	3-Yr.	1993	17.50	18
1990 Old Mother Mouse 573922 - Gilmore	2-Yr.	1991	17.50	20-32
1990 Railroad Repairs 573930 - Gilmore	2-Yr.	1991	12.50	25
1990 Ten Lords A-Leaping 573949 - Gilmore	3-Yr.	1992	15.00	25
1990 Eleven Drummers Drumming 573957 - Gilmore	3-Yr.	1992	15.00	25
1990 Twelve Pipers Piping 573965 - Gilmore	3-Yr.	1992	15.00	25
1990 Baby's First Christmas 1990 573973	Yr.Iss.	1990	10.00	N/A
1990 Baby's First Christmas 1990 573981	Yr.Iss.	1990	12.00	N/A
1991 Peter, Peter Pumpkin Eater 574015 - Gilmore	2-Yr.	1992	20.00	30
1992 The Nutcracker 574023 - Gilmore	3-Yr.	1994	25.00	25
1990 Little Jack Horner 574058 - Gilmore	2-Yr.	1991	17.50	35
1991 Mary, Mary Quite Contrary 574066 - Gilmore	2-Yr.	1992	22.50	33
1992 Humpty Dumpty 574244 - Gilmore	2-Yr.	1993	25.00	25
1991 Through The Years 574252 - Gilmore	Yr.Iss.	1991	17.50	18
1991 Holiday Wing Ding 574333	3-Yr.	1993	22.50	23
1991 North Pole Here I Come 574597	3-Yr.	1993	10.00	10
1991 Christmas Caboose 574856 - Gilmore	2-Yr.	1992	25.00	30
1990 Bubble Trouble 575038 - Hahn	3-Yr.	1992	20.00	24-35
1991 Merry Mother-To-Be 575046 - Hahn	3-Yr.	1993	13.50	14
1990 A Holiday 'Scent' Sation 575054 - Hahn	3-Yr.	1992	15.00	20-30
1990 Catch Of The Day 575070 - Hahn	3-Yr.	1992	25.00	25-35
1990 Don't Open 'Til Christmas 575089 - Hahn	3-Yr.	1992	17.50	18
1990 I Can't Weight 'Til Christmas 575119 - Hahn	3-Yr.	1992	16.50	30
1991 Deck The Halls 575127 - Hahn	2-Yr.	1992	15.00	25
1992 Music Mice-Tro! 575143	2-Yr.	1993	12.00	12
1990 Mouse House 575186	3-Yr.	1992	16.00	16
1991 Dream A Little Dream 575593	2-Yr.	1992	17.50	18
1991 Christmas Two-gether 575615 - L. Rigg	3-Yr.	1993	22.50	23
1992 On Target Two-Gether 575623	Yr.Iss.	1992	17.00	17
1991 Christmas Trimmings 575631	2-Yr.	1992	17.00	17
1991 Gumball Wizard 575658 - Gilmore	2-Yr.	1992	13.00	13
1991 Crystal Ball Christmas 575666 - Gilmore	2-Yr.	1992	22.50	23
1990 Old King Cole 575682 - Gilmore	2-Yr.	1991	20.00	29
1991 Tom, Tom The Piper's Son 575690 - Gilmore	2-Yr.	1992	15.00	33
1992 Rock-A-Bye Baby 575704 - Gilmore	2-Yr.	1993	13.50	14
1992 Queen of Hearts 575712 - Gilmore	2-Yr.	1992	17.50	18
1993 Toy To The World 575763	2-Yr.	1994	25.00	25
1992 Tasty Tidings 575836 - L. Rigg	Yr.Iss.	1992	13.50	14
1991 Tire-d Little Bear 575852 - L. Rigg	Yr.Iss.	1991	12.50	13
1990 Baby Bear Christmas 1990 575860 - L. Rigg	Yr.Iss.	1990	12.00	28
1991 Crank Up The Carols 575887 - L. Rigg	2-Yr.	1992	17.50	18
1990 Beary Christmas 1990 576158	Yr.Iss.	1990	12.00	12
1991 Merry Christmas (Boy) 576166 - L. Rigg	Yr.Iss.	1991	13.00	13
1991 Merry Christmas (Girl) 576174 - L. Rigg	Yr.Iss.	1991	13.00	13
1991 Christmas Cutie 576182	3-Yr.	1993	13.50	14
1991 Meow Mates 576220	3-Yr.	1993	12.00	12
1991 Frosty The Snowman 576425	3-Yr.	1993	15.00	15
1991 Ris-ski Business 576719 - T. Wilson	2-Yr.	1992	10.00	10
1991 Pinocchio 577391 - J. Davis	3-Yr.	1993	15.00	15
1990 Yuletide Ride 1990 577502 - Gilmore	Yr.Iss.	1990	13.50	30-50
1990 Tons of Toys 577510	Yr.Iss.	1990	13.00	30
1990 McHappy Holidays 577529	2-Yr.	1991	17.50	25
1990 Heading For Happy Holidays 577537	3-Yr.	1992	17.50	18
1990 'Twas The Night Before Christmas 577545	2-Yr.	1992	17.50	18
1990 Over One Million Holiday Wishes! 577553	Yr.Iss.	1990	17.50	25-30
1991 You Malt My Heart 577596	2-Yr.	1991	25.00	25
1991 All I Want For Christmas 577618	2-Yr.	1992	20.00	20
1991 Bearly Sleepy 578029 - Gilmore	3-Yr.	1992	17.50	18
1994 Buttons 'N' Bow Boutique 578363 - Gilmore	Yr.Iss.	1995	22.50	23-26
1992 Spreading Sweet Joy 580465	Yr.Iss.	1992	13.50	14
1991 Things Go Better With Coke™ 580597	3-Yr.	1993	17.00	14-25
1991 Christmas To Go 580600 - M. Cook	Yr.Iss.	1991	22.50	23
1991 Have A Mariachi Christmas 580619 - M. Cook	2-Yr.	1992	13.50	14
1993 Bearly Balanced 580724	Yr.Iss.	1993	15.00	15
1992 Ring My Bell 580740 - J. Davis	Yr.Iss.	1992	13.50	14-27
1992 4 x 4 Holiday Fun 580783 - J. Davis	2-Yr.	1993	20.00	20
1991 Christmas Is In The Air 581453	Yr.Iss.	1991	15.00	15-24
1991 Holiday Treats 581542	Yr.Iss.	1991	17.50	18
1991 Christmas Is My Goal 581550	2-Yr.	1992	17.50	12-18
1991 A Quarter Pounder With Cheer® 581569	3-Yr.	1993	20.00	20
1992 The Holidays Are A Hit 581577	2-Yr.	1993	17.50	18
1991 From The Same Mold 581798 - Gilmore	3-Yr.	1993	17.00	17
1991 The Glow Of Christmas 581801	2-Yr.	1993	20.00	20
1992 Tip Top Tidings 581828	2-Yr.	1993	13.00	13

Treasury Masterpiece Editions/Enesco Group, Inc. ORNAMENTS
to Treasury Masterpiece Editions/Enesco Group, Inc.

YEAR ISSUE	EDITION LIMIT	YEAR RETD.	ISSUE PRICE	*QUOTE U.S.$
1994 A Sign of Peace 581992	Yr.lss.	1994	18.50	19
1992 Christmas Lifts The Spirits 582018	2-Yr.	1993	25.00	25
1993 Joyeux Noel 582026	2-Yr.	1994	24.50	25
1992 A Pound Of Good Cheers 582034	2-Yr.	1993	17.50	18
1994 Wishing You Well At Christmas 582050	Yr.lss.	1994	25.00	25
1994 Ahoy Joy! 582085	Yr.lss.	1994	20.00	20
1993 Holiday Mew-Sic 582107	2-Yr.	1994	20.00	20
1993 Santa's Magic Ride 582115	2-Yr.	1994	24.00	24
1994 Santa...Phone Home 582166	Yr.lss.	1994	25.00	25
1993 Warm And Hearty Wishes 582344	Yr.lss.	1993	17.50	18-22
1993 Cool Yule 582352	Yr.lss.	1993	12.00	12-15
1994 Christmas Swishes 582379	Yr.lss.	1994	17.50	18
1993 Have A Holly Jell-O Christmas 582387	Yr.lss.	1993	14.50	45
1994 The Latest Scoop From Santa 582395 - Gilmore	Yr.lss.	1994	18.50	19
1994 Chiminy Cheer 582409 - Gilmore	Yr.lss.	1994	22.50	23
1994 Cozy Candlelight Dinner 582417 - Gilmore	Yr.lss.	1994	25.00	25
1994 Fine Feathered Festivities 582425 - Gilmore	Yr.lss.	1994	22.50	23
1994 Joy From Head To Hose 582433 - Gilmore	Yr.lss.	1994	15.00	15
1993 Festive Firemen 582565 - Gilmore	2-Yr.	1994	17.00	17
1991 Lights..Camera..Kissmas! 583626 - Gilmore	Yr.lss.	1991	15.00	35
1991 All Caught Up In Christmas 583537	2-Yr.	1992	10.00	10
1992 Sweet Steed 583634 - Gilmore	3-Yr.	1993	15.00	15
1992 Sweet as Cane Be 583642 - Gilmore	3-Yr.	1994	15.00	15
1991 Dreamin' Of A White Christmas 583669 - Gilmore	2-Yr.	1992	15.00	15
1991 Merry Millimeters 583677 - Gilmore	3-Yr.	1993	17.00	17
1991 Here's The Scoop 583693	2-Yr.	1992	13.50	20
1991 Happy Meal® On Wheels 583715	3-Yr.	1993	22.50	23
1991 Christmas Kayak 583723	2-Yr.	1992	13.50	14
1993 Light Up Your Holidays With Coke 583758	Yr.lss.	1993	27.50	20-28
1992 The Cold, Crisp Taste Of Coke 583766	3-Yr.	1994	17.00	17-30
1991 Marilyn Monroe 583774	Yr.lss.	1991	20.00	20-24
1992 Sew Christmasy 583820	3-Yr.	1994	25.00	25
1991 A Christmas Carol 583928 - Gilmore	3-Yr.	1993	22.50	23
1991 Checking It Twice 583936	2-Yr.	1992	25.00	25
1992 Catch A Falling Star 583944 - Gilmore	2-Yr.	1993	15.00	15-20
1992 Swingin' Christmas 584096	3-Yr.	1994	15.00	15
1994 Yuletide Yummies 584835 - Gilmore	Yr.lss.	1994	20.00	20
1993 Pool Hall-idays 584851	2-Yr.	1994	19.00	20
1994 Merry Christmas Tool You, Dad 584886	Yr.lss.	1994	22.50	23
1994 Exercising Good Taste 584967	Yr.lss.	1994	17.50	18
1994 Holiday Chew-Chew 584983 - Gilmore	Yr.lss.	1994	22.50	23
1992 Mc Ho, Ho, Ho 585181	3-Yr.	1994	22.50	23
1991 Merry Christmas Go-Round 585203 - J. Davis	3-Yr.	1993	20.00	20
1992 Holiday On Ice 585254 - J. Davis	3-Yr.	1994	17.50	18
1991 Holiday Hideout 585270 - J. Davis	2-Yr.	1992	15.00	15
1992 Fast Track Cat 585289 - J. Davis	3-Yr.	1994	17.50	18-22
1992 Holiday Cat Napping 585319 - J. Davis	2-Yr.	1993	20.00	20
1993 Bah Humbug 585394 - Davis	Yr.lss.	1993	15.00	15
1992 The Finishing Touches 585610 - T. Wilson	2-Yr.	1993	17.50	18
1992 Jolly Ol' Gent 585645 - J. Jonik	3-Yr.	1994	13.50	14
1991 Our Most Precious Gift 585726	Yr.lss.	1991	17.50	18-22
1991 Christmas Cheer 585769	2-Yr.	1992	13.50	14
1993 Chimer 585777 - Zimnicki	Yr.lss.	1993	25.00	10-25
1993 Sweet Whiskered Wishes 585807	Yr.lss.	1993	17.00	17-25
1993 Grade "A" Wishes From Garfield 585823 - Davis	2-Yr.	1994	20.00	20
1992 A Child's Christmas 586358	3-Yr.	1994	25.00	25
1992 Festive Fiddlers 586501	Yr.lss.	1992	20.00	20
1992 La Luminaria 586579 - M. Cook	2-Yr.	1993	13.50	14
1991 Fired Up For Christmas 586587 - Gilmore	2-Yr.	1992	32.50	33
1991 One Foggy Christmas Eve 586625 - Gilmore	3-Yr.	1993	30.00	30
1991 For A Purr-fect Mom 586641 - Gilmore	Yr.lss.	1991	12.00	12
1991 For A Special Dad 586668 - Gilmore	Yr.lss.	1991	17.50	18
1991 With Love 586676 - Gilmore	Yr.lss.	1991	13.00	13
1991 For A Purr-fect Aunt 586692 - Gilmore	Yr.lss.	1991	12.00	12
1991 For A Dog-Gone Great Uncle 586706 - Gilmore	Yr.lss.	1991	12.00	12
1991 Peddling Fun 586714 - Gilmore	Yr.lss.	1991	16.00	16
1991 Special Keepsakes 586722 - Gilmore	Yr.lss.	1991	13.50	1
1992 Cozy Chrismas Carriage 586730 - Gilmore	2-Yr.	1993	22.50	2
1992 Small Fry's First Christmas 586749	2-Yr.	1993	17.00	1
1991 Hats Off To Christmas 586757 - Hahn	Yr.lss.	1991	22.50	2
1992 Friendships Preserved 586765 - Hahn	Yr.lss.	1992	22.50	23-3
1995 Sweet Harmony 586773 - Gilmore	Yr.lss.	1995	17.50	1
1993 Tree For Two 586781 - Gilmore	2-Yr.	1994	17.50	1
1993 A Bright Idea 586803 - Gilmore	2-Yr.	1994	22.50	2
1992 Window Wish List 586854 - Gilmore	2-Yr.	1993	30.00	3
1992 Through The Years 586862 - Gilmore	Yr.lss.	1992	17.50	1
1993 Baby's First Christmas 1993 586870 - Gilmore	Yr.lss.	1993	17.50	1
1993 My Special Christmas 586900 - Gilmore	Yr.lss.	1993	17.50	1
1991 Baby's First Christmas 1991 586935	Yr.lss.	1991	12.50	1
1992 Baby's First Christmas 1992 586943	Yr.lss.	1992	12.50	1
1992 Firehouse Friends 586951 - Gilmore	Yr.lss.	1992	22.50	2
1992 Bubble Buddy 586978 - Gilmore	2-Yr	1993	13.50	1
1992 The Warmth Of The Season 586994	2-Yr.	1993	20.00	2
1993 Baby's First Christmas Dinner 587001	Yr.lss.	1993	12.00	1
1991 Jugglin' The Holidays 587028	2-Yr.	1992	13.00	13-2
1991 Santa's Steed 587044	Yr.lss.	1991	15.00	1
1991 A Decade of Treasures 587052	Yr.lss.	1991	37.50	45-7
1992 It's A Go For Christmas 587095 - Gilmore	2-Yr.	1993	15.00	1
1991 Mr. Mailmouse 587109 - Gilmore	2-Yr.	1992	17.00	1
1992 Post-Mouster General 587117 - Gilmore	2-Yr.	1993	20.00	2
1992 To A Deer Baby 587168	Yr.lss.	1992	18.50	1
1991 Starry Eyed Santa 587176	2-Yr.	1992	15.00	1
1992 Moon Watch 587184	2-Yr.	1993	20.00	2
1992 Guten Cheers 587192	Yr.lss.	1992	22.50	23-3
1992 Put On A Happy Face 588237	2-Yr.	1993	15.00	1
1992 Beginning To Look A Lot Like Christmas 588253	2-Yr.	1993	15.00	1
1992 A Christmas Toast 588261	2-Yr.	1993	20.00	2
1992 Merry Mistle-Toad 588288	2-Yr.	1993	15.00	1
1992 Tic-Tac-Mistle-Toe 588296	3-Yr.	1994	23.00	2
1993 A Pause For Claus 588318	2-Yr.	1994	22.50	2
1992 Heaven Sent 588423 - J. Penchoff	2-Yr.	1993	12.50	1
1992 Holiday Happenings 588555 - Gilmore	3-Yr.	1994	30.00	3
1993 Not A Creature Was Stirring... 588563 - Gilmore	2-Yr.	1994	27.50	2
1992 Seed-son's Greetings 588571 - Gilmore	3-Yr.	1994	27.00	2
1992 Santa's Midnight Snack 588598 - Gilmore	2-Yr.	1993	20.00	2
1992 Trunk Of Treasures 588636 - Gilmore	Yr.lss.	1992	20.00	2
1993 Terrific Toys 588644	Yr.lss.	1993	20.00	20-2
1993 Christmas Dancer 588652	Yr.lss.	1993	15.00	1
1995 Yule Tide Prancer 588660	Yr.lss.	1995	15.00	1
1994 To The Sweetest Baby 588725 - Gilmore	Yr.lss.	1994	18.50	1
1995 Baby's Sweet Feast 588733 - Gilmore	Yr.lss.	1995	17.50	1
1991 Lighting The Way 588776	2-Yr.	1992	20.00	2
1991 Rudolph 588784	2-Yr.	1992	17.50	1
1992 Festive Newsflash 588792	2-Yr.	1993	17.50	1
1992 A-B-C-Son's Greetings 588806	2-Yr.	1993	16.50	1
1992 Hoppy Holidays 588814	Yr.lss.	1992	20.00	1
1992 Fireside Friends 588830	2-Yr.	1993	20.00	2
1992 Christmas Eve-mergency 588849	2-Yr.	1993	27.00	2
1992 A Sure Sign Of Christmas 588857	2-Yr.	1993	22.50	2
1992 Holidays Give Me A Lift 588865	2-Yr.	1993	30.00	3
1992 Yule Tide Together 588903	2-Yr.	1993	20.00	20-2
1992 Have A Soup-er Christmas 588911	2-Yr.	1993	17.50	1
1992 Christmas Cure-Alls 588938	2-Yr.	1993	20.00	2
1993 Countin' On A Merry Christmas 588954	2-Yr.	1994	22.50	2
1994 Rockin' Ranger 588970	Yr.lss.	1994	25.00	25-3
1994 Peace On Earthworm 588989	Yr.lss.	1994	20.00	2
1993 To My Gem 589004	2-Yr.	1994	27.50	2
1993 Christmas Mail Call 589012	2-Yr.	1994	20.00	2
1993 Spreading Joy 589047	2-Yr.	1994	27.50	2
1993 Pitter-Patter Post Office 589055	2-Yr.	1994	20.00	2
1994 Good Things Crop Up At Christmas 589071	Yr.lss.	1994	25.00	2
1993 Happy Haul-idays 589098	2-Yr.	1994	30.00	3
1994 Christmas Crossroads 589128	Yr.lss.	1994	20.00	2

Collectors' Information Bureau   *Quotes have been rounded up to nearest dollar

YEAR ISSUE	EDITION LIMIT	YEAR RETD.	ISSUE PRICE	*QUOTE U.S.$
1993 Hot Off The Press 589292	2-Yr.	1994	27.50	28
1993 Designed With You In Mind 589306	2-Yr.	1994	16.00	16
1992 Dial 'S' For Santa 589373	2-Yr.	1993	25.00	25
1993 Seeing Is Believing 589381 - Gilmore	2-Yr.	1994	20.00	20
1992 Joy To The Whirled 589551 - Hahn	2-Yr.	1993	20.00	20
1992 Merry Make-Over 589586 - Hahn	3-Yr.	1994	20.00	20
1992 Campin' Companions 590282 - Hahn	3-Yr.	1994	20.00	20
1994 Have A Ball At Christmas 590673	Yr.Iss.	1994	15.00	15
1992 Fur-Ever Friends 590797 - Gilmore	2-Yr.	1993	13.50	14
1993 Roundin' Up Christmas Together 590800	Yr.Iss.	1993	25.00	25
1994 Have A Totem-ly Terrific Christmas 590819	Yr.Iss.	1994	30.00	30
1992 Tee-rific Holidays 590827	3-Yr.	1994	25.00	25
1992 Spinning Christmas Dreams 590908 - Hahn	3-Yr.	1994	22.50	23
1992 Christmas Trimmin' 590932	3-Yr.	1994	17.00	12-17
1993 Toasty Tidings 590940	2-Yr.	1994	20.00	20
1993 Focusing On Christmas 590983 - Gilmore	2-Yr.	1994	27.50	28
1993 Dunk The Halls 591009	2-Yr.	1994	18.50	19
1993 Mice Capades 591386 - Hahn	2-Yr.	1994	26.50	27
1993 25 Points For Christmas 591750	Yr.Iss.	1993	25.00	25
1994 Cocoa 'N' Kisses For Santa- 591939	Yr.Iss.	1995	22.50	23
1994 On The Road With Coke™ 592528	Yr.Iss.	1995	25.00	22-25
1993 Carving Christmas Wishes 592625 - Gilmore	2-Yr.	1994	25.00	25
1995 A Well, Balanced Meal For Santa 592633	Yr.Iss.	1995	17.50	18-24
1994 What's Shakin' For Christmas 592668	Yr.Iss.	1994	18.50	19
1994 "A" For Santa 592676	Yr.Iss.	1994	17.50	14-18
1993 Celebrating With A Splash 592692	Yr.Iss.	1993	17.00	17
1993 Christmas Fly-By 592714	Yr.Iss.	1993	15.00	15
1993 Slimmin' Santa 592722	Yr.Iss.	1993	18.50	24
1993 Plane Ol' Holiday Fun 592773	Yr.Iss.	1993	27.50	28
1995 Salute 593133	Yr.Iss.	1995	22.50	23
1992 Wrappin' Up Warm Wishes 593141	Yr.Iss.	1992	17.50	18
1992 Christmas Biz 593168	2-Yr.	1993	22.50	23
1993 Smooth Move, Mom 593176	Yr.Iss.	1993	20.00	20
1993 Tool Time, Yule Time 593192	Yr.Iss.	1993	18.50	15-19
1993 Speedy 593370 - Zimnicki	2-Yr.	1994	25.00	25
1992 Holiday Take-Out 593508	Yr.Iss.	1992	17.50	18-24
1992 A Christmas Yarn 593516 - Gilmore		1992	20.00	10-20
1993 On Your Mark, Set, Is That To Go? 593524	Yr.Iss.	1993	13.50	14-27
1993 Do Not Open 'Til Christmas 593737 - Hahn	2-Yr.	1994	15.00	15
1993 Greetings In Stereo 593745 - Hahn	Yr.Iss.	1993	19.50	20
1994 Santa...You're The Pops! 593761	Yr.Iss.	1994	22.50	23
1992 Treasure The Earth 593826 - Hahn	2-Yr.	1993	25.00	25
1994 Purdy Packages, Pardner! 593834	Yr.Iss.	1994	20.00	20
1994 Handle With Care 593842	Yr.Iss.	1994	20.00	20
1994 To Coin A Phrase, Merry Christmas 593877	Yr.Iss.	1994	20.00	20
1994 Featured Presentation 593885	Yr.Iss.	1994	20.00	20
1994 Christmas Fishes From Santa Paws 593893	Yr.Iss.	1994	18.50	19-24
1993 Tangled Up For Christmas 593974	2-Yr.	1993	14.50	15
1992 Toyful Rudolph 593982	2-Yr.	1993	22.50	23
1992 Take A Chance On The Holidays 594075	3-Yr.	1994	20.00	18-25
1993 Sweet Season's Eatings 594202	Yr.Iss.	1993	22.50	23
1993 Have A Darn Good Christmas 594229 - Gilmore	2-Yr.	1994	21.00	14-21
1994 You Melt My Heart 594237 - Gilmore	Yr.Iss.	1994	15.00	15
1993 The Sweetest Ride 594253 - Gilmore	2-Yr.	1994	18.50	19
1994 Finishing First 594342 - Gilmore	Yr.Iss.	1994	20.00	20
1992 Lights..Camera..Christmas! 594369	2-Yr.	1993	20.00	12-20
1994 Yule Fuel 594385	Yr.Iss.	1994	20.00	20
1992 Spirited Stallion 594407	Yr.Iss.	1992	15.00	15
1993 Have A Cheery Christmas, Sister 594687	Yr.Iss.	1993	13.50	14
1993 Say Cheese 594962 - Gilmore	2-Yr.	1994	13.50	14
1993 Christmas Kicks 594989	Yr.Iss.	1994	17.50	18
1993 Time For Santa 594997 - Gilmore	Yr.Iss.	1994	17.50	18
1993 Holiday Orders 595004	Yr.Iss.	1993	20.00	20-24
1993 'Twas The Night Before Christmas 595012	Yr.Iss.	1993	22.50	23
1995 Filled To The Brim 595039 - Gilmore		1995	25.00	25
1994 Toy Tinker Topper 595047 - Gilmore	Yr.Iss.	1994	20.00	20
1993 Sugar Chef Shoppe 595055 - Gilmore	2-Yr.	1994	23.50	24
1993 Merry Mc-Choo-Choo 595063	Yr.Iss.	1993	30.00	30-35
1993 Merry Christmas, Daughter 595098	Yr.Iss.	1993	20.00	20
1993 Rockin' With Santa 595195	2-Yr.	1994	13.50	14
1994 Santa Claus Is Comin' 595209	Yr.Iss.	1994	20.00	20
1993 Christmas-To-Go 595217	Yr.Iss.	1993	25.50	12-26
1994 Seasoned With Love 595268	Yr.Iss.	1994	22.50	23
1993 Sleddin' Mr. Snowman 595276	2-Yr.	1994	13.00	13
1993 A Kick Out Of Christmas 595373	2-Yr.	1994	10.00	10
1993 Friends Through Thick And Thin 595381	2-Yr.	1994	10.00	10
1993 See-Saw Sweethearts 595403	2-Yr.	1994	10.00	10
1993 Special Delivery For Santa 595411	2-Yr.	1994	10.00	10
1993 Top Marks For Teacher 595438	2-Yr.	1994	10.00	10
1993 Home Tweet Home 595446	2-Yr.	1994	10.00	10
1993 Clownin' Around 595454	2-Yr.	1994	10.00	10
1993 Heart Filled Dreams 595462	2-Yr.	1994	10.00	10
1993 Merry Christmas Baby 595470	2-Yr.	1994	10.00	10-20
1994 Sweet Dreams 595489	Yr.Iss.	1994	12.50	13
1994 Peace On Earth 595497	Yr.Iss.	1994	12.50	13-20
1994 Christmas Two-gether 595500	Yr.Iss.	1994	12.50	13
1994 Santa's L'il Helper 595519	Yr.Iss.	1994	12.50	13
1994 Expecting Joy 595527 - Hahn	Yr.Iss.	1994	12.50	13
1993 Your A Hit With Me, Brother 595535 - Hahn	Yr.Iss.	1993	10.00	10
1993 For A Sharp Uncle 595543	Yr.Iss.	1993		10
1993 Paint Your Holidays Bright 595551 - Hahn	2-Yr.	1993		10
1994 Sweet Greetings 595578	Yr.Iss.	1994	12.50	13
1994 Ring In The Holidays 595586 - Hahn	Yr.Iss.	1994	12.50	13
1994 Grandmas Are Sew Special 595594	Yr.Iss.	1994		13
1994 Holiday Catch 595608 - Hahn	Yr.Iss.	1994	12.50	13
1994 Bubblin' with Joy 595616	Yr.Iss.	1994	12.50	13
1992 A Watchful Eye 595713	Yr.Iss.	1992	15.00	15
1992 Good Catch 595721	Yr.Iss.	1992	12.00	12
1992 Squirrelin' It Away 595748 - Hahn	Yr.Iss.	1992	12.00	13
1992 Checkin' His List 595756	Yr.Iss.	1992	12.50	13
1992 Christmas Cat Nappin' 595764	Yr.Iss.	1992	12.00	12
1992 Bless Our Home 595772	Yr.Iss.	1992	12.00	12
1992 Salute the Season 595780 - Hahn	Yr.Iss.	1992	12.00	12
1992 Fired Up For Christmas 595799	Yr.Iss.	1992	12.00	12-15
1992 Speedin' Mr. Snowman 595802 - M. Rhyner-Nadig	Yr.Iss.	1992	12.00	12
1992 Merry Christmas Mother Earth 595810 - Hahn	Yr.Iss.	1992	11.00	11
1994 Mine, Mine, Mine 585815 - Davis	Yr.Iss.	1994	20.00	20
1992 Wear The Season With A Smile 595829	Yr.Iss.	1992	10.00	10
1992 Jesus Loves Me 595837 - Hahn	Yr.Iss.	1992	10.00	10
1994 Good Friends Are Forever 595950 - Gilmore	Yr.Iss.	1994	13.50	14
1993 Treasure The Holidays, Man! 596051	Yr.Iss.	1993	22.50	16-24
1993 Ariel's Under-The-Sea Tree 596078	Yr.Iss.	1993	20.00	14-23
1993 Here Comes Santa Claws 596086	Yr.Iss.	1993	22.50	35
1993 A Spot of Love 596094	Yr.Iss.	1993	17.50	18
1993 Hearts Aglow 596108	Yr.Iss.	1993	18.50	35
1993 Love's Sweet Dance 596116	Yr.Iss.	1993	25.00	25
1993 Holiday Wishes 596124	Yr.Iss.	1993	15.00	15-20
1993 Hangin Out For The Holidays 596132	Yr.Iss.	1993	15.00	14-35
1993 Magic Carpet Ride 596140	Yr.Iss.	1993	20.00	20
1993 Holiday Treasures 596159	Yr.Iss.	1993	18.50	35
1993 Happily Ever After 596167	Yr.Iss.	1993	22.50	23
1993 The Fairest Of Them All 596175	Yr.Iss.	1993	18.50	19
1994 Christmas Tee Time 596256	Yr.Iss.	1995	25.00	25
1994 Have a Merry Dairy Christmas 596264	Yr.Iss.	1994	22.50	23
1994 Happy Holi-date 596272 - Hahn	Yr.Iss.	1995	22.50	18-23
1994 O' Come All Ye Faithful 596280 - Hahn	Yr.Iss.	1994	15.00	15-75
1994 One Small Step... 596299 - Hahn	19,690	1994	25.00	45
1994 To My Favorite V.I.P. 596698	Yr.Iss.	1994	20.00	20
1993 December 25...Dear Diary 596809	2-Yr.	1994	10.00	10
1994 Building Memories 596876 - Hahn	Yr.Iss.	1994	25.00	25
1994 Open For Business 596906 - Hahn	Yr.Iss.	1994	17.50	18
1993 Wheel Merry Wishes 596930 - Hahn	2-Yr.	1994	15.00	15
1993 Good Grounds For Christmas 596957 - Hahn	Yr.Iss.	1993	24.50	15-25
1993 Ducking The Season's Rush 597597	Yr.Iss.	1994	17.50	18
1994 Twas The Nite Before Christmas 597643 - Gilmore	Yr.Iss.	1994	18.50	19
1993 Here Comes Rudolph® 597686	2-Yr.	1994	17.50	18

YEAR ISSUE	EDITION LIMIT	YEAR RETD.	ISSUE PRICE	*QUOTE U.S.$
1993 It's Beginning To Look A Lot Like Christmas 597694	Yr.Iss.	1993	22.50	23
1993 Christmas In The Making 597716	Yr.Iss.	1993	20.00	20
1994 I Can Bear-ly Wait For A Coke™ 597724	Yr.Iss.	1995	18.50	19
1993 Mickey's Holiday Treasure 597759	Yr.Iss.	1993	12.00	12-15
1993 Dream Wheels/1953 Chevrolet Corvette 597856	Yr.Iss.	1993	29.50	26-75
1994 Gallant Greeting- 598313	Yr.Iss.	1994	15.00	20
1994 Merry Menage 598321	Yr.Iss.	1994	20.00	20-25
1993 All You Add Is Love 598429	Yr.Iss.	1993	18.50	19
1993 Goofy About Skiing 598631	Yr.Iss.	1993	22.50	23
1994 Ski-son's Greetings 599069	Yr.Iss.	1994	20.00	20
1994 Bundle Of Joy 598992	Yr.Iss.	1994	10.00	12-15
1994 Bundle Of Joy 599018	Yr.Iss.	1994	10.00	10
1994 Have A Dino-mite Christmas 599026 - Hahn	Yr.Iss.	1994	18.50	19
1994 Good Fortune To You 599034	Yr.Iss.	1994	25.00	25
1994 Building a Sew-man 599042	Yr.Iss.	1994	18.50	19-24
1994 Merry Memo-ries 599050	Yr.Iss.	1994	22.50	23
1994 Holiday Freezer Teaser 599085 - Gilmore	Yr.Iss.	1994	25.00	25
1994 Almost Time For Santa 599093 - Gilmore	Yr.Iss.	1994	25.00	25
1994 Santa's Secret Test Drive 599107 - Gilmore	Yr.Iss.	1994	20.00	20
1994 You're A Wheel Cool Brother 599115 - Gilmore	Yr.Iss.	1994	22.50	23
1994 Hand-Tossed Tidings 599166	Yr.Iss.	1994	17.50	18
1994 Tasty Take Off 599174	Yr.Iss.	1994	20.00	20
1994 Formula For Love 599530 - Olsen	Yr.Iss.	1994	10.00	10
1994 Santa's Ginger-bred Doe 599697 - Gilmore	Yr.Iss.	1994	15.00	15
1994 Nutcracker Sweetheart 599700	Yr.Iss.	1994	15.00	15
1994 Merry Reindeer Ride 599719	Yr.Iss.	1994	20.00	20
1994 Santa's Sing-A-Long 599727 - Gilmore	Yr.Iss.	1994	20.00	20
1994 A Holiday Opportunity 599735	Yr.Iss.	1995	20.00	20-25
1994 Holiday Stars 599743	Yr.Iss.	1994	20.00	20
1994 The Latest Mews From Home 653977	Yr.Iss.	1994	16.00	16
1989 Tea For Two 693758 - N. Teiber	2-Yr.	1990	12.50	14-30
1990 Holiday Tea Toast 694770 - N. Teiber	2-Yr.	1991	13.50	14
1991 It's Tea-lightful 694789	2-Yr.	1992	13.50	10-14
1989 Tea Time 694797 - N. Teiber	2-Yr.	1990	12.50	14-30
1989 Bottom's Up 1989 830003	Yr.Iss.	1989	11.00	15-32
1990 Sweetest Greetings 1990 830011 - Gilmore	Yr.Iss.	1990	10.00	10-27
1990 First Class Christmas 830038 - Gilmore	3-Yr.	1992	10.00	10-15
1989 Caught In The Act 830046 - Gilmore	3-Yr.	1991	12.50	13
1989 Readin' & Ridin' 830054 - Gilmore	3-Yr.	1991	13.50	34
1991 Beary Merry Mailman 830151 - Gilmore	3-Yr.	1993	13.50	14
1990 Here's Looking at You! 830259 - L. Rigg	2-Yr.	1991	17.50	18
1991 Stamper 830267 - S. Zimnicki	Yr.Iss.	1991	13.50	14
1991 Santa's Key Man 830461 - Gilmore	2-Yr.	1992	11.00	11
1991 Tie-dings Of Joy 830488 - Gilmore	Yr.Iss.	1992	12.00	12
1990 Have a Cool Yule 830496 - Gilmore	3-Yr.	1992	12.00	24-27
1990 Slots of Luck 830518 - Hahn	2-Yr.	1991	13.50	45-60
1991 Straight To Santa 830534 - J. Davis	2-Yr.	1992	13.50	14
1993 A Toast Ladled With Love 830828 - Hahn	2-Yr.	1994	15.00	15
1991 Letters To Santa 830925 - Gilmore	2-Yr.	1992	15.00	8-15
1991 Sneaking Santa's Snack 830933 - Gilmore	3-Yr.	1993	13.00	13
1991 Aiming For The Holidays 830941 - Gilmore	2-Yr.	1992	12.00	12
1991 Ode To Joy 830968 - Gilmore	3-Yr.	1993	10.00	10
1991 Fittin' Mittens 830976 - Gilmore	3-Yr.	1993	12.00	12
1992 Merry Kisses 831166	2-Yr.	1993	17.50	18
1992 Christmas Is In The Air 831174	2-Yr.	1993	25.00	25
1992 To The Point 831182	2-Yr.	1993	13.50	14
1992 Poppin' Hoppin' Holidays 831263 - Gilmore	Yr.Iss.	1992	25.00	25-30
1992 Tankful Tidings 831271 - Gilmore	2-Yr.	1993	30.00	30
1991 The Finishing Touch 831530 - Gilmore	Yr.Iss.	1991	10.00	10
1992 Ginger-Bred Greetings 831581 - Gilmore	Yr.Iss.	1992	12.00	10-15
1991 A Real Classic 831603 - Gilmore	Yr.Iss.	1991	10.00	10
1993 Delivered to The Nick In Time 831808 - Gilmore	2-Yr.	1994	13.50	14
1993 Sneaking A Peek 831840 - Gilmore	2-Yr.	1994	10.00	10
1993 Jewel Box Ballet 831859 - Hahn	2-Yr.	1994	20.00	2
1993 A Mistle-Tow 831867 - Gilmore	2-Yr.	1994	15.00	1
1991 Christmas Fills The Air 831921 - Gilmore	3-Yr.	1993	12.00	1
1992 A Gold Star For Teacher 831948 - Gilmore	3-Yr.	1994	15.00	1
1992 A Tall Order 832758 - Gilmore	3-Yr.	1994	12.00	1
1992 Candlelight Serenade 832766 - Gilmore	2-Yr.	1993	12.00	1
1992 Holiday Glow Puppet Show 832774 - Gilmore	3-Yr.	1994	15.00	1
1992 Christopher Columouse 832782 - Gilmore	Yr.Iss.	1992	12.00	12-1
1992 Cartin' Home Holiday Treats 832790	2-Yr.	1993	13.50	1
1992 Making Tracks To Santa 832804 - Gilmore	2-Yr.	1993	15.00	1
1992 Special Delivery 832812	2-Yr.	1993	12.00	1
1992 A Mug Full Of Love 832928 - Gilmore	Yr.Iss.	1992	13.50	1
1993 Grandma's Liddle Griddle 832936 - Gilmore	Yr.Iss.	1993	10.00	1
1992 Have A Cool Christmas 832944 - Gilmore	Yr.Iss.	1992	13.50	1
1992 Knittin' Kittens 832952 - Gilmore	Yr.Iss.	1992	17.50	1
1992 Holiday Honors 833029 - Gilmore	Yr.Iss.	1992	15.00	1
1993 To A Grade "A" Teacher 833037 - Gilmore	2-Yr.	1994	10.00	1
1992 Christmas Nite Cap 834424 - Gilmore	3-Yr.	1994	13.50	1
1993 Have A Cool Christmas 834467 - Gilmore	2-Yr.	1994	10.00	1
1993 For A Star Aunt 834556 - Gilmore	Yr.Iss.	1993	12.00	1
1994 You're A Winner Son! 834564 - Gilmore	Yr.Iss.	1994	18.50	1
1994 Especially For You 834580 - Gilmore	Yr.Iss.	1994	27.50	2
1992 North Pole Peppermint Patrol 840157 - Gilmore	2-Yr.	1993	25.00	2
1992 A Boot-iful Christmas 840165 - Gilmore	Yr.Iss.	1992	20.00	2
1994 Watching For Santa 840432	2-Yr.	1994	25.00	25-3
1992 Special Delivery 840440	Yr.Iss.	1992	22.50	2
1991 Deck The Halls 860573 - M. Peters	3-Yr.	1993	12.00	1
1991 Bathing Beauty 860581 - Hahn	3-Yr.	1993	13.50	25-3

United Design Corp.

Angels Collection-Tree Ornaments™ - P.J. Jonas, unless otherwise noted

YEAR ISSUE	EDITION LIMIT	YEAR RETD.	ISSUE PRICE	*QUOTE U.S.$
1992 Angel and Tambourine IBO-422 - S. Bradford	Retrd.	1997	20.00	2
1992 Angel and Tambourine, ivory IBO-425 - S. Bradford	Retrd.	1997	20.00	2
1993 Angel Baby w/ Bunny IBO-426 - D. Newburn	Retrd.	1996	23.00	2
1996 Angel w/Doves on Cloud IBO-472	Retrd.	1998	25.00	2
1996 Angel w/Doves on Cloud, blue IBO-473	Retrd.	1998	25.00	2
1991 Angel Waif, ivory IBO-411	Retrd.	1998	15.00	2
1993 Angel Waif, plum IBO-437	Retrd.	1996	20.00	2
1995 Autumn's Bounty IBO-460	Retrd.	1997	32.00	3
1995 Autumn's Bounty, light IBO-454	Retrd.	1997	32.00	3
1995 Birds of a Feather IBO-457	Retrd.	1998	27.00	2
1990 Crystal Angel IBO-401	Retrd.	1993	20.00	2
1993 Crystal Angel, emerald IBO-446	Retrd.	1997	20.00	2
1990 Crystal Angel, ivory IBO-405	Retrd.	1993	20.00	2
1991 Fra Angelico Drummer, blue IBO-414 - S. Bradford	Retrd.	1997	20.00	2
1991 Fra Angelico Drummer, ivory IBO-420 - S. Bradford	Retrd.	1997	20.00	2
1991 Girl Cupid w/Rose, ivory IBO-413 - S. Bradford	Retrd.	1997	15.00	2
1995 Heavenly Blossoms IBO-458	Retrd.	1997	27.00	2
1993 Heavenly Harmony IBO-428	Retrd.	1997	25.00	3
1993 Heavenly Harmony, crimson IBO-433	Retrd.	1998	22.00	3
1993 Little Angel IBO-430 - D. Newburn	Retrd.	1998	18.00	2
1993 Little Angel, crimson IBO-445 - D. Newburn	Retrd.	1996	18.00	2
1992 Mary and Dove IBO-424 - S. Bradford	Retrd.	1997	20.00	2
1994 Music and Grace IBO-448	Retrd.	1998	24.00	2
1994 Music and Grace, crimson IBO-449	Retrd.	1997	24.00	2
1994 Musical Flight IBO-450	Retrd.	1997	28.00	2
1994 Musical Flight, crimson IBO-451	Retrd.	1997	28.00	2
1991 Peace Descending, ivory IBO-412	Retrd.	1997	20.00	2

*Quotes have been rounded up to nearest dollar

YEAR ISSUE	EDITION LIMIT	YEAR RETD.	ISSUE PRICE	*QUOTE U.S.$
1993 Peace Descending, crimson IBO-436	Retrd.	1997	20.00	20
1993 Renaissance Angel, crimson IBO-429	Retrd.	1997	24.00	24
1993 Renaissance Angel, crimson IBO-431	Retrd.	1997	24.00	24
1990 Rose of Sharon IBO-402	Retrd.	1993	20.00	20
1993 Rose of Sharon, crimson IBO-439	Retrd.	1997	20.00	20
1990 Rose of Sharon, ivory IBO-406	Retrd.	1998	20.00	20
1993 Rosetti Angel, crimson IBO-434	Retrd.	1997	20.00	24
1991 Rosetti Angel, ivory IBO-410	Retrd.	1998	20.00	24
1995 Special Wishes IBO-456 - D. Newburn	Retrd.	1998	27.00	27
1995 Spring's Rebirth IBO-452	Retrd.	1998	32.00	32
1996 Spring's Rebirth, green IBO-474	Retrd.	1998	25.00	25
1992 St. Francis and Critters IBO-423 - S. Bradford	Retrd.	1997	20.00	20
1994 Star Flight IBO-447	Retrd.	1998	20.00	20
1996 Star Flight, sapphire IBO-475	Retrd.	1998	20.00	20
1990 Star Glory IBO-403	Retrd.	1993	15.00	15
1993 Star Glory, crimson IBO-438	Retrd.	1997	20.00	20
1990 Star Glory, ivory IBO-407	Retrd.	1997	15.00	20
1993 Stars & Lace IBO-427	Retrd.	1998	18.00	20
1993 Stars & Lace, emerald IBO-432	Retrd.	1998	18.00	20
1995 Summer's Glory IBO-453	Retrd.	1998	32.00	32
1996 Summer's Glory, green IBO-476	Retrd.	1998	25.00	25
1995 Tender Time IBO-459	Retrd.	1997	27.00	27
1990 Victorian Angel IBO-404	Retrd.	1993	15.00	15
1990 Victorian Angel, ivory IBO-408	Retrd.	1997	15.00	20
1993 Victorian Angel, plum IBO-435	Retrd.	1997	18.00	20
1993 Victorian Cupid, crimson IBO-440	Retrd.	1998	15.00	20
1991 Victorian Cupid, ivory IBO-409	Retrd.	1998	15.00	20
1995 Winter's Light IBO-455	Retrd.	1998	32.00	32
1996 Wooden Angel IBO-461 - M. Ramsey	Retrd.	1998	20.00	20

Teddy Angels™ - P.J. Jonas

YEAR ISSUE	EDITION LIMIT	YEAR RETD.	ISSUE PRICE	*QUOTE U.S.$
1995 Casey "You're a bright & shining star." BA-017	Retrd.	1998	13.00	13
1995 Ivy "Enchantment glows in winter snows." BA-018	Retrd.	1998	13.00	13

Walt Disney

Walt Disney Classics Collection-Special Event - Disney Studios

YEAR ISSUE	EDITION LIMIT	YEAR RETD.	ISSUE PRICE	*QUOTE U.S.$
1998 Simba Ornament 41256	Closed	1998	49.00	44-55
1998 Dumbo Ornaments 41283	Closed	1998	50.00	50-55
2000 Thumper: Belly Laugh	Closed	2000	35.00	35

Annual Ball Ornaments - Disney Studios

YEAR ISSUE	EDITION LIMIT	YEAR RETD.	ISSUE PRICE	*QUOTE U.S.$
1999 On Ice 1200909	Closed	1999	40.00	40
2000 Pluto's Xmas Tree 1210003	Closed	2000	40.00	40
2001 Lady and the Tramp 1215-524	Closed	2001	20.00	20

Boxed Ornament Set- Disney Studios

YEAR ISSUE	EDITION LIMIT	YEAR RETD.	ISSUE PRICE	*QUOTE U.S.$
1999 Snow White & The Seven Dwarfs 1204380	5,000		395.00	395
2000 Pinocchio 1209687	5,000		375.00	375

Disney's Enchanted Castles - Disney Studios

YEAR ISSUE	EDITION LIMIT	YEAR RETD.	ISSUE PRICE	*QUOTE U.S.$
1998 A Castle for Cinderella 41293	Retrd.	2001	45.00	45
1998 The Beast's Castle 41294	Retrd.	2001	45.00	45
1999 Sleeping Beauty Castle 41391	Retrd.	2001	45.00	45
2000 Snow White Castle 1209689	Retrd.	2001	45.00	45
2001 Sultan's Palace 1211850	Retrd.	2001	45.00	45
2001 Triton's Castle 1204385	Retrd.	2001	45.00	45

Disney's Enchanted Places - Disney Studios

YEAR ISSUE	EDITION LIMIT	YEAR RETD.	ISSUE PRICE	*QUOTE U.S.$
1997 Cruella's Car 41245	Retrd.	1999	45.00	45
1997 An Elegant Coach for Cinderella 41244	Retrd.	1999	45.00	45
1996 Grandpa's House from Peter & The Wolf 41222	Closed	1996	35.00	35
1997 The Jolly Roger 41243	Retrd.	1999	45.00	45

Mickey's Christmas Carol - Disney Studios

YEAR ISSUE	EDITION LIMIT	YEAR RETD.	ISSUE PRICE	*QUOTE U.S.$
1998 Jiminy Cricket: "Ghost of Christmas Past" 41251	Retrd.	1999	50.00	50
1997 Mickey Mouse: "And a Merry Christmas to you..." 41144	Retrd.	1999	50.00	50
1997 Minnie Mouse: Mrs. Crachit 41145	Retrd.	1999	50.00	50
1997 Scrooge: "Bah-humbug!" 41146	Retrd.	1999	50.00	50

Walt Disney Classics Collection-Holiday Series - Disney Studios

YEAR ISSUE	EDITION LIMIT	YEAR RETD.	ISSUE PRICE	*QUOTE U.S.$
1995 Mickey Mouse: "Presents for My Pals" 41087	Closed	1995	40.00	25-75
1996 Pluto: Pluto Helps Decorate 41113	Closed	1996	50.00	29-50
1997 Chip 'n Dale: Little Mischief Makers 41190	Closed	1997	50.00	30-60
1998 Minnie Mouse: Caroler Minnie 41311	Closed	1998	50.00	50
1999 Goofy: "Tis the Season to Be Jolly" 41368	Closed	1999	50.00	50
2000 Donald Duck: "Fa La La..." 1207742	Closed	2000	50.00	50

Willitts Designs

Orna Magic™ Lighted Motion - Willitts Designs

YEAR ISSUE	EDITION LIMIT	YEAR RETD.	ISSUE PRICE	*QUOTE U.S.$
1999 Angel	Retrd.	2000	15.99	16
1999 Ballerina	Retrd.	2000	15.99	16
1999 Christmas Tree	Retrd.	2000	15.99	16
1999 Colorful Bell	Retrd.	2000	15.99	16
1999 Fireplace	Retrd.	2000	15.99	16
1999 Jack-in-the-Box	Retrd.	2000	15.99	16
1999 Ornaments	Retrd.	2000	15.99	16
1999 Santa and Reindeer	Retrd.	2000	15.99	16
1999 Santa Down Chimney	Retrd.	2000	15.99	16
1999 Snowman	Retrd.	2000	15.99	16

Rainbow Babies - A. Blackshear

YEAR ISSUE	EDITION LIMIT	YEAR RETD.	ISSUE PRICE	*QUOTE U.S.$
1998 Flutterby	Retrd.	1999	28.50	29

Thomas Blackshear's Ebony Visions - T. Blackshear

YEAR ISSUE	EDITION LIMIT	YEAR RETD.	ISSUE PRICE	*QUOTE U.S.$
1997 Little Blue Wings	17,200	1997	28.50	400-450
1998 On Wings of Praise	23,200	1998	29.50	125-250
1999 Peace on Earth	24,200	1999	29.50	125-175
2000 Joy To The World	32,000	2000	27.50	33-99
2001 A Bright & Morning Star	Yr.Iss.	2001	27.50	28
2002 Heavenly Peace	Yr.Iss.		28.50	29

PLATES & PLAQUES

American Artists

The Best of Fred Stone-Mares & Foals Series (6 1/2") - F. Stone

YEAR ISSUE	EDITION LIMIT	YEAR RETD.	ISSUE PRICE	*QUOTE U.S.$
1991 Patience	19,500		25.00	30-35
1992 Water Trough	19,500		25.00	30-35
1992 Pasture Pest	19,500		25.00	30-35
1992 Kidnapped Mare	19,500		25.00	30-35
1993 Contentment	19,500		25.00	30-35
1993 Arabian Mare & Foal	19,500		25.00	30-35
1994 Diamond in the Rough	19,500		25.00	30-35
1995 The First Day	19,500		25.00	30-35

Famous Fillies Series - F. Stone

YEAR ISSUE	EDITION LIMIT	YEAR RETD.	ISSUE PRICE	*QUOTE U.S.$
1987 Lady's Secret	9,500		65.00	70-75
1988 Ruffian	9,500		65.00	75-80
1988 Genuine Risk	9,500		65.00	70
1992 Go For The Wand	9,500		65.00	70-80

Fred Stone Classic Series - F. Stone

YEAR ISSUE	EDITION LIMIT	YEAR RETD.	ISSUE PRICE	*QUOTE U.S.$
1986 The Shoe-8,000 Wins	9,500		75.00	75
1986 The Eternal Legacy	9,500		75.00	95-99
1988 Forever Friends	9,500		75.00	85-125
1989 Alysheba	9,500		75.00	75-85

Gold Signature Series - F. Stone

YEAR ISSUE	EDITION LIMIT	YEAR RETD.	ISSUE PRICE	*QUOTE U.S.$
1990 Secretariat Final Tribute, signed	4,500		150.00	450-500
1990 Secretariat Final Tribute, unsigned	7,500		75.00	75-150
1991 Old Warriors, signed	4,500		150.00	425-500
1991 Old Warriors, unsigned	7,500		75.00	100

Gold Signature Series II - F. Stone

YEAR ISSUE	EDITION LIMIT	YEAR RETD.	ISSUE PRICE	*QUOTE U.S.$
1991 Northern Dancer, double signature	1,500		175.00	250-350
1991 Northern Dancer, single signature	3,000		150.00	150-199
1991 Northern Dancer, unsigned	7,500		75.00	75-99
1991 Kelso, double signature	1,500		175.00	175-250
1991 Kelso, single signature	3,000		150.00	150-199
1991 Kelso, unsigned	7,500		75.00	65-75

YEAR ISSUE	EDITION LIMIT	YEAR RETD.	ISSUE PRICE	*QUOTE U.S.$

Gold Signature Series III - F. Stone

YEAR ISSUE	EDITION LIMIT	YEAR RETD.	ISSUE PRICE	*QUOTE U.S.$
1992 Dance Smartly-Pat Day, Up, double signature	1,500		175.00	175
1992 Dance Smartly-Pat Day, Up, single signature	3,000		150.00	150
1992 Dance Smartly-Pat Day, Up, unsigned	7,500		75.00	75
1993 American Triple Crown-1937-1946, signed	2,500		195.00	200-250
1993 American Triple Crown-1937-1946, unsigned	7,500		75.00	75-95
1993 American Triple Crown-1948-1978, signed	2,500		195.00	200-250
1993 American Triple Crown-1948-1978, unsigned	7,500		75.00	75-175
1994 American Triple Crown-1919-1935, signed	2,500		95.00	80-95
1994 American Triple Crown-1919-1935, unsigned	7,500		75.00	70-75

Gold Signature Series IV - F. Stone

1995 Julie Krone - Colonial Affair	7,500		75.00	75
1995 Julie Krone - Colonial Affair, signed	2,500		150.00	150

The Horses of Fred Stone - F. Stone

1982 Patience	9,500		55.00	95-125
1982 Arabian Mare and Foal	9,500		55.00	125-149
1982 Safe and Sound	9,500		55.00	95
1983 Contentment	9,500		55.00	95-125

Mare and Foal Series - F. Stone

1986 Water Trough	12,500		49.50	149-175
1986 Tranquility	12,500		49.50	95-149
1986 Pasture Pest	12,500		49.50	125-149
1987 The Arabians	12,500		49.50	95-125

Mare and Foal Series II - F. Stone

1989 The First Day	Open		35.00	35
1989 Diamond in the Rough	Retrd.		35.00	35

Racing Legends - F. Stone

1989 Phar Lap	9,500		75.00	75
1989 Sunday Silence	9,500		75.00	75
1990 John Henry-Shoemaker	9,500		75.00	75

Sport of Kings Series - F. Stone

1984 Man O'War	9,500		65.00	149-175
1984 Secretariat	9,500		65.00	125-200
1985 John Henry	9,500		65.00	70-85
1986 Seattle Slew	9,500		65.00	70-85

The Stallion Series - F. Stone

1983 Black Stallion	19,500		49.50	75-125
1983 Andalusian	19,500		49.50	75-120

Anheuser-Busch, Inc.

1992 Olympic Team Series - A-Busch, Inc.

1991 1992 Olympic Team Winter N3180	Retrd.	1994	35.00	20-25
1992 1992 Olympic Team Summer N3122	Retrd.	1994	35.00	20-25

Archives Plate Series - D. Langeneckert

1992 1893 Columbian Exposition N3477	25-day	1996	27.50	25-30
1992 Ganymede N4004	25-day	1996	27.50	20-35
1995 Budweiser's Greatest Triumph N5195	25-day	1996	27.50	25-35
1995 Mirror of Truth N5196	25-day	1997	27.50	25-35

Budweiser Holiday Plate Series - Various

1989 Winters Day N2295 - B. Kemper	25-day	N/A	30.00	55-85
1990 An American Tradition N2767 - S. Sampson	25-day	N/A	30.00	35-125
1991 The Season's Best N3034 - S. Sampson	25-day	N/A	30.00	25-30
1992 A Perfect Christmas N3440 - S. Sampson	25-day	N/A	27.50	25-30
1993 Special Delivery N4002 - N. Koerber	25-day	1994	27.50	35-135
1994 Hometown Holiday N4572 - B. Kemper	25-day	N/A	27.50	25-30
1995 Lighting the Way Home N5215 - T. Jester	25-day	1998	27.50	25-45
1996 Budweiser Clydesdales N5778 - J. Raedeke	25-day	2000	27.50	25-28
1997 Home For The Holidays N5779 - H. Droog	25-day	2000	27.50	25-28

1998 Grant's Farm Holiday N5780 - E. Kastaris	25-day		28.00	25-28
1999 A Century of Tradition N5998 - G. Ciccarelli	25-day		30.00	30-60
2000 Holiday In The Mountains N5999 - E. Kastaris	25-day	2001	30.00	30
2001 Holiday at the Capitol N9000 - G. Ciccarelli	25-day		30.00	30

Civil War Series - D. Langeneckert

1992 General Grant N3478	Retrd.	1994	45.00	20-30
1993 General Robert E. Lee N3590	Retrd.	1994	45.00	25-28
1993 President Abraham Lincoln N3591	Retrd.	1994	45.00	25-28

Collector Edition Series - M. Urdahl

1995 "This Bud's For You" N4945	25-day	2000	27.50	25-30

Man's Best Friend Series - M. Urdahl, unless otherwise noted

1990 Buddies N2615	25-day	N/A	30.00	55-100
1990 Six Pack N3005	25-day	1992	30.00	35-75
1992 Something's Brewing N3147	25-day	1994	30.00	25-30
1993 Outstanding in Their Field N4003	25-day	1995	27.50	25-30

Armstrong's

Commemorative Issues - R. Skelton

1983 70 Years Young (10 1/2")	15,000		85.00	100-155
1984 Freddie the Torchbearer (8 1/2")	15,000		62.50	50-65
1994 Red & His Friends (12 1/4")	165	1994	700.00	1000-3500

Freedom Collection of Red Skelton - R. Skelton

1990 The All American, (signed)	1,000	1990	195.00	400-600
1990 The All American	9,000		62.50	50-75
1991 Independence Day? (signed)	1,000	1991	195.00	250-375
1991 Independence Day?	9,000		62.50	50-65
1992 Let Freedom Ring, (signed)	1,000	1992	195.00	250-350
1992 Let Freedom Ring	9,000		62.50	50-75
1993 Freddie's Gift of Life, (signed)	1,000	1993	195.00	250-350
1993 Freddie's Gift of Life	9,000		62.50	50-60

The Golden Memories - R. Skelton

1995 The Donut Dunker (signed)	1,000	1995	375.00	525-800
1996 Clem & Clementine (signed)	1,000	1996	385.00	420-600
1996 San Fernando Red (signed)	1,000	1996	385.00	375-500
1997 Jr., The Mean Widdle Kid (signed)	1,000	1997	385.00	375-500
1997 Cauliflower McPugg	1,000		295.00	295

Happy Art Series - W. Lantz

1981 Woody's Triple Self-Portrait, (signed)	1,000		100.00	200
1981 Woody's Triple Self-Portrait	9,000		39.50	40
1983 Gothic Woody, (signed)	1,000	N/A	100.00	200
1983 Gothic Woody	9,000		39.50	40
1984 Blue Boy Woody, (signed)	1,000	N/A	100.00	200
1984 Blue Boy Woody	9,000	1992	39.50	40-50

Pro Autographed Ceramic Baseball Card Plaque - Unknown

1985 Brett, Garvey, Jackson, Rose, Seaver, auto, 3-1/4X5	1,000	N/A	150.00	150-250

The Red Skelton Porcelain Plaque - R. Skelton

1991 All American	1,500	1993	495.00	1000-1500
1994 Another Day	1,994	N/A	675.00	750-1000
1992 Independence Day?	1,500	1997	525.00	575-685
1993 Red & Freddie Both Turned 80	1,993		595.00	1000-1500

The Signature Collection - R. Skelton

1986 Anyone for Tennis?	9,000	N/A	62.50	85-125
1986 Anyone for Tennis? (signed)	1,000	1986	125.00	500-850
1987 Ironing the Waves	9,000	N/A	62.50	90-125
1987 Ironing the Waves (signed)	1,000	1987	125.00	200-500
1988 The Cliffhanger	9,000	N/A	62.50	65-100
1988 The Cliffhanger (signed)	1,000	1988	150.00	350
1988 Hooked on Freddie	9,000	N/A	62.50	65-95
1988 Hooked on Freddie (signed)	1,000	1988	175.00	350

Sports - Schenken

1985 Pete Rose h/s (10 1/4")	1,000	N/A	100.00	295-395
1985 Pete Rose u/s (10 1/4")	10,000	N/A	45.00	75-99

Collectors' Information Bureau   *Quotes have been rounded up to nearest dollar

YEAR ISSUE	EDITION LIMIT	YEAR RETD.	ISSUE PRICE	*QUOTE U.S.$

Armstrong's/Crown Parian

Freddie The Freeloader - R. Skelton

YEAR ISSUE	EDITION LIMIT	YEAR RETD.	ISSUE PRICE	*QUOTE U.S.$
1979 Freddie in the Bathtub	10,000	N/A	55.00	144-200
1980 Freddie's Shack	10,000	N/A	55.00	83-175
1981 Freddie on the Green	10,000	N/A	60.00	50-150
1982 Love that Freddie	10,000	N/A	60.00	25-89

Freddie's Adventures - R. Skelton

1982 Captain Freddie	15,000	N/A	60.00	25-89
1982 Bronco Freddie	15,000		62.50	30-75
1983 Sir Freddie	15,000		62.50	60-95
1984 Gertrude and Heathcliffe	15,000		62.50	80

Armstrong's/Fairmont

Famous Clown Collection - R. Skelton

1976 Freddie the Freeloader	10,000	N/A	55.00	320-600
1977 W. C. Fields	10,000	N/A	55.00	75-150
1978 Happy	10,000	N/A	55.00	143-150
1979 The Pledge	10,000	N/A	55.00	115-150

Artaffects

Club Member Limited Edition Redemption Offerings - G. Perillo

1992 The Pencil	Yr. lss.	1992	35.00	75-150
1992 Studies in Black and White (Set of 4)	Yr. lss.	1992	75.00	100-149
1993 Watcher of the Wilderness	Yr. lss.	1993	60.00	60

America's Indian Heritage - G. Perillo

1987 Cheyenne Nation	Closed	N/A	24.50	65-99
1988 Arapaho Nation	Closed	N/A	24.50	65-99
1988 Kiowa Nation	Closed	N/A	24.50	65-99
1988 Sioux Nation	Closed	N/A	24.50	65-99
1988 Chippewa Nation	Closed	N/A	24.50	65-99
1988 Crow Nation	Closed	N/A	24.50	65-99
1988 Nez Perce Nation	Closed	N/A	24.50	65-99
1988 Blackfoot Nation	Closed	N/A	24.50	65-99

Chieftains I - G. Perillo

1979 Chief Sitting Bull	7,500	N/A	65.00	275-349
1979 Chief Joseph	7,500	N/A	65.00	90-150
1980 Chief Red Cloud	7,500	N/A	65.00	112-149
1980 Chief Geronimo	7,500	N/A	65.00	70-149
1981 Chief Crazy Horse	7,500	N/A	65.00	69-149

Chieftains II - G. Perillo

1983 Chief Pontiac	7,500	N/A	70.00	85-149
1983 Chief Victorio	7,500	N/A	70.00	150
1984 Chief Tecumseh	7,500	N/A	70.00	150
1984 Chief Cochise	7,500	N/A	70.00	80-150
1984 Chief Black Kettle	7,500	N/A	70.00	150

The Colts - G. Perillo

1985 Appaloosa	5,000	N/A	40.00	40
1985 Pinto	5,000	N/A	40.00	56
1985 Arabian	5,000	N/A	40.00	56
1985 Thoroughbred	5,000	N/A	40.00	56

Council of Nations - G. Perillo

1992 Strength of the Sioux	Closed	N/A	29.50	45-55
1992 Pride of the Cheyenne	Closed	N/A	29.50	40-55
1992 Dignity of the Nez Perce	Closed	N/A	29.50	40-49
1992 Courage of the Arapaho	Closed	N/A	29.50	40-49
1992 Power of the Blackfoot	Closed	N/A	29.50	40-60
1992 Nobility of the Algonquin	Closed	N/A	29.50	40
1992 Wisdom of the Cherokee	Closed	N/A	29.50	40-55
1992 Boldness of the Seneca	Closed	N/A	29.50	40

Indian Bridal - G. Perillo

1990 Yellow Bird (6 1/2")	Closed	N/A	25.00	39-49
1990 Autumn Blossom (6 1/2")	Closed	N/A	25.00	39-45
1990 Misty Waters (6 1/2")	Closed	N/A	25.00	30
1990 Sunny Skies (6 1/2")	Closed	N/A	25.00	30

Indian Nations - G. Perillo

1983 Blackfoot	7,500	N/A	140.00	350
1983 Cheyenne	7,500	N/A	set	Set
1983 Apache	7,500	N/A	set	Set
1983 Sioux	7,500	N/A	set	Set

March of Dimes: Our Children - G. Perillo

1989 A Time to Be Born	7,500	N/A	29.00	15-29

Motherhood Series - G. Perillo

1983 Madre	10,000	N/A	50.00	75
1984 Madonna of the Plains	3,500	N/A	50.00	75-85
1985 Abuela	3,500	N/A	50.00	75
1986 Nap Time	3,500	N/A	50.00	75-85

Mother's Love - G. Perillo

1988 Feelings	Yr.lss.	1988	35.00	75-125
1989 Moonlight	Yr.lss.	1989	35.00	65-100
1990 Pride & Joy	Yr.lss.	1990	39.50	95-100
1991 Little Shadow	Yr.lss.	1991	39.50	55-100

Native American Christmas - G. Perillo

1993 The Little Shepherd	Yr.lss.	1993	35.00	55-65
1994 Joy to the World	Yr.lss.	1994	45.00	45-55

Nature's Harmony - G. Perillo

1982 The Peaceable Kingdom	12,500	N/A	100.00	125-299
1982 Zebra	12,500	N/A	50.00	50
1982 Bengal Tiger	12,500	N/A	50.00	60
1983 Black Panther	12,500	N/A	50.00	70
1983 Elephant	12,500	N/A	50.00	95-125

North American Wildlife - G. Perillo

1989 Mustang	Closed	N/A	29.50	35-55
1989 White-Tailed Deer	Closed	N/A	29.50	30-50
1989 Mountain Lion	Closed	N/A	29.50	30-50
1990 Timber Wolf	Closed	N/A	29.50	35-55
1990 Polar Bear	Closed	N/A	29.50	30
1990 Buffalo	Closed	N/A	29.50	35-55
1990 Bighorn Sheep	Closed	N/A	29.50	30-50

Perillo Christmas - G. Perillo

1987 Shining Star	Yr.lss.	1987	29.50	70-85
1988 Silent Light	Yr.lss.	1988	35.00	80-100
1989 Snow Flake	Yr.lss.	1989	35.00	75-100
1990 Bundle Up	Yr.lss.	1990	39.50	75-100
1991 Christmas Journey	Yr.lss.	1991	39.50	50-100

Portraits of American Brides - R. Sauber

1986 Caroline	Closed	N/A	29.50	45-150
1986 Jacqueline	Closed	N/A	29.50	30-95
1987 Elizabeth	Closed	N/A	29.50	60-85
1987 Emily	Closed	N/A	29.50	75-85
1987 Meredith	Closed	N/A	29.50	75
1987 Laura	Closed	N/A	29.50	45
1987 Sarah	Closed	N/A	29.50	45
1987 Rebecca	Closed	N/A	29.50	65

Pride of America's Indians - G. Perillo

1986 Brave and Free	Closed	N/A	24.50	45-85
1986 Dark-Eyed Friends	Closed	N/A	24.50	25-65
1986 Noble Companions	Closed	N/A	24.50	25-55
1987 Kindred Spirits	Closed	N/A	24.50	25-55
1987 Loyal Alliance	Closed	N/A	24.50	42-93
1987 Small and Wise	Closed	N/A	24.50	25-55
1987 Winter Scouts	Closed	N/A	24.50	25-55
1987 Peaceful Comrades	Closed	N/A	24.50	25-75

The Princesses - G. Perillo

1982 Lily of the Mohawks	7,500	N/A	50.00	175
1982 Pocahontas	7,500	N/A	50.00	100
1982 Minnehaha	7,500	N/A	50.00	100
1982 Sacajawea	7,500	N/A	50.00	100

Proud Young Spirits - G. Perillo

1990 Protector of the Plains	Closed	N/A	29.50	75-100
1990 Watchful Eyes	Closed	N/A	29.50	55-65
1990 Freedom's Watch	Closed	N/A	29.50	45-65
1990 Woodland Scouts	Closed	N/A	29.50	35-45
1990 Fast Friends	Closed	N/A	29.50	35-45
1990 Birds of a Feather	Closed	N/A	29.50	30
1990 Prairie Pals	Closed	N/A	29.50	35-45
1990 Loyal Guardian	Closed	N/A	29.50	30

Special Issue - G. Perillo

1981 Apache Boy	5,000	N/A	95.00	175-399
1983 Papoose	3,000	N/A	100.00	125
1983 Indian Style	17,500	N/A	50.00	50

PLATES & PLAQUES

YEAR ISSUE	EDITION LIMIT	YEAR RETD.	ISSUE PRICE	*QUOTE U.S.$
1984 The Lovers	Closed	N/A	50.00	100
1984 Navajo Girl	3,500	N/A	95.00	175-250
1986 Navajo Boy	3,500	N/A	95.00	175-250

The Thoroughbreds - G. Perillo

1984 Whirlaway	9,500	N/A	50.00	250-399
1984 Secretariat	9,500	N/A	50.00	350-499
1984 Man o' War	9,500	N/A	50.00	150-250
1984 Seabiscuit	9,500	N/A	50.00	150

War Ponies of the Plains - G. Perillo

1992 Nightshadow	Closed	N/A	27.00	27-40
1992 Windcatcher	Closed	N/A	27.00	27
1992 Prairie Prancer	Closed	N/A	27.00	27
1992 Thunderfoot	Closed	N/A	27.00	27-40
1992 Proud Companion	Closed	N/A	27.00	27-40
1992 Sun Dancer	Closed	N/A	27.00	27-40
1992 Free Spirit	Closed	N/A	27.00	27-33
1992 Gentle Warrior	Closed	N/A	27.00	27

The Young Chieftains - G. Perillo

1985 Young Sitting Bull	5,000	N/A	50.00	100-250
1985 Young Joseph	5,000	N/A	50.00	75-150
1986 Young Red Cloud	5,000	N/A	50.00	75-125
1986 Young Geronimo	5,000	N/A	50.00	75-150
1986 Young Crazy Horse	5,000	N/A	50.00	75-150

Bing & Grondahl

American Christmas Heritage Collection - C. Magadini

1996 The Statue of Liberty	Yr.Iss.	1996	47.50	48-69
1997 Christmas Eve at The Lincoln Memorial	Yr.Iss.	1997	47.50	29-69
1998 Chicago Water Tower	Yr.Iss.	1998	34.50	29-79
1999 At Mount Rushmore	Yr.Iss.	1999	37.50	38-69
2000 Christmas at the Alamo	Yr.Iss.	2000	39.50	40
2001 Christmas Eve at the White House	Yr.Iss.	2001	39.50	40

Centennial Anniversary Commemoratives - Various

1995 Centennial Plaquettes: Series of 10-5" plates featuring B&G motifs: 1895, 1905, 1919, 1927, 1932, 1945, 1954, 1964, 1974, 1982	Yr.Iss.	1995	250.00	240-300
1995 Centennial Plate: Behind the Frozen Window - F.A. Hallin	10,000	1995	39.50	39-63
1995 Centennial Platter: Towers of Copenhagen - J. Nielsen	7,500	1995	195.00	195

Centennial Collection - Various

1991 Crows Enjoying Christmas - D. Jensen	Annual	1991	59.50	60-90
1992 Copenhagen Christmas - H. Vlugenring	Annual	1992	59.50	60-90
1993 Christmas Elf - H. Thelander	Annual	1993	59.50	63-72
1994 Christmas in Church - H. Thelander	Annual	1994	59.50	63-90
1995 Behind The Frozen Window - A. Hallin	Annual	1995	59.50	30-60

Children's Day Plate Series - S. Vestergaard, unless otherwise noted

1985 The Magical Tea Party - C. Roller	Annual	1985	24.50	7-28
1986 A Joyful Flight - C. Roller	Annual	1986	26.50	16-48
1986 The Little Gardeners - C. Roller	Annual	1987	29.50	23-60
1988 Wash Day - C. Roller	Annual	1988	34.50	30-48
1989 Bedtime - C. Roller	Annual	1989	37.00	30-79
1990 My Favorite Dress	Annual	1990	37.00	20-45
1991 Fun on the Beach	Annual	1991	45.00	32-48
1992 A Summer Day in the Meadow	Annual	1992	45.00	35-64
1993 The Carousel	Annual	1993	45.00	45-105
1994 The Little Fisherman	Annual	1994	45.00	44-67
1995 My First Book	Annual	1995	45.00	48-144
1996 The Little Racers	Annual	1996	45.00	45-60
1997 Bath Time	Annual	1997	45.00	47-56
1998 Little Vendors	Annual	1998	34.50	32-75
1999 The Little Concert	Annual	1999	37.50	32-45
2000 Don't Tell	Annual	2000	39.50	40
2001 Be My Valentine	Annual		39.50	40

Christmas - Various

1895 Behind The Frozen Window - F.A. Hallin	Annual	1895	.50	4750-7200
1896 New Moon - F.A. Hallin	Annual	1896	.50	1950-3183
1897 Sparrows - F.A. Hallin	Annual	1897	.75	975-1872
1898 Roses and Star - F. Garde	Annual	1898	.75	799-966
1899 Crows - F. Garde	Annual	1899	.75	950-2247

YEAR ISSUE	EDITION LIMIT	YEAR RETD.	ISSUE PRICE	*QUOTE U.S.$
1900 Church Bells - F. Garde	Annual	1900	.75	750-1425
1901 Three Wise Men - S. Sabra	Annual	1901	1.00	425-663
1902 Gothic Church Interior - D. Jensen	Annual	1902	1.00	350-570
1903 Expectant Children - M. Hyldahl	Annual	1903	1.00	340-500
1904 Fredericksberg Hill - C. Olsen	Annual	1904	1.00	140-219
1905 Christmas Night - D. Jensen	Annual	1905	1.00	150-279
1906 Sleighing to Church - D. Jensen	Annual	1906	1.00	100-144
1907 Little Match Girl - E. Plockross	Annual	1907	1.00	120-160
1908 St. Petri Church - P. Jorgensen	Annual	1908	1.00	85-125
1909 Yule Tree - Aarestrup	Annual	1909	1.50	80-123
1910 The Old Organist - C. Ersgaard	Annual	1910	1.50	75-120
1911 Angels and Shepherds - H. Moltke	Annual	1911	1.50	95-120
1912 Going to Church - E. Hansen	Annual	1912	1.50	75-120
1913 Bringing Home the Tree - T. Larsen	Annual	1913	1.50	95-100
1914 Amalienborg Castle - T. Larsen	Annual	1914	1.50	95-105
1915 Dog Outside Window - D. Jensen	Annual	1915	1.50	125-200
1916 Sparrows at Christmas - P. Jorgensen	Annual	1916	1.50	80-100
1917 Christmas Boat - A. Friis	Annual	1917	1.50	80-108
1918 Fishing Boat - A. Friis	Annual	1918	1.50	75-95
1919 Outside Lighted Window - A. Friis	Annual	1919	2.00	75-90
1920 Hare in the Snow - A. Friis	Annual	1920	2.00	75-96
1921 Pigeons - A. Friis	Annual	1921	2.00	70-85
1922 Star of Bethlehem - A. Friis	Annual	1922	2.00	59-87
1923 The Ermitage - A. Friis	Annual	1923	2.00	70-90
1924 Lighthouse - A. Friis	Annual	1924	2.50	72-100
1925 Child's Christmas - A. Friis	Annual	1925	2.50	70-96
1926 Churchgoers - A. Friis	Annual	1926	2.50	80-90
1927 Skating Couple - A. Friis	Annual	1927	2.50	90-114
1928 Eskimos - A. Friis	Annual	1928	2.50	70-80
1929 Fox Outside Farm - A. Friis	Annual	1929	2.50	75-100
1930 Town Hall Square - H. Flugenring	Annual	1930	2.50	90-108
1931 Christmas Train - A. Friis	Annual	1931	2.50	80-120
1932 Life Boat - H. Flugenring	Annual	1932	2.50	80-110
1933 Korsor-Nyborg Ferry - H. Flugenring	Annual	1933	3.00	70-90
1934 Church Bell in Tower - H. Flugenring	Annual	1934	3.00	80-107
1935 Lillebelt Bridge - O. Larson	Annual	1935	3.00	80-120
1936 Royal Guard - O. Larson	Annual	1936	3.00	80-100
1937 Arrival of Christmas Guests - O. Larson	Annual	1937	3.00	100-110
1938 Lighting the Candles - I. Tjerne	Annual	1938	3.00	145-201
1939 Old Lock-Eye, The Sandman - I. Tjerne	Annual	1939	3.00	175-200
1940 Christmas Letters - O. Larson	Annual	1940	4.00	175-222
1941 Horses Enjoying Meal - O. Larson	Annual	1941	4.00	190-309
1942 Danish Farm - O. Larson	Annual	1942	4.00	174-290
1943 Ribe Cathedral - O. Larson	Annual	1943	5.00	175-237
1944 Sorgenfri Castle - O. Larson	Annual	1944	5.00	90-134
1945 The Old Water Mill - O. Larson	Annual	1945	5.00	90-225
1946 Commemoration Cross - M. Hyldahl	Annual	1946	5.00	65-120
1947 Dybbol Mill - M. Hyldahl	Annual	1947	5.00	90-170
1948 Watchman - M. Hyldahl	Annual	1948	5.50	65-160
1949 Landsoldaten - M. Hyldahl	Annual	1949	5.50	65-148
1950 Kronborg Castle - M. Hyldahl	Annual	1950	5.50	95-123
1951 Jens Bang - M. Hyldahl	Annual	1951	6.00	93-132
1952 Thorsvaldsen Museum - B. Pramvig	Annual	1952	6.00	75-100
1953 Snowman - B. Pramvig	Annual	1953	7.50	85-100
1954 Royal Boat - K. Bonfils	Annual	1954	7.00	90-120
1955 Kaulundorg Church - K. Bonfils	Annual	1955	8.00	80-128
1956 Christmas in Copenhagen - K. Bonfils	Annual	1956	8.50	95-196
1957 Christmas Candles - K. Bonfils	Annual	1957	9.00	115-180
1958 Santa Claus - K. Bonfils	Annual	1958	9.50	95-120
1959 Christmas Eve - K. Bonfils	Annual	1959	10.00	115-180
1960 Village Church - K. Bonfils	Annual	1960	10.00	120-210
1961 Winter Harmony - K. Bonfils	Annual	1961	10.50	90-132
1962 Winter Night - K. Bonfils	Annual	1962	11.00	71-110
1963 The Christmas Elf - H. Thelander	Annual	1963	11.00	61-156
1964 The Fir Tree and Hare - H. Thelander	Annual	1964	11.50	23-55
1965 Bringing Home the Tree - H. Thelander	Annual	1965	12.00	30-69
1966 Home for Christmas - H. Thelander	Annual	1966	12.00	21-60
1967 Sharing the Joy - H. Thelander	Annual	1967	13.00	25-50
1968 Christmas in Church - H. Thelander	Annual	1968	14.00	19-50
1969 Arrival of Guests - H. Thelander	Annual	1969	14.00	15-35
1970 Pheasants in Snow - H. Thelander	Annual	1970	14.50	14-30
1971 Christmas at Home - H. Thelander	Annual	1971	15.00	9-27
1972 Christmas in Greenland - H. Thelander	Annual	1972	16.50	12-27
1973 Country Christmas - H. Thelander	Annual	1973	19.50	16-40
1974 Christmas in the Village - H. Thelander	Annual	1974	22.00	18-27
1975 Old Water Mill - H. Thelander	Annual	1975	27.50	20-39
1976 Christmas Welcome - H. Thelander	Annual	1976	27.50	20-33

YEAR ISSUE	EDITION LIMIT	YEAR RETD.	ISSUE PRICE	*QUOTE U.S.$
1977 Copenhagen Christmas - H. Thelander	Annual	1977	29.50	20-30
1978 Christmas Tale - H. Thelander	Annual	1978	32.00	25-35
1979 White Christmas - H. Thelander	Annual	1979	36.50	24-45
1980 Christmas in Woods - H. Thelander	Annual	1980	42.50	23-33
1981 Christmas Peace - H. Thelander	Annual	1981	49.50	18-42
1982 Christmas Tree - H. Thelander	Annual	1982	54.50	30-54
1983 Christmas in Old Town - H. Thelander	Annual	1983	54.50	30-42
1984 The Christmas Letter - E. Jensen	Annual	1984	54.50	25-42
1985 Christmas Eve at the Farmhouse - E. Jensen	Annual	1985	54.50	24-42
1986 Silent Night, Holy Night - E. Jensen	Annual	1986	54.50	25-57
1987 The Snowman's Christmas Eve - E. Jensen	Annual	1987	59.50	34-57
1988 In the Kings Garden - E. Jensen	Annual	1988	64.50	34-60
1989 Christmas Anchorage - E. Jensen	Annual	1989	59.50	44-72
1990 Changing of the Guards - E. Jensen	Annual	1990	64.50	60-93
1991 Copenhagen Stock Exchange - E. Jensen	Annual	1991	69.50	65-90
1992 Christmas At the Rectory - J. Steensen	Annual	1992	69.50	65-93
1993 Father Christmas in Copenhagen - J. Nielsen	Annual	1993	69.50	69-87
1994 A Day At The Deer Park - J. Nielsen	Annual	1994	72.50	59-96
1995 The Towers of Copenhagen - J. Nielsen	Annual	1995	72.50	59-105
1996 Winter at the Old Mill - J. Nielsen	Annual	1996	74.50	48-85
1997 Country Christmas - J. Nielsen	Annual	1997	69.50	68-90
1998 Santa the Storyteller - J. Nielsen	Annual	1998	69.50	55-105
1999 Around the Christmas Tree - J. Nielsen	Annual	1999	72.50	73-150
2000 Ringing at the Bell Tower - J. Nielsen	Annual	2000	72.50	73
2001 Playing in the Snow - J. Nielsen	Annual	2001	72.50	73

Christmas Around the World - H. Hansen

1995 Santa in Greenland	Yr.Iss.	1995	74.50	75-95
1996 Santa in Orient	Yr.Iss.	1996	74.50	75-90
1997 Santa in Russia	Yr.Iss.	1997	74.50	59-75
1998 Santa in Australia	Yr.Iss.	1998	69.50	70
1999 Santa in Europe	Yr.Iss.	1999	72.50	59-73
2000 Santa in America	Yr.Iss.	2000	72.50	73

Christmas In America - J. Woodson

1986 Christmas Eve in Williamsburg	Annual	1986	29.50	39-150
1987 Christmas Eve at the White House	Annual	1987	34.50	36-75
1988 Christmas Eve at Rockefeller Center	Annual	1988	34.50	35-60
1989 Christmas In New England	Annual	1989	37.00	37-57
1990 Christmas Eve at the Capitol	Annual	1990	39.50	40-57
1991 Christmas Eve at Independence Hall	Annual	1991	45.00	45-65
1992 Christmas in San Francisco	Annual	1992	47.50	48
1993 Coming Home For Christmas	Annual	1993	47.50	48
1994 Christmas Eve In Alaska	Annual	1994	47.50	48-66
1995 Christmas Eve in Mississippi	Annual	1995	47.50	39-48

Christmas in America Anniversary Plate - J. Woodson

1991 Christmas Eve in Williamsburg	Annual	1991	69.50	73-100
1995 The Capitol	Annual	1995	74.50	75

Jubilee-5 Year Cycle - Various

1915 Frozen Window - F.A. Hallin	Annual	1915	Unkn.	199-250
1920 Church Bells - F. Garde	Annual	1920	Unkn.	99-149
1925 Dog Outside Window - D. Jensen	Annual	1925	Unkn.	180-300
1930 The Old Organist - C. Ersgaard	Annual	1930	Unkn.	210-275
1935 Little Match Girl - E. Plockross	Annual	1935	Unkn.	450-900
1940 Three Wise Men - S. Sabra	Annual	1940	Unkn.	1795-2400
1945 Amalienborg Castle - T. Larsen	Annual	1945	Unkn.	90-249
1950 Eskimos - A. Friis	Annual	1950	Unkn.	90-259
1955 Dybbol Mill - M. Hyldahl	Annual	1955	Unkn.	210-250
1960 Kronborg Castle - M. Hyldahl	Annual	1960	25.00	120-199
1965 Chruchgoers - A. Friis	Annual	1965	25.00	59-75
1970 Amalienborg Castle - T. Larsen	Annual	1970	30.00	15-30
1975 Horses Enjoying Meal - O. Larson	Annual	1975	40.00	18-69
1980 Yule Tree - Aarestrup	Annual	1980	60.00	48-60
1985 Lifeboat at Work - H. Flugenring	Annual	1985	65.00	75-89
1990 The Royal Yacht Dannebrog - J. Bonfils	Annual	1990	95.00	85-125
1995 Centennial Platter - J. Nielsen	7,500	1995	195.00	125-199
1996 Lifeboat at Work (released a year late) - H. Flugenring	1,000	1996	95.00	60-95
2000 Star of Bethlehem - J. Achton Friis	Annual	2000	100.00	100

Mother's Day - Various

1969 Dogs and Puppies - H. Thelander	Annual	1969	9.75	250-450

YEAR ISSUE	EDITION LIMIT	YEAR RETD.	ISSUE PRICE	*QUOTE U.S.$
1970 Bird and Chicks - H. Thelander	Annual	1970	10.00	14-35
1971 Cat and Kitten - H. Thelander	Annual	1971	11.00	14-35
1972 Mare and Foal - H. Thelander	Annual	1972	12.00	15-25
1973 Duck and Ducklings - H. Thelander	Annual	1973	13.00	20-25
1974 Bear and Cubs - H. Thelander	Annual	1974	16.50	18-25
1975 Doe and Fawns - H. Thelander	Annual	1975	19.50	10-25
1976 Swan Family - H. Thelander	Annual	1976	22.50	23-25
1977 Squirrel and Young - H. Thelander	Annual	1977	23.50	23-34
1978 Heron and Young - H. Thelander	Annual	1978	24.50	15-28
1979 Fox and Cubs - H. Thelander	Annual	1979	27.50	15-30
1980 Woodpecker and Young - H. Thelander	Annual	1980	29.50	28-35
1981 Hare and Young - H. Thelander	Annual	1981	36.50	28-35
1982 Lioness and Cubs - H. Thelander	Annual	1982	39.50	24-45
1983 Raccoon and Young - H. Thelander	Annual	1983	39.50	25-45
1984 Stork and Nestlings - H. Thelander	Annual	1984	39.50	25-45
1985 Bear and Cubs - H. Thelander	Annual	1985	39.50	28-45
1986 Elephant with Calf - H. Thelander	Annual	1986	39.50	27-55
1987 Sheep with Lambs - H. Thelander	Annual	1987	42.50	49-83
1988 Crested Plover and Young - H. Thelander	Annual	1988	47.50	52-83
1988 Lapwing Mother with Chicks - H. Thelander	Annual	1988	49.50	63-90
1989 Cow With Calf - H. Thelander	Annual	1989	49.50	40-63
1990 Hen with Chicks - L. Jensen	Annual	1990	52.50	62-93
1991 The Nanny Goat and her Two Frisky Kids - L. Jensen	Annual	1991	54.50	65-75
1992 Panda With Cubs - L. Jensen	Annual	1992	59.50	55-75
1993 St. Bernard Dog and Puppies - A. Therkelsen	Annual	1993	59.50	75-114
1994 Cat with Kittens - A. Therkelsen	Annual	1994	59.50	58-120
1995 Hedgehog with Young - A. Therkelsen	Annual	1995	59.50	45-95
1996 Koala with Young - A. Therkelsen	Annual	1996	59.50	56-90
1997 Goose with Goslings - L. Didier	Annual	1997	59.50	60-133
1998 Penguin With Young - L. Didier	Annual	1998	49.50	50-70
1999 Rabbit - F. Clausen	Annual	1999	49.50	49-68
2000 Dolphin with Calf - F. Clausen	Annual	2000	54.50	55-74
2001 Seal with Pup - F. Clausen	Annual	2001	54.50	55

Mother's Day Jubilee-5 Year Cycle - Thelander, unless otherwise noted

1979 Dog & Puppies	Yr.Iss.	1979	55.00	42-89
1984 Swan Family	Yr.Iss.	1984	65.00	65-100
1989 Mare & Colt	Yr.Iss.	1989	95.00	89-112
1994 Woodpecker & Young	Yr.Iss.	1994	95.00	89-95
1999 Panther with Cubs - L. Jensen	Yr.Iss.	1999	95.00	70-95

Olympic - Unknown

1972 Munich, Germany	Closed	1972	20.00	10-30
1976 Montreal, Canada	Closed	1976	29.50	57-59
1980 Moscow, Russia	Closed	1980	43.00	79-87
1984 Los Angeles, USA	Closed	1984	45.00	250-359
1988 Seoul, Korea	Closed	1988	60.00	49-87
1992 Barcelona, Spain	Closed	1992	74.50	59-87

Santa Claus Collection - H. Hansen

1989 Santa's Workshop	Annual	1989	59.50	59-120
1990 Santa's Sleigh	Annual	1990	59.50	55-90
1991 Santa's Journey	Annual	1991	69.50	59-120
1992 Santa's Arrival	Annual	1992	74.50	59-90
1993 Santa's Gifts	Annual	1993	74.50	59-90
1994 Christmas Stories	Annual	1994	74.50	59-90

The Snow Fairies - K. Seeberg

2001 The Snow Fairies	Annual		75.00	75

Statue of Liberty - Unknown

1985 Statue of Liberty	10,000	1985	60.00	49-100

The Bradford Exchange/Canada

Big League Dreams

1993 Hey, Batter Batter	Closed		29.90	50-58
1994 The Wind Up	Closed		29.90	57
1994 Safe!!!	Closed		32.90	90-99
1994 A Difference of Opinion	Closed		32.90	100
1994 I Got It, I Got It!	Closed		32.90	80
1994 Victory	Closed		32.90	69

PLATES & PLAQUES

The Bradford Exchange/China

Dream of the Red Chamber

YEAR ISSUE	EDITION LIMIT	YEAR RETD.	ISSUE PRICE	*QUOTE U.S.$
1994 Pao-Choi: Precious Clasp	Closed		29.90	35-65
1994 Hsiang-Yun: Little Cloud	Closed		29.90	38-45
1994 Yuan-Chun: Beginning of Spring	Closed		29.90	36
1994 Hsi-Feng: Phoenix	Closed		29.90	100
1994 Tai-Yu: Black Jade	Closed		29.90	45-100
1994 Tan-Chun: Taste of Spring	Closed		29.90	69

The Bradford Exchange/Russia

The Nutcracker - N. Zaitseva

YEAR ISSUE	EDITION LIMIT	YEAR RETD.	ISSUE PRICE	*QUOTE U.S.$
1993 Marie's Magical Gift	Closed		39.87	40-45
1993 Dance of Sugar Plum Fairy	Closed		39.87	45-52
1994 Waltz of the Flowers	Closed		39.87	50-69
1994 Battle With the Mice King	Closed		39.87	48-50

Songs of Angels - Vladimirdvich

YEAR ISSUE	EDITION LIMIT	YEAR RETD.	ISSUE PRICE	*QUOTE U.S.$
1994 Heavenly Hearalds	Closed		29.87	30
1994 Divine Chorus	Closed		29.87	30
1995 Springtime Duet	Closed		32.87	33
1995 Mystical Chimes	Closed		32.87	33

The Bradford Exchange/United States

101 Dalmatians - Disney Studios

YEAR ISSUE	EDITION LIMIT	YEAR RETD.	ISSUE PRICE	*QUOTE U.S.$
1993 Watch Dogs	95-day		29.90	30
1994 A Happy Reunion	95-day		29.90	30
1994 Hello Darlings	95-day		32.90	33
1994 Sergeant Tibs Saves the Day	95-day		32.90	33
1994 Halfway Home	95-day		32.90	33
1994 True Love	95-day		32.90	33
1995 Bedtime	95-day		34.90	35
1995 A Messy Good Time	95-day		34.90	35

Aladdin - Disney Studios

YEAR ISSUE	EDITION LIMIT	YEAR RETD.	ISSUE PRICE	*QUOTE U.S.$
1993 Magic Carpet Ride	Closed		29.90	66
1993 A Friend Like Me	Closed		29.90	30-35
1994 Aladdin in Love	Closed		29.90	30-35
1994 Traveling Companions	Closed		29.90	45
1994 Make Way for Prince Ali	Closed		29.90	31-36
1994 Aladdin's Wish	Closed		29.90	49
1995 Bee Yourself	Closed		29.90	33-35
1995 Group Hug	Closed		29.90	35-39

Alice in Wonderland - S. Gustafson

YEAR ISSUE	EDITION LIMIT	YEAR RETD.	ISSUE PRICE	*QUOTE U.S.$
1993 The Mad Tea Party	Closed		29.90	39-47
1993 The Cheshire Cat	Closed		29.90	69-75
1994 Croquet with the Queen	Closed		29.90	69-73
1994 Advice from a Caterpillar	Closed		29.90	65-71

America's Famous Fairways - D. Day

YEAR ISSUE	EDITION LIMIT	YEAR RETD.	ISSUE PRICE	*QUOTE U.S.$
1995 Pebble Beach	Closed		34.95	50
1995 Augusta Beach	Closed		34.95	65
1995 Cypress Course	Closed		34.95	150-300
1995 Medinah Course	Closed		34.95	60-64

America's Triumph in Space - R. Schaar

YEAR ISSUE	EDITION LIMIT	YEAR RETD.	ISSUE PRICE	*QUOTE U.S.$
1993 The Eagle Has Landed	Closed		29.90	27
1993 The March Toward Destiny	Closed		29.90	24-27
1994 Flight of Glory	Closed		32.90	42-45
1994 Beyond the Bounds of Earth	Closed		32.90	63
1994 Conquering the New Frontier	Closed		32.90	40-44
1994 Rendezvous With Victory	Closed		34.90	67
1994 The New Explorers	Closed		34.90	65
1994 Triumphant Finale	Closed		34.90	55-58

Ancient Seasons - M. Silversmith

YEAR ISSUE	EDITION LIMIT	YEAR RETD.	ISSUE PRICE	*QUOTE U.S.$
1995 Edge of Night	Closed		29.90	30
1995 Journey of Midnight	95-day		29.90	30
1995 Winter Sojurn	95-day		29.90	30
1995 Mid Winter	95-day		29.90	30

Autumn Encounters - C. Fisher

YEAR ISSUE	EDITION LIMIT	YEAR RETD.	ISSUE PRICE	*QUOTE U.S.$
1995 Woodland Innocents	95-day		29.90	30

Babe Ruth Centennial - P. Heffernan

YEAR ISSUE	EDITION LIMIT	YEAR RETD.	ISSUE PRICE	*QUOTE U.S.$
1994 The 60th Homer	Closed		34.90	45-48
1995 Ruth's Pitching Debut	Closed		29.90	52-80
1995 The Final Home Run	Closed		29.90	53-90
1995 Barnstorming Days	Closed		34.90	69

Baskets of Love - A. Isakov

YEAR ISSUE	EDITION LIMIT	YEAR RETD.	ISSUE PRICE	*QUOTE U.S.$
1993 Andrew and Abbey	Closed		29.90	26-32
1993 Cody and Courtney	Closed		29.90	30-41
1993 Emily and Elliott	Closed		32.90	64
1993 Heather and Hannah	Closed		32.90	35
1993 Justin and Jessica	Closed		32.90	40
1993 Katie and Kelly	Closed		34.90	44
1994 Louie and Libby	Closed		34.90	89
1994 Sammy and Sarah	Closed		34.90	35-79

Battles of American Civil War - J. Griffin

YEAR ISSUE	EDITION LIMIT	YEAR RETD.	ISSUE PRICE	*QUOTE U.S.$
1994 Gettysburg	95-day		29.90	30
1995 Vicksburg	95-day		29.90	30

Beary Merry Christmas - S. Sherwood

YEAR ISSUE	EDITION LIMIT	YEAR RETD.	ISSUE PRICE	*QUOTE U.S.$
1995 Loving Tradition	Closed		29.95	30-55
1995 Moment/Treasure	Closed		29.95	30
1995 Romantic Ride	Closed		29.95	30
1995 Wreath of Love	Closed		29.95	30
1995 Topping on the Tree	Closed		29.95	30
1995 Under the Mistletoe	Closed		29.95	30

The Bunny Workshop - J. Maday

YEAR ISSUE	EDITION LIMIT	YEAR RETD.	ISSUE PRICE	*QUOTE U.S.$
1995 Make Today Eggstra Special	Closed		19.95	20

By Gone Days - L. Dubin

YEAR ISSUE	EDITION LIMIT	YEAR RETD.	ISSUE PRICE	*QUOTE U.S.$
1994 Soda Fountain	Closed		29.90	60-63
1995 Sam's Grocery Store	Closed		29.90	45-84
1995 Saturday Matinee	Closed		29.90	35-85
1995 The Corner News Stand	Closed		29.90	45
1995 Main Street Splendor	Closed		29.90	32-45
1995 The Barber Shop	Closed		29.90	50

Cabins of Comfort River - F. Buchwitz

YEAR ISSUE	EDITION LIMIT	YEAR RETD.	ISSUE PRICE	*QUOTE U.S.$
1995 Comfort by Camplights Fire	Closed		29.95	30
1995 Lantern Light	Closed		29.95	30-40
1995 Reflections in the Moonlight	Closed		29.95	30
1995 Tranquility	95-day		29.95	30

Carousel Daydreams - N/A, unless otherwise noted

YEAR ISSUE	EDITION LIMIT	YEAR RETD.	ISSUE PRICE	*QUOTE U.S.$
1994 Swept Away - Mr. Tseng	Closed		39.90	79-85
1995 When I Grow Up	Closed		39.90	115-200
1995 All Aboard	Closed		44.90	85-100
1995 Hold Onto Your Dreams	Closed		44.90	125-149
1995 Flight of Fancy	Closed		44.90	90-190
1995 Big Hopes, Bright Dreams	Closed		49.90	60-145
1995 Victorian Reverie	Closed		49.90	119-200
1995 Wishful Thinking	Closed		49.90	125-175
1995 Dreams of Destiny	Closed		49.90	125-130
1995 My Favorite Memory	Closed		49.90	100-195

Charles Wysocki's American Frontier - C. Wysocki

YEAR ISSUE	EDITION LIMIT	YEAR RETD.	ISSUE PRICE	*QUOTE U.S.$
1993 Timberline Jack's Trading Post	Closed		29.90	30-75
1994 Dr. Livingwell's Medicine Show	Closed		29.90	28-42
1994 Bustling Boomtown	Closed		29.90	28-48
1994 Kirbyville	Closed		29.90	30-35
1994 Hearty Homesteaders	Closed		29.90	40
1994 Oklahoma or Bust	Closed		29.90	55

Charles Wysocki's Hometown Memories - C. Wysocki

YEAR ISSUE	EDITION LIMIT	YEAR RETD.	ISSUE PRICE	*QUOTE U.S.$
1994 Small Talk at Birdie's Perch	Closed		29.90	60-73
1995 Tranquil Days/Ravenswhip Cove	Closed		29.90	60-260
1995 Summer Delights	Closed		29.90	50-150
1995 Capturing the Moment	Closed		29.90	55-60
1995 A Farewell Kiss	Closed		29.90	54
1995 Jason Sparkin the Lighthouse Keeper's Daughter	Closed		29.90	55-150

Charles Wysocki's Peppercricket Grove - C. Wysocki

YEAR ISSUE	EDITION LIMIT	YEAR RETD.	ISSUE PRICE	*QUOTE U.S.$
1993 Peppercricket Farms	Closed		24.90	45-48
1993 Gingernut Valley Inn	Closed		24.90	50-54
1993 Budzen's Fruits and Vegetables	Closed		24.90	47-49
1993 Virginia's Market	Closed		24.90	45-50
1993 Pumpkin Hollow Emporium	Closed		24.90	55
1993 Liberty Star Farms	Closed		24.90	48-50
1993 Overflow Antique Market	Closed		24.90	48-50
1993 Black Crow Antique Shoppe	Closed		24.90	54

Cherished Traditions - M. Lasher

YEAR ISSUE	EDITION LIMIT	YEAR RETD.	ISSUE PRICE	*QUOTE U.S.$
1995 The Wedding Ring	Closed		29.90	30-71
1995 The Star	Closed		29.90	50
1995 Log Cabin	Closed		29.90	40-49

*Quotes have been rounded up to nearest dollar

YEAR ISSUE	EDITION LIMIT	YEAR RETD.	ISSUE PRICE	*QUOTE U.S.$
1995 Ocean Wave	Closed		29.90	50-60
1995 Dresden	Closed		29.90	30-70
1995 Goose on the Pond	Closed		29.90	71-80
1995 Starburst	Closed		29.90	74-80
1995 Grandmothers Flower	Closed		29.90	80-85

Cherubs of Innocence - Various

1994 The First Kiss	Closed		29.90	35-74
1995 Love at Rest	Closed		29.90	30-45
1995 Thoughts of Love	Closed		32.90	35
1995 Loving Gaze	Closed		32.90	35-57

Choir of Angels - Toole, unless otherwise noted

1995 Song of Joy - Unknown	Closed		34.95	35
1995 Song of Peace	Closed		34.95	35
1995 Song of Hope	Closed		34.95	35
1995 Song of Harmony	95-day		34.95	35

Chosen Messengers - G. Running Wolf

1994 The Pathfinders	Closed		29.90	21
1994 The Overseers	Closed		29.90	22
1994 The Providers	Closed		32.90	48-50
1994 The Surveyors	Closed		32.90	50-53

A Christmas Carol - L. Garrison

1993 God Bless Us Everyone	Closed		29.90	47-58
1993 Ghost of Christmas Present	Closed		29.90	66-69
1994 A Merry Christmas to All	Closed		29.90	50-59
1994 A Visit From Marley's Ghost	Closed		29.90	77-89
1994 Remembering Christmas Past	Closed		29.90	62
1994 A Spirit's Warning	Closed		29.90	96
1994 The True Spirit of Christmas	Closed		29.90	87-89
1994 Merry Christmas, Bob	Closed		29.90	58-139

Christmas in the Village - R. McGinnis

1995 The Village Toy Shop	Closed		29.95	20-50
1995 Little Church in the Vale	Closed		29.95	30-49
1995 The Village Confectionary	Closed		29.95	52-57
1996 The Village Inn	Closed		29.95	30-55
1996 Goodnight Dear Friends	Closed		29.95	55-65
1996 A New Fallen Snow	Closed		29.95	55-65

Christmas Memories - J. Tanton

1993 A Winter's Tale	Closed		29.90	25-35
1993 Finishing Touch	Closed		29.90	43
1993 Welcome to Our Home	Closed		29.90	59
1993 A Christmas Celebration	Closed		29.90	57

Classic Cars - D. Everhart

1993 1957 Corvette	Closed		54.00	55
1993 1956 Thunderbird	Closed		54.00	55
1994 1957 Bel Air	Closed		54.00	103
1994 1965 Mustang	Closed		54.00	100

Classic Melodies from the "Sound of Music" - M. Hampshire

1995 Sing Along with Maria	Closed		29.90	47-49
1995 A Drop of Golden Sun	Closed		29.90	60
1995 The Von Trapp Family Singers	Closed		29.90	70
1995 Alpine Refuge	Closed		29.90	50

Classic Roses - L. Moser

1995 Beauty in Bloom	Closed		34.95	35-100
1995 Pretty in Pink	Closed		34.95	35
1995 Precious Purple	95-day		37.95	38
1995 Magic/Mauve	95-day		37.95	38

Classic Waterfowl - J. Hautman

1995 Mallards	Closed		29.90	30-55
1995 Black Bellied	Closed		29.90	30-45
1995 Wood Ducks	Closed		29.90	30-45
1995 American Wigeon	Closed		29.90	30-45
1995 Canvasbacks	Closed		29.90	30-45
1995 Blue Wing Teals	Closed		29.90	30-45
1995 Mergansers	Closed		29.90	30
1995 Golden Eye	Closed		29.90	30-35

The Costuming of A Legend: Dressing Gone With The Wind - D. Klauba

1993 The Red Dress	Closed		29.90	30-60
1993 The Green Drapery Dress	Closed		29.90	48-50
1994 The Green Sprigged Dress	Closed		29.90	32-40
1994 Black & White Bengaline Dress	Closed		29.90	41-45

YEAR ISSUE	EDITION LIMIT	YEAR RETD.	ISSUE PRICE	*QUOTE U.S.$
1994 Widow's Weeds	Closed		29.90	45-49
1994 The Country Walking Dress	Closed		29.90	45-48
1994 Plaid Business Attire	Closed		29.90	35-48
1994 Orchid Percale Dress	Closed		29.90	35-42
1994 The Mourning Gown	Closed		29.90	75-90
1994 Final Outtake:The Green Muslin Dress	Closed		29.90	70-75

A Country Wonderland - W. Goebel

1995 The Quiet Hour	Closed		29.90	30
1995 First Blush	Closed		29.90	30
1995 Sunrise Serenade	Closed		32.90	33
1995 Dawns Early Light	95-day		32.90	33
1995 Soft Morning	95-day		32.90	33
1995 Dawns Golden Warmth	95-day		32.90	33

Cow-Hide - P. Casey

1995 Incowspicuous	Closed		34.95	35-65
1995 Incowgnito	Closed		34.95	35-45
1995 Cowmooflage	Closed		34.95	35-75
1995 Cowpanions	Closed		34.95	35-50

Currier and Ives Christmas Collection - Currier & Ives

1995 Early Winter	Closed		34.95	35-45
1995 American Homestead	Closed		34.95	35-50
1995 American Winter	Closed		34.95	35-45
1995 Winter Morn	Closed		34.95	35

Deer Friends at Christmas - J. Thornbrugh

1994 All a Glow	Closed		29.90	38-42
1994 A Glistening Season	Closed		29.90	30-32
1994 Holiday Sparkle	Closed		29.90	30-34
1995 Woodland Splendor	Closed		29.90	35
1995 Starry Night	Closed		29.90	32-44
1995 Radiant Countryside	Closed		29.90	30

Desert Rhythms - M. Cowdery

1994 Partner With A Breeze	Closed		29.90	30
1994 Wind Dancer	95-day		29.90	30
1994 Riding On Air	95-day		29.90	30
1994 Wilderness	95-day		29.90	30

Diana: Queen of Our Hearts - J. Monti

1997 The People's Princess	95-day		29.95	30

Divine Light - Stained Glass Windows by Causland Studio

1996 Savior/Born	Closed		34.95	35-55
1996 Blessed/Child	Closed		34.95	35
1996 Birth of a King	Closed		34.95	35
1996 Praise Him	Closed		34.95	35

Dog Days - J. Gadamus

1993 Sweet Dreams	Closed		29.90	63-110
1993 Pier Group	Closed		29.90	59
1993 Wagon Train	Closed		32.90	65
1993 First Flush	Closed		32.90	50-60
1993 Little Rascals	Closed		32.90	125
1993 Where'd He Go	Closed		32.90	90

Dreams Come True: The Tale of Snow White - Disney Artists

1995 Wish Come True	Closed		49.95	50

Elvis: Young & Wild - B. Emmett

1993 The King of Creole	95-day		29.90	55
1993 King of the Road	95-day		29.90	50
1994 Tough But Tender	95-day		32.90	33
1994 With Love, Elvis	95-day		32.90	33
1994 The Picture of Cool	95-day		32.90	33
1994 Kissing Elvis	95-day		34.90	35
1994 The Perfect Take	95-day		34.90	35
1994 The Rockin' Rebel	95-day		34.90	35

Enchanted Charms of Oz - M. Dudash

1995 No Place	Closed		34.95	35-65
1995 Wonderland Wizard	Closed		34.95	35
1995 Can't/Scarecrow	Closed		37.95	38
1995 Fresh/Brush Up	Closed		37.95	38

Faces of the Wild - D. Parker

1995 The Wolf	Closed		39.90	70-140
1995 The White Wolf	Closed		39.90	148
1995 The Cougar	Closed		44.90	97-100
1995 The Bobcat	Closed		44.90	118-130

YEAR ISSUE	EDITION LIMIT	YEAR RETD.	ISSUE PRICE	*QUOTE U.S.$
1995 The Bear	Closed		44.90	55-125
1995 The Fox	Closed		44.90	75-139
1995 The Bison	Closed		44.90	88
1995 The Lynx	Closed		44.90	150-200
1995 Royal Ascent	Closed		29.90	30

Fairyland - M. Jobe

1994 Trails of Starlight	95-day		29.90	30
1994 Twilight Trio	95-day		29.90	30
1994 Forest Enchantment	95-day		32.90	33
1995 Silvery Splasher	95-day		32.90	33
1995 Magical Mischief	95-day		32.90	33
1995 Farewell to the Night	95-day		34.90	35

A Family Affair - C. Brenders

1994 Den Mother	Closed		29.90	75-118
1994 Rocky Camp	Closed		29.90	47
1994 Watchful Eye	Closed		29.90	49
1994 Close to Mom	Closed		29.90	40-50
1994 Mother of Pearls	Closed		29.90	30-49
1994 Shadows in the Grass	Closed		29.90	30-59

Family Circles - R. Rust

1993 Great Gray Owl Family	Closed		29.90	28-36
1994 Great Horned Owl Family	Closed		29.90	50
1994 Barred Owl Family	Closed		29.90	40
1994 Spotted Owl Family	Closed		29.90	50

Field Pup Follies - C. Jackson

1994 Sleeping on the Job	Closed		29.90	26-35
1994 Hat Check	Closed		29.90	107
1994 Fowl Play	Closed		29.90	40
1994 Tackling Lunch	Closed		29.90	125-149

Fierce and Free: Big Cats - G. Beecham

1995 Snow Leopard	Closed		39.90	75
1995 Cougar	Closed		39.90	40-74
1995 Jaquar	Closed		39.90	40-66
1995 Black Leopard	Closed		39.90	54-75
1995 Tiger	Closed		39.90	75-90
1995 African Lion	Closed		39.90	75-150

Fleeting Encounters - M. Budden

1995 Autumn Retreat	95-day		29.90	30

Floral Frolics - G. Kurz

1994 Spring Surprises	Closed		29.90	34-80
1994 Bee Careful	Closed		29.90	50
1995 Fuzzy Fun	Closed		32.90	48
1995 Sunny Hideout	Closed		32.90	50

Floral Greetings - L. Liu

1994 Circle of Love	Closed		29.90	30-40
1994 Circle of Elegance	95-day		29.90	30
1994 Circle of Harmony	95-day		32.90	33
1994 Circle of Joy	95-day		32.90	33
1994 Circle of Romance	95-day		34.90	35
1995 Circle of Inspiration	95-day		34.90	35
1995 Circle of Delight	95-day		34.90	35

Footsteps of the Brave - H. Schaare

1993 Noble Quest	Closed		24.90	13-24
1993 At Storm's Passage	Closed		24.90	37-42
1993 With Boundless Vision	Closed		27.90	24-32
1993 Horizons of Destiny	Closed		27.90	31-40
1993 Path of His Forefathers	Closed		27.90	30-46
1993 Soulful Reflection	Closed		29.90	32-44
1993 The Reverent Trail	Closed		29.90	25-44
1994 At Journey's End	Closed		34.90	45-49

Forever Glamorous Barbie - C. Falberg

1995 Enchanted Evening	Closed		49.90	34
1995 Sophisticated Lady	Closed		49.90	45-86
1995 Solo in the Spotlight	Closed		49.90	55-60
1995 Midnight Blue	Closed		49.90	80

Fracé's Kingdom of the Great Cats:Signature Collection - C. Fracé

1994 Mystic Realm	Closed		39.90	39
1994 Snow Leopard	Closed		39.90	50
1994 Emperor of Siberia	Closed		39.90	75
1994 His Domain	Closed		39.90	50
1994 American Monarch	Closed		39.90	40

YEAR ISSUE	EDITION LIMIT	YEAR RETD.	ISSUE PRICE	*QUOTE U.S.$
1995 A Radiant Moment	Closed		39.90	40

Freshwater Game Fish of North America - E. Totten

1994 Rainbow Trout	Closed		29.90	48-52
1995 Largemouth Bass	Closed		29.90	55-69
1995 Blue Gills	Closed		32.90	69
1995 Northern Pike	Closed		32.90	68-85
1995 Brown Trout	Closed		32.90	80-90
1995 Smallmouth Bass	Closed		34.90	45-125
1995 Walleye	Closed		34.90	65-78
1995 Brook Trout	Closed		34.90	74-125

Friendship in Bloom - L. Chang

1994 Paws in the Posies	Closed		34.90	37-40
1995 Cozy Petunia Patch	Closed		34.90	40-85
1995 Patience & Impatience	Closed		34.90	40
1995 Primrose Playmates	Closed		34.90	70

Gallant Men of Civil War - J. P. Strain

1994 Robert E. Lee	95-day		29.90	30-45
1995 Stonewall Jackson	95-day		29.90	30
1995 Nathan Bedford Forest	95-day		29.90	30
1995 Joshua Chamberlain	95-day		29.90	30
1995 John Hunt Morgan	95-day		29.90	30
1996 Turner Ashby	95-day		29.90	30
1996 John C. Breckenridge	95-day		29.90	30
1996 Ben Hardin Holm	95-day		29.90	30

Gardens of Innocence - D. Richardson

1994 Hope	95-day		29.90	30
1994 Charity	95-day		29.90	30
1994 Joy	95-day		32.90	33
1994 Faith	95-day		32.90	33
1994 Grace	95-day		32.90	33
1995 Serenity	95-day		34.90	35
1995 Peace	95-day		34.90	35
1995 Patience	95-day		34.90	35
1995 Kindness	95-day		36.90	37

Getting Away From It All - D. Rust

1995 Mountain Hideaway	Closed		34.90	35
1995 Riverside	Closed		34.90	35
1995 Mountain Escape	Closed		34.90	35
1995 Weekend Refuge	95-day		34.90	35
1995 Homeward Bound	95-day		34.90	35
1995 Evenings Glow	95-day		34.90	35

The Glory of Christ - R. Barrett

1995 Ascension	Closed		29.90	30
1995 Walks on Water	Closed		29.90	30
1995 Christ Feeds	Closed		29.90	30
1995 Wedding at Cana	Closed		29.90	30
1995 Christ and the Apostles	95-day		29.90	30
1995 Raising of Lazarus	95-day		29.90	30

Gone With The Wind: A Portrait in Stained Glass - M. Phalen

1995 Scarlett Radiance	Closed		39.90	49-54
1995 Rhett's Bright Promise	Closed		39.90	80
1995 Ashley's Smoldering Fire	Closed		39.90	90-150
1995 Melanie Lights His World	Closed		39.90	100-120

Gone With The Wind: Musical Treasures - A. Jenks

1994 Tara: Scarlett's True Love	95-day		29.90	30
1994 Scarlett: Belle of/12 Oaks BBQ	95-day		29.90	30
1995 Charity Bazaar	95-day		32.90	33
1995 The Proposal	95-day		32.90	33

Great Moments in Baseball - S. Gardner

1993 Joe DiMaggio: The Streak	Closed		29.90	110-124
1993 Stan Musial: 5 Homer Double Header	Closed		29.90	28
1994 Bobby Thomson: Shot Heard Round the World	Closed		32.90	20-24
1994 Bill Mazeroski: Winning Home Run	Closed		32.90	26-28
1994 Don Larsen: Perfect Series Game	Closed		32.90	29
1994 J. Robinson: Saved Pennant	Closed		34.90	39-55
1994 Satchel Paige: Greatest Games	Closed		34.90	30
1994 Billy Martin: The Rescue Catch	Closed		34.90	73-75
1994 Dizzy Dean: The World Series Shutout	Closed		34.90	47-50
1995 Carl Hubbell: The 1934 All State	Closed		36.90	50-60
1995 Ralph Kiner	Closed		36.90	65

*Quotes have been rounded up to nearest dollar

YEAR ISSUE	EDITION LIMIT	YEAR RETD.	ISSUE PRICE	*QUOTE U.S.$
1995 Enos Slaughter	Closed		36.90	65

Great Superbowl Quarterbacks - R. Brown

YEAR ISSUE	EDITION LIMIT	YEAR RETD.	ISSUE PRICE	*QUOTE U.S.$
1995 Joe Montana: King of Comeback	95-day		29.90	30

Guardians of the Wild

YEAR ISSUE	EDITION LIMIT	YEAR RETD.	ISSUE PRICE	*QUOTE U.S.$
1996 Jaguar	Closed		34.95	35
1996 Tiger	Closed		34.95	35
1996 Black Jaguar	Closed		34.95	35
1996 Leopard	Closed		34.95	35

Guidance From Above - B. Jaxon

YEAR ISSUE	EDITION LIMIT	YEAR RETD.	ISSUE PRICE	*QUOTE U.S.$
1994 Prayer to the Storm	Closed		29.90	50
1995 Appeal to Thunder	Closed		29.90	50-55
1995 Blessing the Future	Closed		32.90	50-70
1995 Sharing the Wisdom	Closed		32.90	50

Happy Hearts - J. Daly

YEAR ISSUE	EDITION LIMIT	YEAR RETD.	ISSUE PRICE	*QUOTE U.S.$
1995 Contentment	Closed		29.90	35
1995 Playmates	Closed		29.90	30-85
1995 Childhood Friends	Closed		32.90	35
1995 Favorite Gift	Closed		32.90	40-45
1995 Good Company	Closed		32.90	40
1995 Secret Place	Closed		34.90	40-44

Heart to Heart - Various

YEAR ISSUE	EDITION LIMIT	YEAR RETD.	ISSUE PRICE	*QUOTE U.S.$
1995 Thinking of You	Closed		29.90	30-70
1995 Speaking of Love	Closed		29.90	30
1995 Whispers in Romance	95-day		29.90	30
1995 Tales of Fancy	95-day		29.90	30
1995 Affection	95-day		29.90	30
1995 Feelings of Endearment	95-day		29.90	30

Heaven on Earth - T. Kinkade

YEAR ISSUE	EDITION LIMIT	YEAR RETD.	ISSUE PRICE	*QUOTE U.S.$
1994 I Am the Light of/World	Closed		29.90	38-50
1995 I Am the Way	Closed		29.90	38-55
1995 Thy Word is a Lamp	Closed		29.90	38-60
1995 For Thou Art My Lamp	Closed		29.90	38-55
1995 In Him Was Life	Closed		29.90	38
1995 But The Path of Just	Closed		29.90	38-75
1995 For With Thee	Closed		29.90	38-100
1995 Let Your Light so Shine	Closed		29.90	38-74

Heaven Sent - L. Bogle

YEAR ISSUE	EDITION LIMIT	YEAR RETD.	ISSUE PRICE	*QUOTE U.S.$
1994 Sweet Dreams	Closed		29.90	94-125
1994 Puppy Dog Tails	Closed		29.90	98-150
1994 Timeless Treasure	Closed		32.90	40-48
1995 Precious Gift	Closed		32.90	33-85

Heavenly Chorus - R. Akers

YEAR ISSUE	EDITION LIMIT	YEAR RETD.	ISSUE PRICE	*QUOTE U.S.$
1994 Hark the Herald Angels Sing	Closed		39.90	40-55
1994 Angels We Have Heard on High	Closed		39.90	40
1994 Joy to the World	Closed		39.90	40
1994 First Noel	Closed		39.90	40
1994 Come All Ye Faithful	Closed		39.90	40
1994 Little Town of Bethlehem	Closed		39.90	40

Heirloom Memories - A. Pech

YEAR ISSUE	EDITION LIMIT	YEAR RETD.	ISSUE PRICE	*QUOTE U.S.$
1994 Porcelain Treasure	Closed		29.90	149
1994 Rhythms in Lace	Closed		29.90	65
1994 Pink Lemonade Roses	Closed		29.90	75-80
1994 Victorian Romance	Closed		29.90	69-74
1994 Teatime Tulips	Closed		29.90	70-75
1994 Touch of the Irish	Closed		29.90	75-100

A Hidden Garden - T. Clausnitzer

YEAR ISSUE	EDITION LIMIT	YEAR RETD.	ISSUE PRICE	*QUOTE U.S.$
1993 Curious Kittens	Closed		29.90	45
1994 Through the Eyes of Blue	Closed		29.90	39
1994 Amber Gaze	Closed		29.90	38-45
1994 Fascinating Find	Closed		29.90	34

A Hidden World - R. Rust

YEAR ISSUE	EDITION LIMIT	YEAR RETD.	ISSUE PRICE	*QUOTE U.S.$
1993 Two by Night, Two by Light	Closed		29.90	48-50
1993 Two by Steam, Two in Dream	Closed		29.90	36-55
1993 Two on Sly, Two Watch Nearby	Closed		32.90	38-40
1993 Hunter Growls, Spirits Prowl	Closed		32.90	35-50
1993 In Moonglow One Drinks	Closed		32.90	64
1993 Sings at the Moon, Spirits Sing in Tune	Closed		34.90	63-70
1994 Two Cubs Play As Spirits Show the Way	Closed		34.90	55-70
1994 Young Ones Hold on Tight As Spirits Stay in Sight	Closed		34.90	80-105

Hideaway Lake - R. Rust

YEAR ISSUE	EDITION LIMIT	YEAR RETD.	ISSUE PRICE	*QUOTE U.S.$
1993 Rusty's Retreat	Closed		34.90	21
1993 Fishing For Dreams	Closed		34.90	38
1993 Sunset Cabin	Closed		34.90	36
1993 Echoes of Morning	Closed		34.90	50

Historic Home Runs

YEAR ISSUE	EDITION LIMIT	YEAR RETD.	ISSUE PRICE	*QUOTE U.S.$
1995 Carlton Fisk	Closed		49.95	125

Home in the Heartland - M. Levne

YEAR ISSUE	EDITION LIMIT	YEAR RETD.	ISSUE PRICE	*QUOTE U.S.$
1995 Barn Raising	Closed		34.95	38
1995 Auction	Closed		34.95	35
1995 Apple Blossom	Closed		34.95	35-50
1995 Country Fair	Closed		34.95	35-60

Hunchback of Notre Dame - Disney Artists

YEAR ISSUE	EDITION LIMIT	YEAR RETD.	ISSUE PRICE	*QUOTE U.S.$
1996 Touched by Love	Closed		34.95	35
1996 Topsy Turvy	95-day		34.95	35
1996 Dance/Enchantment	95-day		34.95	35
1996 Good Day to Fly	95-day		34.95	35

Hunters of the Spirit - R. Docken

YEAR ISSUE	EDITION LIMIT	YEAR RETD.	ISSUE PRICE	*QUOTE U.S.$
1995 Provider	Closed		29.90	30-45
1995 Seekers	Closed		29.90	30-48
1995 Gatherers	Closed		29.90	30-45
1995 Defender	Closed		29.90	30
1995 Hunter	Closed		29.90	30
1995 Keeper	Closed		29.90	30

Illusions of Nature - M. Bierlinski

YEAR ISSUE	EDITION LIMIT	YEAR RETD.	ISSUE PRICE	*QUOTE U.S.$
1995 A Trio of Wolves	Closed		29.90	43
1995 Running Deer	Closed		29.90	30-34

Immortals of the Diamond - C. Jackson

YEAR ISSUE	EDITION LIMIT	YEAR RETD.	ISSUE PRICE	*QUOTE U.S.$
1994 Babe Ruth: The Sultan of Swat	Closed		39.90	67
1994 Lou Gehrig: Pride of the Yankees	Closed		39.90	67
1995 Ty Cobb: The Georgia Peach	Closed		39.90	75
1995 Cy Young: The Winningest Pitcher	Closed		39.90	90

Kalendar Kitties - Higgins Bond

YEAR ISSUE	EDITION LIMIT	YEAR RETD.	ISSUE PRICE	*QUOTE U.S.$
1995 Oct/Nov/Dec	Closed		44.95	45-85
1996 Jan/Feb/Mar	Closed		44.95	45
1996 April/May/June	Closed		44.95	45
1996 Jul/Aug/Sep	Closed		44.95	45-100

Keepsakes of the Heart - C. Layton

YEAR ISSUE	EDITION LIMIT	YEAR RETD.	ISSUE PRICE	*QUOTE U.S.$
1993 Forever Friends	Closed		29.90	30-32
1993 Afternoon Tea	Closed		29.90	32-36
1993 Riding Companions	Closed		29.90	35-40
1994 Sentimental Sweethearts	Closed		29.90	38

Kindred Moments - C. Poulin

YEAR ISSUE	EDITION LIMIT	YEAR RETD.	ISSUE PRICE	*QUOTE U.S.$
1996 Forever Friends	95-day		29.90	30
1995 Sisters Are Blossoms	95-day		29.90	30

Kindred Spirits - D. Casey

YEAR ISSUE	EDITION LIMIT	YEAR RETD.	ISSUE PRICE	*QUOTE U.S.$
1995 Eyes of the Wolf	Closed		29.95	30
1995 Spirit of the Wolf	Closed		29.95	30
1995 Songs of the Wolf	Closed		29.95	30
1995 Prayer of the Wolf	Closed		29.95	30
1995 Guardian of the Wolf	Closed		29.95	30
1995 Quest of the Wolf	Closed		29.95	30
1995 Memory of the Wolf	Closed		29.95	30
1995 Hope of the Wolf	Closed		29.95	30

Kingdom of the Unicorn - M. Ferraro

YEAR ISSUE	EDITION LIMIT	YEAR RETD.	ISSUE PRICE	*QUOTE U.S.$
1993 The Magic Begins	Closed		29.90	30-34
1993 In Crystal Waters	Closed		29.90	41-47
1993 Chasing a Dream	Closed		29.90	60-65
1993 The Fountain of Youth	Closed		29.90	50

Land of Oz: A New Dimension

YEAR ISSUE	EDITION LIMIT	YEAR RETD.	ISSUE PRICE	*QUOTE U.S.$
1984 Emerald City	Closed		39.90	40

Legend of the White Buffalo - D. Stanley

YEAR ISSUE	EDITION LIMIT	YEAR RETD.	ISSUE PRICE	*QUOTE U.S.$
1995 Mystic Spirit	Closed		29.90	30-35
1995 Call of the Clouds	95-day		29.90	30
1995 Valley of the Sacred	95-day		29.90	30
1995 Spirit of the Buffalo	95-day		29.90	30
1995 Buffalo Spirit	95-day		29.90	30
1995 White Buffalo Calf	95-day		29.90	30

Lena Liu's Beautiful Gardens - Inspired by L. Liu

YEAR ISSUE	EDITION LIMIT	YEAR RETD.	ISSUE PRICE	*QUOTE U.S.$
1994 Iris Garden	Closed		34.00	34-74

PLATES & PLAQUES

YEAR ISSUE	EDITION LIMIT	YEAR RETD.	ISSUE PRICE	*QUOTE U.S.$
1994 Peony Garden	Closed		34.00	55-72
1994 The Rose Garden	Closed		39.00	75-120
1995 Lily Garden	Closed		39.00	67-99
1995 Tulip Garden	Closed		39.00	66-99
1995 Orchid Garden	Closed		44.00	72-109
1995 The Poppy Garden	Closed		44.00	55-80
1995 Calla Lily Garden	Closed		44.00	84-150
1995 The Morning Glory Garden	Closed		44.00	84-100
1995 The Hibiscus Garden	Closed		47.00	47-99
1995 The Clematis Garden	Closed		47.00	70-100
1995 The Gladiola Garden	Closed		47.00	73-96

Lena Liu's Holiday Angels - L. Liu

1995 Rejoice	Closed		29.95	30
1996 Glad Tidings	Closed		29.95	30
1996 Celebrations	Closed		32.95	33
1996 Yuletide	Closed		32.95	33
1996 Noel	95-day		32.95	33
1996 Jubilee	95-day		32.95	33

The Life of Christ - R. Barrett

1994 The Passion in the Garden	Closed		29.90	49-54
1994 Jesus Enters Jerusalem	Closed		29.90	46-50
1994 Jesus Calms the Waters	Closed		32.90	56
1994 Sermon on the Mount	Closed		32.90	55-66
1994 The Last Supper	Closed		32.90	57
1994 The Ascension	Closed		34.90	60-80
1994 The Resurrection	Closed		34.90	69
1994 The Crucifixion	Closed		34.90	66

The Light of the World - C. Nick

1995 The Last Supper	Closed		29.90	30
1995 Betrayal in the Garden	Closed		29.90	30
1995 Facing the Accusers	Closed		29.90	30-40
1995 Prayer in the Garden	Closed		29.90	30
1995 Jesus and Pilate	Closed		29.90	30
1995 Way of the Cross	Closed		29.90	30-35

Lincoln's Portraits of Valor - B. Maguire

1993 The Gettysburg Address	Closed		29.90	30-60
1993 Emancipation Proclamation	Closed		29.90	49
1993 The Lincoln-Douglas Debates	Closed		29.90	35
1993 The Second Inaugural Address	Closed		29.90	60

The Lion King - Disney Studios

1994 The Circle of Life	95-day		29.90	30
1995 Like Father, Like Son	95-day		29.90	30
1995 A Crunchy Feast	95-day		32.90	33

Little Bandits - C. Jagodits

1993 Handle With Care	Closed		29.90	57
1993 All Tied Up	Closed		29.90	60
1993 Everything's Coming Up Daisies	Closed		32.90	43-50
1993 Out of Hand	Closed		32.90	43
1993 Pupsicles	Closed		32.90	58
1993 Unexpected Guests	Closed		32.90	28

Lords of Forest & Canyon - G. Beecham

1994 Mountain Majesty	Closed		29.90	45
1995 Proud Legacy	Closed		29.90	27-32
1995 Golden Monarch	Closed		32.90	35
1995 Forest Emperor	Closed		32.90	48
1995 Grand Domain	Closed		32.90	50
1995 Canyon Master	Closed		34.90	40

Loving Hearts

1995 Patient/Kind	Closed		29.95	30
1995 Beauty/Splendor	Closed		29.95	30-75
1995 Unselfish/Giving	Closed		29.95	30-50
1995 God's Gift Divine	Closed		29.95	30-50

Lullabears - M. Scott

1995 Sweet Dreamin	Closed		29.90	30
1995 Rock a Bye Read	95-day		29.90	30
1995 Story Tellin	95-day		29.90	30
1995 Wishin on a Star	95-day		29.90	30

Marilyn: Golden Collection - M. Deas/C. Notarile

1995 Sultry/Regal	Closed		29.90	39
1995 Graceful Beauty	95-day		29.90	30
1995 Essence/Glamour	95-day		29.90	30
1995 Sweet Sizzle	95-day		32.90	33
1995 Fire/Ice	95-day		32.90	33

YEAR ISSUE	EDITION LIMIT	YEAR RETD.	ISSUE PRICE	*QUOTE U.S.$
1995 Satin/Cream	95-day		34.90	35
1995 Shimmer/Chiffon	95-day		34.90	35
1997 Frankly Feminine	95-day		34.90	35
1997 Forever Radiant	95-day		34.90	35
1997 Radiant/Red	95-day		34.90	35

Me & My Shadow - J. Welty

1994 Easter Parade	Closed		29.90	40
1994 A Golden Moment	Closed		29.90	35
1994 Perfect Timing	Closed		29.90	45
1995 Giddyup	Closed		29.90	39

Mewsic For The Holidays - Spangler

1996 Purrfect Harmony	Closed		34.95	30-35
1996 Kitten Tree	Closed		34.95	35
1996 Frosty the Snow Cat	Closed		34.95	35
1996 Santa Claws is Coming to Town	Closed		34.95	35

Michael Jordan: A Legend for all Time - A. Katzman

1995 Soaring Star	Closed		79.95	550-625
1996 Rim Rocker	Closed		79.95	87-99
1997 Slam Jammer	95-day		79.95	80
1998 High Flyer	95-day		79.95	80

Michael Jordon Collection - C. Gillies

1994 91 Championship	Closed		29.90	94-120
1994 Comeback	Closed		29.90	30
1994 92 Champions	Closed		32.90	33-150
1994 82 NCAA	Closed		32.90	33
1995 93 Champions	95-day		32.90	33
1995 88 Slam Dunk	95-day		34.90	35
1995 86 Playoffs	95-day		34.90	35
1996 Rookie Year	95-day		34.90	35
1996 Shot	95-day		34.90	35
1997 91 Eastern Finals	95-day		34.90	35
1997 Record 23/Row	95-day		34.90	35
1997 Career High 69	95-day		34.90	35

Mickey and Minnie's Through the Years - Disney Studios

1995 Mickey's Birthday Party 1942	95-day		29.90	30-55
1995 Brave Little Tailor	95-day		29.90	30
1996 Steamboat Willie	95-day		29.90	30
1996 Mickey's Gala Premiere	95-day		32.90	33
1996 The Mickey Mouse Club	95-day		32.90	33
1996 Mickey's 65th Birthday	95-day		34.90	35

Mickey Mantle All American Legend

1997 Triple Crown King	Closed		79.95	120

Miracle of Christmas - J. Welty

1995 Little Drummer	Closed		34.95	35-45
1995 Holy Night	Closed		34.95	35-68
1995 Angelic Serenade	Closed		34.95	35
1995 Shepherd of Love	Closed		34.95	35

Moments in the Garden - C. Fisher

1995 Ruby Treasures	Closed		29.95	30
1995 Shimmering Splendor	95-day		29.95	30
1995 Radiant Gems	95-day		32.95	33
1995 Luminous Jewels	95-day		32.95	33
1995 Precious Beauty	95-day		34.95	35
1995 Lustrous Sapphire	95-day		34.95	35

A Mother's Love - J. Anderson

1995 Remembrance	Closed		29.90	30
1995 Patience	Closed		29.90	30
1995 Thoughtfulness	95-day		29.90	30
1995 Kindness	95-day		29.90	30

Musical Tribute to Elvis the King - B. Emmett

1994 Rockin' Blue Suede Shoes	95-day		29.90	75
1994 Hound Dog Bop	95-day		29.90	30
1995 Red, White & GI Blues	95-day		32.90	33
1995 American Dream	95-day		32.90	33

Mysterious Case of Fowl Play - H. Bond

1994 Inspector Clawseau	Closed		29.90	40-48
1994 Glamourpuss	Closed		29.90	55-87
1994 Sophisicat	Closed		29.90	50-75
1994 Kool Cat	Closed		29.90	75
1994 Sneakers & High-Top	Closed		29.90	125-140
1995 Tuxedo	Closed		29.90	125

Collectors' Information Bureau   *Quotes have been rounded up to nearest dollar

YEAR ISSUE	EDITION LIMIT	YEAR RETD.	ISSUE PRICE	*QUOTE U.S.$
Mystic Guardians - S. Hill				
1993 Soul Mates	Closed		29.90	30-34
1993 Majestic Messenger	Closed		29.90	25-28
1993 Companion Spirits	Closed		32.90	38
1994 Faithful Fellowship	Closed		32.90	35-38
1994 Spiritual Harmony	Closed		32.90	35-60
1994 Royal Unity	Closed		34.90	38
Mystic Spirits - V. Crandell				
1995 Moon Shadows	95-day		29.90	30
1995 Midnight Snow	95-day		29.90	30
1995 Arctic Nights	95-day		32.90	33
Native American Legends: Chiefs of Destiny - C. Jackson				
1994 Sitting Bull	Closed		39.90	45-64
1994 Chief Joseph	Closed		39.90	40-64
1995 Red Cloud	Closed		44.90	57-65
1995 Crazy Horse	Closed		44.90	85-240
1995 Geronimo	Closed		44.90	100-175
1996 Tecumseh	Closed		44.90	75-149
Native Beauty - L. Bogle				
1994 The Promise	Closed		29.90	30-59
1994 Afterglow	95-day		29.90	30
1994 White Feather	95-day		29.90	30
1995 First glance	95-day		29.90	30
1995 Morning Star	95-day		29.90	30
1995 Quiet Time	95-day		29.90	30
1995 Warm Thoughts	95-day		29.90	30
Native Visions - J. Cole				
1994 Bringers of the Storm	Closed		29.90	72
1994 Water Vision	Closed		29.90	44
1994 Brother to the Moon	Closed		29.90	45
1995 Son of the Sun	Closed		29.90	45
1995 Man Who Sees Far	Closed		29.90	45
1995 Listening	Closed		29.90	35
1996 The Red Shield	Closed		29.90	45-53
1996 Toponas	Closed		29.90	35
Nature's Little Treasures - L. Martin				
1993 Garden Whispers	Closed		29.90	30-60
1994 Wings of Grace	Closed		29.90	30-98
1994 Delicate Splendor	Closed		32.90	33-80
1994 Perfect Jewels	Closed		32.90	33-59
1994 Miniature Glory	Closed		32.90	33-85
1994 Precious Beauties	Closed		34.90	35-56
1994 Minute Enchantment	Closed		34.90	94-100
1994 Rare Perfection	Closed		34.90	35-65
1995 Misty Morning	Closed		36.90	35-95
1995 Whisper in the Wind	Closed		36.90	39-85
Nature's Nobility				
1995 Buck	Closed		39.95	40-82
1995 Pronghorn	95-day		39.95	40
1995 Dall Sheep	95-day		44.95	45
1995 Mule Deer	95-day		44.95	45
1995 Big Horn Sheep	95-day		44.95	45
1995 Mountain Goat	95-day		44.95	45
New Horizons - R. Copple				
1993 Building For a New Generation	Closed		29.90	19-30
1993 The Power of Gold	Closed		29.90	28-30
1994 Wings of Snowy Grandeur	Closed		32.90	30-33
1994 Master of the Chase	Closed		32.90	34
1995 Coastal Domain	Closed		32.90	38
1995 Majestic Wings	Closed		32.90	33
Nightsongs: The Loon - J. Hansel				
1994 Moonlight Echoes	Closed		29.90	64-70
1994 Evening Mist	Closed		29.90	58-69
1994 Nocturnal Glow	Closed		32.90	65
1994 Tranquil Reflections	Closed		32.90	40
1994 Peaceful Waters	Closed		32.90	75
1994 Silently Nestled	Closed		34.90	85
1994 Night Light	Closed		34.90	69
1995 Peaceful Homestead	Closed		34.90	57
1995 Silent Passage	Closed		34.90	70
1995 Tranquil Refuge	Closed		36.90	80
1995 Serene Sanctuary	Closed		36.90	60
1995 Moonlight Cruise	Closed		36.90	64
Nightwatch: The Wolf - D. Ningewance				
1994 Moonlight Serenade	Closed		29.90	30-52
1994 Midnight Guard	Closed		29.90	35-39
1994 Snowy Lookout	Closed		29.90	30
1994 Silent Sentries	Closed		29.90	40
1994 Song to the Night	Closed		29.90	47
1994 Winter Passage	Closed		29.90	45
Northern Companions - K. Weisberg				
1995 Midnight Harmony	95-day		29.90	30
Northwoods Spirit - D. Wenzel				
1994 Timeless Watch	Closed		29.90	48
1994 Woodland Retreat	Closed		29.90	40
1995 Forest Echo	Closed		29.90	42-45
1995 Timberland Gaze	Closed		29.90	40-48
1995 Evening Respite	Closed		29.90	50
1995 Fleeting	Closed		29.90	50
Nosy Neighbors - P. Weirs				
1994 Cat Nap	Closed		29.90	30-75
1994 Special Delivery	95-day		29.90	30
1995 House Sitting	95-day		29.90	30
1995 Observation Deck	95-day		32.90	33
1995 Surprise Visit	95-day		32.90	33
1995 Room With a View	95-day		32.90	33
1995 Bird Watchers	95-day		34.90	35
1995 Board Meeting	95-day		34.90	35
1995 Lifeguard	95-day		34.90	35
1995 Full House	95-day		34.90	35
Notorious Disney Villains - Disney Studios				
1993 The Evil Queen	Closed		29.90	34-40
1994 Maleficent	Closed		29.90	50-74
1994 Ursula	Closed		29.90	40-45
1994 Cruella De Vil	Closed		29.90	35-38
Old Fashioned Christmas with Thomas Kinkade - T. Kinkade				
1993 All Friends Are Welcome	Closed		29.90	38-65
1993 Winters Memories	Closed		29.90	38-110
1993 A Holiday Gathering	Closed		32.90	41-50
1994 Christmas Tree Cottage	Closed		32.90	41-75
1994 The Best Tradition	Closed		32.90	41-124
1995 Stonehearth Hutch	Closed		32.90	41-99
Our Heavenly Mother - H. Garrido				
1995 Adoration	Closed		34.90	35-40
1995 Devotion	Closed		34.90	35
1995 Faithfulness	Closed		34.90	35
1995 Constancy	95-day		34.90	35
1995 Purity	95-day		34.90	35
1995 Love	95-day		34.90	35
Panda Bear Hugs - W. Nelson				
1993 Rock-A-Bye	Closed		39.90	60
1993 Loving Advice	Closed		39.90	60-66
1993 A Playful Interlude	Closed		39.90	60
1993 A Taste of Life	Closed		39.90	60
Pathways of the Heart - J. Barnes				
1993 October Radiance	Closed		29.90	40-50
1993 Daybreak	Closed		29.90	75-80
1994 Harmony with Nature	Closed		29.90	56
1994 Distant Lights	Closed		29.90	75
1994 A Night to Remember	Closed		29.90	50
1994 Peaceful Evening	Closed		29.90	50
Paws in Action - M. Rien				
1995 Playful Dreams	Closed		34.95	35
1995 Sweet Slumber	Closed		34.95	35
1995 Nestled Wrestled	Closed		34.95	35
1995 Rise and Shine	Closed		34.95	35
Paws in Play - M. Rien				
1995 Cuddle Buddies	Closed		34.95	35
1995 Bedtime Tails	Closed		34.95	35
1995 Break Time	Closed		34.95	35
1995 Wake up Call	Closed		34.95	35
Peace on Earth - D. Geisness				
1993 Winter Lullaby	Closed		29.90	35-52
1994 Heavenly Slumber	Closed		29.90	44-48

YEAR ISSUE	EDITION LIMIT	YEAR RETD.	ISSUE PRICE	*QUOTE U.S.$
1994 Sweet Embrace	Closed		32.90	75
1994 Woodland Dreams	Closed		32.90	45-50
1994 Snowy Silence	Closed		32.90	48
1994 Dreamy Whispers	Closed		32.90	40-75

Picked from an English Garden - W. Von Schwarzbek

1994 Inspired by Romance	Closed		32.90	50
1995 Lasting Treasures	Closed		32.90	39
1995 Nature's Wonders	Closed		32.90	125
1995 Summer Rhapsody	Closed		32.90	100-125

Pinegrove's Winter Cardinals - S. Timm

1994 Evening in Pinegrove	95-day		29.90	30
1994 Pinegrove's Sunset	95-day		29.90	30
1994 Pinegrove's Twilight	95-day		29.90	30
1994 Daybreak in Pinegrove	95-day		29.90	30
1994 Pinegrove's Morning	95-day		29.90	30
1994 Afternoon in Pinegrove	95-day		29.90	30
1994 Midnight in Pinegrove	95-day		29.90	30
1994 At Home in Pinegrove	95-day		29.90	30

Pocohontas - Disney Artists

1995 Loves Embrace	Closed		29.95	30
1995 Just Around the Corner	Closed		29.95	30-38
1995 Moment/Touch	Closed		32.95	33-40
1995 Listen/Heart	Closed		32.95	33
1995 Fathers Love	95-day		32.95	33
1995 Best/Friends	95-day		34.95	35

Portraits of Majesty - Various

1994 Snowy Monarch	Closed		29.90	41
1995 Reflections of Kings	Closed		29.90	44
1995 Emperor of His Realm	Closed		29.90	48
1995 Solemn Sovereign	Closed		29.90	48

Postcards from Thomas Kinkade - T. Kinkade

1995 San Francisco-California Street	Closed		34.90	55-68
1995 Paris	Closed		34.90	47
1995 New York City	Closed		34.90	47-50
1995 Boston	Closed		34.90	44-50
1995 Carmel	Closed		34.90	50
1995 Market Street	Closed		34.90	56-76

Practice Makes Perfect - L. Kaatz

1994 What's a Mother to Do?	Closed		29.90	52
1994 The Ones That Got Away	Closed		29.90	30-60
1994 Pointed in the Wrong Direction	Closed		32.90	54
1994 Fishing for Compliments	Closed		32.90	55-60
1994 A Dandy Distraction	Closed		32.90	48-50
1995 More Than a Mouthful	Closed		34.90	60
1995 On The Right Track	Closed		34.90	67-71
1995 Missing the Point	Closed		34.90	55-59

Precious Visions - J. Grande

1994 Brilliant Moment	Closed		29.90	30
1995 Brief Interlude	Closed		29.90	30
1995 Timeless Radiance	95-day		29.90	30
1995 Enduring Elegance	95-day		32.90	33
1995 Infinite Splendor	95-day		32.90	33
1995 Everlasting Beauty	95-day		34.90	35
1995 Shining Instant	95-day		34.90	35
1995 Eternal Glory	95-day		34.90	35

Promise of a Savior - Various

1993 An Angel's Message	Closed		29.90	48
1993 Gifts to Jesus	Closed		29.90	56-58
1993 The Heavenly King	Closed		29.90	40-45
1993 Angels Were Watching	Closed		29.90	61
1993 Holy Mother and Child	Closed		29.90	44
1994 A Child is Born	Closed		29.90	52-58

Proud Heritage - M. Amerman

1994 Mystic Warrior: Medicine Crow	Closed		34.90	27-30
1994 Great Chief: Sitting Bull	Closed		34.90	35
1994 Brave Leader: Geronimo	Closed		34.90	40-54
1995 Peaceful Defender: Chief Joseph	Closed		34.90	35-44

Purrfectly at Home - M. Roderick

1995 Home Sweet Home	Closed		39.95	40-45
1995 Kitty Corner	Closed		39.95	40
1995 Cozy Kitchen	Closed		39.95	59-66
1995 Sweet Solice	Closed		39.95	70

Quiet Moments - K. Daniel

1994 Time for Tea	Closed		29.90	37-46
1995 A Loving Hand	Closed		29.90	27
1995 Kept with Care	Closed		29.90	27-45
1995 Puppy Love	Closed		29.90	28-45

Radiant Messengers - L. Martin

1994 Peace	Closed		29.90	30
1994 Hope	Closed		29.90	30
1994 Beauty	Closed		29.90	30
1994 Inspiration	Closed		29.90	30

Rainbow of Irises - S. Rickert

1995 Alluring Amethyst	Closed		34.90	35-50
1995 Pink Pastoral	Closed		34.90	35
1995 Polonaise	Closed		34.90	35
1995 Lyrical Lavender	Closed		34.90	35
1995 Violet Vision	95-day		34.90	35
1995 Perfect Peach	95-day		34.90	35

Realm of the Wolf - K. Daniel

1996 Midnight Harmony	Closed		29.95	30-50
1996 Night Watch	Closed		29.95	30
1996 Evening Song	95-day		29.95	30
1996 Night Sentries	95-day		29.95	30
1996 Moon Shadow	95-day		29.95	30
1996 Moonlit Phantom	95-day		29.95	30
1996 Shadow Spirit	95-day		29.95	30
1996 Moonglow	95-day		29.95	30

Reflections of Marilyn - C. Notarile

1994 All That Glitters	95-day		29.90	30
1994 Shimmering Heat	95-day		29.90	30
1994 Million Dollar Star	95-day		29.90	30
1995 A Twinkle in Her Eye	95-day		29.90	30

Remembering Elvis - N. Giorgio

1994 The King	95-day		29.90	30
1995 The Legend	95-day		29.90	30

Royal Enchantments - J. Penchoff

1994 The Gift	Closed		39.90	75
1995 The Courtship	Closed		39.90	60
1995 The Promise	Closed		39.90	75
1995 The Embrace	Closed		39.90	80

Sacred Circle - K. Randle

1993 Before the Hunt	Closed		29.90	38-49
1993 Spiritual Guardian	Closed		29.90	59-65
1993 Ghost Dance	Closed		32.90	50
1994 Deer Dance	Closed		32.90	70
1994 The Wolf Dance	Closed		32.90	50
1994 The Painted Horse	Closed		34.90	50-56
1994 Transformation Dance	Closed		34.90	49-65
1994 Elk Dance	Closed		34.90	55

Santa's Little Helpers - B. Higgins Bond

1994 Stocking Stuffers	Closed		24.90	30-40
1994 Wrapping Up the Holidays	Closed		24.90	40-50
1994 Not a Creature Was Stirring	Closed		24.90	35-39
1995 Cozy Kittens	Closed		24.90	60
1995 Holiday Mischief	Closed		24.90	35-39
1995 Treats For Santa	Closed		24.90	25-29

Santa's On His Way - S. Gustafson

1994 Checking It Twice	Closed		29.90	45-50
1994 Up, Up & Away	Closed		29.90	52-55
1995 Santa's First Stop	Closed		32.90	75
1995 Gifts for One and All	Closed		32.90	80
1995 A Warm Send-off	Closed		32.90	80
1995 Santa's Reward	Closed		34.90	110

Seasons on the Open Range - Zabel

1995 Dog Tired	Closed		29.95	30-60
1995 September Bulls	Closed		29.95	30-38
1995 Outfitters	Closed		29.95	30
1995 Season/Gold	Closed		29.95	30

Signs of Spring - J. Thornbrugh

1994 A Family Feast	95-day		29.90	30
1995 How Fast They Grow	95-day		29.90	30
1995 Our First Home	95-day		29.90	30
1995 Awaiting New Arrivals	95-day		29.90	30

Collectors' Information Bureau   *Quotes have been rounded up to nearest dollar

Silent Journey - D. Casey

YEAR ISSUE	EDITION LIMIT	YEAR RETD.	ISSUE PRICE	*QUOTE U.S.$
1994 Where Paths Cross	95-day		29.90	30
1994 On Eagle's Wings	95-day		29.90	30
1994 Seeing the Unseen	95-day		29.90	30
1995 Where the Buffalo Roam	95-day		29.90	30
1995 Unbridled Majesty	95-day		29.90	30
1995 Wisdom Seeker	95-day		29.90	30
1995 Journey of the Wild	95-day		29.90	30

Sitting Pretty - K. Murray

1995 Cats Make a House	Closed		34.95	35-39
1995 Cats Add Love	Closed		34.95	35-50
1995 Little Paws	Closed		34.95	35
1995 Home/Cat	Closed		34.95	35

Soft Elegance - R. Iverson

1994 Priscilla in Pearls	Closed		29.90	45-50
1995 Tabitha on Taffeta	Closed		29.90	50-52
1995 Emily in Emeralds	Closed		29.90	45
1995 Alexandra in Amethysts	Closed		29.90	49

Some Beary Nice Places - J. Tanton

1994 Welcome to the Library	Closed		29.90	37-40
1994 Welcome to Our Country Kitchen	Closed		29.90	55
1995 Bearennial Garden	Closed		32.90	35
1995 Welcome to Our Music Conserbeartory	Closed		32.90	46

Soul Mates - L. Bogle

1995 The Lovers	Closed		29.90	30-125
1995 The Awakening	95-day		29.90	30
1996 The Embrace	95-day		29.90	30
1996 Warm Interlude	95-day		29.90	30

Soul of the Wilderness

1996 One Last Look	Closed		34.95	29-35
1996 Silent Watch	Closed		34.95	35
1996 Chance/Flurries	Closed		34.95	35
1996 Winter Solstice	Closed		34.95	35-60
1996 Storm Runner	Closed		34.95	35-60
1996 Winter Whites	Closed		34.95	35

Sovereigns of the Sky - G. Dieckhoner

1994 Spirit of Freedom	Closed		39.00	30
1994 Spirit of Pride	Closed		39.00	70
1994 Spirit of Valor	Closed		44.00	54
1994 Spirit of Majesty	Closed		44.00	65
1995 Spirit of Glory	Closed		44.00	75
1995 Spirit of Courage	Closed		49.00	60
1995 Spirit of Bravery	Closed		49.00	60
1995 Spirit of Honor	Closed		49.00	85-90

Sovereigns of the Wild - D. Grant

1993 The Snow Queen	Closed		29.90	37
1994 Let Us Survive	Closed		29.90	36
1994 Cool Cats	Closed		29.90	49
1994 Siberian Snow Tigers	Closed		29.90	30
1994 African Evening	Closed		29.90	31-45
1994 First Outing	Closed		29.90	30-34

Star of Hope - H. Garrido

1995 Most Precious	Closed		34.95	35
1995 Gifts of the Magi	Closed		34.95	35-50
1995 Adoration of the Shepherds	Closed		34.95	35
1995 Rest/Flight	Closed		34.95	35

Star Trek Ships of the Galaxy

1995 Enterprise	Closed		59.95	70-95
1995 Klingon Battle	Closed		59.95	90
1995 Romulan	Closed		59.95	80-100
1995 Shuttlecraft	Closed		59.95	100

Study of a Champion - B. Langton

1995 Loyal Companion	Closed		29.90	30-55
1995 Trusted Friend	Closed		29.90	30-50
1995 Devoted Partner	Closed		29.90	30-45
1995 Faithful Buddy	Closed		29.90	30

Superstars of Baseball - T. Sizemore

1994 Willie "Say Hey" Mays	Closed		29.90	35-59
1995 Carl "Yaz" Yastrzemski	Closed		29.90	50
1995 Frank "Robby" Robinson	Closed		32.90	59
1995 Bob Gibson	Closed		32.90	54-65
1995 Harmon Killebrew	Closed		32.90	49-60
1995 Don Drysdale	Closed		34.90	74
1995 Al Kaline	Closed		34.90	74
1995 Maury Wills	Closed		34.90	100

Superstars of Country Music - N. Giorgio

1993 Dolly Parton: I Will Always Love You	Closed		29.90	34
1993 Kenny Rogers: Sweet Music Man	Closed		29.90	29
1994 Barbara Mandrell	Closed		32.90	33
1994 Glen Campbell: Rhinestone Cowboy	Closed		32.90	24

Tale of Peter Rabbit & Benjamin Bunny - R. Akers

1994 A Pocket Full of Onions	Closed		39.00	80
1994 Beside His Cousin	Closed		39.00	58-85
1994 Round that Corner	Closed		39.00	50-95
1995 Safely Home	Closed		44.00	75-100
1995 Mr. McGregor's Garden	Closed		44.00	50-150
1995 Rosemary Tea and Lavender	Closed		44.00	60-125
1995 Amongst the Flowerpots	Closed		44.00	90-100
1995 Upon the Scarecrow	Closed		44.00	150

Teddy Bear Dreams - D. Parker

1995 Catch a Falling Star	Closed		49.95	69-86
1995 Thank Heaven	Closed		49.95	60-90
1995 Let Me Be Teddy	Closed		49.95	50
1995 Fly Me To The Moon	Closed		49.95	50

Terry Redlin's America the Beautiful - T. Redlin

1995 Oh Beautiful	Closed		34.95	35
1995 Amber Waves	Closed		34.95	35
1995 Purple Mountain	Closed		34.95	35
1995 Fruited Plain	Closed		34.95	35
1995 America	Closed		34.95	35
1995 God Shed His Grace	Closed		34.95	35

That's What Friends Are For - A. Isakov

1994 Friends Are Forever	Closed		29.90	40-67
1994 Friends Are Comfort	Closed		29.90	75
1994 Friends Are Loving	Closed		29.90	45-48
1995 Friends Are For Fun	Closed		29.90	65

Thomas Kinkade's Illuminated Cottages - T. Kinkade

1994 The Flagstone Path	Closed		34.90	43-100
1995 The Garden Walk	Closed		34.90	43-150
1995 Cherry Blossom Hideaway	Closed		37.90	46-125
1995 The Lighted Gate	Closed		37.90	46-200

Thomas Kinkade's Lamplight Village - T. Kinkade

1995 Lamplight Brooke	Closed		29.90	38-80
1995 Lamplight Lane	Closed		29.90	38-50
1995 Lamplight Inn	Closed		29.90	38-50
1995 Lamplight Country	Closed		29.90	34-38
1995 Lamplight Glen	Closed		29.90	38-50
1995 Lamplight Bridge	Closed		29.90	30-79
1995 Lamplight Mill	Closed		29.90	35-38
1995 Lamplight Farm	Closed		29.90	35-38

Those Who Guide Us - H. Garrido

1996 St. Francis	Closed		29.90	30-42
1996 St. Joseph	Closed		29.90	30-45
1996 St. Jude	Closed		29.90	30
1996 St. Anthony	Closed		29.90	30

Through a Child's Eyes - K. Noles

1994 Little Butterfly	Closed		29.90	65-70
1995 Woodland Rose	Closed		29.90	45-50
1995 Treetop Wonder	Closed		29.90	35-50
1995 Little Red Squirrel	Closed		32.90	60-65
1995 Water Lily	Closed		32.90	65
1995 Prairie Song	Closed		34.90	65-70

Thunder in the Sky

1995 Mighty 8th Coming	Closed		34.95	35
1995 D-Day	Closed		34.95	35
1995 Home/Dusk	Closed		34.95	35
1995 Winters Welcome	Closed		34.95	35

Thundering Waters - F. Miller

1994 Niagara Falls	Closed		34.90	30
1994 Lower Falls, Yellowstone	Closed		34.90	61
1995 Bridal Veil Falls	Closed		34.90	60
1995 Havasu Falls	Closed		29.90	55

*Quotes have been rounded up to nearest dollar   Collectors' Information Bureau

YEAR ISSUE	EDITION LIMIT	YEAR RETD.	ISSUE PRICE	*QUOTE U.S.$
Timberland Secrets - L. Daniels				
1995 Sweet Dreams	Closed		29.90	30
1995 Gentle Awakening	Closed		29.90	30
1995 Good Day to Play	Closed		29.90	30
1995 Wintry Watch	Closed		29.90	30
1995 Moments Pause	Closed		29.90	30
1995 Tranquil Retreat	Closed		29.90	30
To Soar With Eagles - P. Clayton Weirs				
1995 Cascading Inspiration	Closed		32.95	33-38
1995 Crystal Mist	Closed		32.95	33-50
1995 Turbulent Tide	Closed		32.95	33-50
1995 Soaring/Greater	Closed		32.95	33
Trains of the Great West - K. Randle				
1993 Moonlit Journey	Closed		29.90	31-36
1993 Mountain Hideaway	Closed		29.90	45-50
1993 Early Morning Arrival	Closed		29.90	48-52
1994 The Snowy Pass	Closed		29.90	43-48
Tribute to Selena - B. Emmett				
1996 Selena Forever	Closed		29.95	250
Tribute to the Armed Forces - B. Dodge				
1995 Proud/Serve	Closed		34.95	58
Triumph in the Air - H. Krebs				
1994 Checkmate!	Closed		34.90	59
1994 One Heck of a Deflection Shot	Closed		34.90	38
1994 Hunting Fever	Closed		34.90	89
1995 Thunderbolt	Closed		34.90	65-74
Twilight Memories - J. Barnes				
1995 Winter's Twilight	95-day		29.90	30
Two's Company - S. Eide				
1994 Golden Harvest	Closed		29.90	86-90
1995 Brotherly Love	Closed		29.90	88-149
1995 Seeing Double	Closed		29.90	88
1995 Spring Spaniels	Closed		29.90	110
Under A Snowy Veil - C. Sams				
1995 Winter's Warmth	Closed		29.90	30
1995 Snow Mates	Closed		29.90	27
1995 Winter's Dawn	Closed		29.90	30
1995 First Snow	Closed		29.90	30-50
Under the Northern Lights - D. McCaffery				
1995 Running/Light	Closed		29.90	30
1995 River of Light	Closed		29.90	30
1995 Monarchs Light	Closed		29.90	30
1995 Catching the Light	Closed		29.90	30
Untamed Spirits - P. Weirs				
1993 Wild Hearts	Closed		29.90	39
1994 Breakaway	Closed		29.90	50
1994 Forever Free	Closed		29.90	33-49
1994 Distant Thunder	Closed		29.90	70
Untamed Wilderness - P. Weirs				
1995 Unexpected Encounter	95-day		29.90	30
Vanishing Paradises - G. Dieckhoner				
1994 The Rainforest	Closed		29.90	40
1994 The Panda's World	Closed		29.90	70
1994 Splendors of India	Closed		29.90	60
1994 An African Safari	Closed		29.90	79
Visions from Eagle Ridge - D. Casey				
1995 Assembly of Pride	Closed		29.90	30
1995 Generation	Closed		29.90	30
1995 Freedom	Closed		29.90	30
1995 Stately Summit	Closed		29.90	30
1995 Wings of Honor	Closed		29.90	30
1995 Legacy/Liberty	Closed		29.90	30
Visions of Glory - D. Cook				
1995 Iwo Jima	Closed		29.90	57
1995 Freeing of Paris	Closed		29.90	59-98
Visions of Our Lady - H. Garrido				
1994 Our Lady of Lourdes	Closed		29.90	37
1994 Our Lady of Medjugorje	Closed		29.90	30-57
1994 Our Lady of Fatima	Closed		29.90	47-50
1994 Our Lady of Guadeloupe	Closed		29.90	54-63
1994 Our Lady of Grace	Closed		29.90	30-35
1994 Our Lady of Mt. Carmel	Closed		29.90	70-74
1994 Our Lady of La Salette	95-day		29.90	30
1994 Virgin of the Poor	95-day		29.90	30
1994 Virgin of the Golden Heart	95-day		29.90	30
1994 Our Lady of Hope	95-day		29.90	30
1994 Our Lady of Silence	95-day		29.90	30
1994 Our Lady of Snow	95-day		29.90	30
Visions of the Sacred - D. Stanley				
1994 Snow Rider	95-day		29.90	30
1994 Spring's Messenger	95-day		29.90	30
1994 The Cheyenne Prophet	95-day		32.90	33
1995 Buffalo Caller	95-day		32.90	33
1995 Journey of Harmony	95-day		32.90	33
A Visit from St. Nick - C. Jackson				
1995 Twas the Night Before Christmas	Closed		49.00	57-65
1995 Up to the Housetop	Closed		49.00	65-67
1995 A Bundle of Toys	Closed		54.00	65
1995 The Stockings Were Filled	Closed		54.00	55-70
1995 Visions of Sugarplums	Closed		54.00	65-75
1995 To My Wondering Eyes	Closed		59.00	65
1995 A Wink of His Eye	Closed		59.00	75
1995 Happy Christmas To All	Closed		59.00	75
A Visit to Brambly Hedge - J. Barklem				
1994 Summer Story	Closed		39.90	70
1994 Spring Story	Closed		39.90	68
1994 Autumn Story	Closed		39.90	90
1995 Winter Story	Closed		39.90	90
Warm Country Moments - M.A. Lasher				
1994 Mabel's Sunny Retreat	95-day		29.90	30
1994 Annebelle's Simple Pleasures	95-day		29.90	30
1994 Harriet's Loving Touch	95-day		29.90	30
1994 Emily and Alice in a Jam	95-day		29.90	30
1995 Hanna's Secret Garden	95-day		29.90	30
1995 Henrietta's Floral Fantasy	95-day		29.90	30
1995 Charlotte's Summer Harvest	95-day		29.90	30
1995 Sophie and Pearl's Garden Delights	95-day		29.90	30
Welcome to the Neighborhood - B. Mock				
1994 Ivy Lane	Closed		29.90	52
1994 Daffodil Drive	Closed		29.90	50
1995 Lilac Lane	Closed		34.90	50
1995 Tulip Terrace	Closed		34.90	50
When All Hearts Come Home - J. Barnes				
1993 Oh Christmas Tree	Closed		29.90	60
1993 Night Before Christmas	Closed		29.90	60-73
1993 Comfort and Joy	Closed		29.90	45-69
1993 Grandpa's Farm	Closed		29.90	78
1993 Peace on Earth	Closed		29.90	77-86
1993 Night Departure	Closed		29.90	72
1993 Supper and Small Talk	Closed		29.90	60-63
1993 Christmas Wish	Closed		29.90	60-75
When Dreams Blossom - R. McGinnis				
1994 Dreams to Gather	Closed		29.90	30
1994 Where Friends Dream	Closed		29.90	32
1994 The Sweetest of Dreams	95-day		32.90	33
1994 Dreams of Poetry	95-day		32.90	33
1995 A Place to Dream	95-day		32.90	33
1995 Dreaming of You	95-day		32.90	33
Where Eagles Soar - F. Mittelstadt				
1994 On Freedom's Wing	Closed		29.90	32-35
1994 Allegiance with the Wind	Closed		29.90	30
1995 Pride of the Sky	Closed		29.90	50
1995 Windward Majesty	Closed		29.90	32
1995 Noble Legacy	Closed		29.90	35
1995 Pristine Domains	Closed		29.90	40
1995 Splendor in Flight	Closed		29.90	32-60
1995 Royal Ascent	Closed		29.90	63
Whispers on the Wind - K. O'Malley				
1995 Ruby Throated	Closed		44.90	45
1995 Annas	Closed		44.90	45
1995 Allen	95-day		44.90	45
1996 Broad Billed	95-day		44.90	45
1996 Rufous	95-day		44.90	45

Collectors' Information Bureau   *Quotes have been rounded up to nearest dollar

YEAR ISSUE	EDITION LIMIT	YEAR RETD.	ISSUE PRICE	*QUOTE U.S.$
1996 Blue Throated	95-day		44.90	45
Wild Pagentry - F. Mittelstadt				
1995 Flight of the Pheasant	Closed		49.90	50
Windows on a World of Song - K. Daniel				
1993 The Library: Cardinals	Closed		34.90	45-57
1993 The Den: Black-Capped Chickadees	Closed		34.90	32
1993 The Bedroom: Bluebirds	Closed		34.90	31
1994 The Kitchen: Goldfinches	Closed		34.90	52
Wings of Glory - J. Spurlock				
1994 Pride of America	Closed		32.90	31-34
1995 Spirit of Freedom	Closed		32.90	38-50
1996 Portrait of Liberty	Closed		32.90	34-42
1996 Paragon of Courage	Closed		32.90	34-40
Wings of Love - L. Liu				
1997 Tender Hearts	Closed		29.95	30-48
1997 Precious Gift	Closed		29.95	30-48
1997 Tender Hearts	Closed		29.95	30-48
1997 Sacred Promise	Closed		29.95	30-48
1997 Sweet Dreams	Closed		29.95	30-48
1997 Bright/Light	Closed		29.95	30-48
Winnie the Pooh and Friends - C. Jackson				
1995 Time For a Little Something	Closed		39.90	260-525
1995 Bouncing's/Tiggers do Best	Closed		39.90	83-130
1995 You're a Real Friend	Closed		44.90	31-50
1995 Silly Old Bear	Closed		44.90	38-50
1995 Rumbly in my Tummy	Closed		44.90	44-49
1995 Many Happy Returns of the Day	Closed		49.90	44-64
1996 T is For Tigger	Closed		49.90	51-69
1996 Nobody Uncheered w/Balloons	Closed		49.90	50-93
1996 Do You Think It's a Woozle?	Closed		49.90	71-200
1996 Fine Day to Buzz with the Bees	Closed		49.90	45-69
1996 Pooh Sticks	Closed		49.90	50-70
1996 Three Cheers For Pooh	Closed		49.90	55-80
Winter Evening Reflections				
1995 Twilight Falls	Closed		39.95	40
1995 Down by the Stream	Closed		39.95	40
1995 Shadows Grow	Closed		39.95	40
1995 Day Fades	Closed		39.95	40
Winter Garlands - S. Timm				
1995 Winter Spirits	Closed		34.95	35-39
1996 Jewel in the Snow	Closed		34.95	35-45
1996 Crisp Morning	Closed		34.95	35
1996 Frosty Season	Closed		34.95	35
Winter Shadows - Various				
1995 Canyon Moon	Closed		29.90	30-38
1995 Shadows of Gray	95-day		29.90	30
1995 December Watch	95-day		29.90	30
1995 Broken Silence	95-day		29.90	30
1995 Vigilant Companion	95-day		29.90	30
1995 Moonlight	95-day		29.90	30
1995 Trackers	95-day		29.90	30
1995 Icy Dawn	95-day		29.90	30
Wish You Were Here - T. Kinkade				
1994 End of a Perfect Day	Closed		29.90	38-60
1994 A Quiet Evening/Riverlodge	Closed		29.90	38-125
1994 Soft Morning Light	Closed		32.90	41-85
1994 Forest Lake	Closed		32.90	41-75
1994 Evening in the Forest	Closed		32.90	41-75
1994 Simpler Times	Closed		32.90	41-90
Wolf Pups Young Faces of the Wilderness - L. Daniels				
1995 Tomorrow's Pride	Closed		29.95	30-42
1995 New Adventure	Closed		29.95	30
1995 Morning Innocence	95-day		29.95	30
1995 Call/Future	95-day		29.95	30
1995 Early Aspiration	95-day		29.95	30
1995 Rosy Beginnings	95-day		29.95	30
Woodland Tranquility - G. Alexander				
1994 Winter's Calm	95-day		29.90	30
1995 Frosty Morn	95-day		29.90	30
1995 Crossing Boundaries	95-day		29.90	30
Woodland Wings - J. Hansel				
1994 Twilight Flight	Closed		34.90	55

YEAR ISSUE	EDITION LIMIT	YEAR RETD.	ISSUE PRICE	*QUOTE U.S.$
1994 Gliding on Gilded Skies	Closed		34.90	80
1994 Sunset Voyage	Closed		34.90	60
1995 Peaceful Journey	Closed		34.90	35-75
The World Beneath the Waves - D. Terbush				
1995 Sea of Light	Closed		29.90	50-100
1995 All God's Children	Closed		29.90	70
1995 Circle of Light	Closed		29.90	45-58
1995 Reach/Dreams	Closed		29.90	50-65
1995 Share the Love	Closed		29.90	30-59
1995 Follow Your Heart	Closed		29.90	60
1995 Long Before Man	95-day		29.90	30
1995 Miracles of the Sea	95-day		29.90	30
The World of the Eagle - J. Hansel				
1993 Sentinel of the Night	Closed		29.90	34
1994 Silent Guard	Closed		29.90	48
1994 Night Flyer	Closed		32.90	50
1995 Midnight Duty	Closed		32.90	81
A World of Wildlife: Celebrating Earth Day - T. Clausnitzer				
1995 A Delicate Balance	Closed		29.90	29
1995 Europe	Closed		29.90	89
1995 Africa	Closed		29.90	40
1995 South America	Closed		29.90	50
WWII: A Remembrance - J. Griffin				
1994 D-Day	Closed		29.90	30
1994 The Battle of Midway	Closed		29.90	39
1994 The Battle of The Bulge	Closed		32.90	47
1995 Battle of the Philippines	Closed		32.90	58
1995 Doolittle's Raid Over Tokyo	Closed		32.90	50
1995 Operation Torch	Closed		34.90	68-71
1995 Italian Campaign	Closed		34.90	68-80
1995 Liberation of France	Closed		34.90	90-105

Cherished Teddies/Enesco Group, Inc.

The Cherished Seasons - P. Hillman

YEAR ISSUE	EDITION LIMIT	YEAR RETD.	ISSUE PRICE	*QUOTE U.S.$
1997 Spring-"Spring Brings A Season of Beauty" 203386	Open		35.00	35
1997 Summer-"Summer Brings A Season of Warmth" 203394	Open		35.00	35
1997 Autumn-"Autumn Brings A Season of Thanksgiving" 203408	Open		35.00	35
1997 Winter "Winter Brings A Season of Joy" 203416	Open		35.00	35

Cherished Teddies - P. Hillman

YEAR ISSUE	EDITION LIMIT	YEAR RETD.	ISSUE PRICE	*QUOTE U.S.$
1997 We Bear Thanks 272426	Closed	1999	35.00	38-42
1999 Eskimo Holding Stars 534196	Yr.Iss.	1999	37.50	38
1995 Sculpted Irish Plaque "A Cherished Irish Blessing" 110981	Closed	N/A	13.50	14
1992 Signage Plaque (Hamilton) 951005	Closed	N/A	15.00	24-50
1992 Signage Plaque 951005	Open		15.00	15-17

Cherished Teddies Mini Plates - P. Hillman

YEAR ISSUE	EDITION LIMIT	YEAR RETD.	ISSUE PRICE	*QUOTE U.S.$
1997 Joann "Cup Full Of Love" 269840	Retrd.	2000	25.00	25-27
1997 Jordan "Cup Full Of Joy" 269832	Retrd.	2000	25.00	25

Christmas - P. Hillman

YEAR ISSUE	EDITION LIMIT	YEAR RETD.	ISSUE PRICE	*QUOTE U.S.$
1995 "The Season of Joy" Dtd 95 141550	Yr.Iss.	1995	35.00	35-50
1996 "The Season of Peace" Dtd 96 176060	Yr.Iss.	1996	35.00	28-35
1997 "The Season to Believe" Dtd 97 272183	Yr.Iss.	1997	35.00	35
1998 "The Season of Magic" Dtd 98 352764	Yr.Iss.	1998	35.00	35
1999 Christmas Dtd 99 534196	Yr.Iss.	1999	37.50	38

Easter - P. Hillman

YEAR ISSUE	EDITION LIMIT	YEAR RETD.	ISSUE PRICE	*QUOTE U.S.$
1996 "Some Bunny Loves You" Dtd 96 156590	Yr.Iss.	1996	35.00	35-80
1997 Springtime Happiness Dtd 97 203009	Yr.Iss.	1997	35.00	35

Mother's Day - P. Hillman

YEAR ISSUE	EDITION LIMIT	YEAR RETD.	ISSUE PRICE	*QUOTE U.S.$
1996 "A Mother's Heart is Full of Love" Dtd 96 156493	Yr.Iss.	1996	35.00	35-65
1997 Our Love Is Ever-Blooming Dtd 97 203025	Yr.Iss.	1997	35.00	35
1998 Mom-Maker of Miracles 303046	Closed	1999	35.00	35

PLATES & PLAQUES

YEAR ISSUE	EDITION LIMIT	YEAR RETD.	ISSUE PRICE	*QUOTE U.S.$
Nursery Rhymes - P. Hillman				
1995 Jack/Jill "Our Friendship Will Never Tumble" 114901	Closed		35.00	35-42
1995 Mary/Lamb "I'll Always Be By Your Side" 128902	Closed		35.00	35
1995 Old King Cole "You Wear Your Kindness Like a Crown" 135437	Closed		35.00	35
1996 Mother Goose & Friends "Happily Ever After With Friends" 170968	Closed		35.00	35
1996 Little Miss Muffet "I'm Never Afraid With You At My Side" 145033	Closed		35.00	35-42
1996 Little Jack Horner "I'm Plum Happy You're My Friend" 151998	Closed		35.00	35
1996 Wee Willie Winkie "Good Night, Sleep Tight" 170941	Closed		35.00	35-42
1996 Little Bo Peep "Looking For A Friend Like You" 164658	Closed		35.00	35-42

Delphi

YEAR ISSUE	EDITION LIMIT	YEAR RETD.	ISSUE PRICE	*QUOTE U.S.$
The Beatles Collection - N. Giorgio				
1991 The Beatles, Live In Concert	Closed		24.75	35-37
1991 Hello America	Closed		24.75	48-54
1991 A Hard Day's Night	Closed		27.75	45-59
1992 Beatles '65	Closed		27.75	65-69
1992 Help	Closed		27.75	78-94
1992 The Beatles at Shea Stadium	Closed		29.75	40-48
1992 Rubber Soul	Closed		29.75	47-79
1992 Yesterday and Today	Closed		29.75	44-48
Commemorating The King - M. Stutzman				
1993 The Rock and Roll Legend	Closed		29.75	26-55
1993 Las Vegas, Live	Closed		29.75	35-40
1993 Blues and Black Leather	Closed		29.75	29-52
1993 Private Presley	Closed		29.75	34
1993 Golden Boy	Closed		29.75	27
1993 Screen Idol	Closed		29.75	32
1993 Outstanding Young Man	Closed		29.75	29-37
1993 The Tiger: Faith, Spirit & Discipline	Closed		29.75	35
Dream Machines - P. Palma				
1988 '56 T-Bird	Closed		24.75	13-50
1988 '57 'Vette	Closed		24.75	14-50
1989 '58 Biarritz	Closed		27.75	19-35
1989 '56 Continental	Closed		27.75	21-35
1989 '57 Bel Air	Closed		27.75	25-50
1989 '57 Chrysler 300C	Closed		27.75	22-35
Elvis on the Big Screen - B. Emmett				
1992 Elvis in Loving You	Closed		29.75	54
1992 Elvis in G.I. Blues	Closed		29.75	70
1992 Viva Las Vegas	Closed		32.75	50-90
1993 Elvis in Blue Hawaii	Closed		32.75	35-38
1993 Elvis in Jailhouse Rock	Closed		32.75	35-38
1993 Elvis in Spinout	Closed		34.75	30
1993 Elvis in Speedway	Closed		34.75	30-32
1993 Elvis in Harum Scarum	Closed		34.75	22-24
The Elvis Presley Hit Parade - N. Giorgio				
1992 Heartbreak Hotel	150-day		29.75	30-35
1992 Blue Suede Shoes	150-day		29.75	35
1992 Hound Dog	150-day		32.75	35
1992 Blue Christmas	150-day		32.75	33-38
1992 Return to Sender	150-day		32.75	33-35
1993 Teddy Bear	150-day		34.75	35-38
1993 Always on My Mind	150-day		34.75	35
1993 Mystery Train	150-day		34.75	35
1993 Blue Moon of Kentucky	150-day		34.75	35
1993 Wear My Ring Around Your Neck	150-day		36.75	35
1993 Suspicious Minds	150-day		36.75	37
1993 Peace in the Valley	150-day		36.75	37
Elvis Presley: In Performance - B. Emmett				
1990 '68 Comeback Special	Closed		24.75	29-75
1991 King of Las Vegas	Closed		24.75	39-85
1991 Aloha From Hawaii	Closed		27.75	34-46
1991 Back in Tupelo, 1956	Closed		27.75	38-44
1991 If I Can Dream	Closed		27.75	48-59
1991 Benefit for the USS Arizona	Closed		29.75	39-52
1991 Madison Square Garden, 1972	Closed		29.75	49-67
1991 Tampa, 1955	Closed		29.75	45-60
1991 Concert in Baton Rouge, 1974	Closed		29.75	39-85

YEAR ISSUE	EDITION LIMIT	YEAR RETD.	ISSUE PRICE	*QUOTE U.S.$
1992 On Stage in Wichita, 1974	Closed		31.75	50-6
1992 In the Spotlight: Hawaii, '72	Closed		31.75	36-3
1992 Tour Finale: Indianapolis 1977	Closed		31.75	32-3
Elvis Presley: Looking At A Legend - B. Emmett				
1988 Elvis at/Gates of Graceland	Closed		24.75	35-4
1989 Jailhouse Rock	Closed		24.75	34-5
1989 The Memphis Flash	Closed		27.75	27-4
1989 Homecoming	Closed		27.75	44-5
1990 Elvis and Gladys	Closed		27.75	34-5
1990 A Studio Session	Closed		27.75	22-4
1990 Elvis in Hollywood	Closed		29.75	30-3
1990 Elvis on His Harley	Closed		29.75	49-5
1990 Stage Door Autographs	Closed		29.75	25-3
1991 Christmas at Graceland	Closed		32.75	45-5
1991 Entering Sun Studio	Closed		32.75	35-4
1991 Going for the Black Belt	Closed		32.75	32-3
1991 His Hand in Mine	Closed		32.75	42-5
1991 Letters From Fans	Closed		32.75	35-4
1991 Closing the Deal	Closed		34.75	45-5
1992 Elvis Returns to the Stage	Closed		34.75	58-7
Fabulous Cars of the '50's - G. Angelini				
1993 '57 Red Corvette	Closed		24.75	29-3
1993 '57 White T-Bird	Closed		24.75	5
1993 '57 Blue Belair	Closed		27.75	40-4
1993 '59 Cadillac	Closed		27.75	4
1994 '56 Lincoln Premier	Closed		27.75	4
1994 '59 Red Ford Fairlane	Closed		27.75	4
In the Footsteps of the King - D. Sivavec				
1993 Graceland: Memphis, Tenn.	Closed		29.75	20-2
1994 Elvis' Birthplace: Tupelo, Miss	Closed		29.75	40-4
1994 Day Job: Memphis, Tenn.	Closed		32.75	28-3
1994 Flying Circle G. Ranch: Walls, Miss.	Closed		32.75	23-3
1994 The Lauderdale Courts	Closed		32.75	24-2
1994 Patriotic Soldier: Bad Nauheim, W. Germany	Closed		34.75	47-6
Indiana Jones - V. Gadino				
1989 Indiana Jones	Closed		24.75	14-1
1989 Indiana Jones and His Dad	Closed		24.75	3
1990 Indiana Jones/Dr. Schneider	Closed		27.75	20-2
1990 A Family Discussion	Closed		27.75	23-2
1990 Young Indiana Jones	Closed		27.75	3
1991 Indiana Jones/The Holy Grail	Closed		27.75	5
The Magic of Marilyn - C. Notarile				
1992 For Our Boys in Korea, 1954	Closed		24.75	30-5
1992 Opening Night	Closed		24.75	4
1993 Rising Star	Closed		27.75	38-4
1993 Stopping Traffic	Closed		27.75	42-5
1992 Strasberg's Student	Closed		27.75	34-8
1993 Photo Opportunity	Closed		29.75	26-3
1993 Shining Star	Closed		29.75	24-3
1993 Curtain Call	Closed		29.75	25-3
The Marilyn Monroe Collection - C. Notarile				
1989 Marilyn Monroe/7 Year Itch	Closed		24.75	40-5
1990 Diamonds/Girls Best Friend	Closed		24.75	37-5
1991 Marilyn Monroe/River of No Return	Closed		27.75	58-7
1992 How to Marry a Millionaire	Closed		27.75	44-7
1992 There's No Business/Show Business	Closed		27.75	39-5
1992 Marilyn Monroe in Niagra	Closed		29.75	50-6
1992 My Heart Belongs to Daddy	Closed		29.75	48-6
1992 Marilyn Monroe as Cherie in Bus Stop	Closed		29.75	33-4
1992 Marilyn Monroe in All About Eve	Closed		29.75	34-5
1992 Marilyn Monroe in Monkey Business	Closed		31.75	33-4
1992 Marilyn Monroe in Don't Bother to Knock	Closed		31.75	39-5
1992 Marilyn Monroe in We're Not Married	Closed		31.75	35-5
Portraits of the King - D. Zwierz				
1991 Love Me Tender	Closed		27.75	30-4
1991 Are You Lonesome Tonight?	Closed		27.75	26-5
1991 I'm Yours	Closed		30.75	47-4
1991 Treat Me Nice	Closed		30.75	50-6
1992 The Wonder of You	Closed		30.75	3
1992 You're a Heartbreaker	Closed		32.75	35-3
1992 Just Because	Closed		32.75	4
1992 Follow That Dream	Closed		32.75	4

Collectors' Information Bureau

*Quotes have been rounded up to nearest dollar

YEAR ISSUE	EDITION LIMIT	YEAR RETD.	ISSUE PRICE	*QUOTE U.S.$
Department 56				
A Christmas Carol - R. Innocenti				
1991 The Cratchit's Christmas Pudding 5706-1	18,000	1991	60.00	42-110
1992 Marley's Ghost Appears To Scrooge 5721-5	18,000	1992	60.00	42-65
1993 The Spirit of Christmas Present 5722-3	18,000	1993	60.00	40-42
1994 Visions of Christmas Past 5723-1	18,000	1994	60.00	68-72
Edwin M. Knowles				
Aesop's Fables - M. Hampshire				
1988 The Goose That Laid the Golden Egg	Closed		27.90	9-28
1988 The Hare and the Tortoise	Closed		27.90	12-25
1988 The Fox and the Grapes	Closed		30.90	18-28
1989 The Lion And The Mouse	Closed		30.90	21-32
1989 The Milk Maid And Her Pail	Closed		30.90	27-30
1989 The Jay And The Peacock	Closed		30.90	27-30
American Innocents - Marsten/Mandrajji				
1986 Abigail in the Rose Garden	Closed		19.50	13-18
1986 Ann by the Terrace	Closed		19.50	20
1986 Ellen and John in the Parlor	Closed		19.50	13-20
1986 William on the Rocking Horse	Closed		19.50	24-27
The American Journey - M. Kunstler				
1987 Westward Ho	Closed		29.90	20
1988 Kitchen With a View	Closed		29.90	8-11
1988 Crossing the River	Closed		29.90	25
1988 Christmas at the New Cabin	Closed		29.90	11-22
Americana Holidays - D. Spaulding				
1978 Fourth of July	Closed		26.00	10-25
1979 Thanksgiving	Closed		26.00	10-26
1980 Easter	Closed		26.00	10-26
1981 Valentine's Day	Closed		26.00	13-26
1982 Father's Day	Closed		26.00	10-35
1983 Christmas	Closed		26.00	12-33
1984 Mother's Day	Closed		26.00	12-30
Amy Brackenbury's Cat Tales - A. Brackenbury				
1987 A Chance Meeting: White American Shorthairs	Closed		21.50	14
1987 Gone Fishing: Maine Coons	Closed		21.50	26
1988 Strawberries and Cream: Cream Persians	Closed		24.90	43
1988 Flower Bed: British Shorthairs	Closed		24.90	14
1988 Kittens and Mittens: Silver Tabbies	Closed		24.90	15
1988 All Wrapped Up: Himalayans	Closed		24.90	36
Annie - W. Chambers				
1983 Annie and Sandy	Closed		19.00	5-15
1983 Daddy Warbucks	Closed		19.00	5-10
1983 Annie and Grace	Closed		19.00	8-10
1984 Annie and the Orphans	Closed		21.00	9-24
1985 Tomorrow	Closed		21.00	10-12
1986 Annie and Miss Hannigan	Closed		21.00	11-14
1986 Annie, Lily and Rooster	Closed		24.00	17-50
1986 Grand Finale	Closed		24.00	10-20
Baby Owls of North America - J. Thornbrugh				
1991 Peek-A-Whoo: Screech Owls	Closed		27.90	16-23
1991 Forty Winks: Saw-Whet Owls	Closed		29.90	20-27
1991 The Tree House: Northern Pygmy Owls	Closed		30.90	28
1991 Three of a Kind: Great Horned Owls	Closed		30.90	23-25
1991 Out on a Limb: Great Gray Owls	Closed		30.90	19-25
1991 Beginning to Explore: Boreal Owls	Closed		32.90	45
1992 Three's Company: Long Eared Owls	Closed		32.90	42
1992 Whoo's There: Barred Owl	Closed		32.90	54
Backyard Harmony - J. Thornbrugh				
1991 The Singing Lesson	Closed		27.90	25-69
1991 Welcoming a New Day	Closed		27.90	32
1991 Announcing Spring	Closed		30.90	43-49
1992 The Morning Harvest	Closed		30.90	42
1992 Spring Time Pride	Closed		30.90	45
1992 Treetop Serenade	Closed		32.90	51-60
1992 At The Peep Of Day	Closed		32.90	42-45
1992 Today's Discoveries	Closed		32.90	43-45

YEAR ISSUE	EDITION LIMIT	YEAR RETD.	ISSUE PRICE	*QUOTE U.S.$
Bambi - Disney Studios				
1992 Bashful Bambi	Closed		34.90	35
1992 Bambi's New Friends	Closed		34.90	50
1992 Hello Little Prince	Closed		37.90	43-50
1992 Bambi's Morning Greetings	Closed		37.90	35-39
1992 Bambi's Skating Lesson	Closed		37.90	55-59
1993 What's Up Possums?	Closed		37.90	60
Biblical Mothers - E. Licea				
1983 Bathsheba and Solomon	Closed		39.50	22-25
1984 Judgment of Solomon	Closed		39.50	19-25
1984 Pharaoh's Daughter and Moses	Closed		39.50	22-25
1985 Mary and Jesus	Closed		39.50	28-45
1985 Sarah and Isaac	Closed		44.50	37-40
1986 Rebekah, Jacob and Esau	Closed		44.50	35
Birds of the Seasons - S. Timm				
1990 Cardinals In Winter	Closed		24.90	30-55
1990 Bluebirds In Spring	Closed		24.90	31-55
1991 Nuthatches In Fall	Closed		27.90	15-35
1991 Baltimore Orioles In Summer	Closed		27.90	17-40
1991 Blue Jays In Early Fall	Closed		27.90	22-40
1991 Robins In Early Spring	Closed		27.90	20-35
1991 Cedar Waxwings in Fall	Closed		29.90	24-40
1991 Chickadees in Winter	Closed		29.90	35-55
Call of the Wilderness - K. Daniel				
1991 First Outing	Closed		29.90	33-53
1991 Howling Lesson	Closed		29.90	54-95
1991 Silent Watch	Closed		32.90	39
1991 Winter Travelers	Closed		32.90	33-35
1992 Ahead of the Pack	Closed		32.90	34
1992 Northern Spirits	Closed		34.90	39
1992 Twilight Friends	Closed		34.90	35-44
1992 A New Future	Closed		34.90	35-50
1992 Morning Mist	Closed		36.90	37-44
1992 The Silent One	Closed		36.90	37-46
Carousel - D. Brown				
1987 If I Loved You	Closed		24.90	10
1988 Mr. Snow	Closed		24.90	10
1988 The Carousel Waltz	Closed		24.90	11-23
1988 You'll Never Walk Alone	Closed		24.90	12-20
Casablanca - J. Griffin				
1990 Here's Looking At You, Kid	Closed		34.90	16-20
1990 We'll Always Have Paris	Closed		34.90	23-27
1991 We Loved Each Other Once	Closed		37.90	23-25
1991 Rick's Cafe American	Closed		37.90	30
1991 A Franc For Your Thoughts	Closed		37.90	31-34
1991 Play it Sam	Closed		37.90	40
Castari Grandparent - J. Castari				
1980 Bedtime Story	Closed		18.00	20
1981 The Skating Lesson	Closed		20.00	10
1982 The Cookie Tasting	Closed		20.00	10
1983 The Swinger	Closed		20.00	5-29
1984 The Skating Queen	Closed		22.00	10-25
1985 The Patriot's Parade	Closed		22.00	16-22
1986 The Home Run	Closed		22.00	14-22
1987 The Sneak Preview	Closed		22.00	10
China's Natural Treasures - T.C. Chiu				
1992 The Siberian Tiger	Closed		29.90	13
1992 The Snow Leopard	Closed		29.90	22
1992 The Giant Panda	Closed		32.90	38
1992 The Tibetan Brown Bear	Closed		32.90	30
1992 The Asian Elephant	Closed		32.90	58
1992 The Golden Monkey	Closed		34.90	45
Christmas in the City - A. Leimanis				
1992 A Christmas Snowfall	Closed		34.90	37
1992 Yuletide Celebration	Closed		34.90	50
1993 Holiday Cheer	Closed		34.90	60
1993 The Magic of Christmas	Closed		34.90	53-55
Cinderella - Disney Studios				
1988 Bibbidi, Bobbidi, Boo	Closed		29.90	35-65
1988 A Dream Is A Wish Your Heart Makes	Closed		29.90	30-43
1989 Oh Sing Sweet Nightingale	Closed		32.90	38-45
1989 A Dress For Cinderelly	Closed		32.90	45-58
1989 So This Is Love	Closed		32.90	47-50
1990 At The Stroke Of Midnight	Closed		32.90	43-53

YEAR ISSUE	EDITION LIMIT	YEAR RETD.	ISSUE PRICE	*QUOTE U.S.$
1990 If The Shoe Fits	Closed		34.90	45-54
1990 Happily Ever After	Closed		34.90	34

Classic Fairy Tales - S. Gustafson

1991 Goldilocks and the Three Bears	Closed		29.90	30
1991 Little Red Riding Hood	Closed		29.90	40
1991 The Three Little Pigs	Closed		32.90	42
1991 The Frog Prince	Closed		32.90	50
1992 Jack and the Beanstalk	Closed		32.90	47
1992 Hansel and Gretel	Closed		34.90	70
1992 Puss in Boots	Closed		34.90	44-48
1992 Tom Thumb	Closed		34.90	45-59

Classic Mother Goose - S. Gustafson

1992 Little Miss Muffet	Closed		29.90	19
1992 Mary had a Little Lamb	Closed		29.90	39
1992 Mary, Mary, Quite Contrary	Closed		29.90	38
1992 Little Bo Peep	Closed		29.90	34

The Comforts of Home - H. Hollister Ingmire

1992 Sleepyheads	Closed		24.90	34-50
1992 Curious Pair	Closed		24.90	25-35
1993 Mother's Retreat	Closed		27.90	32-35
1993 Welcome Friends	Closed		27.90	26-45
1993 Playtime	Closed		27.90	36-50
1993 Feline Frolic	Closed		29.90	35-40
1993 Washday Helpers	Closed		29.90	35-45
1993 A Cozy Fireside	Closed		29.90	42-60

Cozy Country Corners - H. H. Ingmire

1990 Lazy Morning	Closed		24.90	34-50
1990 Warm Retreat	Closed		24.90	32-36
1991 A Sunny Spot	Closed		27.90	30-34
1991 Attic Afternoon	Closed		27.90	40-50
1991 Mirror Mischief	Closed		27.90	40-46
1991 Hide and Seek	Closed		29.90	30-40
1991 Apple Antics	Closed		29.90	54-62
1991 Table Trouble	Closed		29.90	40-52

The Disney Treasured Moments Collection - Disney Studios

1992 Cinderella	Closed		29.90	38-45
1992 Snow White and the Seven Dwarves	Closed		29.90	45-48
1993 Alice in Wonderland	Closed		32.90	45-49
1993 Sleeping Beauty	Closed		32.90	40-47
1993 Peter Pan	Closed		32.90	43-54
1993 Pinocchio	Closed		34.90	58-64
1993 The Jungle Book	Closed		34.90	38-45
1994 Beauty & The Beast	Closed		34.90	45-50

Ency. Brit. Birds of Your Garden - K. Daniel

1985 Cardinal	Closed		19.50	15
1985 Blue Jay	Closed		19.50	13-15
1985 Oriole	Closed		22.50	13-15
1986 Bluebird	Closed		22.50	15
1986 Robin	Closed		22.50	15
1986 Hummingbird	Closed		24.50	20-25
1987 Goldfinch	Closed		24.50	15-18
1987 Downy Woodpecker	Closed		24.50	19
1987 Cedar Waxwing	Closed		24.90	16-19

Eve Licea Christmas - E. Licea

1987 The Annunciation	Closed		44.90	25
1988 The Nativity	Closed		44.90	35
1989 Adoration Of The Shepherds	Closed		49.90	46
1990 Journey Of The Magi	Closed		49.90	45
1991 Gifts Of The Magi	Closed		49.90	50
1992 Rest on the Flight into Egypt	Closed		49.90	65

Fantasia: (The Sorcerer's Apprentice) Golden Anniversary - Disney Studios

1990 The Apprentice's Dream	Closed		29.90	40-48
1990 Mischievous Apprentice	Closed		29.90	80-90
1991 Dreams of Power	Closed		32.90	28-70
1991 Mickey's Magical Whirlpool	Closed		32.90	35
1991 Wizardry Gone Wild	Closed		32.90	28-53
1991 Mickey Makes Magic	Closed		34.90	30-35
1991 The Penitent Apprentice	Closed		34.90	19
1992 An Apprentice Again	Closed		34.90	20-23

Father's Love - B. Bradley

1984 Open Wide	Closed		19.50	10
1984 Batter Up	Closed		19.50	10
1985 Little Shaver	Closed		19.50	10-29

YEAR ISSUE	EDITION LIMIT	YEAR RETD.	ISSUE PRICE	*QUOTE U.S.$
1985 Swing Time	Closed		22.50	19-29

Field Puppies - L. Kaatz

1987 Dog Tired-The Springer Spaniel	Closed		24.90	33-40
1987 Caught in the Act-The Golden Retriever	Closed		24.90	25
1988 Missing/Point/Irish Setter	Closed		27.90	21
1988 A Perfect Set-Labrador	Closed		27.90	18-34
1988 Fritz's Folly-German Shorthaired Pointer	Closed		27.90	18
1988 Shirt Tales: Cocker Spaniel	Closed		27.90	15-55
1989 Fine Feathered Friends-English Setter	Closed		29.90	20
1989 Command Performance / Wiemaraner	Closed		29.90	15-40

Field Trips - L. Kaatz

1990 Gone Fishing	Closed		24.90	18
1991 Ducking Duty	Closed		24.90	20
1991 Boxed In	Closed		27.90	16
1991 Pups 'N Boots	Closed		27.90	20
1991 Puppy Tales	Closed		27.90	15
1991 Pail Pals	Closed		29.90	29-32
1991 Chesapeake Bay Retrievers	Closed		29.90	25
1991 Hat Trick	Closed		29.90	23-25

First Impressions - J. Giordano

1991 Taking a Gander	Closed		29.90	29-39
1991 Two's Company	Closed		29.90	30
1991 Fine Feathered Friends	Closed		32.90	35
1991 What's Up?	Closed		32.90	42-44
1991 All Ears	Closed		32.90	48
1992 Between Friends	Closed		32.90	35

The Four Ancient Elements - G. Lambert

1984 Earth	Closed		27.50	19-38
1984 Water	Closed		27.50	30-42
1985 Air	Closed		29.50	27-30
1985 Fire	Closed		29.50	30-59

Frances Hook Legacy - F. Hook

1985 Fascination	Closed		19.50	5-45
1985 Daydreaming	Closed		19.50	5-40
1986 Discovery	Closed		22.50	5-40
1986 Disappointment	Closed		22.50	5-40
1986 Wonderment	Closed		22.50	5-40
1987 Expectation	Closed		22.50	5-40

Free as the Wind - M. Budden

1992 Skyward	Closed		29.90	40-50
1992 Aloft	Closed		29.90	50-55
1992 Airborne	Closed		32.90	35-50
1993 Flight	Closed		32.90	45-68
1993 Ascent	Closed		32.90	40-55
1993 Heavenward	Closed		32.90	45-75

Friends of the Forest - K. Daniel

1987 The Rabbit	Closed		24.50	15-41
1987 The Raccoon	Closed		24.50	25-29
1987 The Squirrel	Closed		27.90	15
1988 The Chipmunk	Closed		27.90	15
1988 The Fox	Closed		27.90	14
1988 The Otter	Closed		27.90	11-14

Garden Secrets - B. Higgins Bond

1993 Nine Lives	Closed		24.90	38-55
1993 Floral Purr-fume	Closed		24.90	38-53
1993 Bloomin' Kitties	Closed		24.90	41-47
1993 Kitty Corner	Closed		24.90	47-50
1993 Flower Fanciers	Closed		24.90	49-59
1993 Meadow Mischief	Closed		24.90	56-60
1993 Pussycat Potpourri	Closed		24.90	48-70
1993 Frisky Business	Closed		24.90	40-55

Gone with the Wind - R. Kursar

1978 Scarlett	Closed		21.50	100
1979 Ashley	Closed		21.50	35-59
1980 Melanie	Closed		21.50	20-40
1981 Rhett	Closed		23.50	15-24
1982 Mammy Lacing Scarlett	Closed		23.50	27-32
1983 Melanie Gives Birth	Closed		23.50	35
1984 Scarlet's Green Dress	Closed		25.50	25-31
1985 Rhett and Bonnie	Closed		25.50	32-44

*Quotes have been rounded up to nearest dollar

PLATES & PLAQUES

YEAR ISSUE	EDITION LIMIT	YEAR RETD.	ISSUE PRICE	*QUOTE U.S.$
1985 Scarlett and Rhett: The Finale	Closed		29.50	31-37

Great Cats Of The Americas - L. Cable

YEAR ISSUE	EDITION LIMIT	YEAR RETD.	ISSUE PRICE	*QUOTE U.S.$
1989 The Jaguar	Closed		29.90	38
1989 The Cougar	Closed		29.90	35-38
1989 The Lynx	Closed		32.90	37-39
1990 The Ocelot	Closed		32.90	16-23
1990 The Bobcat	Closed		32.90	13-15
1990 The Jaguarundi	Closed		32.90	17
1990 The Margay	Closed		34.90	15
1991 The Pampas Cat	Closed		34.90	14-16

Heirlooms And Lace - C. Layton

YEAR ISSUE	EDITION LIMIT	YEAR RETD.	ISSUE PRICE	*QUOTE U.S.$
1989 Anna	Closed		34.90	24
1989 Victoria	Closed		34.90	25-30
1990 Tess	Closed		37.90	43-45
1990 Olivia	Closed		37.90	58-80
1991 Bridget	Closed		37.90	62
1991 Rebecca	Closed		37.90	63

Hibel Christmas - E. Hibel

YEAR ISSUE	EDITION LIMIT	YEAR RETD.	ISSUE PRICE	*QUOTE U.S.$
1985 The Angel's Message	Closed		45.00	26-28
1986 The Gifts of the Magi	Closed		45.00	48-52
1987 The Flight Into Egypt	Closed		49.00	47-59
1988 Adoration of the Shepherd	Closed		49.00	45-75
1989 Peaceful Kingdom	Closed		49.00	40
1990 Nativity	Closed		49.00	119-123

Home Sweet Home - R. McGinnis

YEAR ISSUE	EDITION LIMIT	YEAR RETD.	ISSUE PRICE	*QUOTE U.S.$
1989 The Victorian	Closed		39.90	28
1989 The Greek Revival	Closed		39.90	27
1989 The Georgian	Closed		39.90	18
1990 The Mission	Closed		39.90	23

It's a Dog's Life - L. Kaatz

YEAR ISSUE	EDITION LIMIT	YEAR RETD.	ISSUE PRICE	*QUOTE U.S.$
1992 We've Been Spotted	Closed		29.90	29
1992 Literary Labs	Closed		29.90	19-28
1993 Retrieving Our Dignity	Closed		32.90	50
1993 Lodging a Complaint	Closed		32.90	34-44
1993 Barreling Along	Closed		32.90	35-50
1993 Play Ball	Closed		34.90	34
1993 Dogs and Suds	Closed		34.90	32-35
1993 Paws for a Picnic	Closed		34.90	34-39

J. W. Smith Childhood Holidays - J. W. Smith

YEAR ISSUE	EDITION LIMIT	YEAR RETD.	ISSUE PRICE	*QUOTE U.S.$
1986 Easter	Closed		19.50	8-20
1986 Thanksgiving	Closed		19.50	11-22
1986 Christmas	Closed		19.50	10-22
1986 Valentine's Day	Closed		22.50	15-25
1987 Mother's Day	Closed		22.50	10-16
1987 Fourth of July	Closed		22.50	13-25

Jeanne Down's Friends I Remember - J. Down

YEAR ISSUE	EDITION LIMIT	YEAR RETD.	ISSUE PRICE	*QUOTE U.S.$
1983 Fish Story	Closed		17.50	5-29
1984 Office Hours	Closed		17.50	7-29
1985 A Coat of Paint	Closed		17.50	5-29
1985 Here Comes the Bride	Closed		19.50	10-20
1985 Fringe Benefits	Closed		19.50	7-20
1986 High Society	Closed		19.50	10-29
1986 Flower Arrangement	Closed		21.50	7-29
1986 Taste Test	Closed		21.50	7-29

Jerner's Less Traveled Road - B. Jerner

YEAR ISSUE	EDITION LIMIT	YEAR RETD.	ISSUE PRICE	*QUOTE U.S.$
1988 The Weathered Barn	Closed		29.90	10
1988 The Murmuring Stream	Closed		29.90	10-14
1988 The Covered Bridge	Closed		32.90	19
1989 Winter's Peace	Closed		32.90	22
1989 The Flowering Meadow	Closed		32.90	22
1989 The Hidden Waterfall	Closed		32.90	23

Jewels of the Flowers - T.C. Chiu

YEAR ISSUE	EDITION LIMIT	YEAR RETD.	ISSUE PRICE	*QUOTE U.S.$
1991 Sapphire Wings	Closed		29.90	18
1991 Topaz Beauties	Closed		29.90	39-42
1991 Amethyst Flight	Closed		32.90	19-21
1991 Ruby Elegance	Closed		32.90	24-56
1991 Emerald Pair	Closed		32.90	33-39
1991 Opal Splendor	Closed		34.90	29-57
1992 Pearl Luster	Closed		34.90	47-51
1992 Aquamarine Glimmer	Closed		34.90	28-30

Keepsake Rhymes - S. Gustafson

YEAR ISSUE	EDITION LIMIT	YEAR RETD.	ISSUE PRICE	*QUOTE U.S.$
1992 Humpty Dumpty	Closed		29.90	29-35
1993 Peter Pumpkin Eater	Closed		29.90	50-59
1993 Pat-a-Cake	Closed		29.90	60-71
1993 Old King Cole	Closed		29.90	73

The King and I - W. Chambers

YEAR ISSUE	EDITION LIMIT	YEAR RETD.	ISSUE PRICE	*QUOTE U.S.$
1984 A Puzzlement	Closed		19.50	7
1985 Shall We Dance?	Closed		19.50	8
1985 Getting to Know You	Closed		19.50	7
1985 Set	Closed		78.00	78
1985 We Kiss in a Shadow	Closed		19.50	7

Lady and the Tramp - Disney Studios

YEAR ISSUE	EDITION LIMIT	YEAR RETD.	ISSUE PRICE	*QUOTE U.S.$
1992 First Date	Closed		34.90	40-59
1992 Puppy Love	Closed		34.90	50
1992 Dog Pound Blues	Closed		37.90	32-35
1993 Merry Christmas To All	Closed		37.90	44-47
1993 Double Siamese Trouble	Closed		37.90	35-37
1993 Ruff House	Closed		39.90	30-34
1993 Telling Tails	Closed		39.90	65
1993 Moonlight Romance	Closed		39.90	70-125

Lincoln, Man of America - M. Kunstler

YEAR ISSUE	EDITION LIMIT	YEAR RETD.	ISSUE PRICE	*QUOTE U.S.$
1986 The Gettysburg Address	Closed		24.50	9
1987 The Inauguration	Closed		24.50	10
1987 The Lincoln-Douglas Debates	Closed		27.50	12-18
1987 Beginnings in New Salem	Closed		27.90	25
1988 The Family Man	Closed		27.90	25
1988 Emancipation Proclamation	Closed		27.90	19-30

The Little Mermaid - Disney Studio Artists

YEAR ISSUE	EDITION LIMIT	YEAR RETD.	ISSUE PRICE	*QUOTE U.S.$
1993 A Song From the Sea	Closed		29.90	25-36
1993 A Visit to the Surface	Closed		29.90	33-40
1993 Daddy's Girl	Closed		32.90	25-29
1993 Underwater Buddies	Closed		32.90	47-50
1994 Ariel's Treasured Collection	Closed		32.90	50
1994 Kiss the Girl	Closed		32.90	108-143
1994 Fireworks at First Sight	Closed		34.90	53
1994 Forever Love	Closed		34.90	47-53

Living with Nature-Jerner's Ducks - B. Jerner

YEAR ISSUE	EDITION LIMIT	YEAR RETD.	ISSUE PRICE	*QUOTE U.S.$
1986 The Pintail	Closed		19.50	23
1986 The Mallard	Closed		19.50	23
1987 The Wood Duck	Closed		22.50	23
1987 The Green-Winged Teal	Closed		22.50	25-27
1987 The Northern Shoveler	Closed		22.90	27-35
1987 The American Widgeon	Closed		22.90	20
1987 The Gadwall	Closed		24.90	27-30
1988 The Blue-Winged Teal	Closed		24.90	30

Majestic Birds of North America - D. Smith

YEAR ISSUE	EDITION LIMIT	YEAR RETD.	ISSUE PRICE	*QUOTE U.S.$
1988 The Bald Eagle	Closed		29.90	9
1988 Peregrine Falcon	Closed		29.90	10
1988 The Great Horned Owl	Closed		32.90	10-12
1989 The Red-Tailed Hawk	Closed		32.90	10
1989 The White Gyrfalcon	Closed		32.90	10
1989 The American Kestral	Closed		32.90	15
1990 The Osprey	Closed		34.90	13
1990 The Golden Eagle	Closed		34.90	20-27

Mary Poppins - M. Hampshire

YEAR ISSUE	EDITION LIMIT	YEAR RETD.	ISSUE PRICE	*QUOTE U.S.$
1989 Mary Poppins	Closed		29.90	30-44
1989 A Spoonful of Sugar	Closed		29.90	25
1990 A Jolly Holiday With Mary	Closed		32.90	20-23
1990 We Love To Laugh	Closed		32.90	22-30
1991 Chim Chim Cher-ee	Closed		32.90	20
1991 Tuppence a Bag	Closed		32.90	35

Mickey's Christmas Carol - Disney Studios

YEAR ISSUE	EDITION LIMIT	YEAR RETD.	ISSUE PRICE	*QUOTE U.S.$
1992 Bah Humbug!	Closed		29.90	28-30
1992 What's So Merry About Christmas?	Closed		29.90	39-45
1993 God Bless Us Every One	Closed		32.90	35
1993 A Christmas Surprise	Closed		32.90	35
1993 Yuletide Greetings	Closed		32.90	27
1993 Marley's Warning	Closed		34.90	45-50
1993 A Cozy Christmas	Closed		34.90	59
1993 A Christmas Feast	Closed		34.90	54

Musical Moments From the Wizard of Oz - K. Milnazik

YEAR ISSUE	EDITION LIMIT	YEAR RETD.	ISSUE PRICE	*QUOTE U.S.$
1993 Over the Rainbow	Closed		29.90	40-64
1993 We're Off to See the Wizard	Closed		29.90	69-80
1993 Munchkin Land	Closed		29.90	43-45
1994 If I Only Had a Heart	Closed		29.90	54-76
1994 Ding Dong The Witch is Dead	Closed		29.90	90-129
1993 The Lullabye League	Closed		29.90	64-69

PLATES & PLAQUES

YEAR ISSUE	EDITION LIMIT	YEAR RETD.	ISSUE PRICE	*QUOTE U.S.$
1994 If I Were King of the Forest	Closed		29.90	50-74
1994 Merry Old Land of Oz	Closed		29.90	66-69
My Fair Lady - W. Chambers				
1989 Opening Day at Ascot	Closed		24.90	10
1989 I Could Have Danced All Night	Closed		24.90	10
1989 The Rain in Spain	Closed		27.90	15-20
1989 Show Me	Closed		27.90	17-23
1990 Get Me To/Church On Time	Closed		27.90	15-18
1990 I've Grown Accustomed/Face	Closed		27.90	30-48
Nature's Child - M. Jobe				
1990 Sharing	Closed		29.90	21-30
1990 The Lost Lamb	Closed		29.90	30
1990 Seems Like Yesterday	Closed		32.90	34
1990 Faithful Friends	Closed		32.90	42-45
1990 Trusted Companion	Closed		32.90	47-50
1991 Hand in Hand	Closed		32.90	45-50
Nature's Nursery - J. Thornbrugh				
1992 Testing the Waters	Closed		29.90	45-50
1993 Taking the Plunge	Closed		29.90	45-49
1993 Race Ya Mom	Closed		29.90	40-46
1993 Time to Wake Up	Closed		29.90	38-45
1993 Hide and Seek	Closed		29.90	36-45
1993 Piggyback Ride	Closed		29.90	30-43
Not So Long Ago - J. W. Smith				
1988 Story Time	Closed		24.90	16-25
1988 Wash Day for Dolly	Closed		24.90	15-25
1988 Suppertime for Kitty	Closed		24.90	26
1988 Mother's Little Helper	Closed		24.90	20-25
Oklahoma! - M. Kunstler				
1985 Oh, What a Beautiful Mornin'	Closed		19.50	5-9
1986 Surrey with the Fringe on Top'	Closed		19.50	10-35
1986 I Cain't Say No	Closed		19.50	12-20
1986 Oklahoma!	Closed		19.50	11-35
The Old Mill Stream - C. Tennant				
1991 New London Grist Mill	Closed		39.90	24-40
1991 Wayside Inn Grist Mill	Closed		39.90	31-40
1991 The Red Mill	Closed		39.90	30-40
1991 Glade Creek Grist Mill	Closed		39.90	40-50
Old-Fashioned Favorites - M. Weber				
1991 Apple Crisp	Closed		29.90	74
1991 Blueberry Muffins	Closed		29.90	75
1991 Peach Cobbler	Closed		29.90	105
1991 Chocolate Chip Oatmeal Cookies	Closed		29.90	74-188
Once Upon a Time - K. Pritchett				
1988 Little Red Riding Hood	Closed		24.90	14
1988 Rapunzel	Closed		24.90	10-16
1988 Three Little Pigs	Closed		27.90	19-35
1989 The Princess and the Pea	Closed		27.90	11-23
1989 Goldilocks and the Three Bears	Closed		27.90	37-39
1989 Beauty and the Beast	Closed		27.90	28-32
Pinocchio - Disney Studios				
1989 Gepetto Creates Pinocchio	Closed		29.90	30-41
1990 Pinocchio And The Blue Fairy	Closed		29.90	47-75
1990 It's an Actor's Life For Me	Closed		32.90	38
1990 I've Got No Strings On Me	Closed		32.90	24-45
1991 Pleasure Island	Closed		32.90	23-45
1991 A Real Boy	Closed		32.90	36
Portraits of Motherhood - W. Chambers				
1987 Mother's Here	Closed		29.50	15-30
1988 First Touch	Closed		29.50	30
Precious Little Ones - M. T. Fangel				
1988 Little Red Robins	Closed		29.90	13-30
1988 Little Fledglings	Closed		29.90	22-30
1988 Saturday Night Bath	Closed		29.90	27-39
1988 Peek-A-Boo	Closed		29.90	28-32
Proud Sentinels of the American West - N. Glazier				
1993 Youngblood	Closed		29.50	49-55
1993 Cat Nap	Closed		29.90	67-70
1993 Desert Bighorn Mormon Ridge	Closed		32.90	45-50
1993 Crown Prince	Closed		32.90	60-63

YEAR ISSUE	EDITION LIMIT	YEAR RETD.	ISSUE PRICE	*QUOTE U.S.$
Purrfect Point of View - J. Giordano				
1992 Unexpected Visitors	Closed		29.90	24-30
1992 Wistful Morning	Closed		29.90	29-45
1992 Afternoon Catnap	Closed		29.90	41-50
1992 Cozy Company	Closed		29.90	33-35
Pussyfooting Around - C. Wilson				
1991 Fish Tales	Closed		24.90	22-25
1991 Teatime Tabbies	Closed		24.90	20-25
1991 Yarn Spinners	Closed		24.90	20-25
1991 Two Maestros	Closed		24.90	25-30
Romantic Age of Steam - R.B. Pierce				
1992 The Empire Builder	Closed		29.90	23
1992 The Broadway Limited	Closed		29.90	32
1992 Twentieth Century Limited	Closed		32.90	40
1992 The Chief	Closed		32.90	60
1992 The Crescent Limited	Closed		32.90	73
1993 The Overland Limited	Closed		34.90	48
1993 The Jupiter	Closed		34.90	50-59
1993 The Daylight	Closed		34.90	40-54
Santa's Christmas - T. Browning				
1991 Santa's Love	Closed		29.90	33
1991 Santa's Cheer	Closed		29.90	33-36
1991 Santa's Promise	Closed		32.90	65
1991 Santa's Gift	Closed		32.90	45
1992 Santa's Surprise	Closed		32.90	60
1992 Santa's Magic	Closed		32.90	54
Season For Song - M. Jobe				
1991 Winter Concert	Closed		34.90	42-57
1991 Snowy Symphony	Closed		34.90	40-54
1991 Frosty Chorus	Closed		34.90	50-60
1991 Silver Serenade	Closed		34.90	55-63
Season of Splendor - K. Randle				
1992 Autumn's Grandeur	Closed		29.90	29-38
1992 School Days	Closed		29.90	38-44
1992 Woodland Mill Stream	Closed		32.90	59-63
1992 Harvest Memories	Closed		32.90	50-65
1992 A Country Weekend	Closed		32.90	60-75
1993 Indian Summer	Closed		32.90	59-70
Shadows and Light: Winter's Wildlife - N. Glazier				
1993 Winter's Children	Closed		29.90	34-42
1993 Cub Scouts	Closed		29.90	50
1993 Little Snowman	Closed		29.90	45-50
1993 The Snow Cave	Closed		29.90	36-48
Singin' In The Rain - M. Skolsky				
1990 Singin' In The Rain	Closed		32.90	35-52
1990 Good Morning	Closed		32.90	50
1991 Broadway Melody	Closed		32.90	32-37
1991 We're Happy Again	Closed		32.90	50
Sleeping Beauty - Disney Studios				
1991 Once Upon A Dream	Closed		39.90	20-39
1991 Awakened by a Kiss	Closed		39.90	64-70
1991 Happy Birthday Briar Rose	Closed		42.90	35
1992 Together At Last	Closed		42.90	40
Small Blessings - C. Layton				
1992 Now I Lay Me Down to Sleep	Closed		29.90	24
1992 Bless Us O Lord For These, Thy Gifts	Closed		29.90	27-34
1992 Jesus Loves Me, This I Know	Closed		32.90	32
1992 This Little Light of Mine	Closed		32.90	28-30
1992 Blessed Are The Pure In Heart	Closed		32.90	37
1993 Bless Our Home	Closed		32.90	35
Snow White and the Seven Dwarfs - Disney Studios				
1991 The Dance of Snow White/Seven Dwarfs	Closed		29.90	30-65
1991 With a Smile and a Song	Closed		29.90	24-36
1991 A Special Treat	Closed		32.90	28-40
1992 A Kiss for Dopey	Closed		32.90	38-45
1992 The Poison Apple	Closed		32.90	35-46
1992 Fireside Love Story	Closed		34.90	30-45
1992 Stubborn Grumpy	Closed		34.90	24-29
1992 A Wish Come True	Closed		34.90	38-57
1993 Time To Tidy Up	Closed		34.50	38-48
1993 May I Have This Dance?	Closed		36.90	36-46
1993 A Surprise in the Clearing	Closed		36.50	40-49

*Quotes have been rounded up to nearest dollar

YEAR ISSUE	EDITION LIMIT	YEAR RETD.	ISSUE PRICE	*QUOTE U.S.$
1993 Happy Ending	Closed		36.90	50-63
Songs of the American Spirit - H. Bond				
1991 The Star Spangled Banner	Closed		29.90	19
1991 Battle Hymn of the Republic	Closed		29.90	20-39
1991 America the Beautiful	Closed		29.90	31
1991 My Country 'Tis of Thee	Closed		29.90	60
Sound of Music - T. Crnkovich				
1986 Sound of Music	Closed		19.50	7
1986 Do-Re-Mi	Closed		19.50	10-12
1986 My Favorite Things	Closed		22.50	13
1986 Laendler Waltz	Closed		22.50	13-15
1987 Edelweiss	Closed		22.50	19-30
1987 I Have Confidence	Closed		22.50	15-17
1987 Maria	Closed		24.90	19-22
1987 Climb Ev'ry Mountain	Closed		24.90	19-25
South Pacific - E. Gignilliat				
1987 Some Enchanted Evening	Closed		24.50	7-25
1987 Happy Talk	Closed		24.50	7-25
1987 Dites Moi	Closed		24.90	9-25
1988 Honey Bun	Closed		24.90	9-25
Stately Owls - J. Beaudoin				
1989 The Snowy Owl	Closed		29.90	12-14
1989 The Great Horned Owl	Closed		29.90	28
1990 The Barn Owl	Closed		32.90	15
1990 The Screech Owl	Closed		32.90	15-22
1990 The Short-Eared Owl	Closed		32.90	19
1990 The Barred Owl	Closed		32.90	16-24
1990 The Great Grey Owl	Closed		34.90	27
1991 The Saw-Whet Owl	Closed		34.90	25-29
Sundblom Santas - H. Sundblom				
1989 Santa By The Fire	Closed		27.90	12-15
1990 Christmas Vigil	Closed		27.90	15-24
1991 To All A Good Night	Closed		32.90	40
1992 Santa's on His Way	Closed		32.90	40
A Swan is Born - L. Roberts				
1987 Hopes and Dreams	Closed		24.50	25
1987 At the Barre	Closed		24.50	23-25
1987 In Position	Closed		24.50	30
1988 Just For Size	Closed		24.50	40
Sweetness and Grace - J. Welty				
1992 God Bless Teddy	Closed		34.90	35-45
1992 Sunshine and Smiles	Closed		34.90	35-47
1992 Favorite Buddy	Closed		34.90	45
1992 Sweet Dreams	Closed		34.90	60
Thomas Kinkade's Enchanted Cottages - T. Kinkade				
1993 Fallbrooke Cottage	Closed		29.90	50-90
1993 Julianne's Cottage	Closed		29.90	35-89
1993 Seaside Cottage	Closed		29.90	59-90
1993 Sweetheart Cottage	Closed		29.90	85-90
1993 Weathervane Cottage	Closed		29.90	72-74
1993 Rose Garden Cottage	Closed		29.90	85
Thomas Kinkade's Garden Cottages of England - T. Kinkade				
1991 Chandler's Cottage	Closed		27.90	50
1991 Cedar Nook Cottage	Closed		27.90	43-47
1991 Candlelit Cottage	Closed		30.90	49-57
1991 Open Gate Cottage	Closed		30.90	32-36
1991 McKenna's Cottage	Closed		30.90	34-44
1992 Woodsman's Thatch Cottage	Closed		32.90	40-60
1992 Merritt's Cottage	Closed		32.90	50-60
1992 Stonegate Cottage	Closed		32.90	50-60
Thomas Kinkade's Home for the Holidays - T. Kinkade				
1991 Sleigh Ride Home	Closed		29.90	39-44
1991 Home to Grandma's	Closed		29.90	35-37
1991 Home Before Christmas	Closed		32.90	44-54
1992 The Warmth of Home	Closed		32.90	41
1992 Homespun Holiday	Closed		32.90	39-42
1992 Hometime Yuletide	Closed		34.90	38-47
1992 Home Away From Home	Closed		34.90	49
1992 The Journey Home	Closed		34.90	45
Thomas Kinkade's Home is Where the Heart Is - T. Kinkade				
1992 Home Sweet Home	Closed		29.90	50-80
1992 A Warm Welcome Home	Closed		29.90	44-50

YEAR ISSUE	EDITION LIMIT	YEAR RETD.	ISSUE PRICE	*QUOTE U.S.$
1992 A Carriage Ride Home	Closed		32.90	36-48
1993 Amber Afternoon	Closed		32.90	40-70
1993 Country Memories	Closed		32.90	39-78
1993 The Twilight Cafe	Closed		34.90	43-60
1993 Our Summer Home	Closed		34.90	60-79
1993 Hometown Hospitality	Closed		34.90	65-110
Thomas Kinkade's Thomashire - T. Kinkade				
1992 Olde Porterfield Tea Room	Closed		29.90	30-35
1992 Olde Thomashire Mill	Closed		29.90	24-46
1992 Swanbrook Cottage	Closed		32.90	76-80
1992 Pye Corner Cottage	Closed		32.90	35-44
1993 Blossom Hill Church	Closed		32.90	55
1993 Olde Garden Cottage	Closed		32.90	48-58
Thomas Kinkade's Yuletide Memories - T. Kinkade				
1992 The Magic of Christmas	Closed		29.90	83-100
1992 A Beacon of Faith	Closed		29.90	40-45
1993 Moonlit Sleighride	Closed		29.90	30
1993 Silent Night	Closed		29.90	65-75
1993 Olde Porterfield Gift Shoppe	Closed		29.90	45-70
1993 The Wonder of the Season	Closed		29.90	49-52
1993 A Winter's Walk	Closed		29.90	55
1993 Skater's Delight	Closed		32.90	35-52
Tom Sawyer - W. Chambers				
1987 Whitewashing the Fence	Closed		27.50	25-35
1987 Tom and Becky	Closed		27.90	25-35
1987 Tom Sawyer the Pirate	Closed		27.90	25-35
1988 First Pipes	Closed		27.90	23-35
Under Mother's Wing - J. Beaudoin				
1992 Arctic Spring: Snowy Owls	Closed		29.90	38
1992 Forest's Edge: Great Gray Owls	Closed		29.90	35-40
1992 Treetop Trio: Long-Eared Owls	Closed		32.90	45-50
1992 Woodland Watch: Spotted Owls	Closed		32.90	50-55
1992 Vast View: Saw Whet Owls	Closed		32.90	50
1992 Lofty-Limb: Great Horned Owl	Closed		34.90	50-55
1993 Perfect Perch: Barred Owls	Closed		34.90	45
1993 Happy Home: Short-Eared Owl	Closed		34.90	50
Upland Birds of North America - W. Anderson				
1986 The Pheasant	Closed		24.50	10
1986 The Grouse	Closed		24.50	7
1987 The Quail	Closed		27.50	8-10
1987 The Wild Turkey	Closed		27.50	14-28
1987 The Gray Partridge	Closed		27.50	10-14
1987 The Woodcock	Closed		27.90	14
Windows of Glory - J. Welty				
1993 King of Kings	Closed		29.90	30-51
1993 Prince of Peace	Closed		29.90	74
1993 The Messiah	Closed		32.90	33-73
1993 The Good Shepherd	Closed		32.90	33-59
1994 The Light of the World	Closed		32.90	33-75
1994 The Everlasting Father	Closed		32.90	33
Wizard of Oz - J. Auckland				
1977 Over the Rainbow	Closed		19.00	35-40
1978 If I Only Had a Brain	Closed		19.00	30-35
1978 If I Only Had a Heart	Closed		19.00	38
1978 If I Were King of the Forest	Closed		19.00	40-48
1979 Wicked Witch of the West	Closed		19.00	40-56
1979 Follow the Yellow Brick Road	Closed		19.00	56-59
1979 Wonderful Wizard of Oz	Closed		19.00	50-52
1980 The Grand Finale	Closed		24.00	54-60
Wizard of Oz: A National Treasure - R. Laslo				
1991 Yellow Brick Road	Closed		29.90	31-48
1992 I Haven't Got a Brain	Closed		29.90	35-44
1992 I'm a Little Rusty Yet	Closed		32.90	40-44
1992 I Even Scare Myself	Closed		32.90	52-55
1992 We're Off To See the Wizard	Closed		32.90	80-100
1992 I'll Never Get Home	Closed		34.90	59-65
1992 I'm Melting	Closed		34.90	80-83
1992 There's No Place Like Home	Closed		34.90	68-90
Yesterday's Innocents - J. Wilcox Smith				
1992 My First Book	Closed		29.90	44-64
1992 Time to Smell the Roses	Closed		29.90	48-55
1993 Hush, Baby's Sleeping	Closed		32.90	38-50
1993 Ready and Waiting	Closed		32.90	50-60

YEAR ISSUE	EDITION LIMIT	YEAR RETD.	ISSUE PRICE	*QUOTE U.S.$

Fenton Art Glass Company

American Classic Series - M. Dickinson

YEAR ISSUE	EDITION LIMIT	YEAR RETD.	ISSUE PRICE	*QUOTE U.S.$
1986 Jupiter Train on Opal Satin	5,000	1986	75.00	75
1986 Studebaker-Garford Car on Opal Satin	5,000	1986	75.00	75

American Craftsman Carnival - Fenton

YEAR ISSUE	EDITION LIMIT	YEAR RETD.	ISSUE PRICE	*QUOTE U.S.$
1970 Glassmaker	Closed	1970	10.00	20-60
1971 Printer	Closed	1971	10.00	20-60
1972 Blacksmith	Closed	1972	10.00	20-60
1973 Shoemaker	Closed	1973	10.00	20-60
1974 Pioneer Cooper	Closed	1974	11.00	20-60
1975 Paul Revere (Patriot & Silversmith)	Closed	1975	12.50	20-60
1976 Gunsmith	Closed	1976	13.50	20-60
1977 Potter	Closed	1977	15.00	20-60
1978 Wheelwright	Closed	1978	15.00	20-60
1979 Cabinetmaker	Closed	1979	15.00	20-60
1980 Tanner	Closed	1980	16.50	20-60
1981 Housewright	Closed	1981	17.50	20-60

Christmas - Various

YEAR ISSUE	EDITION LIMIT	YEAR RETD.	ISSUE PRICE	*QUOTE U.S.$
1979 Nature's Christmas - K. Cunningham	Yr.Iss.	1979	35.00	35
1980 Going Home - D. Johnson	Yr.Iss.	1980	38.50	39
1981 All Is Calm - D. Johnson	Yr.Iss.	1981	42.50	43-45
1982 Country Christmas - R. Spindler	Yr.Iss.	1982	42.50	43-45
1983 Anticipation - D. Johnson	7,500	1983	45.00	45
1984 Expectation - D. Johnson	7,500	1984	50.00	50
1985 Heart's Desire - D. Johnson	7,500	1986	50.00	50
1987 Sharing The Spirit - L. Everson	Yr.Iss.	1987	50.00	50
1987 Cardinal in the Churchyard - D. Johnson	4,500	1987	39.50	40-45
1988 A Chickadee Ballet - D. Johnson	4,500	1988	39.50	40-45
1989 Downy Pecker - Chisled Song - D. Johnson	4,500	1989	39.50	40-45
1990 A Blue Bird in Snowfall - D. Johnson	4,500	1990	39.50	40-45
1990 Sleigh Ride - F. Burton	3,500	1990	45.00	45
1991 Christmas Eve - F. Burton	3,500	1991	45.00	45
1992 Family Tradition - F. Burton	3,500	1992	49.00	49
1993 Family Holiday - F. Burton	3,500	1993	49.00	49
1994 Silent Night - F. Burton	1,500	1994	65.00	65-95
1995 Our Home Is Blessed - F. Burton	1,500	1995	65.00	65
1996 Star of Wonder - F. Burton	1,750	1996	65.00	65
1997 The Way Home - F. Burton	1,750	1997	85.00	85
1998 The Arrival - F. Burton	2,500	1998	75.00	75
1999 The Announcement - F. Burton	2,500	1999	79.00	79
2000 The Journey - F. Burton	2,500	2000	85.00	85
2001 The Celebration - F. Burton	2,500	2001	89.00	89

Easter Series - Various

YEAR ISSUE	EDITION LIMIT	YEAR RETD.	ISSUE PRICE	*QUOTE U.S.$
1995 Covered Hen & Egg Opal Irid. Hndpt.- M. Reynolds	950	1995	95.00	95-120
1997 Covered Hen & Egg Opal Irid. Hndpt.- R. Spindler	950	1997	115.00	115-135

Mary Gregory - M. Reynolds

YEAR ISSUE	EDITION LIMIT	YEAR RETD.	ISSUE PRICE	*QUOTE U.S.$
1994 Plate w/stand, 9"	Closed	1994	65.00	65-75
1995 Plate w/stand, 9"	Closed	1995	65.00	65-75

Flambro Imports

Emmett Kelly Jr. Plates - D. Rust, unless otherwise noted

YEAR ISSUE	EDITION LIMIT	YEAR RETD.	ISSUE PRICE	*QUOTE U.S.$
1983 Why Me? Plate I - C. Kelly	10,000	N/A	40.00	215-400
1984 Balloons For Sale Plate II - C. Kelly	10,000	N/A	40.00	215-275
1985 Big Business Plate III - C. Kelly	10,000	N/A	40.00	215-250
1986 And God Bless America IV - C. Kelly	10,000	N/A	40.00	100-200
1988 Tis the Season	10,000	N/A	50.00	120-175
1989 Looking Back- 65th Birthday	6,500	N/A	50.00	250
1991 Winter	10,000	1996	30.00	35-175
1992 Spring	10,000	1996	30.00	35-99
1992 Summer	10,000	1996	30.00	35-99
1992 Autumn	10,000	1996	30.00	35-85
1993 Santa's Stowaway	5,000	1996	30.00	30-90
1994 70th Birthday Commemorative	5,000	1996	30.00	90-150
1995 All Wrapped Up in Christmas	5,000	1996	30.00	30-65

Fontanini/Roman, Inc.

Fontanini Annual Christmas Plate - E. Simonetti

YEAR ISSUE	EDITION LIMIT	YEAR RETD.	ISSUE PRICE	*QUOTE U.S.$
1986 A King Is Born	Yr.Iss.	1986	60.00	60
1987 O Come, Let Us Adore Him	Yr.Iss.	1987	60.00	65

YEAR ISSUE	EDITION LIMIT	YEAR RETD.	ISSUE PRICE	*QUOTE U.S.$
1988 Adoration of the Magi	Yr.Iss.	1988	70.00	75-110
1989 Flight Into Egypt	Yr.Iss.	1989	75.00	85

Fountainhead

As Free As The Wind - M. Fernandez

YEAR ISSUE	EDITION LIMIT	YEAR RETD.	ISSUE PRICE	*QUOTE U.S.$
1989 As Free As The Wind	Unkn.		295.00	670-775

The Wings of Freedom - M. Fernandez

YEAR ISSUE	EDITION LIMIT	YEAR RETD.	ISSUE PRICE	*QUOTE U.S.$
1985 Courtship Flight	2,500		250.00	1300-1500
1986 Wings of Freedom	2,500		250.00	1300-1500

Goebel of North America

Pocket Dragons - R. Musgrave

YEAR ISSUE	EDITION LIMIT	YEAR RETD.	ISSUE PRICE	*QUOTE U.S.$
1997 The Astronomy Lesson	1,250	1998	35.00	35
1997 Bedtime	1,250	1998	35.00	35

Goebel/M.I. Hummel

Century Collection Mini Plates - M.I. Hummel

YEAR ISSUE	EDITION LIMIT	YEAR RETD.	ISSUE PRICE	*QUOTE U.S.$
1999 Chapel Time (1986)	Open		30.00	30
1999 Pleasant Journey (1987)	Open		30.00	30
1999 Call To Worship (1988)	Open		30.00	30
1999 Harmony in Four Parts (1989)	Open		30.00	30
1999 Let's Tell The World (1990)	Open		30.00	30
1999 We Wish You The Best (1991)	Open		30.00	30
1999 On Our Way (1992)	Open		30.00	30
1999 Welcome Spring (1993)	Open		30.00	30
1999 Rock-A-Bye (1994)	Open		30.00	30
1999 Strike Up The Band (1995)	Open		30.00	30
1999 Love's Bounty (1996)	Open		30.00	30
1999 Fond Goodbye (1997)	Open		30.00	30
1999 Here's My Heart (1998)	Open		30.00	30
1999 Fanfare (1999)	Open		30.00	30

M.I. Hummel Annual Figural Christmas Plates - M.I. Hummel

YEAR ISSUE	EDITION LIMIT	YEAR RETD.	ISSUE PRICE	*QUOTE U.S.$
1995 Festival Harmony w/Flute 693	Closed	1995	125.00	100-150
1996 Christmas Song 692	Closed	1996	130.00	98-150
1997 Thanksgiving Prayer 694	Closed	1997	140.00	140-150
1998 Echoes of Joy 695	Closed	1998	145.00	145-150
1999 Joyful Noise 696	Closed	1999	145.00	150
2000 Light The Way 697	Closed	2000	150.00	150

M.I. Hummel Annual Plates - M.I. Hummel

YEAR ISSUE	EDITION LIMIT	YEAR RETD.	ISSUE PRICE	*QUOTE U.S.$
2000 Garden Splendor 921	Yr.Iss.	2000	198.00	198
2001 A Afternoon Nap 922	Yr.Iss.	2001	198.00	198
2002 Bumblebee Friend 923	Yr.Iss.		198.00	198

M.I. Hummel Club Exclusive Celebration - M.I. Hummel

YEAR ISSUE	EDITION LIMIT	YEAR RETD.	ISSUE PRICE	*QUOTE U.S.$
1986 Valentine Gift (Hum 738)	Closed		90.00	120-190
1987 Valentine Joy (Hum 737)	Closed		98.00	120-190
1988 Daisies Don't Tell (Hum 736)	Closed		115.00	120-190
1989 It's Cold (Hum 735)	Closed		120.00	120-190

M.I. Hummel Collectibles Anniversary Plates - M.I. Hummel

YEAR ISSUE	EDITION LIMIT	YEAR RETD.	ISSUE PRICE	*QUOTE U.S.$
1975 Stormy Weather 280	Closed		100.00	55-295
1980 Spring Dance 281	Closed		225.00	44-124
1985 Auf Wiedersehen 282	Closed		225.00	163-250

M.I. Hummel Collectibles Annual Plates - M.I. Hummel

YEAR ISSUE	EDITION LIMIT	YEAR RETD.	ISSUE PRICE	*QUOTE U.S.$
1971 Heavenly Angel 264	Closed		25.00	414-600
1972 Hear Ye, Hear Ye 265	Closed		30.00	32-52
1973 Globe Trotter 266	Closed		32.50	52-124
1974 Goose Girl 267	Closed		40.00	50-65
1975 Ride into Christmas 268	Closed		50.00	40-78
1976 Apple Tree Girl 269	Closed		50.00	40-72
1977 Apple Tree Boy 270	Closed		52.50	39-72
1978 Happy Pastime 271	Closed		65.00	30-52
1979 Singing Lesson 272	Closed		90.00	20-90
1980 School Girl 273	Closed		100.00	35-110
1981 Umbrella Boy 274	Closed		100.00	33-100
1982 Umbrella Girl 275	Closed		100.00	84-195
1983 The Postman 276	Closed		108.00	130-228
1984 Little Helper 277	Closed		108.00	39-117
1985 Chick Girl 278	Closed		110.00	49-137
1986 Playmates 279	Closed		125.00	90-245
1987 Feeding Time 283	Closed		135.00	224-520
1988 Little Goat Herder 284	Closed		145.00	90-165
1989 Farm Boy 285	Closed		160.00	117-293
1990 Shepherd's Boy 286	Closed		170.00	180-224
1991 Just Resting 287	Closed		196.00	140-228

YEAR ISSUE	EDITION LIMIT	YEAR RETD.	ISSUE PRICE	*QUOTE U.S.$
1992 Wayside Harmony 288	Closed		210.00	240-300
1993 Doll Bath 289	Closed		210.00	180-247
1994 Doctor 290	Closed		225.00	180-312
1995 Come Back Soon 291	Closed		250.00	180-254
1998 Echoes of Joy 695	Closed		145.00	109-145
1999 Joyful Noise 696	Closed		145.00	150
2000 Light The Way 697	Yr.Iss.		145.00	150

M.I. Hummel Four Seasons - M.I. Hummel

1996 Winter Melody 296	Yr.Iss.	1996	195.00	195
1997 Springtime Serenade 297	Yr.Iss.	1997	195.00	195
1998 Summertime Stroll 298	Yr.Iss.	1998	195.00	195
1999 Autumn Glory 299	Yr.Iss.	1999	195.00	146-195

M.I. Hummel Friends Forever - M.I. Hummel

1992 Meditation 292	Closed	N/A	180.00	163-195
1993 For Father 293	Closed	N/A	195.00	156-205
1994 Sweet Greetings 294	Closed	N/A	205.00	163-205
1995 Surprise 295	Closed	N/A	210.00	163-210

M.I. Hummel Little Music Makers - M.I. Hummel

1984 Little Fiddler 744	Closed		30.00	39-125
1985 Serenade 741	Closed		30.00	33-125
1986 Soloist 743	Closed		35.00	39-125
1987 Band Leader 742	Closed		40.00	46-125

M.I. Hummel Special Millennium Edition - M.I. Hummel

2000 Star Gazer 920	Yr.Iss.	2000	198.00	198

M.I. Hummel The Little Homemakers - M.I. Hummel

1988 Little Sweeper (Hum 745)	Closed		45.00	50-125
1989 Wash Day (Hum 746)	Closed		50.00	50-125
1990 A Stitch in Time (Hum 747)	Closed		50.00	50-125
1991 Chicken LIttle (Hum 747)	Closed		70.00	125

Gorham

(Four Seasons) A Boy and His Dog Plates - N. Rockwell

1971 Boy Meets His Dog	Annual	1971	50.00	215-510
1971 Adventures Between Adventures	Annual	1971	Set	Set
1971 The Mysterious Malady	Annual	1971	Set	Set
1971 Pride of Parenthood	Annual	1971	Set	Set

(Four Seasons) A Helping Hand Plates - N. Rockwell

1979 Year End Court	Annual	1979	100.00	94-200
1979 Closed for Business	Annual	1979	Set	Set
1979 Swatter's Rights	Annual	1979	Set	Set
1979 Coal Season's Coming	Annual	1979	Set	Set

(Four Seasons) Dad's Boys Plates - N. Rockwell

1980 Ski Skills	Annual	1980	135.00	80-225
1980 In His Spirits	Annual	1980	Set	Set
1980 Trout Dinner	Annual	1980	Set	Set
1980 Careful Aim	Annual	1980	Set	Set

(Four Seasons) Four Ages of Love - N. Rockwell

1973 Gaily Sharing Vintage Time	Annual	1973	60.00	175-195
1973 Flowers in Tender Bloom	Annual	1973	Set	Set
1973 Sweet Song So Young	Annual	1973	Set	Set
1973 Fondly We Do Remember	Annual	1973	Set	Set

(Four Seasons) Going on Sixteen Plates - N. Rockwell

1977 Chilling Chore	Annual	1977	75.00	100-125
1977 Sweet Serenade	Annual	1977	Set	Set
1977 Shear Agony	Annual	1977	Set	Set
1977 Pilgrimage	Annual	1977	Set	Set

(Four Seasons) Grand Pals Four Plates - N. Rockwell

1976 Snow Sculpturing	Annual	1976	70.00	147-150
1976 Soaring Spirits	Annual	1976	Set	Set
1976 Fish Finders	Annual	1976	Set	Set
1976 Ghostly Gourds	Annual	1976	Set	Set

(Four Seasons) Grandpa and Me Plates - N. Rockwell

1974 Gay Blades	Annual	1974	60.00	124-150
1974 Day Dreamers	Annual	1974	Set	Set
1974 Goin' Fishing	Annual	1974	Set	Set
1974 Pensive Pals	Annual	1974	Set	Set

(Four Seasons) Life with Father Plates - N. Rockwell

1982 Big Decision	Annual	1982	100.00	100
1982 Blasting Out	Annual	1982	Set	Set
1982 Cheering the Champs	Annual	1982	Set	Set

YEAR ISSUE	EDITION LIMIT	YEAR RETD.	ISSUE PRICE	*QUOTE U.S.$
1982 A Tough One	Annual	1982	Set	Set

(Four Seasons) Me and My Pals Plates - N. Rockwell

1975 A Lickin' Good Bath	Annual	1975	70.00	91-115
1975 Young Man's Fancy	Annual	1975	Set	Set
1975 Fisherman's Paradise	Annual	1975	Set	Set
1975 Disastrous Daring	Annual	1975	Set	Set

(Four Seasons) Old Buddies Plates - N. Rockwell

1983 Shared Success	Annual	1983	115.00	150
1983 Endless Debate	Annual	1983	Set	Set
1983 Hasty Retreat	Annual	1983	Set	Set
1983 Final Speech	Annual	1983	Set	Set

(Four Seasons) Old Timers Plates - N. Rockwell

1981 Canine Solo	Annual	1981	100.00	125
1981 Sweet Surprise	Annual	1981	Set	Set
1981 Lazy Days	Annual	1981	Set	Set
1981 Fancy Footwork	Annual	1981	Set	Set

(Four Seasons) Tender Years Plates - N. Rockwell

1978 New Year Look	Annual	1978	100.00	87-225
1978 Spring Tonic	Annual	1978	Set	Set
1978 Cool Aid	Annual	1978	Set	Set
1978 Chilly Reception	Annual	1978	Set	Set

(Four Seasons) Young Love Plates - N. Rockwell

1972 Downhill Daring	Annual	1972	60.00	138-275
1972 Beguiling Buttercup	Annual	1972	Set	Set
1972 Flying High	Annual	1972	Set	Set
1972 A Scholarly Pace	Annual	1972	Set	Set

American Artist - R. Donnelly

1976 Apache Mother & Child	9,800	1980	25.00	35-56

American Landscapes - N. Rockwell

1980 Summer Respite	Annual	1980	45.00	65-80
1981 Autumn Reflection	Annual	1981	45.00	60-65
1982 Winter Delight	Annual	1982	50.00	70
1983 Spring Recess	Annual	1983	60.00	75

Barrymore - Barrymore

1971 Quiet Waters	15,000	1980	25.00	25
1972 San Pedro Harbor	15,000	1980	25.00	25
1972 Nantucket, Sterling	1,000	1972	100.00	100
1972 Little Boatyard, Sterling	1,000	1972	100.00	145

Bas Relief - N. Rockwell

1981 Sweet Song So Young	Undis.	1984	100.00	100
1981 Beguiling Buttercup	Undis.	1984	62.50	70
1982 Flowers in Tender Bloom	Undis.	1984	100.00	100
1982 Flying High	Undis.	1984	62.50	65

Boy Scout Plates - N. Rockwell

1975 Our Heritage	18,500	1990	19.50	80
1976 A Scout is Loyal	18,500	1990	19.50	55-75
1977 The Scoutmaster	18,500	1990	19.50	80
1977 A Good Sign	18,500	1990	19.50	50-75
1978 Pointing the Way	18,500	1990	19.50	50-75
1978 Campfire Story	18,500	1990	19.50	25-75
1980 Beyond the Easel	18,500	1990	45.00	45-75

Charles Russell - C. Russell

1980 In Without Knocking	9,800	1990	38.00	65-75
1981 Bronc to Breakfast	9,800	1990	38.00	75
1982 When Ignorance is Bliss	9,800	1990	45.00	75-95
1983 Cowboy Life	9,800	1990	45.00	95-100

China Bicentennial - Gorham

1972 1776 Plate	18,500	1980	17.50	35
1976 1776 Bicentennial	8,000	1980	17.50	35

Christmas - N. Rockwell

1974 Tiny Tim	Annual	1974	12.50	45-140
1975 Good Deeds	Annual	1975	17.50	50
1976 Christmas Trio	Annual	1976	19.50	30
1977 Yuletide Reckoning	Annual	1977	19.50	45
1978 Planning Christmas Visit	Annual	1978	24.50	30
1979 Santa's Helpers	Annual	1979	24.50	30
1980 Letter to Santa	Annual	1980	27.50	32
1981 Santa Plans His Visit	Annual	1981	29.50	30
1982 Jolly Coachman	Annual	1982	29.50	30
1983 Christmas Dancers	Annual	1983	29.50	35
1984 Christmas Medley	17,500	1984	29.95	30

PLATES & PLAQUES

YEAR ISSUE	EDITION LIMIT	YEAR RETD.	ISSUE PRICE	*QUOTE U.S.$
1985 Home For The Holidays	17,500	1985	29.95	30
1986 Merry Christmas Grandma	17,500	1986	29.95	65
1987 The Homecoming	17,500	1987	35.00	45
1988 Discovery	17,500	1988	37.50	45

Christmas/Children's Television Workshop - Unknown
1981 Sesame Street Christmas	Annual	1981	17.50	18
1982 Sesame Street Christmas	Annual	1982	17.50	18
1983 Sesame Street Christmas	Annual	1983	19.50	20

Encounters, Survival and Celebrations - J. Clymer
1982 A Fine Welcome	7,500	1983	50.00	80
1983 Winter Trail	7,500	1984	50.00	80
1983 Alouette	7,500	1984	62.50	80
1983 The Trader	7,500	1984	62.50	63
1983 Winter Camp	7,500	1984	62.50	75
1983 The Trapper Takes a Wife	7,500	1984	62.50	63

Gallery of Masters - Various
1971 Man with a Gilt Helmet - Rembrandt	10,000	1975	50.00	50
1972 Self Portrait with Saskia - Rembrandt	10,000	1975	50.00	50
1973 The Honorable Mrs. Graham - Gainsborough	7,500	1975	50.00	50

Gorham Museum Doll Plates - Gorham
1984 Lydia	5,000	1984	29.00	79
1984 Belton Bebe	5,000	1984	29.00	65
1984 Christmas Lady	7,500	1984	32.50	33-50
1985 Lucille	5,000	1985	29.00	35-50
1985 Jumeau	5,000	1985	29.00	65

Julian Ritter - J. Ritter
1977 Christmas Visit	9,800	1977	24.50	29
1978 Valentine, Fluttering Heart	7,500	1978	45.00	45

Julian Ritter, Fall In Love - J. Ritter
1977 Enchantment	5,000	1977	100.00	100
1977 Frolic	5,000	1977	set	Set
1977 Gutsy Gal	5,000	1977	set	Set
1977 Lonely Chill	5,000	1977	set	Set

Julian Ritter, To Love a Clown - J. Ritter
1978 Awaited Reunion	5,000	1978	120.00	120
1978 Twosome Time	5,000	1978	120.00	120
1978 Showtime Beckons	5,000	1978	120.00	120
1978 Together in Memories	5,000	1978	120.00	120

Leyendecker Annual Christmas Plates - J. C. Leyendecker
1988 Christmas Hug	10,000	1988	37.50	30-50

Moppet Plates-Anniversary - Unknown
1976 Anniversary	20,000	1977	13.00	13

Moppet Plates-Christmas - Unknown
1973 Christmas	Annual	1973	10.00	35
1974 Christmas	Annual	1974	12.00	12
1975 Christmas	Annual	1975	13.00	13
1976 Christmas	Annual	1976	13.00	10-15
1977 Christmas	Annual	1977	13.00	14
1978 Christmas	Annual	1978	10.00	10
1979 Christmas	Annual	1979	12.00	12
1980 Christmas	Annual	1980	12.00	12
1981 Christmas	Annual	1981	12.00	12
1982 Christmas	Annual	1982	12.00	12
1983 Christmas	Annual	1983	12.00	12

Moppet Plates-Mother's Day - Unknown
1973 Mother's Day	Annual	1973	10.00	30
1974 Mother's Day	Annual	1974	12.00	20
1975 Mother's Day	Annual	1975	13.00	15
1976 Mother's Day	Annual	1976	13.00	15
1977 Mother's Day	Annual	1977	13.00	15
1978 Mother's Day	Annual	1978	10.00	10

Pastoral Symphony - B. Felder
1982 When I Was a Child	7,500	1983	42.50	20-50
1982 Gather the Children	7,500	1983	42.50	20-50
1984 Sugar and Spice	7,500	1985	42.50	20-50
XX He Loves Me	7,500	1985	42.50	20-50

Pewter Bicentennial - R. Pailthorpe
1971 Burning of the Gaspee	5,000	1971	35.00	35
1972 Boston Tea Party	5,000	1972	35.00	35

Presidential - N. Rockwell
1976 John F. Kennedy	9,800	1976	30.00	65
1976 Dwight D. Eisenhower	9,800	1976	30.00	35

Remington Western - F. Remington
1973 A New Year on the Cimarron	Annual	1973	25.00	35-50
1973 Aiding a Comrade	Annual	1973	25.00	30-125
1973 The Flight	Annual	1973	25.00	30-95
1973 The Fight for the Water Hole	Annual	1973	25.00	30-125
1975 Old Ramond	Annual	1975	20.00	35-60
1975 A Breed	Annual	1975	20.00	35-65
1976 Cavalry Officer	5,000	1976	37.50	60-75
1976 A Trapper	5,000	1976	37.50	60-75

Silver Bicentennial - Various
1972 1776 Plate - Gorham	500	1972	500.00	500
1972 Burning of the Gaspee - R. Pailthorpe	750	1972	500.00	500
1973 Boston Tea Party - R. Pailthorpe	750	1973	550.00	575

Single Release - F. Quagon
1976 The Black Regiment 1778	7,500	1978	25.00	58

Single Release - N. Rockwell
1974 Weighing In	Annual	1974	12.50	75-150
1974 The Golden Rule	Annual	1974	12.50	30-40
1975 Ben Franklin	Annual	1975	19.50	35
1976 The Marriage License	Numbrd	1985	37.50	79-95
1978 Triple Self Portrait Memorial	Annual	1978	37.50	50-95
1980 The Annual Visit	Annual	1980	32.50	50-70
1981 Day in Life of Boy	Annual	1981	50.00	50-80
1981 Day in Life of Girl	Annual	1981	50.00	50-125

Time Machine Teddies Plates - B. Port
1986 Miss Emily, Bearing Up	5,000	1986	32.50	35-50
1987 Big Bear, The Toy Collector	5,000	1987	32.50	35-45
1988 Hunny Munny	5,000	1988	37.50	35-45

Vermeil Bicentennial - Gorham
1972 1776 Plate	250	1972	750.00	300-800

Hackett American

Sports - Various
1981 Reggie Jackson (Mr. Oct.) h/s - Paluso	Retrd.	N/A	100.00	695-750
1983 Steve Garvey h/s - Paluso	Retrd.	N/A	100.00	150-175
1983 Nolan Ryan h/s - Paluso	Retrd.	N/A	100.00	595-750
1983 Tom Seaver h/s - Paluso	3,272	N/A	100.00	200-300
1984 Steve Carlton h/s - Paluso	Retrd.	N/A	100.00	200-250
1985 Willie Mays h/s - Paluso	Retrd.	N/A	125.00	395
1985 Whitey Ford h/s - Paluso	Retrd.	N/A	125.00	200-250
1985 Hank Aaron h/s - Paluso	Retrd.	N/A	125.00	375-395
1985 Sandy Koufax h/s - Paluso	1,000	N/A	125.00	450
1985 H. Killebrew d/s - Paluso	Retrd.	N/A	125.00	275
1985 E. Mathews d/s - Paluso	Retrd.	N/A	125.00	275
1986 T. Seaver 300 d/s - Paluso	1,200	N/A	125.00	200-250
1986 Roger Clemens (great events) d/s - Paluso	Retrd.	N/A	125.00	595-750
1986 Reggie Jackson (great events) d/s - Paluso	Retrd.	N/A	125.00	200-250
1986 Wally Joyner (great events) d/s - Paluso	Retrd.	N/A	125.00	200-250
1986 Don Sutton d/s (great events)- Paluso	300	N/A	125.00	200-250
XX Gary Carter d/s - Simon	Retrd.	N/A	125.00	50-150
1985 Dwight Gooden 8 1/2" u/s - Simon	Retrd.	N/A	55.00	40-55
XX Arnold Palmer h/s - Alexander	Retrd.	N/A	125.00	200
XX Gary Player h/s - Alexander	Retrd.	N/A	125.00	200
1983 Reggie Jackson (500 HRs) h/s - Alexander	Retrd.	N/A	125.00	200-500
1983 Reggie Jackson (500 HRs), proof - Alexander	Retrd.	N/A	250.00	1000
1986 Joe Montana d/s - Alexander	Retrd.	N/A	125.00	600

Hadley House

American Memories Series - T. Redlin
1987 Coming Home	9,500	1998	85.00	85
1988 Lights of Home	9,500	1994	85.00	125
1989 Homeward Bound	9,500	1996	85.00	85
1991 Family Traditions	9,500	1998	85.00	85

Annual Christmas Series - T. Redlin
1991 Heading Home	9,500	1994	65.00	225

*Quotes have been rounded up to nearest dollar

YEAR ISSUE	EDITION LIMIT	YEAR RETD.	ISSUE PRICE	*QUOTE U.S.$
1992 Pleasures Of Winter	19,500		65.00	125
1993 Winter Wonderland	19,500		65.00	125
1994 Almost Home	19,500		65.00	125
1995 Sharing the Evening	45-day		29.95	30
1996 Night on the Town	45-day		29.95	30
1998 Racing Home	45-day		29.95	30

Country Doctor Collection - T. Redlin

1995 Wednesday Afternoon	45-day		29.95	30
1995 Office Hours	45-day		29.95	30
1995 House Calls	45-day		29.95	30
1995 Morning Rounds	45-day		29.95	30

Glow Series - T. Redlin

1985 Evening Glow	5,000	1986	55.00	250-325
1985 Morning Glow	5,000	1986	55.00	130-150
1985 Twilight Glow	5,000	1988	55.00	130-388
1988 Afternoon Glow	5,000	1989	55.00	100-129

Lovers Collection - O. Franca

1992 Lovers	9,500	1997	50.00	50

Navajo Visions Suite - O. Franca

1993 Navajo Fantasy	9,500	1998	50.00	50
1993 Young Warrior	9,500	1998	50.00	50

Navajo Woman Series - O. Franca

1990 Feathered Hair Ties	5,000	1994	50.00	50
1991 Navajo Summer	5,000	1998	50.00	50
1992 Turquoise Necklace	5,000	1998	50.00	50
1993 Pink Navajo	5,000	1998	50.00	50

Retreat Series - T. Redlin

1987 Morning Retreat	9,500	1988	65.00	160
1987 Evening Retreat	9,500	1989	65.00	175
1988 Golden Retreat	9,500	1990	65.00	150
1989 Moonlight Retreat	9,500	1993	65.00	110

Seasons - T. Redlin

1994 Autumn Evening	45-day		29.95	30
1995 Spring Fever	45-day		29.95	30
1995 Summertime	45-day		29.95	30
1995 Wintertime	45-day		29.95	30

That Special Time - T. Redlin

1991 Evening Solitude	9,500	1994	65.00	95-103
1991 That Special Time	9,500	1993	65.00	95
1992 Aroma of Fall	9,500	1994	65.00	95-112
1993 Welcome To Paradise	9,500	1997	65.00	65

Tranquility - O. Franca

1994 Blue Navajo	9,500	1997	50.00	50
1994 Blue Tranquility	9,500	1997	50.00	50
1994 Navajo Meditating	9,500		50.00	50
1995 Navajo Reflection	9,500		50.00	50

Wildlife Memories - T. Redlin

1994 Best Friends	19,500		65.00	65
1994 Comforts of Home	19,500		65.00	65
1994 Pure Contentment	19,500		65.00	65
1994 Sharing in the Solitude	19,500		65.00	65

Windows to the Wild - T. Redlin

1990 Master's Domain	9,500		65.00	65
1991 Winter Windbreak	9,500		65.00	65
1992 Evening Company	9,500		65.00	65
1994 Night Mapling	9,500		65.00	65

Hamilton Collection

1974 Beginning Days! Panorama Plates - R. Tanenbaum

2000 A Rookie Debut!	Open		39.95	40
2000 Following Dad	Open		39.95	40
2000 Beginning Days	Open		39.95	40
2000 Winning!	Open		39.95	40

All in a Day's Work - J. Lamb

1994 Where's the Fire?	28-day	1994	29.50	30-69
1994 Lunch Break	28-day	1994	29.50	30-40
1994 Puppy Patrol	28-day	1994	29.50	30-40
1994 Decoy Delivery	28-day	1994	29.50	30-40
1994 Budding Artist	28-day	1994	29.50	30-44
1994 Garden Guards	28-day	1994	29.50	30-44

YEAR ISSUE	EDITION LIMIT	YEAR RETD.	ISSUE PRICE	*QUOTE U.S.$
1994 Saddling Up	28-day	1994	29.50	30-44
1995 Taking the Lead	28-day	1994	29.50	30-44

All Star Memories - D. Spindel

1995 The Mantle Story	28-day		35.00	35-39
1996 Momentos of the Mick	28-day		35.00	35
1996 Mantle Appreciation Day	28-day		35.00	35
1996 Life of a Legend	28-day		35.00	35
1996 Yankee Pride	28-day		35.00	35-39
1996 A World Series Tribute	28-day		35.00	35
1996 The Ultimate All Star	28-day		35.00	35
1997 Triple Crown	28-day		35.00	35-45

The American Civil War - D. Prechtel

1990 General Robert E. Lee	14-day	N/A	37.50	65-80
1990 Generals Grant and Lee At Appomattox	14-day	N/A	37.50	50-75
1990 General Thomas "Stonewall" Jackson	14-day	N/A	37.50	50-85
1990 Abraham Lincoln	14-day	N/A	37.50	50-65
1991 General J.E.B. Stuart	14-day	N/A	37.50	50-59
1991 General Philip Sheridan	14-day	N/A	37.50	44-65
1991 A Letter from Home	14-day	N/A	37.50	50-65
1991 Going Home	14-day	N/A	37.50	45-50
1992 Assembling The Troop	14-day	N/A	37.50	50-75
1992 Standing Watch	14-day	N/A	37.50	80-85

American Water Birds - R. Lawrence

1988 Wood Ducks	14-day	N/A	37.50	40-54
1988 Hooded Mergansers	14-day	N/A	37.50	40-54
1988 Pintail	14-day	N/A	37.50	40-45
1988 Canada Geese	14-day	N/A	37.50	45-50
1988 American Widgeons	14-day	N/A	37.50	50
1988 Canvasbacks	14-day	N/A	37.50	40-54
1988 Mallard Pair	14-day	N/A	37.50	50-60
1988 Snow Geese	14-day	N/A	37.50	40-45

The American Wilderness - M. Richter

1995 Gray Wolf	28-day	N/A	29.95	27-45
1995 Silent Watch	28-day	N/A	29.95	30
1995 Moon Song	28-day	N/A	29.95	27
1995 Silent Pursuit	28-day	N/A	29.95	30
1996 Still of the Night	28-day	N/A	29.95	27
1996 Nighttime Serenity	28-day	N/A	29.95	30
1996 Autumn Solitude	28-day	N/A	29.95	30
1996 Arctic Wolf	28-day	N/A	29.95	30-45

America's Greatest Sailing Ships - T. Freeman

1988 USS Constitution	14-day	1991	29.50	55-60
1988 Great Republic	14-day	1991	29.50	55-60
1988 America	14-day	1991	29.50	55-65
1988 Charles W. Morgan	14-day	1991	29.50	27-95
1988 Eagle	14-day	1991	29.50	30-60
1988 Bonhomme Richard	14-day	1991	29.50	50-60
1988 Gertrude L. Thebaud	14-day	1991	29.50	45-60
1988 Enterprise	14-day	1991	29.50	50-65

Andy Griffith - R. Tanenbaum

1992 Sheriff Andy Taylor	28-day	1994	29.50	60-100
1992 A Startling Conclusion	28-day	1994	29.50	60-90
1993 Mayberry Sing-a-long	28-day	1994	29.50	85-90
1993 Aunt Bee's Kitchen	28-day	1994	29.50	60-95
1993 Surprise! Surprise!	28-day	1994	29.50	60-85
1993 An Explosive Situation	28-day	1994	29.50	45-110
1993 Meeting Aunt Bee	28-day	1994	29.50	60-85
1993 Opie's Big Catch	28-day	1994	29.50	45-75

The Angler's Prize - M. Susinno

1991 Trophy Bass	14-day	N/A	29.50	55-85
1991 Blue Ribbon Trout	14-day	N/A	29.50	33
1991 Sun Dancers	14-day	N/A	29.50	30-40
1991 Freshwater Barracuda	14-day	N/A	29.50	30-36
1991 Bronzeback Fighter	14-day	N/A	29.50	30-40
1991 Autumn Beauty	14-day	N/A	29.50	30-60
1992 Old Mooneyes	14-day	N/A	29.50	30-40
1992 Silver King	14-day	N/A	29.50	33

Beauty Of Winter - N/A

1992 Silent Night	28-day	N/A	29.50	30-40
1993 Moonlight Sleighride	28-day	N/A	29.50	30

The Best Of Baseball - R. Tanenbaum

1993 The Legendary Mickey Mantle	28-day		29.50	30-65

PLATES & PLAQUES

YEAR ISSUE	EDITION LIMIT	YEAR RETD.	ISSUE PRICE	*QUOTE U.S.$
1993 The Immortal Babe Ruth	28-day		29.50	33-45
1993 The Great Willie Mays	28-day		29.50	30-55
1993 The Unbeatable Duke Snider	28-day		29.50	30-45
1993 The Extraordinary Lou Gehrig	28-day		29.50	30-42
1993 The Phenomenal Roberto Clemente	28-day		29.50	30-42
1993 The Remarkable Johnny Bench	28-day		29.50	30-42
1993 The Incredible Nolan Ryan	28-day		29.50	30-59
1993 The Exceptional Brooks Robinson	28-day		29.50	30-42
1993 The Unforgettable Phil Rizzuto	28-day		29.50	30-42
1995 The Incomparable Reggie Jackson	28-day		29.50	30-42

Bialosky® & Friends - P./A.Bialosky

1992 Family Addition	28-day		29.50	33-40
1993 Sweetheart	28-day		29.50	30-40
1993 Let's Go Fishing	28-day		29.50	30-40
1993 U.S. Mail	28-day		29.50	30-45
1993 Sleigh Ride	28-day		29.50	30-40
1993 Honey For Sale	28-day		29.50	30-40
1993 Breakfast In Bed	28-day		29.50	30-40
1993 My First Two-Wheeler	28-day		29.50	30-40

Big Cats of the World - D. Manning

1989 African Shade	14-day		29.50	42-55
1989 View from Above	14-day		29.50	40-55
1990 On The Prowl	14-day		29.50	30-55
1990 Deep In The Jungle	14-day		29.50	30-55
1990 Spirit Of The Mountain	14-day		29.50	30-55
1990 Spotted Sentinel	14-day		29.50	30-55
1990 Above the Treetops	14-day		29.50	30-55
1990 Mountain Dweller	14-day		29.50	30-55
1992 Jungle Habitat	14-day		29.50	30-55
1992 Solitary Sentry	14-day		29.50	30-55

Bundles of Joy - B. P. Gutmann

1988 Awakening	14-day	1991	24.50	90-95
1988 Happy Dreams	14-day	1991	24.50	80-90
1988 Tasting	14-day	1991	24.50	45-95
1988 Sweet Innocence	14-day	1991	24.50	60-75
1988 Tommy	14-day	1991	24.50	75-80
1988 A Little Bit of Heaven	14-day	1991	24.50	75-99
1988 Billy	14-day	1991	24.50	60-65
1988 Sun Kissed	14-day	1991	24.50	75-90

Butterfly Garden - P. Sweany

1987 Spicebush Swallowtail	14-day	N/A	29.50	30-55
1987 Common Blue	14-day	N/A	29.50	30-55
1987 Orange Sulphur	14-day	N/A	29.50	30-55
1987 Monarch	14-day	N/A	29.50	30-55
1987 Tiger Swallowtail	14-day	N/A	29.50	30-55
1987 Crimson Patched Longwing	14-day	N/A	29.50	30-55
1988 Morning Cloak	14-day	N/A	29.50	30-55
1988 Red Admiral	14-day	N/A	29.50	30-55

The Call of the North - J. Tift

1993 Winter's Dawn	28-day	N/A	29.50	30-40
1994 Evening Silence	28-day	N/A	29.50	30-40
1994 Moonlit Wilderness	28-day	N/A	29.50	30-39
1994 Silent Snowfall	28-day	N/A	29.50	30-40
1994 Snowy Watch	28-day	N/A	29.50	30-40
1994 Sentinels of the Summit	28-day	N/A	29.50	30-40
1994 Arctic Seclusion	28-day	N/A	29.50	30-40
1994 Forest Twilight	28-day	N/A	29.50	30-40
1994 Mountain Explorer	28-day	N/A	29.50	30
1994 The Cry of Winter	28-day	N/A	29.50	30

Call to Adventure - R. Cross

1993 USS Constitution	28-day	N/A	29.50	30-40
1993 The Bounty	28-day	N/A	29.50	30-40
1994 Bonhomme Richard	28-day	N/A	29.50	30-40
1994 Old Nantucket	28-day	N/A	29.50	30-40
1994 Golden West	28-day	N/A	29.50	30-40
1994 Boston	28-day	N/A	29.50	30-40
1994 Hannah	28-day	N/A	29.50	30-40
1994 Improvement	28-day	N/A	29.50	30-40
1995 Anglo-American	28-day	N/A	29.50	30
1995 Challenge	28-day	N/A	29.50	30

Cameo Kittens - Q. Lemonds

1993 Ginger Snap	28-day		29.50	30-50
1993 Cat Tails	28-day		29.50	30-50
1993 Lady Blue	28-day		29.50	50-59
1993 Tiny Heart Stealer	28-day		29.50	49

YEAR ISSUE	EDITION LIMIT	YEAR RETD.	ISSUE PRICE	*QUOTE U.S.$
1993 Blossom	28-day		29.50	30-50
1994 Whisker Antics	28-day		29.50	30-50
1994 Tiger's Temptation	28-day		29.50	30-50
1994 Scout	28-day		29.50	30-50
1995 Timid Tabby	28-day		29.50	30
1995 All Wrapped Up	28-day		29.50	30-55

Childhood Reflections - B.P. Gutmann

1991 Harmony	14-day	1990	29.50	60-80
1991 Kitty's Breakfast	14-day	1990	29.50	50-60
1991 Friendly Enemies	14-day	1990	29.50	35-80
1991 Smile, Smile, Smile	14-day	1990	29.50	35-95
1991 Lullaby	14-day	1990	29.50	50-60
1991 Oh! Oh! A Bunny	14-day	1990	29.50	50-60
1991 Little Mother	14-day	1990	29.50	35-85
1991 Thank You, God	14-day	1990	29.50	35-65

Children of the American Frontier - D. Crook

1986 In Trouble Again	10-day		24.50	40-45
1986 Tubs and Suds	10-day		24.50	30-45
1986 A Lady Needs a Little Privacy	10-day		24.50	45
1986 The Desperadoes	10-day		24.50	28-40
1986 Riders Wanted	10-day		24.50	35-45
1987 A Cowboy's Downfall	10-day		24.50	28-40
1987 Runaway Blues	10-day		24.50	28-40
1987 A Special Patient	10-day		24.50	35-45

A Child's Best Friend - B. P. Gutmann

1985 In Disgrace	14-day	1990	24.50	30-125
1985 The Reward	14-day	1990	24.50	35-135
1985 Who's Sleepy	14-day	1990	24.50	39-135
1985 Good Morning	14-day	1990	24.50	39-135
1985 Sympathy	14-day	1990	24.50	60-135
1985 On the Up and Up	14-day	1990	24.50	34-145
1985 Mine	14-day	1990	24.50	60-99
1985 Going to Town	14-day	1990	24.50	39-145

A Child's Christmas - J. Ferrandiz

1995 Asleep in the Hay	28-day		29.95	30
1995 Merry Little Friends	28-day		29.95	30
1995 Love is Warm All Over	28-day		29.95	30
1995 Little Shepard Family	28-day		29.95	30
1995 Life's Little Blessings	28-day		29.95	30
1995 Happiness is Being Loved	28-day		29.95	30
1995 My Heart Belongs to You	28-day		29.95	30
1996 Lil' Dreamers	28-day		29.95	30

Civil War Generals - M. Gnatek

1994 Robert E. Lee	28-day	N/A	29.50	35-45
1994 J.E.B. Stewart	28-day	N/A	29.50	40-80
1994 Joshua L. Chamberlain	28-day	N/A	29.50	40
1994 George Armstrong Custer	28-day	N/A	29.50	40
1994 Nathan Bedford Forrest	28-day	N/A	29.50	40-80
1994 James Longstreet	28-day	N/A	29.50	40-80
1995 Thomas "Stonewall" Jackson	28-day	N/A	29.50	40-45
1995 Confederate Heroes	28-day	N/A	29.50	36-85

Classic American Santas - G. Hinke

1993 A Christmas Eve Visitor	28-day		29.50	30-55
1994 Up on the Rooftop	28-day		29.50	30-65
1994 Santa's Candy Kitchen	28-day		29.50	35-55
1994 A Christmas Chorus	28-day		29.50	30-35
1994 An Exciting Christmas Eve	28-day		29.50	30-75
1994 Rest Ye Merry Gentlemen	28-day		29.50	30-40
1994 Preparing the Sleigh	28-day		29.50	35-55
1994 The Reindeer's Stable	28-day		29.50	33-35
1994 He's Checking His List	28-day		29.50	30-35

Classic Corvettes - M. Lacourciere

1994 1957 Corvette	28-day		29.50	65-95
1994 1963 Corvette	28-day		29.50	30-95
1994 1968 Corvette	28-day		29.50	65-95
1994 1986 Corvette	28-day		29.50	30-95
1995 1967 Corvette	28-day		29.50	30
1995 1953 Corvette	28-day		29.50	30
1995 1962 Corvette	28-day		29.50	30
1995 1990 Corvette	28-day		29.50	30

Classic Sporting Dogs - B. Christie

1989 Golden Retrievers	14-day	N/A	24.50	50-75
1989 Labrador Retrievers	14-day	N/A	24.50	50-65
1989 Beagles	14-day	N/A	24.50	30-60
1989 Pointers	14-day	N/A	24.50	50-65

Collectors' Information Bureau   *Quotes have been rounded up to nearest dollar

YEAR ISSUE	EDITION LIMIT	YEAR RETD.	ISSUE PRICE	*QUOTE U.S.$
1989 Springer Spaniels	14-day	N/A	24.50	50
1990 German Short-Haired Pointers	14-day	N/A	24.50	50-60
1990 Irish Setters	14-day	N/A	24.50	40-60
1990 Brittany Spaniels	14-day	N/A	24.50	48-60

Classic TV Westerns - K. Milnazik
1990 The Lone Ranger and Tonto	14-day	N/A	29.50	80-100
1990 Bonanza™	14-day	N/A	29.50	60-99
1990 Roy Rogers and Dale Evans	14-day	N/A	29.50	45-75
1991 Rawhide	14-day	N/A	29.50	50-85
1991 Wild Wild West	14-day	N/A	29.50	50-110
1991 Have Gun, Will Travel	14-day	N/A	29.50	45-80
1991 The Virginian	14-day	N/A	29.50	50-85
1991 Hopalong Cassidy	14-day	N/A	29.50	75-85

Cloak of Visions - A. Farley
1994 Visions in a Full Moon	28-day		29.50	30-55
1994 Protector of the Child	28-day		29.50	30
1995 Spirits of the Canyon	28-day		29.50	30-55
1995 Freedom Soars	28-day		29.50	30
1995 Mystic Reflections	28-day		29.50	55
1995 Staff of Life	28-day		29.50	30-55
1995 Springtime Hunters	28-day		29.50	30-55
1996 Moonlit Solace	28-day		29.50	30-55

Close Up Collection #24 - M. Lacourciere
1998 Champion's Ride	Open		35.00	35
1998 Practice Makes Perfect	Open		35.00	35
1998 Rainbow Rocket	Open		35.00	35
1998 The Champ!	Open		35.00	35

Close Up Collection #3 - M. Lacourciere
1997 Ready To Race	Open		35.00	35
1997 Like Clockwork	Open		35.00	35
1997 Black at Light Speed	Open		35.00	35
1997 Lightning Quick	Open		35.00	35
1997 Night Ride	Open		35.00	35
1997 Reflections	Open		35.00	35

Close Up Collection #94 - M. Lacourciere
1999 Burnin' Up The Track!	Open		35.00	35

Colors of the Sea - A. Jones
1997 Sealife At Sunset	Closed	N/A	39.95	40
1997 Moonlight Sonata	28-day		39.95	40
1997 Dolphin's Paradise	28-day		39.95	40
1997 First Breath	Closed	N/A	39.95	40
1997 Peaceful Tropics	Closed	N/A	39.95	40
1998 Tropical Sunrise	Closed	N/A	39.95	40
1998 Return to Paradise	28-day		39.95	40
1998 Aquatic Dance	28-day		39.95	40

Comical Dalmations - Landmark
1996 I Will Not Bark In Class	28-day		29.95	30-40
1996 The Master	28-day		29.95	30
1996 Spot At Play	28-day		29.95	30
1996 A Dalmation's Dream	28-day		29.95	30
1996 To The Rescue	28-day		29.95	30
1996 Maid For A Day	28-day		29.95	30
1996 Dalmation Celebration	28-day		29.95	30
1996 Concert in D-Minor	28-day		29.95	30

Coral Paradise - H. Bond
1989 The Living Oasis	14-day		29.50	30-40
1990 Riches of the Coral Sea	14-day		29.50	30-40
1990 Tropical Pageantry	14-day		29.50	40
1990 Caribbean Spectacle	14-day		29.50	30-40
1990 Undersea Village	14-day		29.50	40
1990 Shimmering Reef Dwellers	14-day		29.50	40
1990 Mysteries of the Galapagos	14-day		29.50	30-40
1990 Forest Beneath the Sea	14-day		29.50	30-40

Cottage Puppies - K. George
1993 Little Gardeners	28-day		29.50	30-40
1993 Springtime Fancy	28-day		29.50	30-40
1993 Endearing Innocence	28-day		29.50	30-40
1994 Picnic Playtime	28-day		29.50	30-40
1994 Lazy Afternoon	28-day		29.50	30-40
1994 Summertime Pals	28-day		29.50	30-40
1994 A Gardening Trio	28-day		29.50	30-40
1994 Taking a Break	28-day		29.50	30-40

YEAR ISSUE	EDITION LIMIT	YEAR RETD.	ISSUE PRICE	*QUOTE U.S.$

Council Of Nations - G. Perillo
1992 Strength of the Sioux	14-day		29.50	45-55
1992 Pride of the Cheyenne	14-day		29.50	40-55
1992 Dignity of the Nez Parce	14-day		29.50	40-49
1992 Courage of the Arapaho	14-day		29.50	40-49
1992 Power of the Blackfoot	14-day		29.50	40-60
1992 Nobility of the Algonqui	14-day		29.50	40
1992 Wisdom of the Cherokee	14-day		29.50	40-55
1992 Boldness of the Seneca	14-day		29.50	40

Country Garden Cottages - E. Dertner
1992 Riverbank Cottage	28-day		29.50	30-40
1992 Sunday Outing	28-day		29.50	30-40
1992 Shepherd's Cottage	28-day		29.50	30-40
1993 Daydream Cottage	28-day		29.50	30-40
1993 Garden Glorious	28-day		29.50	30-40
1993 This Side of Heaven	28-day		29.50	30-40
1993 Summer Symphony	28-day		29.50	30-40
1993 April Cottage	28-day		29.50	30

Country Kitties - G. Gerardi
1989 Mischief Makers	14-day		24.50	55-75
1989 Table Manners	14-day		24.50	55-85
1989 Attic Attack	14-day		24.50	35-75
1989 Rock and Rollers	14-day		24.50	35-40
1989 Just For the Fern of It	14-day		24.50	35-65
1989 All Washed Up	14-day		24.50	45-75
1989 Stroller Derby	14-day		24.50	40-50
1989 Captive Audience	14-day		24.50	45-65

A Country Season of Horses - J.M. Vass
1990 First Day of Spring	14-day		29.50	30-55
1990 Summer Splendor	14-day		29.50	30-55
1990 A Winter's Walk	14-day		29.50	30-55
1990 Autumn Grandeur	14-day		29.50	30-55
1990 Cliffside Beauty	14-day		29.50	30-55
1990 Frosty Morning	14-day		29.50	30-55
1990 Crisp Country Morning	14-day		29.50	30-55
1990 River Retreat	14-day		29.50	30-55

A Country Summer - N. Noel
1985 Butterfly Beauty	10-day		29.50	30-40
1985 The Golden Puppy	10-day		29.50	30-40
1986 The Rocking Chair	10-day		29.50	30-40
1986 My Bunny	10-day		29.50	30-40
1988 The Piglet	10-day		29.50	30-40
1988 Teammates	10-day		29.50	30-40

Curious Kittens - B. Harrison
1990 Rainy Day Friends	14-day		29.50	30-45
1990 Keeping in Step	14-day		29.50	30-45
1991 Delightful Discovery	14-day		29.50	30-45
1991 Chance Meeting	14-day		29.50	30-45
1991 All Wound Up	14-day		29.50	30-45
1991 Making Tracks	14-day		29.50	30-45
1991 Playing Cat and Mouse	14-day		29.50	30-45
1991 A Paw's in the Action	14-day		29.50	30-45
1992 Little Scholar	14-day		29.50	30-75
1992 Cat Burglar	14-day		29.50	30-45

Dale Earnhardt - Various
1996 The Intimidator - S. Bass	28-day		35.00	35
1996 The Man in Black - R. Tanenbaum	28-day		35.00	35-45
1996 Silver Select - S. Bass	28-day		35.00	35-45
1996 Back in Black - R. Tanenbaum	28-day		35.00	35
1996 Ready to Rumble - R. Tanenbaum	28-day		35.00	35-45
1996 Always a Champion - R. Tanenbaum	28-day		35.00	35
1996 Look of a Winner - S. Bass	28-day		35.00	35
1996 Black Attack! - S. Bass	28-day		35.00	35

Dale Earnhardt II - S. Bass
1998 Rising Son!	28-day		35.00	35
1998 Hooked Up!	28-day		35.00	35
1998 Finally First!	28-day		35.00	35
1999 Man On A Mission	28-day		35.00	35
1999 Blast From The Past	28-day		35.00	35
2000 Hot Property!	28-day		35.00	35

Dale Earnhardt II "The Future Is Now!" - Panorama Plates - S. Bass
1999 Red Rocket!	28-day		39.95	40
1999 Black Bullet!	28-day		39.95	40

PLATES & PLAQUES

YEAR ISSUE	EDITION LIMIT	YEAR RETD.	ISSUE PRICE	*QUOTE U.S.$
2000 New Journey!	28-day		39.95	40
2000 Leading The Way!	28-day		39.95	40
2000 A Heart On Fire!	28-day		39.95	40
2000 A Heart Of A Legend!	28-day		39.95	40

Dale Earnhardt Vertical Panorama - D. Sivavec

2001 The Mind of a Champion	Open		39.95	40
2001 A Champion's Heart!	Open		39.95	40
2001 Champion & Machine	Open		39.95	40
2001 Foundation of a Champion	Open		39.95	40

Dale Earnhardt, Jr. - Various

1999 A Tradition Begins - B. Tanenbaum	Open		35.00	35
1999 Finishing First! - M. Lacourciere	Open		35.00	35
1999 Red Hot Ride! - B. Tanenbaum	Open		35.00	35
1999 Born On 5/30/99! - M. Lacourciere	Open		35.00	35

Dale Earnhardt, Jr. Close Up Plates - M. Lacourciere

2001 Tearin' Up the Track	Open		35.00	35

Dale Earnhardt's Great Victories Collection -T. Treadway

2001 D Day	Open		35.00	35

Daughters Of The Sun - K. Thayer

1993 Sun Dancer	28-day		29.50	30-40
1993 Shining Feather	28-day		29.50	30-40
1993 Delighted Dancer	28-day		29.50	30-40
1993 Evening Dancer	28-day		29.50	30-40
1993 A Secret Glance	28-day		29.50	30-40
1993 Chippewa Charmer	28-day		29.50	30-40
1994 Pride of the Yakima	28-day		29.50	30-40
1994 Radiant Beauty	28-day		29.50	30-40

Dear to My Heart - J. Hagara

1990 Cathy	14-day		29.50	30-50
1990 Addie	14-day		29.50	30-50
1990 Jimmy	14-day		29.50	30-65
1990 Dacy	14-day		29.50	30-50
1990 Paul	14-day		29.50	30-50
1991 Shelly	14-day		29.50	30-50
1991 Jenny	14-day		29.50	30-50
1991 Joy	14-day		29.50	30-50

Dolphin Discovery - D. Queen

1995 Sunrise Reverie	28-day		29.50	30
1995 Dolphin's Paradise	28-day		29.50	30
1995 Coral Cove	28-day		29.50	30
1995 Undersea Journey	28-day		29.50	30
1995 Dolphin Canyon	28-day		29.50	30
1995 Coral Garden	28-day		29.50	30
1996 Dolphin Duo	28-day		29.50	30
1996 Underwater Tranquility	28-day		29.50	30

Dreamsicles - K. Haynes

1994 The Flying Lesson	28-day		19.50	20-35
1995 By the Light of the Moon	28-day		19.50	25-29
1995 The Recital	28-day		19.50	30
1995 Heavenly Pirouettes	28-day		19.50	40
1995 Blossoms and Butterflies	28-day		19.50	30
1995 Love's Shy Glance	28-day		19.50	20-30
1996 Wishing Upon a Star	28-day		19.50	20
1996 Rainy Day Friends	28-day		19.50	20-22
1996 Starboats Ahoy!	28-day		19.50	40
1996 Teeter Tots	28-day		19.50	30
1996 Star Magic	28-day		19.50	20
1996 Heavenly Tea Party	28-day		19.50	22-30

Dreamsicles Christmas Annual Sculptural - K. Haynes

1996 The Finishing Touches	Closed	1997	39.95	40-50

Dreamsicles Heaven Sent - N/A

1996 Quiet Blessings	28-day		29.95	30
1996 A Heartfelt Embrace	28-day		29.95	30
1996 Earth's Blessings	28-day		29.95	30
1996 A Moment In Dreamland	28-day		29.95	30
1996 Sew Cuddly	28-day		29.95	30
1996 Homemade With Love	28-day		29.95	30
1996 A Sweet Treat	28-day		29.95	30
1996 Pampered And Pretty	28-day		29.95	30

Dreamsicles Home Sweet Home Sculptural - K. Haynes

1997 We Love Gardening	Open		39.95	40
1998 Homemade From the Heart	Open		39.95	40

YEAR ISSUE	EDITION LIMIT	YEAR RETD.	ISSUE PRICE	*QUOTE U.S.$
1998 Love Is the Thread of Life	Open		39.95	40
1998 We Love Sharing	Open		39.95	40

Dreamsicles Life's Little Blessings - K. Haynes

1995 Happiness	28-day		29.95	30-40
1996 Peace	28-day		29.95	30
1996 Love	28-day		29.95	30
1996 Creativity	28-day		29.95	30
1996 Friendship	28-day		29.95	30
1996 Knowledge	28-day		29.95	30
1996 Hope	28-day		29.95	30
1996 Faith	28-day		29.95	30

Dreamsicles Love & Lace - N/A

1997 Stolen Kiss	Open		19.95	20
1997 Sharing Hearts	Open		19.95	20
1997 Love Letters	Open		19.95	20
1997 I Love You	Open		19.95	20
1997 Daisies & Dreamsicles	Open		19.95	20
1997 First Love	Open		19.95	20
1997 Perfect Match	Open		19.95	20
1997 Hand In Hand	Open		19.95	20

Dreamsicles Ornamental Mini Plates - K. Haynes

1996 The Flying Lesson	28-day		19.95	20
1996 By The Light of the Moon	28-day		set	set
1996 The Recital	28-day		19.95	20
1996 Heavenly Pirouettes	28-day		set	set
1997 Blossoms and Butterflies	28-day		19.95	20
1997 Love's Shy Glance	28-day		set	set
1997 Wishing on a Star	28-day		19.95	20
1997 Rainy Day Friends	28-day		set	set
1997 Starboats Ahoy	28-day		19.95	20
1997 Teeter Tots	28-day		set	set
1997 Star Magic	28-day		19.95	20
1997 A Heavenly Tea Party	28-day		set	set

Dreamsicles Sculptural - N/A

1995 The Flying Lesson	Open		37.50	38
1996 By The Light of the Moon	Open		37.50	38
1996 The Recital	Open		37.50	38
1996 Teeter Tots	Open		37.50	38
1996 Poetry In Motion	Open		37.50	38
1996 Rock-A-Bye Dreamsicles	Open		37.50	38
1996 The Birth Certificate	Open		37.50	38
1996 Sharing Hearts	Open		37.50	38

Dreamsicles Special Friends - K. Haynes

1995 A Hug From the Heart	28-day		29.95	30
1995 Heaven's Little Helper	28-day		29.95	30
1995 Bless Us All	28-day		29.95	30
1996 Love's Gentle Touch	28-day		29.95	30
1996 The Best Gift of All	28-day		29.95	30
1996 A Heavenly Hoorah!	28-day		29.95	30
1996 A Love Like No Other	28-day		29.95	30
1996 Cuddle Up	28-day		29.95	30

Dreamsicles Special Friends Sculptural - K. Haynes

1995 Heaven's Little Helper	Open		37.50	38
1996 A Hug From The Heart	Open		37.50	38
1996 Bless Us All	Open		37.50	38
1996 The Best Gift of All	Open		37.50	38
1996 A Heavenly Hoorah!	Open		37.50	38
1996 A Love Like No Other	Open		37.50	38
1997 Cuddle Up	Open		45.00	45
1997 Love's Gentle Touch	Open		45.00	45

Dreamsicles Sweethearts - K. Haynes

1996 Stolen Kiss	28-day		35.00	35
1996 Sharing Hearts	28-day		35.00	35
1996 Love Letters	28-day		35.00	35
1996 I Love You	28-day		35.00	35
1996 Daisies & Dreamsicles	28-day		35.00	35
1997 First Love	28-day		35.00	35
1997 Perfect Match	28-day		35.00	35
1997 Hand In Hand	28-day		35.00	35

Drivers of Victory Lane - R. Tanenbaum

1994 Bill Elliott #11	28-day		29.50	40-55
1994 Jeff Gordon #24	28-day		29.50	30-40
1994 Rusty Wallace #2	28-day		29.50	30-40
1995 Geoff Bodine #7	28-day		29.50	26-40
1995 Dale Earnhardt #3	28-day		29.50	30-40

YEAR ISSUE	EDITION LIMIT	YEAR RETD.	ISSUE PRICE	*QUOTE U.S.$
1996 Sterling Martin #4	28-day		29.50	30-40
1996 Terry Labonte #5	28-day		29.50	26-40
1996 Ken Scharder #25	28-day		29.50	30-40
1996 Jeff Gordon #24	28-day		29.50	30-40
1996 Bill Elliott #94	28-day		29.50	40-55
1996 Rusty Wallace #2	28-day		29.50	30-40
1996 Mark Martin #6	28-day		29.50	30-40
1996 Dale Earnhardt #3	28-day		29.50	30-40

Earnhardt Championship Plates - S. Bass

YEAR ISSUE	EDITION LIMIT	YEAR RETD.	ISSUE PRICE	*QUOTE U.S.$
1999 The Magnificent Seven!	Open		37.50	38
2000 7!	Open		37.50	38
2000 Black Gold	Open		37.50	38
2000 Take Five!	Open		37.50	38
2000 Four To Go!	Open		37.50	38
2001 3 To Get Ready!	Open		37.50	38
2001 Top Gun	Open		37.50	38

Easyrider Close Up - M. Lacourciere

YEAR ISSUE	EDITION LIMIT	YEAR RETD.	ISSUE PRICE	*QUOTE U.S.$
1997 Brotherhood of Honor	28-day		35.00	35
1997 Sounds of Freedom	28-day		35.00	35
1997 Alamo Sundown	28-day		35.00	35
1997 We The People	28-day		35.00	35
1997 Dawn's Early Light	28-day		35.00	35
1997 Harvest Cruise	28-day		35.00	35
1997 Gambler's Ride	28-day		35.00	35
1997 Brother To Brother	28-day		35.00	35

Easyrider Mini Plates - D. Mann

YEAR ISSUE	EDITION LIMIT	YEAR RETD.	ISSUE PRICE	*QUOTE U.S.$
1998 Brotherhood of Biking	Open		12.95	13
1998 Ghost of the West	Open		12.95	13
1998 Ghost of the Round Table	Open		12.95	13
1998 Ghost of the North	Open		12.95	13
1998 Ghost of the Moutain Man	Open		12.95	13
1998 Ghost of the Sea	Open		12.95	13
1998 Ghost From the Past	Open		12.95	13
1998 Easyriders 25th Anniversary	Open		12.95	13
1998 Silver Anniversary Tribute	Open		12.95	13
1998 Ghost of the Saloon	Open		12.95	13

Easyriders - M. Lacourciere

YEAR ISSUE	EDITION LIMIT	YEAR RETD.	ISSUE PRICE	*QUOTE U.S.$
1995 American Classic	28-day		29.95	30-65
1995 Symbols of Freedom	28-day		29.95	30-55
1996 Patriot's Pride	28-day		29.95	40-55
1996 The Way of the West	28-day		29.95	30-55
1996 Revival of an Era	28-day		29.95	30-55
1996 Hollywood Style	28-day		29.95	30-55
1996 Vietnam Express	28-day		29.95	30-55
1996 Las Vegas	28-day		29.95	40-60
1996 Beach Cruising	28-day		29.95	30-55
1996 New Orleans Scene	28-day		29.95	30-60

Enchanted Seascapes - J. Enright

YEAR ISSUE	EDITION LIMIT	YEAR RETD.	ISSUE PRICE	*QUOTE U.S.$
1993 Sanctuary of the Dolphin	28-day		29.50	42-57
1994 Rhapsody of Hope	28-day		29.50	30-75
1994 Oasis of the Gods	28-day		29.50	30-75
1994 Sphere of Life	28-day		29.50	30-90
1994 Edge of Time	28-day		29.50	30-42
1994 Sea of Light	28-day		29.50	30-85
1994 Lost Beneath the Blue	28-day		29.50	30-95
1994 Blue Paradise	28-day		29.50	30-100
1995 Morning Odyssey	28-day		29.50	30
1995 Paradise Cove	28-day		29.50	30-100

English Country Cottages - M. Bell

YEAR ISSUE	EDITION LIMIT	YEAR RETD.	ISSUE PRICE	*QUOTE U.S.$
1990 Periwinkle Tea Room	14-day	N/A	29.50	60-75
1991 Gamekeeper's Cottage	14-day	N/A	29.50	60-80
1991 Ginger Cottage	14-day	N/A	29.50	60-65
1991 Larkspur Cottage	14-day	N/A	29.50	45-60
1991 The Chaplain's Garden	14-day	N/A	29.50	33-60
1991 Lorna Doone Cottage	14-day	N/A	29.50	45-60
1991 Murrle Cottage	14-day	N/A	29.50	36-60
1991 Lullabye Cottage	14-day	N/A	29.50	30-60

Eternal Wishes of Good Fortune - Shuho

YEAR ISSUE	EDITION LIMIT	YEAR RETD.	ISSUE PRICE	*QUOTE U.S.$
1983 Friendship	10-day		34.95	35-50
1983 Purity and Perfection	10-day		34.95	35-50
1983 Illustrious Offspring	10-day		34.95	35-50
1983 Longevity	10-day		34.95	35-50
1983 Youth	10-day		34.95	35-50
1983 Immortality	10-day		34.95	35-50
1983 Marital Bliss	10-day		34.95	35-50
1983 Love	10-day		34.95	35-50
1983 Peace	10-day		34.95	35-50
1983 Beauty	10-day		34.95	35-50
1983 Fertility	10-day		34.95	35-50
1983 Fortitude	10-day		34.95	35-50

Exotic Tigers of Asia - K. Ottinger

YEAR ISSUE	EDITION LIMIT	YEAR RETD.	ISSUE PRICE	*QUOTE U.S.$
1995 Lord of the Rainforest	28-day		29.50	30-40
1995 Snow King	28-day		29.50	30-40
1995 Ruler of the Wetlands	28-day		29.50	30-40
1996 Majestic Vigil	28-day		29.50	30-40
1996 Keeper of the Jungle	28-day		29.50	30-40
1996 Eyes of the Jungle	28-day		29.50	30-40
1996 Sovereign Ruler	28-day		29.50	30-40
1996 Lord of the Lowlands	28-day		29.50	30-40

Familiar Spirits - D. Wright

YEAR ISSUE	EDITION LIMIT	YEAR RETD.	ISSUE PRICE	*QUOTE U.S.$
1996 Faithful Guardians	28-day		29.95	30
1996 Sharing Nature's Innocence	28-day		29.95	30
1996 Trusted Friend	28-day		29.95	30
1996 A Friendship Begins	28-day		29.95	30
1996 Winter Homage	28-day		29.95	30
1996 The Blessing	28-day		29.95	30
1996 Healing Powers	28-day		29.95	30

Farmyard Friends - J. Lamb

YEAR ISSUE	EDITION LIMIT	YEAR RETD.	ISSUE PRICE	*QUOTE U.S.$
1992 Mistaken Identity	28-day	1994	29.50	30-40
1992 Little Cowhands	28-day	1994	29.50	30-40
1993 Shreading the Evidence	28-day	1994	29.50	30-40
1993 Partners in Crime	28-day	1994	29.50	30-40
1993 Fowl Play	28-day	1994	29.50	36-40
1993 Follow The Leader	28-day	1994	29.50	30-40
1993 Pony Tales	28-day	1994	29.50	30-40
1993 An Apple A Day	28-day	1994	29.50	30-40

Favorite American Songbirds - D. O'Driscoll

YEAR ISSUE	EDITION LIMIT	YEAR RETD.	ISSUE PRICE	*QUOTE U.S.$
1989 Blue Jays of Spring	14-day		29.50	40-55
1989 Red Cardinals of Winter	14-day		29.50	40-55
1989 Robins & Apple Blossoms	14-day		29.50	40-55
1989 Goldfinches of Summer	14-day		29.50	40-55
1990 Autumn Chickadees	14-day		29.50	40-55
1990 Bluebirds and Morning Glories	14-day		29.50	40-55
1990 Tufted Titmouse and Holly	14-day		29.50	30-55
1991 Carolina Wrens of Spring	14-day		29.50	30-55

Favorite Old Testament Stories - S. Butcher

YEAR ISSUE	EDITION LIMIT	YEAR RETD.	ISSUE PRICE	*QUOTE U.S.$
1994 Jacob's Dream	28-day		35.00	35
1995 The Baby Moses	28-day		35.00	35
1995 Esther's Gift To Her People	28-day		35.00	35-75
1995 A Prayer For Victory	28-day		35.00	35
1995 Where You Go, I Will Go	28-day		35.00	35-75
1995 A Prayer Answered, A Promise Kept	28-day		35.00	35
1996 Joseph Sold Into Slavery	28-day		35.00	35
1996 Daniel In the Lion's Den	28-day		35.00	35
1996 Noah And The Ark	28-day		35.00	35

The Fierce And The Free - F. McCarthy

YEAR ISSUE	EDITION LIMIT	YEAR RETD.	ISSUE PRICE	*QUOTE U.S.$
1992 Big Medicine	28-day		29.50	30-45
1993 Land of the Winter Hawk	28-day		29.50	30-40
1993 Warrior of Savage Splendor	28-day		29.50	30-85
1994 War Party	28-day		29.50	30-40
1994 The Challenge	28-day		29.50	30-40
1994 Out of the Rising Mist	28-day		29.50	30-45
1994 The Ambush	28-day		29.50	30-43
1994 Dangerous Crossing	28-day		29.50	30-42

Flower Festivals of Japan - N. Hara

YEAR ISSUE	EDITION LIMIT	YEAR RETD.	ISSUE PRICE	*QUOTE U.S.$
1985 Chrysanthemum	10-day	N/A	45.00	45
1985 Hollyhock	10-day	N/A	45.00	45
1985 Plum Blossom	10-day	N/A	45.00	45
1985 Morning Glory	10-day	N/A	45.00	45
1985 Cherry Blossom	10-day	N/A	45.00	45
1985 Iris	10-day	N/A	45.00	45
1985 Lily	10-day	N/A	45.00	45
1985 Peach Blossom	10-day	N/A	45.00	45

Forging New Frontiers - J. Deneen

YEAR ISSUE	EDITION LIMIT	YEAR RETD.	ISSUE PRICE	*QUOTE U.S.$
1994 The Race is On	28-day		29.50	30-39
1994 Big Boy	28-day		29.50	30-39
1994 Cresting the Summit	28-day		29.50	30-40
1994 Spring Roundup	28-day		29.50	30-40
1994 Winter in the Rockies	28-day		29.50	30-40
1994 High Country Logging	28-day		29.50	30-40

PLATES & PLAQUES

YEAR ISSUE	EDITION LIMIT	YEAR RETD.	ISSUE PRICE	*QUOTE U.S.$
1994 Confrontation	28-day		29.50	30
1994 A Welcome Sight	28-day		29.50	30

Four Seasons of the Eagle - S. Hardock

1997 Winter Solstice	Open		39.95	40-80
1997 Spring Awakening	Open		39.95	40
1997 Summer's Glory	Open		39.95	40
1997 Autumn Bounty	Open		39.95	40
1998 Winter's Flight	Open		39.95	40
1998 Spring's Journey	Open		39.95	40
1998 Summer's Splendor	Open		39.95	40
1998 Autumn Nesting	Open		39.95	40

A Garden Song - M. Hanson

1994 Winter's Splendor	28-day		29.50	30-45
1994 In Full Bloom	28-day		29.50	30-45
1994 Golden Glories	28-day		29.50	30-45
1995 Autumn's Elegance	28-day		29.50	30-45
1995 First Snowfall	28-day		29.50	30-44
1995 Robins in Spring	28-day		29.50	30-46
1995 Summer's Glow	28-day		29.50	30-44
1995 Fall's Serenade	28-day		29.50	30-46
1996 Sounds of Winter	28-day		29.50	30-40
1996 Springtime Haven	28-day		29.50	30

Gardens of the Orient - S. Suetomi

1983 Flowering of Spring	10-day	N/A	19.50	20
1983 Festival of May	10-day	N/A	19.50	20
1983 Cherry Blossom Brocade	10-day	N/A	19.50	20
1983 Winter's Repose	10-day	N/A	19.50	20
1983 Garden Sanctuary	10-day	N/A	19.50	20
1983 Summer's Glory	10-day	N/A	19.50	20
1983 June's Creation	10-day	N/A	19.50	20
1983 New Year's Dawn	10-day	N/A	19.50	20
1983 Autumn Serenity	10-day	N/A	19.50	20
1983 Harvest Morning	10-day	N/A	19.50	20
1983 Tranquil Pond	10-day	N/A	19.50	20
1983 Morning Song	10-day	N/A	19.50	20

Glory of Christ - C. Micarelli

1992 The Ascension	48-day		29.50	50-75
1992 Jesus Teaching	48-day		29.50	30
1993 Last Supper	48-day		29.50	30
1993 The Nativity	48-day		29.50	30
1993 The Baptism of Christ	48-day		29.50	30
1993 Jesus Heals the Sick	48-day		29.50	30
1994 Jesus Walks on Water	48-day		29.50	30
1994 Descent From the Cross	48-day		29.50	30

Glory of the Game - T. Fogarty

1994 "Hank Aaron's Record-Breaking Home Run"	28-day		29.50	30
1994 "Bobby Thomson's Shot Heard 'Round the World"	28-day		29.50	30
1994 1969 Miracle Mets	28-day		29.50	30
1995 Reggie Jackson: Mr. October	28-day		29.50	30
1995 Don Larsen's Perfect World	28-day		29.50	30
1995 Babe Ruth's Called Shot	28-day		29.50	30-39
1995 Willie Mays: Greatest Catch	28-day		29.50	30
1995 Bill Mazeroski's Series	28-day		29.50	30
1996 Mickey Mantle's Tape Measure Home Run	28-day		29.50	30-35

The Golden Age of American Railroads - T. Xaras

1991 The Blue Comet	14-day		29.50	50-80
1991 The Morning Local	14-day		29.50	60-75
1991 The Pennsylvania K-4	14-day		29.50	70-95
1991 Above the Canyon	14-day		29.50	62-95
1991 Portrait in Steam	14-day		29.50	62-80
1991 The Santa Fe Super Chief	14-day		29.50	84-110
1991 The Big Boy	14-day		29.50	60-100
1991 The Empire Builder	14-day		29.50	75-95
1992 An American Classic	14-day		29.50	60-75
1992 Final Destination	14-day		29.50	40-75

Golden Discoveries - L. Budge

1995 Boot Bandits	28-day		29.95	30
1995 Hiding the Evidence	28-day		29.95	30
1995 Decoy Dilemma	28-day		29.95	30
1995 Fishing for Dinner	28-day		29.95	30
1996 Lunchtime Companions	28-day		29.95	30
1996 Friend or Foe?	28-day		29.95	30

Golden Puppy Portraits - P. Braun

1994 Do Not Disturb!	28-day		29.50	30-75
1995 Teething Time	28-day		29.50	30-35
1995 Table Manners	28-day		29.50	30-75
1995 A Golden Bouquet	28-day		29.50	30-35
1995 Time For Bed	28-day		29.50	30-35
1995 Bathtime Blues	28-day		29.50	30-35
1996 Spinning a Yarn	28-day		29.50	30-35
1996 Partytime Puppy	28-day		29.50	30-35

Good Sports - J. Lamb

1990 Wide Retriever	14-day	1994	29.50	45-65
1990 Double Play	14-day	1994	29.50	50-65
1990 Hole in One	14-day	1994	29.50	45-65
1990 The Bass Masters	14-day	1994	29.50	45-75
1990 Spotted on the Sideline	14-day	1994	29.50	40-65
1990 Slap Shot	14-day	1994	29.50	40-65
1991 Net Play	14-day	1994	29.50	34-65
1991 Basketball	14-day	1994	29.50	40-65
1992 Boxer Rebellion	14-day	1994	29.50	35-65
1992 Great Try	14-day	1994	29.50	40-65

Grateful Dead Album Covers - S. Mouse

1999 Cats Under The Stars	28-day		35.00	35-99
1999 Cyclops	28-day		35.00	35
1999 Terrapin Station	28-day		35.00	35
1999 Mars Hotel (part 1)	28-day		35.00	35
1999 Ice Cream Kid	28-day		35.00	35
1999 Mars Hotel (part 2)	28-day		35.00	35
1999 Rainbow Foot	28-day		35.00	35

The Grateful Dead Art by Stanley Mouse - S. Mouse

1997 One More Saturday Night	28-day		29.95	30-65
1997 The Grateful Dead Family Album	28-day		29.95	30-75
1998 Sunset Jester	28-day		29.95	30-65
1998 Lightning Rose	28-day		29.95	30-79
1998 Europe 81	28-day		29.95	30-89
1998 Timeless	28-day		29.95	30-89
1998 Dancing Jester	28-day		29.95	30-165
1998 Rose Photographer	28-day		29.95	30-125

Graveriders - D. Mann

1999 Flyin' Flamin' Phantom	Open		35.00	35
1999 Skull Rider	Open		35.00	35
1999 Dead Mann's Hand	Open		35.00	35
1999 Dem Bones Dem Bones	Open		35.00	35
2000 Breath of Death	Open		35.00	35
2000 Death's Ride	Open		35.00	35

Great Fighter Planes Of World War II - R. Waddey

1992 Old Crow	14-day		29.50	40-48
1992 Big Hog	14-day		29.50	40-48
1992 P-47 Thunderbolt	14-day		29.50	30-35
1992 P-40 Flying Tiger	14-day		29.50	30-38
1992 F4F Wildcat	14-day		29.50	30-35
1992 P-38F Lightning	14-day		29.50	30-40
1993 F6F Hellcat	14-day		29.50	35-40
1993 P-39M Airacobra	14-day		29.50	30-35
1995 Memphis Belle	14-day		29.50	30-35
1995 The Dragon and His Tail	14-day		29.50	30-43
1995 Big Beautiful Doll	14-day		29.50	30-75
1995 Bats Out of Hell	14-day		29.50	30-75

Great Mammals of the Sea - Wyland

1991 Orca Trio	14-day	N/A	35.00	40-65
1991 Hawaii Dolphins	14-day	N/A	35.00	45-55
1991 Orca Journey	14-day	N/A	35.00	40
1991 Dolphin Paradise	14-day	N/A	35.00	45-49
1991 Children of the Sea	14-day	N/A	35.00	45-60
1991 Kissing Dolphins	14-day	N/A	35.00	50-95
1991 Islands	14-day	N/A	35.00	45-60
1991 Orcas	14-day	N/A	35.00	45-50

The Greatest Show on Earth - F. Moody

1981 Clowns	10-day	N/A	30.00	35-50
1981 Elephants	10-day	N/A	30.00	30-45
1981 Aerialists	10-day	N/A	30.00	39-45
1981 Great Parade	10-day	N/A	30.00	30-45
1981 Midway	10-day	N/A	30.00	30-55
1981 Equestrians	10-day	N/A	30.00	30-55
1982 Lion Tamer	10-day	N/A	30.00	30-45
1982 Grande Finale	10-day	N/A	30.00	30-45

YEAR ISSUE	EDITION LIMIT	YEAR RETD.	ISSUE PRICE	*QUOTE U.S.$
Growing Up Together - P. Brooks				
1990 My Very Best Friends	14-day		29.50	30-40
1990 Tea for Two	14-day		29.50	30-40
1990 Tender Loving Care	14-day		29.50	30-40
1990 Picnic Pals	14-day		29.50	30-40
1991 Newfound Friends	14-day		29.50	30-40
1991 Kitten Caboodle	14-day		29.50	30-40
1991 Fishing Buddies	14-day		29.50	30-39
1991 Bedtime Blessings	14-day		29.50	30-40
Guidance of the Soaring Spirit - J. Pitcher				
2001 Let Your Spirit Soar	Open		29.95	30
The Historic Railways - T. Xaras				
1995 Harper's Ferry	28-day		29.95	30-45
1995 Horseshoe Curve	28-day		29.95	30-45
1995 Kentucky's Red River	28-day		29.95	30-45
1995 Sherman Hill Challenger	28-day		29.95	30-45
1996 New York Central's 4-6-4 Hudson	28-day		29.95	30-45
1996 Rails By The Seashore	28-day		29.95	30-45
1996 Steam in the High Sierras	28-day		29.95	30-45
1996 Evening Departure	28-day		29.95	30-45
The I Love Lucy Plate Collection - J. Kritz				
1989 California, Here We Come	14-day	1992	29.50	120-225
1989 It's Just Like Candy	14-day	1992	29.50	160-275
1990 The Big Squeeze	14-day	1992	29.50	165-250
1990 Eating the Evidence	14-day	1992	29.50	200-295
1990 Two of a Kind	14-day	1992	29.50	140-200
1991 Queen of the Gypsies	14-day	1992	29.50	140-195
1992 Night at the Copa	14-day	1992	29.50	150-200
1992 A Rising Problem	14-day	1992	29.50	140-225
James Dean Commemorative Issue - T. Blackshear				
1991 James Dean	14-day	N/A	37.50	100
James Dean The Legend - M. Weistling				
1992 Unforgotten Rebel	28-day	N/A	29.50	100
Japanese Floral Calendar - Shuho/Kage				
1981 New Year's Day	10-day	N/A	32.50	33-75
1982 Early Spring	10-day	N/A	32.50	33-75
1982 Spring	10-day	N/A	32.50	33-75
1982 Girl's Doll Day Festival	10-day	N/A	32.50	33-75
1982 Buddha's Birthday	10-day	N/A	32.50	33-75
1982 Early Summer	10-day	N/A	32.50	33-40
1982 Boy's Doll Day Festival	10-day	N/A	32.50	33-40
1982 Summer	10-day	N/A	32.50	33-75
1982 Autumn	10-day	N/A	32.50	33-75
1983 Festival of the Full Moon	10-day	N/A	32.50	33-75
1983 Late Autumn	10-day	N/A	32.50	33-75
1983 Winter	10-day	N/A	32.50	33-75
Jeff Gordon - Various				
1996 On The Warpath - S. Bass	28-day		35.00	35
1996 Headed to Victory Lane	28-day		35.00	35-45
- R. Tanenbaum				
1996 Gordon Takes the Title - S. Bass	28-day		35.00	35
1996 From Winner to Champion	28-day		35.00	35-45
- R. Tanenbaum				
Jeff Gordon 3-Time Championship Plates - S. Bass				
2000 Simply The Best!	Open		35.00	35
2000 Golden Year!	Open		35.00	35
Jeff Gordon Celebration of Victory Plates - D. Sivavec				
2001 The Desire To Win!	Open		35.00	35
Jeff Gordon Championship Plate - R. Tanenbaum				
1998 A Champion's Year	Open		35.00	35
1998 Challenge of a Champion	Open		35.00	35
1999 Shades of a Winner	Open		35.00	35
1999 Practice Makes Perfect	Open		35.00	35
Jeff Gordon Panorama - B. Tanenbaum				
1999 Look of a Warrior	Open		39.95	40
1999 Heart of a Warrior	Open		39.95	40
1999 A Warrior's Ride	Open		39.95	40
1999 Foundation of a Warrior	Open		39.95	40
The Jeweled Hummingbirds - J. Landenberger				
1989 Ruby-throated Hummingbirds	14-day		37.50	45-60
1989 Great Sapphire Wing Hummingbirds	14-day		37.50	45-50
1989 Ruby-Topaz Hummingbirds	14-day		37.50	45-50

YEAR ISSUE	EDITION LIMIT	YEAR RETD.	ISSUE PRICE	*QUOTE U.S.$
1989 Andean Emerald Hummingbirds	14-day		37.50	45-50
1989 Garnet-throated Hummingbirds	14-day		37.50	45-50
1989 Blue-Headed Sapphire Hummingbirds	14-day		37.50	45-50
1989 Pearl Coronet Hummingbirds	14-day		37.50	45-50
1989 Amethyst-throated Sunangels	14-day		37.50	35-45
Joe Montana - Various				
1996 40,000 Yards - R. Tanenbaum	28-day		35.00	35-89
1996 Finding a Way to Win - A. Catalano	28-day		35.00	35-89
1996 Comeback Kid - A. Catalano	28-day		35.00	35-55
1996 Chief on the Field - Petronella	28-day		35.00	35-45
Kitten Classics - P. Cooper				
1985 Cat Nap	14-day		29.50	30-60
1985 Purrfect Treasure	14-day		29.50	30-60
1985 Wild Flower	14-day		29.50	30-60
1985 Birdwatcher	14-day		29.50	30-60
1985 Tiger's Fancy	14-day		29.50	33-60
1985 Country Kitty	14-day		29.50	33-80
1985 Little Rascal	14-day		29.50	30-60
1985 First Prize	14-day		29.50	30-80
Knick Knack Kitty Cat Sculptural - L. Yencho				
1996 Kittens in the Cupboard	Closed		39.95	40-85
1996 Kittens in the Cushion	Closed		39.95	40
1996 Kittens in the Plant	Closed		39.95	40-99
1996 Kittens in the Yarn	Closed		39.95	40-99
The Last Warriors - C. Ren				
1993 Winter of '41	28-day		29.50	35-85
1993 Morning of Reckoning	28-day		29.50	35-85
1993 Twilights Last Gleaming	28-day		29.50	35-40
1993 Lone Winter Journey	28-day		29.50	35-45
1994 Victory's Reward	28-day		29.50	30-40
1994 Solitary Hunter	28-day		29.50	35-40
1994 Solemn Reflection	28-day		29.50	35-40
1994 Confronting Danger	28-day		29.50	35-40
1995 Moment of Contemplation	28-day		29.50	35-60
1995 The Last Sunset	28-day		29.50	35
The Legend of Father Christmas - V. Dezerin				
1994 The Return of Father Christmas	28-day		29.50	30-40
1994 Gifts From Father Christmas	28-day		29.50	30-40
1994 The Feast of the Holiday	28-day		29.50	30-40
1995 Christmas Day Visitors	28-day		29.50	30-45
1995 Decorating the Tree	28-day		29.50	30-44
1995 The Snow Sculpture	28-day		29.50	30-45
1995 Skating on the Pond	28-day		29.50	30-44
1995 Holy Night	28-day		29.50	30-40
Legendary Warriors - M. Gentry				
1995 White Quiver and Scout	28-day		29.95	30
1995 Lakota Rendezvous	28-day		29.95	30
1995 Crazy Horse	28-day		29.95	30
1995 Sitting Bull's Vision	28-day		29.95	30
1996 Crazy Horse	28-day		29.95	30
1996 Sitting Bull's Vision	28-day		29.95	30
1996 Noble Surrender	28-day		29.95	30
1996 Sioux Thunder	28-day		29.95	30
1996 Eagle Dancer	28-day		29.95	30
1996 The Trap	28-day		29.95	30
Let Freedom Ring (Landscapes) - S. Hardock				
1999 Land of Liberty	95-day		39.95	40
1999 Land of Reverence	95-day		39.95	40
1999 Land of Independence	95-day		39.95	40
Let Freedom Ring (Monuments) - S. Hardock				
1999 Liberty	95-day		39.95	40
1999 Reverence	95-day		39.95	40
A Lisi Martin Christmas - L. Martin				
1992 Santa's Littlest Reindeer	28-day		29.50	35-49
1993 Not A Creature Was Stirring	28-day		29.50	35-55
1993 Christmas Dreams	28-day		29.50	35-55
1993 The Christmas Story	28-day		29.50	35-55
1993 Trimming The Tree	28-day		29.50	35-95
1993 A Taste Of The Holidays	28-day		29.50	35-49
1993 The Night Before Christmas	28-day		29.50	35-55
1993 Christmas Watch	28-day		29.50	35-55
1995 Christmas Presence	28-day		29.50	35-55
1995 Nose to Nose	28-day		29.50	35-49

PLATES & PLAQUES

YEAR ISSUE	EDITION LIMIT	YEAR RETD.	ISSUE PRICE	*QUOTE U.S.$
Little Fawns of the Forest - R. Manning				
1995 In the Morning Light	28-day		29.95	30
1995 Cool Reflections	28-day		29.95	30
1995 Nature's Lesson	28-day		29.95	30
1996 A Friendship Blossoms	28-day		29.95	30
1996 Innocent Companions	28-day		29.95	30
1996 New Life, New Day	28-day		29.95	30
Little House on the Prairie - E. Christopherson				
1986 Founder's Day Picnic	10-day	N/A	29.50	60
1986 The Woman's Harvest	10-day	N/A	29.50	60
1986 The Medicine Show	10-day	N/A	29.50	60
1986 Caroline's Eggs	10-day	N/A	29.50	65-75
1986 Mary's Gift	10-day	N/A	29.50	60
1986 Bell For Walnut Grove	10-day	N/A	29.50	60-125
1986 Ingalls Family Christmas	10-day	N/A	29.50	60
1986 Sweetheart Tree	10-day	N/A	29.50	60
Little Ladies - M.H. Bogart				
1989 Playing Bridesmaid	14-day	1991	29.50	45-106
1990 The Seamstress	14-day	1991	29.50	45-95
1990 Little Captive	14-day	1991	29.50	45-95
1990 Playing Mama	14-day	1991	29.50	45-95
1990 Susanna	14-day	1991	29.50	45-55
1990 Kitty's Bath	14-day	1991	29.50	45-95
1990 A Day in the Country	14-day	1991	29.50	45-95
1991 Sarah	14-day	1991	29.50	45-105
1991 First Party	14-day	1991	29.50	45-105
1991 The Magic Kitten	14-day	1991	29.50	45-65
The Little Rascals - Unknown				
1985 Three for the Show	10-day	1989	24.50	30-49
1985 My Gal	10-day	1989	24.50	25-49
1985 Skeleton Crew	10-day	1989	24.50	25-49
1985 Roughin' It	10-day	1989	24.50	25-49
1985 Spanky's Pranks	10-day	1989	24.50	25-49
1985 Butch's Challenge	10-day	1989	24.50	25-49
1985 Darla's Debut	10-day	1989	24.50	25-49
1985 Pete's Pal	10-day	1989	24.50	25-40
Little Shopkeepers - G. Gerardi				
1990 Sew Tired	14-day	1989	29.50	30-45
1991 Break Time	14-day	1989	29.50	30-40
1991 Purrfect Fit	14-day	1989	29.50	30-40
1991 Toying Around	14-day	1989	29.50	35-40
1991 Chain Reaction	14-day	1989	29.50	40-50
1991 Inferior Decorators	14-day	1989	29.50	40-45
1991 Tulip Tag	14-day	1989	29.50	36-40
1991 Candy Capers	14-day	1989	29.50	36-40
Lore Of The West - L. Danielle				
1993 A Mile In His Mocassins	28-day		29.50	30-45
1993 Path of Honor	28-day		29.50	30-45
1993 A Chief's Pride	28-day		29.50	30-45
1994 Pathways of the Pueblo	28-day		29.50	30-45
1994 In Her Seps	28-day		29.50	30-45
1994 Growing Up Brave	28-day		29.50	30-45
1994 Nomads of the Southwest	28-day		29.50	30-45
1994 Sacred Spirit of the Plains	28-day		29.50	30-45
1994 We'll Fight No More	28-day		29.50	30-44
1994 The End of the Trail	28-day		29.50	30-45
Love's Messengers - J. Grossman				
1995 To My Love	28-day	1994	29.50	40-45
1995 Cupid's Arrow	28-day	1994	29.50	40-45
1995 Love's Melody	28-day	1994	29.50	40
1995 A Token of Love	28-day	1994	29.50	40
1995 Harmony of Love	28-day	1994	29.50	40-45
1996 True Love's Offering	28-day	1994	29.50	40
1996 Love's In Bloom	28-day	1994	29.95	40-45
1996 To My Sweetheart	28-day	1994	29.95	40
Loving Lucy - M. Weistling				
1997 We're Having a Baby	28-day	1999	29.95	30-85
1997 Soaking Up the Local Color	28-day	1999	35.00	30-85
1998 Million Dollar Idea	28-day	1999	29.95	30-85
1997 Chatter Box Ricardo	28-day	1999	35.00	30-85
1998 Wanted: 'Sperienced Chicken Farmer	28-day	1999	29.95	30-55
1998 Caught in the Act	28-day	1999	29.95	30-55
1999 Parisian Potato Sacks	28-day	1999	29.95	30-55
1999 Lucy Chills Out	28-day	1999	29.95	30-55

YEAR ISSUE	EDITION LIMIT	YEAR RETD.	ISSUE PRICE	*QUOTE U.S.$
The Lucille Ball (Official) Commemorative Plate - M. Weistling				
1993 Lucy	28-day	1994	37.50	175-250
Lucy Meets The Stars - M. Weistling				
1997 L.A. at Last!	28-day	1999	35.00	35-75
1997 Tennessee Ernie Ford Visits	28-day	1999	35.00	35-79
1997 Lucy Meets Harpo Marx	28-day	1999	35.00	35-85
1998 Lucy Meets Orson Wells	28-day	1999	35.00	35-75
1999 Lucy Meets Red Skelton	28-day	1999	35.00	55-155
Madonna And Child - Various				
1992 Madonna Della Sedia - R. Sanzio	28-day		37.50	38-50
1992 Virgin of the Rocks - L. DaVinci	28-day		37.50	38-50
1993 Madonna of Rosary - B. E. Murillo	28-day		37.50	38-50
1993 Sistine Madonna - R. Sanzio	28-day		37.50	38-50
1993 Virgin Adoring Christ Child - A. Correggio	28-day		37.50	38-50
1993 Virgin of the Grape - P. Mignard	28-day		37.50	38-50
1993 Madonna del Magnificat - S. Botticelli	28-day		37.50	38-50
1993 Madonna col Bambino - S. Botticelli	28-day		37.50	38-50
The Magical World of Legends & Myths - J. Shalatain				
1993 A Mother's Love	28-day	1994	35.00	35-55
1993 Dreams of Pegasus	28-day	1994	35.00	35-45
1994 Flight of Pegasus	28-day	1994	35.00	35-45
1994 The Awakening	28-day	1994	35.00	35-45
1994 Once Upon a Dream	28-day	1994	35.00	35-45
1994 The Dawn of Romance	28-day	1994	35.00	35-45
1994 The Astral Unicorn	28-day	1994	35.00	35-45
1994 Flight into Paradise	28-day	1994	35.00	35
1995 Pegasus in the Stars	28-day	1994	35.00	35-45
1995 Unicorn of the Sea	28-day	1994	35.00	35
Majestic Birds of Prey - C.F. Riley				
1983 Golden Eagle	12,500	N/A	55.00	55-85
1983 Coopers Hawk	12,500	N/A	55.00	55-60
1983 Great Horned Owl	12,500	N/A	55.00	55-60
1983 Bald Eagle	12,500	N/A	55.00	55-60
1983 Barred Owl	12,500	N/A	55.00	55-60
1983 Sparrow Hawk	12,500	N/A	55.00	55-60
1983 Peregrine Falcon	12,500	N/A	55.00	55-60
1983 Osprey	12,500	N/A	55.00	55-60
Majesty of Flight - T. Hirata				
1989 The Eagle Soars	14-day	N/A	37.50	60-70
1989 Realm of the Red-Tail	14-day	N/A	37.50	40-70
1989 Coastal Journey	14-day	N/A	37.50	38-70
1989 Sentry of the North	14-day	N/A	37.50	38-70
1989 Commanding the Marsh	14-day	N/A	37.50	38-70
1990 The Vantage Point	14-day	N/A	29.50	38-70
1990 Silent Watch	14-day	N/A	29.50	48-70
1990 Fierce and Free	14-day	N/A	29.50	38-70
Man's Best Friend - L. Picken				
1992 Special Delivery	28-day		29.50	30-45
1992 Making Waves	28-day		29.50	30-45
1992 Good Catch	28-day		29.50	30-45
1993 Time For a Walk	28-day		29.50	30-75
1993 Faithful Friend	28-day		29.50	30-45
1993 Let's Play Ball	28-day		29.50	30-45
1993 Sitting Pretty	28-day		29.50	30-45
1993 Bedtime Story	28-day		29.50	30-45
1993 Trusted Companion	28-day		29.50	30-45
Mickey Mantle - R. Tanenbaum				
1996 The Mick	28-day		35.00	50
1996 536 Home Runs	28-day		35.00	45
1996 2,401 Games	28-day		35.00	45
1996 Switch Hitter	28-day		35.00	30-52
1996 16 Time All Star	28-day		35.00	45
1996 18 World Series Home Runs	28-day		35.00	45
1997 1956-A Crowning Year	28-day		35.00	45
1997 Remembering a Legendary Yankee	28-day		35.00	45
Mike Schmidt - R. Tanenbaum				
1994 The Ultimate Competitor: Mike Schmidt	28-day		29.50	30
1995 A Homerun King	28-day		29.50	30
1995 An All Time, All Star	28-day		29.50	30
1995 A Career Retrospective	28-day		29.50	30

Collectors' Information Bureau

*Quotes have been rounded up to nearest dollar

YEAR ISSUE	EDITION LIMIT	YEAR RETD.	ISSUE PRICE	*QUOTE U.S.$
Milestones in Space - D. Dixon				
1994 Moon Landing	28-day	N/A	29.50	45
1995 Space Lab	28-day	N/A	29.50	30
1995 Maiden Flight of Columbia	28-day	N/A	29.50	30
1995 Free Walk in Space	28-day	N/A	29.50	30
1995 Lunar Rover	28-day	N/A	29.50	30
1995 Handshake in Space	28-day	N/A	29.50	30
1995 First Landing on Mars	28-day	N/A	29.50	30
1995 Voyager's Exploration	28-day	N/A	29.50	30
Mixed Company - P. Cooper				
1990 Two Against One	14-day	N/A	29.50	36-55
1990 A Sticky Situation	14-day	N/A	29.50	35-45
1990 What's Up	14-day	N/A	29.50	30-45
1990 All Wrapped Up	14-day	N/A	29.50	35-45
1990 Picture Perfect	14-day	N/A	29.50	30-45
1991 A Moment to Unwind	14-day	N/A	29.50	33-45
1991 Ole	14-day	N/A	29.50	33-45
1991 Picnic Prowlers	14-day	N/A	29.50	35-45
Murals From The Precious Moments Chapel - S. Butcher				
1995 The Pearl of Great Price	28-day		35.00	35
1995 The Good Samaritan	28-day		35.00	35
1996 The Prodigal Son	28-day		35.00	35
1996 The Good Shepherd	28-day		35.00	35
Mystic Warrior Shield Collection - C. Ren				
1996 Deliverance	28-day		39.95	40-45
1996 Blue Thunder	28-day		39.95	40
1997 Mystic Warrior	28-day		39.95	40-49
1997 Windrider	28-day		39.95	40
1999 Morning of Reckoning	28-day		39.95	40-55
1999 Winter of '41	28-day		39.95	40-52
1999 Sun Seeker	28-day		39.95	40
1999 Peacemaker	28-day		39.95	40
Mystic Warriors - C. Ren				
1992 Deliverance	28-day		29.50	55-75
1992 Mystic Warrior	28-day		29.50	40-75
1992 Sun Seeker	28-day		29.50	40-85
1992 Top Gun	28-day		29.50	40-85
1992 Man Who Walks Alone	28-day		29.50	30-85
1992 Windrider	28-day		29.50	30-75
1992 Spirit of the Plains	28-day		29.50	40-85
1993 Blue Thunder	28-day		29.50	40-75
1993 Sun Glow	28-day		29.50	40-75
1993 Peace Maker	28-day		29.50	45-85
Native American Legends - A. Biffignandi				
1996 Peace Pipe	28-day		29.95	30
1996 Feather-Woman	28-day		29.95	30
1996 Spirit of Serenity	28-day		29.95	30
1996 Enchanted Warrior	28-day		29.95	30
1996 Mystical Serenade	28-day		29.95	30
1996 Legend of Bridal Veil	28-day		29.95	30-40
1996 Seasons of Love	28-day		29.95	30-69
1996 A Bashful Courtship	28-day		29.95	30-39
Nature's Majestic Cats - M. Richter				
1993 Siberian Tiger	28-day		29.50	40-75
1993 Himalayan Snow Leopard	28-day		29.50	30-65
1993 African Lion	28-day		29.50	30-75
1994 Asian Clouded Leopard	28-day		29.50	30-75
1994 American Cougar	28-day		29.50	30-65
1994 East African Leopard	28-day		29.50	30-75
1994 African Cheetah	28-day		29.50	30-65
1994 Canadian Lynx	28-day		29.50	30-75
Nature's Nighttime Realm - G. Murray				
1992 Bobcat	28-day		29.50	30-45
1992 Cougar	28-day		29.50	30-45
1993 Jaguar	28-day		29.50	30-45
1993 White Tiger	28-day		29.50	30-45
1993 Lynx	28-day		29.50	30-45
1993 Lion	28-day		29.50	30-45
1993 Snow Leopard	28-day		29.50	30-50
1993 Cheetah	28-day		29.50	30-45
Nature's Quiet Moments - R. Parker				
1988 A Curious Pair	14-day	N/A	37.50	47-60
1988 Northern Morning	14-day	N/A	37.50	40-55
1988 Just Resting	14-day	N/A	37.50	40-50

YEAR ISSUE	EDITION LIMIT	YEAR RETD.	ISSUE PRICE	*QUOTE U.S.$
1989 Waiting Out the Storm	14-day	N/A	37.50	38
1989 Creekside	14-day	N/A	37.50	38
1989 Autumn Foraging	14-day	N/A	37.50	38
1989 Old Man of the Mountain	14-day	N/A	37.50	38
1989 Mountain Blooms	14-day	N/A	37.50	38
Newsom Santa Takes a Break - T. Newsom				
1995 Santa's Last Stop	28-day		29.95	30
1996 Santa's Railroad	28-day		29.95	30
1996 A Jolly Good Catch	28-day		29.95	30
1996 Simple Pleasures	28-day		29.95	30
1996 Skating On Penguin Pond	28-day		29.95	30
1996 Santa's Sing-along	28-day		29.95	30
1996 Sledding Adventures	28-day		29.95	30
1997 Santa's Sweet Treats	28-day		29.95	30
Noble American Indian Women - D. Wright				
1989 Sacajawea	14-day		29.50	50-125
1990 Pocahontas	14-day		29.50	40-125
1990 Minnehaha	14-day		29.50	65-125
1990 Pine Leaf	14-day		29.50	65-125
1990 Lily of the Mohawk	14-day		29.50	60-125
1990 White Rose	14-day		29.50	55-125
1991 Lozen	14-day		29.50	55-125
1991 Falling Star	14-day		29.50	55-125
Noble Owls of America - J. Seerey-Lester				
1986 Morning Mist	15,000	N/A	55.00	45-100
1987 Prairie Sundown	15,000	N/A	55.00	55-100
1987 Winter Vigil	15,000	N/A	55.00	55-100
1987 Autumn Mist	15,000	N/A	75.00	60-100
1987 Dawn in the Willows	15,000	N/A	55.00	55-100
1987 Snowy Watch	15,000	N/A	60.00	60-100
1988 Hiding Place	15,000	N/A	55.00	55-100
1988 Waiting for Dusk	15,000	N/A	55.00	55-100
Nolan Ryan - R. Tanenbaum				
1994 The Strikeout Express	28-day		29.50	50-69
1994 Birth of a Legend	28-day		29.50	25-35
1994 Mr. Fastball	28-day		29.50	25-35
1994 Million-Dollar Player	28-day		29.50	25-35
1994 27 Seasons	28-day		29.50	25-35
1994 Farewell	28-day		29.50	25-35
1994 The Ryan Express	28-day		29.50	25-50
Norman Rockwell's Saturday Evening Post Baseball - N. Rockwell				
1992 100th Year of Baseball	Closed	N/A	19.50	20
1993 The Rookie	Closed	N/A	19.50	20
1993 The Dugout	Closed	N/A	19.50	20
1993 Bottom of the Sixth	Closed	N/A	19.50	20
North American Ducks - R. Lawrence				
1991 Autumn Flight	14-day		29.50	30-40
1991 The Resting Place	14-day		29.50	30-40
1991 Twin Flight	14-day		29.50	30-40
1992 Misty Morning	14-day		29.50	30-40
1992 Springtime Thaw	14-day		29.50	30-40
1992 Summer Retreat	14-day		29.50	30-40
1992 Overcast	14-day		29.50	30-40
1992 Perfect Pintails	14-day		29.50	30-40
North American Gamebirds - J. Killen				
1990 Ring-necked Pheasant	14-day	N/A	37.50	40-75
1990 Bobwhite Quail	14-day	N/A	37.50	50-100
1990 Ruffed Grouse	14-day	N/A	37.50	40-75
1990 Gambel Quail	14-day	N/A	37.50	38-42
1990 Mourning Dove	14-day	N/A	37.50	38-50
1990 Woodcock	14-day	N/A	37.50	38-50
1991 Chukar Partridge	14-day	N/A	37.50	38-50
1991 Wild Turkey	14-day	N/A	37.50	38-50
North American Waterbirds - R. Lawrence				
1988 Wood Ducks	14-day	N/A	37.50	45-60
1988 Hooded Mergansers	14-day	N/A	37.50	50-60
1988 Pintails	14-day	N/A	37.50	40-50
1988 Canada Geese	14-day	N/A	37.50	40-50
1989 American Widgeons	14-day	N/A	37.50	45-60
1989 Canvasbacks	14-day	N/A	37.50	45-60
1989 Mallard Pair	14-day	N/A	37.50	45-65
1989 Snow Geese	14-day	N/A	37.50	45-50

PLATES & PLAQUES

YEAR ISSUE	EDITION LIMIT	YEAR RETD.	ISSUE PRICE	*QUOTE U.S.$
The Nutcracker Ballet - S. Fisher				
1978 Clara	28-day	N/A	19.50	36-50
1979 Godfather	28-day	N/A	19.50	20-25
1979 Sugar Plum Fairy	28-day	N/A	19.50	45-70
1979 Snow Queen and King	28-day	N/A	19.50	25-45
1980 Waltz of the Flowers	28-day	N/A	19.50	20-25
1980 Clara and the Prince	28-day	N/A	19.50	25-50
Official Honeymooner's Commemorative Plate - D. Bobnick				
1993 The Official Honeymooner's Commemorative Plate	28-day	N/A	37.50	135-275
The Official Honeymooners Plate Collection - D. Kilmer				
1987 The Honeymooners	14-day	N/A	24.50	155-225
1987 The Hucklebuck	14-day	N/A	24.50	165-200
1987 Baby, You're the Greatest	14-day	N/A	24.50	165-225
1988 The Golfer	14-day	N/A	24.50	165-225
1988 The TV Chefs	14-day	N/A	24.50	125-225
1988 Bang! Zoom!	14-day	N/A	24.50	165-225
1988 The Only Way to Travel	14-day	N/A	24.50	165-225
1988 The Honeymoon Express	14-day	N/A	24.50	200-275
On Wings of Eagles - J. Pitcher				
1994 "By Dawn's Early Light"	28-day		29.50	30-39
1994 Winter's Majestic Flight	28-day		29.50	30-40
1994 Over the Land of the Free	28-day		29.50	30-40
1994 Changing of the Guard	28-day		29.50	30-40
1995 Free Flight	28-day		29.50	30-40
1995 Morning Majesty	28-day		29.50	30-40
1995 Soaring Free	28-day		29.50	30
1994 Majestic Heights	28-day		29.50	30
Once In A Lifetime - Earnhardt & Jr. Panorama Plates - B. Tanenbaum				
1999 The Mentor	Open		39.95	40
1999 Classic Red	Open		39.95	40
1999 First Black	Open		39.95	40
1999 The Protégé	Open		39.95	40
Our Cherished Seas - S. Barlowe				
1992 Whale Song	48-day		37.50	38
1992 Lions of the Sea	48-day		37.50	38
1992 Flight of the Dolphins	48-day		37.50	38-42
1992 Palace of the Seals	48-day		37.50	38
1993 Orca Ballet	48-day		37.50	38
1993 Emporers of the Ice	48-day		37.50	38
1993 Sea Turtles	48-day		37.50	38
1993 Splendor of the Sea	48-day		37.50	38
Petals and Purrs - B. Harrison				
1988 Blushing Beauties	14-day	N/A	24.50	55-60
1988 Spring Fever	14-day	N/A	24.50	38-55
1988 Morning Glories	14-day	N/A	24.50	45-55
1988 Forget-Me-Not	14-day	N/A	24.50	36-55
1989 Golden Fancy	14-day	N/A	24.50	30-55
1989 Pink Lillies	14-day	N/A	24.50	30-55
1989 Summer Sunshine	14-day	N/A	24.50	50-55
1989 Siamese Summer	14-day	N/A	24.50	50-55
Pillars of Baseball - A. Hicks				
1995 Babe Ruth	28-day		29.95	30-35
1995 Lou Gehrig	28-day		29.95	30
1995 Ty Cobb	28-day		29.95	30
1996 Cy Young	28-day		29.95	30
1996 Honus Wagner	28-day		29.95	30
1996 Rogers Hornsby	28-day		29.95	30
1996 Dizzy Dean	28-day		29.95	30
1996 Christy Mathewson	28-day		29.95	30
Portraits of Childhood - T. Utz				
1981 Butterfly Magic	28-day	N/A	24.95	25-50
1981 Sweet Dreams	28-day	N/A	24.95	25-50
1981 Turtle Talk	28-day	N/A	24.95	36-50
1981 Friends Forever	28-day	N/A	24.95	35-50
Portraits of Jesus - W. Sallman				
1994 Jesus, The Good Shepherd	28-day		29.50	30-39
1994 Jesus in the Garden	28-day		29.50	30
1994 Jesus, Children's Friend	28-day		29.50	30
1994 The Lord's Supper	28-day		29.50	30-35
1994 Christ at Dawn	28-day		29.50	30
1994 Christ at Heart's Door	28-day		29.50	30

YEAR ISSUE	EDITION LIMIT	YEAR RETD.	ISSUE PRICE	*QUOTE U.S.$
1994 Portrait of Christ	28-day		29.50	30
1994 Madonna and Christ Child	28-day		29.50	30-40
Portraits of the Bald Eagle - J. Pitcher				
1993 Ruler of the Sky	28-day		37.50	40-55
1993 In Bold Defiance	28-day		37.50	40-55
1993 Master Of The Summer Skies	28-day		37.50	40-55
1993 Spring's Sentinel	28-day		37.50	40-55
Portraits of the Wild - J. Meger				
1994 Interlude	28-day		29.50	30-40
1994 Winter Solitude	28-day		29.50	30-90
1994 Devoted Protector	28-day		29.50	30-40
1994 Call of Autumn	28-day		29.50	30-40
1994 Watchful Eyes	28-day		29.50	30-40
1994 Babies of Spring	28-day		29.50	30-40
1994 Rocky Mountain Grandeur	28-day		29.50	30
1995 Unbridled Power	28-day		29.50	30-45
1995 Moonlight Vigil	28-day		29.50	30-45
1995 Monarch of the Plains	28-day		29.50	30-45
1995 Tender Courtship	28-day		29.50	30-40
Precious Moments Bible Story - S. Butcher				
1990 Come Let Us Adore Him	28-day		29.50	30
1992 They Followed The Star	28-day		29.50	30-55
1992 The Flight Into Egypt	28-day		29.50	30
1992 The Carpenter Shop	28-day		29.50	30-70
1992 Jesus In The Temple	28-day		29.50	30
1992 The Crucifixion	28-day		29.50	30-65
1993 He Is Not Here	28-day		29.50	30-80
Precious Moments Classics - S. Butcher				
1993 God Loveth A Cheerful Giver	28-day		35.00	35-40
1993 Make A Joyful Noise	28-day		35.00	35-40
1994 Love One Another	28-day		35.00	35
1994 You Have Touched So Many Hearts	28-day		35.00	35
1994 Praise the Lord Anyhow	28-day		35.00	35
1994 I Believe in Miracles	28-day		35.00	35
1994 Good Friends Are Forever	28-day		35.00	35
1994 Jesus Loves Me	28-day		35.00	35
1995 Friendship Hits the Spot	28-day		35.00	35
1995 To My Deer Friend	28-day		35.00	35
Precious Moments of Childhood Plates - T. Utz				
1979 Friend in the Sky	28-day		21.50	50-70
1980 Sand in her Shoe	28-day		21.50	22-35
1980 Snow Bunny	28-day		21.50	20-35
1980 Seashells	28-day		21.50	38-55
1981 Dawn	28-day		21.50	22-35
1982 My Kitty	28-day		21.50	36-55
Precious Moments Words of Love - S. Butcher				
1995 Your Friendship Is Soda-licious	28-day		35.00	35
1996 Your Love Is So Uplifting	28-day		35.00	35
1996 Love Is From Above	28-day		35.00	35
1996 Love Lifted Me	28-day		35.00	35
Precious Portraits - B. P. Gutmann				
1987 Sunbeam	14-day	1991	24.50	60-80
1987 Mischief	14-day	1991	24.50	60-80
1987 Peach Blossom	14-day	1991	24.50	60-80
1987 Goldilocks	14-day	1991	24.50	55-95
1987 Fairy Gold	14-day	1991	24.50	40-80
1987 Bunny	14-day	1991	24.50	30-80
The Prideful Ones - C. DeHaan				
1994 Village Markers	28-day		29.50	30
1994 His Pride	28-day		29.50	30
1994 Appeasing the Water People	28-day		29.50	30
1994 Tribal Guardian	28-day		29.50	30
1994 Autumn Passage	28-day		29.50	30
1994 Winter Hunter	28-day		29.50	30
1994 Silent Trail Break	28-day		29.50	30
1994 Water Breaking	28-day		29.50	30
1994 Crossing at the Big Trees	28-day		29.50	30
1995 Winter Songsinger	28-day		29.50	30
Princesses of the Plains - D. Wright				
1993 Prairie Flower	28-day		29.50	32-45
1993 Snow Princess	28-day		29.50	40-65
1993 Wild Flower	28-day		29.50	30-45
1993 Noble Beauty	28-day		29.50	35-45
1993 Winter's Rose	28-day		29.50	30-45

YEAR ISSUE	EDITION LIMIT	YEAR RETD.	ISSUE PRICE	*QUOTE U.S.$
1993 Gentle Beauty	28-day		29.50	30-45
1994 Nature's Guardian	28-day		29.50	40-45
1994 Mountain Princess	28-day		29.50	30-45
1995 Proud Dreamer	28-day		29.50	40-45
1995 Spring Maiden	28-day		29.50	30-45

Proud Chieftains - N. Rose

YEAR ISSUE	EDITION LIMIT	YEAR RETD.	ISSUE PRICE	*QUOTE U.S.$
1999 Spirit Quest	28-day		39.95	40
1999 Sacred Journey	28-day		39.95	40

Proud Indian Families - K. Freeman

YEAR ISSUE	EDITION LIMIT	YEAR RETD.	ISSUE PRICE	*QUOTE U.S.$
1991 The Storyteller	14-day	N/A	29.50	40-45
1991 The Power of the Basket	14-day	N/A	29.50	30-45
1991 The Naming Ceremony	14-day	N/A	29.50	30-45
1992 Playing With Tradition	14-day	N/A	29.50	30-45
1992 Preparing the Berry Harvest	14-day	N/A	29.50	30-45
1992 Ceremonial Dress	14-day	N/A	29.50	30-45
1992 Sounds of the Forest	14-day	N/A	29.50	30-45
1992 The Marriage Ceremony	14-day	N/A	29.50	30-45
1993 The Jewelry Maker	14-day	N/A	29.50	30-45
1993 Beautiful Creations	14-day	N/A	29.50	30-45

Proud Innocence - J. Schmidt

YEAR ISSUE	EDITION LIMIT	YEAR RETD.	ISSUE PRICE	*QUOTE U.S.$
1994 Desert Bloom	28-day	N/A	29.50	30
1994 Little Drummer	28-day	N/A	29.50	30-44
1995 Young Archer	28-day	N/A	29.50	30-45
1995 Morning Child	28-day	N/A	29.50	30-44
1995 Wise One	28-day	N/A	29.50	30-45
1995 Sun Blossom	28-day	N/A	29.50	30-44
1995 Laughing Heart	28-day	N/A	29.50	30-45
1995 Gentle Flower	28-day	N/A	29.50	30

The Proud Nation - R. Swanson

YEAR ISSUE	EDITION LIMIT	YEAR RETD.	ISSUE PRICE	*QUOTE U.S.$
1989 Navajo Little One	14-day	N/A	24.50	50-75
1989 In a Big Land	14-day	N/A	24.50	35-60
1989 Out with Mama's Flock	14-day	N/A	24.50	40-50
1989 Newest Little Sheepherder	14-day	N/A	24.50	50-65
1989 Dressed Up for the Powwow	14-day	N/A	24.50	35-50
1989 Just a Few Days Old	14-day	N/A	24.50	50-65
1989 Autumn Treat	14-day	N/A	24.50	30-50
1989 Up in the Red Rocks	14-day	N/A	24.50	60-85

Puppy Playtime - J. Lamb

YEAR ISSUE	EDITION LIMIT	YEAR RETD.	ISSUE PRICE	*QUOTE U.S.$
1987 Double Take-Cocker Spaniels	14-day		24.50	60-80
1987 Catch of the Day-Golden Retrievers	14-day		24.50	50-80
1987 Cabin Fever-Black Labradors	14-day		24.50	40-69
1987 Weekend Gardener-Lhasa Apsos	14-day		24.50	35-75
1987 Getting Acquainted-Beagles	14-day		24.50	30-75
1987 Hanging Out-German Shepherd	14-day		24.50	40-75
1987 New Leash on Life-Mini Schnauzer	14-day		24.50	45-69
1987 Fun and Games-Poodle	14-day		24.50	30-75

Quiet Moments Of Childhood - D. Green

YEAR ISSUE	EDITION LIMIT	YEAR RETD.	ISSUE PRICE	*QUOTE U.S.$
1991 Elizabeth's Afternoon Tea	14-day		29.50	45-50
1991 Christina's Secret Garden	14-day		29.50	36-40
1991 Eric & Erin's Storytime	14-day		29.50	30-40
1992 Jessica's Tea Party	14-day		29.50	33
1992 Megan & Monique's Bakery	14-day		29.50	36-40
1992 Children's Day By The Sea	14-day		29.50	30-40
1992 Jordan's Playful Pups	14-day		29.50	33
1992 Daniel's Morning Playtime	14-day		29.50	30-40

The Quilted Countryside: A Signature Collection by Mel Steele - M. Steele

YEAR ISSUE	EDITION LIMIT	YEAR RETD.	ISSUE PRICE	*QUOTE U.S.$
1991 The Old Country Store	14-day		29.50	36-55
1991 Winter's End	14-day		29.50	36-40
1991 The Quilter's Cabin	14-day		29.50	45-50
1991 Spring Cleaning	14-day		29.50	36-40
1991 Summer Harvest	14-day		29.50	30-40
1991 The Country Merchant	14-day		29.50	36-40
1992 Wash Day	14-day		29.50	30-40
1992 The Antiques Store	14-day		29.50	33-40

Realm of the Majestic Eagle - Rigby

YEAR ISSUE	EDITION LIMIT	YEAR RETD.	ISSUE PRICE	*QUOTE U.S.$
1997 Winter Watch & Winter's Call	28-day		70.00	70
1997 Spring Flight & Spring Pursuit	28-day		70.00	70
1997 Summer Guard & Mother's Nest	28-day		70.00	70
1997 Autumn Soar & Autumn Splendor	28-day		70.00	70

Realm of the Wolf - A. Agnew

YEAR ISSUE	EDITION LIMIT	YEAR RETD.	ISSUE PRICE	*QUOTE U.S.$
1997 Midnight Serenade	Open		39.95	40
1997 Free as the Wind	Open		39.95	40
1997 Guardians of the High Country	Open		39.95	40
1997 Lords of the Tundra	Open		39.95	40

Remembering Norma Jeane - F. Accornero

YEAR ISSUE	EDITION LIMIT	YEAR RETD.	ISSUE PRICE	*QUOTE U.S.$
1994 The Girl Next Door	28-day	N/A	29.50	50-85
1994 Her Day in the Sun	28-day	N/A	29.50	50-85
1994 A Star is Born	28-day	N/A	29.50	45-70
1994 Beauty Secrets	28-day	N/A	29.50	50-70
1995 In the Spotlight	28-day	N/A	29.50	50-65
1995 Bathing Beauty	28-day	N/A	29.50	45-60
1995 Young & Carefree	28-day	N/A	29.50	45-50
1995 Free Spirit	28-day	N/A	29.50	50-55
1995 A Country Girl at Heart	28-day	N/A	29.50	45-55
1996 Hometown Girl	28-day	N/A	29.50	50

The Renaissance Angels - L. Bywaters

YEAR ISSUE	EDITION LIMIT	YEAR RETD.	ISSUE PRICE	*QUOTE U.S.$
1994 Doves of Peace	28-day	N/A	29.50	30-65
1994 Angelic Innocence	28-day	N/A	29.50	36-65
1994 Joy to the World	28-day	N/A	29.50	30-65
1995 Angel of Faith	28-day	N/A	29.50	30-65
1995 The Christmas Star	28-day	N/A	29.50	30-65
1995 Trumpeter's Call	28-day	N/A	29.50	30-65
1995 Harmonious Heavens	28-day	N/A	29.50	30-65
1995 The Angels Sing	28-day	N/A	29.50	30-65

Rockwell Home of the Brave - N. Rockwell

YEAR ISSUE	EDITION LIMIT	YEAR RETD.	ISSUE PRICE	*QUOTE U.S.$
1981 Reminiscing	18,000		35.00	55-60
1981 Hero's Welcome	18,000		35.00	55-60
1981 Back to his Old Job	18,000		35.00	55-60
1981 War Hero	18,000		35.00	35-55
1982 Willie Gillis in Church	18,000		35.00	55-60
1982 War Bond	18,000		35.00	35-55
1982 Uncle Sam Takes Wings	18,000		35.00	55-80
1982 Taking Mother over the Top	18,000		35.00	35-55

Romance of the Rails - D. Tutwiler

YEAR ISSUE	EDITION LIMIT	YEAR RETD.	ISSUE PRICE	*QUOTE U.S.$
1994 Starlight Limited	28-day	N/A	29.50	30-50
1994 Portland Rose	28-day	N/A	29.50	30-50
1994 Orange Blossom Special	28-day	N/A	29.50	40-45
1994 Morning Star	28-day	N/A	29.50	30-50
1994 Crescent Limited	28-day	N/A	29.50	30-50
1994 Sunset Limited	28-day	N/A	29.50	30-50
1994 Western Star	28-day	N/A	29.50	30-50
1994 Sunrise Limited	28-day	N/A	29.50	30-50
1995 The Blue Bonnett	28-day	N/A	29.50	30-50
1995 The Pine Tree Limited	28-day	N/A	29.50	30-50

Romantic Castles of Europe - D. Sweet

YEAR ISSUE	EDITION LIMIT	YEAR RETD.	ISSUE PRICE	*QUOTE U.S.$
1990 Ludwig's Castle	19,500		55.00	55
1991 Palace of the Moors	19,500		55.00	55
1991 Swiss Isle Fortress	19,500		55.00	55-75
1991 The Legendary Castle of Leeds	19,500		55.00	55-65
1991 Davinci's Chambord	19,500		55.00	55-65
1991 Eilean Donan	19,500		55.00	55
1992 Eltz Castle	19,500		55.00	55
1992 Kylemore Abbey	19,500		55.00	55

Romantic Flights of Fancy - Q. Lemonds

YEAR ISSUE	EDITION LIMIT	YEAR RETD.	ISSUE PRICE	*QUOTE U.S.$
1994 Sunlit Waltz	28-day	N/A	29.50	30-45
1994 Morning Minuet	28-day	N/A	29.50	30-45
1994 Evening Solo	28-day	N/A	29.50	30-44
1994 Summer Sonata	28-day	N/A	29.50	30-44
1995 Twilight Tango	28-day	N/A	29.50	30-44
1995 Sunset Ballet	28-day	N/A	29.50	30-44
1995 Exotic Interlude	28-day	N/A	29.50	30-44
1995 Sunrise Samba	28-day	N/A	29.50	30-44

Romantic Victorian Keepsake - J. Grossman

YEAR ISSUE	EDITION LIMIT	YEAR RETD.	ISSUE PRICE	*QUOTE U.S.$
1992 Dearest Kiss	28-day	N/A	35.00	40-58
1992 First Love	28-day	N/A	35.00	52
1992 As Fair as a Rose	28-day	N/A	35.00	50
1992 Springtime Beauty	28-day	N/A	35.00	35-55
1992 Summertime Fancy	28-day	N/A	35.00	40-50
1992 Bonnie Blue Eyes	28-day	N/A	35.00	40-50
1992 Precious Friends	28-day	N/A	35.00	50
1994 Bonnets and Bouquets	28-day	N/A	35.00	35-55
1994 My Beloved Teddy	28-day	N/A	35.00	50
1994 A Sweet Romance	28-day	N/A	35.00	40-50

A Salute to Mickey Mantle - T. Fogarty

YEAR ISSUE	EDITION LIMIT	YEAR RETD.	ISSUE PRICE	*QUOTE U.S.$
1996 1961 Home Run Duel	28-day		35.00	35
1996 Power at the Plate	28-day		35.00	35
1996 Saluting a Magnificent Yankee	28-day		35.00	35
1996 Triple Crown Achievement	28-day		35.00	35

PLATES & PLAQUES

YEAR ISSUE	EDITION LIMIT	YEAR RETD.	ISSUE PRICE	*QUOTE U.S.$
1996 1953 Grand Slam	28-day		35.00	35
1997 1963's Famous Facade Homer	28-day		35.00	35
1997 Mickey as a Rookie	28-day		35.00	35
1997 A Look Back	28-day		35.00	35
Santa Takes a Break - T. Newsom				
1995 Santa's Last Stop	28-day		29.95	30
1995 Santa's Railroad	28-day		29.95	30-69
1995 A Jolly Good Catch	28-day		29.95	30
1995 Simple Pleasures	28-day		29.95	30
1996 Skating On Penquin Pond	28-day		29.95	30
1996 Santa's Sing Along	28-day		29.95	30
1996 Sledding Adventures	28-day		29.95	30
1996 Santa's Sweet Treats	28-day		29.95	30
The Saturday Evening Post - N. Rockwell				
1989 The Wonders of Radio	14-day		35.00	40-50
1989 Easter Morning	14-day		35.00	60-65
1989 The Facts of Life	14-day		35.00	35-45
1990 The Window Washer	14-day		35.00	45-50
1990 First Flight	14-day		35.00	54-60
1990 Traveling Companion	14-day		35.00	40-60
1990 Jury Room	14-day		35.00	40-50
1990 Furlough	14-day		35.00	40-55
Scenes of An American Christmas - B. Perry				
1994 I'll Be Home for Christmas	28-day		29.50	30-45
1994 Christmas Eve Worship	28-day		29.50	30-45
1994 A Holiday Happening	28-day		29.50	30-44
1994 A Long Winter's Night	28-day		29.50	30-44
1994 The Sounds of Christmas	28-day		29.50	30-45
1994 Dear Santa	28-day		29.50	30-45
1995 An Afternoon Outing	28-day		29.50	30-45
1995 Winter Worship	28-day		29.50	30-45
Seasons of the Bald Eagle - J. Pitcher				
1991 Autumn in the Mountains	14-day	N/A	37.50	40-63
1991 Winter in the Valley	14-day	N/A	37.50	55-80
1991 Spring on the River	14-day	N/A	37.50	40-63
1991 Summer on the Seacoast	14-day	N/A	37.50	40-70
Serenity at Sea - A. Jones				
1998 Sunset Ballet	N/A		39.95	40
1998 Peaceful Journey	N/A		39.95	40
1999 Graceful Duet	N/A		39.95	40
1999 Morning Majesty	N/A		39.95	40
1999 Sunset Splash	N/A		39.95	40
1999 Riding the Waves	N/A		39.95	40
1999 Journey Home	N/A		39.95	40
1999 Moonlight Splendor	N/A		39.95	40
Sharing Life's Most Precious Memories - S. Butcher				
1995 Thee I Love	28-day		35.00	35
1995 The Joy of the Lord Is My Strength	28-day		35.00	35
1995 May Your Every Wish Come True	28-day		35.00	35
1996 I'm So Glad That God	28-day		35.00	35
1996 Heaven Bless You	28-day		35.00	35
Sharing the Moments - S. Butcher				
1995 You Have Touched So Many Hearts	28-day		35.00	35
1996 Friendship Hits The Spot	28-day		35.00	35
1996 Jesus Love Me	28-day		35.00	35
Single Issues - T. Utz				
1983 Princess Grace	21-day		39.50	50-79
Small Wonders of the Wild - C. Frace				
1989 Hideaway	14-day		29.50	35-56
1990 Young Explorers	14-day		29.50	35-48
1990 Three of a Kind	14-day		29.50	40-62
1990 Quiet Morning	14-day		29.50	35-45
1990 Eyes of Wonder	14-day		29.50	35-45
1990 Ready for Adventure	14-day		29.50	35-45
1990 Uno	14-day		29.50	35-42
1990 Exploring a New World	14-day		29.50	35-45
Soaring Spirits Shield Collection - J. Pitcher				
1999 Majestic Sunrise	N/A		39.95	40
1999 Watchful Eye	N/A		39.95	40
1999 Royal Flight	N/A		39.95	40
1999 Riding the Wing	N/A		39.95	40

YEAR ISSUE	EDITION LIMIT	YEAR RETD.	ISSUE PRICE	*QUOTE U.S.$
Space, The Final Frontier - D. Ward				
1996 To Boldly Go...	28-day	1998	37.50	45-95
1996 Second Star From The Right	28-day	1998	37.50	40-85
1996 Signs of Intelligence	28-day	1998	37.50	40-59
1996 Preparing To Cloak	28-day	1998	37.50	40-65
1997 Distant Worlds	28-day	1998	37.50	40-60
1997 Where No One Has Gone Before	28-day	1998	37.50	40-62
1997 Beyond the Neutral Zone	28-day	1998	37.50	40-78
1997 We Are Borg	28-day	1998	37.50	40-45
1997 Cataloging Gascous Anomalies	28-day	1998	37.50	38
1997 Searching the Galaxy	28-day	1998	37.50	38
Spirit of the Mustang - C. DeHaan				
1995 Winter's Thunder	28-day	N/A	29.95	30-35
1995 Moonlit Run	28-day	N/A	29.95	30-35
1995 Morning Reverie	28-day	N/A	29.95	30-42
1995 Autumn Respite	28-day	N/A	29.95	35-40
1996 Spring Frolic	28-day	N/A	29.95	30-35
1996 Dueling Mustangs	28-day	N/A	29.95	35-48
1996 Tranquil Waters	28-day	N/A	29.95	30-35
1996 Summer Squall	28-day	N/A	29.95	30-40
Sporting Generation - J. Lamb				
1991 Like Father, Like Son	14-day	N/A	29.50	40-75
1991 Golden Moments	14-day	N/A	29.50	48
1991 The Lookout	14-day	N/A	29.50	40-48
1992 Picking Up The Scent	14-day	N/A	29.50	48
1992 First Time Out	14-day	N/A	29.50	42
1992 Who's Tracking Who	14-day	N/A	29.50	40-55
1992 Springing Into Action	14-day	N/A	29.50	35-55
1992 Point of Interest	14-day	N/A	29.50	35-55
STAR TREK® : 25th Anniversary Commemorative - T. Blackshear				
1991 STAR TREK 25th Anniversary Commemorative Plate	14-day	1998	37.50	250-325
1991 SPOCK	14-day	1998	35.00	95-225
1991 Kirk	14-day	1998	35.00	125-265
1992 McCoy	14-day	1998	35.00	40-90
1992 Uhura	14-day	1998	35.00	40-130
1992 Scotty	14-day	1998	35.00	40-90
1993 Sulu	14-day	1998	35.00	40-90
1993 Chekov	14-day	1998	35.00	40-90
1994 U.S.S. Enterprise NCC-1701	14-day	1998	35.00	40-125
STAR TREK® : 30 Years - T. Treadway				
1997 Captain's Tribute	28-day	1998	37.50	50-98
1997 Second in Command	28-day	1998	37.50	45-150
1997 Starfleet Doctors	28-day	1998	37.50	45-85
1998 Starfleet Navigators	28-day	1998	37.50	38-125
1998 Starfleet Security	28-day	1998	37.50	45-125
1998 Women of Star Trek	28-day	1998	37.50	50-125
1998 Engineers Tribute	28-day	1998	37.50	45-125
STAR TREK® : Captain James T. Kirk Autographed Wall Plaque - N/A				
1995 Captain James T. Kirk	5,000	N/A	195.00	195
STAR TREK® : Captain Jean-Luc Picard Autographed Wall Plaque - N/A				
1994 Captain Jean-Luc Picard	5,000	N/A	195.00	175-200
STAR TREK® : Deep Space 9 - M. Weistling				
1994 Commander Benjamin Sisko	28-day	1998	35.00	50-69
1994 Security Chief Odo	28-day	1998	35.00	50-68
1994 Major Kira Nerys	28-day	1998	35.00	75-92
1994 Space Station	28-day	1998	35.00	68-75
1994 Proprietor Quark	28-day	1998	35.00	50-68
1995 Doctor Julian Bashir	28-day	1998	35.00	50-68
1995 Lieutenant Jadzia Dax	28-day	1998	35.00	75-92
1995 Chief Miles O'Brien	28-day	1998	35.00	50-68
STAR TREK® : Deep Space 9 The Episodes - D. Blair				
1997 The Way of the Warrior	28-day	1998	39.95	40
1997 Emissary	28-day	1998	39.95	40
STAR TREK® : First Contact Sculptural Plate - J. Eaves				
1998 Maiden Voyage	28-day	N/A	49.95	50
1998 Resistance Is Futile	28-day	N/A	49.95	50
STAR TREK® : First Contact: A New Dimension - J. Eaves				
1998 Borg Cube	28-day	N/A	55.00	55
1998 U.S.S. Enterprise NCC-1701-E	28-day	N/A	55.00	55

STAR TREK® : First Contact: The Battle Begins - M. D. Ward

YEAR ISSUE	EDITION LIMIT	YEAR RETD.	ISSUE PRICE	*QUOTE U.S.$
1998 U.S.S. Defiant	28-day	N/A	39.95	40-50
1998 Borg Cube	28-day	N/A	39.95	40-50
1998 U.S.S. Enterprise NCC-1701-E	28-day	N/A	39.95	40-50
1998 Borg Sphere	28-day	N/A	39.95	40-150

STAR TREK® : First Contact: The Collective - K. Birdsong

YEAR ISSUE	EDITION LIMIT	YEAR RETD.	ISSUE PRICE	*QUOTE U.S.$
1998 Duty vs. Desire	Closed	1998	19.95	20
1998 The Borg are Back	Closed	1998	19.95	20
1998 Locutus of Borg	Closed	1998	19.95	20
1998 First Contact	Closed	1998	19.95	20
1998 Forward to the Past	Closed	1998	19.95	20
1998 Klingon Honor	Closed	1998	19.95	20
1998 Remember the Prime Directive	Closed	1998	19.95	20

STAR TREK® : First Contact: The Fourth Dimension - S. Wurmser

YEAR ISSUE	EDITION LIMIT	YEAR RETD.	ISSUE PRICE	*QUOTE U.S.$
1998 The Queen of the Hive	Closed	1998	45.00	45
1998 The Collective	Closed	1998	45.00	45

STAR TREK® : First Officer Spock® Autographed Wall Plaque - N/A

YEAR ISSUE	EDITION LIMIT	YEAR RETD.	ISSUE PRICE	*QUOTE U.S.$
1994 First Officer Spock®	2,500	N/A	195.00	195

STAR TREK® : Generations - K. Birdsong

YEAR ISSUE	EDITION LIMIT	YEAR RETD.	ISSUE PRICE	*QUOTE U.S.$
1996 The Ultimate Confrontation	28-day	1998	35.00	50-75
1996 Kirk's Final Voyage	28-day	1998	35.00	50-75
1996 Meeting In The Nexus	28-day	1998	35.00	50
1996 Picard's Christmas In The Nexus	28-day	1998	35.00	50
1996 Worf's Ceremony	28-day	1998	35.00	50
1996 The Final Plot/Duras Sisters	28-day	1998	35.00	50
1997 Stellar Cartography	28-day	1998	35.00	50
1997 Act of Courage	28-day	1998	35.00	50-82

STAR TREK® : Life of Spock - S. Stanley

YEAR ISSUE	EDITION LIMIT	YEAR RETD.	ISSUE PRICE	*QUOTE U.S.$
1997 Spock Reborn	28-day	1998	35.00	35-99
1997 Amok Time	28-day	1998	35.00	35-99
1997 Voyage Home	28-day	1998	35.00	35-49
1997 Wrath of Khan	28-day	1998	35.00	35-45
1997 Unification	28-day	1998	35.00	35-55

STAR TREK® : Ships in Motion - N/A

YEAR ISSUE	EDITION LIMIT	YEAR RETD.	ISSUE PRICE	*QUOTE U.S.$
1997 Full Impulse	Closed	1998	49.95	75-80
1997 Set a Course - Warp 5	Closed	1998	49.95	50-125
1997 Warp Speed	Closed	1998	49.95	50-59
1997 Maiden Voyage	Closed	1998	49.95	50-59

STAR TREK® : Starships Mini Plates - K. Birdsong

YEAR ISSUE	EDITION LIMIT	YEAR RETD.	ISSUE PRICE	*QUOTE U.S.$
1997 U.S.S. Enterprise NCC-1701	28-day	1998	25.90	26-35
1997 Klingon Battlecruiser	28-day	1998	set	32
1997 U.S.S. Enterprise NCC-1701 D	28-day	1998	set	32
1997 Romulan Warbird	28-day	1998	set	35
1997 U.S.S. Enterprise NCC-1701 A	28-day	1998	set	set
1997 Ferengei Marauder	28-day	1998	set	35
1997 Klingon Bird of Prey	28-day	1998	set	set
1997 Cardassian Galor Warship	28-day	1998	set	set
1997 Triple Nacelled U.S.S. Enterprise	28-day	1998	set	39
1997 U.S.S. Excelsior	28-day	1998	set	set
1997 U.S.S. Defiant NX-74205	28-day	1998	set	set
1997 U.S.S. Voyager NCC-74656	28-day	1998	set	set

STAR TREK® : The Movies - M. Weistling

YEAR ISSUE	EDITION LIMIT	YEAR RETD.	ISSUE PRICE	*QUOTE U.S.$
1994 STAR TREK IV: The Voyage Home	28-day	1998	35.00	75-90
1994 STAR TREK II: The Wrath of Khan	28-day	1998	35.00	75-92
1994 STAR TREK VI: The Undiscovered Country	28-day	1998	35.00	75-90
1995 STAR TREK III: The Search For Spock	28-day	1998	35.00	75-100
1995 STAR TREK V: The Final Frontier	28-day	1998	35.00	75
1996 Triumphant Return	28-day	1998	35.00	75
1996 Destruction of the Reliant	28-day	1998	35.00	75
1996 STAR TREK I: The Motion Picture	28-day	1998	35.00	75-85

STAR TREK® : The Next Generation - T. Blackshear

YEAR ISSUE	EDITION LIMIT	YEAR RETD.	ISSUE PRICE	*QUOTE U.S.$
1993 Captain Jean-Luc Picard	28-day	1998	35.00	100-180
1993 Commander William T. Riker	28-day	1998	35.00	75-130
1994 Lieutenant Commander Data	28-day	1998	35.00	75-120
1994 Lieutenant Worf	28-day	1998	35.00	75-125
1994 Counselor Deanna Troi	28-day	1998	35.00	75-120
1995 Dr. Beverly Crusher	28-day	1998	35.00	75-95
1995 Lieutenant Commander Laforge	28-day	1998	35.00	35-125
1996 Ensign W. Crusher	28-day	1998	35.00	35-95

STAR TREK® : The Next Generation 10th Anniversary Mini Plates - N/A

YEAR ISSUE	EDITION LIMIT	YEAR RETD.	ISSUE PRICE	*QUOTE U.S.$
1997 Captain Jean-Luc Picard	28-day	1998	25.90	30
1997 Commander William T. Riker	28-day	1998	set	75

STAR TREK® : The Next Generation 5th Anniversary - M. Weistling

YEAR ISSUE	EDITION LIMIT	YEAR RETD.	ISSUE PRICE	*QUOTE U.S.$
1997 Guinan	28-day	1998	35.00	55

STAR TREK® : The Next Generation Mini Plates - T. Blackshear/ K. Birdsong

YEAR ISSUE	EDITION LIMIT	YEAR RETD.	ISSUE PRICE	*QUOTE U.S.$
1997 Counselor Deanna Troi	28-day	1998	25.50	26
1997 Dr. Beverly Crusher	28-day	1998	set	set
1997 Lieutenant Commander Data	28-day	1998	set	set
1997 Lieutenant Worf	28-day	1998	set	set
1997 Best of Both Worlds	28-day	1998	set	set
1997 Encounter at Far Point	28-day	1998	set	set
1997 Lieutenant Commander Geordi Laforge	28-day	1998	set	set
1997 Ensign Wesley Crusher	28-day	1998	set	set
1997 All Good Things	28-day	1998	set	set
1997 Yesterday's Enterprise	28-day	1998	set	set

STAR TREK® : The Next Generation The Episodes - K. Birdsong

YEAR ISSUE	EDITION LIMIT	YEAR RETD.	ISSUE PRICE	*QUOTE U.S.$
1994 The Best of Both Worlds	28-day	1998	35.00	50-99
1994 Encounter at Far Point	28-day	1998	35.00	50-99
1995 Unification	28-day	1998	35.00	50-80
1995 Yesterday's Enterprise	28-day	1998	35.00	50-60
1995 All Good Things	28-day	1998	35.00	50-99
1995 Descent	28-day	1998	35.00	50-60
1996 Relics	28-day	1998	35.00	50-60
1996 Redemption	28-day	1998	35.00	50-60
1996 The Big Goodbye	28-day	1998	35.00	50-60
1996 The Inner Light	28-day	1998	35.00	50-60

STAR TREK® : The Original Episodes - J. Martin

YEAR ISSUE	EDITION LIMIT	YEAR RETD.	ISSUE PRICE	*QUOTE U.S.$
1996 The Tholian Web	28-day	1998	35.00	50-99
1996 Space Seed	28-day	1998	35.00	50
1996 The Menagerie	28-day	1998	35.00	50
1996 City on the Edge	28-day	1998	35.00	50
1996 Journel to Babel	28-day	1998	35.00	50
1996 Trouble With Tribbles	28-day	1998	35.00	50-65
1996 Where No Man Has Gone	28-day	1998	35.00	50-125
1996 Devil in the Dark	28-day	1998	35.00	50

STAR TREK® : The Power of Command - K. Birdsong

YEAR ISSUE	EDITION LIMIT	YEAR RETD.	ISSUE PRICE	*QUOTE U.S.$
1996 Captain Picard	28-day	1998	35.00	75-150
1996 Admiral Kirk	28-day	1998	35.00	75-120
1996 Captain Sisko	28-day	1998	35.00	50-110
1996 Captain Sulu	28-day	1998	35.00	50
1996 Janeway	28-day	1998	35.00	50-150
1996 Khan	28-day	1998	35.00	50
1996 General Chang	28-day	1998	35.00	50
1996 Dukat	28-day	1998	35.00	50-59
1997 Captain Kirk and the U.S.S. Enterprise NCC-1701	28-day	1998	35.00	75-125
1997 The Borg Queen and the Borg Sphere	28-day	1998	35.00	50-97

STAR TREK® : The Spock® Commemorative Wall Plaque - N/A

YEAR ISSUE	EDITION LIMIT	YEAR RETD.	ISSUE PRICE	*QUOTE U.S.$
1993 Spock®/STAR TREK VI The Undiscovered Country	2,500	N/A	195.00	195

STAR TREK® : The Voyagers - K. Birdsong

YEAR ISSUE	EDITION LIMIT	YEAR RETD.	ISSUE PRICE	*QUOTE U.S.$
1994 U.S.S. Enterprise NCC-1701	28-day	1998	35.00	50-120
1994 U.S.S. Enterprise NCC-1701-D	28-day	1998	35.00	50-120
1994 Klingon Battlecruiser	28-day	1998	35.00	50-95
1994 Romulan Warbird	28-day	1998	35.00	50-95
1994 U.S.S. Enterprise NCC-1701-A	28-day	1998	35.00	60-120
1995 Ferengi Marauder	28-day	1998	35.00	35-95
1995 Klingon Bird of Prey	28-day	1998	35.00	50-95
1995 Triple Nacelled U.S.S. Enterprise	28-day	1998	35.00	50-60
1995 Cardassian Galor Warship	28-day	1998	35.00	50-60
1995 U.S.S. Excelsior	28-day	1998	35.00	50-60

STAR TREK® : Voyager - D. Curry

YEAR ISSUE	EDITION LIMIT	YEAR RETD.	ISSUE PRICE	*QUOTE U.S.$
1996 The Voyage Begins	28-day	1998	35.00	50
1996 Bonds of Friendship	28-day	1998	35.00	50
1996 Life Signs	28-day	1998	35.00	50
1996 The Vidiians	28-day	1998	35.00	50
1997 New Beginnings	28-day	1998	35.00	50

YEAR ISSUE	EDITION LIMIT	YEAR RETD.	ISSUE PRICE	*QUOTE U.S.$
1997 Basics	28-day	1998	35.00	50

Star Wars 10th Anniversary Commemorative - T. Blackshear

1990 Star Wars 10th Anniversary Commemorative Plates	14-day	1998	39.50	175-200

Star Wars Heros and Villains - K. Birdsong

1997 Luke Skywalker	28-day	1999	35.00	35-169
1997 Han Solo	28-day	1999	35.00	35-175
1997 Darth Vader	28-day	1999	35.00	35-175
1997 Princess Leia	28-day	1999	35.00	35-125
1997 Obi-Wan Kenobi	28-day	1999	35.00	35-199
1998 Boba Fett	28-day	1999	35.00	35-199
1998 Yoda I	28-day	1999	35.00	35-195
1999 Emperor Palpatine	28-day	1999	35.00	35-195

Star Wars Heros and Villains - Treadway

1999 R2-D2	28-day	1999	35.00	35-49
1999 Chewbacca	28-day	1999	35.00	35-49
1999 Jabba the Hutt	28-day	1999	35.00	35-225
1999 Lando Calrissian	28-day	1999	35.00	35-355

Star Wars Plate Collection - T. Blackshear

1987 Hans Solo	14-day	1999	29.50	190-250
1987 R2-D2 and Wicket	14-day	1999	29.50	85-250
1987 Luke Skywalker and Darth Vader	14-day	1999	29.50	70-250
1987 Princess Leia	14-day	1999	29.50	130-275
1987 The Imperial Walkers	14-day	1999	29.50	105-200
1987 Luke and Yoda	14-day	1999	29.50	95-200
1988 Space Battle	14-day	1999	29.50	210-325
1988 Crew in Cockpit	14-day	1999	29.50	175-250

Star Wars Space Vehicles - S. Hillios

1995 Millenium Falcon	28-day	1999	35.00	46-75
1995 TIE Fighters	28-day	1999	35.00	50-65
1995 Red Five X-Wing Fighters	28-day	1999	35.00	50-65
1995 Imperial Shuttle	28-day	1999	35.00	50-65
1995 STAR Destroyer	28-day	1999	35.00	50-65
1996 Snow Speeders	28-day	1999	35.00	50-58
1996 B-Wing Fighter	28-day	1999	35.00	35-58
1996 The Slave I	28-day	1999	35.00	50-58
1996 Medical Frigate	28-day	1999	35.00	50-65
1996 Jabba's Sail Barge	28-day	1999	35.00	60-75
1997 Y-Wing Fighter	28-day	1999	35.00	50-69
1997 Death Star	28-day	1999	35.00	50-69

Star Wars Trilogy - M. Weistling

1993 Star Wars	28-day	N/A	37.50	115-250
1993 The Empire Strikes Back	28-day	N/A	37.50	115-255
1993 Return Of The Jedi	28-day	N/A	37.50	115-255

Starships of the Next Generation - B. Eggleton

1996 Engage	28-day	1998	39.95	85
1997 Enterprise of the Future	28-day	1998	39.95	40-75
1997 Resistance is Futile	28-day	1998	39.95	40-90
1997 All Good Things	28-day	1998	39.95	40-75
1997 Klingon Defense Force	28-day	1998	39.95	40-90
1997 Unexpected Confrontation	28-day	1998	39.95	40-95
1997 Searching the Galaxy	28-day	1998	39.95	40-75
1997 Shields Up	28-day	1998	39.95	40-75
1997 Yesterday's Enterprise	28-day	1998	39.95	40-75
1997 Earth's Last Stand	28-day	1998	39.95	40-75

Summer Days of Childhood - T. Utz

1983 Mountain Friends	10-day		29.50	30-50
1983 Garden Magic	10-day		29.50	30-50
1983 Little Beachcombers	10-day		29.50	30-50
1983 Blowing Bubbles	10-day		29.50	30-50
1983 Birthday Party	10-day		29.50	30-50
1983 Playing Doctor	10-day		29.50	30-50
1983 Stolen Kiss	10-day		29.50	30-50
1983 Kitty's Bathtime	10-day		29.50	30-50
1983 Cooling Off	10-day		29.50	30-50
1983 First Cucumber	10-day		29.50	30-50
1983 A Jumping Contest	10-day		29.50	30-50
1983 Balloon Carnival	10-day		29.50	30-50

Symphony of the Sea - R. Koni

1995 Fluid Grace	28-day		29.95	30-35
1995 Dolphin's Dance	28-day		29.95	30-35
1995 Orca Ballet	28-day		29.95	30-39
1995 Moonlit Minuet	28-day		29.95	30-39
1995 Sailfish Serenade	28-day		29.95	30-35

YEAR ISSUE	EDITION LIMIT	YEAR RETD.	ISSUE PRICE	*QUOTE U.S.$
1995 Starlit Waltz	28-day		29.95	30-35
1995 Sunset Splendor	28-day		29.95	30-35
1995 Coral Chorus	28-day		29.95	30-35

Those Delightful Dalmations - N/A

1995 You Missed a Spot	28-day		29.95	25-30
1995 Here's a Good Spot	28-day		29.95	25-30
1996 The Best Spot	28-day		29.95	25-30
1996 Spotted In the Headlines	28-day		29.95	25-30
1996 A Spot In My Heart	28-day		29.95	25-30
1996 Sweet Spots	28-day		29.95	25-30
1996 Naptime Already?	28-day		29.95	25-30
1996 He's In My Spot	28-day		29.95	25-30
1996 The Serious Studying Spot	28-day		29.95	25-30
1996 Check Out My Spots	28-day		29.95	25-30

Timeless Expressions of the Orient - M. Tsang

1990 Fidelity	15,000		75.00	95-100
1991 Femininity	15,000		75.00	75-80
1991 Longevity	15,000		75.00	75-80
1991 Beauty	15,000		55.00	55
1992 Courage	15,000		55.00	55-60

Treasured Days - H. Bond

1987 Ashley	14-day		29.50	70-90
1987 Christopher	14-day		24.50	35-50
1987 Sara	14-day		24.50	35-45
1987 Jeremy	14-day		24.50	29-50
1987 Amanda	14-day		24.50	35-50
1988 Nicholas	14-day		24.50	40-50
1988 Lindsay	14-day		24.50	29-50
1988 Justin	14-day		24.50	40-50

A Treasury of Cherished Teddies - P. Hillman

1994 Happy Holidays, Friend	28-day		29.50	30
1995 A New Year with Old Friends	28-day		29.50	30
1995 Valentines For You	28-day		29.50	30
1995 Friendship is in the Air	28-day		29.50	30
1995 Showers of Friendship	28-day		29.50	30
1996 Friendship is in Bloom	28-day		29.50	30
1996 Planting the Seeds of Friendship	28-day		29.50	30
1996 A Day in the Park	28-day		29.50	30
1996 Smooth Sailing	28-day		29.50	30
1996 School Days	28-day		29.50	30
1996 Holiday Harvest	28-day		29.50	30
1996 Thanks For Friends	28-day		29.50	30

Unbridled Spirit - C. DeHaan

1992 Surf Dancer	28-day	N/A	29.50	30-45
1992 Winter Renegade	28-day	N/A	29.50	30-50
1992 Desert Shadows	28-day	N/A	29.50	30-45
1993 Painted Sunrise	28-day	N/A	29.50	30-50
1993 Desert Duel	28-day	N/A	29.50	30-40
1993 Midnight Run	28-day	N/A	29.50	30-45
1993 Moonlight Majesty	28-day	N/A	29.50	30-45
1993 Autumn Reverie	28-day	N/A	29.50	30-39
1993 Blizzard's Peril	28-day	N/A	29.50	30-50
1993 Sunrise Surprise	28-day	N/A	29.50	30-40

Under the Sea - C. Bragg

1993 Tales of Tavarua	28-day	N/A	29.50	40-48
1993 Water's Edge	28-day	N/A	29.50	40-45
1994 Beauty of the Reef	28-day	N/A	29.50	40-45
1994 Rainbow Reef	28-day	N/A	29.50	40-45
1994 Orca Odyssey	28-day	N/A	29.50	30-40
1994 Rescue the Reef	28-day	N/A	29.50	36-40
1994 Underwater Dance	28-day	N/A	29.50	36-40
1994 Gentle Giants	28-day	N/A	29.50	30-40
1995 Undersea Enchantment	28-day	N/A	29.50	30-40
1995 Penguin Paradise	28-day	N/A	29.50	30-40

Undersea Visions - J. Enright

1995 Secret Sanctuary	28-day	N/A	29.95	30-45
1995 Temple of Treasures	28-day	N/A	29.95	40-45
1996 Temple Beneath the Sea	28-day	N/A	29.95	40-45
1996 Lost Kingdom	28-day	N/A	29.95	30-40
1996 Mysterious Ruins	28-day	N/A	29.95	30-40
1996 Last Journey	28-day	N/A	29.95	30-40
1996 Egyptian Dreamscape	28-day	N/A	29.95	30-40
1996 Lost Galleon	28-day	N/A	29.95	30-40

Unity of Spirits - R. Alfredo

2000 The Farewell	Open		39.95	40

YEAR ISSUE	EDITION LIMIT	YEAR RETD.	ISSUE PRICE	*QUOTE U.S.$
Utz Mother's Day - T. Utz				
1983 A Gift of Love	N/A		27.50	35-38
1983 Mother's Helping Hand	N/A		27.50	28-35
1983 Mother's Angel	N/A		27.50	28-35
Vanishing Rural America - J. Harrison				
1991 Quiet Reflections	14-day		29.50	40-50
1991 Autumn's Passage	14-day		29.50	40-50
1991 Storefront Memories	14-day		29.50	30-50
1991 Country Path	14-day		29.50	36-40
1991 When the Circus Came To Town	14-day		29.50	36-40
1991 Covered in Fall	14-day		29.50	40-50
1991 America's Heartland	14-day		29.50	33-40
1991 Rural Delivery	14-day		29.50	33-40
Victorian Christmas Memories - J. Grossman				
1992 A Visit from St. Nicholas	28-day		29.50	35-42
1993 Christmas Delivery	28-day		29.50	40-51
1993 Christmas Angels	28-day		29.50	30-35
1992 With Visions of Sugar Plums	28-day		29.50	30-65
1993 Merry Olde Kris Kringle	28-day		29.50	35-65
1993 Grandfather Frost	28-day		29.50	30-35
1993 Joyous Noel	28-day		29.50	35-45
1993 Christmas Innocence	28-day		29.50	35-80
1993 Dreaming of Santa	28-day		29.50	40
1993 Mistletoe & Holly	28-day		29.50	35-40
Victorian Playtime - M. H. Bogart				
1991 A Busy Day	14-day		29.50	45-65
1992 Little Masterpiece	14-day		29.50	45-65
1992 Playing Bride	14-day		29.50	85-90
1992 Waiting for a Nibble	14-day		29.50	45-65
1992 Tea and Gossip	14-day		29.50	55-65
1992 Cleaning House	14-day		29.50	45-65
1992 A Little Persuasion	14-day		29.50	45-65
1992 Peek-a-Boo	14-day		29.50	45-65
Voyages of the Starship Enterprise - K. Birdsong				
1997 NCC-1701-E	Closed	N/A	24.95	50
1997 NCC-1701-D	Closed	N/A	24.95	50
1997 NCC-1701-Refit	Closed	N/A	24.95	50
1997 NCC-1701	Closed	N/A	24.95	50
Warrior's Pride - C. DeHaan				
1994 Crow War Pony	28-day	N/A	29.50	30-40
1994 Running Free	28-day	N/A	29.50	30-40
1994 Blackfoot War Pony	28-day	N/A	29.50	30-40
1994 Southern Cheyenne	28-day	N/A	29.50	30-40
1995 Shoshoni War Ponies	28-day	N/A	29.50	30-45
1995 A Champion's Revelry	28-day	N/A	29.50	30-45
1995 Battle Colors	28-day	N/A	29.50	30-45
1995 Call of the Drums	28-day	N/A	29.50	30-45
WCW Sting Plate Collection - N/A				
1998 Sting	Open		35.00	35
1998 The Stinger!	Open		35.00	35
1998 The White Knight	Open		35.00	35
1998 Mystery Man	Open		35.00	35
The West of Frank McCarthy - F. McCarthy				
1991 Attacking the Iron Horse	14-day	N/A	37.50	60-65
1991 Attempt on the Stage	14-day	N/A	37.50	45-55
1991 The Prayer	14-day	N/A	37.50	55
1991 On the Old North Trail	14-day	N/A	37.50	50-55
1991 The Hostile Threat	14-day	N/A	37.50	45-50
1991 Bringing Out the Furs	14-day	N/A	37.50	45-50
1991 Kiowa Raider	14-day	N/A	37.50	45-50
1991 Headed North	14-day	N/A	37.50	39-45
Wilderness Spirits - P. Koni				
1994 Eyes of the Night	28-day		29.95	30
1995 Howl of Innocence	28-day		29.95	30
1995 Midnight Call	28-day		29.95	30
1995 Breaking the Silence	28-day		29.95	30
1995 Moonlight Run	28-day		29.95	30
1995 Sunset Vigil	28-day		29.95	30
1995 Sunrise Spirit	28-day		29.95	30
1996 Valley of the Wolf	28-day		29.95	30
Winged Reflections - R. Parker				
1989 Following Mama	14-day		37.50	38
1989 Above the Breakers	14-day		37.50	38
1989 Among the Reeds	14-day		37.50	38

YEAR ISSUE	EDITION LIMIT	YEAR RETD.	ISSUE PRICE	*QUOTE U.S.$
1989 Freeze Up	14-day		37.50	38
1989 Wings Above the Water	14-day		37.50	38
1990 Summer Loon	14-day		29.50	30
1990 Early Spring	14-day		29.50	30
1990 At The Water's Edge	14-day		29.50	30
Wings of Freedom - S. Hardock				
1999 Coming Home	28-day		39.95	40
1999 Noble Watch	28-day		39.95	40
1999 Glorious Flight	28-day		39.95	40
1999 Regal Sanctuary	28-day		39.95	40
2000 Windswept Return	28-day		39.95	40
Winter Rails - T. Xaras				
1992 Winter Crossing	28-day		29.50	40-45
1993 Coal Country	28-day		29.50	30-65
1993 Daylight Run	28-day		29.50	30-65
1993 By Sea or Rail	28-day		29.50	30-65
1993 Country Crossroads	28-day		29.50	30-65
1993 Timber Line	28-day		29.50	60
1993 The Long Haul	28-day		29.50	30-65
1993 Darby Crossing	28-day		29.50	30-65
1995 East Broad Top	28-day		29.50	30-65
1995 Landsdowne Station	28-day		29.50	30-65
Winter Wildlife - J. Seerey-Lester				
1989 Close Encounters	15,000		55.00	55-60
1989 Among the Cattails	15,000		55.00	55-60
1989 The Refuge	15,000		55.00	55-60
1989 Out of the Blizzard	15,000		55.00	55-60
1989 First Snow	15,000		55.00	55-60
1989 Lying In Wait	15,000		55.00	55-60
1989 Winter Hiding	15,000		55.00	55-60
1989 Early Snow	15,000		55.00	55-60
Wizard of Oz Commemorative - T. Blackshear				
1988 We're Off to See the Wizard	14-day		24.50	150-215
1988 Dorothy Meets the Scarecrow	14-day		24.50	150-210
1989 The Tin Man Speaks	14-day		24.50	90-210
1989 A Glimpse of the Munchkins	14-day		24.50	150-200
1989 The Witch Casts A Spell	14-day		24.50	150-250
1989 If I Were King Of The Forest	14-day		24.50	125-200
1989 The Great and Powerful Oz	14-day		24.50	150-200
1989 There's No Place Like Home	14-day		24.50	150-250
Wizard of Oz-Fifty Years of Oz - T. Blackshear				
1989 Fifty Years of Oz	14-day		37.50	175-300
Wizard of Oz-Portraits From Oz - T. Blackshear				
1989 Dorothy	14-day		29.50	160-325
1989 Scarecrow	14-day		29.50	140-265
1989 Tin Man	14-day		29.50	130-249
1990 Cowardly Lion	14-day		29.50	135-249
1990 Glinda	14-day		29.50	150-270
1990 Wizard	14-day		29.50	110-225
1990 Wicked Witch	14-day		29.50	175-290
1990 Toto	14-day		29.50	225-350
The Wonder Of Christmas - J. McClelland				
1991 Santa's Secret	28-day		29.50	30
1991 My Favorite Ornament	28-day		29.50	30
1991 Waiting For Santa	28-day		29.50	30
1993 The Caroler	28-day		29.50	30
A World of Puppy Adventures - J. Ren				
1995 The Water's Fine	28-day		29.95	30-55
1996 Swimming Lessons	28-day		29.95	30
1996 Breakfast Is Served	28-day		29.95	30
1996 Laundry Tug O' War	28-day		29.95	30
1996 Did I Do That?	28-day		29.95	30
1996 DeCoy Dismay	28-day		29.95	30
1996 Puppy Picnic	28-day		29.95	30
1996 Sweet Terrors	28-day		29.95	30
The World Of Zolan - D. Zolan				
1992 First Kiss	28-day		29.50	30-110
1992 Morning Discovery	28-day		29.50	30-95
1993 The Little Fisherman	28-day		29.50	30-75
1993 Letter to Grandma	28-day		29.50	30-85
1993 Twilight Prayer	28-day		29.50	30-85
1993 Flowers for Mother	28-day		29.50	55-80

YEAR ISSUE	EDITION LIMIT	YEAR RETD.	ISSUE PRICE	*QUOTE U.S.$

Year Of The Wolf - A. Agnew

Year Issue	Edition Limit	Yr Retd	Issue Price	Quote
1993 Broken Silence	28-day		29.50	30-55
1993 Leader of the Pack	28-day		29.50	30-40
1993 Solitude	28-day		29.50	30-40
1994 Tundra Light	28-day		29.50	30-40
1994 Guardians of the High Country	28-day		29.50	30-40
1994 Free as the Wind	28-day		29.50	27-55
1994 Song of the Wolf	28-day		29.50	30-35
1995 Lords of the Tundra	28-day		29.50	30-40
1995 Wilderness Companions	28-day		29.50	30-45

Young Lords of The Wild - M. Richter

Year Issue	Edition Limit	Yr Retd	Issue Price	Quote
1994 Siberian Tiger Club	28-day		29.95	30-45
1995 Snow Leopard Cub	28-day		29.95	30-45
1995 Lion Cub	28-day		29.95	30
1995 Clouded Leopard Cub	28-day		29.95	30
1995 Cougar Cub	28-day		29.95	30
1995 Leopard Cub	28-day		29.95	30
1995 Cheetah Cub	28-day		29.95	30
1996 Canadian Lynx Cub	28-day		29.95	30

Hamilton/Boehm

Award Winning Roses - Boehm

Year Issue	Edition Limit	Yr Retd	Issue Price	Quote
1979 Peace Rose	15,000		45.00	100
1979 White Masterpiece Rose	15,000		45.00	75
1979 Tropicana Rose	15,000		45.00	63
1979 Elegance Rose	15,000		45.00	63
1979 Queen Elizabeth Rose	15,000		45.00	63
1979 Royal Highness Rose	15,000		45.00	63
1979 Angel Face Rose	15,000		45.00	63
1979 Mr. Lincoln Rose	15,000		45.00	63

Gamebirds of North America - Boehm

Year Issue	Edition Limit	Yr Retd	Issue Price	Quote
1984 Ring-Necked Pheasant	15,000		62.50	63
1984 Bob White Quail	15,000		62.50	63
1984 American Woodcock	15,000		62.50	63
1984 California Quail	15,000		62.50	63
1984 Ruffed Grouse	15,000		62.50	63
1984 Wild Turkey	15,000		62.50	63
1984 Willow Partridge	15,000		62.50	63
1984 Prairie Grouse	15,000		62.50	63

Hummingbird Collection - Boehm

Year Issue	Edition Limit	Yr Retd	Issue Price	Quote
1980 Calliope	15,000		62.50	80
1980 Broadbilled	15,000		62.50	63
1980 Rufous Flame Bearer	15,000		62.50	80
1980 Broadtail	15,000		62.50	63
1980 Streamertail	15,000		62.50	80
1980 Blue Throated	15,000		62.50	80
1980 Crimson Topaz	15,000		62.50	63
1980 Brazilian Ruby	15,000		62.50	80

Owl Collection - Boehm

Year Issue	Edition Limit	Yr Retd	Issue Price	Quote
1980 Boreal Owl	15,000		45.00	95
1980 Snowy Owl	15,000		45.00	95
1980 Barn Owl	15,000		45.00	80
1980 Saw Whet Owl	15,000		45.00	75
1980 Great Horned Owl	15,000		45.00	60-75
1980 Screech Owl	15,000		45.00	75
1980 Short Eared Owl	15,000		45.00	75
1980 Barred Owl	15,000		45.00	60-75

Water Birds - Boehm

Year Issue	Edition Limit	Yr Retd	Issue Price	Quote
1981 Canada Geese	15,000		62.50	65
1981 Wood Ducks	15,000		62.50	65
1981 Hooded Merganser	15,000		62.50	65
1981 Ross's Geese	15,000		62.50	65
1981 Common Mallard	15,000		62.50	65
1981 Canvas Back	15,000		62.50	65
1981 Green Winged Teal	15,000		62.50	65
1981 American Pintail	15,000		62.50	65

Imperial Ching-te Chen

Beauties of the Red Mansion - Z. HuiMin

Year Issue	Edition Limit	Yr Retd	Issue Price	Quote
1986 Pao-chai	115-day		27.92	12-30
1986 Yuan-chun	115-day		27.92	14-30
1987 Hsi-feng	115-day		30.92	15-35
1987 Hsi-chun	115-day		30.92	15-35

Year Issue	Edition Limit	Yr Retd	Issue Price	Quote
1988 Miao-yu	115-day		30.92	15-35
1988 Ying-chun	115-day		30.92	15-35
1988 Tai-yu	115-day		32.92	21-35
1988 Li-wan	115-day		32.92	21-35
1988 Ko-Ching	115-day		32.92	24-35
1988 Hsiang-yun	115-day		34.92	24-35
1989 Tan-Chun	115-day		34.92	24-35
1989 Chiao-chieh	115-day		34.92	15-35

Blessings From a Chinese Garden - Z. Song Mao

Year Issue	Edition Limit	Yr Retd	Issue Price	Quote
1988 The Gift of Purity	175-day		39.92	19-40
1989 The Gift of Grace	175-day		39.92	20-40
1989 The Gift of Beauty	175-day		42.92	17-43
1989 The Gift of Happiness	175-day		42.92	28-43
1990 The Gift of Truth	175-day		42.92	35
1990 The Gift of Joy	175-day		42.92	23-30

Flower Goddesses of China - Z. HuiMin

Year Issue	Edition Limit	Yr Retd	Issue Price	Quote
1991 The Lotus Goddess	175-day		34.92	15-35
1991 The Chrysanthemum Goddess	175-day		34.92	19-35
1991 The Plum Blossom Goddess	175-day		37.92	27-38
1991 The Peony Goddess	175-day		37.92	25-38
1991 The Narcissus Goddess	175-day		37.92	37-50
1991 The Camellia Goddess	175-day		37.92	26-38

The Forbidden City - S. Fu

Year Issue	Edition Limit	Yr Retd	Issue Price	Quote
1990 Pavilion of 10,000 Springs	150-day		39.92	10-40
1990 Flying Kites/Spring Day	150-day		39.92	25-40
1990 Pavilion/Floating Jade Green	150-day		42.92	21-43
1991 The Lantern Festival	150-day		42.92	17-43
1991 Nine Dragon Screen	150-day		42.92	18-43
1991 The Hall of the Cultivating Mind	150-day		42.92	22-43
1991 Dressing the Empress	150-day		45.92	33-46
1991 Pavilion of Floating Cups	150-day		45.92	30-46

Garden of Satin Wings - J. Xue-Bing

Year Issue	Edition Limit	Yr Retd	Issue Price	Quote
1992 A Morning Dream	115-day		29.92	30-35
1993 An Evening Mist	115-day		29.92	28-36
1993 A Garden Whisper	115-day		29.92	36-40
1993 An Enchanting Interlude	115-day		29.92	34-40

Legends of West Lake - J. Xue-Bing

Year Issue	Edition Limit	Yr Retd	Issue Price	Quote
1989 Lady White	175-day		29.92	19-30
1990 Lady Silkworm	175-day		29.92	29-50
1990 Laurel Peak	175-day		29.92	32
1990 Rising Sun Terrace	175-day		32.92	15-33
1990 The Apricot Fairy	175-day		32.92	17-33
1990 Bright Pearl	175-day		32.92	14-35
1990 Thread of Sky	175-day		34.92	17-35
1991 Phoenix Mountain	175-day		34.92	18-35
1991 Ancestors of Tea	175-day		36.92	23-37
1991 Three Pools Mirroring/Moon	175-day		36.92	23-40
1991 Fly-In Peak	175-day		36.92	40-48
1991 The Case of the Folding Fans	175-day			

Maidens of the Folding Sky - J. Xue-Bing

Year Issue	Edition Limit	Yr Retd	Issue Price	Quote
1992 Lady Lu	175-day		29.92	34-38
1992 Mistress Yang	175-day		29.92	35-58
1992 Bride Yen Chun	175-day		32.92	40-65
1993 Parrot Maiden	175-day		32.92	70

Scenes from the Summer Palace - Z. Song Mao

Year Issue	Edition Limit	Yr Retd	Issue Price	Quote
1988 The Marble Boat	175-day		29.92	12-35
1988 Jade Belt Bridge	175-day		29.92	15-35
1989 Hall that Dispels the Clouds	175-day		32.92	25-33
1989 The Long Promenade	175-day		32.92	20-39
1989 Garden/Harmonious Pleasure	175-day		32.92	23-33
1989 The Great Stage	175-day		32.92	26-33
1989 Seventeen Arch Bridge	175-day		34.92	18-35
1989 Boaters on Kumming Lake	175-day		34.92	16-35

Lalique Society of America

Annual - M. Lalique

Year Issue	Edition Limit	Yr Retd	Issue Price	Quote
1965 Deux Oiseaux (Two Birds)	2,000		25.00	1250
1966 Rose de Songerie (Dream Rose)	5,000		25.00	75
1967 Ballet de Poisson (Fish Ballet)	5,000		25.00	95
1968 Gazelle Fantaisie (Gazelle Fantasy)	5,000		25.00	67-75
1969 Papillon (Butterfly)	5,000		30.00	50-55
1970 Paon (Peacock)	5,000		30.00	70
1971 Hibou (Owl)	5,000		35.00	50-75
1972 Coquillage (Shell)	5,000		40.00	73-75

YEAR ISSUE	EDITION LIMIT	YEAR RETD.	ISSUE PRICE	*QUOTE U.S.$
1973 Petit Geai (Jayling)	5,000		42.50	100
1974 Sous d'Argent (Silver Pennies)	5,000		47.50	95
1975 Duo de Poisson (Fish Duet)	5,000		50.00	139
1976 Aigle (Eagle)	5,000		60.00	87-100

Lenox China

Colonial Christmas Wreath - Unknown

YEAR ISSUE	EDITION LIMIT	YEAR RETD.	ISSUE PRICE	*QUOTE U.S.$
1981 Colonial Virginia	Yr.Iss.	1982	65.00	76-110
1982 Massachusetts	Yr.Iss.	1983	70.00	93
1983 Maryland	Yr.Iss.	1984	70.00	135-185
1984 Rhode Island	Yr.Iss.	1985	70.00	82
1985 Connecticut	Yr.Iss.	1986	70.00	75-95
1986 New Hampshire	Yr.Iss.	1987	70.00	75
1987 Pennsylvania	Yr.Iss.	1988	70.00	75
1988 Delaware	Yr.Iss.	1989	70.00	140-155
1989 New York	Yr.Iss.	1990	75.00	155
1990 New Jersey	Yr.Iss.	1991	75.00	78
1991 South Carolina	Yr.Iss.	1992	75.00	75
1992 North Carolina	Yr.Iss.	1993	75.00	155
1993 Georgia	Yr.Iss.	1994	75.00	155

Lenox Collections

Boehm Birds - E. Boehm

YEAR ISSUE	EDITION LIMIT	YEAR RETD.	ISSUE PRICE	*QUOTE U.S.$
1970 Wood Thrush	Yr.Iss.	1970	35.00	94-130
1971 Goldfinch	Yr.Iss.	1971	35.00	35-50
1972 Mountain Bluebird	Yr.Iss.	1972	37.50	40-50
1973 Meadowlark	Yr.Iss.	1973	50.00	24-45
1974 Rufous Hummingbird	Yr.Iss.	1974	45.00	39-68
1975 American Redstart	Yr.Iss.	1975	50.00	27-50
1976 Cardinals	Yr.Iss.	1976	53.00	39
1977 Robins	Yr.Iss.	1977	55.00	39-49
1978 Mockingbirds	Yr.Iss.	1978	58.00	35-55
1979 Golden-Crowned Kinglets	Yr.Iss.	1979	65.00	73-90
1980 Black-Throated Blue Warblers	Yr.Iss.	1980	80.00	75-90
1981 Eastern Phoebes	Yr.Iss.	1981	92.50	80

Boehm Woodland Wildlife - E. Boehm

YEAR ISSUE	EDITION LIMIT	YEAR RETD.	ISSUE PRICE	*QUOTE U.S.$
1973 Racoons	Yr.Iss.	1973	50.00	75
1974 Red Foxes	Yr.Iss.	1974	52.50	70-75
1975 Cottontail Rabbits	Yr.Iss.	1975	58.50	60-75
1976 Eastern Chipmunks	Yr.Iss.	1976	62.50	75
1977 Beaver	Yr.Iss.	1977	67.50	75
1978 Whitetail Deer	Yr.Iss.	1978	70.00	60-75
1979 Squirrels	Yr.Iss.	1979	76.00	46-75
1980 Bobcats	Yr.Iss.	1980	82.50	83
1981 Martens	Yr.Iss.	1981	100.00	100
1982 River Otters	Yr.Iss.	1982	100.00	100

Lightpost Publishing

Kinkade-Thomas Kinkade Signature Collection - T. Kinkade

YEAR ISSUE	EDITION LIMIT	YEAR RETD.	ISSUE PRICE	*QUOTE U.S.$
1991 Cedar Nook	2,500		49.95	50-75
1991 Chandler's Cottage	2,500		49.95	50-75
1991 Home to Grandma's	2,500		49.95	50-75
1991 Sleigh Ride Home	2,500		49.95	50-75

Little Angel Publishing

All God's Treasures - D. Gelsinger

YEAR ISSUE	EDITION LIMIT	YEAR RETD.	ISSUE PRICE	*QUOTE U.S.$
1999 All Things Bright and Beautiful	95-day		39.95	40
1999 All Creatures Great and Small	95-day		39.95	40
1999 All Things Wise and Wonderful	95-day		39.95	40
1999 The Lord God Made Them All	95-day		39.95	40

An Angel's Light - D. Gelsinger

YEAR ISSUE	EDITION LIMIT	YEAR RETD.	ISSUE PRICE	*QUOTE U.S.$
1998 A Little Hope Lights the Way	95-day		29.95	30
1998 A Little Love Lights The Heart	95-day		29.95	30
1998 A Little Faith Shines From Within	95-day		29.95	30
1998 A Little Kindness Shines Through	95-day		29.95	30
1998 A Little Joy Lights Your World	95-day		29.95	30
1999 A Little Tenderness Enlightens The Soul	95-day		29.95	30
1999 A Little Harmony Lights The Day	95-day		29.95	30
1999 A Little Joy Shines Within	95-day		29.95	30

Christmas Blessings - D. Gelsinger

YEAR ISSUE	EDITION LIMIT	YEAR RETD.	ISSUE PRICE	*QUOTE U.S.$
2001 Silent Night, Gentle Night	95-day		29.95	30
2001 Season of Giving	95-day		29.95	30
2001 Gift of Peace	95-day		29.95	30
2001 Evening's Light	95-day		29.95	30

Garden Blessings - D. Gelsinger

YEAR ISSUE	EDITION LIMIT	YEAR RETD.	ISSUE PRICE	*QUOTE U.S.$
1996 An Angel's Touch	95-day		29.95	30
1996 An Angel's Guidance	95-day		29.95	30
1996 An Angel's Gift	95-day		29.95	30
1996 An Angel's Care	95-day		29.95	30
1996 An Angel's Warmth	95-day		29.95	30
1997 An Angel's Spirit	95-day		29.95	30
1997 An Angel's Tenderness	95-day		29.95	30
1997 An Angel's Grace	95-day		29.95	30
1997 An Angel's Gentleness	95-day		29.95	30
1997 An Angel's Love	95-day		29.95	30

Nature's Heavenly Guardians - D. Gelsinger

YEAR ISSUE	EDITION LIMIT	YEAR RETD.	ISSUE PRICE	*QUOTE U.S.$
1997 Gentle Guidance	95-day		29.95	30
1997 A Wondrous Discovery	95-day		29.95	30
1997 Making New Friends	95-day		29.95	30
1997 A Gift of Love	95-day		29.95	30

Our Loving Guardians - D. Gelsinger

YEAR ISSUE	EDITION LIMIT	YEAR RETD.	ISSUE PRICE	*QUOTE U.S.$
1998 Someone to Guide The Way	95-day		39.95	40
1998 Her Perpetual Embrace	95-day		39.95	40
1999 Her Blessed Gift	95-day		39.95	40
1999 Heaven's Helping Hand	95-day		39.95	40
1999 Heaven's Little Wonders	95-day		39.95	40
1999 Her Bountiful Blessing	95-day		39.95	40
2000 Heaven's Eternal Gifts	95-day		39.95	40
2000 Heaven's Guiding Guardians	95-day		39.95	40

Prayers For Little Hearts - D. Gelsinger

YEAR ISSUE	EDITION LIMIT	YEAR RETD.	ISSUE PRICE	*QUOTE U.S.$
2000 Joyful in Hope	95-day		29.95	30
2000 Believe and You Will Receive	95-day		29.95	30
2000 The Eyes of Your Heart	95-day		29.95	30
2000 Faith is Certain	95-day		29.95	30

Lladró

Lladró Plate Collection - Lladró

YEAR ISSUE	EDITION LIMIT	YEAR RETD.	ISSUE PRICE	*QUOTE U.S.$
1993 The Great Voyage L5964G	Closed	1995	50.00	50
1993 Looking Out L5998G	Closed	1998	38.00	38
1993 Swinging L5999G	Closed	1998	38.00	38
1993 Duck Plate L6000G	Closed	1998	38.00	35-38
1994 Friends L6158	Closed	1998	32.00	32
1994 Apple Picking L6159M	Closed	1998	32.00	32
1994 Turtledove L6160	Closed	1998	32.00	32
1994 Flamingo L6161M	Closed	1998	32.00	32

March of Dimes

Our Children, Our Future - Various

YEAR ISSUE	EDITION LIMIT	YEAR RETD.	ISSUE PRICE	*QUOTE U.S.$
1989 A Time for Peace - D. Zolan	150-day		29.00	10-15
1989 A Time To Love - S. Kuck	150-day		29.00	30
1989 A Time To Plant - J. McClelland	150-day		29.00	12-29
1989 A Time To Be Born - G. Perillo	150-day		29.00	15-29
1990 A Time To Embrace - E. Hibel	150-day		29.00	22-35
1990 A Time To Laugh - A. Williams	150-day		29.00	14-29

Marigold

Sport - Carreno

YEAR ISSUE	EDITION LIMIT	YEAR RETD.	ISSUE PRICE	*QUOTE U.S.$
1983 Mickey Mantle-handsigned	1,000		100.00	695-895
1983 Mickey Mantle-unsigned	1,000		60.00	195
1984 Joe DiMaggio-handsigned	325		100.00	1495-1795
1984 Joe DiMaggio f/s (blue sig.)	10,000		60.00	250
1984 Joe DiMaggio AP-handsigned	25		N/A	2900-3900

Memories of Yesterday/Enesco Group, Inc.

Dated Plate Series - Various

YEAR ISSUE	EDITION LIMIT	YEAR RETD.	ISSUE PRICE	*QUOTE U.S.$
1993 Look Out-Something Good Is Coming Your Way! 530298 - S. Butcher	Yr.Iss.	1993	50.00	50
1994 Pleasant Dreams and Sweet Repose 528102 - M. Atwell	Yr.Iss.	1994	50.00	50
1995 Join Me For a Little Song 134880 - M. Attwell	Yr.Iss.	1995	50.00	50

Museum Collections, Inc.

American Family I - N. Rockwell

YEAR ISSUE	EDITION LIMIT	YEAR RETD.	ISSUE PRICE	*QUOTE U.S.$
1979 Baby's First Step	9,900		28.50	48

PLATES & PLAQUES

YEAR ISSUE	EDITION LIMIT	YEAR RETD.	ISSUE PRICE	*QUOTE U.S.$
1979 Happy Birthday Dear Mother	9,900		28.50	45
1979 Sweet Sixteen	9,900		28.50	35-45
1979 First Haircut	9,900		28.50	45
1979 First Prom	9,900		28.50	35
1979 Wrapping Christmas Presents	9,900		28.50	35
1979 The Student	9,900		28.50	35
1979 Birthday Party	9,900		28.50	35-45
1979 Little Mother	9,900		28.50	35
1979 Washing Our Dog	9,900		28.50	45
1979 Mother's Little Helpers	9,900		28.50	45
1979 Bride and Groom	9,900		28.50	35

American Family II - N. Rockwell

1980 New Arrival	22,500		35.00	45-50
1980 Sweet Dreams	22,500		35.00	38-45
1980 Little Shaver	22,500		35.00	40
1980 We Missed You Daddy	22,500		35.00	38-45
1980 Home Run Slugger	22,500		35.00	45
1980 Giving Thanks	22,500		35.00	55
1980 Space Pioneers	22,500		35.00	35
1980 Little Salesman	22,500		35.00	45
1980 Almost Grown up	22,500		35.00	45
1980 Courageous Hero	22,500		35.00	38-45
1981 At the Circus	22,500		35.00	38
1981 Good Food, Good Friends	22,500		35.00	38-45

Christmas - N. Rockwell

1979 Day After Christmas	Yr.Iss		75.00	75
1980 Checking His List	Yr.Iss		75.00	75
1981 Ringing in Good Cheer	Yr.Iss		75.00	75
1982 Waiting for Santa	Yr.Iss		75.00	75
1983 High Hopes	Yr.Iss		75.00	75
1984 Space Age Santa	Yr.Iss		55.00	55

Norman Rockwell Gallery

Norman Rockwell Centennial - Rockwell Inspired

1993 The Toymaker	Closed		39.90	60-65
1993 The Cobbler	Closed		39.90	45-70

Rockwell's Christmas Legacy - Rockwell Inspired

1992 Santa's Workshop	Closed		49.90	51-60
1993 Making a List	Closed		49.90	65-84
1993 While Santa Slumbers	Closed		54.90	60-85
1993 Visions of Santa	Closed		54.90	60-110

Precious Moments/Enesco Group, Inc.

Beauty of Christmas Collection - S. Butcher

1994 You're as Pretty as a Christmas Tree 530409	Yr.Iss	1994	50.00	50-85
1995 He Covers the Earth With His Beauty 142670	Yr.Iss	1995	50.00	50-85
1996 Peace On Earth...Anyway 183377	Yr.Iss	1996	50.00	42-50
1997 Cane You Join Us For A Merry Christmas 272701	Yr.Iss	1997	50.00	42-50
1998 I'm Sending You a Merry Christmas 469327	Yr.Iss	1998	50.00	50

Christmas Blessings - S. Butcher

1990 Wishing You A Yummy Christmas 523801	Yr.Iss	1990	50.00	50
1991 Blessings From Me To Thee 523860	Yr.Iss	1991	50.00	50-85
1992 But The Greatest of These Is Love 527742	Yr.Iss	1992	50.00	50-85
1993 Wishing You the Sweetest Christmas 530204	Yr.Iss	1993	50.00	50-85

Christmas Collection - S. Butcher

1981 Come Let Us Adore Him E-5646	15,000		40.00	34-42
1982 Let Heaven and Nature Sing E-2347	15,000		40.00	38-45
1983 Wee Three Kings-E-0538	15,000		40.00	38-45
1984 Unto Us a Child Is Born E-5395	15,000		40.00	34-40

Christmas Love Series - S. Butcher

1986 I'm Sending You a White Christmas 101834	Yr.Iss	1986	45.00	57-85
1987 My Peace I Give Unto Thee 102954	Yr.Iss	1987	45.00	73-85
1988 Merry Christmas Deer 520284	Yr.Iss	1988	50.00	50-85
1989 May Your Christmas Be A Happy Home 523003	Yr.Iss	1989	50.00	48-85

The Four Seasons Series - S. Butcher

YEAR ISSUE	EDITION LIMIT	YEAR RETD.	ISSUE PRICE	*QUOTE U.S.$
1985 The Voice of Spring 12106	Yr.Iss.	1985	40.00	60
1985 Summer's Joy 12114	Yr.Iss.	1985	40.00	57-75
1986 Autumn's Praise 12122	Yr.Iss.	1986	40.00	37-44
1986 Winter's Song 12130	Yr.Iss.	1986	40.00	37-44

Inspired Thoughts Series - S. Butcher

1981 Love One Another E-5215	15,000		40.00	34-40
1982 Make a Joyful Noise E-7174	15,000		40.00	34-40
1983 I Believe In Miracles E-9257	15,000		40.00	34-40
1984 Love is Kind E-2847	15,000		40.00	34-40

Joy of Christmas Series - S. Butcher

1982 I'll Play My Drum For Him E-2357	Yr.Iss.	1982	40.00	60-85
1983 Christmastime is for Sharing E-0505	Yr.Iss.	1983	40.00	63
1984 The Wonder of Christmas E-5396	Yr.Iss.	1984	40.00	40-85
1985 Tell Me the Story of Jesus 15237	Yr.Iss.	1985	40.00	86

Mother's Day Series - S. Butcher

1981 Mother Sew Dear E-5217	15,000		40.00	34-40
1982 The Purr-fect Grandma E-7173	15,000		40.00	34-40
1983 The Hand that Rocks the Future E-9256	15,000		40.00	34-40
1984 Loving Thy Neighbor E-2848	15,000		40.00	34-40
1994 Thinking of You Is What I Really Like to Do 531766	Yr.Iss.	1994	50.00	42-50
1996 Of All The Mothers I Have Known There's None As Precious As My Own 163716	Yr.Iss.	1996	50.00	50

Open Editions - S. Butcher

1982 Our First Christmas Together E-2378	Suspd.		30.00	30-45
1981 The Lord Bless You and Keep You E-5216	Suspd.		30.00	28-38
1982 Rejoicing with You E-7172	Suspd.		30.00	30-40
1983 Jesus Loves Me E-9275	Suspd.		30.00	30-40
1983 Jesus Loves Me E-9276	Suspd.		30.00	30-40
1994 Bring The Little Ones To Jesus 531359	Yr.Iss.	1994	50.00	42-50

Precious Moments - S. Butcher

1995 He Hath Made Everything Beautiful in His Time 129151	Open		50.00	42-50
1997 Love One Another 186406	Open		35.00	30-35

Prizm, Inc./Pipka

Decorative Art by Pipka Plaques - Pipka

2001 The First Christmas Nativity 11614	Open		45.00	45
2001 Mary, Queen of Roses 11613	Open		35.00	35
2001 Midnight Visitor 11607	Open		25.00	25
2001 Sinter Klaas 11611	Open		50.00	50
2001 Star Catcher Santa 11609	Open		25.00	25
2001 Starcoat Santa 11608	Open		25.00	25
2001 Starlight Santa 11612	Open		50.00	50
2001 Sylvia, The Song Angel 11610	Open		25.00	25

Reco International

Alan Maley's Past Impressions - A. Maley

1997 Festive Occasion	95-day		29.90	30
1997 Sleigh Bells	95-day		29.90	30
1997 Summer Elegance	95-day		29.90	30
1997 The Recital	95-day		29.90	30
1999 Summer Romance	95-day		29.90	30
1999 Elegant Affair	95-day		29.90	30
1999 Romantic Engagement	95-day		29.90	30
1999 Secret Thoughts	95-day		29.90	30

Always With You Calendar - S. Kuck

1999 January	95-day		29.95	30
2000 February	95-day		29.95	30
2000 March	95-day		29.95	30
2000 April	95-day		29.95	30
2000 May	95-day		29.95	30
2000 June	95-day		29.95	30
2000 July	95-day		29.95	30
2000 August	95-day		29.95	30
2000 September	95-day		29.95	30
2000 October	95-day		29.95	30
2000 November	95-day		29.95	30
2000 December	95-day		29.95	30

YEAR ISSUE	EDITION LIMIT	YEAR RETD.	ISSUE PRICE	*QUOTE U.S.$
Amish Traditions - B. Farnsworth				
1994 Golden Harvest	95-day		29.50	30
1994 Family Outing	95-day		29.50	30
1994 The Quilting Bee	95-day		29.50	30
1995 Last Day of School	95-day	1998	29.50	30
Angels All Around Us - S. Kuck				
2000 Angel's Gentle Touch	95-day		29.95	30
2000 Angel's Loving Message	95-day		29.95	30
2000 Angel's Soft Whisper	95-day		29.95	30
2000 Angel's Peaceful Wonder	95-day		29.95	30
Barefoot Children - S. Kuck				
1987 Night-Time Story	Retrd.	1994	29.50	54-60
1987 Golden Afternoon	Retrd.	1996	29.50	36-55
1988 Little Sweethearts	Retrd.	1995	29.50	39-50
1988 Carousel Magic	Retrd.	1996	29.50	65-70
1988 Under the Apple Tree	Retrd.	1995	29.50	50
1988 The Rehearsal	Retrd.	1995	29.50	60-85
1988 Pretty as a Picture	Retrd.	1993	29.50	65-70
1988 Grandma's Trunk	Retrd.	1993	29.50	50-70
Birds of the Hidden Forest - G. Ratnavira				
1994 Macaw Waterfall	96-day	2000	29.50	30
1994 Paradise Valley	96-day	2000	29.50	30
1995 Toucan Treasure	96-day	2000	29.50	30
Blessings From Heaven - D. Martelli				
2001 Faith Plaque	Open		20.00	20
2001 Hope	Open		20.00	20
2001 Charity	Open		20.00	20
Bohemian Annuals - Factory Artist				
1974 1974	Retrd.	1975	130.00	155
1975 1975	Retrd.	1976	140.00	160
1976 1976	Retrd.	1978	150.00	160
Carnival Collection - R. Lee				
1998 Wheelin'	2,500		29.90	30
1998 Clown-Air	2,500		29.90	30
1998 Runaway Train	2,500		29.90	30
1998 Horsin'	2,500		29.90	30
Castles & Dreams - J. Bergsma				
1992 The Birth of a Dream	48-day	2000	29.50	30
1992 Dreams Come True	48-day	2000	29.50	30
1993 Believe In Your Dreams	48-day	2000	29.50	30
1994 Follow Your Dreams	48-day	2000	29.50	30
A Childhood Almanac - S. Kuck				
1985 Fireside Dreams-January	Retrd.	1991	29.50	35-59
1985 Be Mine-February	Retrd.	1992	29.50	45-59
1986 Winds of March-March	Retrd.	1994	29.50	59
1985 Easter Morning-April	Retrd.	1992	29.50	60
1985 For Mom-May	Retrd.	1992	29.50	35-59
1985 Just Dreaming-June	Retrd.	1992	29.50	60-65
1985 Star Spangled Sky-July	Retrd.	1995	29.50	39-60
1985 Summer Secrets-August	Retrd.	1991	29.50	65
1985 School Days-September	Retrd.	1991	29.50	59-75
1986 Indian Summer-October	Retrd.	1991	29.50	60-65
1986 Giving Thanks-November	Retrd.	1995	29.50	59-70
1985 Christmas Magic-December	Retrd.	1995	35.00	68-75
Children of the Sun - V. Di Fate				
1998 Mars The Red Planet	95-day	2000	29.90	30
1998 The Bright Rings of Saturn	95-day	2000	29.90	30
A Children's Christmas Pageant - S. Kuck				
1986 Silent Night	Retrd.	1987	32.50	75-90
1987 Hark the Herald Angels Sing	Retrd.	1988	32.50	65-69
1988 While Shepherds Watched...	Retrd.	1990	32.50	39-55
1989 We Three Kings	Retrd.	N/A	32.50	55-59
Christening Gift - S. Kuck				
1995 God's Gift	Open		29.90	30
The Christmas Series - J. Bergsma				
1990 Down The Glistening Lane	Retrd.	1996	35.00	35
1991 A Child Is Born	Retrd.	1996	35.00	35
1992 Christmas Day	Retrd.	1996	35.00	35
1993 I Wish You An Angel	Retrd.	1996	35.00	35
Christmas Wishes - J. Bergsma				
1994 I Wish You Love	75-day	1998	29.50	30-35
1995 I Wish You Joy	75-day	1998	29.50	30-35
1996 I Wish You Peace	75-day	1998	29.50	30
Clowning Around - R. Lee				
1998 Beware of Snakes	5,000		29.90	30
1998 Duck Crossing	5,000		29.90	30
1998 On The Edge	5,000		29.90	30
1998 Almost There	5,000		29.90	30
Days Gone By - S. Kuck				
1983 Sunday Best	Retrd.	1984	29.50	38-60
1983 Amy's Magic Horse	Retrd.	1985	29.50	23-50
1984 Little Anglers	Retrd.	1985	29.50	39-70
1984 Afternoon Recital	Retrd.	1985	29.50	60-70
1984 Little Tutor	Retrd.	1985	29.50	20-55
1985 Easter at Grandma's	Retrd.	1985	29.50	18-60
1985 Morning Song	Retrd.	1986	29.50	20-45
1985 The Surrey Ride	Retrd.	1987	29.50	23-60
Dresden Christmas - Factory Artist				
1971 Shepherd Scene	Retrd.	1978	15.00	50
1972 Niklas Church	Retrd.	1978	15.00	25
1973 Schwanstein Church	Retrd.	1978	18.00	35
1974 Village Scene	Retrd.	1978	20.00	30
1975 Rothenburg Scene	Retrd.	1978	24.00	30
1976 Village Church	Retrd.	1978	26.00	35
1977 Old Mill	Retrd.	1978	28.00	30
Dresden Mother's Day - Factory Artist				
1972 Doe and Fawn	Retrd.	1979	15.00	20
1973 Mare and Colt	Retrd.	1979	16.00	25
1974 Tiger and Cub	Retrd.	1979	20.00	23
1975 Dachshunds	Retrd.	1979	24.00	28
1976 Owl and Offspring	Retrd.	1979	26.00	30
1977 Chamois	Retrd.	1979	28.00	30
Eagle of America - S. Barlowe				
1996 Land of The Free	96-day	1998	29.90	30
Enchanted Gardens - S. Kuck				
1998 Tea For Three	95-day		32.95	33
1998 Sweetest Delights	95-day		32.95	33
1998 Wildflowers of Love	95-day		32.95	33
1998 Innocence Shared	95-day		32.95	33
Everlasing Friends - S. Kuck				
1996 Sharing Secrets	95-day		29.95	30
1996 Sharing Dreams	95-day		29.95	30
1997 Sharing Beauty	95-day		29.95	30
1997 Sharing Love	95-day		29.95	30
1998 Sharing Harmony	95-day		29.95	30
1998 Sharing Stories	95-day		29.95	30
Everyday Heroes - B. Brown				
1998 Out of the Blaze	95-day		29.90	30
Fishtales - R. Manning				
1997 Rainbow River	76-day	2000	29.90	30
Four Seasons - J. Poluszynski				
1973 Spring	Retrd.	1975	50.00	75
1973 Summer	Retrd.	1975	50.00	75
1973 Fall	Retrd.	1975	50.00	75
1973 Winter	Retrd.	1975	50.00	75
Friends For Keeps - S. Kuck				
1996 Puppy Love	95-day		29.95	30-50
1996 Gone Fishing	95-day		29.95	30-50
1997 Golden Days	95-day		29.95	30-50
1997 Take Me Home	95-day		29.95	30-50
Furstenberg Christmas - Factory Artist				
1971 Rabbits	Retrd.	1977	15.00	30
1972 Snowy Village	Retrd.	1977	15.00	20
1973 Christmas Eve	Retrd.	1977	18.00	35
1974 Sparrows	Retrd.	1977	20.00	30
1975 Deer Family	Retrd.	1977	22.00	30
1976 Winter Birds	Retrd.	1977	25.00	25
Furstenberg Easter - Factory Artist				
1971 Sheep	Retrd.	1973	15.00	25-100
1972 Chicks	Retrd.	1975	15.00	60
1973 Bunnies	Retrd.	1976	16.00	80
1974 Pussywillow	Retrd.	1976	20.00	33

YEAR ISSUE	EDITION LIMIT	YEAR RETD.	ISSUE PRICE	*QUOTE U.S.$
1975 Easter Window	Retrd.	1977	22.00	30
1976 Flower Collecting	Retrd.	1977	25.00	25

Furstenberg Mother's Day - Factory Artist
1972 Hummingbirds, Fe	Retrd.	1974	15.00	45
1973 Hedgehogs	Retrd.	1974	16.00	40
1974 Doe and Fawn	Retrd.	1974	20.00	30
1975 Swans	Retrd.	1976	22.00	23
1976 Koala Bears	Retrd.	1976	25.00	30

Furstenberg Olympic - J. Poluszynski
1972 Munich	Retrd.	1972	20.00	75
1976 Montreal	Retrd.	1976	37.50	38

Games Children Play - S. Kuck
1979 Me First	Retrd.	1983	45.00	50-75
1980 Forever Bubbles	Retrd.	1983	45.00	48-65
1981 Skating Pals	Retrd.	1983	45.00	48-65
1982 Join Me	10,000	1998	45.00	45

Gardens of Innocence - S. Kuck
1997 Heavenly Hideaway	95-day		32.95	33
1997 Sweetly Swinging	95-day		32.95	33
1998 Gently Giving	95-day		32.95	33
1998 Precious Party	95-day		32.95	33
1998 Highest Harmony	95-day		32.95	33
1999 Perfect Place	95-day		32.95	33
1999 Peaceful Prayers	95-day		32.95	33
1999 Heaven's Blossoms	95-day		32.95	33

Generations - B. Brown
1997 Passing On The Faith	95-day		29.90	30
1998 Guiding the Way	95-day		29.90	30
1998 Learning To Imagine	95-day		29.90	30
1998 Loving Time	95-day		29.90	30

Gift of Love Mother's Day Collection - S. Kuck
1993 Morning Glory	Retrd.	1994	65.00	75-85
1994 Memories From The Heart	Retrd.	1994	65.00	75-85

The Glory Of Christ - C. Micarelli
1992 The Ascension	48-day		29.50	30
1993 Jesus Teaching	48-day		29.50	30
1993 The Last Supper	48-day	1999	29.50	30
1993 The Nativity	48-day		29.50	30
1993 The Baptism Of Christ	48-day		29.50	30
1993 Jesus Heals The Sick	48-day		29.50	30
1994 Jesus Walks On Water	48-day		29.50	30
1994 Descent From The Cross	48-day		29.50	30

Great Stories from the Bible - G. Katz
1987 Moses in the Bulrushes	Retrd.	1994	29.50	30-45
1987 King Saul & David	Retrd.	1994	29.50	30-45
1987 Moses and the Ten Commandments	Retrd.	1994	29.50	38-45
1987 Joseph's Coat of Many Colors	Retrd.	1994	29.50	30-45
1988 Rebekah at the Well	Retrd.	1994	29.50	35-45
1988 Daniel Reads the Writing on the Wall	Retrd.	1994	29.50	45-65
1988 The Story of Ruth	Retrd.	1994	29.50	35-45
1988 King Solomon	Retrd.	1994	29.50	35-45

Guardian Angel Collection Plaques - C. Lael
2000 Angel of Goodness - January	Open		20.00	20
2000 Angel of Peace & Tranquility - February	Open		20.00	20
2000 Angel of Comfort - March	Open		20.00	20
2000 Angel of Power - April	Open		20.00	20
2000 Angel of Loveliness - May	Open		20.00	20
2000 Angel of Wisdom - June	Open		20.00	20
2000 Angel of Protection - July	Open		20.00	20
2000 Angel of Praise - August	Open		20.00	20
2000 Angel of Light - September	Open		20.00	20
2000 Angel of Healing - October	Open		20.00	20
2000 Guardian Angel - November	Open		20.00	20
2000 Angel of Wonder - December	Open		20.00	20
2001 Angel of Strength	Open		20.00	20
2001 Angel of Victory	Open		20.00	20
2001 Angel of Love & Beauty	Open		20.00	20
2001 Angel of Promise	Open		20.00	20

Guardians Of The Kingdom - J. Bergsma
1990 Rainbow To Ride On	Retrd.	1993	35.00	40
1990 Special Friends Are Few	17,500	1998	35.00	35
1990 Guardians Of The Innocent Children	17,500	1998	35.00	35

YEAR ISSUE	EDITION LIMIT	YEAR RETD.	ISSUE PRICE	*QUOTE U.S.$
1990 The Miracle Of Love	17,500	1998	35.00	35
1991 The Magic Of Love	17,500	1998	35.00	35
1991 Only With The Heart	17,500	1998	35.00	35
1991 To Fly Without Wings	17,500	1998	35.00	35
1991 In Faith I Am Free	17,500	1998	35.00	35

Guiding Lights - D Hahlbohm
1996 Robbins Reef	96-day		29.90	30
1996 Cape Hateras	96-day		29.90	30
1997 Cape Neddick	96-day		29.90	30
1998 Split Rock, MN	96-day		29.90	30

Haven of the Hunters - H. Roe
1994 Eagle's Castle	Retrd.	1996	29.50	30
1994 Sanctuary of the Hawk	Retrd.	1996	29.50	30

Hearts And Flowers - S. Kuck
1991 Patience	Retrd.	1999	29.50	33-55
1991 Tea Party	Retrd.	1999	29.50	33-55
1992 Cat's In The Cradle	Retrd.	1999	32.50	40-45
1992 Carousel of Dreams	Retrd.	1999	32.50	23-33
1992 Storybook Memories	120-day	1998	32.50	35-55
1993 Delightful Bundle	120-day	N/A	34.50	35-42
1993 Easter Morning Visitor	120-day	N/A	34.50	35-56
1993 Me and My Pony	120-day	N/A	34.50	40-56

Heavenly Kingdom - C. Micarelli
1997 The Blessed Child	95-day		29.90	30

Imaginary Gardens - S. Somerville
1996 Pussywillows	76-day		29.90	30
1996 Dogwood	76-day		29.90	30
1997 Cowslip	76-day		29.90	30

In His Loving Care - S. Kuck
2001 Heaven's Little Guardian	95-day		29.95	30

In The Eye of The Storm - W. Lowe
1991 First Strike	Retrd.	1996	29.50	30
1992 Night Force	Retrd.	1996	29.50	30
1992 Tracks Across The Sand	Retrd.	1996	29.50	30
1992 The Storm Has Landed	Retrd.	1996	29.50	30

J. Bergsma Mother's Day Series - J. Bergsma
1990 The Beauty Of Life	Retrd.	1996	35.00	35-38
1992 Life's Blessing	Retrd.	1996	35.00	35-38
1993 My Greatest Treasures	Retrd.	1996	35.00	35-38
1994 Forever In My Heart	Retrd.	1996	35.00	35-38

Jesus And The Children - N. Mc Naulty
1998 Come Unto Me	96-day		29.90	30

King's Flowers - A. Falchi
1973 Carnation	Retrd.	1974	85.00	130
1974 Red Rose	Retrd.	1975	100.00	145
1975 Yellow Dahlia	Retrd.	1976	110.00	162
1976 Bluebells	Retrd.	1977	130.00	165
1977 Anemones	Retrd.	1979	130.00	175

King's Mother's Day - Merli
1973 Dancing Girl	Retrd.	1974	100.00	225
1974 Dancing Boy	Retrd.	1975	115.00	250
1975 Motherly Love	Retrd.	1976	140.00	225
1976 Maiden	Retrd.	1978	180.00	200

Life's Little Celebrations - C. Tait
1997 The New Baby	96-day	2000	29.90	30
1997 An Apple For The Teacher	96-day	2000	29.90	30
1997 School Bell	96-day	2000	29.90	30
1997 Graduation Smile	96-day	2000	29.90	30
1997 Celebration of Love	96-day	2000	29.90	30
1997 I Love You	96-day	2000	29.90	30

Little Angel Plate Collection - S. Kuck
1994 Angel of Charity	95-day	2000	29.50	30
1994 Angel of Joy	95-day	2000	29.50	30

Little Professionals - S. Kuck
1982 All is Well	Retrd.	1983	39.50	65-95
1983 Tender Loving Care	Retrd.	1985	39.50	55-70
1984 Lost and Found	Retrd.	1995	39.50	45-65
1985 Reading, Writing and...	Retrd.	1989	39.50	50-65

*Quotes have been rounded up to nearest dollar

YEAR ISSUE	EDITION LIMIT	YEAR RETD.	ISSUE PRICE	*QUOTE U.S.$
Little Wonders - A. Grant				
1998 Safely Through The Night	95-day		29.90	30
1998 First Friend	95-day		29.90	30
1998 Cherished Toys	95-day		29.90	30
1998 Tender Moments	95-day		29.90	30
Loving Hearts - S. Kuck				
2001 Love Is Gentle	95-day		39.95	40
2001 Love Is Sweet	95-day		39.95	40
2001 Love Is Tender	95-day		39.95	40
Magic Companions - J. Bergsma				
1994 Believe in Love	48-day		29.50	30
1994 Imagine Peace	48-day		29.50	30
1995 Live in Harmony	48-day		29.50	30
1995 Trust in Magic	48-day		29.50	30
Majestic Spirits - G. Perillo				
1999 Nature's Might	5,000		29.90	30
1999 Noble Spirit	5,000		35.00	35
1999 Freedom's Thunder	5,000		29.90	30
March of Dimes: Our Children, Our Future - Various				
1989 A Time to Love (2nd in Series) - S. Kuck	Retrd.	1993	29.00	30
1989 A Time to Plant (3rd in Series) - J. McClelland	150-day	1993	29.00	12-29
Marmot Christmas - Factory Artist				
1970 Polar Bear, Fe	Retrd.	1971	13.00	20-60
1971 Buffalo Bill	Retrd.	1972	16.00	55
1972 Boy and Grandfather	Retrd.	1973	20.00	50
1971 American Buffalo	Retrd.	1973	14.50	35
1973 Snowman	Retrd.	1974	22.00	45
1974 Dancing	Retrd.	1975	24.00	30
1975 Quail	Retrd.	1976	30.00	40
1976 Windmill	Retrd.	1978	40.00	40
Marmot Father's Day - Factory Artist				
1970 Stag	Retrd.	1970	12.00	40-70
1971 Horse	Retrd.	1972	12.50	40
Marmot Mother's Day - Factory Artist				
1972 Seal	Retrd.	1973	16.00	60
1973 Bear with Cub	Retrd.	1974	20.00	140
1974 Penguins	Retrd.	1975	24.00	50
1975 Raccoons	Retrd.	1976	30.00	45
1976 Ducks	Retrd.	1977	40.00	40
Memories of Childhood - C. Getz				
1994 Teatime with Teddy	75-day		29.50	30
1995 Bases Loaded	75-day		29.50	30
1996 Mommy's Little Helper	75-day		29.50	30
Moments At Home - S. Kuck				
1995 Moments of Caring	95-day		29.90	30-50
1995 Moments of Tenderness	95-day		29.90	30-50
1995 Moments of Friendship	95-day		29.90	30-50
1995 Moments of Sharing	95-day		29.90	30-50
1995 Moments of Love	95-day		29.90	30-50
1996 Moments of Reflection	95-day		29.90	30-50
Moser Christmas - Factory Artist				
1970 Hradcany Castle	Retrd.	1971	75.00	170
1971 Karlstein Castle	Retrd.	1972	75.00	80
1972 Old Town Hall	Retrd.	1973	85.00	85
1973 Karlovy Vary Castle	Retrd.	1974	90.00	100
Moser Mother's Day - Factory Artist				
1971 Peacocks	Retrd.	1971	75.00	100
1972 Butterflies	Retrd.	1972	85.00	90
1973 Squirrels	Retrd.	1973	90.00	95
Mother Goose - J. McClelland				
1979 Mary, Mary	Retrd.	1979	22.50	65-69
1980 Little Boy Blue	Retrd.	1980	22.50	25-35
1981 Little Miss Muffet	Retrd.	1981	24.50	8-30
1982 Little Jack Horner	Retrd.	1982	24.50	10-45
1983 Little Bo Peep	Retrd.	1983	24.50	10-38
1984 Diddle, Diddle Dumpling	Retrd.	1984	24.50	10-45
1985 Mary Had a Little Lamb	Retrd.	1985	27.50	15-30
1986 Jack and Jill	Retrd.	1988	27.50	19-23
Mother's Day Collection - S. Kuck				
1985 Once Upon a Time	Retrd.	1987	29.50	60-65
1986 Times Remembered	Retrd.	1988	29.50	45-60
1987 A Cherished Time	Retrd.	1987	29.50	60-70
1988 A Time Together	Retrd.	1988	29.50	60-70
Noble and Free - Kelly				
1994 Gathering Storm	95-day	1998	29.50	30
1994 Protected Journey	95-day	1998	29.50	30
1994 Moonlight Run	95-day	1998	29.50	30
The Nutcracker Ballet - C. Micarelli				
1989 Christmas Eve Party	Retrd.	1994	35.00	30-35
1990 Clara And Her Prince	Retrd.	1999	35.00	35
1990 The Dream Begins	Retrd.	1999	35.00	35
1991 Dance of the Snow Fairies	Retrd.	1994	35.00	35
1992 The Land of Sweets	Retrd.	1999	35.00	35
1992 The Sugar Plum Fairy	Retrd.	1999	35.00	35
On Angels Wings - S. Kuck				
1999 Angel Kisses	95-day		29.95	30
2000 Wings of Wonder	95-day		29.95	30
2000 Heaven's Secrets	95-day		29.95	30
2000 Blossoms of Love	95-day		29.95	30
2000 Heaven's Gentle Touch	95-day		29.95	30
2001 Heaven's Peaceful Starlight	95-day		29.95	30
2001 Always With You	95-day		29.95	30
2001 Angels Wonder	95-day		29.95	30
Oscar & Bertie's Edwardian Holiday - P.D. Jackson				
1991 Snapshot	Retrd.	1996	29.50	30
1992 Early Rise	Retrd.	1996	29.50	30
1992 All Aboard	Retrd.	1996	29.50	30
1992 Learning To Swim	Retrd.	1996	29.50	30
Our Cherished Seas - S. Barlowe				
1991 Whale Song	48-day	2000	37.50	38
1991 Lions of the Sea	48-day	2000	37.50	38
1991 Flight of the Dolphins	48-day	1999	37.50	38
1992 Palace of the Seals	48-day	2000	37.50	38
1992 Orca Ballet	48-day	2000	37.50	38
1993 Emperors of the Ice	48-day	2000	37.50	38
1993 Turtle Treasure	48-day	2000	37.50	38
1993 Splendor of the Sea	48-day	2000	37.50	38
Out of The Wild - S. Barlowe				
1996 The Pride	76-day		29.90	30
1997 Graceful Giants	76-day		29.90	30
Plate Of The Month Collection - S. Kuck				
1990 January	Retrd.	1996	25.00	28-50
1990 February	Retrd.	1996	25.00	28-50
1990 March	Retrd.	1996	25.00	28-50
1990 April	Retrd.	1996	25.00	28-50
1990 May	Retrd.	1996	25.00	28-50
1990 June	Retrd.	1996	25.00	28-50
1990 July	Retrd.	1996	25.00	28-50
1990 August	Retrd.	1996	25.00	28-50
1990 September	Retrd.	1996	25.00	28-50
1990 October	Retrd.	1996	25.00	28-50
1990 November	Retrd.	1996	25.00	28-50
1990 December	Retrd.	1996	25.00	28-50
Precious Angels - S. Kuck				
1995 Angel of Grace	95-day		29.90	30
1995 Angel of Happiness	95-day		29.90	30
1995 Angel of Hope	95-day		29.90	30
1995 Angel of Laughter	95-day		29.90	30
1995 Angel of Love	95-day		29.90	30
1995 Angel of Peace	95-day		29.90	30
1995 Angel of Sharing	95-day		29.90	30
1995 Angel of Sunshine	95-day		29.90	30
Premier Collection - S. Kuck				
1991 Puppy	Retrd.	1993	95.00	125-200
1991 Kitten	Retrd.	1992	95.00	145-300
1992 La Belle	7,500	1996	95.00	95
1992 Le Beau	7,500	1996	95.00	95
Protectors of the Wild - M. Wood				
1998 Moon Song	95-day		29.90	30

PLATES & PLAQUES

YEAR ISSUE	EDITION LIMIT	YEAR RETD.	ISSUE PRICE	*QUOTE U.S.$
Protectors of the Wild - R. Frentner				
1998 Genesis	95-day		29.90	30
Quinceañera - C. Micarelli				
1999 Quinceañera	Open		30.00	30
Reflection of Love - S. Kuck				
1999 Mother's Love	95-day		35.00	35
2000 Mother's Gentle Touch	95-day		35.00	35
2001 Loving Steps	95-day		35.00	35
Romantic Gardens - S. Kuck				
1997 Emma	95-day		35.00	35
1997 Alexandra	95-day		35.00	35
Royal Mother's Day - Factory Artist				
1970 Swan and Young	Retrd.	1971	12.00	80
1971 Doe and Fawn	Retrd.	1972	13.00	55
1972 Rabbits	Retrd.	1973	16.00	40
1973 Owl Family	Retrd.	1974	18.00	40
1974 Duck and Young	Retrd.	1975	22.00	40
1975 Lynx and Cubs	Retrd.	1976	26.00	40
1976 Woodcock and Young	Retrd.	1978	27.50	33
1977 Koala Bear	Retrd.	1978	30.00	30
Royale - Factory Artist				
1969 Apollo Moon Landing	Retrd.	1969	30.00	80
Royale Christmas - Factory Artist				
1969 Christmas Fair	Retrd.	1970	12.00	125
1970 Vigil Mass	Retrd.	1971	13.00	110
1971 Christmas Night	Retrd.	1972	16.00	50
1972 Elks	Retrd.	1973	16.00	45
1973 Christmas Down	Retrd.	1974	20.00	38
1974 Village Christmas	Retrd.	1975	22.00	60
1975 Feeding Time	Retrd.	1976	26.00	35
1976 Seaport Christmas	Retrd.	1977	27.50	30
1977 Sledding	Retrd.	1978	30.00	30
Royale Father's Day - Factory Artist				
1970 Frigate Constitution	Retrd.	1971	13.00	80
1971 Man Fishing	Retrd.	1972	13.00	35
1972 Mountaineer	Retrd.	1973	16.00	55
1973 Camping	Retrd.	1974	18.00	45
1974 Eagle	Retrd.	1975	22.00	35
1975 Regatta	Retrd.	1976	26.00	35
1976 Hunting	Retrd.	1977	27.50	33
1977 Fishing	Retrd.	1978	30.00	30
Royale Game Plates - Various				
1972 Setters - J. Poluszynski	Retrd.	1974	180.00	200
1973 Fox - J. Poluszynski	Retrd.	1975	200.00	250
1974 Osprey - W. Schiener	Retrd.	1976	250.00	250
1975 California Quail - W. Schiener	Retrd.	1976	265.00	265
Royale Germania Christmas Annual - Factory Artist				
1970 Orchid	Retrd.	1971	200.00	650
1971 Cyclamen	Retrd.	1972	200.00	325
1972 Silver Thistle	Retrd.	1973	250.00	290
1973 Tulips	Retrd.	1974	275.00	310
1974 Sunflowers	Retrd.	1975	300.00	320
1975 Snowdrops	Retrd.	1976	450.00	500
Royale Germania Crystal Mother's Day - Factory Artist				
1971 Roses	Retrd.	1971	135.00	650
1972 Elephant and Youngster	Retrd.	1972	180.00	250
1973 Koala Bear and Cub	Retrd.	1973	200.00	225
1974 Squirrels	Retrd.	1974	240.00	250
1975 Swan and Young	Retrd.	1975	350.00	360
Sandra Kuck Fan Collection - S. Kuck				
2000 Summer Outing	65-day		30.00	30
Sandra Kuck Mothers' Day - S. Kuck				
1995 Home is Where the Heart Is	Retrd.	1999	35.00	35-56
1996 Dear To The Heart	Retrd.	1998	35.00	40-80
1997 Welcome Home	Retrd.	2000	35.00	35-55
1998 Wings of Love	Retrd.	2000	35.00	35-54
Sandra Kuck's Journey Through Life - S. Kuck				
2001 Foot Print in the Sand	95-day		34.95	35
2001 Serenity	95-day		34.95	35

YEAR ISSUE	EDITION LIMIT	YEAR RETD.	ISSUE PRICE	*QUOTE U.S.$
Sculpted Heirlooms - S. Kuck				
1996 Best Friends (sculpted plate)	24-mo.		29.95	30
1996 Tea Party (sculpted plate)	24-mo.		29.90	30
1996 Storybook Memories (sculpted plate)	24-mo.		29.90	30
1996 Patience (sculpted plate)	24-mo.		29.90	30
Single Issue - T. Gronland				
1997 Happiness In Heaven	95-day	1998	29.90	30
Sisters Love Forever - S. Kuck				
2000 Sister's Touch	95-day		29.95	30
2000 Wonders To Share	95-day		29.95	30
2000 Basket of Love	95-day		29.95	30
2001 A Cup Full of Love	95-day		29.95	30
2001 Growing in Love	95-day		29.95	30
Songs From The Garden - G. Ratnavira				
1996 Love Song	76-day		29.90	30
1996 Rhapsody In Blue	76-day		29.90	30
1997 Hummingbirds In Harmony	76-day		29.90	30
1997 Golden Melody	76-day		29.90	30
1997 Spring Serenade	76-day		29.90	30
1998 Ode To The Oriole	76-day		29.90	30
The Sophisticated Ladies Collection - A. Fazio				
1985 Felicia	21-day	1997	29.50	30-45
1985 Samantha	21-day	1994	29.50	35
1985 Phoebe	21-day	1994	29.50	33-45
1985 Cleo	21-day	1998	29.50	30
1986 Cerissa	21-day	1994	29.50	33-45
1986 Natasha	21-day	1994	29.50	33-45
1986 Bianka	21-day	1994	29.50	33-45
1986 Chelsea	21-day	1994	29.50	33-45
Special Occasions by Reco - S. Kuck				
1988 The Wedding	Open		35.00	35
1989 Wedding Day (6 1/2")	Retrd.	1996	25.00	25-45
1990 The Special Day	Retrd.	1996	25.00	25
Sugar and Spice - S. Kuck				
1993 Best Friends	95-day		29.90	30
1993 Sisters	95-day		29.90	30
1994 Little One	95-day		32.90	33
1994 Teddy Bear Tales	95-day		32.90	33
1994 Morning Prayers	95-day		32.90	33
1995 First Snow	95-day		34.90	35
1994 Garden of Sunshine	95-day		34.90	35
1995 A Special Day	95-day		34.90	35
Tidings Of Joy - S. Kuck				
1992 Peace on Earth	Retrd.	1995	35.00	29-55
1993 Rejoice	Retrd.	1996	35.00	35-70
1994 Noel	Retrd.	1995	35.00	65-100
Totems of the West - J. Bergsma				
1994 The Watchmen	96-day		29.50	30
1995 Peace At Last	96-day		29.50	30
1995 Never Alone	96-day		35.00	35
Town And Country Dogs - S. Barlowe				
1990 Fox Hunt	36-day		35.00	35
1991 The Retrieval	36-day		35.00	35
1991 Golden Fields (Golden Retriever)	36-day		35.00	35
1993 Faithful Companions (Cocker Spaniel)	36-day		35.00	35
Treasured Songs of Childhood - J. McClelland				
1987 Twinkle, Twinkle, Little Star	Retrd.	1990	29.50	38-49
1988 A Tisket, A Tasket	Retrd.	1991	29.50	38-45
1988 Baa, Baa, Black Sheep	Retrd.	1991	32.90	38-45
1989 Round The Mulberry Bush	150-day	1998	32.90	33
1989 Rain, Rain Go Away	Retrd.	1993	32.90	38-50
1989 I'm A Little Teapot	Retrd.	1993	32.90	38-45
1989 Pat-A-Cake	150-day	1998	34.90	35
1990 Hush Little Baby	150-day	1998	34.90	35
Up, Up And Away - P. Alexander				
1996 Rally At The Grand Canyon	76-day		29.90	30
1996 Gateway To Heaven	76-day		29.90	30
1997 Boston Balloon Party	76-day		29.90	30
1998 Through The Golden Gates	76-day		29.90	30
Vanishing Animal Kingdoms - S. Barlowe				
1986 Rama the Tiger	21,500	1996	35.00	35

Collectors' Information Bureau   *Quotes have been rounded up to nearest dollar

YEAR ISSUE	EDITION LIMIT	YEAR RETD.	ISSUE PRICE	*QUOTE U.S.$
1986 Olepi the Buffalo	21,500	1996	35.00	35
1987 Coolibah the Koala	21,500	1996	35.00	35
1987 Ortwin the Deer	21,500	1996	35.00	35
1987 Yen-Poh the Panda	21,500	1996	35.00	35
1988 Mamakuu the Elephant	21,500	1996	35.00	35

Victorian Christmas - S. Kuck

1995 Dear Santa	72-day		35.00	35-50
1996 Night Before Christmas	72-day		35.00	35-50
1997 Wrapped With Love	72-day		35.00	35-50
1998 Christmas Day Joy	72-day		35.00	35-66

Victorian Mother's Day - S. Kuck

1989 Mother's Sunshine	Retrd.	1990	35.00	85-95
1990 Reflection Of Love	Retrd.	1991	35.00	90-95
1991 A Precious Time	Retrd.	1992	35.00	80-90
1992 Loving Touch	Retrd.	1993	35.00	75-90

Western - E. Berke

1974 Mountain Man	Retrd.		165.00	165

The Wings of Nature Collection - W. Mumm

1999 Royal Courtship	95-day		29.90	30

Winter Wonderland - S. Kuck

1999 Magic Sleighride	95-day		35.00	35
2000 Bringing in the Xmas Tree	95-day		35.00	35
2001 Holiday Wishes	95-day		35.00	35

Women of the Plains - C. Corcilius

1994 Pride of a Maiden	36-day	1999	29.50	30
1995 No Boundaries	36-day	1998	29.50	30
1995 Silent Companions	36-day		35.00	35

The World of Children - J. McClelland

1977 Rainy Day Fun	10,000	1977	50.00	55-75
1978 When I Grow Up	15,000	1978	50.00	55-75
1979 You're Invited	15,000	1979	50.00	55-75
1980 Kittens for Sale	15,000	1980	50.00	55-85

River Shore

Baby Animals - R. Brown

1979 Akiku	20,000		50.00	50-80
1980 Roosevelt	20,000		50.00	50-90
1981 Clover	20,000		50.00	50-65
1982 Zuela	20,000		50.00	50-65

Famous Americans - Rockwell-Brown

1976 Brown's Lincoln	9,500		40.00	40-75
1977 Rockwell's Triple Self-Portrait	9,500		45.00	45-75
1978 Peace Corps	9,500		45.00	45-75
1979 Spirit of Lindbergh	9,500		50.00	50-70

Little House on the Prairie - E. Christopherson

1985 Founder's Day Picnic	10-day		29.50	45-100
1985 Women's Harvest	10-day		29.50	45-65
1985 Medicine Show	10-day		29.50	45-65
1985 Caroline's Eggs	10-day		29.50	45-65
1985 Mary's Gift	10-day		29.50	45-65
1985 A Bell for Walnut Grove	10-day		29.50	45-65
1985 Ingall's Family	10-day		29.50	45-65
1985 The Sweetheart Tree	10-day		29.50	45-65

Norman Rockwell Single Issue - N. Rockwell

1979 Spring Flowers	17,000		75.00	125-145
1980 Looking Out to Sea	17,000		75.00	175-195
1981 Grandpa's Guardian	17,000		80.00	75-80
1982 Grandpa's Treasures	17,000		80.00	75-80

Puppy Playtime - J. Lamb

1987 Double Take	14-day		24.50	35-45
1988 Catch of the Day	14-day		24.50	25-35
1988 Cabin Fever	14-day		24.50	25-35
1988 Weekend Gardener	14-day		24.50	25-35
1988 Getting Acquainted	14-day		24.50	25-35
1988 Hanging Out	14-day		24.50	25-35
1988 A New Leash On Life	14-day		24.50	30-35
1988 Fun and Games	14-day		24.50	30-35

Rockwell Four Freedoms - N. Rockwell

1981 Freedom of Speech	17,000		65.00	100-149
1982 Freedom of Worship	17,000		65.00	100-125

YEAR ISSUE	EDITION LIMIT	YEAR RETD.	ISSUE PRICE	*QUOTE U.S.$
1982 Freedom from Fear	17,000		65.00	100-200
1982 Freedom from Want	17,000		65.00	200-425

Rockwell Society

Christmas - N. Rockwell

1974 Scotty Gets His Tree	Yr.lss.		24.50	88-140
1975 Angel with Black Eye	Yr.lss.		24.50	34-65
1976 Golden Christmas	Yr.lss.		24.50	30-45
1977 Toy Shop Window	Yr.lss.		24.50	21-40
1978 Christmas Dream	Yr.lss.		24.50	15-45
1979 Somebody's Up There	Yr.lss.		24.50	10-45
1980 Scotty Plays Santa	Yr.lss.		24.50	10-50
1981 Wrapped Up in Christmas	Yr.lss.		25.50	9-26
1982 Christmas Courtship	Yr.lss.		25.50	8-30
1983 Santa in the Subway	Yr.lss.		25.50	10-50
1984 Santa in the Workshop	Yr.lss.		27.50	11-45
1985 Grandpa Plays Santa	Yr.lss.		27.90	11-45
1986 Dear Santy Claus	Yr.lss.		27.90	13-45
1987 Santa's Golden Gift	Yr.lss.		27.90	12-45
1988 Santa Claus	Yr.lss.		29.90	17-45
1989 Jolly Old St. Nick	Yr.lss.		29.90	12-40
1990 A Christmas Prayer	Yr.lss.		29.90	16-50
1991 Santa's Helpers	Yr.lss.		32.90	13-35
1992 The Christmas Surprise	Yr.lss.		32.90	20-35
1993 The Tree Brigade	Yr.lss.		32.90	18-33
1994 Christmas Marvel	Yr.lss.		32.90	20-45
1995 Filling The Stockings	Yr.lss.		32.90	44-54
1996 Christmas	Yr.lss.		32.90	44-49

Colonials-The Rarest Rockwells - N. Rockwell

1985 Unexpected Proposal	150-day		27.90	6-28
1986 Words of Comfort	150-day		27.90	8-28
1986 Light for the Winter	150-day		30.90	7-31
1987 Portrait for a Bridegroom	150-day		30.90	8-31
1987 The Journey Home	150-day		30.90	10-31
1987 Clinching the Deal	150-day		30.90	9-31
1988 Sign of the Times	150-day		32.90	12-47
1988 Ye Glutton	150-day		32.90	9-15

Coming Of Age - N. Rockwell

1990 Back To School	150-day		29.90	10-55
1990 Home From Camp	150-day		29.90	21-55
1990 Her First Formal	150-day		32.90	19-75
1990 The Muscleman	150-day		32.90	33-40
1990 A New Look	150-day		32.90	31-55
1991 A Balcony Seat	150-day		32.90	12-33
1991 Men About Town	150-day		34.90	13-35
1991 Paths of Glory	150-day		34.90	13-55
1991 Doorway to the Past	150-day		34.90	17-35
1991 School's Out!	150-day		34.90	25-30

Heritage - N. Rockwell

1977 Toy Maker	Yr.lss.		14.50	41-125
1978 Cobbler	Yr.lss.		19.50	30-70
1979 Lighthouse Keeper's Daughter	Yr.lss.		19.50	13-50
1980 Ship Builder	Yr.lss.		19.50	8-45
1981 Music maker	Yr.lss.		19.50	7-55
1982 Tycoon	Yr.lss.		19.50	6-45
1983 Painter	Yr.lss.		19.50	7-45
1984 Storyteller	Yr.lss.		19.50	9-45
1985 Gourmet	Yr.lss.		19.50	8-40
1986 Professor	Yr.lss.		22.90	9-40
1987 Shadow Artist	Yr.lss.		22.90	11-23
1988 The Veteran	Yr.lss.		22.90	16-47
1988 The Banjo Player	Yr.lss.		22.90	21-40
1990 The Old Scout	Yr.lss.		24.90	30-45
1991 The Young Scholar	Yr.lss.		24.90	19-35
1992 The Family Doctor	Yr.lss.		27.90	43-52
1993 The Jeweler	Yr.lss.		27.90	22-30
1994 Halloween Frolic	Yr.lss.		27.90	35-40
1995 The Apprentice	Yr.lss.		29.90	30-38
1996 Master Violinist	Yr.lss.		29.90	60-73
1997 The Dreamer	Yr.lss.		29.90	50

Innocence and Experience - N. Rockwell

1991 The Sea Captain	150-day		29.90	14-30
1991 The Radio Operator	150-day		29.90	22-30
1991 The Magician	150-day		29.90	49-51
1992 The American Heroes	150-day		32.90	19-35

PLATES & PLAQUES

YEAR ISSUE	EDITION LIMIT	YEAR RETD.	ISSUE PRICE	*QUOTE U.S.$

A Mind of Her Own - N. Rockwell

1986 Sitting Pretty	150-day		24.90	12-26
1987 Serious Business	150-day		24.90	15-35
1987 Breaking the Rules	150-day		24.90	21-23
1987 Good Intentions	150-day		27.90	20-40
1988 Second Thoughts	150-day		27.90	22-37
1988 World's Away	150-day		27.90	20-37
1988 Kiss and Tell	150-day		29.90	13-30
1988 On My Honor	150-day		29.90	34-40

Mother's Day - N. Rockwell

1976 A Mother's Love	Yr.Iss.		24.50	37-70
1977 Faith	Yr.Iss.		24.50	35-50
1978 Bedtime	Yr.Iss.		24.50	25-34
1979 Reflections	Yr.Iss.		24.50	10-25
1980 A Mother's Pride	Yr.Iss.		24.50	11-30
1981 After the Party	Yr.Iss.		24.50	9-25
1982 The Cooking Lesson	Yr.Iss.		24.50	7-29
1983 Add Two Cups and Love	Yr.Iss.		25.50	12-30
1984 Grandma's Courting Dress	Yr.Iss.		25.50	10-26
1985 Mending Time	Yr.Iss.		27.50	11-35
1986 Pantry Raid	Yr.Iss.		27.90	13-28
1987 Grandma's Surprise	Yr.Iss.		29.90	11-30
1988 My Mother	Yr.Iss.		29.90	14-24
1989 Sunday Dinner	Yr.Iss.		29.90	18-30
1990 Evening Prayers	Yr.Iss.		29.90	10-45
1991 Building Our Future	Yr.Iss.		32.90	9-33
1991 Gentle Reassurance	Yr.Iss.		32.90	17-33
1992 A Special Delivery	Yr.Iss.		32.90	7-35

Rockwell Commemorative Stamps - N. Rockwell

1994 Triple Self Portrait	95-day		29.90	44-56
1994 Freedom From Want	95-day		29.90	109-120
1994 Freedom From Fear	95-day		29.90	40-50
1995 Freedom of Speech	95-day		29.90	35-65
1995 Freedom of Worship	95-day		29.90	45-56

Rockwell on Tour - N. Rockwell

1983 Walking Through Merrie Englande	150-day		16.00	6-16
1983 Promenade a Paris	150-day		16.00	30
1983 When in Rome	150-day		16.00	7-16
1984 Die Walk am Rhein	150-day		16.00	7-16

Rockwell's American Dream - N. Rockwell

1985 A Young Girl's Dream	150-day		19.90	10-40
1985 A Couple's Commitment	150-day		19.90	16-40
1985 A Family's Full Measure	150-day		22.90	15-40
1986 A Mother's Welcome	150-day		22.90	14-23
1986 A Young Man's Dream	150-day		22.90	17-40
1986 The Musician's Magic	150-day		22.90	14-40
1987 An Orphan's Hope	150-day		24.90	20-40
1987 Love's Reward	150-day		24.90	20-27

Rockwell's Golden Moments - N. Rockwell

1987 Grandpa's Gift	150-day		19.90	10-40
1987 Grandma's Love	150-day		19.90	20
1988 End of day	150-day		22.90	20-30
1988 Best Friends	150-day		22.90	25
1989 Love Letters	150-day		22.90	27
1989 Newfound Worlds	150-day		22.90	12-23
1989 Keeping Company	150-day		24.90	12-40
1989 Evening's Repose	150-day		24.90	10-25

Rockwell's Light Campaign - N. Rockwell

1983 This is the Room that Light Made	150-day		19.50	9-55
1984 Grandpa's Treasure Chest	150-day		19.50	9-50
1984 Father's Help	150-day		19.50	9-45
1984 Evening's Ease	150-day		19.50	9-40
1984 Close Harmony	150-day		21.50	8-45
1984 The Birthday Wish	150-day		21.50	9-55

Rockwell's Rediscovered Women - N. Rockwell

1984 Dreaming in the Attic	100-day		19.50	7-45
1984 Waiting on the Shore	100-day		22.50	8-45
1984 Pondering on the Porch	100-day		22.50	10-45
1984 Making Believe at the Mirror	100-day		22.50	18-25
1984 Waiting at the Dance	100-day		22.50	15-40
1984 Gossiping in the Alcove	100-day		22.50	15-25
1984 Standing in the Doorway	100-day		22.50	10-40
1984 Flirting in the Parlor	100-day		22.50	14-40
1984 Working in the Kitchen	100-day		22.50	14-40
1984 Meeting on the Path	100-day		22.50	15-45

YEAR ISSUE	EDITION LIMIT	YEAR RETD.	ISSUE PRICE	*QUOTE U.S.$
1984 Confiding in the Den	100-day		22.50	19-45
1984 Reminiscing in the Quiet	100-day		22.50	25-38
XX Complete Collection	100-day		267.00	267

Rockwell's The Ones We Love - N. Rockwell

1988 Tender Loving Care	150-day		19.90	11-45
1989 A Time to Keep	150-day		19.90	14-17
1989 The Inventor And The Judge	150-day		22.90	18-29
1989 Ready For The World	150-day		22.90	15-23
1989 Growing Strong	150-day		22.90	18-25
1990 The Story Hour	150-day		22.90	20-30
1990 The Country Doctor	150-day		24.90	12-25
1990 Our Love of Country	150-day		24.90	12-25
1990 The Homecoming	150-day		24.90	18-48
1991 A Helping Hand	150-day		24.90	15-25

Rockwell's Treasured Memories - N. Rockwell

1991 Quiet Reflections	150-day		29.90	12-30
1991 Romantic Reverie	150-day		29.90	27-30
1991 Tender Romance	150-day		32.90	14-33
1991 Evening Passage	150-day		32.90	9-33
1991 Heavenly Dreams	150-day		32.90	25-33
1991 Sentimental Shores	150-day		32.90	19-33

Roman, Inc.

A Child's Play - F. Hook

1982 Breezy Day	30-day	N/A	29.95	39
1982 Kite Flying	30-day	N/A	29.95	39
1984 Bathtub Sailor	30-day	N/A	29.95	35
1984 The First Snow	30-day	N/A	29.95	35

A Child's World - F. Hook

1980 Little Children, Come to Me	15,000		45.00	49

Frances Hook Collection-Set I - F. Hook

1982 Baby Blossoms	15,000	N/A	24.95	39-45
1982 Daisy Dreamer	15,000	N/A	24.95	39-55
1982 I Wish, I Wish	15,000	N/A	24.95	75-85
1982 Trees So Tall	15,000	N/A	24.95	39-55

Frances Hook Collection-Set II - F. Hook

1983 Can I Keep Him?	15,000	N/A	24.95	25
1983 Caught It Myself	15,000	N/A	24.95	25
1983 So Cuddly	15,000	N/A	24.95	25
1983 Winter Wrappings	15,000	N/A	24.95	25

Frances Hook Legacy - F. Hook

1985 Daydreaming	100-day	N/A	19.50	39-49
1985 Disappointment	100-day	N/A	22.50	39-49
1985 Discovery	100-day	N/A	22.50	39-49
1985 Expectation	100-day	N/A	22.50	39-49
1985 Fascination	100-day	N/A	19.50	39-49
1985 Wonderment	100-day	N/A	22.50	39-49

March of Dimes: Our Children, Our Future - A. Williams

1990 A Time To Laugh	150-day	N/A	29.00	14-29

The Masterpiece Collection - Various

1979 Adoration	5,000	N/A	65.00	65
1980 Madonna with Grapes	5,000	N/A	87.50	88
1981 The Holy Family	5,000	N/A	95.00	95
1982 Madonna of the Streets	5,000	N/A	85.00	85

The Millenium® Collection - G. Ho

2001 Heaven On Earth Oval Plaque	Open		39.50	40

The Millenium® Collection - Sr. Mary Jean Dorcy

1992 Silent Night	2,000	1992	49.50	80-175
1993 The Annunciation	5,000	1993	49.50	100-175
1994 Peace On Earth	5,000	1994	49.50	75-110
1995 Cause of Our Joy	7,500	1995	49.50	50
1996 Prince of Peace	15,000	1996	49.50	50
1997 Gentle Love	Yr.Iss.	1997	49.50	50
1998 Rejoice	Yr.Iss.	1998	48.50	49
1999 Heaven's Blessing	Yr.Iss.	1999	48.50	49
1999 Joyful Promise	2-Yr.	2000	48.50	49

Roman Memorial - F. Hook

1984 The Carpenter	Closed	1984	100.00	135

Single Releases - A. Williams

1987 The Christening	Closed	N/A	29.50	30

YEAR ISSUE	EDITION LIMIT	YEAR RETD.	ISSUE PRICE	*QUOTE U.S.$
1990 The Dedication	Closed	N/A	29.50	30
1990 The Baptism	Closed	N/A	29.50	30

Valencia, Story of Jesus - G. Ho

2000 Last Supper	Open		45.00	45

Rosenthal

Christmas - Unknown

YEAR ISSUE	EDITION LIMIT	YEAR RETD.	ISSUE PRICE	*QUOTE U.S.$
1910 Winter Peace	Annual		Unkn.	550
1911 Three Wise Men	Annual		Unkn.	325
1912 Stardust	Annual		Unkn.	255
1913 Christmas Lights	Annual		Unkn.	235
1914 Christmas Song	Annual		Unkn.	350
1915 Walking to Church	Annual		Unkn.	180
1916 Christmas During War	Annual		Unkn.	240
1917 Angel of Peace	Annual		Unkn.	200
1918 Peace on Earth	Annual		Unkn.	200
1919 St. Christopher with Christ Child	Annual		Unkn.	225
1920 Manger in Bethlehem	Annual		Unkn.	325
1921 Christmas in Mountains	Annual		Unkn.	200
1922 Advent Branch	Annual		Unkn.	200
1923 Children in Winter Woods	Annual		Unkn.	200
1924 Deer in the Woods	Annual		Unkn.	200
1925 Three Wise Men	Annual		Unkn.	200
1926 Christmas in Mountains	Annual		Unkn.	195
1927 Station on the Way	Annual		Unkn.	135-175
1928 Chalet Christmas	Annual		Unkn.	185
1929 Christmas in Alps	Annual		Unkn.	225
1930 Group of Deer Under Pines	Annual		Unkn.	225
1931 Path of the Magi	Annual		Unkn.	225
1932 Christ Child	Annual		Unkn.	185
1933 Thru the Night to Light	Annual		Unkn.	190
1934 Christmas Peace	Annual		Unkn.	190
1935 Christmas by the Sea	Annual		Unkn.	190
1936 Nurnberg Angel	Annual		Unkn.	175-200
1937 Berchtesgaden	Annual		Unkn.	195
1938 Christmas in the Alps	Annual		Unkn.	195
1939 Schneekoppe Mountain	Annual		Unkn.	195
1940 Marien Chruch(girl) in Danzig	Annual		Unkn.	200-225
1941 Strassburg Cathedral	Annual		Unkn.	200-225
1942 Marianburg Castle	Annual		Unkn.	300
1943 Winter Idyll	Annual		Unkn.	300
1944 Wood Scape	Annual		Unkn.	300
1945 Christmas Peace	Annual		Unkn.	400
1946 Christmas in an Alpine Valley	Annual		Unkn.	240
1947 Dillingen Madonna	Annual		Unkn.	985
1948 Message to the Shepherds	Annual		Unkn.	875
1949 The Holy Family	Annual		Unkn.	185
1950 Christmas in the Forest	Annual		Unkn.	185
1951 Star of Bethlehem	Annual		Unkn.	450
1952 Christmas in the Alps	Annual		Unkn.	195
1953 The Holy Light	Annual		Unkn.	195
1954 Christmas Eve	Annual		Unkn.	195
1955 Christmas in a Village	Annual		Unkn.	195
1956 Christmas in the Alps	Annual		Unkn.	195
1957 Christmas by the Sea	Annual		Unkn.	195
1958 Christmas Eve	Annual		Unkn.	195
1959 Midnight Mass	Annual		Unkn.	75-125
1960 Christmas in a Small Village	Annual		Unkn.	195
1961 Solitary Christmas	Annual		Unkn.	100-200
1962 Christmas Eve	Annual		Unkn.	75-150
1963 Silent Night	Annual		Unkn.	75-150
1964 Christmas Market in Nurnberg	Annual		Unkn.	225
1965 Christmas Munich	Annual		Unkn.	185
1966 Christmas in Ulm	Annual		Unkn.	275
1967 Christmas in Reginburg	Annual		Unkn.	185
1968 Christmas in Bremen	Annual		Unkn.	195
1969 Christmas in Rothenburg	Annual		Unkn.	175-220
1970 Christmas in Cologne	Annual		Unkn.	175
1971 Christmas in Garmisch	Annual		42.00	100
1972 Christmas in Franconia	Annual		50.00	95
1973 Lubeck-Holstein	Annual		77.00	105
1974 Christmas in Wurzburg	Annual		85.00	90-100

Nobility of Children - E. Hibel

1976 La Contessa Isabella	12,750		120.00	120
1977 La Marquis Maurice-Pierre	12,750		120.00	120
1978 Baronesse Johanna	12,750		130.00	140
1979 Chief Red Feather	12,750		140.00	180

Wiinblad Christmas - B. Wiinblad

YEAR ISSUE	EDITION LIMIT	YEAR RETD.	ISSUE PRICE	*QUOTE U.S.$
1971 Maria & Child	Undis.		100.00	750
1972 Caspar	Undis.		100.00	290
1973 Melchior	Undis.		125.00	335
1974 Balthazar	Undis.		125.00	300
1975 The Annunciation	Undis.		195.00	195
1976 Angel with Trumpet	Undis.		195.00	195
1977 Adoration of Shepherds	Undis.		225.00	225
1978 Angel with Harp	Undis.		275.00	295
1979 Exodus from Egypt	Undis.		310.00	310
1980 Angel with Glockenspiel	Undis.		360.00	360
1981 Christ Child Visits Temple	Undis.		375.00	375
1982 Christening of Christ	Undis.		375.00	375

Royal Copenhagen

Christmas - Various

YEAR ISSUE	EDITION LIMIT	YEAR RETD.	ISSUE PRICE	*QUOTE U.S.$
1908 Madonna and Child - C. Thomsen	Annual	1908	1.00	2750-6000
1909 Danish Landscape - S. Ussing	Annual	1909	1.00	192-360
1910 The Magi - C. Thomsen	Annual	1910	1.00	130-285
1911 Danish Landscape - O. Jensen	Annual	1911	1.00	144-259
1912 Christmas Tree - C. Thomsen	Annual	1912	1.00	150-300
1913 Frederik Church Spire - A. Boesen	Annual	1913	1.50	147-207
1914 Holy Spirit Church - A. Boesen	Annual	1914	1.50	175-249
1915 Danish Landscape - A. Krog	Annual	1915	1.50	120-198
1916 Shepherd at Christmas - R. Bocher	Annual	1916	1.50	105-165
1917 Our Savior Church - O. Jensen	Annual	1917	2.00	105-147
1918 Sheep and Shepherds - O. Jensen	Annual	1918	2.00	105-147
1919 In the Park - O. Jensen	Annual	1919	2.00	105-147
1920 Mary and Child Jesus - G. Rode	Annual	1920	2.00	105-150
1921 Aabenraa Marketplace - O. Jensen	Annual	1921	2.00	100-135
1922 Three Singing Angels - E. Selschau	Annual	1922	2.00	100-148
1923 Danish Landscape - O. Jensen	Annual	1923	2.00	94-135
1924 Sailing Ship - B. Olsen	Annual	1924	2.00	95-168
1925 Christianshavn - O. Jensen	Annual	1925	2.00	95-162
1926 Christianshavn Canal - R. Bocher	Annual	1926	2.00	130-162
1927 Ship's Boy at Tiller - B. Olsen	Annual	1927	2.00	99-213
1928 Vicar's Family - G. Rode	Annual	1928	2.00	98-147
1929 Grundtvig Church - O. Jensen	Annual	1929	2.00	100-165
1930 Fishing Boats - B. Olsen	Annual	1930	2.50	134-150
1931 Mother and Child - G. Rode	Annual	1931	2.50	140-186
1932 Frederiksberg Gardens - O. Jensen	Annual	1932	2.50	113-180
1933 Ferry and the Great Belt - B. Olsen	Annual	1933	2.50	188-250
1934 The Hermitage Castle - O. Jensen	Annual	1934	2.50	210-280
1935 Kronborg Castle - B. Olsen	Annual	1935	2.50	240-357
1936 Roskilde Cathedral - R. Bocher	Annual	1936	2.50	254-357
1937 Main Street Copenhagen - N. Thorsson	Annual	1937	2.50	250-447
1938 Round Church in Osterlars - H. Nielsen	Annual	1938	3.00	425-575
1939 Greenland Pack-Ice - S. Nielsen	Annual	1939	3.00	525-720
1940 The Good Shepherd - K. Lange	Annual	1940	3.00	525-720
1941 Danish Village Church - T. Kjolner	Annual	1941	3.00	500-579
1942 Bell Tower - N. Thorsson	Annual	1942	4.00	300-822
1943 Flight into Egypt - N. Thorsson	Annual	1943	4.00	625-999
1944 Danish Village Scene - V. Olson	Annual	1944	4.00	350-498
1945 A Peaceful Motif - R. Bocher	Annual	1945	4.00	475-810
1946 Zealand Village Church - N. Thorsson	Annual	1946	4.00	240-375
1947 The Good Shepherd - K. Lange	Annual	1947	4.50	190-414
1948 Nodebo Church - T. Kjolner	Annual	1948	4.50	260-336
1949 Our Lady's Cathedral - H. Hansen	Annual	1949	5.00	275-369
1950 Boeslunde Church - V. Olson	Annual	1950	5.00	230-450
1951 Christmas Angel - R. Bocher	Annual	1951	5.00	395-650
1952 Christmas in the Forest - K. Lange	Annual	1952	5.00	170-219
1953 Frederiksberg Castle - T. Kjolner	Annual	1953	6.00	150-213
1954 Amalienborg Palace - K. Lange	Annual	1954	6.00	145-240
1955 Fano Girl - K. Lange	Annual	1955	7.00	225-270
1956 Rosenborg Castle - K. Lange	Annual	1956	7.00	195-294
1957 The Good Shepherd - H. Hansen	Annual	1957	8.00	125-175
1958 Sunshine over Greenland - H. Hansen	Annual	1958	9.00	158-234
1959 Christmas Night - H. Hansen	Annual	1959	9.00	145-240
1960 The Stag - H. Hansen	Annual	1960	10.00	85-261
1961 Training Ship - K. Lange	Annual	1961	10.00	115-231
1962 The Little Mermaid - Unknown	Annual	1962	11.00	194-336
1963 Hojsager Mill - K. Lange	Annual	1963	11.00	82-99
1964 Fetching the Tree - K. Lange	Annual	1964	11.00	35-99
1965 Little Skaters - K. Lange	Annual	1965	12.00	35-75
1966 Blackbird - K. Lange	Annual	1966	12.00	22-65
1967 The Royal Oak - K. Lange	Annual	1967	13.00	19-60
1968 The Last Umiak - K. Lange	Annual	1968	13.00	15-50

YEAR ISSUE	EDITION LIMIT	YEAR RETD.	ISSUE PRICE	*QUOTE U.S.$
1969 The Old Farmyard - K. Lange	Annual	1969	14.00	20-58
1970 Christmas Rose and Cat - K. Lange	Annual	1970	14.00	22-55
1971 Hare In Winter - K. Lange	Annual	1971	15.00	16-35
1972 In the Desert - K. Lange	Annual	1972	16.00	16-35
1973 Train Homeward Bound - K. Lange	Annual	1973	22.00	24-40
1974 Winter Twilight - K. Lange	Annual	1974	22.00	16-50
1975 Queen's Palace - K. Lange	Annual	1975	27.50	16-27
1976 Danish Watermill - S. Vestergaard	Annual	1976	27.50	16-36
1977 Immervad Bridge - K. Lange	Annual	1977	32.00	20-35
1978 Greenland Scenery - K. Lange	Annual	1978	35.00	25-70
1979 Choosing Christmas Tree - K. Lange	Annual	1979	42.50	35-96
1980 Bringing Home the Tree - K. Lange	Annual	1980	49.50	20-55
1981 Admiring Christmas Tree - K. Lange	Annual	1981	52.50	26-39
1982 Waiting for Christmas - K. Lange	Annual	1982	54.50	55-75
1983 Merry Christmas - K. Lange	Annual	1983	54.50	45-80
1984 Jingle Bells - K. Lange	Annual	1984	54.50	49-60
1985 Snowman - K. Lange	Annual	1985	54.50	75-129
1986 Christmas Vacation - K. Lange	Annual	1986	54.50	60-96
1987 Winter Birds - S. Vestergaard	Annual	1987	59.50	55-118
1988 Christmas Eve in Copenhagen - S. Vestergaard	Annual	1988	59.50	90-120
1989 The Old Skating Pond - S. Vestergaard	Annual	1989	59.50	96-125
1990 Christmas at Tivoli - S. Vestergaard	Annual	1990	64.50	160-255
1991 The Festival of Santa Lucia - S. Vestergaard	Annual	1991	69.50	125-144
1992 The Queen's Carriage - S. Vestergaard	Annual	1992	69.50	75-135
1993 Christmas Guests - S. Vestergaard	Annual	1993	69.50	180-414
1994 Christmas Shopping - S. Vestergaard	Annual	1994	72.50	72-111
1995 Christmas at the Manor House - S. Vestergaard	Annual	1995	72.50	250-414
1996 Lighting the Street Lamps - S. Vestergaard	Annual	1996	74.50	69-127
1997 Roskilde Cathedral - S. Vestergaard	Annual	1997	69.50	72-95
1998 Coming Home For Christmas - S. Vestergaard	Annual	1998	69.50	70-225
1999 The Sleigh Ride - S. Vestergaard	Annual	1999	72.50	73-113
2000 Decorating The Tree - S. Vestergaard	Annual	2000	72.50	73
2001 Watching The Birds - S. Vestergaard	Annual	2001	72.50	73

Royal Doulton

All God's Children - L. DeWinne

1978 A Brighter Day	10,000	1984	75.00	75-100
1980 Village Children	10,000	1984	65.00	65
1981 Noble Heritage	10,000	1984	85.00	85
1982 Buddies	10,000	1984	85.00	85
1983 My Little Brother	10,000	1984	95.00	95

American Tapestries - C.A. Brown

1978 Sleigh Bells	15,000	1983	70.00	70
1979 Pumpkin Patch	15,000	1983	70.00	70
1981 General Store	10,000	1983	95.00	95
1982 Fourth of July	10,000	1983	95.00	95

Behind the Painted Mask - B. Black

1982 Painted Feelings	10,000	1986	95.00	175-200
1983 Make Me Laugh	10,000	1986	95.00	175-200
1984 Minstrel Serenade	10,000	1986	95.00	175-200
1985 Pleasing Performance	10,000	1986	95.00	175-200

Burslem Artwares - C. Noke

2001 Qingdao Charger Plate	200		1160.00	1160

Celebration of Faith - J. Woods

1982 Rosh Hashanah	7,500	1986	250.00	300-400
1983 Yom Kippur	7,500	1986	250.00	250
1984 Passover	7,500	1986	250.00	250
1985 Chanukah	7,500	1986	250.00	250

Character Plates - N/A

1979 Old Balloon Seller	Closed	1983	100.00	120-125
1980 Balloon Man	Closed	1983	125.00	125
1981 Silks and Ribbons	Closed	1983	125.00	140
1982 Biddy Penny Farthing	Closed	1983	125.00	125

Charles Dickens Plates - N/A

1980 Artful Dodger	Closed	1984	65.00	65
1980 Barkis	Closed	1984	80.00	80-95
1980 Cap'n Cuttle	Closed	1984	80.00	80
1980 Fagin	Closed	1984	65.00	65
1980 Fat Boy	Closed	1984	65.00	65
1980 Mr. Micawber	Closed	1984	80.00	80

YEAR ISSUE	EDITION LIMIT	YEAR RETD.	ISSUE PRICE	*QUOTE U.S.$
1980 Mr. Pickwick	Closed	1984	80.00	80-95
1980 Old Peggoty	Closed	1984	65.00	65
1980 Poor Jo	Closed	1984	80.00	80
1980 Sairey Gamp	Closed	1984	80.00	80
1980 Sam Weller	Closed	1984	65.00	65
1980 Sergeant Buz Fuz	Closed	1984	80.00	80
1980 Tony Weller	Closed	1984	65.00	65

Childhood Christmas - N/A

1983 Silent Night	Yr.Iss.	1983	35.00	75
1984 While Shepherds Watched	Yr.Iss.	1984	39.95	75
1985 Oh Little Town of Bethlehem	Yr.Iss.	1985	39.95	40
1986 We Saw 3 Ships A-Sailing	Yr.Iss.	1986	39.95	40
1987 The Holly and the Ivy	Yr.Iss.	1987	39.95	40

Children of the Pueblo - M. Jungbluth

1983 Apple Flower	15,000	1985	60.00	150-195
1984 Morning Star	15,000	1985	60.00	150-195

Christmas Around the World - N/A

1972 Old England	15,000	1979	35.00	35-80
1973 Mexico	15,000	1979	37.50	38
1974 Bulgaria	15,000	1979	37.50	38
1975 Norway	15,000	1979	45.00	45-80
1976 Holland	15,000	1979	50.00	50
1977 Poland	15,000	1979	50.00	50-80
1978 America	15,000	1979	55.00	55

Christmas Plates - Various

1993 Royal Doulton-Together For Christmas - J. James	Yr.Iss.	1993	45.00	50
1993 Royal Albert-Sleighride - N/A	Yr.Iss.	1993	45.00	45
1994 Royal Doulton-Home For Christmas - J. James	Yr.Iss.	1994	45.00	45
1994 Royal Albert-Coaching Inn - N/A	Yr.Iss.	1994	45.00	45
1995 Royal Doulton-Season's Greetings - J. James	Yr.Iss.	1995	45.00	45
1995 Royal Albert-Skating Pond - N/A	Yr.Iss.	1995	45.00	45
1996 Royal Doulton-Night Before Christmas - J. James	Yr.Iss.	1996	45.00	45
1996 Royal Albert-Gathering Winter Fuel - N/A	Yr.Iss.	1996	45.00	45

Commedia Dell Arte - L. Neiman

1974 Harlequin	15,000	1979	100.00	125-195
1975 Pierrot	15,000	1979	90.00	125-145
1977 Columbine	15,000	1979	80.00	80-95
1978 Punchinello	15,000	1979	75.00	75-80

Family Christmas Plates - N/A

1991 Dad Plays Santa	Closed	1991	60.00	60

Festival Children of the World - B. Burke

1983 Mariana (Balinese)	15,000	1986	65.00	35-65
1984 Magdalena (Mexico)	15,000	1986	65.00	35-65
1985 Michiko (Japanese)	15,000	1986	65.00	35-65

Flower Garden - H. Vidal

1975 Spring Harmony	15,000	1981	80.00	80
1976 Dreaming Lotus	15,000	1981	90.00	90
1977 From the Poet's Garden	15,000	1981	75.00	75
1978 Country Bouquet	15,000	1981	75.00	75
1979 From My Mother's Garden	15,000	1981	85.00	90

The Grandest Gift - Mago

1985 Reunion	10,000	1986	75.00	100-150
1985 Storytime	10,000	1986	75.00	100

Grandparents - Mago

1984 Grandfather and Children	15,000	1985	95.00	200-250

I Remember America - E. Sloane

1977 Pennsylvania Pastorale	15,000	1982	90.00	90
1978 Lovejoy Bridge	15,000	1982	80.00	80
1979 Four Corners	15,000	1982	75.00	75
1981 Marshland	15,000	1982	95.00	95

Jungle Fantasy - G. Novoa

1979 The Ark	10,000	1984	75.00	75
1981 Compassion	10,000	1984	95.00	95
1982 Patience	10,000	1984	95.00	95
1983 Refuge	10,000	1984	95.00	95

*Quotes have been rounded up to nearest dollar

YEAR ISSUE	EDITION LIMIT	YEAR RETD.	ISSUE PRICE	*QUOTE U.S.$
Log of the Dashing Wave - J. Stobart				
1976 Sailing With the Tide	15,000	1983	115.00	115
1977 Running Free	15,000	1983	110.00	120-150
1978 Rounding the Horn	15,000	1983	85.00	85-95
1979 Hong Kong	15,000	1983	75.00	75
1981 Bora Bora	15,000	1983	95.00	95
1982 Journey's End	15,000	1983	95.00	150
Mother and Child - E. Hibel				
1973 Colette and Child	15,000	1982	500.00	500
1974 Sayuri and Child	15,000	1982	175.00	150
1975 Kristina and Child	15,000	1982	125.00	150-195
1976 Marilyn and Child	15,000	1982	110.00	140-195
1977 Lucia and Child	15,000	1982	90.00	90
1981 Kathleen and Child	15,000	1982	85.00	150-195
Portraits of Innocence - F. Masseria				
1980 Panchito	15,000	1987	65.00	95-250
1981 Adrien	15,000	1987	85.00	65-120
1982 Angelica	15,000	1987	95.00	65-120
1983 Juliana	15,000	1987	95.00	75-120
1985 Gabriella	15,000	1987	95.00	75-120
1986 Francesca	15,000	1987	95.00	195-210
Ports of Call - D. Kingman				
1975 San Francisco, Fisherman's Wharf	15,000	1979	90.00	90
1976 New Orleans, Royal Street	15,000	1979	80.00	80
1977 Venice, Grand Canal	15,000	1979	65.00	65
1978 Paris, Montmartre	15,000	1979	70.00	70
Reflections of China - C. Chi				
1976 Garden of Tranquility	15,000	1981	90.00	90
1977 Imperial Palace	15,000	1981	80.00	80
1978 Temple of Heaven	15,000	1981	75.00	75
1980 Lake of Mists	15,000	1981	85.00	85
Victorian Era Christmas - N/A				
1977 Winter Fun	Yr.Iss.	1977	55.00	55
1978 Christmas Day	Yr.Iss.	1978	55.00	55
1979 Christmas	Yr.Iss.	1979	25.00	25
1980 Santa's Visit	Yr.Iss.	1980	30.00	30
1981 Christmas Carolers	Yr.Iss.	1981	37.50	38
1982 Santa on Bicycle	Yr.Iss.	1982	39.95	40
Victorian Era Valentines - N/A				
1976 Victorian Boy and Girl	Yr.Iss.	1976	65.00	65-75
1977 My Sweetest Friend	Yr.Iss.	1977	40.00	40-65
1978 If I Loved You	Yr.Iss.	1978	40.00	40
1979 My Valentine	Yr.Iss.	1979	35.00	35
1980 Valentine	Yr.Iss.	1980	33.00	33
1981 Valentine Boy and Girl	Yr.Iss.	1981	35.00	35
1982 Angel with Mandolin	Yr.Iss.	1982	39.95	40
1985 My Valentine	Yr.Iss.	1985	39.95	40

Seraphim Classics®/Roman, Inc.

Seraphim Classics® Faro Collection - Faro Studios

1994 Rosalyn - Rarest of Heaven	7,200	1994	65.00	65-175
1995 Helena - Heaven's Herald	7,200	1995	65.00	65-125
1996 Flora - Flower of Heaven	7,200	1996	65.00	65-150
1997 Emily - Heaven's Treasure	Yr.Iss.	1997	65.00	65-90
1998 Elise - Heaven's Glory	Yr.Iss.	1998	65.00	65-85
1999 Gwydolyn - Heaven's Triumph	Yr.Iss.	1999	65.00	65

Seraphim Classics® Oval Plate - Seraphim Studios

1996 Cymbeline - Peacemaker	2-Yr.	1998	49.95	50
1996 Isabel - Gentle Spirit	2-Yr.	1998	49.95	50
1996 Lydia - Winged Poet	2-Yr.	1998	49.95	50
1996 Priscilla - Benevolent Guide	2-Yr.	1998	49.95	50

Sports Impressions/Enesco Group, Inc.

Gold Edition Plates - Various

1990 Andre Dawson - R. Lewis	Closed	N/A	150.00	100-150
XX A's Jose Canseco Gold (10 1/4") 1028-04 - J. Canseco	2,500	N/A	125.00	100-125
1987 Brooks Robinson F/S - R. Simon	1,000	N/A	125.00	125-150
1988 Brooks Robinson, signed - R. Simon	Closed	N/A	125.00	150-250
1987 Carl Yastrzemski, signed - R. Simon	1,500	N/A	125.00	100-150
1993 Chicago Bulls 1993 World Championship Gold (10 1/4") 4062-04 - B. Vann	1,993	1994	150.00	100-150

YEAR ISSUE	EDITION LIMIT	YEAR RETD.	ISSUE PRICE	*QUOTE U.S.$
1992 Chicago Bulls '92 World Champions - C. Hayes	Closed	N/A	150.00	150
1987 Darryl Strawberry #1 - R. Simon	Closed	N/A	125.00	100-125
1989 Darryl Strawberry #2 - T. Fogerty	Closed	N/A	125.00	100-125
1986 Don Mattingly - B. Johnson	Closed	N/A	125.00	125-150
1991 Dream Team (1st Ten Chosen) - L. Salk	Closed	N/A	150.00	495-750
1992 Dream Team 1992 Gold (10 1/4") 5509-04 - R. Tanenbaum	1,992	1994	150.00	150-200
1992 Dream Team 1992 Platinum (8 1/2") 5507-03 - C. Hayes	7,500	1994	60.00	95
1991 Hawks Dominique Wilkins - J. Catalano	Closed	N/A	150.00	150-195
1990 Joe Montana 49ers Gold (10 1/4") 3000-04 - J. Catalano	1,990	1991	150.00	195-250
1986 Keith Hernandez - R. Simon	Closed	N/A	125.00	150-175
1991 Larry Bird - J. Catalano	Closed	N/A	150.00	195
1988 Larry Bird - R. Simon	Closed	N/A	125.00	275
1990 Living Triple Crown - R. Lewis	Closed	N/A	150.00	150
1993 Magic Johnson - T. Fogerty	Closed	N/A	150.00	150
1991 Magic Johnson Lakers Gold (10 1/4") 4007-04 - C.W. Mundy	1,991	1991	150.00	225
1992 Magic Johnson Lakers Gold (10 1/4") 4042-04 - R. Tanenbaum	1,992	1994	150.00	175
1991 Magic Johnson Lakers Platinum (8 1/2") 4007-03 - M. Petronella	5,000	1992	60.00	75
1989 Mantle Switch Hitter - J. Catalano	Closed	N/A	150.00	225-275
1992 Michael Jordan Bulls (10 1/4") 4032-04 - R. Tanenbaum	1,991	1992	150.00	225
1993 Michael Jordan Bulls Gold (10 1/4") 4046-04 - T. Fogerty	2,500	1993	150.00	150-175
1991 Michael Jordan Gold (10 1/4") 4002-04 - J. Catalano	1,991	1992	150.00	200
1991 Michael Jordan Platinum (8 1/2") 4002-03 - M. Petronella	1,991	1993	60.00	95
1995 Mickey Mantle "My Greatest Year 1956" 1229-04 - B. Vann	1,956	N/A	100.00	100-195
1991 Mickey Mantle 7 - B. Simon	Closed	N/A	150.00	150-195
1986 Mickey Mantle At Night (signed) - R. Simon	Closed	N/A	125.00	250-395
1995 Mickey Mantle double plate set, Platinum (8 1/2") 176923 - T. Treadway	2,401		75.00	75
1987 Mickey, Willie, & Duke (signed) - R. Simon	1,500	N/A	150.00	195-395
1988 Mickey, Willie, & Duke, (signed) 1041-59 - R. Simon	2,500		150.00	150
1992 NBA 1st Ten Chosen Platinum (8 1/2") (blue) 5502-03 - J. Catalano	7,500	1993	60.00	95
1992 NBA 1st Ten Chosen Platinum (8 1/2") (red) 5503-03 - C.W. Mundy	7,500	1993	60.00	95
1990 Nolan Ryan 300 Gold 1091-04 - T. Fogarty	1,990	1992	150.00	150
1990 Nolan Ryan 5,000 K's - J. Catalano	1,990		150.00	150
1995 Profiles in Courage Mickey Mantle Platinum (8 1/2") 1231-03 - M. Petronella	Open		30.00	30
1990 Rickey Henderson - R. Lewis	Closed	N/A	150.00	125-150
XX Roberto Clemente 1090-03 - R. Lewis	10,000	N/A	75.00	75
1993 Shaquille O'Neal Gold (10 1/4") 4047-04 - T. Fogarty	2,500	1994	150.00	150-195
1994 Shaquille O'Neal, Rookie of the Year - N/A	Open		100.00	100
1987 Ted Williams (signed) - R. Simon	Closed	N/A	125.00	450-495
1990 Tom Seaver - R. Lewis	Closed	N/A	150.00	150-200
1986 Wade Bogg (signed) - B. Johnson	Closed	N/A	125.00	150-175
1989 Will Clark - J. Catalano	Closed	N/A	125.00	100-150
1988 Yankee Tradition - J. Catalano	Closed	N/A	150.00	195-200

Villeroy & Boch

Flower Fairy - C. Barker

1979 Lavender		21-day	35.00	125
1980 Sweet Pea		21-day	35.00	125
1980 Candytuft		21-day	35.00	89
1981 Heliotrope		21-day	35.00	75
1981 Blackthorn		21-day	35.00	75
1981 Appleblossom		21-day	35.00	95

Russian Fairytales Maria Morevna - B. Zvorykin

1983 Maria Morevna and Tsarevich Ivan	27,500		70.00	70-140
1983 Koshchey Carries Off Maria Morevna	27,500		70.00	70-150
1983 Tsarevich Ivan and the Beautiful Castle	27,500		70.00	70-125

YEAR ISSUE	EDITION LIMIT	YEAR RETD.	ISSUE PRICE	*QUOTE U.S.$
Russian Fairytales The Firebird - B. Zvorykin				
1982 In Search of the Firebird	27,500		70.00	88-100
1982 Ivan and Tsarevna on the Grey Wolf	27,500		70.00	90-118
1982 The Wedding of Tsarevna Elena the Fair	27,500		70.00	100-200
Russian Fairytales The Red Knight - B. Zvorykin				
1981 The Red Knight	27,500		70.00	30-66
1981 Vassilissa and Her Stepsisters	27,500		70.00	40-50
1981 Vassilissa is Presented to the Tsar	27,500		70.00	45-71
Villeroy & Boch - B. Zvorykin				
1980 The Snow Maiden	27,500		70.00	75-100
1980 Snegurochka at the Court of Tsar Berendei	27,500		70.00	80-97
1980 Snegurochka and Lei, the Shepherd Boy	27,500		70.00	100-200

V-Palekh Art Studios

YEAR ISSUE	EDITION LIMIT	YEAR RETD.	ISSUE PRICE	*QUOTE U.S.$
Russian Legends - Various				
1988 Ruslan and Ludmilla - G. Lubimov	195-day		29.87	12-30
1988 The Princess/Seven Bogatyrs - A. Kovalev	195-day		29.87	15-30
1988 The Golden Cockerel - V. Vleshko	195-day		32.87	15-33
1988 Lukomorya - R. Belousov	195-day		32.87	18-33
1989 Fisherman and the Magic Fish - N. Lopatin	195-day		32.87	15-33
1989 Tsar Saltan - G. Zhiryakova	195-day		32.87	15-33
1989 The Priest and His Servant - O. An	195-day		34.87	20-35
1990 Stone Flower - V. Bolshakova	195-day		34.87	28-35
1990 Sadko - E. Populor	195-day		34.87	30-40
1990 The Twelve Months - N. Lopatin	195-day		36.87	40-48
1990 Silver Hoof - S. Adeyanor	195-day		36.87	47-55
1990 Morozko - N. Lopatin	195-day		36.87	61-70

W.S. George

YEAR ISSUE	EDITION LIMIT	YEAR RETD.	ISSUE PRICE	*QUOTE U.S.$
Alaska: The Last Frontier - H. Lambson				
1991 Icy Majesty	Closed		34.50	19-35
1991 Autumn Grandeur	Closed		34.50	23-27
1992 Mountain Monarch	Closed		37.50	30-39
1992 Down the Trail	Closed		37.50	35-39
1992 Moonlight Lookout	Closed		37.50	48-52
1992 Graceful Passage	Closed		39.50	59-60
1992 Arctic Journey	Closed		39.50	55
1992 Summit Domain	Closed		39.50	45-60
Along an English Lane - M. Harvey				
1993 Summer's Bright Welcome	Closed		29.50	41-50
1993 Greeting the Day	Closed		29.50	53-60
1993 Friends and Flowers	Closed		29.50	60
1993 Cottage Around the Bend	Closed		29.50	53
America the Beautiful - H. Johnson				
1988 Yosemite Falls	Closed		34.50	26-29
1989 The Grand Canyon	Closed		34.50	16-29
1989 Yellowstone River	Closed		37.50	18-30
1989 The Great Smokey Mountains	Closed		37.50	18-30
1990 The Everglades	Closed		37.50	19-42
1990 Acadia	Closed		37.50	15-20
1990 The Grand Tetons	Closed		39.50	25-32
1990 Crater Lake	Closed		39.50	10-28
America's Pride - R. Richert				
1992 Misty Fjords	Closed		29.50	38
1992 Rugged Shores	Closed		29.50	30-36
1992 Mighty Summit	Closed		32.50	37-45
1993 Lofty Reflections	Closed		32.50	60
1993 Tranquil Waters	Closed		32.50	33-50
1993 Mountain Majesty	Closed		34.50	33
1993 Canyon Climb	Closed		34.50	49
1993 Golden Vista	Closed		34.50	35
Art Deco - M. McDonald				
1989 A Flapper With Greyhounds	Closed		39.50	40-48
1990 Tango Dancers	Closed		39.50	48-50
1990 Arriving in Style	Closed		39.50	47-70
1990 On the Town	Closed		39.50	48-56
Baby Cats of the Wild - C. Fracé				
1992 Morning Mischief	Closed		29.50	34-41

YEAR ISSUE	EDITION LIMIT	YEAR RETD.	ISSUE PRICE	*QUOTE U.S.$
1993 Togetherness	Closed		29.50	42
1993 The Buddy System	Closed		32.50	59
1993 Nap Time	Closed		32.50	55-65
Bear Tracks - J. Seerey-Lester				
1992 Denali Family	Closed		29.50	30
1993 Their First Season	Closed		29.50	30-49
1993 High Country Champion	Closed		29.50	30-51
1993 Heavy Going	Closed		29.50	30-49
1993 Breaking Cover	Closed		29.50	30-47
1993 Along the Ice Flow	Closed		29.50	30-50
Beloved Hymns of Childhood - C. Barker				
1988 The Lord's My Shepherd	Closed		29.50	28-39
1988 Away In a Manger	Closed		29.50	23-45
1989 Now Thank We All Our God	Closed		32.50	17-29
1989 Love Divine	Closed		32.50	14-26
1989 I Love to Hear the Story	Closed		32.50	14-21
1989 All Glory, Laud and Honour	Closed		32.50	12-29
1990 All People on Earth Do Dwell	Closed		34.50	20-35
1990 Loving Shepherd of Thy Sheep	Closed		34.50	25-38
A Black Tie Affair: The Penguin - C. Jagodits				
1992 Little Explorer	Closed		29.50	40-50
1992 Penguin Parade	Closed		29.50	45-49
1992 Baby-Sitters	Closed		29.50	50-60
1993 Belly Flopping	Closed		29.50	50-53
Blessed Are The Children - W. Rane				
1990 Let the/Children Come To Me	Closed		29.50	39-45
1990 I Am the Good Shepherd	Closed		29.50	29-33
1991 Whoever Welcomes/Child	Closed		32.50	29-32
1991 Hosanna in the Highest	Closed		32.50	34-40
1991 Jesus Had Compassion on Them	Closed		32.50	40-45
1991 Blessed are the Peacemakers	Closed		34.50	52
1991 I am the Vine, You are the Branches	Closed		34.50	41-45
1991 Seek and You Will Find	Closed		34.50	35-45
Bonds of Love - B. Burke				
1989 Precious Embrace	Closed		29.50	23-30
1990 Cherished Moment	Closed		29.50	25-30
1991 Tender Caress	Closed		32.50	35-51
1992 Loving Touch	Closed		32.50	25-33
1992 Treasured Kisses	Closed		32.50	32-40
1994 Endearing Whispers	Closed		32.50	34-45
Charles Vickery's Romantic Harbors - C. Vickery				
1993 Advent of the Golden Bough	Closed		34.50	33-42
1993 Christmas Tree Schooner	Closed		34.50	50-60
1993 Prelude to the Journey	Closed		37.50	55-68
1993 Shimmering Light of Dusk	Closed		37.50	150-160
The Christmas Story - H. Garrido				
1992 Gifts of the Magi	Closed		29.50	37-45
1993 Rest on the Flight into Egypt	Closed		29.50	50
1993 Journey of the Magi	Closed		29.50	30-43
1993 The Nativity	Closed		29.50	50
1993 The Annunciation	Closed		29.50	30-51
1993 Adoration of the Shepherds	Closed		29.50	50
Classic Waterfowl: The Ducks Unlimited - L. Kaatz				
1988 Mallards at Sunrise	Closed		36.50	15-39
1988 Geese in the Autumn Fields	Closed		36.50	11-50
1989 Green Wings/Morning Marsh	Closed		39.50	10-42
1989 Canvasbacks, Breaking Away	Closed		39.50	12-42
1989 Pintails in Indian Summer	Closed		39.50	10-42
1990 Wood Ducks Taking Flight	Closed		39.50	17-42
1990 Snow Geese Against November Skies	Closed		41.50	20-45
1990 Bluebills Coming In	Closed		41.50	15-42
Columbus Discovers America: The 500th Anniversary - J. Penalva				
1991 Under Full Sail	Closed		29.50	30
1992 Ashore at Dawn	Closed		29.50	20-35
1992 Columbus Raises the Flag	Closed		32.50	24-30
1992 Bringing Together Two Cultures	Closed		32.50	34-39
1992 The Queen's Approval	Closed		32.50	25-33
1992 Treasures From The New World	Closed		32.50	35-50
Country Bouquets - G. Kurz				
1991 Morning Sunshine	Closed		29.50	47
1991 Summer Perfume	Closed		29.50	31-35
1992 Warm Welcome	Closed		32.50	44-47

*Quotes have been rounded up to nearest dollar

YEAR ISSUE	EDITION LIMIT	YEAR RETD.	ISSUE PRICE	*QUOTE U.S.$
1992 Garden's Bounty	Closed		32.50	44-48

Country Nostalgia - M. Harvey

YEAR ISSUE	EDITION LIMIT	YEAR RETD.	ISSUE PRICE	*QUOTE U.S.$
1989 The Spring Buggy	Closed		29.50	15-20
1989 The Apple Cider Press	Closed		29.50	20-28
1989 The Vintage Seed Planter	Closed		29.50	29-55
1989 The Old Hand Pump	Closed		32.50	43-50
1990 The Wooden Butter Churn	Closed		32.50	30-40
1990 The Dairy Cans	Closed		32.50	23-28
1990 The Forgotten Plow	Closed		34.50	19-21
1990 The Antique Spinning Wheel	Closed		34.50	20-24

Critic's Choice: Gone With The Wind - P. Jennis

YEAR ISSUE	EDITION LIMIT	YEAR RETD.	ISSUE PRICE	*QUOTE U.S.$
1991 Marry Me, Scarlett	Closed		27.50	30-75
1991 Waiting for Rhett	Closed		27.50	30-75
1991 A Declaration of Love	Closed		30.50	30-75
1991 The Paris Hat	Closed		30.50	31-79
1991 Scarlett Asks a Favor	Closed		30.50	35-45
1992 Scarlett Gets Her Way	Closed		32.50	29-39
1992 The Smitten Suitor	Closed		32.50	39-55
1992 Scarlett's Shopping Spree	Closed		32.50	35-50
1992 The Buggy Ride	Closed		32.50	56-69
1992 Scarlett Gets Down to Business	Closed		34.50	32-45
1993 Scarlett's Heart is with Tara	Closed		34.50	50-75
1993 At Cross Purposes	Closed		34.50	50-65

A Delicate Balance: Vanishing Wildlife - G. Beecham

YEAR ISSUE	EDITION LIMIT	YEAR RETD.	ISSUE PRICE	*QUOTE U.S.$
1992 Tomorrow's Hope	Closed		29.50	33-50
1993 Today's Future	Closed		29.50	43
1993 Present Dreams	Closed		32.50	30-39
1993 Eyes on the New Day	Closed		32.50	21-43

Dr. Zhivago - G. Bush

YEAR ISSUE	EDITION LIMIT	YEAR RETD.	ISSUE PRICE	*QUOTE U.S.$
1990 Zhivago and Lara	Closed		39.50	22-40
1991 Love Poems For Lara	Closed		39.50	30-40
1991 Zhivago Says Farewell	Closed		39.50	38-45
1991 Lara's Love	Closed		39.50	45-50

The Elegant Birds - J. Faulkner

YEAR ISSUE	EDITION LIMIT	YEAR RETD.	ISSUE PRICE	*QUOTE U.S.$
1988 The Swan	Closed		32.50	35
1988 Great Blue Heron	Closed		32.50	20-28
1989 Snowy Egret	Closed		32.50	17-21
1989 The Anhinga	Closed		35.50	36
1989 The Flamingo	Closed		35.50	24-27
1990 Sandhill and Whooping Crane	Closed		35.50	23

Enchanted Garden - E. Antonaccio

YEAR ISSUE	EDITION LIMIT	YEAR RETD.	ISSUE PRICE	*QUOTE U.S.$
1993 A Peaceful Retreat	Closed		24.50	25-40
1993 Pleasant Pathways	Closed		24.50	53
1993 A Place to Dream	Closed		24.50	25
1993 Tranquil Hideaway	Closed		24.50	25

Eyes of the Wild - D. Pierce

YEAR ISSUE	EDITION LIMIT	YEAR RETD.	ISSUE PRICE	*QUOTE U.S.$
1993 Eyes in the Mist	Closed		29.50	50-57
1993 Eyes in the Pines	Closed		29.50	26-30
1993 Eyes on the Sly	Closed		29.50	45-51
1993 Eyes of Gold	Closed		29.50	30
1993 Eyes of Silence	Closed		29.50	30-40
1993 Eyes in the Snow	Closed		29.50	30-120
1993 Eyes of Wonder	Closed		29.50	30
1994 Eyes of Strength	Closed		29.50	30-50

The Faces of Nature - J. Kramer Cole

YEAR ISSUE	EDITION LIMIT	YEAR RETD.	ISSUE PRICE	*QUOTE U.S.$
1992 Canyon of the Cat	Closed		29.50	45
1992 Wolf Ridge	Closed		29.50	34-45
1993 Trail of the Talisman	Closed		29.50	45
1993 Wolfpack of the Ancients	Closed		29.50	35-45
1993 Two Bears Camp	Closed		29.50	35-45
1993 Wintering With the Wapiti	Closed		29.50	35-45
1993 Within Sunrise	Closed		29.50	35-45
1993 Wambli Okiye	Closed		29.50	35-45

The Federal Duck Stamp Plate Collection - Various

YEAR ISSUE	EDITION LIMIT	YEAR RETD.	ISSUE PRICE	*QUOTE U.S.$
1990 The Lesser Scaup	Closed		27.50	15-28
1990 The Mallard	Closed		27.50	26-33
1990 The Ruddy Ducks	Closed		30.50	19-23
1990 Canvasbacks	Closed		30.50	19-31
1991 Pintails	Closed		30.50	24-29
1991 Wigeons	Closed		30.50	24-29
1991 Cinnamon Teal	Closed		32.50	25-33
1991 Fulvous Wistling Duck	Closed		32.50	36-44
1991 The Redheads	Closed		32.50	45-54
1991 Snow Goose	Closed		32.50	33-39

Feline Fancy - H. Ronner

YEAR ISSUE	EDITION LIMIT	YEAR RETD.	ISSUE PRICE	*QUOTE U.S.$
1993 Globetrotters	Closed		34.50	32
1993 Little Athletes	Closed		34.50	49
1993 Young Adventurers	Closed		34.50	45
1993 The Geographers	Closed		34.50	50-65

Field Birds of North America - D. Bush

YEAR ISSUE	EDITION LIMIT	YEAR RETD.	ISSUE PRICE	*QUOTE U.S.$
1991 Winter Colors: Ring-Necked Pheasant	Closed		39.50	41
1991 In Display: Ruffed Grouse	Closed		39.50	31-40
1991 Morning Light: Bobwhite Quail	Closed		42.50	43-46
1991 Misty Clearing: Wild Turkey	Closed		42.50	65-74
1992 Autumn Moment: American Woodcock	Closed		42.50	48-50
1992 Season's End: Willow Ptarmigan	Closed		42.50	50-54

Floral Fancies - C. Callog

YEAR ISSUE	EDITION LIMIT	YEAR RETD.	ISSUE PRICE	*QUOTE U.S.$
1993 Sitting Softly	Closed		34.50	45
1993 Sitting Pretty	Closed		34.50	46-65
1993 Sitting Sunny	Closed		34.50	45-79
1993 Sitting Pink	Closed		34.50	45-79

Flowers From Grandma's Garden - G. Kurz

YEAR ISSUE	EDITION LIMIT	YEAR RETD.	ISSUE PRICE	*QUOTE U.S.$
1990 Country Cuttings	Closed		24.50	33-40
1990 The Morning Bouquet	Closed		24.50	29-35
1991 Homespun Beauty	Closed		27.50	30-35
1991 Harvest in the Meadow	Closed		27.50	35-37
1991 Gardener's Delight	Closed		27.50	40
1991 Nature's Bounty	Closed		27.50	36-44
1991 A Country Welcome	Closed		29.50	45-55
1991 The Springtime Arrangement	Closed		29.50	39-50

Flowers of Your Garden - V. Morley

YEAR ISSUE	EDITION LIMIT	YEAR RETD.	ISSUE PRICE	*QUOTE U.S.$
1988 Roses	Closed		24.50	20-25
1988 Lilacs	Closed		24.50	44-59
1988 Daisies	Closed		27.50	18-35
1988 Peonies	Closed		27.50	18-35
1988 Chrysanthemums	Closed		27.50	10-39
1989 Daffodils	Closed		27.50	22-28
1989 Tulips	Closed		29.50	15-30
1989 Irises	Closed		29.50	30-34

Garden of the Lord - C. Gillies

YEAR ISSUE	EDITION LIMIT	YEAR RETD.	ISSUE PRICE	*QUOTE U.S.$
1992 Love One Another	Closed		29.50	37
1992 Perfect Peace	Closed		29.50	32-38
1992 Trust In the Lord	Closed		32.50	33-46
1992 The Lord's Love	Closed		32.50	33-43
1992 The Lord Bless You	Closed		32.50	33-45
1992 Ask In Prayer	Closed		34.50	35
1993 Peace Be With You	Closed		34.50	35-45
1993 Give Thanks To The Lord	Closed		34.50	35

Gardens of Paradise - L. Chang

YEAR ISSUE	EDITION LIMIT	YEAR RETD.	ISSUE PRICE	*QUOTE U.S.$
1992 Tranquility	Closed		29.50	37-52
1992 Serenity	Closed		29.50	33-50
1993 Splendor	Closed		32.50	40-64
1993 Harmony	Closed		32.50	35-66
1993 Beauty	Closed		32.50	40-76
1993 Elegance	Closed		32.50	35-56
1993 Grandeur	Closed		32.50	65-82
1993 Majesty	Closed		32.50	50-71

Gentle Beginnings - W. Nelson

YEAR ISSUE	EDITION LIMIT	YEAR RETD.	ISSUE PRICE	*QUOTE U.S.$
1991 Tender Loving Care	Closed		34.50	18-40
1991 A Touch of Love	Closed		34.50	39-43
1991 Under Watchful Eyes	Closed		37.50	51-76
1991 Lap of Love	Closed		37.50	43-49
1992 Happy Together	Closed		37.50	59-68
1992 First Steps	Closed		37.50	40-93

Glorious Songbirds - R. Cobane

YEAR ISSUE	EDITION LIMIT	YEAR RETD.	ISSUE PRICE	*QUOTE U.S.$
1991 Cardinals on a Snowy Branch	Closed		29.50	15-18
1991 Indigo Buntings and Blossoms	Closed		29.50	14-18
1991 Chickadees Among The Lilacs	Closed		32.50	18-20
1991 Goldfinches in Thistle	Closed		32.50	10-23
1991 Cedar Waxwing/Winter Berries	Closed		32.50	17-44
1991 Bluebirds in a Blueberry Bush	Closed		34.50	21-40
1991 Baltimore Orioles/Autumn Leaves	Closed		34.50	39-60
1991 Robins with Dogwood in Bloom	Closed		34.50	33-45

The Golden Age of the Clipper Ships - C. Vickery

YEAR ISSUE	EDITION LIMIT	YEAR RETD.	ISSUE PRICE	*QUOTE U.S.$
1989 The Twilight Under Full Sail	Closed		29.50	15-30
1989 The Blue Jacket at Sunset	Closed		29.50	15-30
1989 Young America, Homeward	Closed		32.50	17-33

*Quotes have been rounded up to nearest dollar

Collectors' Information Bureau

YEAR ISSUE	EDITION LIMIT	YEAR RETD.	ISSUE PRICE	*QUOTE U.S.$
1990 Flying Cloud	Closed		32.50	24-30
1990 Davy Crocket at Daybreak	Closed		32.50	21-35
1990 Golden Eagle Conquers Wind	Closed		32.50	27-33
1990 The Lightning in Lifting Fog	Closed		34.50	30-50
1990 Sea Witch, Mistress/Oceans	Closed		34.50	35-40

Gone With the Wind: Golden Anniversary - H. Rogers

1988 Scarlett and Her Suitors	Closed		24.50	25-75
1988 The Burning of Atlanta	Closed		24.50	25-75
1988 Scarlett and Ashley After the War	Closed		27.50	25-75
1988 The Proposal	Closed		27.50	40-89
1989 Home to Tara	Closed		27.50	24-50
1989 Strolling in Atlanta	Closed		27.50	26-55
1989 A Question of Honor	Closed		29.50	24-65
1989 Scarlett's Resolve	Closed		29.50	31-90
1989 Frankly My Dear	Closed		29.50	33-85
1989 Melane and Ashley	Closed		32.50	20-55
1990 A Toast to Bonnie Blue	Closed		32.50	30-65
1990 Scarlett and Rhett's Honeymoon	Closed		32.50	30-80

Gone With the Wind: The Passions of Scarlett O'Hara - P. Jennis

1992 Fiery Embrace	Closed		29.50	35-50
1992 Pride and Passion	Closed		29.50	48
1992 Dreams of Ashley	Closed		32.50	35-50
1992 The Fond Farewell	Closed		32.50	38-50
1992 The Waltz	Closed		32.50	48-63
1992 As God Is My Witness	Closed		34.50	68-79
1993 Brave Scarlett	Closed		34.50	34-69
1993 Nightmare	Closed		34.50	35-65
1993 Evening Prayers	Closed		34.50	39-50
1993 Naptime	Closed		36.50	37-55
1993 Dangerous Attraction	Closed		36.50	59-70
1994 The End of An Era	Closed		36.50	37-50

Grand Safari: Images of Africa - C. Fracé

1992 A Moment's Rest	Closed		34.50	30-35
1992 Elephant's of Kilimanjaro	Closed		34.50	47
1992 Undivided Attention	Closed		37.50	42
1993 Quiet Time in Samburu	Closed		37.50	38-49
1993 Lone Hunter	Closed		37.50	35-38
1993 The Greater Kudo	Closed		37.50	25-38

Heart of the Wild - G. Beecham

1992 A Gentle Touch	Closed		29.50	18-30
1992 Mother's Pride	Closed		29.50	37
1992 An Afternoon Together	Closed		32.50	46-50
1993 Quiet Time?	Closed		32.50	33-50

Hollywood's Glamour Girls - E. Dzenis

1989 Jean Harlow-Dinner at Eight	Closed		24.50	12-55
1990 Lana Turner-Postman Ring Twice	Closed		29.50	16-50
1990 Carol Lombard-The Gay Bride	Closed		29.50	18-30
1990 Greta Garbo-In Grand Hotel	Closed		29.50	26-45

Hometown Memories - H.T. Becker

1993 Moonlight Skaters	Closed		29.50	23-30
1993 Mountain Sleigh Ride	Closed		29.50	39
1993 Heading Home	Closed		29.50	54
1993 A Winter Ride	Closed		29.50	40-50

Last of Their Kind: The Endangered Species - W. Nelson

1988 The Panda	Closed		27.50	17-50
1989 The Snow Leopard	Closed		27.50	17-40
1989 The Red Wolf	Closed		30.50	13-31
1989 The Asian Elephant	Closed		30.50	18-35
1990 The Slender-Horned Gazelle	Closed		30.50	11-31
1990 The Bridled Wallaby	Closed		30.50	14-31
1990 The Black-Footed Ferret	Closed		33.50	21-34
1990 The Siberian Tiger	Closed		33.50	21-34
1991 The Vicuna	Closed		33.50	17-34
1991 Przewalski's Horse	Closed		33.50	19-32

Lena Liu's Basket Bouquets - L. Liu

1992 Roses	Closed		29.50	30-39
1992 Pansies	Closed		29.50	44-50
1992 Tulips and Lilacs	Closed		32.50	50-55
1992 Irises	Closed		32.50	41-46
1992 Lilies	Closed		32.50	35-39
1992 Parrot Tulips	Closed		32.50	36-40
1992 Peonies	Closed		32.50	38-45
1993 Begonias	Closed		32.50	38-67
1993 Magnolias	Closed		32.50	40-95

YEAR ISSUE	EDITION LIMIT	YEAR RETD.	ISSUE PRICE	*QUOTE U.S.$
1993 Calla Lilies	Closed		32.50	49-57
1993 Orchids	Closed		32.50	44-59
1993 Hydrangeas	Closed		32.50	49-65

Lena Liu's Flower Fairies - L. Liu

1993 Magic Makers	Closed		29.50	48-57
1993 Petal Playmates	Closed		29.50	45-102
1993 Delicate Dancers	Closed		32.50	55-100
1993 Mischief Masters	Closed		32.50	84-109
1993 Amorous Angels	Closed		32.50	60-140
1993 Winged Wonders	Closed		34.50	60-125
1993 Miniature Mermaids	Closed		34.50	60-105
1993 Fanciful Fairies	Closed		34.50	85-99

Lena Liu's Hummingbird Treasury - L. Liu

1992 Ruby-Throated Hummingbird	Closed		29.50	40-50
1992 Anna's Hummingbird	Closed		29.50	55-65
1992 Violet-Crowned Hummingbird	Closed		32.50	70-80
1992 Rufous Hummingbird	Closed		32.50	65-74
1993 White-Eared Hummingbird	Closed		32.50	68-75
1993 Broad-Billed Hummingbird	Closed		34.50	60-84
1993 Calliope Hummingbird	Closed		34.50	60-85
1993 The Allen's Hummingbird	Closed		34.50	80-117

Little Angels - B. Burke

1992 Angels We Have Heard on High	Closed		29.50	39-55
1992 O Tannenbaum	Closed		29.50	55-60
1993 Joy to the World	Closed		32.50	50-64
1993 Hark the Herald Angels Sing	Closed		32.50	55-65
1993 It Came Upon a Midnight Clear	Closed		32.50	50-60
1993 The First Noel	Closed		32.50	45-60

A Loving Look: Duck Families - B. Langton

1990 Family Outing	Closed		34.50	19-35
1991 Sleepy Start	Closed		34.50	20-35
1991 Quiet Moment	Closed		37.50	22-43
1991 Safe and Sound	Closed		37.50	29-40
1991 Spring Arrivals	Closed		37.50	34-38
1991 The Family Tree	Closed		37.50	36-50

The Majestic Horse - P. Wildermuth

1992 Classic Beauty: Thoroughbred	Closed		34.50	35-54
1992 American Gold: The Quarterhorse	Closed		34.50	45-50
1992 Regal Spirit: The Arabian	Closed		34.50	60
1992 Western Favorite: American Paint Horse	Closed		34.50	54

Melodies in the Mist - A. Sakhavarz

1993 Early Morning Rain	Closed		34.50	39
1993 Among the Dewdrops	Closed		34.50	34
1993 Feeding Time	Closed		37.50	36
1994 Garden Party	Closed		37.50	55
1994 Unpleasant Surprise	Closed		37.50	40
1994 Spring Rain	Closed		37.50	40

Memories of a Victorian Childhood - Unknown

1992 You'd Better Not Pout	Closed		29.50	30-40
1992 Sweet Slumber	Closed		29.50	35-41
1992 Through Thick and Thin	Closed		32.50	31-34
1992 An Armful of Treasures	Closed		32.50	52-57
1993 A Trio of Bookworms	Closed		32.50	52-57
1993 Pugnacious Playmate	Closed		32.50	55-60

Nature's Legacy - J. Sias

1990 Blue Snow at Half Dome	Closed		24.50	10-12
1991 Misty Morning/Mt. McKinley	Closed		24.50	13-18
1991 Twilight Reflections on Mount Ranier	Closed		27.50	20-30
1991 Redwalls of Havasu Canyon	Closed		27.50	16-20
1991 Autumn Splendor in the Smoky Mts.	Closed		27.50	18-28
1991 Winter Peace in Yellowstone Park	Closed		29.50	24-30
1991 Golden Majesty/Rocky Mountains	Closed		29.50	25-27
1991 Radiant Sunset Over the Everglades	Closed		29.50	31-35

Nature's Lovables - C. Fracé

1990 The Koala Bear	Closed		27.50	30
1991 New Arrival	Closed		27.50	16-30
1991 Chinese Treasure	Closed		27.50	35
1991 Baby Harp Seal	Closed		30.50	26-31
1991 Bobcat: Nature's Dawn	Closed		30.50	22-31
1991 Clouded Leopard	Closed		32.50	24-33
1991 Zebra Foal	Closed		32.50	30-33
1991 Bandit	Closed		32.50	35

Collectors' Information Bureau   *Quotes have been rounded up to nearest dollar

Nature's Playmates - C. Fracé

YEAR ISSUE	EDITION LIMIT	YEAR RETD.	ISSUE PRICE	*QUOTE U.S.$
1991 Partners	Closed		29.50	24-30
1991 Secret Heights	Closed		29.50	21-30
1991 Recess	Closed		32.50	20-33
1991 Double Trouble	Closed		32.50	18-33
1991 Pals	Closed		32.50	20-33
1992 Curious Trio	Closed		34.50	35
1992 Playmates	Closed		34.50	31-35
1992 Surprise	Closed		34.50	24-35
1992 Peace On Ice	Closed		36.50	40-44
1992 Ambassadors	Closed		36.50	35-40

Nature's Poetry - L. Liu

YEAR ISSUE	EDITION LIMIT	YEAR RETD.	ISSUE PRICE	*QUOTE U.S.$
1989 Morning Serenade	Closed		24.50	10-55
1989 Song of Promise	Closed		24.50	24-55
1990 Tender Lullaby	Closed		27.50	28-55
1990 Nature's Harmony	Closed		27.50	29-55
1990 Gentle Refrain	Closed		27.50	21-55
1990 Morning Chorus	Closed		27.50	32-55
1990 Melody at Daybreak	Closed		29.50	21-55
1991 Delicate Accord	Closed		29.50	20-55
1991 Lyrical Beginnings	Closed		29.50	30-55
1991 Song of Spring	Closed		32.50	27-55
1991 Mother's Melody	Closed		32.50	33-80
1991 Cherub Chorale	Closed		32.50	44-85

On Golden Wings - W. Goebel

YEAR ISSUE	EDITION LIMIT	YEAR RETD.	ISSUE PRICE	*QUOTE U.S.$
1993 Morning Light	Closed		29.50	38
1993 Early Risers	Closed		29.50	44
1993 As Day Breaks	Closed		32.50	45-64
1993 Daylight Flight	Closed		32.50	45-75
1993 Winter Dawn	Closed		32.50	33-60
1994 First Light	Closed		34.50	50-59

On Gossamer Wings - L. Liu

YEAR ISSUE	EDITION LIMIT	YEAR RETD.	ISSUE PRICE	*QUOTE U.S.$
1988 Monarch Butterflies	Closed		24.50	21-30
1988 Western Tiger Swallowtails	Closed		24.50	28-45
1988 Red-Spotted Purple	Closed		27.50	30-35
1988 Malachites	Closed		27.50	18-20
1988 White Peacocks	Closed		27.50	20-30
1989 Eastern Tailed Blues	Closed		27.50	16-30
1989 Zebra Swallowtails	Closed		29.50	19-22
1989 Red Admirals	Closed		29.50	18-30

On the Wing - T. Humphrey

YEAR ISSUE	EDITION LIMIT	YEAR RETD.	ISSUE PRICE	*QUOTE U.S.$
1992 Winged Splendor	Closed		29.50	19-29
1992 Rising Mallard	Closed		29.50	28
1992 Glorious Ascent	Closed		32.50	33
1992 Taking Wing	Closed		32.50	40
1992 Upward Bound	Closed		32.50	40
1993 Wondrous Motion	Closed		34.50	40-48
1993 Springing Forth	Closed		34.50	55-60
1993 On The Wing	Closed		34.50	65

On Wings of Snow - L. Liu

YEAR ISSUE	EDITION LIMIT	YEAR RETD.	ISSUE PRICE	*QUOTE U.S.$
1991 The Swans	Closed		34.50	23-35
1991 The Doves	Closed		34.50	35-40
1991 The Peacocks	Closed		37.50	34-40
1991 The Egrets	Closed		37.50	38-49
1991 The Cockatoos	Closed		37.50	25-36
1992 The Herons	Closed		37.50	38

Our Woodland Friends - C. Brenders

YEAR ISSUE	EDITION LIMIT	YEAR RETD.	ISSUE PRICE	*QUOTE U.S.$
1989 Fascination	Closed		29.00	15-30
1990 Beneath the Pines	Closed		29.50	20-30
1990 High Adventure	Closed		32.50	20-33
1990 Shy Explorers	Closed		32.50	29-33
1991 Golden Season: Gray Squirrel	Closed		32.50	25-33
1991 Full House: Fox Family	Closed		32.50	33-45
1991 A Jump Into Life: Spring Fawn	Closed		34.50	27-35
1991 Forest Sentinel: Bobcat	Closed		34.50	22-34

Petal Pals - L. Chang

YEAR ISSUE	EDITION LIMIT	YEAR RETD.	ISSUE PRICE	*QUOTE U.S.$
1992 Garden Discovery	Closed		24.50	33-44
1992 Flowering Fascination	Closed		24.50	40-48
1993 Alluring Lilies	Closed		24.50	25-37
1993 Springtime Oasis	Closed		24.50	25-30
1993 Blossoming Adventure	Closed		24.50	38-40
1993 Dancing Daffodils	Closed		24.50	25-30
1993 Summer Surprise	Closed		24.50	30-36
1993 Morning Melody	Closed		24.50	31-40

Poetic Cottages - C. Valente

YEAR ISSUE	EDITION LIMIT	YEAR RETD.	ISSUE PRICE	*QUOTE U.S.$
1992 Garden Paths of Oxfordshire	Closed		29.50	32-35
1992 Twilight at Woodgreen Pond	Closed		29.50	70
1992 Stonewall Brook Blossoms	Closed		32.50	53-65
1992 Bedfordshire Evening Sky	Closed		32.50	41
1993 Wisteria Summer	Closed		32.50	48
1993 Wiltshire Rose Arbor	Closed		32.50	48
1993 Alderbury Gardens	Closed		32.50	56
1993 Hampshire Spring Splendor	Closed		32.50	59

Portraits of Christ - J. Salamanca

YEAR ISSUE	EDITION LIMIT	YEAR RETD.	ISSUE PRICE	*QUOTE U.S.$
1991 Father, Forgive Them	Closed		29.50	75-83
1991 Thy Will Be Done	Closed		29.50	50-56
1991 This is My Beloved Son	Closed		32.50	45-54
1991 Lo, I Am With You	Closed		32.50	44-60
1991 Become as Little Children	Closed		32.50	30-49
1992 Peace I Leave With You	Closed		34.50	40-55
1992 For God So Loved the World	Closed		34.50	35-54
1992 I Am the Way, the Truth and the Life	Closed		34.50	35-58
1992 Weep Not For Me	Closed		34.50	55-58
1992 Follow Me	Closed		34.50	55-65

Portraits of Exquisite Birds - C. Brenders

YEAR ISSUE	EDITION LIMIT	YEAR RETD.	ISSUE PRICE	*QUOTE U.S.$
1990 Backyard Treasure/Chickadee	Closed		29.50	20-30
1990 The Beautiful Bluebird	Closed		29.50	18-30
1991 Summer Gold: The Robin	Closed		32.50	19-33
1991 The Meadowlark's Song	Closed		32.50	25-33
1991 Ivory-Billed Woodpecker	Closed		32.50	25-33
1991 Red-Winged Blackbird	Closed		32.50	19-35

Purebred Horses of the Americas - D. Schwartz

YEAR ISSUE	EDITION LIMIT	YEAR RETD.	ISSUE PRICE	*QUOTE U.S.$
1989 The Appaloosa	Closed		34.50	14-20
1989 The Tenessee Walker	Closed		34.50	22-27
1990 The Quarterhorse	Closed		37.50	37-39
1990 The Saddlebred	Closed		37.50	20-38
1990 The Mustang	Closed		37.50	33-38
1990 The Morgan	Closed		37.50	25-33

Rare Encounters - J. Seerey-Lester

YEAR ISSUE	EDITION LIMIT	YEAR RETD.	ISSUE PRICE	*QUOTE U.S.$
1993 Softly, Softly	Closed		29.50	35-45
1993 Black Magic	Closed		29.50	43-50
1993 Future Song	Closed		32.50	45-60
1993 High and Mighty	Closed		32.50	50-58
1993 Last Sanctuary	Closed		32.50	33-40
1993 Something Stirred	Closed		34.50	35-50

Romantic Gardens - C. Smith

YEAR ISSUE	EDITION LIMIT	YEAR RETD.	ISSUE PRICE	*QUOTE U.S.$
1989 The Woodland Garden	Closed		29.50	23-30
1989 The Plantation Garden	Closed		29.50	20-30
1990 The Cottage Garden	Closed		32.50	25-33
1990 The Colonial Garden	Closed		32.50	22-33

Scenes of Christmas Past - L. Garrison

YEAR ISSUE	EDITION LIMIT	YEAR RETD.	ISSUE PRICE	*QUOTE U.S.$
1987 Holiday Skaters	Closed		27.50	18-24
1988 Christmas Eve	Closed		27.50	21-30
1989 The Homecoming	Closed		30.50	17-30
1990 The Toy Store	Closed		30.50	30-40
1991 The Carollers	Closed		30.50	30-40
1992 Family Traditions	Closed		32.50	28-30
1993 Holiday Past	Closed		32.50	57-62
1994 A Gathering of Faith	Closed		32.50	50-58

The Secret World Of The Panda - J. Bridgett

YEAR ISSUE	EDITION LIMIT	YEAR RETD.	ISSUE PRICE	*QUOTE U.S.$
1990 A Mother's Care	Closed		27.50	18-30
1991 A Frolic in the Snow	Closed		27.50	20-30
1991 Lazy Afternoon	Closed		30.50	18-31
1991 A Day of Exploring	Closed		30.50	30
1991 A Gentle Hug	Closed		32.50	35
1991 A Bamboo Feast	Closed		32.50	50

Soaring Majesty - C. Fracé

YEAR ISSUE	EDITION LIMIT	YEAR RETD.	ISSUE PRICE	*QUOTE U.S.$
1991 Freedom	Closed		29.50	10-30
1991 The Northern Goshhawk	Closed		29.50	17-30
1991 Peregrine Falcon	Closed		32.50	21-33
1991 Red-Tailed Hawk	Closed		32.50	20-33
1991 The Osprey	Closed		32.50	20-33
1991 The Gyrfalcon	Closed		34.50	30-35
1991 The Golden Eagle	Closed		34.50	27-35
1992 Red-Shouldered Hawk	Closed		34.50	24-35

Sonnets in Flowers - G. Kurz

YEAR ISSUE	EDITION LIMIT	YEAR RETD.	ISSUE PRICE	*QUOTE U.S.$
1992 Sonnet of Beauty	Closed		29.50	27-34
1992 Sonnet of Happiness	Closed		34.50	40-65

*Quotes have been rounded up to nearest dollar

Collectors' Information Bureau

YEAR ISSUE	EDITION LIMIT	YEAR RETD.	ISSUE PRICE	*QUOTE U.S.$
1992 Sonnet of Love	Closed		34.50	35-55
1992 Sonnet of Peace	Closed		34.50	50-55

The Sound of Music: Silver Anniversary - V. Gadino

YEAR ISSUE	EDITION LIMIT	YEAR RETD.	ISSUE PRICE	*QUOTE U.S.$
1991 The Hills are Alive	Closed		29.50	14-23
1992 Let's Start at the Very Beginning	Closed		29.50	16-25
1992 Something Good	Closed		32.50	40
1992 Maria's Wedding Day	Closed		32.50	40-60

Spirit of Christmas - J. Sias

YEAR ISSUE	EDITION LIMIT	YEAR RETD.	ISSUE PRICE	*QUOTE U.S.$
1990 Silent Night	Closed		29.50	15-30
1991 Jingle Bells	Closed		29.50	17-30
1991 Deck The Halls	Closed		32.50	18-33
1991 I'll Be Home For Christmas	Closed		32.50	25-38
1991 Winter Wonderland	Closed		32.50	20-33
1991 O Christmas Tree	Closed		32.50	30-35

Spirits of the Sky - C. Fisher

YEAR ISSUE	EDITION LIMIT	YEAR RETD.	ISSUE PRICE	*QUOTE U.S.$
1992 Twilight Glow	Closed		29.50	30-40
1992 First Light	Closed		29.50	60
1992 Evening Glimmer	Closed		32.50	67-74
1992 Golden Dusk	Closed		32.50	35-45
1993 Sunset Splendor	Closed		32.50	33-45
1993 Amber Flight	Closed		34.50	42-75
1993 Winged Radiance	Closed		34.50	49-60
1993 Day's End	Closed		34.50	35-75

A Splash of Cats - J. Seerey-Lester

YEAR ISSUE	EDITION LIMIT	YEAR RETD.	ISSUE PRICE	*QUOTE U.S.$
1992 Moonlight Chase: Cougar	Closed		29.50	30-50

Symphony of Shimmering Beauties - L. Liu

YEAR ISSUE	EDITION LIMIT	YEAR RETD.	ISSUE PRICE	*QUOTE U.S.$
1991 Iris Quartet	Closed		29.50	41-48
1991 Tulip Ensemble	Closed		29.50	30-45
1991 Poppy Pastorale	Closed		32.50	42-50
1991 Lily Concerto	Closed		32.50	44-48
1991 Peony Prelude	Closed		32.50	38-48
1991 Rose Fantasy	Closed		34.50	45-51
1991 Hibiscus Medley	Closed		34.50	36-45
1992 Dahlia Melody	Closed		34.50	37-50
1992 Hollyhock March	Closed		34.50	33-35
1992 Carnation Serenade	Closed		36.50	33-45
1992 Gladiolus Romance	Closed		36.50	40-52
1992 Zinnia Finale	Closed		36.50	40-50

Tis the Season - J. Sias

YEAR ISSUE	EDITION LIMIT	YEAR RETD.	ISSUE PRICE	*QUOTE U.S.$
1993 World Dressed in Snow	Closed		29.50	26-35
1993 A Time for Tradition	Closed		29.50	34
1993 We Shall Come Rejoining	Closed		29.50	30-40
1993 Our Family Tree	Closed		29.50	35-40

Tomorrow's Promise - W. Nelson

YEAR ISSUE	EDITION LIMIT	YEAR RETD.	ISSUE PRICE	*QUOTE U.S.$
1992 Curiosity: Asian Elephants	Closed		29.50	39
1992 Playtime Pandas	Closed		29.50	38
1992 Innocence: Rhinos	Closed		32.50	59
1992 Friskiness: Kit Foxes	Closed		32.50	36-39

Touching the Spirit - J. Kramer Cole

YEAR ISSUE	EDITION LIMIT	YEAR RETD.	ISSUE PRICE	*QUOTE U.S.$
1993 Running With the Wind	Closed		29.50	48-60
1993 Kindred Spirits	Closed		29.50	34
1993 The Marking Tree	Closed		29.50	43-46
1993 Wakan Tanka	Closed		29.50	30-63
1993 He Who Watches	Closed		29.50	47-50
1994 Twice Traveled Trail	Closed		29.50	41-45
1994 Keeper of the Secret	Closed		29.50	30-50
1994 Camp of the Sacred Dogs	Closed		29.50	70-89

A Treasury of Songbirds - R. Stine

YEAR ISSUE	EDITION LIMIT	YEAR RETD.	ISSUE PRICE	*QUOTE U.S.$
1992 Springtime Splendor	Closed		29.50	33-39
1992 Morning's Glory	Closed		29.50	37-49
1992 Golden Daybreak	Closed		32.50	41-54
1992 Afternoon Calm	Closed		32.50	39-49
1992 Dawn's Radiance	Closed		32.50	45-59
1993 Scarlet Sunrise	Closed		34.50	55-60
1993 Sapphire Dawn	Closed		34.50	50
1995 Alluring Daylight	Closed		34.50	60-65

The Vanishing Gentle Giants - A. Casay

YEAR ISSUE	EDITION LIMIT	YEAR RETD.	ISSUE PRICE	*QUOTE U.S.$
1991 Jumping For Joy	Closed		32.50	12-33
1991 Song of the Humpback	Closed		32.50	12-33
1991 Monarch of the Deep	Closed		35.50	17-36
1991 Travelers of the Sea	Closed		35.50	15-40
1991 White Whale of the North	Closed		35.50	26-45
1991 Unicorn of the Sea	Closed		35.50	17-38

The Victorian Cat - H. Bonner

YEAR ISSUE	EDITION LIMIT	YEAR RETD.	ISSUE PRICE	*QUOTE U.S.$
1990 Mischief With The Hatbox	Closed		24.50	23-30
1991 String Quartet	Closed		24.50	24-34
1991 Daydreams	Closed		27.50	30-35
1991 Frisky Felines	Closed		27.50	36-60
1991 Kittens at Play	Closed		27.50	30-60
1991 Playing in the Parlor	Closed		29.50	55-60
1991 Perfectly Poised	Closed		29.50	49-80
1992 Midday Repose	Closed		29.50	50

Victorian Cat Capers - Various

YEAR ISSUE	EDITION LIMIT	YEAR RETD.	ISSUE PRICE	*QUOTE U.S.$
1992 Who's the Fairest of Them All? - F. Paton	Closed		24.50	30-45
1992 Puss in Boots - Unknown	Closed		24.50	28-39
1992 My Bowl is Empty - W. Hepple	Closed		27.50	28-40
1992 A Curious Kitty - C. Van den Eycken	Closed		27.50	19-29
1992 Vanity Fair - C. Van den Eycken	Closed		27.50	22-29
1992 Forbidden Fruit - H. Blain	Closed		29.50	41-50
1993 The Purr-fect Pen Pal - A. Tucker	Closed		29.50	30-40
1993 The Kitten Express - L. Huber	Closed		29.50	30-60

Vieonne Morley's Romantic Roses - V. Morley

YEAR ISSUE	EDITION LIMIT	YEAR RETD.	ISSUE PRICE	*QUOTE U.S.$
1993 Victorian Beauty	Closed		29.50	30-48
1993 Old-Fashioned Grace	Closed		29.50	30-50
1993 Country Charm	Closed		32.50	54-65
1993 Summer Romance	Closed		32.50	35-75
1993 Pastoral Delight	Closed		32.50	38-53
1993 Springtime Elegance	Closed		34.50	49-60
1993 Vintage Splendor	Closed		34.50	45-55
1994 Heavenly Perfection	Closed		34.50	35-49

Wild Innocents - C. Fracé

YEAR ISSUE	EDITION LIMIT	YEAR RETD.	ISSUE PRICE	*QUOTE U.S.$
1993 Reflections	Closed		29.50	32-35
1993 Spiritual Heir	Closed		29.50	30-55
1993 Lion Cub	Closed		29.50	43
1993 Sunny Spot	Closed		29.50	44-55

Wild Spirits - T. Hirata

YEAR ISSUE	EDITION LIMIT	YEAR RETD.	ISSUE PRICE	*QUOTE U.S.$
1992 Solitary Watch	Closed		29.50	32-35
1992 Timber Ghost	Closed		29.50	35-50
1992 Mountain Magic	Closed		32.50	28-35
1993 Silent Guard	Closed		32.50	31-45
1993 Sly Eyes	Closed		32.50	43-49
1993 Mighty Presence	Closed		34.50	30-35
1993 Quiet Vigil	Closed		34.50	45-50
1993 Lone Vanguard	Closed		34.50	32-35

Wings of Winter - D. Rust

YEAR ISSUE	EDITION LIMIT	YEAR RETD.	ISSUE PRICE	*QUOTE U.S.$
1992 Moonlight Retreat	Closed		29.50	30-35
1993 Twilight Serenade	Closed		29.50	33-40
1993 Silent Sunset	Closed		29.50	36-40
1993 Night Lights	Closed		29.50	30-40
1993 Winter Haven	Closed		29.50	35-47
1993 Full Moon Companions	Closed		29.50	30-48
1993 White Night	Closed		29.50	30-50
1993 Winter Reflections	150-day		29.50	30-35

Winter's Majesty - C. Fracé

YEAR ISSUE	EDITION LIMIT	YEAR RETD.	ISSUE PRICE	*QUOTE U.S.$
1992 The Quest	Closed		34.50	26-35
1992 The Chase	Closed		34.50	29-35
1993 Alaskan Friend	Closed		34.50	35
1993 American Cougar	Closed		34.50	30-35
1993 On Watch	Closed		34.50	43
1993 Solitude	Closed		34.50	48

Wonders Of The Sea - R. Harm

YEAR ISSUE	EDITION LIMIT	YEAR RETD.	ISSUE PRICE	*QUOTE U.S.$
1991 Stand By Me	Closed		34.50	31-35
1991 Heart to Heart	Closed		34.50	25-35
1991 Warm Embrace	Closed		34.50	37
1991 A Family Affair	Closed		34.50	31-34

The World's Most Magnificent Cats - C. Fracé

YEAR ISSUE	EDITION LIMIT	YEAR RETD.	ISSUE PRICE	*QUOTE U.S.$
1991 Fleeting Encounter	Closed		24.50	31-40
1991 Cougar	Closed		24.50	30-45
1991 Royal Bengal	Closed		27.50	25-30
1991 Powerful Presence	Closed		27.50	23-30
1991 Jaguar	Closed		27.50	25-35
1991 The Clouded Leopard	Closed		29.50	20-30
1991 The African Leopard	Closed		29.50	17-30
1991 Mighty Warrior	Closed		29.50	30-45
1992 The Cheetah	Closed		31.50	35-72
1992 Siberian Tiger	Closed		31.50	35-60

YEAR ISSUE	EDITION LIMIT	YEAR RETD.	ISSUE PRICE	*QUOTE U.S.$

Waterford Wedgwood USA

Bicentennial - Unknown

YEAR ISSUE	EDITION LIMIT	YEAR RETD.	ISSUE PRICE	*QUOTE U.S.$
1972 Boston Tea Party	Annual		40.00	40
1973 Paul Revere's Ride	Annual		40.00	115
1974 Battle of Concord	Annual		40.00	55
1975 Across the Delaware	Annual		40.00	105
1975 Victory at Yorktown	Annual		45.00	53
1976 Declaration Signed	Annual		45.00	45

Wedgwood Christmas - Various

YEAR ISSUE	EDITION LIMIT	YEAR RETD.	ISSUE PRICE	*QUOTE U.S.$
1969 Windsor Castle - T. Harper	Annual		25.00	95-125
1970 Trafalgar Square - T. Harper	Annual		30.00	15-35
1971 Picadilly Circus - T. Harper	Annual		30.00	19-30
1972 St. Paul's Cathedral - T. Harper	Annual		35.00	35-45
1973 Tower of London - T. Harper	Annual		40.00	60-90
1974 Houses of Parliament - T. Harper	Annual		40.00	40-45
1975 Tower Bridge - T. Harper	Annual		45.00	40-45
1976 Hampton Court - T. Harper	Annual		50.00	35-40
1977 Westminster Abbey - T. Harper	Annual		55.00	35-40
1978 Horse Guards - T. Harper	Annual		60.00	40-60
1979 Buckingham Palace - Unknown	Annual		65.00	40-65
1980 St. James Palace - Unknown	Annual		70.00	59-70
1981 Marble Arch - Unknown	Annual		75.00	75
1982 Lambeth Palace - Unknown	Annual		80.00	80-90
1983 All Souls, Langham Palace - Unknown	Annual		80.00	80
1984 Constitution Hill - Unknown	Annual		80.00	80
1985 The Tate Gallery - Unknown	Annual		80.00	80-150
1986 The Albert Memorial - Unknown	Annual		80.00	80
1987 Guildhall - Unknown	Annual		80.00	200
1988 The Observatory/Greenwich - Unknown	Annual		80.00	90
1989 Winchester Cathedral - Unknown	Annual		88.00	88

Willitts Designs

Our Song - B. Joysmith

YEAR ISSUE	EDITION LIMIT	YEAR RETD.	ISSUE PRICE	*QUOTE U.S.$
1999 Madonna with Flowers (Bas Relief)	9,500		45.00	45
2000 Time Honored (Bas Relief)	9,500		37.50	38

Thomas Blackshear's Ebony Visions - T. Blackshear

YEAR ISSUE	EDITION LIMIT	YEAR RETD.	ISSUE PRICE	*QUOTE U.S.$
1997 The Madonna	7,500		35.00	35-75
1997 The Protector	7,500		35.00	105-155
1998 The Storyteller	7,500		45.00	85-125
1999 The Guardian	7,500		50.00	45-50

STEINS & JUGS

Anheuser-Busch, Inc.

Anheuser-Busch Collectors Club - Various

YEAR ISSUE	EDITION LIMIT	YEAR RETD.	ISSUE PRICE	*QUOTE U.S.$
1995 Budweiser Clydesdales at the Bauernhof CB1 - A. Leon	Yr.Iss.	1996	Gift	150-230
1995 The Brew House Clock Tower CB2 - D. Thompson	Retrd.	1996	150.00	210-795
1996 The World's Largest Brewer CB3 - A. Leon	Yr.Iss.	1996	Gift	60-150
1996 King - A Regal Spirit CB4 - D. Thompson	Retrd.	1997	100.00	185-275
1997 Pride & Tradition CB5 - J. Turgeon	Yr.Iss.	1997	Gift	45-150
1997 The Budweiser Girls-Historical Reflections CB6 - D. Curran	Retrd.	1998	100.00	110-200
1998 Old World Heritage CB7 - J. Turgeon	Yr.Iss.	1998	Gift	45-150
1998 Early Delivery Days CB8 - D. Curran	Retrd.	1999	100.00	100-200
1999 The Golden Age of Brewing, Circa 1898 CB10 - J. Turgeon	Yr.Iss.	1999	Gift	40-200
1999 The Anheuser-Busch Collectors Club 5th Anniversary Stein CB13 - A.Busch, Inc.	Retrd.	2000	40.00	40-50
1999 The Anheuser-Busch Collectors Club 5th Anniversary Stein Charter Member CB13C - A.Busch, Inc.	Retrd.	2000	40.00	40-80
1999 Clydesdale Stable CB11 - D. Curran	Retrd.	2000	100.00	90-125
2000 Born To Greatness CB14 - J. Wainwright	Yr.Iss.	2000	Gift	30-45
2000 A Celebration of Anheuser-Busch Achievements CB15 - D. Thompson	Retrd.	2001	125.00	105-125
2001 Living The Legacy CB17 - J. Wainwright	Yr.Iss.	2001	Gift	N/A
2001 King of Beers CB18 - M. Sinovcic	4/02		125.00	125

YEAR ISSUE	EDITION LIMIT	YEAR RETD.	ISSUE PRICE	*QUOTE U.S.$
2001 The Budweiser 125th Anniversary Stein CB20 - A-Busch, Inc.	4/02		170.00	170
2002 Busch's Inn CB21 - J. Wainwright	Yr.Iss.		Gift	N/A
2002 Bevo Mill circa 1918 CB22 - D. Thompson	4/03		140.00	140

Anheuser-Busch Collectors Club-Anheuser-Busch Heritage Series - A-Busch, Inc.

YEAR ISSUE	EDITION LIMIT	YEAR RETD.	ISSUE PRICE	*QUOTE U.S.$
1998 Bevo Mill CB9	Retrd.	1999	120.00	110-200
1999 The Bauernhof CB12	Retrd.	2000	120.00	100-130
2000 The Brew House CB16	Retrd.	2001	120.00	95-130
2001 Equine Palace for Adolphus Busch CB19	4/02		120.00	120

Anheuser-Busch Collectors Club-Evolution of the A&Eagle Series - A-Busch, Inc.

YEAR ISSUE	EDITION LIMIT	YEAR RETD.	ISSUE PRICE	*QUOTE U.S.$
2002 1872 and 1886-1889 CB23	4/03		85.00	85

A & Eagle Historical Trademark Series-Giftware Edition - Various

YEAR ISSUE	EDITION LIMIT	YEAR RETD.	ISSUE PRICE	*QUOTE U.S.$
1992 A & Eagle Trademark I (1872) CS201, tin	Retrd.	1993	31.00	75-130
1993 A & Eagle Trademark I (1872) CS191, boxed	Retrd.	1993	22.00	25-60
1993 A & Eagle Trademark II (1890s) CS218, tin	Retrd.	N/A	24.00	50-85
1994 A & Eagle Trademark II (1890s) CS219, boxed	Retrd.	1994	24.00	35-60
1994 A & Eagle Trademark III (1900s) CS238, tin	20,000	1994	28.00	60-80
1995 A & Eagle Trademark III (1900s) CS240, boxed	30,000	1995	25.00	30-45
1995 A & Eagle Trademark IV (1930s) CS255, tin	20,000	1996	30.00	35-75
1996 A & Eagle Trademark IV (1930s) CS271, boxed	30,000	2001	27.00	27

America The Beautiful Series-Collector Edition - Various

YEAR ISSUE	EDITION LIMIT	YEAR RETD.	ISSUE PRICE	*QUOTE U.S.$
1997 Smoky Mountains CS297 - A-Busch, Inc.	50,000		39.95	40
1998 Grand Canyon CS334 - H. Droog	50,000	2000	39.95	40
1999 Yellowstone CS376 - H. Droog	50,000		39.95	40
2000 Everglades CS420 - H. Droog	50,000	2001	39.95	40

American Bald Eagle Series - Collector Edition - B. Kemper

YEAR ISSUE	EDITION LIMIT	YEAR RETD.	ISSUE PRICE	*QUOTE U.S.$
1999 Winter CS293	50,000		35.00	35
2000 Spring CS365	50,000		35.00	35
2001 Summer CS452	50,000		35.00	35
2001 Fall CS453	50,000		35.00	35

American Originals Series-Collector Edition - A-Busch, Inc.

YEAR ISSUE	EDITION LIMIT	YEAR RETD.	ISSUE PRICE	*QUOTE U.S.$
1997 Black & Tan CS314	5,000	1997	75.00	75-350
1997 Faust CS330	5,000	1997	75.00	75-300

American Songbird Series-Collector Edition - C. Brenders

YEAR ISSUE	EDITION LIMIT	YEAR RETD.	ISSUE PRICE	*QUOTE U.S.$
2000 Bluebird CS424	20,000		60.00	60
2001 Robin CS434	20,000		60.00	60
2002 Red-winged Blackbird CS435	20,000		60.00	60

American Wildlife Series-Collector Edition - J. Raedeke

YEAR ISSUE	EDITION LIMIT	YEAR RETD.	ISSUE PRICE	*QUOTE U.S.$
2001 Whitetail Deer CS446	20,000		65.00	65
2002 Moose CS508	20,000		65.00	65

Anheuser-Busch Founder Series-Premier Collection - A-Busch, Inc.

YEAR ISSUE	EDITION LIMIT	YEAR RETD.	ISSUE PRICE	*QUOTE U.S.$
1993 Adophus Busch CS216	10,000	1996	180.00	125-195
1994 August A. Busch, Sr. CS229	10,000	1996	220.00	170-195
1995 Adolphus Busch III CS265	10,000		220.00	220
1996 August A. Busch, Jr. CS286	10,000		220.00	220

Animal Families Series-Collector Edition - C. Brenders

YEAR ISSUE	EDITION LIMIT	YEAR RETD.	ISSUE PRICE	*QUOTE U.S.$
1998 Fox Family Den CS366	25,000	2000	45.00	45
1999 Wolf Family Lair CS368	25,000		45.00	45
2000 Bear Family Cave CS369	25,000		45.00	45
2001 Cougar Family Camp CS489	25,000		45.00	45

Animals of the Seven Continents Series-Collector Edition - J. Turgeon

YEAR ISSUE	EDITION LIMIT	YEAR RETD.	ISSUE PRICE	*QUOTE U.S.$
1997 Africa CS308	100,000		49.00	49
1998 Australia CS339	100,000		49.00	49
1999 Asia CS349	100,000		49.00	49
2000 Antarctica CS377	100,000		49.00	49
2001 North America CS425	100,000		49.00	49
2002 South America CS462	100,000		49.00	49

YEAR ISSUE	EDITION LIMIT	YEAR RETD.	ISSUE PRICE	*QUOTE U.S.$

Archives Series-Collector Edition - D. Langeneckert

YEAR ISSUE	EDITION LIMIT	YEAR RETD.	ISSUE PRICE	*QUOTE U.S.$
1992 1893 Columbian Exposition CS169	75,000	1995	35.00	28-95
1993 Ganymede CS190	Retrd.	1995	35.00	95-200
1994 Budweiser's Greatest Triumph CS222	75,000	1996	35.00	75-85
1995 Mirror of Truth CS252	75,000	2001	35.00	35-40

Birds of Prey Series-Premier Edition - P. Ford

1991 American Bald Eagle CS164	25,000	1995	125.00	125-175
1992 Peregrine Falcon CS183	25,000	1996	125.00	99-175
1994 Osprey CS212	Retrd.	1994	135.00	675-950
1995 Great Horned Owl CS264	25,000	1997	137.00	99-175

Budweiser Anglers Edition Series-Giftware Edition - D. Kueker

1998 Largemouth Bass CS270	Retrd.	2001	24.95	25
1999 Rainbow Trout CS338	Open		24.95	25
2000 Crappie CS412	Open		24.95	25

Budweiser Champion Clydesdale Series-Premier Collection - J. Wainwright

2001 Hitch Prospect CS459	10,000		125.00	125

Budweiser Classic Car Series-Collector Edition - M. Watts

1998 '57 Chevolet Bel Air CS304	50,000	2001	49.00	49
1999 '57 Chevy Corvette CS340	50,000		49.00	49
1999 '59 Cadillac Eldorado CS403	50,000		49.00	49
2000 '48 Buick Roadmaster CS418	50,000		49.00	49
2000 '64 1/2 Ford Mustang CS440	50,000		49.00	49
2001 '56 Ford Thunderbird CS484	50,000		49.00	49
2002 '57 Pontiac Bonneville Convertible CS503	50,000		49.00	49

Budweiser Holiday Series - Various

1980 1st-Budweiser Champion Clydesdales CS19 - A-Busch, Inc.	Retrd.	N/A	9.95	120-189
1981 1st-Budweiser Champion Clydesdales CS19A - A-Busch, Inc.	Retrd.	N/A	N/A	200-250
1981 2nd-Snowy Woodland CS50 - A-Busch, Inc.	Retrd.	N/A	9.95	215-325
1982 3rd-50th Anniversary CS57 - A-Busch, Inc.	Retrd.	N/A	9.95	75-100
1983 4th-Cameo Wheatland CS58 - A-Busch, Inc.	Retrd.	N/A	9.95	30-50
1984 5th-Covered Bridge CS62 - A-Busch, Inc.	Retrd.	N/A	9.95	20-40
1985 6th-Snow Capped Mountains CS63 - A-Busch, Inc.	Retrd.	N/A	9.95	20-40
1986 7th-Traditional Horses CS66 - A-Busch, Inc.	Retrd.	N/A	9.95	30-50
1987 8th-Grant's Farm Gates CS70 - A-Busch, Inc.	Retrd.	N/A	9.95	21-45
1988 9th-Cobblestone Passage CS88 - A-Busch, Inc.	Retrd.	N/A	9.95	20-39
1989 10th-Winter Evening CS89 - A-Busch, Inc.	Retrd.	N/A	12.95	18-30
1990 11th-An American Tradition, CS112, 1990 - S. Sampson	Retrd.	N/A	13.50	12-25
1990 11th-An American Tradition, CS112-SE, 1990 - S. Sampson		N/A	50.00	50-69
1991 12th-The Season's Best, CS133, 1991 - S. Sampson		N/A	14.50	12-30
1991 12th-The Season's Best CS133SE Signature Edition, 1991 - S. Sampson	Retrd.	N/A	50.00	29-69
1992 13th-The Perfect Christmas, CS167, 1992 - S. Sampson	Retrd.	N/A	14.50	12-30
1992 13th-The Perfect Christmas, CS167SE Signature Edition, 1992 - S. Sampson	10,000	N/A	50.00	29-69
1993 14th-Special Delivery, CS192, 1993 - N. Koerber	Retrd.	N/A	15.00	20-35
1993 14th-Special Delivery, CS192SE Signature Edition, 1993 - N. Koerber	10,000	N/A	60.00	95-140
1994 15th-Hometown Holiday, CS211, 1994 - B. Kemper	Retrd.	1994	14.00	12-25
1994 15th-Hometown Holiday, CS211SE Signature Edition, 1994 - B. Kemper	10,000	1994	65.00	85-140
1995 16th-Lighting the Way Home, CS263 - T. Jester	Retrd.	1997	17.00	14-29
1995 16th-Lighting the Way Home, CS263SE Signature Edition - T. Jester	10,000	1995	75.00	75-103
1996 17th-Budweiser Clydesdales, CS273 - J. Raedeke	Retrd.	1998	17.00	13-20
1996 17th-Budweiser Clydesdales, CS273SE Signature Edition	10,000	1996	75.00	75-100
1997 18th-Home For The Holidays, CS313 - H. Droog	Retrd.	1999	19.00	15-29
1997 18th-Home For The Holidays, CS313SE Signature Edition - H. Droog	20,000		75.00	75
1998 19th-Grant's Farm Holiday, CS343 - E. Kastaris	Retrd.	1999	19.00	15-30
1998 19th-Grant's Farm Holiday, CS343SE Signature Edition - E. Kastaris	15,000		75.00	75
1999 20th-A Century of Tradition, CS389 - G. Ciccarelli	Retrd.	2000	19.00	18-25
1999 20th-A Century of Tradition, CS389SE Signature Edition - G. Ciccarelli	15,000	2000	75.00	64-150
2000 21st-Holiday In The Mountains CS416- E. Kastaris	Retrd.	2000	19.00	19-30
2000 21st-Holiday In The Mountains CS416SE Signature Edition - E. Kastaris	10,000	2000	75.00	75-85
2001 22nd-Holiday at the Capitol CS455 - G. Ciccarelli	Retrd.	2001	19.00	19
2001 22nd-Holiday at the Capitol CS455SE Signature Edition - G. Ciccarelli	10,000		75.00	75

Budweiser Label Series-Giftware Edition - A-Busch, Inc.

1989 Budweiser Label CS101	Retrd.	1995	14.00	3040
1990 Antique Label II CS127	Retrd.	1994	14.00	20-35
1991 Bottled Beer III CS136	Retrd.	1995	15.00	20-50
1995 Budweiser Label CS282	Retrd.	2001	19.50	20-30
2000 Budweiser Millennium Label CS423	Retrd.	2001	23.00	23
2002 2002 Budweiser Label CS515	Open		19.95	20

Budweiser Military Series-Giftware Edition - M. Watts

1994 Army CS224	Retrd.	1995	19.00	45-155
1994 Air Force CS228	Retrd.	1997	19.00	30-69
1995 Budweiser Salutes the Navy CS243	Retrd.	1997	19.50	20-69
1995 Marines CS256	Retrd.	1997	22.00	22-60
1997 Coast Guard CS294	Retrd.	1997	22.00	25-55

Budweiser Opera Card Series-Premier Collection - A-Busch, Inc.

1997 "Martha" CS300	5,000	2000	169.00	169
1998 "The Hugenhots" CS331	5,000		169.00	169
1999 "Siegfried" CS373	5,000		169.00	169

Budweiser Racing Series - H. Droog

1993 Budweiser Racing Team CS194	Retrd.	1995	19.00	19-35
1993 Bill Elliott CS196	25,000	1995	150.00	110-150
1993 Bill Elliott, Signature Edition, CS196SE	1,500	1995	295.00	175-275

Budweiser Salutes The Fire Fighters Series-Giftware Edition - A-Busch, Inc.

1997 Fire Fighter's Boot CS321	Retrd.	2001	32.00	32

Century In Review Series-Premier Collection - D. Curran

1997 1900-1919 CS311	5,000	1999	279.00	237-299
1998 1920-1939 CS335	5,000	1999	279.00	249-279
1999 1940-1959 CS342	5,000	2000	279.00	249-279
2000 1960-1979 CS383	5,000		279.00	279
2000 1980-1999 CS387	5,000		279.00	279

Civil War Series-Premier Edition - D. Langeneckert

1992 General Grant CS181	25,000	1995	150.00	120-180
1993 General Robert E. Lee CS188	25,000	1995	150.00	135-200
1993 President Abraham Lincoln CS189	25,000	1995	150.00	135-200

Classic Series - A-Busch, Inc.

1988 1st Edition CS93	Retrd.	N/A	34.95	145-150
1989 2nd Edition CS104	Retrd.	N/A	54.95	120-145
1990 3rd Edition CS113	Retrd.	N/A	65.00	60-85
1991 4th Edition CS130	Retrd.	1994	75.00	55-75

Clydesdales Series-Giftware Edition - A-Busch, Inc., unless otherwise noted

1987 World Famous Clydesdales CS74	Retrd.	N/A	9.95	24-55
1988 Mare & Foal CS90	Retrd.	N/A	11.50	55-85
1989 Parade Dress CS99	Retrd.	N/A	11.50	65-100
1991 Training Hitch CS131	Retrd.	1993	13.00	20-38
1992 Clydesdales on Parade CS161	Retrd.	1994	16.00	25-55
1994 Proud and Free CS223	Retrd.	1997	17.00	15-45
1996 Budweiser Clydesdale Hitch CS292	Retrd.	2000	22.50	23-42

YEAR ISSUE	EDITION LIMIT	YEAR RETD.	ISSUE PRICE	*QUOTE U.S.$
1999 Clydesdales At Home CS386 - J. Wainright	Open		28.00	28

Collector Edition - A-Busch, Inc., unless otherwise noted

YEAR ISSUE	EDITION LIMIT	YEAR RETD.	ISSUE PRICE	*QUOTE U.S.$
1994 Budweiser World Cup CS230 - J. Tull	25,000	1994	40.00	50-95
1997 The Official 1998 Olympic Winter Games CS350	Retrd.	1998	50.00	40-45
1998 Bald Eagle Character CS326	50,000		99.00	80-125
1998 NASCAR 50th Anniversary CS360 - J. Wainright	25,000	1998	60.00	60-149
1998 Ohio University CS363 - D. Thompson	Open		59.95	60
1999 Celebrating The Millennium CS414 - D. Curran	10,000	2000	150.00	150
1999 Kenny Bernstein Anniversary CS406 - C. Hayes	20,000		50.00	50
2000 Separated at Birth CS421 - H. Droog	25,000		40.00	40
2000 Dale Earnhardt Jr. CS450 - J. Wainwright	25,000		75.00	75
2000 The University of Missouri CS431 - D. Curran	Open		70.00	70
2000 American Olympic Team 2000 CS460 - D. Thompson	Open		90.00	90
2001 "Celebrating The Challenge" Salt Lake City 2002 Olympic Winter Games CS454 - D. Thompson	10,000		65.00	65
2001 Budweiser 125th Anniversary "A Tradition of Excellence" 1876-2001 CS496 - J. Wainwright	20,000		75.00	75

Discover America Series-Collector Edition - A-Busch, Inc.

YEAR ISSUE	EDITION LIMIT	YEAR RETD.	ISSUE PRICE	*QUOTE U.S.$
1990 Nina CS107	100,000	1995	40.00	35-50
1991 Pinta CS129	100,000	1995	40.00	40-49
1992 Santa Maria CS138	100,000	1995	40.00	45-75

Ducks Unlimited, Waterfowl Flyway Series-Collector Edition - A. LaMay

YEAR ISSUE	EDITION LIMIT	YEAR RETD.	ISSUE PRICE	*QUOTE U.S.$
1999 Mississippi Flyway CS384	25,000		50.00	50
1999 Pacific Flyway CS397	25,000		50.00	50
2000 Central Flyway CS410	25,000	2001	50.00	50
2000 Atlanta Flyway CS429	25,000	2000	50.00	50

Endangered Species Series-Collector Edition - B. Kemper

YEAR ISSUE	EDITION LIMIT	YEAR RETD.	ISSUE PRICE	*QUOTE U.S.$
1989 Bald Eagle CS106 (First)	100,000	N/A	24.95	270-375
1990 Asian Tiger CS126 (Second)	100,000	1993	27.50	75-100
1991 African Elephant CS135 (Third)	100,000	1995	29.00	45-60
1992 Giant Panda CS173 (Fourth)	100,000	1996	29.00	40-50
1993 Grizzly CS199 (Fifth)	100,000	1996	29.50	30-50
1994 Gray Wolf CS226 (Sixth)	100,000	1997	29.50	30-40
1995 Cougar CS253 (Seventh)	100,000	2000	32.00	32-40
1996 Gorilla CS283 (Eighth)	100,000	2000	32.00	32-46

European Castle Series - Premier Collection - A-Busch, Inc.

YEAR ISSUE	EDITION LIMIT	YEAR RETD.	ISSUE PRICE	*QUOTE U.S.$
2001 Castle Neuschwanstein CS473	5,000		199.00	199

German Holiday Series-Premier Collection - A-Busch, Inc.

YEAR ISSUE	EDITION LIMIT	YEAR RETD.	ISSUE PRICE	*QUOTE U.S.$
1999 St. Nicholas CS413	5,000		150.00	150
2000 Santa In His Sleigh CS443	5,000		150.00	150
2001 Santa Settles In CS488	5,000		150.00	150

Giftware Edition - A-Busch, Inc.

YEAR ISSUE	EDITION LIMIT	YEAR RETD.	ISSUE PRICE	*QUOTE U.S.$
1992 1992 Rodeo CS184	Retrd.	N/A	18.00	20-55
1993 Bud Man Character CS213	Retrd.	1996	45.00	80-175
1994 "Fore!" Budweiser Golf Bag CS225	Retrd.	1995	16.00	16-35
1994 "Walking Tall" Budweiser Cowboy Boot CS251	Retrd.	1998	17.50	20-35
1995 "Play Ball" Baseball Mitt CS244	Retrd.	2001	18.00	18
1995 Billiards CS278	Open		24.00	24
1995 Bud K. Schrader N5054	Retrd.	1997	25.00	25-39
1996 BUD-WEIS-ER Frog CS289	Retrd.	2000	27.95	28-35
1996 Indianapolis 500 N6003	Retrd.	1999	25.00	25-39
1996 "STRIKE" Bowling CS288	Retrd.	2001	24.50	25
1997 Budweiser Salutes Dad CS298	Open		19.95	20
1997 "Let Freedom Ring" CS305	Retrd.	2000	24.95	25
1997 Budweiser Tool Belt CS320	Open		29.95	30
1997 Budweiser Boxing Glove CS322	Open		35.00	35
1998 Budweiser Black Cowboy Boot CS347	Retrd.	2001	20.00	20
1998 Budweiser Golf Bag II CS362	Retrd.	1999	24.95	23-25
1998 The Budweiser Lizards Louie & Frank CS372	Retrd.	2000	29.50	30
2000 Ferret Takes Center Stage CS422	Open		29.50	30
2000 Dale Earnhardt Jr. - 2000 CS428	Retrd.	2001	19.95	20
2001 Dale Earnhardt Jr. - 2001 CS483	Retrd.	2001	19.95	20
2001 Dale Earnhardt Jr. - 2002 CS502 - J. Wainwright	Open		19.95	20

Great Cities of Germany Series-Premier Collection - A-Busch, Inc.

YEAR ISSUE	EDITION LIMIT	YEAR RETD.	ISSUE PRICE	*QUOTE U.S.$
1997 Berlin CS328	5,000	2001	139.00	139
1998 Munich CS346	5,000	2001	139.00	139
1999 Cologne CS388	5,000	2001	139.00	139

Historic Budweiser Advertising-Giftware Edition - A. Busch, Inc.

YEAR ISSUE	EDITION LIMIT	YEAR RETD.	ISSUE PRICE	*QUOTE U.S.$
1998 Stein and Tin I CS359	Retrd.	2001	36.00	36
1999 Stein and Tin II CS390	Open		36.00	36
2000 Stein and Tin III CS408	Open		36.00	36

Historical Landmark Series - A-Busch, Inc.

YEAR ISSUE	EDITION LIMIT	YEAR RETD.	ISSUE PRICE	*QUOTE U.S.$
1986 Brew House CS67 (First)	Retrd.	N/A	19.95	40-75
1987 Stables CS73 (Second)	Retrd.	1992	19.95	35-75
1988 Grant Cabin CS83 (Third)	Retrd.	N/A	19.95	20-100
1988 Old School House CS84 (Fourth)	Retrd.	1992	19.95	35-75

Historical War Series-Collector Edition - M. Sinovcic

YEAR ISSUE	EDITION LIMIT	YEAR RETD.	ISSUE PRICE	*QUOTE U.S.$
2001 American Revolution CS447	10,000		85.00	85

Honoring Tradition & Courage Series-Collector Edition - C. Hayes

YEAR ISSUE	EDITION LIMIT	YEAR RETD.	ISSUE PRICE	*QUOTE U.S.$
1999 Army CS357	50,000	2001	35.00	35
1999 Air Force CS378	50,000		35.00	35
2000 Navy CS381	50,000	2001	35.00	35
2000 Marines CS398	50,000		35.00	35
2001 Coast Guard CS417	50,000		35.00	35
2001 National Guard CS456	50,000		35.00	35

Horseshoe Series - A-Busch, Inc.

YEAR ISSUE	EDITION LIMIT	YEAR RETD.	ISSUE PRICE	*QUOTE U.S.$
1986 Horseshoe CS68	Retrd.	N/A	14.95	50-75
1987 Horsehead CS76	Retrd.	N/A	16.00	35-78
1987 Horseshoe CS77	Retrd.	N/A	16.00	35-70
1987 Horseshoe CS78	Retrd.	N/A	14.95	50-79
1988 Harness CS94	Retrd.	N/A	16.00	70-100

Hunter's Companion Series-Collector Edition - Various

YEAR ISSUE	EDITION LIMIT	YEAR RETD.	ISSUE PRICE	*QUOTE U.S.$
1993 Labrador Retriever CS195 - L. Freeman	50,000	1996	32.50	85-160
1994 The Setter CS205 - S. Ryan	50,000	1996	32.50	35-75
1995 The Golden Retriever CS248 - S. Ryan	50,000	1998	34.00	40-60
1996 Beagle CS272 - S. Ryan	50,000	2000	35.00	35-60
1997 Springer Spaniel CS296 - S. Ryan	50,000		35.00	35

Lighthouse Series-Premier Collection - B. Morse

YEAR ISSUE	EDITION LIMIT	YEAR RETD.	ISSUE PRICE	*QUOTE U.S.$
2001 Cape Hatteras CS448	10,000		150.00	150

Limited Edition Series - A-Busch, Inc.

YEAR ISSUE	EDITION LIMIT	YEAR RETD.	ISSUE PRICE	*QUOTE U.S.$
1985 Ltd. Ed. I Brewing & Fermenting CS64	Retrd.	N/A	29.95	95-195
1986 Ltd. Ed. II Aging & Cooperage CS65	Retrd.	N/A	29.95	42-65
1987 Ltd. Ed. III Transportation CS71	Retrd.	N/A	29.95	45-50
1988 Ltd. Ed. IV Taverns & Public Houses CS75	Retrd.	1994	29.95	40-45
1989 Ltd. Ed.V Festival Scene CS98	Retrd.	1994	34.95	45-55

Logo Series Steins-Giftware Edition - A-Busch, Inc.

YEAR ISSUE	EDITION LIMIT	YEAR RETD.	ISSUE PRICE	*QUOTE U.S.$
1990 Budweiser CS143	Retrd.	N/A	16.00	16-25
1990 Bud Light CS144	Retrd.	N/A	16.00	16-25
1990 Michelob CS145	Retrd.	1993	16.00	16-20
1990 Michelob Dry CS146	Retrd.	1994	16.00	16-20
1990 Busch CS147	Retrd.	N/A	16.00	16-20
1990 A&Eagle CS148	Retrd.	N/A	16.00	16-20
1990 Bud Dry CS156	Retrd.	N/A	16.00	16-20

Man's Best Friend Series-Collector Edition - S. Ryan

YEAR ISSUE	EDITION LIMIT	YEAR RETD.	ISSUE PRICE	*QUOTE U.S.$
2000 Labrador CS379	25,000		45.00	45
2001 German Shepherd CS458	25,000		45.00	45
2002 Golden Retriever CS504	25,000		45.00	45

Marine Conservation Series-Collector Edition - B. Kemper

YEAR ISSUE	EDITION LIMIT	YEAR RETD.	ISSUE PRICE	*QUOTE U.S.$
1994 Manatee CS203	25,000	1997	33.50	35-65
1995 Great White Shark CS247	25,000	1999	39.50	36-60
1996 Dolphin CS284	25,000		39.50	40

Michelob PGA Tour Series-Collector Edition - A. Leon

YEAR ISSUE	EDITION LIMIT	YEAR RETD.	ISSUE PRICE	*QUOTE U.S.$
1997 TPC at Sawgrass CS299	10,000		59.95	60
1998 TPC of Scottsdale CS329	10,000		59.95	60
1999 TPC of Tampa Bay CS380	10,000		59.95	60

Muscle Car Series-Collector Edition - D. Curran

YEAR ISSUE	EDITION LIMIT	YEAR RETD.	ISSUE PRICE	*QUOTE U.S.$
2001 1969 Chevrolet Camaro SS396 CS486	10,000		69.00	69

NHL Team Steins - A-Busch, Inc.

YEAR ISSUE	EDITION LIMIT	YEAR RETD.	ISSUE PRICE	*QUOTE U.S.$
1998 Boston Bruins CS382BOS	50,000		42.00	42

YEAR ISSUE	EDITION LIMIT	YEAR RETD.	ISSUE PRICE	*QUOTE U.S.$
1998 Chicago Blackhawks CS382CHI	50,000		42.00	42
1998 Detroit Red Wings CS382DET	50,000		42.00	42
1998 Florida Panthers CS382FLA	50,000		42.00	42
1998 New York Islanders CS382NYI	50,000		42.00	42
1998 New York Rangers CS382NYR	50,000		42.00	42
1998 Philadelphia Flyers CS382PHI	50,000		42.00	42
1998 Pittsburgh Penguins CS382PIT	50,000		42.00	42
1998 St. Louis Blues CS382STL	50,000	2001	42.00	42
1998 Tampa Bay Lightning CS382TBL	50,000		42.00	42
1998 Set of 10	50,000		420.00	420

Oktoberfest Series-Giftware Edition - A-Busch, Inc.

YEAR ISSUE	EDITION LIMIT	YEAR RETD.	ISSUE PRICE	*QUOTE U.S.$
1991 1991 Oktoberfest N3286	25,000	N/A	19.00	25-35
1992 1992 Oktoberfest CS185	35,000	1996	16.00	16-30
1993 1993 Oktoberfest CS202	35,000	1995	18.00	19-35
1996 1996 Oktoberfest CS291	Retrd.	2001	24.95	25-30

Olympic Centennial Collection - A-Busch, Inc.

YEAR ISSUE	EDITION LIMIT	YEAR RETD.	ISSUE PRICE	*QUOTE U.S.$
1995 1996 U.S. Olympic Team "Gymnastics" CS262	10,000	1998	85.00	50-85
1995 1996 U.S. Olympic Team "Track & Field" CS246	10,000	1998	85.00	50-85
1995 Bud Atlanta 1996 CS249	Retrd.	N/A	17.00	17-25
1995 Centennial Olympic Games Giftware CS266	Retrd.	1997	25.00	15-25
1995 Centennial Olympic Games Premier Edition 22" CS267	1,996	1996	500.00	850-1000
1995 Collector's Edition Official Centennial Olympics Games CS259	Retrd.	1996	50.00	50-60

Olympic Team Series 1992-Collector Edition - A-Busch, Inc.

YEAR ISSUE	EDITION LIMIT	YEAR RETD.	ISSUE PRICE	*QUOTE U.S.$
1991 1992 Winter Olympic CS162	25,000	N/A	85.00	30-75
1992 1992 Summer Olympic CS163	Retrd.	1994	85.00	40-75
1992 1992 U.S.Olympic CS168	50,000	N/A	16.00	15-20

Porcelain Heritage Series-Premier Edition - Various

YEAR ISSUE	EDITION LIMIT	YEAR RETD.	ISSUE PRICE	*QUOTE U.S.$
1990 Berninghaus CS105 - Berninghaus	Retrd.	1994	75.00	55-85
1991 After The Hunt CS155 - A-Busch, Inc.	Retrd.	1994	100.00	69-85
1992 Cherub CS182 - D. Langeneckert	25,000	1996	100.00	105-110

Post Convention Series - A-Busch, Inc.

YEAR ISSUE	EDITION LIMIT	YEAR RETD.	ISSUE PRICE	*QUOTE U.S.$
1982 1st Post Convention Olympic CS53	23,000	1982	N/A	165-185
1982 2nd Post Convention Olympic CS54	23,000	1982	N/A	135-175
1982 3rd Post Convention Olympic CS55	23,000	1982	N/A	165-195
1988 1st Post Convention Heritage CS87	25,000	1988	N/A	60-100
1988 2nd Post Convention Heritage CS102	25,000	1988	N/A	50-125
1989 3rd Post Convention Heritage CS114	25,000	1989	N/A	50-125
1990 4th Post Convention Heritage CS141	25,000	1990	N/A	50-125
1991 5th/Final Post Convention Heritage CS174	25,000	1991	N/A	25-125
1992 1st Advertising Through the Decades 1879-1912 N3989	29,000	1992	N/A	45-75
1994 2nd Advertising Through the Decades 1905-1914 N3990	31,106	1993	N/A	45-75
1995 3rd Advertising Through the Decades 1911-1915 SO85203	31,000	1994	N/A	35-75
1996 4th Advertising Through the Decades 1918-1922 SO95150	31,000	1995	N/A	35-75
1997 5th Advertising Through the Decades 1933-1938 SO95248	31,000	1996	N/A	75-95

Premier Collection - A-Busch, Inc., unless otherwise noted

YEAR ISSUE	EDITION LIMIT	YEAR RETD.	ISSUE PRICE	*QUOTE U.S.$
1997 Bud Ice Penguin Character CS315	10,000	2001	199.00	199-220
1997 Budweiser Frog Character CS301	10,000	2000	219.00	185-220
1997 Louie The Lizard Character CS344	25,000	1999	99.00	99-125
1998 World Cup Soccer CS351	10,000	1999	99.00	65-99
1999 Frankenstein™ Character CS323	10,000		125.00	125
1999 Bud Man 30th Anniversary Character CS401	25,000		100.00	100
1999 Dalmatian Character CS324	10,000		220.00	220
1999 One Thousand Years of Progress, 2000 A.D. - J. Wainwright	2,000	1999	800.00	795-900
2000 Spuds MacKenzie Character CS445 - T. Buttner	10,000		199.00	199
2001 Salt Lake 2002 Winter Olympic Games CS485 - J. Wainwright	2,500		750.00	750
2001 Budweiser Draught Tower CS461 - J. Wainwright	5,000		150.00	150
2002 Anheuser-Busch Pre-Prohibition Beer Stein CS501 - J. Wainwright	10,000		85.00	85

Sea World Series-Collector Edition - A-Busch, Inc.

YEAR ISSUE	EDITION LIMIT	YEAR RETD.	ISSUE PRICE	*QUOTE U.S.$
1992 Killer Whale CS186	25,000	1996	100.00	85-100
1992 Dolphin CS187	22,500	1996	90.00	65-85

Specialty Steins - A-Busch, Inc.

YEAR ISSUE	EDITION LIMIT	YEAR RETD.	ISSUE PRICE	*QUOTE U.S.$
1975 Bud Man CS1	Retrd.	N/A	N/A	425-625
1976 A&Eagle CS2	Retrd.	N/A	N/A	110-145
1976 A&Eagle Lidded CSL2 (Reference CS28)	Retrd.	N/A	N/A	176-225
1976 Katakombe CS3	Retrd.	N/A	N/A	195-300
1976 Katakombe Lidded CSL3	Retrd.	N/A	N/A	295-350
1976 German Tavern Scene Lidded CS4	Retrd.	N/A	N/A	50-75
1975 Senior Grande Lidded CSL4	Retrd.	N/A	N/A	650-790
1975 German Pilique CS5	Retrd.	N/A	N/A	350-450
1976 German Pilique Lidded CSL5	Retrd.	N/A	N/A	400-550
1976 Senior Grande CS6	Retrd.	N/A	N/A	450-600
1975 German Tavern Scene CSL6	Retrd.	N/A	N/A	195-250
1975 Miniature Bavarian CS7	Retrd.	N/A	N/A	200-695
1976 Budweiser Centennial Lidded CSL7	Retrd.	N/A	N/A	295-395
1976 U.S. Bicentennial Lidded CSL8	Retrd.	N/A	N/A	325-395
1976 Natural Light CS9	Retrd.	N/A	N/A	200-300
1976 Clydesdales Hofbrau Lidded CSL9	Retrd.	N/A	N/A	179-235
1976 Blue Delft CS11	Retrd.	N/A	N/A	1200-1520
1976 Clydesdales CS12	Retrd.	N/A	N/A	275-325
1976 Budweiser Centennial CS13	Retrd.	N/A	N/A	225-350
1976 U.S. Bicentennial CS14	Retrd.	N/A	N/A	300-350
1976 Clydesdales Grants Farm CS15	Retrd.	N/A	N/A	145-189
1976 German Cities (6 assorted) CS16	Retrd.	N/A	N/A	1410-1590
1976 Americana CS17	Retrd.	N/A	N/A	225-300
1976 Budweiser Label CS18	Retrd.	N/A	N/A	450-595
1980 Budweiser Ladies (4 assorted) CS20	Retrd.	N/A	N/A	1200-1308
1977 Budweiser Girl CS21	Retrd.	N/A	N/A	350-375
1976 Budweiser Centennial CS22	Retrd.	N/A	N/A	245-285
1977 A&Eagle CS24	Retrd.	N/A	N/A	360-395
1976 A&Eagle Barrel CS26	Retrd.	N/A	N/A	75-145
1976 Michelob CS27	Retrd.	N/A	N/A	125-150
1976 A&Eagle Lidded CS28 (Reference CSL2)	Retrd.	N/A	N/A	195-200
1976 Clydesdales Lidded CS29	Retrd.	N/A	N/A	175-225
1976 Coracao Decanter Set (7 piece) CS31	Retrd.	N/A	N/A	492-500
1976 German Wine Set (7 piece) CS32	Retrd.	N/A	N/A	450-550
1976 Clydesdales Decanter CS33	Retrd.	N/A	N/A	980-1600
1976 Holanda Brown Decanter Set (7 piece) CS34	Retrd.	N/A	N/A	1012-1250
1976 Holanda Blue Decanter Set (7 piece) CS35	Retrd.	N/A	N/A	415-750
1976 Canteen Decanter Set (7 piece) CS36	Retrd.	N/A	N/A	500-890
1976 St. Louis Decanter CS37	Retrd.	N/A	N/A	275-300
1976 St. Louis Decanter Set (7 piece) CS38	Retrd.	N/A	N/A	900-1022
1980 Wurzburger Hofbrau CS39	Retrd.	N/A	N/A	99-300
1980 Budweiser Chicago Skyline CS40	Retrd.	N/A	N/A	85-149
1980 Busch Gardens CS41	Retrd.	N/A	N/A	125-219
1980 Oktoberfest - "The Old Country" CS42	Retrd.	N/A	N/A	165-200
1980 Natural Light CS43	Retrd.	N/A	N/A	225-300
1980 Busch Label CS44	Retrd.	N/A	N/A	225-250
1980 Michelob Label CS45	Retrd.	N/A	N/A	45-75
1980 Budweiser Label CS46	Retrd.	N/A	N/A	45-75
1981 Budweiser Chicagoland CS51	Retrd.	N/A	N/A	35-75
1981 Budweiser Texas CS52	Retrd.	N/A	N/A	45-60
1981 Budweiser California CS56	Retrd.	N/A	N/A	39-55
1983 Budweiser San Francisco CS59	Retrd.	N/A	N/A	130-199
1984 Budweiser 1984 Summer Olympic Games CS60	Retrd.	N/A	N/A	10-22
1983 Bud Light Baron CS61	Retrd.	N/A	N/A	45-55
1987 Santa Claus CS79	Retrd.	N/A	N/A	75-145
1987 King Cobra CS80	Retrd.	N/A	N/A	105-395
1987 Winter Olympic Games, Lidded CS81	Retrd.	N/A	49.95	60-105
1988 Budweiser Winter Olympic Games CS85	Retrd.	N/A	24.95	25
1988 Summer Olympic Games, Lidded CS91	Retrd.	N/A	54.95	40-80
1988 Budweiser Summer Olympic Games CS92	Retrd.	N/A	54.95	20-40
1988 Budweiser/ Field&Stream Set (4 piece) CS95	Retrd.	N/A	69.95	225-295
1989 Bud Man CS100	Retrd.	1993	29.95	80-120
1990 Baseball Cardinal CS125	Retrd.	N/A	30.00	50-80
1991 Bevo Fox Stein CS160	Retrd.	1994	250.00	250-279
1992 Budweiser Racing-Elliot/Johnson N3553 - M. Watts	Retrd.	1995	19.00	15-35

Sports Action Series-Giftware Edition - J. Whitney

YEAR ISSUE	EDITION LIMIT	YEAR RETD.	ISSUE PRICE	*QUOTE U.S.$
1997 "Play Ball" Budweiser Baseball CS295	Open		29.00	29

YEAR ISSUE	EDITION LIMIT	YEAR RETD.	ISSUE PRICE	*QUOTE U.S.$
1998 "Touchdown!" Budweiser Football CS325	Retrd.	1999	29.00	25-29
1998 "Swish!" Basketball CS333	Retrd.	2001	29.00	29

Sports History Series-Giftware Edition - A-Busch, Inc.

1990 Baseball, America's Favorite Pastime CS124	100,000	1992	20.00	30-45
1990 Football, Gridiron Legacy CS128	100,000	1994	20.00	18-35
1991 Auto Racing, Chasing The Checkered Flag CS132	100,000	1995	22.00	30-40
1991 Basketball, Heroes of the Hardwood CS134	100,000	1995	22.00	18-40
1992 Golf, Par For The Course CS165	100,000	1995	22.00	15-65
1993 Hockey, Center Ice CS209	100,000	N/A	22.00	25-36

Sports Legend Series-Collector Edition - Various

1991 Babe Ruth CS142 - A-Busch	50,000	1995	85.00	60-95
1992 Jim Thorpe CS171 - M. Caito	50,000	1995	85.00	70-95
1993 Joe Louis CS206 - M. Caito	Retrd.	1994	85.00	85-155

St. Patrick's Day Series-Giftware Edition - A-Busch, Inc., unless otherwise noted

1991 1991 St. Patrick's Day CS109	Retrd.	N/A	15.00	55-75
1992 1992 St. Patrick's Day CS166	100,000	N/A	15.00	18-39
1993 1993 St. Patrick's Day CS193	Retrd.	N/A	15.30	40-65
1994 Luck O' The Irish CS210	Retrd.	1995	18.00	15-45
1995 1995 St. Patrick's Day CS242	Retrd.	1995	19.00	15-45
1996 "Horseshoe" 1996 St. Patrick's Day CS269	Retrd.	2001	19.50	20-25
1997 Luck O' The Longneck 1997 St. Patrick's Day CS287	Retrd.	2001	21.95	22
1998 Erin Go Budweiser 1998 St. Patrick's Day CS332	Retrd.	2001	22.95	23
1999 "The Bud That Got Away" 1999 St. Patrick's Day CS385	Open		24.00	24
2000 "Leapin' Leprechauns" 2000 St. Patrick's Day CS411 - T. Buttner	Retrd.	2000	24.00	24
2002 "Tradition and Heritage" 2002 St. Patrick's Day CS516 - S. Noble	Open		24.95	25

Upland Game Birds Series-Collector Edition - P. Ford

1997 Ruffed Grouse CS316	5,000	1997	75.00	90-145
1997 Pheasant CS319	5,000	1997	75.00	75-125
1998 Turkey CS327	5,000	1998	75.00	75-150
1998 Prairie Chicken CS337	5,000	1998	75.00	75-125

Wolf Pack Series-Collector Edition - A. Agnew

2001 Run For The Moment CS471	15,000		65.00	65
2002 Generations CS506	15,000		65.00	65

Working America Series-Premier Collection - A-Busch, Inc.

1997 The American Worker I CS318	10,000	2001	209.00	209
1998 The American Worker II CS336	10,000		209.00	209
1999 The American Worker III CS353	10,000	2000	209.00	209

Anheuser-Busch, Inc./Meisterwerke Collection

American Heritage Collection - Gerz

1993 John F. Kennedy GM4	10,000	2000	220.00	220

Animals of the Prairie Series - N. Glazier

1997 Buffalo GL11	5,000	1997	149.00	149-175
1998 Wild Mustang GL15	5,000	1998	149.00	139-160
1999 Mule Deer GL19	5,000		149.00	149
2000 Elk GL20	5,000		149.00	149

Collectorwerke - Various

1993 The Dugout Stein GL1 - A-Busch, Inc.	10,000	2000	110.00	110
1994 Winchester Stein GL2 - A-Busch, Inc.	10,000	1995	120.00	125-150
1995 "Saturday Evening Post" Christmas #1 GL5 - J.C. Leyendecker	5,000	1997	105.00	90-105
1996 "Saturday Evening Post" Christmas #2 GL6 - A-Busch, Inc.	5,000	1997	105.00	89-139
1997 "Saturday Evening Post" Christmas #3 GL13 - J.C. Leyendecker	5,000		105.00	105

Collectorwerke-Call of the Wild Series - J. Rideout

1996 Wolf GL9	10,000		139.00	139
1997 Grizzly GL12	10,000	1999	139.00	108-139
1998 Mountain Lion GL17	10,000		139.00	139

Meisterwerke Collection - A-Busch, Inc.

1994 Norman Rockwell-Triple Self Portrait GM6	5,000	1997	250.00	189-250
1994 Mallard Stein GM7	5,000	1996	220.00	129-250

YEAR ISSUE	EDITION LIMIT	YEAR RETD.	ISSUE PRICE	*QUOTE U.S.$
1994 Winchester "Model 94" Centennial GM10	5,000	2000	150.00	135-175
1995 Giant Panda GM8	3,500	1997	210.00	129-250
1995 Rosie the Riveter GM9	5,000	1997	165.00	125-175
1997 Norman Rockwell-Do Unto Others GM21	7,500		189.00	189

Meisterwerke-Early Transporation Series - T. MacDonald

1997 Train GM28	5,000	1999	179.00	189-202
1998 Train II GM29	5,000	1999	179.00	145-179
2000 Train III GM30	5,000	2001	179.00	179

Meisterwerke-First Hunt Series - P. Ford

1992 Golden Retriever GM2	10,000	1999	150.00	79-190
1994 Springer Spaniel GM5	10,000	2001	190.00	190
1995 Pointer GM16	10,000	1997	190.00	169-190
1995 Labrador GM17	10,000	1998	190.00	125-190

Meisterwerke-Holidays Through the Decades - A-Busch, Inc.

1996 Holidays: Decade of the 30's GM18	3,500	1997	169.00	139-173
1997 Holidays: Decade of the 40's GM23	3,500		169.00	169
1998 Holidays: Decade of the 50's GM26	3,500	1999	169.00	169-179

Meisterwerke-Winchester Hunt Series - A-Busch, Inc.

1996 Pheasant Hunt GM20	3,500	1997	215.00	150-225
1997 Duck Hunt GM24	3,500		215.00	215
1998 Quail Hunt GM27	3,500		215.00	215

Meisterwerke-Winchester Rodeo Series - A-Busch, Inc.

1996 Rodeo Calf Roping GM19	5,000		179.00	179
1997 Rodeo Bull Riding GM22	5,000	1998	179.00	152-185
1998 Saddle Bronc Riding GM25	5,000		179.00	179

Saturday Evening Post Collection - J.C. Leyendecker

1993 Santa's Mailbag GM1	Retrd.	1993	195.00	225-249
1993 Santa's Helper GM3	7,500		200.00	200
1994 "All I Want For Christmas" GM13	5,000	1997	220.00	160-195
1995 Fourth of July GM15	5,000	1998	180.00	139-180

Anheuser-Busch, Promotional Products Group/Licensed

Coca Cola - Various

1999 COKE on Ice CS393 - D. Curran	Open		30.00	30
1999 Vintage Holiday Vending Machine CS392 - D. Curran	25,000		60.00	60
1999 Santa Character CS394	10,000		270.00	270
2000 Musical Christmas Tree CS419 - D. Curran	15,000		85.00	85

Coca Cola Early Illustrators Series - Various

2000 First Edition CS400	25,000		55.00	55
2001 Second Edition CS491	25,000		55.00	55

Coca Cola Historical Slogans Series - Various

2000 First Edition CS399	25,000		65.00	65
2000 Second Edition CS451	25,000		65.00	65
2001 Third Edition CS490	25,000		65.00	65

Coca Cola Holiday Series - Various

1998 Candy Cane CS391 - J. Turgeon	25,000	1999	50.00	43-78
1999 Santa's Reward CS402	25,000		50.00	50

Elvis Presley - Various

1999 '68 Comeback Special Collector Edition CS375	25,000		65.00	65
1999 '68 Comeback Special Giftware Edition CS374	Retrd.	2000	30.00	30
2000 Elvis Jukebox CS396	25,000	2001	65.00	65
2000 Elvis Gold & Platinum Records CS395 - J. Wainwright	10,000	2001	85.00	85

Elvis Sings The Blues Series - D. Thompson

2000 Blue Suede Shoes CS404	15,000		65.00	65
2001 Blue Hawaii CS497	15,000		65.00	65

Hamilton Collection

Mickey Mantle - R. Tanenbaum

1996 The Legendary Mickey Mantle	Open		39.95	40

The STAR TREK® Tankard Collection - T. Blackshear

1995 U.S.S. Enterprise NCC-1701	Closed	1998	49.50	50
1994 SPOCK	Closed	1998	49.50	50

STEINS & JUGS

YEAR ISSUE	EDITION LIMIT	YEAR RETD.	ISSUE PRICE	*QUOTE U.S.$
1995 Kirk	Closed	1998	49.50	50
1995 McCoy	Closed	1998	49.50	50
1995 Uhura	Closed	1998	49.50	50
1995 Scotty	Closed	1998	49.50	50
1995 Sulu	Closed	1998	49.50	50
1995 Chekov	Closed	1998	49.50	50

Warriors of the Plains Tankards - G. Stewart

1995 Battle Grounds	Closed	N/A	125.00	125
1992 Thundering Hooves	Closed	N/A	125.00	125
1992 Warrior's Choice	Closed	N/A	125.00	125
1992 Healing Spirits	Closed	N/A	125.00	125

Royal Doulton

Character Jug of the Year - Various

1991 Fortune Teller D6824 - S. Taylor	Closed	1991	130.00	225-350
1992 Winston Churchill D6907 - S. Taylor	Closed	1992	195.00	225-265
1993 Vice-Admiral Lord Nelson D6932 - S. Taylor	Closed	1993	225.00	225
1994 Captain Hook - M. Alcock	Closed	1994	235.00	235-525
1995 Captain Bligh D6967 - S. Taylor	Closed	1995	200.00	140-275
1996 Jesse Owens, lg. D7019 - S. Taylor	Closed	1996	225.00	225-255
1997 Count Dracula, lg. D7053 - D. Biggs	Closed	1997	235.00	250
1998 Lewis Carroll - D. Biggs	Closed	1998	195.00	195
1999 Shakespeare, lg. D7136 - R. Tabbenor	Yr.Iss.	1999	205.00	205-209
2000 Oscar Wilde, lg. D7146 - D. Biggs	Yr.Iss.	2000	245.00	245
2001 Queen Victoria D7152 - R. Tabbenor	Yr.Iss.	2001	245.00	245
2002 Sir Walter Raleigh D7169 - R. Tabbenor	Yr.Iss.		285.00	285

Character Jugs - Various

1993 Abraham Lincoln - M. Alcock	2,500	1994	190.00	230-295
1991 Airman, sm.- W. Harper	Retrd.	1996	75.00	75-115
1996 Albert Einstein, lg.- S. Taylor	Retrd.	1996	225.00	225-250
1995 Alfred Hitchcock D6987 - D. Biggs	Retrd.	1997	200.00	238-275
1997 Angler, sm. – D. Biggs	Open		132.50	145
1990 Angler, sm. - S. Taylor	Retrd.	1995	82.50	83
1947 Beefeater, lg. - H. Fenton	Retrd.	1996	137.50	145-200
1947 Beefeater, sm. - H. Fenton	Retrd.	1996	75.00	40-138
1998 Captain Scott - D. Biggs	Retrd.	2000	195.00	195-205
1975 Catherine of Aragon, lg. D6643 - A. Maslankowski	Retrd.	1981	N/A	100-200
1981 Catherine Parr, lg. D6664 - M. Abberley	Retrd.	1989	N/A	190-265
2001 The Chef D7103 - D. Biggs	Open		145.00	145
1989 Clown, lg.- S. Taylor	Retrd.	1995	205.00	300-370
1991 Columbus, lg. 6891 - S. Taylor	Retrd.	1997	137.50	138-145
1995 Cyrano de Bergerac, lg. 7004 - D. Biggs	Retrd.	1997	200.00	210
1983 D'Artagnan, lg.- S. Taylor	Retrd.	1995	150.00	200
1983 D'Artagnan, sm.- S. Taylor	Retrd.	1995	82.50	149-175
1995 Dennis and Gnasher, lg.- S. Ward	Retrd.	1999	212.50	235
1995 Deperate Dan, lg.- S. Ward	Retrd.	1999	212.50	235
1991 Equestrian, sm.- S. Taylor	Retrd.	1995	82.50	83
1997 General Custer, lg.- S. Taylor	Retrd.	1999	237.50	238
1982 George Washington, lg. - S. Taylor	Retrd.	1994	150.00	140-195
1994 Glenn Miller - M. Alcock	Retrd.	1998	270.00	330-340
1971 Golfer, lg. - D. Biggs	Retrd.	1995	150.00	250
1997 Golfer, sm. - D. Biggs	Retrd.	1999	132.50	133-155
1993 Graduate-Male, sm.- S. Taylor	Retrd.	1995	85.00	85
1986 Guardsman, lg.- S. Taylor	Retrd.	1999	137.50	125-155
1986 Guardsman, sm.- S. Taylor	Retrd.	1999	75.00	65-85
1990 Guy Fawkes, lg. - W. Harper	Retrd.	1996	137.50	138-150
1975 Henry VIII, lg. - E. Griffiths	Retrd.	2000	137.50	125-190
1975 Henry VIII, sm. - E. Griffiths	Retrd.	1999	75.00	85-115
1991 Jockey, sm.- S. Taylor	Retrd.	1995	82.50	83
1995 Judge and Thief Toby D6988 - S. Taylor	Retrd.	1998	185.00	225
1959 Lawyer, lg. - M. Henk	Retrd.	1996	137.50	135-175
1959 Lawyer, sm. - M. Henk	Retrd.	1996	75.00	50-90
1990 Leprechaun, lg. - W. Harper	Retrd.	1996	205.00	210-225
1990 Leprechaun, sm. - W. Harper	Retrd.	1996	75.00	75-85
1986 London Bobby, lg.- S. Taylor	Retrd.	2000	137.50	160-250
1986 London Bobby, sm.- S. Taylor	Open		75.00	90
1952 Long John Silver, lg. - M. Henk	Retrd.	2000	137.50	130-190
1952 Long John Silver, sm. - M. Henk	Retrd.	2000	75.00	70-110
1965 Mad Hatter, sm. D6602 - M. Henk	Retrd.	1983	N/A	103-190
1989 March Hare, lg. D6776 - W. Harper	Retrd.	1991	N/A	190-400
1960 Merlin, lg. - G. Sharpe	Retrd.	1998	137.50	155-340
1960 Merlin, sm. - G. Sharpe	Retrd.	1998	75.00	68-105

YEAR ISSUE	EDITION LIMIT	YEAR RETD.	ISSUE PRICE	*QUOTE U.S.$
1990 Modern Golfer, sm.- S. Taylor	Retrd.	1999	75.00	83
1961 Old Salt, lg.- G. Sharpe	Retrd.	2000	137.50	155
1961 Old Salt, sm.- G. Sharpe	Retrd.	2000	75.00	85
1955 Rip Van Winkle, lg. - M. Henk	Retrd.	1995	150.00	125-150
1955 Rip Van Winkle, sm. - M. Henk	Retrd.	1995	82.50	71-90
1991 Sailor, sm. - W. Harper	Retrd.	1996	75.00	83
1984 Santa Claus, lg. - M. Abberley	Retrd.	2000	137.50	160-240
1984 Santa Claus, sm. - M. Abberley	Open		75.00	90
1993 Shakespeare, sm. - W. Harper	Open		99.00	125
1973 The Sleuth, lg.- A. Moore	Retrd.	1996	137.50	249-275
1973 The Sleuth, sm. - A. Moore	Retrd.	1996	75.00	55-120
1991 Snooker Player, sm.- S. Taylor	Retrd.	1995	82.50	70-90
1991 Soldier, sm. - W. Harper	Retrd.	1996	75.00	75
1991 Town Crier, lg. - S. Taylor	Retrd.	1994	170.00	130-210
1993 Winston Churchill, sm.- S. Taylor	Open		99.00	125
1990 Wizard, lg. - S. Taylor- S. Taylor	Retrd.	1996	175.00	185-225
1990 Wizard, sm.- S. Taylor	Retrd.	1999	75.00	85
1991 Yeoman of the Guard, lg. 6873 - S. Taylor	Retrd.	1997	137.50	145

Great Artists - D. Biggs

2000 Monet, lg. D7150	Open		205.00	205
2000 Van Goch, lg. D7151	Open		205.00	205

Great Composers - S. Taylor

1996 Beethoven, lg. D7021	Retrd.	2000	225.00	250
1996 Chopin, lg. D7030	Retrd.	2000	225.00	250
1999 Elgar, lg. D7118	Retrd.	2000	195.00	195-205
1997 Handel, lg.	Retrd.	2000	237.50	238-245
1996 Mozart, lg. D7031	Retrd.	2000	225.00	250
1996 Schubert, lg. D7056	Retrd.	2000	225.00	250-260
1996 Tchaikovsky, lg. D7022	Retrd.	2000	225.00	250

Limited Edition Character Jugs - Various

1992 Abraham Lincoln D6936 - S. Taylor	2,500	1994	190.00	295-550
1994 Aladdin's Genie D6971 - D. Biggs	1,500	1994	335.00	395
1996 Angel Miniature - M. Alcock	2,500	1996	77.50	78
1995 Charles Dickens D6939 - W. Harper	2,500	1997	500.00	500
1993 Clown Toby - S. Taylor	3,000	1996	175.00	225-250
2002 Duke of Wellington D7170 - R. Tabbenor	1,000		285.00	285
2000 Edward VII D7154 - R. Tabbenor	1,000	2001	310.00	310
1993 Elf Miniature D6942 - W. Harper	2,500	1994	55.00	85-110
1997 Explorer Tinies, set/6 - S. Taylor	2,500	1997	495.00	495
1993 Father Christmas Toby - W. Harper	3,500	1996	125.00	125
1996 Geoffrey Chaucer, lg. - R. Tabbenor	1,500	1996	800.00	850
2002 George VI and Queen Mother Pair D7167/D7168 - V. Annand	1,000		565.00	565
1995 George Washington - M. Alcock	2,500	1995	200.00	225
1995 George Washington, lg. - M. Alcock	2,500	1996	200.00	200
1990 Henry VIII - N/A	Retrd.	2000	150.00	150
1991 Henry VIII - W. Harper	1,991	1992	395.00	1200-1400
1991 Jester - S. Taylor	2,500	1996	125.00	150-185
1994 King & Queen of Diamonds D6969 - J. Taylor	2,500	1994	260.00	260-275
1996 King and Queen of Hearts Toby - S. Taylor	2,500	1997	275.00	275-295
1997 King and Queen of Spades Toby - S. Taylor	2,500	1998	275.00	275
1997 King Arthur, lg. D7055- R. Tabbenor	1,500	1997	350.00	380
1992 King Charles I D6917 - W. Harper	2,500	1995	450.00	495
1994 Leprechaun Toby - S. Taylor	2,500	1996	150.00	150
2001 Lord Kitchner D7148 - D. Biggs	1,500	2001	310.00	310
1999 Merlin, lg. D7117 - R. Tabbenor	1,500	2000	310.00	310
1992 Mrs. Claus Miniature D6922 - S. Taylor	2,500	1994	50.00	121-130
1993 Napoleon, lg. D6941 - S. Taylor	2,000	1994	225.00	225
2001 Noah D7165 - D. Biggs	1,000		295.00	295
1994 Oliver Cromwell D6968 - W. Harper	2,500	1994	475.00	475
1996 Pharoah Flambe, lg. - R. Tabbenor	1,500	1996	500.00	500
1991 Santa Claus Miniature D6900 - M. Abberley	5,000	1993	50.00	100-130
1988 Sir Francis Drake D6805 - P. Gee	6,000		N/A	100
1997 Sir Henry Doulton, lg. D7054 - W. Harper	1,997	1997	285.00	285
1992 Snake Charmer - S. Taylor	2,500	1992	210.00	250-275
1994 Thomas Jefferson - M. Alcock	2,500	1995	200.00	175-225
1994 Thomas Jefferson - S. Taylor	2,500	1996	200.00	225
1992 Town Crier D6895 - S. Taylor	2,500	1995	175.00	175-200
1992 William Shakespeare D6933 - W. Harper	2,500	1994	625.00	625

Collectors' Information Bureau   *Quotes have been rounded up to nearest dollar

Notes

Notes

Notes

Notes